A DELICATE BALANCE

A DELICATE BALANCE

Joy L. Esterby, Editor

THE NATIONAL LIBRARY OF POETRY

A Delicate Balance

Copyright © 1995 by The National Library of Poetry
as a compilation.

Rights to individual poems reside with the artists themselves.

All rights reserved under International and Pan-American copyright conventions. No part of this book may be reproduced, stored in a retrieval system or transmitted in any form, electronic, mechanical, or by other means, without written permission of the publisher. Address all inquiries to Jeffrey Franz, Publisher, P.O. Box 704, Owings Mills, MD 21117.

Library of Congress
Cataloging in Publication Data

ISBN 1-57553-001-5

Proudly manufactured in the United States of America by
Watermark Press
11419 Cronridge Dr., Suite 10
Owings Mills, MD 21117

Editor's Note

In the art of sculpture, the artist is often taught to refine, smooth the rough edges, and work diligently with the raw clay until a masterpiece of flowing lines and curves is created. The poet works in much the same way, whittling down ideas, exchanging words and rhythms, until just the right image with just the right sound emerges. The finished product should be able to spare not one word, nor add anything superfluous. The reader must then study every syllable, every connotation, every nuance to understand the living, breathing mystery of the poem. I am continually challenged to unravel the mysteries of the words, lines, and stanzas which lie in the pages to follow. Often they teach me new lessons and create strong emotions. A poem, no matter how short or long, has the potential to produce some kind of change within its reader, and this is a power which is to be highly admired and respected.

Many of the poems in this anthology are debut works: some are written by children; others by adults who have never before tried to write creatively; many are inspired by first love, a death in the family, or national tragedy such as the Oklahoma City bombing which occurred in April of 1995. Many new poets in this anthology have discovered they have something to say and that poetry is one of the most effective ways to express their thoughts and ideas. More seasoned writers continue to refine their talents, experimenting with different poetic forms, creating new words, employing fresh imagery, and re-examining timeworn topics and themes in a new light. I salute all of the poets represented here for their accomplishments, and I sincerely urge all of them to continue in their poetic endeavors.

Kingsley Harrop-Williams' Grand Prize-winning piece, "Unrest's Sure Abode," is a shining example of accomplished elegance that meticulously carves out a disturbing image of the United States as experienced by all minorities. Harrop-Williams' words are deliberately chosen from beginning to end, and each line seems to be another piece in the puzzle which reveals the poem's grave message. For instance, the first letter of each word in the title spells out "U.S.A," and in line 6 the "huddled light" is a veiled reference to the "huddled masses" whom the Statue of Liberty welcomes. At first glance, on the literal level, the poem is about three young men on their own, living in a house of three floors which they have constructed:

> *When George and Ben and Thomas broke free from their father's side,*
> *They built a house of 3 floors for freedom to reside.*

Washington, Franklin, and Jefferson, here mentioned by only their first names, were the founding fathers of the United States. After breaking free from England's rule, they built a country ruled by the three branches of democracy, and promising life, liberty, and the pursuit of happiness to all its citizens. The extended metaphor of the house representing the U.S. and its government is consistent throughout, from the cellar where darkness resides, to the parlor with the transparent ceiling, to the upper room where decisions are made.

In an effective display of irony, the second two lines of the poem illustrate the mistreatment of the Native Americans and the slaves -- two groups of people to whom the newfound freedom did not apply:

> *They packed the base with the native blocks, burying all prior claims;*
> *Then dug a cellar for darkness and refastened all its chains.*

Harrop-Williams employs light and dark imagery to paint a clearer picture of the segregation of races in the United States. The darkness in the cellar most likely refers to the black men, women, and children who were brought to America as slaves. In the second stanza, the "xanthous rays at the western wall" represent the Asian immigrants. Finally, the "[s]ilhouettes from the arid south" symbolize the Mexican immigrants crossing the border into the U.S.

Once the scene is set, Harrop-Williams addresses the racial issue of today:

> *Now in the age of a new millennium, what with Pretoria's open gate,*
> *One would think that darkness everywhere would meet a welcomed fate;*
> *But on the wedge that freed some darkness to be cohorts with the light,*
> *A contract from the upper room "Keep that door shut tight."*

Although the Civil Rights Act of '64 ("the trying wedge inserted in 64") has demanded desegregation, and although the last bastion of apartheid has fallen, the United States still holds on to its prejudices, whether enforcing quotas for immigrants or maintaining "glass ceilings" for minorities in the business world. The underlying connotation of the image of darkness is evil and fear, and Harrop-Williams seeks to destroy this misconception.

Perhaps most impressive about "Unrest's Sure Abode" is the cohesive whole it displays. Though the poem rhymes, the rhyme seems more incidental than intentional, and both the poem's rhythm and rhyme enhance rather than distract from or undermine the poem's serious purpose.

Another highly exemplary, highly refined work is Rafique Kathwari's "Halcyon Day With My Brother Farooq" (p. 552). Like Harrop-Williams, Kathwari is aware of the importance the title holds for the poem, as it is the title which sets the tone. The word "halcyon" refers to the mythological woman who grieved so after her husband Ceyx's death that she jumped into the sea, where she was transformed into a kingfisher. The kingfisher was said to be able to calm the sea and the wind. Thus the word "halcyon" indicates tranquility, but hints at the storms which preceded it and which will come. The reader is warned that something is not quite right before even reading the first line. Kathwari's images are unique in that they create a tone of unrest and intrigue:

> *Sister Mahmuda lobs solo on the clay court,*
> *her shadow crawling towards the net.*
> *Farooq's Madras shirt is starched,*
>
> *Bleeding hues glaze his face.*
> *The only wind is our breathing,*
> *urging the past out of its pockets of silence.*

It is unnatural for Mahmuda to be playing solo tennis; she seems somehow affected. Farooq is wearing a shirt made of crinkly material which has been intentionally starched. The hues of the plaid or striped Madras shirt often do bleed, however Kathwari breaks the stanza in such a way that the bleeding hues are more connected to Farooq's face than to his shirt, and the reader is alerted to Farooq's underlying pain. There is no wind except for the brothers' breathing, and the stillness is so complete it is eerie. Farooq then comments about the mental illness he perceives in both his sister and his brother, yet he, who has lost his 21-year-old son, suffers equally, though differently. In the end, perhaps it is the larger problem of a family uprooted and misplaced in a land far away from its heritage which contributes to the anguish or "madness" of these siblings. Perhaps this is why the narrator says, "two alphabets grate against my clenched teeth." He recognizes the wisdom and suffering of a mother who waits in vain for her children to return to their true home.

Jill Hammer seeks to avert the impending tragedy in her poem "To a Young Near-Suicide" (p. 462). Hammer delivers an impassioned plea to a young person who has bought into the notion that death is romantic. Hammer's words are concise and abrupt; a strong sense of urgency is conveyed:

Wait. Death smells like the mouse
we found in the swimming pool one spring
in gray pieces. Don't taste it. Don't go any closer.

There is no mincing of words; the message, and not its vehicle, is most important. Aside from the first stanza statement, Hammer's stanzas are split into three lines, yet each stanza ends in the middle of a sentence which is then picked up by the following stanza. Therefore, even the poetic form impresses upon the reader the idea of continuity, reinforcing the author's message about life.

Hammer also uses vivid imagery to lend perspective to the youth's situation:

...and you, pale delicate moth caught up
in blue-fizzling electric light, turtle infant
staring with innocent eyes at the diving hawk,

are mesmerized by the energy of destruction.

By comparing the youth to a weak, defenseless insect attracted to the light rather than to the death which will be found there, Hammer hopes the youth will snap out of his trance, will see the painful talons of the hawk before they sink into and destroy his innocent life.

In his poem "Venice Sun," (p. 89) Gregory Kemp also describes the pain of death. The narrator of this poem is profoundly affected by the tragic death of a fawn, ending his lament:

> *I knew what made me cry that day*
> *I felt pain with every tear.*
> *And as cascades of sorrow fell*
> *I knew what I held, dear.*

Kemp's clever use of double entendre at the very end gives readers pause to consider the tragedy of an animal's senseless death and then appreciate the fleeting moments of their own lives.

On a lighter note, Ann Barrett's "Petunia" (p. 6) is a well-written, humorous display of originality which celebrates life's possibilities. A rebel petunia has escaped from the garden prison to begin life again in the limitless bounds of freedom:

> *Now she emerges like a pinprick of blood in the back yard,*
> *Rising brazenly from the unkept lawn and moldering acorns--*
> *A hussy in bright red and strong perfume*
> *With leaves bent saucily like hands on hips.*

The image of the petunia is comical, yet distinctly authentic. The humor of the poem is effective because its description is based on reality; it is simply taken from a different perspective.

The readers will find many other treasures within this anthology. Listen to the throbbing sound of Ruth Young's "Primitif" (p. 521); hear the quiet grief of the stream in Page Coulter's "Elegy in Winter" (p. 553). Visualize the images as Marian Trotter and Lisa Aylish experiment with the arresting color of red in "Fire in the Kitchen" (p. 393) and "When She Wore Red" (p. 554) respectively. In addition, don't miss Mrs. R. Thornton Wilson's captivating work, "The View From Cap Juluca" (p. 69), Stass Andrews' "Apostasy From Decay To My Youth" (p. 3), and "My Grandmother" by Anca Pedvis (p. 448). There are so many more I wish I could mention. I hope you take as much pleasure in the pages which follow as I have. Congratulations to all who have contributed.

I would also like to thank the many individuals who helped in the publication of *A Delicate Balance*. The judges, editors, assistant editors, graphic artists, layout artists, office administrators, and customer service representatives have all brought their talents to bear on this project, and I am grateful for the contribution of these fine people.

Joy L. Esterby
Editor

Grand Prize

Kingsley Harrop-Williams / Reston, VA

Second Prize

Stass Andrews / West Columbia, SC
Lisa Aylish / Phoenix, AZ
Ann Barrett / Needham, MA
Patricia Best / Clifton, VA
Page Coulter / Guilford, CT

Jill Hammer / Middletown, CT
Rafique Kathwari / New York, NY
Lacey Marsac / Long Beach, CA
Anca Pedvis / New York, NY
Erik Roberts / Northampton, MA

Third Prize

John Ahern / New York, NY
Stephen Anderson / Chicago, IL
Muhammad Awais / River Vale, NJ
Neill Barham / Monterey, TN
Wallace Benepe / Huntington Beach, CA
Thomas Bradley / W. Conshohocken, PA
Lucy Bradshaw / New Bern, NC
Kris Brothers / Rapid City, SD
Elizabeth Buckingham / Ashland, NE
Brett Bukowsky / Naperville, IL
Robert Crane / Scottsdale, AZ
Aaron Davies / Wynantskill, NY
Gloria Deckard / Philadelphia, PA
Robert Dodson / Dallas, TX
R. F. Farkas / Suffern, NY
William France / Harlem, NY
Mary Gagliano / Rockford, IL
Alexandra Ghosh / Danville, PA
Joseph Harding III / Swedesboro, NJ
June Harlow / Palm Bay, FL
Lisa Harrison / Peabody, MA
Andrea Hendryx / Grand Prairie, TX
Kenneth Hoffman / Convent Station, NJ
Jim Coffin Howard / Belmont, CA
Jayne Jackson / Florence, AL
Marv Johnson / Denver, CO
Dixie Johnson-Elder / Boulder, CA
Gregory Kemp / Cortlandt Manor, NY
June Lamberg / Jobstown, NJ
Anne Lee / Canoga Park, CA

David Leeds / Beverly Hills, CA
Karen Lemieux / Nashua, NH
Louise Lisenby / Zanesville, OH
Debra Lord / Chicago, IL
Nancy Lutz / Woodbridge, VA
D. Jayne McPherson / Fulton, CA
Lianne Meinzinger / Ford, WA
Susan Miller / Lexington, KY
Fernando Morales / Islandia, NY
Louis Mulkern / New York, NY
Janeen Musselman / East Lansing, MI
L. Palincas / Torrance, CA
J. Prout / Glendale, NY
Shawn Rahier / Ogden, UT
Girsh Reznikov / Richmond Hill, NY
Sara Riola / Lakewood, NJ
Floyd Ross / Santa Barbara, CA
Sandra Schneiders / Berkeley, CA
Barbara Schoenberg / New York, NY
Roy Shults / Beverly Hills, CA
Carolyn Sorensen / Cody, WY
Marian Trotter / La Jolla, CA
Kyle Turner / Hamilton, OH
Robert Warren / Bronx, NY
Gus Wilhelmy / Chicago, IL
John Williams / Clementon, NJ
Mrs. R. Thornton Wilson / Newport, RI
Ruth Young / Enid, OK
Michael Zack / Malden, MA

Grand Prize Winner

Unrest's Sure Abode

When George and Ben and Thomas broke free from their father's side,
They built a house of 3 floors for freedom to reside.
They packed the base with the native blocks, burying all prior claims;
Then dug a cellar for darkness and refastened all its chains.

Shamefully, the time-worn bonds cracked with a costly fight,
And an opening placed on the eastern side welcomed the huddled light.
From dun to deathlike the lightness weighed on the basement door,
While xanthous rays at the western wall slithered in through a bore.

Silhouettes from the arid south stealing through the cracks do fall,
But the unhampered hue to the frozen north blends with the light in the hall.
Above the parlor a ceiling transparent from the penthouse floor
Zooms down on the trying wedge inserted in 64.

Now in the age of a new millennium, what with Pretoria's open gate,
One would think that darkness everywhere would meet a welcomed fate;
But on the wedge that freed some darkness to be cohorts with the light
A contract from the upper room "Keep that door shut tight."

—*Kingsley Ormonde Harrop-Williams*

Rejuvenation

The first yellow jacket flew into the room today.
It wasn't so large, and it didn't seem too focused
Because it meandered more than darted. However,

It did the job: some kids screamed, others hid
Their heads under books or hats and one
Entrepreneurial spirit said. "For fifty cents each,

I'll kill it with a rubber band." I walked
To the lights and turned them off. The insect sensed
The change and went out the window. Spring's here, I guess.

Anthony Sipp

Untitled

This torch I carry proudly in secrecy
in the darkness is my unrequited love;
But the absence of your emotions that is the dark
Leaves me lost and bears down on the light
I shine in search of you;
And even now the strength of my flame
cannot penetrate the blackness in which I wander;
Even now as I search in oblivion,
the fire consumes me;
And as I scream in agony it bares my feelings true
and strips me of my dignity.
There is nothing left;
And the words I whisper in my final breath are of my dying wish
for you...

Carl Joglar

Night

Breathe. Do you smell that?
The fresh air of night time.
All the stars are out
To light up the way.
There goes the big dipper and the small one too.

Where's the moon?
There she is,
Looking down at us,
Protecting us,
Even smiling at us.

What's that orange streak in my night time sky?!?
Where are my moon and stars?
Oh no, here comes day with its vibrant colors!!

Chrissy T. Oriol

Mid-Morning Enlightenment

Mid-morning,
darkness prevails,
dew glistens, rain falls,
transparent grey clouds hang so low,
my heart is enlightened
there is the scent of change in the air.

Mid-morning,
windswept rain clears the landscape,
makes way for the change upon the way,
my heart is enlightened
on this dark dreary day.

Mid-morning,
a deep breath to observe the great feeling,
awareness, tremendous senses
take a drive in your mind,
darkness, rain
what a great day
my heart is enlightened.

Frederick K. McRae

On a walk along the beach...

On a walk along the beach, I stopped and listened,
the gentle breeze brushing across the ocean foam,
tenderly caressing its waters.
and smelled-
the strong aroma of salty fish,
followed by the sweet smell of sunshine.
and tasted-
bitter juice, from a sea of fruits,
quickly souring my mouth and throat.
and touched-
cool grains of hope, slivering through my fingertips,
like gentle snowflakes.
and looked-
heavily and divine, fragile glass easily shattered,
Reflecting the sun as only a vision.

Erica Coleman

Squirrels

Chattering, scattering.
Leaping like acrobats, acting like aristocrats.
They pause to rest, poised paw to chest.
Waiting, debating.
Bounding blindly, landing square, giving the birds a scare.
Feasting regally, flicking their tails imperially,
Chattering, scattering.

Carly Anne Davis

Apostasy From Decay To My Youth

I rip at the wind
only 110 an hour
float by deadened stretches
once sweet, now sour.
Many have I known
little have they shown
one self do they serve,
tear around this curve.
Many cities have I seen
all seem the same, xy2
crave azure crowned fields of green,
floor the pedal to that place spared.
Refuel in the Badlands with peyotian dreams,
toehold on a butte, touching heavens, I scream,
"Hey Old Man! Show me a way!
I plead just a sign! Where this soul a'shines!?"
Through eroded gorges and crumbling ravines
the banshee wind falls...with faith... to nothing.
In Wakpaetowan chant, a shimmering sight,
of centuries before heinous barb'ric might
an infinite deciduous metropolis abound,
no money, tyranny, or protest found.
Swan dive from now godless earth free
aphelion soul chokes to breathe
as wolf, ant, cedar, bison,
as once all was... and will be again.

Stass Andrews

Spring Party

A
weeping willow
shed unseen tears of joy
when she learned the sky was planning
a shower to celebrate the birth of her new leaves.
She bent low and listened as other trees whispered the glad
tidings, and thunder clapped a welcome to hasten the silvery rain.
Then with greening arms she lovingly encircled the festive lawn table
spread for her party. A late crocus sprung from its bed and began
sipping droplets of the delicious punch as they trickled from the
sky's misty punchbowl.

I. Renie Peterson

Mother's Love

When you were born there was something about you that made you different. That laughing smile you gave me when I held you in my arms, the beauty of your baby skin, so soft in touch. I knew you were going to be special.

As a child you were going to do anything your heart desired, anything you wanted to do. Your style of dress is nothing new. Dress up was fun to you. You created new fashions with mom's clothing. You wanted a design of your own. Unique you may be, but my baby, I am proud of you, because you remained different.

My baby is growing into a woman now, and she needs me again, to show her that there is still someone who loves her forever and evermore.

I cried when you were born and when you graduated from high school, yet I do not stop there. I cried when you went away for college and when you graduated I will cry again. I will cry when my baby leaves life's door. I love my special Woman, a baby in my eyes.

Cheka Pedescleaux

The Greatest Gift

God's gift is faithful and true, unselfishly given to me and you;
Not awarded for deeds we've done,
but to create a family to live as one;
Accept this gift full and free, and in return,
that's the way ours should be;
Not a gift that's sure to smother, but having compassion for one another,
A kind gift that suffers long-not here today, then tomorrow it's gone;
Within this gift, there is no jealousy, neither will it rejoice in iniquity;
It cannot be puffed-up or proud, by behaving unseemly and loud;
Seeking its own, it cannot do, but rejoices only in that which is true;
It bears, trusts, hopes and endures, because the gift is perfect and secure;
This gift can never fail or end, along with faith and hope to create a flawless blend;
Without this gift abiding in you, you are deficient and destitute too;
if you didn't catch the clues from above, it's the greatest gift, unconditional LOVE

Demetress M. Hughes

The Paradox Of Survival

The brilliance of the snowy road is dazzling, as we slowly drive with shackles to the lodge. We dismember our union and find our shelter and prepare the way for our elected fun.

Gazing through the small and modest window, it is beautiful and dangerous, this view. My memories mold into one emotion as I remember what it was to be with you.

A lonely tear trickles down my cheek, as I stand and face the mammoth mountain peak. It is breathtaking and wondrous as is our life and again I think of you, my mind in strife.

It's hard to face the past now and the future. What was once a happy memory now hurts so. Can I push the memories to a distance? Can I? Or will I always feel this low?

My mind recalls the touches and the whispers; neglecting all the lies and the deceit. Can we be friends when we were once part of each other? Can we still keep our secrets but never meet?

Resenting you assists in my survival, in this ruthless world from which I have borne distrust. The metamorphic change is an illusion and I see how we transform comme Bestial...

This paradoxical situation is ironic. In my bid to turn the corner I have adorned his way of thinking and of understanding and become what in himself I did abhor.

Looking out this small and modest window, the frosted coat slowly melts away. My vision is, without awareness, magnified and I see the horizon of a brand new day.

Edel Flannery

Christmas Memories

As Christmas saunters in the door, my memories take to before; recalling when there were many faces, missing now, the table has empty places.

Grandma started baking in November, and those 'luscious smells, I can still remember

Our hearts back then were light and gay, as we all looked forward to Christmas Day.

Grandpa lit the fires to keep it warm and cozy, baking pies made our cheeks aglow and rosy.

Mother wrapped the presents with glitter, trying hard to hide my new red sweater.

Elvis sang of Christmas cheer, the weather man hoped that it would clear.

Hoping to catch a glimpse of Santa's flight, I knew that it would be another sleepless night.

Oh, what I'd give to go back then and see my loved one's faces once again.

The innocence of youth recaptured, midnight mass, our heart's enraptured.

Dear Lord, please give them a message for me, to send their spirits to the Christmas tree, our voices entwined once more in mirth, to praise the blessed baby's birth.

Oh yes, and one more thing Lord, I know you're busy, but this isn't hard.

There's only one thing I ask this year,
Give me a stronger faith, Lord, and still my fear!

Bonnie Wright

Childhood

Childhood is the flicker of a candle,
a golden beam of light.
Childhood is the dream we all shall treasure,
for the rest of our life.
Childhood is a brand new bike,
a brand new answer to a complicated question.
Childhood is confusion between friends.
Childhood is the flicker of a candle.

Jenna Notti

Daydreaming In The Dark

Purple quietly absorbs the sunset spectacle,
enfolding light into its regal gown.
Dreams escape from daylight's grasp,
transforming is and was into what should.
I pull the blanket of the night around me,
finding comfort in the cover of its black.
Now night reveals what light has missed,
and past re-shapes itself to truth.
New paths, from turns I never made,
are trod to lovely might-have-beens.
As time rewinds in night's elastic band,
old lows contract, new highs expand.

Here's where the winning games are played,
where arguments once-lost are won;
Where arms untouched by day embrace.
Listen, as my unmoving mouth preaches
Lipless words to an all-attentive void; the applause is deafening.
But black tick-ticks its way to grey, and muscles tense against the day.
So thrust the coverlet aside; night has lost its place to hide.
Light presses on the window pane; dream's curtain must be pulled again.

John H. DeViney

"A Heavy Heart"

Though your heart's made of steel
167 innocent people were killed,
There were mothers, fathers, sisters and brothers.
Among the dead there were Grandmothers,
Grandfathers, children and others.
Why won't you talk, Mr. McVeight?
You are the accused that's carrying the weight.
Why won't you tell, who's John Doe #2.
He's the accused that was seen with you.
On that day the bomb went off.
If you all are guilty of setting off the bomb,
Your hearts are very cold

May God have mercy on your souls
Carlene Taylor

"Life"

Man comes into the world at dawn
A baby cries - A child is born
From mother's womb, he has departed.
An independent life has started.
His eyes have opened - he sees the light
A wondrous world - - Oh, what a sight!
His body grows, his mind does too.
He's now a teen with much to do.
The clock says noon; it's half the day
Some time to learn, some time to play.
Evening approaches; waste no time!
Strive, build, work; he's in his prime
A family's started; his heirs have come
To finish the work he has begun.
The sun goes down. He feels night's chill.
There's no escape, it is God's will.
For what is life? Just one full day
From dawn to night, and then away.

Gloria Deckard

Seemingly

Seemingly, there is always a beginning;
A boy, hardly the age of five.
   His first crush, with the girl next door;
     His first theft, a one-cent piece of bubble gum.
   His first kiss, on the lips of a beautiful school girl;
     His first fight, a trip to the school principle.
   His first awakening, a girl who finds him attractive;
     His first cigarette, a look of disapproval by his parents.
   His first dance, a fire ignites his life;
     His first hang-over, a discharge from life's fun.
   His first caress of a woman's inner soul, a veil lifted;
     His first joy of indica, a dismissal from honest work.
   His first realization that he is extraordinary, a light;
     His first time in jail, a mistake not necessary.
Seemingly, there is always an end,
Yet in truth, there is only continuance.

John M. Johnston

Women Are Different

Two out in the ninth. The score is a tie.
A burly batter hits the ball clear up to the sky.
The crowd is tense. Will it reach the fence?
My wife says, "Look at that—
That woman in the first row wearing a horrible hat!"
I look and nod "It sure is that.
A truly horrible, horrible hat."

Oh why does my beautiful, talented wife
Pick this particular time of my life
To comment on a horrible hat?
Can anyone give me the answer to that?

Hilon Hendershott

"Imagery"

The spider maneuvering a web at dawn.
A Cardinal's aria, the messenger of morn.
The syrup of the fog, lying prostrate on the ground.
The commotion of the city, an intoxicating sound.
The moon is on a junket, still looking for the man.
The sizzling dance of butter, squirming on the frying pan,
The ocean casts its sorcery, for all to gaze with delight.
The mystery locked inside a tomb, that we all know as night.
The cologne of earth, the cry of rain.
The laughter of children, like bubbling champagne.
The disorganized motion of a leaf on wing.
The babbling in the air, after summer had its fling.

These hallmarks are immortalized like a flame that never fades,
And the Robin's song slowly disappears, as do life's
brief charades.

Harvey Frank

"A Life Broken"

A baby cries...no one hears
A child cries...no one listens
A teenager filled with pain....no one cares
A lover....the pain is covered
A wife...the pain is hiding
A mother...this new life is heard and loved
The old pain wears a mask
It attacks...it doesn't go away....it attacks again....
It doesn't go away
A woman....a girl......a child....they all cry out
They hurt....they hurt......God, how they hurt
But no one hears
A life broken
A new life comes
Her child —— she hears
Her child —— she loves
Her child — is love
Love...pain
Pain....love

Debra Bevinetto Hirsch

Conquistador

The pioneer and the pathfinder
A commander in the hierarchy of English
Commandeering all those who fall under his literary shield.
Stalwart in his defense of the English language, defender of its tongue.

Into the battle he leads his young recruits,
Surging forth to unknown paths of word discovery
Setting his own limitless boundaries in pursuit of literary excellence.
His lance poised to do battle with those who dare profane the tongue,
And poised to seek yet another battlefield of minds,
Sweeping away the dregs, the dross, the chaff
That lay waste to the spoken word,
Clearing the forest so that the word,
In all its glory and elegance and history,
Becomes the flower on the hill—
Unscathed and pristine.

Like their leader, the new beneficiaries of
The journey through the etymologies of time,
Have now become the conquistadors and aficionados
Of the spoken word.

Alice Ishkanian

A Desert

While heading through the desert one day
A day I had set aside to pray
I was suddenly aware of my surroundings
With flowers and trees abounding

I looked around at this scenic splendor
And I truly had to wonder
How the scenery blended in
And the sudden peace I felt within

God must be in this place
One could almost touch his face
This is a place of awesome splendor
This place, the desert, I'll always remember

Barbara F. Spencer

Bird up in the Sky

Yesterday there was only me, a single grain of sand
A drop of water on an endless Sea that never would touch land.
And then one Day a Little Bird Appeared Across a Sky so Blue.
She laid a path through a golden Sun, and brought me here to you.

AND YOUR HEART IS LIKE THAT BIRD UP IN THE SKY!
I've searched in silence for that Rainbow's end down narrow Streets of Gold
I've walked that Circle that had no end, and did what I was told.
And if anything was learned at all, I Know now It's a lie - It's
Not the things you hold in your hand, It's forever in her Eyes.
Now my Heart is like that Bird up in the Sky.

John Karagovalis

Growing Pains

She started her life one early winter morn.
A feisty little child since the day she was born.
Years one, two and three kept me going night and day.
The fourth....Grandpa passed away.

At five and six learned to swim in her pool.
Seven and eight brought high grades in school.
Trophies for soccer and bowling ages nine, ten.
Eleven years old and forced to move again.

The twelfth she insisted on having house keys.
Thirteen I gave in ... saying take these please.
Fourteen and fifteen started staying out late.
Her life nearly over at sixteen - what a terrible fate.

Memories of seventeen have now started to fade.
Eighteen and pregnant about to have a babe.
Nineteen and a new mother, she's starting to see....
Late hours, diapers and formula - is this all there can be?

At twenty she's adjusted to the little one.
Twenty-one - back at school and under the gun.
Twenty-two moved out and is on her way...
To becoming a very independent lady, I'm happy to say.

Desiree A. Hayes

The Power Of Love

What can love hold? Love can hold
a great amount of power. Love can build
dreams, love can build a life.
When two people share love, there is a
power that overwhelms the heart and controls
the soul. But what happens when half of that
love is torn away, suddenly; hatefully? If the
other half is still there, the love will continue
till the end, when both halves are joined again..
Where the power of love will overwhelm the heart
  and control the soul....
    Again....

Abbie Pender

Mother Earth, Our Only Home

I look around and what do I see,
A free country with opportunities for him, her and me,
Your beautiful rivers, lakes and ponds all tarnished from man's corruption making them almost gone,
Your precious animals are hunted for fun and games,
no one coming forth to take the full blame,
Yet, all they can do is complain and complain
never realizing that you are in pain,
What promises we had for a better tomorrow are now held onto by a mere glimpse of hope,
They all fail to realize your job has been done,
It's now up to us to build the pulp of our love for you
in the years to come, our dear Mother Earth.

Blanca I. Kuar

Petunia

She's a rebel flower,
A fugitive from the manicured garden in front of the house,
An escapee from white picket prison.
She busted out
Right out from under the nose of the stone rabbit guard.
Must have been an inside job by the squirrels.

Now she emerges like a pinprick of blood in the back yard,
Rising brazenly from the unkept lawn and moldering acorns—
A hussy in bright red and strong perfume
With leaves bent saucily like hands on hips.

She knows it's a tough life on the run,
A jungle
Of dandelions and crabgrass
And predatory beetles:
A flower can get used up fast on the outside.
"I'll never get pinched back again!" she vows.
She's planning to go wild.

Ann Barrett

I Am Free

"Today, today," the eagle cries
A high voice singing,
While other birds fly all about.
The snowcapped mountain crowned with pines
Sits in peace, calling to me.
Calling...
Calling...
I must go now, to the forest.
Feel its beauty and the grace of the tall oaks,
Hear the wind whistle in my ears,
Surrounding me.
Swirling my hair with a life of its own, it seems.
Listening to the music of the stars:
The moon's melody,
The trees' harmony,
And Nature's rhythm.
I am free.

Caroline Sturges

Morning In The Night

I dream of a place called Morning in the Night
A place of creeks, streams and rivers of dreams.
The Sun with its beams, the Moon with its gleams,
Skies of blue, clouds of white.
The hood of an owl darkened by night.
The stars in the sky bold and bright,
They twinkle like diamonds scattered on white.
I waken and see it is the same,
The place I just left is the place from which I came.
Morning in the Night.

Juanita Lorraine Eubanks

This Thing Called Me

I search in desperation for a glimpse at what should be
A hope that there is purpose within this thing called me
I would Love the emotion of the depths of life's appeal
To clasp in both my hands it's full to break these chains of will
I hear a plea within my heart a fear I may not see
A choice that I may let slip by that was my destiny
To make a choice from good or bad to choose from right or wrong
May not produce the perfect note I wish for in life's song
If I take a road I know is wrong then I'm not really lost
It's when there is no warning and all good roads are crossed
I reason in my heart foresight may not be mine
That I may never be quite sure and go through life as blind
If the reason for my life is met and somehow finds its way
I guess I don't really have to know what is there left to say
I need to go to the warehouse and fill my cart with care
The stronger fabrics of life that will not easily tare
Give me plenty of commitment a will to pay the price
How about some of that dedication PLEASE! Fill that one twice
When I can - I will choose my currents, when I can't, we will see
But in all I do there is hope in this thing called me.
   John B. Strange

A Short Farewell

Slowly I bend my head to kiss your lips.
A kiss that so many times I gave to you.
To say hello, goodbye, or on happy occasions.
This kiss that I am giving you is very special.
A kiss that must forever last.
A kiss that marks a lifetime.
A lifetime of joys and tears.
A lifetime of fond memories of a warm and always helping heart.
A heart that could never say no - to those in need.
This kiss that I am giving you will last only a few seconds,
Yet, wishing that time could be stopped -
   that it could be turned back.
Wishing this kiss was not being born.
It is hard to believe how full of life and happiness you were one day,
Then the next day you were gone forever.
My lips will be touching yours knowing that yours will never feel mine.
How cold your lips are.
You will forever be in my heart.
Till we meet again,
May you have eternal rest....MOTHER....
   Eduardo Quezada

Thinking Loudly

As I sit here pondering,
A lady and her daughter happened by me,
Laughing and enjoying each other's company.
My eyes followed them with such envy,
For my own mother's company.

At age ten,
I missed the way she combed my hair.
I missed her voice, first thing in the morning
At night, I missed her lips on my forehead.
As she pulled the blanket over me,
"It's time for bed," she said.

At thirty something, funny, I miss the same things.
I can't hear her laughter. I wish I could.
When I converse with her in solitude,
I hope she sees my growing pains,
And hears my laughters of joy.
   Celestina F. Abejon

Elusive Dream

An eternity since I've seen your face;
A lifetime since I've felt your touch;
Lurking around every corner;
Yet, a million miles away.

Always there, on the other side of the mist;
One day we're destined to collide.
But now, so much time has passed;
Will I know you,
Will I recognize
The laughter and tears
That breathe life into your soul.

Yes, it was I who no longer wanted you
And banished you into oblivion;
But now, I search for what I once felt
And will know you the instant you appear.

For you are the dream of a lifetime-
An elusive dream called
LOVE.
   Dawn E. Roode

Why Am I Here

A bundle of joy, my parents to bless.
A little girl baby, to love and to dress.
A schoolgirl learning, doing her best.
A teenager struggling to leave the nest.
Finally, an adult, hope within my breast.
   But, why am I here?

Married young, then motherhood.
Challenges of life both bad and good.
Principles of work grimly understood.
To gain shelter and clothing and even food...
Experiencing love, laughter and a happy mood.
   Now why am I here?

Growing older, experiencing strain.
A sense of accomplishment trying to gain.
Searching for happiness, often in vain.
Trying, ever trying descendants to train.
Then finding God despite the pain.
   That's why I'm here.
   Beatrice Downes Joseph

If Forever Ends

To find a friend in a lover
A lover in a friend
Wounds we inflict upon ourselves
Some hearts will never mend

An empty shell of a man
Without your love to fill me, I've become;
Our short lives are not worth living
If we can't surround ourselves with love

I dream of the sunshine in your hair
The look of love in your eyes
Without you, an empty soul
Without you, everything within dies

A soul that never loved
Is a soul that never lived
Fade away, we fade away
Love is the only thing I have to give

To find a friend and a lover
A lover and a friend
The dreams that we dared to dream
Are nothing if forever ends
   Al Costa

Ease Me

Stuck in a world full of blame,
a mind filled with flames,
I must find an escape,
I don't know how much more I can take,
I can't wash away this horrible dream,
everyday I live the pain grows more extreme,
it is time, time to throw myself in,
as I am the conscious of a mortal sin,
you can kill me ...,
but you can never hurt me,
you can kill me...,
but you can never hurt me,
kill me........,
kill me........,
do me this one favor,
be my only savor.

Dave Marnell

Rainbow End

The rainbow's end has always been
a mystery to all.
You gaze across the horizon,
you walk the land,
you search near and far.
But, the rainbow's end has always been
a mystery to all.

At the end of the rainbow, the story goes,
A pot of gold is to be found.
But, the rainbow end never seems to touch the ground.
It appears in Spring and Summer,
Winter and Fall.
But, the rainbow's end has always been a mystery to all.

This beautiful array of colors
magnifies through the storm.
When nature's at its worst
and the earth seems ready to burst,
this beautiful array of colors, so wondrous to behold,
brings hope and promise for all.
God's beautiful rainbow waterfall.

Harold Wayne Stockton

Dreams

Living in a world where evil conquers good

Where the night never sees day
A never-ending fear
Never knowing what will happen next

Feeling scared and frightened
Knowing it's just a dream but thinking
   it's real

Feeling the pain and anger
Uncertain if you're awake or not
Seeing the worst and not sure if
   you're going to live through it

Hearing screams echo through your mind

Forgetting life's happiness
Thinking you've crossed the other side
Wanting to escape
But it only seems as if you were
   falling in a deeper, deeper sleep.

Damaris Sepulveda

Creation

What a sight to behold in the eyes of beauty.
   A new life in the world, is something
Unique, that our Father has conquered.
As I.
Open up the windows of life in my heart,
   I can see, that God created man,
      in a crystal glass bowl; with all the
loving and care that he so miraculously
Possessed!!
   Hum.....that is why I,
      A creation in this world,
am happy to know,
That all creation was done by...
GOD!!!!!!

Alexandria Tacker

Immortality (A Villanelle)

The sun sets, the end, in a cot, he lay.
A new mother smiles, he opens his eyes.
The sun rises, the start of a new day.

Youthful and blind with life, he goes to play.
Sleep with dreams of candy rule as he lies.
The sun sets, the end, in a cot, he lay.

Open to the influence all will say.
Problems, pressures, mistakes, the teen defies.
The sun rises, the start of a new day.

Grown, he pushes his future his own way.
Food for home and gas for the car he buys.
The sun sets, the end, in a cot, he lay.

Lost dreams and hopes are thoughts, put on delay.
Worn by life he sits, thinks, reflects, and sighs.
The sun rises, the start of a new day.

This journey complete, his grandchildren pray.
Weary, loved, honored, remembered, he dies.
The sun sets, the end, in a cot, he lay.
The sun rises, the start of a new day.

Bobby Rundberg

Longing To Belong

All my life, I've searched for a place.
A place I could call my home.

I've longed to have friends.
Friends, that I could call my own.

I've looked for a family,
Family that I could say was mine.

Hungered for a father.
A father that could stand the test of time.

Now I know, what I did not know.
I know the love of Jesus.

Now, I have a house, a house to call a home.
It's always been a part of me, but not a place I've known.

Now, I have a father, who not only loves me.
But, teaches me to love.

Now, I no longer, long to belong.

For He fulfills all hopes and dreams,
He completes all families.

I have a father that writes the test of love, that only he can pass.

And I'm glad I know him now, for he completes my past.

Cheryl Dodd-Ray

To See Through The Eyes Of A Child

I know a place where you can be free. . .
a place where everything is in perfect harmony. . .
it's in the eyes of a child. . .
where you can be free like a bird. . .
flying through the air after being set out of a cage. . .
all the wonders of the world can be seen without any rage. . .
to see through the eyes of a child. . .
To be a child again with eyes that see good and not evil. . .
to be happy and trusting and sometimes sad. . .
believing in good and never in bad. . .
I think there is a child in every one of us. . .
only we act like wild animals sometimes and forget how to trust. . .
how many wonder what it's like. . .
to see through the eyes of a child again. . .
how many wonder what it's like to be free again. . .
and see through the eyes of a child.

Erin Holder

I Read A Book About Destino (For The Birds)

I read a book about destino
a science
but only you and I would understand

I read a book about destino
a fiction
but only you and I could understand

I read a book about destino
a diary
and now I don't even understand
how you can fly around the world
but only birds seem to find a place to land

Dave Antonio Munoz

Christmas

Christmas time comes but once a year,
A season for loved ones to be near.
The child's mind filled with gifts galore,
A time for Jesus to be adored!

Brightly, colored lights do shine!
Bells ring in rhythmical chime.
Christmas carols fill the air.
Presents wrapped with loving care.

Christmas cards sent back and forth,
Cookies, candies, and sugar canes, of course!
Trees embraced with decoration,
Thank our Lord - for all creation.

Judie Anderson-Madsen

Enchanted Reflections

As the sun rises above the horizon
A shimmering light peers through the trees along a lake
Casting silver shadows amongst the various foliage
Illuminating reflections hovering along the embankment
Gazing at the waves of light one becomes allured by the flickering
rays to know as the sun gives strength to the Earth
It also give strength to one's own self
Entranced by the sounds of the forest
Peace and tranquillity enters the soul
One can find great happiness floating upon a lake
Listening to the birds, the frogs, the animals
rummaging through the forest
One can find wholeness in their life
The strength to hold on to what one has
To what one desires
Giving the endurance to survive the world that we live in
As long as nature can survive, so will we

Asianita C. Gonzales

The Deathhead

Nothing remained but the deathhead-
A shrunken skeletal mask-
And the back-
A piece of purple, over-ripened meat-
All traces of the one I loved had long since vanished
But she still lingered, the spirit hanging on
As even though in that dread state
She could not bear a wrenching from the bones
Which locked her in her shell
I bent to kiss her forehead while others shrank away
If I could only kiss away her pain
And kiss her soul away
It was not the dying that was horrible
But the lingering
Dying in bits and pieces-
And Death was no cruel axe man
But a longed-for black redeemer
Coming to wrap his strong dark arms around her
And tearing her away at last
Away from the deathhead

June Bailey Harlow

Summer

A beam of light dancing,
A slight girl in white gauze
Spinning through fields of buttercups
And tall grass,
With hoofprints and wild tansy.
Plucking berries from brambles
And thorns on her fingertips,
Thorns on her fingers...
She
Imagines herself glamorous, and beautiful,
and liked,
She dreams herself into movies;
Acts, she
Hummms and skips and sings, for
Circling birds overhead.
Circling underhandedly.
She imagines herself beautiful, and
Beautiful, and Buttercups, and
loved...

Comfort Pearson

"Grandma's Baby"

She arrived on a very special day.
   A smidgeon over seven pounds she did weigh.
     Like a kitten her eyes would remain
        closed mostly, 'til strength she could gain;
But soon lovely "blues" opened wide,
   "Cute as a button" she was, even when she cried.
     She took Grandma's heart in tiny hands,
       made her hers with "wedding bands."
Tiny fingers grasp Grandma's thumb
   making her whole being slightly numb.
     Heart-shaped face looks up with a smile;
       Lovely blue eyes promised to beguile.
These two will travel the sands of time;
   One aged, one yet too young to "climb,"
     Joined together by a "band of gold,"
       names the same, to have and to hold.
Something old, something brand new,
   something "borrowed," both with eyes of blue,
     Grandma and grandchild joined with love,
       a special gift, this baby from heaven above.

Grace R. Sosomen

"Snowfall"

It's snowing.
A starless night,
the snow crisps the ground.
The waves crash into each other,
the large devouring the little.
And the snow comes down on the rocky shore.
In the background a bird sings a soft song.
The sun comes up and warms the snow.
The children come out to play.
Snow crystals come down,
each more un-identical and complex than the last.
Balls of snow whizz by to shatter on the wall.
Then everything is silent and still.
It's snowing.
   Jeffrey Bates

One Of Many

A tear is: the thorn of a red, red rose piercing the skin…pain
A tear is: words from a loved one that pull at your heart…sadness
A tear is: memories from the past you wish to forget…anguish
A tear is: the sight of a small puppy being handed to you…happiness
A tear is: the loss of someone very close…sorrow
A tear is: the accomplishment of something so very much earned…
   relief
A tear is: thoughts of past emotions…regret
A tear is: remembrance of words you once said…remorse
A tear is: thoughts of needed love…reluctance
A tear is: seeing someone for the first time in years…joy
A tear is: finding out someone really cares…reassurance
A tear is: thoughts of what life should be…confused
A tear is: thoughts of someone so far away…helplessness
A tear is: thoughts of broken hearts and those who caused them…
   hatred
A tear is: one of many
   Alicia Pitchford

Life's Blessing

I have a daughter …
A thoughtful, considerate little person
Who makes life such a pleasure with her
unselfish ways,
I'm thankful God allows her to share her life with us.
You see, this little "mother hen" who's
so precious to me, is
My daughter - in law.
   Frances B. Frank

Autumn Night Walk

The setting of the sun bringing on a new time
A time of peace and rest
A time to escape the shelter of your home and be free
Follow the glistening of the moon through the trees
It creates a path with its beam of light
Silently walk as if you were a predator of the night
Become one with the world around you
Feel the cool night air freeze your fingers and nose
Let the darkness into your soul
So you can truly understand its purpose.
Find a rock to sit upon, and gaze at the city lights below
Believe in how wonderful this world is to have such unnoticed beauty
As daylight approaches, you must return
Return to the everyday life that will soon change again with darkness
Await it
No one can imagine the beauty until they've been there
Continue on
Night after night
Realize the other side of life?
   Dawn Weinsteiger

An Old Sailor's Lament

Her sensuous eyes, her ivory skin,
   A tiny being was she,
And there I lay, nestled to her,
   For she belonged to me,
It wasn't forever, a period in time,
   And someday we would part,
But in precious moments, we lived that life,
   With one beat of our heart,
And at this hour, my thoughts drift back,
   To those days so very long past,
And wonder what her life must be,
   And if happiness found her at last,
But, alack and alas, as I dwell upon,
   These fading memories of mine,
Will be lost forever to all eternity,
   Diminished by the passing of time.
   Charles F. Sumner

Unknown Soldier

In the bathroom across the hall the faucet drips
a young boy closes his eyes
the drip becomes the footfall of a soldier
he walks through a battle of anger and hatred
those around him don't even see him
someone nearby cries out in pain and he too cries out
each drop of blood spilled in the battle is matched
   by a drop of his own
he watches as those around him destroy each other
   and him in their wake
he feels helpless, smothered by their anger and hatred
those around him don't even notice
he is saddened
in the bathroom across the hall the faucet drips
as the blood of an unknown soldier flows from his wrists
to the bathroom floor.
   Charles Staeven

Accept Me

I am I, do not change me, condemn me, nor put me down.
Accept me for who I am…
No…
You need not agree with me, but accept me.
For I am total in being. I have my faults,
I have my guilts, but that is who I am.
Perfect I will never be, allow me to be uninhibited.
Do not pressure me into feeling what I do not feel.
Accept me when I am flying high as I have accepted you.
Do not put me down, nor make me feel unhappy about me.
I am I and I like being what I am.
Me!!!
   Ieisha M. Melendez

Untitled

A picture is a moment in time;
A memory which endures for years.
It is the witness of important occasions;
happy or sad.
It is the image of people and places,
that never age,
   that are never forgotten,
   that are always loved.
A picture can make one cry and laugh;
It can make one relive feelings from the past.
It can reflect, in an instant, a story.
And it can concentrate, in a moment, a life.
   Esther N. Sanguesa

The Garden

The Garden of Eden was where two people lived.
Adam and Eve had so much to give.

God gave them everything, and He was pleased,
but Satan came along and began to tempt and tease.

He said to Eve, look! look! eat of
the tree over there, but Eve said no! no! I would not dare.

But ole Satan said, why not? If you
eat of that tree you'll be wise and learn a lot!
For if you eat it'll open your eyes.
Don't believe God, no one surely dies.

Adam and Eve, they both ate, only to meet their fate,
Their eyes were opened because they had sinned,
the life they will not want, was now to begin.

God drove them out of the Garden, Cherubim
and flaming sword turned every way,
the Garden was no longer their paradise it
was a place where they could not stay.
Now... out of the Garden, into the world..Adam
to work...Eve to travail, dying a little day to day,
for disobeying God, this was the debt they had to play.

Charmaine Anderson

Aged Vine

To compare one's love one must first have sipped the nectar of
aged wine and walked the fields of vineyard vines with love
and prune all entanglements of love's pride.

Young love is green on Nature's vine.

Then return with eager cups of love to aging vats of golden
wines to purple hues and see what another year that nature
has done to love and wine.

Love's fruit still clings to Nature's vine.

After years of analyzing love's wine, stumbling through life's
path of tangled vines, always striving to improve the lines and
reap the fruits of nature's wine.

Love will never wither on an aging vine.

Fred Luther

"Dairy Products And Other Things"

Wednesday morning, I open the door
Air like Novocaine heavy on my arm
The frost clears and she's there pressed between
the Wonder Bread and the eggs
Motionless, a faded stamp
She does not smile, does not blink
She has that dairy look about her
this low-fat carton girl on my shelf
I grab the grapefruit juice
and she does not scream when I shut the cold door
Where could she be?
The thoughts melts with the butter on my toast
Just another date on the verge of expiration waiting to be recycled...

Alejandro R. Consuegra

The Entreaty

I consider the tree to be much like the human race,
all are diverse, each seeking its special place.
They do not all soar and reach and abound,
some prefer their path somewhat closer to the ground.
None is less or more than the other,
all have beauty and purpose and all are brothers.
When you tread through a forest be it valley or peak,
consider each and all you see special and unique.

John Mariano Nistico

A New Light Of Day

All alone cause no one can see
All I feel inside of me.
I'm always on the outside looking in
In this position you can never win

All that your heart desires,
No matter how simple it may be
I always end up with battered, broken wings.

In all my pain you can never see
A positive outlook of life.
They've ruined it for me

So dear Lord if you have the time
to listen to an old tossed away coat,
turn me into one that can float.

Far, far away from this way of life
Dear Lord I want a knife
to cut me loose from these harsh burdens.
So I can see a new light of day.

Elizabeth Wilson

Darkness

I look into the bone chilling darkness of a moonless night.
All is immersed with the color of death.
The skeleton of a tree seems to be more than that and the leaves on
    that tree seem to beat like a human's heart.
I hear chirping, that of a small, shiny cricket and the lapping of
    waves on the shore of Cat-Tail Lake.
The smell of dewy grass becomes putrid, making me feel like a fish
    out of water.
As I look out onto a scene, once full of color, that is now completely
    filled with black, a feeling of sadness and anger overcomes me.
Black—the color of night, of bad and evil, and of death.
In that vast darkness I see my father's body lying on the ground.
The rustling of leaves, like the beating of a heart, turns into the
    sound of gun shots and the chirping of crickets transforms into
    angry shouts and yells.
The lapping of water on the shore becomes the sickening sound of
    bullets hitting flesh at a rapid speed and in all that blackness
    I see red.
Red, the color of blood, my father's blood.

Becky Rickert

To My Son...

From birth to now you've always been
a point of pride, a Song without end.

First halting steps, then words all your own,
now Man and Scholar, how beautiful you've grown.

We gather together with Joy and with Praise,
as you commence a new Life - start a new phase.

Never forget, there's always a place
for Honor and Courage, Wisdom and Grace

Remember to stop, to ponder and pose
those questions so deep - like what is a Rose

The people you touch, the Paths that you cross
are Healing and Balm in life's Tempest tossed.

The Love that you render, forever returns
a Light never fading - a Candle that Burns.

As we pay homage for Deeds now well Done
I bask in the Honor you've given me, Son.

So I thank God, on this beautiful night,
for the Gift that He gave, a father's delight.

Wherever you go, whatever you do,
be sure of one thing - I'll always Love you.

Bruce F. Kommer

Waves

People moving about make Waves
All living things make Waves
Good deeds, hard work make Waves, as do stress or strife
Physical and mental efforts ripple through life

One Wave can encourage another
Cheerful, kind, trustworthy Waves help each other
Changes in interest alter Wave sizes and speeds
Energy from each Wave brings pleasure, fills life's needs

Waves are in the mind, the sea, the pond, the air
They keep coming in good times or bad, foul weather or fair
Emotions like Waves ebb and flow
Sometimes they come fast - sometimes slow

Waves make rhythmic sounds night and day
Tides bring them closer, then take them away
Storms stimulate their actions up, down, to and fro
Their sounds can escalate, forming a thunderous crescendo

Turbulent souls, like the sea, struggle to be free
At times water changes color, souls we cannot see
Confidence rises, fear falls, life makes its splash
Into shore, out to sea, water too continues its mad dash

Life follows life, like wondrous Waves, part of Nature's bash
David G. Honeycutt

"Mother"

As I sit inside this man made hell.
All my thoughts turn to you;
Knowing I have hurt you mother,
Has made me oh so blue.
I have tried to be the son -
Like the mother you've been to me;
Sometimes that's not possible, when I'm out there running free.
I'm not very good at writing, mother -
These feelings I have inside;
And that is why I run, to find a place to hide.
To hide from all the pain,
All these many years -
To try to find an answer,
For all these lonely tears.
I know that you hurt too mother, I know you have much pain;
But the times are changing
And you lives will be whole again, my time will soon be over
And we will start anew, I would just like to say
Mother, how much I LOVE YOU.....
John Peccerillo Jr.

I Will Help You Finish What Those Two Brothers Began

I will help you finish what those two brothers began,
Give me a million dollars so I can spit in people's eyes as Joe
  Kennedy told Jack his eldest son.
I will help you finish what those two brothers began,
And for Rose and the grandchildren write poems and sing simple songs.

I will help you finish what John and Bobby began,
Like mighty tenacious King David of old, I will toil with my two hands
I will help you finish what those two brothers began,
And when it is over we will sing and say "what the heck; we won."

I will help you finish what those two brothers began,
Not only because they gave new hope to the negro american black man.
I will help you because that is the way I am,
I will help you although I am a simple - simple man.

I will help you because I do believe you also share my dream,
I will help you because like in PT109 you'd give your life for the
  brave and free.
I will help you because those two brothers remain an integral
  everlasting part of my being,
I will help you because John Fitzgerald Kennedy and Bobby Kennedy
  still inspire me.
Keith Locke

Slaughter Of The Innocent

Auschwitz, Bergen-Belsen, Dachau;
All of them madhouses, where the mad rule the sane,
Driving them to the brink of insanity.
Can the story be truly told?
Can we bear to tell it so?

Attila, Hitler, Stalin;
False Gods, all of them,
Presiding over their own sick religion.
Can the story be truly told?
Can we bear to tell it so?

Bundy, Gacy, Kemper;
The dead of soul among the living,
Living demons, bringing a reign of terror with their sacrificial rites.
Can the story be truly told?
Can we bear to tell it so?

Dahmer, Noriega, Hussein;
Shall we call them the new breed?
Will the madness ever stop?
Part of human nature, it continues;
The slaughter of the innocent.
Christopher M. Toulson

"Mother"

Mother, oh mother, why did you have to go -
all of us, left behind, really love you so -
won't you tell me mother, why you couldn't stay -
Is it because, they needed you in heaven, right away -

A bright light is what they needed, to brighten up the place -
and so they called you, mother, hail Mary full of grace -
though you are in heaven, watching over me -
I am very careful, for I know that you can see -

All year long I think of you, and what I should say -
you have always been special, you still are, on Mother's Day -
I shall always miss you, though you are afar-
and you are always with me, for I know just where you are -

One day we shall meet again, and I shall hug you so -
that is when they call me, and I too shall have to go -
I hope my ticket is for heaven, and when they ring the bell -
but if there is a mix up, I could end up in — hell
Harry B. Sherr

Dark Realities

In vain I searched a trace seven decades of my life.
All seems like a chain of dreams, vanishing as echoes of songs.
I took a cruise to catch my youth, watched the foamy waves
behind, Disappearing as years gone by leaving no trace behind.

Alas! Childhood years like dreams are gone with no return,
O', you happy carefree years, you're meant only to rejoice.
Against the arrow death, no shield ever will save you,
Gold, lustrous wealth, have been useless, only good
deeds remembered.

And when I'm gone leaving this world, for the sunrise and for
sunset, Makes no differences to rotating world, whether I'm
walking or six feet deep. World will rotate just the same,
yielding space to new born souls, As fresh victims to deadly
bombs-millions will die for greed and wars.

Hydrogen, nuclear, atomic bombs, will devastate continents.
Before expiring my last breath, I only wish few minutes
To shed my heartfelt tears for millions hungry children
Who will perish before seeing the next spring of their lives.
Ferdinand Kaimakamian

My Day With Calie

I am with Calie
all throughout the day
to talk and to play,
to wile the hours away.

When I get up in the morning
I can hear her purring;
I guess that's her friendly greeting.
Then to the kitchen she comes running.

Up on the counter she jumps
looking for bits and crumbs,
then when she finds some
she winks at me as if to say "thank you, madam."

From room to room she goes
to watch the birds by the window,
on the floor she rolls and rolls
with a crumpled paper as a ball.

Calie is a calico cat
spotted white, brown, and black;
she has such a pretty face
and walks with elegance and grace.

Josefina Mischke

That Moment Of Love

Poets and painters, sculptors and playwrights
All try to capture a moment of love.
When you hold someone special,
Someone who's the sunshine after the rain,
Someone who's the angel sent from above.
When you kiss someone special,
Someone who brings with her the beauty of life.
When such a person is found,
When such a moment is felt,
That moment of love.
Don't try to capture it.
Don't write it.
Don't paint it.
Don't mold it.
Just feel it.
Just embrace it and never let it go.
For when it's gone,
That moment can never return.

Eric Dryja

Ominous Opportunity

I, the desert thunderstorm
Am dark, fierce, furious!
Rip through threatening skies
With jagged bolts of power.
My voice majestic, my warning loud;
Without gentleness I pound and pelt
Against parched, hostile land.

Soak in my every promise of life,
Suck it up through the root of your being.
Survival depends on the ability to
Store each drop wisely.

Sniff the air with the coyote
Savor the fragrance of sweet mesquite;
Slumber silently 'neath its shade
As dust settles to the desert floor.
Lick the rocks, quench your thirst while
Streams of opportunity trickle past.
Rainbows fade to memory
Tomorrow I become
A vaporous mirage.

Barbara Thompson

"Ode To An Animal Killed On The Highway"

I'm sure you didn't understand the danger,
All you wanted,
Was to get to the other side.
Was your family or home over there?
Or was it the quickest route?
I hope you didn't suffer,
And that your death was instant.
I'd like to believe,
That there are animal "guardian angels,"
Who swoop down, from heaven,
And take animal souls to a safer place,
While your carcass just lies there,
On the road.

Char Knowles

I Hurt

I used to sit next to you and watch the expressions on your face.
All your thoughts would show in many different ways.
   The sternness of your jaw,
   The furrow in your brows,
   The sparks in your eyes,
   The smile so sweet and broad.
Now you're gone.
I close my eyes and see your face.
I hurt.
Someday I will close my eyes, see your face,
And your smile will brighten my day.

Faye E. Ressler

"Innocent Angels"

Innocent angels
Alone in this world
Innocent angels
Life tumbles and swirls

No hand to cling on to, no face with a smile.
No soft cuddled moment, no whispers or sigh.

Their head full of bubbles
That burst into pain
That showers like acid
Will drive them insane

No soothing still tummy, how it thunders inside.
Like the angry blue ocean, with no place to hide.

With uncontrollable spasms
Their hands shake and they shiver
Crying out with confusion
Silent pain, silent quiver

Please stop all the sorrow
Please stop all the pain
I'm an innocent angel
Slowly going insane

Carmen Liaga

Snow

They come from somewhere up above
A little child's dearest love
They dance upon the wind and sky
While amazed eyes look and wonder why
And wonder when this magic rain
A lace, a crystal will come again
The joys they get from it they cherish
They hope that it will never perish
But when it does, they will move on
and play with other toys long gone
and when they play with toys most attracting
the snow, of course, it will be watching

David January

Point of View

Oh, once I was a birdie sitting in a tree.
Along come a pilgrim and took a shot at me.
Now I'm just a turkey a-lying in a tray.
Oh what's there to be Thankful for on this
    November Day?
Hubert P. Kelly

Today

Feel the excitement of a brand new day;
Already bright with its sunbeam's ray:
And the unseen wind is finding relief,
As it stirs to dancing each little leaf.

The flying birds are chanting their song;
Providing a melody from early dawn.
The colorful flowers are tossing their heads,
Waving a welcome from their little beds.

Tall green mountains silhouette the blue sky;
A refuge for eagles soaring so high.
However, the true beauty of a day,
Is not determined by nature's play....

But in each heart one must decide,
If Jesus' love is to dwell inside;
For He makes a day purposeful and bright,
By the power He imparts from morning to night.
Doris DeVault

Tribulations To Elations

One year ago today was a special day
  although we didn't know exactly what to say.
Our minds and hearts raced and raced and raced away
  then we knew, "oh yes!" somehow, some way

All throughout the year
  with our soul open and bare.
We had the pleasure to share
  everything, to show each other we care.

Even through trials and tribulations,
  keeping our minds in correlation.
We managed to keep each other in elations
  simply by taking Saturday vacations.

Three hundred and sixty five
  is this next year's supply.
And I'm looking forward to all its surprise
  by golly, I'm glad you're the woman in my eyes.
Elliot J. Dixon III

Tiny World

Up in the sky
Flying free like a bird
Blue sky
Blue-green water down below
Green landscape down below
Tiny house
Tiny cars
Tiny boats
Tiny people
Feel so powerful up in the sky
Feel free
Feel like in heaven
See a group of ducks flying by down below
Look over the horizon
Unbelievable how big the world is
Unbelievable how tiny I am
Marisa Ann Lalomia

Our Special Baby Boy

Oh baby dear, your birthday is here.
Although you are gone, you are still so near.
We loved you, oh so much;
Our hearts are still filled with pain
That only God can explain.
Why did He take you from us
When we had so much to gain?

From your sweet little smile
From such a frail baby child...
We learned so much from you:
How to love and to be loved.
But God loved you too.
We hold your pictures so near;
We feel we have a part of you still.

You were a special baby boy
That only a select few got to enjoy
So on your third birthday, sweet baby,
I just had to write what I felt.
Although I miss you oh so much,
I know you are with God playing and laughing and such.
Joyce Sistrunk

Friends

Friends are those who know you best and love you anyway
Although you may disagree
or act foolishly
Friends are those who stick by you
they won't betray their love for you
or themselves by lying to protect
They tell it like it is
and always wish the best for you
Friends are those who love you anyway
and those who love you are always in your presence
Anastasia Zcats

Life's Journey

The paths we choose are not
always right.
You can walk all day.
You can walk all night.
Trying to find your way.

You face four doors of emotions.
Sadness, happiness, love and hate.
Your decision needs time and devotion.
Before you choose your eternal fate.

We fear the thought of making the wrong one.
Even though it's a human mistake.
The weight of your choice feels like a ton.
Sometimes there are chances that we must take.
Denise Chiasson

"Faith In Him"

As a grain of sand sifts through time
All is lost in my precious mind.
Time is slumbering every day
With nothing to do but hope and pray.
And with each prayer up to Him.
I know He's Listening when the lights go dim!
It may take time, for my prayers to come true
But He will answer, this I guarantee you.
For God Loves us all, always and forever
And to God we are His most precious treasures.
So keep your faith and be strong
And we'll all have our freedom before too long.
John J. Young

Waiting

I will be waiting
always waiting for you to come back to me.

It may be years - and I'll shed many tears
Before your dear face I'll see.

I know that someday I'll see you
As "God" meant it just that way.
Why did he bring us together
If sweethearts we were not to stay
Why would he make me want you - each hour of the day

Why would he make me love you
If he meant to take you away.
I know we were born for each other.
My heart tells me that you see,
Darling I'll be waiting, always waiting
For you to come back to me.
   Eve Huffman

Dreamscapes

I saw you in a dream last night,
An angelic vision bathed in light,
Attired in raiment of the purest white.
The April moon you did outshine.

Sunbeams streamed through my windowpane.
They touched my eyes and stirred my brain.
The goddess of dawn broke Morpheus' chain.
Wakefulness, your form did undermine.

I left my bed with a leaden heart.
From images of love I did depart.
I ate, dressed, and then did start
To Boston town, my hours to confine.

I passed modern buildings of cold concrete,
To Beacon Hill and cobblestone streets.
Remembering that there I did entreat
A kiss, our warm lips to combine.

Night's approach brought me home, and then
Expectations of loving dreams again,
And fervent prayers for that someday when
I shall exchange my heart for thine.
   John J. Feeley Jr.

"SHE LOVED TO DANCE"

She loved to dance - and dream romance -
   An arrow was not straighter -
She waltzed and dipped - one day she slipped -
   To a passion that was greater.

She fell in love - with love itself -
   So vulnerable was she -
To men's seduction - her introduction -
   On a roller coaster spree.

They used, abused, accused her -
   Of infidelities -
Then lied, spied, until she died -
   With haunting melodies.

No one to care - no one would dare -
   Nobody's business - maybe -
But a girl was lost - her death the cost -
   They use to call her - "Baby."

God help those who turn their backs -
   On helpless girls in danger -
Come judgement day - He'll find a way -
   And consider them - "A Stranger."
   Elaine Mc Namara

Onion Patch Blues

I'm a lonely little potato in an onion patch,
an onion patch, an onion patch
When the wayside is rough
And the going gets tough
All I do is cry all day.
Don't you worry, your life is in His hands
He knows and He loves and He understands.
When you are sad He brings such peace
And it's only through the comfort
That a burdened heart can bend.
If you're plagued and vexed with worries
He'll comfort, rest and soothe you.
I'm sure that He's beside you
Every moment of the day.
If you keep God in sight throughout the day Amen.
   Helen Sak

Wordless Presence

Through the lacy pattern of a willow
   and a small fracture in a pane of stained glass,
The wind sang for me.

Whisking past a lonesome doe, grazing in a field
   and rolling with the thunder,
The wind went by me.

Touching the falcons wing with magic
   and lifting her high above the clouds,
The wind touched me.

This alone was the powerful evidence
   that wind existed...
   Andrea Medeiros

The Passing Of Your Last Day

Another day has come and gone
and again I end this day alone.
We took for granted yesterday
until suddenly it was taken away.
So many things were lost this way -
by the passing of your last day...

Each day the sun will rise and set
yet not all of our goals will be met.
People will stop and clap their hands
but for what - no one will understand.
Many debts will be left to pay -
at the passing of your last day...

Love might have been our fate
but the words were spoken a moment too late.
My feelings were kept silent by my pride
until I realized you were no longer by my side.
There was one "I Love You" left to say -
at the passing of your last day.

   I Love You!
   Jennifer McNeely

I Wish I Were A Tree

I wish I were a tree, I would shed my leaves on thee.
And if you did complain, I would do it just the same.
For as the leaves unfold, many treasures you will hold.
The positive approach which is never termed as gross.
The energy to endure which opens any door.
The happiness you need to accomplish many deeds.
The golden gift of love to fill your inner self with
   spiritual great wealth.
The fullness of your being exploding with esteem.
To share the gifts you have and eliminate all sad.
If I were a tree.
   Donna Foy Jones

A Parable Of Love (The Myth Of An Embrace)

When the morning woke, the evening fell to wonder
  and all his thoughts were turned into stone;
why must you always come to me with such wonder
  Please let me have just one little note.

As the morning played, the evening cried out his heart
  for golden light poured his songs into the sky;
why must you only play among the silver clouds
  Will you not look into my house?

So the morning stayed and the evening made some tea;
  but for a pleasant sip, her gaze is made to stray
Why must you ever yearn for love not mine?
  My heart cannot last the scorn you serve!
    Andrew Choung

If I Could

If I could fly, I would soar above the trees,
  and all my fears would float away with
  the breeze...

If I could fly, life would seem complete,
  and I would never have to walk on my tired
  feet...

If I could fly, I could go anywhere,
  and not have to stay in this place filled
  with despair...

If I could fly, I would be a hero,
  and not what people think is sometimes
  a zero...

If I could fly, it would be like magic,
  and then maybe life wouldn't seem so
  tragic...

  ..but I can't
    Audrey McDowell

The Irony Of It All It Begins At Birth

He gasps for air, and coughs a bit -
  and all that adore him will witness it.

He's always in diapers, no hair on his head -
  he cannot walk, spends a lot of time in bed.

He learns to ride a bike, a sneaks his first beer -
  becomes home coming king his senior year.

He goes to college - and takes a wife
Has children and grand kids... he's had a good life.
His hair starts to silver, his memory fades -
  his eyesight is blurry and sickness invades.
He's always in diapers, no hair on his head
He cannot walk, spends a lot of time in bed.
He gasps for air and coughs a bit...
  But there's no one ground
    to witness it.
    Dana Marie Wiggins

Courtship

A wind horsed out of the west last night
And bucked across the sky
Moaning and curling
Whistling and whirling
To woo a tranquil eye
The moon drew behind her cloud curtain of lawn
Disappearing until
Depleted of will
Wind staggered into dawn
    Eleanor Brigid Salmon

That's My Mama!

For all that she is
  and all that she's done.
The hard times she's lived through
  for her daughters and sons.
For the love she has given
  and the wisdom she's imparted,
She'll have my deepest love and gratitude
  'til from this life I've departed.

These thanks I give
  on this special day:
Thank you, Lord,
  for this woman.
Thank you, Lord,
  for Carrie Muriel.
But thank you most of all, Lord,
  for making her my Mama
  and me her little girl!
    Hope Antoniadis

Tangled in Lilies

When the table was laid out
  and all the players at the ready
Then the king gestured
  and his mother laughed
    a short, sharp bark.

Suddenly, from a finger too tense
  the string snapped
    pearls all over the place
  and his eyes
    set on the screen before him
      behind which she lay
    tangled in lilies
    her shade
    the delicate, hectic shadow
      of a cold and wooden Balinese puppet.

At the sound of a sword drawn in the distance
  someone lit a pile of sticks
  and his mother rose
    to mild applause.
    Dixie Elder

Buckle Up To The Wor'd Alpha

(Before The World Without An 'L.)

'I, buckled up one day, as 'I got into my Car-'Nal,
and as 'I started the engine, 'I lit a Ci-Gar,-Smell;

'I, said to myself, as the `Alpha' talked to Me-, 'He-'Hee,
why not place a "Bet" on 'Omega, and take a Spree-', 'She;

As 'I, shifted to 'Alpha, "Bet" said let Hrrr roll-, 'Hoo! Hoe,
for Omega is in 'A'A'R'P; 6000 Yrs. down the road Sow-'Go;

'I, was now doing 70 Yrs; on a freeway at Mid-night-, 'Might,
that is all Christ allowed me, without any Lights-, 'Sight;

It was then 'I, thought 'I had better open mine Eyes-, 'Wise,
but 'I, was '70.00 Yrs. too late, tow-ing a SEMI LIE-, 'Guide;

For in the fullness of our Gentile 'Age, we "Bet the Ment-, 'CENT,
while the Car-'in-'Nal, wondered where the Gentle Sen-t'ence went;

So Alpha said to 'A'A'R'P; your "Bet can-not save the Grave,
as Omega "Toled the Gentile "Count, May'Day, May-Day, May-Day;

Then Omega went back unto Alpha, in 24 Letters of Greek to seek,
why Car-Nal aborted heaven, as Israel finishes it in one WEEK.
    George B. Allen

Jesus Who!

Jesus who watches over me like clouds look upon the earth
And asks who prays to him
Who is a giant and teacher
Who is a lion and lamb
Whose body is made of love
Is too caring to let me down
Who tells me in my heart not to worry
Who tells me I'm right here
Whose words flow freely from his mouth
Who's going to return
When the world has ended
Who died like a forgotten lamb
All for me
A whip that burned
A crown that pierced
Blood that shed
All to forgive sin
Who asks who prays to him
Who praises him who
   Cari D. Griffin

Awakening Fields

The richness of the damp moist earth reddened with clay
and bits of dark brown
gives the appearance of readiness.

The turned soil beckoning submissively and wantingly.
Wanting to be utilized, wanting to produce and give life.

Row after row of revitalized life cries out, it is time.
After lying dormant in the coldness of winter, the earth
is now ready to yield to the farmer's gentle hand.

The rains have softened the dirt and the cultivator of the
tractor has turned each clot with tender care, leaving
waves of fresh nurtured soil waiting.

Waiting for warmth, waiting for the seed, waiting for life.
The soil to give, the farmer to take
life to live and futures to make.
   Bettye W. Ratliff

The Piano

Oh, the sound of the piano caresses my spirit...
and brings a soft smile to my lips.
I close my eyes and lightly lift into the sound.
It carries me to forever.
I am happy.
   Ardyth Brock

"Today"

Today is the day that he Lord hath made
and called us to be His own.
And how we live it depends on whether
we stand or fall.
If we live it according to His word,
We can always stand very tall,
but if we fail to obey His word,
We then are subject to fall.
But God is there, if we stand or fall,
to give us a second chance to obey His call.
So let us then be willing to follow
in His steps and be assured that He is there
to always give us help.
God hears our prayers if we are willing to repent,
that is why His Son was so willingly sent
to save us from our sins.
Then let us live today and leave tomorrow in His hands.
And pray that God will help us all to reach the promise land.
   Ida L. Miner

The Rest Of The Year

Now that the Christmas Season finally is here
And every heart is warm and full of good cheer
I take a look at the year in the past
To see if I've done anything good that would last
I see a blind man searching his way down the street
Trying to sell his brooms to people he would meet
Then I remembered a one legged man on the walk as he sat
Out in the hot sun with all those pencils in his hat
As I see him sitting bare headed in the sun
He never sold a pencil, no not even one
And the man on the corner with the sign over his head
Will work for food is what the sign said
Dear Lord, I pray to you our lives to spare
So I can have another chance to share
My love for them when I shall meet
Them again with their pencils and brooms on the street
I'll feed the man with the sign over his head
And give him some money for more food and bread
I'm going to buy a bunch of pencils and some brooms, too
So when next Christmas Season comes I won't feel so blue
   Joseph Zimmerman

"A Teddy Bear For You"

When the world has got you down
and everything's going round and round

When you think that no one cares
that's the time for Teddy Bears.

He's a friend when one's in need
and he's the very best kind, indeed!

He won't fight back or even hit
and he won't talk back, not one little bit.

So talk to this Bear, he know all the cures,
just squeeze his pot belly that's just like yours.

And don't ever lose this little Bear,
he'll give you a hug when I can't be there...
   Dorothy L. Lindsey

Sights And Sounds Of God's Love

I see the trees gracefully away
And hear the voice of God
In the breeze they do convey.
I see the brightness of the sun,
and feel the radiant heat
When each day has begun.
I see the clouds
That cover the bright blue sky,
and feel the cool dampness
of the rain as the clouds cry.
I see the flakes of snow
That God sends to let us know,
That He has spread a blanket of white
To protect the sleeping plants of the earth
Through the cold long winter night.
I see the tiny buds bursting on the branches,
Making leaves and the forest
Once more it enhances
again to sway in the breeze.
   Florence Needham

My Candidate Girl

I have a girl who's a pearl of a girl
   and her name is Leveda B.
Her eyes are a'glitter with politicking
   vigor for all the world to see

But elections come and elections go
   and voters get kinda fickle
Then comes the day, much to your dismay,
   when supporters are down to a trickle

Bee's pearls are pearls and once out of
   their shells, can never return to the sea,
But my girls curls, full of election
   perils is evermore free to be

So no matter your fate as a candidate,
   let it ever be said of thee
She was some girl, a real pearl
   a pearl of a girl was she!

Ause Brown

Mulatto

   I was walking along a stretch of dirt road
and I came upon a young mulatto woman playing a game of
     chance with five dice
   so I sat down across from her
and I said I would gamble with her
   so she said that if I lost I would have to
     marry her
and I agreed
   so we played the game
and sure enough she won
   so we got married
and neither of us had wedding rings with us
   so she gave me a purple stone
and I gave her a piece of candy
   so we were bride and groom
and I never quite caught her name
   but I loved her.

Bradley J. Fritz

I Am A Poet; Therefore I'm Free

I think or ponder, not to judge.
and, perhaps, this is why by
the poet's pen that I am blessed.

As the sea is quiet before a storm,
so doth the mask of silence enclose me.

Yet underneath that tranquil sea,
churns a storm of unknown fury.
As within me churns a streak of fire.

And when that silence shatters,
explodes a roaring wave of anger, hurt,
fury, fear of the fervor by which I write.

As when my pen moves along its way,
crashing down my hopes, dreams, pride,
or glory.

A burning flame lights upon my heart,
A passion, I myself am awed, by the
power of the poet's prose.
A spark lights my eyes for at
last, I am truly alive!
The sea calms, and I the poet, live on.

Christina Eichelkraut

Causes

As a child I felt ignored and unloved
And I can't remember being hugged
I do remember being told to shut up
Told to get out of the way
Could this be why I have no self esteem today?

I then searched for a connection to the world and found it
Through drugs and alcohol and the life around it
An outward appearance of joy was just an illusion
In reality it was just a ploy to hide my confusion
To disguise the pain of not being good enough
And not let anyone see that I wasn't all that tough.

I want to cry all the time
I don't go out much anymore
I can't believe I can be so hurt
By people who could treat me like dirt
People who should care for me
Family and such
I can't believe at my age it can still hurt so much

Faye St. Jean

I'm Not A Kid Anymore

Oh my rusty body, it's full of ache and pain
And I either stay at home or I use my walking cane.
As my life gets longer, my body gets weak and poor
I used to walk through town, but I can't do that anymore.

When I got older and my health got worse
I had to slow down because my body has that curse.
I keep getting older every night and every day
But that is how my body is and I can't change that way.

When I was younger I would lick an ice cream cone
I never thought there'd be a time when I would grunt and groan.
When I was a young child I would sit on my grandpa's lap
And when I got cold I'd wear a coat and a cap.

In my younger years of life I would work on the apple farm
And I could usually get up with a clock without an alarm.
Now I live off of medicine because my body has gotten sick
And sometimes I wonder when its clock will stop its "tic."

Joe Dunkin

"To Eunice"

"Could we be friends?" You only asked in a sweet and loving way—
And I?? I thought: "Well, sure! Why not? It might brighten up
our day!"

"Just an occasional little note," you said, "Like I write each month
or so to all my loving family, and a couple of friends I know."

"Okay, Miss," was my reply—"The ball is in your court,
But I'm really not much hand to write, and I'm kind of a silly sort—
But I'll go ahead, if you will too"—(Now I wonder, was that smart?)
I little knew what you could do to a dormant, lonely heart!

Or, was it I that stirred a heart that was perfectly content?
Did I move too fast? Did I say too much? Or were you really
Heaven sent?

Did "Mr. Cool" (same as a rule) realize what he had done?
Tables turned—a lesson learned—can there still be fire at seventy-one??

I s'pose the answer comes with time—a true love would know the way—
And a friendship that is this sublime would ripen, rich—not fade away—
Now, I don't care for things that fade—I'd rather see them grow—
'Til, blossomed full, in joy arrayed—we hear, "I love you so!!"

Henry T. Hudson

Mother

When I look in the mirror I see a little girl, naive and sane,
and I remember all the love you gave. As the years passed on,
and times changed, I felt so desperate...
and so alone; too caught up in my own world to recognize my
home. So suddenly everything was changing, where was my
mind, what was I thinking? I lost control.
You carried me through the desperation, and when
we recovered, I realized how much I cared for you.
All I could think was how sweet destiny had brought
us together. Our differences make us stronger...
A common bond between mother and daughter, with the
strength you've given me a change has been brought
before me. A skin has been shed, and I feel weak and
insecure, for this path I have never taken, and the
direction is not clear...but I see you standing beside me,
and I know you'll help see me through. And for that
I thank you.

Jennifer Elaine Harmon

Just Tell Me

Just tell me you know that we're not meant to be,
and I'll rest this desire in my heart here for thee.
So full and complete and so totally true
my very whole life I would surrender for you.

To me you are the beauty of every garden's prized rose.
The essence of flow in all poetry and prose.
That way distant star I reach for at night.
The wind under wing of a sparrow's first flight.

The water of life, on a parched one's dry tongue
the incredible beauty of the first rainbow hung.
I'd give you the moon, and the stars up above,
all substance of life; for such is my love.

I'm a dreamer it's true, I long and I wait,
I'm envisioning you before my heart's gate.
I'd open it now, too, if only I knew,
that you were for me, and I was for you.

I am ready to go, to the end even more,
for a future with you, I would go through death's door.
So just tell me you know that we're not meant to be,
and I'll rest this desire in my heart here for thee.

Jerome Lucki

Grief

I look around and see your tears
and know that you have all my fears

Some somber faces, some with smiles
each one hurting all the while

We've been left behind to carry on
without the loved one who is gone

I thank God for His loving grace
that He has put me in this place

To grieve, to listen and to hear
always knowing He is near

Somewhere in God's glorious plan
He has asked me to take a stand

So I look to the Lord for my strength and my joy
and I trust in His promise my life He will employ

There's a light at the end of this tunnel I know
and after these tears I'll find a rainbow

So don't look to the world for the secret of life
Just reach deep inside and look up with your eyes

Julee Snow

'Round The Bend

In a distant land flows a river,
And in this river is a bend.
With steadied hand and studied eye,
Schooled by daily tide and sudden storm,
The ferryman ferries his passengers
Back and forth from shore to shore
But never 'round the bend.

But once his hire
Be destined 'round the bend,
The ferryman, though sailing the same river
And returning now and then to familiar shore,
May not want to sail again
The charted course
He sailed so many times before.

Edward Zerin

The Ocean

The ocean is big
And it is quite wide
You had better watch out
For an oncoming tide
If you watch carefully
The color of the ocean-blue green
Will appear as the sparkling water
And the true beauty of the ocean can be seen
If you want to see underwater
You can do many things
You can aboard on a submarine
Or swim in the water that the ocean brings
The ocean covers
Three-fourths of the Earth
And if you take some time
You will see what it is worth

Ammara Chowdhry

Change

The confusion cycles constantly in my mind as I search for truth
and knowledge.
The change that has occurred in me is obvious to every passerby.
Although darkness prevails around me, I see the sun shining in the
distance.
My eyes are flooded with tears as I helplessly reach for your hand.
It is not there.
You are not there.
Was the happiness and security just a mirage?
As the snow melts, I count the tiny grains of sand that pass through
the narrow passage of the hourglass.
I realize the dramatic complexity of change.

Debbie Barwick

My Divine Revelation

Silently I look out my open window
   And I am content and at ease.
Before me sweeps his beautiful garden;
   Ah, the grass, the flowers, the trees.
Realization comes to me slowly but surely;
   As sure as a warm summer breeze.
God's love I see everywhere around me;
   In the air, the ground, the seas.
It envelopes my heart and wraps me in warmth;
   His sweet love that I have found.
How forsaken I've felt, seemingly all alone;
   When always about me his arms did surround.
My heart is now free, my mind now clear;
   I am acutely aware of every sound.
It matters not what had gone before;
   Knowing he's here, my heart is unbound.

Irene N. Kessler

Life Is Short

Earth's short years have passed me by
And left me all alone and blue
I do not belong, I know not why
Why in this life, I am not due
Some small token of love and hope.

It is so sad that this world is cruel
That people die and are never mourned.
When one gentle smile, one loving touch
Could mean so much and lift such gloom,
And in this moment, one could be reborn.

As children we either laughed and played
or we were the reverse and screamed and fought.
Why must there be either joy or sadness,
why cannot life hold just a little of both
Just a small ray of sunshine which cannot be bought.

We must open our hearts, our souls, our minds
fill each day to the fullest with joy and love.
Respect our fellow man, share his sorrows and triumphs.
Be a friend and lend a helping hand, if need arises.
Let our hearts be as pure and white as the feathers of a dove.
Glenda M. West

On Mind Control

A mind can make the darkest night as light as brightest day.
And, lift the sorrow from a heart that cannot find its way.
A mind can cause a mouth to speak a million words of choice.
Words that cause the tears to flow or make the heart rejoice.
A mind can change the lives of men—for good, sometimes for bad.
A mind think and work and love and also hate—how sad!
Since every person in the world possesses mind control,
Why is there hate and war and crime and trouble for the soul?
There is no answer to this question—man will never know
What makes some minds soar up above and others fall below.
A mind helps one accept this life—unjust, unfair, unsure.
And, helps the soul outlast the days and through the nights endure.
But, at the end of time we'll see all peaceful minds as one.
And, cruel others in decay for all the deeds they've done.
Geri Coats

The Whippoorwill

One night I stood upon a hill,
and listened to a Whippoorwill.
His call was crisp, loud and clear.
He called his name to who might hear.

Whippoorwill, o whippoorwill!
What is your quest? What is your will?
Whippoorwill, o whippoorwill!
Do you keep moving? Do you sit still?

What is their purpose? Where do they go?
What do they think? I do not know!
But they stay elusive as if in fright,
and call their name throughout the night.

Whippoorwill, o whippoorwill!
Do you know passion, love, or thrill?
Whippoorwill, o whippoorwill!
Why do you call your name so shrill?

Amazed, I simply shook my head.
I was growing weary and longed for bed.
But I am puzzled and will pursue it.
My nocturnal friend - why do you do it?
Ernest L. Akers

Today Son

Son, this is the today you are going away—To face the world
and make your own way—Yes, the call of the man has come
from our child—The call of the world, the call of the wild.

There has been joy as you passed this way, and sorrow and
heartache as we face our today. Our prayers and wishes
plead for success—for whatever you do, our Great God will bless.

Decent rules of the home seemed to bind you too much,
And placed you at arm's length just out of touch...
Son, as you go through that open door—with plans not to
live at home any more—Remember, you can come back inside,
Where love for our son shall always abide.

And Son, here is a motto for you I submit: "A quitter never
wins, and a Winner never quits." This applies to just living—
or running a race—For a college degree—or, just things you
will face.

Our hearts cry out to rub off the rough rocks—that will be a
part of your life of hard knocks—but Son, we can't do this,
We have gone as far as we can...We have walked the way with
our boy...You walk the way of the Man.
Ruth J. Cook

My Son Is No Longer Here

The bicentennial year,
and my son is no longer here
I raised him nineteen years shedding many a tear
We had our ups and downs but good or bad we shared
We made trips galore till his Dad became impaired
Then it seemed he changed and had to explore
I worried when he was late scared of his fate
But all to no avail
as he died, stopped at a red light.
A keep asking, why the car
that hit him traveled
At a high speed rate
didn't the driver
Know, he was tempting fate?
I have no answer, only
faith, that God will hear
my prayers and heal my hurt
For I cannot celebrate this
bicentennial year
my son is no longer here
Eddy Steen

The Final Journey

The ocean runs deep
And my soul reaches down
To the depths of my despair
As the rain falls gently on the window sill.

And my soul reaches down
Like a father to his son.
As the rain falls gently on the window sill
You can hear the sorrow in my heart.

Like a father to his son
The wind scolds the autumn sky.
You can hear the sorrow in my heart
For today I must depart.

The wind scolds the autumn sky
As the train pulls into the station.
For today I must depart
To a distant destination.

As the train pulls into the station
I reflect on how quickly it all transpired.
To a distant destination
I travel on my final magnificent ride.
Alan L. Eid

God's Love

I thought I could walk this world alone,
   And no one would ever care
But Jesus showed me through His love,
   That He was always there.

I thought I couldn't resist this world's temptations
   And would always be in its vice,
But Jesus said if I would only believe, if I would
   only believe in Christ.

Then He would take care of me,
   And never leave my side
All I have to give to Him
   Was myself to be alive.

Dead to the world's evil and strife
   And dead to satan's woe
Is all behind me even now
   While I wait for Jesus below.

I'll wait for the sweet call of Jesus
   When my days on earth are done,
Then the dear one's will rejoice in heaven
   When the Almighty Father has won.
   Donna Wilbur

"My Little Girls"

They say "thank Heavens for little girls,"
and of course, I must agree.
Just having two of them, is most precious to me.

The time we spend together,
watching them laugh and play;
sharing secrets with each other,
hoping that their closeness,
will always continue to stay!

I think about tomorrow and wonder,
who will they be, and what will they become?
Their talents, creativity and uniqueness,
have always been a special gift to me.

The smiles on their faces, and that sweet hello.
Just brings a certain sensitivity of love,
that I would never want to outgrow!

I will always be there,
forever they are in my heart.
God blessed me with two special little girls;
and I'll always thank Him,
from the bottom of my heart!!
   Charlyn O'Brien

Spring

Wake up Mother Earth, Lady Spring is here
and Old Man Winter is gone
Your drab winter dress must be cast aside
for you've worn it much too long

You're sure changing slow, Mama Earth, hurry up
Brother Man's getting eager you know
He's waited so long for you to come out
from under your blanket of snow

Come on, come on, let's rise and shine
I'm not gonna be here long
And I'd sure like to warm your cold old back
ere little Miss Summer comes on

That's better, now here's some green for your dress
and some flowers I'll leave to cheer
So anyone seeing the change you've made
will know that spring is here
   Archie G. Phelps

"Time"

Time was when the heart was young
   And on Cupid's arrows swiftly took flight
But what to do with a heart not free,
   To make known its loving plight.
Should the words be spoken or suppressed,
   When what we feel toward someone
Could mean so much happiness?
   Dorothy Moberly

The Marriage Of Science And Religion

Together they descended Golgotha.
And one asked of the other,
"Well, who created this evolution?"
In response- "Some say it was that guy," thrusting a young finger,
"the one with the thorns."
Still waiting
for Atom and Eve.
Theory, the beguiling mother of rationalism,
the wretched depriver of contentment.
"Inverse relationship!" I scream,
"Circles," I whisper.
Still waiting
in Eden (third Garden from the sun).
Faith, the honest Father of hope,
The glorious giver of life.
   Andrew Noyes

Now And Then

Once I looked upon a sky of blue
And praised the Lord for the work he can do.
I wish to graze through green fields,
and watch the farmers harvest its yields.
Long ago I fished flowing streams,
Happy with its lingering dreams.
I loved the freshness of a spring morning,
and the fowl forever soaring.
I wish today was the same.
But the world got caught in its deadly game.
Now the once proud streams flow free no more!
To my heart it is a great open sore.
I look across great bodies of water
And watch oil slicks needlessly slaughter
the fish and game that therein dwell,
As they are washed ashore by every swell.
I once lived in a proud and beautiful land,
that could have been Eden, created by God's own hand.
   Allen D. Heike

My Death

My death is straight ahead
And around each bend
In certainty I rest within his orbit.
Where in life is safety such as this?

My death shall claim each part of me
Mind, thoughts, and every cell
Nothing of me too grand or too paltry
For his embrace.
Where's a lover such as this?

My death will not reject me for my lapses
Nor praise my excellences.
My death is faithful; I will be welcome home.
How could I wish for more than this?
Death indwelling in my bones.
   Joan C. Anderson

Releasing Thyself

Before I close mine eyes to sleep,
and put away my fears down deep.
I must prepare my mind to meek,
by living my day again for critique.
I've tried real hard to state my piece,
and do I really cause such grief?
That all I've known has gone astray,
and folks I liked, I've pushed away.
It seems to me I've changed my style,
can't be bothered with the "Born to be wild."
A stable life with hopes, as days before,
and when all else fails I know I've matured.
Fret not thyself because of evil doers,
but it's hard to avoid their loving maneuvers
when growing has grown and tall thy be,
the future unknown, uninvolved are we.
Use caution in your words before you say
something uncaring that could cause dismay.
Forgiving all those who have hurt thy pride
the overly provoked spirit will subside.

K. C. Copper

Precious Moment

I wish that I could take this precious moment
And put it in a box all bright and new
Then tie it with a lovely yellow ribbon
And secure it with a little lock or two.

I'd like to keep it in that box forever
Take a peek at it every day or two
This lovely, oh so precious, precious moment
With its joy and hope, to have my whole life through!

Dorothy Ethel Vancil Ward

I Love You

I love your lips when they are wet with wine,
And red with a wild desire.
I love your eyes when the love light lies
Lit with a passionate fire.
I love your arms when the warm brown flesh touches
Mine in fond embrace.
I love your hair when the strands enmesh your
Kisses against my face.
Not for the cold calm kiss of virgin's bloodless love,
Not for me the saints' white bliss,
Nor the hearts of a spotless dove,
But give me love that so freely
Gives and laughs at the whole world's blame
With your body so young and warm in my arms.
It sets my whole heart aflame.

So kiss me my sweet with your wet mouth still
Fragrances with ruby wine.
Stay with me forever my love
And love me till I die.

Andrew Goco

A Cry From A Child

Why have you done this to me, such a sensitive child so weak
and mild. I hurt inside to think of what you've done and
just think you thought that it was fun. I will run away, I will hide
I will go somewhere unto which I can abide. Mama always told me
the grass is greener in the other direction, so that is where I will go
and get all my love and affection, not the way I was shown. To me,
the pain I felt is so unknown, I have fallen but climbed
my way up; I had to undergo so much pressure, I was confused.
I feel so dirty, so I used to pray to the Lord night and
day. Now that my prayers have come true, I hope they will stay.

Dawn Nelson

Descending the "Golden Staircase"
in the Gorge of Palisade Creek

(for Kathy)
Accustomed to the honor
And refusing to surrender it lightly,
The lodgepole pines—stalwart exclamations,
Proud yet reserved flames of dark green—
Strive up the cliffsides,
Contending with rock and snow,
But thinning until at last
Ascendent rises the dominant rock
With her sometimes handmaiden, snow,
To represent the Earth to the Sky.

Dave Hull

Eclipse

We frolicked 'til the early morn
And rode the carousel horse of love
We viewed the magnificent sunrise
It looked so vigorous, warm
I was so alive for love of you
By evening the mask fell, and your frosty words
Told me different
As did the rigid coldness of your hand
The air turned cold, and the fiery apricot
Sunset melted through grey cloud eyes full of tears
I froze, like the frozen tear on my cheek
Sunset in my eyes.

Diana Dolhancyk

"Your Brown Eyes"

'Though I've sailed across the jeweled seas
And seen the setting sun so rare.
Of all the stories, to me have been told -
Of gallant ladies and knights so bold,
There's ne'er been a gem that could compare,
With the look from your brown eyes, so fair.

Dorothy Hunt Love

All The Children

Your tousled hair lies free upon your pillow,
And soft beneath my hand. I would but touch it gently,
If only for a moment, but my hand is stayed by a sigh
And I am content to gaze upon your countenance.
You hold all my worldly treasures in your being, tousled-head.
Guard it well and when you awaken all my joys of life
Will awaken with you. In the interim, I shall guard your
Sleep from wayfarers who would try to share my queen
In her cribbed castle. May God protect you in your sleep
And when you awaken give you strength and courage to
Carry on another day!

Florence Eiser

Shades Of Gray

Some don't see the lessons in the shades of black and gray
And some don't feel that they should learn that hurting is ok
And when their darkest hour comes and they are sad and down,
some ignore the fact that it's alright
To wear a frown
And maybe if they just sat back and learned to face their fears,
they would realize they're alone
but there's no shame in tears
Then when the crying's over and the tears come to an end,
they'd sit back and realize it's ok to smile
Again

Amanda Ferguson

I Miss You

I am lonely without you dear,
and sometimes I often fear;
as if you vaguely appear
in those treasured memories I hold near.

My heart beats while I closely cherish your past presence,
which disappeared through many lessons.
You may be gone, but not forgotten
as life continues and I soften.

I miss your smile and I miss your laughter.
It seems as though I can still see you enter.
I miss your most tender face
and sometimes my heart aches.

I long to see you so I can talk to you.
I want to caress your face like I used to..
As an ascending beautiful white dove,
you had captured my love.

Catherine Garcia

A Bouquet For You

I dug up the ground, early in the spring.
And sowed the seeds, and prayed for rain.

They came up so good, and bloomed so beautiful.
I enjoyed them all through the summer.

And since you love flowers, as much as I,
I picked them and hung them up to dry.

I thought of you, as they dried,
A bouquet of flowers, I give to you.
Because I'm so proud to have a sister like you.

Juanita McIntosh

God Blessed America

Red and white stripes near a field of blue
and stars that seem to marry the two
A tempest march of a Sousa band,
sounds of courage from a promised land
Streams and rivers flowing to fields of gold
sparkled by cities of wealth untold
Different faces anguished with pain
whisper a song of freedoms gained
When young and bold and full of God's grace
we enjoyed the envy of the human race
Time has etched our divine rock
and now the Godless set our clock
Down a road our morals pave
where dreams and visions become enslaved
Down a road our morals pave
to a lake of fire and eternal grave
God blessed America
God Bless America
God save some Grace for thee

Daniel Ray Wilson

"Love"

Like silence whistling in the trees,
and mourning flowing through.
The love that was shared was not to be compared,
for tears were being ruined.
The movement was dynamic,
and spared of truth.
The stings were of rain
and so was the moon.
No one ever knows what to look for.
But now it could become,
as it is like lightning.
That strikes of love.

Jennifer Seiler

Love One Another

I want you to look at the earth from this point of heaven
And tell me if it is possible that I can feel happy.
Look at how the earth is. Does it frighten you?
As you can see, the earth is in a turmoil and is marred
from the fault of your sins.
People have forgotten that I exist and from here, from heaven
I devise all things.
I have given you a commandment, that you love one another
as brothers, but you haven't listened.
You only look at the pleasures of the world that takes you
to self-destruction. You become slaves to sin, staining
your hands by killing your brothers. I sent my Son to the
world to save you. Forgetting your conscience, you act like
animals and give in to sin.

Eugenia Santiago

Don't Take Life For Granted

I awoke this morning to a glorious bright and sunny sky.
And thanked God above for allowing me to see another day pass by.
I considered how lucky I am to have a family and a happy home.
When all of a sudden I had a thought of others less fortunate and
    alone.
How can one not think about the poor when they are living in wealth?
And how can one not think of the sick when they are in perfect health?
Many of us take our lives for granted, thinking this is the way it
    will always be.
Well troubles can plague anyone from a derelict to someone with a PhD.
They say tomorrow is promised to no one, we all know this to be true.
None of us are immune from pain or death; it is something we all go
    through.
Let's not take for granted that things will always stay the same.
Life is like having the sun shine one minute and the next minute
    changing to rain.

Gloria J. Begett

"I Dared To Dream"

My last tear has fallen into his soothing palm,
and the first good-bye has come from these fumbling lips.
    The wish, as always, has failed.
    Underneath the earth I have been placed.
    I only want one chance to explain the hurt left by the
deep mistake that was put in front of a true friend.
    Or so one thought.
    Now it's gone...
    Forever...
    I dared to dream...

Johanna L. Woodward

Untitled

Spring has come —-
And under the remaining crust of winter that
    refuses to let go
Life stir anew.
Leaves burst from their pinned-in shells;
Roots reach out with tiny tendrils exploring
    new territories
The meadows grow green and birds sing
    merrily in mating
Busily building their nests in their
    anticipation...
The jonquils and iris dance in the breezes,
    proudly displaying their gay attire.
Wild things stir from their long dormancy,
Sniffing the air and stretching their legs,
While I, humble at the sight of this great miracle,
Am grateful to be a witness to
    Spring's awakening.

Gladys Starr Campbell

Socks

When one sock in your shoe is red
And the other sock is green
Do you often wonder where
The other red or green has been?

When you put two socks in the washing machine
And only one comes up
Don't you absolutely know for sure
That the machine has gobbled it up?

If you find that sock and it has a hole
Doesn't it make you despair
That when you find another one like it
Two socks with two holes don't make one pair?

I'd like to buy my socks in threes
Or maybe go barefooty
Instead of looking for two of a kind
Now, wouldn't that be goody?

But I am sure that all lost socks
Are hanging out to dry
And you can see them if you look up
They're the rainbows in the sky.
   Joni Sack

To One I Love

I think of you when it is dawning
and the sky is streaked with red and gold,
I think of you, as the first birdling
Wings his way across the painted sky,
And I think of you, as I partake of the air
The dew-scented breath of wild blossoms, and I sigh
With exhaustion, for the morn beauty is indescribable and profound
As is my new-born love for you.
I proclaim my love for you in the morning
because like the sky, newly created, fresh and pure.
'Tis at early day-break that I long to enfold
Your head within my arms, pressing upon
My bosom your noble forehead.
'Tis when the sun illuminates the sky
That I feel enraptured and cry —
"I love you, I love you - my dearest"
'Tis then that I wish to clasp your hands -
'Tis only at early morn, that I desire and long
To kiss your lips, so that you might share the song
That enters my soul with bursting joy.
   Irene Stockman

"Easter"

I walk through a field of Lilies,
and the warmth of each petal I do touch -
there is peace bestowed within me
that I desire so much.
There is stillness in the air,
there is no sound,
but I am not alone,
it is GOD who I have found.

His presence surrounds me, this I do feel-
a light shines through the Lilies,
it is so very real.
This Easter Day he cometh to
show me the way -
to help others who may have gone astray.

He will lead me out of
the field of Lilies and I shall rejoice -
and through me another shall have peace -
another shall hear God's voice.
   Janet E. LaRue

If I Could Change The World

There would be love and peace, not war,
And the world would be a better place than it ever has been before
The hatred would all turn to love, and the hungry would be fed
And all people in the world would have a cozy bed.
The naked would be clothed, and everyone would care.
If this place existed, I wish that I lived there.

If I could change the world, the color of your skin
Wouldn't make a difference, 'cause what matters is within.
Guns would not be needed, there would be no such thing as crime.
People would not rush around, instead they'd take their time.

If I could change the world, the rain forest would not burn,
And the people in the world would finally start to learn,
That the cures for some diseases may be hidden somewhere there
And yet we cut it down as if we do not care.

If I could change the world, abuse would not exist
People would be disciplined by mouth and not by fist,
This world could not be real, but if we all pitched in and tried,
Together we could save the world standing side by side.
   Genienne Betts

Death At Arromanches, France
(Commemorating The Battle At Juno....)

The water is stilled now, the fury has died
And the young blood of England washed out with the tide....
Only the ghost hulls of ships lie here to see
To remind that England, old England is free....
England birthed her young in a sea of blood
Before reaching manhood—there they stood
Before the German guns in the sea they fought....
Thus England's honour and life was wrought...
What more could they give but life and limb....
For their love of home and the British realm?
   Jeanne Aya Duncan

Love

There was a time when we were friends
And then I came to know you,
A side of you which I didn't see,
And now I share a part of you
And you share a part of me...called love.

A love that we share between us
Is nothing the naked eye can see,
Or words can express.
When you look at me
There is nothing I have to guess.

It makes me feel like rainbows, ice cream,
Lollipops, and bells ringing,
And sometimes without the music,
I just feel like singing.

Please hold me close and not to part,
For these words are from my heart.
   Flavia V. Smith

Dad

You were my first
And only love
Always sweet as a dove
A man whose emotions ran deep
Your laugh brought tears to my eyes
Though now you're gone forever
Our memories will never diminish with time.
And so our love for each other will grow
   Joann McGowan

"And Then I Woke Up"

The crowd roared as I jubilantly raised my arms in triumph,
  and then I woke up.
As I stepped up to the podium to receive the Oscar, I...
  and then I woke up.
The sun was blinding as Cindy stepped out of the pool,
  and then I woke up.
I had the enemy in my sights as my trigger finger jerked anxiously,
  and then I woke up.
I reached the summit and the battle was won,
  and then I woke up.
A colorful plume of smoke shot out of the brass lamp as I polished
  vigorously, and then I woke up.
As the alarm sounded, I reached for the snooze,
  and then I woke up.
  Andy Murino

Sounds Of The Night

The trees were swaying in the breeze;
And then they stopped as if to tease;
Pitter, patter go the leaves;
The darkened winds begin to breathe.

The voices chant an endless song;
The notes cut short or they drift on;
In empty fields that look remote;
The sawgrass dance to every note.

Bright yellow dots freckle the sky;
They always stay lit, like a dream that never dies.
The moon looks over us as it drifts;
Like a watchman with night shift.

His light reflects on the rippling wake;
His clone appears in the crescent lake.
Many don't realize what goes on;
So soon before the crack of dawn.
  Caley Winans

Second Chance

Footsteps coming this way, I hear,
and these footsteps are coming for me, I fear.
Could it be that life passed so fast,
or could it be echoes of my past
Shh! I think I hear them at my door,
and now they are coming across the floor
A cold breeze wafts across the room,
could that be the voice of doom.
I ask its presence to grant me a boon.
It answers me, "Alright, not now but soon."
The specter turns around and mutters,
"For granting this boon, I must seek another."
  Curtiss M. Dingess

Prelude To The Annex

At The Bar

Salem was searching that night.
Amongst a jury of his peers he fostered such
Desires as go bodily unquenched, until;

Inadvertently, between courage and prop, he relumes
The guests' young Amphitryon.
Smiling and sweating, also searching, her derelict finds
Shelter from leers.

While crawling from mud on stolen fins, his that was
Charms what is, and seeks to call it love.
As perfect lies are so with truth,
Would she were fooled by a kiss than a smile.
  Jason M. Donnelly

A Softer Bell That Rings

Look to the East to begin the day
And to the West to see it close,
Live a life within each moment
For tomorrow, no one knows.
Yesterday is an old friend;
For absence does spawn fondness
To-day is but a mere acquaintance,
That memory will not caress.
We must whisper pain and cry out joy
Strive to build and not destroy.
Save our saints and praise your honest paupers;
Elect yourself and breathe your breath much bolder.
The East is but a sunrise
That starts another day.
And riches, like beauty,
Come in many ways.
So hold tight your sweet beloved;
Think not upon your purse strings;
Care not what your brother spats;
For yours is but a softer bell that rings.
  David Slack

The Earth

And to each passing day a petal falls,
And us mighty humans aren't caring.
As a wolf barks and calls,
While the Earth is wearing.
And to each passing day a tree is gone,
And more will be leaving soon,
As a hunter shoots a fawn,
While a robin sings a clever tune.
And to each passing day a species is lost,
And we are destroying their home,
As we got down rain forests at a cost,
While the animals that lived there roam.
And with each passing day the problem grows bigger,
And no one seems to care,
As people build their homes and hunters pull the trigger,
While to the Earth this is not fair.
  Carrie Griffin

"Shadows"

I sit here in my easy chair,
and watch the fire lights glow.
The flames cast shadows of faces forgotten
Memories from long, long ago.

I see the face of an innocent child.
it shines with faith and hope.
Then I watch as it slowly disappears,
Into the fire and smoke.

Then there appears a tender young girl,
Wearing her heart on her sleeve.
Plans and expectation shine in her eyes,
She's trying so hard to believe.

then a shadow appears — the largest of all.
it seems so worn and mature,
Looking so serene and familiar somehow,
I'm sure I've seen her before.

She holds her head high, not proud but content.
Smiling at the other faces she sees,
Accepting the faces of change in her life,
I hope it's the shadow of me.
  Jeanette Estep Davis

"Going Downward On An Upward Hill"

Sometimes I ponder who I am, when times are weary and rough,
and what I'd expect to see, when I finally climb the upward thrust.
I know the climb is not as easy as I seem to think,
even though I keep my prospectives high, they somehow seem to sink.

I push, and I pull, striving for the best, sometimes knowing my
efforts are dim, but, I never give up, on my upward thrust,
I might slip and trip on my hem.
Like Jack and Jill going up the hill to fetch a pail of water,
I refuse to fall, because the cause of it all, would be an endless border.

When the climbing seems to cease, and I'm not getting anywhere,
I look towards the HEAVENS, in a moment of PRAYER.

"Lord, I know you're looking down from up above,"
watching over your pathetic child. But blessed Lord, I know you
understand, because you are HUMBLE, MEEK and MILD.

All I can think about is WORLDLY things, and making it to the top,
I don't mean to be so selfish Lord, but it's only a jump, skip and
a hop.

Lord, help me to understand, and strive to know your WILL,
and that you would say, in a loving way,

"IT'S ALRIGHT TO GO DOWNWARD ON AN UPWARD HILL"

Ellie Mitchell

Searching

Am I to sing a song in life
   and what is it to be?
The song of love I sing each day
   in many tunes in many ways.
But still I know so little about so many things.

I reach the sky on this wondrous night
   with its twinkling stars and moon so bright,
and I ask myself will I ever grow
   for there are so many things
I do not know.

If there is a song in life for me,
   I ask myself what it can be.
Perhaps, I am not meant to know.
   But I will learn and I will grow!

Beatrice Held Hart

I Wonder Why?

I often sit and wonder why,
And when I wonder I start to cry,
I wonder if all things wished will come true,
But then a doubt comes and makes me blue,
I wonder if the things I dream,
Will ever come true and be for seen?
I wonder if the picture in my mind,
Will come true and he will be kind?
I wonder also when I meet this guy,
Will he even be worth a try?
I just wonder and hope to see,
If he will possibly marry me?
Maybe I wonder just too much,
But it doesn't hurt when it's the heart that you touch.
Maybe soon someday I will find,
This man who I wonder of in my mind?
The future maybe to far to see,
But I like to wonder what will happen to me?

Julie Granger

Remembrance

I cannot understand when you say it "MOTHER"
and why your eyes turn soft with a knowing smile.
I cannot understand it and I cannot smile it - it's your smile.
Neither can I weep.
Who could weep for what he never really possessed?

I am standing at a grave.
I see dark letters furrowing the harsh brightness of marble
and flowers bowing gravely towards the earth
and I attempt to believe that this grave never was,
instead I would have your smile.
But I cannot.

Sometimes, nestled into the summer grass,
I lie and dream under the blue summer sky.
It is so quiet,
only the soothing, velvety humming of bees.
And suddenly, it seems, a gentle, forgotten melody drifting
   from far, far away,
and eyes are looking at me, loving and warm
and I remember - she had blue eyes - my mother.

Irmgard Parrington

As Snow Reigned Upon A Mirrored Lake

At dawn, we awoke to such a surprise,
And wondered, had God made a mistake?
A chain of mallards swam upstream,
As snow reigned upon a mirrored lake.

The pussy willows took stage of the corner,
Boastfully announcing the coming of spring,
But gazing out of the picture window...
Were stark realities, of another thing!

May was approaching, within a week,
Yet the woods stood dusted, in cotton masses.
Could it be, He wanted one last show...
Before His spring, of bright, green grasses?

Our yellow dog ran for a stick,
While a snowman, I attempted to make,
A scene, once captured, by Currier and Ives,
As snow reigned upon a mirrored lake.

Saddened that I'd forgotten my camera,
To arrest this memory, of time,
Guess I'll store it, somewhere in my heart
And mark it, as one of sublime.

Judith Anne Mergens

My Daughter, My Friend

I could search the world and never find
Another as beautiful, sweet and kind,
A daughter, a friend, so special to me
I pray that's the way it will always be.

Warmth and love exudes from your heart
You're something special, one set apart,
You walk in a room and everything is light
Your smile, like the sun, shines so bright.

The help, the concern, shows always in you
In the things you say and the things you do,
You are always there to lend a hand
Ready and willing with few demands.

For a more perfect daughter I could not ask
You were molded and made, then God broke the cast,
Forever thankful to Him I will be
God was so gracious, He loaned you to me.

Jean Carpenter

A Flower Without A Color

What is the meaning of Color? For it is the aspect of things
apart from the shape, size and solidity.

Yes, a flower without a color, its meaning is beyond its lowest
peaks, its highest mountain, and most of all its greatest depths.
A flower without a color signify beauty, romance, style, and
imagination from within the most inner soul. To see a flower
without a color is an Optimistic view of what our eyes hold
beyond any human imagination.

We all know Roses are red and violets are blue, but to imagine a
flower without a color is the beauty within me and you.
Stop and think ... for a while how extraordinary it will be to blow
a flower and you will see its buds and petals reach far within
many colors of a rainbow and return back to its colorless form.

A flower without a color is the crystal pearl and colorless dreams
of which my fantasy whole. I love beauty, I love peace, I love my
imagination to run free and hope on day I will live to see A Flower
Without A Color

Cheryl C. Prescott

An Ode To Life

In the dark and misty shadows of the night,
Appears a gently lambent flame
Whose glow bathes all with brilliance as the sun does so,
Creating peace and comfort by its light.

It flickers in the breeze with all its might,
Resisting winds that ever stronger grow,
Yet still the flame does ebb, its brilliance slow
And pale calm beauty flickers out of sight.

The passing of the light spreads gloom around
As death devours all sight, all sound, all life,
Or when night, the day in darkness deep has drowned.

When death does come and sorrow then abounds,
One strives to find the path of love where Heaven's found.

Deana Ghiglieri

Life

The city life and sounds of wild living
are exciting, demanding and zestful
The country style is peaceful and serene
Its nature and living life uplift your thoughts
The earth has its experience of lights and darkness
The sky, whether it's day or night, has its own tale to tell.

The spirit of each human and animal as well as
living matter has its purpose and can
tell its own story and can teach each other
of its purpose and its existence
We are here for a purpose and it only matters
that we learn to grow upward in this overall Universe.

Mrs. Grace E. Pratti

"Hope"

When the sun goes down
and the trees become tainted by its rays
darkness begins to surround
and my eyes are scared to look
but they do
and as my eyelids begin to rise
I smile
I see you higher than any bird or cloud in the sky
shining brightly
it comforts me to know
you haven't left my sight
but instead
have left me with your light

Catherine Sin

The Castles At The End Of Time

The castles at the end of time
Are filled with wine
They float endlessly in a sapphire dream of clouds
The sunshine lasts forever when you're there
And rocking horse warriors fight away the fear

The castles at the end of time
Are for lovers
They hold more joy
Than a little boy
Christmas morning
The love you have lasts forever when you're there
And they've taken away all the sorrow
So you'll never ever shed another tear

The castles at the end of time
Are in your mind
They float endlessly in a dream through you and me

Carl Weems

A New Nation A New Rule

Out of the valley between the hills southward turned
Are remnants of ages long forgotten and spurned
Past the battlefields where so many soldiers were slew
Visions of unity of the north and south with little rue

Climbing the hills past marks of American Settlers discovering the west
Gettysburg was the most crucial and severest test
Eastward toward the historic Pennsylvania battle
March the tens of thousands majestically in saddles

Lee descended from Cemetery Hill
Grant at the bottom history would fulfill
Many injured and gone their sacrifices not forgotten
Through history and folklore associated stories were rotten

At Gettysburg President Lincoln did affirm
Many of the most important platforms of his first term
Addressing a young nation courageous and meek
The president envisioned a bright future not bleak

Independence, self-reliance and rule would not fail
Endless striving and leadership were primary first to assail
American forefathers' dreams he would insure
Beyond the borders of neighboring states' doors.

Frank J. Cenna

Parent

Your words and actions survive,
are talked about by your son and his friend
under orange stone cliffs-
soft sand their bed.

Between two sleeping bags
they snuggle, smuggle through the canyons
memories native to his youth.
Memories of when he rose from the soil
and opened petals of person hood
under the sky of you - your weather
giving growth to his new shoots.

And now, below a hidden sky,
resting on the floor of time...
thoughts forced
to a vertical reach,
he whispers to his friend
his recollection
of how he became
the person he is.

Jason Gries

The Anomaly of a Kaleidoscope

The colors of the world,
are the kaleidoscope of life.
Each time the tube is turned,
another flower has blossomed
or an old oak tree is cut down.
The colored pieces of plastic,
are the pieces in the puzzle of life.
Just when you think you're piecing it all together,
the tube turns, and you have to start all over.
The cardboard tube, is the bars,
that hold you back, from fulfilling your dreams.

Ashley Briggs

The Thought Of Poetry

The thought of poetry is more than theme
Around a rhyme or meter and time.
Beyond the heart it goes, and flows its stream
Until its sense another has in kind
The feelings in their hearts that brought it 'round.
A wisp; a smoke, a joke or beauty spied
Not with the mind but with the heart that's wrought
A world of thought and feelings but implied.
And, more the thought does away; and fro is caught
In music but not music all alone
That must be played again - again be heard;
Except, alas it shall be lost and gone.
The thought plays; rises to the air a bird
That flies beyond the sight and touch to song.

Dolph Greer

the universal party ball

salamanders that dance in the moonlight know,
as do toucans toucanning to and fro
and I do believe even the tse tse fly has an inkling
that a rabbit's brassiere wouldn't suit him
just as an elm tree's naked dance with the flirting wind
are naturally
a part of our universal society.
not to mention a sea gull's lust for thermal thrust
or a cockroach's passion for post-nuclear fashion.
just all part of the tapestry,
the intricate web of delicacy
that reflects each living's role
as part of a whole picture that is not to all revealed,
to many concealed,
and yet felt, at one time or another,
to be the truth that resonates,
through and through
in fact, reverberates the dance of life, the path of each,
the joy of all.
the universal party ball.

erica horstmeyer

Our Treasure State

Have you ever been in the mountains camped against a rocky wall,
And watched the sun arising, and watched the sunset fall
While at your feet shimmering lies a lake of azure blue,
And you can smell the wild flowers wet with mountain dew.
You can smell the campfire burning, trout frying in the pan.
You can drink your coffee, hot from an old tin can.
You can see the giant glaciers of solid snow and ice
You know it's God's own handiwork that made this Paradise.
If you have never had occasion to take a line and pole
And go out in the mountains to a favorite fishing hole
Then visit Montana! Don't wait until too late
To view the shining mountains of Montana, our Treasure State

Frances Rollwitz, Age 90

Season's Way

The flowering buds of spring bring life to earth,
As does a mother to her child unborn.
A life which starts for him before his birth,
And then matures with each new passing morn.

As summer comes and child begins to grow,
Just as the fruits and plants. Soon both attain
Their full potential growth, releasing glow
Throughout the early days of autumn's reign.

As fall goes out and winter rushes in,
The snow will fall upon the barren ground.
The life of fruits and plants will then begin
To disappear. Now earth is inward bound.

As every living thing is doomed one day
To die, then let it follow season's way.

Joanne Caruso

My Farmer

I span my eyes across the field
   as far as I can see;
I hear the rattling of the old John Deere
   while he is coming back to me.

He has been up on the dykes checking the rice
   the water has been let in;
In the distance there is a spot of green
   I get excited thinking he will hold me and then...

We can laugh and cry until the day we die
   our excitement doesn't seem to wear out;
He brings me an orphaned little bunny
   I am so happy I could just shout.

The table is set and I can't wait
   for my love to come sit down;
He talks to me with dancing eyes
   He keeps my face from being a frown.

I love this man with all my heart
   we are made with an identical mold;
We look, we touch and our bodies entwine
   and our love will never grow old.

Barbara Nell Smith Dawson

The Condition We Call Love

I went and quit karate, and I had to quit kung-fu,
As for little league baseball, let me just say I'm through.

I was asked by my friends, "Why'd you quit the school play?"
I said that I'd tell them, but just not today.

School got so boring, I had to quit that,
They said go see the doctor, you and he ought to "chat."

The reason for all of this quitting must be
Ever since I met Cindy, life hasn't been easy.

You see, the day I met Cindy, and from then till today,
I've had a certain feeling which won't go away.

My heart's always pounding, my bones always ache,
And my brain sort of sits there, like a three-day-old steak.

Through my confession he sat there, his mind buzzing like a bee,
I asked what was wrong, he said, "Let me see."

The condition that you have is a gift from above,
It's contagious and permanent, it's a condition called love.

David Chapman

Crown Of Thorns

The crown of thorns pressed against his head
  as great drops of blood for us were shed.
They spit on him, mocked him all through the day;
  about this Jesus they had nothing good to say!
The purple robe to his lashed back clung
  at the foot of the cross, where he was hung.
Many hailed him as "The King of the Jews,"
  but other's scorned him, about this news!
Their King was Caesar, they served only him,
  and took the consequences for their sin.
"Crucify Him, Crucify Him" they all stood and cried!
  In agony on the Cross He suffered and died!
Do we stand with the crowd, laugh him to scorn,
  or bless the day that he was born?
Do we accept each day all His loving care,
  then forget to thank Him as we come in prayer?
He's there, waiting for those who will come,
  take up the Cross and all become one.
What greater joy than to walk at His side
  till Heaven's gates swing open wide!
God grant that we draw closer to thee!

Dolly Aumann

In The Midst

Early in the morning
As He taught those gathered there
A web was being woven, a mob of men the snare

A Pharisee?...A Scribe?
No one told his identity
But in the midst - A woman, her shame for all to see

"Stone her!" Someone shouted, "She was caught in the act"
Another tempted, "Come Jesus"
Judge the law, judge the facts

In the midst He turned His face from sin
Stooped down and began to write
They chided, shouted, beckoned, challenged Him to fight

And as the crowd stirred 'round about
(leaving the woman crushed and scorned)
He carved in the ground beneath them
Markings which have never been made known

HE THAT IS WITHOUT SIN CAST THE FIRST STONE,
He spoke. Convicted hearts departed
Some because of what He said... Or was it
what He wrote?... In the midst

Audrey C. Arrington

Human Vs. Inhuman

Anything that is human can be inspiring to the eyes.
Anything that is inhuman can be deadly and cause blindness.
We lived to see the present and future our of domestic lives.
But if we become inhuman our lives could be cut short.
The fighting within our society.
The discrimination against each other.
Because of the color of our bodies.
The neglect of our children, their cries not heard
Wishing for an angelic cherub
To come down and save them.
The killing of innocent people,
Leaving a horrible burden on a family.
People living in poverty, hoping for answers that they can't find;
Because the government traps them in an economic bind.
Our mortals are defeated by immortals.
We have to live and inspire ourselves to continue on,
Spreading the love within us when we were born.
We must become human, not inhuman.

Brent Fitzgerald

Salvation?

I hear the last sermon read
As I count on death's bell toll
Ask for religious amnesty
An inquiry, is it blasphemy

I still hear distant wailing cries
Something had to have gone wrong
Or are they merely whispers in my dreams
So loud they bring up a din in my mind

Scalpels edge outlines the dead
It left incisions in my chest
Leaving a crimson highway from my head to abdomen
Is this my salvation

Mold begins to fill my grave
Morbid dreams consume my mind
My flesh dead and inert, my face pallid and ashen
Here I rest in my perpetual hell enthroning my corpse to be

Now I reside eternally feeling worms crawl through
Impaling my empty shell
One with the earth, I commence my flesh to dirt
Only to rot and lie stinking in the earth

Chris M. Bowden

January 5th First Snow

All misty morning the lonely foghorn whined
As I lay in bed, all cozy and warm
Wishing for loving arms and sweet caresses
To be made love to and feel the fondling of my breasts.
I turned on the radio to listen to talk and songs
It was a very quiet grey morn,
Because my child was away.
This morning seemed endless and quite long,
So I pulled on my winter clothes
To venture down the street amidst the snowflakes and winds
To say 'hello' to anyone,
It's a New Year, 1980's just begun.
What had I left that's still yet to be done
Many places to go
Many new faces to meet
So - locate new places
It's the first snowstorm white.

Jone Wise

Spare A Dime

The cold air hurts, maybe more than my stomach;
As I remember when I could have lived a dream

But I know the dream is just a dream;
Nothing more than a fading memory

Could you spare a dime? Maybe two? I can take away the pain
Just a dime; no more; maybe help a fellow out?

I have nothing more than what is on my back and what travels
Through my mind, day in and day out

Can I live that dream? Do you think? Maybe not;
Maybe so? Could you spare a dime, maybe two?
Maybe help a fellow out?

Most just walk away, ignoring my dream, they don't know;
they just live their own dreams; day by day

How about that dime? Maybe two? I know I could live that dream;
I could live that dream, just like you

C. Huston Wamsley

The Pit

A natural crime a taste of time. A year in the house of hell
as I walked through the doors of division A4 onto a dismal cell. The
mattress is bad, a nightmare I had. I counted devils instead of
sheep. I was awakened by a bell from a dream which was hell. My
door opened with a bang. With a feeling of horror, I walked down the
corridor into the grim faces of a leering gang. A big wide
dayroom, which is really no playroom broken benches and junk in
the bars. Hot dogs and beans, and sick dope fines pimps.
Short stops, punks, and stars. A big wide dayroom which is
really no playroom. A cement floor, and gents, by the score.
Fresh air does not exist. There is a awful stink in the bathroom
sink. The floor is battered with dirt. The days are long the
atmosphere is strong with the scent of bodies unbathed. Suppressed
feeling by all, petty stealing and few fellows that know how to be
hawk. Farina, and otes. We must be goats dry flakes on a Sunday morn.
And a cold cut dish that will make you wish to curse
the day you were ever born. I am still alive, thank God I
have survived, I paid my debt for my theft. But many sit in gloom
and won't leave soon. They have a lot of time left.

John Damascus Spivery

"The Snail"

I stopped this moment to watch a snail
as it dragged its home like a ponderous tail.
The leaf it travelled was withered and alone,
that showed how the cold winter winds are prone.
It moved so slow as not to move at all and
my thoughts drifted to my life, past and future.
In all, I was lost in a world of dreams,
and then I noticed it had moved an inch it seems.
How it moved I could not tell, so slow it was,
not exactly a bat out of hell.
So, why a snail, why is it alive?
Is its only perception to eat to survive?
What does it know? What can it think?
Whom am I to know, for I too will be gone in
a blink.
I love my life dearly but too soon it will end, just
like my slimy and beautiful new friend.
As time races by, the more I dream of the past, and
I suppose my snail believes it is moving forward fast.

Frank J. Pietras

My Little Man

Where are you going my little man
  As you toddle down the street?
Your face aglow with wanderlust
  On unsure little feet.

You seek adventures new to you,
  And many sights so strange.
Preparing for another day
  When far from home you range.

But now your faithful watchers
  Observe your steps with care,
Your every move is censored
  So proceed as you dare.

Each step brings you closer
  To the days you're on your own.
When parents cut the apron strings
  And you face the world alone.

So learn my little fellow.
  Absorb all you can.
So life will treat you kindly
  When you become a man.

Jean Manuell

Why Did I Do It?

The water ran clear, clear as day I could see my life
As it passed away. A tear trickled down my cheek
And lightly fell into the creek.
The memories came back as bright as the sun
I could see the good times all that fun.
Her smile, her laugh, her certain glow
Why it happened I'll never know.
She left me, left me here, left me with
A lot of fear. But I left, left her first but this
This is the worst. I'm back she'll never be
Why it happened I'll never see.
I yelled, screamed, and cursed
I know it hurt her, she almost burst.
I didn't know what I was saying I was so dumb
Now all I feel inside is numb.
I was drunk, we were leaving a bar
She sat in the passenger's side
While I drove the car. The memories flash back
A tear filled my eye remembering the night
I made my friend die.

Jill Linsenmeyer

Nine Thousand, Nine Hundred, Ninety-Nine Lilies

I've always grown a garden of lilies,
As pretty as lilies can be.
So, they were fine enough for me.
But little did I know, there was one shrub I could never see.
That shrub grew a splendid rose that blossomed very slowly.
At its peak I spotted it,
But later, forgot it was there.
As I watched my lilies grow tall around me,
I saw my rose had died.
I sat in that garden and cried.
I now looked at my garden that I once thought was fine,
With a tear streaked face of disappointment.
My lilies, I thought, aren't worth a thorn off that rose bush,
But now they are all I've got.

Beth K. Jergenson

Untitled

If I could unravel the future,
assuredly, I would change nothing.
What makes life so interesting is the WAIT.

Jeff Ross

Untitled

I smelled Freedom
as she lowered her semi warmth
on buildings, trees, water

She did not duck her head,
Freedom placed her hands on Reality
embraced Reality
then led the way

Freedom chose the path not made
and made it
she pulled up stone and rock beneath her
then wiped her bloody hands

Each drop of blood formed a sticky trail
between rocks and sand
life began to form from this precious juice

Raw vegetation popping up in craggy spots
wildly growing and alive
Reality came behind Freedom
and pruned life for its growth.

Erika M. McKethan

"Recipe"

BRONZE COMPLECTED AND SMOOTH AS DARK CHOCOLATE
As slender and firm as his body, what he possesses as a man is inevitable.
There is a gentleness in his look and touch, like the calm of the dawn awakening.
His aura stimulates my presence, his thought process is precarious.
CARAMEL COATED WITH A TOUCH OF GINGER
The sensuous movement he carries pulsates my need for him.
With piercing eyes that entrance my mind, I am captured and destined to be explored.
MAHOGANY STRENGTH HIGHLIGHTED WITH EBONY
Rays of warmth radiate from his skin.
Any embrace is deeply rooted.
The strong pounding of his heart gives out secrets of his passion for me.
HOT AND SPICY, STEAMY BROWN JUICES
I have a desire to be wrapped in the moistness of his arms and smell the aroma of his being.
He is my tantalizing, delectable assortment of love.

Antionette I. Malone

The Fisher's Dream

The silken shadows dance on leaves
as sunlight flickers through the trees.
A twisted branch dips to and fro,
its gnarled tip caught in the flow.
Gently does the water ripple.
The beaver's home — plain and simple.
From grass, and twigs, and trees he's cut,
the master crafts a cozy hut.
Aloft, is heard a lonely loon.
He softly croons a wistful tune.
Beyond the lazy river's bend,
the peaceful current meets its end.
Chill waters spread through marsh and lake —
a home to countless pike and drake.
It's here the fisher casts his line
in hopes for just the slightest sign,
a dazzling lure for him will reap
a splendid creature from the deep.
Ergo, the fisher's dream will be
forever, a sweet memory.

Frieda D. Klotz

The Life Of A Wife No Longer

Be Woman; be woman till you're all over me.
Be Woman, be sweet, hot, rhythmic, woman.

Be Sister; Your brother's in town. Be little sister.
Remember he will tell mom, he always has.

Come to me in darkness, like a ghost, an apparition
of faith, soul with no body, with no flesh

Be a victim.
Be the victim of your own depression,
of the child you bore me, of society's evil ways.
Be that victim who sleeps only to wake and cry.
Be that girl that tries to take her own life, the life of a mother,
a sister, a wife

Remember Brother tells mother and mother will cry
for her lost child.
Father cries for his lost son.
I cry for my wife who is gone,
like that ghost at dawn,
like my son who has died at the hands of one who loves
no longer, who loves no one,
who loves not even her self.

Christopher L. Weston

Poetic Life...

My life is like a poem yet never does it rhyme
As surely each line changes and never keeps to time

The years go by so quickly and things I truly know
Have turned around completely, they say that's how we grow

Now I never say for certain that thus 'n thus is so
'Cause to someone it is different that's all I really know

Well poetry IS different. It varies many ways
and so it is with people...For one life is work
For another life is play

For me life takes some pondering
Like good poetry devised...
Keeps my thoughts a wandering for points that seem disguised

Though others find life different I'm sure you must agree
A poem fits description of a person just like me

Doris J. Dolejs

Burdens Of The Natural Tree

A tree, its seed is sewn, it stands alone
as time moves by day by day forever wanting to grow.

A tree, it spreads its roots into the earth, becoming one,
enveloping rock for its solid base, as it devours its
nutrients in its place.

A tree, it spreads its branches from its base, as if reaching
out into the heavens while basking in sunlight.

A tree, spreading leaves in its array as raindrops toss and
tither, leaves fall to the ground, green, gray and sometimes
withered.

A tree, oxygenates the air and shines on rainbows with its
flair, giving life and breath for all who dare to dabble
with the thought of.....a tree

George R. Bintner

Brucie

I'm a super, electrifying, spit-fire machine
As you can see, I have high self-esteem
I'm better than Swartzenegger and Stallone
Those bar-room girls won't leave me alone
My name is Bruce and I can sing
Just give me a stage and pull the string
If Madonna could catch a glimpse of me
She'd be happy, she's wild and free
'Cause this is how I really think
I do it all without a drink
'Cause in this life you get one chance
And I am going to the dance
And I am first in the human race
'Cause I have such a pretty face
And I'm as slick as greasy slime
'Cause I feel that it is my time
And I am one of the shiniest stars
They know all about my "Gig" on Mars

Bruce Marut

Jealousy

One may cross many perils within the sea of love
Beneath its tallest waves squirms the cruelest-
  Jealousy high above
This fierce wave takes over the mind of man
  Strong or weak
For jealousy destroys loves highest peak
And so my love wait- caring that we step not upon
The sands of broken shells of distrust

Fran McCartney

"World Of Pocahontas"

As I enter a world of imprisonment,
ascending the stairs to my cell,
I long to be out with the singing crickets,
where the birds fly free
and minds are greater than ever,
where no one says no,
and no one says yes;
everything is free, everyone trades.
It's the world of Pocahontas
  before the explorers.
  Angela M. Lecher

Magic Moment

What I would give for just one moment of joy
at an intersection of two wounded souls in parallel paths.
To sense, to feel, to know another's spirit
so that time and pleasure fuse
in a magic moment
that lasts into eternity.

But the dream fades as morning light
takes my awareness hostage
for the journey to mundane.
But the memory is the dream,
or better,
because the enchantment is me forever.

Dwelling in the ecstasy of the dream
transforms my companion, loneliness,
from antagonist to confidant.
And, with the transformation,
I overlook how far I've wandered
along this path or who is with me as I go.
  Carl L. Harshman

Time

What matter if our hopes grow dim—and life's a weary mile,
At best, we live for such a little while.
So, wring from every day the nectar of content,
Good toil, good food, good friends, bring sense of time
  not wasted, but well spent.
And this content, the essence of true happiness, will
  so expand,
That all the world becomes a marble in your hand.
You'll walk in gardens filled with fragrant flowers,
And spend your love in heady, golden hours-
Then, if the darkness which men fear, appears too soon,
Ah well - You've had your pleasant afternoon.
  Dorothy J. Lauletta

A Family Treasure

Dear little Lisa, a treasure of gold
Bringing such happiness to all you behold

Ten dainty fingers and ten tiny toes
Cute as a button - you sure love to pose

Chin with a dimple just like your Dad
Eyes big and blue like your Mummy had

Nose like your Grampie's and a blonde wisp of hair
Ears like a raindrop and cheeks rosy and fair

Nicest of all the girl babies you bet
Just like your Mummy when she and I met

Dear little Princess, with eyes bright and blue
Has anyone told you how much I love you?
  Charlotte B. Rollins

Darkblue Scented Iris

When we see the darkblue scented iris bloom
  at the corner of the studio

We know that Spring has come to Northridge.

The scent is subtle, not unlike lilac,
  but smells more of Spring.

The colors behind the outer petals,
   white to purple to deepblue
      green yellowgreen
   veins and shininess
     and sometimes a yellow that reads as fuzziness.
The look of the reproduced back of these iris petals is the
  closest Tiffany came to nature in his work.

We have shared these rare iris
  when we have them
with close friends,
   they are the banner of renewal
   they are the resurrection after winter
   they are the symbol of love from earth, minerals, and sky.
  Chuck Bowdlear

The Almighty

In the beginning times, he is alone in his great kingdom
At the end will remain; the glorious heir by his wisdom
From the bottom, he raised truly! the high mountains
By the night, he dims the lights for our needful rest
By the day, the sunlight making easier the gold's quest
In the mystical space, he's sustaining the birds and the clouds
Running from everywhere by his order, the wind about! He's proud
Under our weak feet, he solidified the seven lands
We'll be asked about the messengers and what did our hands
And then! Started swearing by the waters of the seven seas
All mankind, will be gathered like those pigeons peas
like curtains, he lay over and above the seven skies
He made love and hope the shields protectors of believers lives
No doubt about! He's ruling the world towards the seven days
Until! Happens the greatest even it history: The judgment's pay
Thus! Will begin the trial of the nations present and past:
From the first to the last by him! The first and the last
As long the sun is running from the east to the west by his glory
As long thanks and praises, remain the blessed anthem of his
victory...
  Bocar Dia

Untitled

And the longer train comes down the track
at the signs of a broken conductor
And tomorrow will I get some rest?
A heavy burden to bear outfoxes me in the dear, wolfish frenzy
she looks up and smiles:
"Can you stay awhile?"
I have to go lose my bodies first
strange to listen; strange to talk
to the stranger I talk and stare and he stares back
"Are you staying awhile?" "Your whole life."
Thunder is running in the nasty hills, so the clown kills
the children in the parade ground and mothers scream
while I live alone in the nothing world
send steel through my invisible head
and then maybe I'll shut up
"So you're not going to stay awhile?"
There is the grave of an unhappy boy;
toss a rose, and jump for joy
that you're alive and he is not
that you move on, and he coolly rots.
  Alex Stiner

Whose

World around good land abounds
Available measure — having pride, survive.
Those turning wheel builds, found
Towering edifice — wondering why

Lying in shadows ghosts
Wanting a loaf, demanding it toast.
Building foundations, tilling the ground
Few help willingly — seldom around.

Divide: Fight to gain pieces of pie
Have and have not killing, innocent die.
Towering edifice crumble and fall
Percentage of nothing is nothing at all.

Charles G. Harding

Evening

Walking along the beach with a soft breeze blowing
  barefoot with shoes in hand.
Hearing the song of the gulls as they dance in the air
  while the waves roll over the sand
The tall grass sways to and fro
  as graceful as can be.
And little fish dance at the water's edge
  while castles are washed into the sea.
The outline of a boat out on the horizon
  drifts silently across the setting sun.
At last a restless soul can find peace
  after a long day is done.

Christopher Dellert

Race, Can It Be Just A Word

Barely able to live
Barely able to believe.
Barely daring to dream.
Barely knowing where to run.

Tired of watching eyes.
Tired of polite no's.
So tired of (I didn't see you).
Tired of that's just the way it is. (God).

Barely able to understand.
Barely able to want to.
Barely daring to look beyond.
Barely knowing what patience will do for me. (To me).

Tired of understanding.
Tired of I don't know what you're talking about.
  Tired so tired. My people. My world.
Please take away that sick feeling.
The hammering in my head.
  God please.
  My people please.
  My world.

Judy N. Baird

Every Day

Every day I think of you,
And wonder if you know.
That what we had was more to me,
Than anything before.
  Now that we are far apart,
  I guess that I now see.
  That what we had meant as much to you,
  As it had meant to me.
Now every day I think of you,
A smile comes on my face.
I know it was fate that brought us together,
And will again some place.

Jody Hale

"Memories Of Daddy"

Fairy tales ordinarily begin with, "Once upon a time," so as not to be different, and stay with the tradition, I have chosen to do so in mine.

Once upon a time, there was a little girl,
a head full of curls, and her Daddy's only Pearl.
He would carry her upon his shoulders,
Should his Princess stumble over rocks or boulders.

Clad in cute little frilly white dresses,
lacy socks and shoes always white,
Satin ribbons always in her hair,
He was her Prince, and she, his delight.

Her eyes would a sparkle, shiny and bright,
the twinkle reflected from her father's sight.
As mirrors reflect, so did her eyes,
of her father's love, that never dies.

Once upon a time, was the yesterdays,
Today, the present, I am writing this,
but tomorrow as I read what I wrote yesterday,
is the proof, that time is ageless.

Dottie Race

Didn't Even Have A Chance

A baby didn't have a chance to run or play,
because its mother didn't want to pay.
A baby didn't have a chance to wiggle its
fingers or toes.
What a choice its mother chose.
A baby didn't have a chance to cry, whine,
laugh, or say its first word,
because its mother didn't want a third.
A baby didn't have a chance to open its eyes
or hear its first sound,
because its mother didn't want to be around.
A baby didn't have a chance to take its first breath,
because its mother wanted to be a thief.
She stole its life and hers,
of the wonders and joys it could have been.
All because she thought it might be too rough,
A baby died because its mother didn't care enough.

Elisa Maldonado

Crying For A Friend

I cried a cry that hadn't been heard,
Because no one wanted to listen.
I apologized for the things I did wrong,
But I will never be forgiven.

People will die, people will cry,
Others just won't care.
I asked someone why,
You know what they told me?
Whoever said life was fair.

So here I am, at the top,
Where I wanted to be.
I actually had friends,
They liked me for being me.

I leave you now,
Knowing you will miss me.
It has happened before,
But it is the way things are supposed to be.

Jennifer Robbins

Untitled

That day you felt so empty, though it's only just begun.
Because you've lost the person in your life who makes everything so fun.
The sacred memories and the image in your head...
All come rushing back to you while laying in you bed.
You sit and think in different worlds;
Staring in a daze.
Suddenly your life seems like a different kind of maze.
"What path do take?" you ask yourself while sitting all alone.
Without his love you wonder how you'll make it on your own.
People keep on telling you "with time" your pain will fade
But you always knew your heart would stay once your love was made.
Even much, much later your life will be as dim.
Because you still contain all the memories within.

Genia Anaya

An Irish Mother's Legacy To Her Child

So many partings you must endure
Before you can stand and face
Your true love
Destined and adapted for you
By struggles conquered.

And so many disappointments shall be weathered-
As the storms of rage and injustice swirl about.
Take shelter in endurance-
And keep bitterness at bay.

For too many stand hypnotized by grief and strife
As a deer is transfixed by light-
Unmoving-unable-uncaring...
But not you.

You, my child, shall be different from the others
You shall be cut as a multi-faceted diamond
By life's rough treatment,
It shall only shine and polish you-
Not destroy you.
Allowing you to be truly beautiful...
A shining example of humanity and legacies kept.

Joy A. Young

My Roots

Two trees not one; not one tree, two trees not one
Beginning me, me beginning, beginning me.

Top one tree me, he top tree two, top two trees we,
Seeing below, below seeing, seeing below.

Moon shining, shining moon, moon shining
She lovely, lovely he, she lovely.

Passing time, time passing, passing time
He up North, down South she, he up North.

Wanting her, wanting him, wanting her
Returns to trees, to trees returns, returns to trees.

He begging, begging he, he begging
Loving her, she loving, loving her.

She thinking, thinking she, she thinking
We waiting, waiting we, we waiting.

Eloping not telling, not telling eloping, eloping not telling
Forever together, together forever, forever together.

Passing time, time passing, passing time
Hugging her, hugging him, hugging us.

Smiling brother, sister smiling, lovers smiling
Two trees not one, not one tree two, two trees not one.

Florence G. Miller,
Daughter of Liz Elliott Grimsley
and James Doderidge Grimsley

"Your Chair"

I miss you sitting in your chair
Believe me about you I really care
My heart full of love goes with you everywhere
Where you are, my love, I am there.

Until you return, home fires will burn
Our bedroom light seems to yearn
Along with me it desires your return
Our love and happiness is my concern.

Your duty I know keeps you away
A job, your profession, that's O.K.
I promised you when our love began
I'd wait with open arms until our end.

Only you, God and I know our powerful love
God sent His love and ours from Heaven above
He gives strength to endure our sorrow
You are not in your chair tonight
I know you'll sit in your chair tomorrow.

Faye Simpkins

You Don't Know What Love Is

I have been down and I've been weak,
believe me baby, I've lost plenty of sleep.
I will not beg and I will not plead,
and I will not lower myself to my knees.

I won't miss your touch half as much as before,
and if I call, it doesn't mean I care anymore.
You keep your love because I don't need it,
it took a long while to make myself believe that.

It's only my heart not the rest of my life,
I'll start all over, but I'll be alright.
Now you think you're back after you've gone and had your fun,
thinking of me as being helpless, and the stupid one.

You admit you've done me wrong, that you won't do it anymore,
you and I both know, I've heard that same line before.
You would say anything to get back into my heart,
but when it comes to love, you don't even know where to start!

Joann Guzman

Picking The Wild Plums

The wild plum thickets grow along an old hedge post fence
Bent and gnarled, the posts still stand
They were set by Grandpa Barrow's hands
To divide his from the neighbor's land

Two tardy butterflies dip wings of parchment
In minute waltz deportment
If I would run, the bees would give chase
They are jealous of the fruit I take
Soon the sugar-sap will make its run
Coursing downward to the root's safe haven

Before the frost tastes the wild plums
I fill my shirt-waist with the sour-sweet fruit
Juice drips sticky sweet
From purple-red ones just out of reach

The ripest ones the thicket tries to keep
Hidden among dark green leaves with purple rust
Bunches of milky-purple globes
Are held fast in a thorny clutch
To be released by my fingers' touch
As August bids the thicket to disrobe

Elizabeth Buckingham

Summer

The feel of wet sand
  between my toes
the sound of waves crashing
  against the shore
the sound of the crowd
  going wild at baseball games
the way the cool water of
a swimming pool feels on a hot day
  the dream of staying up
late, sleeping late
  how a volleyball flies through the air
it all means summer
is here

Ashley Gross

Untitled

Though life binds her with its thorny limbs...
biting;

As her flesh withers and dies, her memory
engraves my heart. It is there that she lives
for eternity.

Gently, she whispers into your heart, the satin
image that love secures us.

Through mine eyes, I cannot see her...
Yet, I see her clearly as she lives on within
my heart.

And I, her child, merely a rosebud, need only yet
to blossom, knowing ...
She loves me still, and forever will.

Diane M. Krall

Little Black Angels

For those of you who are mistaken, confused or blue—There are
Little Black Angels, too!

They come when called, one by one, and sit at his feet. He tells
them of the hope, love and compassion he has for the world and
never to give up because it might be tough.

Then he blesses them, one by one, with his staff and sends them
back to the task—as morning glories, rainbows, sunshine and the
beautiful grass.

So, if there are no Little Black Angels, then there can't be any
rainbows, oceans, seas, horizons, love or peace—Beauty simply
cannot be.

Cynthia J. Miles

God's Gifts

The leaves are scattered 'neath the trees,
  Blanketing the roots from winter's chill.
And limbs sway gently in the breeze,
  While snowflakes drift to my window sill.

It fills my soul with joy and hope...
  To see God's wondrous gifts to me,
The sky, the fields... the entire scope,
  Of all I feel, touch, sense and see.

And soon on trees... buds will appear,
  And flowers and grass will start to grow.
Lambs and calves and fawns so dear...
  Will feed with the ewe... the cow... the doe.

God guards and treats nature so tenderly,
  That I'm filled with awe as I bask in His love.
How much more he must care for and think about me
  As He guides and He nurtures me from above.

Joan M. Velott

Hold The Homophone!

The English language is all wrong! Who's in charge, and who's to blame? So many words spelled differently, yet they're pronounced the same. My *nose knows flour* isn't *flower*, but what of *maul, moll, mall*? It's *cruel*! (Like *crewel* yarn, I'm tied in a *ball* and could *bawl*!)

Queens can be *thrown* from a *throne*, and broken *stairs* can cause some *stares*. Bells can *peal*, but bananas *peel*. I can *pare* a *pair* of *pears*. I can *tint* a *tent*, *jam* a *jamb*, or paint a *pail* that's too *pale*. I *see* the *sea*, but I can't *be* a *bee* nor *wail* like a *whale*.

Ladies wear *furs*; trees are *firs*. *Lead* soldiers must march where they're *led*. *Colonels* eat *kernels* of corn, but all books that are *read* aren't *red*. A *miner* might be a *minor* sailing with *crews* on a *cruise*. Sailors can *peer* from a *pier*, but they cannot get *news* from *gnus*.

I *wrap* a gift, *rap* on doors; *flee* a *flea*; *shoo* flies with my *shoe*. *To* add a *sum* may trouble *some* if *too* high To count's just *two*. *Catch* a *ketch*, see a *plain plane*, or find *sires* who are *sighers*. Songs from *choirs*, paper from *quires*; *liars* playing *lyres*.

My *sole soul* lies *bare* (It can't *bear* more). I'm *grown*, yet I still *groan*. I can't *write right* or call up my friends without a homophone!

Won plane weigh in witch two reed ore right mite bee reel grate two dew, sew aisle prey we mite knot waist moor thyme, butt meat hour knead. Wood ewe?

Barbara Kuhn

Blanket

The big, red raggedy
blanket
sits on my bed...waiting for me to come home.
It has large holes
where the fabric grew thin.
Coming home and enveloping myself
in its warmth
always brings a smile to my face.
Sometimes
when the tears flow from my eyes,
it is there to catch them.
It protects me from all the wrongdoing of others.
When my parents and I are fighting,
or my grades fall,
it listens to all my hate-filled words.
I can curse and scream, but it

Jessica Lessing

The Escape

I must have heard her calling, from deep within my heart;
Bidding me to come to her, though we were miles apart.
It had to be an angel who led me to that place
Where I first laid my eyes upon my Darling Pansy's face.

And though we'd never met before, our hearts were soon entwined
From the first time that I hugged her, I couldn't get her off my mind;
We both threw caution to the wind, and took a lot of chances
From a motel in a nearby town to New Year's Eve slow dances.

There's never been another woman who could make me feel so good
But Pansy came into my heart the way a True Love should;
She showed me how to open up, and trust, in spite of fears,
The way she says, "I love you!" is sweet music to my ears.

I hoped that we could get away before the law could find us;
To settle down in our new love and leave the past behind us;
Then someone made a phone call and the cops came rolling in,
As the T.V. cameras stood close by they returned me to the pen.

Those days we spent together were the best days of my life
But even better days are coming, for now she is my wife.
I'll have to pay for running off but there's one thing I know
My Pansy will be waiting when they finally let me go!

Barry Cutlip

Hurt

I sing of a girl who took my love away;
blond hair, brown eyes, alluring
she took him into her hell
of lies, deceit by her looks,
while I look on and cry.

I sing of my baby who loves me no more,
and lingers in her touch.
His embrace sent love through me
like a mama and her baby,
and two lovebirds who will always love.

With hungry eyes I look on
wishing it was me in his arms.
I think of the love that we both once felt,
now her cold hands have covered him.

With her eyes gazing in his
she stabs me, and watches me bleed to death.
We used to be friend, now we are foe.
Each time I try not to blow,
she took my baby, now I am dead.
    Danielle S. Dean

Innocence

A tragic rose sleeps in a garden.
Blood red - beckoning to all
"Come pick me, come smell my
sweet, beautiful nectar."
What love-sweet, unknowing love.

The tragic rose slept nice and quiet
Alone on the darkest night.
A man tiptoes softly
And springs on the rose wrapping his pale thin
powerful fingers around her delicate
vibrant red petals.
Pulling - wretching - choking all her love.
He took the tragic rose - put her in a vase.
A prison where she lived her last days.
    Julie Lawson

The Wind

Cold waves curl and
blown white surf,
froth and foam,
covers rock with a lacework
of thin, white ice.
A roar in the tops of spruces,
trees battle the unseen.
The chickadee
huddles on heaving branch,
eyes closed against bitter swirl.

Seas part and pointed bow thrusts through,
a plume of spray and snarling wind force
whip exhilarated faces.
Man plunges on, not part of forest struggle,
yet also riding perch of wood.

Feet on wood, gripping, sliding.
One succumbs and falls to forest floor,
yesterday's seed's not enough.
The other lives to test
the wind again.
    David Morse

Untitled

I awoke this morning, dreading the day
blue and gray and felt, reluctant to
be a part of the chill and dampness
without.
The chill and the dampness that conspires
to hold me a prisoners in my house.
But in a little while, I chance to hear
behind the naked gray and wet trees,
the sounds of birds and chipmunks
God's creatures you see - clearly proclaiming
His message to me
One day at a time, the bad with the good.
No prisoner will you be.
For tomorrow promises the sunshine
and the feeling of reprieve.
    Evelyn L. Bock

Reflections

I stand by the window that catches my breath
blurring an image once so clear.

I look beyond me looking back and watch the rain
try to pull memories from the ground.

I hear in the silence the cry of a boy
who wants the leaves to be crisper
and the air to be younger
and the reflection in the window to speak.

I think of a time when words came so easy
and the quiet was much less revealing
and the rain was less greedy
and slower to judge.

I sense the dark as it approaches the window
and my gaze becomes fixed on a man.
There's a tree full of leaves and
a puddle of hope and
a boy with a bittersweet smile in his eyes.
    Jason Brodeur

What Have We Done?

When I look around I see such confusion
Bombs, diseases, litter, pollution
Crime is at an all time high
In a given day hundreds of people die

But not from old age or natural causes
Shootings, murders, bombings...the world silently pauses
For a brief moment we mourn and shed our tears
But all that remains are shattered lives and deep fears

What I'd give to go back to a simpler time
When life had purpose, rhythm, and rhyme

Alas I'm stuck here and must learn to cope
With the world as it is - at the end of its rope
I pray that the children can undo what we've done
And find what it takes to make living fun!
    Jo Kizer

More Than Spoken Words Can Tell

Communication an artful tool
Born of persistence and the golden rule
Continue your mission, do your best
Speak with wisdom - hold in the rest
On bended knee you'll find a way
Hear his counsel, hear him say
Those who listen and listen well
Receive more than spoken words could ever tell
    Janice Lynn Hambrick

"Our Songs Of Silence"

I look at him, he looks at me;
both looking expectantly.
And yet, our eyes avert
as quickly as the dispersing mist
of the night.
I sing silently,
the sweet notes wafting
and floating through
the mystic veil of midnight.
Does he sing to me too?
Why then can I not hear his serenades?
I strain my ears to hear,...
is that a voice vibrating in the night?
I do not know.
I still have to wait for an answering note to my songs.
Wait, now I hear a voice...
the mysterious voice
of silence.

Cherry Lou C. Sy

Picking Softly The Sun

There was an apricot high on a
Branch where the sun said "Mine" and
Held on in possession for the longest time.

Finally, when he could stand it no longer
And he got the ladder and climbed up to possess her,
He reached out afar, and tippingly and tipped,
Over.
But reached her anyway. She, he it squished.
And stunk up his hand. Too long sweet.
Too long grand. Too long a sunning in
the midday sun.

Bruce R. Davis

Chorus

We laugh, we love, we talk all night, until the
break of day, then it's time for me to wake up
inside this prison far away, and soon my eyes
are open, as I look around my cell, then I know
I'll face another day in this prison they call hell.

I'm setting on my bed-side, thinking of these
lonely days, and hoping that tomorrow I will
hear the warden say, it's time for you to pack
up, your release came in today.
You're going home tomorrow, to your baby far a way.

Yes I'm going home tomorrow to my baby far away.

Carson Webb

Children

They are God's gift sent from heaven
  blessed onto mother's and fathers all around...

They are small bundles of love and joy
  which at birth have no limits or bounds

For those of us who want them...
  The Blessed event we await
For those of us who want them...
  sometimes we find out too late

You can give them all the material gifts,
  that mean so very little...
For what they need most of all is love... All unconditional

Time passes by so quickly... They need you more than you know
  for it's when we least expect it, it's time for them to go.

Angela Bava

Akina

Akina was an African Princess, forced to be a slave-
Brought to this country, she bore the burdens to her grave.
Her master sought her comfort many nights, and she bore his sons in
  shame; then to steal and sell those sons, her master one night came.

All night she cried, feeling afraid and alone,
She could not believe her sons were gone.
Later, that very night, her master came to receive her comfort once
  more.
Nine months later, a girl child she bore.

She looked into her child's eyes, and her sullen heart fell-
One eye was the shade of a perfect pecan shell,
The other was the shade of an ocean so blue.
Then her master came to take that baby too.

Her master quickly approached the child.
Empowered with love for her child, yet crying all the while,
The shovel she took to the back of his head.
She looked and saw her master, dead.

Akina ran down to the river bank, to see what she could see
She thought of the pain she had suffered,
and that her child would forever.
Akina held her baby tight, and jumped into the river.
Although her sons she never again did see, Akina and her baby were
  finally free.

Angela Ragin

Oklahoma's Anguish

Concrete slabs, twisted steel
Broken glass, final dreams
They stand out, for all to see
The madness, of man's inhumanity

I hear the screams, the running feet
As concrete crumpled, where once were seats
I hear the wails, the anguished moans,
I hear the gasps, of life that's gone

I hear the shrieking wails, as children cried
And frantic mothers run, with tears in their eyes
As they ran they prayed, Please Lord! Not my baby!
Please keep my baby safe

This cycle of violence, all must see
Is not a solution for the ills that be.
If anarchy is allowed in this land,
The innocent suffer, caught by the violence boomerang

Oh Lord! Why must this be?
My brother's hand hurting me
Must there be no end?
To Cain's evil seeds, striking again?

Joseph Abrahim

Best Friend

My best friend is two people, one in the same
because of them into this world I came
they taught me the meaning of life
My Dad and his wonderful wife
Sometimes I don't realize what friends they are
As I search through this life near and far
No expressions will ever let them know
that I feel as close to them as to my shadow
it's a unique relationship between me and them
it's give and take, both of us bend
I'll never forget who is my best friend.

Frank V. Covacevich Jr.

Jesus On My Mind

Woke up this morning and I was running very late.
Brushed my teeth and combed my hair.
But I did not have time to pray.

I fixed the breakfast and washed the dishes.
The children said that it was quite delicious.
I did not have time to pray.

Took the children to school and found out that the new
school goes by a different set of rules.
On my way home I had a wreck.
As I lay there in pain I remembered that I forgot to pray.

Yet, I heard a voice say, "I am with you.
I woke you up this morning and started you on your way.
I gave you food for your table so that you could be able."

On the roads there are many loops and turns;
This accident is just a little reminder as to the builder of the road.

It made me know that wherever I go or whatever I do,
Jesus is always on my mind.

Janet Levy

In My Heart

Only in this heart of hollowed oak, built from years of love and
Built from years of love and tears;
With every bump and scrape or nasty fall,
Endure each memory, recalled.

Relived at any given moment, this heart, a mother's heart,
My heart, keeps you my children
Inside its tempered walls.

Your perils, pains, loves and dreams;
Much like an attic trunk,
To hold them while they sleep.

And when we meet and time demands;
This heart will spill with joy and grief,
Those moments wakened as if in sleep,
When time allows a peek.

So when you've gone your separate ways,
To forge your fated paths;
This heart, my heart, your mother's heart,
Shall hold for you each memory new,
Inside its ever crowding space.
Dustless in its ageless place.

Charmaine Rochon

Angels' Wings

Don't cry for me in vain
But be my voice in spirit and in mind.
Don't let sadness for me remain,
For I have flown on angels' wings
Toward the sun.
Always know that I am there,
For you do not walk alone—
I am forever by your side.

Let my memory dry your tears
And let my love embrace your fears
For I will comfort you in the quiet hours of night.

Don't cry for me in vain
For I am not sad.
Let me console your pain,
For I do not hurt.
My arms surround the stars,
And my soul embraces the sky
And as I close my eyes, I smile
For I know that I will always be with you
In spirit and in mind.

In Memory of Nicole Brown Simpson
Diana M. Pash

Thoughts Of Love

We both have had battles with love,
  But believe me, my little dove,
    There could be no other—
      For it is *you* whom I give my love!

The day is long and the night so dark,
  'Tis you who makes me happy as a lark,
    Cause can't you see—?
      It's you for whom my heart tolls.

Life is like a tide.
  There's no use to run and hide.
    Can you search your heart and mind
      And believe we'll be together in time?

I love you! I love you, my dearest dear!
  Just as the dark of night adds fear.
    Please have faith in me—
      For I'm so near.

For can't you see it's you
  I need to share my life.
    So we, *together*, can face life's strife.
      I love you! I love you!!

Dennis L. Healy IV

Love Sonnet

I have always thought love poems were trash
Bunch of mush that gives me a red rash
Red as a heart in poison ivy
Its throbbing beats are pretty lively
Always going where it's not wanted
My own bravely remains undaunted
Most people would say it's just a crush
All the same I think you're really lush
I can't cut through the jungle of your mind
A sharp machete is hard to find
You don't need to know how much I care
You'd hate it that I would even dare
On my love life I'm not one to whine
A cat chasing canaries I have nine

Carl Lehfeldt

Summer Rain

Your heart feels like the rain on a cool summer's night, so breathtaking and so intense. Your love is the rain that soaks my soul.
Drenched by emotions of love and desire, the rainbow of my life has never looked so bright. Having a love so real is like looking into the sun. Overwhelming, something you need and just can't live without.
You are the star that makes my rainbow complete.
Happiness, from my head down to my feet.
You are the angel in my life and the reason why I love to go outside, in the rain.

James T. Love Jr.

Heaven Or Hell

Heaven of hell which will it be?
Both were made for someone to see.
Heaven was made for those with faith
In God above, his love, his grace.
Hell's for those who live in vein
Choose to live in threat in pain.
God gave his son, for you for me
Prepared a place for us to see.
The choice is yours, it's real, it's free
HEAVEN OR HELL, WHICH ONE WILL IT BE?

Charles Bonham

"Pop's Old Shed"

It was dark, it was scary, Pop's old shed
but me, I was noisy so I poked in my head...
There were tools, the were boxes, a couple of rakes
but what scared me the most, was I knew there were snakes
Little by little I stepped further inside
it looked like a place where the boogie men hide.
I didn't stay long, there was nothing to see,
"nothin but junk" that's what it looked like to me.
So I ran out of that shed fast as my feet would let me,
still afraid an "ole snake" would jump out and get me.

The years have gone by and my Pop is now dead,
when I went home for his funeral I went into "Pop's shed."
Same old tools, same old boxes, some old wooden tape measures
what I thought was once junk, were really "Pop's treasures."
I stayed in there longer than I ever had before,
then I took one last look as I walked out the door,
Same old tools, same old boxes, a couple of rakes.
I said my good-byes to my Pop and those snakes.

Lynn Marie Gleason

Where Love Is Hidden Fate

It's only for one to think in life
But never should one say
For what might really come by light
Could come another way
And as the world turns by night
Our love might turn by day
For our belief for what is right
Is love, joy, goodness, and happiness I pray
For style that lies in sight
Is romance in ever living grace
For looks will always show a sign
Where love is hidden fate
In destiny and way of life to find
Where stars will always lay
For beauty lies behind in time
But always in its place
For the beauty in my mind
Is true glamour of your face

Leroy James Hendershot

"It Took To Be An Adult To Be Believed"

It took to be an adult to be believed
I had these thoughts as a child and they were pushed aside by adults
But now that I'm an adult they are believed
Is it age that controls belief

When I was a child my thoughts that of an adult
Yet my child intellect hasn't changed
But maybe the majority of adults just a child
Or they couldn't or didn't have the child to believe
Didn't have the child to believe

Did it take adults my entire adolescence
To catch up with my thoughts
Those of which I still believe and use today to make those believe
Predominantly I haven't changed a thing though I'm an adult

I'm adult in disguise and probably will be for a long time now
To get the results I need maybe it's wise
To be an adult in disguise

They've caught up with my thoughts and age the reason
I'll continue my disguise to keep them believing
As a child I could pick those of no self belief
The most difficult belief of all is convincing a child

Frank P. Polancic

An Omen

Your earthly commanders honored you well
As they leveled you low,
With a twenty-one gun salute, straight
Across your bow.
With the first roll of your casket,
oh, how the wind did blow - just a second or so.
It was unlike a whirlwind,
It had its own characteristics.
It was smooth, swift and wild, just a second or so,
Just a second or so.
Oh Goodness, the swiftness of the blow.
Just a second or so. Just a second or so
It was as though "The Greatest Commander Let Us Know"
That a swift and safe journey
Was surely in tow.
Such a magnificent and divine blow
Just a second or so. Just a second or so.

Muriel D. Glaister

The Ties

The ties that bind us are unseen
But always are they felt,

For here's a child that's part of me-
Innocence - so soft, so sweet, and cuddly
It just makes my heart melt.

The ties that bind us are unseen
But always are they felt,

Especially the tragedy of the
hand you seemed to have been dealt.

The ties that bind us are unseen
But always are they felt.

As I cry and yearn to hold you
close, while beside your
tiny grave I am knelt.

Trilby Nunes

I Am Not My Disability!

I am male, I am female,
I am young, old and in between.
I have many faces, I am not a stereotype portrayal;
I am just like you a fellow human being.

You might see me as a person with crutches, walking canes or a wheelchair,
I might have a nervous tick, or utter unusual sounds, or shake or walk unsteady.
You may perceive my limited strength and therefore conclude restricted ability,
But it's not true, so please don't look at me with your piteous stare.

True, I might need some special consideration, on the job or at home,
However, through creative modification, I am efficient, conscientious and viable.
As your fellow worker, don't leave me out, don't make me feel alone.
I am here to stay as part of the work-force, it's the law and no longer deniable!

I am not trying to frighten you or fill you with solemnity.
I am just asserting myself and trying to make you aware,
That regardless of what you think, or how you see me... I am not my disability!
Earnestly try to empathize and comprehend my true meaning... be fair.

I may be hearing impaired or mentally impaired or physically challenged,
Or perhaps, visually impaired or speech impaired,
I hope you'll try to understand that... I am not my disability!
I am like you, a distinctive human being... I am me!

Benito R. Diaz (Nature Boy)

Growing Consciousness

Yet another day goes by
Yet another play
Another flashy musical
From the seeds of yesterday

I memorize my lines
And spill them out on cue
Always saying just the right thing
It's what I'm trained to do

"A little to the left-that's it
Now stand up straight and tall"
"Just do it like we taught you kid
And you're guaranteed to slay them all"

So my motor keeps on running
The myth provides the fuel
But my consciousness just keeps on growing
And one day I'll stop playing the fool

Michael Lackey 11/29/90

Self Affliction

He has broken my heart a thousand times.
I have endured needless suffering,
though the love for him prevails.
My mind is plagued with virulent images.
His captivating blue eyes
are piercing.
His luring deep voice
penetrating.
His charismatic gestures
engulfing.
Thoughts of him ignite
a merciless pain within me.
Still, I ache to be with him.
When will these lethal recollections elapse?
I pray that someday
the malignant memories of him will perish from my
sundered heart.

Nancy L. Mickels

The Search

For that elusive someone who rivets down my soul
slammed to the depths of passions
chained to the hope of love
I'll never compromise my search
For I can't lie to myself
Truth and desire
Inseparable - like flames to fire.

For that elusive someone who tugs upon my heart
pounding in blank admiration
searing at the thought of what could be
We'll heal the gaping wounds of life
Tap the wasted energy
Discovery and relief
Nurtured - like a tree to a leaf.

For that elusive someone who pulsates blood and bone
unbridled, sweaty ascension,
hot, twisted flesh of want
we'll know on first encounter
Forgotten physical revelation
The craving much hotter
Undeniable - like wet to water.

Anonymous

Passengers

The train moves swiftly through the night,
and we are snugly berthed and unaware
of trestles crossed, of mountains to our left and right,
of prairies pierced then quickly left behind.

We are amazed, when morning comes, to find that we
have come so far along a trip so recently begun.

We pass unknowing, mansions, hovels, modest homes,
makeshift lodgings of the homeless.
We do not know the joy, nor feel the anguish in
that stream of humankind through which we rush, removed
by speed, and glass, and steel from neighbors-never-met.

On through another day we fly,
Our way made easy by the work of others —
The labor of geniuses,
And the genius of laborers, assuring our comfort.

The train moves swiftly through the night,
And we are snugly berthed and unaware
A bridge is out around the bend
And we are closer than we know to journey's end!

Raymond F. Rogers

Cameron

From the moment he was born
he had the eyes of an old soul!
Life did not come easy to him
Death was so close you could almost see it.

A monumental will in a tiny tiny body.

First his heart, then his growth,
each step up the ladder a struggle to survive.

But, survive he has, with a wisdom shining
in his large eyes just waiting to be passed on.
And a smile that can break your heart at the
pure pleasure it brings!

What does he have to teach us?
LOVE! SIMPLY LOVE!

Suzanne K. Gary

My Ship And Me

My ship is going under, please don't let me go under.
I fear that more than the roaring clash and thunder.

My ship is flowing over, no one seems to care.
I can stand going down, going under I just can't bare.

My ship is going under, this I surely see.
Someone please take my hand and save my ship and me.

Oh God I know you hear my cries deep into the night.
Lord I've been forsaken, help me make things right.

I call upon you, oh Lord, for only you can see.
For those I trust so very much, have forsaken me.

Just then the heaven beamed a silent light and opened up the sky.
A voice so strong but gently said, "Yea I hear your cry."

For now you know I'm always here when others take flight and flee.
Only I, in the end, can save your ship and thee.

I allowed your ship to go down, you beckoned it not go under.
Feast your ears upon the sound, there is no clash of thunder.

Just then my ship began to rise and look as if it was new.
The Lord looked down and gently said, I present your ship to you.

So now I'll sail from port to port and share my blessing with glee.
Of how the Lord came from above and saved my ship and me.

Thelma Hendrickson

Babies Don't Stay Long...

Dedicated to my brother Floyd, sister-in-law Dorothy, and
their only daughter Debbie...whom I love very much!!
There was a time when our daughter was so small,
We thought she would never grow tall.
Then all at once we look and see,
She has out-grown our lap and knee.
The time has come and she is off to school,
Far too big for her wading pool.
Now, it's boys, a car, and the phone,
My, what little time she is at home.
Our daughter comes...but, we must let her go,
For God meant we should let her grow.
Soon she will marry and be out on her own,
And we will be left all alone.   What's this that we see?
Our daughter is back and has one upon her knee.
All at once we knew the score...
Babies don't stay long...on the floor.
It's piano, dance, and swimming lessons for our treasure,
For we love her without measure.
Our daughter is grown-up and a baby no more,
But, we will hold our granddaughter tight,
For she is on her way out the door.

Vernieca G. Weaver (Aunt Icea)

Dripping Water

Sure wish I could say something, to make you fall in love with me
I know your love is precious, cause in my world of dreams this I did see
Now everything is so real, my dream world is broken down
Just dripping water and a few cars passing by is about the only
   sound

I'd really like to talk to you, try to capture your heart
Because in this real world, I couldn't stand for us to be apart
Couldn't talk to you in my dream world, in this real one you aren't
   around
Just dripping water and a few cars passing by is about only sound

I don't know if I can make it by myself for another day
Wondering where you are at and what would be the right words to say
Being without you is hell, and maybe there isn't another chance
But I'd sure like to take you out to wine, dine, and dance
And try to tell you things, so maybe you would go another round
Can't stand dripping water and a few cars passing by being the only
   sound

Maybe before long you will feel the same as I do
And believe there is such a thing as love being true
Having faith and companionship, that is very very sound
And a house that is anchored like a fortress to the ground
And the noise of happy children running all around
So dripping water and a few cars passing by isn't the only sound

Stewart Hardesty

Happiness

Happiness is knowing:
   a joy and peace within the heart,
   comfort and assurance, only God's love can impart
The strength of his presence, through toil and strife.
The promise, the hope of Eternal life.

   Happiness is showing:
A loving concern for those in need,
   A helping hand or some Good deed.
A pride in home and country too.
   An inner glow that shines right through.

   Happiness is growing:
In grace and faith to keep us strong,
   Ability to resist the things that are wrong
In wisdom and knowledge to understand
   and patience to wait for the Master's plan.

Thelma Hicks

A Bouquet Of Truths

Here are lilac and jasmine grown in the compost of my embarrassments.
Learning has to be fun if we're going to rise from a warm bed to do it.
Seeing the world widens our thirsts so we want to drink more of life.
For the first indescribable weeks with your new baby,
   gather the money to snap your fingers for a hired helper.
Not everyone should have been a parent, perhaps not even yours.
Open to the truth of your own childhood to be truly free of shame.
Forgiveness is a steep footpath; bring cool water for a dusty hike.
TV can be an insidious addiction for us all. Get help for addictions.
Listen to yourself whether you are angry, silly, oppressed or fulfilled.
Share summer sun-warmed grasses letting them tickle your bare feet.
In winter radiant heat from a wood stove is very nearly happiness.
Don't underrate fleeing, moving, daily moments. Love whenever
   possible.
Develop friends who respect you and generally think you're a delight.
Laugh with little provocation; allow yourself to cry. Take naps as
   needed.
Eat wholesome food and rest except for exceptions. Eat when hungry.
What do you keep secret? How is it affecting you? Who could you tell?
Just as they tried to tell us, getting sexual too fast doesn't work.
Have a willingness to let go of what you hold too dearly. Avoid
   ruminating.
Our souls know these truths. We thank us for the reminder.

Leya Aum

Trail Of Tears

Tears on my heart, bloody feet, gaping holes in moccasins, legs
like lead... so tired
Run us from our summer camps, past our winter camps, to other
camps and camps
Around and over snow packed mountains, plunging valleys,
Into freezing waters, through deep forests...
Lies, all lies we're never home.

Oozing sore of grandfathers and grandmothers, babies can't cry.
Too hungry.
Fearless warriors with empty eyes, helping slow walking,
pregnant wives.

Traveling, walking. Where are we going? Why can't we stay here
or just over there?
Everyone is saying a different prayer. Our shamans had omens,
dream visions...
Alien men would come. Our life, as we'd known it, was done.
Racing from the past, running over our ancestors
Soaring to the endless ... trail.

Xennia Gittoes-Singh

My Dad

My Dad is not a rich man,
   A humble shoemaker was he.
A life of hard work he chose,
   To provide for a wife and three kids.

My Dad is not a rich man,
   Lawn mowers he fixes
And electrical switches.

Musical ability—a gift from God,
   Peace and contentment,
He's been blessed with
   Friends too numerous to count.

He shows compassion and love
   To neighbors and friends.
He's cried at the bedside of a loved one,
   Who has breathed his last breath.
He's cried at the feet of his Savior,
   Oh, what an example he has been!

My Dad is not a rich man?
   His life I have misjudged.
He is the wealthiest man I know!

Peggy L. Scott

"Wake Up Men And Women Of America"

Wake up men and women of America; speak out loud and clear before it is too late, stop listening to your crooked politicians with the lies they tell you each day; God gave you five senses, now you must use them before you begin to seal your fate; first, it's social security and other programs they claim that is at fault I say.

They won't tell you the truth of the unbalanced budget they caused so far at hand, they pass it off to anything they choose to call it in their band; they give your money to Israeli and others; when you need help none can be found, with foreign giveaway an overthrow of foreign lands, a government like this I can't understand.

Instead of giving you job opportunity, they gave you an illegal NAFTA for sure. To break up your unions and let big business move to where wages are extremely low the loss of over 200,000 jobs and more to come, walk in the light, the light is pure. Your vote put them in office but the money they get from others, and they never say no.

You must take your Country from those who would gladly give it away for money, and stop letting Israeli decide what museums will be built here in our land; they are the slick-talking politicians that you trust and they think you're funny for the so-called holocaust didn't occur, it was the falsehood of lies and a plan.

Rudolph V. Freeman

U R

U r the brightest star in a purple sky,
1 just has 2 look at your face 2 wonder why
U r an angel sent from the Heavens above,
2 share your smile, 2 discover my love.

U r the rain that washes away my sorrow
U r the color within the lines
U r an aura of mixed emotions
Only 2 be sorted out in time.

It seems all around us is so unfair,
U r light held back by darkness.
My heart with u I try 2 share,
Yet my efforts seem so hopeless.

1 day I believe it will all come true,
I keep hoping day by day
A kiss on the lips, a touch of your hand
And 2 hear u say, "I love you."

If it seems untouchable in the distance
Listen 2 your heart, and u won't have 2 look far
It is u and I who r.

Kelly Kennepp

Bronze Offerings

Lying about like soldiers in rank - except they are horizontal,
A bevy of bronze bodies, arched upward like sacrificial offerings to the Sun Goddess

Somehow I must make my way to the coolness of the ocean, through
These bronze offerings, the sun burning like hot coals beneath my feet

Wishing to remain unseen until I am safely into the water; hopeful the
Offerings will be unaware of the body of white passing among
them - but wait,
A white cloud drifts above - between the sun and bronze offerings now
They are stirring from their repose - I am seen; all eyes riveted on me

My feet will not carry me quickly enough - I have been seen, ah,
Almost there, yes, I am in the cool and safety of the ocean....

Instant relief at last, but wait, those eyes all those eyes, still
watching, no, it cannot be, they are waiting from me to emerge

How long will they watch
How long must I wait

I am sunk!!

Leah R. Moore

"Kitty's Morning"

A dash to the window, to greet the dawn,
A breath of fresh air, and a glimpse of a fawn,
'Hello' to the bird, who lives in the tree,
A sigh at the breeze, and a screech at the bee,
A thump on the bed, and a romp through the covers,
Then tearing downstairs, to wake the others,
Meow to him, meow to her,
A pet on the head, an instant purr.
A wag of the tail, a jaunt back upstairs.
On the bed I feel footprints, two tiny pairs,
A lick on the nose, a paw in my hair,
A faint meow, in my left ear,
Long, soft whiskers, tickle my cheek,
I open my eyes, and take a peek,
And whatever is it; the first thing I see?
It's the cute little puss, of Miss Boo Ki-tty.

Suzanne Goss

Collateral Damage (A Reality Of War)

In a recent high tech war,
a briefing was held to tally the score.
"All strategic targets destroyed,"
stated the general with pride.

Countered a reporter,
"Tell us of the men, women and children who died!"
Moving on to others, the question he tried to ignore.
Then surrendering to the accusing silence,
quote the general;
"Collateral Damage is a Reality of War!"

Troy Conrad

Hurting

As my beloved one departs
A chill runs through my heart
And none shall penetrate this lonely cold
Love is my weakness, ignorance will make me bold
As I look at you from across the room
I start to ache with pain
I hold back my tears, but only in vain
But you have moved on, I'm just a part of your past
If there was only a way to make yesterday last
Forgive me for my rudeness. I mean not to be callous
Forgive my rudeness, my resentment.
I mean not to be jealous
I'm so empty, so cold. I don't even think I exist
Give me something to live for
Because there's none on my list
Another day passes in my life without you in it
The torment is torture and I just cannot stand it
To love I shall no longer succumb
And to my emotions I shall be numb.

Paula A. Colaor

Good-bye

The saddest of all good-byes is that of a dear friend.
A friendship lined in silver and gold, lost within the
    depths of the afterlife.
But for you, a new life begins.
With a higher plane to travel, your spirit grows.
And a heart that overflows with grief is mine to
    see you go.
As time has passed I've come to terms, though my tears
    have yet ceased to flow.
Your pain is gone and you are well again, and happy
    as you may be,
Remember me from time to time and of the love and
    memories we shared a long, long time ago.
If only in heaven, I promise to be with you again.

Suzanne L. Mierisch-Kracke

Steely Dan

I wish I were a steely dan...
A chrome plated steam powered stainless steel dildo -
Would I find acceptance then? Perhaps...
Perchance to sleep or dream,
I sing the body electric!
But do androids dream of electric sheep?
(Small consolation to the auto f**king machine
steam powered-coal burning love machine)
"I don't think so."
Said Mr. Burroughs to Mr. Dick
(Who was listening to Valis)
Bessemer, Schnieder, Carnegie and Krupp
   don't agree.
I believe - thus, I am
Nickel - Colbalt - chrome - flint - steel
My beauty is self evident
Use me for your pleasure
But don't abuse me.
   Ralph Allen

Tip Of The Iceberg

It's a painful storm refusing to blow away
A cloudburst of sorrow streaming down your swollen face
I hear stories of abuse that go against my every grain
No excuses can be made that leave a woman in such pain

It's an eye that turns black from a temper that was lost
It's the bruise on your back from a line that was crossed
Is it meanness or weakness that makes a man lose control
Is confusion in the bleakness why some women lose their soul

An early warning you didn't stop to gauge
His threatening gestures in a fit of jealous rage
Now he smiles, says forget it, simply one of those things
Do pathetic stabs at sweetness make it better where it stings

It's the welts on your arm from a belt or a fist
It's the cries of alarm he ignored and dismissed
What happens inside that turns a man's heart to frost
What happens to a woman when she pays the final cost

From the blood on your lip to a grip that unnerves
It's the power he feels and the fear he observes
When you think it's deserved and the secret's preserved
It's only the tip of the iceberg
   Keith Steinbaum

Love In The Heartland

In the heartland, one bright spring morning
   A dastardly deed - performed with evil intent.
A bomb that explodes, with no warning
   Of the chaos to follow - not even a hint.

Help and aid came, from all the world over,
   To dig and to search - and remove the rubble.
To pray and to save all that they could.
   Then having to accept - and mourn those they should.

In a world being torn asunder,
   One filled with hate, fear, distrust, greed and plunder;
A strength was born - that's healing our world,
   A strength being fueled - by compassion and love.

Angels gathered in heaven above
   To gaze below, at a new world, filled with love.
Love is knitting our hearts together,
   The future to come - shows only fair weather.

God's plan is so all great and mighty,
   We mortals cannot possibly comprehend.
But overall, He's saving our world,
   So that only - He and Love - might reign again.
   Opal Gibson

"Desire"

Drive me wild, like a storm chiseled in the sky on
a deserted night. Allow your emotions to precipitate
in our body movements, and impel this desire to
the limits of time. May you keep your eyes open
and watch the beauty of two people collide in
the battle of love and possession. And within
midnight hours, a fantasy's apparition will
dance gently upon the darkness and among tender
shadows. It won't call for experience - this
moment - for my love is strong enough to devour
the winds produced by God's own breath. Your
touch is a hallucination, I do believe, for it
puts me out of my mind and causes me to love
you endlessly. Rest your dreams in my hands
and let me feel them burn through my skin
until I hold what you hold, and know what you
know. Then the rain can meld our hearts into
one and wash them into eternity's imperceptible
soul.
   Marty Mohr

New Day

I've a feeling of emptiness,
A feeling of sorrow and sadness.
The sound of gone,
echoing through the dawn;
never returning,
gone and forever burning.
Ghosts of the night slipping away,
Leaving to haunt a new day.
Time passes by,
A small light spreads over the sky.
As the night turns to day,
All our fears seem to whisper away.
The ghosts of the dark slowly disappear,
and the brightness of day comes quite near.
Ghosts of the night slipping away,
leaving to haunt a new day.
   Rachel Nichols

Gentle Silence

A gentle, loving hand holds mine,
A gentle stroke upon my cheek
The world's shut out, nor is there any sign,
Or need to hear another speak.
The silence envelops me,
And holds no threat, but gentleness.
Velvet blackness, smooth to see,
Soft to touch; the wind is a caress.

The foaming, booming surf intrudes; it roars
The world's back in, unwanted guest.
The gull spreads its wings with threat of sound and soars,
Borne on the wind, rushing west.
   Marlene Baron

Kitty Kat

Kitty Kat can be asleep in her chair,
A chair large enough to hold just her,
Her round little body fits in there,
And you smile — All for love of Kitty Kat!

Always one ear stands at attention,
The better to hear you with, my dear!
She keeps her world in order - no intervention,
Please. You obey. All for love of Kitty Kat!
   Ruby Nifong Tesh

The Reformation

95 theses nailed to Wittenberg's door
A firm conviction no less no more.
That he was right, on the views he held
Regarding the sale of indulgences, he felt
Let's discuss, and find, where the scriptures say,
To be free'd from sin, all you do is pay.

He knew the scriptures, he had the proof.
What Jesus taught, so he kept aloof
They never got him on the grounds of libel
It was due to his efforts we got the Bible
Now we know, what the scriptures say.
Jesus died for our sins, you don't have to pay.

This is only in part an explanation
What history calls the reformation
Indelibly inscribed on history's pages
To be studied by all in the coming ages
His famous words, will forever stand
I cannot, I will not, I shall not, recant.

Suzanne T. May

Dreams

Streaking, shrieking by,
A glimpse at the window of the speeding train.
A sheer white veil, pale hazy face sheathed in white mesh,
The smell of longing as it floats through,
Then is gone.

Everywhere, my dreams escape,
Flitting loosely across my vision,
Then darting out if sight.
Teasing, daring me, then crying for me.
While I sleep, they crowd my room,
Waiting, a cluster of tiny ants in the corner,
Staring patiently into the stuffy night.

The bold colors of the kite sail high and away in the clouds,
Thick, oozing green colliding with hot deep yellow,
Royal blue skidding into screaming red,
Tearing recklessly across the sky, dragon shape in Joseph's coat.

If there were a way to consume the colors, the dreams they enfold,
Eat them, smooth and condensed like mashed potatoes,
Inhale them, absorb them into my pores,
They would surely not dare haunt me so.

Ruth Rotkowitz

Moving On

The short time you live you go throw
a lot, but you never stop learning
and you use all that you've got, you
learn how to love and to be a better
person, you learn from your mistakes
and try to make them right, and
people will judge and call you all kinds
of names, but you should always
stay strong and love them just the
same, sometime in life you will
experience love and it could be the greatest
experience you ever dream of, but like
many dreams it may come to an end,
and all I can say is you won't always
win, so just try to move on but never
stop loving, because if you do, you
may grow to be old and very lonely, so
always live your life and live it
to the fullest, be independent and
strong and keep moving on.

Robbie Lee McKinney

Oh Sweet World Of The Sky

As I look across a crimson sky,
a horizon watches me as I fly,
I do not fret the stress of tomorrow,
nor do I care of my pain and sorrow,
the darkness below is of no concern,
a glance of the future is not my yearn,
I am living the moment, care-free and strong,
for the moment does not last at all that long,
my mind is not focused on my descent,
for landing is what I mainly resent,
good-bye moment, good-bye skies,
as I enter to a world of lies,
the life below is what's chosen for me,
not a world that is everlastingly free,
I give the sky but one last kiss,
with one last glimpse of this world of bliss

Paul Andrews

My Husband, My Love, My Friend

You are to me a breath of spring
A joyous song my heart can sing
A simple quiet little stream
A keeper of my hopes and dreams
You are my ever constant flame
How proud I am to wear your name
Through all my days and all my nights
You are my guidance, my ray of light
You are my shelter when life threatens harm
A cool safe harbor in the storm
You've never failed to ease my fears
You've been my friend through all these years
And as the years go steadily by
I feel your love there by my side
And as our time grows to an end
I know I'd gladly choose you all over again
My husband, my love, my friend

Marie B. Harris

Untitled

BENJAMIN KUBELSKI at the age of Eighty is dead.
A life of fun and laughter for millions he has lead.
For the last forty-one years he was "THIRTY NINE"
"I WON'T SPEND ANY MONEY" - was his famous line.

As JACK BENNY he was known by one and all;
Remember, when "ROCHESTER" he used to call?
The antics of "MEESTER KIETZEL" and DENNIS DAY
Evoked his humor and chased the blues away.

When on the violin he played his "LOVE IN BLOOM"
The roar of laughter shook the walls of ev'ry room.
And yet, he played with major orchestras throughout
The world and audiences their "BRAVOS" did shout.

The World of Comedy lost a champion by his death,
I wouldn't be surprised, if with his very last breath
He didn't say: "LADIES AND GENTLEMEN, THIS IS JACK BENNY!"
Because with these words he brought joy and pleasure to so many.

When BENJAMIN KUBELSKI was born in Eighteen-Ninety-Four
Who'd dream that as KING OF COMEDY he would rule forever more?
That you rest in Peace, the whole world prays to the Almighty God
"YIS GADAL, YIS GADASH, SH'MO ISRAEL, ADONOI ECHOD!"

William Osten

Wrinkles

What is it that wrinkles really portray,
A life time of living or simply decay.
Does it reflect the joys and sorrows of yesterday,
Or does it just it mean that you're wilting away.
No I think if you're wrinkled you're lucky indeed,
Because your experiences in life, are full of past deeds.
Good or bad, happy or sad, you've been through it all,
Yet remain upright, steady, and tall.
So when you see those wrinkles on their faces,
Remember it means, they have been many places.
And though you may posses a look that is smoother,
You may never live long enough, and end up the loser.
You see, wrinkles are earned, they are not given away,
It takes a lot of living to arrive at that day.
And there's wisdom in wrinkles, you can be sure,
The longer you live, the more you endure.
So be proud of those wrinkles you may display,
Accept them, God gave them, they are really O.K.

Lou Roppolo

Treasure Chest

You came to us one morning.
A little of me,
A lot of he.
Bringing your treasure chest with you,
To which you have the only key.
Each awakening unlocks the chest,
Revealing songs or laughter,
Some smiles and tears.
Baseball champs and pizza delivery, too.
Sometimes a kiss on the leg,
Or a squeezing bear hug.
Playing train, reading books, growling like lions.
Most of all, love emerges from your chest.
Unending, unrestricted but enlightening throughout.
Darkness is closing the chest for another day.
But as you sleep, the love will grow into new treasures,
New treasures that will spring from your chest,
As tomorrow unfolds.

Melanie K. Graves

We Live In Poem

We live in a world of difference
A world of different races which clash.
The cause of violence.

We live in a world of prejudice
A world of a few unaccepting people.
The cause of others looking wrongly upon our nation.

We live in a world of jealousy
A world of rival and lack of affection.
The cause of hatred.

We live in a world of greed
A world of selfish desires.
The cause of poverty.

We live in a world of despair
A world of utter hopelessness and discouragement
The cause of desperation.

We live in a world of power
A world of ability, potential, and strength.
The cause of a better world.

Sarah Szlosek

Fallen Angel

Looking at the top of the world
A living, breathing entity
One out of millions
Such a small part of the vast infinity
I am here, the golden angel
Death comes knocking
Taking ahold of my life, my soul, my being
Destruction is inevitable
There is no escape
Taking away everything I believed in
The golden angel is falling
Seeing life through mournful, saddened eyes
Her black heart is empty, and dark... broken
Feeling only loneliness and sorrow
No more trust
No more respect
No more forgiveness
The golden angel has fallen.

Michelle M. Olson

We Once Had A Love

We once had a love
A love that was strong in its prime
But when this love came to a decline
It was like a beautiful flower dying with time.

This love I speak of was yours and mine
It's just too bad it couldn't stand the test of time.

We once had a love, a love that was real
Our love was special, like something I could feel
I like to think you loved me too
I always thought that our love was true.

But now I look back at it, when I'm feeling blue
And I smile... Oh I smile, when I think about my love for you
Now we're apart, you and I
Like two birds soaring through the sky.

Whether or not our paths will meet again
I want you to remember, I will always be your friend.
    Because... We Once Had A Love

Richard Roderman

Good Bye - Come Home

It's one AM and I'm out of bed
A sixteen hour workday lies ahead

Sixteen hours oh how I dread
I can't wait to get home back to bed

It doesn't seem fair, day in, day out
For forty years, there's no way out

It's rather funny after all this time
Five children in college, all doing fine.

And now the youngest is grown and gone
So weary am I all I could say was so long

All five have given us happiness and grief
All five are still doing well, what a relief

We worry about them, what parents wouldn't?
But they're grown now, I know we shouldn't

The grandchildren are beautiful as they should be
My wife and I vacation each year just to go and see

After all this time we're finally alone
God I wish all five would come home.

Sam Krull

My Mother

My Mother lived a wonderful life,
A loving mother and a devoted wife.

Her friends were many, she loved them all,
And was very gracious when they came to call.

Her sense of humor was such a delight;
She could make a dull day very bright.

She loved to dance, she loved to sing,
And loved a cigar at a gathering.

She could swear like a trooper,
and like a saint she could pray,
In her own angelic or devilish way.

Yes, my Mother was truly fine,
And mostly so because she was mine!

Mary Irvin

A Keepsake For The Heart

H appiness is a love like you,
A lways serene and always true,
P olite and gracious, and sound of mind,
P roper and loving, one of a kind,
Y es, you're special without a doubt,

V aliant and gentle, wherever about,
A true Christian heart, you hold your ground,
L ife is so special, when you are around,
E ver so faithful, with virtue and spice,
N ever submitting to any vice,
T ruthful and proud, distinguished and fair,
I t's always a comfort to know that you're there,
N ow in my heart, forever to stay,
E ven should I be so far away,
S o I thank the Good Lord for all that you are,

D arling and caring, God's shining star,
A nd always remember, for this I can shout,
Y es, you are my true love, without any doubt...

Jose Maria de Jesus

A Fool That Dreamed

My life is a graveyard to broken dreams.
A man living in the shadow of former things.
Reaching for the stars at night,
To wake in the morning full of fright.

I dared to dream the dream of fools,
Only to find that reality rules.
So I shrink back deep inside my soul,
And die each day while growing old.

Born on the wings of an ill wind,
Comes the Grim Reaper slowly closing in.
But I'll fight you, you fallen angel of light,
And I'll win by God and all my might.

Flee my presence and leave me alone,
So I can count my losses and try to go on.
I am a man with lofty hopes and ethereal dreams,
Who knows inside will never reach these things.

But without my dreams there remains only a shell,
A broken man that can never be well.
So shed a tear for this poor broken fool,
And watch him die slowly as reality rules.

Roy Hale

Cowboy Rap

A Cadillac, a cowboy hat and silver mounted spurs,
A Motor home, with seats of foam and rooms marked
"His" and "Hers,"
No roundup fires, no guns for hire, no covered wagon trains,
Our slim hipped rider of the purple sage, has split our golden plains.

Oh! We miss you so, as cowboys go, and as cowboys go, you went..
You swapped "Old Paint" for sixteen wheels and a brand new
"CB" set.

A concrete trail now leads you on, as you modulate with Sal,
she's a washed out version of a dance hall Queen and everybody's gal.

You'll meet each other at the next cafe, you and that gal Sal
You'll lie and brag and talk big plans, but just remember pal,
When the sun goes down and the bright lights shine,
they sure make a pretty sight,
But think of how it used to be when you kiss Ole Sal goodnight.

Adios, old friend, you're on your way, a Westerner, you're not..
For the cottonwood trees on the lone prairie....
lie under a parking lot.

Mary A. Stadtman

An Angel's Visit

The glorious vision appears from above.
A mystical being shrouded in love.
Whispers of softness caressing the sky
pilot the creature's wings to fly.
Slowly descending, radiating great light
the angel approaches nearer to sight.
Shimmering streamers of white and gold -
Oh, what a magnificent sight to behold!
To look at such beauty almost causes you pain
but you thirst for it like a flower does rain.
Ever closer you feel deep warmth and peace.
You wish that the moment never will cease.
The worldly problems crushing your spirit
all seem to disappear as you near it.
Resting a gentle hand on your brow
She calms your restless spirit somehow.
Releasing her gently, she floats ever higher
into the sky like smoke from a fire.
Farewell dear angel, tranquility's your name.
Know that all who behold you are never the same.

Kenlynn D. Amodei

Untitled

Dead grapevines entwined on a weather beaten fence
A new room gray unpainted lifeless
Rounds of wood waiting to be split.
Evergreens bent from white
Brown and green grass clumps
A half-roto tilled strip of dirt with old
Beet stems and carrot tops
Cherry almond and pear trees
Short stunted growth from frost
And leaves of red and gold falling to the ground

A black lab running through leaves
Ricocheting of fences burrowing through
The grapes to the porch and off for
Another round

I am watching this from a bedroom window
For ten years
The plants die and then live
Now I leave this childhood home.

Tim Dunlap

Lightheart Series No. 1

A perfect poem
a perfect home for
the present moment

Framed in peace
a perfect place
to honor grace

Full of ecstatic intention
and loving attention
focused on simplicity and sharing

The writing of poetry is in itself the caring
complete and rewarding
Full.

Norine Lever

Eye Call

Eye carried a raging sight, following it day and night.
A pier danced with wet. A close interject of angry thoughts in
flight. Was it wrong?
They claimed for justification, condemning a young nation.
Borrowing ideas from Fear. What was straight is now
queer with ebullition. But was it wrong?
Laugh hard and care not for the Past is forgot.
Recreate mistakes made in a dramatic nonsensical plot.
Eye soar to ask: Is it right?
In the night and day I see Eye say not with what words can.
Because a war exists as do misfits who keep not a plan.
And the stand to claim righteousness, albeit a sight that just
grows grand.
NAND AND NOR is where they score, killing the core of man.
But is it wrong?
Everyday bloodlines flow further from hips, giving in to
techno-blips. Each hour that's passed, a moment in glass, as men
become microchips. A new war has begun and it's virtually won.
Not by family ties, only metal brides - perfection with a gun.
But was it wrong, my son? Was it wrong?

Robert L. Warren

Bill Kielman

More years than you care to remember,
a quarter century the 13th of December.
But the yesteryears only seem to be
a blur of memories given to thee.
Calls have come and calls have gone,
like blades of grass on your lawn.
To those who know, parts is parts,
but try to get them on those little carts.
Tool cases, scopes dispatch and PT's,
CC that call, to all we appease.
Regions, areas and trading places,
you hope to remember all those faces.
This was just a little note to say,
Congratulations, Bill Kielman, on your day.
We are all glad that you are here,
as IBM's Service Support Customer Engineer.

Karen LaGorio

Shadows Of Me

A Stream running wild
A Mountain reaching high and strong
A Flower providing others with peace and beauty
A Falling star who's journey has ended
A Bird on an everlasting quest
A Child's laughter full of hope
A Baby's cry waiting to be held
A Bird's song being heard

Kelly A. Gracey

Why?

Why?
A question I have asked for centuries.
Why do pressures of everyday life consume our every inch of energy?
Why did someone who I cared about lose his life?
All he wanted was a second chance.
A chance to be free,
Free from an overwhelming society.

Should I feel happy that now he is free?
Is this the freedom he was talking about?
What about his second chance?
Am I the only person who seems to understand the way he felt!

Our friends were together, the class of "94."
While Fitchburg was yelling "Who Cares?"
Monty Tech was crying in tears "We Do!"

Did he drown in tears of sorrow and despair;
Or did I not do enough to help a true friend.
The friendship we had will be there forever.

Timothy, I'll be your friend to the end;
Or has the end already come?
Why?

Martin Valiton

Humanity

Humanity is a passion
a rare essence of beauty.
Like a rose petal in the wind
her beauty can never be seized.
A mere caressing of the mind
a PASSION undefined a
love that must not perish
it is HUMANITY that I will always cherish.

Robi M. Robleau

Without You

Not having you is like standing inside
a river of flames with an endless tide
although I know you'll be by my side
I'll keep on dreaming without you
each memory I hold in my mind and heart
each prayer that I pray that we'll never part
I dream that our love is a true work of art
I'll keep on dreaming without you
and when I finally have you here
I'll want to hold you close and near.
Become part of me - have no fear
because life means nothing without you.

Lisa Marie Kammerer

Attic

   A room with walls is not a room. Walls give limits.
A room with walls could only store what the walls will
allow it to store. But the attic—the attic has no walls.
It will store whatever you want it to store from birth
until death. Antiques are kept in the attic. You could exit
any room with walls at any time, but if you exit the attic,
you enter unconsciousness. In order to illuminate the attic,
the windows must be kept opened. When opened, a draft enters
the attic; sometimes a fresh draft, sometimes a toxic-ridden
draft. It is impossible for the attic to absorb only a fresh
draft. Such attics re found only in Utopia. It is possible
for the attic to absorb only a toxic-ridden draft. If your
attic does, you will either exit your attic, or force others
to leave their attics. Regardless, all of the air unites in
the attic. The wider the windows are opened, the more air
the attic absorbs.

Michael Rosenberg

Mirror, Mirror

The mirror at the dress shop played
a shocking trick on me.
I stared and could not believe
the sight I had to see.
Face to face with something I didn't
want to own.
But then these mirrors are not like
the ones I have at home.
Who wants large mirrors? There's not space
upon the wall.
Shall I mention one that's worse?
A rear view mirror down the hall.
For as I looked back - Guess what
I found?
Everyone of those lost pounds!!

Margaret Kloster

Life

What is life but a mere instance
A sparkle, a glitter in the distance
In the scheme of things, a life can be
But a speck in the eyes of humanity.

Yet wait, watch and see what is there
A life is important to those who care
For caring, sharing and above all love
Brings life like the fig brought by a dove.

We sometimes forget what it is all about
The hustle, the bustle, our feelings in doubt
Yet something will guide us to see the truth
If nothing else to help re-capture our youth.

So I guess all in all life matters so much
Like the warm feeling from a gentle touch
We all must remember, through all the strife
To cherish and keep ourselves happy in life.

J. A. Emerson

Moonlit Night

A moonlit night, no clouds in sight.
A starry night, no city in sight.
The only thing I see at night is Mother Nature in her plight.
Among the moon and stars I see Pegasus flying with glee.
Oh, how I wish that was me flying up there with such glee,
flying round the stars at night, taking in the pretty sight, coming,
going as I please, shouting out with such glee.
Half way round the earth I see, a little among the trees.
I go and see what it could be, and am amazed by what I see:
A little pond with a stream shining back, back at me,
shining back the moonlit night, the starry night and I'm in flight!
Moonlit night, no clouds in sight.
Starry night, no city in sight.
The only thing I see at night is Mother Nature in her plight,
but by my sides I just happen to see two great wings
flapping diligently...

Rebecca Almeida

Snow Outside

There's snow outside my house today.
A winter storm is on its way.
Daddy's dressed all warm and snug as he
Sits by the fire on our red and white rug.
He says, "Let's go out and play in the snow,"
His eyes shining, his face aglow.
We played and we played, we were having some fun,
But Daddy got tired and our playing was done.
As we went inside, snowflakes started to fall.
So I snuggled up in Daddy's lap and said,
"I had the best day of all."

Tiffany Thorpe

Blue Sky Sunday

It's a blue sky Sunday.
A Sunday of white blossoms and cinnamon coffee.
A Sunday where lovers eat pancakes
thick with syrup and the sun seems
to drip with honey.
In your pocket you got lots of money.
It's a Sunday where a sweet sixteen
fashion queen steps into the canteen and
comes out with a bottle of pop.
She gives it to her favorite cop.
You get the feeling that on this
blue sky Sunday, anything is possible.
On this blue sky Sunday, you could
be my dream come true.

You could be my champagne and
bubbles, and everything that marvels.
You could be my luminous sea.
You could be my emerald green island.
On this blue sky Sunday you
could be my dream come true.

Thabo William Nkomo

Essence

The ESSENCE of friendship begins with a tiny thought in your mind.
A tiny thought which you do not want to forget.
A thought which you can't forget
   of a person and of a place,
   that you would like to be.
It also begins with a feeling.
A feeling that starts deep within your heart.
A feeling of excitement each day,
   knowing you're going to see the person is
   sometimes enough.
Sometimes the unspoken feeling reaches mind to mind.
And the other person can tell exactly
   what you are thinking, and feeling,
   without you having to speak a word.
And sometimes, the essence of perfume
   will be enough to trigger a thought,
   a memory, or a feeling.
Whenever we are part, I feel a deep longing
   within my heart and soul.
A longing which only you, BILL, can fulfill.

Louise Kelley

The Ocean's Rainbow

A wave is a light drizzle in the morning dew,
a torrential downpour striking at the stained glass window.
A wave sings the cry of the wild.
It is a feather lightly caressing a rose petal.
A wave roars with sheer power and force,
it ebbs, a puppy with its tail between its legs.
It is a train rounding, the bend, bearing down full throttle...
and leaving, cloud puffs trailing off.
The power of the ancient, the tranquility of a thousand stars,
it rises and falls, pushes and pulls, tears the canvas,
seductively unbuttons the shoreline.
A cool breeze with a gale pounding behind it.
Perfection. Tainted.
An endless seam on the continuum,
it pacifies while it pummels.
Whip cream on a bouquet of daisies drifting to glass.
Forever bound, overlapping, dividing.
Finality, signifying nothing.
Consuming everything.
A wave.

Scott Chambers

Oh, Daughter Of Mine

Oh, daughter of mine lost in the past.
A whisper, a dream. Soft and sweet is she,
A beauty to behold. Silken locks of black
With skin so soft and eyes of fire - strong and alive.
A sparkle in her eyes, innocent and shy.
Where is my love? My first-born child?
A stranger to me, but closer than my beating heart.
A memory. A gleam of hope.
I close my eyes a vision to recall:
The moment of life, a tiny bundle of joy
To all who embrace her, but not mine to be
Because I love her so I will not see her grow
Nor feel her tiny lips on my throbbing breasts.
Not see her first steps nor her walk down the aisle.
I love her so that I will sacrifice my joy
For her future and her chance to succeed.
I may never know if it is to be.
Yet, in my heart and mind I love her so,
Daughter of mine.

Sandra Taylor

Love And Affection

You are so sweet, so very kind,
A woman like you, is truly hard to find,
A simple kiss in the middle of the night,
Makes everything in life seem so very right!

You are a part of my dreams,
You are the object of my hearts desire,
My heart and soul burn white hot like I'm on fire,

I know my feelings are true,
Because I yearn to embrace you,
For that my dear, is my only intention,
To shower you with much love and affection,

To keep you warm when you are cold,
To love you always, even when we're old,
To always hold a place for you in my heart,
And pray that we never, ever part.

Steven T. Keeler

Storms Of Life

Storms may come and storms may go
All kinds of storms in our life you know
Snow, hail, sleet and rain
But the hardest of all is a life of pain.

When a dark cloud is overhead
And you wonder what lies ahead
What's in this life for me you ask
Not seeing that the storm will pass.

But in one's life out comes the Son
Before all the storms in life are done
A rainbow appears in the sky
Blessing us as life goes by.

Once again we are reminded of God's word
One that we as children heard
Jesus loves me this I know
Are words that bring comfort and joy to us so.

As life goes on and you weather the storms
Don't think of them as prickly thorns
But just live each day because
Jesus is your umbrella of love.

Terry Beagle

A Place

I wish this were a world of paradise,
A world without hatred and fear.
And times when you could always have a friend so near.

A place where problems are kept behind
A place for love that you can always find
and a place where you can be happy and never low
with small flowing rivers going to and fro.

Is this place a dream? Only God will know.

I would love to walk a road that would never end.
I would love to watch some flowers grow without
someone tramping them in.
And to let it shower with rain all through the day.
But to wake and see a rainbow the very next day.

I know when I die I'll see this place.
Yes, it's the paradise I call "Homebase."
A place I will always remember.
A place I will never part.

Sherri Kay Phillips

Betrayed

They lie there like slithering snakes
about to strike. They are the most
wicked. No one is safe around them.
We should hate them and run from the
very sight of them. Instead we let
them use us, and actually have
pity upon them.
　Oh, how they sicken me! Their
words are so seductive and pretentious
that they could snare almost any
poor soul in their midst.
　Little did we know when we
befriended them that they would
drain all the goodness from our souls.
Leaving us at first, empty - then
filling us with such hateful venom
and loneliness that no prayer in
heaven could come close to healing us.
　You broke my spirit. You took
my life's blood. I have nothing left inside but pain.

Kathleen Manning

Wanting To Be Loved

Not asking to be born,
Accepting birth into this world.
A child of love, a child of innocence.
Wanting to be loved.

Years go by, step by step,
Reaching out, grasping,
Always determined to do more.
Always wanting to be loved.

A time of change, becoming the mature young adult,
Thinking of life as a major problem.
Pressure from peers, wanting acceptance to be as others,
Wanting to be loved.

On your own, facing the world,
Climbing the mountains, holding on each ledge.
Success a desired need, support a needed guidance,
Always wanting to be loved.

Each day of each new life
These things never change,
The wanting, The need,
The needing to be loved!

Patsy I. Cox

"Night's Calling"

The sun begins to descend,
Absorbed by the distant hills;
Peacefulness.

I rest in the grassy valley,
Lying on my back,
Seeing the stars slowly begin to materialize,
The moon watching over its children,
Bathing the Earth in a pale white.

I can feel my heavy eyes slowly begin to sag,
Yearning to drift away.

I struggle with them,
Not wanting to leave the serenity of the night,
And try to pry them open.

But I can't,
And my eyelids rest upon one another victoriously,
And I fall into slumber.
Sleeping to the sound of the distant owl,
Harbored by the dancing stars.

Tara Koenig

Ashes

When you were born, you began crying
Afraid of life, you wished for dying
You held your mother's hospital gown:
Ashes, ashes, all fall down.

When you were young, everything was new
Curiosity overcame you
Blood from your hand dripped on the ground:
Ashes, ashes, all fall down.

When you grew up, you drove a dump truck
One day, driving, you lost your luck
You crashed it with a mighty sound:
Ashes, ashes, all fall down.

When you died, we built a fire
Burned you on a funeral pyre
It shone from the center of town:
Ashes, ashes, all fall down.

Micah Edwards

Misunderstanding

What if your perceptions of me are wrong
After all, I don't think you know anything of me
I may be black and that's a fact
For my ancestors just like yours are African
But important to say we are of many ethnicities
Please don't misunderstand me

Born on the shores of the Caribbean
Tiny Nevis with its splendor unknown
How can you say that you know about me
My roots have been transformed by European colonies
You must check with the British about my culture
I'm in North America but not from this soil
Please don't misunderstand me

I'm proud of being black and African descent
But don't blame me because of my mentality
It's been transformed by the European cultures
I share in the suffering and poverty of black people
We must strive to change what went wrong
But it's Africa where the biggest change must come from
Please don't misunderstand me

Wycliffe E. Tyson

Susie

I found you curled in a tight circle of fur
Against the cold.
I neared and you peeked up
Your eyes were almond slits of gold.
I reached out and stroked your soft
  striped fur
And heard for the first time
Your rough and joyous purr.
Then suddenly in one quick motion
Of feline grace
You leapt up and I saw
Your tawny little lion's face.

Norma Neilsen

Harriet, Harriet

Harriet, Harriet born a slave
All her life she was brave
Harriet, Harriet worked all day—
She let nothing get in her way.
Harriet, Harriet ran away in the middle of the night,
She wasn't afraid of the cold and fright.
She went back again and again,
To help others freedom to win.
Harriet, Harriet never got caught,
Families together again she brought.
Harriet, Harriet never would mope—
You would always see her hope.
All her life she was a maid,
But when she ran, she was not afraid.
Harriet died at age 93—
But her spirit still lives in you and me

Kourtni Elizabeth Jones

Written Word

God bless and protect
All made by Mankind
He feels this is essential
In this trying time.
Water brings beauty to the Land
As does the Earth to the Trees
When Mankind destroys it all
What will bring beauty to thee?
Today is the day to fulfill his heart's needs
To subdue forever all man's Greed
Release the Anger release the Pain
Shall life itself will bring all that is to gain.
When this time comes to depart
All will fill what's lost in his heart.

Kathleen Haglund

Love

There is a light on this cold dark place,
a feeling so warm and so true;
There is a power with not just one face,
a feeling shared only by two;
There is a chance when the time seems right,
to speak the words of devotion;
There is a time; morning, day or night,
when spring forth the signs of emotion;
There is a flame that starts a fire,
one that burns long and will last;
There is a wind that will take some higher,
but a wind that moves not too fast;
There are those who are wise and smart,
knowing always what to do,
But there's only one thing that comes from my heart,
and that is my love for you.

J. Carlton Likes

Munchkins

Today is the day that she turns eight,
All of her friends have gathered for cake.
After the presents they go down and play,
By the riverside they bathe all day.
The little minnows swim over their toes,
Who will catch one nobody knows.
The inner tube is full and round,
But when it flips, to the water they are bound.
They would play fairies and climb in the trees,
They would heal one another with mud and seaweed.
After the chill of the river is gone,
They head to the house for the day has been long.
Spaghetti was served of white paper plate,
Chef Boyardee they hungrily ate.
Spilled on the table and dumped on their heads,
UFO's were launched which filled Mom with dread.
After the hands and the faces were wiped,
The bed mats were laid, and the living room swiped,
For the movie that they watched on that lively June night.
  Chloe Wierwille

A Perfect Dream

   Gliding over every inch of your mind, body, and soul
All these feelings inside and you hold my happiness as a tool

   Feeling you pulsate with every little breath
Wanting to share so much with you

   All these feelings I can only take to my death
In a weekend I feel as though I have gone through many relationships

   While my insides turn with butterflies as I close my eyes
to dream of becoming one with you by way of your full
beautiful lips

Yet my reality is that I still don't know you the way I
would like too

   And for now this is my fantasy of how I could love and
be loved

All these feelings for someone I had once known as my
feelings have changed and I have let them become estranged

   All my feelings towards you...I hope...I wish...I dream
of a time when your feelings will also die to change
and become estranged
   Michael Weinstein

Street Of Black

   Again in this solitude.
All thoughts floating mindless.
I then wonder what I am pondering.
This room is desolate, though, I will not complain.
The time is an element, outside there is rain.
The trees are being cleansed,
as well as the roses.
Inside here I lie, dry if I may.
Or shall I be cleansed as well?
I run wild,
through the paved streets.
Faces press to glass,
and they watch my mad task.
To be clean and pure,
That desolate chamber is much too dull.
This rain that bares me
refreshes my soul.
This life is really not then so harsh.
In this rain I lie, on top the street of black.
I found my heart here, beneath the black.
   Rosie Rivera

The Battle After

The fighting is over, now the battle is done.
All weapons are silent, every cannon and gun.

The fields that were green are now covered by the slain,
And we who are wounded are miserable with pain.

We relieve our despair with cursing and crying,
After we will pray for the dead and the dying.

Days of steamy agony, nights of icy hell
Both full of tortures and horrors I dare not tell.

Some men are lucky, they recover and go home.
Other men gave up and now sleep under the Dome.

Wellington was right, the battle is a sad place
Where all men are scarred, and others lose in life's race.

Now my own pain increases. My wounds will not heal.
Few are left who would know the suffering I feel.

You there Pale Rider! Won't you stop and be a friend?
Be sympathetic. And to my pain put an end.
  Thomas Newman

My Amazing Heart

My amazing heart is what amazes me so,
Although at times it beats quite low,
Then at other times it tends to really go,
As a matter of fact it amazes me so,
That's okay as long as it goes with the flow,
For I know it's my one and only pro,
As long as it continues to stay on the go,
Whatever you do Dear Lord, just help it to go,
And as time goes by you'll be glad I didn't go,
You'll be proud you made this heart of mine go.
It's one amazing organ that beats as it flows.
My amazing heart is what amazes me so,
As the years go by and the more I grow,
This amazing machine inside me continues to go,
It is called my amazing heart of a pro,
It pumps faster the more I throw,
And when I'm tired it will skip a beat as I throw,
I get scared to death and think it's my time to go,
For it pumps more blood than you'll ever know,
My amazing heart, I need it so.
  Laverne Rhoden

Little Stuffed Buddies

Little stuffed buddies, how kind you be-
Always about to comfort me.
Twenty-four hours, squished and hugged,
No other requirements knowing of.
Warmly you're placed-warm soon to be-
Sharing the warmth emanating from me.
In return, you sure ease the pain-
Comfort of body, to soul even gain.

Others gaze at us, thinking we're cute-
Others think childishness is the route.
Who in this life does not at times
Need someone or something to buff a rough time.
A little security amongst the rustle-
We're all needing such in this life's tussles.

Little stuffed buddies, you're precious to me-
When no one can be there, there you always be
Never alone - a strength so derived-
Hugs of all types keep one alive.
Be it by blood or stuffing, the message is clear-
Little stuffed buddies are in life's perspective dear.
  Lorraine A. Allard

Musings By The First Great Grandchild

Hi - My name is David Timothy - A.K.A. baby Matthew to some,
but always Peanut to Mommy and Daddy - Whew! Don't guess
any baby on Earth ever had so many names - even *before* birth!

I know, dear family, you don't understand why I couldn't stay in
your world - But I think you do understand, as little as I am, when
I arrived the banners of Heaven all were unfurled!

I did enjoy the short time I had riding in my Mommy's tummy - all
nice and warm and comfy - And when you took me to church and
the music began, I would pat my feet and wave my hands -
'Course I can't tell you but you can at least imagine
That I'm in one of Heaven's tiny angel bands -

So - don't you fret and don't you grieve, dear Mommy, Daddy and
  family
Even though for me to stay with you was not meant to be -
One day - some day - you can come be with me!

Written with much love
By Great-Grandmommie
Winona Evans Bean

You Sweetheart

When you are lonely, and feeling blue.
Always remember that I'm lonely too.
The days may drag slowly, the months slower yet,
But you are my darling, don't ever forget.
So, don't worry honey while we're apart, I'm yours
forever, I'm your sweetheart.

Patricia G. Bower

My Moment

Sitting on this green grass,
amazed how life is passing fast.
Looking at the sky so blue,
seeing myself how much I grew.
Here alone just me and the trees.
Enjoying this cool summer breeze.
I have not a care in my moment,
as the stream moves on in calm movement.
Drifting back through the years.
Had some rough times and shed some tears.
Looking at the birds way up high
wondering if they too cry
looking into the stream without a fear
my moment is peaceful and the sky is clear
I wish this could last forever,
like it's said forever is never.
I take a deep breath of this fresh air
will I ever have another moment this fair
or will this just fade away like the rest
my doubt is high, life is good, my moment's at its best.

Rebecca A. Marron

Think Of Today

While life has unexpected endeavors, we must
accept today before the curtains lower and our
play is over. Our performance will live on
to those who know us.

As much as we'd like to stay without
reserve, we must take our final bows.

We leave blinded only to understand
what we hear, but don't fully comprehend,
How can we comprehend the unknown without
experience?

Enjoy what you have remember yesterday
live today and forget about tomorrow.

Lawrence Lombardo

Talking Stones

Brothers, I found your broken arrows,
Amongst the sage and sand.
Shaft is gone, but stone points strong,
Brothers, do you hear them calling?

Sisters, I saw your moccasin tracks,
Snow melt knows your traveled paths.
The platte forever sings your songs,
Sisters, do you hear them calling?

Soaring eagle drops his feather,
Stones speak millions strong.
Red sun blazes behind the Bighorns,
Sending echoes of the great herd traveling.

Shadows on black hills - the point of beginning,
Footprints in the dust, the talking stones scattered.
In wisdom, his hidden heart remains somewhere near.
Do you hear them calling?

Sun rises, flat plain meets the soaring black rock,
Out of the earth, like a beckoning beacon.

Stand! Stand! Faces lifted, songs trilling, hearts united.
They can hear you calling.

Vicki L. Piano

Cry Of The Heart

There is a stillness, like a deep dark cave, that holds no light.
An emptiness, only the soul knows, after it has been rejected by the
  body.
The desperation, in searching for a lost loved one, that holds little
  hope.
The pain, that penetrates the heart so deep, the cry can be heard,
  throughout the heavens.
A love not wanted, and a love not received.
A physical exchange taken, and a commitment burned in vain.
Sailing far across the sea, or climbing the highest mountain, the
  heart cannot escape its torture.
In the deep recesses of the mind, the final act continues to play,
  over and over, longing to find hope, for a better ending.
Have the choices been taken away?
Will there be a sequel?
No answers, only promises, only time.

Patricia Lynn Donovan

Safe At Last

Cloudy skies are hanging over my head
  And a drizzle of rain is falling
Thunder rolls and the lightning strikes
  And I hear my voice keep calling...out your name

I see a vision on the trail ahead
  And for a moment I start to stumble
I catch my footing and continue to move
  But the soil begins to crumble...beneath my feet

The river rises spilling over its banks
  The frigid wind chills my senses
As darkness settles in the valley below
  Ev'ry part of my body winces...from the cold

I try to imagine you holding me
  And my pulse begins to quicken
A warm sensation passes through my soul
  And it causes my blood to thicken...in my veins

I see a light that I begin to walk t'ward
  And my confidence starts to strengthen
My feet move faster, I break into a run
  And my strides commence to lengthen...safe at last

Peggy C. Quijano

When The Moon Follows Me!

When the moon follows me,
An experience appears, a hush to see!

The flair of magic in romance moonlight connects,
Reverses the harsh glare the sun reflects!

A glow shining shapes the shadow of things,
Shows the shimmer the moon following me brings!

Gliding smoothly, bounding between cloudy stretches,
Streaking black shadows the silver light sketches!

A vanishing disappearance absconding through life's dark hills,
Tempos on apparitional reappearance in light's sprawling thrills!

Some say loneliness is inspired gazing at the moon's sight,
Filling the sky to fullness illuminating the night!

The silver silence following the moon seems chasing me,
Watching, waiting in wonderment about everything I see!

So remember a right conscious deliberates all around,
Then the moon wears a smile instead of a frown!

Dedicated to everyone who sees the perfect reflection
of nature's imperfection in themselves!

When the moon follows me!
Roger Pique

The Blessing

The kitchen was dappled in sunlight looking out over an apple orchard, an inviting-looking place. Attila, the goat, roamed the back yard at will looking for his daily requirement of anything and the ducks swam in their pond. The six people who lived there were summoned twice a day, sometimes three to sit in dead silence, each replaying the latest conflict or loudly arguing who had committed the greatest sin. The irony of the surroundings was clear only to those who stayed there. To the priests who came to visit, the grandparents who shared a Sunday dinner, the occasional friends of the children who came to stay overnight, the elderly spinster who was invited to eat on Thanksgiving, not a hint was evident of the great chasm between what appeared to be and what was. But now after 40 years have passed, the abyss is clear with no secrets to obscure it. No kitchen will ever be remembered like that one. My kitchen now is smaller, with no view and worn cupboards but it shines with a different kind of light that is not extinguished after the meal.
Susan McDonnell

Fresh Batteries: Shine On

In the dusty volumes of forgotten verse.
Ancient poet's balladry raise voice.
Sappho's eloquent show of love and nature.
Tell me emotions are forever.
As solid as stone.

In the ages of old, Socrates did ask.
As to the awesome powers that be.
Philosophies of life itself did take shape.
Always has there been questions of why.
Into the vast vague.

Confucius did say many eternal truths.
A long life of search for what is sure.
By observing and listening, he did find
Absolutes of life on which to guide.
For gospel we seek.

As does the clock keep up with the march of time.
So does the expression of the soul.
New times and twists of fate only change the words.
The songs of the heart there remain the same.
And to the next age.
Thaddeus W. Kidd

Showdown

On that cloudy afternoon of sixty-four, out came the Navy with a roar
And a mighty aim—to even that score.

Out came the Army with a grin—as if they knew they would win.
They spoke very little before that day, for they came to win, so they say.

As the coin was flipped, the game began
And the mighty teams were off again to victory or defeat
neither knew which it would meet.

And so the first half comes to an end
But on one was sure who would win the score being tied eight to eight
No one was sure what would be the fate

The half-time ceremony is over, everyone is glad
Out come both teams dirty, tired and mad
Back onto the battlefield they came
To finish that long-awaited Army-Navy game

So at the close, as everyone knows
Army defeated Navy as it goes
There'll be another time, another place
For Navy to beat Army's pace.
Patricia Ann Garvin

Reassuring Sky

I look up to the dark sky for answers
and all I see is black dreariness,
but as I look to the night sky longer
I start to see little bright spots,
and those little bright spots stand out more than the big dark one.
The longer I look the more these bright spots magically appear.
Then one of these spots winks at me
and sends reassurance back though me
that someday I will reach that huge bright spot
currently hiding behind the clouds.
Tim Loschiavo

Spring

   While gazing out my window - a peace within me came
and all the air with life was full, though nothing looked the same.
   The trees all reached another inch - into a sky so blue
and on each blade of grass did shine -
   the "diamond like beads of dew."

Flowers grew in places - where before there were none
   they turned their faces to the light as if to kiss the morning sun.
Birds all sang a saintly tune, that to me did bring a smile.
   Why I'll bet that even God himself paused to listen for a while.

Never have I been witness to and yet find the words to say —
   just how different life had looked to me on that fine day.
I look forward to another time - when such joy a morn will bring.
   As God hath given me the eyes to see the miracles of spring.
Walter F. Rej

"One's Need"

One need not look any further than the unconditional love of one's pet
An example in every way of miracles heaven sent.
A reflection of infinite solace lies deep within their eyes
If only we could be like them...no tears, turmoil or anguished cries.
Learn their secret for the peacefulness of time
Enjoying every moment...bringing happiness and being kind.
Giving, not expecting, no more than just love
Likened to the symbol of the beautiful white dove.
Free in spirit, simplistic and content
Satisfied and grateful are their miracles heaven sent.
One doesn't have to look for answers to any truths we seek
For they are in our pet's example and from them we've much to reap.
So, if we're down and out, with feelings of hopelessness and despair
Look for God's answer in our pets' loving message..."Somebody cares."
Mary Anne Binger

'Twas The Night Before Surgery

'Twas the night before surgery
and all through the hospital
the nurses were on duty-doing their night shift
Most doctors were at home resting their miraculous gift
The patients were in their beds
Thoughts of enemas and IV's in their heads
So quiet were the halls
NPO's were all posted on the walls
There was hardly a sound and not a visitor could be found
And all I could do was feel a little blue
When what should I see, but a tiny cat flea
She looked at me closely, her eyes held me near
Then she whispered in a twinkle, "Dear, you have nothing to fear,
you're not alone, just pick up your phone,"
So I did as I was told
And heard a message of gold
It was the voice of God, though a bit sad
Saying, "Don't worry you haven't been bad
Just listen and I'll help you
Your guardian angel and I will see you through."

MaryAnn DeFrancesco

A Reunion In Heaven

Take some time and think
about the Reunion going on in heaven.
They are all there—All the relations that we have known!
I wonder if they are sitting around a picnic table
Eating potato salad, pork and beans,
Hot Dogs and cake.

Listen to the laughter as they all reminisce.
"Remember when this happened, remember when that happened?
Remember when this was that?

Bet they talk about all of us and how much they miss.
They probably long to see us as much
As we long to see them.

Do the men play horseshoes? Do the women play cards?
Are the kids playing baseball? Are they in someone's yard?

Well, if you don't like Reunions here on earth,
Don't think that when you pass this life
They are over...... They probably are not......

Pamila Gale Vaughan

An Illusion Due South

Nations honor mortal crimes
And I am restricted by one score
"I don't want to be here"
   Says the boy who has his troubles served to him on a golden platter
Romancing the dead is all I would do
If I only could have smiled
If I only could have succumbed with them
Then maybe ... then maybe
Parades keep our forbidden spirits high
But a shattering notion denies our hopes
DENIES OUR FEARS WITH KNIVES IN THEIR HANDS AND WAR IN THEIR EYES
Hold on for the last day that will never come
Knowing that I never cared for the previous twenty-three years
Knowing that I will never care because I only met your brother in passing
It was a dark and stormy night
And with cliches and anticlimactically moments abound
I scream out a now passive name into an absorbing heaven
And slowly realize that I am an illiterate cartoon

Muhammad J. Awais

The Honored Dead

In the day the guns boomed high
And blew to pieces in the sky
And fell among the honored dead
Who gave their lives in the country's stead

The night seemed just as bright as day
The guns gave light in burning rays
Cries were heard and men fell dead
Falling in their bloody bed

When Armistice came the Church bells rang
The firing stopped and the soldiers sang
This war was won, but by the dead
Who in Flander's field now lay their head.

Robert F. Cook

Darkness

Sometimes I close my eyes and all I see is blackness full of blood and death is coming over me all full of pain and fear and then those screams of pain are all I hear I panic and my heart is racing toward my only path of escaping from his brutal pain he gave me all those nights so long ago he robbed me of my life and raped me of my pride and so I'm left with all this pain inside that no one seems to understand or want to face as all I want is to erase this memory all made of dark, dark dreams. Will I ever learn to sleep?

Michelle Weller

Mere Words

Don't say "I love you"
   and fail to be there in my time of need.
Don't say "I'll be a good father"
   and deny ever planting this seed.
Don't say "I'll promise you the world"
   and have not one thing to give to me.
Don't say "I'll never raise my hand"
   when bruises upon my skin I see.
Don't say "I'll never leave you"
   when during intimacy you're calling her name.
   For it's not the mere words you say
   it's the actions that aren't the same.

Keturah J. Miller

In A Dream

I saw your wan and anguished face last night;
And faint I heard your plight and helpless plea;
This vision told me clear as eagle's sight;
The fruit of sacrificial love could be.
Why come in portrait etched in air so deep;
And why with deathly pall which I can't bear.
Your skin-bone wraith did end my quiet sleep;
For love's eternal secret dreams laid bare.
What scared me was Life when I saw you last;
Was mute beside you as you try to laugh;
I prayed for healing, comfort, strength of heart;
And will of steel and grit that's di'mond tough.
Awake long hours, and memories persist;
Must see you now, must see you now, no longer I resist.

Rolando Bartolome

Winter

It's time for animals to go to bed,
And for birds to hide their cold little heads.
Some birds stay out and feed on seed,
Squirrels go out and get what they need.

Robin-Louise Burkitt

Dancing Sunbeams

Have you ever watched the sunbeams dance
And given them more than a passing glance?
Their lively capers are most amusing
Although the patterns are often confusing.
One short hour is all you need
From the swift path of life we all do lead.
Time to stop and time to ponder
Time to dream and time to wonder.
Do the sunbeams really dance with glee
Or are they merely laughing at me?
I'm the one who works all day
But sunbeams dance and joke, they say.
   Rose Ule

By The Shore

I see the sun come up over the ocean
   and hear the gulls calling
   are they calling me?

As I walk on, it is a beautiful
   new dawn!
The sky's so blue and the ocean is too!
I feel calm, quite happy!
My face feels that cool ocean air,
   I walk on.

Now I come to a beach house
My lady awaits me
I come to the door
She answers
That smile, those eyes and light brown hair

I know I'm safe
   with my lady at home, by the shore!
   Robert J. DiGennaro

Cupid's Bow

Cupid shot his bow today
And his arrow hit its mark
With lightning speed it came to me
and went straight through my heart
It opened up a whole new world
And let my eyes see you
Your smile, your warmth, your friendliness
And things I never knew
So on this day of love
I pledge to make you mine
Today, tomorrow and always
Please be my Valentine
   Maude Storey

A Child's Best Friend

A beautiful garden of colors bright and gay.
A little girl following a butterfly got lost
one day. It flew from flower to flower as she
watched and traveled on fascinated by its beauty
and birds singing their song.

Not realizing she was getting far from home, lost
in the garden and all alone. Her mother was frantic
and looked everywhere, but no lead could she find,
until the girl's little puppy started to whine.

He wanted in on the search and followed through,
when he came upon her little shoe. From the shoe
he followed her footprints and at last his search
was over. He found his little playmate still
watching the butterfly as it lit on a bed of clover.
   Mamie Hodge

I Am The Girl...

I am the girl from the city
And I am the girl from the town
And I am the girl who usually wears pants
But dreams of a red velvet gown
I love loud music but enjoy ballet
I accept sun in December
And rain in May
I am the girl from the city
And I am the girl from the town
And I am the girl who has an angel cry
And wonder what happens after you die
I am the girl from the city
And I am the girl from the town
A girl who grew up with the sun
But always wishes it would snow
A girl who's scared she'll be unprepared
Someone who welcomes friendly faces
From unknown places
I am the girl from the city
I am the girl from the town
   Kim Schwartz

"I Wonder"

Life is but a minute pause, in an eternity of time
And I can't help but wonder, Lord, just what I've done with mine
Will all the things I've tried to do be forgotten when I die?
Or have I tried to do those things worthy of another's try?
Will all the words I've spoken fade as quickly as their sound?
Or were those words "Here, take my hand" as help a friend I've
   found?
My footprints on the sands of time, will they quickly wash away?
Or on my journey through this life, did I teach a child to pray?
To a world filled with sadness, did I bring a little cheer?
Have I left some small reminder, Lord, to prove that I was here?
When my life on earth is over, when I hear the final call
If I haven't helped someone, somehow I haven't lived at all.
If I haven't helped someone somehow, I haven't lived at all.
   Raymond L. Roberts

"As The Years Unfold"

People say that I'm strange
and I guess that I really am,
because I do those things
that they don't quite understand.

I take walks in thunderstorms,
and I like to sit by my fire and dream...
of those far-away exotic places
that I have never seen.

I will probably never get there
to see these wondrous sights first hand,
but I shall not be discouraged from dreaming
by those who don't understand.

Those who do not dream are fools,
who know nothing of life or of living.
For most of these self-doubters,
they get through life with only misgivings.

Who really knows what sights I'll see,
or what wonders my eyes may behold?
I only know the real beauty in dreaming
is in watching the years unfold.
   Timothy D. Mullis

Goodbye My Love

It was the end of October, nineteen-sixty-eight -
and I had to go; but I wanted to wait.
It was hard for me to leave my wife
knowing that soon, I may lose my life.
I will never forget our last kiss goodbye -
and her wiping the tears from her eyes.
But I was in a hurry - so we had to let go.
Why? Because Uncle Sam said so.
He said that he wanted me, and needed me bad —
and I was so proud even though I was sad.
So, goodbye my love — and dry your tears.
I will only be gone for a year.
Then I turned and walked toward the plane.
My heart was filled with pride and pain.
I took one mare look at that pretty young girl -
in tight blue jeans, and her hair in curls.
Then I blew a kiss from my hand -
and wondered if I would see her again.
Then I flew from Flint to Detroit - from
Detroit to Seattle. In a few more days I would be in the battle.

Larry Blevins

A Lazy Afternoon

I had fixed up my hammock between the oak trees
And I lay there content, swinging gently in the breeze.
I had a feeling to open my eyes
And I looked up into the blue, blue, skies
A hawk was hovering and watching with care...
A little mouse... that had scurried out on a dare.

But suddenly the hawk felt a current of air
And soared higher and higher with his wings spread in a flair.
I didn't want him to fly away...
I wanted to be part of him that day.

The hawk was soaring with grace and ease
While I watched him from my hammock..slung between the trees.
He glided away with ease and grace
And I felt the warmth of the sun..shine on my face.

He dipped and swooped and a part of me
Though how wonderful it was to be free
As I lay in my hammock..and watched a bumblebee.
Oh yes...life is wonderful... when you are free.

Madeleine Short

Eve

You are so beautiful Eve,
And I love you with all my heart.
But now it seems that we shall have to part.

Because you TOUCHED! that tree, how could you do it love?
When we were told not to by our FATHER above.

Why did you it woman? why did you TOUCH! that tree?
The serpent TRICKED! me Adam, the Serpent talked to me.

Said we would be like Gods!, become very WISE!!
The tree then began to look pleasant! to my eyes.

The Serpent DECEIVE! you, while I was away.
Now you're going to LEAVE! me all alone one day.

GOD made you for me darling, FLESH! Of my FLESH!.
Made you to be with me, and both of US HE BLESSED!!.

Don't want to LIVE! without you Eve,
Can't be ALONE, and BLUE!
Don't want to LIVE FOREVER!
If you're not LIVING TOO!!!.

Lee Ette Robinson

Lalitha

If, after a summer's rain had fallen softly upon the earth
and I were to travel the path of God's promise,
'twould be my prayer to find thee at rainbow's end.

For gold compares naught to the riches thine smile brings
unto my life.

The birds sing, as they perch upon the branches of green-leaved
trees, yet they could ne'er match the musical softness of thy
voice so melodious and true.

And though the sun may shine with all its brilliance upon my
brow, 'tis within thine smile that my soul finds warmth.

From within thine eyes I do find the love that gives me light to
pass through a world clouded with the darkness of despair.

For truly, I say unto thee, there be no greater gift in life than
that of a lady's heart, who's beauty is as great as time is eternal.

I shall love thee always.

Otis A. Mardres

Wishing

I wish I could hold you in my arms
and keep you safe from all harm.

I wish that you feel the way that I do,
knowing how much I truly love you.

I wish that the future will bring you in my life,
to spend eternity together as my love and my wife.

To share the joys of raising a family and watching them grow.
To make our lives complete as we grow old.
To share the bitter, the sweet as the future unfolds.

I wish for you. I wish for love.
I wish so much. I wish.

Richard T. James Jr.

Sweetheart

You came to live with me when you were just a kitten

Such a tiny fellow; you weren't much bigger than a small child's mitten!

Of all your brothers and sisters, it was you who leaped onto my lap
and looked anxiously at me with those big bright eyes
Begging for a chance to spend with me every remaining minute of
your nine lives!

Soon you became much more than a pet to me—I will forever think
of you as my baby!

Our time together went by so quickly; today you've been gone for
a year and I still shed many a tear!

My beloved Sweetheart, Heaven is your home now, but you will
always have a home in that special place reserved just for you in
my heart!

We both know that we will never truly part!

Everyday I think of you and remember how adorable you were and
how much I loved our life together; to me, you were wonderful!

Somehow you could always tell when my spirits were falling and
you knew just what to do to give them a much needed uplifting pull!

Sweetheart, I know you haven't forgotten me, either; I sense your
presence in my life and know you've been watching out for me
from your beautiful home in the sky above guiding me through
each day with your eternal love!

Although you are always near, I still miss you!
The love I feel for you, Sweetheart, will be everlastingly true!

Patsy Zimmerman

Staring At The Sun

If you've ever been outside on a sunny summer day
and looked up to the sky, you'll know
If you've ever taken off your sunglasses
and opened wide your curious eyes, you'll know
If you've ever been sucked in
flying towards a myriad of wonderful colors, you'll know
If you've ever been lost, unable to come back
and grasp reality as your eyes melted away, you'll know
If that warmth and shine and heavenly glow
that entered your soul through your eyes still remains, you'll know
If the light that you saw and felt and experienced
is the last thing you've ever laid your eyes upon, you'll know

The brightest thing I've ever seen.
Randal Ivor-Smith

"The People Could Fly"

We were brought here, to this new land
And made to work for an old white man.
They treated us like animals
And the way we were fed, you'd think we'd
   have been cannibals.

They beat us almost to death, Oh my!
But little do they know, some of us can fly!
Soon, on one clear blessed night
We'll fly up and out of sight.
We'll fly to where we want to be...
Some place where we'll be truly free!!
Taniesha Tolbert

Dreams

If I could give sweet memories...
And make all dreams come true...
If I could give the sound of music...
Angels singing high in the sky...
If I could give good health...
To be strong in the coming years of age...
If I could fill one heart with joy and peace...
To last a lifetime...
If I could close my eyes...
Make a wish and have my dreams come true...
There would be love, peace, and joy...
In the heart...
And I'd give my dreams to you.
Sandra L. Dotson

Just Give Me Time

Do not deny that I am older now,
and in the veins the blood runs colder now,
and yet I have a million miles to go;
so much to see, to touch, to taste, to know.
Give back to me those years I felt behind.
I do not wish to wrinkle like a prune;
or die; or lie abed whilst noon
creeps on to dusk, when nurses spectral white
flickers before my eyes unseeing sight
with nothing left to think with in the mind.

Quietly accept old age, I will not do:
Sit in my chair and rock, I will not do:
For I have books to write, new friends to make.
So many skies to fly so much at stake.
I will not ask for youth, just give me time,
day-dreams, quick blood, a chance to be reborn
that I may ride the nigh-owl to the dawn,
to know why stars go out, to see the cloud
gold tipped with rising sun, to cry aloud
in !ove with life. Dear God, just give me time!
Stella M. MacKintosh

"A Single Ray Of Sun"

Beaches stretch out endlessly for miles around me,
And my mind lets loose thoughts to be caught by the breeze.
The silence is broken only by the tide from the incoming sea;
I close my tear-filled eyes and fall helplessly to my knees.

Encased in self-imposed darkness, I taste the salty air with each breath I take....
Digging my fingers into dampened sand, I am suddenly aware of the feeling from which I cannot awake...
Despair and helplessness surround my heart, laying the foundation for a wall of pain
That fills my soul with frustration and anger that threatens to drive me insane.

Dark clouds hanging above thunder open and flood the depressed sky
Mocking the pain and emptiness of my lonely wilting cry.
Waves rise, crash and break in chilling formation around me,
Snapping me back to the reality from which I so desperately want to flee.

Shocked by the cold, I open my weary eyes to face the cruelty of the imposing shroud;
But to my surprise I am greeted by a single ray of sun breaking through the dark clouds:
One that fought through the cold and rain to light the world in its own small way...
I dry my eyes and stand tall, filled once again with the hope and promise of a new day.
Michael C. Owens

"Revenge"

Revenge; a dish best served cold, or so I was told when I was young.
And now that I'm old it can finally be told
That I've served my share of dishes that now rest heavy on my soul.

I will admit that some of the dishes I served
Were ones that I felt were well deserved, and of those I remember all.
But I, too, will have to admit with a sigh that some servings went awry...
Oh God!
But then again, people, like everything else in this world,
Someday, too, must die.

So now here I sit in this room trying to shake the impending doom
which soon will be upon me.
Wait...listen...I must take my leave of you now.
I can hear footsteps in the hall and by the smell I'd guess it was my
final meal that I will ever eat within this cell.

I hope it's hot because I told them to bring it hot;
Very, very, very hot.
Because I am not
one
who accepts any dish...
Cold.
Paul H. Corcoran

Peace

Peace, a word meaning tranquility
A word we throw around like a ball
Do we really know what it means
Crime, hate, murder a dangerous game to play
Through a child's eyes this must seem so insane
For they do not do what we say, but what they see
Will they learn from our mistakes or continue them
Will the fear ever end?
Bodies of the innocent lying in the streets
It seems like such a dead end
The scars that cut this world so deep
For the promises we did not keep
Will our children have the power to make this end
Or do they face the same dead end!
Yvette Dorn

Grandma's Day After

'Tis the day after Christmas
And "Oh" what a mess
Papers all over
And a non fitting dress

The children have gone
Took all the loot home
And here I am all alone
Some couldn't come
Too far away
I hope they will come some other day.
The grand kids are all grown
And homes of their own
Some will have Christmas in their own homes
It's nice knowing they are there
I can reach them by phone
When we are talking
I'm not all alone.

Mildred Sanders

Designer Leaf

Once in a garden there was a tile in relief,
   And on its surface a painted leaf.
I thought, "That artist really painted with guile
   And tried to fool me with a flamboyant style.
That shape so perfectly symmetrical
   To exist in nature would be heretical,
And a pink like that has never been seen
   Or peachy wine or that lavender-green!"
While thinking my thoughts, (I had more to say)
   A wind came along and blew it away.

Kenneth Hoffman

The Beauty Of Dreaming

Beauty lies where you find it and what you'll find is pure
And opinions may try to change that, but they can't if you are sure
Sure of yourself and of your dreams that you want to follow
If you aren't sure of these things yet, inside you may feel hollow.
But don't be scared if hollow describes the way that you feel
Because as long as you attempt to dream, happiness can be real
Think about what you want to do in life and who you want to be
And your reflection in the mirror will be one you're glad to see
And if you can, try to find your place in this imperfect world
Dream until you find your perfection as I have found in my girl
This girl is the one I've searched for who has also searched for me
And on that day when we first met we clicked so naturally
Others said, "Don't fall too fast or she might break your heart"
But when in love all that matters is never being far apart
Soon we were joined in matrimony and the angels began to sing
Happiness overwhelmed us as the wedding bells started to ring
I gazed into her eyes once more to see the treasure I had found
And as I stared I swear I felt my feet lift off the ground
It was as if I had reached heaven and an angel was mine to keep
She makes me feel like I am dreaming even when I'm not asleep

Sean Dennison

Last Chance Romance

I just want to slow dance all night long,
  and be held in the arms of a brand new song.

The excitement and desire of a long, soft kiss
  is something that I need and sincerely miss.

I yearn for the touch of a new love's hands,
  and to be caressed by the one who understands.

The loves of my past have been torn and tattered;
  my life, it seems, has been completely shattered.

As time passes by, I dream of the last chance
  to be lucky in love with a new, true romance.

Lillian L. Johnson

A Price For Freedom

Today our President declared war on Iraq,
And our brave service people will do all they can,
To free Kuwait from Iraq terror,
And console the children with loving care.

Which part of "out" does the Iraqi Government
Not understand?
All we ask for them is to leave
And give Kuwait back their land.

Many people demonstrate against this war.
Go ahead and knock on the Iraqi door.
If the demonstrators do not support our Government
Then I'll give them a positive hint.
(This is what really meant)

Hurry and catch the first flight out
And live with the Iraqi Government and learn what
Their Government is all about.

All must pay a large fee,
Support our Government to keep America free.
Love it or leave it
Is my solemn plea.

Mary Laverty

Endless Train To Venice

Slowly, single dark travelers pass,
And push through slumped dreamers in aisles.
Stop by stop, we watch them end
And begin the adventures of their lives, which we know nothing of.

Click, clack, we grind to a halt as their bags brush by,
Blowing old-laundry and basil scents
Over our faces watching grass and vines
Slow, through a soot-draped window.

In and out of sleep you drift, restless but hopeful;
Just as the train, straining to open heavy eyelids
From town to town, yearning for real rest
In the city of lovers.
Silently, your blue eyes dance on the strings of an old man's
Soft Mandolin, strumming in time with click-clack rails.

You dream again, and the tears flow freely;
For, as I glance once more at golden fields,
I see only flowing hair of our future children,
Their bright eyes and dreams, and I love you so deeply
And long as our journey. I rise, heart not in thumps.

But click-clack, click-clack, click-clacks.

Paul Dobransky

Storm

When all the sky is dark and clouds appear
And sail across the heavens in majesty,
And lightning rips the firmament to sear
The clouds with fire, and branches as a tree
Upon the ever darkening earth below;
When winds are rushing by at violent pace
That bear the mighty peals of thunder low
To all awaiting ears with awesome grace;
'Tis then my heart rejoices at the sound
And, feeling light, leaps up to conquer all!
'Tis then the laughter of my soul is found
And, being freed, has freedom to enthrall!
In this exultant hour my feet are shod
With wings which soar in jubilant praise to God!

Marita J. Lowell

At Journey's End

As time draws near I walk deserted streets
and search empty dreams.
I voyage through misery, which has consumed my being.
My soul has wandered endless nights,
yet her call beckons me forward.
I cross oceans of sorrow, which I have made.
My uniqueness among creation has imprisoned me.
I drift past solitude who is awaiting my arrival.
I breach the boundless heavens, only to find reality.
I hold onto hope, my only companion.
I have searched the world over
and discovered not even myself.
At journey's end I find her,
the one who was there all along
The other to make me complete.
Together we walk on happiness
and float past harmony.
At journey's end we become one
and enter the currents of time
which take us away.

Todd Szewczyk

Earth's Greatest Beauty

When God created the universe
   and set this world in motion
He planned the beauty of it all
   from the mountain tops to the ocean

From the lovely flowers of springtime
   to the colors of leaves in the fall
The one who created beauty
   in his Majesty made it all

By far the most exquisite beauty
   he planned from Heaven above
Was the everlasting magic
   of a man and woman in love

As Bride meets Groom at the alter
   and they place a ring on each other's hand
May they rest assured in the knowledge
   they are simply completing God's plan

May the lifetime they share together
   be centered upon his will
and in sunny or stormy weather
   he their hearts with happiness fill

Otto Phillips

Alone

The wintry snow comes down in blasts,
and smites the drawn green shutters.
The timbers groan with an ancient rasp
while the shaded lamp's flame flutters.
The fire roars like a troubled sea, lashed by an angry gale
while I sit here with a restless mind,
like the wind on the snow-white vale.
I smoke my pipe and browse my book.
I feign to half recline, but I am the only one here to fool —
myself and the endless time.
I raise the window high, and hurl the shutters wide.
The snow blows in; the lamp goes out.
The clock rings out its chimes.
The silent tears stream down my face.
My grief I try not hide.
She is gone, she is gone, she is gone beyond that silver lea beneath a
cross and a rounded mound of shifting snow and frozen ground, and
here is darkness, winter, and wind engulfing all there is left of me.

O. Clinton Spence

"He's Expected"

Unique…Yes he surely will be, this baby we are all expecting.
And so beautiful too!

He'll be so loved, like all babies are born to be loved.
But this baby boy will never doubt that he is loved!

Wonder if everyone believes that before their baby arrives?

Each of us awaiting this child, has our own idea just what
Has our own idea what he will be like.
But we can't really know,
For he comes from many peoples.
German, English, Irish, Swiss and even more,

Including Native American.

Our little boy could be fair or tawny,
Eyes of blue or brown.
Curly blond hair or brown and straight.
He'll have a personality with a capital "P,"
Whether quiet or playful and noisy…it'll be his alone.
Lots of genes, DNA, etc., have gone into this Creation of God.

So, God we pray for a peaceful and loving world,
For "our" baby boy and for all the children and people of the World!

Maydell Seibert

Circus Memories

The trucks move slowly down the street
And soon the tents led out two by two
The animals are led out two by two
The lion, the elephant, and the kangaroo

They face back and forth in their wire cage
As they wait for the show on that giant stage
The man in his tall hat and carrying a cane
Smiles as he walks by, saying something 'bout rain

Here comes someone with balloons on a string
Bright colors flying high, I can hear him sing
He is closer now, I can see his face
All painted up, why it's quite a disgrace

His hair sticks out and the looks so funny
As he smiles at me and calls me honey
His big red nose looks like a cherry
No wonder he makes the children so merry

His feet are so big with curled up toes
And he's squirting water out of a rose
Tomorrow it will all be gone,
But the memory of the circus will linger on.

Verda M. Gingrich

Thankful

I am thankful for the sea and the sky,
And the beautiful mountains that are so high.

I am thankful for my friends who care,
And teachers who are always fair.

I am thankful for the winter, spring, and fall,
But I love summer most of all.

I am thankful for my Mom who is a lot of fun,
Except when she asks if my homework is done.

I am thankful when the door opens, and there is my dad;
But when he sees my room, he sure gets mad.

I love my parents even though at times they're short;
I am glad when I was to be born, they chose not to abort.

Because the world is such a wondrous thing,
Just think what to the world I alone could bring.

William Keith Hawley

Meet Me

Meet me where time has no memory
and spirit transcends your existence.

When you look upon me, let it be
through the magnificence I was created.

Open mind, open heart, open beauty.

Meet me where your lovin' runs strong.

Let us walk to the beat of truth
constant and ever flowing.

So you may lay in the arms of fulfillment
where my lovin' grows strong.

Meet me where innocents begins
and want has endless boundaries.

Where the pool of passion runs deep
and happiness reins eminent, allowing
peace ever-lasting.

Meet me where, the reflection of you
becomes a rush.
Meet me, just meet me.

Sharon A. Jones

When Lilacs Bloom

In April when the lilacs bloom
And spread their musky, sweet perfume
Across the green, awakening land...
I think of you...and try to understand

Why you left me here alone...
Oh, how sad my heart has grown!
And then I smell the lilac bloom...
In a China vase across the room.

The vase we bought, so far away
On a trip we made one April day.
I laughed and called it my "dresden" vase...
You smiled and lovingly touched my face.

I feel that touch when breezes sigh...
And lilacs scent an April sky.
I walk alone this Spring-drenched day...
Oh, why did you have to go away!

If lilacs bloom there up above...
My darling pick one "with my love."
Reach out so I may touch your hand...
It may be then I'll understand.

Margaret L. Speakman

Why Kurt?

Toiling for years, the going was slow
And then people became aware four years ago
Of you who hailed from the Pacific Northwest
And arrived to put pop music to the test
Accompanied by shrieking guitar and feedback
You finally gave us great rock' n' roll back
And bearing angst-ridden tidings on tracks
About teen spirit, heart-shaped boxes and beeswax.

The world suddenly opened up to you
We understood your message too
But trouble loomed over the horizon
Mounting problems began to weigh a ton
You sought desperately to escape from the pain
And now somewhere in Washington you are lain
Andy Rooney dismissed you as a loon
Tell me, Kurt, why did it have to end so soon?

Robert J. Brown

A Loud Cry

I'd like to say why I'm so sad,
And that dirt and filth makes me mad.

I beg and plead for the world to change,
But corruption and gambling still remain.

God's earth, so wondrous to behold,
With billowy clouds more beautiful than gold.

Flowers and birds and so many greens,
But the Lord's purchased souls wear ragged jeans.

The sun, moon and stars, the air we breathe
Not enough; drugs and liquor are the squeeze.

The oceans and tides all finely tuned,
But many disgrace God, being indiscriminately mooned.

Our bodies, the temple of the Holy Spirit,
Oft times smells and shows little merit.

I wish I could say that I detect,
A heaping measure of respect.

But no; not for self, for me or others,
Hope only is our Savior and mothers.

Shirley M. Holden

The Little Old Church

The carpet in front is ragged and worn,
And the Hymn books have pages that are tear-stained and torn.
The rich and the poor, the feeble and old,
The glad and the merry, their presence behold.
Oh, the church bells ring on, loudly they hail,
From the village, the town, the country, the dale.
Ring louder and louder to shut out the noise
Of the roar of the cannon, the cries of our boys.
Dim out the shrill of bombs bursting in air,
Dim out the cries of our boys over there.
'Til the cannons have ceased and we've lost all our fear,
And the world's at its peace and we've heard the "all clear."

M. E. Leuliette

I Use - I Lose

It has taken away my freedom
and the meals I used to choose
they've arrested my addiction
Crack Cocaine, where I'd always lose

I know there will come a day
when they will have to set me free
I'll have to walk the straight and narrow
a change of life for me

I'll beat this damn insanity
which they call Crack Cocaine
the craving and the guilts will go
only then I will be sane

Crack is very sneaky you see
it sleeps, sits and waits
then drags you through a burning hell
and tells you it's the pearly gates

Crack you took me to my lowest
I'd steal anything to sell
Crack you really ruined my life
so with that, you can go to HELL.

Ted Colclough

Waiting Heart

The rain comes mostly at night it seems
  and the melancholy sigh of wind and leaves
    whispers from the deep throat of a starless sky.

Thunder drifts slowly away
  the distant echo of a far horizon
    weakly pulsing with sometime flashes.

The wind dies, trees are stilled, rain patters
  a sentinel night holds breathless watch
    for a sleepless, waiting heart.

Thomas Pentecost

Misty Dawn

The days of glory are forever gone,
And the morning brings a misty dawn,
The rose petals have decayed and fallen,
Taking with them love's last calling,

My heart was buried in the winter snow,
Joining my mind of long ago,
The clarity of which is never to be found,
Leaving my hands tied and tightly bound,

The dreams of yesterday are better not remembered,
As I turn to a new page of my life coming in December,
Leaving behind a major part of myself,
Adding more stock to an already cluttered closet shelf,

All of the nights have grown much colder,
As the day of my life have much older,
And the summer of my life is almost gone,
As I still face a misty dawn.

Karen L. Williams

Renewal Of Love

As darkness fell upon us last night
And the night before
So too did my fear into the dark
Stumble its weary presence into thought
History you can review
But pure energy will come from the present
And this you make the best of
Then the future must be left to build on
From this new energy of the present
Will come a glow of light
Shining through hearts that beat as one
And into this light will night travel
Quietly and restfully into morning
Where a stronger sunshine will embrace us
And always prevail
And so too will come the future
Step by step by step
With family and happiness forevermore

Stephen C. Kerr

Untitled

Yesterday the skies in my heart clouded over,
and the rain began to fall.
When will my Rainbow come back to brighten the day with her smile?
Today the sun peeked through the clouds,
and I caught a glimpse of what's been missing.
My Rainbow has begun to shine again.
Tomorrow my Rainbow will be there in all her beauty
to keep the clouds away.
Gladly I would give up all the memories of yesterday and today
to spend tomorrow in her arms.
Rainbow, save the tomorrows.

Stephen Siodlarz

For Loneliness

He opened his arms for Loneliness
  and the sky was lit
    with a glowing torch of brightness
      for her.
To please her, He fashioned the spheres
  for a game of catch
    to pass their time away.
The distance of their toss was great
  and the game being new
    She clumsily played.
In fear she could not play
  Her tears fell, full of life, soft but bitter...
    full of life...
      soft,
        but bitter...
    Dampening some of her new play things.

Victoria Ruggiero

My Prayer

After another day is done;
  and the sun has found its nesting.
I lay upon my bed and think while I
  am resting.
I think awhile as there I lay and then
  I close my eyes of pray:
I pray to God who is up above,
  to be very near the one's I love.
To be very near them in every way,
  in their work and in their play.
To watch over and keep them day and night
until we are bound far heavens flight
  Amen.

Kay Asbury

The Lover In My Dreams

I want you
  and think of you much
And in my dreams I feel your touch.
To yearn for you
  I'm in deep despair
my broken heart in need of repair.

Please come mend my broken heart
and think of the life we could start,
Together.

To you would belong my soul
And my heart your gentle hands would hold;
forever.

Oh, how happy we will be
  someday you will see;
But until then I will sing
  to the lover in my dreams.

Tammy S. Poynter

Soul Saver

The world is succumbing to the will of the devil
And we can't do anything to make it right
Evil is ruling the world that we live in
Who's gonna save our soul tonight
Soul saver - is sent down from above
Soul Saver - rules with an iron glove
Power -
Soul saver - and the license to kill

And you think this can't be for real?
A savior riding down on a steed of steel
But down He comes with His sword in hand
To make peace across the land.

Lona Mitchell

Baby Love

Even though we had our differences,
   and we didn't plan our lives this way.

There is no reason or explanation,
   why you ignore your little girl.

You may have harsh feelings or words for me,
   but to take it out on your child, you see.

It's cruel and unfair to all who see.

Cause all your life, through your troubles and pain,
   good times and bad times.

She'll love you just the same.
   Susan Scarpa

Untitled

We'll meet again in another life my love
And we'll fly away to the heights of the stars.
Meanwhile, don't let me go or wander too far...
I'm always with you, heart and mind
Continue your look, hopefully me you will find
There I'll be, waiting for you with open arms and soul
Willingly with me, you will go
But of the look must go on
You can always find me
In the heights of the stars.
   Laurie Presby

Happiness Is...

Happiness is joy,
and when people don't annoy.
Happiness is caring,
and also sharing.
Happiness is anything good,
and doing everything you should.
Happiness is coming home to your family after a long day,
and when your hardships all go away.
Happiness is a good feeling,
sometimes it even helps in healing.
   Matthew Bai

I Thought Of You

I gazed upon wickedness from the heavens so blue,
And with heaviness in my heart, I thought of you.

I descended from divine glory to show you the way,
And to free you from sin so the price you wouldn't pay.

When they hung me on the cross I was certain what I must do,
And with tears in my eyes, I thought of you.

I asked for your forgiveness from the Lord up above,
And when my job was finished, God poured out His love.
   Wendy M. McMillian

The Joy Of Jesus

The Joy of Jesus is always there
and with his Love I know he cares
Just put your trust in his hands
give your problem to him he will understand
even though we sometimes fall
trust in God he knows it all
Just walk in the spirit with Jesus alone
and find out how close you two have become
Jesus gave his life to redeem men
so we don't have to live in sin
if we confess with our mouth salvation is made
call upon the Lord you shall be saved.
   Maggie McCray

I Have No Memory

I have no memory when I was born;
And yet my conscious reveals the story.
The infinitesimal reflections of dim bits,
of immortal glory. Of 3 billion years
or more in making of homo sapiens,
immortal taking.
I have no memories, I am mortal!
   Samuel L. Chapman

Caring Confusion

Do you wonder sometimes if you'll ever get through,
And you ask, "is it really worthwhile?"
Those times when it seems your world's breaking in two,
And you can't even force out a smile.

While others are standing beside you,
Who care but don't know what to say.
Should they joke or be solemn and cry too,
Stick with you or just go away?

Well, whatever the reason you're somber,
Be it sorrow or plain lack of rest.
One thing you should always remember,
And this you can put to the test.

Please tell me the path I should follow;
Just say "Stay," or "Get out of the way."
Although being apart would feel hollow,
It's worth chasing your grey clouds away.

I'd rather the answer be — Stay by my side,
Because two will be stronger than one.
And I'll be someone in whom you can confide,
'Til you know that the battle is won.
   Travis Burr

"Till Death Do Us Part"

Just a few bruises at first —
And you did apologize;
Even forgave me for making you hit me!
Remembering "Till death do us part,"
I forgave myself — and stayed.

Black eyes, contusions, a fractured jaw,
Cracked ribs and far too many broken bones;
All this and more — yet I stayed,
Never once understanding what I was doing wrong;
But I understood "Till death do us part."

Then one night, after a particularly savage attack,
I watched, horrified, as you turned to our children,
Lashing out with deadly intent —
Consumed with a mother's love,
And fueled by years of contained rage,
"Till death do us part" didn't merit a thought —
Only that my children remain safe!

Now you lie dead — at my feet;
And I? — May God have mercy on my soul,
I stayed — "Till death did us part!"
   Louise Simmons Thomas Spell

Johnny Castaway

Johnny sits on his island alone
And picks his teeth with an old fish bone.

Day by day the boats float by
He sits and wishes that he could fly.

And if he could fly he'd go to a land
Where there's more to do than just sit in the sand.
   William Allen McGrady II

Someone Does Care

Though your pain is deep
And you don't know
If you can trust anyone again,
I'll be there for you.

You smile when you only feel anger.
You give love but are afraid to accept it.
But no matter how you feel,
I'll still be there for you.

When your soul creams out
To free its gift within
And all you can do is cry from frustration,
I'll still be there for you.

And if your battered heart
Can give you the strength
To reach out once more,
You'll know I've always been here for you.

Mark Arniola

Just Rely On Your Faith

When life seems to get you down,
   And you don't know where you're bound,

When the devil throws obstacles in your way,
   And your troubles seem to multiply and seem like they are here to stay,

Just rely on your faith to carry you through,
   Through prayer and God's love, you'll know what to do,

When it's sunny outside but you're cloudy within,
   And the situation you're in, seems there's no way to win,

When family problems seem to tug at your heart,
   And your life seems to be falling apart,

Just rely on your faith to carry you through,
   Through prayer and God's love, you'll know what to do,

When life seems to have you down for the count,
   And the pressure and tension on you just seems to mount,

When tears you feel could go on forever,
   And going through the day is a major endeavor,

Just rely on your faith, to carry you through,
   Through prayer and God's love you'll know what to do...

Sandy McMurtrie

Happy Birthday "Mom"

Well another year has passed, so you go the same old way;
And you say to yourself again, well it's just another day.

There is no reason for you to have these kinds of feelings;
You must realize when at times it's hard to believe, life does have all its meanings.

You're the best mother anyone could ever have, this is why I love you so much;
Because you've got that special smile, good advice and a kind touch.

Try to live a happy life, throughout your future years,
Think of those wonderful memories and clear out the tears.

You've still got a long way to go, and many things to do;
This little poem I'm writing is my way of saying, "MOM, HAPPY BIRTHDAY TO YOU!!!"

Starlet Martin

Prelude

I had a dream last night—
Angels in white silken dresses gathered in
Forest of Arden
And created darling Dream:
   Birth of Her—
Wild roses held their
Wine-red buds high for her,
And soft wind carried their scent:
   "Ambrosial!"
On the emerald leaves was
Crystal dew of Mysteries—
Tarrying, glittering, tenderly.
When her small snow-white fingers
Touched one of the sleek crimson petals,
I heard the angels—with heavenly smiles—toll
   The luscious bells of exultant Life
Brimming the lapis-blue sky with echoes...
As I woke up, I felt in my arms
   Her sweet sweat.

Takashi Kozuka

Idiosyncrasies Of The City

In the wee hour of the morning I awake
Angels of clouds open up to day break...
The feathery birds are happily chirping
The brilliant red cardinal sounds the first note.
Mewing at my front door is a stray cat
Neighbors' dogs are barking
Oh well, that's the city.
People of the city are bustling about
Scurrying for the taxi - honking horns.
Fire engines roaring past my house
With the loud clanging of the bell
Hoping they save another life
Oh well, that's the city.
The city weather is moody
Bright sunshine, gray clouds, feathery snow
Plenty of angry winds too!
Oh well, that's the city.
God lets me share these treasures every day.

Naomi Hulme

"Timber"

I think that I shall never see
Another man as great as he.
Standing straight and tall as could be,
Not unlike his beloved pine tree.

In nineteen eighteen he left this tree to mature
So tall and sturdy, it was a beauty for sure.
He was justly proud of his favorite tree;
Children he guided so they might see.

He loved every pine cone and each fragrant spill
Of this King of the Forest growing high on a hill.
As years passed by, the man and the tree
Fell victim to disease; it was God's will to be.

Each had lived a long life giving shelter and joy
To all who had known them, every girl and boy.
The man, like the tree, had been looked on with pride,
A symbol of strength and love at our side...

Until the year nineteen seventy-four
When God whispered, "Timber" and opened the door.

Marilyn H. Bowers

Counsel Of Creation

Have you ever heard your name on the wind?
Answered the call of the wild...
Found yourself lost in laughter with the moon?

Shared secrets with the stars?
Felt the kiss of a wild rose
Whose thorn pricked your soul?

Have you ever embraced a wide open field?
Danced with a sunbeam to music in your heart...
Comforted by the caress of a tear on your cheek?

Then you have heard the voice of Truth.
Listen to the counsel of creation...
The very breath of life sings the love of God.

Una-Melina M. Everroad

Dreams And Memories

Dreams of the future
Are memories of the past
Some are just fleeting dreams
Dreams become memories that last.

Some memories we would like to forget;
Others we hope will never go away,
The ones that come in a moment
In the passing of one's day.

Most people know what they want
When they grow up, I guess
Riches - marriage - homes,
Love and happiness.

Dreams give us a goal,
To climb upward and fulfill.
Believe in your dreams
You will find they are not mountains - only hills.

Ruby Button

Honored

Mirrored in your eyes
are my hopes and aspirations
you give to them encouragement
that they could all come true.
I speak my mind, you let me
vent my wrath, opinions too.
And then you hold me calm, within your clasp.
The knowledge that shoulders there
to be strong for one another
To support or lean upon makes ourselves
Complete, and yet, a better pair.
If I could mirror for your eyes
I think you know just what you'd see
your hopes and aspirations
are reflected
held by me.

Sharon Grove Mack

On the night of your departure

To my *"Sunshine"*:

  As I know that it is not the warm sunshine,
felt upon my face, that causes the cold, empty darkness of night,
I know that you are not the cause of my sorrow and pain.

  Rather, it is your absence which reveals
to me the overwhelming and inherent sadness of my heart that,
like the darkness, disappears in your light.

                    Eternally yours,
                        Darkness

Mark Sarojak

Simple Things

Simple, simple things,
Are what I long to see;
A gentle summer breeze,
A sparrow in the tree.

A quail with young-uns close behind,
Scampers 'cross the trail;
A squirrel poised high upon a rock,
Shows off his fury tail.

A mother sings a lullaby,
A child plays pat-a-cake;
Two children wish upon a star,
Grand wishes they will make.

A man stands 'neath an old oak tree,
And seems to hear it say;
"Won't you take some time to chat with me,
Won't you take some time today?"

While pondering these simple things,
My struggles seem to cease;
A ray of light fills my soul,
And points the way to peace.

Pamela Komarek

"Passion On Compassion"

Passion, enfold your loving arms
Around my unworthy being.
My thoughts are shamefully alarming
Me thinks of it as sensual calming.

God made it thus for all kindred lovers.
Passion so true, a most rewarding union
Perfect compassion, lasting peace, it all covers.
Oh, that the world could experience such communion.

Love, not misgiving state of compunction,
Will someday turn lives of destruction,
To an ultimate world void of international constrictions.
God, we pray, bless, lead and provide such production.

Sybil S. Myers

"Wisdom"

Learning never ceases, error persists ever.
As a child I sought the wisdom of adulthood.
Such a thought now brings a twinge deep within.

Through growing I have found how much I lack.
An improvement in one area startlingly points out a lacking in another.

If I begin to feel I have mastered my goals,
My own humanity is brought swiftly into perspective.

In growing and learning, I have come to understand
That wisdom involves encompassing knowledge gained
With the strength to be open enough to still learn.

Truth often lies beneath a well veneered surface.
I look beyond the spoken word, to the eyes which
Find truth harder to conceal.

Wisdom will travel across many
Miles of mistakes and shattered dreams,
Just to find an occasional oasis of truth and true knowledge.

Through wisdom I am learning to accept my mistakes,
In order to be less judgmental of the mistakes of others.

Wisdom has taught me a sense of humility,
And yet, comfort in continually trying to be all I can be.

Patricia Wolf DeSanti Chapman

Troubles

Just read a paper, or watch T.V. it's there
as big as life, for everyone to see.
You try to put it out of your head.
But, you can't forget all those people, who're dying, or dead.
You say this is none of your business.
It's nothing you can do - unfortunately you're probably right.
It's probably very true, but just think if everyone
thought in the same self-serving way.
Not caring what's going on around them,
Just living from day to day.
How long do you think we could exist?
Before everything starting falling apart?
So wake up before it's too late, and start thinking
with your heart.
  William E. Ward

The Ocean

The ocean
as fierce as a roaring lion
that calls to me in the middle of a dark haunting night.

The ocean
as gentle as a cute little bunny rabbit
that calls to me on a sunny day to come pet it

The ocean
as different as the sun and the moon

The ocean
as graceful and beautiful as a ballerina
as tough and violent as a brown bear
  Nicole Hilton

Love

A most popular subject - this feeling of love
As fleeting and evasive as the flight of a dove
There is, of course, a love of all kinds
The word "love" brings what feeling to our minds
Just a soft word spoken or a gentle caress
So simple a gesture; yet, love they express
To ease the burdens of one we hold dear
With no restrictions of when, why, or where
It remains ever present in sickness or in health
Existing in days of poverty or in days of wealth
Love knows no boundaries or limits to show
From it perpetual fountains of emotions do flow
The actuality of love and of hope
Forms a haven of safety for those in its scope
  Sarah Dempsey

A Prayer For The Little Ones

I closed my hands in prayer today
  As I knelt down on the floor,
I prayed for the little ones
  That they will hurt no more.
I prayed for them some happiness
  For that's the way a child's world should be,
I prayed for parents to understand
  And see the way that child sees.
I prayed for God to guide them
  And to keep our children strong,
Especially for the hurting ones
  I prayed for them a song.
I prayed for them some laughter
  When things are going bad,
And I prayed for them some sunshine
  When their little hearts are sad.
  Susan Hasche

Untitled

Another day has gone by
As I prepare my heart to die.
As I am willing to give you my soul
My heart easily ceases and lies low.
I try not to think of the pain soon to come,
and I try not to think of the good-byes
  that are soon to be said and done.
I imagine my face with tear-filled eyes
and imagine my life left
  with many unpeaceful cries.
Why do you have to leave me like this?
Your love I'm really going to miss.
I won't be happy without you by my side
I can see it, and I can feel it, I am
  going to have to live with it;
But you'll be gone; and our hearts
will be wondering what went wrong,
As we live our memories.
  Memie Zimmerman

The Bird In The Old Apple Tree

My grandchildren play around me and sing,
As I sit here to-day in the old porch swing.
My mind wanders back down memory lane
To the thirties, the depression and so much pain.

At this time on our farm I was a young bride.
And worked in the fields by my husband's side.
There was no electricity so we used wood
To heat our home and cook the food.

I canned vegetables, fruits, jellies and jam,
Made our sausage, cured the shoulders and hams.
I made our clothes and learned to trim hair.
While making soap I gave up in despair.

Lonely and tired I sat in the old porch swing
Wondering what else life to me would bring.
Then I heard a note so pure and free.
From a little bird in the old apple tree.

He sang the joy of life, the blue, blue sky
Fleecy white clouds drifting by.
The beauty of Nature God gives and it's free.
Thank God for the bird in the old apple tree!
  Katie E. Edwards

I'll Always Care

Raindrops splash the puddles at my feet
As I walk along this lonely street
The sky is darkening; night is due
But I have nothing to return to
So I will just walk this lonely street

My love and I had a silly fight
And I thought it would be only right
For me to pack and be on my way
And maybe come back another day
I don't know where I will stay tonight

It's raining harder, or is it tears
Damn, we've been through a lot all these years
I can't believe this happened to me
This is not what I wanted to see
To be alone with all of my fears

I can't let pride get the best of me
I'm going back home where I can see
If she is still waiting for me there
Because, I know I will always care
And I'll always need her beside me
  Lary L. Wallace

Reminiscing

It's soo quiet in these ruins
As I walk through this town,
I feel stone crumbling under my feet
and I see smoke for miles around.
It's enough to make me weep,
All that remains of the main street.
It used to be on Saturday
Dogs would be roaming and children playing,
But it's changed now -
Winter turned on the old town.
Buildings emptied as people ran,
Winter came and stole the land.
If we could return to when
   this town was green,
When the trees were growing
   and the air was clean.
I guess it's too late to restore the
   old town,
For nature has come and knocked
   it down.

Salvatore Corso

Tears

The tears of joy now filled with sorrow,
as I weep in the coldness of a familiar place,
for yesterday will always drift into the darkness
of tomorrow. I have yet to see a tear tear
Through my skin and pierce my heart, like a
jagged dull blade; but if knew then what I know
now, my tears would never have fallen.

Rossinia Sarmiento

Time

Time is of the essence
As it dictates our presence
And ensures our sense
Of what love represents

Time moves meticulously slow
Or swiftly as sunshine melts the snow
Yet if spent well and so completely
Never lost in a forgotten memory

Time is a gem as precious as gold
More priceless in quality as we grow old
Slips through the fingers of our aging hands
As through the hourglass of sifting sands

Be careful with time and don't forget
Nurture it wisely each second you get
May time stand still while spending it well
And be kind to you as it bids farewell.

Pat Tonelli

An Important Day In My Life

My Mom and Dad let go of my hand
As I slowly walked to the door
It was time for me to take a stand
I would not need them anymore

The door shut with a click behind my back
I now stood there feeling bold
I stepped quickly past the towel rack
Because the tile floor was cold

All the practice I now enhanced
And I soon became quite drained
I stood up proud and pulled up my pants
I now was toilet trained

Nicholas Holtvluwer

My Summer's Child

Oh come to me, my summer's child,
as leaves turn red, and winds are wild.

Shed your cloak, like leaves that fall,
while geese in azure skies do call.

Drape your arms, around my chest,
then pierce the heart within my breast.

Silken maiden, reflect the sun,
with skin that flows, through, blouse undone.

These thoughts that pierce your silken vale,
flows down your legs, to feet so frail.

Chilly storms in distant skies,
send bashful breezes, down your thighs.

Oh come to me, my summer's child,
I am the one, you have beguiled.

Let me hold you, in lustful arms,
let me feel your love, your fragrant charms.

Radiant hand, with golden skin, fraught with pleasure, for hungry men.
And I no less, am free from sin, oh carnal fruit, so sweet within.
Beware the frost, beware the cold,
and come with me, we'll ne'er grow old.

Richard Lawrence de Gallegos

The Window

The man is a window
As lucent as glass
Seeing through his lies and stories.
Still he has women draped around him like curtains
Hanging by threads of mercy.
His blinds hold back the truth,
But soon, like a lightning bolt,
The sun will shine through.

You can see his breathing
Pushing back the curtains.
And what it left behind were his icy words
Like frost on a cold day,
Saying, only as he could,
"I need..."

Shandi Fuller

Sit

Sit here awhile and I'll tell you why,
As many live and several die,
A few more moments will pass you by,
And you ponder nothing more than why fish swim and birds fly;

Sit upon no mighty throne,
For the scars you'll bear are not your own,
They are coming from the heart's unknown,
And still you ponder of things not shown;

Sit in memory of youth's sweet bliss,
When life is that of innocence's kiss,
These are times we only learn to miss,
And you continue to ponder to endlessness;

Sit here still, even after I leave,
Yet stop the pondering, it has you deceived,
The lie you feel is no longer yours true,
For no man is greater or less than you;

That is the reality that you must face,
While you sit in this simple little space.

Keelan Jones

"Hard Climb Through Life"

Another stone has been placed upon the large wall of life,
as my body tries to climb the unending fortress.
Pebbles fall briskly beneath my weary legs
advancing slowly upward with much duress.

The final point for myself to arise at
will be that one remaining stone beneath my feet.
However there are many more tasks in life to be accomplished
along with the many goals which I must eventually meet.

Only then will that fortress be completely built,
as others can view the effort in it from a distance.
The trials and emotions will be shown proudly in that great wall,
with a hope to make a difference.

Upon viewing the glorious structure which I so carefully constructed
for the whole world to eventually find,
knowing in my heart that I have greatly fulfilled a dream,
and left a proud past behind.

Michael F. Backes

Life Between The Avenues

There's a crushed beer can mating with the bricks
As the man with brown teeth pushes his cart.
Two yellow cats are performing alley tricks
While the old lady is waiting for life to depart.

There are two avenues which may lead to wealth.
The unpaved life in the middle is pitifully rotten.
There is no such thing as good times or good health
Because the alley people are too often forgotten.

While the Marines battle in far away lands
The alley population fights roaches and lice.
The people of the avenues dance with the band
While the sounds of the alley are scurrying mice.

The rich and the powerful think they are so good.
There's something I wish I knew.
They are so blind to the hideous fact
That there's life between the avenues.

Mark Cubic

I Am Life

My eyes cannot hear or smell,
But, do I not need to see?
Though there are those who are prettier and wiser,
Is there no place for me?

The sun, the moon, and stars above,
I observe and admire your peace.
For chaos and hurt attempt to dismantle my life;
I'm a prisoner with faint hope of release.

I travel through the valley of the honeybee,
And dwell in the meadow of the lamb.
Yet, I can't share greatly in their freedom, you see
Simply, because of who I am.

I see bombs, bullets, knives and things
All made for good and used for harm.
I need to awaken from this nightmare;
But my clock has no alarm.

You see, I love life because I am life,
With no need to deceive or connive.
I want to share the pure joys life can bring;
But, I'm told only the strong survive.

William L. Brown Sr.

Mother "Beautiful Roses Of My Heart"

The rose is known for beauty with its petals soft and smooth,
As we look upon God's nature, to the eyes, the rose does sooth!

But just like life, a natural thing—it has some thorns on there,
But if they weren't on the rose, we'd not handle with such care!

A mother is just like a rose, the child is like the thorn-
The mother wraps soft petals, round the child when it is born.

As the child gets older, and life has run its test
To pierce that thorn into the heart of the rose, who's done her best,

It often takes a little while, of growing through the years,
To see that all the thorn has done, is left the rose in tears,

So Mama now I say to you, this thorn has seen the light,
She realizes so many times her rose was oh so right!

Now Mama, let me tell you, though thorn and petals so far apart,
You've been to me, throughout my life, beautiful roses of my heart!

Ruby N. O'Haver

Passing Through...

Life is like a house with many rooms.
As we pass from one to another, we pass through stages of life.
Sometimes we travel alone, sometimes with a crowd;
But always passing through.

Sometimes we would like to stop life for awhile,
And re-live a "special" moment.
But that is impossible.
We must always be passing on from room to room.

Sometimes we would like to speed up our pace, and quicken life.
But, this too is impossible,
For we must walk moderately and take life as it comes;
But always passing through.

The restrictions are many,
And the privileges few, in this house of life.
Sometimes I feel as if I can't go on.
But then I remind myself that you are in the next room,
And that makes the passing on, easier.

Someday we will reach that room that meets
And we will pass through the rest of the house, the rest of life,
Together.

Robbyn Hancock

Friends

I don't want today to ever end
because I was with you, my friend.

It touched me when you played for me
and sang those songs both serious and silly.

I loved the beauty of the mountains
and the sun beating down on me.

I like to talk with you; I like to be with you.
I ask myself, "Could it be true?
Could he like you just for you?"

You make me feel both shy and pretty
and full of fun and laughter.

You make me remember that life is good
and how the real me used to be.
When things were simple and I was free.

You might know that I want you; that might be clear.
With that desire there is also fear.

Fear of hurt and fear of caring,
Fear of pain and fear of sharing.

But, I'll take my chances maybe, anyway,
because once again you made me love today.

Shayne Steeby

Lost And Found

The lake calm, serene gives me peace within.
As we stand on the boat deck, watching
the harvest sunset, suddenly no longer
there with its beauty so rare.

I am saddened, at a total loss, for pure
natural things are often unsought.

You caress me, understanding my emptiness,
my pain.

As tears escape my eyes, flowing down, you
hold me tight, for we both know the time is right.

Our lives are worlds apart, this I knew
from the start.

Things happen for a reason, this I truly
believe, now that the time has come for you to leave.

Fate has a way of tossing us about, this
I have no doubt.

I await your return, like the sunset, this
I will not mourn.

Please make it soon, I am lost without you,
with you I am found.

Sharon Kaye Allred

Sea Shore

I love the sea shore - it's God talking to me
As we walk hand in hand, to the tune of the sea

The wind blows my hair and it's cool on my cheek
And my thoughts tumble out, in this calm that I seek

The waves roll on in with a firm steady pace
And the sea gulls cry out as they hang in one place

As the mist settles in and the clouds move along
The ocean sings loud its continuous song

When the darkness sneaks in, there's a feeling of peace
And my worries fly off and my cares all release

If you doubt there's a God, on a cool winter's eve
Just look all around, you can't help - but believe

Marlene Van Metre

Dance!

Dance! Dance with your heart and your spirit shall soar,
   ascending to heights never dreamed of before!
Dance! Dance, little angel, on gossamer wings,
   and soon you'll discover such wonderful things:
   emotions of joy and jubilation,
   arising from hard work and dedication;
   the aesthetic expression of feelings you'll find
   in the grace and the movement of body and mind!
Dance! Dance as the butterfly springs from its chrysalis
   with courage, charm and a strength so few possess;
   a perfection of motion with power and zeal,
   yet delicate and pure as an essence ethereal.
   And remember, in life any effort worthwhile
   may bring heartache, laughter, tear or smile.
   Embrace every moment at zenith or nadir
   with energy, patience, and conscience so clear.
So, dance! Dance with your heart and without hesitation,
   for it's then you attain your supreme destination;
   the confidence and pride to perform any song
   with the poise and the passion you had all along!

J. Wilkins

The Eagle

A cashmere fog wraps the valley in gray dampness.
Ascots of fog cling to the throat of the canyon.
On his aerie perch the monarch sits in the sun-drenched morning,
Scanning his vast domain.
A raven croaks in the Valley fog;
The eagle screams in the morning sun—
Worlds apart.

Orrice E. Adler

Swimmers In The Dark

There were twice two swimmers in the dark, fighting for first place.
At different times they swam like Olympians, not for fun,
but for life they raced.
Who knew what impact they would make, to me,
the man with the starting gun.
Who knew what feelings they would create, once the race was won.
God did not see fit to allow me the words with which to express
The enormity of the gift of me, of love once the swimmers drew breath.
I am, of course, talking of a common thing, that of giving birth.
But no one prepared this Daddy of the feeling and the worth.
The gift of my sons is when my own journey of love embarked.
Oh, if I knew then what I know now, when they were just swimmers
in the dark.

William J. Basten

Unconditional Love Dianetics Style

When I look into your beautiful clear eyes
at first, I become mesmerized and then,
I disengage my reactive mind
and I am no longer emotionally blind
Your clear eyes have become my spiritual guides
allowing me to see your God
and I feel my creative energy unclog
eliminating all reactive mind fog.
I learn how to become one
with you and your God
who is love unconditionally
for all eternity
and forever and always clear.

Vincent A. Cappello

The Ending Of Pain

Hurt may be caused by a million things on any day
At home, in a car, while at work or at play,
A cut, a burn, a splinter, or a speck in the eye,
Sickness in your body, a bomb from the sky,
The death of a loved one, the birth of a child,
A headache, a toothache - no matter how mild
Rejection, divorce, the betrayal of a friend,
A heart that is broken and will not mend.

And yet no matter how great the pain,
God gives flowers, sunshine and rainbows after rain.
Our Precious Father God in heaven above
Promises strength and salvation and much much love.
GOD gave his "Own Son" for you and for me
To shed His blood and give His life on Calvary's Tree.
That one day when our life is all finished here
Heaven eternal will be ours forever to endure!

We must ask forgiveness - Trust in Him - And believe
Then God's love, hope, joy and mercy are ours to receive.
PRAISE GOD! Sing Hallelujah! JESUS is your friend!
One day - In heaven - ALL PAIN WILL END!

Nell Jean Barnett

The View From Cap Juluca

Absolute tranquility. A crescent of powder sand rims an azure sea.
At my feet a gown is flung, fit for a wedding.
Scalloped lace smooth over cream satin.
Can I walk on water, or do I just feel that way?
The storms of hurt and betrayal are past.
I've navigated to safe harbour and shrugged off regrets with my
  winter cloak.
I'm at peace, suspended in time.
Weightless, translucent, insubstantial as foam.
But buoyed up with hope for the future.
Between my lashes butterfly-wing colours swirl.
Aquamarine, deepening to emerald, all shimmering with sequins
  where the hot sun strikes.
Streaks of purple meld beneath ageless mountains,
brooding below their benediction of clouds.
I hasten my steps where the sporting surf carves chasms on the
  coral point,
and a wave leaps to throw a bridal wreath high overhead,
showering drops of diamonds on my expectant face.

Mrs. R. Thornton Wilson

Dream

As the Dawn is breaking
At the crossing of the day
Here am I
Coming out of a sweet dream

Smack uncovered into a river
When the spirit of the waters is making merry
Into the arms of a Nereid of Turquoise

While the waves are rolling
Up and swelling down

Here am I
Laying on the flower-bed
Settings of the reefs

In ecstasies over your silhouette
That spins out slyly
Upon the crest of a glassy stream

When my legs intertwine into your legs
As the Dawn is breaking
At the crossing of the day.

Yvan Jean-Pierre

When Does The City Sleep?

When does the city sleep? When can it say its work is done?
At the end of a busy day, can it nod its weary head?
No, for then the workers of the night must earn their daily bread.
Not then can the city sleep.

When does the city sleep?
At midnight can it sink into slumber deep?
No, then the bright lights of Broadway claim their part of the busy
throng, who try to forget their cares in revelry and song.
Not then can the city sleep.

When does the city sleep?
Perhaps in the hush of early morn, just before a new day is born,
it can rest its weary head.
No, not then - a hospital room must blaze with light
as doctors and nurses work to save a life.
Not then can the city sleep.

When can the city sleep?
When can it close all its twinkling lights and rest?
When that last trumpet sounds and time shall be no more,
When He who rules the universe proclaims life's day is o'er.
Then and only then will the city sleep.

Pat Kelm

The Healer

His healing touch
awakens deep feeling
as my eyes adjust to the darkness
and my third eye sees the light.

His hands rest lightly, reading my most inner energies
drawing me deeper within, ever aware of
the warmth of the room
the rain on the window
the hands on my face
the face in his hands
the faith in his hands.

I heal closer and closer to the truth, my truth
my reluctant shadows and my most glorious being.

Today, as I felt that cloud lift before my eyes
I felt words well up inside me over and over, gently, insistently:
"You are a special child of God."

My own innermost affirmation
a gift I gave myself through his healing hands
to keep in my mind
long after his touch has faded.

Sandi Kimmel

Waiting

Pacing up and down the floor
Back and forth he can't take it anymore
He's waiting, waiting, pacing, pacing
Wondering what will it be.
Will it be a cute baby girl?
Or a handsome little boy
Whatever it is I will love it just the same
Because it will belong to me.

One hour, then two, what's going on in there?
Then he said "This just isn't fair!"
Then the nurse came out and he knew it was time.
To find out what kind
She walked very slowly coming toward him,
And finally said "Congratulations, it's twins!"

Teresa Soldyn

Weighted Flesh

I take a look into my past
back when the sun had fallen fast
it was too dark for me to see
just what he was doing to me.

His weighted flesh had held me down
every time I had come to town
it was this weight that would not lift
and then was gone my treasured gift.

He said things were just what they weren't
it's here my heart was being burnt
all at once, my flowers wilted
life had turned and become tilted.

So much he did to kill my youth
all actions taken were uncouth
I began to regret my birth
I blamed myself for all my worth.

I finally saw that this was wrong
and I blamed him before too long
I want revenge is all I know,
even though this was long ago.

Marianne J. Decker

Untitled

I've come back from where I was yesterday
Be at peace with me for I am your beauty
I conquer my enemies like day conquers night
may I take charge with you? May we lead this fight?
Ra lives for millions of years, His flames enlighten your faces
and blaze in your hearts - are you, offspring of the first man
to lie down without movement? Rise and your future will live forever
Your enemies will fall, you have life strength so rejoice
   when we rise, we live.
What is ours is within us - our power is in our hands
You cannot be held by the hand but you are we who can hold us in
   our hands
we are not the children who walk the path of yesterday
But we are today for untold nations
Our hour rest with you - we are a bind, a judge for the children
who shine and walk in light, a light which remains in our presence
That brings light to the dark which dovetail the enemies who live with us.
I am art, the children, the people!
(a se em hen her heh)
One man in return for millions.
   Morrison Washington

Lucky

One's lucky to live, and lucky to give.
Be lucky to share, be lucky to care.
To have all your wits! And if you should fall,
Lucky to get up, no breaks not at all.

Lucky to see; share laughs with a friend.
Walk down the road to the tree at the bend.
To have a nice dog with whom you can play.
A small garden to tend, a new path you can stray.

Lucky to see the sun paint the skies
New hues each morning and hear the birds' cries.
Lucky to sing, and easy to weep,
To have wondrous memories, forever to keep.

To feel the soft breezes, and hear the wind moan.
As it rattles the tree tops as you stand there alone.
Lucky you are, to see a good rain
As it fills the ground, again and again.

Life is still thrilling with a family to love
With music to listen to and the Lord's kind love.
Lucky you call it? No, you are royally blest,
Just share some compassion, God will care for the rest.
   William B. Wilbur

TRUTH

   The VERDICT has been WRITTEN, now let it
be said.

   As for many of us the SPOKEN TRUTH is
something we often dread.

   It is our MINDS from which we often
BLAME.

   We have suppressed our GUILT deep into the
subconscious, if this is not the answer we
must be INSANE.

   The JUDGE was ready to give the VERDICT
as he stood proud.

   "The JURY has found you GUILTY as
charged", as the JUDGE voiced it out loud.

   Am I DREAMING, no I must be AWAKE;
the TRUTH has been SPOKEN, there is no
MISTAKE.
   Kevin M. Brown

Wappapello

You were named after a proud Indian chief.
Beautiful Lake Wappapello, glistening in the silver moon light,
You truly live up to your name.
   Dear Wappapello, you hold my heart, a feeling I can't shake,
Memories of you bring me peace, in this world of turmoil.
   I hear you call to me, someday I shall return.
   Oh, my Cherokee ancestors, look down on me, send down the
gentle breezes and cool my aging brow.
   This Lake Wappapello, named after one of your own, when I stand
by you, holding my face up toward the heavens, I seem to sense
others long gone.
   Wappapello, in the state of Missouri,
Where the sun shines warm and sweet,
And the wind is soft and clean.
It's where my Mom and Dad lie sleeping,
Hold them close with sweet love forever.
   Ms. Willie-Dean Bartlett

I Remember Momma

I remember Momma, though she took ill when I was six months old;
   Beautiful things of her I've been told.
She held me gently upon one knee;
   And embraced me within her heart so graciously.
Through her eyes, she expressed tender love;
   She kept her faith to sweet God above.
Her time here with me was sad and brief;
   Since I know she's in Heaven I share no grief.
She suffered with MS for ten long years;
   But she always smiled beyond her tears.
I'll never forget that glorious day;
   When God took precious Momma home to stay.
Love and peace nestled all over the place;
   Beauty and tranquility shimmered upon Momma's face.
Some said that I was too young to understand, so I kept my
feelings to myself;
   They never knew how much I understood about life or about death.
Sweet memories of Momma in my heart forever remain;
   For I know through "Sweet Jesus," I'll be with precious Momma
again.
   Yes, I remember Momma!
   Linda Thames-Walton

Innocent Seductress

Something in her face, a grown woman, yet still a child,
beauty lying inside her, eyes growing increasingly mild.
A certain magical power exists inside her fingertips.
A peaceful serenity endures at the soft touch of her lips.
The luscious curve of her mouth portrays the impossibility to
   forsake.
The gentle tilt of her head expresses a vow she would not break.
to look upon her face creates a mysterious spell,
captivating the angels in heaven, the demons in hell.
The grace of her laugh, the touch of her skin,
is enough to drive you mad, sending you to the lion's den.
The power of her being reaches far, better known than the most
   distant lore,
controlling the waves beating against that far away shore.
Moving as a woman, she creates a tumultuous desire,
with a touch of her hand she'll take you ever higher.
Into the ever existing skies, for pain to never meet,
you will become entangled inside her web of deceit.
She opens her mouth, emitting a delicious sweet breath,
which, unknown to her victims, is the scent of death.
   Mary Hurry

Retirement

When you are young you can hardly wait
Because not working would seem to be great
You long to retire, get away from the strife
Do whatever you want for the rest of your life
I wish I had known some things in advance
Unfortunately you don't get a second chance
I spent all my time working and chasing the buck
Now it's too late, I've run out of luck
I'm left with no hobbies, no friends, no ambition
I don't even know how or care to go fishing
I'll tell you a secret, it's hell to get old
Your hands and your feet always seem cold
Your skin shrivels up, your hair gets much thinner
You fail at things that once were a winner
The days seem much longer, your memory dims,
The change in the weather can be felt in your limbs
It seems like the world is passing you by
You just can't keep up so why even try
Just when you think things couldn't get worse
Think of the guy who just went by in the hearse

Russell J. Coddington

The Distance

Time has past in the distance,
Because prayer has changed my circumstance.
I felt my life falling apart,
Then that glorious day, I asked
Christ into my heart
And there was such a peace, I never had felt before—
Now I shall not ever be alone anymore
During whatever comes down my pathway.

Luthia Shaw

Amelia Earhardt

I began take-off without my grandmother's clearance
Because two snake-wielding demons were on my tail
I propelled to the top of the tree fueled by fear
But just as I reached the highest altitude
The branch bent then snapped
I began to descend quickly in a downward spiral
I no longer feared the little demons
Only the pain of crashing into the rugged, solid ground

Monique Alexander

Change

Before a flower is a flower, first it's a thorn.
Before a butterfly is a butterfly, first it's a worm.

Springtime, it gives new birth to
remarkable changes of a wonderful kind

Within each spring season its splendor
ceases not, nor grows moldering, rather
it is rejuvenated by way of God.
His marvelous works I am beginning to
take less and less for granted.

Indeed there are extraordinary changes,
changes that change with the time like
now in the lovely months of April and May.
Things change, people change at
different times in different ways.
How we can be glad and rejoice for
the better most that there is one who
still remains unchanged.

God never changes. He's the same today,
yesterday and forever.

AMEN

Willie Owens

Woodwork

There's a beauty in her woodwork
Behind its painted shell,
And there's a loving person
Locked in a lonely cell.

In winter, flowers go away,
And the leaves fall from the trees;
But with time and love and care and faith
We move past bad memories.

The woodwork will take labor
To see the grain shine through,
But a broken heart takes love and time
Before you can trust it to tell you what to do.

The flowers always bloom in spring,
Behind a cloud the sun can't stay,
And the woodwork's bare behind the couch
Where she's peeled the paint away.

Thomas Maiden

Mother's Garden

Midst lovely stones so neatly placed
Behind my mother's home,
Is a gentle sloping garden
Where oft she loved to roam.

There, bold orange poppies bragged all day
To slender hollyhocks,
And dark blue English violets
Surrounded smaller rocks.

The multi-colored asters watched
Japanese lanterns nod,
Their sunlit magic mirrored on
the leafy goldenrod.

Though mother now lives in Heaven,
her garden lives in stone,
With lovely flowers in this place
She dearly called her own.

Shirley A. Nuottila

Cloud Shadows

Sun beams from blue skies bump into puffs of
   billowing white clouds
Casting cloud shadows on the land below.

Cloud shadows creep along the earth wending their
   way like silent giants
Following the pathway of each cloud.

Cloud shadows, silhouettes formed by clouds,
Their patchwork clutches mountains, fields, and rivers.

Cloud shadows retreat from where they lie
When sunlight fades or the wind sweeps clouds away.

Nannette Bauer

Good Morning

Wake to the sounds morning can bring
birds near and far, together all sing.
Song is the key to this special time
Making you feel very good inside.
Squirrels run around, it's play time for them,
Running, chasing each other like friends.
The air is pleasant, nice little breeze,
Leaves getting full, green are the trees.
With all of this beauty just right out the door,
How can one ask for more?
Take in this magical feeling they share;
Stop once in a while and just listen -
you're there.

Mark Turnbull

"I Wonder"

I stand in the shadows,
Behind the many faces and wonder.
I don't stand out like the others
I'm plain. I'm simple.
I melt between the crowds (or is it hide?)
And yet I wonder if you see me.
I stand next to you and wonder
Can you feel that slight touch of hand? Did you?
I did. And it felt like shock waves washing over me.
I wonder if you feel me.
On days when boldness is in my grasp
I stand in plain sight and open my mouth to talk.
Do you hear? Or just ignore? I wonder.
Sometimes I think
Yes! You see me.
Yes! You feel me.
Yes! You hear me.
And yet deep down in the darkest corners of my heart
I still wonder.

Sabeen Edwin

"To You"

Merry Christmas to you from me,
being with you I am as happy as can be.
Red, blue, green, silver and gold you're one Christmas
present I'd love to hold, here's a card you can unfold.
Cold air, piney smells, Christmas is in the air,
soft music, happy music, shiny lights
so many delights.
Wreaths with ribbons of red and green with little
bells that ring jingle, ling, ling, and
trees with cute little things and stockings full of treats
that make me want to peek. Boy!
 I'm so excited I want to sing jingle-ling-ling
 Merry Christmas to you from Me.

Myra Velasquez

Untitled

Anne ate eight ants at Amy's apartment.
Ben bobbed Billy Bo's bottom badly.
Christina chased Chris cat calmly.
Dan's dog did his duty.
Emily's elephant eats enormous amounts of eggs.
Fran's fanny flew fancifully.
George gulped green gatorade.
Henry Hamburger hated Harry hare
Ian is an Iguana in Israel.
Jo jumps joyfully and plays jinga.
Kate kangaroo can kick camels.
Lisa lamb likes licking lollypops.

Nicole Grant

The Kill

Teeth tear into the flesh.
 Blood drips. The mortal screams.
Two hearts simultaneously beat
 one slows then fades out.

Teeth refract and the limp body falls,
 smashing into the ground.
Dawns almost here. Running as the wind it
 tears through the night.

Unseen and unheard,
 to sleep through the day
and make the next night,
 to feast only upon those that fear.

Theresa Payne

The Soul Of Life

Love is known as the soul of life.
Between mother and child,
between husband and wife.

For a life without love is one without meaning.
Like an old hollow sea shell
or a bird that's not singing.

We all here on earth need love in our life.
To survive in this world that
can cut like a knife.

So try to give love in any given way.
Life needs love
each and every day.

Hold it precious and try to love others
like God loves his children
and children love mothers.

Stephanie Colleen Cook

Dream Interrogation

Some dreams can't be distinguished
Between reality and fiction;
Others are clearly pure creations of the mind,
Not possible.

Do people in general dream in reality;
Even if they don't live it, or are
Their visions in their sleep related to only
Fantasy which they believe is real?

Is a dream just another state of mind,
Or is it an actual dimension in which
Your soul diminishes to during one's slumber?

How can the brain get thoroughly rested
If the eyes are moving rapidly,
Catching visions of the brain's fantastical stories?

Perhaps, it is to keep the brain conscious
So that it might not slip into a deeper rest...

Suzanne McSwain

Long Ago, And Today

Long ago I was that black man
brought here from a far away land.
Bound and chained, I was in a lot of pain.
They beat me, until I could no longer see.
When I had reached that land unknown to me,
I'd never thought this is where I
would someday be free.

My heart had been broken, but not a word had been spoken
About the emptiness I felt deep
down inside.

Today I'm still, still that
black man. But I am living free,
just look at me!!! I'm able to
read, write, and think on my own.
I have a wife and some kids.
And a place I call home.

The clothes that I wear, not one little tear. My shoes
shine, and fit mighty fine.
Today, I'm a black man, an educated man, a business man.
But most of all I'm a free man.

Mary E. A. Perkins

I Remember A Little Girl

How do I remember thee!

I look lovingly at a picture on my desk. A little girl with long blond hair filtered by bright rays of golden sunlight, glowing impish full cheeks that held a bright smile filled with energy and eagerness.

Star War figures, Unicorns...always drawing and painting from those dreams that filled your head.

Going on hikes together, climbing mountains, fishing in ponds. Oh, they were adventures of bonding of young and older spirits.

That was a long time ago but not to me!

Where has the time gone?
You are an adult now!
At times I still remember thee fondly as that little girl.
A proud Father's prerogative!

Robert W. Hamel

Oklahoma Bomb

Death of Babies
Blood, doom, unexpected sonic boom
On a Wednesday - before noon
Why? Who?

Blame a nation, far away
They were guilty the other day
They don't understand "fair play"
Why? Who?

Murderous slaughter, extremist revenge
Cultist survivors - on a binge
Some of our own from the fringe
Is this who? Is this why?

Rules of court, jurors evidence
Must we allow them a defense, the law for them makes no sense!
Who? Why?

But - Procedures and Order
Create a way, better than a bomb - a - day
Better than a power play, two wrongs don't make a right; we say
It stops because we refuse to play
We are Who. This is Why.

Trip Smalley

"Over The Countryside"

Over the highways, over the bridges that lead to the sea,
Bo travel roads together just sweet little you and good ole me.
See all the wonders America offers would be a good ride,
She shows all of her beauty, has nothing to hide.

Over the deserts and on to the sandy beaches,
Through the dusty prairies, to the fields of ripe peaches.
On the roads of old cattle drives like a cowboy drover,
To the blue grass of Kentucky and hills of green clover.

Over the hills to the snow cap of high a mountain,
Quenching of thirst of fresh water from a stream or a fountain.
Visit military forts where "old glory" still wave,
Then to Grand Canyon which mother nature had to save.

Over the roads to the east where the sun shines so bright,
Then back to west and see a harvest morn at night.
Travel roads through Texas will take a full day,
Out west to California to San Francisco Bay.

Over the mountain to the top, gaze at the giant redwood tree,
Breathe in fresh air, that is given by God to us for free.
Everything you've seen was ever so, purty
Just like the poems I dedicated to you, my darling Verdi.

Kenneth R. Kitchens

Barrel Racing

Alas, for many years I found myself alone
bobbing around out at sea in a sawed off barrel
struggling continually to get my balance
doing whatever it took to right myself
sometimes coming so close to drowning
that I visualized death and wished it would take me,
but somehow stabilizing just before
the undertow sucked me down and united me
with all the debris that could not escape it.

All those endless days I paddled frantically
with my one pathetic chipped oar.
My strength increased very gradually.
My arms slowly adapted to the roughness around me.
Each day that went by that I did not die
I became a little more alive.
And finally, now, by default, I have crashed into the shoreline.
I stand up on my shaking feet and step out of my cocoon
A whole new set of mazes to find my way out of in front of me.
But, I live.

Louise Claudia Cody

La Rosa

Suave y colorante.
  Bonita todavía
deceptiva.
  ¡Ten cuidado!
No es tan inocente
  como se mira.
causa dolor,
  como muchas cosas en la vida.
  No dejas que le haga sangrar...

The Rose

Soft and colorful
  Beautiful and yet
deceptive.
  Watch out!
It is not as harmless
  as it looks.
It causes pain,
  like many things in life.
Don't let it make you
  bleed...

Marie Bassi

Endless Love

The thought of loving again,
Brings my heart to an end.
The feeling of being left behind,
Makes the future look blind.
The memories from the past,
Make me wonder how long we'll last.
Deep feelings touch my soul.
A needful heart wanting to let go.
I speak to you in my dream,
Trying to hold on to what seems,
To be love at first sight.
But I walk blindly to your light.
Speak with soft whisper through the night,
And try not to put up a fight.
Nothing's sweeter than the look of your smile,
Than the words you speak, so wise.
Your instincts are telling you to give me one chance,
And that this will never be our last dance.

Rebecca Sharp

The Seizure

A four year old's body trembled
As did her mother in fear
Frantically she called 911 for help
While her sister watched through innocent eyes
They knew not what to do
For nothing had caused this
No grievous sin
Yet the suffering began

Kimberly Gainey

Death's Last Grip

Death can be such a sudden thing.
Brings with it, its hashes sting.

Dragging along sadness, bitterness and hate.
With dreaded darkness circling you and locking its gate.

Alas! When you can no longer bear,
Its cloud, slowly begins to tear.

A small light begins to appear,
ever growing and becoming clear.

Warmth and peace will soon abide.
It's nice to know, God is still by your side.
Donna M. Bell

Untitled

I sit on a stiff chair drinking my seltzer water.
Bubbles form and explode in my mouth.
A beam of sunlight stroked the doorway like a soft hand to a baby's face.
Muddy boots sit.
I noticed that summer pushed spring aside when sweat beads formed on my hairline.
When I stepped outside, my memory of her increased with the heat.
She's gone.
The seltzer pushed itself down my throat when my emotions choked my soul.
Another day forgotten already.
The sounds of a noisy world tapped my shoulder.
Fishing gear lay beside the shack, I was ready to go fishing.
Kelley Corner

Truth

   Modest spring, mother nature peers through the rain, with budded trees, and tiny white flowers.

   She's grown old, or can she? The time is upon us, when her entity may fade, and she will not awake to take her beautiful new birth!

   She has grown sick, or can she? We a nation, must nurse her back to health, before it's too late!

   Our nation, united, will realize we are of one race:
the human race!
Neil W. Woods

My Birthplace, New York City

City of concrete, of iron and steel,
Buildings scraping a leaden sky:
Smokestacks belching; church bells peel,
Traffic sounds muffling a baby's cry!

The poor, the powered, walk side by side
Sharing some space every hour each day.
The city is fertile with dreams and pride
And aspirations that have gone astray!

A pulsing lady, this city, it seems,
Showing her multi-faceted face:
Birthing inventions and crushing dreams,
A wonderful, awesome, yet vibrant place.

To be born in this city and part of its life
To be a New Yorker and call it by name
Is to feel its vibrations, its toil and its strife,
Is to share in her glory, her power, her shame!

In the cauldron called living she has for-ged my soul:
Oh wantonly mistress, Madonna and shrew,
Adversity gave me a feeling of "whole,"
New York, I am proud I was once part of you!
Marge Roddy

Fore!

Reminiscently driving down the fairway of life,
Bunkers on the left and roughs on the right,
I recollected an eagle, familiar, in strife.

Her sleekness and regalia high above the green,
Catching glimpses as far as eyes could see,
Brought enthusiastic hope to a frivolous scene.

Eminence and pride overcome me so,
I refused to admit flaw
And list not to the foe.

On, no! She's hooked to the left!
Off course! They cried. Anticipation, I felt.
The eagle was wasted.... squandered...bereft.

The mighty power once represented in air,
Had experienced a stroke of human err
And puttered rapidly to a dark, aqua lair.

A challenger she was, and now, is no more.
Treasures unclaimed still lay up in store,
For no one — no one— cried out, "Fore!"
Teresa Crouch

"The Little Darlings"

The little darlings of my life
Are Treasures I inherited,
When I took a wife.

They are so adorable, loveable and sweet,
The next thing I knew,
They're stomping on my feet,
Saying, daddy, I love you!

One rolls her eyes filled with tears
And pouts as she looks up at me.
She knows I'll buy her any thing she wants
And she wants everything she sees.

Her little sister is fast learning
All the tricks of the trade.
People ask, am I happy?
I stick out my chest and proudly
Tell 'em, Happy! Man! I've got it made.
Merle Ann Schneider

Sunset

When the tide is low is the time to go
Around the bend and clear to the end of the island.
The marigold sun has already begun
To sink at the edge of the sky.
Such a radiant magic fills the air that you wonder why
You never before came there.
Quickly the night comes down, a misty dark, a veil, a shroud.
But there's the first star!
You wish on the star, a longing wish for one who is near
Yet who is far, as far as the star is far.
The magic is gone, forlorn alone, you turn and run
Back from the island's end,
Away from the wish that is not to be.
Back to the world of reality,
And your heart tells you why you must never return
Nor wish for that love again.
But more fool I, to keep on wishing
Till the day I die.
Olive P. Gay

Grandmother's Parlor

I have so many memories of my dear Grandmother Hill,
   But among all the memories that I hold close to my heart,
Sitting in the cool, almost reverent, solitude of my Grandmother's parlor,
   Is always the one that my mind and my soul refuses to let part.

The room was always chilly, because there wasn't central heating.
   I remember all the furnishings as though they were still there,
From the old mahogany piano to the grand old blue glass mirror.
   The sugar-starched, crocheted basket and Grandpa's favorite chair.

She had a special old scrapbook kept especially for children who came,
   It had all the greeting cards given her on special occasions in her life,
And my cousins and I could sit for hours and through this book thumb and thumb,
   And my cousin vowed he would have a book like this, if ever he had a wife!

And the smells in that room that comes to mind, were really quite unique.
   Slightly musty ones from the room being so closed-in and always roses
Grandmother had a rose garden, the loveliest that you just might ever find,
   Almost right outside the parlor, and those scents always tickled our noses.

I yearn to sit again in that room and feel once more my Grandmother's essence,
   I know those slow, lazy days of childhood are gone, just stored in my mind,
But the memories are there to recapture and the nostalgia's so wonderfully strong
   That my Grandmother's almost sitting with me, her smile so loving and kind.

Marlene T. Julian

Elephant Love

The dermis of a pachyderm is thick, hair-sprigged and rough,
But elephants, for one, believe the tissue wondrous stuff.
Though rather badly wrinkled skin, it's sensitive and tough
And offers each humongous beast protection quite enough.

An elephant can call a mate across ten thousand feet
By sending out a rumbling sound that humans cannot meet.
They come together purring like two kittens, soft and sweet
Then start to sway in rhythm to a pachydermial beat.

A pair will gently twine their trunks, caress each other's side,
Then flap great ears and slowly move in shuffle, dance and glide.
In time, the loving message gets beneath each thick, gray hide
And both the massive mammals choose together to abide.

Sally Miller

Spring Of Darkness

Spring is here a good thing for most
But for me it brings darkness
And no hope
I feel trapped in spring's sunshine
And green
The flowers and bees
  The way the birds sing

     I hide from spring as if I'm scared
     There is something to be feared
     It smiles to let me know it's there
     I don't smile back; I can't bring myself to care
     It would make them too happy to let them know I dared
     To listen, be happy, joyful and not scared

  I step outside and expect to find everything bare
But much to my surprise there is life and new growth
THERE! I begin to feel scared
Looking in wonderment at the sky I realize it's turning grey,
Some begin to cry, but me, I just smirk and nod my head
  When MISERY comes again I might be DEAD.

Lisa Trautwein

But I Can't Remember

Mother's Day is here again,
but I can't remember-
All those wonderful childhood moments,
but I can't remember-
Being safe and secure in your embrace,
but I can't remember.
All I feel is emptiness and the pain of years gone by,
the helplessness, the despair as you slowly faded away.
So many things I never got to ask, so much I'll never get to say,
The grandchildren who will never know you.
You were the best person I shall ever know, and
I will always love you,
but there is so much lost, that I wish I could remember.

Theresa A. Couzo

Who Would Be First

I thought we'd be together forever
   but I guess I was wrong.
One day you are here,
   the next day you are gone.
I tried to find you,
   but got lost in the search.
Now I am waiting for one love to return
   and searching for a new love.
Which should I wait for first,
   the old or the new love.
I get so lonely that I cry,
   I don't want to betray one love for another.
I must live my life either waiting or
   looking for the love of my life.

Sharon M. Lopes

Thy Will

Thy will be done we often pray,
But it didn't make sense, until that day.
My baby girl was close to death,
The machines were giving her her breath.
To have her stay was our hope,
But God was there to help us cope.
We finally prayed, "Lord, Thy will be done,"
And it wasn't long until He took her home.
They removed the tubes and many wires,
And for the first time I saw her smile.
An infant face so pure, so sweet,
Her tiny hands and her tiny feet.
I held her close and kissed her face,
And thanked the Lord for His wondrous grace.

Rhonda L. Fassett

Thank You

You are the woman who taught me to walk.
You are the woman who taught me to talk.
You are the woman who dries my tears.
You have stuck with me through the years.
I know I should thank you, but I'm not quite sure how.
All I can do is write for you now.
I can't say "I love you", I can't form the phrase.
My admiration for you grows through the days.
When I need comfort, I trust in you.
All I can hope is you trust in me, too.
I may disagree or put up a fight.
But I always am sorry later that night.
If I didn't have you, how would I live?
You taught me to love, you taught me to give.

Jessica Dunmire

rhythms of peace

fresh greens
fresh whites
snowy rhythms
fall in peace

silver icing
silver voices
spoken rhythms
talk of peace

festive lights
festive meals
remembered rhythms
live in peace

red ribbons
red smiles
new rhythms
call for peace

golden hearts
golden wishes
rich rhythms
walk in peace

Courtney Rouse

TOUCH OF SAND

The slender shadow of a woman
walking slowly along the sands of time
is reflected in the waves.

A woman of importance
possessing a soul of fire and
a heart of warmth.

She has a peaceful smile on her face
and a shine in her eyes...
as she sinks down in the sand
as if trying to live there for a moment.

She touches the sand
swirls it around in her palms
and gazes towards the waves.
She wonders...

One can only dream
what a woman of importance
possessing a soul of fire and a heart of
warmth
thinks about
while feeling the touch of sand.

Angie C. Thomas

Trapped Inside Your Darkness

I was trapped inside your darkness,
A prisoner of your lies.
I had many eager questions,
You had many false replies.
I was captive of your evil,
I was lost amongst the black.
I was in too deep and out of luck,
And there was no turning back.
My mind, it tried to rescue me,
My heart, it wished to stay.
My mind, it sensed the darkness,
And my heart pushed it away.
I was trapped inside your darkness,
I received your mental rape.
I was captive of your evil,
But I managed to escape.

Jade Lambert

Leaving

A
drifting
leaf
meets
me
at
your
feet
as
I
weep

Beth Borgman

Violence

Violence:
A DNA renegade
With blighted control;
Cloned at will
Within a weakened soul;
Threading with force
Without a plan;
Destroying fertile minds
Within any clan.

Violence:
Needing but a thought,
To deliver instant death
For any life within its path.

Violence:
A DNA blight,
Destroying humanity
With uncontrolled might;
For reasons so slight
With a DNA script
Unable to heal.

Agnes Holton

In Torment

A fanciful feeling
A fickle heart,
  faded emotions.

A hopelessness
A helplessness,
  haunting despair.

A dark road
A dark night,
  desolation.

A wounded soul.

Belinda Gross

Memories

A fading memory
A forgotten place
A picture you remember
An expression on a face
A very small moment
That is captured in time
It stays with your heart
But fades from your mind
An emotion you felt
A story recalled
A moment of happiness
A person you saw
They'll stay with you now
They stayed with you then
You'll never forget
How, where, and when.

Dana Edwards

To Be A Deputy

Oh how I loan to be
A Franklin county deputy.

To have a badge
Shaped as a star
And drive around
In my squad car.

In my uniform (two shades of brown)
I will patrol along
From town to town.

I will pull over other cars
And break up fights at bars
Go on small raids
And attend other crusades.

Yes I can already see
That is the life for me.

Andrew N. Trogolo

It Is

Love is the lightest blow
A giant can give;
Love is what we two build
With our melting bricks;
Love is the metal
Fastened to the magnet;
Love is like closed eyes,
Yet they're looking;
Love is gasping for breath,
Searching through the sweet
Crumbs around the doors.

Ann W. Dyer

My Little Corner Of The World

A bear came to visit me
a gorgeous sight to see
only a glass door separated it from me
I stayed there, with thumping heart
but soon he decided to depart

I love to roam outside my home
the trees reaching toward the sky
give me a feeling "on high" -
brook trout jumping in the pond -
that's beyond the beyond -
heron, mink and other come in spring
to have a choice taste of "my offering."
As the American flag I raise to unfold
over my little corner of the world -
I feel the liberty, "as it applies to me"
God's gift are more than eyes can see.

Edith T. Morcy

Our House

My Dad, he built a house for us,
  a house of logs you see.

A house with many windows,
  to enjoy the scenery.

The moose, they browse outside our door.
The eagles fly on high.

At night I watch the Northern Lights
  flash bright across the sky.

The sunsets' blazing colors
  dance around Mt. Redoubt's face.

And I really want to thank you Dad
  for building us this place.

Diane J. Thompson

Fantasy II

From the marble slab
  a human form emerges
smooth, sensual, seductive.
Angular lines chipped away
  to form the gentle curve
of muscle, body, face.
Its cool exterior
  touches interior warmth.
Explosive recognition
  of love sexual and sublime
and the fantasy lingered on.
George Da Roza

For Men Only

If after church your chance to see,
a lady pretty as can be,
Just say to her "How do you do?"
She'll smile and say it back to you.
To make her happy all the day,
and really win her heart you say
"I like your hat, it's beautiful."
All other words will seem quite dull.
She'll always think of you as such
a darling man she likes so much.
A pretty girl, you can be sure,
about her looks she is secure
Believe me Sir - I'll tell you that
she's never sure about her hat.
Doris B. Deriso

Dandelion

What is a dandelion?
A leaf or two,
then many more,
a tall straight stern
with bud on end.
a ruffle of green
to frame serene
a puff of golden sun,
a graying head
  a burst of stars,
to fly to some new place.
Dying limbs
a barren face
to earth return
   GONE!
To be born again.
Anne Benso

The Way Opens... An Ode To Tolerance

A telephone rings
a letter arrives
a siren wails
and so do I

  A retreat inward
    the silence beckons
    and deep within
      where all is gathered into All

The wailing subsides
and a new I comes forth...
the Way opens.
Ellen E. Howie

Halloween

H appy little boys and girls
A ll dressed up on Hallowe'en
L ike witches, goblins, cats and ghosts,
L aughing clowns, or dragons green.
O n each arm a paper bag
W here everyone can store his treats
E yes are bright and footsteps light
E cho softly down the streets
N earing home, the children say,
"'Tis Hallowe'en, Hooray, Hooray"
Elizabeth S. Park

Father

Father of hope, love, and care
A man of strength
The man of mankind
He works hard for his family
either, sick or well, his is
There for you
Rich or poor he is a hard-
Working man, to please
His family.
Joann Turner

Love Freeway

A simple hug I never felt
A mother's embrace I never knew
Just zig-zag roads with
Narrow squeaky bridges
A perfect highway, I was told.

Emotion of tears of joy
Connective advice
Are alien signs
On this love free-way

Siblings had what I yearned
Road signs made of
Chocolate chip cookies
Vanilla Ice cream
Little white dolls and all.

I clutch straws
Of dreams of fulfillment
Not a faded sign of love
Just another drowning man.
Carla Lawrence-Martin

Untitled

I thank the Lord for things unsung,
A neighbors hi, a washing lung
The blessing of the rain and sun
A rosebud, nurtured to full bloom
A husbands presence in the room
Children grown, long gone from home
Miss us so much they telephone
These things to some may common be
But Lord they near the world to me,
Thanks for everything Lord.
Charlotte Powers

A Place

There is a place I go to think
A place that holds only peace.
A place where I can go to rest
A place where I am the very best
A place I pray about the passing of time.
I come here often; it's in my mind
Jessica Kerr

Seattle

I looked up and found
A rainbow over the sound
Slowly it faded away
As if fearing
Its right to stay
Sky rainbow, sky rainbow

Appear again for us
in all your splendor
I think that you are
Heavens beauty vendor
Henry Vincent Scott

The Rainbow Of Friendship

We live in a rainbow.
A rainbow of doubt.
Doubt about friendship.
Friendship somehow.

We need more friendship.
Friendship without a doubt.
Friendship from other nations.
Friendship from other lands.

Children would bring that friendship.
Friendship from other lands.
Children are our salvation.
Salvation without a doubt.
Eva Saumell

Anonymous

Of neither flesh nor blood conceived:
  A rascal, just the same;
Since birth and death, you've refereed,
  In this, life's transient game.

'Tis by decree, who's born to be
  Among the human race;
Yet, even more decisively:
  The color of one's face.

Truly, you decide who'll live or die,
  And what matter takes up space;
Or when things cease, as years go by,
  What form shall take their place.

As servant of our Lord,
  You sit at God's right-hand;
Thus, it's with divine accord,
  All judgements, you command.

Our destiny's not left to chance:
  Your will does dominate;
For, though you have no countenance,
  Thy unknown grace is Fate.
George E. Pointon

Untitled

Eyes of tinted glass stare out
A mirror of others' souls
Picture perfect countenance
Emotions that find no holes

Stages filled with memories
Of curtain calls and encores
Her photo albums playbills
Now strewn upon rotting floors

The final act has been played
And her last bow swiftly nears
The theater is now empty
And silence is all she hears
Jacqueline Downey

"The Devil's Gain"

A promise to keep
A secret to hide
A distressful cry
Of a molested child
A mortal bond broken
Beyond repair
A burden to carry in life
We all share
A deep rooted problem
Carried with illusion of shame
A killer of the soul
The devil's gain
A time that is here and now
A guest to help the children
And give them faith in the human race

Charlotte Whitaker

What's Life

A resurrected tree in springtime,
A smell of sap of dead one,
A seed that dreams to be awakened,
A night that ends in dawn,
A wind that's born in sea,
A wind that whispers love to me,
A sip of brandy, a kick in ass,
An anger, curse, rebellion, revolution,
Compassion, tenderness and sweat of love,
Intolerance and frolic thoughts,
An esoteric sense of wisdom,
A walk at night and loneliness,
Desire, children's laughter,
An omnipotent will to live.
This endless inventory -
Does it belong to me?
I still don't know…maybe.

Helena Rozbicka

Life Goes On

As I watch today go by
A tear wells up in my eye
Because you see
the roads that I've traveled
I made some wrong turns
The roads that are left
I've got a lot to learn
And when my life is close to an end
I'll have another tear in my eye
Because my son
You have roads to travel
And you too will make wrong turns.

April Lolley

Shots

Buck, buck, is what I hear
all day.
While smoking hunts around
the way
things are getting hectic, it's a
mini Vietnam.
Got to survive this war so
brothers are armed
Buck buck buck, there it
goes again
another young brother gone
with the wind.

Eric Pastor

"As Season's Change As We"

To everything there is a season,
A time of gladness, grief and cheer,
Smiles of laugher, sadness of tears,
For every sunset there's a sunrise.
There is no rainbow without the rain,
No summer time without the spring,
Golden days and frosty nights,
Icy winds throughout the days,
With winter's newly fallen snows.
Whose years are like the seasons,
Let the future hold no doubt,
There'll come a change of scene,
With rainbound skies of hope and love,
I have seen your different faces,
Life is like the changing seasons,
   Upward always climb,
   As the seasons change as we,

Deborah M. Vanderwood

Nights

Nights…
A time to reflect
On things that happen
Long ago
memories
That haunt my very soul
Dreams
That bring back horrible sights
How I dread the dark of night
And yet I sink into deep despair
Fighting memories that are still there
Will darkness of night hide my thoughts
Will daylight bring relief
Or will I continue to dwell
In this nightmare of grief
To reflect on things, that will remain
As I dwell with torture and pain
And contemplate the nights to come
On things that cannot be undone

John E. Hatcher

A Silent World

My little boy has never heard
a train, a plane or even a bird.
With his hands he speaks to me,
much worse would be if he couldn't see
the sky, the sea or even a dove
I have to thank the Lord above
for giving me this love and joy.
Thanks again for my little boy.

Alma Martin Leboeuf

Thanksgiving Day Feast

My mother has been cooking
a turkey all day long.
I have been helping mother cook
the stuffing and the pumpkin pies.
When we get the cooking finished.
And the turkey is done too,
We can all sit down to a great

big meal and give thanks to the
Father above.
Yum!
   Yum!
      Yum!

Amber L. Hagan

Silence

Only in the silence she would see it
   A vision of a little girl
   Sweaty hands clutching a doll
   A doll made from a man's sock
   Its button eyes hanging by a thread
   Its yarn hair messed and tossed
   Its cloth dress ripped and torn
A girl sat clutching a doll
   Her eyes staring blankly ahead
   Her mouth unable to speak
   Her mind unable to think
   The faint shadow of a man
   The smell of blood in the air
   The haunting silence he left behind
A woman sat clutching a doll
   Her eyes staring blankly ahead
   Her mouth unable to speak
   Her mind unable to think
Only in the silence she would see it.

Cathy Pezzuti

The Child Who I Am

When I think
About myself
I remember the dreams,
hopes,
and prayers
of my past,

And the beliefs that were
Innocent and
carefree,

And my goals that were
so close and
Barely out of reach.

When I think
about myself,
I think of the child
That I used to be
and who
I will
always remain
to be.

Jessica Josephson

This My Love

The unspoken promise of Life and Love
Adoring, Compassionate, Unselfish Lover
Mistress of my thought
Needed, Wanted, Desired

   This my Love
Hair like the finest silk
Eyes far bluer than the sky
Lips, delicate, yet firm but yielding
to the touch - unleashing a passion,
yet to be known

   This my Love
Softness of voice, smoothness of body
Coolness of untouchable beauty
A precious Jewel - untarnished by the
passage of time
   This my love

Donald A. Sharon

"Love And Happiness"

Love and happiness is what you gave me
After fifteen years of marriage.
Though we married thrice,
And divorced twice,
You finally filled my life
With love and happiness.

Without love there is no happiness.
Without happiness there is no love.
But combined the two
To make a glue that
Will bond two together, forever.

Love and happiness is what we have
Few find it, others can never have it.
How lucky we've been,
To be given again, the chance
To find love and happiness.

Janita Valdez

Word

A word can tell a thousand tales
A word can have a thousand meanings
A word can cause a thousand feelings

One word can bring joy
One word can convey love
One word can break a heart
One word can tear you apart

One word may start a war
One word may bring peace
One word may save your spirit
One word may never hear it...

Yet words can tell a thousand tales
And words can have a thousand meanings
But those who choose not to listen
Have not yet felt a thousand feelings

Ida M. Pogue

This Too Shall Pass

She asked—
"Am I the one, is it really me?
What has become of my sanity?"

The Empty, The Ache, the Pain.
The Joy had become her bane.

She asked—
"Where do I go from here?"
My heart and mind are full of fear.

Her intuition told her to "Get Out"
So alone was what it was all about.

The Hurt, the Anger, the Flame—
She'll not look for one to blame.

"Am I the one, is it really me?"
Now she'll search for who to be.

Part of life are Loss and Pain
Flowing through all toward the gain.

She was reminded by a dear friend—
"Be gentle with yourself—all will mend"

"Joy may be next in view.
So much depends on you!"

Celia Bolyard

One Life Ends

The darkness of the eyes
All can see the hidden lies.
The blueness of the cheeks,
Only as death tries to peek.

The body yesterday was no wimp,
But now look as it lays limp.
The shadow of darkness now lurks,
Waiting for the body's last jerks.

Many shall gather only to see,
This body of what it use to be.
Nothing has become of this time,
Only to walk a very narrow line.

The breeze becomes a gale,
Is this the soul up for sale?
The gamble is heaven or hell,
Only the lived life shall tell.

The soul now drifts through the air,
Somehow this seems not so fair.
Body and soul hopes for a true call
Then finally a tear shall fall.

Debbie Jacobs

From A Farm House Window

As I look out the window the grass
all covered with dew.
It looks like many diamonds as
the sun comes shining through.

It's that time of the year that the
leaves start to fall.
Soon a blanket of snow will
cover it all.
The fence post will be snow
capped all up and down the lane
Jack Frost will paint his pretty
pictures on each window pane.

When it squeaks with each
step you take in the new
fallen snow it is zero out
side or even below.
That deer child of God is
the time to go where the
warm breeze blow.

Jacob W. Van Wyk

"A Mother's Day Thought"

Be grateful for your mom that's here
and don't be afraid to hold her near.

To tell her how much you love her so
and never, ever want her to go.

The day will come when she'll be gone
and then your heart will truly long

To say the words, "I Love You"
and "Happy Mother's Day" too.

Gwen Radt

In My Life

In my life I know it can be
A treasured time for you and me
A time for love and not for hate
I know we all are not too late
So take the few that have this dream
To show the others how life can be

Debbie McCullough

All Was...All Is!

Emerald waters have vanished
 All is lost!
Periwinkle skies are blinded
 All is unseen!
Crimson roses crinkle
 All is ugly!
Violet ribbons smooth the night
 All is forgotten!
Bittersweet kisses poison the snow!
 All is deceased!

Sapphire seas have risen in triumph
 All is found!
Clear heavens gleefully awake
 All is seen!
Peach blossoms open with thanksgiving
 All is beautiful!
Diamonds adorn the resting sun
 All is remembered!
Pure rains welcome a unity in rainbows!
 All is ALIVE!

Jennifer Rose Yantis

"Forgotten"

One nice spring day I took a walk
 along a country road;
'twas turning dusk; my shadow stretched
 long-legged as I strode.
Amused, I watched the giant as
 it crossed a rye-grass nook,
when suddenly I had to stop
 and take a second look!
A tombstone jutted through the grass!
 Another! Are there more?
I struggled through the tall dry fronds
 and counted near a score -
some tall, some short, all old and worn
 from years of wind and rain;
the etchings were as faded
 as the mem'ries of those there lain.
I wonder of these people,
 how did they live and die?
Some old, some young, some gone too soon,
Forgotten in the rye.

Joann Ryan

Searching

What are we searching for,
 along the pebbled beach,
A special shell, a gem-like stone,
 a twisted tree-root, borne upon
The waves from distant shore?

Perhaps a piece of seaweed, or
 a starfish stranded high and dry,
Or a horse-shoe crab whose carapace,
 unchanged for lo! these many eons,
Echoes forth the mystery of life.

What we may find in all our searching
 is peace of mind, the peace of union
With all the family of Earth,
 the living remembrances of both
The change and the eternity
 that are present in our "now."

The wind is gentle, the water calm,
 its ripples tickling the shore,
We are all one.

Barbara D. Schriever

Mindfulness

I flew
Along the shoreline.
I watched
As sea played with sand.
I saw
Water kiss Sandpiper feet
And then retreat.
I heard
The world sing
As waves moved
In rhythm
With the earth.
I gave
Thanks for beauty.
I knew
Peace.
Helen H. Susky

The Turkey

The turkey is a happy bird
Although his looks are quite absurd
And no he's not a soaring eagle
And no he's not a singing lark
And no he's not a noble puffin
But in defense he's great with stuffing
Colleen A. Frank

Untitled

I've loved you for so long,
Although you never knew.
I tell myself it's wrong,
To keep on loving you.

I can't tell you who I am,
Though I long to let you know.
I want you to hold my hand,
And help me make it through.

I dream of you by my side,
As we walk hand-in-hand.
In the moonlight we have nothing to hide,
Walking barefoot through the sand.

But we all must wake,
And all dreams must end.
My happiness is fake,
And my wounds will never mend.

I say I'll give up,
And that my obsession has died.
Yet all you do is look up,
And I know that I have lied.
Amber Machalk

Clouds Or Sunshine

Today the sun's behind the clouds.
Am I sick, or just plain lazy?
To feel like this just drives me crazy.
It's hard to separate the two,
Which one makes me feel so blue?
Can't get going, life's flavor lost.
I feel at sea, by waves I'm tossed.

The phone just rang, the nurse's voice,
My tests are in - Can I rejoice?
"Biopsy clear, things can't be hurried.
Healing still, so don't get worried
Take your pills, and you'll discover
It won't take long, you will recover."

I'm not out of the woods, but I can see
Tomorrow the sun will shine on me.
Hazel McAllister

Abyss

Moving like a shadow
Amongst the unknown
Winds stirring the emptiness
Of dreams only half grown

Memories like fluffy clouds
Unchained melodies floating asunder
Question of what could've been
Only repetitions of hopeless wonder

Love like desert winds
Scorched and barren, left in despair
"What if" on threads left hanging
Ball and chain of everlasting disrepair

The abyss lies open and yawning
Another hopeless soul it seeks to take
Yours becomes a ghost of past desire
A nightmare forever left in wake
Dawn Boone

Everything Reminds Him

In the foggy mist
An aged, crippled man
Leans on a cane.
He wears all black,
And his cold, white face
Is in his hands.
He cries for his love.
He stands on sharp rocks
In a rugged field
That reminds him of his painful past.
The sky is a light shade of blue
Streaked with dark, gray clouds
Almost ready to burst
Into tears of rain.
The clouds cover the cruel memory.
He can still see
The bullet take his wife's life.
Birds disappear into the trees.
He tries to forget,
But everything reminds him.
Amy Flahave

Peaceful Darkness

When the lights go out
And children are sleeping
Traffic outside is slow
All is calm

The night is my time to think
Everything is quiet
My mind is clear
Thoughts are easy

Problems aren't so tough
Solutions are possible
Handling them one at a time
They disappear

A few moments of silence
To sort out my thoughts
Hours of restful sleep ahead
To finish off the day

I feel closer to God at night
His answers are easier to hear
Together we share the peace of the darkness
And tomorrow is greeted with a smile
Carla Mayer

Anger

My body lies restless
　an anger in me persists
My hands and legs quiver
　an anger which insists

My eyes I cannot see
　an anger that lives in front
My mouth I cannot speak
　an anger I must confront

I'm afraid to leave the house
　an anger seeps through my pores
I'm afraid to sleep alone
　an anger cries for more

My soul rests tenderly
　an anger leads to anxiety
My heart pounds rapidly
　an anger faces reality
Christina Day

Untitled

Rejected, but included,
An empty feeling, but full,
So alone, but not lonely,
How I feel, not complete.

An outsider, but in,
Far away, but still around,
Shut out, but closed in,
Who I am, not myself.
Janelle Muscarella

Phantasma

P hantasma is a dream, a vision
　an illusion of the brain
H overing in our minds, fluttering
　in our souls
A spired by our deepest thoughts,
　clinging to our dreams
N otable by the way we act and
　feel toward others
T olerated because we can't
　distinguish dreams from reality
A llowing us to explore new
　adventures and paths in life
S howing us the way to be free,
　to be bold
M aking us see weird and
　meaningful things that should be seen
A rt in the making of our minds,
　the phantasma just began.
Courtney Huber

Papaw

Take heed the man who is simple,
And labors all his days;
For he keeps his eyes and ears wide open,
And gives knowledge in a phrase.

He seeks not fame or fortune,
He wants no prize nor pay;
For life is just a riddle,
To be answered day by day.

His passing came like many,
Sudden and unjust;
But he leaves behind a legacy,
For wisdom ne'er turns to dust.
Clinton C. Seybold

I Wish

If I had wings of an eagle
and claws of a bear
I could claw through rocks
and fly anywhere.
If I had eyes of an eagle
and muscles of a bear
I could pick up a tree
and see anywhere.
But the way I am is good for me.
But if I could,
I would,
have wings of an eagle
and eyes of one too,
claws of a bear
and muscles of one too.
But if I can't,
I want to be
ME.

Cassie Jo Cleere

Statue Of Liberty

She held aloft her flame
   And from the world they came.
Born of compassion and need
   She accepted the world's seed.
Now these illegals this land do roam
   Over this country they call home.
Murder, rape, and jail
   Tell a sorry tale.
We have our own sick and poor
   Those for whom we should do more.
Time to get tough.
   Enough is enough.
Do what is right.
   Blow out the light.
Give us back our glorious land.
   Time now to take a stand.
Keep your hungry and poor.
   We want no more, no more!

Betty E. Stisser

* * * *

I sit in the park
and God the Father
is there.

The little trees
are just beginning
to shed their leaves

And I am with
this Person.

I am glad
to be with Him.

John Cronin

I Love Jesus

Yes I love Jesus
and I know he loves me.
He loves me when I'm happy.
He loves me when I'm sad.
He loves me when I'm good.
And he loves me when I'm bad.
He always likes to see me happy
And never see me sad.
Likes to see me good
and never see me bad.
This is why I love Jesus.
And I know he will always love me.

Florence Meling

Picking Up The Pieces

We're picking up the pieces now
And going on with life somehow...
Pressing ahead, not looking behind
We must go on, make up our mind.

We must now fill this empty space
And, bit by bit, this pain erase.
These tears we must now put aside.
For too long now, we've sat and cried.

Things are getting brighter. You'll see.
Now, there's only my son and me,
The image of your father's face
But with a sad look in its place.

The most precious of souvenirs,
You have his hair, his nose, his ears;
But you are you; and he was he.
Yourself he would want you to be.

Your father's dead, but we are not
Even though we miss him a lot,
He would want us to find a way
To be happy again someday.

Connie S. Crum

Untitled

She struggled through the hours
   And haunted by the nights
The memory of his footsteps
   The fear of his very sight

The pain and fear that he instilled
   Could never be forgotten
She lay upon her bed and prayed
   As she held her daddy's shot gun

"Take my life, oh please dear Lord
   for I have been betrayed
I cannot live my life this way
   I'm dirty, ashamed and afraid."

The Lord came to her in the night
   And held his child with all his might
"I'm here my child, I have not gone
   You stay with me and you won't be wronged"

She now shined through the hours
   At peace with every night
The strength with in His footsteps
   And the love within His sight

Amy L. Beaupre'

The Main Effort Is Explosion

His mind is in confusion.
   And he likes an intrusion.
The main effort is explosion.
   This is his religion.
His thoughts are all hate.
   And you can see the trait.
He knows no goodness sake.
   This is not in his mate.
His efforts are all terror.
   And he is a real big swearer.
The action is opposite of fairer.
   This is meant to be horror.
His main goal is to kill.
   And he will never tell.
The action is not to kneel.
   This is the road to Hell.

John H. McNally

No Greater Love

Jesus wore the crown of thorns,
And heard the jeering mob.
Why did He bear the pain and shame?
That man God's love might see.

They cruelly nailed Him on the cross.
"Father, forgive." He prayed.
It wasn't the nails that held Him there.
It was His love for me.

Christ was crucified for all,
And not for me alone.
Angels could have taken Him down
Except for his love for thee.

Our savior died upon the cross
To save mankind from sin.
What was the thing that held him there?
Love for humanity.

Christ rose from death on the third day,
And how blessed are we
Who give our thanks for the wondrous love
That held him on the tree.

Esther Brotherton

"A Mother's Prayer"

Thank you, God, for this day,
And helping me in every way
I'm sorry for the things not right,
But Lord, Please help me sleep tonight.

Oh God, You're Great and good to me.
I thank You for our family
Please help us love and serve you too,
And help us see that we need you.

My husband is so good to me,
My favorite on our family tree.
He works so hard and helps me too,
We have so many things to do.

We try and do the things we should,
And be to others kind and good.
We love you God, and as we pray
Please help us with another day!

Cyril M. Welles

Rosebud

You are like a rose,
And I like the morning dew,
That ever longs to touch your petals,
Just to be with you.

Amy Lanzendorfer

Spring

When the snow begins to melt
and the grass starts peeking through,
when we hear a pretty robin sing
and he then hops into view.

When the trees begin to bud again
and the crocus soon appear,
we know that spring is here again
what a lovely time of the year.

It's a time for many miracles
that only God can bring,
it's a time for hope and a time for love
this magic time called Spring.

Bea Hanson

The Mouse

I'm just a little girl
And I live in a great big house
'N sometimes when I go to bed
I hear a little mouse.

A gnawin' and a scratchin'
And maybe biting too.
N gosh oh gee I get so scared
I'm almost black and blue.

N I cover up my head
and hope he can't find me
I wouldn't want him in my bed
Right this close to me.

N Sometimes if I'm real brave
I throw my oldest shoe
And if the old one isn't there
I throw the one that's new.

I don't never call my Daddy
Cause he makes such fun of me
But I guess I'm just a woman
Cause all I yell is e-e-e-e-e-

Anna V. Shore

Flying With Love

Love asked me to fly with it again,
And I tried running, but it caught me.
It swept me into the heavens,
And carried me across the stars,
Into a euphoria I never thought possible.
Only to let go of its grasp,
And watch me crash to the ground.
Love revels in my pain, as I lie there,
Begging to fly again.
It laughs at me, and taunts me.
Someday, when I fall out of love's hold,
And shatter into pieces on the earth,
The pain will vanish.
And I'll soar higher
Than love or I have ever been.
No longer subsisting,
And with no one noticing
That I have gone.

Deborah Emery-Gigliotti

"Unfinished"

You walked into my life
  and into my heart, smiling.
When you asked my name,
  our hearts and eyes connected.
Two lonely people whose lives
  had been bruised
Found each other as though
  Brought together.
Years of sharing that love
  Basking in its comfort.
You told me ours was a love
  that was meant to be,
Safe, secure, content.
  And then, the world darkened -
Your strong heart stopped beating!
  And mine stood still -
In disbelief.
  How am I supposed to go on -
without you?

Chris Heitman

How This Daughter Really Feels

She has brown hair and blue eyes,
and is very kind and nice.
She never cheats nor lies,
and is more than sugar and spice.

She takes me where I want to go,
and never complains.
She let's me drive her car,
and used to take me on trains.

She gave me my first teddy bear,
and bought me my first bike.
She has a piece of my baby hair,
and she's everything I like.

Who is this unknown source?
My Mommy of course!

Cheree Mayes

Hold Fast To Dreams

Hold fast to all your dreams my friend,
and keep them safe from men of spite.
For one day you will see them rise,
but for right now you'll have to fight.

Fight to keep them all alive
or soon you too will fade.
Never let them give you gold,
and say it's even trade.

For what your heart and soul both offer
cannot be weighed or measured,
and feelings that you have of life
are always yours to treasure.

Don't bury all the love you have
behind a wall of scars and tears.
Hold fast to dreams so they may live
within the coming years.

Cathy Juarez

The Hardest Love Is
What We Go Through

We've been through rough times,
And the hardest may be yet to come.
You and I have seen each
other at our best and worst and
still we remain friends.

Past hurts and angry words have
not built walls between us, changes
must sometimes be made and we
must not be afraid to make them.

In the darkness of those
nights I see you in my mind and
I can feel the love we share.

Andrew Slaughter

Untitled

Sun is shining
And the snow is on the ground
Wood in the woodshed
And not too far from town
Venison in the freezer
And beans in the pot
Cold outside but inside it's not
I'm thankful for these blessings
But wish you were here
So we could see your face
And have a little cheer

Frank T. Ryther

Summer Leaves

When summer leaves
and leaves fall,
some don't think it's
good at all.
I think it's nice to
sit and watch,
when summer leaves
and leaves fall.

John Harper

Brotherhood

I stood on the mountain peak
And looked down the valley low
I shared some harvest seeds with those
Who live in the valley below

Why shouldn't I help my brother
So he can help another
Along the way to sing happy songs
When things seem to go all wrong

Some of my brothers have greater needs.
So why not help when I succeed.
No greater joys in life to me
Than sharing with others blessing seeds.

The joy I feel is all so real
When those who succeed help those
in need
Brotherly love will have power enough
To battle life's storms when raging and
rough.

Hannah Forsyth Dixon

Enjoyed

I enjoyed the moment of your smile.
And moments never last.
We shared it for a little while
And now it's turned to past.

So think better of tomorrow
And have treasures in the past.
For each moment begins to be followed
As a reference to the last.

John Slaga

The Four Seasons in Haiku

Spring

The rains wash the world
And leave the air and the earth
Fresh for a new year.

Summer

Blossoms burst open
To share their richness of scent
And perfume the air.

Autumn

Winds whirling about
Calling for a lull in life
Put the world to sleep.

Winter

Soft snow swirls around
Fluttering fluffily down
Resting on the ground.

Debra Sunukjian

Endless Future

As the days turn into future
and my conscience is my guide,
my soul turns into star dust
and it drifts on through the sky.

My heart beats out a rhythm
and my mind floats on the breeze,
my ears seek words of wisdom
and my eyelids part to see.

There's no time for confusion
or to waste the time of day,
with meaningless involvements
as we journey down life's way.

Life is too short and precious
in so many little ways,
so take my hand and walk with me
and we'll laugh and dance and play.

We'll frolic in the sunshine
and we'll drift out on the wind,
as the days turn into future
and just hope it never ends.

Helen L. Scarborough

How I Felt Yesterday ... Today ...

I felt like running to the church
and rolling on the carpet of the church
floor.

I felt like crying out to God. Lord,
what is this? What is ... happening
to me?

I'm laughing when deep inside I
wanna cry ... .

I'm smiling when things I see and hear
make me want to roll over, roll out,
and faint ... .

I feel this way, today ... .
I feel like I wanna faint! Lord,
I feel like I wanna, faint!!!

*Donnie Pearlethia Delores
Pendarvis Davis*

After The Rain

She looks at the water
And sees clouds in repose.
An inverted street lamp,
The roof and side of a shop.

A child on a bicycle
Rides through the puddle
Erasing the picture.
All is quiet again.

She looks down now
And sees her face:
A young woman, short curly hair,
Wearing a white cardigan sweater.

Who is this woman?
What are her innermost
Hopes and dreams?

She stands and meditates on the
Reflections
After the rain.

Dorotha Loewen Dory

Cactus Man

A sticky white film
and sharp points at each end,
protecting their soft green middle
from outside intruders.
But for him they let down their guard
and allow his faithful touch
to bring soft petals to their buds.
They take on new shape,
stretching to the light,
letting out new flowers
of orange, red and yellow.
Their deadly spines
do not prick him
and his long black hair
flows around them
and in return
they whisper slow songs to the wind,
carried in stories of the cactus man.

Heather Grinstead

Seaside

A sea gull cries overhead
   And soars into the heavens.
A sandpiper scurries by,
   Always in a hurry.

As the waves crash below me,
   I view nature through glazed eyes.
The glaze of tranquility;
   The silent reverence of peace.

I am in a world that knows no pain;
   A world that sets my heart free.
Free to be whole.
   Free to be me.

Some day this world will be mine.
   A world that wants only to be simple;
Filled with sunny days
   And turquoise waters.

But until then,
   I will always return to the seaside,
And dream of the day
   When this world will be mine.

Benny Harden

Intuition Fulfilled

A new day dawns, light as whisper,
And softly nudges me awake.
Soft grey fingers of the dawning
Points me toward a new daybreak.

Like a summer cloud, my mind flies
As I lie here thinking, thinking—
Ah, the wondrous potential in
The day and I interlinking.

I close my eyes and think ahead,
In quiet anticipation,
To the promises promised by
A twinkle of intuition.

The golden day gently unfolds,
Inviting me to step inside,
And there I find, to my delight,
The faith I had was justified.

When day is done and I lie down,
I like to think myself to sleep
Reviewing each precious moment
As a treasure I want to keep.

Ellen Wheeler

"Prayer Power"

Every problem can be solved,
And solved right if you pray;
Practice thinking about Jesus,
For a few minutes every day.

Pray using simple natural words,
And tell Jesus what's on your mind;
Concentrate on His Holy presence,
And pray for all of mankind.

Pray throughout the business day,
But don't always ask when you pray;
Instead affirm Jesus' Blessings,
And give thanks in this special way.

Pray that Jesus' love and protection,
Will surround both family and friend;
Pray with the sincere belief
That His will shall be done in the end.

Be willing to take what Jesus gives you,
It might be better than your request;
Practice putting everything in His hand,
And for the ability to do your best.

Frank Olivencia Jr.

To Heaven

He takes us through the darkest night.
And takes us to that wonderful light.
No hate in his eyes.
No sin in his heart.
He's all full of love,
ever since the start.
And if you let him in your
heart you'll then see why
he died for you and me.
He shed his blood, he rose so high.
To make a haven in the sky.
That haven is heaven.
The world of the Christ
The world for the saved
The world of the nice.
The world you will go to
if you believe in Christ.
So ask yourself am I naughty or am I nice.
Then be saved, and rise so
high to that heaven in the sky.

Jayme Salvanish

God Cares

I thought of you today
and said a little prayer,
I asked the Lord to bless you
and keep you in his care.

May his hand reach out and help you
Each hour of the day;
May the sunshine of his smile
Brighten and guide your way.

May you feel the love
That is sent to you today,
May you know that God Cares
in a very special way.

As we count our many blessings
May we always be aware.
That God in all his beauty
Really, really cares.

Anna F. Turpin

Someone

I know that Jesus died for me
And that He hung upon the cross.
How could I possibly forget
And think that I am boss?

I know the plan He has for us
Is for a certain reason,
And each will do what he must do
And reap when it's his season.

To follow Him is my desire,
To let my light shine bright!
But myself gets fully in the way -
And blinded, I lose sight

Of the One who makes life worth living,
The One who loves us so.
And that is when He sends me someone -
Someone who has His glow.

A friend who shares His love and will
With encouragement and care.
The friend is you who always seems
To cheerfully be there.

Joanna Showers

Autumn Love

When the leaves fall
And the birds call
As they ever southward fly,
Then, alone, my dear,
I wish you were here
And I softly breathe a sigh
For a love gone wrong,
So I sing my song,
Of my love for whom I cry.
For I love you still
And I always will,
With a heart that wants to die.

I'll love you forever
I'll forget you never
For when Autumn comes
And my love song hums
To forget you I still try,
But it's just no use,
My heart takes such abuse,
And I can only wonder why.

Anna M. Wiest

A Matter Of Territory

I enjoy visitors
And the comforts of my home gladly share,
But I always feel uneasy
When guests sit in my favorite chair.

Arlyne Calloway

Who Are We

  Who are we, the man in torn
and tattered clothes; sleeping on
a bench or the woman all dirty
and taunt lying under a bridge
in a cardboard box for shelter.
  We are the people who you
laugh at and look away from.
  We are the people who you call a bum.
  We are the people you say you
spend your tax dollars on.
  We are the people who you say
the country can do without.
  Who are we; we are you.

Diana L. McElroy

Morning Meditation

How lovely, Lord, your trees
and the cooing of the dove,
   your clear blue sky,
   the winds that sigh

in the pine trees by our door.

In gratitude I fall to my knees,
my heart overflows with love.
   How can it be?
   That you'd love me
as much as that and more!

Every doubt I had swiftly flees
and my arms reach to heaven above.
   To thank you, Lord
   in deed and word.
Let my life show you live in me.

Doris Chapman Phillips

Going-Going-Going-Gone

First their eyes meet
And they quickly look away.
Shy and unsure they look back
Attracted by a simple glance.
Now they are going.

Now their hands meet
Timidly seeking togetherness.
Asking and answering questions
Posed by their silent hearts.
Now they are going faster.

Now their lips meet.
Captured and now happily alive
Searching for the glorious future
Each desperately dreams of having.
Faster and faster they now speed.

Now their hearts meet.
Love finds its way into their minds
Seeking sweet true meanings to life.
Searching, finding, then committing.
Deep into love they are now gone.

John Fitzpatrick

"A Generation Gone By"

I hold her hand
As I kiss her at night.
I love her like a band
Around her finger tight.

She takes a breath
Could it be her last.
My heart skips a beat
As our lives go past.

I pray to God
Don't take her away.
I couldn't live on
No, not another day.

Her life goes out
As another comes in.
I hold her tight
As my daughter's life begins.

Years go by, as I hold her hand
She kisses him this night, as she takes his band.
But I still know I am holding them tight
On this night, by this fire light.

Dolan G. Newell

My Son

I raised my boy from childhood
And watched him grow into a man
Then one day his country took him,
He was needed in Viet Nam

I watched him don his uniform
My heart was swelled with pride
And prayed he come home safely,
For the Lord was on his side

The days turned into weeks
Then months and into years
My heart was very weary,
I was filled with terrible fears

I had a terrible premonition
That I would never see my boy alive
I prayed to the Lord above,
To please let my boy survive

One day my fears were realized
There was a knock upon my door
A messenger stood with a telegram
Stating I had a son no more

The Lord only loaned him to me
I guess that was His plan
He served both God and country

And went to God like a man

Anthony R. Scelzo

Farewell Journey

Our paths crossed,
and we walked,
together for awhile.
Each step we took,
I knew would be
one closer to good-bye.
And still I went,
treading happily,
with you by my side.
Enjoying your touch too much,
loving you too deeply,
knowing the road would turn,
and there would be
separate routes for us to follow.
Hoping the pleasure of the journey
might outweigh
the pain of the parting,
and believing the memories
could comfort forever.

Janice Flauto-Hayes

Someone In Need

I only see you once a week
and wonder, "Does it matter?"
Do I offer hope for what you seek
or only idle chatter?

Will the time I spend make any dent
in the days ahead for you?
Would my efforts be much better spent
in some other rendezvous?"

I innocently gave my time;
I was doing a good deed.
But, having shared, I find that I'm
the someone who's in need.

Barbara A. McDowell

Outside The Window

Look out from the window
And what do you see?
There's a world out there
For you and for me.
The old maple tree
So broad and so tall,
The hills and the meadows
The color of fall.
Our road curves away
Over to the side,
Jed Brown's bright red barn
Cow-full and wide.
Far away you can see
Mountains of blue
At the corner the brooklet
You waded with Sue.
Our look is most over,
Sky's losing its light,
Back into the room
For here comes the night!

Charlotte Flood

After Thoughts

Ahead in the darkness
Are things I can't see
Out there lies a man
He is waiting for me

He is lonely and cold
As he breaths the night air
His constant companions
are fear and despair

The same painful thoughts
Race through his head
Many tortured memories
Of friends lying dead

Only death can end
These visions of hell
He could have been my brother
I know him so well

Early in the morning
Will come the battle cry
One of us will live
The other has to die

Harold Ewing

Springtime

Gentle lambs at springtime's smile,
And mother goats at kid;
Floral heads will nod their praise,
Whenever breezes bid.

The winsome gleam of earth's delight,
Spews life into growing things;
And trees, new burden in their arms,
Rejoice at tiny wings.

The beaver shows its labored dam,
A leaping salmon all its might;
Awakened bears will wade the stream
To catch an early bite.

With all the color blossomed now,
The sun repeats its glow,
It warms the hearts of frigid man,
To rid him of all woe.

Arnold L. Norris

First Things First

Wool socks on a winter morning
Are wonderful to wear.
Warming the feet that walk on sleet;
Making it easy to bear.

God made the feet and also the sleet,
But first He made the sheep
Whose wool will keep
Warm the feet in the sleet.

Now this may sound silly to you,
But it wouldn't if you only knew
How God in creation proceeded
To supply the need before it was needed.

Forrest A. Mauldin

Butterflies

Butterflies are:
as delicate as porcelain
as soft as silk
as pretty as the stars
as prim as a princess
as gentle as warm milk
yet tiny.
God, how did you do that?

Ella Jane Moore

Precious Words

I hold it in my hands with gentle care
as I whisper a quiet, loving prayer
I caress the extremely worn cover
I cherish it, as I would a lover

As I open it, a tear forms in my eye
looking at it, I begin to sigh
slowly, I move my fingers over the pages
touching words that have lasted for ages

I read the words that are so revealing
freedom expressed, hope, joy and healing
words that were spoken so many years ago
still showing me things I need to know

Oh! How precious these words are to me
when I need an answer for my anxiety
when I am dealing with sorrow and strife
I read of hope - of eternal life

This book so eternal, so full of mystery
words that have lasted throughout history
a book blessed with a heavenly nod
this wonderful book - is the word of God

Connie Huffman

Rainbow Universe

Kaleidoscope of hues and shades
As if projected from
Harmonic sequences

What gravity is to black pigments
Helium gasses are to colors

All of the juices' flavors
Catch the tongue like
A prism's refracted
Sunlight rays
Catch the eye[s]

Vicariously travel in adventures
At the very sight of
Rainbow colors

Howard Falk

Underprivileged?

There are no underprivileged children
As long as teachers people the world
With their love of learning
And their love of opening doors
To the great outside world of
The wonders of nature-
The thrill of learning a new word-
The joy of stepping eagerly into
The captivating pages of a book....
There are no underprivileged children
As long as love of boys and girls
Matches the teacher's love of learning.

Christine McGlasson

God's Complete Rainbow

Rainbows are deceptive
As many things can be
Here on earth when we look up
It's only half you'll see
However, if by chance some day
You'll fly above the clouds
Perhaps if elements are right
You will exclaim out loud!
I never knew, was never told
The rainbow is complete
A circle perfect as can be
Around God's Holy Feet
When cares of day come your way
Think of clouds above
Up there is a circle rainbow
Of God's unending love.

Isabella M. Simon

Pentless Sonnet

The hands do turn a perfect shape,
As orbs in dark and gracious sea.
Adornéd muscle of crimson be,
Soon wary of the ally's rape.
And gentle more of hope to take,
With tumbling whim on bending knee,
Thrown amaurotic recklessly,
Of faulty mind or moral break.
A bloodless breast is left to rot,
Upon the heart it hoped to find.
Lack of loot the problem not,
Thought avarice of other kind,
Cause moiety to lay in rest,
On scales of languid emptiness.

Jim Coffin

Stage 93 - My Brother Be

A hissing bottle there I see
Behind the great, grand bonsai tree.
The precipice so wide to bridge.
White buffalo standing on the ridge.
Give me the strength, so far is near,
To hold the things I see as dear.
The time has come to make a stand
The powers of all at my command.
To choose the path I've come upon
Or search the seas of armatron.
I'm here, I'm me, I really am
The grand result of all my plans.
So see me as I really am.
A spirit soars inside this man.
I can't be held, you cannot bind.
My life is formed inside my mind.
So see me as I really am
Or say goodbye. I say amen!

Danella Opela

First Snow

The first snow makes me reason
as the air fills with its white.
The changing of the season;
autumn days to winter nights.

Dead leaves' smoke and burning
signal the end of summer light.
The rain as it is turning
into snow on a winter night.

The mountain trees are naked;
they retreat for the coming blight.
As the cold air shows its hatred
in the chill of a winter night.

The field corn stands are rustling;
huddled together against its might.
Men gathering firewood are hustling
to beat the winter night.

The first snow of November
brings memories back to light.
Scenes of home that I'll remember;
safe and warm on a winter's night.

David E. Montgomery

Christmas Prayer

Let us truly thank you, Lord
As we look around and see
With all the many things we have
Those less fortunate than we.

Let us thank you for our Children
Our Husbands and our Wives
Our Families, Friends and Neighbors
With your mercy, bless our lives.

We pray for peace and happiness
That all of us near and far
May look into the Heavens, Lord
To see your brightly shining star.

Let us know the joy of giving
As we travel along life's way
And as we wake each morning, Lord
View each new dawn as Christmas Day!

Bobbie L. Stringfellow

"The Wonder Of It All"

Within the depths of my darkness
Beneath the calm exterior
Presented towards the world
Liquid heat lies, gentle waves building
Wash over within, again and again
Feel the warmth grow to fire
Rise with it on higher.
The loneliness of nature,
Bring faith my desire
To be complete with another
To at last know a lover
Fires abate they never subside
The depths are but waiting
The glorious roar of the thunder
A flash flood of nature
Deny me not the storm within
Waves crashing the banks of desire
Again and again... I am but waiting.
I seek not justification, but oneness
You must look, within, to find me.
You must look within to find me,
for here am I.

Jacki Davis

"The Love Of Music"

To get me through this world of Hate
At least it is Peaceful and beautiful
I sure am glad I have my Music

Where did Howdy Doody go?
And Kaptain Kangaroo
What put the Hate in this world
I'd really like to know!

I sure am glad I have my Music
to get me through the day
the world is so full of hate
Where did it go wrong

Where did peace and love go?
I'd really like to know
It's a scary thing, this hate
I'd really like to know!

I feel sad for today's children
they didn't yet see what we did
Where are the roller skates and Hula Hoops
but I do have my music
that is love and they can't take that away!

Ginny Barker

"The Accident"

He was on his way home
at one-forty-five,
his friend and his gal
gave him a ride.

They drove over a hill
and driving in their lane,
there was a drunk man
driving insane.

They crashed at the top
it was instant death,
for, Jason, my friend
as he took his last breath.

His friend's gal lay
in the hospital bed,
in critical condition
and also brain-dead.

But, his friend was okay
With some stitches and things;
I'll remember that day
and the memories it brings.

Amy Wood

True Friends

As I look around me now
At people I have known,
I think of all the happiness
And love that we have shown.

Together we had good times,
Together we had bad,
Rejoiced in the happy,
And lived through the sad.

We helped each other live,
We helped each other grow,
Gave each other reason,
Gave each other hope.

But the final test came,
And we had to let go.
True friends will come back,
In my heart - I know.

Alayne M. Courts

Is It Dust?

It's showing again
at this mystical hour
eliciting a sigh

Amber rays of a mirror
off a window
surrender themselves

These two hearts cannot capture
words, have no light to invade
and these dreams only sense with
fingertips awakening

Shower offers a respite
words import
more pull, push, and measures

Too much for this sun
this time, this place, this hour
this solitary 'armageddon'
must dry from the inside
instead

Is it dust?

Joan M. Kowalsky

Major

Hassles in the morning,
Attitudes in the afternoon,
Mood swings in the evening,
Misunderstandings in the night.
It's all part of the wonderful world
that we call marriage.

Don't take me wrong,
There are the good times,
When you finally do something right,
And there is peace in the house.
Even with your spouse!

Fred Murphy

Dream Travelers

Were we travelers, you and I
Aware of you, you of I
Spoke, we not a word
Departed, continued on our way

Met again on this road of life
Knew your face, as you did mine
Again we spoke, no words heard
Separated, went our ways

Resting now in an artist's shop
Create the words, let them flow
Presence all around, cannot prescind
Appear, disappear, laughter knows
The tears

Were we travelers, you and I
in the sequence of the dream
You were black, I was white
You were young, I was old
Under the skin, we are but one
Between us the story was told...

Celestine H. Smith

Hope

Once a shining flame,
burning brightly — Rekindled.
Now only ashes.

Athena M. Markos

"Burial At Sea"

Don't bury me in the cold, cold ground,
Away from the light of day.
Nor, burn me up in a fiery flame,
for Hell is not my way.
But, place me in the ocean blue,
with the whales, and the fish,
'til someday, when the future comes,
I shall become your dish.

Gary Saint Martin

Reminiscing

Away from concrete cities,
Away from their bustle and din,
Away from their painted ladies,
Away from their perpetual sin.

Into a flowered landscape,
Into meadows of grasses green,
Into fields of honey and grapevines,
Into the tranquility of a dream.

Cool breezes waft the fragrance,
Cool breezes from the hills,
Cool breezes with remembrance,
Cool breezes bring me chills.

One deep grave, memories to keep,
One deep grave, far from the mills,
One deep grave, for her to sleep,
One deep grave, it haunts me still.

Away from concrete cities,
Into a flowered landscape,
Cool breezes waft the fragrance
One deep grave, memories to keep.

Harold Sampson

Forever

Walk with me and talk with me
Be my friend for eternity
And when you're feeling down and blue
You know I'll be here to listen to you
As I know you will always be
Here with me for eternity
For you're in my soul and in my heart
No matter if we are far apart
So walk with me and talk with me
Be my friend for eternity
For even when we are not together
I'll be with you forever and ever

Amy Fowler

Keeping Right

It's not about who's
black or white.
It's all about what's
wrong and right.
It's not about if we
should fight, but that we
fight for what is right.

It's not about our
leaders' might, but us
staying in God's loving sight.
For in that sight
there's a precious light
that will keep us strong
and keep us right.

John Edward White Sr.

Precious Time

Meghan Ann, a child, age of eight
Beautiful, standing tall and straight
So proud her mother this special day
For those who come to kneel and pray
Her first holy communion to partake
In front of GOD for Jesus' sake

David F. Blanch Sr.

To Love

To love is to know that within us all,
  beauty can always be found.
It is to know that someone is there,
  who will never let us down.

To love is to feel the pleasure,
  when someone holds you tight.
It is to feel the happiness,
  when everything feels so right.

To love is to hear a bird's sweet song,
  as he is perched atop a tree.
It is to hear sounds rarely noted,
  though we knew that they must be.

To love is to see the lovely sky,
  with cotton clouds aloft,
It is to see things never seen,
  though this is the beauty we have sought.

To love is to make a union,
  between a woman and a man.
It is to make a wonderful life,
  to live and love the best you can.

Dani McCollum

There Is No Hope For You Today!

Oh baby, my darling, don't you cry,
because in a few days, you will die.

It isn't my fault, that you were made.
There is no hope for you today!

When I found out that you were in me,
I told your father and he began to see.

He didn't have a responsibility,
so then he ran away!

I cried and cried for many days,
I blamed myself for his run-away.

I started getting crazy,
and also very lazy.

I blame you for being made.
Honey, there is no hope for you today!

June Ramirez

Buck

Around me always;
Before bedtime,
After dog-tiring school.
Inside a cage usually is he
During the witching hour,
Among the wolves' howls
Beneath the full, yellow moon.
In my mind my dog is howling
With the wolves.

Elizabeth Whitehead
Fall, 1994
Age 11

Listen To Your Heart

Listen to your heart
before you tell me goodbye.
Listen to your heart
your heart won't lie.
You said you love me
If you do, listen to your heart,
your heart won't lie.
What have you got without my love?
What would your heart say?
Listen to your heart,
you can't go wrong.
Listen to your heart,
your heart won't lie.

Amy White

Eternity

To imagine Eternity.
Begin with things of Earth.
Count joys and tears with scrutiny
And start with your day of Birth.

Then count each star up in the sky,
Each grain of sand here below,
Each blade of grass which grows to die,
Earth's waters which ebb and flow.

And when all your counting is done,
You will come to comprehend,
Eternity has just begun,
"Forever will never end."

One day just for "you" death will send,
And you will remember then.
Your eternity will depend
On how you lived "Here" Amen!

Eternity with God brings "Peace."
Without God, spells "Disaster."
Those joys or sorrows never cease.
You build Here - your Hereafter.

Joseph Blanchfield

Bonds Of A Forever Friendship

Invisible boundaries
Between Heaven and earth
Conceal experiences
Preceding birth.

Yet, fond, familiar feelings
Of unfeigned love and care
Intimate of knowing you
Before somewhere.

Our prized association,
So seemingly to me,
Will warmly be abiding
Eternally.

Carolyn Joyner Freebairn

Me In My Land

Let's take another ride
And walk along beside
The body that I once owned
I wish I could have known
The pain that I feel
And how nothing is real
If you were mine
I could take the time
To help you understand
Me in my land

Emily Henry

Red Waves

Sandy beaches
bloody waves
the whale breaches
harpooned by knaves.

Thoughtless actions
dreadful deeds
violent reactions
the mammal bleeds.

Near extinction
o' graceful whale
No more distinction
as humans fail.

We that kill
We kill ourselves
Murderous thrill
for a trophy shelf.

We prove we can
We're species one
the death of man
Thy will be done.

Helen Grahl

A Spring Clock

Magnolias in
blossom mime cups of tea.
They're reawakening.

Blossom cups are in
flight with spring in mind.
Soon a leafing out at this time.

Some butterflies edge
to the lips of the blossoms
on a hot spring day.

The loosening of
a flower in bloom cracks
its own gentility.

Teacups are breaking,
and they drift under the trees.
Petals curl too soon.

Blushes mix with gasps
and dry out to clock in pure
disintegration.

Barbara Schoenberg

Bluebird

Blue is the sky
blue is the sea
a baby bluebird stuck in a tree
longs to be free
as his bluebird brothers fly
fly fly away
on such a nice day

Jemmy Chen

Makayla's Sonnet

Her soul's as pure
as a mountain lake,
Her parents look upon
the angel's face.
Their child whose love
they both shall share,
A beauty to which none can compare.
Not flower, nor painting, nor rising sun
shall ever match this little one.

Jamie Reynolds

The Four Seasons

Spring

Laughter sings
bluebells ring
little birdies chattering
baby robins on the wing, it's Spring!

Summer

Warm rays of sun
Summer has begun
and pretty soon,
it's done.

Autumn

School is here
apples fall
it's getting chilly
winds blow, it might snow!

Winter

Make a snowman
skate on ice
Christmas is coming
that is nice!

Emily Wang

A Car Poem

A car you can drive any
Body that is able to.
When you are able to remember
That a drunk one
Is a done one, a smart one has
Just begun.

Gabriel V. Buldra

We Met On The Roads Of Laughter

We met on the roads of laughter,
both careless at the start,
but other roads came after
and wound around my heart.
There are roads a wise man misses,
and roads where a fool will try
to say farewell with kisses,
love, touch and say goodbye.
We met on the roads of laughter
how wistfully roads depart,
 for I must hurry after
 to overtake my heart.

Jessica Constantine

Chanting

The sweet sound of chanting
 charge the universe.

Excited by the sound
 the moon dances
 between the clouds.

The happy rain
 feeds the earth
 where flower beds await
 the dawn.

The sweet sound of chanting
 has the power of love
 and
 my soul rejoices
 hearing the sound.

Janet R. Oshiro

Wind

The insanity of greed,
breezes the fowl scents of
sour depths,
freezes the waters falling
from the skies,
blows the treasures of the shining,
and drifts loose emotions to
the front of your thoughts,
I can imagine the spite
of the still, and the black
dove that chills upon your window sill.
Does he lurk to find what
reasons your heart has to
leave your soul?
Dark desires slip and slide
through the cracks between
your destiny and maintain
the disbelief in your heart
so your self respect will
continue to flow with the wind.

Bong-Ye'

The Greatest World

Look around and see what God made
Bright light and dark shade
Look around at the stars so bright
Shining there every night

Look up way in the trees
Can't you see the honey bees?
Look around you what do you see?
The greatest world that could ever be

Rushing streams and beautiful flowers,
And don't forget pretty rain showers
And look at the animals—what a sight!
Running around with all their might.

Just look at the world a second time
The world is not sour like a lime
The world is a wonderful place to be
And there are wonderful things to see

Just look around you a second time
What do you see?
The greatest world that could ever be.

Crista Fuentes

Ode To Harmony

A quiet walk by a mountain stream.
Brilliant sunlight reflecting on
untrodden snow.
Crackling cedar logs in a winter
bonfire.
Endless lapping waves touching the
shore of a sheltered sea cove.
Holding the hand of someone you love.
Images of peace.
Brings tranquility to the soul.
Mirrors serenity.

Dixie L. Aliamus

The Captain's Farewell

From the China Sea to Gibralter Strait
Ever westward to the Golden Gate,
The sun counts cadence on time and fate
Eight bells toll; the day is through
My watch is over, the wheel to you!

Joseph F. Madeo Jr.

Ichthus

Lord Poseidon
Bring back your fish!
Surely you have the power.
Fulfilling a lifelong dream
I snorkeled around the tour boat
in the Aegean Sea
beneath your Temple:
Empty water!
Oil spills have killed your fish.
Later the guide showed us
fisheries along the coast
Happy Gulf of Corinth!
Hope for future anglers
snorkelers and gourmets.
Barbara R. DuBois

Memories

In the winter the frost and snow
bring memories of a love which
is long gone
When all alone in the dark of
night
The winds sing a lonesome song
My love for you brings sweet
dreams
of times we've had together
I can't forget our life my
love.
It's like a fire burning ever
The winter's winds sing of
long ago
My heart is slowly dying
For my life without your love
Is like the flowers when
snow is falling
Joyce Simmons

Windwail

She wails as she sweeps past my window
bringing with her the salts of many seas
and the scent of a child's rose
pounding her fists on the fragile glass
leaving a dusting of freshly fallen snow
and the scent of a child's rose
I open the window and invite her in
Elaine Johanson

You Said

Scattered pages, tossed
aside, left in a heap

You said you
sent me poems
I've never seen — who
cares if words
don't rhyme, who
cares if silence reeks
of your words simply
wasted, words
shouting from some
corner, a room
I never enter
anymore

Why gather words
put away
for never —
collected in dust?
Diane Nelson

Venice Sun

A fallen fawn, where winter's lawn
  brings the crimson from mere red,
Lay streaming bold, a liquid, cold
  from where the heat had fled.

I'd found the fawn, when the dawn,
  Drew the curtain of the night,
And tragedy lay next to me
  In swirls of red and white.

I lifted up the lifeless pup,
  Its form now permanent.
As I carried her, I knew the fur
  Once warmed the innocent.
I brought her back to my humble shack
  The walls of my father's rule.
He asked, "What sort of twisted soul
  Could ever be so cruel?"

I knew what made me cry that day
I felt pain with every tear.
And as cascades of sorrow fell
I knew what I held, dear.
Gregory L. Kemp

A Child

Let me be a child
Building castles in the sand
And feel the ocean water
Make them crumble in my hand.

Let me walk the shore
(A barefoot boy am I)
Who dares to meet the monster
A rush, and then a sigh.

Let me be alone
A dreamer by the sea
And let my future plans
Come reaching out to me.

Perhaps I'll be a fireman
Or build a house with dad
Or I could be the president
The best we ever had.

Let me take your hand
Don't push, don't shove, be mild
And I shall climb life's ladder
But first let me be a child!
Anne B. Currier

Split Personality

I'm two people
but both are me
I'm two people
to all that know me
At school I'm quiet as a mouse
except when I'm with my friends
At home I yell and scream and shout
with glee and happiness
with anger and spite
I'm two people
for all to see
I don't try to make friends
but I do
I don't try to be myself
but I am
Me and myself
we're two people
but both are me
I'm two people
to all who know me
Connie Lytle

Patience

Sometimes the road ahead seems long
But faith and courage keep us strong
To travel that road every day
To achieve goals set so far away.

With patience life's a success game
A store-house of fortune and fame
Just keep focused and learn every rule
Victory comes, it begins at school.

So build a future, explore your mind
Be marketable for every kind
You have the power, you hold the key
Go right ahead shape your destiny.
Grace Batson

"Fallen Stones"

This is not just another cry for help
but for the awareness of
where we are going

And that we somehow
have lost sight of life
each one of us
just a little

Because if we stopped
for one minute to think
what it's all about

Why we want so much
to give back nothing

Why we don't demand
the powerful to feel
their conscience

Yet we slowly join them
as we scrape our way
up their hill

Thinking that a fallen stone
will bring us happiness
Carolann Marino 8/22/93
©1995 Carolprose Ltd.

My Friend

I don't hear from you often.
But I know you're my friend.
You may not be able to reach out to me.
But I will always reach out to you.
You did not feel well today.
And you may not feel well tomorrow too.
It's Christmas now.
I got your card in the mail today.
It is good to hear from you.
I am happy you're here
To share another year.
Jenny Block

Black Hawk

My mind flutters in a rage,
beating uselessly against the cage.
Growing stronger with age.

Wild wings—powerful and free—
pounding on, but they are not the key.
Something is there to see.

But not for my soul to grieve,
my mind is trapped, ever can it leave?
To be free is a need.
Alice Huyler

Destiny

Avon's Bard didn't say it,
But it's the true poet's fate;
"To slaughter sacred cattle
And tweak noses of the great."

David P. Fowler

Life

In time and strife, we live this life
but morsels on the sand.
God looks down, from the heavens round,
and lifts them in his hand.
We cannot explain the sudden pain,
when the spirit flits away.
We must go on, into the dawn
of the ever coming day.
To ponder why, man should die,
is left to the population.
Poor man I fear, did not hear
the truth in its revelation.
To happen again, and yet again,
a thing that will never cease.
For man is weak, so miserable and meek,
God's burden to release.
It seems a shame, that man's so lame,
but how else could we take his measure.
For man is grand, on the one hand,
comparison makes it a treasure.

John S. Haynes

The Homeless

I cried out for people to listen,
But no one would listen to me.
I cried out for peace,
but no one would care.
I cried out for work,
but no one would hire me.
I cried out for food,
but no one would
share with me.
I cried out for love,
but no one would love me.
I cried out for mercy,
but no one would shed a tear.
I cried out for help,
but no one would help me.
I cried out,
but no one would hear me.

Eileen C. O'Rowe

Untitled

Once I had a wonderful friend
But now he is gone and I pretend
That someday I will find another
One as nice or like a brother
For I am only in my nineties
That love and life are only endies

Jessie Elaine Parone

Love

Love is something that
burns in your heart.
Love is the longing for
that special person in
your life who will always be there.
Love is the unique magic
between two people forever.
Love is unconditional.

Jodi Halverson

Praise

It's not a big word, as words go
But put to use, it seems to grow.
The more you praise, the more you get.
You use the word without regret.

A motivator word, it's true.
There's nothing that a man won't do
When praised for that which he has done,
It spurs him on from sun to sun.

Oh, what a little praise can do
To someone who is feeling blue.
It picks them up, and gives them hope,
And makes it easier to cope.

With all life's wearisome demands.
A little praise can take these hands
And turn them into willing tools.
Two motivated working fools.

But without praise life is a bore,
An endless, hopeless, weary chore.
So why is praise so hard to give,
When it's a need for all who live?

Edna P. Fehrmann

Hope

The pain is searing,
But the heart beats true.
Let forth the flowing hope,
For it comes from you.
No pain is greater,
Than hopeless despair.
Remember me,
A friend out there.

Derek Neal

The Way It Used To Be

Strong the fortress used to be,
but then the walls they tumbled,
the foundation had been rocked,
and with the walls it crumbled,

deeper is the grave I'm digging,
trapped in parts unknown,
I have lost my dignity,
life's taken all I own,

I fought for my beliefs,
a soldier I became,
I fought with everything I had,
now I only have my name,

on I push through life,
my future so uncertain,
I fear to see the end,
as death slowly draws the curtain,

I saw the reaper in my sleep,
my heart his claws did severe,
I lay here on this earth,
I fell asleep forever.

Ben Penrod

The Giant

Judge the size of a man
 by the wake he leaves in his passing
And this one was a Giant I never saw
But I see him now, reflected,
In the eyes of a crowd that show his size
A Giant not of Evil and Hate
But of Smile and Heart

Jacob Daniel Schimming

Fears

I say "Hello," as I walk by
but they don't see the pain inside.
The hurt, the guilt for many years
that when I'm alone bring out the tears.

They see a smiling, happy face
that always has everything in place.
A person who has grace and style.
A mother bringing up her child.

They never guess that when I'm alone
I cry.
Because of all the things that go on
outside.

The fears, the insecurities,
that as a child have built in me.
I pray each day for help with these.
That I may someday live with ease.
And not be scared of the unknown.
And never, ever be alone.

Elba Lallave

Life

Man is afraid of many things.
But true fear is life itself.
To be nothing more than grains
of sand twisting and shifting under
the pressures of the world.
Never knowing where you'll end up
or what you'll end up as.
Everyone wanting to be something
else for fear they will not be accepted
by the sea of the public.
And those who are accepted, get
pulled back into the never-ending
tides of society's watchful eye,
life is just a challenge of the
mind, and if think you can over-
come the world's struggle and
you have accomplished more than
you'll ever need to survive the crashing
waves of the earth and the tumbling
troubles that shape and carve the future.

Amanda Jordan

Lonely Time

To-day I am lonely
But why should I be
When I know that I have
Such a loving family.

This ache in my heart
Deep down inside of me
I don't understand
Why must it be.

It must be something
In the past
Some loving bond perhaps,
That didn't last.

I've thought about it
through and through
Can't seem to sort it out
I know what I will do.

I'll take the time
I spend alone
To think about
My loving home.

Dorothy Ryan

Daddy We Love And Miss You

It broke our heart to lose you
But you didn't go alone.
A part of us went with you.
The day God called you home.

Each time we see your picture.
You seem to smile and say
Don't cry I'm only sleeping.
We'll meet again some day.

When we think of you in silence.
Secret tears do flow.
For what it meant to lose you...
No one will ever know.

Our thoughts are always with you...
Your place no one can fill.
In life we loved you dearly.
In death we love you still.

We feel you walk beside us.
And when our life is through.
We pray that God will take our hand.
And lead us straight to you.

Evelyn T. Tallman

The Bar-Flies

She
Buxom at bosom
Big in the fanny
Hat on one eye
One drink too many.

He
Draped on the counter
Propped by the rail
Sappily grinning
He's everyone's pal.

Clarice F. Pollard

Golden Dreams

Where wild plums grow
By an old spanish fort
Their lies a treasure galleon
Of to port

With iron held high
Under lightning sky
The great ship bore
To the ocean floor

While one king wept
Over empty chests
The sea king sat
With treasure in store

Gerard C. Minihan

Trash R.I.P.

I'm wasting in a world of wastefulness
Can't you see I have use
But yet you bury me
And try to forget what I am

So now I'm in darkness
And I wait for my time
Because the more you bury me
The closer I come to my revenge

But now I rise to haunt
For there is no more room
And as I destroy the place you live
You try to find a use for me

Daniel Imberi

One Man's Heart

One man has a heart like others,
by this heart he has a life to live
within this life which is his own,
one man has love to give.
One man's heart may be rejected,
if he loves what could be wrong
but one man's love, like any love—
can be love, just as long.
One man has a heart like others,
a body, a soul and a mind,
within this man, like any other
a heart is what you will find,
One man's heart can be rejected
when he loves he will understand,
that the ability of one woman,
one man's heart can love a man.

Jonelle Jenkins

Trust Me

"Fear thou not for I am with thee,"
   Came his word so soft and clear,
"Be not dismayed, nor be discouraged"
   For your God is lingering near.

I will strengthen thee and help thee
   All thy needs will I attend
And uphold you while you're sleeping
   With my strong and mighty hand.

He presence lingered, oh so sweetly
   Watching o'er me all the while
Gently whispering, "Trust me, dear one.
   I will heal you, you're my child."

Yes, I knew his grace sufficient
   Had been with me through the day
For I claimed his Holy Spirit
   As my loving guide and stay.

What a friend I have in Jesus
   Joy and peace o'er flows my heart;
He has saved me, kept me, filled me,
   healed me;
   Ne'er from him will I depart.

Ella Duckworth

The Attic

Unorganized thoughts
clutter my brain
as I stumble past dreams
I cannot explain.

The bookshelves are empty,
the scrapbooks are torn.
Personalities flutter
on the rack by the door.

Lyrics float past me
as the melodies fade,
and the shadows still taunt me
from happier days.

My tea set is broken.
My Barbie is dead.
And etched on the walls
are the words left unsaid.

The dollhouse is vacant.
The cheerleader's gone.
I thought that I knew me...
I guess I was wrong.

Barbie Dockstader

"Allowed To Love You"

Does love have great consequences
cause I believe so.
Am I allowed to love you
do you want me in your life.
Let me in your world
do you dream about me
do I lie in your mind
your book of history
can I read the story
perhaps you'll let me in
an I'll promise I'll stay
forever with you
together someday
will remain and not be broken
until it is time to move on
to another destination.

Desiree Gordon

Fiery State

Catching characters of life
Changing energy
Gilding shadows

Sacred scatterlings
Earth portraits
Gather form
Balance time

Moving prayer
Feeding fire

John D. Gerut

Mindless Fatality

Sound of blades, axes -
Chopping - cutting - killing
Crack! Snap!
Majestic beauty
That once stood tall,
Topples.
Falls to the forest floor -
Silence...
One tree fell - now lies dead.
After a hundred years of life -
Humans cause yet another -
Mindless Fatality

Cortney Lamprecht

That Christmas Tree

Christmas trees
Christmas trees
Light them up on Christmas Eve.
Decorations, what temptations!
Ornaments of animation.

Presents to people,
Under the steeple.
It's a time for laughter,
And a time for tears,
Not to worry, instead just cheer.

Janell Kotrice Goudeau

Good Intentions

Good intentions in brilliant array,
Dancing like fireflies in the night.
Much too strong to be kept at bay!
Sadly, found dead in the morning light.

David Gamble Moore

Yesterday's Gone

Yesterday's gone
Clouds in my mind
Memories linger
All the time
My heart stopped beating
When you said goodbye
Are you receiving
The tears I cry
Al Cooley

"Of All The Places We Had Gone"

I remember sanded beaches of night
cold dune grasses tickling my calves
chilled fingers and sandied bodies
Then, the suspenseful drives
the movie theatres
and back road rides
of course, the shimmer of the moon
on the rippling waves at ten o'clock
And no one existed but you and I
Jennifer Dopkin

Dream Work

Clowns with funny faces
Come to me at night.
Comical, with traces
Of pathos, rage and fright.

Dressed in rags and tatters
Which magnify their flaws,
Propriety in shatters,
Inanity their cause.

Horns and trumpets clashing
Chase the truth away.
Reality goes crashing
And chaos comes to play.

When the night is over
With order back in place,
It's then that I discover
Myself in every face.
Alice Townsley

Your Face

Is the one, I want to see
coming through the door.
  The way you cocked your head at me,
parted lips and smiled, eyes as wide as
they could be,
  Cheeks blushing red for me,
Oh how I long to see, you
standing here in front of me,
  But that will have to be
in my fondest memory,
your face coming through the door.
Andrea F. Coulson

Lost Treasure

I once had a stone
  Crystalline and brilliant
But
  I was cut by its jagged edges
So
  I threw it away
Not knowing it was a diamond in the rough
Jeanne V. Gill

Rachel

Joy, like music from within
  copper mane - pale skin —

Tell me where your soul has been.

Did starspirit pierce when you were born?

Or resting nighttimes in dark skies,
  does it rise with you each morn
  dancing life till daylight flies?

Oh, sprite - young, wild,
  come, sit - a moment mild -
  my child's child.
Barbara Shapiro

Yearling

Once and once only
Could be a rewarded gift
First of all we need
To sift and shift
When this is known
We will be more grown
An acquire a name
of our own.
When the little
Words fall in place
We have found our way
Which is the reverse
Of dismay.
The march forward
Might be slow
Therefore you have
To watch the undertow.
It could be a fright
but after all-
It could be a delight.
Edward T. Philpitt

Birds

The birds are wonderful
  creatures
With shiny wings and
  handsome features
Magnetic tongues and
  glorious songs
Singing joyously all
  day long.
Helen Urban

Majesty

As the brilliance of the morning sun
...crimson red
...with awe and splendor
...heralds the new day...
all the majesty of unfaltering steps
...to seek a new way...

In your presence to behold the miracle
...another day
...to be as you will
...as we walk with you
In the warmth of your sunshine and sight
...to see from your view...

As the brilliance of the evening sun
...golden red
...with royal wonder
...draws nigh on the bay
You hold us near in the palm of your hands
...to greet this new day...
Joedy A. Yule

A Doomsayer's Poem

The walls of time
Crumbled in the face of eternity
Where life and death are the same
No tears, no pain
Only a Heaven.

"Neath lay the Stygian darkness
Of Hell and Satan
Where sin and damnation
Marked the fallen.

On earth
Mere mortals breathed and bore
The scourge of borrowed moments
Not seeing Light nor the coming of Night.

How sad if the world should end
And we all by Fire consumed.
Genida Tan-Trapp

Cain and Abel

SMACKING, GRINDING, BLACK.
CRUSTING RED.
CLOTTING BLUE.

Alluring, waving, white.
Smoothing pink.
Calming green.

BASHING, seductive, WAR.
GUTTING peace.
RIPPING love.

VICARIOUS VIOLENT VOYEURS.
Jaidene Anderlini

Untitled

Can you hear your lover
crying in the night?

Or are you too busy
thinking you were right.

Listen very carefully,

You can hear your lover's
teardrops fall

Like raindrops
on a forgotten wall.
Cindy Fleck

Clouds Of Life

It's light as a feather,
drifting in the wind.
My mind shoots to the sky,
as it begins.

Making pictures of you,
up in the clouds.
My heart beats faster,
and I'm feeling so proud.

I can see memories,
inside the clouds.
Like a movie in the sky,
many scenes floating by,
in the air.

Making a dramatic movie,
in the sky.
I hope I finish it,
before I die!
Byron Lee Golden

Mind And Soul

Mama had good advice when she said
   daughter guard your mind,
He'll search your being deep within
   but your soul he mustn't find.

Remember through misfortune
   please stay in control,
For if he has your mind dear
   he surely has your soul.

There is nothing more precious than
   a mind that can think clear,
If you lose the power of sanity
   you'll gain a heart of fear.

Mama assured that God would help
   through my times of need,
He is the root she always used
   to plant this vital seed.

Don't forget these simple words
   and let them be your goal.
For if he has your mind dear
   he surely has your soul!
   Cathy M. Strong

Old Phantoms

Old phantoms invade the mind,
Deceiving perception.
Is this reality -
Or just some reverie
Of a dead dream I see?
Old phantoms are hard to find,
They palter detection.

Old phantoms infest my thoughts,
Denying rejection.
Is this my honesty -
Or just some travesty
Of an old lie I see?
Old phantoms, like juggernauts -
Destroy my perfection.
   Donald J. Bayman

Love

Stare deep,
Deep into his eyes,
They are fire,
Fire on ice,
The waves crashing on the beach,
They are silently calling,
He is out of reach,
Like the sun on the ocean,
Shining,
Sparkling,
Reflecting,
Me, love, life,
Forever.
   Amber Dudley

Mangroves

As though their beauty weren't
   enough to justify their being:
They shield the birds, feed the
   fish and cleanse the waters.

May God protect the mangroves
   the cool green forests of the sea.
The vast and pristine
   wetlands, from man,
   the enemy.
   Brenda M. Waddell

Time

Black nights.
Diamonds trace the sky.
The moon shines down on the waters
below.
Crystal clear is the beauty.
Chilling winds whisper lullabies.
As the clouds cover the child.
Lonesome is he that sees the night.
All seems calm.
Falling diamonds from heaven,
As few stare in amazement.
Time does this,
and not the days.
Some pass by.
But not the lonesome man,
He that peers over the night.
   Danielle Sedlacek

Did You?

Did you take cupids arrow?
Did you spear it to my heart?
Did you lower the clouds so I
could lightly walk?
Did you repaint the rainbows
to color in my world?
Did you enter in my dreamtime
so I could share the night with
thee?
Did you warm my days with golden
sun with which you shower me?
Did you touch the mighty ocean
for it to call out my name?
And even if you didn't you
can take all the blame.
   Annette Maria

Freedom

When the sun is setting
distant in the sky
the colors blooming
I wish to go there
When the sky is a pale shade
of blue and the clouds
like magnificent white islands
I wish to go there
When the sky is deep and endless
billions of stars suspended
I wish to go there
To be unseen soaring through the
colors and clouds and many stars
To be free!
   Dyana Bailo

A Soldier's Gone They Say

Can you hear the bugles play
Do you hear what they say
A soldier's gone, he's passed away
A soldier's gone they say
He learned to fight day by day
Then they shipped him to a foreign land
Where he fought hand to hand
A soldier's gone, he's passed away
Can you hear his mother cry
Can you hear his widow asking why
As she wipes her baby's weeping eyes
Can you hear the bugles play
A soldier's gone, he's passed away
   Henry Magee Jr.

Old Age

I have seen it all beginning to end
Do I have Problems I'll not pretend
Pains and ache my body cries
My memory slides and vanishes by
Teeth no more store bought ones
Food to eat soft like buns
A little walk to the corner store
Half way there can't walk no more
A hearing aid helps me hear
Misunderstanding is what I fear
Cyclops glasses I now wear
Upon my Head I have no hair
It sure is great retiring
Took up art to be inspiring
Colors fade and thoughts are mixed
Now how do I get that fixed
There must be something that's worthwhile
Only Social Security makes me smile
   Frank Salzano

"The Whispering Voice"

Do you hear it
Do you acknowledge it
Sometimes rough and demanding
Sometimes sweet and refreshing
Sometimes hateful and sometimes loving

Who's to tell where it comes from
Maybe from the sky
Maybe from someone speaking to you
Maybe it's your imagination

But don't be alarmed
Because it is within you
It is your personal guidance
To where, what when and how you move

But how do you grasp it
Just acknowledge it's you
A personal guidance to see you through

Through rough and good times
It will be there for you
Because this voice is your inner you.
   Brendolyn Reid

Untitled

Time has no meaning
Distance has no miles...
   for friends
Small things awaken thoughts,
Loving memories resurge...
   for friends
Secrets stay well hidden
Tears are sometimes shed...
   for friends
Talks well into the night,
Long walks taken...
   for friends
A warm hug given,
With a soft caressing kiss...
   for friends
Twinkling eyes, joyous smiles
And laughter...
   for friends
Sunrises and sunsets,
Now and forever are...for friends
   Joanna Lannin

Come Fly With Me

Come fly with me.
Don't be afraid.
My wings are strong.
They'll never give way.

We'll soar through the air,
Like birds in spring.
And nature will show us
Everything.

We'll fly near the ocean,
Then up through the clouds.
We'll experience life
And nothing left out.

Our love will carry us
Through every storm.
And when the winds come
We'll keep each other warm.

So let yourself go
And hear my plea.
I just want you
To come fly with me.

Dawn J. Cawrse

Ego Go Away

You there!
Don't come down so hard on me
We are alike
Maybe from the same tribe
Our skin has the same hue
Our hair the same thickness
Our lips are full
Our nostrils wide
Our backgrounds similar

Don't fly so high that we cannot meet
Don't stand so far away from me
Don't talk at me

Share with me
Fellowship with me
Know me
Look into my eyes -
See my soul

You there meet me where I am
So that we both might grow.

Eileen S. Berry

Always

Don't you cry for me,
Don't you shed a tear.
Do not live in my pain,
Do not live in my fear.
I will not forget you,
I will always remember
The love that you gave me
With each dying ember.
Please don't cry,
Don't cry for me,
For I will not die -
My soul will live on, always,
In your memory.

Diana Lomonte

Miracle Of Morn

At the break of day,
Dewdrops dance and shine
On the face of the lily,
White and solemn.

Dorothy Murakami

Your Answer Please

How many times must a man fall
down before he realizes he is in need of
a friend? Your answer please?

How many times must we say, I'll
do this tomorrow before realizing for
some tomorrow will never come?
Your answer please!

How deep must the hurt of our hearts
go before we realize we are in need
of tender love and care?
Your answer please!

How far in this life must we travel
before we know there's an end to
what we have started?
Your answer please!
How long? How long can a man go
onward in this world before
he learns his soul has to spend eternity
somewhere? Where is your soul's
resting place? Your answer please!

Elizabeth A. Harrison

"That Which Reaps"

The sun lays
down its rays,
upon the mountain peaks

    The sprawling breeze
    and shaded trees
    where the languor,
    wind speaks

        Beckoning the rushing seas
        and harvesting the earth's
        degrees
        the rain does flush with
        streaks

            So wonderful the homespun
            field
            silence casts the seeds;
            that yield
            which Mother Nature reaps

Helen McKenna

Boooooo!

The time we fear is
Drawing near,
The time of spooks and
Goblins;
They leer at you and peer
At you and set your
Courage wobblin'.

The witch will zoom upon
Her broom.
Accompanied by her cats.
And pumpkin eyes will
Show surprise, you might
Even see some bats.

Wolves will howl and
Cats will yowl,
And you'll sit rigid
With fright,
So be prepared cause
You'll be scared on
Coming Halloween night.

Ginger Gordon

My Love

Fantasies are fun but,
  dreams come true,
For you stole my heart,
  the first moment I laid eyes
    on you

Or was it an answer to a prayer
  from somewhere in my past,
That brought you and happiness,
  into my life at last.

Well my love one thing is certain
  and from my heart so true,
As long as I live I'll always,
  L-O-V-E Y-O-U.

Damon Craig Guillory

Ghost Of You

I think I thought I saw a ghost
  Drifting through the trees
A pale blue light on a moonless night
  Floating on the breeze
An ancient arch stood watching
  From beneath the leaves and twine
Eavesdropping on a long lost love
  A love that once was mine
But time crawls by and seconds roll
  Into some secret place
There remains no time to pay the toll
  We have fallen far from grace
But now is not the time to dwell
  On emotions spent in vain
Find me shelter in the wine
  From the falling of the rain
For I think I thought I saw a ghost
  Once hidden from my view
Yes I think I thought I saw a ghost
  Saw a ghost of you

Jason K. Gardner

Shades Of Everglades

Peaceful glow of rays shine the
effervescence shadowing the mist
of the everglades in motion. The
night swarms over me cooling the
days work resting my will. Freedom
of bliss comforts me capturing the
beauty touched by hands unknown
appreciating the unquenched love
of cool shades of everglades.

Charlie Hyatt

Lions

He has no cares this moment,
enjoying the savanna's view
He's cast aside all torrent,
enjoys his lioness in lieu
They've hunted with pride,
but not today. They've taken
time and set all aside
instead resting, half wakened
He's aware of life's dire straits
Bitter ends of wild beast's strife
Oblivious to that fate,
he's vowed to enjoy this life
Lying in the sun-baked shade,
as the lion licks his mate

Daniel Gibboney

Still Is She

The lake lies still and quiet
Enjoying the sun's gentle
touch
Until the wind turns towards
her
And stirs her surface.
Ripples dance across,
Disturbing her peace.
What is his reasoning for doing
what he does
And why doesn't he turn to
stay?

Cari M. Bacon

Untitled

Sensationalize,
Enterprise
This is your life
bound by ties.
You see through naked eyes
opened up to funky disguise.
capitalize,
materialize
The river dries.
Economize,
Monopolize
Poverty cries
have become stealth for the wise.

Gina Foster

It Doesn't Matter

I am happy I have you
Even though you're not here now
Every day I'm dreaming
And it's definitely of you

It doesn't matter
If this all shatters
Nothing lasts forever
But I'm praying
That we're staying together

I am warmed by your friendship
Even when you're far away
But when I'm asleep I want somebody
Who will kiss me tenderly

It doesn't matter
If this all shatters
Nothing lasts forever
But I'm praying
That we're staying together

Joy R. Whittemore

"Sea Song"

Splash into these waters and see,
down within the aquas deep -
The mysteries of an ardent sea,
to design, an immortal keep.

Where troubled souls dart and dash,
clinched in chains of inebriate force -
and time is but a scaly flash,
forever seeking the forgotten course.

Voyage deep; beyond the realm,
to witness the most amorous part -
the lonely whales that cry and swim,
the depths of a labyrinth heart.....

Clifton Cates

Tunnel

I had to build a tunnel
Ever since my body fell apart.
First it was my knees
Then it was my heart.

This body has grown old
and quite decrepit, as you can see.
Climbing mountains of life's problems.
Is much too hard for me.

In solving my many problems
I find I must tunnel through
If ever I'm to find solutions
It's the best I can do.

So what I can't climb over
Or even go around
I must tunnel with all my effort
And trust the answer
will be found.

Bonnie Waller

Mary's Art Class

Fill in your masses first.
Everyone is too uptight.
Leave your art work,
And take a walk.
Dorsetti's horses had many legs,
But only two that counted.
Oh! Marie, are you happy with it?
Yeah, I'd leave it.
Listen everybody,
Did anyone find my attendance cards?

Helen A. Hoffman

Stillness

Some days
Everything
Speaks
So loudly -
Today,
There is just
The silence
Of being -
Transparent,
Radiant,
Still.

Edda H. Hackl

The Flame And The Mind

It is late at night
Everything is calm.
Everything but something
Burning in my mind.

The stars in the sky
As usual are shining
Remind me your face
When you are smiling

Dear, you are the night
And the shining stars
You are the one I love
Wishing you were mine.

You are all I need
To fulfill my dreams
Yes, you are the flame
Burning in my mind.

Eduardo J. Leyte-Vidal

What Girls Are Right Down To Love's Soul

Sugar and spice and
everything nice they
say that's what
girls are. All yet
of love's dream, like
peaches and cream
Their love yet is
born through life's door,
and their inspiration
that they give to man
From the way in which
they have grown
It tickles man's heart
right down to his bones
As choirs yet echo love's song
In three words "I Love You"
yet words from their hearts,
which are also words from time's
door, in all their compassion
and deep inner soul is equally
thus what girls are.

Barry C. Hunter

Glass

Personality's shadowed smoke,
evolving smoldering mystery.
The soul kept in a bottle.
How the fires temper me.

Greeting the morning with embered song,
beyond the skin, the bone,
beyond all hopeful stardust,
beyond the waiting stone.

Statues within the sunset hill,
more statement than reward.
Ancestored memory is lost,
beneath the tired sword.

The soul, heavy with matter,
embracing the world with order.
The heart's glass hands will shatter,
the mind escape the border.

All my days have wondered,
in the nights, anticipating.
The soul in prismed embryo.
Encasement, I am waiting.

James E. Danielson

A Quiet Place

There is a quiet place
Far from the rapid pace
Where God can soothe my
troubled mine
Sheltered by tree and flow'r
there in my quiet hour
with him my cares are left
behind
whether a garden small
or on a mountain tall
new strength and courage
there I find
then from the quiet place
I go prepared to face
A new day with love for all
mankind

Erana Hodges

Celebration

Butterfly,
Favor me your soft
Umber wings.
And in this moonlit hour
Let me hear you sing.
There is no sin
Within this love;
Only passion, true and real.
A heart once blue with ice
That once again can feel.
What a cold and lifeless world
A colorless world would be.
No place for rainbows;
Or lovers, like you and me.
So close your eyes,
Butterfly,
And fold me in your wings.
Nothing else could be as sweet
As what the night will bring.

Hal Wright

Dreams That Are Kept Inside

That no longer you can hide,
feelings that are buried deep inside,
the treasure heart can only fly,
dreams that can come alive
only when you see a butterfly
and a rainbow in the sky.
Then let your spirit shine
like a diamond in the sand.

Angelica Panduro Martinez

Chances Missed

Dreaming of that perfect soul.
Finding perfection is the
ultimate goal.

Wishing to call perfection
their own.
Acknowledging what it is
like to be alone.

Searching day by day for
the "one."
Admitting to oneself what
has been done.

Discovering that perfection
does not exist.
Counting all the chances
missed.

Wanting to take a chance
with a special soul.
Crying because perfection
is their ultimate goal.

Caryl Weber

Amy

Her face, so glowing, innocent
Eyes so very clear and blue
Her body fresh and beautiful
Her young soul so pure and true

Please Lord, let her grow up wisely
Learning and doing and full of grace
Let her life unfold securely
A rose that blooms at God's own pace.

Jewel Fisher

Ode To Friday

Friday bird, Oh Friday bird
Flap your wings once more
Fly with me
To ecstasy
Beyond this trepid shore

Friday bird, sweet Friday bird
Spread your wings of grace
Fly me there
With tender care
Where your sweetness I embrace

Friday bird, faithful Friday bird
Whose wings are the love we share
With beauty rare
beyond compare
Where hopes and dreams find us there

Joe Allen Smith

Lifegiving

Awaken by morning, the sun bursting out.
Flowers blooming, ready to shout.
Trees a budding, green as can be
Alive and talking, just to me.
Skies of beauty, radiant blue,
Emerald green grass, covered with dew.
Birds and insects, singing a song
Majestic operetta, choir in throng.
Vast world of beauty, wonder to see
Picture view of life, diversity.
A wondrous gift of God to all
Prior to our boarding call.
Transformation of life, always there
All the world to equally share.
Prominent feelings, this world is mine
So majestic and divine.
Oh! Thank you God for all to see.
Great wonders of earth given so free.

Jack A. Rogers

Love In Nature

Trees glisten
Flowers glow
And grass
Is a carpet

Shrubs are
A gathering place
For bird's gossip.

The moon
Reflects the
Sun's power,

Parks are holy
In highest beauty
With nature singing.

Carl R. Miller

Love Hurts

You made my heart skip a beat
For thus I thought we'd never meet.
You used my heart and played it well.
For I thought love was bound to be there.
Now my aches have slowly healed
for my love is burning for you
somewhere, somehow -
should I enter or beware

Debbie L. Trejos

"Maiden Of Shadows"

A lonely wolf treads her path,
 following invisible footsteps
 of her clawed ancestors.
Her silver hair is crowned with ice,
 and her dim blue eyes
 a bleak reflection of the sky
 turn from side to side.

Like a lost maiden of shadows,
 she wearily lies in the
 bed of winter treasures,
 waiting for the darkness to come,
Far from the blinding, cold light.
To the darkness of her realm.

Esther Lin

"When And Where"

My soul is searching
for a bright light-
Where I find it
I know not-
I must look,
I must listen,
I must wipe the tear
from my eye-
and try to find
the rainbow,
That tries to find me.

Bernadine King

Young Hunter

My barefoot boy goes hunting
For bear and deer and things-
His small toy gun beneath his arm;
His pocket full of strings.

He has the keenest eyesight
Of anyone I know.
He finds the hippos in the trees
And tiger tracks in snow.

And down beside the river
Where tree roots are quite bare
He spied a cave and peered within,
And found a rhino there.

Joyce A. Truchinski

Patiently I Await

Thank You, Almighty God,
for creating this little one,
for allowing her to live,
to learn, and to love.

Thank You for caring for her
with divine gentleness,
to teach her how to listen to You
and to respond with immediate
and trusting obedience.

Thank You for encouraging her
to keep in mind
the everlasting life
following this temporary existence.

Oh! How wonderful my hope
to actually see and be with
forever
my Creator, my Redeemer, and
my Sanctifier!

Mary Frances

My Daily Prayer

Lord, I'd like to thank You
For giving me today -
I also want to thank You
For listening while I pray.

Forever being patient
With a lonely soul like me,
For You forgiving daily sins
That only You can see.

For courage, strength and hope
You instill within my heart,
Of life with You in Paradise
When from this earth I part.

For blessings You send me
On the wings of a dove,
I humbly give You
My undying love.

Helen May Rocha

Tommy

I cannot give you money
   for I have none to give
I cannot grant you wishes
   or tell you where the river bends.

I cannot give you royalties
   nor diamonds in your hand
I cannot give you luxuries
   or you own beach with glazing sand

I cannot promise you glory
   I cannot give you fame,
I cannot send you around the world
   or promise you a world that's tame

I'll do my best to make you happy
   to cheer you up when you are down
I'll do my best to comfort you
   when you are not so sound

I will not go on with things I cannot give
   All I can offer is my heart, my
soul, faithfully yours, for as long as I
   shall live.

Amy Light

My Heart

My heart is a place where birds fly,
fish swim in clear waters, where
flowers never die.

My heart is a place of friendship and
kindness, where trees never stop
growing taller and taller.

Inside my heart there is no such
thing as nature growing smaller.

Inside my heart there are waterfalls
where all of the weakness is
covered by walls.

Wherever you go there is loving
and caring, and there is also a lot
of sharing.

Where wind is always ready to blow.
Where miracles are always falling
from the sky.
Where birds are always ready to fly.
Where love is always ready to show.

Brian Pugach

To My Children On Mother's Day

This house is my castle
   for in it remains
My whole life's hassle
   with happiness and pain.

The treasures within
   are not measured by cost
But by echoes resounding
   and memories not lost.

From the memory of tears
   to the lilt of their laughter
The sounds of my children
   resound from the rafters.

For God gave us children
   to love and to cherish
For what greater wealth
   could any Mother wish.

Dorene J. Mowatt

Untitled

X'mas is a anxious season
   for the little children, you see
endless waiting, wanting, hoping
   till the time day of glee

X'mas is a holy season.
   with services at midnight
listening to ancient carols
   and witnessing the advent light

X'mas is a happy season
   camouflaging winter dreads
school is close, and if it snows
   testing brand new sleds

X'mas is a sad season
   I mean in reference to fire
many a home has gone up in smoke
   from trees becoming drier

James J. DeMartinis

On The Brink

Maddening frustrations fill our life,
From choice of husband or of wife.
And how to lift our children's strife,
And whom to curse for wretched life.

Love life. And in a second breath,
Hope for the calm and peace of death.
Shall God be subject of our wrath,
For having willed our troubled path?

The blame lies with our foolish sires,
Made thoughtless by female desires.
Drawn by shape of limb and breast,
And thus drawn forth is our unrest.

Soothed senseless by a warm caress,
Through longing for sweet tenderness.
Our mothers lease their guarded heart,
And there the misery will start.

Through weakness in the man or dame,
Or whatsoever we shall blame.
We're glad though poor - without a name,
That to this grief we briefly came.

Joseph A. Rush

"Too Young"

Why does life have to end
For those so young?
Life should be long
And full of love.

They say lives that end early
Have the most purpose
But they leave the biggest heartache
For those they leave behind.

Life, as it is
Is too short.
For it to end too soon
Is what hurts the most.

Denise Smith

For You

For you I'd do most anything
For you hold my heart on a string
I would walk upon a thin wire
Just to see if you would smile
For my love is true
As I am with you

So church bells will ring
As I will sing
Make love to me
I sing to thee
But if harsh you will be
Then my love will flee
From you, my love
And like a pure white dove
Our love shall fly
High in the sky
And in the wind it shall blow
But if there is no wound
Then our love shall glow
Like the bright shining moon.

Bambi Merrifield

Free

You fight, and fight, and fight
   for your right to be free.
So now that you are free you feel
   alive,
and nothing can go wrong.
And then came knowledge,
and it kept you prisoner to your
beliefs.
That's when you realize you can
   never be free.
Unless you are blind and shut
your mind off.
Close your eyes to the world and
the wisdom must leave.
And then you will feel free...
Free to be a fool.

Abby Jane Large

Vows

Today I say my vows.
For today I will marry a man.
A man I will love for years.
Flowers, people, food, and dresses.
So much to think about.
But inside I feel happy.
For today I will marry a man I love.

Amy Smith

I Have Walked

I have walked through storms of winter
   fought wild and blowing snow
Just to find a place where I was welcome
   And to let my Lord know
He has my heart in the palm of his hands
   My love is his to keep
   My soul is his forever
Until my burden he puts to sleep
I have walked the sands of summer
   Across dry and barren land
   Just so I could reach out
   And pray with my fellow man
I have scuffed my feet in dry leaves
   When the grass was turning brown
   Just to find a store front church
Where my soul I could put down
I have walked in all kinds of weather
   from the summer to the fall
   To let my Lord know
He is the greatest of them all.

Anita Jackson

Timeless Words

I wish I was free
Free to express what I feel inside
To say what I hold within
to open my heart and speak the words
speak the words

I can't
It's a problem of time
measured in years
years spent and still awaiting
the difference in our time

If time and years
held no importance
if I could speak the words

Would she listen?
Would she hear?
Would she understand?
Would her heart be filled
With the joy they convey?

Would her lips
speak the words?

James L. Ringe

"Our Vows"

For better, for worse
for richer, for poorer,
in sickness, and in health
'til death do us part.

Over forty-one years ago
we stood and made those vows,
now we stand the testing
that life allows.

Progressive disease-
there is no cure,
yet, my love, through it all
my vows to you are sure.

My arms and heart will hold you close
whatever future time may hold,
our love will still endure
until our heavenly Father takes you safely
to His fold.

Sue Brock

Grand Canyon Trip

From Las Vegas to Arizona
four hours trip.
Twenty-one passengers were
on the mini flight.
And even a worm will turn.
Forty-five degrees turn like
greased lighting upset my stomach.
Sixty degrees and I felt
as quiet as a wasp in my nose.
Only one who got airsick.
Failure!
Bad luck me!
Try again next time!

Becky Fung

Triumph

I think I'm sure
for there is no cure.
I want to believe not
but it's something I've got.

Clear but obscure
is this fearful thing.
Which has me like a ring
forever more
till my heart beats no more.

I cannot run.
I cannot hide.
This is just something I must decide
to accept true
no matter how new.

This will be forever
so I will do whatever I endeavor

Oh God, I still want to cry
it is not that in life I did not try.
I want to fly, fly and be free
forever and ever soaring above the sea.

Valerie D'Angelo

The Flight

The pilots waited in anticipation,
For the big moment to arrive
The runway was cleared
The plane began to roll

Up, Up, the plane flew
Into the darkness around
Just the moon to the side
Lights of a city below

What a sight it was,
So quiet and serene
Not a bird was flying
Clouds here and there

Suddenly! There it was
The city below was seen
The plane began to descend,
To meet the runway below.

The plane touched the ground,
So gently and with ease
Once again, the pilots waited
This time for passengers to leave.

Marilyn Carlson

Bless The Children Of Oklahoma

Bless the children
for they'll never understand,
the senseless hatred
of a supposed trusted man.

Bless the children
their innocent lives too short
unfulfilled dreams
they were forced to abort.

Bless the children
for they are now
in a much better place
of endless carefree days
with little known haste.

Bless the children
as we search for gentle peace
let us reach upward for guidance
and pray that the senseless hatred will cease.

Sharon Walters

Untitled

Life
For what do we owe this Honor?
To make as many mistakes as we can,
to experience as much as we can.
For what?
In a world where heroes are forgotten,
corruption is rewarded,
and it doesn't pay to be a good man.
For who do we owe his honor?
To be happy, to be content,
then watch it all fall apart.
In a society that is less than average.
Less than average?
Compared to what?
To our dreams?
Life is built on dreams....
A fallacy indulged by generations.
Life is built on Reality.
Sad, sad, realty.
Life, for what do we owe this honor.

Ryan Lykins

The Peaceful Death

Come ye place where I do lie,
For you are now where once was I.

Up along the dawning brink,
I now have found the missing link.

I approach like the rising sun,
Then fade away, my life is done.

Katie Casale

The Auction

I do not mingle with the crowd
   for I'm not here to buy
They see me standing at the edge
   And think I'm passing by.

My heart is like a battlefield
   but I'm stoic as a monk
As I listen to a hawker sell
   the things I love as junk.

Soon the bidding is over
   with their treasures they move on
And though it was not marked "For sale"
   The heart of me is gone.

Mildred Brown Duncan

"Fear"

Everybody has something to fear
But fear for me has come true
I feared that my friends would fade away
And one by one surely they went away
I don't understand what went wrong
I thought I could be strong
So now I'm all alone in time
For I have been alone for a long time
It doesn't get easy or better but you
Feel like you're the only person in time
I should know I've been alone for a long time
People said the pain would go away
And now I wish I would fade away
But if I fade away will the pain fade away with us
The fear still lives in most of us promise me
You won't let the fear destroy your life
And you won't let the fear come true
And run your life through and through
Angela Caudill

Ad Astra Per Ardua

"The road is long," the young man led,
But his father's voice within his head
Said,
"Go for it!

The road is strewn with storms and squalls,
With pain and prejudice and walls
That make you falter on the way,
Plod on, plod on, push back the fray.

The scorching sun will soon go down,
The night will wrap you all around,
And in the darkness there afar
You will reach your distant star."

"The road is long," the young man led,
But to his father's voice within his head
Said,
"I'll go for it!"
Dorothy A. Butzer

"The Future And The Past"

I know that I can't let my future depend on things in the past
But I can't stop wishing that those times would have last
Things didn't always go the way that I planned
But I am proud and not afraid to take a stand
I want the best for myself and my friends
And the things I love I'll always fight for and defend
I've always believed in trying hard and doing my best
So I'll just do that and let my Heavenly Father take care of the rest
Casey E. Wisner

To The People

I've tried endlessly to runaway
   but all of a sudden, there's nothing
     left except the busy street.
Where did all the green go?
   It's brown now.
     Where did all the beautiful sounds go?
Their gone too.
   This is my home
     can't you see, but you're just taking
it all away from me.
   I have nothing
     left, except tree stumps.
Now my family and friends
are gone by those big noisy things in the street
where did it all go?
Tara Scardina

The Lord's Work

The Lord had a job for me,
But I had so much to do
I said, You get somebody else
Or wait 'til I get through'.

I don't know how the Lord made out,
He seemed to get along.
I felt kind of sneaky,
Knowing I had done God wrong.

One day I needed the Lord myself,
Needed him right away.
But He never answered me at all.
Down in my accusing heart -

I could hear Him say, I got too much to do,
You get somebody else, or wait 'til I get through'.

Now, when the Lord has a job for me
I never try to shirk,
I drop what I have on hand
And do the Lord's work.

My affairs can run along or wait will I get through'.
Nobody does the job that God's marked out for me and you.
Eva Popejay

Untitled

I know it seems as though we have drifted apart,
But I want you to know you're still close to my heart,
One would think that we have lost touch,
But I know our friendship means too much,
In actuality our souls are still together,
And I hope this will be true forever and ever.
Heather Lee

Mother's Flower Garden

Mother, we told you good-bye many years ago,
   but in spring I like to drive by and see your flowers still grow.

In my mind I can still see you there,
   wearing your apron and the bonnet over your hair.

When I hear someone say be good to each other
   it always brings memories of my Mother.

She always said God wants us to do good deeds.
   If you only look, you'll find folks in need.

I remember how she did much more than her share.
   If I can make it to Heaven, feel sure I'll find her there.

So, if only in my mind, it's great to drive by the farm,
   knowing there's nothing left but the old barn.

Except in spring I can still see Mother's tiger lilies and sweet peas
   So going back in time brings sweet memories to me.
Holly DeBerry Turner

Untitled

It is a Beautiful Day
For such a miserable life
not a raindrop
but sorrows storming forth
give dark clouds to this
Beautiful Day
and sorrows bring forth
bloomin' impatience
to see the feeling free
to smile in the sun
for
a face which reflects no light
shall never become a star
Catherine Lynn Riberdy

Good-bye

"I love you" is such a simple phrase,
But it has a deeper meaning.
It provides a warmth that lasts for days,
And it sets your thoughts a reeling.

But the pain it brings when you say good-bye,
It hurts so very much.
You miss the look in his eyes,
His soft and gentle touch.

But without good-bye, there cannot be hello.
Some good can come from the pain.
And no matter where he may go,
In his heart you will always remain.

So, do not despair when he says farewell
For one day he shall return.
And though times without him may seem like hell,
It's a lesson we all must learn.

Ariana Caboni

Emerald's Longing Shared

It was a stormy night, tornado like,
But it was our last night to share the light
Of candles' fire and her last love desire.
Her long longing hands holding tight to her first love's sight.

Her emerald green eyes holding back her cries
Which she never lets anyone hear not even through a tear.
Why can't I ease that pain that is driving her insane?
Him not holding her near was her one and true fear.

Her long hair which extends far contains the colors of the stars.
Her laugh is like the happiness of a blind man's sight.
But where is that laugh, why was it cut in half?
Why was the candle light not there to take his darkened sight?

So now she is healing that desperate feeling.
The feeling of loss that she has tossed
Into one bleeding bad dream in which she won't remember how bad
   it all seemed.
So now it is he that has to pay the cost, it is he who lost.

She has the strength to go on even though they are done.
She has the strength to bleed without having to need
His love or his words which seemed as powerful as swords.
He ashed their fire's feed but she will not forever bleed.

Elizabeth Blair Livingston

The Lamb Of God

A virgin Birth? Who'd dare believe.
But it was so...yes, he was the seed
That bruised the serpent and mankind redeemed.
He was destined to be, the lamb of God.

A man with a mission, he was ahead of his time.
To live among the oppressed, was he assigned.
A Nazarene, some say...a wine bibber,
He didn't mind being a friend to a sinner.
His short life span affected every man.
He was elected to be, the Lamb of God.

His life was the ransom, our debt paid in full.
The eternal sacrifice, no more sheep, goats or bulls.
He was reproached, scourged and suffered.
Without a blame, but not once did he mutter.
He endured the cross, wanting none to be lost.
The anointed one, the Lamb of God.

This Lamb of God, in Gethsemane travailed.
Accepted the bitter cup, on Golgotha was slain.
In three days he arose; death, the grave and hell could not oppose.
Who is he? This son of man! He's Jesus Christ, the Lamb of God.

Colleen Van Horne

Maybe I'll Try

I say I'll try something,
But maybe I won't.
I'll try something else,
Think of the do's and don'ts.
It may be fun,
Which I want it to be.
I'll try it with you guys,
Come on and see.
What do you want to do,
Climb a mountain, cross the sea,
Or even just talk in an old oak tree?
Maybe I'll try to give ideas, a lot,
But take them seriously, you're all I've got.
You need good friends to understand you
when you're sad,
And so far you guys are the best I've ever had.
Maybe I'll try for you,
After all you did for me!

Anneke Bosma

Cousin's Love

A brat at first is what I thought of you,
But now I hold a different view.

Although they want for us the same,
The time has come when we must change...
For our own style we must obtain.

We've grown a lot, though they hate to admit,
But with the changes, we've made a true friendship.

A friendship that few will ever know,
For only we have a special home.

A home in which we've learned to achieve all
that our minds are able to dream.

And with those dreams, we've learned to love,
For that is where our special bond comes.

A bond that's true no matter where we go,
For a cousins love will never grow old!

Amanda Tracy

A Lost Cause

He had wanted to look into the light
But his mother had told him to look away,
Reluctantly he had turned to the night.

When people told him he was too uptight
He would unconsciously think of that day.
He had wanted to look into the light.

He then thought of days, that could have or might
But yet turned out in such horrible ways.
Reluctantly he had turned to the night

When he broke in the house, ending her life,
This act that would decide; The night or day?
He had wanted to look into the light.

He now lies in his cell, thinking of flight,
And how his mother said to look away,
Reluctantly he had turned to the night.

This man who as a child had dreams so bright,
In this prison a lifetime he now stays.
He had wanted to look into the light,
Reluctantly he had turned to the night.

Christopher S. Robertson

The Love Lost

I use to love you with all my heart,
But now I seem to be torn apart!

You told me you love me, how dare you lie,
You hurt me deeply you made me cry!

Now all I see is a cloud of gray,
I wish you were here like yesterday!

You was always so pushy and I mean all the time,
I guess that's why I'm here of course—I did the crime!

I never stood up to you to make you stop,
I guess it all happened because I was so shocked!

I really do miss all the fun,
But on that crazy night, I just had to load the gun!

I felt like you gave me no choice,
And now I just can't stop hearing your voice!

I don't think I have the kind of heart for regret,
So you're just THE LOVE LOST that I once met!

Estelle M. Billiot

It Used To Be

It used to be beautiful,
but now it is just wasteful.
It used to be drug-free,
but now people doing drugs is all we see.
It used to have rain, snow and fog,
but now the weather is mixed with smog.
It used to be where people were just sick,
but now sickness causes people to die so quick.
It used to be when kids were really sweet,
but now their violent from their head to their feet.
It used to be where there was plenty of food,
but now there isn't enough, and people get into this mood,
It used to be so good in the past,
but now everything is changing so fast.
It used to be like petting a cats fur,
but now you should start thinking how worse it will be in the future.
It used to be like ocean sprays,
but now the world was so weird these days.

Dezarai Hanway

A Choice

God made a perfect world for mankind,
But sin soon entered in, we find;
This sin causes eternal death to all
Who receive not Jesus, but fall.

But to those who accept Christ as their Lord,
God has wonderful riches and untold blessings stored
In that heavenly home on high
Where no one shall ever die.

We have a great choice to make
Do we realize what's at stake?
Peace in our life and for eternity, you see,
Or separation from God it must always be.

Then don't we owe it to others
To ask them to be our brothers?
By becoming the children of God today
And living for Christ always.

God gave each one some talent for his service to use,
Which he asks each Christian not to abuse;
So ask God to help find his plan for you
Then willingly live as he asks you to.

Jeanette Beck

A Mother's Plea Of Love

The days seem dark and cloudy.
But someday the sun will shine and shroud you.
It will enhance your black beauty.
You are the extension of Mother Sun.
It takes time to grow and mature
Feed your mind and soul.
Build a foundation of creative talents.

The blossom that will someday bloom
will stand among many weeds
strong and everlasting.
Displaying her Black Beauty from within.

Remember O' daughter of mine,
always make love to your mind
and body for this is the key to success.

REACH! REACH! my child for a star.

Hildred P. Mack

Friends

Saying good-bye isn't easy,
but sometimes it has to be said;
It may seem painful to be
leaving, but your friendships won't be dead;
Moving on, reaching out to
higher places we go;
Opening up, trying new things
just so we will know;
That, new people and new places
may cause us to do wrong;
New situations, which bring,
challenging choices along;
Sometimes life can be confusing,
but through this you'll always know;
Friends stick together no matter where they go.,

Jennifer Szasz

Forever Love

I've been searching all my weary life,
but still I long to find
    That special guy I'll love so much, the one I can call mine.
    Sometimes I feel I won't succeed
my mind tells me it's true,
    But in my heart I do believe
he's searching for me too.
    He may be far, or may be near,
only God knows where he lies
    He could be a million miles away,
or right here before my eyes.
    I don't know what the future holds,
I don't have the slightest clue,
    But I do hope that someday I'll find the one that will be true.
    Right now the way I feel inside is so hard to explain
    It feels like I'm the only one who's dealing with this pain,
    Whoever he is, wherever he's at,
he'll be sent from up above,
    He'll be the one I'm searching for,
the one I'll forever love.

Charity Lively

Butterfly

Butterfly, butterfly you fly so high,
butterfly, butterfly you can touch the sky.
Butterfly, butterfly you are so colorful,
butterfly, butterfly you make a flower look dull.
Butterfly, butterfly you are so free,
sometimes I wish I could fly with thee.

Brian Kenneth Eitelmann

Self

I am a person, not unlike many others.
But still I'm unique, not a clone of another.
I am my own person, not another man's puppet.
Inside, I am a complex labyrinth of feelings and emotions.
I'd rather think for myself than follow another man's notions.

I am like the hawk, going where I may,
soaring through the heavens, each and every day.
Looking all around, I see struggles of every kind,
and I know the solution is in learning to use our minds.

I am a poet at heart, a scholar in mind,
a collector of electronics and things of that kind.
but none of that will mean anything,
if I fail to fulfill my dreams.

John Cunningham

Tick, Tock

Tick, tock, tick, tock, as I try to sleep,
But the clock wants me to stay up and weep.
Time may be on your side, but it's no friend of mine.
As the seconds tick by, tears fall down my face in a steady line.
You asked if we could talk, but you ended up yelling.
I thought this time would be different, but with you there's no telling.
I thought you wouldn't hit me this time.
I give you everything, but you'd never give me a dime.
Tomorrow you'll be apologizing, down on one knee.
Begging for forgiveness, saying you don't deserve someone like me.
I'll agree with you this time, because I'm sick of all the fights.
It's time for a change, so I'll be the one putting out the lights.
The flame has gone out, says the clock.
Tonight I'll finally be able to sleep, tick, tock, tick, tock.

Elizabeth McPherson

The Land Of Make Believe

I can feel the world attention,
But not enough to win the fame;
I'm maybe a wandered soul across the braves land
Or maybe I'm just an invisible faith.

Some people see me as an awakened giant
Pouring some light within the doubt and the flame;
Some said I was too scared to tell the truth when hit the engines,
But was not afraid, was more than energy
running wild my veins and set the freedom of speech.

I'm a believer, I'm a God messenger
I hate the gossips that ruin my green,
This is your planet and not a battlefield
This is the land of make believe.

Bamil Gutierrrez Collado

Talk To Me

Talk to me Lord, what would you have me do?
Close my eyes that I may hear,
Close my ears that I may see,
Open my heart that I may feel.

Talk to me Lord, what can I do for you?
Send me a message that I can hear,
Send me a sign that I can see,
Open my heart that I can understand.

Talk to me Lord, where are you?
I listened at the cross, you weren't there,
I looked in the tomb, you weren't there,
I opened my heart and found you there.

Jo Anne Peters

Just A Stone's Throw Away

With each passing moment, the past seems more distant
But the memories of yesterday will live on
And though certain details will be lost
The feelings of yesteryear will never fade

Memory lane is a lonely road without you
But it seems that I sometimes must take a stroll
And each time I regress into a nostalgic trance
My thoughts about the past become clearer

I know that what I felt for you was true
And I think that you felt the same
The past is just a stone's throw away
There's still time to recapture what we had

James P. Snow

Spiritual Strength

The World is a big challenge,
But the spirit need not be daunted.
With a strong mind,
Encouraged by spiritual strength,
All obstacles can be overcome,
And encouragement surface to sustain the spirit,
Advancement and growth take place,
And the Light shines on the right path.

Dorothy Ogihara

Untitled

She is pretty shy
But with her friends she opens up
They possess the key
To get her open
Her mind keeps thinking,
Travelling over many thoughts
she thinks
Seeing her with her hair as gold or maybe more gold than any treasure
ever found
And her eyes greener that a cat's
You'd never guess that her spirit, her thoughts, and her whole mind
can be so free,
so wild, so uncontrolled
Nobody could know, or ever guess how her plotting mind works
She thinks and thinks
When she writes the thoughts that she thinks end upon paper
that's how this poem was written.

Jaime Semensohn

This Mind Of Mine

Purple flowers, green sun, red skies, yellow sea,
black birds, singing out of key.
Blowing wind trying to hurt me, what are you saying?
Are you yelling at me?
You wrap me in your coldness, hurting me with your boldness.
I see all the hate you have for me, why do you hate thee?
Why won't you understand?
Why won't you let me comprehend?
Won't you please let me live on your unhappy land?
Won't you please say I love you and reach out your hand?
Falling... falling in a deep black hole and where I go
I do not know.
Where is my body, not within me, for me soul lies not within, thee.
It belongs to a force that isn't mine,
for a land I have to find and when I do...
I will define it all to you, this world, this hell of mine...
This land, this hand, this mind of mine.

Sophia A. Sonoqui

"I Was Taught To Read, But My Eyes Could Not See..."

Learning is eighty-percent (80%) sight,
but your vision is an acquired skill;
and if your eyes don't function properly,
reading will always stand still.

I remember I was taught to read,
but my eyes could not see;
the words would double and blur,
the teachers would always blame me.

I knew inside I was intelligent,
even though I was "labeled" ADD;
others called me lazy,
but time would tell it wasn't meant to be.

A reading specialist suggested,
an Optometrist for me;
Vision Training was my answer,
so my eyes could finally see.

My school grades have greatly improved,
and I love to pick up a book and read;
my vision has been corrected,
making learning life's greatest seed.
David U. Burke Jr.

The Eternal Dance

The man saw his wife lying asleep,
By the doorway he stopped, to take just a peek,
He brushed back her hair, with his hand, by her ear,
And he thought to himself, "Those were the years."

The woman awoke, and spoke not a word,
But kissed her fair prince, all wrinkled and worn.
In position, he placed her, and danced her around.
They needed no music, they made not a sound...
Like a school girl she felt, as he twirled her around.

Moments did pass and their bodies did slow,
But in spirit they danced as they did long ago.
Their marriage had lasted through many a year,
Their love had lasted through many a song,
They knew in their hearts, this was where they belonged.

Marriage is made by ones who love
It is blessed and kept by God above.
Adair Powell

Where Do I Belong?

I'm of the sea of humanity. One of many, yet of none.
Caught in the currents of my existence,
Flowing with everyone, yet alone.
Trying to find a niche I can call my own.
Yet, I'm a prisoner of all around me, and all that's unknown.

Emotions, words and music have all been silenced
For no one understands the language I speak.
No one feels the turmoil of what I wish to say,
And no one cares the knowledge I would seek.

For I wish to know the why, and wish to know the wherefore.
I'm seeking the serenity this knowledge would bring.
I keep hunting patterns
That bring all together
For there's a master plan beneath everything.

The rivers keep flowing. Winds keep blowing.
Yet no one listens to their song.
Sun, moon, and stars keep glowing.
There's knowledge hid from knowing.
Still, I seek the place where I belong.
B. LUE

Verses To A Farmer

[Meditation on the tombstone of Ebeneezer Hubbel, Easton, CT; d. 1774, aged 98 years]

How sad: the azure sky above
Can never share a farmer's love
For earth and field and summer sky
And winds that weep when farmers die.

Or how the green grass beneath my feet
Does cover where the farmer sleeps
In moldy earth, in cold clay keeps,
Or where the silent spider sleeps.

How sad it is that time's not lithe,
But is quick and unforgiving:
He beckons death's hands to his scythe
To lay low and reap the living.

The farm's stone walls are lichened green,
Silent, save the spring rain's patter,
And what was once the farmer's dreams
Falls to ruins and hangs in tatters.

Death and time (old friends) went walking
Out, just to view their handiwork:
Dusty death's mouth does no talking
As time turns farmer into dirt.
Daniel Blythe Gilmore

Dreaming? A Young Soldier's Nightmare In Viet Nam

Could it really be me standing here?
Can this frightened boy be the man I was?
Are the things I'm seeing really there?
Or am I dreaming?

Does life begin and end with this gun?
Is this the only way I can survive?
Am I ever again to see a peaceful setting sun?
Or am I dreaming?

Is this a different side of me?
Have I always been like this?
How could I kill and still feel free?
Am I dreaming?

I feel the fear surging through me
To kill is the key to my existence
Do, lest it be done unto thee
I AM NOT DREAMING

I see the enemy coming now
As cold sweat runs down my brow
I'll pull the trigger, I am the killer
Was I ever dreaming?
Carlene A. Knights

Looking

   By looking at a single person you can't tell anything. They may look happy, they may look sad, but on the inside it could be different than portrayed.
   You can't tell what their thoughts are about, good or bad. For most cover them all too well.
   You can't tell if they're hurting inside or extremely joyous. They just leave you to wonder.
   By looking at a single person you can't tell what they've been through in their lifetime, so don't portray you do.
   When looking at a person you see what's on the outside, never the inside. Some may be dying to ask for help, but just don't know how, and you just don't see.
Dana Johnson

The Glory Of Trees

The trees with their leaves in bloom,
carry the glory of spring to start.

Birds fly by for a place to nest,
while squirrels look for a place to rest.

The leaves in colors of green and red.
Some with flowers that smell perfume.

The Lord sure knew what to do,
when he made the trees for shade and beauty

To use to build a home for all,
the tree sure is a useful plant

To give us fruit and nectar pure,
what other plant does even more?

Can anything replace the tree?
Not anything that I can see.
Frances Bean

Ponderings

While walking through the wooded land, amongst the beautiful trees
Catching glimpses of the sunlit sky, feeling the gentle breeze
Inhaling the freshness of the air, enjoying the warmth of the sun
Wishing I had many lives to live, knowing mine is near done.
Years to enjoy the beauty and savor the sweetness of this land
Years to add to my knowledge to help me understand.
To help me understand the mysteries of this life
The hills and the valleys of emotion and strife.
Mysteries that are held within the land, sky and sea
And the analysis of how it all came to be.
So many diversified creatures that live within our sphere
From what minute components are they and why are they here.
Well, the science, breadth and depth of this is all too deep for me
Since my life is so very short, I'll leave these mysteries to my
  posterity.
Eva K. Holbrook

Here To Stay

Behind my eyes, there lies a face,
Calling himself Despair.
His dark lenses glare inside me
As a dagger embeds deep in my heart.
He stares into the depths of my soul
And sees none other than his own reflection,
Realizing a treacherous victory.

Blue rain drops drip down my cheeks.
My desperate tears feed his hunger
His hunger for control of my being,
Lying in a bed of my fallen roses,
Never will he disappear.
Jennifer Meagan

Figure Of Stone

To you I am strong
But really I am weak
A figure of stone with a heart of gold
Let me come close to you, be so near
Our warm breath meets in motionless air
And let you murmur softly into your ear
Tell you things you need and want to hear
And when I go, you will know
That I do have a heart of gold
Even though I am a figure of stone.
Dawn Dabbs

Mothers Make A Difference

Mothers make a difference - that's clear by God's own word.
'Cause it's often from our mothers where first his word is heard.
With mother's arms around us, while in her lap we're laid,
We feel God's peace and comfort - no more are we afraid.
From this infancy we struggle and grow through adult years,
Then realize how our growth was nurtured with mother's love and tears.
The perfect way to send a savior; God truly understood,
Delivered by way of labor's stress, he glorified motherhood.
Yes, mothers make a difference when they carry out God's plan.
They impart to us God's strength and love as only mothers can.
Curtis Crawford

The Beauty Of Life

One beautiful day I was
celebrating my birth.
When I found out what life
is truly worth.
The love of your family,
good times with your friends;
That is where the beauty begins.
The ocean so blue
The clouds so white
The sparkling stars in the darkness of night,
You look and see the tranquility around.
A blackbird takes off from the ground,
a beautiful and moving sight.
The birds flying around in the sky above
show you that we are
surrounded by love.
You see the sun when you rise.
The lion roars as the eagle flies.
Akima Mayo

Dreams

   I watch the world
change and grow. I see the
world through high and low.
I wonder what tomorrow brings
I dream of the most amazing
things. I blow a kiss to a shooting
star. Away, away, so far, so far, I dream
about amazing things I dream of
what tomorrow brings, I said
it twice to make it clear, that sometimes
dreams are so near so near.
Ean Jenkins

Miss Trust

The soothing touch of a foreign hand
caressing my soul within its boundaries
enrapturement tasted, indulged in demand
pretextment deterred by desultory
Love is thus spoken through rhymes of reticence
petals flittering about me
Angels kiss my eyes in assurance
painted devils concealed appropriately
The hand doth twist and grab a hold
my soul is raped unknowingly
Introverted emotions become exposed
the fragrance of betrayal throughout me
my trust does shudder and dissipates
descending upon the atrocity
I crumble to ashes upon burdened weight
retroversion to hate, transposed of such piety
Insomnious slumber, emotions entranced
unfeeling upon my amazement
desolation discerned, deception thus danced
confined to the depths of estrangement
Fernando Morales

Memories Of Yesterday

Looking back at the years of yesterday,
my fondest memories are of children at play.
I was one of those children and so were you,
As we learned and explored each day something new.
We were more than just classmates, neighbors or friends,
We were bonded like siblings that nothing could bend.
Sometimes we fought over games that were played, but soon we'd
be laughing the madness away. Between lemonade stands and
garage sales galore, we had lots of fun though our profits were
poor. We were trying too hard to grow up too fast, and were all
unaware of how quickly time passed. Among curfews, chores,
homework and tests, we were sure that the worst would soon bring
the best. During winter, spring, summer and fall, together through
time we weathered it all. We shared all our secrets, our hopes and
our dreams. "Together forever!" Was just how it seemed. We
experienced happiness, sorrow, and pain, though time heals all
wounds, the loss still remains. We're all moving on the best that
we can, to follow those dreams that a child once had. If just for a
moment I could go back in time, to the memories that still are alive
in my mind. For looking back at the years of yesterday, my
fondest memories are of children at play.

Jennifer M. Brewer

Song Of The Sick Poet

Waves beat on the shore, as they count out the minute,
Clock ticks out the hour-and we have to be in it.
Time is of the essence to all mortals bound.
We are here on a track that goes round and around.
I'd like to stop and ask to get off.

So I have time to see you and love you enough.
Or where can we find us the timeless zone.
Forever and ever we will be there alone.

Carolyn S. Gray

Blue Bird At The Window

Bird in the window—how beautiful you are
Close enough to touch, but ever too far
With wings spread, I flit, flutter, and fly
You do as I, but never join me—why?
How wonderful it would be—for you and me
Flying together—quick and free.

David A. Clark

Grandpa

I went through the days so brave and strong
but that didn't last for long.

As the days went on,
it was hard to believe you were gone.

I swore I'd never cry
but then I saw where you lie.

So still and lifeless, like a statue.
I still couldn't believe that was you.

As I burst into tears on that cold breezy day,
they put your coffin in the cemetery.

Where it would forever lay.
You were mean and bitter,
and not much of a sitter.

You were strong and loyal,
but it seemed your heart was in a coil.

You were a man with a dream,
and now a man of the past.

But our memories of you
will forever last!

Dawn Schlauger

By The Grace Of A Favorable Sun

When on the bed I lie, six inches from your face with my pillow eye
closed, my left eye drinks you in. I feel your body heat soothing
close to mine. All time disappears in the features of your face as
I study your contour roll and lazy blue eyes staring into mine dreamily.
You make me smile

When working morning 'til night, determined to be satisfied with our
hours together, my beard is ever growing. I know it hurts,
snuggling against my bristling chin. All those unkempt days are
but a flash and forgotten as I shave clean, knowing you will stroke
my cheek and say, "You look like a lit-tle ba-by bird!"
You make me smile.

When curled up dreaming, your wild lucid nights filled with surreal
possibilities, the black cats fly and cling to your back. I am
mystified by the terribly credible in your night's eventuality, all
sensuous absurd shapes confounded by grotesque, oft doomed plots, as
you whirl towards some desperate metaphysical mission. Then you
roll over, tell your story, and give ME a hug?
You make me smile.

When thinking of moments that comprise your life, your special
art of living both maddening and beautiful, I am touched completely.
Without doubt, I believe that all days in your presence are presents
from a favorable god. As light warms our lives by the grace of a
favorable sun, so you also provide the warm growing spirit of my life.
You make me smile.

Donald D. Andersen

Released By Forgiveness

Unforgiving heart needing time and space to heal
clothed in layers of bitterness inability to feel...

Belief this is sole shelter while vulnerable and frail
Unknowing peace comes only with the layers you unveil...

Locked within the soul reside deep love, a bond, emotion
wall built high, heart struggles with the strength of
love's devotion...

Then comes a time of forgiveness, a beauty to behold
heart and soul released in peace, fit together in one mold...

Christine Dawn Legros

Questions My Child Questions

*I wish to dedicate this poem to my son, Joseph David, who
reached out with courage to "The Lonely Woman" and pulled
her from a darkness she was blindly sliding into.*

Where are you My Child? Born into darkness,
confined to the shadows by an untrusting people,
an unbelieving land. Why do you feel alone -
so alone in this dim crowded world?

Where are they My Child? Your guardians, the
loving people, your laughing friends, your teachers?
Have they abandoned you to this fate of loneliness?
Why do you feel so lost - lost and alone in this crowded world?

Where is the light My Child? The wisdom, the words to bring
knowledge and comfort? Is nothing real, sacred, reachable?
Why do you see only darkness - darkness between yourself and
others in this sad crowded world?

What is the emptiness inside My Child? This painful emptiness
that lingers, this thin shadow of fear that constantly surrounds
you, that haunts you. Why are you so afraid - afraid, alone, lost,
captured by this relentless grip of fear.

Oh! My Child, I know you wish to be free - free to laugh,
to cry, to create, to sing, to dance. Free at last to live and love.
I saw a weed today that had the beauty and majesty of a
beautiful flower - the darkness faded, I saw you.

Clare B. Gerber

The Tragedy In Oklahoma

'Bye Momma, I love you,' a child's last words,
'C'mon, let's get outta here!!' a killer's cry of glee,
An explosion shakes the ground,
half of the building comes crashing down,
The whole world turns to a broken city,
'It's not supposed to happen here...' but it did,
'My baby is in there...'
A fireman holds a crushed child as we look on,
'Help me, please.' A woman's strangled plea,
Heroes come to help, but there's only so much one can do,
The tears will never stop flowing,
The lives of innocent children and workers are gone,
Broken children lie in the rubble, their parents heartbroken,
"You certainly have not lost America."...I sure hope not, Mr. President.
  Jennifer Klausner

Collection

My spare parts
collected on Thursday mornings;
to the bellow of whining motors
and the trash men laugh. They see my pocket
full of mischief and eyes seeping with
conceit.
I've been thrown away.
Apparent disregard for my shackles, rather they
exile me and my ignorant pursuit of materialism.
My spare parts
thrown in the decaying heap of life;
I'm left to drown in the dead sea of the city.
No one wants to visit,
No one cares to see my foul institution.
Everyone is gone.

We were never important.
I've been thrown away.
  Amanda L. Holcomb

The Procession

California Firestorms
She is God's Angel
Come to purge a city's sinfulness.
She is Satan's Mistress,
Jealous and demanding equal glory.

The hem of her royal red gown
Cascades gracefully, effortlessly
Down the canyon staircase.
All eyes are fixed.

She consumes simple sagebrush as greedily as museum delicacies.
Her palate never cleansed from one course to the next.
Winds play in her hair-she feels refreshed.
Sparks fly as she snaps her long fingers-she feels impatient.

Only her mercurial mood
Grants access to her intrigue or flight from her wrath.
Your anxiousness amuses her.
Her vulgar beauty is scorched in your memory.

And you wait...afraid to look her in the eye.
And you wonder...what will she demand of you?
Only your all, your irreplaceable.
  She passes and never looks back.
  Anne W. Lee

A Prayer

Thou oh infinite spirit divine
Come unto me so refined

Also, in ignorance I must confess
you leave my mind confused and distressed.

For 'tis tangible evidence I seek
Subliminal is my finest attribute

A base and debased nephs that is as
the turbulent sea

Forever searching to commute to
higher planes
  of conscious intellect.
  Alice Coutee

How I Need You

How I need you. God must have really known. So small but such a comfort. A comfort to my soul when I'm sad, blue, suffering with a bug or just simply need a hug. When I hold you, a warm feeling caresses my body as no hands of anyone bigger than you could ever do. When I feed you, it's such satisfaction as I could never find dishing a plate to any one bigger in weight. When I clean your little body, it's a feeling I could never get while cleaning any other. I kiss your cheek, so tiny and so sweet. I hold your feet, so beautiful and warm with your own little heat. How I need you. How God must have known that a mother needs a baby just to feel some sense of own. When I sprinkle you with powder, you kick and smile with all your little power. You calm my soul with your every roll. You alone make me know I have a strong purpose here on earth. What a feeling of such great and grand worth. God truly knew how much I needed you. How I need you. How I need you.
  Annie Dantzler

Marriage

Friction, tightness, a warm familiarity.
  Conflict, change, a passion for desire.
    Comfort, comfort, forgiveness and reprisal.

I grow, we share, a new beginning tomorrow.
  Your heart, your heart, my soul I try to follow.
    Life, life, life a narrow passage way.
As one, we are, our being, never borrowed...
  James H. Woodard

Thoughts

A continuous nonstop circle
Confused - without a clue
Love keeps me thinking
Lies keep me drifting
The feeling of being used keeps me crying
Thinking, drifting, crying
Love is what does this
Why does it have to be so hard?
Why can't it be the way it used to be?
Peaceful, loved, secure
I'll never know the true meaning of love
I tried so hard to figure it out
I'm clueless.
I can't let go of the feeling
The feeling of which I devour
With emotion and insecurity
At the same time wishing it would be easy
It's not. Love's not
Life's not
Love keeps me thinking...
  Julie Lapides

"C-Ing Is Believing"

Crying crystals, cleansing, clearing the collective
conscience;
Contemplating creation, the cosmos, constellations;
Clouds, condensation, climate, crawling, creeping,
climbing, constructing civilizations.

Clans, community, caring couples, chastity,
commitments, church, ceremony, children, a circular
continuum of comfort.

Compassion, charity, counsel for cancerous, corrupt,
callous, cruel, cowardly, criminal colonization by
creed, color and class.

Control, competition
Cold, chilling computerization,
Commiseration in concentration camps.

Cauldrons of clashes for centuries, climax, crescendo;
catastrophe;
Conclusion of chapters, conflicts;
Charred carrion in a corroding cesspool; divine comedy.

Cooling, Ecclesiastical calm — Christ!
Danica L. Jones

What If?

Upon my demise a floppy disk
   could be extracted from my skull

Is there anything useful for posterity
   related in there?

Or could they sift and glean and find
   a pearl of wisdom?

Maybe the computer was down at times
   leaving empty spaces

Or were there happy times expressed
   in eerie laughter

I hope the darkest secrets reveal themselves
   in undecipherable code

I keep adding to this mass of info
   because it's fun for me

But seen by anyone?
   That I'll never know
Evelyn T. Ericson

Ultimately

Fingers of tightness
Clutching, squeezing, gripping
With a terror to chill one's soul
Pain dark and terrifying
Ripping one's breath away

Next time calm acceptance
Of the fate long desired
Not so sharp and painful
Dull pain that eases you
Into out of life swiftly

Beckoning, gently opening
The loving arms of death
Only so many stays can be granted one
When time laughingly trots outside your reach
Close enough to desire

Yet forever
Unattainable
Chantal Spring-Dupres

Fantasy Land

I really do live in a great fantasy land,
Could be I was touched by a Prophet's hand.
I can conjure up tales of love and romance,
Graceful as a fairy, I am able to dance.
I know all the music and popular tunes,
I have made love under silvery moons,
At the Bali Ritz I have checked my cape
The Opera House you know was first rate.
Gentlemen bedecked me with jewels at my door,
Vacations in Europe, on yachts and much more.
Walking on beaches and riding the surf,
I guess I have been every place on this earth.
I'm sure you can tell by this, I have been most everywhere.
Of course it is just dreaming from my old wheelchair.
Jeanne Beckett McMaster

From Earth To Eternity

From the graves they meet pulsing in my veins
Coursing through history to this time.

I have lived before in their happiness and pain
My ancestors all formed me to be what I am today.

The tanner, the preacher, the artist, the father
Of course, I have been there before!
That feeling of deja vu is true.

I've lived in those castles, fought on the heather,
Died on the battlefield, cried on the plain.

And I will live on in those who come after me
My blood forming their features and talents.

Among them will be perhaps pilots, space engineers,
Designers, mothers of the Exploration Age.

They'll be born on distant planets
Growing flowers in asteroid dust
Watching the earth shine in the sky at night.

When they come here to vacation
On green grass under blue skies
They'll say "I have been here before!"
Catherine Overstreet Boutz

Mildred

Mildred, you're home now!
  Cradled in God's Almighty arms, safe from any human harm.

Mildred, you're home now! The fields of heaven wait.
  You're free! So much to see, so much to be!

No more murkiness of sight that once had dimmed your night.
No more stiffness and pain on days of mist and rain.
  You're free! So much to see, so much to be!

The fields of heaven wait!
Mildred, who's that watching by the gate?
Why, it's Mother Reubie standing tall-just listen to her call.
  "Mildred, ah, Mildred, my child
  It's been such a long, long while."
And Daddy Leslie's standing by with a smile so big
  it lights up the sky!

Mildred, you're home now
  wrapped in God's all-glorious light
    no more darkness, no more night

Mildred, you're home now!
Carolyn Grigereit

Promises You Can't Keep

You said that when you saw me first, the thought that
  crossed your mind,
Was that I was the one for you until the end of time.
You said that if you lost me, you'd take your life right then,
You said that I was perfect, forgetting all my sin.

But then you turned away from me, leaving me in tears,
Your reason wasn't very clear, unlike your doubts and fears,
So I stood there all alone, remembering as I wept,
All the itty-bitty things you've promised and not kept.

So I'll tell you dearest darling, one thing you taught me well,
If something ever troubles me, find someone to tell.
So, I thought you said you'd love me, never causing me to weep,
Or was that just another promise that you couldn't keep?

Christen Rae McGaha

Untitled

Reveille broke the morning sky,
crusted eyes slowly waking,
darkness all around.
Screams echoed in my head
darkness all around
a sudden shift on a downward spiral.
CRASHING!
Silence screaming.
Daisies bloom under the reveille broken sky,
never to be seen.
Darkness falls over our sleepy town
darkness forever.
Tear-filled eyes slowly close
never to open again.

Charles Swint

Honor Mother

Though Mother's Day comes but once a year
Daily reminders continue our cheer...
That your health is stable and your heart is strong.
You've made living a challenge to obey and rely on
Jesus for guidance and
His father for grace
While the Holy Spirit eases a day's
  hurdles and race!

Diann S. T. McDonald

Where Are The Children; Where Have They Gone?

Where are the children? Where have they gone?
Death hovers from conception and feeds upon crack and cocaine
that is supplied in the womb
Wee cries go unheard, it follows the innocent when born,
Watching them experiencing withdrawal as they try to hold onto life,
with each agonizing breath
Bombs explode, babies die, parents abuse and kill, stifling their cries
The cold reality of the world smothers the small flickering candles;
some only dimmingly, while others are darkened forever
Carry knives and guns to school, bully the weak, protect your turf
at all costs Child pornography, molestation, gangs, and teenage
pregnancy run rampant; along with the graffiti and blood of the streets

Substitute a mother's love for a key that fits a door, but never opens
a heart or home. Food stamps, welfare, a parent who swears, yells,
drinks, and sometimes hits a lot, is my world.
Along with role models that play roulette with the devil's advocate
"AIDS," spilling over for me to inherit the suffering

God must surely cry, as his precious gifts are thrown in the trash,
Discarded with the garbage, whether born or unborn
Where are the children? Where have they gone? Where is the
laughter? Where is the love?

Joyce Sowers

Words Of Power

Mist Covered Mountains, a faded memory,
dance across the paths in my mind.

All the stones I've stepped across,
all the ones I've missed;
linger through the air in the cold, dark night.

As deep as the ocean,
as deep are my thoughts;
that no man will ever know or see.

The sun pierces through the trees,
its light jumps swiftly upon the leaves;
blinding my emotions.

The waves crash against the stones,
the sky quickly turns gray;
its clouds burst into tears.

The winds whistle,
lightning flashes in the distance
as shadows of my past appear before me.

Up high on the hillside shines a glimmer of light,
the rains slowly subside, a gentle breeze blows
and deep in my soul are words of power.

Dayna M. Haraczka

For You

As the sun sets on another lonely day, the soft glowing light
  dances in your warm, tender eyes. You comfort me.

I feel a strength growing in my soul. There's a spark inside
  me that is dying to burst into flames.

With your simple kindness and your attentive ear, you are
  filling a void in me — a new and exciting friendship
  that I so desperately want.

I would be there for you, but I need you to lend me the key
  to the fortress that guards your soul, your heart, and
  the all thoughts racing through your mind.

I would love to get closer to you, but that key is in your
  hand. I promise not to pressure you, but please
  know and understand: I am here
For you.

Diana M. Shemansky

The Daffodil

A bright yellow daffodil, on her merry ways.
Dancing and dreaming, that's how she spends her days.

The yellow little daffodil forgot her one main care,
While she danced and dreamed, all the others would prepare.

Winter was coming, weather turned cold.
The flower forgot that she was getting old.

One day her mother told her, that she had to get ready,
For winter was coming soon and steady.

Her best friend the daisy,
Was driving her crazy.

She was constantly telling her to pack,
And song and dance, did the daffodil lack.

The daffodil didn't mind,
She still tried to find

A place where she could dance and sing,
A place where it was always spring.

One day her father said.
"It's time for you to go to bed."

"One last song I'll let you sing,
Then underground you'll go for spring."

Jane Porter

One Moment

You were too young to die
dear friend, you had so much
potential only to have it stolen
from you in one swift moment...

    Your life had only begun,
    so young, so lively were you.
    You always were there ready to
    offer your assistance to anyone
    yet in one swift moment you were gone...

I saw you that day, you were so alive
and dwell and happy. Imagine my shock
only hours later to hear an accident
stole you away in your prime from those
who loved you..

    We know our lives will be empty now,
    so very lonely without you.
    Our main comfort now is our certainty
    that one day we shall be together
    in a better place.....
      Angelique M. Philips

The Recipe

Join hands and embark on the road to happiness
Decide that you are on the same team—
Erase all the competitiveness towards each other
And focus on the great attributes each possess.
Agree that both are very precious
And should be treated with the utmost respect and tenderness.
Allow your partner to be the best—
Praise and believe in each other.
Know that peace and contentment
Only comes when total trust is present—
Give 100% to the other.
Forgive and let go of any resentment you may carry,
It will only hurt you and each other
Love, laugh, look for rainbows
    Ann S. Walsh

The Next Chapter

Wings of freedom in the west,
Deep down I know this really isn't the best.
Seed of Life inside,
This is something I can no longer hide.
Sharing the news with all,
Lifts the burden and opens the soul.
The desire of my roots burns strong
I'll soon be with my family, it won't be long.
    Christine Strub

"Little Eagle"

As we drove along this road
By which a roost was built
My eyes drank in the beauty
And my heart beat faster still
There he was, so bold and proud
The "little eagle" stayed
His head, it showed his bright white crown
That surely God had made
He never moved, now flew away
From all the sights and sounds
He seemed to enjoy just sitting there
Surveying all around
The "Little Eagle" gave me peace
Deep within my soul
He was made for all to see
Until God calls him home
    Janice R. McCovey-Kelly

My Dearest Daniel J

I'm not real sure how to start explaining how I feel
Describing my emotions is hard, please know that they are real
This feeling I have of peace and content I know is from the Lord
And the rules for living a fulfilled life I'm finding in His word
He tells us time and time again, who and how to love
And He tells us that if we need more strength to look to Christ above
He reminds us not to worry but to trust in Him alone
To rest in His power and might instead of in our own
When I think of all He's done for me I can't help but want to cry
Then I think of how He suffered and how He had to die
So I tried each day to live my life the way He'd want me to
When all of a sudden out of the blue, His gift to me was you
At first it might not have seemed that way, just working side by side
I wanted to get to know you better, you only wanted to hide
Well it seems that God had something planned because here we are today
Starting our lives in His name and our living in His way
God has done so much for me by putting you in my life
He's made me ready for caring and sharing, I'm ready to be your wife
It's time for me to finish this so we can say our vows
Besides if I know my mom, I'm sure she's crying by now
    Joanne P. Morris

Roses For The Lady

Roses are for the lady whose lips are cherry red
Diamonds are for her eyes for they see ahead
Her skin is as soft as the music they play
Her hair blows freely on a cool summer day

The smile is a gift all on its own
With your love I will never be alone
I have searched for a long long time
Now it has ended because you are mine

In a room full of strangers you are all I see
Your heart plays such a sweet sweet melody
I make a wish upon a star
To be with you wherever you are

If you should cry I will cry a little more
And hold you closer than I did before
This is my heart that I give to you
These are my words that remain true

Roses are for the lady whose lips are cherry red
Diamonds are for her eyes for they see ahead
She is the reason my reason in life
Like seasons change she has changed my life
    Gregory Ruckman

Considering

Consider all of the times that you've had fun,
Consider those times when there was work to be done.

Consider what life would be like if you were totally free,
Consider life if only blank walls you could see.

Consider the joyous times you've had,
Consider what it would be like if all were sad.

Consider the time that you now stand,
Consider the days that slipped through your hands.

Consider the things that touch your heart,
Consider also those that tear it apart.

Consider the loved ones that you hold dear,
Consider a world without them near.

Consider all of the best things in life,
Consider finally your everyday strife.
    David McCoy Jr.

Untitled

I sit looking out upon the desert, while a red tailed hawk floats and dips through the sky. This desert once untouched and so peaceful and now the sounds of tractors and bulldozers at dawn. And I just keep asking why? Can we not leave the tranquility to be? Its only sounds, those of nature's creatures, the true inhabitants I used to see. Oh those incredibly peaceful mornings. Awakening to the luscious warbling and tweeting of so many birds. And oh those wonderful coyotes. Baying at the moon and howling and yipping outsidemy door. It's difficult to add to this symphony the proper words. But of course progress must win once more. So that all the wood and glass and steel will take away this precious desert floor. And then they say those darn Coyotes they're right in my backyard. They're eating my cats and dogs and they are so bold. Well dear Sir and Madame you see, no one told them that their property was sold. Sold right out from under their feet because you chose to uproot this land that never should be touched; the original inhabitants have nothing to eat So this is progress these developers will say, and so the city council lets them have their way. To my little friends in the desert whose home will no longer be, I wish deep within my heart that I had control of this land so that you could stay and sing and howl for me.

Donald S. Kalton

Heart Of Hearts

No, I understand

> Don't mistake my sad face and tears for disbelief and a need to cling to you.

Yes, I hurt

> My heart aches at the realization that my best wasn't good enough to sustain you.

No, I reflect

> But appreciate your candor and honesty, I wish you well.....

My Friend

My Lover

My All

Charlene Hardy

Horizon's Turn

I come quietly to the sea and watch the dark
   distance - barren and empty.
The moon, with its meager light, is a shattered
   dance on wet marble.
With it, the night separates into sea and sky.
There is no lighthouse, or buoy's tolling bell...
   only the whispering waves.
Beneath my bare feet sand drifts, scatters,
   spreads - a small summer avalanche.
Time slowly ebbs by as I stand and wonder.
Sleepy sea gulls stir, and begin their ascent to the
   air with soft cries filling this solitude.
Morning rises out of night when colors of the
   forming sunrise bathe the horizon...reaching
   out fragile fingers of blues and pinks, grasping
   the sky and erasing the emptiness that once was.
I watch in awe...such beauty is the reward of
   night's long holding hope that such vibrancy
   and life can be created out of such utter
   lifelessness.

Christine M. Guyler

Independence Day Reflections

As the day of July 4th draws near
Do you hear the voice of Paul Revere
What if he had not made that midnight ride,
Be thankful Americans and smile with pride.

We glorify the day, with loud celebration
Let's thank our God for this great nation
Be humble and proud but sound the alarm
We still must be alert to keep this country from harm.

Let's bow our heads and whisper a prayer
For the blood, toil, and tears
Of those who were there.
If some had not fallen in death for this land,
We would not be able to hold out our hand,
And say to America, the land of the free
Thank God for this country
It's where I want to be.

Joan Heskett

Reality

What is this world coming to?
Does anyone know? How about you?
The violence still keeps climbing high,
and lots of people are going to die.
Isn't anybody going to do anything?
We'll have to see what these elections bring.
Will any of this violence stop?
And will these death rates eventually drop?
Is it that people don't care about their earth?
What does it matter? What is it all worth?

Jamie Kirk

The Things Of Beauty

He said, "I take note the things of beauty."
Does he see the morning glory spread its petals in first light?
....Or the tulip stretch its cup towards the noon day sun?
....Or the lengthening shadow of the rose as the sun goes down?

He said, "I take note the things of beauty."

Can he feel the cool air as the sun goes down?
...Or the calm night around him?
...Or the crispness in the early morning just before the sun comes up?

He said, "I take note the things of beauty."

Does he hear life waking up at the break of day?
...Or the locust singing his song in the noon day heat?
...Or the owl's praise of the day gone by?

"Does he take note the things of beauty?" Said she.

...The brilliant light in my eyes?
...My heart reverberating in my chest?
...My breath close to his ear?

Carolyn H. Jensen

"My Husband"

Quietly you stand, in your blue,
duty and honor are the shield.
Bearing the symbols of your pride,
A star of brass and a ring of gold.

Each day leaving to do what's sworn,
Uphold the law and protect your fellow man,
Each night returning home,
With tales to tell and a silent thanks.

A goal long held in heart and soul,
this one thing, the only thing to be.
Though the reality isn't quite the dream,
You stand boldly in your blue.

Julie A. Petty

Lost Love

Where does love go when it is lost?
Does it cling to the windows of your heart
Like the remnants of winter's old Jack Frost?

Or does it hide itself deep in your mind
until a memory stirs it up for you to find.

Does it listen for that lilting song of long ago
waiting breathlessly for you to recall and know

The meaning of that song's refrain
and to remember the joy as well as the pain
of that parting moment so long ago.

The years may come and memories dim
still in your thoughts you picture him

Your mind will see him standing there
for the love still clings, and you still care

A love once found is never really lost
but softly, gently released and tossed

Into the back roads of our mind
silently waiting for that time

Our hearts will bring it to the fore
and keep it there forevermore.
Elaine Brown

Ode To A Dream

What's in a dream — can we ever really know
Does our mind hold a secret — of times long ago
Or maybe it's a yearning — to see what lies ahead
I see and hear a vision — while lying on my bed
Old men often ponder — on things that might have been
If only they had followed — their vision to the end
Oh what a time to wonder — oh what a time to care
My time is growing short — it just isn't fair
But these are not — the times to sit and weep
The only time I see them — is when I'm fast asleep
James W. Davis

"God Be My Back-Up Partner"

Dear God, don't let me tarnish, this shiny badge I wear
   Don't let me be a villain, don't let me be unfair
Keep my weapon holstered, and pray that I won't need
   Such force that could be deadly, or termed a foul deed
Don't let me use this power to crush my fellow-man
   Let me show compassion, in cases where I can
Make me ever mindful of people and their plights
   And pray I always honor basic human rights

Should my life be threatened by those who won't conform
   Be my "back-up partner," protecting me from harm
Pray with me for loved ones, who worry about me
   Give us hope and courage to serve mankind and thee
As we pray for comrades, who die for you and I
   In honor of their memory, help keep our standards high
Dear God, don't let us tarnish, these badges that we wear
   Don't let us be the villains, don't let us be unfair
Earl J. Picard

Futile Efforts

In a vain attempt to please the masses
Conforming over to the nameless and classless
A life that is oozing at the rate of molasses
From the mold and die society has cast us
This sickening routine that never passes
Drinking forever from their half-empty glasses
Becoming lost in the uniform vastness
In a useless attempt to be one of the masses
David Winterfeldt

The Brilliance Of Death

What is the sky to you?
Don't you see how essential it is to know
what the sky means to you? Or the moon?
  A giant sphere of isolation, heated by phantasm,
  glooms of light, our fears —
  or just the definition of night
  and everything else just shadows in its spine
  controlled by witches. Every life, every need
growing deeper and deeper in the boil in mother's soul
until the child wakes! And leaves, feeling guilty
then is smacked by the father and made to breath
the new air and sun, then told to shine
and you never die —

So what is the sky to you? What is the earth?
What are the stars, the sea, but afterbirth
of the womb and mind of time.
And what are we in life but the brilliance of death
trying to live again — with only the dead star of hope
to guide us out, back into the light
the scar of light in my dreams and life
Carlo Fiore

Puppy Love

A little stray puppy went wand'ring
Down the road on small feet that were sore.
He came to a large fancy mansion
And whimpered in front of the door.

From within came the voice of the master,
"I've no time for a mongrel like you!"
"Go away from my fine stately mansion."
And the little stray puppy withdrew.

On feet that were swollen and tender
He wandered alone in the night
'Til he came to a shack by the river
Where within he could see a dim light.

Once more at the door he did whimper.
As it opened he cowered in fright.
But the voice said, "My friend, are you lonely?"
"Come share my poor fire tonight."

His small grateful heart full and bursting,
The puppy curled up by his chair.
At last he had found his own mansion
And a kindly old master to care.
Evelyn Bjelland

Dreamt Of You Last Night

I dreamt of you last night
Dreamt of the next time we will meet
Remembered the first time
The first time I touched you
It seems like yesterday when my life changed forever
I can't picture life without you
Without you I am weak
With you I am stronger than any man
And no man will love you like I do
I swear my love for you always and every day
Every day you will know how much I love you
Because love is what I found
So come to me, come to me now
Love me like I've never been loved before
Bring me down,
Down to your soul
I want us to be one,
One we will grow old
Old you are as beautiful as my dream
Did you know I dreamt of you last night?
Joseph Juliano

October Lady

October is a lady
dressed in fiery flaming colors
flamboyantly seducing those
who longingly embrace last summer's warmth.

Breezy afternoons...
Captivating rains...
Indian twilights...
Songbirds sweet dalliance...
Each its own celebrated merriment.

Night beckons swiftly restoring restless mortals
sleeping to a finely tuned lullaby
of rustling, whispering, whirling leaves.

He who wakes the dawn
spreads gifted streams of shafted light
slipped through silvery tree tops
comforting faded bare branches.

Eyes, a thousand eyes aroused by pointed lights
held in disbelief
upon exquisite frosted dazzlement
softly blanketing a now subdued October lady.

Eleanor Nappa

The Zephyr

The slender, silver Zephyr
drew its line
across the sleeping Nebraska prairie.

Daily
the monarch of the C B and Q
paraded across the plains
from Denver to Chicago
and back again.

Its blaring whistle
trespassed the boundaries
of one small life.

1995 A.D. - Amtrak
slightly delusional
surrogate King with
tarnished crown
clatters along the lonely rails

while one small life
cradles the illusion
it has grown.

Jean Peterson

The Broken Circle

I wait to be born, a feather in the wind
Drifting on and on till the clouds unfold their wings
And with a mother's doting nudge, cradle me to the earth
On the wind's warm breath.
I nurture in the bosom of budding intellect—
The succulent pure milk quenches my thirst
And with fruits of this bearing I cultivate a stream of conception—
The quintessence of soul imagination.
We become the circle—the perpetual bond of pulsing fervor—
A life force
Spinning eternally and again. Then my lungs collapse.
Dark scratches out my sight. I feel the blade upon the throat.
The skin splits like a blister, pops open along the thin red line.
Sucked out through the fissure, I am a spot on the floor-
Scrap cast out to Oblivion's dogs.
Now I crouch, cowered in the corner, adopting a home of filth.
The offal of humanity. Debased. Belittled.
Raped by reason and diseased by its lover's kiss. Conformity.
I am art. A whisper on the breath of youth.
My executioner—the world.

Alexandra Ghosh

Daydreams

I lie in the green grass on the top of a high hill. I begin to drift off, not even realizing the objects near me. My one true concentration is high above my head, fluffy and white. Yes, I am watching the clouds. They capture my thoughts in their billows and mist. I cannot help daydreaming as they pull me into their airborne silence.

I am a bird, a dove, soaring so high. I have my eye on the world, and I watch out for all creatures. I spread peace and happiness wherever I fly. And I am an eagle, with a sparkle in my eye. The clouds below me are like snowcaps. I soar high above all mankind, not a bird of paradise, but wonderful in my own way.

I am the snow that falls in the wintertime. I know that once I fall, my beauty will be gone. I shine like glitter as I daintily flutter to the ground. The wind that blows me and urges me to fall faster is a dragon, fierce and mean so that he can become the most powerful.

Now I am the sun rising in the sky. My color deepens with each inch I rise. I turn from red to orange, orange to yellow. Now I am golden and high above all else and I know that neither the wind nor clouds nor birds soaring below are equal to me.

I awake from my daydreams on the hill, under the clouds and sun and birds and understand more about what each thing in life means. The doves to spread peace, the eagles to soar high and show freedom, the snow to add beauty and the wind to be powerful. And the sun to add liveliness and color to all of the creatures under its umbrella of light. And I realize that the world is a better place because of them.

Erin Jeannine Leverton

Two Worlds

While we eat millions starve,
During our sleep,
tens of thousands seek shelter.
As we learn children labor.
A tumor is removed,
and a child dies of diarrhea.
We eat to our fill,
as a prisoner crunches a cockroach
between two pieces of bread.
A millionaire is massaged on his bed;
a prisoner whipped on a wall.
One man skips lunch and complains of hunger,
yet another man lies awake in agony -
having eaten nothing all week.
Hundreds see the pain of these and ignore it
while three men bring sandwiches and clothes
into the city for the homeless.

Brian L. Wood

Schoolhouse

The old schoolhouse is gone;
  Dust are the walls and rafters.
Of the children naught remains
  But the echo of their laughter.

Gone also are the sidewalks
  Where the children skated,
Before school and during recesses
  While their lessons waited.

Steel wheels on concrete made
  Music accompanied by flying tresses.
Boys were in knee pants and
  Girls in gingham dresses.

Many decades have passed as these
  Friends scattered across the nations' byways,
But the memories of those
  Happy days will remain always.

Gerry Monfore

To A Friend

Time moves swift as angels
Each moments dance her last,
And I, like a sullen gossamer
Am afraid and tremble to ask.
Will you be my love for this moment?
We can make the sand grains freeze.
We can hold each other in embrace and float
Like a feather on a springtime breeze.
We can paint the skies a Castillian Blue
And the trees a Spanish Green.
We can melt the snowflakes with burning kisses
That none, but us, have seen.
Ours, a song of love's sweet longing
That shall forever be sung
By a tender princess and a prince
Amid virgin meadows young.
Jyotsom Ganatra

Untitled

A thousand listless dreams dance through my mirrored life,
echoing over the memories that touch me,
piercing forward to forever wonder of the consummating
choices that encompass my being.
In a small shelter stuck in time I rest my mind,
putting to sleep the wonder.
Melting into the night lurks my passion,
partaking in the touch of spiced silence.
God it tingles, the comfort the time, the time with you.
Brett R. Bukowsky

A Thermostat — Not A Thermometer!

I want to be your THERMOSTAT, Oh God.
Emotional climates change upon this sod.
I'll use a calm and understanding life,
Defusing anger, showing optimism,
Working now to cancel people's strife.
Please help me, Lord, to keep away from criticism.

THERMOMETERS respond to fevers of emotional nature.
These fevers go around them matching anger
For anger, fear for fear or blow for blow.
Let me be a THERMOSTAT to lift the spirits
Of the fearful or unhappy ones and not incur
Depression that will pull me down so low.

Let me support, encourage those who faint,
Because the fevers of emotions taint
Surrounding areas where the people live—
Help me take forward steps to them and give
Just what they always need from day to day.
Please Lord, show me now just how to walk your way!
James A. Stoddard

"Impatience"

Let me go! Let me free! I will be who I will be
despite your pleading and ordering I am me always

You hold back, you cry "wait!"
You cling to the past but I must go

I want to run free, to ride the wind
To touch the stars, to take a risk

You are afraid, it is in your eyes
You remember the child but see the woman

You think things through while I plunge headlong
You are cautious and slow while I run heedless

If you will not let me run, I will break my leash
I will rush ahead without your well-thought consent
I am a woman, let me go
Ann Wamsley

"Soul's Flight"

Timeless, eternal, across the Galaxies of the Universe;
Entering life as innocence to inhale the existence of man.
Some remain a long span while others are taken in an instant;
Yet each imparts this world with curiously wonderful gifts.

Through some souls we learn tolerance and forgiveness;
From others we change laws, impart sentences, portion reform.
Love and compassion are the silent dictates of many;
While monsters of hate in the few remind us we are not perfect.

We are transcendent beings, our souls live on in an endless state.
How we live our lives ascertains the state of our next existence.
Every action in Nature brings about an equal and lasting response.
Choose honor, good will come; choose evil, depravity triumphs.

Yet often, we do not see the end results of our encounter.
We battle to endure, only to flounder at another time.
How can beings, so marvelously created and enduring,
Struggle a lifetime and never discern the flight of the soul?
Clara Marie Cook

Nature's Yearly Fashion Show

Nature is dramatic with her year-round fashion show.
Ermine is in shadow when compared to Winter's snow.
The soft, white glow of hills and dales is fashioned in one night.
The river's frozen surface, like jewels, sparkles bright.

The warming sun casts its spell as fields of flowers gleam.
Their colors dance and sway to catch the sunlight's brightest beam.
There's blue and yellow, pink and red, purple, green and white.
Nature has dressed for Spring. Oh, what a glorious sight.

The lazy days have settled in, pools of shade beneath the trees,
The songs of birds, the crickets call, the humming of the bees,
Invite the dreamer pause and see what nature has to share,
The music of a rippling brook, the summer skies so fair.

Then vibrant Fall bursts forth, with leaves of brilliant hue.
Jack Frost helps paint the foliage bright, and waters it with dew.
Creeping vines display their fruit and grains in golden robes stand high.
Trees dominate the scene with fruit and nuts against the cool blue sky.

Oh, who can choose from such a show; one choice is far too small.
From Nature's store of beauty, I guess we'll choose them all.
Janice P. Gates

Sometimes

Sometimes, I think of you, wondering where you are... or
how you are. Many years have gone by, but, there is...
this thought at the back of my mind, I wonder... what would
it be of me, of us, if I would stay in my hometown

I do not know if I am doing right thinking of you when...
I have already my own life, but, you were the first to kiss me,
to hug me under that shining moon, so... bright, I won't
forget that night... You know, I was scared, feeling so...

I will say, different by your side, it is the truth... I won't
lie, but wait, that is now just a thought, do not forget that.
You and I were so much apart, the magic ended due to the lack of
time. Now memories bring everything to life, now...

I find myself confused, let me tell you, I wish I could go back
in time and... enjoy every minute by your side. We were fourteen,
I know that, but, we were happy discovering love for the first
time, at least that is what I felt, no worries, no knowledge of life...

Sometimes, it is better that way, you seem to enjoy yourself out,
ignoring people, time and living each day like it will be the last,
what would it be of me now, without those memories... they kind of
kept me alive when I found myself so sad.
Rosa M. Lopez

Swing Set

At dark a swing set glows,
even in the rainy days, it holds
A body of stories to be told
An observance, just a toy.

Swing too high and touch a cloud.
I know silk-stocking will catch me now.
Blend freedom of Robin, Lark or Dove.
Stave, a tear, though lessens in love.

Towering hours for aging and days
This long staring through windows gaze,
Remembering children's shoes on my feet.
Wrinkled skin souls told of wind and wheat.

Hours on end I can remember
Of grandpa's spun fine tales.
Now grandpa sleeps a lonely September.
Outside the house swing set turns paler.

Heath A. Cole

The Sands Of Time

The sands of time, like the dunes of a desert,
Ever moving, ever lasting, ever changing.
There are breezes blowing through them,
Reshaping, reforming, rearranging.

One human, like one single grain, is lost amidst it all.
No one will ever know his name; he'll never stand up proud and tall.
But walks hunched down beneath his load,
Down the ever-winding road,
Not knowing what he shall behold,
His future yet to be foretold.

The road to fame is red with blood,
And with tears is soaking wet.
Those who fall down lie in the mud,
Amidst the tears and human sweat.

The sands of time, like the dunes of desert,
Ever moving, ever changing, ever lasting.
So fragile on the inside,
And on the outside, so majestic.

Elisabeth Genn

There's A Ghost In Our House

There's a ghost in our house, that only I've seen,
I know she's there, though she stays in between.

The first time I saw her, I was new to this house.
The sound of her startled me, I thought her a mouse.

It soon became clear she was checking me out,
Not sure if she approved my presence about.

A flutter caught at the corner of my eye,
Kept me alert she was always nearby.

I had a feeling she waited to know of my heart.
To make sure I was the right one, so she could depart.

In a house this old, a lot of things neat,
Most people a ghost not wanting to meet.

The warm feeling I get, tells me she cares.
I've seen her in the kitchen, I've seen her upstairs.

A spinning wheel came to live at this farm,
Learning to spin, with her at my arm.

If these walls could talk, the history they'd tell,
Of the two hundred years under her spell.

One day I realized she was no longer there,
She's gone, and left her house in my care.

Honey Vaine

Why?

Did you ever wonder why,
Everyone must die?
Why tragedy must strike,
Like a thief in the night,
Why it must rob us of our precious Life?
No matter if it's a child, a husband or wife,
Death has no hour, so they say,
It comes night or day;
Why can't death be beautiful?
Why does it have to be so awful?
Why can't death be planned?
Why does it jump up and grab our hand?
Why can't it give us a warning,
To prepare those who will be mourning?
Why does it leave such an impression on our mind?
Why can't it be something we can put behind?
Death is something I know nothing of,
I guess it's a calling from Above;
Maybe someday, I'll know the answer Why,
Just like all the others, when it's my turn to die!

Dotty Spinosi

Love Is A 4-Letter Word

Love is what makes the world go square.
Love is something people fall in.
Love is what makes all mothers seem like good cooks.
Love is what, in spring, a young man's mind lightly turns to thoughts of.
Love is Hell, too, but more fun to make than war.
Love is what you should have for your neighbor instead of his
  lawn mower. Love is emotion's sickness.
Love is something you send in a letter when what you'd really like to
  send won't fit in the envelope.
Love is one of the few kicks you can experience anymore without
  getting busted.
Love is why people get married - when it's not for the sake of the
  children.
Love is like running down the street naked; you can be forgiven for it
  on the grounds of insanity.
Love is butterflies in the tummy and ants in the pants.
Love is finding the answer and losing sight of the question.
Love is the soy sauce on the chop suey of life...
Love is a warm place.
Love is a thing you like to give even more if you think you can get it
  back.
Love is the subject of this clever writing, but writings based
  on other 4-letter words are more popular.
Love is thinking about someone, even if you don't know you're
  thinking about them.
Love is sweet nothings whispered in the ear that mean everything.
The End? Love is the beginning, but always goes beyond the end.

Jon Coffman

"The Jaguar"

In the jungle heart at night,
Every creature lies in fright
Wondering if the Jaguar is near.

Leaves will rustle, then quiet again
With animal fears and fears of men.
Look up with dread to see the view
When demon eyes stare back at you.

Suddenly, the jungle comes alive
With blinding pain and death cries,
Glowing eyes pierce the night
And still the jungle lies in fright.

Nothing here can match his speed.
With stealth and will, he commits natural deeds.
The night is long for those who fear.
Hush...the hungry Jaguar is near.

Alexander McRae

Life's Window

Thinking of you all the days through.....
Everything that's beautiful reminds me of you.....

Looking through this window a tree I can see.....
It reminds me of how things are, and how things could be.
As I watched it blossom from the buds to the leaves...
It made me realize how things grow from such tiny seeds.
Like the trees and things great and small.....
Together we can make it from the spring to the fall.

'Cause if we cling to the branch that we grew.....
There won't be anything we can't go through.

Though the high winds, downpours and rains.....
Through life's weather of heartaches, downfalls and pains.
Like leaves we come on and grow for a season.....
Then we fall off.   But fall for a reason.
Some fall in the water some in the mud.....
But we can thank the Lord there's a new bud.
Away to come back.   Bright shiny and new.....
That's the way I think he planned for us to do.
   Darrell Lee Nichols

October 25, 1994

Scared and unsure ...
Excited and happy ...
Feelings of joy and pain blending together,
Moments ticking by seemingly forever.
Months and months of anticipation,
The moment finally arriving.
Hopes and dreams being fulfilled,
Blankets and bunnies awaiting your appearance.
Many hearts already molded,
Love overflowing ...
Then ...
There was hair ... brown, I think,
A pink little nose,
A voice rebounding your arrival,
Ten fingers and ten toes,
Perfect in every way!
Tears and smiles of love and joy filled the room,
God blessed our family and the world
with the gift of sweetness and spunk,
Miss Rhea Ashley Walsh.
   Cathryn L. Walsh

The Things My Mother Has Taught Me

A recognition of intangible power in the common
exerting where I can yet knowingly
a benign participant in the plans of God
an attendance every day to what and to whom is loved
with sentiment, amusement and diligence
wafting balls into desired orbits
rotating for balance within the fragile ether
a layer upon layer of small movements
in the life game of Finesse.

More salient than any chased accomplishment
are these brushes with virtuosity
alive in the mosaics of ordinary form and function
where Spirit unwittingly attains
what Mind wishes it could consciously manifest
each detail a devotion so quiet
it usually passes without calling attention to itself
or to its creator
the ephemeral reality given substance
in acts of infinite subtlety:

the things my mother has taught me.
   Carolyn C. Coffman

Senior Citizens' Plight

Looking our the window and as
  far as the eye can see

Ice and snow covered our entire community—

There was no transportation-
  No cars, no trains or bus

The storm has made prisoners of us

Our homes and apartments have
  become our jail

And we can't be released for any
  amount of bail

However, let's try to enjoy our hibernation
  without fear

Winter will soon be gone and Spring is near.
   Bertha Pitkofsky

Chains Of Silk

Restless spirits lashed with silken chains
Fashioned secret strands of hidden fears
Knots tied to keep safe from harming selves
To anchors set in bedrock of the proven past
Secure in binding boredom they are cast

So soft the comforts of these traitor bounds
With time their grip grows ever tighter still
Strong coils enveloping the freedom to believe
Which choke the faith in visions yet unseen
And still the hope that dwells in future dreams

Soul's courage to undo the filaments we weave
And live the happy danger that a life must be
Grasp uncertain freedom and the fear it brings
To unleash the spirit to soar wide and free
And rip forever all the silken chains that be
   Adrian Caraceni

Memories

  As the moon took its place so peacefully in the sky
my heart started to ache and a tear feel from my eye,
  The love I had for you I knew could never be the same,
the way you made me feel now all I have is shame,
  That night we took our stroll along the moonlit beach
the man who pulled his gun and took you from my reach,
  I kneeled down beside you and held you close and tight
you wanted to stay with me and fought with all your might,
  Though fate took its place on that warm moonlit night
the love I have for you is just as strong tonight,
  Now I live this world without you by my side
it has taken me six years to learn that I can't hide.
   Bill Symons

"My Favorite D.J."

(Johnny Randolph)

  You play the songs I love to hear -
Every Saturday night; without fail,
  A voice to count on -
  A song to be played - on my couch I lay;
  being taken away, to another place,
  another time.
I love to hear the songs you play;
  my favorite D.J.
A toast to you and your sexy, soothing voice;
  not just a lot of noise-
A toast to you - from me,
I hope you enjoy as much as I.
   Andrea Moore

Grendel

He does drink from the blood of the multiple sinner
Feasting from the cornucopia of lies,
Gorged and greased, slick and sallow abdomen
Distended and shaking, social indigestion
Grubbing forward on oily, putrid flesh
Not the Vampire of olden corruption and beauty,
The degraded night terror, belly to the ground.
Legions twisted carcass, unbelievably animated
Barest glinting humanity shimmers, belying dull eyes
Lillith's sociopath son, Adam's first wife and child
Dwelling below the comfort of the Blood Pond
His breath the foul bubbles, rising, erratic,
Lending vague credence to theories of boiling earthen arteries
Arise, Fear Grendel, to plunder and rend the night anew
Bold in this plated age, 'fore no gentle deceiving
Beowulf has turned near blind, heroic eyes
To the population's plight, raised his great sword to journey
And end your reign again.

Amy Harmon

The Glowing Candle

Desperation, fear, sorrow,
Feelings of frustration.
Sometimes the pain does not ever seem to cease.
The hurt and anger inside starts to consume.
The hopelessness envelopes your entire being.
It creates a power which allows you no control.
Sadness descends and contains no release.
Dreading the day after tomorrow,
Helps you forget today.
The light at the end of the tunnel never seemed so far away.
Yet it guides you to safety.
A haven you've never known.
The suffering dissipates,
Leaving behind someone special.
Agony no longer allows itself to grow.
Its job has now been completed.
And all you needed was a spark to get it started.

Jennifer Hahn

Your Voice

Your voice touches me like a cool hand on a
feverish brow

Like a hot cup of tea on a snowy wintery
evening

Like the comfort of a loved-one's arms,
wrapped around you, welcoming you at the
end of an unkind day

Like the calm that comes right after
the storm

Yeah...your voice...

Annise Lucia Chapmon

War

Eyes peer upon humanity,
Figures judge our so called sanity
From the hour glass falls the sands,
All of life he holds in his hands
Guns, tanks, missiles, knives
How we take innocent lives,
He wonders, he doubts, he dreads, he dreams,
And our world goes to war with savage screams.

Chris Reed

Brown Eyes

Our government took our red brother's land,
filled them with promise from our great Uncle Sam.
They live in poverty on these promised reservations,
we silently stood by and watched as a nation.
The buffalo which once roamed plenty, now face extinction.
Our once clean rivers and lakes take on a whole new dimension.
We see now through "brown eyes".
Great spirit in the sky, how long will our world survive.

Christine S. Smith

Song for America: "My Country 'tis of Thee"...

"My country 'tis of thee"
Filled with crime and infamy
With "dreams deferred" and dreams denied
We must act now to turn the tide

Each of us must look within
That is where we must begin
Nothing can change for us until we change
Our hearts, our thoughts we must rearrange

And as we change for the good
So will our world and neighborhood
Our transformed lives will give new birth
To Love, to Light, and Peace on Earth.

Delia Destinee

Peeling An Onion

As I take the onion in my hands, I search for obvious imperfections.
Finding none, I begin.
I make the first cut at the end closest to me. Roots are severed.
Next I pull off the first, hard layer. I find another hard layer.
This will not be easy.
After the brown, brittle layers, I find firm white flesh.
I make another cut and peel back this first soft layer.
Tears begin to sting my eyes.
More layers are peeled, more tears come.
They blur my vision and stream down my cheeks.
Can I continue? It's so hard. Why don't I just stop?
Do I really need to do this?
Slowly I peel more layers. I put down my knife to wipe my eyes.
I find more layers, more tears.
Soon this will be over. I will uncover all the layers.
Soon this onion will be peeled and in the center I will find
it wasn't an onion I was peeling,
It was my life I was healing.

Janis Metzler

True Love

Even though it was fate from the start, for when I met you,
I felt it as I do now a tug at my heart for you,
Within tear-stained eyes and our hopeful relation,
Your love made me think, cry, and smile.
I cried just for all your fears, hurts, and because I loved you.
When you felt all of this, I felt it too.
When you cried, I cried.
Somehow I knew everything, all the stories, lies, and
I cried for the pain and sorrow in your life.
But what made me happy and shed tears of joy which
ran down my face was, your love.
And how I could tell was, the way you spoke and
the way your beautiful eyes looked.
Couldn't you just reach and touch your soul and feel what I could feel.
The reason of all this I knew there was, and hoped you could do,
and say the same.
I love you, all questions were never answered.
And I wish they could be.

Melissa Copeland

He Plunges His Hand Into The Stars

He veered from the barrage of naked steel,
flares scattered like exploding stars.

He remembers her face
in his locket, his name
on her bracelet.
Her face reflected against a banana leaf.

Where is the heart?
The moments he remembered —
Love curled hands, scent of spring ferns,
and lettuce seeping through fertile loam.
the moments he remembered —
plodding through torrid fields
of yams, and sun on peanut patches,
and flame of red birds in the dawn.

A hand, a shadow,
a machete wedged in bone.

There is so much to lose in dying.
His breath bursting — he plunges
his hands into the stars
and feels heaven.

Emma Crobaugh

The Sweet Season Of Spring

The sweet season of spring, enlightens my thoughts
Flowers bright scarlet and like the sun
Mesmerized by their beauty, the brilliance of each flower intrigues me
What pleasure they hold in their delicate petals of spring
A sight to see, more detail than the eye can capture
Fragrant and regal are the spring flowers
One of God's precious gifts, like the rainbow
we sometimes see at the end of a storm
Another miracle of life the Lord has sent forth
With a scent as sweet as heaven, the flowers embrace my soul
Colorful and bright, their radiance glows
The sweet season of spring makes me feel many things
A feeling of contentment and happiness
A feeling of being thankful
Thankful for all the wonderful things in the world the Lord
has given to us to enjoy.

Ellen E. Kohlhepp

"The Reaper"

He is coming, he is never late.
I do fear him so, this escort to the
world of the damned. He is so ugly,
and evil. I see him standing in the corner
laughing at me as I wait to die and to be taken
to his domain where I will spend eternity
in pain.

As he steps out of the shadows I can
see his horrible, fleshless, bony face
and his red eyes. Oh! those eyes,
so full of death and pain, and something else,
age, he was here in the beginning and he
will be here in the end.

He is coming closer and I can see his hands.
They are green with death. He is grabbing the
end of the sheets and pulling me closer
to him. With one final
Breath I give up and all is forgotten of me in
This world, in the next I will be in pain. But
Alas! My soul will not be the only one there.

Russ Dollar

Reflecting On Flowers

Flowers to brighten a dismal day
Flowers that show sunny faces in May.

Flowers for buzzing busy bees
Flowers bursting in bloom on trees.

Flowers for hummingbirds to gather nectar.
Flowers for friends to show we care.

Flowers carefully chosen and picked.
Flowers to send to cheer the sick.

Flowers for that special day
Flowers for the bridal bouquet.

Flowers emitting a fragrant perfume.
Flowers displayed in a living room.

Flowers of every spectacular hue
Flowers created by God for me and you.

Angeline Daniel

The Caretaker's Memorial Day

Poised in the sun a white-winged angel,
Flowing with beauty like ballet grace,
Crowns the headstone standing close
To fitzers trimmed with a fine-cut green
Where poppies brushed by the sibilant winds
Bend and sway on fresh-mown graves
And a caretaker, stooped by the ache
Of years and the drag of a rusting rake,
Pauses by soldier-biographies to murmur
Prayers for "buddies" his heart holds near;
While off in the distance through wrought-iron gates
A Cadillac, simonized white, enters
Glinting in afternoon sun bringing
Silken complacency toward one grave
To pay her respects, her yearly homage,
Then leave behind an angel of marble
And a caretaker whispering aves,
Who cherishes each forgotten story
Carved in stone, not just for the day,
As epitaphs held as long as his years.

Gus Wilhelmy

The Park

While sitting in the park one day, the world came rushing in.
Flying birds, buzzing bees, and I heard a cacklin' hen.
The sun was high up in the sky as children played around.
Dogs were barking at running cats, and bugs walked on the ground.
I saw the sights and heard the sounds, then something stirred inside.
How many times have all these things made me go and hide?
I was afraid to be seen out in the morning air.
I thought the world would laugh at me, because of my wheelchair.
But now I see that I was wrong, and in the park I'll play.
And watch the world go rushing by until the close of day.

Dianna Murphy

Complicated

Wherever I was before I wasn't
I felt no pain happiness or blame
I didn't ask to come and be
All of a sudden, wasn't was me
Whenever I wasn't, before I was
I had no worry or memory
This place earth her bittersweet cup
Brought forth what wasn't and I was
Why couldn't I stay? After all I wasn't before I was
Somehow I guess I was just to be, for whenever I wasn't I was

Sandra Lacy Robertson

Hammers Song

Now my hammer sings against the stone
For all my life I will toil
Lord! Let me rest these weary bones

Never again will I see my home
Anger and heat make my blood boil
Now my hammer sings against the stone

In my lost youth I did roam
Now I pray for a return to the soil
Lord! Let me rest these weary bones

Momma used to say before I was grown
Boy, you got dreams no one can spoil
Now my hammer sings against the stone

My freedom was taken before my seeds were sown
Shackles and chains around my ankles coil
Lord! Let me rest these weary bones

The cold wind blows and my spirit moans
To you great father I will remain loyal
Now my hammer sings against the stone
Lord! Let me rest these weary bones

Douglas Taylor Jr.

Friendship

Color our friendship as an early spring green,
For continual growth with from the beginning until infinity,

For care and protection as the shroud of an aged spreading oak,
For tranquility and peace like a forest of towering redwoods,
For willingness to share as a branch with a perched, singing bird,
For wisdom to yield to nature's frequent storms as tender young
Branches do,
For enjoyment as young leaves in a cool breeze under a brilliant
Sky of blue...

Ernie Hooks

Anniversary Tribute

In 1988 on the 26th of May
For Court Street it was a very Special Day.
Pastor Mark James Montgomery became the Pastor here,
And to our hearts, he has become very dear.

He has remained true to the precious Holy Word
In every message our ears have ever heard.
It's great to have a Pastor who speaks the Truth unerring,
And also to have a man so helpful and so caring.

We love his family which is loyal and devoted
Even though sometimes their names are "quoted!"
We would be remiss if we failed to state
His musical talent - we think it's great!!

So Pastor Mark, "Happy Anniversary Number Seven."
And we know you give the glory to our God in Heaven
Keep preaching and teaching the Biblical Way
And seven more years we your salary will pay!

Jane Nash

"Treasured Friendship"

Each day I think and wonder "What Might Have Been"
For each passing day, it is the same thought
of the loved one
The loved one who slipped away
For he is gone and might not return
But the friendship we have shared will not die
until the end of time
For this friendship means more than he will ever know
Our friendship is a great and wonderful treasure
for all to know

Jeanmari Michael

Rudy

Jumping lightly from perch to perch,
For food and water he doesn't search.
Grooming golden plumage, what does it matter?
He's not in the mood to play on his ladder.
But the bars of his cage are bent from his beak,
Breaking from his capture, his freedom he seeks.
Longing to be with the birds in the trees.
Chirping and flying in the morning breeze.
He longs to soar up and push the clouds away,
Beating his wings, no longer caged where he stays.
Such a sad bird he rings on his bells,
He vows to get out, but no one can tell.

Catherine Vera Menn

Untitled

Sleep now, my love,
For morning comes.
And the drums that throbbed have
    ceased their ancient call.
This passion given first within your bed
Has fled the creeping light upon your wall.
But I will stay a moment more,
For from this tranquil shore
I know
That I must go.
If indigo is blue
My love is true
But I must come again no more.

Cheryl Knarr

Sounds Of The Night

As evening creeps upon us,
    daylight disappears.
The sounds of evening time
    is music to my ear.
Frogs are making noises
    which ring within the car.
I can hear the sounds of crickets
    though cars are very near.
The moon is shining bright,
    lighting up the sky.
"Where are the stars? Oh,
    there they are scattered about the sky."
A calm and peaceful quiet time -
    after a very busy day.
Makes me restful and sleepy now.
    I really like it that way.

Nicholas Angelo

Snow

Like little pieces of lace,
Floating down on to your face.
It covers the ground with a blanket of white,
To me this is a very lovely sight.
Children go outside, and they play,
They build snowmen and they sleigh.
They know they are supposed to keep the snow outside,
For this is a rule every parent has tried.
Still that one snowball finds its way in,
This is how most snowball fights begin.
The children have their fight in the cold,
This is a very funny sight to behold.
For the children are slipping and sliding with glee,
While they are praying "I hope no one hits me."
Then all too suddenly that snow filled day ends,
And everyone has departed, once again friends.

Greta M. Haar

My Favorite Star

I've been waiting for this moment
for such a long time
and now you are finally mine
I've always thought of you as a star up in the sky
a star I'd never be able to reach no matter how hard I tried
This moment will always be a dream coming true to me
but hey let's face it, this is reality
My life was so confusing and I wouldn't know what to do
But now things are changing all because of you
I used to think that dreams never could come true
But I must have been wrong because I am now
together with you
You'll always be a part of me that's hard to let go
and that's basically all you should know
Hey wait there's one last thing that's not easy to do
But all I wanted to say is "I love you!"

Amanda Boyer

"The Cane Cutters"

They never see over the distant hills.
For the cane fields hide their view.
They pick mangoes from the trees
And oranges are green and easily reached.
They stare through dark piercing blind eyes.
They told me there is seldom rain.
Yet it's rained since I've been here.
The fog hides the nearby hills on either side.
Ravi just came now, but must go to bring the cattle in.
Twenty one days in a row under the burning sun.
Cutting cane for eight dollars a ton.
One hundred and twenty dollars for this long run.
Not much to feed a family of four.
No electricity and little flour.
The cutting season's just begun, the trucks are moving
This desolate place is now alive.
With no sugar they would not survive.
Off they march with their cane knives on their shoulders
Like an army moving towards disaster
For their faces show this their fate until hereafter.

Bill Horan

Love

I'm grateful to my Father and Mother
For the gift of five sisters, also a brother.
The last of the seven was allotted to me.
Six to look up to and to look after me.

We never were wealthy, oft times were poor.
No fancy wall hangings, no rug on the floor.
But one thing was certain with a God fearing Mother.
She instilled in each of us to love one another.

If we misbehaved, or when we lied
A peach tree switch would tan our hide.
"Bring up a child in the way he's to go
When he is older, he'll hoe the right row"!

Each of us loved our Mother and Dad.
When death took them home it was so sad.
But soon we realized we had each other.
A bonus a large family brings one another.

Love is what makes the world go around.
And in our family there's love to be found.
Love one another as God has loved you.
The love for my family is ever so true.

Bobbie Jean Williams

For The Love Of The Game

I would practice from dawn till sunset
For the love of the game.
I would practice outside while it was raining
For the love of the game.
I would play in the NBA for free
For the love of the game.
There is no other game I'd rather play
I love this game!

Anthony King

The Winter Is Past

The winter is past and the time has come
   for the singing of the birds.
The beauty of God's spring
   can't be expressed in words.

The crocuses, with great enthusiasm
   pushed through winter's snow;
Setting the stage for hyacinths and
   daffodils to grow!

The lilacs and tulips and forsythia appear,
And colorful azaleas return every year.

Violets springing up amid a carpet green;
Trees sprout new leaves and blossoms can be seen.

Our feathered friends of every hue
   harmonize in celebration;
All nature joining in a
   hymn of adoration!

Our gratitude can never equal
   each season's bounteous presence.
God's gift of love comes shining through
   with joyful effervescence!

Ellen Rice

Our Rewards

If we count our rewards given could we say they were of man,
For the things I speak of are not carried in man's hand.

For I find my greatest treasure is not in what I see,
But it's the breath of life that God gives you and me.

For he rewards the soul and not the outer flesh we wear,
But in him I find comfort and know I'm in his care.

He is a friend that never leaves you as sometimes others do,
But he is always there to comfort and he will see you through.

His mighty hands have held us as we go about our way.
He is always there to lead us as we go from day to day.

So lean not to our own understanding and fall by stumblings of man,
But let us turn to the treasures God offers for they are carried by
   Gods hands.

Dennis Manuel

Despair!

Where are the dreams of yesteryear?
   Has bitter life dissolved them into dust?
The bright, fleet hopes of youth are gone,
   The deeds undone, lie mouldering in rust.

What quirk of fate engenders disillusionment,
   When leaping flames fade into ashes gray,
When eager spirit wills — but helpless flesh cannot
   Endure the night, nor tolerate the day?

I have not lived — I have but failed!
   In endless ways I have been proven wrong!
No tribute grand shall grace my lonely tomb,
   When welcome death shall still my wailing song!

Marian L. Glover

Therapy

A fire-side chat
for the years of life
letting them free for ponder.
Each one open to different sights
from those years of yonder.
To keep in darkness for so long
those thoughts of inhibitions -
each of their own
in time and place
each kept alive from their own conditions . . .
One might say,
what's past is gone, do not reopen the womb.
But isn't it better to help friends be strong,
than to watch them build a tomb.
  Cameron S. Landis

Winter Reflections

Lights of the far northern skies gleam on the
Forest crowned with crystals, and flame upon the
Shimmering habitat of arrogant nature, where the
Harp of life vibrates over the vast native land.

Stars smile in the grand canopy above, shedding
Fires of the frigid heavens on the distant trees
And plains, while kindling the golden music of
Welcome among the bright cords of flora's wake.

The flight of a lone eagle hovers over the cold,
Broad standard of dream's robust beauty on earth,
Gliding across showers of sunbeams in minion's
Snow blushed day of constant blaze and liberty.

A silent feast of deep snow covers the landmass,
While the heart of man seeks pleasure in calm
Sighs of the pure foliage breeze in the chilling
Air of the firmament's sublime moonlit scenery.

Showers of bright light sound a victorious tear
On the immense white ground; winter embers of the
Soul herald a distant revival of hero's freedom,
As the primitive luster of a jubilant dawn breaks.
  Donald M. McIntyre

The Hero

Silently strong, discreetly aware...
Frightens the fearless his presence there
Stalks with grace on reverent ground
Roars with pride; justice abounds.
Nurtures the young with song unsung,
Courage doth peak to defend the weak.
Loyal in love, life's passion doth ring,
The secret be told, fit to be king.
  Eileen Hogan

Drugslug

Darkness surrounds my cold, pale body,
Dampness,
Sweat trickles down my cheek.
My mouth feels dry, so stale, so bleak.
Is this what I get?
Such dreams which were not met?
I have now a black room,
And then there's me
Sitting alone
Waiting to see...
Where are the beauties, the wonders, the life?
I feel as though I were stabbed with a knife.
Movement is forgotten,
Paralyzed forever,
I won't do this again,
Never, never, never!
  Aimee Moo

Mary Lee Magdelane Neal

The night when I First met her, I Knew she would be the one.
From a feeling deep within me knowing, at last my time has come.

She was oh so beautiful, her attire so precise.
we dined in dimly lit comfort, she seemed so very nice.

She spoke of a serious illness she had, and a love who had broken her
  heart.
I knew she was hurting and deep within me, I too was coming apart.

So I asked her to dance and took her hand, then held her gently in
  my arms.
I knew I was falling for Mary; she had elegance, grace, and charm.

I saw her only one more time, we spoke about the same.
Then she called me three weeks later, and my world fell apart again.

For she said she had found another, this I could not understand.
I felt things were going oh so well, but I guess I was wrong again.

Well now I am left in limbo, to start my search over again.
And try and find the one true love before my time will end.

For my love belongs to Mary, and I have been hurt so it seems.
Now the only time I can hold her close, is when we're together in
  my dreams.

Though my heart won't let me forget her, for what little time we shared.
I will always think of Mary, and just how much I cared.

Her big blue eyes, her fragrant scent, the softness of her skin.
Yes, I will hold her memory oh so dear and look back remembering
  when.
  Daniel R. Malo

A Personal Request

I had a call the other day
  From a shy, expectant mother;
The need she outlined I will say
  Was for temporary shelter.

The place of her home
  Was daily disturbed by
A faithful postman's delivery;
  Her mother nest, her very best—private security.

How sweet the sound baby birds
  Make to any intruder;
How wise the labor of parent-birds
  To fulfill their role as mother.

No chirping sounds I now can hear
  No more incessant chatter,
No inconvenience at all to me,
  No disturbance—no matter!

But, Mother bird, please come again
  To be my welcomed guest;
An honored host you'll be to me
  Accept my one request.
  Earl W. Johnston

Forget To Remember

I forgot to remember to forget:
forget the color of a man's skin.
I forgot to remember to forget the hate of a man's race.
God help me to remember to forget:
cruelty of hate and persecution of all that are different:
so God let me not forget to remember to love life.
And all of God's people and help me not to forget
that the light of the angel's will bring us love of all people:
for love is God and God is life.
  DeWayne M. Weaver

Roses And Gold

Everyone has their story of Pain and Woe,
from an aching Head to a Swollen Toe.
Just listen to each as they Always Complain.
"Look at me" hear my "self-pity"
   Such a boring refrain.
  God gave you a marvelous Soul,
   to experience the Joy of the
   Universe again and again.
Don't Focus on your Body. The
  "Great Healer" is in you today.
Be Loving and Giving. The urge
  to Complain vanishes away.
People often turn their back on
  you if you "Whine," but they
  will come to Love you when you
  show them you are a part of the
  DIVINE—-
Everyone has their story, I'm told.
  Just never complain; then your
  Life will unfold like Roses and Gold.
    Elaine M. Adams

Since I Met You

Many of us travel any avenue with hope of escape
  from our lost empty life.
Yet, we are the cause of the emptiness, and must face
  reality for nothing is solved by such a dash.
But, as we search the face of man, we sense the need
  a cry for a helping hand.
When and where did we make our mistake to turn man into a thing
  of hate.
But since I met you the clouds cleared, the rain stopped,
  the stars are exceptionally bright, and the world
  had a clean smell.
Since I met you the things that seemed to be the weight of
  the world has become weightless.
The dark hours have become bright moments of happiness,
  since I met you.
My cloudy thoughts have changed to clear sharp
  thoughts I once knew.
Now I know that life is useless, unless shared with someone.
All this, since I met YOU.
    Charles W. Hall

The Snow

As I stepped to my window I was awed with delight.
For God had painted a picture sometime in the night.
The trees were all laden
  boughs hanging low,
Everything glistened like diamonds
  with the new fallen snow.

I heard children laughing
  stomping and shouting with glee.
They glanced up to the window
  and waved to me.
They were all bundled up
  in hats, scarves, and mittens
Frolicking and rolling
  like a litter of kittens.

Ah! I wondered would it be fittin' for an oldster like me
Who can't skate, or even ski
  If I done my wraps all buttoned up tight
And went to join in their snowball fight
  Laughing and shouting so full of glee

To be part of that picture God painted for me.
    Edna A. Swan

"Hearts And Flowers"

Flowers of every shade and hue;
From springtime pastels to crystal blue,
The flowers of children like me and you;
God bless them all, so innocent and true.

Heart to heart and hand to hand.
The circle of love stretches across the land;
From every race, from every clan,
We focus our hearts to the Son of man.

Hearts and flowers never wither and die,
For God heals the broken in heart,
O blest be the binding tie!
For he will bear you up on eagle's wings;
Up to his home in the sky.
    Jeanette A. Weaver

Isn't It Wonderful?

Isn't it wonderful, all the things that God has made?
Fruits and vegetables for food and trees to give us shade.
Birds, fish and animals, all for the use of man;
And He gave each of us a brain, with which to think and plan.

He gave us hens to provide eggs, to make many a delicious treat;
And cows to give us milk and cream, so many good things to eat.
He gave us mountains, valleys and shady nooks,
Fields and woodlands, with rivers and babbling brooks.

He gave us lakes, large oceans and seas,
And He gave us the refreshing Canyon breeze.
He gave us sunlight for the daytime, moonlight for the night,
Also beautiful, twinkling stars, to increase the dim light.

These are just a few of the things, that are given for our pleasure;
But there are so very many more, which are given in full measure.
He gave us the ability to serve, the best of all He gave us LOVE.
So how can we ever give thanks enough, to our dear God above?
    Jennie W. Madsen

Small Surprises

The wings of brimstone is coming soon
God's beauty in the month of June

The white edges of the soft Adonis blue
Come shining pale colours through and through

God's smiles are in delicate disguises
Like spring the nature of small surprises

Even the green of a marbled white
Makes a denizen meadow a pretty sight

For their colours are soft and shy
Sprinkled on the wings of the butterfly
    Tracy Turpin

What?

My thoughts are twisted
I feel as thought I do not exist, yet I do
In a world of horror and crime
I feed on extremes as a monster, I am
Madness overcomes pity in this twisted world if mine
I sit, I sit and waste my time away
I could advance, but I don't
I am not worthy
I am of a race full of hatred and horrific thoughts
I exist.. I am.. I sit.. I think
I think those twisted thoughts away
I think and sit, forever and never
In this twisted world of mine
I do, I live and I die
    Marie Prokopets

The Only Gift

Of all the voices none has ever been more in harmony with the fruits of life than the voice of The Mother. For her song is heard from every corner of the world, and its music is recognized by all peoples as the sweet lullaby to which the strongest of them all will bend and fold their knees.

The wise men have said that there is but one mother and that all mothers are one. In the heart, she is the tavern wine, and in the mind, she is the riddle of our vision. Time and time she is star dust and earth fire. She is the first breath of the golden seed and the last wave of the silver sea. The mother is the ever changing beauty of nature with justice under one arm and fate under the other. It is also said that the mother always veils her wisdom, but in the end she offers herself as freedom. All of this she is and nothing less, but of what is said I know for sure that this life was given to me by one mother, my mother, the mother of my reality. This gift is all that I am, and this life which no man or woman will ever taste but me is the greatest gift in eternity.

The mother's voice, the one we all hear in the primordial waters of the womb, a voice pure and sublime, is a kiss born with passion and eternal forgiveness. Let us not lose this music from which we all come from. For she, The Mother, is all that there is and will ever be. Love your mother the way she has always loved you for centuries. Her love is unbound and thus free, this love is the only true gift, a gift for all children like or unlike you and me.

Amir Khademzadeh

America....A Dream?

America...a paradoxical image of paradise
Gems of lofty dreams and opportunities,
Inspire anyone to wander his mind.

But wait - even the powerful
Flock to your enticing scent and mystic name,
Embrace all culture you pioneer.
Dreams of you when will they end?
Capture minds and hearts in a global way,
Forget identities and precious lands.
Beyond your image there's more
Your superpower talent and fame,
You're the world's paragon: a myth?

America...a dream or reality
What is it that attracts a foreign soul?
Clings his cultured mind to your way.

Evil image of you is also known
Drugs, vicious gangs violence and crime,
Racism - all parts of your magic charm?

Yet, amidst all these you shine
on everyone - far or near you ... stand!

Aida E. Espiritu

Branchwood Towers

Branchwood Towers in back of Clinton Park
Has a neat exterior where tenants sit 'til dark.
Its young trees and flowers so friendly in spring
Make thoughts come and go like birds on the wing.
The interior is spacious, cheerful and bright;
The tenants are gracious, friendly and polite.
There's a library; activity room,
A lounge and community room.
We dance, we exercise-all the family meets
For activities, clubs, fun and special treats.
I feel we're a family here at Branchwood Towers
Living in sunshine, not sadness and showers.
I am a new tenant telling about today.
'Couldn't have been different before-
No way, no way.

Evelyn W. Fields

The Lover

The sea caresses the land as a lover -
Gentle, though forceful one upon the other.
Giving, loving, it comes in with the tide -
Taking, leaving all away in its stride.
Cunningly once more it forms its web
To attack the shore and take it to bed.
The soul of the sea entices the quest,
Pulsating the waves that never rest.
They roll and break with a rhythmic roar
Exploding in laughter as they hit the shore.
In white foaming beauty they parade their passion.
Then mesh together with love and compassion.

Carole M. McCloskey

Dying As He Grew Up

A rich kid away from his parents' home for the first time
gets a job at the local cafeteria.
Fellow addicts laugh about it.
Another dreamer is subdued.
Groomed to appreciate destruction.
Blackout-
allowing ones self to become trapped to be accepted.
Love starved.
Living in a nice house but homeless.
Succumbing to his tendencies.
Fading into the curtain of the spectacular show that he imagined he
would be as a child.

Graham N. Rich

Beanstalk

The same, but different.
Getting roses, striking poses, blowing noses.
Red roses, pretty poses, raw noses.
The same, but different.
What, may I ask, is wrong?
What, may I ask, is going on?
And WHY CAN'T I FIX IT?

Abracadabra! Hocus Pocus!
Ah la peanut butter and jelly sandwiches!
- Reappear!... You're not here.
I miss you.
WHAT ARE THE MAGIC WORDS?

The same, but different.
Jack had a beanstalk that sprouted
From some magic beans.
FEE! FI! FO! FUM! I -
That's not what I need.
I need the magic words.
WHAT THE HELL ARE THE MAGIC WORDS?

Jean Hopkinson

Never Be Lonely

Never be lonely, you're never alone
God watches over His loved and His own
Feel His presence in Spring's first bloom
A ray of sunshine across the room
Sudden Summer storm with strength and might
God is our defender and all is right
Autumn's aroma, its crispness, its hue
God's grace is as bountiful as the harvest is too
And the peace of God, which is wondrous to know
I sincerely sense in the Winter's snow
So look around you day by day
God is there in many a way!

Carole B. Loughran

Clouds

Thin as a whisper, using moisture as a thread.
God's patchwork of patterns always changing with the wind.
Some like pillows, or an angel's bed,
Look surreal almost, as they dance above your head.

The horizon may turn dark, the earth shrinks beneath its form.
Thunder rumbles as a lion waiting to be fed.
Lightning explodes as a rocket hurled down to the earth.
Searing what it touches regardless of its worth.

Rain begins to fall, as if in deep sorrow were they,
Blocking the sun as a canvas, keeping warmth at bay.
With liquid as a prism, soon a rainbow forms.
Bringing the hope anew that follows every storm.

At sunset, as a peacock, the sun's rays spread as feathers.
Brushing each cloud with a portion of its splendor.
Each day is a masterpiece, each cloud a work of art.
Bringing the beauty and power of heaven to everyone on earth.

Amy L. Crockett

Strike

A treasure once was lost to me
Gone was its brilliance, its simplicity, its purity
To gaze upon it had been to be
Oh where was the joy that had come for free
Was my treasure lost though it I could not see?
It truly was not, only it was more dear to me.

David J. Wedgbury

Empty Scenes

Your silent house,
graced faintly by sweet perfume.
Two white chairs,
reflected side by side in the bright April moon.

My unmade bed,
untouched since we last kissed goodbye.
This lovers refuge,
silent now of our whispers, our sighs.

Your presence alone,
gives life to these empty scenes.
Your love alone,
moves my heart and makes it sing.

Donald R. Brady

Broken Heart

The birth of a child is a mother's joy,
Great hopes for the future she has for her boy.
The first step and word give her heart a glow.
She watches her boy to a young man grow.

As the time quickly passes - try as she may...
Her handsome young son wants to go his own way.
Like a thief in the night through his window he goes
To seek excitement and fun.
Where? - God only knows!

It's easy to steal from his mother's purse
To support his habit which is now a curse.
The last chance to start over has come and gone.
His life is slowly slipping...
He's all alone.

"I'm sorry, mother!"
Is all he can say,
"Though I broke your heart,
Forgive me, I pray..."

Gay Gaisma Newman

Winter

Deep is the chill that cuts like a knife laden heavy over the
ground without the sun to warm the soul.
Everything is dressed in dormant attire as the biting wind
whispers around every corner.
The frosted windows seclude the storm as the snowflakes
wrestle violently without a sound.
Grayish smoke moves slowly through the frozen hickory scented air.
Sidewalks and streets are nowhere to be found, nor living creature,
except for the footprints left behind.
Only eyes can be seen beneath the heavily wrapped bodies as
their blades cut swiftly across the ice.
Children laughing as their bright colored sleds tumble quickly
over the pillowy sculptures of snow.
Such delicate masterpieces created by nature.
A sight to be seen by mid-afternoon when a ray of sunlight allows
prisms of color to dance through the ice suspending from roof-tops.

Belinda Szwarc

The Written Word

T houghts borne on waves of vocal vibration,
H ave little to say for each generation,
E xcept to express communication.

W ords that are written, prod Man to his dreams,
R ide him to heaven and hell with his schemes,
I ncite him to anger and fill him with fear,
T rouble his truth and make him sincere,
T each him to love and provoke him to fight,
E xtol his virtues but praise him for might,
N urture his mind with thoughts to shed light.

W ords that are written are scraps of Man's soul,
O beying his impulse to strive for a goal,
R eadable thoughts etch love, hate and glory,
D eep in the heart of life's endless story.

Celeste Wessel

Genetic Syntax

Playing God could be dangerous, I think, as I
   hack at dead dried branches of dormant crepe myrtle:
   what if they still harbor a tender thread of life
   enough to nourish even a few new leaves?
Pausing to ponder implications of arboreal murder
   I study a squaw tree's slender vertical blossoms
   whose yellow throats abrim with golden nectar
   seduce thrumming humming birds
A shaman wise in ways of our universe once told me
   that determined squaw volunteers marshaled each spring
   in my garden are so named because the burden
   of their proliferating leaves forces them
   to lean lower, lower arching toward the earth
   with the weight of age while sowing seeds
   to affirm nature's edict: continuation
My sharp shears nip off another node
   for my modest knowledge tells me
   that the old must make way for the new
   even as generations nourish one another
Ongoing spiral of energy evolution enlightenment.

Barbara F. Kovner

Feelings Grow

   My feelings for you grow greater everyday like the blades of
grass during the month of May. The contrast images that crowd my
mind are but so real words cannot describe the way I feel. As I
sit and stare through the window into the past I can only help to
think and hope that the memories will last. What the future
holds is only up to us whether it be broken hearts like shattered
glass or living futuristic memories of the days we share now and
forever.

DebraLee Strandahl

"My Little Dani"

No more than seven pounds she was in my hands,
Hair so dark and skin so pale,
She was my creation with the man
Whom she would learn Daddy to tell.

And Daddy she did tell everything special to her,
But I was the one who first told Dani
About the daffodils growing on the curb
And of the enchantment she did carry.

Daddy's girl she seemed,
Cars, motorcycles she liked fast,
But when boys came into her dreams
It was Momma she ran to ask.

Long and bright, just like mine,
Her hair is her given glory,
It shown when it was her wedding time,
And never will I be sorry
For all the days it was mine.
Diana L. Gooden

Requiem

Sitting quietly in parched grey earth
hands slowly crushing clumps of dirt
sifting soil through calloused fingers

Tired to the core from working in these fields
I let the busy ants crawl over me as
they search doggedly for something sweet or wet

Sun red hot, hovering relentlessly,
my eyes closed, nose dry with dust
mindless reaching for relief in darkness
When I hear the fluttering, my eyes open to the sound

An injured bird fallen upon sun-baked soil
brown breast feathers matted, wet with blood
broken wing stretched out for balance
final piercing squeak from open gasping beak
Rising to my feet I quietly approach

The bird has lost the strength
to shriek its fear but struggles still
I lift my boot as high as it will go
and crush the tiny head into my silence
envying the freedom and the peace I give
Joanne Conrado

Santa And The Nativity

Santa came to our house last night.
He brought the holy family,
Joseph, Mary, and a babe lying in a manger.
That babe was Jesus, who loved us so much he died for us.

Santa came to our house last night.
He brought Angels, who told of a wonderful
Baby King lying in a manger.
That babe was Jesus, who loved us so much he died for us.

Santa came to our house last night.
He brought Shepherds who saw a star,
And came to worship a babe lying in a manger.
That babe was Jesus, who loved us so much he died for us.

Santa came to our house last night.
He brought wise men three, who traveled afar,
To see a babe lying in a manger.
That babe was Jesus, who loved us so much he died for us.

Oh come to the manger, come to the manger
to see the Angels, Shepherds, Wise Men three,
Holy family and a babe lying in a manger.
That babe was Jesus, who loved us so much he died for us
Beatrice Van Deest

You Do Not Walk Alone

Each of us now drawing breath
  has known of hurt, loneliness, grief, and death.

In life's misery we suffer not as one,
  only as a unit of much suffering that is done.

Each of us has a story that could be told,
  and each one to be voiced is ancient—very old.

To live us to suffer and suffering is surely done,
  throughout the world, known in every tongue.

So where does this leave us? We send up our cry,
  we oft beg of each other and plead the way.

No one has the answer and all that I know,
  is that you do not walk alone my fellow soul.
Carolyn Schwartz

Sonnet For Elizabeth

Who tends a tree within her garden walls'
Has much delight and many joys for sharing.
Here, airy transients, weary of their faring
Find rest within its quiet and leafy halls...
Here, as the seasons slip away, there falls
The summer sun, the winter rain, ensnaring
So much delight, so many joys for sharing.
Who tends a tree within her garden walls
Learns patience best of all...how life, contriving,
Brings leaves from loam and beauty from the dark;
Learns when to labor, when to cease from striving.
Here the gay mocker tunes his mimic flute
And shy small plants that fear the sun, take root.
Blest be the garden where a tree is thriving.
Josephine Siple

Take A Little Walk With The Lord

Take a Little Walk with the Lord,
Have a Little Talk with the Lord.
You will find
Peace of mind
When you have a Little Talk with the Lord.

Pray on your Knees To The Lord.
For it's you, who sees in the Lord
Open your eyes
Look up to the skies
And have a Little Talk with the Lord,

Put your trust in the Lord
For you must be just with the Lord
you will see
That it's Heavenly
When you have a Little Talk with the Lord

Reach out your hand to the Lord
Walk hand in hand with the Lord
Life can be an eternity,
When you take that Little Walk with the Lord
And have that Little Talk with the Lord.
Joseph Motta

A Fox's Lies

  A fox runs through the midnight light
Gasping for air in the dark, dark night
Help me! Catch me! Please don't die
Because the only reason you are to suffer
is for lack of knowledge I shall not lie
Wisdom is used to better understand one's mind
But without someone understanding their own
selves how are they supposed to get another out
of a bind
Erica Campbell

Warnings

I've been around better than four score;
Have left very few footprints on the ground I've trod.
In poetic form, I'm thanking my Mom and Dad
For their teaching and belief in the Almighty God.

America morally is at its lowest tide;
Doubting Thomases have invaded our Nation.
Daily He keeps reminding the skeptics
This world is of His own creation.

Floods, tornadoes, hurricanes and bombs;
Towns and families literally torn apart;
Could someone be loudly proclaiming
Please put God back in our hearts?

Other Nations have grown and prospered;
Sinned violently — now no longer exist.
Can our multi-cultural, immoral society understand
We are taking historically proven risks?

The Bible's been around for many year's
Loved by many and scorned by a few.
I've firm belief in the Ten Commandments.
Your beliefs are up to you.

Edwin C. Baker

"Memories Of Love"

I have kept these memories inside of me,
have not let them out none.
I have not abandoned the feelings you gave
nor shared them with anyone.
I heard our loveable love song, one I shall always hold
nothing can break our foundation or the universe
deep within our soul.

These memories are more precious than any gold
under heaven's skies, these memories you have
given me I hold with tears in my eyes.
You taught me to have patience, how to share
life together, showed me the joys of life, and faith
will be forever.
We have communication in spirits and hold our
seasons tight, those memories of you are so
beautiful that I sleep with them each night.
I've kept your feelings in my thoughts,
they will be forever true.
These memories are fulfilling as this rose
I give to you.

Aaron Horne

And It Came To Pass...

To Mom and Dad on his day of birth
He brought love...and it came to pass,
He grew to a child filled with mirth,
Brought laughter - and tears...and it
   came to pass,
Puberty brought problems, some small, some great,
He experienced the world...and it came to pass,
He chose a mate, children were born,
Stung by divorce that left him forlorn...and
   it came to pass,
A love so pure, all his he found,
Together in spirit for always were bound...
   And it came to pass,
The great spirit called, and separated these two,
But their hearts were entwined...and it came to pass,
One day in the great milky white way,
Two lovers will join forever and a day,
It is said no one on earth who passes this way,
Is ours to keep, it is merely a stay....
   For we come to pass.

Jennie Robinson

My Grandson Dylan

When I see you, I wonder of God's divine love, for when He molded
you, He created a perfect baby body with His huge Almighty hands

When I look into your sky blue eyes, I wonder of the love that I
see and of the unknown wisdom and talents that live within you

When I smooth your hair, I wonder if God spun your curls from
fields of wheat and colored your hair with the sunshine of His love

When I hug you and you hug me, I feel true exhilaration and wonder
if you feel my heart swelling with joy and melting into yours

When I am not with you, I pray that God and His loving angels will
guide and protect you, and I wonder

When I hold your little hand and you wrap your tiny fingers around
one of mine, I wonder of the power of your unconditional love

When I am with you, I am in wonder of your innocence and realize
that I would do anything humanly and spiritually possible for you

When I kiss you, I am in wonder of the feelings you arouse within
me as my soul stirs with childlike love when you kiss me in return

When I think of the gift of love and all of God's beauty, I think
of you with wonder, my grandson Dylan

Gloria J. Bojanowski

A Tribute To Sgt. Franklin D. Fisher

Most of his life he worked for Uncle Sam
He even served two terms in Vietnam
As a soldier, he was brave and bold
But underneath the surface was a "heart of gold"

He has traveled all over this land
Lending our country his "helping hand"
Those that knew him called him a "true friend"
Because on him, they could always depend

He never met a person that he didn't know
And he met many people while on the go
Happiness to him was helping others along the way
His "sense of humor" seemed to brighten everyone's day

This soldier picked a "mean guitar"
He could sing as good as any star
With a unique strum of his hand
He was a welcome addition to any band
"Family Bible" was his most requested song
On the chorus—everyone would sing along

This special soldier is missed by family, friends, and country
But he lives forever in our hearts through each memory

Anne T. Fisher (sister-in-law)

You How My Heart

Do you know God above created you for me to love
He picked you out from the rest, because
he knew I loved you best.
I had a heart and it was true, but now
it has gone from me to you.

Take care of it as I have done,
For now you have two and I have none.
If I'm in heaven before you're there
I'll call your name on the Golden Stairs
So all the angels there can see how much
My darling means to me.

If you're not there before judgment day,
I'll know you have gone another way.
I'll give the angels back their wings,
and golden harp and other things.
And just to show you what I'll do,
I'll even go to hell for you.

Eva B. Murray

The Gift

He asked me to do this, He said that I would
He gave this to me because no one else could
How could I be so selfish to think
The gifts that He gave were mine to keep

He said to share what I have and give freely
Without hesitation, I must give completely
Some have the gift to share a song
Those who are weak get gifts from the strong

They pull them through bad times and stay to the end
These are the gifts one gets from a friend
Some have the gift of verse and thought
Some receive the gift of being taught

Taught to be kind, humble, and meek
The gift of caring, the gift to teach
Whatever the gift He has given to you

Don't keep it for yourself
You see, the gifts He gave were always meant
To be shared with someone else

Agatha T. Williams

Blind Seeker

The man looked out his window, the sun was setting fast.
He gazed into the future, and longed so for the past.
He'd searched the world for wonders, had sought the far, unknown;
His quest for secrets of the world had left him all alone.

He set his mind to ponder, all the times afar and near,
And from the corner of his eye fell one regretful tear.
As darkness drew so close he wished for someone by his side;
But those who'd cared he turned away with greed, conceit, and pride.

In searching for his life, he had left it far behind.
Only thoughts of coming glory had dwelt upon his mind.
He had his precious wonders, countless riches to defend;
But in obtaining glory he had gained a lonely end.

Jared Prazen

Shawn

Why the boy so young?
He had so much to live for,
 so much to see and do.
But God came down and
said his time had come.
The Lord and the boy went to heaven.
The Lord said this is your new home
 you will be safe here.
But in every tear
 I remember the boy and
all the joys we shared.
So when I lay down to sleep
 I think of him, but know he is safe and happy.
Every move I make,
 the boy will be watching over me.
So all I do is look up and
Keep the memories close to my heart
 and he will never leave again.

Dianne Schaller

Mommy

Her smile animates my soul like the dancing sun.
Her immense height making me feel as if she's on top
of the world.
Comforting eyes fill me with care.
When I need her for help, she is always there.
Helpful actions towards me, make me feel important.
She fulfills my needs,
That's my very special Mommy.

Gary Riggs

Prince

"Good night, sweet prince," the angels said -
He lay there in the dust, quite dead -
A scene that was, in truth, not bad
For look at all the fame he's had!
For me, I stumble through this life
With human joys and human strife,
And when I die, they'll let it be,
No angels mourning over me,
No poet bright to cast a verse
To grant me peace - it could be worse!
 I am me and he was he -
 A prince of men I try to be!

Gerald B. Frank

Eternity

He comes down upon us to reap the souls of our dead,
He moves in silence, never to be seen,
With the smell of death the only signal,
He is eternity, he is the catcher of souls,
No one may escape,
The poor, the rich or the powerful will fall into his arms,
He is eternity, he is everywhere,
He cares for no one,
He is alone,
He is eternity,
He takes the souls of the living dead,
Those who crave nothing,
Those who die but live, the lonely,
He is our fear of nothing, yet he is more,
He is eternity.

Jason Van Riemsdyk

Our Newsboy

Our Newsboy is very polite.
He rides a motor instead of a bike.
He doesn't throw our paper in the yard.
He doesn't throw it against the door real hard.
Instead, he politely hands the paper to my mother.
Well, you see, our newsboy is my brother.

Frances S. Jackson

Mommy, I'm Scared To Die

In memory of my son Anthony

Oh mom, why has this happened to me
Have I been so bad that I could not see
All the love I have right here
Is just where I want to be

I'm afraid to go away to a place I don't know
I'll miss you so much, 'cause I love you all so,
Brothers and sisters, nephews and nieces
I've cried my heart out and just go to pieces

I wanted a house, little kids running about
Some horses and fences and family there
I want to get up and get out and shout
Why has this happened, it just isn't fair

I love you so much, I'll miss Dad too
I don't want you to cry, God will care for you
I'm afraid to go away to a place I can't see
Oh mom, why has this happened to me

It's time to go now—God's waiting there
Thanks for all your love and your care
God told me heaven is where I'll want to be
I'm all forgiven and now I see

Irma Fiscella

Untitled

The first child rose up to the top—the highest point and then,
He slowly stopped, began to drop, touched ground and rose again.
The second child did much the same for both went up and down.
But rising-falling through their game, neither made a sound.
Until child one said to child two "I like the ground far more,
It's stable, safe and free from view—besides, the game's a bore."
He left his place, and walked from there, it seemed the game had stopped;
But hark, child two, still in the air, still played, and down he dropped.
And yet, without the first child's weight, his fall, not smooth nor slow
Summoned up his final fate, and crushed him with a blow.
Perhaps in this then, life is fair as one must touch the ground
To hold another in the air, or else he'll tumble down...

Dalin T. Error

"Satan"

Satan, like a man; "come to work for a day!"
He spread forth his tools, in a varied array,
Deceit, jealousy, hate and also fear,
With these controlled men, afar off and near.

Eve he slew first, and at maddening price,
And on Cain; he turned Adam's heart as if ice.
And Cain wandered the earth, and scattered his sin,
And deceived most of the earth, with his power through men.

He sent forth his word, to a generation of men,
And went through the earth, causing all men to sin,
And nourish his seed, of awful deceit,
And to worship him widely, and establish his seat.

He caused Tubalcain to make weapons for war, to cause strife,
And covetousness of men's livings, families and life.
Merrymaking and drinking, all the pleasures of sin,
And brought man to the terrible shape he was in.

So god made clouds, and the fierce thunder rolled,
And put into men, a fear not yet told.
Taught how to live, they thought it just jive,
Then fought and swam to live, but drowned and died.

Joseph R. Lewis

Butterfly

High in the sky I see colors.
He spreads his wings and they flutter.
Beautiful by sight, he makes his flight.
When the butterfly lands, his wings will fan.
He's gentle by touch, so be careful.
He can slip right out your fingers,
and parts of him might linger.
Injured by a hand, his wings will still fan.
Fly away little butterfly.
And I will see you another day.

Bernadette Harper

Elegy - 1/14/93

Elegy,
   Had I known your life was meant to be,
   Sad and lonely,
   and you made yourself be free.
   It was not the answer
   but you ran from agony.
My Elegy,
   If I'd told that I loved you when you lived,
   would you have run to life?
   And love would you forgive?
   But you could not take the torment and the pain.
   So you ended life to not face life again.

Jamie Crone

Penances Of Loneliness

Alone for so many centuries
He walked the streets of New Orleans
In search of true companionship.

Then out of the mist, came this stranger.
Although, stranger did not feel right, friend and soul mate did.

His every feature was of pure elegance.
Skin luminous and milky white, like that of my own.

Unlike me, his other features were dark:
Eyes of deep brown, with flecks of amber,
Lips full and stained dark with blood.
The final touch was the coal, black hair
That fell upon his shoulders.

Compared to my light blond hair,
Emerald green eyes, and mildly rose-hued lips,
We were the perfect symbol of lightness and darkness.

Although I knew he offered
An eternity of happiness, I could not stay with him.

I still had penances to pay for my betrayal.
The only way for me to pay them is alone.
Alone for all eternity.

Jaime Ingram

"Daddy Short-Legs"

He was a quiet man in so many ways.
He wasn't very old, least that's what I have to say.
But he was sad because his wife passed away.
His life fell apart, he counted the days.
He grew much weaker with each passing day.

We'd sit by his bedside, talk, laugh, cry, the hours away.
Then one day, "Daddy Short-Legs" awoke
Wanting to go home for one more day,
So I drew him a picture; the front of the house
Now this made him smile, he said, draw something else?
I did and that made him laugh.
My last picture I drew made him cry,
Then he reached out to touch my face
He told me not to be sad,
So "Daddy Short-Legs" was preparing me
Then he told me, "I'm going to die."
"So don't look so sad," is what he said,
Just before he died.
It was hard for us to accept at first,
That "Daddy Short-Legs" died from a broken heart.

Frances Kelly

Life's Crooked Way

Friends keep passing, day by day,
Headed down life's narrow, crooked way.
Some of them stopped, and stayed for awhile,
And some of them even made me smile.

Some took more than they left behind,
While others left a good memory, of some kind.
Friends may come and go, some in fun, some in strife,
And some of them are responsible,
For a lot of pain in my life.

We all need friends,
It helps us to grow, day by day.
Without friends and loved ones,
Our lives would be so drab and gray.

So hold out your heart and hand,
To everyone that comes your way.
For it is better to give, than receive,
And it will help you to find your way.

Catherine Reeves

Maria — A Lyric Essay

Perhaps you always knew, I would daydream the years away.
Hearing a sound, a beat, a song, that — only in my head — only in my
heart would play. And yet my dreams, not unlike your own, would make
the heart grow quick, from beauty in seeing, feeling or hearing a tone.
Trembling in anticipation, from a borrowed soaring sound —
The aching, unfilled, loneliness of violins in a swell of tenderness
drowned. But because of you — knowing a fog horn in Bremen —
A lonely voyage, across a grey, foggy sea. Understanding now, the
anguish of the strange, the new, the sometimes unlovely.
Understanding too, the swelling of your love, and its diminishing,
now and again in the hard cold bitterness of reality. But, "Oh!" —
all you gave to live by and remember! To love a glistening, drop of
early morning dew, a dripping, sticking cone in hot mid-afternoon —
To look and really see a cold winter moon, wearing the ring of a new
bride — together, a breathless swim in a star-filled summer night,
Moving soundless, side by side. How can one say thank you, for
nameless indescribable joys, for wordless thoughts, for soaring
flights of fancy and feelings, that live their lives alone in my soul.
Because you taught me to live — and give.
Because you showed me how to love.

Irene H. Peterson

"Mountains Of Rubies"

Mountains of Rubies, Rivers of Light,
Heart of the Smokies, Great Spirit's Might,
Whenever I wander too far from home,
I look to the landmark of Clingman's Dome.

Mountains of Rubies, Riches untold,
In warmth of the Summer, Or Winter's cold,
It matters not, the time or the season,
My Love of these Mountains needs not a reason.

Mountains of Rubies, Lakes of Pure Gold,
Sequestered throughout this Land, We're Told,
Like vintage wine, or wild mountain honey,
These splendors take time, not more money!

Mountains of Rubies, Home of my Heart
Splendor and Beauty, How Great Thou Art!
When my eyes grow dim and no longer can see,
These mountains, I know, will still cradle me.

Eve Connestee

The Pioneers

The pioneers were brave and strong,
Helped build a great new land;
They worked and sweat and fought and slaved,
with little but their hands.

They traveled west by wagon trains
through wilderness and forests,
They gave their strength, and some their lives,
to open new lands for us.

This country now, from coast to coast
is far beyond their dreams,
For now above old wagon trails,
the jet's white vapor streams.

Alma Ilene Gough

Home

The wisp of hair that falls into my eyes,
Carelessly blows in the wind.
It hasn't anywhere to go except back to its place atop my head.
That is where it belongs.
Many people are like that wisp of hair;
Blowing and wandering away from home,
Only to find that they are rooted there, by their hearts.
That is where they belong.

Katherine Hall

When Nellie Blew Up

I was breakin' this filly up north of Ford
Her back was as wide as a 2" x 4" board
The spunky little gal's name is Nellie
She had spindly legs and a little pot belly
I's a ridin' along spending some "Quality Time"
When all at once she decided to unwind
We were lopin' along, I'm thinkin' there's nothin' to it
Then she started bucking like she's used to doin' it
She planted all four and headed for the sky
I shook hands with a flock of geese as they flew by
The bottom fell out and we headed for the ground
When my backside hit the saddle it made a loud slappin' sound
Well she packed her bags and again up we went
She was going to meet her maker, on this she was hell-bent
By now my air was gettin' thin
I was passin' out and comin' to, and I didn't know where all we'd been
One last time she jumped for the moon
I'm thinkin' "please Lord let it be ever soon"
We hit the ground again and I braced for the worst
Then she started lopin' like she had been at first.

Dale Loder

Jungle Justice

Rat! Tat! Tat! Boom!
Here comes the sound of doom
Blood, bones, guts spilled like water
Peace and tranquility shattered like China Glass

Oh, Billy what has thou Done? Love your neighbour said the Bible
But reward my friends and destroy my enemies said the Priest

But killing him? He is an enemy; arrogantly rich
Alas, the son of man is as poor as church rat
What worse enemy can be poor man ask for?

But killing him? Exploitation and stealing was his game
Robbing and taking from poor
But killing him? He is a sinner and the wages of sin is death
Billy, who made you a judge?
Judge not so that you will not be judged. Said who? The Bible.
Thou shalt not steal says the Bible too

But killing him? Good riddance of bad rubbish you might say
But it's a case of the pot calling kettle black
Two wrongs don't make a right

Abimbola P. Oyewole

"Alone I Sit"

Somewhere deep inside a hidden part of me lies,
Hidden because romance is something to share.
Our most important search is for that special person,
The one with whom you tell everything if you dare.

Falling in love can be a most complicated thing,
It can be wonderful and joyous or cut like a knife.
If someone special loves you back there's nothing better,
But when they don't, the pain can last for life.

Why is fate sometimes so merciless and cruel,
To let you fall in love with someone that can't return it.
To let you find someone so special but never be close,
These are the questions I ponder as alone I sit.

The pain of a special love that is not returned,
Is greater than any pain I have ever known.
No crop or love in this world can ever grow,
If the seeds you have can never be sown.

David H. LaRue

Sounds Of Darkness

The fiery sunset gives a fleeting
hint of darkness.
Then the sun finally bleeds its last colors
And there is a moment of silence as
darkness encircles the Land.
Then the sounds of night begin.....
The echo of wolves singing
of their hunger,
Owls hooting,
The murmur of crickets,
And the soft wind rustling
in the leaves.
Ihuoma Onyeali

Beneath The Chinaberry Tree

I see a small boy beneath the Chinaberry tree, day-dreaming in the grass.
His eyes are lost in distant thoughts as the hours slowly pass.
The tree from heaven is fully dressed, in her spring-time green leaf gown.
A breeze rustles the Chinaberry leaves, to echo a soothing sound.
The sound of peace, the sound of love, or the sound of flowing streams.
It seems to beckon the mind away, to grandeur thoughts and dreams.
A moment or chance to talk to God, while nature is silent and soft.
To converse with him, who reigns above in the cloud struck
   heavenly loft.
I know the child who yonder lies, beneath the Chinaberry tree.
God guide the child and guard his heart, because I am the child
   you see.
It seems to be that no matter where, my feet may tend to roam.
God plants for me a Chinaberry tree, and it makes me feel at home.
Beneath it, I lie and rest my body; my heart, my soul, and mind.
I listen to God and feel his peace, and let the world leave me behind.
So if I'm asked, "what do I do? I'm as troubled and hurt as can be."
Please understand when I reply, "Go find a Chinaberry tree."
D. Andrew Liles

God's Eyes

The tears in his eyes are the sea,
His heart keeps caring for me.
The black in his eyes are the night,
That he made to come after the light.
The white in his eyes are the day,
That he made to show us our way.
The colors in his eyes are the trees and flowers,
They grow for hours and hours.
The Love in his eyes are the creatures,
And they all have special features.
Jessica Ann Henry

I Found My Friend

I have a friend in my mother.
I have a friend in my grandma too.
I have a friend in my family. Do I have a friend in you?
They gave me birthday presents. They gave me Dr. Suess.
They gave me the chance of understanding. Is my friend you?
They took me to the movies. They took me to the zoo.
They took me to the park. Could my friend be you?
They took care of my broken arm and when I had the flu.
They visited me in the hospital. Can you tell me if it's you?
They took me to my meetings. They watch me perform what I do.
They watch me play basketball. If it's not them over there is it you?
They care a lot about me and never make me choose.
They love me and my poetry. I think my friend is you?
They ask me about my problems, even when they're new.
They ask me who my friends are. Do I tell them you?
I've asked and asked and even searched; now I know who.
I have found my friend.
My friend is you.
Ashley Stoner

Our First President

George Washington was a truthful lad who lived in Mt, Vernon with
   his Mother and Dad
One fine day little Georgie cut down his father's cherry tree
yet, with all his honesty, told his Dad that it was he.
A few years later the Father was dead; this left the family to strive
   on ahead,
George's life was an outdoor one, he was continually eager for
   sporting and fun -
In the army, Washington had taken command; he was equally good at
   surveying the land -
George married Mrs. Custis when she was twenty seven, and after that
   life seemed like Heaven!
Then on to the battle went brave honest George, with a cold, starving
   army to Valley Forge -
Time came and he said "Goodbye" to his dearest of friends with a tear
   in his eye
Thus he said to his officers true, "With a heart full of love I take
   leave of you."
George then traveled for away to become president one fine day,
Then, of course come the inauguration, which made everyone happy
   throughout the nation!
After many long years which came and went, ended the life of our first
   president.
Bernadette C. Doyle

"Our Fathers"

A Father is a gift - sent from Above...
His whole purpose - is to show us love...
He cares for us - and he watches us grow...
And picks us up - when we're feeling low...

The one we depend on - through thick and thin...
To help us and correct us - now and then...
He's there to teach us - right from wrong...
To stand on our feet - and to become strong...

Then one day - our fathers are gone...
That's the way it was arranged - all along...
God never gave them to us - only lends them awhile...
So we should cherish the memories - and all the smiles...

Fathers and daughters - have a special bond...
They give of themselves - to us they belong...
When they're gone it's an emptiness that nothing can fill...
But in time - God will help us - to make it heal

You have to be strong - and remember one thing...
Just look to the sky and when the moon has a ring...
Our Daddies are up there - encircling it with love...
So when we pass on - we will join the circle above...
Angela Redman

The Dreamer

When I was young, as I was told,
I had my dreams - a million-fold.
But as I grew, I came to see
I had to live in reality.
It was a shock and quite a bother,
Having to work like Mother and Father.
But work paid off, as I can see,
I have beautiful children - all three.
It makes me happy to watch them play and scream;
To see them try to live their dreams.
And now I'm old, and so it seems
I have more time to think of dreams.
Some have come true, and some may not,
But I'm very happy with the dreams I've got.
And when I die, they all can say
"Dreams kept her happy, night and day."
Cathy Riesbeck

Runaway

Runaway from the pain.
Hold the pain inside you, never letting it show.
Runaway from the pain.
The pain is greater when some one stabs you at the source of it.
Runaway from the pain.
Love has no meaning anymore, did it ever? Will it ever?
Runaway from the pain.
When you run away, the pains gets
  so strong it kills you.
The pain is so strong I can't take it.
When the pain tries to kill you... let it.
You can never win.
Now, you don't have to run away from the pain.

Betsy Stratton

We Used To Be

We used to be like a pin
Holding things up and holding
things together
Always being put together
But now I'm alone
Fighting my way to make it on my own
Like a fierce lion with its claws
How could you just stand there and do nothing?
I thought our love would last
But I was wrong
How could you break my heart?
I guess it'd be better if I
was alone
Wouldn't it?

Holly Wojciechowski

Abyss

Lost in an ocean of swirling iridescence,
Hopelessly bewildered
I grasp at a crystal shard of water,
But it slips through my fingers
As if it had never been.

Helplessly I flounder in a never-ending sea,
The frenzied currents pull me further away,
Groping, groping for a solid form
On which to rest my defeated body.

Twisting and turning to my immortal destiny,
A beaten path to a black void,
But an atom of my being resists.

  And then—

Far above me a shimmering vision appears,
How quickly it flies!
Boldly, gracefully, swoops down, pulls me up
And wings me back to yesterday I remember.

Cheryl Walker

Madness

Lying on the boundaries of reality and the nether world he cries.
  His world is a vast darkness...
    consuming all who are near.
Demons and angels dance
  He runs through the passage ways.
    The hall connecting realms
Truth and lies, myths and facts lose any relationship.
  The creatures and demons wail horrific screeches in his pale face.
    His eyes widened, sagging and red.
      These grayish eyes
        tell tales of torture and pain.
          So he sits,
            crying, almost laughing in agony
              for he is lost in his own mind.

John Matthew Estock

The Seasons Change

When snowflakes fall; bitter winds blow, snow drifts bile high; one hour of time. Biting frost, the ice melts against my door.
The Seasons Change

Flowers of color swaying in the breeze; rain drops on the trees, grass grows strong and tall, reaching high above the wall.
The Seasons Change

Sunny days ahead; hot, humid and wet, brighter days before. I can hear the laughter and the roar.
The Seasons Change

Golden leaves, yellow, brown or green. Pumpkin seeds lay on the ground, chilly nights ahead, the sky turns red.
The Seasons Change

Elissa Johnson Francis

Oklahoma

Debris and tears fall from the sky,
How can anyone stand not to cry?
Adult's and children's lives are lost,
Whoever did this will pay the cost.

Parents left their kids in Day Care,
Thinking maybe they'd be safe there.
'Till Tim McVeigh drove up in his truck,
By the end of the day they'd all be stuck.

Under falling rods and wires,
Through the thick and dense fires,
All is lost and nothing won,
Very few shall ever again see the sun.

I feel for those in Oklahoma City,
I send them all my hope and pity.
Now I too must live in fear,
In fear that this could happen here.

Dawn M. Toomey

"Letting Go"

Oh mother bird please show me how you teach your young to fly
How is it when they flee your nest, you never seem to cry?
Is it only Humans then that cling so to their young?
And when they go out on their own, wonder what went wrong?
With all our hearts we want what's right, and that's our only care
Yet when it's time for them to leave, why do we then despair?
If only I could be like you and urge them on their way
Instead of aching so inside, because they cannot stay
To be a mother bird right now, how simple it would be
to watch this "offspring" take his "flight" into his own new Tree
The day he leaves I'll try real hard to hold back on these tears
But tell me what will fill the "Void" he's filled for 19 years?

Dorothy Christensen

Dreaming

When I dream, I fly,
I fly through the air with a big smile on my face.

Dreams are wishes,
When my mind needs to get away,
to think,
to fly.

Dreams let me relax,
Dreams let me sleep, and
Dreams let me retreat from reality.

Dreams make me happy,
Dreams make me sad.
Dreams let me be anything I want to be.

Anything I want to be.

Angela Johanson

Bombing

You try to think how it would be,
how it would feel to lose someone.
You won't believe and just can't see,
How it would feel to lose someone.
I can't believe what people do,
How they can kill the innocent.
I don't know why, I have no clue
How they can kill the innocent.
How can someone hate so much,
To destroy the lives of children?
They did in just one little touch,
They destroyed the lives of children.
How can you possibly explain, explain the deaths to the families?
There are so many who are slain, explain those deaths to the families.
I pray that justice will be served let God deal with all the guilty
I pray to God, no laws curved, let Him deal with all the guilty
My heart cries out to loved ones lost,
To all of those who have lost them
let pain be healed that someone cost
I pray for families who lost them.
Erin Vallier

To Mother

Mother's Day in Heaven—
How lucky the Angels are
To have you there to help them
Light the Morning and Evening Stars.

Your gentle smile is sadly missed
By your children this Special Day.
Not to have you here with us
Seems to get harder with each passing day.

So special still is this day for us
Because of you, Dear Mother.
We wish to let all who read this
Know that you were like no other.

The example you set in your daily life
When you walked upon this Earth
Will serve as a guide for us to follow
To teach our children their worth.

All the values you taught us are well in place.
We will do our best to remember.
For all the Love and Care you gave us while you were here—
WE THANK YOU — DEAR, SWEET MOTHER.
Jacqueline D. Scott

Thoughts About Oklahoma

I wish that I could change what I don't understand
How one can justify inhumanity to man.

The man that lacks respect for another's point of view
and takes it way beyond what seems right to me and you.

I understand the flaws among the human race, but the
intensity and action cannot be erased.

They live forever in the hearts and souls of those affected
and especially in the child who thought he was protected.

The sad and evil thoughts that somehow get out of hand
will multiply so swiftly if we cannot take a stand...

To do as much as we can do to protect our precious lives
with respect and love and kindness so that everyone survives.

Is it too much to want or try to ask for these...
that man must simply stop the hate and learn to live in peace?
Billie S. Besinger

Changes

Occasionally I see the rain, I often see the storm.
However, the world is live in you wing the weather.
There's never a time you feel at ease,
to get away at your time of need.
Nothing ever seems at all right when you are to
live the life of the weather.
It alters as the days elude, the clouds, the rain,
the darkness, the moon.
A pinch of sunshine may burst through a storm of clouds,
While the darkness of the night takes over the crowd.
There's always the sun to come when all else fails,
To brighten the world despite all the hell.
The storm is the virus that causes us to hate,
that pinch of sunshine is that pinch of faith.
As the storm discontinues the rain will surely fade,
to let your feelings of LOVE guide you the way.
Felicia A. Powell

Strength

I'm young and thin and leaning west,
I am a haven under which you rest.

My leaves show love as they sway in the breeze,
Whenever the wind chooses to sneeze.

The sunlight filters to the ground,
Through my leaves, jagged instead of round.

My skin looks smooth to the sight,
But feeling the roughness sets you right.

Willowy and weak I may appear,
But I will protect you when you are near.
Dixie D. Karlson

The Embrace Of.....Divine Love

Oh, joyful and glorious day!
I am a sparkling bubble being blown to as yet
undiscovered heights within the gentle, warm BREEZE
of Divine Love.

Gleefully I shimmer, calling to whoever wishes
to share my soul's journey.

Come! Come!...everyone into LOVE'S LIGHT—Never-ending,
All-Encompassing, Forever Faithful.

Yes! Our Creator has made me a whimsical bubble; ever-
dancing, ever seeking, always finding His Heartbeat of LOVE.

I am HIS lowly bubble floating....and boldly
trusting.....that the grace of HIS GENTLE BREEZE will
not let me burst on the ground of despair.

I float....not knowing where, or why, or how, but do I care?

I surrender....with bubble-like freedom to HIS WILL,
HIS WHERE, HIS WAY......

Delightedly my face becomes like the SON,
my sparkle is consumed within the BREEZE,
I am breathlessly one with the LIGHT.....
Janet Bodell

Untitled

Sun's brightest light, glaring over the icy crystals
Creating beauty amidst the winter's cold
Leaves a warm feeling in the coldest of hearts
Bringing hope into the darkest of shadows
Leaving a balance through the wonder of the morning.
Robin Martucci

"Who Am I?"

"Who am I?" I ask. No answer.
I am an intelligent girl.
I wonder what I'll be when I grow up.
I am my own role model.
I want to travel around the world.
I am hoping for a better life in the future.
I pretend to be an important model for others.
I am Hispanic and stand for it.
I feel like the queen of the universe.
I am fully trusted upon myself.
I worry about the nuclear bombs.
I am only one person, who just wants to be herself.
I cry when I see someone dying.
I am beautiful.
I understand the poverty in Earth.
I am my own.
I feel that everyone should be treated equal.
And then I get these answers.

I am proud of who I am...
Jeannette Navarrete

In Loving Memory

I am only a child but
I am getting older, almost an adult
At least to have a pet

It is mine to take care of
To love
To hold and to feed

Sometimes it's a pain
But a bigger pain called death
Is worse

Not even a tear can bring my friend back
No longer am I a child
It's hard to call me one
When my mother is sitting next to me
Shedding a tear for the companion I have lost

My dad does not say much
But he is next to me
Willing to hold me
When I need a hug
And to be there to help
With the burial ceremony
Harold Colon

I Am

Often they've said I don't know who I am
I am woman
I am pleasure, I am pain, I am woman
I'm serenity, I am strain, woman I am
I am aggression and submission
I am anger, I am love, I know who I am
I am darkness in the light
I am sorry after fight
I am liquid, I am mass, I am bosom, I am ass
I am satisfaction, I am frustration
I am stamina, I am gestation
I am mommy, I am lover, I'm alone
I am grown
I am yours, I am mine
I am distant, passing time
I am success, I am fame
I am sincere, not your game
I am honest not lame
I am your future unfold
a story untold
Phylli Walker

My Silent Prayer

Heavenly Father full of grace,
I ask of you to keep my family in its place.
There once was five, but now there's three,
soon this family will be left with only me.
My Mom and Dad now aren't together,
I ask of you not to let it last forever.
It hurts to know that holidays won't be the same,
because this family of mine has gone down the drain.
I used to think this family of mine was so special
and nothing could ever lead it astray,
but Satan intervened and tore it away.
God, I love this family of mine with all my heart,
and I pray you will lead it back to a brand new start.
So God, I hope you've heard this silent prayer,
because this is my family and I really care.
Dara Rebecca Miller

Color

Hard cold sweat pours down my face like a lion on a rampage.
I breathe deeply, waiting for relief.
Hot searing pain runs through my body.
I am a cattle, weak and helpless in the night,
praying, hoping for the pain to stay away.
The hot searing steel plows into my side and I shriek in agony.
A circle with a p inside is forever branded into my heart.
The p is for Powers, or perhaps it stands for pain.
My gut taunts and twirls like a storm raging its anger upon the earth.
My body is thrown from side to side, limp from exertion.
I crawl back into the space in my mind where peace and dignity remain.
Colors are all around me. I speak to them. One is blue.
His name is Jerry; He is my soothing relief.
Then Frank, a crimson red, comes to me.
He brings me to the edge of my thoughts and anxieties,
where the pain remains.
I shout at him, but he does not listen.
The pain envelopes me again.
Emma Littman

The Sun

Desperately you wait for me each morn,
I bring beauty to your day.
My warmth brings a glow to your face,
Your day is filled with hope and peace.

On those days that I decide to sleep,
and gloom fills your sunless day,
you are weak.
You wish for a sunny tomorrow,
to make your life complete.
To give you courage to face another day on this earth.

So, I decide to grant your wish,
I arise and fill your world.
You are happy once again.
What would you do with out my warm beam and bright light?
Would you simply fade away?
Helen Polanco

When God Made You

When God made you he put the sun in your smile and after that he walked an extra mile and got some stars from the skies and put them in your sparkling eyes. He picked a red-red rose and gave you its beauty from the top of your head to the tips of your toes. For your heart he walked to the ends of the earth and the edges of the universe and gathered everything of worth- and with these ingredients he began to start and after days of hard work he finished your precious heart. After his work was all through and he made you-he discovered the ingredients of a perfect mother.
Christian Curtis Torres & Christopher Curtis Torres

"Depression"

I want to walk, my head held high
I cannot do it, I don't know why
My mind is veiled behind black curtain
I'm all alone, of this I'm certain
Nails raw to the quick, blood on my hands
From trying to dig out of depressing sands
I fight and fight, but just sink deeper
Mocking voices in my mind; "Keep her, keep her"
Opening my eyes, surrounded in black
Slowly realizing I'll never get back
To the child I was, so long ago
Big eyes, bright smile, and far to go
When was it that I fell off this path
To land here, now, in the aftermath
I suppose in time the pain will fade
But for now I lie in this bed that I've made
And all that I've hurt will turn their heads
Sometimes I think I'd be better off dead
But I'm too weak to face it, too weak to go
Over the edge of life, into what I don't know

Christina Jay

Then Suddenly, A Vision!

Whoever said life is but an empty dream
I cannot fathom what it means
Living life itself is full of sense
Be it a nice car, a sweetheart, or good friends
Fulfillments, goals, heartaches, or happiness
Get an honest look at your life, unless,
You really understand what destroys your confidence
And holds you back from making a change.
And then I wonder what my purpose be
I toil, I seek, I reach and want to see
What is in my heart that tears me up
In a world chaotic that I cannot drop
The pessimism and emptiness that I fear
Cannot be dropping out of life even if I will
Be steered to real life righteousness in me.
What then this emptiness in me so real
Until one day I shouted out very clear
GOD! GOD! come to me and set me free
From this my life no purpose be
And suddenly, a vision! GOD IS ALL I NEED IN ME

Brenda Garma

The Revenant

Mother was gone but scarce a week.
I deep in slumber lay,
Much wearied by the circumstance
And sorrows of the day.

Then, sudden, she appeared to me
In her own rocking chair;
There was a brightness in the room
And whispers in the air.

"Mother...your diary...we must find...
Can you remember now...
We know your wishes were inscribed...
If you can speak somehow...."

She strove to speak, but scarce her lips
Would move. Then a great wind
Rushed through the house, and she was gone,
An empty chair behind.

When I awoke, I marveled;
In grief I smote my head
That I should speak to her, and leave
So much of love unsaid.

Ed Johns

Fatherhood

I have become a creator, a bridge to the past and the future.
I contemplated my rebirth; looked upon the darkness and pierced it
with the movement of my word and caused the breaking of nothingness
with an explosion of LIFE!
I watch as this universe expands, its parameters easily within my grasp.
I was there when my creation sprang forth from the darkness into the
light and the breath of life ignited its soul.
I look into the eyes of my future and reconcile my demise.
I have not forsaken my purpose, for the Will from which I am fashioned
guides my path. I have not forsaken my struggle, for the toil of
my forbearers sustains me.
I have not succumbed, nor will I ever submit for my creation shall
nourish me long after my flesh is gone.
I have fashioned life in the image of the Ancient
and assisted in its journey.
I have kept balance in the universe.

I am protector.
I am nurturer.
I am complement.
I am re-created.
I am more of that which I am.
I am a creator, sustainer of life.
I am Father.

Byron J. Harris

Miss Carry

All I do is mourn, Miss Carry, the death of the girl embryo I held.
I couldn't hold her, God I couldn't (blood spots on white cotton)
I couldn't hold her in.

I felt her move through me, slip through my cavity,
Leave traces and essence inside me.
I heard her wails and felt her fingers claw at my womb
Desperate for something to cling to.

I felt her slipping and what could I do?

Oh Lord, Miss Carry, she's gone from me now.
She's left me hollow and sickly orange like a rotten pumpkin.
Found her remains, she took me with her.
She took her shadows, marlboros, and playthings.

Would that I could've squeezed my legs shut, even as I saw her life
   blood dripping from me.
Would that I could've resolved myself to her sins and made her pure.
And pray that it wasn't her soul
That slipped past my knees and into the cold.

I've lost myself, God. I've lost myself in What was.
She's a fleeting tendril of mist and blood,
laced with my knowledge of who she was.

Elizabeth Borghi

"American Angels"

The eyes of my mother's wisdom rest upon me.
   I am not alone.
The strength of my mother's courage invigorates me.
   I will never be alone.
The depth of my mother's love spirals into time with me.
   We are still together.

Palm Sunday was for Jesus. This Sunday is for you.
   A blessing lies upon me. I send one to you, too.
Each year I see you clearer—
   We share the daily news....
You tune me into heaven and describe the lofty views.

Please, God bless our country, and mother bless it too—
   Kiss all the little children who've just arrived to you.
They have your sweet protection, the way I always had;
   But give a special ray of love
To our heartlands tears of sad.

Elizabeth LaFrance

The Sea

The music of the sea brings hope and joy to me.
I dance with the sea gulls in their flight until
Their wings are folded for the night.
Does my existence bring purpose to this life, as
I need not perish only in strife.

I walk amongst the littlest footprints,
Pelicans dip and soar;
Sand castles left upon the shore.
The sea breeze carries my thoughts as it flows
Amongst the dangers and calm of the winds' bellows.

Where does the sky begin; where does the sea begin?
Where do I exist between these mighty forces?
Little sand crab in such a hurry
Mussels and clams ashore
Star fish with radiating arms
Sea horses with bony plates
Silver dollars on the oceans floor
Oh the sea life, I so adore.

Deborah Elizabeth Merriman

To A Purple Pansy (On Picking It Up)

Sweet little flower of royal hue,
I dedicate this verse to you;
You cause more gladness in my heart
Than sculptor's skill or painter's art.
Your skin of velvet, smooth and soft
Enraptures me, and yet how oft
We mortals heedless of your charm,
Neglect your beauty, do you harm.
Had not I picked you from the walk—
Some careless foot, perhaps by chance
A man's or else in playful dance,
A child's had crushed you 'neath its weight;
Praise be, I saved you from that fate,
And as I held you close to me,
Your purple head so glad to be
In safety in my hand, it seems
Expressed that gladness by the beams
Of radiant light from eyes of gold,
If you had words, your thanks you'd told.

Harold G. Schoenthal

Fate

I don't blame God for making the sun.
I don't blame God for making the moon and stars.
I don't blame God for crime, poverty or a TV that shuts me out.
I don't blame God for making me
But I'll make it through the best way I know how.

Julius Theodore Fields

Bobby

I received a call my father had passed away
I had to go, I couldn't say;

When I arrived it was very late
I stayed with a friend but I remember the day;

Early in the morning I looked at a vision
My brother was an angel
And he was looking at me
He had a strange smile but comforting too
I knew in my heart it was you;

Later I knew my dear brother was gone
I saw him for a moment
But that moment has been long
It dwells within my very soul
A wonderful angel is his current role.

Dee Shoemaker

Bread

I can't buy a loaf of bread because I don't have any money
I don't have any money because my job doesn't pay well
My job doesn't pay well because my company cannot compete otherwise
My company must compete because I need a job
I need a job because I need capital
I need capital because I need purchasing power
I need purchasing power because I need input in the supply/demand system
I need input in the supply/demand system because I need to have my needs supplied
I need these particular needs supplied because the government ignores my needs and spends my tax money on defense
The government spends my tax money on defense because I don't have enough purchasing power to input enough input in the supply/demand system
I don't have enough purchasing power to input enough input in the supply/demand system because I can't even buy a loaf of bread
I can't buy a loaf of bread because I don't have any money

Dave Gerardi

I Don't Know

I don't know how to talk to you
I don't know what to say.
I'm paralyzed with fear,
Afraid of what you'll do;
Afraid you'll turn away.
The only one I love is you
But this game of yours I just can't play.
It's like you're the master, and I'm the slave.
But shouldn't you be my knight in shining armor
For when it's me you'll save?
To you this game is amusing,
And yes you have the right.
To me this game is agonizing, And I'm too weak to fight.
You say you love me, And yes I believe it.
But every now and then I find myself wondering:
Do you really love me, and do you really mean it?
I want to play this game with you.
I guess I'm just crazy.
I have but one more thing to say:
As you go on in life, just please don't forget me.

Becci Nebeker

Dream

I am walking and walking.
I don't know where I am,
Although this place is familiar.

No one is around,
All is silent.
The wind dare not make a sound.
I am not afraid.

Trees line both sides of the road, I am walking.
It is fall.
The leaves are beginning to turn.

Dusk is upon me,
Shadows are cast from the setting sun.
Still unsure of where I am or even if I am me.

A fence made of fallen branches stands to my left.
Whether it is to keep in or keep out is not a worry.
For I have a fence of my own I am climbing,
Keeping me from what I used to know...

All is white,
I have woken, a sigh.
It was all a dream.

Erin J. Setzer

Untitled

In the stillness of the morning, away from all the noise
I feel the peace enfold me as it moves, without a voice.

It flows down from the mountain and across the crystal lake
It understands no barrier as my tension it seeks to take.

It steals me from my anger and puts my mind at ease
And I'm aware of nothing but this still, small, quiet peace.

It moves me beyond the words I watch flow from my pen
And I feel a certain gratitude; this peace is my best friend.

I do all I can to protect it and I cherish the time we share
And as I watch the sunrise, it's for peace I say a prayer.

Oh Lord, please give to everyone who is going through some pain
A portion of this joy within; may peace forever reign!
Julie Ann Fricker

War

The gases erode my eyes,
I cannot see.
The streets are full of burnt gunpowder and rotting corpses,
I cannot smell.
The alkaline dust rises from the street into my face,
I cannot taste.
The bombardment of the planes and the stomping of the troops' feet
  is deafening,
I cannot hear.
The figures of huddled masses and what once were people rise from the
smoke and I try to help them even though I'm burnt and bruised.
I cannot see. I cannot smell. I cannot taste. I cannot hear.
Yet I can feel.
Garrett Ericksen

Lullaby

Ah, my babe, so innocent and sweet,
(I have played 'mid the stars and sat at God's feet),
Your rosebud mouth and shell-like ears,
(I have heard God's secrets for a thousand years),
Your dimpled hands hold my heart strings,
(I have held sunrays and ridden moon beams).
Where were you, my babe, before you came to me?
(I heard the songs of angels and slept on God's knee),
Will you love me, my babe, when you know me?
(Ah, Mother, I have always know thee,
  thy name is Love).
Jane Scoggins

Your Flag

I am your National Emblem.
I emerged out of a bitter war for Independence.
My color is red, white, and blue.
I have been adopted as your special flag.
Through almost two centuries I have been called a "Living Flag."
For as I ripple in the breeze I breathe out,
Proclaiming man's freedom and his right to life,
Liberty, and the pursuit of happiness.
I grow as our nation grows.
I have ridden the seven seas; been carried into many battles.
Waved over lonely islands and floated over high mountains.
I inspired our fighting men on to battle.
A famous song was written for me, "The Star Spangled Banner."
I fly at half-staff to honor our heroic dead.
Full staff shows that the Nation lives;
And the flag is the symbol of a living nation.
I stand for the gains, hopes, and ideals of my people.
When I am passing in a parade or a review,
Please stand at attention and salute.
Be proud as your flag passes by!
Evelyn Hamilton

Friends

To one of those of a chosen few,
I give all my love and respect to thee.
For the thought of you brings a touch of bliss,
And your gentle touch makes my life complete.

Total strangers from two different worlds,
Who fulfilled their destiny to collide.
Bringing together an inseparable pair,
The devil himself could never divide.

You came and saved me from a dying soul,
With a love as true as a child's prayer.
Giving me a chance to live once again,
With the help of someone who truly cares.

You were given to me as I to you,
As the gift of mercy that only God sends.
We established a bond of the strongest love,
Shared by, those of a chosen few I myself call...

...Friends.
Edward Joseph Jachimiak

Spring Day Optimism

It was early in the morning on a cold, rainy spring day
I got out of bed, feet on the floor, I heard the weatherman say,

"It's going to be hot one, sunshine and not a breeze,
but take heart, the pollen count is down," while I heard him muffle
a sneeze.

I put on warm clothing, got ready for work and put on rain gear galore.
Rain bonnet tied tightly with umbrella in hand, went out the
kitchen door.

Got in my car, turned the ignition key, and what to my puzzled surprise?
Was that frost on the windshield or were my eyes playing tricks?
What was I to surmise?

The rain came down hard as I drove to work and I dodged puddles
and potholes galore.
"Where's that sunshine and warmth as promised this morn?" I
thought as great shades of winter lingered o'er.

"Something's wrong here!" I thought aloud. "That weather report
can't be for today.
Maybe he knows something better is coming." I live in hope and I pray.

Such optimism is great if you stop and think that one day soon it will be,
hot and humid, sunny and bright. Summer's truly coming. You'll see!
Geraldine E. Schafer

My Dream

Oh, how fast the years go by,
I have so much to do before I die.
I'd like my life to be worthwhile
And leave my name with lots of style.

I'd like to make someone happy,
make their life full of joy and love.
Keep them honest and truthful in every way
May they always learn to stop and pray.

May the love of God be with them,
as through life they go.
Trust them to love one another,
and go to Heaven some sweet day.

When our turn comes to leave this world,
May we go with a song in our hearts.
And know we are loved - like all the rest,
With God beside us it has to be the best.
Gertrude G. Howieson

Fathers Should

Fathers should do this, Fathers should do that;
But not all fathers can do this and that.
You may think your father interferes, but only because he cares.
Fathers should take you to the park or even baseball games;
But some are ill of just don't care.
My father does share; my father does care.
He may not take me to games because of his uncontrollable pain.
My father's dying from illness—too unbearable to confess.
My father's great and has an inquisitive mind;
If only he had more time. But I won't worry just yet,
I still have him every day. Well,...until that painful day.

Now that day has come; my father's now with the Heavenly Father,
Bonded and together, and will not part ever.
My father is remembered by numbers of people,
He, himself, has contributed and touched everyone around him;
He is in the light, for he has finished his part in life,
And he has left us with the forever puzzle, for he has done his part.
And in my heart, we'll never part,
For our relationship is strong and will not wither,
Eternally and forever.

Margo McNeeley

Beauty In Winter

The winter wind blows with its penetrating cold,
but somehow your radiant gaze keeps me warm.
like a fresh dusting, of the softest and purest, of white snow,
you sparkle in a different light...
ever changing, with each shift of the season's cool breezes,
and the reflective rays of a shimmering golden sun.

With each simple glance, it seems I'm frozen in time.
how will you know...
if only you could see inside,
what grows stronger with the passing of time.
your crystal blue eyes are like mystical frozen pools,
and frozen are mine, as I admire their wonder and beauty.

Quietly, the sun begins to melt away the crystals of winter's ice,
with its unrelenting heat.
unknowingly, you slowly melt a once concealed heart.
protective barriers of ice begin to crack and falter...
dissolved rivers of past love, flow gently at our feet.
finally, two captive hearts...
released together, in warmth and tenderness.

Michael G. Price

A Wishful Yearning

There is a land my eyes have never seen,
But which my heart knows exists,
Across the vast ocean,
Beyond the ethereal mists.

The forests there are old and remember the times
When children and kings would stand and look upon
Them in silence, wondering if the trickling streams
Within flowed through the faery lands, anon.

Beyond those woods lay lush grassy fields,
Rolling and peaceful, in places harbouring grazing sheep.
Beneath the grassy roots lay broken swords and splintered shields
of noble men; for blood runs hot and at times, sadly deep.

The mountains of this land are of all highlands most grand,
For when the sun shines bright the mountains fairly glist.
At times the clouds creep into the valleys, enshrouding the land
Below while the mountain tops float like islands in the mist.

The surrounding seashores are broken and rough,
And the grey sky above is filled with the gull's mournful cry.
Gazing across the land, atop a tall craggy bluff,
Someone is standing alone, brushing a tear from his eye.

Robert T. Addison

The Peanut Man

The peanut man has a wooden leg
But yet he gets around
He pushes his cart from house to house
Unshelled peanuts heaped in a mound

The maid and the children wait by the gate
As the peanut man crosses the road
His daily visit an afternoon treat
For the maid, her happiness shows

The hot Texas sun makes his black face shine
As he fills the small paper sack
Five cents a bag is all that it costs
To weary his leg and his back

Annie's in love with the peanut man
She waits for him every day
As she leans on the fence to pass the time
Her small charges run off to play

Peanut shells and broken dreams
Lie scattered on the ground
Annie the maid and the peanut man
Speak love without a sound

Marilyn Hohn Vaglia

Darkness

I have travelled far and wide,
But yet I have not travelled at all.

I have searched endlessly,
But yet I have looked nowhere.

I have been covered with darkness,
And that darkness will overcome me.

And I will have contributed nothing to life,
Or to the living.

Yes, I travelled,
But I could not see.

And I searched,
But I could not find.

E. C. Walker

Parody To Life

It's been eight years since you died,
  But you are as alive to me now as then.
I see your face, hear your voice,
  My fingertips still sense the feel of your skin.

To survive the cold waters,
  Loss and loneliness are confined deep inside;
Work, with no respite, keeps me afloat
  In a turbulent grief that will not subside.

Today, the dam that held my pain sustained a break,
  And, once again, tears poured through the breach.
They washed in waves over the pieces of my heart,
  As I struggled for a lifeline to reach.

Death is final, death is absolute;
  At least it's portrayed that way.
But, in truth, it's a parody to Life,
  It lives, and continues to mock those that stay.

Who, or what, will rescue my soul?
  And leave you, and me, at peace.
Will it be someone with love anew?
  Or death that causes the turmoil to cease!

Patricia Nicole Fultz

Your Blood Flows Through Me

No one understands. No one sees the things I see.
By force of nature, your blood flows through me.
Part of myself. The same flesh that I am made of.
Placed together, by the higher power from above.

I sit and watch you die, unsure of what to do.
No physical pain, but me, I ache too.
I knew that I would lose you. I should have said goodbye.
I wanted to hold you. I knew that you would die.

I pray at night, that you'll see the light of day.
I cry alone, 'Please God, don't take her away.'
Why you? But my tears are all in vain.
Unable to move. I watch you live in pain.

I can't stop thinking - your blood flows through me.
But you let go. Free yourself from agony.
"Hold on and fight!" I cry out in despair.
Hope for the best, but for your death I prepare.

But on this day, we say goodbye.
Not understanding why you had to die.
I'll forever love you. In my thoughts you'll always be.
Part of myself, for your blood flows through me.

Renee Husk

"Light"

Humility is a conscience of reverence and respect.
By grace we are saved; Jesus name alone is all that is need met.

A personal relationship is answers, when none can be found.
But we all shall see, when we leave this ground.

Grace is my debt to you,
For we live not in a zoo.

Life partner to have is dear,
To bless your other half.

So have no fear,
Christ's rod is your staff.

Stephen Bringhurst

Love

Love is something that has to be made,
by people that have a friendship that will never fade.
Love isn't some toy that you can play with,
and it is not just some myth.
Love is true,
but only for people who want it like some do.
Love is something that won't fade away,
as long as you keep it like the very first day.
Love is a feeling that two must hold,
not just one can form a loving mold.
Love is something that isn't a joke,
because some couples love can never be broke.
As I said before and again,
love is something that begins with two very special friends.

Rachel Hill

Afro American Woman Still Hope In Believing

To hope is to believe. To believe is to dream and to dream is to conquer. In a world of color there is madness and in a world of madness there is light and that light is belief. At times the light may flicker but as long as the flicker of light is present there is still hope. Another time, another place, hope was not known, only doubt. My word, what a world we live in. To hope is to believe and doubt is no longer a ghost that walks side by side. My sisters, continue to still hope, for it is only then that you will believe and when you believe you have won.

Pamela Caldwell

Death In The Family

A dream began
by the ghost
of a star's light.

With painted hands
they carried the drowned boy
in a coffin black as the wind.

A bride stood naked; her breast wild
and shaking with convulsions of pure hate.

Strange music as bullets
whistled crescendo
and candles tortured
romantic nights.

Then summer brought salt
to the earth and the sky turned
away from morning.

While we made an altar
in a haunted house
and watched memories
disintegrate like glass.

Louis Mulkern

The Worth Of A Child

The worth of a child can only be told
  by the one who gives life and cradles the soul,
by the one whose hand he'll hopefully hold
  whose feet he will follow in paths yet to unfold.

But many the child eyes full of despair
  whose hands hold no food and whose feet go nowhere,
no hope for the future and no one to care - just
  looking and looking for someone to share.

So please won't you help them - tell them you care,
  there's someone who loves them - no need to despair.
Yes, give of your wealth, deposit it there,
  in the life of a child, a treasure most rare.

The worth of a child is quite clear don't you see
  to the one who proclaimed, bring the children to me,
the one who gave His own life on the tree
  that life more abundant for all might be free.

    Red and yellow, black and white, they are
      precious in His sight.

Rebecca W. Engle

My Special Man

We have something special, it is easy to see
By the way that you act, whenever you are with me

And though we live many miles apart
You have taken a space deep in my heart

I have never met a man like you
You have taken control over everything I do

Not a day goes by that I don't think of you
How you make me feel, even when I'm down and blue

You put the hop back in my step
You give me hope and much confidence

In the way I feel about myself
And how I perceive everyone else

My love for you continues to grow
And this is something that you have to know

You are the best, you are my little clown
And it is my hope, that you'll stick around.

Suzanne Williams

The Ocean

The waves crash themselves against the shore fading into short calm waters crawling gently up the sand
The seaweed floating in these waves gently glide against the legs of excited children with laughs and happy screams echoing in the salty air
The sand beneath the water carpets the ocean floor with shells and rocks, some with tiny animals crawling inside
The coral reef is dazzling with a color of its own to show out in the clear blue waters
The sun's reflection in the rippling ocean sparkles far and wide making lots of glittering stars float in the sea

Lindsay Kumpf

April 16

You who are at peace with your world,
   Came into my life bringing sunshine and happiness.
Offering a good friend to be.

We talked of allowing time to let us grow,
   Giving space and room to be sure of ourselves,
That would be the best for you and me.

But time is an illusive thing,
Who are we to judge or understand,
All things take time to grow,
Yet time has its own measurement,
Whether an instant or an eternity,
We all leave footprints in the sand.

Would that I could be all you would like me to be,
   For I feel safe and secure in your hand,
Loving you means I am free to be me.

Melody Montgomery

I Hear Footsteps

   I hear footsteps coming closer. I hear footsteps coming closer. Can it be my mind, doing it one more time? Is it my lady or sister Sady? It is you Lord? Coming closer?
   You see lately, I can't sleep at night. Just me and my needle, with my belt tied tight. And I hear footsteps coming closer. Is it you Lord? Coming closer?
   My face filled with sweat, as I suck in my need. As I try not to think of the death and deceased. That has brought me this thing that keeps me alive. As I float on a cloud, in the Heavenly sky.
   And I hear footsteps, coming closer, I hear footsteps, coming closer. Is it you Lord? Coming closer? You see these sleepless nights are gettin' me all uptight. But it's crystal clear and all I hear are those footsteps, coming closer, I hear footsteps coming closer. Is it you Lord? Coming closer?
   Is it my brother Fred? That they shot in the head? Is it the man in the paper? Pulling another caper? Is it a warring? Coming early this morning? Is it you Lord? Coming closer?
   I hear footsteps coming closer. I hear footsteps coming closer. Coming closer. Coming closer. Coming closer.

Tyrone E. Woodward Sr.

Alone

I sit here quietly hiding behind my fears,
can no one see I shed real tears?
Nobody knows the real me,
my friends, teachers, and family.
Lie after lie to cover the truth,
Sometimes I wonder if I'll ever have
proof.
Maybe someday my lies can all come to
a close,
but for now I sit alone,
where nobody knows.

Shannon Anne O'Dell

Life Spring Love

The spring brings new life,
Can it bring new love?

It brings forth the flowers.
It calls out the bees.
It makes the sun brighter, on the new budding leaves.

It brings out the newborn.
It awakens the sleeping bear.
It melts away the last remains, of winter's icy lair.

It rings with the bird song.
It adds color to the land.
It washes away wintery thoughts with the sweep of its
   magic hand.

Will it bring out the excitement?
Will it awaken forgotten dreams?
Will it melt away the pain we've known, like a
   mountain's winter streams?
Has it rung with a new hope?
Has it added the chance to share?
Has it washed away the doubts I had, about whether I'd love or care?
The spring brings new life, and it brought a new love!

Troy D. Renault

A View From The Kitchen Window

The view from the kitchen window
can never be surpassed;
too bad these lovely colors
cannot - ever - last.

We look forward to the change of seasons;
it's a gift to us each year.
One morning we will awaken and
our winter will be here.

The trees have never been more gorgeous;
it is a study in black and white.
It has been just a few short weeks
since the colors were gold'n - bright!

The limbs are so very heavy
the winter snow has come;
the ice that came behind it
is that which troubles some!

Our fairyland will soon be gone;
we are looking now to spring.
Mother Nature has been busy;
the WEATHER is her THING!!!

Wilda Kathryn McVeigh

Cockroaches

Raid, shoes, and even bombs,
Can't kill these bugs that fit in your palms.
You can step on them; you can freeze them cold,
but they can't be killed, I was told.
They don't know the meaning of "nothing to eat"
They can eat anything, even 5 year of meat.
Papers, erasers, glue, and paint thinner
Are all served at a cockroach dinner.
Even worse these things can FLY! Trust me, I do not lie.
I found this out the hard way when I saw this roach right on my pen.
I moved slowly and grabbed a book,
Not a sound I made; not a breath I took.
Then just before my hand went down,
It spread its wings and turned around.
It took off straight towards my dad.
I heard him scream, what I laugh I had!
But then it started heading south.....
.....right into my-uh-open mouth.
The rest of this story I will not say,
But if I see a roach, it'll PAY!!

Robert Hyun Wook Woo

Afterthought

People have asked
Can't God see? Can't God hear?
How can He let this be?
Why does He not care?

But far away (but not far enough)
in a corner of the universe
sits He who carries the heaviest weight of all
and God hears, and God sees
and God feels
but shackled by the gift of free-will given
He is stricken
He can do nothing
only man/woman can
only you can
He can only watch and hope
as man uses/misuses His gifts

And there in the folds of endless night
huddled down amongst the scattered stars
waiting for us to grow up

God weeps
Wim R. Sweerman

Facing Fifty

Left my billfold in the store.
Can't remember to shut the door.
Wonder what this key is for?
Menopause makes me stupid!

Broke the mirror on my van.
Cannot sleep without my fan.
Burned my finger on a hot cake pan.
Menopause makes me stupid!

Can't remember my cousin's name.
Forgot my daughter's baseball game.
Am I the only one who's sane?!
Menopause makes me stupid!

Organization is no more.
I buy the wrong things at the store.
Someone - help me - what's four plus four?
Menopause makes me stupid!

For several years it's been this way.
There'll be more, or so "they" say.
You better not laugh, 'cause one of these days,
Menopause might make *you* stupid!
Linda Perero

She Is...

Like a country road beneath a cloudless velvet night
casting shadows with the silvery blue moonlight,
she helps me see when once I could not.
Wherever I travel upon this earthen plane,
incognito to protect myself from this world's pain,
yet always knowing she has given me a safe haven in which to stop.
Like a rain soaked forest on the edge of nowhere
sustaining with life-giving richness to spare,
I feel her hand of help though I may never see.
Knowing far less than pretention should dictate,
the facade crumbles like so much sandstone under a mountain's weight-
still she teaches me the one thing that will be true endlessly.
Like a jester playing beneath scornful eyes in the King's court,
or a buck skinned scout posted in the splintery tower of the soldier's fort
she keeps me alert to make the most of my life.
Feeling incomplete, like a puzzle with too few pieces,
I searched 'til I found one who could iron out my stubborn creases.
She is all I desire and more - she is my wife.
R. Kevin Hughes

A Carefree Summer

Mornings of hungry anticipation for what summer's mugginess will bring
Carefree and vibrant with energy naturally
But how today?

The friends arrive as the mercury pushes farther
They don't carry much
Only bright coverings to contrast their bronzed skin

Ker-plunk! Plunge!
The water's glass is broken
Changes from sweat to refreshed is almost euphoric
Smiles grow from the relieved and are passed to spectators
Ker-plunk! Plunge!

A top is down on a misty white '68 Camaro
"All Aboard!" shouts the driver
Three long locks of flaxen hair whip about carelessly
as the sun changes hue

The sun leaves but refuses to take the humidity
Psssss, the feel of cold relief
Solarcaine becomes indigenous with the evening.

"Ready for tomorrow?" the girl asks her friend
"You bet!"
Kristin Kae Zaun

Real Life

Down and out feelings fill a crowded bus stop
Children fight in empty, dusty lots
And Charlie routinely searches through the refuse
Beneath my bedroom window with a view

Cars honk angrily at one another in the deep night
A starless sky stares at the violent city
And as usual Mr. Robles closes the "tienda" very late
Across from my bedroom window with a view

The sun-drenched park contains all types of citizens
High schoolers wander the streets for answers to life
And there's the ice cream truck pied-piping along the block
Beside my bedroom window with a view

Shadows dance and flaunt their ambiguous forms
A barking dog and bright threatening moon serve as scenery
And here I am again sleepless and annoyed
As I lay underneath my bedroom window with a view
A. K. Garcia

Just After Midnight

The solemn night
creeps around my door.
The occasional creak of loose boards
and the wind slightly, almost hollowly
whistles over the teeth of the shingled rooftop.

The moon is bare
polished over by raindrop prisms.
Brilliance screaming over the slick
saturated street, sleek like a winding black asp.

The air is unfamiliarly cold and empty.
Hollow is the roadside, all wandering shadows
have retreated to the bedrooms, reciting poetic motions
and provocative ritual, Yes, that is where shadows are.

The solemn night
closed up the neighborhood.
The occasional drunk stumbles aimlessly to his home.
He curses while his boots stagger and
tromp through and around loosely scattered
puddles of liquid moonlight.
Matt Gooding

Market Day

Fragrant cargoes of cardamon, cumin,
cinnamon and spice fill
the sultry morning air.
The sweet decay of overripe papaya,
passion fruit, and pineapple
is sticky with flies.
Fish, chicken, and goat entrails
hang blooded, limp.
Jasmine, orchids, and
freshly cut roses —
aromatic, drench the air.
Dark-skinned merchants with shiny black hair
bargain from simple wood tables,
crowds shuffle, throbbing with sweat.
The echo of Hindi startles me,
"Baksheesh, Baksheesh" — a deal is struck.

Peter Quinn

Baby's First Snowfall

Snowsuit, scarf and boots, size two.
Clip-on mittens, soft and new.
Glowing cheeks and shining eyes.
As he looks at the snow with great surprise.

He builds a snowman, mini-style.
He plops right down to rest awhile.
He catches snowflakes on his tongue.
So innocent, so very young.

He tumbles face first to the snowy ground.
Chuckles of laughter, the only sound.
Soaked to the skin, he is carried inside.
Pampered and powdered and towel-dried.

Content, he drifts off to sleepy land.
Sucking the thumb of his tiny hand.
A baby is beautiful, make no mistake.
If he can find joy in a single snowflake.

Sandra Marie Jensen

"Dear Little One"

You came to visit grandma last night,
   clutching your dolly with fist clinched tight.
We lit the lamp in your "special" room,
   and peeked out the window for "our" moon.
Now time to create shadows on the wall -
   scary creatures of great-others small.
We shared make-believe; some wishes too.
   Our secret world stood still - for me - for you.
Your green eyes laced with blue and brown
   captured by a face with a golden crown,
soon fell heavy without a fight -
   and as slumber crept in and stole the light,
I felt your breath of life kiss my face -
   like a wispy butterfly in haste,
building precious memories for grandma to hold -
   more priceless treasure than any gold.....

Maxine Haddox

My Dream

My dream is to fly away
from the sadness of each day
I dream so long
daydreams and night dreams about all the wrong
I dream about my life and theirs
even though we aren't all pairs
My dream is to stop all the sadness
Even though I might not pass it

Maria Lombardi

"A Little Hug Will Do"

I was feeling rather low.
Cold November winds had begun to blow.
It was really getting me down.
I'd even wondered why I'd gone to town.
Then all of a sudden at my side I felt a tug.
You whispered, "Could I ask you for a hug?"
I'd almost forgotten the warmth of friendship.
Yet in a moment in your arms I was off on a long, long trip.
You'll never know the joy you brought.
Happiness which I promise will never be forgot.
But anytime, my friend, you feel you need a squeeze,
You may ask me if you please.
Perhaps a little hug is the thing I miss most in life.
It's so hard to go on alone in a world so full of strife.
And yet, I forgot to thank you, dear,
For bringing me so much cheer.

Rodger Diederich

Spreading the Sand

"Wait!" the people cried.
"Come back here, or you shall die!"

George and Lennie did quite the contrary.
They ran to a place that was quite far away.
They slaved, and they prayed
That they might have a house some day.

Until one day a lady asked Lennie to play with her hair;
Which he did ever so fair
'Til she gave a frightful scream.
Then she was no more.

Lennie ran far, far away;
George tried to keep up just the same.

George shot Lennie in the head;
Then Lennie was no longer living—because he was dead.

All their dreams of living off the fat of the land
Had all disappeared in the spreading of the sand.

Melissa Wagner

Reality 2

Often do I wander here and there,
Communing with my Love in silent speech.
The air alone is witness, as we bare
Ourselves and dream as far as we can reach.

We need no words to herald our pleasure,
We need no voice to sing love's glorious songs.
My soul retains all beauty without measure
While reveling in life's rights, but ne'er its wrongs.

I summon scenes I wish to contemplate.
Sadness is always there! Why waste thoughts on it?
I choose to think the thoughts I love, not hate,
Much as I choose the rhymes to write this sonnet.

   Reality, for me, includes the skill
   To pause and linger at a window sill.

Sidney L. Teitelbaum

Rusty Memories

Pictures of my childhood fluttering through my mind,
entering unbidden at unwanted times.
An invaded memory lying below the surface of reality.
Sounds stolen from the past and preserved to rise to the top of
bubbling consciousness.
A bubble of memory increasing to a point of realism.
then busting, leaving me once again with only
RUSTY MEMORIES.

LuJuan Bartlett

Dealing With It

Pain is uncontrollable
Control is manipulation
This is something most people desire
The truly smart folk know
That manipulation is an illusion

Then there are those who seek solace
They want rest and ease from fantasy
This apparition is like a drug
This toxin causes pain, obsession, insanity
Too much of this narcotic can lead to Death

Death also cannot be controlled
Nor is it a manifestation
So. What is Death?
   Death is a path
     The path to the ultimate
        R E A L I T Y
There you will find your ANSWER!!
Thomas J. Bean

Babylon

Got that rhythm and it makes me lose
control, just rock and roll on the
radio—it ain't nothing more

My music has the rhythm to make you
lose control, dust 'n bones—to live
and let die, they're right next door to
hell, and you'll think that nothing matters,
it's just the rhythm of your mind—
Mr. Tinkertrain was in the dope you smoked,
Gee.....I wonder why?

Babby's been heard, he's in the air—
his power only comes in the chanting
of his words

-so if you smoke and listen, you've
chosen his conditions—to make the
trade, a wish for your soul

You may not know but eventually you
will care, Baby's been playing with your
head, you're sanity's left on the line—so
wake up, it's time to get scared.
Robert Lloyd Correia

"Ode To The Four Seasons"

I love the seasons in Missouri,
Especially spring, when all things are new
You're never really all alone,
'Cause nature practically talks to you.

Summer has its special days,
Like barbecues and fishing.
With friends and family's laughing ways,
In winter, I'll be missing.

As autumn's leaves of green and gold,
Drift slowly down and cover the ground,
It signals the end of the summer sounds,
Waiting for the winter's shivering cold.

Shadows of oak trees fall upon the ground,
Like great giant sticks, but without a sound.
The snow falls gently 'round their base,
Softening their fall with elegance and grace.

But I love the seasons in Missouri
You never know what to expect.
I might say, "show me something different,
That you haven't shown me yet"……
Margaret H. Bills

A Gift To You

If you've ever walked a sandy beach
  cool wind blowing in your hair,
Make note of timeless dreams
  sure to have taken you there.

If you've ever stood before a rush of falling water
  exploding at its base,
Then remember a feeling deep inside
  as its mist embraced your face.

And if ever meadows of green
  or mountains of steep
Have held you by stare,
  Thank God for his gift that he gave
For all to share.
Robert C. Counselman

The Best Things In Life

What are the best things in life?
   Could it be watching the fiery morning
   sun come up over the horizon?
   Or maybe watching the multicolored evening
   sunsets?
   Could it be watching the moon's
   shadow shimmering over a still lake.
   Or enjoying a blazing fire
   in the hearth of a fire place
   could it be enjoying a delicious
   meal in a fine restaurant
   maybe lazing around a campfire
   high above in the mountains
   could it be savoring the love
   of a beautiful man or woman.

   Could it be all of these things?

What are the best thing in life?
Wallace J. Schexnyder

The Promise Of A Heart

Have I written my own fate?
Created my own star?
Is this moment very far?

How long must I wait?
How long must I wonder?
When will I find out what spell I am under?

Is my heart broken? Is it being mended?
Is salvation still free to all those yet repented?

Should I fall again?
Should I stay?
Will she push me over when it comes the day?

Is it worth the pain?
Is it worth the sorrow?
Will the sun shine upon my heart tomorrow?

What went wrong before?
Who was to blame?
Is she calling out my name?

Should I learn from the past?
Should I make a new start?
Can I hide behind the promise of a heart?
William Joe Lister

The Star In My Life

As the darkening of the sky was moving across the heavens, like a creeping shadow, chasing off the last ray that the sun has absently left lingering behind. And the round, golden bronze, orange color of the sun had finally sunk down for the night to a slumber of sleep. I was sitting high on a grassy hill, where the grass still carried the lingering smell of a fresh cut. The crickets were singing, whistling, hopping and skipping for their mates, while the fire flies were flashing their small but encouraging light to lead the way for romance. The air was crisp and there was a rising of a breeze that gently blew across the trees to do nothing but ruffle and shuffle the leaves. And then it happened — someone was sprinkling handfuls of glitter across the sky. They were flashing, twinkling, glinting, shimmering, gleaming and glistening in the cloudless night. Then one of them caught my attention — it was the one that was competing with the others, to see if it could glow brighter than a electromagnetic radiation of any wavelength. The brightness and the clearness was so splendid, until it was just a shining and blinding white light. As I sat there, staring up at the star that out shone the others, surrounded by the velvet midnight blue of the sky, a striking resemblance of your face came to mind. The star must have known, as it illuminated the starling reflection of you. Then it hit me, out of all the sparkling, twinkling, dazzling stars in the sky, the one star that radiated its brilliant, luminous, incandescence of light, was the one that could forever shine in my life.

Rachalle Denise Jackson

Jesus

Everyone has an angel of their very own, all because of the cross and the crown made of thorns.

All of God's angels watch us. We could be anywhere, even on a bus. One day back on Calvary, they killed Jesus, some people, not everybody.

Jesus' angels help to keep an eye on us. If we're doing good we probably would get an A+.

God is the creator; he created you and me. Without him in your life you're nothing. Can't you see?

All of God's first angels didn't have a choice, but when he made us, he made us with rejoice.

When you pray to Jesus and you live in a bad area, pray to him that you'll wake up the next day. And maybe you'll hear a message that everything is going to be okay.

Keep Jesus in your head and in your heart. Stay close to him, don't get far apart.

So when you pray to Jesus, pray real loud. Don't worry he'll get the message even through those thick, thick, clouds!

Tamika Lane

You Whose Painful Diadem

You whose painful diadem
Crowned the son of God.
You whose bladed, piercing stem
Lifts itself from out the fertile sod.
You whose ivory and scarlet cousins
Enticed the nobles to clash.
You whose beauty conceals your sins
And whose endurance recreates you from scorched earths ash.
You who would taint the innocence
Of a child's wandering hand with blood,
Represent the harbored love of hearts and hence
Would be greeted with the tears of a ladies eyes who flood
Your petals with the essence of joy or grief.
No doubt so many worship you with the tender passions of belief.

Miguel Angel

Mommy

Someone's always getting up in the middle of the night
Crying, "Mommy, I need to go to the bathroom" or
"Mommy, I'm thirsty, get me a drink" or "Mommy, I'm frightened by my bad dreams."
I don't lose my head, holler, burst or scream.
I can hardly remember a thing.
I'm always in a comatose state.
But I'm the mommy and I love them.
I'm there to combat their childhood fears and kiss their salty tears.
I'm there to get out of bed, hold them close, and caress their head.
I'm the mommy and I love them.
Someone's always getting in trouble and into fights.
Crying, "Mommy, the other children aren't nice."
"Mommy, kiss my boo-boo and bring me some ice."
I'm there to combat their childhood fears and kiss their salty tears.
I'm there to listen and teach them how to play fair.
Every night when I rest my weary head I pray:
Our children are the future and we are their guiding light.
For as long as I am their Mommy and I love them they will turn out all right.

Stacy L. Carner

Beloved Baylee

I imagine you brought joy to your parents when you came into the world Curiosity ruled when you learned to crawl and be free to explore the house. That milk and apple juice tasted better than pureed spinach and carrots. You cried and wanted held as many times as you saw Mom come and go in your room. You uttered your first word but made unsuccessful attempts on your first step.

I imagine your first days in pre-school hiding behind your mother's skirt and refusing to let go. Making friends, playing games, learning ABC's, singing aloud your favorite nursery songs. Your baby tooth fell and the Tooth Fairy gave you a quarter. Your senior prom and great adventures as you leave home for college.

I will not be able to imagine what color your eyes were. Shut close as your small lifeless body hung limp in a rescuer's arms. Your clothes were full of dirt and blood gushed out of your tiny head. A poignant picture of a man-made disaster meant to kill flashed across the country. A feeling of loss and sadness around the world for you and those who perished that day left us all wondering why this had to happen, why Oklahoma City? Why us?

Your parents will never see your goal oriented years of two. A senseless vindictive idealist took your young life away. Today and forever we will remember you and those who died in our prayers. God Bless You Baylee, may your soul rest in peace.

Sonia M. Janecki

The Forever Living Rose

There is a forever living rose. It's the memory of a
dear friend, which lives in our hearts and grows
when we talk of them in that remembering way
I knew someone special I turned my thoughts to today
If that friend leaves or has passed away.
They live as a forever rose in your heart
and will be with you each day.
And when a crisis comes, and Death has taken the toll
No one need ask, for whom the bell tolls
For in each heart alive today, will remember the awful days
But those who have passed aren't gone, in my heart as a rose
live on. Goodbye is but a worn out phrase,
that people tend to overuse these days
For if you remember they truly aren't gone
And you see them again in a breeze or in a song
I'll remember those who've cried and sadly I'll remember
those who died if I only know a relative's
tears. I'll remember that through the years
And if still, you forget this prose
I'll never forget the forever living rose.

Wendy R. Kephart

Desolate

Dying is all a part of life, but I crave death
Death is a desired yearning to go far away
Every living person has a hole inside them
This hole is filled with thoughts
Once you find this hole, you know your true
definition of death
To see him again
To hold his hand once more, that would be heaven
I cry for him, for thing I wish he could see
He will never see me graduate
He won't be here to walk me down the isle
We won't ever go hunting together at the
farm on Christmas
I won't ever see him laugh again
I'm going to miss the little sayings he always said.
But he never told me he loved me.
I guess he thought I knew.
There is a land of the living and a land of the dead,
and the bridge is love,
The only survival, the only meaning.

Teresa Ezell

Do You Hear My Voice?

The world around us so different from the one I knew.
Death is on the run with our youth.
Value of life seems now uncouth.

I know that people and things must grow.
Can we afford to take our hands off before they know.
Children smiling, carefree and gay is not how they live today.

Self-worth must be instilled in our youth or they will pay.
The price is DEATH in spirit and soul.
  DO YOU HEAR MY VOICE?

It's the voice of pain and rejection
For children have too few who seem to care.
We must put aside our material values and let them see
The rewards of spiritual ones.
  DO YOU HEAR MY VOICE?

Yes, we have a choice.
Turn back the hands of time to a place where love
and values and hope were a part of youth.
There's no reason for our children to say,
  DO YOU HEAR MY VOICE?

LaVerne Chamberlain

"Death By Understanding It"

I don't care how old you are, trying to understand
death plagues everyone, both young and old, alike!
Someone that you've known for years could be alright
one day and dead the next. So the next time you're
around your favorite friend or relative, express your
feelings towards that person...maybe go to a good
movie together, go horse back riding together, go shopping
for a new outfit or go out to lunch or maybe dinner;
whatever your interests are just make it a positive one!
suffering from long time illness, people sometimes never
ever get better so take lots of pictures so that the memories
will not be forgotten! So that many years after they are not gone
we can gather around that old kitchen table and talk about the
nice times we had with them on this particular day or that day.
Choosing the right coffin and making sure it's the right
size for the person that just died, also making sure that it
goes along with the color that the loved one liked. Plus
staying with the mortuary that was so friendly to us when grandpa
died last year and remembering those visits to the cemetery.

Robin Marie Walsh

Lines To A Physician

Dedicated to Dr. H. C. Mayer
His golden craft was more than skill alone.
For few have worn the mantles of his art
Who dared to look beyond the flesh and bone -
And understand the sorrows of the heart.

And yet, I think it was the love he gave
That healed as certain as the surest knife,
And there could be no finer calling save
The skills that pushed aside the foes of life.

Henceforward now, we'll walk a sterile hall
Without his wisest judgement to transcend,
And there are some who won't be strong at all
As none can compensate a cherished friend.

Leisures now are his, that every day may bring,
And we are sworn to fond remembering.

Rosemary Muntz Yasparro

Six Little Feet Under The Table

The night is cold and the chill winds blowing
Deep crunchy snow on the patio, and it's still snowing.

The six little feet have just rushed in the door.
To receive the warm good food as they'd done before.

Damp little plaid stockings, and round toed shoes,
Over restless little feet and cold, cold toes.

The six little feet, now around the ample table,
To eat the warm food, and listen to a story or fable.

Blond curly heads, now are ready for slumber
As the story time's over, and the mantel
clock chimes the right number.

Wondering tonight - Where are those little feet?
Are they hungry, sad, lonely or cold?

Now that they've grown, and I'm growing old,
trusting all to God, as this story is told.

Marian G. Weber

Angel Alert

Throughout the Bible it is plain to see,
  God created angels to watch over you and me.
God has many angels that go unaware,
  You may meet them as strangers, you know not where.

Some come to you on a beam of light,
  Others make their presence all dressed in white.
When you first see them it almost seems,
  You are just having one of your dreams.

You may wonder where angels are to be found,
  When God's children are in trouble there they abound.
An angel stopped Abraham's upraised hand,
  Saving Isaac's life for that of a ram.

And after Jesus with Satan his battle won,
  Angels gathered and ministered to God's only son.
They also troubled the waters, of the pool where the sick did cram,
And will be blowing their trumpets with the return of the great "I Am"

Angels are trained to give special care,
  To help God's children who are in despair.
So always be watching and never have fear,
  If trouble comes to you, your angel is near.

R. W. Nelson

Housefire

I bit down hard upon my soul, denied myself the tears,
Denied me let to think, forget, denied it all these years.
But three dead kids will not let me forget them, then or now
Tears not yet cried won't be denied. I'm not yet certain how

I need to deal with smoke-rough voice: "I got a live one here!"
And how we saw them reaching up to one last child so dear,
She turned her head and then was dead ... we all had lost the race,
The Loo just stood and held her, grief's carvings on his face.

I remember three dead children, lying still beneath their sheets,
Their resting-place upon the grass their mother mowed so neat.
I remember how their house burned. I remember most the smell
Of smold'ring dampened cloth goods, and the roasted flesh of hell.

I remember three dead children as I knelt by them in prayer,
Coat open and my helmet off, I drank of smoke-stained air.
I marvelled that they could not move, throw off their sheets and play,
To taste with me the hell-stained air....
....that dead they'd always stay.
   Linn Keller

Painted Feet

Lying on the floor, he scans his surroundings,
desperately searching for some excitement.
Suddenly, he spies a living canvas—
his sister's foot, soft and fleshy,
resting within his reach.
While she's sleeping soundly, he grabs
his new paint set and gently works her toes
into five rolling waves. Next, a beach appears
with miniature crabs scampering to find shade.
With a splash of brown, and streaks of lime,
her ankle becomes a palm tree
gently blowing in the breeze.
Upon completion, his artwork done,
his sister is awakened.
Expecting praise, he's disappointed.

"MOTHER!" my sister screams.
But I'm not scolded,
for Mom's too busy laughing.
"No one move," she tells us both,
"I'll run and get a camera!"
   Quinn Weber

"Tell Me Mommy"

Tell me mommy is it true what they're saying
did those guys really go to the moon
were they shot into the sky 'round the middle of July
and it's so far, how come they made it back so soon.

They must have had to use a giant road map
to find their way up there and back again
Weren't they afraid that they'd get lost and how much did it cost
they must have had a lot of nerve, those men

Tell me mommy what it was that they found up there
is it true that it's really made of cheese
did the man in the moon hate to see them leave so soon
and when he asked them to come back, did he say please

I heard them mention something 'bout the dark side
did they find out why there wasn't any light
did they forget to pay their bill and tell me if you will
How long before they make another flight.

Now Mommy if you'll answer all these questions
I'll gladly close my eyes and try to find
some way to say a prayer and thank the Lord up there
that they took that giant leap for all mankind.
   Walter R. Brown

We Are Still One

From the time of our creation we have been one.

Sharing a common land. As tribes we set out in different directions, East, West, North, South, and those in-between.

And we are still one.

Creating nations of various names. Even our tongues are foreign to one another.

And we are still one.

We possess skin color that varies from one another, caused by geographical climate.

And we are still one.

Unfortunately, the masses fail to realize — we are still one.
   Renaldo Raeheim

Magic Of Morning

Crispness cuts with morning light,
Disembowels the cold, still night,
Sweet souls pause from endless flight,
Heavenly morning, such a glorious sight.

With eyes closed, we leave our scholars behind,
For but a moment, we close our mind,
All lonely children can then be so kind,
What humanity paints is not all we find.

Truthfulness awakes, and then we pray,
Cleansing dew of grace, on the grass it lay,
Birds rejoicefully singing, always find their way,
Lovely magic of morning, brings another day.
   Terrance R. Giddens

What Might Have Been

Do you think of me now? Did you think of me then?
Does your mind go back to way back when?

Are you ever at work, or an evening of play, and
your thoughts take you to that time and that day?

When you're with someone, and her scent is the same
as what I once wore, do you call her my name?

Would you change what you did, or change what you said,
to keep our love from now being dead?

Would you choose with care your words and your deeds,
because you now know where that road leads?

What would you do, what would you have done,
to make our failed union of two into one?

Do you think of me now? Did you think of me then?
Do you ever wish for what might have been?
   Talitha Eastridge Norris

Springtime

Flowers, flowers smell the air
Cheerful flowers everywhere
Sun a-shining oh so bright
Makes you feel all warm and light

Here the birds tweet their song
Listen to them all day long
Watch them in their tree so tall
Sitting, looking, no care at all

If you feel so mad and sad
Read this poem you'll feel glad
This one's made just for you
So please try to read it when you're blue
   Shelby Matheson (8-17-1980 / 2-3-1994)

"Our Country Is Calling You Dear"

Though our country has called you, dear,
Doesn't keep me from wanting you here.
But if all our boys should back off
And lag, it would cause us to
Lose our good old freedom flag.

But darling since all this war has started
I stay at home all broken hearted.
So darling do your best to keep our
Stars and stripes waving over our
Land and I'll send up a prayer to
God to guide you with his mighty hand.

And when our country's freedom you
Boys have won on land and sea
I'll send a prayer to God for your
Safe return to me.

Linda Smith

"For Stacey"

Thinking of you!
Don't blame yourself for the situation you're in,
for it isn't you that committed the sin.

You've had a tough life for sure,
Which no one but me is aware of it more.

Be kind to your children when you are crying,
They will give you support and love and are trying,
To comfort you with their love and concern,
That you will not have to continue to earn.

Those three precious boys are as anxious as you,
Because their future is uncertain too.

You need to have strength to deal the pain.
That has returned to be with you again.

Because you're low and so sad,
The days that are to come can't be as bad.

So pull your own strings and get up and get busy,
kicking Tracey's butt all around that tin lizzy!

Kay North

Angry At God

Dear God, Why Did You Take Him?
Don't you know that we weren't through?
They say that you know all, Ahh but I don't think you do.
Because if you did you wouldn't have taken him so soon.
My dear God who art in Heaven, well did you make a big mistake?
And did you take the wrong one?
For we'd had plans that we'd told no one
Well if you have it in your heart to bring one back
would you let it be him?
So we could watch the rising sun, do a little fishing and
have some real fun.
Well they say that you know all, Ahh but I don't think you do
Because if you did, you wouldn't have taken him so soon.......

Priscilla Emory

Mama

About my Mama, there could never be -
enough words or phrases to express her beauty.
Always there when you need her, never caring of herself,
she'll try to do the impossible - and do it very well.
When I was younger, I didn't appreciate
all the things she did for me, and that was a mistake.
For now that I am older, and understand her kind of love,
I'm sorry for all the days I missed returning the above.
This is for you, Mama, though it may be late,
I love you and I'll always care in my very special way.

Susan M. Buckley

The Rain

The raindrops slide silently
down the window,
Like the tears that slide
down my face.

The rain beats a crazy
pattern on the tin roof,
Like the beat of life dancing
inside my head.

The skies are gray,
lifeless and cloudy,
Like the dark and gloomy corners of my mind.

The leaves hang limply on the trees
from the weight of the rain,
Like my spirit so tired of the burden I must carry.

The rain seeps deep into the ground,
Like the loneliness seeping deep into my soul.

Still the rain continues until it floods all,
and nothing can be seen but pools of dark still water.

And still I continue until the bleakness and sorrow
overflow from my mind and I see nothing but a dark silent future.

Veronica Einhellig

I Used To.....

I used to be in first grade,
Drawing and cutting and pasting,
But now that I'm in sixth grade
Time I can't be wasting!

I used to be in second grade,
Scared witless of the lunch line,
But now that I'm in sixth grade
I get along just fine!

I used to be in third grade,
And I thought that boys had cooties,
But now that I'm in sixth grade
I found out, I like those cooties!

I used to be in fourth grade,
And boys were handing me chewed-up gum,
But now that I'm in sixth grade
I found out, that they've grown up some!

I used to be in fifth grade
And I thought I got a lot of homework,
But now that I'm in sixth grade
I found out that I liked that easy homework!

Laura Lyon

Shadows, Others Have Spoken

Others have spoken of your footsteps,
but one night I saw something more,
as I walked alone, cold, and tired
as I prayed for one step more.
   The light shone over my shoulder,
and looking I saw two shadows;
one short like mine and one tall
as if intertwined, one leading the other.
   The next step came after the other
until the door I entered was warm and lighted
and the cold was no more.
   The shadows were one; the tall one
had not gone but merely been waiting to be called upon,
out of love He came, shone His light and then was gone;
but only by sight for like most great things
that are not seen but only felt, remained.

Julia Love

"Dreams"

Dreams, what you always wanted!
Dreams, "Future"! Dreams, one couldn't live if we didn't have them!
Dreams, there's no life if I can't have my dreams!
Sometimes it is better to keep it like that, so that we have something
  to dream about!
Dreams, so that we can sleep as a feather, and not as a rock!
Dreams, what you always wanted, but you just can't have it!
Dreams,
Keep it like that so that you won't get bored with dreaming in
every night!
Dreams,
Sometimes, as bad as we want our dream to come there, we just can't!
Dreams,
Why? Because they are dreams and that's what makes our
sleeping so delightful as the real world!
Dreams,
Because, we as humans, compare dreams with real life, and that's
so wrong.
Dreams, think about it! God gave us all a mind to think.
Dreams should not interfere with real life.
  Shantal Gonzalez

Spring In Virginia

Every yard is aburst with beautiful blooms
  Each one is a sight to behold
With azaleas in pink and purple and white
  And forsythia - fireworks of gold!

The tulips so daintily push their way up
  With an irresistible force
They've been primping all winter long
  To be there for the show, of course.

The sparkling white dogwood towering near
  Look like heaps of snow, piled high
Their cross-shaped white blossoms almost appear
  To be tatting, starched, hung out to dry.

The potted geraniums sit on the steps
  And they nod at each passing breeze
The faithful old lilacs bring year after year
  Sweet fragrance - and sweet memories.

There are places on earth with beauty to spare
  We've seen some and heard of the rest
But for eye-popping, heart-stopping glorious sights
  Virginia in spring is the best!
  M. M. Bales

"The Bells"

Float in the sound of the Bells
ear to the ground, hear the Bells.

Hear the drums and the horns
see the vines filled with thorns
and listen now, to the Bells.

Here presented to you are the Bells.
Drawn from grace that I drew,
see the Bells.

Above all that I've sold—
more that silver and gold...
are the sounds, oh the sounds of the Bells.

Close your eyes and smile...
see the Bells.
In your mind for a while...
are the Bells.

Of the Light and Divine
(which can never be mine!)
is the rich, high pitched sound of the Bells.
  Rebecca H. Smith

Youth

How slowly life travels, it seems, as a child.
Each second an hour, each inch is a mile
And the fusing of days, all ones like the rest.
All endless tomorrows, there is no past.
But slowly the tempo increases its pace.
You started out walking, but now it's a race.
The future is coming, much faster, it seems.
There isn't much time, to complete all your dreams.
Then nature takes over, with a saving device.
It whispers its song, with some timely advice.
Your life is a minute, when traveling through time.
But it'll leave impressions, for others to find.
  Raymond J. Mendez

My Grandson

HE finally arrived one bright April Day!
Eagerly welcomed and loved from the start,
Kevin, my grandson, found his place in my heart.
He grew with rosy cheeks, big brown eyes
(and oh! Those endearing smiles).

A delightful child, a handsome boy, shy in many ways,
Sensitive, caring and sometimes belligerent
Forming his personality, that makes each of us different.

He struggled through his early teens,
At odds with some of his fears
That follow the young in their growing-up years,
To a tall, handsome, virile young man leaving his childhood behind
To take up life's challenge; to see what awaits
It's such a big step, closing those gates.

My hopes and prayers will be following him,
As he leaves this era to go on to another
For the big world out there is his, to discover.
  Loretta Gillis

Pain And Death

Drowse days, sleepless night.
Can't fall asleep, just turn off the light.
The problem here too far and low,
My mind won't reach - so I don't know.
The status of my being is too much to fully withstand,
When I fall, on my feet, is how I hope to land.
The tears are only drowning me,
And the lying on the side.
Is the only place I find that is somewhat safe to hide.
The synthetic feeling that I dare to share with all,
The reason why I use them is to cover up what's raw.
The glass eye that I looked out through saw the murder of my own.
It wasn't my eye so I can't testify for your high and unworthy throne.
  Suzanne Sword

Her Laughter

Her laughter rose on throaty trills of glee;
Drawing me to realms of risk, it set my spirit free.
A traveler in rare atmospheres of space,
My soul floated on a chord beyond my earthbound place.
Her eyes laughed along; sparkling sapphire bright,
They enveloped me in fiery embers of delight.

Now that she has gone to another realm,
I search for my own humor; my hand is at the helm
To plot the curious charting of my way.
Still, her essence fills me with the wonder of the day.
With the crisp new dawn and the morning star,
A treble spark erases time. Reaching from afar,
Joy sweeps a tufted seed its breezy way,
And her laughter finds my heart to trim with warmth today.
  Mary Lee Friesz

Seasons

The view I have shows color anew —
Early fall bringing early hue.
I ponder calendars — months and years —
And suddenly find I'm full of fears.

To look behind, so long ago —
I now know much I did not then know.
Events have come, events have gone —
Memories I'll hold for long.

To look ahead, God knows the path —
I wonder what, for me, He hath?
So many dreams, so much desire
To stay always for Him on fire.

Suddenly, reality sets in —
Will I use these years as I did those then?
Trials and joys I have yet to face —
May I pass through each aware of His grace.

To learn from mistakes, to not regret,
To live each day as I haven't yet —
This I wish, but one thing most —
To always glorify the Lord Of Hosts!

Mary Bainter Bishop

The Decision

Can't decide, haven't chosen yet
Endless safe choices, nothing but regret

Do something right, decide now
Fall in line like the rest, I don't know how

Answer the call, so much expected
Unfulfilled potential, future unprotected

Do your best, pass the tests
The good life is there
Choose your fate despite what's great
Life is hardly fair

It's done, you're on your way
The green flag's waving, it starts today

A new career and life's begun
Now you're set, but have you won?

What you do is who you are
Unfair condition
Consistent urging pressures
Make the decision.

Scott G. Gutheil

The Road Builders

Great, dirt eating, iron dinosaurs,
Engines inside them instead of blood and life.

Rumbling, grumbling along uneven ridges,
They eat great chunks of dirt and rock out of the earth,
while others of another variety,
push the earth out of their way so they can continue on.

These prehistoric monsters
have riders sitting loosely, almost casually upon them;
sunburned men with dirt on their faces
and dust in their nostrils.

One pair of eyes, to guide both machine and man,
squinting eyes, with creases at the corners,
varied colors and shapes, these eyes that control,
and push the machines on and on,
building the roads that weave
in and out and around the world
where once the real prehistoric giants walked.

Shirley L. Anderson

Mood Shifts

Anger bites. It really does.
Especially when it's you it strikes
And persists without a cause.
You don't know why, but are sure you detest
This feeling of hatred
That rushes through your chest.

This triggers the tears,
angry and searing they be,
That flow from your inability to express
All the aggression locked up in your chest
That beats against the walls to be free.

The strength and power of what's locked inside
screams to get out, and attacks your will and reason.
It attempts to release this terrible force
At those nearest you, whose fault it is not, of course.

Anger is powerful, the strongest emotion of all.
Trying to stay calm and sane is
like trying to break, with your head, a brick wall.
If something is done with this emotional thrust,
You could move mountains or turn them to dust.

Sienna Keown

The Words Truest

She read the lines written so long ago,
etched by her own hand
and full of the emotions that had lain in her breast.
The words were full and bold
and scarcely written in any color except black
and every line - she remembered -
seemed as though
it tumbled out swifter than she could possibly write.
The lines were her passions
locked away and stored
and freed and exulted;
the writing was her own self -
captivated and bewitched,
the soul and essence of all.
Lying about her was her past,
the lines of her life
with letters that curved and dipped - like life itself -
and somehow it was everything;
what she felt now,
she felt then.

Stephanie M. Holcomb

Wrong Numbers

My telephone rang last Sunday —
Even this moment I feel the skip, the
abnormal beat of my heart at the happy sound.
"Oh, a call. I wonder who it is!"
Excitedly, the possibility making my feet
very light, I ran to the phone.

It was just another wrong number.

My phone pain - three attacks this week!
"Am I speaking to Jane?" "Is this Sally?"
"Is John there, please?"
Oh, why do I still live here when
my friends are so far away?
I'm so busy making new friends, and —

No, no there's the phone ringing again;
I'll not answer it this time.

It's probably just another wrong number.

Opal M. Cessna

Forever Valentine

- I know you are my Mr. Right
Even though we sometimes fight

- We've grown a lot through the years
I hope you don't have many fears

- Words will never say
The way I feel for you today

- I'll be proud to be a Blais
Until I reach my dying days

- I know we'll have a happy marriage
I can't wait to be pushing our baby's carriage.

Lisa L. Lockwood

Somebody Cares

God never closes a door on us
   even when stillness is just a hush.
He is always there when we call
   and will never, never let us fall.

The beauty all around us can be found
   from high above down to the ground.
Roses, tulips, all the rest we may see
   and know God has them just for you and me.

When we look across the green, green field
   We think of just how great the yield.
We can know that everything is from God
   and that it started with seeds in sod.

Our thoughts must be kind and pure
   and leave evil out of our minds sure.
True prayer must rise to Heaven above
   and be sent from hearts full of love.

Thelma A. Bess

My Friend Sam

Sam was a friend of the four-legged breed
Ever so friendly and eager to please
No one could ever have a truer friend
Than Sam was to me right till the end
When I'd come home feeling weary and small
It was always Sam at my beck and call
He'd run to greet me with love and great haste
And plant a kiss right on my face
For eleven great years Sam and I were together
Until that dreadful day in September
He was weak and in pain but did not complain
He just looked at me with his eyes full of pain
We tried to help Sam all that we could
But his going must have been God's will
Sam was so special that he must be in heaven
And I'll never forget him and what we shared together

Mary Ann Bruni

Redwoods

Redwood redwood oh so big
carried by a heavy rig

They cut you down in big big chunks
but everyone knows that you're a hunk

They carry you to a lumber mill
And a guy cuts you up who's name is Bill

The wood is used to make a table
but it is also used to make a stable

Oh the table and the stable are so strong
cutting down redwoods is wrong

Shawn Michael Jehs

"My Dad"

My Dad is the most courageous person I know,
Everyone calls him Mr. O,
To find one like him is very rare,
I never once thought he didn't care,

In the Major Leagues he could've played baseball,
Instead he choose to catch me so I wouldn't fall,
He gave his baseball glove to me,
When I hold it, it makes me so happy,

He knows he made the right decision,
When he sees me through his vision,
He gives me so much more and more,
He'll give me till we are poor,

He gives me a roof to sleep under,
What life would be like without him I wonder,
He would teach me how to play,
But he can't, he works all day,

That's my Dad being the best he can be,
I guess everything he does he's doing it for me.

Lindsay O'Connell

Untitled

Jesus is jubilant, justly, and jovial.
Everyone praise the Lord as every beat pumps within our chest.
Surely the Lord God will rescue His children in a matter of time.
Unite together in prayer, feel His beautiful presence.
Sing with a joyful song unto our precious Creator.

Open the heart of the soul, our minds and the Holy Bible (the book
   of direction)
Uplifting, the heavenly Father will do to you and I.
Ruler of all people, creatures, the heavens and the lands.

Safely in His presence, as the Lord watches o'er us.
Almighty is He, the Fathers' home will be a peaceful place to be.
Virgin Birth by the Holy Ghost is born our Lord Jesus Christ.
Immutability (unchangeableness) is our God making a difference in
   our lives today.
Omnipotence, Omnipresence and Omniscience is his nature.
We, as the people of this world, are to have a relationship with our
   Lord God.
Resurrection of Jesus Christ!

Thelma Mae Woodall

Battlefield

Stretching far and wide
Expansion tells of the misery of an era gone
Memories no longer live
Though, the field yet is not forgotten
Trampled on and obstructed by the visions of those today

Buried is the tale of what went on
Material is the only detail left
To be the eye of tomorrow, the tongue of yesterday

Lost lives, dead sons, loves gone
A man's war, fought for freedom
Brother against brother, loyalty shines on the faces
Even as blood stains and death reigns
Smiles come and go, songs are sung
Friends help friends, although
Fighting in different colors

One last short rings out, one last cannon is dropped
One last boy has to die
A battlefield becomes a remembrance
A war becomes a tragedy of a lost generation
The history of a new generation.

Sabrina Atkeson

Song of the Wind

Listen carefully ... can you hear
Faintly in the distance ... as though an echo drawing near
Whimsical drifting without a care
Quietly approaching the inland fair

On nighttime's waking brow
A whisper subtle, yet comforting somehow
From the calm the immensity grows
Graceful as a ballerina ... Tippy toe, Tippy toe

Silent as midnight's candor
Gentle breezes on their course meander
Creating harmony unique and clear
Voices ... of the whispering winds drawing near

From all directions the voices come
Their prelude soothing as a distant hum
Limbs and bows their talents lend
Rushes and reeds their fluted strains send

With one last finale the chorus ends
Onward the conductor his performers sends
Quiet once again, the breezes gone away
Leaving the memory of the song of the wind in echo's way

Kristine Frost

The Loves Of My Life

Newborn babies; freshly cut grass; the first
Fallen snow; fuzzy-furry cats; family and friends
At Christmas time; and the sweet scent of the
Everlasting pine; the smell of the seasons;
Summer, autumn, winter, and spring; all the
Flowers the rain does bring; the colors of the
Sunset skies; the way an eagle soars and flies;
The warm sun shining on my face; a dress made
Of silk and lace; magical-mythical beasts with
Their beauty within; the awesome feeling of
A victory I strived to win; energetic children
Who play all day, not one worry would cause
Dismay; the feel of jewelry around my fingers,
Neck, and wrists; the sweet taste of a chocolate-
Mint twist; the love I receive from my mother
And sister. I don't know what I'd do without them.
 These are the loves of my life that I will
Cherish and hold to my heart forever.

Khriscinda M. Freije

When Fear Came Knocking at My Door

(Knock, knock!) Who's there?
Fear!
Fear who?
Fear ye not, for most know not what they fear!

Fear knocked at my door and politely said,
"Hello!" I backed away!
Fear stepped inside my door showing the utmost concern
and asked if I was okay!

Fear grabbed my hand and surprisingly said,
"I mean you no harm!"
I gathered my thoughts and realized that fear
had a sense of cleverness and charm.

Fear came and left
with grace and style
Fear made me forget what I
feared the whole while!

Don't lock yourself in fear, for fear will take over you
Stand tall and look fear in the eye,
So when fear comes knocking at your door
You can kiss your fears goodbye!

LaMonica Yarbrough

A Christian Mother

Of all the gifts that I've received from my Heavenly Father above,
I think that I'm most thankful for a Christian Mother's love.
A vessel used by God above to extend His loving hand,
To offer comfort to the broken heart; if it's just to understand.
Much like Jesus, she's a loving friend who understands our fears.
And somehow grows more precious with all the passing years.
In times of disappointment, she would never turn away.
Instead she'd wipe away the tears and teach me how to pray.
A priceless gift God's given me; a gift unlike any other.
A home filled with joy and harmony, and the love of a
Christian Mother.

Madelyn Weigand-Wood

Missing You

Wading along the shore
feeling the soft of the sand
and the soothing cool of the water.
A gentle cry comes from
a sea gull gliding above,
and from the night sky
come streams of light
beaming out of the moon.
As the wind encloses me
in a hug of warmth,
I envision myself in your arms
caressing my neck with breaths of love,
embracing a lonely soul
which has longed for your touch.
My cheeks are soon moistened by bitter tears.
as I open my eyes
and find you not there.
Suddenly I feel alone;
with only my memory, imagination,
and dreams to feast upon.

M. P. C. Paye

Mother And Father

Oh my mother, oh my mother, the world's so different today it
feels stranger every day; and I love you and I still love you.

But you just don't understand that things are different today
Than when you drifted all along in your dreams of yesterday,

That the changes are something you cannot understand. And
That people just have a different way... of understanding.

Oh my father, oh my father, life is sad on this day; you may see
this as just another day, but the real drift is just the other way.

Ronald Kaisen

Autumn

The setting sun shone on the water
Fiery orange was its hue
This breezy evening in Autumn
Here I sit thinking of you.
The rustling of long forgotten leaves
As they tumble across the lawn
Makes my heart silently grieve
Summer now is gone.
The sun is slowly sinking now
The frost begins to bite
In the dusk, trees seem to bow
As if to say, "Goodnight."
In the darkness of this lovely night
I look up to the sky
Amidst the clouds, the stars shine bright
Autumn passes by.

Shelli J. Gray

Fill My Cup Of Life

Sunshine, like golden liquid
Fills my cup of life.
I sit and gaze over Glorietta steeple top
At pinon and juniper covered mountainsides
Climbing up away from me.

Hope has come again;
Like Spring, it melts the Winter snows;
Warmth again at the hearth
Replacing dark cold stone ...
And I turn to see your face.

What's it like to dream again?
To feel excitement flowing
From the very sense of knowing
Tomorrow will finally come once more
... And you'll be there.

Flowing ... temples throbbing ...
Like a river pounding;
White water, rushing like adrenalin;
The liquid gold of your smile;
Flowing ... to fill my cup of life.
Lou Storm

The World's End

Children cried out frightened of doom
Flower gardens begged for rain to bloom
Nightfall so gentle covered pain and despair
Since for children and flowers there was little care.

Mankind created to tend to this place
Could not comprehend how to keep up the pace
Of nurturing nature of compassion for gender
How could in affect these humans be tender?

The mark of the devil was soon to appear
That day of destruction was finally here
No regrets and escape from this fate was expected
this world was so hopeless and badly infected.

Remorse did not save what was destined to die
And nightfall came one more time to the sky
To conceal the sorrow and protect from the pain
Of losing all senses when going insane.

Tears of sorrow fell slowly and blinding
And man who thought that creation was binding
To the one that created the heavens and earth
Now saw that man's making should have started at birth.
Renate Rooney

Spring Symphony

Songs of hidden birds aloft blend their melody.
Flowers birth to rapture hearts and join the harmony.

The sun bestows a warming ray upon the seeds fair growing.
Knowing well that everywhere a singing brook is flowing.

A forest path gently curves to capture morning light.
Velvet crests of violets dressed in purple lavish sight.

Softly shadowed wild blossoms gladden a meadow vista.
Petals ruffled by the breeze shed floating in a whisper.

Woodland balm spreads its charm amidst the lofty trees.
The rhythm of the crickets' song keeps choir with the bees.

Bountiful profusions reap of pink and yellow hue.
Gently grace the regal grass sprinkled by the dew.

A tender rain delights the leaf and garnishes the buds.
Nature's sweeping majesty sends message of God's love.

Heaven's blue adoring sky stills the early rain.
The changing season's symphony of spring comes not in vain.
Marilyn Maddalone

The Wonder Of The Falls

As it cascades down the mountain side;
flowing like the tension from your body as the
tranquility reaches your mind,

Its beauty calls to you as the sun glances
among the threads of water, sparkling like
brilliant diamonds — Yet the power makes
you hesitate as you long to meld with the
wonder of the falls,

Your adventurous soul beckons to go beyond
the wall of water; to find a brightness of light
so blinding, the whiteness empties your mind,
and the roaring power reverberates through
your ears down to your toes.

Then you step through the white wall to find
yourself wet and refreshed as you cross into
the present reality of more adventures to come.
Karen M. Danchenko

The Beginnings

Life, the beautiful thread that binds the earth
fluttering shadows flying free like a bird

Everyone should have a sweetly scented vision
because life is the ultimate gift

Some see thunderous clouds
and shivering cold winds as a part of their lives

"Why" sway to the dark side?
Stay in the light, enjoy!
No matter how, that's the way you're brought in
And "the end" is only
the beginning
Tanisha Hurdle

Our Flag

I stood one day and watched our flag.
Flying high and proud.
And felt the arms of super strength
Surround me like a cloud.
I heard the voice of men of yore,
Who fought for Liberty
Say, "we gave our lives, that you might live
In free prosperity."
I know I owe my life to you, and
Of you I will brag.
And never let them trample on
For you're a "GRAND OLD FLAG."
Larie Nelson

The Phoenix

The fire swirls and dances around the bird enticing the animal to death,
Its rib cage rising and falling, forcing out its raspy breath.
Death is coming, it lingers like the echoes of the bird's cries of pain.
Fear is etched in her amber eyes, now yellow and blinking
steadily as she waits to die.
The flames stop dancing and now begin to consume,
The bird realizes her struggle is in vain and surrenders to ever
present death that looms in the air.
Her wings, burned and charred, breath no longer present,
Her eyes wide open staring into the flames with fear.
Then the fire stirs and rustles and the flames have been disturbed
And now fire dances in the outline of a magnificent bird.
She blinks her eyes and begins to stir,
Her body and soul rejuvenated by what has occurred.
So the flames that had seemed so deadly provided new life
And the Phoenix stretches out her new wings and takes off into flight.
Timothy Allsopp

My Mother's Jewels

If God puts a jewel in each Mother's crown
For all the good deeds she has done,
Then there is one thing of which I am sure
You, Mom, will have the brightest one.

You will wear a jewel for each child you have
Though a jewel I'm not worthy of.
A jewel for each of those you have helped
And a jewel for your friends whom you love.

I could go on for hours with a long list of things
For which a jewel you have earned up there,
But space won't permit to tell them all
So I'll just tell you that I care.

As I see the angels around the great throne
When my life in Heaven I've won,
The angel wearing the brightest crown
I will recognize as - my Mom.

Lillie Scruggs

A Mother's Joy

Of all the gifts that God has given, *one* gift is far the best,
for even if at times he's trouble, my pride outshines the rest.

I gazed upon him in his cradle and glowed from ear to ear,
and knew I'd done *just one* thing right throughout my foolish years.

He cooed and cried for special needs, that only I could give,
and when I held his hand in mine...I'd found my goal to live.

...A gentle soul that needed love and gave back *endless more*...
He'd teach me things I'd never known and open brand new doors.

I thought...gee, maybe God has sent an angel in disguise...
to show me how to sacrifice and love and yet be wise,

Wise enough to guide *my son* through different paths of life...
and hope he'd be a righteous man and choose a righteous wife.

My life has weathered fairly well and I've been blessed each day,
in knowing I have somehow given life along the way.

Yes, God has showered me with gifts and given me such joy,
but none could ever be compared to *this* love for *my little boy*.

Susan Troesch

"A New Song"

(Inspired by reading Psalm 98)

Oh, sing unto the Lord a new song and sing it loud and clear..
For He has done such marvelous things...Oh, tell it far and near!

He hath sent forth His salvation; His righteousness has been
  brought down;
His holy arm hath gotten Him the victory! His right hand hath
  gained Him the Crown!

Mercy and truth are with Him; He extendeth it to all the world..
The whole earth is full of His glory.. let all the banners be unfurl'd..

Make a joyful noise to God; rejoice all ye ends of the earth!
Sing praises unto the Lord of Hosts... and glorify the Saviour's birth!

Let the seas roar, and the world roar, and all that dwell there in!!
Let the floods clap..let the hills rejoice...for the Saviour cometh again!

He cometh to judge the earth with His great righteousness..
His equity He will show to all mankind, and His great tenderness..

So, rejoice, and again I say, rejoice... Oh, sing a new song unto Him..
For He cometh in clouds of great glory... with all his saints again!!

Marie Bass

Children

I gave them everything I had,
for I couldn't see small children sad,
Children without parents to call their own.
Many kids are from broken homes;
to see their tiny faces,
And to wonder in what places
They had lived before,
Children not yet four,
I'd like to take them all home,
Each and every one of them I'd adore;
I'd give them things they never had before.
I'd like to see them all get parents
They could call their own,
For in this world with all its glory
Would be the end to a happy story.

Ron Donovan

Let Me Embrace You, Mom

Let me embrace you, Mom, for your loving ways,
  For I have realized the importance of affection.
Let me embrace you, Mom, for your expression of compassion,
  For you have opened my heart to others.
Let me embrace you, Mom, for the gentle smile upon your face,
  For I have learned sadness is only fleeting.
Let me embrace you, Mom, for your swift sense of humor,
  the exuberant laughter from your heart.
  For laughter will forever keep me young.
Let me embrace you, Mom, for the wisdom you have shared,
  For I can see beyond any obstacle that may stand in my way.
Let me embrace you, Mom, for sharing of yourself so unselfishly,
  For you have shown all of us how beauty seems to radiate,
  when one is warm and kind.
Let me embrace you always, Mom, just for being You.

Pat Campbell

Ode On My American Car

Malibu, Malibu please remain as my sled
for if I need to go somewhere, you point me straight ahead.
Fecal brown your color is, dents and wrinkles show your age,
Three hundred dollars I got you for, not a bad weeks wage.
In the cold you start right up, coughing up grey smoke.
The stories you have are to be revealed, only if you spoke.
Elvis, Shakespeare, even the massive Fabio,
have never driven in my car-io.
In the freezing winter months your seats can get rock hard,
yet your beauty and comfort remain all but unscarred.
The people whom I travel with
can only be my friends
for I do not subscribe to the myth
that gas money makes amends.

Pete Dever

Fantasy Land

Help me save me for I am lost, for it's so cold here, cold as frost. For let me run, run away and pray that it won't like today. Pray for me as I run and hope where I go will be more fun. I will go to a fantasy land where there is no snow but a lot of sand and the sand will be by a great big pool, and there will be sun but there won't be school. But I don't care what it will be and how school means nothing to me. It only means so much to me to have a friend as you can see, but that won't be, that won't. So I will sit by the pool with the sand on my feet and be able to take the very hot heat. Oh how it feels so good to me to be in the sun and get stung by a bee, and it may hurt others but it won't hurt me, no it won't hurt me to be stung by a bee. Oh how I wish this could all be true to sit by the pool with who? Nobody but myself.

Melissa O'Gara

All Mother-In-Laws Are Mother

My mother-in-law is a mother to me,
  for my mother isn't with us;
  she is in heaven, you see.
If you have a mother-in-law that's a pleasure like mine,
You couldn't say bad things you say sometimes.
She is so good and kind to me.
I try to treat her like she was my mother, you see.
Oh! Yes, she lived with us eight years or more.
We never had a fight or became sore.

I'm not saying we never disagreed on anything at all,
but there is a difference in disagreeing and having brawl.
It takes patience to do this from both sides,
but I can honestly say this with pride.

what kind of a mother are you?
If you have married children you are
  a mother and a mother-in-law too.
I hope and pray I can be the mother, and
  mother-in-law to my daughters and sons-in-law
That my Mother and mother-in-law was and is to me.

Edith Williamson

Hope For A Candle In A Window

A warm embrace but never a trace
For never the twain shall meet.
And sorrow and grief was a big separator
But at long last never mind defeat
Hope for a candle in a window.

But as the story goes on and on
The blame game was the order of the day.
And the sins of the father shall visit
Down upon three then four generations.
Hope for a candle in the window.

Old traditions die hard but not impossible
For a wall of oppression shall crumble.
If I lay it all at his feet.
And never, no never, mind defeat.
Hope for a candle in a window.

Pride goes before a fall and destruction soon to follow.
And life is dearly too short
For Heaven is close as tomorrow.
But never, no never, mind defeat.
When I hope for a candle in a window.

Marlo Dean Vockrodt

It Was Love

It was love that planned salvation's plan;
  For God is love to everyone in every land.
It was love that made Jesus lay down his life for us:
  That we may stand before God in his righteousness.

It was love that made me surrender my life to him:
  Though, all the time my understanding was dim.
Now, I know it was his agape love
  That could come from only God above.

It is love that sustains me day by day:
  On this Jesus road, for it's his way.
And his way is right and always best;
  Because, if we'll be totally committed, we'll be blessed.

On this Jesus road, the Holy Spirit will teach us;
  And He is the best of all, to guide us.
And He is the only one to convict us
  Of our sins, and lead us into righteousness.

Mary Blair

The True Vision

Things have been kept hidden,
for now I cannot, I have been beauty stricken.
You, the subject of my surmise,
I couldn't hide the dwelling sleep.
You, the rebirth of beauty, someone of whom I will reap.
I cannot contain myself, for so long have I wondered
just what it is that makes you my vision.
You becharm me,
when you are in my sight, I can hardly look away,
knowing, I drop what I'm doing and leave.
I just couldn't bear to leave this alone,
for you have enchanted my soul
and released the anguish of a faceless heart.

Michael Fitzpatrick

A Laugh

A laugh is the greatest cure on earth
  For something wrong with the soul;
It makes the hardened heart grow weak
  And the timid one grow bold.
A laugh is a pleasant affliction
  That spreads with every ring,
It's the smile of the voice that appeals to you
  Whenever you hear it sing.
A laugh is the vintage of life
  That sparkles whenever it flows:
It pours from the fountain of blissfulness
  And floods through the passage of woes.
A laugh is a pillar of fortitude
  That strengthens the peace of mind:
A laugh is the ruler who abdicates
  All the kingdoms of troubles I find.

Robert T. Baxter

The Tiny Sparrow

I watch the busy sparrows as they hunt so diligently
For sprigs and twigs and grass, to weave together lovingly
A nest unique and special, of warmth and coziness
Where they can house their young ones, with joy and happiness.

In time I hear the chirping of little birds so sweet
I watch the parents cheerfully fly out for food to eat
The babies wait in eagerness, with each mouth open wide
For food of God's provision that the parents place inside.

Wilma De Hoop

The Visit

I was coming home
For the first time in a year.
I felt a little anxious
With a slight touch of fear.
My mother was waiting with welcoming arms.

My brother was smiling
With his own sort of charm.

I felt a relief that I was here,
And it was still the same,
Though I was gone a year.
It was a long, hot journey,
Those seven hundred miles.
But it was worth it,
Just to see my mother's smile.

Now I am waiting to go back the next day.
I'll have to say, "Goodbye, It's been a pleasant stay."
I've got to go back to Houston
To be on my own.
Back to Texas, the place I call home.

Suzanne Oviedo

Oklahoma Bombing

Tears fall,
for the Lord has made his call.
Parents tears,
all those fears.

Imagine the surprise in my eyes,
the fear in my face when the phone was for me.
I collapsed and started to cry.
Why'd my baby have to die?

All the pain those children endured,
this is what the parents have feared.
They blew up the building with a bomb.
Girls and boys calling, "Help me, Mom!"

My rage is stronger.
I can't last much longer.
They've killed too many,
they've harmed plenty.

You're gone today.
I'll see you someday.
We'll love you for eternity.
Believe me, the bomber won't go free.

Marybeth Replogle

"Lost Love"

I am not in your heart the way that you are in mine
For the reality of it happening is a dream I will never find

I don't know what else to do, I don't know what else to say
But I get a real strong feeling that you don't want me to stay

I have to make a decision should I stay or should I go
For my dream to make it work doesn't seem like it will grow

So many emotions - so much hurt,
It all seems to be so very much in vain
Whatever happened to the saying "no pain—no gain"?

For all the pain I am feeling there should be so much gain
But the only feeling I have is of tremendous stress and strain

Often sorry for loving you to the degree that I do
For it makes me unhappy and sometimes very blue

I do my best to make you happy with a feeling that it is to no avail
I might as well be on a search for the original Holy Grail

Deep down inside I will always love you, Oh so very much
I just hope that as we both grow old we will be able to keep in touch.

Paul Whitfield

Seize The Day

Leaves fall to the ground, the air is crisp;
Deer run into the forest devoid of color.
Winter is near, everything can feel its presence
As the bright sun falls; the pale moon rises.
Children going straight home instead of running
Through the fields along the way.
They hear a voice coming from the wind blowing
Through the trees.
It whispers to them - Carpe' diem.
At first they do not understand.

After years of wondering the children now adults,
Understand, Carpe' diem means - seize the day.
Life is short and days are few, even when moments
Are bad. Days go on and life goes by.
Listen to the voices in the trees; your friends and
Family whispering to you. Do not run inside away from
Change; seize the day, every day.

Melissa Gary

The Way

God has a great and vast plan,
for the world he gave to man.
He alone knows all and nothing is hidden,
even the greatest secrets and things forbidden.
No need for pain, grief and evil wallow,
if the ten great laws of the Lord we follow.
Our days could be happy and bright,
if we would only walk in the Lord's light.
No need for gold and riches,
Jesus wore rags and stitches.
He don't ask for much - just honest love,
give Him that and receive the kingdom above.

Shari Williams

The Immortals

The time has come for the final battle.
For us, the immortals, to end it all.
To finish a war waged long ago.
Before the beginning of life.
Before the beginning of time.

We shall finally answer an age old question.
We shall discover who will be the ultimate ruler of the universe.
Thus, we will therefore discover where our followers shall come from.
Whether it be Heaven or weather it be Hell.
We are complete opposites.
I have created good, you have created evil.
Thus, we have been and shall always be mortal enemies.

I am God, you are the Devil.
Life shall not bind us, death cannot stop us,
and time will never touch us.

We are The Immortals and we are doomed forever.

Kevin P. Michaels

Wishes

Wishes are the ones that stay
Forever deep in your heart.
Wishes are the ones that play
Never ever, ever to part.

I wish now for the stars
I wish now for the moon
I wish now for the planet Mars
I wish for a fluffy caterpillar curled up in a cocoon.

Wishes can be beautiful
Wishes can come true
Wishes can be meaningful
But only yours to you.

So use your wishes sparingly
But if you happen to run out
Just look over at a friend caringly
And think of all the wonderful things
you won't have to do without.

Lauren Anderson

September

The cusp of autumn welcomes
crisp, light air.
a fragile eggshell sun,
a drizzle of orange and yellow leaves
dabbed with morning dew.

Summer laughter echoes
through football cheers
then rides south on the wings of eager birds.

Daylight dwindles
romance lingers in the face of the moon.

Lisa Stiffel

Love Awry

They stalk you with their perpetual gaze,
foul, evil things with hearts full of ill riches.
Jealousy well hidden behind so much praise,
words are cheap coming from b****rds and b**ches.
Actions speak volumes that are never written
and actions give voice to so much contradiction.
They try to call it love, when by hate are bitten,
for many loves carry hate as a main addiction.
And through the hell of all their dirty deeds,
rooted in insecurity and so much self-doubt,
rage is a strength, that only evil grows and breeds,
eating from within with fear of being without.
I can but think that cupid's arrow went astray
for no one should live to see love that way.

Manuel Rosa

"If I Could Give The World A Gift.."

It would be a very big shift
From hate to love and war to peace.
People wouldn't fight over a month's building lease.
There would be no evil and no pollution,
Two common subjects to which we cannot find a solution.
Some people care, but not enough,
What others say is just a bluff.
Police would be good and true,
Defending the red, white, and blue,
But hopefully they would have nothing to do.
Gangs would listen to the law,
Unlike today, which is societies' flaw.
Students would speak, "Good is what we know—
If you don't like it, you're free to go."
People would use money, not waste it like trash,
For if they did, they'd get no extra cash.
On racism there would be no movies or sequels,
For whether you're black, white, or in between, we'd all be
considered equals.
If we today had the courage and strength
Maybe, just maybe, tomorrow we could stop violence's endless length.

Kumar J. Kayastha

From A Seed

True love grows so gracefully
From seedling to a flowering tree

The source is planted unaware
And sweetly grows with gentle care

A whisper soft, a friendly smile,
Add sunshine, faith, and wait awhile

Love flowers in gardens least expected
In hearts and souls thought long neglected

You must welcome both the sun and rain
So love's ripe seed can sprout again

Sheri Carden

Alone

Shards of fog swirling, clutching with dark tentacles.
Eyes unable to pierce the encroaching cloud:
Senses dulled by deafening silence,
Reality obliterated.

Alone in a gray, vaporous world,
Landmarks obscured from sight, sound, touch, smell, life.
Where, when, how—escape!
No one there, nothing, only you.

Reaching out, fingers clutching at nothing,
Droplets, clammy on the skin; moisture seeping down.
Senses screaming, heart pounding, ears ringing,
Emptiness, deserted by all, alone.

Lois K. Cronin

In My Mother's House

As I open the door and go inside there's a place for me
from the world to hide. A gentle hand lips softly into mine,
an understanding look, a nod of her head,
without one word I know what she's said.

The memories of yesteryear hang on her wall,
not paintings of sunsets, or mountains so tall.
But pictures of her children she proudly displays
that can't be recaptured or ever replaced.

A place at her table is always set, she still says to me,
"Eat your supper child, don't fret."
There's a fire to warm by, a soft bed to lay.
Scratches on her furniture where her children once played.
Chipped cups and broken hearts could be fixed by her
gentle hands, no one but Mama could never understand.

This house holds her treasures, not crystal, nor gold,
but treasures of a mother that can't be bought or sold.
And this house is more priceless than all that you see,
but without my mother just a house it would be.

Linda Gayness

The Keeper

The beauty of the light is in its distance
From those whose wayward courses it illumines;
Spare me the proximity of their need;
Their broken shells astride my cloaking crags;
If die they must, let it be out to sea
But more than that, ever beyond my view.
No refugee camps disturb my solitude;
There are no ethnics here to cleanse;
In the hardened recesses of my heart
The guns of Sarajevo lie silent;
Rwanda's anguished children cry unheard.
Safely dry-eyed in my salt-sprayed fastness,
Vague prompt of tears no longer shed...
The beauty of my light is in its distance.

Roy L. Shults

Vickie

God sent an angel to me
from where I did not know
She took me by the hand to lead me
at a time when I felt so low
She came to my world when life looked dim
and I needed a friend for more than a whim
She cared for me as a mother would a child
her tone never critical, her manner so mild
She restored my self-esteem and pride
through love and patience, she became my guide
She tutored me in waters uncharted
her conviction and confidence unparted
She grasped my heart with her caring
and now we count on each other for sharing
God sent an angel to me
from where I do not know
And just for me, God did send
Vickie, now my closest friend.

Linda White

Senior Static

It sounded like a drop forge factory, pounding day and night;
  had there been an invasion?
The constant din was driving me bunkers;
  truly, an intolerable situation.
Since when, I asked myself, was this residential area
  zone for industrial thumping?
After an intensive check, I found to my surprise
  that it was only my heart pumping!

Val Palmer

Garden Of Lost Childhood

Crystallized memories upon the grass.
Frozen all at once to be looked upon at last.
Marigolds sink sadly, deathly old.
They've grown too fast, the weathers too cold.
The trees tower over, blocking the sun.
Forming a shady wall, that keeps out every out everyone
Tears trickle down the stem of a flower
Filled with immense sadness power
the power of love, wanting to hold
the feelings of being, young, opens and bold
Wishing to survive, to remember if they could
Instead of being the garden of lost childhood
Tina Magan

For The Love Of Children

I step outside and what do I see
Gangs and violence and drugs on the street.

Children are dying and what do we do? We
sit and watch it on the news. No one will
help us to find the key to solve the
problems we all see.

Children are dying every day for the lack
of love we don't pay. How many children will
it take to get your attention. So love your
children before it's too late.
Kesa Rager

The Shawl

(for Helen Mikulak)

When my mother passed away at 68, her lifelong friend
gave me a white shawl she had made, gifting me
with it at the hall where we ate following the
burial. Our three lives, and that of her daughter,
were knitted together like the weave of the shawl.

As I sit on my porch on a cool Mother's Day in May,
I wrap our lives around me in memories and stories,
partly as soft as cotton, partly as springy
as nylon, full of electricity against my flesh.

I cannot pass through the doors to a bygone time
and place—doors with delicate glass covered with
white lace, but I can wear the shawl with its great
threads, entwined like strings of years, wrapping me
in a full circle.

If I should wear the shawl beyond my porch into the
fullness of the weather, I wonder if I will be able
to feel the same warmth against the same breezes
that my mother and her best friend felt when together.
Will I feel in the material of the shawl the dreams
they once dreamt if the moon glistens upon the cotton?
Yvonne Lubov Rusiniak

Untitled

There's a special spot, I often remember
Concerning your body, so smooth and tender
It's something I've seen, and never been told
Of what I am writing is a tiny mole

It sits just below your silky white shoulder
It's part of your beauty that never grows older
Now let me ponder, I believe it's the left
About five inches up from your lovely firm breast

I dream in the night more often than not
Of pressing my lips to that beautiful spot
But for now it's just a wish I pray will come true
It's just one thing I long for when my heart's missing you.
Scott B. Matthews

Guide Me Lord

Guide me, Lord, as only you can do;
Give me strength and boldness to follow through.

Help me, Lord, to do your will;
And walk in your guidance Holy Spirit filled.

Guide me with the right words to say.
Show me the right thing to do.
I want to walk in your perfect way.
Guide me, Lord, please guide me.

A willing vessel am I, dear Lord,
To complete your perfect plan.
Even if it means sitting still...
And watching...
And waiting...
... for the move of Your Mighty Hand.

Guide me, Oh Lord, guide me.
Lena Ford

Minds Metamorphosis

Words and ideas dapple dance across white pages
Giving substance to thoughts from beyond words reach

Sweet release from emotions' confines
Anger takes wing and comes to rest on stark white
Extinguished and serene

Trials and troubles of every day's rhythm
Disappear in the syntax of soul and printed word
Life leaps to the page and reveals itself

The power of words dispels my darkness
Proclaiming me messenger
Earth bound wasteland to elysian fields

To God I pay homage for this inheritance of grace
And fervently pray when moon reigns o'er night's tide
All that is me is my offering
If only allowed to retain the gift of "wonder"
Margaret Bell Moore

Deeply Moved

Sweet little Liana, a fallen angel, indeed
God wanted you back, a huge mistake we all agree
We wanted you here, not there, to attend parties all pretty in pink
To laugh and have fun in skating rink a supreme power (Oh no!)
another huge mistake added to a long list oh darling little one,
You ought to be here for all to hug and to be kissed
This adorable child was not given a chance
   to live, love, pray and to dance
Oh Lord you made a terrible mistake!!
To snatch this little fragile-like child, so tender and mild
I am angry and so full of rage
like a "Never to be fixed" ripped page
You ought to be here to be forever hugged and kissed
You will be so very very surely missed
God, you made a horrible mistake!!
To enjoy her siblings and friends, Liana was cheated with no amends
What a large waste, I cry no matter how I try
Day after day the suffering is about to be put to rest
Her parents, what a humongous and a cruel test
God!!! You made an indescribable mistake!!
Reba R. Kramer

Teaching And Learning

Teaching is learning and sharing your news.
Giving your discoveries to whomever you choose.

Learning is toiling and laboring long
Testing and trying learning sometimes you're wrong.
La-Goldia Williamson

No Plan

Hey, no plan what are you
going to do?

When the police show up
you gone be through,
Thought you was big and bad trying,
to stop me from doing good,

Trying to sell that junk
that's why you about to get dumped,

Hey, no plan, man you caught
there ain't no way you're gonna get loose
from those cops,

Throw down the dope
cause you don't have a plan nor escape route,

Look at the guilt trip on your face
you should have stayed in school,

Sometimes I care and sometimes I don't
but it hurts to hear my generation
getting smoked, I know one thing for me,
I got a plan to look forward to and
that's staying off the streets!

Shenek Hollins

The Cookie Jar

The cookie jar is empty, as it sits upon the table
Granny had filled it for many years, as long as she was able.
First for her little ones, then as they grew
Their friends and neighbors little ones too.

As the parade of children came on the hour
They headed for the jar to get two or more.
Some were chocolate chips, butterscotch or peanut butter
"It doesn't matter which you get" you could hear them mutter.

And now and then you would see a grown up hand
Reach in the jar and chew to beat the band.

But now the jar sits empty, it almost makes you cry
As no more little ones are left to pass by.
They have all grown up and moved away
And won't be coming home again to play.

I hope someone will take the jar home with them to stay
And keep it filled again, so some little ones will be happy and gay.

As Granny has gone home, I hope to heaven
And is passing out cookies to little angels, by the dozen.

Minnie Freeland

Magic In The Mountains

I have been touched by a spirit
greater than any I've ever imagined
a presence
which lay all about me as I sat so high above
majestic glacial peaks
glistening brilliant white
in the sunlight
elks grazing quietly
in the bubbling river below
black birds
graceful shadows
gliding effortlessly through the sky
the chiming of the wind whistling through the pines
standing so proudly on the mountainside
I have been touched by a spirit
that beckons me to stop and listen
to be at one
within its comforting arms
I am at peace
I am home.

Sue Wasserman

Sweet Louise's Ring

Sweet Louise's Ring
gripped tightly to her long, bony fingers
Attached to her crossed arms.
That crimson hoop with the desecrated stench
made me close the casket in fear,
But her thin, skeletal branch levers up in a swift motion, cracking
Her joints as she stops the falling casket lid.
That ring I tell you, it's got to be that ring!
She stares at me with noxious clouds and manages to point at me
with her haggard fingers.
Her legs creep over the casket's edge and stagger to me
With a festered grin as if blaming me for her tortured cadaver,
But fall at my feet as all her bones are crushed leaving silvery
    fragments.
Outside, a loon screamed in the bitter darkness.

Matthew Geide

A Red Rose

I wish I were a red rose so fair, for you to pluck and wear in your hair. A red rose without the thorns that stick. To make it easy for you to pick. A red rose for your jet black hair, for a wonderful girl, a girl so rare, that wears the rose for all to see, and knows she always thinks of me. But then the red rose begins to decline, as time takes its toll on a red rose once so fine. From the jet black hair the red rose has departed, wilted, faded, thrown aside and discarded. Perhaps another red rose to take its place? To adorn the jet black hair and the pretty face. For the red rose has meaning, from the very start. For a girl to wear with a sincere heart. The red rose, a symbol throughout the ages, of an inner feeling, that so often rages, within the hearts of two, so much in love. But the red rose does fade as the sun above. A new red rose will bud, blossom and appear, for the pretty girl to wear in her jet black hair.

Walter Ladonis

Mother's Hands

My mother's hands gave me so many things, I look at her hands and say. She fed me with those hands, She clothed me with those hands, She sheltered me with those hands and she disciplined me with those hands. But the thing I remember most about those hands is She loved me with those hands. You never realize how important mother's hands really are and we take them for granted everyday But I would give anything for one more touch of those loving and caring hands today.

Stacy Villarreal

Rhapsody Of The Trees

The white-frilled arch of His vast temple's ceiling
Hangs serenely above, His eyes in the sun's eye,
His hand tracing billows in the blue deep, revealing
Majestic and gentle ideas, unfathomable to them.

They reach their arms up, stretching, yearning for the fair
but their poor tired feet hold fast the dirt.
Gales of the spirit caress their fingers and lift their hair,
And they sing their mournful hymns while they hold fast to mortality.
They whisper, and chuckle, and rain tears on the Earth
they sway together in thundering mirth
The sky grows dim, their company grows more fair
Lovers of dirt, now lost to their sight is the soul of the air.

They push in their folly, they cry in the dark
And how He smiles yet, lovingly painting the arch
Golden, red, pure white sun, sprinkled with stars
Waiting on His children to remember His art
Still He pours from the sun's eye bright blessings, and yet
Their arms do mount skyward, while their hearts do forget.

Mary Ann Honaker

A Fly Fisherman's Tale

The anticipation of what is to come
Happens with the early morning reddish sun.
Quiet thoughts of the last visit dominate
As my senses settle on the quiet lake.

Ripples on the surface indicate a hatch
As a rising trout engulfs its morning catch.
Hurriedly I rush into my fisherman's garb
Hoping the wader ritual ain't too hard.

Gold-ribbed elk hair caddis is the one
For it seems alive in the glittering sun.
Long smooth eleven to one waves of line
Bring the caddis to the surface on time.

A large cutthroat trout engulfs its prey
Only to find himself mercifully at bay.
And so the half hour battle is on
But in just a heartbeat the trout is gone.

All of a sudden the lake's a mirror
And not even the fish care if I'm here.
I'll go back home trying to get it straight
Hoping maybe next time I'll get a break.

Kenneth V. Salazar

Loss of Lucrece

Lucrece will know and my desperate chance
Has come for her to know that in sorrow
I arrive to watch her breathe at one glance
Again; just knowing that day tomorrow.

That day slowly came, but faster it had gone.
It was from the letter I had left post
To hurry to my wife before she was done
And save her from harm which I thought was lost.

So fidgety fast I had grabbed her words
Though the ones I kept, in mind they had stuck.
Again came the screeching cry cutting like swords.
My control, my strength, my joy it did pluck.

"Beautiful Lucrece, why O why is this?"
She allays the terms with Father and I.
Then, leaving us stone-still in mindless bliss,
She cuts her life out, waking up my eye.

I bet the audience knows now my mind
In how it worked; shameful for what they find.

Turhan Caylak

The Window

I often wonder if my window
has eyes - maybe even a heart.
  For year after year the window
has become my beacon of life.
  I go to the window for possible
hope - often to return, so hard to cope.
  Where are they? If only my window
could speak - and give my spirit some relief
  A school bus - Don't be late - Oh
Window he has grown at such a rate -
  The first car so by the window I wait.
And then the girl so pretty and sweet
  I keep my windows so neat
Lace curtains with even a pleat -
  Oh window my friend -
They are all gone - they are all gone -
  But still I come to the window
and often I long for the time gone by
  When I wondered if my window
had eyes.

Louise Moser

Down The Road

A stainless steel tongue
has sliced and sliced ... and sliced
like an uncontrollable electric carving knife
had sliced the fleshly wood
Now, human fragments lie in bleeding pieces
where a hyper-sensitive man once stood

Words, part-sins ... part faults, part mindless-things
Yet, part-truths. So to run.

Run from human faults - that keep you running
'til you don't know whether you're going or coming

While down the gravel road a tired old man has stopped to smoke
and perhaps to rest (but for him there is no rest)
He hears the broken man running ... coming
So he stops to put on his cloak, then sits and waits

Down the gravel road he runs, spewing behind restless dust
and stones - like bleeding fragments of broken human bones

Now the trees go flying by - to whisper, to talk, to sway
To get out of the way (of this messenger of death)
But before they open up their path to him
They preach, as if to say: "From yourself ... you cannot run away."

R. T. Tsuji

"Distrust"

Child let go of your fears
Have faith in yourself and in your tears....
Is the strength that you've been searching for all this time
what it is is nothing and all in your mind

There are fools who hate and fools who love
And people blindly preaching of a mighty God above
But behind their words and their hand clenched crucifix
They cringe for their next fix
It could be a drug or sex with a whore
Whatever it is it makes them fiend for more
More and more of human decay

And then there're those people who you think of as friends
Those people you blindly trust, love and defend
But those people you see, themselves they lack
They'll lead you astray and stab you in the back
And some of them hold their heads proudly high,
And some pretend they know,
But most wearily stagger by
In bitter scorn they keep their eyes low

Tim Marshall

True Friendship

  Friends are special to me and I
have many, but if you took your friendship
away the others wouldn't be worth a penny,
because friends are friends and brothers are
brothers, but in you I have both and that
puts you above all the others.
  We've been friends for many many
years and we've shared times of happiness and
we've shared times of tears, but you've always
been there to keep my spirits up and even when
I'm thirsty you're there to fill my cup, and
I want you to know I would do the same for
you, because there is nothing I wouldn't give
you and nothing I wouldn't do.
  I wrote this to tell you how much I've
appreciated your friendship over the years and
we've gone from having sodas and playing cars to
drinking beers and going to bars; and though I may not
say it, I know it to be true - I will never have
another friend as good as I have in you.

Tim Van Zile

"It's Up To Us"

All the children of this world
Have us to thank for their domain
We're the ones who did it
And we are the ones to blame

They don't miss a thing and they learn what they live
They watch us take when they should see us give

So let's all turn around and go the other way
A better world we'll find if we're aware of what we say

The children, they're so innocent
And they don't know any better
We can teach them how to walk
And to pronounce each letter

But our lifestyles and our actions
If we'll just stop and think
They're what really matters
And that's the most important link

So to those of us who care
I think we'll really listen
And to those of you who don't
It's your fault their morals are missin'

Marshall D. McGuyer

Untitled

Can I escape the odds?
Having millions of cells,
if only one rebels,
contaminating others, willing
to spread bacilli, spilling
contagion through me,
finally killing.
What am I to do?
Seek medical prognosis,
develop a neurosis
from each infinitesimal ache or pain.
Commercial exhortation compels us to be afraid.
To expand each symptom into a terrifying experience.
Fight cancer with a check-up,
give to help fight heart disease,
give to support research.
if I must give let it be
any traitorous extensions of myself.

Robert G. Yost

Blue Eyes

He had big blue eyes and rosy cheeks,
   He always gave me a kiss with a squeak.
His dumplings were great, I've never had better,
   And the belly he got, he said, was sewn into his sweater.

My Grandpa had strength and a will that wouldn't quit,
   He passed these to his children, and believe me, they use it.
My Grandpa had a heart bigger than the whole world round,
   Not a finer man will ever be found.

He loved his large family, each and every one.
   We remember with love that his new life has just begun.
I imagine his entrance to heaven, Grandma's standing there,
   They exchange a look, a smile and a hug stronger than a bear.
They're together now, watching and guiding us,
   Surrounded by God's love that we know and trust.

We'll never lose Grandpa, he'll remain in our heart,
   From beginning to end, from stop to start,
We love you, Grandpa, and always will;
   We say goodbye with great memories still.

Renee M. Rauscher

Forget-Me-Not

As he walked through the isles in the Antique store
He came across things he had seen before
A pair of skates an old girl friend had
A baseball glove like he shared with his dad
A figurine from his great aunt's parlour
Afraid to touch for fear she would still holler
Mother's favorite dish that he once broke
As she held back a tear she still made a joke
"It is only a thing," was all she did say
But to her it was a memory of some special day
An old bike was the next thing down the line
He remembered outgrowing when he'd turned nine
One other thing in the Antique store he did see
Did not bring back such a fond memory
So when taking a walk down a memory lane
You sometimes have to stroll with a little pain

Robert A. Volpe

Innocent Woman

The river runs slowly downhill;
He decides that soon he will kill.
The river rushes over grasses and rock;
He goes inside and fastens the lock.
The river glides into many streams;
The baby cries; the woman screams.
The river flows into a lake;
He decides it's her life he will take.
The river bubbles and goes back down;
The blood flows all over the ground.
The river silts the sandy bed.
She lies on the ground; DEAD.
The river flows any which way;
Innocent people are murdered every day.
The river runs slowly downhill;
The woman is dead because his heart didn't feel.
The river runs free from anyone,
But the woman lay dead; killed by her son.

Whitney Parks

Grace's Plight

Grace, a loveable malamute,
   Enjoys playing, especially, with 'fowl'.
One day, she, launched her 'shoot',
   As she, sharply, used her paws and 'Jowl'.
She abounded right out of her pen,
   Shooting out around the domicile,
Scared, Glory, the kitty, 'up a den',
   A tulip poplar, in just a little while.
But, Grace could not climb abreast,
   And Glory could not make the descent,
So, the good man, came out of rest,
   To retrieve Glory, without accident.
Today, all things appear real sound,
   As the gate stays tied real tight;
You could say, divinely, 'bound',
   As is, also, grace's plight.

Jean Stephen

Reflection

I can see this girl — she's talking.
   I've heard her voice before.
I can see this girl — she's laughing.
   I've heard her laugh before.
I can see this girl — she's crying now.
   But I don't know why.
I reach out to touch her, to comfort her somehow.
   But I can't.
The mirror is in the way.

Brandi Brockinton

His Life

She feels like a hitchhiker on the side of his life
He does not see in the blind spot stands his lover, his wife

He has driven his family and his friends away
He lives for the moment, he lives for the day

She has tried to warn him of the curve ahead
He has not listened to anything she has ever said

He has taken and used and never given back
He refuses to admit the end of the tunnel is black

She cannot apply the brakes to stop and save this man
He races on with his life toward a gulf too wide to span

She has to let him go, the husband she loves and adores
He crashes never understanding why she could not give any more

Rosanne Holley

Shelley

My daughter, Shelley, is an angel, sent from God above;
He filled her with His greatest gift...that is the gift of love!
If someone isn't feeling well, you know she'll be right there.
A smile or a gentle hug, to let you know she cares.

And if you need a helping hand, though she's running all the while,
She'll set aside her busy time and greet you with a smile!

My little angel, as a child, had pep and energy,
When I was ill or feeling down, she'd be right there for me.
And now she's grown into a woman, a mother and a wife,
Unselfish love she gives to those who share a part of her life.

Her house is always spotless... a dust ball cannot hide,
She'll hunt it down and wipe it up, with all her womanly pride.

As her Mother, I'm so proud, of this angel from above,
God has truly blessed me with her very special love.

Sharon Julian

Christ Is With Me

He is with me when I am happy
He is with me when I am sad
He is with me when I am at the top of the mountain.
He is with me when I am at the bottom of the mountain.
He is with me in health
He is with me in sickness
He is with me for better or worse
He is with me when I am lonely
He is with me when all others forsake me.
He is with me during the good times
He is with me during the bad times
He is with me during spring and summer
He is with me during autumn and winter
He is with me when I feel good
He is with me when I feel bad
He is with me when I fly a plane
He is with me when I am at the helm of a ship
He is with me when I am rich
He is with me when I am poor.
He is with me forever... *He is*.

Robert Edward Gaskin

Not Rich But Happy

My treasure is not rubies and gold
Having money is being rich, so I'm told.
A diamond is glass if you're as rich as I
What good is money if you're not happy
When you die?
My dream is not having a jewel for every day,
Thought it would be nice to live half that way.
But without happiness it wouldn't mean a thing,
I only want the love it all would bring.

Recina Staplins

Son Of God

When God was creating us, He knew what would be
He knew there would be some sin, so His Son came to set us free
He was born in a cattle stall, where shepherds came to bow
He knew he was sent to die, so that we may live now
All his life He preached the Word, to all those big and small
He preached that He would save each of us from our fall
It all ended on a Friday night, when they nailed him to a tree
To His Father He cried out "why have you forsaken me?"
Three days later the tomb was empty, "Was Jesus really dead?"
People then knew He was the Lord, for He had risen as he said
He then ascended into Heaven, to sit at God's right hand
Now sooner than we really think, in front of God we will stand
He made for us a perfect world, we gave it all away
One thing that will help save us is to bow our heads and pray.

Nicole Kindschy

The Eclat Whip

The geldings hay was drawn the night before
He knew-tomorrow who would be whipped some more
His churned up stall looked a sight
He had paced throughout the night

The whip is punishing often cruel
In the stretch it's a whipping duel
Only the horse suffers the pain
As jockeys go slashing down the lane

Michael Guldemann

Destiny And Fate

He rode into town that day, on a horse as black as coal.
He looked at me with fiery eyes that burned into my soul.

He said, "My name is Destiny," I felt my knees grow weak.
I tried to say, "My name is Fate," but found I could not speak.

He smiled at me and turned to go, I guess that broke the ice.
I offered him a lemonade, he said, "That would be nice."

I asked what brought him to our town, for people seldom came.
He said, "I was born here and I've come home again."

I remembered the story of long ago, from my sisters Hope and Fame.
How Misery had given birth and left the town in shame.
I asked him if the story was true, He said it was indeed.
He'd come home to find his dad, whose name he said was Greed.

I took him to his father and he spit upon his grave.
He said, "I hope you rot in Hell for all the pain you gave."

Five years have passed, we're married now and moved onto a ranch.
Our family's grown with children two, their names are Luck and Chance.

Someday when they are older, oh I can hardly wait,
We'll tell them both the story of how Destiny met Fate.

Phyllis A. Kramer

He Is Alive! Christ Lives!

No sightless idol He,
For lo, He sees and seeing my distresses
Brings relief to me.

No deafness stops His ears
From hearing when I cry to Him of wrongs,
Injustices and fears.

No heart of stone in Him
To cause Him to ignore my private pains,
My wounded faith grown dim.

And so, on Easter morn,
Because Christ lives, my faith again swells large
In confidence, no more forlorn.

Loie P. Knight

"My Soul Is Free In Jesus"

When I saved, it was when Jesus saved me,
He loosed the chains of bondage and he set my soul free!
My soul, my soul, the immortal part of me,
My soul, my soul, has truly been made free;

My soul was locked up like a prisoner in jail,
But King Jesus came and snatched it from hell,
Old Satan thought he had me, but by grace I got away,
He had used me and abused me, and left me for prey;

Oh! As the one sheep who was lost from the flock,
The Lord, who is my shepherd, heard my soul crying out;
My soul, my soul, belongs now to God,
My soul, my soul, longs for heaven afar.

It is God's will that I am saved from all of my sins,
He's cast them in the forgiving sea, never to rise in this world again.
So when the Devil tries to bring the past up in my face,
The holy ghost within my soul, puts him in his rightful place!

I thank Jesus for the blood, the covering for my soul,
You see it's the blood of king Jesus, that worth more than pure gold
My soul, my soul loves god and him alone,
For it's my desire to serve him until I'm called home! Amen
Nancy V. N. Baker

The Most Unlikely Couple

She's fat, He's skinny
He plays cards, she can't remember numbers
She likes air conditioning, He likes none
They both are Trekkies, Sci Fi, Movie Addicts
He's a retired Postal Employee, she's a retired Nurse
She dresses well, it's just not important to him
They both like jazz and all kinds of music
He's not as thoughtful as she would like
She's kind of pushy about certain things
She likes to cook, He enjoys the meals she prepares
He can do puzzles, she can figure out "Wheel of Fortune"
She likes to dance, he accommodates her
School is her thing, the discipline of learning and ideas
Bowling, Pinochle, and Poker are enough for him
He holds her hand and caresses her face
She responds with soft tender kisses
He says "I love you"
She says "I love you too."
A most unlikely couple!
Maxine Spilton

"The End"

As the color of life left his face,
He took his last breath,
Their youngest yelled, "Good-bye Dad,"
As he passed from life to death.

She laid him to rest as he would want,
The way he would usually dress,
In his jeans, shirt, and cap,
Not in a tie, suit, and vest.

She put a pack of cigarettes in his pocket,
And didn't forget his lighter and knife,
A sign in his coffin said, "Gone Fishin',"
She wasn't a widow, just a fisherman's wife.

He was proud of his military years,
So National Cemetery was where he'd be laid,
The Gun Shot Salute rang through the air,
And tears filled her eyes, as taps was played.

He'll always be with her,
In heart, mind, and spirit,
And when she talks to him,
He will hear it.
Patricia A. Averette

Untitled

Many years ago, God put you in our care,
He trusted us as parents, with a gift so sweet and rare.

A daughter small and beautiful, a perfect little girl,
an angel given human form to illuminate our world.

Each year was something different, you always made us smile,
you taught us to appreciate what makes our lives worthwhile.

So many things have happened to create the bond that we share,
we will always stand beside you, and we will always care.

You've brought us so much happiness, more than most have ever had,
We're really very lucky to be your Mom and Dad.

We'll always have our battles, there will always be fences to mend,
But even if you were not our daughter, we would choose you as a friend.
Paige B. Denham

epitaph to my brother Newman

Methodically (not slowly)
he was ever there.
Smiling with a sly
always ready for it -
if it's the sky!
There was no limit
To his inner resources
to meet a need.
Lovingly, he
easily understood and freely gave
until the end when his written word was honored.
His deeds were done at God's speed in God's name.
Remembered for all above and even more
because of his great love for God and man,
he stood out to all who within his reach were
captive to his winsome store and now
forever share his heavenly peace.
Thelma C. Norton

He Is Here

A child is born of Virgin Mary.
He was her baby - a son so dear.
With only swaddling clothes to wear,
In the manger, shepherds found them there.

The wise men came with gifts to share.
They viewed a mother with loving care,
Holding a babe in her arms so very near,
She was whispering love in his ear.

Then he grew to manhood year-by-year.
There were times he lived in fear.
He knew a time - a place for prayer,
That God would meet him there.

Hear the voices singing loud and clear,
Ringing out through the air.
A time to listen, a time to care,
A time to celebrate the birth of love
Yes, he is everywhere, HE IS HERE!
Lynn A. Monroe

For The One Man I Will Always Love

He holds me tight, when I am scared.
He wipes my eyes, when I am sad.
He give me hugs, when I am lonely.
He lends me an ear, when I need to talk.
He makes me laugh, when I am down.
He tells me he loves me, when no one is around.
He says that he'll always be there, and I know it's true.
When we dance together, I'll always remember
The one man who'll always love me, is my father.
Laura Maltese

Untitled

I saw God outside my window today.
He was there when the first break of dawn arrived
He was there when the flowers drooped their heads
From the chill of night;
He was there when the sun burst forth
And dispelled the coolness of the breath of morning
I saw Him among the tulips,
Whose foliage was fast breaking through
The cool brown earth.
I saw Him too as the branches swayed
Beneath the rollicking sound of the robin's merry tune.
I saw Him again down by the brook;
The ripples seemed to chant His promise,
"Something for everyone, go find it."
It is the song of the bird,
The blossom of a flower,
The whisper of the wind,
The green of the grass.
In every bud, in every sound
We can find His promise.

Stella M. Fries

"On The Pier"

He left me standing on the pier
He whispered something in my ear
My ship is waiting in the Bay
Don't cry Dear, I'll be back some day
I watched him far as I could see
Then said a prayer for him and me

Day after day I sit and wait
My ship isn't in, it must be late
At last I see the smoke, my ship is here
I must meet him on the pier
I stood there with tears in my eyes
And watched the sailors passing by

After hours of waiting, everyone had gone
I started walking slowly back home
I heard a voice from behind me
Is it him, could it be
With tears on my face
Again, his sweet embrace

Margaret R. Potts

7:03 P.M. 13th Of May

No baby/no lover/acquaintances many/friends few/little money
hear me I'm not complaining
other gifts have been given me,
what you may wonder?
For starters composing a poem
on the 13th of May at 7:03
while listening to Verdi,

For now I say it's enough,
No! Not merely enough but plenty,
this tumbling love I've for
children/opera/poetry
Lo!
Wake up Larry!
You've been spared the curse of babbittry,
wake to your gift of compassion
wake to the door of your soul/always open
letting all who dare entry in!

And might I dare even wake
to the celebration that this is my very first
Whitmanesque hymn?

Laurence C. Schwartz

My Turn

Pat him, hands low. Talk to him, keep him slow.
Heels down, away we go. This is fun!
First jump, keep him straight. "Please, horse, don't hesitate."
Jump number two is bigger than one! But remember, this is fun?
Going over three lost a rein. Jump number four, remember the mane.
"Reach. Get forward. Not that far. The horse has to see
where you are." The neck can hold you if you need it. "Are you
sure he uses a snaffle bit?" Cleared five and we're still alive.
Number six took two tries. Maybe if I'd open my eyes.
Number seven we went through. Fifteen jumpers and I got you. Push!
Popped over eight like cereal shot from guns. Horse, let's go back
to one. Now for nine, show no fear. What the heck am I doing here?
Cleared ten like a champ. Why is the back of my lap so damp?
May I be excused?
Over eleven straight as an arrow. I needed shin guards,
it was so narrow. Here comes twelve. Gee! It's tall. Horse,
why are you suddenly so small? Over thirteen he didn't falter.
Lost the bridle, steer with the halter.
Aim for fourteen, off course! Cleared fifteen, missed the horse.
Wasn't that fun? Next!

Marilyn Morong

Hello-Goodbye

Goodbye - home,
Hello - camp, goodbye - parents
Hello - coach, goodbye - junk food
Hello - health food, goodbye - free time
Hello - training, goodbye fat, hello - muscle
Goodbye - relaxation, hello - soreness
Goodbye - social life, hello - hard work
Goodbye - camp, hello - olympics
Goodbye - training, hello - dream
Goodbye - hard work, hello - gold metal
Goodbye - average, hello - fame
Goodbye - goals, hello - accomplishment
Goodbye - striving, hello - glory
Goodbye - good, hello - trouble
Goodbye - house, hello - streets
Goodbye - morals and values, hello - cults and gangs
Goodbye - money, hello - drugs
Goodbye - law and order, hello - fly high, goodbye - stopping
Hello - addiction, goodbye - fly high
Hello - death

Shannon Ward

Untitled

Someday you'll need to talk about it, to someone who'll
help you deal with what you will not face today

Maybe you'll be lucky then and know someone who'll
help you find the answers for your troubled life

But, if you wait, you may not know the truth about
the way it was. The one with all the answers died,

or maybe they gave up on talking cause they couldn't
pierce the wall that keeps you sep'rate from your pain

Oh my mother won't you tell me what your life was like
back then. When daddy used to come home drunk

Dad, I know you had some demons that you could not
exorcise, but why would you not share your pain

Alone you must decide if they are blamed for
screwing up your life and will that make a better day

When you've made the final judgement they won't suffer
from the verdict. Condemnation clouds your mind

Thomas Culver Hill

Joker's Privilege

Galloping through the pasture,
her beautiful white mane blowing in the breeze.
She grazes in the pasture,
eating the grass and buttercups.
Her majestic beauty,
that placed her second in the show,
is hidden by the mud in which she rolls.
Now she is pregnant and ready to bear her young.
I am unable to ride her,
but she is still my closest friend,
Joker's Privilege.

Kari Jasper

The Goddess

She walks with a light step seemingly weightless.
Her beauty proceeds her and lingers still after she's gone,
Grace is her ally, charm is her weapon,
With them she rules the world. Her name is Love,
Her kiss is soft as the summer breeze.
Her eyes are gentle as a newborn fawn.
Enchanting is her personality;
She'll trap you unaware. Her name is Love
Once she catches you there's no escape.
She'll hold you till you give your life to her.
Then, with a twist of fate, she'll turn on you.
Her game has just begun. Her name is Love.
When she leaves she'll take your heart and soul with her.
To try to make her stay is suicide.
She'll tear your flesh and laugh as she watches you bleed.
She's wicked as a serpent. Her name is Love.
Once she's gone you're left alone with nothing,
But the pain and scars that remain for the rest of your life.
You're determined to never let her get close again,
But then it's too late, she's there. Her name is Love.

Monique Parker

The Woman

She extracted my heart's alluring lust;
Her golden tann'd complexion seems priceless
Eyelids reveal caramel- virtuous
Countenance like island ken of sunsets.
Satin skin rubs mine; feather locks I touch;
Rose color'd lips, succulent, I must taste
Hourglass structure, curvaceous is such
I must see inward; I'm sure she's as chaste.
I attempt; flying colors; accurate-
Justifiable fantasy; she's all.
Adore and cherish; I won't hesitate
Respect and not neglect, I will not fall.
Eye the looking glass, for in it she'll see
My image of love, for infinity.

Kason Reeves

A Unique Design

The foundation is square and level,
Equality of thought and mind;
When oneness is reached in a marriage,
It's by God's unique design.

It's built by faith and trust,
Unswerving loyalty and just being kind;
An inseparable union drawn together by God,
Permanent, lasting by God's design.

Completed by giving and sharing,
Prompted by love divine;
A happy union: solid, established;
Unique by God's design.

Theodore Hill Jr.

The Confessions Of An Abused Child

She cries in the night
Her mom dies of fright
For when she doze
No one knows

She only sometimes sees a light
And only sometimes is it lit
She is tired of being hit.

She'll strike back one day
And then we all must pray
For she will die
For that try
With a gun, it is done
To the brain, he has gone insane

I saw past the bruises
The killer is the true one who loses
I loved her more than any other
I did this because I am her mother
I left him far too late
I should have left before the death of Kate

Taylor H. Earnest

Immigrant Eyes

They look at me with their immigrant eyes,
her mother, my grandmother, lost to us both.
A picture taken in 1916 shows my grandparents
proud, stern, unsmiling as befit the day.
Born in Finland, each came here alone.
You with your ancient eyes, Asian bones,
Vilho yearning for land, Emma longing for
home, mouth even then curved down in defeat,
regret tumbling through your face as if
hope would crack your flesh in pieces
leaving a husk, a mannequin in its place.
I learned how you died, at grandpa's grave.
My mother, your Ellen wept in wracking sobs,
on her knees, clinging to your gravestone.
Emma, she found you hanging in the barn!
At sixteen, what a wretched thing to find!
My mother reviewed this scene again, again.
You three are smudges in a tiny graveyard
with God holding you in His broad hands.
A legacy of your eyes shines from my own.

Nancy Cronin

Untitled

Her eyes so warm,
Her smile so bright,
No matter how far she is
She's never out of sight.

Her hands so soft,
Her touch so kind,
And if that wasn't enough,
Her body so fine.

She's always nice,
To you she can do no wrong.
She's perfect in every way,
And she always seems to look better each day.

You're always trying to impress her,
But it doesn't always work.
She might just ignore you,
Or even call you a jerk.

But you keep trying every day,
Hoping you can be together.
It doesn't always turn out that way,
But you dream that she'll love you forever.

Richard Petts

What The World Needs Is: Great Arm-Chair Quarterbacks

There he is the WINNER of each game.
He's the WINNER of each and knows no fame.
The GENERAL, a PLAYMAKER,
He CONTROLS each call
From the CENTER to his HANDS.
He's got the BALL!
Now all he needs is the PLAY to continue,
With his POWER to psych the follow through.

Will the VIKINGS on December 17th
BEAT the "SNAKE"?????
Only if the ARM-CHAIR QUARTERBACKS
Are there to CREATE.

The Replays will tell all to THEM
The PLAY, SELECTIONS, the OFFICIALS' CALLS.
Only if the ARM-CHAIR QUARTERBACKS will
CARRY the ball!!!
In the living room, a lamp may be BROKEN,
From SPIKING the BALL and being OUTSPOKEN.

He called the PLAY and the T.D. was made.
THE ARM-CHAIR QUARTERBACKS SHOULD BE PAID!!!!!

Samson Daniels
December 1978

The Squirrels

Abigail's nemeses live in the trees,
High in the branches above her head.
They scamper along limbs ignoring her bark,
As playful as children bent on a lark.

Abigail's nemeses dine in one tree,
Munching on corn put there by me.
They take turns with the kernels and the cob they're on,
Despite Abigail's protests, voiced from the lawn.

Abigail bristles as they run through the garden,
She watches their antics, her hostilities harden.
Her hackles on end, she charges the spot
Where, all of a sudden, the squirrels are not.

Abigail's nemeses each have their own tree
To which when they're chased they know they can flee.
Abigail roars her frustration, reminding her quarry
That one of these days it is they who'll be sorry!

Pat LoCascio

Birds

How can so many birds fly so high,
Higher than the great, golden blue sky?
How can so many birds create such grace,
That they fly so free without a trace?

Topping the trees and lacing the leaves,
Fleeing the states and taping the seas.
Capturing the sights with all their might,
Touching so many without a fight.

What is it like to create such bliss,
Making such music with their soft- hearted kiss?
Chirping songs about their loves they miss,
Why do they feel such terminal bliss?

Caught in the flames of the burning dames
Who do they blame for the tragic games?
How do they react when destruction's the name?
What do you do when they have such pain?

Who is to say they're wise and clever?
Who is to say that wisdom is forever?
Many may think they're crazy and weak
When they have little life left to seek.

Tara R. Wight

Expression Of Love

A precious baby boy with eyes of blue,
His big sister of three says "I love you."
His proud mommy, daddy, grandparents, aunts and uncles,
And cousins too....
All love this precious baby boy with eyes of blue.
As only a sister of three could say....
As she sits on the lap of her mother,
"Thank you mommy for giving me a baby brother."
As Mother's Day approaches, it makes me think back,
To when my own two precious blue eyed girls,
Were as little as that.
How the years flew by from toddlers to teens,
With many happy memories in-between.
Now all grown up with loves of their own,
Each with two little ones to call their own,
Makes this grandma proud to say...
"Have a Happy Mother's Day!"

Phyllis Kittinger

Daydream Father

I stop and watch, try not to be noticed. A father tenderly takes his daughter by the hand.

Dreams cloud my mind, rust aches my heart.
Feelings of emptiness. Something that will never be.
I sit down and close my eyes bringing my daydream father to me.

Pull of dream from my mind, a feeling from the soul.
It is I now, my father and me walking by the sea.
Tenderly he takes me by the hand, leading the way in the sand.

Just as a hawk in flight after his next meal capturing the moment, I feel at peace, a fulfilled soul, carefree.

"Daughter," he says, "life is only but a moment, a spirit that can be captured but has to be set free."
"Father," I say, "I can't let go, you should have been a part of me. Is not the heart to be the true spirit of need?
If I let you go, my heart shall break and die."
"Daughter," he says, "I'm only a desire of your heart, for an ache that was never filled. It's not I who is your father, just a dream on a never ending carousel, forever affinity."

Theresa C. Baker

The Sweet Silence Of His Love

Without an utter, not a single word, not a whisper of his love is heard.

Without a kiss, without a single sound, I can hear the the silence of his love.

He is cool for he is sensitive, so quiet is his love.

When the kiss comes, and his hug follows,
It's like a storm a comin' to the silence of his love.
I feel a tremble in my heart, when he touches me.
A love so strong, I feel the breeze as he brushes his lips against my cheeks,

He holds me close, the rain starts to fall, the
lightning is seen, but it is not heard,
felt in my heart as he thunders, a tremor a spark,
the sweetness of his love.

I can feel the quiet storm inside of me, so strong is his love.

Sweet his touch
silence his love

Like the silence, in a quiet storm...

Linda Coaker

My Friend

There is one who is my friend.
His love for me will never end.
I had been feeling down and out,
But then he turned my life about.
He's made me see and hear once more,
And all I had to do was answer his knock at my door.
He is wise and has taught me much
And he has added to my life a sparkling touch.
I now realize I often do wrong,
But with him my heart is able to sing a song.
He saved me from a terrible fate,
And directed me towards Heaven's gate.
Yes, my friend is Jesus, Lord to all.
He will be your friend too if you'll just answer his call.

Valorie Thies

A Blessing

Your Grace, O Mother Earth grant me one wish,
Hold me in your embrace.
Set my sole free, aloft on your wings,
Allow me to flow with your tides,
Rivers, brooks and springs.
Declare me born again,
Give me flight on your winds
Race me through your trees and valleys.
Share with me sacred beauty,
Show me wonders beyond my eyes,
Allow me to carve out a mountain,
Or cloud over an otherwise brilliant sky.
Rest me on meadows,
Explore with me every cave,
I return to you with one wish,
I wish to be your slave.
Take hold my hand Mother Earth,
Lead me on our way,
I am no longer me with you,
With you, I will forever stay.

Randy Miles

Untitled

Come, walk beside me through paradise.
Hold my hand as gently as you hold my heart.
Let me see this new world through your eyes.

Come, walk beside me through paradise.
Let me reside in a quiet corner of your heart,
Let me be as much a part of you, as you are of me.

Come, walk beside me through paradise.
Give yourself to me holding nothing back.
Let our two hearts beat as one.

Come, walk beside me through paradise.
Together we will survive through all eternity,
For love can never die.

Mary Theresa Salazar

'Beyond Belief'

Distant thoughts, wild and freely I dream
Hopeless and out of reach is what they always seem
Romance and happiness in a land so far away
Is there such place, longing to be there one day
Don't awaken me, for I'm in a far away land
Palm trees, coconuts, hot moist clinging sand
Fantazise in my dreams is what I always do
Maybe in another time, it will all come true.

Macksine Johnson

Late March In College View Northern Illinois

Rugged, rough, irregular.
  Hopkins' pied lawns: swatches of grass
  Old gray-brown blended into a new lime-jade,
  Like patterns in crocheted lap robes.
All are pregnant.
  Trees with swollen trunks and bud-pierced branches.
  Thickening shrubs.
Bursting-at-the seams golden sun in clear blue sky
  Chased by bone-chilling, drizzle-filled days.
Ugly, black birds needle-beaks hemstitching
  the thaw-loosened ground in the deserted,
  soon-to-be worked backyard.
In the air a teasing, promising, slight smell
  of the annual resurrection.
Ragged, rough, irregular.

Lillian Renecke

Untitled

When I was a boy I was taught God is love and the church was the house of the Lord up above
And taught by my elders Mom and Dad to obey, and to love thy neighbor 'cause that was the way
The priests, preachers and reverends and such-took care of God's work, preaching and the church
But now we read it and it's quite often said, he spoke at a political rally or a protest he led

And in the midst of rioting, looting and burning, a churchman you'll see placard in hand, God spurning
But it's all for the Lord, you'll hear them proclaim, and say it's God's will and we're not to blame
But how can one love and respect his fellowman and in rioting and looting shoot him down because he can
And every day we read that in some foreign land a "holy man," a priest, is out leading his clan
In a bloody uprising his fellowman to kill, and call it a holy war and proclaim it God's will

But my God that I worship I'm proud to say, is the one that teaches that love is the way and looks with contempt at those men today that mix in politics and war and let "God's Word" go astray
But all that I was taught when I was a kid, has long been abandoned "And the whole world's backslid" —————!

Lyken L. Warren

What Life Is About

You will find when you walk through our door, an old farm house with unscrubbed floors, cluttered up cupboards, worn out rugs toys everywhere and stains on the couch.

You will find when you walk through our door, a bright burning candle with treats on the bar, spills in the refrigerator, garbage not taken out, a VCR playing and children walking about.

You will find when you go upstairs, six unmade beds and stuffed animals everywhere. Dresses so packed that the drawers don't close, night-light still shining and pajamas on the floor.

You will find when you walk through our door, a mom and dad who live for this all. A ')ving little Louie, a cheery Charlie Brown a happy Miss Hillary and more babies to come.

And we all know when we walk in our old house,
our love and our happiness is what life is about.
For our greatest asset is our family and our love,
and we thank our Dear Jesus in the Heavens above.

Mary Jane Hengesbach

I Hope You Love This Like I Do!

I wish I could explain to you,
How beautiful our world is.

The pretty, soft and bright green leaves,
The way the wind blows through the trees,
I HOPE YOU LOVE THIS LIKE I DO.

I wish I could explain to you
How wonderful our nature is.

The birds and the grass and the golden bright sun,
The way the flowers seem to have fun,
I HOPE YOU LOVE THIS LIKE I DO.

I wish I could explain to you
How sweet of a song the wind sings.

The way the leaves crunch beneath your feet,
And how there's not a car or street,
I HOPE YOU LOVE THIS LIKE I DO.

I wish I could explain to you
How very lucky we should feel.

To have such a special place to come,
When we are feeling low or glum.
I HOPE YOU LOVE THE NATURE LIKE I DO!!!!
Marcy Del Monte

Let Love In

How can you laugh.
How can you cry.
When all your feelings are frozen inside.

You must allow the ice to break.
Allow the sorrows to melt away.

If the ice doesn't break it is you who will pay.
Your potential to love will soon dissipate.

You're facing dilemmas only you can fight on your own
We all have to do this, it doesn't mean you're alone.

You're having to make choices, not knowing what's right
Because the fears have set in, and they've clouded your mind.

You want to do what's right and true.
You want to be loved and be loved for you.

So don't let one more day go by feeling lonely and lost inside.
Find those demons and cast them aside.
Let yourself live; let yourself fly!

You are a person who deserves to be loved.
Just let down the guards and it will come.

Trust your heart and it will be true.
When nourished with love, it'll take care of you.
Tammy L. Wright

'If Love'

If love is a many splendid thing,
How come it ain't splendid to me?

If love can make you feel high in the sky,
I got both feet on the ground.

If love can put a smile on a face,
How come I wear a frown?

Nothing but pain and sorrow
Awaiting me tomorrow
And where will you be?
No where
'Cause love ain't a many splendid thing
To you and to me
Marla Lynn Pluck

Alcohol, Oh, Alcohol

Alcohol, Oh, Alcohol
   How I know your call

At times, from me,
   You have taken all.

You make my best friends
   want to break my jaw.

Just to have you in my hand,
   Changes the entire man.

You made me believe I had to alter my mind
   in order to be able to have good time

Alcohol, Oh, Alcohol,
   You will not make me fall.

The only way to fight you,
   is not to touch you at all.

So now I saw goodbye my friend,
   For I know that this must end.
Mitchell Wayne Layman

Heart Beat

As I listen to you Mother Ocean I'm taken back to the womb
how I remember that time when your love surrounded me so

The wind through your mist echoes in my heart
your precious song again
it was unmasked in my darkness the passage to betake

You denote as I flow into each crevice I ingest
my consummation with nature in knowledge I give birth

I know you oh Mother
I was formed from your depths

I am also a flick of my Father
the passionate and lustful Sun

I've come to walk on this nourishing Earth
I was given my lessons from the Telling Wind

And when the darkness of Night enshrouds me
the Moon appears in the Heavenly Sky

As a promise of love
the reflected memory of warmth that will always be mine

This is renowned with each beat of my heart
and this is the essence of my very soul
Roberta Harydzak Daer

Anthony

I have a little Miracle, he's cute as he can be,
He's my little Grandson, and his name is ANTHONY.

He has a little curl, that sits on top his head,
I know he gets it naturally, he gets it from his dad.

He likes to stand down on the floor, and bounce himself up and down,
He likes to stand on my shoulder, and glance all around.

I like to play with him a lot, I like to make him laugh,
I wear him out, and myself too, till he's ready for a nap.

He's such a joy for me, I never though it would be,
That I would be a Grandma, at the age of forty-three.

It's wonderful, it's marvelous, it's joy beyond belief,
To see this little miracle, several times a week.

I pray that as the years go by, his mom will get a treat,
To feel what I feel now, with his little miracle at her feet.
Grandma K. Wilson

Life

Oh, that my life could be different,
How many times have I thought that?
But what do I do to make it so?
I just sit back and let it go - no more, no more.
Dear God give me the wisdom
To go straight from the heart
That would be a good start!

I keep so much to myself
And yet I talk so much
Not saying what I really want to say
"Life is so short," my mother always said that!
Help me to know another's feelings,
and please help me to let them know mine!

There is so much hurt,
Why must there always be hurt and tears?
The tears flow like rain
My tears, how many others have tears and
misunderstandings?
Well, let my life change, I am the one
it has to start with!

Marion V. Mitchell

A Daughter's Love

I don't think I ever told you,
how much I appreciated the things you do!
You've always been there when I cried,
and always spotted when I lied!

You've cleaned my wounds when I got hurt,
punished me when I played in dirt!
You were always there to kiss me goodnight,
you always knew how to make things right!

You are my inspiration Mom,
I love you very much!
I can't imagine what it would be like,
without your loving touch!

You will always and forever be first in My Heart,
It won't matter a bit how far we are apart!
Mom, I haven't told you,
I don't know where these words have been!

YOU'RE NOT JUST MY MOTHER
YOU'RE FOREVER MY BEST FRIEND!!

Robyn C. M. Calhoun

Destiny

Wee babes are we; so innocent and sweet
How peaceful and undisturbed is their sleep.
You look upon the world so kindly.
When you wake, smiles form your rosebud mouth,
When you behold God's clean sky,
And kindly faces of those who love you.

Then on to happy carefree childhood
Too quickly it travels by toward adolescence
When first we begin to feel the trouble and strife,
That lies ahead in the pathways of life.

Yet eagerly we rush forward with hopes and joys
To embrace our destiny. Have we not often said,
"Could I have foreseen the future,
I would have," and cry aloud against
God's wisdom that he does not let us see
Where our faltering footsteps tread.

For should we see, would we not flee
In terror from our own stupidity?
So protect not his kindly wisdom, but thank him each night.
He does not let us see what fools we mortals be.

Vivian Van Lennep

"Another Kind Of Love"

In the hustle of the noonday,
how quietly tranquil we remain.
Not a care nor worry could render our budding hearts,
for Cupid's arrows have found their victims,
and the sweet ache of love caresses our unprotected souls.
How we gaze into the depths of each other's eyes,
becoming merry on the fruit of life!
Our cups have run over now, and
fully satiated, still
we ask for yet more.

Melissa R. Luznicky

Oklahoma City - The Heartland

On Wednesday morning the world would see,
How the heartland of America would come to be,
A tragic, and gruesome, and broken place,
With terror and shock upon our face.
We came together and worked as one,
From coast to coast and sun to sun.
We wait, we listen, we pray to hear,
A cry for help from someone dear.
And then the word comes that we all dread:
"I regret to inform you, your baby is dead."
This tears out our hearts, and makes us ask why,
These innocent people were slated to die.
The world waits and watches, in true disbelief,
As the stories are told in the eyes of our grief.
We pray in our hearts, and hope it's today
The terrorists are caught, with strict prices to pay.
And that's how on Wednesday, the whole world would see
How the heartland of America would come to be.

Sandra L. Robins

Twenty One!

Lo and behold, my daughter is twenty one!
How the time has flown
It seems only yesterday that you were small
How anxious I was — and still am.
You've done so much and gone so far,
I sometimes feel estranged
But when you return, we start anew
Not always eye to eye
We see each other as we really are
Not as we pretend to be
No perfect mother
No perfect daughter
But we can still draw close and whisper,
"I love you!"

Susan Marchand

The Time Of A Love

We are all individuals - different and unique
How wonderful life is while I imagine you in my world
You never will be though
You have your world and I have mine
And there are many many many other worlds
Maybe our paths cross momentarily to be shared
But they are only paths
They started in different places
And they travel in different ways
And they have different destinations
They all do - There are no exceptions
And the rule is, there are no rules
It was my good fortune to have met you

Marlene Preziose

Cornered

He's alone, old, two generations from me.
Humped over, pushing forward in a wheelchair.
Waiting for death, loved ones gone.

A cave inside of him
Once filled, empty now, pulled away
by death's evil hand.

This home, but not his home.
Here are caring people, who don't care.
Trapped inside a cage of iron.

Put away, forgotten,
waiting
they will never come.

Giving up,
gave up,
gone.

Micah Strait

Hand In Hand

I desired something unknown to me. Nothing satisfied the
hunger. I searched and searched.

Unexpectedly, I got my first glimpse of her. I was captivated
by her stare. Gently, she held my hand in hers. I was
no longer afraid.

Together we discovered a love unimaginable, love that cannot
be duplicated with another. Passion others will not
understand.

Together we developed a bond that would join our lives
forever. I was filled with happiness, overcome with peace.

Lost in my desire, I did not see her fear, I did not feel
her hand leave mine.

I'm reaching out to her. Will she hold my hand once again.
This time, to never let go.

Yvette Pinazza

Dictionaries

My fifth grade teacher said they were your friends;
I agree with her now and then.
They tell me how to spell everything, every day,
A million for one of them I could pay.
Because they are one of my best friends,
They will be for now and until the time ends.

Winston Veeraprasert Woan

Untitled

  Slide into the temptations
I am frustrated
    along my side is fear and shame
The secret of passion
  stash this away with the needs
    never look at the Emerald stones and vines
My figure of this dimension is dying - without
with- my love holding hands with lust
   I can be
  My mind can think, I can create
  Night is born and free I fly...
When morn breaks I must leave
  in shackles and chains of leaves,
Nature sets its jury opposing me,
    strong as I am I must plea
Sentences for eternity
  My conscience is blackmailed
    forever to know

Rita Sylvia Miller

Great and Mighty King

My Great and Mighty King I hear your call
I am here, I await your return
Lead me, that I may follow
It is You I serve and no other
May I do right by You
You protect me and keep me
You guide me in light
Your presence is with me always
Praise and honor and glory be to You
King Jesus, Lord of all
Holy is your judgment and truth
I strayed from You but You never falter
You took me back and restored me
How wondrous are Your ways
Though all is unstable around me
I fear not, for You are here
My enemies are beyond number
But no harm befalls me,
Your truth and Holy judgment shall endure forever
May I always be with You

Michael William Edison

Somewhere Inbetween

   Please listen to what I am saying for this is who I am.
I am not who I seem to be...but am who I am not. It is not
all that hard to understand....it is just who I want to be, I
want to be secure and confident and perhaps someday I shall be
but now....right now it's a mask I shall wear...a game I must
play. I don't want to fail....for rejection is my fear. I am a child
but an adult, somewhere inbetween and I am lost in a world of
uncertainty. I am trying to get better day by day....and yet
there is still some game I must play.
   A left turn or right one....it is all up to me...that is why
I hide behind my mask....for there are still so many questions to ask.
   I want to get better for you and me, reach a little bit higher...
...and yet higher. I want you to remember the little things I
do as well as the big ones....for those are more special in certain
ways. Each little thing leaves a mark....I don't want to be
known for what I am...but for who I am....and yet what
I am to become.

Stephanie Nicole Schock

Us

I have tomorrow, the dream of today.
I am the future, I'll find a way.
You are the memories fading one by one.
Today when I saw you, I remembered our past.
We shared something wonderful, but it just didn't last.
I can't stay any longer.
I have no move on, to find tomorrow,
Because yesterday is gone.

Lindsay Lagoe

Trust

Hold him close... but not too tight
He makes you feel... but not just right
Opened wide... but closed up tight
He'll hurt you soon... with all his might
Gave it all... he's given none
Scream real loud... you've come undone
What he's made of you he'll break
What he can salvage he will take
Cut up inside as your outside thrives, unwind slow.
You're down as low as you can go, cut and dried.
You've been skinned alive, give up everything.
Slide deep inside, feelings gone.
Nerves are severed.
Your punishment now is to live forever.

Keetah Simonds

I Am The Sea

I am the ocean
I am the sea
Delve into the depths of me
Explore, beneath each grain of sand, behind every stone
Leave no drop of water untouched
Pick up each shell, letting your fingers slide across its smooth surface
Sail on my crests, ride on my waves
Let me carry you into the unknown
Let my waters of life cleanse you
Let my waters of death overcome you, finally giving you solace from
Empty glasses and fading moons
Let me release you
Caress, surround, fill you
Swim into my caves, until you disappear inside of me
Hide, my waters are endless but you cannot drown
Stay in me forever, float always on my currents
Your glistening body, sweat running down your back
Like the trail of seaweed left in the sand
I am the sea
Swim into me.

Marcy L. Solomon

Changing World

Staring out of my window in dismay
I began to wonder without much delay;
Where are the friendly faces who used to say,
"Hello my friend, how are you today?"

The world is changing right before our eyes
Days are too often spent in silent cries;
Gangs are running around in a rage
Papers are filled with violence from page to page.

Friends are turning against each other
There is little love for one another;
Mothers and fathers have lost control
And kids have become so very bold.

People are not safe on the streets anymore
The value of one's life isn't important as before;
What is this old world coming to
What are the innocent people to do?

How nice it would be to turn back the hands of time
When there was less fear and very little crime;
When families could go out and enjoy an evening of fun
Or spend a nice day of relaxation in the sun.

Myrtle Wilson

"I Cry"

I cry because I'm happy
I cry because I'm sad
I cry because I fail
I cry because I achieve
So, I ask myself when will the crying stop.
How can it, I say when I'm surrounded
with sorrow, and hearts that no longer
feel or need.
I cry when I go outside. "Why?" they ask.
Because of all the hatred and envy
I'm faced with out there.
I cried for the robbers and
giggaboos too.
I cried for the newborn
I cried for the one 6 ft under
I cry for my mother, for all her
obstacles she has won.
But tonight I'll make one last cry,
that cry will be for me
to stop my eyes from burning with fever.

Nadia N. Keating

Eliza May

Eliza May stood on judgment day facing those pearly gates.
"I came to see St. Peter. What's holdin' him up he's late?"
"Eliza May" boomed a voice that day, "your wait will be a long one."
"I know my name's in that book," she exclaimed. "Hurry up it's hot in the sun!"
"Please go away Eliza May, St. Peter doesn't need to see you."
"I'm here to stay," said Eliza May. "Open up, I'm comin' through!"
With a roar and a crash the gates opened at last, and Eliza May strutted in.
But the figure she saw wasn't Peter or Paul, but the devil who said with a grin.
"You humans it seems can be pushy and mean when you aim to have your way."
"Glad you came to stay Miss Eliza May. Heaven's gate is the other way!"

Lisa Teague

Walk With Me

Old wonderful life what you can give me.
I cannot find under a tree.
For the branches are hanging over me.
Trying to stop the sun from shining through me.
That warm my heart to my soul.

All wonderful life come walk with me,
For we can see just how wonderful our life will be,
And to understand what you mean to me.
For there will be rain and there will be dew,
But you can make it if only you would walk with me.

I gave you my life, I gave you my soul,
I gave you my sun light to let you know
Just how wonderful your life will be,
If only you will continue to walk with me.

Mattie Wolfe

Mother's Prayer

In the middle of the quiet still night
I can remember hearing my Mother cry,
Down on her knees she would stay
And I could hear my Mother pray,
Ten small children she would say
You gave them all to me to raise,
Now I have been left all alone
With ten small children and no home,
They have no clothes or shoes on their feet
Lord, where will I get them something to eat,
I need a job, she would say
Lord I know you will find a way,
Then she stood on her feet
She went to bed and fell asleep,
All she had was her love for us
And in God she did put her trust,
Over the years she taught us to pray
And every day for us God made a way,
I will always remember that day
My Mother on her knees did pray.

Viola Jane Tabor

Untitled

Oh God, I have sinned and my heart burns
hot with the grief of it.

Even now as this pen moves, I see no end
to my torment.

And yet, while all that is good cries out
to me

I turn my wretched soul toward hell,
and weep...

F. Norris McKinney

"A Thousand Words Is What I'm Feeling"

I don't know you - yet you've touched me
I cannot recall ever feeling so much ANGER - FURY
- ever feeling so much of everything
oh, what those who are close to you must be feeling
lying there so undignified
representing nothing
never being able to come home
and I hope you'll never know what became of your body
- may your soul be experiencing tranquility
I can't seem to concentrate on what I'm supposed to be doing
have they no humanity
can one achieve peace with violence
can one make a point with savagery
is there anything to achieve
is there a point to be made
will I be able to get this picture out of my mind
for someone I've never met - you've certainly touched me
and since I've seen your picture
a thousand words is what I'm feeling...

Laura Anne Lord

I Wear A Mask

Each morning when I rise there are tears and sadness in my eyes;
I can't let anyone see the hurt that is there inside of me.
I put upon my face, a mask to get me through the daily tasks -
A cheerful cloak; so no one knows - my heart is broke.

The mask I wear is painted fine but the smile that's on it isn't mine.
As the days, the weeks and months go by I ponder over the question,
   why?
No one knows the grief inside, because the mask does hide
the pain within my heart I feel, that time has so far failed to heal.

You see my daughter died... they say it was a suicide.
No note, good bye, not a clue; it just wasn't in her character to do.
But within my heart I know, as the happenings do show,
and by the facts of the event, it must have been an accident!

Daughter, I miss you so! Why, oh why, did you have to go?
I know you're in a better place, surrounded by God's warm embrace!
"Time heals all," as they say. So, maybe I'll find, some day,
an easy way to shed this mask I have upon my head,
The painted smile replaced and my own back on my face.

I'll keep your memories in my heart where you'll always be a part,
and some day when I can no longer cry I'll let you go and say goodbye.
In my heart you're still alive! As life goes on, I will survive!

Renee Godberson

"Dream About Tomorrow"

As I watch the sun rise over the mountains,
I contemplate this new day.
I hope this will be the day I triumph,
That I finally get out of it what I put in.
I believe that my hard work will be praised,
And that I will get credit for what I have accomplished.
But as the hours slowly pass,
My achievements go unnoticed.
The extra mile I have gone seems worthless.
I feel cheated and taken for granted.
As I drive towards home, my heart feels heavy,
My soul cries out for recognition.
As day turns into night, I reflect.
The dreams and hopes of today are over.
No one has made me feel significant,
That I must do for myself.
As I watch the sun set over the mountains,
I dream about tomorrow
And I know it will be a better day.

Ronda G. Viars

In My Heart A Bliss Of Sorrow Bears

No hope for chains of tomorrow.
I continue my journey deeper remorse.
The grip of life's noose has freed me,
"The host," for life is a parasite feeding on my soul
leaving only tattered remains no longer a whole.
Wondering lost in my castle every passage way is cold
every room a frozen dream from this life I behold.
Darkness rules supreme and after eternity will be there,
ready to embrace the final remnants of the last of light's heir.
I have met my eternity, my future is dark.
I once had candles which flickered a warmth in my heart!

Sean Woodcock

Story-Telling Session

Her loving eyes looked intently into mine with clemency
I conveyed my account of the occurrence by the sea.
As the tale ascended to her ears
Her onyx eyes rapidly filled with tears.

She philanthropically embraced me when my story was done
And kissed me on the cheek with love meant only for a son.
Mom expressed her congenial attitude for my droll yarn
As we perched in the hayloft of our musty-fragrance barn.

Then came her turn to humbly narrate.
Although her chronicle was obsolete it was amusing at any rate.
She fervently told of Brer Rabbit with mispronounced words
In our story-telling session up high amid the chirping birds.

William K. Young

On The Death Of An Infant

I just stopped by to say hello.
   I couldn't stay; I had to go—no time to spare.
With so much left to do and say,
   We'll talk and play some other day, sometime, somewhere.

You thought I ought to stay, I know,
   So you could watch me learn and grow with passing years.
But I have found a place quite fair,
   So beautiful and free from care—no pain, no tears.

And while my visit here was brief,
   There will be joy beyond belief when next we meet.
Everything a lifetime brings,
   Plus a host of undone things will be complete.

Although it may not seem that way,
   A thousand years are but a day—God made it so.
My stay seemed short? I'll tell you why:
   On angel wings I just stopped by to say hello.

Owen E. Humphrey

"The I Am"

He quietly enters a room; someone asks,
have I met you? The "I am" came
alive and began to speak "I am"
the beginning and the end. I have
come to forgive all your sins. To have
the presence of the "I am" in your
life, you must die to this world, and
ask the "I am" to come alive in your life,
to lead, guide and direct you, a light
to shine so bright. The "I am" will bring
you out of darkness, dark as night. Trust
the "I am" to be with you. He will forgive you
for your sins. He says "Lo I am with you even
to the end. Who am I? I am the beginning
and the end. I have come to forgive you of all
your sins, "Jesus Christ."

Mary Lee Caldwell

Goodbye

The moment that you said goodbye,
I didn't know if I should laugh or cry.
   The thought of losing you was too much to bear,
If I went on living I didn't care.
   You always told me how you loved me so.
I don't understand why you let me go.
   You hurt me so bad, In so many ways.
Now I find myself just counting the days.
   Counting the days since you said goodbye.
Now it's time for me to dry my eyes.
   I know in my heart it's what you had to do,
But there will never be a day I won't think of you.

Teri Haney

"What Are Mothers?"

I have no special knowledge, nor insight more than you,
I do have some ideas, and I guess you have some too,
   So, here, I'll make a list of mine, and pass them all along,
My list of course is personal, and may be short or long.
   For mothers are a host of things, all aimed at doing good,
Most prominent in family care, you knew just where she stood.
   For she was cook, and baker too, and keeper of the nest,
She'd decorate or paint the house, and always gave her best.
   When sickness, pain, or injury, would come to trouble you,
She was the source of total care, the nurse and doctor too,
   And mothers are a storehouse full of talents I have missed,
Too many to be a written down and make a single list,
   But when there was a problem, or job you had to fill,
Your mother had that special gift, so sure to fill the bill.
   "Some mothers" sure have all of this, and maybe even more,
"All mothers" sure have some of this, and that we're thankful for.
   For mothers are as many things as we can think to name,
They all are in-di-vidual, perfection is their aim.

Richard Baird

Flower Song

A flower grows, in my backyard, on this lovely day in spring.
I do not know the kind it is, that is such an incidental thing.
The beauty of this golden flower lies in its representation,
It was a gift given me, by a friend, without any hesitation.

A flower grows, in my backyard, on this lovely day in spring,
I appropriately call it, Lisa, a feminine little thing.
This flower chose to grow and bloom without intimidation.
Another sign that friendship grows despite any trepidation.

A flower grows, in my backyard, on this lovely day in spring,
It was given with love and planted with love, no accidental thing.
This flower required, from both of us, yet a little modification,
To make our friendship grow and bloom without any nullification.

A flower grows, in my backyard, on this lovely day in spring!

Patricia S. Leonard

A Dark And Stormy Night

It was a dark and stormy night, and the sky was turning from light gray to black. The clouds were rolling in overhead, covering the moon that was trying very hard to find a crack to peek through. Suddenly the lightning flashed in the west, making the darkness light up with an eerie glow, the thunder rumbled, and then there was a silence for a short time as the storm gathered force and once again rolled across the heavens. The lightning snapped, and the thunder crashed so loud it shook the earth. The rain poured down, beating at the window where I sat watching. The beauty was beyond words, and no one would ever be able to capture on film the majestic wonder of the breathtaking splendor of a summer storm in the blackness of the night. I could sit here in my window seat and watch all night, but for the duties that tomorrow would bring.

Barbara B. Keetch

Mommy?

Mommy, I gots a boo boo
I falled at de play ground today.
Will you come out and kiss it bedder?
Please, Momma make it ok.

Mommy, why don't you answer?
How come you went away?
Gramma says you're wiff Jesus.
Are you comin back out today?

Oh Momma, why can't I see you?
Why don't you open this door?
Mommy do you still Love me?
Do you love Jesus more?

Hey, why are they putting you into the grown?
Stop! My Momma's in there!
She can't breve, let her out!
Daddy help! Daddy shout!

Hey daddy, why do you cry?
What does that mere?
Daddy, what does that mean?
When you tell me that mommy died?

Rachel Mellon

Untitled

I feel Angry
I feel Like...
   A caged animal in the zoo.
   A storm cloud rolling high,
   destroying things with the rain.
   A cold blizzard, blowing across the land.

I feel Carefree
I feel Like...
   A kite flying high in the sky.
   A deer frolicking in the meadow.
   An autumn leaf dancing with the wind.

I feel sad
I feel Like...
   A drop of dew falling from a dying rose.
   A raindrop falling from the sky.
   A lost cub wandering in the forest.

Michelle Renee Munson

Heart Strings

In the light of day or the darkest hour
I feel your presence surrounding me
Searching, reaching, to feel your touch
Can it be, will it be, you I see.

Your smile I remember quite well
The hand that held mine so tight
Wishing upon a star so high in the sky
Can it be, will it be, this beautiful night.

Wind blows calling you home
Raindrops falling against the window pane
Music playing our favorite song
Can it be, will it be, calling your name.

Few moments alone once again
Two hearts together, one beat
United from heaven to earth
Can it be, will it be, you I greet.

A heart that longs to open doors
Letting eternity come to stay
Once again I light the fire
Can it be, will it be, you find the way.

Sandy Hill

Untitled

Through the eyes of a child,
how innocently they look at the world,
with kindness and love,
they wonder with open eyes,
reaching out to touch and to feel,
ready to explore an unknown world,
so willing to learn,
ready to hold your hand,
watching every move you make,
waiting to be taught,
how simple it is to them,
through their eyes,

Stacy Lynn MacKail Davis

THROUGH CHILDREN'S EYES

A Tribute to Oklahoma City

And the rubble came down
As our treasures were found
And our minds do explode
At the thought that our hopes
For the future of the world
Could go up in a "whirl"
'Cause the children are our dreams
This we realize through the screams
What we all have come to
If the children have lost value
We must look once again
Then forgive...then begin
To evaluate our lives
Looking through children's eyes
For the causes are not right
If we senselessly destroy life
It's for the children change is made
Just view the past until today
And the world spins round and wise
If we look through children's eyes

Tammaryn Alston-Goodwill

Tiger And Baby Too

A baby is coming,
A baby is near
A time for joy,
And a time for fears.

But love will guide,
And see you through,
Down each street
And avenue.

And when the pain
Has come and gone,
And a baby is snuggled
In your warm arms.

And you've counted
Ten fingers, ten toes,
Then you'll surely
Have to know.

God gave you a miracle,
one to love,
one to cuddle
And one to hug.

Appreciate this special gift
Don't take it for granted,
This miracle has chosen you
To be a special parent.

Rick Tomlinson

Untitled

In a starry lavender filled sky.
A beam of light comes from way up high.
Burning through the darkest clouds.
From a moon of cobalt blue.
Falls upon a sea of gold
and lights the glow of waves
of living blue.
And in the waves where the
dolphins play, singing songs of
love along their way.
With a passion lit bright within
their eyes, they swim a joyful
dance in their undersea life.
What they see who can say
but what a better world it
would be if we all could see
that way, so on this day of
valentines, I ask of you to be my valentine!

Tyron Chad Hamilton

The Park

Close to the building of elder adults
a beautiful park is located
are elm trees and oat trees inside
near the lake situated.
   People from nearest places
like in the park on the bench to unwind
or with some of their neighbors
are walking around the park.
   When plenty of people are in the park
it looks so cheerful and bright,
but without the people
it has a boring sight,
   Its view is now another
not like it was at the first
and it remains us of mothers
abandoned in their empty nests.

Mira Brokhin

Disaster Strikes

Suddenly, horror strikes,
A bomb explodes,
Buildings crash down to the ground,
Innocent people dying,
Police come in,
Tearing away all the debris,
Looking for people alive,
But finding dead ones instead,
They are giving up,
But suddenly they find someone alive,
All their hope is up now,
They go on,
Tired, hungry, thirsty, SCARED,
But still they go on,
In hope of finding another,
Suddenly they see someone,
But they are already dead,
They rise to a better place now,
Where there is no more pain and suffering.

Laura Phillips

Time

I wish I could slay time with a slash of
a sword, and make the seconds bleed
for eternity. The days would never
end. Damn that would be mad fun!

Michael Lopez

Summer Lost In '94

The warmth of the summer sun tapers off
A crisp nightfall breeze picks up
Autumn is on the horizon
As I sit watching emptiness
The scene parallels a ghost town
Plastic bags drift like tumbleweed
Clinking cans clatter like rattlesnakes
What was innocent is now lost
What was sacred is now sacrificed
Excitement lost
Tradition lost
Summer lost
The consequences can be felt everywhere
This travesty does not discriminate
Emptiness lingers about
And although the pigskin has been offered
as a substitute
Nothing can replace the sound of cowhide
on ash

Terry Allen Lipshetz

Love Is

Love is...
A daisy,
yellow,
a sweet smell,
a little girl picking it up,
and saying
"he loves me not",
a prayer,
that your heart screams
out loud.
A dream,
that's in your mind,
then the water
turns warm,
and that
daisy
drifts away
into the
sunshine!

Rossilyn Sanson

"The Beauty Of Life"

Do you expect too much from yourself,
a family, great job and good health?
Don't get discouraged if you can't see
what life has to offer you and me.

If sometimes you're feeling down,
Stop! and take a look around.
Life's not all that bad
There's more to be happy about than sad

Every day is not a dream come true
Some are happy, some are blue.
Show someone a smile, lend a hand
on your feet you will land.

If you think positive and live right,
the beauty of life will grow in sight.
Each one of us has something to give
that makes our life worthwhile to live.

Life is all in what you make it,
take some steps, just a little bit.
You'll see what you have before your eyes
and be thankful of your will to survive!

Paula Moore

Ouch

An elbow to the ribs.
A fist to the chin.
A foot to the thigh.
Oh what a position I'm in.

I must stay to the finish.
There's no escape from it.
I'm bruised but not bloody yet.
Gosh if just still she'd sit.

A wrestling match?
A boxing bout?
No. Just in the back seat with Sarah
Traveling about.
Marianne Sardino

Slumber

Her trips are
A gas chamber
And the smell from the stove
Her hands are all empty
And she grips them alone
She sees the priest walk behind her
And her mother beside her
Reciting her last rights

Her dreams are the last to slumber
A soft light of blue glow
Time loses its hold on her
The fall begins slow

The echo of footsteps
Down the hall
For someone else
And there is no call

The quiet comes
And the smell from the stove
Her hands are all empty
And they open alone
Katrina Perrault

Life

A full moon.
  A hairy baboon.
And.
    Rhubarb on the trail
Walter I. West Jr.

A Hero At Home

A Hero at home
A Hero away
That's what Mr. Donald Ellis is today
He went to the war
with a gun in his hand
he was with a lot of others
they were all in demand
he fought and was wounded
he may have hurt a few
but in this kind of situation
what would you do
caring for others
not thinking of himself
the medals for his mission
now sit on a shelf
the war is now over
and he is back home
he cooks for handicapped men
who have not a home
Rodney Bee Neal I

Betrayal

Betrayal-
A jagged
Weapon,
Contaminated
With germs of
Greed-
And self,
Inflicting
A wound-
Unparalleled
In pain,
And leaving
Scars-
That may
Remain,
For a
Lifetime!
Roland L. Crosby

God's Highway

I walk along God's highway,
a journey full of grace.
There's a angel on my shoulder,
and a smile upon my face.

My days are filled with wonder,
as I travel on my way.
I follow my heart's pleasures,
as I live from day to day.

"There are no fears worth fretting,"
An angel told me this.
"So let your spirit run free,
and live in Heaven's bliss."

My journey's just beginning,
There's so much more to see,
I thank God for every moment,
I'm to free to "just be me."
Lauralyn T. Mohr

Forever

Forever is tomorrow.
Forever is today.

Forever is where you go,
When you go away.

Forever is the time we spent,
Just sitting there together.

And the thought that makes me happiest
Is you and me forever.
Sarah Gilman

At Thirty-Six

Regrets — opportunities — choice
  for better or worse.
Life through halting steps giving voice
  to current values.

Peering through a glass darkened by
  the unknowable,
a hardened heart can only try
  to reclaim its way.

In the end, will one, can one, see
  patterns in chaos?
Only saints have epiphanies —
  mere men must face facts.
David R. Grace

Lonely

A lonely heart
A lonely soul
A lonely woman
Losing control
Wanting you
Missing you
Loving you more
Wishing and waiting
Just open the door
You're running scared
Of this I'm sure
Stop and look
See what you've found
A love with no boundaries
A heart that does break
Star crossed lovers
Joined by fate
Torn apart by reality
A sad and lonely life
This does make.
Rene S. Reidenbach

Joy Of Life

Life can be a joyful thing,
A lovely poem, a song of spring,
A painting hung upon a wall,
A scene of beauty we recall.

Life can be a rose of radiant hue,
As sunbeams glitter on the dew,
Or become an ecstasy of delight,
As twinkling stars come out at night.

Life can be a mirror clear,
Reflecting day by day each year
Happiness of days now past,
Those days are gone, that joy shall last.

Life can be a vision fair
For us to cherish everywhere,
From now until eternity,
A source of comfort constantly.
Ruth E. Powderly

Untitled

A shortened breath
a meaningless death

Darkened scars
brightened stars

Blood flowing
wind blowing

Powerful mind
two of a kind

Flowing hair
straight stare

Closed eyes
white lies

Hatred burns
as the world turns

Victory won
burning sun

Meaningless talk
solid lock

Tiny key
washed to sea.
Lisa Stayner

Untitled

We make
a naked
poetry,
a metaphor
undressed.
The words
are merely
simile...
our sense
is in
the flesh.

Paul Wittenberger

A Mother's Fearful Reflections On Life With A Child With A Genetic Disease

Wide-eyed beauty—baby boy
  "A perfect child, like a toy!"
    "Let me see him one last time
    before they take him away."

Nine-pound first-born, blonde and proud
  Always sick, cloaked in a shroud
    "Let me kiss him one last time
    before they whisk him away."

Failure to thrive—one heart arrest
  Shades of blue—a moral test
    "Let me hug him one last time
    before they wheel him away."

Rife admits, grand mal seizures
  Fainting spells, never leisure
    "Let me hold him one last time
    before they take him away."

Lisa R. Benedict

"On Getting Older"

Sometimes I feel
A piece of sad,
Recognizing
I'm no more a lad.

But considering
What I've done and had,
It makes me feel
A piece of glad.

William E. Engbretson

Shooting Star

A fractured second,
A piece of sky,
A fizzling flash—
Tear in your eye.

That streaking light,
Gravity's fission;
Terminated flight,
Aborted mission.

Wade Reynolds

"Life Is Precious"

Life is precious, as we all know.
A gift from God, for us to show
that we can love all mankind
and to keep looking until we find
peace and harmony here on earth.
And someday soon it will be worth
all the years that we are here.
That's why we hold life so dear.

Russell J. Bennett, II

Heavenly Gardener

A bud the Gardener gave us,
A pure and lovely child.
He gave it to our keeping,
To cherish undefiled.
But as the bud was opening,
To the glory of the day.
Down came the "Heavenly Gardener,"
and took our bud away.

Ronna Adler

There Is A River

There is a river of dreams
a river of potential
a river so priceless
it is strictly confidential

It flows with grace
beauty and peace
with strength only to be imagined
its waters shall never cease

With elegance unknown
beautifully undefined
drinking of it
will turn evil to kind

A river of love
where the angels dwell
with black magic's code
it will cast a spell

I dream of this river
so wonderful and pure
if one was lost without love
for this would be a cure

Toye E. Watts Jr.

Daydream

I wish I could visit
a room in your silence
that has not been dusted
with flecks of memory,
nor has known
any tears
that have fallen and dried.

I wish I could call
out a name
that enters in you
a place
so far away new
that it feels like
a Sunday
of red leaves and hope.

Michael B. Zack

Untitled

Vulnerability
alone, single
yet the need for love and compassion
is always there

Venturing
into the world
bravely tackling all that's new
so frightening

Independence
its joy and strengths
the move into your own space
affirmation of self

Ruth Morris Luthi

Alone

Stuck in a locked room.
A room with black walls,
no windows, no doors, and no way out.
I can't see you, I can't hear you.
You can't come in, I can't get out.
There's no way out.
Locked away forever.
Alone.
No one to talk to, no one to listen.
Nothing to do but think.
Alone.
Can't see anything, can't hear anything.
Can't speak, I want to get out.
I wish I hadn't come in.
Maybe if I could have thought twice.
Maybe if someone could have helped me.
There's nothing I can do now.
Nothing anybody can do.
All I can do now is think.
No one here, only me, all alone.

Nicole Ardolino

Mon Petite Fluer

She put a gleam in my eyes,
a smile upon my face,
even caused my heart to race.

But now she's gone,
gone without a trace,
left behind only sweet aroma,
bits of fine white lace.

Mon petite fluer (my little flower),
she has gone and left me,
left me alone,
alone the world to face.

Willi Wolfschmidt

Daybreak

Early morning awakening - beside you;
A special feeling -
Of love, gentleness, and tenderness.
Watching the peace
Written upon your sleeping face
Brings joy and warmth to my heart,
And I reach out
To caress the source of my happiness,
Half afraid to disturb such beauty.
You stir, and with fluttering eyes,
Awaken -
And all my fantasies become reality.

Philip A. Eckerle

Binocular

A far, far world the eyes embrace,
a strange, elusive world brought near,
a single star in Heaven's space
among a myriad, made clear,

where greener grasses cannot be,
no snowy mountains reach so high,
where Earth unfolds her symmetry
of trees against the vault of sky,

where keener image none can deem
than holding in a clasp of hands
deep lenses ground to seek some dream
conceived beyond familiar lands.

Margaret Hellewell

"The Beginning"

His body, decaying,
A tree once flourished, green, life
No more, No more...

The soul searches, bodies ache
The spirit agonizes, free
wants to be...

Once there are life, now death
Darkness overtakes the heart
Nearly torn apart...

He flies to the sky
Like the dove to his Master
He goes faster.

Through the clouds, he reaches
Someone takes his hand, it is He
The place where everyone wants to be...

He is home, pain, suffering
Things of the Earth mean nothing
No more, No more...

Kevin O. Beasley

Precious

I stood up proud and made you mine
A trembling virgin, pure and fine
With lips that taste like sweet red wine
As we embraced in love divine.

I held you as you bore my child
With brightest eyes, and skin so mild.
I learned to love that little one
And then you bore a little son.

You are my wife, my only flame.
They say the tongue no man can tame.
If you're with me - I'll be just fine
With rocking chairs, and love divine.

No rockin' chairs, no streets of gold,
But when you're here I'm not so cold.
In beauty now we're growing old
With love that can't with words be told.

In life, in death, and in between
Together always we'll be seen.
Your lips still taste like sweet red wine,
And I'm still proud to call you mine.

Robert Marlett

"Whisper In The Wind"

A daisy in the spring flowing in a pond.
A weeping willow weeping right
before the break of dawn.
A smile to up-lift you when the
day seems so long and blue.
A walk within a garden sprinkled
with the morning dew.
A beat within your heart, reserved
only I hope for me.
A baby calf just born opening its
eyes to see.
Like a storm with enormous strength
hold me close in your soul within.
Listen with your heart and hear
my whisper in the wind.

Vanessa Rodgers Tracy

Lost Daffodils

I would like to tell you a story,
about daffodils in their yellow glory.
These are not real in flower and stem,
but are plastic without and within.

In my flower garden today
I planted them so gay.
To charm the passer-by
and reflect the beauty of the sky.

The real bulbs survived the snow
but not the rodents who loved them so.
Those nasty, naughty creatures you see,
they dug them up and ate them up on me.

And then right here in true day light,
my plastic daffodils so bright.
Succumbed to a flightier fate,
for they were stolen instead of ate.

Shall I ponder on this void estate,
or dismiss it as a neutral mistake?
Plant some stinky blossoms instead,
in this my lonely flower bed.

Rosie Sandra Lannoye

"Us"

I've done a lot of complaining
   About the muss and fuss.
But the old house was comfortable-
   When it was filled with US!

I've rattled around this morning,
   Though I know there's work to do!
But the lonely is so deafening-
   I long for YOU and YOU and YOU!!

Thank goodness the "little one"
   Is gone for just a day;
And the "wanderers" in 2 weeks
   Will be around to stay.

And maybe then Big Son-
   (the one who lives away)
Will find himself some spare time-
   And come and spend a day.

And then How I will wallow
   In all the muss and fuss!
This house will be a "HOME" again-
   When it is filled with "US"!

Norma Bodkin

Against Entropy

She silences her trout
alarm at 4:30 hours before predawn
woods and streams at Salem Pond

April fools collected
feathers, bits of fur poured
molten lead homemade sinkers, her

Bicycle laces through meadows
gorges with split bamboo rods
strapped to a leather case

Hand-tied flies where Argentinean
twenty-inch browns rainbows leapt
on a dry run not as steelhead

In shadows forage oversized waders
floating line bucolic moving in
and out of mythological gill.

D. Jayne McPherson

Thoughts Of Love And Time

My thoughts, they swiftly travel
Across thy space and time
To rest upon your mind

Your thoughts resound in harmonies
Past love have left behind

Our thoughts entwine, combine
And time, once again, is yours and mine

Terry W. Huffhines

Left Me

How could you do this,
after all I sacrificed
for you?
Everything I heard, saw, hoped for
was you.

Now you drown me
in the tears
you made me cry.

Why?

Hope is too far away.
A bright and sparkling light
charging onward into
the endless emerald night,
leaving me behind
to drown,
still loving you.

Nineveh J. Marceau

To My Grandchildren

Oh a breath of fresh air
After the stale smoke
Of light-filtered cigarettes

A renewed sense of being
Belief in life and myself
As I once was long ago!

I wipe the tears from my eyes
And remember my youth
As I relieve it through you

So often now I feel
Past sensual remembrances
A fragrance means so much

And as the past unwinds
I think of you and hope
You'll always think of me.

Russell Cappo

Little Children Come Unto Me

"Some would gather money
Along the path of life.
Some would gather roses
And rest from earthly strife.
But I would gather children
From among the thorns of sin;
I would seek a golden curl
And a freckled, toothless grin.
For money cannot enter
Into the land of endless day,
And roses that are gathered
Soon will wilt along the way,
But oh, the laughing children,
As I cross the sunset sea,
And the gates swing wide to heaven
I can take them in with me."

Louise Lisenby

SAGUARO CROSS

Silhouette
Against crimson sky,
Silver shimmer moonlight,
Pale, promised dawn,
Noonday burning glare;
Arms reach out
   in appeal-
     forgiveness-
      welcome-
All the long day of life.

Beauty blooms
   in peace-
     wonder-
      hope.

Sap assuages
   pilgrim thirst-
     strength-
      for the journey.

In shadow,
   love sleeps secure.

M. Thomasine Steel

Autumn

Yellow rimmed leaves
all balanced,
tipped along branches and stems,
a rotunda twirled
turning titian

Descend in varying textures,
a painterly spectrum,
on shades of burgundy
and orange and red

All aglow,
slip down wind

Dispose in
a fall conundrum:

Batches of brown ablaze
ascend in hickory ash,
a rejuvenation.

Michael E. Bennett

A Special Game

Today was played, a special game
and everyone there knew it.
A Little League game, a little boy,
and those who said he'd never do it.

He was born with a disability,
doctors said he wouldn't overcome.
He could walk, they told his mother
but he'll never be able to run.

He won't be like other children,
he can't do the things they do.
He'll need braces just to walk,
and a lot of help and love from you.

Well, his mother wouldn't accept it
and her son, he proved them wrong.
Because today he ran onto the field
with legs that were quick and strong.

He helped his team get outs they needed
and at his turn up to bat,
He ran around all the bases
as his mother cried, "See that!"

Margaret Mary Dunn

In Memory

When I think about you,
All I feel is the pain
Trapped deep inside of me.
When I close my eyes
It is only you I see.
If only I could see you alive again,
I would feel so happy then;
To hear your voice,
See your smile and
To feel your love.
But now you are gone
And I am here.
So until the day
That we meet again,
I will miss you,
My beloved friend.

J. R. O'Neil

Happiness

Everyone thinks that happiness is
All the nice things that money can buy;
They are nice - I must agree,
But true happiness is this to me:
A little boy playing catch with Dad,
and later telling the fun they had.
A little girl in Sunday best,
And baby birds tucked in their nest.
A gentle smile, wrinkled with age,
A canary singing from its cage.
Watching the sunrise, bold and bright,
Then fading away in a pretty twilight.
And watching a snow fall,
Soft and cold,
Are some happy things, seldom told.

Rosemary Parrish

Kids

Kids, kids, kids
we are all
alike in many
ways and different
in many ways.
Our actions maybe
different. But we
all want the
same out
of life, and
that is love.

Roy McClain

I Am A Whale

I am a whale who swims
across the ocean,
like a giant rock floating by.

I sing to myself, a high strong hum,
that makes the water swirl
like a tornado.

When my friends hear me sing,
they come
and join me in song.

Our sounds fill the ocean
with playful mischief,
and forever
lasting peace.

Xsabeida L. Ramirez

Santa (Mom) To The Rescue

'Twas the day after Christmas when
   all through the house
The gloom was abounding because
   of that louse — The Landlord.
The wrappings were scattered; the
   house was a mess
The spirit of Christmas seemed
   less and less
The vet must be paid — the bills are
   all due
There's only one answer — "Santa to the
   rescue"
Her eyes were sunken, her shoulders
   were sagging
Her spirit was dampened, her duper
   was dragging
But I heard her exclaim as her Toyota
   streaked by
"Mi Casa es su casa — 'til relief
   is nigh"

Marjorie Frazer

Dancing With Her Eyes

She came to us in her 70's
   already crippled with arthritis,
She loved to dance and sing
   what a rug she would cut -
The music "let her do it"

By her early painful 80's
   she was wheel chair bound,
But she could sway her torso
   and tap her feet in rhythm -
The music "let her do it."

In her late 80's barely vocal
   she still had that happy smile,
An appreciation of life that
   would put most of us to shame -
The music "let her do it."

And finally the twilight 90's
   completely crippled and immobile,
She never missed a dance because
   she danced "With her eyes"!
The music "let her do it."

Wayne Field

Father From A Distance

I can hear your little voices
   All the laughter and the joy
All the games you played with Daddy
   How you held a favorite toy.

With the clouds we had the sunshine
   And I never will regret
Once I shared your every sigh,
   If you cried...my eyes were wet.

Does a Daddy's heart stop beating
   To a daughter's happy tune?
Will the cold of winter fade
   If I come to you in June?

This is what we will remember:
   Hop on Pop! and Hide and Seek;
After dusk we watched the embers
   As we camped beside a creek.

From the trials of life I'd shield you.
   On this cosmos there is strife,
Yet not we but He who lives within us
   Guards our love and gives us life.

Mark Reginald Rogers

Wife

I finally have God in my life,
Also, a very beautiful wife.
Her eyes are like two shining stars,
That's how I seen her from afar,
When I saw her,
I knew it was love,
Because I saw a beautiful dove,

I'm so happy you're my wife,
I want you around,
For the rest of my life.
Even when God comes down,
We'll go up and do the town.
God says, the streets are made of gold,
Phyllis our love will never get old,
Phyllis I love you,
All so sweet,
I'm so glad we got to meet.

Vanice Guidry

Love

No love, an inertia of protracted custom,
Although custom conveys predictability.
Predictability casts its own phantom,
But love sets forth sincerity.

Love bears infinite reliability.
Love is the mirror of the heart,
A heart full of love reflects God.
Love carries vow and responsibility;
And that - sets forth ultimate totality.

F. Sadeghpour

Drive And Ambition

Drive and ambition
Ambition and drive
These are the things
'Twill keep you alive.

Courage and strength
Are mighty nice too,
But drive and ambition
Will see you through.

Drive and ambition
Ambition and drive
These are the things
'Twill keep you alive!

Nancy Aldridge

Kwanzaa

Kwanzaa is a young holiday
An African-American celebration
A festival of seven days
It's spreading all over the nation.
Kwanzaa means harvest first fruits
And family, friends and community
Celebrate African roots
December 26 to the first of January.

Welcoming this new time of joy
For joy encompasses all races
That search for the truth of their being
At the core of their cultural genesis.
The ethnic milieu of this nation
Contributes so much that is good
And Kwanzaa adds it celebrations
To the cultural fabric of our national
neighborhood.

Velma G. Warder

Mr. Buck

Mr. Buck...
An appropriate name
Hunter of hunters
Master of the game
The thrill of the chase calling his name
Mr. Buck...
Once his kill has been made
The thrill of the hunt beckons his name
Mr. Buck...
So blessed by the heavens to have
never been his prey
Just remains of a haunting scent
forever calling his name
Mr. Buck...

Stacy Ervin

Mental Hazard

Third green water hole
An easy six iron shot
Swing - plop! Damn.

William Usher

"A Prayer For Home"

God bless this home
   and all who dwell within
Make it a haven of peace and grace
   free from care...void of sin

Let none o'er the threshold pass
   anger's thoughtless words to bear
Preserve within its sheltering walls
   faith aglow...love to share

God bless this home
   the friends who enter here
Make them feel who close the door
   sweet repose..the Savior near

May each day be filled with happiness
   each night give perfect rest
Preserve within the recess of its frame
   in Thy will...all that's best

Lorna E. Delancey

Sincerity

Oh, won't you fly away with me
And be my valentine?
We'll fly on wings of gossamer
Above this worldly clime.

Across the skies, above the clouds
On wings of beaten gold,
And I will tell you of my love
Of passion strong and bold.

My love for you shall know no bounds
It sweeps and soars above
And ev'ry heartbeat sings a song
Of endless, endless love.

Down through the vast depths of space
And corridors of time
Our love shall march forever, if
You'll be my valentine.

But if you cannot give your love
Because there is one other
Give back these verses right away
I'll try them on another.

Sandra M. Findlay

Peace

Silence floats up to the clouds,
And bounds around and down.
It seeps from out the cacti
And wells up from the ground.
It folds up past and future,
And lets me live today
With quiet heart - so grateful.
"My God!" is all I say.

Mary A. Mertz

Children

Children make noise
And children leave toys
Scattered all over the floor.
You feed them and then
They come back again
Saying they're hungry for more.

Children outgrow all the clothes
That you buy
Before they are noticeably worn.
And the ones that they don't
You can bet that they won't
Because they are hopelessly torn.

But smiles from little faces
And hugs from little arms
Make up for any small lack
And when they leave us
For school, job, or marriage
We will always welcome them back.

Ruth Olimpio

The Tree That Cries

She sits at its roots,
and cries.
Letting her tears fall to the ground
and be scuffed into the dirt
by her torn canvas shoe.
The tree's limbs reach out
for her,
to climb up into
and be lost in the green leaves.
But she sits,
and blows her nose
on her sleeve
and cares not for the trees' branches
to hide her tear streaked face.
She feels a drop on her head
and looks up into a cloudless sky
and wonders
if it's going to rain.

Karla Renee Tull-Esterbrook

Untitled

We think and think everyday
and forget half of what we say,
  But that one thing is so sweet
that nothing else can compete.

We think of it in the morning
as a special kind of warning,
  To remember it at night
for it's such a lovely sight.

We all should know it by now
it's your own sweetheart and gal,
  It could be none other
then your own sweet MOTHER.

Robert H. Ferguson

Do You Want To Dance With Me?

Take me into your arms
and dance with me tonight.
Pale and bare, the sound-
of a thousand candle lights.

Take me into your eyes
and wipe away the tears.
Tall and elegant, our bodies
spinning ever so near.

Underneath heaven's night
you dance in a silken dress.
Above and below, a thousand candles,
and I dance in a dark vest.

Stir around the floor
for the sullen band to see.
I'm lost in a lover's daze-
Do you want to dance with me?

D. Christian Clauss

Night Wind

Night is a time of darkness,
And for some a time of fear,
Yet some folk find it peaceful,
Very restful to the ear.

The hurried world has slowed now.
And the night wind takes it flight.
But in our minds our deepest thoughts,
Are brought out to the light.

Words that seemed important,
Only clouded up our sight.
But in this peaceful hour,
There is wisdom in the night.

Yet if we know inside our heart,
That wild flowers still grow,
Then we have opened up our soul,
And everyone shall know.

Robert J. Zec

True Love

I remember the first time I saw you
And from then on I knew it was true

Your smile was the greatest
and your eyes were the brightest

Whenever I looked into your eyes
I knew I was in paradise

If ever I needed an ear
you were there to take away my fear.

The first time we kissed
I knew I had been blessed

When you hold me in your arms
I feel nothing can do me any harm.

If anyone ever mentions your name
I feel I am going to go insane

When I'm away from you
I feel down and blue

I think of you all through the day
no matter what anyone can do or say.

I guess what I'm trying to say is
you're my true love
and everything I've ever dreamed of.

Nicole Harrison

Confused

I wanted to reach out
and give you a hug.
I stopped myself.
I don't want to now.

I wanted to reach out
and give you a slap.
I stopped myself.
I don't want to now.

I wanted you
To give me a hug.
I stopped you.
I don't want you to now.

I want
I don't want
I stopped wanting.
Now what do I do?

Lee Robertson

Boil And Broil

The earth opens up
and gives birth to a perfect life
it's a still birth
it's unearthly
it's worth nothing
they boil and broil
the inner oils
turning into soil
Wrap up in tinfoil
before I spoil

I am the mighty roil
toil with my emotions
coil with me

Make me turn red inside
to match my outsides
boil and broil my inner oils

Sally A. Luger

Samuel

If I could only touch your face,
and hold your hand once more.
If I could only kiss your cheek,
and hug you like before
my tears still flow.
My heart still aches,
I know you understand.
I love you and I miss you son,
the very words you spoke.
I keep in mind those words of love,
It gives me strength and hope.

Margaret Coleman

Day-To-Day

Monday is a regular John
And I am its servile whore
Selling my weathered soul again
Can't remember the price anymore

My well-known stranger comes
He is ever the faithful contender
I kneel before him or climb on top
Too willingly my services are rendered

Holes and scars and missing parts
He creates before leaving my room
I'm patiently waiting for Tuesday
Unsettled, unmartyred and doomed

Monique M. Randall

Warm And Fuzzy

Slowly my eyes open,
And I blink the sleep away.
I look around my room, and know
It's time to face the day.

I feel so warm and fuzzy,
But reality lies ahead.
I contemplate how it will be,
And want to stay in bed.

The dreams I had were wonderful.
My covers feel so good.
I hug my pillow tight, and say,
"I'd get up, if I could."

I stare up at the ceiling,
Hoping for more rest.
I think about a ton of work
Sitting on my desk.

"It won't get done today," I say.
"It will have to keep."
I call my boss, "I won't be in,"
And snuggle back to sleep.

Karon Billheimer

For Just A Moment

I blushed at what you said,
and I gave you a smile.
Our eyes met and the gaze was long.
For just a moment,
I had fallen.
My heart opened and you got inside.
You gave me that look,
and slowly you moved closer.
Our lips touched gently;
my heart began to melt.

Tina M. Busch

The Black Dream

I wrote
and I had
no pen.

I spoke
and my voice
said nothing.

I looked
and only darkness
quickened.

I listened
and my heart
was quiet.

I cried
and my tears
flowed not.

I felt
and only satin
met my touch.

Robert DeGraw

Life And Love

Life starts at a beginning,
 and grows until its final end.
Love is everlasting,
 just like the peaceful night wind.

Melanie Phillips

But Not At The Same Time

If you had loved me less
And I loved you more
Life would have been different
For we cared not for each other
At the same time in the same way
What a pity.

Yet deep between us we did care
In our own peculiar way
Yet went on hurting each other
A long time with careless indifference
Regretfully we broke away from
Each other to seek new loves.

For a while it was enough
And then not enough as we drifted
Back to each other
Not to love but to again hurt
And hurt, so came the end
You went your way and I mine.

Yet you were niched in my heart
And I in yours, but not at the same time.
Tillie Lewis Kaplan

Object Of Desire

You want my attention
And I seem drawn to you
But dare I touch you
Only to discover we may not be in tune?
There's a bond between us
As if I've known you all my life

Neck in hand I gently caress you
And at the sixth moment
You are released
With a strum of my hand
Only to hear you leave
As an echo in the night...
Linda L. Galiza

A Violent Breed

At night I come alive,
and I wait up in the dark.
You cannot see me, hear me, smell me.
If you look upon me,
you will see an angel.
An angel who'll bring death.
You look into my eyes and see heaven.
I feel your pain.
I will touch you, feel you, hold you.
You are mine!
With a single kiss,
I take your life.
You feel it slipping away.
Your life warms me, you are gone.
For you I shed but a single tear.
A tear of blood.
I am sacred,
I am a violent breed,
I am a vampire.
Shane D. McNaughton

Diversion

Man refashioned wild perfection,
And with vigilance
Matched nature's ruthless patience,
Guarding his distortions
Down the path of time.
Ron Sissons

Let There Be Roses

My nights and days go on
And I'm found beyond...
Beyond the walls...
Of red roses and sharp thorns
Being beaten by the eye of a storm
I know I'll be reborn
But I'll try...try to go on...
To what may become my destiny one day
I'll seek the rose along the way
But beware of the thorns!
One crowded red rose bush at a time....
Crammed by the sharp thorn
I slowly wilt and dorm
Drained from the world....
Torn in half from life itself
I was young and frail
But my soul shall surely sail...Away...
Far away from here to seek safety and no fear
My soul slowly lifted and planted firmly in
a blanket of secure
Let there be Roses....Not Thorns!
Nicole Ann Lacsina

On The Death Of Ronald Kendall

God planted a seed in a garden,
And it grew to a flower fair;
So sweet was its perfume and radiance
That it charmed all who saw it there.

The Gardener with hands kind and tender
Each day gave it water to drink;
And into the garden it rendered
A Harmony full and complete.

The Master one day needed flowers,
To brighten his mansion inside;
And he plucked this flower so fair
To always with Him abide.

No flower there grew to replace it,
Its place is forever bare;
But I hope for that day when we two
Shall meet in His mansion up there.
Ralph W. Martin Jr.

The Place

There is a place right by the sea
and it's run by Mrs. G.
Michelle Nice

Why The Banana Split

I woke one summer morning
And looked out my bedroom door-
Saw seven ripe bananas
Playing poker on the floor.

One jumped up and hollered
It was time for him to quit.
They all got mad and hated
To see that one banana split.

He slipped out with all the money
Just the way he came
Had to get home to his wife
Chiquita was her name.

When playing poker with bananas
And you suddenly get a hunch
I guess it's wise in a case like this
Not to bet a bunch.
Norman Salome

"Seasons"

It's October now
And it's starting to get cold
The nights are getting longer
And I wish I had you to hold
The leaves will be changing
And beginning to fall
Then the snow will follow
And we can go out to throw snowballs
Then in the spring
It will be time to start again
To throw out the old
And start where we first began
Then summer will come
We can go out in the sun
Lie on the beach
And have a lot of fun
Our life together will be as
Wonderful as the seasons of the year
We will live in harmony
And have no fears!
Susan C. Roberts

Untitled

She used to wipe my hands and face
And kiss away my tears
She was always there when I needed her
In my younger years

When I was in my teens
Not sure what I wanted to do
We would sit and talk
She helped me make it through

She taught me to except things
Whether they were good or bad
To be loving and understanding
She was the best teacher I had

Now that I have children of my own
I realize what she means to me
She is the kind of mother
I would like to be

She adds happiness to my life
She is the nicest lady by far
I am very pleased and proud
To call this lady "MA" Happy Mother's Day
Rena Orlando

Silence

Reach out your silence
And know my nights and days
Are filled with softness
When your eyes lock with mine

My silence screams
That even if two hearts I had
Both would overflow
With that I've begun to feel

Silence is a blanket
Which covers love to keep it warm
    As I wait
        And long to hold you
I clench it tingly under my chin

Lone hours feed me
For weakness melts to nothing
    When I think of you
Then with silence a chilling warmth upon me
I fall into your eyes
    Through a face of such beauty
And my heart is home
Robert Parkinson Jr.

Black Chiffon

Alone, I free it from its wrappings
And let it fall above my head,
A wisp of midnight, from a dream time
Soft, sensuous, in clinging folds
Created to enhance a shadow, and recall
Gently moulding rounded breasts
Like softly budding waterlilies
When half open, tinged with pink.
Then draping softly, Grecian-like,
Small cascades of sheerest black,
Drift to the ankle, but mid-way
Reveal an alabaster thigh.
—The moonlight moves beyond the door
The mirror casts no backward glance;
I let the gown and memory
Return to tissued potpourri.

Winnifred Hiatt Scanlan

Lonely Dreams

If dreams were given to lonely men,
and lonely men's dreams came true,
I'd force myself to sleep at night,
just to be dreaming of you.
If wishes were given to lonely men,
and I were just given two, I'd wish
you'd always love me, and the other
I'd save for you.
If teardrops could write love
songs, before my love song was
through, you'd know just how I feel
inside, and how much I love you.
But dreams are just for dreamers,
and wishes seldom come true. Tear
drops cannot write love songs, they
just keep falling for
you…

Len Bianchi

The Final Time

Stillness, peace surrounds me,
And looking up I see
Faces that were once
Dear to me.

Reaching up I feel their hand,
And suddenly I find I stand;
And then with joy surpassing all,
I find that I answer the call.

Tears are shed, not rightly so;
For only when it's time to go
Can one really comprehend
The glory that comes
When one ascends.

Norma J. Rupp

Baldness

The guy has no hair on his head,
and it shines in the glistening sun
like buttered bread.

I stopped him one day and asked;
"Do you need your head shined today?"
but as he hit me on my chin,
I laughed, smiled and grinned,
because I will ask him again and again.

Trey Stevens

Seventy-Five

When I'm seventy-five
and my joints all ache
I'll live with my wife
on a secluded lake

Into our golden years
staring back at the past
time is now the vine
so slippery in our grasp

There will be no mortgage
no smog
and no phone
Just me and my love together
at last alone

Robert W. Mayes

Forbearance

You gave up drink
And now you think
Some health you have regained

…And cigarettes are on the list
From which you have refrained

Now only if from gambling
And woman you could abstain

I wouldn't be a bit surprised
If you couldn't be ordained

William Michael McGinty

Fellowship

Have Fellowship together
   and one with another

And let us consider Friendship or
   affection toward each other

And staying prayerfully steadfast
   within the Holy Spirit from above

For it will bring forth peace,
   joy, happiness and love

We shall all walk together in the
   same light as Jesus is in the light

Because we as fellow Christians
   know that this is only right

So we shall come together and
   come on one accord

Let us all remember to have
   fellowship in goodness of
The Lord.

Rebecca Renay Spears

Our Home

Our home, a shelter
And protection from the elements.
Cozy, secure and serene.
Children growing to maturity
Healthy and strong.
To meet the world.

Days of fulfillment,
Nights of comfort and rest.
Holidays with family and friends
Gathered within our walls —
A feeling of loving arms enfolding us.

Stella Manaker

Untitled

Still
and still

Quiet
   motionless
      calm

Until now
   even yet
nevertheless

You remain in me.

Karen R. Larson

Your Compassion

You have taken me into your confidence
And taught me from above

Giving yourself as a Gift
Patience - Peace and Love

I will remain
I will obey
With Joy I am complete

Secure in your faithfulness
I rejoice - Your word is sweet

Roanne Bonomo

"Just Wait For Us There"

We knew you were going away
And that you had to go alone
We were honored to have loved you
But now Father has called you home.

Your pain has left your body
Your spirit fills the air
Now an angel called up yonder
Will you wait for us there?

When you arrive to meet Jesus
No more burdens will you bare
We all wanted to go with you
Could you wait for us there?

It's hard to let you go
But we know it was your time
We will always miss you, Granny
Just look what you left behind.

You graced our lives with love
In the years that you were here
And till we all meet in heaven
Would you just wait for us there?

Melody Wright

"You"

You said that you loved me,
and baby this is true.
Because you are the one,
I fell in love with too.
You are very special to me,
and baby that's a fact.
Now that I'm in love with you,
there is no turning back.
You have made me very happy,
for this I cannot hide.
You are the one I really love,
and want by my side
My love for you grows,
each and every day.
Hopefully you will say yes,
and be my wife someday.

Marcel Forte

What The Future Holds

Violence has torn the world in two
And the future is between me and you
We must learn to care
And make things fair
Change all the greed
To help those in need
End all war and keep no score
Do what's best to pass the test
Make things bright
Without a fight
Share our joy with a little boy
Tell a joke or just a poke
Cheer one in fear
And be there to hear
Never let down and you will have found
What it takes for a heart to pound
If you show your love
In all of the above
The world won't become
Another slum.

Vanessa Lichon

The First Zephyr Train

The hum of bright steely tracks
And the stir of the pregnant air
Tell us, a wayfaring pair,
Toting our humble packs,
Of the rise of a thunder-head there
On the well traveled tracks.

The heat waves dance as we stand
On the pulse of the giant's road,
Feeling him change the mode
Of the rural scene. The land
In a tremor translates its code
Into shock where we stand.

Our packs we move to the trail
As the silver monster bears down,
Rearing his armored crown,
And snaking his high-powered tail
Around curves. We, pensive, frown
At his meteor trail.

Robert J. Cordell

Shadow Folk

Nameless streets on hollow nights
Are passageways through time.
Ghostly forms 'neath halo'd lights
Speak wordlessly in rhyme.

A flash of fire. A puff of smoke.
A dialogue's begun.
A deaf man listened as a mute man spoke
Till the cigarette was done.

The swirling fog, and midnight rain
Enfold discarded dreams.
The begged of beggar gives his gain
To live below his means.

Yet, don't dismiss these shadow folk,
Whose lives are ifs and whens.
They see more clearly through the smoke
Than we through crystal lens.

For I have stood among the horde
Who set themselves so high,
And learned the words I most abhorred
Were me, myself, and I.

Thomas A. Bradley

He Sent Me An Angel

Though the road ahead is long
and the times are sad and blue
And you think you would be better dead
than to go through what you're going through
But the Lord he smiled down
for he knows that I am true
So he sent me an Angel, It's you!

Though the times may still be hard
and the pennies we must save
things just don't look so bad
With all the gentleness you gave
And I thank the Lord above
each and every single day
For he sent me an Angel, It's you!

Linda Teabout

Love For A Child

I looked in the eyes of a child today
And there I saw unfold
The very soul of the world so wide —
The very soul of the world.

I saw the mark of lessons learned
As man long and patiently filed
Down through the ages, day by day,
There in the eyes of a child.

I saw the wonder of moon and star,
Of the vastness of the sky,
A flight to the great unknown and back
In the twinkling of his eye.

I saw an understanding heart,
A caring for each other,
A sensitivity to need —
To share with one another.

I looked in the eyes of a child today
And saw the soul of the world.
I knew why my love could boundless be —
'Twas wrought in the soul of a child.

Neva G. Smith

Harboring Guilt

No one wants to admit a wrong,
And this is mankind's continuous song;
But human flesh is not so strong,
And cannot hide it very long!

What awful, dismal, terrible pride
Can cause a willful act to hide;
To only fester and reside,
And grow, ripen, gnaw inside.

Guilt becomes a person's plight
Because a wrong was not made right;
So everything that's done in sight
Becomes a "careful" deed of fright.

Be sure that sin will soon be found
When one's iniquity does abound;
For truth one day will come around,
And crush the secrets to the ground!

Only then will lies decrease
Through one's repentance, sin's release;
No other way can conscience cease,
Be put to rest and have its peace!

Michael Baxter

"Sneakers"

I've learned to put my sneakers on,
And tie them real tight.
There's only one small problem,
I can't tell left from right.

I think I'm oh so careful
as I place them on my feet,
they turn themselves around.

The right shoe on my left foot
and the left on my right.
I'll have to take them off again,
I may be here all day.

My sneakers are a naughty pair,
they trick me and confuse me.
Guess that's why we call them sneakers,
those silly, sneaky sneakers!

Kristina Calandro

The Others

Malcolm stood aside
and watched the other children play,
and, when they asked him would he join,
he slowly turned away.

Later, when the others laughed,
and gaily went to dances.
Malcolm leaned against the wall
and looked with shyish glances.

The others married and moved on
to many different places,
attending to this job or that
with hope upon their faces.

They sometimes wrote him letters,
or called him on the phone,
but Malcolm rarely answered,
he preferred to be alone.

When old age came, and touched them all,
the others were prepared,
they met together, holding hands,
but Malcolm - just was scared.

Lillian Geller

And The Journey Continues...

Another tragedy touches the day
another heartbreak comes our way
no understanding to be found
and the news goes round and round

Some say hatred is the key
some say are they really free
yet we all should value life
so little love yet so much strife

And the children what do they say
when adults they act this way
as the day brings the rising sun
should our lives turn to our guns

Understanding and peace is the plea
but it is too late for you and me
for this life is a journey you see
and its purpose not determined by thee

Will our land ever really heal
on the journey can we learn how to feel
a hope and vision and maybe a dream
the flow of love like ripples of a stream

Patricia A. Fudge

The Sun

I sit and watch the glistening sun
And wonder when the day is done
Where has it gone this light of ours
That has so many wondrous powers
Has it descended to the ground
Or maybe turned itself around
To become the moon which shines at night
Or maybe stars that shine so bright
Will it return to us tomorrow
If not our day will turn to sorrow
For we need the sun to light our way
To keep us warm throughout the day
To help the trees and flowers to grow
To give the earth that special glow
Just think how dark would be our way
Without the sun to light each day
Rebecca Small

Untitled

The days have gone too fast at times,
and yet too slow to mourn
and tally all the errors made
the day when I was born.
I tried so hard to make it work
not to hurt, not to evoke
the petty grievances of life
that come one's way most every day.
Have I succeeded or have I failed?
Who knows, who keeps the score?
Or do I really want to know
or keep it secret forever more
Ludmilla Evans

Existentialist

I was thirsty
And you gave me chalk to drink.

I was hungry
And you fed me myrrh.

I was bleeding
And you sucked me dry.

I asked for love
And you gave me gall.
Katherine Gates Runkle

Lost Love

Your grave stands before me
As my tears fall so fast
Before I say one precious word
I think about our past...

I think of our love
And the times we spent
The smiles and laughs
And the places we went...

The future before me
I wanted you to be there
But now that you're gone
It just isn't fair...

Why did you leave me
Is a question I know
Cannot be answered
By the tears that I show...

I plant three roses
To say you are missed
As I walk from your grave
I blow you a kiss...
Mandy Felks

Jesus

Jesus, you're my best friend.
And you're always at my side.
You're always there for me to talk to
When I'm down and no one will listen.
No matter what I do, good or bad,
you're still there for me.
You always forgive me.
I guess the only thing I can say
Is 'I love you!'
Kelly Herbst

Thoughts

How to let go, one so dear.
Answer found in the heart of a tear.

Precious moments shared, oh too rare.
The graying of my father's hair.
And little one so innocent and small,
I pray God's Grace to ease your fall.

Come little teardrop and share your song.
The depth of Love, loneliness long.

Goodnight for now, silence come.
Revelation found in God's own Son.
Tears he cried with sweat of blood.
Eyes now see but not by mud.

How do I let go of one so dear?
Answer found in the Heart of His tear.
Scott Phillips

Yes Virginia

In the pre-Barbie Age and in
ante-Belle
Ante-Simba, Aladdin and also
Mattel
The Oldsters knew what
Christmas meant
And it wasn't the "Age of
Increment"
Home-made goodies, fruit cakes
and candy
Patch-work quilts from goods
that were handy
scarfs for the kids and for
Grandma a shawl!!
"Merry Christmas, My Dears,
God Bless You All"
Marian K. Francis

I Lie Awake, Though Sleeping

A lie awake, though sleeping
as I did, I started dreaming
I rose high, above my bed
angels surrounded my head

I started to cry, though I
didn't know why

I thought for a bit
I was sad
I never said
I love you, Dad

Although you've been gone
Twenty-two years
I say I love you, Dad
though through my tears

I lie awake, though sleeping
Rose M. Schuldt

"Something To Remember"

In a dark sea a long time ago,
  Appeared a gem that wouldn't glow.

A drought came and strickened the land
  Everything turned to dust and sand.

In the land the dandelions and bees died,
  Nature seemed lost and began to sigh.

Creatures viewed green as a lost hope
  Until an unselfish gem did approach.

Unleash the gem was an emerald green,
  For the color of hope could be seen.

Looking at this the creatures knew
  They had to stick it through.

They had faith in their heart
  That this drought would soon depart.

The emerald continued to shine
  The clouds gathered in a line.

Rain fell through the abyss;
  Clouds and creatures formed a kiss.

This is to be remembered my dove,
  That this emerald represents my love!
Mark Witherington

Laura

All the stars in heaven
Are in her eyes,
There's nothing else I can see.

So much in her gaze,
An eternity in a glance,
Once saw my reflection
In her eyes.

Beneath the stare,
She hides her fears.
She looks beyond help or
Understanding.

Sensuous,
Licentious,
Need to forget
The glimmer in a lover's eyes.

Past the wishing,
Still holding on,
I close my eyes.
Foolishly thought I deserved
As much as I gave.
Peter Ternes

To Ease The Pain

He stood amidst the rubble
  and the pain of lives disrupted
a heartfelt passion to correct
  a wrongful sin.

They saw his dew-filled eyes
They heard within his voice
  a promise
That it would never happen again

He gave them hope
  to ease the pain.
This President named Bill
  Hugged Oklahoma.
Mercedes Conner

"The Soiled Earth"

Childlike thoughts of adults
are seldom spoken aloud
To admit all our faults
we break our promises vowed
Innocence is now soiled
there is dirt upon its name
Eating away every day
it preys on us all the same
No one is perfect
neither I nor you
can cleanse the wounds of Earth's core
We can't wash away
soil under the skin
that's not what we're put here for
We cannot undo
and we can't start anew
this will only end in time
We must unshackle from the shadows
or our lives are pointless decades
valued at less than a dime

Nicki Becker

Spring Paintings

Hills of dappled hue
Are webbed with golden threads
of sun.
Skies of sapphire blue
float clouds that drift by- one
by one.

Silhouettes in green,
Of stately pointed form-
The pines-
Ranged in dewy sheen
Along a mountain ridge
In lines.

Velma A. Pooley

Streams

Streams, why do you move so fast?
Are you not full of bass?
Coming into the glory from above
Filled with trouts and salmons of love
Streams, why do you move so fast?
Alas now is the time of swiftness
Move from glory to glory
for God created you to flow
So there could be many to come
And you could be able to open the door
of God's divine nature

Linda Tindal

Seasong

You laugh and I cry
as we step towards the sea

And dance to a music
heard only by you
and by me

The waves pound
against us
our hearts pound
within

Keeping time to the rhythm
in love's ocean
we swim

S. Lyric Watson

Just A Friend

Each day I see your smiling face,
As happy as you can be;
And maybe it is just the place,
But you seem so carefree.
I watch you walking past me,
I can even smell your cologne;
Although somehow you can't see,
I'm feeling so alone.
The love inside your heart,
Is coming to an end;
And now you get a whole new start,
And say I'm just a friend.

Kelley White

Changes

Here is not the same
as here is now
as was before

No moment lives
beyond a moment
through time
like times ago

Go and then
come back again
to once you
were before

Now it is a
different time
unlike the times
once so

So the place of once
when back before
can never be no more

Rick Jones

"Suffering"

The silence swept in the darkness,
As I lay there waiting for you.
You left in such a hurry,
And said "Don't worry, I'll come back
For you. Days are passing by,
And I am growing old, with wrinkles on
My face and whiteness in my hair.
One day somebody came, and I was blue
And cold.
I waited for you every day, but you,
You never showed.
You left me there to die alone...
You made me waste my SOUL.
But I am gone and I will see,
That you will live in AGONY.

Priscilla Lee Brooks

The Path Of Possibilities

A feather drifting,
Appearing aimless,
With care and chance,
Without destination or destruction,
Quick to rest,
Eager to continue its journey,
Delicate,
Sometimes pure,
Avoiding nothing in its path,
Knowing,
Only existence leads to possibilities.

Virginia L. Ganley

Joyful Memories

All aboard the memory ship
As I recall these joyful quips!
A lifetime joy cannot be priced
As I go gliding on the ice.

For perfect attendance at
Sunday school
I was awarded a precious jewel.
A pair of ice skates was the prize.
Black figure skates just my size.

Miles to the rink we walk
It seems like a minute as we talk.
With smiling faces couples sail by
Inspiring success if only I try.

Holding hands with my friends
Slowly around the rink we spin.
By myself some spills I take
Having fun learning to skate.

Precious memories cherished dearly
As winter scenes appear so clearly,
Then my heart with pleasure fills
And I go skating enjoying thrills.

Shirley Conway Brigham

Entering Insanity

Creeping in the tall grass
as I search
for my demons.
The sweet smell of the ground
enters my senses
and when I find my demons
I am taken to their sacred place
and left there forever

Megan K. Chicoine

True Friends Are Few

True friendship is as hard to find,
as one to love for a lifetime.
Scores of friends we can have,
but who can one count on in the end?
It is the one who listens the longest,
holds you the tightest and doesn't
try to shut you up during the final cry
and at last the hiccups.
Friends are people who will be there
no matter what, if they screen their
calls they'll always pick-up.
Friends are people who let you use
their fireplace for emergency purposes,
when the day has been long and all
has gone wrong, it's a cure for all
of life's bad excuses.
When the headaches occur and life's
A big blur - you'll know who'll have
the cure, a true friend, for sure.

Laurie Beth Blanchette

"My Cat"

Her eyes at night
are ruby bright,
her day eyes sapphire blue.

I think the sun
she traps by day,
at night comes sparkling through.

Rachel LaVoy

The Wind And The Chimes

The morning so quiet
As she awakens.

Her yawns bringing
Many single solos.

She does not like
The sounds she hears.

She says to stop,
But they begin to tune.

Her voice raises,
They start their piece.

She commands them,
Yet they play on.

She begins to yell,
A full symphony erupts.

She can't help screaming,
Now they break up.

She must calm herself,
Their playing will cease.

Silence has returned tonight,
But another song will play tomorrow.

Stephen Johnson

What Went Wrong

I sit in the still silence
As the darkness folds in around me.
All sound is smothered.
All light is gone.
I sit alone and stare
And wonder what went wrong.

The sun used to shine all day.
The moon would light the night.
The light of the sun,
And the light of the moon,
Have all vanished and gone.

My world is cold and empty.
My soul is all alone.
As I sit and stare in the darkness,
And wonder what went wrong.

Lindsay Sydney Van Houten

Christmas Whispers

The silent joy that dwells within,
as the first whisper of Christmas and
the frosty season begins.

The cradle of snow that is yet to
come, is a gentle reminder of Christ,
God's only son.

The pillow of softness will blanket
the ground, like the feathers of a dove
so white and downed.

The songs of peace that all love
to sing, and the smiles of children
Christmas always brings.

But the child that's alone in the
season's bliss, their faces forgotten
and their smiles not missed.

The silent cries that no one will
hear, the faith that our Lord holds
those special ones dear.

Mary Ann Skinner

One-Winged Heart

Time sheds a tear
As the heart does a flip-flop
The look outside the window pane
Is one of envious joy
But beneath the secluded clouds
And the roaring, thunderous storms
Far beyond the ends of the world
Is a shrilling sound of prevalent pain
From a little speck of brown spots
that can no longer take flight.

Patricia Fullerton

Memphis 1968

I heard the shuffle,
as they marched along.
The shouts the jeers
they were not there
I heard the silence,
it spoke so loud.
The tears the sobs
his work is done
He lies alone.

Lena H. Anderson

Our First Time

I remember the night
as though it were yesterday.
Just you and I,
it felt so right.

Looking at the city lights,
smooching in the breeze.
I knew it then;
I wanted more of these nights.

I decided during a kiss
that tonight would be the one.
We shared laughter early on,
The next moment was too strong to miss.

Our times together have been few,
but that night is memorized.
Now when I look at the city lights,
I think exclusively of you!

Lora Dreibelbis

Mother's Love

Mother's love is strong - without end,
Beginning long before birth.
More precious by far than silver or gold
Nothing can measure its worth.

Mother's love is blind
To red hair or brown, big ears or small
A boy or a girl,
It doesn't matter at all.

Mother's love rocks the cradle,
Walks the floor - dries a tear.
Loves childhood chatter,
Holds a hand - calms a fear.

Mother's love sees the best,
Prays God's best and stands by.
Quick to forgive and forget,
Building confidence to try.

Protecting and guiding,
Believing and free...
Mother's love - the example
Of Christ's love for me.

Nona Norgaard

Ila's Verse

I held your hand
as you remembered
all the smiles and fears
of all your years

When the man came
in my minds eye
I saw you pass through

All the loved ones around you
cried, each for a different
reason in their hearts

But I will remember you
for the stars in your eyes
the beauty in your smile
the wisdom of your words
and the wonder of your life

Keri McPike

Where Are You

I talk to the wind,
Asking for an answer to my prayer;
A prayer that the mighty wind
Blow my empty soul
into your arms above,
I look to the clouds,
like when very young,
And painfully try to shape
your lovely face
With their image;
Instead they drift apart,
and become disfigured;
I no longer find comfort in springtime,
I've become winter;
When rain comes,
I know the wet is your tears;
I will them to drown me,
But you stop crying;
I am the confused, tiny bat
In a cave of bright sunlight.
I am lost,
Where are you?

Susan Moneyhun

Colors Of Sadness

The leaves that brighten
At winters first breath
Grieve at their frightening
Flight into death
And cry in their colors
To pigment the ground
And die with the others
With never a sound

Walter Westergaard

Katherine

Funny, nice, happy, and
Aunt of Ashley and Colin.
Lover of Mom, Dad, JTT and soccer
Who feels happy, responsible and good
Who needs family, love, food and friends
Who gives friendship, time, and fun
Who fears death, meeting new people
Who would like to see people stop
fighting and killing.
Resident of Carrollton, Texas.

Katherine Uding

Untitled

Sitting to a rescue death,
awaiting the annihilation bed.
Morbid is the claim,
Sentimental is not the value.
Rejection is to your own cowardice,
Only the "One" knows....
the understatement of reliability,
cutting over and over the dead skin
only proves the same.
Washing of the hands,
only a temporary cleansing.
There's no hiding-
The dirt no matter how deep
it is,
Seemingly it climbs to the surface.
 Tony Colon

The Berry Picker

We were on the second
basket, several berry-layers deep,
when he saw it.
It was a bird, he said,
with golden breast and head,
-the wings were silver-
maybe striped?

The others laughed,
He was the dreamer, after all,
the one who weaved through
summer's tissued sounds
who listened to the heat.

I didn't laugh.

He always knew
where berries were
And fastest filled his pail.
 Kenneth Holihan

Battered Woman

Battered woman with sunken eyes
Battered woman, no one hears her cry
The scratches on her chin and cheek
The bruise above her lip
She came into this marriage blind
She never pictured this
911 —— They took too long
With the help of a knife
Now he's gone
She doesn't regret what
She's done you can see
Because she says,
"It could have been me."
 Keyana Jones

The River Of Life

The river of life can
be harsh and cruel or
gentle and caring. One
day it could be your
friend and the next
thing you know it stabs
you in the back. It can
protect you from enemies
and then be your worst enemy.
It can help you when you're
bleeding and then be the cause
of your bleeding. My advice to
you is watch your back because
someone could be watching yours.
 Robin Ann Burnam

Come On, Stay Well

Stay well
Be healthy and strong
Be happy and show concern
Don't think of children as
Something to keep you down.

Come on and make it happen
We are needed as parents,
Our children need us.

Stay well
Be strong for the children's sake,
But communicate with others
And make this world a better place.

Come on, keep us all together as one
Be thoughtful and lovable
For we have to care for all
The good things God put on this earth
Like humans, animals, birds, insects all.
 Yaminah Maxey

Strings

Strings of our golden harp
Be not separate nor silent any longer.
Once dismembered
And scattered to the winds.
Now through healing hands
All attached and playing
Together in perfect harmony.
Never give up golden harp
For some strings are like rare orchids
Slowly developing
And blossoming almost in secret.

Help us healing hands
To uncover our sacred purpose,
Allowing spirals of energy
To vibrate through our strings,
Irradiated with golden light,
Through poetic sound,
Singing together a song of hope
And reclaiming our destiny.
 Mary Ann Gagliano

Me

I will do what I want to do,
Because that's what I want done,
I will say what I want to say,
Because that's what I wish said,
I will go where I want to go,
Because that's what I want to do,
I will be what I want to be,
Because that's left up to me,
Everything I do comes down to one person,
And that one person is me.
 Nicole Arnold

Untitled

I am a child in limbo
Behind a darkened wall
Hidden, inside myself
With nowhere else to go.
When I am told to open my inner gloom
There are little few who see my doom.
Can I hide longer?
I've nothing to give.
Deep within, my hunger
For life to live.
 Robin Elise Call

Justice

Her eyes of blue
behind the dark
she can see through
your soul into your heart
Her touch as soft
as gentle as the kiss of spring...
Those same hands
can crush a rock...
 Susan Gottfried

Your Own Private Hell

He was born the cutest baby
Big brown eyes and shiny hair
Given birth by a lady
Who thought you truly cared

But you said you were not ready
To be a husband or a dad,
Because you were so selfish
You lost what most men pray to have.

At night you lie and wonder,
"What has he grown to be?"
Tossing, turning, without slumber.
Asking, "What does he think of me?"
And, "If I went to meet him,
Could he forgive my mistake?"
"Could he ever learn to love me?"
As you lie there still awake

You left to make your fortune,
Thinking you would do so well,
When all you have created
Is your own private hell
 Sharon Hall

My Class Ring

Encircling the days of my schooling,
Binding the good and bad.
Reminding me of times gone by,
Emotions, happy and sad.
This band I wear exhibits
I have triumphed through the years.
I have fallen, then risen to be my best.
I have managed to conquer fear.
Influences; friendships; memories;
And all life's lessons they bring,
Make my finish become a beginning,
Like the circle of my class ring.
 Misty N. Stone

"Mr. Poe"

 Dark cold days,
 Bitter nights,
Scared of dying!
  Afraid to fight!
 Fatherless child,
 A bastard's life,
Abuse and torment!
  No visions of light!

 Insane fears,
 Hellish sights,
Opium cures
  Alcohol rights

 Buried alive!!
 Terror Bestowed.
Catacombs wandering,
  No friends... all foes!!!
 J. Patrick Cowan

Untitled

Meant to be a hippie,
Born 30 years too late.
A real loner by choice,
Never even wanted to date.
Always alone, no one understands.
Undeniably strange,
Really dig those 60's bands.
Janis-the white blues singer.
Jimi-The guitar God.
Jim-The poet with the soul of a clown.
A friend is a stranger,
A stranger is a friend
Janis-Heroin,
Jimi-sleeping pills.
Jim-who knows?
Died before I was born,
Heroes are all dead.
Wrong generation,
Nothing left to be said.

Rhonda Carol Howton

Dante

Dante, Dante
Born one fine April Day
To Patrick and Vicki
It was a very happy day!

She has brought a lot of happiness
To her mom and Dad.
She thinks they are the best parents
That a baby ever had.

Soon she will learn to crawl
Then she will began to walk.
And mark on the wall!
Oh, how she loves to talk!

When she starts going to school
She will show them all,
That she's nobody's fool.
Around the boys she acts so cool!!

Nora Atkins

Welcome My Child

I saw you take in your first
breath; I cried, I knew you were fine;
  Welcome my child

I watched you skin your
first knee; I cried. I knew
you would be alright;
  I love you my child

I watched you graduate from
school; I cried, I knew you were ready;
  I'm proud of you my child

I heard you say "I Do";
I cried, I knew you were happy;
  I'll miss you my child

I could feel your pain deep
in my soul; I cried,
I knew we're frightened;
I will always be here for you my child.

I saw you take in your
last breath; I cried, but
I knew you were fine. Welcome my child.

Linda K. Ross

The Dead Man's Lyric

The lyric of the dead man
breathes life into his soul.
His body forever wasted
his mind no longer on the goal.

This day has passed forever,
new thoughts will begin anew.
No eyes are on the dead man
his children have grown few.

But then against the ear,
the song of heroic praise,
the dead man is dead no longer,
for his lyric soaks this song.

So as the dead man withers
and life begins anew.
Remember to write your lyric
and remember
that your song sings too!

Ludwig Otto

Longing For Your Touch

My feelings for you are
burning desires, desires that
can't be expressed or shared,
emotions that torment my
very being from happiness.
I can only hope that our
feelings and desires we
share for each other can
one day be released openly
and begin to grow from that
day forward.

Natalie

"The Stare"

The eyes stare.
But I don't dare,
to see their scary stare.

The eyes stare.
I clearly care,
if they stare.

The eyes stare.
I can't bare,
their striking stare.

The eyes stare.
It frankly isn't fair,
that they stare.

Shiloh Richardson

Our Wedding Day

Our moment is here
But I have no fear
As I take you as my bride
And walk down the isle by your side

Under the Huppa we will stand
I'll put the ring on your hand
Our vows will be said
And we will be wed

There will be dancing, joy and fun
Then 10 days of basking in the sun
I know that I'll be merry
Being married to my one true love Sheri

Mitchell A. Levinson

A Retiree's Dilemma

It would be easy to be an alcoholic,
but I knew I had to keep my pride.
I could have been a gamboholic,
however, luck never was on my side.
I might have been a drugaholic,
but I vow to never take that ride.
I could have been a girlaholic,
but that involved many dollars and cents.
I could have been a workaholic,
those times were just experiments.
So, I'll keep trying all kindaholics,
until I find one that makes sense.
Maybe, you may call me a hobbyholic,
and for now, that won't be past tense.

Raymond Venettozzi

Reflections

I look into the mirror
but I see to my surprise
A whole different person
looking deep into my eyes.

The carefree little girl I saw
when I was four or five
has now become a young woman
fighting to survive.

It's really sort of scary
that time has gone so fast
For what I call the present
has now become the past.

I look into the mirror
and looking back at me
Is a beautiful young lady
where a little girl used to be.

Sarah Miller

My Friend

My friend I hate to do it,
but our friendship just can't last.

The times we shared together
have faded to the past.

I told you it would happen
our friendship wouldn't last.

Please don't disagree, but try
to understand, that time can
change two people like the
tides can change the sand.

Our friendship has been lovely
but you see it has to end, for
I look at you in a different way,
I've fallen in love with you
my friend.

Stephanie Brown

Untitled

We gave birth to our happiness one night
Conceived of a love so pure.
We nursed it until it starved to death
And no longer could life endure.

I filled a cup shaped as a heart
With the juices of love's tender tears.
I watched my light of happiness
Grow dim throughout the years.

Linda E. Ochenduszko

Side By Side

We walk together side by side
but our lives are not defined.

We have no direction in which to go
so we go to and fro.

One day we heard a voice that said
the way is narrow but he lead.

He lead us to the tree
that stood on calvary.

At that place we could see
that Christ had die for you and me.

To the grave we did go
but to see just a hole.

Christ had risen from the dead
now He guides us straight ahead.

Now we're walking with the Lord
his commandments to perform.

Little time left to go
so speak to others of the goal.

That Christ has died and paid for sin
that all who receive Him may come in.

Virgil Freels

You Look At Me

You look at me
but you don't see me
You walk with me
but you don't walk by my side
You talk to me
but you don't talk with me
you love me but
you're not in love with me
You listen to me
but you don't hear me
You look at me
but you don't see me
You still look
Why?

Laurie L. Farda

Memories Of Vision Past

Upon some past ethereal shore
By ocean's rushing, mighty roar
In gusting wind, by waves that soar
On rocky ledge by nature wore:
    My love and I have met before
    Have met again—but nevermore.

Her countenance so pure and bright
A pose like Helen's classic form
Diana's soft and tender light
Renews her beauty morn to morn:
    My love and I have met before
    Have met again—but nevermore.

A golden queen and goddess fair
Sings tender song so soft and sweet
Cynthia's song so sad and rare
Flows from her lips with rhythmic beat:
    My love and I have met before
    Have met again—but nevermore.

Paul O. Forsberg

Ocean

O mnipotent part of nature
C utting through the earth
E xpanding the horizon
A dorned with life
N atural in its form

Kevin Shapiro

Love

  Love is a feeling no one
can explain.
  It can make skies turn blue
when there's rain.
  Love is a feeling that comes
from the heart.
  And when you're in love your
souls never part.
  Love is a feeling that never
fades.
  Sent from beautiful heaven
that's where it is made.
  Love is a feeling one gives
to another.
  Even if only your father
or mother.
  There's only one man I
will ever love.
  Our hearts locked forever
in heaven above.

Rebecca P. Schuh

Suicide

Will I or won't I
Can I or can't I
Commit an ugly scene
Oh why am I a human being

Everyday I look so mad
When really inside I'm always sad
For some reason I never can tell
About my life here in hell

People say they understand
And they'll always be a friend
But when it boils down to it
They say good-bye and split

So there's really no one who can help
Never till the day I cry out
And all my troubles seem to stop
When all I can see is the devil on top

Rudy Amador

Thunder

Why does the Thunder
Break the silent earth
The rain falls gentle
Caressing beauty's life
A crack of lightning
Lights the dark sky
All is quiet. Your
Thunder disrupts our hearts
The rain falls heavy
With blackened skies
Then your Thunder crashes
through, bringing pain
Soon the rain will end
But the Thunder rolls forever
Unbound by life. Thunder
Never ending; growing until
There is no more—

Susan Lantz

Mother

Your lessons are like a chisel,
carving in my mind forever.
Your words are like a stamp,
for when I choose to endeavor,
they will be in my mind forever.

Your steps are like a map,
a map to my future.
for when I am grown,
your steps will be the only known
for me to follow.

Your song so softly sung,
the song of your life,
the song that I will hear,
when you are not near.

Patricia Rhea Ward

A Boy's Day

Six a.m. and wide awake,
catching fish out in the lake.
Strolling down an unpaved lane,
sweet honeysuckles after a rain.
Swinging on a backyard gate,
rounding third to make home plate,
rolling in a field of clover,
reading comics over and over.
Teasing sister to no end,
building tepees with a friend.
Soap box car with steering wheel,
apple pie with evening meal,
catching fire flies in a jar,
wishing on a distant star.
I knew the boy that lived this day,
and with me the memory will always stay.

Wayne Skinner

The Children Are Crying

The children are crying
'Cause their fathers are dying
In a war that they didn't start.
Is it too much to ask
For the fathers to come back
To the ones that have broken hearts?

Is it only the young ones
That have lost their loved ones
To the sound of bloody bullets?
No, there are others
Referred to as mothers
That cry to the photos of their vets.

Sarah Jean Schwickerath

The Flower Bloom Forever Now

The flowers bloom happily
'cause there's no more pain.
I feel her with me-
she's reassuring.

I cry in her arms-
for she is strong now.
I hear her telling me-
she whispers in my ear.
She'll always be here-
her warmth won't leave.
I'm stronger now-
'cause she is.
Yet now we cry together,
my grandmother and I,
They're happy tears.

Lisa Bosse

Colors Die

Gray are the skies
'Cause you're not by my side

Black be the nights
With not a twinkle in sight

Red is my eyes
From times of cries

Blue I will be
For you I will not see

Brown were the leaves the day you went
Angels took you, from him they were sent

Yellow flowers draped all around
Choir made joyous sounds

Green the pastures you now lay
To see someday I hope and pray

White the tears rolled and fell
Memories of you I'll always tell

Orange the sun next day rose
Smiles I remember precious as gold

Purple a color not so bad
I'll always love and miss you, Dad
Wilbur Sampson

Changing

Little bird learns to fly
Changing slow and fast
Soaring in the sky so high
Changing slow and fast.

Little seedling, small and weak
Changing slow and fast
Towering oak, like mountain peak
Changing slow and fast.

Changing is what all creatures do
Every change is fun and new
Some are small, some are vast
Changing can be slow and fast.
Sara Saye

Untitled

A wind begins the storm,
   Clouds will drop the rain
Lighting blinds the sight,
   Thunder racks the brain

Tears flow down your face.
   Emotions spin through flight
Cries will have their place,
   Deny then cause a fight

When you have this feeling,
   Your eyes now look at me,
It is simple in revealing,
   You cannot blame a tree

Next time you wonder why,
   You may not realize then
With every little lie,
   You fall deeper into pretend

Dogs you're hearing bark,
   Cause a lion inside to roar
When you ignite my spark,
   Your friend will be the floor!!!
Dopeman

Listen

Not from around,
comes the voice of God
but from within.

Not in stereo sound,
from heart and mind,
but as a whisper of wind.
Norman K. Motter

Light

Have you ever felt
confused, lost, scared, and alone
like you're in a maze
an endless maze
no beginning, no end
every turn
makes you more lost
then you're falling,
falling
into an endless pit
a pit of despair
and when you land
you're in a cave
a dark, damp cave
you walk for years, months, weeks
and then
after all the tears, sorrow and
pain
you see the light
Samantha Makar

From An Airplane

As I look out my window
cotton balls float below;
So gentle and soft,
moving ever so slow.

Quiet, very calm
way up here in the sky.
Perhaps it's heaven,
To find out when I die.

Heaven? I doubt.
For heaven's where I want to be
and where I want to be
is here; you with me.

Wouldn't it be funny,
when that day should come,
we find out heaven is where we're from?
Roger D. Harrison

"Fall Forward"

An extra hour today
but what good is an extra hour
without you
to fill it
with your gentle touch
your loving glance
your tender smile.
Without your hand reaching out
to touch my face
caress my hair
warm my heart.
Even an extra second
in an empty day
is too long without you
to share it with me
Sheena Ross

A Fool's Game

When I was a young man by measure
courting a girl was a pleasure
I saw quite a few and then said adieu
always in search of new treasure.

Their chambers of love did I seek
wanting for ecstasy's peak
pretending to be of great chivalry
then off I would be in a streak.

I persisted in playing the game
which young men mistake for fame
portraying the cad as though it were fad
in time I acquired a name.

It wasn't too long before
the ladies would see me no more
they felt that I… was just being sly
and I was thereafter ignored.

I acted like I didn't care
rejection was nothing to bear
I stayed at home…close to the phone
and learned how to play solitaire.
Lenny Ellis

Worth

The dark shadows
Cover me tonight
Shall I bear the pain
Or take my life

Why can't they see
beyond their face
Why can't they see
the truth in me

Why do they have to fall
Fall for me physically

There is more
so much more
more inside to show

There are years
of tempering
grace and flair
see me, see me

My worth is there
Marcelle Rabinovich

Inner Peace Found Love

As she walked
down this path
not knowing what's ahead
Dawn was coming
faster than her thoughts.
At one time
she felt no future.
Day was starting
to break through.
The emptiness
that consumed her deeply
was fading rapidly.
As she turned to the east
The sun was shining on her face.
This was a beautiful being
That would show her
a love she had never known.
This, after all
was the inner peace
she thought she would never find.
Stephanie Nilles

"Christmas Time - Family Time"

Snow falling, icy roads,
crowded stores, presents by the loads.
Christmas music, bright lights,
Smiling children,
What a beautiful sight.
Mistletoe and Christmas trees,
Big red bows on merry wreaths.
Christmas bulbs and Nativity scenes,
"Peace on earth," do we know
What this means?
Church bells ringing,
Families gather from far and near.
The choir singing,
"Do you hear what I hear?"
This is a time to share, to love,
A time to worship God's Son
from above.
A time for you and me.
This is Christmas time,
A special time for family.

L. Clark

Final Jeopardy

animal on the road. two
crows pick at its outer
detached extremities. it
could have died asleep

in the flowers. yet premonitions
of sunlight warms
the lovely asphalt. did you
have fun both living and dying

for someone else, Saviour?
was it worth knowing the
answer when the question
remains "who is who?"

Mark Steudel

Undying Love

Crucified!!
Crucified!!
How many of us would have died?
Would we hang there on the cross,
Would we believe all was not lost?

Our mother looking on,
Trying to be strong,
Knowing since our birth,
It would end like this on earth.

Nail scarred hands
Mangled back and feet
What will you say to Jesus
When you finally meet?

Traci Noe

Untitled

I heard a girl speak of me
Just as I walked by
About this elusive cowboy
and the look in the eye.

A stare with cold blue eyes
Under a black hat with a gaze
He's been a rodeo cowboy
and will for us this day

I wish I could touch him
to feel where he's been
mom said those cowboys
are filled with life and sin.

Robert Nichols

Untitled

Diamonds sparkle - their
cut perfect and refined,
a precious gem,
You are my diamond.

The Moon glows,
a mysterious wonder,
a nightly vision,
You are my Moon.

The evening Wind,
gentle breezes,
caressing my skin,
You are my Wind.

The Stars twinkle,
like your eyes,
a gentle glow,
You are my Stars.

You are these things,
and so much more,
you are my World...

Victoria Lakatos

Daniel's Dream

Not so awfully long ago
Daniel Scott Smith entered a race;
There were thousands of contestants,
But of fear Daniel showed no trace.

He was a winner and he knew
That he could walk off with the prize;
He only had to train himself
By eating right and exercise.

His eyes shone like a million stars,
Sparkling at the thought of winning;
Faster and faster would he go,
While his parents stood there grinning.

So - at long last came that great day -
Daniel stood at the starting line;
His dad down at the goal shouted,
"Come on, son, you're gonna do fine!"

"Go!" the boys were off in a flash,
Their feet pounding the ground like mad;
Then - with a smile, Daniel said,
"I sure did run, didn't I, Dad!"

Mary L. Shelton

"My Dark, Dark Secret"

I have a dark, dark secret,
darker than the dark blue ocean,
darker than the dark, dark sky,
when I think about it, it makes me
feel like I'm going to cry, and sigh,
sigh, sigh, I can't tell anyone this or
else I'll feel like I'm going to die.
I can't stand it; I've held it in for a
very, very long time. I wish I hadn't
held this dark, dark secret in my
mind, it hurts so bad in the bottom
of my heart, it feels like a big black
dart right in my heart. I wish it
would part but that wouldn't get me
anywhere, I would still have this
very, very bad feeling in my heart and
in my mind remains that dark, dark
secret I've kept for this long, and from
this day on, I wish I never kept this secret.

Rachel Palmer

Silent Cry

Shake my hand
dear old friend of mine
Haven't seen you
in such a long time.

Could it be,
I've forgotten what to do
I don't know,
Maybe I'll take just a few.

I recall now
how we became such friends
I do regret
we never made amends.

Here's to you,
my friend from time gone
You're smiling,
you know you have won.

Lawrence I. Winchowky

"Death"

Death is different from life.
Death is cool, it rules.
You can't cry, smile, lie, or laugh
when you're dead.
You can't think, or kill, or hate.
You are dead and rotting.
You can't love, walk, or hear the
Beat of your heart when you're dead.
Death is darkness without memory or
any idea who you are or who you
loved or looked like. It is like an
Underground prison you can't escape.
Death is something everyone fears
because...
... death is another world nobody
can explain.

Melissa Snouffer

Freshman Year

I swim in loneliness and despair!
Deep down there are so many fears.
My heart aches.
But yet I dare to fake

False smiles
All the while
In great pain
Though I may act vain

Lonely in a crowded university
That will give you great history?

Yes I scream.
As I Feign...

For a hand to hold mine
Until I have time
To adjust
To all the fuss.

Roxanne Harvey

Shades Of Light

Shades of light
can you hear,
can you see?

Turning grey to light, light to grey!

Brave the time you have
To turn the shade to BRIGHT!

Marsha Strand

"Rest Home"

In a rest home for the aging,
deeply nestled in the pines,
I saw a lonely lady,
half hidden by the vines.

Her face was filled with worry,
her body stooped with gloom.
For being old and helpless.
is this to be her doom?

Oh Lord! How far we've fallen,
Our lives so full of greed.
We've cast out this lovely lady,
And forgot the love she needs.

God Bless this lovely lady,
give her peace divine,
But for the Grace of Jesus,
that Mother could be mine.
Lavonia Gilleland

Shadow

I sleep beside a shadow
Deja vu of a person I once knew
Confused by the altering light
Swiftly changing from day to night
  then back to day
Leading me astray
Sense of reality getting hazy
The shadow redefines the view
  what was me is now you
How to reach the shadow
  and break loose from its hold
How to unlock its tentacles
  reforming the human mold
Sneaking out to grasp
  in the seductive silence of the night
Blighting the innocuous spirit
  of the child within
Instilling the infectious gene of ugly
humanness
The dark side of the soul - its shadow
Pushing out the light to another place and time
Phyllis Ilene Tonkin

The Holocausts

When in the course of human events
Demons rise and spew the scents
Of putrid fear and greed and hate
Their brutal hunger seek to spate
Hatred spawned in cruelest strife
Of race and faith and way of life
Extermination is their cry
Destiny reason for foe to die
Camped by force of soldier's rifle
Starved in rags to spirit stifle
Shot and slashed with bloody vigor
Left to die in frozen rigor
Stripped to cleanse in lethal gas
Graved in ditch in mangled mass
One bristled monster did or let
Crimes of horror ne'er to forget
Then there's the one who said
The only good Indian is a dead Indian
And left the natives dead.
Tom Crowder

"At The Hands Of Destruction"

In the early dawn,
destruction came knocking at the door
filled with rage,
as never before.

The lives of precious children,
have been taken away
hearts filled with sadness,
there is only darkness today.

Overwhelming sorrow that has,
spread worldwide
'til there is nowhere to run,
no place to hide.

People filled with fear,
they live as if in a cage
at the hands of destruction,
there's a terrorist,
who carries a heart filled with rage.
Patricia M. Ramos

A Mother's Hope

He's my child, I know it
Difficult as it may be, I must show him

Cutting glares erased by my prayers
helps me get by day by day
I say, it's up, He says, it's down
We communicate round by round

He's my child, I know it
They say it's puberty and I must allow
Oh Lord, help me not disavow
Victoria Ribbron Baker

Up In Smoke

Who are you?
Do you know?
Can you only think of
What you just smoked?

You parents question;
then they cry,
they know what you put in your eye.

You feel real good
and know it gets worse.
It made you broke
get in your mom's purse.

It's taking over
your body and soul.
Who are you?
Do you know?
Lane Kingsbery

Idyllwild California

Fingers of smoky snow
curl down the mountainsides,
dewy damp decorated
pine-trees shine white bright
in the afternoon's embrace.
Amidst the misty cabins,
piled-high hard-soft snow
crunches underfoot
and black back-tracks
snake hither and yon
to tiny tidy yard shops
of precious power jewels,
ancient arcane artifacts,
and cunning coyote crafts.
Steven Porter

Reflections

Morning comes too soon-
  Down the hall, out the door,
    Over the fence,
      It disappears in the noonday sun.

Afternoon-
  Long shadows on the grass,
    Longer thoughts of
      What, where, why and why not?

Evening-
  Everywhere promises,
    Scent of roses, candle glow-
      Joy!

Night-
  Dark and warm,
    Soft wings enfolding the spirit
      Love!
Marion Jane Mattes

Shoulder To Shoulder

He had blond hair
Draping over to one side
It covered one blue eye.
A black loose sweater,
Hanging neck-line,
Youth exposed.
Ivory skin showing.
As if welcoming a meeting,
A smile savored the sight,
Glimpsing into eyes
Seldom gazed upon.
The heat between the two
Rose, as feelings came to.
Maria S. French

Untitled

Slowly the wax
drips down the candle
just as my life
melts away
making me smaller,
yet stronger,
and like a candle
I shine brighter
and then fade
into nothingness
Michelle A. Triolo

Pencil

Yellow school bus
Driving over paper
Leaving skid marks
Tommy Hill

Life's Journey

Sweet traditions and old things
Comfort the heart of one who dreams

Caring friends and tender hearts
A thoughtful eye makes a spark

Time is fragile within life's frame
use it wisely and make someone's day

Show in life that you know what's best
And give a smile to all the rest.
Mary Catherine Moores

Red Sun

Red sun,
  Dry air, dusty road,
    path so long
    mouth so dry,
  Woman carrying child out of womb.
  Feet wrapped,
  Can walk no where,
  Man in control,
  Country will not surrender,
  Water sparse,
  Child cries, woman must flee,
  Area open so many miles to cross,
  Abandonment not by woman,
  Reasoning set to ensure security,
Red Sun.
    beating down,
    mouth so dry,
  Woman's breath shallow,
  Defeat up the road
  Must still concentrate on each step.

Sage Michaels Pembeltan

Let Me Make A Difference

Let me make a difference Lord
each and every day ...
Lead me to someone who is lost
and does not know the way
to the happiness, the peace and joy ...
that only you can give ...
Let me tell them Lord just how you
died ... so that we may live.
Let my life reflect the perfect love
that made you leave your throne ...
to walk that road to calvary and
die there all alone.
Lord, of this love and sacrifice
give me the words to tell.
Let me make a difference Lord
and keep someone from Hell!

Ned L. Mathis

Lifetime Dreams

Now that we are united
Family as one together
As it was written in the book
United before our time

  Lifetime Dreams
Thank-you Lord! You heard my prayers...
  Lifetime Dreams

Years lost — memories made
Stories remembered and recorded
Family history is marked in time
Growing generations-Family treasured

  Lifetime Dreams
Thank-You Lord! You heard my prayers...
  Lifetime Dreams

No byes need be said!
The love shared—Remembered
We shall live on as one in heaven
  Thank-You Lord!

Lifetime Dreams-You heard my prayers
  Thank-you Lord!

Sharren Ann Paulick

Delomie

  The cool wind blows from the
east against her bath filled

  With water, lifting her black
flowered printed hem
    from the ground,
twisting her long dark shiny hair
    to the heavens while she
rests her weary body down on
    the platform chair,
her voice heals my wounds inside
slowing down and tuning down
    the ocean's tides
while her hands rapped tightly
    around my poor lonely heart the
drizzling rain slowly began to start

  As her golden body picked itself up
from the chair I heard a whisper
    from God that said grandmother
really cares

Rhea V. Jeffrey

Flight

Is this the landscape of heaven?
Endless Sahara of vapor
And no oasis?
What hand stops the fall?

Mary Ann Rice

The Journey To Wholeness

The arm of one,
ends;
The arm of another,
begins.
There is a wholeness,
between the two.

They fit together perfectly,
like two pieces of the same puzzle.
Separating means incompleteness.

They came from one mold,
split in the beginning of time.
The years of searching have ended,
wholeness once again.

The process of connection,
long but not tedious.
The end result,
eternal life as one.

Kimberly Jones

Lost Sibling Ere Disease Meant Sin!

Disease isn't constant; but
Fatalism fuels more than
Brimstone and coke - cook - barriers!

There is always a ninety-year-
old woman....keeping a
Doddering old husband's
Sneaking against...Traffic
signals —— to begin
the quest.....for...where....?
Eternity begins!

If not — It's the
Him, itself....at fault - not
Zeus!

Richard C. Miller

Enlightenment

I turn to look and see nothing,
Except the gleaming knife.
At once I know what I must do,
So I take the knife with gentle hate,
And slash across my arm.
I see the blood flowing from the cut,
It reminds me of your hair.
At that thought I see your face,
But I'll never be close to you.
I slash my knife across my scalp,
So I'll have your hair.

Bradley

"A Faceless Stranger"

Throughout life, we meet them, every day,
Faceless strangers going their way,
But in time of need and pain,
a hand reached out to me, one day,
a person, I had never known,
Before this hour, of deep forlorn,
a smile; a touch; some shared remorse.
Made me walk, a steadier course,
Things a stranger did for me,
When my life felt so empty,
For in this world of fear and strife,
It might just happen once in life,
Little acts of kindness shown,
From a "faceless stranger."

Patricia McCarty

The Passenger's Window

I think it was on Interstate 75...

She was standing
Facing me
On the other side of the room
With her clothes lying by her feet
She moved forward
Tantalizing me
Her bold eyes
Beckoned me
Her endless curves
Captivated me
And as the night continued to exist
Her body, heart and soul
Made love to me

The mile markers and guard rails
Flashed past my dormant eyes
And I caught my mindless expression
Reflecting off the window.

Tyler Spencer

A Distant Memory Unlocking

To know the love,
that was present,
to feel the pain,
that was caused,
to know the wrong,
that never became right,
with regrets now carried,
and stories now told,
life could be all over,
for someone might have known,
to your knowledge,
you were not aware,
of the many things,
that weren't there.

Stephanie Burch

To Love Again

The lonely teardrops of the heavens
fall upon the roses so red,
as I awake in the morning,
peer into a mirror,
and see your reflection on the bed.

I begin to think as I stare
and gaze into my eyes,
of why you were sent to me
from such beautiful skies.

I search the thoughts of my soul
and I still cannot see,
the reason why you stayed here to
make love to a man like me.

All I know is you've set my heart
on fire and finally made it bend.
So please, let me love you forever,
for teaching it how
   to love again.

Kenneth Prygon

Tears

Raindrops of sadness
falling
down
my face because of YOU.
Sitting in the window seat
tasting the
tears of love.
Why do I love you?
Remembering the times
sitting outside
on the porch
talking, laughing, and
staring into each other's
eyes.
Now everything
that we had is just a
memory.
As if a crowd of
leaves has just blown
us away forever.

Nikeishia M. Moore

Dedicated To The Brave - 1921's

Footsteps - healing footsteps
  Falling softly on the tired earth.
Gentle footsteps bringing kindness,
  Bring peace and love and mirth.

Faithful footsteps never weary
  Though the day is bleak and long,
Friendly footsteps making cheery -
  Making others tall and strong.

Courageous footsteps walking boldly
  Through the valleys dark and dim
Walking in those stronger footprints -
  Footprints that were made by him.

Other footprints now are silent
  Though their message lingers on.
They speak to us of victory.
  They have won the marathon.

Your living footsteps through the years
  o'er hills and dales have trod
You follow in the Master's steps,
  You blaze a trail to God.

Sarah Mooney

Endless, Nameless

Oh, the burden of light
falls on us all.
Faith must be restored.
The time is here, we must act.

Move our energy to the source.
The heavens open up,
Our eyes reflect the wonders
To our soul,
lest there be anyone left

The power of the age is critical.
Oh, the changes we are about to see.
The wonders of the unknown awaits.
We are part of the flow.

Endless, nameless
the surge is beyond words.
We must not falter.
lest there be anyone left.

Woody Liggett

In Time

I look yonder
Far away
No longer
For the love of lovers
To me my other
I wipe away my tears
For a life that grows near
And in the end
There's just me
And no other

Maureen M. Green

My Window

I would like to tell you, my
Favorite spot, in our home,
is sitting and looking out
my Windows. It's like a mirror
to my soul, so peaceful, I see so
many things, of mother nature,
Created by God, to live and grow.
Beautiful Birds flying to and fro.
Rabbits hopping across the lawns,
The Green Trees, so tall, weaving in
the breeze. Pretty Flowers blooming
Butterflies fluttering through the
air, Beautiful, little Hummingbirds
Drinking the sweet Nectar. My friends
and neighbors driving up or down
the road, a smile, or a wave as
they go. Looking out my window,
I can see so very much of God's
Creation. I'm so glad, he created
me, and someone built a window.

Lucille Burke Imel

Summer

Silent walks along
deserted roads.
Tall glasses of sour,
yellow lemonade.
Soundless evenings on a porch
in a rocking chair.
Daffodils, dandelions, daisies
dancing together in the soft breeze.
Quiet strolls on
the beach, barefoot.

Kim Johnson

I Know No Other

I know no other who makes me
Feel the way you do

I know no other who makes me
Put pen to paper the way you do

I know no other who can reach
Inside my heart and create such a spark

I know no other to say
I wish we weren't so far apart

I know no other that can gaze
Into my eyes and see a gem

I know no other who said "Thank God-
I've found him"

I know no other who loves me
The way you do
I know no other

Kevin L. Palmer

The World Is Dying

The world is dying,
Fighting an endless disease
Everyone's laughing and not caring
Not a moment to seize
It's a virus that's winning
Tearing each soul apart
This virus is called hatred
It's filled every heart
Maybe no one notices
Or maybe no one cares
But the blood on the hands of a killer
Makes everyone aware.

Stacey Bradshaw

Untitled

Sitting here
  flipping cards
    watching them
flutter.

Like snowflakes
  falling through
    my endless
existence

Looking through
  my mind's eye
    watching life
pass.

Not accepting
  my mortality;
    holding onto
youth.

Sitting here
  flipping cards,
    escaping from
reality.

Sarah Kleeb

Wind, Sand, And Stars

O what chagrin
For the genius of man
Who finds
Immortality
Merely a tan.

L. Saunders

Untitled

You say I'm the one to blame
For all the fights and all the pain
Look in the mirror
What do you see
You see nothing but you and me
All we can do is sit and pray
That there will be another day
We fight to keep this love alive
It seems nothing but a lie
We go in circles to seek the truth
When all we do is make an excuse
To try to keep this love alive
Will break us apart even more
Let's just say our goodbyes
For there will never be another day
Remember I will always love you
Look in the mirror
What do you see
You see you
But not me

Yvette DeCaro

Where Cometh The Wind?

Where cometh the wind,
for I cannot see it,
But I feel it on my skin.

Where cometh the wind, yet
I look at the sky, the
clouds use the wind to pass by.

Where cometh the wind, I gaze
at the ocean, does it move the seas?

Where cometh the wind, see the grass
and trees swaying with the breeze.

Where cometh the wind?
The North, South East, the West.

Where cometh the wind?

Kevin G. Lewis

Untitled

While in the night I sleep
My soul slips away to the
Softness of the night
And visits the stars
The moon and God.
Says hello to the sun
As it comes back to me
And I awake.
Some night my soul
Will slip away to the
Softness of the night
And visit the stars,
And the moon and with
God I will stay.
What a wonderful thought
Such a lovely way.

Harriet O. Kidd

Peace on Earth

Pray for it
Even give it a chance
A calm before unknown enhance
Casualties no more for the ambulance
Everyone take a stance.

Larry Laub

The Rose

I see it now,
for it is easily seen.
You just couldn't miss it some how,
for it is colored emerald green.

The pedals are bright red,
it's easily seen in snow.
The black writing from what was said,
the wind began to blow.

The picture was painted,
it's perfect in every way.
The lady just fainted,
she was so gay.

It is cold outside,
just look at the lady's nose.
We just got back from a sleigh ride,
now look at the rose.

Mary Theisen

My Heroes

The price is very high,
   for knowledge,
   righteousness,
   justice.

For all who subject themselves,
   to any of these loves,
The road is long,
   unpaved,
   almost untrodden.

They are only recognized,
   when they are dead,
   if ever.

They are the true
   unsung heroes.

Sara Wineland

Peace

Thank you God for peace of mind
For lonely avenues of time
For tranquil days and sunny skies
For little birds and butterflies
For the beauty of the trees
And lonely sails on spaceless seas
For love that reaches out to me
And you my God...
I long to see.

Loretta M. Wismer

Over Again

Burning with guilt
Dying of shame
Kiss me over and over again

Make me forget
Be rid of regret
Kiss me over and over again

I want this. I need this.
I'm hungry within
I'm giddy. I'm dizzy.
My head's in a spin.

So take me and make me
So glad to give in
Then kiss me over and over again

Maria E. Foster

House of Glass

A house of glass is what I spin,
For looking out; not letting in.
The doors are made from gold that shines
Made for me to hide behind.

Built with all the finest things,
Held together with brass rings.
The halls, they are all diamond lined
Made for me to hide behind.

My windows frosted to perfection
So I may look without detection
Curtain spun from silk so fine
Made for me to hide behind.

This house I've built so very grand
Piece by piece with my own hand
A better house you'll never find
Made for me to hide behind.

Marie Frisco

I Thank You God For This Amusement Park

I thank you God for this amazing park:
for the leaping green spirits of trees
and a blue true dream of sky; and for
everything that's natural and infinite

I who have died am alive again
and this is the star's birthday; this
is the birthday of animals and of nature,
and of the gray great happening of earth.

Sylvia Dande

Grandmother

I will always remember you
For the things you did do
You were always there
Because you did care.

With a smile upon your face
Your arms held out to embrace
With an ear to always lend
On you I could depend.

I can't understand why you had to go
It hurt me more than you'll ever know
My heart is filled with much sorrow
Because I won't see you tomorrow.

To forget you, I will never
I'll always love you forever and ever
Because there will be no other
Like you, my special grandmother

Tina L. Poland

The Zoo

Animals are everywhere
Birds and geese way over there
There are some lions and some bears
Pink flamingo, zebra too,
Everything is at the zoo
Tall giraffes and a reptile cage
There are tigers roaring in rage
Hippos swimming, monkeys climbing
Dolphin shows and turtles staring
All these things are fun to see
but now it's time to go to sleep
As we dream of the things we've
done this day.

Rebekah Meyer

Eternal Love (lost)

I am weak but I can manage
  I have suffered tremendously but healed my damage
dishonesty, deception, mistrust and deceit
  I have been crippled... then bent...but remain on my feet.
If my journey through your life can be covered by experiences yet to
  come then let it rain blood that will coat and stench every
    footpath through your Life that has denied my existence and
    ignored the destruction of a man.
Black queens have knelt before me... not to be circumcised of their
  dignity, but to become the fluid of my life...my River Nile.
If the memories forged by my sculptured efforts
  can be cast as small birds on iron-feathered wings
    or shattered as the stones beneath my trembling weight
then I will wobble through life on the cane that you have carved for
  me from my own torment
yet I remain Enraptured...Captivated...Blinded by Outrage
  deafened by the screaming truth screeching the fluidity of youth to
    a crippling halt destined to wobble through life on the cane you
    carved for me from my own torment
yet to love you still.......and wish for nothing more.

    Gary McIntyre

Wedding Bells

Somewhere in the distance, there is something I hear
I have tried to recognize that sound, but is still not clear.

I know what I would like for that chiming sound to be
Wedding Bells! because I am getting married in July, you see.

Even though I am a bit apprehensive to say the words "I Do"
I know that I have chosen the right man, that much is true.

As the time passes, and the happy date draws near
I experience excitement and of course, some fear.

Somehow I know this nice man is so perfect for me
Therefore, I will keep looking forward to becoming Ms. B.

In a few short weeks I will become a bride
To a precious man in whom I take great pride.

The man with whom I've chosen to spend my life
Will certainly inspire me to be a good wife.

I cannot wait for that exciting date in July
When my true love makes that final, committed reply.

I must admit that I don't anticipate anything but the best,
This positive thought is good, so I will forget the rest.

Then after the Wedding Vows, we'll claim each other's heart,
And remain as man and wife 'til death do us part.

    Azzie Lee Stroble

A Desert Around The Bend

He knows the time is old,
He does not have to be told.
The money may be poor,
But still no one comes to the door.
No family or even a friend,
A desert around the bend.
The air is sickly,
But death is coming quickly.
Afraid he lays,
And wishes he could play.
Alone, sad, and sorry about things he could have changed,
But to him people are out of range.
Now it is black,
Breath he now lacks.
He sees light ahead,
He sees a gate, that is to be said.
He weeps no more,
He is now with the Lord.

    Katherine Chase Barrett

Life

I have two eyes to watch all the colors.
I have two ears to listened to the sounds.
I have one nose to smell all the fragrances.
And I have one mouth to wash it all down.

I have a brain that years for knowledge.
I have a heart that leaps and jumps.
I have bones that hold me together.
And I have fingers that clink and thump.

I am lucky, for some people can't see.
I am lucky, for some people can't talk.
I am lucky, for some people can't listen.
And I am lucky, for some people can't walk.

I have all my senses.
I have all my organs too.
I am fit and healthy.
So I must honest with you.

I take these things for granted.
I do not stop and think.
I do not appreciate these precious gifts.
Each time I smile, jump, or drink!

    Bethany Freedman

Breecher

I think about the rain
I hear its cold wetness
It's coming near
I hope every day it'll rain some
But no one listens
I'm stuck in the sun
I wish the brightness would go away
I wanna get outta this place
And play in the darkness of raining grace
I wouldn't hesitate to get outta here
I know not many would miss me dear
I wish the brightness would go away
I need some rain to have some fun
I need to get away from the sun
I hope someday it'll be gone
Just bring the rain, just bring it on
I wish the brightness would go away
So I could be the one having a nice day

    Amber Pfeifer

I Am A Person I Am A Bird I Have To Fly!

I wonder how to fly
I hear the birds
I see the clouds as they float slowly by
I want to fly! I want to fly!
I am a person I am a bird I have to fly!

I pretend to fly
I feel the sky
I touch a rainbow soft and sly
I worry I will fall
I cry I can fly! I can fly!
I am a person I am a bird I have to fly!

I understand it's not possible I took flight the other
night but...
I say I flew! I flew!
I dream that I will fly again
I try to return there
I hope to reach the sky. I'll climb the stairs up to the roof.
I'll jump off there, I'll fly!
I am a person I am a bird I have to fly!

    Colleen Perris

Pain

I cry so deep with sadness;
I hear the echo of my heart.
Inner tears, so hardened with pain - they will not flow
For they are afraid to weep,
As I fear they will sweep me into a river of non-existence,
Never to be again.
Judith D. Connell

The Old Trees' Secrets

Lying in my bed at night
I hear the roar of the wind in the trees.
With the music of clicking leaves
I am desperately trying to sleep.

It is a soothing, comforting sound
With a hint of wildness to it.
I tell my children to listen closely
The trees are trying to tell them secrets.

Think of the stories the old trees could tell,
Of past lives of humans come and gone.
Think of the things the old ones have seen,
The Indians and their campfires and song.

The stories they could tell of the buffalo
Running together - so many - in great herds.
The white men in their wagon trains
Coming to settle this land with their hopes and fears.
Jeanette Haskett

Silent Thoughts

I see you often, I hear you speak
I hear your laughter, I see your smile,
much brighter than a sunny day
these feelings I have for you, can I ever let you know

I hope to be a part of your life someday
if only in some small way
another watchful eye, a helping hand,
a shoulder to lean or cry on

Will I be able to contain my thoughts and feelings
as time marches on, never ceasing, never blinking
always wanting more, always feeling more
but always caring more than either

If you go away, to some place I do not know
if you go away, without ever knowing what I know
are you better off than if you never knew
how very much a certain someone cares for you

And if that day should ever come
when there appears no place for me in your life
I hope I can carry on with the void I will surely feel
content to have my thoughts of you, silent and so real
Garrett Vaughn

Is It My Lord

As the sky cracks the light falls on me
I drop to my knees asking myself,
"Is it my Lord?" No! It can't be as I tell others.
Is this not the third time I've seen the
signs; the sky is telling me not long,
not long before you're home. I have neither seen
the bloody moon, nor heard the trumpet sound
but I look up into the Heaven and see a figure,
"Is it my Lord?" No, the time has not come;
I must stay and suffer a little while longer;
for only then can I go home.
Maranacci Madison

"Shadows Of You"

Autumn, leaves fall gracefully to the ground;
I heard a crunch in my path, it's such a soothing sound.
Winter, white flakes fall like angels from the sky;
A footprint in the snow beside mine tells me you're nearby.
Spring, the sun is so bright and new;
It took my eyes to squint when I thought I saw you.
Summer, splashes of water echo in my mind,
The heat on my head has me searching for someone,
   but only to find.
Shadows of you in the sky at night,
A bright twinkling star, what a comforting sight.
The times of the seasons;
Give me so many reasons.
Why I loved you dearly;
The world above and the ground below
Offer contentment and relief to know.
A shadow of you will always be near me.
Cynthia Kay Keele

"Mama's Girl"

My daughter has left me; I know not to where.
I hope somewhere peaceful, I wish I was there.
I hear her saying to me, "That's our Lord's way."
"He'll call for you soon Mama, on your chosen day."
I hear her asking me, "Mama, why must you weep?"
"I'm happy as your angel, protecting your sleep."
I hear her begging me, "Mama please try to smile."
"I didn't leave you forever, just for awhile."
I love you dear daughter; I miss you so bad.
"I miss you too, Mama; don't be so sad."
"There are others that need you Mama, while I'm away."
"A place by my side will be ready some day."
It's my turn to question her, "Why did you die?"
"I love you dear Mama; it just was my time."
Life is not eternal; death is always near.
Treasure our children, as long as they are here.
Connie Kay Zaffino

"Recycled Tears" (Partings)

Frozen tears,
I keep them in a golden ice cube tray...
And every so often,
When touched by a need...
I take one cherished cube
And hold it to my heart...
(it warms from the love that lives there.)
The memory melts...
And leaves me with the tear...
And I keep it in
A golden ice cube tray.
Christine E. Kersch

Amnesia

He says he knows me,
  I know him not.

He says he once loved me,
  Love for him I do not feel.

He says that once I was his,
  Was he mine? - I think not.

He says he cried a million tears for me,
  My eyes are dry.

He says he died when he lost me,
  He is still breathing.

He says he will die if I don't remember him,
  I do not remember.
Heather Sanders

In Giving

I wish I were the one to be and take your pain away,
I know not what is right to do nor the words that I should say.

But...

If you stumbled and hurt your knee I know what I would do,
I'd treat it with a kiss so soft and bandage it like new.

If your wagon lost a wheel and no longer would it tow,
I'd find a spare to set it right and then I'd watch you go!

If your chair broke out from under and no longer would be fit,
I'd mend its leg with wood so strong forever you could sit.

If your balloon escaped from hand and floated towards the sky,
A kite I'd make and teach you how to fly it twice as high!

If your kitty ran away or she came no longer round,
I'd search the night and the day until she could be found.

If your sun no longer shown with golden warmth so bright,
I'd give to you the moon and stars that fill the sky at night.

I've searched within my heart to find how to comfort and to heal
The wound that's pierced your soul so deep, the sadness which you feel.

I found no magic nor a fix, only me if that would do,
Sincere and true a friendship held, in care so much for you.

Ann Micheli

A Mother's Goodbye

The day you were born to your dad and me,
I learned the meaning of the world, "family."

My heart swelled with pride
As I held you at my side.

As you learned to run and play,
Your laughter could fill the day.

I watched you become a wife and mother.
And you did it better than any other.
You raised your girls so well,
My heart would just swell.
I've loved you since the day you were born,
always know that with the start of every new morn.
I'll always keep a watchful eye on you,
What else would a mother do?

As I say goodbye,
go ahead and cry.
Just remember over the years,
I'll still be there wiping your tears.

Cheryl F. Jorgenson

You And I

I can remember the smile upon your face
I long to feel your warm embrace...

Separated... physically apart...
Yet so close... for you are in my heart

In my dreams visions of you flash...
My mind is spinning, my thoughts race fast

Of hopes and dreams we wish to share...
You and I, a perfect pair...

When I think of happiness I think of you
Of days to come with skies of blue...

Shell covered beaches, you and I hand in hand
As we leave footprints in the sand...

Someday soon we'll be together...
I love you now... Always and forever.

Deveron B. Jackson

The Hill - The Perfect Little Hill

I sit on a hill overlooking my world...
I look and see everyone and everything.

I see the fly talking to the toad peacefully
I see the black man talking to the white man peacefully.

I see no conflicts, no riots and no deaths...
I sit on my hill—my perfect little hill

I see peace as far as I can see here.
I sit where the sunlight dances on everything
I sit where the clouds rain joy and peace,
I sit where no other sits
I sit on my hill—my perfect little hill
overlooking my imperfect little world
knowing that tomorrow will come.

Fiona Walsh

Rare That I Dream

I sat under a tree, with its shadow over me
I looked to the sky, with a tear in my eye.
I rose with my arms, closed unto harm.
And smelled the fresh air, that comforted me with care.
I was happy and calm, at least it did seem.
I softly revised a psalm, but it's rare that I dream.
"Yet mad I am not" and my heart won't rot.
It's as if sometimes I just can't help
But to wander off, and I'll never tell.
My eyes look soft, I thought I saw
My love with open arms.
My head feels weak, so I sneak a peak.
It seems almost too far.
Then I snap out, and it seems almost mean.
That's why it's very rare, that I ever do dream...

Arika Kantlehner

My Love Poem

Day to day, I think of you. For all the trouble we go through.
I love him and he loves me. For the future we will see.
When we marry, time so great. Just to think that we used to date.
The time is now and now is for the loving touch I adore.
And when I die I'll never go. For I'm the one who loves him so.
Our daughter was born; we were so gay.
We had waited nine long months for this day.
Who was to know that our son would be born in just one year.
On the same day we hold so dear.
As we watch them grow we have to teach them right from wrong.
And as the years go by this will make them strong.
There might be some problems as we grow together,
but I think these will be problems we can always endeavor.
So this is our family as it might grow, the one thing I
Want you to remember is I love you all so.

Darlene Bogart

"I"

I know who I am,
I know where I've been
I know where I'm going,
I know what I've seen.
You say you're ok, maybe you are,
You say you're ok,
but I think you know better.
I know I love me,
I know I love you,
but how can you love me,
if you don't love you?
Oh, yea, says you; oh yea indeed, says me
until you love you,
don't say you love me!

Alan R. Kestin

My Grandmother

They say you are old, but in my eyes you are young.
I love you, and I will love you through all the pain of each day.
You are kind and have been kind through the eleven years of my life.
I will love you on and on and take care of you forever.
Brittani W. Lewis

Us Or My Beloved

The nights are cold, the days are gray
I miss you so when you're away.
I miss your hands in soft caress,
Your lips so warm, upon my lips
I miss your heart beating close to mine,
Your thoughts and words with love entwined.

Be still my heart, your step I hear,
my soul cries out for you are near.
Together again, as we should be,
your love shines forth, it covers me

All fears are calmed safe in your arms
the world is ours, my life is charmed
my only wish, and it would be,
just you with me, through eternity
Elizabeth O'Donnell

"Face In The Mirror"

Stay out of my Gethsemane
I need to think for a while
So when the walls come crashing down
There'll be a whole man here to smile.
Let me put on the noble, thoughtful face
And hide the thief and liar
The smaller one hides in the weeds and grass
While the bolder covers up his traces in the briar.
It all seems much clearer once I've some time to breathe
In time I'm able to find a lie and keep all things in hand.
And yet I'm lying, even now. Lying to myself
Lies come easier than this truth. Lies I understand.
So now I know that I'm a lie
I wonder now what I'll do
How can I distinguish between
What is false and what is true?
For in my fear and desperation
I've lost who I really am
When I look in the mirror, I see a face,
A face I don't understand.
Dave Wake

"Journey Of Faith"

   On the road to recover,
Faults and liabilities I have discovered!
Locked inside and never released,
That's why the drinking never ceased.
A lot of things I did and said
Because the "alcohol" controlled my head
The things I thought, the more beer I bought
Created a world of my own, seeds of doubt
I have sewn. Out of control and really insane!
loved ones I've hurt and caused lots of pain!
Here alone I quietly sit,
I'm an "alcoholic," I truly admit
Oh heavenly Father, God above!
I cry for help! For you I love!
Give me the strength and courage I need
To remain sober, with the prayers I'll succeed.
Through AA and family recovery,
My life becomes a joyous discovery.
Putting the past behind,
What the future holds is but "One Day At A Time."
John Pifko Jr.

Ode To A Little Girl

Before I was grown I had traveled the world
I never saw nothing as precious as my little girl

And, yes, it amazed me
How happy you've made me
With your smiles

I will never ever leave you
I will always be beside you
Across the miles

For words can never be put
Oh how I love my sugarfoot

I get excited just thinking of you
Please don't let this dream ever end
You can bet that I'll always be true
Because a best friend will never bend
David Mauldin

Murder Mother Nature

Shatter the sun,
I now see by a soft white bulb.
Silence the ocean waves,
I've bought their sound on compact disc.
Block the wind,
I installed fan propelled AC.
Dam up the rivers,
I am, powered by electricity.
Blast down the mountains,
I already have them on wallpaper photography.
Serve the world's horses on a platter, no matter,
My car takes me where I want to go.
Burn all the books,
I found them on my home computer library.
There's no need for a rain forest anymore,
I can see it on my TV.
In fact..., murder mother nature,
I live in Modern Day Society.
          Sincerely,
          Technology
The Black Bird Brandon L. Holley

Three Rules Of Life

Nothing is forever, I guess that is true
I once had happiness, now I am blue
All of my joy has now turned to sorrow
This happened in a day, what of tomorrow

Never admit to anything, that I will not do
But I must admit, I do miss you
Were not very far apart, I see you everyday
So tell me why I feel you're miles away

Anyone can be replaced, Ha what a lie
Without you I think I'd rather die
What have we done, neither of us has sinned
So tell me why is it here, THE BEGINNING OF THE END.
Chris Castlebury

Dogwood Petals Danced

Turning into my homeward lane,
I saw a tiny flash of white.
I chanced to see Dogwood petals dancing.

Fallen from the tree, the petals rejoiced in newfound freedom.
Gleeful Dogwood petals danced a waltz.
The ballroom street opened to the swirling wind,
Lifting the party to full swing.
Whirling, Dogwood petals danced.
Jonell W. Williams

"Adrift At Sea"

As I awake this spring day so fresh and new
I ponder all the tasks that I must do.
Should I go to work my daily chore
Knowing exactly what waits in store.
Life's heavy burden thrust upon me
Wishing I was ADRIFT AT SEA.
I mull around my house so slow
As the sun from East begins to grow.
Still wondering what this day will bring
I can faintly hear the ocean breeze sing.
Unchain the binds that shackle me
I yearn to be ADRIFT AT SEA.
To the skies I stand up and reach
I'm thinking mostly of a warm sandy beach.
I now realize which way I'll go
Down to my dory and start to row.
I set my course out to middle bay.
It is here I choose to spend the day.
There is nothing there to trouble me
When I am ADRIFT, ADRIFT AT SEA.
John B. Gleason

The Open Cupboard Door

It stood wide open, that cupboard door.
  I raised too quickly and felt I'd soar,
The shock made stars flash by the score.
  To stifle pain was an ugly chore.

It hit my head, that pesky door,
  'most knocked me to the floor.
I held my hand right on that sore,
  I felt like cursing that open door.

It hurt so much I almost swore.
  I tried to count: one, two, three, four.
My tongue spat words right at that door.
  It spitefully hurt me to the core.

I tried to work with pain galore.
  I felt so angry at the door.
Open doors, to me, are such a bore,
  I'll hate that door forevermore.

My advice to you, I solemnly implore;
  Never hit your head on an open door!
Uncomely words you should deplore
  'cause "Imps" grin behind an open door!
Benita Slawson Welebir

Blossom

She's only a little grey dog that I found.
I really didn't want to have her around.
I thought she'd be trouble and I didn't have time.
But all of a sudden, Blossom was mine.
The kids said, "Please Mom, she's so cute and so small.
We'll take her out and feed her and all."
But the newness wore off in time
And lo and behold Blossom was mine.
She stays by my side wherever I am
And sleeps on my bed through the night.
She looks with worried eyes if I have to go out,
She can't stand me out of her sight.
Her slippers, her toy,
And her only trick is to shake it.
Her bark is sharp, but we know she just takes it.
The love and loyalty I receive from her
I can't give back in kind.
But when somebody says what a cute little dog
I say yes, she's Blossom, she's mine.
Doris Russell

For The One I Love

As I lie here and think about you
I recall all the wonderful things you do.
When I remember the day that we met
I break down inside, into a cold sweat.
I think of you every moment of the day
Wishing I could be next to you if I could find a way.
If you could look into this heart that makes me live
You would see all the love I have to give.
You're sweet, gentle, tender and kind
Everything I've dreamed of and now it could be mine.
I would never let this chance go
Because I want to see our relationship grow.
No matter what happens, I'll be by your side
Even when it hurts and you've started to cry.
I want to tell you how I feel
Because these feelings are for real.
Douglas J. Leitzke

First Love

I think about love, I think about you,
I remember the good times that we've been through.

And now that our time has reached its end,
I only still wish you had left as a friend.

I guess two years was just too long,
I thought you loved me and I was wrong.
My parents used to say you'd never settle down,
that you were still momma's boy and still foolin' around.

There was a time though that I really loved you,
And deep down inside I know I still do.

You always used to say that someday we'd marry,
And sometime after your baby I'd carry.

All of our dreams that we once had,
I think of them a lot and it makes me sad.

And when I think about love, I think about you,
I remember the good times that we've been through.

And now that our time has come to an end,
I only still wish
You had left as a friend.
Julie C. Mercier

Lullaby For A Missing Father

Yidele, Yidele. Tatete, Tatele.
I remember you I remember your white hair
Sitting on a chair in the sunlight on a Sunday

Yidele, yidele. Tatele, Tatele.

On a Sunday you do not work on that day
I climb all over you kiss you and tickle you
I comb your white hair and sing aloud in the air

Yidele, Yidele. Tatele, Tatele.

I wind a scarf around your neck
Your favorite color, white
I pinch your cheeks and pull your ears

Yidele, Yidele. Tatele, Tatele.

I climb on your knees and you embrace me
Sing me a lullaby and I fall asleep
In the warmth of your love

Yidele, Yidele. Tatele, Tatele.
Your arms around me keeping the outside world away
Just you and me now I embrace the cold air
And you are not there

Yidele, Yidele. Tatele, Tatele.
Greta Herensztat

Aligned

The silhouetted voices against the cavern walls of my soul.
I rise from death to see the sky, to eat the summer sun.
Like clouded days, my soul darkens. My heart is void;
My mind is a chasm where the River carves into my life.

All seems aligned in silent skies, with clouds that hide
the moon and stars. I walk the green maze alone,
alone to my home.
Peace and sleep await me in the darkness of my pictured dreams.

The houses aligned along the road have lights that creep
and slip away. Weary souls that are slaves to death sleep
beneath the shadowed grave.
We wake at night to see the dark, our lovers breathing rage.

Like pain of heart, the silence spoke.
I lie awake to see my dreams of solitude.
I am aligned with death tonight, sweet peace covers me.
At the edge of it all....
Jon M. Pritt

Thanks To Uncle Fred

Thanks indeed to Uncle Fred
I said to him as I turned Red!!
I thanked him for my bow and arrow
My big stuffed dog and my big blue barrel
He said he wouldn't stop buying me things
Until my bird grew new wings!!
So thanks again to Uncle Fred
I said to him as I turned Red, again
Then down the road came the U-Hall truck
And out of it popped Big, Fat Buck
He said to tell Uncle Fred thanks again
Oh no, I said as I turned RED!!!
But what I got was mighty fine
A telephone and a fishing line
So thanks again to Uncle Fred
I said to him as I turned Red!!
Oh darn, I said those dreaded words again!!
Casey L. Russell

This Must Be Love

I woke up this morning, with a smile that was true
I said to myself, is this really you?
Is this the person who always wears a frown?
No, now that you're here, my love has come down.
You lit a fire within me that burns oh so deep
I can't eat in the morning, and at night
I can't sleep, this must be love in my heart
that makes me feel so alive; I now have
a reason for living, a reason to strive.
I'll take each step with tender loving care
because I know that for you, I'll always be there.
Cathy Lee Irvin

My Daily Prayer

Now I lay me down to sleep,
I pray to God your love I'll keep.
Deep inside me all the way,
'til the end of every day.
I long to hold you in my arms so tight,
I want to share my bed with you at night.
All day long I think of how things will be,
me loving you and you loving me.
One day soon you'll make me your wife,
then together we shall spend the rest of our life.
Forever we shall stand hand and hand,
forever and always you'll be my man.
Angela Rowe

"Sprinkling Of Snow"

Peeking out the kitchen window one clear frigid night,
I saw a lovely wintry scene emerge as icicles hung from the eaves.

There was a sprinkling of snow, the shiny and sparkly kind,
as on a Christmas card, it was spread over the sleeping garden.

The moon had just risen above the carriage house,
the light of the moon made the snow glitter and shine,
even in the shadows.

I wondered if Jack Frost had made his rounds quietly scattering
moonbeams and sequins about the snow covered yard.

Maybe tiny snow fairies dance and prance atop crystal drifts
through the night till the moon is dismissed by the dawning sky.

One more look as I held the door ajar to see the frozen scene,
to hear the North wind embrace the bared old maple trees.

At the kitchen stove the kettle was whistling softly that it
was time for tea, so I settled in near the warmth to enjoy
a pekoe brew.
Claire Makl

Whisper I Love You

Whisper I love you
   I saw your face — you were grieving —
   I heard your words — how deceiving...
  Oh, I just couldn't go on believing...
Whisper I love you
   I saw your face — you'd been crying
   Did I feel your heart — maybe you'd been trying —
  Oh, why couldn't you let me know
  Oh, why couldn't you let it show

And eyes can tell what words can't say
I never would have gone away...
I had to deceive you —
It got too hard to see you —
   I had to hide, too...
Oh, whisper I love you
  If you could have, there'd have been no reason
   for my leaving —
  The warmth, the cold, the cruel, the nice —
   the deceiving...
    ah, the believing...
Andrea Cavalier

Worldly Sight

In my eyes, I see myself,
I see a world of fear without wealth.
My present, past, and yet to be,
I fear, I fear what I do not see.

It's too much, I look away,
What I see is shocking, make of it what you may.
But curiosity takes hold and I look back,
The sight would make a sane man crack.

It was not a sight but more like a feeling,
The world, the heart, and all the healing.
A sense of what was real,
It's something amazing that you feel.

All these worlds that I saw,
A world of fear, loveless hate, the breaking of the law.
All were one, and one were all,
Babies born while leaders fall.

Our world is grand and we must take care,
For everyone everywhere.
For our world isn't perfect, but we must try,
Or civilization will cease, and our world will die.
Joe Atkinson

My Home In The Woods

Early mornings when I arise
I see God's wonders before my eyes
I pour my coffee and go to the Deck
The hummingbirds are a nervous wreck
The feeders were filled only yesterday
But many hummers came to drink and play
Some days they light by three's and share
Next day they fight and fly just over my hair
Occasionally one hovers, looks right in my face
As if to say, "Move over, this is my special place"
The grass is green — freshly laden with dew
The morning-glories are a heavenly blue
The trees are tall reaching up toward the sky
And many beautiful birds come flying by
Cardinals stop at the feeder to eat a bite
While other birds seem afraid to light
In my piney woods home there is a peaceful feel
And in the beauties of nature I know "God Is Real."

Imogene Wiley

"Don't Cry Mommie"

I look down through the blanket of clouds.
I see mommie crying out loud.
She is crying for me.
She is wondering why this is to be.
I am happy up here, but don't know why,
'cause mommie is still going to cry.
Don't cry mommie, don't cry.

I look down and there are people still searching for me.
Rescue workers are praying.
All the children have stopped playing,
Everyone pauses in silence to try
and understand what has occurred,
But no one understands 'cause their vision is all blurred.
Everything is quiet and I don't know why
all I can hear is mommie cry.
Don't cry mommie, don't cry.
It isn't your fault I had to die,
so don't cry mommie, please don't cry.

Chandra Hildabrand

The Day The Angels Came

A soft spring breeze and I were walking along,
In my heart was a happy new song.

The warm and lovely tropical breeze,
Embraced and entranced me as it pleased.

Spring had erupted with all its glorious flowers,
The trees were once again green and thirsty for showers.

Birds were busy building their homey nests,
Chirping and calling to their mates - let's rest.

All was fine and I was at peace in my mind,
When suddenly two angels embraced me from behind.

They moved silently and swiftly, not uttering a sound,
They lifted me ever so gently up from the ground.

We soared over mountains, valleys, and seas,
Then with a quick thrust upward, I became weak in the knees.

The trumpets were sounding, the light was so bright,
I had suddenly found Heaven; it was right there in my sight.

What a glorious place, I saw Jesus waiting patiently,
With His outstretched arms He welcomed me.

I was safely home, no more tears, pain, or sorrow,
I now had the promise of God's eternal tomorrow.

Caroline F. Nunamaker

Childhood Memories

Childhood memories are precious to me;
I sit and remember how things used to be.
As I look back and recall what we shared;
I'm thankful for knowing how much we all cared.
Although there were bad times along with the good;
I treasure the thoughts of my childhood.
Mamma worked hard to take care of us all;
She is my friend on whom I can call.
We spent time together, just daddy and me,
And I'll cherish those moments in sweet memory.
The death of a loved one brings us much sorrow,
But Christ gives us hope of a brighter tomorrow.
Brother and sisters, our bond it is strong;
It's a family in which I am proud to belong.
Sometimes we would argue, but deep down inside
Our love for each other would always abide.
We are now older and living apart,
But we are together in each other's heart.

Donna M. Berry

That Time Of Day

Late in evening, and early in morning,
I stand on a hill to watch the mist forming,

To smell the freshness, to feel the cool,
That time of day I keep free as a rule.

The colors of silver, of blue, green and grey,
The colors of mist, not here to stay.

On that hill alone, at that time of day,
That time of my own, that I use to pray,

To dream, to think, to watch the mist forming,
Late in evening and early in morning.

Barbara E. Bogucki

Untitled

Why do you care what I wear
I still breathe the air

Why do you care what I say
It doesn't matter if anyone is gay

Why do you care what I do
I still have to live in this world with you

Justin Henderson

The Sea

When the pressures of life start getting to me,
I jump in the car and go down to the sea.

There's a calming effect when the ships sail by,
Even though sadness has brought a tear to my eye.

As I watch the waves roll in to shore,
My problems don't seem so big any more.

The light on the water is such a beautiful sight,
It makes me feel that things will turn out right.

With the ocean breeze upon my face,
I can't imagine a more wonderful place.

As on the shore I walk and wander,
In my heart and mind many things I ponder.

The marvelous smell of the clean salt air,
Is so hard to describe, it's beyond compare.

The sound of the waves on the rocks and the pier,
Make me feel serene and it clams all my fear.

These sights, smells and sounds are like a symphony;
And they're the reason I love to go down to the sea.

Barbara A. Switzer

My Bairns

Oh, my Lord,
  I thank thee
    for this beautiful being
      so tender and trusting
        for mine to keep.

If thou allowest me to continue to keep,
  I shall protect, provide
    and cherish
      until the end of my days.

For, I do not know of thine great boundaries,
  I shall not bow to thee again.

But, now, I bow to thee
  not to thank thee
    but to promise mineself
      that my bairns shall have
        all that I can give.

Junko Geddes

Shelly's Story

"When I grow up," said Shelly,
"I think I'll be a star.
I'll sing and dance upon a stage
and drive a fancy car.

The people will come from miles around
just to hear me sing.

They'll jump and dance and clap their hands
what joy to them I'll bring.

My dad will turn the volume on the T.V. way up loud.

And when he sees my song and dance,
he'll be so very proud.

Fans will buy my records and play them time and time again.
Even though they do not know me,
I will kind of be their friend.

When folks ask for my autograph I will be so very nice.
I'll sign my name so thoughtfully,
I'll even sign it twice.

I will always smile and fill the world with lots of
love and cheer.
And everyone around me will be glad that I am here."

Vonna Moody & Ebbie Noyes

Grandma's House

From days of young my senses flare
I think of grandma's home so fair
The kitchen warmed with essence full
Tea tables, lace, and sunlit rooms
Tall beds of cotton, with clouds of wool
Cookie jars, aprons, and old corn brooms
So sweet those days of which I knew

With joyful eyes I would awake
It's grandma's house there's no mistake
Sweet morning glories fill my head
For her touch only...could make this bed
An angel's kiss...to this room flew
So sweet those days of which I knew

Reflecting back on days gone by
Of young times shared...Hello's...Goodbye's
It's grandma...who had made that place
And God who carved her from His grace
As time goes by...I know well true...
So sweet those days of which I knew

Dennis Charles Garberino

Granny

When I think of Granny
I think of reading stories late at night
  and snuggling close all up tight
I think of playing cards and laughing till it hurt
  and playing in the sand, filling lunch trays with dirt
I think of sweet rice, cream corn, Morgan gravy, and of
  course, salmon patties cooked just right
Coming to my "second home" after school for all these
  delicious treats
Playing old maid, our favorite game, we laughed till we cried
  and we played all day
Feeding cows, when I was younger
These are all memories that I hold dear
When at last it's time to say good-bye
I don't worry for soon we'll play again for your love will
never end.

Craig Morgan Seekamp II

The Thought Of You

  As I sit here alone in my room,
I think of you,
Though I know the love I feel is destined to doom.
I pray that you are thinking of me too.
  I dream and hope,
That some day you will be mine.
If you turn me away my heart will have to cope.
If only you would show me a sign.
  Like a lost sailor welcomes the sight of shore,
I too float lonesomely in the stormy sea of love.
Waiting to see a glimpse of love in those eyes I adore.
As I sail I look for a flicker of sunlight through the gray clouds above.
  What words can I say to prove that my love is true.
They are not yet known to man.
For tonight my thoughts of you are through.
I have said all that I can.

Jennifer S. Tate

"Black, My Race"

I love my race, my race is quite beautiful.
I think the large eyes, the wide noses, thick
full mouths

My race is quite beautiful I say.
I say thick and full is the hair against being called unattractive.

My race is quite beautiful; the way they carry
themselves is quite nice

Now if our brothers and sisters could be more God fearing,
every race could love us more.

If our race could be more loving, parents, children,
sisters and brothers caring more and more, hate not.

My race is quite beautiful when they are God fearing.
My race is quite beautiful.

Constance Carter

A Divine Definition

"Who is God?" of you I asked,
  "Is He mortal, or is He masked?
What does He think of life on Earth;
  Was He the creator of its birth?"

God is a symbol of life's motivation;
  Expressed by many with pure elation.
Denied to none, is His love;
  We are His children on Earth and above.

Clinton T. Yamasaki

Untitled

We danced to the music of the wind.
I took your hand and followed you
Through garden path, and over rocky hill.
I had no thought, that you would go
Some unexpected day,
Now, your absence, like the chill of winter
Seeps into my being,
The sounds of the day
Fade into silence;
The shadows of the evening
Lengthen into darkness;
And the sleepless hours of the night
Are distorted by the long ago past.

Bonnie Cohu Campbell

"It Seems"

I'll never see you again it seems,
I toss and turn 'cause I see you in my dreams.

The night, how can I make it through?
How in the world did I ever lose you?

I miss your laugh and soft silky hair,
I turn and look in the shadows but you are not there.

I'm so lost without you it's like I'm in hell,
Thoughts of you run through my mind as I suffer alone in my cell.

I'm telling you how I feel,
But I don't know where to start.

This love I feel is real,
And we shouldn't be apart.

Me without you is like a flower that's dead,
As memories of us go through my head.

A tear drops from my cheek to my chin,
And I wonder if I'll ever see you again.

Dominic Carbona

The Man I'd Like To Be

When I left home the first time I was nearly twenty-three
I traveled this world over to see what I could see
I got so tired and lonesome I nearly lost my mind
I was starving, slowly starving and down to my last dime
So I called on my Papa to help me if he could
Papa sent me money just like I knew he would
He met me at the station, he took me by the hand
We walked home together a young boy and a special man
Papa you're the kind of man that I'd like to be
Why you put up with someone who's as wild as me
I'll never understand it, but I'm glad you do
Even if I never say it, Papa, I love you

Ernie Shoemaker

Lonely Souls

Lonely are the souls that cry out a silent cry.
Imprison thee with thoughts of love so sweet,
For it is solitude that beckons a life love so long ago.

Remember moments when laughter echoed fortress walls,
Mind and body were one and strong.

Challenge the death of the living,
Bear the candle's dimming light.

Ask not to be taken in vain -
For you truly loved and are greatly loved by others.

Johndrue Mabb

Myself

I have to live with myself, and so
I want to be fit for myself to know,
I want to be able, as days go by, to always look myself in the eye;
I don't want to stand, with the setting sun,
And hate myself for the things I have done.

I don't want to keep on a closet shelf
A lot of secrets about myself.
And fool myself, as I come and go
Into thinking that no one else will know
The kind of woman I am; I don't want to dress myself up in shame.

I want to go out with my head erect.
I want to deserve all man's respect.
But here in the struggle for fame and wealth
I want to be able to live with myself,
I don't want to look at myself and know
That I'm bluster and bluff and an empty show.

I can never hide myself from me, I see what others may never see;
I know what others may never know,
I can never fool myself, and so, whatever happens, I want to be
Self respecting and conscience free.

Jessi Gardner

Conundrum

Now listen, girl, and listen good;
I want to make this understood.
This advice could mean your death or life
Whether daughter, sister, lover, wife.
Have I now got your mind and ears?
Listen, and I might ease your fears.
First: how familiar should you get
With your human being, love-mate pet?
Do you always hurt the one you love?
Sure — the closest one is the one you shove.
So, keep your distance — hunker down — be content,
'cause familiarity breeds contempt.
And never tell all — it will come back to haunt you;
He'll long for new stories, and no longer want you.
Now, listen, girl, and listen good;
I want to make this understood.
Don't play the weakling, the "patsy," the pawn;
Those girl-beaters are cowards under that brawn.
Just play it cool, baby, cool, and you'll never be used;
And chances are you won't be abused.

Helen Estes Seltzer

"Why Do We Pretend?"

Why do we hide behind lies?
Everything is not always okay
Very rarely does anyone understand.
Seeing life through dark glasses
Only hearing the noises, the sounds, the laughter.
A hollow mockery of life..... is not really living it.
Everyone is so fake, so dark and secretive,
afraid to let someone in
fearful of ourselves, afraid to find out
who we really are.
So we go on,
making jokes and fitting in,
until everyone's the same
and we all forget to be
fearful and no one remembers
what it's like to be afraid
and then we forget
who it was we were really hiding from.

Jennifer Keith

"Today Is Very Boring"

Today was very boring,
I was at the beach all day,
A surfer dude came my way,
He discovered a blue smurf on the sand,
He arrived on shore on a boat with his band,
The smurf was very stern,
So the surfer put him in a urn,
He found a rubber tire,
Stuck inside was a big, fat, chubby, baseball umpire,
The umpire bounced across the turf,
When he heard the terrible scream of the
Little, blue, old, ugly, smurf,
At ten o'clock, a herd of elephants traveled through,
A signal that it was the surfers' curfew.

Ella Smith

Legend Of The Village Butterflies

I have lived a thousand lifetimes.
I was born of unlimited spirit and brilliant light.
The blood of Kings and Queens flows through my veins.
Light gave me direction to guide the way,
Spirit gave me wings to reach my dreams.

With wings spread I soared into life!
My journey was long my wings got tired.
I stopped to rest and was captured along the way,
I was scared and alone I was leaving my home.

Over land and sea there were others with me,
We had color in common, but we weren't all the same.
Farmers, Warriors, Merchants and Scholars,
We were different Tribes brought together by chains.

The Journey was rough some of us died,
Some got sick, others cried.
At Journeys end we flew from the bowels,
We took spirit with us, the light was our guide.

The Blood of Kings and Queens flowed through our veins.
We were born for flight, Spirit gave us new wings.
The legend continues, we can survive anything.

Barbara Miller

When Love Found Me

Love found me one day when
I was least expecting it, I've been in love ever since
and this feeling will probably never quit
This little voice inside me said
listen to your heart and take it from there.

I'm happier than I have ever been before,
you know, you're in love when you
don't care if your companion's rich or poor.
It's the love they give that matters,
I'll love my friend forevermore.

I love it when he holds me
close, sometimes he never lets me go,
I feel so safe within his arms,
Our friendship, boy has it grown.

It all started one day when I saw him from a distance,
When he looked at me my heart began to dance.
People say I think of him too much; they say I'm always in a trance.

To my friend I've given of my heart the key,
He didn't ask and nor did I, it just happened one day
when love decided to find me!

Jennifer Diamond

God's Mourning Dove

Early in the morning a dove nestles in a lovely tall tree.
I watch with delight wondering if this beautiful dove
senses me.
The feathers seem to be untouched as the dove remains silent
I feel the peace and solitude from the dove.
Is God's dove here for me to enjoy and feel peace in my heart?
The answer lies in the face of God's mourning dove.

Crystal A. Snow

Grandmother Of Mine

I put a rose upon your casket with love,
I watched dirt put in your grave,
Because I promised you, I would do these things for you.
And a part of me was buried with you that snowy-windy day.

I know now you couldn't stay with me, your
pain was just to much to bear.
I miss the talks, stories, rides in the car,
together and much more than I can say.
I still shed tears when I remember
All the warmth and closeness that we shared.
I will always love you and care for
your resting place.

Clara Oscie-Ola Stewart

I Wake Up In Pieces

I hate myself
I will not allow for any pleasure
My self esteem was forced out of me like a balloon which has a
hole in it,
I have a deep hole of which I think is my soul
I never felt safe
I nervously and constantly keep an eye behind me waiting for attack,
Afraid to look back
Close my eyes, endure the pain and it will go away
Make believe that I am not here
My childhood remains an empty swing on a rotted pine tree
Pine cones, like daggers, pierce through my heart.
Pools of blood flood over the promise of the green grass
that all children are supposed to be given
Tortuous nightmares awake me in horror, screaming, sweating
Reality/unreality, which is it?
My identity has been stripped from me layer by layer,
Rotted skin inside. Smells of smoke and alcohol follow me around
I can't escape the feelings of hands on me, of hot, out-of-control,
dirty breath on me, breathing rapidly. Is it something I did?
One wrong stroke
And I got broke
And the pieces got taken from me

Ann Marie Genovese-Buck

Untitled

The days they all went by so fast.
I should have known it wouldn't last.
I gave my love to him too soon.
I tried to give him the stars and moon.
I gave my love to him for free,
but he couldn't give his love to me.
Today I think about him a lot,
although I should be happy with what I've got.
It's been a while since we broke up.
You'd think I would have had enough.
I know I shouldn't torture myself this way,
but I think of him each and every day.
I told him I loved him, I love him still.
I love him now and I always will.
I know I should try my hardest to forget,
but I don't know how, and I haven't yet.

Erica Jenkins

I Am

I am a crazy guy who makes no sense.
I wonder if donkeys really kick hard.
I hear men fighting in a bar.
I see myself tying my shoes.
I want to lick a horse's nose.
I am a crazy guy who makes no sense.

I pretend to see a big thing with 7 ears.
I feel cold toe nails on my back.
I touch the brain of a dog.
I cry when I am not fed.
I am a crazy guy who makes no sense.

I understand that what I have said wouldn't even please an armadillo
I say to myself "Hi Brian."
I dream that a pitchfork is fake.
I try to wake up.
I hope I have a war in my basement.
I am a crazy guy who makes no sense.

Brian Merel

The Battle

As I lay there, sprawled across the cold damp table,
I wonder why I am here.
He says nothing, for me he is nothing.
As I feel the pain and anger thrusting through my body,
I think... Why me?!

Now the pain surges down to my toes,
Making it as hard as my bones.
My feet start to lock up, the joints harden why me?!
The table gets softer and softer as my way of life drifts away,
My Body, my blood, my soul drifting away helplessly.

Now the human touch is gone, enslaved by the sleep of my body.
Now I drift away.
Why me? It was him who did it!
The pain charging through my heart, launching it fierce blows,
My senses start to fade away.

Now I go into deep sleep,
I feel my eyes gradually closing,
No, don't go! It is too late to fight,
The pain governs my body and my soul,
I have lost the battle.

Matthew Kuberski

Why?

As the breezy wind blows in my face,
I wonder why it blows the way it does,
As the shinny sun shines down on me,
I wonder why it shines the way it does,
As the prickly thorns scratch my feet,
I wonder why it scratches me the way it does,
We may never find the answers to these questions,
but we will know that the wind will always blow,
the sun will always shine,
and the thorns will always prick.

Alicia Young

Conclusion

Life without love of fellow man
Is empty, devoid of plan,
Except for striving, selfish gain,
A race for fortune, gold or fame.
Such is the greed that sows the seed of future wars.
But a continuous search to understand
Our common bonds, and a helping hand,
Revive the souls of the ones who give
As well as the ones who need.

Florence M. Mink

"Our Mother"

Mother is a gentle word full of kindness that is sweet.
I would lay all of this world's treasures lovingly at my Mom's feet.
You deserve the best in life all that this world has to hold.
You're more precious to us, Mom, than diamonds and rubies or gold.

I hope in the years ahead, Mom, that I can only be
half as good a Mother as you are, Mom, to me.
Words alone could never say what I'm trying to express
But as for being a good Mother you are the very best!

There are so many things, Mom, that I would like to say to you
Feelings of childhood memories that will last a lifetime through.
I know I could never repay you for all those wonderful things
It would be like trying to pay the robins for the beautiful songs
they sing.

I know it's not said enough, Mom, but believe me for it's true
There has never been a Mother as wonderful as you.
If it were at all possible, here is what I'd like to do
I would buy up all your hopes and dreams and your wishes would
all come true.

Donna C. Storms

"If I Had Another Chance"

If only I had another chance to start my life anew,
I would start from a new babe just crying in mother's arms.
Just to feel the love of a mother's tender care to her new born
 baby.

If only I had another chance to go through school again.
I would study hard to pass my grade so mother would be pleased
 with the marks I made.

If only I had another chance to go through college age.
I would not study foolish things, I would turn to God and
 trust in all His ways.

So now I am grown in age, but I am just a babe.
It seems like only yesterday Jesus came in and saved.

So why not be born again and start life anew.
If you can only trust in Jesus, He will take you through.

Hester Wilson

The Merry-Go-Round

Please let me off this merry-go-round
I'm tired of riding this thing,
I'm weary from going around and around
Trying to catch that crazy ring.

It looked like fun from where I was standing
With so many different rides to choose;
The glitter and the bright lights
Soon gained another fool.

I should have realized the smiles were painted
And the ring was securely bound
The lights were artificial
People went nowhere, just round and round.

In time it finally dawned on me
This was all a ridiculous game;
Like the donkey chasing the carrot
The merry-go-round was the same.

I'm still going around in circles
Even though it's lost all its fun;
I no longer reach out to grasp the ring
I just pray for this ride to be done.

Bobbi LaMonte

Untitled

When I was young I used to pray
I'd ask the Lord above -
When did people stop believing
Why don't they believe in love?
It's not that hard to figure out
Still people run and hide
Afraid to give their souls away
And let someone else inside
It's not supposed to cause a fear
That put up walls of stone
For those who live behind that wall truly live alone
It seems to me love's a fairy tale
And I may be a fool
Just believe that I'm your hero
Sometimes fairy tales come true.

Don G. Scarsella

Little Boy Of Three

Little boy of only three
I'd like to hold you on my knee;
Cradle you and squeeze you tight,
Cling to you with all my might.

But you have other plans today,
To yell, to climb, and mischief play.
Yet, when you're sleepy, toward the night,
You might consent to my delight.

Someday, when you become a Dad,
You'll understand the folks you had,
Our love for you will always be,
From now through all eternity.

So little one, please understand
We take our loving when we can,
For time is short, and days go fast
But rest assured our love will last.

Betty L. Haire

I'd Never Thought

I'd never thought I'd be like this
I'd never thought I'd care
I'd never thought my life would be in so much despair.
I see the little children looking up at me, for I wonder why.
My goals have not reached me yet
I might as well quit trying
I know that's not the answer for me for I know that is not right.
One day I wish to reach my goals and fly as high as a kite.

April Steele

Untitled

If I were an element,
I would be a noble gas
and turn up my nose
at casual associations
and invading advances.
Fulfilled in my aloneness
I drift unconcerned through crowds
while others scramble to mate.
Firmly protected by my own radiance
I spread freely through space
fitting the shape of my cage
while others fret against the walls.
Neighborly elements who react without scruples
I scorn your unprincipled alliances.
And keep myself to myself.
Needing no one, wanting nothing
I am satisfied, alone.

Jennifer Bloustine

Home On The Hill

Your home in the country is the perfect spot,
Ideal to unwind and get rid of the knot
That's been strangling you for so long now!!
Where your closest neighbor is a friendly cow.

You wake in the morning to the song of birds,
The view is a picture, too lovely for words.
The fields, the trees, and the rolling hills,
Take you far away from the bustle and bills.

The folks you meet, the salt of the land,
Are always there, to lend a helping hand.
Be it milking, mowing or chopping wood,
You seldom meet people this good.

The stars that shine in the heavens at night,
Seem closer here, and twice as bright.
You know in your heart that it's worth the strife,
You really believe there's no greater life.

Be happy - in your home on the hill,
It was meant to be, so I know you will.
Live in peace, harmony and love,
With special thanks, to the Lord above.

Ida F. Graham

"Homeless, But Still Alive"

"What would you do
If I sat next to you?
What would you say,
if you had any money to pay?
What would you feel
if you had to steal?"

"When I sat next to you
you got up and moved down two.
When I asked you for some money,
you looked and laughed, like it was funny.
But you don't have to steal.
You don't know now it feels
to sleep in the snow,
a family you'll never know,
to eat out of a garbage can,
to get a sick look from every passing man.
I am not alive in your eyes.
A once burning candle in my house dies,
because people stopped believing in me,
I am not a show to see."

Heather Goodman

Where Are You?

I call your name and wait.
In the distance
I hear the echo of my voice calling your name—
hollow and flat,
like a ceased and guilty heart
that never fought to keep the body alive.
So is my voice that knows
there is no reply—
just the echo of my voice
calling your name;
my soul darkening,
my senses becoming dull
and flat
and hollow
like the memories that keep my mind alive,
if unable,
to find the light,
brighten the soul or sharpen the senses.
I call your name and listen
to the echo of my voice calling your name.

Jessica Kostopoulos

A Whispered Cry Too Late
Dedicated to the children of the "Oklahoma Bombing"

From laughter to cries, I wonder
if I will die under a desk between
a floor, will they hear my whispered
cries, I wait and wait holding on to
my dear life and begin to think I
Will die, soon I shut my eyes,
Never to shiver, never to wake.
  Dominic E. Gutierrez

Love...That's What It Is

If love is not accepting her for who she is, then what is?
If love is not sharing, then what is?
If love is not tucking her in, then what is?
If love is not using your own time to teach her how to ride a bike,
then what is?

If love is not worrying about her, then what is?
If love is not trying to make her smile when she is sad, then what is?
If love is not believing in her hopes and dreams, then what is?
If love is not being understanding, then what is?
If love is not coloring with her, then what is?
If love is not letting her tag along with me and my friends,
then what is?
Love is my little sister... that's what is it!
  Dana Billman

Security

My job is large — not difficult but huge
I'm at the smaller site tonight, only fifty-one kept here
All standing on end, a little more than waist high
Seven rows of seven and two more standing off to the side

It's those two I watch
Though the other forty nine are clearly in view
I cannot take them in

It's like statistics in the news
When the tragedy gets too big for personal accounts
The numbers, while accurate, take the truth away

I can hardly imagine the damage two of these would do
I measure the value of my own life by them
And I would lay it down to keep them here, harmless

The word "bombs" is never used here... they are simply "devices"
I have even heard them called "The Ladies"
A vain attempt to make them seem less dangerous
Or is it because of their seductive power
I've seen some men filled with lust as they enter here
That lust is what I fear the most

My job is large
  Brad Batchelor

My Imagine That Poetry

Imagine that
Imagine that pigs had wings,
Birds flew upside-down and
Whales spoke French
Imagine that people had feet on their head,
And if pencils stayed sharp all the time it would be a blast,
What if the ocean was peppery
And goldfish needed walking?
Wouldn't it be strange if we walked on our noses,
Or pizzas ate us
Or computer mice ate cheese
Or pens would unwrite instead of write.
Imagine that.
  Jack Eby

Can This Be......

Can this be.....
I'm in love with you,
instead of me.
My heart is open for you to see
there is no room to hide,
for you are always by my side.

Can this be.....
I hear words of melodies, whirling around
inside of me.
My soul is behind looking at you,
I touch you and I can see,
All the beautiful things I want to be.

If only in a dream that has come true,
I knew I would always feel this way about you!
  Connie Campbell

"A Mother's Prayers"

The world thinks I'm unimportant
I'm only a wife and a mother;
But God said I was special
And made me like none other;
I gave birth and raised our children
I did it with great pleasure;
These children are our gifts
In love we cannot measure
And in return is all I ask,
Respect, kind words, and love,
Our home will be filled with peace and love
And blessings from above.
  Carole A. Pahl

Sunshine

"Do you know what you search for?" I asked.
Impossible relationships are quite a task,

Searching for understanding, comfort, love,
Trusting our Lord above,

Warm was your smile, assuring me,
Come into my life, believe, and let it be

Willingly, you gave of yourself to me,
Drawn together like magnets you see,
closer and closer our need seemed to be,

Inevitably, emotionally, our lips meet,
My temperature rising increasing my heartbeat,

Do you have any idea what you do to me?
Suddenly dreaming of how sweet it might be,
Falling in love unconsciously,

Beauty that shines from your eyes I can see,
A light radiating inside of you and me,

Undeniably real, these feelings we share,
we've come to believe we really do care.
  Anna Leon

Mother

She always leaned to watch for us, anxious if we were late
In winter at the window, in summer at the gate
Although we mocked her tenderly, who took such foolish care
The long road home would seem more safe, because she waited there.

Her thoughts they were so full of us, we never could forget
And so I think, that where she is, she must be waiting yet
Waiting until we come to her, anxious if we are late
Looking out of Heaven's window leaning over Heaven's gate.
  Douglas Morrison Wallace

The Butterfly's Slap

The surface stands sticky from pelting sun drops
Imprints are stolen as predator slinks to stance
As crunchless snaps of lifeless twigs flop
The fluttering vibrancy floats without hesitance

With ears pinned back and body lurched frozen
Fangs grit whetted to clench on the unlikely
And carefree wings of colorful brazen
Tempt felonious claws of frustration perpetually

Legs coil and flex to slash after a spring
Sprightly sparks of ridicule emanate from
Waving hands of the insuperable butterfly king
Our feline friend's ego has been masterfully overcome

You try your hardest, you give it your all
It was not meant to be, rejected you fall.

Justin Fay

A Stranger

When all the goodnight's are said and our precious children are tucked in bed we say "sweet dreams" as we all look forward to our lives' dreams.

No detector, no warning, you won't live to see morning, for tonight black smoke fills the room.

Who's to save us from this shadowy grim but a stranger in armor and a hat with a red rim.

He comes as a stranger, but he's a messenger God sent, for a fireman knows death's scent.

He's as quick as a call and doesn't grumble at all, for he is as proud as an angel when his duty calls.

To save a life, is but an honor, he braces death in his protective armor.

Is it an angel or stranger that enters your home in search for our lives with dreams to fulfill?

From the darkness of smoke's death the fireman brings forth life's breath.

Is it a stranger or angel God has sent near? It's time to give thanks for the lives saved this year.

Carmen L. Honeywell

Words

As long as there is life on earth
I'll love you more and more.
   When this shall end and we are gone
   It's you I'll still adore.

As long as there are sunny days
I'll hold you in my arms.
   When all the clouds should block the sun
   No one can do you harm.

As long as there are mountains
That reach up to the sky.
   My love for you will pass them
   And never will it die.

As long as there are raindrops
That fall upon this ground.
   A stronger love for anyone
   No doubt will not be found.

As long as there are rivers
That run so far and deep.
   It's you I want beside me
   To love, respect and keep.

Carolina Petrides

An Afterthought

Death comes for us all, always with a grin.
In different shapes and sizes but I'll never let her win.
A lonely warrior is where I stand, I shall never take the fall.
No matter how many kicks or punches I'll continue standing tall.
I'll still be that solid rock when my family begins to go.
My shoulder for them to cry on, but I will not let my feelings show.
No tears trickling down my face, nor will my body shake,
Nor goose bumps on my skin, or even my heart begin to ache.
Physically they're in their graves, yet they'll never leave this place.
For they'll always be alive in your memories of their face.
A memory is a life force though it isn't counted one.
Death is but a phase, and life is never done.

James Lacasse

My Room In My Mind

As the wizard traps a fairy
in his enchanting Crystal Ball
The wolf draws back to serenity
'neath the luminous waterfall
The magic unicorn cuddles
with the forbidden persian cat
and the majestic lion gambles
with the savage loyal rat
I listen to the harp's
peaceful melody of the sky
Played on her pastel rainbow
as she swiftly flies on by
The mighty tiger's watchful eyes
glare at the lightning's slow demise
The dolphins play with the bubbles of the sea
This mystical place of harmony found inside of me

Crystal Erickson

In His Image

God tells me in His word that He created me,
In his very image He wanted me to be,
With capacity to give, accept, forgive, receive,
To be creative, and in Him only to believe.

And now as I live my life each day,
I try to reflect His image in every way,
Reflect His light, His peace, His compassion, His love,
His balance, His wisdom, His hope from above.

And some day ahead, uncertain the time,
I'll pass through God's rainbow of promise, sublime,
I'll bow before Him, imperfections all past,
I'll stand in His image, perfected at last.

Doreen K. Rice

"His Birthday"

Jesus was born upon this day,
In a lowly manger on a bed of hay.

The shepherd's awed the beautiful sight,
The star that shone in the sky so bright.

Three wise men came from far away,
To see the place where the baby lay.

The angels heralded his coming then,
With "Peace on Earth, goodwill toward men."

Yes, Peace on Earth throughout the land,
Where people love and understand.

And won't forget what "Christmas" means,
That it's not just the tinsel and the evergreen.

But that He was born upon this day,
In a lowly manger on a bed of hay.

Helen DomDera

The Fortune Teller

Peer into my crystal ball and see your future
in its all, Tell me what you think you see
In the fog and mist of me? Do you see you
future wife Or the end of a very gracious
life? Look into my gleaming eyes then ask
me where your future lies. Ask me all you
wish to see And watch your future come to
me. Peer into the magic scene and see your
future as it beams. Now sit and wonder how
I knew and if I tell you what is true.

Do you really want to see, the consequences
that may be? Or will there be a mystery
Inside my crystal eyes of glee? Would you
be afraid to see your future as it comes to
me? Would you like to see your days as
they come into my gaze? Would you wonder
if they came From the depths of the crystal
pane peer into my crystal maze and see your
future in a haze now peer into my crystal
eyes. The fortune teller never lies.

Emanuell Sinclair Franklin

The Garden Key

My garden sits, and waits for me
In my hand I hold a Key
I'm looking for something in front of me

I look, and look, but cannot find
surely I might loose my mind
It's somewhere in front, not behind!

I found this key, but will it fit?
Here is my garden, where I am to sit
Inside the gate lies the ground
In my pocket are seeds I've found

I will not falter, I will not wait
I will plant these seeds, no time to waste
Place the key inside the lock
I will try, I cannot stop

I tried the key, this one is it!
This key in front seems to fit
It turned the lock, and opened the gate

I'm glad I tried, and I did find
I was looking ahead, and not behind
Without my garden, I would loose my mind

Debbie Metz

One Day Love

One day love, it will be you and I
In our hearts, our love continues to grow
Mighty strong, with a roaring sound
In our minds, we must hold on
It is I who loves you
In a very special caring way
The true love of your life that awaits you
One day love, it will be you and I
Together as one; until then, we keep holding on
To faith, trust, and understanding of one another.
Good things come to those who wait, so we wait
until our day comes. One day, love, it will
be you and I, the love we share will be
beautiful and bright, our dreams and goals
will turn out right. We believe in each other.
Our love will continue to grow stronger with a
roaring sound that echoes from all around.
One day love, our day will come. I'll take you
for my husband, you'll take me for your wife
We'll be happy in love for the rest of our lives (One day Love)

Elaine N. Matthews

I Remember...In Silence

I remember seeing you when we first met,
in silence those moments in time I will never forget.
I remember sounds of joy and laughter of how things used to be
in silence the only sound that can be heard is an echo of my plea.
I remember you said you would always care,
in silence my heart is breaking I look for you but you're not there,
I remember being with you, I was free of worries and fears,
in silence I am slowly drowning in my own tears.
I remember little things you'd say that really touched my heart
in silence I watch as my world falls apart.
I remember you vowed to stay forever at my side,
in silence I am forgotten, no one is seeking while I hide.
I remember how you used to hold me and whisper things in my ear,
in silence I am lonely wishing you were near.
Most of all, I remember your wonderful smile,
in silence I wonder what I did wrong and why you did not stay awhile.

Anna Melissa Manaloto

"To Prove This Captivation"

When at first my eyes beheld thine outer beauty glow,
In stunning silence I stood gaping, breathless as time froze.
For ne'er hast been seen through all the faces from my past
A countenance of which description could not grasp.
Motionless, but for slight movements made to maintain sight
Of one who captured my heart spellbound, stirring warmth inside.
Beyond dreams light from inner workings of my mind,
In truth before me held the vision sought to find.
Should the timeless journey end with this angelic face
Mine gratitude begins forever, deathless thanks and praise!
For all search high and nigh their one true love in life,
But many pass the way without that shining light.

So be ye that which quench my thirst for love eternal?
This fluttered heart yet still doth echo, deeply from my soul,
Pounding rapid with each closing step approacheth
Louder still until upon my face your breath
A kiss... for which to open intertwining passion
Answers any questions left to tell - speechless we are one!
These hard-pressed eyes, delightful sighs and loving looks
Were all the signs I needed, ... and a kiss was all it took!!!

Bill Brown

"For Faith In God Is Mightier Than My Fears"

At times this splinter-covered cross that I willingly carry
is too much for one common man to endure.
I ask for God's help through prayer bent down on one knee
but my thoughts are frozen in the frigid temperature.
Giving up is something I cannot let occur.

Like darkness creeping in from far and wide
hardships come but my strides onward will not subside.
Far beyond is a glimpse of light beaming and serene.
This hopeful sight lives year-round like the sharp needles of an
    evergreen.
My mind will not allow past doubts to intervene.

Suddenly flowers blissfully dance and sway on the green lawn.
The spring that nurtures the living is the bright light of dawn.
Dark ominous clouds clear away
because it is a new and invigorating day.
Birds chirp in praise by the fruit trees ready to spawn.

The elders of the animals are again adolescent.
I realize the meaning of those trying times I spent
because now at this time, there is not room for torment.
The effervescent wind dries my wet tears
for faith in God is mightier than my fears.

James Tieng

A Poem Of Love

I love the way you make me smile,
in the morning when I see you, you
smile at me and I began to blush,
I turn pink at your every smile.
When I see you leaving I start to cry,
because I know the sun won't shine.
You see me smile and start to smile, your
lips are so perfect.

When I see you at night your rays are strong,
your aura is gleaming so,
you blind me with the look you give,
I start to melt when you start to breathe.
Your kiss is so soft, like the mid summer bloom,
your hair is like silk it blows with the wind,
your mind is like Confucius' it knows what to say
I love you, I love you all of the day.

Christina A. Glover

You'll Be Ok

So you've taken some knocks
In the past was able to rebound
Just would dust yourself off
Take a close look all around

So this time the blow was harder
You took it square on the chin
Spilled a little bit of your blood
But it's no place you ain't been

So I hope this time it sinks in
Sometimes you're better off to duck
Don't be such an easy target
In the course could change your luck

So you know there's no way to avoid
And remember this probably won't be the last
Some things just go 'round in a circle
It'll happen again what occurred in the past

So no matter what they say
I know you'll be OK
It may be hard some days
But I know you'll be OK

Gary L. Havranek

Yesterday's Tears

We were young and dancing
  in the street
The smell of youth was
  alive and sweet.
We roamed the parks
  with laughter in the air.
No time to remember yesterday's tears.

We smiled as we said good
  morning ma'am
but we never really gave a damn.
All a part of the master plan
  grooming to become a man.

That time of life has come and gone
  so fast, he who was once first is now last.
Just a shadow of the past.

Maybe we will meet on the road
  somewhere old and gray,
but better from the years
we will rejoice and shed our fears.

No time to remember Yesterday's Tears.

David Moore

Miscarriage

I grieve for the child that never was,
In whose eyes curiosity never leapt,
The child I wanted so desperately
Who never dreamed as he slept.

Time has passed, the memory alters,
And now I have another,
A child of love, and cries, and laughs,
Of mine, and like no other.

Yet still in a secret corner
Of my mind I do remember
The grief that's borne for a child unknown,
A wound that remains, ever tender.

Jill Rose

Philosophy Of A Marriage

The life of a marriage is like the life of a pearl. It takes two individuals like a special grain of sand and a special oyster to find each other on the vast ocean floor. When they do find each other they join together, as time passes and with a lot of effort they form a pearl. It's small and rough at first but as the years go by the pearl will grow and the rough edges will smooth out. That pearl will then become beautiful and priceless.

You both have found each other in this huge world of individuals. Today you have joined together to form your own pearl, which you will both need to work on the pearl together. No one said it would be easy but a lot of LOVE, PATIENCE,
and UNDERSTANDING
you will work out the rough edges, and as the years pass your pearl will become beautiful and priceless.

Clayton Onnen

Window Blinds

The window blinds create a fine barrier between outside and inside. When they're closed you can't see within, when they're opened your vision widens, widens to all the things that were hiding within.

As the sun pours in people wonder what happens within when no light can pass through this barrier between me and you.

Window blinds are like a state of mind. When you close them, you will find yourself in a world undefined. But, when you open your state of mind, things and treasures of any kind you definitely will be able to find!

Femaarta Momo

Abused

A whimper from a dark corner and a sudden intake of breath at the sound of approaching footsteps mark this child.

A plea for love and understanding to unhearing, unsympathetic ears cause great billowing tears to form in the eyes of this child.

A pair of outstretched hands begging to be held, if only for a moment, brings the agony of hell to the very soul of this child.

A small, soft cry in the night for uncaring parents who ignore the sounds, and a sniffle lost in the soft folds of a pillow, damp with tears, identify this child.

A pair of drooping shoulders and eyes that have forgotten how to smile are characteristic of this child.

This "Child", although neither visibly scarred nor marked with bruises, is "abused."

James W. Duncan

Untitled

To write is to set shifting thoughts
   into the permanence of ink
Arrogantly, yet dutifully
   exchanging pencil for pen
Frightfully rising to stand
   amidst opposing perspectives
   on the "turf" of past artists and intellectuals
The thoughts must be conveyed through time
What vehicle might safely arrive with her cargo intact?
What word or phrase will not erode
   in the face of society's scoffs and sneers?
What idea will find refuge in the hearts of man
   and narrowly evade the "cleansing" fire?
What wit will echo persistently through the minds of men
   and compel the flow of ink
   onto a page of tomorrow's history?
The pen must be freed with conviction
   when granting words to a speechless soul

   Joshua D. Smith

American Family

Ideal to the world
Is a home with two parents
But so often now, we find only one
Ideal to the world
Is someone who is always there
But so often now, is an empty house

Long ago the family consisted of a mother and a father
Divorce, a seldom used concept
But in our growing world things have changed
With both parents working or apart
Children come home to an empty place

This is the American family of today
A war zone in our homes
A place of hate instead of love
Separation and divorce

We teach our children to love each other
But go against our words
When we fight with each other
The marriage vows are a promise to love always
A promise that too often now we break

   Elaine Staggs

Reflections Of A River

The first flood approaches, is it a dream?
Is a question so clear as water appears.
My thoughts intertwine and overflow in a stream,
Not grasping reality until it is here.

Serenity threatened by swirling anxiety,
Feeling though life has ceased, time is still.
Awaiting final destruction from the almighty,
Leaves me breathless, no mind and no will.

Holidays pass as though never existing.
Has destiny met me with such demise?
Harsh spirits soon lift that were once drifting.
What a lesson this is of life that applies.

Anticipating the crest from dawn until dusk,
Torments one's soul until you know.
If only for a moment our lives were untouched,
Is a ridiculous thought as the water grows.

A trial not over, this is the beginning,
With memories stored in the banks of my mind.
I will never forget but continue remembering,
Reflections of a river not hard to find.

   Janice W. Schramm

Despair

One thought and one image
Is all you have
Pushing you
Deeper and nearer to what you call home
Your mind cannot focus any more
Your heartbeat has had its toll
All you can hear is the thumping in your ear
All you think about is how to stop it
Stop it
Stop it
You crawl closer to the light
It begins to feel better
Closer and closer
It calls you with a sweet welcoming
As you touch it, it fades away
You hear it draw away with laughter
The light tricked you and disappears
And you watch yourself
Falling to your destiny.

   Ghassan Hassan

Love

"What is love?"
Is it what one feels for a man or a woman they are about to marry?
Is it a favorite song or dance?
Is it the way someone looks at you from across the room at a party?
Is it the way a Mother cares for her child?
Or is it the way some people are kind to other people
for no reason at all?

"I have the answer: it is all these things and more, much more.
It is everything you care about or care a lot about doing.
But it is one thing above all others,
A teardrop that falls from the face of someone who lost their
family or friends.
By them dying so did a part of that person.

That above all others is love, a tear pure of heart, and pure of mind.
Sliding slowly down the check of someone who cared deeply,
about someone who died.
That is love."

Love is not something you can hold, touch, or grasp.
It's something more real
It's something you feel.

   Gina Harmdierks

Are You Listening?

Listen to the wind blow...do you hear the name it calls?
Is it yours or someone else's, or are you listening at all?

Listen to your mind...when the day has just begun.
Listen to the good inside, don't listen with your tongue.

Listen to your voice within...what's it telling you to do?
Are there opportunities inside you, or have old one turned to new?

Listen with your heart, at times, when your ears are tired and weary.
Is it love you hear within you, or can you not quite hear it clearly?

Listen to the ocean as you walk along the sand.
Have you ever listened with your feet, or maybe with your hands?

Do the sea shells talk your language, or do they only hum?
Have you ever tried to listen to the moon or to the sun?

Listen to the older ones and the stories they relay.
Do you hear their wisdom speaking, or are you too smart to say?

Listen to the children...they have no fear to tell
About loneliness inside them, when grownups start to yell.

Becoming a great listener is what life is all about...
Whenever we stop listening, the lights will all go out!

   Joni Clark

A Closed Loved

My love for you,
Is like a big black hole.
So far in depth I am not able to get out.
No ladder to climb.
No wings to fly with.
Sometimes I wish I had those things.

For you hurt me so much.
The first time I let it slide.
The second time I told you not to do it again.
The third time I'm leaving.
I hope you see what you've done to me.
Hurt me in so many ways I can't even imagine.
You don't know what you've done.
Destroyed is the word to describe.
I Love You meant nothing when it came from your mouth.
When it comes from my mouth,
There is a meaning and many feelings.
And my love for you,
Is like a big black hole,
That's now been closed.

Camille Smiley

The King Of The Remote Control

The King of the Remote Control
Is my brother dear.
And when he has the control
I always shed a tear.
Because I know I have to watch a very gruesome tale
About a dead sailor on his very last sail.
I love to watch cartoons
On weekday afternoons.
King Control watches whatever he pleases.
He'll be king 'till he croaks or wheezes.
He annoys me when he tells me what to do.
But when I get mad, he has no clue.
He is always such a pain,
That he may drive me soon insane.
However, after all is said and done
I love my brother next to none.
He is a very special guy
Even though he sometimes makes me cry.

Diana Williams (9 years old)

Ultimately Alone

We are all ultimately alone in this cruel world,
just think about it hard;

Everyone plays their deceitful games, holding and
strategically placing their Ace Card—

But, if you ever dare to cross someone, deliberate
or not, whether family, friend, or foe,

You will quickly realize and learn that in the end,
there is no one left to go—

So, the best of luck to you survivors, through to
your long and hard journey's end;

I really wanted to be the best kind of person,
a loyal, caring, and loving friend—

However, I've become cynical regarding life, as life
is not just, and life is not fair;

Therefore, I suppose God's plan for all of us,
was many, many crosses to bear—

For you and I came here ultimately alone, and so
ultimately alone we will die,

Because we all know if it came down to you or I,
it would have to be I!

Gail Tanksley

Longing For A Lid

They say, "There's a lid for every pot."
Is that really true?
How do they know?
If it is, where is mine?

Maybe it's been misplaced,
Marched from the kitchen in a one-man, one-drum band.
It's possible my lid was switched at a pot-luck.
(Could have been it wasn't well-labeled.)

Perhaps it is forgotten,
Hidden from sight in the back of a cupboard,
Behind the unused, seven-year-old condensed milk and soy sauce,
Or sitting in a cobwebbed, dust-covered box in a basement.

In any case, it hasn't yet been seen,
Or noticed anyway.
Hopefully, it'll show up soon,
Before the soup gets cold.

Brooke Van Engen

Life

What is sacred to you,
Is what you will sculpt out of your life.
That which lies within your soul,
Is what you must heed and honor.

As your heart beats with a reverence,
So you must listen to its rhythm.
This is where creativity is born,
Where wisdom bears radical amazement.

Engage in your journey of growth,
Embrace it, caress it, and nurture it.
Offer your uniqueness with no regrets,
So too, the oceans obey the cosmos.

Your ultimate spirituality is revealed in creativity,
As the origins of life are revealed in the rock.
Your primordial yearning is to be liberated,
And liberation requires action and opportunity to become expressed—to
become born.

Elizabeth R. Trusel

The Main Little Button

Our lives are like a pretty TV.
Just sitting there catching dust,
Its face is dark, there is no light
And it doesn't even make a fuss.

OH! It is plugged onto the socket
From whence the power comes,
THE Antenna and all wires are in place
But still there is no hum.

You can push every button on it
And turn the dial all day every hour,
But, there's still no light nor sound
Until the ONE is turned that brings power.

When you turn that ONE LITTLE BUTTON,
It lights up and sound is in the air,
SO ARE WE AS THE CHILDREN OF GOD,
OUR MAIN BUTTON IS THE ONE CALLED PRAYER.

Let us PRAY FERVENTLY with a righteous heart,
For GOD said it availeth much,
Let us not be like a plugged-in TV.
BUT THE MAIN LITTLE BUTTON, WE NEVER TOUCH.

Doris T. Bowie

Peace

Plethoran societies, unitarily bonded as an
   isolated Utopia.

Everlasting reigns of friendship subdue
   a totalitarianistic civilization.

Afflictions of outright maliciousness,
   overwhelmed by an abundance of
   love and unification.

Capitalistic bureaucracies outrun
   by the capabilities of the congruency
   of mankind.

Endless imagery of a nation without
   war, a world without
   grief and hatred, and a universe of
   eternal love.
     Jason Wingerter

A Pool Of Blood

A woman sees a pool of blood and thinks
"It could have been a baby,
but the time is not quite right, I'll try again."
And even after she has had her children
she is still reminded every month
that blood should be respected.

A man does not experience this.
To him a pool of blood is either his
or it belongs to someone else.
If it belongs to someone else
he feels that he has won;
if it's his own, then he has lost.

If man was not so arrogant
then he could learn from woman
that blood should be respected
and the world would be a better place.
     Alice Hinshaw

Life's Challenges

So what you are born of color,
It doesn't mean you are less fortunate.

So what your grandma is sweet,
But your mother is a b****.

So what your dad is an alcoholic
And can't keep a "real job."

So what your brother has a master's degree,
But is a drug addict.

So what your sister is a doctor with a life,
And is too good to call the hood home.

So what your favorite cousin is always mad
Because he thinks that life isn't fair.

Life is full of so what's, but I challenge you,
What are you going to do?
     Cecelia Henderson

Me

The sun is my happiness
It shines when I smile
It's not there when I am sad

The rain is there in its place
The thunder shouts my anger
The rain is my tears when I am confused

And the fog covers my eyes so I can't see reality.
     Erin Whitney Elio

Get Well Mama

When you are down, it seems like no one is around
It feels so depressing to cry, but no one hears your sound

After years and years of taking the load on your shoulders
You body and emotions feel the battle wounds that were hidden,
but left over

Being the strongest person and standing up for what is right
Having feelings of guilt and trying to pray until the LORD shows
you the light

Praying that the LORD will lift the heavy burden off your chest
Changing from day to day, never seeming to progress

But you must lift your head up and keep the faith
know that you are a strong loving MOTHER and your life hasn't
been a waste

Only look ahead and build your life better than the way it use to be
With the right attitude things will work out, you will see

The LORD, LOVE, and a SINCE OF WORTH are all you need to
get well
If that is all you need, you can find it in your baby son,
DONTRELL!
I LOVE YOU MAMA!
     Dontrell Deas

A Rose

A rose with its beauty reveals no imperfection,
it follows the sun when it seeks direction.

A rose with its beauty does not disclose its pain,
You will only catch a shimmering droplet
disguised as rain.

A rose with its beauty always seems to have room to grow,
but it will never divulge its roots for all to know.

A rose with its beauty gracefully withers away,
it will not allow its feelings of shallowness
to be seen in such a way.

A rose with its beauty wears its thorns with pride,
in itself only of its disappointments it will confide.

A rose by any other name
I believe that's what they say,
A rose unlike any other exposed is me today.
     Jane Schilling

Untitled

Music is beautiful
It goes Ding Dong Ding
It sounds so much better than a telephone ring.

Music is beautiful be it
Percussion or flute or sung by our children
We all think so cute

Or listen to a combo or our local Junior High Band
And clap till did hands hurt
To heat the band

Music is beautiful just listen to a choir
A cappella or Mother's Day same tears in their eye

Music is often a gift from God
Some never study it
Just walk on the sad
Yet, they learn the pitch
and pick and toot

All the instruments their souls desire, many
land up performing in a choir

Music is beautiful the sky the limit I'm
gonna try it myself in a minute
     Argatha Hamilton Merchant

The Phoenix
(For "Tigger")
What was once but a bird became, and it was a bird no more.
It had burst into three, burning white hot, fanning its peacock's tail
Into a blazing storm of the hearts of hours, clipping time
As it went, seething in the blinding heat's ashes. Out it soared,
Ripping through the blue skies and the great fire filled firmament,
Searing through the nine choirs of angels burning them all down
Out of man's great heavens; the sky, moon, universals: et Dei
This great new prince of the highest nightly universal's bent
Contemplations, was reborn, more beautiful than before, draped
In the colors of day: sweet sorrow and soft, bitter sour,
Blue, red, yellow, and Green, all with the candle-light eyes of hours.
I was one among the many who looked at, and became wrapped
Up in the sublime sight as the great gods all fell in and through.
It then blinded our orbs with its brilliance, opening our hearts.
The celestial sun's ray then caressed my brain, fanning thoughts
Over the calming scents of home, hidden beneath the ashes:
Days, and nights. Its beak then descended, touched my heart,
and my mind.
It then bent down low and whispered into my ear: "I have died."

Aaron Davies

My Bicycle
I have a GT bicycle; It's not like any tricycle.
It has two wheels that spin around, on the dirty, dusty ground.
You can hit jumps, or little bumps.
If you want a thrill, go down a real steep hill.
But if you wreck, you can hurt your neck.

Brian Baigis

My Sister
Everyone's got a cross that they must bare.
It is more than I can handle-I swear!
Hard to believe that life can be so unfair.

Leave an impression, nobody forgets my name.
They seek my advice, but they don't let me play the game.
Don't even realize how they cause me such pain.

You call me up when he's made you cry,
lean on my shoulder and ask me why.
All the while, inside I'm the one about to die.

I cherish our relationship for what is, hate it for what it's not.
You drain me emotionally of everything I've got.
My mouth has gone dry, stomach's tied up in a knot.
He's gonna put that ring on your finger, then I'll be forgot.

She could never see me in any other way.
I gotta move on, got to get to the next day,
Gonna believe that tomorrow will be O.K.

We're not related but you fit the part.
You wanted it that way from the very start.
You have got no clue what you have done to my heart. But then again,
you never were very smart. Yeah, then again, I never was very smart.

Jeff Casey

No School Today
A voice I hear so loud and clear
It is Mother calling get up my dear
I open one eye and what do I say
I think I will have a headache today
My mother's very hard to convince
But she has to agree when a jar makes me winch
But something went wrong because the radio plays
And stops to announce there is no school today.
So boys and girls, I give you this warning
When you don't want to get up in the morning
Be sure there is no school before you start faking
It's hard to explain why your head just stopped aching.

Jeannette Bennett

Emotion
Emotion is a very strong thing to me.
It is one of the forces that controls our destiny.
What you say, what you think, is spirited by
our harmonies.
Love, pain, happiness, lust, can be heard, can be felt, can be seen.

What about emotions! Man must eat, man must breathe.
What are emotions to me?
What are clouds to the sky, are eyes any good if you
cannot see.
Cupid without his arrows, helps the world,
as no emotions would help thee.

Burn in rage, burn in flames, Satan's hell would not
watch the pain, if no emotion flowed in my veins.
Sadness, pain, sorrow, give all these things to me.
I would rather feel these wounds into my heart, than
not feel anything.

Read my lines, read my words, understand, and you shall see.
Man must fear, man must quake, if my emotions are allowed to
breathe.

Inkuk Yi

In Remembrance Of A Revolutionary
If and when a revolutionary passes on,
It is to another world beyond knowing,
That's where his ancestors are waiting.
Don't call it death but just passing,
for a warrior is not the dying type,
Revolutionaries don't die but pass on
Revolutionary spirits to other generations.

> If and when he is no more, let there be no big deal about it,
> For people come and go, and so do lives,
> Let there be no wailing and weeping for him,
> For revolutionaries don't cry over lost life,
> Let there be renewal and dedication to fight on
> Because his remains only serve to fertilize revolution.

As for those remaining, hold on!
Keep the flag flying and struggle on!
Don't waiver but be fortified even more!
For the future and the land are yours galore.
Hang in there, for the prize is sweetest!
Freedom is the only prize for the boldest!
Izwe Lethu - the land is ours all the time.

Bojana V. Jordan

The Beautiful Rain Bow
God put a rainbow of many colors
in the Great Blue Sky one time
It comes after a rain has fallen
It's so beautiful there as it shines

Noah saw the beautiful colors of the
Rainbow and knew it was a sign
That the earth would be destroyed not
By water but by fire next time

How peaceful it looks there in the sky
As it smiles on everyone below
When the clouds hide it from view
No one can see where it goes

God put a rainbow of many colors in the sky
just so mankind could see
A sign to let him know of things ahead
That are sure to be

Ervin Sams

Today

Today is mine,
It is unique.
Nobody in the world has one exactly like it.
It holds the sum of all my past experiences and all
my future potential.
I can fill it with joyous moments or ruin it with
fruitless worry.
If painful recollections of the past come unto my mind,
or frightening thoughts of the future,
I can put them away,
They cannot spoil today for me.
Annie Willard Nixon

My Little House

My house is not just a roof and walls to me,
It is where my family and I dwell, you see.
It serves to protect us and keep us from harm;
In the winter it keeps us dry and warm;
The doors and windows let in the light.
My house keeps us snugly locked in at night.

It is little and white with yellow trim around,
Inside is a place where love and joy abound;
The floors held the little ones learning to walk,
Its walls ring with the sound of laughter and talk.

My house has the smell of cooking and bak'n,
It often looks quite forsaken;
I can understand why people do not like to sell,
A little house they have loved so well;
If I someday with mine should part;
The memory of it will stay in my heart.

Ann Hungler

God's Artistry

I saw a picture in the cobalt blue sky,
it resembled the "Garden of the Gods,"
Redrock cloud formations were beauty to the eye,
awe-inspiring and a special sight,
Truly was God's painting for everyone to see,
It appeared once more in early night.

God uses all colors his Glories to portray,
an artist paints a colorful sunset,
Some say it couldn't look that way,
Flowers are lovely and they attract the bee.
In autumn the leaves have many hues,
beauty is all around if we have eyes to see.

Dorothy Moshier

Sister Love

Sisters love
is a forbidden fruit
hidden beneath the dark... sarcastic shell
she calls her heart.
We're not that close...
She hides in her room
mocking my sensitivity
with the cold... dark... rain... she considers to be her friends...
I think I'll embrace her
let her kick and scream
maybe then her sunshine... would chase the cold... dark... rain away
no... I believe the only thing to do
is to cut her open.. crawl inside her heart
search for signs of compassion and trust
destroy the demons... plagues.. and insults
crack the dark... sarcastic shell... she calls her heart
fall back from the sudden impact
rejoice... for finally I've gained...

Jason Turner

My Desire

Glassy, stormy, calm, billowing, or choppy
It rises, it falls, it glides, it crashes
Blue, green, brown, or clear
Inhabited by many creatures fierce and meek.

Man has taken a board and become one with it
Risen with it, fallen with it, glided, and crashed
Stood in awe of the majestic blue, green, brown, and clear
Always respected its inhabitants, fierce and meek.

Rising, falling, gliding, and even crashing
Becoming one with that blue, green, brown, or clear
Sharing that place with the fierce and meek
That's where I want to be.

Jessica Churder

A Moon Lit Bliss

A moon lit bliss rowing anxiously across the sky.
  It seeks out the sun and lets out such a cry.
A love song was shared when once they were together,
  But split into night and day still seeking forever.

As sunrises and sunsets go slowly by
  They reach out to one another as though they were to die.
Inside this lonely arch of love
  is the earth looking up to the stars above.

So when I look into the sky
  I see you there and I start to cry.
And knowing that broken hearts will mend
  For now to you these words I send.

So I'll sit and wait every night that goes by
  To let you know
I am that moon lit bliss
  seeking you in the sky.

Jennifer Dearing

Fire

While ashen pieces flutter up to meet

A twirling quarrel of blackened smoke and air,

A downward whiff of drafty cold pokes fun.

Ignited murmur burning low, now lights.
It flickers tossing to and fro, and snorts
A puff of rage against the taunting chill.

With dives and leaps and a brazen prance, retorts
The blaze as cracking, crashing conqueror
Throwing wildly a handful of flaming sparks
That scatter, whirling frantically about.

They fall, submitting, and smolder lying still
With patient embers and realize, no need to fight.

Heather L. Doty

Music

Would you dance with the Devil in the pale moonlight?

I saw you look up above,
In your eyes the glint of love.
When you sway to the beat,
I see your eyes burn with heat.
The heat to dance at the "ball,"
I know music has its call,
The call of passion, and of love-
It's said to be carried on a dove.

So I ask you again, in the middle of the night,
Would you dance with the Devil in the pale moonlight?

Jessica Gill

"Never Forget You"

Sometimes, just out of the blue, I start crying, crying for you.

And even though it hasn't been long,
it seems like forever and still moving on.
(one day you were here, and the next you were gone.)

And never knowing whether to laugh or to cry, the good
and bad times we had you and I.

Not a day has gone by I've not thought about you.
I'll tell you one thing I know is true:

You'll always have a special place in my heart.
And no matter how long we are apart,

I know one day I will see you again, and until that day,
until the end, I look at your picture and see the face of a friend.

And although our lives were filled with hardships
and trial, you always seemed to come out with your wonderful smile.

And until that day that I see you again, I'll never
forget you, never, my friend.

Arin Cain

"The Lease On Life"

Life is such a precious experience that most people don't enjoy
it to its fullness.

Going though hard times, sad times and happy times are part of
that experience.

We sometimes forget the good times which are many and remember
the negatives of life which are few and far between.

Just remember that there are people out there who have it worse
than you do.

Count your blessings and make a mark in life by helping your
fellow man.

'Cause someday your lease on life may expire when you least
expect it.
It cannot be transferred, nor can it be renewed.
Your lease on life is only as good as you make it to be.
Therefore be positive in your lifetime for you have the greatest
gift of all — THE LEASE ON LIFE.

Glenn W. Fujita

Pray For God's Blessing

Once I stood alone—and prayed—
It was a moment I'll never forget
That instant I was forgave
The moment is still there yet

The Holy Spirit is a funny thing
With it, you rejoice, with our Lord Himself
But, it takes our mind and flesh to rejoice
And without rejoicing, you are left by yourself

How long since you knelt on your knees
And knew our Lord would answer you
He will always be your friend
"Do not"— wait till you are blue

I rejoice with you
In our Lord Jesus' name
For your confession is true
You will enter the gates of heaven

You can now be one in Christ
He will now live in you
Most people will always thirst
But only you can make this true

David L. Becher

The Room With A View

There you were, the room with a view,
  it was just us two.
We spent much time there
  sharing the beauty of it all with each other,
  what each new day brought.
The days turned into weeks,
  as I enjoyed your company.
Then it happened, I was given the eviction notice.
I was only renting, I hadn't bought you.
Reluctantly, I've gathered my things,
  as I took one last look
  from the room with a view
I would never get to look from there again.
I hope the new occupant takes care of you.
I miss you, room with a view.
I often wonder, do you miss me too?

Donald M. Jackson

World Without Tears

A world without tears means no longer being in the eye of the storm.
It will be a place where sickness and death
cannot reach out and touch us anymore.
Where perfect health and eternal life will be the norm.
Where the beauty of paradise will enrich the quality of our lives,
and will instill upon us the peace and security we've never felt
before. Wickedness will not exist here, only righteousness will
thrive. In the land of many pleasures we will come to know
true happiness. We will give praise to Jehovah God who made this
all possible, and every day will shine upon us, bringing even more
happiness into our lives. In this world of plenty we will eat to our
heart's satisfaction. The finest foods that the earth has to offer
will fill our bellies with laughter. Before, I was filled with tears
of sorrow when my parents were laid to rest; but then, the tears
that I shed will be tears of sheer joy at the sight of their
resurrection from the grave. "What happiness" God will give his
people in this "world without tears."
He will spread out his tent of loving-kindness and provide us with an
abundance of all good things for all eternity to come.

David Leslie Spence

5:45 On The Clock

The sun rises and filters through the blinds.
It's 5:45 on the clock.
Unknown to the family of nine and the cocker spaniel
Sleepin' on the cot.

The neighbor next door is up on this dawn.
Takes an outstretch hearty yawn.
While coffee percolates in a pot.

Things to be done. So up and at 'em!
It's 5:45 on the clock.

A long day lies ahead pickin' corn,
Countin' heads.
It's all in an honest day's work:
Family, the farm title, it's all in the Bible.

It's 5:45 on the clock.
Unknown to the family of nine.
And the cocker spaniel sleepin' on the cot.

David R. Lewis

Untitled

Cute face, adorable smile, it all seems to drive me wild. Good looking is the best. Frankie is better than the rest; Frankie's the greatest as everyone knows; his friends stick by him wherever he goes. Now that my poem is finally done, you can see why my friend Frankie is and always will be number one.

Laurie Ceppos

The O. J. Simpson Murder Case

We learned a lot this summer about justice and the American way.
It's a great civics lesson; we learn something new each day.
Simpson is charged with murdering his ex-wife and a friend.
The jury will decide who is guilty in the end.

Simpson has the best legal defense that money can buy.
He told the judge "I'm not guilty..." and looked him in the eye.
O. J. said he didn't commit the brutal murders,
He was out of town, he has hired the best lawyers to turn things around.

O. J. Simpson is a famous athlete, he could run with the ball.
Now he is in a nine by seven foot cell, with his back against the wall
He has offered a $500,000 reward for the real killer of his ex-wife
Some believe there is more than one killer, and more than one knife.

People are hungry for news about Ronald, Nicole and O.J.
They watch T.V. for hours, and buy the tabloids the next day.
The Simpson case has drama, suspense, mystery and murder too,
It's like "Murder She Wrote," someone did it....but who?

We know the best things in life are sometimes free.
Money can't buy happiness for you and me.
You may be a millionaire with glory and fame.
But nothing is better than peace of mind, and a good name.
   Isaac J. Olds

Put My Mind To Sleep

Everything is distant everything is gone
It's all forgotten when there's no more sun
The far off cries of yesterday have faded like a dream
Hold me for a whisper so I won't have to see

The wind slides 'cross the waves like your hand across my face
I breathe a sigh of deep relief you've put my mind to sleep

Everything is calm, everything is bliss
Nirvana surrounds me like an early ocean mist
Early morning rises and flows with the tide
I fall a little farther when you open up your eyes

The wind slides 'cross the waves like your hand across my face
I breathe a sigh of deep relief you've put my mind to sleep
   Gary E. Havel

Family's Sonnet

My family is fake.
It's an act we put on for the world.
Perfect we are to them;
Outside we look flawless in our actions.
Inside we are beasts outraged
spitting violence and anger.
A family without compassion towards one another.
Where is the love?
God is the only answer;
The One who will bond us together
With the Bond of love.
Pray for strength and wisdom
To care for your family,
As God cared for you.
   Christy Shelton

"Speak My Heart"

Speak my heart, say what you feel.
Look how beautiful the world around us is,
the sky, so blue, with its racing clouds.
Take a look at those tall mountains,
standing so high.

Speak my heart, run free and fast, then
walk slowly, take time to see the beauty
of our world. The rivers, trees and flowers,
so many things to see. Let's share all of it together.
   Acie Patton

My Turn

A hope for love, romance and commitment has alluded me once again.
It's an empty feeling when you lose at love, it's rejection,
   disappointment and loneliness rolled up in one.
And then, someone hurls it at you with perfect aim never missing
   the mark.
Once again your heart is broken, your dreams and fantasies
   shattered not understanding why, you find yourself asking why can't
   someone give me love, devotion and commitment I'm not so
   bad, I'm a nice guy.
But you ask yourself am I so good, am I so nice
Maybe, maybe not.
Well, whether I'm good or bad, one day, yeah one day
It'll be my turn
   C. Orlando Parker

"Spirit Wings"

I have closed my eyes to this troubled world, and left
its burdens behind me.
The times that I would sit and cry and thought no one
had heard me.
Trying to live a better life and raise my family.
There were lots of fears and lots of pain so many
times I felt so strange.

But now these things have passed me by, and I can see
all things through the twinkling of God's eye.
And now my spirit wings can fly,
And I can soar through heaven's sky.

There's a street of gold and gates of pearls,
and aqua seas of blue.
I'll save a special place for you so when we meet again
our spirit will soar all through the sky,
The spirit wings of you and I.
   Dona J. Kendricks

Waiting for the Day

My heart is filled with so much sorrow,
It's hard for me to face tomorrow.
Sometimes I pray that I won't wake,
Because each day becomes harder for me to take.

I can only hope and pray at night,
That with each new morning's light.
I'll find a way to make it through,
So that maybe one day I can begin anew.

Because, who knows, someday there might be
Someone who loves me just for me.
No more pretending to be what I'm not,
I'll finally be happy with what I've got!
   Deborah A. Borhman

Spring In The City

Spring
It is spring
Neighbors glare the heated stare of spring
Sidewalk stairs become a balcony
All else a stage,
Within the maze
A maze of window hanging eyes
A stage of phases
Luring by way places
Teeming hi-rise havens,
Graced in sun
A lover's wish from winter
Winter's mask withdrawn
The breath of summer
A season of passion.
   Bruce A. Tates

The Fishing Hole

As the sun rose to reveal the fishing hole,
Its rays glimmered over the crystal clear water,
And yet it had a twinkle in which no other had,
This is a special hole that no-one knows about,
It is my dream world;

The world where only the crystal waters know,
The fish shining in the many sparkles,
They are the only ones in my fishing hole,
Who understand what I'm thinking,
They are part of my dream of the fishing hole;

So if you do find this hole,
You will experience the same crystal waters,
If you are intending to find this place,
First you must believe in dreams coming true,
And you must have a big imagination,
If you're lucky, you might find the rusty pole to fish,
out the fish of dreams, in my fishing hole.

Jesse Powers

Adrienne

The name "Adrienne" is, oh, so sweet
It's the one word that makes my heart beat.
When I look at her eyes, there is much to see,
The love and comfort, hopefully, waiting for me.
With puppy-dog eyes and brownish-black hair,
She makes me feel as if I'm walking on air.
When I look and see her beautiful smile,
It makes me glad I'm with her all the while.
When I catch myself holding her hand,
That's when I know I'm the luckiest man!
I'm so glad to see her at my side,
Whose love and beauty she cannot hide.

Jason Harris

Another Angel

How can I say goodbye when your life has just begun?
I've barely said hello.
I waited so long with such anticipation just to have you taken away.
When I held you in my arms all my dreams seemed to have come true.
But you knew then didn't you?
On the last day when I touched you and talked about the
future a single tear rolled down your cheek; then I knew.
You were so beautiful and perfect from head to toe...
It's hard to believe a problem heart would take you away.
You touched so many other hearts during your very short life,
and a piece of all our hearts are still with you.
You are now safe, no more pain or suffering will ever touch you.
God needed another angel and he picked you.

Judy Hannaman

Violence

Where do we go from here?
Is our end drawing near?
So much violence, it's all we ever see,
In our lives and on t.v.,
It's not the shows or the movies that we see,
It's the evening news that glorifies these deeds,
A man found dead at this home in the city,
Was there for a week, no one knew, what a pity,
A cab driver shot in the back of the head,
Worked so hard to end up dead,
A ten year old boy with a gun robs a store,
His dad's a drug addict, his mother's a whore,
Life today isn't what it was years ago,
Is today your last day? No one knows.

Debi Leiter

Center Stage

I've scared myself by feeling things I have no right to feel.
I've caught myself revealing things I never should reveal.
I can see myself in later life filled with harsh regrets,
And who's to say that I am wrong and cannot hedge my bets?

I dream a dream and live a lie and go my merry way,
Pursuing goals I can't attain, and throwing time away.
I'm standing here on center stage, the crowd awaits a sign,
As I scan the eyes of every face and realize they're all mine.

The critics choice, that's what I'm called, but don't they understand?
Shakespeare said, "to thine own self" and only I can be that man.
I'm not so proud of who I am and yet my head's held high,
For I know within my heart that we all live in a lie.

And my own lies are nothing worse than needing something more.
A reason for existence is what we all are looking for.
My own lies are nothing less than what I would become,
If I were granted just one wish, what would I become?

Geraldine Watson

The Questions Of Sorrow

I watch the world with saddened eyes,
I've seen people fill it with screams and cries.
Can't we all just learn to be friends?
Will this pain and madness ever end?

Do people realize the crime and hunger?
Does anyone care, I often wonder.
The ones who have that are never pleased.
Do we stop to think of the homeless and diseased.

Why can't we live in a perfect place?
Where there's no more racism and human disgrace.
The times of war and nuclear weapons.
Will this world ever learn from its lessons?

The soon forgotten and uneducated
People should be loved instead of hated.
Too many questions and not enough answers.
Not enough stories that end happily ever after.

But this is not a story, yes this is real life;
We have to learn to love and sometimes sacrifice.
So when I wake, and see the light of day,
I have hope the children of our future will find a better way.

Angie May

"Every Mother's Fear"

As my children began to grow
Just thinking about the problems I know
Do I teach them to take the blow
Someone please tell me, because I don't know

Why are our children killing each other
People off the streets, being called their brother
Wanting to hide them, wanting to cover
Wanting to change it, because I'm their mother

Everyone searching for someone to blame.
always wanting that someone's name.
Trying to realize it's not just a game
For my children I feel the shame.

Our children's future looks grim and sad
Trying to raise them to be like their dad
Teaching them good, hiding the bad
We're raising our children in a world gone mad.

Hoping our children can win at life's race
Can they stay at a steady pace
Not wanting them to become another court case
Then praying they aren't found dead some place.

Janette Kimbrough

Oklahoma City

What do you want out of life? The horoscope asks.
Just a peaceful heart, that's all, liberation
From clenched jaw and gut, pain and nightly
Phantasms spawning viruses of personal sorrow,
A monkey mind agonizing over petty worries.
Just some peaceful rest, that's all,
Instead of ritual twisting and trembling.

Dawn and the morning news carry me
Into broader worlds, eclipsing mightily my puny sphere,
Shocking scenes of violence and death—
Bosnia, Rwanda, Chechnya, Oklahoma City,
Brutality, tragic suffering and loss,
Desperate people also craving
A full measure of peace and rest.

May I offer my share to them?
Joseph Petulla

"Our Long Distance Friend"

If some days or nights, you are lonely or alone,
Just dial up a Christian friend, on the telephone,
It doesn't matter if they are close to you, or very far away,
You can be an encouragement to them, or even help them pray,
You don't have to be well versed, or have the gift of gab,
To help them through their trial in life, just be there to confab,
And if you are ever at a loss for words, then the Word discuss,
And you will always find a subject, that will be a plus,
For when we talk about the Word, it's not just ink on paper,
But the very words of life, that will help and strengthen us,
  if we savor,
So if at times you need to talk, and there is no friend home,
Just dial up Jesus in your heart, not on the telephone,
He's always there to talk to you, at morning, noon or night,
He'll tell you that He loves you very much, and that He is the light,
You don't have to have a reservation, or even make a date,
Or worry about Him being asleep, even when it's late,
He will supply just what you need, to get you through the day,
And you will never get a bill, or even have to pay,
For He paid one time on the cross, a debt for you and me,
That we might have sweet fellowship with Him, throughout eternity.
Ernie Hitchcock

Children's Rain

It was a time of rain and sorrow;
Just how long I don't remember.
I guess it really doesn't matter;
Not at all.

Puzzle pieces;
Some are missing.
Some don't fit that well together.
Could I just be making big of something small?

Memories deceive;
Changing time will tend to brittle picture pages.
What you see now might be faded;
Colors turned to yellow
All those faces on the wall.

Long ago emotion follows throughout life
And leaves us never; if at all.

Have you ever watched the ocean?
Just to listen won't relieve that secret pain.

There are things I have remembered;
Best forgotten hidden memories;
Children's Rain.
Joelle Magliano

Mother - Child

A friend I hadn't seen for a while
just lost a child, a son -
The hardest road for a mother to travel
but, God's will must be done!

I am also a mother
and my heart bleeds for her so -
Where does she get the strength to carry on...
such a heavy load of sorrow, I don't know!

My mother used to say -
when they are ready to fly - let them fly!
That seems almost easy now...
but, please God - never let me live to see them die.
Elisabeth Wind von Rummelhoff

A Poem To Evelyn

Dear Evelyn,
Just thinking of you and the things that we say
Makes me love you even more with each passing day
Your smile, your grace, the way that you walk
Your eyes in the moonlight when we start to talk
I think of you and I feel no pain
For when I am with you our love's not in vain
So let's take it slowly for when you are near
I cherish each moment as if they were years
And when you hear this, please think of a thought
That reminds you of us and all we have got
Love, Fred

The Enemy Within

For. . . I am my worst ENEMY, it is I who
Keeps me from succeeding,
I deprive myself of life and its meaning.

I give myself reasons for
Not doing what needs to be done
In hopes of pursuing.

It is I. . . who am at fault
For my actions, I am the one who knows
What's best for me, for I am the one to
Blame you see.

To feel the pain and grief inside,
I often run and try to hide, to hide away from the
ENEMY within, trusting God to forgive
Me for all my sins. . .

For if this ENEMY I cannot condone,
I will weep in sorrow to be left alone,
To reminisce of my past you see,
What could have been and should have been,
But will never be. . .

For I did not succeed in defeating my ENEMY.
Cordy Stegall

War Zone

Its roots were extracted,
Leaving shadows upon shadows in the blinding sunlight.
There is no sign of life,
But there is existence among the rubble.
They put nice pink curtains up and flower pots on the fire escape.
Frustration has eaten away at the cracks in the walls,
So they should fall down,
But they won't.
Words, like bombs, blow things all out of proportion,
Exterminating the environment.
And in the dirty dark corners, the Lower Planes are satisfied,
Here in the South Bronx.
Jeff Edmond

"Across The Miles"

The sky above, the earth below
Keeps reminding me how I miss you so
All the feelings, love and caring
Breaks my heart, 'cause we're not sharing
As I think of you and your happy face
Those precious memories I'll never erase
My darling, my darling
Believe me when I say
My happiest moment was when you came my way
Remember one thing, no matter how far
Always stay as sweet as you are

   Because I Love You
      Always and forever Grandma
Joanne Tamuccio

Untitled

I sat quietly, and a butterfly
   landed on my finger.
It was there that it sat,
   allowing me to
   admire it, enjoy it,
   and love it a little,
   if for but a short time.
And when it gave me all that it could,
   it took flight, knowing
   I would benefit more
   by its short visit,
   rather than if it had stayed with me.
I was more touched by
   that one butterfly
   that flew away,
   than by all of the ones
   who had stayed.
The memory is forever.
And that is enough.
Danielle K. Ungaro

The Coming Of Spring

O, how cold you are, the final winds of winter!
Last snow, how brightly do you glitter!
But fear and confusion I can sense
As Winter's making ready her defense.

Yes, everything is ready for a change!
From somewhere beyond my senses' range,
Somewhere hidden from my ears and my eyes,
I feel the rising waters smashing ice.

Below, in the whitened, frozen earth
The grass is only waiting to spring forth;
And up above, still in the snow sleeves,
The branches are all set to bring forth leaves;

And, in suspense - a tightened bowstring -
The whole world is ready for the spring!
Dmitry Turovsky

My Child

Mother, yes Farrah
Mother, I am happy that you're my mom.
Oh, I was blessed with you my child,
Oh dear, look at you...
You are like a sweet dream:
Your big eyes brighten every room around,
Your footsteps are like musical taps,
Your sweet smile is but so innocent,
Your little fingers are like little bells,
Oh, child it's you who makes this home alive!
Cynthia C. Myers

Broken Path

  Down a broken path of brush and briars we've both traveled, leaving scrapes, cuts and scars on flesh and hearts. Some, leaving scars so deep, they even seem too mar the edges of our souls. Exhausted, bloody and confused, we arrive where our paths meet .
.
  Here we collapse, each facing one another, together sharing our pain without need of a spoken word. Closer we are drawn as need for physical unity calls to us, a call we can neither resist or ignore. In our touch there is more communicated than any words could ever explain, in our kiss is more need than any heart can ever reason. Our emotions' burning like the open wounds from our journey and our tears bathe our broken hearts and soothe our aching spirits. As time passes we decide to join together to begin down the path once more, knowing each has lost others at different lengths of the trail now behind. Each with no reason to trust the other (and yet we do). So with only our memories, hopes and fears to guide us, we return to our journey once more ...
  ...along the broken path.
Carl D. Hudson

"Drug Free"

Mommy! Daddy! Hear my voice
Let drug-free living be your choice
Let me live in smoke free air,
Around our home, while we are there.

Life is short, we're just passing through
I love you, and you love me too.
Take my hand, show me the way
To drug free living, every day!

We are clay in the potter's hand
A drug free temple is in his plan
A heart that loves with all its might
With armour on, keep up the fight.

Away with needles, smoke, and booze
All to gain, nothing to lose!
A life, a home, a family dear
No longer made to live in fear

I have a right to live and see,
A world created to be drug free!
Mommy! Daddy! Take my hand
Lead me through a drug-free land!
Dot "Pittman" Holbrooks

Thinking Of You

Life sometimes is just so sad
Many times we feel so bad
It's hard for us to keep going on too
Yet, we must not get overly blue

Because we know of our hope ahead
When only happiness will be our stead
So we go on and do our best
Even though the world is at unrest

We are so different, with no fear
Because we know the New World is near
We look forward to everlasting life
Where no more will there be heartache or strife

Oh yes, the Bible tells us of a time
Under God's Kingdom, blessings sublime
Through Jesus Christ our King, we'll see
A new world to last eternally

It's great to know you have friends galore
Who care and wish they could do more
A prayer, a wish - a card - or two
Remember, we all wish the best for you.
Ann R. McCartney

The Springtime Of The Heart

Does the bleakness of winter still linger within?
Let it out! Let it wither and die!
Away with the crushing burden of sin,
The hour of new life now draws nigh!

Does it still feel like winter deep down inside?
Look around you! The world is abloom!
Rid yourself of the doubts you feel you must hide,
Put an end to the darkness and gloom!

The spirit of Easter has now taken hold,
The gray of the skies turns to blue,
Let go of the past! That has grown old!
Take the path that leads to the new!

Now is the time for your true rebirth,
Do it now! Let the old ways depart!
Then just like the newly green earth,
You'll know the springtime of the heart.

Gregory M. LaBrake

LIFE IS LIKE A DREAM

Life is like a dream;
Life began with an infant's cry,
Perhaps it knew it was born to die.

Life can be a nightmare;
With pain and oh, such nasty fare,
As tho' a demon has access there.

Life also resembles sweet dreams;
With blissful love from God's good grace,
Desired by most all the human race.

Yet, there is one thing the living have in common
And most mortals dread to look forward to,
It is what the crying new born perhaps knew.

However, it has been said "when a life on earth is over,
Like a heavenly dream life begins anew,
With it everlasting and having eternal peace too."

But alas, it has also been said,
"Like a hellish dream a life on earth is over,
When one's six feet, under-ground topped with clover?

Ida Pat Cain

The Holocaust

I lie in the fields,
listening to the birds chirp
as they fly overhead.

Then all is silent.
All is peaceful.

Suddenly the beauteous
leaves start to rustle throughout the trees.

The fight for survival
has begun.

The winds slowly take them down,
to their burial grounds.

The leaves run and hide,
trying not to be evicted.

They know they can't hold
on much longer, and they give up.

They descend into their
Cemetery, joining their decaying families.

The fight is over.

The wind moves on to catch
its next victims.

Christina Fiore

"Words Not Spoken"

Through good times and bad memories to last a lifetime
Life gives many a task one in which all will not pass
But our friendship has proven time and time again
That we will be there for each other... till the end.
Family exists in one's heart
One that no one can tear apart
You are one that cannot be replaced
An individual ... a shooting star
One that will go very, very far
I never imagined us so far apart
But I guess I knew in my heart
That our paths someday would part
You've helped me grow and learn
To even think twice before I turn... and bridges burn.
Even though things sometimes were rough
You never turned away or said that's enough... and I thank you

Julie M. Conrad

Life

Life is a game we must all play.
Life is infinite both night and day.
To waste time, is to waste life.
Life is what we live for.
Not the work, not the chores,
Not the rumble of a slamming door.
Each of these one in its own.
The definition of all together is unknown.
To cheat yourself of life
Is to cheat yourself from love.
Life doesn't come easy,
it isn't always sweet.
But, without it where would you be.
The presence of life, the presence of love.
Can only be given by God up above.
So if you must waste time,
Do not let it be mine.
For life and love
I find divine.

Hazel Helgen

"Life Is Like"

Life is like a rose, with its thorns along the way,
Life is like a flower, its beauty you can't repay.
Life is like a river, not knowing where you're bound,
Life is like a mystery, a treasure not yet found.
Life is like a bird, soaring without a care,
Life is also fragile, be careful it doesn't tear.
Life is like the sunshine, when it blinds you by the light,
I hope I can succeed to make my days seem bright.
I'll hold a hand for courage and strength along the way,
Remembering friendships won't last, if I require pay.
With friends things won't seem so bad, as I will learn to see,
But mostly, I'll feel good about myself and be all that I can be.

Jan Paquette

Dying

People come and people go,
Like water, high tides and low,
They lay in a hospital bed, temperature low,
Their body is there but their soul left some time ago,
Just a lifeless body with little color or to their skin,
Surrounding them are a bunch of hospital bins,
So they can take their last drink of water,
Or spend their last moment with their daughter,
When their finally arrived in heaven,
They think back on their life when they were eleven,
Happy thoughts is all they see.
As tears come to their eyes as they think of what they could be.

Daisy Minthorn

When I Think Of You

When sullen and sad, the day growing dark
Life swelling ominous, like autumn to a lark
One glance at a picture of beauty anew
And the shadows vanish, when I think of you.

When the day blooms bright and waxes of joy
The sky is blue, the man becomes boy
I cast my eyes at poetry so true
A storybook setting! When I think of you.

Why is this so? I'm betwixt and between
How thoughts of you make real each dream
It baffles the wits to conjure a clue
The riddle is solved, when I think of you.

In days to come, in nights to pass
In ethereal bliss and always, fair lass
When want takes flight, I'll always imbue
The sun never sets, when I think of you.

Bart Rippl

Fleeced

I wait for spring.
Life will be better then.
My ship will come in
with the robin red's wing.

Spring is here. I wait for summer.
Life will be better then.
My ship will come in
with the soft summer wind.

Summer is here. I wait for fall.
Life will be better then.
My ship now feared lost
Surely will come on the night of a frost.

Fall is here. I wait for winter.
Life will be better then.
My ship will glide through the snow from the sea,
A great gilded gift by the Christmas tree.

Winter is here.
A small sinking yawl, my ship has come in.
With deep sadness I ponder,
Was not life better then?

Daphne Kaylor

Child Within

Waking in the darkness, a chill comes over me,
Light from the lantern, release my spirit free.
Silently disguise the pain, my trembling hands,
I must refrain.

Flashing across the room, reflections from a knife,
Held in his hand; evil piercing me with his eyes.
   "Daddy stop, you're scaring me!"
   Soundless screams echoing.

Years drift by, lost in fear and disgrace,
Cries unheard, satin pillow covering my face.
Tears gently splashing to the ground, marking memories;
The story told without sound.

A woman aged now, yet from the child within,
Silent cries remain disguised; a new life begins.
Knowledge and wisdom show beauty and light,
Even through the darkest night.

After a storm life blooms and grows,
Like a breath of spring, after winter snows.
Paying for love with your flesh and bones,
Turn anger and pain to stepping stones.

Jeri Klausner

Spring

I wait for spring
   like a woman in her last weeks of pregnancy

   Anticipation....

   Anger at the irritants which
   remind her that the time is not yet.

I hunger for nature to spread her thighs,
   pushing winter out like a mucus plug
   allowing the first waters to break
   cleansing and lubricating the earth,
   making way for new birth.

I coach her through her labor.
   "Breathe, let your warm sighs
   drift across the land, like
   Southern winds, melting the
   last remnants of winter."

"Sit up earth", I encourage, "change the position
of your body. Allow the sun's comforting touch
to stir your roots, prompting the buds and
sprouts to emerge, like the head of new born."

   Aah! Listen... the cry of spring.

Bob Boyd

Wilderness

Stones lie silent in the desert far as I can see,
Like bones of life's temptations scattered by the enemy -
   Satan's snares to capture Me...in the wilderness.
My body's famished when a voice comes whispering through my head:
"Since You're the Son of God Almighty,
turn these stony rocks to bread."
Rebellion's angel tempting Me...in the wilderness.

Wilderness, wilderness -
Place to be feared or place to be blessed?
Wilderness... "It is written" in the wilderness.

In a blinding instant all the kingdoms of the world appear.
"I will give You all their glory if You'll bow to me right here."
Devil's choices pressing Me...in the wilderness.
Suddenly I am in David's city atop the temple there.
"If You are God's own Son throw yourself down to angels waiting near."
   Evil's cunning testing Me...in the wilderness.

Wilderness, wilderness -
Place to feared or place to be blessed?
Wilderness... "It is written" in the wilderness.

Barbara G. Stephens

My Best Friend

In memory of Stephen Parden

   When he left me, my heart
left with him.
   His life was taken; I called it a sin.
   Taking their time to search,
when we all knew he lurked,
   Lurking to find his spot,
   a place to run and hide!
      It's too late now; it came as no surprise.
His life was taken from this earth,
And now they quiet their search.
Let him lie in his bed to rest, rest in peace,
It's all over now. Your life is gone, you're
not around, But in my heart I see not a frown,
But my best friend still
smiling an acting like a clown.
There is still a vague memory of when you were around.
I'll never forget my best friend;
when he left, when he was gone and now.

Danielle Scott

Here Comes The Rain

Hear the fist come beating down
Like rain on a tin roof
Not quite hard enough to dent
Not quite hard enough to chip the paint
Just enough to sting
Just enough to remember
These are the things that are always on my mind
These are the things that are carved in my soul
This is why I fear you
This is why I cry

As the lighting strikes
The thunder screams
Here come the fists beating down
Just enough to sting
Just enough to remember
Brae

Trust Of The Soul

It is tapped from the heavy heart -
Like sap sucked out of the damp honey tree.
Or maintained like a winter coat that has
not lost its style nor function.
It is a way of life.
"Survival!" It screams.
Progressively growing into a standard and then a
reward for the bright and athletic.
Able to produce a list of charmers or a single
being, who can ring down a cement hand when need be.

Trust of the soul.
Can be counted on.
Will be counted upon.
And.
Oh! Yes!
Stay reliable.....like an intriguing novel.
Davied J. Peoples

Angels

Whispers of truth lie in the air
like specters of dawn waiting to appear.

Silently radiant these spirits define
the wonder of life a dimension of mind
that few can behold or then understand
what really matters so each comprehend

that central point they seek to find
while others observe intuitive behind
this glimmer of light that suddenly shines
sighting the child who was until then blind.

They shake from the soul a cloud of despair
with a truth now in hand that always was there.
Charles G. Albrecht Jr.

Death Can Be Lonesome?

   Death comes for you in the dead of night, doing this
job for what he thinks is right. To take a soul and deliver
it to hell, just like throwing stones into a bottomless well.
On a pale horse in the dark night he rides, killing in scores
and taking in strides. With wings of death and a skull of lies.
A face of pain with fire for eyes.

   It's a job of sorrow and a life full of pain, riding the clouds
endlessly living in vain. Our faith will fail and the nightmares
will come true. Love will be lost when death comes for you.
Beware of the night when death will come. He will strike down
an unbelieving sum. Heed this warning and make no mistakes, for
when he comes your life he'll take. And when he does, just hide
your face. These are his words, "You're taking my place!"
Andi Holeman

My Heaven

A small log cabin nestled in the wood
Little wild critters scurrying where they would
A huge pine forest all about
A mountain lake with jumping trout
White tail deer drink from placid ponds
Turbulent growth of fern and fronds
Tiny squirrels climbing forest giants
Hawks patrol in grand defiance
A busy beaver builds his dam
Working on the virgin land
Survey the meadow and delight
For only God could paint this sight
A trillion colored perfumed flowers
Song birds sing from leafy bowers
Honey bees buzz their special music
My eyes grow misty, please excuse it
I bow my head and bend my knee
And tell my God, my thanks to thee
Give me the world my God created
It's here, I feel my soul elated
Bob Strauss

Life Is Poetry

Face the tears that greet you each day.
Live the life that only you may.

Fulfill the promises you make yourself,
living for love and truth instead of riches and wealth

Live not in the sorrows of the past.
Rather, look to the tomorrows, where all your possible futures can last.

Take the paths that are never taken.
Only then, will your deepest wants awaken.

Follow these words with utmost devotion,
and you will that life really is poetry in motion.
Jason Buck

The World of Children

I'm gonna live in the world of children, just for a
little while. I'm gonna take me a child's lesson on
how to laugh and to smile.

Cynical heckler, hard nose skeptic, don't follow me,
stay away. And there's no lust in a playground, only
one more happy day.

Then I'm gonna give to all the children, my kind of
wisdom, I'll say, if you kids could learn to preserve
your innocence, there'd be a new dawn and day.

We could do away with so much confusion, give out
with the love, not an illusion. I'm gonna live among
the children today.
Conrad D'Ampolo

The Dreamer's Dream

Winding down a narrow path
Lay each dream from years gone by
As dreamers dream of pensile wrath
And auricles newl to a distant cry

Skyward bound each thought is hurled
And blameless found it shall be
As timeless jewels of words unfurled
End the dreamer's searching key

For sounds of time bound alone
As dreamers dream and dreams are born
While new thoughts sound the pensile tone
And man? Again yields to scorn!
Gene Larrimore

Life's Passing Parade At The Cafe' De La Paix

The parade has no beginning, as, too, it has no end.
Lives that have been broken. New lives on the mend.

Travelers in exotic dress from many a far-off land.
Lovers seeking romance, walking hand in hand.

Heading for a carriage ride as daylight turns to dark,
And the twinkling lights come on again in famous Central Park.

Here comes a former Ziegfeld girl in tattered, faded gown,
Talking softly to herself as she wanders through the town.

Across the street in the jewelry store precious gems sparkle
    and gleam.
While' neath the windows on the sidewalk below,
    a weary traveler rests to dream.

Now a limousine pulls to the curb, and out step the bride and groom.
They're whisked to their wedding reception in the rooftop
    Sky Garden Room.

So here's a toast to the passing parade -
    there's no drum - or flag - or fife.
Whether rich or poor, young or old, they're all a part of life.
   Eleanor Michael Henry

Untitled

We started out our marriage
Living in a rented room
We worked and saved the best we could,
I, the bride, and he, the groom.

Eventually, we got a car
And then we had a son
We tried to buy a house but
Of established credit we had none.

In time, we had our credit, with
An A-1 standing, I might say,
Then we bought our house and made
Our lovely garden to display.

We were blessed with good and loving boys
Who can only be described as joys,
And my husband is the best there is,
What more can anyone ask than this?
   Eileen M. Diaz

Disintegration

I would be a walnut
Lying on a mound of leaves underneath a walnut tree
My shell is tough and hard and cannot be penetrated,
From the beginning, this was fated to be.

I smell the ferns, the moss, the trees
I do not mind my new sanctuary,
I feel the leaves stir, the wind sigh
Am reminded of other times, long gone by.

The sun bakes the earth
I've never felt so warm before.
My nest is safe, a small round hole -
What harsh spirit could knock on my door?
What harsh spirit could touch my soul?

Time slips by - I am afraid.
Winter is coming; what plans have I made?
The wind grows stronger
The leaves flutter and cover me
I am cold no longer.

I lie very still, be still I must
For if I am still enough, I will turn to dust.
   Diane Volkhardt

Fourth Of July 1936

I close my eyes. I see...

My mother dressed in a Gold Rush costume.
Long purple gingham dress,
matching sun bonnet with black velvet ribbons.
She is planting fat brown tiger lily bulbs
that we found growing in the woods.
She pats the red soil
around the long white roots.

We are waiting to go into town with my Dad
who is trimming his dark beard of four months
for the Whiskerino contest.
Then he'll march in the parade with the veterans of World War I,
wearing his overseas medal and his blue cap,
carrying a United States flag with 48 stars.

Next comes the picnic and the free beer.
It is the fourth of July in Grass Valley.
I hope he doesn't get drunk.
   Diana G. Browne

Love

Love can hurt, love can feel
Love can help, love can heal
Love is sweet and love is kind
But sometimes it can blow your mind

Sometimes it can last forever
Sometimes it comes maybe never
It's something that's felt in the heart
And it is cherished right from the start

Love can be jealous, love can be mean
It's the strangest thing I've ever seen
To those who have it; it is gold
But it's nothing to those it doesn't hold

There are times when it can be confusing
You sometimes feel as if you're losing
Just when you think you have figured it out
Something happens and fills you with doubt

Love is young and love is old
Love can even make you bold
People wonder if love is real
Well, I only know what I feel
   Jennifer DuBois

Red And Blue

Heat can be a good thing
It warms the soul on a cold day
like a lover's touch on an intimate evening when passion melts
slowly into pleasure
Its invisible red presence can only be experienced,
never seen as can be desire on someone's face
Rich humidity worships the skin
yearning for the sweet moisture generated from body heat
On this subject lovers have devoted a great deal of study
And when they've completed their test,
they bathe in the refreshing delight that is the essence of
sensual satisfaction
The cool feeling of erotic fulfillment brings serenity into
the souls of event the most rapturous of people
Dissipating their lust with its benevolent blue radiance,
before carrying them away on comforting currents of calm coolness
to places only thought of in splendid dreams of unbound bliss
A realm where only they exist
and our fantasies are their reality
   Diori J. Thomas

Love

Love is a devotion deep and true,
Love is shared between me and you.
Love can strengthen or break your heart,
But love will never tear us apart.

Love cannot be bought or sold,
But love can be shared with the one you hold.
Love spreads joy, happiness, and cheer,
Love is felt every day of the year.

Through the good and the bad throughout the day,
Love has the power to find the right way.
The power of love is rare and grand,
Love is shared from heart to hand.

Love happens to those who wait for it,
Love isn't something that comes in a kit.
A rare, strong, and true gift is LOVE,
Love is sent to us from above.

Janea Scheck

The Challenge

Like the game of Golf;
Loving you all these years
has been a great challenge,
But if we had scored a hole-in-one each time,
We would have gotten bored;
And that would not have been any fun.
A double bogey occasionally throws us off,
But...it always makes us work harder.
Thanks for being there for me,
Through all the sand traps of my life.
It makes me proud to be your wife,
And when we both score seventy-five,
We'll still be together holding hands through life.

"I love you"

Bonnie A. Smith

Live Your Life

Live your life with dreams of a future
Live your life with hopes from the past
All we are is all we dream
All we are is what we've been
So, live your life with dreams of a future
Live your life with hopes from the past
Tell someone the secrets for loving
Tell someone the wisdom of life
All we are now are dreams of a future
All we live are hopes from the past
Someday when our lives are through
We will know all that is the truth
But now we live our future and our past

Cheryl Lynn Chang

Na Hoku Elua (Hawaiian: The Twin Stars)

Born the day after Spring had turned to Summer.
  Lights and shadows seen through tiny eyes with
  a sense of astonishment and wonder.
Twin Stars shine like diamonds in the sky.

Children of the moon - sisters of the sea,
  Venus signs a lullaby - tidal Harmony.
And now another Spring has turned to Summer.
  Another year passed in the twinkle of an eye.

Memories of when you both were so much smaller,
  Twin stars sparkle in the darkened sky.
Na Hoku Elua!!

Jaime Sutherlan-Chun

The Roads Of Time

Before me are the roads of time,
Made long before I ventured here:
Some soon end dead,
While others, far beyond where I can see.
Yet all hold in their grasp
The aftermath of storms long past.
They break the smooth unbroken lines
To which I have so warmly come accustomed,
And lead me to a land I have not known.
Still, they exist,
And as I trace their wrinkled course
I wonder what their cause might be
Frown not, my love,
For all these roads are so unknown to me.

Heidrun M. Dias

The Lover

It was just that one kiss that
made me understand, that I wanted
to be with you to walk hand and hand.
We had a lot of good times and
some fusses here and there, but no
matter what I stayed giving you tender,
loving care.
   Three years had past and I thought
it would last, I loved you more than
anyone, more, than a mother loves, her son.
   You wasn't happy so you left, I
guess it was for the best, because our
love could not stand strong when it
was put to the test.
   If I ever get one wish, I'll
wish to be with you, to be in your
arms, under your charm, and saying:
   I Love You.

Crissie Fulton

Untitled

She sits in the corner,
looking past the smoke filled room.
Lost in thought, she remembers the harvest moon.
She feels the chill of the fall, night air,
remembering the breeze blowing through her soft,
   blonde hair.
The stars shone brightly down upon the city;
she stood up on the stone wall until she felt dizzy.
Then she laughed aloud,
   feeling warm and proud.
Above and beyond the pain,
her memories rest deep inside her brain.
Now, smiling to herself, she returns to the smoke
   filled room;
only to gaze out the window at the bright Harvest Moon.

Claire Cody

I Am Carried

In my weakness and despair I am lifted up.
My Father, The Good Shepherd, has reached this helpless one —
so helpless and grieved in my spirit,
unable to see for tears,
fallen to the ground,
mocked and tormented.
I am now gently cradled in the bosom of my Lord.
So close to the Master.
In my weakness I cling.
In his arms of love, so safe and secure.
Who will laugh at this helpless one now, for I am resting in the
bosom of the Christ, savior of all.

Carol A. Mohler

Amira

Loving you, can only be a dream
Made of fine fabrics, sewn tight at the seam
Stronger than man, more worth than money
Better than sugar, sweeter than honey
Loving you only brings better times to the mind
Love in the heart, you can't always find
Looking outside, in only hell's delight
Looking in the world, staring in the night
Many often wonder, and they often stare
How is it that they are blinded by a midnight glare?
Is it true that love is always around?
In hell? In night? Where it shouldn't be found
Many times love is there, everywhere, all around
This is why I write this, as not to say a sound
To the ones who can't find, or don't know where to look
For the love they can only find in a storybook
So I will keep you a secret, and be glad you're here
Because it's your love that I cannot share
Referring way back, to the very first line
When I wake up, I hope you'll be mine.
Jamel Smith

Keeping The Bully At Bay

(Carried by six, or judged by twelve)

Bully badger starts early to frighten and frustrate
Make you cower and cry, keep you down so they can be high.
Tests strength and toxic tone in schoolyards,
Keep you weak, so they can be strong.

Grown bullies, cloaked now with velvet,
Smooth tones masking true intent.
Keep you stupid, so they can be smart
Keep you poor, so they can be rich.

Batterers, rapists, killers, sharpen skills,
Leaning, forcing, wooing and winning.
Bedeviled and betrayed,
laws no shield against the bully.

How does one learn to move from defense to offense
'gainst a tyrant who would separate you from your life?
Use strategy instead of fists, that's politics
Use strategy instead of sticks, that's politics.
And if that doesn't work,
Get a gun, and use it!
Grace R. Welch

"50 Years" 1945-1995

Fifty years ago, you said "I do"
Mama 19, Papa you were just 22.
Life had just begun for the both of you.
Years passed and your family grew.
Papa worked and did odd jobs too.
Mama stayed home
Her job was not new
Being a "Mom" is a job very difficult to do
Just ask anyone they'll tell you it's true.
Papa the "Portofino Singing Chef"
Helped his family live a dream, with love and respect.
Together you've built a family
With years of memories
Mama and Papa - "50 Years" — no regrets please.
You've been the very best you ever could be;
Not one grandchild would disagree.
We've all been privileged
Of being twice blessed
With love and friendship
Something that you do best.
Happy "50th" Papa and Mama!
Ann Fagliano

Looking Back

I would rather die than be your slave,
Many of my ancestors went to a watery grave.
I have their blood running in my veins, my ancestors pave the way,
They worked in your cotton fields all day.

I can feel their spirits soaring high,
You got away with a lot, but not with I.
Looking back, I see the tears running down their faces, and the men
  feeling so out of place,
Not human, you say, because they are of the black race.

Lie peaceful, rest, and we will finish the test,
No more hot sun on your faces, no more feeling out of place.
No one will sell you ever, because you're on a planet in heaven.

I have my ancestor's blood running in my veins, I can feel their
  spirits soaring high.
You got away with a lot, but not with I.
Betty J. Garner Johnson

Looking For True Love

I'm looking for true love in a world full of sin;
many offer facsimiles, but true appreciation, I aim to win.

I looked for true love in the world of fantasy;
but while I found lust fulfilled, there was no enchantment
for the real me.

Singles bars and other such places, I tried them all; I even went to
church on Sundays, only to wind up feeling small. For it seemed no
matter where I went or who I'd meet,
it wasn't me they were interested in, but how much money I made.

So to God Almighty I left my fate;
believing in Him, and Him alone, to help me find my mate.
And miracles of miracles, what did I receive?
I received a bride named Tina, whose heart proved true to me.
While many I met cared only about physical things;
my bride left everything dear to her, to take on my unworthy name.

What did she see in me? Your guess is as good as mine;
but for Tina I'll do what I can to keep her happy, even if it takes
the rest of my life. For I was looking for true love in a world full
of sin; now, thanks to God Almighty, my quest has finally come to an
end. I love you Tina.
David H. Berry

Thoughts Of My Dad

As I remember back through the years
Many thoughts of my Dad ring in my ears
When I was young and just a little girl
He'd take me in his arms and give me a whirl.

I grew older and I remember quite well
All the fascinating stories he loved to tell.
Stories of him and his kin when he was just a little boy
Some of them were sad ones, some were filled with joy.

I became a teen, graduated, and off to college I did go
He was so proud; I was the first of his family to do so.
Then I got married and eight grandchildren I gave to him
You talk about love; he loved each and every one of them.

But then on January 23rd in the year of 1994
He was struck with a stroke, paralyzed and much more.
This was very hard for me to take and for me to understand
Because my Dad had always been a very active, strong man.

He's now in a nursing home where often I go to visit him
It's hard for me but must be much harder for him.
Trying to remember all the things of the ages past
But, you see, God has blessed me with memories that will last.
Carolyn M. Wilson

"After"

...And then he weighs and ceases to amaze at the wandering masses of children, gazing into unforeseen futures, not knowing where it lies and of the days that will pass them by.

Carol Hofhine

A Wedding Blessing

May your heads always rest on matched pillows,
May your lives always rest in God's love,
May your love always rest in each other,
May your new life be blessed from above.

May each sunrise bring days of contentment,
May each sunset bring peace for the night,
May your partings be slow and reluctant
And your greetings be pleasant and light.

May your sorrows be few and be feeble,
May your joys be increased every day,
May your love for each other grow stronger,
As you live with each other day by day.

May your hearts and your minds blend together,
For this journey that you have begun.
May this day be one always remembered,
As the day that the two became one.

Diane Goold

Maybe...Today

Today....
    Maybe.
        Today, maybe I'll find a flower
        near my path, worn
        by walking green grass to grains.
        Bloodied my feet.
        Worn holes in my shoes.
        Sometimes crawled;
        picking through grass to find my four leaf.
        I've sat on creekside.
        Stared into shallows;
        cooled my feet and slaked my thirst.
        But, always, I've forgotten
        my simplest, best and favorite remedy:
        you, the one with me and beside me.
        I'm reminded
        when I look at you
        One day I'll remember before searching.
    Maybe...
Today.

John Mark Sherbert

Transcending The Resistance

I looked through the sky resting on my side
Looking through ripples of honeysuckle-scented water

Then I saw myself just a ripple in series
Sliding past the rocks I rested on, conforming to their shapes

Flowing through trees, the fluid reflection of me
Through squirrels and birds flying things of all kinds
Dripping hues, gliding sun

The muck and mire beneath
Pulsing with primitive life
And my dog's footprints of yester moment

Just a ripple flowing by a surface so shallow
Yet so deep in many reflections of being
Just a note, bent by the forces
To be Melodious in Harmony

Dell Dorenbosch

To Dianne

If I could catch a rainbow,
Maybe I would find you there.
I stand crying in the darkness instead,
My spirit somehow dancing into oblivion
While I wait night and day
For the search to end.

The past and future have crashed head-on,
And life is shattered
Into a jagged edge—
Cutting the heart that once held
Silent dreams, and cutting the hands that try
To piece the Dream back together.

You and your dreams
are just out of reach,
but not quite out of sight...

Nightflight and Moonshadows
Whisper softly your name;
With tears glistening in the starlight,
I lift my hands and fly away to where you are,
My memories creating an invisible song.

Deana Truman-Holliday

Pollution

Mr. Factory with your machines so green. Why are you so cruel and mean? Look at what you are doing to our gulfs and streams. Am I cruel? No, I'm not. I just give you what you want. I give life to new industry. No! Mr. Factory can't you see. You are causing an intrusion and that can't be. You are upsetting our ecology! Stop and take a look around. The trees were green and the air was clean. Look at the smog and stream, and look at what you have done to our natural green. The birds in the air will soon disappear...and the fish in the ponds will all be gone. Do you want the people of this land not to be? Can't you clean the air so we can see? No! Man polluted the land in which he lives, he started this before he invented me. Man is responsible for what happens to thee. For I am a machine and you made me. For you put me here, and here I shall stay till the end of man and the end of day. I cannot change the will of man. I am a machine can't you see! I have no way of helping thee. But there is a chance if man can see. For man changed the world once when he invented me and he can change the world again if he wishes it to be, if man doesn't want the world he has, then he might as well get started and do whatever he can. That is all I can do; if man doesn't heave, he'll soon turn blue. Maybe just maybe someone will lend a hand and help preserve this land, for I cannot, can you? For it will take many to clean this land and have it fit and grand.

Blanca Estela Gonzalez

After The Storm

The wind has quieted,
Lulled by the ending storm.
Time passes, lost, as the endless rainfall
Befits my justification for
Awaiting the sun.
Never searching, fearful of finding
A new storm.
Remaining safe and challenged
In the comfort of the drizzle
   After the storm.

As I walk in the complacency
of my discontent,
Eluding downpours, never risking the thunder
To find a bridge above the water.
Then truly I have and will continue to miss -
The glory of the sun and the warmth of its days
A beckoning rainbow, a spectrum of color
And the magnificence of a sunset
   After The Storm

Carol Mitchell

My Princess' Breath

A thousand nights have gone
Melting into distant memories
They are, for me
The finest collection of art, ever...

Encompassing a rainbow of time
Splashing colors tall, some wide
Striking reds, bouncing yellow
Tunnels of darker blues ending one maze...

Beginning another
...I have locked in the fragrance
Of pink beaches and grey shadowed parks
A potpourri of children add scent
To my deja vu

Impossible to have drawn on my own
The catalyst was you
My Princess, your breath
Forever alters my view

Ingrid Carretero

The Long Walk Home

As I walk through silent night, I see shadows of days of old.
Memories and nightmares of stories never told.
I see myself and family there in tears and broken smiles.
I wish that I could help them all, but how can I stop such
an inevitable fall.
I put forth my hand but it cannot reach.
I can feel the tides of time ebbing away.
Their faces are like some great sculpture made of sand and
with each new wave they fade away.
Until finally I see nothing more than simply sand beneath the waves.
No longer can I hear their cries.
They are not dead you understand, only born again in a better life.
There are only four now though the fifth has flown away.
Pushed away by the hand of Satan.
Kept away by the grace of God.
Slowly now I begin the long walk home, passing by lost
and broken dreams.
To the place where I feel safe, with my new family, them and me.

Jeffery Ray Campbell

Hal

My husband's body was dead; a much crueler fate awaited his mind and memory—THEY survived for 18 years;

The man I loved was in there, of that I was certain. That proud, talented, outgoing man reduced to a shape man handled into a chair on wheels;

It was hard to look into his eyes, the eyes that had given me so much pleasure when they laughed with me and followed me-dark black pools with lashes women envied, now dull until some little thing awakened them;

The tongue slept too, with only memories of speeches made and awards won, of jokes he played and stories told to children gathered 'round, of loving words spoken, conversations over coffee, the songs he sang to entrance us all, forever gone.

His dog, the family dog, but his alone in truth, mourned his voice and touch as much as the humans in his fold — his mother left this world with a broken heart at the loss of her only child — his father collapsed into a world of tears and opened his arms to Alzheimer's;

He suffered all the indignities possible in this world, including the disgust on the faces of upright humans — they dropped him and broke his leg. Hal died, and left me with my nightmares.

Arlene Johnson

Memories

As I sit and ponder thoughts of another place and time
Memories of my childhood flow gently through my mind
I remember special places, the hills, the creeks and trees
And the apple orchard north of home where the bee man kept his bees
The sounds of clucking chickens as they scratched the ground for seeds
The corn cob fights we had as kids and the spears we made from weeds
I can hear the sounds the winds made as they whispered through the trees
And see the fuzz from cottonwoods dancing softly on the breeze
I can even close my eyes and smell the smell of fresh mown hay
And hear the coo of the rain dove on a lonely summer day
I remember the fall when ducks flew south and leaves began to brown
The walnuts that us kids picked up and tried to sell in town
I can see Mom in the garden pulling weeds between the rows
And standing in the front yard hanging out our clothes
Sometimes I even hear her voice and it echoes through my mind
I can hear her calling to us kids, "Come home, it's supper time."
I remember when I went to bed and everything was still
I used to drift away to sleep to the song of the whippoorwill
And someday when I'm dead and gone, on that old farm you may see
A crow, a dove or a soaring hawk, and who knows, that might be me.

Allan W. Pfaffly

You Still Do

As I lay in the darkness alone in my bed,
memories of you start filling my head. I think of a
time when our love was brand new, you held the key
to my heart, and girl, you still do...

There was no way of knowing that our love would
end, you were more than a lover, you were also my
friend. Time can never erase my memories of you,
you held the key to my heart, and girl, you still do...

With the passing of time we grew far apart, but never
one time did you stray from my heart. The moments we
shared were so precious and few, you held the key to my
heart, and girl, you still do...

I've always loved you and have from the start, if only
I'd told you what I felt in my heart. Give me a chance
to prove that these words are true, you held the key to my
heart, and girl, you still do...

You hold the key to my heart, now it's all up to you...

Donald Anderson

Life's Memories

Roll back the years when we were young
Memory of the past still lingers on.
Our hearts were young our spirits gay
Cares and worries of the times seemed far away.
Peaceful days rolled on with happiness
Daily life was free our hearts content.
We loved and laughed in freedom's light
Time filled with gladness day and night.

The memories of those years linger on and on,
Acceptance of our lot with love and song
Made problems of the times seem lesser still
Than any care of troubles stubborn will.
Then duty called, war was begun,
Our hearts were heavy with endless fear.
Fathers, sons and all our friends sincere
Called to serve the land we all hold dear.

The time rolls on with memories dear
Of loved ones gone and far and near.
Yesterdays are passed, life must go on
To complete the span from dawn to setting sun.

Juanita A. T. White

Untitled

Four wall with no windows and no doors;
Men pretending to watch me but only caring for themselves.
Their backs towards me;
I'm alone.
I do what I'm told;
But I do it my way.
The men turn toward me;
They don't like my way;
They want it their way.
I tell them I'm not them.
They don't listen;
They don't care.
There's only one way;
That's our way, they say.
My four walls close and I get smaller.
I disappear as they grow;
Don't look for me because I'm gone.
I did it their way.

Ilana Gurevich

Voices In The Night

I have heard voices in the night.
Muted voices from times long past
Now speak as aftermaths of dreams,
Or still within the dreams are cast.
And faces that with daylight powers
I cannot see nor e'en recall,
But which in quiet of night's small hours
Form sharply etched scenes that enthrall.
A boon of age—the stores from which
Dreams are retrieved: first love's shy kiss,
An elephant ride in Rajasthan,
My mom discussing Genesis,
Much more than these. I bless the night
That lets brain cells unlock their cage,
And long-stored memory's fires re-ignite
And shed a light on mind's half conscious stage.

Harry H. Sisler

Someday

We will meet again someday, I know,
My faith and hope have always told me so,
No matter where you are,
No matter how very far,
We will meet again someday.
Although my heart is still not entirely free from pain,
I can see rainbows through the rain,
And somehow I know because faith and hope are
  telling me so,
That we will meet again someday.

Frieda Dolinko

"Pollution... Is No Solution"

Living on this earth and feeling fine
means cleaning it up and making it shine.

Automobiles and factories too
make cleaning it up very hard to do.

Trash on the ground, rivers, oceans and lakes
can make our earth ugly for goodness sakes.

Try picking it up and throwing it away;
let's try to keep it clean starting today.

Walking, bicycling and roller blading too
can make our air cleaner, feeling like new.

What I'm trying to say to get to my conclusion
is pollution...is no solution!

Chenee' Schutz

Open Sky

As a shadow moves along side
My car down the road my thoughts
Of a love trail behind like the
Drifting away as a boat does at sea,
Man's only abode.
I roamed down a road past the point of return
Just to watch the clouds shift to a
different angle below my feet the grass
grow only to be mangled by the sense of time.
It takes me back to my lost love
and I rejoice my mind to the open sky.
My spirit feels like the cold wind blowing
through the trees in late fall.
As I look I can see my lost love by
my side and the air so pure that time moves
Slower as the deepest thoughts within me
are caught up in the open sky.

Jody Wilson

Today Is The Day

Today is the day
My dog ran away and my cat got hit by a car
That my sister Eileen turned our blue pool green
And my brother got stuck in the tar

Today is the day that it's snowing in May
And my mother's car got stolen
That we had to pay bail to get my dad out of jail
'Cause he was speeding on the way to bowling.

Today is the day I can't go and play
'cause my grandma wants to come over
That my uncle's wife Midge fell off of a bridge
And I swallowed a poisonous clover

Today is the day my hair turned gray
And I got warts all over my body that all of my uncles
Broke all of their knuckles
And I got a new little sister named Dotty

Today is the day I was able to pray
And to thank God for the worst day of my life
But I have to admit all of that wasn't it
I also married my six thousand pound wife.

Chris Solberg

Stepping Out

The rain falls heavy, yet
my eyes blink intermittently.
I can still hear that sporadic noise
behind my wall of sound
   drip, drop

Lulling, therapeutic, enchanting,
continual-security. Memories evoked by
the smell of wet leaves always interrupted
at just the wrong time.
   drip, drop

I am dry, inside, if I were not
I would be interacting with natural harmony
But the drip, drop of water rolling
off the roof of my house keeps me from myself.
   drip, drop

I am afraid of stepping out.
I am afraid of becoming
a little wet.
I force myself to endure
   drip, drop

Christopher Kachur

Mother's Day

My love for you is like a breath of fresh air
My heart is full of love just for you
You are like the star above that shines so bright
You gave me part of yourself
I am full of joy that my life has been good
Because of you, my mother
You taught me to be the best that I could be
Thank God; Without your love I might have been lost
But you have always been there for me
My words for you are
What I feel for you, Mother, comes straight
from within my heart
I want to let you know
I love you so much, Mother
I send you a stamp of a thousand kisses
Just for you
Kiss, kiss, kiss, kiss

Elizabeth Rodriguez

Today

Today is like no other day
My father has passed away
As I wipe away the tears
I am overcome by my fears
There are so many decisions to make
What if I make a mistake
My father was a man who always gave
This man's life they could not save
I have my memories that can't be taken away
how I wish I could have him just one more day
He did not live a long enough life
He left behind two children and a wife
you left this world to lead the way
Your family will be with you again some day
I wish I could do something other than cry
Daddy I miss you I love you goodbye
Today is like no other day
My Father has passed away

Dominique Baker

Untitled

I'm soaring high in the sky.
My feathers have finally healed.
It is my time to try and fly.
Chances are I'm going to crash and burn.
Why then do I take the risk?
It is so I can for once have my turn
I can see the light shining up ahead
The light is so bright I cannot see the mountain
It is not too late to turn away, so they said
It may be true that crash and burn I may
But the fire has not totally burned me yet
No matter what happens, I will remain
So what if my feathers get scorched again
Forever has to end one of these days
When it is all over, once more will I begin
It is not certain anymore what I fear
More than likely it is time to crash and burn
But once it is all over, everything will be clear.

Baq Emadi

Color Me

Bringing brightness and light into my life.
The most indelible ink,
Is the memory of you plastered on my mind.

With shades of an autumn leaf
Falling from an oak tree,
Color me.

TTW

An Empty Room

As I sit in this empty room,
My body fills with awful gloom.
This is where my sister stayed,
This is where my sister gazed
Out the windows among the trees,
Wishing she could sail along the seas.

As I sit down on the bed,
Wishing she were here instead
Of flying in the sky, away up soaring the clouds on high.
She cannot be on this earth anymore,
What, oh, what did she leave me for?

As I walk around this empty room
Which now is just a dungeon of doom,
Thinking of how bad I wanted this place,
Or how many times I wanted to open that case,
I think I won't now, so I can remember her beautiful face.

As I walk out through that door,
I don't think I will ask for anything more.
For now this horrible, wonderful dungeon of doom,
Will stay in this house as an empty room.

Ashley Jarratt

Sunsets

In the twilight of my after-years,
my face will be lined; paths for tears.

As the day of reckoning draws near,
I will face my end, but not with fear.

I will stand; arms open wide,
With my hands stained where innocent blood dried.

As the love I felt begins to burn,
and happiness begins to turn.

I'll walk away with a tear in my eye,
and find another blood red sunset over which to fly.

Clayton Norman

"Love Should Be Known"

Let the world know our love
let the world know we care.
As we walk together from land to sea.
Hand in hand a smile that shines so bright
all will know that everything is alright.
Let it start with you and me for the world to see -
show our love to whoever it may be,
every hour of each day, be grateful,
the Lord has blessed us on our way.
Hand in hand, our love must show,
will make a better world for all of us to grow.
Love and caring, sharing too,
will prove these words are very true.
We are all brothers and sisters on our Father's land.
So let you and me walk hand in hand, and
show our love for all to understand.

Arlene Barton

Deep Thought

Shine! Shine!
Let your light cast a shadow in this dark, dismal thought of rejection.
Let your voice ring loud and clear in my ears.
For whom only your voice can hear,
Love Telegraphy
Touch my thought of you when you feel me near.

Kenneth Williams

Give Me My Flowers While I'm Living.....

I would rather have one little rose
From the garden of a friend
Than to have the choicest flowers
When my stay on earth must end,

I would rather have a pleasant word
In kindness said to me than flattery
When my heart is still, and life
has ceased to be.

I would rather have a loving smile
From friends I know are true
Than tears shed 'round my casket
When to this world I bid adieu.

Bring me all your flowers today,
Whether pink, white or red;
I'd rather have one blossom now
Than a truckload when I'm dead.

Joyce Ann Davis

Antagonist

Cities are ant hills,
full of people.
Houses are ant caves,
filled with modern things.
Highways are ant trails,
buzzing with cars.
Cars are the workers,
carrying their loads.
People are the ants,
hustling about.
Children are the eggs,
the future generations.

Jonathan Floyd

Very Understanding

They say you are very understanding
Full of wisdom and gracious ways
For the future you are planning
You seem to know the soothing and
fitting things to say.

When my heart is dreary and my
spirits are running low,
You come along with words so cheery
You let me know my confidence in you
I can show.

Such friendships so loyal, true and kind
are seldom and few.
It's worth its weight in gold
cherished, remembered for the whole world
to behold.

Grace L. Sullivan

A Whisper Of My Soul

It is the wind   A thief of
I hear at night   My mind
A light   It is for all
To the eyes of   It is for you
My heart   It is a tear
Opening the wall   That I hear
Closed to love   On my pillow
Closed to you   In the night
It is lonely   Drowning sorrow
In the dark-   Drowning love
A keeper of   All for you
My life   All for nothing

Dawn Marie Hunter

Red

Red is the juicy taste of a
gigantic strawberry straight from
the field.

Red is the heat of a crackling
flame from my fireplace on a cold
winter day.

Red is a lovely rose from my garden
opening up on a sunny day.

Red is the first beautiful red robin
flying on a warm spring day.

Red is the symbol of the ones
I love on Valentines Day.

Jon Koch

Jesus Shadow

I have a little shadow who
gladly comes along;
And though I never ask him to,
He follows all day long.

If it's to the left I go,
He always does the same.
Or if it be the right, I know
He will play my game.

"Jesus loves me, this I know.
For the Bible tells me so!"
I want to do His will for me
then Jesus' shadow I will be.

Judith Wright

"To My Mother"

To my mom that I love
God be with you from up above,
He's with you always,
    right from the start.
He'll always be strong
    in your heart
He gives you strength,
    forgiveness too
He teaches to love our
    enemies through and through
Who is this man we cannot see,
Who promised he'll always be with thee,
He's the Holy Spirit, the risen king,
He helps us through everything,
I love this man who loves us back,
And will lead us through any attack!

Joseph A. Jordan

An Eagle's View

Flying
Gracefully through the air
If I had an eagle's view,
I'd fly along the airways
Every few hours I'd come to
A river
I'd come down and get a fish
A fish the colors of the rainbow
A fish with eyes the color of
The glistening moonlight
As for me, I'd be sparkling
Gold all over
Yes,
That's what I want to be.

Dale Swartz

Creation

I think a billion years ago
God took a brush in hand,
and with his colors he began
to decorate our land...

He chose a thousand shades of green
to paint the grass and trees,
and with his many shades of blues,
he formed the lakes and seas...

He used the shades of black and grey
to conjure up the night,
then added shades of yellow,
to bring in sun and light...

He came upon the desert,
and painted brown the sand;
you'll never guess what happened
when the brush slipped from his hand...

The colors spattered everywhere,
all o'er the rocks and ground,
and made the painted desert,
silent beauty, endless bound...

Jeanie Bishop

Sunset

A gentle wind
Goes floating by:
The clouds above
Fill up the sky:
The sun is low,
Low to the ground:
It slowly moves,
Without a sound:
Sunset's colors
Appear, then fade:
Purple, yellow,
Orange, pink and jade:
The moon comes out,
And then the stars:
Darkness touches
Near and far:
Night is coming,
It's here at last.

Amanda Rogers

Mom

Hands wrinkled, but still tender
hair flecked with grey,
She's wonderful and gentle,
In her own, special way.

Wrinkles on her forehead
From worrying once in awhile,
I've seen her sad and crying,
But I'll never forget her smile.

She yells sometimes
We give her cause to
after all it's not easy,
When kids do what they do.

She turns tears to laughter
With a touch of her hand,
Everything becomes brighter,
All over the land

I'll miss her terribly
When she's gone away,
I should tell her I love her
yes I'll do it today.
I love you, Mom

Fanny Lee Baker Shaw

The Sun Is Setting

The sun is setting, leaving rays of
   gold to cast comforting
   shadows of light upon the earth.
Light turns to darkness as the moon
   takes shape in the colorless sky.
The comforting shadows I once saw
   are no more.
Only frightening blackness surrounds
   me as evil lurks in the crevasses
   of every tree.
I take to flight as I strive to leave
   this place I once knew as safe.
My aching limbs hit the ground as I flee.
Suddenly radiant light consumes my body.
I am frozen in time, helpless to the
   power which embraces my very life.
I can resist no longer, I am one
   with the earth long before my
   body rests on it for eternity.

Heather Burchill

Originally Heavy Horses

Co workers
good morning Dick, Maude,
Rusty, Jane.
No answer, just a snort, or
soft nicker and the toss of a
proud head.
"Not polite!" you say.
Perhaps not, until you
understand and love
draft horses.

Harry W. Herron

The Sunset

The sunset looks as if a
   great painter painted it.

The bright colors of the evening
   sky make me feel happy inside.

The bright oranges, reds, pinks,
   and purples.

The colors I see,
   The colors I feel,
     That is why.

I wish that I could just pull
it right out of the sky and put
it in my living room for all to see.

So that everyone can feel the
   happiness that is
     inside of me!!!

Courtney Krajeski

The End

I was dreaming of yesteryear
How often one is prone
And then so suddenly
I shed a tear
But soon—so soon it was gone
And why do you think I cried my love?
Could you even guess
From sheer exhaustion and blessed relief
I'm free from you at last!

Coralou K. Malcom

Winter Morning

The blooming African violets
greet the winter morning light,
unfolding their new blossoms
to meet the day-star rising
in the cerulean sky.

The illumination of the room
reveals the lingering solitude,
so intimately woven with my
sapphirine mood, but
I no longer cry.

In acceptance of this early
morning ally, I might paint
my room the most splendidly
brilliant and radiant hue.
Since I'm awakened by the sun
instead of by you.

Jacquelyn M. McClaney

Home No More

Lone and desolate,
Happiness is gone,
Sadness has over swept my face,
Now I'm old and run down.

At birth I was filled with happiness,
A loving family with children,
Running laughing, playing,
Growing old with me.

Children grown and gone,
Parents moved away.
Left all the spirits of the years.

Now on the hill I sit,
Weeping for companionship,
They took my soul and
Left me dusty and old,
Forever more.

Donna Wardlaw

Broken Thoughts

   The picture in the window,
has seen what our minds shall not,
reading the lives of others,
in their souls of broken thoughts,
   Our eyes do not see,
nor do we comprehend our past,
yet we continue walking blindly,
hoping our future will last,
   The world is full of loneliness,
leaving us distraught,
for how can we be peaceful,
when we know love can't be bought...

Bonnie Thurston

"Freckles"

Some little boys and girls I know
Have freckles on their faces,
There's freckles on their hands and ears
And lots of other places,
I wish that I had freckles too
For all the world to see,
I wonder what I'll have to do
To make them
To make them land on me?

Herb Walsh

Untitled

All the Teenagers who have or
haven't already experienced the
reality of life, and anyone else who
reads this.

It doesn't hurt to take a little
advice or time out to think, but
it does hurt to reach out for
your dreams unprepared and lose
someone you deeply love.

So think first and prepare yourself.
Use caution and protection.

Cause it can happen to you!

Candina Malabag

A Rough Time

I'm sorry you are
Having such a rough time.
We have been told there is
A reason for everything.

Now is the time to have faith
In that promise and I
Know that you will.

Things do get better, it just
Seems to come so slowly.
Maybe it is to give one time
To be grateful for one's blessings
Or to prove no one is infallible.

Just know we are here
To help, love, encourage, love.
Offer prayers, love and to
Help tie that knot at the
End of your rope to hang onto.

Bernadette Harris

"The Becomer"

He is a lost boy
   He breathes a raw life
   He dwells his secrets in captivity.

Once, he dies alone
   His spirit unleashes the power
     of a phoney God.
He is unfamished
He kills the blind and borrows
   their hands.
He fails his test
He is distilled.

Dana Maria Veronica Smargisso

Korea

There for the glory of God
   he died in a mud-filled foxhole
   fifteen thousand miles from home.
The bugles blew and the flares flew
   and the artillery boomed
   fifteen thousand miles from home.
The teenaged soldier held his ground
   and fired his weapon
   fifteen thousand miles from home.
The fog lifted and the enemy crept in
   and threw his hand grenade
   fifteen thousand miles from home.
There for the glory of God,
   he died in a mud-filled foxhole
   fifteen thousand miles from home.

David J. Seigle

He Hadn't Time

He hadn't time to pin a note
He hadn't time to cast a vote
He hadn't time to sing a song
He hadn't time to right a wrong

He hadn't time to love or give
He hadn't time to really live
From now on he'll have time on end
He died today my busy friend

Jessica Liguori

Untitled

Why do I fret and fumble?
He is not mine to raise
I am so quick to anguish
He needs soft words and praise.

Idle moments are far too many
His rashness torments me so
The mind ever so fragile
Needs fresh ideas to grow.

He steps on stones and stumbles
When the sand is loose and free
He divides and crumbles
When the whole is meant to be.

Oh to grasp the golden moments
And banish those swirls of gloom
Extend your thoughts beyond the now
Unravel the bindings and let your spirit bloom.

Helen J. Ford

My Pastor

My pastor is strong.
He is spiritually strong.
He knows all about the Bible
And what God says is right.
He is physically strong.
He rides horses, big and tall.
And he bales hay with all his might.
He is mentally strong.
He knows how to make you feel good,
And never gets into a fight.
My pastor is strong.

Jessica Wiederkehr

He Is

He is the light unto my path
He is the bright of day
He is called the great "I am"
He is the truth, the way.
He is the healer of my heart
He is the open door
He is the giver of all life, and
He holds what's in store
The giver of all perfect gifts
Sent from the Father above
He is the one that turns my heart
Renews me in His love.
He is my hope of tomorrow
The one who fills my dreams
He is the one I run to -
For all else fails, it seems.
He is, of course, my Savior
He's filled with power and might
He is the rock I stand on
And He makes all things right.

Faith Stevens

The Run

Into the box you back your horse
He is willing, no need to use force
Not much pressure with this run
Just get it right and you've won
You get set, the header is set too
Both know what you need to do
Header gives a nod for the gate
The steer is fast, you're out late!
Header catches and makes a left turn
Now the heels are your only concern
Your horse is in the perfect spot
Throw a loop and see what's caught
In the trap there are two back feet
Pull slack and dally, ain't it sweet
Your partner turns and you face up
Just made an amazing run on this pup
Check the flagger; it's a finished run
Tell each other now that's how it's done

Jody Hampton

Surrender

Sizzling sun in shimmering sky
He lifts his face to feel its flames
Chill instead creeps cross his flesh
Within its wake no warmth remains.
Mist of memory, glimpsed then gone
Savory sweet the brief caress
Swallowed up by seeping shroud
A mantle made of hopelessness.
Sensing soon the soul's surrender
Taste of tears his taunt reply
Resisting not the nameless chasm
He yearned to live, yet dared to die.

Debra H. Landis

"What Is A Baby Boy"

"A baby boy is such a Joy."
He plays around and throws his toys.
He smiles and giggles and tries to talk.
Then he's going to learn to walk.
He wobbles and stands so tall, but
then he going to start to fall.
He smiles and laughs and tries to sing.
He's trying hard to do everything.
He's loved a lot and such pure joy.
Thank you God for this Dear Boy.

Charlene Booth

Untitled

God whispers a secret with each sunrise
He repeats it with each sunset
He does this from now till eternity
Can you hear him
I can
Listen closely and you might

Emily Tinsley

The Old Timekeeper

As I stand in front, and wind this grandfather clock that I have wound 4,000 times in my life, my mind asks!

"Will this be my last? Will the new time keepers know their weekly task, or will this grand old clock fall silent at last?"

Charles M. Bailey Jr.

Untitled

A rose for your thoughts
He said in a whisper
I can't tell him
He'll laugh or leave
Or say he agrees
I dare not say
That I feel this way
I was just thinking
How much I love you
I said in a whisper

Angela Keithline

Sammy's Song

Mounted on wings of an eagle,
He soared over poverty and shame,
And rose to the highest pinnacles
of wealth, fortune and fame.
He was a young man from Harlem.
Sammy, Sammy was his name.

Weary from mountains of prejudices,
He found strength in his father's love.
It was the wind for his journey,
To overcome prejudice and hurt.
Small in stature, only four feet tall,
Sammy looked up to no man.
Timidity never made him fall.

God game him a special talent,
A voice and a song in his heart.
He shared his love for the people.
With a smile that brought him to fame.
Now we feel his love from heaven,
Which, with choirs of angels, he sings.
Sammy, Sammy is his name.

Dorothy B. Geiger

Second Chance

When he was dying, so young and handsome
He told me not to be afraid
Softly, reassuringly he said.
    "The light are just going out"

Now watching another he
I wish that he will be
    ....not afraid......
As the lights slowly fade out.

Ellen F. Harlow

Open Ends

She felt weak - ask her why?
HE was the shadow of Summer
....in the mist....
Beneath her sleeping Winter
She ached for THE VISION,
    drunk through Mother's breast
And this raw void crushed
    her elaborate dream
Together - never -
Robbed - of the purple garden for two.

The rain thundered
    "Go!"
Spring into the delicious
Smell within the petals of self.
Watch.
The majestic colors.
Fall....
The symphony of life.

Alice Pyle

Autumn Of My Heart

Here I stand with only my broken
  heart in my hands, just the cold
  lonely wind at my side.

The sight of a single green blade of
  grass fighting for its withering life
  seems so familiar.

Echoing sounds of shattering hopes
  and dreams ring in my ears, I know
  it's the brittle dying leaves beneath
  your feet.

Never before this day have I felt the
  bitter isolation of the winter sun as
  its icy rays freeze my heart.

Must I once again wait for the warmth
  of my next chance meeting with spring
  before my heart will thaw.

Franklin Reed

"Second Chance"

The mask smothered, as I
held my arms across, and my
body lay still -

The sound held whisper warning
to my soul -
I screamed prayer quietly as the
deadly feeling entered within -

I left body to the masked
men as I laid still on the
Wooden Cross -
The mask smothered me as
the flesh flowed red blood -

Seven Hours of Crucifixion,
Seven Hours of Hell,
Seven Hours of Resurrection
Seven Hours of Heaven,
Seven Hours,
Before I was pulled from the cross
and taken to Room 334-B
Washington, D. C.
Seven Hours

Anne Carr Kirkpatrick

Grandfather

He is kind, loving, and caring
Helpful and always sharing
Loved by everyone big and small
He is the greatest one of all

Stories coming out of your ears
About all experiences over the years
Tales of adventure, family, and history
But never a dull story

Lots of wisdom to share
With everyone who cares to hear
The words of an old friend
Spoken so dear

A grandfather is a good friend to have
For he will always be true
And cheer you up
When you are feeling blue

Enjoy his friendship while you can
Help him through good and bad
For there will be a day when you wish you had
Shared your time with this wondrous man

Carolyn Moore

Untitled

Her beauty hides behind
  her forgotten face
Knowing not much of this
  horrible place
Never hiding behind
  pain or gold
Waiting for another story to be
  told
She sits in a corner
  wondering if it's true
That someone always
  loves you
Feeling left out of the
  games they play
Telling herself
  that will be me some-day

Billie-Jo Bishop

Grandma's Goin' To College

Her mind is made up and set
Her goals are all in line
Lots of things to go and get
Books to buy and forms to sign
Grandma's goin' to college

Supper will just have to wait
Socks and underwear pile up
Chores will now be done late
No fresh coffee in Grandpa's cup
Grandma's goin' to college

Paper, pencils, books, and such
Clutter the table and the chair
Her head is buried in books so much
There's hardly time to curl her hair
Grandma's goin' to college

No more drop-in baby sittin'
No more nights out on the town
No more wastin' time on knittin'
She's got to wear that cap and gown
Grandma's goin' to college

Betty Brown

"Treasures Of His Love"

Long ago, in only six short days
  He made things on this earth.
Can you recall the last time
  you enjoyed their precious worth.
We seem to forget just what they are
  in our disgust and in our haste,
So here's a list I made for you,
  to appreciate what God has made.

We have birds and bees and apple trees,
  butterflies and snakes,
cats and dogs and new mown hay,
  and cows and pigs and sheep.
Our children, bless their little hearts.
  They're angels from above.
Best of all we're made by God
  and we're the treasures of his love.

Yesterday, as I walked down the street, a
  blind man passed my way,
and I realized that I could see, and hear and
  smell and taste.
My legs aren't bound in braces, and my
  arms and thoughts are free,
Why can't we thank the Lord each day,
For the world is at our feet.

Darlene R. Hatheway

"Where's Grandma's House"

Her bones are so soft, so fragile
her hair blue gray in the sunlight
Her life gone by was so wonderful
Now she lies all alone in the night
A broken hip was causing her pain
Her mind has lost its power
So she waits in her room
Hoping someone will untie her.
She heard this must be done
It's for her own safety
Her self-esteem, she has none
How can this really be
She counts the dots on the wall
She hears them talking in the hall
A nursing home will be her life
Oh no! My home, my heart, how can they?
I cannot bear such strife. Oh! Lord God I pray
Let me close my eyes to thee
And take me to your shore
Please will you accept me; I simply cannot
take anymore.

Helen C. Gould

The Family Album

If you really want to know someone
Here is what you do
Go through the family album
The pictures give the clue

The pictures in this album
Are certain memories
Of special times and places
With friends and family

Go through the pages
The book upon your lap
See the past and present
Starting to unwrap

Look closely to the pictures
Don't be surprised to see
One too many nuts
Hanging on the family tree

Connie Lee Hale

Oh!

Oh! Look how the rain is coming down.
I guess we will go to the town.
They buried my aunt in a beautiful gown.
Now my uncle goes around with a frown.
Oh! The earth is still big and round.
My brown dog is a cute little hound.
Be that way till I'm in the ground.

Donald Finch

"In Love Too!"

My heart is imprisoned by the love
  I have for you.
I don't know why, I only know it's true.
I would do anything you asked,
  Including set you free.

The love I have for you is stronger
Than any love should be.

This is why I'm still with you,
When most would let it be.

  You see!!!
I don't just love you
I fell "in" love too!

Connie Agnew

"A Single Mother's Prayer"

God Bless this little boy
He's brought me such love and joy
Every night I put him to rest
I pray to you I give him the best.

I know our life will be rough
But make him grow to be strong and tough
You who was nailed by hand and by feet
Please let him never to feel beat.

For already I know he is strong
But I pray nothing will go wrong
Please watch over his sleep at night
For then I know he will do what's right.

Jennifer C. Skaggs

The Irony Of Dogs

My brother is bad
his dog is black.
I am tainted
my dog is white with two black spots.

Others believe my brother to be bad
his actions reflect their opinions.
Others believe me to be without flaw
they cannot see my mistakes.

Others cannot see
that I deserve my brother's dog.
Others cannot imagine
the darkness of my sins.

Anthony Craddock

Oh, That My Love Was The Moon

Forever there,
His face in my memory.
Deceptively near,
Cruel distance separates.

Icy blue,
His eyes pierce my soul.
Softly glowing,
His smile comforts my thoughts.
A breeze flirts across my lips,
His sweet kiss blown from afar.

Staring into the night sky,
Eternally there.
Oh, that my love was the moon. . .
That I may gaze upon him every night.

Christine C. Irelan

Love

Love
Here one day
Gone the next
Comes in as a kitten
leaves as a flame
some take it lightly
Others take it harder
Sweet as sugar
mean as a snake
Sharp as a knife
dull as an unsharpened pencil
can be a best friend
or a worst enemy
soft as a pillow
hard as a rock
smooth as silk
rough as sand paper
Love

Julie Burke

Old Man

The old man stands on the corner
holding a sign
that says, "Will work for food."
He hides under the brim of his cap,
ashamed.
His skin is darkened
from a lifetime of hard work.
The lines in his face
tell of happiness
and heartbreak.
He doesn't want to be there,
but he sees no other way.
Weatherbeaten and stooped
he accepts change
from a man
in a passing car
who hopes never
to be standing on the street corner
holding a sign that says,
"Will work for food."

Gwendolyn M. Sullivan

Life

Life is a beautiful rose
how it blooms,
No one knows.

Life is a bright summer sun
Full of light
Full of fun.

Life is a small baby's cry
Sometimes we hurt
And don't know why.

Life is a brand new car
If you do good
You can go far.

Life is a cold winter day
When our time comes,
We still wanna stay.

Life is a new fallen star
Some are near,
Some are far.
MOTHERS GAVE LIFE

Amy Sweeney

Miracles

I believe in miracles!
I have to, for I see
God made a million things that way
Especially for me.

He promised I need never fear,
Just trust, obey and rest,
And open up my heart to hear
The way to live my best.

I believe in miracles!
For when I sinned and fell,
He never once deserted me,
And I have learned it well.

He took my unrepentant soul
And taught me to replace
My sinful, scattered, painful life
With one of joy and grace.

I'll stand beside his glorious throne,
And claim the victory.
For I'm the living proof of it -
The miracle is me!

Joan L. Green

I Believe

Today, I spoke to a daisy
I asked if you loved me true
As the petals fell one by one
The last one said you do

Oh daisy, with your wisdom
Your colors gold and white
How you made me happy
Oh, how I hope you're right

For you above the mighty rose
God made it very clear
That you would be, instead of she
The flower propheteer.

Though some prefer a crystal ball
Or leave their love to chance
I'm glad I asked a daisy
My flower of romance

Esther E. Wallace

Untitled

Pain deep within
I avoid telling, showing
Afraid of what people may know
A bird humming
A tree growing
Deeper the roots of the soul
Into the ground they grow
Lost in my heart
I cannot find
The peace of me
I've thrown around
Love does not know
It's lonely and cold
Searching for the colors
I cannot show.

Jill McWhirter

Romantic Self (At Eighty)

R.S., Remembering you,
I can clearly see your face;
And though your voice is silenced
 In my heart,
Wonder still lives in my soul.

Geraldine P. Trory

Untitled

Love is a'coming my way
I can feel it in my dreams
Love is a'coming my way
at least that's the way it seems
I give love to little things
then they grow and go away
and come back with angels' wings
promising to stay.
Snowflakes in the winter
rainbows in the summer
what it takes to win her
is to be much dumber
because she is so innocent
and my mind is twisted so
it would at least be decent
to let him run and go
and we could meet again
around the corner of my life
let the Great Spirit determine when
to ask her for my wife.

Bill Kenney

"There Goes My Allowance"

I am the master of the universe,
I can unleash any curse,
I can defeat the alien mother,
and its deadly brother.

I am the ruler of planet Mercury,
I have fought Hercules,
I almost beat the wizard Vorters,
But, I just ran out of quarters!

Brian Kerg

Love Is Blind

I've often sat and wondered how
I could have been so blind,
to all the love and comfort offered,
as well as peace of mind.

The fact that God has created us
and sent His only Son,
has inspired more awareness
of just how it all begun.

He could have simply forgotten us
and let us die in sin,
but He's expressed His love abounding,
and can cleanse us from within.

It only takes an open heart
and a willingness to admit,
that Jesus Christ has sacrificed
His life that we may live!

Holly M. Bell

Life

Since childhood's death,
I could not see.
I was one and others me.
I saw deceased,
Upon the fall,
Which clung to me, induced us all.
As others sang - I could not.
As others sung - I would not.
My spirit moved among me slow,
But will rest, immortal hollow.
Death thus departs - creation begins
And I will see tomorrow's endless sins.

Armando S. Bevelacqua

Childhood

Tension.
Fluid fear.
Anxiety drips like
icicles in spring thaw.
Anger is a shark.
Circling.
Hungry.
Pain smothers.
Terror rips free
like a scream.

The Self
.....
   fractures.

L. F. Ricka

Haiku

Water is pretty
Crystal clear and pure to drink
Coming from the earth.

Matthew Strenth

My Last Breath

Did you hear me breathe?
I did, but you didn't hear me
My life was over
In a split second

I heard a noise
And I looked around
And I saw a shadow
I recognized it
But it said nothing

I saw a knife
And I felt it on my throat
The pain was so severe
And I saw darkness
Nothing but darkness

I wasn't dead yet so, I did feel
Stabbing after stabbing but I had no strength
So I couldn't cry

In my last breath my God, my God
My Jesus, my Lord, my children I love
My children I love

Benjamin Perea

Home Away From Home

Where is your home, my child?
I don't know. What's a home?
Well, let's see…It's a place
Where hugs and kisses are, and fun
Where Papa is, and Mama

What's a Papa? I never had that
And Mama. I know that name
But when I say it nobody comes
You know what? I think home's
A kind a dark scary place with
Loud noises and fights and things
And smells that make my nose itch
Look! Look at the twinkle lights!
Is that a home? Is it? Is it?
No, dear child, that isn't a home

Neon lights wink, blink, off, on
YOUR NEIGHBORHOOD BAR-
HOME AWAY FROM HOME
Come in and join the party
Have a drink, let's have some fun!

Irene Prater Dell

A Day's Dream

I dream of the future
I dream of the past
Of the memories to come
And the moments that will last

I follow my heart
To where happiness hides
A place where I can dream
And no one ever lies

The past is behind me
But it's still with me each day
With thoughts of the friends
That have gone away

But my future is bright
With the birds that will sing
There's one thing I will always have
And that's a day's dream

Bridgette Morris

Untitled

Beneath the ashen floor
I dwell
Seeking the light I once knew
Entwined with the air I once breathed
Now I am still
And yet full of the dance of life

Sorrowing befits you
Not me
For I am disposable
And easily thrown away
I am willing
And you aren't sure
So I dwell quietly
Beneath your curled up toes

Dan Ray Noyes

Mother Love

With tears in my eyes
I gaze at the skies
And wonder why
He had to die,
The child I nurtured on my breast
With mother's love, I can attest
The depression we did survive
With love abounding in our lives
As the years have flown,
A new generation has grown —
Grandchildren who are dear,
Extend their love from far and near.
God who does not forget, has blessed
Our lives with hope —
As we strive and cope
Until we reach our rest!

Ellen M. Kindred

A Piper's Day

When you lay me down to rest
I have only one request
That along with the stars and stripes
Have them play the highland pipes
Let me hear the drum and drone
So I'll find my way back home
To another time and place
Where I'll see again my father's face
And there we'll pipe along
Playing English and Scottish song

Edward Wallace

Paradise

As I stride towards paradise,
I hear eternal music within.
   Entering, I see you,
   Pretending, to be unaware,
Of my presence.

Quietly, I move behind you,
   to gently touch your silken hair,
   and savor your closeness,
And let you know, — I'm there.

Drawing you into my arms,
   Pulling you into the hollow,
   Reserved for you alone,
We Kiss, — and say hello.

And the music of love plays,
   In my heart,
   My soul,
And my mind, — in paradise.

James J. Occhiogrosso

Violence

As I lie in bed at night,
I hear the sirens roar.
  Was someone wealthy hurt?
Or was it someone poor?

Why was that person hurt?
Did they do something wrong?
  Or were they just a victim
for no reason at all?

Why do people hate?
Why do people kill?
  No one knows the answer,
and I guess I never will.

Jaime Dymond

talking ants

there was a time when i was young
i heard the talk of ants
my ears and heart were both in tune
and as i lay upon the ground
i heard the talk of ants

there was a time when i was young
i saw animals in the clouds
my eyes and heart were both in tune
and as i lay upon the ground
i saw animals in the clouds

there was a time when i was young
i made angels in the snow
my body and heart were both in tune
and as i lay upon the ground
i made angels in the snow

there was a time when i was young
i dreamed i was a bird
my soul and heart were both in tune
and as i lay upon the ground
i flew

Jacqueline Babbage

Untitled

Good morning little one
I hold you near my heart

I knew that this would be beautiful
I knew this from the start

There have been some challenges
I didn't think I'd get through
"If" it weren't for your daddy
I wonder what I'd do?

I keep on wondering....

Wondering what you're doing?
When will the contractions start?

I wonder what you look like or
How big you really are?

I wonder if you have dark or light hair
I just wonder what it will be?

I wonder if you'll have blue eyes or
Big brown ones like me?

I know it won't be long until I get to see.

Until that day keep kicking to let me
Know you're here

Gina Marie Sample

God Is With Us....

God is with us today,
I know because I heard him say,
We should kneel down and pray,
For soon it will be judgement day.
Yes, God is with us today.

God is with us today.
I know because I heard him say,
Satan has made a foray!
The good will go and the bad will stay.
Yes, God is with us today.

God is with us today.
I know because I heard him say,
That we should rejoice and play,
For it's the Easter Holiday.
Yes, God is with us today.

Cathy L. Long

Untitled

I shall die.
I know not where; I know not when,
But I shall die.

Once before, in my mother's womb,
It looked like death—
That exit from my tiny room.

The head so big;
The door so small;
Strange I exited at all.

That death meant undreamed-of things—
Laughter and tears,
Ice skating and cold ears.

It was all a gift—unsought.
Will death be a boon-unthought?
Will earth-time worry be for naught?

One desire—
Will some child say, "He lived. I felt his hands;
I saw his prints on forest paths and ocean sands?"
Remembering, will some face wreathe into a smile?
I hope so; I'll be gone in just a while.

Arthur Eikamp

School

All my books
I learn a lot.
From A to Z,
and 1,2,3.

Heather J. Arscott

Untitled

Nina,
  I kiss her good morning
    Comforted by her touch
  Her smile, her eyes
    Show acceptance
  She smiles to avoid tears
    I'm encouraged by her strength
  I feel only sadness my
    Courage may not last.
  I feel her touch, I awaken
    I'm alone
  I missed her kiss goodbye.

Arla Thomas

Shadows Of Midnight

In the darkness of midnight
I lie alone in my bed,
While fears of the unknown
Creep into my head.

The blinding fear of midnight
Keeps knocking at the door,
But if faith is strong
Fear will vanish for evermore.

Suddenly I realize
There is no need to fear,
For there is someone special
Who is always near.

Lo and behold
I glance through the window,
And I see from afar
A bright and beautiful morning star.

The shadows of midnight
Are now out of sight,
For the darkness has past
I see only the light.

Ella Ivey Powers

The Way I Feel

There is a woman that I treasure,
  I long to hold her ever so near;
To get to know her is my pleasure,
  her smile fills me with happiness and cheer.

She has blue eyes and blonde hair,
  she's sexy in every way;
to her none can compare,
  that's why I say the things I say.

You ask me "Who can she be?"
  Just keep reading and you will see;
these feelings are very true,
  and this woman...well she is you.

James Newsom

Gossamer's Wings

A desire to reach the stars
Hopes of fulfilling hopes
To rise up with success
From life's thin ropes
To bounce back with ardour
From the deep wells of sadness
To hold onto moments
That run on ethereal threads
Rhythmic keys of brotherhood
To destroy destruction itself
A world with no ugly threats
A Utopia in which to dwell
But alas! This dream, like all others
Flying on Gossamer's wings
Slips through the fingers of reality
With tiny, deceiving links.

Batul Jeddy Abbas

Loving You

I love you much, can't you see?
I hope your love's the same for me.
  My love for you keeps growing strong
and may it keep forever long.
  Things don't work the way they should
But when they do our love's so good.

Judy Strom Truman

"Missing You"

I miss your talks
I miss your smiles
for you I'd walk
a million miles
I miss your eyes
I miss your face
I especially miss
your warm embrace
I miss your walk
I miss your touch
I never knew
I could miss you so much
I miss the evenings
we would spend
holding each other
until the end
I miss your kiss
and your hugs too
I only hope
you miss me too

Jennifer Schaler

Can You....

Can you love me the way
I need to be loved?

From my head to my toes
UNCONDITIONALLY......

With mental kisses of knowledge
here and there

Embrace me with the strength
of your heart and the kindness
of your hands

Tickle my thoughts with chocolate
tasting forget-me-nots

Talk to me with a smile and a sensual
stare

Bathe me in songs from way back,
among candles and incense.........
I SAY AGAIN CAN YOU LOVE ME
THE WAY I NEED TO BE LOVED?

Dedra W. Hunt

Where Can I Go?

Where can I go, to escape this pain.
I often feel sorrow of tainted rain.
Where can I go totally free from
crime.
With a vision of drugs and guns left
behind.
A wonderful place where birds fly high.
In this place rain never falls from the
sky.
Where can I go, nowhere it seems.
Now nothings left but broken dreams.
It would have to be a magical place
No fear, No worries, only love, not
hate.
Where can I go to be by myself.
In this land everyone's dealt with
good health.
I need a place where I can grow
but I often, ask myself
Where can I go?

Jason K. Grimes

Lord, Please Help Me Find My Way, I Pray

Lord, please help me find my way,
　I pray.
I may stumble, I may fall,
　but it is my call.
In deciding what to do,
I haven't very many clues.
Which way to go? Which way to turn?
My head and heart must discern:
What I should do, what I should be.
Lord, please help me find my way,
I pray.

Carolyn Salley

Jodie I

I hope she knows I love her.
I really do...
From her big brown eyes
Right down to her chubby little thighs.

She's always taken her time;
But, my, she catches up to the heart
With gold and silver treasures.

She's always had time for a hug and kiss.
How did I live without her?
What did I miss?... perhaps love.
And how can I tell her.
　She's cherished beyond, always loved,
　　very lucky we have each other.
Every night I watch her tiptoe
down the hall as she goes
to lounge at her days end.
Tucking her in.. I look around
and hope with all my heart
that she never passes away.
　Goodnight, Jodie!

Cindy Trice

Over The Hill

Over the hill
I saw a skunk,
Playing with a cute
chipmunk.
They were playing
A game of hide and seek.
The chipmunk said,
"Do not peek."
The skunk said,
"I'll always be a friend
Right to the end.

Bonnie Boisvert

Loose

　I hear your winter;
I taste your rain;
　I've failed you, summer,
but feel no pain.

　I feel you fade away;
I watch you drown in rain;
　I've given my love away,
but feel no pain...

　You were my lover
and sweet, little angel.....
　... but now we're all over,
and our only memoir is a dead skyline
　and dying rainbows...

Jeremiah Brewton

Dear George

I see you when the clouds roll by,
I see your face, I see your smile.
Perhaps nobody else can see
But there you are, so clear to me.
And when the sky seems low and dark,
With thunder sounds and splash of rain,
I know you're there, you feel my pain.
Our life was happy all those years
With smiles and laughs and also tears.
I miss you dear, so very much
With heartfelt memories of your touch.
And so, I watch the sky for signs
In walk-abouts you're on my mind.
I'll always miss the life we had
The emptiness is very sad.
But we must go on separately
Until the time God calls for me
And we're together eternally.

with love,
Ethyl Biles

Twenty Three Years of Service

Another day at this dump
I sit at my chair and slump

I feel so uninspired
I'm just waiting to get fired
So I can display
One of the bumper stickers that say
retired.

Ellen Schneider

Unspoken Silence

I listen without a word
I speak without a sound
Does not matter to me
How I feel, what I see
Whatever! You just agree
Wouldn't care, couldn't know
What does not matter to you
Shouldn't possibly matter to me
I'll be something for you
What shall it be
First you choose,
then leave it up to me
Just let me know
That's what I'll wish to be.

Angi Sedlock

Untitled

Once upon a castle
In a town far away
We dance with kings and queens
On a mystic winter's day
Where the icicles hang from willow trees
That sparkle throughout the night
We twirl around a fountain
Till the rise of the morning light
Fairies come and join us
With diamonds in their eyes
We laugh and wish and play
Among the stars high in the sky
But soon the days of love and fun
Come swiftly to an end
And all there is to do my friend
Is dream you are young again!

Jody Reed

"Chances"

We've been the best of friends so long,
I thought we'd stay the same,
I thought we knew each other well,
But then stronger feelings came.

Every time I looked at you,
When I looked into your eyes,
I felt a sudden change in me,
Something deeper than what lies.

I went on day by day,
With emotions growing stronger,
I had to let it out,
I couldn't hold it any longer.

So then I told you everything,
How long I felt this way,
The reasons for my actions,
All the things I had to say.

I took that only chance,
One I never will forget,
And no matter what the future brings,
It's a moment I won't regret.

Cynthia Takahashi

Woe To Be Loved By Time

Bound to this life, it won't set me free
I try to escape and feel ties
force me back to the home and world
where I don't want to be

I pursue another path diligently
Five years of striving to be,
what I think I want to be
I am so near, I my mind I see me there
Yet so far, I haven't reached the door

The past won't let me go
The present lingers on
and the future chants hello
Woe to be loved by time
can anyone begin to know.

Ellen Ibert

Untitled

My daddy's little girl
  I use to be
He would sit and
  bounce me on his knee.
He made me feel safe
  and secure at night
He taught me what was
  wrong and what was right.

Now that I'm grown
  and have children of my own
as trials come my way
  my Daddy will still lovingly say
"Daughter, here is my shoulder
  let me carry that heavy boulder."

I thank my Heavenly Father above
  for filling my Daddy's heart
with His love, so that when the storms
  of life start to whirl
I can still feel like I'm
  My Daddy's "Little Girl."

Gale Odom Coleman

In The Eyes Of Love

Surrounded by love
  I walk to you
Through the petals of love
  with wisdom by my side

As our eyes embrace
  and our hearts touch
We join our hands
  to follow our hopes
  and dreams.

With each whisper of love
  we begin our journey
Faith as our guide
  and nature as our Mother

Our hearts and heavenly bodies
  now intertwined
We become one
  in the eyes of love.

Jennifer L. Matheny

Epitaph

When you wake and find me dead,
I want no mourning, no tears shed,
For you must live each long day through,
I've made it, I should weep for you!

Diane Saccocci

Reclamation I

No one explained to me why! why!
I was being taken down there.
The steps were steep and bare.
Each step was warm and glow'd
by others descending the stairs.

A single bulb whirled and stared,
the light was dim down there,
a dot—swinging on a golden chain.
The light from which I came
grew dim, as I slowly pass'd away.

The years slowly went and came.
I heard the flight; felt the plight;
saw the land parch'd with white.
Saw a naked stranger standing near.
Felt his love, I drop'd a tear.

I found a word, found a frame.
Looking up! I felt the rain.
It fell upon my tattered head
washing away the aching stain.
His tear wash'd away the pain.

Frank Anthony

Reverie Before A Retreat

Grasping the hand of my Saviour
In my search for His infinite truth
I find myself turning and wondering
Whatever happened to Ruth

No matter how far I may wander
Enthralled with God's wonderful charms
I find the pursuit cold and lonely
Unless I return to her arms

Dear Lord keep her safe in your favor
She is troubled when I leave her door
But in loving who treasures me dearly
I find myself loving You more.

Edward B. Schulze

"Happy Birthday Darling"

Happy Birthday Darling
I wish you joy and happiness
All my wishes are for you today
I want to wish you the very best

I wish you many more birthdays
In our golden years to come
We will be so happy together
As we count them one by one

When we are old and gray my dear
We will reminisce about the past
We will talk about our binding love
And what we did to make it last

We will talk about the good old days
When we were so very young
The time I kissed your tender lips
Our true love thus begun

Now back to you my darling
On this your happy day
Excuse me while I dry my eyes
I must have been carried away

John A. Vines

Patterns

I used to dream of wishing wells,
Ice cream cones, Christmas bells.
Feath'ry skies all painted blue,
And pictures that the angels drew.

I used to dream of gentle rains,
Choc'late bunnies, candy canes,
Endless roads all paved with gold,
They do exist, so I've been told.

All that happened long ago
When I was young and didn't know
Dreams are rambling fantasies,
Empty as the summer breeze.

Now I'm older and I know
Life is not a picture show,
Our patterns change from year to year
And childhood dreams just disappear

Elio Desiderio

"Clouds"

If I were a cloud
I'd be puffy and white;
I'd float through the sky
Through day and night.

But when it becomes stormy
I will become gray;
The sky will turn black
And you won't want to stay.

You will see lightning,
You will see rain;
You will want to hide
Under the window pane.

After the storm is done,
You will be amazed
At the beautiful rainbow
Being raised!

When you walk out the door
Look up in the sky;
See all the beautiful clouds
Passing you by!

Amanda Lee Reiter

Remembering

I wonder what would happen
If she would have said yes.
Would we be happy?
I can only guess.

What would have happened,
If she would have chosen me?
Would never carved our initials,
In that old pine tree?

I can't help but wonder,
But that's all I can do.
Because instead of me,
She has chosen you.

I still fantasize,
About those summer nights.
In the middle of a field,
With hardly any lights.

Those days are gone,
But the memory remains.
The pain is only soothed,
By those cool winter rains.

Christopher M. Cowgill

Together We Stand

It matters not that we are free
If we let things happen to you and me
These terrorists that use the bomb
Will try to break us, in our aplomb
This just can't happen in this land
  When together we stand.

Let's not for a second relax
Our thoughts and loves they'll try to tax
To cause discontent and aggravation
But they can't harm this great nation
'Cause we are walking hand-in-hand
  For together we stand.

Do not listen to their smooth talk
Remember to say, "Take a walk!"
Stand together and you will find
That a fool has uttereth his mind
He has given himself a brand
  "'Cause together we stand."

Yea, we can conquer all our fears
As we're doing all through the years,
Then we will roll in the clover
Truly our cup will runneth over
As we keep this country grand
  Together we stand.

John M. Antonucci

The Day The Pickles Fell

Pickles do an Irish jig through my head.
I'll never rest or go to bed
With the pickles of a Whopper
Jiggling before my tired eyes.
Pickles—green and sour on top of
Whoppers and cheeseburgers.
Oh, no! Where're my pickles?
Ruby red tomatoes with green middles
Cover the pale green and white lettuce
As the confused kitchen crew tries to—
Ketchup, all over the place.
Oh no! The slimy pickles are escaping.
Quick! Pick them up and wash 'em off!
Throw them back on!

Carlene Cogshall

Memory Lane

I don't need a mirror to see,
I'm not the girl I used to be.
The wrinkled face and snow white hair,
And the laughter that's no longer there.
The dulling eyes that used to glow,
And a pace that now is very slow.
But deep in my heart will always be,
A special love that only I can see.
It carried me through heartache and pain,
And was with me when life seemed in vain.
So may my thanks as my years end,
Be to one special, special friend.
Who never knew of my trouble and pain,
But was always there through memories...
Down Memory Lane

Alice Carlson

My Final Journey

  On a golden sunny day
I'm waiting my final journey
there no apprehension about
moving to my final home

  You see the China is all clean,
furniture is waxed, floors
are mopped, boxes labeled
for Susie and Johnnie.

  Everything's done you see
I'm just waiting to reach
my final destination;
no apprehension just joy
to reach my new home

  When suddenly being there
on that golden sunny day
my destination is reached
in that changeless eternal
home called Heaven

Ardelia Young

Darkness

In the darkness I lay down.
In a gloomy room, there is nothing
but doom.
I can't resist
some kind of brightness
in my heart.
As it glows, it lights up
the dark gloomy room.
There is nothing,
not even doom.
The heart was there with me
in that very same room.

Courtney Anne Chiarella

Agony

Agony smells like metal warming
  in a noon sun

It tastes like the cut on your lip that's
  gushing blood

It sounds like the whimpering cry of a
  wounded puppy

It looks like a ripe bruise turned puffy
  and purple

But it feels like a fist coming hard down
  down against a child's skin
  hitting over and over and over...

Jennifer Schlief

Freedom

A long, long time ago
In a place I do not know
I was captured and put in jail
My heart was filled with storming hail.

Then one day the sky was blue.
And a man that I once knew
Came along with a key
And said, dear friend, now you are free!

Amanda Radandt

My Morning

I will marry a sunlight morning,
In a quiet forest clearing.

With air still soft,
from morning mist.

Sunlight's heated arms
enfolding around me,

Protecting me from snow, storm
and burning words.

The smell of vibrant life
soaking into my soul.

The sound of laughter
forever in my ears.

I live here in happiness,
and die, a smile on my lips

My morning will remember me.
Flowers will bloom on my grave.

Jessica Verburg

The Way

Almost two thousand years ago,
in a stable He did lay,
and still today millions pray,
Because, He is The Way.

The Way to the love and peace
we share on earth to this day,
The Way to hope and eternal life,
That rose from a bale of hay.

Can't you see Him in your mind
and feel Him in your soul,
that sweet, sweet little boy Jesus
That Mary loved to hold.

Can't you sense the beat of His heart
the warmth of His caring eyes,
the touch of His gentle hands,
And His love that fills the skies.

How blessed are we to celebrate,
His birth again this year,
To share His love, hope and joy,
With those we hold so dear.

Judith Evans Leftwich

Perfume

Whisper in an otherwise silent room,
In secret though we do not speak...
Our words are like perfume;
Not too strong, not too weak.
Slowly they pervade our senses;
Soft innocence in a fragrant air.
A glimpse of heaven in the confidences
And quiet words my love and I share.

Hope L. Russell

Strawberry Patch

I went to pick strawberries,
In a strawberry patch,
I slipped and fell,
On some of them.
But I did not get up too fast.

I sat and ate the ones not squashed,
Till I was full of gas.
There were none left,
When I got done.
In the strawberry patch.

My folks got mad,
But don't understand.
I'm too sick to pick
Strawberries from the other patch.

Gladys E. Walker

Untitled

Bugs crawling over his body
   in and out of his eye sockets
   and mouth,
They do not care that it is flesh
   that they eat
it is just and ordinary day,
Bad news for this skeleton of a
   soul
I guess it will be the dirt and bugs
   for company
      tonight,
He didn't need his soul any way
the bugs seem to know it wouldn't
   do any good
   for them either,
I guess
easier to be soulless
   and cold
When you are surrounded by
   greedy bugs and dirt.

Carla A. Lowe

The Softest And The Loudest Sound

One sound is the softest sound
In despairing souls it is found
No one can hear the agony
Except the one in misery
But to that one the sound is heard
Much louder than the spoken word
To the one under despair's cloud
No other sound could be so loud
And thus in despairing soul is found
The softest and the loudest sound.

Erin Magee

Anger

The hollow blackness
inside your heart

A bitter taste comes
out of your words

You smell smoke as
you look into the
gleaming red eyes

Frustration comes out
of the bellowing words
that burn your heart
and soul to dust.

Christy Clark

I Want To Be Like Jesus

I want to be like Jesus,
in every way I can.
By following his example,
and not the way of man.
To care about all people,
without discrimination.
And pray for all their needs,
in daily supplication.
To purify my thoughts,
and resist the evil one.
So I can truly say,
"His" will I've surely done.
Through trials and tribulations,
and every kind of sorrow,
I'll keep my trust and faith in "Him,"
and look for a bright tomorrow.

Dorothy Radcliffe

The Light

The light that went before me
In every way was you
Soft and sweet, you brightened paths
And led me to the truth

The finer things you showed me
The simpler some would say
Grass and birds; music and words
The color, not the gray

So now I've lit my own light
And you have gone from me
I travel down new pathways
I help the others see

But if someday I flicker
Or light from me should drain
Thoughts of you will keep me warm
Despite the coldest rain

Carolee M. Calvin

Untitled

I speak
   in footforms
along the ocean edges,
   pressing into waters
that 'round some distant world's corner
might this moment enclose you
     now spray
     play
   upon the dark tan of your body.

It has only been one short wile
   after another
that draws me to this sea
in a rush to drown toescars
   in waning watercrests
hoping to share with you
   in these short touches
the confinement and the freedom
of waves.

Debra J. Lord

Old

Sitting ─────-
In my wicker chair at sunset,
Waiting for the dark of night,
That goes too quickly
In my dreams of youth.

David C. Stark

A Young Boy's Cry

I seen a young boy with tears
   In his eyes
I asked him, young man why are
   You sad, why do you cry,
He said, sir, it's my father, I don't
   Understand, why did he die?
I asked, did he read the word of
   God, did he believe in him?
He said, yes sir, he was saved, he
   was saved from sin.
I said, young man you should be
   Happy, don't cry no more.
Your father is with Jesus, our
   savior, our Lord.
He said, thank you sir for helping
   Me see.
Now I understand, the Lord has
   set my father free.

Joseph Martin Miller

Tiny Angel

(In Memory of Michelle Hamdan)

Did God need an angel
by his side...

When he called you
to him that day.

Did he see in you
something special...

In your tiny perfect
way.

He left us know
you briefly

And set our hearts
awhirl.

We never will forget
you.

Our beautiful baby
girl.

Diana M. Day

Maple Tree

   She sheds her colorful ornaments
in October. Gently, her trinkets
swirl to the ground.
   Naked, she stands alone in
isolated silence. She raises her
black majestic arms up to the heavens
praying to God to spare her life.
Her black clawed hands shrivel in
the breeze. She has accepted her
temporary death.

Doreen Muscoe

Anguish

A wandering thespian
In a world without stages

Pondering passages from
A book with no pages

Running from yesterday
at a marathon pace

Yet oppressed by tomorrow
Still losing the race

Charles D. Padrick

Believing

Hear your voice calling me
  in soft wind
    during my afternoons
      perhaps your days

Must be there alone, thinking
  but me too
    during my nights
      I hear you

Feel you sometimes
  at dawn of new day
    and caress your spirit within me
      I miss you

Awakened I grasp out
  as breeze of you withdraws from
    me, haunted by emptiness
      and yet rewarded from your presence

Hear you, then, me
  and touch at you sometime
    knowing time, now, is an ally
      to draw us together

Charles Washington

"Wealth Of Home"

My home is not a fine chateau
In some far distant land.
It is not built of mud or bricks
Upon the shifting sand.

It is a place within my heart
Where there is order and bliss.
My home is an earlier heaven
That brings me happiness.

It speaks of God and family ties
This place that is home to me.
It has that glowing atmosphere
Where I rest so peacefully.

I do not need power or splendor.
I don't need a Lordly dome.
I need beauty, love and contentment
For this is the wealth of home.

Frances Ely Wood

To My Love On Father's Day

If my love could be measured
In terms of cups or pints,
You'd need a water tower or two,
And still that wouldn't suffice.

If one could measure your wisdom
In terms of inches or feet,
I'd have to encircle the whole darn globe
And still 'twouldn't be complete!

Your wisdom can't be found in books
On tapes, records, or VCR.
It's like the Wisdom of the Ages;
(God gave you an extra jar!)

I love your very demeanor...
Ever kind and patient and dear.
When I'm a trial and a tribulation
You can fill me with good cheer.

So always know that I love you,
Through all times, good or bad,
Just thinking about you, dear husband,
Makes me feel cozy and glad that God
made you!

Gayle Tebay

The Rain

In the evening breeze
in the moonlit mist
They shared one special,
lasting kiss
Remembering when
they first had met
In a small cafe
trying not to get wet
From the rain falling
down down into the street
It was nature's intent
that they should meet.
But tonight was different,
so warm and still
As they laid on the grass
at the top of the hill
Staring up at the sky
and the stars above
Thanking God for the rain
that had first brought them love.

Jackie McGinnis

Those Who Wait

Those who wait
In the sickroom and outside
Die a thousand deaths
Before the loved one has died.

Those who wait
Grapple with yesteryear
Minus the morphine
With dry eyes that tear.

Those who wait
Home is four walls
Pill or position? Drink or condition?
And endless recalls.

Those who wait
must be willing to take
The power reluctantly relinquished
And then extinguished.

Oh, the weight!
Of each day and minute
for
Those who wait.

Jeannine Randolph

Allan

Everyone
including me
hates to be in Allan's company.

He insults people
he talks non-stop
he is bright
but
no one can stand him.

Allan quietly sat
at my kitchen table
stared into his coffee cup
looked shyly into my eyes
looked back at the cup
and said
I have become my father
and I hate myself.

Allan sat there
naked in his skin.

Evelyn Lambert-Dannen

"Loser"

In the silence of my lips,
In the stillness of my heart,
I gasp, "Love, where have you been?"
I heard nothing, but the howling wind.

The gloom that has been in me for ages
Has seeped from inside out;
The waiting, the fight, is o'er,
Now, just the tossing of the dreams.

I'm the wanderer who knew no sleep,
No rest, but aching limbs,
I'm the child who lost,
The 'loser', preordained.

George Isaac

The Forest's Ruins

Deep beneath a hollow log,
In the water of a forgotten bog,
Where children once played,
In a pond, nature made.
There lies some secrets,
And a different world,
From the forest's ruins,
A history box is swirled.
Some ants have taken over,
The log's inside.
Where once there was a squirrel,
When the tree was alive.
The bog is now misty,
But someone else is at home,
A family of geckos,
With a place to roam,
So all the other places,
That are forgotten and still,
Still buzz with life,
Silent, strong, and shrill.

Annette Adams

An Interlude With Peace

As I sit in my chair
in this world full of despair
I encounter an Interlude with peace.

The blue sky
The elegant butterfly
The birds, the bees
The spectacular trees
A gentle breeze
The scent of a rose
Just a few moments of repose
Some silence
in an aura of global violence

Cynthia K. Chapman

Winter View

I know this road most every day.
In torrid heat and driven cold
  I pass this way.

Yet -
I never saw that house before.
With lush, green life before its dour,
It hid from passers-by.

But-
Now with all growth brown and bare
a snowy carpet everywhere -
Is bid us from our path to see
The beauty of the barren tree.

Dorothy Therese Reilly

Solitude

To proffer blow for blow,
In war of field and fortress,
Toward the great King's army,
Marched on a mighty foe!
Few sing the victor's paean -
For hill and battle-plain,
With dying men and stain,
Grew mountain-heights of pain,
And mine is boundless woe!
How shall I meet my fate,
When sires grown old in sorrow,
Ask of the unreturning
For whom they vainly wait?
Few sing the victor's paean!
On hill and battle-plain
Alas, the many slain,
The mountain-height of pain,
That won on the fortress-gate!

John Juji Hada

Untitled

Looking at the beauty I see
in you. A heart of caring and
love. Shining so bright with a
halo of life. That stands out
with hope and strength. Seeing
the peace you possess in your
soul. At a time of being off in
the distance. Your face with a
glow of being loved. To share a
wonderful gift given to me.
Feeling loved is an experience
to be able to say how much I
need and miss you.

Joseph Irwin

Purple

Purple is the taste of plum dripping
in your mouth.
Purple is the smell of violets blowing
in a garden.
Purple is the feel of me curled up
in my favorite sweat shirt.
Purple is the sound of a kid chewing
bubble gum.
Purple is the sight of a crayon laying
on a piece of paper.

Danielle Yielding

Spring's Debut

Spring is just around the corner,
isn't it grand?
Makes you want to sing and shout
let's strike up the band.
Get yourself together, take a walk
out in the sun,
it would be terrific, not to mention
it's fun.
Daffodils and Tulips will be
coming up soon,
time to dig the garden and to mow
the lawn too,
Hyacinths and Crocuses will be
coming into view,
Spring is making its debut,
just look around you,
Spring is making its debut.

Catherine A. Miller

Reflections

There is a mirror in our minds,
into which we sometimes peer,
to see where we have been
and to remember times so dear.

But the mind's mirror also tells
of times we've stumbled, too,
as we travelled life's pathway
and if we were not true.

But memory is a selective thing
and we tend to concentrate
on times when we did kinder deeds
and accomplishments were great.

Ah, but History has a mirror, too,
and records life as we live,
and though we manipulate our minds
from History, we get just what we give!

Frank Sweeney

Seasons

Summer never comes when you want it
It waits until you can't stand anymore
Snow and sleet and mush
And walking in the slush
And shoveling the sidewalk to the door
Summer never leaves when you want it
It waits until you can't stand anymore
Sitting in the school
When you should be in the pool
And in the shade the temp is 99.4
Neither Spring or Fall
Are any help at all
In stopping this ugly chain
'Cause as soon as Winter's over
Spring bursts out all over
And all we want is summer back again

Julie Woulfe

Untitled

The first time I saw your smile
 it was not for me.
The second time I saw your smile
 it was at me.
Friends we were for a while
 at first.
And then our hearts met and
 love was our thirst
We gave ourselves to each other
 in the most ultimate way
God I love you more and more
 each and every day
Our children are proof of the
 love we share
So perfect and innocent and
 without a care
Like the graceful white dove
 who flies in the heavens above
Our love will soar.

Juli Hallowell

Earthly Mirror

The earthly mirror will never break.
It will never fall,
for it has no glass at all.

The earthly mirror is the key.
To another place,
for us to see.

Justin Lee Sharp

"Love Is Like The Twine"

Love is like a piece of twine,
interwoven into the minds.
Of lovers who seek and find divine,
when working upon their skeins...

The grape you drink is red and sweet,
like these old and ancient streets.
When couples doth seek to meet,
the weavings of the twine...

Roses are red, so is the heart,
the dance of chance to make a start.
Lovers sow, and then depart,
their love is like the wine...

And to prove the work they've done,
in truth to love the two are one.
A child of life has met their love,
in the meeting of the minds...

Under the roof of God the true,
who predestines couples to come into.
With the needle he weaves anew,
lovers of the rhyme...

Christopher Ardanuy

Angel In Our Midst

God sent an Angel unawares
Into our lives one day.
Oh God, we cried with flowing tears,
Why torture us this way?
This girl of ours will never be
Like other children are,
To romp and play and bring such joy,
A bright and shining star.
We nursed and fed this little girl
And every day we prayed
That God would heal our precious one
As in her crib she lay.
But in His wisdom from on high
God touched our hearts with love
To help us know that he had sent
This Angel from above.
And truly God has blessed our lives
Throughout these many years.
Her loving heart has touched our souls
And washed away our tears.

Jeffa P. Hill, Jr.

Are You There?

I whisper deep
Into the air
I wait for a reply
But you are not there.

I listen close
Undo the sounds
But it's complete emptiness
And you are not found.

I reach out
Upon human souls
I try not to pour
But it's like walking
on hot coals.

If you are not here
And they say you're not there
Where can you be
But nowhere?

Guadalupe Mendez

Somewhere In The Pacific

Somewhere in the Pacific
  Is all that you can know,
Not where I've been to
  Or where I yet must go,
But this much I can tell you
  That all censors will O.K.,
You are my lady
  And I love you more each day

You are my lady
  Half a world away,
But never mind, my darling,
  For there will come a day
When the Rising Sun will be darkened,
  Then I'll come back to you
And we'll pick up where we left off
  And start life anew.

Alma LaMothe Smith

A Kingdom In The Sea

A kingdom in the sea
is calling me
In the day and in the night
Don't let them take me
Hold me tight
If you listen hard enough
You will hear them too
Voices from another world
Begging to join you
Hold me tighter, can't you hear?
They're coming closer, they are near
They're coming for me
How can this be?
The kingdom in the sea
is calling me

Camden McClintock

Where I Like To Sit

I like to sit in certain places.
indicated by tradition or emotion.
In church near the back of the room
because the seats up front are
for those of serious devotion.
Which I am not.

The side aisle in a cinema
where the exits are
or used to be.
Sometimes used as entrance doors
for kids without the access fee.
Which was often.

I like to sit and review
my life that has gone before
and wonder why the important things
were hardly ever done.
Can I even the score?
Maybe!

Arthur Russell

Friendship

  Friendship is like a
knot that never gets untied.
Friendship is like two turtledoves
that never leave the sky.
Friendship is when you're with
your friend and having lots
of fun. Friendship is like a
hot dog never separating from
its bun.

Brandon Johnson

Unsounded Shame

This unsounded motion
is not heard, but seen
it is the victim's call
solicited long before
they are made
shed no more
once the betrayer has them secure
as the victim complete

The silent warning is made
with scars to delete
with silence unattended
vocalization runs to retreat
time, a non-factor
a soul already shackled by its raptor
forever's hope is replaced
the continuum, a shame-filled embrace

Joseph Dziadosz

My Love For You

My love for you
Is oh so true
But you couldn't see that
You were so cruel

I tried my best every day
To show you my love in every way
I hate that you could never see
What you and me could really be

A love like you I'll never find,
'Cause you are just one of a kind
If you and I could ever be
I'd make it last for eternity

I'll never find a love like you,
Because my love is oh so true!

Cindy Castro

Untitled

Tears of pain
Laughs of joy
So close together
Confusing all around
Relinquish the love
The end may be the beginning
Nothing said you hear
A fate worse than hate
I sit alone in serenity
but my hypocrisy goes only so far

Adam J. Keemon

Sweet Pea Teddy Bear

Sweet Pea Teddy Bear
My friend
Soft, huggable, warm
Your face rests against mine
Waiting for a kiss.

Keeper of my secrets
Guardian of my slumber
More than a toy
Polar bear.

Silent and attentive
Always a good listener
The only price you ask
Is a hug and a smile
My teddy friend.

Cher MacQueen

Reality

Reality, though plural in appearance,
Is singular.

We each in truth
Inhabit our own world
Peopled by our own imagination,
Ever changing—
Ever moving in a perpetual dance
To a tune only we hear.

Oh, Reality, Thou product and reflection
Of my mind...
Tune the strings of Thy existence
To the tenor of my heart.
Help me to know
That Thou and I are one.

And if Death must perchance come,
Let me be reborn
Into a new and wondrous realm
Where the eternal dance
Begins anew.

Carl Jordon

The Color Of Misery

The color of misery
is steel grey at the
jagged edges
shot through
with cobalt blue
at the
frozen core,

Frozen
because
anything warmer
would release
all the
blood red
pain.

And that
just
won't
do.

Frances R. Goldstein

What Is The Meaning Of Life?

There is not a simple answer.
It is a very deep question.
Why are we here?
What is our purpose?

The continuation of the species,
Might be the main reason.
It is not wrong to ask,
Is that all there is to it?

Religious people would say,
That we are God's test.
To learn right from wrong,
And save our souls.

Others would say,
We are here for experience.
To accept pleasures and pain,
and then we are gone.

There is not one answer,
For there are many reasons.
The nicest reason of all,
Is to make it a better place.

David K. MacPherson

Love

How can
it
be shared
by only
two
cannot comprehend
what it is
they
are sharing

Deborah R. Peruski

Love

Love is like the sun
It burns so bright
And lasts until we die

Love is a pure white dove
It at times soars so high
And it is beautiful to behold
But lovelier to feel

Love is a child
It starts out unexpectedly
And grows into a priceless treasure

Love is like the atmosphere
It is all around us
Just waiting to be noticed
And to bring happiness to us all

Courtney Doolin

The Sun People

The sun is bright.
It doesn't show at night.
It makes it hot!
And makes a beautiful day.
It makes the people happy.

Jade Buehler

Some Love

Some love is like a river;
It flows fast and strong;

Some love is like a bird;
It sings the sweetest song;

Some love is like a mountain;
It reaches its highest peak;

Some love is like a baby;
It is born helpless and weak;

But this love I am sure
beats the more.

April All

Early Morning Trip To The Airport

My son falls asleep
in the car seat as we pass
a graveyard where shadows
are being entombed.

Rain begins to beat on the car
like desperate prayers.

The airport lights pierce
the growing storm, and,
for a moment
my son's sleeping face
is light.

Charles A. Startup

Hair

Everybody has hair
It gives flair
Or they will be bare
It is mostly rare
Then you use hair that you wear
That won't be fair
Most people care
It could be cut like a square
Not necessarily on a chair
After it is washed
Dry it with air
It can be in pigtails
So you get a pair
If you cut too much
Don't you dare
You might get a big scare
So there
I declare hair
Everywhere
Maybe I am a bear

Edward S. Quirk

In Review

When I look at the past again,
It gives me always some small pain,
To think of mountains never seen,
Of eyes deprived of valleys green.
Too much I think of seas uncrossed,
The thousand subtle paths unwalked.
There are a million things undone,
So little time and space to run.

But what a useless thing it seems
To rue and pine and dredge up dreams.
It isn't boundless this fruit of life.
We cry and laugh and bear the knife
And march and drum and play the fife.

John Morrissey

"Soldier's Wish"

Is this ever going to be over?
It goes on and on.
I lose all control.
My sanity is gone.
The main man commands me to shoot,
shoot to kill.
He says there's no need to worry,
it's a thrill.
There must be someway out of this,
it's my wife I want to be with.
I don't want to be here,
it's my children I want to be near.
He commands me to fight,
to destroy.
He tells me to be brave,
not to be a boy.
Suddenly there is a pain,
pain in my head.
My sight blackens,
now I'm dead.

James Eric Johnson

"Love"

Love is like an Umbrella
It goes up and it goes down
When you need it the most
It's never around:

Frances Collins Kasdan

Balance

Shifting... turning...
it is the constant movement of mind
which brings men large and small to
their knees....
The sides crumble at the first glimpse
of light and the center divides itself
at will; if you can find a way to stand
still and witness both day and night
with steady eyes (blinking is death),
the dream of living inside the flow
does seem possible.

Dylan Jaymes

I Couldn't Think of a Poem for You

I couldn't think of a poem for you
It must be writer's block.

I really tried very hard too,
But my creativity has a lock.

I'm sorry I couldn't think of anything
To write or say or do,

I guess it's just not my day
But I can still say —
    I love you!
    Happy Birthday!

Jessica Simon

It's A Great Day

It's a great day to praise the Lord
It's a great day to praise the Lord
let us praise our Lord almighty
let us praise his name today

It's a great day to praise Jesus
it's a great day to praise Jesus
let us praise His precious name
let us praise His name today

It's a great day to praise the father
It's a great day to praise the father
let us praise His holy name
let us praise His name today

David Shade Hoover

The Road That I Must Follow

   The road that I must follow
is short from side to side
it is very rocky
and it isn't very wide.

   Sometimes it gets so dark here
that the path I cannot see
so I have to trust his wounded hand
to be the light for me.

   My heart seems to compel me
his spirit lets me know
that I must keep on going
the farther on I go.

   The road that I must follow
is less traveled it is true
but maybe as you watch me walk
you'll want to follow too.

   On the road that I must follow
over hills and mountains high
I must press on to reach the goal
by the grace of GOD go I.

Heather Swanson

"You and Me"

You love me,
It's easy to see.
Everything,
Is what you mean to me.
Together,
We were meant to be.
Forever,
Our time together will be.
You and Me,
Happy as can be.
Little P,
Yes that's Me.

Barbara Clark

Untitled

My heart is like a red balloon
It's fragile when it's full
It can take a little playfulness
It can stand a stretch and pull
and your words were like the wind
as they filled me up with air
I was floating and I was bouncing
then suddenly you weren't there
your lies were like a pin
a knife you drove into my heart
you popped my red balloon
you ripped it all apart
now you can try to pick up the pieces
and throw away the pin
but my heart is like the red balloon
it can't be fixed again.

Christina D. Amtmann

Nightmare

Through the night the thunder rumbled,
Its hardened wheels of iron rolled on.
The lighted path aglow before it.
The horses sound of hoof on stone.

Blackened with the clouds of heaven,
Lighted with the lamps of God,
Pangs of fear in every heart beat,
Trembling blades of grass on sod.

Then the north unleashed its weapon,
Gusting wings of wind unfurled.
Beating drops of cooling moisture,
Quenching thirst on the dusty world.

In the barn the dumb brutes huddled,
Stables filled with dampened straw.
Dew drops from the realms of heaven,
Resting on their troubled brows!

In the morning clouds have lessened.
Rays of heat have just begun.
Branches stretched in mere rejoicing,
Glowing red, it is the sun!

Garry L. Henderson

"In My Sister's Sorrow"

Tho' sorrow and hurts come to us all,
it's the good things I recall.
The happy times of childhood funs,
the memory of laughter comes.

Oh Lord, I pray, you'll quiet her fears,
and give her spirit trust.
And she will know your love
and ways are always fair and just.

Jean White

Just The Two Of Us...

Let's run away together
It's not such a silly idea
We could run away
To the islands of nowhere
where
no one would
disturb our privacy
we can share a lot of love
and
see a lot of dreams
for as far as the love
in our hearts
will take us

Denise Marie Wahnon

Good Advice

I've heard this story often,
It's one I won't forget.
"A stranger's not a stranger,
It's a friend we haven't met."

It could be that they are so shy,
That's why they seem so cold,
They cannot make the overture,
So walk up, bright and bold.

Introduce yourself to them,
And say a word or two,
The next time that you see them,
They'll say "hello" to you—

Helen H. G. Evers

Untitled

It's time.
It's time to go now,
said the jury and judge
You have to go,
there's no need to push and shove
You have nothing,
You have no love.
Everyone has a time,
Everyone gets prime
But this is you,
You have committed many crimes.
The judgment has been made,
Your final day has been played.
You've lasted this long,
You've stayed.

Carrie Kramer

Cast Away

Like a ravenous vulture stalks
its vulnerable prey
in a desperate fit of rage
so does my pain rush in
swallowing each tangible
asset of mine.
My original essence
lives on in memory
through the many miles of blizzards
and stifling arid sands.

I, once bright,
am nothing more
than a ravaged bleeding corpse,
plucked away by life,
whose carcass lies cast
on a seemingly barren desert
away from my reach.

Helen T. Spear

A Goodnight Prayer

One night I watched my little son
    Kneel still beside his bed,
And it seemed to me that I could see
    A halo round his head.

His tiny hands were folded,
    His head bowed reverently
As from his baby heart he prayed
    With faith and piety:

"Dear God, pwease bless my Mom & Dad
An' brothers Ned and Joe.
An' pwease take care of little Spike,
He's my puppy dog you know!

An' pwease to keep on watchin'
My baby sister Flo,
An' kinda keep ol' Spike in line,
He's my puppy dog you know!

An' I promise, God, to be the bestest
Boy you'd ever like,
If you sorta keep my dog from harm,
You know, his name is Spike!!"

Dody Houk

Trust

To master anything you must first
    know its True name.

To learn its True name you must first
    know its True nature.

To know its True nature you must first
    be in rapport.

To be in rapport you must first...pace.

To pace you must first...know its world.

To know its world you must first
    know the True nature of all things.

To know the True nature of all things
    you must first trust.

To trust you must first
    be in rapport with all things.

To be in rapport with all things
    is to know your self.

To know your self
    is to know your True name.

To know your True name
    is to be the Master of all Things.

Carl Lagle

Piece

To leave this place would be
like leaving a piece of me.
Though I was never there
I can pretend
my Books give me the key
to go to that place and see
that same Piece of me.
I have known the blood and gore
just from those Books I read
just from what my mind sees
just from the TV screen
just from those people who were
really there.
I am not one of those
but I still know

Aleksa Moss

Worship

There sits little Sammy, communing.
Legs crossed like a lotus, eyes
Glazed and unfocused, ears hear
Every word. The pulpit squats
Beneath the stuccoed wall, glowing;
Blue nimbus lights up Sammy's face,
Leaving his head's back black and dark.
With only his face in the glow,
He is happy. The scene shifts,
Though not much, and Sammy's
Eyes reflect red—the color
Of passion, color of the heart —
Wrenched from live broadcast.
He smiles, and his crooked teeth
Shine crimson like his Kool-Aid;
Tongue licks lips. What his
God wants, he will do.

John M. Williams

Time

If I could stop one moment in time
Let it be you who stand before me
If ever a song could remain in my heart
Your words would be my melody
If I could capture a feeling
It would be your touch
No promises, no lies
Just a dream as such
If when I awaken my moment is released
Walk with me.
   Talk with me.
      Touch me.
Forever in time

Deborah A. Brooks

The Elders Way

Let the blind man teach you to see
Let the deaf man teach you to hear
Watch the prisoner to know freedom
Listen to the wind to know destiny
For you are a vessel holding nothing
Therefore containing everything
For the void encircled us once
But then it opened
Releasing us into the light
The blinding glare of birth
Leaving us frightened and alone
Severed from the warmth of Uroboros
Projected into the cold all
To begin the Elders Way
And struggle for the infinite
Searching without seeking
To find all of nothing
Within the shell of everything

Jeffrey C. Thompson

Thoughts

Sitting on the hearth by the fire
Makes you think.
Think about the good things
And the bad things.
Is it because of the flickering flames
Dancing around in your head?
Or is it the warmth on your back
After playing in the crystal-like snow?
It's probably the calm and serene world
That always seems to be
As you sit by the fire.
Yes, that's what it is.

Bart Braunger

As A Child

As a child
life outside
was the real world.
Our lives were dramas.
Life was filled with a
bottle of hope.
Every day was
a walk down
a narrow dream.
But soon the
day was over
with a sudden thud.
We sulked and
whined our
way inside.
To stay outside
forever was our faith.
But now our
love-free days are over
as we look outside.

Christy Oelslager

Suicide, Oh!

Take a chance, oh, what the hell.
Life's too long, oh, anyhow.

Do it now while you are young.
It's your life, oh, anyway.

Take the trip, don't hesitate.
It'll be fun, oh, it'll be fast.

It'll be great, oh, it'll be grand.
Far away from here and now.

You'll go where you've never been.
You'll see things you've never seen.

Take a gun and blow your brains.
Take a knife and plunge it deep.

Take a glass and slash your wrists.
Take a dive and break your neck.

Take a pill and open wide.
Take a match and light the fuse.

Take an axe and chop your head.
Take a swim and drown yourself.

Do it now, oh, do it quick.
Now's that time for you to click.

Joe Baratelli

Joy

The joy of the Lord is in me
  It makes me smile
  It makes me hug
  It makes me reach out

Thank God for the joy
  You are wondrous
  You are joyous
  I thank you

Your joy is with me
  Thank you, Thank you
It makes me so happy
And contentment fills my soul

I want to spread the joy
It feels so good
Let me help others in my joy
How joyous is Your word

Hilda E. Ward

I'll Show You What You Missed

Tears are falling from my eyes,
Like rain drops from the skies.
You know you're in my head.
I keep thinking about what you said.
I know you care for me.
But is that how you want things to be?
I dream about you every night,
When I close my eyes you're in sight.
I can still feel your lips on mine.
My mind is in such a bind.
I can picture your arms around me,
This is not how I want to be.
Why don't you say you love me?
Why don't you say it's so?
Don't you even want me to know?
I wish you were mine.
We would be together all the time.
It doesn't have to be like this,
Just give me one kiss
And I'll show you what you've missed.

Jeannie Scott

Echoes Of Pain

As we sat under the stairs
like so many times before,
we could only hear echoes of
pain; our parents screaming and
fighting, it was driving us insane.

They taught us children to love,
but we only saw their hate, how
were we supposed to understand the
mixed feelings that grew so great?

Their hatred brought us close,
their selfishness tore us apart,
the only thing that was growing was
the pain inside our little hearts.

The pain will never leave, always
to be there; not only are we lost, but
we're all so scared. To stop the fighting
would be such a cost; we children were
separated and our futures together were
lost.

Gene Wayland Jr.

The Old Couple

They huddled, together for many years,
Like two spare lean-tos,
Each supporting the other.

When one should fall down to earth
The other knew the gravity of things
Would bring the other down -
Bosom to bosom, together again.

Joseph S. Ragno

Pictures

  Pictures hold a lot of memories,
movements, thoughts, and ideas. They
show expressions; happy, sad, mad,
glad, achievements, and goals reached.
  They show life and how different
people live it. Maybe even life
coming or going. Battles won or lost.
  The future being changed for
all eternity. But most of all they
show you and what you are.

Jacqueline Santos

Petals And Thorns

A dozen red roses
long stems and all
were offered for love
in the middle of fall

The roses are dying
and soon they will wither
Close at hand
is the beginning of winter

The next offering
for me he gave
was a rose wreath
for my cold lifeless grave

He returns each year
in the middle of fall
with a dozen red roses
long stems and all
   Glenda K. Jackson

Our Children

Listen to our children
Look into their eyes
They are here by destination
Can't you hear their cry?

Look into their faces
How long must they be torn?
Can't we just love them?
Can't we just love them?
   Joyce Ann Nash

Within Me

Look deep within me
Look through my eyes
See the real me
the me that I despise

See the world wrapped up in lies
Rise and fall behind my eyes
Look at all the ants that live and die
All behind my eyes

Look deep within me
Look through my eyes
See the real me
The me that I disguise

See the hues caused by the sunrise
Sweep the mind behind my eyes
I see the people and hear their cries
All behind my eyes

Look deep within me
Look through these eyes
See the real me
As I make my own demise
   Donna LaRosa

Keepsake

A small keepsake
Lying close to my heart
A gift given unknowing
It holds so many thoughts
To touch it, is to remember
...looking up at it...
...looking across at it...
...looking down upon its
   smooth, shiny face
   a small tear or
   the sparkle of her twinkling eyes...
   Jeaninne McIlvaine

Little Lady Bug

Little, little Lady Bug
Looking for someone to hug,
Sitting in the tall, tall grass
While the others rush right past.

Who will ever see you there
When you only sit and stare?
Open up your wings and fly
To meet the others in the sky.

Little, little Lady Bug
Sits so quiet and so snug,
Looking for someone to love
While the others fly above.

Who will ever see you there
When you only sit and stare?
Open up your wings and fly,
Meet the others in the sky.

Little Lady Bug will try
To open up her wings and fly;
There she goes, up in the sky
Now true love won't pass her by.
   Elizabeth A. Catuzza

I Think

Love for the less fortunate
Love for those who don't know
Love for justice for all
Love to help and share from the heart

From the heart is what matters
From the heart makes sense
From the heart I share goodness
From the mind it makes sense

I think what is right
I think reality present tense
I think I need necessities to live

I think I help others
Look back at mistakes
I think I need dreams
For future undertakings

   I think
   Don Goodman

Love

Love is fear
Love is hate
Some are lucky enough
For love is fate

Love is dreams
Love is will
Some are lucky enough
For love can fulfill

Love is trust, love is care
Some are lucky enough
For love they share

Love is chemistry, love is real
Some are lucky enough
For the love they feel

Love is friendship, love is a vow
Some are lucky enough
For love to be allowed

Love is true, love is gay
Some may fall hard
For love sometimes...drifts away.
   Diane Burke

LOVE

Love circulates through blood,
Love invades thoughts,
Love helps the heart beat,
Love heats a sweaty palm,
Love pulsates through dreams,
Love thrives on life.
   Cassandra Maida

Reverie

I remember lying...
lying cheek on hand, eye
near the autumn
floor and sun's warm
gold rays moting tiny
worlds
from musty carpet.
And old paint cracked
candelabra-ed mantel.

Mind leaps back to those
simple days,
those glorious moments of
innocence.
Of leaf littered
almond orchards
Of faint blue tendrils
of smoke
curling through a
frozen morning.
   Floyd Ross

Verb Sanctity

Small lies.
Maiden shies.
Soft sighs.
Limpid eyes.
Passions rise.

Cautious tries.
Sacred ties.
Straining thighs.
Weak cries.
Passion dies.
   John D. Conklin

Love

Love is a bond of beauty that is rare,
Love is a sign of trust and care,
Love is what we need to survive,
So keep your eyes open and wide......
To all the things you can find,
Dwelling in the back of your mind....
   Cara Simms

I Look Upon The World And Cry

I look upon the world and cry.
Man is destroying man
by his own hand.
The once clean rivers,
and oceans are now
polluted, and sick.
The weeping willows never
stop crying,
while others are dying.
The rain pours clean tears no more,
for now the rain's
a pitcher of polluted tears.
I look upon the world and cry.
   Anne McComas

Prayer

Lord,
make me a cup of your love,
shoot of your life,
object of your grace,
herald of your truth,
instrument of your power,
reflection of your wisdom,
example of your justice.
You, the Love - me, your cup;
You, the Grace - me, your object;
You, the Life - me, your shoot;
You, the Power - me, your instrument;
You, the Truth - me, your herald;
You, the Wisdom - me, your reflection;
You, the Justice - me, your example.
Guido Feliz

Mentor

Wisdom and strength
Love and understanding
Discipline and teaching
Patience and trust
Firm and concerned
Generous and kind
Fearful and attached
Caregivers and advisors
Your shoulders to cry on
My mentors
I have been blessed by these
   two special people
They are my parents...a
   precious gift from God!
Evelyn Kennedy

We Three

There's a mystery of joy at our house
My wife and I are just two, you see
But there is always another person
So, abiding at our house are three.

Yes, there's one that resides here
That can't be seen with the eye
But He's for real, far more than we
When we need Him He's ever nearby.

He dines with us at our mealtimes
He's our precious and dearest friend
We should always make Him welcome
For neglect or a slight will offend.

No, He's not a guest, He lives here
And He gives to us our daily bread
When trials come in, He protects us
And by His hand we are gently led.

Friend, do you know of whom we speak?
Do you understand, or know our story?
Yes, if you love Him, you will know
He's Christ Jesus, the Lord of Glory.
Clyde Matthew Taylor

Untitled

Onceaclan
Now drifted apart
What was the string
that
held
us
together?
Antonella Maria Padula

He Is My Protector

As I struggle through this life
May my soul be free from blame
May I always see your love
As one eternal flame

The Lord is my shepherd
With him I will abide
For there will be good pasture
Somewhere on a green hillside

And when you want to drink
Go to the crystal sea
Then you can just look around
And the Saviour you can see

You will be in a place
Where storm clouds never roll
And everybody will rejoice
For there is joy untold

I am longing for that day
When I see you wave your hand
May I be in your flock
Somewhere in the promised land
Johnnie Estle Willyard Sr.

Eyes of A Clown

The giggling eyes of a clown
Mean more than you think
For the make-up means nothing
It's what's in his heart that sinks

It sinks into your mind
And shows you what's true
The painted smile or frown
Is shown only for you

You are what makes his eyes smile
Frown, laugh, or fill with pleasure
Your reactions and words
Fill his heart with treasures

These treasures are your enjoyment
Of his passion-filled act
For when the show is over
Your laughter shines through a crack

The crack of his eyes understands it all
The beckon of your request
Laughing for more, shows that...
This giggle, is the lasting effect
Christina Rose

My God

He is a teacher teaching the great
mysteries the universe holds.
and he is taught, learning how to
Live life here and now.
He is gentle, like a whispered breeze
blowing by.
And he is fierce, like a storm if
aroused to anger.
He is clever, wise, and intelligent
and he is naive, ignorant, and unknowing
He is the light, bringing life, warmth
and compassion
And he is the dark, enforcing law,
righteousness and power
He is good, and he is evil, the perfect
balance, God-like, a sheer divine creature
and I love him.
Heather Hummel

Waves

Waves, softly gently
   Mesmerizing with
Moonlight, balmy evenings
Taking cares away
Soothing and promising
For more and better days.

Waves with moonlight
Reflecting a restful
   Peaceful night
Promising - at least -
   Hopeful at best
That events will turn
   Out right.
Barbara Meyer

Michelle

Little lady blue eyes...
   Michelle, your given name,
total of Michellettes
   gives heavenations claim.

One Michelette I see,
   A starship of I drink,
a flood from above fill
   trill, reality, think!

Another one stardrop
   Has a sounding sea
of resonance echo!
   Live! Personality!

Thoughts of stairs I do climb,
   to reach your pedestal'd feet.
In that clime is a starship,
   lifting Michelettes sweet!

Don't say I'm a writ wit!
   Writless, witless witness
if I left your eyes aside,
Your Michelettes caress!
Henry Bezner

Untitled

River
Moist and winding
Meanders through rock paths
Hoping to reach its destiny
Traveler
Cristina Arriens

Mom Is.......

Mom is special,
Mom is sweet,
Mom is gentle,
And always on her feet.

When Mom goes shopping,
She thinks of me,
And brings back something,
That I need.

Mom is brave,
Mom is caring,
Mom is determined,
And always understanding.

She goes out of her way,
If I feel sad,
To give me a hug,
And make me feel glad.
Danielle De Caprio

Diamond Girl

You are Grandmom's little girl
more precious than gold
more special than gems
no one can place a price
on my Diamond girl.

   You give Grandmom joy
   you give Grandmom love
   More love than ever known
   You are so very special
   for you are Grandmom's
     Diamond Girl!

You are more karats than the Hope
more rays than the sun
more jewels than the stars
for you are my Diamond girl.

   A Diamond like I never had
   more precious than your name
   A diamond with more meaning
   than the jewel for which you are named
   for you are Grandmom's Diamond Girl!

Cheryl D. Brown White

Spectral Voices

Screaming,
Mortally wounded.
The visibly defiant,
Hold their words only until,
The first possible moment,
When they can be seen.

Never alone in this standing abyss,
Clawing at the sharpened obsidian walls,
Death is a cheap but healthy release,
Fear is wasted on the timorous,
Religion catches you like a barbed hook,
In the back of your neck,
Waiting patiently for eternal release,
Your soul screams vengeance.

Screaming, visibly wounded.
The mortally defiant, hold the moment
only until,
The word is given, when they can be
forgotten.

Dean A. Jones

hopeless

you probably know me
most people do.
you all think i'm fine
but if you only knew

i wake up each morning
with tears in my eyes
but i always make sure
you don't hear my muffled cries

i put on my fake smile
will i make it through the day?
i am beginning to hate myself
and this pain won't go away

nobody understands me
you don't even try
so i don't even care anymore
and i will just say good-bye

my hurt is escaping me
and i see a glimpse of hope
not that i am left hanging
from a noose in this rope

Amanda D'Angelo

If I Could

If I could, I'd wipe away all of
my baby's tears.

I'll create a clean environment
so people could live.

I'd wipe out any violence, crime
and pain, the word racism
would have no name.

Everyone would have food,
money, a place to live. I
would give, give, give.

Although for now this is how
Life must be; the devil created
sin in the world, not me.

These are the things I'd do if
I could.

Angeline Holmes

Untitled

As the candle flickers,
my body sweats...
... cold...
... beads thicker...
... clothes drown in the pool...
... drenched...
... regret, desperation
(A fool?)

As I begin to shiver,
my heart dives...
... Quicker...
Teeth chatter, love splatter...
... Doubt, anticipation
(The End?)

As my limbs quiver,
I see the river...
... beauty...
... flows...

As my cigarette
Scorches...
... my fingers the pain is painless
Soul at one, it lingers
light I can see

Errol Bergadon

The Folly Of The Genius Brain

You wonder of my moods, my heart,
my clouded brow of reflection?
I'm a child of a renaissance
who can't express his passion.
The folly of being human,
left to the measure but not the means;
the inadequacy of words
relating of what only seems.
Mere symbols placed upon a page
are no justice for a genius brain.
'Tis the reason of Van Gogh's shots:
My confined soul makes me insane.
For those content not to understand
and accept the mean but not the be,
you never need to free your soul.
I envy your simplicity.
The folly of the genius brain
is limited capacity,
and for this I shall always grieve:
what's locked in my mind cannot be free.

Emily Turner

My Dreams

My dreams come to you by me
My dreams come to everyone
My dreams are everybody else's

Julian Warren Bell

"I Know"

"I know as my life grows older
My eyes have clearer sight;"
And under each wrong doing
There lies the root of right
"I know each sinful, action
As sure as night brings shade,"
Is sometime, somewhere punished
Though the hour be long delayed
"I know there are no errors
In the great eternal plan:"
For all things work together
For the final good of man
"I know as my life speeds onward
In its grand eternal quest,"
That soon we shall all look backward
And know, "God's way is best."

Helen J. Chandler

I Call To The Ends Of The Earth

I call to the ends of the earth
My heart and soul I would trade for
a moment of warmth in your arms
for just one day. I lay in a darken
place of bricks and surrounded by
metal gates as I lay down and
pray. I hope the passion of love
with unstoppable faith would bring
Back those days were I could
truthfully say I love you. In your
arms I lay with my heart and soul
already set for trade. As I lay back
In the comfort of your soft arms
and hands wrapped around my face
I set a smile before you and the
last breath I whisper to your lips how
about one last kiss. As my eyes closed
My heart stopped and my soul fled
but my love for you never left.

Ely Blu Escobar

Helpless In The Flame

Fire burning in the haze
My lungs feel the smoking blaze
With my life in my hands
I enter the fire.
Now I pray to the God of all lands
To help me put out this sparking wire
While my life flashes before my eyes,
I hear the scream of a child.
Now I see him as he tries
To escape the wild
Inferno in his room.
This little lad will never see
The day he will be a man,
Here I stand as helpless as he.
Now the baby boy takes the raft
To his new resting place, unlike me.
Here I must stay
To feel the guilt and pain
Of leaving my son
Helpless in the Flame.

Justin E. Brewer

Abandoned Voyage

Looking into the eyes of life,
My mother gently cradled my soul
Then forced upon me a voyage
To find my identity.

When I was a younger man,
I walked along the wooded edge
Searching for my identity.
It was not there.

The uncertainty grew as did I,
While escaping reality to pursue myself,
Ever watching my identity elude me.
What have I become?

Lights flickering where my eyes
Once saw the world for what it was,
Never grasping my identity.
Who was I?

Douglas Everett Lewis

Love

For my sword was drawn,
My shield was up
and my armor was new.
But oh how worse
this sickness had become.

For now
My sword is broken,
My shield is gone
and my armor is torn
My wounds drip with blood

I am down on my knees
and I admit
I love you.

Jeremy Strickland

Angel Of The Damned

Low and behold
My singular soul
Has arrived in hell for a visit.

Bitchy the sin
And judgmental the name,
How remanding and oh so exquisite.

For as they say,
"Judge not lest ye
Be judged for your wrongs one day."

But sad is the fool
That heard no complaints,
For this he will dearly pay.

Jeffrey P. Bill

Be Still!

Wind, wind, in the pines, be still!
Murmur no more today,
I cannot bear to hear
These things you seem to say.

Be still, lest I recall,
Too long, one child at play
Beneath a pine that sang
Its twilight song your way.

Oh, wind, the angel child
Has gone, beyond knowing —
Still I hear her cry, when
Winds through pines are blowing.

Helen Milburn Hodges

Naked Truth

I stand before an audience
naked with knowledge

Audience is not pleased
Hands reach out and grab

Hands grab my hair, clear
skin, clear eyes and clear body

They pull skin, pull hair
scratch eyes, scratch body

Stop! hands let go of hurting
hands now are smooth against my
tender skin, comforting me suddenly

I stand before an audience
pulled and scratched from knowledge or
is it ignorance?

I stand tall before an audience;
naked as a man
naked as a child
naked as a woman
naked truth.
Audience is pleased.

Alexandra Velez

Losing Freedom

The gentle trickle
Of a mountain stream,
Creates a solemn dream.

Bubbling and gurgling,
Swirling and slushing,
Endlessly moving;
Through a course
Meandering.

The trout know you as home,
The birds quench their thirst;

Yet,
Man in his wisdom
Fills you with dirt,
Dams you and crams you,
Calling you his
Until you must hurt!

Brady C. Harness

Neophyte

I remember my thoughts at twenty —
Narrow, shallow streams
Trickling over a rocky bed,
Occasionally going dry
When the sun was at noon —
Not pouring over
But around
The obstinate debris
To come to an abrupt end
Underground.

There forms an ocean,
The shifting depths unplumbed.
Each new tide brings increasing currents
Which churn the waves
To effervescence
To hold their peaks but a moment
Then gently break to return to
The great source —
Forming nourishing tributaries
To a hungry land.

Abby Morris

Mothers And Mother Nature

Mothers are like Mother
Nature because they care
for their children even
when their lives are full
of pain from the dark clouds
of the winter and fall rains.

Mothers are like Mother
Nature because they teach
their children to thank and
praise God above when the
summer and spring months
fill their lives with love.

Mothers are like Mother
Nature because they never,
ever leave their children
in this world alone. Mother,
Mother Nature:
They pair with their children
as the love doves.

Gwendolyn Wilen

Missing Out

She is facing the window's
network of perfect squares
armed with shovels
digging up dirt on themselves
preventing each
buzzing question from
gnawing a hole through
the first sign of spring
a gardener's glances are
piling up to eye level
with her seclusion
both imagine ideal weather
from opposite sides
of a common screen
brilliance is reheating
their senses
drying out any motivation
to hatch another black hole
preparing no one for the loss
of precious ground.

Christine Bjorkfelt Behrman

One Day's Life...

For I am
Not what I see
The way you are
Not what you want to be

For you are not
What you ought to be
The way I am, for how you see
The way you see I need to be
The way I will never be
So long as there is eternity.

Now I am eternity
The way I was meant to be
For I am and no longer will be
The way you thought I ought to be

Too many things that we both see
Are in one day's life
Like you and me

Me and you, you and me
For the way I see you
And for the way you see me...

Gregory Jones

My Brothers

My little brother Fred,
never goes to bed.
He cries and whines too much,
with all his antics and such.
He wakes me up at night,
and gives me terrible fright!
Although he is a pest,
My brother's still the best.

My older brother Harry,
his brain is kind of airy.
He makes himself look good,
like a brother should.
He always likes to party,
that makes him very tardy.

My brothers make me see,
how fun life can be.

Adam Salmen

Never Looking Back

A carousel spinning around
Never leaving her track
Bumping up the loose pieces
Never looking back
A midnight awakening, a peace of mind
Searching but never found
Destiny pushes her best effort in
But who shall see the result?
No one can escape it
A boundary is not found
Leaving the past in memory
Never looking back
An image is set before the throne
Immense power is released
The magnitude of radiance burns the soul
Let it go...it's over...the choice is made
Never look back.

Bonnie Lynn Hinchey

Crazy

My eyes are crossed
My brain is scrambled
My hair is gone
All I do is babble

There are voices in my head
They say weird stuff
I take medication
But it isn't enough

My heart is filled with goodness
I accomplish what I can
To you it may be easy
But, all I can do is clap my hands.

Andrea McCartor

"Not Doing Nothing"

Not doing this, not doing that
  Not doing nothing.
Pulling the tail of the old house cat
  but he's not doing nothing.
Sneaking a lick from a freshly iced cake
  Playing in bed with a frog or a snake
Praying "Please Lord my spinach take."
  But he's not doing nothing.
So sad when childhood disappears
  adulthood brings some lonely years.
And we forget all the fun we had.
  "Not doing nothing."

Eva L. Rodgers Becker

I Had A Dad

I had a Dad, who NEVER was bad
no matter what he did.
Sitting in his chair
he ruffled my hair
an idol for any kid.

I had a Dad, who cried and was sad
when we had aches and hurts.
But, with a laugh and smile
he'd enchant and beguile,
as happy times came in spurts.

I had a Dad, who related as a lad
and never showed his age.
Always thinking young
whence many dreams sprung,
he WAS a loving sage.

Oh! I loved my Dad!
"The BEST that God had"
who gifted me his life!
His courage and guts
Helped me over the "ruts"
on the road of living strife.

Eugene F. Schmidt

My Feelings

Everyone ignored my cries for help
No one understood the feelings I felt
In my mind I feel a great pain
A pain that can make me lose what I gain.

A sadness lurks behind the shadow
Like a child in a meadow
Happiness has a power that is great
Happiness can be the soul's mate

The one that understood is now gone
I feel as though I'm all alone
Like I'm the only one left on earth
It almost is like a curse

Amanda Barnett

Giving Up

The lights went out that winter day,
no understanding words could I say.
A growth occurring in my brain,
satan is tightening his worldly reign.

I search and search for his healing word,
till all in my mind is just a blur.
I finally relent and give into faith,
and let him know his peace I will take.

The morning is bright, my mind so clear,
his peaceful presence I feel so near.
Life or death what will come,
all I know is that I have won.

The battle is over, satan has lost
and what you ask was the cost.
It was paid in full,
by his blood on the cross.

Janis Gordon

Statue Of Liberty

She feels not the caress of the wind
Nor in prayer do her knees bend
Her bloodless lips, they do not speak
Why? thoughts of liberty we seek
Pointing upward, her torch defined
Burning compassion, for all mankind.

Judith Tucker

When Love Walks In

I found my future.
No words are spoken.
Just thoughts of him,
and to me, a small token.

For our souls in harmony,
never to part,
Longing for memories,
given to the heart.

Unseen to explore the secret,
the beauty remains the same.
We rise to our feet.
We whisper each other's name.

So let us sway to music;
love has walked in.

Debra Theresa Biela

Mountain

Glimmered diamonds fall
  not silently
Through fingers outstretched,
  taut in the sun

Reaching up and back
  to catch this moment,
And days past and passing,
  holding memory suspended.

The many colored coats
  crimson and gold
Raced headlong down the hill,
  the palest reminder of

History's ancient rites so
  solemn in their color and glory;
Holy songs of another place
  and a time long past.

The child's delight in cold
  diamonds in the air
Recalled on nights warmed
  with the patina of age.

Carolyn Kelly

Winning

Our road has been cast
Now let's make it last
For only you and I know it's winning

With our trust
We must
Help the other
Like a brother

Knowing now
Winning is our game
Let's help the other make it our fame

What a treasure
In every measure
Winning, living
Oh what pleasure

Christine A. Pineo

Death Wish

Drink of the sun.
O' dream no more
of love on some halcyon shore.
Where morning kissed
the tears away.

Glenn Craig

This Place

Once we were one,
now we are many.
Once we were frugal,
now we have plenty.
And there we are.

Once earth was robust,
a cradle for life.
Once life was tranquil,
now there is strife.
And there we are.

Once we were bound,
by a natural order.
Now we're unbridled,
We've breached every border.
And there we are.

Joseph Glenn

Gangs

P utting lives in danger
O wning trouble in this society
W illing to give up your life
E nrolling those who are bored
R ioting only for fun
F illing the U.S. with more crimes
U nbelievable to our society
L etting others give up because
  - you do.

T rouble goes on everyday
R arely gangs stay out of the way
O nly stir up trouble for others
U neasy things happen every day
B uilding - up in our society today
L iving with a troubled country
E ven when we love one another.

Christy Cain

With A Door

My soul is bruised,
My heart is broke,
My strength is used,
He took it all in one stroke

Hoping he is dead,
I need of the pain to be lost.
As a thought runs through my
  head,
To be loved there is a cost.

I paid the price,
And got the love that hurt.
I rolled the dice,
And got dropped in the dirt.

The love I asked for,
I soon shut out with a door.

Erin Crow

Self - Imprisoned

What a muddled maze,
of anticipatory, unfulfilled days.
Will we succumb to errors of the past,
unrecognized by praise?
Let us proclaim our disdain,
for the feelings we must contain.
Open your heart, your soul, your veins,
of the life giving fluids they retain.
For only in so doing will you break
that self-imposed custodial chain.

Beth J. Pauley Wagner

To Dream

Lying in my bed at night
I wonder what I'll dream about.
A handsome prince? A fairy tale?
Something that keeps the world out?

I'll make a world of my own
And share each vision first with me.
I'll dream of happy things to do
Happy things to think and be.

I'll let my mind go on and on.
No limit can be set for dreams.
No one to say "impossible"
To all my silly girlish schemes.

I close my eyes, I say a prayer
I wait for sleep to call.
The sun comes up, I rise from bed.
I did not dream....at all.

Dani Burckhardt

Transfer Of Power

How did it happen
How is it so
The subtle transfer of power
I was the last to know

'Twas an arduous trip
Joys, heartaches and woes
It came like a silent messenger
I was the last to know

Heading onward the last mile for some
He will come to meet us I know
But how come
I'll be the last to know?

Lucille L. Warren

What Love Is

Love should be clean and fresh
  Like newly fallen snow;
Love should be nurtured and fed
  So that it can grow.
Love should have feelings
  Of happiness and pain
Love should be shared
  And not kept for selfish gain.
Love between a man and woman
  Is truly meant to be;
The love that they share
  Is for the whole world to see.
Love brings happiness
  Even during the saddest times;
Love makes music
  As beautiful as a churches' chimes.
Love should be spread
  Like a farmer spreads his seeds;
Because love can solve all of the world's needs.

Mark Vincent Harvey

Shadow's Beyond

Golden Gate
Misty skies
Bring teardrops to my eyes
Pleasant memories to recall
Will not fade or will not fall
Fading away in the skies
Are my teardrops and mystery eyes.

Lou Lazzareschi

A Villanelle: Ballerina

She flows by with breaths of grace,
Leaving valleys in her wake,
A picture stained with lace.

A perfect, easeless, airy pace
She keeps, and in the music's wake
She flows by with breaths of grace.

A thought encompassed in her face
Reminds one of an icy lake:
A picture stained with lace.

Stiff and still, her skirt erase!
Its cold, unfeeling harshness take!
She flows by with breaths of grace;

In swirling steps she pleads a case—
Sad scenes for some poor lover's sake—
A picture stained with lace.

She has won, it seems, her race:
But stone will softness overtake.
She flows by with breaths of grace,
A picture stained with lace.

Lisa Brand

Simple and Common Too

Bring me the simple and
Let me hear
What they desire to say
That I might embrace
The spirit of God.
In a joyful and childlike way
I've heard the teachers
And scholars in common
And read most books well versed
Yet still my soul cries out to God
Your simple perfection
My unquenched thirst

Sherry Smith

Flowers

Flowers, flowers everywhere, come see;
Let me show you the beautiful flowers;
Oh, how beautiful are they!

Katherine M. Schaeffer

Kingdom By The Moon

In our kingdom by the moon
let us melt in
each other's arms; smile
like lovers should

Love was the first word

beneath shady canopies
of timber,
beside whispering moonlit
waters, our lips
gently entangled like

soft vines of
roses.

Golden musical winds
are playing

for you and I

as we dance
with eternal joy inside

our kingdom by the moon.

Karl Julian

Reminiscing

As I stand here at my window waiting for the storm outside to quit
I find my mind wandering back through the years a little bit.
When I was young it was so great to watch the coming of a
  summer storm
And to see it approach with gray-blue clouds of every form.
My eyes would fill with the mystery of the lightning flashing far
  off in the sky
Then I'd count the seconds 'till I'd hear the thunder rumbling
  softly by and by.
The wind would start blowing gently swirling dust and leaves around
But as the storm grew nearer the gusts were more profound.
The rain drops would strike the ground merrily without fail
And sometimes bouncing among the drops would be little balls of hail.
Once the fury was finally spent and the storm had moved on past
The clouds would open up and let the sun come out at last.
Then in the sky would be displayed the most wondrous sight of all!
A rainbow would appear from where the rain did fall.
I wish I could go back to those days of old again
And recapture the excitement of a storm as I did then.
Somehow life seems different now—when it changed I don't even know.
The fires of childhood have died down with time and their embers
  are just a glow.
Now sometimes storms of different kinds appear but I don't care
Because at their end as in my childhood days I always find a
  rainbow there.
  LaVerne M. Purkey

At The Local

He slid into the red booth facing my direction.
I glanced down quickly hoping for an introduction.

She sits there, nibbling intently on her dilly bar.
"Did she just glance up? Or am I reaching for the stars?"

Did he see me peeking as he sips his Mr. Misty?
I hope he speaks first. Or am I being too insisting?

She's almost finished I can see most of the stick.
How can I let her know? Oh, no! She took the last lick!

Is it me he's adoring or just the last of this dilly?
Goodness here he comes and I feel so silly.

He stopped at her table.
She looks up and grins. Would he be able? Then he said:
"You have chocolate on your chin."

Oh God, she thought and wiped it clear.
"I'm so stupid!" he exclaimed.
"It's okay," she replied sincere.
"Then may I inquire your name?"

She said hers. He gave his
From then on it was just those two,
the romance that began at the local D.Q.
  Sally J. Harris

Forever Free

I was so lost never to be found.
I had sinned never to be heaven bound.

I was so sure you could not love me.
But you made me see, perfect I could not be.

I did not have to earn the love you had given me.
A sinner I would always be.

Our father, you have opened
up my eyes and made me see.
Your love was always free.
Our father's love will be forever free,
Forever free for you and me.
  Sue Swain

Storm Is Gone

I broke my little boat
I grasped a small log
My half dead body reached the coast
Storm is gone, storm is gone
You won't be my island
you won't share your hand
You want to care, little sand!
Storm is gone, storm is gone
I burned my children, I call them my poems
Reason, reason is still alive
Watching my boat with angel's eyes
Storm is gone, storm is gone
Moving counterclockwise
The result is in the hand of dice
My dice show six
Steam of love, steam of love makes me mix
Storm is gone, storm is gone
Passing road twenty six
My dreams are again fixed
  Mehrdad Zarreh

Grandmother's Tears

I saw the tears in Grandmother's eyes
  I had never seen before
I had never seen my grandmother cry
  Though I knew the pain she bore

But, that day, I did understand the tears
  I never saw before
For I know that on this day, Her son
  was being sent to war,

My grandmother was a child of God
  and she prayed every day
for the safe return of her dear son
  She just believed that way!

God answered her prayers
  and her son was returned
    still a perfect boy
Again I saw my grandmother cry
  But this time tears of joy.
  Pat Canady

Being A Mom

Now being a Mom is quite a job, it's one I take most serious
I have my good days, I have my bad, at times I'm even delirious!

That very first time you hold that babe the reward is in your arms
You feel so proud, so special too, you recognize their many charms.

The trying times of cutting teeth will seem so never ending
Little do the books tell you your trials are just beginning.

The sleepless nights the diaper changes occur more than you can guess
You think you can't survive, till you learn this isn't yet stress!

Soon it's off to school they go, tears will stream down your face
You wonder how you coped before, how did you keep this pace?

That day they leave from elementary to head to junior high
You tell yourself their growing up, and you heave a little sigh.

It's during these years you ask yourself what happened to my baby
Will we make it through these times, I can't say for sure but maybe.

Alas they're now in senior high then marching through the college door
It's at this age they think of you as nothing but a bore!

The day that you've been striving for, they're finally on their own
All their problems are over 'til the next time they're on the phone.
  Sandra J. Henry

Nothing

I have nothing to write
I have nothing to say
I am still reasoning why
I am still searching for the way
People walk around with their
heads in the sky.
I look around and reason why?
Why are we here? Why does it matter?
In many years, after many tears
the human race will still be full of fears
of the unknown, the known, but
basically themselves
the wars will continue, the fighting won't stop
people will kill as the farmer reaps the crop
there is no rhyme, there is no reason
then the cycle will begin a new
the fire won't go out, it fuels off our hate
look at man, so civilized in their primal state
judging each other, no regard for humanity
If I reason anymore I'll lose my sanity.
   Sebastian Natera

No One Cares

As I have lived in this country for many years,
I have seen many Americans shed many tears,
People are dying and the streets need repairs,
But in reality, no one cares.

Crime and corruption are ruling our streets,
And politicians' only answer is a speech,
Go to the crime areas, they wouldn't dare,
Because in reality, they don't care.

Practice safe sex was the talk of the town,
As we saw Magic Johnson's career go down,
AIDS was the diagnosis and it seemed unfair,
But after two weeks, no one cared.

More and more people end up in jail,
No chance of reform as they are denied bail,
They go to court and in the judges' eyes they stare,
Judges' state "life without parole" because they do not care.

Children are the future as we claim,
But it is tough being positive with a life full of shame,
Kids killing kids is a thought hard to bear,
Because in reality, I care!
   Tim Slade

To My Love

   You don't understand how truly loved you are;
I haven't felt like this for anyone else before.
   When I wake up and see you lying next to me,
I have to thank the Lord above for bringing you to me.
   As the years go by, and when all is said and done,
I hope that in the end I will have been your one true love.
   When they lay me to my rest, the sky will be so blue,
for in the end I will always have loved no other soul but you.
   Yvonne Stokes

Untitled

As we part and go our separate ways
I remember all the help and kindness
You have shown throughout the years
You were always there when I needed you
With a shoulder to cry on and a hand to comfort
I thank you for your love
   C. L. J. Wicker

On A Monday Night

On a Monday night I was all alone
I heard a ring and he was on the phone
Our love used to be so very strong
That nothing was ever going to go wrong
We got off the phone and I thought more and more
Then all of a sudden I heard a knock on the door
We began to talk and our love drew stronger
Then he kept saying he could wait no longer
He got on his knees, and began to sing
Then he took out of his pocket a diamond ring
He slid it on my finger so that I could see
Then he begin to say "Will You Marry Me"
   Monica Thompson

Thoughts From Grandma

I tiptoe to your crib and marvel at your beautiful face and then,
I inhale the smells of your room and dream of another time and place.
You have captured my heart with your beautiful and easy smiles and,
I am taking that image with me across many many miles.
I watch your mommy always playing and singing with you and,
I think "shouldn't that be me instead trying to make you coo?"
It seems like only yesterday she was looking into my eyes
while nursing on her bottle and,
it seems like only yesterday when she took my outstretched
hands to first learn how to toddle.
But time has flown and now my child has become a mother and so,
The time has come for me to be called "Grandmother."
I dream of the day when I hear you call "Grandma, please
come, I miss you so!"
The miles will not hold me back because Grandma loves you so.
   Patricia Dene

Mother...

What a pleasure to have a mother...
I just came to the earth, is cold;
Few minutes later somebody,
Will warm and feed me with her body and her soul,
I will look at her eyes.
She will look at my eyes.
At the beginning so elementary
At the end so essentially
"Eye to Eye Contact"
Beginning of Love, beginning of concentration,
Beginning of thrusting and appreciation
As well as rewarding at the end of the journey...
Then, what will be the key?
To maintain the bondage, that at times;
could not be seen or palpated...
What takes the success?
Math, Chemistry, Material things and commodity
College tuition, competition or just
"Eye to eye contact"
Mother.....will give the answer.
   Natividad Nazario

"Metamorphosis"

Falling off the brink of yesterday,
Leaning on the surface of tomorrow,
I have thoughts of each new day
believing there will be more happiness than sorrow.
There must be reasons for the Almighty's plans,
He says "Do not forget the past," but
Put the future in his hands.
And so as time heals my heart so slowly each mile,
I shall emerge from my cocoon each day,
not with a frown, but with a smile.
   Theresa Hubbard

A Boy And A Man

Am I a boy, am I a man
I just don't know, don't understand
When is the time we take the staff
Point our feet down life's tortuous path
To be a boy, that seemed a breeze
Now I'm a man and not at ease
What are the rules, the path to follow
Too many ways, in my angst I wallow
My friends and loved ones try to guide
Still, I don't know the way, so I hide
Put on my false face, show the world my mask
Communication, spoken word, is that the best?
Can we be sure, how better to express
I will carry on, still no simple plan
Do what I'm able, be a boy and a man

Timothy E. Larson

Cathy's Pain

She called me at midnight. I knew what it was of.
I knew how she was aching. I knew he called it love.

She told me he hurt her. The walls were closing in.
I recognized those painful eyes. I used to be with him.

Why do we remember pain for so long?
Can the heart of hurt learn to be strong?

Why does anger hang around?
and where's the peace I thought I found?

Where's the peace I thought I found?

I went and I listened as tears began to flow.
I tried to find if they were hers or mine, but which, I didn't know.

He told her he loved her. But time was running thin.
I felt the same familiar pain I used to feel with him.

Why do we remember pain for so long?
Can the heart of hurt learn to be strong?

Why does anger hang around?
And where's the peace I thought I found?

Where's the peace I thought I found?

Where's the peace?

Lauren Lane Powell

Sunshine And The Rain

When I see the raindrops, fall from the sky,
   I knew it was teardrop's from Jesus's eyes.
And when the sky went from light to dark
   I knew the world had broken Jesus' heart.
That's when the rain, it did start.

All the stars left the sky, then the dark clouds came rolling by,
I looked up with a heart so sad, I said to myself
   Why is the world so bad?
And then the sky lit up with a light,
   I knew Jesus was there with me in sight.

When the thunder it did roar, Jesus's voice I did hear
   He was saying to his children "Do not fear.
I am your savior, and I'm here, trust in
   me and I'll always be near."

And when the wind came speeding by, Jesus
   said unto me, "Oh do not sigh, I do not forsake
You, it is you who forsakes I."
   Then I looked up, the sun was shining bright
I knew, Jesus was holding me tight,
   Jesus loves me, this I know, when he died he told me so.

Reba LaSure

In Memory Of Ruby

Heaven must be beautiful,
I know because you're there
The love we shared is everywhere
In all we say and care
We know that you are happy now
In your new home above
That you are now in God's good hands
And that you share His love
I know some day that I'll join you
There in that great home above
And that I too will have a chance to share
His Everlasting Love.

Ralph Warren Martinez

Love

When the sky shines,
I know love is on your mind.
Everything is good and strong,
Because insides of you had nothing wrong.

You laugh and share,
All those moments you remember that you care.
Love can be found in many different ways,
And that's something never goes away.

I love my family and friends,
But not the same as I will love my boyfriend.
When you first look into each other,
What do you feel for one another?

Love can hurt sometimes,
But life passes by.
Something will go away,
But love always stays.

Love is around us,
In heaven and earth.
Love can be found in anyone's heart,
You just have to know in what part.

Sarah Huang and Carolina Kishimoto

Ode To You

If I will my thoughts to you, will you feel them?
If I will my strength to you, will it heal you?

If I tell you I won't leave, will you believe me?
If I call you unexpectedly, will your heart take heed?

If my intentions and heart are pure, who will be the judge?
Only you...only me, and God, high above.

I imagined I heard you outside my door; your voice fading, inchingly.
I didn't have time to say "goodbye;" you fled almost instantly.

Now I sit here pondering, attempting to find solace in words.
Yet, my heart continues to murmur, "I love you, dear friend."

If I close my lids and cup my hands over my eyes.
Your face appears, striking radiance encompassing me.

Sucking, wet sands encase my feet; waves lap, licking softly.
Surging from the ocean bed, a man's history ebbs ahead.

Destiny brought you to me; the milk of friendship filled your needs.
Refills bring you back intermittently; energy surges to you from me.

Gray mist of my nighttime dreams, three years prior sought my steed.
Waking exhausted, I've done my best, burying the memory
   in heady dust.

Questioning the purpose I now play; you continue to take my
   breath away.
Perhaps that's the reason we are bound, to give the breath of life to
   each other before we drown.

Ruth Dreher

Starve For Pleasure

I like the agony, the thought of you that comes in my mind
I like the pain that tortures me
When I'm hollowed out from my insides
Decide when I want to fill myself with unnecessary needs
I like the growling anger that calls from within
The pain that virtually rips from under my skin
My innards revoke my sources of life
So I throw forth my needs
Enjoy my disgusting pain that tortures me
But it's a pleasure that I love
It's a pain that I love
It's a nothing that I love
My insides shrink with disgust; I laugh and burn
My stomach is about to burst with decay
Rotting entrails fill my bowels
I feel o.k.
I unearth my insides every single day...

Misty Pang

"Is It You?"

I was told you would come to me
I listened, and yet, I didn't believe in my own destiny
When I first saw you at the river's edge... by that old gnarled tree
I still doubted. "Is it You?" I asked. "Is it?"

In that instant, something happened to me
Time had no meaning; my life had forever changed
As the days passed, all traces of doubt were erased
Your precious love and gentle embrace...
I have never known such sweetness

If only the future had been mine to see
Our time together hopelessly brief... every moment was to be savored
A glimpse from your past took you from me and I was left alone in
my world "Come back to me!" I cried.

And, now, there is merely a golden pocket watch to prove you were here
Our love was timeless; it reached beyond the limits of mortal existence
All I cherished had vanished
I knew I must find you... Somewhere in Time.

I know now, as I knew then, the answer to my question
It was you... it had always been you
Only in eternity were we to be reunited; and,
In our destiny there was no longer any need to ask... "Is it you?"

Linda Guyan

My Secret

You are on my mind and in my heart,
I long for you when we're apart.

This love of mine cannot be told;
It's you, my love, I yearn to hold.

Your lips I need to feel on mine,
Your touch I need for all of time.

I dream of you when night is here;
Daytime, too, I dream you're near.

I have you only in my dreams.
I'm dreaming my life away, it seems.

Maybe one day, oh when? Oh where?
I'll awake and find you there.

I'll have you for time untold,
You'll be mine to have and hold.

My life at last will be worth living;
Our love will last, each sharing and giving.

But until that day, I continue to weep;
My love is a secret that I must keep.

B. Jeffery

Message From The Sea

Walking upon a sandy beach, one bright and sunny day,
I looked down and there I found, a bottle floating my way.
I looked inside and to my surprise, was a letter from the sea.
It was addressed to everyone, everyone, including me.
The note said "Won't you please, please help me?
Humans are killing the life inside me.
My coral's been stripped, my water is cloudy.
The life inside me is crying out so loudly,
Please, take your papers, glasses and gunk.
Throw them in trash cans, or even the dump.
Fish cannot breathe, nor turtles swim.
The plants have been ripped limb by limb.
The sun is so cheerful, warm and bright.
Please, keep me clean, so we can see the light.
Then I'll be here for years and years,
Animals, fish and plants,
For you and yours to really enjoy,
Generations of girls and boys."

Mary L. McCord

The Grandeur Of Our Land

I love the snowcapped mountains and the jeweled sapphire sea;
I love the miles of sweeping plains and what they mean to me.
I enjoy the emerald splendor of the rugged mountain ranges
But I ponder still the mystery that brings each season's changes.

I hold dear the mountain streams and the lonely babbling brook;
I observe with keen intrigue each rugged course they took.
I adore the Blue Pacific with its miles of sandy beaches,
Still I wonder with amazement at just how far it reaches.

I give ear to pounding surf with its constant, frightful roar,
But sense a lonely, moanful cry deep within its stormy core.
I gaze with awe at majestic sea while charting each testy wave;
I watch with focused scrutiny to see how each behave.

The enticement of the sea draws me often to its shore,
Tho' I drink its generous gifts, I'm left... always... wanting more.
The glitter of our harbors where the sea caresses sand
Portray with enchanting grace the grandeur of our land.

Oh, the beauty of her splendor as the waves at shore unfold,
Its power is ever present but its secret left untold.
Survey the magnitude of America as Old Glory proudly waves
Displaying still her graceful stature for all the world to gaze.

Ruth C. Demetral

"You Will Always Be"

Listen to me, I love thee is all I can say,
I love you more and more each and every day,
My heartstrings pull whenever you go away,
I just wish that you could remain and stay
Even if it's just for the day.

Who could have known that this would happen to us
I think this is love and not just lust.
You know that I wear my heart on my sleeve
And I hope that you will never deceive.
Because in you I put my trust.

It just seems to be untrue to me
That I could be in love with you too.
I thought I was smart, but this is tearing me apart.
I don't know how much it can take my heart.
I just hope I'm not played for a fool.

You see my dear, what I fear, is some day we'll part
We're in a fix and I feel all mixed up.
But in my heart you will always be a part.
This is something that you can't stop when it starts.
You will always be in my heart.

Teresa Jachimowicz

Remember Me?

My name is Gossip. I have no respect for justice.
I maim without killing and I break hearts and
ruin lives. I am cunning and malicious and
gather strength with age. The more I am quoted, the
more I am believed. I flourish at every level of society.
My victims are helpless, they cannot protect themselves.
I have no name and I have no face.
To track me down is impossible. The harder you try,
the more elusive I become. I am nobody's friend.
Once I tarnish a reputation it's never quite the same.
I topple governments and wreak havoc on marriages.
I cause heartache and sleepless nights.
I spawn suspicion and generate grief.
I make innocent people cry in their pillows.
Even my name hisses. I am called Gossip.
I make headlines and headaches.
Before you repeat a story, ask yourself,
Is it true? Is it fair? Is it necessary?
If not, keep it to yourself.

Kristine Escoto

Teach Me

Teach me now, oh mighty Lord, show me how
I may live my life for You, what to do
Using gifts You've given me, help me to see
What is real, what is clay, and how to pray.

Lead me on, oh precious Lord, You alone
Are my Guide, my trusted Friend, You transcend
All else. The destiny You have for me
Lies ahead. Help me find the road assigned.

Grant me faith, oh gracious Lord, to believe
What comes my way is for best, You have blessed
My life. No evil, no dire duress
That besets breaks that bond. You see beyond

My weakness. Oh loving Lord, the bleakness
Has been lifted. I know now that somehow
There's something I must do, must give to You.
Let me serve, Oh Holy One. Thy Will be done.

D. G. Cox

Star

The day I was born, the Lord had seen,
It would take place three days before Halloween.

An only child to my mama and papa,
Four years later out came Joshua.

I don't know what it was, it must have been fate,
Over a year had passed, and there was Nate.

Some people thought, "Three children for heaven's sake!"
But that wasn't enough for us, so we had Jake.

And now our family is complete,
Raising four children is quite a feat.

But now I am eighteen, sweet and sincere,
Soon I must leave my family, so dear.

I feel I am in my greatest time of need,
Realizing I am no longer a nurtured seed.

As I start to head my way out the door,
I realize I want to stay with my family more.

I want to succeed, I want to be strong,
When I walk out the door, will you come along?

No matter where I go, near or far,
My family has already made me a star.

Monica Barber

A Dimension Unknown

Steadfast I move through time and space into a dimension yet unknown
I move into another world—into the infinity of time, the boundless
of space - I've passed into a dimension unknown.

I'm caught up in the winds that blow - a sparkling ray of sun
the twinkle in a distant star, I'm a part of the moon's beam...
the gentle breeze that blows.

I'm not here—I'm there, there in the rustle of the trees, the cry of
a new baby born,
a melody that's sung... the rush of a flowing stream,
the echo of a sound that passed.

I'm not here — I'm there,
there in the morning mist, a storm cloud that grows
the crispness of a sudden rain, a flake of fallen snow
the fragrance of fresh bouquets... I'm all of these — and more.

I am not here — I've gone
into a dimension to you unknown,
an infinitesimal part I might have been
but oh what a part I was!

I am infinity now — it awaits us all.

Lloyd L. Royston

"The Fix"

I need a piece of pizza!
... I need a life!
I'm 49 years old today.
What does this say?
... Aahhhhhhh!
I need a piece of pizza!
Ummmmmmm.
...But pizza doesn't last.
And the past is still past.
It hasn't a NOW.
W-O-W!
I need a piece of pizza...
Like I need a cow!
It's a fix
And full of tricks,
But for a little bit... I'm O.K. it's O.K.
Gimme, gimme, gimme some!
I need a piece of pizza!
Yum!!!

Mary Smith

My Name Is Katie

I love to play soccer, and baseball.
I like pizza.
I love Jesus.
Jesus loves me.
I like to learn more in school.
I love Sunday School.
I love to draw.
I have two brothers, one named Parker
And one named Zack-attack. I love them a lot. (And they love me)
My Mom and Dad love me very much, and I love them.
I am a very loved person.
I have a special friend named Nick, and another named Emily.
I am a brownie girl scout at St. John's School.
I love Mrs. Hoyt, she is my 1st grade teacher.
I love my Grandma, and my Nana and Papa.
I love to swim. I have a lot of friends.
They are all nice.
I have a Godfather who lives in the state of Washington.
His name is Dan Woolsey.
He loves me. And I love him.

Kathleen Elizabeth Crehan

Smith

I am no longer afraid of burning in hell.
I no longer pray for my soul to be saved.
I no longer believe in death.
I no longer believe in life.
I no longer believe.
I simply accept my role as sinner and witness
to another existence, devoid of conscious compassion
or organized religion.
We are alone in our actions and reactions.
We are not defined by God or government.
We are free and some of us will kill the innocent,
while others will put them to death and become killers.
There is no after-life.
Hell is the creation of man.
And the first rape, which was of Eve, makes Adam
our savior and corrupter.

Robert E. Hurley

untitled

everyone has hopes and dreams and fears
i only have fears and my lonely tears
i cry from time to time
and walk on the graves
of those who have not yet died
please just leave me alone
to cry on the shoulder of an angel
that i seem to know
i borrow her wings and visit the heavens
fall to the cold ground beneath
i call for help when no one comes
lay there until i hear the drums
down swoops the dove from above
killing the man with the drums
i lie there beneath his shadow
as it picks at my scars as i bleed to death

Kelly Clark

An Old Friend

My journal's cover is yellowed with age.
I open it tenderly and turn the page.
It knows all about me — my laughter and tears.
After all, it's been with me for so many years.
All of my secrets are locked up inside.
Especially the ones that I wanted to hide.
I read my journal for a while,
then close it up, hug it, and give it a smile.
It's nice to know that I have a friend.
One that's been with me from beginning to end.
So as I leave my journal on the shelf,
I know that I'm leaving a part of myself.

Sonja Skrovanek

My Twinkling Star

I counted your fingers, I counted your toes
I kissed your soft lips and your round button nose,
I looked down in my arms thinking this can't be true
My baby in pink and my baby in blue.
Through so many years of sorrow and grief
My feelings for God became disbelief,
My adopted son came from God up above
Now my beautiful twins conceived through our love.
And now as I kiss my family good-night
From out of the window is a very bright light,
That shiny bright light that I see from afar
Is my baby I lost, she's my twinkling star.
I now understand you must give to receive
I gave him my first born and he gave me my three,
As I crawl into bed and I turn out the light
Her star shines above; she's our little night light.

Shelly Ramirez

Now Look What I've Done!

Hey world, now look what I've done:
I quit my job and I'm on the run.
I left my home, friends and familiar life
I have even quit my role as wife.
As the dotted black ribbon continues to unwind
Conflicting thoughts flit through my mind.
Have I really really done the right thing?
Have my heart and soul began to take wing?
The boys, Hank and Lanny, have done their best
To cheer me up while driving west.
Their youthful humor could be a pain.
A normal person would have gone insane.
But then, who's normal at fifty three
To pull up stakes and wander free?
So many things for me to decide.
And by that special word, time, I'll now abide.
Each day, each step I'll carefully take.
All the mistakes will be mine to make.
I'll test my wings and fly away free.
I'm slowly learning what it's like to be me.

C. Martine Maetzold

"Mother's Eyes"

As I look in my daughter's eyes,
I realize the same kindness that embraced me as a child,
Will repeat itself, I smile inside.
Because I know her innocence, I've seen that look before,
As a child.
My daughter is innocence, pure, happy, knowing no other
feelings than joy,
Her strength, spirit, and kindness are all things,
That I have seen before,
In my mother's eyes.

Timothy Hernandez

I Am A Lover Of Life

I am an active participant of dreams not yet realized or accomplished.
I receive great pleasure from watching my fellow man doing what gives him the ultimate High,

Even though he might not even know it...the gardener, organizer, the dedicated humble teacher/educator, lecturer, the janitor, the grocer and modest helpful soul

They produce, render, bestow knowledge, present, contribute, deliver, relinquish...services to others as needed

Because something within induces them to.

They have a reason for living and sharing it with others.

They are lovers of life as I am.

Michele Grimes

Dreamer

Wanting to get away from the dirt and the grime
I relax and I ponder, I begin to unwind.

My mind starts to wander to the land of the dreamer
A place where the land and air seem much cleaner.

Traveling the land where love and peace are the times
Harmony among men gives off sounds of the chimes.

Sharing and giving among sisters and brothers
Giving love and respect to all fathers and mothers.

Where understanding and compassion are as precious as air
Loving the land, not living in fear.

Cause in the land of the dreamers there's no cause for tears
As I pray to my God, please take away my fears,
I enter the times of reality, and much better years.

Lynn Marie Lekhlifi

So Far Past

'Twas a day far past that I saw your face
I remember it well such a puzzled look
You were so young yet so mature
For a young lad of ten to have experienced so much.

It was war time we were in and it seems too much
That we were just children to be interested
Yet what we saw and we heard was
To unspeakable so we must not believe
What we saw so far past.

Now years have been good and bad since those
Days and we have gone on separate paths
You chose good and I the one of turmoil
Yet we cross once again on this planet called games.

We have been through quite a lot these past decades
And yet you do look serene for such times
I have seen you better and I such a loss
You still remain my friend as I never forgot
that my strength comes from so far past.

Marcella K. Leaton

The Venetian Lagoon

Like the city of Venice,
I remove the striped poles of my lagoon
When strange ships come near.
Appearing completely open, unprotected,
Vessels run aground
In my shallow bays
With no markers for the single, narrow channel.

I have allowed you into the trough
And you have stayed in the deep waters.
By firmly holding your hand to the tiller
You have sailed
Into the ancient kingdom
Where nobles, merchants, artists, and frisky nuns
Mingle,
Wearing masks even in the daylight
So no one knows
Of their ardent trysts.

Rebecca Curtis

"Emotional Hang-Over"

A bowl of wilted flowers -
I sat and gazed upon for hours -
and dwelled upon there fallen crest -
Dangling faded, as a worn-out dress.
Once their beauty glowed and shown -
Now tired and ugly, about to be thrown -
Will lie upon the ashes heap -
So incredibly useless, it makes me weep.
A sadder, more sympathetic sight, I'll never see -
The feeling of comparison, between them and me.

Norma J. Haines

The River

I stand at the river as the cool breeze blows.
I see a smooth crystal blanket as it flows.

I touched the satin sheet to cool my hands,
Amazed at the journey it takes to carve
a path in the land.

Where does this glass come from? where does it goes?
As I kneel to see a reflection I realize;
God put this river here as a mirror for my soul.

At night our body must rest our souls never sleep.
So like-wise the river stands still to run deep.

Teresa A. West-Fields

Stool Pigeon

As I was walking through the school,
I saw a pigeon on a stool.
It flapped its wings and flew away,
I began to chase it, it lasted all day.
   Yes it did, yes it did, yes it did.
I chased it through the water and woods,
Until I came to men wearing hoods.
I asked them about where I was,
And they said I was in the town of Buzz.
   Yes they did, yes they did, yes they did.
I walked around for many an hour,
Until I knew I needed a shower,
After I was clean and not very dirty,
I went around to look for that birdie.
   Yes I did, yes I did, yes I did
I found some money on the ground,
And then I ran away from a hound.
I decided to go back to school,
And who was there? That pigeon on a stool.
   Yes it was, yes it was, yes it was.

Noah Kory Hardin

Beauty

As I looked up in the sky
I saw the world's beauty slowly go by
The sun was passing through a cloud
I though what beauty and I felt proud.

I felt the presence of God so near
I had no aches I had no fear
I looked upon the earth so green
I thanked God for the beautiful scene.

The trees in the woods stood tall and so still
Yet on my bare arms, a wind I could feel
Beauty to me is what God gave us
To love and to cherish without no fuss.

Beauty is not a diamond crown or a gorgeous face
But something God created as a heavenly place
A field of flowers, a clear blue sky
That something to think about as time goes by.

Kay Kelly

The Cellar Door

As I sit against the cellar door, that once I never knew,
I think of my family, I am scared.
I am worried, I am afraid of death.

As I sit against the cellar door, I am starving and weak.
I see another woman, grabbed by soldiers, taken away.
I know it is her time to die, and I know my time will come soon.

As I sit against the cellar door, I see children,
horrified and bloody.
I am sad. I pray for them.

As I sit against the cellar door, I try to be brave,
but I know I can't.
I close my eyes and remember when I could be brave,
so many years ago.
I think, I am too young to die. I shouldn't be here.

As I sit against the cellar door the Nazis grab my arm and drag me away.
It is my time. I see my life pass me by in an instant.
I think of so many things, I can't concentrate.

I begin to cry, but I am not scared.
I cry because I think, anything is better than staying here.
At least, when I die, I won't see any Nazis in heaven.
When I die, I can be happy again.

Natalie Karmo

Nightmare

Falling through the dark bleak world of deception
I scream but no one hears me
My voice is absorbed by walls of lies
Every lie from my past haunts me
As I sink into the inferno
I wish to take it all back
Start all over but, I can't
I see demons and they're laughing
Laughing at me and the torture I'm going through
Please God help me
I don't want to die
I see a bright light
It calls me from far away
I open my eyes to see it was all a nightmare?
Yet it was frighteningly real.
Keith D. Estes

Look Into The Future

As I look into the future,
I see a gruesome sight.
A planet of neglect and waste,
that mother earth's too weak to fight.

Not only is there pollution,
but other problems, too.
Such as gangs, violence, and drugs,
just to name a few.

I wish my vision could be different,
a world of knowledge, perfection, and fresh starts.
Where there isn't racism or ignorance,
just intelligent people with big hearts.

There is one small hope for the future,
to look into the present and recognize our past mistakes.
Help by educating and caring for others,
can ease the damage others make.
Mandy Gohman

Lost

Am I lost, or just lonely?
Like there was a cost, that I paid solely.
In this prison that I have made.
Is there a hole, is there a cave?
Some way out, some way clear
Of all these thoughts, of all this fear?
This is just a faze, some would say.
Some sort of haze, blocking my way.
As if I'm too immature to know what I say.
But this is real, it's happening to me.
This is the way I feel, can't you see?
I am lost, not just lonely.

Release me,
From these bonds I've made.
Release me,
Or just make it fade.
Dylana Radke

My Family And Me

I thought I was what they could see.
I tried to be anything they'd want of me.
I'd look in the mirror and what would be,
Someone else - but no not me!

I look in the mirror and what do I see?
I see the one they want me to be.
Oh when will I look in the mirror and see,
The me that I want me to be?
Lorraine Holzer

I See

As I walk through the path of life,
I see all the obstacles you
face, as a parent, husband, and wife.

I see the world changing so very fast,
some of us have no morals,
putting our children last.

We never want to stop and take any time,
when our family values are on the decline.

I see life as a challenge of making the right choice.
But just open your heart
and listen to your inner voice.

I see what is happening to mankind,
So let's stick together
and keep this in mind...

There is a lot of love out there.
Just stop... and take time
and say a little prayer.
Sylvia A. Pengelly

I Can Still See You...

I'm the star that twinkles in the sky.
I see and hear everything you say and do.
Now we are no longer together,-
and I miss you and you miss me.
I can hear you, but you can't hear me...
I can hear your wishes for happiness ahead,
and your wishes for forgiveness.
I can see you...and you see me,
as a shiny star above you.
You're sad I'm gone...
but I'm in a small land where I'm safe.
I am happy and I don't suffer anymore.
But I still wish I were with you!
Kristine Lynn Flandreau

Be A Teacher

As I look into the eyes of the children staring back at me,
I see each one's individuality:
The happiness, the sorrows, the befriended, the lonely, the eager,
   the apathetic.
For channeling, challenging the energies and abilities
   in his, her own special way
Is rewarding and fulfilling every day.
Amassed within these bodies are treasures they store,
Awaiting the teacher to arouse and implore.
Dormant many memory banks lie,
Longing for knowledge for life to apply.
A golden chance,
A mind to enhance-
be a teacher.

Help form the mind
To be one of a kind
And create a tie that forever will bind—
Be a teacher.
Ron Fogle

Friends

You are my inspiration throughout the night and in my days, in the things you say and ways you do. My strength comes from the constant thoughts that you have given me to think about. No one has or ever will be the kind of friend I have found in you. In ways that even I may not know, I hope that I also have been the same to you. It is very rare to find that kind of friendship with a person, and know they will always be there when needed.
Friends
forever and always.
Maxine Talley

"My Dad Is Free At Last"

I see him in nature soaring as a bird
I see him in the trees swaying freely in the wind
I see him in the wild flowers in the field,

I hear him in the whisper of the wind
I hear him in the laughter of the raindrops.
I hear him in the lonesome sound of a train.

I feel him in tears of joy for a life that he loved.
I feel him in tears of sadness for this life he had to leave.

At long last - I see him, hear him,
and feel him in another realm.
At long last - no sadness, no tears, only peace.
My Dad is free at last!
   Nel Selfridge

Who Am I, If Not Me

I breathe - therefore I must be...am I?
I see - therefore I must be...am I?
I think - therefore I must be...am I?
I touch - therefore I must be...am I?
I feel - therefore I must be...am I?
I hurt - therefore I must be...am I?
   Why am I?
   Who am I?
Am I the creation of a Mother and Father,
Or, of some Higher Power?
Am I not told to be Me?
Who is Me? Molded by parents and society to be
   anything but Me.

   I AM? ME OR AM I? ME
   Marie Spaulding

Muttonchops

Frankly don't look like the food at all.
I should know. I had them growing on my face.
Although my friends told me "cut 'em off,"
I didn't listen, 'cause, well, I liked 'em.
At a time when most felt caught
between big kid and young adult,
I had my muttonchops to keep me from slipping
into the vast mass who suffered from plain faces.
I thought that they suited me very well.
They were very long, and fairly thin.
The short stubbly hair sloped itself towards my jaw line,
darting out three inches or so, towards my
chin, which was then bare. I kept them well trimmed.
I had to, 'cause if I didn't, the whole point would be ruined.
What good is a security blanket if it doesn't make you secure?
And furthermore, what good is a security blanket at all?
It allows you to hide from your fears. Rather than
facing up to my own insecurities and doing something constructive,
I tried to cover them up with hair. Long since now, I've lost the 'chops.
I'm older now, so I have a little goatee.
   Michael Wade Silberstein

The World

Maybe this world wouldn't be so bad.
If people didn't always look so sad,
Some people have it all.
Others just want to go to the mall
People in this world are so cheap.
They won't even give the homeless a sheet
Maybe if there wasn't so much crime
People could afford to give the homeless a dime.
Nobody knows how bad it really is out there
But does anybody really care?
   Rebecca Domis

Down By The Stream

From the bank,
I sit and stare
At the frogs and ducks and all the hares.
I watch the water running slow
And see the fish swimming below.
In the view, I see the sun's glare
Brightly shining, as its rays seemed to flare.
From the bank,
I sit and think
About how much joy the stream brings.
   Valen Alane Burke

Untitled

In the wee hours when everyone else is sleeping,
I sit here in the rocking chair and enjoy this quite time with you.
As I rock at a slow pace my heart is racing with excitement.
I feel your little body moving inside me and my heart feels the
excitement of the day that is soon to come.
I sit here wondering if you will have my eyes,
your Daddy's smile or maybe even your grandma's hands.
As I sit here wondering all these things about you,
I know no matter what color hair you have or how much you weigh,
you will be the most beautiful baby in the world to me.
God has blessed me and your Daddy with you.
Now go to sleep my baby, we need our rest for the days ahead.
   Rhonda Smith

Very First Date

I spoke of my heart, maybe not all too late
I spoke of my heart on our very first date
Shivering cold was I in a lonely dark dream
But I didn't mind uneasiness ebbed with time
Conferring utterance about my consumed whims
It was hard to conceal
I thought all was said, but maybe not enough
Dwelling only on the joy that embodied me
Starry eyes..., I could only see the twinkle, the gleam
If I should enhance a smile then I'll know the time shared
Was all worthwhile when time had passed
Much too fast, in a lonely dark dream
Lull I became as eventide deferred my delight
I spoke of my heart but there was so much more
As my dream was ending with every trice
The rhythm of my heart became prominent
I gave into the tranquil eve..., I could not wake
As we prattled with each other I could have touched the stars
Just hoping that all wasn't too late
When I spoke of my heart on our very first date
   Mary Esther Farrell

That Was Then

I don't hold any grudges dear;
I still want you for my friend.
Life goes on you know, time is short.
This is now, and honey, that was then.

We all from time to time I'm quite sure,
Utter hurting words that we don't really mean.
But as we grow and learn about ourselves,
We know others aren't as bad as they had seemed.

You see, my dear, we can't afford to linger,
On past pains and hurts and things that we regret.
The life we've yet to live is still before us,
A destiny demanding it be met.

Let's give each other a great forgiving hug,
And allow our wounds a little time to mend.
The mistakes we made no longer will we dwell,
For this is now, and honey, that was then.
   Saundra L. Washington-Peeples

His Love

In reverent meditation, in hushed repose and fear,
I talk to One Who Knows my inner guilt,
My faltering failings in earth's stormy sphere,
And my desire to have my life rebuilt.
I rely upon His given pledge, His word;
To ask is to receive; to seek, one surely finds;
And though He be a justifying Judge, a Lord,
He is as well a loving Sire, Who binds
The wearied heart and gives it rest.

His Son, Who walked this way for mankind's sake,
Endured, perceived more mental anguish and more woe
Than ever I could suffer or could take.
Thus, he can sense and see my plight, the path I go,
And love me nonetheless - indeed, will love me more.
For tenderly, He looks upon the prodigal, beaten, tossed,
And will prepare the "fatted calf," all former joys restore.
He cares intensely for the sheep that's lost
And holds it to His sacred breast.

Susie M. Jenkins

Untitled

When we kissed that day,
I thought our love
was going to be an everlasting one.
I couldn't help it
and went crazy about you.

When we kissed that day,
I thought our love
was etched in stone.
I could swear that we were
created for each other.

When we kissed that day,
I heard the greatest symphony ever written.
Like an omen from heaven
I thought the magic
was going to last forever.

Now that I see you sometimes
glancing at me with indifference,
taking our love for granted.
The magic is gone
and MY DREAM runs down.

Ronald Fils-Aime

"Blue"

You had to seek the sea.
I should've known by its reflection in your eyes.
Your blue gaze splashing me.

But, I'm losing you in the sea.
You sail into the mist-evaporate-your soul soaring
Until blue is all that's left me.

Deep blue sea.
Wide blue sky.
Wise blue eyes.
For a time I can see them shine!
Then blue merges with blue-horizon lost.
I cannot follow past that line.

The sea seethes with our tears.
While you are bathed by blue
I am consumed by it,
And submerged beneath my fears.

The wind is our pulse now.
It blows kisses and whispers confidences.
It is the only thing we share over such a chasm of blue,
While I wait endlessly for you.

K. Leigh Leonard

Betrayal

Times spent together were better than ever,
I try to forget but all I do is remember.
I can't fight the feeling, it's too strong to hide,
just being with you made me feel so alive.
I will never regret all the memories made,
but I know that someday they'll all start to fade.
it's hard to describe all the feelings inside,
my mind started working, my heart just died.
You can never imagine, the hurt and the pain,
the tears I have cried, almost made me insane.

I cannot explain why I feel this way,
but I know in my heart you will too someday.
I thought I knew you from loving so long,
but what you have done proved me entirely wrong.
You told me you loved me, I believed it was true,
but now I see, you care only about you.
I would have given up my dreams and my life,
to one day in the future become your wife.

Rebuild my dreams, I have started to do,
but never forget how much I love you!!!

Marcia Santos

Silent Screams

Tears roll down my face so smooth.
I try to run but my feet won't move,
almost as if it were a dream.
I close my eyes and my heart starts to scream.

No one hears my cries,
and inside, part of me dies.
My throat vibrates with what seems to be
a single silent scream.

I'm all by myself in a roomful of people.
Looking at life from behind a door, through a peep-hole.
Never seeing the whole picture,
unless someone opens the door.

I've learned it doesn't matter anymore,
all alone and crying.
While somewhere outside the rain teams,
and I'm doomed hearing silent screams.

Wendy Thomas

A Day With Granddad

When I was a little boy, I'd visit with my Granddad.
I'd go to stay down on his farm, of this I'm very glad.

Oh, what fun we had together, my Granddad and I,
All he would do down on his farm, I would surely try.

We called the cows in from the field, and put them in their stall.
We milked them while feeding them, and then released them all.

If you think our day was done, I'll tell you, you're mistaken.
This was just the start of day, but first some eggs and bacon.

After breakfast, we went to work on the chores that day.
We cleaned the barn, collected eggs, and even raked the hay.

Then came the time to get the corn and tie the stalks together.
We did this all the afternoon, being mindful of the weather.

Then came six and time to go and get the cows again,
They had more milk to give to us and get it we did intend.

Tired we were at end of day, but happy to be through,
We ate the meal in silence, as our weariness grew.

Sleep we did with peace of mind, for the good work we had done,
Granddad and I had worked together. He said, "Well done, Grandson."

Thomas J. Ridgway

Shadows Of The Past

I visited our place of long ago.
I walked where we walked.
I sat where we sat and everywhere
I saw your ghost and felt your presence—-
In the flickering flames of the fire,
On the path where we walked hand in hand,
On the bed where we lay
Wrapped in each other's arms,
In the hot tub where we sipped champaign.
I am here—but where are you?
There is only the shadow of the past.
I thought I saw you standing there.
The wind was blowing through your hair.
I reached out to you and found only air.
My heart felt sad and heavy with loss.
Oh! My love, my love - it's not fair
That I am here all alone.
Alas! It is only shadows of the past.
I am here—but where are you??
Marjorie S. Foster

I Want You To Know You Have A Friend

When challenges seem to come up, and alone you can't cope
I want you to know that you have a Friend, full of hope

When at times you feel so all alone, and don't know where to turn
Know that you have a friend, who will always be right there

When you need someone with whom to share your fears
Know that you have a Friend who will never condemn

On this Friend you can depend,
'Til the end this Friend will defend

To this Friend you can cry freely,
and still be loved completely

This Friend your secrets will keep,
because your friendship was etched in concrete

No longer searching for someone to share
your joy,

With this Friend your life will forever be enjoyed
And who is this Friend?
I AM
Michelle Davis

Life

Just as king, I once had a dream
I wanted to be all I could possibly be,
But some negative things happened to me and
I kinda got knocked off course
Since then it seems, I just went downstream
And I still ask myself, what does it all mean?

Well, although life is tough, the measures are rough
We must stay strong and keep it together,
For if we don't, then this life won't
Be everything it can be

Life on earth, for what it's worth,
Has been interesting for the most part,
You learn a lot about this mystery
Pot, we as humans are spawned from

I try to stay positive in a negative environment
While trying to figure out what it all means.
I'm focusing on mine, but I think it's been
Enough time, when will my break come, when will It be?!

The thing I know for sure, a thought we should
All adore, and that is, we've got to stay positive in this
Negative world
Valerie R. Banks

Untitled

She was never a secret the whole world knew.
I was a secret no one knew.
I was the secret in my husband's life.
I was the secret in my lover's life.
I was the fool in all their lives.
Manipulated, used and abused by the other guys.
I woke up one day and I opened my eyes.
I'm too nice a person to put up with those guys.
I am no longer a secret in anyone's life.
Everyone felt better except for the other guy.
His ego has been damaged.
His reputation scarred.
The chance of her discovery, he will always be on guard.
He will live a life of lies to be true in her
eyes, to be between her thighs.
Because of his lust for the other he failed to respect my feelings.
His promise to me had been broken.   My promise to him was broken.
My broken promise has set me free. No longer a secret must I be.
Because he cannot see the logic of my reasoning.
I will always be his secret for eternity.
Suzette Harsh

"That Bee Put A Buzz On Me"

As if I didn't have enough trouble already,
I was feeling as though I was ready for "Freddy."
A bee buzzed right into my home
Having the audacity to feel free to roam.
My heart so tender wouldn't harm a flea
That is, until that bee put a buzz on me.
My mode has changed, I'm armed to the gill,
Patiently waiting to have my thrill.
With swatter and spray,
I'll have my day.
'Cause that dad-blasted bee
Put a buzz on me.
Kathryn R. Grice

I Wish You Were Sitting Here Next To Me

I wish you were sitting here next to me
I was hoping that you wouldn't have to leave
I knew it was coming in a matter of time
Now that you're gone I just can't get you off my mind.

I wish you were sitting here next to me
I was praying that you wouldn't have to leave
But now that you're gone I now see
Why this just could not be.

I now know why you're not sitting next to me
You have always wanted to be set free
I understand you want to be alone
That is why I am now gone.
Rachel Loyd

Why I Love Jesus

Once upon a time, not so long ago
I was lost in sin, living on death row
As I saw my life coming to a tragic end
I fell to my knees and asked the Lord to mend

From heaven above the Lord heard my desperate plea
That was the day, the day He saved me
He looked beyond my faults and saw my every need
How wonderful a Savior Jesus Christ is to me

Now my life is filled with peace, joy and happiness
The Lord promised He'd do nothing less
He's my best friend, He's everything to me
I love Him with all my heart, because He set me free
D. Lynn Coleman

Drug Result

The beats and the bruises make me wish
  I was on a boat trip of cruises.

The hurt and the pain tells me to say,
  it's not all in his brain.

The crying and the fears show he's been
  doing drugs for years.

The lies and threats reveals another
  man I have not met.

The nights he walks the floor; looking
  for drugs more and more.

The warrants I take out make him turn
  his head about.

The thoughts of him cured has me shoveling
  horse manure.

The prayers and hope in Jesus; releases
  me closer to Jesus.

Patricia C. Dorn

My Mother

Coming into the world,
I was unaware of the dangers.
Someone was always there,
And she helped me through
the times we share. She is my mother.

When I was sick she was beside me.
When I was in trouble, she helped me.
When I was hurt, she comforted me.
When I needed someone to talk to, she was there.
She is always there for me, she is my mother.

She brought me into this world.
She gave me life and happiness.
I hope to spend years with her.
I hope I'll never lose her.
She is a special person, she is my mother.

I'm glad to have her, she is strong.
She knows when something is going wrong.
People say that we are somewhat alike,
In more ways than one.
I hope so, because she is my mother.

Kristi Rogowski

Faces

*Dedicated to the men who lost their lives
on Hamburger Hill #937 May 10-20, 1969*

Vietnam veterans 6th Reunion Melbourne, Fl. 1993
I went to on this fine day
Drove some 110 miles or so
Just to hear what they had to say.
Went there not knowing
What all would take place.
Ran into some "Screaming Eagles"
I was looking for one face.
An old friend and brother
That I haven't seen in 25 years.
For three long days I searched
Till my face turned to tears.
What I found wasn't my old friend and brother
Who in Vietnam had fought by my side.
But faces of other brothers, sisters, and families
To honor those who fought and died.

Roy J. Moore

Untitled

I am Chitty Chitty Bang Bang!
I wonder if there will not be another gang.
I hear the wonders of the Spring.
I see the sights of the Summer.
I want to hear the wonders of Fall.
I am Chitty Chitty Bang Bang!

I pretend to be a character.
I feel the dog and the pog.
I touch the chicken.
I worry about my brother.
I cry if I smother.
I am Chitty Chitty Bang Bang!

I understand the wondrous world.
I say hello to the birds.
I dream of the candy man.
I try to feel the air and breeze.
I hope that I will get a job.
I am Chitty Chitty Bang Bang.
I am Trevor.

Trevor Chitty

The Future, The Past And Now

I am a friendly nature lover
I wonder what I'll be doing in ten years,
I hear the world crying,
I see pollution rising,
I want to appreciate all the goodness of living,
I am a friendly nature lover.

I pretend students are learning about me in history,
I feel God's presence,
I touch the hearts of others,
I worry about my country,
I cry for the unfortunate innocent,
I am a friendly nature lover.

I understand no one lives forever,
I say more people should smile,
I dream about traveling to other galaxies,
I try to treat others fairly,
I hope for a hate-free world,
I am a friendly nature lover.

Sara Leon

Our Futuristic Memory

Dedicated to Morgan Nitz

I sit by the window at night, in this town,
I wonder what it would be like, with the sky upside down.
The ocean, now beach, the stars, you could reach.
Time will stop and cease to exist. The Earth's rotation will
not be missed. We will all live together, but then you and me,
will fly down through water, and into the sea.
Dark, it will be, into the sea, but who needs much light,
when you've got you and me. No wars, no fights, just days, and nights
Peace and some rain, love and no pain.

This is a dream, a futuristic memory,
no one understands, except you and me.
I've sat by the window, minutes ticking away,
the half and whole hours, maybe a day. Thinking of you, smiling too.
Staring at space, getting out of this place.
When I'm with you, I feel my dreams have come true.
They all will someday. When we're out of school's play.
The world needs discovering, but when I do,
I'd like some company, can it be you?

For now we dream, in this large town,
about what it would be like, with the sky upside down.

Lauren Afinowicz

I Am

I am a ball.
I wonder what little kids would do
without me.
I hear things as I hit the ground.
I see the ground close-up and far away
I want to rest a bit.
I don't understand and why they do this to me.
I feel there is no gravity, for a second......
or two.
I touch the cement then the clouds.
I worry it will never stop.
I cry as I am put to rest because I know
it will not stop.
I understand why they like me.
I say "I have no life, just up and down."
I dream it will stop, but it is just a
dream.
I am a ball.
Matt Ross

Moonlight Thoughts

The moonlight shines through the window
I wonder "will I ever go home?"
His face I will always remember
on which the moonlight had shone.

The darkness of night falls upon us
I wonder "will it soon be dawn?"
I wake up early next morning,
Only to find he is gone.

The stars in the sky up above us,
Shine like crystals of light.
The same stars that shone on us last night,
Will shine on him once more tonight.

The clouds swirling around the moon
Remind me of days that have passed.
I know that my love for him grows stronger
My love that will hold steadfast.
Sarah Garfield

Untitled

I'd love to give Mom a whole load of flowers
I'd love to give her a hug and a squeeze
And say thanks for a million memories, Mom.
But if I went home today Mom wouldn't be there
Though the house is still standing so lonesome and bare
She's in her other home—so beautiful—and rare,
But if she were home, she'd want all of her children together once more.
So we'll all get together, Mom, this Mother's day.
But will never say what we were thinking about
Mom's not here with the family she loved
But I know you'll be here Mom.
So I'll close my eyes and I'll see you again
And I know you'll be smiling, when you hear me say
Happy Mother's Day, Mommy way up there in heaven.
Pearl Bozell

Dreams-Visions-Future

As a child I dreamed of castles and dragons,
Indians, cowboys, knights and kings,
fearless deeds, beautiful maidens, pure and noble was me.

I grew and my dreams turned to visions,
still noble, more practical, some still unreachable,
of who I would become and for others would do.

I've learned that the dreams and the visions of child and man,
combined with doing produces the warp and woof,
the weave, the fabric of our nation's future and the world.
D. C. Riggs

Candy

Wouldn't it be dandy
If all our food was candy?
Chocolate, caramel, peanut butter
No finer words can one utter,
As dear to me as my own mother.
When you're feeling blue
Just grab a chew
Of something filled with chocolate goo.
Start your day with a Breakfast sweet.
Grab yourself a donut to eat.
I have a hunch
That for lunch
You would be happy with a
Chocolate-y munch. For your dinner
You'll feel like a winner (though you won't be much thinner)
With a slice of cheesecake
And a strawberry shake.
So when you're happy
Let your spirits soar
Hop on down to the candy store.
Nicholas Beyrle

True Love

I sit and wonder into the night
If I will ever find my true love and if I do
will it last forever or will it be a dream I had
will it ever come true or do I sit and wonder if it will ever be real
Sometimes I think to myself it was a dream and if it ever comes true,
Will I be here to meet my true love
or will I find someone else to fall in love
Or could the man of my dreams be my best friend, can it be real?
If my true love was my best friend
would it last forever or just be in the past
and when I do find my true love, will it be a dream or real?
but when I do find my true love will he love me the way I love him?
Will he cheat on me, or lie to me,
will he tell me everything is going to be all right
and will he be there for me no matter what?
Because if he is my true love he will never let me go
but if my true love won't be there for me
I know it was never meant to be
and I will find my true love
will he be true as me?
Shannon Parker

If Only

The "if only's" of our lives...what a way to live,
If only this, if only that, what do they have to give?
Life itself is full of choices, some good, some bad,
It's the dwelling over the "if only's" that makes life sad.

If only he could have loved me, they way I wanted him to,
If only I could have been the woman he wanted too.
The world is filled with "if only's," it seems to me,
If only we could get past them and live life as it should be.

If only I were stronger, more able to take care of myself,
If only people didn't hurt one another, caring only for themselves.
God gave us the gift of life, and watches us to see,
Just what we do with it...of what we will be.

To lose someone you love is such a desperate feeling,
To feel rejected and unworthy of love should not fill our
   lives so completely.
If only we could put into practice what our minds tell us to do,
Instead of listening with our hearts and souls to all of the
   "If only's" like fools.
Linda L. Brummette

Pride

I could be close
If only you would let me.

I know the strength inside
But you hide.
Only to reveal a coward
That's not who you were meant to be.

Is it that I cannot forgive you
Or is it that I cannot forgive myself
For loving someone
For loving the something that was not there
Something missing
I knew all along.
You hid it inside
Until you had to run
But still I wept
For the secret that is still kept.
Keri-Ann Cole

If There Was Love

If there was love the hungry would be feed.
If there was love no one would be sleeping
on the street all would have A bed.
If there was love no unkind words would
be said if there was love gossip would never spread.
If there was love there would be no need to lock
the door. No thief would enter in no one would
be found murderer lying on the floor.
f there was love all would live by the
golden rule. If there was love there would be
no problems in our homes churches or schools.
If there was love that A wonderful world this
would be. Lord fill the world with your love
beginning with me.
Ruby Ingram

Come

If you are in need of a friend, a foe, come here.
If you have lost your way, come here.
If you are a slave to the arts, the small sounds; if the
moon rays set free from the last red rise that pierce the
surface in the dips and curves of the earth at night let you
see all the hues in dimmed form; if the out of doors calls
your trees to come and play and you go with them every
time; if you see peace when you look at the moon in the
sea, come here.
If you have no home, come here. If you need, but do
not want, more than you get, come here.
Come if you are afraid, if you do not know, if you must
find out... but do not come if there is perfection in your life.
There is flaw in all that touches the earth, even here -
but flaw will change one and add another as it leaves.
Come as you are, as you might have been; you will not
be the same if you come out again.
If you dream, if you need, if you ache, if you roam, if
you have hidden fears that cannot be crushed, if you
want nothing but endless space......Come.
Kristen Van Dam

Dreams

At night I came to you in your dreams.
In your mind I dwell.
I coarse through your veins.
I am your soul.
You would not be possible without my existence.
At night we seal our fate with the dream
route we take.
The night you dreamt of me was to be a night
of eternity.
Lisa Diana Kimmer

Keep Fighting

If your arms feel weary,
If your feet feel just like lead,
Just keep looking for the rainbow
And you're bound to get ahead.

If everyone seems to be against you,
If the big fellow keeps calling you a runt,
Just keep tugging and plugging
and you're sure to wind up in front.

If the going keeps getting tougher,
If you can't keep up the pace,
Just try to smile, for at least part of the mile
and you're bound to win the race.

If things look very black,
If you think the end is near,
With all your might keep up the fight
and you'll never stay in the rear.
Morris Rosen

Jehovah My Peace

Show me your God and the things he builds,
I'll tell you of mine and point to the hills.
I'll show you the sky and clouds above
And tell you of his eternal love.

Show me your houses your beats and things
And I'll tell you how my glad heart sings.

Tell me of all the things you own and how
You managed to get the loan. How hard
You work and how much you owe and I'll
tell you what I learned long ago
That all these things will pass away and you
Will be left with a bill to pay. For when all
is totaled you can't be free. Until you
have paid for eternity.
Show me your Gods of silver and Gold
I'll show you the shepherd and sheep in the fold.
Luvena Spratt

Saying Goodbye

Saying goodbye is hard to do,
If only for a week, or even two;
But saying goodbye forever and ever,
Is like taking the color out of a feather.

The last goodbye, yes that's the one,
That shatters your heart, and eclipses the sun;
These roses are meant for you, only you,
That you might fondly remember our last rendezvous.

Never forget, please please never,
That I will always love you, forever and ever.
William A. Bodine

Beauty Of Night

The light of night
Is an old beauty falling asleep
And the cold death waits

The still red light comes
And the wind flows with peace
People in their dreams fast asleep

But the cold rain night will soon go away
For the light of the sun will come
And the sky with birds will fill the air,
sun will cover the mountains
All nature will awake
Rocio Mendez

The Rapists

They are raping my lady.
I'm enraged.
This frustrating helplessness begins at my gut and radiates
as an internal malevolence throughout my body.
What is there to do?
My lady bore me and those I love.
Throughout my years she has graced me with;
   Suns setting and rising with beauty so intense
   that I taste the sweet pleasure with a subtle
   yearning for the next taste,
   The honest affection of creatures that know no
   malice but live to love,
   The sights, smells and random colors of the flora,
   The awesome displays of power as the weather changes its wraps.
   These things that might have been forever but for the
   savage attacks of the rapists.
My lady struggles to no purpose. To be so abused by one's own.....
This penetration will bear no product.
Will the rapists know what they have done and will we
cry together with arms outstretched?

   Louis Katz

Withered Rose

I am a flower ruffled by a spring breeze
I wonder why the elements have abandoned me
I hear no birds chirping in the blue sky
I see no creatures scurrying chatteringly by
I would like some love to nourish my roots
I am to be trampled by man's big, clunky boots

I pretend to be a rose, blossoming pretty
I feel that others look upon me with pity
I touch those around me, but they do not see
I worry that I'll forever be only with me
I cry when I hurt and am exposed to the hand
I am a flower with no spine to stand

I understand why others are ashamed to tell
I say I am fine when I'm really in hell!
I dream of a better day with birds and sunshine
I try to pretend that he's all in my mind
I hope for a life not bitter or hostile
I am an abused child.

   Ragin Jennings

Flowers In Spring

Flowers! Flowers! God's creation!
I'm only the gardener. He is the Creator.
How beautiful they all are.

I look out the window and see all different kinds-
Tulips, daffodils, hyacinths and crocus-
All surrounded by a small, white boarded fence.

You can see rows of yellow, orange
White, red and pink tulips
Reaching toward the sun's rays
And then quietly sleeping while their
Soft delicate, fragrant petals close at night.
Yellow daffodils are still blooming
Even though they are at bloom's end-
Stalks of hyacinths and leaves of crocus
Are spreading and growing into the tulip's path

While they gently wave in the warm breeze,
I quietly saunter like a cat over to the flowers
To breathe in their faint, perfumed scent.
God knew what He was doing when He gave us flowers.
They are so lovely to enjoy.

   Susan Rice

Finally Found

I've finally found what you needed me to find.
I'm still unsure about some of the things that I need to do.
I'm on the road leading to my expectations, taking myself,
with your help, to better places where I can learn and grow.
Teaching me to be the best I can be and helping along the way,
you show me the light that will brighten even my darkest day.
The pressure that was there is gone and a feeling of greatness that I
cannot describe takes its place helping me to get by each night,
setting my goals as a little higher each time.
Reaching my destination with you by my side, for one has faith and the
other hope, each knowing that I will make it to the one place in life
that I want to go.
Keep the faith and hold on to your hope
some day I'll thank you for all the help you've given me and for
keeping faith, for pushing me along the way, giving me the strength
to go on, and holding on to the hope, for you I'm grateful....

   Melanie Traverse

What's A Mother's Day Without My Mother

It's a day that breaks my heart in two, every day I'm missing you!
I'm still wondering how you could leave me.
When we had so many things left to do.
We used to fight, you'd make me so mad!
Then I'd realize you truly were the best thing I had.
When the chips were down, and my world was ready to fall apart,
I always knew I could call you, and you'd mend my heart.
You never could stand to see me cry, it just tore you up inside.
I hope wherever you are, when you look down and see me cry,
That it doesn't hurt you, and you just understand why!
I want to sit with you on that great big swing, and simply
talk about nothing. Let's go shopping from dawn to dusk, and
how about one of those great T-Bone steaks, that only you
could make to taste that great.
You always said, you were a tough old bird, nothing would
happen to you, you'd never leave me. But, you did!
So I'm sitting here wondering how can I have a
Happy Mother's day, without my mother here with me?
I'm in so much pain! But, wait, I've forgotten
something Mom. I have two sons of my own,
I have to go on!

   Sherry Aginah

God's Country

We said it couldn't happen here
  IT DID!

Not in our quiet, non-militant, Bible Belt
  IT DID!

On a quiet morning, with a boom and a puff of smoke
  In just a minute, we lost hundreds.

Where are our eyes? Hearts?
  Where are our government's eyes?
Why are we so naive?

We are part of God's world,
  And in many countries this is a way of life.

WAKE UP! Put God back in this nation.
  How many innocent children, men and women have to die?

WAKE UP AMERICA! It is here!

Wake up - realize we are already in Gun's country,
  Instead of God's country.

WAKE UP AMERICA - while we can still be saved

Put your eyes and hearts on God again
  Before revelations is upon us

   Pat Booze

Looking Back

Today, I found a picture
In an old magazine.
I wondered what my grandmothers
Would have thought of such a gaudy thing?

They didn't have a lot of things
This world says you must own;
To make their lives more enjoyable
In their simple, country homes.

They didn't have microwave ovens
Or carpets upon their kitchen floors.
Yet, they went about their country kitchens
Doing their daily chores.

Their old wood-burning cookstoves
Were unique in their own way.
For upon them, my grandmothers
Cooked many things I still remember to this day!

They, always, made my favorites
And, of course, pinto beans and good old-fashioned cornbread.
When we came a visiting,
Sat at their tables and were fed.
Sara N. Kernal

Once There Was A Nation, A Country So Proud

The war had ended, the Nation was proud
In downtown New York there was such a crowd

The Germans have gone down in defeat
American solders marched to the beat.

Women and children danced with their feet.
Husbands, dads coming home, what a treat

Our Industries' whistles blew with a shrill
We have just the job for you at our Mill

Crisp was the air as they marched down the street
The clip-clopping of the animals' hoofs to the beat

The coffin with an American flag was in retreat
A woman and two children marched to the beat

Another was ended after so many years
A nation divided with anger and tears.

Once there were industries all over the hills
Many have left us with no way to pay bills

Once there was a Nation, a country so proud
Once there was a Nation, a country so proud
Lois Nichols

Untitled

As I stop to take some time to explore my inner mind,
I wonder what awaits me when I leave this world behind.
As I stand and stare out over the edge of eternity,
I have no more fear of what flesh can do to me.
Looking back over my life all the stories I can tell,
of times as sweet as paradise, and days of living hell.
When comes the savior I've heard about that will end this
torment and pain.
For distress falls down around me as a storm of heavy rain.
I've searched the skies from pole to pole in hopes someday to find.
But never have I come across a cloud with silver line.
Many have said what I've endured is a product of chance and such.
But I can't believe that lady luck
could hate someone so much.
As I gaze into the skies at stars so far away,
Someday peace shall overcome my heart, on this I hope and pray.
Timothy Horsley

The Case Of The Moth-eaten Merkin

A moth-eaten merkin was found
In most disreputable repair.

It had been chewed on and gnawed on and so on,
In fact, most of it wasn't even there.

The detective in charge of the case
Avowed it a terrible disgrace,

That a once soft and lovable merkin
Should end up as holey as lace.

Finally, however, it was discovered
There really hadn't been any crime.

For the moth-eaten merkin, though tattered,
Had been worn by Mrs. Moth at the time.
Vincent S. Hopkins

Despair

Despair follows me wherever I go.
In my head and heart it seems to grow.
Since I was a child I'd always know.
Despair follows me wherever I go.

As a child it was there, in a small way.
It left me without a lot to say.
People who knew me did not understand.
People who loved me did not lend a hand.

I grew and grew and there it was still.
It would not let go went against my will.
It made me different and to give it a name,
Most people thought I was quite insane.

Now I am older, guess what it's still there.
It's become a problem, I no longer can bare.
But bare it I must, that's all that I know.
Despair follows me wherever I go.
Marcia S. Wells

My World

I am in my world and I don't want to leave.
In my heart this world is easy to achieve.
One has told me it's a world of fantasy
I declare unequivocally, it's sheer ecstasy.

A world where we worship, praise and pray.
There is always time for work, laughter, and play.
Love is expressed with willingness
And the least problem is needing to be caressed.

A world full of joy, peace and love
Can only be a world sent from God above.
A world with time with someone who knows how to care
Someone with whom you can your joys and sorrows share.
Someone with whom you can feel at home
The one you look forward to no matter when he may come.

When the rest of the world has kicked you around.
A house is a home because there healing can be found.
Healing from alienation to a welcome warm touch;
A gentle voice, a pleasant smile that means so much.

Fantasy? I proclaim it's ecstasy! I don't want to leave "my world."
I must stay in "my world." May I, please?
Willerma Frazier-Means

True Emotions

Colors and joys collide then part, but your vision stays
in my heart. You are the sun that makes my grey skies stay
behind. Your voice is the angel that rings clear in my mind.
Your eyes are like gems that no one can stain. You are the one
who in my mind on the highest plateau reigns. When I am having
a rough day your laughter and joy give me a reason to stay. My
emotions normally do not show true, but when talking to you
my love can come through. You are my port, my good luck
charm.
It is you I will try to keep from all harm. You are my port
in the storm of the world's cruel pain...With you I hope to
forever remain. You are the tree that shades me from the heat.
Your love I probably will never reach to meet. These are the
reasons I tell you true that I think the world of you.

Sean Reid

Through Vampire Eyes

During the day I sleep, lying restless
in my room, my little box of darkness where
I sleep alone. No one to wonder what I
do when I'm out at night. No one to feel my
loneliness, see the pain in my eyes, or sense
the despair in my heart as I drain them, my
innocent victims, of the life God has given them.
Am I evil? If not, why has the Devil, this
Prince of darkness, claimed me as his slave?
Why has he taken away the light and the warmth I
so long to feel once again against my now heartless
body? The darkness, now my brother, keeps my heart
and mind captive allowing nothing, not even hope or
faith, to reach my decaying heart. Is there no one
to help me, to take me away from this damned place?
No one to help me find my love, to finally feel the
warmth that love brings and know I was put here for a
reason? No one. Not now, for I know it is too late
for my lost soul to find love, love... which lives in
the light.

Siobhan Serra

Insomnia

Restlessness brings me to this place
In quiet hours while the world sleeps
Alone in the vastness that is night
With only the stars for company
Even Luna hides her face in slumber
Cicadas surrender their voices to silence
The hum of stillness almost deafening
The darkness void of warmth
With no thoughts to comfort me
I cannot dare to dream

Tracy L. Savo

Sonnet Number One

The one I love has given me his heart,
In return, I have given him my hand.
Our love shall last until death do us part.
On my finger, he slips a golden band.
His strong arms embrace my complete being.
Yet, at times, he stands far away from me.
Watching others for my safety, seeing
All the evil around us. On his knee,
Teary eyed, he asked me to be his wife.
He wants to protect me, hold me near.
To be only his, the love of his life.
And now, at last, our dream will soon be here.
It is sad to say, I will be leaving soon,
But he knows I'll return, like a fortnight moon.

Shannon Markey

Untitled

The desert flowers dance
In solitude upon gleaming sands.
Everywhere it is silent, watchful.
The cactus does not dare bend its spine.
Its needles are sentries guarding the plain
While overhead a single cloud is there.
In all this endless present
God enters as a lizard shaking
A blade of dry grass.
Now He is a horny toad.
He is a species almost extinct.
In His furtive ways He can
Hardly be seen.
But when He stops,
He blends into all that's there
And unless you know Him,
You would hardly recognize
Such life could exist.

Robin Keeler

A Mother's Prayer

A Mother came to church one day, her two sons stood by her side.
In stony silence they stared ahead, as their Mother softly cried.
Oh Lord, I bring my boys to you, upon this hurtful day,
One wears a coat of Union blue, the other wears confederate gray.
I ask that you reach down to them, and touch each beating heart,
Please fill their souls with family love, before we're torn apart.

I ask that you watch over them, as each one takes a different way.
Don't let them meet on the battlefield Lord, for this I humbly pray.

Another Mother came to church, but no sons stood by her side,
She'd already lost them to the streets, and this is why she cried.
Oh God, my boys are gone from me, as if they both were dead,
For one proudly sports the color blue, the other wears crimson red.
I beg you Lord, don't let them fight, upon some dirty street.
Please hear this Mother's prayer, Oh God don't let them meet.

I ask that you watch over them, as each one takes a different way.
Don't let them meet on the battlefield Lord, for this I humbly pray.

Two Mother's prayers, separated by more than a hundred years
United in time as they prayed to God, and mourned with bitter tears.
My Mother's prayer is for a world, where our hearts don't have to break,
And sons won't have to fight and die, for the choices that they make.

S. J. Marion

The Darkened Unforgiving

It is finished.

I told you I would wait by the ledge,
  in that wooded uprising hidden by our past.
    Water, vexing its sadness, clears then
brightens - it shall never be. Suffered wisdom follows the Lamb.

I did not show you the wolf of the Steppes,
  the one that had lost its way and strayed
    into the life of the herd, crucified there
      by its self-contempt.
It reminds us of faith in our High Estate;
  we are born for solid earth. One day,
  in the weeping water, the wolves shall drown.
    Tamed.

I could not entrust you with my release, so I slipped
  away from the whisper - this deeper sorrow carving vessels
  of joy, a self-chosen hunger and thirst.
Distasteful enrichment, my blessed bounty.
  Silent, unclaimed joy.

Robert Crane

Ponderings

My thoughts do not keep pace with my heart
in the acceleration of expression
of beautiful words and phrases -
would that it were otherwise

There are so many roads to traverse-
the intersections of by-ways
the preludes of decision
the ebbing of tides
the channelling of corners to be turned-
the waiting threshold beckons

Eyes are privileged to feast on the splendors
of morning's dawn, sunlit skies
rainbows of undiscovered, yet refracted colors
evening's sparkling reflections
the cast of billions appointed and apportioned
under night's universal constellations
- the watching of starry skies -

All are melodies of Splendor and Majesty,
All amid lovely sounds of silence
The bounty of meanings, yet unperceived!
   William J. McCormick

Midnight Meditations

It is not easy to meditate
In the heavy noise of day;
But when night closes in,
Confusing sounds fade away.

Thoughts so vague all through the light
Come to focus around midnight.

That's when I think more calmly,
And meditate upon my thoughts;
That's when I see more clearly
The lessons life has taught;
That's when I realize wearily
That sometimes my work was all for naught;
That's when I face the truth and ask,
"Have I missed the goal for which I sought?"

And then I think more comfortingly
Of the many blessings life has brought;
Of the gifts to man by His hands wrought.
   Mary F. Bagley

My Lady Doctor

I first met her ten years ago
   In the hospital Intensive Care.
She was studying my heart x-ray.
   I couldn't help but stare.

The bright colored dress to her ankles,
   The dark hair hung to her waist;
The keen black eyes held great compassion
   Deep concentration, no sign of haste.

Surely this woman should be home "mothering"
   Not here among white coated men.
Could this possibly be my doctor?
   Doubtless another they would send.

A decade has come and gone.
   Now we are together again.
She is dressed in the latest fashion
   And ready to be my friend.

Skill in her profession
   And lengthening my days of living
What more could one ask of a person
   Than what "my lady doctor" has given.
   Ruth Wofford Miller

Gone Forever

One minute we were here together
In the next, you're gone forever
You truly were my best friend
You promised you'd be here to the end

You said you would never go away
Why couldn't you spare my feelings and stay
Think of me wherever you are
Wait for me, don't go too far

I find myself wandering far away
Trying to find you, don't fade away
You're fading, fading, fading fast
Please don't make me relive the past

For the past is too much for me to bare
You were someone for whom I cared
Now you're just a memory
Of someone who I wanted to be

I know you're watching over me in heaven up above
Correcting all of my mistakes, your heart still full of love
I know that you cared for me, I understood it clearly
As long as I remember that, I'll always love you dearly
   Tia Nashay Prince

Of Love and Hate and Freedom

Sometimes this little cage bursts open as a painted balloon
in the sky; colors flap their wings at each other
flying high their restless embrace,
then spread, becoming soul blue
like looking you in the eye-
sometimes music breaks away from these strings
beating the drum chests, coiling the song,
shouting in the ear of freedom
sometimes trees throw their burden of leaves off their backs
to be swallowed by the thirst below
sometimes this heart holds its hands up
and cries over the fence into another universe;
sometimes this child, the unborn, grows out of my clasp
straight back into death and mother
stands out of my memory and weeps over me as if I were gone;
sometimes hatred is just a striped veil over love
and soft hands torture it to say otherwise.
   L. Palincas

On Seeing Claude Michel's "Nymph and Satyr Carousing," A Maquette in Terra Cotta

*"To model in clay, one uses a well-prepared clay,
... it is the hands with which one starts and which
bring the work farthest along. The greatest practitioners
use their fingers..." Diderot's Encyclopedie (1765)*

Exultant nymph and lusty satyr join
in exuberance. His arm behind stays
their tumble, another enfolds her play-
ful rush. She lifts her chalice to anoint
his upturned, open mouth. Bacchants purloined,
bear still their maker's prints in flesh of clay.
Bacchus heeds Midas's greed, his dismay,
then his terror to prove the humbling point:

How much more is passion than desire
or more possession. See them! Shibboleths
that vex all humankind—our births and deaths
our sex and loves—all these unfamiliar.
For us of clay and orgiastic fire,
how many gods must breathe immortal breath?
   William N. France

God Speaks

God speaks
   in the soft clouds that ride the sky,
   in the mournful wail of a newborn's cry,
     in the silence of a restful night,
   and in the splendor of a bird in flight.

God speaks
   through the babbling of a little brook,
     in the reading of a magnificent book,
     in the purity of new-fallen snow,
   and in everything with desire to grow.

God speaks
   through everyone one you've ever met,
     in the blaze of a Spring sunset,
     in lightning that splits the sky,
       and even in a lover's sigh.

God speaks
     but do you hear?
   Shirley R. Piersen

Revival

The tapestry of life woven
in threads of varying hues
Is reminiscent of the eternal pattern
of birth, life and death;
For the scenes depict joy, sorrow, hate and love,
lending vitality to the heavy cloth.
Renewal and rebirth, symbols of the phoenix and butterfly,
underline the multi-colored designs.
Elegantly draped on the wall the richness of the shades and decorations
re-echo immortality ...
   Nellie Agostino

Friends

Who is that special person - always there
in times of joy - happy moments we can share

We can call and feel so good by just
talking and listening to each other
almost like a sister or a brother

When something sad occurs we know
our conversation will still be warm
and oh so helpful to lessen undue alarm

Even without contact just thoughts of
all my friends - here or in another state

Reward me with a feeling - I'll just simply call "great."
   Robert Nicholson

From My View

From my view up on a hill,
I saw a row of trees.
They were filled with golden leaves;
Their trunks were made of silver,
When I saw those trees I dared not shiver!

From my view up on a hill,
I saw a little cottage among the trees.
I asked myself;
Was that the cottage of Snow White and the Seven Dwarfs?

I saw sixteen peach blossoms lined up near a waterfall,
And behind was a women playing her harp of love.
When she ended her song with a shout.
I woke up and my view went away.
   Rebecca Liao

A Lesson Learned

There have been too many times
   In which I have been deceived
I thought I knew everything
   There was nothing I didn't believe
I was so blinded by my feelings of love
   I could not recognize
All the hurt that he would cause me
   Amounting from all of the lies
Hidden behind a sincere, kind face
   Lives a cold beatless heart
It took nothing more than some words from him,
   He was finished acting out his part
It was a cycle that I went through
   Now long gone in the past
And I promise myself to rise above
   To make sure my next love lasts
This is what makes the world spin 'round
   The mere beat of a heart
The most beautiful treasure is to possess
   A true love that will not part.
   Melissa Fox

Ink And Paint (The Poet/The Painter)

The poet paints a picture with his pen
   In words descriptive
In a most fashionable color of rainbow songs

   The painter writes a poem
With the brushes and the strokes therein
   Bring out true feelings
Of a landscape coming to life

   Combined they create the Masterpiece
Of epic proportions untold
   Meandering thoughts mingle
With the jeweled oiled colors that unfold
   Theresa Marie Wilson

Beyond The Casualties

Beyond the casualties did you find life?
   Innocence, despair, and the sacrifice...
Irrelevant to the noble and earthly elite,
   the few who are merited by their faith and belief.
Bound to matter of realities, do you still seek your release?
   While grasping for possessions and deserting precious memories.
Alone, your choices blaze your own bridges and trails.
   To each, their own, in these ironically termed, "common affairs".

Fading dusk echoes, fleeing a question its answer has escaped.
   Dawn finds the mourning, reveals a light and births a new fate.

   Beyond the casualties the sun shines, breathing life...
   Ronald J. Hill

2 A.M.

The moon is a cold sphere reflecting an icy light over the land
In the distance a coyote band yips and yaps as they chase their prey
The night holds it breath, it senses the stillness of Death as he comes
across the sand dunes, through the Juniper trees, looking for me
I, too, hold my breath thinking to elude Death by being silent
But he knows I am there waiting and he smiles as he sees me
He raises his arms as if to say, "Come," but I turn away and run, run, run
And he laughs, the echo of his speaking seeping into my consciousness
as he says, "I love you, don't run, I am freedom," and die as I scream
because he is suddenly all around me like a shroud, a choking cloud
And I frantically awake, gasping and sweating from the dream.
I know he will come for me soon, the moon will be cold.
   Warren J. Adams

A Grave Matter

Up on the hill, in the narrow moonlight,
Is a lone cemetery, breathing in the night.
When no one is there, the silence is loud,
the dead leaves cover the earth like a shroud.

A brisk wind, every now and then, passes through.
A smell of rain, a smell of earth, in a sky so darkly blue.
Insects scurry upon the dampened leaves,
a tree branch twists within the breeze.

One lone stone seems to stick out,
a dark silhouette, so prominent and stout.
No one cares what is written on its face,
nor if it's upright and in its place.

Not many have read, what's written on the stone,
nor care about the grave, that's standing all alone.
From the side of the road, not many can see:
"I'll remember the world,
but the world will forget me."
   Wallis A. Myers

Teen-Age Love

My heart is like a saddened song sung from dust till dawn, My love
is a tortured soul that lost control. My life will only live for
   love, that is
hard for me to feel. My love must carry on like a sad love song,
   that will
never cease. To feel love would be the best thing for me, for love
is often not there. To give love is easy, to show love is hard,
To receive love is the worst thing of all. To know love is there,
but just out of reach, is very confusing to me. To know I could
just reach out and it would be there, is so much for me to share.
To know I could hold it and feel some warmth there, is just too much
to bare. Do I dare take a step towards a few sort hours of relief?
Will I ever take that last step open my heart to one who
is always there? Will he take my heart and keep it near or throw it
away after some use.
   Nicole Melvin

"My Lover, My Friend"

A romance like ours,
Is an endless glory,
For my love is real,
And yours is a story...
Like a bright, burning amber,
My love goes on.
But your love is here,
And then it is gone..
Your lips say I love you,
But your heart, says no.
And like a fool,
I pretend that it's so...
I've cried and cried myself to sleep,
Because my love for you is deep...
And if someday, our love should end,
We'll never be lovers, but always good friends...
   Peter Torruella

She Cries

Late at night she cries, and doesn't know why.
Is it because she lost a really close uncle?
Or a really good friend? Is that why she cries?
Maybe it's because her dad is in jail or her
favorite cousin is gone forever. Is that why
she cries? Could it be that she just broke
up with her boyfriend? No I think it's just
because she just wants to talk to somebody.
Is that why she cries?
   Kristy Smith

Fuchsia Roses

My Heart-
Is as soft as the fuchsia roses I sent my desire.

The Rose-
Shows the warmth of the heart I hold for him.

Holding-
Patiently, waiting for a chance to unfold myself into his heart and
his soul.

My Soul-
Is more patient than time can imagine, waiting, yearning for his
touch and acceptance.

Accept-
My love as true and find the excitement of bringing our hearts
closer, sending ourselves to heaven.

Sending-
The season of Spring for us to explore our love.

Love-
Me as I love you.
   Susan M. Collins

To Dead Lovers

Sadness envelopes me - what might have been
is long gone, but never forgotten.
Wisps of memories dance fleetingly through my mind,
stopping on my tongue, my eye, my ear,
reminding me!!

I savour each thought - repeating words
heard through the mists of time
and long forgotten melodies deafen and blind
me to sights recaptured,
ever reminding me!!

Never again shall I see the face
of that tortured soul; saddest of men
who played the horn with such life and pride
who wished only to die.
Again, reminding me!!

Gone is the boy of a man
from this place, echoes alone remain
in my mind's eye, keeping this dead love alive
to survive once again,
to remind me!!
   Kathleen M. Hall

Crying Rose

A tear is shed.
It falls from beauty.
This is for the others.

Another falls.
It is for their mortality.
They are foolish.
They will perish.

Another falls.
It falls for their society.
Their advancements will be their own undoing.
It rests near the other tears.

The final tear falls
It falls from loneliness.
There are none more like it.
Now there will be no more.

The tears come from the last rose.
It cares not about itself.
It weeps.
It weeps for us.
   R. J. Kingston

"Coping"

Sometimes it seems the best we can do
Is never quite good enough.
Each of us handle it in a different way,
Some "gung-Ho," some shy and some bluff.

We all seem to arrive at the same place on time,
Even though we travelled different streets;
Using different equipment and speeds by each traveler,
Some victories and some defeats.

I think life tries to test us at times,
Making it sometimes hard to cope.
We challenge ourselves with difficult tasks,
Confiding with our spouses, our preacher and even the pope.

We don't understand everything that happens,
Some weird, some good and some not;
We just keep trucking the best we can,
By taking our very best shot.

Most everyone helps in their own special way,
Offering encouragement and some type of hope;
We can deal with it in our own way,
By simply trying to cope.

J. R. (Bob) Smith

The Senses Of Love Of A Soul Mate

You are smelling the fragrance, the aroma of the flower which
is so dear to you and draws your attention to your love's presence.

You are seeing the flower in bloom, as your love draws magnetism,
the beauty from within your eyes as no one else can.

You are tasting the flavor of love, wanting more and more, for
the addiction is so powerful as you have never experienced before.

You are feeling the spiritual energies as they engulf you in
the powers of God's veil.

You are hearing the precious words which are so sacred and so
meaningful that they captivate the heart.

You are sensing the closeness of a soul mate, the symbiotic
that creates a special internal bond which no one can break.

Mary Ann Rensch

* * * * * *

Yes, I'm fat, I'm ugly,
Loud and lazy,
Don't fit in and don't watch my words.
I'm too direct, too demanding;
I am compulsive.

I'm a Jack of all trades
But a master of none.
I'm insecure,
I'm self conscious,
I'm too exacting and too picky.
I don't set the example I expect of others.
I try to solve everyone's problems,
I can't solve my own.

Mary Jane Langeloh

The Rose

The rose stands in the Ground.
It shows the outstanding color "Red."
Red is a color that shows that the rose is healthy
and taken care of by God.
God gives the Red Rose light, water, soil, and air.
During the fall the Red Rose sheds the outstanding
color of its Red petals; during the spring the
Rose will grow its petals over again and the
color Red will soon stand out on, "The Rose."

Ryan P. Peterson

Another Day?

He won! showed those experts of wall street how it's done! And now he
is the richest one. Life is not just money and fun! Time marches on!
You see - He lost another day!

She won - all the Olympic games - and is the greatest athlete of her day!
But wait - she lost - another precious day!

He was elected speaker by a whopping score.
And maybe an encore they say!
But he too lost - another day!

She won the nod and became a member of the highest court!
But alas she lost - could not vote on her loss of another day!

And now for the children - they win our hearts every day as they play
And play - too young to understand the loss of another day.

We all dream of winning every day - but it is no dream!
We all will lose another day!

M. D. Morrow

Prelude To Summer

That persistent sound… ding-a-ling… ding-a-ling….
Is there anymore delightful sound than the bell of the ice cream
wagon in early Spring? A harbinger of the coming Summer… baseball
games… hot dogs with onions… cold beer… penciled programs
and always the fun of extra innings. The sputtering sound of
lawn mowers, reluctantly starting and stopping…a few garter
snakes…darting across the lawn…wading pools being filled
…and of course children being told not to track grass into
the pool (this of course is always ignored)…the beautiful
birds, robins, cardinals and sparrows…pulling fat worms from
the flowers beds…hyacinths…in purple and pink…
like a little girls outfit in the Easter parade….
Evening thunderstorms…and the sweet coolness that followed
All of this trails the ice cream wagon…like the pied piper
ding-a-ling….ding-a-ling……
Doesn't it make you shiver with anticipation?

Pauline E. Johnson

"I"

I look to the heavens above.
I think of my life.
I want to live in a world that is hate free.
I cry for the baby with no love.
I touch the hands of all that have ever suffered.
I dream of a better world.

I hear soothing music in a distance.
I close my eyes.
I feel the warmth of the sun.
I try to imagine happier days.
I dream of a better world.

I worry about what the future will bring.
I understand that life has its ups and downs.
I pretend that everyone lives in peace.
I dream of a better world.
I hope that one day my dream will come true.

Ryaja Johnson

Friendship

Friendship is like an apple tree
It starts out as a seed
If given the right soil it will blossom
Water it with understanding and it will grow
Give it love and care and it will sprout
Eventually with time it will grow to be a beautiful apple tree
Take care of it and it will give you apples

Teara Parker

Torquemada

Can it be God's will that I follow?
It can be no other, for I hate the devil and will see him burned.
Burned and despised and cast down into eternal torment.
I see him tempt me in the face of every Jew and heretic in Spain.
I will not bear it; I know my God is testing me.
Will I give in to every plea for mercy?
Every face of every witch whose lust has shamed the flesh
    she shares with Mary?
Will I yield to see my soul endangered by the very evil it despises?
I know what God intends.
I see His wisdom and His power and His might.
God can mete out mercy in His time,
But men like me He meant to carry out the law.
I can but cleanse their putrid erring souls,
These heathen non-believers,
And send them purified to meet their God.
This earthly life is short.
The soul's eternity is all we should consider:
A moment's pain against His Paradise forever.
I am an instrument. I carry out His will.

Victor Barranca

Smoking It Up!

Smoking is bad, though it feels so good
It destroys from within as though working under a hood!
Smoking is for fools who try
   to fit in, their two fingers
   become symbols of a cry
   for help and attention.
Smoking is a sin - a disease
   of the heat - it's wrapped, and
   packaged and sold by the carton.
Smoking kills - it's been proven
   so many times - even insects know
   it - flies, mosquitoes, moths, dogs,
   cats, birds, animals know it.
Smoking is for humans whose
   brains lack the smallest basic
   instinct of survival - all living
   creatures must have this instinct!
Why do humans smoke?

Terry Reece

"Rhyming Time"

When I hear a rhyme, that I think is sublime,
   it brings music to these aging ears.
It's been on the scene, since I was a teen,
   and has followed me, down through the years!

One has to repeat, that rhythmic beat,
   of this I'm perfectly sure.
You need that old rhyme, at the end of the line,
   to keep your poetry pure!

It's funny, but when, I pick up a pen,
   to drop my kids a short note,
if I write it in rhyme, they think it's just fine,
   they really 'dig it', quote dash unquote!

Now, I'm not a poet, as most people know it,
   I'm more of a 'rhyme-an-eer'.
I write just for fun, to please anyone,
   but mainly, for folks whom I hold dear!

As I reminisce, I'm not sure if this,
   is a poem, an ode or some verse.
'Cause this old mind of mine, has run short of rhyme,
   and seems to be stuck in reverse!

Richard E. Nickel

The Empty Stage

The Empty Stage
It draws me to it
With its majestic beauty
And echoes sounds of past triumphs
With silent applause and curtain calls

Stories of forbidden love and stubborn will and such
Drew crowds of millions to the stage
Where I stand now in silence

No more Shakespeare plays here now
No more standing ovations
Silence now will reign here
On the Empty Stage

Rebecca Culp

"When I Fell In Love With You . . ."

When I fell in love with you so sincere,
It flowed from my heart bringing forth a tear,
I watched you move to a catalysis of sound,
Arousing tones, and those eye pleasing twirls
Brought out my secret, my senses astound.
'Twas once hidden, and it all now unfurls,
My heart's dam was cracked by passion's moment,
Unbridled that time we were love making,
Emotionally when it started breaking,
And this all feels as if 'tis atonement.
At first, my love for you was a drop in form,
But growing fast, a lovely unending storm
Brewing, love and beauty is now advancing,
When to lovely music you were dancing!

Michael John Ortiz

"Confusion"

Spinning. Swirling. Spiraling down upon me.
It happens every time we look at each other.
We try to act indifferent. Unsuspecting.
What a delusion! What a lie!
The truth, however, reveals itself in our eyes.
Our deep, unflinching eyes. They know the truth.
Why, then, do we continue the deception?
Why not throw ourselves headlong into each other?
I want for it to happen and so do you.
One kiss is all it would take. One innocent kiss.
I suppose there is no such thing as an innocent kiss, though.
Why should that matter any? Especially to me.
I have nothing to lose but much to gain.
I believe that the same applies to you, also.
These intense looks have grown old.
And they hurt. The pain of a missed opportunity.
I want our pain to end. To cease.
I want this confusion to leave us.
One not-so-innocent kiss is all it will take.
Then the real confusion can begin for us.

Patrick James Cheatham

Creative Kindness

Creative Kindness
   Is the channel through which
   One's creative thoughtfulness of others,
   Wends its quiet, unpretentious way
   To the awaiting shore of another's heart;
And there
   With a gentle touch of kindness,
   In word or deed,
   Speaks to that heart of
   Sincerity, warmth, and tenderness.

Thomas E. Tindall

Submersion In The Infinite

I come naked making an offering of myself
it is a small body compared to yours
but it is restless and stirring in time
with your infinite momentum
embrace me
I ask only to submerge myself in your deep blue womb
to let the darkness become a solid entity against my skin
to run my hands along your coral spine
and feel life firing like synapses around me
if I open my mouth I will rejoice in the pressure of my throat
all water gushing inward to quell my human voice
a new sound will bubble from my lips
it will echo my subterranean metamorphosis
I will become a whale growing fins and two blow holes
and weigh thirty tons
a presence in the world at last
   Lynn M. Jones

The Light

I look out the window and I see a white, bright light.
It is coming down on me.
I am scared.
It is calling me.
I won't go.
It is louder and louder and coming closer and closer.
Now I am really scared.
It's still coming, so I run away.
It is still following me.
I scream for help, but nobody comes.
I am by myself.
I scream again.
It picks me up above the clouds.
I float.
This time I can't get away.
Help!
   Melissa Fuentefria

Thoughts

Spring has a great meaning.
It's a season for a new beginning.
The first rain with babbling sound,
feeds the hungry roots in the ground.
The naked trees—it is still winter gloom
but when the sun gives the earth a warm embrace,
the earth will bring forth beautiful greeneries and
clusters of bloom.
Spring brings love and cheer,
everything is full of life when spring is here.
   Mary Pollack

In May

In May the flowers probably say,
"I thought you were going to drown me yesterday."
This is what they'd say to the rain all thirty days before May.
May is a month of hope.
The news has more positive things to say:
"It's Mother's Day, Spring is here and graduations are under way."
In May. May is short and sweet.
Abbreviations don't need to accommodate May.
May can be a name or a month, asking is so much more pleasant
when it begins with May.
May is a time full of peace, is gay.
Sometimes I wish May would never go away.
School's almost out, the kids are more than ready to play.
"All right, okay, just this time" the teacher would say - in May.
The world would be a better place if it were more like May.
May - please stay.
   Sara S. Cooks

"Life's Greatest Gift"

When a gift is given,
It is given with love,
Especially if it comes from above,
It solves all our misery and our strife,
A gift that could change your entire life.

Give to the Lord whatever you can give,
and in the glory of God you can live.
Forever and ever in his love,
Living in the glorious heaven above,
Live for the Lord our God himself,
Dwelling forever in spiritual wealth.

Blessed are those who truly believe,
Strongly in what their eyes can't receive.

And let us be one with Christ as a nation,
And pass on life's greatest gift which is salvation.
   Tom J. Balzamo

This Magic

When the magic comes to those of the ancient
It is said to be wisdom
When the magic comes to those of the young
It is said to be evil
The magic comes to all who call
Yet no value can come from it
No one can see this magic
No one can buy this magic
There is no way to control it
But when it hits you, all shall be understood
It is not evil
It is not wisdom, no...
For this magic comes blessed by the
Young lips of a small child and the
Innocence of every child is in it forever
Now do you wish to call upon the magic's power
Remember it shall grow stronger every hour
Be careful never to fall
For you will destroy yourself
   and the magic all
   Nushabe Kazimov

Self Analysis

I'm too sensitive,
I'm kind,
I'm faithful and loyal.
I'm devoted and love too much.Cedar Creek
The best time I remember
is sitting on the creek bank in December

There was not a cloud in sight
as I watched some geese in flight

Towering rocks forming bluffs so bold
holding so many secrets that can't be told

A little cabin sits on the mountain top
with a view that will make your heart stop

Soon there will be snow
and the cold winds will blow

No matter what the weather may bring
winter, summer, fall or spring

And no matter what day of the week
I can always enjoy Cedar Creek
   LaVerne Clayborn
   Fort Smith, Arkansas

Life's Journeys

Life is full of wonders;
It is what thunders in your heart.

Leading you through bright or dark pathways;
Even though you know some were a plot.

Life is more than a riddle, and being mislead is just one part.
Living it to the fullest, but still having a willing heart.

Bringing to one joy, otherwise, to be still playing your part.
Life is full of wonderful things; consequently, some break us apart.

LaShunda James

Shelly Has A Name

Shelly has a name and it isn't "kick me."
It isn't "degrade" or "abuse me" or even
"punching bag judy."

Shelly has a name - one that is worthy of
respect, kindness and gentleness.

Her name is filled with strength, honor, energy,
love and lots of youthfulness.

Shelly has a name but he stole it when he
punched her with his fist.

Karen Humphreys

Morning Dew

When I hear the breeze rustling thru' the trees,
   it makes me think of you,
and when I dream about our love,
   it's as fresh as the morning dew...

It's in the flowers that bloom with light,
   it's in the coolness of the night.
Smiling thru' the sun, shining down on me,
   brightening my life with clarity....

Sometimes storms rage, clouding the way
   our seas becoming choppy and rough,
but when they subside, dawn a new day,
   we see "together", life's not as tough...

So let the breezes blow, warming our life,
   scattering the hardships, troubles, and strife,
and in the morning, when there's dew....
   LET ME ALWAYS THINK OF YOU.......

Paula J. Dibble

A Passing

I travel a road where death passes me by.
It is a road that travels in the opposite direction of my life.

At first, its presence is not made known or apparent . . .
But then between the silence of my heartbeat . . .

The distant, dark horizon is broken by its warning beacon of
heavenly light . . .

To which I encounter a slow-moving procession
where death passes me by.

Its momentary presence -
   Solemn . . .
      Somber . . .
         Untimely . . .
Much like that of a passing storm cloud.

For now . . .
Without invitation or deadline . . .

I travel a road where death passes me by.

Shelley A. Topham

One More Ride

"Here comes the bus!" I exclaim with a smile.
"It must have traveled at most fifteen miles,"
This was a city bus, everyone knew,
With a driver and the children that made 62.
As I stepped on the bus, on that bright summer day,
I looked up and saw the smiling face of Ms. Dray.
Her personality flowed and her character, a rhyme,
It was 2:30 p.m., she was right on time.
As the kids crowd inside, she gives them a grin,
But I get smile that I'll treasure within,
I went to my seat, and let out a long sigh,
And prepared myself for the extremely long ride.
Yes, it is true, I was the last one off,
It was very tiresome, the weather was hot.
But the end of the ride was so special to me,
For I'd move to the front, to get a cherished treat,
Ms. Dray and I would talk, and laugh like old friends,
And I dreaded the time the ride would end.
Now Ms. Dray is gone, I have nothing to hide,
And I wish, now, I could have just one more ride.

Stephanie Paige Sanders

Beware

There was a songbird, who liked to sing.
It sang and sang about everything.

This songbird, it had two songs.
One was good and one was wrong.

The good song was sung to its fellow birds;
Friendship, friendship and trust they heard.

The other song was to the big hungry cat
About fellow birds doing this and that.

One day while the other birds were playing on the ground,
Songbird sang to the cat where they could be found.

Now that all its friends are gone,
There's nobody around to hear its song.

Let's hope no one else will come to hear,
'Cause it's not the cat but the songbird they fear.

Raymond E. Metcalf Jr.

One Bum Knee Meets Five Physical Therapists

My left knee hurts sometimes
It seemed like time to check it out.

The place
to go for chronic
knee problems
is physical therapy.

Physical therapy is as much art as science.
I am in good health, active, 31 years old.
What should I do?

Russel Silver says I am loose ligamented.
Carol Greenberg says I fell down as a little girl.
Debra Goldman said it was cycles of pain.
Valerie Harris says I have an alignment problem.
Marjolein Unger said one leg was longer than the other.

So far no one has guessed the truth -
Someone whom I have treated badly
Has put a curse on me.

Lisa Miller

The Ice Lily

She kissed the wind as it went by —
It seemed to her she heard it sigh;
Hands outstretched she cupped a cloud —
And almost thought it cried aloud;
As cradled palm stilled quaking leaf
her tracing finger calmed its grief;
In close embrace of rough-barked tree
Did it whisper "... forever hold me..?"
Barefoot she flowed on wet-lipped grass —
Each blade not wanting to let her pass;
Mirror pool in still forest place —
Without a ripple received her grace;
A lily lingers even winter there —
A lily in ice with those who care.

Stuart D. Lenz

What A Glare

The moon twinkles with a glare.
It shines in dark nights,
That represents life and it not being fair.
The moon stands still as motion surrounds.

But the black man has a spirit in the midst.
It cries from injustice through
voices that appear to be non-existing in sounds.
Why is the moon twinkling with that glare
that allows the black man's spirit to grow, as
he lives a life full of great fear and despair
no one but him and other black man can hear?

Shine moon shine!
Exist with a hopeful stare,
instead of your empty glare!

Torrance R. Harvey

Yesterday

It seemed like yesterday I held him with one arm
It sure felt like yesterday I didn't need an alarm
Time went so fast
Only pictures of his baby face past
Where did all the time go; I'm sure it was only yesterday

I waited on him at every whim
Especially when he made an awful grin
A priceless gift from God;
people would give a smile and a nod
where did all the time go; I'm sure it was only yesterday

Now with him being a little older;
I don't care to tell you about him being a little bolder
His independence is growing strong
All his punishments hurt and feel wrong
What will the future hold compared to yesterday

I pray to God to be with us through this trying time
I don't want him to grow up making mischief and doing crime
This is the most precious job;
it definitely won't be without a sob
What will the future hold compared to yesterday?

Wendy J. Horner

I Quit!

I set the pencil down too near the edge;
It toppled to the floor, metallic sheath
In tight-lipped aim against two pallid specks
Who'd dared to litter—that somehow I had missed.

I removed the specks, and set the pencil on a ledge
Beside the weighty list I'd strained beneath
All day, then picked it up again—flexed
My wrist, and set a period to the list!

Mignon T. Brinton

Memory's Touch

I saw a little girl riding high atop her father's shoulders
It touched a memory of days gone by and far away.

I saw a lovely young girl strolling hand in hand
with her lover beneath a moonlit sky
It touched a memory of days gone by and far away.

I saw a smiling young mother holding her infant close
It touched a memory of a laughing child against my
breast in days gone by and far away.

I saw a woman and her mate of middle years
sitting on a summer's swing holding hands and whispering
It touched a memory of lying close with the man I loved,
days gone by and far away.

I see an old woman rocking alone on her front porch
gazing into the past
I am what's left of days gone by — I am the memory!

Suzanne Woomer

Untitled

When the World began
It was a closed flower
Dormant - Still - Quiet
Awaiting the Sun's caressing hour

Slowly each sun-kissed petal
Opened itself for all to see
Stretching - Extending outward
To its full capacity

It Consumed all the light - All the water
Greedily - Carelessly - Ignoring Consequences
It took until it was sated and nothing remained
Yet in its Lust It never Replaced

The flower awoke to the Bareness one day
And it wept with Regret - With no place to turn
Why didn't it Think or Care - But it was too late
All that was left was to Close its petals - wither - and Die

Rayna A. Vause

Your Embracing Touch

Gently I bear my heart to you,
Kiss it ever so gently, for I am blue.
I will be incomplete until we share each remembering
moment,
For whisper not your refreshed breath,
Let your essence walk unto me.
For without you, who am I?
Half of a friend, half of a soul, half of a mate to know.
Ever so softly I will kiss you, as your soul envelops me.

Scott Martin Berry

"Death/The Memories"

Something very real and deep in what you feel,
It's an accident that happens and it's just that way,
It's something that happens each minute of every day,
People don't quite understand, how our lives move so fast,
and from the time of their death they're a part of the past,
So many feelings bottled up inside,
It's like a fast roller coaster, or a bumpy ride,
It's something that happens,
You'll get through it, you'll see,
Because you have something special
that nobody else has...
"The Memories"

Paula Burr

Untitled

This morning I woke up and felt the need for some fresh air.
It was cold and snowy outside, but I didn't care.

I walked to the beach hearing the cold murky water crashing
with a thunderous roar and sometimes a quiet swoosh.

Stopping to listen, a young Bald Eagle flew over me with wings
spread quietly soaring on the wind,
I watched it fly around the rugged bluff bend.

Without a doubt I wanted to shout, thank you God for letting me
share in part of what you put in man's care!

With the crunching of my foot steps in the crispy white snow, I
continued my walk on home, as the wind began to blow.

I stopped for a moment thoroughly enjoying the brisk morning
chill, noticing the frosts crystal-like pattern on the window sill to sill.

With the bark from a dog, I went on inside, crawling back into bed,
knowing my mind had quietly been fed.
Karla Shervanick

Viet Nam Diary

I came to town to see the wall again,
It wasn't the Berlin wall, crumbling to refrain of freedom,
nor was it the wall of defeat
in the last mile of the marathon.

It was a black wall with many
names on it, swallowing the ground
in the horizon.

It made me cry, and I looked
for my name.
I saw that I did not die,
as I was wallowing in Viet Nam shame.

I felt submerged with an orange
chemical burning in my brain,
and I felt small when
I saw the Washington monument
in the distance.
Tony Tripodi

Why?

Why would someone who's usually smart
Let someone take over and control her heart?

Why would she allow the pain he inflicts
Upon her, which causes such stressful conflicts?

Why would she keep being mistreated and abused
When inside she feels so dirty and used?

Why would she continue to be so forgiving
When he's altered the way she goes on living?

Why would she repeat such stupid mistakes
When with every action, her pride he takes?

Why does she seem to take it in stride
But continue to struggle with turmoil inside?

Why won't she get the help that she needs
And put an end to his obsessive greed?

The answer lies with the guilt in her heart.
The guilt that is slowly tearing her apart.

She knows that often she has done wrong.
She should have said, "No!" rather than go along.

She feels that she has no right to complain
So she'll continue to live with the grief and the pain.
Kelley Northam

The Truckee

I'm going to live by a river.
It's called the Truckee.
It's up in the mountains
Where I want to be.
It's cold in the winter and wild in the spring.
In the summer it's cool and best for swimming.
In the fall it's home for birds on the wing;
And for fish in its waters it gives everything.
I love this river they call the Truckee.
It reminds me of what wild animals should be.
And what is that you might ask of me...
It's because, best of all, it's wild and free.
Mac Barton

"Do We Belong"

It's not a matter of right or wrong,
It's do we belong?
Do we have the same path,
Are we looking for the same growth?
Look into your heart and what do you see.
Is it somebody or is it me?
Only we can decide if we...together... are right or wrong,
But me must be truthful whether we really belong.
Sharon E. Khoury

A Precious Life

There's nothing that's cleaner than the breath of a stream.
Its ever growing life feeds all the unseen, from the fish in the
water to the birds in the trees, to the Bears in the thatch who
share their luncheon of leaves.

The world that surrounds us, are we to blind to see?
But the animal's that live here run wild and free.
Only the sky has no boundary, to float with the breeze,
to fly like an eagle so proud yet so free.
To dart on the pray only his eye can see, then soar through the
heavens in command of his world. But soon comes defeat from a
creature called man who see's not the proud life the world's
creatures would lead if given the chance to even complete.

For they are the life the way it was all meant to be!
And with man's greed and great hate our children will be lucky to see,
a trout filled creek or one lonely tree!
Or a sun set that glisten's on our wondrous sea.
So I ask you all brother's and sister's as well to put down your foot
so they don't create hell!
To think of the future the way it would be, when our children would
die never seeing a tree!
Richard E. Allen II

Watching Mallory Grow

I know this pretty little girl, as smart as she can be.
It's hard to guess this pretty miss, can possibly be just three.
She is a little angel, that God loaned us to love.
We should thank him every day, for sending her from above.
She brings joy to all who know her, she fills each day with fun.
She never stops from morn till night, she's always on the run.
Her dad and her are special pals, they talk about things good and bad.
And as she grows much older, he'll be the best friend she's ever had.
She looks so much like her mother, their voices are the same.
She'll be her mother's daughter even after she's changed her name.
I am known as grandma, but I live so far away.
I miss so much the things you do, and all the things you say.
You grow and change from day to day, a special person you will be.
I only hope when you are grown, that you remember me.
Remember me the grandma that wrote this poem for you.
And maybe when you're all grown up, you'll have a daughter too.
Someday you'll be a grandma like me, and then you'll finally know,
how much fun it was for me to watch my Mallory grow.
Lucille Newcombe

Tomorrow

When I stop to think about life,
Its joys, its pains, and sorrows;
I fall down upon my knees and thank God for my tomorrows.
I know that what I face today will become a memory,
And at that moment of truth I realize that God has set me free:
Free to understand that I cannot change the past,
Free to appreciate that true love is long last,
Free to use my life as an example to those whom are to come,
Free even when I feel overwhelmed to know that I must go on.
I know that obstacles will continue to block my way;
So with that thought in mind I enjoy life day by day.
It is with gratitude that I confront what is to be,
And at the same time I have learned to make tomorrow work for me.

Lula M. Walton-Barnett

The Magic Globe

My son gave me a present....Oh! The love it hold's for me
It's made of crystal and of snow...A globe of "Use to Be"

I hold it in my hands...And dream of yesterdays
When he was a baby...When he was at play...

I see him small and not too tall... A sweetness in his soul...
A little boy with a little toy...Made of crystal and of snow...

He gently tips it upside down....And watches the snow fall...
His eyes are bright and shining...His look is one of "awe"

I hold the globe, he gave me...My heart then skips a beat....
And for an instant only...Our past and present meet....

Patti Ann Griffin

On Childhood

Childhood is wonder, adventure and daydreams.
It's tantrums, tooth fairies, and mischievous schemes.

Childhood is playmates, imagined and real.
It's a pre-school diploma with a shiny gold seal.

Childhood is Fairy Tales and nursery rhymes.
It's a piggy bank full of quarters and dimes.

Childhood is a big hug and kisses so sweet
For grandparents who bring a special treat.

Childhood is hopscotch and climbing trees.
It's jumprope, hide-and-seek and skinned knees.

Childhood is a time to laugh and play
And behold the excitement of each new day.

Childhood is the best time of life, some say...
But for some strange reason it soon slips away.

So live it to the fullest, immerse yourself in it.
As the years fly by, it will seem but a minute.

Rita Bryant

Flame That Burns Within

He walks along the edge of time,
In step with the flame he hides inside.
He feels its heat within his soul,
Burning like madness with each thrust of the coal.
He tries to look innocent, caring and kind,
Just as the heat is starting to rise!
He is running from evil that is not far
behind, so he banks to the left and does a great dive!
Then plummets in darkness with tremendous
speed, which was his passing or that's what it seemed.
His mind threw out pictures in front of
his eyes, of the crash where he once had died.
Just as the last picture faded away he
realized as he gave his last cry,
"OH, MY GOD IT'S MY JUDGMENT DAY!"

Suzanne Eva Gardner

Nickels And Dimes

All my life
I've always asked
for what I knew
I could get.

I would ask for five dollars
instead of ten.
I was always under-requesting.
Asking too little
all of my life.
Not a good way to live.

At my present rate, at my funeral, it will look like this:
A fat balding man, looking over my body, saying:
"Now there's a man who could have done better.
He could have died with a dime, instead of a nickel."

In other words,
do what you can't
not what you know you can do.

Patrick Sherrick Moore

— Never Ending Story —

"Just Another Page From The Book Of Love"

I've been through the thick,
I've been through the thin...
Don't know where I'm going,
But surely know where I've been.
The story of my life
Is here within my heart.
In the past, the characters cast
Helped to build the plot.
With those chapters,
Came the raptures,
That now tear me apart.
Pages turned, bridges burned.
All that I've learned, as my heart yearned...
Is what makes a new chapter start!

Richard A. Graham

Don't Look Back

As I walk down the pathways of life.
I've encountered many trials and tribulations.
But as I continue moving forward, I tell myself,
"Don't look back."

Many weeks, months, and years go by.
My life has felt many happy moments.
So there is reason I must say.
"Don't look back."

I know the world itself doesn't stand still.
And the heart..and headaches can and
Will be felt, only I say life is still wonderful
So please remember this if you will.
"Don't look back."

Lee E. Sawyer

A new bird
kicked out of his nest
soft muscles but strong
like a baby's soft but can grip your finger like an eel
his wings kinda know what to do
the collision of wingwithwind sickens him so he has to
sing
launches self onto a current,
current wacks him onto a branch,
he grips it like a huge parent's finger,
decides to risk wings again
and really flies

Neal Buccino

"Never Too Late"

What a pity, what a shame
I've only played at life's passing game
But rather to stop awhile and take in
All that surrounds you from God's great pen
The middle ages are right upon me
What used to be is no longer there to see
"If only" is heard within my mind
But now it's too late and I'm left behind
I think of all I should have asked
But failed to because I was a self-centered lass
Oh how I long to sit with my Mom and Dad
Asking them questions which would reveal of their lives
The things they loved and felt inside
And then you realize how swiftly time flies
So much you've let go down the slide
If only you could reach the younger generation's heart
Warning them, it's not too late to start
So why not make the most of your time
To drink in the beauty of God's great design

Mary Katherine Pattillo-Newman

Communicable Patterns

I could have killed her
Just as she murdered me with neglect
Oh no, she didn't dismember me with a
cold sterilized wire

But my blood gushes out and stains her thighs
She is drowning in my plasma
Generations, covered in cancerous platelets
Every malignant ancestral word,
Dripping from her lips

Spilling a legacy of abuse and broken promises
Destroying what could have been healing
And instead choosing
What is infectious

I wear my blood like a decorated soldier
My purple heart of pain
Intact and contained

I simply choose to
Remain in remission

Raine A. Carson

Christmas Joys

Stockings full of toys,
Just for little girls and boys.
The Christmas tree stands tall,
And underneath love gifts for all.
Creeping down the chimney comes a big fat man,
He is wearing red and white and has a sack in his hand.
He swiftly tiptoes over to the tree,
And pulls out what he has in store for me.
I close my eyes, I can't wait to see,
Just what this man plans to give me.
I open my eyes and see the most beautiful thing of all,
Snow is falling in a tremendous downfall.
I ran to the window and started to stare,
Then all of a sudden I see a bright glare.
It is so bright I can hardly stand it,
I look up at it, and it is the moon brightly lit.
I see a sleigh and reindeer fly by,
Then I see a man in the sleigh, and he politely
  waves goodbye.

Kristin Williams

Why Can't I

Why can't I
  Just once, be the tail that
    wags the dog?

Why can't I
  Just once, skip being the tadpole
    and be a frog?

Why can't I
  Dream the impossible dream and
    make it come true,
      Reaching all those goals attained
        by few?

Why can't I
  Help end much of the suffering and strife,
    that's plagued mankind through
      most of his life?

Why can't I?
  Well, you can,
    You can win
      all you have to do is begin.

R. C. Rimel

I Never Wanted Much

I never wanted much from life
just what most young girls dream of:
a house, a car, and a couple of kids
and a kind, sweet man to love.

I wanted to marry and hove my children young
to watch them make their way through life,
and have my husband stand proudly beside me
as he whispers "I'm glad you're my wife."

I wanted so much to be a grandmother
and see reflections of me as they grew,
to have them wrap their arms around me,
and say "Sweet Grandma's like you are few."

I wanted to grow old with my husband
to be content in our Golden Years
and the only tears I'd ever shed
would be happy and contented tears!

I've never really wanted much
as I made my way through life
I just wanted to be what's important to me
a grandma, a mother and a wife.

Lonnie Carr

Oklahoma Bombing

O Lord, have mercy
K king Jesus is all you need
L Lord have mercy
A all my help comes from the Lord
H have you any rivers that seem uncrossable?
O how I love Jesus, because he first loved me
M make up your mind to follow Jesus
A at the cross where I first saw the light

B because he lives, you can face tomorrow
O taste and see
M my minds made up to serve the Lord
B be steadfast, unmovable, always abounding
I can't stop praising his name
N never along, he promised never to leave you, never to leave you
  alone
G God specializes in things impossible and he will do what no other
  power can do!

Lucy L. Williams

Free As Butterflies

Don't be unhappy...Don't shed a tear
Know that I am watching you from here
Please understand I did not want to leave
  but know there is no more pain....
Think of me when you rise with the morning sun
When the moon rises and you see the first star of the night
  know it's me winking at you in the twilight....
In the spring plant my favorite flowers watch and you will
  see clusters of butterflies gather around, take a good look
  and see they're watching you and know one is me....
In the summer as the long hot days pass....
When you're eating watermelon don't forget to spit
  some seeds for me...
When the trees turn color and the birds fly south...
When the cold winter days seem like they'll never go away...
Remember the years we had even though they were so short
  it meant the world to me to grow and share things with you
I will see you again one day soon and then we'll both be
  Free As Butterflies...
   Nancy A. Hertz

Freedom Chance

They call this land America, home of the brave
Land where people dwell for the freedom they crave
They come from great distances and many places
Setting aside their past, leaving no traces
Many come only with one thing
Hope for a new beginning or whatever God's goodwill might bring
Once here, they struggle just to make it from day to day
It's sad and ashamed people choose to live their lives in this way
Some beg, while other turn to a life of crime
Leaving them behind bars doing time
A few unfortunately end up six feet deep
Giving their souls up for someone else to keep
Though there are a few who make the effort to make it through the day
Educating themselves and working hard for an honest day's pay
These people only came for a chance at freedom and happiness
Many of them end up with the freedom but also with sorrowness
So I guess it's true in life that nothing is for free
At least that's what these people see
   Thomas K. Post

Love's Journey

Come run with me through fields of newly mown hay.
Let me feel my hand in yours;
Share the gladness of the day.
Come sit by me in quietness;
Enfold me in a warm embrace.
Fill me with a confident joy;
Touch my lips and caress my face.
Speak to me of gentle things, of secret dreams,
of hope and fear, of joy, of love, and laughter,
of deepest thoughts.
And in our sharing and our knowing,
We'll find our tender love is growing.
   Nathan Holtzclaw

Fragment (9:19) Saturday Night

Brake lights never turning on,
like Zebedee's boys lost to the sun,

A sure sign she is never coming back,
crayolas my heart the color black.

Her car speeds off in veiling light,
and tragedy is alone again on this autumn night,

A grove at Gethsemane where her ocean once flowed,
now left behind are soiled pools of oil and failed gardens of gold.
   Patrick Toney

Can It Be!

Feel my emotion; hear what they say
late last night, or was it the night before,
  I tossed and turned
   like a lost soul in hell condemned to burn!
Can it be!
  The night won't let me be.
  Because the passion that swells within me
   longs to be set free
So I close my eyes just to be with you
If what I feel is true
I wonder will your heart do
What I want it to, you gentle lover, you angel child.
Who am I to believe that I'm any more than you
as I look into your eyes they're so enchanting
It melts my heart
  and love is born
   sweet as the morning dew
   falling from me to you.
   Parish Blake

"Time For My Dad"

1945 We rested, watched the clouds,
Laughed, different shapes, floating,
Chubby babies, clowns, animals,
My dad, caring and fun.

1947 Salt lake City's 100 year parade,
Dad made sure we made the parade,
The bus was our only transportation.
Dad found a way to buy our first bikes,
mine was the most beautiful blue ever!
1954 Dad was very ill. - Not physically —
Chemical imbalance in the brain —
friends weren't friends anymore, that
old social "stigma."
I let him down when he needed a place to live.
1969 Dad wanted so much to see 1st man
on the moon. He died may 1969 - man on moon
2 months later. I hope he had a bird's eye view.
"I love you - Dad" - (1904-1969)
   A. Heusser

You!

My love for you-
  leads me to tell everyone of your extraordinary beauty,
  and think of you on only two occasions, day and night!

Because I love you-
  my appetite often escapes me when we're apart.
  My heart has convinced me to resist other women.
  I'll excel in all endeavors!

You make me-
  wild and crazy!
  Happiness is my mother, and desire, my father!

I want to grab-
  the future and bring it here...now!
  You!

Thank you-
  my love!
  my life!
   Norman D. Davis

Unconscious Destinies

In the realm of distorted perceptions lies a truth called reality
  Its bounds are undefined and surpass themselves over and over
In the unconscious destinies of the world.
   Julie Carey

Corporate Games

Join a firm, expect to stay.
Learn to do the company way.
Pledge your life, your brain and skill.
Rewards will come, you know they will.
Promises kept, promises made.
All good hard work will be repaid.
Just do your best each day by day.
Corporate games I learned to play.

Times have changed, it's not the same.
They changed the rules, they changed the game.
With mergers made or things downsized.
Some lose the game, some win the prize.
Some retire before their time.
Loyalties change for an extra dime.
Perhaps I'll go, perhaps I'll stay.
Corporate games I've learned to play.

Lois Renker

Empty

The wind whistles through dancing shadows
   Leaves rustle under dragging feet
Cold air burns as it caresses my face
   Sadness chills my broken heart
     I walk alone.
A solid course rock
   The only comfort I find
My numb, tired body rests upon
   Pondering restless thoughts and shattered dreams
     I sit alone.
The night sky slowly swallows
   The last light of day
Darkness encloses me in its chilled embrace
   Feeling empty and broken
     I cry alone.
Angels mourn for another lost soul
   Tears from heaven fall
Trapped in a black hole
A world all my own
Lost in hopelessness and despair, I am alone.

Mary E. Kremer

Game Of Life

Life is full of mysteries,
Leaving us with many memories.
Some that we all regret,
Others we don't want to forget.
No one really understands the meaning,
Yet we all have the precious gift
of living.
At times life guides us in the
wrong way,
But in time we all learn it's our
heart we need to obey.
Our heart knows what is true,
and always knows exactly what to do.
As we all grow up and realize
what life is really about,
and we finally find the one we can't
live without,
our heart begins to grow for that special
someone.
And from there on the game of life is won.

Shannon Thayer

"Carnival In Paradise"

They sing and dance in jubilation
Legs akimbo, hands in the air.
Costumes colorful visions of imagination
Butterflies, fishes, birds - the focus of everyone's stare.

Down the street they tramp
To the sweet melody of calypso.
Tall Moko Jumbies entertain - bodies damp
And the children.....how they love it so.

Tummies grumble under the sun
As the air fills with pates and fries
Eating guava tarts, having fun
Later, at night fireworks illuminate the sky.

Exhaustion overcomes me
As I claim my warm bed.
Vibrant figures in my dreams I see
And they remain through the days ahead.

Neela Sookdeo

This Place.....

Here's my hand, take it.
Let me lead you to this place...
I'll take you step-by-step, hand-in-hand
I'll be your guiding light.
Let me lead you to this place...

This place is where we can discover
each other's inner beauty
This place is where we can express ourselves
openly and freely.

This place can be so wonderful and exciting
It can be so innocent and pure, but also
intriguing.

Let me lead you to this place...
that's built on trust, honesty,
communication and dedication.
This place... you can bond as "one"
This place... is "LOVE."

Theresa S. Herrejon

The Shoe

To want what's not again and again,
it'll drive a man like me to sin.
What once was there is gone today,
sacrificed away to stay.

Those pallid few too skewn to share,
forsake their own without want or care.
Or give to one - unfaithful mind,
and break my heart too weak to bind.

Bring this circle at once to end,
find the one whose caring mend.
Search long and hard 'till interest arouse,
that lonely heart I still espouse.

At times long end when the looking is through,
you'll find my love like and old sock, or shoe.
Too tattered to wear yet somehow warm,
Something sheltered and protected from the storm.

If today was yesterday as chance may be,
might you find a place for me?

Robert D. Lewis

Nature's Touch Of My Love

When we are apart,
let nature caress you as I would.
Let the sun kiss you gently upon your face.
The warm gentle breeze be my whispers of love,
The gentle rain be my tears when we are apart,
and the thunder the beat of my heart.
When you lie upon the cool green grass,
let the firmness of the Earth be our bodies touching.
When you look up into the light blue sky,
imagine you're looking into my eyes,
and you'll see the love I have for you.
Hear the stream's waters rushing by
for it is the time passing
until we can be in each other's arms again.
Nancy Ann Anderson

Untitled

The sweet desires of life
  lie in the depths of one's mind.
To taste one's lips
  just to find delicate flavor,
    of aged wine within.
To touch one's skin
  just to have known the softness,
    is as that of a rose petal.
To hear one's voice
  just like the whispers,
    of a gentle breeze.
And to smell the aroma of one's presence
  is enough to bring all the wonderful memories;
    brought to you,
      by the one you love.
Naomi Carius

Love's Light

Shadow to eyes, deep of mystery,
Lies of sweetness, passions from the light,
treating this heart to satin,
Thunder from rain's poetic drop,
hearing of sighs, pain's wind of mood,
the sentinel's light fading to the eave,
making love under its realm,
sanity's time rocks to the passions,
riding a wave on emotion's delight,
rarity to this love,
sanctuary to its depth,
sounds the wave to early sun's light.
William Pringle

Just A Picture On My Wall

The sun's a soft warm glaze
In a pale blue sky.
Giving me its last rays
Do you appreciate it as much as I?

The wind dances through my hair
Feels good against my skin.
Yesterday could not compare
I've already given in.

I walk along the edge
Gathering sand between my toes.
Gone is the champagne in my glass
Don't want to leave, does it show?

The water is so enticing
Soft waves embrace my legs.
There's no-one here, I should go swimming
Won't be long before I fade away...
Lisa Patterson

Life Is Real

Life can be lonely, life can be sweet.
Life can be sensuous, life can be neat.
Life is common sense and more.
Life, it's your open door, hoping to have a whole lot more.
I know life special decorated with details.
Life can have you walking on sea shells.
Life is a gamble, life is a race.
Racing towards my career in place.
Life will be special, pure and real.
Life is the kind of cards you wish to deal.
Life is a trade, living, giving, and caring.
So make your choice, make yours today.
Because tomorrow isn't promised.
But it will be another day.
Give life a score, a point, a chance,
a remembrance of me.
Live life, it's living and dying.
Live it and see.
Life, it's you; life, it's me.
Marcella Thompson

The Circle

We all began as one, in harmony and balance
Life was so simple, the laws soft and gentle.

We were part of the greater whole
Co-equals existing in nature's balance.
With no one above the other, each respecting the other's place.
Man, animal, plant, all interdependent
And respectful of the Creator and the beauty created.

But something happened along the way,
The old ways were forgotten, new ones entered, the balance shifted.
Laws of power, laws of control replaced the old.
The completeness of the whole gave way
To the puzzle of the parts,
Lines and boundaries reduced our vision
We become educated, but we lost our knowledge.

The sun has risen and the birds are singing.
The winds move the clouds, the branches wave.
The raccoons scurry for a rest,
and the eagle shouts its call.

We are in harmony, we only have to see.
Steve Christian

Easter Dawn

The cold wind whistles, 'round the headstones now,
Light glows, then glistens, o'er the brittle bough.
My loves, will you wake, stir to hear me weep?
Feel my breast shake, or lie you fast asleep?

Sleep not, my loves, such ends I cannot bear,
Take flight, sweet doves, entombed do not rest there.
Lie not you by these stones, through long cold night,
Fly away, sweet doves, to bask in His light!

Rise, sweet doves, flee the buried box of bones,
Glide high above, o'er this cold yard of stones.
Behold his dawning day, as it grows bright!
Light bathes your souls, accompanies your flight!

Though I stoop to stones, I long for the air,
In fancied flight, to greet my sweet doves there.
So hover doves awhile, 'bove the dewed lawn,
Linger for me there, I'll meet you at dawn.

Then my soul unshackled, by Him sprung free,
We will embrace, and soar eternally!
Richard Bridgford

Best Friends...

Best friends always stick together
like a bird to its nest. Best friends tell
each other secrets that they would
not dare tell anyone else. You
know that during a crises in your life, your friends
will always be just around the corner
waiting there for you. And later in your
life, you part from your friends like
a bird - ready to leave its nest - and learn how to fly away
You hope you can still be
best friends, but through the days, months,
and years you change and you meet new
people, or new best friends. But through
life's heartbreaks, and with all your
memories you still remember that
one person who stuck with you...
your best friend.

Kathleen Craig

Where I Lie

I lie in the cold dark, the tangible blackness enveloping me
like a lover.
It invades me, rapes me, caresses me with its tainted touch.
I reach through the delirium, blinded by the vertigo.
I'm so alone.
My life has become a laughing stock.
Who do I think I'm kidding?
My wanderings have led me to Hell.
Someone should be getting a kick.
I see my enemy; he's on the other side of the mirror.
He smiles when I do. He cries when I do.
Loser. Fiend. A**hole.
I turn from my reflection ...back to the dark illumination
but I do not remember peace anymore
images in my mind wrack at my sanity.
Pain; no more than pain... torture
at least in the veil of inky blackness, I cannot witness the rapist
who is in the throws of passion.
How he must love his job.
Somewhere I drift away... to a dream...
is this an escape or is this the next iron maiden?

Rob Evans

Time

Time will never end
Like impulsive youth with an abundance to spend

A joyous succession of childhood days
Endless hours blessed by sunshine's rays

The window of puberty agonizes so slow
Impetuous wanna-be thrusting to go

Love won and lost; time soothes rended hearts
Which runs fleetingly as offspring start

Ambitious adults toil to get ahead
Fast they go but behind instead

Worldly labors earn a replenishing glow
A rewarding respite resisting life's flow

Like shadows tasks are longer, but time won't wait
Resolute we march on with hampered gait

An eddy in time conjures vestiges of fame
While tracing painful moments of shame

With clouded mind we clearly see
Visions of past blend with reality

During our golden era reflections pass
Only to know time won't last

Larry Hagethorn

'Video Game Pimp'

Going to market with the newest rage,
Like some long traveling sage.
Selling a little mortal combat where pixels get hurt,
So to let the youth have their killing flirt.

The Mario Brothers flatter a turtle,
While an earthworm blows wind.

It is a joy to be a new age pimp,
Turning the high-minded child into a chimp.
Hitting the controller so as to kill a menacing blip,
While on a Snapple they will slowly sip.

A ninja tears out his opponent's spine,
While screaming girls run about in a night trap.

They're the new age of American culture,
The mindless, circling vulture.
Here comes the world's final stage,
As I leave and the world an unwanted sage.

N. Jonathan Dennis

Pieces

The time for talking has come and gone
Like the snow that falls in the wintertime
Words are everywhere much like the snowflakes
Everything accumulates but specifics are hard to find
An eerie white blanket steals any spotlight
With a naivete and maliciousness rolled into one
Neither gaining the upper hand, too bland
From where does it all come?
High above, in a dense cloudy obscurity
Tiny building blocks begin their lives
Unknowing as to a final destination
Finding out where they are only after they arrive
Pieces of time float aimlessly down
Searching only for a final resting place
A grand finale for an anonymous beginning
Existing in the long loneliness of space
But that perhaps does not have to be
As a difference is made even by one small piece
The strongest of chains can be broken
By the resourcefulness of the very least

Paul Novak

Leaf

Golden-brown, heart-shaped, like a
little canoe, she drifts in autumn wind.
Dust on her flat face, web on her boney back,
she travels in the wind with destination.
Once, she stopped, thinking of the green
youth she spent by that running brook.
Blue birds had sung for her on spring mornings;
a little spider had built her home on her back.
Yet she is falling and withering in autumn wind.
No one remembers her young face.
Perhaps her mother would recall her past,
but she wouldn't tell.

As I watch the leaf floating in the air,
I remember mother's long hair in the wind.
Now I understand the bitterness in her eyes
when she sent me off to another land.
Ten autumns have carved the wrinkles on my face;
ten winters have planted mother's sorrows on her forehead.
While I'm searching for a better life,
mother's beautiful hair is turning white.

Yi-Wen Chan

Save The Children

The sad face children with dirty clothes and hands
Live in a collapsing wooden shack
A trail of tall grass leads to the well out back
The children, mother and father are unemployed,
The food runs out before the end of the month,
They are hoping for a bag of food
The children have hunger pains
They cannot play, they have not eaten all day,
They have a painful infection called poverty
There are no sewers, no water, no electricity, no jobs, no hope
Every passing day ends with the reality of diminished hope

Maxcine Fuller

The Little Mermaid

Deep in the ocean, way out about a mile —
Lived a little mermaid, with a magical smile.
She swam among the fish-e-e-e-s, she dived among the stars
She'd tickle the jelly fish, and nap on the sand bars.
But then, one day a ship sailed by, with a lonely crew
The little mermaid swam right up, out of the blue!
The sailors were astonished, they could not believe their eyes
The lovely creature from the sea, was such a big surprise!
The crew paused and pondered, what fate to them had come —
But the thought of a mermaid, began to sound like fun!
The mermaid climbed upon the front, and perched her pretty tail —
"Ahoy, mates!" she called out, "It's time to set sail!"
The crew sailed for many day, the mermaid as their guide —
But alas, when the voyage was over, into the sea she dived!

Margaret Roberson

Times That We Spend

The times that we spend bring memories to lend
living each day blessed with a friend

The moments of laughter and those of despair
Someone to listen, understand and care

Sharing the joy, feeling the sorrow
having a friend always brightens tomorrow

Cherish the trust, always return the lend
Forever a treasure, the love of a friend.

Randolph McFadden

The Medium

The ghosts and spirits of people who were once
living, I believe are here. Speak to me or give me
a sign that you spirits are near or that you are here.

Speak to me tell me the truth, don't tell me a lie
for you see that it's only the truth that I am able to hear.

You are a faint colored mist without feet that
slowly, begins to speak there is nothing that
I can say I am humble and meek.

The ghost is a blasts from the past. I remember now
he was once an artist called Rembrandt.
It's not my fault that I was born with this gift where
at the drop of hat I start to glance and go into a
Mediumistic trance.

The voices of those who are no longer here it is their
voices that i hear and yes those people are still very Dear.

I'm not small, I am not large either for it's only mediums
like me who can at a glance just go into a trace. I am a
receiver that's true, I won't deceive you.
I'm not buoyant because I am clairvoyant.

Sheryl Hanna

Christian Woman

Wonderful, wonderful, wonderful me,
Living life so happily,

Living life through the Spirit above,
Living life fully through Christ's love.

Wonderful, wonderful, wonderful you.
What I do you can, too.

Jesus is the path to take.
Do it for your Salvation's sake.

You will find happiness you never dreamed,
Unlike anything the world has schemed.

Wonderful, wonderful, you and me
When we open our hearts to the Christ we see

Life as intended by God above
Filled with health, and Joy, and Eternal Love.

L. Mila Warn

Perfect World

You could try and control the devil in me
lock it up and deny it of free

You could try and stunt the growth of my will
the passion in my reverence
that is often halted to a stand-still

I could moan and would cry
because my memories are stale
wasting away in my mal-nourished head dying of hunger
and an insatiable appetite for things left unsaid

I could wait in confusion or just end it all
I could live an illusion or nothing at all
I'd like to hide under my bed
or rather the tiny asylum
that exists inside my head

You make me want to adore myself
and extinguish myself simultaneously
I rush to fast forward these times
but all too soon I'm dying to rewind

I'd like to stay here in my perfect world
the one that never existed, only in the eyes of this little girl...

Laurel Parisi

Walls Of Steel

Locked up, blocked shut, bars of steel. Cold is how I feel,
Locked up in this cell, locked up in this hell. And each day
I sit and stare, something we all share. The world it
passes me by, this is no lie. I can't even change this
if I try. I sit and stare through my despair I long for freedom,
like a mole from his hole. But I know in time I'll be
set free. But until this day I'll wait and see. So here
I stand, a naked man in this place, with only time to
face. You and I share the dream, a dream of life and
nothing more. And of this I do adore. So here I sit
and wait, for this is my fate, I'm finding out too late.
This world is a beautiful horizon with gold bars afar
from mine, convicts in line. So this is my life, and
this is how I live it. Pity me not, for I've been caught.
You don't ever want to come to this place, you don't
belong here. So heed my warning.
Drugs you dare and the crime is unfair.
If you can't do the time, commit no crime.

Richard W. Pexton

Lost

I hear the night sounds
Loneliness surrounds me, closes in.
I wander without direction or cause
There is no purpose to life without you.

The empty days and nights stretch into eternity.
My sanity balances on a precipice.
I am alone, without you
Yet, you are my reason for being.

Reach out to me, touch me
Before the distance becomes too great.
Do not condemn me to this wandering
Lost with no one waiting.
   Maxine A. Merry

"Without You"

You've been there every step of my way
Long as I can remember
With a love that wrapped around me like no other

When I have up you came in
With a strength I couldn't find within
I miss you-

Without you each day is hand to her through
Without you each night I wonder
What am I gonna do without you.

The comes a warmth a familiar feel
A touch I can remember
I wake up - you're gone

And the feeling inside starts to grow old
The crying in your heart starts to make you cold
Why'd you do away -

Maybe I'll tear up the town - point up the cry
Find someone who can make me forget about you
Each day is hard to get through
Without you each night I wonder
What am I gonna do without you
   Marie Adele English

Infinity

"You have suffered, haven't you, my child," she questioned gently,
long robes lifting with the breeze, golden hair melting in the sunlight.

"All souls have chosen their own Karma. You have been here before,
have lived different destinies, forged various paths.

You have close the first part of this life
to complete old business, settle old hurts.

It is now time to begin experiencing
the joy within your days, the love within your heart."

"But hurts!" she cried.
"they have turned from me once, I could not bear twice.
You cannot ask if of me and I cannot bear the pain a second time."

Silken strands of hair wrapped lightly around her body,
holding her in a loose embrace.

"You have the strength," the soft voice promised,
"to anticipate the future with joy.
You have the strength," she insisted, "to be truly happy."

Her whispers hung in the air,
reverberating to a music of their own making.

Perhaps.
   Tawnie M. DeGrange

Gangs

They're not all that.
Looking at the gangs, they act so tough,
But...they're not all that.
They deal in guns and drugs...
But without all that...they're not all that.
Listening to the gangs all you hear is Bang-Bang.
But...they're not all that.
They wear their colors and tilt their hats.
But...they're not all that
So let's make a pledge not to join a gang.
Because in reality...gangs are nothing but a fatality.
So it's just the fact,.. they're not all that.
So I pledge to stay drug and violence free.
So if that's what being all that is...
I don't want to be all that...
  Just me.
   Ryan Marie Konen

Looking For...

Running in the night
Looking for something in the darkness
No human around but still being watched
Something in my hand
But don't have the strength to look down
In the far a light appears
It's dim but bright enough to see
I finally reach the source of the light
A wooden door
With the light shining through the key hole
The key was in my hand
Slowly I opened the door
On the other side the end of my journey
So I turned and walked away
   Rafael Gomez

"Between The Two Rivers"

Between the two rivers, where they become one,
Looking towards heaven, stands an Indian's son.

No sound from his mouth, and no blood in his veins,
Unchallenged he stands, the keeper of the plains.

His arms are uplifted, his head is held high.
He offers a prayer to God in the sky.

His prairie has vanished, his Buffalo too.
But he leaves a message, for me and for you.

That Great Spirit in heaven listens to all.
So ask for His guidance, when on Him you call.
   Leon Simmons

Love Addiction

I had a habit, oh! for so long.
Knowing all the while, it was wrong.
Hating the fact it controlled my life
And admitting it when I lost my wife.
The treatment I sought is God sent I'm sure.
For arresting my illness, there is no cure.
In the place of booze, my main addiction
I've replaced with love as my conviction.
Love addiction, is like a wall
of defense against my boozing past.
Without this wall, I cannot last.
I love the world and all that's in it
Without this love I cannot win it.
   Nelson Joseph Simmons

Love Conquered My Soul

Encourage my heart...with nice and easy kisses of joy.
Love generates beauty and wisdom.
My soul needs your pretty help.
Your wonderful help-lotion sprays my heart
with gentle beauty and truthfulness.
Love makes life "so easy." I adore your soulful smile.
Yes! My soul needs genuine help.
Yes! My mixed up heart desires your beauty and excitement.
Love caught me. Please! Easy does it.
It's easy to fix-up my "soulful dreaming"
...so help repair my sad heart...use your
soft beauty and enchantment. Love is my goal
and love is indeed..."easy to take"...can
my heart understand your help?
Can you coax my soul to merge with beauty?
Can this new beauty merge with heaven?
Love won me...with easy-smiling ways.
My soul understands your helping warmth.
...Keep my heart...near your easy...
helping...beautiful-heart.
"Love Conquered My Soul".... ....

Bill Fox

Love Is

Love is not just a feeling;
Love is giving;
Love is sharing;
Love is caring and forgiving.

Love is what keeps my life going;
It helps me and my family to go on living.
Having ups and downs, we still keep on going;
Still going on living and striving.

So many times, we have misunderstandings;
So many times, we have each other's shortcomings;
So many times, we hurt each other's feelings;
But still we keep our love growing.

With love no matter what you do,
With love no matter what you go through;
Always keep it within you;
And let it grow and glow.

This I will say to you,
Love is what you keep;
Love is what you cherish;
For love is the greatest.

Placida C. Mencias

"What Do You Need?"

The fruits of the Spirit are listed below,
Love, joy, peace, and long suffering,
Gentleness, goodness, faith,
Meekness and temperance are given by the King
To all who need them so.
Is your problem hatred?
If so, you need love.
Maybe you are bitter,
And need joy from above.
Do you have long suffering? Christ did.
Maybe being gentle and good
Is your problem too.
Everyone has faith,
But God can increase that faith in you,
And help you to fight the devil as you should.
God will give these gifts to you,
If you accept Him and His grace,
And ask Him into your heart,
And then of your sin there will be no trace.

Tobias Gerber

Explanation Of The Lonely Star

When you see her eyes in the dark glistening
Like two lost stars shining together but separate
Don't scream because you think she's a demon
Stop and pet this mysterious creature
If it bites your hand off
Don't worry you've got another
Just as she 'had' two eyes
Maybe next time you'll pause just a moment
When you see this one eyed creature
Staring back at you in the dark

Robert B. Berlin Jr.

"One Painting Ahead"

We are the artists in the gallery of life.
Life is the painting of reality where we
express our feelings and emotions in a
mandala of colors. After the painting
is completed, we let it dry and hang it
on the wall of forever. So, do not retain
your anger or pain. Every time we gaze at
our painting we will experience those
feelings anew, but with greater understanding
and knowledge, since we have
been rewarded with the value of wisdom.
Each day we paint again, employing the same
mandala of colors, but with a different technique.
Then we may comfortably remember the past,
because each painting reveals our hand-print,
which is the signature of our souls.

Maria Covas

Precious Liberties

The Stars and Stripes - The Red, White and Blue;
It is sacred to me. Is it to you?
There are those who would step on it, even
 set it ablaze.
Where is the pride? Where is the praise
For those who gave their lives in
 bygone days,
So this symbol of freedom could still be raised?
Will we lose these precious liberties so rare—
To salute Old Glory and bow our heads in prayer?
God said he would not always strive with men.
Will we lose our freedoms because of our sins?
We must return to the Shepherd's fold,
And begin again as in the days of old,
To make God, our neighbors and this land of
 the free,
Uppermost in our minds, our top priorities.

Lela Dyer

The Fog

The fog comes creeping, creeping into the streets
like a thick blanket of white mist shrouding the ground.
Hiding all the familiar landmarks hidden from view

The street lamps shining like cats eyes seeing in the dark
In and out of the creeping fog I go. Running, running
Playing hide and seek, looking for the answer.

Looking for my last love, lost to me forever.
The witness of the fog hides my tears.
For all the lost feeling I have had.
In the goodbyes long ago I said.
To my lost love never to return.

We had our goodbyes
now only the tears are left,
 In the bay.

Sara Cook

Fantasy Flight

I traveled to wondrous places last night
It was a most delightful flight
I visited lands far and wide
All on a magic carpet ride
I ate fine foods from plates of gold
And danced with noblemen both young and old
I clothed my body in shimmery silken sheets
While crystal slippers adorned my feet
I accented my fingers with glossy pearls
As glistening gems entwined my curls
I never thought all this would last
But everything moved much too fast
I did not notice the small flash of light
Until it grew enormously bright
The sun had invaded my special place
As daylight streamed across my face
I could no longer resist the sun
It was time to end my fun
But I will return to my fantasies
Gee! I am only thirteen

Margaret G. Fleming

A Mother Memory

To my mother who has gone home to be with the Lord
looking down on her daughter with such tender love
saying, God, protect my child in such a special way,
and let her know that I loved her each and every day
Remember the times you played with your doll, or most
of all when we went to the park.
You always had that special smile on your face,
whenever you wanted to go out and play
I watched you carefully as you played in the yard, then
I looked up to heaven and said, thank God for my child
Who else will love you as much as I do, except for
Jesus who's precious to us too.
So don't cry, my child, when Mother's Day comes
instead call on Jesus; He will comfort your heart
O death, where is your sting, no more pain or suffering
I have taught you, my child, good values in life
so go on in Jesus, and try to live right
and make me proud of you, each and every day
because your mother loves you in such a special way.

Theresa McKeever

Happiness

Happiness is - - -
  The ability to rise and face each new day,
  To spread sunshine and cheer along the way;
  To watch the sun set and slowly sink out of sight,
  To see the moon and stars appear to usher in the night.

Happiness is - - -
  To take a stroll beside a babbling stream,
  To momentarily forget your problems and daydream;
  To read a good book, to go on a hike,
  To play a game of croquet or ride a bike.

Happiness is - - -
  To hear the laughter of children as they play,
  To know you've done your best at the end of the day;
  To hear the pitter-patter of a summer rain,
  The assurance of knowing that time eases pain.

Happiness is - - -
  Elusive when it is searched for,
  One of Aesop's fables, a tale out of folklore;
  Interest in those who've been put on the shelf,
  A way of life for those who forget self.

Evelyn Knouse

The Spiral

Rage of a wolf or the silent of a
Lamb? Alone from night to night you
will fine me. Too weak to break
these chain that bound me. I sit by my window, and see no
flowers. I need not no the time
nor the hours. Alone from night to night you will find me.
Look around no sound. Children make
you laugh, than they make you
weep. Were are my brother, mother,
sister and father? Ship at a
disdain has everyone wish on board. I sit by my window;
and see no sea. Only the lonely no me. Alone from night to night
you will find me, to weak to break these chain that bound me.
How long has it been? How long will it be?
Love, Love, show thyself to me.
Why must the weak be? Alone from
Night to night you will find me,
Sitting by my window; if only I could see who speaks.
Rage of a wolf; silent of a lamb.
Rage of a wolf, silent of a lamb.

Lee Martin

Tall Wall

I had built up such a wall
it must have been at least 10 feet tall
made of solid brick and stone
I thought I'd never have a love to call my own
I often thought I was meant to be alone
but you somehow tore that old wall down
by showing me you'd always be around
you've done something for me that no one
else could. I never felt anything
that ever felt this good by just
being you you've taught me how to be me,
to live, to love, and to be free
by simply giving me your love
you've given me all that I will ever
need. Love is a flower and you planted
the seed and now with that old
wall all gone there's room for it to
grow on and on.

Shannon M. Bowles

A Special Guy

You're the greatest guy in the world,
The best gift from heaven above,
but if you weren't here...
My heart wouldn't have anyone to love.

The day you came into my life,
You brought Sunshine to my eyes,
No more rainy days,
or the search for fine guys.

The sound of your voice makes my heart rejoice,
To feel your touch sends chills through my spine,
When I look at your face,
I am proud to say you are mine.

Your dark sparkling eyes,
and your smooth black skin,
No one could replace you
My love they could not win

On another happy day,
You'll be wearing a wedding ring,
because I am a queen,
and you are my king.

Candace Thomas

Untitled

Hither comes the raging river
forward comes the running sun
do you see me in the trees
for I am not the only one.

We live among these giving trees
we give these trees our love in return
those who do not make our trees burn.

The trees are our souls we live among
them all.

Virginia Zampella

The Effortless Error

How many times have you and I
Found ourselves in a shrugging sigh.
Seeming to say "Oh what the bother,
This will pass and bring on another."

Each mistake accepted so,
Insouciant, blah, and oh, so-so.
Our minds closed, blank and narrow -
Welcoming in the effortless error.

What, if after each mistake
We would take a 'learning break';
Something deep inside would pause,
"For this mistake, what was the cause?"

With real effort and decision,
Minds open, sure clear vision,
Lessons learned are silent mirrors,
Reflecting hard on future errors.

W. Neil Hohmann

Little Jamal

He is as big as age
four and a half,
and as long as a two and a
half size shoe.
As he alights onto his
grandmother's lap with a plop,
his eyes take on a crafty hue.

They carefully reveal
a mind so quick
as he selects the next
thing to conquer,
while his grandmother
places candy inside his pocket
hoping to forestall his rancor.

Having scaled the room
with scant success
he slides down unwittingly
on grandma's dress, and plants
a kiss upon her cheek, accepting
her candy, as an offer of peace.

Luqman A. Magied

Friends

Friends are always there,
Friends will always share,
Memories from long ago.
In everlasting time,
you'll have to keep in mind.
That I will always love you,
and never forget you.
You will always be with me,
know matter where you are!

Tiffany Haines

Reflections

Fragile, fleeting memories,
From a youthful frame of time,
Flicker 'cross my consciousness,
Forming into rhyme.

Spider lilies growing, blowing,
Waving heads of red,
Glimpse of an old fall afternoon,
Shines clearly in my head.

Then winter shadows on a shade,
Of trees all bare of leaves,
A childhood sunny old cold day,
A lasting picture weaves.

Gardenias worn in the hair,
On the way to school in spring,
Reminders of brief innocence,
To my heart now bring.

These reflections, bittersweet,
And called upon at will,
Allow me to relive old days,
That linger with me still.

Rebecca Hogue

Foreign Love

O' lovely flower,
From 'cross the sea,
That washed ashore,
Just next to me,

Your gentle hand,
I've reached to find,
On sunlit trails,
We've left behind,

What charming smiles,
You've sent to me,
On moonlit nights,
Gave cause to be,

Come closer now,
O' friend so fine,
 and place
Your tender soul,
Just next to mine.

William H. Scott

Deck Time

We struggle to break out
from the narrow lines
of our daily planners
and reshape them into lounges
we can settle into on the deck.

We recall from somewhere
the lazy wash of yellow sun,
the sparkle of wine coolers,
the curls of smoke—
once harmless and simple rings

that could carry us
to flexible diving boards
from which we could
jump up to heights and down,
to splash around in meaningless gossip.

We could dry off
into sparkling rainbow stripes,
seriously considering
only the shapes of the puffy clouds
and flight patterns of the birds.

Paula Rozan Gassmann

Gumdrops

Gumdrops are falling
from the sky.
Grab one quick,
before they fly by!
Some are green and
some are blue,
they taste like cinnamon,
and bubble gum too!

Kristen Renee Braun

Memorial! Well Remembered

Picking broken pieces
from the tragedy
though unsafe
to continue
the search

Rescuers give
up hope
prayers continue
in memorial
for the lost

Heavier equipment
must take over
till the damage
it is cleared
though families
stay close by
even though it is over

While angels never leave
sending out
a glow

Roy C. DuRant

Winter Ocean

Winter Ocean, so vast, so cold
from your wintery waves
 to your frothing foam
Your never-ending onslaught
 is awesome to behold
You take from shore
 and give back sometimes more
ageless yet older than life
 what secrets you must hold
Winter Ocean, so deep, so old
 colors of friendly blue
to death-like grey
 you give life and take away
Not knowing nor caring, how cold
 Yet the harvest from your watery womb
Helps to feed a hungry world.

Martin J. Kerins

Forgotten Past

Looking beyond the present
Frightened by the unknown
Vulnerable in lonely silence
What was once suppressed is now released
Bits and pieces fall together
Secrets are revealed
Feelings intensify with time
Knowing the truth of a forgotten past
Comfort for the fragile soul
Always yearning yet never receiving
Wanting but needing to wait
Desiring more than empty words.

Lauren Odman

Mother

You are like a rose
Full of grace, beauty and life
Grand, alive with change
Like the mountains
Shining like a beacon light

A memory of a rose
Or a mountain is forever
And we who understand
Know your image
Shall diminish never

A rose born from strains
Pure, vibrant, beautiful
Filled with a virtuoso's
Voicing the highest aim fulfilled

Blooming every spring
A progeny measured in genes explodes
Breaking forth in a splendorous song
Singing a magnificent ode
This is Sarah, the mother -
The mother of us all ...

Samuel Rich

Not Enough Knowledge

Sitting meekly,
Gazing intently,
Watching every
Physical movement.
Learning all about life, gaining
Not enough knowledge
To understand the world.

Tiffany Powell

Loneliness In The Night

I lay in bed
gazing out the window.
I felt the loneliness
of the world.
I noticed the calm darkness
of the night.
One bright star
a lonely puppy
tall trees reaching out
the silent darkness in the room
a tear rolled down my cheek

Rhonda Rehm

The Rose

The rose has soft
fragrant petals, many thorns and
there sitting in the dirt with its
green green leaves sits

J. Chavez

Mango

The orange savory taste
gives a blissful feeling inside.
Round, smooth, and sticky skin
fits perfectly in my palm.

Oh, how sweet the mango is,
freshening my mouth
with juicy fragrance floating through,
the aroma is released.

Young Mi Kim

Horizon

On the horizon
  Genetic prediction,
sorting out people
  born with affliction.

Sorting out people
  lesser of mind,
Sorting out people
  according to kind.

A drop of blood
  lays-out my tomorrow.
A drop of blood...
  a feast for the beast,
    holding the key
  to what I shall be.

A new game for evil to play.
  A game for the greedy
  A card up their sleeve,
    holdin' the blue-print
    for Adam and Eve

Michael Hill

Searching For Sanity

Sanity, who has it and where did they
Get it. Did they buy it at a store, or
send off far it. Maybe it was a gift.
I need to know. I've lost, my
I checked the usual places, under the
bed, in the closet, I just can't find it.
I really need to get it back. When I
lost my sanity along with it were
love, happiness and peace. I really
need to find my sanity, it's a matter
of life and death.

Lisa Chase

The Potters Choice

'Tis precious clay the potter bakes
henceforth to make his molds
and yet it is his choice alone
to claim and save our souls.
Almighty God is just and true
to all that he creates
Let not your heart be troubled
if some he does not make
to understand
his wisdom
and listen to his
voice
Oh' blessed hand of mercy
still
'Tis the potter's choice.

Walter M. Horton

Untitled

To My Sister:
Her blonde hair glistens in the sun,
Green eyes,
Twinkling like the stars,
Show us happiness.
When she smiles,
Anyone who is near,
Will smile too.
Radiating love,
Warms my soul.

Rosia Anderson

God's Monarch

On wings outspread to
  Giving light
Adrift upon a sunbeam
Compelled to seek
  Their parents' memory
They flutter in majestic glory
  Above, below, beside.

Sharing their journey
With grace and certainty
  Of the path.
Each generation becomes a century.

Still, their purpose remains clear
  As the histogram upon their wings.
Tomorrow another hundred miles to go
Another soul to enrich with radiance
  Another mind to engrave with
Beauty's compassion stored
In the resonance of a billion
  Flying wings.

Marilyne V. Mabery

Little Children

Little children; precious treasures
Giv'n by God in love unmeasured.
Little minds to teach of Him
Who died for each and every sin.
Little eyes to show the way
To live for Jesus every day.
Little lips to sing His Glory.
Little ears to hear the story.
Little hands to teach to labor
In the witness of the Savior.
Little feet to walk in Light
Tho' the world be dark as night.
Little children, every one,
Giv'n by God to us, on loan.
Ours for just a little while;
Innocent and with no guile.
That in them Faith, we may instill;
God's great Commandment to fulfill.
So, let us work to do our part
to win to God their little hearts.

Kathy Floyd

A Little Child

A little child is someone
God has loaned us for a while,
To love, to live and play with
To cherish each tender smile.

For what could be more wonderful
Than to take a child upstairs
To kneel beside him by his bed
To help him say his prayers.

To linger by his bedside
When he is fast asleep.
To tuck the covers round him
And kiss him on the cheek.

To know each precious moment
As you look at him and smile,
That God has placed him in your hands
Just for a little while.

As you leave his room so softly
And you stop and say a prayer,
Thank you God for trusting
A little child within my care.

Kathleen N. Cates

Listen

Listen all you little ones.
God has sent us Christ, His Son.

Believe in Him and you will see,
He has come to set us free.

Listen, listen, when He calls,
Some may stumble, but will not fall.

Jesus loves us everyday;
give your heart and go His way

Jesus, Jesus is the one'
gave His life, now all is done.

Those of you who do believe;
in His kingdom you will be.

Lisa Jackson

Lamentation

America, America,
God shed His grace on thee.
You shed His grace,
Now in its place
There reigns insanity.

I saw the children you have killed
In the name of choice.
Oh land, lament,
For life unspent
In death without a voice.

America, America,
Land of adultery,
Of broken homes
And aborted wombs
From sea to shining sea.

I saw your eagle bow its head
Not in prayer, but shame.
Devoured alive,
It slowly died
And yes, it died afraid.

Roxanne Maree

All My Children

God gave us all
Guardians angels
He blessed me with 5
my children
You have been my angels
You take care of me
I wish every mother could be
Blessed like I am

Thank you for loving me
Thank you for caring
I will love you forever
Love, your Mama

Lucy Parra

"So Far Away"

Here I am, all alone
Have to get back to my family.
Special days come and go
Have to get back to my family.

Smiling faces, loved ones
Haunt my memory.
Have to get back, will
 get back to my
 dear sweet family!

Margaret Crowell

A Black's Point Of View

I hear...
 guns, shouting,
I see...
 wars, fighting,
I smell...
 fires burning,
I feel...
 heat, hurting,
I touch...
 dead bodies,
I want...
 my kingdom to be
 free.

Lauren I. Rugani

Untitled

The leaf on the ground
has lost its face
But I can
still see the veins
It's dying,
blowing away-
never to be seen again.

Marc Brandon

"Help!" A Mother's Prayer

That energy is bursting loose-
he just can't hold it in -
Lord give me patience that I need
and help "me" not to sin.
He's a just shaken bottle of soda
whose lid is popped off quick;
his energy is bubbling fast
I think I'm getting sick!
I can't keep up with him, you know,
he's on the go both day and night -
I know he's just a little boy,
help me to do what's right.
Help me to show him how to be
like you Lord, every day;
and help me, too, to be like You.
so I can lead the way.

Nancy Grace

Long Distance

He's kind, and
He's considerate;
He's older than me.

He's tall, and
He's strong;
He's from Tennessee.

He's funny, and
He's sweet;
He's witty, for sure.

He's warm, and
He's wonderful;
He's what I adore.

He's giving, and
He's caring;
What can I say?

He's huggable, and
He's lovable;
He's too far away.

Nancy J. Jacoby

The Day He Died

The day he died
He lay in peace
While I lay in fear
The day he died
his eyes were closed
while mine were all of tears
The day he died
he went somewhere far away
While I stay standing by his side
I don't now why he died
but that was the day he died.

Molly Maeder

Grandpa

My grandpa's death lead me to weep,
He lays there silent and fast asleep.
He looks so different laying there,
I couldn't help it but to stare.
My sadness wandered within my heart,
I never thought we would be apart.
Sometimes I still will shed a tear,
I love him so much I wish he was here.
I think about him everyday,
How much I miss him I cannot say.
Now he lies there still and cold,
Yet there are only memories to be told.
I remember the day I said goodbye,
For this is the end until I die.

Ashley E. Stansberry

Gordon

His eye moves my way.
He moves like a drunkard,
To be dead very soon.
He is polluted and can move no more.
The chills are getting worse,
Pressure, Pressure, Pressure!
But heat is what he needs.
He is dead.

Zach Stroud

Untitled

My dad's name is Rob
He never seems to sob

Sue is my mom's name
Loving is her game

Tresa is my sister
I have never kissed her

Charlie is my brother
I don't have any other

His twin is Christine
she is never mean

My Grandpa's name is Donnie
He seems a little scrawny

The other one is Dallas
He sure doesn't live in a palace!

My mom's mom is Janet
She's always clean and at it

Then there is Betty
Who is always ready

My family that is
Boy, that was a whiz!

Tiffany Slayton

Untitled

The other day I met a man,
He smiled at me and took my hand.
He seemed to want to walk awhile,
I questioned him, he only smiled.

And as we walked content flowed in
So I looked up and smiled at him.
As I smiled it came to me,
The key to life is just to be.

To live each day, no false pretense,
No lies, no need for self-defense.
And with these thoughts to lead me on,
I turned to smile - the man was gone.

Sherry Scrivner

"Gone Home"

One year ago tonight,
He took a "remarkable" flight.
A place we all long to be,
But some may never see.
A journey into the "Son",
A battle dad finally won.
Some would say "that poor man",
His life snuffed out by cancer,
But for all those who believe that,
Don't know "Christ" is the answer.
Yes he's gone and yes we cried,
But at least I know where he went,
The day my father died.

Patsy A. Durmer

The Grunge Poet

He was a grunge poet,
He was alienated,
He was loved.
He was OD,
He was a grunge poet,
He was gay,
He was made fun of,
Never again to be gay,
He was a grunge poet,
He was married,
He was a father,
He was a husband,
He was a grunge poet,
He was a great musician,
Played guitar,
But now he's dead,
He was a grunge poet,
He was Kurt Cobain.

Katie Kuster

The Child Waits

The child waits up against the bridge
He watches the cars slowly pass
Excited that one day they will find him.

Closely he watches for cops
Hiding under the bridge homeless
In the dark the shadows freeze
Lowly the child shrinks to hide
Down under the child bleeds

Wanting to die he still hides
And waiting for a car to find him
In thoughts, he waits in life he hides
Too shy to leave he waits to die
Starving and cold the child waits

Margaret Rausch

The Man Of Change

The man of change,
He will change all things,
He will stop the hate.
He will stop the hurting in us,
He will stop the tears,
From rolling out my eyes,
And down my face,
He will,
Yes, he will.

Tara Lee Baker

The Love Of My Life

The love of my life
he will never know
  My love for him
will always grow.
  The love of my life
is so far away
  So it is hopeless for
me to even pray.
  The love of my life
is so very great
  My love for him
will always wait.

Pam Swinford

Love Versus Friends; Impossible

Love aches,
  Heart Breaks,
  For the one,
Who none of these appear.
  Friends last,
  Minds blast,
  To have fun,
When friends are near.
  Friends forever,
  Love whenever,
  Love last forever,
But friends last an eternity.
  Love sweet,
  Heart treat.
  You and the one,
Become won.
  Friends best,
  Minds test.
  The strength between,
You and the world.

Samantha Slater

Untitled

A man with a
  heavy step and
    sore feet.
He's worked his
  Heart to the bone
    and has little to
      show by it.

He looks too old for
  His age and his
    movements are tired.
He looks forward to
  the little shack He
    calls home...
For that is what it is,
  And that is what
    makes him happy.

Shana Looney

My Wish

Had been to see my sister,
her mind had gone afar.
While driving home on new 19,
I saw a falling star.
Had to make my wish and fast!
Didn't want my chance to pass.
Before I had the time to think,
my wish I made within a blink.
I wished Diane could somehow get better,
the way she was when Johnny Mac met her.

Melanie Norman

The Great Awakening

Deep inside my mother's womb,
her voice but a whisper.

Her warmth enveloped my very being.
My soul had been washed clean.

All she had she gave to me,
so pure and so inviting.

I took it all and wanted more,
this thirst, I could not fight it.

I did not know the full intent,
of this I had accepted.

A spiritual change was in effect,
no man would dare to stop it.

A transformation! A great event!
But...there was no announcement.

And then my birth.
O what a day.
This day of celebration.

Out of the darkness I emerged
and into the light of SALVATION.

Mary Coleman

Marathon Man

His life a marathon.
He's turning 26.
Next year a triathlon,
It will be even better than this.

Because he's getting stronger,
He's not weak at the end of the race.
It's just a preparation.
You can see it in his face.

He's not running from anything.
Getting everywhere fast.
New York, Boston, London.
He was there the year before last.

Look at him go!
Look where he's been.
He's ahead of us all.
He always seems to win.

But pay attention to his gate,
For he doesn't run but walks.
Lucky for him—usually straight.

Patrick R. Searles

Self Image Me

I was born a cinderella
Grew up like snow white
Took a bite of the forbidden
Apple! And turn out to be
Like Adam's wife.

Sue Scheuer

Little Bird

Oh little bird I see you there,
   hiding beneath the bow bent tree.
What keeps you keeping to yourself?
   A fear of being free?
Oh little bird take flight today,
   spread your wings and fly away.
A open mind is an open door
   fly through it and fear no more.
Find new places, see new things
   enjoy what every new day brings.
Take my advice, not because it's free
   but because in you I see me.

Sandra L. Burksaze

The Love Of A Mother

Fresh crisp air, bright shining sun.
Hits her face. Her eyes twinkle,
as a mother will do.
Lips set firm but, will turn
upward when needed.
A few wrinkles and gray
hairs begin to appear.
Hands that worked so hard
to raise her children.
Oh the patience a mother has.
She was there when she was needed.
Laughter lives within her.
Someone you can trust.
Thank you for the love, Mother.

Karen Ross

Salted Paper

Salted paper does not
hold images or things
remembered, brought
up from the past
and spat out into
the present like
Jonah from the whale,
but is a landscape
of words and
feelings sprinkled
liberally into the making
in the way some pages
don't exist until
written on, leaving
a taste
dissolving in your mind.

Leif Sorensen

Imagine

I can't see you smile
I can barely hear the
   laughter in your voice
I can't feel you or see
   the expression on your
   face when you say
   "I love you"
I can only imagine.
   Imagine
that's all I can do.
Imagine you're here
Imagine how you feel
Imagine how you smell.
   Imagine
My imagination can only
go but so far.
I wish I didn't have
   to imagine.

Shavonne Brown

Escape

The day was
hot
but the water felt
cool.
The girl nestled herself in her
towel
as the
Steaming, Summer Sun Shone
on her body.
The sweat
poured
down her forehead
and her body was
changing
color.
She got
up
and dove into the
pool
again.

Lina Orfanos

Little Ones

Little ones, little ones
How nice to watch you grow!
Little ones, little ones -
You're very sweet ya know!

Some days you are grumpy,
You push and play too rough.
Sometimes we aren't happy,
'Cause life's just kinda tough.

But little ones will grow taller
And wiser as they age.
Little ones change daily -
Like the turning of a page.

Today everyone's happy
(and that makes me smile too!)
Tomorrow brings the frowns.
Having a bad day are you?

Lots of toys, lots of noise-
Don't ask me to complain.
For with little ones, there are always times -
When the sunshine's worth 'some' rain.

Rhonda Susco

That Winter

When Aunt Harriet taught me
How to bake
Oatmeal cookies for Valentine's Day
She advised:

   Avoid Churchmen
   They brag, they boast
   But can't wonder
   about life in an orphanage
   'cause they've never known
   a disadvantaged life

   These HOLY MEN
   Can't dream, either
   For their hearts
   Are within white Mercedes
   in some parking lot

Don't have any other anchor

D. A. Dawn Stegenga

Child Of The Lord

I am a child of the Lord.
How wonderful to be,
a child of the Lord,
When a child of the Lord,
he is watching over me.

As I am the Lord's child,
he has blessed me daily.
As a child of the Lord,
he takes care of me.

As a child of the Lord,
he will watch over me, sending
angels to guide and protect.

What a wonderful Lord,
who always knows my needs.
I am a child of the Lord,
O what a blessing I see.

As a child of the Lord,
he sends angels to guide and protect.
Just try being his child and,
you will see what a blessing it is.

Nellie M. Brand

Little China Doll

Precious little china doll
how your face is the same,
I laughed and I cried
and your face never changed.

Your face is as porcelain
so white and clear,
somehow I hold on to
your face so dear.

I dreamed that you smiled,
in your fragile glass case,
but I opened my eyes
and my thought did erase.

The smile wasn't there
but it was in my heart,
and no foreign language
would keep us apart.

We are similar in many
different ways except for,
the porcelain like face
that never does change.

Sue Southard

The Spirit Within

I, am body,
I, am spirit
I, am man.
In God's name
The I, am I, am I, am.

I, have a heart
I, can feel pain
But I am somebody
In Jesus "Christ."
Holy Name,

I, have the patience
I, weep and I, pray,
I, am the radiance of light,
I, am God's "bright day."
"Please Father,
Bless Me, bless the way.
Remember me Lord,"
Your faithful child O. J.

Virginia Forsythe

Baby Fingers

New little fingers,
hurry up and count.
A smile and sigh.
He has the right amount.
Little wrinkly hands,
softly moving in the air.
Lean over gently
and kiss them with care.
Little furrowed palm,
filled up by mommy's finger.
Chubby little hand closes
in grasps that slowly linger.
Amazing little hands,
searching for a touch.
Whisper in his ear,
"Mommy loves you very much."

Ruth M. S. Van Dyke

A Wife For Life

Stop YELLING at me.
I am not a little
Child with no courage to
defend myself so STOP
YELLING at me.

Stop HITTING me.
I am not a punching bag
on which you beat out
your infantile frustrations so STOP
HITTING me.

Stop KILLING me.
I am not the answer
to whatever makes you
question your obsessive
manhood so STOP
KILLING me.

Naomi R. Jacobs

"Epitome Of Hate"

I care not of your fate
I am the epitome of hate
Join my legion 'fore it's too late
I am the epitome of hate
Deny me not a date
I am the epitome of hate
Satan is my mate
I am the epitome of hate
I guard hells gate
I am the epitome of hate
Don't you know my wrath is great
I am the epitome of hate
I'll slay you with a broken plate
I am the epitome of hate
And your death certificate will state
Killed by the epitome of hate

Nathan Argilan

Promise Of The Heart

I am a part of you,
I am your thoughts and imagination,
You can trust me, I don't lie.
I am your beliefs and feelings,
You can tell me anything,
It will be safe forever.
I am your conscience,
I will tell you right from wrong;
I am your heart.

Patricia Clear

One

I saw You from a distance;
I came upon You - slowly.
You wrapped Your arms around me.
You whispered... I listened,
and then You showed me.

Though Your eyes, I looked
With Your heart, I felt
And with You, I embraced
You whispered again
Again, I heard
I asked a question: "What is this?"
You told me: "This is ALL, this is ONE."

"You are ready to SEE this;
You are ready to KNOW;
At times it may seem fast,
But I will go slow.
First, you will SEE,
Then you will KNOW.
Next, you will shed in order to grow."

"Keep listening"

Suzanne M. Nye - 1992

Forever

When I look into your eyes
I can do nothing but smile
For I can see your love glowing
I feel the need
I feel the want
For when you're not around, I feel your
loves arms wrapped around me, I can't
escape it, for I feel no need or want
to escape. For you are my destiny! You
have filled my whole world with joy and
happiness and no one person has really
been able to capture my love until now,
and my love, that is you!
For you can see it in my eyes,
in my smile and in my heart and no
one could ever destroy it, not even you
my love, for it has taken me over.
Heart, mind, and yes, I have married
you in my soul and you are forever

Ruth Bloom

"A Boy Lost"

Is anyone out there
I need to see
Got to find
The person in me

Look at the inside
To see who I am
Not at the outside
Of what really is

So come inside
And be by my side
Look at me for who I am
Not what I can be

Just a young man
Looking up and out
Reaching and wanting
Just to be heard

Is anyone out there
Yes, I believe
Come reach out and find me
And let me be me

Linnea M. Bell

I Love Poetry

I love poetry
I can feel it flowing through my
mind making me half blind.
You can hear it from a distance
having a lot of persistence
Making rhymes and riddles
getting very little
Feeling it, and tasting it
reading it bit by bit
I love poetry, it's very close to me,
it's very flowing and very loving
It has a life, it has a heart
that's very close to me and
that's what makes me free!

Kathy Stockman

Are You There?

My time is almost over,
I can feel my spirit floating.
Drifting in and out of life,
My mind fills with curious foreboding
   Are you there?
There's a picture on the wall,
And even though it's dark.
I shine my flashlight on the frame
Its comfort leaves a mark.
   Are you there?
Please hold my hand tightly!
I lost my fight for life,
Lead me toward the peaceful light,
And soothe my precious wife.
   Are you there?
In memory of my brother - Bernie Ertman

Lillian Wisniewski

A Hand And A Voice

Smile, dear;
I can hear my singing
   in your dreams,
I can boast a song
   and a lie.

Those reckless noises
   on your hands
Defy my tears
Dare me to spite.

I cannot forget:
Rain,
Laughter,
And a hand
   wrapping my voice
   around the night
And your dreams
   around my fears.

Mansour J. Ajami

Window

Looking out a window
how beautiful it looks
mountains are still
sun is yellow
skies are blue
trees are green
it looks like a picture
then winds start blowing
trees start swaying
birds start flying by
it's not a picture it's life
how beautiful life can be.

Katherine J. Pino

The Love Of God

Who is God really?
I cannot tell this clear
I only believe He's near
And also very dear.

I can't realize He's with me.
I only know He's real
Like the "good book" says.
The love of God I feel.

At times I remember a verse
And it soothes my fretful soul.
"I go to prepare a place for you,"
For heaven is my goal.

My heart and soul know
I'll one day be in heaven so bright.
I only know to "only believe,"
But this seems hard, but so right.

Sharon Elisabeth Bradford

Strapped To A Wheelchair

"I wanna walk,
I can't.
Come to me.
I love you.

What have I done
To hurt you?
Nothing.
Come to me,
Please."

Martha Gerritz

Evermore

I look into your eyes and
I can't help but wonder what I did to
deserve your tender care I've been put
under.

I see your smile and in
my soul this new feeling is making me
whole.

I sit with your arms
around me and my heart begins to soar
and I know we'll be together... evermore.

Laura R. Hazen

"Breakwall"

If I could make the world go away,
I could be happy here,
with the eagles flying overhead,
and the ocean crashing at the breakwall.

So then...let us go there together
in the imaginary of our minds;
On a Sunday morning, when the
world is in deep stillness,
the grey sky dripping rain,
and the leaves rustling gently
in the dawn breeze.

Yes! I will meet you there,
and later in the evening,
in front of a warm fireplace,
we will await day break at
breakwall again and again
and again.

Patricia Mattei

Solitary Confinement

On an open desert plain
I crouch
And hold my head in my
Shaking hands
And I'm so thirsty my tears
Are dry
And the wild wind knows my
Name....
But why must the wild wind call me?
Why can't a young man hide in the dark?
Why can't my parents just hold me?
Why does this race have to start?

Michael S. Staub

I Cry For Me

Why do you cry?
I cry to let out the old and new me.
I cry because I know no one else will
do it for me.

I cry for the good and the bad that
was done to me.
I cry for the cleansing of the inside
and outside of me.

I cry for the part of my spirit that
was lost to me.
I cry because I feel no one loves me.

I cry because this is part and all of me.
That's why I cry.
I cry for me.

Shari L. Williams

What You've Done

Dedicated to Jack Dougherty

When I came to visit you
I didn't realize,
That the last time I saw you
Would be the last time forever.
I didn't realize,
That last hug
That last kiss
Would be the last one forever.
The one that said goodbye
I'll miss you
The one that said
I'll always remember you
I'll remember everything
You've done,
For me
For my family,
And for anyone who knew you.
I'll always remember
Everything you've ever done.

Tricia Warren

Thoughts

When we were young
I fell in love with you.
I love you even now
that we are older.
My feelings are deep
and your eyes reflect to me
deep feelings of many bonds.
My heart strings play a melody
of sincerity and joy.

Mary Muckle

Patience

Patience is a virtue
I do not have.
You have so much
may I share some?

Understanding to me
is just another word.
You practice it ——
Will you teach me?

Kindness is a word
we use too freely.
you live it.
You'll be my example.

Robert Lundgren

Misery

My heart is dying
I don't know why
I couldn't cry
It's stuck inside
I sit in a maze
Yet total silence
My soul has died
There's no denying
The pain I'm feeling
There's no understanding
Of the world I live in
The world of misunderstanding

Stephanie Leiteritz

My Secret

When I awake at morning's light,
  I feel renewed with rest of night.
Joy comes in knowing you have
  a new start.
Try sharing with someone the
  love in your heart.

Love comes in many forms, you know,
  a smile, a helping hand, a kind
  word or two.
Share someone's pain and you help
  bring joy to life again.

I've found you cannot do enough,
  For some life seems so tough.
Just reach out and do the best you
  can.
For you see My Secret is "God is
  holding my hand."

Wynona Jacobs

The Nightingale's Song

Who taught the Nightingale
how to sing - gave it
what it needs... its everything.

It sings so beautifully all
through the night - bringing
brightness, when hidden
is the light.

The one who created its
melodious song, has given
it flight.

It is good to hear the
Nightingale sing.

Rose-Marie Spratt

Left Wounded

I have found a love today
I found a love for hate
If you don't see it my way
Chances are I am too late
I am sorry for your madness
I am sorry for your lies
But I can't find an answer
When I look into your eyes
A mystic blue attracts me
But I have one more destination
to fulfill my final part
I need to find the one true key
that leads into your broken heart

Rodney Duane Lewellen

Knowledge

I have seen him!
I have been there.
I sat on the edge of
his brook and
smelled him in the air.
I saw him in the trees.
I smelled him in the leaves.
I saw him in the
bright sunlight
and tasted him in the
waters so pure.

For ages and ages
are but cosmic past
but the soul and spirit
will forever last!

Mira Holman

Fun With Dolphins

I like dolphins,
I hope they like me.
They live in the ocean
or the sea.
They twist and turn
and learn and learn.
Oh! I like dolphins,
I hope they like me!

Michelle Wick

Untitled

When death came rapping at my door
I kindly showed him in
His long black cloak embraced my body
Mortality was what had been.

He spoke no words, the time was now
For us to leave this place,
His thoughts spoke to me from his eye
The eye which claimed no face.

He led me to the Redwoods
We strolled amongst the trees,
We listened to the birds cry
The song of eternity.

And then we paused before the place
Where I was meant to lie
The sun went out, the clouds blew in-
Darkness filled the sky.

It seems just now since death has come
Although all time has passed
Since he gave my body to the earth,
Eternity comes so fast.

Kirsten Thomas

Alone Again

You're a lonely child
I know it to be true
Tell me how to reach your heart
For I am lonely too.

We're both afraid to let it show
For lonely hurts so bad
You think that only you feel pain
But I feel just as sad.

Maybe we were meant to be
Together we could grow
Perhaps if we were not afraid
What love we both might know.

But you stand there and speak no word
Oh glance at me please do
Take the chance to say hello
And I'll speak back to you.

Michelle George

Today There Will Be A Miracle

Today, there will be a miracle ....
I know it's a fact, you see ....
For I have asked God, In Jesus' name ..
  To set my loved ones free.

My brother died by another's hands ...
Our hearts are filled with grief .....
But I prayed to God, In Jesus' name ..
  To send us all relief.

Today, I prayed for a miracle ....
And I know it's on its way ....
I realized not, when it happened .....
  But it happened——Today.

Today, I prayed for a miracle ....
And left him in God's hands ....
He said, "Ask, and it shall be given."
  In Jesus' name, AMEN.

Linda S. Wilson

To Mother

I have some flowers for you today
   I know they're not much
But here's what they say
   I love you Mother
Each day in the year
   Even when to your eye
Comes a tear
And I will try
   All of my life
To make all your days
   filled with joy and not strife
And so on this day of all
   the year
I thank God you're my mother
   And I'm grateful I'm here

Mickey

Someone Special

When I look around,
I know you're down,
You can come to me,
Because we can be
Happy together
Forever, and ever
Because you're that someone special.

Melanie Zogg

Angels

Where are the angels?
I look up to the sky.
Where are the angels?
Do they like to hide?
Where are the angels?
I can sense they are near.
Where are the angels?
Who loves us so dear.

I know that the angels,
guide all of our lives.
I know that the angels,
hear us when we cry.
I know that the angels,
watch as we sleep.
I know that the angels,
gives us peace.

So, where are the angels?
I ask you again.
They're all around us,
you just need to look again!

Marissa Simons

The Only One

Please don't go, don't leave me behind
I need you,
need you by my side
to give me strength
to hear my cries
to feel my sadness
to help me chase these blues away
for they won't die

You're the only one who understands,
who knows what I'm going through
you can save me
for you give me hope
you give me your strength
to help me cope
with what I'm struggling through
each day of my life

It gets harder and harder each day to get up
for me to survive
knowing that someday
you will go far away

Michele DiPrima

"Until You"

I never knew the love I might miss
I never knew that only one kiss
could make my heart sing
from the joy it would bring.
No, never, not until you.

I never knew the love of a man
I never knew the touch of a hand
could set me on fire
with a heartfelt desire.
No, never, not until you.

I never knew that love was so sweet.
I never knew the warmth of loves' heat
could burn deep in my soul
to make me feel whole.
No, never, not until you.

I never knew in darkness of night
I never knew a feeling so right
could capture my heart
as if did from the start.
No, never, not until you.

Sheila Drake

Blind Love

I walk beside a lonely man
I only wish he could hold my hand
I see him smile when he looks at me
But it's only me he can't see
I turn the page to chapter 4
He's all I want
Couldn't ask for more
I don't ask why as I start to cry
I need to feel his love so real
It's now page 99, when will he be mine
So long, it took as I closed the book
I reach out for you, you're not there
If you could only see
If you would only look.

Nicole Webbert

Smiley-73

In the morning, when I arise
I open the door, to the morning sunrise
The sweet smell of lilacs in the air
I gaze at a dark haired beauty
Her hair blowing in the breeze
A smile soft and gentle
She is five-foot two, eyes of blue
I am greeted with a hug and kiss
Lips that taste like honey
Pretty little girl, in the yellow dress
You stole my heart away
I must confess

J. Byrne

You

All the time I see you,
I really don't know what to do,
I wish I could be the one,
But yet I never know when I'm done,
Done thinking of you.
I really don't know who,
Who you trust within,
I always try to begin,
Start saying "hi,"
But never wanting to say "bye,"
Can't you see how I feel,
I'd cook you an entire meal,
While thinking of you,
And never knowing what to do,
I really don't know who,
I wish I could be the one,
The one who always brings you
    all the fun!

Zuzana Slobodnikova

Channel 7

The 11:00 news ran a special.
I sat trembling
breathless
left hand to my lips
right hand still clutching the remote
but I wouldn't change the station
and I couldn't walk away
from watching footage of that hospital
of what would happen between
when everything went black
and when I'd wake up shrieking
and groping for my glasses.
It's no wonder
they wouldn't release the records.

I curled up and tried not to vomit.

R. F. Farkas

Happenstance

To the rainbow's end
I search for my pot of gold
Seeking no fortune
but the answers it may hold

Intrigued with the mysteries
of time and space
what is my purpose
where is my place

Will it matter tomorrow
that I was here today
did I make a difference
in some unique way

I would like to believe
I have touched someone
On their darkest days
I'd bring the sun

Is there a reason for being
or just happenstance
Do I follow the road of certainty
or walk through the valley of chance?

Wendy Lynn

I Saw The Light

As I lie in my bed,
I see a sudden light,
I am greeted by my father,
glowing in the night.

The light brightens as it nears,
as it stands before my soul,
I have fears of leaving my mother behind,
because her life will turn black as coal.

But my father stares at me,
and he speaks with his eyes,
I must follow his footsteps,
before the light dies.

I walk over to my mother,
to kiss her before I go,
I drop a tear upon her lips,
so my love she will know.

My father opens the gate,
and leads me to God's land,
he holds me close and cries,
but he never lets go of my hand.

Rachel Walters

Surroundings

As I walk upon this earth,
I see all types of birth.
Birds are in the trees,
Feeding their chickadees.
Babies on breast,
Kids passing tests.
All these surroundings,
With surroundings,
Surrounding them.

A tree here an insect there,
Some people have lice in their hair.
Animals are all around,
Sometimes gofers are in the ground.
Mechanical objects all over this earth,
Even Technology had a birth!?
All these surroundings,
With surroundings,
Surrounding them.

Scott Axelrod

In This Child Of Mine

In this child of mine
I see the stars shine.
In her eyes they shine so bright
I see the everlasting light
In this child of mine, so young, so new,
I see all my hopes and dreams come true.
In the distant future,
In the near past,
I see how my days will last.
In this child of mine, when she is grown,
I hope that it is known
How much she filled my heart
Right from the very start.
In this child of mine,
Oh! How the stars shine.

Theresa Torre

The Haunting

In other smiles
I see you
On the street
I smell you
Pulling my pillow close
I feel you

You're with me always
in my mind,
my words

Through the pain
It keeps me going
The dream of a better tomorrow
dream boy
tomorrow never comes

Timothy Janis

Excuse Me

I spat
I shat
I belched
and flat-

I slurped
and burped
my belly chirped

My body functioned
all in time
I beg your pardon
in a rhyme

Zane Carriker

The Man Who Died For You And Me

The rain beat down
like the tears and blood from
the man who died for you and me....

The thunder serves as a reminder
of the hammer beating against
the nail driving it through
the flesh and
the bones of
the man who died for you and me...

The lightening is like
the tear in his heart
from people who don't care
about the man who died for you and me...

Theresa Hite

Summer

I smell summer in the air,
I smell summer everywhere.

Summer smells fresh,
Summer smells sweet,
Summer feels hot beneath my feet.

And the wind that blows softly
through my hair,
Makes me think of summer everywhere.
Todd Mason

Dreams

My early years were full of dreams,
I spent them writing by the reams,
Of lovers many and far between,
Of lanes they trod that none have seen,
In meadows soft, and oh, so green,
Along a pretty, rippling stream
As the moon in the sky brightly beamed
They walked side by side in that
  glorious beam,
Forgetting all that's bad or mean,
They'll live in a world of their dreams.
  Happy forever!
Rozella D. Ashbaucher

The Sea

The sea has been my mother,
  I suckled at her breast.
Sailed with many I'd call brother,
  From far, far east to west.

I've crossed her wide expanses,
  In ships both great and small.
Done hornpipes - sailors dances,
  Held in her sweet thrall.

I've seen her aspect alter,
  From calm to roarin' wild.
She never let me falter,
  She knew I was her child.

I've felt her strength and powers,
  She's gently rocked me too.
I've spent many blissful hours,
  In her cradle, deep and blue.

And now my sailing ended,
  My tide is at the flood.
Her treasures I've defended -
  Her flow is in my blood.
Robert Simmons

Remember

I remember as a child the simple games
I used to play.
In summers warm and winters mild.
Never caring of the day.

Never knowing that someday
No more summers warm and
winters mild.
No more simple games to play
But getting older by the day.

Closer, closer death draws near
That's the day that I fear.
No more simple games to play
No more caring of the day.
Monica Allison

When I Think Of You

When I think of you
I think of red roses with raindrops
all over them that have just sprung
I also think of you and me dancing
to the most romantic song.

When I think of you
I think of romance and passion
I think of a waterfall flowing
downward with endless motion
and I think of us on a moonlit
walk with the wild animals
walking around with their bright
yellow eyes, making mysterious noises

When I think of you
I think of a stream flowing so soft
with the wonderful taste of clean water,
and again the rose that is now a
rose bush so beautiful and delicate
Nicole Carr

You

The night I met you
  I thought it was too good to be true;
You were what I was looking for,
  and everything more;
You have a smile,
  that can glow for a mile;
When your eyes set my way,
  I knew you would be mine someday.
The night you asked me to be yours,
  it was like my heart fell to
  the floor;
When you said you loved me,
  my soul was set free;
What I'm saying to you,
  is I'll never make you feel blue;
Because I love you.
Susan Young

Reward And Punishment

It hurts so much not to know why
If others are rewarded, but only I
For my whole life, has gone nearly by
Once I must learn why, before I die
Where do they lie, the sins of mine?
Marc C. Modaressi

Rainbow

Can there be a wish
if there's no life
Can there be a dream
if there's no strife
Can there be a future
if there's no past
Can there be a way
if there's no hope to last
Can there be happiness
if there's no pride
Can there be courage
if there's nothing to hide
Can there be hate
if there are no fears
Can there be joy
if there are no tears
Can there be love
if there's no pain
Can there be a rainbow
if there's no rain
Melissa Siebers

Four

One:
I thought you would take
me to my destination.
But now we are both lost.
Two:
When I was searching for independence,
I did not realize it is another
form of dependency.
Three:
All these years I kept
my heart open to feel
the beauty of love.
But it never came to me.
Four:
Far away from here maybe
there is a golden pond.
Sati Mohan Das

Twenty Five Years

A secret I have kept
I want you to know
for almost twenty-five years
I have loved you so.

The first time I saw you
as you towered high above
down the high school hallway
I knew instantly - it was love.

You didn't know and I wouldn't say
for almost half my life
with our paths crossing along the way
secretly, I have loved you.

The secret of my past is no more
as I hold you lovingly in my arms
I love you now as I did before
my secret of twenty-five years.
Mary E. Andreko

"When That Star Fell"

I saw a star falling bright
I was with my love that night
We were close arm in arm
When that star fell; we were alarmed.
Wishes were made, but never came true
When that star fell, I lost you.
Dreams were lost, but we couldn't tell
Till that night when that star fell.
We were dreaming of marriage that night,
We thought our love was so very right.
I thought to myself, all is well
Till after that star fell,
Hopes and dreams faded fast
Like that star, we didn't last.
That one night, no one can take,
It belongs to us; it felt like fate.
Do you remember and will you hold tight?
That falling star we saw that night.
Louis Costanzo

Ocean Fun

If I lived in the ocean,
I would have a lot of fun.
I would play with the walrus.
Will you come and play with us?
We could swim, and play a game.
Won't you please tell me your name?
Lindsay Crouse

"The Rose"

The Rose you gave me
I will always keep because I will
always miss you, but you hurt
me so deep; I can never take you back.
   You wanted my body,
I wanted your heart. Now it's all
over, we're torn apart.
   When the rose bleeds,
I start to cry because I fell
in love with the wrong guy.
   That's all over now, I have to
go on. Just leave my life and
try to be strong.
   What's done is done, there's
no use turning back.
   The Rose you gave me
is now; black.

Mary Dunn

The Field Of Tranquility

In this field of tranquility,
I will forever rest.
Peacefully, I will slumber,
In my infinite castle.

Comfortable and motionless,
My stately body lies.
The silence that I hear,
In solitude, I will endure.

Above my dwelling place,
The whisper of the wind,
A peaceful, gentle breeze,
Softly whispers my name.

A solemn sound of movement,
I hear and gently feel,
Where I lie, deep and alone,
In my eternal resting place.

In this mansion where I dwell,
My soul departed, the sun never rises.
Days are lasting nights,
Darkness prevails and will forever.

Oclides Tenorio

"All"

How uninteresting the world would be
If everyone thought the same,
All had identical features
With all the same last name
Yet all are created equal
And capable of love,
We are each other brothers
And children of God above
You have your faults, I have mine
No doubt there's good points too,
So remember when all is going wrong
Part of that "all" is you

Lilly Miller

Living Water

When water flows from heaven
In a narrow waterfall,
Love can shape a broader flow
In answer to life's call.

Churning water of deepest green,
A part of nature's scheme
To stir again the dormant life
At rest in winter's dream.

Neva Dawkins

Wouldn't It Be Nice?

Wouldn't it be nice
If feelings were like ice
Mere temperature change
Solidifies and perfection remains
A solid feeling when it's crushed
Remains on tape, cannot be hushed
In times of strife it's sure to compute
Throughout this life, why can't it be
Stay Mute?

Marge Anderson

Dreams Of Mine

I slit my wrist to see
If I still bleed
Feel the pain of life
And the joy of illusion
Any of these open doors
Leads to shattered thought
Help me fade away
To my dimension of sleep
As dreams clear the soul
And my mind drifts away
You could have it all
But you choose my ways
For reasons of yours
And dreams of mine

N. Granfeldt

The Muse Says

Pump to stalling,
If you will success,
Visioning the end game
Before crafting any movement,
Then...
Cancel,
Replace,
Affirm,
Focus, and
Train every day
To checkmate the ironies of living.

Robert D. Becker

A Hand-Me-Down

Crafting an heirloom through the eve
   I overcasted by her side.
While she fed teeth against the weave,
   Grandma tailored stitches in stride.

Ribbons of seams sewn in her hands
   Starting to fray at raw edges.
Fibers of her life she amends
   Looping lace over the ridges.

Threads of time I bobbed in between.
   Tension, turned on by a dial
      Forwards —
   Backwards—

Yards of fine cotton, silks, and wools
   It's just the fabrics of her time.
By hand she etched her initials
   Passing on her labor, as mine.

Grandma designed the tapestry,
   I remember it, as her last.
Adoring it most lovingly,
   It's my cameo of the past.

Karen Jean Lemieux

Compromise

You kill my dog
I'll kill your cat!
Now where on earth
Do we get that?
Being human
We humanize
With head -
Or with heart -
Often - unwise -
Why not use them both -
And compromise -

T. R. Nelson

Love

I love you
I'll tell you why,
You are a diamond in my eye,
You love me,
I love you too.
My heart will always
belong to you.
From day to night,
from calm to fright
I will always love you
When you travel around the world,
I will always be your girl.
And when the day comes
and you give me the ring
and we plan our wedding in the spring.
When we're on our honeymoon
dancing to our favorite tune
we will think about the years to come,
and have our children
one by one.

Kristina DeVivo

Please, No Labels

No —
I'm not a caretaker or a caregiver
Sounds too much like a maintainer of
grounds, gardens, or a museum.
When a surgeon's knife sentenced him
to a wheelchair
PERMANENTLY,
it did not sever our vows.
Though it changed our days in
a multitude of ways,
smoldering rage honed our courage,
our understanding, and our
capacity to cope.
Fusing us in a special way so
PLEASE, NO LABELS.
I am his wife
for all of his life.

Mary Stuve

Blame

It wasn't me who told the rain to fall
I'm not the one who built the wall
I've never fought in a war
I've never asked myself "What For?"

That doesn't mean I don't feel the pain
And I too look to hide my shame
I might not have told the rain to fall
But I blame myself for it all.

Merrideth A. Lindsay

Feelings Of Pain

In a world of anger,
In a world of hate,
can't escape the horrors that haunt
and burn your fate.
In a world of violence,
In a world of fire,
can't escape the people that burn
and crush desire.
In a world of no control,
In a world of no faith,
can't feel love,
can't feel joy,
just feel the pain.

Melissa Kass

Reflections Of Me

Feeling peace transcend
In bountiful amounts
A softly winged hand to lend,
Every bit of heaven counts -

Help is never far away
Just a tiny prayer each day
I am loved, as are you
Know this always to be true

If you look across your shoulder
Feel comfort in your glance
I am with you forever
By fate, not chance

Sarasvati Lorion Hess

California Rain

A year ago
In drought days
My thirsty ears drank in
The silver sound
Of pre-dawn rain
Blessing the dry brown world

Now
In monsoon months
I awake to
The monotonous thud
Of pre-dawn rain
Beating the helpless earth

The ears of the heart
Are as fickle — or faithful —
As rain

Sandra M. Schneiders

"For You"

For you
I would swim the deepest ocean
For you
I would cause all kinds of commotion

For you
I would run four hundred miles
For you
I would do nothing, but smile

For you
I would give all my sorrow
For you
I would love like there is no tomorrow

For you
I would make the waters part
For you
I would open up my heart

Lisa Tallent

Decisions Of Life

There comes a time
in everyone's life
To pick a road.

Is it the right one?
Please the parents,
or please thy self?

Decisions of life
on a lonely road,
You can't decide
as life passes you by

You wait
You wonder
As life crosses you under

You hesitate
You try to relate
But it's gone…

Your life
It's over.

Terri Batcheller

There's Always Hope…

Why can't we all live
In harmony and peace
Live with one another
Trusting
Working side by side
Lending a helping hand
After all
That's the sole purpose
We've been put on this earth
Not to cause
Pain, suffering, destruction
We can strive
To make a better future and environment
If we but try
After all there's always hope…

Monique Zivkovic-Torres

The Wedding Ring

Down foggy beach
in sun I go -
clear cut patterns
lost beyond -
a loosely harnessed
Vagabond.

Velma Ilsley

The Two Me's

I walk in memory's long, long lane
In sweet remembrance's smile -
The worn and fragile shell remains,
Waits for me awhile.

I open gates to other years
Where dreams are fresh and new -
Roses there are wet with tears
In place of morning dew.

I see the faces loved and fair
And clasp once more a hand.
We talk of other times and scenes
A different place and land.

But time goes on and memory's book
on dusty shelves, lies bare -
I slip into the old, old me
To wait in silence there.

Mildred B. Simpson

"A Ride Through Heaven"

In the marshmallow clouds
in that infinite sky,
Like the meadowlark of Kansas
I did fly.
A feeling of freedom like I never knew,
And oh those moments of splendor too!

So close to heaven I never felt,
All my troubles simply melt.
As the wind hit my face
so cool and crisp,
Like the dew on the flowers,
it can't help but be missed!

Yes, in the marshmallow clouds
in that infinite sky,
Like the meadowlark of Kansas
I did fly!

Roni Rochester

Heart Threads

My son lies beside me
in the dark hours of morning,
awakened by bad dreams

His warmth reminds me
how fragile the bond of loving,
shattered by old hurts

The tender needs of a child
in his early years of living,
demand all my heart

He comes to me, a little boy
smelling of warm things sleeping,
needing a mother's love

Strong ties corded by years
of hopes dared, dreams of loving,
pain shared and life lived

The threads wrap around my heart
and hold, bring thoughts of staying
where I don't want to be.

Vicki L. Dawson

Life's Pathway

We must choose life's pathway
In the days of our youth
With our hearts full of hope
Our minds blind to the truth

As we travel this pathway
Down through the years
We gain knowledge and wisdom
Amid our laughter and our tears

We make many wrong turns
In this journey through life
We may reap good fortune
Go through troubles and strife

If we learn from our misfortunes
We can better our lot
We need never feel envy
Of what others have got

Near the end of life's pathway
When we turn and look back
How much clearer our vision
From this end of the tract!

Ruby Coggins Gordon

In Your Dreams

As I sit and watch you sleep
In the early hours of the morn,
Wondering if you dream of me
Or the roses full of thorns.

Do you dream of times of past
And all the happiness you had,
Or are they dreams of loves you've lost
And all the things that made you sad.

Are they dreams of happy times
Do you wonder now and then,
What our future will hold in store
Or what the future could have been.

I wonder what you dream about
In the place where only you can go,
Is the place a darkened room
Where your demons only show.

Do you ever dream of me
In the darkness or the light,
For my love I think of you
Every day and every night.

Tracy Fowler Anderson

"Grandma's Morning"

Walking with my grand kids
In the early morning dew
Watching daytime come alive
Nature starts its day anew

The sun shines very bright
On a lake of softest blue
Sheep grazing on a hill
Say 'good morning to all of you'

Oh! there are some ducks
We stop to feed them a treat
They glide quickly over the water
Paddling their little webbed feet

As we head back for home
Along the flowered path
There are robins and blue jays
Enjoying a splashy bath

I truly cherish these morning walks
Teaching them life's true joys
A quiet, glorious time
Away from stress and noise

Mary Ellen Bird

Un-Masqued Ego

Born of innocence
in world of
wonder, enchantment and learning...
seduced too soon
by indulgent path of ego
a life designed
of pain and yearning...

Hidden self
in maze of possessions,
status and pseudo-science..
constant seeking
        admired image...

Ego un-masqued
spirit free
to be or not to be..
invokes
a powerful essence
of enduring
        self-reliance...

Veronica Theuma

Green

Green is a lime
In the fridge.
A pine needle
In the fall.
The fantastic smell of apple pie
And sour dough rye.
Green is leaves blowing
In the summertime breeze,
Spring in the morning.
The smell of dew
Rises from the grass.
Tops of trees
Reflect in glass
Of a nearby skyscraper.
And in the city pound
A dog looks
On the ground
And sees hundreds of
Clovers all around.

Matt Rosenthal
Age 10

"The Mark"

I hear a dog bark,
In the park,
In the dark...

I hear the song of a lark,
I hear the moan of the tree bark,
When lovers cut in their Mark!

I hear the babies' laughter,
The oldsters' halting steps falter,
And the flight of two ducks,
Striving to fly higher and higher!...

I hear the grass endlessly growing,
Forever stepped on,
But forever trying!...

I feel so terribly alone,
But only for a while, I remember...
I'm only the inch, in a mile!

I heard a dog bark,
in the dark.........
And I made *my* small Mark

Marcelle Gaffney

A Lifetime Of Smiles

A boy runs with his puppy,
in the park, on a sunny day,
while a little girl blows bubbles,
and above her they float away.
To see an elderly couple,
holding hands, and walking alone,
it makes you think of what they share,
and the love that they have shown.
Two little things, that by chance,
you may see once in a while,
these are the kind of things
that bring out that certain smile.
The nicest things to happen,
always seem to involve you and I,
and how I always look to tomorrow,
as each day with you passes by.
When I think of all that's nice,
for me what seems to be true,
is that there is a lifetime of smiles,
in an afternoon with you.

Michael J. Tieri

Lonely Little Boy

A little boy is digging with a shovel
  in the sand.
"Why won't she come and play with me,
  I just don't understand.
There's time to do the dishes,
  mop the floor and feed the baby.
And if there's time to do all that,
  there's time for me just maybe.
But what is that, oh here she comes,
  oh joy and victory!!!
I'm just so very thankful
  when my mom takes time for me."

Phyllis Johnson

Old Man

Old man sitting
  in the silence dark
Staring blindly into winter
  cold and stark
Outside, howling,
  are the angry winds
Inside, embers grow
  lifeless and dim
Old man see's clouds
  scream by the moon
He knows his life is ending,
  he knows it will be soon
Pouring out memories
  like grains of sand
Old man sitting
  with face in hands

R. Brian Coleman

Token Of The Heart

Standing by a fountain
In the warmth of the afternoon
I weighed a penny in my palm
As if a gold doubloon

And noticing the coins
That sparkled in the sun
Thrown by other dreamers
A wish upon each one

I wondered if the chance
Of my dream coming true
Depended on the value
Of the chosen coin I threw

Then, I realized the penny
Was just a token of my prayer
For if I gave full value
'Twould be my heart in there.

Marcia C. Smith

Beauty

Beauty lies in the eyes
In the eyes of the beholder
With some, beauty is in the heart
With others, beauty is in the mind

Beauty lies in the open meadow
And in the river that runs through it

Beauty lies in the sun
The sun that oranges our sky

Beauty lies in the moon
The moon that lights the nights

But most of all, beauty lies in the eyes.

Thomas B. Turner Jr.

My Favorite Place

I am a girl.
In the woods,
Picking flowers with my Grandmother.
I can see trees and flowers and branches
In the woods.
I hear branches moving.
I can see trees and flowers and branches.
The birds are chirping.
I hear branches moving.
I feel happy.
The birds are chirping.
I feel glad.
Picking flowers with my Grandmother.
I see trees and flowers and branches.
I am a girl
In the woods.

Leslie Lincoln

Crisis In America

Take a look around you
In these United States
People need to take a look
Before it is too late.

There are people being shot at
By gangs in East L.A.
Violent crimes are on the rise
Each and every day.

There are people killing babies
With no remorse at all
Is America really on the rise,
Or heading for a fall?!

What happened to compassion
And love for one another?
Those days, it seems, were long ago
When we all cared for each other.

If you see someone who needs a hand,
Don't turn and walk away
Don't let your heart be hardened
And turn a dingy grey.

Theresa Marie Logan

The Mimosa

I love the Mimosa,
It comes from Formosa;
How lovely it does look,
I could write a whole book;
It looks like a fan,
and it's prettier than
anything I've seen thereafter.

Linda Frakes

The Crying Clouds

I sit in my window
I see the rain
The clouds, they cry
They cry for me
They cry for my pain
they cry for you
They cry for what you do not see
There is so much I want to tell you
I just don't know how
So I join the clouds....
I cry.

W. Paugh

Loneliness

Am so alone
  in today's
  world
Nowhere
  to go
No one
  to turn to
Each day I
  look into
  the mirror
All I see
  are the memories
  I possess
  inside of me

Rebecca Ruby

Watch Me Drown

At sea I'm lost, I'm going down
In your arms I am bound
A sea of blood is where I tread
This is where I make my bed.

Take my breath with a kiss
I want to sink in your abyss
Pull me under, pull me down
Hold me under, watch me drown.

I see my death within your eyes
I take the knife, hear my cries
Water churns about my feet
So cold, so clear is your heat.
Secrets are rushing without sound
Waves are crashing, they pull me down
You lick my body with your lies
Taste me now, with your eyes.

This is where I want to die
My sea of blood, you and I
Pull me under, pull me down
Hold me under, watch me drown

Lisa Marie Tews-Newsome

Grandmother

Grandmother I love you, the pain
in your eyes bring those tears to
my eyes.

Grandmother I love you, you have
been there for everybody and I'll
always be there for you don't ever
forget.

Grandmother I love you, you will
always be a hero in my heart.

Karen Cosaert

Etherea

From the tears of angels came the rain,
Indicating displeasure with us mortals.
From Satan came the pain,
Before passing through Hell's portals.
From the sun came the warmth and sight,
Stirring the senses and emotions.
From the moon came the delight
And the surge of oceans.
From God came, like no other,
A feeling of ethereal bliss;
But on earth, From Mother
Came a sweet, sweet kiss.

Laura Davis Vickrey

Ode To Sycamore Canyon

There's a canyon dressed in sycamore
  Inside my dreams
Where flowers stay forever young
  And dragons dance on fountain-springs

Hummingbirds contend with butterflies
  For nectar sweet as summer rain
While spiders skate across the glass
  Like sentries in a timeless chain

There's ringtail' cat beneath a stump
  Where tiny purple mushrooms grow
And if you think to let them
  They'll steal your heart and more!

Between these canyon walls I hear
  The echo of a distant past
Tales of Lost Apache Gold
  And dreams of always coming back

To see the white-tailed buck again
  Crashing through the rocks above
Where the fawn and doe behind me ran
  And Mother Nature fans her love.

Mark Colyn Meacham

Purple Passion

Purple passion
intense and sweet
shivers down my spine.

Sweat smells
wrapped in sheets
bodies intertwined.

Burning mouths
melt to touch
toes curled in climax.

Entities in another
world, leaving
all behind.

Tenderly, slowly,
only now
exists.

Regina Hawk

Prayer Of Thanksgiving

Thank you Lord for blessing me
In such a mighty way;
For rescuing this sinner, Lord,
Who had been led astray.

Thank you for the cross of Christ
Who died on calvary;
Who rose again on the third day
And won the victory.

Thank you Lord for blessing me
With such a Godly man...
With him I find great joy;
We both worship the lamb.

The lamb who had been slain
For your sins and mine.
His blood is the atonement
Which suffices for all time.

And when the Lord returns,
(This is not an allegory!)
He will take his children back
To live with Him in glory!

Nancy I. Smith

A Sonnet Of The Stars

I like to lie at night and gaze
   Into the starry skies;
'Tis then I see the wondrous sight
   That falls before my eyes.
I realize then how good God is,
   How thankful I should be
To think in all this great, wide world,
   That He loves even me!
He watches o'er me through each night,
   And guides me through each day;
He always sees that I do right
   And never go astray.
Oh! I'm so glad the stars will light
   The way to each new day!
Marilyn Ruth Dahlgren

Death Isn't The End

Some feel death
Is dark and dreary,
Leaving earth
In such a hurry.

But with death
You can find
Peaceful eternity;
It's one-of-a-kind.

I feel death
Is another start
For those we cherish
Close to our heart.
J. Yano

While Angels Watch

Each time alone
Is heaven sent
A chosen moment
Of our consent
Our pasts recede
As oddly spent
Our futures bloom
With loves ascent
All despair within
Now abruptly went
To leave us here
Both quite content
While angels watch
With rapt intent
Matthew J. Storey

Bright Moon On A Dark Night

The mountain/the valley
is illumined
by the bright moon
on a dark night.

I drive the open road
81/66
back and forth
to my abode
hazy/hot/humid days
cold/cool/chilly nights.

Morgan ford
dismal hollow
narrow passage
distance to destination soon
I glance/the bright moon
on a dark night.
Larry L. Smith

The Words of Poets

IT is written in the stars,
IS immortal to the mind,
THROUGH the ages and the wars
THE truth is common to the times...
WORDS in verses say it all,
OF the soul's rise or fall when
POETS told them how to love,
THAT love alone might be enough, while
GOD keeps silence to the wise,
CONVERSES just behind their eyes
WITH soft unspoken poetry, Oh!
MANKIND should not be so blind, for
It is through the words of poets that
God converses with mankind!
Rio Bates

Ecstasy

Who has taught you how to make love?
Is it a gift from the Lord above?
Have you learned it from our romance?
Or is it by mere coincidence?

When with your fingers you touch my body
You put me in a trance, into an ecstasy.
My blood boils with happiness
Under the fires of your caress.

When with your lips you kiss my face
And in my hands, I hold your face
I can't help say to you, my treasure
You fill me with intense pleasure.

When with your body you cover mine
And try to keep me on a straight line
I lose all sense of direction
Under the spell of your passion.

When with all my heart I say I love you
It is not just for only a day or two
For, you are my world, my fantasy
And I am yours for all eternity.
Maxime Duchard

"Torn Love"

A torn petal
Is like love torn apart,
But once it's torn
It will never be in your heart.

You can never keep a petal
For a every long time,
Once you let it die
It's like committing a crime,
Sarah Martin

Homeless-Loveless

He sits on the curb
In the light of day
This poor man
All alone
With troubles on his mind
His outstretched hand
Asks for help
But people just walk on by
He bows his head in sorrow
In sadness and pain
Why won't anyone help me
Does anyone even care
He covers his face
To hide his tears
As the people walk on by
Sarah R. Miller

My Dog Benny

My little dog.
Is my best friend.
His name is Benny Frog.
Benny don't like fat men.

We two together one the bet of pals
Every day around them we go for a walk
When Benny gets tired he sat and growl
Sometimes I think he can talk

Today he's laying in his bed
With one eye looking straight a me
He covers his body except his head
I love dogs I had three

Benny plays ball- and soccer too
Rain Hale are shine
What he likes best is my old shoe
This little dog is mine
Mary Leon

Carma

What you do
is never through
even when it's done.
Through partial moons,
and skies of grey
and many speckled suns.
It comes
and comes
and comes
for you
even when it's done.
Paul Baymiller

My Best Friend

My best friend,
is Stephanie Bellson.
I hope our friendship will never end.
It's like we are one.

We laugh and cry,
I don't know why,
but we are friends.
And it never ends.

Through thick and thin,
and bright and dim,
we are friends
and it never ends.

I give her advice,
and she is nice.
We make a pretty good team.
Together we hope and dream.

We are glad,
and we are sad.
Together we make it through,
I like her and she likes me too!
Nicole Holly

Untitled

Inside my mind
is the
   slender hope;
if I reach out
to touch
   you won't disappear.

Yet nothing is certain,
except that which is not.
Laura Lee Silverman

Experience

To travel through experience
Is to walk within one's calendar
Looking for a map of direction
To the lessons of life.
The one who has found meaning
Has learned
The one who has not
Shall remain.
To travel through experience.

Michael H. Moler Jr.

The Other Side Of Silence

The other side of silence,
is very dear indeed;
but if we could hear it all,
we would never succeed.

The sound of a fallen tree
when no one is around;
the sound of the seed germinating
way beneath the ground.

If we were to hear everything
from a fish's gill to a bird's soar;
I agree with the man when he says,
"We would die of that great, great roar."

Vaché Blagmon

Life Is Like A Butterfly

Life is like a butterfly-
It begins in the womb - we are larva.
The womb is our cocoon.

We live our early growing stage,
attached to a life giving sustenance.
We are born - we grow.

We feed off that sustenance;
We grow, we do, we age.
If we are lucky, we have learned-

Some have evolved into beauty-
all through the learning process.
If we are lucky, we are free.

We are free to fly away-
A beautiful, spirited creature.
Life is like a butterfly.

Patricia Trzyna

Nature's Dance

When out alone
In the woods am I
High up in a tree
Beneath blue sky

The wind is blowing
Through the branches
Bending, swaying
Pine tree dances

In unison moving to and fro
Like ballerinas in a row
Bending, swaying, slow and soothing
Pine trees dance to nature's music

Nature's dance
Never twice the same
Performed just once
Never seen again

Kenneth D. Baker

Dreams

An imaginary screen,
 it comes in the night.
When senses aren't keen,
 visions take flight.

Like bubbles I float,
 soft music drifts round.
Run catch a note,
 but never hit the ground.

It seems I can't wake,
 yet submissively I talk.
Deep breaths I must take,
 as on cloudy grounds I walk.

The magical assault,
 on fears buried deep.
Repressed memories are fought,
 as unconsciously I weep.

Turning thoughts deep within,
 to reality it would seem.
The lifeline is thin,
 in the world of a dream.

Natalie Rossi

To A Very Special Lady (Veronica)

That you are a gentle woman.
It does set you apart.
Yes you are a special person.
Who has the kindest heart.
A heart that's full of love,
With a definite inner peace.
Something all of us should have.
Because it is within our reach.
That you share this love and peace.
In my heart there is no doubt.
You share it with your loved ones.
And you share it all about.
I've seen the sun-rise many times,
Seen a lot of sunsets too.
The glow of both of them.
Make me think a lot of you.
That you are a special person.
It surely would lay a long bet.
For I've yet to meet a gentle woman.
Who could out do you, no not yet!

Lawrence C. Kirkwood

Research Research

I work in a computer Lab
It's the sweetest job I've ever had
All day long I work so hard
That every evening I come home tired.
I do research, research, research
All I do is research, research, research

I get my supper and go to bed
I've seen that my kids and dog are fed.
No time to play
While in the hay.
I do research, research, research.
All I do is research, research, research.

All week long I sing my song
I'm stuck up-on this fork-ed prong
My routines mean
I'm losing steam.
Doing research, research, research
Doing research, research, RESEARCH.

Nathan Z. Bridwell

The Sun

The sun is bright
It gives off light
It warms the earth
With all its might

It shines down on us
Through the day
It brings us joy
Some might say

The sun is there
In the sky
As each day goes by
I look and wonder why

Then it comes to me
And I almost cry
It's God's way
of saying Hi

Robert E. Austin

Mind Games

There's a room in my mind -
It holds all my clues
This place I can't find -
I don't know what to do.

There's a room in my mind -
Where my thoughts can be found
This place I can find -
But I don't here a sound.

There's a room in my mind -
Here, conscience runs free
This place I can't find -
And it really scares me.

There's a room in my mind -
In which feelings lie
This place I can find -
with my tears, when I cry.

Throughout the empty corridors -
the shadows of unconsciousness -
A light, burning from a key hole, seen,
Unknown, the key. In my pocket, buttoned

Shannon Lynn Stevens

Kyle's Poem

It is rough, it is tough
It is played in a rink
The players are fast
So don't dare to blink

You can pass, you can shoot
You can score many goals
You can pass through the class
Of the players that snore

If you have luck, with the puck
And the crowd starts to roar
You outsmart the goalie
And eventually score

It feels good, like it should
And if you're not late
You score again
And it feels great

When the game is all over
The score's Two-to-One
You take the victory lap around the rink
And all have some fun!

Kyle Lierman

Friendship

Friendship is a precious thing
it is life fulfilled
enough to make hearts sing

Earthly pleasure comes and goes
bringing with it
life's highs and lows

Yet, through it all
the steady even keel
is a loving bond
that seals
a friendship
rare and true
as the one
shared with you.
Mary A. Lewandowski

True Love (Ode To Kelly B)

True love is forever
It knows no limits,
No faults, no shame
Nor humility but
it does know pain
and when the love has gone astray
and you, my love, go your separate way
I know the pain of true love's feel
There is sorrow and a rain of tears
But in all despair there is a light
Somewhere shining in future bright
I know we will meet again somewhere,
Sometime, in some unknown year.
When this time shall come to be
God will praise my love for thee,
All will see true love is... Forever
Stephen Leon Wells Jr.

Why Do I Feel The Why I Do?

Why do I feel the way I do?
It must be from loving you.
Just seeing you every day,
Makes all my worries go away.
I love you so very much,
But you seem so far from my touch.
So many wishes to be with you,
And I'm hoping they all come true.
So many questions, are they true?
But one simple question,
Why do I love you?
Stacey Best

Entrance Of Spring

As I listen I hear the robins singing,
In the distance church bells ringing.
How I long for a day so fair,
Will spring ever be here?
Is that the sun I see peeking out
It won't be long I have no doubt
Rain comes and the flowers bloom,
Love between a bride and groom.
In spring new life unfolds,
Tulips stand so tall and bold.
In the boxes on my window sill,
Starting to bloom are the daffodils.
As I lift my eyes toward the blue sky,
I tell old man winter good-bye.
Tracey Overby Garner

The Card

A card for Carol I need to send.
  It must be sent today.
No card I have, no car I drive
  must be another way.

A pen and pad is all I need
  and they are here at hand.
My thoughts I'll write to you my dear.
  You Carol will understand.

Twice is too much to loose a mate
  and all his daily charms
So God has sent the comforter
  to fold you in his arms

So you can cry your lonesome tears
  and cleanse your bleeding heart
So that new strength will fill your soul
  each day that you're apart.

God has His plan for you to do
  He'll gently lead the way
To face the world while you're apart
  until your rapture day.
Mildred Clauff Jemison

'A Lonely Hearts Comfort'

It lies here right beside me
  It never moves an inch
    Except when my heart's lonely
      When I feel sad within.

Then I hold it to my chest
  I hold it oh so tight
    I cry upon its cover
      And keep it through the night.

When I awake still lonely
  Holding it to my chest
    I remember love that only
      Filled its place instead.

I wish I could have kept it
  The love that was so strong
    Instead of having only
      This pillow to hold on.

The warmth that came from you
  It cannot be replaced
    By something soft - yet cold
      With no arms to embrace.
Kirsten Amy Barlieb

Trapped

I wish it was an angel;
It used to be an angel,
The spirit inside of her.
But the angel left,
Now she was empty,
no spirit inside of her.
She was weak and vulnerable,
free to all spirits;
Satan jumped at the chance,
of a new follower;
He'd been working on her for years.
Finally she gave in,
and drove the angels out.
Satan sent his demons,
to take over her body.
Now she was trapped,
no where to go,
except back to the Lord:
but no!
Kelly Moyers

"Easy"

It was easy to say "Goodbye, dear,"
It was easy to say "we're through,"
It was easy to love another,
Oh so easy, for you!
It was easy for me to love you,
And I miss your sweet kisses so-
Though I prayed from the start
We would never part,
It was easy for you to go-
It is easy for me to remember,
And easy for you to forget,
Though you're gone from me
In my memory
It is easy to love you yet!
Mildred L. Holbrook

Musings Of A Convalescing Man

It's gone now, I'm healing.
It won't be the same.
They've cut out my prostate
To save me, they claim.

Now hear this, they tell me
The margin is nil.
Perhaps there's invasion
of cancerous spill.

We wait now with watching,
Its psa read.
It must be unmeasured
or treatment we need,

If reading is nothing
Four years in a row,
we'll claim it a victory
and on life will go.

So that's it, my story,
a short one to tell,
but for me it's longing
to wholly get well.
Ralph E. Adams

A Long Day's Journey Into Night

As the dubious day dawns
Its dreary head
Republicans and democrats
Pondered their fate
Will it be ours
Will it be yours
As tedious minutes
Turn into tedious hours
As a long day's
Journey turns into night
The polls are finally closed
And each one asks
"What Now?"
Novia McGregor

Emotion

From afar I can see the sky
  It's so beautiful and so blue

From afar I can see me say bye
  It so happens to be my cue

It's a different one ahead
  And a scary one too
Teresa R. A. Patri

He's Gone

The sun has lost
its glow
and time goes so slow

What so many dreams and hopes
How will I ever cope

He's now at God's
right hand
I guess where he
needed him to stand

Now only memories
remain
Although it'll never
be the same

Marilynn Watters

Visions

I gaze through the window of my mind;
Its opaqueness
Turning copper-colored dreams
Into gold,

And making carbon-copied wisps of mist
Into sparkling statues of the future.

It is good the frame is one
Through which I may see
But still not touch -

For to reach these swirling clouds
Of wishes not come to pass,
Would return the gold to copper
And the statues into dust.

So I watch, with inward eyes
Through the pane of my soul,
At transforming shadows of men and time
Until no longer is there vision
And I am blind.

Lisa Harrison

Untitled

Relationships are hard these days
it's so easy to walk away
from vows we whisper in the night
from bitter words in broad daylight
from temptations, real or not
we're all afraid that we'll get caught
in a place where we don't want to be
so instead we set ourselves free
leaving broken hearts behind
for some unsuspecting soul to find
and make them realize we did
what we had to do to live

Tami Jo Landrum

Missing You

Even though you're away,
It's so nice to have someone to miss,
To miss you brings you closer,
  I can smile.
Thoughts of you are happy,
Thoughts of you are warm,
And as time passes on,
That special feeling grows,
And when you return,
My heart bursts with gladness,
It's been so nice missing you.

Peter Vallas

Through These Times

Through these times
I've come to Find...
A jewel so rare
One of a kind

Through these times
I've come to cherish...
Without her
I would truly perish

Through these times
I've come to love
This woman so strong
My angel from above

Through these times
I've reached my goal
By destiny's Fate
We are one in soul

Mark A. Barno

The Beginning

Since I met you
I've had nothing better to do
I can't stop thinking about you
You're always on my mind
Every day and every night.

You're always in my heart
Even when we're apart
And nothing makes me happier
Than to hear your voice
And to be with you almost everyday
As I look at the stars above
You're the only one that I dream of.

I'm glad we're together
I hope it's forever
Because my love for you
Will always be true.

Martha M. Bass

Oklahoma

Oklahoma, Oklahoma
It is not only you,
whole world, fell in shock,
        and coma

What an explosion, what an impact
What emotion, what a caution
Took place in this act

Cement, steel, flesh, hand,
smoke, flame, mixed with the scent

Still counting one by one
Man, woman and children,
        and my own son

Name them John, Kelly and Kevin
Last I heard, one hundred sixty seven

Oklahoma, Oklahoma
Tell my dad and my mamma
You know it was bad and odd
We are now in heaven
        with the GOD
Clear your face, let it be dry
Pray, smile, but no more cry,

We are off the shock, horror
        and the coma
Love you more than ever
Sweet Oklahoma.

M. N. Ozdaglar

A Mother's Love

I loved you when you were born,
Just a babe in the storm.

You toddled through the years
I loved you when you had tears.

At four and five, I loved you when
You always liked to pretend.

By eight to ten, you did show
Your independence start to grow.

In the early teens, it was tough,
I loved you then, when things got rough.

From a child to a woman you are,
By sixteen you had a car.

Now at eighteen you must spree,
Off to college for your degree.

No one is more proud of you than I,
I love you more than the sky.

Enjoy your life, as you go,
Remember Mom's love will always grow.

Ruth McMasters

Rain

The rain started slowly,
Just a few drops,
Falling onto the page.
But soon the droplets came faster,
Turning into a downpour,
And soaking the letters.
The droplets became rivers,
Fast moving and strong,
Swiftly moving across the ink.
The words turned into streaky smears,
Their meanings lost forever,
In rivers across the page.
So I closed the book forever,
And tossed it into the flames.
And slowly,
The tears stopped.

Rebecca Snyder

Where Has God Planted You?

Are you doing your duty or
   just running away to hide?
If you continue denying
   your duty, He'll leave your side.

Just remember He still loves you,
   He'll never leave nor forsake;
And as long as you are in His
   will, your problems He will take.

What if the sun would not shine here
   in our state at any time;
Yet it would be shining somewhere
   else where other church bells chime.

Imagine a dark gloomy day
   if the sun gave not her light;
So when you are absent, do you
   think it makes the church grow bright?

If God has planted you in a
   place, be ready, don't be late;
Do your very best, give your all
   for someday you'll meet your fate.

Mary Lafary Seitz

The Words "I Love You"

I know the words I love you
just seem like everyday words,
but they are from me to you
with all my heart.

I love you dearly even
though I have only known
you for a short while.

You seem to be always
on my mind and have
all of my time.

I hope you feel the same
for me as I feel for you!
'Cause dear!
I love you!

Kimberly Stephens

Never Wanted Anything

I never wanted anything,
just to escape my own torment
an inner wyrm... writhing... twisting
a lament for what never was.
Try to be good
try to be right.
I just can't do it
my life, my fight.
Hope to see you later
if I don't fall into my own open grave
hope to have you accept me
don't send me outside into the rain
...like all the times before.
But then I never wanted anything
only escape from my circumstance
never wanted anything
just to be a hero for a single day
escape the towers and the turrets and the wall
escape what I was fashioned into
escape from them all.

J. H. Garner

Good?

I mean you don't know what's good.
  Just where is that yellow brick road?
    Every stop I take...
      in this direction...
        and that one...
    NEVER
    Unfolds their mystery...
      until I fall;
  The tragedy I must face
    crawls up my back
      in the stillness of the night,
        as carefully as
A PREDATOR HUNTS FOR PREY,
      to sting me with
        reality...
I mean you just don't know what's good!

Leslie A. Leal

Courting Times

When green grown grass is moist with dew,
It's early for a swain to woo;
It's early when the morn is new.
O, sleeping she can't sigh that soon.
O swain, she is more apt to swoon
When she is under evening moon.

Pierce Stith Ketchum

Certain

Shut my eyes to hear the rain.
Keep my lids closed as thought
prospers through my mind of someone
certain.

Every thought puts a smile on
my face.
A smile that's like a glimmer
of sunshine that breaks through
every drop of shiny water.

One, two, three drops count
every reason my cheeks grow
larger.

Crazy about the rain as I am
of that someone certain.

Tamiko Y. Dodson

Not Gotty Money

Two men knock
knock on my screen door
their faces clean
fingers manicured
they sell insurance, life insurance

No gotty money, Apá says
in broken English

But Señor, the nice dressed man says,
everyone needs life insurance
for your family

Yo no, Apá says
no gotty money

But if you die,
your family can live comfortably

No no, says Apá
waving his long arms,
so another hombre enjoys mi dinero?
No gotty money.

Yolanda Aldap

The Sun Rises, The Sun Falls

Where an unknown path
leads to a dark, damp,
dreary woods; where the
sun rises, the sun falls
from the east.

Running away from a
bright light, suddenly
there came a bony branch.

Grabs hold,
Pulls in

The sun rises,
The sun falls.

Katie L. Grable

A Place in Time

I've seen you in the winter snow
I've seen you in the summer's glow
I've walked the lilies of your fields,
played in the waters of your stream.
You are a child born of nature,
but a lover sent to me,
for I caress you in my heart,
though forever apart.

Kathy Scarbro

Untitled

The sound of water
  Leaping over small pebbles
Brings peace to my heart.

The sound of raindrops
  falling on top tin roofs
Brings thoughts of childhood.

The years, for me, have gone too fast
  but sounds have no age
And so with joy I relive the past.

Lorri Lee

Melting Tears

Beneath a glacier of frozen tears,
Lie the cause of our deepest fears.
Intertwined with memories of the past,
Wondering if we are truly free at last.
The crumbling of inner walls,
Causes the melting tears to fall.
Releasing the pain of another day,
While clearing our hearts for today.
With the warmth of love inside,
You realize you need no longer hide.
As the glacier is melted slowly away,
You understand you are free today.
You can truly be yourself at last,
While putting away the unkind past.
The tears of love, concern and care,
Are the kind which are now found here.
Love that touches a heart so deep,
It causes dry eyes to weep.

Teresa Kaye Marshall-Terry

Essence

At the center of every flower
Lies a captivating stillness:
  A PRESENCE
Revealing the essence
Of identity
In relationship with Divinity.

Lynette Y. C. Char

Mother's Day

On Mother's Day past
I've always shed a tear
Longing for my mother
To be ever so near

Always thinking of you
On this very special day
I knew you thought of me
Your daughter, who was away

You were always remembering
Keeping me in your heart
Wondering if forever
We would be apart

But God always had a plan
And now we can see
He never forgot us
He's returned you to me

On our first Mother's Day
You will no longer fear
I am forever your daughter
I will always be near

Tammy Golliday

Try To Understand

Bruised and beaten
life has its effects.
Try to understand,
somehow it should be better-
Imagine - peace
someday it will come,
try to understand,
feel my pain,
hear me
speak for me - as I cry,
in sorrow.
Try to understand,
I live for you-
I am me-
expect nothing more,
try to understand - it's me!

Sabrina Heady

What Is Life

Life is the beginning and the end
Life is broken hearts to mend
Life is sharing, loving, and giving
Life is caring and being understanding
Life is being happy and laughing
Life is being sad and crying
Life is sometimes very demanding
Life is living and dying.

Susan Charlene Cox

Life's Extremes

To know about
life's extremes,
Of lost youth
and shattered dreams,

And the devastation
that's always a part
Of forgotten love
and a broken heart,

Is to know about
emotional pain
That runs too deep
to ever restrain,

Desperately needing
to find release.
So your troubled soul
can again have peace.

Roger K. Salyers

Mother's Love

A mother's love grows each day,
Like a beam of sun rays,
Always striving to hold on,
To help her children to grow up
Strong,
Her love endures her whole
Life long,
Just like a magical song,
She guides with such delight,
Always wanted in our sights,
She whispers like the wind,
"Stand up my child,"
"Fight and win,"
My love will carry you,
Until the end,
For all to see,
A mother's love,
Was always meant to be.

Valerie Breedy

His Scheme

His words shot through the air
Like a dagger through my heart.
Is he really being sincere?
Or is he just playing his part?

When he says the word "love,"
What does he really mean?
I'm not completely sure.
Is it just part of a scheme?

If he plays his cards right,
He knows I'll take the bait.
He knows I'm a little naive.
He knows I think it's fate.

He's set his trap
With lies and deceit.
He knows it's only my hesitance
He'll have to defeat.

As he waits for his plan
To fall into place,
He washes away all the doubts
And puts a smile on my face.

Sharon Ann McCoy

The Tide's Message

I sit alone beside the sea
 listening to the tide,
As it rolls in from the deep
 and stops by my side.

It always has a message
 that it brings to me.
It tells of one who lingers
 on yon side of the sea.

Oh gentle tide, please carry
 across the sea so blue
A message to my sweetheart
 saying, "Darling, I love you."

More I would have told you
 but you have no time to stay.
Only for a second
 and again upon your way.

Lester H. Balentine Sr.

What You Are to Me

You are my knight in armor.
It may not be shining,
And you may have lost the fight,
But you did it with all your might.

You are my heart...why...
Because I can feel the love
You pump through me.

You are my friend, because
You're always on my side,
Whether I'm right or wrong,
There you will always abide.

You are my lover, because
You love me.
You'll be my lover in life,
As you are in my dream.

My knight, my heart, my friend,
My lover, those you'll always be.
Most of all you are very special
To me.

Monicole L. Washington

Hmmm?!*!

Wondering, a blank stare out the window.
Lonely world of pain.
Still I love, forgiving,
seeking existence's reason.

Love, apathy's lesson,
truth revealing, a glimpse,
O' non-tangible "Universe,"
my thoughts, a universe
inside another, inside another...

...Endless opposition for
peace and unity,
awakened choking,
allowed a quench of happiness.

Unknown, origin, destination
reality, dream,...

...A pinch, waking still more pain...
...Hmmm?!*!

Patti J. Rackley

Tasting In The Deep Woods

White blossom heads of sweet Sisally -
Long, juicy mahogany stems
I chew to savor the licorice -
As I gather golden buttercups,
 for my bouquet.

The Jack in the pulpit —
 I cannot reach,
My bare feet would sink in the mire,
At a distance, I stand and gaze,
Not to possess, but to admire!

The rhubarb discovery proves -
 bitter burdock
To elude poison ivy, I step aside,

There in a clearing, by Nature's plan,
Wild strawberries, pull down the sun
To provide me a feast,
When their work is done!

Lilia S. Huston

"The Hill"

I'm out on the hill,
Lookin' for something to kill.
Maybe a nice 8-point buck,
Or even a big, fat duck.

There it went,
Without a dent.
What a buck
And me without my luck.

Out on the hill, nothin' in sight,
It's getting near night.
So, then off the hill,
Without a kill.

It was a pitiful sight.
That long, long night.
Because I had no kill,
Out on that big, big hill.

All the other kin,
Just had to rub it in.
For they had a kill,
Out on that big, big hill.

Shawn T. Laughlin

A Double Treat

I stand here in awe
looking at Vermont maples,
which are the prettiest trees of all.

The leaves turn fire red,
on a cool fall's day,
I wish this would never, never, go away.

But I look forward to what happens next,
they give us syrup, that is the best.

It's amber gold and oh so sweet,
now, wouldn't you agree,
this is a double treat.

And so next year,
one thing is sure to be clear,
you can bet,
I'll be standing right here.

Marlin M. Clouser Jr.

Unbroken Chain

Love can come in tears of pain,
love can come from a smile.
Love can come from a tender kiss,
and love can end in a rile.

Hate can come from a bitter past,
hate can come from a friend.
Hate can come from a horrible fend,
but love can cause hate to end.

Love makes hate, and heat breaks love.
An unbroken chain, you see;
but who controls this love and hate,
no one, but you and me.

Melany Kearns

Empire Remembered

We loved all your people
  Loved all your lands
We sailed on your oceans
  And walked on your sands.

How proudly we vanquished
  So silent and few
It comes from within us
  The way that we grew.

Our island is safety
  Our England is bold
We'll love you forever
  You'll never grow old.

So fondly we cherish
  So fondly we dream
Of fields that stay pasture
  With river and stream.

John Harrison

Dusk

The waves roll into the shore,
Making noise like wind through trees
The sun is going down
In the sky: the color red-like a rose
The fishermen going home with no fish,
And a frown on their faces-
The dark sky of the night:
Taking over the light of the day,
The water is calm, the moon is shining
Like a diamond in the dark,
All of the day is over;
Everyone has gone home and all is quiet.

Steve Hansen

At Sunset

Golden Palette in the azure sky -
Melting, molding into itself -
Gold its only color -
And dripping, oozing, gliding
Into a golden urn,
Painting itself into becoming
The Gold Sun disc on
The horizon -
The Eternal God of Egypt -
Bidding us good-night
Until tomorrow,
And leaving us with
Only beautiful golden
Afterglows
In our hearts.

Ruth Seeliger

"The Lonely Whittler"

　　He sits in a room filled with
memories as he whittles on a piece
of wood.
　　He wonders how life could have
been if he had chosen a different
path.
　　His regrets and disappointments
cloud his head like a hazy fog
when he remembers what he could
have had.
　　Past images of the woman that
could have changed the way his
life turned out, but he is to blame.
For he was the one who pushed
her away.
　　Now he is just a lonely
whittler that whittles all day.

Sherri Blanton

Subway Home

She was standing
merely standing
gazing into the abyss
She was dreaming
barely dreaming
of a soft and gentle kiss

There was motion
rushing motion
silver chariot appears
she was walking
quickly walking
destination filled with tears

She was listening
truly listening
silence was the only choice
she was longing
sadly longing
for the sound, a lover's voice.

Kitty Murphy

Woman's Curse

Today she feels mature and clever,
Like having been around forever.
Imagining she's Mother Earth
Founder of her own universe.
　But...
Tomorrow she feels like a child again
On small ground, struggling in pain.
Searching anew for yesterday's universe
Sadly realizing her woman's curse.

Liesel Hildreth

From Birth To Death

Mother, Sister, Girlfriend, Wife.
Mom understands her Baby,
Childhood with her, what a life!
Without her, an annoying bee
Our Adolescence will be.

Raised otherwise, our sister
Often envies her brother
For having tacit okays
To experience all plays.

Girlfriend creates fantasies,
And daydreams without worries.
Indeed our heaven on earth,
Also called the lover's turf.

Elected Wife to become,
Loving Spouse and caring Mom
Our Woman has no equal,
Without her, life is fatal.

Yves Bien-Aime

"Anticipation"

　　As the sun greets the
morning blue, green and dew, my
heart also awaits the time of
our meeting and caressing. The
birds fly high and slide across
the horizon then return to rest
on a branch of a tree below
singing a song so beautiful and
pleasing to the ear. Such as my
heart is in anticipation of our
rendezvous. So are your words
to me when you speak and as your
hair brushes against my face
when we kiss.

Peter Mijatovic

Walk With Me

　　Walk with me and hold
my hand as we walk the
shores of life.
　　Let's walk together and
find each other and love
everything in our sight.
　　Let's walk the banks of
rivers and the shores of oceans
and seas.
　　Let's walk among the stars
so bright, if only in our dreams.
　　Let's walk the paths that
others have walked and know
that we'll make them our own;
and when we walk past the
path of life, then God can
call us home.

Nancy L. Gayler

Life's Light

Life has lost its light.
There's no will to feel cause
there's no life that feels real.
The light of life grows dim.
When the life's light dies within.
For life to die within would
cause it to be a sin.
As life has lost its light.
Life will soon lose its sight.

Bridgette Burford

Just For Fun

I've never had much money,
My home is very plain.
I don't have fancy clothing,
I don't buy by brand name.
Elite do not invite me
To share their cake and tea.
I wouldn't know which fork to use
They're all the same to me.
I've never been to Paris
I've never been to Spain,
But when it comes right down to facts
I'll match them with my brain.

Laura Shelton Thurmond

Soul Of Iron

I look at you each and every day
Knowing we would go our own way.
Not knowing if we would be back,
  to see the next day.

From where I stood,
I could feel the earth dampen;
I went as far as I could,
Not knowing if I should.

I drive by,
And think that I
Need to make a difference,
so I save your life.

At the end,
I show I care,
By saying these words that
Mean so much,
I love you.

Sarah Clark

Wonderings Of Wartime

Long days of waiting,
Lonely nights of wanting,
Constant hours of wondering,
Will my soldier ever return?

War is a must:
A result of greed and lust.
But families are tortured by wondering,
Will my soldier die in vain?

To protect is a duty;
An honor born in good men.
So, we at home pray; wondering,
Will my soldier really win?

With the span of miles between us
And uncertain events to forego,
I want no room left for wondering;
My soldier is my hero.

Karen B. Carroll

Shoestring

You are born on a shoestring
Tied in knots all your life
Left dangling
Stepped on
Played with
Twisted
Swatted
Dragged through the mud
Never expected to snap

Jeff Gottermeyer

Loneliness

I heard of loneliness
It means depression, no care,
no laughter,
no acceptance

It means restraint
Of feelings
It is cloudy, confusing,
Feeling alone

Loneliness is a life without a purpose
Loneliness is conspiracy
Loneliness is a loving heart being
Closed from the world.

Phillip Koon

Still Life

The fingers seem longer —
more transparent —
plucking at the blue blanket
rhythmically. Strumming
the silence between us.

Removed from me now,
these hands made life for me.
Impotent now
They waver in the space between us.

I want to ask her remote face
above the blue field —
serene as a moonscape
and as a silent —
if she knows who I am.
But the question is cruel
considering our shared blood.

The shock of her eyes,
accepting,
is the reason
I am here.

Yvonne Linden Elshout

Can You Find Me??

  I heard you were
Looking for me today
  I did not travel far
I was watching as
  You searched around
For me

I heard you say
  To someone, "Where
Has she gone"!
  I went nowhere
That you could not
Go
I am here where
  You left me
Home is where
  You left me
Come home and you
  Will find me.....

Susan S. Mitchell

Untitled

Dancing in the smoke
The water-dropping chopper
Like a dragon-fly

David C. Butterfield

Spirit Filled

Twilight time appears once more
  moonbeams begin their dance.
Lights flicker and candles roar
  souls follow in the trance.

Look and see what others don't,
  strength and courage to the brim.
Your eyes turn back, yet you won't.
  Unlock the door, enter Him.

Think with your heart and not your mind
  the soul is hungry, nurture it.
You'll be amazed at what you find,
  continue forth, quietly sit.

To be is the Spirit's greatest prize,
  go now to listen, learn, surmise.

Robin Kirby

I Need You

Snatches of time
Moments of togetherness
in this fast paced world
never seem enough.

Time seems to crawl while we're apart
Flit so fast when we are near.
I know your love is there, always,
but when you are not here,
far away each night and day,
there is such ceaseless pain
I cannot bear much longer.

I need you near.
I need you forever.
Our short moments together
never seem enough.

Sandra Marion

Stairway

Lasting scents and
Lingering glances
Hopeful fears
Of second chances
While dancing in
The evening rain
Rose petal torn and
On the ground lain
The soothing sound
Of raindrops falling
The whispering echoes
of nightingales calling
Calling our for all
to hear
That you are the one I love
My dear

Mary Caraway

Here

Here comes the king.
We all bow down.
Here comes the queen.
She wears a jeweled crown.
Here comes the prince.
Why does he frown?
Here comes lowly me.
Must I always be the clown?

Edna V. Roberts

A Heart Felt Journey

When I was young and full of fun
My heart went out to everyone.
My heart was happy, but oh so fleet
For fear of capture with every beat.

Then one day,
I lovingly gave my heart away.
It was filled with love and flourished well
For 25 years I'm proud to tell.

But then, I must confide
My poor heart was cast aside.
It was ripped, and torn, and battle scarred
How could the one so loved become so hard?

It took eight long years of tears and strife
To mend my heart — renew my life.
But still, my heart is sad and shy.
It no longer goes out to everyone that passes by.

It sits and waits in quiet seclusion
For someone to come, with a soothing, gentle intrusion
And when that day comes, I know I'll pay
Once again, to the heartless one who will steal my heart away.

Augustine J. Russo

Wants And Needs

I want to make you believe
my purpose isn't to deceive
I need to do what's best for me
and not work so hard on what you want me to be
I want to make you happy and give you all my love
without feeling what I'm giving will never be enough
I need to know what I'm giving is all I need to do
to get back the love and respect I'm sending out to you
I want to make you realize I can't be controlled
but I'm feeling weak and these thoughts are getting old
Why have I suffered for so long?
What did I do that was so wrong?
I've tried so hard to make you understand
just exactly how I feel
Now I know what we expect from each other
will never be real

Darcy Roberts

Greenyears

Once I was single and shy, twenty-three.
My Springs and my Summers were happy and free.
I had lots of money and an automobile,
And I loved all the girls I could borrow or steal.

But in the fall the cold wind would blow,
And along would come winter and three feet of snow.
Then I'd get the chill-blains and miseries untold,
Because in the Winter my feet would get cold.

Then I met a woman with a figure divine,
Her lips were like honey, her kisses like wine.
I met a woman, the warm-blooded kind,
I took that woman and I made her mine.

Now my Springs and my Summers are no longer free.
We live in a shanty in deep poverty.
We've got thirteen children and heartaches untold.
But in the Winter my feet don't get cold.

Once I was single and shy, twenty-three,
My Springs and my Summers were happy and free.
Now I am tired, and I'm growing old.
But in the Winter my feet don't get cold.

Howard F. Walter

"Alone No More"

Although I have left your earthly place, way before
My time, please don't worry and please don't cry, because
I am just fine.
You see, I talked to Jesus, he understood I felt alone,
So I guess that he decided he should come and take
me home.
Don't worry now that I have sinned and God wouldn't
Let me in, you see I prayed and he forgave, then rescued
me before I sinned again.
I'm sorry I can't be there to see the future plans, but
Just the same I'm happy, Jesus has me by the hand.
To my children I'll be watching, making sure that
They're alright, and if they should feel the need to
Talk, they can look to heaven in the night.
Right above their precious heads they'll see a distant
Star; there I'll be shining down, shining love
Wherever they are.
So until that time of judgement, let not your hearts
Be sore, and understand that I am fine, I feel alone
No more.

Dolly Dailey

I Miss You So!

Never a day goes by without my thoughts of you,
Never a night passes by when I don't dream of you.

Never a dream is dreamed when you're not there with me,
Never a song is sung, without my wishing what should be.

Never a happy moment is spent without your name
Remembered in all times we shared, love's meaning still aflame.

Never a sad situation when I don't wish you by my side,
To guide my steps and tell me how to turn the teeming tide.

Never a New Year passes that I don't wish your tears
Could be wiped away by my own hands and calm your every fear.

Now I've grown into adulthood, as most young people do,
And I think you'd be real proud of me in everything I do.

I never had you long enough to tell you how much I cared,
You left too soon and made my life a burden hard to bear.

But I can't forget the memories and I can't erase the pain,
Of being without you, Mother, 'cause I'm missing you again!

Barbara Ball

Children Of The Bomb

Blessed are the children of the bomb
Never ever did anyone harm
Never had a chance to go to school
All because of some idiotic fools
Never learned to swim or play sports
Never got to go fishing or camp out in the woods
Never had a graduation or a prom
All because of the terrible bomb

To all the people who lost someone dear
God took them with him, never fear
To be your guardian angel
To watch over you all through the years
So look up toward heaven and you will feel calm
Knowing they are safe now from anymore bombs

I am a mother and a grandmother too
And want you to know my heart aches for you
Blessed are those children of the bomb
For they are the kingdom of Heaven

Betty Samulewicz

Reflection In Black

No political division
no ethnic division
no race, no sex, no class
no prejudice, only names.

I did not know any of them,
but I knew them all.
They are, every one of them.. us.
For you stand before them,
their names cover your image... a shield.

Too many, names upon names, upon names.
They did not ask why, but only did; Die.
Too many.. and yet enough
to cover all of us, forever,
who stand before them.. who stand behind them,
our shield

Gregory L. Pentecost

Addiction

There are no Sundays when you work every day.
No frisking about in the sheets, feckless, while outside
   the scuttling wind scythes the scent of ripened hay
     and thrusts it through our curtains like the tide.

Now your smile is stripped of its shine by deadlines, eyes
   glazed by the shades of pleading alarm
     clocks, telephones, satellites —clamoring
       and wheedling with needless, never satisfied commands.

Do you see, ever, the moon progress the silver rim of the world?
   Measure her quickening against the still quiver of starlight?
     No stopwatch, no brittle ticking can cradle time so—
The devil's bright devices will not fracture this sweet night.

Jan Chorlton Petersen

True Love

I have you treasured deep within my inmost heart,
No one would dare to steal you from that sacred spot
Where from the very start
Dan Cupid sent his precious dart.
From you to me.
From me to you.
To last down through the ages,
To stamp itself upon the pages
Of eternity.
You're mine.
I'm yours.
No one can take from us the hold
Our hearts have tied with strings of gold,
And twined each golden thread
Two souls——————

Ellouise Moore

Gentle Beauty

   To thou who art so lovely
near by chance, but by eternal hand from above
   Thy sweet goddess, love are thou
your tender way you dost give freely
Do what e'er thou wilt, gentle beauty
Your loving touch to soften thine soul of man
Thy body possessed with magical charm
With crystal eyes aglow with infinite vision
Your wisdom and grace to mold destines
Natures bequeath, thou makes ones heart pure
Your heaven, treasure like some secret Eden
Never its warmth shall be forbidden
Still live so sweet, fair goddess of the stars
For then the world it shall rejoice

Donna Costic

You're The One

You're the one who sees me at my worst -
Not always at my best;
You're the one who knows the faults I have,
And loves me none-the-less.

You're the one who adds encouragement
To times that have gone bad;
You're the one who helps me with the load
'Till I'm no longer sad.

You're the one who does such thoughtful things
My heart just overflows;
You're the one whose kindness makes my love
Just grow and grow and grow.

You're the one who makes my day complete
From beginning to the end,
And I'm grateful to you darling -
You're my husband, lover, friend.

Evelyn M. Howard

Wild In The Pantry

I've taken up digs with a mangy old bear
Not due to the lonely, nor out of despair
She brings something to me, I know what it is
The call of the wild, she's pedigree grizz

She don't cook much, takes most things raw
Settles our fights with a flick of her paw
But I know that she loves me righteously so
By that deep hungry look as she nibbles my toe

She does all the cleaning and most of the chores
Hook her up to the buffer to polish the floors
I'd ask her to marry and give her some cash
If I could just get her to take out the trash

She sleeps most the winter and most of the fall
Ain't much trouble, hang her right on the wall
She's smaller than me but a tuff bunch to lug
So mostly I use her just as a rug

Now I've always felt huntin' grizz was a sin
Still my baby bear's got a price on her skin
Shot at or not, being wild, runnin' free
Beats eatin' popcorn and watchin' TV

Blaine Lowe

The Rain Barrel

It's like rainwater in a barrel, sometimes I think.
It trickles down from a prearranged
Rut in the roof to a pipe leading down to the barrel.
There it sits and collects and when
The well is dry, everyone dips in their cups,
Their ladles, their pots and pans,
And their wash basins.
They cook, clean, and drink from that collection of rainwater.
They swim and bathe in the river or lake or pond,
But when the time comes to wash face and hands,
They go to the rainwater.
And while everyone recognizes its usefulness,
And even its necessity,
When the rain falls down heavy and hard,
They complain about the leak in the roof,
And about how dismal the rain makes them feel.
I sit back and stare into all the
Empty and contrite and preoccupied faces,
And sometimes I genuinely think:
It's like rainwater in a barrel.

Sharon Hodgson

"A Chance"

God, we sit before you with our heads hung low.
Not from shame or asking for forgiveness,
Instead, it's a bow of thanks. What for, do you ask?
There is only one thing we can thank you for
and that is a "chance."

A "chance" to do what we know is best.
A "chance" to make happiness for all.
A "chance" to stretch out beyond selfishness and despair.
A "chance" to love.
A "chance" to make love and a "chance" to be loved.
A "chance" to make and mold the world around us.
A "chance" to pray.

Every time we are given these opportunities, we know that they are miracles in action and they happen every day.

We have opened our eyes and we will do our utmost to give each "chance" a chance.
Daniel B. Mattingly

Atelier

That's the way I used to be...
Not just any rock or stray boulder
left by a distant glacier, but
something else, rather like a Henry Moore:
massive, but with a definite shape...
forms hidden within a form.

The next layer revealed a Picasso:
more line, but still peasant-sturdy.

I needed more motion
to my beauty, though:
Carl Milles, I thought.
More speed, less strength.
Lithe limbs, tapered fingers holding
fragile instruments.

There are no layers left after
Giacometti: he and his man
pointed back to the past
where I had left
stone and tools and ideas
in a heap.
June Lamberg

"The Answer"

Did you ever feel like you were at wit's end
Not knowing which way to turn?
Have you ever been tired of your hum-drum days
And fulfillment is what you yearn?

There is One Who cares and One Who shares
He knows just what is best,
His Word is so true, the words are so new
He will give you such sweet rest.

This One is my Lord, so faithful is He
The Bible is His book,
Such precious thoughts contained therein
If you will only look.

Such joy to behold as the pages unfold
His promises can be so sweet,
Your life becomes new in all that you do
So come and sit at His feet.

He longs for you to completely rely
On Him for your every need,
So feed on His Word and be assured
Blessings come in following His lead.
Jan McClintock

Swan Song For "Old 62"

There stands the lonely semaphore, the tracks and ties are gone...
Not like it was in days gone by when trains ran from dawn to dawn...
A passenger went whizzing by and blurred the folk within,
My how we'd wave, we'd get the smell of coal dust, oil and steam!

Upon the tracks, three blocks away, whistles would toot, bells would ring...
On summer nights, the sound would blend with the squeak of the old porch swing.

Remember how we used to put a penny on the track?
When we picked it up, it was always hot and very, very flat!
I can almost smell the sulphur and feel the cinders fly,
And hear the mournful whistle as smoke trailed the winter sky.

Now I miss those sights and sounds and smells,
The Mammoth engines, the hiss of steam...
Are all a part of my memory, thank God that we can dream!
Louise W. Primmer

The Sea

Feel the sand, it's quite nice,
not like the ocean, cold as ice.

I had an idea I'll set sail, so
I got in a boat and set afloat.

While at sail I spotted a whale.
When it sprayed water at my boat,
I was really thankful I was wearing
a raincoat.

I'm looking at the sunset while smoking
my pipe, it looks like an orange, sweet and ripe.

The moon rises and casts a silhouette on the
gently waving water. I go to sleep
without a peep.
Josh German

"Silent Dream Walk"

As we walk hand in hand
Not saying a word to each other
Everything was so quiet and beautiful
Listing to the water trickling under a wooden bridge
Violets and all kinds of beautiful flowers on both sides
Interminable looking into each other's eyes
Silently, smiling tenderly
Yes, a silent dream it was
The kind you wouldn't want to wake up from
But one has to get back to reality
The warm and tender feelings
Will always be there in heart and soul
Elizabeth Nichols

Mother

As I wonder of all the things I could have been,
My mind gets all dull and cloudy.
My ambition went away
the day I saw my children's faces.
For each time I had a child
I knew my life was worth while.
For all I ever truly wanted to be was their mother.
For no job or career can pay me more than the price
I receive when my children say,
"I love you Mom" or "I need you Mom."
Their kisses to me are priceless.
So thank you my children for letting me be your mother!
Gloria Faucher

Violence

America, home of the beautiful, proud, and brave
Not true, it's a place where violence takes you to an early grave
Violence is everywhere, you can't run or hide
It's in everyone, it's buried way deep in our minds
It's in our house, our heads
Our T.V., even our kids
Violence is a result in every hospital and every grave
It's in someone's life you just can't save
Violence is like a drug needed by some
Violence is in the woman's voice screaming you've just killed my son
Violence knows no race, nor color; it's white, black, Chinese, Mexican
It's when a stray bullet sends an innocent life straight to heaven
Violence is in every gun, drug, even beer
Violence persuades a person 'cause it knows we fear
What's the use of lawyers, juries, judges, even cops
When all the bad guys just get off
Violence is when bullets cry out, and people drop
Violence is a big madness that needs to stop!

Brande Johnson

Reflection

It happens at no certain time,
nothing in particular leads me to the thought of you;
you just come and go
pausing briefly on my mind
like butterflies on the flowers outside my window,
catching me unaware
and sending me strolling bittersweet-ly
down memory lane.
Acclimation isn't easy
yet I live with my decision to leave you.
In retrospect I now see that:
while you and I wasted precious moments
waging non-essential wars of words and
foolishly allowed outside forces to penetrate our world,
that we created a space just wide enough
for love to slip away.

Bridgitte Figueroa

Man-Made

You're all the same
No wonder why
You have the same makers

You believe everything you see and hear,
The senses often deceive you
Your insides haven't told you that,
Because you shut them off before you were born

We all go through that,
But few overcome it

Look into the burning flame,
There is no pattern
It's not controlled
Be free with its smoke
Fly as free as it does.

George Shanahan

My Love

My love where were you when the hurt was so deep
my soul and body would lie down and weep.

Visions of you so near made my body ache
Only to find I was dreaming, not really awake.

So many faces and the travels were long
as I journeyed each day in search of my song.

I despair, the answer I could not see
My love, my life, thank God that you found me.

Billie Kelly Bucinski

Life

When I was young I was quite a flapper.
Now I am old and gray and not so dapper.

My memories of yesteryear are long gone past.
If there was only a way to make them last.

My lovely neighbors are wonderful and always near.
When I need them, they are the first to be here.

When storms in my life arose I shed a tear.
But I knew real happiness was so near.

There are so many things that cannot be bought.
Faith, love, compassion and a good clean thought.

Five times I have seen our boys answer the call,
They fought long and hard and our nation did not fall.

When I go away no tears or sorrow.
For each of you will still have tomorrow.

One by one you will come to the splendors of heaven above.
I will meet and greet you with a new found love.

While here on earth we must give thanks and pray.
For that puts sunshine into each new day.

Alta Dill

I Have Let Myself Free

I have let myself free.
Now I am one with the wind.
We visit our friends the moon and the stars
And create the nighttime chill.
We escort the springtime bride and her beauties.
When she is shy, we sweep the clouds away
And wrap you in our warmth.

I have let myself free.
I am now one with the brook.
Making the grass green
And quenching your thirst are our prides.
We take you to your dreamlands.
We supply you with fantasies and thrills, both at once.

I have let myself free.
I am one with your soul.
You confide in me your hopes and your fears.
I alone can take you everywhere.

Christine V. Filter

Untitled

Twisting turning colors are flying at my face
Now I stare up into an endless burning space
I try to stand up now but I'm stuck to the floor
I think I'm going crazy; I can't take it anymore
Everything is black now and I am all alone
This never would have happened if only I had known
The colors seem so pointless, my life comes to a halt
Show me no pity or remorse for everything's my fault
On one side there is good, on the other there is bad
On one side are the things I want; on the other, the things I've had
And I stand in the middle, not down below or up above
Those who stand below show hate, but up there they show love
Still I stand in the middle with either way to go
To my right side I have a friend, to my left I have a foe
Up above me it is safe, but there's danger down below
So I'll just stand here patiently and watch the world go by
And only when I die I'll know will I burn or will I fly

Becki Early

Sean

Why did you leave me?
  Now what will I do?
Who will I turn to,
  if not to you?

Was God so short of angels
  He had to take you?

With you being there,
  Heaven will never be the same,
But with your laughter and high spirits,
  no one will complain.

But there is one thing I am sure will be true,
  Whenever the sun is shining
I'll know that God is smiling at you!!
    Eleanor Rennhak

Gold, Silver, And Bronze

Six men commence upon the track,
Numbers placed upon each back.
Cleats sparkling clean a foot to run.
Cinders black and hard and tough.

Get on your mark. Get set. Bang! Go!
Twelve legs stampede, all in a row.

At the quarter two falter quick. Number Two and number Five.
All others press, the tape the goal.

Halfway the race, two more a fade.
Number One and number Six join Two and Five.

Three quarters through, numbers Three and Four
Abreast they be, needing air and more.
The tape is broken by but one.
Number Three is first; Four comes in second. One comes in third.

Who gets the gold, the silver, and the bronze?
Alas, only three and three will suffer.
But wait, let's be as fair as fair can be.
Give gold to all, no losers, see.
Five men are happy. One man is sad.
Why run at all, if the gold is already had?
    Frank Di Giovanni

Untitled

No thoughts come when I think.
Obscenities pour from your mouth,
When you look at me—every time you speak.
I am speechless—look at me!
What do you see?
What do you think?
You molded me this way, like a ceramic doll
with no room to grow.
Stuck inside this caramel mold,
I'm dying young.
My heart has grown old.
    Gina DeRose

Longings

  Times slips by but my youth lives on in the images
of my mind.
  I pull out different days at random, only to find
the blurred figure of a child I knew so many years ago.
  My heart cries out - change places with me for a
few moments
  Let me feel again the happiness and faith only a
child can know.
  The child never hears but keeps on playing in the time
that used to be.
    Helen Madge Clark

My Beautiful Dreams

The most beautiful places that I've ever been, the most perfect loves of a lifetime dreams, I've lived them all as they came to me in my beautiful dreams.

Love has no time setting or scene. I've been a pauper and I've been a queen. I've been down many highways since time began in my beautiful dreams.

I've swam in the ocean at sunset. I've climbed mountains with snow tipped caps. I've danced in the ballrooms with kings and queens, flew over mountains with golden wings.

If you are unhappy and want to be free just close your eyes and dream along with me. We can be anywhere we want to be, swinging on a star or lying by the sea.

The most beautiful places that I've ever been, the most perfect loves of a lifetime dreams, I've lived them all as they came to me in my beautiful dreams.
    Jeanette Herring

"The Girl In The Park"

Wasn't she pretty and ever so sweet, so right in a setting of beauty and peace. Her dress was yellow, and her hat was straw; she shared her lunch of fruit and cheese and displayed her sketch of a squirrel near a tree.
Just an hour or so, many years ago her name, forgotten now, but he will always remember the Girl in the Park.
    Ann Miraglia

Untitled

Some say their mother is a PAIN —
Of course she is —

The PAIN started just before you were born — it's called "LABOR" —
She went through PAIN when you were a baby and couldn't tell
  her what you were crying for —
She went through PAIN when you cried and couldn't tell her
  where you hurt —
She went through PAIN when she saw you wanting a certain
  toy that she could not afford —
She went through PAIN when you started school and she had
  to work and couldn't be your room mother —
She went through PAIN when at sixteen you wanted a better car than
  she could buy —
She went through PAIN when you didn't get home on time —
She went through PAIN when you broke up with your
  "first love" —
Now you are grown and the PAIN hasn't ceased —
Because that PAIN is a "Mother's Love" —
    Betty Starke

Years Pass Quickly

Seems like yesterday it was me and Dick Clark
Now it is as though I'm falling apart.
Hair color can cover the gray on my head.
But what can you do about middle age spread.
It takes fifteen products to do my face,
It's time consuming and my husband began to pace.
All in all, life's been good to me.
Let me get my glasses, I need them to see.
the magic bra can lift and squeeze.
The bladder gets weak, I notice when I sneeze.
Thank God for support and control top hose.
It would take a miracle to help with my nose.
There's also those terrible hot flashes, that's menopause,
The mood swings, I'm like an animal with sharp claws.
So let's party on down, it's really nifty,
Let's all celebrate before I realize I'm fifty.
    Brenda S. Buchanan

Clearing Out The Barn

The difficult task
Of finding the buried wetsuit
Under boxes and piles of stuff
Gathered and saved by the Old Man-
The extra tools, the odds pieces of wood,
The spare parts from five different engines
And the model A truck from '29.

There was no rhyme or reason to this madness-
It's simply his life.
And two days later
We had cleared everything from the barn.
Fending off the threat of trips
To the Dump or to Goodwill,
The Old Man shared
Himself with me
In that dream-filled yard.

A barn, like any soul,
Needs a good cleaning now and again.
And so
We returned everything to its place.
Benjamin Bartlett

My Doctor's Eyes

Since childhood, warnings haunted me of punishment by fire
of impure acts that stem from lusty pleasures of desire.
And even natural practices of cleanliness and health
must not be pleasant or enjoyed, else lose the soul's pure wealth.

And as maturity advanced I met from time to time
a man or two with glaring eyes and hands more quick than mine.
Embarrassed and ashamed I learned to turn my face and hide.
For forty years I held these fears, suppressed, deep down inside.

Until I met a kindly man, intelligent and wise,
with gentle voice, and soothing touch, and caring, loving eyes.
It's said the eyes are windows to the soul, and this must be,
Despite his jokes and quips and barbs, he cares, that's plain to see.

He sees the terror in my eyes, and feels the pain I bear.
He may not understand just why, but still, he is aware.
He quickly blinks a moistened eye, and turns his head away
at some inadequate expression I might try to say
to tell him of the feelings welling deep inside my heart,
But words cannot express emotions, nor the soul impart.

So look into my eyes and learn the secrets that are there.
No Father ever gave his daughter more than what we share.
Barbara J. Loriaux

The Testimony Of The Roman Whip

What have you to say for yourself
O merciless whip that bruised my King?
Dare you inflict that bite into this flesh
And feel no sorrow for the one you sting!

"Listen and I shall tell you today,"
Said the merciless whip of yesterday.
"Roman Soldiers taught me all I know
And sometimes I hate hurting others, though"

"When they brought me the one called King of Kings
And stripped His chest bare for me to sting
I shall never forget that look on His face
As the soldiers compelled me to step up my pace"

"My job was to carry out that Roman decree
Of beating my victims till they could hardly see.
But I'm so amazed at this King of Kings
Who withstood every one of my stings!"
Dixon Weaver Jr.

My First Grandchild

Baby boy Hettiger is finally here
   Now the anxious waiting can disappear.
Family and friends are drawn near.
   Aaron Michael is so precious and dear!

Mom and Dad won't get much sleep,
   But that's okay because you are so sweet.
Even though all you do is sleep and eat,
   Watching you is really a treat.

Holding you in my arms, I realize my feelings for you go very deep.
   In fact, it is the best feeling I have had in many a week.

My first grandchild, you are so special to me
   and always will be!
Brenda Kardatzke

Kill Of The Day

The tiger sneaks upon the helpless prey;
   Now the tiger is ready for the kill of the day.
Over a rock under a tree,
   Too fast for the poor prey to see.
Only now does the prey hear.
   Off it goes fast as a deer.
The chase will now begin;
   Who is going to win?
The death run is very fast;
   For the prey it may be its last.
The tiger leaps at the prey,
   Looking for the kill of the day.
The tiger's jaw locks on the prey's neck,
   Faster than you can spell "check."
The tiger's lunch is downed,
   The bone breaking with a terrible sound.
He then fills his tummy,
   Licking his lips as if to say "yummy."
The tiger then walks away,
   Away from the kill of the day.
Josh Cowdin

The Golden Rule
(Philosophy of an "Old Man")

As a child, most were admonished from first cognizance of right or wrong,
Obey the "Golden Rule" in our lives, we'd prosper, get along.
Somehow that admonishment lost its meaning and our trust,
For blindly we strive to achieve, excel our fellow man, forgoing all, in our lust.

We exist in a "state of war" in our homes, our cities, and abroad,
With small consideration to the real reason: Basic humans are flawed.
Imperfect, we extol the virtues of "equality" in wealth, well being and laws.
Yet do little to attack the failure of "family values," the ultimate cause.

Everyone talks of wrong doing, crime, ill will and personal right,
Still failing to re-establish family cohesion, and tend the "light,"
Of the foundation of Christianity, its purity of purpose: God's foresight.
Thus, selfishly we go our way in pursuit of self fulfillment; it's their plight.

The world grasps at straws, forming opinions on perfecting mankind,
High sounding programs, actions, restructuring: Well meaning, but mis-aligned.
They forget those basic precepts of Christianity in which love is found,
That we're all his children, made in His image, by His law, bound.

Surely even God grows inpatient, that all civilization has strayed,
Yet His wrath and just retribution for our actions can be stayed,
If we but accept His one solution to re-right world and self—it's true,
"Do unto others, as you would have them, do unto you!"
Calvin T. Gibson Jr.

If Houses Could Talk

The house I grew up in could tell quite a story
Of laughter and tears and the fight for Old Glory.

It war truly majestic with a stone wall so strong
A tribute to pioneers it had lasted this long.

Seventeen fifty-nine was inscribed on the chimney so wide
That it encircled three fireplaces which were inside.

The main fireplace housed an oven which I know
Had baked numerous loaves of bread from fresh dough.

The colonial people must have really been small,
For the door frames were low-barely six feet tall.

It was rumored that George Washington had once spent the night.
Was he on his way North to engage British in a fight?

In the back was a stone barn which could tell its own tale,
With iron bars on the windows to signify a jail.

For here silent movies had been a success
With Fairbanks and Pickford and others known less.

From colonies to country, through bad times and good,
Through hurricanes and blizzards this old house has stood.

And now it's a New England historical site.
It stands as a guardian of all that is right.
   Elizabeth S. Gill

My Own Savior

You have opened my eyes and have shown me the light,
  of the faith which I struggle and fight.

You strive to save me and show me you care,
  it is that love I wish I could share.

When I'm confused to the point of tears,
  you assure me you also have doubts and fears.

I want to help you through your hard times,
  but I need you more when I have mine.

When I look at my life I wish I were you,
  for the faith that is with you will always be true.

I thank you the most for helping me see,
  that to be more like you I must be more like me.
   Christen Kyre

"Our Separation"

When it's time to let go
of the one you love so much,
just remember it's not the end
and try to keep in touch.

The nights will be so very lonely
and you will feel so all alone,
you wish you had a magic wand to make that happy home.

With so many things to sacrifice
and so many things to change,
you must keep reminding yourself you're not the only one to blame.

It's so very hard to understand
why you need to have your space.
But when you are home or walk through the door
the unhappiness shows upon your face.

If there's anything you could do
just to make me understand
it would be to reach out very far and give me your helping hand.

If you could learn to respect me
just a little from each day.
I promise you I would do the same so we could both be on our way.
   Brenda Chavez

Outrage

Sometimes, my brain is like a seething caldron
of tormented precepts, frustrated emotions.
The culprit, old age
like the venom of a poisonous serpent
an elixir that sours the endeavors of my life space.
So hard to believe, impossible to conceive that loneliness,
honed sharply by old age, to me would befall,
disconsolate Yes! Acquiescent NO!
Listen, do not ignore me
I will not be taken for granted,
My spirit is unwilling to be a passive ball of wax,
to evaporate into an evanescent nothingness.
Yet, the frailties of advanced years prevail,
My protests to no avail.
Deep within me an inner voice, Silence!
Maundering old man, broken dreams,
You have had your day.
Reason, and you will know
that it is time to fade away.
   Carl Arguello

"Our Right To Life"

As I sat down to ponder
of what words to put into verse,
I turned my very thoughts into words
of no rehearse.
The reason for our being here
is so simple and so clear,
That the almighty let us choose for ourselves,
God and his way, reason for being here.
Open your hearts and minds, people.
And know that time is almost at an end
for love, giving, sharing and caring,
for some have not thought to begin.
For we are as an entity of time.
A blink of an eye, a sentence of rhyme.
Our days are numbered, our nights are long.
I spend my time wondering what I did wrong.
As I stand before my maker and am asked to explain,
I will say I fought a good fight Lord!
And I tried to make a grand stand.
   Josephine S. Butler

Beauty

Beauty is ubiquitous but paradoxical
Often it is quite quixotical

Consider the case of the toad
Who is in reality a prince.

Is his a more difficult road
Than the prince who is really a toad?

Tragedy lies in their lack of success.
Neither could win the favor of the princess.
   Irving Kaufman

Untitled

My heart rides the rails
Often unsuccessfully
Losing grip with bump and speed
I've found it has nine lives
Well, maybe fifty
Having been caught naked before
Surprisingly, it doesn't hesitate to undress
With the moon overhead, sometimes it bares all
With neither foresight nor care of repercussion or consequence
Love is a dangerous weapon
After all, it's an arrow cupid shoots through the heart
   Julie Rae Carrigan

Lament

Cursed with crossed wires
(oh help me)
I mourn sweet kittens and yellow daffodils;
sing sorrow at weddings;
dissolve in a melt-down of orgasmic sadness;
cry Easter tears.

Irene Thorne

Loneliness

No one to listen, or hear what you say.
Oh it's ever so lonely today.
The sun is shining, there's no cloud's gray;
Why am I so lonely today?

I set by myself, the T.V. humming,
hoping for someone a'coming,
To bring a sweet smile, on a face so becoming.

To chase away bad dreams, monster and such,
Maybe bring flowers, I hope quite a bunch.
Yellow or blue, I don't care much,
As long as there's also, a hand I can touch.

Judy Elsea

Dream On

Dream on, dream on
Oh, pleasant one
For now is just the beginning
Forget and forgive
And you shall live
Forever and ever dream on

I dream of a beautiful sky
I shall never lie
For the sky is so pleasant and blue
It seems to ask how are you?
The rainbow that appears
Always wipes away your tears

I dream of the beautiful flowers that bloom
It always will take you out of your gloom
Blue flowers, Red flowers
All are special
For you and also others
Flowers are beautiful and your heart can be too.

Dream on, dream on
For now is just the beginning

Jemilia Harrison

Miracles Are Performed In Mysterious Ways

Miracles are performed in mysterious ways,
   often by use of "angels unaware."
They perform their miracle and then suddenly
   vanish, we do not know where.

The angels come into our lives as strangers
   unknown to us and our friends.
But the miracle is an answer to our prayers
   and brings happiness in the end.

We may have ignored the stranger, not knowing
   he was an angel when we passed.
And when we begin to realize a miracle has
   happened, the why's we start to ask.

This not knowing often leaves us bewildered
   in the following days.
We accept these miracles and the happenings
   as His mysterious ways.

Ada Stein

Ode To Murrah's Own

The midst of spring sees the sun shine down.
On a glowing tranquil Oklahoma town.
As buildings stand and deflect the breeze.
Murrah prepares for hellish seas.
A cross the square its shadow cast.
Through guilded portals its workers pass.
Some to wield the bureaucracy.
Others to the record floor nursery.
Unsuspecting are and all.
That here hell's minions will come to call.
For all of the horrors that man hath seen.
Lead not to learning from what hath been.
The fires of malice consign to ruin.
As two-thirds their own doth they consume.
An eye for an eye, a tooth for a tooth.
Murrah's and Timothy, Lincoln and Boothe.
A militant here, an assassin there.
Strife begotten without a care.
America the brave, land of the free.
What shall thy intolerance bring unto thee?

Christopher E. Skoog

Poetry On Reading

Blessed is the gift that God has given me
On granting me the ability to read already
Which on any given occasion it will serve me
To bring me closer as an illustrator.

Our world has been transformed
Our culture is now advancing
For in learning how to read,
We have won....
In studying much is gained.

Reading is my true advisor
Always my colleague and companion
Because it is an efficient
Educator of reality.

By reading...I can always transfer
Into fiction when I want,
Or approach my ideal knowledge.

Genaro Camorlinga-Romero

My Little Boy And Me

I can see him there by the water's edge
On that very warm summer's day
The stick that he got and threw in the stream
And we laughed as it floated away.

We were sailing ships on the open sea
And the world was ours for the day
Together we conquered a world of dreams
In our own quiet world of play.

There were minnows to catch and crawcrabs to chase
And bare toes to squish in the sand
Rocks to skip and treasures to find
And hold out in grubby wet hands.

We lingered as long as the sun would allow
Then followed it home for the night
Taking our treasures boldly we went
As pirates filled with delight.

So there on my window sill sits a small jar
Filled with snail shells, pebbles and dreams
Memories of a warm summer's day
My little boy and me.

Cora Jean Allan

Crestfallen

The black shadows play
on the living room walls.
The trace of her slender figure
barely noticeable.
The grandfather clock resounds
And owls hoot in reverence to the night sky.
He waits in the corner
Temptation.
His gray robe draped casually across his shoulder
A wicked grin upon his handsome face.
Her scent signals her presence
Slowly, he pushes the box
across the sleek, wooden table
the ornate chest placed carefully by the gods
Her frail hands slowly lift the heavy latch.
Her worries soon become the worries of all mankind
with hope, trailing slowly at the end.
Pandora clutches her ivory dress
and tries her best
to blend into the darkness.

Betty Chu

To Love Is To Serve

In the course of events, I feel myself whole
On the periphery change, assuming a role;
Challenging plans, projections, and polls;
Challenging power that plugs up the holes.
As a moment arrives, I'll look in its eye
And decide if it's proper to laugh or to cry—
To sympathize, empathize, listen, or wait
For the One-in-Charge to move up to the plate,
And strike with the flash of a radiant light,
Sending His love at a time that's just right.
I'm not really sure how I'll handle the case
Of the person on the way to my office in haste.
I'll just stay loose and get on the hot line
To the Source of my strength who heals in His time.
A pilgrim I am, and a pilgrim I'll be,
Diffusing the love that permeates me.
Not planning, just loving, and letting life flow,
Comforting, healing faint hearts as I go
To a life that is richer and God-filled with joy—
As one tiny instrument in the Master's employ.

Charlotte Bruck

Where Love Has Gone

Love is the essence of the soul flying high
on the wing of a cloud,
soaring to the ultimate heights of infinity
in an eternal union of body and spirit.
The ecstasy therein permeates the body and
lives forever within the heart,
to remain in indelible waves of whispers of
love on the edges of a dark night, in the
serenity of a morning sunrise, in every
crevice of the psyche.
It lives in the minute moment of time and in
the sleep of the unborn in the eternal threads
of life.
To have loved, to have been loved remains
inexplicably in your soul.
It is never lost.
It is never forgotten.
It is never gone.
It is!

Dorothy Norman Cooke

"His Promise"

All alone here I stand,
once a boy, now a man,
I face the world defending all,
save myself I soon will fall.
My every prayer stands at my side,
In her love my heart does hide
This love so honest, true and pure
for this promise I shall endure.
An embrace of gold to change her name,
Yet my love's true face remains the same
He for she and she for he, together my love,
We will always be!

Daniel Richard Savage

Soul Search

I guess you won't like me
once I lose my looks and figure this out:
There is more to madness than a facade
pleasing to the eye in your face
the facts because they won't change, I won't change.
Face up to that to because hope is a killer
of small children and round furry animals in my hand
you my heart, you chew it and spit it back out
of your reddened mouth those words to me.
Please pretend like you mean what you
say to me all this time
I believed you and I believed in you and I believed.

Christina Sfekas

Eden's Run

I
Once more do escape on velvet winds
To lush emerald midnight banks; breathless,
Parched heart in hand to rest where welcome
Garbs me with repose, and trust dissolves the mask
Between twin lacy willows; there to gaze into
The sapphire mystery of the crystal stream: reflections
Of tranquility wherein breathes life, harmony. Of ageless
Calm and wondrous depth extending refreshment to my
Thirsting soul, it serenades me with the symphony of peace
Inviting me to enter the waltz.

My willing spirit drains the cup, arising
To take up the dance embraced by unseen arms;

Enfolding the way in my heart, I return content
To love my life with all its turmoil, where still
There is beauty: for through the seventh
Gossamer veil I see anew that
In all is The Life, One Eternal
Compassionate Truth. Jesus
Christ.

Carol Nicastro

My Sisters

A smile, a tear, a hug or two,
Oh! what a joy to be with you,
We'd run and play and just pretend,
Of places we had never been,
I really thought you were here to stay,
Never, thought of parting and going our way,
But, God in Heaven had plans too.
He wants to be with me and you.
I'm so thankful I had you for a while,
But Oh, how much I miss your loving smiles
 I love you Sisters.

Evelyn J. Pierce

Tears In The Wind

A whisper of the wind against my skin
Once more you are there from my memories
With sandy hair and quick flash of a grin
The smell of your cologne faint in the breeze

A cloud drifts blocking out the shining sun
The shadows bearing thoughts of suffering
The day of your death was the hardest one
As the reality dawned of your passing

A crack of lightning breaking the still air
Ideas of my loneliness abound
I can't cry though it is so much to bear
The smothering pain making not a sound

The thunder rolls as rain pours from the skies
My heart pounds as the tears stream from my eyes
   Amber Dawn O'Daniel

"Mirrored Images"

Once upon a time - there was a me
once upon a time - I was free
Time came - time went
But I stayed the same
Parts of us have come
Parts of us have gone
but I have stayed the same
The others taking any blame
For my shame - for my pain
They must never leave
so now I will hide, deep down inside
She now will live my life
without constant strife away
Away from all the eyes searching lurking
Slipping down down-inside inside I must hide
If I did not
I'd have died
Now to fade fade away
Someone else
To save the day…
   Ann M. Williams

Who's Nature

Through life its attractive nature has killed me.
One of which gave me a luscious sense to live for
has parted me. Don't we learn to love our
nature. Like little drops of rain that one peak of
sun fades. Life's nature has stolen from me, my
red and my innocence of purity. But most of all the
heart which nature gave existing pain as blood
stain streams. Where has my nature in me gone?
Heavens without any shine I am like you. Why
not take me away from this nature for it was
never to be. As I sit and try to reason why
doesn't nature sacrifice. I am dying like a flower
thirst for water. Oh! nature, take me, take me for
your nourishment. Veins of my heart are rending
of blood like nature's leaves on weeds and die on
nature's earth. Myself the rose of any of your
color you desire. I'll carry it off like a wealthy
nature girl. Why my love of nature have you
forsaken me? For if you knew who my nature is
to be.
   Asma Razaqi

I Feel Terrific

I FEEL TERRIFIC……..It's a brand new day
One that I've never seen before
Tho' it may be filled with ups and downs
I'll use them to make me grow…………..

I FEEL TERRIFIC………….I'll wear a smile
There's no reason for me to complain
For I'm like a flower…I get my strength
From the sun……………..and from the rain

So…Adversity, to me, is a stepping stone.
I face it………..and I will survive
And each day I'll say…………..I FEEL TERRIFIC
Because…….I am alive!!!!
   James O. Price Jr.

Sorrow

Sorrow is a lonely place where all of us must go,
One time or another we all pass this way we know,
Although the feelings are overwhelming and unfair
The circle of life rotates as others are left here,
Loneliness is a feeling we wish we didn't have to know,
But life is made up of all different experiences which we need
   to help us grow,
Deal with situations as they come your way,
Cause in time new ones raise and the old ones go astray.
   Irene Gruber

The Necessity

Love the necessity for true human existence.
One who has never had such a feeling,
is truly a pity.
For he is not whole.
It is the dream in everybody's hearts
to be held, to be praised, to feel beautiful, to be loved.
Such a simple need, such a simple answer
Yet it will never be fulfilled
For the word has been polluted, with the evils
of humanity.
It is no longer the word of promise as in our dreams.
It is used as a weapon, a tool of cruelty-
It is no longer safe to believe.
Now we all share the pity.
For even the most beautiful word of love
can be the most dangerous.
What would you say
If I told you
I love you … would you believe me?
   Christina Sandoval

Child In Your Garden

Feel softness of petals, hold this rose
in your hand—give no love, press hard as you can.
Crush this little rose, push future aside—
no space to grow, soon will wither and die.
Damage when born, so early it seems—abused
flowers are unable to gleam.
Hug this same small rose, give precious care—love
oh so gently, sunshine to share.
A child is fragile, will become very bright—
like a rose in your garden, shall bloom overnight.
Note: Child abuse, is a rose garden, already dead.

Child's Coping Well
Children have coping wells, bad seeds grow in souls of tears—
Beyond shadowing, hiding personal trials and fears.
Each drop of love in their well, hope shines children bright—
Bless them, help that child in your sight!
   Maryellen Worsham

Ode To My Wife

I met a girl from Tennessee
Oneita is her name
and since I met this lovely girl
I have never been the same.

I asked her if she would be my wife,
and she finally did agree.
I have often wondered since that time
why the Lord was so good to me.

We have been together many years
and seen times good and bad,
but the support I get from this lovely girl
is the best I have ever had.

She provided me lovely children.
They are the pleasure of my life,
and whom do I have to thank for this
but the Lord and my lovely wife.

If Heaven is any more pleasant,
that is where I want to abide,
if the Lord will grant me the favor
of her there by my side.
Henry C. Higgins

Death

It is something unexpected
Only God knows when it is time
We are waiting to get into heaven
That is a big wish of mine.

Some people die from diseases
Or because God needs some company,
This is something that comes unexpectedly.

This something includes prayer
And eternal peace forever
But then there is a second life
One with God forever.

Death is not something to be afraid of;
But be prepared and ready.
Erin Ernst

The Last Minutes

What will the last minutes of the world be like?
Will people join hands and unite,
Or draw weapons and fight?
Maybe they'll loot and riot,
or pray in the quiet?

Will the earth crack and split?
Will geologists know about it?
Will volcanoes explode,
or just erode?

Will disease be spread,
and leave behind dead?
Will people go insane,
from all the pain?

Will animals run free,
or disappear mysteriously?
Will aliens leave,
or come and see?

There is one question on our mind
whose answer no one will find,
When will the last minutes occur?
Maybe sooner than you and I prefer.
Josh Kawka

Don't Let Go

Take me not to the ends of the world,
Or fantasy isles where life is unfurled.
Rather, take me to where no other can go.
Take me into your heart and don't let go.

Tread not too lightly when dealing with me.
Act not with fear or with uncertainty.
Compare not our lives with others we know.
Just give me your hand and then don't let go.

Shelter me not from the threatening rain.
Stop not, what together we may attain.
Simply take me to where no other can go.
Take me into your heart and don't let go.

Seek not gifts you can shower upon me.
Value not our love with things others see.
Give me your touch, a love I'll always know.
Just give me your hand and then don't let go.
Elizabeth A. Melchiori

An Ode To Rusty

How can we tell you how much we cared
or how precious the moments we shared

Your life was short, not even four years
but your going has brought an ocean of tears.

You came to us, just a frightened pup
but, oh, how we bonded as you grew up.

Your coat would glisten in the sun
as proudly we would watch you run.

Just walking our dog it would seem to be,
but a family member we would see.

You showed such love in your eyes of brown,
but if we did wrong, I declare you would frown.

Thank you dear Rusty for the pleasure you gave
though you are gone, we've many memories to save.

You've really made of us a believer
the best dog of all is a Golden Retriever.
Fran Bailey

My Daughter

I didn't change her diapers
Or rock her to sleep each night
I didn't go to the P.T.A.
Or referee a childish fight

Her little dresses, skirts and bows
Were not sewn by me
Her first word I did not hear
But it must have been D-D-D-A-A-A-D-D-D-Y-Y-Y.

She came to me along with her dad
When she was in her fourteenth year.
The next few years were turbulent
Emotions running...joy, confusion, fear.

We had the usual problems
And a few that we invented
While the years have swiftly flown by
Our relationship has cemented.

We lost her Dad suddenly last year
And the grief is still a crushing blow
But I know I have my daughter to help me
Survive, strengthen and grow.
Amanda S. Malone

Will You Marry Me

Some marry for security
Others for love like thee and me
Those who marry for security
Rarely find love like thee and me

Those who marry for love alone
Soon discover that they can't live on love alone
And part company
After agreeing not to marry for love alone again.

Some marry for companionship
But companionship without love
Is no companionship at all

So what will it be?
Security, companionship,
Or my love for thee,

Or do you seek all three?

That will never be.
Arthur Reidel

Sign Of The Times

This is the ballad of Bobby Lee heard all across the land
Our boy's gone bad, say Mom and Dad
How could it happen to such as we?

We work so hard for Bobby Lee as anyone can see,
Look at this house, the grass so green,
A car for every driver, it's not for us,
it's not for show, it's all for Bobby Lee.

We run on schedule, nerves drawn tight, to give you
things we never had; we'd rather spend our time with
you, You know it's true, our Bobby Lee.

You wear a frown, you sneer at us, you break the rules and wear us
down. We tell it right, you don't agree, what happened to the child
we knew? You're someone else, not Bobby Lee.

The ones in charge go on and on, we'll save our youth somehow,
they say, but nothing's done, they rattle on,
While teachers look the other way.

The fault is theirs, someday you'll see, the guilt their own,
it wasn't us, dear son, our Bobby Lee.

the drum beats ever louder,
A mournful melody
It fills the earth, the sky, the sea,
It sounds for Bobby Lee.
Barbara Danielsen

Empty Arms Of Society

Mothers who gave up their children are mothers
of pain and sorrow.
But able to go on and with the hope to see her
children again someday.
Society says a mother is one who raises and
cares for her children.
Then what about us mothers who gave birth and
live with empty arms.
Are we not important too! Are we not also mothers?
We cry for the lost children our arms ache to
hold them close.
We want to raise them and care for them also.
And we did this the day we signed them over.
We cared for them, we loved them and we wished
them happiness.
We are mothers too! For we gave birth, we cared
for and loved our children and this is what a
mother is.
Is it not?
Irene LaVerne McCartney-Cutshaw

Earth Angel

With feathery wings and a heart full of love
our dear Earth Angel watches from Above.
She greens the trees and keeps the waters blue
Her care for our planet is nothing less than true.
Alas, our Angel is but one
and cannot do everything alone.
She will guide us well and show us the way
but we must help to save our earth today!
Carol Drzewianowski

"The Loss Of A Loved One"

As we go through so much pain and bitter sorrow
Our loved ones are in our lives one day, and gone tomorrow
But God has a purpose for them in the beautiful heaven above
We lose them here on earth, but never forget their gentle love

We look back and cherish what we had throughout each day
And understanding is hard, but we know they have a better way.
There will be no more tears of misery and pain
Now they just begin to live their lives, with so much to gain

God looks upon the earth and selects his very special few
Even though he takes them from us, he gives us something new
A peace within our hearts, and serenity within our souls
And his holy spirit, that we can forever have and hold

I know it's hard to lose someone that is so near
But don't you worry, let him take all of your fear
They're in good hands, and in that very beautiful place
As they follow the stairway to Heaven, and pass through.
The Pearly Gate.
David Tiner

Relationship

Don't lie to me
or else I will flee

I am confused
and right now I feel used

My heart is aching
I hope I am not mistaking

A relationship relies on trust
And that is definitely a must

You say you care, but I am in doubt
Every time you lie, it makes me want to shout...

Liar, Liar, Liar you are
This relationship will never go far.
Dot Lee

A Teacher's Tribute

I may not ever fly through space
Or campaign in a presidential race.
I may not ever soar and fly
Or build a building towards the sky.
You might not see me curing pain,
Or on Wall Street counting loss and gain.
I may not be in a court of law
Or on the stage holding people in awe.
I might not be there when AIDS is cured
Or when universal peace is secured.
I may not be the one who tries
To comfort the needy and ease their cries.
I may not be famous in government
But my grasp on the future is evident.
Tomorrow's promise is within my reach
Through the minds of children today. I teach!
DeAnna Drake Sampson

The Looking Glass

As through a looking glass our lives go by
Our memories forever captured in time
It is infinite and finite, we know not why
A mystery like a dream sublime
As through a looking glass our lives go by
We cherish the moments dear to us
Like a child who tries to capture the sky
Life unfolds, surprising as it does
As through a looking glass our lives go by
Each treasure is but once told
As the sun rises and sets we must try
To grasp each and take hold
As through a looking glass our lives go by
Unknowing when it starts or ends
This life of many joys and sorrows
Grateful for the time it lends
As through a looking glass our lives go by
A bright reflection of ones' soul
That illuminates the way for us to go
And shows each of us our role

Iris Moya

The Apple Tree Speaks

Home on break my last year of college
Out jogging 'round our block in May
A block of 4 miles around rural homes and farms
Some apple orchards and a florist shop
Considering — with plenty of time to think
My future — still unknown — but LOOK UP!!
I gaze at an apple tree and
Wonder
As the buds begin to bloom this warm spring day
I become aware of a creator who brings the birds
Leaves of shade from summer heat
And takes them away in winter coolness so
They can soak in every available sun ray for heat
Then I knew, I, too
Would be taken care of as well
As I head into the unknown future
No more fear, but rather a celebration of JOY.
Now 20 years have come and gone and many trials and travels
Where I can look back and say for sure,
This lesson I learned from the apple tree: 'TIS TRUE!! 'TIS TRUE!!!

Deborah A. Nitsch

Soulmates

Into a garden let us stroll
Out of the mundane world
Into a place of celestial beauty
Where everything is perfect, nary a care exists.
Into the ocean let us swim
And float in a sea of love.
Rainbows surround us and doves fly above us.
Let us take each other's hand and walk together silently
In perfect harmony.
You and I, as God had planned
Became soulmates long ago. Now we have found the love
We'd searched for ever so long.
Let us sing, rejoice, and play
And be happy that we have today.
As our hearts beat to the same drum
Let no one come between us.
Dance with me, my lover. I am your beloved.
Into the spacious realm of dreams come true
Let us fly, higher than the sky.
Together, forever, in Peace, Love and Harmony, you and I.

Carol L. Epstein

"My Shoes"

I think about what I'm going to do with and what I'm going to make out of this gift I've been given called the Miracle of Life.
So I look at the floor and close my eyes because it's time to open my mind.
I see a family with a husband and children and myself.
Our eyes are sparkling and happy.
I see myself finding a cure for every incurable disease there is.
I can do this without getting paid because the last thing I care about is myself.
I see myself looking in the mirror and falling in love like Narcissus.
I love myself because I am myself.
I see myself as president and the U.S. never has wars anymore.
Ultimate peace is achieved because I decided I liked it that way.
I see myself creating Utopia. Everything is perfect because it leaves people time to enhance their souls.
Then I open my eyes and see my dirty old Keds.
I promise my shoes in a whisper, "You and I can walk anywhere we want."

Christina L. Calabro

Out On The Road

Just me and my Mom
Out on the road.
There's nothing to do
You can't even see one toad.
Only trees to see, grass to watch grow,
And mountains to admire.

After two hours of darkness and night,
We drive up the mountain to one frightening height.
Then we see a lovely sight!
"City lights, Mom, city lights!"
She looks over, but she can't see.
She's too focused on driving me.

Just me and my Mom
Out on the road.
Thinking our thoughts together
As we go.

Clara Rose Rucker

Emily

One of our neighborhood little sweeties - Emily is her name,
Ran into Grandpa Wern outside and over to our house she came.

Although we are neighbors, she had never come in and met,
Grandma June's collection of stuffed animals, puppets and her marionette.

She checked out the toy animals that were placed over the house.
And gave a kiss to the Computer Room guardian - "Mr. Mouse"!

Emily operated the puppets easily - letting her hands control,
But a marionette run by strings was something she didn't know.

Tito the Clown is the marionette's name, and though he is fragile and old,
He's enchanted all age children and adults, from the shy to the very bold.

Because his strings have grown thin from use and are very, very worn,
Emily felt sad that she might not learn how to make Tito perform.

But Grandpa Wern told her not to worry and to erase that frown,
Said he'd quickly restring Tito and get him ready to dance around!

While waiting Emily found a picture of a cute clown marionette,
She colored it so neat, then cut it out, what a present for us to get!

Tito was repaired so Emily was called - said she'd be there soon,
To begin learning how to operate him with help from Grandma June.

Watching her work Tito, stirred up memories that seemed to have no end,
Of the pleasure the same marionette had given to our kids and many a friend.

June M. Ruopp

The Act

A lonely figure on a darkened stage, surrounded by shadows with outstretched hand,
reveals to us through hollow eyes all that cries upon the land.

Revealing horrors to our ears through a charcoal mouth drawn wide and low;
wearing a costume so deprived no hand could design it so.

The character stands in a shaft of light, so thin and pale it shakes and cries;
lamenting about the life it knows, tears streaming from its eyes.

The monologue drains to a faint whisper; we all lean forward and strain to hear.
The shaft of light slowly fades, the end is obviously near.

We all rise from plush theater seats praising this magnificent show.
With thundering applause we approve this Act, and now it's time for us to go.

Turning slowly on the stage, as we disappear from its penetrating view,
the character stands in a blackened shroud waiting for a final Act..from you.

Deborah Stambaugh

Untitled

My mind, often times
packed with pornographic frames
square and black white.
They are me
I am the squares.
The square.
Tonight- the frames a triptych.
3 boxes
one box- a girl
she is yellow and dressed but her skin is soft
and everywhere.
The distance plays havoc lately.
All I want is to be easier.
Complications surface.
The remaining boxes
now infinite
to the right and left
change frequently.
3 second intervals out of sync.
Random unpatterned flashes.

Ian Roop

Why Did He Have To Go?

I stare at his picture on my wall
Placed beside my bed so I can remember all
I still wonder to this very day
Why did he have to go
And leave me here betrayed
I loved him more than anything in this whole entire world
The way he talked to me
And treated me
I wish it wasn't he that had to leave
And go to heaven
But I know that it was his time
And that there was no mistake
But why did he have to go in pain, and suffer all that he did
At least we were expecting it
It wasn't a sudden let down
But I still can't believe
That he is really truly gone

Elizabeth Buvinger

My Favorite Place

I'm an artist, I draw, I paint a
picture to relate to my favorite place.
When my painting is finished I sit back and reminisce.
I enjoy the time I used to be there.
My favorite place was when I swam on the beach.
I was only five, the beach was empty except for my mother and brother.
The water was green and warm, the gulf stream ran close to the shore.
The deep water was dark blue and colder farther away from shore.
They say that Ponce de Leon was looking for the "Fountain of Youth"
I found it in the Atlantic where the island's in the stream.
The gulf stream when the precious water that kept me and my body so young. No one believes my age, because I look so young.
The gulf waters on the shores of Miami Beach I left when I was eighteen. I miss my beach, I miss the water, I miss the sand and Palm trees. My figure is still the same, when I left at eighteen.
Thanks to Ponce de Leon and the Fountain Of Youth. Looking at me you wouldn't believe it's a myth. Because when I was a child I swan in the Gulf and today I have continued I keep my youth. So I believe that I have found the "Fountain of Youth."

Hilda Barbara Siegelman

Fallen Twig

A slight breeze rustles through the trees
Pitter, patter, the drizzle begins to
Tap gently against the window
As I watch the storm rise very quickly
The drizzle turns into a downpour
Each rain drop races to the ground
Lightning dances across the black sky as
I count the seconds between the sounds of thunder
Then as fast as the storm came it is gone
It occurs to me that the storm
Was very symbolic to my life
My happiness much like the sunshine
The drizzle creeping in like sorrow
Finally the storm rushes in like anger and rage
Then the thought slips away as I watch
The blue jay gather fallen twigs
While his beautiful song
Greets the sun once again

Carrie Jo Krebes

Child Within

Dedicated to my children Charles, Jacqueline and Philip

Deep beneath the surface, in a dark and hidden place...
Lies the lonely frightened child oh' please come show your face.

I want to whisper to you "I'm sorry" for all the wrongs been done...
For if you can forgive me we will smile and see the sun.

So many precious moments were lost among the tears...
I so tenderly want to hold you and push away your fears.

Oh' child within please hear my words of sincere apology...
Come here and let me hold you tight and sit you on my knee.

My heart will only beat with joy when I can see you smile...
For from now until God calls us home is just a little while.

Please hear my voice and hold my hand, let us understand each other...
For I love you now as I loved you then, I am your loving mother.

Florence Jones

The Mushroom Mafia

As the dawn of our age begins its ascent,
plans are in order for the Mushroom Mafia.

Amazing, the art-elite-chic-beautiful people
Hang with the down-and-out-ugly-no-good-
bedridden-I-don't-give-two-sh**s-lowest
forms of human beings.
At one time, they were locked in a vicious circle of hate.

Now, they sit and talk, as the lion and lamb
were prophesied to lie with each other, creating new forms.
All walks of life know the value of a good trip.
It possesses them with motherly ferocity
as the waters of peace cleanse their minds.

A 90's, hip sort of jazz baby fountain of youth,
or a nemesis of Christian evil?
A sort of melodious music to calm the beast,
or a drunken decadent idol of hell?

It is the start of a new age.
The circle has begun to revolve.
As Lewis Carroll once said,
"Eat Me."
Bryan Bear

Peanut Butter

Possessed by the fragrance of your beauty.
Possessed by the memory of what once was.
The memory of your body and soul lying next to me.
The feel of your breath on my neck.
The beating of your heart on my chest.
The tickling of my nose nestled in your hair.
Reminiscent of the way my hands formed to your waist.
My whole life I've been possessed by the dream of you.
Could you hear my heart beating faster?
While for an instant that dream came true.
Now I'm possessed by the reality of what once was.
Could this be the cause of my tears?
To hold a dream, to have touched my angel of mercy,
While blood still pumps through my veins.
Now I know the true meaning of King for a Day.
But I'm back to my original role of playing the fool.
Always for eternity will you possess me.
Always for eternity will you haunt my every dream.
You are my angel of mercy.
Come again and take me away from everything.
John Basham

Breaking Through The Storm

The rain has stopped and the sun is
Out, peaking through the clouds.
A ray of light, a ray of hope, breaking

Through the dark clouds of the storm.
That's what I think of when I see
your smile. Knowing that you're the

One for me. Even the sparkles in your
eyes, are brighter than the lightning
that flashed in the storm. The storm

Is over and the clouds are no longer
In the sky. It's true the land needs
Rain, just like I need you. The storm

Is gone, but there will be other ones.
But that's alright, for you are my sunshine
That breaks through all of the storms

To lead me through.
Daryl Nathan Woolard

The Handwork Of My Lord

I saw the handwork of my Lord today,
pray you may have also, in much the same way.

I saw it in the clouds that softly fly,
I felt his presence as the wind whispered by.
I saw it in the flowers that bloom,
each petal so wonderfully designed,
They were not made just for me
Oh no, but for all mankind.

I saw his love in the smile of a stranger,
I met along the way.
Would be nice if someone saw it in you and I today,

I saw it in the trees, and the fruit they bear,
in the creatures both large and small,
You surely must know that our Lord God
created them all.

He is everywhere, higher than the sky, deeper than the sea,
wider than the earth,
He has made it all for you and me.
Christine Moneymaker Ashley

Counting Blessings

First we count the days, then the weeks, the months, the years,
pretty soon we count the wrinkles and the tiny graying hairs,
next we count our fortune and we are busy gathering wealth,
soon the only thing important is to count on our health.
if we count our friends, our health and the good times spent together,
we are luckier than most, we are blessed beyond all measure.
Inge Lankeit

The Statue Of Liberty

Oh! Lady of Liberty how graceful you stand!
Proclaiming your welcome to all of our land!
With your flaming torch, held so high
Its beauty enhanced by the sea and the sky!

Welcoming those of our own — strangers too
With the flag we respect in its red, white and blue!
Oh! symbol of freedom how graceful you wave
O'er the land of the free — the home of the brave!

May the vision of caring for one another
Be encouraged by the viewing of another brother
Who pauses to honor and respect your goals
That all o'er the world the message be told —

Of brotherhood — on land and on sea
As our Lady of Liberty, in beauty we see
Thanks for the vision! Thanks for the light!
That beckons weary travelers in day and in night!
Alva M. Thompson

Ode To Rainbow Girls

With the glow and sparkle their name implies
   Our youthful women search out the skies.
And with their friendly, eager hands
   They reach to grasp the golden sands
That shift and move in rainbow-hued heights
   Among the promise of heart-warming lights.
They search not for that pot of gold
   The fabled rainbow's end would hold,
Nor any sort of hidden wealth
   Except perhaps the gift of health.
Their aim: To try to warm the cold;
   To lead by example the young and old.
Our RAINBOWS ask only "Please lift our hearts,"
   With the love and joy that TO SERVE imparts.
Celia and Jessy Stokes

Did You Ever Really?

Make dandelion curls or eat sheep shower?
Propel water wheels by their own power?
See the castles of Jack Frost on a window pane?
Or sail paper boats barefoot in the rain?

Ever been stung by a hornet? Kicked by a cow?
Fall from a horse then put up a row?
Ever find any money or see the work of bees?
Spy a mud-puppy or a tadpole with knees?

Ever hear a bull frog croak or drown a sack of cats?
Rob a birdie of its eggs or kill a snake or rat?
Ever bury your best doll, your dog or pet bird?
Find a four leaf clover of which you often heard?

Does she love me, does she not with a daisy petal?
See a Jack-in the pulpit sit there very subtle?
Drink the cold spring water, that gushed up from the earth,
Or sip it through a fresh wheat straw at harvest July first?

Tic-tac a window? Lost? Fall so mad in love
That you were certain he was sent you from above?
I admit all these things, even tho' it's silly-
But, have you ever done these things, now, really?

Dora Griffith Sanders

On One Heartbeat

At age seventy-eight, one heartbeat
Propels me on Eternity's Sea,
For each day's dawning and vesper time,
Gifts from the Prime Mover Unmoved—
The One keeping tab on how many
Of my few days remain to marvel
At the wonders of His creation.
O how precious and wonderful is
That one heartbeat to this mortal man!
At Dawn, when neighbors ask: "How are you?"
I'll say: "Fine! I woke up this morning!"
To see a sparrow push a crumb and
Chirp his song of gratitude is no
Vacuous interlude—aware
The Giver of the crumb propels
The feathered wings that fly and marks
The spot where sparrows die.
Ergo, Man, take one day at a time
And rob each second of its beauty—
And say: "I woke up again today!"

Jefferson D. Yohn

View

The audacity. The pain produced. Ashamed describes the most pungent feelings that should be seeping from the earth which embodies so unenlightened graves. The man, the man what man. The word's definitions couldn't and shouldn't be tainted with the false pretenses of such bunk.

Who really owned who? Who wronged who? The Lord has already made an unknown decision. Did the man once own your blood? Such a concept is unobtrusively vile. Proud, no relieved is a concept that I bear for my ancestors hadn't crossed the tumultuous waters yet.

Freedom, only a state of mind. I think not. It is a mere reflection of the mind, along with the body, soul and...circumstance.

Stripped of their names which eluded to the core their being. All for the most powerful and sought after creed. In God we trust.

Lives wasted under the sun. Too late to open those doors now.
Be wary. From up above the all knowing and merciful eyes can penetrate facades to feel the true warmth of a human heart. Use the ... circumstance ... as an example to learn from and love all. Exude the aura of a being who is one with itself and God.

Christopher L. Berardi

Commitment

Confidence is like a piece of clay;
put it into the right hand and it becomes a masterpiece.
The greatest sign of trust is to give your body to another.
Can you keep a secret, I mean not even tell a soul,
no matter how strong the urge?
Do you have faith, love and hope, joy and peace? You have faithfulness.

Leave a tape in a hot car and you'll ruin the music; CDs are an
improvement but keep the dust off them.
An unmarked street corner creates uncertainty but a friendly guide
shows you how to get to your destination.
Constant attention and helpfulness make a bold statement;
but anonymous benefactors fortify unity.
Performers often cover-up discontented faces with warm smiles and
affirming hugs; but loyalty is expressed when your back is turned.

A masterpiece is never seen by the visionary, it just happens.
Diamonds only have value when there are no sparks. Sharing
confidential information with "trusted friends" always edifies the
soul. How to be loyal: Never take action in response to your
commitment, sacrifice to satisfy yourself, take delight in
your accomplishments and ask, "what's his real motivation?"

Donald L. Parker

Ben Bug The Bed Bug

Bit a bug while in bed. He was big and he was bad.
Put that bug in a big brown bag; buried that bag in a berry bog.
Got back home and bid on a box. It had a bow and was full of rocks.
Emptied the rocks out of the box and there was the bug in the big
  brown bag.

Said the bug, "My name is Ben. I'm a boy bug, big and bad.
Bet your boots or buy a bat; I'll still be by, sitting on your hat."
Put the bug back in his bag, slipped the bag back in the box.
Filled the box with all the rocks, closed it up and tied the bow.

Took the bug in the big brown bag in the box with the rocks with
  the bow,
then scurried off to the berry bog and buried it deep, 30 feet below.
There was that bug when I got back in bad! I was so mad I bit off
  his head.
He squealed loud "I never sat on your hat or bet on your boots or
bought a black bat. Don't send me away, please let me stay.
Don't send me away, please let me stay. Honest, I will, I will behave!"
So I gave back his head (it's on the mend) & he sleeps on my bed,
  up by the head.

And he does behave, the bug named Ben. He's not so big, nor
  terribly bad.
His head is on backwards but he doesn't know. He just walks
strange, and terribly slow.

Connie Worden Leslie

The Peace Rose

His gift appeared full, yellow and fragrant,
quickly old, too heavy for its stem;
Awhile it endured showing silent beauty,
bending softly toward earth's grime;
Once life-giving sun wilted its petals,
they fell, scattered by evening's breeze;
Each bruised segment retained gratitude,
until smashed by introspective boots;
Midst unconcerned time and growing disorder,
glorious fiber perished in the dust;
Lament not for decayed life's darkness,
its moment was praiseworthy and immortal;
Senses fail yet memory claims our past,
rose still speaks serenity to imagination,
wherein remains its beatitude.

Gil Gunderson

Untitled

He exclaimed, pish, posh and phooey
Quote: "I've stepped in something gooey!"

Sticking and adhering, to his very best shoe
He shouted and stammered, "what must I do?"

So searching and searching, to do the neat trick
The best he could find, was a very short stick

It's hard to believe, this mouth-watering chicle
Was once chewed and chewed, to the state where it tickled

Of course it's impossible, to remove completely
He limped on home, likened to a crippled trick-knee

To clean this mess, would be short of magic
For ending in the carpet, would be sadly tragic

He wanted to scream, expletives after expletives
But not with the room-full, of family and relatives

His wife tried to console, while the kids were in laughter
The memory of this event, will be remembered forever

Clyde Wilson

Love Always

One summer evening came the gift of life
Rachel Maureen was our first delight.
Soft and sweet with her beautiful glow.
Our love for her continues to grow.
In all her wonderful ways, the best of which I'm not sure
To bear her hearty laughter or see her expression, so pure.

I never dreamt I could feel so complete
Until I was blessed with a child so sweet.

One spring morning, not two years later
When I thought my love could grow no greater
Came our second gift - Marisa Frances,
With her heartwarming smiles and starry-eyed glances.
A radiant personality in her possession she holds,
And to all in her presence she glitters like gold.

I never dream I could fee so complete
Until I was blessed with children so sweet.

All of our lives we must adapt and rebound
From the changes that affect us, both ups and downs.
And although I'm not certain what God has in store,
Both Rachel and Marisa I will always adore.

James K. Aiello

Mother

As I walk along cold damp pavements, I remember the warmth and radiance that was reflected from your ethereal face.
Cold and wet weather convey breezy winds and droplets of rain against my flesh and I feel it's you embracing me again after all these years.
Washed away remembrance is soaked and carried to shore.
Memories have drowned....
Memories have died....
Navigate along the passage of my thoughts, they compose in harmony, can you hear the synchronized sound they offer the caged bird? A gift of reassurance for its desperate plea.
But it was you who taught it to soar high and it was you who kissed its freedom.
Early mist and golden sunsets harbor perturbed and restless sentiments, and for a few moments I am aware of our miraculous existence.
Soar like a mighty bird above high plains and embrace nature with wide arms, never cease to exist without passion, without romance, and I promise...
I will find you

Christa Deyanira Urraca

Hands

Are these the hands of a child
Reaching upward for life above
Or are these hands
The hands of your child
Reaching out for your warmth, strength and love.

You say you're too busy to wonder
I say are you even aware
That a child's hands will do
What the mind tells them to
If you don't care to be there

The first call might be the police
The second might come from a neighbor:
I'm sorry to inform you
Shots were fired from the hands of a child
Description fits the one you had labor

Are these the hands of your child
Do they even seem familiar to you
If you are not there
Then you should beware
That child might end up like you

Annette C. Brown

The Non-Born Son

Looking at a sky of many big fluffy clouds
   reflects as a castle in the water
   but above it's just a cloud - far the prettier that way

Clouds in perfect 3-D as they fade into the haze
   as an inverse canyon, suspended above a chasm
   or inverse floating flattop islands, in a sea of air
   a beautiful woman dressed in a fancy dress
   but in her heart an image fading of a man, or is it you?

In the distance mountains not yet landed
   and look, over there it's starting to rain,
   and the sun shows through it, not the clouds just the rain
   looks kind of like a silver screen between me and the distance

A far distant mountain with something on top of it
   A circus tent, a seal on frozen sea?
   No, half a fish on the shore -
   with a frog in the water looking at it
   and those are rocks in the background
      I can almost really see it, but I know,
      it's just a cloud

Brian Clasby

Mind Control

When I feel like I'm losing control and my mind is about to explode. I must dig for that inner source, to release the ugly negative force. I alone know myself, better than anybody else. So here I sit, searching for the calm to negate the storm. Mind control is the key, like the dove that flies oh so free, I must struggle through self-imposed tension, find my own redemption. Others cannot bear the crown I should wear. 'Tis my grief and I shall find the answers for relief. One will always have trials and tribulations. Many days of high expectation, sprinkled in with moments of jubilation, I cannot let anger prevail, If I do I'm doomed to fail. Mind control is learning to deal with life on life's terms. Knowing the thing that you can change means knowing the things you cannot. One will never learn all the things that one should do, but what one learns is the things not to do. Life is a series of highs and lows, one must ride the crest, because the fall is a mess. Life's reality is dealing with adversity devoid of any animosity. To maintain mind control one must be at peace with self with an air of serenity and newfound certitude, replacing old habits of ineptitude.

William R. Willis

"The Best Friend I Ever Had"

The best friend I ever had was always there beside me;
Remaining silent, supportive, and strong,
Guiding me through all my wrongs
She was there, even when I couldn't see.

The best friend I ever had is always on my side;
When I let myself down or take a wrong turn;
When life's scratches and scrapes begin to burn -
Only my best friend's along for the ride.

The best friend I ever had will always be there for me;
Because of her I know to be strong
I must write the words today for tomorrow's song.
The best friend I ever had is one I'll never see;
Because all along my best friend was here- it's me.

Jennifer A. Whalen

Broken Heart

If I die it will be of a broken heart,
Remembering all those times you've torn my heart apart.
You ask me why I cry but to me it's plain to see.
Your actions justify the fact that you don't really love me.
So I broke away and found that person inside that I had known,
But as time passed on I wept silently because I was alone.
If I were to die tonight of a broken heart it would be because
I am sad,
For I am alone today and I'm not able to say,
"Look at the love I had."

Erin Baker

The Black Wall

She stood at the memorial, alone, filled with tears,
Remembering the father she had not seen for years.
The massive wall was granite—a blackness unfolding.
Each inscribed name added to the pain she was holding.
A butterfly, by nature, who loves softness and light,
Was silently commanded to divert from its flight.
It gently rested freely upon black polished stone;
Beautiful colors reflected on one name alone.
   A prayer hung in the air.
   After a silent "Amen,"
   Graceful wings fluttered—
   That swiftly—it was gone again.

Unseen by the mourners at this long black granite site,
It flew into the Heavens on its most precious flight.

Bonnie Gerhard

Tourists

Lately, the sour apples pall and wrinkled faces
remind the dancers of the old music.
She held her spine straight as Trajan's column
in that faded autumn we met.
Already too old for cartwheels, beyond candor,
we added the days, parcelled out moments.
The wine was thin, but we drank
as if remembering a life we never had.

Oh, Rome, give us the princes of your catacombs,
the saints we need to stir our maudlin souls.
We had one chance to turn the lock on regret.
Staying the croupier's hand, we played our last bet.
Later, on the Via Flamina, we had a hope.

Tomorrow rushed past to another
tomorrow and heaven's answer.
Come back, she pleaded, our hands are icy
and we do not need the bells or towers,
the gory passions of these streets.
We have amputated the city's enchantress.
We have become common, literal as flesh and fire.

John Ahern

"The New Year"

The New Year is here and we make a fresh start;
resolutions are made with joy in our hearts;
our intentions are good; to keep them we try,
but we fail to trust in our Father on High.

We grumble and fuss when things don't go right;
instead of singing, we all get "up tight."
To make things better, we all need to pray
that our Father in Heaven will show us the way
to a happier life and His service to do;
and our faith will grow stronger all the year through.

When at the end of life's road we come,
we will stand accountable for the deeds we've done.
Won't it be wonderful to hear Him say,
"Welcome my child to a bright new day?"

Dorothy Vanzant

Post-Modern Liberty

The pops and scratches of one man's record
Reverberate in spinning, echoing onto
The wet evening sidewalk street of empty-hour alone.
The factory bids one more life farewell.
And he sleeps here one last night.

A cat sounds his respectful mourn
From the wooden fence across the street
Among the scratching sounds of other
Patriot mourners coming up to join him.
The king of the night-wind oversees his territory.

A man, long out of the factory,
Long gone from jobs at McDonald's,
Strokes his cat and falls asleep against
The dark and familiar brick wall.
The great mourner merely purrs underneath his hands.

Craig Collier

Falling Apart

My world is falling apart
Right before my eyes
The bricks and stones that were once carefully placed
Have now tumbled into a pile of ruble.

I have lost the love of my life
I've lost everything I once had.
The love I once had for you is much stronger now,
And can never be taken away.

The world can be such an evil place,
So hard and so complicated to understand;
I worked so very hard to get you to love me,
But someone, just one person, had to take you away.

Jessica Hill

Sitting On The Couch With You

Is even more fun than going to the South of France, London,
Amsterdam, Rome, Madrid
Or being sick to my stomach on a gondola ride on a canal in Venice
Partly because in your worn t-shirt you look like a better,
prettier St. Tropez
Partly because of my love for you, partly because of your love for MTV
Partly because of the sound your laughter takes on in front of me.
It is hard to believe when I'm with you that there can be
anything outside the window,
Like streets crowded with people, taxis, smog,
When right in front of it in the afternoon
in the warm New York apartment building we are drifting back
and forth between each other.

Gia M. Rokeach

As My Heart Speaks

The thought of you is like the sweet sensation from a scent-filled
rose, for it lingers within me in perpetualness, echoing through my
mind, never escaping, like water forever trickling down a river,
like waves infinitely crashing onto the sand.
To me you are the sun, forever shining, forever bringing light into
  my life.
Looking into your eyes I loose myself, my heart soars high into the
  heavens.
When in your presence I am a cloud, hovering over all the earth, I
forget all and in my mind remains only you.
In my heart shall you always be, as the stars shall always shine.
You are my life, for without joy, life is empty, as my heart was
  without you.
To you I give my love everlasting. And in your hands lay my fate.
Like the air around you by my love shall you always be surrounded,
for my everlasting love will live on forever, like souls travel'n on
  in eternity.

Gino Belarmino

Life's A Beach

All we really need to do in life
is the same thing we do at the beach.
Run. Have fun.
Relax. Look at the sky.
Watch where you step.
Feel the warm sun on your face.
Play in the sand. You'll feel better.
Use sun screen.
Pay attention to signs.
Breathe in the fresh air.
Walk slow and hold hands.
Don't get in over your head.
Smile and laugh.
Walk in the water in your bare feet.
Lay down, close your eyes and breathe deep.
Remember the old and new flow in
and out like the ocean water.
When the sand is taken away,
new sand is brought in.
Friends are like that too.
If we lose one, we'll find another.

*Cheryl Yeoman and 4th grade students
at Medlock Bridge Elementary School,
Alpharetta, GA*

"Star Of Lost Courage"

Every night, she looks out the window,
She talks to the "man on the moon,"
She tells him, "I'm going to be a star;"
She wants to be a star.

Looking up at the sky,
Can't you see the pain and anger in her eyes, that lurks inside;
Everything's still the same;
Nothing has changed.

She lies in bed and waits for sleep.
She dreams the impossible dream,
But lives the impossible life.
She closes her eyes from the tender night,
Still; as she's lying there.

"Give me the courage to live:" she says,
"Give me the courage."

The pain that is held inside,
Soon melts away as she closes her eyes;
Into the quilts on her side.
Where soon they'll return, when the sun will rise.

"Give me the courage to be again; Give me the courage."

Judite Garbrielle Santos

Pilgrimage To Rome

I stood - awe-struck - 'fore works of
saint and sage
Who labored to pour forth their paeans of praise
To God or gods - Whatever Age they be -
or concept of immortality.

To think that I in poem or prose, forsooth
could e'er hold their noble grasp of Truth!
What arrogance that wells within My breast
To reach the heights of their artistic quest!

Yet - not to strive would but negate the call
of Cosmic Mind to battle or forestall
that thought which brings to flesh such ennui
and questions Faith - "To be or not to be"!

But Challenges still the Man of every Clime
To rise to higher plane or realm sublime
that earlier sage of brush, or knife, or pen
had never thought to see or enter in.

So, guilt from guttered gauntlet now has fled.
Another fool has taken muse to wed.

Jeanette Holmes Babin

Our Daughter Lois

Many girls make splendid daughters,
  So our daughter is not alone.
So all the years in passing,
  Prove there is no daughter like our own.
In childhood she was our shining star,
  We and only we were her delight.
And her reassuring presence,
  Made our small world calm and bright.
Adolescence may be trying,
  But she put up with our spanks.
She gave us what we asked for,
  Though she often received no thanks.
Adulthood brought us new pleasures,
  New adventures to unwind.
New relationships as warm and real,
  As we might hope to find.
The many bonds between us,
  Have all multiplied and grown,
So there is no daughter like our own.

Orville M. Steele Sr.

Happiness? When?

I am scared Lord!
Scared of everything; scared I won't win, scared I will fail,
scared that something worse will happen.
What The Heck Do You Want Me To Do?

I ponder to your word, for it is probably the only thing that can
help right now. In a Psalm, it talks about happiness and how
confiding in you makes it all better. Yet still...

I look around and watch my parents, how hard they have it.
How can I possibly be happy and rejoice when my parents are
fighting the good fight and are being shot down?
They pray to you for guidance, and sometimes you help, but
sometimes you don't seem to.

Yet you say that you will make it alright.
I pray you are correct.
Then I will be happy for an eternity.

Better yet, I'll start now, could this be what you want?
Either way I'll be happy, or at least try.
It's hard, and sometimes I feel that you just don't understand,
even though you claim you do. But I'll be happy, and I'll just keep
on praying that you make everything alright. AMEN...

Fred Pilarczyk

Who I Am

Nobody knows who I really am
Satanic? No, but still they say I'm damned
Every time I make a friend it's always the wrong guy
A troublemaker who smokes, drinks, and gets high
They say look at him again with another troublemaker
When I try to be nice, they say I'm a faker
I wish someone could see deep down the real me
But I'm always afraid to show it you see
'Cause I'm the bad guy, the class clown
A troublemaker just being pushed around
Hey it rubs off, I'm as bad as my friend
That's what they'll say from now to the end
But I'm trying to be good. I'm trying to get free
From this body who won't let my heart be me.

Anthony R. Gennari

Renaissance

  On Friday nights he'll be in the big game,
Saturday, it's to the theater.
  He loves Theisman......And Byron
Nobody calls him a wimp,
  Yet he's not afraid to cry.
On Friday nights, he's ready to stare death in the face,
  Saturday, he's ready to stare into your eyes.
He loves the Raven.....and the Babe
  Deep down, he's the one you wish you were more like,
Deep down, he's the one I'm looking for.

Amy C. Egger

A Walk In The Rain

Warm rain swept my face as I walked the lonely road. With the
Scent of sweet honeysuckle capturing the moment.
The birch trees sway gently in the wind summer rain, and
Visions of childhood appear without refrain.
Sound of thunder roll across the sky overhead.
In a clearing the lightning bolt strikes the near meadow's edge.
I've always loved the rain and never knew why.
Perhaps it was the surrendering of farm work as a boy that first
Caught my eye.
Fond memories of rainy days have never eluded, as I continue
My walk down this tranquility so secluded.
As I near the crossroad and simultaneously the sun now emerging,
Cast its brilliant rays through the dissipating clouds and trees.
A rainbow soon visible in all the captivating colors, looking like
A giant shroud across the summer sky.

As my walk came to an end down this remote country road, so did the
Rain. Without it I would have missed a wonderful journey down memory
Lane.

Allen T. Hunt

I Am Mad

Yes I am mad, no I didn't say
sad, no it's not a fad. You heard what I
said. My stomach is light, food I don't get before bed,
I live with no Dad. Mamma I know not, is she that woman on the
block? She lives her life for that ole base rock. I didn't say sad,
I am mad, oppression heavy on my head,
I don't wish to be dead, I want a home with a bed,
poor old mom and dad. I can only imagine the life
they had. Me, I am a mom and dad.
My child I just had, this life we live,
I trust in God, life he gives.
Mad with him? No, he gave me not this deal,
the system I say, you're the one for my ordeal.
I am not sad, I am just mad, wonder what kinda life I
could have had, if all had gone well
for dear ole mom and dad.

Bobby Flowers

Flight Of The Innocent

Take me away from the maddening bustle of the crowded cities and screaming people with mud on their faces and hate in their eyes.

Take me away from the cry of the unborn children and the confusion of the unwed adolescents for whom no one sheds a tear - only scorns.

Let me out of this sinful hell where no one knows why they came or what they're here for.

I must escape the questions that have no answers and the reasonings that are only rubbish, leaving puzzled looks on the faces of fools who could never begin to understand.

I will run far, far away, let my mind wander recklessly, and live forever in the simplicity of my own innocence - blocking out all forms of intrusion from this impossibility entitled "Life."

Carolyn Wright

"Sweet And New"

Softly, you stretched unseen fingers around my life
Seeking to surround my very soul without strife.
Slowly moving across, like early morning dew,
You reached out, making everything so sweet and
new.

With quietness like fluttering wings of a dove,
You captured my frozen heart with kindness and love.
You accomplished what has been done by only few;
Moving, oh so sweetly ... my soul cried out to you.

Calmly and cautiously, you moved around my world;
Lifting my heart like music so softly unfurled.
Never asking me to do anything for you —
You have reached me - Now everything is sweet
and new!

June Keener Allen

It's You

Mixed emotions describe it best
Seem as I'm taking a stringent test
I'm lost for words, and don't know what to do
It's difficult to decipher what's false or true
My heart says yes, but my mind says no
It's a weighty decision, I know not where to go
So I'll ask a friend, to see what they will say
Upon their shoulder, a burden I'll lay
But low and behold, what is this here
My friend is the one for whom I care
My tongue is tied and voice gets weak
I move my lips, not a word I speak
So all I possess is yet still on delay
For another time, my thoughts, I'll let slip away

Eric Lamont Mickens

Meaning

Let the four winds blow freely
  over the insecure existence of all.

Their touch, whether soft or not,
  will only for a fleeting moment
  attempt to change that upon which they fall.

And cautiously descend within
  that inviting cradle of substance and form

That will lift and carry you grandly
  with bold distinction of meaning forlorn.

Ah, but what is the relevant meaning
  of all those things you pass

If you have only to wonder
  at their color and whether they will last.

Jack Napier

The Train

How could something so mundane as fifty miles of track,
Separate two worlds, one out front, one out back?
Two worlds totally different, apart like night and day,
The first so rich and gleaming, the second black and gray.

The lives of those who live there, one bright, alive, robust.
The other dark and gloomy. No hope, just coal and dust.
The miners and their families, their lives, their schools, their shacks,
A hundred years away from us, but fifty miles of tracks.

Just fifty miles from our homes, these lives and their travails,
These nameless proud we do not see, distanced by the rails.
We may never know the hurt, the death, the tears, and pain.
One, however, sees their world. That witness is the train.

The train which daily hauls away the harvest of the strife.
That puffing giant passes through the grim, nocturnal life.
The crucial link, the only link that moves the precious ore,
From colliery to marketplace. Its life is nothing more.

The train, six hundred tons of steel is only but a slave.
To money, men, and anthracite, its might and strength it gave.
Connecting two eternities, the gleaming and the black.
With fifty miles of ties and spikes, and fifty miles of track.

Daniel R. Hiltz

Where Are We Going?

In a view from a distance it was clear the train was headed for the set of tracks that led over the cliff.

"Somebody listen," was the cry. "Hit the switch track to save the train."

No one could hear the plea over the countless other happenings, all of which seemed more important to the journey of life.

SOMEONE LISTEN!

Then a small voice cuts through the roar, "Switch the track? How?"

Anthony Hendricks

Sold Out My Life

I could have been a star; didn't think I could reach that far
Settled for a replaceable job, plastic man's suit and tie
I will endure the yoke, daily don the outfit till I die

What happened to my dreams
I gave it all up; trivial plots, grand schemes
Gave in, all for the taking
Sold it all out, my life
Everything for a buck; meekly forsaken

Outwardly you get to choose
Try something different with an increased chance of abject failure
Abandon everything for a safe rut; else you'll lose
Take the prize behind the well-worn curtain badly labelled
Safe, secure; or is it despair?

We all have to determine our selling price
Decide what cost is acceptable for mediocre security
Getting nothing of value in return for your life

Bob Connors

Quiet Cathedral

We enter the nave of the cathedral is search of
solitude and the tranquility of the mountains.

As we headed for one of the many chapels the we
will visit below the arched ceiling and the spires.

To climb some of the buttresses and to look through the
stained windows to see the sun going down behind
Blackfoot Mountain.

At last we left through the portals of the cathedral
with some of the peace and quiet we hoped to find.

Eric Whiteman

The Ones Left Out

She sits by herself, lonely and blue,
She doesn't have friends, not even one or two.
She's always the victim of a joke, prank, or gag,
and is almost positive her life is a drag.

His life is miserable, he doesn't have a friend,
He's planning to make his life come to an end.
A pull of the trigger was all it would take,
And right before he died, he knew he'd made a
Mistake.

The pain they had, they tried to hide,
But way deep down it was aching inside.
People around them didn't seem to care,
That the way they were treating them was cruel and
Unfair.

People despised them, they didn't know what for,
Then they came to a decision, they didn't want to live
Anymore.
Their parents didn't know what the suicide was about,
But you and I know, they were the ones left out.

Holly C. Bibb

"Life With My Children"

There was a young woman who lived in a shoe.
She had five children and she knew just what to do.
She kept them well fed and clean as she could.
And was always around doing what she should.
They were happy little children with their ups and downs,
But nothing was so bad that a remedy was always found.
But as time went on and they grew big and strong
the shoe was too small, and then things seem to go wrong.
Each one of them was ready to make their own flight
One at a time they left the shoe from their sight.
Each one started up the big mountain to discover new ground.
Praying as they started up, they wouldn't fall back down.
But as they grew older, the tap wasn't easy to reach.
Falling back to the bottom is something we cannot teach
I did my part, what happens now I cannot stop.
It's rough, it's hard, it's tears, it's grief
and in the end there is no relief.
I know I did the best I could
It's up to them to do what they should
I would feel I had reached the top if only this grief would stop.
Now I'll leave this in God's hands and let him lead them to the top.

Barbara Burton

Wisdom, God's Sabbath And Rest

True wisdom does not finally rest in the Greek Sophia or Philo.
She sings her praises among her people, Zion, God's goal.
Wisdom comes from the mouth of the Most High on a pillar cloud.
She sought a resting place to see what God allowed.
Then God gave Her a spot for Her tent.
This is in Genesis Two, the New Eve and Adam, not of the serpent.
This is Mary, the virgin, Our Mother.
She has given us Her Son, Our Brother.
To the chosen city, Zion, God has given rest.
They enter into the marriage of the Lamb: THE BLEST.

Then the Creator of all gave me this command
as He who formed me, chose the spot for my tent
saying: "In Jacob make your dwelling. In Israel make your descent."
Before all ages, in the beginning, YAHWEH created me,
and through all ages I shall not cease to be.
In the holy tent I ministered before him,
And in Zion I fixed my abode without sin.
Thus in the chosen city, He has given me rest.
In Jerusalem, Our Mother, I have struck root among the glorious
people, in the portion of the Lord, his heritage: THE BLEST.

Helen Lowman

Mom

Mama had a little jar she kept on the sideboard shelf
She told us it was magic and only for herself
She pulled from it myriads of things like picture show dimes and fifteen cent rings
When I kept complaining that I needed shoes, she pulled out four bits and ended my blues.

Yes, Mom was a wizard without hat or rabbit
But we all knew it was just her usual habit.
Once when I had a big hole in my stocking, Mom stifled a grin and just kept on rocking.
She said, "My dear child, that's nothing new—one hole in your stocking is better than two."

Her wisdom never seemed to cease. The more problems we had, the more it would increase.
At times we all laughed and often we'd cry
But our love for Mom grew as time went by.

If only all mothers could be just like ours
We all could be blessed with sunshine and flowers,
And God would fill us with His grace
And the whole world would be a much better place.

Bonnie Kerr Amy

Somehow Tomorrow

Somehow tomorrow she'll still be in sight
She walks through the sand as her body feels light
Hands so intense, they seem very cold
Maybe someday she'll have someone to hold
Somehow tomorrow. I hope she can smile
Whenever she frowns, nothing's worthwhile
Her eyes so blue, they formed from God's tears
Or maybe her mother as she's grown these past years
Somehow tomorrow there's always something new
Somehow tomorrow I'll keep loving you

Jason C. Miller

Somebody Else's Child

He must be somebody else's child
A total stranger he is to me.
But I knew him before he turned thirteen
As close as Mother and Son could be.
And now he won't clean his room
This child of mine makes me wanna scream.
Throw his clothes all over the floor
As if it's a new carpet which only he adorns.
He talks on the phone for hours and hours
Because time to him just don't matter.
He must be somebody else's child.
He has music blaring and blasting
I have nightmares of it lasting.
He leaves rings around the tub,
Throws his towel where they don't belong.
Drops his cut hair on the floor, and then figures there nothing wrong.
Until no words are finally said then he'll try to
Act just like he totally deaf.
He tries to argue and argue again until no words are finally said.
He must be somebody else's child but whose could he possible be?

Kimberly Dykes

Black And White

What is black and white? Man see's it as
Skin color, but God see's the black as dark
and gloomy, and white as the light, to see
the beautiful things that he has created,
see in the eyes of God, there is no color,
that we are all equal, and that is the way
He want's us to see it.

John S. Roblyer

Where Is My Place?

She sat staring out into space,
she was wondering where is my place?
A lot of people ask that question,
others ask do I really exist?
Some end to thank that suicide is the way,
but I say not today or any other day.
How many things can I be,
what do other see in me?
Many thoughts are flying through my head.
I think that it is time for me to go to bed.
I may go to bed, but still people are awake,
some are real and some are fake.
Tomorrow I still will not know my way,
but I think I can make it though another day.
The wind is blowing,
the lights are dimming.
The room is getting quite dark,
I think I can hear a dog bark.
I fade into sleep,
as my mother takes a peep.

Bradley Taylor

"Quest"

More than less this era diminished
Shattered goes what kind of joy
Leverage why struggle it is finished
Battered comes hope despair to deploy
Kindle ash trails through paths once used
Only where tropical breezes and rivers flowed
Blended emotions splint hearts once abused
Oddly tainted nepenthe despondency gleefully grows
Mirrored blunders mire hearts once forgiving
Fondled aspirations show a pitiful glow
Mimicked retractions quietly stalk meander discipline
Mindless violations blench the heart and soul
Carefully a clear picture is made
Boasting not afterwards the errorless shoot
Blistered still the past may fade
Love can return as abiding youth

David L. Faison

Carpenter's Carol

I love the feel of wood in my hand, as it turns from rough to smooth
The wood's as hard as life in this land as HE shapes us from rough to smooth.

And who is this child I'm pledged to marry
Her eyes look beyond me; her sweet name is Mary.

I work my trade from dawn to last light, turning the rough wood to smooth
Praying my work is just in God's sight; hoping the rough wood will smooth.

And who is the Babe I know her to carry
In the night of my dreaming they sang, "Hail Mary."

I'll try as I know to honor the law HE made to shape rough men to smooth
And feel through the day HIS hand on my saw as I turn the rough wood to smooth.

And I'll love this child as the dream voices told me
Why see I a rough cross rear darkly above me?

My mind cannot grasp why all this must be, as I work the wood of the land.
I can only believe that somehow the wood will all turn to smooth in HIS hand.

George T. Bedway

Our Mom

Our Mom works hard both night and day,
Showing us her love in every way.
Three days a week to our school she runs,
To teach computers to the little ones.

To the skating rink each week we go,
If we want to take friends, she won't say no.
When we ask friends to spend the night,
She may be tired, but she says, "All right."

Our Mom is great, she is the best,
And many times she's been put to the test.
With last minute this and last minute that,
From a cowboy suit to a Daniel Boone hat.

So, Mom, on this, your special day,
We wanted to take this time to say,
"We think you're great; we think you're neat,
As a super Mom, you can't be beat!!!!

Jason Adams & Shawn Adams

Knowing

Natives beating on the water
Smells of their feast
Gathering for the slaughter
Of the virgin beast

She knows, she knows, she knows she's gonna get it
For some made up God's relent
The crow, the crow, the crow watches in amazement
And they know, they know, they know 'cause they believe it

The torch man slowly paces
Fire touches lumber
Brightens up their faces
Virgin's last number

She knows, she knows, she has already seen it
A young girl's life cheaply spent
And so, and so, and so who relieves it
Know one, know one, know one because they believe it

James Blalock

Picture Of Hatred

Evil look in the eyes, forehead in a deep frown;
Smile turned upside down.
Lips in a pout.
This is what hatred looks like on the human face;
What s disgrace!
A pleasant countenance can be
Made ugly
By this vile emotion.

Glenna Weber

"Missouri Country"

From my travels north and south,
Shore to shore, I've many friends.
There are good people in every part of this country.
But it must be true that home is where the heart is,
'Cause I always want to come home to Missouri Country.

There's nobody like Missouri country people
It's no matter how far and wide I roam.
When I want to be welcomed by some real fine people,
Missouri country makes me feel at home.

'Spent my childhood in the suburbs,
Programmed to that city life.
My uncle's farm was a place we visited once a year.
Well, I grew up and fell in love with a man from the country,
So at home in Missouri I am here.

Esther St. Louis

Doxology Of A Sparrow

Dear Lord, I heard a bird at dawn
singing praises from my lawn.
He sang of sun, of flowers, of earth,
of trees, of nest, of love, of birth;
He sang of rain that drenched his wings
and snow that left him shivering.

No Chorister, nor seraphim
ever sang so sweet a hymn.
And as his song flew over me,
I joined in his doxology.

And instantly I seemed to know
the source from which all blessings flow -
blessings that I recognize,
that lift the spirit and dry the eyes.

So, you who mourn the Sparrow's fall,
bless the little bird, so small, so small -
who does not know the trials of day
but sings his praises anyway.

Betty V. Barnes

We're Dying For Peace

I will always be discontent with my
situation here, in this place.
With all that this place has
to offer me...
Up and down motions;
moving people standing still,
and dreams that never came true.
Clinging to hope... fighting for change...
praying for salvation... dying for peace.
I sit crying, but no tears can fall.
Lifeless words spoken from liars' mouths,
about how the world can rid itself
from this disease called poverty.
Finding hope in our demise,
created by the selfish fools
whose love for vanity has displaced
love for mankind, and fear of God.
Nevertheless, we still stand here, motionless...
Clinging to hope... fighting for change...
praying for salvation... dying for peace...

Franklin P. Berry

Song Of Daisies

A note and the song.
Sleep lying peacefully between thy,
riding on time as the daze of now
passed by.

Light and then darkness.
Walking above the pale blue water.
Sailing upon fluffy clouds of white.
Watching the cool breeze merge
  with the warmth of my breath.
Listening to the dance of bright
  colors above the tree tops.
Caressing a melting being in the
  tracks of a beast

The creator and verse.
Tomorrow is gone, yesterday is yet to come.
Don't worry, my a sweet child,
for you belong to me, and me to the song.
Come and take a trip;
An adventure you'll never forget.

Chandra Kunnemann

It Is All Like A Dream...

And you are here with me...and our
Smooth skin touching gives off such warmth and energy...
And I stroke your soft silken hair as your head so gently
Rests over my happy heart...and you lie listening
To the breathing and the beats as if they
Are your symphony...with muscular arms
So securely surrounding me...and you say
It has been so long for you...and
It has been so long for me...to feel...and so I whisper...
Don't leave...please don't leave...but as I wake up
I can now clearly see that
   you are only a beautiful balcony dream...

Anna Allen

Pain, Pain, I Have A Great Pain

I had my left leg amputated above the knee
so as to take the pain away.

But the pain does not go away.
Pain, pain, I have great pain.

They call it Phantom pain
but the pain is real.
Pain, pain, I have great pain.

I live each day in great pain
but life must go on with or without pain.
Pain, pain, I have great pain
But my life is worth great pain.

Anthony F. Boni

Mother

Mother, so humble and gentle, like a saint.
So dainty and so quaint.

So quiet as a mouse.
Cleans this big old house.

No time for sighing
Because the baby's crying.

They need love and care
Only in mothers' hearts, so rare.

Thank you for doing so much for me.
You even helped me find my key!

The Best Mothers
Make the best huggers
Because they don't smother.

Whenever we went for food, you held me in the cart
I love you and you will always have a place in my heart.

Bernadette Melissa Sarlo

Field Of Dreams

In a field of dreams,
where the flowers are my thoughts,
and the sunshine is my energy,
where the trees are my home,
and the clouds are my blanket.
I dream wonderful dreams
where someone doesn't expect to go,
what someone doesn't expect to see.
Wonderful dreams.
My head like a balloon filling up
slowly, slowly.
I might burst!
My field of dreams
my own special pleasure.

Arlene Rodriguez

Death

As night fall approaches,
So do those ghastly sounds.
Those of whirling and swirling,
Like a ghost crawling in the dark.
And as the stars in the sky
Become slowly dim,
Covered by the vigorous grey clouds,
So does a man's life,
When he finds himself living his last moments,
And fearing what is knocking at his front door.
His heart pounding, louder and louder,
As he realizes he must go soon.

It comes on this winter's night,
And soon his dreams of life will fade quickly.

His body lying in his bed,
An island never to be found.
So he closes his eyes,
And as the darkness grows,
His life fades and eventually vanishes forever.

Andrea Calvo

"It All Comes Home Today"

So many "trip ups" along the way
So many "nights out" in which to play
I hope the test comes out okay
Now I wait: It all comes home today.
From night through early morn I searched the stars
Prayed and hoped that God would forgive my wrongdoings,
And give love and forgiveness for those selfish longings.
As I wait; it all comes home today.
Tomorrow's reports may be my dismay.
No.. more... anything I do will be okay.
For now, all my friends, they ran away.
I cry my tears, it all comes home today,
I know what counts, through all this hurt.
Too late I find who really cares
Tears that flow are truly yours
My home and comfort, are to contend
And home's love is there to the end.
Too late I find my true, true friend
Forgive me love, it all comes home today.

Frances M. Howard

Sisters

To both my sisters - the best to ever be
So proud of you I am
More than you'd ever believe
And even though I failed you
I got it together now for no longer
Am I, running all around
So now we can do - all we should have done
To make life beautiful - a very happy one
To go to wonderful places
and do all kinds of things
To stick together - be together
The way sisters are supposed to cling
And even though mommy is gone
I bet she's feeling really proud
for now we stand as one
And scream to the world aloud
"Hey we're sisters"
And together we survived
the best three - to ever be
Making it side by side

Charlene Graham

Oh, Puppy Of Mine!

Sir Zipper the streak - oh, puppy of mine!
So small and frail from head to tail.
Oh, puppy of mine!
When first I saw you with sad eyes crying
as they looked into mine.
Eyes begging to go home, never again to be so alone.
I grabbed you up in my arms to hold
And you kissed me with a wet, cold, nose.
Oh, Puppy of mine!
Now you're older and wiser too,
Our love for each other, oh, how it grew!
I look into your eyes now, to see only
Love and thanks from you to me,
Oh, puppy of mine!

Helen Hilborn

Until Today

Your skin is so soft I'm afraid to touch you,
So soft that even the softest touch would bruise.
Your beauty burns an everlasting image in my mind.
When you pass, your smile brings the
needed warmth to my cold and lonely heart.
Your touch is so gentle.
Your words are so kind,
like petals of a blue rosebud, a rarity to see.
But if only for a moment,
our lips could meet so soft and delicate,
warm and sweet.
I love you more than you will ever know,
More than I could ever show
never before have I felt this way,
never before. . . Until today

Bryan Talley

My Valentine

You are my love and my best friend,
so this Valentine to you I'll send.
We've been together for 38 years,
many times of joy, and yes some tears.
It seems like only yesterday,
that we were "Oh so young."
With a busy life and four small kids,
hard work but also fun.
Through the years we've had a few discussions that were heated,
but they were settled with a kiss, 911 was never needed.
When day is done and darkness falls,
and you say come on to bed honey.
I wouldn't trade what we have,
for a rich man and all of his money.
I'm happy we're together,
and so glad that you are mine.
And I hope that you will always
want to be my Valentine.

Gail McClelland

A Star

I don't want to be a star
stars belong in the sky.

I don't want to be a naughty child
to worry my mother when I cry

I don't want to be a cloud
that crosses over the blue
yonder or a storm or wave on a raging sea
because Lord,
just because it is hard
just being me

Gladys Turner

Darkness

There's no darkness in those hills
so very far away,
and adventures it conceals
must wait another day.
There is coldness in this land
unlike the warmth down west,
where the great mountains stand tall
and birds make their summer's nest.
They lament and cry for me,
from inside those mighty hills.
The sun's warmth I do not see,
and my heart with longing fills.
The sun will never shine upon my face,
and never will I see this warm and lovely place.

Andrew Bednarski

Childhood is...

Childhood is being afraid of the dark
So your parents can buy you a night light.

Childhood is getting more toys
So your parents can take them away later.

Childhood is playing games
And not having to do work.

Childhood is having fun
Because you won't be able to later.

Childhood is having no worries
Like you will later in life.

James T. Mitchell III

Sensitivity

Touching, caressing,
Softly, gently...

Understanding, feeling,
Sincerely, deeply...

Wanting to know what I feel, inside,
Caring and sharing my feelings to
the bone, sensitivity...

Not tearing down, but building up
my strengths, my good qualities...

Forgiving weaknesses, my insecurities,
realizing my feelings run deep, and are
true...

From the best of me, comes my love for you...

Touching, caressing,
Softly, gently...
Understanding, feeling,
Sincerely, deeply...
Oh, how I long for sensitivity...

Elaine Smith

My Dreams

When I lay my head down to sleep,
Some of the dreams I dream I keep.
It seems like in my head there is a little drawer,
And it can hold more and more.
But some of those dreams freeze like ice,
And most of those dreams were not very nice.
But most of the dreams I cannot keep,
Felt very good when I lay down to sleep.
I miss them so very much,
But I cannot keep them in my clutch.

Amy McCleese

A Rose

Beauty, and admiration it combines.
Solemnly, and courageously destines
the ever all thorny paths.
Often eluded, by both the desolate
　and joyous hearts.

Smooths, grieves and takes sorrow away.
Thanks, congratulations, and sympathy
　it conveys.
Anoints understanding into realities.
Cushions, the impacts of certainties.

Presents and represents absence.
Always of goodwill and in consonance.
For by patience and tolerance it cultivates.
Out of which, pride and smiles proliferate.

Dependable, trustworthy and always responsive.
Propriety, determined, tough and positive.
Its duty and responsibility never of proposition
Because it's versatile and beyond limitation.
Baljit Singh

A Friend

Throughout my life, I have met many different people
Some I loved to be with; others, well, I tried
But, I have learned that friendships are important to me
And it shouldn't be taken for granted
For often times I'll come and see
That I fall into a situation
That I lost a friend because of me.
Friendship should be a 2-way street
I love them and they love me.
But that is a difficult task,
For we must be giving to each other
But at the same time, we must love one another.
And I have realized that there is one friend
Who always cares for me
And loves me more than I love Him.
But there are those times when I do abandon and forget Him
And somehow, somewhere,
He is still there as loving as He has ever been.
So friendship, to me, is something that I'll always treasure
And it is a love that is too great to measure.
Brian T. Castaneda

Family

Most are born into this world alone.
Some, like me, came with a "clone."

The egg split and became two.
It is hard to tell who is who.

Striving to be different, not alike.
The exact genetic make-up was a strike.

On special events the spotlight is shared.
Being selfish is not how twins are reared.

The same clothes, car, grade and such
All definitely seemed a bit too much.

What once at times left me sad
Now I see as what luck I had.

Being born a "clone,"
Meant I'd never be alone.

Friends have come and gone,
As the bond of sisterhood remains strong.

Blood is thicker than water,
My friends forever are my parents and their other daughter.
Audra Woods Ulrich

My Precious Moments

Among my precious moments are
　some loved-filled reflections
Of childhood and grown-up memories
　With tender recollections.

With reverence and love.
　My parents, I did idolize,
I thought of them as saintly souls,
　And very, very wise.

They taught me how to cope with life,
　And encouraged me to success,
And what I owe to them today,
　I certainly will bless.

How tenderly, when I was ill,
　They nursed me back to health,
Why! I wouldn't trade them - not one bit -
　For all the worldly wealth!

I believe that He above had
　Guided my folks so -
That life for me is stronger now
　And continues on the grow.
Evelyn Hilliard

Differences

People are like shadows, as shadows fall...
Some shadows are big, and others small...
Yet in this grand existence of wonderful life, those that
are in between have struggled with strife!
For there are certain shadows, who need to do
things that other shadows don't want to... Because
then they seem... out of the crowd, a blemish, a zit, yelling out loud
Hey! all you shadows, exactly alike!
Take a look at this, a better way of life!
Look at all this stuff that can be made by people who don't ridicule
and who don't hate! The T.V., the microwave, the Personal PC, they
all came from people who wanted to be...
Different!
Daniel Davis

Shall I Compare Thee To A Ballet?

As the warriors stride gracefully towards their ballet slippers,
The audience observes with their erroneous prayer.

Petite frames enclose acute, enthralling minds
That exhibit their flair at the conductors whim.

As they meticulously settle into the slippers,
I's are dotted, t's are crossed.

The kow-tow is complete
The song has been sung.
Gentlemen, start your engines.
Gregory Jezarian

Nemesis

Within my heart lies a door
that time nor God can open,
for it is I alone who possess
the key. The incessant
screaming, growing trepidation,
and measured animosity
remain hidden from passersby.
Unknown to them is the secret tryst beyond the door,
its deceptive negotiations near closing. The dream of
serenity remains lost, snatched by the turbulent tides
of life.
Jennifer Cox

Someone Who I Care For

Someone who I really care for, someone I adore
someone that cares for me and does much, much more.
She does everything for me and when I'm sick she even brings me tea.
She's always there when I need her the most
and even though she has many talents, she never dares to boast.
A very sweet person she is,
so sweet she should be called Princess, Miss or Ms.
Many people asked, who is this person, the one that does everything,
who even cleans the windows and the curtains?
In answer I reply, my favorite person in the whole world,
the one whose hair is curled. Sweet, kind, loving and caring is she.
This person is a good friend and most important of all is the mother of me.
Yes she is my mother, caring, sharing and kind
and in her personality love is what you will find.
What is her name? You will never hear the same.
Even though she is not as rich and famous as Tina Turner,
her name is nothing other than Patricia Werner.
Her smile opens up on a nice sunshiny day.
That is wonderful and fine but I really, really love her
this wonderful mother of mine.

Christina M. Werner

"Love And Friendship"

Through the years we've always stayed in touch
Sometimes it was only - in such a rush
Who'd ever dream things would change so much
And at the same time create such a fuss

To this day I say I have no regrets
Even with the obstacles that come our way
We'll continue to handle them and on we'll go
For I believe our feelings are here to stay

The time were together it means so much
Feelings that have come with just a touch
Now our emotions are starting to show
How were we to know we just couldn't let go

As we go on there's something I want you to know
No matter what happens I'll love you so
But there is one thing that we both shall bear
Our "Friendship" is something we'll always share

Diane G. Muyleart

Wounded Bird

His sun drenched arms reach out to signal his dear beloved
Sparkling eyes penetrate through me, how I wish he were my love

Someone else upon the pier, this spectral man surely recognizes
I look for his lost companion but not a blessed soul arises

A sudden grip from behind brought this soaring question to land
A turn of my head and a sudden smile because of his hand

I have waited so long, I fear that you are only a premonition
Of a love I'll never know with a face like that of a vision

It is me, he is sure, who has harbored such dubious emotion
As I sailed to this foreign place, across many a rough ocean

A wounded bird did find solace upon my weathered bow
And as thanks guided my ship to a love worthy of my vow

Please know that I am real and pray now for just one thing
That after you are mine the Lord heals this little bird's wing

His kindness makes her behold there is so much at stake
Her drop of love has run dry but now he offers a lake

Cascading tears of rapture run down her flushed cheeks so round
To be dried by the gentle lips of the fine helmsman she has found

And at the very moment she admits someday in his arms she'll die
They see the little bird ascend singing, then away she does fly

Joanne L. Owens

Untitled

She walks near the moon, her light glowing
Sorrow and tears, is what she's showing
She rides a rainbow of cosmic dust
I search for her love and for her trust
If she did, she would not know
To be hurt, happy, what feeling to show
If she loved me, it no longer exists
For the hand of fear grabs my neck and starts to twist
I look out at the finite twilights, long dead
I don't see her, I see a flower instead
A flower I think, maybe she once wore
She walked with the wind, through the sky she soared
She's far, far away, maybe she found her peace
and maybe some quiet night soon
I'll experience her again, near the moon.

Dan Evans

Last Of The Morning Coffee

So broken engulfed in the sand, I lie here,
  spread like Jesus on the cross.
My eyes so desperately trying to reach behind the sky.
  Another night of glorious hopeful thoughts all soaked
Within a drunken wisdom has hit and run.
  Our dreams left dangling to be kidnapped by today.
The ocean, so silent with its silver cloak just
  stares with disgust.
My best friend, not that I care, I need you
My worst enemy, not that I care, I hate you.

II

The sun 'tis rising now as I am kissed by the
morning's breath.
I feel these tears all drip from dreams and those eyes,
  so numb only stare at me.
And for all the things I thought meant nothing
  I crave and pray and beg.
Those memories, those friends, pushed aside, ache
and pull at my heart.
When the angels cry I'll say goodbye.
  I shall be on my way.

John Doyle

Mr. Grinch

Creeping through the grass
stalking grasshoppers and colorful
butterflies,
spying goldfish in a small pond,
watching squirrels through the bay window.

With a certain look in his eye,
thinking:
"Oh, come just a little bit closer"
curling up in front of the
fireplace,
dreaming of a place where
birds can't fly and
the streams are flowing with milk.

Geoff Winn

What Have We Come To?

Reach for the rush of the drink,
Something stops the sensation, strangling the mind.
Struggle for a smoke of slow suffocation,
Believing breaks the binge from a brink.
Charge for a chomp of chew - any kind,
Dilation doesn't damage determination.
Kneel for the needle - not nicotine no more
For seconds forgot future ...
Forever.

Alice Johnson

"Unchained Heart"

As I stand near the river
  Staring down at the stream,
I often wonder aimlessly
  About my broken dreams.

What if I could have travelled
  Down that straight and narrow way,
Would my life be different
  But who am I to say?

Many moons have fallen
  Since you became my life,
Without you in my world
  Emptiness would pierce my heart like a knife.

For years I spent in bondage
  Behind cold gray prison walls,
To come home to your love precious
  Makes it worth it all.

Adjusting to the freedom
  Please help me with my part,
And beautiful I will love you
  With all my "unchained heart"
    Billy Williamson

Reconnection

The sun set upon my heart;
Stars melded with city lights
and I could not discern a difference
in the blinding brightness.

Questions backlogged and collected interest.

Hopes, dreams and wishes
fell from atop skyscrapers in the night...
gathering speed...wanting to dance,
yet acknowledging the fall.

Gravity ended just before impact,
Creating reflective moments in time
to reconsider options.

I fell another way.
Chose another landing...
Giving love a second chance.

Then I met you.

The splash has made me smile,
Offering journeys
to places never been before.
    Grace C. Chrystie

Priceless Gifts

This priceless thing that caused for me to plow the fields of our love started with the day our hearts crossed paths. A branded day paused for a moment. The seasons rolled into one.
A seed was planted on the plowed fields of much needed love. True blessings came about: Spring arrival, whispers of the heart only we could hear, a true friendship formed, and tranquil moments as if we became that oneness that had GOD smiling. The time of my life arrival like the seasons: Winter forever solid, sleeping while waiting for the sun of your kiss. Spring brought forth reborn of already undying love to a joyful heart. Summer our field showed how we planted, watered, nurtured, and shared our love's blossoms for all to see. So strong our rooted love that the sun wasn't needed to make it grow, only the reflection of our faces. Wasted not a single hour on letting anyone tear it apart or trample on our field or spoil it at any time. Then fall, during almost autumn where our love turned over a new leaf and the changing of color brought about a glow of GOD'S rainbow of praises which in turn brought again the PRICELESS GIFTS of FEELINGS.
    Clarice Hall

Summer Pastures

My quiet ascent to undulating hills
Startles the hare and piques whippoorwills.
Rivulets well from the entangled deep
And criss-cross the path far from the neap.

Gowans and feathered flowers spot the heather
And lend a cast despite foul weather.
Even when gathered in armfuls to preen
They timidly, searchingly peek from the green.

My shoes are thin. I feel the rocks.
The remains from sojourners cast a pox
Of gum wrappers, cigar butts and tissue,
The spore of despoilers with whom I take issue.

And I stray beyond where there's no trespass
And spy a hoof, not that of an ass.
The cloven foot leads me quiet as death
Beyond church bells that toll Sabbath.

Aging patriarchs with gnarled root
Bathe their feet and charm the newt
And wiggled their toes in the silent pool.
It's not protocol, but it's certainly cool.
    John W. Ceder

Song Of The South Building

There at the far end of the hall, a wheelchair parked with its stately back towards emptiness, and the empty rooms scattered all about, with faces everywhere.

The voices echo far into the night and early morning, telling stories to the walls of how it used to be, and mourning.

Stories of the days when sounds of activity resounded in every corner - the silent noise of pain and sometimes joy, of friends and brotherhood, and life and even death that compasses some without much warning.

This was the Home of printers that labored long, with insight into the future, seeing grandpa time elope with independence, and knowing help existed there when needed.

But now the story concludes - and birds keep right on singing and all the while the walls lay silent, keep on dreaming, and for this structure, time exists no more - yet time goes on eternally, unheeded.

This is the song south building sings.
    Coralie Heldman

Carey

She's the best friend, that never goes home.
She's the music maker for sleepless nights.
She is the foreteller of dreams and weaver of truths
She makes the shadow puppets roar
She's the one with lingering clasps,
after the house lights have died down
She's the high seas tide,
that crashes the shore and pampers the sand
She's the Lion's grip that bears me,
When I fight to hide my feelings.
She's on the other side of enhanced conversation
She's the strawberry patch among the demolished evergreens.
Her identity lying in my heart-shaped locket,
and her legacy is rampant on the tongues of timid yet outspoken gentry.
She's the midnight proofreader,
of conjunctions wrapped up by week's end
and She's the deliberating voice of season
that echoes in my sanctuary of ambition
She's my savior, my angel, my sister.
    Janice Ciesielski

Stephanie

Stephanie, do sit down here with me.
Stephanie, do drink a warm cup of tea with me.
For a gentle while, let me admire your
lovely brown eyes. The bold sun way up
high in the blue skies.
This is a lovely tranquil day
With more sunshine on its slow way.
Stephanie, have I told you about the banquet?
A banquet just for you and I.
Certainly, there will be others there.
But miles away from our loving care.
Stephanie, a gala party for just you and I.
A party that will be remembered by and by,
The photographer will take your photo.
And place it in their keen rota.
The whole world will know I love you so.
Say hello to the populace as the time goes.

Henry J. Dugan

Suddenly

If tomorrow never be
stopped in time suddenly,
what would be the words unsaid
never to rest within your head,
forever clouds the ties that bind
words unsaid leave doubts behind,
if a lesson's to be learned
never bridges should be burned,
always say what's on your mind
loving thoughts and words real kind,
because we never know what tomorrow brings
so speak now of love and gentle things.

Gale Croft

The Refuge

Loneliness engulfs you and you run deep within
Strange awareness of being nothing sets in
   and then flees.
Only sixteen wondering "if" I have sinned?
Waves crash the shore - the sky grows very dim.
Back to the sea my mind drifts again.

Confusion meanders endlessly each passing day
Twenty four wondering "If" I have sinned?
Back to the sea my mind drifts again
Slowly the sun smiles behind the dark clouds
Strange awareness of my youth echoes at loud?
Forty approaching and wondering "if" I have sinned?

Back to the sea faith flourishes - I find me!
Freedom breaks flawed chains and they bend
Water magnifies calmness and dances in my head
Goodness triumph while God visits me
Back to the sea my soul shouts "I'm free!"

Barbara Pierson

My Flag, I See

Into the mirror of my flag, I see
Stripes of red, stripes of white
and a constellation of beautiful
white stars, in a field of blue.
Battles, with courage, tears, fears and joy.
How beautiful my flag looks waving
on high, in the breeze.
I hope and pray that my mirror of my
flag shall never break,
So that I can always see my
flag of red, white and blue.

Joe Loin

A Bow In The Sky

Every time I see a rainbow,
  stretch forth across the sky,
I'm reminded of a promise made,
  that reached to you and I,
A promise from our Father,
  that we can trust His care,
And despite our circumstances,
  He always will be there.

Through winds so fierce and rains so long,
  there never seems an end,
But then He sends the rainbow,
  like a long awaited friend.
And I'm so glad He made it,
  and set it there you see,
For it stands as a reminder,
  of love eternally.

Debbie T. Barefoot

Our Pond

If you wish upon a star;
Such a beauty to reach afar...
I wish I were a fish; swimming among them as I wish.

As I watch them go by...
Slowly wiggling their tail so high;
Especially the butterfly Koi...
Which we named the Little Mermaid Koi.

Ariel is her real name; Big Bertha is another one for fame...
Plain and spotted mollies in schools;
Growing goldfish, as well in the pool.

Shimmering water makes magic...
It fills our yard as well as our heart with music;
Cascading slowly over the rocks...
It gives you treasures to grow and keep in stock.

Blooming and dancing water lilies; take away your worries...
As jewels of the pond; it sparkles when it blooms with the full sun.

Nature really is a beauty...
As long as you appreciate and protect its bounty;
It will fill your heart and soul...
To make your life content and full.

Joseph Hoffmann

Knowing One's Life

There comes a time in life when all that's good will
Surface, when all that's love will show, when all that's
true will fall upon one's heart.

At this time you've become that good love that's adorned
my heart.

Your spirit of challenge, fearlessness, confidence and
adventure has sparked a flame in my soul that has become the
very essence of my respect for you, my admiration for you,
my love for you.

The silence of my heart aches with the words that I cannot
say, with the feelings I cannot express, with the love I
cannot give — for my heart is frightened to beat in
conjunction with yours.

I leave with you this thought...

Pace your love for the steps you may take
cannot be erased.

Search your soul — for the moment may confuse it.

Know your heart for it gives best
When it's best known.

D'Eitra O. Bryant

Better Than Roses

Roses are so beautiful soft and bright,
   Taking in God's sunshine, reflecting the light.
Beautiful as they are, they soon fade and die.
   There they will fall; and there they will lie.

When God created the soul of man
   He meant great things in His perfect plan.
And when on this Earth we've spent our time,
   Our soul moves on in this plan sublime.

The beautiful rose and God's marvelous creation
   Cannot reflect a human heart's loving sensation.
It takes a born again heart of thankful love
   To reflect God's redemptive love from above.

So better than roses or any gift for me
   Would be this love, in you, for me to see.
Do not wait until death comes to claim my soul;
   But let His love from you continually roll.

Helen Ruth Ewing

At The Wall

We stood in the cool November dusk, looking at the
tapestry of death: white names carved in black marble.
The wall was warm to the touch, mellowed by the sun.
It seemed to be throbbing with the life blood of the
remembered dead: those who had been slain in Vietnam,
many of them sons of fathers who had survived World War
Two. Withered leaves, like dead dreams abandoned there
from hopeless hearts, clung to the base of the wall.

I turned to my grandson, who stood beside me, tall
at fifteen, taller than I, and I smiled and said,
"If you should die before me, I will not see your
name on a wall. I will see you alive and well in
heaven, living there with God, and angels all around!
I will see you visiting planets and playing lead
guitar with the heavenly choir."

He looked at me and grinned and gestured, his way,
thumbs up, and said, "Right on, Grandma." And we walked
together, hand in hand, through the night, toward
the shining, white light of the Washington Monument,
that pierced the dark—and pointed straight to heaven.

Barbara Hudson

No Room At The Inn

Joseph and his wife, Mary, live in Judea.
Taxes have been levied and they journey to
Bethlehem to pay them.
It is time for Mary to be delivered and
There's no room at the inn.
There is no room at the inn. No. No.

Mary is tired and weeping;
Joseph is praying silently.
The keeper of the inn lifts his lantern
And reads the pain in their faces.
Compassion fills the innkeeper,
And he offers rest in the stable.
There is no room at the inn. No room.

The lantern light reveals a manger filled with hay.
The animals in the stable are contented
As they chew their cuds and bray.
The little town of Bethlehem is sleeping-
Never knowing a King is soon to be born,
And there's no room at the inn. No. No.
No room at the inn.

Alyce Trimm Williams

Tears Of The Butterfly

I see the tears of the butterfly.
Tears of pain cascade gently from those dark, glistening pearls.
Tears that speak of tenderness, loss of love, and hunger for life.

Oh my sweet butterfly, I feel your tears pierce your soul.
Tears that glow of crystal and diamonds, yet sting of a scorpion's
deadly bite. With each bitter-sweet descent, your tears fray to douse
the fire within.

Butterfly, butterfly. Why has your cloak of colorful silk become broken?
You must have fought unsettling winds which dared to show no mercy.
Your tears have weakened your strength; and once again, your
wounds are exposed.

Listen, butterfly. Listen to the gentle taps of your tears fall upon
your broken, silkened, colorful cloak. Those tears tap as gently as
your dance in the air. Your dances. Your beautifully, unrehearsed
dances emanated love beyond a shadow of a doubt. Your dances
were so carefree, yet so eloquent to behold.

My precious butterfly. Your tears have weakened your cloak,
your cloak has weakened your spirit, and your spirit has weakened
your dance. Few are your dances. Frequent are your tears.
Ruined are your wings. For you shall know love no more.
Is that why you weep, butterfly?

I know your tears, butterfly. I have lost my love and my heart is
broken. My tears are many and my dances are few. I, too, shall
know love no more. I know why you cry, sweet butterfly.
I know why you cry.

Camilla L. Stewart

The Answer

When we pray, sometimes it seems
   The answer is awfully slow;
Could it be that because it isn't what we asked for,
   We refuse to "know"?
Although we think we know what's best for us,
   It might be all wrong!
Then He, to protect us from ourselves,
   Leads us down the path where we belong.
It isn't always easy to accept
   That his answer might be no;
Yet his love and wisdom
   Is best for us I know!
So I try to accept his will,
   And follow without fear,
Knowing when I need him
   I will find him near!!!

Betty O. Mason

Communicate

You communicate with people, some are very smart
   Sometimes you have to dredge the bottom of your heart
You have to show how it's done, besides explain
   And so you think dull people are a pain

There is a wrong way to do anything, and a right
   At your discretion, trying with all your might
You can learn the right way, and do it well
   So the product you make will be an easy sell

So you think you have bad luck
   All your life that hard work you ducked
Now you're convinced all of your luck is bad
   That's what I call really very sad

Somebody said, "enjoy yourself when you're young and bold
   you won't be worth a tinkers dam when you get old
Old age is supposed to be your crowning glory
   Now I'm inclined to believe it's a different story.

Edward L. Pearlman

A Double Edged Sword

Johnny sat near an old oil drum, that crackled into a roaring fire,
Telephone lines were hung with icicles from every wire. Huddling
Huddling alone his body stiff, ridged, cold as a stone,
The flames licked upward, sparks a-flying..in the shape of a cone.
The bottom of the barrel was vented and so hot was the glowing heat,
The snow turned to shiny rivers flooding about his soleless feet.
Johnny drew up his collar, muffler over his face and throat, a masked disguise,
His eyes, dark, narrowed, he searched the alley way for a victim to surprise!
To steal a wallet, scarf, a coat, then disappearing into the frozen shadows to gloat!
He was evil to the core! Many hates towards the world to score, poverty to emote.
But it would be he this awful night would see distorted in agony and horror!
Muffled footsteps, soft spoken words nearby…"Ah, Me," came a sigh, then more.
A strange figure in bright attire made its way silently to Johnny's fire
"Your..name is..Johnny, I'm told,.." the voice was old, wise, cold, "a thief, a liar!"
Dressed in blood red satin, smokey grey his cape, gold buttons reflecting the flames,
From His pocket came a sack of gold coins…a parchment scroll spattered with stains.
A plume great in length he took from His hat, then into His palm, as a pen it sat,
"Wealth I have, a compensation, in exchange.." His eyes burned yellow like a cat!
The pen poised, the scroll unrolled with a snap! Johnny signed…
He smiled with satisfaction
"A rich man am I, for it is your soul away you signed, and forever without retraction!"

D. H. Boyd

"The Battle Of The Bulge"

I step on the scale, and what do I see?
Ten extra pounds have crept up on me!
I've got to start working, on shedding some weight;
Maybe tomorrow I'll have salad, and fruit on my plate.
I've got to work hard, and I've got to be good;
I'll start a strict diet; next Monday sounds good!
I have good intentions, really, I do;
But that one piece of chocolate, always turns into two.
To be overweight, I've always been prone;
Hey, can I help it if I have big bones?
After one month of dieting, I step on the scale;
I look down at the number, and you see my face pale;
How can this be, I've gained some more weight!
It must have been the ice cream and cheesecake I ate.
To heck with this dieting, who needs the grief?
In "The Battle of the Bulge," I'm Commander-in-Chief!

Jessica Kirchner

It's Time

The pain is always more
than anyone could take.
While memories reflected moments of reality.
To be a slave
to one's own thoughts
not life.
Trying to leave
a mark
somewhere in time.
A different piece of nonsense
Which we call tomorrow.
Thinking we have prepared for the day.
We all are some kind of manifestation
How you like your new form now.

Calvin Bland

"My Mother's Heart"

I never could have been more loved
Than by my mother when she was here
Her thoughtful, caring, soothing way
Her image remains so clear

Gentle hands, brilliant smile
Comforting words to ease the pain
Clearing the unmarked path ahead
Encouraging support with modest restrain

The only face I saw in the crowd
Fulfilling a child's selfish needs
Her love was boundless while on this earth
I received a gift in all her deeds

Now when I'm cold and all alone
An emptiness that tears me apart
I wrap inside the memory
And live again inside her heart

Joey Cupp

On The Power Of Love

What more fitting way to end this story
Than to speak of God in all His Glory
And to look at the Heavens shining down from above
That God created and say….God is love

We speak masterfully of priesthood power
And how it can save us hour by hour
The priesthood can do so many things
It can heal and ordain and even bring

Back to life those who are dead
And in the Bible it is even said
That if one has the faith of a mustard seed
The mountains will move and the oceans heed

And I know in my heart that these things are true
As I gaze out into the skies of blue
And realize the power that God must have had
To create the Heavens, it drives me mad

Not to be able to comprehend infinity
Or the true force of our own divinity
But there is one thing I know as a gaze up above
That our Heavenly Father….God….is love.

Calvin Reed Brown

Remembrance - Mother Dear

Time ran out before I could say,
thank you for giving birth to me that day.
While I stumble through life to learn,
you were always there with concern.
Those were the greatest days,
you showed me love in so many ways.
Now, death has pulled us apart,
and a spear went through my heart.
My soul cries out to you in vain,
take away this awful pain.
Why aren't you near,
to kiss away a tear.
Heavenward I'll turn, and pray, Jesus, let her hear,
I love you Mother Dear.
Daily, I close my eyes, and sense your presence near,
and feel your touch like soft kisses near my ear.
While I work and play with your grandchildren here,
I hear your voice in the wind, and know you are near.
So, I whisper
"I love you Mother Dear."

Francine Bakker 03/18/1995

Common Nails—Uncommon Love

For the want of a nail, the story goes,
That a brave rider's horse lost a shoe;
but the ripples felt from that one small loss,
Toppled a crown and the kingdom too.

But there was no want of the common nail,
At the place we call Mount Calvary;
Where the common nail met uncommon love,
And sealed forever our destiny.

The battle raged fierce that infamous day
Those common nails pierced his tender skin
But love won the day! What more need be said?
Now the kingdom of God dwells within.

For 'twas love, not the nails that held him fast,
To the arms of the old rugged cross;
Failure to attain love's saving power,
Is an incomprehensible loss.

That others might know of uncommon love,
Graciously poured from coffers above;
Oh let me be, just an uncommon nail,
Displaying heaven's uncommon love.

Clarence A. Diller

Life

Oh great weeping willow with twigs,
That are so green, so early in spring
Putting forth your signs of life
Ignoring the winter's ice.
Soon your buds will mature into little green leaves,
Swaying in the gentle breeze.
Majestic today you stand rooted deep in the ground,
Just as a tree is from the earth,
Our spirit is from God, our second birth.
From Him our spirit came and to Him it shall return.
So much He will teach if we want to learn.
He always comforts and never spurns.
We see His love every way we turn.
Indeed God will supply our every need and our hungry souls will feed.
In love and compassion too, He will strengthen me and you.
No matter how dark it may seem to be,
We are safe if we walk where He leads
We do not know the way
But I know He will lead us day by day.

Hattie Glass

I Am The Wind

I am the wind....
   That eagles ride and clouds caress
     I move through boundless halls of air,
   From yesterday beyond tomorrow.

I slant sunbeams to touch the sea
   And paint rainbows after rain,
My clouds descend to fog at dawn
   And sprinkle dewdrops after dusk.

I make blue skies orange when day is done
And polish each star one by one,
   I carve caves of stone
     Where I have blown,
I have the thundering fury of hurricanes
Or whisper breezes through summer rains,
   With every sunset made sublime
     Along the corridors of time.....
For.....I am the wind.....

Charles R. Clark

Uncle

You can tell by the way he talks
That he'll live life for all its worth
If you watch the way he walks
You'll see he'll leave his mark upon this earth.

His voice is hard and strong
Yet inside his heart is warm
His hands are very firm
But he means no one any harm.

By himself he shall stand
Until he finally lets someone in
Still he's more of man
Than any boy will have ever been.

Barbara J. Bilbrey

My Childhood Swing

It was outside in my childhood swing
That I first heard the bluebird sing
I thought of all times I had sat here
And shed many a tear
It was here that I fell and skinned my knee
On the side of this big old tree

It was outside in my childhood swing
That I first heard the bluebird sing
I thought again of my childhood sweetheart
How we swore, standing by this swing, we would never part
Even then as he gave me the ring
I was thinking of my childhood swing

It was outside in my childhood swing
That I first heard the bluebird sing
Now I stand alone by the tree
For he is no longer with me
I know we promised to love and obey
But you see, he was buried just yesterday

Diana Bell

Untitled

Far into the virgin forest stood the stoutest of oaks
Soaking up the buttery sun.
Gently, slowly inhaling the ever so sullen silence
As a brand new glorious day had just begun.

In the clearing was an array of verdant finery on display
An implacable harmony of flowers intermingled with a canopy of pines.
Where even animals entered with trepidation.

Mother nature's sleeping sanctuary concealed on a vast hilltop;
A solemn spectacular meadow peppered with flourishing samples
of raw beauty;
An aura of peace presided over the sloping acres,
Allowing a panoramic view of the heavens.

Holly Draudt

Untitled

The path of life has many turns
Sweet is mixed with bitter
Many times, easier it seems
For a man to be a quitter

Shall we duck,
Recline a little
Or dare we face foursquare,
And give our all to fight, though we be brittle

The best within us answers thus:
Take life on the chin —
And when you can, with gusto,
Kick it in the shin!

Carmine T. Vigorito

"Glass Porch"

There's a Special Glass Porch at a Cabin up North,
That is so dear to me,
From this little Glass Porch along Kitchie Shores,
I see special memories,

I remember the time in my Grandfather's arms,
He was carrying me along the shoreline,
How I fiddled and fussed as we walked through the brush,
To some clear water sand splashing fun,

Oh, I look at a tree where a swing used to be,
And see Grand mother pushing me,
How I kicked my legs high with my toes to the sky,
And watched lilac branches passing me by,

As I look around the room where many memories loom,
I feel a chill in the air,
There are books along the wall where preacher stored then all,
And a chair that we use to share,

Oh, this special glass porch is worn and torn,
And there is no way to repair,
When the roof caves in and the porch falls down,
Part of me will be gone.
George Allan Meissner

Goodbye

We've known each other for so long,
that it's hard to say goodbye.
  And though I know you have to leave,
the tears still fill my eyes.

  Places we've gone and things we've done,
I never will forget.
  Your warm and loving heart I've treasured,
ever since the day we met.

We've been through many things together,
some struggles and some trials.
  But our faith in God and in ourselves,
has kept us going for miles.

  The days alone will seem like weeks,
and the weeks will seem like months.
  But in our hearts we both will know,
just what the other wants.

  We'll be waiting for the day to come,
for us to meet again.
  So that we can start right where we were,
when we were the best of friends.
Christy Boyd

Lonely Road

The road of life stretches out lonely,
so many things left to be done.
Someone had gone on before me
I was left to travel the road alone.

Of course now I could do all I wanted,
I could travel to Venice or Rome.
But when it came down to what mattered
I only wanted to stay at my home.

The flowers and birds were one answer,
they filled a void that some have not known.
Pencil and paper beside me
lead to adventure supreme and my own.

Soon I'll have to put pieces together
and in my life take a stand.
Whatever I do I hope it's the answer,
that I can meet life and deal a fair hand.
Florence L. Miller

The Nature Of Man

God started nature for it was fate,
That man would start to communicate.
Bringing together the whole universe,
Starting with man in a single burst.
He thought that this species would help a lot more,
Instead all these species came to war.
War over land or colored skin,
All man brought was sin after sin.
Peace was brought for a very small time,
Then man crossed the peaceful line.
If only the people could come to a conclusion,
There'd be no wars no death or pollution.
People think power is having the biggest sword,
They all are wrong, it's having the Lord.
Jason Schiffman

"Anointed Peace"

There is a peace that passeth all understanding
That peace that washes over the soul of man;
It comes in like a flood and calms the storm
Your body feels it ever so warm,
From the crown of your head, to the soles of your feet.
In deepest despair, you know that I am there
Crying out come, come to the shelter of peace.
What is this peace that is so sweet?
It is a gift that is meant to be
A gift from on high that is given to thee.
Joyce Nadine Williams

Being Blessed

Don't say it's a weakness or a fault, some are just born with answers
that require no experience or thought.

You can't buy it - there's no money involved, there is no guarantee
all your problems will be solved.

The heart should control all feelings, not the mind - if this happens
to you, please don't be confused, it's only a sign.

Tis always a blessing to forgive, just be sure and remember,
never judge whomever it is.

Always go with and trust the doubts, in the long run,
you'll realize what really counts.

Everyone is different no matter where you've been,
not everyone is gifted, it's ashamed to pretend.

Being blessed means you're able to hear,
and never forget the memories you hold most dear.

By now you should know if you are or not,
either way you read this
to me is good, so thanks a lot.
Benita J. Patty

A Small Child

A small pair of feet,
that awaken you while you sleep
A small pair of hands,
that will soon touch the outside land
A small pair of eyes,
That will soon look up at the skies
A small pair of legs,
that will soon crawl into bed
A small pair of knees,
that will soon be crawling trees
A big pair of eyes,
that will soon once more cry
as you remember how he'd crawl into your lap to sleep
without as much as a peep.
Brianne Petit

Ballerina

The ladies dancing leapt in sweeping lines
That shamed my awkward smile and held our backs
In rapt attention at their daring grace.
Piano tingled, tickling in my ear.

As we walked home, I stumbled on the stone
sidewalk that twisted up beneath my feet.
My knee was torn, expanding red on jeans
My friend was worried that I might pass out.

The hospital was full of dancing girls
With trays of medicine and bandages.
They weaved their way through blood and weary groans,
And smiled at me with grace like falling stars.

As my nurse twisted swishing from my room,
I wondered if perhaps I should applaud.
   Heather M. Sias

Love

All through my life, I have treasured
that special feeling that couldn't be measured.
I do believe that the sun was made to shine.
I do believe that the clock was made to tell time.
The flower that grows in a garden is a pretty sight.
The moon that glows in the dark to bring the light.
When the birds began to sing in the spring and the leaves began to fall.
I think of you most of all.
As days go by and the sky is clear
oh how I wish you could be near.
If I were a king and had all the riches that money could bring,
I would not be happy because I would not have the most important thing.
If I were a prince and you were a princess
I would feel like I had accomplished a great success.
There were good times, there were bad times.
There were times I thought we would come apart.
But the power of love kept us together in our hearts.
This is what I say in every way, the fact is to be true.
God created me just for you.
   Harvey Edgar

Columbia Cafe!

I flew to Columbia to
Taste the ground bean.
Just a few cups, Whan Valdez and me.

It was so strong so fresh and hot,
I added some sugar and milk just a spot.

We drank to our health our future and someday.
Then he said buenos dias have a nice day.
   Charles W. Orsini

The American War!

The bullets and blood are taking us away,
Someone is killed in America every day.
Crime in America is taking its toll,
Killing the young and the old.

The bullets are strong, but the heart
is weak, the mind has to be strong
to walk away, to live and see another day.
The bullets and blood are taking
the American flag from the streets
into a body bag.
No matter if you're black or white
what's right in America hasn't shown
its strength, crime has gone beyond
its length.
   Desiree L. Miller

"Primal Spring 1995"

'Twas two springtimes past
That the patriarch's charges
Men encased in steel
Worthy of the distant father
Smote the heretics in their most strange temple
Smashing the infidels at their impudent altar
Those driven by some unknown creed
But - we loved them not anyhow.

In Aries month past
The Sooner plain torn asunder
A firestorm from the bowels of hell
Eye for eye, tooth for tooth
The god of the iron age rages
As he has for two times two thousand springtimes past
Since the banishment of our earth mother
Expelled by our heavenly father.

Lo! Is it the metamorphic butterfly
I spy on my window ledge
Peering shyly for seasons to come
As it was in the primal spring?
   Enn O. Koiva

A Whisper On The Wind

Alas, I have caught that whisper on the wind,
That was thought to be beyond my grasp,
I now caress it with ever such a delicate grace,
Hoping it shall never taste the wind's breath again.

O how I've longed for this glorious day,
For the whisper had drifted by me many a time,
Leaving me with only a distant, empty embrace,
And arms full of sorrow and longing again,

Now with an utter content I can surely say
Joy has brightened the trail of anguish to my heart,
Allowing me, once again, to look myself in the face,
While silently wishing the wind won't take my love again.
   John Douglas III

Untitled

A fierce battle plagued this land
that what was once a hamlet
but had been transformed into
the scene of armageddon.
It was a brutal battle —
one of which both sides were victorious.
Now it is but a grassy lawn
sewn with tears of heartache.
The sadness has transpired into euphoria.
And all that was annihilated has flourished
not into a daisy — but into a rose.
   Erin Thompson

The Road Of Life

Life is a road.
Sometimes it can be rocky and rough,
Often we feel like we've had enough.
Or it might be smooth and flat,
Then you'll feel better, just like that.

Life is a roller coaster.
Sometimes fast, sometimes slow,
Up, down, and back we go.

Why is life this way -
Different almost every day?
There's only one thing I can say to you,
"If you try your best you'll make it through."
   Carrie-Ann Begnaud

Perfect Love

If there could be a perfect love
that would never be broken in two
I'd be with you.

If a dove could to eternity fly
then on white feathers
there'd be you and I.

If the heav'ns showed from their majesty
just what endless love really could be
our love amidst the clouds would beam.

And if the stars searched through every heart
looking to find the one true pair
they'd shine on us forever, from up there.

Yes, if you'd give me your hand
all these dreams would come true
because with a perfect love, I love you.
   Benjamin Gary

Nature Is Everywhere

In a way nature is beautiful in everyone's eyes.
The animals, plants, and the spacious skies.
Look up at the sun, so warm and bright,
With birds fluttering by.
Look back down upon a rose and see a butterfly.
Under the sea clear and blue,
Swims a great blue whale;
Back on land, a horse awaits, swinging its beautiful tail.
Deep in the jungle, exotic and green,
A tiger sneaks up on its prey.
And up in the trees, a monkey swings, trying to get away.
On the forest floor, a fox runs
To warn, his family of one of nature's cruelest designs,
Which is wiping out the animals of the world,
It is called mankind.
   Dazel Mary Roberts

A Special Rose

A special rose that blossomed in the spring took wings amid the Autumn leaves and fluttered into flight above the orbit and into the night...
As spring came, the petals unfold, lending beauty to behold. Hosting fragrance to accent the ever presence of the rose, enriching life with pure delight until each petal falls from sight.
When siphoned by the summer's blight, the petals lie devoured by night. Devoid of energy and of life. Succumbed by nature's stormy might.
Yet, far into the winter's chill, there remains a token still. A thorn nestled in the sand to remind us of the beauty of a special rose.
   Bettie Withers Edwards

"Friendship Is"

Friendship is life's finest treasure
So much more than simple pleasure.

It's caring and sharing in some small way
The hopes and dreams of each passing day.

The smile you can bring to someone's face
Is a joyful feeling you can't replace.

And if someone does all these things for you
Happy you'll be if you return them too.

The sky's the limit as you will see
And that is what friendship is to me.
   Alice S. Guzay

Friendship

He says that friendships come and go
That, like the tide, they ebb and flow,
That they happen "as they will"
As if we humans had not skill
Nor strength of character to build
Loving kinships amongst ourselves.

I disagree, it isn't true!
True friends are far between and few.
Not at the whimsy of the tide,
We choose whom we will stand beside.

A single strand may start the weave
That, like a spider's web
Grows stronger and more beautiful
As we add each shimmering thread.
Till bonds have formed so strong and fast
They've forged a friendship that shall last.
   Joanne Roberts

What Makes My Day

They say it's the little things in life
that makes a person's day, but I think not,
'cause when my little girl came into my life
it was the biggest thing in my whole world and that made my day.

So sweet and innocent and beautiful, full
of life that she stole my heart away, and that made my day.

The way she danced and jumped in her own
little way, singing with a voice that would
scare all the birds away, and that made my day.

When I would leave to go to the store, she
would run up to me, and say, "daddy, where
are you going? Can I come? Can I come?" and
what could I say, 'cause that made my day.

Now that she is going to school, and in
the morning as she is getting dressed, I can
hear her from my bed, combing her hair and I
look at her and say, "you know you make my day."

Then at night, before going to bed, she would say,
"give me a kiss daddy, God bless you and I love you," and you
probably guessed by now, what makes me say, "yes, she makes my day."
   Arthur Torrey

A Daughter

Ribbons and bows and tickle toes
That's what a young daughter means
A ride on a swing, a flower she brings
A daisy, a clover, a rose!

And the years how they fly
and we ask ourselves why
This daughter is so un-aligned
She's happy, she's sad, she's good and she's bad
At times we think she's lost her mind!

Then the teen years appear
It's loud music we hear
A shout "Did anyone call?"
Lets go to the movies, do something groovy
Have a party or go to the mall!

So, ah, now she's grown, her time is her own,
She's left in the physical way
But she's not really gone, cause when she comes home
We hear... GOTTA DO LAUNDRY, O.K.?
   Barbara Swan

"The Outdoors"

Sing to the tree, the flowers blowing in the breeze
The birds sing their favorite song
As the children below hum along
To the squirrels gray and nutty
Are the chippies brown and muddy
Like the bats that fly at night
To the children with kites

Deer are free to roam
The bears that are overgrown
Rattlesnakes that bite
To the porcupines that prick
To a caterpillar on a slick
The night crawlers in the mud
To the glow worms in the air
For the feelings that we share

Jessica Baughman

The Fairies Party

The fairies had a party once upon a summer's night.
The breezes all were blowing, and the stars were shining bright.
And all the little fairies had on their Sunday clothes -
The boys in green and yellow and the girls in blue and rose.

At first, they danced the fairy dance and sang a fairy song.
And while they all were dancing, the Fairy Queen came along.
Her hair was long and shining, and her dress was silvery white.
She carried a candle in her hand that shone like gold in the night.

She joined in the dance but it soon was o'er, and the fairies sat
  down to dine.
They ate ice cream and fairy cake, and they all drank blue grape wine.
And then when the fun was over - while the moon and the stars still
  shone -
They said good night to the Fairy Queen,
And the fairies all went home.

Dorothy Farrell Obecunas

Oklahoma

A time to mourn the passing lives of youth-
  The building lies in heaps upon the floor
  In a nation known for preventing war.
It is a sight to see the working sleuth.
Who tried to find the answers based on truth.
  One bomb's brief blast can shake us to the core:
  As Oklahoma fell, our nation tore.
We saw its jagged edges on the roof..
Militia brought a nation to its knees.
  The bomb that blew broke deep into our souls
  And cast the fallen dead into its hole.
To see the victims weeping as they flee!
  Reports recount the number slain by tolls
  But cannot replace the life the bomb stole.

Bryan Robert Black

A Lament of a Deceased

Look at the place you left me to bore, no window, no door,
unable to breath or snore, pitch dark no pore, lying stiff
in a gore, decaying on a dirt floor, as if I was never able
to make love and spore.
Dear O dear it is lore, the same is waiting for all flesh in store.
We are all mortal, one later one before,
it is incarnated in life's core, but while we live we toil and roar,
one makes less the other makes more, but the end evens the score.
So let us not be sore, not be against each other but for,
help our neighbors instead of making war, violence abhor,
rudeness deplore, be placid and life explore,
time given us do not ignore, but do appreciate and adore.

Jacob Haruvi

Imagination

There was a tiny piece of string attached to
    the carpet
that particularly caught my attention,
and as any curious individual would do,
I pulled it,
    and I pulled it,
        and yet, I pulled it.
But as I pulled it,
    the string changed colors,
        widths
        and textures.
After my arms were tired and ready to fall off,
I looked at the lifeless pile of stuff that
was so large that I couldn't see beyond,
then I looked to my right, and realized that
    half the world was gone!

Jamie Jedlicka

Where Do They Go?

There's an unsolved mystery at our house
That makes me just irate.
It's how those sly and clever socks
Can always lose a mate!
I put two stockings in the wash
And they swish and slosh about,
But when I stop the wash I only get one out.
Where did the other meet its fate?
Did it go down the drain?
Could it be in the dryer hid?
Or in the washer still remain?
No? It's just as I have feared,
That sock has up and disappeared.
Now if dissolving was the cause
Then both would then disintegrate,
But that is not the case, just one evaporates.
Could it be? Would it be?
That stocking eat their mates?

Alathea Hansen

For Jeff

It's been too long since we've seen your smile,
many times it's hard to travel life's lonely miles,
without our son, our brother, our friend,
whoever thought so soon we'd see the end
Of your joy, your laughter, your shining eyes,
much too soon we had to say goodbye.
God knows how much we love you,
but He loved you more,
and now you're an angel
waiting at Heaven's door,
for the day when we'll see your smiling face again,
and the tears we'll be crying will be of joy, instead of pain.

Sherri T. Dickerson

Little Precious

A poke in the tummy, a kiss on the ear
Makes my love grow - so deep - so clear.
I fetch my toys, and wiggle with glee
When my ball comes bouncing back to me.

I love to kiss, I love to cuddle
Only those baths put me in such a muddle.

I'm 20 lbs. of cute and adorable fun
I'm happiness and love, all rolled into one.

Sassy Lady's my name - a girl Schnauzer, you see
And just as precious as I told you I'd be.

Rosell W. McLean

The Butterfly

A selfish man fearful of loneliness captured himself a butterfly.
The bait he used were lies dripping in honey and nectar.
His desire was to own her body and soul, so he held both wings.
She squirmed and screamed, but her cries echoed on deaf ears.
Poor-r-r-. poor-r-r, butterfly.

And when that didn't work, he held her prisoner with words.
Words to control her, pin her; weapons lashing her flesh daily,
Words meant to humiliate, debase, demean, to rob her soul.
When he had hurt her enough; hopeless; and wanting to die,
She would then spin a cocoon, where inside she'd heal herself.
But, when she emerged, she was a little lovelier than before.
This only incensed him, because he couldn't destroy her essence.
The hate and anger inside him grew until it oozed through his skin,
Spreading like a web; the ugliness now showed for all to see.
The butterfly continued to change over and over again;
Each time emerging more beautiful and stronger than before.
She knew to be free from him, she also had to fight herself.
She flew harder and harder against the barriers, breaking through,
And with her heart racing, and wings fluttering off she darted,
Fly-y-y butterfly, fly,
 Beverly Stanczyk

Savor The Moment

Colors of every hue
   The blue sky the billowy white clouds
Spring is here that is our due.
   After all the months of cold snow mounds.

You see the forsythia and lilac bush
   The sweet smell comes from the earth
Gazing at the clouds you dream and feel a rush.
   It is nature in all its mirth.

I sit and wonder and slowly let the earth
    sift through my fingers,
   Do I deserve all this beautiful bounty
My mind is going through a wonderful faze
    and I let the earth smell linger.

My joy at being alive and well
   Don't sit still another moment
I feel a song in my heart swell
   Spring is here! Savor the moment!
 Helene Christopher

Where Are They Today

What happened to our families, did we fail in some way?
The children are still here, but they have drifted away
How and when can we bring them back home,
In spite of the fact they choose to roam?

We all have been given a cross to bear
The scripture's the same, nothing can compare
So, bring in our lost ones, although they did stray
Our Heavenly Father longs to faithfully guide the way!

Could we dust off our Bibles and pull up a chair?
Our God is alive and still answers prayer
So, put another log on the fire and a family together we'll see
Trusting in Jesus, how great that will be

I remember the precious memories of long, long ago
So, turn your life around, you have to let go
Remember, whatever you sow now, in the future is what you will reap
"Let us all prepare our lives, that someday in Heaven we'll meet!"
 Emogene Johnson

The Harsh Realities Of War

Where do we go from here in these troubled times of war,
the bombs explode right in our ear but yet it seems so far,
nuclear and atomic weapons seem to be our most and recent encounters.
Sirens and smoky filled skies lie above our heads,
people lying on the sidewalks shriveled and dead;
civilians go from day to day their stomachs filled with dreads
no one dare to venture outside not even for their breads.
They have become prisoners, prisoners of their very own homelands;
little children are forced to wear a gas mask
even for an adult it's a very tough task.
Some people say it didn't have to be
while others said it's just reality,
yea they say lets take the bull by the horn.
Fist tightly clenched and face with look of scorn;
I stand aside not a hint of strife, ready to fight, to fight
for what is right, what do you think is right, my friend?
Peace and let it begin with me.
 Evelyn Corinthian

Now At Peace

He was so strong. He was so brave
So brave he even faced the grave
He's gone on ahead. He's led the way
I cannot forget what He would say.

"I lost my mom some years ago
I thought of her as I prepared to go
I lost my dad, He's waiting too
Now I'm waiting, waiting for you

There was nothing left for me to do
I helped you all, I saw you through
Of all of you I am so proud
From heaven I'll whisper out loud

Take care of my wife I love so dear
She'll need you now so stay near
Comfort each other I'm with you still
Draw close to God and line His will

Praise God, He cares so much for you
Lean on Him He'll see you through
He's in the small things of your life
Even with you in times of strife

I couldn't have made it without Him
As my years my life were growing dim
He is the light that leads the way
Stay with Him and I'll see you one day."

 written by Lil
 daughter of Richard
 but created by the Father
 inspired by His Son and sent to
 me by the Holy Spirit, as I sat in
 tears of grief. I soon felt high and
 lifted up on the wings of His love for me.
 Lil Webb

Untitled

My mother is like no other
She's smart, she's sweet, she's really true,
She's always there with 'I love you.'
Her charm, her wit, her caring ways,
Have helped me through some trying days.
Her advice is helpful, it will never end,
That's why she'll always be....
   ....My Best Friend!
 Valerie Ulbrich

"Air"

Air is something we all need.
   Of course you all know why.
We use it, and pollute it
   And even in it fly!

Once, when I was in the sky
   a "pocket" I did hit.
I thought that there was no more air
   And nearly "took a fit."

But as I sat about to cry
   I started breathing deeply
Until I saw a bird fly by,
   Climbing oh so steeply.

And then I realized that there was
   Enough of what I needed.
So with a sigh I settled back
   To level flight succeeded.

I thought about the air we have
   And how we make it smoky
Until my darling came to me,
   And sweet and gently-woke me.

Herbert Needlman

Sailing...

Sailing past the innocence
of everlasting smiling skies
I listen to the wind and rain
where tomorrow holds no surprise

Having an open mind, I rush ahead
past all living, past all dead
past all dreams I left behind
Part of life and love
Part of dreams which feel no pain
Part of yes and no, smiling in the rain
Always dancing, never seeking gain
Part of how,
Part of now
Part of thoughts which never die
Part of you and I, always ready to try
And with this I say so long, goodbye
Ave Atque Vale!
Hail and farewell!

Bernard Lipsius

Big Blue

Our town has been so very proud
of music made by blue
we wanted to remain on top
and prayed it would come true.

For weeks they practiced hard and strong
with their drums beating loud
nobody could steal their dream now
for soon they would be proud.

To North Agusta they would march
their hearts were full of glee
when their award time came to pass
they wanted to see victory.

But up against big Burns they fell
the second in the State
to the heart of loyal Walterboro Fans
the Big Blue would always be great.

A year away they'll try once more
with their hearts beating proud
and when their time comes again
we'll be cheering loud.

Jean Lyons

Human Sin

The ancient curse
of human sin
let loose upon the earth

desecration and destruction
the price of human birth

Infiltrate into the system
A wrench in the machine

Subtly changing the way we live
Subliminal desensitizing

Values and morals
Twisted around
Life and death unclear

Chaos in the future
The end is very near

Charles Rich III

Run Together...

Lovers linger by the side
of life's eternal shore
Tossing pebbles into space
Taking chances with their fate.

Strolling side by side
Lover's hearts and hands entwine
Sketching dreams in shifting sand
Watching tides erase their plans.

Run, run - Oh - break away
Before the crashing waves destroy
All the sweetness of the dreams
Filling lovers' hearts with joy.

Run together, beat the tide
Lest the ebbing waters wide
Wipe away those dreams held dear
'Ere too late to run together, ever!

Gayle Lockwood Fell

Luna Sea

I was dreaming
of my love of velvet
as the moonlight washed through
my window
and lit up my feet in silver
I felt your breath
you were in my soul

Dell Dorenbosch

"Age"

Age is life's recorded message
Of our minutes, days and years.
Hopeful Morning, busy Noon-time,
Evening, hinting rest is near.

In our morning, hope inspires us;
By ambitious youth we're led
Ever strong and striving onward,
Eager for each task ahead.

Age at Noon-time will remind us
We have traveled half the race;
Social climbing, job declining...
Friends and children join the pace.

Evening comes, and now our message
Shows the value of design.
God's own hand and good, unmeasured
Guide this life to one divine.

Bo Buice

Whispers

Certain things that I see...
Of people, places dear to me,
Ghostly pictures in my mind...
Now, but memories of that kind.
I could not write you,
   to explain...
There are no words,
   no words to name...

But in dreams, of all,
   if you listen...

You might, sometime,
   hear me...whisper.

Jerome Paul Salazar

Sail On...

Don't harbor your vessel on the shore
of self defeat
Instead, sail it on the open sea, with
the rest of the fleet
for life has its billows and waves
trickles and streams
So cruise your vessel onward
ever looking forward
Cheer up! For life isn't always
what it seems.

Julie A. Fisher

Changes

Now instead of flecks
of your ashes in the grass
there are flecks of
new white paint.

The house needed it anyway
and Raymond wanted the work.

Did I think the old paint job
would always be good enough
or that my children
wouldn't grow up and go away
or that you
could go on living?

Claire L. Steiger

"At Jesus' Feet"

Oh how sweet to sit at Jesus feet,
Oh what fellowship divine!
Just to leave the world behind.
Oh how sweet, for He is mine!

Once I was lost in sin,
Then my dear Savior entered in.
Saved my soul and set me free.
Born to live with Him in Eternity.

Darlene L. Cory

The Soldier Boy

I asked him when we climbed the hill
Oh, what, my dear, are you after
His sweet reply, I hear it still
Your love, your life, and your laughter

War's cannon called, and he marched away
And love and laughter was over
Life followed soon, the unkind day
They buried him in the clover

Florence Pearson

Together

It rained that afternoon,
on a cool, late September day.
Wishing I could stop your tears,
there was nothing more to say.

Although I must be leaving,
my heart remains with you.
A promise of my return,
knowing our love is true.

Hours turn to days, days to weeks,
missing your smile, your touch.
Loneliness now a constant reminder,
of your love I need so much.

I have cried many times,
to help reason and understand.
The road we must travel,
to have our destiny at hand.

But alas, we are united,
together, you and me.
Sharing our hopes and dreams,
together, forever, we will always be.

Charles R. Archer

Meadow Dreams

In a country, far away,
On a golden pond of shiny light,
Circled by white lilies and tall grass,
My dream mind takes flight.

I recall a pretty girl in white,
Dressed all in ribbons and bows,
Handsome, tall, dark-haired stranger,
A fantasy dream only she knows.

She sees a meadow, runs to him,
Held in his strong arms so tight,
Just wanting to be there, forever,
Never wanting to let go for dear life.

Looking up, their faces move closer,
Time seems then to stand still,
Lost in a breathtaking moment,
Lips touching, kissing at will.

As time passes with each day,
She waits forever it seems,
Hoping that she'll meet him,
In reality, and not in her meadow dreams.

Danita Sawler

Three Crosses

One cross between two others stood
On a hill overlooking the City.
Two wrong joining the Right.
The Right leads to the narrow gate,
The crooked way made by wrong.
"No wrong have you done," said one,
The other laughed.
The wrong was received unto Right,
While the other mocked in scorn.

He asked forgiveness for all,
They not knowing the wrong they do.
He died for me,
He died for you
That me might live again.
Our sins He bore with Him to take,
That someday we will see our mistake.
And like to the thief He will say
"We are wrong come unto Right."

Elisabeth Haylee Knox

Haiku

The hummingbird sat
on air waves and sipped from
red hibiscus cups.

Exel Dyar Winn

"The Skies Were Weeping"

Even the skies were weeping
on that day
we were sadly parting
in the summer rain.
Only the fates could tell when
we would meet again.

And still our hearts are aching,
we're apart.
We'll continue hoping,
praying for that day,
when the nearness of each other
steals the tears away.

The skies are ever weeping
but we dream -
sunny days ahead,
the two of us together.
Skies are blue, no raindrops fall,
just you and me forever.

Jean C. Barks

Heartprints

Man has left his questing footprints
on the moon, and on earth's crust.
You can trace the Pilgrim Fathers
by their footprints in the dust.

Man has left his fateful handprints
on our laws, and on our creeds.
You can trace the Founding Fathers
by their handprints on these deeds.

Man has left the depth of footprints,
by the measure of his press.
Man has left utopic handprints,
by his plumb of righteousness.

Yet, the trail I find climactic
are man's heartprints, as they fall.
Tears, so weightless, so unpublished,
leave the greatest print of all.

Flora Turbyfield Porter

My Guy

Together we walked in the park,
On the trees we left our mark,

As he held my hand,
He could never understand,

The love I feel for him,
I thought he could never win.

Sometimes I think of days gone by,
I wonder how I got this guy.

The time that we first met,
I could never ever forget.

I was standing, eating a pear,
And all he could do was stare.

Now as I stare into his big brown eyes,
I know there could never be another guy.

Christine Rodriguez

Say A Little Prayer

Say a little prayer for me,
On this day it would be
A comfort to my soul.

On certain days like this one,
When everything is going wrong,
Say a little prayer for me.

When in my soul is a terrible ache,
And my heart feels as though
   it will break,
Say a little prayer for me.

My heart can feel no sympathy,
And in my life there is no harmony,
So please, say a little
prayer for me.

It's nice to have
People who care
People who will
Say a little prayer.

But I'm the one who needs to kneel and pray
Keeping up hope for a brighter day.

Candy Swope

My Sweet Little Renee

My sweet little Renee
One day you came to stay
How I loved you from the start
And I didn't want to part
My sweet little Renee
I love you more and more each day
You have such a lovely smile
That makes my life worth while
My sweet little Renee
You're like a blooming flower
Changing by the hour
Your sparkling eyes that shine
Each time you look at mine
What more can I say
But thank you dear God
For giving us Renee
Protecting her with all your love

Elizabeth Aslanian

Freedom

We open our arms to the world
one generation, one century, two.
A nation like none other is born
we are strong, vast, unhindered
by cultures and practices left behind.
Opportunity for all, Freedom.

As we start our third century we fall
from strong to wrong.
60,000 young men dead
Freedom mourns.

To be us is not enough
we have opportunity
we have freedom
we are idle, the frontiers conquered
and we imagine we want
the very lives we left
so many centuries ago

Folly is the monument of rose-colored nostalgia
Freedom forged in blood and sacrifice
blithely lost in ignorance and prejudice

Guy J. Ricci

Struggle To Live

Killing in the name
only for the game
leaving your mortality
entering your soul.
Like an elevator
up or down
the soul goes up
the body goes down.
Jumping, trying to catch yourself
falling
while your soul moves up
Feeling no more
Scared no more
Your soul leaves peacefully.

Andrea Lynn Miller

Symbolic Thought

Today we walked a path together,
Only minutes before we had to part.
A bouquet of flowers we gathered,
To relieve the sadness in our heart.

Safe in memory will be our footprints,
Although the path be dust,
Not night nor storm will ever wrench,
Our thoughts of love and trust.

When duty releases our bonds of time,
We'll walk this path some morrow.
This flower, symbolic thought of mine,
From God's creation I'll borrow.

Though lost of color this flower may be,
So unlike my love for you.
You've only to close your eyes to see
This beautiful bloom in glistening dew.

Bill Lee

Take The Time

Do you feel my pain
or even see it in my eyes...
When you turn your head
till you can quickly pass me by?

Maybe I remind you
of what you've left behind...
Still I don't know why it's so hard
to be a little kind.

To those a lot less fortunate
who don't have very much...
And sometimes all we need to feel
is a loving touch...

To know that there is something more
than just pain and despair...
Is it really just that hard
to show someone you care?

For there but for the grace of God
we all could be someday...
So maybe you should take the time
to help someone today.

Brendalyn Crudup Martin

Rain

Rain on my window.....
Pitters and patters,
Like the beat of drum,
In the grand parade.
The rain marches down,
Down my window pain.

Danean Mezynski

"If There Be Love"

If there be love
Our world would be
a better place for you and me

If there be love
People would care
foregoing the hate willing to share

People today must be told
When one another grows selfish and cold
Love is a difficult treasure to hold.

If there be love
who cares what life brings
Love can overcome anything.

To these add one
for you and I know it can be done.

Brianne Liwaj

Ode To The Leopard

Sinuous, lithe, you glide and run,
                outstripped by none.
Making your way with feline grace
                at deadly pace.
High in a tree you sleep away
                all through the day.
Your spotted fur blends in the light,
                hidden from sight.
You come alive when day is past,
                dark comes at last.
Your eyes, great cat, in black night seem
                like agate's gleam.
Your padded tread is seldom heard
                by beast or bird.
Triumph of Nature, very few
                are match for you.

Eleanor Hepburn Noall

Home

The sun's shining bright,
Over the lakes and streams.
The river and waterfalls throw,
Their mist into the air.

The trees wave endlessly,
In the wind, as if to
Say "Hello!" to the angels that
Watch over us.
This is the home in my heart.
Though it be in my mind,
I will always be welcome.
Whenever I close my eyes,
I am home.

Dustin K. Hawkins

Hypocrisy

I sit and look out...
On a world calling for peace,
But fighting for war.
On a world calling for love,
But from its pores seeps hate.
On a world of people seeking acceptance,
But giving only rejection.
On a world of pain and suffering
Hidden by a facade of joy.
"All the world's a stage,
And all the men and women
Merely players."
But we never play ourselves.

Jessica Petit

Spring

S is for Spring
P is for pouncing in puddles
R is for rain that make flowers grow
I is for imagination
N is for nice weather
G is for God who made the earth
   Spring, spring is the perfect
season to ask somebody one good
question. Do you like spring?

Jason Taylor

The Screamin' Eagles

They sped up the middle
passing a little
Till an eagle spotted a hole
and promptly kicked in a goal.

Up and down the field they soared
moving the ball at their own accord.

They scampered to and fro
controlling the ball toe to toe
unwilling to yield to the foe.

As they drew nearer to the fore
another eagle eyed an open door
and in went another score.

That was the end of the game
and where the losers failed
the winners prevailed
so they all left from whence they came.

So if perchance you see a
sea of sea gulls on a soccer field
you're not seeing sea gulls
it's the Screamin' Eagles.

David T. Chavez

Kitty Ditty

"Little cuddle kitty with a
Peach-fuzz nose,
A peach-fuzz nose,
A peach-fuzz nose,

Little cuddle kitty with a
Peach-fuzz nose, and I
Love you so."

Donna Parker

Pen In Hand

When I take pen in hand,
   perhaps,
I can make you understand.
It is not to arrange words,
   but to reveal,
what I have heard.

A way of sending forth
   my thoughts.
Not those sold or bought.
Feelings from deep within,
   can be shared,
only with a pen.

The tongue hesitates.
Vocal cords refuse to state.
The truth that lives within.
Of the places and the people,
I have been.

Jan Couch

The Answer To Life

We won't know all the answers,
Perhaps not until the time we die.
    And even then we may still not know
All the answers to life.
    For as life goes on
For those left behind,
    Many more questions
Still will arise.
    Yet in all the beings
That survive,
    The best answer may lie
In the love kept alive.
    St. Paul said it better, I know,
In his Epistle on Love.
    But for all that we write
Only actions count most
    And the words thus seem lost
When in Love we create life.

Horatio Costa

Graced Beautifully

Rays of sun glimmer, on the sand
Pieces of driftwood dot the land
Beyond lies a sparkling, clear sea
Nature has graced this land beautifully
As the sun sets over
The tide gets lower
Night joins the sea
Nature has graced this land beautifully

Jenica Rodriguez

Changes

I gather dried leaves
Placing them carefully
In a plastic bag

I miss the winter season
Moving to my new home
Sun-filled with palm trees
And tropical vegetation.

Returning to visit on a winter day
With gloved hands I collect leaves
I plan to take them to my tropical home
As part of my past life remembered
My winter now facing me.

I look again at the gathered leaves
They seem drier and more withered
Too fragile for migration.
I scatter the leaves upon the cold ground
Awaiting a threatening snow.

Some things cannot be moved easily
Cannot accept change easily
And should be left . . . alone.

Edith Soffler

"Star Watch"

Perched on bluffs'
rocky mound
like eagles' resting nest
watched from here
'top solid ground
travelers of a quest
Arch shaped roll
of falling fire
blazes past a wish
to grant a lover's still desire
of happiness once missed.

Constance E. Radin

"Love In The Deep"

I am a powerful dolphin cavorting
Pluming the depths of the
    deep
        blue
            sea
Searching, poking my snout about
The coral reef and under
    the
        rocks
For a treasure
A love beyond measure.

I caught a glimpse of a noble prize
Powerful, speedy
    like lightning
        rumbling
            like thunder.
If I could snag this stimulating specimen,
Sam would yell "Uncle"
Searching for his smooth,
    sleek submarine.

Elizabeth Lambrecht

Spite

Spiteful spicules,
poison tipped,
pierce the thin tissue
of my breast.

Hsst...hsst...
splinters sent,
streak! Streak!
To split my flesh.

Tiny pointed barbs,
strings of heartless wit,
venom spit
with spider spite,
to sear crisp
with laser light
my soul in flight.

James R. Estes

Night Sounds

Night sounds.
Quiet whispers.
Cool mist.
Early gray.
Dawn breaks.
Birds sing.
Rising up.
Another day.
Turning in.
Failing light.
Midnight moon.
Night sounds.

John Czopek-Knight

When The Earth Turns

A lone man and horse made shadows
Over the newly plowed ground
As they broke the furrows down
In ceaseless movements.

Birds followed close behind silently
Picking up worms and seeds
This is one of their happy feeds
Each spring when the earth is turned.

Adelee Bonadurer

Untitled

Barnacles of fear
quiver slowly the underworld
water of stagnant pools in my mind.
Thieving is the whitened dust,
for fear is of the craving kind,
to suck pain-pleasure from the rusted rind.
My bottom in the ocean murmurs forces
in the tide,
through which the dim cry for light
never will subside.
The daily night of the motive world
for whomever can see,
a blackened labyrinth to shine
in the realm of the deep.

Jennifer DeRyck

Rainbows

Rainbow
Rainbow
Rainbow
in the sky
Rainbow different
colors. We don't
know why. Maybe
it is exciting and
maybe it is bold.
Maybe it don't have
color do you even
know. So if you
see a rainbow
come and tell me
Please so I can
Put it on my paper
you just wait and
see.

Amber Hill

Old Wine

You are like old wine.
Rare and red as the
Red blood in the cask of your body.
I have not tasted your
Bittersweetness for years.
But your kiss is a sweet
Remembrance in dreams and waking
dreams.
A shot of heady spirit
Never forgotten
But tightly plugged up.
A half-drunk ancient bottle
Thrown overboard a shaky
Ship.
A rare burgundy was your
Body's sweetness.
A sunken bottle
Half-empty
Never again to be enjoyed.

Irene Seymour

"Rainforest"

Humid, hot, warm, moist
So green, so tall, thick and lush
    Peace, so, so still
Wildlife voices everywhere
Not so far, man and machine.

Danielle Frizalone

Golden Heart

Thy golden heart encircles my being
reaching, touching, igniting my love.

Your gentle caresses touch my soul
feeling, seeing, beyond control.

Two souls dancing in the night
to the rhythm of Gods delight.

One eternal song of love,
one eternal pounding heart.

One breath of love,
one inner light.

Good night my love,
our souls unite.
Bonnie Fisher

Double Date

She gazed
right through me
and straight into
your eyes
a gesture meant
to sting me
but falling somehow empty
as I sat outside
my body
knowing all the history
I gathered
my androgyny
and felt giving
through the distance
now created by your demons
she's politically expedient
and we all must choose
our wardrobe...
although green is not my color
I wear dignity quite well
Barbara Lee Jewell

Early Morning On Saint Simons

Solitary, grizzled old sea gull
ruffled and weathered,
aged and stoic...
Watching? Waiting?
Perhaps a sentinel!

Sea gulls and Sandpipers
work the surf
in early morning light.

White hulls nestled
on the horizon...
Winged booms reaching side to side...
Every present shrimpers
silently tend the net.
James L. Johnson

Peace

Bought a gun today
So I could play
Called my friends so they could
Come and play
We argued and fought, fought and argued
I pulled out my gun as big as it was
I said today is my birthday glad you
Could come
I pulled the trigger
Off it went with a loud report
We had fun with my toy gun
Gary Croson

Nothing More

whisper sweetly; scream, yell
say a prayer; witch spell
walk into walls; splinter in your eye
speak of the truth; tell a lie
open a window; slam a door
one serving; twice as more
down a hill; vertical climb
empty pockets; dollar and dime
purple youth; orange golden age
agree with everything; filled with rage
tears of joy; sobs of depression
like a lamb; lion aggression
book's cover; countless pages
like a bird; closed cages
Jacqui Cooper

Terror

Terror builds with destruction, its
screams bring reality,
tears drown understanding,
left to fumble unheard.

Terror explodes without letting, its
cries bring loss,
sound drowns comfort,
left to search unfound.

Terror hurts without reason, its
wounds bring pain;
weeping drowns peace,
left to fall uncaught.

Terror unites with commons, its
helplessness eases hatred,
togetherness drowns fear,
left to bond unrestricted.

Terror dies without emptiness, its
loss brings relief,
time drowns memory,
left to sit unforgotten...
Hope Ziemkiewicz

Summer

Smash the dazzled eye with sun,
sear its cringing inner night,
bleach out shadows one by one
& leap into a world of light!
The yellow, baking, blinding sun
beats blue enamel, hard and vast;
while reddened children scream their fun
in arcs of joy on pounded grass.
Come celebrate the crude — the strong!
Embrace the heat! Adore its brand!
Sing lushness into greenest song —
All Welcome Beast Bananaland!
   And revel, revel, revel free
   in summer's brute fecundity.
Jay Chollick

Gleaming

   The tears on my pillow fall so light,
so I don't wake you in the night.
   I see you lying over there,
sleeping so gently without a care.
   I will hold you with a gentle touch,
hoping that it's not too much.
   I'm feeling a gleam in my eye,
and I pray that I don't cry.
Ina Bowen

Happiness

Happiness is
   Seeing you standing
   Smiling at me.

Happiness is
   Being next to you,
   Feeling you near.

Happiness is
   To talk to you,
   To listen to you.

Happiness is
   What wakes me up
   What sends me to sleep.

Happiness is
   What brings me through
   The trials of life
   And I attribute it all to you.
Christopher M. LaPorte

Song Of The Serpent

Dragons aflight on leathery wings
Serpent speaks of magical things.
Things of life, and things of light,
of these the Serpent always sings.

Hydra cries in villainous rings
Eerie light the moonbeam brings.
Things of death, and things of sorrow,
of these the Serpent always sings.

Fairies sleeping in innocent dreams
Nightlight glitters on their wings.
Things of beauty, and things of worth,
of these the Serpent always sings.

Gold medallions and silver rings
Rich Emperors and wealthy kings.
Things of royal, and things of charge,
of these the Serpent always sings.

Devilish creatures who haunt our dreams
Good and evil in separate teams.
Things of nether, and things of poison,
of these the Serpent always sings.
Jason Wilkins

Woman And Child

She brings to me a child.
Set at my feet
a girl
-small girl-
of eight, maybe nine,
but very small

and crippled.
Stolen, the light,
from this child's eyes.
Stunted legs- polio.
Swollen limbs- kwashiorkor.

Stolen light-
retarded from malnutrition.
Disappointed that I am helpless,
mother grasps the child's wrist
and lifts her from the ground,
transporting her back
into the manyatta.

This child without a light
is a burden.
Christine Jost

Alienation

Separated from you with a slash,
Sharp and clean,
And only then to know the pain
Of a large and open wound.
I called to you
Across a room of broken dreams
While a demon fumed in counterpoint.
Your hands were warm
As they caressed me,
And your voice,
Hushed and tender,
But the knowing look was not there.
You could not understand.
And then,
With my loneliness like a weight,
I began to sink,
Deeper and deeper into myself.

Cheryl M. Lodico

My Mother

I love my mother, don't you see,
She is always there for me,
I come first I am told,
She's there ready to enfold.

When my world gets cloudy,
And I get real pouty,
Mom's there ready to console,
When I'd like to crawl in a hole.

Asking that we always do our best,
At each and every little test,
As our model and our teacher,
She seems like a preacher.

Sometimes we ask to have a guest,
She just adds them to the rest,
Mom thinks what's one more,
There is still room on the floor.

A mothers love is plain to see,
She always has plenty for me,
You can bet she loves you all,
And I know that's a good call.

Beverly J. Wormald

Emily

A lady with a brood of seven
She never left the 'nest'
　　to wander
Always there to answer…
　　to question… the seven

Seven girls around her apron
The strings stretching -
　　as elastic
The bands at times - retracting
　　close enough to smile at her…
　　　to wave… to sing to her

While basking in her 'owlish' ways
The seven grew wiser…
　　she mistook
Soon to conquer what their
　　vision directed…
Left Emily …..
　　the beautiful….
　　　Mother of seven

Deloris Lightfoot Jackson

My Sister Plays Piano

My sister plays piano.
She smiles playing,
A beautiful prelude by LISZT
Called "LIEBESTRAUME."
She is so relaxed and so magic
playing that daring music
that she forgot herself completely.
So all the jurors noticed
that she's smiling,
all the audience is happy.
All the floor is happy.
The security guard, the street,
the buses are happy.
People which are waiting for the bus
are exquisitely happy
that they don't have to wait
any longer.

Gabriela Gurgui

Saturday's Seat

　February mid morning hanging sun
shines on the naked tree and branch
sending its long shadow down the gorge
to blend with those below

　　each crystal of fresh fallen snow
　　is a minute mirror reflecting
　　the radiance of existence,
　　each messenger of frozen sky
　　a testimony and evidence
　　to what is only seen
　　as a backdrop to
　　what we really need

and the tracks are but a trail
through that which needs no path
the road just a highway
for the coming and going
of man

　　the shadows
　　　on
　　the snow.

David Griffy

"Our Special Star"

There's a new and ever brilliant star
Shining high above,
It illuminates the skies each night
And sends us so much love.
And tucked within that special star
That's just begun to shine,
Is so much love from here on earth
I know… 'cause some is mine.
You were so much a part of us
Of each and every day,
We had no indication
That you would go away.
You were the very best
The fairest of the fair,
Part of us went with you
Please know we'll always care.
When we look up to heaven
Knowing that you're there,
We wish upon our special star
And remember you in prayer.

Ethel M. Sandstrom

Silence

The leaves fall
Silently.
The evening falls
Calmly.
I come to meet you
And slowly
Give you a kiss
Tenderly.
We are sitting closely
hand in hand we have no voice,
But our hearts beat
Sweetly.
The woods hold their breath,
The crickets hold their songs.
Silence, silence everywhere,
Our soul is floating here, there
　　In the silent night.

Henry Tuoc V. Pham

On My Mind

Daily at work and at play asleep awake.
Simple smile
From miles away,
deep felt love
in hand and heart
mind and soul,
"together" as one
Tell you I love you
always have always was.

Excuse my shortcomings
though they are many
the past is now gone,
forgotten - not hardly
the future is tomorrow
not yet that I've seen
all that I have is today.
With you - in my dreams
so let it be said
and written here
I love you!

Donald J. Brill

A Year

Has it really been a year
since I last saw your face?
Time is slowly healing me
but the pain it won't erase.

It seems like just yesterday
I softly touched your hand.
I told you that I loved you
and I tried to understand.

I strongly held back the tears
I tried to keep my faith.
I whispered a Silent Prayer
Please don't take him away.

Standing patiently at your side
I knew I had to set you free.
I held onto you extra tight
Wanting to keep you here with me.

I gently closed my eyes as
I felt you slip away.
Even though it's been a year
You're still missed each and every day.

Betty Baker

Carousel

Big children
small children
black children
white children
mild ones and
wild ones how
I love the sound.

Dancing and
prancing on
bright painted
horses how
happy the
music this
merry-go-round.

Jean Carol Ramsay

Mystic Impressions

She brushed by me, the
smell of sweet perfume still....
Lingering in the air. I did
not see her, but knew, she
was still there. As I looked
onward, still hoping to see her
her image was gone.

Today... tomorrow... and everafter

I think of her still, of her
presents in the air, the sweet
fragrance of romance, still...
Lingering in the air.

Cindy Reinier

My World

Crime is running rampant
   Smog fills up the air
Syringes on the beach
   Children in despair
Crooked politicians
   Homeless everywhere
This is the world you left me
   But you don't seem to care

Prison overcrowding
   Murderers set free
Cutting down the forests
   Garbage in the sea
Ozone disappearing
   Violence on TV
You had your piece of pie
   Now there's none for me

Jason Wayne Cochran

Shady Lane Ranch

Two hay eaters
side by side,
Roaming the pasture
Sometimes they hide,
Under the trees
Where the shadows grow,
Or down in the hollow
Where cool waters flow.
Race in the meadow
Hear their hooves pound
Manes wildly tossing,
As they cover the ground.
Pinto And Brown.

Della Bicking

Untitled

Sometimes I feel like an opal...
Smooth and cool
Milky white and round.
But when you look closer...
A fiery spark of red,
a surprising burst of energy and passion,
A small glimmer of bright yellow,
radiating sunshine and warmth,
A tiny speck of cool green,
calming and peaceful,
A few spots of orange,
anger and bitterness,
And a shining glint of blue,
thoughtful and serious;
Those are just a few facets
of my sparkling personality.

Faith Scrivano

Sons Of Man

He comes as quiet as soft falling
snow to gird us sons of man,
for the trails that will show
we're not worthy of thy name

Still our faith abounds on earth
when it beckons to our mother,
yet our vessels will not berth
for we sail without a rudder

The almighty in all his wisdom
tries us in the court of honor,
that we may enter his kingdom
in consort with our Father

May we be worthy of Thee, O Lord
moving blindly through the night
we vow to drop our sword
for we have seen your might

We, the sons of man O Lord
are ready to accept your nod,
brothers all in sweet accord
we now know we're sons of God

Abe M. Peña

"Little Pig"

Little pig, Little pig
so cute and stout
with your floppy ears
and funny snorting snout

What are you doing
cuddling in your pen,
just tumbling over
again and again

Then you jump right up
just like a stud,
look at you
you're covered in mud!

With your short little legs
and curly little tail,
woe is me
you sure do smell!

All I can say
that we must do,
is hope for rain
so it'll cleanse you.

Barbara Collins

Children In Trauma

Catastrophe in Oklahoma.
So many innocent lives.
Some lie in a coma.
As volunteers work and strive.

One year to date.
The Waco Davidian burned.
Many children suffered their fate.
Have any of us learned?

Emotions put on hold.
As we gazed into the screens.
Broadcasters' stories are told.
What we imagined in our dreams.

We the American people
Need to make time for our children.
Go to our church or temple.
The American people cannot remain
hidden.

Love thy neighbor.
Give from your heart.
Precious are those that labor.
They share by doing their part.

Donna L. Zuar

Beautiful Surroundings

I've got beautiful surroundings
So peaceful and worry free
Beautiful surroundings
That's what Jesus gave to me.

There are no problems, no troubles
I see
In these beautiful surroundings
Here with Jesus and me.

I've got beautiful surroundings
So peaceful and worry free
Beautiful surroundings
Right here on earth you see.

I don't have to wait for heaven
There with Jesus to be
I've got heavenly places right here
In the church you see.

Beautiful surroundings
So peaceful and worry free
Beautiful surroundings
That's what John Chapter 14 means to me.

Dora Johnson

God's Masterpiece

This precious gift rests in my arms
So perfect and so sweet
Abound in love and happiness
With ten little toes on its feet.
This treasure is mine from above
It brightens my entire day
Thank you, God, for sending
This masterpiece my way.
Each rhythmic heartbeat I feel
As it lies against my chest
Is something you have given me
And you've accomplished your very best.
My dream is fulfilled
My life is complete
The ecstasy of motherhood
Is a feeling that can't be beat.

Donna K. Grandinetti

Love Is One, But Never Twice

I thought you said you loved me,
So you say you do.

Your actions are so transparent
I can see them through and through

You stay out all night long
When I ask you where you been,
You sing the same old song.
When you do spend time home with me
You never want to be

You're in one room
I'm in the other
You're really avoiding me

I know true love suppose to last
It's really in the past
A wife loves her husband
A husband loves his wife
May love me once
And only once
But never loves me twice.

Agnes M. Brown

Eternity Of Wonder

Flying upon a wind-broken sky,
Soaring but never catching an eternity.

Riding the waves of fantasy,
Beached at reality.

Hoping for the world,
Living with the scars.

Reaching for the sky and beyond,
Fated only so far.

Wishing upon the night,
Living with the day.

Running with the tide,
Never one with the bay.

All things are connected,
You are your dreams.
Never, never give up hope
To change the world from what it seems.

Anna Moody

Warfare

This world has always been a battlefield.
Some battles to lose and some to win.
Some are for greed and for power.
Some for the freedom of man.

There is a Christian battle on.
They are soldiers of God you see.
It gives the promise of redemption.
And also of love and peace.

When the battle of life is over
God will call his soldiers to rise.
The battle cry of the resurrection
Will shake the earth from its ties.

There will be no more warfare.
No more sin or grief.
But peace shall reign in eternity
And God shall reign supreme.

Dorothy Moore Black

Nature

The beauty lies within,
Some may never realize
how important it is to us.

Some people never have
looked close enough
to see the difference
between the ant and the antelope.

All we can do is hope
that someday, somewhere, someone
will care enough to say
We have to help restore
what we have torn from our planet.

Maybe one day our
world will change,
Maybe one day it will
be as it was meant to be.

All we can do is hope!

Jan Haussmann

Friends

Friends are forever
Some people say
But a friendship is fragile

Friends need reassurance and allegiance
Love and understanding
Otherwise something may be lost

Once it's gone, it can never be the same
You may always be friends
But the friendship will change

Friends are your personal treasure
Insure them against loss
For your own protection.

Barbara C. Crawford

Someday

"Someday" is wishes and dreams
"Someday" I say to him—and to me
"Someday" can become all it seems
All my mind wants it to be.

"Someday" is almost a prayer
Wishing for dreams to become reality.
An illusive hope to dare;
A door awaiting the right key.

"Someday" is a circle, never-ending,
Of wishing and dreaming
We need someday in our lives
To go on with today.

Dorothy Wilson

Early Dawn

Early dawn sun
Shall rise.
Everyone opens
their eyes to
the sunrise
high in the sky.
Every night the
sun will set
with you by
its side, waiting
waiting, waiting,
until again the
sun will rise.

Crystal Crawford

Have Mercy Upon Us Dear God

Have mercy upon us dear God!
Someday we will understand
   that you alone are God
   and we are only man,
created for your divine pleasure
   molded by your holy hand.

Have mercy upon us dear God!
   The seed of Abraham
As withering grass stands
   upon parched, dry, enemy, sand.
Have mercy and let us be
   the remnant, humanity,
bringing glory and honour to thee.

Have mercy upon us dear God!
Blow not billows of wrath
   from your fan
upon children of wayward man.
Save us as only you can;
cleanse our hearts and remold us again.
I thank you, Father. Amen!

Dorothy Phyllis Garrett

Plant Talk

Take me to someone
Someone who knows my beauty
One that can see with the heart
One who touches with love

Pick me gently
Lay me into water
Let me drink of life
For I live with your tender care

Keep me shaded and cool
Fresh as the day I bloomed
For my joy is the happiness
In the one I was picked for

Be swift sacred carrier
For time in this form is short
Let my life story be sung
My beauty be heard

The songs I sing with my colors
Arranged by the Great Spirit
Feeling Love at my very presence
From the ones who will see

John Foree

Child Abuse

The chill
Of his mother's voice
Pierced the boy
Imprisoned in the corner

Mother raved, hit
And hurt her babe
As he murmured
Stop! Please, you're hurting me

Sitting crying
Knowing not what to do
Mother beats him
And watches him agonize

Ignoring the bruises
And scars she inflicted
Mother fiercely raged
As private anger lured
Her on and on

Jennifer Beckstrom

Where Did The Yesterdays Go?

What did I do with the yesterdays?
Something has happened to them.
It seems the older I grow,
The yesterdays grow more dim.

Precious memories of yesterday
come to us now and then.
Wouldn't it be wonderful
to live them over again.

Though most of our yesterdays
were happy, sadness sometimes came along.
Scenes of our yesterdays flash
through our minds and
plant in our hearts a song.

Let us be thankful for those
songs in our hearts.
Tomorrow may never come.
Let's reflect now and then on our blessings,
forgetting our pain and woe.
I would not exchange my place
in life for any ones I know.

Anna Lou Biggs

Flotsam

A wave advances towards the sand,
Sometimes gentle, sometimes grand,
Pushing out and pulling back,
Scheduled on a steady track.

The rhythm of its heartbeat
Set by lunar face,
And winds unseen by mortals,
But felt in noticed pace.

Watch the whitened crest
Breaking on the sand,
Leaving many treasures,
Taking contraband.

Am I like the ocean's wave,
Purpose set from birth to grave,
Born again in ocean's floor,
Just to make the trip to shore?

Taking all life's contraband,
What will I leave upon the sand?
Something to delight and treasure,
Or a sadness without measure?

Florence Dweck

Why, Oh God

Why, oh God,
Should I love
Not to be loved,
Give, and not receive,
Desire, without fulfillment?
The time has come
For me to soar like an eagle
Up in the sky
Hopefully, I will find
That special someone.
The thought of meeting you
Feels like the first day of Spring
I try to tenderly touch you
But darling, you are never there.
I always wish
But haven't achieved
Why, oh God, why?

Joseph K. Ernest

Love

Love is beautiful, sweet and kind
Sometimes it is very hard to find.
But as you can already see
That is the only way to be.

Love is not foolish or selfish in a way
That it would stop someone from having
  a good day
I know history sure will tell
How countries grew, and countries fell
But history books could never describe
How God made and created our lives
And how we received this wonderful
  LOVE
That we got from the heavens above.

Devyn Wray-Scriven

40 "And" A Grandma

39 and counting, oh my!
Soon to be 40, what to do.
How will I feel?
Will my body go to pieces?
With a look over the hill?
40, oh my.
What's that you say?
You're what?
I'm going to be a what?
A grandma?
But wait!
I can't be a grandma, I'm going to be 40!
A grandma in February and 40 in April!
Oh me, oh my!
What am I to do.
A grandma you say?
A grandma you say.
Wow! A grandma and "only" 40.

Anita L. Radakovich

Untitled

Life's so immortal
souls trapped
wanting to be set free

The young wanting to be old
the old wanting to be young
never satisfied just to be

Life's so challenging
wanting death —
wanting to be freed

Darkness surrounding
excitement, anxiety

To be afraid of death
is to be afraid of life
the afterworld wanting
to believe

Joanne K. Hill

Not Work, But Worry

It is not the work, but the worry
  That makes the world grow old,
That shortens the years of many
  before half their life is told.
It is not the work, but the worry
  that places on life a brand,
The cares and fears that flood the years,
  that break the heart of man.

Christopher Blanchard

Spring

Spring is here
spring is here
everybody cheer
everybody cheer

Flowers grow
no more snow
spring is here
everybody cheer

Sun shines bright
sun shines bright
all day and night
all day and night

Spring is here
spring is here
everybody cheer
everybody cheer

Rainy days all
go away

Summer's
coming soon

Ariell Joiner

Untitled

Silence broken by sound
Stillness by movement
Forms fade to shadows
While wealth and poverty mingle
blindly in the social contract.

As darkness and light wrestle
for dominance,
Reality and fantasy flow into
a single stream.

Stormy winds howl
and cold waves rage
Against the steel and glass monument
Where history snakes through modernity.

The world within a few square meters,
Like a multi-colored chess board,
Where pawns, and even knights
Are sacrificed
To protect their puppet kings.

Cherylynne Duncan

"Don't You Become A Fool"

Why would you make
such a big mistake
by going out there
and getting nowhere.
Why would you leave
a house and good food
to go into the streets
and become a big fool.

Think it over my friend
don't you become a waste
don't you give up right now
try hard and try your best.
For it a fool, doesn't know
what is it coming next.
Make an effort, try to reach
don't lose your interest
for it another fool
no difference can make.

Adriana Garcia

One Day's Flowers

Dreary morning, day is forming,
Sun falls from my eyes.
Night is past, walls of sleep collapse,
To fade away in sighs.
Washed out street looks incomplete,
A boulevard of lies.

One day's flowers pass in hours,
Tomorrow's lumps of clay.
Reality of self presented on a shelf,
Saved for a distant day.
Preserved under glass the years to pass,
Sharp tones slowly turn to gray.

Self taught lies, weak alibis
Excuses for missing the start.
The poet's song still rhymes along,
Cold comfort to the heart.
Divided soul is conquered whole,
Eternally apart.

D. L. Bryant

Someone Left The Window Open

The delicate rose petals
sweep to the floor,
The table legs whine
Under the heavy breath of the night.
The clock is restless
above the kitchen door,
It pines away the minutes
until someone stifles the cold.
And the rusty pans chatter in the oven,
saying, "Someone left the window open."

Jennifer Harbeson

Harvest Gifts

Beneath
swirls of
autumn haze
like ashen
wreaths,
beneath
streaks of
cotton-candy,
sunset rays,
stand fields
of corn —
weather dried,
golden stalked,
patiently waiting
to give up
their gifts
of harvest.

Alvin Robert Cunningham

Despair

In grief of the past,
that torturous journey.
Tears shed today for
fears of the future.
Ringlets of time
choking to death
hopes and ambitions
left gasping for breath.
Yesterday's dreams are
shut in a bottle.
Thoughts for tomorrow
dusty and idle.

Deborah J. Claypool

Night Person

You are there,
Tall and straight.
I did not dare to speak.
The hour is late.

The night is dark;
Moonbeams silver your hair.
You stroll in the park
Totally unaware.

You know me not
Though I know you.

Through the night
You pass walking slow.
Coming now is dawn's light.
I live in your glow.

Happiness is your face.
I capture the picture.
You quicken your pace.
Alive, I make my departure.

Georganne G. Tiemann

Peaceful Co-existence

We hunt with our skills
teeth, claws, and muscles.

Man uses none of these
except for guns and for dogs
without muzzles.

If man did not have
these, he would be at a loss

He would then be at my
mercy with my teeth and
my claws.

I would kill him if I
were hungry, I would not
kill him for his teeth or skin.

So let's keep the peace
after all, we are kin.

Julia Marion

The Choice Is Yours

We underestimate the choices
　That confront us every day,
And take for granted risks involved
　In what we do or say.

But there's a great degree of thinking
　That goes on in our minds,
For we're making choices daily
　And their consequences do bind.

We make choices of our homes
　And the merchandise we buy,
Of our friends, and the books we read
　And the knowledge we apply.

We choose our mate with confidence
　And vow with all our heart,
"To cherish, love, and honor
　Until death shall do us part."

The final choice is yours to make
　In any situation,
But be sure you've chosen Jesus Christ
　Who has given us salvation.

Helen Palmer Tucker

"Shining Friend Of Night"

"Shining friend of night,"
tell me how you shine so bright.
　How do you give me that silky feel,
as I watch that sky turn teal?

"Shining friend and night,"
how does that kite take flight?
　Does it fly through the trees,
or does it fly into the breeze?

"Shining friend of night,"
how do you give me that beautiful sight?
　As the sun comes out,
I wonder how that came about.

"Shining friend of night,"
now I have another sight.
　But as the sun came out,
I had a frown about!

Alex Ring

Crimson Tide

Crimson tide growing stronger
　Tell me when
You flow no longer
　Rushing odious and red
Against a black sun
　Claiming all in your path dead
Crimson tide when will you die
　When will there be
Stars in the sky
　I pray some day
You will be banished
　Sorrow and tears
Will then all vanish
　Crimson tide tell me why
Tell me why
　We have to cry
Why can't there be
　Joy and peace
Is there a reason
　We can't be free

Gretchin DuBose

Just Say No

His background a loving family
The future bright and full of hope
He was young and loved to party
So was introduced to dope

Said yes, so got addicted
Stoned when he left home
Hustling on street corners
Trying to make it on his own

Lying in the gutters
Shaking in his tattered clothes
The money that he hustles
In his arms and up his nose

Searching the back alleys
Hoping that he might
Score for the last hit
To make it through the night

He stinks, his body's dirty
Unwashed hair infested with bugs
None of this would happen
Had he just said no to drugs

Joseph L. Mosbacher

Love Is Like

Love is like a fairy tale
that doesn't last to long.
Love within a helpless soul
sings a helpless song.

Love is like angels that
fly away.

Love is like children who
love to play.

Love is a gift that you
can't return.
Love is like a flame
that likes to burn.

Danielle Morin

Enchantment

No, I have not forgotten
That green and sunny noon
When we exchanged our selfish smiles
With haste and shameless greed.
Or how we painted wild the night
With fragile shards of grand illusion,
Splashed the starry skies with laughter,
And gypsy passion born of lies.
For this I pay the beggar's debt
To that tender dalliance past
With tears in buckets brimming over
And constant note of what has gone.

Denise Kemery Brown

Goodbye

Goodbye, dear friend, goodbye.
Take my heart with you, friend,
My smiling eyes to warm you.
Recall what I taught you.
Love yourself forever
For you are the best man.
Trust in yourself always
For your legs are yet strong.
Grow in love for all men.
God hath willed you strongly.
Know the way to come home
For the door is open.
I say goodbye today,
Knowing I will need you
More tomorrow than now
As I lean on your strength.
Goodbye, dear friend, goodbye.
I'll let you go for now.

Corinee W. Guy

No One Realizes

The ones on the street
that have no food or clothes.
The ones on the street
Who don't have any homes.

The ones on the street
who are suffering in the cold.
The ones on the street who
go from young to old.

The ones on the street
Who just don't give a damn.
The ones on the street are
human, woman, children and man.

Gina Raimondo

Don't Let Me Go

Don't let me go to a world
  that is always calling;
teasing with enticing words
  of promise for my worth.
Hold me with your love,
  and like me for who I am.
Loosen the bonds of painful,
  restricting love.
I could never be perfection
  of the image of your desires.
I am an individual, worthy
  in all I have tried to achieve.
Lacking perfection, just as you,
  wanting perfection,
  just as you.
Like me for myself,
  for love does not endure
  the harshness of dislike.

JoAnn Price

"Back Then"

"To be or not to be"
That is the question?
"To have or have not"
"Is not to have at all"
"It's not given to all
It has to be earned
You can work for it"
But it's not for you to have,
"You will not earn it,"
"Nor will it be given to you."
Looking "back" is to "hate"
The future is out of reach
And the past has gone
"Back then"
Will not come, again.

Alphonso J. Hairston
"Crazy Horse"

Blackened Love

  It has always been said
that my heart is of pure gold.
  Yet I continue to deprive my
heart of its fine pride.
  It is no good for my heart
when my life is so tart.
  Coming deep down from inside is
the only whisper of a little cry.
  "Why did she ever have to lie?"
Now it is just sad that my heart
is starting to die.
  All the memories running through
my head, clear and unblurred. It is
obvious to me just how much I really
did love her.
  Now that I have lost my only
begotten love, it is only time that
has blackened the white love.

Jarret D. Winn

"Remembrance"

If by chance we may meet
That time will be pleasures keep
Again will I remember this as
life's thoughts ebbs away
Remembrance is the hope I seek
to met you in memories keep
that promises friendship that I seek.

Jack Wakamatsu

Endless Lonesome

Lonesome is the willow
that whispers secrets to the wind,
lonely is the daisy
that grows upon the hill.

Lonesome is the heart
in which love does not live,
empty are the feelings
when you've nothing left to give.

Endless is the time
where lonely sits to weave,
endless are the tears
that an empty heart cries.

Endless is to lonesome
as stars are to the sky,
while running for tomorrow
you beg for one more try.

To end the endless lonesome
pick the daisy on the hill,
still the whispers of the willow
to give a heart the chance to feel.

Beverly Terrill

A Glimpse Inside

A dense rain forest, lush and green
that world locked in your eyes.
A beautiful and natural creation
under stormy, summer skies.

A smile reaches the wilderness
like light falling through trees.
I feel its warm touch on my face
engulfed in a scented breeze.

Night falls and mystery reigns.
Danger and darkness reside.
Promise, unspoken, lie awake
too frightened not to hide.

Daybreak entices fiery hues
and sounds of hopeful sighs.
Never void of fragile life,
that world locked in your eyes.

Jessica Bowyer

The Gates To Your Imagination

Gates to your imagination
  that's what they are.
They can take you to many places,
  both near and far.

But what are these gates
  that many have opened,
to explore this world,
  including its oceans?

You have probably used them
  often before,
to help and guide you,
  through life's door.

These gates are called books
  which many have found,
lead to adventures
  this wide world around.

So read each book
  with anticipation,
and you will expand
  your imagination.

David A. Broz

The Vigilant Mother

You like to perch behind
the bay window, fogged
like a milky cataract
from radiators tolling
hollow bells,
and clear a porthole
to stand your watch.

I feel you at the edge of sight,
like the shadow of a cloud
not quite overhead.
In a field of fresh snow,
I squash tracks that lead back
That lead back to where I started,
laying the filament
you could reel in,
to keep me close,
in the creel where
you keep the things
you need to hoard.

David Leeds

My Sailboat

One look and it stole one breath
the beauty, the shape
the feel of silk from its lowest point
all the way up to the endless sky

After being tied up, I let it loose
with a single stroke it moved
taking me with it

Oh how much I loved the sensation
on my body as it sailed with the wind
through unknown waters!

As I felt that fresh sea wind
I was lost in thought,
where I had been
where was I going

A ship with no direction
just sailing with the wind

I was happy
no matter where I would turn up
the grip of its wheel
will always lead to my destiny.

Iris M. Mora

Cherished Memories

I knelt at His feet;
  The cross rising up before me.
Through my tear-stained face
  I saw Him in agony.

The cherished memories of the past
  were now flooding my soul
with the words He had said
  about His saving role.

I wanted to scream and shout
  that they had the wrong man,
but my heart knew His place
  was in his Father's hand.

I heard Him breathe His last
  and saw His head hang down.
His lifeless form just hung there;
  silence the only sound.

I knelt at His feet;
  the throne illuminated by His face
because even His mother
  needed His saving grace.

Janet Burger

Mom's Poem

The flowers come out when you're here
The clouds go away when you're near
You make the birds sing,
And every good thing,
You take away all of my fear.

A Mother's Day poem just for you
For all the good things that you do
You're special to me,
All one mom could be,
You make old things seem like brand new.

Erin McLaughlin

Travelling The Corridors Of Time

Travelling down
the Corridors of Time:
Joys abound
God's Providence Divine.

Each appointment
ordained by His hand,
show us part
of His Almighty plan.

May we follow
as He leads:
To those with
unexpected needs.

In minutes, or hours:
Mid-sunshine or showers;
keeping always... on the climb
travelling the Corridors of Time.

Carol Olson

Untitled

In the depth of life
The cunning image of myself
Occurs on liquid mirrors.

My face is water running
Into bowl of hands -
Expression of despair.

What is known form tiny birds -

Unspoken words came into being
Among leaves and grass
Watering my eyes made of day
And keeping dreadful thoughts at bay -

gotta be learned in a hard way
From placing myself on a shaky branch
Suspended in not supportive air.

Oh, strong wind
Sculptured my hands
In despair.

Girsh Reznikov

Fantasy

Remember our first day together?
The drive through the country,
the blanket on the soft green grass,
a picnic lunch, two glasses of wine.

We were new together, fresh, pure,
like the air that cradled us.
Unspoken words, looks of love,
attached and unattached we spent a
day of stolen dreams,
a Fantasy.

Bill Cooper

Gold

Gold is hidden, masked, and fearful,
the darkest shadow of dark night.

Gold is a driving force,
splitting people, rock, and earth.

Gold is the tired sky,
passing the burden to its sister night.

Gold is an autumn leaf,
forced to leave the tree.

Gold is the love we need,
impossible to find and harder to keep.

Gold is something not understood,
deadly, yet desired most.

Gold is what I fear,
the brilliance of the soul within.

Caitlin M. Williams

Baby

My first day on earth,
The day of my birth,
  My mommie and daddy were there.
They counted my toes,
And tickled my nose,
  And brushed back my soft fine hair.

My name!
What's my name?
  Is it Sweetheart, Darling or Love?
They must be confused,
Or are they yet to choose,
  A name that comes from above?

I spit up my food,
When I'm in the mood,
  And mommy's right there with a wiper.
And just when my folks,
Try to relax...,
  I cry and I fill up my diaper.

Harry Minor

I Love You

Being apart isn't always the easiest,
the distance divides, but love can win.
Trying our hardest, doing our best,
looking to find a way to begin.
We fell in love with just a glance,
now you're away, what do we do?
We made a promise and took a chance,
all I can say now is "I love you."
It isn't enough to say all that I feel,
there aren't enough words to say it all.
I want you to know that this is for real,
I never want to slow this fall.

Crystalynn Tanner

Dreams

I look at him
Just a shadow in my mind
Not him but a memory of someone else
Maybe just a thought that lingers on
But eventually that thought will die
I will realize dreams are just dreams
Know that he's just a ghost
A ghost of all that's past
And like all ghosts he will eventually
drift away

Kristen Sarra

Untitled

Reality held in by a fluorescent light,
the dog barks but he doesn't bite
Short fat girl wearing tights
Come along and see the sights
Technology has captured his slaves
Disease and death come in waves
Where are the good times we had
Guess it was just a passing fad
The women we love, the men we hate
When they die it'll be too late
Look around, society's falling
Listen up, 'cause reality's calling.

Duane Leggett

Fall

As I slowly walk through
The dry, cool forest,
I let the crisp breeze
Blow my hair away from
my face.
All around me
The leaves fall from the
trees,
In a whirl of color
Covering the ground
With a blanket of
Vibrant Golds,
Reds,
Oranges,
And yellows,
Above me the sound of
geese wings
Beat out that fall is here.

Jennifer Marie Bennett

Untitled

The crucial moment
The epitome of time

The ancient paradigm
The brutal reality

The beautiful essence
The cruel result

All enfold before thine eye
In the form of an arras
In the guise of mesh

To discern the truth is to know -
To know the truth is to be afraid.

Jennifer L. Kisala

Who Is Needy Among Us?

Earthquakes, flood, fires and such—
that's where the needy are.
Yet most are around the corner,
a distance not so far.
Might I be a channel for them—
not just a storage tank,
Or would I chastely look away,
with expression totally blank?
Could I be caring—or curing—
What kind of person am I?
would I help with a smile—
or run from a plaintive cry?
Help me know my brother's needs,
then reach out and grasp his hand.
Make a difference — be alert to the
plight of my fellowman.

Faith Carol Larson

The Writing Of A Poem

Writing poems is fun.
The feeling of joy when done!
Everything is going fine,
you have just finished another line,
then your mind goes blank.
You simply cannot think!
The frustration and pain,
the agony and strain!
Suddenly the words flow through.
A great relief to you!
Now!
The poem is done!
You feel you're a winner,
You've won!
As you look at your piece of art,
A feeling shoots straight through your heart.
So go and let your mind roam,
and go create a poem!

Carrie Knierim

The William Web

I was locked into your being
the first time you stared at
me with your vampire gaze.
You thought the conquest
would be easy.

No penetration was required
of you as I willingly slashed
and opened my veins for you
to feast upon.

Once my soul had been let,
the walk away from me
should have been a simple one.
But, in your vanity you forgot
that venom works both ways.

You have lost your power,
I have gained your strength.
You are now the bloodied victim.
I will haunt you with my
vampire gaze for the rest of your days.

Carina S. Dieringer

Erutan

The wind stands silent
The trees bow to pray
Boulders skip in the darkness
Leaves dart away
Water rises silently
The moon salutes the day
Clouds struggle noisily
Flowers nap in may
Lightening smiles timidly
Thunder swirls the hay
Snow bangs loudly on the rooftops
The sun has lost its way
Hail tiptoes to the ground
The deserts embrace the bay
Oceans ripple towards the vastness
Rivers are content to lay
Summer shivers relentlessly
The winter's here to stay
It was only a matter of time
Before we had to pay

James H. Vondrell Sr.

Love

Across the room,
The green eyes said:
"You are mine forever,
And I am yours for all eternity."

Across the bed,
The green eyes said:
"You are mine in love,
And I am yours in all ecstasy."

Across the years,
The green eyes said:
"You are mine in truth,
And I am yours in all sincerity."

Across the stars,
The green eyes said:
"You are mine forever,
And I am yours for all eternity."

Irene Urban

My Sister

If I could turn back
The hands of time,
I'd wish to be with my sister
with her hand in mine.

As time goes by
I realize more and more,
How precious my sister was
before she passed through heaven's door.

My sister fell prey to cancer
and God called her home,
and now deep inside
I feel so alone.

They say the pain won't last forever
and she'll always be in my heart
and someday I, too, will go to heaven
and there, we'll never part.

Donna D. Smith

Child Of Demeter

Forsythia is
The harbinger of spring.
The messenger of Demeter,
Bringer of joy to the Earth.
A saver of mankind
From the desolation of winter.
That is forsythia!

Each little blossom
Is a trumpet announcing spring,
Shining out into the hearts of others
With their golden radiance,
Living forever.
That is forsythia!

Charles J. Klement

Stressing "Stress"

It's stressing to be stressed about
  the stress that caused my stress
It seems I can be stressed without
A clue to my "Distress".
Distress is caused by all the stress
That comes from being blessed
With home and family no less
I'm stopping this I'm under stress!

Eris M. Orton

Family Lie

Lightning strikes, the pain it grows.
The heart will hide its joy down low.
What sorrow could this young man know?
Two years apart and best of friends,
a comradeship came to its end.
His older brother, and closest tie,
was brave and honored when he died.
This would be the family lie,
his death was ruled a suicide.
The young brother knows not why.
His pain and sorrow grows inside.
Joseph K. Russell

Waving Summer

Faded, not yet bright
The hues of gum and maple;
Air so crisp in autumn light,
Wispy trails from chimney gable.

Color through the scenic meadow
Leaves of brown and red and yellow;
Sunlight dimmed by hazy mist,
Wilted blooms the frost has kissed.

Preface to dead winters cold,
There comes the black skies, overcast;
Cattle huddled in the fold
Awaiting pastures newly grassed.
Eirlys E. Bailey

Autumn

The summertime is waning
The leaves are drifting down
A frosty chill now fills the air
The grass is turning brown

Across the hills and meadows
Which once were truly green
One can slowly close their eyes
And pictures life's long dream

No, it's not the grand finale
Of mother nature in her jest
Indeed, it's just another way
She passes a great test

Each and every one of us
Have tests we must endure
Sometimes we do not understand
And wonder what's the score

But if we live as God has chosen
Through all our cares and strife
He surely promised one and all
An everlasting life
Ann Porter

"Dying Wishes"

She slowly slit open the envelope
That held memories from so long ago
This was her way to find release
When she felt she missed him so.
She studied his scrolling script
Confessing his love for her
His death had torn her to pieces
Leading her health to deter
But soon her day would come too
She felt sure of this
And they could fly together
Totally in Bliss.
Christina Sones

A Sunrise

Today I watched a sunrise
The most glorious one as yet.

I can't describe the splendor
Upon which my eyes were set.

I stood in trance like wonder
And held my breath just still.

I watched the full ascension
Knowing God is real.

For man can never accomplish
The marvel I have seen.

In a day's beginning
Erasing yesterday clean.
Delia Powell

The Man Inside

What do you do with the man inside
the one who Feels the Pain
Sorrow of a Joy not known
a Fear he can't explain
the one who knows the Love you feel
Dr. Jekyl and Mr. Hyde
a Stoic warrior is the guise put on
by the Whimpering Child inside
there is a beggar constantly there,
he Begs of you today
once a king, but now to rags
you constantly Turn him Away
society Smiles at the masks we wear
but inside I want to Cry
the Poems we write, the Dreams we dream
like a flower Wither and Die.
Grant Wilcock

The Owl's Night

When everything's dark
the owl comes out.
He flies like an airplane
very sleek without sound.
Whooo, whooo, whoooo
that's his sound when
he finds food
Whooo, whooo, whooo
He catches it!
That's it for the rat!
Julianna Marquez

Our Heavenly Kin

No greater person can there be
than He who reigns above,
Yet while on earth He suffered so
To save the ones He loved

He felt the pain and sorrow,
the loneliness and fear,
of being just a human
for which we hold Him dear.

He understands your heartache,
The loss that you must feel.
He also knows that only time
will allow your heart to heal.

So in your midst of sorrow,
stop and think of Him,
for He is there beside you,
your closest "Heavenly Kin."
Jeanne Setters

Cat's Paw

Never underestimate
The power of
The paw:

It can diddle
Sort of fiddle,
Push things lightly
Oh, so slightly
Back and forth,
South or north,

Then hang poised
Pat gently,
Pop out claws,
And kill.
Christopher Young

The Words Of Eleven

Expected to be a poet
the reputation that I blew
I want to be judged differently
from my frantic point of view.

the proportions that I'm in
for myself I want to judge
and also the attention
for which I always budge.

as nights and days race
straight before my eyes
I hear the possessing songs
and the innocent cries.

the effective poems
that the true masters made
for me, my dream is different
before my soul they fade.

my touching, infinite poems
are already quite cold
as I'm in the eye of war
at eleven years old.
Igor Norinsky

"Love Of A Friend"

There are many degrees in love
  the strongest degree of love
is the love for our Creator
  without the love of our Creator
there would be no love at all
  the love one friend has for
another, is greater than the love
  of Lover's in love, it is an
inseparable love that only
  friends will know the real
feeling of that kind of love
  I've been in Lovers love before
but nothing comes close to the
  love that I have for
  My Friend Marie
James Glucksman

Untitled

Measure in your mind's space now
the subtle drift and sway
of the sailboats lying anchored
at their moorings in the bay

Though myself I see no sun, no sails,
no wind to make them fly
some latent longing for the waves
will drive them by and by
Janet M. Lumkes

"Darlene"

A garden of roses
the sweet smell of clover
the beginning of new life
each time spring starts all over
long ivy vines
that cover the walls
crystal clear water
rolling over the falls
the call of the wild
being played in the wind
long country roads
that twist, wind, and bend
a large flock of sheep
a small herd of goat
an old time castle
with dungeon, drawbridge, and moat
I love all these things
so gorgeous to see
girl, their beauty is excelled
only by thee!

Denis C. Leverington

"Why"

As I sit here alone soaking in my tears,
The tears of pain and loss.
I wonder why? Why did you have to go?
Why?
Was it something I said,
or something I did?
For I will never know.
What it was that made you leave.
I hope and pray every day,
that the love we once shared,
would be reunited,
and strong enough to survive,
life's long and twisted paths,
I hope...

Jessica Balderston

Lonely

It's quiet now
the fog hangs still,
A tender breeze
breathes like a soft caress.
Not daring now..
but then again
like a shy lover touching.

The muffled sound of waves
stealthily approaching
to drench the waiting sand.

A far out squeal..
A sea gull.
Its longing cry not answered.
Lonely..

John L. Coppejans

Morning Dew

As I walk along a hillside in
the morning dew, spiders have built
webs with a sparkle of new, sometime
in the night they mastery spun, a work
of art for the dew and the sun. The
light of the day shines through the
web to brighten the dew, the morning
has left. As I walk along a hillside
in the morning dew, the spiders at rest,
and the sun and dew are at there best.

Brenda Murphy

Life Exposed

Well, thinking that I should become
The thing I ought to be
My mind drifts back to former times
My memory wants to flee.

The past reminds me, oh so well,
Of things I've tried to do.
And then my brain reels to and fro.
What's this? I've lost a shoe.

I limp along, my foot's on fire,
The pavement stings my skin,
I know the pain black asphalt brings,
My socks are getting thin.

The naked foot knows pleasantries,
Because it dares to bear.
When open we can know the same,
Our life a must to share.

Pain may come when you're exposed,
But God will take that too.
You'll never know the joy that's there,
If life is in a shoe.

David Babcock

The Mystery

The mystery of it all...
The things that I can see,
The grass, the trees, the flowers,
The you, the him, the me.

The wonder and the majesty,
The strength that all possess.
The ecstasy of wanting,
And the awesome knowingness.

The silence of eternity
That sleeps in all that is -
The need of seeing all of this,
And still the need to give.

The passion and the sorrow,
The hurt, the joy, the tears -
The ever-present meaning
Of each one's hidden fears.

Yes, all things are so wonderful
Yet still it's hid away.
Why do we have to steel ourselves
From what we want to say.

Geri Cohen

Windows

The door closes, the room begins
    the time-warped journey
(Alone) the dark mind moves in
    cyberspace.
The chips, like stars, bits of flight
    like the night
    with light years, sparkling.
Polypheme corneal glows in place
Waiting to search upon command
The galaxies of virtual man.
Once was the soft needle tap
    on crystal the mystic
    potential of human possibilities
When Marconi held his sounds in the pin
    scratch snatched from the batch
    of the great surround.
What ship now in the odyssean kenoma
    What Aegean sea guides
    Our wanderer in the net to what port?

Herman S. Geller

It Could Be Me

The hurt, the anguish,
the turmoil of life,
occurs to every soul.
Some hold it inside striving
for self control.
  Seek rainbows and bubbles,
with someone who cares,
and shares your troubles.
  This person will be honest
and true, their efforts will
be for you, ultimately, perhaps
for two.
  It could be helpful,
let them in and be hopeful.
  If it feels true,
let it be... Dear Lady,
  It could be me.

Jim Allen

Love And Caring

Love and caring seem to share
The unseen edge of moving air

Yet the art in loving can make it last
Far beyond the iron they cast

Caring is the key
Sent from the soul

Holding the parts
For hearts to be whole

The meaning in
These moments spent

Can keep from life
The time we rent

Gary Freebody

The Silent Serenade

Surrounded by the sounds of inadequacy
The voice that taunts and reminds her
    "Not good enough,
    Not good enough"
This is the haunting
That takes away her right to live.

It seems that others have entitlement
But she is left with nothing.
She thinks there's proof,
She notices how well they look
How perfect their world appears to be!

She is separate from them
She feels it deep within,
For even when the voice is quiet
She hears its silent serenade.

Janice Brown Krolack

Mogieman

The mogieman can't dance
The mogieman can't sing
The mogieman can't see
The mogieman can think
The mogieman can dream
The mogieman works all day
And drinks

Darlene Davis

Fabric Of The Sky

Torn and ragged clouds descend
the wind has ripped - how can they mend?
they twist and roil and fiercely rend
the fabric of the sky

Broken clouds are hard to tend
like awful battles between friends
left drifting fragments at the end
of friendships new or old

Torn and ragged clouds descend
Who's right this time? Will no one bend?
will we no further message send
and hope that one will hear?

Refusing to give in to trend,
refuse to leave - a path to wend
reconcile and thus defend
against the lonely sky

Torn and ragged clouds ascend
the fabric of the sky
the wind that ripped them lifts and mends
the day for you and I

Alice J. Thomas

Angel Of Death

First great pain
then numbness comes,
death does reign,
your shell succumbs.

Your soul flies forever free
and to the skies you do flee.
Embrace the angel of sweet death
as your spirit takes deep breath.

To the stars you do soar
to see forever heaven's core
like a vision of pure love
floating as a dove above.

Ever seeking divinity's light
while soaring ever celestial heights,
you in space and time retrace,
you embrace God's giving grace.

Your spirit screams in deep delight
as with God you do unite.
The Lord rewards the very best
as this is life's last request.

Allan H. Lambert

Through The Child's Eyes

Through the child's eyes,
there is no black or white.
Through the child's eyes,
racial differences have no place in life.

Through the child's eyes,
rainbows are more treasured than gold.
Through the child's eyes,
a wish or a dream will never grow old.

Through the child's eyes,
life is a carnival of fun.
Through the child's eyes,
you can see the bright summer sun.

Through the child's eyes,
hate and war have no place.
And through the child's eyes,
people are simply one, great human race.

Jacqueline Grunau

Future Perfect

God closes the window,
Then opens the door;
It's new and it's frightening,
Never seen here before.
Oh, life was much safer
Behind those old panes,
But this newest adventure
Could be strewn with new gains.
Old ruts promised comfort.
Let's stay there instead,
For this portal before us
Seems framed with a dread.
Now wait, pause a minute;
We are in God's hands.
He's a reason for opening
This new door to new lands.

Jo Piper

Spring

The flowers in the spring are blooming,
there goes one and another one,
all the colors blooming bright,
all the stars sparkling in the night.

Beauty surrounds me
Beauty surrounds me
Beauty surrounds me

Baby animals drinking from a stream,
wondering how it is to dream.
Rainbows sparkling bright in the day,
rainbow please don't go away.

Beauty surrounds me
Beauty surrounds me
Beauty surrounds me

A dark night, no rainbows in sight,
no flowers, no sparkling stars, no baby
animals.

Beauty surrounds me
Beauty surrounds me
Beauty surrounds me
This is what is beautiful to me.

Ashley Russian

Reading

Exciting trips to old world countries,
Thoughts traveling to unknown boundaries.
Upon fantasy's enchanting wings,
A wealth of pleasure reading brings.

So many journeys there are to take,
Over oceans, seas and lakes.
To outer space or back in time,
To exploring the regions of the mind.

Hard at work are imaginations,
Researching ideas and situations.
To take the reader on joyful flight
To an adventure or mystic night.

Writing truth or rousing fiction,
Thoughtful poems or sound predictions.
Authors' writings open doors,
To peaceful sittings or raging wars.

So turn off the computer and the T.V.,
To yourself pledge a decree
To find a quiet, special nook,
Just for you and a very good book.

Jerry Reisner

Have Faith

Gun fires, echoes in the night.
There is no moon or stars
To see tonight
The sky lights up.
And one million souls
Leave the earth.

The earth trembles with fear
At the sound of death
I only hear
Tears of blood
I only cry
As I watch my children die.

I kneel and pray
And say onto thy Lord
When will you end this day.
And thy Lord said
Have faith
I will be there at heaven's gate

Freddy Nowbath

Untitled

In the beginning
there was no love or life
no church to say what's right
only instinct
pure delight
they say we've evolved
but that's not right
and in the end
when the story's been told
then you die
or just grow old
what will you be left with
besides your soul

David McCallum

Shadows

My son gave me the blue and white bowl,
the Wedgwood one
he carried back home
after his summer in Wales.

Only after,
ten years after his death,
did I look at the bowl
closely enough to notice
all the figures were women dancing.

Why
didn't I see more clearly
when he was with me
offering his love?

Joan Reynolds

Untitled

In our hearts
There is majestic beauty and truth,
Serenity beyond compare,
A silence who's unspoken words
have meaning...
A place where love's brilliance stirs
Silently, gracefully, intensely,
In fervent passions
burns our destiny.

Jessica Kelly Ebright

My Memory's Preserves

In the maze of my mind
there's a dark place I find
where I can be all by myself,
And the memories I find
in that place in my mind
are like preserves that I put on a shelf.

Each one has a label
and I find I am able
to take them all out, one by one,
And I examine with care
the sweet joys I find there...
the memories of love and of fun.

Like preserves held to light,
they're a wonderful sight...
All clear and glowing and new;
And when I'm all by myself
I reach onto my shelf
And examine, with love, one or two.

Claudette M. Mogle

"Someone Cares"

In all of life's problems
There's someone who cares,
Just reach out and touch Him
For He's always there.

He died on the cross
To redeem us from sin,
This "gift" He has given
For a "new life" to begin.

Our Savior is waiting
To bless you and me,
Just make Him your Lord
And from sin you'll be free.

He'll never forsake you
He'll always be true
If you ask, you'll receive
Because He cares for you.

Just praise Him and thank Him
And show Him your love,
And your life will be blessed
From the Father above.

Carmela Sanfilippo

To See

Their faces are angry,
  they're mad at the world.
They think learning is stupid,
  their thoughts of life a blur.

One try isn't successful,
  two go unnoticed.
    A third brings tears,
    the fourth - a friend that knows.

Knowing isn't everything,
  but trying should count for something.
I want to show you - my angry one,
  that failure, means nothing.
If you try and don't succeed,
  this means you're much like me.
For I have tried so many times,
  just for you to see.

TO SEE that what you think
  is not always what will be.

To make the best of every try,
  to spread your wings and try to fly.

Jennifer D. Jason

"The Time Of Indecision"

When I was very young.
They told me not to play with guns.
Later on, in my years,
They wanted me to kill.
  And the time of indecision
does grow near.
  Old enough to kill and die,
and never know the reason why.
  Still too young to drink or vote.
On a pad you're just a note.
  And the time of indecision
does grow near.
  When I was very young.
In my hands they put a gun.
Old enough to kill and die,
and never know the reason why.
  And the time of indecision
is here!!!!

Alvin R. Chappel

A Moment's Triumph

I can feel the excitement
  Thinking of how we met
That day I finally understood
  What I really wanted to get
After getting to know you
  Life has changed so much
I need to be real close
  And feel your warm touch
I miss you each moment
  You are not beside me
Without your endless love
  There is no life to be.

Arja Marttinen

The Wedding Gift

Though the marriage long over
  this kettle's now used
A happy reminder
  that I did not lose.

Perking hot water
  the cups are untold
Long hours of writing
  as stories unfold.

Grateful to have a beautiful pot
  whose water is boiling
  so my coffee stays hot.

My pen is my speaker
  my paper a map
But my pot full of water
  never takes naps.

Brenda Sue Ball

Super Hero

I ran away but just for the day
They asked me where I was going
but I didn't reply
It was an adventure
I sailed ships on roaring blue oceans
I walked across vast deserts
I fought fire breathing dragons
I swam with blue dolphins
I beat up our school bullies
I was a Super Hero
I ran away with my imagination

Callie Hammer

Bad Day

Today is a bad day for me.
This morning I could hardly see.
I couldn't even find my shoes.
I almost felt like singing the blues.

My shirt got ripped by the door,
and I had to go change once more.
Then my hair got in a knot,
and I burnt my hand on the coffee pot.

I have a headache and can't get it out.
My hand still hurts and I'm about to
SHOUT!

I'm having one of those bad days,
and I've been a terrible jerk.
The only thing that went right today
is that I remembered my homework.

Andrea Falk

A Bullet Has No Eyes

"Give them all guns," seems to be
  This nation's battle-cry,
Yet we all seem to forget
  That a bullet has no eyes.

You can accidentally kill someone
  Could be a friend that you meet,
Or it could be a passerby
  Who's strolling in the street.

You may be shooting at someone
  That you hate and despise,
Remember this word of caution
  A bullet has no eyes.

"I'm sorry," will not suffice,
  Though in deep contrition said;
Because of unthinking hasty action
  An innocent victim lies dead.

Guns are not the answer
  To the problems of your life,
Because you fail to remember
  A bullet has no eyes.

Eugene L. Cowen

I Heard It For The First Time Today

I heard it for the first time today
This new sound sneaking into my head.
It came softly into my mind to play
But I felt there was nothing to dread.

I heard with my eyes, ears and soul
Transported far beyond this place.
I stretched to reach a higher goal.
New horizons and a more gentle pace.

I heard the white clouds touch the sky
And seeds slowly growing in the ground.
I even heard time as it passed me by
And the sun as it made its rounds.

I heard the rain as it congealed to snow
The sound of wind before it was born.
The breathing of trees all in a row
And the music of quiet, I didn't know.

I stand on this bit of fine green earth
My spirit wanting to take wing, fly away.
What are the deeds of man worth?
I heard it for the first time today.

Harold Reider

Untitled

It runs into a dam
This river in my heart
I see tomorrows memory
Floating into parts

Rehearsing lonely messages
That only go so far
I look into my wisdom
Wondering how to start

Passages grow wider
And thinner while I walk
Leading to that river
I cannot even talk

Time is a natural weapon
It serves to no regard
Moving fast for nothing
Toward the river in my heart

Anne Buss

A Simple Smile

This action could change someone.
Though it's quite small on your part.
The most important thing about it
Is that it must come from your heart!

There could be someone hurting
Or facing a deep woe,
It only takes a small effort
But many blessings it could bestow.

This small action could encourage someone
To go the extra mile.
There are no limits to what you could do.
With just a simple smile!

April Keeton

The Wounded Heart

The wounded heart still bleeds,
Though just a drop or two.
A touch of sorrow lingers there
Quite hidden out of view,
Until the key called memory
Unlocks the door of time,
And for a brief eternity
You've crossed that fragile line
That separates the present
From yesterdays long ago
When sorrow first visited
And then refused to go.

Darcy Terpening

Footprints In The Sand

In the sand his footprints lie,
  Though many years have slipped away.
And in my mind, I look to see
  The shadows of where he used to play.

The echo of his laughter sounds
  As clearly as I heard him last.
The sweetness of his look and mien
  Are in my mind held safe and fast.

The earthly part of him—now gone,
  But mem'ries are mine, upon demand.
He's here—but not—yet part of me,
  As are his footprints in the sand.

Diane Elliott

God's Gifts

Faith is believing,
  though you can't see,
Hope is a yearning,
  for dreams yet to be,
Love is the greatest,
  God's gift from above,
Let's treasure all three
  faith, hope and love!

Trust is important,
  it comes from the heart,
Honesty is a whole,
  Not just a part,
Patience is necessary,
  You must not give up,
It takes all these
  To fill up a cup!

Dora Lee Campbell

Separation

  We've been together for years,
thought I knew the real you.
After all of this time,
I thought you knew me too.
  When we first met,
the small gestures we made.
A warm special feeling
inside us they gave.
  The years have gone by,
hard lessons we've learned.
The bridges we've passed,
are now bridges we've burned.
  All the time that it took
to make us feel like we do,
can't be erased
with a gesture or two.
  Even though we are parting,
who knows for how long.
The life that we had,
as it was, can't go on.

Crystal Liddy

A Turning World

If this world should turn on me.
This planet fade away.
Will you still love me, darling,
Forever and a day?

If people spurn and chastise
And weeping willows sob.
Will you still love me,
Darling my treasure not to rob?

Will you turn your face away
With coldness in your eyes?
Or will you grant your tender ways
And sweetness of your sighs?

If another world should beckon me
And God should call me near.
Would you bend and pray for me
And shed at least a tear?

I know that I should miss you, dear
If all these things were true
But for now, Sweetheart, I'll trust
In my great love for you!

Carole Fisher

Shackled

A poet's curse is dark and deep
Thousand secrets I must keep
Alone I wander on this path
Wrapped within word's cold wrath
Gypsy lines swirl in my mind
Seeking solace I cannot find
Ink pen running off the page
Fragments chase in fits of rage
Laughing muse holds all the powers
Enslaved, I toil and write for hours
Shoving me, snatching sleep
Shivering, alone I weep
In deep twilight I am drained
Blotches of ink the floor has stained
Servant left obeying master
Sweet delight embrace disaster
Ill control of ill defenses
Shackled to the heightened senses
Virus pillages through my skin
Inside an ending, I just begin...

Janeen Musselman

Falling Asleep

A sudden darkness
Through exhausted eyes.
A body at rest,
A mind at work,
Thoughts become a
Sky of visions.
A cloud of questions
Form in this atmosphere,
You Ponder thunderously
For answers.
The winds of thoughts
Drift you further on
Through unconsciousness.
Because of today,
What will become of tomorrow?
What will I do?
Where will I go?
What will happen to me?
What time is it?
What.............

Daniel Barker

No Time

  I am busy, very busy,
there is so much to be done.
I am busy, oh so busy,
I work from sun to sun.
I have no time to stop and chat.
I have no time to pray.
I am busy doing this and that.
I simply have no time today!

  So many tasks, so many chores.
Bake the bread, clean the floors.
Do the dishes, wash the clothes.
No time to stop and smell the rose.
Feed the stock, spin the flax.
No time to rest, no time to relax.

  I am busy, oh so busy,
I dare not pause to rest.
I am busy, very busy,
my life must pass God's test.
Somehow I must go on, each mountain
I must climb.
I cannot stop, I cannot rest,
for I do not have the time.

Janis L. Miller

Pumpkin Face

The candlelight flickered
   through the cut-out eyes,
The teeth were jagged
   and large in size.

The shiny orange head
   was big and round,
With a nose carved out
   like that of a clown.

It comes to life
   just once a year,
Its characters vary
   from smiles to fear.

The features start out
   with a good sharp knife,
Put a candle inside
   and it comes to life.

On a porch or a window
   you can find a place,
To show the world
   your little pumpkin face.

April Hawkins

The Wolf

Green yellow eyes
through the darkness
waits.

Listening for noises
that will not come
rests.

Odors flash past
the sensitive nose
searching.

One of many
the wolf howls
silence.

Driven by fear
and scents of blood
runs.

Never to return.

Gail A. Fox

Eulogy

Although I am just passing
through this world
I hope
that I can
leave behind
something
to remember me by.

For
If I came
went through
and left
there would be

Even if I am here today
and gone tomorrow
and I left a trace
of love
and laughter
in someone mind
then it is indeed
all worthwhile.

Charles M. Hempel

Cemetery

Let this be our home
'Til time be all gone
Cold is the ground
That lies upon.

'Til the day break
'Til shadows do fall
'Till all that are gone
Meet once and for all.

So shall we be silent
So shall we be free
We lie here in darkness
While waiting for thee.

Take your time coming
Your dreams be well meant
We will be here waiting
Cause ours have been spent.

Arthur L. Duteau

Little Guy, Little Guy

Little guy
tiny and white
brown eyed
and bright.
Wandered by
me in the
mid morning light.
Helpless and bewildered
of people in sight!
Touched the heart
of a passer-by
where and how
should such a
pet stray?
Little guy
Can't believe why,
such a poodle in
sight was
around to be found!

Dorothy Stamm

Dear Love

I sit here alone,
under the starry sky.
Thinking about us,
As the hours fly by.

Wondering if we can make it,
through the stormy weather.
And wishing on every fallen star,
that we will always stay together,

I broke your heart,
When we tried this before.
I only hope and pray,
You're not out to even the score.

This love that I feel,
is sincere and true.
And all that I have,
Will be given only to you.

I won't ask you to love me,
the way that I love you.
But, the one thing I ask of you
Is to always be faithful and true.

Holly Peterson

To And Fro

Our bodies sway
to and fro
please stay
please don't go.

Dancing with you
to this beautiful tune
nothing I can do
you must leave me soon.

Together we pranced
like flakes of snow
together we danced
to and fro.

Alun Harris-John

Be A Friend

No man should lie by the wayside as if
to be a mere discarded article.

Be my tender - receive my spirit,
make me once again happy.

Remove the cloud that hovers in my mind,
so I may see the right way more clearly.

Feel my presence and remind me of my
gentle touch.

Repair the worn edges of my woven will
with oh so easy kind words.

Nourish my humor with the simplest
of jests.

Reward me these pleasures and I
promise you indeed.

I'll be right beside you in your
time of need.

Greg Stevenson

Lord Send You An Angel

Lord send you an angel
To be by your side,
As you begin your journey -
May God be your guide.

As day begins to darken
And dusk turns into night,
May you follow the tunnel
To God's holy light.

May God bless you and keep you
In the palm of His hand,
As He leads you to -
His promised land.

Dorothy Plant

Pencil In Hand

Pencil in hand,
thought on your mind,
write the words
you wish to rhyme.

Inspirational thoughts
from a peaceful soul,
writing of heavens
and mountains of gold.

Dreams that escape
that make peace on the page,
flow through the hands
of the innocent age.

Jenifer Owen

Loneliness

To be lonely is wonderful,
to be lonely is horrible!
Sitting alone
under
the sun, the summer sky,
the darkening evening sky
full of stars, the moon
and the reddening sky
from the evening sun.
Sitting alone
listening,
the wind blowing, whispering
on evenings on the days of fall,
telling about dreams
and better days.
Seeing the snow touch
the white beauty of the mountains,
Hoping for the spring...

Gertrud Szeless

To Wait

I have to wait, I was told,
To be sixteen to drive a car.
I have to wait, I was told,
To be eighteen to go into that bar.
I have to wait, I was told,
To be twenty-one, they changed the rules.
I have to wait, I was told,
To send my children off to school.
I have to wait, I was told,
For the empty nest, left at home.
I have to wait, I was told,
For the Grandchildren, I was so alone.
I have to wait, I was told,
For Social Security to kick in.
I have to wait, I was told,
To see what the extra job would bring.
I have to wait, I was told,
To take charge, and be bold.
I have to wait, I was told,
I did. Now I am too old.

Judy Gregson

Reflections On A Summer Night

I wandered out one summer night
To see the August moon so bright.

The stars seemed few and far away
Because it was as bright as day.

The night was peaceful and serene
As moonlight bathed the entire scene.

The air smelled sweet with new mown hay,
A sign that Fall was on its way.

Off to the south were thunderheads
Flashing yellows, oranges, reds.

They were no doubt a somber warning
That rain could come before the morning.

Or perhaps they'd take to flight
And dissipate by cool of night.

The countryside was quiet and still
Save for a lonesome whippoorwill.

Long stood I there in awe and wonder
And listened to the distant thunder.

Man cannot copy tho' it be his whim
This splendid grandeur wrought by Him!

Fred Wagner

"Ebbtide"

"A dream conceived of life
to bear: to hold and mold.
To love and teach
The child within my reach.

A bat, a car, a job.
A toy, a trip, a boy
A smile away.
I cry in vain that day.

A doll to dress, a prom.
A kiss, the falls and calls
Of joys and tears.
Somehow we lost the years.

A forest, a clearing, a beach
To harbor love beyond my reach."

Jo Maschino

Silent Wonder

As the snow falls so silent
to blanket the earth;
I hear God whisper; "sleep
until spring, I'll give you new birth."
My old body aches as I lay down
and look to heaven above;
oh God! Dear God! "Will you show
me such love?"
When these tired, weary eyes
close for the last time;
will I awake to such beauty
divine?
When I enter the cold earth below
and I'm covered with this blanket
of snow;
I wonder if I will know.
Or will I lay there all dreary
and cold?
Never to see my rebirth; and
God's wonders untold.

Amy Bafford

"The Truth"

The beginning are from dying.
To fly, don't mind the wings.
The poorly guide who like the King.
Look for invert research the thing.
Tear of cry inside laughing.
Million of pounds found in shilling.
Lost of finger dreamer the ring.
Who was to leaved that is living.
Who close beside to hide the link.
Hardest outside, in vibrating.
Kinetic power offer rising.
Energy supply of mind living thing.

Choochai Rittiluechai

Untitled

How sad, when I became four decades old,
To know that I had been so cold
To people in my younger days,
To souls I viewed as enemies;
But oh! What joy to realize
As finally I am more wise,
And walk with people more warmly,
And they respond so beautifully,
That it is true; I know it, then,
People treat you as you treat them.

Dennis Ewen

The Pathway

He gave me the sun
To keep us warm
He gave us the moon
To light up our way
He gave us a pathway
To guide us to Him
He's waiting to see me
Running to him
I see Him smiling
Waiting for me
His arms are reaching
Reaching for me
He has a shelter waiting for me
My heart will guide me
Guide me to Him
Waiting, waiting, waiting for me
Running, running that's what I'll be
Running, running, running to Him
I'll make it, I'll make it
I'll make it to Him. Hallelujah, Hallelujah,
Amen.

Helene D. Piernowski

The Rose

How foolish of me
to liken love
to a rose.
How could I forget
that its petals wither
and the fragrance
is lost in time.
Oh, beautiful rose
that now is dead.
Take with you the thorns
in my heart.
That I may renew
my strength of love,
and seek it among the lilies
that leave no scar.

Elva D. McFarland

Dreams Don't Die

I had a dream
To live and die
In the country
Where I came to life
It's small
It's not rich
but has a sunny
And blue sky
I had a dream
To raise my child
In my country
Of blue skies
It was a dream
And dreams don't die

Francisco J. Sotolongo

Rhyming With War

The red in this Autumn's turning
Was not sufficient mourning.
The colloquy on why
Defeats the eye.

Color of another hue
Disturbs the view.
Is grey the shade of brain
Or just...
Of rain...pain...stain?

Edwin Charles Turner

Partial

All around me it crumbles
to my feet it falls
I try to pick up the pieces
they are scattered, they are shattered
into the eternal blackness they are cast
never to be retrieved again
I need them back
without them I am not whole
but maybe partial is better.

Whole with a hole
to be filled by images
times remembered, times lost
good times forgotten
or were there none
forgotten is good
to remember is to hurt
with nothing I am at peace
whole with a hole.

Chris Haley

Missing You

I wish I could call you,
to remind you, that I love you.
But I know you're asleep,
and I won't dare wake you.
I know it seems silly,
but I miss you so much
and just to hear your voice,
gives my heart your caressing touch.
It's so hard to sleep,
When I get that urge to call,
I know it wouldn't bother you,
you wouldn't care at all.
But I can't stand the thought
of disturbing your dreams,
So I just hope and pray
that they're made of you and me.
So Baby, sleep tight,
And remember I love you.
And keep in mind
that I'm always thinking of you!

Cindy Owens

What A Gift He Gave

People gathered around,
To see the awful sight,
Some out of sorrow,
Others out of spite.

No one seemed to realize
The sacrifice he gave.
They had no idea
He would go beyond the grave.

With holes in his hands,
And cracks in his heart
He opened the door
For salvation to start.

He saved our lives
On that glorious day
This is a debt
We never can repay.

This is a symbol
Of God's eternal love,
He's watching over us
From somewhere up above.

Jennifer Milhoan

"It's The Time Of Year"

It's the time of year, again,
To spread joy and good cheer;
Christmas carols and ringing bells,
Christmas day will soon be here;
It's the time of year, we know,
For special praise and deeds;
To help those in spirit low,
And those we find in need.

See us standing here in prayer,
Bending low in humble praise;
Bless our friends that they too share,
Joy and happiness from each prayer;
For one little gift, he gives you more,
It's love and kindness He has in store;
Yes He multiplies the deeds you do,
With joy and happiness He gives to you.

Anna L. Rodgers Blincoe

I Want To Be A Writer

I want to be a writer
To write a book one day
Sell a thought, idea
And, perchance, get paid

I want to be a writer
To see my name in print
Write the words, the stories
All the others didn't

I want to be a writer
To be someone, someday
Make the public happy
With what I have to say

I want to be a writer
I'm reaching for the moon
I'll write my books, my sonnets
And make the women swoon.

Douglas C. Schnitzler

"Say A Prayer For Me"

I may not be important,
To you or any others,
But I treat you as family
Like a sister or a brother,
I include you in my prayers,
Before I go to sleep,
So do the same as I,
And say a prayer for me.
It may not seem cool,
You may not even pray,
But if by chance you do,
Include me every day,
So when you're in church
Or praying on your knees,
Remember these words,
And say a prayer for me.

Daniel Raymond Munjak

Tears From Heaven

The only day the angels cried
Was the day Jesus died.
He died for you;
He died for me;
To save our souls eternally.
So next time that you see it rain,
Remember the hurt and the pain
The angels felt the day it rained.

Sheyenne Star

Life

Just you and me
Together
What a feeling
To love
To live
To help with healing
To share
To grow
To spend together
To dream the life
We'll have forever
And ever

Douglas Gray

Sixteen

Surly lips and hostile eyes
Unkempt hair and baggy clothes
Inertia and arrogance
Disdain and contempt
Reign.

Gone sweetness and honesty
Compassion and energy
Laughter and hope
Plans and dreams
Pain.

Cheryl C. Anderson

Growing

Life is like a pinwheel
that goes very fast.
You can't see any colors
and impressions don't last.

When the pinwheel slows down
you can see it very clear,
the colors, the shape,
the beauty that is there.

That's how we learn to love life.
We need to slow down,
before we can rest long enough
to take a look around.

Deborah Stoeckel

Years

Years are lovely fragile things
Treasures that I'm glad I own
Fruits growing near the Springs
From seeds that I have sown

They lie behind me sharp and clear
The years that I have spent
Their messages concrete and clear
Help me today to live content

They stretch before an endless road
To which I cannot see the bend
By which the Master lifts a load
Helping me to meet the end

The year I'm living in today
I hope will be the best of all
To make the past a more pleasant way
The future a vision to enthrall

Years are lovely fragile things
Treasures that I'm glad I own
Fruits growing near the Springs
From seeds that I have sown!

Helen O. Atkins

The Rose

A bud, it grows.
Up tall, into a rose.
It blooms, out bright.
Each day, each night.
It's picked, and placed.
It's watered, and vased.
Time passes, it grows.
Into a tall, and beautiful rose.
But soon petals, begin to fall.
And the smell, doesn't smell at all.
After weeks, petals dry.
The smell returns, it didn't die.
It has been now, one more year.
That I've held this rose, so very dear
And its memory makes me cry.
For now I know, it will never die.

Gina Marie Lunel

I Am Just A Puppet

There I stand
waiting for your command.
You will pull the string
and my heart will sing.
I'm all aglow, ready to go.
Given the chance
my feet will dance,
my body sway
to music gay.
Full of love and dreams
to last forever, it seems!
No thought of fear
or life so dear.
Suddenly the dance is over!
The strings broken, do not hover!
I stumble, then crumble
with a broken heart.
Just a puppet pulled apart!

Dorothy Baigle Schlesinger

My Prayer

Dear Lord, I sit in silent prayer
Waiting for Your direction.
The worries of my inner self
Need the peace of benediction.

In the peace and quiet of this room
I think of problems that I see.
The solutions do not seem to come
So I wait for word from Thee.

In this quiet prayer vigil
There is peace within my soul.
It's something that I've needed
To make myself feel whole.

Will you be with me, Lord,
As I go along my way?
Will You stay beside me
Through every coming day?

With You walking beside me
I can do the work to be done.
I'll look forward to the day
When a golden crown is won.

Frances E. Tolson

One Time

One time I was
walking on a hill and
wonder is there life to line,

One time I was
walking in the woods and
wonder is there life to live,

One time I was
taking to my sister and I
asks her is there life to live.

One time I was
taking to myself and
said yes there is.

Courtney McCranie

The Letter

A young couple
Wants a child
Their hearts are true
Their love is wild

They know everything
That they need to know
Or so they think
But it goes to show

That they know how
To love each other
And take advice
From their mother

A baby to us
Is all too new
We need to grow some more
And maybe get married, too

Perhaps to wait
Would be much better
But I still love you,
Said the letter

Catherine Wathen

Summer Heat

Summer suns beat down
upon my pastures, heat.
Summer touches create
and cool the dewdrops heat.
Summer breezes bring
the scent of roses, heat.
Summer heat waves felt
through hills and valleys heat.
Summer storms release
the building tension, heat.
Summer sunsets close in
dreaming languid sleep, heat.

Denise LeCompte

Reflections

Look in the mirror....
    What do you see?

A reflection of you
    Not of me.

I look in the mirror
    And I see too...

A reflection of me
    Not of you.

Christine Martin Jungels

Untitled

The one eyed monster
was on the prowl.
He peered out
through
his turtle neck
at all the gals
around.

His two swinging
friends who
accompany
him everywhere
wondered
where would he
strike tonight?
Would he find
a mound
in
some
uncharted
ground?

George T. Zane

Gifts From My Dad

Did you ever chase a sunbeam?
Watch the dust just settle down?

See a blade of grass with sparkle
From the dew that's on the ground?

Did you ever see a rainbow
Through the sparkling drops of rain?

Let it lift your heart to Heaven.
And forget its worldly pain!

Janet Washington

At The Shore

The sweet, soft sun does glisten
Waves beat against the shore,
They say that if you stop to listen
You'll always come back for more.
Today there are few quiet places
As peaceful and perfect
Here you'll see no anguished faces,
Things are all they seem to be.
The sun is slowly setting
The clouds are pastel hues.
I can feel the rippling water
Slapping against my sandals
Suddenly the spell is broken,
I snap back into reality
As I turn to leave the shore behind,
I leave a piece of me.

Crystal R. Gonzalez

The City

Come to the city and you will see
what a wonderful place it can be.
They have pollution you can see,
smoggy air and hardly any trees.
There's a lot of love but a lot of fear.
If you come to the city you can see
the people living off the streets.
They have no home to call their own.
They beg for money just to get along.
So come to the city; it's my home made
up of buildings, cars and telephones.

Amber Hansen

Who We Are

We got soul.
We be rhythmic.

We flow with our stride,
We flow with our words,
We flow.

We're artist.

We sing with our voice;
We paint with our thoughts;
We create with our hands.

We're endurance.

We've survived the past,
We survive the present,
We'll survive the future.

We're black.

Black as in ebony,
Black as in bronze,
Black as in BLACK.

Ernest F. Pettus

In A Moment

In the brief course of our gathered days
We do not often see what shines
In an instant, like a brilliant ray
Of sunlight peeking through the blinds.

These golden moments pass us by
With just the slightest whisper
It pleads, "lift up your shaded eyes"
My glory soon will wither.

But not to hear we often choose
In times so unrelenting
for all the things we fear to lose
hours lost we're left regretting.

Still, sometimes by chance we lift
our bowed heads from the ground
and risk our bleared gaze to drift
upwards to endless skies abound

And in that moment all is right
the world lies with a cloud
and on the wings of birds in flight
our hopes may shout aloud.

Carrie Olsen

Children's Prayer

Dear Jesus of Divine Mercy!
We don't know a lot about you,
but we know,
You are Truly God.
  You are the Savior and have
  angels singing at your throne,
  You are the King,
  the thorns in the crown.
We need you, Jesus,
Like flowers need rain,
We need you, Jesus,
to hush our crying and pain.
  Give us your Holy Grace,
  over the bad things we meet,
  Bless us dear Jesus,
  this is the most we need.

Bless our homes and country,
from sea to shining sea,
Let us trust in you, Jesus,
of Divine Mercy.

Irene Trippod

Yearbook Memories - Edition II

Twenty-five past years ago
We each chose different ways,
Not knowing how our lives would change
Beyond those "Senior Days."
Our morals, values, faith, and dreams
Were all put to a test
Throughout the years that followed
As we reached, to grasp our quest.
Tonight, as we drift back in time
Another memory's born,
Another channel from the past
Begins to take its form.
This form, will "shape" our memories,
to bond, throughout our lives,
For even when we're not in touch,
Our connection never dies.
A connection of these "moments,"
Small fragments, etched, so bold,
Of hearts sharing some memories
Form the days of "Wine and Gold!"

Glenda Willis Shelton © 1995

To Be Another

In our humanness
We long to be another,
With Fame or with fortune,
Had we our druthers.

To be as they
Along life's road,
No cares, no worries,
A lessen of load.

But should we rise
To take their place,
It's not as it seems,
This different pace?

The pain and suffering
That lies within
This struggling soul
Has made us kin.

But what is irony
In this I see,
It was I myself,
They longed to be.

Elizabeth A. Arnold

Life

Life is like a rose
we start as a bud
and slowly grow.
Our petals
so velvet soft
show us a life
to have, we ought.
But as the velvet
so soft to the touch,
starts to spread, and such.
We understand
that thing called life.
That once so beautiful
and sweet to sight
will shrivel up and
die without the light.
We start as a bud
and slowly grow
and that, my friend, is why
Life is like a rose.

Candice Eberhard

"Church On Sunday"

We have come to
welcome our waveless
soldiers. We have
grown content and
have found solace
in patriotic silence.
The greeting of
the windless flag
is nostalgic in
its peaceful lay.
Who stirs up
the chaos, where
is one guilty of
wrong. Evil America
blessed by media
power in their infamy.
Local hero lost in a column of
a small town newspaper
next to a bad movie review.
America's cup is half full.

Don Tjernagel

Untitled

My feelings for life,
were stopped at age seven.
Became afraid to be a wife,
and didn't want to go to heaven.
Pain, and fear was no way to mine.
They held me prisoner, for a long time.
To stand and commit,
was hard for me to do,
until chock made me submit,
and strong love, me woo.

The key wasn't found,
until a chock to the heart,
made rhymes the sound,
and songs take part.
Now, I'm in another world,
Where I can let go.
I feel like a young girl,
with a future to sow.
It might be a new fresh start,
that has finally caught my heart!

Elena Kristina Reese

Memories That Last

My parents taught me right from wrong,
  Were there to understand,
Then I had children of my own
  To proudly hold their hand.

I look back to those by gone days,
  Great visits to the zoo.
Camping trips away from home,
  Boat rides and fishing too.

Carnivals, candy and ice cream cones,
  'Tho wealth was not our style,
But we were richer more, by far,
  We had each other's smile.

The precious, good things I recall
  And as the teardrops start,
Our souvenirs of happy times
  Remain within my heart.

While gazing through my pictures
  With fond thoughts of years gone past,
For generations down the line
  Will have, "Memories that last."

Edith M. Kennedy

Dreams

Dreams.
What are dreams anyway?
Are they something that you want?
Are they something that you need?
Are they there to comfort you?
There to tell you somehow
That you will succeed?
Will they be good?
Will they be bad
Will they just tease you,
about something you wish you had?
Or are they there to guide your way,
through this horribly dark world?
To make sure you don't get lost?
Make it to the other side,
And without ever saying a single word?
Dreams.
Do you really need them?
I would say you do.
Because without dreams,
What on earth would happen to you?
Brandy Fleming

Colors

What does a box of crayons have?
Well look inside
and you will see
the magical land of crayons.
Dragon wings
and big green leaves
Colored in so light
that you can't believe your eyes
so brown like a twig
so high in the sky
that you can see a rainbow
with red, yellow, purple and green,
so if you want to see what
I can see
then open a box
and let your imagination
travel into the world of
crayons!
Jessica Boo

Never Alone

With each footstep I take along the sand,
My prints are washed away behind me.
The waves of the ocean continue to roll in,
And thousands of sea shells are scattered
Upon the nearly deserted beach.

I feel very alone and far away from God.
With each step I have a yearning
For a renewed peace within my heart.

I wonder if I can find a conch shell.
I don't know why I even want one.
The sand is cold, Lord, and so am I.

And then I see a shell, so very small,
A conch shell, perfectly formed.
And then, a few steps beyond,
A butterfly skimming the water.

Oh, Heavenly Father, how great is your love,
To give me a miniature shell for my hand,
And a butterfly for my spirit.
Once again, Lord, you have shown me,
I am never alone.
Susan McAllister

Unwelcome Companion

The night is long, lonely and dark.
My pain is pounding, persistent and sharp.
Sleep would be welcome, but it will not come,
Not till the pain is finished and done.

The hands on the clock are ever so slow.
I'm tired and I'm weary, with no place to go.
The pain overwhelms me, consumes me like flame.
Its power is horrendous; it surely will maim.

Pain's power can be weakened, its hold can be broken,
but it's harder at night when the silence lies molten.
The next pain pill is three hours away.
I hope the last pill will hold it at bay.

I long for the time when it no longer plagues me.
When nights will be restful and I will be pain-free.
No more aching, or throbbing, piercing or such.
Pain, please go away.
I've had more than enough.
Sara Jo Helm

Grandma

Even though it is far in the past,
My pain still lasts and lasts.

I wonder if she's watching me in the bright blue sky,
Trying to comfort me when I cry.

I wonder if she remembers Cumberland,
With its beautiful water and softly blowing wind.

I wonder if she hurts as much as we do,
I wonder if she tries to comfort Grandpa, too.

I wonder if she lives in a happy place,
Where she's an angel dressed in lace.

Maybe she's a teacher up there, too,
Just like what she used to do.

I hope she got to see the pond she started,
If not, I'm sure she's broken-hearted.

Sometimes when I'm up in my favorite Pear Tree,
I look up at the shining stars and say,
"I miss you, Grandma, I wish you were here with me."
Trista Lumpkin

That Woman

I wanna be that woman who will:
    make you smile with thoughts of your destiny,
        shiver inside the breeze of my ecstasy,
            Ah, so next to me. So sweet, so sexy, I hear you say yes to me.

I wanna be that woman who will:
    empty your dreams into reality,
        make you come, ever so delicately...to me.

I wanna be that woman who will:
    follow your lead and not inquire,
        swallow your need with my desire,
            cool you with my fire - icy-hot, until you tire.

I wanna be that woman who will:
    make you call out my name in a whisper not even you can hear.
        but only to my ear is it clear, that you are near.

I wanna be that woman who will:
    meet you more than half-way, insist you say what you may...to me.

I wanna be that woman who will:
    move time ahead one half day to make love to your shadow.
    make you speak without choking, on words unspoken, and say
        "you are that woman for whom I'm chosen."
Michelle E. Ford

Earth Is Hard

Accept the children
love them all the same
carry their tears for them
in the buckets of your heart.

Feed them love
when they starve inside
look beyond what they show
at everything they hide.

We are all children
pupils of the earth
growing up does not mean we stop embracing
we need to feel the waters of love
as we swim our life long streams.

Can we embrace the frightened children in each other?
Before we lose each other
to an earth that won't stop spinning
to a world that won't stop sinning.

Earth is hard
life should be easy
love with all your might, and it will be.

Stacey Handler Gerber

Untitled

The bombers little friends
Luck became their only ally
The bomb drop ability to take flak and
survive - fighter and flak (those who failed their country)
B. M. Bombers Moon, the price of dignity sat that coffee on
make enough for me to share with
It looks like you'll be gettin' out
of here your ability to turn food into
energy your body has to get the vitamins
and minerals it needs peak performance
Which vitamins should you take using a
scientific formula created by a doctor -
Abdominal strength if you're tired of livin'
it's as quick a way as going as I know
It's wonderful what a new sent can
do for a man - sifting our thoughts
through the word of God and using the will
of God - she wasn't much of a cook
but he ate everything she put before him.
He didn't kiss her goodbye because he didn't think of it.

Farrel

God Has Not Forsaken You

Sometimes you are up, sometimes you are Down,
Sometimes it seems as though you are Bound.
It may look as if everything is going Wrong,
Your body feels weak instead of feeling Strong.
But remember your Strength God will Renew,
For God has not Forsaken You.

Yes, sometimes you wonder, has the Lord forgotten You?
You may even say to yourself, Oh well, what's the Use?
You call upon God and it seems as though He didn't Hear,
You look around for a Friend and there is not one Near.
But remember your Strength God will Renew,
For God has not Forsaken You.

You Pray as you go along your Way,
But still feel like a Castaway.
You ask the Lord, Oh Lord, Oh Lord, How Long?
I haven't turned my back to Thee or did Thee Wrong.
But remember your Strength God will Renew,
FOR SURELY, GOD HAS NOT FORSAKEN YOU.

Mary Isabell Coleman

Man And Machine

They don't make them like they used to
Machines were easy to use
When men handled them, then women got confused

We weren't allowed to work out of the homes
But inside, we had to work harder
Machines still run, and men lost their sense of humor

They say it's a man's job
Today women have turned those knobs

Men and machines, it's not that easy
Oil them regularly to keep them rust free

Some men are machines

A faithful dog is a man's best friend
Men and machines break down
And we women gotta pick them up and put 'em back together again

If only he can be at his master's side

So do you still think it's a man's world, 'cause if you do
Make room 'cause it's a woman's world too

Your senses should be keen, about man and machine

Tisa Green

Wind

Wild winter wind within me
   makes a vast grey sky of my soul.
O how I behold with envy
   all of those who have a fire for the cold.

Wild winter wind unrelenting,
   will I ever know that warm days are real.
O how can I help resenting
   all of this bitterness I feel?

For no matter where I go
   all I find is ice and snow
and the howl of this demented wind.
   O where or when will the searching end?

Wild winter wind should I fight you,
   like the limbs on the bleak and barren trees?
Or should I simply invite you
   and surrender to your freeze?

O no! Winter wind, only after
   I have found my summer meadows green
and my heart has melted to laughter,
   not till then may you sweep away my dream!

Robert Alford

Laughing In The Wind

Just standing there the only movement it
makes is the swaying with the wind... tall
with its age there is a knowledge of life
It sees all standing there reaching out into the sky. The secrets
that it knows are a treasure within themselves... if it could speak
what would it say? Sometimes when I'm alone in the wilderness I
sit and meditate trying to find peace with myself,
but then my thoughts are interrupted by a leaf leaving its home and
falling to the earth in despair. Then I feel a tap on my shoulder,
It is a branch.
Is it telling me to leave so once again peace will be stilled in the
forest... And as I sit I hear whispers and voices there saying so
much, but they are so far off in the distance.
Is it that there's nobody there at all?
Is it my conscience speaking to me?
Or is it the tree, laughing in the wind?...

Ron D. Scavone

"Fading"

Mom you've always made all bad things go away;
Making my fears erode like an incoming tide to a child's sand castle.

I need you now to take away my fear.
Fear of my life fading, slowly disappearing.

I stand alone here with my pain. Mom can't save me;
God has forsaken me; Now I must fade.

Fade to a cruel world of indigents and suffering.
Serve my dues with a tainted soul.

How will I tread on, day by aching day?
With love and joy slowly fading away.

Mommy are you there? God do you hear?
No one hears my cry.
Stop the pain, stop the fading; I would rather die.

Jesus doesn't want me for a sunbeam.
Sunbeams aren't dirty like me.

When I was a child, I had dreams to carry my life on.
Clean of pain and suffering, Pure with love and without the fading.

Fog surrounded me. Opened my vision to a future I deserve.
Left me time, Left me pain, Left me tears,
Left me blame, Left me here.

Michael L. Logan

Tears Of Nature

Natures cries, tears resembling ashes
Man destroys, the stal gives way to radioactive steel
Leaves fall as tears, man cuts, burns his existence
Death's thirst is satiated by emptiness
Nature sheds its tears but man exterminates,
Man destroys his life
Smoke billows in the name of predatory capitalism,
In the mane of planet's death, but this is big,
Nature sheds its unending tears
Life does not matter at all, since thirst is bigger,
Blindness is everywhere, man kills...
He seals his self-destruction
Nature sheds its tears in the name of man,
But the human being is blind,
Thirst is big, the world gets small...
Existence slowly dies away, like sunset
Putting an end to life
But the human being annihilates,
Up to the last day when the tears of nature,
Will be shed in his name...

Marcos Tiberio Lima

I Feel Restless...

Tonight I feel restless and pretty soon
the clock will strike about three o'clock in the
morning.
  Dear Lord,
    I really do have a lot on my
mind. But, somehow it's quite difficult to
give you my troubles so that I can get
some sleep.
  Maybe it's because Len and I had
an argument, or maybe it's the fact that
Mom died of cancer about 8 months ago.
  Or could it be that I'm just
lonely for the man that I love?
  It's hard to say, but hopefully
my day of sabbath will be a lot better.
  I'll now close in the name of
your Son, Jesus Christ. Amen.

Deborah Fountain

Man

Of all God's creatures on the Earth
Man stands as the first
He stands on the house top, and in a loud voice he sings
I am the Master, the Ruler, and King.

While the deer may run with accelerated speed
Man with his automobile can him supersede
While the fish may plunge in the might deep
Man with his submarine can with him well compete

While the lion may roar so loud and strong
Man with his radio can be heard in foreign homes.
While the eagle may look the sun in its face
Man with his telescope can see the sun's make.

While the bird may fly through the distant space
Man with his airplane can him overtake
While the tiger can fight with unusual might
Man with his machine gun can him put to flight.

Man can accomplish feats of this kind
Because he is endowed with a noble mind
A mind to think, plan and dream
Because of this He is Supreme.

R. B. Garrett

Between Obsessions

Give me a fetish and compulsive behavior
Mania I can use for some kind of strange savior
A single passion to direct all my care
A person, place, or thing, a bizarre cross to bare

Waiting around for another one to come along
It's gotten a bit dull and feels all wrong
Can't make them come, can't make them go
Like telling the wind which way to blow

I'm stuck in between obsessions
I don't know what to do
My heart and soul is in a recession
I need a fixation to help get me through

Something on which to focus my attention
Blinders in place and extreme tunnel vision
They're never perfected I've tried and tried
Obsession refuses to be satisfied

Do it to death, start and stop
Climb up a mountain without any top
Peaceful and still seems like a depression
Waiting around on another obsession

Rick Sands

We Can Agree

Man, through the ages has always had
Many differences, some good, some bad;
Which he has, in various ways
Tried to solve throughout his days.
And though from time to time we strive
O'er things which matter not, it's drive
That pushes us on in the fray
To become a hero, just for the day.
Then when the battle is finally o'er
We find that our differences are as before;
All the while knowing they mattered not;
Our minds not working, 'cept on the plot.
But when our minds do finally see
That understanding, 'tween you and me,
Would have settled the squabble at the start
It would have changed history, in part.
So as time continues to go on and on
Our thoughts can cover the undertone
Of disagreements, here and there
If with our fellow man we will be fair.

Margaret Good

My/His/Story

My peoples originated from her—the Motherland—a continent which lies many miles across the sea; the land of the warm sun and the Sahara, the fig, and the date free. My great, great grandfather called this land Afrika; but, he did not spell it with a "C"; for that was once our land—the land that belonged to you and me. My ancestors sat along the banks of the Kembe Bolongo and watched the young ones as they quietly played; while speaking tongues long forgotten to us, beneath the Baobobs' eternal shade. Look deep into my face and into my beautiful brown eyes and you will see, my sisters and brothers, where our true history lies. You might gaze upon my Afrikan features and wonder: Are they not unlike his?— My great, great grandfather—the mighty King Osiris? Perhaps my original home was Mali; maybe Tanzania, or might I have come from Morocco? Of one thing I am most certain: I might never ever know. Through trickery, lies, and awful deceit, he entered into her precious lands. And robbed and raped her of her treasures; then destroyed her with his own two hands. Our vast knowledge, this man stole; and our precious history he erased; And as if that were not enough, he then stole us here to this place. He deleted an entire history—our history—which would explain the false smile; And for the greatest crime ever committed, this devil will never stand trial.

Kwakou Casselle

In Memories

May the beautiful sea of life be calm
may the sky be clear above the palm,
and the lust of a sunny day's fashion
strive through the heart in meditation.

Think of these thoughts as the cloudy past.
as the dream, the dreams which always last,
until the midnight clock will strike
and take them for the final hike
from the surface of this aged old earth
into the warm bosom of a grave's heart.

Preserved humanity in vaults?
Though lasting flesh has faults;
but continuing mankind in eternal strive
will speak of a human soul and heavenly life.

The burning flames of many, many lives
flicked through human kindling desires,
until the charcoaled aches lie.
In the path of the wind — away they fly,
oh, mankind's fate to live and die!

Rudolph H. Wahner

Poetry About Still I Rise

You may write me down in history With your bitter twisted lies.
You may trod me in the very dirt But still like dust, I'll rise.
Does my sassiness upset you? Why are you beset with gloom?
Cause I walk like I've got oil wells Pumping in my living room.
Just like moons and like suns. With the certainty of tides,
just like hopes springing high, still I'll rise.
Did you want to see me broken? Bowed head and lowered eyes?
Shoulder falling down like teardrops. Weakened by my soulful cries
does my haughtiness offend you? Don't you take it awful hard
cause I laugh like I've got gold mines Diggin' in my own backyard.

You may shoot me with your words. You may cut me with your eyes.
You may kill me with your hatefulness but still like air I'll rise
out of the huts of history's shame I rise up from a past that's rooted
in pain I rise I'm a black ocean leaping and wide welling and
swelling I bear in the tide leaving behind night of terror and fear.
I rise into a day break that's wondrously clear.
I rise bringing the gifts that my ancestors gave.
I am the dream and the hope of the slave. I rise. I rise. I rise

Tomara Thomas

Reunion

The magic of reunion, as alumni often know,
May well awake emotions fast asleep since long ago.
They ebb and flow, come and go, as each memory we tell
Reverberates and penetrates like a slowly tolling bell.

In and out of time we drift, the living of our stories
Coming nearer, coming clearer, as we dust off faded glories
Of our youth—its foolishness obscured by years
Filled with laughter, filled with tears.

Returning does become our aid in turning back the pages,
Sharing chapter after chapter once closed by passing ages.
We begin to realize, as we pause and do remember,
That this age, too, is passing quickly — fading, as an ember.

As we meet again together and reflect upon the old,
We reaffirm the friendship we should cherish more than gold;
And welcome opportunities to rekindle warmth since ended
With kindness toward those friends whom we once may have offended.

Some are here, some passed on, their images so kind.
We see them as though yesterday, their faces in our minds.
God bless and keep us evermore in friendly, good communion;
May we live and die in fellowship, and look forward to Reunion.

Link W. Llewellyn

The Exit Sign

I softly speak to the presence itself
Me getting the outlook, it disappears
Leaving me with nothing but my integrity,
I cease to make ends meet

Looking up, I pray
That nothing will ever happen that happened today
Turning on my past, dwelling on the future,
I keep looking for that red-blinking EXIT sign.

Leigh Chadwick

Seeking A Friend

Friends are something very dear,
something I'll always hold near,
someone I'll let see the tear,
only if I know they really care.
I seek to find a true friend,
on one I know I can depend,
who will try to help my heart to mend,
and not use me as a passing trend.
I've had many in my life,
through all my troubles and strife,
but they've all carried a knife,
Maybe I'll have to search for the rest of my life.

Sonya Lanier

Fire

Rising in the blue mist sky was a fierce,
Lying, deceiving coward that lay beyond the shadows,
Hiding in fear of recognition. It led us away in a
disguise that we had never seen with such magnificent
surrender. As we looked in the far north we noticed
that this devil had emerged in the dark and made the sky
fill with sadness. The sapphire sky was leaping in laughter
towards the innocence. We knew safety was far, yet the strong
would make it and the weak would have a new home. Then suddenly
mother nature appeared with a roar and the wind arising in
air. With sudden rain the devil would soon be gone. In
knowledge that it had a sweet defeat. As it left in the mist
from where it had arisen. The rain had defeated the devil and
they knew it put up a good fight, yet they knew
nothing about victory!!

Maea Ross

The Victims

For once in my life I felt so complete because of the love you gave to me. You opened my heart to feelings so new and in a short time my feelings grew into something so special, something so deep, you were in my waking and in my sleep.

I gave you my heart so easily, never realizing what pain could be. I now walk through life so cold and alone because my heart is not my own. I gave it to you willingly; there is no one to blame, but the victim is me.

Never once did I think that you would cheat and when I found out, it hurt so deep. I left the present and live in the past. Oh why, oh why did your feelings not last?

You cast me aside for a love not so true but now you believe the victim is you. You say, you want me back, if I can explain why I walked out and left you with pain without any reason, without any cause, leaving you the victim nailed to the wall.

We gave our hearts so easily without realizing what pain could be. We don't walk through life now cold and alone because our hearts are not our own. We gave to each other willingly; there is no one to blame and now we can see, the victim was you and the victim was me.

Patrice Adams

Never

And such pleasant
Memor-ease
Cold reality loses to the
Glowing warmth and found recollection
And if you die tomorrow, it's no
Goodbye
I say hello, I don't need eyes to see you
I have a heart
I say hello because you will always
Be a part within me
Inside forever in thought
I say hello for you shall remain
Immortal in the hearts of your friends
Immortal in the hearts of your offspring
Immortal in the hearts of the many
Who have loved you
Immortal you shall remain
Bodies cease to exist
But you will never die!
Never

Michael Osborne Griffin

Feelings

Tell them to come to a hush,
men say women talk too much
keep them to myself,
  or share them with someone else?
De-emphasize feelings, what to do with these dealing?
God gave Jesus to save
Yet, feelings are to be silent...at times they become violent
Ignore them!
  How long till the end?
Learn to shut them off, or you will be scoffed
Express anger, depress danger
Own not own emotions, my heart's devotion
Surrendering to what can be done
  to only the feelings of the Son
We can... it's God's plan
Don't cut them from who you are,
because it'll drive you far
it isolates, violates
Deal with feelings, even those can be changed
Hurt is exchanged, no longer estranged.

Oneida Higginbotham

O! Jesus

O, Jesus! You came to this earth with a peace message from God.
Came to this earth, to deliver a philosophy of a healthy life. And a way for survival.
You adopt in yourself, but they are,
learned by others, but they are.
But you sacrificed for them.
They break down, not break your philosophy,
theory of principle and make a sweeter way.
You will return to this earth again,
this is true?
Alas! Then they don't recognize you.
Perhaps, they will ask you, who are you?
Where are you from?
Perhaps you will express, a deep sorrow.
And you will say "Why did God revive me?"
Human beings don't know how life began.
Except the creator knows, who created this earth and all galaxies.
This is the time to come back again, O Jesus.
Come back again, come back, O Jesus.

Mohammad S. Arefin

Caught In The Storm

Lightning flashed across a sky that was darker than a half dozen midnights. Thunder roared with the sound of a thousand trains, and I shivered as the cold rain battered me like a giant battering ram. I had no idea that this was the beginning of the end. With numbed fingers I clutched my coat tighter. I was being drenched by the waters of racism, the rains of oppression and the moisture of indifference. As I struggled to open my umbrella of employment which was to provide some shelter against this storm, I realized with horror that the waters of racism had reach flood level. As I screamed for help, Uncle Sam threw me a life preserver made of affirmative action. I slipped it around my neck and I begin to sink faster! Affirmative action had been replaced with quotas. To prevent me from drowning Uncle Sam threw out some more government assistance. As I stretched forth my dying hands to grasp this life saving floatation device, I realized with a horror that was felt in every nerve of my body, he hadn't thrown a flotation device at all, it was a tombstone. I lost all hope of survival. I took one last look at my Uncle and He was smiling. After sinking to the bottom of the sea of racism, I read the inscription on the tombstone. "Here lies another good ni****." I took one last dying breath before succumbing completely to the freezing depths of hatred.

Richard H. Hill

Unaided Brother

My brother was born screaming,
miserable though adored,
by mother, father and me was
that wretched infant, oh wretched infant.

My brother grew taller, thin and handsome
a scholarly student,
friendless boy, angry relative was
that unloveable child.

My brother left home young, college-bound
rarely visiting, seldom calling,
forgiven and missed only by
that poor mother.

My brother returned home degreed and greedy
mother didn't guess, father didn't care,
only I knew
that gay is not happy.

My brother died screaming
denying his diagnosis, mad and in pain,
wanting no family or friend at his side so
that he was still lying, in his coffin.

Marilyn E. Gould

I Love You, Mom

As the sky is blue and the grass is green,
Mom, I see you as my caring queen.
You cared much for me, when I needed you most,
You have been my teacher, nurse, friend and coach.
Not the long and short of time, nor the distance of space,
Can ever destroy our mother-daughter state.
You're a very special lady, and I'm happy to tell you so.
Because I love you, Mom, this I want you to know,
All my childhood memories, both good and bad,
Help me to be grateful for the good mother I have.
Faults and failures, surely, touch us all,
Yet, the great God of love and forgiveness still calls.
Despite hard trials and heartaches that have come your way,
You're able to smile as God blesses you, Mom, day by day.
I will praise the Lord Jesus for and with you now,
Since Motherhood we share, today, before you,
   Dear Mother, I bow!
Verlyn D. Williams

Oh What The Hell!

My childhood was a funny thing.
Mom or Dad never saw me play ball.
They never saw me score a touch down.
They never listened to my Oratorical Declamations.
My mom never liked the girl I liked.
They both said I would never be any good.
Standing tall, I was undefeated in Debate,
Speech and Extemporaneous Speaking.
My girl and I were the best dancers, we looked
like we were made for each other until she
dumped me for a rich guy with a convertible.
Well, my best friend Buddy is now my age.
Our eyebrows have a few white hairs.
My legs creak and amazingly, I've shrunk
an inch, or two, but oh what the hell,
isn't this life?
Michael R. Tully

Reminisce

I never loved anyone quite like you, I cherish the
  moments we spent.
Whenever I see you I can't forget, how together we
  walked hand in hand.
When we walked on the beach in late June or July,
  I remember how our kiss was so real.
How we shared a love of friendship and passion,
  of romancing and often of sadness.
But each moment I spend without you is an eternity
  that is too hard to bear.
My heart aches to see you just one last time even
  if it is only a glance
Our two hearts again will beat as one and we'll
  make the minutes fly by.
I hope and pray that you love me too or these
  feelings don't mean a thing.
If this love isn't shared between us then I might
  as well give-up now, because a couple needs
  more than one love, it needs two loves to be shared.
K. Dukes

Parting

Parting of many years of pleasure and sadness
Memories of success and failure.
Years have passed so long ago, with thoughts
Of tomorrow never ending
As the morning sun shines ever so brightly
The dream of days to come will endure in my
heart and soul
As I look to the future around me.
Myrtle Butcher

The Street

My street was more than a street to me,
More than broad lawn and spreading tree.
In fall, the people went to town
And watched the leaves come drifting down.

The winter brought the soft white snows,
And then the icy north wind blows.
In spring we saw the brand new bikes,
And then went on some late spring hikes.

It's playing in the summer rain,
And now and then a bitter pain.
I remember the night the whole street cried,
The night a small black cocker died.
Marilee Dodimead

Technology Revives Irving Berlin

Dial 1-800—a toll free call.
Morning or evening, any time at all.
Press 1—for information, 2—for registering a
complaint.
3—for explanation of your bill, 4—if 1, 2,
or 3 your problem ain't.
"Our lines are busy," a recording will relate.
Please don't hang-up, you've not long to wait.
Again this message, your patience fleeing.
Will you ever speak to a human being.
This technology has created a mechanical clone.
And you're still "all alone by the telephone."
Mort Friedman

An Angel's Lullaby

Little one, it is time for sleep
May your Father give you dreams to keep
Let your soul now rest in peace
For His Hand is watching over thee

Be not afraid - No, He will not slumber
Just lie down child your sleep will be sweet

Leave all your worries with Him now
By morning they will all be gone
'Cuz He's taking care of thee
His Love is gonna make you free

So dreams your dreams - you can trust Him always
Fret not, my child He'll bless you in sleep

May this one rest easy tonight
Restore her faith - Make all things new
In tenderness, He is smiling at you
Yes, I see You are watching her now
Oh Lord, may her sleep be so sweet...
Louann Leon

Happiness Is...

Going to my brother's house for days at a time
Making up poems that don't have to rhyme
Helping out people along the way
Sitting outside on a bright sunny day
Going out somewhere special to eat
Or just sitting on a comfy seat
Being around the people I love
Staring at the clouds above
Riding in the car for hours
Smelling a bouquet of flowers
Going shopping at the mall
Watching all the snowflakes fall
Sitting in a swimming pool
Sipping a lemonade that's nice and cool
Leaving at one on the last day of school.
Mary Brunswick

A Father On Mother's Day

Despite getting older and grayer
   Mothers still keep taking care -
Of all the sons and daughters
   with fathers they do share -
Yes fathers love and treasure and
   by their kids are always thrilled -
But one seldom sees a father do for kids
   what a mother always will -
From diapering to burping to putting on their clothes -
To kissing all their boo boos to wiping their runny nose -

But a mother's love doesn't stop
   though kids reach 40 plus years of age -
You'll still find "mom" a-mother-in'
   she is just on a different page -

Most fathers try to see that their kids are well provided for -
By going one step further than
   just keeping the wolf away from the door -

But the greatest achievement as a father
   I shall ever reach in life -
Is that I gave my sons a perfect mother the day I picked my wife -

Robert Bowen

Me!

Who sits here alone, unhappy and blue?
Morning and night, thinking of you
With a need to see your smiling face?
All this unhappiness, only you can erase?
ME!

Who missed you more than words can tell
Leaving me alone, in this torment and hell?
Who watched for you, as the dawn awoke
Wishing you here, with a comforting stroke?
ME!

To see tomorrow, knowing it will be in vain,
Unhappiness inside me, a heart full of pain,
To see your laughing eyes, your tender lips,
To know it's you, for whom my heart flips?
ME!

Please come back to me, as quick as you left,
And ease this torment that has set me adrift.
Who will be waiting with open arms?
A happy heart, again to beat calm?
ME!

Ray Regnaiere

All Because I Took The Time

Today I saw a homeless person stranded and alone.
My heart felt heavy and my eyes teared up,
As I passed by and continued on.
I thought of this person later that day, her face,
Her coat, even that silly pack.
Then with one swift jerk I turned my car,
Bought some food and started back.
As I neared that bench not one but three
Were seated in a row.
All wrapped in tattered blankets, each with
A story that I will never know.
So I slowed my car, then stopped it near,
And greeted them with a smile.
I asked if they were hungry, and if I
Could sit and talk awhile.
I think of my friends quite often now, Sally,
Frank, and Joe. And all because I took the
time, bought some food, and said hello.

Robin R. Laflin

Till We Meet Again

Till we meet again be happy be strong and proud: I've gone to a place much higher than a cloud. I stood at a door one morning just before 4 o'clock: I heard a voice say; enter Samuel the door is unlock, I went through the door to see who was there: It was the Lord sitting in a chair. He said welcome Samuel this is your new home: It's peaceful, it's quiet and you're not alone. I said; I enjoyed life with my family it was fun: Working with Sarah to raise Andrea, Denise, Kevin and Avain. But Samuel this is a special place I have for you: To relieve the pain and suffering you went through but what about Sarah will she be fine: Of course she has the Lord on her side all the time. I told Sarah you gave me a second chance that day: Only you knew it would be this way. Andrea my daughter you helped me too: You became a nurse to help others, I'm proud I love you. Denise my daughter you have a very special touch: To work with others children I love you much. I love you, Kevin, I know you'll do right: 'Cause you get on your knees and pray every night. Again my son you have a big and warm heart: Keep praying to the Lord and he'll never part. Stay strong my son he'll see you through: He knows how much I love you. Misan, Malik, Tori, Kevin, Krystal, Deanna, Davon too: You're my seven hearts, Granddad loves you. Son-in-law Tony and Daughter-in-law Grace: You two are in my heart in a special place.
Sisters, Brothers, Nieces cousins be positive and strong: Keep faith in the Lord so you can't go wrong. Sarah my beautiful wife you were loving and also true: I love you to the end and now I'll look over you. My journey on earth is now done: I'm in heaven now with the great one. I am with the Lord my savior my friend: I want you all to remember to stay happy till we meet again.

Kevin O. Gourdine

"Burning Cold"

That summer brought its
music, sunburned laughter,
and you.
The heat scorched with its
excitement and passion; minds
raced in circles, hearts reached
out for one another....
Those were the days when nothing mattered except
being together, when the cool breeze
was welcomed as much as the
thought that this might never end.
Then the heartbreaking truth of
it all, that soon winter would
come and take away those
seemingly endless summer nights,
the bitter cold of faded passion,
the chill of realizing that you
no longer care.

Lori Goodwin

Dead Beat Dad

Anger drives my soul from
my body. It flies around the room
passing Pictures of a more perfect
Life and curtains that hide a view
to a perfect world. Realization that
they will never be stings my very
being, because of a cheating woman.
It comes to rest on a simple light switch,
void of understanding; it is on or off,
Yes or No. A choice is made without
decision, without reason. A life is
over. An abortion of a grown man.
My son is older now and asks,
"What happened"? I search for an
answer; there is none! I reply, "Ask
Mom!" For I am a Dead Beat Dad
an abortion of life in the 90's.

Lee A. Dunkelberger

To Tiger With Love

It's three o'clock in the morning. I've tossed and turned all night.
My Basenji puppy, named Thunder, is snuggled next to me snoring
out right. The problem is I can't forget about Tiger Stripe. You
know, the big brown brindle dog in the middle row. The one that
had his ball in the long run, who was so healthy with his eyes all
aglow. Tiger, I will never ever forget you. I wish there was
something I could do. If I could have things my way, I'd find a
home for you. First, I would find lots of volunteers, to pass the
word and show you about town. To community centers, city
market and other places where lots of people could know you're
around. I'd put your picture real big on the animal control truck,
as well as the city busses that take folk about. I hope they would
read and ask themselves questions and go to your place to seek you
out. I would demand that all news channels give air time so that
all people in the city would know. That if a master couldn't be
found as nice as you, soon it would be.............death row. I try
not to think it's a losing battle as I rant and rave up and down the
streets; as people cross breed and make stupid mixed dogs and let
them run the streets without a leash. Folk talk about teaching
responsibility, to nurture and teach caretaking skills. Instead they
are turning their backs on the problem, pretending all is OK and no
problems exist. Just like one dog in one year makes 12 puppies
and in two years those 12 make 72. I hope the 30 students I
brought to visit you today spread the word of what made your
situation for you. So, Tiger, I wish I could tell you before the
death angel comes. That because I met you, with your ball in the
run, that my world and this world has changed some.

Trunita Miller

To My Grandson On His First Birthday

I saw you born into this old world
My daughter became a mother, no more a little girl.

And I'm so glad that you came to be
A significant part of our family.

It was one year ago, this great event took place
And I thank dear God for His saving grace.

Because He sent you, as an extension of me
To love my sweet grandson unconditionally.

If love were a valley, mine would be deep
If it were a mountain, mine would be steep.

High, wide, big or small
I give you my love, I give it all.

Pamela H. Oglesby

And I Will Grow

Look at me and see the sorrow that I bear.
My hope has been killed and my trust is gone too.
All I had thought was right has deserted me,
Yet I cannot be left alone.
I know that there is better than I have ever had -
That this pain is not all the there is -
But within me I do not feel that to be true.
I need time too heal now
And then maybe someday I will understand a life without pain.
It is strong fault that I have - this holding on to pain
But it is all that I know.
I want to learn otherwise, but before I can grow
I must heal completely, or I can only injure myself more.
Be patient with me and I will grow
Today I am slowly beginning to let go of my pain
And then I can heal... and grow
I am as a rabbit who is hungry
Yet afraid of those who would feed him
Feed me - yet know that I am scared
And I will grow.

Kathleen Keller

Untitled

The seductive pull of madness, I've read of it, never dreamt it.
My imagination stunted by the narrow experience of my life.
Is madness not born from brutality and poverty, alcohol and opium?
These are the children of madness easily seduced.

In my debilitated state, I must appear an easy mark.
He's come to seduce me. Am I lost, forever to be possessed.
I am terrified of succumbing. Having known but moments of terror
Still I recognize the uncontrollable paralyzing power.

Lifeless like the stinging kiss of the vampire,
Rancid as a werewolf's breath,
Loud as the din of dancing skeletons,
Cartoonish images and metaphors I hold in my mind life a talisman.

Standing near a cliff on a mountain I did not climb,
I feel his offer of a pliable warmth luring me to the edge,
Like a line in a bar uttered to seduce.
Where the man's comfort is physical, madness is emotional oblivion.
The hold on emotions is so tight, I could have both by letting go.

Fear protects me.
I create the images and metaphors, therefore I am in control.
In control created by madness to disguise my evaporation.

Kim Michelle Liming

Hephaestus To Aphrodite

I'm no athlete;
   My legs are crippled.
   Many Gods are stronger,
   Richer, powerful,
   More handsome than I.

Yet Mother makes me stand here,
Babbling like a fool.
I am withered and ugly,
A disgrace to my family.
Why should you want me?

   You, created from ocean mist,
   With hair the color of daffodils,
   Deserve better than this hideous creature.
   Surely you are more interested
   In Poseidon or Apollo.

I can make you jewels
To match your eyes...
Was that a kiss?
I should have known.
All you ever wanted was love.

Melinda Roche

The Last Dance

The pale yellow leaves hang limply
   onto the branches of a sycamore tree
as if for dear life
   which will soon be taken away.
Then
   wind comes
the leaves tremble and weaken
   in fear of falling down.
A leaf descends
   slowly tossing and turning
dancing... elegantly
     politely
in the air
   and then it arrives at its final destination-
the ground
   and ends up in a big black garbage bag
with all its other tearful friends
   each never to be seen again
doing its own
   unusual little dance

Yvette Cavalli

Let The Record Show

As I entered the room it filled with light and I heard her calling
my name. Uncertain at first, my steps were quite slow,
but compelled to move onward all the same.

In this room sat a table made of brilliant white stone and I saw
her waiting just beyond. She beckoned me closer and I knew then
and there, that I stood in the house of God.

"Good morning," she said, "Please don't be afraid. There's something
I'd like you to see." "I am called Rebekah, Keeper of the Book -
it's the record of your soul's history."

From beginning to end and every thought, word and deed, had been
kept throughout ages of old. At the top of the page were written
these words: "Forevermore, Let the Record Show."

The good and the bad, every step that I'd made without doubt was
there as my truth, and I knew in my heart for the days still ahead,
there was more in my life yet to do.

With a smile from the heart she looked into my eyes, "Go in peace
and the record will show, that today you have learned a precept of
God - Man Will Reap That Which He Sows."

"Live sincerely each day, planting seeds where you can,
For the world needs these truths as you know.
Then take peace in the fact that you did all you could
And that's what the record will show."
Rita Richardson

One Torn Piece Of Cloth

My name? It's not important, I left it long ago
My only friend is the doll I carry with me
Other than that I'm all alone.

Who really cares about a homeless kid today?
If I were to ask for help,
I'd be teased because I have no place to stay.

Life is often meaningless and sometimes it seems cheap
Instead of suicide, I cry myself to sleep.

The only link to my past is one torn piece of cloth
The one my mother gave to me
Before she died and my soul got lost.

My Dad left us long ago, and Mom was never quite well
When she finally gave in and died, I found myself in Hell.

Tomorrow is my birthday,
  the same day Momma died,
I'll be seven and I'll always keep
  that one torn piece of cloth,
Which holds all the tears I've cried.
Shannon Struwe

My Christmas Angel (With All My Love, Mommy)

'Twas the night before Christmas and all through the house
not a child had stirred not an echo heard.
All snug in their beds the angel's miracle began.
The tree in its stand the garland abound,
the glow of the lights ornamented each branch
The masterpiece complete with the topper on high.
She flew through the room wrapping and taping
with bows tied tight.
Each present with a tag and wrapped with pride.
All deeds accomplished and off to dreamland night.
I awoke from my sleep and sprang from my bed
to discover a treasured wonderland created for me.
Treats in her hand and face all aglow
brought truth to my heart.
Embraced with a hug, I whispered so low,
  "I love you my Christmas Angel!"
Rosemary Andrews-Sibbering

When Is Tomorrow?

I cannot see the time to be - it worries me
My thoughts do soar - to that I will say
I have sailed calm waters - the stormy sea
I crawled - I walked - I climbed - I lived a day

I am left a curse - again approaches a tomorrow
There's no path - this curse - it's always there
My head is bent with the sorrow of tomorrow
I face with hope - a wish - for some other where

I looked at starlight - there is no place to be
I plod - I struggle - what direction is the day
To find a harbor in tomorrow - to be free
I do not beg - I do not pray - that is not my way

I do not believe I can borrow a tomorrow
It comes - it goes - unseen - a misty thought
Oh! Yes I am sure today is never tomorrow
Though priceless it can't - by me - be bought

What is to me - this strange - this tomorrow
Do I see this curse - a collapsing universe
The cosmic fires - not eternal seem to know
All can gaze - alas - at the coming of tomorrow
Primio Tiberi

"A Sinner's Prayer"

I come to you in prayer, Dear Lord, for your guidance is what I yearn,
my troubles are many and I have grown weary, I know not where else to
turn. You've given your love to me graciously and being a fool my
head is like that of stone. Now I'm down on my knees asking
forgiveness, Lord, because I know I can't make it on my own. Your
servants called upon me having news of your great Kingdom to come,
teach me how to walk your path as I pray your will be done. You have
taken me down to the pits of sorrow and it overflows my filling cup;
no earthly man can fulfill my needs and now I must lift my eyes up.
Yes up to the heavens where you dwell so far and high up above, teach
me how to praise thy name, teach me how to love. For I am just a man
lost without direction, no destination to bear, steer me to your path
of righteousness, Dear Lord, show me that you care. My words are not
spoken easily, for I've never knelt down to pray, let your Holy
Spirit guide my thoughts, let it show me the way. And if I fall
short in all my efforts to stand beside your heavenly throne, let
your love take over me and please let it bring me home.
  Amen
Timmy R. Wilkins

When You're Not Near

When I'm alone and you're not near,
my body aches, my spirit dies.
Energy drained I feel so queer,
with saddened heart and watery eyes.

With my mind's eye I see your face,
so beautiful, so soft, so wonderfully mine.
Your tender touch, your warm embrace,
your sweet fragrance, a rapture so fine.

I'm sad and gloomy, a lonely depressed man.
My thoughts, emotions, movements, all in strife.
I can't eat or sleep, only dream as I can,
of your nourishing presence and sweet breath of life.

The comfort of your arms is what I crave,
the song of our hearts beating harmonic power.
With you I am strong, confident and brave,
your life-giving radiance as sun is to flower.

I wait for your return with great expectation,
I miss you, I want you, I need you here.
This as described is my preoccupation,
when I'm alone and you're not near.
Michael Maddi

"Gimmicks"

A warm bottle and a diaper make
my world complete.
Now there's a combination which
nothing else can beat!

Dad has his shot of whiskey to
make his life sublime.
He also uses vitamins to keep him
in his prime.

Mom exercises madly to keep her feeling fit—
And her astounding beauty comes
in a little kit.

Sis starves herself at breakfast
to stay so nice and trim.
Brushing a hundred strokes at
night is her other whim.

Brother's really muscle-bound
from lifting heavy weights—
And grooms himself quite nattily for his heavy dates.

Our whole family uses gimmicks—
one kind or another.
I feel my best with a bottle at one end,
And a dry diaper at the other!

Maxine Untch

Mount Saint Helens

Hell I've raccoons 'n' cats to feed
'n' the birds 'n' the bear 'n' the deer
besides in the lodge is all I need
Hell I think I'll stay right here

To the spirit of the lake I'm just a slave
and of the mountain I've no fear
nor the moanin' of the ghost - of the Yakima brave
Hell I think I'll stay right here...

Near Helens' crown the Aspens quaked
twelve hundred Fahrenheit
through the mud banks down the rivers snaked
while the day turned sudden night

And stilled most living things
and ashen masked you in a tomb
with the bears 'n' the deers 'n' sparrows' wings
immortalized by - Helens' plume

Wallace Lee Benepe

Crying Out

Powerless without a thought of destiny and of fate, of destruction and misery. Powerless and limp, behind the controls of this falling plane behind the controls of this endless shame. No power, no help no words to say just emotions I want to express but cannot say. Tears of fear role down in dread tears of fear fall. I cry out to her in the wind of my breath I cry out to her to stop. But all which is heard in return is the voice of denial the voice of insecurity, anxiety, pressure, false bearings and attacks of drugs and cigarettes of insanity. She takes up the offer to inhale a bowl thinking over the consequences but only for a second. So she drifts off into a world not of her own. Only of impaired hearing and thought impaired vision and mind. She feels so light she sees no colors no birds nor toasters, just feels the nature and the relaxation of the new toy she has found. Like a child once again with no worries no problems just some Velveta and a sandbox to play in. The sand quickly slipping through her fingers the cheese digesting in her stomach. While she talks with her sand pal and shovel talks with her new toys surrounding. Without many lights without many turns without many comforts she sits there and talks. Therapy, medication, treatment and care so much of this has been neglected so much forgotten for my friend.

Zack Scott

"That Healing Touch"

Won't miss your water till your well runs dry.
Never felt its meaning till I looked him in his eye.

He's always been there through thick and thin.
Please Lord, this time, won't you let him win?
Always worked two jobs just to make ends meet.
Friends, often laughed at his car's broken seat.
He didn't care, just kept going mile after mile,
Doing what he had to with a big old smile.
Many days tired and filled with pain-
How do you help a man who never complains?

He's my dad, you see, I love him oh so much.
I'd give anything to have that healing touch.

Those eyes that taught me so much through the years,
Were now looking back all filled with tears.
"Tell me how to pray," he said, "how can I fight back?"
Talk to Dr. Jesus, Dad, He'll put you on the right track.
If I could hug you and the sickness could go into me,
Then I'd be assured of God's victory! But if after all that and you still have to go, I won't like it but I'll understand. You're just walking ahead, getting things ready, for "us," once again!

Linda Dianne Stewart

Dare To Discover

As you uncover the pages to an exciting and wonder-filled book;
New worlds unfold as each door is unlocked with every look.

Endless and magnificent opportunities abound for learning, discovery and hope,
Notable knowledge, experimental ideas, aspired dreams are all within your scope.
Characters transcend your expectations, imagination and fantasies,
Heroes, villains, and sorcerers act out scenarios with dramatic ease.
A scientific formula, a biography, a historical essay are all within reach;
Nowhere else can you find such diversity and unlimited potential to teach.
Theatrical images are painted on the open canvas of your mind,
Every possibility is explored; nothing imagined is left behind.
Dynamic encounters with exceptional models of humanity are common place.

Where else can you find caring, compassionate and creative members of every race?
Only in a fictional novel, a short story, a captivating tale, in essence a book,
Reality is based on an author's visions, feelings, or maybe a chance he took.
Lives can be forever changed by one's perception of the written word,
Dare to discover the power of silent reading, that is virtually unheard.

Tanya Lukasik

Seasons

No winter's wind is as cold my inner fears.
No summer breeze is as warm as the flow of my compassion.
No spring growth is as verdant as my hope.
No autumn leaf drop is as emptying as my sadness.

The seasons of life are reflected in the seasons of my days,
Each becoming my favorite upon approach.

No winter wind is as clearing as my self-acceptance.
No summer breeze is as humid as my confusion.
No spring growth is as exciting as my new insight.
No autumn leaf drop is as solemn as my solitude.

The rhythms of my day are mirrors of a larger life,
Each teaching me a new song.

William J. Weber

"Paul"

I've sailed on ships against conquering foes, I've walked by the River Niger;
I've seen the nights of a thousand stars, and prayed on a pagan alter.
I've walked with kings and loved many rogues, I touched the hand of Jesus;
I've known the peace of a child unborn, and sang the executioner's song.

I've felt the strength from my manly loins, the passion from my breast as woman;
I've felt the fear of a night with no dawn, and pain from the viper's venom.
My soul belongs to the total one, my path belongs to all;
who I am and what I've been is the struggle since mankind's fall.

Listen to your silence, hear it in the heart of man;
I tell you now for all to hear, feel it if you can.
I am Ra, I'm the son of man, I am the breath of fire;
I'm the river through the sands of night, I am essence and desire.

The whole of me is the sum of you, I am and have been all;
I am the tree,
I am the rock,
I am a man named Paul.

Linda Lanier Eller

Buttercup

Wild you grow, buttercup
No careful cultivation
Your soil not rich or treated
Tumultuous winds tossed you about
Bending, altering your upward growth
but not halting it
Nearly plucked up, unanchored
By anonymous fingers
Circumstances and chance oft' threatened your existence
Nature's crude concoctions
Weathered, withstood.
You thrive
petals now unfurled
trusting the sun to nourish
Your brilliant saffron hue attracts.
Compare not to the rose or orchid
delicate and pampered relatives
Take pleasure and pride
in your lusty, roadside habitat
No freedom in a showcase.

Linda Carpeno

Jockey Hollow

The name sounds light,
No trace of night
In it. No argument.
Instead, merriment.
But things that seem to be
Rarely add up to reality.
So look past the shadows of those gaunt gray trees
And try to make out what the inner eye sees.
The fame
Of Jockey Hollow is not in the name
But in what came
Of men's blood on the snow
And happenings that did not show.
No shots fired here were heard 'round the world,
Yet in this hollow a glory unfurled
As waiting, frustration and pain
Yielded a gain
That all men and women could see:
From endurance, liberty.

Martin Goldman

The fingers shall clench stiffer yet
no longer in the light of day
pains that they never will forget
beneath the cold and heavy clay

Life is a fire of pain and rage
and flesh is broken on Fate's Wheel
the grave, a cold and mocking cage
that binds with pain more cold than steel

Weariness chokes the soul's vain will
freedom, the goal of all, dangles
from careless mockery of Ill
to taunt our souls, as they strangle

How like the living dead we are!
Hesitation and fear curdle;
regret, despair, and shame flee far
from pain, to haunt grave and cradle!

Anonymous

Here's The Recommendation

When you don't have a lot of time,
No matter how far you roam,
From the hills, from bridge to ridge, beyond the rainbow,
A thousand points of light from a different point of view,
Half empty or half full.
Generation after generation,
We could go on and on,
Even with paradise waiting,
Some will be tempted to stay on board.
Pulling back the walls to the art of love,
Tired of being the forgotten, A Grand Entrance!
To think we used to come up here only twice a year.
There may be more shelter here than you think.
Don't miss a thing, drive carefully,
The seats are fit for a Lord.
Who says. It will change the way you think.
Giving new life to the spirit,
Which ties together old and new...
The treasure house beyond the love,
Is never ending.

Sara Maria Beardsley

To Doris

My love is not like a red rose,
Nor can it be compared to a summer's day.
And she may not like my classical bent,
Yet I sincerely do I love her in many countless ways.

She may not be a ravishing beauty,
Nor an Athena of old Greek lore.
But she's thoughtful, kind, and considerate,
lavishing praise on me, could anyone ask for more.

She's my Lara of Dr. Zhivago,
The Beatrice of Dante and much more.
She's all I need to make life worthwhile,
And every day so eventful, and not just a deadly bore.

Her face may shows signs of aging,
A few wrinkles may show here and there.
Yet I see so much beauty in her visage,
She's so delicate, so sensual, so fair.

How to describe that angelic look,
While her sweet rhapsodic grin holds me in sway.
With her dainty, enchanting, and engaging smile,
And her chastely winsome way, makes me love her more each day.

Thomas Granowitz

Untitled

You will never know the joy of giving birth
Nor the touch, the smell, of fresh rained earth
You will never know a pain so sharp, so deep, that doesn't stop
Although you are asleep you will never see this pain in my eyes
that holds and caresses me more than you'll ever realize
You will never keep the promise,
"to grow old" you've already
been there so I've been told.
How could you not want what life is all about
Maybe one day soon I will figure you out.
G. Theresa Jones

Looking Back

Looking back, so long ago;
not a nice sight to see.
 I wasn't even there, yet it
seems so close to me
 His cup was so full, it ran
over the side, plain to see his love cannot
hide
 With his pain, he set me free,
oh, no one can steal my Saviour's love
for me
 Nailed to a cross, He saved
my soul, He died for us; pain untold
 Sin of the world envelopes
me, oh, no one can steal my Saviour's
love for me.
 Sin, it is too hard to bear, he
arouse for me; arouse up there
 His love - how didn't start?
Jesus is with me, within my
heart.
Kaleigh Murphy

Death

It happens to all of us
Not because were bad, and not because were good
It is a stage we all go through, just like the terrible twos

We are born, we live, then die
It all goes so quickly, we live like time bombs
So we better do what we want, and do it today
Don't wait until tomorrow, because it might never come
Live out your life, because you only have one

If you love someone, let them know
Remind them, and don't let them forget
Say the word love all the time
Because once you're gone you say no more
So say love often, enough to last them a lifetime

Love the ones that love you, and not the ones that don't
When you're gone everyone mourns, but when you're around nobody's there
So when you're alive and living, show the ones that love you that you love them too

Live your life to the fullest, and forget your faults
The past is the past, and the future is awaiting
Sabrina Licari

No Child Should

No child should have to be afraid that they might not see another day.
No child should have to watch another life go down the drain.
No child should have to face the knife.
And watch someone take another life.
Valerie Carter

Images On Wings

Death circles overhead on ebony wings,
Not death itself, but that which off death feeds.
Keen, searching eyes soaring high in silent flight,
Seek after the weakened, maimed or fallen.

Shattered hearts, damaged spirits, wretched men,
Delectable morsels for scavenging.
Clothed in a happy mask of promised relief,
Satan spawns death, then devours his child.

Earth bound, smitten, cursed with viper bruised heel,
Wilderness fasting, tempted sore, He came.
Keen eyes searching the silence of a soul's depths
Finds wounded, broken, and heart-sickened man.

Bridegroom banqueting with a Magdalene sort,
Unmasked and true, metes living water fresh.
Nude, nailed, dead, entombed, a vulture's spectacle,
Risen Christ birthed life. Christ's child soars God-ward.
Stiles T. Watson Jr.

A Grandparent's Love

A grandparent's love is like no other,
not even matched by a mother;
They protect and defend the grandchild's view,
no matter what the child may do;

As parents they seem so tough and hard,
unwilling to bend or let down their guard;
As grandparents though they are now set free,
to give their love unconditionally;

As time goes and generations pass,
there is one thing that will always last;
The memories that are left behind,
will be shared with grandchildren down the line.
Tammie Kay Murphy

The Keeper Of My Heart

I gave my heart away one day,
Not knowing if he would have it to stay,
He nurtured it, and kept it near his;
Just for me, and he did not give it away.
Love's a funny thing, I know,
It takes time to let a feeling grow,
And as many years went by,
My heart was still near his,
Kept warm, safe, and dry,
I could not ask for it back,
So there I left it to stay,
To add many warm memories and love in anyway,
The love in his heart would then add with mine,
To build a wonderful friendship over time;
Whenever I feel lonely,
When I feel the sun will never shine,
I know my heart is in a safe place,
His entangled with mine.
Paula R. Pearson

My Wings; My Dreams

What would these wings be?
My loved ones said my dreams could never be.
If it were so, what would become of me?

During the day I polish their might.
Then I touch my heart and pray at night.

What would these wings be?
Could I fly them someday?
Someday we will see.
Raquel Abella

I'll Work For Food

I feel base.
Not the base of a drug addict, but that of utter disgust and nothingness.
Betrayal and deceit are my friends, while I anger at love and hope.
Despair drenches me in her alluring essence, as all the while I cry for death to be upon me.
Anger is so fierce inside of me that not even the longest scream can diminish my intensity.

The world seems to me a corner in a squalid project, as a mouse-like man cannot even get cheese.
Beyond anger is my rage, for years its suppression has been strong.
Reckless is my mind as it wanders into depths unknown.
While I sleep good omen elders salute me and I them.
In reality I have nothing.

The pain inside is deep.
I am the brother on the street - Angry; Hungry; Misread; Misunderstood.
This is a rage that has been consumed by the belly of the beast at its most base level.
Misery and Hell are as one, intertwined in a dance that is forever.
I repent all my sins, bow down to God on my knees and desperately beg...
HELP ME - I'LL WORK FOR FOOD!

E. Cameron Mitchell III

Graffiti

There is an artist that I admire —
Not your usual sort at all —
For he writes his message at the back of a parking lot
On an old, slightly tumbled-down wall.

Whoever drives past that wall will see it,
And many do,
For it's a busy street there.
And they'll read his message and be reminded,
And, hopefully, will begin to care.

And when the wall is painted over,
In an effort to beautify, I suppose,
The graffiti message always seems to reappear.
It's as if, somehow, the artist knows.

And the message that is written is important enough to him
To risk being caught in the night.
For it brings to us a persistent reminder
Of an increasingly common plight.
The message is a simple question,
"What does it take to make a home a right?"

Vicki L. Volkman

Indifference

My house I cleaned today
Of cobwebs and of dust;
I swept the dirt from the corners,
And washed clear the smudges on the window pane.
The dishes dirty from yesterday
I scrubbed and put away;
My house I cleaned today.

From my garden I plucked the weeds,
And the flowers looked much brighter;
I even bathed the little dog
That runs around the place.

And tonight—

Tonight when he came home—
He said,
"What have you done today?"

Mirth B. Langer

The Desert Wild

The open desert there once laid
Now only lies roads of new homes
By a big business getting paid
Where will life in the desert roam?

They say the city benefits from the growth
They're only looking as far as today
From nature's view people broke an oath
To be aware of our actions, so to not relay
our misfortunes, but to share our world as we know it
With generations to be and as not a memory of yesterday

If we only took time to appreciate the desert wild
We would see more than our monetary gain
If we could see the desert through eyes of a child
We would then hear the cries and feel the pain
Of all that's a part of the diminishing desert biological chain

Big business will continue to expand
While people continue ways of, "Sell upon demand"
For the Sonoran desert only will their lie
An evolving city, leaving the desert to die.

Kathleen Jacobs

Good-Bye My Love

You have been my solid rock through all these years
Now that you are gone all I have are tears.
You said our love could withstand anything
I remember those words each time I look at my wedding ring.
The preacher said till death do you part
I didn't think much about his words at the start.
I thought we would be together forever.
Did I think you would ever leave me? No never!
Now the time has come for me to say good-bye
And as I do a part of me will die.
But someday I know we will be together again
When that day comes my broken heart will mend.
Your love will always be with me even though you are gone
And because of your love I know I can go on.

Good-bye My Love, May You Rest In Peace

Mary Jo Hammonds

I Wonder Why God Put Me Here

I wonder why God put me here
O heavenly father reply
I wonder why God put me here
As I look to the blue and snowy white sky

I wonder why God put me here
O Heavenly father look upon me
I wonder why God put me here
Focus my eyes so I may see

I wonder why God put me here
Wasting the summer hours in doors
I wonder why God put me here
Washing windows and scrubbing floors

I wonder why God put me here
Will I be some one great
I wonder why God put me here
I better shout up and wait

Because God is greater than man
Which no human can understand
He is the father, this is his land
He has the blue print, and the master plan.

Leon Sergio Cox III

The Man Unknown

Faded yellow and fainted images are all that remain
   of a man... the man unknown

Scenes once lived and painted bold seem strangely dim
   held in a silver frame now constrained to be his home

Did she love him then in her starched white dress
   pressing tight their darling dear

And is it love that fills his laughing eyes and boyish grin
   for her for me for us for what we would become

Or does fragile clay see only what it longs to see
   knowing not what lies ahead

And like the colored images then bright and bold
   pale to shades of lesser hues

Was the different path hard to follow and difficult to see
   lined with shadows of another so close by

And was the new canvass brushed with sounds of laughter
   splashed aflame with brilliant colors of new loves and dreams

As for me my path was filled with faint images of another nearby
   and a canvass needing colors from yours

So here's to you my man unknown the one in the silver frame
   I missed you then and I miss you still
   R. M. Trammell

Seasons

Joy and laughter live in the hearts
Of all the ones who saw the Spring start.
Passion and fun are given to the ones
Who know the wonder of the Summer sun.
Sober and saddened are the ones in the Fall.
Eternally iced is the winter one's call.
   Lisbeth Sweet Frank

The Walk

Have you ever walked among the wood and heard the sounds
of crackling leaves and twigs beneath your foot?

Have you ever walked among the wood and smelled the fall smells
of drying leaves and moss and pine needless and decaying limbs
and twigs?

Have you ever walked among the wood and seen the sight of leaves
of gold and tan, rust and red dancing in the warming morning air,
swirling through the branches as they descend upon the ground?

Have you seen sparrows darting among the hedge, pecking at some
seeds and squirrels busily scurrying up and down the trunks of trees?

Have you ever seen a blue-bird light on a blueberry patch,
peck the few berries that are left, while just below there appears,
in full winter coat, a brown rabbit with his twitching nose,
nibbling on a sprig of grass?

Have you ever walked among the wood, among the oak, among
the elm, among the cluster of birch, spruce, and pine?
Do it now, take that walk, there's so little time.
   Richard Solo

Hatred

Hatred looks like a red flaming devil coming up the golden stairs
   of Hell.
Hatred tastes like a frog in your dry, sticky throat.
It sounds like long, sharp fingernails scraping against a foggy
   chalk board.
It feels like hot, boiling water scorching your tongue.
Hatred smells like toxic gas escaping the sewer floors.
   Melanie Zucker

What Ever Will Be

If things that happen weren't meant to be
Nothing would happen in this world, you see
Whether it's meant to be bad or good
It always turns out the way it should
When you might think it was better some other way
What has happened is here to stay
Change is something that's uncontrolled
For some of us our hearts grow cold
We know there are situations we just can't stop
It'll make us feel we're so far from the top
Just when you think the world is crashing down
and there is no love to be found
A white knight will ride into your town
And put your feet back on the ground
For nothing is ever bad enough
to be overcome and make you tough
So grab some dignity and show some pride
And get your life out from that downward slide
Everyone has hope, let go of despair
Hope is a chance, show <u>YOURSELF</u> you care
   Tim Tommaney

In Memory

When I was just a little lad,
Mother taught me good from bad.
She taught me to always honest be,
And to piss against the wind was not for me.
Mother taught me to read the Bible each day
And not to forsake Webster's dictionary.
Now that I am old and lame and gray,
Mother's lessons follow me to this day.
   Marion D. Handly

Why

   I don't know what to say to you.
One minute happy the next blue.
I think that I should go away.
Tomorrow will be a new day.
   I need to be by myself for a while.
So I walked down the road that would never end.
You're in my heart and in my head.
The warning sign I should have read.
   That was something I couldn't do.
I didn't want to go away from you.
But you opened the door and I came in.
This is a game I can't win.
   The day will come and I must go.
Back where I came from a while ago.
Time will heal the hurt and pain,
And dry the tears that fall like rain.
   Shelly Corey

Sentience

When life has come to a point of endlessness
One must turn inward and know where the cardinal
focus of life sojourns

It remains a curious burden to all of us
Yet we will continue to maintain its character
through social detachment

It is only when we gaze into the amaranthine
That we free ourselves to the peace beyond

May we raise our level of consciousness to that level
Before the encumbrance engulfs us all
   Wayne Spickerman

On The Song Of Moses

They sing a song, these lovers,
of him, so great and glorious, a psalm
of Yahweh, praise and sea,
of horse and rider flung into the sea,

Of Pharaoh's chattel they ring
the sound (like stones sinking in sea)
of stubble and anger, and depths
scabbed over by the right hand, by Yahweh.

They sing - a breath, strange power,
uplifted arm, hand outstretched,
a psalm for a striding pillar,
for a cloud of freedom, for a holy land.

The chosen child, go on
to the mountain, on to the sanctuary
where lives strength and mercy,
where dwells the aging Lord.

Murray C. Bradshaw

Alpha And Omega

Alpha and Omega, the beginning and the end. Jesus Christ taught
of himself, to show endless love toward men.
He took upon himself the sins of all mankind and bled from every pore,
to satisfy the law you see, in the Garden of Gethsemane.
On Calvary He sacrificed himself to rescue and deliver us from Satan's
lies that destroy, blind and bind.
In this world of sorrow we wander and perish in sin, if we don't
receive His guidance to a new world tomorrow. I pray we let Him in.
While in the tomb, His spirit hastened to visit His other sheep. So
grand and glorious were His words, that they wept and fell before
  His feet.
"He is risen," "He us risen"; Resurrection describes Christ's rising
from the dead. A message of hope to the righteous, to the sinner a
message of dread. Apostles saw Him so splendidly transfigured on the
Mount. Joy consumed their thoughts, mere words wouldn't tell about.
He is Alpha and Omega, the Apostles knew, and then they went to
spread the Gospel near and far across the land.
Alpha and Omega, make me quake at the thought, I pray this glad
message personally be sought. Alpha and Omega, these words echo
from on high, will be Life Eternal in the Mansions in the sky.

Sara D. Colebrook

Aunt Julia's Lace

Lace: A delicate network of threads
   of linen, silk, cotton, etc

The old tablecloth held many a hole
With stains here and there as does sometimes my soul.

But the love that was shared as the table was set
Was worth all the work to repair its torn net.

As I thought of Great Aunt who had sewn it with care
Does she know this old lace is becoming quite rare?

So I clipped and I tied till it looked rather nice
Then I washed and I bleached which I had to do twice.

Like the old tablecloth God's still working on me
And I'm hopefully becoming what He wants me to be.

He's repairing the threads that were broken with strife
And He's filling the holes that have crept into my life.

He's washing me clean as I've asked Him to do
And when He comes back I'll be just "good as new."

So we'll use the old cloth and I'll pass it along
To my children who don't know my Great Aunt who is gone.

But I'll tell of the love that went into this lace
And some day we'll all meet in a wonderful place.

Rosalie A. Keene

He Died

He died, and gone forever is a part
Of me that no one else can ever know.
He died, and yet there lives within my heart
A remnant of him that only I could know.
I used to dream we'd meet again someday
When we'd grown old. And I had rehearsed
The roles we'd play, exactly the words we'd say.
But cancellation of that meeting by death is coerced,
My fantasy doomed never to occur.
No time to cry for words unsaid. Today's
Demands won't allow it. Yet remains here a blur
To be focused only by dream's sweet maze.
   Death and Duty, unanswered Inquiry,
   And *lost* forever is a part of me.

Ruby L. Calkins

Loretta's Rainbow

When I first look at a rainbow, I feel sad because it reminds me of my Aunt Loretta who just died.

It reminds me of her because she was always happy and smiling, just like a rainbow, bright and shining.

When I look at the same rainbow a second time, I feel good because I know that Aunt Loretta is up in Heaven with God. So when I see that rainbow, I know that my Aunt Loretta is looking down from Heaven above, keeping an eye on the ones she loves.

Maureen MacDonald

The Journey

Caught in the catacombs
of my mind,
ever searching for the answer,
the walls in this place
seem to close in ever closer.

Do not worry, they say,
you will find your answer.

There is no light
at the end of these tunnels
only deep darkness, and never ending twists.

It's the joy of the journey
they say.
I see no joy,
only despair.

You must not stay too long,
they say,
or you'll surely go mad.

Mad?
We have never heard of the word,
the catacombs of my mind and I.

Lisa Rooney

No Return

The trees are ablaze with colors
of orange, reds, and browns
while the children play on the rolling
hills of burnished colored ground.

Beyond the hills lie a field of death
without their knowledge or concern
closer and closer on course they stray
as time slips by with no return.

And as it dawns on these children of old
while slowly they pass through this field of death
they remember the rolling hills of burnished gold
weeping for lost time they didn't want to forget.

Renee Baggarly

Eulogy

There's a memory that lies just out of reach
of the rock and sand of the nearest beach,
of moon mirrored pool and dark lagoon
and the flesh of scales in the light at noon.

That memory lives in the heart of me
and forever calls me back to the sea
from whence the siren's clarion call
echoes and rings over each landfall.

I am drawn to the days of my youth at sea.
The cry of the gull is like music to me.
One day I'll go to return with the tide.
Those who don't know me will say "He died."

Those I have loved and closely held
will know I rejoice in each knell of the bell
as tolls out the word that I'm gone once again
to the ocean, the current, the sea without end.

Ocean Shackleton

Irish Rose

I have strolled the garden
Of this precious irish rose
Reaching out I touched the petals
As I wandered through the rows
Strange I feel I have been here before
A long long time ago
Perhaps in another dimension of time and space
Back a hundred years or so
Each twist and turn's sheer pleasure
There's treasure beneath my hand
Though often very painful
Times there are ecstasies unplanned
Each week I visit this beautiful garden
At least a time or two
Spending sweet precious moments
Lately that's all I want to do
I'll stroll forever in the garden
Of this priceless irish rose
Until she fails to come and see me anymore
When is that? Only heaven knows

Richard Kenyon

Of What Is Missed

Looking out upon this
Of what is missed
With other situations that exist
Situations which persist
But completely unlike what is quite listless
The unreachable beauty of the lovely peace of bliss...

Stephen Muldrow

Whosoever

  Here I lie in my hospital bed,
Nothing to do for my T.V. is dead.
  I'm far more than restless, yet calm and serene,
For faith my life will never end.
  Early this morning I spoke with a pastor,
He told me with confidence God is my master.
  He then showed me a Bible and what did I see,
I saw the love of Jesus for you and for me.
  I then bowed my head and said Lord above,
Save me from wrong and give me your love.
  I lifted my head with tears in my eyes,
I thought about Satan and his final goodbyes.
  I now have the love I've so long craved,
And whosoever calleth upon the Lord
   shall be saved!

Ruby Faye Crews Price

(A Moment In Time)

(Yesterday), it's only a moment in time, a blink of a eye. One little thought of yesterday sends one back in time, to a time when time itself seemed to say, I'm in no hurry, I'll wait for you. A week seemed to hold a summer time when one had youth. A month seemed like a year, a year seemed to be without end, but little did we understand or care to understand, that time we thought was waiting for us was passing with every moment, with every breath.

Time like a river, never stopping, always flowing, carrying you with it, not waiting for you to reach the shore carrying you on. Your life caught in the current passing before you. Sometimes you come to a spot where the water, like your life, seems content and out of the current, but time, which is your life, like the river is passing, just a moment in time. When you reach the other shore, time has passed, your life has moved on, you now have reached another season, headed to the winter of your life.

The acorn that fell to the ground when you were born, now is a beautiful oak tree that has recorded the time and changes in your life. Each ring of growth tells a story of time, now gone forever only a moment in time. Take the time when you're young not to let a moment of time slip away. One day later in life, you'll look back on yesterday and suddenly the day you thought would never end, has passed, only a moment, a blink of an eye in time, for time moves on, never stopping, waiting for no one. When you reach the winter of your life, you'll look back in time to yesterday, now long gone, but seeming like only yesterday, but in time is your life, gone forever in a moment in time. Yesterday is a moment in time, a reference in time to your past, now gone forever.

Norris D. Gulsvig

Voices

Gardener, gardener, how do your flowers grow?
Oh cried the Gardener, my Red Rose
is wilting and hasn't long to go.
Gardener, gardener, how do your flowers grow?
My white rose is a beauty, so I've been told;
she could win a ribbon as she unfolds.
Gardener, gardener, how do your flowers grow?
With the Lord's blessing and so I do pray
my Sunflower seeds will not blow away.
I followed the directions and gave it
water and sun and rich earth
to grow in and plenty of love.
Gardener! Gardener! Some advice to you,
don't cut down your Red Rose for she
will re-bloom.

Lee Hollis

Glass Enclosure

Between a world, one which speaks a tongue of reality,
one which speaks the breath of red waters.
Holding on, with the brink of sanity,
closing eyes shadowing everything
but the ability to see things which are tangible.
Across the white - stained doors, closed by imperfection.
In the depths of the animal, breaking, no escape,
only the shatter of glass fragments
across the floor which breathes the breath
of life and the outer barren world of the living.
Someone reaches, touches the outer edge of you,
pushing, you try to move from the touch.
Impossibility strikes you and you are falling...
Hitting the world of reality, you break from the confines
of the music, over and over, the glass, turning the twisting,
you are there, sitting looking up,
like a new child borne but a few minutes before,
curiosity steaming from the way you had known your
existence, away from the natural course.
In a world of collection, in glass without courage to escape.

Stacy Renee Lauzonis

The Wonderful Gift

Our Lord has given us many gifts as we walk down life's long ol' road. But one gift I'll always be thankful for is that wonderful gift to love.

I just want you to know before we leave how much your friendship means to me.

This is something I'm sure you know in your heart and I pray we'll never grow far apart.

I'll love you forever and that's a long time. I know you'll always be on my mind.

No matter where we go from here I'll feel your presence very near.

So please take care and may God Bless one of the wonderful people of whom I'll miss.

Phyllis Maxwell

Life Of A Rancher

He woke to find no sunrise and then headed for the barn
  Ole Poke was awake and ready, but he probably thought, "oh darn!"

Another spring upon them and cattle to calve out
  They'd ride in amongst the herd taking the shortest route.

They had a job to do and it was their livelihood,
  The job was raising cattle so vigilance was understood.

Getting the calves into the world to make it until fall
  Then it was off to the market place to hear the auctioneer's call.

It is a constant cycle, the years are good and bad
  But it's the life of a rancher as it was the rancher's Dad.

Shane R. Batey

"The Stranger"

I ride with the wind
  on a pale lit night.
The wolf is my companion.
My only defense is nature.
The rose is my heart;
  never breaking,
  always filling,
  fragrant endless perfumes.
My voice is those of birds whose
  pain has made sorrow.
I walk painted trails of reminiscent years.
There are no answers to the puzzling
  thoughts I might quote.
Though no one has found the
  endless search of my crying soul.

Michelle Gilreath

"Night Life"

The darkness approaches as the sun goes to sleep.
One by one stars come out from their sleep.
Popping up one by one, the earth begins to spin, the darkness sets in.
I sit out and watch as everything falls including the walls.
They trap me from freedom, who needs it?
As people cry to survive, the evil fulfills the sky.
God is there only if you care, you have to believe to succeed.
You scream for silence as you try to hear the footsteps of laughter as they come near.
Our children grow faster than lightning, it's extremely frightening
Your life goes quickly it's very sneaky.
You learn to live above abyss where all mistakes take place.

Melissa A. McCroy

Day Of Infamy - '95

Without any warning, under blue skies,
on April nineteenth in ninety five,
a terrorist's bomb blew a building apart,
with intent to strike fear within our hearts.

The debris and dust settled over all,
the men, the women, the children so small.
Then silence profound, and feeble cries
were heard nation-wide under blue skies.

Symbolizing hours of rescues logged,
was a fireman leaning on his rescue dog,
head bowed and saddened; a moment of rest.
They had searched for hours and done their best.

Our star-spangled flag was flying that day,
'till someone attacked, and tore it away.
But in our hearts remains freedom's peel,
which never will buckle under evil's heel.

Instead it will serve as a rallying cry,
with trust in our God as in battles gone by.
We must strengthen our vigil and refuse any blight
trying to darken freedom's bright light.

D. Randall Stack

Rainy Camp

A rain in camp can focus all routine
On keeping warm. That means we give much thought
That backs, and hands, and shins, and food stay hot.
So, if there's company, a fire can mean
The day succeeds by piling logs to lean
Against a shooting flame the rain cannot
Defeat.
  But if you have a cot you've fought
To hold away from damp, the way is seen
To hide yourself all snuggled toe to head,
And ponder in the depths of questions' store
And swirl the answers slowly at your ease.
Then too, you listen to the sounds that seize
The night and swell your being in the roar
Of nature happening around your bed.

Rod Clark

The Horse With Wings

One night as I sat
On my bed,
I looked out the window.

Alas what I did see,
Was a gallant, white horse;
But after shaking my head,
For I thought I was dreaming,
I noticed the horse had wings.

She beckoned me to come with her,
I couldn't not,
So off we went,
And in a few seconds did see,
A bear talking, walking,
And waving to me.

My horse with wings landed on the ground,
But before we went home,
I talked to Mr. Zebra, Little Beaver,
And even old owl.

As I grew old no longer taking these trips,
I learned, sadly, it was only the wings of imagination.

Kristina Allen

Too Depressed

I put on my brown sweater, it has three holes, one for every attempt
  on my life.
Now I shall add one more.
To speak to someone would be wrong, so I leave the house to be alone.
A train is in the blistering distance, a small light peaks through the
  branches.
Closer it comes, farther I go. Standing on the tracks I can hear the
  howls it blows.
Vibrations in my feet grow stronger and now I am ready to go.
Approaching with increasing speed, a picture comes to mind. It is of
  the one I lost and now I shall find.

Melissa S. Dykstra

Sins

Bright-colored clothes
on the line of my youth.
My Ma's face framed in the sunlit morn.
With clothespins upright they freshly flap,
in the breezes of my memory.
Her chapped hands washing dishes worn.
She had us six kids all in a row.
We treated her forgetting,
what it took to be born.
Like dominoes standing,
in all the old pictures.
We posed there on church day,
'til dad blew the horn.
"Respect her," he'd say tightly,
waving calloused hands.
We'd bow heads in shame,
our little hearts torn.
Bright-colored clothes,
on the line of my youth,
Summoned in the coffee-scented morning air.

Sean C. Griffin

Evening's Last Search

Seeking shells—whole though void inside,
On twilight's fragment-littered beach.
First tossed ashore by Neptune's seas,
Then crushed beneath man's careless breach.
Each shard a dusky memory,
Of ecstasy once found intact.
Unbroken curves, pearl-colored swirls—
Radiance arrested.

Susan S. Miller

Once Upon A Time I Hurt

Now graduated, now liberated, still educated.
Once hurt.
Once counseled from the pain of 15 years.
The years have hidden much mental,
Much physical strife.
Once beaten, once slapped, once punched.
Once cut, once thrown, once kicked.
Once confused. The voices talked, I listened.
Once abandoned. The voices, my only companions.
Once abused. By my hands and others'.
Once split between the feelings of the people inside.
I emerged.
Once weak, now strong.
Once obese from pain, now healthy from love.
Once shackled and chained,
Now free.
Free to move.
Free to love.
Free to live.
Free to be me.

Keomia

Inspired By A Garden

I have a sun porch garden that I love.
Once in a while it looks perfect.
All the watering, feeding, pruning and love
add up to a moment of beauty.
Then I think...if only I could keep it this way;
preserve this moment forever.
But my garden is alive.
Time and seasons bring changes.
All living things must change.

Every life has its garden.
Perfect moments can be had,
but not preserved, except in memory,
My garden inspired this thought,
not new but durable...
Each of us are living beings that will change.
If we can accept these changes, we can accept ourselves.
When we accept ourselves, we can all enjoy the changes,
and the beauty of the changes in the garden of life.

W. A. Hollenbach Jr.

The Exotic Land

An exotic land
Only dreamt of, barely seen
Through tall trees and dim photographs

With a glorious bridge, towering redwoods
A crashing sea hidden
By the creeping mist and persistent rain

This is the unknown land
Where love breathes and the future waits
Patient, ignorant
Of who is his destiny

In this peculiar land
Of breathtaking vistas and impressive trees
My portion awaits my lingering arrival

I will be his mate, even though I
Am a little unsure of the how and when,
Sometimes even why

But in that secret place within a human heart
Is unwavering certainty, unexplainable surety
Of my future home
In the exotic land

Rosie Hoskins

Color's Please

You can't choose your father.
Only God can do that for you.
But my God you can choose the colors you like.

Tikoyo Wright

The Best And The Brightest

Today started so sunnily,
only the restless breeze belied the coming
of that cold, cold day.

When we awoke, none were the wiser
suspicion alone fielded guesses as to why
hearts suddenly weighed too much.

I did not know him well, but I knew him;
and he knew me - we shared a common bond
of soldiers and of men.

So now we pass unbidden through our doorway
and our arch, with its shiny words
now dulled by sorrow's tarnish.
The best are not so bright today.

Kevin Kilpatrick

Dead ———-

Imagine, a beautiful baby,
only ten months of age.
A precious gift to its parents,
but it's infected with AIDS.

Only sixteen years old (young),
already packing a gun.
Suicidal to the people,
but he thinks that it's fun.

I thought this was America?
The home of the great.
The land of the free.
As I write, another mother is being raped.

Let's not forget our fathers,
that sat at home all day bored.
Drinking six packs of beer,
but yet he's unemployed.

Tell me, what's the solution?
Before I loose my mind...

Should I commit suicide?

Or beat the DEAD LINE?
 Klever Ken

The Mayflower Boat

On the Mayflower the Pilgrims came
Onto America's land from out of Spain.
The Mayflower did sail on high seas,
For to have their own religion was the key.

"I see land," one Pilgrim said,
While other Pilgrims were already dead.
They smelled fresh air one day,
And vowed that on land they shall pray and pray.

Very soon these Pilgrims landed on Plymouth Rock,
Where many Indians around them did flocked.
Together they worked, together they lived in peace,
They ate what they reaped and gave thanks with a great feast.

This was how they celebrated the holiday of Thanksgiving.
They were thankful for the crops they brought in.
 Loretta Martin

Beds

Some folks perish in burning fire,
others by touching electrical wire.
There are those who exit by smoking gun,
and those who depart while having fun.

Many pass on in a violent way,
for crimes they committed, they have to pay.
More have died in defense of their land,
or in various ways they had not planned.

But there's one known fact we all must face,
a comfortable bed is a dangerous place.
For that is the place where most of us leave,
our loving families to weep and to grieve.

Now this is my plan, I think it wise.
A way to prevent our certain demise.
If you want to avoid waking up dead,
never, no never, get into a bed.

This is the only way, try as we can,
to prevent the death of each woman and man.
Destroy all the beds, and then evermore,
simply lie down and sleep on the floor.
 L. J. Ernster

A Method Of Measure

Comfort comes not from fluffy pillows
  or down comforters
  or a cushioned easy chair,
But rather from a peace found within ourselves.
Accepting life with its flaws,
  but willing and eager to look for and savor
  the gifts of life -

A breeze across a front porch swing
  a sweet tune, or a rousing melody at just the right moment
  a few good and loving friends

We may share these bounties with a partner
Or we may look for life's offerings one on one.
And when we find ourselves enriched
  with the path we have chosen,
Then we have found blessed comfort.
 Lisa G. Kersting

Do I Ever Cross Your Mind

Do I ever cross your mind, does my memory come to haunt you,
or has time helped you to forget.
Tell me my love does your heart harden when my name is
mentioned does it turn to stone, has my face become a face in the
crowd you see everyday, and the love you had for me, has it flown
from your heart, and has old man time healed the emptiness and
the pain you shed over me?
Tell me have the dreams of me turned to nightmares and life been
unbearable? Let go and rest my dear, for my heart is dying and it
remains the same, in love with you.
 Paulette Cain

Love

Can love be an addiction
Or is it an affliction
Can it be too strong
Do you really belong

For love has a tremendous power
You feel on top of the highest tower
Trying to direct it in the proper way
Can often times lead it astray

For love has no straight and narrow course
Thinking that way leads to much remorse
Open up and let it take its path
Therefore no one has to share the wrath

Love is a wonderful feeling
True love is forever healing
What is meant by true love
It's unconditional, unselfish and as pure as a white dove

So let it spring forth and fly in the air
Let it be said that it's two who care
And most of all, let there be trust
With that and this, love never goes bust
 Keith R. Sorgeloos

Evening Quietness

I can see millions of stars
On a clear dark night
See the fire flies with their lights so bright.
Smell the roses and honeysuckle so sweet
Feel the cool damp grass beneath my bare feet
Hear the wind blowing in the trees.
Hear the soft buzzing of honeybees
I listen to the sad cooing of doves
Settling for their night's rest
I pray this day I have done my best.
 Mary P. Johnson

Anything

I'd climb the highest mountain,
or sail the biggest sea,
I'd walk the longest dessert,
or pay the largest fee.
There's nothing that could stop me
from seeing or being with you,
'cause I'd do anything just to be closer to you.

Melissa Mercer

"Brass Feathers"

I do not know which I miss more, the memory of you
or the memory of those passed.
It has been too long, the bud of your youth gone... stolen.
That flower is ever present in my mind.
Thoughts fade and falter as the initial bloom departs.
But a cruel conscious will not allow your absence.
You shall thrive in eternal spring as long as I shall love.
I am left alone with remnants, the bloody carcass of the albatross.
We once walked together through mazes of golden corn.
You can no longer walk. You can no longer stand.
Within those fields we were Kings and Knights, criminals and protectors.
Where are you now? Where is that place we call recognition?
When shall you rise from that sickbed, that funeral slab, that mortuary?
When shall you rise above that shroud of death and demand your life back?
Do not allow life to wax and wane like the dying swan my beautiful bird.
Remember that boy and bird are creatures of God who could swim,
but who choose to drown because wing and neck are broken.

Teal S. Crawford

A War On The Infant

There's a war going on, our own mothers are in charge, she gives the order to kill us for a crime we have no control of. Why do we have to pay? We are just miniature copies of your self that you don't want to face.

The reason why you want us to die is because you don't have the time. There's no place in your life for us. You say you are too young to raise a child; now you give the order for the infant to die. Mothers, did you for once ever stop to think before you said yes. Which one of us would pay for the choice that you made.

There's a war going on, our mothers are in charge. Why do we have to die for the crime she made? Kill infant so I won't have to pay. Kill it before it even breathes or has a brain to think for it self. Why should it live? When I'm the one who will pay. Destroy this infant today.

Toni Lee Dillard

Untitled

Sometimes I feel like crying
  other times I laugh out loud.
   I feel as though my world is dying
but everywhere there is a crowd
   This dream I'm living in
makes no sense at all
   My world is caving in
the ceiling, the floor, the walls
   When I'm sleeping in the night
it's as though I'm awake in the day
   I pray it's going to be all right
but here I cannot stay
   I used to think that there was hope
but now I know there's none
   At times I turned to using dope
And the hope I found... Well, there was none
   And now it's time to realize
I should just stop trying
   No matter how much I fantasize
everywhere my world is dying.

Neh

We Did Forget

In Flanders Fields our fathers lie,
  Our sons and brothers had to die.
To save mankind; that's what they say,
  With blood and pain we had to pay.

They fought a war for what they believed,
  While many families cried and grieved.
And in the end it made no sense,
  For the human mind is awfully dense.

We did forget; it's sad to say,
  For the terrible price God made us pay.
Lost souls cry out from many a grave,
  Wake up; wake up; our world we must save.

World War II, Korea and Vietnam,
  The Atomic age of forgotten man.
WE DID FORGET; I am sad to say,
  Now — in God's name - we all should pray.

Kenneth A. Johnston

"The Hope For Another Sun"

I have seen many a sunrise up, and then set
Over and over, the seasons I have met.
I have smelled the lilac with its heady perfume
And watched the bright tulips burst into bloom.
I've seen the robins arrive in the spring
And watched the majestic eagle spread its wing.
I have seen the trees turn brown,
And watched their leaves float to the ground.
I've heard the North wind's mournful cry
While fat snowflakes go drifting by.
I've seen many machines that do marvelous things,
And the cures for diseases, such as I've never dreamed.
I have known the joy of the birth of a babe
And felt the loss of a beloved face.
My heart has been full, empty, and torn
In a body now worn.
I am now awaiting my time,
For I know it must come.
Yet, I hope for another morning
To see another sun!

Ozelle Conway

Death Of A Butterfly

Wings of a rainbow, pure and bright,
Radiance of beauty, raptures my mind.
Aurora Borealis; engraven image of light,
Flight of the Papilionidae, unravels and intertwines.

Crowning of the new Monarch,
Pennants waving for the Red Admiral.
Dance of a Zebra Swallowtail; dusky and dark,
Painted Ladies, skip and race, tango and twirl.

The gentle curtsey of a Lady Diana Fritillary,
The punctuality of a Green Comma and a Question Mark?
A glimpse of a Mourning Cloak ghostly and wary,
Great Purple Hairstreak; a heavenly shark.

Hues of radiance confining troves of treasure,
Living wildflowers flowing in a mountain meadow.
Golden luster, Blue diamond, Green pasture,
Black Ambrosia; glisten and glow.

Reflected prism of life,
To some incidental tragedy.
Trifle struggle and strife,
Catastrophic catastrophe to me!

Rodney W. Davis

Austin's Riverside

Three little ducks idling, paddling,
  paddling and idling water by the dock;
innocent and happy, their little necks extended,
  six little eyes in a feathered flock
    await tidbits from passers-by.

Hear a little boat paddling, paddling,
  straddling and paddling water towards its stern.
Busy chatting tourists sit watching, watching
  the gleaming water slide on by.

Three little ducks drifting, drifting
  into the maw of a paddle-wheel boat;
yipes, increasing currents alarm an escaping
  as the inevitable paddle goes whirling by.

Hey Ron, ducks underneath calling he calls
  from the moored tourist-twin by the dock.
Wow, into reverse the wheel churns, turning;
  count three little ducks paddling out
innocent and happy, little necks extended
    awaiting tidbits from passers-by.

Louise Bruce

Seasoned Spices

Autumn -
  Paprika, saffron, parsley, mustard, cayenne,
  Lavishly dashed across the landscape,
  Falling gently earthward, leaves of color.

Winter -
  White pepper, salt, a sprinkled downpour
  A splendor in white
  Turning to black pepper, harsh to eyes
  Unwelcome in its tang, turned to mush.

Spring -
  Alerting the taste buds of life
  With a spread of mint leaves and chives
  Among tender celery shoots
  Ready to burst into the glory of

Summer -
  Dusky with all spice
  Satiated with a mixture of bouquet garni
  Yet perky, like chervil, but making us indolent in
  The tastes, sights and smells
  Of the fullness of life.

Rowena B. Lawrence

I Once Was Alone

  As I walk down the straight and narrow path, I think back of all the deep love that has been in my life and the love that is now here, is it going to stay?
  You left me and now my life is a rainy day filled with tears, you'll never know how I loved you or the happiness you put in my life, but now you're gone and you're not returning.
  You've gone on to a different life without me in it, and now I'm so alone. We've had good times and bad. The good we will always remember; the bad we will wash away with the deep love that we share.
  The past is the past and the future is the future, so why don't we make the best of the upcoming years of the love and happiness we still have to share, and I promise that neither of us will ever be alone again.

Staci Estes

What's Happening And Why

Life should be getting better, but it's getting worse. Our young people are steadily being killed as I write this verse. They say that it's because of all the drugs in our streets. I say that it's not being careful whom you've had between the sheets. It's this new breed that has taken us back to our beginning. These drug gangs are like tribes hooked on winning. It's not enough just to be getting paid. That is until the raid. Then all the gangs are trying to be the first To turn state on the others as I write this verse. What happened to the unity that took us so long to get? Are we going to let drugs make us all into misfits? Or are we going to get our people back together. Back to where it's safe to offer a stranger in out of the weather. We must try to regain the unity we once shared. Get back to the times when people showed they cared. It's not the violence in the movies or on T.V.'s that have us so far apart. It's the lack of understanding from the start. In our homes where discipline is the key, that's the beginning of what any child would see. And that's the cast to set the mold. The making of a lost or found soul. The key is in love and understanding. Something that should come natural and not be so demanding.

Robert Golden

A Sleeping World

Sleepy world, wake and sleep no more!!
People of the Universe, take heed and make a stand!!
Lest this monstrous tyrant crush in his hand
Our children. A bloody hand it is and cold.
Each cracked and bleeding knuckle a story will unfold.
Each swollen joint a country from out whose heart they tore
The fathers, the mothers, and the worth sons they bore.
The tainted palm bulges with the fat of conquered nations.
Oh God! Can we not strike that fatal blow to cease
This unholy strife, these sacrifices and starvations.
Bring to this sad earth once more tranquility and peace.
Return to these wretches their right to live, to die, to love
Their loved ones once again. Power we need from the One above.
  For man now destroys what God hath created.
  Beware lest he destroy what God hath mated!!

Richard C. Griggs

Watch-Dogging

Never think you can sneak a lone peanut
  or grab a grape on-the-run,
Never try to chew-up a cookie
  you'll be spied before you are done.

For pups are eared to the crackling
  of wrappers—of foil and of pulp,
And latches and lids that are opened
  bring them fast on-their-paws with a yelp.

So accept that "watch-dogging" your sneak-food
  is healthful: you love it! it's fine!
And soon you'll be fitting in outfits,
  that haven't fit right for some time.

priscilla whitaker

Fears

Will I have to go through pain again?
Or will everything turn out okay?
Will my problem be completely gone?
Or will I have to live with it always?
Will this effect my social life in any way?
Or will I just go on like a regular teen?
Will any new people I meet next year understand?
Or does anybody understand what I am feeling?
Will anybody know the real me...
  the me with all of these problems and fears.

Lisa Naucke

The Gull

A gull sits stately
Perched atop a rock
Jutting from the ocean
In a desolate spot.
A quiet sentinel, all alone
As the pounding waves swish around his throne.
He watches as other friends fly by;
As a gull's shrill scream splits the daytime sky.

Do you wonder why?
Verna Von Steen

Images

Images of your loveliness flow continuously through my mind;
Pleasure and joy erupt thinking you will be mine.
Unto that special moment when reality can flourish;
My imagination will cheerfully create and nourish.

Until fate releases me from this protection,
Magic illusions are run with total recollection.
Feeling the emotions of a school boy and a man,
Mystic powers from above to this princess who only can.

Fantasies of you cause my spirit to surrender;
Then hearing your voice "patience and discipline," I remember.
At this tender stage know my intentions are sincere;
What seems so far away, in reality is actually quite near.

Although it's difficult to deal with such a notion,
The feeling from my heart and soul is one of devotion.
My body trembles at the image of your lips on mine;
Oh!! How the best things come in images and then will "Our Time."
Toff B. Garcia

Showers

A light rain is falling. As if for my amusement, tiny circles eclipse one another, on the waters surface.
Where have these clouds been, I wonder.
Soon they will depart, slip away on the silken sky.
The sky darkens. The circles become obscure. Where one ends and another begins, I can no longer see.
A glistening streak of light appears. Leaves and petals become perfect settings for raindrops, that appear to be diamonds.
Calm is returning. I hear a gentle song, as the graceful feathered inhabitants of my garden make an appearance.
They will dry their wings and celebrate the life giving showers.
Do they wonder why the woman in the hat, is this day on the other side of the window.
I watch, as if peering through a keyhole, at a world so much larger and grander than anything I could imagine.
I too celebrate.
Katherine Crinklaw

"On A Quiet Night"

The moon hangs low like a vanquished pinnacle
patiently watching the lovers' reflection
mingle with its own. Side by side,
together seeming to glean an equal
support from one another, they
ripple and meld with the moon:
good night. They feel like letting
go; into the freedom of comfortable
loneliness. They move,
shadows merge; moon watches from up
high. Sometimes it's the secret
uneasiness, underneath the heavens,
far from the light of days, we need.
Matthew Timothy Frazier

The Joy Of Gardening

You may find me in my garden most any time of day
Plowing, raking, planting, or hoeing weeds away.
Working in my garden is a pleasure I am told
That will keep me young and active even as I'm growing old.

It is a joy and wonder to see the sprouting seeds
And to watch them form their blossoms so I can tell the flowers from weeds.
I grow juicy red tomatoes and my corn gets very high;
The insects can't resist them I don't believe they try.

I spray them, swat them, stomp them, and my pumpkins were doing fine
Until I saw brown beatles chewing ravishingly on a vine.
My flowers will bloom profusely if I can kill off all the slugs
But if I can't the flowers they leave will become a lunch for bugs.

I have little choice but to share my corn with worms and flocks of birds.
But must they gorge on my tomatoes, then for dessert devour my herbs?
I guess I'll go on fighting with hoe, and rake, and spray
Then harvest what they leave me, that's the price I'll have to pay.

So tell me true, if you can decide, is gardening a joy or need?
But while you ponder, please excuse me, I see another weed.
Leslie A. Cole

Poetry

Poetry reality, fantasy, or make believe.
Poetry is whatever you want it to be.

Poetry is a work of art from which is done by only one
Poetry is from the heart deep within your soul.

Poetry is something that is done by
the master, it takes time as if it
was a masterpiece coming from a shelf.

Poetry is a work from within us, it's
something that you have and that you do not lose.

Poetry is like a song with beat and rhythm.
To me there are two kinds of poems,
one from the heart and then make believe.
Leslie Taylor

Would That I But Love Thee

Would that I but catch one stolen glance from thine wondrous
pools of deep reflection, once called eyes,
for that act doth touch my very soul to its depth and breadth
with the essence of thy being. Would that I but love thee...

And would that I but savor one lingering touch from thine
silken limbs of grace and charm, once called hands,
for that act doth fortify my very soul to its foundations
with the strength of thy being. Would that I but love thee...

And would that I but breathe one sigh of misty spring from
thine parted scarlet ribbons, once called lips,
for that act doth lift my very soul to its grandest height
with the mystery of thy being. Would that I but love thee...
William C. Peter

Untitled

The eyes of innocence shed tears of blood.
Pools of sweat drown the hope.
Beams of light engulfed by darkness.
Purity severed and torn apart.
Devil's breath penetrates your soul... no hope.
And as the angels cry you scream.
Your screams dissolve to nothing.
Nothing can save you!
Nichelle Anne Cranston

Untitled

Staring at a blank page, lines seem to
protrude off the edges racing on and on.
Stare hard; they move. Squirm.
Imagine what could be written; strength, life, death.
It could be powerful, could be weak,
could be a quote, memorized by everyone in a college
literature course or scribbled words, meaningless, Ink, black
as death on white life. Taking over man's thoughts. Is there a
point? Not in what is written. Change is inevitable, going
to happen. Optic sense surrounded by inky
pools. The lines are barriers. Don't leave them they say.
In the lines or behind a cage? Restricted to a language
if to mean something, What? Don't know,
no one does. The longer you stare the
more angry the lines become, the harder
they bind the mind creating false hopes
of greatness. Some write their souls on
paper, between lines, drops of blood oozing from their pens.
Until they're engulfed, struggling to free themselves.
Screaming silent screams; helpless.
All this, staring at a blank page.
Kimberly Fleming

Gloomy Saturday

The grey days continue,
pressing gloom on my mind
like a workman clamps an instrument.

There is no hope in our world-
only wispy dreams of past encounters.
No future-
only the heavy, oppressing moments of now.

I've been running-
aching to dance along star-lit mountains,
and you just don't get it.
I run farther away from you now, faster-
and your footsteps pursue me in heavy heartbeats.

A maze, that's what it's like
My emotions bump into the walls and bruise.
Broken, I try a new direction.
What lies in wait at the end?
Freedom and another chance at loving?
Or the Grim Reaper?
Kit Leamy

My Dream

The LAND - beautiful, remote with trees and hills,
Peaceful, serene where time stands still;
No tomorrows, no yesterdays; just the present - always.

The LAND - enter the gates of eden; follow the winding path;
Seeking truth and wisdom; searching for what God hath.

The LAND - where peace, harmony, and unity fills each and every soul;
Where God's grace is given freely for all there to behold.

The LAND - awakens the senses; awakens the mind;
Awakens the joy bound up inside.

The LAND - the birds sing, the winds blow, the clouds drift,
And the flowers grow.
The stars shine, the moon glows, the sun sends warmth to all below.

The LAND - lifts the spirit, enriches the mind,
Heals the bodies of those dwelling inside.

The LAND - is life, is ecstasy, is freedom, is joy, is hope.
Is faith, is love, is truth, is forgiveness, is strength.

The LAND - the manifestation of God on Earth,
I yearn to dwell there forever.
Rose Ann Bedell

A Daughter

How tiny you were when you were born
Pretty long fingernails
And so inquisitive and bright.
I never wanted to let you out of my sight.
I wanted everything for you to be right.
What love you brought into our home.
You were never one to roam
Now you have a home of your own.

I pray that you will seek God's grace
In every storm that you will face.
The highest honor you could give to me
Is that you feel the love God has for you.
For all the rest is temporary you know
But God's love is forevermore.
Patricia A. Bradford

The Romance Writer

On mists of dusk, sweet yearnings rise
promises of mystery and romances unfulfilled
one's mind travels among the dew-stained hills
the wind brushes my face as the breath of
a stolen kiss.
Would I close my eyes and feel the
warmth of you next to me
I can almost believe you standing there
the depth of your eyes, but not the
color of your hair
in my mind you and I are separated
by great expanses of time and space
yet - if I but hold my arms out to
the moon, I may embrace you here
by night fall.
Susan Fisher

Puber

Hmm...
Puber is his name.
His life is an empty cage-
School is even worse.
They try to teach him
  but it's like a curse.
Are his parents old-fashioned?
  His sister is a tease!
He finds himself better than all the rest
  at their best.
The radio-
  Music loud as can be -
  that's him.
The whole world seems to be against him -
  poor boy!!
Puber is his name.
Wilma Bylsma

Tulip's Dream

In a flash of darkness the brilliance came,
  Purple burning bright without a name.
Born within a tulip's dream,
  Dark slivers of black in its seams
Edges aglow with a burst of light,
  Turning circled edges dipped in white.
Wonderings of dangers of deeper thoughts,
  Spilling from touches and talks.
The flower shows things to be,
  With promises fulfilled, the spirit leaves.
Linda Richardson

"Heroes"

Walk away Joes—throw away Jills.
Rap, no longer a signal—a language.
Weapons speak angry words.
Smoke spirals upward—
Dusting off
Walk away Joes—throw away Jills.
Shooters' veins throb with ice-cream chills.
Cracked minds create "crack babies"—
their legacy—
Walk away Joes—throw away Jills.
Awareness—drifting
Honesty—scorned
Responsibility—unanswered.
Love—feared.
Ambling along—Jill becomes Joe
and Joe becomes Jill.
"Heroes" of our Society.
Marguerite Brosnan

Neighbors In The Hood

I had an alarming thought today, more often than I should, a heartfelt
reaction, quite bothersome, accounted from...some neighbors in
the hood.

So, just who are our neighbors, neighbor, living in our neighborhood?
Living as wolves, meek as sheep, living as scoffers, because they could.

In my mind, I witnessed the fatherless, there's the slothful,
the idle, and feeble.
I thought of murders, molesters, seducers, heady,
and high-minded people.

And so, I thought of the many lives...that were here,
now come and gone.
The causes, and effects, the fruitless deaths...'Twas a nightmare,
barely won.

I could see homosexuals, and vagabonds, harlots, wizards, and liars.
I remembered the peacemakers, the servants, the priests....,
and the stranger, meet for hire.

So neighbor, good neighbor, evil neighbor, I have determined it
fairly good.
Every good and evil neighbor is from our neighbors in the hood.
Lillian J. Grigsby

Untitled

Searching the world for the meaning of life,
Reading, watching, listening.
Conquering only enough to fulfill,
The ambitions that strike us like lightening.

Whenever we travel to far away lands,
That hold the keys to survival,
Somehow, empty handed, as we return home,
Our hearts ache for more constant revival.

The simplest of pleasures, walking down a street
People greeting us in return.
Their smiling faces, heartfelt love
A feeling we needn't discern.

Dreaming, disoriented we dally,
Among the throng of onlookers, seeking the same;
Loving our neighbors as ourselves
Won't earn us an ounce of fame.

Above the anger and anguish,
Isn't that all we really need and want,
To be recognized and loved and love in return?
Aye, there's the end of the hunt.
G. O. Perri

Our Wedding Day...

As I walk down the aisle and see you waiting for me,
Realizing we are two, yet we are one.
Along this walk I think of things to come,
You and I, home, children, days yet to come, and growing old
with you.
Going to pledge my love and faith to you,
and place it on your hand in the form of a gold band.
Before I take the first step of our life together,
my mind draws a blank.
I look up and see you for the first time.
Kimberly S. DeCair

"Fire In The Kitchen"

I am doing reds today, the "no" signs, toxic and inflammable cast outs.
Red is the color of bad, of fire in the kitchen, paprika and tobacco,
salsa and Tabasco, a red hot pepper brother told me was a piece of
candy.

Red is the color of the match she warned me not to play with.
It is the color of my explosion, of my disruption and exile.
At five, I blew up the kitchen. Does anyone ever ask about me?

I, of bald sockets wearing a red facial bandanna, am the self-anointed
curator of a sculpture garden, a red conveyor of tinkling, clattering
tin concussions of used metal, of breaking glass. The floor is a
concrete slab.

The sky, domicile blue linoleum. Walls, heat waves like cellophane,
distort a cardboard city, a starving dog, drowned kittens,
an amputated limb sealed in a metal bin. What don't I have here?

I don't have a mirror, a match, a circle of gas or a suicidal thought.
Marian W. Trotter

Beyond A Dream

If you're lost,
remember everything you have and you will be found.

If you have nothing,
remember your dreams and you will be happy.

If you do not know how to dream,
look up into the sky and let a star carry your mind away
and you will see what you really are.

For what you have is your life,
and your dreams are merely what you see.
Nicole Braddock

My Spring

The times when someone can
   reach into your life and touch your soul
   are rare.
The intimacy of that action transforms
   and you can never again look upon that
   person as a stranger.
They hold a piece of you,
   whatever their awareness of that
   hold might be.
To the heart, so exposed, there is
   both liberation and fear of
   revelation.
Emotions though forgotten are suddenly
   fresh — newly felt,
   full of sting and promise.
Tears pour to cleanse old wounds
   and nurture the budding
   new life hiding beneath them.
Winter has passed — it is spring.
Thank you for seeing me.
Penelope H. Addy

Love

When love has faded and your world seems to end,
Remember there is always someone that will help your heart mend.
So open your mind and think what's ahead;
Instead of gloom and wishing you were dead.
Use your mind to think with and your heart to feel,
And you will never be alone,
Again.
Melanie Nielsen

Feelings

Two minds, side by side,
reminiscing -
of little songs sung together on a
scrubbed, clean porch.
of little games played together
with broken pieces of china,
discarded only because they couldn't
be used on the table anymore -
of bare feet dancing
to the rhythm of the old accordion,
and papa singing softly -
Two minds, side by side,
reminiscing -
sharing the inside of each other's hearts,
letting love flow,
through the hands that suddenly were holding together,
happy that this moment was here.
Maude Ancelet

Rest In God's Hand

Rest in God's hand, and you'll never complain;
   Rest in God's will - He'll never change.
God is the one to whom we must go,
   God's will is perfect - we know this is so.

Jesus died and rose again-
   It was in God's perfect plan.
Jesus is with you, and always will be
   Your strength, your song, and your victory.

Rest in God's hand, and He'll do the rest,
   Rest in the fact that He'll do the best.
He'll always be there when trouble comes;
   He'll be there to help you to overcome.
He knows just what you're going through,
   He'll help you, and guide you, and be with you.

"Rest in My plan, for I know what is best
   You're in My hand, and I'll give you rest.
The rest you desire is here within Me-
   I love you so much, and will give it to thee.
Look unto Me in the midst of these tests-
   Even within them I'll give you rest."
Susan Wendt

Take Not For Granted

Have you ever felt the softness of a red maple leaf?
Or caressed the neck of a kitten ruffled in distress?
Ever notice how slowly the shape of a cloud may change?
Or how the brilliant colors of a sunset can quickly dim and fade?
Why are people in such a rush? They take no time to see,
Ignoring Mother Earth, her beauty and mystery.
The scent of a fresh cut lawn and lilacs in full bloom,
The sound of far-off thunder foreshadowing the storm.
These awesome gifts of nature were given to you and me,
But they don't even notice, their eyes too blind to see.
I thank God every day for the air in which I breathe,
Appreciate the little things, not as little as they seem.
I also thank Him for keeping me alive another day.
Take not for granted what the Lord has given, for He can take away!
Robert J. Stewart

Lost

I want to imagine his breath on my skin, want to close my eyes and rest in his absent arms,
I want to brand his image on my heart's memory, yet to flush it from my soul through yearning tears would be to treat the wound.
No. It is only a bandage on blind eyes, for it is incurable.
The laugh that haunts is sweet but sharp, its echo floods me with a warmth, yet twists in my side.
The vision of those crystal pools of sky burn icily into my being, chasing all thoughts from my mind's realm.
Something anxious flutters inside my stomach, courses through my veins deliciously tingles in my head until I am faint and I feel weakened and vulnerable when soft and perfect lips part to form the crooked grin that snatches the very life from my breast, and holds it, guides it into a cavernous abyss of mystery and secret, imprisons it captive guest under hypnotizing charm.
I remember all with painfully distinct detail, it brings a smile to my lips and a tear to my eye, it fills me with a longing ache, leaves me numb except for the cold shudder of regret, a chill that far surpasses any physical feeling.
Empty hope begs for life's soft caress on flesh once more.
Nicole Haag

Sunrise/Sunset In Seattle

Dawn sets the sky aflame with lovely soft hues
Revealing silhouettes of the city and mountains around,
And creating reflections of this beauty
Off the waters of lakes and Puget Sound!

This scene offers a peaceful morning drive
Midst the workday's traffic congestion,
As sweet music comes from the car radio
Providing a time to review one's convictions.

The evening drive home repeats this view,
As the sun slips slowly down.
Ah! Such awesome beauty and serenity
Showing the presence of God's love abound!
Maxine C. Howe

Memories Are Forever

   My dear, I knew that you loved me
Over the years, through bad times and good
   We were a great team together, you see
and always did the best that we could.

   We gave our children a very special love
Raising them up, knowing right from wrong
   Because God gave us wisdom from above
Through Angels' spirit, their love and song.

   You will always be within my heart
With memories that will live forever
   Someday, we shall never be apart
In heaven, with a brand new endeavor.

   When God sends his Angels for me
I'll be coming with a great big smile
   Just anytime will suit me to a tee
Because my life has been so worthwhile.
Mattie Dee Kinnison

Spring

Slowly the rain finds its way through the
Proud bold clouds from winter's day.
Rain falls lightly, almost as a mist.
Irises awaken from a long winter's sleep, as they peek
   through the last of winter's snow.
New growth springs up everywhere,
Giving us the sweet smell of spring.
Ryan McGlynn

14 July: Bastille Day — Independence Day
For The French

Virginia, I kneel down and kiss your slick, slimy mud.
Rich soil fertile with lush greenery.
Your steamy air wraps loving hugs around my wounded heart.

California, your dry breezes whisper promises
of camaraderie, family-love.
But your wooing no longer answers my dreams.
The price is too great to pay.

Tear out my heart and let the birds pull it apart.
Fly the strings on those sterile breezes.

Pry open my squinting eyes that shield me from
your mis-shapened images of love.
Pry them open with your angry, sharp words and
fill them with your salty tears of frustration.

Hammer my sleeping naivete on your cold anvil of guilt.
Mold me into your image of a loyal daughter.
Scorch my brain with your searing screams of guilt and pain.

I will venture of the land of (mother's) milk and honey only when
I have turned to stone.

Patrica Best

The Mind Of Man, America

A mind unshackled, free and sound,
Rid of fetter, fate and folly,
Sailed the earth's unbounded sea
And wedged itself in history.

A mover of men, it moved us all;
Its courage, its goal, its purpose, its soul
Led us to a brighter place,
Where freedom shined and minds could race.

The Founding Thinkers, wise and bold,
Full of richer rights and reason,
Used their minds to mold a son—
A model state to look upon.

Enduring the death, subduing the pain,
They challenged their nature; gave it a name.
Freedom is Man; His mind is free.
Denied your rights, a slave you'll be.

Bloody battles Man has fought
For the contents of His thoughts—
Wars to be remembered by
The future movers of the mind.

Sean Green

A Gift Of Rest

A blanket of sleep
Quietly spreads its billows free,
Its presence unknown, its purpose hid
To all except the earth who sees
With open arms and weary limbs
The gift of rest that winter brings.

Her own adornments are now at rest,
Her trees, her flowers, have done their best,
But now their warmth is already gone,
Their life was short, they now belong
To soft white snow, and cold north winds
That cover her body, and turn her gentle ways to grim.

But she must wait, too tired to struggle
From the comforting realm of sleep.
And so she rests, and makes her plans,
Knowing soon that winter must go,
And, for a time, she will live again.

Peggy J. Poole

Shackled Man

Catch a glimpse of people frowning,
rows of saddened sheep
Dreams they have, dreams too late
Never living out... only locked in
Accomplishments thrown into non-existence
Persistence towards emptiness... aching skulls... pain
Survival depends on this, a mind device
Trapped within the confines of civilized hell
Endless routines within a routine, an empty field
An orange ball behind a range
Thoughts racing, thinking about an alternate present
So hard to find the inner glow.. living by
preconcocted ideals
Recanted by they
Thinks of they... they have kept him locked in
He is they...only now there is no they
Only him, frightened for so long... only him
Fear slowly drifts... the man breaks the chains
Not the chains of they... his chains... only his
It was never they... only him
Sets out into the field
Behind him... old rusted chains
Someone else can have them... It was always him
It still is

Tory Mondragon

Legacy Of Man

Long ago, giants lived here,
Ruling a kingdom, stretching from Great River to Mighty Sea,
A peaceful nation flowered, each member with a purpose,
Then Man came, from across the sea,
No one minded, for the bounty of the giants was great,
But man's relentless hunger for power, was intolerable,
The armies of the bear, wolf and cougar resisted,
The giants sadly watched, as war developed below,
The green kingdom was consumed by bitter carnage,
Terrific battles were fought, brave souls perished,
Nature and man struggled for control,
As the clouds of war cleared, man stood alone,
Nature's noble resistance, lay prostate forever,
Today, where giants once stretched green limbs,
Stand homes, malls, and parking lots,
The legacy of man.

Kevin Dodge

We Never Finished The Dance...

The music still plays... the melody
reverberates in the places of my heart and
soul that finds you there.

We never got a chance to finish the song
that we started many years ago, but
maybe, just maybe, there should never be
closure. Why bring closure to hearts
that remember cherished moments never
to be forgotten... love that has endured...
feelings that tug at the heartstrings...
and friendship that will be forever new and alive?

We shared a song, but now we have
different arrangements, in our lives.
I miss when we were on the same page,
cord, and beat... I miss those moments...

Tomorrow,... the music will continue to
play and the dance will live on forever.
We may not be on the same page, cord or beat,
but the music we made will never be silenced.

I hear you.....

Larry Dawson

Screaming In Silent Complacency
(Rodney King's Tears)

List all my depravities,
Sanctimonious bloated weasels concealed in sacrosanct garb.
Swallow your vices.
Regurgitate the black secrets in your hollow existence,
For the sake of pecuniary compensation.

Mire my neurotransmitters with pseudo intelligentsia
Fabricated by media source.
Affront my ethnic culture with legal indignities
And social alienation.

Forge a continuity of enslavement through glass ceilings,
Silent recriminations and blatant persecutions.
Enlist my children into a battalion of ignorant zombies
Generated by apathetic money herders and electronic gurus.

And when it's all complete, look me in the eyes,
Spit into them, and tell me my eyes were menacing.

Shelly Todd Velox

The Lonely Man

A quaint old man, with a long white beard
  sat on the dock of a rundown pier.
He looked dejected, lonesome, and full of despair,
  His eyes seemed to say, "won't somebody care?"

He traveled and trudged through this life, filled with woe,
  raised up a family, watched them all grow.
Some of them married, some passed away,
  He was left all alone, needless to say.

He sat by himself, looking out to the sea,
  At the foam on the white caps, on the beach, the debris.
He folded his hands, which were gnarled with old age,
  Bent his head low, and thought with a rage.

Why do I sit here, waiting for death,
  To struggle, and gasp for each little breath.
God in your mercy, take pity on me,
  Don't let me sit here to look at the sea.

His face became peaceful, his eyes filled with love,
  As our good Lord embraced him, in heaven above.

Lorraine Anzalone

Freedom

She titled her head toward heaven,
  Scanned the blue-domed, cloud-fleeced sky;
Surveyed her celestial domain, her kingdom,
  Where her eagle kin did fly.

They plucked her powerful wings,
  Brought her to earth to languish, to die;
"N caged her in a cruel metal forest,
  Not willing that she should fly.

Nobility brought low in bondage,
  Her home now a metal cage;
Corn 'n carrion from the hand of man
  Her food, her sustenance, her wage.

She's a pleasure to man in her beauty,
  Elegant, steel-clawed, regal;
Symbol of raw strength and freedom,
  The noblest of birds, this eagle.

Could she speak with the tongue of man,
  "Excelsior" would be her one word cry;
But the selfish spirit of shallow souls
  Won't let the eagle fly.

Reuben L. Hilde Sr.

The Blackboard

I see a blackboard in my mind,
Scribblings, pictures of every kind.

Confusing, twisting, in different directions,
Needing to make many corrections.

An image of an eraser wipes it clear,
The words and the faces
Reappear.

Disturbing, mayhem, not making sense,
I need to take some kind of defense.

I erase and erase trepid with fear,
The words and the faces
Reappear.

The eraser is worn, it's lost its fight,
The blackboard now
Is totally
White.

Vita T. Falzone

Peace At Our House

To each other we look for strength
Searching for it we go to a great length

It is not easy to forgive sins of another
Even if it is a husband, wife, sister or brother

We may have into troubled times fell
In our complex thoughts we believe it is Hell

With peace in our house to others we are able to tell
Before the troubles out of hand swell

In our house that certain peace of mind can be felt
Those outside troubles began away to melt

It had seemed our nerves were to the very edge
But that peace we have at home drove in relaxing wedge

Without a peace in your house to stop troubles from being fed
You find hopelessness within you being spread

Yes, a peace in a home takes lots of work to make it flow
But for a happy family it brings a closeness and a bright glow

A home without peace makes us sad
Thank you God! For we have a home with peace and we are glad

A peaceful home and a happy family makes the heart of the USA
Don't kid yourself as long ago, it is just as important today

Keith E. Sheldon

A Discontented Life

Youth spent dreaming, yearning, hoping
Searching, seeking,
Something always elusive
Longing, desiring things not known
Aspiring to even greater horizons
Achieving but not content
Craving that which would ease the torment
Fill the emptiness in the soul

Bygone days are gone forever
Now regretting, reliving
Grieving, lamenting that which is over
Despairing, despondent, opportunities unheeded
Never knowing, always wondering
Choices made
Good and bad, lost in the past

Finally accepting
Appreciating today
Too late! A life wasted.

Lillian K. Lynch

"A Boy's Puzzle"

A young soul of curiosity,
   searching the heaven for answers;
His mind full of questions,
   screaming words of challenge to anyone.

Winds of time gone by,
   blowing its realm of wisdom;
As the young child listens,
   hearing great knowledge to digest.

Clouds reap with visions,
   using vivid images to foretell;
While eyes so immature,
   viewing only tales transform to humor.

Nature with scenes of beauty,
   scheming to brighten one's imagination;
Youthful frustrations of envy,
   refusing guidance known to existence.

Life wild with mystery,
   making responses with much perplexity;
As the youth grows,
   realizing life is but a puzzle.

Leonard T. White

Dedication To Love

Just one look at you and my world turns blue.
Seeing you is like a dream come true.
When you smile my heart goes wild.
My greatest moment is walking with you on the lawn.
Your charms are so warm, it's like the breaking of dawn.

Mental disturbance of my brain,
Backed by a broken heart, shattered by pain,
Love can bring joy, it can also bring pain
But my love can never be wild and bare like Pedro Plains.
If you are sick in any manner I will give the love frame.

Just to be honest dedicated and true to you
Just to let our dreams come through
You might say I've got a girl friend or two
But you alone make me feel for nothing new.
When you are sad, I feel your sad state and your hunger too.

My empty loving reservoir you do fill,
Also my ocean of emotions stand still.
My moments of loneliness make me feel like going up a hill.
Dearest our love can never change, no never.
My sweet baby my love will always be true forever.

Leslie E. Hyde

Garden Of The Simple Statues

I turn into her now, long elegant shoulder,
rounded bulb, bent elbow I slide into the frozen gesture
of the hand, the stopped palm, the fingers up
toward heaven, their flesh gray and
flecked mixed with black grain of earth.
I become him also on his trophy pedestal,
big solid calves, the curves of the heavy hips
the repetitive power of his drive gone away,
the boulders of the pecs lying like stone
when it waits to be broken and sandblasted.
I understand this now.
I understand the cement sac of the balls, the rock penis,
the elliptic shape of the polished head,
I understand the other one too, the face turned away in disgust,
the thick smoky hair over the iron nipples
of the dry milk breasts,
the hand on the hip like a fashion statement. I see her place,
an escape passageway from the dark belly to the world of light,
where the phantom children cry,
where the two used to fit.

Mehdi Ouni

Bless Thy Woman

Not where I want to be,
Seems as if no one at all loves me,
Places to go and things to see,
everything's the same to me,
The dark, the light, evening shade before the night,
Phase of the moon, as the sun shines high in the afternoon
Bless thy Woman in uniform as she walks by,
"I look at all of them and want to cry!"
Everything's the same, and everything will die,
No matter how many times she walks by,
She does not know,
She does not care,
She has her money, and all is fair,
As a soul lies clean beneath filthy skin,
lying out under the sun,
She sees only dirt and filth,
Not true beauty outside the wealth,
Not everyone is rich or beautiful on the skin,
but souls are clean and accepting of all, no matter how bad you fall.
KILL THY WOMAN IN UNIFORM!

Sarah Martley

Hope Everlasting

The World is a "Stranger," with its "misses" and "hits,"
Seems the longer we live here, the stranger it gets.
Some actions get irksome, and matters misused,
There's really no wonder we're often confused.
When awful things happen, and hope appears dim,
God, alone, holds the answer, so we leave it to **Him**.

Richard M. Shaffer

Untitled

Servants of the most high God we are
   Sent to bring healing
   For a world reeling
     To another holocaust.

In hands and hearts there is compassion
   Meant to be feeling
   Illnesses' depths, depression's power,
     Awake to need and to respond.

Lord, for all failures and transgressions,
   We plead for pardon
   And beg Your mercy
     That forgiven we may serve.

Lord, redeemed by Christ's most precious blood
   Let us be Your hands,
   Your feet to go the rounds,
     To meet the crying needs we see.

May our fellowship give You glory
   As, in the company
   Of those redeemed by grace,
     We crave Your blessing and Your peace.

Robert W. F. Harms

Christmas, Christmas In The Night

I can imagine love and snow and mistletoe
rhyming in the night
Santa Claus and happiness together in the night
ornaments and joyfulness
just being together without fright
standing together, with a friend, may be the only
thing you want
until then, sugar plums might dance in your head
until Christmas time you should imagine,
try to at least,
because there are so many things to love.

Paul Nicholas Panza

Parents Love

Parents will be parents, different each day
Set in their minds, in their own way
Trying to show us the best life to live,
Giving us all they could possibly give
We may not agree with them all the time
As our parents, their answers need no rhythm or rhyme
The love they have for their children, is like no other
Different from the love between a sister and brother
Teaching us about life and hoping they're right
They pray to God as they kiss us good night
As kids they're all we know
Always standing beside us, helping us grow
They tell us when we're wrong,
Praise us when we're right,
When we disagree, it will cause us to fight
As time passes by, the older their children grow
Parents hope that they're right,
In passing on what they know

Lisa M. Chiuchiolo

If There Had Been A Day....

If there had been a day,
seven years from today
When the sun could come out and play,
just for an hour would be okay
All day yesterday, we read about the sun,
oh how hot and fun
The sun can be a pretty flower,
only blooming for about an hour
It's as if the red devil himself has taken over,
I wish I could find a 4-leaf clover
I'd wish for the sun to come out forever,
the sun, I think, should have all the power
So it will come out for more than an hour,
this time
I'd even pay a dime,
maybe the sun would say a verse that can rhyme
Maybe even a spooky one,
yeah that would be fun
But only, if there had been a day.

Michelle Meyer

A Father's Love

Being a parent is never easy to do
So many things you face, with each day that is new
In order to survive we must give and take
We will never be perfect as we learn from mistakes.

When you have children, you give them a name.
And though they are different, we try to treat them the same.
We try to provide the same for each one
Seems it is never enough when it's all said and done.

Sometimes we argue and disagree, late at night,
But because we are parents doesn't mean we're always right.
To have their respect, this we must earn
No matter what age we're not too old to learn.

Some things we do they may not understand
I hope they know we will be there; if they need a helping hand.
Sometimes they may think that we are unfair
But the love that we have will always be there.

Most of the time they make our hearts sing,
But some of the time they pull at our heartstrings,
We can't put it aside or do away with this love
Because as parents it is sent from above.

Ricky Ray Roe

Circle

Breath to breath
sex to sex
heat to heat
our hearts beat a rhythm even Gods can't dance to
yet I pray to no God but this one I can touch
to feel trembling before me
and whose eyes I see shining by the fire
my tongue has wrought

Mind to mind
hand to hand
myth to myth
you tell me your lies yet I know who you are in your bones
two such as us cannot be kept by one mind yet
we are strangers in body only
I find the shadows of your past liven you and
as you rise to greet me I am fulfilled that
yes I know you.

William Lawrence Bowen

Hearts In The Rubble

For Oklahoma's Mothers

Sleeping mats scattered, hopes and dreams shattered
Shards of Barney records intermingled with bricks.
Quiet peaceful naps and delighted hand claps
Lost to horrific silence permeating rubble and sticks.

Puffs of dust curling, drifting and swirling
Echo tiny feet that once danced on this floor.
A dolly's left arm, cows and pigs from a farm
Broken toys strewn about, to be played with no more.

Empty arms ache, voices stumble and shake
As prayers and amidahs are mumbled in pain.
All the tears from our faces cannot wash clean these places
The Lord's merciful rain cannot wash clean the stain
Hateful revenge and inhumanity strike us again.

Robin Haseltine

Gone

A dove flying alone calls out for one to
    share the skies with him,
As he flies, tears fill his eyes,
    I think of my life without you.
A stream continuously flowing in a circle,
    goes nowhere.
Glistening its beauty lost, no one sees or
    seems to care.
It goes on forever lonely, like my life
    when you're not there.
A beautiful flower, living happily, is torn
    away by the storm's rain.
In the mud it lies, lifeless, its petals
    full of pain.
When you leave, it rains in my heart like
    a storm I never knew.
My life feels the pain of really losing you.

Mark A. Warren

The Bag Lady

Day after day the bag lady makes her sad journey
She stops now and then to rest
People hurrying by look at her with detest
She knows her hair and clothes are dirty
There's a sad and hungry look on her face
Now the bag lady is walking at a much slower pace
She feels that no one cares
I'm giving her my sandwich. Maybe I'll need help someday
Smiling and thanking me the bag lady goes her way.

Sandra Cannon

M-O-T-H-E-R

M is for my MOM who gives me much loving care.
  She always takes me to school and places everywhere.

O is for the OUCHES I often feel many days.
  My Mom helps my hurts and OUCHES go far, far away

T is for the TIMES that Mom gives me a special TREAT.
  Mom really loves me from my head to my feet.

H is for my HAPPY HOME where Mom always loves me.
  She gives me HUGS if I hurt my hand, head, or knee.

E is for the extra EATS Mom fixes all the time.
  They are so very yummy and they don't cost me a dime.

R is for my ROOM where Mom helps me RELAX and REST
  and when I put these letters together,

MY MOM IS THE BEST!!!
Sister Loretta Fick

Who Is She?

She is the cooling breeze on a hot day,
She is the laughter heard in children's play,
She is the blanket that covers the cold,
She is the strength given to the bold,
She is the mountain that overlooks the valley,
She is the light that brightens a dark alley,
She is the sun that rises every morning,
She is the eagle that is always soaring,
She is the star shining through the night,
She is the wing that keeps the birds in flight,
She is the peacemaker of all bad wars,
She is the lion with meaningful roars,
She is the medicine that helps heal,
She is the love that all may feel,
She is the unreplaceable, there is no other,
She is the wonderful woman I call
My Mother.
Tara Voors

Love And Pain

A rose is the seed of eternal life which becomes to be the fatal light
So much love I give out, yet none has been returned
The feeling of pain is sweeping over me, but nothing can I do about it
I feel lost and forgotten in this pain that is taking over me
All love for me is gone, as is everyone else's love for me
These memories of pain come back to me and seem to haunt me through the night.
The memories of you and me and all the love we had for each other
But I must end this pain somehow and go on with life without you
My love for myself is gone again as it was before you came into my life
But I must regain it. How? I don't know, but I do know
the memories of us will never be forgotten.
Rebecca Switzer

Thanks

Close your eyes,
See the dream.
Look to the skies,
Look to the stream.
Think of all the days of old,
When kings would wear Great Crowns of Gold.
Queens and Maids with Golden Hair,
Knights and those for whom they fare
Open your eyes, return to this place,
Look in the mirror at your face.
Thank the Lord for what you've got,
Thank the Lord for something you did not.
Nicholas Serre

The Tragedy

I looked over and saw the tears on the old woman's face.
She knew this was the end of her race.
Her skin was so tan-its appearance was like leather.
Yet when she spoke her thoughts, her voice was light as a feather.
I died inside when I saw her tears fall to the ground.
They fell steadily down her face, never making a sound.
She sat there so straight and so very proud.
She never heard the battle raging so loud.
She went back in her mind to when she was a child.
She respectfully helped her mother as the boys ran wild.
Suddenly she was brought back to the present as she felt great pain.
She looked to the sky and it started to rain.
As her life ran out of the gaping hole.
She started a chant to guide her soul.
An evil white man stood over her body as she lay dead.
Wondering what price he would get for her head.
There are so many spirits still wandering around.
Because the Indian Spirit cannot leave if the body is face down.
Terri Hailey

A Choice

As she walked gracefully along the shore
she thinks of thoughts she once ignored
so confused seems all alone
no one to guide her, no one to hold
ocean so calm, stillness in night
stars so bright, to light a blind man's sight
wind so cool against her breast, moon
was full as she undressed.
A dip in the water, toes tipping the top
a plunge would be nice, this she thought
all alone, as alone could be
there with the thought of what should be.
Time on one hand, nature on the other
maybe sixteen years or younger
an answer needed before to long
not knowing if it's going to be right or wrong
the moment of truth had finally arrived
the feeling of love from deep inside
the thought of a being only in mind
now has become a reality of time.
Tamra Lanum

Child

The child in me decided one day
She'd come to my rescue, she'd come out to play
She'd teach me that living's what makes life a joy,
That we should forever, remain girl or boy.

She told me I'd never be happy or free
If I always did what you say makes "me" me,
If I never listened to my inner guide,
If only on you and on others relied,
Then life would be joy-less, depressing and sad
I'd end up unhappy, betrayed, raving mad.
She said: Let me be your partner in fun
Let me come out and play, enjoy rain, snow and sun.
If you're constantly working and speaking of doom
We'll both drown in sorrow, in darkness and gloom.

Abundance and life has been purchased for us
Accept it, embrace it, don't count it as loss.
Forget rules and orders that freedoms deny,
'Tis compassion and love that must drive you and I.
Praxcedes Gonzales

Regarding Jenny - Grandma's Thoughts

Jenny's no longer a baby -
She's approaching the terrible two's.
Gone is the little darling
Who only sleeps and coos.

Now she comes in like a whirlwind -
Sweeps things in her path away.
Her word list is growing - her favorite's "no"!
She finally reached doorknobs today.

A joy to behold and one of a kind,
Her vices and virtues are many.
She's sweet as sugar - but lots of spice.
You really can't quite describe Jenny.
Margaret H. De Mar

Jennifer

Jennifer is gone,
She's far, far away,

She has left,
And I've had to stay,

She's gone to Tennessee, California and more,
She's had fun, fun galore,

She's having a good time with friends and family,
While I'm stuck here in Lee County,

One day she'll realize her friends are back here,
Then she'll come home to her friends so dear,

I remember that day not so long ago,
She left but I couldn't go,

Jennifer's my best friend,
And always will be,

Even if she never returns,
She will be in my memory.
Stephanie Midkiff

Babe

"She is sure something," I'll tell you Joe.
"She's young so sweet, and don't you know
She loves me too! I'm years too old.
"But that," say she, "is a story not told."
"Age is a sense of time, not years."
Old is a word, often softened by tears."
Love is the truth, not ever lost."
"She sticks to her guns at any cost."
"I'm curious, says I, "who is this gal?"
"You know me to be your trusted pal."
"You won't believe," he said with a smile.
"Your baby sister is this gal!"
Maurine I. Truitt

On Dying Young

I learned from one.
Quickly he passed
passion extended
dreams on sleeve
breathe the world,
   taste the world,
     embrace the life....vile, ugly, beautiful life
that does not last
nor final hour tell.
How did he know?
...Now it seems
but a dream,
the one who passed so quickly.
Mindy Duncan

Asperse

Violence rises like the sun,
Shining its hate onto everyone.
  Complete destruction is near,
All hearts and souls are filled with fear.

  Wars break out throughout the land,
All hopes for peace and love are banned.
  People mourn and pray to God.
  People mourn and pray to God.

  Time is running out, tick-tock, tick-tock,
Many people lie in deep states of shock.
  The undesired reality grows day by day,
More and more people turning astray.

  It's time to waken before it's too late,
To end all the fighting, killing and hate.
  Put the world back together the way it should be,
A place for all people to be happy and free.
Michael Perez

Untitled

It's Memorial Day
Slowly, I walk through the graveyard
Heavy dew lies on the grass as if the night has wept

Two men I love rest here so alone I come
To visit them once more: a young rebel who made me feel alive
And the man who gave me life

From my father's grave I see his black headstone
Glistening in the morning sun I close my eyes
As tears begin to fall
I remember their smiles and their laughter

I sit in silence, touching my Father's cold granite headstone
While a tiny flag waves I speak softly, hoping he can hear

Other visitors are coming I see their solemn faces
As they hurry to place the flowers by each grave

But, I sit quietly a while longer with my Father
Then silently I go to his grave
Kneeling, I touch his name

I am in no hurry today for as I sit here
I know, the only thing I can give them now
Is my time and love and flowers
Cairo W. Adams

Love Everlasting

Love is a blessing,
So they say,
But will it be as strong today,
As it was yesterday?

Life has its problems,
Distressing as they may be,
But what does it take,
To keep love alive,
Or can we foresee,
What will be?

As we follow the path of life,
With the one we love, along its way,
We hope there will always be a new tomorrow,
Brighter than yesterday,

So, as the days come and go,
Like the tides of the sea,
We hope the love we knew in the past.
Will forever be.
Lynn Edelman

"The Sun Came Across The Water"

The sun came across the water,
shone over the beach, and the storm was over.
As the waves moved my shell. Only part of me
survived. My other shell lost.
The water pushed me up on the beach. I no
longer felt the wetness of the sea. The sand
and salt drying and sticking to my shell.
Soon a pair of feet were facing me. A hand
gently reaching down and picking me up.
Smiled at me.
She was so happy to see me. Often told me
how much she loved me.
To my surprise! I was placed in a bucket
next to my other shell.
Oh, how the little girl surprised us!
Now we have a home growing up with her.
Glued together forevermore.

Randall Ardeane Hilbert

"Melancholy Mood"

Another day gently passes
Signaled by browning grasses
Another day slides on by
into the blue back-dropped sky

In life's full circle life's re-arranged
In a mix of trees slowly colors change
Squirrels scurry gathering winter's food
It comes with the fall, my melancholy mood.

A crisp breath of air blew by memories
of pouncing children in piles of leaves.
A symphony of squeaking swings sound.
Thoughts riding leaves as they glide to the ground.

Soon snow will cover them without a trace
Like the many smiles on a person's face.
Only one left hanging, so with the tree I'll grieve
"Melancholy mood" mourns the death of the leaves!

Keith Duane Curtis

Dawn Of The Dusk

The dawn of evening hours
 signals the ebb of daylight's powers;
now is the time, as nighttime begins
 for forgetting all hassles, the whole day's chagrins.

The peace and serenity of the night
 unfolds, the sunset's a beautiful sight;
subtle pink hues, pale yellows and blues
 help obliterate sadness you saw on the news.

Nighttime enfolds you, arousing your senses;
 your eyes start to wander from well-worn park benches
to nature's own beauty; the flowers full-blooming
 are scenting the night air for fireflies swooning.

The whippoorwill rises with sweet melodies,
 so glad for an audience, eager to please.
The crickets awaken and, taking their cue,
 join in with the wildlife to serenade you.

The air becomes lively with nature's night-song
 as they herald their God-head, so proud and so strong,
to thank Him profusely, each in his own way
 for the dawn of "their" nighttime at the end of the day.

Therese Baxter

Sarah's Faith

It's Sarah's first birthday, one year has gone
Since a premature infant cried in the dawn.
Struggles and surgery just to survive
Caused many to ask how she stayed alive.
Her heart was repaired—one chamber to four—
But numerous upsets resist any cure.

A congenital challenge also holds sway,
Affecting each future and present day.
Innocent eyes in this most perfect face,
Tell an age-old story no one can erase.
Mischievous and blue, they sparkle so bright,
But a slant portends shadows upon the light.

When life is beset with troubles, don't run,
Some suffering and pain comes to everyone.
Experience is needed but more must inspire,
Man's courage to kindle or put out a fire.
Like the innate faith that Sarah holds dear;
You too can believe and erase your fear.

Louise Wright

"Singing A Song For You And Me"

Little cardinal perched in a tree
Singing a song for you and me
along came a little bee, buzzing by,
Oh, sang the cardinal, come hum with me.

Oh, no, no, hummed the little bee
I'm too busy making honey, you see
Off to his nest, the Cardinal did fly
Singing sweetly a song of goodbye

Down upon a flower, the little bee flew
Oh! said the flower, what do you want with me,
I want some nectar, nectar sweet
To make my honey, I'm a Honey Bee

Little bee, little bee, take what you need
That's why God created us indeed
Beauty of flowers and nectar to give
Honey for man to enjoy as he lives

Taking the nectar, away the bee flew
Off to the beehive, deep in the woods
Where other bees were gathered too.
Making honey, God's plan to do.

Mary Dorothy Hall

Catching A Moment of Tomorrow Today

Inside a thoughtless room,
sitting alone,
looking out to a distant world,
seeing no path to follow,
just destiny leading the way.
Experiencing lost hope,
sometimes joy,
but always dreams and God
which make way for times like these
when in the distance, in a now frozen picture
of being alone, lost, unknowing...
But through prayer,
one seeing and believing
will catch this moment again.
Sitting in a room with a glow,
full of life, peace, and answered dreams,
it seems I've moved again.

Catching a Moment of Tomorrow Today.

Leonard Guy Papania

A Poem To My Friend

My dearest friend,
Sitting at my window,
looking at the sky.
Thinking of your faithfulness,
made me realize:

No matter how much wrong I do,
no matter If I lie,
no matter how much pain I cause,
no matter if I cry,

You'll always comfort me,
and lend a helping hand.
You'll always smile and pat my back,
and say you understand.

Sitting at my window, looking at the sky.
Thinking of your faithfulness, made me realize:

No matter how much wrong you do, no mater if you lie,
no matter how much pain you cause, no matter if you cry,

I'll always comfort you, and lend a helping hand.
I'll always smile and pat your back,
and say I understand.

Sarah A. Brack

A Little Girl

Behold her there, with those golden locks,
Skipping on the sidewalk,
Kicking up her heels,
A little, blithe spirit,
A bundle of joy.
Her neat-cut features, moulded by angels,
Through the eons of time.
Free as a bird, on the wing,
Like a swallow, skimming through the trees,
On a Summer's eve,
As the Sun slides down,
Relentlessly,
Like it has done, for a billion years.
All part of a Universe,
Fashioned by God,
And controlled by his electricity.
Mary Rose, I said, you're a living doll!
No, no, she protested, I'm just a little girl.
And, everywhere, there's God.
And, everywhere, there's His electricity.

Patrick Walsh

"They Will Never Know"

They were very little, tiny, innocent and
small, now missed by mommies and daddies most of all.
Never to see another sunrise, watch the
clouds and stars above in the sky.
Never to hear the birds sing,
watch the butterflies spread their wings
Never to play at the beach in the sand,
Not know what it's like to build a snowman.
Never to feel the wind in their face, not even feel a warm embrace.
Never again to get hurt at play, not know
mommy would kiss their boo boo away.
Never to ride their first three wheel
bike, never to go into the woods on a hike
Never again to say, "Mommie and Daddie, I love you,"
just had to leave them with hearts of blue.
Never know their mama and papa who
gave them teddy bears, just hoping and crying and shedding tears.
Now roll the hurt away, let the guilty pay.
Please God, America and Oklahoma, let them
pay on judgement day.

Martha L. Mathes

Precious

Precious is the lamb that was
Slain for our sins to be cleansed
away, and made pure this day.

When in doubt give a shout
he'll surely help you out.

I thank God for the two, but I
So love you I pray every day for
him to make a way to have a
precious one of you.

Precious are the birds that wake
us singing it's a new day beginning.

Precious are dreams, they can be so
serene; we should be thankful to be
living as rich human beings.

For in the presence of hope, faith
is born, and in the presence of love
Miracles happen and they are happening
every day.
I will expect them and praise you for them
Amen

Patricia Rivers

Untitled

Laughing
Smiling
Talking
Crying
That was all her time was buying
I remember being told she didn't make it she didn't make it
I remember the pain and I still can't take it.
They said it was already her time to leave
That's a fact I didn't want to believe
I would do all I could to get her life back.
It's her beautiful smile
That we all lack. I miss her glowing happy face
That no-one can ever replace
I feel so bad you're probably wondering why
It's just the simple fact
I never said good-bye
Her death has left us
In such deep sorrow.
But we've got to realize
There's no promise for tomorrow.

Tabitha S. Davis

A Bloom Amongst The Brambles

Amidst the thorns of tribulation,
　Snarled by worried weeds of woe,
Hidden by the bristling brambles,
　You'll see a flower grow.

Could roses thrive in the desert,
　Or strawberries bloom in frost?
Yet she thrusts her haughty petals high,
　Unaffected by a winter lost.

She tastes the warmth of summer sun,
　And sips the rain as though 'twere wine;
Renewed by nature's rich repast,
　She shares it with the choking vine.

So we, ill-used by life's sharp stabs
　Can reach between the tangled tare,
Entrusting all to God's own plan
　To find a flower there!

Marie Matthews Hackney

The Falling Snow

How beautiful is the falling snow,
  So clean, so pure and holy white.
Like a blanket of ice just starting to grow,
  It cloaks everything in sight.

Oh, how I wish I were out there
  Running and sliding all about;
Breathing in the cool, clear air;
  Blowing smoke-like rings out.

Just as the snow falls everywhere
  And covers all that it sees,
I, too, could go without a care
  And do anything I please.

Marie A. Melaro

"Barry, My Love"

The cloud so dark, I the center
  So dense, so stark, no one to enter
    This web of life, so cold, so lonely
      The pain, the strife, the load mine only.

Until by chance, a stranger met
  His hug so warm, my heart he kept
    A light so bright, the dark did lift
      True love on sight, from God a gift.

My cloud so clear, we the center
  This man so dear, my life did enter
    His gentle touch, his kiss so fine
      I thank the Lord, this man is mine.

Pansy Cutlip

The Life Cycle Of Man

A gasp, a cry and it is done, a brand new life has just begun.
So helpless, needing oh such care, he has no teeth and little hair.
He eats soft foods for quite while, he cries a lot then learns to smile.
He learns to crawl and then to walk,
he coos and gurgles and learns to talk.
He goes to school, learns what he can, then out into the world, a man.
He takes a wife, he's not alone, and soon has children of his own.
Now he is strong and at his peak, but soon he finds he's growing weak.
He's back to soft foods as before, the teeth he had, he has no more.
His hair is getting thinner too, he just can't do what he used to do.
Now he needs help once again, it's back just how it all began.
A helpless child of many years, I see a smile shine through the tears.
Thinking of the life he's led, another gasp and he is dead!

Roma Menke

Angels

Sixty-three years they spent together; lives so intertwined
She insisted on attending all his last services in a record heat wave
Against all admonition, she was there to say good-bye

Vision dimmed and losing hearing, depending on others for daily living
Bravely she spent the next year and a half as a frail old widow
Enduring live-in care-givers, small substitute for her life-long love
I want to die but if I live will there be enough money?

Oh, it was all worth it she exclaims
Now on her death-bed in a brand new nursing home
"Nurse, can you give me enough morphine
That I won't wake up again?"
The struggle to die sometimes harder than the living.

  I believe in guardian angels and a life here-after
  I know my parents are re-united again
  With each other, family and friends of long ago
  Now they know our joys and sorrows, sins and generosity
  Perhaps they become new guardian angels?

Marie D. Lychak

Why, Oh Why, Can't We Fly?

The sun, the moon,
So high in the sky.
Why? Oh why can't we fly?
Over the mountains,
And through the trees?
Why? Oh why can't we fly with the breeze?
Like an eagle that soars on high,
Or like the stars suspended in the sky?
Why? Oh why can't we fly?
Way up high to reach the sky,
With the stars that all float by
High, high up in the sky?

Travis Williams

Different Kinds Of Weather

I love when there's a sunny day,
so I can go outside and play.
I like to see the snow flakes fall,
then I can make a snowman Tall.
Rain, rain, what a pain!
I wish it would go down the drain.
Lightning, lightning, it's so frightening,
up in the sky it comes down striking!
Thunder, thunder, I hear the "BOOM"!
It makes me want to hide in my room.
When it's windy I fly my kite,
Uh oh, it's out of sight!
The weather is different as you can see,
you never know what it will be.

Kristen Engels

I Have...

I have seen the rainbow's colors,
So I know what peace is.
I have felt the golden rays of the sun,
So I know what warmth is.
I have seen my mother's caring eyes,
So I know what love is.
I have heard the blue bird sing,
So I know what joy is.
I have seen the flowers bloom,
So I know what beauty is.
Now I have enjoyed these wonderful things God created,
I know what wealth is.

Serena Chen

The History Of The World

My words must be much louder and much more clearer:
so if anyone has any suggestions, please, let me in.
Welcome my children,
welcome to the Nuremberg night.
God has been seen with dancing bears, leading the tribe, with
placid warriors revising freedom.
The ancient archives has brought me knowledge and shall serve
as wisdom in my created procession.
Listen, to the sounds of the Indian shaman.
My visions inscribe symbolic reasoning for all the history of the world.
Serpents crawl,
and water falls.
Death by lack of courage, renown glory, a controversial
ending.
The world stands alone, as selfishness and chaos
reflect evolution.
Disclosure of the senses.
A conclusion of mystery, panic, fantasy,
(nothing else but a dream).

Sean King

A Special Lady

Who is this lady? She's one of a kind.
So many memories of her to cherish in our minds.
She loved it outdoors, with her garden and flowers.
Her faith was in God, and all of His powers.
She held nothing back from family or friends.
Her love came natural, she would never pretend.
She was smart and resourceful, creative, and bright.
If she wanted to do it, she would give it all her might.
She was a daughter, a sister, a wife, and a mother.
But wait, there are a few others.
A grandmother and great-grandmother were important as well.
All the wonderful things she did as these, we could never tell.
As a grand-daughter who loved her, oh so much,
All the memories and love that she gave to me,
will always stay warm from her special touch.
Linda K. Hunter

The Gift

Beach, golden rays of sun send messages,
So silent are the stories, I can see
But not hear them. Sun's rays, red-oranges,
Golds, peaceful colors—wonder how the sea
Can be like that, so calm, so cool, alone.
People, sad ones, some lonely, walk by,
As if the ocean were a quiet zone.
They don't walk slow enough to see the sky,
How beautiful life is on earth with all
The splendors of one life, that's all I need
For happiness. Some people have the gall
To say, "How pretty," then walk off, agreed?
  The ocean is a gift; treat it like one.
  No one can copy it; really, no one.
Lauren Cooley

Fall

Fall is ambivalent to me.
September is hot. Before October,
the nights begin to cool. Slowly, leaves
emit a petulant whine, loath to change.
Then green becomes gorgeous red in the Northeast.
A few glorious shades of gold intermingle with
the early signs of autumn. By Halloween,
blankets emerge from cedar chests. Early frost is predicted.
Foliage twitches with anticipation by All Saints Day.
It's cold! Suddenly warmth returns for one last moment,
awakening memories of summer. Coats are shed but
early dusk returns then to chilly shoulders. Hurry!
Cover the plants, frost is due, and it arrives in the night.
The golden burst of trees turn brown.
Listlessly, they shed their burden.
The earth receives them.
Margene Betts

Corridor Poets

A veritable legion of hate mail from the disenchanted
Populates the corridor; scrawls
Protest capitalism, government, avarice
Only coldness here;
The bitterness of the dissenters
Parades in technicolor across stone-cold indifference
Striving for some revolutionary form of justice

A peculiar debauchery -
Anonymous exiles from the status quo
Pause to offer their legacies;
Amidst the anarchy
One lone voice admonishes in the corner,
Black on gray,
"Honor thy superiors"
Kristin Sunshine Arena

A Birthday Prayer

The years they come, and years they go
So swiftly they pass us by
From toddling feet, and elbows skinned
With tears of anger or pain,
With a little care
The smiles of joy and happiness return again
So as the years went by,
And you grew older day by day,
I held your hand, when you were glad, and
in your sadness I wiped your tears away.
The years passed by so swiftly
It seems like only yesterday.
My hair is turning silver,
and my eyes grow dim and weak
I will always have the memories of you
In my heart to keep
I want you to know that I still care,
and it does not cost a penny for a prayer
So as you read this today, I pray
you will have a happy birthday.
Virgie Mae Davis

Somewhere In Time

Somewhere in time a dream lives on.
  Soft as a melody, bold as a song.
Floating through both time and space.
  Holding on without leaving a trace.
Reaching in to sweep me away.
  In the midst of my mind I'm left at bay.

Somewhere in time a love is still there.
  Reaching out for someone who cares,
Slipping in through the dark of night.
  The dreams of love fill my sight.
Bringing both joy and happiness to my mind.
  Though only in my dreams is this love that I find.

Somewhere in time we are joined as one
  In castles of stone the dream has begun.
The love we share you and I.
  The dreams of love in days gone by.
I am yours and you are mine.
  The dreams we share somewhere in time......
Mistie L. Williams

A Tribute To Mothers

Mothers are the very best
they always meet the test
Mothers are always on the go and never seem to rest

Mother are so precious,
and they are so dear.
When things are dark and lonely,
A mother makes them clear.

When we are lost and stumbling,
and can't seem to find our way.
A mother is there to guide us
and tell us it's okay.

Mothers do so very much and never ask for pay.
It's only just plain fair and right
That they have a special day.
She tells us when we are wrong
She stands for what is right.

Mothers are a special gift
God sent down from above.
We owe our mothers everything
but most of all our love.
James Sanders

The Bombing

Early one morning in an Oklahoma town,
some unknown people blew a building down.

The bombing took place in a U.S. city,
now the whole country feels shame and pity.

They drove a large truck and no one knew,
the unspeakable damage it was going to do.

Digging, digging, and digging is such a pain,
I'm afraid the search is all in vain.

This incident made many people soften,
as many of the victims are in their coffins.

A few days later they gathered at the fair,
to pay their respects and show that they cared.

Nathaniel Bacon

Mending Malls

Something there is that doesn't love a mall,
Some would rather not shop there at all.

Why queue with a hustling cloud of people?
It makes one yearn to climb up a steeple.

The clerks know little about their wares,
From sheer boredom, they emit their vacant stares.

I'd sooner go visit an old-time shoemaker,
Than pick through shoe boxes and pay a change maker.

Have we lost the individual shopping touch,
As we push our shopping carts around so much?

Outside the mall, an artist carved an oaken salad bowl.
Now that was a sculptured work, with lots of soul.

I bought the bowl and took it home to table.
That's how I'd shop more if I were able.

Ralph H. Stearns

"From A Health Aide's Eyes"

   The sights I see, I sometimes wonder why
something that I see wants to make me cry,
God puts us here with a purpose in mind,
some of us are thoughtless and some are kind.
   He watches over us, gives us something
to strive for, nothing less and nothing more.
I cannot see what will happen to me, but
life is as precious as it can be.
   Some people abuse and some really care
if all people only realized that God's really there.
   For the young and the old we're knowingly told
their dependance is always needed.
The sick and the weak and those who cannot speak
also need to be needed.
   Yet we seemingly struggle for independence
and self-worth before God takes us back to
the earth.

Oleta Braley

Two Flying Washcloths

Two flying washcloths charge playfully into a summer bath.
Two flying washcloths dodge defiantly dirt's double duty aftermath.
Two flying washcloths, will they stop their airborne flight?
Two flying washcloths, "No!" declare our daughters with ever
  girlish might!
Two flying washcloths, watch them launch and land in bath time's
  silly roar.
Two flying washcloths, they're a footnote to the summer - a highnote -
  now and forevermore.

"A merry heart maketh a cheerful countenance." Proverbs 15:13

Chris Schneider

Tomorrow

I went to call a friend of mine, who, I'd not called in quite
sometime, but somehow as the day went by it just seemed to slip
my mind. "Oh well," said I, "it does not matter...For there
is always tomorrow."

I started out to visit my family who lived some miles away when
suddenly I felt so tired and decided I'd go another day. "Oh well,"
said I, "it does not matter... For there is always tomorrow."

Today I thought I'd go and volunteer my help where needed, but tired
I grew so decided just to snooze. "Oh well," said I, "it does not
matter... For there is always tomorrow."

This morning I awoke to a phone call that came my way, I'm told my
friend, an accident did claim. Another call late that day, my mother
says to me my Dad has just passed away. Toward evening my
mind grew deep in sorrow and I awoke in this strange place.

I sit every day waiting for someone; someone to please come my way
just to say a word or hold my hand, I don't understand; no one has
the time; and when I ask is anyone here for me, I hear, Oh well, it
does not matter... For there is always tomorrow.

Shirley Harriman

When I Get Weary

Lord I do get weary; my troubles seem too much to bear
Sometimes I feel like screaming
Does anyone hear me? Is there anybody there?
At these times when I don't know
where to go
I am gently reminded that I am
not in control
There is a power at work that is greater
than mine
And I don't see it now, but things will work
out in time

Like a child in rebellion, I fall flat
on my face
But you pick me up with your
redeeming grace
When I feel too burdened and am at a loss
Your voice whispers,
"Child your burdens will never be greater
than my SON'S on the cross."

Ursula Scanlon

"The Night I Cried"

As a kid I used to think that men weren't supposed to cry.
So, in prayer one night I asked the Lord "why?"
Why must men be afraid to shed their tears?
Why musta a man hold in the pain for many years?
When times get hard and the road seems long,
Why is it that a man is told to be strong?
When the sea seems too deep and mountain seems too high,
Why must I keep climbing and still not cry?
Still unanswered the question I ask is why
can't I cry when performing my task?
That night a tear fell and I ran to hide.
No one must know that "Tonight I Cried."
If my friends knew, they'd say I wasn't a man.
They'd tremble and gloat over the ground I stand.
I guess I can't hide it, the Pain is too strong to bear.
I can't seem to run or hide anywhere.
Must I put my pain aside and keep marching on with pride,
Or shall I be the man and not hide "The Night I Cried"?

Ramon McDonald

The Old Man

The walls are as grey as the sky today.
Rivulets of years worn down like tears.
Layers peeling toward earth - green underneath pink underneath
　brown underneath gray.
Covering cement brick structure like bone.
There are no soft curves, only sharp angles, steep angles.
Small tiny windows that offer no light.
Empty of life it stands abandoned, with no place left but decay.
Boarded up for safety against strays, homeless bands seeking shelter.
A fortress impenetrable.
Someday the men will come. They will open the padlock on the
　old rusting iron gate.
They will bring their hacksaws and hammers and wrecking balls.
And all the ghosts of all of the memories that echo within its
　dripping, mossy, cold walls will rest forevermore.
Finally destroyed into peace.
　　Staci Greason

Think Twice

Hurts are the tears that fall like rain,
Showing inner feelings of emotional pain.
They ask how much can one endure
When tension strikes - not much, I'm sure!
Cruelty goes on from parent to child;
Without learning control, they're destined to run wild.
To calm the anger, you must count to ten.
Think! And say, "I'm sorry, let's start over again."

This hurt that wrecks one's self esteem,
Can be turned around working as a team.
You must think twice before you say
Something that could ruin not only one day.
Perhaps to be harbored their whole life through,
Be sure what you say, you'd want said to you.
Put away the arrows that cut to the core.
Say nothing that hurts, hearts can't take anymore.
　　Marlene Guerin

The White Lyon

Splendid is the tail of love
Rushed into my ear
Hidden is the reason
For which the big cat roars

Ice cold is his stare
Like the blood that runs from a playful scratch
Cut deep into the heart of matters
He sees me and I'm aware that he knows

Chewing through the string once dangled before him
Now tangled and wet about his proud mane
Determined to get through without the use of the claws
That have claimed the loves of so many lives

Choosing not to eat the weak
Because of the screaming
Determined to go on...
In spite of a painful thorn
　　Kirk A. Burton

Howling

Howling, calling into the wilderness.
Untamed, unchanged, unwilling to stop.
Must not touch, must not spoil, this call from the wild.
A message or warning, howling, calling from the wild.
But is it calling, or is it responding
To the call of the wild.
　　John Ferraro

Untitled

　Place to place I hear the ring, the call of darkness and shadows sing.
　In my dream, I see the light of a small city under layers of ivy and cries of mortality.
　Fire rises from the cup of death with a crack, blood runs over my hands and all over my body.
　The teeth slowly enters into my flesh, they cut, and what you see, feel, and here is silent.
　Nothing can replace the taste, the eagerness of being as no death can say, forever.
　The sweetness of the bite into a new victim calls out in a song. For this life, life must live.
　The pain is short, but the felling is infinity, forever.
　As the spirit speaks to the night, the dreams never ends but what was known as life is gone.
　Unity of darkness, blood, and a new happiness is alive.
　　Megahn Elizabeth Dimmette

The Life Of A Book Moth

Small brown spiders drop from the ceiling
Trailing silver strings to intercept my flight.
　　Words caught by the wings.
Beating resultlessly against the fears
Sticking in my eyes and binding my feet.
The web tells me how life is
And to worry about the future.
Bitten and dragged,
I let myself be covered, spun round,
With what they wish to make of me,
　A dried out snack for later.
Twitching spindly legs,
I dangle over the floor
Still believing that I'll fly.
　　Jim Dawson

The Remains

We each live the life of a peregrine,
Until on this earth we are a "has been."
It's a quick trip between earth and heaven,
Then my song is sung by some other kin.

My river flows remembering nothing,
My tree of life is dry and is kindling.
I remember, I sigh, again I sigh.
What fame! What glory! In the grave to lie.

The river still flows, the mountain's still high,
Apple blossoms still bloom with their own cry.
Frail silver petals fall and there they lie,
I stand on my helm, I hear river sigh.

We sit together; you, the mountain, me,
Until only two remain, me and Thee.
　　Duane Mastrangelo

Such A Short Life

Falling faster and faster to the ground
Tumbling and twirling-freedom bound
I twinkle with a radiant shine
But only for a moment in time

Oh, how wonderful I feel to be falling
As if the earth, my name is calling
I have the urge to feel the surface below
I want to kiss it before I go

No one will take the time to see
All the beauty that lies in me
For in a moment my heart will break
Short was the time of my being...being a snowflake
　　Cathy Bowman

"Come Be With Me"

Come share my life with me,
My house on a country road.
Come share a love with me,
And it will lighten your load.
Come give me your heart
And you shall have mine.
For I'll be true forever.
Though we're old we'll stop time
And when you are troubled
I will hold you tight
Just be here for me
in the dark, lonely night
I will never judge you
for perfect I'm not
just glad that you came
glad for what we've got

Margaret McGuire

If Ever I Die

If ever I die
my life smouldered in burning leaves
not in spring or summer
flush with fragrance
or winter's sleep unscarred by dreams
If ever I die
and the choice is mine
tired of the throb of my heart
let it be in October
and life stops racing
as mine may well do
let it be in October
not in April's flower
if ever I die
and still can choose
when to expire

A. H. Perlow

Light Years Above

Late morning,
My longing,
Mingling up there
With the breeze,
Barely tree leaves
Shimmering there
Before her balcony
When she appears.

Freshly bathed,
The beloved,
Fluffing her hair
In the breeze,
Shimmering there
Beyond my hopes,
My hands aching for
Fistfuls of lush black silk.

Kalman Gayler

My Love For You

How do I love thee.
My love goes as deep
as the biggest tree.

My love goes as wide
as the ocean tide.

My love is as true
as the deepest blue.
And this Father's Day,
I send my love with delay.

Lottie Hopkins

Love

Moments of touch
my love,
coalesce solstices
of my heart.

Darkness and lightness
orb as one,
love's boundless power
for me to become.

Roaring seas, in distance-shaped,
whisper to the outstretched shore
murmuring sweet
our secret song.

Hand in hand we search the sand
and skim a heart-shaped stone
surf hurls to the sky
our swirling silver star.

And then I write in velvet sand
for tide to take - for time to keep
the truth of your touch is
the touchstone of my love.

Mort Sobel

Untitled

Oh Lord,
　My memory contains
The unwritten pages of my life.
The lines and creases
　Of my hands and face
Speak a story few can read.
Scars, Long Forgotten, Mark
　This vessel that contains
My child-like spirit.
　The child that laughs
And loves....accepts with a smile.
Arms open wide in anticipation
　Of hugs of love and comfort.
I am beautiful,
　I am the apple of God's eye.
　　I am Loved.

Penny A. Hart

A Repentant Sinner

I sat alone in my silent room.
My mind was torn asunder.
My past and future filled the gloom
While my sins I tried to number.

Anguish, misery and regret
Rushed into my soul.
I wished that death could pay the debt
When counting out its toll.

I bowed my head in grief,
My weakened knees did bend.
In prayer I sought divine relief;
My wrongs I tried to mend.

With a spirit full of shame
My soul did intercede.
I asked forgiveness through His name;
For mercy did I plead.

When my wrongs I had confessed
I saw a light; a glimmer.
I knew my Saviour had blessed
A repentant sinner.

N. N. Reid

Fate

My fate of doom
My quiet room

No noise in
No noise out

Sunlight dims my sight
Darkness completes my life

Candlelight feels right
My life follows the depths of night

His sight calms me
While his touch frightens me

My quiet room
My fate of doom.

Tiffanie Saltsman

A Spouse's Parting

I have gone to a place very far away
my soul rests in pain
longing to see you happy again
I'll always be close to your heart
Even though it's come time
for our lives to part
I will remember you as you
have remembered me
So have no agony
for together we will always be

Sarah Taylor

"Recruiting Evils"

Beautiful Satan used to be,
Near and close to God was he.
He fought a war and that he lost.
His trust, respect, and soul the cost.
His mind still keen, his senses kept,
this enemy is not gone yet.
He feels that his great debt is paid.
He feels that his amends are made.
He hopes that we will find this true.
He hopes that we will join him too.
The sequel comes, the war will rage
The student duels eternal sage.
The day will come, the time will end.
A tear the needle cannot mend.
The sage will give part of himself.
He will come divide the wealth.
The war will rage within the world.
The moon will crash and waves will curl.
Inside the universe I fear,
The end of time may be quite near.

Shane Farthing

Love, The Untold Story

　Like a cold hard silence,
nothing breaks.
　With each breath of life,
that it takes.
　Like, a song unheard,
like, a story untold.
　What will tomorrow hold?
　Fore, this disease that ills our mind,
no cure can we find.
　With each day we throw away,
the innocence, we take away.
　With the laughter we once heard,
the past is gone, without a word.

Summer Rogers

Broken Heart

Broken heart
Never to mend
Ever hurting
Ever yearning

Broken heart
Never to dream
Ever hurting
Ever yearning

Broken heart
Broken life
Ever hurting
Ever yearning

Broken heart
Broken me
Ever hurting
Ever yearning

Oh my love, why?

Kathleen A. Kelso

Wake Up America!

There's a stillness in the nursery,
no childish laughter heard.
Teddy bear looks sad and lonely
for his friend no longer there.
A pair of sneakers by the bedside,
looking so out of place,
a mother sits with empty arms,
tears streaming down her face.
Church bells tolling sadly,
midst the strains of Amazing Grace.
They toll for those who were sacrificed
in this American Holocaust.
How many more lives will be slaughtered
before such acts are curtailed?
How many more hearts must be broken?
How many before right prevails?
It's time we heed the warning,
it's time we took a stand.
It's time to bring America,
safely back into God's strong hands.

Madeline Chapman Fish

A Reason For Living

I've found myself upon this earth,
  not knowing whence I came.
Just where I was before my birth,
  I really can't proclaim.

This planet is so grand and fair!
  I'm glad I did not miss
A chance to see, and have a share
  of its terrestrial bliss.

Why God created me a man,
  may seem a bit obscure,
Indeed, for me, he had a plan.
  of this, I'm very sure.

I wonder what's the reason why,
  the favor granted me
This lovely globe to occupy.
  I think that it must be

To make the world a better place,
  to help my fellow man.
With this priority by grace
  I'll do the best I can.

Theodore Archibald

No More

No more tears
No more pain
No more wind
No more rain

No more masks
No more lies
No more guilt
No more cries

No more hopes
No more dreams
No more despair
No more screams

No more confusion
No more hate
No more fear
No more wait

No more...

J. E. Loy

The Angel

No one is there
no one cares
there is no help
where help is needed.

On the edge
confused and alone
reaching out
but no one is grabbing.

Looking around
someone is there
peering around the corner
watching closely, from a distance.

Approaching you
the angel appears
close to your soul
showing you the path to support.

Rachel Hannon

The Price

How cruel you are,
now we're apart.
I have the scare,
within my heart.

No laws, you find,
will change my mind.
I'm just a man,
without a crime.

You made believe,
that you were mine.
I fell for thee,
I paid the time.

So fly from me,
and let me be.
The gifts I gave,
are in your grave.

I shot her twice,
revenge is nice.
I took her life,
It's worth the price.

A. Joseph Templett

In Christ

I feel pounding in my heart;
no where else is it received.

Crucified on frames like art,
hung in all who had believed;
resurrection of the graves,
is assured from nail torn hands,
sealed by faith is that which saves,
those In Christ whom He commands.

All are deceived by darkness;
many will never accept;
everlasting life's promise,
nurtured by redemption kept.

Lindsey Haskins

"The True Pity Of War"

Weep not for the fallen man,
Nor give to any grief;
Suffer not a wounded heart,
Nor beg for death's relief.

Wish not for the gentle times,
Nor dare bring them to mind;
Pity not the fallen man,
But her who's left behind.

My dearest love, your death was mine,
Though not with gun or knife;
My death is in remembering...
The rest...
    ...of all...
        ...my life.

Sandra L. Zuckerman

Fields Of Dreams

There is a sight,
not all of us get to see
A life we don't all live
To feel the breeze,
See the leaves rustling
Hear the birds chirping,
See a field mouse
Running from a fox
Hear the cattle calling one another
See the horses run through the fields,
Watch the sun rise or set
See the animals enter the barn
Get their feed,
Only hearing sounds of tractors
Heading home from the fields
No crime, no pollution, no hassles
Country people,
Living simple
Quiet,
Proud.

Monica Pastula

Solitude

It is often desired,
Not always available,
Forever cherished,
That's undeniable,
Muchly appreciated,
When in a multitude,
Too soon vacated,
This moment of
Solitude.

Ruth Ellen Fross

No Wonder

When I'm awake and you are
not at my side, I still see you.
I wonder why. When I am
asleep I see you, and I wonder why.

When I look into the sun I see
you in each ray of light, I look
upon the night sky and I see you. Why?

Everywhere I look I see you,
awake or asleep, into the light
or upon night and I wonder why,

So one day I decided to look
into a place I had never looked,
into my heart and soul and you
were there. I now know why I
see you everywhere; it's because

I love you and it's no wonder.
To my husband Terry L. Birge
Nancy R. Birge

Time

Only hours I have known thee
Not days nor months nor years
Yet time alone cannot be judge
To share all joys and tears
I saw you for the first time
And pondered what might be
An un-requited love, not knowing
That you shared love for me
Paul Solimene

Encircled

The back of this worn hand,
not gnarled but gloved in curing rind
(a scar or two as remnant
signs of ventures found remiss),
is chammy foil subdued
in homage to a lustrous band
with sequent nicks that moondust
long ago absolved in bliss.
Stephen Anderson

Untitled

I close my eyes
  Not to sleep
  Only to dream
  For in my dreams I'm free
Free to fly to where
  My true love waits
  With gentle words
  That comfort me
His hands caress my skin and
  My emotions was over me
  Like the wind blown waves
  Wash over the sandy beach
He looks into my eyes and
  Touches my soul
  My whole body trembles
  All my fears are washed away
I close my eyes to dream this dream
  To laugh
  To live
  To love
Tania L. Rose

Inner Truth

O why?
O why deny
the bitter cry
that lurks amidst my soul?

Better embrace
than to erase
this bit of gall
long past and cold.

What worth it be
if truly free
of hidden rot
inside the heart to moon?

Only through pain
can one retain
the belief
that he is his own.
Karen Butler Jenkins

Dream Deferred

In the '54 Olds
Of copper and creme
Three ripe vital virgins
Out to fulfill a dream.

In the '54 Olds
Of copper and creme
Plans were made
Flawless they seem.

In the '54 Olds
Of copper and creme
The gas tank went dry
"Not now" was heard in a scream!

In the '54 Olds
Of copper and creme
Tears were shed
For the vision that been supreme!
Kerry Eisenmenger

Teach Our Children

Teach our children -
Of God up above
Teach our children -
Respect and love
Teach our children -
Against discrimination
Teach our children -
Hate will be our ruination
Teach our children -
Carrying guns might make him bold
Teach our children -
What happens when he loses control
Teach our children -
Violence won't make him brave
Teach our children -
Violence can only get him an early grave.
Maggie L. Cannady

Where Time Stands Still

I found a place
On a plane closer to the stars
Where time stands still
Valleys and mountains
Untouched by human beings
Beauty beyond words
The soul reaches to those stars
And can feel the valleys and mountains.
Mary Raseley

Nudity

I love the naked body
of my little boy.
Jay J's squeal of pleasure
to be free.
The cheerful chase,
diaper in hand.
His eyes twinkle,
"No Diaper!"
I love the joy
lighting his face.
Running circles,
till we breathlessly
fall down.
I think,
"No Diaper!"
let him go.
Dance
little creamy body
running through the house.
Nikki Belk

The Seasoned Us

You cannot be certain
of my <u>red</u> madness.
It defines you,
yet it consumes ME.
He somehow finds a way
to say it is wrong,
so some close their charcoal nerves.
NOT ME!
The dawn will come
when my eyes are bronzed
and you will have said it all,
but for one falling reason
you'll never leave.
I don't have the strength
enough to kick your branches.
So when the sky runs from blue
to black,
you and I will surely
admire our place in the wind.
Kris L. Brothers

Untitled

A name is a name
only words on a page,
to be used in happiness,
sorrow or rage.

It's nothing too fancy
nor is it too drab,
it's only a name
like Taxi Cab

Some make you laugh
and some make you cry,
but most stay with you
'til the day that you die.

A name is a name
and no one knows why,
I guess it's just something
we have to go by.
Kathie Churchill

Memories Of Red Roses At Dawn

Few loves are unending
Or hearts as true as they claim;
A month can be a lifetime,
It also can chill a flame.
Nan Garcia Hicks

Jenny Wren

She is such a tiny bird
of that there is no doubt,
but you don't have to see her
to know when she's about.

She has such a cheerful song
it's sure to fill your heart;
you may even sing along
she'll let you do your part.

A busier bird I've never seen
there is so much to be done,
what's so very strange is
she makes it seem like fun.

If she can face this big wide world
with spirits oh so high,
please won't someone tell me
why, oh why, can't I?

Ruby Nohren

A Child's Smile

A child's smile is genuine
of this I know not why.
It's filled with the age of innocence
enough to make you cry.

You know how much they love you
when you see their precious face.
Anger, hate, or malice
of this there is no trace.

Try not to be upset with them
they must learn right from wrong.
And keep in mind that someday soon
they will be grown and gone.

A child's smile is genuine
pictured forever in your heart.
Always keep them close to you
and you shall never be apart.

Lynn Belk

"Beneath The Stars"

If you have ever had your dreams
  Of touching God, his hand, his brow,
To know His truth is what it seems,
  To pray He comes in Glory now.

With the rosy glow of the blushing bride,
  The ashen here of the groom;
Your Grandson's first live pony ride;
  An Easter Lily in full bloom.

We mourn at the gravesite of our kin
  And reach to God for love,
To cleanse our hearts and souls of sin,
  We yearn to gain His Home above.

But to really know of touching God
  Climb high on a grassy hill,
Succumb in supplication,
  Look up: Accept God's will.

His face will glow, and more
  From deep in the blue of the sky,
The touch you longed and looked for
  Will come to you where you lie.

F. Satterfield

Thoughts Of You

The sun shines like the glow
  of your smile.
Ribbons of the rainbow are the
  many colors of your personality.
When the sky is bright blue, I'm
  reminded of your brilliance and
  the way you tell me you love me.
I feel the wind blow through my
  hair and I'm swept away by your
  passionate kisses.
With each evening, the sun sets
  low in the horizon and the day
  ends with thoughts of you.
I smile.

Tanja S. Thomas

"Division"

Where have I been?
Oh, to other towns, to other places,
seeing other things and other faces.
But I was not where I have been,
for you see, I was not with him.

Where have I been?
Oh, to rest, to sleep,
to work and house to keep,
but I was not where I have been,
for you see, I was not with him.

Where have I been?
Oh, with him, with him.
Can this joy be such a sin?
because where I am is where I have been,
for you see, I was with him, with him.

Mary Hervey

Untitled

Death came to the valley
on a spring afternoon
and blossomed into fires
of blood and despair.

Death came to the valley
on a spring afternoon
and blossomed into a shame -
so rare

Death came to the valley
on a spring afternoon
and the people rose
to the echo of its moan
on a spring afternoon

Ruth Carney

Things I Feel

I feel like talking to you God,
Of things I feel within my soul.
Of the vastness which You gave the sky,
Of the beauty in the mountains' roll.

I'd like to talk with You of trees,
Of gardens, colors of Your choice,
Of birds whose songs are music sweet
Of a Church whose silence is Your Voice.

God, help all know such things as these,
Do away with wars and such,
Make us proud that we can live
Beneath the glory of Your Touch.

Roberta B. Simmons

We Planted A Plum Tree

We planted a plum tree
  On a warm December day—
Watered and fed it and
  Stroked its fragile limbs.
Tiny leaf buds on extending
  Branches whispered, "Spring".
Blooms metamorphosed into
  Purple fruit of summer
Satisfied the palate and the soul.
  A brooding storm violated the
Petalous branches of the aging tree
  And sapped its life in slow degrees
As often happens at Autumn time.
  Full circle now - a quick demise
And all is cruelly destroyed
  Except for one aging branch and
Three developing green shoots.

Natille P. Lindsey

Three Grace Notes

Driving south on the Outer Drive
  On certain nights
    At sunset
With Lake Point Tower
A lone silhouette to the left
Crowned with molten gold

Walking the sawdust paths
  At the Clearing
    In Door County
Footsteps cushioned and hushed
Sunlight sifting down
Through a lacework of green

Watering the geraniums
  on my balcony
    At mid-morning
Lake Michigan a deep cobalt
Light-suffused clouds floating
Across the sky
The cottonwoods murmuring
Among themselves

Polly Flynn

One Wish

If I could have but one wish,
Oh what would that wish be,
For strength to face the trials
And temptations placed on me?

Or would I wish for knowledge
'Tis something I can keep
But then what good is knowledge
In that everlasting sleep?

Perhaps I'd wish for happiness,
For all the long years through,
But that would be too selfish
Not to think of my friends too?

Oh no dear friend 'tis none of these,
could satisfy my need,
But I would wish that every day
I'd do a golden deed.

A deed to make life richer,
For someone else you see,
Would make my life seem brighter
That's what my wish would be.

Phyllis D. Yeatts

Untitled

The death sentence
on communism
Is passed
For in total destruction
It can
Only die
But as a hindu,
Moslem,
Buddhist,
Jew
Or Christian
Are you afraid
Of death
Not I.

William Davis

Summer Shower

Capricious sun, intent
on some new whimsy
turned its head,
in that indulgent moment
a dew-filled cloud
hung there instead.

Rain drenched, a startled
dove winged its way
amidst green leaves
while earthbound things
looked heavenward and
seemed to breathe.

Sara Hewitt Riola

The Commuter Dragon

On winter morns I ride to work
On the back of a big red snake.
Its head lies far beyond the hills.
It never sleeps, always awake.

The body shines bright through the dark
And threatens all who see its glow.
It often bites and sometime kills.
The number dead I do not know.

Far behind me the tail glows white.
A flame, a torch, is what I see.
This fire burns not a tree or bush,
But always seems to follow me.

I can't avoid the crimson snake,
For off to work I go each day.
At night I ride that snake again
And drive myself towards home and play.

Leon T. Ross

"A Wedding Poem"

Today is a very special day,
One to remember
forever and always
You and I united as one
Memories of joy for years to come
Tears of Joy
from the Bride's eyes
And from the Groom
a big, bright smile
Remember this poem of
Wedding memories always
Because these memories
Will last forever and
always

Shelia Cox

Pear Trees

There are too many blossoms
on the old pear trees today,
too many for me, too many for you,
too many for the trees to shake,
too many for the wind to take,
too many expectations
of the perfect fruit cloud our view
of the boughs at the swaying core—
those darker ones
we have lost sight of before
or simply chose to ignore.

Why trouble with too many
when we have need of only two?
One from me and one from you—
a leaner bouquet, that's true
but enough for the trees to keep
and enough for the wind to sweep
enough given to expect our due
without making us drop away
from the pears our blossoms now renew.

Tim Markey

Untitled

As you are confirmed,
On this your special day -
You have chosen a life with the Lord,
And promise to walk in his way.

   He will be there when you need him
   to guide and give you strength -
   just pray and ask for guidance,
   and he'll answer at great length.

He will never let you walk,
Where he has not yet been -
So in him put your faith and trust,
And always follow him.

   So live your life as he would,
   be kind and strong and true -
   go out and be a disciple,
   and great things will come to you.

May your faith grow stronger everyday,
With every step you take -
The Lord bless and keep you,
With every choice you make.

Nancy Carol Mascaro

Sisters Are Friends Forever

Dedicated to my sister Wendy Brooks

The years have passed
One day at a time,
And it's too complex
For a simple rhyme.
You've aged,
You've grown,
Your future
Is sewn.
You're letting go,
And flying away,
For inside you know
Here you can't stay.
We wish you luck
In all you do,
And wherever you go,
We'll always love you.

Tara Mitchem

In The Final Analysis

Sun comes up, sun goes down,
One man's smile is one man's frown,
One man born while one man dies,
Why not his sights 'fore my eyes?

One day clear, next falls rain,
One man's loss is one man's gain,
One man's win is one's defeat,
Why not his shoes on my feet?

Summer warmth, winter snow,
One man's high is one man's low,
One man falls while one man stands,
Why not his gloves on my hands?

Peacetime plow, wartime gun,
One man's toil is one man's fun,
One man lives while one is dead,
Why not his hat on my head?

Lifetime body, death time dust,
No more wants, no more lust,
All return to one same place,
Need I his smile on my face?

Rachel Rubel

Moment

Only the moment...to waste
one must lament on how one's
life is spent
Action now, ever more
To win with oneself one cannot
ignore.
Reach high and wide with ears, eyes,
heart and sinew
every breath used to renew
procrastination never more,
one moment to explore.
Look not where you came
but where you are is to gain
with every moments wish
let it sustain
   moment
      moment
         moment...

Kenneth Foley

Beach

The place to go where people think
or to lay out in the sun
some look for the missing link
while others wish the day is never done

The sand is all around
with shells and broken glass
some people build mounds
all with a lot of class

In the summer the waters aglow
from the sun's golden rays
it's a place where everyone wants to go
and spend a pleasant day

In the winter months the beach is alone
because of the cold winds that blow
the waves, due to the storm have grown
and people wish winter would go

The beach is a great place to ponder
and figure out what to do
it gives you a place for your mind to wander
and think of only of you

Marc Kemler

Strength

A big hand holds a little hand
one soft hand, one strong
one hand offers guidance
one hand, and the pain's gone

One small hand in a big hand
one experienced hand, one new
hold my hand, help me stand
as I reach out for you

One hand held for security
one hand held for love
one hand held out to me
one hand can mean so much

One hand held for friendship
one hand trusting, one deceived
one hand held for the strength it gives
one hand gives reason to believe

Mark James Ammerman

Santa's Visit

Our cheerful, happy Santa
   Only comes but once a year.
He travels in a bright, red sleigh
   that is pulled by eight reindeer
His beard and hair are silvery white
   and he's always dressed in red
He never comes to visit you
   until you're snugly tucked in bed
His pack is bulging and mysterious
   filled with goodies, games and toys
He fills the neatly hung stockings
   of all good girls and boys!
You can almost hear his chuckle
   as he quietly slips from sight
He laughingly calls out "Merry Christmas"
   And to each and all a good night!!"

Shirley Gillenwater

Silence

Winter has now come.
Snow is falling on the damp earth.
Summer's blossoms sleep.

Matthew Chisholm

"Children In The Snow"

Only a few inches
or maybe just two;
Never the matter
if it covers your shoes.

Children are watching
and waiting for it;
The white falling snow
and noses, frost bit.

All bundled up
not to be cold;
Their on coming journey
ever so bold.

Their fearless and daring
not a care in the world;
Sliding down slopes
these young boys and girls.

Young, they all are
no difference age makes;
We all are just children
for goodness sake!

Louellen Whitton

"Did Rhyme"

We were once very close
   Our feelings we did expose
Times together seemed not be much
   Our bodies they did touch
When arms and hands had bound
   News of us did sound
A many missed, broken, a good-bye
   Looking a past I did sigh
Lost of confusion, you may, why
   In silence, the mind it did cry
To miss all I now know
   Make you walk I did so
Our eyes caught deep stare
   I need say I did care!

Stacy Hintz

Times That I Will Remember

On December 18, 1993,
Our school principal died.
He was very nice to me.
When I heard he was gone, I cried.

We had good and bad times,
Through these four and a half years.
But his sudden death,
Caused us many tears.

I loved him,
But I knew to show respect,
Or on the red bench
I would sit.

As I look back on the happy times,
His smiling face made me glad.
And I find myself missing,
The best principal I ever had.

Zack Sparks

Wilderness Night

Engulfed by fog
Our tent
Is wrapped in silence.

Moon glow reflects
Off our
Beached canoe.

Rocks weave foaming
Trails on the
Restless river.

Lips bind.
Arms
Entwine.

Our bodies
Surge in
Arced waves.

A frog
Croaks us
Asleep.

I. Herbert Gordon

First Kiss

Love so great
so fine, so pure
an everlasting mist
that surrounds our
hearts as one
when first we
ever kissed.

Maria Arghiere

Alone Again

He came walking toward me
Out of no where.
He was every thing that
I had ever dreamed of.
He came to me and held me.
I knew then at that moment
We were made for each other.
He stayed there at
My side for a long time,
Until one day he decided to
Leave me there, with
My heart broken
And the feeling that
I could never love again.

Margaret M. Steele

Winter Lace

Once again the snow decorates the
   Outside like a big frozen
   Sheet that is open wide.

The white snowflakes fall to
   My nose and tickles it ever so
   Gently when the wind blows.

The trees' branches trimmed in
   White, look like delicate
   Lace, when they shine in
   The sunlight.

The rooftops gleam under the
   Night's full moonbeam.

The big white sheet will soon
   Melt away, and it
   Will just be another
   Sunny day.

Natalie Kelly

The Promise

Beauty of The World
Overshadowed Pearls
Thorn - ed Fruits
Hurled upon Truth
Random
Seemingly
Fall Aground
So Many Found
NECTAR Saddened Rain
Sprinkled upon that which remain

Linda Rose

Destiny

Sailing on a sea
on a long summer day
smoking a joint
and flying away
when I felt a breeze
I started to freeze
I hear a loud sound
I got a little scared
when I turned to look down
the boat started to flood
it started to sink
the only thing I could do was think
so I looked in the sky
when I started to pray
that was the last thing I remember
about that long summer day

Lacy Stracener

Burial By Sea

The white hot sand
Padded my steps
As I walked on the beach

This was our spot
Where we used to go
Where we'll go no longer

Though it was not your fault
Fate played a hand
He won, and death was the payment

I mourn you now
As I mourned you then
And as I'll always mourn you

My life is incomplete
You were the final piece
I shall never forget you

Good-bye, as I toss your ashes
Among the rolling waves
And see you, never again

Sarah McGregor

Love And Trust

Love is like a dagger,
painful and deep in your
heart;
   It goes further in with
every tug to pull it out.
   Trust is like a light bulb,
which shines bright and then
goes dim.

   Only he who is
sincere in heart,
can pull a dagger
and avoid the hurt—
or change a bulb
and not get burned.
   He has to be special
to pass the test;
and prove that for
you he is the best.

Suzanne Prince

The Fluffy Cloud

I lay my head in this cloud
So fluffy and soft.

I think I could lie here
for hours, months, even years
maybe just maybe I'll get up
in a thousand years.

Rachel Boik

"Remember Me"

Remember me when I cry out.
Remember me when you see that
Innocent child.
Remember me when you see the
Rivers run deep.
Remember me when you see a
Bird flying free.
Remember me always for I will
Always remember you.

Renee Pietila

"Teaching"

Being a teacher takes
patience, kindness, and will power.
Hoping every student will
Shoot up like the Eiffel Tower.

We learned so much from you,
Yet, so very little.
Together we solved every problem,
and almost every riddle.

We know you'd rather be someplace,
the Keys or the Bahamas too.
But we're really glad you didn't (yet),
Or we'd have never known you.

Teaching is a good job.
It shows that you care
About our education.
You're a precious stone that's rare.

Susan Y. Ru

Remembering You

Thoughts of you are like the moonlight,
peeking through the thick summer trees,
or reflecting off calm and still waters,
at times engulfed by a crashing wave,
only to reappear, pretending to sleep
upon a cold winter's snow,
silently weaving in and out
of the footprints we left behind.

Karen Marie Calvacca

People

People walking in the streets,
People at the market buying beets.
People driving in flashy cars,
People sadly standing behind bars.
People resting in their homes,
People styling their hair with combs.
People scattered here and there,
People are surely everywhere.

Paige Walus

Space

The sea gulls as though sitting ducks
Perched along the water's edge
With friendly gaze
All but a smile
To feel the peaceful atmosphere
Settling upon this earth
And only you to reach out to me
In a tender warm embrace
The air so crisp
The breeze so cool
The moment treasured
With you I share this space

Shirley R. Broude

Sepia

The other day I found an old
photo. It was brown and tan.
Smiling up at me were my mother
and father younger than I am now,
their eyes full of hope and
unabashed innocence. I smiled
back at them. Then I cried.

Harriet Tipping

Alone Is The Heart Of Love

Ablated is the heart
pierced by cupid's ire.

Coveted by one hundred hopes
defeated by one desire.

As love called upon me
undeservedly I claimed its prize.

Wore the frilled embellishments
that moved the poet's of mine.

Strengthen by the blood of fate
contained within its fire.

Imperfect to the love I quest
despatches into quietus mire.

Roberta A. Barrera

A Note To Remember

The beat from your heart
Plays a melody to my soul,
While the rhythm in my mind
Caresses your thoughts.

Our dreams sing in harmony
And passion heats intensely
in time we'll be together
as one.

My being revolves around
The rapture of your existence.

For you are the music of my life,
The song of my spirit,
And I long to spend forever
with you.

C. A. Grant

Prayer Of Love

Lord visit at Eltrio Way,
Please come today O Lord I pray,
Attend to those who tend to stray,
Bring back your peace to Eltrio Way.

A sweet little girl, a sweet little boy
need you to bring them love and joy.
A mom, a dad, to make the day a joyful
one at Eltrio Way.

Thank you Lord for this little prayer,
May your answer come with love and care
for those who dwell from day to day
in the little home on Eltrio Way.

Mattie P. Siggers

Precious Things

Precious little things
priceless jewels shine
and twinkle in their eyes
their little prize

Precious little things
intricate works of Master
delicate art that bleeds
art that lives and breathes

Precious little things
no currency or coin
or certificate of gold
just someone warm to hold-

Precious, precious little things.

Michael Kraemer

This Moment

This moment will never be again.
Precious and fragile...ephemeral.
It guides us into the future.
It is unique in all of time.
Never has it happened before,
Nor will it come again.
That is, in itself, reason enough
To appreciate, to question,
To explore, to experience.
For every moment is unique,
And every moment, fleeting.

Mary Hilaire Tavenner

Willow In The Wind

There's a willow tree as
pretty as can be! The limbs
dangle to the ground all the
way around! And on a
windy day it whistles
in the wind, as it weeps
it whistles a "beautiful tune"
"It's as beautiful as the moon!"
So listen to a willow in the wind.
and your dream may begin.
"When you hear a willow
whistling in the wind."

Marjorie Dempsey

The Veteran

Daily he walks sign in hand
protesting, I suppose.
No words are written
no words are spoken.
Back and forth he travels
like a timeless pendulum.
Void of things that represents life.

We all are guilty of
speculation
giving his plight a name.
Feeling better now that his
pain has a reason to exist.
We shake our heads
in avoidance
go home to sleep
wishing him well.

Maxine Thompson

Growth

Intimacy; in its most
Prurient Guise
Often takes place as
Physical communication.
Oft called less Poetic phrases...
does not lesson the
inevitable beauty
of
life's' own Language.
As in first meetings;
there are
traditional blunders, slips and
silences.
Yet, they foreshadow the
caresses and delicious
tastes of Sleepy
intimate growth

Thomas Bender

The Chance

Slowly, quietly, the flowers bloom.
Quickly, loudly, the people are crying.
Things that we never think about
will soon be real.
And everything we fear
Will be no more.
Things will change.
Everywhere, things will change.
Everyone changes when they've
Been given the chance
And their lives they do turn around.
"Soon, before it's too late!"
You'll miss it....
"Hurry up, you'll miss it!"
Oh, you missed it.
Slowly, quietly...
You left without the chance
And unchanged.

Mindy Liedecke

Red Earth

Amongst this dry
red and white earth, runs a vein,

A powerful medicine...
Ansel Adams captured it with camera.
Georgia O'Keefe with a brush.

These voluptuous mountains
reaching skyward, as a child
to its mother.

Where clear water runs from
The black mountains,
Rich with history and wisdom.

I have walked these hills and
ravines, the red earth sifting
through my fingers...

I felt the insurmountable
power beneath me, stopped... listened...
And heard the earth's heart beat...
barren though it be
my soul finds peace here...

As the eagle soars high...

Yvonne M. Schmidt

I Pause...

To reflect and to see
Reflections of twisted
Trees dancing over the
Frozen earth.

Gray and chill
The tombstones stand,
A mute, stark vigilance branches,
And the last vines of Autumn
Whistle wintery tunes for the
Names on the grave stones.

All of nature naps
As I think how often I
Played here in the summer.

I wish for that summer as I
Leave with cold and older

Footsteps...

Sharon H. Neel

Memories

Memories of loved ones gone
Remain within our hearts;
We miss them still and always will,
It is sad to be apart.
Yet memories can keep us close
At times loved ones seem so near;
somehow we sense their presence,
You feel that they are here.
But then you come to realize
That death has come between;
And what you see and feel
Is only a beautiful dream.
You feel so bruised and broken,
The loss is oh, so great!
But we have hope to see them again
When we enter Heaven's gate.
But for now we must take courage
And through our tears we carry on;
Holding precious memories deep within
Of those we love who are gone.

Virginia C. Blaich

Little Cloud

Little cloud you're floating free,
Riding over home and tree.
Little cloud high in the sky,
Watching birds go by.
Little cloud dipping low,
Watching time go very slow.

Little cloud of many colors,
You see many brothers.
Little black cloud growing tall,
Waiting for rain to fall.
Little cloud of grey,
You will chase the sun away.
Little cloud of red or yellow,
You will make the sunset mellow.

Little cloud changing shapes,
Becoming lions, dragons and apes.
Little cloud a friend of wind,
Raced across the sky again.
Little cloud and wind
Are swirling and twirling around again.
Little cloud and wind and sky,
Yours is not to reason "Why?"

Lynsey Drybrae

"Hello....."

Talk to me someone
Right now I'd like to hear
Another voice, to interrupt my own.
Say something someone, speak
Break the silence here within me;
Stop the hurting, comfort me.
I feel so lonely and confused.
I'm a ship, battered, weary,
In such a vast blue ocean
Of endless, used emotion
But talk quietly. Talk calmly.
Talk of anything.
I just need someone now
To be a friend
But not to sound false.
I want to know you too,
So that if things get turned around
I can be there, the same for you.

Kate Simmonds

Winter Ski Vacation

Snow scant, ice clogged streams
road rises, voices shrill
tensions tight, spirits sizzle
expectations, tales tall
views charm, food fills
and snow's assured.
Fidgets frequent, choices fret
destination doubtful,
suddenly,
resolved.
Explosion of activity!
Doors slam, poles jam
faces freeze, fingers numb
pulses leap, guts wrench
air cold, sun bright
snow white
and
we're off...
Sonia Wilson

Patriot's Song

Red is the color of rubies
   rosy cheeks
   juicy apples
   robin's breasts
   fragrant roses
stripes on the flag.

White is the color of snow
   puffy marshmallows
   vanilla ice cream
   picket fences
   milk for babies
stripes on the flag.

Blue is the color of the sky
   singing birds
   a pretty girl's eyes
   denim jeans
   lakes and streams
the backdrop for stars.

All as American as mom's apple pie.
America - I'm proud of you!
Marjorie Christiansen

Autumn I.

Gilded leaves, glitter gold.
S-L-O-W-L-Y..... One-by-one
  each a precious coin
    t
     u
      m
       b
        l
         e
    s hushed
  and crinkles brown crisp
  muted with the wind song.
They blithely dance
  swirling, twirling, fluttering
  in the frosty air — until,
  gold dust; summer smoke,
  autumn haze.
Gilded leaves
    passing
       on.
Paula Slade

Who Is He?

Who am I?
Said Jesus one day
He asked His disciples
Who do men say?

Some say Elias
Or a prophet, one of them.
Some say John the Baptist
Come alive again.

Jesus then asked them
Who am I say ye?
Thou art the Christ of God,
Said Peter to me.

Jesus asks you and me today,
Who am I do ye say?
Is He Lord of your life?
Or have you turned him away.

Who is He?
He is God's beloved Son.
Begotten of the Father,
The only one.
Nora Shutt

Time And Space

I wake up to colored beams of light
scattering through the window's dew.
Still clutching at the pillow
that all last night was you.

Though the night was cold,
with tender thoughts in bed I lie;
as I slept my dreams of you
would keep me warm inside.

The brightness of morning
brought sudden reality;
that instead of the one I love
lies a pillow next to me.

Tonight when I go to bed
my thoughts of you I'll keep;
someday I'll be holding you
as I awaken from my sleep.

Until the time comes that will allow
us to touch and embrace;
we share a comfort knowing
we'll overcome this time and space.
Ronald E. Conroy

Living This Lie

I'm drowning in a
sea of sorrow,
living this lie.
Living this lie
as I die.
I watch the darkness
closing in on me,
all the while,
as I live this lie,
waiting to die
As I leave you, I shall
be unrelenting.
Keep me not in
your retrospection;
I am not worthy
of it.
But, as I die,
do not forget
that I willingly
lived this lie.
Rebecca McMillen

Awakening

I spent my youth, and half my life
seeking elevation -
In lightning flashes and thunderstorms...
awaiting revelation -

It's true that Nature humbles,
and yes I too was led -
down pleasant pathways by my heart -
but never by my head ....

Never once did a trumpet sound on high,
nor an earthquake split the ground -
for the answer that eluded me -
had not been lost, I found -

Its truth was far too simple,
delaying me from seeing -
the august beauty manifest,
In myself - a human being!
Michael D. Ferguson

Ashes

Ashes will be my final word
Particles of history of who I am
Of who I dream of being.
Awakening alone unto ourselves
Fragments are who we are
Clinging to daily ritual
Longing for daily spontaneity.
Fragments held together in human bodies
By loving, by compassion
By energy from dreaming.
Fragments threaded by a mind
that knows the heat will come
The fire will consume, transform
My particles to something new.
Will my ashes lie tenderly in your hands?
Will they fly in the wind
Or swim on the crest of a wave?
Lift up your hands, let my ashes go
Just keep me in your heart.
Lynn Marie Nereo

Destiny's Daughter

She's Destiny's Daughter
  Society's orphan child;
She's Gossip's conversation
  And satisfaction's smile.

She works on the corner,
  Selling her body and soul.

She has to make a living...
  Gotta stay warm from the cold.

She's destiny's daughter,
  A victim of life.

She'll be anybody's baby,
  But seldom anybody's wife.

She could be your daughter or sister,
  But she's also a child of God;

She also needs his comfort,
  With his staff and rod.

She's destiny's daughter,
  Destitution child's her name;

She gives herself to others,
  And others only give her shame.
Sarah Thomas Hendricks

Rage

Dark clouds gathering— unseen—
   Seething tempest within
   Force building-
   Seeking release

Power—
   Coiling - coalescing-
   Compressing into
   White fire

Striking out—
   Searing all in its path
   Blinding-
   Deafening with its release

Leaving those in its wake
   Blackened and
   Bloodied—

Fearing when next it may strike.

C. R. Davis

"Cowboys"

Cowboys
Serious men
Branding cattle all day.
I love to watch them rope and ride.
Ranch hands.

Trevor Powe

Mother

I will always remember Mother dear,
She always wiped away my tears.
She would hold me real tight,
Then everything would be alright.

No one will ever take her place,
I can still see her loving face.
Though she has passed away,
I think of her about every day.

You will never know how I miss her,
Since she is gone, I shed many tears.
Wish I could tell her I love her so much,
It would be nice to feel her warm touch.

Someday I will see her again,
Then it will be all the same.
Happy, loving, like it was before,
Never ever to be apart anymore.

Raymond M. Wiesenmayer

Bid My Heart

Bid my heart tick unheard
So that I be still
I am attendant on those
Skipping beats and extra sounds
So void of harmony
Would that my sense of comfort
Return to obscurity

I do not need proof
Of a fallen heart
Once I was indifferent
It was on its own
The Orator in my cavern wall
Must make a final choice
The muscle is his own

Max V. Kaplan

The Rope

Tink's dead
She dead
  Tinkerbell's dead
They're crying

Tink's dead
She's dead
  And they watched her
Softly dying

On the stage that was black with fear
Where she faded swiftly near
  She fell from a sky that was not a sky
But a space.

  And no-one dared to clap
  Hands folded in their laps
While Tink lay, bloody streaming,
    ever near.
    ever dear.

Sherri Davidoff

America

She beckoned to me
She set me free
She gave me a home of my own.

In a country so vast
I enjoy at last
The peace I never had known.

Mildred J. Katemopoulos

My Love For You

My love for you,
Shines bright each day.
Next to you,
Each night I lay.

My hopes my dreams,
They all came true,
My life so grand
Because of you.

Comfort and love
You give to me.
I see how wonderful
Our life shall be.

Happiness and joy
I give to you.
Together we bonded,
Together we grew.

I'll always cherish
The love we share.
The love we have,
A love so rare.

Richelle M. Freeman

Primordial Dawn

Soft wind brushes the cheek of dawn.
Rain crow calls.
Night shadows echo
Lingering in unseen places,
The veil lifts.
Brightness breaks.
Blinding, erasing all vestiges of night.
Gaudy brilliance reflects,
mirroring stark shadows.
Hidden eyes

Sharron Chason

My Own World

People of all types
sitting on the grass
the tears he wipes
he no longer lets pass
numbing voices float around
many chairs around the tables
let us lie on the ground
to hear the untold fables
bodies so lifeless
no point to what we do
there is one that I miss
this one is you;
someone you used to know
but they went far away
they wanted you to follow
but that was an insane request to say
a dark shadowing presence
that will never let me be
a long drawn out sentence
that only leaves you guilty...

Lisa Stayner

"Angels In That Other Land"

Yesterday we laughed with you,
So beautiful and young
We held you near,
You were so dear.

But in the light
Without pair or fright
Your soul took flight
To a better land.

Today we must not weep
Though you have gone away,
Nor sadden your tomorrow
With our sorrow,
Nor question the things
We cannot understand.

You were so fair!
And our love we now must share,
With angels there,
In that other land.

Lisa K. Hefner

Spring

How grand it is to be alive
So early in the SPRING,
To see the bees swarm in the Hive,
And hear the Robins sing.

Oh what a time to live and fish,
The Sportsman sure will say,
To cast his line to hear it 'swish',
Spells spring the best of ways.

Throughout our nation many feet
Go on their merry way
To Ball parks where teams compete
In Baseball, day by day.

Along the wooded pathways green
Such gorgeous wild flowers grow
Spring's magic carpet here's seen
In contrast to the snow.

In City Town or County dell
Like nature we are free,
We love this way of life so well
Long live DEMOCRACY.

Ruth N. Hannah

The End

Letting go
So easy to say
So hard to do
Why?
True love
It only comes once
Once it's gone - all is gone

Laurie L. Smith

The Four Musketeers

She was one of us
so efficient and exciting,
she organized and set up
our Elderhostel trip to Arizona,
for Nelwyn, Betty, and me
And of course for Gerry,
our first Musketeer.
She loved every minute from
the new faces and places
staying at a Cottonwood motel,
or soaking in a hot tub
by the light of an Arizona moon,
to celebrating my birthday
at Sedona, amid the towering red rocks,
with a cathedral peeking out.
Yes, life was a bowl of cherries.
Now we are only three
but if I know Gerry,
she is musketeering in heaven
for the three of us here on earth.

Pauline B. Roth

In Pedias Mess

Always contented to be with me
So elegant in her grace.
Sharing my life so peacefully
Oblivious to life's rat race.

I let her down one dreary morn
I did not go with care.
Life's darkness got the best of me
There's treachery out there.

The nurses shrugged at my dilemma
They seemed so unconcerned.
Indifference can be so cruel
When will I ever learn?

When venturing out into the world
One must sometimes go so slow.
If not you see you'll be like me
And break your little toe.

Mary Edwards

Happily Ever After

Happily ever after
So the story goes,
Happily ever after
No one really knows,

That happily ever after
Is each and every day,
That one gets to journey through
As they pass along the way

Towards the rivers and
Where the waters are most calm,
And happily ever after
Has come and now is gone.

D. O'Connor Salazar

My Home Town

Mississippi is a State
So often criticized.
But the people there are full of pride,
And love and care abide.

Mt. Olive, Mississippi is my home town,
Of 800 maybe more.
That human touch is surely there,
They smile with joy, galore.

"Everybody knows everybody else,"
Is a saying that is true.
There they live a happy life
In that small town that's true blue.

If ever you're visiting down south
Let Mt. Olive be on your agenda,
And you will love our small little town
'Cause they'll treat you, O so tender!

Precious M. Funches

It's Never Too Late For A Miracle

It's never too late for a miracle.
So, open up your heart.
And as you see God's truth unfold,
you'll make a brand new start.

In light of what He'll do for you,
the past grows strangely dim.
'Cause God knows
it's never too late for Him.

Lori Allert

"O' Righteous Ones See"

When you take a sparrow,
So young and free,
And you plan and trap him,
then put him in a cage.
So you say he is safe and protected.

But behold him now, for
you have killed his spirit
and hurt his mind.

Lena Ciulla

Limerick

Errors in ads are grammatical.
Some of which I am fanatical.
Anchor persons on TV
Say "Where it's at" - annoying me.
Me thinks they need a sabbatical.

Mary Shaw Rowland

Lonesome

I count the minutes, hours, days,
That I'm away from you;
When I come home I'll stop the clock,
So my dreams will all come true.

The time no longer will I count,
I'll never let you get away.
Just keep you always close to me
For all times and a day.

My love for you is now pent up;
I want to let it go.
Just enfold you in my arms
And let my true love flow.

Leroy Springstead

Someone to Love

We need someone to love
Someone who'll be there
  on rainy days
Someone to comfort you
  when you're down
Someone who'll be your
  protector
Someone who'll be your
  guide
Someone who'll take away
  your pain
Someone who'll pick you
  up when you fall
Someone who'll wipe your
  tears when you cry
What we really need is
  someone to spend eternity
  with.

Melanee Norgaard

"Heart Beats"

Dedicated to "My Grandchildren"

The first time that I saw you,
Something happened to my heart.
How could such a little thing
Be tearing it apart.

Before I even knew it
You were living deep inside
It was then I knew the feeling
Of a Grandma's pride.

When you're not with me
And I can't hold you to my heart.
I always feel my heart beat
And know we're not apart.

If someday I leave you
and I've gone you know not where.
Just put your fingers to your heart,
You'll always find me there.

Sharon Hemphill

Untitled

Someday,
somewhere,
in some far off spring
soul will dance
and soul will sing
and march to the dream
of Martin Luther King.

Monica Johnson

For The One I'll Always Love

With you I've known
such happiness,
And found a love
so real;
I only wish I knew
the words to tell you
how I feel.

With you I've watched
my dreams come true,
Hoping that you knew
what joy you bring to
everything
Whenever I'm with you.

Sequoia Wise

Death

Neither far nor near, death will
Soon appear; it could be today,
it could be tomorrow; you shouldn't
drown yourself in sorrow; life lives
on day after day, so pray to
God he will keep your fears
away.

Nicole Allen

Take Heed

The king of all kings
  Soon will appear
Our ruler is coming
  To resume his place here
Take heed is the plea
  As they open the seals
Releasing the beast
  To ravish its pray
Tainting or wasting
  Everything in its way
Causing fear for the faint
  And the wicked to flee
Take heed and receive
  For the trumpets will blow
Sending fear through the land
  Before screaming the woes
His judgement has started
  With no place to go

Kenneth L. Taylor

Human

Time upon time
  Space upon Space .....
None can ever
  Be erased.

Our time here
  is so small
we hardly know
  we're here at all.

Write a book
  make a bomb ......
Man himself
  is undone.

Bend your Back
  for bread and wine.....
Bend your mind
  to worthless time

To be in history
  engraved in stone........
Without love
  we're all alone.

Gerald A. Valenta

Justyn

A Wondrous Joy!
So quickly transformed
Into a semi-mechanical form.
And as such, a prayer
On the lips of thousands.
And now, only a name,
A photograph, a word,
A thought, an enigma,
A tear, a spot of God's green earth,
A bitter-sweet memory.

Ruth P. Thrash

Life Ought To Be

Beside the brick wall
Stood a stage, a star
And a waterfall -
Flowing pure and free
The way life - ought to be.

Life ought to be
Like the peaceful sea
Flowing over the bank
And through the trees-
Tender like the leaves
Hanging on a tree.

Energetic like the woman
Who climbed the mountain
To reach the peak-
Reaching for the sky
Of endless dreams.

Mary Stevenson

Untitled

Sweet
Substantial underneath
A kiss
Succulent almost tasted
Perfume of strong rum
Without the choky bite
White stiff Bristol RSVP
  For us
White soft flannel furled uncased
  For me

J. Prout

Like Matter For Nine

Spring with soft rain
Summer and warm days,
May and August
Both days
Cool shadows, light showers.
What's the matter,
Nineteen and twenty-nine
Lives change with nine
Does it really matter?

Earth, God matter,
Fixes the date,
Planets dancing the Milky Way
Rejoice with one of the nine.
Expanding universe
Gravity's curve of love,
Reaching across the stars
Like flowing wine,
Embracing two lives
Twice confirmed and blessed
Signed by the nine.

Thomas P. Keevey

The Hunt

The day is just dawning
The air is cold and crisp
As white tales gaily frisk
for they know 'tis too cold
for the hunters to be about
You can almost hear them shout
come out, come out, 'tis safe.
There are no hunters here about!
But as the day warms 'neath the sun
The white tales seem to vanish
from the hunters darting too and fro
and acting crazy and mannish.

Mary R. Finch

The Groaning Of Rebirth

'Tis the energy of this moment
Swaying to and fro
An axle pivoting, grating, groaning
Spurious reconciliation of life and love

The spirit of hope
A tangible glitter
Rebounding as from a star
A galaxy in force
Come hither a breath of freshness
Across the earth it blows
Spring time of renewal
The rains they fall to cleanse to grow

The heart of man beats to begin
In fellowship of harmony; a song
Filled openly of melodies
Unsung - but heard

Wisdom excites explosion of truth
unveiling layer upon layer
The corridors of thought -
the groanings of man; of rebirth!

Lahoma Vivian Guinn

The Midnight Dream

The cool breeze of the summer's night
Sweeps gently through my hair;
And as I lift my weary eyes,
The moon and stars shine there.

The stillness of the darkened eve,
When all life's fast asleep,
Implores my mind to linger close
To memories cherished deep.

The softness of your manly lips
Are felt upon my own.
I melt and feel your tender touch.
My body yearns . . . I moan.

With open heart and eyelids closed
I bring you into view
To cling within your precious arms
And give my love to you.

So secret one, my silent dream,
Be kind as kind can be.
Please send the love that heaven blessed
To warm and comfort me.

Patricia A. Fauci-Morosky

"Pass Over"

Pass over me
  sweet angel of death
    let the morning come
    smelling of sugar cane
    and damp grain.

Pass over the blue sky
  darkened by the poison
  ink of night.

In a populous, polluted age
  the angel of death passes quickly
  like "McDonald's" at rush hour.

The earth lies silent
  carved and criss-crossed
    with highways
  and air waves
    only angels know.

Rosena Simon

Sunken Treasure

Love, like a sunken treasure
Swim deeper and deeper
Until you run out of air
You're drowning slowly
Trying to save something
So precious and beautiful
Only to find out someone else has it
You wait your whole life
For that one big break
Only to find out you're breaking yourself
You have to have an air supply
Or someday you'll die
No one can make it alone
I guess that's why
There will always be love
Without it we'd be lost
But with it
We seem more lost than ever.

Melissa Oliver

"The Fisherman"

I once knew a fisherman
tall and lean
Handsomest man I'd ever
seen.
Eyes as blue as a crystal blue
sea
Arms big and strong
Just to hold me
Kind of shy a real sweet guy
I'll always love him till the day I die.

Lisette Y. Tripp

Dandelion

Yellow flowers invading the grass
Taraxicum dens-leonis enmasse
Nobody's helping, no one is paid
Growing by millions without any aid.

"Stop world famine" people all pray
Begging the Lord, "Stop it today!"
They fret and worry—clothing is rent
May I suggest, He's already sent.

Offering guests dandelion wine
Often is called manners divine.
Cooks boil leaves in their stew
Others dry roots for a tasty brew.

I agree without any guessing
This weed is a great blessing.
On my lawn, I have a bunch
I never poison—if you need lunch.

Muriel Pettett

A Day Begins And Ends

Arise Sir Sun and with your work
Tell how the day begins
When the rooster crows and sound flows
That is when the day begins.

Then at noon the sun is high
and now the workman's lunch begins
Whistles blow, midday begins.

When at night the moon goes up
and now the dark light begins
Your heartbeat's slow, now you know
How the day does end.

Tara Nichols

Reflection

The world is a swirling
tempestuous sea
But nothing is as great a miracle
as a child can be.

He looks at me, wanting to be older,
wanting to be me.
I smile when I watch him
and wish I could be three.

There is not a penny you could give me,
not a way that I could part
with the sparkle in his eyes
nor the magic of his heart.

As he looks up at me
with love in his eyes
I look down at his innocence
and know he is wise.

Nikki Lopez

The Winner

The Jockeys line up side by side
Tensing for the long hard ride
many fences in the race
Can they hold the cruel pace?

The jostling starts, the flag is down!
At the racetrack at the edge of town
Becomes the one and only place
For each revealing anxious face,

Well combed manes, curled just right
Of those great creatures well in flight,
And cheering from the massive crowd
Fills the air, both long and loud!

The Jockeys' shirts a rainbow streak
The Tic-Tac man, the punters seek,
The lead horse with panache and style
Thunders down the last half mile.

First past the post, now standing there
Trembling! steaming! chestnut fair,
Takes one more accolade of fame,
And adds "wonder" to his famous name.

Marie D. Taylor

Mr. Clown

He has a sense of humor
That can erase a cloudy day
He'll put a smile upon your face
And chase the blues away
He does the funniest things
Healing minor pain
Removing the inner tension
That brings about the strain
He can eliminate your stress
A smile replaces a frown
He has that special way
Performing like a clown
He's a belly full of laughs
Being upset is just taboo
Laughter is the remedy
This clown prescribes for you
Whenever there is that need
Just to bring about a lift
Look for Mr. Clown
He'll deliver his laughter gift.

Robert J. Pool

Loves Past

What is this cloak
That comes
Without warning,
That seeps through the
Flesh
And weaves a cage about
The heart.
What can this power be
That overcomes the
Wonders
At our sides.....
And turns life
Into a nonexistent
Form.
What is it
That can make a smile -
A frown
A joy - a tragedy
A forgotten memory
To reappear.....

Richard J. Schotts

A Child Of God

A child of God! How can it be,
That God so shed His love on me?
He made my mind and heart rejoice,
That I might cry with lips and voice,
"Abba Father, hear my prayers,
I bring to Thee my joys and cares."

A child of God! Oh grace divine,
What a privilege now is mine!
I dwell in peace from day to day,
Because my cares are wiped away,
For I may come before His throne,
And make my needs and wishes known.

A child of God! Amazing love,
Flowing down from heaven above!
He makes snow white my scarlet sin,
And washes clean my heart within,
That I might stand in nothing less,
Than clothed in His own righteousness.

I know Him now through faith and prayer,
But soon His presence I shall share.

Mary L. Kress

Too Young To Die

You were too young to die
that is all I can say.
You were too young to have been
taken or to have ever gone away.
I never thought we would ever
have to part.
I never thought I'd have to
say goodbye.
Now there is so much pain in
my heart.
I never thought that the young
could die.
You had a whole lifetime ahead
to live.
So many challenges you have not
gone through.
You had so much love to give.
Now time is the space between
me and you.

Michele Ambrosini

Verse And Reverse

Have you heard the story
That is going around town,
About the backword poet
Acting like a clown?

His work is all scrambled:
It couldn't be much worse.
Each time he writes a poem,
The lines are in reverse.

His topics are of interest.
He works both day and night;
When reading the next verses,
Start reading from the right!

Person that is poet the
Immerse to ability the with
Phrase to prose condense and
Verse of form the in arranged

Expression mere is work his
Led nature which life the of
Agree must we form in projected
Said beautifully certainly is

Nelson D. Bartlett

A Tender Rose Bud

Once I entrusted a tender rose bud
That is watched with loves and care
To a loving, children's couple
Each others home and life to share.

I didn't try to escape a duty
or long to go fancy free
I just didn't care to bruise this flower
That was given unto me

I pray this little rose bud
When it has washed full bloom
Will retain the same old sweetness
As while in the nursery room

May it bring abundant pleasure
To those who guide its life
Let it be worthy of their efforts
May it never cause then strife

When we find a rose among the thorns
It should best be set apart
Transfer it to a more futile soil
Bring sunshine in round its heart.

Ruth Klessen

Over The Hill

So now I hear you're 40 too
That makes me feel just great!
Because we'll have much more to share
We truly can relate!
We'll WALK around the jogging track,
And color our gray hair,
We'll try to win at bingo games
And travel here and there.
We've made the climb, we're at the top,
We've reached the crest of life!
And now we start the downward trend,
No more hard work and strife.
We'll take the walk together
And we'll move a little slow
'Cause when we reach the bottom now
I'm not sure where we go!
At any rate I'm glad that we
Can work together still
'Cause misery loves company
And we're BOTH over the hill.

Kathy Piazza Hammond

Mom

I don't know how to show
That my love for you is true,
I guess our busy lives
Have to do with it, too.

We will sometimes disagree,
That's normal for us,
Thanks for putting up with me,
Well, I just like to fuss.

The bond that we have shared,
Will never break apart,
You will always have a place,
Right inside my heart.

For everything you've done with love,
You, I wish I could repay,
And I will show my love for you,
This wonderful Mother's Day.

Kristen Riccardi

Hidden Messages

Life is like a dream
that passes by so quickly.
Life is like a bird
that flies so free and swiftly.
Life is like a rainbow
full of color and light
Life is like the morning sun
shining down so bright.
Life is like a gift, sent from
up above
Life is like a baby, full of
joy and love.
Life is like a snowflake, each one
is never the same
Life is like a heart, sometimes
full of pain.
Life can be so many things,
it depends on who you are,
Life can be a fresh raindrop
or a brightly shining star.

Sonia Munoz

Bridget

A childhood hell
That she survived.
A twisting of her mind
And emotions.
Battling Gods and men
At every turn.
Trying her best to remain
Afloat in a sea of sorrow
Where the waves crashed
Over her and promised
To pull her under.

Admire her?
Love her?
My God, how could you
Do anything but!?

For the world has crashed
Down on her shoulders,
And she has found
The strength to
Rise and walk.

Thomas J. Kern

In A London Shop

It wasn't her long auburn hair,
That spilled about her shoulders fair,
Nor knowing eyes of sapphire blue,
That I was first attracted to.

And when she smiled, the heavens danced,
But that would not divert my glance.
Her figure, those delightful curves,
Were wasted on me, unobserved.

A silken blouse, her shapely hips,
The touch of rose upon her lips,
The way she moved about the store,
Took little effort to ignore.

No, none of these, I must attest,
Caused any stirring in my breast.
But when she sang, "Good morning, luv!"
My heart belonged to her, thereof.

Martin H. Ornstein

"Time, Life And Love"

Yes, time is that silent force
That starts then controls our course
    Try as we may
    There's just no way
To bring back one moment that's passed

So, treat time and love with care
Though things get too hard to bear
    When all goes wrong
    Stand tall and strong
Remember your troubles won't last

    Life's road is a bumpy highway
    No signs to ensure each turn
    Avoid every tempting by-way
    That's one thing we all must learn

With you by my side each day
I know that it's safe to say
    We'll face our trials
    With courage and smiles, I'm sure,
Our love will keep us secure,

Tag: May time, life and love, long endure.

Raymond S. O'Riordan

Dad

Maybe it's the twinkle in his eye
that will stay with me,
Or maybe the sweetness of his voice
it will always be,

Perhaps his gentle, knowing face
will visit me at night,
Or perhaps it's his memory
that makes me feel all right,

Whatever it will be
that sparks my thoughts of Dad,
The warmth of his love
will overcome those sad,

As I hold my children
with one upon each knee,
There is a touch of Dad
in each one's face I see,

But, you're there too, Mom,
giving us all your love,
And Dad is with us
content now up above

Martha Marienthal-Baumgartner

Initials

If I had one wish
   that wish would be
To wander and roam
   to the giant oak tree
Through meadows of heather
   o'er hillsides of green
Under sunlight a smilin'
   or moonlight serene
Hand in hand, together,
   my true love and me
And carve our initials
   for the whole world to see

J. R. Gallagher

A Prayer For Peace

Let us bow our heads and pray
that world peace will come someday
all this hatred, war and strife
is taking its toll upon our life
I humbly ask you for world peace
will all this fighting never cease
war and fighting, don't you see
will only destroy you and me
so, let us bow our heads and pray
that world peace will come our way

Sharon J. Boyd

"The Dream Goes On"

There is no limit to a dream
   that's born within the soul -
It's nourished there with rich ideas
   until it's strong and bold.

Then it goes out with powerful acts
   accomplishments to bring -
Rewarding one for sending forth
   this very special dream.

Mary Jo Sherlin

Closed Door

In our life we find a door
That's never left open

So don't be shattered or depressed
If the key is stolen

You'll come across a challenge
For you that's not hard to achieve

But you must remember if you don't
Conquer it
You'll never be able to leave

So before you find that stolen key
That's been held by many before

Know it's not the key but your heart
And mind
That will unlock the closed door.

Shakira Badilla

The Uniqueness Of Man

What manner of man am I
Surely not more than flesh and blood
Not more than a star in the sky
Yet unique in a mind that is boundless,
Unfettered, soaring, free
To vanquish all the legions of
Life's Adversity.

R. James Lyons-Colichio

Reaching Out

I am reaching out
That's no doubt
I wanted to play
But I couldn't stay

When I was young
I bit my tongue
Reaching out
No doubt

When you don't know the right people
You become a casualty and a steeple
Reaching out
No doubt

Attain a stride in your pride
Don't reach out on your ride
Do it on your own
Without thinking it's a bone

That's the old fashion way
Just work for it today
Reaching out is no doubt
Making on your own is the right tone

Michael A. Martin

Untitled

I sit and watch the sun go down
The chatter of the birds
As they eat their evening meal
I wonder what they think of me
As a friend—a provider of bird food
First the screaming blue jays
As a loving family
The fire red cardinals
The little orioles and chickadees
The shy exotic pheasants
They all arrive
They eat together
But in the end, each kind separates
To their nearby nests
To sleep and wait till dawn
And then again to eat together
Until they separate again
I wonder if the little birds
Can teach us about life and family ties
Which so many have forgotten.

Pat Palmer

The Gift

As the still, gray light of dawn
Slowly exposes another day,
We lie somehow always touching.
The softness of your skin,
Its radiant warmth a lure,
The scent of our love lingers;
Your gentle beauty shining
Even as you sleep.

Though we will soon part again
My heart remains calm;
The now familiar longing soothed
By the gift of these few moments.
My thoughts are of a time
When dawn will always find us
Lying together, somehow touching;
Our love exposed.

Kenneth K. Wiscomb

Building Memories

Having few memories,
The child daydreams,
Builds sand castles
Of expectations,
For the keeper
Of the dreams.

Lucie Glenn

A Time For Blessing

The violent storm is passing
The clouds no longer threatening
The worried brow de-stressing
It is a time for blessing.

The joy will come in the morning
I can feel the anguish leaving
The sun is almost shining
It is a time for singing

The day has been long in coming
The night was so unrelenting
The search for truth revealing
It is a time for healing.

My soul was desperately longing
For a touch - a gentle anointing
The darkness is finally dissolving
It is a time for evolving.

God brought me through the testing
Through times that were so depressing
On a higher plane I'm now resting
It is a time for blessing.

Thelma Lee Ayers

One Day Gone

The day has passed
   the cool night air has crept in
a calmness approaches,
   a sacredness,
a time for all to rest.

Up in the trees
   the leaves quiver
with the approaching breeze,
   a most astonishing quietness,
calm, almost deathly.

Darkness is here
   the dampness, coldness
the silhouettes, reaching upward
   the pine needles whistle
limbs cracking,
   now, a stillness.

Timothy A. Glass

Symphony

I heard the high pitched notes begin,
The crying voice of violin,
And thought it strange to music sense
In such a crowd of people dense.

Still, on it went, the horns fell in,
And cello joined the violin,
Was woodwinds next, the sound divine,
Then, full orchestra on line.

I spun and turned to learn the source,
Found no musicians there, of course.
But, as our eyes met, it came to me,
Your beauty was that symphony.

Richard C. Enger

"The Day!"

The day begins with sunlight,
  the day ends with dark.
The day brings new comings,
  the day brings new friends.
The day brings you love...
  and then it ends.

Renee Latimer

The Voice

Silence
The far away ringing of the phone
Your tender voice
Caressing my ear
Sending sensual vibrations
In my ear
Turning me on
To you
Far away
I hear a phone ringing
Reaching across
And retrieve you
From the cradle

Tracy Autry

Animus

The results of desire
the flash of flame
losing control with inarticulate cries
the fear of solitude, dark isolation
the coming and going of touch/
countertouch

Merging and moving
together, alone
always afraid to break free of the past
how far to feel, how much to take
wanting to know but
unable to ask

Hidden eyes and heart
burning the night
shielding, coveting what the body screams
desire moves us, flings us wide
then leads us home
in chains

Tammie L. Pollard

Eternity

To taste the fruit
the fruit of eternity
that alters my mind
my heart, and my soul
like a gentle sip of the
everlasting fountain of youth

To be the one
the only one
to taste the sweetness of eternity
to live with the everlasting
wealth and royalty of each day

Each day, as people die
to remain
until all is gone
and the dreadful back isolation engulfs
the lonely body
seeping into the core
draining any love, warmth, or feeling
that's left

Eternity is not so sweet

Lily Tippin

Untitled

The world is falling apart,
The gangs are getting worse,
The crimes are increasing,
There is nothing nobody can do.
No matter what anyone does,
It seems not to help.

Everyone imagine of a better world,
A world that is peaceful,
Like back in the old days.

Drugs are getting worse,
Younger kids are using them.
How can we stop everything like that?
I guess the only thing that is able
To be said about it is —
   That's reality.

Sabrina Stanley

God's Love

The ducks so sweet and small,
The giraffe so very tall,
The buffalo big and brown,
And the pigeons you see in town,
Both great and small,
God loves them all.
The dolphin with its tricks,
The dog with its loving licks,
Even the pink dogwood tree,
Both you and me,
Now don't you see,
God loves even me.

Rebekah N. Torresson

The Last Glance!

I remember the last glance
The glance that made me cry
My heart was torn apart
I thought I was going to die.

I remember in November
When I got her
She was my early X-mas present
  from my dad
When day by day went by
I was so happy then
For this I cannot lie.

We played in the grass together
We snuggled like birds and their fathers
Then she did something bad
And made my dad really mad.
Day by day I prayed
because I didn't want to
  give her away.

Rebecca Middaugh

Falling Apart

All alone no where to go
The love and laughter will always grow
Being strong is hard to do
When someone you love is gone for good
The anger inside keeps building up
The pain inside won't break apart
Seeing his face will never fade
Tear drops fall as I walk away
He will always be with me
Where ever I go
One more look and time to go

Nicole James

Heaven

The skies are so blue
The grass is so green
The mountains are so beautiful
The air is so clean
There are no wars
There are no fights
There is no prejudice
Just peaceful nights
The people are happy
The world is at peace
The color of skin
Doesn't matter the least
A place like this
Is hard to find
But the place is there
In the back of my mind.

Kimberly J. Diaz

Wake Up!

How can we forget our ancestors' cries
The history we've been taught,
Of how they were stolen from their land
Transported, sold, and bought?

Their intelligence could not be shown
Given ignorance as a guise,
Servants, slaves they were
Only their master to be wise.

How can we forget their dreams
For which they struggled day by day,
For freedom and equality
Their descendants might see one day?

How can we become successful
Filled with pride and greed,
And forget the constant struggle
Of others to be free?

Kim M. Talbert

The Blessing

Bless the smiling face,
the kind eyes,
the gentle words,
that sometimes, but not often,
arrive just when needed most.
When your spirit is crushed
and your ego deflated,
when you are tempted to cry,
but do not have the strength;
bless that sweet someone
who cares.

Rhonda Moreno

A Dream Come True

The beauty of the mountains,
The cacti, rocks and sand
Mean more to me than
The trees, grass and snow
I do not cherish snakes or lizards
But since they are essential
To the desert terrain
I accept them as they are
When some people see the desert
They do not care for it at all
For some people the desert
Truly has to grow on them
But for me the desert really
Is a dream come true

Linda Swart

A Priest

At mass a priest I see
The love of God and man
His face aglow as each day
Hands blessed the host caressed
Warm and gentle a pact with Christ
Giving of his all
Help for the weary
Comfort for the afflicted
Untold compassion for the sinner
A guiding light for those in darkness
A prayer for one and all
Gifted beyond compare
Through him God speaks to us
Words of wisdom and love
God bless and keep you as you are
So like my Christ
The chosen of the Lord

E. Ruttner

Demons

From the boiling entrails grow
The massive beasts of high and low,
Living in a life of death,
Dying from a life of less,
Something from their life amiss,
Less the others, less the rest,
Sorrow hangs from iron chains,
But life will fall and burn in vain,
Mourning daze will long remain,
Never leave, but come again.

Matthew Bustard

Love Is

Love is like a rose,
The more you care for it
The more it grows.

Be kind and gentle
and give it only
pure and healthy
nourishment,
It will bring beauty
to those who Cherish it,
And last a very long time.

Kathy L. Garleb

She Came

She came to me softly in the night
The mystery of her presence there
so gentle, oh so right

She came to me so early in my spring
I could not understand that she
Such heavenly bliss could bring

She came with all her lovely charms
Carried me to lofty heights unknown
So softly cradled in her welcome arms

She came to me and I was swept so high
I knew that I would never feel again
The beauty of her softly murmured sigh

She came and I could hardly see
Was she real or just a myth
Or was she really here with me

She came to me all beauty and aglow
I clung to her and couldn't let go
She came to me, I know was heaven sent
She came to me, came to me, then went

Vaughn Guthrie

Family

The young ones give the memories
The old ones give the laughs
You must give from deep inside.
all the lessons to pass.

Penny Lee Kessler

What Happened To Our Tears?

What happened to our tears?
The ones that made our eyes
moist when we listened to the
stars and stripes forever.
The little drops we wiped
away at a marriage or graduation.
The tricklets we sometimes shed
for ourselves - because we
thought no one cared. The
rivers that ran down our
cheeks when we honored
a friend at his or her
final resting place.
What happened to our tears?
they are still there, in
God's eyes!

Robert B. Thomas

The Ocean

I watch the ocean's endless waves
The rise, the swell, the crash,
I contemplate all that it means
A teardrop bathes my lash.

What beauty nature did create
Our maker led the way
Now that I'm growing older
It delights me more each day.

I listen to the ocean's roar
Such comfort from those sounds
To know it always will remain
The swish and swoosh abounds.

The ocean does call out to me
Jump in, cool off, get wet
But I must still be cautious
Or my match, I will have met.

I'll consider all the dangers
But I won't let them spoil
My enjoyment of this ocean
Placed here to guard the soil.

Norma Dubbrin

Untitled

The sky is blue
The earth is sad
The earth is like a ball of fire
The sun is as warm as the light
The earth is over heated with anger
The sun shines with love
Love is what this earth needs
Love love love
To find is to seek
The life of one's self is to love
To love comes with the heart
The heart can only love
Love is the message we bring
To bring in is to give the world peace
Peace is the everlasting word
The words come from God.

Ursula M. Post

The Roads

Here my son, I show you
  the roads
I tell you the life
  of a man's loads
I show you the tears,
  the pains, the fears
Of a man whose searched
  the roads for cures
We come and go
  each child you know
And leave behind
  the roads to show
What lies ahead
  I think I see
I see the light
  that's come for me
I'm old and grey
  and wrinkled too
But my son
  the roads I give to you

Larry G. Wilson

For You

The sky is blue for you
the roses are red for you
the violets are blue for you, and the
hearts are you and me, I love you.

Metallica Uddley

A Teacher's Lament And Joy

The same car,
The same road,
The same snow,
The same load

Of school work, of home work,
Of duties that do lurk
On desk tops, table tops,
Counter tops and chair tops.

They seem the same, my routine ways,
But each glad thought renews my days.

The same car - my trusted steed,
The same road - a link I need.
The same snow - earth's flaws erased.
The same load - my choice embraced.

Marianna K. Staples

Go To Sleep

We've been tucked in together,
the sheets are nice and clean,
  so close your eyes,
and we can start to dream.

The cows have left the corn crib,
  a long, long time ago,
the sheep have left the meadow,
they're standing here, you know.

They're filling up the bedroom,
  those tired little sheep,
they wish that you would count them,
  so they could go to sleep.

The sandman's also waiting,
  he's got a job to do,
and he can't stand here half the night,
  and wait for me and you!

Tara Kinsey

Untitled

The touch of a hand
The smile on a face
The sight of a child
in a warm felt embrace
The sound of a bird
on a sunny spring day
nature's beauty in the midst of May
Words of love expressed from the heart
Loved ones together and never apart
Peace and tranquility
throughout the universe
Emotions never shattered
Life not a curse
Only good memories lasting within
Thinking of what will be,
Not what could've been
Everlasting happiness
fills a future so bright
So let me close my eyes
And dream this dream tonight...

Lisa Marie Bonfiglio

"Vietnam War"

Surrounded by unknown wilderness,
the soldiers were alone.
Fighting for their lives,
miles away from home.
Afraid of dying,
most did not want to go.
For us they fought their hardest,
but did they receive any celebrations
or awards in their honor? - No!
Now we recognize you,
even though it is rather late.
For all of your bravery,
we at last congratulate!

Korin Stefko

The Waltz Of The Wind

Softly, sweetly, through the night
The strains of music float -
Wafting lightly through the trees,
This waltz the angels wrote.

Gently now, up to the moon,
The whispering notes will rise -
Moving velvet leaves to dance,
Caressing as it dies .....

Rosemary P. Youngquist

A Rainy Day

The blue skies have disappeared
The sun has gone to hide,
The white clouds have turned gray;
Making ready for a rainy day.

A rainy day is needed,
To cleanse the air we breathe;
To water crops in a farmer's field
And make the flowers grow.

It gives us time to slow our pace.
Allow the rain to hit our face -
Children's eyes as large as pools
Watching the rain come down and cool.

Anxious to see the clouds roll by,
The blue returning to the sky -
And when the sun appears again,
The world is all aglow.

M. M. Calderone

Untitled

I walked into your world
The sun was in your soul
Yet shadows that remained
Left secrets yet untold

Love guides a ship along
What guides a ship to shore
Does anyone really know
What the future has in store

I'm headin' towards a place
A place I've never been
Love will take me there
And bring me back again

I need you to help me
To help me make it through
Like actors on a stage
It's your turn to take the cue

Take me for what I am
Not for what I must be
And I'll love you for you
Knowing you and knowing me.

Stan Yamaguchi

Now I Lay Me Down

The stars are out and shining bright,
The sun's gone down and now it's night.

The moon is shining bright and clear,
The fear I feel is drawing near.

I close my eyes and try to sleep,
I see the beast and start to weep.

The cold, damp darkness has come again,
What's in my mind is deep within.

They've come again to claim my soul,
Nightmares are a deep, black hole.

It's just a dream I try to say,
As I wake to face another day.

I go about my daily grind,
Try not to think of what's in my mind.

I wash and clean and run to town,
Try not to let it get me down.

I've kissed the kids and put them to bed.
It's bedtime again, oh, how I dread.

Now I lay me down to weep,
I pray the Lord my soul to keep.

Michelle Cline

Man?

Are you a pawn of FATE?
Then hold you tongue and wait.

Are you a mouth for bread?
Then eat until you're dead.

Are you a monkeys seed?
Then defecate and breed.

Are you a flame of LUST?
Then dance whenever you must.

As any of these, at best
You're nothing but a pet.

But if you kneel and pray
To crush you will away
There isn't much to say.

Louis Paolucci

Azaleas

Now winter's icy blast has gone
The trees bloom forth in grand array,
Like some grand march of infantry
Their colors to display.

How welcome are the flowers red
And pink and white, against the sky,
To show forth, each to crown their own
With beauty from on high.

So swiftly bloom, so swiftly pass
And soon their beauty ends
But for the moment, brings a joy
To each heart it befriends.

We're grateful for this loveliness
That now so swiftly seen
Is but a passing fancy, now is gone
And soon becomes a dream.

Winnifred Dixon Redd

Nature

Nature, the gift of life.
The trees, the stars,
the moon, the ocean.
How gorgeous it is to gaze
at the glistening sand at the beach,
watching the clouds overhead
changing their forms.

The sun shines bright,
yet, my visions remain black.

Nature is great.
Nature is beautiful.
But nature alone will not comfort man,
for man will remain lonely.

Nature, the gift of life.
But what beauty can I conceive
from this gift,
when it's my loneliness and despair
with which I share
this gift of life?

Mother Nature - God damn you!

Marc Wiener

Drifting

I am drifting, drifting at sea
The waves keep tossing endlessly
I'm way off course, I have no port
Won't someone show the way to Thee.

All my life, I have been adrift
A lost, lonely abandoned ship
No one has ever set me right
I have just drifted, all through life.

When I leave this old world behind,
Heaven's bright port I want to find
And climb the winding, golden stairs
That reach high above, in the air.

Point the way, before it's too Late
Set me on course and keep it straight
Steer me away, from all temptations
Guide, help me find my salvation.

For I'm drifting, drifting at sea
The waves keep tossing endlessly
I'm way off course, I have no port
Someone, show me the way to Thee.

Monettia Phillips

True Love

You could never understand
The way I feel about you
My love for you is so deep
It almost seems untrue
I see you once a week
but that's not enough
The pain of knowing you
don't feel like me, is real enough

You're different from me
but that I understand
The only thing I can't is
why you won't be my man
you said you don't love me,
but my love will never die.
Just see if you can stop it,
just go ahead and try

Michelle White

Flowers, Wind And Water

The flowers
The wind
The drips of water
Flow softly
To their places,
No destiny
or
Shame
Finally they rest in peace
And settle down to lie

Veronica Chase

Oncology Nursing

Their eyes reveal the story,
Their eyes reveal the pain,
Comfort measures given
sometimes seem in vain.

Their eyes reveal the story,
Their eyes reveal the fear,
Prognosis is uncertain
as death lingers near.

My eyes in turn reveal to them
compassion, kindness, hope.
My arms stretched out, enfold them,
support and help them cope.

Rewards are in the sparkle
of their eyes when I am done.
Guided by their light
to help another one.

Marcia E. Berg

True

I woke up one day and knew
that to myself I had not been true
I tried and tried to be another
procrastinating
needing to be stronger
absorbing knowledge, never knowing
my true potential steadily growing
I found a savior inside of me
the talent to write poetry
and so I rise with every day
greet myself with a smile and say
goodbye to the girl I thought
I knew
hello to a woman who now
knows how to be true

Tracy McReynolds

Ember Of Love

The fire rages like an inferno
then it cools to the embers.
Is it gone away forever?
It is benign below the cool crust?
Does the daily routine smother it?
Where is that raging excitement?

It does not go out.
It is always there.
Still at times, but there.
A touch, a nudge, a tickle.
A smile, a hug, a kiss.
There are the kindlings of love.

Our love burns differently.
Sometimes soft and warm;
Sometimes hurriedly and tepid,
Sometimes long and hot;
Sometimes raging to our souls.
But always it burns deeply.

King V. Turney

Ode To A Nursing Home

Hope the home will not smell bad,
    Then you will not be sad.
Pray that there will be plenty of love,
    Within and from above.
Guide the staff's feet,
    And hope they can stand the heat.
Smell the home cooking,
    The residents all looking.
While some drink Zebra-aide,
    Some need an aide.
They remember yesterday,
    But have a hard time with today.

Nelson C. Montague

So Close

So close within my heart,
There is a silent cry,
it is not a cry of pain
but that of a yearning...
a yearning for companionship,
for that of love and friendship,
to be touched,
to be held,
not only for awhile
but for an eternity.
    So close,
is what I desire,
for a gentle saying,
upon my ears to be heard...
but what is heard is the wind;
    So close,
is what I yearn to be,
with the comforts of a true friend.

Willbends Baptiste

Light

In the long dark tunnel of night
there is always light at the end.
Find the light and keep it in sight.
Find faith. Find God.
Find the inner strength to keep your
head and let your heart follow.
In the long dark tunnel of night
there is always light, however dim,
it burns eternal.

Melanie A. Seitz

Apology

Normandy, Okinawa, Occupier of Japan
There you now sit a shadow of the man.
Arm crippled by trauma,
Tongue numbed by disease,
Dispatch you, I cannot
Even though you scrawl please.

J. E. Lynch

Secret

Want to know a secret?
There's a thing about poets,
when we bleed, it's not blood.
It's words,
Flowing across a mystic paper.
My heart pumps the messages out of me.
Scabs are writers block,
but when allowed to heal,
they are new avenues for mind.
My cells are forms of letters,
the combined cells are words.
Gradually these form sentences.
I am the living poem,
my body is a sentence.
My mind is a ripple in the universe.
Are we not small indeed
compared to:
The planet?
The universe?

Ty Patzer

Stormy Visit

Today angry clouds fill the sky.
These gray rainmakers hover for a
    moment and then race on.
The wind is anxious to be rid of them
    and hurries them on their way.
Sibilant gusts give us all warning.
The sun's rays are prisoners tucked
    tightly behind this steely curtain.
The lofty intruders start to disperse
    showering upon us their disdain

Lucy C. Bradshaw

Time

Tender years are given but once,
their moments now so fleeting
bountiful then, a memory now
one wonders to where life is leading

Manacled in time's cruel grasp
once taken without a fight
now I struggle to savor today
...struggle with all of my might

I sit and I stare at years gone by
relieved again and again as I lay
then I realize I am guilty again
for I have wasted an irreplaceable day

Useless it is, my nostalgic dream
...useless to all but me
I now confess to time that I've wasted
but that no longer be

With half of my life expended
I still learn through word and song
this very moment proves what I say now
too late already.....and forever gone

Richard Vincent Brigidi

Untitled

Skinny puppy to dark park
These words float over me
Like songs from a lark
"ReffineJ" brought me to this land
Where every sight, every sound,
even my hand is grand.
The black dog glares
-But not evilly
It's as if to say, "get up here with me!"
Up in the trees with
Dandelions and daffodils
And willowy wisps of wonder,
Floating across paper lakes
in boats of ink.
Listen to my sight
If only you could
Because love flows through my toes
-And joy comes through my little fingers.

Michael L. Anderson

Broken Rose

They broke her spirit
They broke her will
But they did not
Break her soul
They took away her
Freedom to grow
On the clinging vine
Plucked away from
Her life's cord
She can no longer
Sway in the wind
Or bow her head
In the bright sunlight
All she can see is
Fear and darkness
Waiting so patiently
It seems
She is the broken rose
begging to be free

Stephanie S. Canonica

They Forgot

To all our Viet Nam Vets
They forgot what you had done
You were there when they said come
A battle that came, was not declared war
For people had died more and more
To our Vets I know you were there
Doing things others wouldn't have dared
Fighting for their country
People here did not see,
You risked your lives
To set others free.

Tracy M. Palmer

Storm

A storm is going on outside!
The thunder roars.
We feel safe, but know that
We can never really be safe.
A storm is going on outside.
Suddenly . . .
    Lightning!
A storm is going on outside.
It is almost over.
I run outside
To find the end of the rainbow.

Nicole Cline

Words

Ornery little devils
they huddle in the wings
when the curtain opens
they forget their lines
come on stage for the wrong scenes
and stumble through the music

The dress rehearsals go so smoothly
every character in place
I guess they just get stage fright
or maybe the spot blinds them
perhaps they enjoy
making a fool of the director
tittering behind closed doors

It's better to pin them down
in their places on paper
so they can be rearranged
replaced
erased
(and with a crumple, taken back)

Nicole Brown

Retirement

When they put me out to pasture
They took away all the laughter
They took away all my hope
Left me nothing to do but sit and mope
Until the Lord Jesus to me spoke.

Lift up your head my child
Come work for me a little while
I have some seed you can sow
Plant enough seeds and some
Will surely grow.

So I'll just work a little faster
And leave the harvest to the master.
Then when at the pearly gate we meet
My life will then be complete.

Tommie Bostick

Mr. Nix

Some people say when they grow old
  They'll wear purple and learn to spit.
As for me, you'll hear my story told
  As on the porch I'll daily sit.
  About the day I went to town
    With Bassett Buckley Nix—
  A man, just one T away from a hound!

Yvonne Edwards

Heaven's Gate

Carry me,
  through the perils, Oh Lord.
Watch over me,
  when carrying the beat of my time.
With your wink of motion,
  I will follow.
To a place
  where peace heavenly reigns.
In time to step
  with angels.
To put all
  the suffering at rest.
Please dry your tears,
  my dear ones.
'Cause my pains
  were washed away!

Rhonda Gooding

Terror In The Heartland

In the devastation left behind
This becomes the trying time.
Middle America was blind.
Now they try to find
Those who have no respect for life.

The dealers of death
Who stole society's breath.
Reality caught them by surprise
They took so many lives.
Those left behind
Will ever try to find
Reason's for this gruesome crime

So many tears they will shed
For those not long dead.
Some who had just begun to live
They killed so many kids.
Do they realize just what they did?

Mike Crandall

Untitled

Lord, without pride you find me in
This earthy frame so scarred by sin.
I beg you survey what's here within
Don't grade me for my discipline.

Forgive apparent shamelessness.
Propagation of such extensive lists;
Rebellious acts, perfidiousness,
Time not spent in prayer like this.

But now, here kneeling I beg relief.
As sure as Adam under his leaf
Empty. Causing soul to grief;
Revolt, condemning me for unbelief.

An unworthy heart, yet genuine
In rhythm beats this phrase within:
"Remove from me the stains of sin,
Forgive. Walk and talk with me again"

Struggling, grasping for your hand.
Alone. Alone I cannot meet demand.
Give Adam's son, a heart to stand,
Soul committed, at your command.

Samuel J. Brown

Our Wedding Day

She could not be more beautiful
This loving bride of mine today.
She walked engulfed in tenderness
To my side forever to stay.

Her appearance in love and faith,
Her loving self behold all mine.
The shadowed giving of her trust;
An unseen light to me does shine.

Forever will I love you, Dear.
Forever will I tell you so.
Please take my hand and hold me near.
My need for you God had to know.

The bells of love in wedding told.
A new line upon life's long leaf.
You look at me; I look at you;
And, in that look, beloved belief.

Together hand in hand we'll walk
Through love and life thus long we pray.
As wrinkles form; youth is no more.
Still, Dear, 'twill be OUR WEDDING DAY.

Michael A. Cicon Jr.

Silent Vision

Today God has sent forth
This miraculous creation to us
She carries innocent wisdom
And a new vision of life
Her visions are silenced for now
For she cannot speak
But as she grows
She will learn
How to voice her thoughts
Maybe this child
Will hold all the secrets
the world is in search for
But the answer is not clear
We must cherish this soul
And help her to grow
Until that precious time comes
That she is filled with sweet music
And allows it to escape from her lips
The vision of life
Will then be heard and seen

Renettia K. Quillen

Daybreak

The sun was a great phenomenon
this morning at the break of dawn.
The sky lit up with a wondrous glow;
it made you thrill from head to toe.
Watching as colors came into view,
there were oranges in every hue.
It seemed to creep across the sky,
and became mottled before your eye.
The light spread in every direction;
it was like a special resurrection.
God had awakened a sleepy earth,
giving a new day a spectacular birth.

Susie Barter

"Another Absynthe For Mr. Van Gogh!"

You were a blaze
those last three years.
Your flame dancing
like mercury in a
barometer riding
rapids down the
leeward side of
the Dolomites.
Drunk on the
heated air of the
haunting scirocco,
spitting paint
in manic ecstasy,
hastened by petulant
gales of pride.

Neill Winston Barham

The Child And Simple Things

To love as a child
The simple things
Like a flower growing wild
Or a bird on its wings.

To love the moonbeams
And feel the breeze fair
To still have some dreams
If we dare.

These are from God who loves us so
Whatever we do, wherever we go.

Virginia Skinner

Castles Of Dreams

I can dream of castles,
Though I may never see;
Except through imagination,
That God has given me.

I can dream of other lands,
Their quaintness —
Each their own,

I may sail the seas,
I dream of,
Where warm waters deeply flow —

See ships high upon the waves,
Sailors going home.

Dreams very seldom ever
Come true —-
That's why they're called —
Castles in air.

And if you dream on,
Often enough —
They're around you,
And everywhere!

Lucy N. Stroman

Mom

Mom you mean the world to us,
Though sometimes we make quite a fuss.
You are the one we will always trust.
Even if your beautiful lamp we bust.

You stayed up nights and worked all day,
Doing it all without any pay.
Knowing that we wouldn't always stay,
Soon we will be on our way.

You picked the clothes for us to wear,
Time you had none to spare.
We both know that you care,
You have always been there.

You deserve a long vacation,
In the heart of relaxation.

Though we may not always show,
We thought that you should know,
We love you.

Laurel E. Veit

Teacher Tamer

Like hungry lions,
They await the moment
Their trainer's back is turned
To POUNCE!

But they miss-
Not to the surprise
Of the lion tamer.

He has survived twenty years
Of attacks
And can fight
The sharpest of claws
And the fastest of assaults.

The master cracks his whip
To line up the lions
And no matter how they grumble,
They submit
For they are hungry for the meat
The master has not yet handed out.

Meggin Kahn Silverman

Ronnie's Song

I'm trying to get over you
Thought you'd be happy to know
It will be a long process
And it will be slow

I still miss you
Sometimes I still cry
When I hear that certain song
And realize we've said our last goodbye

I don't know how this started or why
They say for everything there's a reason
My heart will always ache for you
No matter what the season

You said everything just went too fast
And it would be best if we'd part
Now all I can do is hope and pray
That I'm somewhere in your heart

Rebecca J. Hamilton

"Tell Me A Story"

Tell me a story where my
thoughts will fly,
Tell me a story where the words
go by and by.
Tell me a story that will make
my imagination go wild,
Tell me a story with a very
courageous child.
Tell me story with a magical
place,
Tell me a story with no problem
a person has to face.
Tell me a story where nobody gets hurt,
Tell me a story where nobody is
left in the dirt.
Tell me a story that is glorious
and vane,
Tell me a story where each
person has something to gain.
Just please tell me a story.

Morgan Milford

Living Limbo

Whispering sadness drowns out sorrow
Thundering heartbeats fill the head
Voices encompassing logic
For fantasy is found to be dead

The days grow shorter
Although the minutes drag on
Time is dislodged
And reality becomes strong

Close your eyes to resurrect the lost
Spending life energy no matter the cost
The mystic memories start to resurface
So hold onto them for the endurance

Music regains its missing meaning
Life moves on in existence
Stories get told with feeling
Death is misplaced with hesitance

Slipping, slipping into depths
The subconscious taking control
The heart slows down
Into dream after dream you stroll

Thomas M. Wright

Untitled

The laughter... the sadness...
Time has no meaning
  Shadow grow darker
The smiles... the tenderness
Day turned into night
  Shadow grow colder
The pain... the hurting...
Midnight has descended
  Shadow... no longer.

Lily T. Wu

The Last Drop

I cup my hands
To catch the last drop.
It filters through my fingers.
The white glare
Burns my eyes.
I turn to stone
As the green vision fades.

Louis M. Kousin

Tools

If I gave you a spade
To dig up my heart
You would see how it died
And how it would start

If I gave you a knife
To carve out my brain
You could see how crazy it is
To act like the sane

If I gave you a key
To open my virtue
I think you would be pleased
To know I could love you

If you gave me a compass
To show me the way
I would go astray
And be lost for days

Until I noticed
The needle points to the attractive not true
Like my mind to the distractions
And my heart right to you

Scott Coley

My Brother

Who comes with the tray
to eat at the table
all alone?
It is my brother.
Slowly and carefully
does he clean his plate,
only fleetingly will he smile.
Does not one care?
He is my brother!
Talk to him, share your food!
But no one does, not even me
and he leaves.
"Come back!" I cry
yet he is already gone.
No! Do not come by
and wipe his crumbs away
as if he is no more.
I loved him, I'll remember him.
He was my brother.

Merry Condon

White Rose

Growing tall
to face the sun
Soft velvet petals
awake in the dawn
A fine fragrant song
for all to see
That beautiful blossoming
rose is me.

Sarah Pope

"He Cometh Soon"

On a white stallion He cometh soon,
to greet some with love, and others
with doom.
Let our hearts and minds be open now,
to live for the dawn, or face the trial.
For he is the mighty one, mercy He hath,
some will endure His everlasting wrath.
Hear oh hear what He has to say, for He
cometh soon, to share His love, or bring
some of us dismay.
I cannot stress enough with angels by
His side, there's need to pray, or
forever engage in strife.

Wanda Elizabeth Tillwach

Maggot

I know how you taste me
  to hate me
  to waste me
I know I deceive you
  believe you
  conceive you
I now know the path toward the truth
Inside me, you live inside to use

You know you deprave me
  enslave me
  to save me
I know I offend you
  pretend to
  defend you
You will die inside and all alone
Yes it's true the seeds of hate are sown

The maggots are inside to die
The pain I feel, I want to cry
Darkness in the womb, I now bleed
You will live as they plant their seed

S. Ethan Barrett

A Royal Line

From a royal line HE came
to heal the blind
to heal the lame

Now we can see
we understand
salvation comes
from GOD'S LAMB

Daily
we must bare our cross
we've been redeemed
no longer lost

Yes on the cross
JESUS bore our sin
HE gave HIS life
that we should live
AMEN!!

Richard Lee LeBahn

People, There's A War Going On

Everyone should do their parts
  To help combat this war.
Stop blaming other people
  At home is where most evil starts.

Society has made a great mistake
  It's all a great big fake.
When you try to keep up with it
  It'll make your poor heart ache.

Parents are held accountable.
  For what their children do.
But when you try to punish them
  They call it child abuse.

God, we truly need you
  To step into the plan.
Something is surely missing,
  We need to "love" our fellowman.

Lois Jean Brown

"Laguna"

To the ocean one goes
To listen deeply
Quietly
To the voice within

To the ocean one goes
To cleanse their tears
To open the wounds and
Let them heal

To the ocean one goes
To take their power
To remember their love
Commitments

To the ocean one goes
To listen
To learn
To love
To forgive
To know.

Rosemary Alderete

It's Snowing At Last!

Little Meg woke one day,
to find a big surprise!
She went down the stairs,
peeked out the window,
and cleared her little eyes.
To her amazement, snow was falling,
falling very fast.
She shouted
Hurray! Hurray! Hurray!
IT'S SNOWING AT LAST!!!

Kelly Garone

Elegant Irony

Plush pillows of white
thickly frame inside walls
Puffs of pleated velvet
like rolling clouds
cushion the closing lid
Soft feathers of dove
snuggle beneath smooth silk
for comfort

The elegance of wealth
which had only been dreams
Came true
in my final resting place

Peggy Collier

Mother

My mother is special, so special
to me.
There is no other person that
could ever be.

She's there for me when I need
her in good times and bad

With her around I never get
sad, just glad.

She teaches me everything
a teenager should know.

And that is just one of the
many things that has helped
me to grow.

And that is why my mother
is so special, so special to me

Melissa Leech

Yesteryear

Deep into your mind you search
   To reach a hollow part
Where still you hear the chorus
   Of the hoping of the heart.

Where dreams were somehow answered
   In a child's wishful way
And daytime meant a time of joy
   To laugh and sing and play.

Where kisses from your mother's lips
   Could wash the tears away
And hugs from your best teddy bear
   Made everything okay.

The "memories" of the "Good ol' Days"
   Our imaginary pasts....
Create illusions in our minds
   That last...
     And last...
       And last...

Susan L. Yancey

A Dozen Unbruised Roses

A Dozen unbruised Roses
To scatter at the edge of shore.

My eyes libation weep, at this place,
My broken love, here,
   Sought her a keep.

"Waters! she said,
   Embrace my secret sorrow,
     For I desire no other morrow."

"I would go out known as strong,
   Never helpless or forlorn."

"My mind has brought me thus far,
   But I would bear no more alone
     Deep sorrows scar".

With willful gulp, and sorrowful swill,
   the waters to my love did fill.

The body shudders, the heart does quake,
The willful death, it's forced to take.

But, do pure to keep, the water purged her
from its deep.

The body hidden, would not remain,
But returned, to our world profane.

Miles Wells

His Children

As a parent it is amazing
To see what children do,
It matters not what they look like,
Nor where they wander to.
They give us so much joy,
And sometimes cause us pain,
But they're still our precious children,
And we love them just the same.

To Jesus - it is amazing
He offers us his best,
Though we try him to the limit
And put him to the test.
He's truly the Great Father,
Who loves us - come what may,
He keeps his faith in us once more
He's forgotten yesterday!!

Ruth Williams

A Rose

You open up
The petalet folds
To form a cup
We call a rose

Queen of flowers
Colorful and scent
Those magic powers
Thorns do defend

Like a kitten
Softly yet bold
So it is written
So it is told

Sebastian

A Ray Of Hope

Dawn, a horizon of expectations.
Thoughts unspoken, words unheard,
a canvas of pure and perfect white,
still unexposed to the colors of life.
No green of envy, spite, or jealousy.
The blue of broken hearts not yet seen.
And the black of death held back
by the red of love.
The future is yet unwritten,
our paths have not been set.
The opportunity is yours.
So grab your dreams and hold on tight.
As the sun begins to rise.

Liz Morphew

Love

Every time you look into my eyes,
You should always know that
My love is no disguise.
When you feel
that times are going bad.
Always remember
the good times we've had.
The feelings we share
with one another,
Is stronger
than any other Lover.
No matter in the future
or in the past,
Our love is the one
that will always last.

Erica Shima

The Little Yellow Flower By The Road

Little yellow flower peeking up from
the grass,
As if to say,
I have grown taller at last,
Watching the world passing by,
Wishing at times it could fly,
The ability to soar through the
heavens above,
From that view,
Easily falling in love,
Knowing as a flower,
This can never be,
Yet even flowers can dream as we,
Soon this flower will be a memory
this Spring,
Arriving each year with falling rain,
Hopefully leaving pleasant memories
this year,
Departing from each of us with a
small sigh and tear.

Willie C. Williams

A Parent's Pride

Time so short
Time so dear
Take some time for the growing years.

Forget the spills
Remember the thrills
Advance them toward the hills.

Let them embark.
Oh no, it's not dark
They're ready for the sharks

Looks with regal
Oh my, how they appeal
They're soaring like eagles

Time so short
Time so dear
Take same time for the growing years.

Pat Mohr

Mother, You're As Sweet As A Rose

I love you mother
   You're as sweet as a rose
You brought me up right
   From my head to my toes

You've lead me away
   From sin and from harm
Never raised your voice
   Or shouted with alarm

I love you greatly
   For your clean, Godly ways
And bringing me to God
   And teaching me His praise

From healing up a scratch
   To the care of a broken arm
You are the best there is
   Your love and all your charm

With a tear your children left
   And all your love still flows
All ten children look back at you
   You're still as sweet as a rose

Betsy Betz

Once Upon A Time

Once upon a time the Light came to the world.
The darkness had to leave for it shone so bright and clear.
There was a power from the Light that could enter into souls.
This power drove out hatred for the name of it was Love.
Love was stronger than the meanness of cruel sinful men.
It endured the pain and ridicule to win a soul and friend.
Many came to know this Love but many more didn't understand.
They wanted it to stop so sought to bring it to an end.
Truth set out to meet them but it wasn't recognized.
The good and perfect Gift of Love had been replaced by many lies.
After all it was believed that Love was painful and a joke.
So humanity deprived the entrance of it to their souls.
Love knew that what was needed meant a deeper sacrifice.
Salvation would require death in order to suffice.
For even from the mouths of babes perfect wisdom can be found.
And little babes have understood what became of Love.
The rejection of a gift required mercy from the Giver.
So Love was crucified to bring life to the transgressor.
Separated from creation, to the depths of hell, the sins remain.
Back from the grave, and within, man and Love are born again.

Delores Feinberg

"Who Will Say, I'm Sorry?"

My love, we have fought and my life is distraught,
The days are long, and oh so weary.
Now our hearts have come to a standstill,
We've been together, oh so long, and still you are a handful.

I married you clearly out of love and wanted nothing more...

Can't we be friends, when hardship ends,
Why must we go on pretending to hate and wait,
Anticipate when love will come again.

Life is too short, to waste the thought, of loving you tonight...

I miss your warmth, under my sheets, our bodies touching,
So come back to me, and let's be friends.
Although you never go, you need not leave for me to grieve.

My darling, I miss you so...

We made a life together, two children we carried from year to year,
Now they are grown and we're on our own,
needing each other more than ever.

So let's not pretend,
We will love until the end, even if it means I have to say...

I'm sorry.

Jennie Soriano

The Bombing

I turned on my TV, Lord what did I see
The devastating destruction of Oklahoma City
Whoever bombed that building should surely die
We must show no mercy and don't ask him why
Our little ones died, had no chance to live
He had nothing but hate and no love to give
America is in mourning, it's terrible you see
To see all the hurt the sadness and agony
Make sure the one who did this pays the cost
Have mercy Lord the ones we have lost
Those left behind must call on God for relief
He will ease the pain and heal your grief
America this is a terrible wake up call
To protect our citizens we must run with the ball
Let the terrorist know when he hits our shore
He will be punished and that's for sure
Take one day at a time, let God help you through
My prayers are with you, my tears too

Georgia Rose McLane-Collins

Minds In Captivity

Values no longer count; there is no right; there is no wrong.
The door has slammed on decency and morality.
Once there was an edge — a danger zone with clear taboos.
But that edge has receded to infinity on the far horizon.
With the speed of light and the force of wind,
A legion of people took charge,
Commanding an arsenal of electronic weapons wired to human brains,
Flooding family rooms with obscenities, raw sex, and violence.
Writers, entertainers — and make-believe Platos on talk shows
Became modern Pied Pipers leading people to a land where
anything goes
Implanting confusion in the void where once man's
Conscience chose to dwell.

We ring our hands. Decry the much, the filth, the death,
But strangely ignore the watershed that feeds the pools.
Are we deaf to the cacophony of obscenities blaring around us?
Are we blind to the destructive force of cruelty and flaunted sex?
And in deafness and blindness, are we afraid to be
Davids in Goliath's realm?
Teachers distribute condoms in the public schools,
But are forbidden to display the Ten Commandments on classroom walls.
We wave white flags to those who hide their trash
Behind a facade of free expression.
Meanwhile, the Pied Piper takes his pay: celebrity adulation,
Outlandish profits, and power to enslave the human mind.

Bill Turner

Cheer Up My Friend

Here I lay, silence all about me
The door's locked, I without a key
There was laughter outside my door
That I truly did want to see and explore
With curtains drawn and a small peak of light
The laughter I heard made things so bright
Then I heard whispers of someone in the night
Saying cheer up my friend
You know it could have been the end.
So ease your mind from all the difficult things
Bind them altogether in your dreams.
There, I lay with silence all about me
The door's locked, I without a key
Now I know how it feels to be locked and bound
You see now I have a friend and I am found
With a smile on his face, I know I've gone the race
For he assures me that I will be fine
That it will take a small amount of time
So silently I wait to hear from him saying
Cheer up my friend, it's not the end.

Dorothy Warren

Together

Did you ever see the waves crash
upon the lonely rocks;
and know that deep in your heart
the two could never part?
Can you ever imagine life
without love
or lips never being kissed?
Did you ever wonder, when your heart beats loud,
can it be heard in a thick, thick crowd?
Did you ever see snowflakes fall
upon misty cliffs;
and realize it can be blown away in a whiff?
Well, my dear friend, remember this,
love must be always sealed with a kiss.
Whether it's snow, water or lips,
the love of nature is sealed with a kiss.

Elizabeth Russolesi

Nevermore

He could not take it any more
The drugs had taken control
The pressures mounted one by one
Stress had taken its toll

Thoughts raced madly through his mind
He brought the gun to his head
And for some odd reason he thought to himself
That he'd be better off dead

A bead of sweat rolled down his brow
His finger numb and tense
He looked back on his life and thought
It hadn't made much sense

He pulled the trigger fast and sharp
The sound rang loud and clear
And in his cold blue eyes there stood
A single saddened tear

His body limp and lifeless
Fell hurtling to the floor
Put an end to all his suffering
Nirvana nevermore
Christina Terry

"Childhood Dreams"

My Easter basket was never filled.
The Easter bunny never came to my house.
I never had a pretty dress, little
patten leather shoes, white gloves or an Easter bonnet.
The Easter eggs were never colored with
red, purple, green and yellow.
It always rained on Easter. The clouds were so dark.
The wind would blow our candles out.
My Easter was of sadness, despair and gloom.
I'm still waiting on the Easter
bunny to fill my Easter basket. It
doesn't have to be the Easter
bunny anymore.
Cathy Offenberger

A Special Place

Great-Grandfather's hill is a special place for me.
The ethereal sky promising that dreams may be touched.
The abandoned well, forgotten by time, cries out its loneliness,
But the surrounding hills warn you are not alone.
Through the woods, images of long gone children playing
are seen in my mind.
Their voices can be found in the songs of the birds.
Serenity dwells in every tree creating an ease of mind.
The lone pear tree revives the memory of a once thriving orchard.
The hill is a place where peace and perfection can be found.
A place where problems are unknown.
A place where history is told by the fossilized rocks
that were left behind.
A place where joyous memories can be found.
Casie Walukonis

Moon Dancer

I float on my window sill looking out at the full moon.
The grass is wet and in the middle of a meadow glows a rose
that reflects the gleam of the moon. I go out to get a
closer look at it and the rose is wet from dew and the moon-
light dances on its petals. I am soon hypnotized by its
sparkles and how it transforms its beauty to the most
splendid sights ever gazed at by the blindness of human eyes.
Its beauty beckons me closer and closer. I reach out to
touch its petals. Now I find myself soaked from the water
in the pond. The rose was nothing but an image in the water.
Jeremy McMurry

"Spring"

I think today I'll write about spring
The excitement in the air makes my heart sing.
It makes me feel like nothing can go wrong
Like nothing can ever take away my song
The Robins are chirping, the tulips peeking through
And early in the morning, the earth's covered with dew,
Oh, the beauty of God's great earth
How grateful I am that I was given birth,
To be able to walk among the trees and flowers
There's no boredom here, only happy hours,
Yes, even the toil and sweat of the brow
Brings a feeling of contentment and joy, somehow,
For, when I get weary and need the shade of a tree
I can feel the sweet presence of God, right here with me,
Oh, Thank you dear Lord for the beauty of spring
Today I'll give thanks and not worry about a thing.
Faye Calhoun

"A Daughter, As I"

A poem such as this could never reveal
The feelings as "I," a daughter, could feel.
With a loving mother by her side
Trying to help and to be her guide.

A daughter, as "I," takes for granted
The love and admiration that she holds,
But when we are grown and out of her midst
The love once shunned, suddenly grows.

When we are young, and depend on her so
Life seems to be easy and full of fun,
But after we are married and out on our own
Her "fun" appears to be few or none.

A daughter, as "I," will never forget
The things my mother has done for me.
The thoughtfulness of buying a vase
When only she could possibly see.

My mother will always be a part of me
No matter when her life shall end,
For God has blessed her with "Special" love
And a love of this kind will never end.
Debby Schryer Riley

Soldier Boy

Soldier boy,
what are you running from?

You are a fierce warrior yet,
at times you cower
From your own anger-

Embrace your anger; embrace your own anger
It is your own
Is your own, just as your eyes

To fear your own anger is to panic and run
from your own shadow

Soldier boy of Innocence
Soldier boy of Anger
Soldier boy of Fear

Fighting for no reason-
Hold your head up high
but not until you've faced your fear
deep seated
in your fierce warrior eyes

Soldier boy
The war is over
Perika

Remember

I remember walking through the park thinking of
　the fight I had with my brother.
I remember talking to a man full of sorrow and
　loneliness.
I remember him telling me about his wife, of the
　food she made, how it melted in his mouth.
I remember the picture of his wife he held in his
　hands.
I remember asking him, "Why are you telling me this?
　Why are you speaking of her in past tense?"
I remember him saying "All I have is her picture in
　my hands and the warmth of her in my
　heart."
I remember that day for the rest of my life trying
　to figure out what he was trying to say.
But now I know...since I now, too, am a
　person with only a picture in my hand
　and the warmth of my brother in my heart.

　　Suzanne Ramirez

Missing In Action

The American had anchored and the Marines had gone ashore.
The fighting was over for me forevermore.
For I had been wounded and left for dead.
A pack for my pillow and a rice patty for my bed.
The guerrillas found me and took me away.
And made me a prisoner of war so they say.
But God in his mercy was with me one day.
The wire was cut and old Josiah got away.
To the old home, my sweet wife to see.
The home I built for my darling and me.
The door I opened and there on a stand.
I saw a picture of her and another man.
The clothes she was wearing told me the sad tale.
My darling was wearing a new bridal veil.
Then I found a letter and these words I read,
Missing in action, she thought I was dead.
So I kissed her picture and whispered "so long."
A Marine dreamer forever I'll roam.
The face of my darling no more shall I see.
For missing in action - I will always be.

　　Josiah Barrow

Spoon of Content

I sip the spoon of content, and sit
upon my ocean floor in feverish expectation.
No day will pass me by before I
have held it to my breast and shouted out
　　an oath; that I will return again
　　the very same way again

Then will my time be complete,
I caress the dreams of children, locking away
each gentle vision, until all is forgiven
to God, and children can grow to seed.
　　Then rest will I against the tide
　　and dream of my own dreams

Casting their mark on God.
I take what offers comfort me, and wash
away the rest. With a mere twitch
of the wrist, I can bring the night
closer. Or double a day. With a simple whispering
and will, tempt the demons to my door.
　　for love has touched me and to my
　　core, brought promises of never more...

　　Cailin O'Connor

Turbulence

See dark clouds meet and gather in the East.
The flags of warning flutter, and the least
Of winds will leave a sign that they've been here
To mar and break and fill the heart with fear.
The winds, though strong or gentle, leave a trace
Of broken limbs that we cannot replace,
And tides that fiercely beat against the shore,
Amidst the raging wind and deafening roar,
Must change the sand and beach and take away
A portion of the beauty meant to stay.

But all things move and then must change their course
By wind, or rain, or by some other force.
A fool it is who says that life must be
Unchanged and fixed in mute simplicity.
He best will weather storms by heeding signs
And great with strength, instead of plaintive whines,
This savage fury tearing life and heart
That scatters pieces shorn and pulled apart.

　　Dorothea A. Kneher

To Our Wonderful Son At His Beautiful Fiancee's Bridal Shower

As the mother of the groom, I'm giving you a present, too!
The gift is from both Dad and me - for all you are; for all you'll be.
It's a gift we hope you'll like; it's special, and you might
Enjoy it with your lovely bride; she, too, views you with pride.

There's so much more we want to say about the man you are today.
Our first-born child, a groom-to-be; now grown, our little boy, you see.
For since you were our baby boy, you've always brought us so
much joy.
We're blessed to have you for our son. Thank God for you. We
truly won!

Reflections of some days gone by; your beliefs so strong. You
never lied.
Injustice always bothered you - you'd fight for it, no matter who.
"A different drummer," as it were, was who you are and what you heard.
You are a parent's dream-come-true; it wasn't others leading you.

Your loving way persuaded us that you were different from the rest.
You always travelled to your song of what was right and what was
wrong.
"We have no greater joy to know our children walk in truth," and so,
Our respect you certainly have earned. We had so much from you
to learn.

We give your "wings" to you in love, and as you journey on in life,
May God always guide you from above, as husband and as wife...

　　Jacqueline Carchide

Americans Together "In Oklahoma"

Great are the people who came to help
the day the building in Oklahoma was blown up
The people came from far and near to
help to save the people here.
No one gave a second thought as they offered their lives
to do what they knew they had to do
to save the lives of those buried here and
as they dug through the rubble
they put their lives on the line
to save those they hoped could be found
alive
as they did their best and no one
could ask for more.
When this is over we must stand and give a
cheer for all those
AMERICANS
who stood together here.

　　Jimmy Jenkins

A Vision Of Love

There is so much love and peace in your eyes.
The glow is pure, magnificent and yet so comforting.
The embrace of your outstretched arms is sublime.
I feel the essence of life flowing through me with every breath.
I played my favorite music to recapture
the beauty of this exquisite feeling.
But it only distracted the sensation.
There is no need for outside interferences
to enhance what is already perfect.
Your existence is the purpose of my being.
I cannot contain my heart and my soul from pouring out to you.
The frailty of my humanity bounds my spirit.
Time affords us the opportunity to share.
I often feel your presence but seldom pause to realize it.
An introspective glance at your eyes reveals that which I seek.
I can see my reflection in your eyes as they capture an
infinitely expanding universe, bound only by love.
I falter at times but you are always there to reassure me.
It's been a while since I've talked to you.
You look at me, and I know why I am here.

José Alvarez

lunacy

waters roll continuous along the strand,
the green waves envelop themselves in aquatic
madness, the sea crashes; birds skim its edge
without being devoured by its encompassing lunacy. i
am afraid. afraid that i have gone mad. the
sea calls me with every blow. each ebb, each flow,
tell me my life is unset, i am going mad, my grip
is like the sand, slowly being taken out to sea.
millions and billions of waves, calling me, damn the
sea, damn the sea. the horizon is endless, it ends with
my own reflection at the other end, i see
myself across the sea, waiting, waiting, patiently
for me. the waves recede, i can at last
breath, small breaks, patting the coast. the
sea has lost. i have won. ha! i have won. but
the sea gull still flies, still screams, higher and
higher, away from the ocean's grasp. she
is gone, so am i. i am not mad, the ocean
                         still roars.

Jonathan Kidd

My Tree

The backyard I see you in

Barren and brown, wilted and withered
The ground all around you is spotted white
The birds have long since lost their chirp

Time turns and time churns

The sun peaks out of the clouds
The birds have found their chirp
Your buds peep out, your flowers bloom

Time turns and time churns

Your buds mature
Apples hang from your long twisted arms
Your flowers are no longer here

Time turns and time churns

The wind from the North grows mean
Your brothers and sisters are all sick
The birds have once again misplaced their chirp

You have caught their illness, slowly brown you grow
Your summer umbrella falls to the ground
Yet majestic you still stand

Time turns and time churns

Joshua L. Rix

What About Me?

You left us so long ago
The hardship and pain
You refused to know
You turned your back on mom and me
It was so clear but you didn't see
You left me to face my life alone
Only hate and fear to call my own
Sometimes at night I cry out your name
But you don't hear, it's not the same
But to my heart dad, you still hold the key
So I ask you this question,
"What about me?"

Dannielle Weller

Light

As I lay down to sleep one night,
the heavens opened and I took flight.

A little voice calls to me from near,
the sound so delicate her message quite clear.

I turn to look and what do I see?
My guardian angel looking at me.

A glowing light surrounding her presence
gave away her everlasting innocence.

A cherubic smile and glimmering eyes
showed me the way through the holy skies

We danced and flew for most of the night,
pushing stars down, making a glorious sight.

She lay me back down in my snug little bed
taking the worries right out of my head.

When I awoke I remembered all
for that was the night I discovered my soul.

Julia Pritt

Worried Are You?

Confined in the maze the cheese worried from fear
The holes in the swiss are sweating skin pores
The odor of the cheese smells as if it had had an over-
Drawn work out
The piece of cheese then screamed in terror as a white
Mouse turned the corner
He new it was over; slowly the mouse came toward
Him
Every step seemed to last an eternity
Suddenly out of nowhere a large hand grabbed the
Mouse
Then saving the cheese, placing it back into the
Refrigerator
Unknowing to the cheese, he must live with this for the
Rest of his life…

Jeremy Moore

Things I Have Never Told

I never told anyone about the mark on the wall
the stain on the carpet or the mud in the hall.
I never told anyone about the crack in the vase, or the
scratch on the floor, the hole in the sofa or the dent in
the car.
I covered up the mark and hid the stain under the rug.
I blamed the mud on the dog and said the cat cracked
the vase.
I sewed up the hole and pretended not to know a
thing about the car.
I just hope no one finds out about the things I have
never told.

Jennifer Hampson

The Old Oak Tree

Many moons ago Dad spoke of that old tree.
"The Indians must have known it."
'Twas that ancient he had said.
Its stature is high with arms long and
   branching,
Their gnarled digits clutching those
   bronzed Autumn leaves.
Like a mother bird's reluctance to relinquish her nestlings,
The old oaken tree holds its leaves in a panic
Lest it lose its last vestige of splendor.
Yet I see that old tree in all its naked
   glory all winter,
Knowing new life is even now stirring
   in its venerable self.

Now I am ancient, yet renewal
   is upon me —
For eternal life stirs
   in my own aged self!

Florence Vining Thomen

Heaven

Heaven, what a beautiful land that will be;
The jasper walls, 'round this city fair,
The pearly gates beyond its crystal sea,
The streets of gold we find so rare.

Imagine sitting on ground of gold,
Friends gathered both left and right,
Listening to stories from the saints of old,
Listening to them tell of God's great might.

In Heaven, no longer shall man see sin,
And, no more shall death be known.
In Heaven, no battles to lose or win,
And, no more shall man be alone.

But imagine how beautiful it will be up there,
When we meet our Saviour up in the air.

Andrew J. Miller

What Is Love

Love is the aura that surrounds me
The joy of being complete
The ecstasy that is felt with your presence
The winding path
The rocky road
The raging river
They become a conglomerate of life
As love spills over it is swept up in the pool of ones eyes
It is passed on only to be entrapped by the enticement of the heart.

Debra Baerwolf

The Devil's Curse

I close my eyes, I must not watch
the fiendish things the devil taunts.
Love is hard to find these days
just dirty love, the devil's way.
People think in ways of wrong
like they don't know what's going on.
They hide their thoughts, their fear, their pain,
as they lie they lie, they lie in vain.
As you know, and as I'll say
he takes our feelings all away
He makes us cry and do things wrong;
that's why so many die so young.
To feel hurt in many ways,
to know that you've been stripped away,
to do the things you know are wrong,
the devil's curse is all too strong.

Beth Baumgartel

Untitled

Jerusalem, Jerusalem, look what you have done
The killer of the prophets, even God's son
They took my Lord, hung Him on a tree
He shed His blood for both you and me
They insulted and mocked Him, spat in His face
Exposed Him to the world, a human disgrace
The day He died, God had raised
His beautiful Son for His glorious praise
Sitteth at His right hand, for righteousness to dwell
Took with Him the key, even the key of hell
Who will concern Himself with His days
The things He suffered and the price He paid
He forgave our sins, even the past
Makes our hearts new, like tender green grass
He is the Father of the celestial lights,
The spirit that illuminates darkness, the darkness night
Ciaphas, Ciaphas, you wicked high priest
Brought my Lord to pilate to have His life cease,
Found in Him no fault, so He washed His hands
My Lord was taken and severed from the land

Frank J. Laieski Sr.

All Is Lost

All is lost, and I'm only yesterday.
The last flicker of light has gone from
the evening star. The morning sunrise
has perished into a cloud-filled day,
and gone is the bird that sang from the
tree on the hill.

All is lost, and I'm only yesterday.
The morning has faded into a shadow.
The storm has driven the calm from the land,
and the butterfly is gone from the
flower in the field.

All is lost, and I'm only yesterday.
Darkness creeps in at a swifter pace.
The bush is still, for the lion don't roar,
and on the morrow I won't arise;
I am nothing; I am no more:
I'm only yesterday.

Gerald Cagle

Concerto

Loom of Volcanic Doom did bring
The loss of Joy, whilst Fullest Spring;
Shroud of the Blackest Cloud then lay,
O'er Love and life in Brightest May.

Up the rise of American Mount,
I climb to quench from some Freshet Fount
And there, midst boreal Shine and Shade,
Find haven in its Sierran Glade.

Clyde Pointer

Summerlove

On hot, sticky, summer nights,
Underneath the pale, blue lights.

You sit on your motionless swing,
Thinking of how love can sting.

Sting like your feet on hot beach sand,
Holding a tissue instead of his hand.

It seems like a nightmare,
but it's only a dream,

That love only lasts like the foam from the sea.

Jessica Clague

The Master's Music

In the very beginning before time began,
The Master created the universe but had not yet made man.

Every planet, ocean, and star was given a musical note,
And every day they'd play a song that the Heavenly Father wrote.

The music resounded throughout the universe
A glorious, heavenly music without word or verse.

The Father's heart was so filled with love as each crescendo rang
With a divinely magical beauty that even the angels sang.

Everything was perfect until envy came along
And shattered the perfection of our Master's lovely song.

God's heart was so broken that He commanded the music to end;
So with the entrance of envy the silence began.

Now, as I stand alone on the edge of a sandy beach
My heart cries out to hear the music just out of reach.

As the waves roll in, I thought perhaps I heard a tiny note
Left over from the music that our Heavenly Father wrote.

On certain days, I think I hear a whisper of a magical sound
When wind goes by and kisses leaves or thunder begins to pound.

And as I strain to listen, I can understand God's pain
Envy took away the beauty that will not be heard again.
   M. Faith Gordon

OUR DREAMS ARE

Memories of peace from the color of the sunrise
The music of angels bouncing off the walls where heaven lies
Small children feeling darkness but not in themselves
A vision of a world that no one knows
When you reach your dreams it never slows
Peace in the heart and when its darkness
Is the differences in the rainbow which colors enlighten
The risk of your goals being like a incredible sunshine
Shining in your heart forever like a celebrated time

OUR DREAMS ARE

The storms of fear bursting out into the hands of the gods
The cries of a small child brings darkness to the air
Reaching for what is not there
The rainbows of walls bringing peace to the world
Let us all pray in our hearts and deep in our souls
   Chanel Narcissus Chandler

How Will You Know

How will you know what life will hold,
The mysteries and challenges you've yet to unfold?

Don't look for an answer in black and white,
What you long to know, may not be clear in sight.

Instead, pass your days with care and love,
And use your gifts given from Above.

Use the knowledge you gain from day to day,
To clear your path and make your way.

Be true to yourself and be a friend who cares,
And the riches of life will be yours to share.

When you've done your best and given your all,
You'll be filled with pride and stand very tall.

If you live and learn and play your part,
You'll find the answers you need come straight from your heart.

Then for your life you've much to show,
Love and happiness are how you will know.
   Julie E. Schantz

House of Mirrors

In my house of many mirrors lie secrets never told
The pain of many memories haunt the depths within my soul
Like a javelin in flight its mark is swiftly found and the
Deep and ending thrusting yet but gnaws its wretched pain
Can my house of many mirrors block the anguish and the pain
Can its inner wall so gleaming thrust the demon from within
And end this constant teeming from within its fragile walls
Can my house of many mirrors bring forth a spot of light
To end my ailing spirits and bring instead some rest
Where I pray within this house of mirrors can the answer be?
I search in all the inner walls the answer must lie there...
Have I not the will for better within these mirrored walls
But tho' I search its coiled depths I find no peace or calm
But I'll gather all my forces and will that it be so and I
Know my house of mirrors will somehow find a way to calm
This inner torment and make me whole again
   Ann Hoffman

The Nightingale's Cry

O nightingale, sing to me your song of the moon.
The people will stop, animals too.
Your song can stop the busy raccoon.
The frog, dog, and farmer, all listen to you.
"What a beautiful song," they all seem to say.
No one would think of doing you harm.
With such a beautiful song you make new friends every day.
You can win anyone over with your lovely charm.
You earn almost everyone's respect.
With the songs that you sing every night.
You can always try to know what to expect.
All the violence will stop and no one will fight.
But, o nightingale do be careful.
For the cats also think you are delightful.
   Brian Ellis (1995)

Forenoon Grandeur

In the image of God created he him
The mirror reflected
Six days I did the earth form
Thousands of years to sway the giant redwood
Alpha and omega, beginning and end am I
Oh to be young again retorted the old woman
The light shall I be separated from darkness
Youthful play leads toward eternal rest
No other Gods 'cept I shall you have
Behold beauty with a smile
My only begotten son gave I
One love for all love
Resurrection
From a caterpillar to a butterfly
   Joseph Mark Johnson

They Said

They said
The mind is stronger than the body
They never said
We can only use three percent of our brain.
They said
Listen and learn from my words of wisdom.
They never said
Experience and curiosity are
The true teachers of wisdom.
They said time heals all wounds
They never said it would leave a scar
Have faith in God.
They never said
Have faith in yourself.
   Eric M. Carnahan

The Bundy Double Murder

The date was June 12, 1994
  The police had something to explore.
It was getting late and very dark,
  That's when the dogs started to bark.

The neighbors were worried something was wrong,
  Because the dogs barked all night long.
The police were called to investigate,
  At first they didn't see the blood on the gate.

One body was found on the ground,
  It was believed to be Nicole Brown.
It was O.J.'s ex-wife,
  Cut with a knife.

Just a few feet away Ron Goldman was found,
  In a pool of blood flat on the ground.
Ron put up a struggle, he fought for his life,
  That's when he was stabbed with a knife.

The police tried to contact O.J.,
  To tell him the news that happened that day.
They went to his house, they called him by phone,
  But O.J. wasn't at home.

Evelyn Baskin

Human

They cry from their human eyes,
The same human eyes as Nazis.
They scream from their human mouths,
The same human mouths as Nazis.
They smell death from their human noses,
The same human noses as Nazis.
They hear sorrow with their human ears,
The same human ears as Nazis.
They feel lonely with their human hearts,
The same human hearts as Nazis.
They starve their human stomachs,
The same human stomachs as Nazis.
They understand with their human minds,
The only differences between Jews and Nazis.

Amy Kelmenson

Untitled

The ignorant sun rises, even if hopes are crushed in despair,
The scent of sweet love laced with the autumn day, comes and goes.
Fire burns in the hearts of those who dare to play the most dangerous game.
Flames that are put out all too soon for some...

A sweet disguise of gentle, loving arms embraces a new player,
A face full of hope and wonder comes shyly toward the end.
A long lasting pain that wraps around an unsuspecting heart.
The soul that cries through the night knows the next event.

Like soldiers coming home from war, like strangers in the night,
Passing unaware of lost love, through eyes of foolishness,
Lovers come, lovers go, lovers who dare play the game.
Lovers who dare play the most dangerous game.

Chi Nguyen

"Blind Perception"

Speak to me only with your eyes...
The magical gaze of deception.
Words that are filled with lies.
A tainted soul,
  releasing a vision of luscious strawberry delights.
Spoiled by a taste that isn't as sweet as it looks.
A blind desire.
A false belief.
A victim of perception becoming more important than reality.

Dean Tamborello

"A Schooner's Goodbye"

Magnificence - exhilaration!
The schooner tosses her mystifying beauty,
into the arms of her awaiting beau.
Icy winds kiss her tattered sails,
as her innocence is given to the night.
Hues of midnight, blue and snowy white
are blended into a concoction of an enchanting elixir,
causing innocent eyes to fall prey to the sea's endless delirium.
Clouds of grey, come roaring by, on a track upon the milky way.
Dark reflections of her gentle body, shine like a blazing fire
upon the blackened waters, as the atmosphere is given
analogousness of ghostly terror, yet - the deck remains desolate.
She reaches her final point of refuse, as bolts of white light
flash across the sky. At once a doomful hand stretches
across the heavens, reaching for her ivory locks of purity.
There, in the brief second, where time and eternity meet,
her ties are severed, and as she plunges
down into the cold, dark, arctic underworld,
she screams out goodbye.

Andrea Hendryx

From Jersey Shore To New York Sky

Entranced, I gaze above, envious of the gulls' flight.
The shore reaches the embankment at the curve of a hook.
Surrounded by thick and heavy sand from manmade water-breaks,
  I can peer to the farthest point.
The slight image of two twin figures cut through the cloudy haze.
I can barely recognize our lady fair, but by her formed shape.
The soft gleam of the colorful state overshadows our meek sea-
  sprayed coastline.
My view is shallow and glib compared to that of the thermal swept
  wings.
How jealous I am of the view of you from above.
If only for a day to be perched on the tower's point overlooking the
  coast, the city, and the hook.
I have often built a bridge in my mind and crossed over to your
  exciting shore.
That shore where lights of crimson, sapphire, emerald and white burst
  into bloom against an ebony night.
For angels doth possess wings of such grace which ascend in such fluid
  splendor.

Dorcas H. Delfyett

Lift Off

On a quiet Thursday morning at Pad 39 D
The shuttle was sitting there as quiet as can be.

The people were watching with telescopes.
They were happy, excited, and had high hopes.

I looked over at the launch pad; it was just the same.
I sat back in my lawn chair. This was so lame.

Suddenly the voice on the loud speaker says,
"T. minus two minutes and counting." So I ate a Pez.

I admitted this was exciting.
So I came out of hiding.

I walked by the car and looked at the pad
Thinking again that I had been had.

Then the loudspeaker said, "10...9...8...7..."
Soon the shuttle would shoot up to heaven.

Then the shuttle has its power.
It was more poetic than a flower.

With the power of this flight.
I will dream about it each night.

Brandon LaRue

Global Warming

We, at EPA, frequently hear about "global warming,"
The situation is scary and really not charming.
But there are little things we all can do
To prevent "global warming" and the future "woo"!
Let me give you some very simple tips,
They are too easy, like reading my lips!
Conserving energy will reduce the trend.
If in doubt, call EPA, the earth's best friend!
Saving money through the lower utility bill
Gives the key to "warming" a second chance to kill!
Cleaning the air filter once a year
Will provide clean air without the dust fear!
Turn off the lights when not in use
To reduce the heat and load on the fuse!
Cleaning A/C and heat furnace every year
Will reduce the "warming" and "high priced" tear!
Well, read my tips above and implement them,
You will be ahead of "global warming" game!
Let me thank you now for reviewing my tips.
You will thank me later for reading my lips!

Hillol Ray

"Christine"

The eldest of the younger
the softest little flower
watered by God's
tears of joy and quiet sorrow
you have been a flower true
through the many winter frosts and storms
friends came
and went
but you were heaven bent
you danced your way into my heart
a gentle wind of humble love
for your Lord and savior
and now I give to you what little my hands
and heart
can give - a poem and a picture
a tribute to the dance you live.
Love, your big
brother dave

Dave Cragnale

Deep Inside The Velvet Light

Resting in the arms of Silence
the orphan child falls unaware
of the muse tiptoeing its idle feet through the air

Quivering at the brisk chill of Winter's humor
his HEAVENLY body lay naked beneath the empty blanket of emotions;
he is but a mute witness to his own imperfections

Once touched by Love's warm breath
who (colored his pale cheeks with an unwonted fever)
gently drifted away...the last he ever felt (of Her

grace) surrounded by worthless reminders which hold him still,
he sits in loneliness but the respected act of Silence
has served to be his FAITHFUL companion ever since

singing in solitude as he stares up into the starlit sky, no
remembrances
picture so sweet as whisper in the evening breeze
or the quiet dance and rustle of autumn leaves

taking pleasure in the purity of simple things
it is the innocence of the Divine that holds the young boy tight
as his body blends deep inside the velvet light.

Carrie S. Waterman

Emily's Spirit

A soul meant to happen, a soul meant to be
   The spirit is changing, from it into me
It's so unexpected, yet known all along
   So many wonder and ask when and why
When it all really happens...in the wink of an eye.

I strive for the future and push to be free
   I just want to flourish, I want to be me
The future is coming, it's faster each year
   I want them to listen, but most just don't hear
I race down the path and don't stop to ask why
   And soon I am gone...in the wink of an eye.

In a place where I wonder, in a place where I am
   It happened so fast, I can't understand
I was happy to be, I was happy I'd been
   From soul back to spirit, it truly did fly
And it all really happened...in the wink of an eye.

David U. Thomas Jr.

Someone Special

There once was a guy I used to be with,
The story between us seems like an ancient Greek myth.
We used to love to be together day and night,
Until one day he went out of my sight.
People told me he just didn't like me,
But I knew there was more to that, I just had to see.
He was seeing other people and didn't want to break my heart,
From that day on I still know we can't be apart.
I sent him my picture with a letter,
But I guess he doesn't want to know what's for the better.
I know this is the matter of my opinion and mind,
But he treated me like gold and was always oh, so kind.
I always thought I was the only one,
Until one day he called and told me we were done.
If he ever reads this poem one day,
Just to let you know, there is still a way!

Cristina Madaffari

Papa Edwards

He was a businessman with many strengths.
The strength of his heart was kindness and giving.
His mind worked like a clock....always ticking.
He was a man with courage,
He had no fears.
If you asked him a question....it was more
Than just an answer you'd hear.
If you'd tell him what to do....you'd get some advice....
"Don't tell me what to do!"
He'd make you laugh.
He'd make you smile.
If he liked you enough...he'd make you fish.
Though he is gone now and God took his soul,
He left us his heart forever to hold.

Amy Schintzius-Wilt

Expectations

As I walk through the meadow and up to the sky,
There shown a bright light as I turned to wave good-bye.

In a midst all this wonder
For a moment I stopped to ponder

No more hurt or tears
No more sorrow or fears

Only joy and laughter
In what is known as "the hereafter".

Cynthia Wells

Sweet Dream Song

Night has come, my little one, don't be afraid
The sun has gone to China so other kids can play
China is an ancient land far across the sea
I'm glad that you're not far away - I want you close to me

Now just for you A SWEET DREAM SONG
To comfort you the whole night long,
And when the gentle moon is almost gone
You still will know A SWEET DREAM SONG

Night has come, my little one, it's getting late
The baker's baking muffins for your breakfast plate
The cows are giving fresh milk to fill your captain's cup
And the sun will get back home as soon as you wake up

You can count the silver stars up in a sky of blue
I just count my blessings since God blessed me with you

Now just for you A SWEET DREAM SONG
To comfort you the whole night long
God bless my little girl (boy) and keep her (him) strong
And as you grow you'll always know
Mommy loves you, Daddy loves you,
Kiss goodnight.

Dean Alexander

Another Day

I wake up in the morning, another day begins
The sun shines through the trees and the birds peacefully sing.

The way people act today, it's just not right
I turn on the news to see what happened last night.

Reports of killings, people left dead
I turn off the T.V. and go back to bed.

I stare at the ceiling and think to myself
And say a little prayer thanking God for my health.

I think about the funerals I've been to
Back to my grandparents, and the boxes they put them into.

And wonder about why they had to die
Either I'm going to stay strong or simply break down and cry.

I wish I could go back to the days
When there was no such thing as diseases like Aids.

Back to a time when there were no guns
And people didn't kill others just for fun.

Back to a time when fathers gave hugs
Now they are found dead, overdosed on drugs.

A tear drops on my cheek, why is it this way,
As I lay in my bed, it's just ANOTHER DAY.

Chad L. Carlson

Memories

I breathe the humid, salty air and I remember those days:
   The sweet, lingering taste of the warm, ocean waters,
     while I snorkeled in their clear, blue essences.
   The fish and sea life held me captivated with their range
     of colors, from red to blue to purple.
   The sun above was bright and hot, scorching my back
     as I swam.
   I didn't realize until later just how strong the sun was.
   But I didn't mind, much, for the fun that day was worth a
     bit of pain.
   I walked the deck the night before I had to leave, the
     humid night air was nice and warm.
I hated leaving the paradise I had found to return to the
   real world, For the time spent there had been too short.
But Someday I know - I WILL RETURN.

Jennifer Erhart

Loneliness

"Are you ever lonely?" the old man said to me.
The tears glistened in his eyes as I could plainly see
"No-one to tell my troubles to or talk to all day long,
I wonder what will happen should anything go wrong.

I dread the winter evenings with the darkness and the rain,
when the wind is howling is when I feel the pain.
Money isn't worth a lot; it doesn't buy one friends,
for if it could then I'd willingly every penny spend."

"Tell me what it's like," he said, "to be wanted, needed and loved."
But I just couldn't answer as my tears overflowed.
I wept in vain for this old man and all the countless others
Who are neglected and alone, with whom nobody bothers.

A warning voice it whispered, "Take heed now while you may,
Don't let your life just slip by, don't live just for today.
You never need be lonely, for all this you can mend
If you just cherish your loved ones, family and friends."

Ann Harris

Two Battles

The guns have ceased the pounding of our fire.
The terrible destruction is complete.
The atoll shows that it has been delivered.
We celebrate a Japanese defeat.
Tarawa's isles are still tonight, and now
Pacific wind stirs not a single leaf.
The fight is o'er, but just offshore, how red,
How bloody red the cursed coral reef!
  And so,
Five thousand miles I've come to Saipan's shores
To cast my lifeless body on its hill.
My rifle lies beneath my hand unused.
My flesh is riddled, lifeless, useless, still.
But gladly do I now accept my lot-
A losing bout with Death's ambassador.
I suffer it with one undying prayer-
That I have fought the War to end All War.

Harold A. Lane

January 1986

Today, January 28, 1986
The world stood still as
Seven souls continued their
Flight to Heaven
And as the world stood still,
People prayed, children watched in awe,
And in one swift second, realization
Swept the world of man's frailties in the
Scheme of time.

Bettie M. Magee

Matt

My life was torn and taken away, I wondered how long the pain could stay.
Then I Found you and my life began to change, You showed me happiness and everything I had to gain.
You made me happy and filled my life with hope,
You've been a support for me and showed me how to cope.
Through times of heartache, pain and many tears, You committed your life to be with me all the rest of your years.
I realize someday you'll leave and go miles away,
You'll take my heart with you leaving me to stay.
I know deep down soon you'll be mine and we'll be together till the end of time.
But until that day comes I'll be here waiting for you,
Patiently until our dreams come true.

Derenda Gentry

Just Mileage

Our youth is a series of remembered happenings both pleasant and bad,
The things we accomplished were rarely very sad,

We took for granted those that were routine,
Like playing competitive sports was really keen.

As proceeding through life our reflexes slowly age,
Unable to maintain an edge can ignite our rage.

Having items frequently slip and drop is not of our wishes,
Unaware that the lost natural hands oil is from years of washing dishes.

Command of our speech and good vision was a part of our youth,
Then to later be unable to see what we are saying it's because we lost our eye tooth.

Once trim bodies are misshapen with fat,
A gaze in the mirror prompts the question, "who is that?"

In the eyes of a mother, a boy will always be youthfully her son,
Who will ask himself why he can no longer maintain that style saying, "why not, I'm still the same person."

Remembering a loaded wagon of life, how you used to pull it,
Now you know that you are no longer faster than a speeding bullet.

So in looking at life to maintain an edge,
Don't say you're getting older, it's just mileage.
John Fratis

What Is Time?

Time. What is time?
    The tick of a clock, a cycle of the moon
    Solstice to solstice, the turn of a century
    Heartbeat to heartbeat, the blink of an eye.

Measurements, yes.
What time is
Still eludes me
Still baffles me.

Time lives in starbursts, flows in rhythms
Rushes and dances over waterfalls
A life full of love is too fleeting, too swift
Hate slows time, distorts time, pains the fabric of life.

My time is precious
I choose my time carefully
Time is past, it is present
There's a world full of time.

Now, I exist
I am time
I am timeless
Now, I am.
Jessica C. Saunders

Nostalgia

Waking up to the sound of rain, to the croaking of the toad
Playing "saul" on a moonlit night between water-marked lines on the road
Christmas days with pepperpot, everyone bright and gay
Restless hours from noon 'til three in church on Good Friday
Boarding the choo choo train for school, bedecked in uniform colors
Marking time in the colonial office, waiting for that four o'clock hour
Long afternoon walks in empty field with cow's dung piled in a mound
Looking up in the endless skies where childhood dreams are found
Memories of days long past that never leave, somehow
Treasures that we hold on to in this crazy here and now.
Grace Glinton

The Duffer

How cool the breeze this summer morn.
The trees and greens, all just reborn.

The scent of fairways drifting about,
And the day's first foursome has just gone out.

There's coffee brewing in the clubhouse.
Across the way, a field of grouse.

Yesterday's drive lies in yonder pond.
My 'one' wood I've found, is no magic wand.

I oft' times wonder why I play this game.
Each drive turns out about one and the same.

I've lost clubs, bent 'em, slammed 'em to the ground.
But, I guess forever to this mistress I am bound.

My joints soon grow weary and my breath gets so short.
By the 'eighteenth' I'm looking for some sort of support.

The golf cart, I left. The battery went dead.
It sure will feel good to get home to bed.

Approaching the clubhouse, the sun's hangin' low.
My back just gave out. That's why I'm walking so slow.

I'd sell my clubs and ease all my sorrow,
but I need the damn things for tee time tomorrow.
Alan Plummer

To Be Me

Oh, how I wish that I could see
The very innermost part of me.
To understand the workings of my heart;
To make me feel whole, rather than part;
To know why I do the thing that I do,
And say the things that I say to you.
What am I seeking - what will I find
In the unconscious recesses of my mind?
My dreams, my wishes - are they -
Really mine or only a scene in a play?
Am I being totally honest with me,
Or is it like others, I'm trying to be?
I turn to you Lord, for the answer I pray.
from the pathway of light I often do stray.
Yet I know my real self is somewhere inside-
Only from you - myself cannot hide.
And so Dear Lord, I have but one plea-
To be what I am - I want to be me.
James H. Stark

If Today Was Yesterday

Father, some years ago our good-bye was said,
The tears fell as you lay in your eternal bed.
As you stand by God in his eternal grace
I still miss the smile of your sweet face.
Each day I pray that I am what you hoped me to be
Memories of what was, is what I see.
Even though I must live for today, and forget the past
All that you taught me shall forever last.
Life without you was never planned
When you were gone, it became harder to stand.
With you gone the children were mother's shoulder
We are here when she doesn't have your arms to hold her.
Our family has bonded as one,
Through loss we have truly won.
There is still one thing I wished I could do
On final thing for me to tell you.
If I had one final moment, you know what I'd say?
I love you, Daddy, but only if today were yesterday.
Jeremy Mansanales

Ode To The Familiar

Let that comment slip by, because there will be another.
The war may be leaning to one side but the battle is far from over.
Wish you could see, all I want is the familiar.

How many nights have I wakened in clenched fists and unstoppable tears?
Dreaming of memories and "took for granted" years.
Wish you would see, all I want is the familiar.

Do you think it's foolish not to live a life, not living?
I have found the answer behind the question you keep giving.
Wish you could see all I want is the familiar.

No need to waste your happy moment, wondering why I can't smile.
Next season might be warmer, I'll just walk the extra mile.
Wish you could see, all I want is the familiar.

You don't know what I go through to get through every day.
The first has left the building, the second is on her way.
Wish you would see all I want is the familiar.

Blue waters washed away many footprints, that were dug deep in the sand.
But the sea will not drown me, for I have reached out my hand.
You will never understand, why you can't see.
   All I want is the familiar.
   Brook Morrison

The Stranger

It was on Friday night
the weather was just right
Bells going off in my head
So finally it was time to answer.

The sidewalks were moving slow
and the bus arrived on time
But, the train took the winding back roads
Finally, we arrived at the beach.

The sounds of the wind bouncing
off the walls, the sand got in my
hair. The temperature steadily rising

There was a pause...
I find us face to face.
   Deborah A. Pierson

Coincidental "Pantoum"

I sat on the bench in the hall, wondering if I smelled.
Then some woman walked by
and hacked, coughed and sputtered.

Wondering if I smelled, I read of Nichomachean ethics
and hacked, coughed and sputtered.
I'd inhaled a fruit fly.

I read of Nichomachean ethics, wondering about the oversimplification,
I inhaled a fruit fly,
one that could have lived forever.

Wondering about the oversimplification, I saw a parakeet being poked with a pencil,
one that could have lived forever
if it hadn't died of sorrow.

I saw a parakeet being poked with a pencil and contemplated my intentions.
If only she hadn't died of sorrow,
there on the bottom of the cage.

Contemplating my intentions, some woman walked by
there on the bottom of the cage
and so I sat on the bench in the hall.
   Erik Roberts

My Humble Home

The air is full of fright,
The wind hits the trees with such might,
It blows the leaves so fiercely and strong,
If you just listen for a while,
You could pick up a song.

I whistle a little hymn to myself,
As I walk down the deserted street,
The wind is blowing in my hair,
And the leaves are blowing at my feet.

I then turn to go into my humble home on the hill,
Where I will soon sit all alone, but still,
How I wish I had you back in my arms to hold,
But then my thought runs away, my thought is sold.

Every night, I pray on my hands and knees,
That you will come back to me,
But I know you can't and you never will,
That is why I always return to my humble home up on the hill.
   Christopher Jones

That Night

One night I was walking on the beach,
The wind was blowing out of the east.
I looked out toward the sea.
To see what I could see.
I had to say it was a beautiful night.
The moon was shining just to give enough light.
I saw the first star in the distant glee,
I wished on it most carefully.
The moon I noticed gave me a wink,
Almost to say just believe and think.
Singing was in my ear that night,
As I thought, oh that was a lovely sight.
If my wish shall truly come true,
I hope to share my wish with you!
   Julie Clark

Pegasus

As the beautiful winged animal took flight,
the wind whipped through the many strands
of her mane, so bright.
The beautiful animal flew like a free bird in Spring.
It swooped down and tumbled all around.
My grip grew stronger, as did the blowing winds.
Then, when I could not stand it much longer,
a soft soothing voice called out to me.
I opened my eyes and there was my mother.
She stood next to me, trying to wake me.
I sat in my bed and said, "It was only a dream."
I went to my window and stared up at the stars.
As I stared at them, they began to move.
When they stopped, they made an image of the most
beautiful animal I ever saw, a Pegasus,
with a form so perfect and skin so white.
   Jennifer S. Amos

Granddaughters

A Granddaughter is a special child
They're not like boys, they're not so wild.

From birth to twelve as they age in years
They're not like boys, they still shed tears.

Thirteen is a magical year for them
They're not like boys, they've become a gem.

When they're out of school; with lots of pride
They're not like boys. They become sweet brides.
   Gerald J. McFarlane

Open Up

Open your mind that you may be,
  The wonderful person God wants to see.
Open your ears that you may hear,
  The music of birds, the cricket and lyre.

Open your nose that gives you the power,
  To smell the fruits, the berries and flowers.
Open your eyes that you may see,
  The beautiful flowers God make for thee.

Open your feeling to the world 'round you,
  To the green and the red, the flowers of blue.
Open your life to your neighbors and friends,
  And see what a wonderful world you're in.

Open your heart to our wonderful world,
  Join hands with God and give it a twirl.
Open your soul to our God up above,
  And He will fill it with His wonderful love.
    John R. Henry

Untitled

Nature's dark veil weighs heavily on my eyes.
The world as I know it begins to crumble and fall;
My mind goes to shambles as I listen to their lies
And learn that good turns to evil after all.

The heart of the wind turns angry with time,
As it waits for the peace that love would bring.
Its rhythm is broken only by a rhyme,
Sung by a lonely rainfall in spring.

The soul of the earth looks burnt to emptiness.
I shiver as I search for a reason to live;
I look towards the sky for a sign of forgiveness,
But the persistence of time has no patience to give.

Now the time has come to make my decision,
But maybe I could hold out for one more day.
I have used much strength pondering with precision;
Do I follow the Devil or use the Lord's way?
    Beth Schultz

Rosary Of Tears

At every prayer time I grope for answers
To the secrets each bead holds in my rosary of tears -
I find instead in its dewy bead I touch
The sorrows of yesteryears.
I dream of you at every prayer time;
Then dream each bead along the watery chain.
Somewhere - just somewhere - I end up at the Cross
and find nothing there!
    Constancio R. Montera Sr.

The Man In The Moon

The moon was shining bright this evening.
The man in the moon, his smile was beaming.
"Tonight," he said, "people will fall in love,
And it's me they'll see as they look above.
Romance has a smell so sweet,
Oh please tonight let there be no deceit!"
"Too late," whispered the wind,
as it brushed through the trees
"For broken hearts will always be.
Love hasn't the strength to struggle or survive.
There is so little forgiveness to keep love alive.
Too many young hearts have already been broken,
From words that a lover thought must not be left unspoken.
So turn out your bright light Mr. Man in the Moon,
And maybe we can stop the hearts from breaking so soon."
    April Minteer

The Coming Of Humankind

When the sun comes up and raindrops fall,
The world seems beautiful to us and all.
When the moon and its gloom cast over the land,
How the earth seems grand.

But when you look outside and all you see is pollution,
You wonder if there really is a solution.
The earth seems grand and tall.
But if we don't clean it up there'll be nothing at all.

A world may not exist for the generation of tomorrow.
And not even rain or shine will wipe away our sorrow.
Buds of blossoms, leaves of fall,
There's a deeper story to it all.

Nations of peace, nations of war,
It seems all so much more.
Tall grass prairies, a world carefree it seems so much,
But it's just a dream, left untouched.

Pioneer days to modern days, just a recollection of the past.
But just how long will humankind last?
When we realize the problems and the earth starts to die,
We will also slowly lose humankind ties.
    Colin Dawson

Prissy Lou

She was just an alley cat that strayed to our yard one day,
then Grandma'd always feed her so she wouldn't go away.
She was such a pretty cat, a calico at that.
Soon Grandma thought that she should have a name.
So we called her Prissy Lou, she was always tried and true.
Well, she moved into the house, so we'd never have a mouse.
That's what Grandma'd say, as she smiled and watched her play.
But we knew that little cat had come to fill the gap
that Grandma'd felt since Grandpa'd passed away.
She was Grandma's joy and pride, she was always by her side.
As a hunter, she could never be surpassed:
when a bat got through the door, we knew our Prissy'd score
and she even caught a snake out in the grass.
Now many years have passed, and they both have gone to rest.
But their memory will always linger here.
Like that day in early spring, I can still hear Grandma sing
the jingle that is music to my ear:
tried and true, tried and true Prissy Lou.
    Evelyn J. Swenson

Empty Seasons

We loved too quickly,
Then you shied away.
Where have those precious moments gone?
Oh, but very few.

Was it only a dream,
That touched my aching breast?
Or the passion of the summer heat,
Swiftly, swiftly going by the wind?

The blowing leaves here and gone,
The cold emptiness of Winters remembered,
Then the birth of Spring's freshness adorned,
And all seems new each year.

The seasons come and go,
Ah, but I captured one moment in Summer,
Too quickly past,
A glimpse of joy, of love once.

What newness are the seasons for me?
Where have they gone?
For they have not repeated
That fullness in my heart.
    Joyce M. Morocco

Nothing Dies In My Garden

Nothing dies in my garden, the plants, they all live.
There is fruit and beauty and shelter they give.
But among all in my garden, no flower ever dies,
Between God and the gardener, no flower leaves our eyes.

The gardener's care is rewarded each day,
As I inspect each growth, I reap all my pay.
From the vegetables I harvest, my body will stay strong,
and the fruits that I eat are as sweet as a song.

But the flowers I view give me nourishment as well,
For they soothe my mind and make my heart swell.
One rose bush is tall and prominently placed,
With firm, stout branches - standing southerly faced.

It gives the biggest blooms, with petals folded bright,
And thorns have protected them from intruders in the night.
The rose bush in my garden has started a new season,
And will continue to bloom, if for only one reason:

The gardener loves the beauty that comes from this rose,
So he'll continue to protect it from all of nature's woes,
As the rose bush will always be, fragrance and beauty to give,
Because nothing dies in my garden, the Rose will always live.
   Greg D. Kubiak

Cynthia

Looking back and remembering...A day unlike any other day
There she was...Her beauty is as ageless as the sands of time
Skin as soft, like the gentle breezes
Her strength stands tall from within, lighting up a room
Her smile captivates hearts but, caught only one suitor...Suddenly!!!
She touched my spirit
Uttering soft spoken thoughts and wise words of wisdom
Never holding back her tongue, always speaking the truth
I was intrigued with her uplifting soul and tranquil eyes
Which loom over everything with interest
Being with her for a day is very refreshing!
Like a spring day in April, Cynthia, the word echoes like a love song
A beat with uncontrollable dimensions...a river gone wild!
She's very extraordinary, a jewel in the Nile to everyone around her
Even at a distance you are swept off your feet!
That you can see wherever you may be
Sitting here smiling as the sun goes down beneath the clouds...
I reminisce? Looking back and remembering...
Compassionate, warm, loving, that she is... Cynthia!
   Joanne Beaubrun

We Two

I cannot do it alone;
   the waves run fast and high
And the fogs close chill around
   and the light goes out in the sky;
   but I know that we two shall win in the end
Jesus and I
I cannot row it myself
   the boat on the raging sea
But beside me sits another
Who pulls or steers with me
And I know that we too shall come
   safe into port
      His child and He
Coward and wayward and weak
I change with changing sky;
Today so eager and brave
Tomorrow, not caring to try
But he never gives in;
   so we two shall win
Jesus and I
   Deborah D. Harris

A Whole World Of Happiness

There's a whole world of happiness for you and for me.
There's a whole world of happiness if you'll look and see.
There's the moon and the stars and the sun's shining light,
There's the flowers and trees and the birds colored bright.
It's the small things of life that bring joy to the heart.
It's the old apple tree and the brook through the park,
It's the creaky old mill with its wheel going 'round,
It's the woods in the spring where violets abound.

There's the family reunion and baby's first cry,
The laughter of children and the contented sigh.
There's the choir in the chapel that longs to be heard,
There's the love of a child and the song of the bird.

There's thanksgiving and Christmas, the fourth of July,
There's our fathers and mothers on whom we rely.
There's a whole world of happiness to see and to hear.
There's a whole world of happiness in all we hold dear.
   Hazel V. Kemp

Thanks To Your Lord

There are not many words which could express my thanks to You Lord,
There's no way that I know to begin to show how much You are adored,
But I'll write this heartfelt verse for You and I'll pray that You will see,
How much love that I have pouring out to You from deep inside of me.

There were times of doubt when I'd scream and shout "listen to my plea,"
I felt deep within when the doubts would begin Your love inside of me,
And then I knew that all the hours of praying had not been done in vain,
I knew what You were saying..."Child, there's no sunshine without rain."

Even the trials I've had don't seem so bad after the blessings given to me,
The lessons I know were to help me grow as the saint You want me to be,
So in the midst of pain and sorrow came Your peace beyond compare,
As I looked forward to tomorrow I saw Your perfect joy waiting there.

You've given much more than I ever hoped for...I praise Your holy name,
It's always been You that pulled me through...it has always been thesame,
It's when my faith can't be tested much longer that You open up the way,
Each time my trust in You grows stronger...I see the need for Your delay.
   Heather Presley

Tulips

Tulips are better than roses or daisies.
Tulips are better than candy or wine
Tulips are better when given sincerely.
Two lips are better when pressed against mine.
   Glenn Farris

Nature's Plea

As blood red skies give birth to fury's fire,
Wicked night winds scream, revealing their age.
Waves break along faded shores of desire,
Nature's chaos flows through a world of rage.

The trees once in bloom and full of power,
Now grow roots of twisted anger and hate.
Silent pleas lie among tainted flowers,
That are left unheard to seal their fate.

Harsh winds caress stars slowly to their death,
Helpless we stand and view their extinction.
To midnight skies they whisper their last breath,
As our fate appears in their distinction.

Nature screams yet we do not see its pain,
For ignorance within our hearts does reign.
   Kelly McEveney

"A Mother's Pain" Being Taken For Granted

Dads are the luckiest people of all,
They aren't on 24 hrs. a day call.
They spoil their kids, and have all the fun;
But, Mom's are the ones who get things done.
Sometimes I feel like a picture on the wall,
When Dads around, it seems they don't see me at all.
Just once, I'd like to feel that I'm important to them
For more than just comforting, when they fall.
For more than just cooking and being a maid,
At least a maid gets rewarded by getting paid.
Plans get made, that I know nothing about,
That really makes me feel left out.
I wish there was a way to make them see;
A "MOTHER" is what I always wanted to be.
I want them to know that I really love what I do.
But, like any human, I want to be respected too!

Gabriella A. Plantz

Friends

Horses can be brown, or white, or black
They can have names like Bucky or Jack

Horses are friends too, though it may not seem true

When something goes wrong, instead of saying "darn"
You know where to go; just go to the barn

Your horse won't always be by your side
So don't let your memories be washed away with the tide

Your horse will always be with you in spirit
When you talk to him he will surely hear it

But when your horse has gone away
A better place where he does lay

When thinking of him, try not to be sad
Just think of all of the fun that you've had

Jacinda Wintrow

Of Life And Limb

I often stand in awe of trees
Their trunks representing the soul
Their branches, a reflection of life's experiences
Large sturdy branches expressing accomplishments
Small frail branches protrude with promises of things to come
Curved sagging branches hang in depression
Fallen branches seemed burdened with promises gone awry
Branches that are lucky enough to produce leaves
seem to dance with excitement
Branches gracing the tree top that have survived the
passing of time
Look down on its roots in hopes of virtual propagation
Urging the continued flow of life and strength

Elaine Jackson

"Solitude"

I find myself in a crowded room and yet I feel so alone,
There's no one to turn to,
No one to call on the phone, I desperately seek a friend in
whom I can confide
These dark lonely feelings that I harbor inside.

No one can see the tears of pain that my eyes have cried.
For all that I lost,
Writing is the only solace I can find.
Loneliness is one of the things that we as humans suffer.
And it makes the quest of finding a true friend even tougher.

I turn and search for somebody to hold me in the still of the night.
But all I find is emptiness,
There is no more comfort when I turn on the light.

Alexandra M. Cansing

The Sixties Moms

Moms were different in olden days
They expressed their love in so many ways.

They worked hard every day to put clothes on our backs
and most of them were made from clean potato sacks.

When food was rationed for just enough for us
Mom would always say I've done ate, I'm about to bust

She would stay awake at night trying to keep our feet warm
She would hug and kiss us in the morning and tell us to get going.

They toiled and slaved twenty four hours a day
Just for a measly wage of fifteen dollars pay

They woke up in the mornings with smiles on their face
put the little food down to us and made us say our grace

Dear Lord, we thank you for this small bit of bread
we are also thankful for our mom who saw that we all were fed

Moms have changed in so many ways
because drugs and booze have taken their children to-day

Gladys Barnes

"The Mercantiles"

The mercantiles in New York are much tougher than others.
They give you tiny bathrooms, tiny kitchens,
Bedrooms barely big enough for a bed and bureau.
You must pay more for these jails.

These mercantiles eat in fine restaurants,
Spend money as if they print it.
They sh— very nicely in big bathrooms.
Cook lavish meals in lavish kitchens.
Sleep like angels in mammoth bedrooms.

They've removed the brain circuit
That would make them feel badly about the
Jails they create
And the rate.
They just go on
Sh**ing, eating, sleeping,
In lots of space.
The guillotine waits.

Bryan Wells

The Troop

Our troop in the woods with 18 boys,
They pitched their tents and made some noise.
We came in the truck with the trailer in back,
And all our grub in a brown paper sack.

With three patrols in several tents,
They would soon make fires if they found their flints.
The food was cooked and eaten soon,
And they washed greasy dishes by the light of the moon.

When cleanin' up they can't get goin',
It's a good bit like the front yard mowin'.
I make loud threats and offer advice,
But to get it done it may take twice.

They went to bed just after nine,
Talkin' still and feelin' fine.
I woke 'em up at the morning sun,
To gather wood and have more fun.

I have camped out with many a group,
But I've had more fun with a Boy Scout Troop.
To any man who's willin' to give,
Go teach a boy the clean way to live.

George E. Statham

Ancestors

They walked out of the past, a proud, noble people.
They were strong so they were used.
Taken from their fertile soil.
Their women raped, their children robbed of the dignity
   they justly deserved.
For years they endured their pain silently.
They were my ancestors.
Their wrongs will be set right
For I am one of the few who will speak
I am the one fortunate to know the unjust treatment.
Four-hundred years have passed.
The cruelty of it all still exists.
Yet it hides behind deceiving faces.
We as a people no longer speak in hushed voices.
Our voices sing out!
Yet there was a time when we endured our pain silently.
I write this not for sorrow, pity, or grief.
I write this solely to try and justify my and all other long
   since departed ancestors.
Thank you for your strength and courage.

Erin M. W. Bradley

The Message

I heard singing bells in the wind,
they were talking to me.
It was the sweet sound of heaven,
an angels choir, singing in harmony.

I heard the stars talking to me
they told of the past and of the future.
The stars shone their heavenly beams on me,
they say I will have good luck, and all shall see.

I heard the Angels call out to me,
they needed to speak, and so they chose to do so through me.
They tell of a time when all will be free.
They tell of a time when peace will ring through, and all will be seen.

Jesus spoke to me, He told me listen.
"Did you hear the wind, the stars, and the Angels speak?"
"They all speak for the creator, including me."
All you have to do is listen!

The message is simple.
The message is true.
Peace will be king again.
But, it must first begin within YOU!

JoAnn Perdue

There Is A God

You say there is no God
Then who made this world of ours?
This world with all its wonders,
The sunshine and the showers.

Who hangs the twinkling stars at night
Or sails the moon across the sky
and makes the flowers bloom in springtime?
It certainly isn't you or I.

No God you say?
Then tell me if you can.
Who gave us life, a mind
And a heart to love our fellow man.

Oh yes, I'm very sure,
He loves and helps us through each day.
And by his grace if we believe,
We are redeemed, for aye.

Inez Spradling Grouf

Slave Dancer

Stranger white people glare and snap at me,
They whip my feet and force me to dance.

Miles of ocean, sails flapping in the wind,
Songs of the flute,
Cries of the babies,
Yells from the whites.

Heat from the blazing sun,
Feet full of pain,
Splinters slicing into my foot.

Anger at the white ones,
Ashamed,
Treated like an animal,
Worse.

Elijah Ceccarelli

God's Gift, Children, Just Children

Children are such precious gifts.
They're sent from God above.
So happy and so carefree;
Just full of so much love.

Boys are so mischievous
And always on the go.
Girls are so very pretty;
With their ribbons all aglow.

But whether boys or girls;
Or whether they're large or small
Children are simply wonderful.
To me, they're God's greatest gift of all.

Bertha D. Johnson

Oklahoma City - In Memoriam

The earth deep below began to shake, then rumbled;
Thick pilings of concrete fractured and crumbled.
Glass windows shattered into shimmering shards;
Nine stories collapsed like a house of cards.
Then screams of pain rent the dust-filled air.
The devil had abandoned his hellish lair,
Watching in glee people trapped with their pain,
Exulting as they cried for assistance in vain.
Some people died quickly, both young and old,
While others, in terror, slowly grew cold.
To heaven above rises an agonized wail
Against Satan's evil, "May justice prevail!"
Disbelievers will tell you that there is no hell,
Don't you believe it! The devil's alive and well!

Janet S. Mayer

I Remember You

On this dark December night,
   The sky is void of all the brilliant stars
     That command my attention
There is a lonely stillness except for the tiny raindrops falling,
   As if each one has a purpose, and its very own place.
As I gaze out my window my thoughts turn to you.
   Before I realize it, the dancing raindrops turn to
     Dazzling snow flakes covering the ground like
       A blanket of crystal,
        The reflection of a rainbow.
         I remember your natural grace of manner,
          Your wonderful laugh,
           Your gentle touch,
            Your strength.
I remember you, and my being is complete
   At this moment.

Arlene Sherma

Nothing So Small, Nothing So Great

One blade of grass, one bud on a tree;
Things so small that you do not see.
A bird flying high, a tear in the eye,
But God sees everything!

There's nothing so small, no, nothing at all
That God can't do for you.
There's nothing so small, no, nothing at all
If you only ask Him to.

Something so big — a huge mountain of strife
Seemingly unbearable that fills your life,
A loved one's lost soul, an impossible goal,
But God sees everything!

There's nothing so great if you only wait
That God can't do for you
There's nothing so great if you only wait
And if you ask Him to.

There's nothing so small, no, nothing at all
That God can't do for you
And there's nothing so great if you only wait
And if you ask Him to.
   Anita S. Ford

Mother

Today I rest my forehead on my thumb
Thinking what you might be doing
There's not much to do down there
Where it's dark and silent, cold and endless

You're used to be doing everything
All day, not a moment to rest
Mother, I love you and wish to touch you
No one will ever see me cry, but when I am alone - I do

When I stumbled, you picked me up
I do remember your laughs and tears
Your loving arms and sweet smile
Why did you leave me so soon?

You are gone
But you have taught me to survive
Your principles and beliefs still live within me
I will carry on in a life which I still cannot understand.
   John Persaud

"The Man Who Holds The Reins"

Where are you taking us?
This road, where does it lead?
The passengers know not where their journeys end.

Yet most, if not all, wonder where this coach is destined.

Looking back at the mountains —
Their peaks frost white with snow,
Their shadows seem to follow —

Elongated as they grow.

Faster! Oh, do go faster!
Your pace seems all too slow.
But wait! The ride is smoother now.
This section of the road is new.
Its serenity, intriguing.
Bright — with a refreshing view.

Slower! May we go slower?
Here, I need more time to enjoy!

Ah, but the man at the reins
He ignores me,
As if I were his toy.
   Ceane O'Hanlon

What Is A Daddy?

What is a daddy?
This I'll never know.
I never really had one
His feelings he didn't show.
I never really cared too much
About what he said or done
I knew he was out living his life
Having lots of fun.
I didn't care what happened to him
Until I watched him go.
They put him down and covered him up
Beside him lay a rose.
A rose that meant I wish you well
And until we meet again.
I'm happy to know you're in a better place,
With your brother and some friends.
I wonder if you're watching me
Crying all alone
Every tear says goodbye, to the father
I've never known.
   Carrie Thrift

A Cowboy's Restin' Place

Makin' his own decisions and being free
This is always the way a cowboy should be.
Generous in possessions and free of heart
It's a better place, by playing his part.

Sometimes brisk in manner and a slow drawl
Touching the lives of one and all.
Loved by many and admired by more
He thinks this is what life is for.

Supporting the weak and admiring the strong
Not caring whether it's right or wrong
But doing it because he feels it's best
And doesn't worry about the opinions of the rest.

So, when a cowboy's called to a higher home,
In God's Holy Pastures where he'll roam
Put him where there's wide open space
'Cause this is how it should be——
  For a Cowboy's Restin' Place.
   Janelle Langham

Shades of Gray

Gray, dark, looming and foreboding
This obsession rules my thoughts like an out-of-control dictator
The only way to continue is by overthrowing
This specter who lives off of my terror

My nemesis is basic but it hurts just to live
I know of the answer to expunge this plague
My problem, however, is that the cure is not mine to give
The disease of loneliness is controlling this stage

I can't comprehend why I am not good enough
For I know that he's lonely too
Stifling the tears in my soul is becoming very tough
We get along so why wouldn't love be the thing to do

This verse is juvenile, silly and unrefined
He said go find someone with whom I'd like to be
Finding someone else couldn't be further from my mind
In my heart I know that he's the one for me

Until I find pure and total love
My life will remain in multiple shades of gray
No happiness in my existence can I find to give
Just another dark, dreary, overcast day.
   Jennifer Storrick

Dawn Light

She holds a dream....her heart is strong
This place is hers....she defiantly holds on
No one dare take....her dream she belongs
Frazzled and torn nerves....she lovingly moves on
With every Dawn light.....she is closer to home

Christopher B. Vahey

"My Dream For You On This Your Wedding Day"

Oh what a glorious day.
This the 20th of May.
As you begin your life together as one,
Everlasting commitment is a challenge that can always be won.
Strong love and respect will transcend all boundaries for you.
Its secure foundation will surely hold true.
May your faith shine forever.
For it to fade—no not ever.
Your marital moments always treasure.
Oh so precious and cannot be measured.
Listen to life's medley, like the wind blowing through the chimes.
Your bond will be nourished over time.
May your dreams blossom from a bud into a full bloom,
Surrounding you with much beauty and security,
As the halo circles the moon.

Angie Grantham

The Lamb Is Risen, He Is Risen Indeed!

The Lamb was led to the slaughter, and grave,
This was a willing act; there were souls to save,
It was gloriously planned from the very beginning,
For Father and Son knew the world would be sinning.

It was the greatest of all heroic deeds,
The Lamb knew well He would die, and bleed,
He had deep concern before His appointed time,
But he said, "**Your** will to be done, not Mine."

Yes, the Lamb was led to the slaughter to stay,
Many signs occurred, and were witnessed that day
Showing the Lamb to be truly the Son of Man,
And how God had moved his Mighty hand.

That day our Lord flooded every home
With Light, that the world had never known,
The Lamb fulfilled every prophesy, every need,
To the angel's chorus, "He is risen,
He is risen, indeed!"

Christy Cumbie

Friend

You came out of nowhere and made
   those sadder days a little brighter.
You even listened to my worries
   on those long and gloomy nights.
You were my friend
I know in that little time we had.
And to tell you the truth it wasn't all bad.
I really just want to say, thanks for it all.
And no matter what would happen,
   I knew I could always call.

You lent an ear, you helped me
   dry those tears, and you always...
You always helped me calm my fears.
You kept me sane in my crazy, mixed up world.
You understood what I was saying
   about being that lonely little girl.
I appreciate you, friend.
Since friends are far and few.
But I'm oh so very thankful,
I could have a friend like you.

Aisha L. Sewell

Milton

You call him blind, who saw so clear
Those truths which veils disguise
For other men; veils which fool the mind.
Blind? Nay! but gifted with a thousand eyes.

So, let him take you by the hand
To soar on rhythm's wing.
The way is sometimes dark
And very frightening.

Other times, majestic light
May threat to blind *your* eyes!
Yet, follow on with him to find
The beauty which in wisdom lies.

Fran Allison

To The Beloved Abroad

The sun is set, the day is dead,
Thou art gone, I live yet.
The cloudy sky, with many a sigh,
Grieve with me, to console try.
Still I laugh, live to love,
And love to live for thee my dove!
I do know, weal and woe
Will come to me in turn in a row,
Like a wheel pass it will
Through ups and downs a good deal.
Thou art mine Deity Divine
O'er my life thou wilt shine
Like a star staying afar
At the pole, my ship steer
In storm and haze, through night and days
With watchful eyes in smiling face.
I am thine, thou art mine,
The sun must rise next morn fine.

Basudeb DasSarma

A Change Of Wind

The wind through the meadows has reached its destiny,
though it cannot stop for as it goes still, the time travels.
It reaches the end of time and wonders where it has been,
for it cannot see what it has passed, only what the wind will bring.
As through a lifetime the wind has accomplished all the wonders of
life, changing, nourishing, maturing, blessing, and the gift of love.
It shows itself that it is time for the world to change once again,
as when the world changes, the wind will also turn its head.
It will now dismiss into an unknown world carrying all of time,
it will follow all that it has traveled with time and time again.
Though it is frightened it will take up its heart and go on,
it will blow and force the world to take the obstacle of life.
Though it is scared it knows it's what is right and what occurs.
A change of wind is the time of lapse in the occurrence of life,
it took a trial of life to mature as does the time of life.

Julie Ann Owens - 16   Mt Pleasant, Texas

Autumn's Sculpture

I'd like to know why leaves begin to blaze
Though they've been green; it seemed that bitter days
Are denied when The Almighty's Woodlands
Bring to bear its bright flames of color-bursts.

Although leaves are left starved and lifeless
Don't have any sorrow for them
For they're truly nature's own brightness;
Days come when lifeblood flows through stem.

In wonderment I gaze at season's change
Knowing that God is surely here to show
That He has an extraordinary range
of leaf sculptures and paintings to bestow.

James S. Harvey

End Of The Road

"I love you," she whispered in his ear,
Three little words that every man fears.
They held each other close and tight,
As they danced with darkness as their light.
"it just won't work," he said again and again,
However, she was determined to win.
When the end of the dance was finally there,
She heard the words that she had always feared.
"I don't have the same feelings," she heard him say,
She couldn't believe all the time she had wasted on him every day.
They pulled away and their hands locked,
All of her feelings, she was trying to block.
"try again," she said in her mind,
"Please," she tried one last time.
Slowly, he motioned his head to tell her no,
Sadly, she said that she had to go.
She ran out of the room with tears in her eyes,
Feeling much hatred and despise.
Moving on was difficult to do,
Because this one time made it two.

Darci McWater

A Lady Waits

The sleepy sea massages a creaking ship which slowly navigates
through blackness the sky emanates and the great Atlantic integrates.
A sailing school of serenading sea gulls dips and dives and celebrates,
and amongst the sea-sick shipmates, a welcome murmur swiftly
  circulates.
A wave of steerage class splashes onto the seaweed-soaked stern
  and congregates
viewing a line of lights which levitates on the horizon it incubates
As fingers point to a distant shore, the name "America!" reverberates.
The salty air invigorates, and the chorus of commotion escalates.
A cry pulls the tide of faces to the rear row of citizen candidates.
Her wind-whipped shawl barely insulates the ravenous newborn
  she placates.
As if Moses were parting the sea, the silent congregation separates.
Gleaming with thanks, she glides through the aisle to the front rail
  the moon illuminates.
Her son's tiny throat pulsates with mother's milk, and through
  lash-locked lids he fixates
on the Emerald Empress whose torch radiates on the dreams she
  consummates.
Beholding the beacon who beckons brave believers, the mother
  boldly states,
"When this restless night abates, the misty morn of a daring dawn elates,
but tonight sleep well my sweet child for across the harbor a lady
  waits..."

Beth Wyler

Untitled

In the little town of Arlington, not so far away;
there lived and evil being, that roamed around by day.

Pillaging and plundering, and beating her roommate;
she kept the townsfolk terrorized, and in an awful state.

Down to the Salvation Army box to see what she could find;
she strapped a couch on her back and a chair to her behind.

She beat the kids with broomsticks, and stole newspapers daily;
then got her old red wagon out and waddled along gaily.

This thing that I'm referring to is no more than Ms. Beagle.
Who's lifetime has been spent by doing things illegal.

When she's around her presence is bound to darken the happiest place;
it looks as if when time marched on it stepped on her face.

If I've told you once, I'll tell you twice, look out for this old bag;
she really is a mean old bat, especially when she is on the rag.

Erika C. McGuire

Rite On The Beach

From right around the vernal equinox
through September, the pilgrims come in flocks
to our seashores, where sun and sea air can
transform their winter-whitened skin to tan.

These dedicated people glorify
the sun. For hours they, in their worship, lie
prostrate upon the altars of their choice,
anoint themselves with lotions, and rejoice.

Through brutal heat and blazing sand, the crowd
performs the sacred ritual unbowed.
Oh, what is the extraordinary bliss
the devout derive from sun's relentless kiss?

Though a number will achieve their desire,
still others will need potions for the fire.
All too many will prematurely age
or be a victim of dread cancer's rage.

These folks would better serve their kith and kin
by simply showing reverence of their skin!

Joseph P. Wechselberger

Our First Anniversary

God is watching us from a distance. The angels are guiding us
through. You are my husband, and I love you.

One day our wishes will all come true, but you are my wish, my
wish come true.

Our love has grown through a lot of thick and thin, but were
still the best of friends.

Dedication is so important to us, towards our relationship.
We have a natural ability to communicate without leaving anything out.
We're strong with our moral character. We're guided by love,
hope, faith, and honesty is our main priority. This is why were
so perfect for one another, because we get along so well.

It's as if God put us here on earth for us to find one another.
Down life's road we passed each other up, but when we met, we
knew it has fate that brought us together.

As we climb life's ladder, there will always be ups, and downs.
But as long as we have each other, life's ladder will become
strong, and sturdy. You are my love, you are my life, it's been
one year today, and so wonderfully nice.

Happy Anniversary Honey. I love you so very much.

Cindy Nord

The Time Side Of Life

The time side of life, where God blesses us with time.
Time to see another day which God has created.
Time to fall in love, time to give love,
Time to share life.
Time to give life and care for the lives given.
Time to stop and think about God's instructions,
Time to go and do according to His will.
Time to open our hearts and minds.
Time to shut out hate and ignorance.
Time to forgive and time for forgiveness.
Time to look to our Father which is in heaven,
Time to look away from Satan on earth.
Time to plan and prepare and time to idly wait.
Time to laugh and time to cry.
Time to say hello, before it's time to say that
final good-bye;
Until we meet again on the side of life where
TIME stands still.

Artee M. Ross

"Will's Summer With The Sheep"

Rocky Mountain spring of the year.
Time for Will to stock up his gear.
Back to hours of hittin' leather. Dusty days of sheep to gather.

His push to the mountain was very hard.
Will packed up the bacon, the flour and lard.
His sturdy ol' sheepcamp wagon,
Gave Will much pride, a source of braggin'.

It kep' him dry. It kep' him warm against that sudden summer storm.
Wagon wheels retraced the track, through prairie sage on his way back.

One camping site that Will would take
'Twas amongst the aspen by a shiny lake.
Going slow for the flock to feed.
Newborn lambs, he'd tend their need.

Pine and sage, the aromas blend, cook stove, campfire also lend.
Daylight spent, he'd come back a-draggin'.
Night would pass in that cozy wagon.

Dangerous coyotes on their evenin' prowl
Caused sheep to tremble at their howl.
But sleep came easy, he felt assured
That ol' dog Bawlly would watch the herd.

Dorothy E. Wilke

The Strangeness Of The Clock

The clock sounds, yet it is not moving.
Time goes by and the hands are still.
The sound of this "time revealer" is oh so soothing.
Yet the alarm is shrill.

This clock puzzles my mind.
Why do the hours proceed?
This clock does not wind.
Actual time exceeds.

I can feel the loss of minutes, yet minutes I cannot see.
The hands remain the same.
Unchanging, the hands exactly.
Is this my insanity speaking? Or is this just a game?

If I trusted the clock, seconds have refrained.
Seconds no longer exist.
Even if seconds don't show to move, time has remained.
What is the meaning of this? I must know, I insist.

The alarm of the clock is sonorous.
I cannot hear from this harsh sound.
This noise is threatening and ominous.
Silence is wished to be found.

Hope Burgess

My Grandmother

She gave me everything in moderation:
time, play, food, her smile
sharp as a sliver of glass
tracing on my face the wrinkles I have now.
She was hard as an ice bank
I unexpectedly hit while swimming about
the Mediterranean of my days
and thinking I was free to convert the world
to paganism and adventure.
Afterwards it was too late for pardon:
I was sentenced to death by indifference
and executed right away.

I was learning to distinguish
the faint signs of love
against the cold, dim sky of her rigor
by shoeing with tears
my heart's free galloping.

Anca Pedvis

"I'm Only Human"

Time past,
time lost,
time remembered,
time loved,

I set and wonder of the time I felt loved.
But there my mind was blank.
There has been so much time passed by.
I've lost the memories of love.
All around me I see hurt and anger.
I wonder if it's me.
But I cry, "I'm only human!"

Helpless and unsure of myself I face the world,
for I'm a woman of my teens.
I make so little for everything isn't free.
Even love has a price to pay, sex or suicide.
But I cry, "I'm only human!"

With no pride or self being,
I cry, "I'm only human!"
Perfect I'll never be.
But I guess that's me!

Dana Michelle Jessee

Spring 1995

Spring is in the air, I'm sure
Time to plan vacations or that special tour.
The days are much longer
And the weather much warmer
Soon green grass will sprout up
And trees will wear a coat of leaves,
Swaying and whispering in a summer breeze.
We'll know that spring has arrived,
Seeing the elderly sitting out on the benches,
Some using canes, many wearing dentures.
Already we've turned the clocks ahead
Though we lost an hour's sleep that night
We've gained an hour more of daylight.
The cold weather is gone and we have survived
So let's rejoice and be happy that we're alive
During this coming spring of 1995.

Irene Kanter

Ode To Potato Chips

Oh, salty friend, how thou tease me with thy flavors
Thy crispy, crunchy sound in my ears do I savour
At a valued price I can have thee for a snack
Thou come in different sizes, even individual packs.

I walk down thy aisle and how it's hard to stay away
Thy tasty neighbors call to me, "Oh, be inclined to play."
How can I say noeth? Thou lookest like so much fun;
My mouth begins to water and I realize I've been won!

But who should I pick first? Pringles? O'Boises? It's insane!
Sour cream and onion? BBQ? Ranch? Or Plain?
When everyone else picks chocolate, thou knowest I'll pick thee out
I'll seek thee out in every store and find thee, make no doubt.

Don't give me those crackers, those cookies, those cakes
No candy bars, or ice cream, just what my heart takes
And if thou hast learned anything, thou knows what I crave
Just give me my Frito, my Dorito, my Tato Skins, my Waves.

Then I'll take thee home and sit with thee as we watch a little TV
And probably share thee with the others who are sitting next to me,
But they shan't appreciate thy talents like a royally can do
But we shall all enjoy your company....my crunchers, here's to you!

Amie R. Ridley

"Changing Of Times"

The faces of Earthling man have changed with times,
To a world of alternating minds,
Where virtue wrapped in haze so dimly shines.

Hands vaguely groping through worlds' fading light,
Of shrouded pictures and unpleasant sight.

Minds that punctured and scared by Mr. Dope,
Specter of hope beyond a clouded scope.

Oh how we wish this world would free its minds,
To think in line of former times.

The life that was simple, just and pure,
Returning once more like an encore.

Carlton Williams

Duel With The Devil

I met the Devil on a one way street. I wasn't about
to admit defeat.

Come on Devil I'll take you on. I'm not about to become
your pawn.

He sneered at me through an evil grin. He said your
life's so full of sin you might as well just come on in.

I'll have your soul before this day is through and
there's really nothing you can do.

It's true I hadn't taken the time to keep the Lord upon
my mind.

But I also knew it was never to late to prepare myself
for that heavenly date when Jesus would open the Golden Gate.

So I looked the devil in the eye and told him he could
kiss this soul goodbye.

My Father waits in a higher place and some day soon I'll
see his face.

Diana Erwin

The Words Go On And On

Is there a solution to convolution or is it a billowing way,
to avoid the truth and find the words to circumvent what we say,
It seems to me and others that the words go on and on
a half truth here, gray area there, sometimes it's hard to see,
are the statements made really true or an ambiguity,
the words go on and on...

John Glynn

Tonight May Be Forever

The night was dark and ominous-The stillness seemed
to be the only sound for miles around; Oh Lord don't
let it be.
A presence there so horrible- Beyond all comprehension;
Too ugly and repulsive, for a mortal soul to mention.
An evil so determined to consume your very soul- That
no force in the universe could overcome its pull.
And then in my delirium I hear the preacher's voice-
And knew I should have changed my ways, while I still
had a choice.

Born in this peaceful valley, where the preacher often
spoke- of the Devil and his demons, that your sins
could well provoke.
And now I screamed in agony, I was suddenly aware
I'd been drawn into the depths of HELL.
It was here or
I was THERE.

Fred J. Huwald

Life's Ill-Design

Life is a maze, a series of traps
To catch the traveler unwary;
A journey for which there are simply no maps,
In which each his own baggage must carry.

Around every corner a crisis appears;
A new battle looms for each that is won.
It's filled with excitement, as well as with fears,
And with things that just never seem to get done.

How I endure this perpetual fight
Is beyond me to clearly explain.
At the end of the tunnel, I see a light,
But it's that of an oncoming train.

If God is so kind, all-loving and wise,
Then why this sadistic charade?
Being omniscient, He must recognize
The terrible mess He has made.

If life by mortal man were planned,
Instead of God on high,
Its ill-design I'd understand,
And I'd not question, "Why?"

Edward G. Pizzella

A Gift To Life - To Dance

Callused feet on the hot desert sand.
To dance, a celebration for the coming of spring.
A prayer for rain.
To dance, to prove one's manhood in a certain tribe.
A new beginning a child is born.
To dance, to celebrate the wedding of an ancient cousin.
The sadness of death as
A weathered feathered elder passes.
Silence.
A lizard warms himself on a hot desert rock.
Fires burn, the sound of drums fill the goat filled mountains.
To dance, as I discover life.
The obsession is gone.
The depression has been lifted.
A new beginning.
As I learn I am free from the demon me
Which used to haunt me.
I am recovering.
To dance, a gift to life.

Joseph Goode Jr.

The Winds Of Time, The Race

Was it so long ago the child within was young
To dance among the flowers to race the beams of sun.
To think all was within me, to capture and embrace.
To feel the warmth of summer, the rain upon my face.
To see the joy of butterflies, the fireflies, I'd chase.
Was it only yesterday! I'd joined the human race?
If only I could go back there and run again the race.
What's that I hear? A babies cry!
A new one will start the race

Elizabeth Lindsay

Your Table

And you, you- we go dancing
through the light like cut out paper dolls,
Brittle in the center, where marrow oozes out,
Nine thousand ways to say nothing.
Light catches your earring—casting light upon the wall.
Come, bring nothing but a place for me
at your table, anywhere, flying, umbrella as parachute,
singing out over the rooftops where
Mary Poppins once flew.

Christina Taft Levy

"Dear Arthur"

Some people don't think about HIV, until it happens
to either you or me; what is this deadly disease
  Bestowed on us, that makes our hearts bleed!

Until it hits home we never understand, no matter
how many tears we shed. None of us yet have to lie in
  Arthur's bed. With open heart surgery, your brain
surgery, where were we? In all your family's misery

We prayed to God you would be alright, not knowing
The HIV virus you soon had to fight. Arthur, you said
"It doesn't hurt" and that you are ok, but we couldn't
feel that being so far away. I know the heartbreak and
  Loneliness, the trouble and despair, God knows I wish
I could be there. But Arthur your time is not measured
  By the years you live, but by the deeds and joy you give.

Now "Arthur Robert Ashe Jr." you're gone, you loved
  To the fullest, leaving nothing undone
it's up to us now to live your dream on
  We won't stop until the defeat of Aids we have won!
    "I love you cousin"

Annette Ashe-Montgomery

The Wedding Poem
("I Take Thee From This Day Forward")

I Take Thee From This Day Forward
  - To embark with me
    in the journey of life!
I Take Thee From This Day Forward
  - To my sleep.
To teach me and gentle me
  uncover the better in me.
I Take Thee From This Day Forward
  - To discover LOVE.
To laugh with and cry with
  receive the gift of "Loving" with.
I Take Thee From This Day Forward
  - To harbor me
from the untamed winds of the world,
  and keep me only on-to-thee.
I Take Thee... for my home, for my spouse,
      to be "ONE" with me!

Anna P. Carvalho

A Wonderful Journey

Put your problems and sorrows away and come with me on an Odyssey.
To explore a different world is like finding a new pearl.
Be amazed by the escapade of delightful adventure full of mystery.
To encounter unique, yet friendly creatures in an exotic land full of unlimited paradise.
In a place where melancholy misery does not coincide with the perfect blends of harmonious happiness.
What a wonderful journey it would be if we took a quick trip to ecstasy.

Carole Simpkins

What's The Point?

Worthless fighting. What's the point? To gain land?
  To feel powerful?
Angry at one another, mad enough to kill the innocent?
  What's the point?
Ruining the lives of others, killing the young men willing
  or not to serve. What's the point?
Save the young men, the women, the children, the old.
  But what's the point?
The guns shouldn't do the talking... we should.
  But again, what's the point?

What is the point of war?

Erin Vice

"Just Listen"

I need to go home for just a little while.
To find out what happiness I've left behind.
The angels have come to tell me different.
Only for me, to make the difference.
My mother has passed on....
But is back to say
Just listen
You can hear for yourself if
you would just listen
Never before would I hear anyone
Because, being stubborn I've always been one.

The time has come only to hear
That my guardian angel has appeared.
Thank you O' Lord for having my time.
To find this right path,
How I've found.
  Believe —
  Pray —
  Follow your dreams.

I'm on my way there.

Jan Francis

That Special Love

People search all their lives for that special prize, of wanting to find someone to share and wanting to love someone who cares.

But thanks to "God" Lord above who taught me about that one great love
to love yourself, respect yourself and only then can you love someone else.

To be true to your soul you can't go wrong; and then and only then you'll find that love.

There's no great secret in the game of love, just help from the heavens, the almighty above.

These words I speak are of no mystery; my prayers have been answered when he brought you to me.

Now I know with all my heart that your soul and mine will never part.

My search is over, I'll search no more, I found that love which I've been searching for.

And so I thank "God" the Lord above in helping me find that one special love, so together we'll be until eternity loving one another in harmony.

We'll take it slow, we'll do this right, we'll build our foundation with all our might because when it's love, you'll know it.

When it's love it shows it. When it's love you'll need it, and I know it's love because I now breathe it.

Denise Hill

"Look Into The Eyes Of Old Millie"

Look into the eyes of old Millie.
They sparkle like a crystal ball.
You can see all the things and adventure she has had.
You can see all the seasons from winter to fall.
She would run in the wind with Huckleberry Fin, and play till
The night would fall.
You can do all the things she use to do.
With a whistle the birds she would call.
She liked to climb trees and sing in the breeze.
She was the loveliest of them all.
You can see the truths and treasures in her eyes.
They twinkle with every surprise.
Inside, Millie really is a beautiful lady dressed in
Mother Nature's wrinkled old disguise.

Anna L. Lewis

I Missed The "Gravy Train"

I worked with all my might, straining every nerve,
To get a ready, clear cut, full panoramic view
Of the "Gravy Train" coming around the mountain curve,
When it was daily scheduled to be due.

What could have caused the "Gravy Train's" delay?
Missing its coveted cargo filled me with disappointment;
Yet procrastination told me there would a future brighter day.
Those thoughts of future success brought me encouragement.

With the sad news, I was very much taken aback,
When the train had met with a terrible fate.
My train of hope and courage had jumped the track,
Leaving its cars in a jumbled, twisted state.

News stated that the "Gravy Train" schedule would soon resume,
But I was exhausted, since I had done my very best,
So there was plenty of time left, I did casually assume,
Procrastinating, I relaxed, and sat down to rest.

During my tiring, long station wait,
Falling asleep, in spite of all that I could do,
Sluggishly I awoke much, much too late,
Already the "Gravy Train" had passed through.

Aileen Fielding

C E O Still

Complexity of life in ninety five alerts me
   To God's plight for
     Saving man's soul
By knowing each hair on each sinner's head.
   To complete that task,
     Monumental to scroll,
Despite whiz kids, calculators, computers
   To crunch numbers,
     All rapid compilers elite,
God alone remains the key for all data
   To enter, whose to save
     And whose to delete.

Carolyn Kelley Sorensen

Live Life Embrace It

A heartbeat, a ponderance, a whisper too quiet
to hear, the echo, a crash and the silence
you fear.
Death to the beginning and life to the end.
As life is so simple, but complicated to mend.
Thoughtfulness is worth the gems of rich men.
Teach words of wisdom, but few will attend
It is hard to help those who won't listen,
while raindrops fall and dew drops glisten.
So in the end when times grow short,
There may be nothing or very little to report.
Many days have fallen, many days yet to come,
Life is threatening it is never humdrum.
So how can you ask why the flowers bloom, the
children laugh and we all meet our doom

Forrest Jones

Untitled

Let us try to develop a world of harmony and peace where we come
To know each other, not for gain or control, but for love and truth.
Let the true brotherhood or nationhood live in us, and then in the
Society in which we intend to see grow. Let the good in all of our
Hearts, day by day be manifest in a world in which men and women
Will come to love and respect each other. Let us take the strong
Hand of God as a lasting force, in a cement bind and let the
atmosphere of tranquility and peace, live with us this day and
this time.

Ishmael Ali

Memories

Your family and friends are gathered today
To help you celebrate! What is this grand and glorious day?
You're 85 - Isn't that great?

I brought to you Jan, a little angel
To pin upon your shoulder.
The birthstone in it is for December,
So wear it as you get older.

As your baby sister I have memories
Of our family in the house in Oak Park.
I had older ones telling me what to do;
I really had to toe the mark!

But I also remember the bouncy chairs..
And high heels... and perfume ...and curls!
(Ernest Hemingway put Elly's in the ink well;
At Holmes School, he teased the girls!)

(Nine more verses of memories -then)

I'm happy to be here to join in the fun,
And we thank your son Jack and Lois today
For inviting us to come celebrate,
And wish you a very HAPPY BIRTHDAY!!

Jean Y. Homan

The Tide

People come from far and near
to leave their footprints in the sand
But soon the tide comes in
and the footprints are no more.

People are building sand castles
a different one each day
But soon the tide comes in
and the castles are no more.

Sea shells are by the scores and hundreds
But soon the tide comes in
and the sea shells are no more.

Life is like that restless tide
In and out each day
and then there is no more.

Joan Lanberg

Dark To Light

All was dark — all that was, but all that was—no eye saw,
   Till that which was—but never saw, brought to light—light for all.
To be with light—all that is, made by that—which no eye saw,
   To dwell in light—forever more, the man, the place—light for all.

Darkness came—despite the light, to bring to naught—light for all,
   The man, the place—light that was, man to dark—the greatest fall.
All was dark—dark for man, the light that was—hid from all,
   The man, the place—all was new, hid from that—which no eye saw.

But, light was from—that which was, dark to light—which had a plan,
   Plan for man—light which was, to bring to light—light for man.
From that which was—no eye saw, son the light—light for man,
   From where light is—like that which was, brought to light—once again.

Man must seek—light which came, from that which was—light to see,
   Dark that is—behold the light, from that which is—light is free.
The man, the place—the light the dark, man to light—dark subdue.
   Light that is—plan for man, life with light—promise true.

The day, the time—darkness gone, the man, the light—all that be
   Darkness gone—light remains, we that are—light to see.
That which is—all is light, now behold—which no eye saw,
   Darkness gone—to be no more—all is light—light for all!

Alan R. Steele

Unmarked Grave

They fall, one by one
to lie upon the cold and damp,
weathering the elements, they slowly rot away.

Hands of time, chase around the face,
the tick and tock, the only sound
noticed by man.

The sun, the moon, the seasons come
showing their names in their times
and heralded by all.

Yet unseen and alone, there they are
the hopes, dreams and desires
of my lonely inward soul.

Lying exposed to all, yet hidden still,
that part of me, known only to me,
buried in the unmarked grave of my heart.

Janet A. Barbour

Moments Of Life

While I was young and looking forward
to live my life with utmost enjoyment,
I wondered through it day by day;
and dreamed and played my life away.

Now that I am looking back;
I see that child I wish I was.
So carefree and happy so winsome and daring.
No pressures of life are her shoulders baring.

If only I could, I'd turn back the clock;
to capture the time as a child I would mock.
The pleasure's of life are just what they seem;
little joys of playing down by a stream.

To know then what I know today;
I wouldn't have squandered a moment away.
I'd take every second, and hold it so tight;
like a child with a puppy who's afraid of its flight.

Instead of just grieving for life's grains of sand;
I'll use the time left the best that I can.
The spans of our lives are precious and few,
to waste but a moment, would be saying adieu.

Janet L. Zebley

Untitled

They've placed the headstone on your grave
To mark the place you lay
But you have never been there
Not even on that day.

Your soul it went to heaven
When you drew in your last breath
We've all been thinking of you
Ever since the day you left.

Now when the moon is shining
Amongst the twinkling stars
I stare off to the heavens
And picture where you are.

I know you're in a beautiful place
Where no one's heart does ache
A place where teardrops never fall
There's no such thing as hate.

There's only joy and beauty
and harmony within
Everything's so peaceful
And life will never end.

Deborah Armentrout

Daharan Air Force Base, Saudi Arabia

To my beautiful wife Pearl Borkoski,
on her birthday February 1, 1952.
There is never a minute throughout the day
   when you're not on my mind
You're always in my thoughts and deeds
   Even in my dreams I find.

I miss you most at the close of day
   It seems just at evening tide
Because that is when I am so weary
   From the weight I feel inside.

But when I wake up each morning
   I feel so different it seems
Maybe it's because we've been together
   And I've held you in my dreams.
But what I really want to tell you
   Is that I love you so
And that you're always with me
   no matter where I go.

So because this is the first of February
   And it's your very special day
I thought that I'd remind you
   I'll soon be home to stay.

Edward A. Borkoski Jr.
Daharan Air Force Base Saudi Arabia

Saint Nicholas

Did you know Santa stopped by our house today
To rest awhile, then be on his way.
He was instructed to find all of God's little lambs.
Said he had gifts for all of them.

The reindeer were restless; they wanted to go,
To carry old Santa above the sleet and snow.
After the rest, he had coffee and cake,
Said he'd better go - he didn't want to be late.

When he picked up his bag, these gifts fell out,
I picked them up to give them to him
I barely could hear him say, "Give 'em to them."
Had it not been for Rudolph with his nose so bright,
I might not have seen them in the dark of the night.

As he passed by the moon that lit up the sky,
I could see him waving a fond good-bye.
And just at that moment I heard him say,
"Have a glorious Christmas on Christ's Birthday!"

Helen Millican

Grandpa

To have a Grandpa to love and to hold
   To tell you tales of his life, when young and old.
A Grandpa to comfort us when we are sad or scared,
   To protect us, besides Mommy and Daddy, just to know he cares!
Our Grandpa became lost; he's not like yours; not on any one day
   Never a nice word; he ridicules; belittles; and controls
   And Grandma's in denial and doesn't even know it, not even today!
The worst and most tragic, is the lives that are tarnished; we are
   Forever burdened with guilt.
Grandpa's pleasure is tearing away the self-esteem we have built.
To molest others, besides us, you show no shame...
   Grandpa has no remorse; he says we are to blame.
We cannot stand your hands upon us, or your looking at our face.
   For it brings back horrible memories of how it all took place!
So...if someone has been blessed with an extra GRANDPA that is not
   wicked and mean,
   Would you, could you lend us one to love; oh that would be so keen!
Just to have a Grandpa to love and to hold
   To tell us stories of his life when young and old!

Bobbi Ruddell

Pornography

Oh courts our friend, thankful you understand the desire lodged within.
To see, to read human anatomy, unrestricted, so zealously proclaimed
The bonds upon my freedoms of speech and inquiry did free my fantasy's
Of so long undo restraint.

As I perused body parts, I wondered if there's more.
No more to see, its plain monotony
Unless I take action of feelings aroused in me.
I stopped short of further conflicts you see which I call morality.
I dare not venture to the baseness of sexuality,
But wondered how many have thought porn sensuality,
And based their world of pornography as their only reality.

The crimes of sex seem to rise with every passing year.
Rape, seduction, molestation increase while victims fear.
While senseless, spineless, hideous sexual perversion everywhere do
appear. I ponder if freedom of speech and expression has gone to far.
While the victims claim degradation, dishonor, disgrace, humiliation
and contempt. Politicians only compromise for political benefit.

As I look to the heavens now as the answer to my needs,
Oh courts to you I plea.
O wretched pornography, be ceased.
   David O. Huseth

Mountain Ambiguity

Too fond of earth I tend when trading low levels for the heights,
To stand at ease 'mid flighty clouds and lovely mountain sights.
My sometime fix on heaven is permitted here, perhaps,
By humble things of lifted earth in early autumn light.

Too fond of earth I tend when shedding town sounds for singing lea,
And hearing well unfettered wings in gay cacophony.
I tune my eager soul once more to deep heaven's key
From this world's joyous music of mountain sonancy.

Too fond of earth I tend when leaving folk for solitude,
Retreating from the fretful fray for prayerful interlude.
I traffic rather with wood creatures who insistently intrude,
Their manners - amiable and innocent - a primal paradise pursued.

Too fond of earth I tend when climbing swiftly toward the sky,
On broad-breasted mountains - gravity defied!
And I touch the rim of heaven, nightly pluck at stars by eye,
Whose neighboring glow reminds me of my source and supply.

Too fond of earth I tend when seeing high earth become the means
For lessoning my soul by glory-ridden scenes.
And real conveys the Real; a paradox it seems,
That matter's Maker shows Himself in mountain-mirrored gleams.
   Eloise K. Schreiner

It's Never Too Late

It's never too late
   To start anew, to build a wall 'tween me and you.
It's never too late
   To act the fool - to play your games - make up your rules.
It's never too late
   You're always told to mend the fence - prepare your soul.
It's never too late
   To live and love - to look for help from up above.
It's never too late
   To spend your days counting time - counting hate.
It's never too late
   To wish it weren't, to make it stop, to just make sure.
It's never too late
   When things cave in, things around are scattered and dim.
It's never too late
   'Till you're old and gray, and mornings stop - no more day.
It's never too late
   'Till you're cold as stone and night has come - you're alone.
Ah-
   But then it's too late.
   Darrius Rains

A Mother's Prayer

Help us Lord with those hands,
To teach them to do the best they can.
Help us to teach them right from wrong.
When they grow up, let them grow strong.

When they need us; let us be there,
Help us to show them we still care.
When years to come for broken hearts,
Help us Lord to know our part.

When marriage happens to come their way,
I'll pray to you, Lord, day by day;
Please don't let us interfere.
And, cause them to lose the one they love dear!

We'll pray for Your Guidance to help us through,
And, in all we may go to do,
Please don't let us make offense,
'Cause Lord, we're for them every inch!
   Freda L. Richardson

"Fond Memories"

This earthly life is but a pathway
To that eternal home above.
Though at times the road may be rough and rocky.
The rewards are great when it's paved with love.

God didn't put us here to be lonely,
Nor to hoard all the blessings we're given.
If we share our love and compassion.
It will surely brighten this world we live in.

A cheery "God Morning", how are you?
To someone lonely, sad or just mad,
Brings a surprising chain of reaction
And even makes you feel glad.

If we carry out our mission
As ambassadors of love,
Just think of the joy in heaven
When we meet our friends and neighbors above.

Though we are deeply hurt and saddened
When, from this earth a friend or loved one departs.
If we remember the good he has done here,
Fond memories will ever remain in our hearts.
   Adele Schrupp

Dreaming

From a passion that's hotter than high-noon in July,
to the soft sensuality expressed in the Casablanca Lily,
a versatile vision of you has been burned into my mind, body and soul
to replace a dream that has now come to life. It's so nice to look
into your enticing grey eyes and to hear sincerity in your voice.
All my life I've dreamed of meeting someone like you, my perfect man
of choice. To find someone so powerfully gorgeous in so many
ways who communicates and listens as well as you do, you're the most
complete man I know; a real dream come true. I have thoughts of
holding you in my arms until you fall asleep at night, only to watch
you sleep, listen to you breathe and wonder what you're dreaming of,
While thinking of a relationship with you that will ride on the peak
of infinity, only to be topped by the happiness on your face when you
awake at sunlight. I hope my thoughts will show you a side
of me, a side that says listen to your words and look at what you see,
a side I'm presenting to a special person that really appeals to me...
I only ask that you be true to yourself and recognize what you see.

I have so much to say from deep inside of me, I couldn't possibly
write it all down, this insight to my view of passion and wisdom
unfortunately must come to an end. I hope you cherish this for its
emotionally true honesty. Always remember, Love is natural and
real when it's to you from me.
   Catherine Hollenbeck

My Love

My Love, my Love,
To thee I give
The treasure of my heart;
Till time shall cease
To be no more
May we never be apart.

To thee I pledge my heart, my soul, my love
Unto eternity
With each sunrise
And each sunset
Made just for you and me

Unto thee I give my love
May it never be taken away
Remember this vow I give to thee
On this our wedding day.
 Janice Moss

Tribute To Those Who Did Not Return

Hats off to our warriors
To those of yesterday and today;
Without them to protect our country,
Our children could not come to play.
Remembering the burial of a Precious Soldier of World War One,
If the war hadn't stopped when it did,
My Father would not have a son.
In my Father's arms, a small child under three,
A big group of people standing under a tree;
I close my eyes and I can see
A man riding on a horse, firing bullets in the sky
For us, that dear Soldier did die.
About twenty years past, World War Two broke out,
Worse than the last.
Then came Korea, Viet Nam and Desert Storm.
God bless the families whose sons and daughters
Did not return.
Our Dear Flag still waves high, reaching out
To those who made their home in the sky.
 "GOD BLESS AMERICA."
 Jessie Taylor

Daisy Fields

I only meant to rest awhile upon
This tranquil blanket of immortal dawn.
But soft...how feathers claim a tired soul!
The weightless bells of silent thoughts do toll
A melody of golden daisy fields
Bejeweled in its morning dew does yield
The fragrant scent of peaceful dreams.
Such bliss...too bold a gesture rising seems.
And so in golden daisy fields I fly
Inspired by rainbow beams of butterfly
Until the warm caress of summer's breath
Does gently waken me from sleep's soft death.
 Diane Gnotta

"DNA"

In coils of mortality there lies a twisted tale,
two ends to meet, a strand complete,
the blueprint of the grail.

In sought cohesion, amnesty, regardless of its fate,
the ladder knows, in code it grows,
Entwined verbose template.

In cyclic meta synthesis, a teeming gang of one,
distinction gene, extinction scene,
and backwards is the pun.
 Joseph James Harding III

"True Love (Ruth Herrington)"

Reminiscing about the way your life used to be, yet can't seem
to understand why some things are meant to be. Turning to the
"Lord" with so many questions, hoping to receive some much
needed answers. Helping others is her "specialty," so they can
better cope with "Reality." "Heart of Gold," is what makes
her so "Bold," to care for so many "living souls."
Even when her day is bad, she'll still listen to what
makes you sad.
"Ruth," you're very special to me, even when you think
I don't see. I remember the time when we first
met, I said to myself, "I'm not ready for this yet."
I feel so comfortable when we're together, I see
that life can really be much better. Now our love for
each other has grown so much "it's hard sometimes
not to stay in touch. Now "Grace" have given us
another chance. Let's make the best of it, so others
can be "enhanced." "Tender at heart," in so many
ways. Optimism in spirit, to share all her days.
Noble as this may sound, sometimes you may wonder,
"Does she ever frown?"
 Isaiah Cobb

Untitled

I am drawn outside by the moonlight
To wander, barefoot,
The sensuous feel of dewy grass
Heightening my mood.

Humming, I dance lightly across the lawn,
Gown lifting and swirling,
My arms reaching out to hold you
As if perchance the wish itself
Could cause you to appear.

Alas! It is not to be!
And yet...
You are here.
I can feel you in the whisper of the breeze,
And the warmth of the earth beneath my feet.
I am surrounded by your love.
I am not alone.
 Jane Jabusch

In Reverence Of The Trail

 To lie upon the cool soil along the mountain trail,
to watch the billowed clouds and see the falcon sail,
to feel the clean spring air wash upon our face,
to hear a soft sweet breeze move by without a trace.

 With reverence tread lightly this beauty not to spoil,
to linger there and savor air filled fragrance of flower,
tree, and soil.

 Softly moving sun calls us to this mother nature's womb,
just as this cycling clock reminds us of the tomb.
It speaks to us of our fading happy times,
and bids us to savor special moments,
and reflect upon our crimes.

 As I leave this scared mountain trail,
the experience reminds me how we are tender, weak and frail.
For this mountain has withstood greater pain than I,
been shaped by rain and noble windy tempest and many a storm-
filled sky.

 Oh if I could remain there and within its rhythm live,
though sweet was my intrusion, with reverence I must ask it
to forgive.
 Dennis Dougherty

Our Future Has Eyes To See

Riding on the wings of yesterday, upon the birth of a new
today, before the appearance of dawn, opens the eyes of
yet another born.

The beauty of creation, the silent, still movements of the wind's
breeze, brings to our conscious state of mind, that our future
has eyes to see.

The future breaths in new life, and with it brings a new day
of hopes and dreams for a better tomorrow -
Never to look back at past pain and sorrow.

As eyes are lifted toward the heaven's blue, beholding a vastness
filled with eternal and unknown destiny -
Life holds fast to this truth, though we see not the things that
lie ahead, we still move forward following our future,
who has eyes to see.
   Bertha Crampton

Untitled

Today I felt your pain....
Today I saw the wreck that was your life
I was washed away by your sea of emotions

I closed my eyes to see your troubles
I saw the man who made you
taste his hatred...
the man who locked you in his
own dark room of despair

You were ruined by the thoughts
of another....
Today you left reality
Today you left behind your past
to rise above
and shine brighter than the sun
   Billy Knisely

"Cliff By The Lighthouse"

Meet me at the cliff by the lighthouse
  together we'll watch for whales.
I'll light my lantern to warm our hands
  we'll count the ships with sails.
We'll bundle up all of our troubles, cast them into the sea.
I'll hold you in the afterglow of the sunset here with me.
Meet me at the cliff by the lighthouse, saddle your pony and go.
Rendezvous there before sunset falls
  we don't want to miss the show
You be my gypsy princess, I'll be your captain ashore;
I'll hold you in the afterglow of this psalm forevermore.
Meet me at the cliff by the lighthouse
  together we'll watch for whales.
I'll light my lantern to warm our hands
  we'll count the ships with sails.
We'll bundle up all of our troubles, cast them into sea
I'll hold you in the afterglow of the sunset here with me.
   David A. Bixby

'Twas My Heart

 'Twas my heart that sank the sun.
'Twas my heart that beat so loud and fast
as the hooves of a thousand pegasus. 'Twas
my heart that caused father Sun to move, not
to the slow ticking of the second hand, but to
the swift beating of my most precious organ
within my chest. 'Twas my heart that hurdled
father Sun into the eastern sea and awoke the
scarred Moon so that through the moon's beams
I might find my way to your balcony.
   Casey Lee Thompson

Today Is Today

YESTERDAY has come and gone,
TOMORROW is yet to be,
But TODAY is TODAY
It's here and now, so pursue it diligently.
Fret not the things that should have been,
nor worry about what's in store.
Just do your best to take care of TODAY,
no one can ask for more.
Let your troubles fall by the wayside,
put a smile upon your face,
lend a helping hand to a neighbor,
and everything will fall into place.
TODAY will soon become YESTERDAY,
and TOMORROW will soon be TODAY.
So open your eyes to a NEW SUNRISE
and ENJOY IT ALL THE WAY.
   Ida Hugenot

The Widower

A veil on the dreams of a broken man
Too lonely to go forward in his search
Too scared to go back to what has been
He closes the door to those around him
And suffers his shame from life in silence
Oh to be young and full of the promise
Of a long life, not thinking of sadness
You know the day will come, you close your mind
As if you can will the years that pass you by
You curse the nature that has embraced you
Your fist raised in defiance, a gesture
Of a feeble life, no hope against it
You cry out, the battle is over
They are upon you, it is your defeat.
   Douglas L. Ely

Friendship Lost?

I lost my best friend the other day
This has me blue the least to say
I guess we're not speaking and this is quite sad
Over something I think that got us both mad
We used to joke and laugh a lot
How I wish those good times would not stop
We knew what the other was thinking before we would talk
As if we were one with each little thought
My life is empty without my best friend
And I shed a tear that it has come to an end
So if it is possible to call a truce
It would cut the pain in my heart loose
I hope to hear from you in any way
And I wait anxiously for that day
   Carol Wolford

Angels In Waiting

They came to play and learn a song;
to socialize away from home.

Mom and Dad came to drop them off
with a hug, and a kiss and smile adieu.

The rain of death struck quick and fast,
with falling rocks and tons of glass;

But Angels nearby caught them up-
"let's soar away to God above"!

With waiting arms of love and care,
a hug - a kiss - a smile - was there.

"Enter in little ones - We care, We care."
Welcome home.
   Artemese B. Jones

Death Of The Wild West

As I walk the sandy road of time
Toward the town I see two men facing each other
I know what will happen. One will rot in the overflowing graveyard.
I turn away. I cannot watch this murder.
Two shots are fired. All is quiet.
Then people begin to bleed out of the woodwork.
They come from the rickety barn, the store, the haphazard
schoolhouse, and the saloon.
I see a girl holding her pet sheep crying. One of the men was her
father.
I look toward the pond and I see flowers rolling across the hills.
How can there be such beauty in such a sad world.

Now people say these days are gone.
They say the Wild West is no more.
But the old days are never gone.
They are remembered forever in the eyes of the children, the old, and
the old-fashioned.
We will never see the Wild West again,
But it will be in our hearts and minds forever.

Cristi Gower

Untitled

Two Women at a bar
transcending, stretching and recreating
the harshness of
just being.

Two queens on a stool
watching one another disrobe.
Cloaks of disguise
evaporating into
the sweet, sweet promises
of a bottle.

Two souls at a bar
courageously dismantling all structures of despair,
while building blocks of hope
rejoicing in periodic
bouts of grandeur.

Two minds soaked in
turpentine.
Shouting obscenities at the neon walls
Blurry faces, blurry lies and dreams.

Two Women at a bar.

Joyce Dunham-Smith

May

My favorite month of spring is May
trees spruce up with colorful blossoms so gay.
It is a time of new beginnings - a fresh look -
flowers on the hill cover every cranny and nook.

The grass is green, oh how the birds sing!
Sounds of children playing have a happy ring -
their laughter comes floating in the wind,
a message of love and hope they send.

Gone is winter with its snow and cold -
sunny days and warm nights we happily enfold.
God's world takes on a look so bright:
in each and every heart comes a glowing light!

May is the month we pay tribute to mothers —
symbols of beginnings, hope and love above others.
Having you for my mother, I'm proud to say -
God has surely blessed me in a special way!!!

Betsy Ross Roth

Pondering Trees

It's cold outside... I stand peering through a window staring at those
Trees with cold and bare branches which stand so still...
A ritual pose... I start to wonder... Do trees possess knowledge?
They're older than I... And have seen so many seasons come and go.
How about wisdom? A world of thoughts... maybe those branches
Can feel... not a single leaf and yet so alive.... It's cold outside.
Those branches are awaiting for Spring to arrive... When the breath
Of Spring will bestow a growing of substance... to dress up the
Scenery with beautiful hues... and to abundantly provide... but, for
Now they await... So sullen and so still... waiting for that moment...
To become fruitful... shadows for coolness... relief from the heat...
But for now those branches lie silent and patiently... in front of
A beautiful background of chilled skies... with a depth which appears
Never ending... then I start to wonder... Do trees think of me?

Benjamin J. Lovato

Regarding Life

I have walked amid the noise and the haste of the universe and
truly there is great joy in silence, but only at the proper
time, and you and your soul can be the judge of a proper time.

Allow no one to silence you if the need to be heard is that
great and the creativity of your mind should be stifled.

Inasmuch as it is most important to stay on friendly terms with
everyone, do not humble yourself to the degree of surrender
or submission.

Friendship is only as good and meaningful as the person who
is offering it, this does not mean the same at all times of
the recipient; they will accept what they want and discard the rest.

Never allow your feelings of a moment's bad heart to clear your
vocal cords and cause spoken words truly meant to be unspoken.

Soft spoken yet clearly stated truths should be the leader of
your mind and the guide for your speech. Do not turn away from
the advice and ramblings of others as they have much to say
and even the most feeble of minds has good ideas and concepts, if
not for your lifestyle then theirs.

Fred Hewitt

A Frame of Mind

Some can laugh and love life
without money on their side.
Others live in mansions, rich, yet ponder suicide.
To pine and lust for fortune
is to miss the point, it's blind—
'cause we are here for living
and life's just a frame of mind.
Yes it's all a frame of mind.

Barry R. Haft

"Imagination"

Even though you can't be free...
Try your best to be happy.
They can lock you up in a cell...
And make your life a living hell.
So they think!!!
But in your heart and in your mind...
You can take a trip of the Grandest kind.
"Imagine" you're walking on the beach...
With a pretty girl, and the warm sand on your feet.
Or cruising down the highway, watching the cars go by...
Because there's no limit!!!
To how high, your "imagination" can fly.
It's as free as an Eagle soaring through the sky.
So open your mind and you will see...
You can be as free as a ship at sea.
So come along and take a trip with me.

Annia Deck

My Father

I'm sitting at my desk,
Trying to study for a test.
The light of the moon,
Shining through the window,
Made a pale white light on my book,
I knew I had to take a look.
Up at the sky,
I asked myself why?
My father had to die,
Then I started to cry.
As a tear ran down my cheek,
My mother came into take a peek.
She asked me what I was doing up this late.
"I'm studying for a test."

"Then why are you at the window instead of the desk?"
"I'm thinking about dad,
And that's why I'm sad."
"Try to remember all the good times you had,
Then you shouldn't feel so bad."

Deborah Lynn Anthony

The Man's Battle: The Child's Triumph

A man who dared to dream, a life that was going so well; then came the turmoil and trials that went with the days, hence came the casting of satan's spell. Two separate identities living inside of one man. One of them was living in the memories of the past, the other one was struggling to remember himself, but he struggled too hard, he struggled too fast. Eventually they would both meet each other in the arena of life, and those of us who looked onward with awe couldn't for one moment comprehend nor grasp the enormity of this final fight. Which one of these men would break this devilish spell, who would triumph this night? One of the men was seemingly violent, but the other one "He Was Mild." The battle begins: They both fight, they both struggle, and in the end they both lose; but during this massive struggle for domination of the soul they give birth to a child. And in this child's last days of walking this earth he walks it as meek and as gentle as a lamb; no longer the struggle, no longer the fight, no longer is pain haunting this man. But finally at last from beyond the shadows came a man with a gun one senseless and horrible night. And those of us who cared and dared to look forward would never have thought it ever would end: "With The Loss Of A Little Boy's Life..."

Brian C. Gordon

The Raven And The Cat

In a long time ago fable, I read of a spat
'Twas I think of a raven and that of a cat
They bored the same space and called it home
On a shingled red roof, they dwelled there alone

In the evening light shed from a sphere of the moon
Light shadows were cast from the figures that moved
Known was their fate and what would lie ahead
And both knew their boundaries, though nothing was said

Turns to the dawn does the darkness of night
And the two feeble bodies they give into the light
Eye contact is made, through the silence that brewed
And a bird that chirped lightly, confirmed the day new

Like a powerful tree that could not be sawed down
Both made their stance, their roots strong in the ground
When one of them nestled and rummaged abroad
The other was king, and his confidence soared

The struggle was constant, and conflicts were spewn
And through the long days they were subdued
Why is it the human race can't be much more like that
And learn to live together like the raven and the cat

Charles Daidone

Granddaughter Marianne Olivia Determan

Granddaughter began acting up around two in the morn,
Twelve days early, and warning all she was to be born.
About four-thirty Grandpa and Grandma were called,
And in the darkness Grandma went gladly enthralled.

At six Mom, Dad and Grandma had to rapidly head out,
For Marianne Olivia was soon due, there was no doubt.
Grandpa arrived as fast from home as he could go
As did the two Aunties with big sister Amy in tow.

Soon a nurse took some reading and ran out in a hurry
Bringing much activity and increased medical scurry.
The delivery scene is new, now being a one-room stint.
From labor to delivery through bath and legal footprint,

The newborn never leaves the birthing room at all.
Those wishing to be present during the delivery call
Are allowed to observe from beginning to baby outcry
Except for an old-fashioned Grandpa who paced nearby.

The birth went breathing and pushing fairly fast
With the usual coaching and coaxing, and at last,
Marianne put in an appearance, amid sighs of relief,
Tiny, wrinkled and red, yet beautiful beyond belief.

Howard H. Becker

My Mother's Heart

My life began in her womb
twenty-five years ago

A reddish glow flowed down from her heart,
serving as the lifeline for my growing parts

From day one, this instrument of her's
has played a vital and consistent role in my life

Over the years her heart has become one of a heavy sort,
since it has been weighed down with many a care, many a thought

However, the branches of her heart extend wider each day
as they touch the souls of many people

This heart of her's continues to pump everlasting love,
although it skips a beat

For I know, that wherever my life may take me
her beat will always be with me

I thank God for my Mother's heart!

Chris Pitchford

True Regrets

I've been living inside you, months add up to eight,
Today is my day and I hardly can wait.
The joys I've encountered, and love that you've shown,
Overwhelms me with peace in my little home.

At night time you lie there so quiet in bed
Talking silently to me from inside your head.
I feel belly caresses rubbing gently and dear,
And my unspoken words I know you will hear.

Elation you felt, tears of joy I did bring
When Dr. Dee said to expect me this spring.
So much you offer will keep you wondering why
You'll not see me smile and you'll not hear me cry.

I've not been born, yet I know what's to come,
I'm deformed and cruel laughter's still given by some.
There are people whose choice was to be born and fight,
And many brave others turn wrong into right.

Feel me leave you dear Mommy and please don't be sad,
The world that you gave me was the best I could have.
Grieve not for me Mommy, for you're not to blame
Though the world's slowly changing, I'll go back whence I came.

Geraldine Hinz

My Angels

The Angels brought to me,
Two babies simultaneously.
There must be some mistake, I said.
I expected one and received two instead.

God makes no mistakes their heavenly voices roared.
And back to the Heavens the angels soared.
I cried, Don't leave them here.
This is much more than I can bear.

Then one angel whispered to me,
You'll be alright, you'll see.
And when I looked at each tiny face,
Everything seemed to fall into place.

When times get tough now and then,
I think of how things could have been.
I smile and thank my lucky stars,
That these two angels are ours!

Janet Salomon

God's Little Image

Ten little fingers, ten little toes,
Two little ears and one little nose.
Two big eyes with mischief aglow,
One little mouth to say Hello.

Two little feet make such sweet patter
Bring him to mother with things that matter.
Two little arms that hug so tight
When tucked away safely for the night.

First there were girls then there were boys
Then the toys and oh the noise.
We bring them up in God's loving care,
First the nursery then the chair.

Off to Sunday school they toddle,
Sometimes before they leave the bottle.
Whom on earth ever did produce,
An image to compare with God's Papoose.

I'm sure you'll agree if there be any other,
It will surely have to be my father.
My father you know is also great
Who on this earth did God first create.

C. Duane Field

I never felt...

I never felt pain
Until I had a life taken away
A life that was a part of my body
A part of my living days

I never felt sorrow
Until I saw my son's face
I never felt shock
Until I held his little body in my embrace

I never felt hate
Until I saw there was nothing I could do
I never felt lost
Until I really could feel and knew

I never felt helpless
Until I held my son in my arms
I never felt bewildered
Until there was no more of his charms

I never realized how short time could be
Until that one night Justin was taken away from me
I never cried so hard in such strife
Until that one night took my son's life.

Cassandra D. Days

One Daring Night

There once was a girl precious and dear.
Until she found out the worlds biggest fear.
She wanted to fit in, just like all the rest.
So she said to herself, being good is a pest.
Then she went in a crowd, she shouldn't have gone in.
Her friends tried to help, but she didn't want to listen.
So they all gave up, and so did she.
That one Friday night, she felt so sick of her life.
So she drank a beer, thought it would make her cheer.
But it wasn't enough.
So she tried what they called "the good stuff."
She smoked fill she couldn't think, and then went totally blank,
Within two seconds she just collapsed.
Her life flashed before her.
That was it! That was her death!
Her true friends will never forget.
They wished they would have stopped her.
They'll always regret!
Except for the crowd that "dared".
And the crowd that she thought really cared.

Charity Zimmerman

A Unique Tree

I'd never seen a tree that the bark on the trunk was spiral,
Until the other day in the yard. Looking it over, the bark
on the trunk spirals from the ground up including the branches.
It has an appealing look, not a forlorn one. How
"God" can take a tree "HE" put on earth and give it a twist,
To give it beauty. What a "God"! The tree so tall, leaves
appearing as spring has sprung. The new life appears for
one to enjoy. Then the tree isn't in a place for many to
see, nor pay attention to. Would like to put a swing there on,
and swing back and forth like a child, to feel the wind
and swing high. Oh what a beautiful tree with its
spiral bark trunk. Makes it unique in itself. As the
spiral bark trunk has seen the weather through the eyes
of its knots. Branches that have been cut off. No doubt
because of disease. Even when it has no leaves. It still
holds its beauty throughout the years. In time "HE" puts
leaves back on the branches to give it a new life. "God"
takes care of it. "HE" waters and feeds. It gives off
oxygen for us. A Unique Tree In Itself.

Charlotte M. Ryan

Mr. Hank

Mr. Hank would set up his tent near the river bank,
until the sun had sank slowly in the west.

Then he'd do
everything that the great fishers taught him to,
and some more he knew, different from the rest.

There he would sit and wait for his catch till the morning came;
Mixing his brew and baiting his lines in the pouring rain.
What a shame.

Solo — Hum

Very kind,
But there's nothing he owned but his peace of mind,
and this he stood behind, every inch of the way.

There he'd be,
set aside in his world for his heart was free,
and even I could see that he lived from day to day.

Now the sun would rise and the clouds would clear for the time
had come.
He would take his fish to the nearby stores and hope to sell them
some, while he'd hum.

Hum — Solo

Jerry Stup

Untitled

Cocaine: "Where would you be if not for me?"
User: "Probably not in all this misery.

A house, some clothes, a car or two
and many miles away from you!

I'd have some meat upon my bones,
and not take my meals at mission homes.

I'd go back to school and learn a trade
and even have the highest grade!

I'd be someone and that is true
if I didn't waste my time with you.

In fact, I do believe I'll quit
for I'm tired of all your daily sh**!

I'm out of here, I'm on my way
to find myself a better day.

And thanks for asking what I'd do
without the likes of a drug like you.

And to think all this time I've been such a fool!
Goodbye to you, worthless tool!"

Charles R. Butler Jr.

Windmills

Come once more, dear solitary night,
  veiled in silvered silent darkness,
  weaving threads of faded dreams.
  Who is this night's abrupt intruder
  scratching at the windmills of my mind?

Innocence's sweet beauty — hope's eternal wonder —
  cradled in the palm of my existence
  fight the darkened grasp of life's despair.
  Emerge triumphant in quixotic state;
  conquer swiftly this inner foe.

Battered windmills need repair —
  now so slowly turning.
  do not let the threads unravel,
  worn and oh, so very fragile —
  do not let the pattern fade into the night.

Blessed peace of night, please enter.
  Softly wrap your arms around me;
  mend my tired, splintered windmills;
  lift me gently — now so gently —
  that my soul might feel the promise of another day.

Frances Marioni

To Our Friends In Oklahoma

Roses are red
violets are blue
we know you are hurting
for we hurt too.

The pain is so real
you wonder when will it cease
and when will there be peace.
The lives of the innocent taken in a flash
I wish we could erase the past.

They came to work to do a job
some visited and some even played there.
Who would have thought we'd have this
great burden to bear.

As you lay your loved ones in the grave
we all know you'll try and be brave
to carry on and remember that you'll
see your loved ones again. They're in a place
where pain and tears will never be seen again.

Gerri Marcum

Eden's Exit

Two towns separated by fate but merged by human nature.

One was grief stricken to the everyday eye. Having to deal with the vicissitudes of eternal darkness kept its contents busy and its right arm hypertrophied. It thrived on the vibes that small children endure after eating too much candy late at night, screaming and screaming, running into their parents' bedroom, looking for a safe haven in which to confide the subconscious pleas for help.

And the other gave of a vibrant light, a place where every whisper was echoed and everyone heard. Never could you get lost for every gate to the mind's eye was opened unravelling the conscious of a new day - fresh and clean with hope. A child's innocence was given as a gift. Everything was understood.

These two towns where separated by fate but human nature merged them.

Frances Hope Brewster

Nothing

A fettered dream withers in forgotten shadows,
Vision dims as the abandoned future darkens,
Empty hopes collapse where love has wearied.
Sparkling trifles steal the truth of love;
Seduced eyes see not the fading light of a new dawn.
Faith and love are robbed by those who hold nothing;
A hollow life is beautiful in the darkness.
Grasped to the breast is exquisite nothing;
Trampled underfoot is tarnished truth.
The void fills us; emptiness gives meaning.
Unwanted truth is happily buried,
And in its place we adore nothing.

Brent M. Bergandine

To Wish Upon A Star

A faded remembrance of your soft
  voice lingers in my mind
It talks to me, says you miss me,
  but how does it feel?
Are there emotions behind those words
  that remain when we hang up?

The miles between us seem so far
  and many
I sit by my window looking out on
  the moonlit night, glaring at a star
Wishing you were here for me to have,
  to love; wishing you were near again
As it glimmers, like a piece of gold
  against a dark black sky, I hope you are looking
  out and seeing what I see....
I pray you are thinking of me...

A faded remembrance of your soft voice
  will always stay with me
It promises my heart that it's you I love,
  wherever you may be...

Julia M. Mancuso

Taught Not To Love

Take a good look at our future, the children.
So often forgotten, overlooked and used.
They come into the world full of hope,
  anticipation and love.
Yes love, they have an over abundance of it to share.
But remember that it is a two way street.
To give and receive are necessity here.
Love comes so naturally...
Until they are taught not to love.
Let them follow their natural instincts,
For they hold our future in their hands.

Lydia E. Thacker

Suicide

For all of you people who want to die
Wait for it to happen, don't commit suicide
If you have a lot of problems and life is a bore
Suicide doesn't solve problems; it creates many more

Think of the things you'll miss in life
If you're young and a bachelor, you won't meet your wife
Think of the guilt your family will feel
And think of their pain because they won't know the deal

When you feel down don't look for drugs
Find lots of people who will give you hugs
How would you know what your future was to hold
What if you were to be an inventor or find your pot of gold

What if you were to be President or savior of the world
What if you were to marry the most beautiful girl
You won't find this out if you're six feet deep
Why would it make you happy to make all your friends weep

I've met the girl who keeps me on my feet
There is no other person that I need to meet
I'll love her forever, or at least it seems
She was twice my girlfriend; now she's only in my dreams

Brian S. Pfaff

Heart In Flight

My heart was patient, it was warm and pulsing,
   Waiting to become a butterfly or moth.
Trembling it hung suspended from a limb,
   Covered in shimmering, silver-spun cloth.

The cocoon was transpired, the world was alive.
Piercing and warming was the lustrous light.
It welcomed my lonely, tender white wings,
   Gasping, disbelieving, they made ready for flight.

My body was lifted, weightless and trusting,
   Quickly it learned pebbled paths of the air.
Fearless, it sent itself playfully thrusting,
   Into the wafts of the wind-whirling dare.

One I became with my ebony branches,
   Sketching the sky like the boughs of the trees.
Soaring as even the sun turned to pillow,
   Clouds tried in vain my passion to ease.

The Night came upon me somber in sable,
   Sending a warning for my spirit to heed.
You can't fly forever, unheavenly creature,
   Tuck head beneath wing, sleep is thy need.

Annabelle M. Moseley

Tribute To My Grandma

This statuesque lady, God's gentle child,
Walked this earth, with a simple style.
You all know her, you've heard her talk.
You can't miss her, she walks with pride.
Her sensible shoes, her purse close by her side.
A hat adorns her head, an umbrella shields her from the sun.
The thing that stands out most, to make her so unique,
In Winter cold or Summer heat,
A long white dress, pressed crisp and neat.
The long cuffed sleeves made the look complete.
A silken scarf, she wrapped around her neck.
On Sunday, white gloves covered work worn hands.
I'm sure somewhere in heaven, the way she did here on earth,
Grandma will plant her flowers and make them grow.
You have left us, for now, those who love you so,
But we'll have you in our hearts and carry with pride,
The memory of this statuesque woman, God's gentle child.

Cassandra A. Smith-Thomas

Longing

I long to be with her, by her side
walking short journeys stride in stride; listening to the ways of the "Olden days." I long for the comfort and understanding of a wise ole woman—Big Ma!

I miss her dearly! For she parted this way some four years ago.
I pick up the phone and realized there is no one to call.
She has no phone.
I go to a place that once was her home; I go to a still odorless house
No laughter, no shouting, no smells of the meal to come.

Loneliness grips my heart. I can hardly breathe.
I must go to her, to her resting place.
The sun shines brightly. The wind blows gently.
I see her in the sun. I hear her in the wind.
I see her rocking in the chair on the front porch.
I hear the tales of the "olden days", day am given hope for the
days to come.
My heart swells with warmth and releases the clutches of loneliness.

I am comforted. Tears roll down my cheeks.
Sobs erupt from my lips, shaking my inner soul.
I must leave her. Longing, longing to be with her more than before.

Brenda L. Foster

Long-Legged Fran

Oh, look at Long-Legged Fran,
Walks down the street as sexy as she can.

Oh, look at the way the men drool and stare,
Everything from her clothes right up to her hair.

She smiles, nods, and gives a wink,
The men stare so hard they can hardly blink.

On the street is the only place she's seen.
One man screams out something obscene.

They make hand gestures, hoot, and holler,
Fran just undoes one more button from her collar.

Today she walks over,
The men slobber and beg to roll over.

She just slyly smiles and gives each a kiss,
They can barely mutter "Thank you Miss..."

Oh, look at Long-Legged Fran,
Too bad the men don't know she's really a man.

Jessica Ciacco

Daybreak

It was the dawn of day and the dew-like spray
was a blanket on the tips of the grass.

I awoke to the hymn of a bird on a limb in a tree
near the bed where I lay.

I sat with a grin and almost joined in, but got
scared that he might fly away.

It was beauty to hear as others gave cheer to
welcome the sunrise that day.

Christopher A. Andersen

Resting In His Arms

Led by the Spirit, the veil I pass,
Velveteen touch rent from above,
woven together with strands of love,
Anchor of the soul, both sure and steadfast,
wrapped in His warmth, He gathers me here,
fragrance of Heaven, His breath so near,
Sweetly He whispers, entereth in,
My Father, My Jesus, My Spirit, within.

Jenny Hann

Heaven Is My Destination

Lost in the wilderness seeking he who is most holy am I. Want desperately to see the light of righteousness am I. Giving praise abundantly every day upon him for all the blessings he has showered upon me. With reverence I pray for the knowledge, wisdom, and understanding that is needed to walk the path of the righteous. Being diligent upon my path, for evil and sin abound. Straight and narrow is the path I choose because the kingdom of heaven is my destination.

David Drinkard

Searching

There sits upon the bench
Warming tired and weary bones
As thoughts go by of years past
Good times revisited like skipping stones
Into the vast memories of the mind
Young girls fancied babies on the knee
Created with love and toil a man past is he
Deep in thought that seems to surround
The fun and joy in his memories abound
Look close and you will see a sparkle in his eye
A twitch in cheek the beginning of a smile
As a good time passes by
Withered brawn and crippled hands, a pile of nothing to do
Fond memories past bring each day something new
A nod of his head a frown in place
With past mistakes upon his face
Gray hair, withered bones, cane are now the mainstay
A life of struggle and toil was the pay
What to do when age creeps in
He breathed a sigh and thinks again

George Ford

In The Eyes Of A Child

Sitting on some rocks overlooking the sea,
Was A very young child no bigger than me.
She watched the sea gulls fly high in the air,
And land in the ocean heaven knows where.
One after the other and in A straight line,
They would bring back A fish time after time.
The sail boats going by with their sails in the air,
Would dance over the waves without even A care.
Down by the bridge so high in the sky,
They would open their gates to let the big ships go by.
There were no houses that she could see,
just mountains of rocks surrounding the sea.
A few little crabs running here and there,
Over bumps of clams that the waves washed bare.
Soon she was gone as gone could be,
The only thing left now was the quiet old sea.

Barbara F. Long

The Awakening Heart

A gentle rose caressed by dew,
Waits upon something new

A piercing light has made its way
To help it through another day

The wind and hail has made a fight,
As the chilling cold..alone in the night

Yet comes morning, and an eastward glance
Bringing the music with which to dance

Not seen in the shadows, to the eye is plain
Fades into the heart as a precious gain

For though each night we bid adieu,
Each day I grow from a part of you.

Charles Godoski

Somebody Cares

It was one of those days that everyone
was confused or upset about something.
No one knew what was going on back there.
As I looked back on that day I wondered how
I could help or change a few things. But,
that isn't possible, for everybody didn't
want to be helped. Somehow, no one really
knew what was their trouble or what they
were getting into. In that group, everybody
wanted help of some kind, but, they didn't open
up to us. Until a girl in the far back opened
up and said what was on her mind. Everyone
was silent and listened with their eyes wide
open. When she was done everyone else started to
voice out their feelings. It was wonderful,
people opened up. They were laughing, happiness
was in the air. Their questions were answered and
there was joy that day. But as soon as everybody
left, it was over. Nobody, was there to comfort them or
listen to them. So, there was sadness that day.

Claribel Santos

The Joy Of Life

The dark and lonely street
Was covered with people.
Men, women and children, such a sad sight.
Their glaring, sad eyes
Wanting a little love and compassion
Stare at you and I
As we walk by, such a sad sight.

Rags, dirty faces, and poor
Was what others thought of them
But no, I did not see that.

I sat on the cold, hard sidewalk
They gathered around me
We played, joked and told stories
Then as I left, the children's eyes looked up
Pleading with me not to go.
I smiled and said, "Don't worry, I'll be back again."

They are the joy of life always and forever
A sad sight? No not anymore.
Please show love and compassion to everyone.

Brooke L. Petersen

My Brother Ernie

He enriched my life ten-fold,
was loved and respected by many I'm told.
He was my protector and teacher for many years.
When I was six he destroyed a snake that frightened me to tears.
Summers he would take me swimming and fishing just us alone
and would give me a piggy back ride on the way home.
Winters he took me sliding and skiing,
but never on days that were freezing.
In my teens he taught me target shooting with a gun
and that was a lot of fun.
When I was fourteen he taught me how to drive a car
but never let me drive too far.
At sixteen he was forced to leave school and go to work
as our father was accidentally hurt.
When I left home after graduating from school,
he packed his bag and left home too.
We stayed real close throughout the years.
He's gone now - but I'm sure when I talk to him he hears.
Right from the start,
he had a tender and sensitive heart.

My brother Ernie - how I miss him.

Dorothea Dunton

"River Of Tears"

I've heard many tales in my travels, but one I remember so well, it was told to me by an old brave, it's a legend he'd heard great braves tell:

Once there was this young brave, who had just lost his young bride and child, so he went off to an old ravine, and there he began to cry.

He cried till his tears started flowage, he cried from the pain deep within, and there he started a river, the river that has no end.

It flows through prairies and valleys, and meadows and canyons below, It seems there's no way of telling, how far the river goes.

Wild life won't drink from this river, and trees won't grow from its banks; it just keeps on flowing with sadness, and showing its sad sad sway,

The water is warm, yet bitter, though it's clear fish won't swim within, it's filled with heartaches and misery, of widows and children and men

There's no way of stopping this river, no sleet nor freezing days, as long as there are men and women to cry in its river bed.

I've told this legend from time to time and now at the prime of my years, I'll tell you the name of this river, they call it the river of tears.

No sand, nor snow, nor winds that blow can stop the river of tears.

Jaybird Raul Strungbow Cantu

My Christmas Thoughts

It is foggy and misty, the night she
watches the waves kiss the sand.
And in the sky, blue gems sleep
while she touches them with her hand.
Though lives linger carelessly,
unpolished, only she remains.
A tear charms her rose,
then without regard, out to sea it wonders.

Through the haze, desert memories
fill her eyes and leave longing
for her sun.
Her shadow, full of image
of misplaced angels, dances like a flame
with the moon;
Whispers to her and caresses her soul.

Treasure that she will not always be
so far away, her heart faithful,
rocks itself to sleep.
She kisses her angels goodnight,
Then tucks them safely away in the wind.

Heather Playford

"A Mother's Regrets"

He stood at the door, so quiet, so small,
  Watching me hurriedly stuff my purse with keys and all.
His big brown eyes filled with tears, and I heard him say:
  "Mommie, do you have to doe to wort today?"

I hugged his tiny body and replied
  "You be a good little boy and I'll be back this
evening and we'll take our little ride."

That little boy that stood at the door so long ago, and
  tearfully watched me leave for work, is now a grown man.
There are times, however, when I catch a glimpse of tears,
  And I long to hug him, in spite of the passing years.

How I wish I could go back in time and erase the memories
  of that little sad face.
I'd say: "No, Mommie will not go to work today, (or ever).
  We'll bake cookies, color books, and make this home
a happy place."

Helen Paulsen

"The Movie"

I am the person sitting in the dark theater.
Watching the screen, sensing the changes, knowing I am
Watching my life. Feeling it rushing past me and perceiving
All I really need to do is to reach out a finger and
Caress its essence, taste its rich taste.
But, all the while knowing if I dare touch the screen I
Will be forever changed. No more will I be able to just
Watch life go by, but now I will have to reach out with
Both hands and drag it from the very depths of its
Essence and make it purely my own.
I must reach out, I have to, but it is so much safer to
Only sit. But, oh! What I'm missing! Love sweet and soft,
Laughter soft as tinkling bells, and tears fresh as dew
On a leaf. Do I have the strength? Can I have the
Will to live, to breathe, to exist? Yes! I will touch life!
I must if I am to grow and achieve and enrich my life, as
well as my children's! But, alas the question I still must
Ask is, "Would you?"

Annemarie Jacobsen

"We," As In "We"

We marched with Martin Luther King.
We clapped when Nat King Cole would sing.

We understood words of Malcolm X.
We knew the days of Tubman were complex.

We cheered on rightfully Muhammad Ali.
We spent time figuring out Mr. T.

We felt the sting of Scott Joplin.
We heard James Brown and our fingers were poppin'.

We read good books by Alice Walker.
We knew 'The Color Purple' would be a talker.

We loved Miles, and Coltrane.
We heard Lil' Richard and went insane,

We supported the trail of Rosa Parks.
We saw our children dying in the dark.

We heard the speeches of Jesse Jackson.
"Where's Gwendolyn Brooks?" the readers are askin'.

We cried through 'Roots' and wiped the tears.
We have struggled for equality for so many years.

We know what happened in the Jordan River.
We must continue believing only God can deliver.

Charlotte L. Easley

To A Young Near-Suicide

Wait. Death smells like the mouse
we found in the swimming pool one spring
in gray pieces. Don't taste it. Don't go any closer.

Death courts like a cocaine God, promising
hieros gamos. An unwary raccoon struggling in the woods
with mask awry found out differently:

death's wedding ring strangles. The gold-
gleaming door leads to torn steaming metal,
the love poem is doused with gasoline,

and you, pale, delicate moth caught up
in blue-fizzling electric light, turtle infant
staring with innocent eyes at the diving hawk,

are mesmerized by the energy of destruction.
Your grand passion is an unrequited love; your offering
will be trampled and spurned. I could tell you to run,

but you, lemming, would only fall over the cliff.
Freeze here. Be a rabbit, and in an hour's time,
the charming wild ash-colored wolf will hunt elsewhere.

Jill Hammer

Reflections

We come, we go, we follow, we lead, ever continuing the ancient deeds.
We greet the morning with hope, we weep as the moon departs,
while uttering silently, stand still my heart.

A smile, a tear, as we ascend the mighty grade; we stretch out our arms while our feet are firmly planted on unsteady ground; pondering the impending harvest while tampering weeds.

The sun becomes bright, the sky a crystal blue, while the great mother "Terra Firma" gives birth, covered with her wet silvery veil as cries of pain and joy emits. With motherly pride she presents her new born son and exhorts all to respond with love. Sounds of the dove; sounds of the mole; lead a thunderous chorus in singing, we do, we do, we do.

Forty years are now past, a new year begins, in the school of life a mark has been made. The ancient deeds continue, eternally old but forever new. The morning is greeted with hope and the moon no longer departs. While the pondering of the harvest continues in the heart.

Joseph M. Steward

The Infamous Weeds

We are the infamous weeds;
We live in your garden, flowerpot and yard.

Damned are we when uprooted;
And angry we become.
Yet as you will soon discover tomorrow noon or night,
We breed and breed and breed.

So strong our love for life,
Our race left us to doom,
But through every storm we stand straight.

They fall those others,
Call them flowers if you must.
Weak, crippled, wanted.

Unwanted are we weeds within a bouquet,
Corruption; we feed.
Dancing through the night in the deceased garden.

Resentment profound,
Crying to daddy dandelion,
The song of strength abound.

Juliana Belmore

Survivors Triumphant

"Kids of the depression" was what we were
We never knew it back then, I am sure -
Everyone took poverty in their stride
No matter what happened we took it with pride!

We never heard of robberies, killings, or drugs
Except from the radio, we'd hear of some "thugs."
The real depression come for us one Sunday
When World War II blackened our way!

Somehow most of us survived it all
And did all the things necessary I recall.
That's why we can never throw anything away
Instead we just save it for a "rainy day."

Through it all, I've pondered it in my mind
How can we have happy memories of those times?
Then I know it was because of our father and mother
Who taught us courage, trust, and love for each other.

I really think, it doesn't much matter
Whether you have steak or spaghetti on your platter
All that it takes is to trust in the Lord
And He'll give you than you could ever afford!

Cora June Dykstra

Memories

She and I were great friends.
We played everyday,
And laughed every night.
We had so much fun,
She and I.
For five years you couldn't pull us apart.
I knew what a best friend was.
Now, the friendship has faded.
I moved away from what we had.
She found new friends,
And I did the same.
Even though the friendship is lost,
The memories will always be strong.

Carin M. Hansen

The Day I Lost My Best Friend

He was my best friend of all.
We played in the leaves during fall.
And in winter we played with snowballs.
He was there through thick and thin,
No matter what happened as a team we would win.
In the spring he loved chasing frogs.
But sadly one night he was hit by a car, in the fog.
So now he is gone.
Boy do I miss my dog.

Bonnie Hart

The Long Race

We race toward we know not what, in our great desire to win.
We race headlong down life's long road, from the moment we begin.

We stumble and fall and jump to our feet, as we race on down the road.
We do not notice the one there beside us, who carries the heavier load

As up hill and down hill we race both far and near.
Never stopping to smell a beautiful rose or a birds sweet song to hear

We pass both friend and stranger, as we bound over brook and stream.
Sometimes we leave our loved ones, just to follow a childish dream.

The longer we race the older we get, the further away are our dreams.
The road goes on and further on, and gets steeper and rougher it seems

So we better slow down 'ere we come to the ridge, daylight fades away.
For over the ridge is a long bridge, a light shines showing the way.

Where our dreams can come true, for Christ waits there for you.
And we will be rich, and prosper in whatever we do.

So watch for the one that might need your helping hand,
As they take their stand, and stumble over steep and rough land.

Then as you reach that land, where you must take your stand,
You will find those called, "God's little band."

For God's angels will furnish the music as we enter God's city so fair
We will shout and praise God and thank Jesus, because we made it there.

Harry D. Palmer Sr.

"Rob"

Biting my neck and stroking my hair
Were just some things to let me know you care
Your humorous ways and insane smile
Are what makes my days all worthwhile
Many of your characters with many a voice
The character of Rob will always be my choice
Long talks on the phone and some crazy beeps
This is a friendship that may forever keep
Whether it be a party or a high school prom
Remember me in good times even when I'm gone
Hershey kisses will someday sog
But those kisses aren't as sweet as the ones by ROB.

Damaris Veguilla

What Are Friends?

Friends we were, but no more.
We shared laughter, tears, and everything.
Things you did made me sing.
We laughed a lot, had things to say.

I'm the one who was hurt;
Your talk was trite and curt.
You found some excuse
For verbal abuse.

I'm the one who always called,
You never answered.
I'm the one who always fell.
You never helped me up.

I'm the one who always wrote,
I never heard from you.

You felt you were owed an apology.
You received it from me,
But you never write or call.
Please help me the next time I fall.
Dorothy E. Trupiano

Goodbye Dear Friend

We shared our laughter
We shared our tears
Our friendship grew throughout the years
Her many stories that filled her life
A caring mother a loving wife
She did her best to always give
And we all know she loved to live
Her many journeys throughout this world will not compare to
This, for in his kingdom he has made
A special place for her
To watch below from Heaven above
To give her soul and share his love
Her body weak her heart so strong
She fought so hard to carry on
For to the end she never let known what her eyes would say
The questions she had the worries she felt leaving all behind
But in my heart I know that now my Sharon's on her way
I hear her voice I feel her touch, I know
She loved you all so much, so goodbye for now
My dear, dear friend for we will all meet in the end!!!
Heidi Sue Post

Vilma

I knew an illustrated Venus.
We struck it rich for a time being.
Might've felt a threat but I felt a thrill.
Dark rum and darker eyes laughing in East Side bars.
Legs sticking out on a Hoboken sidestreet
Face to face with the hothouse flower.
In a peak of prime, I have souvenirs saved.

Seems like I lived my life backwards
It should've been the '50's or in our teens
I'm getting old and you're a mom
You said I was naughty, I bow to that honor
I've always had a passion for cigarette girls.
These were the days of wine and roses.

I was too weak to stay just friends
Damn that Doo Wop night
"Evils of the flesh" claimed a friend, and she was right.
Too short but very sweet
Frozen smile in a frame
I damn the Doo Wop night.
John McDermott

Dream

Come with me into the sinuous twilight.
We will taste the moonbeams
As they break against the moist grass,
And listen to the crickets as they sing in the stillness.

Follow me into the breathless heat of the summer night.
We will walk underneath a star-struck sky,
And feel the earth's seething heart.

I will touch you with the throbbing, half-remembered
   tenderness of fading passions,
You will hold me with the strength
   of forgotten heartbreaks.
We will lose ourselves in trembling fingers and ravenous lips
And our blood will rush to the sound of the rain
   as it moves among silent trees.

In summer's twilight,
Memories lie floating on the green - gold grass
And fling their seeds into the air.
Let us go into the verdant night
And hear the heartbeats of the stars
And gaze forever with sightless eyes.
Anna Krauthammer

"A Kiss For Eternity"

Our friendship grew, right from the start
We'd laugh, we'd smile, and we'd talk a lot
Then suddenly, when all was still
Our lives became entwined
With a gentle, soft and warm first kiss
We brought worlds together, we could have missed
As time went on that kiss did grow
Into all the love of a pure white snow
In all the ways that love grows deep
From the tips of our heads
To the soles of our feet
The years would come and the years would go
Our love just deepened, as the ocean flows
For in my arms he chose to lie
With his gorgeous white hair and his beautiful brown eyes
It wasn't in life that we did part
But in his death, of a broken heart.
Ann Kew

What Happened?

What has happened to America, the "Land of the Brave and Free"?
What has happened to truth and justice, and the values of family?
What has happened to our youth, as we are compared worldwide,
What has happened to this great land, where values did once abide?

I remember a time when a man would walk more than a country mile
To pay a debt, return a favor, and this he'd do with a smile.
There was a time when there was no need to lock your car or door
Where if you tried hard, and did your part, it was no disgrace to
   be poor.

I remember a time, when the flag passed by, one stood straight and tall,
As the band played our national anthem, from the eye a tear might fall
And patriotism was a built-in concept for which a man might die
Remembered by the marching throngs who parade on the Fourth of July.

It's still the greatest country that can be found on the face of the earth
It's still a land of which we can be proud, this land that gave us birth.
It still has freedom, and truth, and justice; we still have our family
But something is lacking, I must confess, now just what can it be?

I think I've got it, I think I know, exactly what we need,
Please listen close to what I say and to this thought give heed.
It's on the coin we use every day and I believe we must
Go back and do just what it says, it says **"In God we trust!"**
Buz Spooner

Reality

What is black and white? A figment or a pigment?
We come seeking success and riches, but only a few
attain anything and millions crowd the streets.
Homeless, runaways, and the addicted lost in a maze
of concrete and uncertainty. Life is a cruel joke
or ice cream on a hot day. What we expected
never existed and what we have we don't want.
Never satisfied and always coveting, it's the American way.
We can't co-exist we just do. Blind and
deaf and sometimes speechless, we march along in
a monotone. In the end we all lie down
in the dirt, and some will smile for what they
did and some will smile for what they left,
but most will smile because they are not here.
Here is where dreams are destroyed by reality and roaches.

David A. Shaw

The Affair

With only a glance setting us aglow
We danced till the other side of midnight's fire
Embraced we'd gone beyond a daydream
Gently melting into shadows
Harboring pleasure, passion untold
Though not binding our rendez-vous
'Twas sustained with a softness
Bringing shared moments of discretion knowing no compare
Flirting in the temptation of romance was emotionally undenied
Although a veil of unspoken words held golden truths
Secretive eye would whisper clearly
Till sealed fate brought a struggle of blinding conscience
The final pull into lightness was heartfelt
All the tomorrows have become innocent
With no bridges burned
Sublime will be the memories without regret

James Martinsson

Remembering Remembering

My friend and I were chatting in the mall.
We drank our coffee as we stopped to rest.
We paused to rest because we did not want to fall,
Exhausted, as we exercised our best.
She had a problem to discuss with me.
She wondered where she put her credit cards;
Could not remember where her watch could be;
"Who was that woman sending `best regards?'
And now you wonder why I'm so upset?"
She said she bought a book on "Memory"
To teach her tricks so she would not forget.
She could not find her keys and jewelry.

"It would not help my memory to look.
I don't remember where I put the book."

Ellen Matilda Hudson

Where Are We Going?

Where am I going? Why am I here?
What does it matter, time's not so dear.
Where are you going? Why are you here?
We're here together, more far than near.
Why not get closer, shed coat of fear.
Let heart unbind you; let fall that tear.

Everyone's needed to do his part,
If we are ever to make a start.
Life's not worth living if no one cares;
If God's the dollar and no one shares.
New days are dawning. Where do you stand?
Will you be yawning? Are you so grand?

Elizabeth A. Radojcic

I Want To Love You

We were formed with the same mix;
welded with guilt bond to hurt us.
So
I sent pure love to warm you
to
feel it cut with doubts and frostbites.

Hurt
I bathed my wounds and still tried,
To have
that trick smile hide your real blades
of mistrust, self-love and twisted thoughts.

I felt cold air from your fan
force me back, yet stop just close enough
for me to be there for you
and taste your thin love offer.

My guilt bonds don't scold me.
They know I want to love you.

Dorothy Randle Clinton

We Who Once Did Love

We have stored our beauty in a vault of aloneness;
We have been thrown aside to be Fate's tools.
Our souls will forever wander homeless:
This world will judge us as pitiful fools.
Yet, once we were crowned by Love's own joys.
We sang with the birds that floated in air -
Ah, now we find we were only toys,
And the nursery is dank and bare.

Once we thrilled to a glorious spring;
We rode with the wind of the open roads;
We whispered soft words where the ivy clings,
And sensed a deep yearning to know Life's code.
Now, ours is only the right to dream:
To set aside for ourselves one hour,
For the cool, soothing waters of memory's stream -
To rest in tall grasses, our love-scented bower.

Evelyn R. Paris

My Beautiful

My beautiful!
The first day of the spring, the world so still,
Blues skies, a cry of color on each hill...
As dreaming, over magic roads we fled,
Not caring where the sun-warmed trail led;
And drunk with rapture felt the vagrant breeze,
So cool on the half-closed eyes, as if to please
My beautiful!

My beautiful!
The first night of the spring, the stars in flight,
The moon so wan in amorous delight...
And then I heard your golden burst of song,
A fluted melody, re-echoing so long
It seemed a dream, an ecstasy apart,
Ah, sing that song against my heart,
My beautiful!

Remy Hudson

The Wind Chime

The clock ticks the passing of time
The breeze gently flows through the wind chime
Creating a lonely sound
The street is empty no one to be found
With the moon full in the sky
The shapes on the chime play as the wind passes by

Linda Praznik

"The Window"

Lady sitting at the window,
   What do you see?
Are your eyes beholding sky
   And grass and trees?
No, I think something different
   May be before your eyes
A little girl is playing underneath
   Past days' blue skies.

Do you see her laughing,
   Unaware of coming rain?
As you sit there looking out
   Can you still feel her pain?
Does she pray and cry
   To see her "momma" once again?

Lady, your window is getting hazy
   And the view is growing dim.
So, I'll meet you here tomorrow
   And we'll look out once again.

June Metzmeier

Look It Up

A smiling girl once asked me,
"What does `antiseptic' mean?"
I think it was my error
to have answered, "Super clean."

A day had scarcely past
before she asked the question twice,
and I decided there and then
replying wasn't nice.

For if she was to earn and own
the knowledge that she sought,
She had to learn that knowledge
was by only effort bought.

And so I answered, "Look it up,"
in tones both stern and true.
Certain that the harder way
was easiest to do.

I didn't get this wisdom
from a book upon a shelf,
but I, too, had a father
who said, "Look it up yourself."

James Timothy Kelly

For Cupid

Were I to ask of you again
What I received so long ago,
You'd maybe think I asked too much.
But surely you can aim once more
And strike an older, colder heart
That needs and seeks
The warmth of mine.

Ethel S. Botnick

Not You

I thought I heard
your voice the other day
but it was someone else.
I thought I saw
your face the other day
but it was someone else.
My heart skipped
at a word
at a glance.
For just a moment it was you.
And then it was someone else.

Dana Freed

Change

Friend of mine,
what is new?
My life's not the same
when I'm not with you!

Things get crazy,
things get strange,
things get weird
when there's a change!

Life changes rapidly,
life changes slow,
but why does it change?
I really want to know.

What is happening?
Anything new?
Have you changed?
I really miss you!

A friend can be old,
a friend can be new,
all I care is that
a friend is you!

Heather Quast

What Of

What of life that I have seen
What of hopes and dreams
What of love that walks away
What of tricks and schemes

What of all that matters when -
A shadow hides the sun
What of all those special things
When that precious day is done

I have much to think about
Of His wisdom do I share
I find His peace and solitude
In knowing someone cares.

Arthur W. Carey

ON READING THE LA TIMES

What the hell's going on, God?
What's it all about?
I'm a Cro Magnon looking up at the stars.
Cold...hungry....wondering.....
I'm a woman with a baby at my breast.
Baby sucking...sucking...sucking...
Is this all there is?
So what's it all about?
God?
The Big Question - not What?
Not When? - not How?
But WHY?
The Big Answer - you don't know either!
You busted out of the Big NoWhere
Into the Big Here
Just like the rest of us!
I'm laughing!
Laughing.....

Don Alva Johnson

Shell Of The Future

In the dark that isn't night,
When hope is but a glint of light;
When paths chosen cannot be changed,
Don't look back nor cross them twain;
For through patience and determined will,
A heart empty will again be filled.

Judy W. Ousley

Hand In The Dark

You're sound asleep in the dark.
When a hand touches you,
Starting you awake.
Voice saying it will be alright.
But you are scared and afraid.
Then you beg, please don't,
No, No please don't,
Tears run from your face.
By morning light.
Your whole world has changed.
You are scarred and,
Changed forever in a way.
Some people can never understand.
You will live in fear.
Never be able to completely.
Trust anyone again ever.
All thanks to one, you used to trust,
And a hand in the dark.

Belinda A. Linkous

The Man Who Gave Me Life

He wasn't around
When he was needed
For many many years
I've grown up feeling cheated
He never called
Never sent a letter,
Or money for support.
Then one day
Out of the blue
I hear a familiar voice
Over my phone,
He says he wants to see me.
What's the point though?
I'm all grown up now
I don't need a father
He left when I needed him
So, all he'll ever be to me
Is "A Man Who Gave Me Life."

Ebony Moore

"The Things God Does For Me"

Silently, he speaks to me,
When my mind is at peace and clear,
He gives words so sweet to me,
It's music to my ear.

He let me know that he watches me,
And knows all the things I do,
And he tells me when things go wrong,
He will always see me through.

He stretches forth his arms,
And I feel his warm embrace,
That he loves and keeps me,
While I run this race.

Annie Mae Monroe

Tomorrow Is Gone

I reach to touch...
Why is it I cannot feel?

I lay and dream...
Which is nightmare which is real?

I sob and cry...
Where are the words I did not say?

Tomorrow is gone...
Why can't I forget yesterday?

Ida Apponi

Spring

I didn't hear a bugle blow.
When spring arrived today.
Nor did I hear the whole world shout,
Along the springtide sound.
Of song birds everywhere.
The gentle breezes, humming bees.
The wild geese in the air,

I didn't see a big fanfare.
When spring came by our way,
nor did I see a festive feast
to mark this gladsome day.
Instead I saw rebirth of life.
A world of blossoming;
oh yes I saw the first spring.
John Joseph Kunco

Faith

Why do we weep and worry so
when things go wrong and troubles grow?
Have we no faith to just believe
when sorrows cause our hearts to grieve?
We may not understand it all
when disappointments come to call,
But GOD has promised to be there
and I call his name in prayer.
We know that he is on our side
for in our hearts he shall abide,
until the rivers cease to flow
and autumn winds refuse to blow.
For GOD is great, his word is true
and there is nothing he can't do.
So rest assured that GOD is near
and wipe away that silver tear!
Georgia Merchant

Tools And Keys

Money is a dreadful tool
when used to measure worth.
Ill-begotten, it rapes our soul
and criminalizes birth.

Love and empathy is a better way
to flow in life's new school.
Give everyone a hope and chance
to grow beyond the fool.

Education is a key
unlocking info's doors.
Each teacher is a student too
in mutually sharing chores.

When opportunity is as free
as Nature's running waters,
we'll see the worth of Humanity
in radiant sons and daughters.
Carolyn Ashe Stokes

To A Robin

Herald of the spring!
With joy and hope and love,
Your clear notes ring,
Conveying thought above
Vain need.

How warmly welcome is your gay intrusion
Upon a world made weary with confusion
Of strife and greed.
Ferne Eikenberry

The Magnificent River

There's a river in the mountains,
    Where I long to be again,
Where the Rhododendron whispers
    As Arbutus past it winds.

'Tis the cherished river "Gauley"
    Where nature seems to smile each day,
And the sunbeams kiss the ripples
    As they hurry on their way.

Ah! You river..How majestic!
    Striving onward toward your goal.
May the tiny brooks that join you,
    Find a haven for their soul.

Now I'm older, time is fleeting,
    In my heart you'll always be,
Another gift of God's creation,
    You will live eternally.
John Young

Horse And Rider

What is this sport they call
Where man and horse run for it all.

With forms of grace and speed
The jockey mounts his steed.

Together they become one
Off to the gates, my son.

With a lurch, forward they go
Hearts a pounding ever so.

Fleeting legs turn the bend
Coming nearer to the end.

The whip strikes its side
In hope of a quicker stride.

Down the stretch they come
But glory only to some.

A bed of roses is their prize
With the motto 'He who tries.'

They will ride again some day
For horse and rider will always stay.
David M. Doonan

Ann

There's a hole in my family
where my sister used to be
and I stumble in that hole
all too frequently

I think I never realized
the importance of her part
as the one that I could turn to
for wisdom from the heart

Will I ever learn to live
without her calming voice
her greater understanding
of life and love and choice

So here I am without her
or so it sometimes seems,
but her spirit still surrounds me
and visits in my dreams

And one day we will meet again
and fly the great blue sky
and she'll be there to act as guide
when it's my turn to die.
Cecilia B. Jones

Hidden Secret Undry

The geography of the white mountains
    where the great basin
is desert cracked and dry
pin stripe snow hidden secret undry

Culture was in shadow of arrow
    the shadow of ancient
clock work of space sophistication
survival voice hidden secret undry

The sea cannot claim
    its lost water untamed
the great basin water
modern hidden secret undry

Voice songs echo
    in remembered and wash
gone and lost forever more
modern hidden secret undry

Lost way up clouds
    seem to guide and summit
leaving us wandering rampart
hidden secret undry
Isabelle Hunter

"Heaven"

There is a place so far away some
where there is nothing but white clouds
and a "Golden Gate"
This place is called "Heaven"
This is the place some people
think where God is, I believe
that this place is to start a new
beginning, there are people you cared
about but now are not with you,
are now waiting for you at
that "Golden Gate."
Like someday I hope to see
my father and both of my aunts
To say how much I love
and miss them so, and to say
I am with them for eternity.
Betty Richardson

Wonderful Earth

The day begins
When the sun comes up
I pour the tea
Into my coffee cup.

As I look out my window
I notice the trees.
It will be a wonderful day
To go along with the cool breeze.

When I walk outside
A smile comes over my face.
I'm very happy to see
This wonderful place.

Now the day has come and gone
It seems it just flew by.
The trees look like they're sleeping
Beautiful stars fill the sky.

I love this place
The home of my birth
I am extremely delighted
To live on this wonderful Earth.
Constance Gibson

Imagine

Imagine
A world of silver and gold
Where you forever stay young
And never grow old.

Imagine.

No drugs, no alcohol, no war,
just peace. If dreams came true
and skies were always blue.

Imagine.

If rain forests were never discovered,
something you lost was always recovered.

Imagine.
Every child born was healthy,
no person was poor or wealthy.

Imagine.

If no one got hurt, killed or raped,
if no one ever made a mistake.

Donna Myles

Black Child

Black child, black child
Wherever you are
Stand up,
Be counted,
You can be a star.

Black child, black child
Do your best in school
Learn to read,
Learn to write,
Don't be anybody's fool.

Black child, black child
Keep climbing to the top
Always keep a positive attitude
Keep on climbing and never stop.

Black child, black child
Always keep your faith
Walk around obstacles
And do whatever it takes.

Celious Binion

For Heather

Hither, thither blows the heather.
"Whether? Whither?" it forever whispers.
"Whither? Whether?" wafts the wind,
Walking lovers on the strand.

Wildly, warily roam forever.
Tentative tethers twine together.
Gather, give her flowers whether
night is silver or is sand.

Dither, waver talk together
over whither and of whether.
Bring each other close together
'neath the light of crescent band.

Quiver, shiver in the heather,
parting once and once forever.
Yet never ever completely severed,
leaving slowly, hand in hand.

Hither, thither blows the heather.
"Whether? Whither?" it forever whispers.
"Whither? Whether?" wafts the wind,
blowing heather on the strand.

Elizabeth Dahm

That Hang On The Vine

War's not in the heart
Which pumps bright blood
Waking up love,
And songs from small children
Who hang on the vine.

War's not in the soul,
Illuminator of man's
Immortality,
Bringing down star thoughts
To hang on the vine.

War's in the belly
Where vile gases stir
Blowing out stink,
Killing fair flowers
That hang on the vine.

And when war is over,
What hangs on the vine?
Strips of flesh and broken bones,
Carrion bait is all
That's left on the vine.

Jack W. Kerr

A Chance at Life

Lacy curtains form shaded pictures
While tear-stained faces grieve
For youth swiftly passing
And mid years yet retrieved

With maturity a dose of mirth
Mixed and plied into form
Of what is coming tomorrow
For the tasks we must perform

Tomorrow's gift is yesterday's promise
Coddled in protective arms
Seeded and growth-inspired
Shielding us from harm

Contentment arrives slowly
Like raging winds turned weak
A haven in life's harbor
Where the strong abide the meek

A view into the future
Do we have the strength to see
Blindfolds neatly placed
Unbound and at last free

Ellen Bernstein

Untitled

Take walk - relax in woods
While your health is right…
While the cold - don't freeze you yet
Or the sun - don't overheat.
While the wind - don't overblow
Or the rain don't overflow!
Weather - controls everyone ..
Without - any plan…
We have plans - that contradict…—…
Hard - to analyze…-
Weather is in charge of you…-
Does not matter - what you do…-
Am walking - in forest
So peaceful is there!
Sun still - shining…
But fading fast here
So lonely - to rest in dark!
Moon will take over
To light Woodland again - to save all from darkness…

John A. Schlesser

Don't Pay Attention To The Preacher

A woman leans over to
Whisper
A sentiment to an old friend.
A note is passed through
Many hands before reaching
To whom it is addressed.
Giggling from the youth
Echoes throughout the
Sanctuary.
Rattling candy wrappers
Supersede the message,
God's message.
Who is more important
Than God?
Not a soul.

Jennifer Jackson

Dark

Some skin is black
Who cares? So what?
You look inside and you think
  and see
"His heart has no hate, unlike
  me"
Look at your own heart, hey wait!
Your heart is covered in violence and hate!!

Dev Priya Ranjan

Ode To A First Nephew

O little man so fair
Who, crowned with red-gold hair
Has up and stolen Auntie's heart
Quite unaware!

Jeffrey David is your name
And ever since you came
Your Auntie's outlook on the world
Is not the same!

Who knew, before your birth
What each new day was worth?
In you I see the very best
Of Heav'n and Earth!

Barbara Z. Myers

Angel In White

There's an angel in white,
Who from heaven was sent.
To keep watch day and night,
Over those, who misfortune has spent.

This maid who so seldom receives,
The glory of fortune and fame.
Yet ever alert, to suppress and relieve,
Those, in whose presence are in pain.

With a noble mind to inspire,
Her work with tender care.
Undaunted, by consequences of tire,
To the cause, she did pledge to bear.

In war, as in peace,
Whether days be dark or bright,
Her vigilance seldom does cease,
This mortal, who I call angel in white.

Edward Winiasz

Untitled

I once had a cat name Tom.
Who loved cats without any harm.
He met up with a vixen
Who didn't want any mixin'
And now Tom's no longer warm.

I once has a dog named Rover
Who played on the White-cliffs of Dover.
He was very brave
As he jumped into the wave
When the ball went over.
Now, it's over with Rover!
Bella Wein

My Joy

I look at this girl
who once was my baby,
she's growing up fast
to be quite a young lady.

Gone are the days
of ribbon and lace,
with little ruffled panties
and a chubby chipmunk face.

Now she's involved
in phone calls and boys,
and driving my car
which has become her new toy.

But time has a way of flying
as swift as the wind,
Soon she'll be leaving
an empty room where she's been.

I think of her now
as I start to grin,
I gave birth to a daughter
but also a friend.
Anna Moore

This Beast

Who is this beast
Who wants to feast
On people large and small?
He is the one who has the mark,
the largest of them all.
He is the one who fights all men
and rages through our towns
He is the one who lies, wants fame
The Beast, that is his name
But people, how nice it seems to be
the wonders of this beast to see,
Let no one step away from God
stay close together, because if not;
you will forever see the flame
and no one else, but you to blame.
Johanna Shastsky

Gone Astray

When the sun goes away,
Will your heart be led astray?
Will you think of me always,
Or am I just another maze?
Just another step for you,
Will you go without a clue?
Will you love me, will you care;
Will you look back, will you dare?
Will I ever see you again,
Or will I wonder 'till the end?
Comfort Ibe

Christ Is Christmas

We thank God for His precious Son
who was born on Christmas Day,
His birthplace not a mansion
just a manger filled with hay.
He grew up in poor surroundings
yet far richer than any man,
He preached, He healed, He suffered
as he traveled on this land.
We will celebrate in many ways
this beautiful Christmas Season,
but no matter how we celebrate
we must never forget the reason.
This firm, but very gentle Christ
left a gift beneath our tree,
A very special Christmas gift
His great love for you and me.
Let us pray this gift of love
will remove the barrier of strife,
Then our Rock and our Redeemer
becomes the Way, the Truth, and the Life.
Dorothy V. Uthes

Little By Little

Little by little...
Who would have known
The changes this world
Inevitably has shown.

From the treasured wisdom of long ago...
To the problems of insolvency
We must now forego.

Little by little...
Will we learn to live
With the pain and misfortune
The world has to give.

From the harrowing experiences
That are left untold..
To the perils of life that do unfold.

Little by little...
Do we turn our face
Or conform to the changes yet to take
place.

From within our hearts the answer deems
For this is still a place
To fulfill your dreams.
Jessica Powers

Let Me Understand

God hates the gut full cry.
Why am I a poet?
Why am I a star?
Why do I have friends so far?
Why do I feel?
Why do I smell?
Why do I cry?
Why do I angry?
Why do I have so much?
Why is there sun?
Why were there Romans?
Why do I know?
What do I know?
Id like to know nothing!
Why do I want?
Why am I still unborn?
Why do I still ignore?
Why am I war?
Let me understand.
Anna Avetissian

I'm Letting Go

Why must this dream come to an end,
Why must we live our life as friends,
I said I love you, now you're gone,
Someday you'll see that you were wrong.

You showed me that you didn't care,
I'd need you and you weren't there,
To give support when I was down,
And now you'll never be around.

I'm letting go, I'm letting go,
Who needs a love that doesn't show;
It hurts so much to see you now,
Thinking of you just brings me down.

My love for you will never end,
Even though you'll only be my friend,
I lived the dream I was your man,
That's why it's hard to understand.

Were we in love or was I wrong,
Remember how we got along,
Two people never laughed so much,
Oh how I still long for your touch.
Charles Hutter

"America"

Oh America, great land of dream,
why should we be so full of greed.
Oh America, great land of opportunity
you stand, yet we as a different nation
failed to unite as you stand for
justice and liberty in the land for
each and every one.
Oh America, so shall your name
ring across the universe to make
our need and greed be at peace.
Oh America, beautiful America,
land of God as you shall always
stand we take no time to understand
how great you are for each and
every one. I love you America, I
hope everyone can understand that you
are that land helping each and
every one.
Elaine V. Morgan

If All The World Knew Leslie

If all the world knew Leslie,
With her laughing, sparkling eyes,
Not many hates or wars
Would be likely to arise.

For how can you hate your neighbor,
Or plot of hurts and harms,
When you feel the warmth and love,
Within those little arms.

If all the world knew Leslie,
Could see her laugh and smile,
The world would be a better place,
If, but for a little while.

The world is full of wrongs and wars,
Of walls and misery,
But if all the world loved Leslie
Just half as much as me,

There'd be no room for walls, or hate,
Or hurt or misery.

Our hearts and lives would just have room
For love and joy and beauty.
Donna Wright

Nocturnal Flights

My dreams are my wings,
wings of the night.
Far away they carry me
from the pains seen in light.

Rain girls dancing,
their sparkling reflections
young and laughing. The city is
beautiful with their blossoming.

And darkness, misty
and damp, things unseen...
Yet with fear I search them out,
and find truth, at least, in their shame.

My wings are my dreams,
dreams of the night.
Bring to me the beauty
of things hidden from sight.

David R. Stanley

The Seasons

There are four seasons,
winter, spring, summer, and fall
there are four seasons,
I love them all.

Spring, on that lovely day
the warm breeze
during May

Summer, the flowers in bloom,
stars in the clear night sky,
during June

The one I love most
winter, rain and snow
during December

Fall, leaves turning color
flowers are dying
during October

So those are the seasons
winter, spring, summer, and fall
those wonderful seasons
I love them all.

Barbara Armstrong

Music On The Breeze

Music on the breeze
Wind in the trees
Whispers among the leaves
   Have you heard them?

Baby birds in a nest
Butterflies at rest
A rainbow in the west
   Have you seen them?

A dog's lick on your hand
The sting from blowing sand
The quaking of the land
   Have you felt them?

Aromas that tickle your nose
The petals of a rose
Snowflakes when the wind blows
   Have you tasted them?

Laundry on a line
Cucumbers pickled in brine
Dandelion wine
   Have you smelled them?

Edna Mae Lowell

Needling Thoughts

A tiny little needle,
with a little bit of thread,
can produce a million thoughts,
from just one little head.

A tiny little needle
with a little bit of thread
can fill a heart with so
much love
I think I will use more thread

Dolores Hale

His Love

God woke me this morning
   with birds singing loud.
A wonderful feeling spread over me,
   making me feel so very proud.

He reached out and told me to listen,
   for he knew the turmoil within.
I stopped, I listened, I heard
   his promise to free me from all sin.

His love is filling the universe.
   His arms and hands open wide.
Reaching, forever reaching for us,
   leaving no one a place to hide.

He smiled down on me this day
   as I reached for his hand.
My heart was filled to its limit,
   like time in the hour-glass sand.

Now my life belongs to Jesus.
   He'll stand by me forevermore.
I know this means through eternity;
   because he has opened Heaven's door.

Bessie L. Likovetz

Walking On The Water

Walking on the water
With Jesus holding my hand
Life can be so troubled
Sometimes, I don't think I can

But like with Peter, He says
Come, take these few steps with me
From the waves of troubles and fears
I will deliver you safely

But the swells of my ocean engulf me
And, I too, begin to sink
My fears too large, my faith too small
I forget to think

All I need to do is trust Jesus
Then I can be totally free
Jesus reached down for Peter
And He will reach down for me.

Jean Loudermilk

The Competition

Sweaty palms, aching muscles.
Your name is called.
The unsmiling judges,
Watch as you walk by.
The time has come.

Exhaustedly you sit down.
Waiting for the score.
Knowing you did
Your very best.

Jacob Barnhill

Regardless

I rest my flowers
with loving care
on your bed of earth
and
over-grown grass

Voiceless is your hollow grave
Nonetheless
everlasting is your presence
since with you
I share a human purpose
Regardless
of what you and I
and all the others
ultimately
would have wanted.

Etty Mainenti

Untitled

Your head pounds,
   with the irreversible illusions
   of reality,
Cooking secretly
   without ingredients.

People assuming
   what others want,
Encompassing total ridiculousness
   when trying to be philosophical.
Idleness streaming
   from every vein of imagination,
   disturbing the apex of prejudice.

Feeling apart
   at the touch of a look,
Pushing away this temptation
   to search for selfishness.

Joyce R. Barnes

Pleasant Folks

Lord let me live
With the pleasant folks
Who have their fun
And crack their jokes

Who sing their songs
And have their cheer
Who are content
With being here

Folks who can laugh
For laughter sake
Nor deem this world
One vast mistake

But take this life
For what its worth
And don't expect
A heaven on earth

Jennie Strayer

To My Wife Helen

years have swiftly gone and yet
you look to me as you did then
when young, and lovely, I first met
your gentleness in the care of men
and women, who looked up and smiled;
Your Irish charm had us beguiled.

Hubert C. Huebl

Bundle Of Love

Beautiful baby girl
With tiny smile so sweet,
You bless our lives
With each and every heartbeat.

Precious bundle of love
With eyes of deep blue,
You light up our world,
Making troubles seem few.

Lovely skin soft as silk,
Hair dark as night,
You fill hearts with pride
And make burdens light.

To each day comes joy,
As lonely lives you touch.
A lusty cry, a quiet sigh,
We love you so much!

Beautiful baby girl,
You bless us with love
Creating visions of hope.
For you, we thank God above.

Dorothy A. Wallace

I Am Alone With You

I am alone with you.
Without meaning words are words alone.
These emanating from my mind
For you
Have a different connotation,
That I am with you and you alone.

I am alone with you.
The very same words
Spoken by my lips,
Passing through my heart,
Are saying: I am alone.
I just happen to be with you
When I am alone.

I am alone with you.
I am alone with you.
Identical words.
You hear: I am alone with you.
I hear: I am alone
With you.

Alberta S. Lynch

Memories

Memories are such a
wonderful part of life.
To remember back what
great times we had.
The love we shared
between each other.
The fun time we
had together.
The unhappy times
we disliked each other.
The embarrassing time
we laughed at each other.
The bad things we did together
The sad times we cried together.
It was fun while it lasted.
but now all we have is
the memories to remember.
Where ever you go, what ever you do
remember, memories are always there.

Ebony Edwards

Me

A baby blanket
wrapped in twine
around a brass statuette
on the mantle
in front of the mirror

Jacquelyn D. Lyons

Is This Life?

Reality obscured by childhood dreams,
Wrapped up in our own little worlds.
No one said they wouldn't be the same.
Hearing but not listening...
Seeing but not believing...

Animosity and oppression all around,
Wallowing in self pity.
Much rather to live in the pain.
Speaking but not meaning...
Breathing but not living...

Fixated with darkness and depression,
Offending harmony and peace.
Life thought of as only just a game.
Living but not loving...
Feeling but not caring....

What's the point of the sun shining,
If we refuse to find good in life.
Love is what sparks the flame.
Hear and see, speak and breathe!
Live and love, feel and care!

Christine M. Schramm

To Arthur

I guess I'm writing from the heart
Writing about Art
He was a great person that I knew
He did all that he could do
Not a person here not a person there
could say Art didn't care
He was an inspiration to everyone
In all ar hearts he was no. 1
To all children big and tall
We can say Art gave us his all
To all his friends and family out there
we can honestly say Art did care
We all know that Art is gone
but he only left us to move on
With Cancer Art has won
and his journey has just begun
Goodbye is what we all must say
and try to move on to another day.

Andrea Fornaro

Fret

I turned to bid you farewell
yet you were gone away
How long I cannot discern
What disregard have I?

Be it that I love you not?
Nay, for I hold great affection.
My belief in your immutable love
was my exorbitant err.

Apathetic was I to your needs
that I should be so callous
Now I suffer for my imprudence
and fret for what is lost.

Jay Vigil

Untitled

Forever in my thoughts
You are constantly on my mind

Take a look in my heart
and there you will find

Memories of you
Together with me

How I wish they weren't memories
If only they could be

The present not the past
And even much more

How I wish we were together
More than before

Please don't forget me
And find someone new

For I'll always have a place in my heart
And that place will be for you.

Adria Archuleta

A Father To His Little Girl

Come here to me, my Little Girl,
You are my sweet, my Little Girl,
You'll never know
How much I love you.

Here is a kiss, my Little Girl;
I'll always miss my Little Girl;
There's nothing in this world
I wouldn't do.

I'd brave a burning fire,
I'd fight a war alone;
I'd never give up or tire,
Until you're safe at home.

Come here to me, my Little Girl,
You are my sweet, my Little Girl,
You'll never know
How much I love you.

Frank Carlomagno

My Friend

So clear in my mind is the day we met.
Your smile, your eyes,
So warm and inviting,
Be my friend, yes, be my friend.

I thought of you constantly.
Saw you in my minds eye,
Your laughter, your wit.
Be my friend, yes, be by friend.

Your touch would go deep,
from the embrace of my shoulder
trailing a path to the heart of my soul.
Your warmth, your sincerity.
I felt it, yes, I felt it.

I have grown since that moment
a child so long ago.
Searching for love
trading it in for affection.
Wanting a partner
happily settling for a friend.
Yes, my friend.

Ann Brown

What's A Daughter's .... Wish

What is my wish, my wish is for
you because I would do anything
just for you, because I love you
and I hope you love me too.
Every little thing I do, you're on my
mind, and I like being around
you time after time.
    You are my mother and I love
you so true, this is what a
daughter is supposed to do. On this
special day my wish is for you.
    So happy Mother's Day and I
will always love you.
Helen J. Waters

Bruce And Brandon

Like father, like son,
You both were very special.
All the hearts to be won.
But, for you it was no trouble.

You reached out to everyone
To lend a helping hand.
Though your time on earth is done,
We'll never forget the man,

The man who showed us strength,
As well as compassion.
You went to great lengths
To stand up for what you believed in.

You fought like the dragon.
With the wisdom of the crow.
Why, so young you were taken.
I guess we'll never know.

The angels took you to heaven.
And now, you can be free.
But my heart is still saddened
For Bruce and Brandon Lee.
Eva King

Lust And Love

You are one the same
You can lead us to ecstasy
You can lead us to shame
You can lead us to triumph or to defeat
You can make us meek, mindless, and weak
You can broaden are horizons
and shower us with joy
You can make us your treasure,
your jewel, or your toy
But it makes no difference what you do
We shall continue to forever be true
Andrew Ingoglia

Be Thankful

Awake in the morning be thankful
You have survived for HIM a new day
Pray for divine guidance to help you
Whatever the command may say

Be thankful for knowing your SAVIOUR
Many have fallen away
They would not heed HIS COMMAND-
MENTS
And now have drifted astray
Jean Wilcox

'Us'

You took me in,
you held me up
I'll always love you...
no matter what.

I'm here for you,
always will be,
the four of us,
make a great family!

Both of us know,
how the other one feels,

Once that's accomplished...
there's nothing that can't be healed.

You were willing to listen,
to what no-one else heard...
you were willing to help me,
when no-one else cared.

I'll love you for always...
I'll always be here,
Together we make a hell of a pair..!
Anita M. Davidson

How Much You Mean To Me

You ask how much you

mean to me
You mean everything on
the world to me
More then the moon, the
stars, the sky, the sun
You mean so very much
too me.
More then the clouds,
the birds, the green grass
you mean more then
the world to me.
Hope McDemmott

Kim

How beautiful you are.
You take care of your hair
You take care of your self
That made you a beautiful person
Connie K. Janssen

Untitled

You tell me that you love me,
You tell me that you care,
And when you put your arms around me,
I say a little prayer,
A prayer that you will never leave me,
As long as the stars shine through,
And when we sit and talk at night,
I can tell your love is true,
Maybe it's the things you do,
Or the little things you say,
But when it comes we say good-bye,
I'll feel sad and cold,
But also blue,
And then we'll go our separate ways,
In hope of finding someone new,
But in the end for I will know,
Our love was always true.
Jamie Bodie

Hanging On

You were here, but now you're gone,
You took my heart and soul.
What to do I do not know,
I'm barely hanging on.
Can't you help just this once,
Then you can go on your way,
And I'll be left alone.
You're gone and I still love you.
Can't you see,
It's not the way I thought it would be?
I'm barely hanging on.
Jennifer Lohry

Peace - What Price

The years have taken many lives,
Young and old alike.
Give up your guns and ammo.
The little children cry.
You fought for Ireland's freedom.
Sentenced you're to die.
The judge shows no mercy.
You will hang tomorrow night.
Before the last breath's taken.
You may hear the people cry.
Ireland's been united.
Go in peace lad, God is by your side.
Christina Morone

Threshold

The end is the beginning,
  young pioneers.
A border draws closer,
  promising frontiers.
A wilderness of feelings.
  explorers unguided.
Many decisions abound,
  with which are we sided?
In every desert trek,
  the last mile is longest.
But an oasis is this,
  for even the strongest.
Stride on to that border,
  on the brink do stand.
There are no engraved ruts,
  in this virgin land.
The caul is now broken,
  the world still unseen.
Push your way to the light,
  the future is green.
John J. Crum

"A Mother's Heart"

    Inside this place
your love shined upon
my face

    Inside this place,
your kindness
molded my soul.

    Inside this
place, your grace,
I'll forever embrace

    Inside this
place, your faith,
it guides my path,
    Inside this
place.
April Haynes

Remembrance

Oh, that I might see once more
your face, with all its joy expressed
in one swift glance. To feel
the dear caress of hands
that love with uttermost perfection.

Only a sea gull's mocking cry
echoes my heart's loneliness
no hour nor moment passes
but remembered thoughts of thee
make fast the agony of my longing.

Would that I might soon forget
the touch of hand, the voice that
now is still. But there is not one
glance, or kiss, amidst the tears
that is not remembered down the years.

Joyce W. Gibson

In Time

I don't hug you enough
   You're growing so fast
But might I ask
   For more
   To restore
The need I have to hold you
   And this day
While you're still this way
   A child

A child now, an adult soon to be
And I dare to scorn
   At time
While you're still mine

I wish you all good things
   ...my love ...my heart
But let me hold you once more
before you walk through that door
   To return no more
   To childhood

Judith A. Staed

Mommy's Bird

The spring flowers are bright
In the morning sunlight
Oh, what a sight to see
And I hear a song
From the heavens above
It must be mommy's bird

For this bird you see
Tells all to me
Without saying a word
This mystic bird I've only heard
And seen now and then

She could be a Finch
Or a white Dove
Because, the melody
She sings for me
Ends with tender love

But, I know for sure
She, comes from above
Because, she comes to me
With Mommy's love

Ruth J. Thornton

Girl

People sometimes say
You're not like all the others.
Why is it you don't walk,
Why is it you don't talk,
The real girl way.

Something just ain't right
You don't look the same.
Your voice and hair are too rough,
The sounds of your outside's too tough,
You just ain't lady like.

What you wear is out of place
Nothing wrong with that I guess.
Out late playing in the dirt,
Bugs and snakes call you flirt,
Never to wear clean, white fancy lace.

I'll show them different
If same is what they want.
Walk with your back up straight,
Talk softly and never be late,
Why is that called girl.

Danyelle Lesch

My Special Sister

You're lying there so silently
Your eyes are softly closed
Your mouth is open just a touch
Your perfect little nose

Your skin is olive color
Your hair is oh so brown
Your ears, oh so tiny
Your face, a little round

You're mommy's little angel
You're daddy's pride and joy
You're frankie's spoiled sister
You're my little toy

You're a gift that's from the heavens
You're a star that shines at night
You're the heart that keeps us pumping
You're a fist that starts a fight

You're a special little girl
You're a petal of a rose
You're adopted to our family
You're the child that we chose

Dara Schlegel

Iran

Far over in Iran
Where all the oil dwells,
Instead of Peace and Happiness,
It's hate, greed and pure hell.

They burned the U.S. Embassy,
And hold our people there,
While Uncle Sam is trying everything,
to make Peace with God, in prayer.

Days and weeks go past
With no hope in sight,
We can only hope and pray
That our hostages are all right.

Perhaps the day will come
When God will intervene
We pray it will be soon
And our people will be FREE.

Ida Espenschied

"I Love You Daddy"

Will it hurt, daddy
when I go away
will you cry, daddy
because I can't stay

Why am I sick, daddy
what did I ever do
do I have to go, daddy
is it really true

I'll see mommy soon, daddy
I'll tell her you said hi
I'll have to hurry, daddy
and say my last goodbye

God will be here soon, daddy
tell sister not to cry
but before I go, daddy
please kiss me goodbye

Chrissy DeSimone

Untitled

To leaves falling from the same tree...
Why do you meet in air?
Dancing together.
Temporary. Unaware.
In concert. A pair
Falling terminally down
To the hard clay.
The curl of decay...
Stillness....

To be inevitably
Turned to dust again;
With hope, to try
On some cosmic plane
To make sense of it all.

Joe Ambrosino

Myself

I am a woman of means
With three sons of my own
My mother is behind the scenes
Letting us live in her home.

When there is love at home
Satan cannot creep in.
You won't give him room
With God your worries all end.

I'm happy with my work
And my boys make me glad.
My duties I'll try not to shirk
I'd rather be good than bad.

Carolyn Thomas

My Silent World

I live in a world that is silent
Where nary a sound is heard
Not even the blast of trumpets
Nor the soft twittering of a bird

For I was born without hearing
Not that I do care
A lot of people have thought
What a great burden I must bear

But I tell you, dear friends
That is absolutely not true
For I can see and talk and walk
Just as well as you

Barbara A. Mongeau

"Frustration"

Frustration is...freedom and justice
Sometimes it seems - not for all!!

Frustration is...feeling as though
We are always standing - against a wall!!

Frustration is...trying to keep up
With our neighbors - at the mall!!

Frustration is...never being able
To reach the one we want - when we call!!

Frustration is...equality...having to
Work harder to be the one - to stand tall!!

Frustration is...paying taxes to a
Government whose control - can appall!!

Frustration is...not having someone
To catch us - when we fall!!

Frustration is...the emotion we feel
When our lives seem to be like - a bouncing ball!!

Frustration is...bafflement that we
Cannot enjoy all of life's
Pleasures - without pitfall!!
Star A. Weidman

Heaven's Lane

Wandering down the lane of time,
Sometimes life can be sublime.

But often times that is not the case,
While in life's race.

Time marches on, along with sorrow and pain.
The days fly by as we meander down the lane.

We look for gladness along the way,
Hoping for sunshine and warmth each day.

Peace and contentment walk hand in hand,
When Jesus the Savoir leads the band.

Keep up the good walk,
But remember to talk.

To the one who can keep us
  on the straight and narrow,
Marching us along toward tomorrow.

To the destination, reached at last,
When time has elapsed.

Heaven's lane ends, and the rainbow
  surrounding the throne you see,
With Jesus waiting for you and me.
Marie Elena Petramalo

What's The Point?

I've been wordsmithing for a long time,
Sometimes serious and sometimes sublime
Yet always I strove for a meaning
In what we now call communicating.

But the process has become so devastating,
Fed by an explosion of mass media relating
That "words" have lost all their meaning
In the cacophony of electronic beaming!

Macluann said: "The medium is the message"
To understand this takes a dedicated sage.
Question is, does the message have a meaning
Or, are there just "words" you are gleaning?

Before this sonnet you anoint
Pray tell me: What's the point
Marshall Hahn

Good Tidings Of Great Joy

I dream of winter, dark and deep
Somewhere inside my spirit when I sleep
Snowflakes fall in silence on the grass
Clear, refreshing memories I keep
Of autumn leaves blowing in the wind
A wind that smelled of gentle, wood-tinged smoke;
A secret sign that winter was around the bend
A whisper, just of heavy woolen cloaks.
Of cozy coats and socks
To dress in for long, refreshing walks;
Eyes a-sparkle and cheeks ablaze with light,
O Blessed day, O Blessed night!
Should Christmas be a warmth of summer sun
Or should it be a coldness soon in passing;
A season of the heart's dearest asking
A prayer for peace and freedom everlasting.
But mine are only dreams of memories of Christmas past
When snow fell lightly on the grass;
And the lake turbulent with winter's soul
And the children, all a-bundled, danced.
Kate Lowell

Mother To Us All

From an embryo of nothingness you came,
Spawned by the great father,
From the darkness into the light,
Born of chaos into order, how great your mystery,
How great your wonder, can I dare ask your name?

Terra is my name, do you not know me,
You drink of me,
You take nourishment from my valleys, waters and sky
You share my breath,
You consume my body at its depth,
Leaving me scarred and even burned,
Is this the respect I have earned?

Some have called me by another name,
You may think it is the same,
No, I think Terra should remain,
For time and chaos will bring the flame,
Leaving nothing untouched, ever changing my flesh and soul,
As I age beyond your time, burning fire, burning cold,
The sands of time are so very old,

I am your mother, treat me well.
Steven W. England

Here Comes The Rain

Here comes the rain
With pride and no pain
Its submissive duties
It just can't refrain
To shower the mountains
Shower the plains and clean down
Every gully, gutter and stream.
The might of the rain.
We just can't forbid
See its drastic effects
In the earth parchy stage
The bloom of the earth it reinstate
the trees that were wilting
their lushness retain.
The flowers that were suppressed
Will fame sweet fragrance again
The birds that were thirsty will
Sing across the plains
Sweet little songs that brings thrill to the brain
And a smile to the farmers who welcome the rain.
Andy George Seafarers

"Connecting"

For everything that happens in life physically, there is a
spiritual connection.

Making known God's will for each of us with this conglomeration.

From one connection to another He is drawing a physical picture
to show a spiritual application.

Connecting daily routines with unexpected interruptions of one
kind or another, and with apprehension.

Bringing about different things and people into our lives to (teach)
show us the way the truth and the life.

Things don't just happen by chance or happenstance. (Ironically)
It is by God's amazing grace that they are enhanced.

In order for you to know and believe exactly what I mean by this,
you will have to experience it to comprehend this same bliss.

Encouragement comes to us more and more from above, as we on
bended knees connect into His throne - room of love.

He is the power source by which we all are connected, one with
another, through His Son.

One has need to be open and ready to receive this assertion,
to apply it to their life for affirmation.

Nora Lee Copeland

Apart

After she hangs up the phone, she sits
Staring at it like she's watching his plane fade into the twilight,
Oh! If he could just be here, she yearns...
   I'd not have my soul put on hold
     But for two brief conversations a week -
With my heart plunged, pulled, and pressed
   Through two hundred miles of telephone wire
To capture as much of his as it can -
     to subdue her...

Until this Godforsaken waiting is over.

What for the restrained anticipation approaching the mail box -
Just something to bring me closer to him! She pleads.

Though love transcends time and space -
   Memory persists.
It is the imp of the soul,
   Insatiable of recollection!
It plagues every thought with reminders of him;
It frolics through the depths of her mind - The Scavenger!
   Retrieving to the consciousness all traces of him...

Until this Godforsaken waiting is over.

Michelle A. Delaney

If I Cry, Should I Lie?

I'm 24, too old to cry anymore.
Yet, sometimes I don't know why,
but my eyes just don't feel so dry.
Did someone say goodbye?
Did someone die?
No, that's not why.
Maybe like a baby, everyone just needs to cry.
And if someone tells you not to cry,
ask them "Why, why not cry.
If out of the blue, I let out a tear or two,
why wouldn't that be okay with you?"
If they can't answer why,
tell them "you see, it's okay to cry."
If someone asks you why you cry,
there's no need to tell a lie.
Do not say there's a bug in your eye.
Because, you see, it's okay to cry.

Robert Pugh

All Drift Away

Staring at a blank and lifeless page
Staring at it, staring at it for days
Thoughts are blank, thoughts are empty
Memories - all drift away

Pain comes over me again
Memories all drift away
Memories of where, memories of when
All drift away
Memories of yesterday
The memories that hold me, keep me from today

Looking up from a blank and lifeless page
Looking up, looking up in a daze
Thoughts are blank, thoughts are empty
Memories - all drift away

Rain comes over me again
Soaking wet, dripping life
Draining, draining by the second
Forming a lifeless pond
Memories all drift away
Without, without anyone to respond

Richard Hussey

One True Love

What happened to this man I loved
Who told me I was his little white dove
He's filling our lives with anger and rage
Me and my children are trapped in this cage
I peak out through eyes of despair
Wondering if anyone out there cares
I think of the words, "to have and to hold"
Before he became so callous and bold
Why have things changed so drastically
I wonder is it him or is it me
Lord help me through this sleepless night
Help me Lord to fight the fight
This man has taken all my will
I've resorted to this bottle and pill
I don't know how much further I can bend
I feel as though I'm near the end
I know my father wouldn't want me to feel this pain
My life should not be such a strain
So I'm turning my heart to the Lord this day
Knowing I have one man who will never betray

Rita Lee Conley-Walters

Untitled

Yes, I am a fledgling
still learning how to fly
You gave me wings, a song to sing
and taught me not to cry.
The journey was not easy,
my future destined, - still,
a need so great, a vision bright,
a dream that was not filled.
By day, my gaze was skyward,
my passions knew the sun,
the nights, like quiet thunderbolts
reflecting duties done.
Then one day you found me, in perfect disarray,
my plotted course from fight to flight
there seemed no other way.
You knew you could not hold me,
but forces did prevail, like,
currents, from above or deep, grew love that could not fail.
Now we are together to fly or be earthbound,
our strengths and tender caring a "home" our hearts has found.

Marie Procopio

Woman In A Red Cap

A woman in a red cap
stood over the ground meat
fingering each shiny pack
until she turned and asked
which one was only a dollar.
Her broken tongue thick.
Her face broad with years of hard work,
She could have been my aunt, just off the boat,
preparing a new life in a new land.
She could have asked for anything.
But she stepped back pressing some cheese in her hand.
Later, at the checkstand, she spread out a few items,
a loose squash, some sour cream.
She reached through the tight neck
of her sweater, into her bra, for a five and a one
but it wasn't enough.
The squash rolled on the counter
pale yellow and bulbous.
She disappeared into the light
hidden, quiet and alone.

Sandra Davis

Oklahoma City

The mind blanks, the body numbs. Terror!
Strikes vital organs; Sleep leaves.

This in not your world we see, oh God?
Your will for us? CERTAINLY NOT!

Destruction real: Twisted girders, dangling cables,
Emptied shell, mute symbols of
Shattered lives, families, fractured heartland.

If we are so connected, that by knowing
six people, we know the world.
Then we are all in grief, all victims
of this carelessness that annihilates!

Help us to breathe again.
To bloom trust amid burying dark evil.
To grow love in the closets of fear in which we want
to hide those we love.
May the tensile strength of our faith in You, O God,
Hold us fast to sanity — and let us pray,
"Father forgive them for they know what they do
And they don't care.

We will love." Amen.

Ronald D. Elly

Forever A Friend, Far After The End

Bigotry, prejudice, and hatred
surrounds us every day,
the thoughts being pressure into our minds.
Then you came and eased the pain
that our minds could no longer endure.
You showed us how to laugh and
showed us that you cared.
You wiped away our pain whenever
it came near.
You changed our lives around
showing us the way.
You gave us all this feeling, we all could
feel is love.
When we were able to handle things and
started to move ahead,
God took your soul in close to him
to tell you you've done well.
Though we've felt the sorrow,
and felt the deepest grief,
a piece of us will always be with you forever, eternal peace.

Stacey McKittrick

A Marble Work

Hammered blows are reverberating through the resistant mass.
Strong arms are determined to overcome the herculean challenge
With passionate energy; painstakingly striving to bring to pass
The unexplainable inner vision of resolute courage embodied.

By defying skeptics, yielding to pride in his prodigious talent,
A seemingly impossible task will become a monumental work
Of incomparable beauty. One man's great artistic genius is intent
To create awe-inspiring magnificence in towering marble.

The chisel repetitively strikes; slowly gouging imprisoning stone
With unerring skill. It reaches inward to find the form of a
Cherished son, whose mission will be a nation's destiny to hone,
With his singular, spirit-guided resistance to tyranny's Goliath form.

His generating is not that of humankind's nine-months gestation,
But a more than two-year effort in bringing him to life full-grown:
A Colossus of manhood, taller than thirteen feet, in contemplation,
Forever fixed in poised readiness by genius hands of Michelangelo.

The naked David, armed with his slingshot and God's protection,
Will always confront the Goliath tyrant; in sculpted example
Of the human spirit's persistent zeal for a free-choice selection
In governance, religion, love, custom, commitment and lifestyle.

Manuel J. Silva

In The Yard

It hangs there, blowing ever so gently in the breeze on meticulously
    strung threads.
Only the correct amount of tension will maintain its architectural
    integrity.
Floating in space between the fence and some twigs,
    it gracefully billows in and out of the shadows.
It waits without movement; patience unsurpassed.
There are many flies zig-zagging to and fro just below it;
    chasing, landing, and flying without suspicion.
Gnats and aphids jostle about unaware of the predator floating in
    the breeze, ever so near, ever so quiet, ever so patient.
Now almost completely submerged in the shadows, the sunlight
    glistens on its spiral threads no longer.
Appearing to defy gravity, it has yet to flinch.
It could strike in the blink of an eye, guided by the vibration of a
    distressed, captured victim unfortunate enough to stray into the net.
I continually glance over at this silent, artful creature,
    anticipating an inevitable capture.
My neck tires from the endless askance.
But, no movement, no change, no capture;
    only the smooth flow of air lifting and caressing the arachnid
    upon its woven seat.
With a sigh and a turn, I close my eyes to face the warmth of the sun.
    Fascinated, I surrender.
Its patience is greater than mine.

Maxwell Lazinger

Time Is White

The great fire spatters memory with its light.
Somewhere a voice is crying, 'time is white.'
A smell of ironed sheets overwhelms the night.

Winter is rising to the window sill,
While shadow birds sing lullabies to chill.
A sheen of crystal holds the moment still.

The lonely rhythm of a rocking chair,
Holds nothing but a battered teddy bear.
The dream he keeps is much the worse for wear.

The boy who played with him seasons ago,
Has hair that rivals January's snow,
But button eyes will never tell him so.

Sandra Fowler

Freedom Our Heritage

Our constitution was based on freedom and brotherly love
Such a set of laws had to be inspired by the Lord above
These freedoms inspired people to come to our shores
Italians, Irish, Polish and others came by the scores
This melting pot of people changed a wilderness to a nation
They worked by the sweat of their brow not expecting rations
They educated their children to become leaders from the ranks
Living in freedom from fear was their reward and their thanks
They fought against slavery and the states became divided
Then came the civil war where this issue was decided
After the war brutality and hatred was created
The assassination of Lincoln was a loss too great to be stated
Our industrial revolution created expansion that unfurled
America kept thriving and was a model for the world
Hitler and Mussolini followed with hate and brutalities
By conquering the world they'd wipe out most nationalities
England and France tried to hold them back with a fight
Then the yanks came forward like a beacon of light
Since then the world has gone amuck; now we hope and we pray
That the people on earth will have the freedoms of the USA

Sidney Levin

Concert Of Fools

Wide-eyed, we waited, seeking songs,
Surely a message for each of us.
What better way to spend an evening?
What better evening to spend?

Nervously laughing, sipping wine,
Surely that look was just for me.
Who had more right to be there in the crowd,
Than his ex-wife, his dear friend, and me?

And me...chatting lightly with his lady,
Holding court by the wall; she had it all.
And me...reminiscing with his old love,
Waiting there for the word, she never heard,
While the old friend worked so hard to pretend,
That everything would be fine in the end.

Sad-eyed, we snickered, juggling jokes,
Surely this next song is just for you.
What better fans than old friends and lovers?
What better lovers than fans?

Louise Anderson

Thoughtlessness

Why are we so concerned about our own feelings,
that we can't see the other's side?
Why do we believe we're always right?
It's just our foolish pride.

Why do we take each other for granted,
and think they'll always be there?
Why can't we see beyond ourselves,
and show that we really care?

The little things that mean most in life,
aren't such a difficult task.
A hug, a kiss, a warm embrace,
are all that you really ask.

With so little time to spend in the world,
don't waste it like a fool.
See that the other one's feelings are real,
and treat them like a jewel.

When we can care more about the others' happiness,
it's such a great gift to give.
Then we can find our own happiness.
And that's the best way to live.

Rocco Martelli

It's A Different World

To ride a different wave to conquer the element of surprise as we hear the free-will people pushing their drugs

Laughter in the alleys and music in the streets are the sound of people committing crime

It's a different world. Why do some people take color as a sign of hate for any black face who is trying to live their life?

Father against daughter, daughter against mother against son is the sound of war that just won't quit

War won't bring life, it only just takes it away

Yes, my brother and sister, it's a different world out there with a cruel mind who tries to get ahead

It's a different world, but it doesn't have to be because everyone needs a little more

Leon Hodge

To Know Me

To know me:
Take a walk in an autumn wood,
Discard your worries, open up your senses,
Awe in the place where the oak once stood.

To see me:
Absorb and indulge in the rustic colors around,
High above your head, draped around your feet
My golden brown is found

To hear my call:
Listen for the bough to moan and creak,
The leaves to rustle and the thrushes to sing,
For these are my voices you seek.

Finally to love me:
Take a moonlit walk in our autumn wood.
Under the shimmering stars lie down,
Down in the place where the oak
Once stood.

S. J. Rowland

The Sun Is Shining

Sun shine on me, down to my bones,
take and heal my weary heart, and empty soul, straighten out my crippled bones,
my source of being and long lived life,

Sun shine on me, down to my soul,
heal my heart that hurts me so,
my friends and family now are all departed,
my soul right for the dust who are soon to get started,
let the earth roar for the soon departed,
here is my heart and bones ready for rotted,

Sun shine on me, down to my heart,
heal it, heal it, it's torn apart,
the blood gushes and soon dries up,
leaving my body to wrinkle and soil,

Sun shine on me, down to my mind,
heal it first, for it will save you time,
without my mind the body is nothing,
the soul can flee, the bones can rest,
my heart will no longer break, and I can be at peace with thee.

Rhoda Conway

Come With Me To A Distant Star, A Distant Land

I am with you
Take my hand
Come with me to a distant star,
A distant land.

Listen to me, and I shall teach.
Walk with me along a beach.
Smile and run free
To any place you want to be.

Walk this way along my path
And even have fun doing math.
Laugh and talk a little funny,
And there will be no need to worry about money.

Hear and see all this and more.
Come on in and open the door.
You can be you, and I will be me.
And finally we will see…

We are at last together
Hand in hand
Going to a distant star,
A distant land.
Thomas Berntsen

Ma, Da…

Sing of old Scotland.
Teach the wee brains that
Sweet song of old.

Sing of moors and heather,
Of plaid kilts and ghosts in the
Mists where swords swing in castles keep,
And Scottish pipes flare on a wedding day,
Where ancient ones with their green eyes
Cast the bones for the fate of the first born,
And fairies rule the mystic land of Loch and Glens.
Sing of old Scotland.

Where Gaelic is spoken from earth to sky.
Sing that sweet, soft song
Of old Scotland.
Sing…Sing!
For Scotland's sake.
Teach the old ways.
For it won't be long
She'll only be remembered
Through your stories and songs.
Mandy Rhea Miller

Tranquility

Reflections in a quiet stream,
   Sunrise in the morning or a lover's dream.
A poem at the end of a busy day,
   When we feel too evil or tired to pray.

A Mother's lullaby to a weary child,
   A peaceful visit or a walk in the wild.
A starry sky on a summer night,
   Or a full moon beaming on snow so white.

Raindrops softly splashing the window pane,
   A smile and gentle touch when we're in pain.
A rainbow at the end of a storm,
   A fireplace aglow to keep us warm.

A Christmas tree with all the lights,
   Bringing cheer on winter nights.
Church bells afar calling us there,
   To leave our woes in His loving care.
Leah Betterly Brotzman

classroom

I interpose on the cot of boredom as the fabrications spew from the teachers mouths,
Musing visions of flipper alternating with Willis from "Different Strokes" on topics such as love and racism zing past my head,
They stop for a twinkling but continue their debate after consummating that it is just me,
For I have travelled this road of tedium infinite times previously,
Unaccompanied countless times yet with you this a first,
For I may seem like the type of being full of rapture and glee,
But fooled you may be if you vindicated it,
'Cause I too have been extracted into this cesspool of ennui,
Pulled from my roots like the flower of love from the garden of actuality,
It is the same for those whom aren't as great too,
So show gratitude towards every day,
For they too endure this life of total banal,
So as my road comes to a stop I shall say adios, arrivederci, au revoir, auf wiedersehen and cheerio.

   For the bell has rung
Paul Zarou II

Untitled

Shattered glass is the shadow from my heart
Tears from my eyes an illusion drip of art
Look in my face tell me what do you see
A hurt young lady how could you do this to me
Anger, rage I can't sleep at night
Anger, rage can't close my eyes without a fight
Pain and misery will not go away
Trying to care to love each and everyday
Forgive and forget that could never be true
How can I ever forget the pain you put me through
I will go on and on until I fall
Only to get back up, baby this ain't all
As I fight through reality a nightmare in its self
As I fight through days of having good health
As I fight through the pain in this world I'm apart
Just remember the shattered glass
Is the shadow from my heart.
Melissa Lee

Mother

Tell me a story, oh, mother dear
Tell me a story to last through the years.
To comfort me and hug me when you're not near.
Tell me a story so there'll be no more fear.
Take me away from the darkness that I fear.
Tell me a story so I'll cry no more tears.
Your story shall guide me all through my life.
Till I come into your loving sight…
Shelby Wood Leroy

Sweet Music

Strange how the birds seem to call a little sweeter this year
Stranger yet is that I can't seem to stop humming their lovely tune which seems to transform my staggering steps into strides of confidence
I am helplessly caught up in this moment
I want to savor its sweetness
For one day I shall wake up dead and this moment will be obsolete
I shall not remember the sweet call of the birds
I shall not remember the long sleepless nights full of frustration
I shall not remember my mornings of emptiness longing for the night so that day might be over
I shall not remember my sweet, lovely tune
Tyresa Spivey

I Keep Seeing This Man

I keep seeing this man in my dreams
telling me about Abraham, it's always in
my mind and it won't go away. If I told
somebody they would think I was; it's
like blackcat and I are talking. It just stays
in my mind maybe I'm going to meet someone like
this. I just want it to stop, I can't concentrate
on my work, without this man badgering me.
It's like he's in my thought process. I wish we
could just meet each other face to face and get it
over with, but if I don't meet him what will I say?
You knew why from the first time you
looked over your shoulder in arch restaurant you
smiled and moved me with your breast and walked
away, you're everything in my life, my only prayer is
three minor changes; I can't live without you:
    You excite me
Pat Blackcat Parker

I Heard The Voice Of An Angel

I heard the voice of an angel, I felt the touch of a hand
Telling me not to worry, there was no need to be sad
I felt a peace overwhelm me, I brushed the tears from my eyes
I knew my friend was in heaven, there was no need for goodbyes

I heard the voice of an angel, I felt the touch of a hand
I know now, that there is a Heaven, a beautiful Promised Land
I know that when life is over, there is much more on the other side
We'll be singing our songs with the angels, there will be no reason to cry,

I heard the voice of an angel, I felt the touch of a hand
Our spirits will go on living, in Heaven the Promised Land
There may be some things in life, some dreams we never knew
But, we'll be dancing with angels in Heaven, on clouds so powder blue.

Karen L. Scheuermann

"The True Friend"

Heat waves make you sweat.
Thank God they haven't got you yet.
Cold waves make you chatter.
Your body crippled, fragile, battered.
Standing up is a challenge within.
Your head's pleasure is to spin.
You try to control it;
But it rebels with a persistent grin.
You brace yourself against something strong.
Or even kneel, but not too long.
Because you've got things to do;
Chores and assignments, to name a few.
You yearn for strength and power,
Not to overtake your neighbor,
But to face all the comments, insults, and cowards.
Finally a loving friend comes to your side
Ignoring their remarks and his own pride.
You think to yourself "How nice,
For him to make such a great sacrifice."

Matthew Ryan Gause

Alone

I am sitting here this beautiful day.
Thanking God for the love He has sent my way.
I live alone but I am not sad.
My eighty five years are not so bad.
Thank You God for everything.
It's your love that
helps me sing.

Mamie Kemp

You Can't Curse Love

You can't curse love even though it brought much pain
That broke a happy heart that will never love again
The hurting and the pain that comes from within
No you can't curse love 'cause it would be a sin

A love so strong it reaches deep into your soul
Why did it leave no one really knows
Yet I wonder why you have nothing to say
About this love that's gone like clouds after a stormy day

Just look around you before it's too late
To have a love so strong and let it turn to hate
I try to forget but the mind wanders at will
Life must go on but time just seems to stand still

Theresa M. Reznik

Happy Birthday Jesus

The little Lord Jesus was born on a day,
That captured the world is a mystical way.
The joy that was felt by all who believed,
Made them all weep and bow down on their knees.
This feeling was felt, miles across miles.
The feeling was love for the small Jesus child.
The chill in the air was warmed by his love.
The stars in the sky shown bright from above.
On this special day all the animals smiled.
And all evils ceased from the birth of this child.
From that day till now, on the same day each year,
We celebrate his birth and live without fear,
And share all our love with those far and near.

    Happy Birthday Jesus
Pamela Witt

Freedom, A Treasure

Liberty, freedom, that very special treasure,
That frees the mind, calms, makes merry the heart,
Much as a healing spring, after winter's cold measure;
Even in a long, long, enslaved land, freedom, can start!
Freedom, first starts its pure, pure flame,
In the individual, then it can grow as a tide,
Lands, as Switzerland, Sweden, freedom is fame;
Great is a people's joy with their own choices decide!
Love, gains the greatest wing span, when it's a spirit free,
Open bright blue skies, comfortable, in warm sun,
proving, practicing, self denial, is not the way to be;
Free society, isn't always easy, but it can be won!
Even today, free man's thoughts do march forward,
Yet to maintain one's liberty, one must duty serve,
Rewards, come by peace's loom, some come by noble sword;
An alert free nation, only the best of secure fate deserve!

Raymond Bradburn

A Mother's Prayer

God, watch over my children and keep them safe in your arms,
Teach them all about this life and spare them any harm.
I pray that they will live each day trusting in only you,
And I pray that they will do the things that you expect them to.
Help me to teach them your word and help them to teach others the same
So that everyone can learn of faith and everyone can proclaim.
Help me to teach them the importance of thanking you each day,
And help me to teach them of your love and the right way to pray.
Help me to raise them in a church with all of those who care,
And show them what good fellowship means and what it means to share.
Help me to teach them to always smile even when things seem bad.
And teach them to work through their problems and never to stay mad.
Help me to teach them all of these things, for I know good Christians they will be
And they will pass these things on to their children and have a happy family.

Linda Lightfoot

The Golden Coffee Cup

Many years ago, my mother gave me this golden coffee cup
That her mother had given to her.
When she handed me the cup,
She told me that it had been passed down
Through many generations from mother to daughter.
And that it holds all the joys and sorrows
Shared by our Family down through the years.
How it had withstood the frigid
winters and sweltering summers.
How it knew all the secrets whispered throughout the house.
How each fingerprint disappeared as a new one appeared.
How it overflowed with abundance when times were good,
And how it was almost sold when times got rough,
How it too rejoiced when a new baby was brought home,
And grieved when someone was taken home to the Father above.
But most of all, it was always filled with love
(Especially from God above)
So now you know why this cup is so dear.
Because it holds all the Family's memories
Down through the years.
   Shelly Welborn

"Equality"

In a hovel on a hillside
The old lady sat and looked

On her lap, opened at her favorite passage
Lay the good book

She was watching the children playing
In the junk heap down the road

Their grimy faces lit with laughter
Forgetting for a little while the hunger and cold

She knew at the time of creation
God meant equality for all of man

But it appeared the distributing had been done
With a dishonest hand

What had been but trash to others
These children shouted over with glee

O' course, along with equality, he promised trials and tribulations
She supposed this was one of the three

Testing to see of what stuff we are made
As each must earn his way

If but one could remember his youth and still keep the faith
There might still be equality some day.
   Patricia A. Bramlett

The Strings That Bind Me

I close my eyes and I can imagine,
that I have no strings that bind me.
I am free of my earthly limitations,
I have no strings that bind me.

I see myself racing down the basketball court,
blocking the oncoming shot and winning the game.
High above, on the shoulders of my teammates,
I have no strings that bind me.

I see myself wrestling in the tall green grass,
overpowered by an excited golden retriever.
I gaze up and feel the wetness of my dog's kiss,
I have no strings that bind me.

An unwanted sound pierces the solitude of my dreams,
and I realize that my mind was playing tricks on me.
The hum of my machine, always by my side,
tells me that I still have the strings that bind me.
   Mary Ann Douglas

"It Seems Just Like Yesterday"

It seems just like yesterday -
That I first held you in my arms,
And promised to always protect you from harm.
Such a good baby - you hardly ever cried,
So my patience you never tried.

It seems just like yesterday -
I kissed and sent you off to school,
And tried to teach you the Golden Rule!
Reading, writing and arithmetic...
And staying at home with you when you were sick.

It seems just like yesterday -
I turned and looked at you to see
You were now the same height as me.
And now I'm not the number one girl in your life;
That place now belongs to your wife!

It seems just like yesterday, I first brought you home.
And now you're living out on your own.
With a wife and kids you're so proud of,
And soon it will be you I hear say —-

It seems just like yesterday!!!
   Pam Tyner

A Promise

This is written to the young woman
that I love, who's soon to be a mother.
And for the little girl who will always be
number one among others.
I just want to say with all my heart.
I'll work hard each day for our new start.
Work hard to get the things that we need.
Work hard to get the things that we please.
For that's what I need to do
So, I can take good care of both of you.
As I close my note I want you to know.
I'll love you both with all
My heart from now until It's time for me to go.
   Mark Somerlyn L. Thompson

Longing

I long for something that will never be
That is for someone to truly love me

I need the closeness - a bonding with one
The way God intended for it to be done

I want a trust so open and strong
That grows even deeper as time goes on

I want a connection - heart and soul
That's more precious to me than all the gold

Someone who knows me inside and out
To me that is what love is about.
   Sharon Lawter

Emotions In Color

   Your color is red,
stained with the blood of the innocent.

   Your color is green,
envy corrupting the government.

   Your color is blue,
the pain of life's problems.

   Your color is yellow,
bright as the sun, that even though your colors
may be tragic, you can still have a yellow day.
   Matt Stone

Time And Love

Farewell to a person I once knew,
that is here but gone.
If remember a time when things were right,
that now are wrong.
Only time will tell the fate of it all.
Only time will tell that went so wrong.
What am I to do while love waves farewell,
but wait to see what time will tell.

Richard Lykins

The Child In Me

I give you, my little one,
That rest untouched in a sacred place,
Away from this ungodly place,
A tiny riddle for you to embrace.

My deepest apology to you I chant, for here you are safe,
For now, and yet I can't deny them your sacred place,
In which will be taken from you with little grace.

For it is my fault I am aware,
All The things you will adhere
There is just little time for me to spare
To spend with my little one without despair.

I am to blame, you see,
For I knew that this world is now Sown with salt.
Though my heart is in such shame,
I will not regret the day,
When you arrive, without dismay.
I give you, my little one, me to blame.

Terri Menser

Weeping Willow

Weeping willow as you cry, please shed some tears for me
that the ground may soak up all my sorrow and take away my misery
then the seeds of life will start to grow and spring into the air,
to catch some rays of happiness so I will feel no more despair.

Susan Cuckler

"Momma"

I remember Momma most when night begins to fall
That was the time of day she liked the best of all.

She would sit in her chair so tired and worn
And think of all there was to do with the coming of dawn

Her work was never done, her hands were never still
All that kept her going was her own strong will.

I'm not very big, but I'm bigger than she
Yet she had four strong sons, my sister and me.

I remember Momma most when night begins to fall
For that was the time of day she loved the most of all.

Pauline E. Bailey

Come Here To Me

Come here to me and set me free.
Take me away to a place where lovers play.
Come lay your head upon my breast.
Make love to me till morning's blessed.
Loving you is all I see.
The two of us in ecstasy.
Don't be afraid to come to me.
Come here to me and take all you need.
Take me away, love me today.
Come kiss me more and forevermore,
true love we'll see.
Come here to me.

Stacey Hunt

This Is My Dream

This is my dream:
That we resolve to make an irrevocable pact,
To let our children grow up with innocence intact;
That when we pick up the paper to pursue the news,
Not one precious child would have been abused.

This is my dream:
That from all social bans, we find permanent relief,
Regardless of color, race or religious belief;
That man would live in unity with man,
In harmony with nature, according to plan.

This is my dream:
That those who suffer may experience some ease,
As a cure is found every debilitating disease;
That 'drugs' will refer only to the therapeutic kind,
Not the harmful substances that unhinge the mind.

This is my dream:
That wars will become a thing of the past,
As we finally discover a peace that will last;
That mankind would realize God's timeless scheme,
Of everlasting life and love—this, is my dream.

Margaret S. Wilson

A New Arrival

I bring you home- not really happy
　　That you are here.
Hesitant, to have you- why this silly
　　fear?
I hide you! No one should know
　　you arrived.
You insist, to accompany me, as my dishes need to be dried,
　　Plants watered, beds made and eggs fried.
Supportive, you are the reason, I am
　　moving about
　　and not getting stout.
Always waiting by my bed, while I sleep
By my side, at the library, supermarket, post office
　　and over puddles we leap
My wonderful new friend, should some
　　day be in the Hall of Fame
My Faithful companion, strong, slender,
　　Firm
　　　"MY CANE"

Margaret B. Reilly

"What Is Love?"

What is love? A special glance,
That goes to my heart like a lance.

What is love? A whispered word,
A sweet name that is nearly unheard.

What is love? But a gentle sigh,
When a girl is kissed by the right guy!

What is love? A bunch of beautiful flowers
That make me remember for hours and hours.

What is love? It is worry, too,
When my guy is upset, moody and blue.

What is love? It's his smile,
To let me know it's been worthwhile.

What is love? A warm, gentle kiss,
When he's gone, it's this I miss.

What is love? A very special song,
That I remember, when the nights are so long.

What is love? It's hard to tell,
Whatever it is, I'm under its spell!

Sandra K. Flemings

Speed Kills!

Five seconds,
that's all that it took.
As I walked down the street,
and talked to my friend,
my life almost came to an end.
The speed of that car,
Oh, speed is an evil deed.
I will be in pain for the rest of my life,
this is the price
No longer can I run,
or have any fun.
Now my friends live in fear,
that my end is near.
Tears that flow down
I want the pain to go away,
so please stop the speed of cars today.

Marie V. Gostel

My Daughter's A Mother

My daughter's a mother
That's plain to see
My daughter's a mother
But how can that be?

As I watch her with her children, I can't help but think
Was it so very long ago, she couldn't reach the sink?

Ethan has an ear infection
Evan scratched his eye
Caden is always eager to help
He's such a sensitive little guy

It seems like time flies as we watch our children grow,
And then in an instant, it becomes very clear, and we know.

My daughter's a mother,
I'm as proud as I can be.

But as I'm watching her,
I think I see me!

Nancy Reichel

Is There Life After Nam

Over a decade ago the cloud of war hovered above
The bugle blew Taps for those whom we love

Finger pointing and name calling was the order of the day
We're Vietnam Veterans, we were ashamed to say

Our handshakes were silent with eyes looking down
Our heads were bowed as we moved from town to town

Life after Nam for some was a cane, wheelchair or a bed
Life after Nam for others was alcohol, dope or a bullet in the head

We were minutemen at Lexington, doughboys in France
A dogface in Germany, but from Nam you gave us no chance

From soldier to civilian, we had to make the change
With blood on our hands, suddenly this world seemed strange

We came back winners, but you made us feel we had lost
No one to talk to, nowhere to turn, Oh what cost

Some of our scars are not seen by the naked eye
Pains of lost buddies, brothers, classmates; at night we still cry

The anger you see is really hurt in a mask
Rejected and dejected, we only did what you ask

Is there life after Nam? We must live it to see
For some, life after Nam was never to be.

Maxey D. Little

Illumination Pulsating In The Night

Watching the porch light slice through the cracks
The embers glow of crescent moons
As Apollo finishes his chariot run
moonbeams cry,
yearning for a home
Post apocalyptic hues of grays,
beating with shades of Michelangelo
Inner agony of vibrant pigments
bursting from days of future past
Poetic justice,
light shining darkness,
Illumination pulsating in the night.

Tony Eng

Grasping For The Wind

A ride in the New York Subway, travelling home.
The ancient question why?
Evokes the timeless trail of men great and small;
Of past, present and future:
This strange passage of time, with all its unanswered whys?
Makes me wonder at many a man's attempts to define
What really is life?

A weary man with dirty clothes sleeping in the train.
No one's near.
The big space around him screams so loud and helplessly;
On the other side,
A well-dressed man in suit and shiny shoes,
With something important to do - his New York Times.

Vanity of vanities. All is vanity?

The meaning of it all seems to slip and slide
Further away from my futile grasp,
And I feel so small, ignorant and appalled,
How can I begin to define...
Truly I do not know...

Vanity of vanities. All is vanity?

Vincent E. Liew

Dedication

The eternal flame was kindled, as we stood in silent prayer,
The anthem blared out in the cold winter air.
Winged birdmen sped across the sky above-
As tears were shed for those we love.
Will his name appear as one to return home-
Or will he lie in oriental grave and remain unknown.
Then the bells tolled five - for many mending a broken heart,
Yet for all the others, this was only a start.
Parted sons - never to return from where they came-
It is for you that we kindle the eternal flame.

Seymour B. Feldman

Scars

He screams again and disappears
The crash of the door shakes my life.
He is gone again.
Maybe this time he won't return...
But he will.
Maybe this time I won't open my door...
But I will.
But for now I fill my being with thoughts of independence.
In vain I swear that this shall never occur again.
I do not miss him
I do not need him
And while I do not need him tears fall down
My once flawless face now covered with
The scars of his undying love.

Misty Dawn

My Picture Window's Picture

The feeders hang for all to view
the birds seem to come as if on queue
to get their fill at least twice a day
the robin, the wren, the feisty blue jay

The finches and the chick-a-dee
the red-headed woodpecker debugging a tree
the cat-bird taking her usual dive
at any creature that seems alive

To protect her young in the nest above
one can just feel this inborn love.
And then when they all have their fill
they fly to the bird bath and down goes their bill

To first get a drink and then take a swim
shake themselves dry and fly to their limb —
the business of God's creatures on wing
oh! the beautiful notes they continually sing

In perfect harmony - what a choir
and harmony is what we all desire
in our daily living - our work, our play
and the birds seem to know the way

  What a lesson I've learned this day!!
    Peggy Byers

Hallowed Glory

The Stars I knew lie in Flanders Fields
The broken, maimed, left lying to bleed
Raising the head to suffer the shorn
Seeing the limb gone! Now a crippled breed

Within earth's holes the dug and deep
The tremble, fearful, praying for each other
A sickened lot amid stain and cries
Giving courage and hand to wounded brother

These heroes I knew came home with the flag
Its draped told of the gallant and the brave
Their last pillow with peace and perpetual
Lowered slowly and solemnly to the grave

The Stars I knew have the sun to their name
The hushed breeze whispers the memorial call
The rain bathes as like tears and embrace
To the beneath, within the gravestones wall

Here! is the stage and uncoveted trophy
White fields! and rows! miles of sacrifice!
None! ever bowed to applause or hollow glory!
Marching toward the sunset! After war's price!

    Vera Ireland

God's Place

There is a tale of a place,
that's known by few but should be known by many.
It's a beautiful place with green, green trees
and skies as blue as the sea.
With valleys deep and luscious
and hills and mountains that touch the skies.
It's a place where no one has a color
and you are welcome anywhere.
Words such as bigot and prejudice do not exist
every one is liked for whom or what they are
because they are all individuals.
For those who know it I know they love it
and for those who don't will soon find out
For to follow God's word
will give you riches more than any
of the world's treasures could give.
The place I speak of is most wonderful you see
for that's the place of God.

    Melanie Williams

Darkness

I am surrounded by Darkness,
The cool Breeze comforts me.
Stars twinkle down on me,
I lift my head and relieve my soul.
The Night is quiet and beautiful,
With time for private thoughts and dreams.

I walk through the Dark, I am calmed.
People are happy in the Day,
And feel threatened at Nighttime.
But for me, the Day is frightening, overwhelming.
The Night has always soothed me with its mysteries.
The Shadows leap as the Trees sway in agony.

I dance to the melody of the Wind,
And as I lift my arms and sing,
I become the Nighttime.
I am calm and fearless, I rejoice all Night.
The navy blue Sky lifts me up,
I am flying.

This is Night, a silent, healing vacation,
From our busy, frantic lives.

    Melissa Smith

Sometimes

Sometimes I don't think at all —
  the days just come and pass.
Sometimes I think of the good times —
  fantasies of bygone smiles.
Then sometimes I think of the times not so good,
  the hurts along the way —
Those great ambitions that loomed so large,...
  the one that was the "one".
Then the days just come and pass,
  and mostly I think of the good times.
Then sometimes I think of the times not so good ---
  sometimes.

    Robert W. Stratton

"Carved In Stone"

As I stood there amidst it all,
The destruction, devastation, death's last call,
I reflected upon special moments from our past,
Then thought about the future, flags at half-mast.

And as I told my troops, that if they should fall,
I wouldn't let them be just names on a wall;
So now I come here about once a year.
To lay down some flowers, to shed a tear.

And as I look around I notice they weren't alone,
They were all men of steel, men - carved in stone;
So now as you read this, I've made myself clear,
Come visit the wall, and leave them a prayer...

    Michael S. Cahill

Will They Know

Will they know my greatest fears
The ones that set off many of tears

Will they know my every thought
like a book on a shelf that you just bought

Will they know my inner feelings
the heart and existence of my very being

Will they know my weakest points
to soar my soul with tease and taunt

Will they know my life's desires
shimmering and roaring like an open fire.

    Valerie M. Cooper

Silent Murder: A Reflection

In the place where "brave" men wander
The devil dances 'round
Planning plots of murder
No life can be found

I see the pain and thunder
Torture with no sound
Bodies torn asunder
I walk the killing ground

Humanity is lost, families broken
Who pays the cost? On the killing grounds

Revolutions turning, with out much sound
The red rivers are flowing, on the killing grounds

The fields are burning, to the ground
Humanity is burning, on the killing ground
As the world keeps turning, with no sound
Humanity has drowned
On the killing ground

Pontus Weibull

Snow Dreams

The glitter of its innocence,
The dream waiting to be cherished
Is put to the back of my mind,
for I am not well.

So in here I remain
Only watching, from the inside out.
Someone help me, I want to play
In the white wonderland.

I want to build dream men
Of no consequence and no personality
Save those we give them.

Out there in the cold lies a world of frozen time.
In the cold they play, with flesh all pink,
All taking for granted
The magic they tread on,
The stuff that fills my dreams,
Cheers me when I am sad,
And brings my family closer together.

They play and laugh
While I sit tortured and dreaming.

Katie McKenzie

Unlock The Magic

Do you dare to discover the magic of the world?
The elegance, the enchantment, and the wonders.
There are so many things in this world, blossoms, trees, animals,
and, oh, so much more.
   Do you dare?
   Do you dare?
   Do you dare to discover?
If you take up the dare and lift the enormous gold key that is
deep in your heart and put it in the lock and turn the key with
all your might.
Your heart will fill with so, so, so, much delight.
   Do you dare?
   Do you dare?
   Do you dare to discover?
So take up the dare and find the enormous gold key that is deep
in your heart.
Unlock the magic in the world and see everything you can see and
be everything you can be.
   Do you dare?
   Do you dare? Do you dare to discover?

Natasha Malasnik

To Yellow

While inner heart hides inner grimace
   The eye turns to the yellow gamin;
Owing nothing, beating with motion,
   She moves with unearthly grace.

Unerring, a prompter airily comes to enlace
   A bit-phrase, a scrap of weightless prose,
Skips over her arch of brow, then lightly goes,
   As relic to the image of her face.

Wayne Nadeau

I'm Real

I wish all my old friends could see
The fantastic, new and improved me

The one they knew has left, I'm glad
She wasn't happy—only sad

She went away where those souls go
After losing love, zest for life and dough

She didn't listen to advice of kin
She moved away, she began again

She fought the panic, loneliness and fear
She even drank some wine and beer

She trusted herself, and that was hard
She always kept up her protective guard

She finally started to settle in
How she'd lived before was a shameful sin

That was then and this is now
I'd like to stand and take a bow

Now her life has steady streams
Of love and laughter and future dreams

Time goes by, broken people heal
For the first time in my life I feel real!

Susan Bowen

Devastation

It struck us with no surprise
The fear in their little eyes
The ones who survived
The ones who died
The ones who aren't known to be dead or alive.
A second floor of beginning lives, terrorized.
Not to mention the lives of all the others, who now have to suffer.
Also all the tension of paramedics,
As they use all their different anesthetics
Trying to keep people alive,
All this is seen since the bombing in Oklahoma
April ninth-tenth, nineteen hundred ninety five.

Windy Ronnell Arzt

Crimson Glory

"The fire and the rose are one." —T. S. Eliot
It has an old fashioned rose odor crushed velvet scent
Victorian ladies dried its petals
To put in their lingerie drawers.
Each lotus like layer unfolds and stretches out to the sun
As full as length and breadth will extend
Exposing the center seed cluster knotted crown.
Responding without question
To a rhythm beyond argument
The flower joys in its awakening
First opening slow then
Increasing insistence
Quickening to crimson flame.

Susan Hartz

Chances

Apart - unable to reach for help because...
The fire sits around me
Yet the river of white runs cold below me.
I can see everyone surviving - surviving on their own
And I wonder how I became trapped -
Trapped in a world of fears and flames
   that never seem to end.
I shall go mad if I stay here any longer,
But I think I shall go mad if I leave;
For too much time has been spent in this hellish ring.
The time has come to take a chance...

As I dive into the water below,
The cool temperatures soothe my burning skin.
All around me the water wails and yet I know that I am safe.
I close my eyes and wait for something better.

I awaken on a sandy shore.
The glorious sun beats down on my pale face
Making my past but a shadow - as black as night behind me
I know now that taking risks is something everyone must do,
   in order to make a better life for themselves.
Laura Bailey

"The First Time"

The first time you held me,
The first time you kissed me,
Was the first time I knew love.

The first time you spoke,
The first time seeing you in awhile,
Brought me back to the first time we met.

The first time there was a rainbow,
The first time there was a gray sky,
Reminded me of our early days together.

Now the times you look at me,
Do you feel the same way you did,
When you first looked at me?

Do you ever think of me,
Like you did when we were younger,
When it was our first time thinking of each other?

Now that we are older,
Will you promise me this one thing,
Act like we did,... the first time.
Rachel Meltz

Houses Don't Crow

It's morning time...the last rooster crows
The last horse whinnies, the last hound croons.
Soon not to be; West Hill has been sold.

Out of my window just last springtime
Mares and their foals did romp on East Hill,
Waving blond tails, nudging their young,
Grazing on sweetgrass, drinking up sun.

Then came the backhoes and graders and dozers,
Raping East Hill, shoving it over,
Pushing it up, loading it down
With rebar and concrete in place of gold wheat.

Parcel by parcel, acre by acre,
Tile, wire, and stucco, glass and hard sidewalks,
Where horses won't tread...hill's nearly dead
With her burden to carry.

Houses don't crow. Apartments don't whinny.
Condos don't croon. Cars don't drink sunshine.
Don't look now, Grandfather. West Hill has been sold.
Turn away and don't look.
Natalie Mitchell Juntz

If I Had Three Wishes

If I had three wishes,
the first would be to fly,
to pack up my things and say good-bye.

If I had three wishes,
the second one would be
to gaze at the world's lovely sights to see.

If I had three wishes,
the third would be best,
to end world hunger and all the rest.

Since I have no wishes,
I'm just plain old me,
I can't gaze at the lovely sights to see.

I can still have fun without wishes now,
beside wishes only happen in books, anyhow.
Scotty Hopper

A Long Night

I sit here smoking a Marlboro Light, Self destruction in
the form of tobacco tonight
Loves lost, Dreams failed, Goals not achieved
Happiness not found, Pumping Iron, Inhaling vitamins,
making dates, making time
Masturbating, Alienating, Compassion, Oversight, Fright
Alcoholic Dad, Religious Mom, Both handing out fright
One with a hand, the other with a book, what a hideous sight
Wondering of there's a power to be, wondering if there's a
lifeline for me
Sinking in sentisium, drowning in mysticism
Climbing out of the hole to fight one more fight
Bloodied, Battered, no end in sight
Passion, Love, Wealth, and bright lights
Impossible to grasp the end of my flight
Ron Broadway

My Children Are Me

My children today, are the true pictures of me tomorrow
the future kaleidoscope of my character, so it may seem
subconsciously sketching my life for each one to follow
dabbing each personality with the colors of my dreams.

Now, I must paint me as a portrait of true value
the image of my every thought, surely a reflection
of my inner being, of everything I now say and do
to depict goodness from evil, a durable impression.

Unknowingly, each child of mine becomes sculptured
by their memories of me, by the spirit of my deeds
hopefully, I've done the best, as each one I've nurtured
with virtuous morals to portray since they were but seeds.

My worth to be brushed as a mural within their hearts
I pray my likeness can save them from anything tremulous
decorating them with happiness and peace from the start
all of my children, the essence of my love so tremendous.
Karie Philomena

Ridgewell, England

The fire crackles and brings me warmth.
The rain drops announce the arrival of Thor.
The thunder sounds, flowers genuflect,
as lightning spells your name across the heavens.
I am in awe of your beauty, alive,
with the pelting of your being.
I hear your voice, and see your face,
as I am caressed.
Richard Mack Jr.

I'm Thankful For

The things GOD gave me so many years ago,
   The gifts to learn to love and grow
The parents sent to teach me so.
   And if by chance I may have learned to
feel for others' souls
   Then I owe that gift to those He sent to
guide and nurture my growth
   You've taught me so much through your life
and now you teach me even more
   So if you can allow it please let me show
you how the gifts that were given have matured
   in value.
I'm thankful for You!
   Kimothy A. Wimer

First Love

First love of mine has been stolen away.
The girl I will love till the last day.
Stolen by hands of a stronger man,
And taken to his castle where she'll stay.
Thoughts of revenge and suicide ache my head.
My depression brands me better off dead.
Your beauty in mind, our future behind,
Leads me to the conclusion I dread.
That I will find another to love.
A girl to raise my spirits above.
And she'll love me true, unlike you,
To allow your memories to be shoved.
On I will live for my heart to give.
But not one will take your place.
Your eyes are with me and will always be,
A place in my heart for your face.
   Matthew D. Kramer

The Reason

The trees whisper in the wind.
The grass swaying along with them.
The birds singing the words so sweet
it's the world performing for you and me.

The ocean flapping waves to shore
the dolphins feeding their baby bores
the sounds of a mother giving birth to a child.
The happiness of the father standing back in the crowd.

The freedom of the forest the oceans, the seas.
Are all gifts given from God to you and me
So open your eyes look and you'll see
the same gifts, only given to the.

God gave us this world and the things you see
take care of them, for they are our children to be.
   Lisa Diane Bakke

"The Bridge"

The bridge is a beacon, all night and all day
The bridge is calling, to take me away
The water below is so dark and still
It brings a calmness, and the pain is nil.

The bridge fills my thoughts and my dreams at night
The bridge is my road to make things turn out right.
The moon and the stars are high in the sky,
My eyes see the beauty, no tears left to cry.

The bridge is empty, no one around
The bridge is here, it won't let me down.
No one is watching, no one will know.
One sigh of relief, and over I go.
   Marian Ruth

The Hatred That Is In Our Land

It is difficult to understand
The hatred that is in our land
The bombing and shooting of the young and old
By those whose hearts must be very cold

They must think that their cause is right
To harm those who are black, brown, or white
They don't care who they kill or hurt
And eventually are buried beneath the dirt

But the outrage that has spread
About the wounded and the dead
Will rectify this injustice
By bringing the perpetrators to justice

And after a period of reflection and mourning
We will all awaken one morning
Realizing that we are united as one
And that those terrorists have not won
   Nicholas Di Maria

I Remember When

I remember the day our eyes met
The heat in the room was growing
And the question was set
I remember when

I remember the nights we talked on the phone
The conversations were so heart warming
The communication was so long
I remember when

I remember our first fight
We were so confused
But we made up that night
I remember when

I remember the last time I spoke to you
That's when our time of love and togetherness
Had gone through
I remember when

I remember when I said I will always love you
It wasn't a lie
I still do
I remember when
   Ne'Kilya Silmon

Until Never

Until the darkness of midnight is dark no more,
The heavens open up and swallow me whole.

Until the light of the day is a forever lasting glow,
I will love you forever more.

Not until the clouds vanish,
and the mountains break open the sky.

The trees stop to watch,
the animals pause and perch.

Not even then, will my love lose strength.
I will love you forever more.

When death becomes you and I,
and our memories are buried,

The angels flock to us
and our souls are realized,
Not then, my love, not even then, will my love falter.

Hold onto me as we rise,
See yourself in my eyes, as I see you.

Hold onto me as we live
our lives adjoined.
   Mara Jacobs

The Magic Bus

As the bright yellow machine parades down the street
The impressionable children conduct their own parade
A parade which should logically be labelled a celebration
The children express their true feelings of liberation
From their so called adamant captors

This magic ride is an opportune time to "let it all hang out"
And the fledgling bastards sure do not hesitate
They know that this is 'their' time
Well, at least this is what they think
Disgusted of enduring screams and harassment, they will now rule

The target of their antics is a welcome new figure
…And the poor bus driver knows what she's in for
Another unforgettable 3 o'clock ride

She opens the door coolly, and offers a sincere hello
The dastardly children are already in full force
Spit balls zoom as paper airplanes fly
But the good old bus driver just keeps on truckin'
Understanding that they will only be children once

Mark S. Schreiner

Senior Citizen's Lament

What's happened to America,
The Land of the free?
Our slogan should say.
I'll help you out, if there's something for me!

We educated our kids,
Right through to College,
They got smarter than us,
They're so filled with knowledge!

Money talks for them all,
For that's what they seek,
As they drug-up and drink-up and step on the weak.

Crime runs rampant, you dare not go out,
Deadbeat fathers and mothers are running about,
No morals or respect for the old or the new.
Lawyers, Doctors, Government workers, to name a few!

Where is our land of the free, home of the brave?
A "Puzzlement" I have, to take to my grave!

Rose M. Homola

Ocean Of Life

As I sit before an ocean of openness, I wonder what is life?
The sun is high in the sky and begins to set with the ending of
a beautiful day

I see the calm waters glistening in the moonlight
I hear the distant sound of creatures in the night

The waves roar like a lion in the wild as they suddenly crash with
instant silence

I feel the cool ocean breeze blowing inland, touching my face,
my hair, my heart as happiness overtakes me

I ask you, is life like a cool ocean breeze, always soothing
and refreshing?

Is life like the swelling tides of the ocean, always challenging and
powerful?

Is life like the setting sun on the horizon, always bright
and rewarding?

I ask you what is life? Life begins and ends every moment of a day,
like the rising and setting sun, a new day begins and ends

We must all appreciate what life brings us and aspire for what
God has given us, for life as we know it is us; man, ocean, sun,
all surroundings of life, and for that we are given our lives to live

Kurt Angst

Fall Leaves

The forest is blazing, blazing with colors so bright.
The leaves on the trees are all aglow with vibrant colors.
The vibrant colors of golden yellow, amber, burnt orange,
  and a deep dark red.
Oh so beautiful, those gorgeous colors coming from the leaves
  on the trees in the forest.
Yes, the forest is blazing with colors burning so brightly.
Burning so brightly, reminding us of marvels of God.

The forest is burning, burning with all the various colors.
The leaves on the trees are all aglow with the vibrant fall colors.
Showing us the majestic work of God, showing us how much He
  loves us in this beauty.
Oh so beautiful, those gorgeous colors coming from the leaves
  on the trees in the forest.
Yes, the forest is burning with colors blazing so brightly,
  reminding us of the marvels of God.

Mary E. Younger

As The Tree Grows

As I sit and watch the tree grow,
The limbs and branches still quite low,
I see the buds that will turn into leaves
And think, "in a few years what a beautiful tree that will be."

The tree's not too short but slightly plump,
Of course it will be easy for me to jump.
Every day I look, not much change is made.
In a couple of months I look and on the ground some leaves are
  laid.

My wonderful tree has grown I thought to myself,
No longer able to sit on a shelf.
As I looked at the tree I thought,
A lesson in beauty God has taught.

Ricky Braddy Jr.

A Reflection In Her Eyes

A lone girl rests high atop a perch of antiquity.
The lolling hills and green grassy meadows are picturesque
in the yawning rays of the sun. Her milky white skin is
as soft as an angel's kiss. Her hair, a shimmering brilliance
of gold, is far more priceless than any ring or chain of the
same. The slender and delicate curves of her body beguile the
true strength in her heart. The loveliness of her lips is
rivaled only by the voice which flows from them. Her eyes,
yes, her eyes! To be the focus of her gaze would be a
baptism of awe and reverence, a blessing. They are bright
orbs with a fierce steel - grey beauty, an overflowing well
of purity that would melt the coldest heart. Her eyes were once
full of love, real love swimming in those angelic radiant pools.
When love comes to swim again, I hope to see my reflection in
her eyes.

Ramon Altamirano

The Rain Falls Up And down

The planet is enchanting when the rain falls down.
The droplets dissolve our greedy, dirty atmosphere
and lock the freaks in their sanctuaries.
The droplets form scenic puddles that reflect solitary peace
in the present, for a moment erasing the noisy past,
So I get lost in a ball called selfland and splash alone.
Then Satan's concerning gaze follows me from book heaven,
And Goofy's welcoming black Nytemare rescues me,
And Dr. Ben's hot honey-touched tea heals me.
Then I smile in the downpour
Until the rain falls up
and the greedy, dirty planet returns to normal.

Sara Sowers

The Man I Once Knew

The man I once knew?
The man is not the same man I knew.

This man used to care,
but now he doesn't care.

The man I once knew loved to talk,
This man is not loving and doesn't talk to me.

The man I once knew used to be fun,
This man is like a stranger.

The man I once knew was interested in how I was doing.
This man is not interested in anything I do.

The man I once knew was my father.
This man is not a father — he is just a man.

Robby Dawson

The Meadow

   They stand, peacefully grazing on the lush green grass in
the meadow of the recesses of my mind.
   The meadow is in a box canyon, rich with wheat and barley fields.
   There are low growing apple trees that are always heavily
laden with fruit.
   Carrots grow up instead of down into the earth and there are
salt blocks that never dissolve.
   An underground spring supplies fresh sparkling water and trees
of all sizes and species abound.
   It is majestic and serene on the meadow in the recesses of my mind.
   The herd is getting restless now, a few pounding hooves, some
shrill neighs.
   They're going faster, running, pounding, neighing,
   They're trying to get loose, they're pounding and pounding,
they're raising their hooves and trying to break the gate.
   The pounding, the gate shaking, the neighing,
louder and louder and louder.
Go back go back go back go back pllleeeeaaasse
   Somedays they try for hours, sometimes they try for days,
but eventually they go back. Back to the meadow. Back to the
meadow in the recesses of my mind

Patricia A. Lloyd

"To Find The Love..."

   The loneliness of a silent cry
the meaning of an empty sigh
   All so obvious, yet all so hidden
but to look into one's heart is not forbidden
   To find the love that lies inside
the love that everyone tries to hide
   The true love we should all share
if only we would learn to care.

Stephanie L. Seibold

Technology

The mouse is replacing your pen in hand...
The monitor is replacing your world and your land...
The hard drive is replacing the memory in your head...
The keyboard is replacing things you have said...
The office chair is replacing your comfortable couch...
The disks are replacing the notes in your pouch...
The software is replacing the information in your brain...
The speakers are replacing the thunderstorm rain...
The modem is replacing the telephone lines...
The Internet is replacing your everyday signs...
The computer is replacing your wife...
Technology is becoming your life.

Tammy Gouker

"My Johnny"

I met a man named Johnny, who's hair was dark like blue
The minute that I saw him, I knew I'd love him true
From hat moment on he became my life
And after six months I became his wife.

He is so gentle, he is so kind
I could search the world over
No better husband could I find.

We have our problems and we have our joys in everything we share
To have a love so rich and full
There's none other to compare.

There are many people who have a wealth of gold
Unhappy with their life
I'm the richest woman by bar
As my darling Johnny's wife.
We take not our love for granted
We simply wouldn't dare -
Our marriage was made in Heaven,
It's a lifetime love affair.

There is no ending to this story as I have a job for life -
The most promising career of all - as Johnny's loving wife!

Mari Schwamberger

Who Will Keep My Clock Wound?

It comes on time once each year
The moment, our arrival, memorably clear
As time passes, the ages march
Our clockwork internal touches the arch

Insignificant the minutes, how wasteful when young
To let them pass, who cares where they run
Relentless and vibrant and reckless and free
The end of time; to youth no plea

Priceless the threshold when youth fades to gray
All too real, our mortality shouts nay
The mirror's faces map lines of experience
Bones rattle and creak, no need for clairvoyance

How quickly it seems as our own lives retreat
Forsaking, forgetting what we'd like to repeat
The seasoning we've gained, the achievements to tell
to all who sit quietly, engrossed under spell

To walk away humbly, to reflect on what's told
To remember with fondness when our own have grown cold
Perhaps they'll recall our brief moments in time
As their own clockwork internal marks the hour to chime

Mazlone Caldwell

Untitled

This is a poem from my heart
The heart I willingly gave to you
And you willingly took when our eyes met
You'll always have my heart
Because of this....
I'm not complete without my heart or you
Be careful with my heart
Please don't hurt it, for it breaks easily
It feels all love that will always last
without a smile and laugh from you it would die.
You keep it alive
Without you my heart is dead
Therefore I'm dead
When we meet again my heart will be filled with love
A love only for you, from me
So keep this as a reminder...
For when the two pieces meet
That is when my heart is complete and alive

Melissa Cloeters

A Picture Of Your Face

I tried to paint a picture of your face one day,
The more I thought about it, the more I felt a need to pray.
It was brighter than the brilliance of the moon,
It was lovelier than a flower in full bloom.
It shone greater than the radiance of the sun.
My heart was overwhelmed, I was undone.

Your hair was golden and upon your head you wore a crown,
And you were girded with a white majestic gown.
Within your eyes I saw the tears you've shed for me.
Your smile was deeper than the vastness of the sea.

Upon your lips was written love,
As can only come from God above.
Within your heart I saw my name,
And I'll never be the same.
It spoke words I've never heard.
And my soul it has been stirred.

It's a picture of your love, your warm embrace,
It's a picture that's too lovely to erase...
It's a picture I can never ever trace,
It's a picture of your face!

Susan Soto

Dawn Of Day That Lights The Soul

In silhouette the mountains stand against the reddened sky
The morning breeze glides softly in and bids the night goodby
Filtered through tall stately trees the sun peeks o'er the crest
Then brightens vales and plains below and stirs within the breast

Oh dawn of day that lights the soul within this land of peace
Beam ever bright from shore to shore that strife may ever cease
Seed the plains with crops of love that harvests may be great
Instill in all a common glow with courage not to hate

Let little ones like sunbeams dance without a thought or care
Warm family life with harmony and keep it always there
Cause understanding light to shine that those who lead may see
And give them courage to direct and keep our liberty

May noonday sun pierce to the hearts of those who harm would cause
Help them to mend, transform their ways, be just, obey the laws
Send rays of hope to those in need and lighten up their grief
Prompt those who have, to share their wealth in bringing sweet relief

Preserve the glow from dawn to dusk and with the setting sun
Bathe souls with radiance that will last until the night is done
Night skies give rise to twinkling stars, a sure and blissful sign
That soon another day will dawn, the sun again will shine

M. Wayne Western

Nana's Angels

Do you believe in angels? I surely hope you do.
We're all assigned an angel, but me well I have two
Little cherub faces, sparkling diamond eyes
Smiles that warm the sunshine, and put starlight in the skies.

A mother's love is special, a grandmother's love unique.
When I realize how much I love them, I find it hard to speak.
Children are a gift from God, a treasure to behold,
Grandchildren are the rewards we reap that turn our treasures to gold.

Angels touch our lives each day, protect us and hold us near.
Grandchildren are our angels on earth, a thought I hold so dear.

I thank you Lord for all my gifts, my children whom I adore,
for Nana's special angels on whose wings I daily soar.
They lift me up to heaven each time I see their face,
They warm my heart and cleanse my soul with every little embrace.

Angels are all around us, this you can believe,
Nana's angels are heaven's gifts, that I am proud to receive.

Fran Lotti

Mother Earth

The rivers are the veins of Mother Earth,
  the mountains are the breasts that never feed.
Mother Earth can only live once.
Mother Earth, like any other living being can die.
We may live happily today, we may live happily
  tomorrow, but Mother Earth is the one that is
  not getting the best of our happiness.
Mother Earth, how can we save you from the
  devastation the white man has caused you.
Mother Earth, your children have been put on small
  reservations plagued with poverty, alcoholism,
  and jealousy.
Mother Earth, it is time to take a stand, the
  Sun Father told us—at the beginning of time—
  to take care of you. We your children are
  being dominated by the white man, so we cannot
  take care of you.
Mother Earth, It is time to take a stand, show the
  white man the harm that you can bring them, if
  they don't start respecting you, Our Mother.

Nolan Laate

The Nazi's Are Coming

The Jews are rushing for shelter
The Nazi's are coming
People are screaming and yelling
The Nazi's are coming
Air raids are destroying Europe
The Nazi's are coming
Jews are in terror and are scared
The Nazi's are taking over.
The Jews are getting destroyed by Hitler
The Nazi's are taking over
The Jews see the smiles on the Nazi's faces
The Jews are frightened
The Nazi's think that the Jews are not people
The Jews are frightened
The Nazi's think that they can rule the world
The Jews are frightened
Six million Jews were annihilated
The Nazi's came!

Kevin Roskom

His Big Bay Mare

They ride into the sleepy meadow.
The new mown hay smells sweetly mellow.

The mare is fresh, but obedient to his touch.
She stands her ground, as a rabbit leaves its hutch.

Which way shall we go, he thinks for a minute?
He looks at his hand, the reign loose in it.

Give her her fancy, let her go where she will.
As he nudges her, he senses a chill.

The afternoon has brought with it a quick shower.
The ground so muddy, the mare slips on a flower.

She falters, loses her balance and comes crashing down.
He falls free, and steps quickly, his worry seen in a frown.

Quiet deafens the air, she seems lifeless lying there.
Gently, he strokes her neck, as he pulls closer, her eyes open and stare.

A twinkle in her eyes gives him a sense of relief.
She moves suddenly and raises to her feet.

The mare stands there, beautiful and free,
and he hopes in his heart that she always will be.

Mary Gerene Lucas

Life's Numbers

They start when a baby takes his first breath,
  The numbers he'll carry from birth 'til his death.
The month, day and year he arrived are first noted,
  Then weight, length, and hours of labor are quoted.

Various weights at various stages,
  How tall he has grown at various ages,
How long he sleeps, how often he eats,
  The dates he performs the usual feats.

The government issues an "old-age" card
  Before it's known if he'll get that far.
Bus numbers, room numbers; school has begun,
  How well can he write? How fast can he run?

Numbered papers soon insure life, car and health
  Numbered, too, are the bankbooks recording his wealth.
Success is measured by what's been attained,
  The number of dollars and goods he has gained.

But when life is over and he's all alone,
  The last of the numbers etched on his stone,
Only one number will really suffice...
  The number of good things he did with his life.
        Marilyn C. Klase

Awakenings

  The earth began to awaken, lightly sprinkled with a dewy mist,
the nymphs rubbed their sleepy eyes, as night and morning gently kissed.
  A finch sang a song to the sun as he rose slowly out of the sea,
an eagle spread its wings and flew to show the earth what it was to be free.
  The sun bid the earth "hello" as he took his place in the sky,
the moon journeyed to the sea for her rest as she bid the earth "good-bye."
  The nymphs and fairies frolicked joyfully underneath the clear blue sky, the sun smiled down upon them and the eagle continued to fly.
  His warm rays caressed the nymphs and fairies as he watched throughout the day,
and he smiled with an indulgent grin as he watched them laugh and play.
  And then it was time for farewell, so twilight and evening met for their kiss,
the nymphs and fairies stopped playing and listened as the sun sank into the sea with a hiss.
        Mandi Mutch

The Sweet Wishes

I wish you were here with me,
the only place I want you to be,
I wish I was the one in your arms,
telling me your sweet charms,
I wish you will take my mind,
with your magic touch "so kind"
I wish I could share with you,
the dreams I've had of us two,
I wish you would whisper, "I love you forever"
in my ear, in the wind, in your mind, "wherever"
I wish all I had to do was try,
but with you it's helpless, "I cry"
my love for one is true,
and the only one is you,
I wish you would relate,
I can't hardly wait,
I don't know what I would do,
If I was without you.
  I wish you knew, how much
    I love you!
        Myra Remster

Enchanted Forest

The forest comes alive by night
The owl, its eyes they glitter
The wolf, it calls to its mate
The bats, you hear them flitter.

Deep within the center
Lies the murky swamp;
The foul smell entraps your brain,
Its odor causing immediate pain.

To lose oneself within its grasp
Is death at once, an easy task.

There is not light, no day
Because the leaves hide the ray
The sun is hidden, it comes not out to play.

Mysterious is this grove of trees
That closes up an area so no one sees.

What lies within these borders
What secrets does it hide
Would you like to go inside?
        Kathie G. Van Schyndel

The Pain That Nobody Sees

In the eyes of the children, there is the pain
The pain that nobody sees
The pain brought upon them, by those who came before them
The pain that nobody sees
The pain that runs deep, deep in the hearts of the children
The pain that nobody sees
The pain caused by prejudice and war
Race on Race
Gay or Straight
Fat or Skinny
Ugly or pretty
The pain that nobody sees
The pain that goes on forever, the pain that never stops
the pain that causes anger
The anger that causes hatred
the hatred that causes killing
The pain that nobody sees

Why must I be
one of the children who's pain is never seen
        Kyla Porterfield

For Dad And Claire

The morning sun, the patter of rain,
The subtle scent of sage carried on a hot summer's breeze.
There are the memories of childhood -
my childhood - my time spent with you.
And you brought these to me
Like gifts brought to an infant king, too young
To comprehend their grandeur,
Gifts far greater than diamonds, silver, or gold.
The smell of coffee, your voices whispering softly in the morning, or
Singing sweet and low to a tune from a Spanish guitar.
Waves pounding, sea gulls screeching,
The babbling of a freshwater stream.
Stars shining in the desert sky like millions of beacons
To guide us in our dreams.
A chipmunk, a snowflake, a thieving raccoon,
A prank, a giggle, tears of joy.
These gifts you have given me, which have molded my heart like
Gentle currents shaping a riverbed.
Would that I could package them as well for my children,
Would that their memories might shine in their hearts as brightly.
        Lianne Ashley Meinzinger

Untitled

A summer breeze never to be felt again.
The passing motions of my pen.
A victim of her own negligence,
now having to live with its morbid sentence.

The beautiful life gone to waste,
crying to be lived out with so much haste.

Time! Time! That insufferable creep.
That always robs us of so much sleep.
Rushing frantically to somehow slow the clock,
hoping and wishing for one last moment with family and friends.
Always with the assurance that the Grim Reaper will someday come and knock.
Brother and sister thrust apart by different lives and habits.
Ironic how I'm a cancer and she has it.

Mark DeCoteau

"Faithful Friends"

So many people take for granted
The people who really care
Never knowing what it's like
Not having someone there

They're not the same as the family you love
Or the friends who just know your name
Or the people who stay when the weather is fine
Or that love you when you're playing their game

The friends that are there despite where you are
Who'll love you and just understand
They're the people who's captured your heart and your love
These precious people are truly my guiding hand!

Matthew W. McCarthy

spring - an ode to the season - after e.e. cummings

rising and bursting through
the petals
unfurling
pushing
hardly without effort
yet mightily forthright
in their tiny stream
a ray is cast
the branch bends now
slightly taut and curvaceous
luscious
this living
out
side
the
husk

nico la follette

Roads Of Time

Walking the lonely roads of time, I face myself.
The puffs of dust gently follow the slight air,
As the grains fall slowly, they echo my despair.
Raising my eyes, misery lies on the shelf.

The pounding in my chest never ceases, ever drumming
hopes of newness unknown, wilting all my joy forever.
Creasing brow tangles the web of larger endeavor.
Cautious moments bloom again into smiles of humming.

Stalking the days of glory on sun-drenched youth,
Seas foaming, calling back to visions once held.
Last images always haunt minds gazing truth,
Praising battles fought in life alone and felled.

Robert Dodson

February

Black with dark reflection
The quiet river slides along
Between the banks-covered
With last week's snow
And striped blue-gray
With shadows.

The old snow lies about
With pock marks from the sun's heat
Widening,
And here and there
The brown green-grass shows through.

The trees that striped the snow with blue
Still stand brown and bare,
But their bark color seems
A so much warmer brown
That spring shows through the snow.

A. R. Vahan

The Lifeguard Stand

As I sat in the darkness of the night
The rain from the heavens came bouncing down.
I watched the rain drops as they floated down,
and thought how sad as they broke into a million pieces on the ground.
As the wind playfully gained its strength
I thought how cruel as it coldly slapped my face.
I felt as if the Gods of the powerful sea
were teasing me to set them free.
I looked far beyond the white caps,
and noticed how beautiful just like a great big bubble bath.
I watched the mighty ships roaring through the sea,
and felt hypnotized by the beams of light bouncing off the sea.
So please believe
That this is all that is sacred to me.

Karen A. Niver

Rain

The rain flowed and so did my tears,
The rain to me seemed like years.
Years of my ancestors, my brothers, my fathers,
Years of young girls bearing young daughters.
I feel their pain, I feel their sorrow
And the rain...it continued to flow.

Tiffany Miranda Brown

Young Memories

I look out the window, the ground is white.
The light is bright. Oh, what a lovely
Sunday night.

The sky is clear from over here.
The snow is blowing and it's growing cold.
Oh, how I wish I wasn't so old.

I'd rush outside and go sleigh ride.
I'd run and play into the night,
And start all over as soon as it was light.

I'd make a snowman with carrots and coal and
wish he'd come to life, like Frosty and glow.
But being a wife, a mother and so,
Make being a child a life long ago.

So what do I do when I wish it was so,
I tell my children go play in the snow.
For youth is short and time is not fair
before you know it, you too will look out
a window and stare.

Linda Johnson

Untitled

Miniature splashes
the rush
down the purple sky
reaching all points
but never hitting
the same spot twice

Covered flesh
reducing the frequency
of cuts caused by
stalk and tassel
irritated by microorganisms

Focusing two miles ahead
to see the clouds and
the ground make love
in electric bursts at 186,000 miles per second

This is the time for song and dance.
D. Alexander Levy

Strangers

I drive all day
The sky is dull, rainy and gray
But, I can still find good people along the way.
People who share and people who care
To keep the boat floating
To open the sail
Strangers can be the most helpful people around.
When everyone else has let you down
They renew your hope, faith and trust
So you don't just settle in the dust
Lately, I've met people like that
And I'm very thankful for that fact
I know it sounds too simple, but true
And I hope I give them something too
That's what makes the world go round
And I've been lucky enough to have found
Strangers I meet along the way
To help me make it through another day.
Sue Pollard

Untitled

Last night was as wonderful as it ever could have been.
The sky was so clear and while I was alone I felt
as if you were holding my hand all night long.
Things just haven't been the same since you left.
Sometimes I feel as if you just left me to start a new life
with someone else.
It's so hard to believe you're gone and that you're never coming home.
I wonder if you miss me from so far away,
because I know I've missed you since the day you went away forever.
This has been the first night I didn't have to cry for help,
because I didn't need anyone else to pretend everything was okay.
But now I know that for myself, I can really let go,
and not feel any pain.
Melisa A. Nusser

Capital Over Head

Dear brethren where we abide
Gathered momentously to decide
Our roofs leak
In bed, at stars we do not want to peak
Gold over the Utah Capitol Dome
Too shiny over our home
Very good, Anaconda copper
Not enough dough in hopper
Something short of tin or lead
Must last till we are dead
Could our solution be
A concoction fire free.
Joseph Rutkowski

Untitled

I knew it was over the morning after.
The smell of cigarette smoke in my hair was
all that I had left, and all that I was given.
It wasn't the seedy underground surroundings,
nor the dancing of intoxicating slow-motion.
It wasn't the dirty secrets whispered in my ear
as I was clenched in a suffocating grasp.

It was the feeling of a juxtaposed heart,
the contradiction of emotion.
Gluttony, but emptiness..
Vampishness, but naivete..
Nothingness...

I was a pawn, when I thought I was a queen.
Yet, there was no manipulation, because there was nothing to be gained.
A bloody mark, the Pharaoh's cursed sea upon my mouth,
my only hope of independence...

All taken away.

And I knew, from that day on, that I could never wear red lipstick again.
Lacey Marsac

God Is There

The freshness of the forest after a Spring rain;
The songbirds with their melodic refrain;
I feel your presence there.

The cool, gentle breeze that bends the trees,
The sweet scent of blossoms, the rustle of leaves,
I know you are there.

The golden sunrise in a red streaked sky,
White fluffy clouds that float quietly by,
You are there.

The soft rippling of a forest brook,
You are at work wherever I look,
I know you are there.

The melody of a rushing mountain stream
These are all things of which I dream,
And you are there.

The little blue violets on the forest floor,
These things and many more,
Tell me God is there.
Rebecca H. Olsen

And There Is Music

Music... the heart of all that breathes —
   the soul of all that loves —
beckons us as it orchestrates turbulent swells of motion —
   peaceful poignant moments, silent reveries of intensity.
As notes are struck
   sounds sing songs of sacred realities
   bringing to life feelings of what it means
     to run - to fall - to rise again.
As its melodies intone - chant - flow into movements of
   symphonic antiphonies
it continues in harmonic peace with an all-embracing panorama
   of sound.
Music is the language that knows no boundaries...
   the tiding of lasting melodies.... rising above and beyond
   oftentimes where no one has dared to go.
It is that voice which encompasses the world
   as its vista opens out into the expanse of time and place
     creating - gifting - soaring in mystery and vision
    in all that breathes - loves - lives - dies - and rises new
into the resounding movements of life!
Rose Garramone

Untitled

The dust has finally settled
The streets covered with red is fading
The echo has finally subsided
But the pain will remain forever...

Our nation has become a prison
We have to be aware of all our surroundings
We are unsafe even in our own homes
When will it all end?

Should I bring a child into this vicious world?
Does he have a chance at survival?
He will be a savior
I must believe
If not, all is gone
We might as well become the remains of the dust.

Shirley Wong

Calmly, As The Day Begins

How calmly does the day begin.
The sun appears above the rim.
It climbs the ladder of the sky
And looks on us like some big eye.
And seemingly floating there above
Sends us rays of light and warmth and love.

If by some chance our lives could be this way
And all could start as calmly as the day
Think what goals our souls they might achieve.
Then nothing is impossible to believe.
If we could slough this mantle of dismay
Behold what wonders we'd perceive each day.

Paul T. Robinson

Paths

Our paths in life lead us every which way.
  The sun lightens the sky and brings a new day.

Make the best of that day, reach for goals in your mind.
  Try to live out those goals to see what you'll find.

It's not very easy, at times you may fall.
  Get back on your feet, stand straight, stand tall.

Now be realistic, don't set goals to high.
  Start with small ones, get bigger as each day goes by.

One day in the distance you'll wake up and see.
  You made it, you did it, you're where you want to be.

Regina Sheppard

Sunset Rock

Far over the ridges and across the town,
The sun peeps from curtains of clouds
Like a person taking one last good look
At the lovely scenes before he lies down.

From a passing train the blue smoke hangs low.
The fields stand out in the twilight;
Night seems so eager to embrace the earth
Before the man-made lights begin to glow.

On the highest hills the beacons blink;
The trees stand still on the mountain.
Do they wish to hear what the people say
Who admire the scene from the rocky brink?

For we two can admire the scenes that be;
We can talk and laugh with pleasure.
And thank in our own humble way
The fates that brought us together.

Thomas W. Carroll

He Will Always Be Near

As I gaze up into the loving sky
The sun shines brightly down in my eye

I wince because the light is near
The sun brings me comfort when he is not here

The bright spotlight is just on me
Up in the distance he looks over me

I realize he watches, he cares
The sunshine is his penetrating stare

Through the sun he says to me
"Don't worry, I am watching, you see?"

"I have not left, so do not cry"
"For I watch you now through a different eye"

I will always know he cares
For the sun tells me he is there

Sara Lynn Womeldorff

The Bomb

On an April day it happened.
The thing that brought the whole nation together.

I can only wonder why such
an atrocity would happen.
And also how something so bad
could bring an entire nation together.

It would indeed be wonderful if
we could all get together without
such a tragedy.

One building one bomb
That is all it took to take
babies and loved ones from
this Earth and their families.

Why did it have to happen?
Again, it comes down to
Can't we get along?

I just hope we can!

D. H. McNabb

The Quest

Throughout the dark and foggy night
The sound of many horses can give you a fright
Is it near, or is it far?

Through the thick of the fog
You can't even see a star
You know you must wait and now prepare
For the breath of the dragon is in the air.

Suddenly through the mist you see a light
It can only be Merlin casting spells in the night
You try to run and you can only hide
For the knights of King Arthur are not far behind.

Finally you hear the chanting of armor and steel
Arthur is wielding Excalibur
So you must yield.

Throughout all of England he has conquered the land
To unite all men and bring flourish to the land

The quest is complete and Merlin must go
From whence he came no one shall know.

Richard C. Ulrick

"Streets Of Gold"

Leaving life so suddenly
the way that you did,
left searing scars on our hearts
the future loomed dark ahead.

No time for teary good-byes
Ever too late for regrets.
unspoken words of love
never able to forget.

Childhood memories of happy days
are constantly flooding my soul.
Small gifts sent us from heaven
sent, possibly, to console.

Memories, however, cannot always suffice
when the wretched heartache won't subside.
Escaping sighs echo lost paradise,
prayerfully ebbing with each receding tide.

"You must go on," she adamantly said.
Death has by One been fully conquered,
Thus before us on the streets of gold
another child will fearlessly tread.

Lora L. Pogue

My Radiant Light

As I sit here by the ocean, looking upward toward the stars
The peacefulness I feel, with my child resting in my arms
The world seems so far away, We left our troubles behind
It's so wonderful to be here
With just the ocean, the stars and my child
As we looked upward toward the stars, Some looking near and far
Nothing could be so wonderful than wishing upon a star
This time we spend together looking at the beautiful stars
It's only the beginning, for my child's life has just begun
My child is like a star, giving off a radiant light
The clouds may sometimes cover a star,
but my arms will cover my child
As the night air comes upon us, the waves are rushing near
It's time to put our sweaters on, and leave our special place
As we walk along together, holding each other's hand
Glancing at our feet, as they make imprints in the sand
And as we journey home, my child and I won't look back
Because we know our special star
will follow us safely home

Wendy Barkley

"Memories Of Days Gone By"

How I long for those days gone by,
Those days of youth that make me sigh,
A time that seemed endless before my eyes,
A time where innocence knew not lies,

Those days of youth have long since gone,
Only the memories remain to carry on,
The hopes and dreams of a time once trodden,
Is like yesterday..... gone but not forgotten!

The years have passed but it has never been the same,
Children have brought me both happiness and pain,
My eyes have grown dim, my step a little slower,
I rest a lot more and stoop a little lower,

Such are the memories that consume my soul,
An elixir for the heart that is tired and old,
The vitality and vigor I once knew,
Is a ghost today in a lonely pew,

The end awaits though I fear it not,
I dream constantly, it remains my lot,
To be young again before I die,
Is why I have "Memories of days gone by."

J. M. Marquette

A Man Of Word

A man of word and not of deed is like a garden full of weeds
The weeds begin to grow like a garden full of snow
The snow begins to melt like a garden full of help
The help begins to peel like a garden full of steel
The steel begins to rust like a garden full of dust
The dust begins to fly like an eagle in the sky
The sky begins to roar like a lion at the door
The door begins to crack like a whip at your back
Your back begins to smart like a needle at your heart
Your heart begins to fail like a ship at sail
The sail begins to sink like a bottle full of ink
The ink begins to write until it is all blue and white

Mary Burnell

"The Thought Of You"

The touch of your hand;
the whispers from your lips,
makes my heart expand
as tho' we have always been connected by the hips.

Your eyes are of gold;
Like the twinkles in the night;
Your caress is like an everlasting hold;
Which is always right within my sight;

A kiss of bittersweet notions;
A tongue full of ocean's misty weatherwinds;
The smell of your alluring love potions,
Makes my heart soar like our winged, feathered friends.

The thought of your touching soul
gives me the beliefs of a brighter tomorrow,
Which I am woman and God broke this particular mold.

Lawrence Gypsy

Apache Tears

The tree dying, the beauty subsiding.
The wind and sky dancing, the children in the rain laughing.
The teardrops of the clouds falling, the tears in her eyes yearning.
The nullness between the thunder, the crackle of the wind, the dying
sound of laughter... The beginning of the end.

Tears of rain, won't smother the fire nor the pain.
The tears in her eyes fall on lost paradise.

Today we go, tomorrow no more.
Tonight we cry, tomorrow we morn.

The land dies, nothing will grow.
The last of her tears fell for the coming snow....

Nick J. Ibarra

"My One And Only, Papa"

Papa, why does it hurt so?
What has happened to you?
I thought you would be with me forever,
But I see, that is not so
We're growing apart and the gap is growing wider each day.
I feel sick in the pit of my stomach
I'm scared- scared because I am losing you
We used to be able to laugh and talk together, but we don't
anymore
The laughter is gone - the smile has faded - your eyes
have lost their sparkle
And our talks no longer have meaning.
Each day that I can hold your hand and you squeeze it back tightly,
I know you still love me and feel the same feelings that
I do, even though you cannot speak the words.
I shall treasure each day that God gives me with you and
I know that someday we'll be together again throughout all
Eternity.

Dorothy M. Geisel

The Ending

"The ending becomes you," said the crow to the dove.
"The wind was always cold and stark.
The walls were always blank and dark,
and I always couldn't see you."

"The ending is peace," said the crow to the dove.
('No life, no living, no lover, no love')
"Our boundaries are set so our goals won't be met,
and you have crossed the line between us."

"The beginning is beautiful," said the dove to the crow.
"But do you know what to do? Do you where to go?
You sing a song of rebellion, violence and strife.
The song is about your fear of life."

"The beginning is here," said the dove to the crow.
"Can you handle the truth?
Can you reach your goals?
If you look at my life, you won't end your own."

"The ending is eternal," said the crow to the dove.
"The ending is permanent," said the dove to the crow.
"But the ending happens to us all," said them both.

Rachael Smith

"Oceans Of Blue"

Seas of blue, skies of gold.
The winds brisk against the faces of strangers,
No movement, no motion from all things surround.
Eyes scanning the seas for something more than it is willing to give.
Rocks still to the outburst of the moving waters.
The tides roll slowly onto the shores as the first
   touch of day happens.
The harder the crash the more the water seems to reach for company.
Waves crashing onto the sands raging with anger,
A sudden splash of water, a quick break in the sky—
   nothing seems right between the times of day.
The drops start to fall from the sky and the ocean seems
   to anticipate their touch.
But peeking around a big puff of white the sun shoots off its
   rays with such radiance the ocean shines
      like a lost star.
Scared to stay the hands of the ocean flow back to be in peace.

Kelly Thompson

Lady Bronc Rider II

Sue came out looking grand...
The women cheered her from the stand!
Chin tucked well down, as was right,
Her bronco really showed some fight!

Her form was correct, it was true,
She showed the Davie boys something new.
They probably gave her just the worst,
To see a girl thrown down, would be a first.

The next dude up, was blonde and tall;
He laughed with his friends to see her fall.
Soon after his bronc did come out,
We women began to have a doubt...

That he could stay on, any better than she!
He hung on perhaps, to the count of three...
He clung desperately to his mount's side...
"Don't let me fall like a girl!" he cried.

But he did finally, bite the dust...
His bronc 'bout trampled him, in his lust.
But Sue's mount did but run away,
So she could return another day.

Shelley Herold

Just A Little Higher

Lift me just a little higher, Lord I'm such too small to see all
the wonder of this world you made for me. I've only fleeting glimpses
and I want to see the whole, bend down a little closes, so that I can
grab a hold.
Lift me just a little higher so I can appreciate the blessings
of each passing day, before it is too late. For though I stand
on tip toe I can barely see the sun. I want to touch a
star or two, before my life is done.
Lift me just a little higher, Lord this little prayer is such a
simple thing for you before I do not weight too much. Lift me
just a little higher, so that I can understand, if you sit me or
your shoulders, I can be a taller woman.

Sabrina Craighead

The Seasons Appeal

SPRING is an awakening of Mother Nature once again,
The woodchuck leaves its burrow, and, of course the bear its den.
Grass starts greening up again, and birds so sweetly sing
Fragrant lilacs and azaleas blossom forth to herald spring.

SUMMER'S drawing nigh, and what it means to the young folks
Is bathing suits and tans from sun the color of egg yolks.
It's their own spot on the beaches, even though there is a mob
But, for me it's looking forward to some fresh corn on the cob.

AUTUMN sees the slowing down of many growing things.
Hears the chirping notes male crickets make while rubbing their forewings.
The dandelions' golden nuggets now raise heads as white as snow,
While the maple trees with their lustrous leaves to slumberland soon go.

WINTER finds temperatures falling, and the air gets crisp and nice.
Skiers-snowmobilers-skaters all delight in snow and ice.
Children happily build a snowman, or, pull along a little sled
But, for seniors it's the season to snuggle up in a warm bed.

Ruth L. Will

Ode To Mankind

Doom entertains, dark bones wane
The World echoes a cold, strifeful guile
Only to be soothe and sectioned by the abbreviate of
Our Conductor's artful wail.

His arms swing wildly with warn
Apprising all creations wavering in concert, concerned.
The curtains swing open, all is silent
Will man's solo ring of an artful, peaceful resolve?

Michael Holman

Shining Lights

Come my little children, I have a tale to tell
The world was once a beautiful place to live to love and dwell

But then came all disruption, people full corruption
Power controlled by greed and hate, I think it is a little too late
To open eyes that cannot see, the world as what it's meant to be

But oh sweet little children, our hope is all in you
with minds so clear, eyes so bright and hearts that shine
through morning light

This sorry generation can only hide in shame
With drink and drug controlling all, who are we to blame

The darker side of evil rejoices in its quest
for it believes it's conquered all that got into its path

But light so bright that shines from you will reveal the truth
this evil has no power over innocents and youth

Sylvia K. Vierra

If I Could Dream

If I could dream
the youthfulness of
sweet rose's down the river line stream
I hope with the captain of his ship floats, away
with the reflection call the moon angle
keeps, on shining on and on.
My heart smile's inside with a defining
character if I could dream once again
in an ever loving moments with you for you
are my dream love for ever so.
This far away lovely dream relievers with in me
and you if that don't beat all beyond life
if I could dream a dream.

Ramona Eve Escareno

An Endless Love

Two lovers walk on an endless beach,
Their hearts and souls are out of reach.
To her, he can do no wrong,
To him, her love is more than strong.
This feeling is without a doubt undying,
they know this, as they hold each other, crying
Like two wings of gold that have taken flight,
Into the stars, the day and night.
Nothing could be as true or mild,
As is also, to an unborn child,
As they recall, "to have and to hold"
A future together, they will faithfully mold
Their endless love to die? It will never
May they live a long life, true and forever

Kristine Patton

"The Life Of Chewing Gum"

First, I was bought from the store by a boy named Nor,
Then, he spit me out by his front door.
Then, his dad came out and I got stuck to his shoe,
And he carried me all the way to 5th Avenue.

Then I rode on a truck's tire all the way through town
And it left me in an alley turned upside-down,
After that, a girl came by with brand new skates,
But she kicked me off by a set of iron gates.

Then I rode on a bicycle down the highway,
And it left me in front of a long, narrow driveway.
Then a boy stepped on me and left me beside a door,
And I realized I was back where I started before.

Stephanie Driggers

Dreams

It started with a look, simple and innocent
Then came the thoughts, more and more as time went by
I looked forward to seeing you, if only once a week
But never more will come of it, as I don't have the courage to say
   "let's get together for a while"

You, the older man - wiser, smarter, handsome, and experienced
Why would you be interested in me?
Me, years younger - barely wet behind the ears, and not even sure
   what I want to do when I grow up
Is there a chance, perhaps, if I could only express how I feel or
   would it be better to continue with my dreams?

Alas, dreams are what would probably be best
If the age difference didn't hurt us, our situations would
One simply doesn't get involved with someone one works with and helps
Then again, dreams can also be the cowards way out or, if something
   is merely hinted at, dreams can come true
There are some dreams with happily ever after

Karen Jansen

Broken Pieces On The Ground

There were three women in my life to whom I gave my heart.
Their mien very different, in fact, miles apart.

The first was young and careless, to say the very least.
After only a few months of courting, she asked for her release.

The second one was older, and wiser as was I
To her I swore my faithful love until the day I die.

We married and raised a family; for a score I was duty bound.
But then one day I saw my heart in pieces on the ground.

So picking up the pieces I went on my lonely way.
Vowing not to love another till my dying day.

But as I on my journey went, something strange I did see.
A woman standing in the path with arms stretched out to me.

She spoke with gentle eloquence, her every word I heeded.
I sensed way deep within myself, she was the one I needed.

She took the pieces of my heart and mended them anew.
And all my shattered dreams somehow, she helped me to renew.

But that's not all she did that day that took me by surprise.
As she offered me her loving heart, the sun began to rise.

So now I've found my one love who means so much to me.
And now I know how beautiful true love can really be.

Samuel F. Peeples

Memorial Day

They are again remembered with glory and thanksgiving.
Theirs is the sigh of pipes, the restless hunt of bugle,
Theirs is the honor, all the solemn splendor,
Yet all they lived for, suffered, toiled and died for,
Still is denied them, There is no peace.

They are again remembered with laurel and with poppy,
So have they been throughout the strife-filled years.
Wars to end wars have come and gone still adding
Crowds to their hosts who cry with anguished pleading,
   Where is thy peace?

They are again remembered and with a new resolve
Men go their ways to Council and Committee,
Talking of peace, but all the while creating
Weapons of slaughter, more and more terrible, groaning they whisper
   There is no peace.

They are again remembered, the clangor rises crescendo-ing.
Atom bomb, missiles and napalm, all nations competing,
Building a Calvary on which the whole universe
Waits to be sacrificed. O, hear them still bleeding and
   Grant us Thy peace.

Pauline Innis

A Deep Red Rose

Such beauty may rose hold to one like you or I.
The symbol of love, life, "Yes" and even death.
Life in which happiness held in which we see the
beauty of this deep red rose.
The rose that we have cherished for so many years.
May there be a great number more in gardens our
homes and in our weather beaten world.
Yet life does not last forever, for there comes a
time for undesired deaths.
What do we choose to cover the casket,
but a deep red rose, to show the love and appreciation.
For that loved one above or below us,
There is "No" flower more full of love and peace
than the deep red rose that we hold so dear.

Malinda Andreasen Dakin

Smoking Crack Kissing Satan

First comes the free one "Hey man try this!"
Then comes the price tag sealed with Satan's kiss!
First it takes your dollars, till you're down to counting cents.
Kissed by Satan again as he takes your common sense.
MORE, MORE AND MORE IS ALL YOU THINK.
You've been up a week, without a bath covered with Satan's stink.
No more caring about how you look.
No remorse for what you've took.
"Took" from loved ones - money, jewelry, home and child, your body and your soul, for THAT NEXT ROCK becomes your goal."
Satan's even kissing our kids, the rich as well as poor, not just the young, yet also the old!
For Satan's rocks are made of Gold!
It takes your remorse, you care not what you do.
And the ones sleeping with Satan NOW ADDS YOU!
So when someone says "try just one" they might as well being saying play Russian roulette and hand you a gun.
The end.
Life is highway, with many dead end roads, so turn around or find the real end.

Lisa Rice

The Hour Of The Violet

The crocus make their early show with colors of bright hue,
Then daffodils and tulips dance, more colorful to view;
Meanwhile, the lawn is greening and beneath its carpet dense,
The shy and quiet violet is growing more intense.

There was a time that Mother and I would pick them, chatting the while
As she was recovering her health, I was searching for meaning and style.
In later years, my daughter and I gathered blooms in fields of new green -
We, too, shared moments quiet but gay; joyful, yet somehow serene.

That little girl is grown up now, and living so far away;
Mother has left the earth we know, but remains in our hearts today;
I miss them both - to share highs and lows- every day of the year,
Remaining thankful for family and friends - so thoughtful, kind, and dear.

But in the spring, as I stoop to pick the shy and humble flower,
The three of us join in spirit and love, and time is lost in this hour.

Mary Wolfe Riley

"Lonely Siren"

When the lonely siren sings from the black depths of a restless night
there are many who long to join her, to find peace
in the hypnotic song that calls tides by the moon's light

Like woman weaving man through undulating spells,
soft silver pours in streams and rays
haunting as sounds drift from where she lays

It is a bewitching sound that trembles on the sea
and breathes with the waves calling through mists that pass through time
beckoning dreamers to the wind caves

There amid rocks and crashing crests she waits plaiting her hair
to the rhyme of the answering sailors, who speak in eyes
their wandering hearts and fear of jailers

Tracing ancient patterns by following stars they journey to her
working rigging and casting nets of spun rope in the direction they roam;
When the lonely siren sings there are many who answer

Dawn splashes on sea birds' wings, the sun born again from water womb,
takes to sky with the day it brings and before the rush of day's new sounds
mermen flash through shadows gathering seaweed crowns

Pat Tierney-Hashimoto

An Empty Spot

Use music and champagne after hours
then surprise her with fragrant flowers.
'Neath the moonlight hold her close while dancing.
She's always in need of some romancing.

She needs to hear how pretty she be
how pleasing to hear and pleasant to see.
She needs to know her hair is just right,
her skin is soft and her perfume light.

There's hope in her and caring and feeling
for any who need some loving and healing.
She needs a man to look and discover
her virtues, and then honestly love her.

She needs to hear that someone cares
when feelings are hurt; that someone shares
her pain with her. Yes, she must know
that she's not alone when times are low.

She needs a man with a void to fill,
an empty spot that aches until
she occupies the space deplete.
See, most of all, she needs to be needed.

Kevin Draper

Unconditional Love

If there is nothing but pain in loving
Then why is there love
You offer your heart to her
But want to claim hers in turn
The madness grows in your eyes
And desires are burning in your blood

He hankers for nothing in the world
Who is in possession of himself
He binds no one nor is bound by anyone
His love becomes free and giving
Like the running brook
Whose water diminishes not after giving

He flies upward to reach great heights
Competing with none, restricting no one's growth
He always lends a helping hand
Giving of himself without being asked
Expecting nothing in turn
That indeed, my friend, is true love

Romi Mallik

Love In A Suit

Well if it's what you wanted,
then you got the whole package.
His ties, his fancy cars,
and luxury that sings for miles.
But honey, where are your smiles?

The ones I use to know when you were
young and sound, I guess that part of you died.

Well if it's what you wanted...
Well I am happy for you,
But I know that your heart would have held out for love.
In your mother's eyes, the world
was full of men in suits.

It does not strike me as odd that
other people marry for money, but you....
you had a poet's soul, and that
could have carried you far.

I wonder, is it worth the price
of a beautiful soul, to please
your mother, to have your suit
come home every night in his fancy car?

Laura Hodge

A Day In L.A.

There are babies in the weeds with no one to squeeze them
There are bums on the street with no one to secure them
We have become a nation of quitters
Are there no exceptions to the rule
Why does the hollow soul give up and die?
Where did hope go, gone before desire
The lust for life absent like a season
Justice only a winners bargain
Freedom only a dead man's charm
simple pleasures smile so fake
Are you honest, so decent serenade
Yesterday is done tomorrow's only begun
and today is wasted on pity
Innocence stolen no remorse
Doubtful am I for beginners luck
Folly forward for future failers
Daisies done dead diseased
gone, gone, gone,
Absent am I

Lydia Mick

What It's Like At Age 72

Now that I am 72,
There are lots of things that I can't do.
My joints all ache, and my head does too,
Why I am no better than a worn-out shoe?

My golf game, it's got so poor
That I'm ashamed for anyone to know my score
Why I even swear I won't play no more,
But then I always do.

But there ain't no need for me to cry,
I still feel just a little bit spry;
And I still like to watch the ladies walk by,
That's about all that I can do.
And that's the way it is when you are 72.

W. Calverin Poff

"The Rose"

Purple, red, yellow, or white,
　There are so many colors, dark and bright.
Soft to the touch with a perfume-like smell,
　People bring them to wish you well.
There's a long stem that you don't want to touch.
　But they are still beautiful, as one or as a bunch.
Wonderful for saying, "I'm sorry" to your lover,
　Only God knows how may times it's helped others!
Yes, there are many nice flowers, I suppose,
　But not one could ever hold a candle to, "The Rose."

Michele Lynn Granger

Naked

I walk naked through the sand,
the water and the sky,
Just to have the wind in my hair,
the water to my thighs
To feel the breeze of innocence,
discover beauty sights.
Have sand travel between my toes,
hear the lovely things.
To see the naked people having graceful fun,
satisfying every need to wish' would over come.
I human this in which I tell.
I say this only once
I shall walk naked through the night
and try to have good luck.

Kara L. Lillethun

Tear

What is a tear? There are many kinds of tears
There are tears of sadness when you are hurting
There are tears of disappointment when something
goes wrong at work or at home
There are tears for someone that you love when they die
There are tears for someone that you need to
spend some time with so you can express
your feelings. There are tears for loved ones
that are sick and in the hospital.
There are tears when your little baby
Takes his first step. There are tears for
little children that have died and gone to heaven
There are tears we have when we are feeling
the pain of others in our heart.
There are tears when you feel the sin of the
world in your heart is getting you down
We have tears in our heart because we
feel Jesus Christ's love in our heart.
Don't be ashamed to cry and show your tears.
Tears come from the heart and the heart is where the love is.

William Pruitt

The Shadow Of Doubt

When I tell you this will you understand
There are times I'm afraid to be a man
No, I'm not talking about sexuality, only the realization of reality

It hurts to know this thought is in my head resting there in its
　featherbed
And it will tuck the covers up to its smirky chin when I feel this
　way now and again
Knowing it's only a day more of things in the wind knowing it will
　come to me again

When I tell you this will you be able to see
This thought doesn't live inside of me
It only comes there upon request from a few bad eggs in the nest

It hurts to see these eggs hatch out, to watch the growing image of
　the shadow of doubt
And feeling the loneliness of an empty hand is something I've
　grown to understand
But when this egg has gone away is there another hidden to take its
　place

When I tell you this will you have known
When a man his full height is still not grown
That wisdom and reckoning will come to him,
　as tomorrow becomes yesterday and they're stored within

It hurts to see the eggs still hatch into the new dark members of a
　new bad batch
But I've heard voices trying to let me know to look through the
　shadows for a place to go
Then I can lie back and grin with covers at fan, as my brain
　receives the signal of a fulfilled hand.

Zane Mills

Blessed The Brave

Many brave men of yesteryears gave all
Their tomorrows for your freedom today.
There may be many days between you and the grave.
There are many reasons that causes men to be brave.
God, country and family, give men courage for each day.
Today is d-day I an. Here with the brave for
Tomorrow many men will be waiting for their grave.
God gives and God take away.
God bless the brave, for he welcomes them, in every day.
Heroes or cowards are for you to say.
Being brave is yours today
So for "All" the freedom bells will be heard loud and clear.
Remember the brave an American flag will be near.

Russell Barnes

The Box That's Gone...

She remembers now that box she once had.
There for a long time, waiting and wanting to share.
Many memories, some good, some bad, some happy, some sad.
Just hoping for someone to love, to touch, to care.

Its room was once bright and full of love.
But slowly grew dark, more each day.
The one who filled it, into a corner they shoved.
Further and further, forgetting it more each day.

Memories and laughter once vivid in the mind.
Now were locked away and new boxes were being filled.
Soon forgotten was the box and its contents in kind.
It was the past that was lost, just killed.

And one day a fire raced throughout this dark room.
The box was engulfed and quickly gone.
She remembers now the memories once in bloom.
For that simple forgotten box, she now longs.

Tomorrow the sun will rise, a new day.
Her life will surely go on.
But she stops, wishing things a different way.
For now she knows she loved the box that's gone.
Thomas L. Hill

Prickly Pear

There, the evil and mangled deed was done.
There, in the heartland of the prairie, where the American pioneering spirit reigns.

There, the lost innocence of our children lies crushed beneath the mounds of steel and dangling concrete.

There, on the Oklahoma red clay soil is soaked with the precious blood of our brothers and sisters.

Thus, the prairie flowers will forever bloom despite the prickly tumbleweed blowing across the plains.

There, the goodness of the human soul like the prairie flowers will forever prevail.
Sandra F. Mitchell

"The Faceless Stranger"

In the twilight hours, when the moon is shining o'er, there is a faceless stranger, who stands upon my floor. He always stands immobile, silent and still, an ominous forewarning, of doom that I will feel. In this desperate hour of despair, I seem to sit and stare, at this nameless stranger, who causes my shivered nightmare.
I think of vast entombment, that engulfs the midnight air, something about this stranger, makes us quite a pair. He stands there watching me, as if I've done him wrong, and often makes my fears, grow into something strong. Again and again I call to him, but he never seems to hear, and I've come to notice, he cries a single tear. A tear that shines and glimmers, with a picture in it to see, a picture of old things, things I use to be. Now I know this stranger, 'cause this stranger use to be me, and he will always stand, and cry a silent plea.
Roger L. Thompson

Peace

I hope that some day in some way
there will be peace
that everyday would be a happy day
And we would come together.

No more fighting, no more screaming
let there be happiest and joy
For people are teaming when others are screaming.
We need peace! We need peace now!!
Michelle Sauder

Last Goodbye

There is a part of me that's dying, every time I hear your name.
There is a part of me
that keeps on trying, when I have only myself to blame.
There are times when
I just want to run but there's no place to hide,
Even though my heart is breaking into a million pieces inside.
I can make believe that none of this is true,
Although I know if
I do that I will never be able to forget you.
There are nights when
I lie wide awake thinking how good it really could be,
Then on other nights
I don't feel worthy of the love you gave to me.
I remember not too long ago we both were here to stay,
But it seems like overnight we just threw it all away.
I can walk away and find things that are new,
But you should know that you are so beautiful
and I will never forget you,
It's too bad we couldn't have embraced for one last while,
Because that would have brought out my last true smile.
Michael J. Queene

Father's Love

My Father's Love is a special part of me,
There is a part of my heart that he can only see.

To me my father is my real best friend,
He has been there for me in the very end.

My Father's Love begins with his heart,
Without him here with me I would fall apart.

If I didn't have my Father's Love around,
That little part of my heart would never be found.

My Father's Love has shown me life as it's meant to be,
It has opened my eyes to the real me.

To me My Father's Love is part of life as I know it,
My life and the meaning I would not get.

My Father's Love is built very strong,
I will have and need his love forever long.

For me to live and go through life without him here,
I will need his love to guide me and keep him near.

My Father's Love will last forever, though he will fade away,
But his memory and his love in my heart, they will stay.

I love my father more than he will ever know,
But for the time we have left together, it will show.
Kimberly Blizzard

Unfaithfulness

The heart keeps crying -
There is no end to pain
When once the seal of true commitment
Is broken by the stain
Of sad betrayal, of loves tried out
On journeys taken - alone - without restraint.

There's no going back
To get again that rapture
Of one who loves you
With a love so pure
No doubt would ever capture.

You live constrained
The ever haunting fact:
You couldn't pass true love's test
By your unfaithful act.
D. Mae Rastetter

Silence

What's that sound
There isn't any noise

It's the sound of silence
It's a lonely sound

The sound of the walls talking
Talking of past memories
Memories with you

It's that hurt inside
The hurt from missing you
The hurt of loving you

It's a sound that can be heard
In the most crowded places
In the destitute places too

The sound that can't be stopped when you are away
The sound that only comes from missing the one I love

Rid me of this sound
This sound of silence
Be with me my love
Today, tomorrow, forevermore
  Randy Adams

Be Happy

Be happy, don't look so blue,
There may be others worse off than you.
Let the sunshine come within your heart,
And give thanks for who you are.

Eyes to see with, ears to hear,
You are able to walk and talk,
These are precious gifts not given to all.

Look around when you're blue,
And try to comfort someone who may need you.

A cheery hello, a friendly smile,
Make someone happy in that small way.
And see how fast your blues will go away.
  Muriel Hoell

The Widow's Cow

A long, long time ago,
There was a farm, by the Cumberland flowing.

The man who owned it, left owing.

The river green and bustling,
Along came the store keeper a-hustling.

He said to the widow Holder, "I cannot lend you a shoulder."

"Your Johnny owed me, I know you cannot pay.
So your only cow I'll have to take away."

There she stood wondering what to do,
Three little children and one overdue.

She said to her little ones, "We won't fuss,
Work real hard and sweat we must."

"We'll farm this land and till the ground,
Proud we will be and take our stand."

Times were hard and times were bad.
Looking old and gray, but never sad.

She sets in her chair by the window and smiles,
Looking back in memory of all her trials.

Now at ninety my grandmother quilts each day
Letting the world know her strong will is here to stay.
  Wanda Lee Gregory

Make Me Believe

Make me believe
There is not such thing as settling
When in reality
The only part of life that means much
Is the actual sacrifice of too much
Make me believe
There will be time to create life
But with the somber truth
We walk away
We walk away
Because knowing what we are supposed to do
Eventually forces one of us to follow through
Empty and alone we will probably be
And somehow survive
But surviving ain't the only thing
Since what counts is generally deemed
Worth all that was lost
  Laura Prather

"Easter, With Thoughts Of You"

Pretty 'n colorful lilies, chocolate bunnies and Easter Bonnets, then there is you, I have known many an Easter, grand 'n bright, but "love" has been few, this divine 'n lovely season, we too, resurrect a specialness, that has always been new. We as God's children, pay homage to his glory, and because so we grew.

When we stare into our memories of Easters past, what a smile of delight we get, because we have found the true love, that many have not come to know yet, in our minds 'n hearts we stroll along life's avenue, in the parade together, being proud, standing tall, and our dreams being as light as a feather.

This Easter, sweetheart, I tip my hat to you, for giving me the chance, to know you, laugh with you and love you, and at each other always stealing a glance with words unspoken and touches so soft, we know what our hearts hold. Because of that gentleness we give, many treasures are yet to unfold.

With sweet 'n tender kisses, I send to you Dearest Easter wishes, hoping that these feelings shared make it special 'n bright, certainly you make mine delicious, there are many ways to spend such a day, and one is to wish it was with thee, to hold you and remind you, that without you what would I be?

So, this Easter, darling, let us rejoice in God's loving light. Because it was his doing, that for us, he made what is right. I love you before, now and tomorrow, that's my solemn promise, dear. I am so thankful that you're in my life and wish you could feel my cheer.
  Maurice Patterson

In The Spring It All Ends

In the spring when skating is over and school has just let out,
There's a part of me that's missing something I just can't
  figure out.
This happens to me every year.
I just can't bear to say good-bye to friends and friendships,
  it's so hard to say good-bye.
No more after school activities,
No more late nights doing homework,
No more early morning competitions,
No more late night practices.
When spring is over,
You just can't help wondering what will happen to those long,
  lasting friendships.
If friends will grow up without you,
Or if your popularity level will sink;
When those long summer days are over
And it's back to school and skating,
You can't help thinking,
What this year will bring,
And if next spring, will this happen again?
  Symone Charles

True Love

The first time I saw you, I fell in love with you,
There was nobody else that could make my dream come true.
It's been so long I've been hiding within myself
the truth no one knew.
Not even you knew, how much I do love you.
There is no other way I can put this in a phrase
Except to say that my eyes stay in a daze.
I don't know why, I don't know how.
How I could keep this within myself.
It's been so long, I've kept this within my heart
I think it's time to tell you the truth, about
how I felt right from the start.
Every time I see you, my feelings for you grow,
My love for you is like a river that will forever flow.
I have been in love with you for so long,
Now I know it can't be wrong.
I know I love you and I want to marry you,
But let's just hope that God wants that too.
I don't know if you love me, but I would like to know
I do know one thing, that I really love you so.
Miriam Catarino

Eternity

There once was a time when everything seemed right.
There were seven of us and we were all very tight.

There was something special about our crowd,
we shared the love like a family and we were very proud.

We would get together to party and celebrate,
we shared our laughter as well as our heartbreaks.

The closeness I felt while I was around these friends,
is a special feeling that I probably will never feel again.

What happened to us, that caused us to now be separate?
Well sometimes it's hard to play with the cards dealt by fate.

Most of us moved to different places,
for one of us, the face of God we now grace.

There was seven of us including me,
and now though we are apart,
our love for each other will last for Eternity.
William Gregory Cleere

The American Dreambug Bite

I've got the American Dreambug bite
There's no anecdote to fight
My temperature is running high
For Mom, country, and apple pie

It's contagious and spreading fast
I want this feeling to last and last!
I have the right to dream these things
A-M-E-R-I-C-A — of thee I sing

I dream of peace, of strength, and health
Of destiny and national wealth
Of freedom and liberty
Of brotherhood and fraternity

From the plains of the great Midwest
To the South where ghosts of Dixie rest
From sunny shores of the Golden Coast
To Eastern harbors our nation boasts

There's little we can't achieve!
In God we trust and we believe
So let the American Dreambug bite
And get a dose of its venom might
Stephen Mathis

The Space Between

Between the "I will" and the "I do"
There's plenty of space for words
Between the Royal Doulton Princeton and the Noritake Turning Point
I want to tell you the wisdom mothers know
Between the Satin ribbons and the pastel floral prints
I want to say don't fear the sorrow
Between the daisy circlets, the September flowers, and the blue hydrangeas
I want to give you the formula for magic
Between the printer's ink and the computer lists
The champagne toasts and the tira mi su
Crammed somewhere between the "I will" and the "I do"
I hope I say, daughter-becoming-wife, I love you.
Therese M. Willis

False Expectations

Misty, rainy, cold, and wet,
These are the images the day has yet to project.
As I look at the weather I can hear the cries
Of others also hurt by the lies.
The lies are passed on from one to another.
Each lie contains something about the other.
The other looks to you expecting you to feel the emotions too.
You sit there quiet, as he waits for a riot,
A riot of your emotions.
But you look to the other next to *you*,
And *you* expect him to feel the emotions too.
Kim French

The Sonoran

I can tell you why
These carefully measured rocks
Are so meticulously placed
As to seem
Crusty offerings of cake

I can tell you why
Ten million briars, thorns, thrusts and stabs
Thorns, thrusts and stabs
Bar a million sandy ways—
Convert the granite spans
Into a checkerboard
Of snelled palaces
so tidily, so fast in secret kept

I can tell you why the sand
Why the rocks
Why the hooks and barbs—

   But
I cannot tell you why
A small white-breasted bird
Chose this point in flight
To descend to die...
Richard Ruppert

Wings

If I had wings upon my feet,
the two of us today would meet.
I would fly right to your side,
over distances, far and wide.
I'd be with you, to sit and talk,
and tell you things I have as yet not thought.
All of these I would surely do,
if I could only make my way to you.
So I will close my eyes, and dream instead,
and let visions of you fill up my head.
I love you oh, so very much
I long for you, and miss your touch.
Stephanie A. Blackmon

Appreciation

When born, you gave me senses like sight and sound and touch
These gifts have brought me happiness; I'm thankful, oh so much!
So often things left taken for granted, though loss is always feared
Conscience tells me persistently: be grateful; kinda weird

A happy couple in the park the day after a flood
Cure for disease that could kill me sends chills throughout my blood
A coon that plays and feeds on ground under my deer stand
shows me I'm not the only one for which you made this land

There are mountains in winter covered in snow with water falls in spring
So awed by these, hard to believe, Lord thank you for these things

The sound of waves at the edge of the sea can flush and cleanse my mind
'Til problems hovering over me seem almost put behind
I hope one day success will come and show that it can be
Until then I say thank you Lord for watching over me.
Michael Scot Horton

Dreams

Dreams are a special gift to me,
They illustrate reality.

Dreams are like God whispering in your ear
Messages only your mind can hear.

Dreams can tell you which way to go,
Teach you things that you didn't know.

Dreams can bring moments back from the past,
To remember, to learn, and forget them at last.

Dreams can explain things you don't understand.
Like a guiding light, they're a helping hand.

Dreams always mean things, surprising or not,
They can't be sold and they can't be bought.

Dreams are the dreamer's but they can't be owned,
Can't be borrowed, can't be loaned.

Dreams are a symbol from God for me,
They tell me exactly which way to be.

Dreams are a special gift to me,
They illustrate reality.
Mica Mojica

Oklahoma Tragedy

They listen for the cries through the night,
They look for a smile in the morning light;
But the bed lies empty, no outstretched arms,
God has taken them home, away from all harm.
No one can ever replace those who died,
Hearts are broken and many have cried.
But there is hope if we trust in God,
We will be re-united when we leave this sod.
Keep in touch with Jesus in prayer,
He'll bring comfort and your sorrows share.
These things happen because of sin.
But take heart, my friend, Christ will win.
Marge Boyce

Words

WORDS are a wonderful thing
They make songs I can sing
They make poems I can read
Tell stories of real and imaginary things
make me laugh
make me cry
Let me say what I really mean!!!
I tell you WORDS
are a wonderful thing.
Mary D. Burns

Dragonflies

Dragonflies lay their eggs in different spaces,
   They really like to lay them close to an oasis.

A nymph comes out and roams about,
   It then grabs its dinner with its shout.

When a dragonfly molts its last molt,
   It has a blast and becomes a dragonfly adult.

It climbs on a stick and its exoskeleton splits,
   It's not down in the pits.

It dries its wings before it can fly,
   Don't worry, it will not cry.

He tries to fly sixty miles per hour,
   Oh no, he ran into a wild flower!
Nathan McKain Noland

My Answer To River Of Dreams

Today I got a letter, it was good news for me.
They really liked my poem, and published it will be.

I can't believe someone heard, the words said from my heart.
For I know not what I'll say with pen in hand I start.

Sometimes I talk to Mom, 'cause she's no longer here.
She always read my verses, and kept each one so dear.

She'd smile at silly things I wrote as if she really knew.
My private thoughts I told her, on a paper as I did you.

Some are to my children, or my husband, who's my life.
Or to God, that I'll be worthy to be called Mom and Wife.

But, only in my secret dreams I dared wish for immortality.
Now when my life is done, someone - will - remember me.
Louise Howard

Braids

My braids are mine; they identify me,
They represent my past and the struggles I see.

The time that it takes to make each row,
Represents the patience that existed long ago.

Each little twist in each little braid,
Reminds me of the number of sacrifices made.

The patterns and designs you've seen on my head.
Are symbols of diversities that still lie ahead.

The constant stares I receive from you,
Reminds me there is still a lot of work to do.

My braids represent me and not my race,
And should not be looked upon in disgrace.

They represent the strength that lies within,
Which society has suppressed since time begin.

My braids are mine; they represent me,
MY HISTORY, MY LIFE, MY IDENTITY.
   Piccola Smith

The Experiencing Tree

His eyes shimmer in the sun,
   they smile at the wispy breeze.
His arms long to finally reach the heavens,
   never quite there, sometimes lost in
   their plight.
His legs dig deep, yearning to reach the fiery
   infernos of the "other sides'"
   holy shrine.
      Why? To quench a life-long thirst.
The purpose? His life is life-giving.
   Suzan Nguyen

Indifference

They Fathom not the reasoning in any devotion.
They seek not the conscience of the soul.
They adhere not to the powers of emotion.
And they want not the love to make them whole.

They are thieves whose treasures are from another.
They are prophets who predict only loss.
They are jokers who bring the fools together.
And they are saviors whose hearts bare no cross.

They wish not to trust in any form of offering.
They believe not in the virtues of sincerity.
They show not the scars from their suffering.
And the possess not a soul redeeming of purity.

They are the clan spawned from indifference.
They are dreamers who gamble with fate.
They are lovers whose hearts show no preference.
And they are the leaders who dictate with hate.

Such are they who profess of great strength.
This meager majority with no soul as hindrance.
They toll with life and greed at great length.
And they conquer love through the heart of indifference.

Melissa J. Sheard

Visiting

Their fragile hands reach out to touch as I walk by -
They smile their vacant smiles -
They know my face - not my name.
They call me - soft voices - "Take me home."
The air is thick with the smell of air freshener, talcum powder,
 mouthwash.
In each room a pink or purple violet, or a red geranium -
A reminder of life and living - outside - apart.
At last I enter her familiar room.
I kiss her soft forehead, hear her say "I knew you'd come."
Then, the nurse with her medicines - the taste so bitter she makes
 a face.
And says "Do I have to?" As if a child again.
I stay - we talk - not conversation - but words -
They satisfy her now.
Then we kiss, smile and say goodbye.
And once again I pass those other fragile hands, calling voices,
 vacant smiles,
And then - once more I leave their world
And promise to return soon — very soon!

Millie Faye Gloyd

Winter Wonderland

I saw some children playing in the snow.
They were as happy as can be.
If they were cold I would never ever know
for they played so merrily.

They rode down a hill on a big red sled,
seated one behind the other.
The ice cold wind made their noses turn red
as they laughed at one another.

They built a fort about three feet tall
and they put a flag in the center.
The igloo they made had a big round wall
and a door so one could enter.

These children sang, they danced, they jumped and ran.
One could hear them a mile away.
They threw snowballs and built a snowman
whose smile just brightened up my day.

I saw some children playing in the snow.
They were singing hand in hand.
If they were cold, I would never ever know
for they played in winter wonderland.

LaTonya Daniels

Declaration Of Absence

Those men, in times when
They were the New Disruption
Could advance with little caution
Against conformity-
Have been quietly omitted from these days.

Words have been disgraced
Absent minds in present times
Caught us on our backs-
No thought
No Mad Thirst
No Kerouac.

This Renaissance is extinct.
Art and its playmates have died
With their passing no one's cried - 1995.

Reason for treason, subject to change
Depends more on the New Science
(conScience)
Than what hangs on the Tomb of the Unpublished Notebook
Scribbles and deletions.

Art died with God, peacefully.

Kyle Turner

A True Friend

A true friend won't let you down,
they'll be there when you need them,
they'll be behind you all the way,
and believe in you for they know no other way.
For a friend like you, anyone would be true,
as much as I am to you!

Rachael A. Roberts

Your Love

The love of most people is shallow and bare.
They'll leave you in bad times, but you're always there.
The love of your mate can truly be good.
But will it last, the way that it should?
The love of a child is great when they're small.
But when they grow up, you'll hardly see them at all.
The love of a pet is mostly true.
But you can't compare that with the love of you.
The love of most friends doesn't last very long.
For the day soon comes when they too are gone.
But the love of your father never will it end.
Forever and always, you're my one true friend.

Mick Winfrey

Our Talking World

As I sit beneath the trees,
they talk to me as friends;
with soft whirling air that blows straight through,
their words all seem to blend.

The birds seem to have their own language,
one I try so hard to understand;
And even through their flight of air,
their words unclear to man.

And last but least, the land itself
seems to roar below;
of words of long lost relatives,
that once lived and now are unknown.

So you see, the earth itself has many ways,
of talking words that glisten;
All one must do to hear these words,
is just sit still and listen.

Therésa C. Stephenson

The Agony Of The Voices Within

I hear them when I'm sleeping
They're there when I'm awake
They tend to always be there
Be Gone! for goodness sake

I'm conscious of their existence
No matter where I roam
I try so hard not to listen
Especially when I'm alone

I long for when they're silent
I yearn for not to hear
But just when I think they're gone
They suddenly appear!

The voices in my head
Are never never dead
They're live as live can be
Yet not for eyes to see

They're truly truly there
But only for me to hear
The battle never ends, it continues all the time
Dear God please hear my plea and grant me Peace of Mind!

Rose Ferrugio

What I Feel For You

In my moments of confusion there are things I say
things I write that are lies that are wrong, that I hate
things I think that are not what I feel.
Did you know, I see you make the same mistakes I made
and every move I make is the opposite of what I want to say.
Are you lonesome tonight, I wonder if you are
my head plays tricks on me since it knows that you don't love me
it knows I've always wanted you since I first saw you
my head thinks, if I only got away that you and I would move apart
but the feelings in my head are not the feelings in my heart.
In my moments of confusion I think you might someday
look up and see the stars I see, the moon I love, the night I sleep beneath
I think that I might tell you what I think,
my thoughts are a quiet avalanche of reason and I think
that my thoughts are my saving grace that keep the really sad
moments at bay,
My head knows there is no answer, no solution, no bridge of white
wisteria we are slaves, we are not destined, neither mythical nor
ethereal, I slave to my mind, you to the dim and blinded words of
your dark world
if you listened to my thoughts with quiet words I would just start
to say, the feelings in my head are not the feelings in my heart.

Sirena Scales

Unrest's Sure Abode

When George and Ben and Thomas broke free from their father's side,
They built a house of 3 floors for freedom to reside.
They packed the base with the native blocks, burying all prior claims;
Then dug a cellar for darkness and refastened all its chains.

Shamefully, the time-worn bonds cracked with a costly fight,
And an opening placed on the eastern side welcomed the huddled light.
From dun to deathlike the lightness weighed on the basement door,
While xanthous rays at the western wall slithered in through a bore.

Silhouettes from the arid south stealing through the cracks do fall,
But the unhampered hue to the frozen north blends with the light in the hall.
Above the parlor a ceiling transparent from the penthouse floor
Zooms down on the trying wedge inserted in 64.

Now in the age of a new millennium, what with Pretoria's open gate,
One would think that darkness everywhere would meet a welcomed fate;
But on the wedge that freed some darkness to be cohorts with the light
A contract from the upper room "Keep that door shut tight."

Kingsley Ormonde Harrop-Williams

The Eyes Of The Devil

Have you looked through the eyes of the devil, have you witnessed the things which he stores?
Have you seen his false sense of satisfaction, that lies beyond his door?
Oh his beauty and admiration, has captured the young and the old.
The things which he has to offer, are trimmed in the finest fools gold. He gives you the drink of destruction, then hands you a plate full of sin. As he binds you into his darkness, he's convincing you all along he's your friend.
As he once told Eve in the garden, you shall not surely die.
His beauty was overwhelming, as his tongue was lined with such lies.
He appears as a sheep soft and gentle, but what you see is only pretend. For he's rugged and wretched and ready, to destroy all that he can from within. The things seem sweet that he offers, but are filled with poison and pain. As he lures towards his evils, he stains your life with such shame. His goal is to gather as many as he can pull from the flock. As he stands at the door of destruction, you can hear that awesome knock. My friends beware not to open, for he's torment dressed in disguise. His home is a pit full of fire, and ready for all who believe in his lies.
So when you look through the eyes of the devil, there's really just death standing near. My children cling close to our father, for through his eyes all things are clear.

Karen Haley Wathen

Jennifer

Imagine a world where no music was playing
Think of a church where no one was praying
Have you ever looked up at a sky with no moon
Then you've seen a picture of me without you

Have you walked in a garden where nothing was growing
Or stood by a river where nothing was flowing
If you've seen a red rose unkissed and all blue
Then you've seen a picture of me without you

Can you picture a heaven with no angels singing
Or a bright sunday morning with no church bell's ringing
Have you ever seen a man with his heart broken in two
Then you've seen a picture of me without you

Salvador Martinez Jr.

Thoughts Of You

From the moment I woke up, all I was
thinking about was you. I try to think
of something else but it doesn't work.
I never really knew that I loved you until
my whole day was spent by thoughts of you.
I really do hope that you know that I
enjoy being with you, even if it's for a
short time. There are so many things that
we need to do (but remember there's little
time!) You are the person who I want
to be with no matter what. I hope
you feel the same!

Sonia Fernandez

Burning

There's a burning rage deep inside the soul.
This fire burns and tugs at the heart.
It causes hate, fear, and frustration.
It blinds love and caring to where the soul is bitter cold.
Each match, each spark kindles the flame until it's a raging fire.
A fire that is impossible to put out.
A soul overflowing with love is the only hope for this rage.
This love is the water and dust that can fight the flames.
Love has brought the raging torch down to a flickering match.
The raging soul has opened its eyes and has seen a beautiful light.
It now sees love and caring it now knows someone really cares.

Veronica Field

A Promise And Tribute

My mother's the very best that there ever was.
This is a fact and I love her because
She works really hard eight to five every day
Then comes home to housework with no time to play
She washes my clothes and makes meal time a feast
She does a wonderful job to say the very least
She always manages to make time for me
No matter how occupied and busy she may be
I love her so much with all of my heart
I'll try hard to show it and do my fair part
I know in the past I've sometimes been ungrateful
But I hope that I've never been down right hateful
I've said it before and I'll say it again
I love my mother through thick and through thin
I hope she realizes she's needed 'round here
She's so very precious and so very dear.

Sarah Bragdon

A Melancholic Rhapsody

A melancholic rhapsody instills the beating of my heart
this soft enchanting rhythm wakes me from the dark
a soothing voice is faint within the serene melody
these charming sounds begin to tear away at the fault inside of me

I repent unto myself and weep softly in the dark
while this melancholic rhapsody instills the beating of my heart
the unrelenting music drives me mad in this bleak, harrowing dark
angrily I repent against myself and my committed crime of the heart

I jump from my bed to my vacant window encased in the dark
to find the silken moon bleeding upon my crude and shallow heart
that once serene voice, now vexing, grows monotonous with the
melancholic rhapsody

I drop to the floor, falling upon my knees
blood is gushing, pounding through my veins as I stare at the floor
hard wooden floor…and nothing more

A melancholic rhapsody instills the beating of my heart
instills the beating of my heart
stills the beating of my heart
As I crumble to the floor…hard wooden floor…and nothing more

Robyn Bordelon

Untitled

I love you dear, love those clear eyes.
  They saw the road to Paradise.
And, on the way together there,
  Lingering, we found that we could share
    The joys of life.

The way is rough, sometimes, I think,
  But let it be! For, when you link
Your arm in mine, the way is smooth.
  My care-worn spirits you can soothe,
    And still the strife.

I ask no more. I care for nought
  Than this true love that you have brought.
Of joys, of cares, let come what may,
  It is enough that I can say,
    "I am your wife"!

Viva M. McComb

What Is A Friend?

A friend is always there for you when you're feeling down.
They're willing to put a smile where there was once a frown.
A friend will always tell you what is on her mind;
She is always honest though may sometimes not seem kind.
A loyal friend will stick by you in all you say or do.
A caring loyal, honest friend is what I have in you.

Pearl Ann Weber

The Cross

The Cross is my strength, to which I hold dear,
This Symbol of hope eradicates fear.
It desolates those who do not believe,
This cross will help, comfort and relieve.
It gives us courage to complete a task,
When in need of help, we can only ask.
We refer to this symbol day after day,
When we are lost, it will help us find our way.
It also symbolizes suffering, humility and pain,
But this was only so salvation we could gain.
When we see this Cross, we should stop and look,
To remember the Man whose life it took.
Our Lord is watching us from above,
Praise Him for giving us this symbol of love.

Kristopher Sheets

Society As One

It's the time of year,
This time I ask you lend an ear.
The lights have shone and the choir has sung.
Can you not hear?

The last time of year,
The last time I asked for a lended ear,
The lights did not shine and the choir did not sing.
Could you not hear?

I saw what you would not see.
I heard what you would not hear.
Will you ask of me what you would not see?

The lights had shone like a blast through our bigotry.
The choir had sung the thoughts of society.
What I heard was the end of our ignorance.
Will you see what I saw?
Will you hear what I heard?

When society lends an ear
It will see the lights that had shone,
It will hear what the choir had sung,
On that day society will be as one.

Martha Vasquez

"River Raider"

Monsoon, paddies, booby-traps,
This was a year that changed life forever.

Death in the air, always pain and suffering,
My heart bleeds for the children.

Night ambush, incoming, First Tet,
When will it all end?

Friends wounded, friends killed,
Will America appreciate our sacrifices?

Fear, mistrust, lots of anger,
No one speaks.

Body count, media, lies….
Families watch, listen, but mostly pray.

Whiskey, weed or brew,
Can't run, can't hide, doesn't go away.

Three months, six months, nine months,
Death or "the World," short timer?

Delta, Mekong, 9th,
A river of blood.

No God, Dear John, futility,
We're all close to the Wall.

Timothy P. Rogan

This World

Is this the good world they say we live in?
This world so full of hatred and sin.
Where people kill because you walk and stare.
And ridicule you to scorn because you have some fear.

Is this the good world they say we live in?
Where in country there's drought and in others famine.
Where people die because others are greedy.
There are so many rich, yet out numbered needy.

Is this the good world they say we live in?
Where poor ones lose, because rich ones win.
This world full of darkness, and little light.
Chaos every day because the wrong says he's right.
                Kristina Shaw

Untitled

When the Rapture of the world is near.
Those whose names are written in the Book
   of Life, will have no fear.
For Our Lord has revealed unto us through
   His Word the way.
Read it, Learn it, Teach it, Live it today.
Oh, what a day it will be when we once
   again gaze upon His holy face.
Only through Jesus's saving grace, will
   that ever take place.
Is your name in the Book of Life?
Have you asked Jesus to come into your
   heart and life?
      IF NOT! —— WHY NOT!
            Kathy Sicklesteel

Existing On Winds Of Fright

Wandering alone in the sill of the night
thoughts turn to you in days of solitude.
Wondering often of the bird that took flight,
haunting from its soft lilting altitude;
Catching the winds, spreading its wings,
only to leave you standing alone.

Finally fleeing the small voice inside me
dreams are of you and nights of frustration.
Cunningly lying to the wind and the sea,
hurting where the pain eludes relations;
Floating on shore, seeming to soar.
A lonely fall from dizzying heights.

Whispering currents on high pine, mountain tips
swept by the whirl wind that oft' remembers
one life complete with silent, dry, trembling lips,
afraid of the fading Septembers.
Scarcely a sound, darkly abounds
and all the years are suddenly gone.
            Michael L. Shaffer

Memories

To thee we pledge our love,
Through all the hard times and sad times,
Because within our heart a candle burns for thee.
This candle never flickers
or burns out.
It burns forever.
Each year brighter and brighter.
Within us there is yet a glow.
This glow stays with us because
It is all the memories you have given us
throughout our life times....
In this verse we vow to remember
you.
      Sheila Gonyea

I Heart

As a river flows softly
through a yielding pleasant valley,
As a mountain that can be climbed to its summit
in time to overlook the brightest of sunsets,
I heart beat for my love,
As a raindrop cannot turn back
but runs quickly to its appointed goal,
As a tree sways gently to and fro
full of blossoms sweet smelling to my soul,
I heart beat for my love,
As a breeze lifts a dove
beauty in flight for my sight,
As the hurricane thunders against the shore,
I heart beat for my love,
As the snow keeps one in
to feel the warmth of the glowing fire
secure from the cold,
As her hand brushes against mine,
I heart beat for my love.
            Yvonne Sass

Someone

At night he peers
Through his lonely tears,
through the ocean that surrounds his fears.

He walks so fast through the dark, lonely
streets, to go find his life somewhere.

But he just has no hope.
He has no one, he needs someone.
But who?

He does not know.
But does anyone know? No!
No one knows. He does not know,
He just goes back to the lonely shore.

He feels the sand, he touches the water
He is going back to the loneliness rather.

His fears surround him, his life is behind
him. He just needs someone. But who?
            Veronica Lameiro

My Everlasting Love

(Dedicated to my wife Suzanne)

As we've grown through all these years,
Through the smiles and through the tears,
There's one thing in my life that's clear:
I LOVE YOU!

As our Seasons come and go,
Through the springs and through the snows,
There's one truth that will always grow:
I LOVE YOU!

As the trials come and pass,
Though our strength seems fading fast,
This the strength that always lasts:
I LOVE YOU!

As our children come and go,
And they grow the lives we've sown,
There's one thing that is always known:
I LOVE YOU!

As we enter life anew,
When our days on earth are through,
There's one truth that's still always true:
I LOVE YOU!
            Stephen Willoughby

A Taste Of Winter Shoes

Damp air cruises 'cross my face.

Splashing water puddles send dabbling cool wetness
through my shoelaces.

An icy breeze tiptoed up a warm spine.
Iron dried clothes turn to soaked dripping slime.

A shower of gutter water spreads a dreadful chill,
the coming ill.

Chattering teeth, ice cubed noses and frozen toes,
from cold winds that blow trees.

Feet too deep in muddy slush.
Between toes a crusty mush.

Dripping wet ooze,
Bubbles bubbling in tennis shoes.

Anger turns to the blues,
in this year's winter shoes.

Samuel Smith

Mirror Reflection

You deceive me into believing I'm something I'm not. My mind, through your manipulative powers, you have stolen from me and dissolved all coherent thinking. And when I kneel in front of you, you spit out an image of a monstrous mass of flesh, with snarled hair and a face like a blank piece of paper. I am now possessed by my mind, which you have transformed into a miniature Hitler. I cannot escape its constant screams TOO FAT, TOO FAT, lose, lose, like a sleepwalker. I find myself gorging massive quantities of food until my belly swells with satisfaction and my mind rests. I run back to you, to show you hoping that maybe you'll like me better this way and restore my thoughts. But, no, as soon as I stand in your reflection you slap my eyes with that monstrous image again. Quickly my mind jumps to attention as I find myself being shoved back into the defecating chambers to be purified. It forces my finger into the door of my throat, expelling all of my energy into the white bowl light headed from this constant torture, I am my own world, I listen. I look but you control me, I cry for death, and you shout back at me, "In time in time."

Lori Wedal

Let's Remember Our Soldiers

Let's remember our soldiers
Those who fought to end the sting of war
We should always remember
Everything their sacrifice was for.

Every gold star parent
Hold your head up high,
With the spouse and children
Of the men who said goodbye.

Let's remember our soldiers
May they not have died in vain.

Let's remember our soldiers
Those who left their loved ones all alone
We should always remember
That they fell on many shores unknown.

Not a soldier fighting
Thought of race or creed,
Side by side in battle
When our nation was in need.

Let's remember our soldiers
Let them rest as God decreed.

Louis A. DePasquale

On Aging Of Dreams

My paths all beckon me back
'till I reach that dark blockade
that shields my mind
from that which dreams are made.

Words flowed like wine
from a pen that made rhyme
of wing and sing; June and moon.
Skies were ever blue;
there was that love so true.
No clouds would hide the sun,
and the river of dreams would forever run.

Where did those dreams go?
Do you know?
Did the wind passing by
Lift them up into the sky?
Are they still there?
Does anybody care?
Or did they go back into the past?
I wonder. Were those yesterdays the last?

Norma Silvers

Lena Maye

On the hilltop lies the poor old soul of Lena Maye
till one dewy morning light
when I saw an amazing sight.
The poor unfortunate soul
has now rose up all ready to go.
Look what the last of life has made.
Beauty in itself you shouldn't be afraid
for she comes in shimmering white
that is soft as candle light.
When Lena Maye is near
you will not find darkness near.
She's back once more to see the world with their new.

Lena Maye thought it be
the world was made perfect for you and me.
Lena Maye brings the sun up the East and Down the West
as she herself rises and sets.
How I came about and found
Lena Maye rise from the ground
Is still a mystery yet,
All I know is I'm glad we met.

Lori Ann Comnick

In Due Time

"...Painting portraits at five a dime; longing for stardom in due time.
Cast a shadow o'er time and space; over a lifetime are these paths traced.

Sweet and simple is all I ask; oh, how enduring and such a task.
Why must this be, shall I venture to guess?
Sudden feelings ascertain this quest.

How, might you say, could this be?
For time will tell, it is so free.
In due time, is this so much too fast?
Love, in essence, is thee test.

When will this take place?
In a word, time will erase.
Deep thoughts entrance my vision,
Regretful guile; to some, religion.
To some, the answer's the solution; to me, this just breeds confusion.
Sometimes my mind borders sublime; yet I will know in due time..."

Phil Harwood

Feelings

There are times when I am weary, times when I am sad.
Times when I am anxious, and times when I am glad.

Sometimes it's hard to please me, I don't know like this at all,
I'm always glad when this is past, and never try to recall.

When my days are all upside-down, and it seems useless to try
I can never do a kindly thing, only to sit down and cry.

But what good would that do, for all the world to see,
I wouldn't want everyone to look exactly like me.

But when I feel happy, and someone I want to please,
I usually find someone that I would love to tease.

When I feel uncertain and I don't know where to go,
It's just around the corner, I'll find someone I know.

When I am dreamy, and I would like to stay in bed,
I have a cup of coffee, and it really clears my head.

When I am so thirsty, that I can hardly think,
I find a friend and say, "Come on, let's have Cola drink."

All of us have feelings, not only in our head,
This is very true of course, otherwise we'd all be dead.

Vi Mendicki

Of Pawns and Fate

Oh sweet elation, jubilation and joy! You have a new baby boy!
'Tis an occasion disposed to mystify.
   Tho' inclined to feel he was 'heaven sent,'
   He's merely the issue from an earthly event.
Even as you and I.

Now you'll plot and scheme to mold him to your dream,
But no matter how zealously you try
   His future life to formulate,
   He will remain a pawn in the hands of fate.
Even as you and I.

'Tis fate that shall decree his ultimate destiny;
Unchangeable, tho' you may desperately try.
   No matter the joy or pain that is felt,
   He must play the cards that fate has dealt.
Even as you and I.

Destined not to know how the future will go,
'Tis a frustration you will surely decry.
   Everyone exist purely by chance:
   A product of fate's capricious circumstance.
Even as you and I.

Tom Jones

Reflection

Pray tell, I say, "Who could this be?"
"'Tis you, 'tis you," echoes everywhere.
But dismayed, this could not be me!
Not me! Not me! Strongly I protest.
I am young, you see, and beautiful too.

Who's reflection is this in my mirror?
"'Tis you, 'tis you," whispers I hear softly.
Not me, not me. Again I protest.
No wrinkles have I; no gray hair either.
I am young, you see, and beautiful too.

A voice softly I hear, "Look closer, my dear
'Tis you, 'tis you, 'tis your reflection.
The wrinkles you've earned, wear them proudly.
The gray hair is yours, your crown you see.
Character and grace are now your reward.
Take your place, oh, so gracefully.
Look closer now, who do you see?"
"'Tis me, 'tis me," softly I murmur.

Marielle Zino

A Friend

A friend is someone to talk to
To be there when you're feeling sad,
A friend will always be there for you
In your good times and bad.

When you have a problem
A friend will always be there to help you out,
She will always be there for you
Without any shadow of a doubt.

Thank you for always being there for me
And listening to me cry and whine,
Thank you for being really caring
Our friendship is truly divine.

I will always cherish
How kind and sweet you were to me,
And I will always remember
Such a caring friend you'll always be.

Maureen Gibbons

What Is Love?

Love is a feeling of complete happiness
To be with someone you adore
It means you'd do anything I guess
You hope to see one more and more
The heart beats fast, the face is flushed
Symptoms cannot be hidden
The voice that sings is never hushed
To deny it is forbidden
True love brings trust and loyalty
Kindness, passion and Oh! such a glow
Its splendor compares as with royalty
A love that climbs both high and low
Whichever way the wind takes course
And still holds firm the constant love
How else can a perfect love endorse?
Two hearts are blessed from God above
Each year in life that we may see
Holds dear the greatest memory
Of those we love and hope to be
As one with God and family

Lucretia A. Gunnett

Pause And Reflect

Morning's come and you're awakened
  To behold the dawn of day.

Did you pause to thank your Maker,
  Did you bend your knee to pray?

In the daily paths of duty,
  With the problems that dismayed.

Did you sow some seeds of kindness
  In the things you did or said?

In the press of mid-day's toiling,
  Someone's fallen by the way.

Did you stop to share his burden
  In a Christian kind of way?

In the hush or quiet of evening,
  Deeds are done and work is wrought.

Did you meet each situation
  In the way that God has taught?

Night is come a chapter written,
  No recall can change a thing.

Ask the Lord for His forgiveness,
  Wait, see what tomorrow brings.

Z. W. Phillips

Don't Say Goodbye To Your Dreams

You walk in fulgent road
   to find fulfillment for your dreams;
But when the road becomes hard,
   you say goodbye to your dreams.

If when hardship comes your way,
   You mustn't give up!
If where the way you go gets tough,
   You must remain and steadfast!

Dark clouds may cover the horizon,
   but the sun will shine through;
So don't give up what you've started,
   carry your beginnings with you.

As long as there is Hope,
   there's no reason to stop dreaming;
As long as there is Life,
   don't say goodbye to your dreams!

Just continue with your journey,
   Someday you'll reach your destiny;
With the help of our GOD ALMIGHTY,
   YOUR DREAMS will turn into REALITY . . .
   Margie Viado Monge

Tribute To Alexis

A little Angel came to earth
To give the world her brand of mirth.
She danced through life, brought joy to all
For this I'm sure was Alexis' call.

She taught us faith, for God knows best
And her little body is now at rest.
For God is near, if we reach out
And embrace each other is what it's about.

He will give us strength to face each day
For we know that Alexis is not far away.
Our hearts are saddened at our loss,
But he had a son that died on the cross.

And because of his gift we are free,
Of the burden he carried for you and me.
So we must be true, to our little one
And love one another as he has done.

Her life was short, but she gave so much
To all the people, her life did touch
Now it's our turn to take up her mirth
That this little Angel carried to earth.
   Margaret E. Haugen

A Letter

A letter is the warmest way...
   To greet a friend far away,
Bringing smiles across the miles...
   brightening up a cloudy day.
Immeasurable strength, courage and news...
   Tucked inside a little envelope,
Reminding our loved ones, in part...
   we are near, in thoughts and hope.
There is magic beneath a postage stamp...
   That defies age or miles,
Written down on pages, fancy or plain...
   Thoughts and news, tears and smiles.
A letter is one of the warmest delights...
   Moments shared, thoughts we send,
An envelope filled with nostalgic warmth...
   To be read, to treasure as an old friend.
   Laurie A. McBroom

Time

The sound of a clock ticking is peaceful
To hear the tick as every second goes by
Or on every quarter of, some chimes playing music so beautiful
So why is it, that time seems so fast?
As the cars and people go by rushing
And why does everyone want to return to the past?
You begin to wonder why time keeps pushing
For some, twenty-four hours isn't enough
For others seven days in a week is too less
Each year goes by quick, which makes it tough
And as each year goes by, time is a bigger stress
If we could stop the clocks
To not have to worry about time
To hear no quarter of music, like that of a music box
To hear no ticking or a beautiful chime
To be able to have enough time on your hands
To be able to go to sleep with nothing on your mind
To be able to have a minute to stand
The world may not be so busy without the word time
Though no matter how nice it sounds,
We'll always have time on our hands.
   Sheri Stahlmann

Untitled

Your words are silk
tickling my mind,
Smothering my brain,
Sending me into a blissful drowsiness.
I'm sick like a dog
In love with you.
My blood runs hot
Burning me from the inside out,
My heart cries out,
"I'm in love with you"
Echoing through this vast empty carcass
Barren without you.
Yet my mouth clamps down,
My eyes stay fixed
On a beauty that has never existed before;
Afraid of losing you.
   Samuel J. Hunt

A Rose

If you want to smell a rose,
   To caress it in your hands...
You must endure the pain of thorns,
   For love does have demands...

You might enjoy a daisy's touch,
   A billion on the land...
But none could match that special feeling,
   Of a rose held in your hand...
   Vincent James Gorge

"To Mom"

As I walk down the valley of life,
Through all the heartaches, trouble and strife.
Sometimes I wonder where I might have been,
If I didn't have you mom for a friend.
All down through life the good and bad,
Mom, you are the best friend that I ever had.
Now that I have grown older, I can look back and see
All of the sacrifices that you made for me.
Now I look out and see your sweet smile,
It makes me want to go that one extra mile.
   Vernon C. Moore

A Daughter's Wedding Day

The months of planning have been done
This joyous day has finally come.

Music, flowers, food and wine
Lovingly chosen with friends and family in mind.

Their self-written vows filled out hearts with love
And a keen awareness of a hand from above.

Dreams for my daughter of love without end
Were fulfilled when I saw her wed her best friend.

So let the celebration begin, the dancing and fun
A toast to my daughter and my new son.

As they continue their lives hand in hand
May God bless the marriage of Holly and Dan.

Patricia O'Brien

A Mother's Day Poem To My Grandmother

To my grandmother, my mother, my sister, my best friend
To a woman who never said I'm too tired or I don't have time
To a woman who gave up or went without to provide me with a life
A life love designed
To a woman who went the extra mile to lend a helping hand
To the woman who never said can't but always, yes I can
To the woman who wiped my tears and cast aside my fears
To the woman who gave me unconditional love and the nurturing and guidance to stand on my own
To the woman who said, as long as your heart is good and knows how to love, you'll never be alone
So, here's to the woman who already sports a halo and wings
I just want her to know I love her for all of these things

Toni Schwartztrauber

Autumn

Autumn is beautiful, the sun shines
through the leaves of many different
kinds of trees.
They seem painted, reddish golden brown.
And hues of purple can be found.
The cold wind blows, and makes them fall,
to decorate the ground.
As if to help, the children scatter them
in piles all around.
And grown ups can be seen, raking leaves
in every part of town.
The crisp, clean air gives us another reason
To be grateful for the autumn season.

Richard A. Granholm

Time

Time goes by, in a strange way.
Time goes by, the more I'll miss you
   each day.
Time goes by, life must go on though.
Time goes by, things are tough, I know.
   The time will come, when you'll have to
   go on your way.
   The time will come, then I'll wish for you
   to stay.
Time goes by forever, you see.
Time goes by forever, as I am hoping
   you will remember me.
Time goes by forever, that's true.
Time goes by forever, forever I'll
   remember you.

Wendy V. Dematas

Sitting Here

Sitting here, thinking of your dark brown eyes.
Think of me, think of my lonely sighs.

Sitting here, missing your touch.
Miss me, miss the one who needs you so much.

Sitting here, holding your picture tight.
Hold me, hold me close with all your might.

Sitting here, wanting your kiss gently on my lips.
Want me, want me there to touch your face with my fingertips.

Sitting here, needing to see your face.
Need me, need me there for you to embrace.

Sitting here, remembering what it feels like to be with you.
Remember me, remember being with me, too.

Sitting here, dreaming about us being together.
Dream about me, dream about being with me forever.

Sitting here, waiting to see you next time.
Wait for me, wait until you are finally mine.

Lisa Evans

Curt

I never saw a dad so proud,
You could almost hear him think out loud.
I've got a son, I've got a son.
Seems like his life has just begun.

Precious little boy,
Long nightie and all.
Front teeth shining.
And not very tall.

How exciting it's been,
Since you came to our lives.
You bring sparkle and sweetness,
and happy tears to our eyes.

You love boots and hats,
Peanut butter and hot tea.
Batman and puppies, and
a little girl named Amy.

Virginia C. Thompson

Ring-A-Ding-Ding

Alexander Graham Bell.
You've made my life a living—well!!
Just get in the tub-Ring! Ring! Ring!
Dashed all wet and dripping to-no ding-a-ling!!!!

Laid me down to sleep last night.
Heard bells ring before daylight.
I dragged out of bed with the chickens
To give Ma Bell the dickens.

Then down to the car and away.
Ring-a-ding-ding all the day.
Oh for the days long gone,
When the air was filled with bird song.

Bells in the steeple,
Calling to the people.
Computers clatter,
People chatter.

Where will it end?
Will we go 'round the bend?
Noise pollution!!!
What's the solution?

Janet Joann Butcher Boes

'A Part Of Me Is Excited'

A part of me is excited
to start this brand knew life,
and a part of me is crying to
leave my past behind.
I am looking toward the future
with all good things in mind.
I know there will be a struggle
but I'm ready to cross that line.
I have set my expectations
on the level of the sky, and
the best way I know to reach
them is to spread my wings and fly.

Sheena Skinner

Ego

I sat, reflecting inward
To take a look at me,
And what I saw within myself,
I did not like to see.
When, suddenly, I realized,
Because this fact was true
That others looking at me
Must have these feelings, too.
My heart became quite heavy
As I pondered what to do,
Then, revelation came to me,
I must begin anew.
If I want to like me better,
And have others like me, too,
I must change within myself
To change their point of view.

Marguerite M. Bailey

Communication

"Whoosh," said the wind,
To the birds.
"Tweet," said the birds,
To the chipmunk,
"Chatter," said the chipmunk
To the fire.
"Crackle," said the fire,
To the ocean.
"Crash," said the ocean,
To the thunder.
"Boom," said thunder!
"Shhh," said God to all His children.

Maria A. Lendacky

Between Worlds

Endless night has called my name
To the place where shadows hide
Cradled in the fallen stars
Neighboring with love's sweet suicide.
Tonight the magic has ended
Secret truths have been revealed
As I talked with broken dreams
That time refused to heal
This night a happiness so sad
Has allowed confusion to embrace me
This life or the next is the decision
Thrust upon me
The night continued
And the stars brightened
Their song rang so true
There was a sign that signaled life;
Lord, tell me,
Was it you?

Stacey Parish

"River Of My Soul"

From the mountains of forever
to the voice of yesterday
to the stream of everlasting
a magnificent display
flows a never ending beauty
that my eyes can e'er behold
this gift of God from heaven
to the river of my soul...

In the distant blue horizon
on the waves of shining seas
in the golden sands of nature
and the grandeur of the trees,
these enters forth a blessing
that they heart here-to enfolds
the stream of living waters
to the river of my soul.

William Poppas

Sherri

Thunderclaps moving the crowd
To unseen music
A dance - a glance
And a trade for future

Twisting and grinding
Birthing the pains
A light - a night
Too soon leaving

Chained in silk
Left in change
A match - attached
Returning at last

Hoping for sun
Each bright morning
At last - the past
To hold forever

Matthew Tait Lifto

My Love

I am still more in love with you
    Today than in the past.
And if you're sure that you love me
    Our love will always last.

I am your own forever
    If forever you will be
The angel in my dreams
    And my exclusive company.

I love you more than all the world
    With riches wrapped in gold.
I want you to belong to me
    To always have and hold.

F. H. Hewett

A Shattered Dream

You find that special someone
Your dreams now seem so real
Months of passion together
Bound with promises of love.
Making plans for the future
Only you two alone will share.
Then without warning
You hit that brick wall
All the dreams of love eternal
Now Shattered and torn.
No longer that feeling of love
Can be dreamt of as before.

Denise C. Fisher

Blending Of Two Hearts, Two Souls

Two hearts, two souls, blend
Together transcend-
Where words need not be spoken,
And promises aren't broken.

There's an acceptance.
Don't need repentance.
An unconditional love,
As free as a mourning dove.

This sincere friendship-
Will not ever rip,
Because of its true meaning,
Will continue succeeding.

Michelle A. Rowe

My Angel's Call

Here I lay presumed dead
Took a gun to my head
Bang, bang, the gun did sound
Then I fell onto the ground
With no I.D., John Doe was named me
Just another suicide
In a bag and off to the lab
Where they put me on a slab
Slice, slice, did the doctor's knife
Said what a way to end a life
No Pa, no Ma, no next of kin
So they buried me six feet in
The funeral was short, dull, and grey
Even took place on a rainy day
Now here I lay, can't really say
Where my spirit will take me away
Either heaven or hell, never can tell
Was I bad, good, or just misunderstood
Hark, hark, I hear the angel's call
Must've had a good life after all.

Thomas Paul Abel II

My Mom

I picture you in a garden
with flowers all around,
surrounded in the beauty
that God has showered down.

You picked a single flower
and added to your bouquet,
a joy you've left for others
when you walked along your way.

You thought no one seemed to notice
those gifts you left behind,
the thoughtful little tokens
that leaves memories on my mind.

Marjorie Carroll

A Widow's Lament

I loved you with my heart, my soul
You loved me too, and there was none
To interfere with all our goals
That we had made in vain, in fun.

But then appeared that awful cloud
As dark as even pitch of night,
To take away my love, my heart
For me it was a wretched fight.

Oh, God, it seems a cruel fate
For two such people as we were
For he to be right at the gate
While for my turn I yet must wait.

Mary Lou Dunn

Sun Child

Sun child
Touch this day, brighter of light
See you walk through the flowers
And you belong.

Earth child
Warm with love, all enfolding
Deep and knowing—
Bring life to me.

My love, take me to you
Let us live as one
Let us feel
The vast space our love has filled.

Fly with me/Journey with me
Share with me/Love with me
Rejoice with me—Together,
You and I
And Eternity.

Maria T. Davis

Hands

Once young and fair
Touched my cheek
Held our child
    Hands
Now old and wrinkled
    but soft
Touch mine
    and lie still.

Mildred P. Farr

"Humble One"

O' why
Tree, against the wind
Do you let nature
Your lovely branches bend
Don't yield!
Stand fast -
Victory?
Yours at last.
When you can stand
With roots entwined
So tall - so tall
Your magnificent head
So proudly enshrined
Your heart -
Only but of wood
A substance
Only meant to be…
To help mankind
O humble - humble tree.

Ronald H. Baarz

To My Son

I used to take your hand in mine,
When you were just a tad.
It was a sign of trust and faith,
And it made me very glad.

I think about the many times,
We'd walk this way; we two.
It seems like just yesterday,
When life was young and new.

Now when you come to walk with me,
And take my hand to guide.
It's my turn now to trust in you
As I walk along your side.

Gerda Turnquist

Adoption

Celebration of perfection
two fluids
both hold all
together
in a spirit dance
they mystify…
a supernatural
a natural
creation
in beautiful pain
she comes
the mystery's unwrapped
then wrapped again
then wrapped once more
in tears
in dreams
in paranoia
in gift paper

Roma Farber

Suicide

Senseless words
unheard
one senseless act
unspoken of
leads to one senseless
death.

Many questions
left unanswered
many tears left
to cry
many hearts left
to hurt.

Many people left
behind
many wounds left
to heal
one body to
put in the ground.

Leslie A. Erickson

Pebbles

All infinity beckons us
Unto restful twilight saunters,
Along winding paths of pebbles,
Near dappling, lapping water.

How curious are pebbles
In tones of sombre earth,
Each patterned through eternity,
As fragments from life past.

Reluctant would we leave them
Without tossing some midstream,
Just to watch encircling ripples - widen
Waving outward to far shores.

Though ripples seem to vanish
Ere they touch upon the sands
Yet they leave enduring patterns
In the building of God's lands.

While upon the surface shimmering
Ripples rolling gently on,
Ideas permeating outward,
Add more beauty in God's world.

Myrtie G. Houpt

"Like A Spirit"

I'm like a bad attitude
    up on tippy-toes,
    like a marionette
    cracked — so gimme
    a break.

I'm like a lonely fly
    never loved, never good,
    just crushed.
    It doesn't matter what
    I do — so gimme
    another chance.

I'm like a wicker basket
    speeding on wheels
    with some silver chain
    linked to a unicorn —
    odd, splendid.
    So gimme time.

Mark Wagner

"The Simple Life"

To touch the drizzle
upon my face

Beneath my bare feet
the earth has grace

To see the sky all white
like lace

To hear the sounds of quiet
embrace

With height and open arms
life is simple

But full of charm and grace

Lucia Coffman

Waiting

I exist,
    vanquished, cold, alone,
    motel prison cell sentence
    from a cynical paranoid jury,
    fearing my eighty-proof jailer.
I bide my time.

You scurry,
    frazzled, frantic, exhausted,
    organizing your heart's world
    to wander wild wilderness
    with a love and trust compass.
Your time runs short.

I wait,
    passion-filled, flustered, anxious,
    pondering perpetual tomorrow's parcel
    containing a rigid reacquaintance,
    my love, my fire, my freedom,
And our forever together.

Russell Johnson

"Purest Love"

Blessed son of God above
Wash me with thy purest love
Remember not my evil ways
Cleanse me for the judgement day
Wrap me in thy robes of white
That I may be holy in thy sight
Casting all my sins away
That I may live with God this day.

Terri M. Settlemyer

Not All Like Me

Our world is full of many others,
Various shades of sisters and brothers.
I value each for who they are,
As wondrous as each shining star.

Each expresses his own belief,
And that is much to my relief,
For no way would I want to see,
Everyone be just like me.

Then only females would abound,
No men would anywhere be found.
No love to hold me every night,
And make my world seem so right.

There would not be any new birth,
Humanity would die off the earth.
If white was the only color of skin,
Ethnic diversity would come to an end.

If we had only a single faith,
Heaven might be a boring place.
But thank God the world's not all like me,
For uniqueness is God's plan for humanity.

Rosemary French

Eviloution

Eons of fire and ice, rock, water.
Vegetation, animals - man!
Walking on two feet -
Wondering, thinking, dreaming.
Killing. Wondering, worshiping,
writing. Killing.
Learning, inventing, building,
Killing.
Playing; worshiping players.
Acting, "play-like" players.
Killing. Killing. Avenging.
Exhorting, posturing, punishing.
Waiting for deliverance.
Invoking God, Christ, Allah.
Buddha, The Great Spirit.
The "Force" to punish
Unbelievers, infidels, barbarians.
Atheists.
Killing. Killing. Killing.

William H. Schulze, Sr.

"Treasure"

You and me.....
walking in the sands.
Happy and always free.
Together our warming hands.

Barefoot walking slowly
hearing the song of the sea.
Was our night of love
happily forever you and me.

Do you remember our dreams?
The shells in the sands?
We had nice and sweet things
when you kissed my hands.

With the sky in our way
and only your love to give
we were happy day by day
forever until we live.

Walking and enjoying the way
with that splendid vision.
We wanted forever to stay
and hear the ocean song!

Dr. Laura Da Vinci

Psychoasis

Here the unsung soldiers meet;
Veterans of those soundless wars
That rage within our guarded souls;
Here we bare our battle scars.

Strangers pause a little while
Here, our wounds to ease and bind;
Understanding fellowship
In every brave, tormented mind.

Sharing tales of fear and woe;
Anger, laughter, triumph, pain,
Losses, loves and broken dreams;
Each some bit of strength to gain.

Soon this little while is past,
Then we're on the field once more,
Facing age-old enemies;
Yet unbeaten, though still sore.

Mary J. Richmond

Untitled

Roses are Red,
Violets are Black,
Do not tell your father
But Wildcat is back.
The love of your life.
The man of your dreams.
The man in all
Impossible scenes.
I have fallen for you
Like Popeye for Olive Oil.
So please say you
Will be my girl.

Michael Applegate

The Brink Of Extinct

Innocence and truth,
virtues of peace... at war.
Blinded faith is given sight
of the destiny in store.

Logic weeps, as hope retreats.
Tomorrow is Yesterday.
A wounded pair of flightless wings
spiraling... down... away.

No longer strong and sure,
intuitive, care-free...
a once heroic spirit
now lies tangled in debris.

Sandra Carol

Our Friendship

People like you are hard to find
too much to say, not enough time.
I try to explain what I can in words
Seldom are listened to
Seldom are heard.
What I am trying to say
to my closest friend.
Is life is too short for
Our friendship to end.
The love that I have for
you there aren't enough
letters to fulfill my words
so I will say it once
and only once more
Life is too short for
Our friendship to end.

Shari Berman

Missing You

I often wonder
Was I always at the mercy
Of the world?

Tear-stained pillowcases,
Wastebaskets overflow
With Kleenex
Transformed into stiff balls
By my loneliness

Encompassed by darkness
I sit on the edge
Of my bed
And miss you.

Love so intense
Comes once in a lifetime

Secure in the knowledge
That I have lived,

I've only one question:

How do I continue living
Without you?

Mandi Eaton

Dreams, Wishes, And Elegance

She moves around the stage,
With much beauty.
And grace.
She intrigues me.
As I sit there watching,
And wishing I could move like her,
I feel the warmth of her arms
　wrapped around me.
Lifting me out of my seat,
Carrying me around the stage,
With little effort.
Now I, too, feel beautiful.
And others are intrigued by me.
I am graceful like the ballerina.
But abruptly the music ends
　and I come from my reverie,
Realizing I was once again touched
　by the elegance of the show.

Michelle Hawkins

Ashley's Song

Oooo I love you Ashley
　You're precious as can be
If I will be good to you
　Will you be good for me

You are such a special child
　Born on Easter day
God has blessed this family
　In each and every way

Our lives have been much brighter now
　Since you came along
Having you within our hearts
　You're just where you belong

No one can take away the joy
　That you have brought this house
You were such a tiny babe
　Smaller than a mouse

Oooo I love you Ashley
　You're precious as can be
God has made my life complete
　Since he brought you to me.

Pamela R. Ryan

Bereft

Standing on a cliff
watching the earth fall
falling apart
parting from you

Letting a rose crumble
forgetting the love
loving a memory
remembering your eyes

Raging like the ocean after a storm
you stood on this cliff with me
and danced to the music of the sea
as the moon usurped the sun

Breaking my body
collapsing in laughter
laughing at the blood
bleeding yet again...

Tara R. Keenan

Twilight Thoughts

Sitting alone at twilight
Watching the shadows fade;
Smoking my pipe in silence,
I vision the face of a maid.

My smoke rings linger around me
Seeming to shape her face;
Then, curling and climbing they wander,
Floating away through space.

For a moment I see her smiling,
Chasing away my gloom;
I hear her laughter around me
Like soft music, filling my room.

My visions fade and vanish
Leaving me lonely here,
As the shadows lengthen to darkness
And the stars begin to appear.

Paul R. Drury

"The Ocean"

I live in the ocean,
Way down in the ocean.
Tied to an anchor way down,
in the ocean.
The fish I see,
Do remind me of me,
Way down in the ocean.
I live off the band,
While I lay on the sand,
In the ocean that's where.

Sean Kaufman

A Wedding Wish

As you start your life together,
When two become as one,
We wish you all the best of things,
True love, good health, great fun.

We hope your future dreams come true,
And stars light up your eyes.
We wish you both great happiness,
And love that never dies.

Remember as you walk life's path,
Your future still depends
On your being the best of partners,
And also best of friends.

Katherine M. Thibodaux

O Whippoorwill

With the parting of day gives
way to night, you suddenly appear.
Calling your sad song whippoorwill -
whippoorwill. The little boy lost
in the Blue Ridge mountains.
Lost in their color, lost in their
depth, lost in their range.
His mother's heart full of
sorrow for surely it was broken.
Praise thee little bird for your
faith. You both are gone but not
forgotten. You both brought joy to
one's heart, you both have found
peace and tranquility with your
creator. For one still hears your
sad song each passing night calling
Whippoorwill - Whippoorwill

Larry L. Wangler

Untitled

Life is like territory
We build our own cities
Ruled by genius minds
And heart-filled committees
Unclaimed land
Our wild frontiers
Soon we discover
Our hopes and our fears
Building our own territories
To states, yet countries
Overcoming the obstacles
That quickly become memories
Growing old
Conquering land
Looking back
To where we once began
Accepting and admiring
What we have done
We realize that the battle
Of life is something we won.

Vanessa Aspen Henderson

Forgiving

Through the grace of God,
we can see far beyond our eyes
length and see into the soul, and
in the soul, the truth allows
forgiving and truly lets us
remember what's important in life...

Theresa DeTonno

The Essence Of Life

Our ears deceive us if in time
We hear no rhythm, hear no rhyme.
The orchestration is so fine.
All sound in mantra.

Tell me, tell me, have you seen
The vast solution, the larger scheme?
Things aren't always as they seem.
All sight is Buddha.

We are each other, yet we divide
Our Selves from Man, our Spirits hide.
The One can lift us ever high.
To be is Nirvana.

Stephen J. Ruberg

We

In this day and age of illness
We need a helping hand
To get us through the rough times
That we never would demand

For with weakness of the body
We are grateful for the care
As the busy world goes speeding by
Some take the time to share

I thank God for all the loved ones
Who gently tend our needs
For without them we would fade away
And no one would give heed

God bless these giving gentle souls
Who sacrifice their day
And hopefully if need arrives
God's help will come their way

Virginia Riley

Journey To Our Writing

Journey can open, but before we write,
we think about the words and make it.
We draw a draft in our though and
throw out it way.

We rewrite our words
journey to our writing,
our souls and feeling into the paper.

Journey is expressing your word.
Can open the world in your hands
and going around the world comes back
in your writing.

But journey find our life's
and tells us how we came to be,
that is why your journey
is important for us.

Lorna Irizarry

The Morning

As the dew touched the grass -
We watched.
As the sun's overpowering light
conquered that of the moon's -
We waited.
As the animals woke up
from a long night's rest -
We listened.
As the breeze swept through the
branches -
We heard.

Sarah M. Powell

Insistence

Crack, crack.
What my dear?
My window is cracking.
Where my dear?
Here.
See my window pane?
I see no crack.
Down in the corner.
It's creeping so slowly.
The crack is creeping.
Oh, I see.
Do not fear.
Winter is almost over.

Kelly Stockman

Carving Our Names

When we were children
We would carve our names in sand
Created so awkwardly
With a twig in our hand
As we grew older
Our names were carved in wood
Chiselled on our battered desks
Left our mark as others would
Then slowly we matured and the sand
Washed away
While our ancient desks from school
Had surrendered to decay
So useless were our actions
So foolish not to have known
That the only way to be recalled
Is to carve your name in stone
  Peggy Jo Smith-Woodmore

Nothing To Eat

Lick, Lick, Lick
What a cold chill
Sitting out on the window sill.
My taste buds felt nice,
Resting on some ice.

Then my sister came in,
On her face was a great big grin.
She grabbed what was in my hand,
Stuck out her tongue and ran.

I was really mad at her
But I went to the refrigerator,
Took out an ice cream and licked.

Then my brother came in
With an even bigger grin
Grabbed what was in my hand
Stuck out his tongue and ran.

Now that there are no more treats,
I'm left with nothing to eat.
  Thuy Nguyen

Memories

Words on paper

What do I do
What do I say

Up in smoke
Lost on the wind

Sometimes

What I want to do
What I want to say

But turned to ash
They are

Like another
Lost thought

Another lost day
  Todd Manning

Nothing is the same
  with this broken heart,
except this feeling that
  won't depart.
It's in my mind now,
  that familiar ache
Oh..tender habit I
  cannot break.
  Peggy Brady

Questions To Ponder On!

What gave us the right to burn?
What gave us the right to kill?
What gave us the right to cut?
What gave us the right to hurt?

Who gave us the power to command?
Who gave us the strength to triumph?
Who gave us the code of memorization?
Who gave us the swiftness of the reflex?

Where did we get the talent of athletics?
Where did we get the power to forgive?
Where did we get the feeling of death?
Where did we get the muscles to fight?

When did we discover our strengths?
When will we solve the puzzles of life?
When did we learn how to destroy?
When will we find peace?

Why are we so powerful?
Why do we think were so cool?
Why are we alive?
Why do we have to die?
  Russ Bahr

The Other Side

I think about her often,
What is she like?
How will she come to me -
In my sleep, sometimes I
catch a glimpse of her
This lady of darkness
But as always
She slips away, away, further
and I am glad again.
  Maria Caroballo

Sabrina

I spend a lot of time thinking
What would it be like
trying to figure out what is best
torn between two, I could have...
how does a person choose?
Either way could lose.
If I had done right - to start
No problems I would have now
But that's destiny, not knowing....
what's going on, wondering what,
will happen tomorrow?
Lost in thought...can't remember...
what is what ...mind going slowly,
very slowly...but going anyway
Why? I have all that is,
all of little importance,
But one thing, the one thing
the only love of my life,
that returns it... Sabrina
  Teri Shrubb

Wait For Heaven

The time shall come
When all battles are won,
And all men shall see
What they were meant to be.
Their wars they'll forsake,
A better world they'll make,
Resisting evil's lure
To embrace all that's good and pure.
  Kathryn Eliza Bensch

Come Live With Me

Come live with me at golden dawn
When all the fears of night have gone.
Come take my hand and lead my way
Onward forward into day.
Together we will thus remain
Through that day of sun or rain,
And then as twilight dims our view
Hold me ever close to you,
Dispel my fears that come with night
And stay with me 'til morning's light.
  Pauline Bender

Easter

Easter is the time of year,
When children wait anxiously for
  Peter Rabbit to appear,

When eggs of vibrant colors are
  found,
By squealing children running all
  around,

Moms and Dads share time and space,
With family and friends as their
  children play chase,

The joy and laughter found this
  special day,
Could never be replaced in any
  other way,

Although the children will not
  always be small,
Let us not forget just what Easter
  means to us all.
  Linda Linde-Gibson

The House

There is a house that I see
when I close my eyes
though I don't know how
and I don't know why.

It is colored with shades
of gray and blue
the windows are so
much like crystal, they're not
really true.

The door is so small
that even if I tried
I could never in my life
get inside.

The inner walls are so unclear
and standing by the
porch is a man with a long beard.

Sometimes I think it might
be God
but is it a ghost or
just a fraud?
  Mollie Knoble

Winter Moon

Light breaks black lines etched in space
Vertical moments shadow-bound
A clarity cold perspective face.
Yet, music melts a moonbeam's mind
Intuitive vibrations that sound
Love to the edge of rippled time.
  J. W. Fosshage

Missing Renae

I miss you, so much..
   When I wake in the night -
Past thoughts of your touch..
   Become absent delights -
I miss you, so much..
   Through the long busy day -
It's tough to be patient..
   When you are so far away -
I miss you, so much..
   When the day is through -
And I reminisce of the wonders
   And fantasies..of you -
I miss you, my darling - all day..
   And especially, at night -
'Cause I miss making love to you..
   And holding you tight -
But what I miss most,
   When we are apart..
- Is that woman I love so deeply..
The one who gave my life - a new start!

Ted Billings

From Bitter To Better

Though our thinking may turn bitter
when our lives sustain a blow
we must trust that things get better
and attempt to ride the flow.
It's no good to have self pity -
optimistic views may pay,
though when seeing this in others
know it's easy just to say.
Nonetheless, this is my feeling
and I think about this fact -
bitter can be changed to better
by this letter-changing tact —
E for I makes bitter better
and can make a right from wrong -
having faith can change this letter
and return to life - its song.

Raymond J. Acosta

My Daughter

I have a daughter Carrie is nine.
When she comes over we have a great time.
She's getting older so I can't
hold her.
I hug her and kiss her and
tell her I miss her.
I'm so glad, she's mine,
I love her all the time
She's always on my mind.

Verla Marlene Groomer

Lonely Chapel

I sit in this lonely chapel
waiting for your death to finally hit,
even though you're gone
I haven't stopped loving you one bit.

My mind is in a wonder,
as I see your lifeless face
your love has not left me,
but it's your spirit I must chase.

Oh man, I'm going to miss you,
as I think about the good times we had,
no more sweet, sweet kisses,
makes me really, really sad.

Matthew Kilts

I Need Your Love

I need your love in the spring,
When the birds begin to sing.

I need your love in the summertime,
When the grapes are turned to wine.

I need your love in the fall,
When the wild geese call.

I need your love to keep me warm
On a cold winter morn.

I need your love wherever I go,
Be it in rain, sunshine, sleet or snow.

I need your love to take with me,
In the air, on land or sea.

I need your love from the start,
To match the love in my heart.

I need your love in every way,
To match my love for you each day.

I need your love wherever I may roam,
To help make my house a home.

I need your love in the night,
To be my guiding light.

Richard R. Lamp

Untitled

Tell me
When the heart beat of life stops...
What will you see
What will you hear
Will you still love me
Will you still care
Tell me
When the heart beat of life stops...
Who will you be
Who will I be
Where is our beginning
Where is our end
I see you fading
I touch you,
but you are not there
Tell me
can you feel me
can you feel this touch
I'm not ready for you to go...
PLEASE...

Thea M. Ruhling

Springtime

I reach out and touch
  your scarlet face
fragile, perfect
  growing in a beautiful place
A soft scent drifts in the breeze
  again you appear
  after the long winter's freeze
A sight to behold
  your color again so bold
Every year
  I wait for this day
  to come into the garden and say
A tulip in your usual flair
  Springtime
  for a moment I haven't a care

Sandy Romer

For You Are My Heart

When the sun stops shining
When the rains don't fall
When the stars are invisible.
And the birds don't call.

When the waves don't wash
themselves onto shore
when kittens don't purr
and lions don't roar.

If all this happens
On one thing, you can depend.
All the love that's inside me
to you, I'll still send.

For you are my heart
the center of my soul.
You're the one I love
With you, I'd love to grow old.

I'll love you forever
'til death do us part
and I can't live without you
for you are my heart.

Randall Snowden Jr.

Cosmic Revelation

When all the deeds of life are done,
When time and space converge as one,
When love and hate are synthesized,
The stars of heaven crystallize,
the soul awakes its nocturne eyes,
enrapt with splendor's diamond skies,
When both our life and death are sealed
our embryonic soul congeals,
to shine its light eternally,
Upon death's dark finality,
The laws of Physics thus repealed,
All God's creation is revealed.

Russell Eyre Shelhamer

When Crops Are In

When the crops are in
With meager means around him
a man sets and cries
For the price he pays is not
what he gets back
For his crops are in and hunger
dwells in the faces of his
children
He worships his God faithfully
and asks why?

Anonymous

Beyond Belief

There is a place beyond belief
Where reigns a constant, even peace
No remorse, nor mortal grief
Secluded far from gnashing teeth.

The people there are perfect.
Their beauty is immeasurable.
Their works are eternal.
All discourse is pleasurable.

Their countenances shine divinely bright
Pure, in the straight and narrow way.
Envision a sea of solid white
I'm going there someday.

Katie Akers

"A Sad Good Bye"

Dedicated to our Uncle Ted

We always wondered how we'd feel,
When your home became the sky,
We always wondered how long we'd pain,
And how many tears we'd cry.
    Sometimes we would listen,
    And think things through you'd say,
    So often you'd never realize,
    How our problems went away.
Your wisdom much amazed us,
A truly brilliant mind,
A man of your integrity,
So gentle and so kind.
    Your strength was like a mountain,
    Which no other could endure,
    Your pain had reached the peak of it,
    And still you handled more.
So no longer do we wonder,
About the tears and pain,
For they never seem to go away,
Each day it hurts the same.

Mary Frank

My Garden

Come sit with me in my garden,
Where flowers are always in bloom.
The dancing colors of a rainbow
Will pass through our afternoon.

Come sit with me in my garden,
I dearly would love you to stay
To see the glory of new roses,
And taste of a warm summer day.

Come sit with me in my garden,
There's a comfort found only here…
In nature's quiet hiding place
She'll calm away every fear.

Come sit with me in my garden,
And find peace in love abound.
The flowers you'll see growing,
Smell so sweet they carry a sound.

Come sit with me in my garden,
Its beauty is free to behold.
Please stop and smell the roses,
A "gift" more precious than gold.

Linda Sue Margroff

"Secrets"

I sit on a barren hill
  where no birds sing the
dark clouds cover my obscure
  body—I succumb to the images

Alone I can share the secrets
  of my heart to the raptured
ear of the heavenly air

A voice of desire sings as the
  landscape listens to the loveliest
of trees bending gently in the breeze

Nature always lends a glimmering
  light and here where life force and
beauty meet a rainbow appears in the sky.

On this barren hill where no birds
  sing the breathing pulse of my heart
finds your tender eyes

Robert J. Cece

A World War II Hill Revisited

I watched the sun go down
  Where freedom's fighters died —
I saw the hill's dark crown
  Aglow in sunset's tide,

And once again I knew
  The naked loneliness
Of standing with the few
  Whom victory came to bless

When cannon ceased to roar
  And snarling guns were quiet
Where splattered pools of gore
  Lay black as hades night,

And once again I thought,
  The rains will wash away
And a time of peace be bought
  Until another day

Shall wake the tyrant's rage
  And greed will once more reign
When memory's fading page
  Reflames in war and pain.

A. E. Holton Sr.

For The People Of Oklahoma City

They died amidst the shattered glass
Where lives and dreams would end
And all about the fury raged
For loved ones child or friend
And waiting killed the hearts of some
Beneath that somber sky
As day on day no answer came
And all the nation cried
While healing was so far away
Clutched in a mother's arms
A bear that was a child's once
Was safe from further harm
And oh the deep abiding loss
That great city knew
But echoed here within ourselves
Your grief is our grief too

R. Sollows Dow

Brother

How dare you call me "Brother,"
When we both know from within,
The only reason you say the word,
Is because of the color of my skin.

How dare you call me "Brother,"
By the selfish life you live,
Always wanting to receive,
But you can never give.

How dare you call me "Brother,"
When you see me on the street,
No place to go in from the cold,
Without any food to eat.

How dare you call me "Brother,"
When each night I'm all alone,
As I wander from street to street,
For somewhere to call home.

How dare you call me "Brother,"
As if it came from up above,
When all I really wanted,
Was for you to show me love.

Paul O. Crowder

The Treasure

I walk beneath the endless sky
  Where ocean meets the land
Till sun surmounts the darkness
  As sea tide beats the sand.

Soaring far above the shadows,
  Reaching through the mind.
Caught up in the faintest murmur,
  Leaving the world behind.

Breathless in its lofty presence,
  I capture destiny
With a peaceful resolution
  Of how it is to be.

To sustain within that moment,
  As fragments on the shore,
A gleam of understanding,
  I seize forevermore.

Stephanie Johnson

Alone

Through wooded paths I walk alone,
Where once I walked with you.
Birds still sing among the trees,
But their songs are not so true.

Among ocean sands I play alone,
Where once I played with you.
Breaking waves still wash the shore,
But the sea is not so blue.

By garden swings I pass alone,
Where once I passed with you.
I search for climbing roses there,
But found they no longer grew.

Past lilac trees I stroll alone,
Where once I strolled with you.
Bushy blooms reach for the sun,
But gone are their scent and hue.

When from this earthly home I go,
On a morning sparkling with dew;
Along misty paths I'll joyfully walk,
Not alone, but once again with you.

Patricia M. Robinson

The Mockingbird

I am the mockingbird
Without a voice of my own,
So I shall steal yours
Every note, every tone.

How bitter my soul must be
To be locked in this curse,
For if I am to sing
You must sing first.

If your song is of sadness
I shall sing it tomorrow,
But I shall feel like a traitor
For I do not feel sorrow.

If your song is ecstatic
I shall sing it with delight,
But inside I'll feel nothing
Does this seem right?

I am the mocking bird
Never alone,
For if I was
I'd be silent as stone.

Paula Calaor

Down In The Old Pine Trees

Down in the old pine trees
Where the man thinks of bees
And the swallows and the crows
On his mind do grow

Down in the old pine trees
Where the kids scrape their knees
The moms do their weekly gossip
The men brag and laugh
As the man walks the path

Down in the old pine trees
The old man not only sees
the swallows and the crows
But the old pine trees
Yvonne De Los Reyes

Raven's Fight In Winter

I sit aloft high in the trees
Where the wind bloweth free
I search earth around
For a morsel to be found.

I caw out to the flock
The swift winds echo, my voice mocks
Ebony wings cover the sky
Like claps of thunder, the ravens cry.

The barren earth is blanketed white
Every tree and mountain that i site
I search below for friend or foe
Before i light upon the snow.

I soar above the forest deep
All nature's secrets it doth keep
Time is of no essence where i stay
A free hearted spirit i live and play.
Ruth Crawford

Sisters

We sisters are always together
   whether near or far
We will love each other forever
   no matter where we are
If one of us is in trouble
   we will help each other out
We will be together always
   no matter what it takes
Our bond is very strong
   and that's the way we belong

   Forever together
   Forever sisters
Samantha Ruggiero

The Mirror

The mirror reflects an image
Which in ignorance
I call "me."
Within the glass
Is a vast being
If only I could see;
A being composed
Of contrasts
Which somehow make
Me whole.
I look again
Into the mirror
And catch a glimpse
Of soul.
Sue Morris

Stat Crux Dum Volvitur Orbis

Man searches vainly for answers,
While God sits on His throne.
Man thrashes 'round and 'round
Thinking he's all alone.

Man stretches mainly for Love
And Peace within his domain.
He wants to be accepted
Knowing his life is profane.

The Cross remains e'er constant
While the World turns in despair
Man calls to God in anger
Wondering if He is there.

God beckons to Man with pity
'Til Man reaches up at last
"Come to the Cross, Beloved,
'Tis there you'll find your rest."
Vera Rush Hill

Red Mountain

The sun sets in red,
While mountain shadows grow long,
In purple divine.
Keith Fiene

Love's Safe Keeping

My heart weeps,
   while my eyes cry tears.
You're so far away,
   but yet so near.
Do you hear my voice,
   as I call out
     softly your name?
Do you feel my fingertips,
   when I touch you
     in my dreams?
It's not the same,
   as you being here.
But, it will have to do
   until you are near.
My love stays awake,
   as my body lies sleeping.
My heart's been reserved,
   for my love's safe keeping.
Melissa G. Buckles

"An Ode To Soviet Psychedelia"

Fighting clouds of laughing clowns,
while pools of kisses come crashing down,
I see you.
licking tongues of smiling suns,
staring at the elusive ones;
happily running up the slide,
lime green jello astroglide;
peeking 'round a monster's cake,
daffodil and safflower steak;
dark as night and black as day,
speaking in seeds of caraway;
felling trees with needle eyes,
running from the mackerel's cries;
tasting tender iron ore;
as you search for one that you adore;
and time remains a ticking dream,
in a constant ebb of butter cream;
as shackled fleas of talent show,
allow you to reap that which you sow;
I see you!
Marv Johnson

Depression...

   Is that
Whirlpool of
        Pessimism,
   That
Choking feeling
         Of
   Hopelessness,
Those   stormy
   Clouds
        That   rain
   On your hopes,
     Smother
Your   dreams,
And
        Leaves you
   Like   a
Rainbow
     ...
        Whose
   Color has
        Been
D
R
A
I
N
E
D

    Out
Sharon H. Neel

There Is A Father Up Above

There is a Father up above,
Who cares for you,
And gives His love.

He sent His Son in Mary's Womb,
To save us all from Devil's Doom.

No need to live like worldly folks,
No need to shame what God has spoke.

No need for crying, shame, and despair,
There's need for shouting, joy, and care.

He took His Son upon the Cross,
And died for us - who's a worthless cost.

So next time when you think to pray,
Take Him in your heart to stay.
Karen Hyatt

Untitled

   It's like looking through a
window you can see my broken
heart. You can tell when I'm hurting
and when I'm falling apart.
   Our love is like no other, and
nothing can replace all the things
that we're been put through on those
cold winter days.
   We've had smiles on our faces and
tears in our eyes, but the trials we
have gone through have brought some
fears to our lives.
   Knowing that it's possible to lose
what we have right now pulls us
back together and holding stronger now.
Krystle Richardson

My First True Love……

I love someone
who doesn't love me.
I guess we weren't meant to be.

I've tried so hard
with all my might,
but still I'll never
win the fight.

The girl he loves,
she is my friend.
Though he will love her to the end,

he'll always be
a special part;
a memory within my heart.

Someday I will
find a new;
a love that will be
oh so true.

But I swear on each star up above,
I'll never forget
my first true love.

Maria Iorlano

My Baby Brother

I have a baby brother
who is always a bother.
I only would sigh
when he would cry.
He is so squirmy
like a little wormy.
He is so brown.
He could walk to town.
He is so big,
he eats like a pig.
He chews on his boot,
he is so cute.
Sometimes he seems stronger than me!
but I laugh at that, hee, hee, hee!
even though he is a bother.
I still love my little, baby brother.

Michal Grace

To My Unborn Child

Who are you?
Who lives now within my womb
and is nourished by my blood?
whose heart beats and who kicks
   and grows beneath my ribs?
What gift will you bring to the world?
What song? What wisdom?
   What insight? What hope?
What wonder has God created
   through your father and me
   to give to the world?
I await your arrival, my child
to see you, to hold you, and to meet you.

MaryAnne Mayne

Dragon

There was a dragon,
who pulled a wagon,
bumped his head,
and went to bed,
and never touched another wagon.

Tyler Mace

Keeping Yourself

Esau was a hairy man,
who sold his soul for pottage.
The hairless one usurped his place
and lives now in his cottage.

If you were born a hairy man,
and wish to keep your birthright,
don't listen to the hairless one
who seeks to blind your sight.

His fancy words and dulcet tones
are nothing more than snares
to take your goods and services
and leave you naught but tares.

If you refuse the hairless one,
he'll hate you without measure.
But you will keep your soul intact,
And he'll not have your treasure.

Lydia E. Morang

Grandfather

There was a man
Who was so dear

Like a father
Always near

I loved him more
Through each year

He was a man so sweet
and kind

A heart of gold
You'll never find

He was so sick
So many times

But not once shed
A tear in his eyes

Now he's gone
Forever more

But in my heart
He rests once more.

Marie Marotta

Unison

I have an guardian angel
Who watches over me
my Holy heavenly Father
made me a living tree
He bore my sin and sorrow
for I could never win
Our Father taught us how to walk
to keep us free from sin.
Look up for Our Father
He lifted you and me
to see life's journey clearly
To know "Truth" keeps us free.
He planted me by water
that I would thirst no more
I help Him call all children
let's open up your door.
Come with me for His Glory
and sing with me a song
we all will sing together
"alleluia," we are ONE

Renate Viseur

Johnny Tremaine

There once was a boy, Johnny Lyte,
Whose hand made a terrible sight.
This lad was a silversmith by trade,
Making goblets and basins inlaid.
On a Sabbath, he worked to his doom,
For his work he could never resume.
But this lad wasn't beaten quite yet.
He delivered the local gazette.
One, if by land, two if by sea,
Lanterns were hung for all to be free.
In Boston, the townsfolk awoke,
To the Redcoats, to muskets, to smoke.
When the haze did finally clear,
"Freedom" was everyone's cheer.

Nicholas A. Gianadda

Who Am I?

Who are you?
Why do I ask?
Who am I, nobody knows!

The sorrow in my days
The difference in my ways
The sadness that I show,
Just makes everyone
Turn and go!

How dreary to be somebody like me.
How scary to be alone and afraid.
To just turn and everyone looks away!

What a pity to keep living
To die would make things easier.

Those people, those friends
That I have so very few of
Would be happy and grateful
Just to see things end!

Ryanne Young

Canute On The Beach

Fools!
Why do they stand there,
Watching, waiting?
What do they want?
What do they hope?

Christ!
What is that at my feet?
What is sucking the sand
From under my throne…

Roger P. Kovach

Earth And Sky

Earth and sky -
   two joys have I.
One in physical beauty bound
   packaged as a planet round.
The other blue, beyond, above
   where does dwell a limitless love.

Manifest wisdom-work of art
   world's apart, yet separate not.
Treasure of wonders and wonders
   joy upon joy altogether.

Love, power, justice and wisdom
   all qualities of God and man.
As created from the dust am I
   breath and spirit - a soul alive!
Forever -
   part earth, part sky.

Linda Williams

Oh Soul Of Mine

Oh soul of mine don't hurt so much
Why won't you let me have some peace?
What is a kiss? What is a touch?

Oh, yes a kiss can mean so much,
but only while it lasts.
A great big hug, a gentle touch
if only I could have.

A soul that bleeds
but no blood flows,
is in this chest of mine.
It's lifeless with a great big hole
and yet no tears I've cried.

Oh, soul of mine don't hurt so much,
my heart can take no more.
It's broken now
and can't be fixed,
for now and ever more.

Rikki Hill

Untitled

These eyes of mine
Will always hide
Hidden secrets locked inside
A tormented mind
May never find
Peace or joy of any kind
All this pain
And unseen rage
Kept within a mental cage
Fighting to escape
Have crossed onto this page
No more am I insane
Just confused

Rich Markey

Suspense

will I be silently alone?
will I be talking on the phone?

will I be drinking wine?
will I be preparing to dine?

will I be at home or on the street,
or heading for land that's meadow-sweet?

will I have business to expedite?
will I be finishing another fight?

will I receive a warning
some night, evening, noon or morning?

when, where, how will it come?
before, will I feel alive or numb?

a certain event catches my breath -
the intriguing wonder of
the when, where, how of death

Virginia Wise

Earth

Great big mother earth,
with her beautiful ocean surf,
with her black an starry sky,
she is asking you just why?

Why do you pollute her ground?
Cans and bottles never found...
Smoke and gases pollute her air
no one seems to really care.

Rebecca Klein

The Break Up

After the rain
Will you feel the pain,
The pain I tried to escape?

Late at night
Will you remember the fate,
The fate you left me to live?

When it's cold outside
Will you feel the warmth,
The warmth I tried to give?

Only time will heal
The scars you left
Until time finds me another
The sun will shine
Leaving the clouds behind
And I will be born again

The love I gave just wasn't enough
Not for a boy who didn't want it

So in time you'll find
The pain I feel
In time, your eyes will cry...

Margaret T. Yasharian

"Soul Free"

I know what to do now
will you take my soul away
my life span is over
but you didn't care...anyway
Thou shall die for
whether right or wrong
life ain't nothing to me
that's why I wrote this song
Lord have mercy
I think the devil's calling me
I can't take it anymore
I gotta let this spirit free
knowing nothing will come
to this future of mine
Lord I have to let you know
my life is at the end of the line
I'll fly away
like the birds in the sky
I'll release myself
and let this soul to die

Landon Iwamura

Morning In Martinique

Gazing at the sea swept shore
with sky so blue
I see right through
her eyes
for miles

I stand alone
with air that drifts
laden with scents
of earth and water

Waves soften
sounds of silence
as they fumble
for the sand

Feeling fascination
I wished to be another
the one
who dreams awake
yet be myself
in dreams without waking
while in the midst of you

M. J. D'Angelo

"winter leaves"

stark and snowless
   winter
pale the wintry sky

biting cold
   the winter wind
thin the clouds
   on high

a sticks-and-branches
   forest
barren Winter trees

but at their feet lay
   springtime's green
and summer's
   fluttering flags

brown and dry
   they whisper
chants of time gone by

but,
softly now,
they sing their song
and prophesy of joy

paul hubert

Father Of The Sky

As the sun sets on the
   winter landscape,
I see the sun pour out
   the colors that dwell inside.
The reds, purples, blues, and
   oranges cover the night time sky.
As the sun finally sets
   what seems to be ink
   spills out and covers
   the heavenly land above.
The stars break through
   the ink, and the moon
   lights up the star filled
   sky, while snowflakes
   trickle down to earth.
During the moons rule
   over the sky - it seems
   to be the father of the sky.

Michael Wesbecher

Sunshine

Summer sunshine makes the flowers grow,
Winter sunshine melts the snow,
Rainy sunshine makes a rainbow,
Autumn sunshine turns the leaves aglow.

Richard Daddona

Her Day

What happened on that day,
With bitter indifference you say.

The sun probably rose,
It most assuredly set.

The stars came out,
The moon probably did too.

My life became a little bit brighter,
On that resounding day.

Although I did not know it then,
That day was the beginning of you.

C. Garland Compton III

Soul-Mates...

On this day we celebrate
with friends and family.
Hand in hand I want to share
just what you mean to me.
You accepted me for what I am,
Because of you I'm a better man.
You accepted my children as your own,
opened your heart and shared your home.
You touched my soul and healed my heart.
In you I have found my split-apart.

I promise my love will never end
For my lover, wife, and my best friend.
To hold your hand and kiss your lips
And share our lives till my last sunset.
With this ring I thee re-wed.
With all my heart and soul I pledge.
To cherish each new day with you
and appreciate the things you do.
I give this ring, as I gave my heart,
Still lost in love with my split-apart....

Keith Tucker

The Cry

Along the road he walked one day
with his clothes torn;
his eyes were red with blood;
his face looked sad and furious.
He was hardly moving.

The asphalt below his feet was
blazing with fire;
I could not stand to look at him
I moved on,

But there was a cry; a cry for help
I still moved on, and every step that
I took the cry got louder and louder.

I stopped, I took another route; but the
cry was still there, it was in my head.
I turned back, I looked for that man
the man in patchy clothes;
I could not find him;
I was now beginning to get sad;
because that cry, that cry never
leaves me.

Keresia Taffe

Fate

The low hanging willow
With its spreading sprays of green
Touch the brown fruit pillows
Of life cushioned on Earth unseen.

Under that yonder willow,
Solitary and alone
Sits an old man
With his fishing pole.

On a stump, damp with moss
Slumped in tiredness, he sits,
His youthful powers of life lost
To time, bit by bit.

From early dawn to starlit night
Quiet and alone, he seems to wait
Not only for the fish to bite but-
To be called "Home by Fate."

Vivian Archie Mathews

Primitif

I cover massive turbulence
With nonchalance...pacific calm,
Cordon off in some remote recess
The muffled sound of jungle drums,
Never silent... only distant,
Amoral, savage and insistent.

Correct and cool, unruffled, tame
Am I, until they sound your name
Begun in whispers...rising slow
To muttering, rumbling thunder low,
Primeval, sultry, heavy beat,
Jungle drums in fever heat,
Mad crescendo, swelling, throbbing,
Deafening roar... subsiding, sobbing.
Your name in pulsing rhythm comes
On the receding sound of jungle drums,
Torrid, savage and insistent
Never silent.... only distant.

Ruth Young

The Wanderer

Monarch butterfly,
you should have fluttered free,
kissed again blossoms sweet
with nectar. Young, beautiful,
with perfect wings, you
floundered instead
on my cobblestone walkway,
gave blossoms of stone
your final kiss, became still
in the summer sun, turning
brittle as an Autumn leaf.

Sandy Fink

I Had A Friend

I had a friend
    Who couldn't hear a word you say
I had a friend
    Who couldn't see the games you play
I had a friend
    Who had regressed
I had a friend
    Who was depressed
I had a friend
    Who hated going outside
I had a friend
    Who committed suicide
I had a friend.

Scott Carter

Untitled

As I soar over the
deep blue cloudless sky, I
remember the time when I
was a young boy, forever waiting
to grow older. I remember
the hard ships, the special moments,
and the secrets left untold. This
was my life, but now
it's over. As the buds
of flowers bloom into beautiful
petals, I slip away. I'm
dying, I'm dying , but I
have no control. The mirror
does not lie, I'm growing
old.

Jennifer Jefferson

Heaven's Tapestry

Lord, when my earthly walk is through
    with quickened pace I'll run to You
And when I see You face-to-face
    in heaven's realm we shall embrace!

And then, in awe, I'll clearly see
    the workings of Your tapestry;
The testings of my faith shall be
    woven into memories.

I'll understand Your gentle "No"
    when I preferred instead to go;
I'll see the wisdom in the "Wait",
    and in the "Child, don' hesitate."

But, for now, just let me be
    content with blindly serving Thee
Until the present joins the past
    and all is heavenly at last!

Kathy Cirello

Untitled

I dreamed it and hoped it all day,
With the imagined scent of you...
The touch of your lips on mine.
So anxious to see you....
The magic is like a fragile bubble,
So glorious in its right,
Felt so seldom in such abandon
The thrill like a child's delight.
Inside I wanted to jump and clap my
hands with glee.
Laughter in a smile,
Eyes that shine a big bright light
The joy, the anticipation...
But all to be forgotten,
The day that followed the night.
The magic is like a bubble,
That broke before its flight.

M. Sue Benner

Untitled

Fly high, my friend
With the life you once knew
And remember us
As we'll remember you
Stand tall and strong
Don't ever cry
And in our hearts
You'll never die
Walk on, my friend
And leave the pain
The memories we have
Will forever remain
Soar towards the clouds
And reach for the sky
Fly high, my friend
Fly high...

K. O'Hearn

Untitled

Life is like a lake,
with its little ripples,
and occasional waves.
I am an island,
and the waves wash upon my shore,
and take a little sand away,
until I am no more.

Richard L. Carr

Inner Peace

As I walk along this path filled
with wild flowers, leaves rustling,
birds chirping, and small animal sounds,
I stand still to listen to the many
different sounds that nature makes.
As I stand there I look up to the sky
and it's the brightest blue
that I have ever seen.
It feels so peaceful as I stand there.
The feeling of inner peace
comes over me.

Orena Orr

Dichotomy Tales

It's an awesome gathering of patients
Yawning, fainting femme fatales,
Gandy dancers, with white shark teeth,
Puerile games, yet no one is laughing.

Amoebas at best,
Crawling up the walls,
Slowly as unnoticed ivy,
Blurred by prestige.

Quizzical ambition?, Duty?, Denial?
Tentacle lies from the demigods.
Tossed like lots, unsure answers,
Does "je ne sais quoi" say it all?

Corporate molding clay,
Death defying acts.
Blood droplets of deception,
Stain the carpets.

Who is your trusted one?

R. Strehle

Colors

I see colors, the colors of life.
Yellow; the son of every man.
Orange, the daughter.
Red; of every parent's anger.
White; of everyone's smile.
Blue, for every tear shed.
Purple; of the flowers.
Black; of the dead.

Norman L. Obremski

We Are A Part

Are there gay trees.
Yes there are.
They're in the forests.
And on the highway.
And on our streets.
Right there with the straight trees.
And when God lets it rain,
They all share equally -
And when there is fire,
They all get burned.
And when there is disease.
They all get it.
And God, men, women and kids
Do everything to cure 'em
And help 'em grow back again.
So let us all help,
And they will be able
To help us someday.
That's the way it is supposed to be.
So come with me.

Paul Leech

To Dylan

The day that you came to our lives
　you brought love, and hope, and tears.
You filled our lives with such great joy
　that it overcame our fears.
For nine long months we waited for you
　to make our lives complete.
And when you finally came to us
　you charmed us off our feet.
We've been told so many times
　that you would never be.
We'll help you grow into a man
　for the whole wide world to see.
To mom you're her "little bundle of joy"
　to dad "His little man"
To you we'll be your protectors
　for as long as we possibly can.
Dylan, you're so special,
　you make us both so glad.
We'll be there through thick and thin
　We love you, Mom & Dad

Michael Crouse

Untitled

Through all,
You can conquer
through all,
you deceive.

Life a pity,
take no mind,
why at least?

Take the will and courage,
You get what you deserved

But if Providence hinders
it is bygoned.

No one to be sympathetic,
no one to care
who would?

You made well,
You made bad,
It's you who shall.

Xining He

Within The Heart

Love is given
to those who find its treasure-
in honor, duty.

To those who look
within the breast of affection
and see its beauty.

The same beauty
on your countenance fair
when sleep reigns o'er the night air.

And the purpose
in your eyes of peace
when understanding sends release.

In matters of the heart
where life etches its most sacred trusts

No invader can stalk its gates
to keep lovers apart.

In matters of the heart
where joy sketches its gifts of mem'ry

No tear can strain the bonds
if love remains...within the heart.

Victoria G. Nicholas

Who Will I Be If I Tell You...

The way I was
You don't know the way I was.
If you knew the way I was,
then you'd understand why that
if I told what happened to me,
then I would no longer be who I am.
If I am no longer who I am,
then I'm just back to being
The way I was.

Susan J. Impink

Desolation

In my desolation
you found me

My broken heart restored,
my tears washed away
my faith renewed again

Those who made me suffer
were ashamed, pity them,
they have no faith

Through the tunnel of life,
I saw the guiding light
My heart content
to meet you there

Miriam Andujor

Little One

Oh Little one, oh little one,
You glow so tenderly.
And every time I look at you,
What wonder do I see!

A little one who's just begun
To grow so gracefully,
That every time I hear you smile
I know who you will be.

'Cause ever since this small one came,
My heart has been set free.
You've brought me to tears and laughter;
You mean everything to me.

So little one, oh little one,
Upon my bended knee,
I thank the Lord of love above
For sending you to me.

Vickie Young

Casting Out Syllables

You hear it on the radio
You hear it on TV
You hear it from the Pulpit
Or wherever you might be.

"Comftorble" can't sound at all
The way it's meant to be:
The coziness is lost at once
As one can plainly see.

"Deteriate" cannot depict
"Impair" or "make worse."
"Unfortunely" might convey
"Disaster" or a "curse."

Take heed of the syllables
That make the common sense,
Or what you say may come out
As blasphemous offense!

Vera Snyder

Untitled

Thoughts of you come often through time in my heart and in my mind,
What is it that I foresee? A view of the future pertaining to me,
Time of past is over and done experience all learned bad and fun,
The future too hazy for me to ponder through bad or fun I often wonder,
In the past never a miss always a love I wouldn't diss or a love I couldn't do without,
A friendship is easy though with you I doubt,
We can communicate by phone or by mail cuz in person my foolish heart would prevail,
Stop this thinking I play a fool for no man a spotless record to maintain the best I can,
Though with images of you lie awake at night wanting almost pleading to hold you tight,
Be real I tell myself hurting would come new not to all but to you,
But your eyes your face to feel your skin all the treasures I want again,
Confusion of what to do not to bid or carry through,
General info I pass on sure I am the best of me for only one man,
Of whatever we amount to be, let honesty be our basis, a mutual guarantee

Denise Greene

What Makes a Man a Guy?

What makes a man a guy?
What makes a guy a man?
Is it the tie, the shirt?
Or is it the pants that fit tightly around his butt?
Is it the way he walks, the way he talks?
Or is it the way he looks, him and his bad self?
Is it the way he turns a girl on, sweeps her off her feet?
Or is it the way he holds her, kisses her, loves her?
Is it his passion, his personality?
Or is it his sensitivity?
A woman may never know!

Crystal Alaway

Tribute To Baby Baylee

A symbol of our grief
You touched our hearts
Never, will we be the same

Emotions burn from deep within
How could this happen
Maybe, you are our lesson

A reminder of what could be
If we learn to live in peace
Forever, you will be remembered

A symbol of our love
A symbol of our hope
A symbol of what could be

Susan Medeiros

Freedom

In my moments of humblest endurance,
when the tears of reflection attest
to the sorrows, the guilt and the penance
so deceitfully covered with rest,

I will think of you, ever so noble,
with your heart open, free as the wind,
spewing forth all your goodness, ennobled
by the fact that you cannot but win.

You're my strength, my love, my support,
and in gleeful rejoicing, I'm proud
of the fact that you've lifted my spirits
and dissolved my sorrowful shroud!

Judith Acevedo

Dreams

Dreams, what are they made of?
What makes them appear?
Are they thoughts of the day,
Or of things we hold so dear?

Is the Lord trying to speak to us,
In the quiet of the night?
Are we just mentally disturbed,
And our nerves are uptight?

Is it our sub-conscience,
That awakens, when we are asleep?
Is it a glimpse of the future,
Maybe an appointment, that we're to keep?

It sometimes makes me wonder,
When I go to sleep at night.
What kind of journey will I take?
Will I awake to see the light?

Betty E. Mercer

I Hate Shopping

A daily chore, this going to the store.
   What to have for supper — choices galore.
Spaghetti or roast or chops or fowl,
   Beans or pasta? Oh, I want to howl.
What do I need? Let me see now,
   Milk, eggs, bread? I have oregano
Salad, of course; lettuce, onion, tomato
   But do I have mayonnaise? I just don't know.
Ah, chicken wings on sale, I'll need a little flour,
   But I think I have oil for the supper hour.
What about dessert? Hmm, a strawberry shortcake
   With a little whipped cream is easy to make.
There, my menu's planned and I'm all but beat.
   Oh, the phone — What? We're going out to eat?

Joan M. Hudzietz

"You"

If I had my life to live all over again
What would I do about you?
I wouldn't change, but only one thing
I'd love you even more than I do.

You've been my joy and my laughter
And been the greatest past of making my life so happy
Right from the start.

Your time was cut short
Why? I don't know
I'd do things that we missed
This, I don know.

If I had my life to live over again
I'd turn my head to heaven
Give thank for your love
Because that I kind of love
I'll not find - ever - again.

Barbara S. Bost

Passion

Buried deep within the mind lies an abyss of darkness where passion lives on the brink of release......

With only a sliver of soft light, a rippling wave begins to build into a raging storm out of control like the pull of the moon on a thousand seas....

As the screaming passion explodes, it ignites the fire that lights the way and burns in the heart of the one who holds the key.

Donna L. Welch

Chosen People

When God created man, or man made God
When earth was young and loved war,
A fateful wrong scourged the world.
Man's God on a sad day chose one people
Above all others, heirs to a fruitful land.
A blessing and a burden, a promise and a curse.
Now does God see the folly of this way,
And gives a message of new meaning to the world.
Thus says the Lord:
"Now let all men be equal in my eyes.
All races and all creeds commingle.
Let all mankind be one great people.
Let there be no more baptisms and circumcisions.
Let all the righteous people of the earth
Be chosen.
Charles J. Shagoury

The Apocalypse

You think the Apocalypse is
When entire world is collapsing.
No! The Apocalypse is
When a woman begins to cry,
When a child doesn't know
What is father's love
The Apocalypse is
When your neighbor is
Going to buy the drugs on the corner.
The Apocalypse is
When you are so lonely in a big city.
The Apocalypse is
When the finger of somebody
Has pulled a trigger...

Remember: The Apocalypse is near you always!
See and hear!
Time and time again
The Apocalypse has knocked on your door...
Do you hear?
Alex Komanetsky

A Day At The Beach

The odd photograph taken on a happy occasion
When everyone was posing and unconcerned,
Will somehow survive.
Like the odd leaf that evades the fall rake
And is gusted out weeks later to be picked up
And book-pressed for the next hundred years!
Decades later when the ebullient egos have
Long quieted someone will pick that photograph up
And in an instant, feelings, emotions long dormant,
Will flood the mind as it returns to that fond
Moment long ago when every day was
Like a day at the beach!
Harry W. Gordon

There

Way beyond the deep blue sky
where all living creatures prepare to die
in a place where the sun never shines
where evil lurks behind the pines
the smallest trace of happiness
would be all so rare
all that can be heard
are cries of utter despair
the darkness the blackness
everyday
why will it never go away
Brett Coppol

The Promise Of Springtime

The time of year is here again
When hearts are stirred anew.
His Presence - oh how It surrounds us
As all nature and life renew.

Trees covered with buds, the robins return
Spring flowers all peeping through.
They are all signs of God's commitment
His promise of a New Life for you!

How can we mortals repay Him?
The answer is not simple but true.
He laid down His guidelines in the Bible
Now how shall we follow them through?

Not by living a free and easy lifestyle
Not by following the "in-thing" to do.
But by keeping our end of the commitment
And "to thine own self be true."

Make "morally right" the Right Choice!
Always ask yourself what would He want me to do?
Keep in personal contact with Father God daily.
He will always come through for you!
Joan Schipper Robb

Buried In Your Heart

Why do you seek Me in the world
   when I am buried in your heart?

Why do you take this killing pace
   and keep Me buried in your heart?

Do you not know that I desire
   to speak to your heart?

I desire to give you a heart
   that is tender toward Me.

Take in the food that will
   feed your spirit and nourish your heart.

I love you and accept you
   right where you are.

Move toward Me, your Lord,
   and allow Me access to your life;

For I will come only with your consent.
   I will come upon invitation, only.

I await your willingness to let Me
   be resurrected in your heart.

I look to your choice to let Me
   unbind your heart and set you free.
Florence Bullis

"Under The Stars"

Sometimes I lay out under the stars
when the sky is all so black.
I relax and think of all kinds of things
Till the point when I don't want to go back.
Back to the world of hurt and pain
And sadness that can't be forgotten.
I just close my eyes, out under the stars
To numb the wounds that are rotten.
I toss a stone out into the lake
Next to the tree where I lay
And watch the ripples circle around one another
And hope tomorrow's a better day.
I use the leaves that fall from the tree
To help bandage up the scars
All these things may not help,
But it's soothing under the stars.
Carl Schaum

Days Away

There was a day not so long ago-
When I felt of young and not so old.
I never felt an added year a birthday brought-
The wrinkles around the eyes weren't even a thought.
I felt there wasn't a problem I couldn't handle-
I even tried the burning of both ends of the candle.
Loneliness I knew not of-
I knew only of flowers and of love.
Now I feel the added years the birthdays have brought-
And unwrinkled skin is always sought.
The gray has slipped into my once dark hair-
My makeup is heavier and always there.
I feel there are problems I cannot handle-
And never again could I burn the candle.
I have come to realize it is time to grow old-
But with dignity and pride my head I will hold.
Now don't misunderstand the meaning of this-
A good, healthy and happy life I haven't missed.

Barbara A. Primrose

Just A Vet

It was snowing, cold and wet as I recall that day,
When I first saw the hills in Korea so far away.
Just a kid, from home wanting to play on a team,
Thinking he was grown when he is only seventeen.

When all at once a thought came to me,
About my loved ones who were far across the sea.
The sounds of General Quarters caused shivers up my back,
Because that meant that soon we would start the attack.

With all of us now in place at our battle stations,
It was "God bless America and the United Nations".
With the ship's guns firing both far and near,
Trying to be so brave and yet full of fear.

That was my first time to experience this sorta thing,
But, in my ears those sounds will forever ring.
Now, that it's all past to become a memory,
I give thanks to God because he took care of me.

All Vets have their stories they will never forget,
That's why the folks at home just call us Vets.
So, when you think of Viet Nam, Korea, Wars I or II,
Remember the Veterans that fought and died for you.

Clyde R. Averitt

Life

When the Red of the Sun lights the day.
When the Moon comes out to shine.
You will hear a sound of joy!

What is this sound you ask?
What makes it seem a joy!
Only you alone can tell.

Others may not hear it, the way it sounds to you.
Because in every person, Every living thing
Life is lived in a different way.

As time goes on, many experiences come your way.
Different people and places make life more exciting
in each passing day.

Sometimes you're happy, Sometimes you're lonely,
But there will always be someone,
Something that helps you live on.

You smile when your sad, laugh when you cry,
What makes you want to love, and be loved?
These and many more questions entire you life.

When the Sun Lights the day, and the Moon comes out to shine.
You will live on until, Time—Passes—On!

Ethel J. Sladek

I Need You

When I'm in trouble, you're always there,
When I'm going crazy, you're the only one to care,
   When I need to feel special, you make it that way,
When I need to feel loved, you love me every day,
   You are the one, the only one,
And if I loose you, my life will be done,
   So please stay and never go,
Never leave me, and make sure I know,
   Make sure I know when you are there,
Make sure I know you always care,
   Make sure I know I can be happy too,
Make sure I know I'll always have you.

April St. Pierre

A Rainy Day

The rain feels cold and wet
When it showers down on me,
I walk carefully, trying not to slip and fall
The branches of the trees thrash wildly,
Like a fish out of water,
I try to avoid puddles of water
But sometimes I splash in them
causing water droplets to fly in all different directions,
I want to avoid the mud
but I fall right in
The soft oozy mud surrounds me,
I get up and realize I look like a werewolf,
So I run home where it's safe and cozy,
And I promise not to walk on a rainy day.

Diya Banerjee

Best Friends

Young girls, Karen and Jana were sitting on a log
When Karen, chuckling, said to Jana, "Have you ever kissed a frog?"
Jana looked at Karen with bright eyes and knowing smile
And said, "I can't recall, but if I have, it has surely been awhile."
About that time there came along two big old happy toads.
They daringly approached the girls sitting there at that crossroads.
"Hey Frank," said that one named Jesse, "Have you ever kissed a girl?"
"Not that I remember," he said spinning in a twirl.
"Let's give those two a try then," said Jesse with a croak.
Frank thought that Jesse liked his fun, and really loved to joke.
Into the air those toads did jump, their goal a comfy seat,
And those girls with wide-eyed wonder, went scrambling to their feet!
They say that frogs and toads are fast and often mighty slick,
But they were no match for those two girls, for those two girls
   were quick!
Karen bolted to the left, Jana bounded to the right.
And all there was remaining on that log was bright sunlight.
Frank turned and looked at Jesse, and Jesse gave him a grin.
And they warmed there in the sunshine, best friends on their log again.

Dick Sherman

Autumn's Gold

Days I remember, not so long ago,
   when living in places where northern winds blow.
October's bright lesson was yearly retold,
   as cool winds changed leaves all about me to gold.

Those flashes of color, so lovely to see,
   proved that life's ever changing, for even a tree.
Yet beauty is written in all of God's plans,
   and we, like those leaves, can be gold in His hands.

Change! Ever change! Autumn leaves seem to say.
   You can't own the past, or even today.
Hold fast, though the winds may seem bitter and cold.
   Your God is the painter of autumn's pure gold!

Caren Ippolito

To Smile Again

When words and touches are no consolation at all
When no tomorrow holds a sun.
When the pain is so deep and so wide and so tall
Then death has stolen a loved one.

Run to nature at its very best
Look deeply into a flower.
In that cup of solemn beauty rest
From all creation there comes power.

Or stand alone beside a lake
Let all of nature touch you.
From your aloneness you will wake
As the life cycle of everything is true.

Not the wind now but Hallowed Spirit and comfort blow
Dwelling on completeness is a new call.
Deep within us strength and hope begin to flow
Then we understand! God is the artist within us all.

Charlotte Vogel

And Satan Slithered In

Life was normal the day was blue
When Satan slithered through...

No one noticed, all seemed fine
When Satan slithered through.
With quickness and flash he appeared at 9:00 a.m. in Oklahoma City

And Satan slithered through, the earth rumbled
The glass propelled, the concrete crumbled
Many lives were lost when Satan slithered through.

Smoke and fire, screams and panic
disbelieving, the walls came tumbling down.
Confusion...oh sweet Lord what is going on?
When Satan slithered through, in a truck set to
destroy lives, the babies and the workers,
Many were not spared... when Satan slithered through
Then the good Lord appeared in the guise of people
helping strangers, lending a hand in the wake of
such senseless destruction, strangers came from
all over to help and pray.
The day Satan slithered through...

Jean Regina

On Marriage

   How quiet is love
when we may touch hands with unspoken words,
and feel the closeness and warmth flowing through.
Or silently beckon with eyes that reveal,
adoration - undeniably true.

   How understanding is love
when we may know of our imperfections,
yet never admonish or create a doubt -
But faithfully, lovingly help one another,
by talking and working things out.

   How exciting is love
when we have that wonderful feeling,
of accomplishing projects that must be done.
Eagerly sharing and working together,
as our hearts and our minds act as one.

   How beautiful is love
as we step through this marriage together,
as we walk in his light, hand in hand,
may we never lose sight for a moment,
of the meaning of our wedding band.

Cynthia S. Marasa

Reaction

You search your soul to get an answer,
when the doctor tells you, that you have cancer.

You try to tell yourself that it must be a lie,
because your first reaction is to deny.

Up to this point life has been a breeze,
you've solved all life's problems with such ease.

After you've had time to realize and think,
this is just one of life's little bumps and kinks.

You go through treatments with a feeling of despair,
but your worst fear of all, is your loss of hair.

No one knows the pain you have to go through,
until they have walked the same road too.

You trust your doctor with all you can give,
even though you're tired, you do want to live.

Charles L. Allen

Untitled

Let us go then you and I.
When the evening is spread out against the sky.
Let us talk of things that will soon have no part in our days.
Let us go through certain motions, then be on our way.

And people may travel different streets.
That follow a path of opposite beats.
But do not ask 'what is it?'
Let us just go and make our visit.
And would it have been worth it after all?
Was it worth it?
After the corruption and the falls.
And this now - there is so much more to it.
Do we really try hard enough to say what we mean?
Or is it just easier to just slide back into our own lives and give
   our faces back their screens?
Was it worthwhile, I ask this question of you.
I know the answer for myself.
But for now we must do what we have to do.

Erin E. Byrne

Introspection...

Shall I first know
who You are...
why You are...
what You are...

Or shall I know only that I am known to you...that You call to me...
that something in me would move mountains to get to You...
if I would let it...

I am at war with my own self...with the many versions of me
who question the indwelling of Something
unseen...unheard...unfelt...
unexperienced by the conventional five senses by whose witness
we test the reality of most things...

How do I free the so small, so frail...and yet so very insistent part
of me...that wants desperately to give itself to You?

How does that small yearning bit of me drag the rest of my reluctant
soul into the inexorable vortex that You are?

How do I free that shred of myself that knows beyond doubt that
I belong to You...from time out of mind have always belonged to You.

Oh my God...
gather in my splintered selves...
unite them...and be Lord of the whole.

Barbara C. Stanley

Tara

Tomorrow's tears you finally shed.
When the light changed its shade to gray
And the laughter grew louder
until the pain was put to silence,
You loved your life who cannot be seen again.

Because, yesterday I felt your sorrow
When the air turned to rain.
I heard your cry from the deepest corner.
I watched as you buried pieces of your heart
When the sky began calling the wind.
In your most vulnerable moment
I saw through your eyes and you were weak.
I yearned then to steal you away from the shadows.
But unable to find my way
lost
I was weaker.

Elena Plass

Sunday Morning

Oh, the beauty of the early dawn
When there's nothing but the sound of the bird,
Enjoy it now as the sun slowly rises
Nothing has been spoken, not even a word.

Thus as the day opens like a budding flower
Time goes on; none can hold it back.
Memories and sounds of old-time when family was together,
Skies seemed bright and in food no lack.

What a precious thing is memory
Scenes of past flash before my mind,
Like music and pictures of God's love among us
It seems His smile was on all humankind.

Oh! That we could just recapture, relive a few old scenes
That God would allow us to play and replay
The records that we so enjoyed together
Before he takes us into this day called today.

Dora Reimer

Family Reunions

Those family reunions come once every year,
When relatives gather from far and near
To meet once again the family clan,
To eat and have fun and for next year to plan.

The years roll by fast, as time marches on;
New names are added, like Sally and Ron.
The officers change, but the routine is the same:
Election is held—a chairman they name.

The minutes are kept with meticulous care,
A collection is taken for expenses to bear.
A door prize is given, but beans must be guessed;
Then good food and games make the picnic a fest.

Alice Marie Imig

Rock of Gold

I was walking my dog outside
When I looked down on the ground
There! and behold! was a rock of Gold
It glistened and shined in the day seen rays.
It had a sparkle with Gold and Silver
The sight of the rocks was a delight
Where was the rainbow? Where
was the pot of gold? Everyone
knows the pot of gold at the
end of the rainbow. A
leprechaun said NO ____,
It's just the blarney stone!!

Hilda Barbara Sugelmar

Did I Forget To Say "Thank You"

You brought me over shackle and chained
When we landed you gave me a new name
Laws were passed so I could not learn
But the thirst of knowledge and perseverance within me burned
I knew I was from families of wealth
A pride I had to keep buried within myself
In spite of this I want you to know
I have a heritage that continues to grow
Scientists, doctors, lawyers, to name
Politicians, actors and actresses of fame
There are many things I can point to you and hate
But that will only hinder my fate
Yes, you tried to destroy Gods' seeds
What God has planted no man can decree
But I feel I must say something, something to let you know
How proud and beautiful I am to be
An African-American Woman
So thank you, thank you, thank you for your miss misdeeds.

Estelle C. Baker

Feathers And Gold

Feathers and gold just can't be compared
When weighed in the balance of time,
Affliction with feathers is not very heavy
But brings forth the gold that's refined.
Our moments of sorrow, temptation and testing
Our trials too many to tell
Our heartaches and pain, all our fears and frustration
Are feathers that can't tip God's scale.

The gold He brings forth from the trial of our faith
Is possessed of a weight all its own.
Precious, eternal, exceedingly heavy
The substance of things not yet known.
So take comfort dear loved one, endure every hardship
Your scourging with feathers will pass
And there in its place, you'll find priceless treasure
Eternal rewards that will last.

Oh help us dear Jesus to look at these trials
With heavenly vision from you
To go for the gold in our moments of suffering
And give all the glory to you.

Carol Simpkins

I Miss You, I Love You

I miss you, I love you, what more should I say?
When we're not together, you feel so far away.
I miss your smile, and your loving embrace,
I miss your warm words, and I miss touching your face.
I think about you every minute, and pretend that you are near.
Remember the things you say to me, things I long to hear.
You are so sweet to me, it makes me want to cry,
Each night that I am with you, it's just so hard to say good-bye.
I try to keep busy, and think of things to do,
But nothing feels right, unless I am with you.
The time I am without you, just passes by so slow,
I miss you, I love you, what more should you know?
And I hope that when we're apart you miss me too,
Do you think about my smile, and things that we can do?
Do you miss my hugs, or my sweet kiss?
So tell me, when you're away, what is it that you miss?
I love you so much, my baby's the best,
I'll love you forever, and forget all the rest.
So now you know how I feel, when you are away,
I miss you, I love you, what else could I say?

Elaine Goncalves

Destiny

Look beyond the hills of life and what do you see.
when you reach that plateau, you see the visions
of your goals pass before your eyes. You look
around to find the lost dreams, to determine if
it's truly gone.

You search and search for that feeling you had;
before you made the climb up. Looking through the
horizon, you realize your dreams are not gone,
but just beginning.

The open space you see, is the non-existing
limitations of what your life can be.

So never quit dreaming, for someday it will be
gleaming with happiness and prosperity for the
rest of your life.
John Shin

The Quiet House

I often return to this quiet house,
Where ageless seasons of youth I spent.

I am older now.
Youth vanished long summers ago.

You are no longer here -
Nor yet am I.
We are ourselves ghosts of our own recollections.

The dust on the table is settled
And undisturbed by the passing of some carefree soul
Who in a moment of whimsy
Swipes a pattern without breaking stride.

With a strangely aching heart,
I see that
No one passing would ever know,
Just looking at this quiet house,
What sweet companions we were long ago.
Joan Ashton

"The Beauty Of Magic"

In the land of enchantment
   where everything is magical
Comes a song from a nightingale
   from a high willow tree
Blending so softly from their silvery nest
   a pair of white doves
Singing a celestial duet
If you listen very closely,
   you will hear
Songs through the tree tops
   to enchant your heart.
Doris Mahon

Communion

O Goddess, hopeless
wailing, crying, grieving
as the land lies spent
wallowing in winter waste.

The Goddess within
whose heart leaps joyously
as Circe's sweet songs
lure sailors to their doom.

Our Goddess triumphant
as the blood red moon
laughs in exultation
as the battle cry resounds
and She reclaims her own.
Kathleen A. Muja

America, Where?

Where is that great nation in which we once lived?
Where is that great American Dream?
As we grow up in life we are often reminded of our past.
A past in which we lived safely, not knowing the viciousness of today.
A past where we once slept with doors unlocked and windows open.
A past where boys and girls at school fought with their fist,
not chains, not knives and not guns.
Where is that great nation in which we once lived?
A nation where dad went to work and mom stayed home.
A nation where one income was enough.
Why did we change that dream for drive by shootings, crack, cocaine,
gold chains, expensive sneakers, and dirty money that absorbs
so many of our young people?
We have become victims of our own world, and each other. This
is our America Today! Our America, a country shamed more than
  proud.
When's the last time you were mugged or
someone that you knew was a victim of a car jacking,
drive by shooting or a family mourning the loss of a loved one
who was in the wrong place at the wrong time? America,
the land of the free and the home of what? It's an American
Thing! And we all should try to understand!
Debra Larregui

The Journey

Let me take you on a journey to the center of my soul
where many have gone before and felt there was no hope
To a world that has no color, only black and white
where the sun is just a glimmer and the days are black as night

I crawl around in darkness, my legs too weak to stand
with the tiny hope that somehow I may leave this desolate land.
I choke from all the emptiness my heart feels deep inside.
as my strength begins to drain and my soul continues to die.

In one last attempt, I cry out in pain
for the love I once felt but could not retain
My voice becomes hoarse and my lips have turned dry
unable to hold back the tears in my eyes.

I hang my head low and start to give in
'Cause I know in my heart, my time's at its end.
my body lies lifeless, my face in the sand.
and my last breath of life just slips through my hand.

My quest is now over and my life's been renewed
For it wasn't me who died that day, only my love for you.
Daniel Ford

Where Do Old Fireman Go?

My heart has need to know ..beyond all gossips doubt,
Where do old fireman go? When flames of life die out.
I've ask my Lord to bless these men...day out, day in,
Some—where near a child of tender years is looking up...
To them.. perhaps in search of a friend.

I believe my Lord aware of old firemen by heart
He knows old firemen have faith to meet each task
I believe when old flames of life depart
Another lifetime starts
A path of ease to follow by Journeys tracks
Dues were paid, when firemen prayed
Answers to all needs..forever were unmasked!

My heart has need to say before we start each day
We all should stop to praise the firemen's job
And even as we pray.. give thanks for dying embers
Unto God for members..and keep alive our memories
Where old firemen go..when flames of life have lost their glow?
Elveda O. Pritchett

Dixie Evermore

Down in the Southland
Where people are real and good
Working for a living, believing in God
And doing what they should
Oh, they had slaves and the slaves had masters
all of that is true
But there came a time when the North
wanted change, and made ol' Dixie blue
Self determination was the right that made
them fight and bleed and die
But all those men lying in their graves
must make us all wonder why
But men will flight for what is right
Until the end shall come
Let all men pray for the day that victory
will be won

Charles E. Houchins

The Good Land

There is a land so good to know,
   Where wooded streams bright ebb and flow
Accent the air with a music, sweet—
   Where mountains dip their giant feet
Into lakes which grace that land
   Like multi-jewels—ever grand.
Great forests rise tall toward the skies
   Like sentinels, with piercing eyes,
In everlasting quest for light-
   Observing birdlings eager flight.
The lovely land pervades the heart
   With quiet joy—and feelings start
To fill the corners of the mind
   Until, at last you come to find,
That here where Patriots once trod—
   You too, are walking close to God!

Dorothy L. Black

Love, The Heart And Soul Of Dance

Love guides the soul through each motion
Whether it be the uplifting joy it brings
To the soft pointed pink shoes of the ballerina
As she gracefully floats across the stage
Like a fluttering butterfly ever so filled
With an undeniable and unselfish love.

But the deniable love can wreck the heart
And tear the soul leaving the dancer
To beat her fists upon the stage
Twisting her body
And pulling herself across the dance floor
Trying to relinquish her soul to the answer
No knowing that the answer is waiting to be
Accepted by her heart.

Cyndy Carrasco

Heartache

Heartache is a war between the mind and heart,
Which turns into an art, of struggle.
It causes the pulse to race,
as the mind tries to embrace,
and in the heart burns the face of a lost soul.
Letting go of that face is the hardest thing
for one who tries to trace the cause of pain,
which pours down like rain,
onto one with a heartache.

Angela Michelle Turner

Faraway

From memories seated in far yesterday
Whether real or imagined, yet, no one can say
There is an island which stands to this day
'Tis a magical paradise called FarAway

No mist of time has e'er dulled its call
through the eyes of my childhood I bring to recall
That mystical realm that is called FarAway
Where all things fare better with each passing day

No ship in hurricane e'er stood its cay
Nor pirate chest hidden, no, not to this day
For quickly as sighted, it doth steal away
In the depths and remembrance of each yesterday

Oh, how my heart aches for just one getaway
To savor each moment for all time, this day
to dabble unfettered in that virgin cay
Who'd not purchase the passage to sail there today?

Please,...could you come with me, oh....,
would you come with me, to show me the way
To that FarAway Island of our yesterday?

Charles D. Bolen

Untitled

Woman...
Which way do you go?
Sitting silently, pondering the thoughts that are yours alone,
Trip on the sound of your needles knitting the scarf for no one,
   dragging tails of yarn in the sand.
Tonight, the moonlight shines on your shoulders, coppered sand,
   footprints of a man,
His sand-signed signatures are all your world tonight.
   the children never born
   the man you couldn't keep
   the father unknown
   the God unloving
Sounds of a scraping lake, a harsh and brittle cracking, the shrieking
   spirits in the ice.
And you shiver with desire, for this is your home, your mother,
This is where you shall return and you know the way.
Leave your half-knitted scarf, the skeins of tear-crystalled yarn
   for me to finish
   ...too late.

Cathy Schickedanz

The Hawks

Blue skies upon the horizon,
while Hawks soar and are soon gone,
only to light upon tree or fence post to stare,
wondering at the fanfare swiftly passing by,
not knowing soon it may die.
Little creatures upon the ground,
Meant for food of birds of prey.
Come after the long close of day.

Flora Beth Weber Sargent

Untitled

   I walked the sandy beaches of Jamaica
while I sat alone in Atlanta.
   I shared harmonious wedding vows,
   with the man I love —
as I passionately kissed a beautiful woman.
   Happiness grows within my soul,
   day by day —
as I sit in the darkness,
viciously slicing my already scarred wrists.

Allyn L. Williams

A Light Of Hope

Some days bring us laughter,
While others bring us pain.
Inside our hearts we strive to capture
That sunshine always follows rain.

This world is deeply troubled,
With violence, hate and sin,
But our strength is daily doubled,
With the knowledge that it will never win.

For all the pain we are given,
And the times we are let down,
The Lord says "It is written...."
"For each hardship there is a crown."

Sadness fills one's heart,
Smiles hide one's pain.
Remember, all who are set apart,
Will be together again.

No matter how dark our lives seem to be,
Or how alone we may feel,
A light of hope is sent to thee,
With God's love as its seal.

Josephine Sandoval

A Veteran's Prayer

Oh, Lord, I pray to you as I lie here upon my hospital bed
While the thoughts and prayers of my life pass through my head.
I pray to you that you hear my call and the call of those who died.
And that with your loving heart by our wishes you will abide.

Stop this war that has taken part of my life from its being
And make the ones who continue to fight stop not seeing
The harm and infliction upon our world it has done
By its thunderous blast and boastful gun.

Stop the killing and destroying of lives as if a natural thing
War should not be a song for our future generation to sing.
I pray that my son will not have to kill and be killed
And that by the time he is old enough the hate of the world will be stilled,
I have given a part of myself for my country and loved ones
So I pray that the battle call will not reach my sons.
Hear me, Oh Lord, as I pray and plea.
Open the world's eyes so the agony of war they can see.

Angela White

The Mirror

When I look into the mirror,
who do I see?
Is that a stranger looking
back at me?

Who's the man behind
the face?
Is it me - or someone else
in my place?

Curse this mirror that shows
us who we are!
There's no place to run, no
matter how far.

We can hide from people and many other things.
But we can never hide from ourselves,
no matter what danger knowledge brings.

So, when you look in the mirror, do it
with an open loving heart.

Being able to face yourself honestly is
where an understanding of life really starts.

Floyd R. Weeks

"My Two Boys"

I've two mischievous little boys
Who bring me many, many joys.
And - being a parent, I'm very fond
Of one brunette and a little blonde.

There are days when they're very good
And always do everything they should.
But - there are days when they are bad.
Those are the days that make me sad.

But tho' they aren't always at their best
I wouldn't trade them for all the rest.
They may fuss, complain, and sometimes fight,
But they look like angels when they sleep at night.

No matter what they grow up to be,
I'm happy that God sent them to me.
They're "my two boys" and I love them so
That I want the whole wide world to know.

Audrey E. Polleck

"For The Bravery Of Men"

Nature beams on the bravery of men,
Who fought in wars, and never gave in;
As the red bird chirrups softly above a flower strew mound,
The wind echoes through the silent ground;
The old sun peeps from an azure sky
As a gentle dove sends forth its cry;
The moon is ever faithful too,
As it shines above the boys in blue;
A blanket of stars softly roam the sky
As they pay tribute to the boys who had to die;
There's a garden of memories, where poppies grow,
Where our loved ones lie sleeping, row after row;
Sweet forget-me-nots sway in the breeze,
As they come springing up among the trees;
Deep shadows are hanging low in the darkness of the night.
As they too, remember the boys who had to fight;
These sentiments of Nature are for the bravery of men;
Who fought in wars, and never gave in.

Cleta Williams

Slim, Strong, Swaying Tree

Tree, tall and slim, you reach up to Him
Who hung upon a tree for me.

Tree, strong and still, teach me of His will,
That I may learn to stay and pray.

Tree that bends and sways, teach me of His ways.
For I must learn to bend and mend.

George Jacob Adams

Eurealie B. Hicks

Word of mouth praises Eurealie B. Hicks
Who runs a repair service up in the sticks.
There's nothing you name that Eurealie can't fix.
Your car shines and purrs when she gets in her licks.
She's got the best glue to mend breaks in your bricks,
And a just-right remover for furniture nicks.
She's a Jill of all trades and a mistress of tricks.
Her numbers are winners for lottery picks.
She can inc-you-a-bator for hatching your chicks,
Or dish you up devil or angel food mix.
She can help one to click in the fashionable cliques
Or can even get votes for political slicks;
And where others count progress by so many ticks,
What they do in seven she'll manage in six.
So for anything you may need someone to fix
The fixer to see is Eurealie B. Hicks.

Clifton J. Noble Sr.

The Gray Brigade

Lord, bless all missionaries, please,
Who take your word across the seas;
And bless the people whom they teach,
Obeying Christ's words, "Go and preach." BUT WE WILL STAY.

They leave their homes and safety here
To spread the gospel, make it clear
That Christ loves every soul that lives,
And tender invitation gives: "JUST COME TODAY."

"Come unto Me," our Lord has said,
And precious ones to Him are led
By those who hear the mission call,
Trusting His grace, giving their all. FOR THEM WE PRAY.

We who are "up in years" and gray
Can't go to places far away,
But we can help; we give and pray.
What power we can wield each day! YES, WE CAN PRAY!

Don't count us out! We say it clear—
We'll do what WE can do, right here!
Others evangelize far afield
But still a mighty pow'r we wield— WE STAND AND PRAY!

Elinor Stuyvesant

The Bearded Man

People still speak of the dark bearded man,
who walked these streets with a Bible in his hand.

He lived his life by the scriptures he taught,
for eternal life is what the bearded man sought.

Material possessions were not his goals
only seeking the lost and the saving of souls.

He was always there to show his love; to show his care.
His hand constantly extended to this whole town.
For the bearded man would never let you down.

Children loved him and held his hands,
even the smallest of babies smiled at the bearded man.

From birth to death; from young to old,
tales of the bearded man continue to be told.

Amazing grace, how sweet was the sound
of the bearded man who walked this town....

Connie Jackson

To The Children

When innocence is shattered like panes of slivered glass
Who'll pick up all the pieces of a child's life just smashed?
When memories haunt and echo and fill the night with fear
When emotions slice like razor blades betrayed by loved ones dear

When tiny, helpless children wear scars inside and out
And have no voice to scream for help — No way to cry or shout
When eyes once bright with wonder now fight the tears of shame
And live with scars and shadows — having never been to blame

Who will be their voices, who will mend the broken hearts
Of countless, shattered children — victims slashed apart?
What tenderness can soothe a life wrenched with anger, rage and pain?
What hands can wipe a million tears — for risk and not for gain?

Who are the unsung heroes unprotected by the law
Standing in the silence, sometimes giving all?
The gain is not for riches — not for fortune nor for fame
The gain is for the children — saving lives from untold pain.

The gain is for a future — every child needs a home
A safe and healthy haven — a place to call his own.
Though the effort may be costly, how can we put a price
On the lives of precious children so worth the sacrifice!

Donna M. Gallagher

My Lost Rose

There was once a rose I grew,
who's beauty was beyond compare.
Along came a freezing rain and wind,
that blew the rose to who knows where;
only thorns remain on the bush now,
a bleak reminder of what once was;
as it sleeps under a wintery blanket of snow.

The robins in spring will come and sing a song.
Everything will be in green again,
flowers of all colors will show their heads,
the rose will awaken from its bushy bed;
my lost rose will bloom once more,
only more beautiful than it was before.

Helen Hastings

Untitled

What you need is a gentle man
whose heart is filled with love
  Blessed with tender loving care
from our father up above
  Who would honestly love your children
as if they were his own
  Who loves to work hard every day
to take care of his family and home
  Not someone who thinks he owns you
or places himself above
  But a man who sees you as equal
and is thankful for your Love
  Who spends his time off with his family
because they are his pride and joy
  Whose big heart melts, when he sees the smiling faces
of your little girl and boy
  I hope someday you find him
and your life is filled with love
  I would be happy to see you achieve
the life that I'm dreaming of

John W. McPherson

Untitled

I've seemed to notice you've been kind of down.
While often I look to you for smiles,
Reminiscent of those from a clown.
When I turn and they're not there,
I can't offer much, but I offer my prayers.
And if with you my happiness I'm unable to share,
To me this world just wouldn't seem fair.
If I'm correct, and you're feeling blue,
Then I hope this gesture will be good for you.
If I'm mistaken, please don't correct me,
Just accept this gift, graciously.
And all I ask in return, is the slightest smile,
Which would result in this being,
Well worth my while.

Gary D. Travis

Untitled

What spirit haunts my heart
Who rips my facade of happiness
And drops me into cold truth
Will the tears come tonight
My lost friends
Come to me tonight
Let me feel my hurt, my screams in the warm darkness
My companions in my trek of sadness
I'm alone with my thoughts and there she is
My ethereal beauty, out of reach
As my soul creeps to meet her I'm gone
Alone again to cry inside

Jason Mulholland

Where Can I Find Peace?

Where can I find peace?
Why can't I find it in our love?
Someone once told me,
Love is the cure for all things.

Where can I find God?
Why can't I find Him in you, love?
Someone once told me,
God is in everyone.

Where can I find me?
Why can't I find me in you, love?
Someone once told me,
You get to know yourself through someone else.

Where can I find peace?
Why can't I find it in our love?
Is it because, someone else just told me,
I have to look inside myself.

After one look, I can tell you.
Peace, I will never reach.
   Angela P. Spegal

Why Did You Take Her?

My grandma died when I was in 3rd grade,

A non-curable disease, no not AIDS.

It was cancer a deadly disease. Answer me God,
Why did you take her? Please?

Smiling, laughing, all the time she was.
No reason, just because.
She didn't deserve this,
Don't you see?
Answer me God, why did you take her from me?
Always wanting to care for everyone else,
My grandfather, our family, not herself.
The most caring person in the world.
Answer me, God, why did you take her?
We loved and cared for her every last minute,
holding her hand, not a lost hope in it.

She believed in me, cared for me;
why did her breath leave? Answer me God,
Why did you take her? Please?
   Bree Whybark

The Urchin Pond

Live within an urchin pond and of lowly life you
will grow fond...
Where lizards crawl and light is dim, escape from
this comfortable place seems grim.

The urchin way is effortless, all surroundings
mirror the pace...
No spark of stimulation hides behind each
thoughtless face.

Amidst this aimless way of life an elfish craves ascension...
Wondering how it happened, was it karmic intervention?

If it is true, we choose our path and the lessons that will be...
Then may I request another view from far atop a tree?

Or has a bigger plan been laid to begin beneath a rock,
And strive to be the wizard by some imaginary clock?

Alas, these questions far removed, rehashed by many a scholar...
Are to remain unanswered, even by the man of collar.

Because you see, the way it is, the search is never ending...
Elusive answers, drive each soul... continuous transcending.
   Debbie Black

Untitled

They came so unexpected
why I'll never know
yet when they are here
they take up all my time
then they are gone
somehow I never know
but what is this I see
again they've come to visit me
Mr Pain, lady shame, and their child suffering...
   Arthur Rodriguez

Cluttered Room

What's all this clutter?
Why it's memories my dear.
I dig it all out and just don't put it away.

No it's not very tidy,
and it's not very neat,
But it's a room I love to go to each day.

There are pictures, there are books,
there's music there too,
and then there are the memories
I won't throw away.

Contentment doesn't come
In a dust free room,
There's nothing in it to do.
   Eva Wilkerson

Life And A Mosquito Bite

I brushed the mosquito from my arm and it gently flew away
"Why not smash him flat?" Asked the child at play.
"Do you to get smashed flat when you pull carrots from the earth?"
   I asked in reply.
"Oh no, not at all" Said my child
   as he looked about with question in his eye.
I looked at him and said "Like that chicken for lunch,
   or that mosquito on my arm,
Sometimes to get along in life we have to do a little harm.
So when we have a sick friend,
   or we are just out for a walk in the wood
We need to make up for it and do a little good."
He sat and he looked and he pondered as if in question,
So I asked "How do you feel about this little life lesson?"
He then answered, "I am glad I am not a chicken,
   and how do you feel?"
I said, "I am glad I'm your Dad,
   and not a mosquito with you for my next meal."
   John R. Morris

"What Is Forever For?"

Someone asked me once,
What is Forever for?
As the years have gone by,
I have thought about it more and more.

Forever is for sharing things important,
Like memories of days shared.
Having someone special to be with,
And knowing for you, he has cared.

Forever is for remembering places gone together,
Favors that was done with no bother.
And though miles separate two in love,
Their hearts and thoughts can be on each other.

Forever is always being a part of one another,
Even though life's changes aren't always for the best dealt.
Together always you might not be,
But the presence of each other can Forever be felt.
   Fern Rector

Signs Of Spring

Said the Giant Oak to the Stately Pine,
"Why so sad—old friend of mine?
All winter long—you've been sighing,
It grieves me much, to hear you crying."
The pine tree bowed its stately head,
Waved its arms and softly said,
"To see you naked in this cold
Grieves my very heart and soul."
Said the Giant Oak to the Tall Pine Tree,
"I thank you for your sympathy,
But listen sweet friend, don't you hear a note
Of music rare in the air afloat?
That's my buds, just beginning to grow,
And I'm so happy you must know;
These cold winter days will soon be over,
Then a fine green mantle will be my cover;
Little birds will sing their sweet songs to me,
And squirrels will play on my lap with glee;
So cheer up sweet friend, be happy and gay,
And live in hopes of a brighter day."
Ora Lewis Bradley

"To My Mother" From My Heart

Will you ever know, how much I care
Will I ever know, how much you care

You watched me grow up, my burdens you shared
I never stand alone, you're always there
You give me love, you let me know you care

You wiped my tears when I could not bear
My burdens of life, more often you bore

When I'm on my knees, and pray to the Lord
Father in heaven, bless this mother of mine
And when her time comes, I pray you will
Be there, to take all the burdens, she
Chose to bare

Her heart is pure gold, so keep in mind
You'll be getting an angel, one of a kind
Carolyn Carroll

Like Wine

          I am aging
          Wine in cuve
          Not vinegaring
          But mellowing

     You must not
     More than sip,
     Now and then —
     Never long drafts,

  Down too eagerly!
(Lest heady turning
    Unbalance you
    And you fall)

Taste and know
  How I love you
    Delicious
    Fully

        Redolent of grape
        And sweet summer
        Sun windwarm
        Starnight lit.
              Lovingly...
Herman J. Creary

The Artist's Response

Venture a trail of creative expanse
with a brush and a beat and a puppet
who'll dance top your head. On a stage,
on the screen, on a whim, for the love
of it all, for the joy that's within.
Just let go, let it out, don't hold back,
keep it in. Walk away from the one who
would tell you, "You should stop," hold you
down, snuff you out, sign off, kill you
now and for good. Shut forever your mouth
and your heart and your soul. Be without, if
you fall for the lure and the trap of denying
your call of the wild. Yes, you're wild.
Please be wild. Make me wild by your child
that still lives...that still lives...
that still lives. Yes, she lives and he lives...
How we live!
John Yano

My Deepest Secret

She comes to me each and every night,
With a love that's complete and out of sight.
She opens my heart and walks right in,
like a little girl lusting in eternal sin.
I feel her arms, her warm embrace,
I gaze into her eyes, her pretty face.
Holding her tight never wanting to let go,
pulling her deeper into my very soul.
We make passionate love throughout the night,
a love that shines ever so bright.
Our sweat flows freely through the fury of love,
like two birds in flight, like two white Doves.
The night is short and we soon go to sleep,
we lie drained from the ecstasy without even a peep.
I thank the Lord for this wonderful love,
full of fire and compassion, and for all the above.
I often think that she will leave me one day,
but then I awake to a brand new day.
David Franco

Lost In A World

Lost in a world of Hopes and dreams
wondering if life is all it seems.

Wondering what it all means.
Is it so much to ask.

Is there a place for all lonely
souls who ask, to be free from
heartache and shame, with all life's pain.

Is it all the same to be free, from life and all its misery.

Lost in a world of fear, will it always be there.
Is this the world we come to know, as we learn to grow,
should everyone know.

I want to go to a place that's near that's heaven so dear.

Is that so much to ask, or is this world my task.

If this is so, the world will come to know
of children laughing free from pain, from
people starving, what a shame, is life's
disease all in vain.

With sun filled days of mountain haze, blue
skies and meadows of green and peaceful ocean
scene, and all God's creatures to be seen.
Catherine M. Morgan

God Needed An Angel

God needed an Angel, we know not why,
   With auburn hair and dark brown eyes.

An Angel was here as he looked down from above,
   An Angel, our Marcy, so full of love.

So he called out to her in his loving way,
   Come to me, Marcy, I need you today.

The Garden of Heaven is waiting for you,
   I need you my child there's so much to do.

The most beautiful place you have ever seen,
   With no pain or sorrow you'll find here with me.
You've carried a cross that was hard to bear,
   Sometimes I'm sure you thought I didn't care.

But you've earned your place in heaven with me,
   So come to me, Marcy, and you shall see.

That life everlasting is what waits for you,
   Everlasting peace and eternal love too.

So with these words she said goodbye,
   God needed an Angel, we know not why.
    Dalene Hansen

Home

Behind this wall of mortar and wire
with freedom my only desire
I ran a race with the devil and thought I could win
Look at the mess he left me in
Where I live is not much fun
I took a life with a gun
Now, everyday I must pay
I've even started to pray
If I had started to pray at an early age
I would not be on the devils stage
Each day I perform just to stay alive
where I live only the strong survive
I moved in rent free
take a good look at me
it's not a place I want to be
I listened to the devil and what he had to say
now my life is wasting away
people on the out side looking in
judge me not,
I could be you or your next of kin.
    Joe W. Hardy

The Skies Are Silent Today

Nothing but soft cumulus clouds playfully pushing towards the sun,
while at loftier levels a few scattered cirrus stand.
But my memory jolts back more than half-a-century, as drizzle
swept airfields return and our bombers race down ghostly runways.

As I sit on my terrace, smoking a fine cigar, no flak and no
fighters shatter this azure blue.
Then, once again, we are some four miles high, turrets turning and
firing as the Luftwaffe stalks.

Contrails are now friendly, made by passenger-filled jet airliners
peacefully roaring from city to city.
Long ago contrails marked our place in hostile air, and enemy
cannon shells spit their agony at us.

Yes, I survived, but there again go bursts of orange from forests
below as their steel explores up high.
The great air battles are dim now, as Schweinfurt, Berlin and the
Ruhr Valley are tamed.
The skies are silent today.
    Joseph Broder

A Father, An Oak

He is standing amidst all of the oaks
with gentle smile and subtle jokes
casting shade when the sun is high
providing shelter to keep us dry

His roots that spread so far and deep
to gather substance as we would sleep
towering high above most other things
revered, respected among kingdoms and kings

His children laughing and playing games below
look upward in admiration as they would grow
this oak, a stellar example of what to be
a loving, wise, near perfect tree among trees

Certainly planted on Earth to administer God's plan
It is hard to imagine him as merely a man
for as we have grown to cherish that childhood we had
this oak, a marvel, that we call our DAD
    Dennis Pruitt

Andrea Gayle

Andrea Gayle of the sea who holds the key to eternity
With hair of gold and of brown
Life with her, you're never down
For with her crown she creates peace and harmony at her place
Some come from far, others are close by
Few may go but many stay, a world of mystical magic
Prevails a path to precede neither of riches nor of gold
Can cease the wisdom she unfolds
Andrea Gayle, a mighty missionary is she
Protecting friend or foe indeed
To stride with strength teaching traverse tales
Or listening to weeping wails
She is like an angel sent from above
Sometimes she wanders to a cove where splendored smells often are
Water lilies of white and lavender lie
Where a sea shell to an ear
Hums a song, one of care and concern
Just like the sparrow's song, sad, but often true
Sings a last lullaby when slumber soothes
A depletion with a devout devotion
    Brenda Durden

Just Two Rooms

We packed up and left on a warm Saturday,
with left no choice, it was harder this way,
too many beers, and so many tears, I
knew I just couldn't stay.
"Just two rooms", is what my little girl said,
I was just worried, how they'd get fed.
Tomorrow is school. So kiss me goodnight,
I held my daughter as I turned out the light
I try to sleep, but my mind won't rest,
did I do the right thing, is this best?
My son looks at me, he wants to go home,
who will feed his lizard, he's all alone...
This is my chance, we must start a new,
to make a better life, for all including you
it's difficult at first, but in time you'll see
change is for the better, were always a family
"Just two rooms", is what my little girl said,
with all our possessions, a roof over our head,
tomorrow will be better, there's help on the way
just give me a hug, and love mama today
    Denise Rae Wright

Shadow Reflection

I'm miserable people, a murderous mass;
with loving thoughts does my life pass.

Destroying the earth in my seething greed;
she's being devoured 'cause of all that I need.

I'll spend a few moments inside of myself;
take a long, long look; do I need help?

Selfless solutions implode in my head,
for a chance to survive when this world is dead.

Sweep it under the rug, it'll go away;
lying to myself that all is okay.

My world is it hurting, can I still feel;
put a bandage on it to help it heal.

That's how I deal with it, the mess I made;
see it, then deny it; the truth I evade.

Am I the stable one, am I the waif?
Obsessed with rationality, is anyone safe?

I want to write of love but the words won't flow;
reality creeps in and it takes control.

I want to go home, get me out of this place.
I need another chance, signed the human race.

Cathy De Laney

The Look

There she stood looking more beautiful than words could say.
With my eyes, I held her close.
I gently touched and caressed every inch of her,
Overwhelmed by her beauty,
And thrilled that my eyes had the pleasure to behold.
She looked my way and I held the glance, but just for a brief second.
I knew not what to do, how to act, or what to say.
I stood there frozen in a moment of time,
Feeling myself melt with every tenth of the second that passed.
And just as quickly as she looked at me,
And filled me with a lifetime of joy,
The look was gone.

Herman Solis

Inside Out

If I dressed from the inside out, how naked I would be
with my feelings on the outside for everyone to see.
My heartbeat would be clear to give away my stress,
And my deepest wounds uncovered of anger long repressed.

There are no hidden thoughts of happiness and aire,
For they have been my shield, the clothing that I wear.
They cover me for now and protect my humble pride.
But oh how I wish that they could clothe me on the inside.

Bradley S. Krigbaum

The One Who Fell

What is this sorrow, this aching pain.
Why do I feel there's nothing to gain.
Why am I standing here alone in the cold.
Where is my heart so precious and bold.
I am lost, lost deep in the rain
and all of my thoughts are strictly in vain.

I wish I could run, run from the fear
run from the hate and each little sneer.
Why do I feel there will be no end.
Why is it me they are going to send,
to the pit of sorrow, the deepest hell.
For I am the angel, the angel who fell.

Chris D'Antonio

Reflections

I glance at you - then hesitate, and look at you once more
With open, wond'ring eyes as if we'd never met before;
"Who are you?" I might whisper, but your lips would ask the same
And give me no reply except for what from me first came.

I raise a finger cautiously to feel your cold, hard face;
I know that you're not real but I must touch you, just in case,
For though I'm used to seeing you when everything is fine,
Sometimes your eyes surprise me and I wonder if they're mine.

You look as if you want to cry, but cannot find your tears.
You look much older to me, too; much older than my years
And I feel so uncomfortable that I wish I were gone.
I only meant to check my hair. I'll do it later on.

Depression, disappointment, and confusion find their place;
I knew them well but never dreamed I'd see them in your face...
"How much of this do others see?" I ask you, in reproof
But your expression vanishes and now you seem aloof.

I'm angry with myself for letting feelings go so far;
You're just my image in a mirror. That's all you ever are.

Esther Cope

Ode To A Summer's Fancy

Pure at heart was this maiden so fair,
with ribbons of blue she wore in her hair,
So soft and gentle was her touch
like a cool summer breeze you long for so much.
The sweet fragrance of flowers freshly in bloom
seem to fill the corners of my tiny room
as thoughts of this maiden' dance in my head.
I peer through my window while perched in my bed
was she sent from God in heaven above
down to thee to be my true love.
How long must I wait
Please give me a sign
for I long for the day when she's forever mine.

James M. White Jr.

"You Can Do It"

A happy smile, a handshake too,
Will make some people think well of you.
Try your best to be a man,
Do the very best you can,
Then things will surely come your way,
The dark clouds in your life will roll away.
Take each criticism with a grain of salt,
You'll find that most of them ain't your fault.
So smile and the sun will glow,
Because it knows you're on the go.
For brighter things that will be done,
By one of America's favorite sons.

Griffith Morgan

The Disabled Man

I sit on the sidewalk with a bowl at my side asking for money,
with no legs with no arms and I am deaf. The only thing I can do
is see and talk. People pass, people pass, and pass, please help me,
please help me. I cry. My face turns red as the color red
I freeze like a meat that had years and years in a refrigerator and no
one to check on it. I yell for help but everyone passes by as if I do
not exist. Hungry and frozen I am, but still no one helps.
I try to move from where I am but I cannot get too far. The cold
froze my blood. I stay on the sidewalk like a Statue. My only hope
is to ask for the help of the LORD. So I close my eyes and pray to
the LORD. He is the only one who feels and sees my pain. The LORD
puts his hand on me and hides me from the cold. When I wake up
I find myself warm. I pray to him more and he gives me food. It
is then I see how hard the human Heart has become.

Francois Petit Levy

Brandy And Me

We first met in winter
With snow on the tree
It was love at first sight
For Brandy and me

The first year was rough
For both her and me
Somehow we survived
My Brandy and me

For many years it was us two
Constant companions, and our love grew
She could read my mind, this gentle soul
She knew she was loved, or so I am told

I miss her so much, but life goes on
I still have her collar, her brush and her comb
I always remember, and sometimes with glee
How life was so good then
For Brandy and me

Carl W. O'Donnell

Play For Me

There you came seemingly out of nowhere
With wrists of steel and fingers of air - a touch as
Light as an angels kiss - play for me
Drummer boy, show me what I've missed

Today is all we have, tomorrow's not for us
We're different moments in time, destined
Like Haley's Comet, to briefly shine just once in
This lifetime. So play for me baby, play like
You've never played before

People are opinionated about what's right or what's wrong
And if you listen to people you die before you've lived
And it won't take long - so play for me baby, let
Your beat become mine, suspend me in time
For just this moment, this increment of time

And when our beat has stilled and we've begun
Our descent - Pause- Listen - Reflect - and grant me
One wish: When your drum begins to roll for
Someone else - Remember when you made my heart
Soar! You played for me baby, like you
Never played before.

Dee Fowler

A Measure Of Time (For Carol Ann)

Time...
  with you...
  is the joy of a running stream.

Time...
  without you...
  is the slow, grinding of a glacier retreating from the sea.

Time...
  with you... there is never enough.

Time...
  without you... there is always too much.

But all my time...
  would I spend with you,
  without ever feeling blue;
  doing as God wills, ever Loving You.

Time...
  with every beat of my heart,
  with every breath I take.

Time...
  in all its forms is...
  to measure my Love and need for Thee.

James E. Smith

Triceratops

You lumbered peacefully through the fields
without any fears or worries.
Why did you ever become extinct?
Many have come up with theories.

Your titanic build has served you well
through days and days of feasting
without fear of odontoids
or anyone perceiving.

You simply can't help being laggard,
corpulent and ample.
But haven't yet, that I perceive
let T-Rex get a sample.

I puzzle at why you had to be
so aggressive and so slow.
And why you met with your demise
without a single foe.

Ann Erickson

After The Laughter

After the laughter, the music was gone.
Without any music, it sounds all wrong.
But when Jesus calls me I will go home.
He'll give me the laughter, and the music to his new song.
I'll sing with the angels, praise God, I know.
You've made fun of Jesus, and you've made fun of me.
I'll just let it be.
I'll keep on singing for eternity.
If I hit the wrong note
Your ears will be ringing.
I'll sing for Jesus here on this earth.
I've been singing his praises
Almost since my first birth.
If one gets a blessing, I'll sing 'till the end.
Then I'll begin the new song with Jesus again.
This is my song with no laughter or music.
And I can sing it to Jesus, 'cause he told me so.
I don't have to worry about the tune or the notes,
Because there are none that go to this
little song I just wrote.

Angie Daveler

God

Without GOD there wouldn't be life.
Without GOD man wouldn't have a wife.
GOD is the creator of all living things.
We give thanks to him for the many joys that he brings.

We love GOD, we truly do.
You should allow GOD into your heart too.
We give thanks to GOD everyday.
Some people give thanks to him by reading the Bible and others pray.

Andrea N. Welch

Think About It

If I could do it all over, some they say
Without really knowing, it'd be the same ole way
A person must learn from mistakes he's made
Through heartaches, tears, the price he's paid
If the ability I mention, is what you're lacking
Then a ghost through life is what you're tracking
To fight with a loved one, mother, father or wife
Should be the last thing you do, for the rest of your life
This story I'm telling, ain't meant dirty or nice
Just a few simple words of friendly advice
So whether you're prayin' for peace, or prayin' for beans
Keep prayin' you don't live it, to know what it means

Dwaine L. Honea

Yet Redeemable

Redeem me from thou grave ominous depression,
woes that come in waves of succession.
from exceeding heavy ties that bind
true love, true joy, true peace of mind.
Redeem me from the fiery tongue
that effects grief to innocence come.
From all the weary burdens bore,
a careless tongue spat out much gore.
Redeem me from the jealous heart
whose raging envy played its part,
unfounded hate it did disperse,
unwarranted revenge its heart did nurse.
o' lie, o' lie, o' gruesome lie,
all truths you invariably will deny.
Redeem me from one void of compassion,
discharged emotion, birthed devastation.
But most of all redeem the one
that wrought hurtful pain and ill-deeds done,
redeem the barren and tormented soul
who steered a life that lost control.

Billie A. Toney-Regusters

The Destiny

Children are laughing, toys are crackling
Women are gaffering, men are gabbling
The crowd is clacking, the lifts are clanging
The demons are clattering, Fluttering their wings

Cars are streaking, planes are roaring
People are strolling, kids are running
Sun is glowing, moos is hiding
Demons are hovering, deriding the crowd.

Oklahoma City, the prime city of Sooner State
A city of peace, the city of tranquillity
A transport of death moved through the city
Sulphur fuming demons, furiously guided the van

The death van is moving, Crackpots are riding
Culprits are craving for craven crime
Demons are riding, the guardians of evil
The death van is moving, the time bomb is ticking.

The fight is on between demons and angels,
The demons won, and the angels are blocked
The time bomb exploded, and the death toll climbed
The children are crying, America is mourning.

Jefreys K. Samuel

For My Best Friend

Our love was unspoken
Your eyes spoke to me so many times
Always I saw love in your eyes even in the last day

When you knew I'd be okay without you, you left
Peace came for you when you knew I was ready
Ready to let go
Your eyes said, please, remember me as
Your knight in shining armor, your protector
I love you, I never want to be a burden on you
It's time for me to go

Our spirits are one
Death only makes the love stronger
Walking on the beach I know you are still beside me
At home I know you are still here
I cannot see you but I feel you
The bond between us will never be broken

You were a gift from God
Thank you, God, for such a loving gift
I love you, Rusty Tin Tin
Good night until we meet again

Kathleen E. Kosack

Tears

Drop Drop sprinkle
Worrying brings wrinkles
Drop drop drop
After Chest it seems it never stops
Drop Drop Boom
You're the center attraction of the room
Boom Drop Sprinkle
The Joy in your eye starts to twinkle
Tears show gladness as well as sadness
Tears show happiness as well as madness
No matter how frequently or often they drop
If they are of joy let them roll, or even of pain they'll stop.

Demarko Bennett

"Be Prepared"

Have you ever wondered if you
would be the next, for death to
come and rise upon and invite you for a rest?
You'll find out when He finds
you, He'll bring you up to Kingdom Come,
Your life will be a whole new
wonder if you open up just some.
You'll find Him in your prayers
from the bottom of your heart. We
haven't always been angels but
right now can be a start.
This is the time for our voices
to be heard. Live your life well for
life's short on earth. Do what you
can before you don't get a chance
and remember that life can be a dance.
Look around, what will you see?
A new world blooming brightly. You'll
be thankful for God above us and
what He's done for thee.

Jennifer Steffek

The Legend

All the dreams no time has found
would melt the sun without a sound.
Like ships in flight with wings of fire,
they pierce the night until my self's desire
has been slain ... by love's guiding light.
We all feel its presence and we know the feeling's right.
Though I sometimes bow to shadows where the self will have its way,
I can also rise in the sunlight where I need no choice today.
For as we dare to dream into love's living light
the process begins... the surrender comes down
... and we witness freedom's flight.

Ben S. Nelms

Man In The Moon

She sleeps tonight with dreams of fear,
yet, nothing harmful is anywhere near.
Wondering if she'll awake the next day,
each night, before rest, she kneels to pray.
She prays to God, but not the way you do,
she prays to him through the moon.
"The Moon Child" is who she is,
for the man in the moon owns her, she is his.
He pleases her with gifts no other can give,
he gives her every reason to live.
Some say that he's make believe and not real,
but that won't change the way she feels.
She's fallen in love and doesn't know what to do,
she's fallen in love with the man in the moon.

Jessi Gerstenkorn

Happy Birthday

A tiny baby was handed us that day.
Wrapped in a pink blanket like a
flowery bouquet.
The relatives all gathered to see and
to praise.
Our own baby to love and to raise.
Our baby grew as babies do...
and we sang, "Happy Birthday" to you!
From toddler, to teen, to full grown.
All those years, how quickly they've flown.
Now you have a wee one all your own.
Cherish each moment, for in the blink
of an eye he will be an adult and saying
'Good bye.'
That's how the circle goes,
now you watch how he grows.
Hold him dear to you, your little tiny son.
As his "Happy Birthdays" come,
one, by one, by one.
Barbara Crankshaw

Untitled

I feel like one of those plants.
Ya know — the kind that the owner takes good care of until
  he gets lost in his own life again — forgetting those
  that have grown to need him.
And you're the owner.
When you first picked me off that shelf of many,
You fed me...
not with food, but with
sweetness,
compliments,
kindness, and
care.
I felt your warm rays and extended my stems of love to you.
But now...
it seems as if you're out of that food.
My stems are drooping and my leaves are disintegrating to the
  brittle ground below.
Would you please feed me?
Just a droplet will do more than you could ever imagine.
Elizabeth Buehler

The Answer

My knees begin to hurt, I have prayed so long,
  yet the only subject stressed has been your woeful self.

It hurts me much to watch you fall apart so fast.
Remembering your strength and seeing this new weakness scares me
all too much.

But still I sit beside you, with my loving eyes.
Your blank gaze back breaks away my sides.

Again I kneel to pray, hoping that soon they may get
you out of this undeserving pain.

I don't understand why it has "rained" so hard on you.
But I pray it will leave just as quickly as it came.

I try and keep my spirits up for you, talking about our memories
  and good times,
But it's getting hard to even animate my smile.

I watch your body lie there limp and think of the pain your
innocent soul is going through.

I kneel down beside your bed and once again I pray.
And this time when I opened my eyes,
I knew my prayers were answered,
I knew He had taken you.
Jennifer Bell

"Ya Left Me As A Child"

Daddy why did ya go, and leave these ways?
Ya left alone in my childhood days.
Now I've grown older, and still I wonder why?
Ya left me as child, and I still want to cry.

I wondered as a child where I went wrong.
Ya left me as a child because you weren't very strong.
Now I've grown older and I still don't know the fact.
Ya left me as a child, so lets leave it at that...

I've come a long way, all on my own.
Ya left me as a child to be all alone.
Now I've grown older, people say I'm crazy and wild.
People say it's because you left me to wonder as a child.

My childhood days are gone in the past.
Ya ;eft me hurting with a memory to last.
Now I've grown older and learned to live with the fact.
Ya left me as a child to live with a new knock!
Donald Johns Canning

One Of These Days

You pretend it's not yours
Yet accept all the praise
God knows she'll laugh back
One of these days.

The queen has taken her king to the throne,
  Mockery takes hold of her face
Lashing a scar that no time can erase
  For no time has found time to take place.

You pretend it's a dream, and live both the pains
  Each child's role to search for remains.
Return to the field
  And make love for the yield
Was only yours to find.
  The truth was left behind.
For those you love will destroy the Way
  To welcome you into a different day.

You pretend it's not yours
Yet accept all the praise
God knows she'll laugh back
One of these days.
Donna Blythe

Centuries Past

Centuries have passed since we last met,
Yet through all the time I didn't forget;
The places we'd been, the things we'd done,
The people we touched, each and every one.

The Royalty of Paris, a foggy London night,
A thousand deaths can't hide from my sight,
The roar of the waves against a distant seashore,
Reminds me of the past, forever and more.

I remember the sky in its bluest hue,
I remember the touch of the morning dew,
I can feel the chill of an autumn rain,
I can sense the motion of a midnight train.

In my thoughts it seems so clear,
How very long we've all been here.
Like endless day and endless night,
We continue on this endless flight.

As for my loves, there've been a few,
But none I remember as well as you.
In my heart you've lived, my every life,
A friend, a companion, a lover, a wife-

   And I remember.....
Anthony Perin

My Heart's Cry

It's my turn! I know — it even sounds selfish to me
Yet, I glide the highs and stride the lows;
But it's all for others, you see

I listen to every waning sigh; I wipe their tears when they cry
When they give up, I tell them try; but it's all for others, you see

I bear the cross that weighs them down; I fill the gap when no one's around
I try my best to not let them down; But it's all for others, you see

I open my heart and let them in; In a losing battle, I let them win
When the chips are down, I am their friend
But it's all for others, you see

Yet in the stillness of the night, my heart speaks quietly
You've given him, you've given her; But what have you given me

Like a soldier, you stand by their side; Under your wing, you let them hide
A confidant, in you they confide
But what have you given me

The sun has risen and set again; The storm has come and gone
The tree has cast her figs again; And now you're all alone

And now my heart doth scream aloud, and relentlessly it yearns
Where are all those people now
It's my turn! It's my turn! It's my turn!

Deborah D. Lacey

Contemplating In A Box

I gaze through the filthy window, the world appearing so immense-
Yet so minute.
No one sees my anguish, but neither can I see theirs.
We all live to die, they say,
But shouldn't we live to live instead?
Through the window I view the bliss and exhilaration I have never
Felt, as never have I been free.
I long to break out of this Box that I have built around myself.
I stare at the others around me in the Box, also viewing the world
With pessimistic eyes.
They claim to understand and believe me,
But I doubt them just the same.
They teach me that the Box in which we have lived is a protectorate
Against the outside, and I used to believe them.
They say we must all live one way,
Think one way,
And believe one way.
But I surprise them all;
I open the Box.

Jennifer Culp

The River

A snake slithers across the river top,
While an eagle watches for shadows moving under the river water.
The shadows peek their heads out of the water
Eating the mosquitoes which are everywhere now.

A bear pounces on the creatures,
In hopes of catching and eating one.
Not far off, a doe drinks from the river,
As her fawns hide in the shade of a tall redwood.

The tall grass around the river
holds many insects like grasshoppers.
A Blue Jay leaps from its nest in one of the tall redwoods
As it spots one of the grasshoppers.

As the Blue Jay eats, two wild boars jolt out of the grass
One-hundred yards away;
These creatures come here because they are protected
From man in this forest of heaven.

Kevin Isetta

Don't Leave

You say you won't be here much longer,
yet the love I have for you in my heart gets stronger.
Why would you want to leave me behind,
with thoughts and memories of you in my mind.
You can go from the world but not from me,
In my heart you'll always be.
I've loved you since the day you walked into my life.
Now I'm begging you please put down that knife.
If you love me as much as you say you do,
You'll be smart and walk away too.

Colleen Dillen

A Golden Arrow

You are a knock, you are a feather
You are a shaft, you are a point
You are a golden arrow.
The Lord sent you here on a one way path
This path the straight and narrow,
Your mission to achieve a special goal
The goal of everlasting exaltation
You as a golden arrow must sail swift and strong
You must choose good from evil, right from wrong,
Over come obstacles in your way.
Seek for truth and don't ever stray
And never let temptation or anger pull you away,
Always listen to what the Lord has to say,
Keep shooting forward and never delay,
And you as the Lords golden arrow will hit the
Center of the target one day
You will have achieved your mission, your goals,
And your destination, your journey is through,
    You have pierced exhalation!

Chad Allen Nation

My Only Love

Dear, when your blue eyes shine
You bring so much love to this heart of mine,
When I'm unhappy, and feeling blue,
You share your love with me so true,
I often wonder what would I do,
If in my life I didn't have you,
As years go by, and you look at me
I'm so happy your wife to be,
All rolled into one, you are lover and friend,
I'll always love you, 'til life doth end,
Remember dear, we vowed from the start
Only death will part us, dear heart,
So take my hand, dear, through the remaining years,
We'll walk together through happiness and tears,
Thank you dear through the life we've made,
Though our hair is silver, and blue eyes fade,
When God doth call, and life's path may we part
Remember this, dear, you will remain in my heart.

Eloise N. Callin

Birdbath

```
                                                    Y
                                                   A
                                                  W
   Sitting, sipping            Flapping, flying  A
     Sweetly singing           Dripping, drying
       Hopping, hoping         Puffing proudly
         Splashing, soaking    Perching, pruning
           Feathers fluttering Tail wagging, clean
             Freely frolicking Ruffling, reveling
               Dipping, diving Happily, heartily
                 Making a scene Swishing, swimming
```

Carol Sharp

A Poet

They say that composing poetry is a labor of love
You can write about a pigeon or a beautiful dove.

Put happiness in a song and cover it with words
Describe beauty of the world with flowers and birds.

A poem can take away a frown, replace it with a smile
Help everyone forget their troubles for a little while.

You can phrase special wishes in a greeting card
To tell someone you love them is not very hard.

A poet can express his feelings in so many ways
He can look up at the sun and conquer its rays.

Glance into the dark and paint a picture of the moon
If he explores the night, the dawn will come soon.

Put value on pleasures for what he thinks they are worth
He knows there's a purpose for everything on this earth.

Words are special instruments that rhyme in his heart
Laboring together they play a very challenging part.

Talent placing thought into verse is what a poet will need
Friends will cherish his work and enjoy what they read.

Howard Golley Jr.

Old Days

Remember the days when you were little and free.
You couldn't wait until your dad came home
   so you could ride on his knee.

When you could lie all day in bed.
And a worry never popped in your head.

When all you did all day was have fun.
You played outside and would just run in the sun.

When you thought, when I grow up
I want to be just like my mom and dad
You always wanted everything they had.

When all your dreams seemed with in reach.
And you didn't think about all the things
The world still had to teach.

When life had no problems or so you thought
All the dumb lies you bought.

When everyone was a friend.
You thought these good days would never end

Now as you lay in bed this night.
You look at the poem and think "Yeah right."

Jessica Blaszczyk

"Mother Forgiveness"

She howls at darkness, opens the night
with a voice that cracks the sky,
stealing precious light from shadows.
She walks the pitch, dragging nets stretched
collecting stars from death.
Singing songs that came before words.
Wailing the ancient sounds older than stones,
she knows.

She knows of the forsaken and forgotten souls.
She knows those never claimed, or mourned, or buried.
And she carries those with names never mouthed
with offerings of gentle mercy.
Reclaiming the weak, she calls them her own.
She walks the blackest skies
piecing together fragments and bones.
Forever singing the wails of a wind unleashed.
Calling her children home.

Jayne Anne Jackson

Untitled

At first I was a Mother, so happy and so blessed ....
You filled my days with sunshine, my nights with peaceful rest ....

To me you grew quite swiftly, and one day I did see
No longer my small baby, who snuggled close to me ....

Much like a full blown orchid, quite lovely in and out
My baby girl no longer, of this I had no doubt ....

In later years you married, I cried with tears of joy
I had not lost my baby girl, I'd gained a baby boy ....

Now in my Autumn years am I, grateful I have lived to see
A grandchild of my very own, so much a part of me ....

So remember my Daughter in years to come, the love I have for you
For the day will come, when you yourself, will tell you Daughter too..

Elaine Trotter

Just A Condo Small

"You had such a huge place, 20,000 feet square, wasn't it?
You had cherry trees, and maples and even evergreen!
And the birds you used to see fly by:
Robins, orioles, blue jays (So they are raucous) and even woodpeckers.

All that myriad of natural things and you sold it for what?"

I'll tell you for what:
For no worries about the roof leaking; for the grass growing
too fast; for the termites boring into the perimeter of the house.

Now we have a sliding glass door,
that overlooks other peoples' problems.
And we have our own personal squirrels that rap on our door.
We have a hanging wall of flowers and a colorful border box,
We have our own personal robins, blue jays, cooing doves and
some birds we don't even know.
We feed them and they strut fearlessly before us and in the winter
they look to us for life.
they are not fly-byes. They are live-ins, live-with.

Better yet, someone we don't even know cuts our grass, shovels
our snow and even waves to us.

And, Oh Yes, there's the money left over from the old house.

Charles Patterson

Friendships

Friendships can be so weird
you have a friend
and then you don't
You hate a friend
and then you won't
There are your pals and your best friends
the ones who are just there and your boyfriends
or some who care
Why do people fight
Why do people love
Why are they there
and why...
I just shrug

Heather Gullett

My Climbing Tree

My climbing tree, just him and me.
You can climb up in it and watch the bees.
Or as the days go by you can watch the birds
that are ready to fly.
While you're up there high, shaded from the sun,
you hear a faint voice that sounds like, "Come."
So now I leave my climbing tree to you,
and I hope you love it as much as I do.

Jessica Prewett

Ode To A Spider

Hello little fellow with phalanges of eight,
You may not be large, but your numbers are great.
There are thousands of you in each of Earth's acres,
What a testimony to the wisdom of our Maker!
You sit there so patiently at your web-station,
Waiting for the sweet feel of some vibration.
It comes and you scurry after the source,
Hoping that dinner is served of course!
The hapless victim is struggling to get away,
But you wrap him in silk and welcome him to stay.
Once he is suitably prepared it is time to eat,
You always eat with a straw - tidy and neat.
Nary a drop is spilt while you dispose of this treat,
Now it's time to clean the web and hope for a repeat.
The trash has been put out and night has come,
But you never sleep - always on guard for a
tasty little crumb.
Good night my little friend, sweet dreams to
you until the next one comes!

Bruce E. Francone

After First Hearing Sam Fischer Play

Oh sweet, tender music; haunting, haunting melody.
You pierce my weakened heart with your passion,
you wield your violin like a great knight pushing forward into battle.
To posses such a talent the power of ages must reside in your soul.

So quicken your bow
and gently move my body over those strings.
Lay me across the bridge
and hear how you make me sing too.
Let me feel each cord vibrate through me.
You capture my scenes and jolt them into perception.
I feel each of your finger tips press against my mind,
as you conquer my intellect.

I stand at the shore to await the waves of your invasion and as each
note reaches me, I invite you to these shores to be conquered.
As I wade out to you my lungs are filled with the azure waters
that are the creative fervor of your soul.

Do not cease your playing for I fear that I might die.
Too quickly you have plunged your sword in my breast
that to remove it now would kill me.
So take me with you, I freely surrender!

Anisa Abeytia

The Visit...

Thank you for the visit Lord
You promptly answered my prayer,
You entered my room and my heart that night
And allowed me to see you were there.

I saw the lap of your robe, Lord
As you stood by my bed touching me,
I did not see you come, Lord
Hear the door or the turn of a key.

I'm sorry that I was afraid, Lord
I meant no offense toward you,
I wasn't aware all at once, Lord
That you were doing as I'd asked you to do.

I truly am grateful you came, Lord
So soon after hearing my plea,
Next time I plan to be ready
So you can visit much longer with me.

I know for sure you were here, Lord
Felt the warmth and the touch of your love,
For I know I've received the best gift of all
A visit from you, from above...

Anita A. Viney

The Deer People

Nowhere to go
You provide suburbanites with natural entertainment
Nowhere to grow
your children take in the waste of those intruders
    who pushed you out
Trapped in a maze
which is so vast it even confuses its creators
The power of your gaze
makes me want to do something
    but I myself am an intruder
How could a million years of fawn-speckled,
fleet-footed survival fail you now?
    "We have the technology."

David Singer

The Treasured Heartland

Heartland, dear heartland, how we treasured thee
You stood so long for peace and tranquility
But on a spring day in April 1995
Despicable madmen struck in the name of liberty..
    sheer insanity

Now we are left with our terrible sorrow
And try to make sense of this brutality
All the little children taken so sudden and viciously
Rest in our beloved heartland for all the world to see

But no matter what may befall us
We will overcome every adversity
And these dear children will live on forever as martyrs
Who gave their lives for you, me, and our precious democracy.

Audrey R. Kachelriess

The Dream

At times when you are feeling bad, you look at it and smile.
You think about the time you've spent, and know it's all worthwhile.
When you received it, and felt upset, and maybe even cried,
You know that somewhere in your heart, the judges haven't lied.
It may seem the disappointment may never go away,
But you know that once again you'll be up there someday.
On your chest a bright blue ribbon, you'll really want to wear,
To have the happy feelings that the crowd will want to share.
The applause, it will be deafening, never ending it may seem,
And the vision that you'd had in the past will be more than a dream.
You'll feel the shiny piece of pride, silky to your touch,
To the crowd and to the team, you'll say thank-you very much.
At times when you are feeling bad you'll look at it and smile,
You'll think about the time you've spent, and know it's been
worthwhile.

Jennifer Epting

Just For You

Psst!!!

I heard from a lovely unknown source
Whose name I won't reveal, of course
But those lovely words that I was told
Implied that you are another year old

I was told at the last minute, so I'm a little miffed
Boy!!! I really wanted to buy you a special gift
But since you work uptown and I work downtown
This message of cheer will be sent all around

I am sending lots of good wishes, only your way
And I'm asking God to bless you, on this special day
And may All your Special days never come to an end
Just remember that these wishes for a Happy Birthday
Are for a Very Special Friend

HAPPY BIRTHDAY

Janie L. Ragland

Love Is Gone

When someone you love,
you think is gone,
you remember the nights,
you had with this one.
You remember the hello's
you remember the goodbye's,
But wish there was a kiss
for good old times.
Even a hug, or even one word,
Is better than a fight,
or yell to be heard.
You wish you said, "I love you"
for the last time, so in his memories,
he'll know he's mine. And never forget me,
'til the day he dies,
cause I'll remember him,
for all the times.

In the days to come, and the days to go,
as the world turns round, I'll still know, I love him.
Too bad I didn't tell him so...

Crystal Franco

Dream

You looked at me and I smiled at you.
You thought of me and I dreamed of you.
What will happen now that you have found another?
Between my heart and you, my life has shattered.
In all my life I may never find another as special as you.
I may look my whole life and still dream of you.
Do you still think of me? I still dream of you.

Beth Hall

Dreams

The first day I saw you my cloudy skies turned to a sun so bright.
You took the darkness out of my life,
And replaced it with a shining light.
I thanked God every day, for giving me someone like you
And if he ever took you away from me, I don't know what I would do.
But now you left me to go on without a friend
You gave so much and then just let your life come to an end.
You always told me that success was one step away,
If I wanted it bad enough
But I see you couldn't handle it, when your going got tough.
I cared so much for you, I gave so much of me,
Now you left me nothing, just by myself-so lonely.
And once again my cloudy skies are here to stay,
Your absence leaves my sun without a shining ray.
All of our dreams are over.
They meant not a damn thing to you,
I've thought about doing what you did,
But I realized it's just not the thing to do.
You've given up on your life, and I've lost a really good friend
All because you couldn't handle it, you let our dreams come to an end.

Dena M. Yurenda

"Happy Mother's Day"

Across the miles, there's a mom who's
loving, gentle, kind and sweet. Who is
dear to my heart. I can feel your
warmth and caring arms around
me. I feel your hugs and warm
kisses all the way into my heart.
As you read my poem to yourself
this past Mother's Day. I can somehow
feel the glow upon your face
as you read my poem to yourself
and that you are smiling and I'm
smiling back at you.

Joan H. DuBose

Untitled

Dear Father, up above, you called our Randy to your Garden of Love.
You wanted him to share with us things created by you alone.
When night falls and the stars appear, I know my Randy is always near.
The moonlight is his sign to me that he will always watch over me.
As the soft winds blow, he moves across the sky,
down through the trees,
And over the flowers, just to tell me his life is eternal.
And when the rain drops fall from above,
Randy showers me with his kisses and his love.
He says, "This is from your son up here to you mom on earth below,
I love you so."
And after the rain, the rainbow appears,
And Randy is saying, "Please mom, no more tears."
When the snow covers the earth, and cold and dismal days are here,
Randy's love takes over then, and warms my heart and soul.
He prays for me to carry on, and do the best I can.
When the sun shines way up high, Randy smiles and says,
"I love you mom forever, and until we meet again,
be courageous and strong.

Annetta Parfitt

Lost Love

From the moment that I saw you I felt our love was right
You were as plain as the day and you were as dark as the night
you were filled with mystery.
And I was filled with fright
You wiped away my tears
helped case me of my fears
You seemed quite wonderful in most of your ways
I thought you were true cause you promised you'd stay
Where did it go wrong
Our love was so strong
We had so many plans
but they dissolves in our hands
I loved you more than anything in life.
And hoped one day to become your wife
Our love was torn apart
I wish we could find a new start
things we'll work out alright
but until then it's just a might but until that day
I hope we can always be friends
and see what will happen in the end.

Jessie Madsen

Young Life

Life could be so difficult.
Your so desperate to find, to know things
that people or a spite wants to hid.
People just think that life is so easy.
They don't know that you have to work hard
to survive in this harsh and cruel world.
There are people that are dying because they
don't have clean water to drink or food and shelter.
There are so many disease that you can catch.
But some people don't get it.
They just think that there life stinks or sucks.
Maybe we all go through bad and good times.
But there are a lot of people that are suffering and need help.
I guess we all are going through a crisis at home or in a job.
There are a lot of wars and the soldiers that
are in those wars don't know why they are fighting for.
They are doing what they are told.
A soldier may get hit and die. Others may get hurt.
Their wounds may heal but their memories are still inside.
Out in the streets their gangs and people are fighting.
Drugs are being exposed to many young people and they are getting
  hooked on it.
There are many disasters to life and its world.
We have to move on and be better in things and our selves for a
  better future

Corinne Marquez

Baby Food

Sometimes I could just eat you up
You would be a luscious and divine meal
Of sweet skin so fair and clean, smelling of talc and baby oil
I run the outside of my fingers
across your rosy cheeks
Feel the plump smoothness
of your little arms
I want a bite
Not to break the newborn skin
or cause you to wince or cry out
Only to feel the fattened newness between my teeth
So I run my hand across my own cheek, my flesh
Wondering exactly when I lost my palate-ability
When was it that I lost my bite-ability?
Looking back at you, I take an arm, sink my teeth in softly
While you giggle from my tickle fangs
"Silly girl," I tell you,
"Ma Ma," you coo back
You are so luscious and divine
I could just eat you up
Britta Anderson

If Only You Could

If only you could feel what I feel,
You would understand my fears;
If only you could feel what I feel,
As you wipe away my tears.
If only you could see what I see,
You would see the gray skies turn blue;
You would feel all the love I give to you
Is all sincere and true.

If only you could see what I see,
You'd see why towards some memories I am blind;
You would only see the light shining brightly ahead,
And leave the darkness behind.
If only you could feel what I feel,
When I look upon your face;
If only you could feel what I feel,
When I'm in your warm embrace.
If only you could see what I see,
As I search for answers in your eyes;
You would only see that my love for you
Truly has no disguise.
Julie Cheung

Amber Eyes

Oh amber eyes, how I miss you so.
  You'd perform many tricks,
as you'd put on a show.
  A proud maine coon cat
from her garden she'd hunt.
  Hounds couldn't chase her,
for she was no runt.

A carefree life we shared
  in our woods and home.
With her by my side I was never alone.
  But a heart attack struck her,
and I knew through her cries,
  that I'd seen the end of ole amber eyes.

Now I'm getting married and moving away.
  But when my thoughts wander,
I reflect back to the day of a maine coon cat,
  who illuminated my way.

An era has passed.
  And I say with a sigh,
bye my good friend, bye amber eyes.
Gary Hooven

My Tree

I love this little tree, every day, every season;
Young, strong, perfect, standing for a reason...

Stretching far and wide, its predecessor was a mighty Elm,
Its shade and beauty covering always our busy realm....

We enjoyed it and life, for a score of years;
Then came disease and strife, our loss - our tears.

A tree is rather like a life, here for a little while;
Then no shade, no beauty, no father, no husband for a wife.

But time goes on and with each year passing;
This new tree and my family has filled a void, never erasing...

Spring, summer, fall and winter, the seasons come and go;
David, Donald, Julie, Paula, I love you - this you must know.

This little tree and my children, as they grow, will always remember;
A home, love, parents, a son, cars, faith, good times by the number.

My wish for all of you, be strong, happy, sheltering many;
Giving, loving, caring, no heartaches - not any.

Each stay close to our Creator, each in his own way;
Our family and our angels will meet again, one sweet day.
Elizabeth Dietrich

Woman

Woman, where art thou to shelter this storm that awaits me,
your arms to comfort the weary person that I am;
your words to command my troubles away;
your eyes to behold the trial that awaits me?
Woman, where art thou to calm these angry waves hungry to crush
my tender bones like a starved lion upon its prey?
where art thou to drive these dark clouds away,
command the rain to end its fury, the sun to dry the weeping eyes?
can't you see the beauty of the land is no more, and the children
no longer are at play?
Woman, where art thou to enfold me in your arms in this my hour of
need, my weary head to rest upon your comforting breasts, my
heavy burdens
to lay upon your attentive, ear, your loving eyes to behold my despair?
where art thou woman, that your radiant smile may spread over me
like a gentle heart? Where art thou to grant me peace, love and
tranquility, can you not feel my need of you, Woman?
John Sentino

Peal Out The Bell

I have lived with a thing I have not known,
Yet I feel it here, in my heart and bone.

It is gentle and wild, savage and sane,
It was our loss and it was our gain.
It was the goodness of people and their kindness, too -
(God, rest their souls in heaven above with you!)
It was evil and proud and an open sore -
It's over. Let it rise no more.

I have lived with these hearts, the good and true,
And live with them yet, the Grey and the Blue.
I stiffened with their anger, rejoiced in their pride,
Cursed with them and at them, blessed those who died.
I cheered them marching, held fast to their hand,
Helped dress their wound, joined the foraging band.

We have cried and rejoiced; we sing and we weep
For something that is past - and something we keep.
Oh, I've lived with a thing I knew not well -
The War is over! - Peal out the bell!
Fay Ernestine Gillespie Pickett

Untitled

Dear little Maxine I'd just like to say
Your cheery hello sure makes my day
But for health sake, I follow a diet of low fat
So please "Eve" don't ask me to change from that
Come sun, come rain or came storm
You really don't need to reform
Miss Hines our so correct English teacher might say
To rhyme your verse you sure need a better way.

Arthur A. Long

To My Daughter On Her Graduation Day Master's Degree

In the sky you are a bright star
Your dream took you high that far
You reached your destination
With a sound determination.

Like an eagle in the sky
You fly fast and high
I am proud you know why
You fight, you win when you try.

My heart is above the cloud
because of you I am so proud
before you could crawl on the ground
Beauty and talent in you I found

My congratulation for your award today
I can't find the right words to say
How much I love you, I can't measure any way
It is bigger than the whole Milky Way

Your way of life is to be free
to decide what you want to be.
Your love to us deeper than a sea
On the ground you are a strong oak tree.

Ellis Wheby

The Magic Of Your Kiss

When we kissed this is the way I felt ——-
your kisses thrilled me so much that my heart started to sing.
I am your pretty, black Cleopatra queen
you are my tall, black, African king.

Kissing a man such as yourself
unleashed desires in me that I had forgotten.
My wildest fantasy wishes were laid bare
now all I want to hear is that you really care.

Your kisses drove me wild and mad
You have won my heart and soul, aren't you glad?
I am now your angel and you are my king
this love I have for you is much more than a careless fling.

Anita C. Smith

Typhoid Mary

If Typhoid Mary lived today
With our laws we'd have to pay

To keep her freedom at any cost
Even if more lives were lost

She could work in fast food
Move as free as a breeze

   To handle the menu
   To cook and to sneeze

We'd all wear masks and wash our hands
As she traveled about to many lands

Protecting her rights would be top priority
While taking the lives of the silent majority

Barbara McClure

The Secret Of The Night

Why do you weep and fear the night alone?
Your limbs are weak and worn and old your bones.
"Listen" and hear the secret of the night.
"I" the night die gladly into dawn.
For dawn is just a passing until another night is born.
The petals on a flower will wilt and bend.
The seed will fall and there will be no end.
"So let your spirit flow into the wind."
To blend into the clouds in search of him.
His arms outstretched to meet you.
The gates will open wide.
"And then" "Just then" you'll know the secret of the night.
That is to die from darkness to the light.
Your life begins.

Ethel Searson

To An Easter Lily

Hail Easter Lily, Joy of Spring!
Your trumpets happy tidings bring.
Your life is like a blissful duty
That greets bright spring as a thing of beauty.
You choose for color white's lone hue!
You dance with wind; you welcome dew.
You grow with grace from sun and shower.
You deck stage, pulpit, home, and bower.
You garner smiles from youth and age.
You bow with thanks for poet's page,
Like pretty rose, azalea fair,
You banish thoughts that woo despair.
You listen to "The Easter Story"
That blesses earth with love and glory.

Abna A. Lancaster

Dolphin Child

Return to the sea my dolphin child
your untamed spirit must run free
don't look back to this bridled shore
it's not where you're meant to be

You're care-free by nature my dolphin child
as you dance through the break in the waves
you run with your kindred to the open sea
for the venture your playful heart craves

Be aware of the season my dolphin child
when it's time to return from the game
to find someone who will share your desires
and ignite your silent heart flame

Don't be afraid my dolphin child
though life comes with no guarantee
when you find unlimited, undying love
you'll know what it's like to be free

Jeffrey A. Rayner

The Door

An open door is always there,
you have to sense it in the air,
where birds fly through and wind blows in,
the door is there for future dare.
When you are in a lonely state,
the door is there for you to stare,
the time is right for you to sight,
the other options in your life,
and when the time is right for you,
the door will open just for you,
and if you dare to follow through,
all your wishes will come true.

Beatriz Marcano

A Dream

You thought your dream wasn't coming true,
your whole life had suddenly turned on you,
but still you looked up to the sky,
with a little twinkle in your eye,
you saw something you've never seen before,
it was your hopes, dreams, wishes, and more.
Suddenly you knew your dream of world peace would come true,
and you knew what you had to do,
so make a little time for friendship,
make a little time to show the world you care,
you know your love for the world will always be there,
make a little time for wishes,
make a little time for love,
if you think your dream isn't coming true,
turn to the sky above,
it will tell you what to do, so your hopes,
dreams, and wishes come true.
And if your dream doesn't seem to stay, find your star,
in a shining bay.
   Danielle Holtz

Dream World

Our two lives will soon become one life
You're my dream come true, my best friend and wife
Stronger and stronger my love ever grows
I cherish the life we both chose

More precious than any diamond or gem
More beautiful than any rose and stem
Your eyes release your beauty within
And spark the passion of a heart so loving

For you I'll be planning a great surprise
I love feeling your excitement from the look in your eyes
Our life together is about to unfold
Uncovering those surprises yet untold

One kiss from your lips ignites a fire
And opens the door to my heart's desire
Thinking of my life with you is inviting
Being with you is all the more exciting
   Jeff Plickert

Victory Is Yours

Sometimes your trials get you feeling kind of down
You're no longer smiling but have somewhat of a frown
Victory seems to be nowhere in sight
But I pray that somehow you may see the light
Although it seems as dark as night could be
I know that sometime soon you will be able to see
Satan will be defeated just as he was before
He will not keep you feeling down anymore
So look to the Lord and He will give you power
For the victory is yours at this very hour
   Andrea V. Garcia

May God Bless You

Love is the reason for Christmas -
To look at all the growing you've done,
To share and to care, and always to have prayer,
In honor of God and His Son.
So forget about all those fictitious wishes,
And the pile of dirty dishes!
Look up above, and remember the Dove...
For He's the only Creator of Love.
Remember the Rainbow in all of your Days,
That many things are just a Faze.
Be who you are and Love who I Am.
I Hope You Like This CHRISTMAS GRAM!!!
   Karen Hanneman

"One Day I Will Join You"

You left and went away by God's choice not
yours, and left me to be alone through the years.

I loved you so much and now it's all gone,
And now by myself I must carry on.

Your spirit will always be by my side,
And even in death you'll still be my guide.

Once a love is born, it won't really die,
Just put to rest by that man in the sky.

I know you're looking down from above,
And trying to help me with all of your love.

Your laughter surrounds me through all of the
days, and even by night as I kneel and pray.

One day I will join you in heavenly peace,
in God's holy graces together as one,
hand in hand through eternity looking down at the sun.
   Dennis Tuttle

On The Night Of Snow

My friend, if you go outdoors you must walk in the snow.
You will come back with little shoes on your feet,
   little white slippers of snow that have heels
   of sleet.
Stand by the fire, my friend, sit down, do not go.
See how the flames are leaping and hissing low.
Stay with me my friend.
Outdoors the wild winds blow and dark is the night.
Strange voices cry in the bare trees.
We're hearing strange sounds, and more than we move,
   lit by our eyes' sparkling light.
On silent feet where the frozen meadow grasses
   hang bound -
My friend, there are portents abroad of magic and might,
   and things that are yet to be done by the beautiful light.
Please, my friend, stay still, here, with no worries,
   on this snow glistened night.
   Christine Lavoie

Kick 'Em When They're Down

Back page, small-print: Clerics meet half a world away
To set up a village kangaroo court in Bangladesh,
Where, a man raped a fourteen-year-old girl — someone's daughter.
The men crimp for court, but I count her terror and her tearing.
Men find the girl-victim guilty for having unlawful sex.

How can I empower her against the cleric-clash?
Do we provide a domestic shelter for a whole country?
Writing these words — will it help?

The girl's mother should not wear lipstick, men use a razor blade
   to her lips.
They will not feed her for days; then, her daughter receives eighty
   blows from
Toughened Bamboo canes — but she faints after only thirty-five.

I wonder about women in such countries, and in our own country.
I ponder the plunder-loss of women's art.
You can't think about art when you're hungry.
You can't think about art when you're trying to get up
And the thick, leather shoe smacks you in the face again.

I mention these things to light a lamp
Of observant love on the human condition,
Because I consider the unpainted canvas. (The paintings we won't see)
I think about the lyrical links. (All the voices we won't hear.)
   Kathryn Kimbro

First Entry Into 1988

Assumed the watch, lines tied in such a way
to keep us tied safely at Naval Station, Norfolk V.A.
Pier 7, Berth one by number
The watch is on deck while shipmates slumber.

From the pier various services are in receipt
including power for lights and steam for heat.

In the harbor are ships of the Atlantic Fleet
most like us have anchors under feet.
USS Stump, a destroyer of the line,
is outboard to starboard at this time.

SOPA is Vice Admiral Larson, by rank and name,
or if you prefer, COMSECONDFLEET - they are one and
   the same.

The Captain and XO are ashore tonight
as 1987 fades out of sight,
for people everywhere and especially for you,
As tonight's CDO, on behalf of the entire Yellowstone Crew,
Among wishes of good cheer
hope for peace on Earth and wish all a
   HAPPY NEW YEAR!!
   F. M. Hutto

Things I Wish For

I wish I was a little star suspended in the night
To look down on the earth and once find all things right
I wish I was an astronaut flying into space
Like a beautiful white swan with all its poise and grace

I wish to be like Santa Claus and bring to girls and boys
Lots of clothes and lots of toys
I wish that I was rich and with lots of money to spare
I'd buy houses for the homeless to show them that I care

I wish to be an elm tree to provide the yard with shade
While people in their lounge chairs are drinking lemonade
I wish I was a teacher to teach English or Histories
Or be a writer like Gardner and write Perry Mysteries

I wish I was an Angel from heaven up above
To look down to the sky and watch a flying dove
I wish I were the President for only just one day
I'd give the people back the things the government has taken away

I wish I were a movie star with fame and fortune too
To entertain and make you laugh if only for an hour or two
But I know that I am special, as special as can be
And I guess it was in God's plan to make me be just "Me"
   Rose W. LaLone

The Key

A gateway to the inner soul, a passageway to the deep within.
To look in them, is to forever get lost in their secrets.
A small fire burns in the background.
As you look harder, the flame grows, as does the passion they convey.
They are the key to the heart.
Slowly unlocking the thoughts so long constrained.
To close them is to front a shield,
But to open them is to allow another to see all.
The pains, the triumphs, the concerns, the joys.
They swallow everyone with a single glance.
Once a prisoner of their depths,
Never again shall you be freed from their influences, their intensity.
But it is worth the burden.
For once you hold the key, the flame burns higher and brighter.
As the warmth overwhelms the soul of the spectator,
The beholder too is warmed,
And they are one.
   Lindsay Siberry

A Hug In The Morning

When I hugged you this morning
To say bye - you were leaving for work;
As my palms ran over your back
There was a lump in my throat.
My beloved's back isn't straight anymore
Straight as a ballet dancer's that was
There was a semblance of a slight bent
Bent with age? No - not age;
For me, you will always remain
Forever young. But, all the work
That you have put in
At the hospital - behind the microscope
At home - looking after me
And our beloved girls
All the cooking, all those delicious meals
All else; Has taken its toll
My heart goes out to you
My darling - you have done more than you know
And we -the girls and I
Love you - more than you know.
   P. Thayaparan

I Miss You

I have something to tell you, and this is my way,
to say that I miss you and wish you had stayed.

I'm lost without you and feel torn apart,
I must rebuild my life, but where do I start?

there's part of me missing-it was you.
We were together so long, now everything's new.

But God, with his wisdom, saw your strength had drained,
now you're with Him in heaven and out of your pain.

You're happy and well and I should be glad.
Then why do I feel so lost and sad?

Everything's different 'cause you're not here to share.
We did everything together-now I don't care.

You were my life, my love and my dreams,
now who do I turn to, on who do I lean?

On God, that's who. He's carrying me now.
I know it, I feel it, to His will I shall bow!

He'll lead me and guide me every step of the way,
Till he takes me to join you, it's here I shall stay.
   Lois Blaser

The Eagle

Their wings are clipped and their lungs unable
to soar o'er peaks and the mountains table.
Deprived by their fear, they will never see
the sights of wild beauty in a land that is free.
They risk very little, and fearfully strive
to prolong their years, though they're hardly alive.
The winds ne'er hurl them o'er mountain or plain.
The storms never buffet with cold sleet and rain.
Magpies gloat while gathering their scraps,
but the eagle will scorn the lure of soft traps.
Rain strikes a rooster and he droops his way through.
Storms make an eagle seek heights great and new.
Humans shouldn't droop through life with a moan.
Challenge the heights though you go there alone.
It will demand, of course, courage, never offer much ease.
There'll be no assurance of which moment to seize.
Yet, if you find a challenge appealing.
if you don't fear risks; want a life with no ceiling;
then open your heart and heed the wild call
of the One who can lead you, the lord of them all:
The Eagle!
   Ronald R. Hamilton

Daddy

I tried to put in words how much you mean to me
to say to you I love you and will through eternity
yet words seem so little to let you know I care
so I pledge my love eternal to my Dad who is so dear.

When you are old and feeble
I will hold you like a child
our hearts will beat as one
as I stroke your tender smile
I will kiss your pain away
and put your fears to rest
as I gently rock you back and forth
with your cheek against my breast
I will rub your furrowed brow
till the creases go away
and peace replaces pain
upon your weathered face.
  Linda Little Caudle

The Plantation

Retired at last - to find 'Peace of Mind'
to search for a village, one of a kind
we found a plantation far from town
Serenity from dawn 'til the sun goes down
the day starts with a smile, the birds sing
a good way to wake, and one more thing
most people are friendly and kind
in the big city today - it is a hard find
one can bike for miles and walking too
most of the time the sun smiles with you
there are no gangs, there is no fear
even a sick person will feel better here
had we known a place like this before
we would have retired five years ago or more.
  Karl Schaffner

Dream

In fall I share the dream of many
to seek a warmer place.
To leave the cold and dark behind
for love in my heart and a smile on my face
On the wings of love I soar above the highest bird
on some unchartered course over land, time, and sea.
But then I reach the golden shore where you lay.
The heartbreaks have come and gone.
There is one question in my mind -
was it worth the pain?
  Yes!
  William R. Armes

Without A Warning

Without a Warning I was called away
To Serve my Lord in another way
So quiet, So sweet, So all alone
My Lord said, Scarlett, I am sorry but Come on Home

The voice, The vision, I had no choice
I took the steps to Heaven at Jesus' choice
I am sorry, but the Lord led the way
He promised to stay with me all the way
Hearing those words made me choose

No Time to Think, No Time to Lose
I had no choice, but to go on Home
To rest with my Father on His Heavenly Throne
No pain, No suffering
No tears, No goodbye
I will see you again, but I will be flying up high
As Angels do up in the sky
  Machelle D. Wormley

Our Love

Our love is what you gave to me! Our love was
to set us free!. Our love was there and we both cared. Our Love
was always shared, our life wasn't never messed up. Because
our love was never out of touch.

Our feelings was always there. Our heart never
had no fear. Our friends was never strong. Once it came to
love our friends were gone.

Now our love is stiff and strong, because if
it wasn't for you and me our love would be gone. So let's always
make our love last, because a person like you make me laugh.

So it seems to me you may understand that you're
not the average boy; excuse me I mean man". So since our love
last and last, I think that you're not the average man.

So our love is really strong and if it wasn't
for you I wouldn't never held on.
  Nakia Evans

Does Success Come Easy?

Is the eye of a needle
To small for a thread
To pass through to grasp?

Will success swallow you up
As in the eye of a hurricane?

Does belief in God become arduous?

Are the fruits from his trees
To high to attain?
Would you risk the anguish
To reach them?

As birds gather the fruit that falls
What shall be left for the others?
God promised He would feed the birds

Is the one who starved necessarily hungry?
  Larry Blumberg

Two Hearts

Two hearts all alone side by side.
Two hearts never showing what hides inside.
Perhaps they don't know the feeling it hides,
Or perhaps they're afraid of the on looking eyes.

Two hearts all alone side by side.
Two hearts afraid of showing what hides.
Perhaps they don't know what the other heart hides,
Or perhaps they're afraid that the other heart lies.

Two hearts all alone side by side.
Two hearts never showing what hides inside.
  Sharon Elizabeth

Love Reigns

Tempers flare, harsh words and criticism fill the air
Two loving hearts turn dark
Tears well up behind the eyes
Throats choke up
Happy plans take second place to loathsomeness and anger
Time ticks slowly
Agonizing moments slip into hours
Eyes meet
Hands touch
The warmth of forgiveness rushes through two bodies
Devotion brightens the hearts
Bleak ego of indignation fades
The sweet smell of affection returns
Love Reigns!
  Marie Richard

Thank God For Another Day

Every day is a new beginning
To start this day I thank God for life.
That he has kept me throughout the night.
To let me wake up another day
to be able to feel whether it's hot or cold.
Whether the sun is shining or it's snowing
Whether there be aches or pain
or sometimes just despair.
But with all my heart I thank
God for this day.
To put aside yesterday's mistakes
and to start another day
  M. Ernstine Carson

My First Friend, My First Love

From the very first breath I took
To the moment I opened my eyes
To the very first beat of my heart
That was a moment I had realized
There was a warmth of love surrounding me
Never to leave, but to remain within
Never to question, but to accept
The sacrifices that come with time
Every minute, every hour, use to the fullest
Struggling to deal with reality
Our time was limited
But my memories were not
From you I became strong
And from you I shared my strength with others
My tears from you are never limited
You're worth every drop
The warmth of your very first presence
Will always remain within me
You were my first friend, my first love
You are my Mother!
  Ronald Lavington

"Listen My Little Ones"

Listen my little ones
to the wind and rain,
as they rattle and patter the window pane,
and rustle through the leaves and weeds
Scattering tiny seeds.

Listen my little ones
as the birds chirp and sing,
In the early morn,
on a clear day of spring,
Making music for the day
That's coming your way.

Listen my little ones
As you hear these things
That nature freely brings,
Listen my little ones
With the love in your heart
to all things of which you are a part.
  Nancy Mathews

Tunnel Of Love

Tunnel of love.
Tunnel of love.
Where art try tunnel of love.
Is thy hidden in the mouth of a dove.
Or is thy gone far and faraway to the bottom of the world until hatred
comes to its senses and depart.
Come back tunnel of love.
Come back.
If only I could feel you then I might wait for your return.
  Kesiwaa Nebblett

Our Dedication

Since the very beginning you were there
To urge us onward with a word of care

We met in fourth grade, made acquaintances through sixth
And in those few grand years our friendship was fixed

Through reading and acting you opened our minds
Through the days of hard work we came so to find

That we needed you there to help us along
And correct us with love when we did wrong

You taught us our skills, what we needed to know
And though we are leaving, Good-Bye isn't so

Now our time has come to move on away
We'll love you two forever, Your One Act Play
  Rakel Thigpen

To Whom It Concerns

To whom it concerns I am the shortest one in my class
To whom it concerns I lack a lot of mass
To whom it concerns I don't plan ahead
To whom it concerns I have trouble with my pants
To whom it concerns I am not a sports fan
To whom it concerns I am still not a man
To whom it concerns I am not 100% pure
To whom it concerns I am sometimes not sure
To whom it concerns I always want more
To whom it concerns I am very poor
To whom it concerns this poem is for you
To whom it concerns I hope you understand too
To whom it concerns I hope you know how I feel
To whom it concerns this poem makes my hopes seal
  Paul Mushiana

Fear

As I lie here in semi-darkness I can feel a foreboding wind.
Tomorrow this wind will be a storm that is going to pick
me up and carry me to the lair of fear. I hope the coming years
do not abound with the torture this night has brought me.
I look into the eyes of those around me and hear the question
booming in my ears: "Why are you so frightened?" The answer
is so simple: "I am being taken by the wind instead of flying
my kite in it. I look upon the morrow with dread, but in my
soul and deep in my heart I know I will get over this fear.
The night will be long and the day endless, but when it is
all over there will be people there to comfort and help me.
  Paul Mikulski

The Rainbow

The rainbow—a spectrum of light
touches the earth
  and changes it into colors.

The children mesmerized by its beauty
stare in awe.
Busy fathers and mothers take a moment
to observe the astonishing array of colors.

Somehow the rainbow sparks the light...
  for new beginnings...
    a time to ponder one's life...
To remember moments: Good and bad.

The warmth causes the heart's temperature to rise,
  The spirit to soar,
The soul to glow,
Brings peace of mind...
The rainbow.
  Leizel Ching

A Leaping Lizard And A Living Legend

Hear me my fellow friends, sit upon the ground of gravel,
Truth is the timeless tale my tongue tells of my travels:

A feverish fiend was formed, by fear, from the flames of fire,
A brutal beastly being boiled its bubbling brew of dark desire.
In the depths of the deadly dungeons a dangerous dragon breathed,
And every mere mortal of mud took to their holy heart the heed.

The dark demon of the doomed arose from his dirty devilish den,
Devouring into dust all that dammed his destructive path of sin.
The crushed kingdom called for the crown's conquering command.
A champion came to cure the cursed country, by his holy hand.

Sounds of a song shone from his shimmering sword of salvation,
It summoned the sacred spirits of shadows for the transgression.
The fiery flames of fury, the fire fighter was fiercely fed,
But the bellowing battered beast became bloody in his black bed.

Who can unlock the mighty mystery of the symbolic story?
Who is the sacred one, swelled with spiritual grand glory?
What is the symbol of the destructive demonic dragon?
What is the symbol of the crown's conquering champion?
Marcus Max Cozmos

Our Little House

Our little house sits all alone,
'tween trees and watery run.
Amidst the green grasses and pretty wild flowers,
It glistens, our home in the sun.

It sits up upon a knoll nestled in,
A hollow, or valley quiet steep.
The vistas presented, canvas of nature,
In my heart's eye I do keep.

It's not all that large, but space there is much,
For friends and family profuse.
The best part of our house is the love that's within it,
And how it's all put to use.

For it's here all can find the piece and respite,
Deserved by us one, and us all.
It's here I would die, though I'm not in a hurry,
To answer that last, final call.

It's a place, no, a feeling, of belonging and love,
A place we can call just our own.
It's not just a building. It houses our love.
It's our, yours and mine, little home.
William R. Smith

What Successful Means To Me

S Spiritual guidance, to be led by the Spirit in all that we do
U Using our gifts, talents, and knowledge, in positive ways
C Confidence in our parents, our teachers, and our leaders,
   confidence in ourselves.

C Commitment, committed to the task of preserving our Royal heritage
E Excellence in education, excelling by simply doing our best
S Social involvement, becoming involved in positive social activities,
   such as, church choirs, spelling bees, boy scouts and sports.

S Surpassing stumbling blocks, identify life's little setbacks as
   challenges and work through them as we march on to success
F Faithful to our Creator, our parents, our teachers, and our role
   models, and not letting their work be in vain
U Unselfishness, help those who may lose sight of the goal for
   success, rebuilding and in some cases, establishing their hope and faith
   FINALLY
L Love live! Live the life that our ancestors have laid the
   foundation
   for us to live!
Margaret Spencer

Five Keys

The first key to a heart is to respect and adjust.
Understanding is a definite must.

Number two you see is to love with your own.
Then you will learn how love is truly shown.

The third key is very simple, you must never doubt.
Trust is the word, don't hesitate to let it out.

Lucky number four is not ever to deceive.
If you do, only then will doubt relieve.

Rule number five is the simplest of these.
Just follow the others and you've got the five keys.
Shelly Musgrove

They Call It "Recovery"

It's beginning to look like the recession is waning,
Unemployment is down, and the Dow Jones in gaining.
We seem to have more in our pockets to spend,
And the banks also have more money to lend.

They call it "recovery," a word bringing hope,
That the economy is better, and we're able to cope.
Interest rates have come down, and now we can buy,
What we couldn't afford, 'cause the price was too high.

But still, there are many who haven't found jobs,
And where there are openings, they show up in mobs.
For those who have been out of work for a year,
It's hard to pay bills, and buy food for those dear.

We've heard the word "deficit" mentioned so much,
And "freezes on hiring," cut backs and such,
Does this mean "recovery" is not really here?
It's becoming a fact that is causing some fear.
Margaret Hatfield

Harmony

Come and sing my song with me,
You who in my very key
Are written,
And whose every note
Might, in the issue of my throat,
Find echo,
Or might gently blend
In tones of sweet concord, my friend.

Or come with me a silence keep
Of music that is but asleep;
A perfect harmony unsung,
For the heart can sing although the tongue
Be mute. Let this our refuge be
Against the world's cacophony.
Adele Gerber

Our Golden Promise

A promise was made many years gone by -
To love, honor and cherish without asking why.
It would last forever - our golden promise.

In the years that followed, many tears were shed,
Many words were spoken that should not have been said.
Dying slowly was our golden promise.

Soon love was replaced by hate, honor with deceit
And poor cherish lost to silence with defeat.
Gone forever was our golden promise.

I often wonder how it happened and have to question why.
There must have been some good reasons - Did we really try?
It should have lasted forever - our golden promise.
Ostap M. Mohyla

Searching For Flying Saucers

The love that touched us in the past
unfurls around me now like a flag
caught up in a sudden gust of wind.
We would wrap that flag of ecstasy around us.
Afterwards I would lie with my head
upon your breast like a little child.
We sent our love out like a signal flare
arching up into the stars.
We held it up like an offering,
it became a sacrificial lamb
seeking redemption from some unknown, unreachable God.
My sins have become too numerous to count.
I wish they would stop haunting me.
I fear the sounds of my prayers are falling upon deaf ears.
I remember the night we sat and tried to count all the stars,
We made wishes every time we saw one falling
while we secretly searched for flying saucers.
Tonight the stars somehow seem to be closer than normal
and even though you're gone I'm still here
I'm still here searching for flying saucers
and missing you.
Robert Evans

Dream Land

Drifting deep within a dream land sleep,
unknowing to the outer world of the close yet distant life beat,
Allowing the mind to seek as the eye captures a visual peek,
Composing the mind to be diamond strong, not weak.
Untouchable to the hand for dreamland surface where the eye and
    mind meet,
But all cannot open their blinded eyes to enter and see,
The exposed images of surrealism surrounding thee,
For the absorption of time carries an awakening ray,
Stating life is more than just foolish play,
Realization of today and tomorrow are built by trails and error of
    yesterday,
Not allowing the ability of my mind's imagination to mold,
For only the ambitious survive life's burdens and heavy load,
For inside dreamland one constructs the beauty of their own road,
Expressing I am the maker and keeper of my priceless treasures
    during the hot, warm, or cold,
Realizing in dreamland knowledge is life's precious path to gold,
For dreams turn into goals and goals construct life's planning load,
Reaching and elevating the dreams that were once not able to be seen
    or told,
But let it be known dreamland regains power inside both young and old,
Stimulating and motivating the soul...
Robert Rhodes Jr.

Spring

I like to hear the birds singing in the trees,
Up among the new green leaves.
Then I know that spring is surely here
Bursting forth with new buds so near.
And God in His heaven looking down,
At all the new life and beauty around.
This world of ours will be filled with beauty,
And each of us has a given duty,
to keep it thus,
It's been given to us,
To cherish and to love,
Like a new born baby dove,
So smile and give thanks today,
For all the beauty that comes in May.
Then summer will come in on wings
Capturing beauty in all things.
So enjoy life with smiles and laughter,
Some day we'll meet again in the hereafter.
Live and love your whole life through,
Much happiness and love will come back to you.
Muriel Watson

Music Man

For sixteen years, this man
unknowingly reached out his hands
through his music to me

Taken from this man
the knowledge to understand that
independence is the key
the path less journeyed only for me

Oh! Mighty soul, this man's
passion no other could know
shared through colored eyes
the heart, the whole with me

Honesty, this man
Thine eyes, as life
changing not fearing, laughing and tearing
always believing in me

For he is in my thoughts, this man
For he can reach out
not only with the touch of his hands
but with his words of wisdom,
his song, his voice, and his heart, this man
Sherry L. A. Bartosik

Father's Day

Father's day is like a normal day for me.
until one night I had a dream
That you couldn't be with me.
Thinking about all the good times I had
Just me being with you
Not ever thinking one day I'd wake and you'd be gone
Crying all night and the next day thinking you're coming home
Waiting for the next time I could hold you in my arms
Even though through so many year we drifted far apart
I just want you to know, I share my love in tears
Father's Day is a special day for you to be recognized
Being a role model in all our lives
knowing that you've influenced some type of career
We know you're not with us forever, but Lord knows we
wish you were
Even if you were gone, I'd remember you always
Because you'd be in my heart.
LaToya R. Hill

Don't Forget Home

One day, as we stare up the ice cliffs of Miranda framed against a
velvet sky, or sail past the terrible jets of SS433,
let our thoughts linger on the place from where we came.

Back there, so far away, a troubled sphere full of contention.
Where the first child cried,
always tugging our heart's desire.

Hear the whispers from far away.
Don't forget us, we are of you and you of us.

If by chance we grind the soil beneath our boots
of some warm moist world in a starry vastness that we have ventured,
let us pause.

We'll raise our domes and plant ourselves, then one night
sleep beneath bright flecks strewn across eternal night.

Look up before your eyelids close.
The heavy curtain of sweet fatigue drifting off to slumber's rest.

One of those... was ours!
Lost behind a field of lights lies one, remote, in a desert realm.

In empty space it turns silent round,
the lands drift cross our field of view.
Which one did we come from? Which one?
Ricky Ascher

The Heavens

The Heavens are a wonderful place,
up in the big blue sky.
A place where harking angels,
play their harps and fly.
A place where there's always time,
oh wonderful time to go by.

The Heavens are a happy place to be,
A place where you can laugh and be free,
A place full of friendly people you see,
The Heavens are the most wonderful place in
the world to me.

Laura Paterson

Let Thy Rivers Flow Through Me

Dear Lord let thy rivers flow through me!
Use me Lord so that I may see
What my purpose is, Lord Heavenly Father.
When the people of the church cry out, "Oh Abba, Abba,"
Let the rivers of wisdom, joy, peace and love flow through me.
And people of the church shall see me as a living sanctuary.

The river of wisdom shall flow from my head and I shall teach your word,
The river of joy shall flow from my hands and feet and I shall praise you;
The river of peace shall flow through me and everyone shall see you
The river of love shall flow through me and I shall live your Word.
All four rivers shall flow through me from every direction.

If the people are willing to receive, I'm sure thy will shall be done.
The river of wisdom shall flow from the North.
The river of joy shall flow from the West.
The river of peace shall flow from the East.
The river of love shall flow from the South.
Use me Lord so that I may see,
Lord let thy rivers flow through me.

Keyana McNeil

In My Eyes

Imagine a world with no war,
Vegetation is luscious and people aren't poor.
Good riddance to violence, poverty, and power,
The world is as clean as a morning flower.
No more racism, everybody is as one,
Everyone helps and people have fun.
If the world had no president, governor, or mayor,
everybody is equal, everything is fair.
With no anarchy, or cops with busts,
a peaceful earth for which everyone lusts
Get rid of inflation, debts, and jail,
everyone is someone and we can't fail
peace on earth, it's the way it should be
never will I rest till everyone can see
so look in my eyes and you will find
a peaceful place to expand your mind

Torrey Wallace

Children

Suffer the children to come unto me
What a wonderful verse for eternity.
They're the world's greatest treasure, I have no doubt.
For aren't the children what the world's all about?
Sometimes they are sassy, unruly, even bad.
But they're usually good and that makes you glad.
They bring laughter, tears and a love like no other.
Which makes you so proud to be Father and Mother.

Nadine Standfield

Family Reunion

Is the most exciting day of summer
vehicles lined up for miles
flags flying to designate the spot
the aroma of ribs barbecuing on the grill
the scent of freshly cut grass
hugs and kisses of relatives greeted
the sun's rays beaming down on my head
the chaos of everyone speaking at once
the musical sounds of the Motown era
ice cold watermelon on my tongue
and the creamy frosting on grandma's
famous "Coconut Cake".

Virginia Howard

What Is A Mother?

The question is asked, what is a mother? A mother is someone who is very loving and caring towards her children. She is the only one who carries the child and nurtures it way before he/she is born. She is the one who is tender to the needs of her children and supplies their wants as well. Mother, a child's first teacher. She is the one who sets the example for her children, the role model. Mother, she teaches her children to become independent and loving. She instills in her children values and morals in order to make the world a better place. For the children are the future and in order to make the world a better place, our children must be taught that Education is the key. Mother, someone who stands up for what is right and scolds her children when they're wrong. Mother, praises her children when they accomplish something good and not dwell on failures. A mother shows her approval of her children's success and supports her children in their life's endeavors. Mother, someone who makes her children feel safe and secure in this upside down world. A mother will not turn back on her children, but will steer them in the right direction. Mother, someone who teaches her children to have faith in God and to Pray. Mother, a smile, a touch, a warm embrace. Mother, greets her children with a smiling face. Mother, A Perfect Gift From God!

Sharon Robinson

The Eyes Of Ancient Lovers

The eyes of holders of ancient love
Twinkle down on us from above.
Their vision watching over us
Like a lonesome white dove.

Every time that we flight
Another star fades from the night
Hoping that we will once again allow it to restore its light
By joining our hearts and overcoming the blight
Once again casting our love to the ever fading night.

I love you, and you love me
Together we will be all that we can be.
You just wait and see
Because I love you, and you love me.

Kevin Kutac

Choices

The choices we make are reflections of past,
   voices we hear let us make some too fast.
Without knowing the outcome of what we choose,
   instead of fixing, we settle to lose.
We all make choices that we didn't think we had
   and continue to live by them, even when they're bad.
Reflecting back on the choices that you've made,
   wondering at what price have you paid?
The paths and directions of which you decided;
   your eyes, your feet, your heart, of which were you guided?
But as those junctions in your life did you really stop to say,
   What's the outcome of the choices being made on this day?

Marti Wooff

Some People

Some people said that I'm crazy and some that I'm not
very smart.
Some people didn't mean to hurt me while some aimed
straight at my heart.
Some people sensed I was hurting, while some didn't
see it at all.
Some people said "God will help you for he's always
there when you fall."
Some people wanted to help me and then did all that
they could.
Some people showed God's love to me when there alone
I stood.
Some people said they were sorry and want to start
anew.
Some people will always be there whenever I'm feeling
blue.
Some people know that I love them and they have made
life worthwhile.
Some people show that they love me too, for I can see
it in their smile.
Linda L. Jones

She (Riot Grrrl)

Independent! She states-very strong
Victim! I scream, but am not heard
Influenced and under their spell
she screams-Independent!
Her own woman-or so she thinks
and I try to understand-and suddenly it is clear
how this strong-minded woman
has become brainwashed
She says-Independent
I know better than she
thought she may think that this is not so
her actions and words reveal.
To go into detail and complicated, technical verse
A victim is she-of a figuratively misunderstood and overdone
women's liberalism movement taken to the extreme.
Standing around, sipping coffee
they interpret the women's movement-but wrongly
and this (so-called) interpretation leads to harm
as it is spit into her ears, and she stands...
believing every word.
Melissa Vilaire

Halcyon Day With My Brother Farooq

We sit on the chaise textiled by impatiens
under the sanctuary of the beech tree
I helped him plant two decades ago.

Sister Mahmuda lobs solo on the clay court,
her shadow crawling towards the net.
Farooq's Madras shirt is starched,

Bleeding hues glaze his face.
The only wind is our breathing,
urging the past out of its pockets of silence.

He says, "Mahmuda has inherited Mother's
paranoid schizophrenia. And so have you.
Ask a doctor for drugs to make you well."

As Mahmuda comes within earshot,
Farooq's shaded eyes turn upon me
two alphabets grate against my clenched teeth.

I inhale a sorrow stronger than
the death of his 21-year old son,
the sadness, of mother herself in Kashmir

Waiting for her mad children to return.
Rafique Kathwari

"For Tatiana"

I will always remember that picture of you
wading in the East River,
baby keeps peeping above the ripples—
standing rigid, like they did, long ago, for the camera.

You carried the wounds of a defeated Russia in your eyes,
the resignation of a people both worn and exalted by suffering.
It was an ancient look of lost empires
disturbing to see in the face of a child.

It gave you power, that melancholy patience,
which many mistook for cowardice.
Even I learned too late the magnificence of your solitude,
and I pitied you. You never fought back.

Now, the husband and daughters who once disdained you
—said you had no fire—understand where their strength has gone
when they remember how you met your death
with that Mona Lisa smile.

Gentle woman with the immovable will
I felt your soul rush past me in the night
like the laughter of a child
splashing and dancing across the river.
Nancy M. Lutz

The Girl From The Mist

Here I sit,
Waiting,
For the girl from the mist,
Whom I kissed, just yesterday.

It's been a long time,
Is she not coming,
I love her madly,
Yet waiting for her is a burden,
Stacked with the others in my brain,
Slowly gnawing away at my sanity.

I remember, yesterday,
Her soft pink lips,
They met mine for a time of only two seconds,
Yet I couldn't wait to kiss her again.

She is coming,
The curves of her beautiful naked body entice my emotions,
Our lips meet.

I know I'll always remember, the time that I got kissed,
By that lovely girl from the mist.
Max J. Miller

Waiting... For An Only Love

Waiting... is an infinite time.....
Waiting... is an indefinite time.....
It is a time of awakening reminiscences.....
A time when tears flow, when you have no one near.....
Nor here..... nor there..... nor anywhere.....
Gathering your philosophical energies.....
Remembering those wonderful ones.....
The only ones..... perhaps, the only one
That is somewhere, oh so near:
When your whole spirit inside you gathers like a storm.....
And rids of all those unwanted thoughts—
And discards them to the winds.....
The tears..... are like the rain.....
That washes that time away,
And brings the clear road to focus.
That renewed hope and love.....
The only one existing and worthwhile:
What a wonderful renewal..... feeling.....
Waiting...... wondering..... waiting.....
Just waiting..... for an infinite love.....
Rozaly Osi

Time

Time continuously moves forward,
Waiting not for advancements to take place,
Leaving humanity an inconsistent path,
Upon which their problems they try to face.

How great can one lifetime then be,
When challenges are so diverse,
And one cannot live or visualize all the future,
When time is as vast as the universe.

Even when each moment is lived to the fullest,
Time cannot be made up for humanity,
Because each lifetime cannot be stretched
Beyond its boundaries to exist into eternity.

Lisa Fishman

That Guy

I was sitting in a room full of familiar faces:
Waiting to see something new...
Something bright... someone special.
More special than the rest.
Where is that person?
The one that could be a special friend, one
To hold me, caress me, make me smile.

I scoped the room and noticed one unfamiliar face
Is that the one?... Is that the guy?

I began to look deeper. I saw the sensitivity, the hurt,
The pain and uncertainty He was feeling,
At that moment I decided. I was to be the special friend to listen,
Hold and caress him.
How Luck I am!!!
If only everyone could experience these special feelings
But it was I, I was the one... the one to notice "That Guy."

Suzanne Sasson

Journey

... to my wife

As every one of us, I'm a traveler,
Wandering around every world I can find in my way.
Caressing the grass and the sun
During the day,
Breathing the dust from the stars
During the night....
Blending each drop of my life
With the fires and the waters and the jewels I step on.
But this above all,
Dreaming about you
As my priceless treasure
On a little island in a shape of a hand.

Traian Alexander Balan

"Pain"

The pain I did not
want to feel has come.
I thought into each rain,
there is sun.
You think I am not sincere.
But I think of this feeling I can't hide,
it's deep inside.
The more I think of good times,
I know you will not forget.
You were once mine,
but you are gone out of my life.
Yes I will think of you always.
From now until the end
you will be my friend.
With heart and soul until I get very old.

Timothy Arnold

What Is Next

Watch the news to see what life means,
war and starvation, the shattering of dreams.
Nations will crumble with self-imposed defeat,
while madness rules over the homes and the street.
Justice that was is a glimpse from the past,
it is today's tragedy that justice did not last.
While we were living, the world took a fall.
The blame, you see, was meant for us all.
So you think the blame was not on me,
take a look in the mirror and tell me you are free.
The freedom you had was the world from the past,
it is such a shame that world did not last.
The world of today is not like before,
so hold onto your dreams and enter the door.
In the world of today there are visions to see;
it is not too late for all to be free.
Hope springs eternal and is that not true,
the future is waiting, so what will we do?

Ken Kunz

Elegy In Winter

What astonished her in the sub-zero temperature of her cabin
  was how the pine and ash seemed not to notice,
  how the sky was neither a deeper nor shallower shade of blue,
  how the snow let go of itself across the springless fields,
  how the earth underneath lay silent and intact.

What astonished her was the way the ice held itself
  over the stream with neither breath nor scorn,
  ignoring the shuffling of silvery dace and minnows below,
  the way firs stood stalwart with deference to angels
  and mountains and Gods.

What astonished her was how the trees kept a grip on things
  even when the neighbor's daughter died,
  holding the snow in place as if each flake were a place card
  carefully set out, how the stream burbled
  like women's gossip over a quilt:

Did you hear? Did you hear? Oh yes, how sad, oh yes,
  oh yes, did you hear? Oh yes, oh yes, hear, hear, sad, yes;
  how the ice reached across, housing deep, humming caves.

And she wondered how the spider sun could spin back,
  over pine, ash, mountain, grave and snow.

Page P. Coulter

Mother

Mother,
Where does your pain come from?
Does it tighten your chest or make your stomach feel big and bloated?

I go into the bathroom at night and I can smell the herbs that
  you've burned.
You open a window, but it is winter so I close it again.

Silver needles stick out of your body charging up your pressure points.
Every part of the foot, they say, corresponds to a different organ.

Don't go around the house barefoot, you tell me.
It's very bad for your feet to be cold.

I often wonder if it's all in your head.
Western medicine could never diagnose your pain
And yet you are sick. You do suffer.

I want to take you jogging.
I want to throw that apple-shaped body of yours that you hate so much
into a pair of sweat pants and sneakers and run with you,
Pull you and push you
Until you start to pant and your face turns hot pink,
steaming with sweet rivulets of sweat
And you fall down,
Shaking with the undiscovered power of your own body.

Te-Yi Lee

The Coming And Going Of Saudi Arabia

The day I came to Kentucky to see you, I
Was so happy to see you and to feel the
Love between us that the months apart
Tried to take from us, I felt like crying
When I tried to touch you.

When I looked and saw you standing there
I thought my heart would burst, I had
Thought my love was the same, but I found
Out it had grown to ten times more.

The day I left Kentucky and I left you
Standing in line, I thought my heart
Would stop beating, but what kept me
Going on was that I knew I would see
You again soon, and I knew that Jesus
Would take care of you.
Pamela Woodson

When She Wore Red

Her hair, though there were areas of patchiness,
Was thick compared with the whiteness
Streaking through. When she wore red,
That salvaged her skin, the dark portions
Like coffee stains, whitened with bleach.

In her gold mirrored tray glittered
Her only scent, 'Chantilly' and powdering
The nape of her neck, her life, she says
Is like wicker, that used to be brass
But motioned to something softer and mimics
The sound of her bones when she sits.

She is, she says, while chewing a 'mint pastille'
Like aged wine. A good year Chianti perhaps,
But at times, a light Chablis, on days when she still finds her
Eyebrows intact and her cheeks still hold some color.
Days when she trades in her bathrobe, desiring something blue.

She says that this last season will set aside for her
Its whitest whites, its fiercest yellows
Its reddest velvet sash, to tie up her hair
Or tie around her neck, whichever she might choose.
Lisa Ane Aylish

When I Close My Eyes

The wind lifts me from solitude, feeling so free...
Watching the world far below me.

Flying with the birds, breeze through my wings...
Singing and dancing, just the simple things.

Building confidence as I head for the sun...
Finding my soul, life has just begun.

Swaying side to side, wind in my face...
Never stopping, enjoying this place.

Smelling the flowers, feeling content...
Having no worries, wondering where they all went.

Over the ocean and above the hills...
Nothing but good my heart fills.

Landing on the ground, opening my eyes...
Feeling so warm and fulfilled inside.

Smiling to myself, approaching reality...
Holding onto the freedom, increasing vitality.

Just a moment of time, believing in me...
When I close my eyes, there is nothing I can't see.
Michelle Barreiro

The Willow

Smooth, gentle blowing breeze,
way beyond the water seas,
Breeze goes in,
Breeze goes out,
Breeze comes out of the willow's mouth,
for granted is the willow taken,
young, strong, hearts it will be breaking,
Breeze goes in,
Breeze goes out,
Breeze comes out of the willow's mouth.
My mother which the willow takes,
and breaks my heart and though it makes
The Breeze go in, and
The Breeze go out,
my heart is aching for my
mother to come out.
Kate Laberge

Two Strangers

There are no words of love between us now.
We are as two strangers who once moved together
like waves that bowed upon the shore,
and which now separate
as they clash against the beach no more.
There is no passion in the slightest
touch of your fingers now,
we are as two strangers
who once made love together
like two flowers that opened their petals
to the warm caress of the sun,
and which now are parched petals of a haunted love.
We have shared what most lovers have not known,
the satisfaction of being one person so closely united.
There will be no forgetting,
even though we are as two strangers now.
Patricia Leavey

"The Sacrifice"

Dear Lord,
We gather our hearts and souls today
In remembrance of your son's passing away.

We know you took him from this earthly place
So that he may see you face to face.

You sent him here to pay for our sins
So that we may have the chance to be born again.

We pray that our special little ones
Will grow up to know why you sacrificed your only son.

For Easter is not about funny bunnies and stuff
But that your son died on the cross is plenty enough.

Thank you Lord for this food that has been prepared
And for all the blessings that continue to be shared.

Thank you that you live within us
And that you've allowed your grace to be sufficient enough.
Melony Von Hallmark

Love And Commitment

If love and commitment were forever
What a wonderful life it would be.
We would solve all our problems and endeavor
To build toward happiness — it is free.

Strive to be positive and cheerful
Look for the good in each day.
Give a thought to help others
And happiness will find its way.
Marple E. Peterson

Compukids Online

Between the work at work and work at home,
We grab some time for all our kids,
When everything is happy fun,
And homework is already done,
As we enjoy this break which is our own.

So often we'll compute away the time,
A game or book or teaching tool,
That's somewhat cool,
But not quite school,
As we connect with services online.

These compukids as they now call themselves,
Are pleased to have this special time,
It's really sweet,
That they can peek,
And climb into the mind where magic dwells.

Our time seems swift to go and slow to start,
Quick laughter and a hug or two,
The hour moves on,
Our time's now gone,
But compukids or not, you've got my heart.

Kathleen Garcia

It's Time

There's so many problems in the world today.
We hope and pray they will go away.
The trees, the streams, the mountains, the beaches,
All made by God as the bible teaches.

We destroy, we build, we pollute the land.
We go, go, go, just as fast as we can.
With no regard for mother nature's family.
We just use her up because she's so handy.

But what will tomorrow bestow for our kids.
will any be left after today's bids.
We all want power, riches and wealth.
Doesn't anyone care about their health?

Some people say our health is what matters.
So why do they continue climbing those ladders?
Their stuck in the rut of today's rat race.
Letting someone else worry, about the problems we face.

We're all on this planet sharing it together.
But no one can say it will be here forever.
Take time people and show that we care.
For we must leave our children something to share.

Todd M. Jacobs

The First Day-To My Dad

I remember hunting with you the 1st day,
We jumped in the truck and we were on our way.

Just like we did every year,
Out to get that elusive deer.

I didn't know how much it meant,
That precious time we both spent.

As we left the house together that day,
I didn't know the price I would pay.

God took you from me that afternoon,
The pain and emptiness came too soon.

I guess I should be grateful the way you left,
You were doing the thing that you loved best.

I miss you, Dad, every year,
As your grandson and I go after that deer.

To hunt with you again would sure be nice,
But I'm not strong enough to lose you twice.

Roy A. Cook

My Little Sister And I

When Nancy and I were about four and five,
We lived in the country, cows and chickens come alive.
We stood on the back porch, threw the feed in the yard,
Knowing very well our punishment was hard.
I, being the oldest was brave and so bold,
I defended my sister, neither of us told.
Our parents were loving, our home so a'bliss,
But Nancy and I sometimes went amiss.
In the month of April, we were born within a year,
She depended on me, she grew up with little fear.
Confidently, big sister would not leave her behind,
Even in school, the two of us you would find.
My little sister hugged and tugged at my skirt,
The boys had not even a chance to flirt.
Although, my little sister was younger and shy,
As we grew up, a lot of times I made her cry.
And now I'm still biggest and oh, so bold,
Little sister and I, in love as we grow old.
Together, we have conquered to the very end,
She is my sister and I am her friend.

Wanda Hicks

Sidelined by Mr. Muller

The black circuit line was in the back by the pummel horse.
We made sure our seven-year old bottoms sat on the black line.
That's how Mr. Muller wanted it.
The normal kids sat smooshed together on the far right as if we
were contagious. There was a gap.
Mr. Muller refused to identify the cause.
He picked two captains, (one from the left and one from the right.)
Standing authoritative, he jingled his extensive keys which hung
from his Catholic plaid pants.
I hate this class.
Picking people to be on your team, was like picking those you
accepted and those you refused. To Mr. Muller it was just Dodge ball.
I was picked last, and my throat felt like I had swallowed a
large pudding stone.
It was lodged stubbornly, and when I tried to speak it only
grasped the lining of my esophagus with a firmer grip.
I used to dream about being captain and picking Mr. Muller last.
I fantasized about pulling one of the keys from his Catholic
plaids pants and stretching the latch until it snapped back at him
with the pain of a gun shot wound.

J. Stolting

Angels In The Barn

I remember the barns,
we used for both work and play ...
All were very well kept,
painted red, not weathered gray.

I remember the fields of wheat,
their waves such a beautiful gold ...
We'd lay between the rows of soybeans,
when I was not so very old.

I remember the lofts of hay,
so fragrant in the mow ...
The storms with thunder and lightning,
that we grew to enjoy somehow.

I remember summer days,
dancing barefoot in the grass and I'd believe ...
There were angels in the barn,
not just sparrows in the eaves.

I remember all these treasures,
as a little girl with not so many toys ...
But my memories of the farm,
truly bring me the purest of joys!

Karen S. Watson

True Friend

One night I was set up, to be a willing victim.
We met, we talked. We talked, we walked
along the mountainside.

The joy I feel of being near one
who doesn't drain the tank.

The one way street of giving has grown very old,
you give back and leave me full;
I feel a lot more bold.

Your thoughts, your heart, your life are all
for you to have. The moments that we share are
good; as friends, together should.

The times you come and take me to
beaches that seem so far. The feelings
and the music, the place is just the car.
The shining light of life, soft lips upon my skin
Your brown eyes full of presence
our time is spread too thin.

When you go, I'm happy, we have shared each other's soul
I have no expectations; no nights
as black as coal.

Rosemary J. L. Barry

Hand In Hand

Though our paths seem harder with each passing day,
  we must believe in our hearts to guide us,
    show us the way,
although our lives have been lonely and full of fear,
  a thought of you brings a smile,
    and a tear
we haven't had much time to spend together,
  but my heart tells me,
    there is always forever.

Love and happiness are the goals in my life,
  every second with you feels so right!
The love I feel in your presence is immeasurable,
  the pain in your absence, unbearable.
To gaze into your eyes is worth a king's ransom,
  to touch your essence makes life,
    worth living, at last!
Hand in Hand we walk down life's path
  considering the future
    building on the past.

Robert K. Lanham

Untitled

I love to lie with my face to the sun
Upon the grass on a lazy day.

I love to hear the birds whistling in the trees
Serenading me in the open sphere.

I love the smell of crisp, fragrant flowers
Enticing insects to rest upon them.

I'm all alone among the heavens
yet this space around me is full of beings.

The stillness about me is quite rejuvenating
Nothing else could be so peaceful.

Hark! I hear a sound!
The rustling of an underbrush.

Is it a bird, a squirrel, or some other creature?
No, it is just the wind.

The day slips by with creeping shadows
Closing that day to rest for another.

Lisa Parker

The Old Scout And The Taos Trail

I rode with Kit and along the way
We reminisced of a "bygone" day
The Buffalo roamed and the Indian showed
As the trail climbed high and the moonlight glowed.

I rode with Kit and the sun grew hot
Our lips were parched and the "battles he'd fought"
Scanned many moons and many a trail
That let to Taos and down the vale.

I rode with Kit, that controversial scout
And I wondered...what really, was he all about
Friend to the Indian or spy for a foe
From tales that he told, it was hard to know.

I rode with Kit from the long ago
But the Kit I saw, had neither rifle nor bow
He scanned the trail and with capable hands
Brought the "Bronco 4-wheel" to Enchanted Lands.

Yes, I rode with Kit Carson, not of old time fame
But "his" was from a more modern name
We enjoyed the "Old Scout" of the "long ago" time
Then we bid him "farewell" and continued the climb.

Zettie Painter Garcia

"Love That Lasts Forever"

As we looked in your eyes,
We saw a love, that would always last forever.

You were so tiny when you were born,
We couldn't wait to bring you home.
To put our loving arms around you,
To keep you safe and warm.

To see your little arms rise,
Bought tears in our eyes,
And love in our hearts.
We'll always be together, and we will never part.

Your sparkling eyes, and gorgeous hair,
Your little rosy cheeks, your skin so fair.
You've opened up our hearts, to a love that's deep and true,
An unconditional love, that will always be shared with you.

You're our little girls, the most precious gifts of all,
Sent from the heavens above, for mom and dad to love.
Thank God for our little girls,
The most precious gifts in the world.

We'll always love you, we'll always be there,
We have so much love to share.

Karen Bouchard

A Memory Of Life

I remember what it meant to be alive
To run in the sun
And dream with the moon;
To receive the first glance
From love's fair eyes

I remember what it meant to be alive
To be among others,
A constant companionship;
To breathe morning's sweet air
Through an open window

I remember what it meant to be alive
For remembrances are all that I have
In afterlife's cold dark;
Memories that color the obsidian void
Into which all that is living will soon descend

I remember what it meant to be alive
And so will you.

Jamie Carlson

Is Love Worth The Pain?

If we are to open our hearts to love;
We shall be tested of our faith,
Our loyalty, our respect and our honor
To one another.

For we cannot know the answers and
The way seems lost to us.
We are blind in our grief

Where do we begin? How do we think?
How do we know? If love is the question?

We have opened our heart and now we are in pain.
To begin, we must accept the pain is part of the truth of loving.
Do we only accept that which feels good in love?
When sorrow and trouble come - do we close our heart
To love and turn away?

But if we can find the strength, the faith,
within ourselves - to look past the pain,
to a brighter day - we find our truth in love.
Then and only then is love worth the pain.

Sharon D. Munoz

Rainbow Of Colors

Colors are what we see.
We shouldn't look at the color as a bad thing.
 The color of our skin,
 The color of the sky.
I ask why do we look at the skin when it's the
 inside that counts.
Does it matter if you are black, white, yellow
 or brown.
We are a rainbow of colors so we should be
 proud.

Michelle Smith

Sisters Of The Heart

Sisters born of the same mother and of the same heart.
We spent a childhood together, seldom apart.

Now we are adults with separate lives to lead.
But still we come together when there is a need,

For companionship and guidance only a sister can provide.
It is destiny's wish that we remain side by side.

The bond that we share is strong and is true,
Yet it doesn't begin to explain how much I love you.

Nola K. Meyers

My Wedding Vow

In the midst of God's wonderful creation
We stand before Him united as one
As witnessed by our children and friends
We also give thanks and praises to God the Son

For without Him we have no strength
It is He that gets us through each day
My love for you, Wanda, flows from my heart
That's why it's so easy for me to say...

I promise to always be here for you
To cherish, to hold and to care for you
I will be faithful, trusting, giving and loving
Forever through eternity, this I vow to you

I will wipe from your eyes tears of happiness and joy
I will hold you during times of sorrow
I will never leave you, I promise my love...
Our lives together will always see
Yet another tomorrow

Randy L. Brunette

"Place My Heart Upon The Moon"

My eyes are weary, and my knees are
weak; as I stride along in desperate seek.
My heart is pounding as the cold sweat
drips from my brow.
Wondering where my life will lead me now.
My masquerade has gotten so old
it feels like my saddened soul has
been sold.
To the prince of darkness; the ruler of
pain, my instincts seem insane..
Now my heart seems to go slow as I
fall to the earth and see the sun trickling
beneath the horizon.
Myself and everything around me seems
barren, as each beat of my heart
seems eternal and everlasting.
My heart is still, as I place my heart
upon the moon, and send sweet
wishes to the stars.
As I feel my life dripping away from me.

Susannah Jorgensen

The Joy Of Being At The Beach Again

Hello, you soaring, pristine sea gulls,
Welcoming me to the beach once more.
Too long it's been since I last saw you.

The cadence of the pounding surf,
One of nature's most wondrous sounds,
Is glorious music to my ears.

I revel in the feel of the warm sun on my skin
As I lie on the beach,
Or walk through the sand and surf, all cares left behind.

Oh, how I've missed the unmistakable uniqueness
Of the seaside air, so wonderfully breathable,
And its gentle, caressing breezes.

Moonlight shining on the water can take your breath away.
How I've longed for this visual delight,
And to be a child again as I gather sea shells in the mornings.

I feel a kindred spirit with the poets of the past
Who had the same feelings about the seashore as I
And also felt the desire to express them in verse.

Lois A. Ruckman

Dandelions

I often think of those backyard-summer days. I'll never forget the fun we shared, high in the willow's green grown of leaves. Nothing could stop us from climbing our old friend. Like a guardian angel, our tree would hold us in her branches and whisper stories to us. I remember how free we felt, how much a part of nature we were— our own grove of escape in the forest of life.

Now the tree stands alone.

That summer I was a queen and he a king, wearing costumes as glamorous as our seven-year-old minds could allow.
I wish I still imagined such things.
But the summer flew away, and so did he, soaring south for the winter.
"Friends Forever!" we promised not to forget.

So every summer I return to the backyard, climb our tree, and remember the adventures we shared. Then I lie in the grass, hypnotized by the buttery smell of the tawny-colored dandelions. As drops of sunlight, they invade that backyard, reminding me that nothing will ever be the same. They surround the tree whose branches now hang limp on the ground—our tree, our branches, our dreams. I experienced another world during those back-yard summer days—a world that no longer exists.

Lori Fuhriman

Endlessly Searching

The building blocks for creatures of the world
Were all in place when flight of time began
When Earth from distant galaxy was hurled
And thus commenced the mystery of man.
Great spirit force that rules the universe
Shares secrets sparingly with humankind;
Man works with zealous haste to sate the thirst
And satisfy the longing of his mind.
He scans the skies and maps the Milky Way,
Through telescopes he views a distant star
And sends machines to fly light years away
To ascertain what planet markings are.
   Before we all are placed beneath the sod
   The most of us will call the spirit GOD.
   Lois Graf

The Flood Of 1993

There was no place to go to escape it
Were the prayers that we said all in vain
Could the banks of the river be raised quick
Would the flood walls hold torrents of rain

There were questions we never had thought of
While the Congress still argued our fate
In the levees they built stood a fortress
Sand castles protecting our stakes

There were people who came to the river
Armed with muscle and sweat on their brow
They were bowmen who filled but sand quivers
On the banks of the river they plowed

There they aimed at the mighty Mississippi
While the guardsmen stood watch to protect
Neighbors fought those assaults desperately
From the east...lost hope saved the west
   Thomas R. Groll Jr.

The City

The city at dawn
wet, bustling, hazy
the masses begin to stir
it begins...

The city at noon
hot, sweltering, confusing
the pavement is calling, steaming
the masses in a rush to go nowhere, nowhere they are going...

The city at night
cool, colored, dangerous
headlights, horns and sirens penetrate the soul
the soul of the city...
   Steve Hauber

The Search

Why do I feel empty?
What am I looking for?
The whole world is at my fingertips
I can go anywhere
do anything
with anyone I choose -
why do I sit still and do nothing?
The small comforts I take for myself
never really fill the emptiness -
never really kill all the pain.
I pick myself up
to start a new life's calling
Just to end up where I started all over again.
Or did I ever really leave?
   Michelle Jeanne Hanson

Friends For Life

We've had our differences, yet we remain friends
We've had our moments of spoken and unspoken anger
But we still remain friends.

We've come to each other for the other's advise
Indeed we are friends.

At times we have different views and opinions
concerning each other's life, but we remain friends

We've said and done things that we later regret, still
we remain friends.

We may not always express our love for each other, but
indeed there is nothing less than love between us...
We're friends.

Our lives, one day, may go in opposite directions,
but, for a life-time we'll remain friends
There is a special bond between us that even the strongest
grip can't break...

We're friends for life.
   Kamar Ali Niblet

Linda

Linda, Linda,
What a pretty name!
If it was anything else
It wouldn't be the same

A terrific Mom, a terrific lady
Who did a fine job raising a baby
A person who is loved, a person who loves others
A person who is the finest of all Mothers.

Born a leader, born a motivator
Solves her problems now if not later
A successful person throughout her career
A special person no one could come near

Linda, Linda,
What a pretty name
If names never did exist
She would still be first on my list
   J. R. Paredes

Now And Then

Many times in my life I have paused to remember
what I have done, where I have travelled and have been.

I sometimes review in my mind the earliest things
I remember: the what, the where and when.

Then it occurs to me to wonder about my ancestors,
and sometimes ask
Where and how did they live,
and what was their daily task?

Were they wanderers and hunters,
or tillers of the soil?

Did they live in a cave, hut or cabin
lighted by the fire from an open hearth
and candles or a lamp fueled with oil?

Often I think how enlightening it would be,
should a written record be kept
for those who follow to see.

No longer need one wonder about those left behind
for a written record immortalizes people and happenings
for centuries in time.
   William Alan Hawkins

Fleeting Moments Of Time

I wish I knew where time went
what did I do with it, how was it spent?
Gone in a snap, a blink of the eye
while here I sit just wondering why!
A fleeting moment lost now
it happened so fast I don't know how
a child was I just a short time ago
now a bit older but not too much though
another passing moment and my hair has turned snow white
I'm starting to get weary, losing the fight
now old and frail I look back on my life with a thought,
did I finish it all, do everything I ought?
I may not know where time went
what I did with it or how it was spent
but I know there wasn't enough time for me
as my eyes grow dimmer and I can barely see
I now know where it is headed, where time is going
as the vigor from me is swiftly flowing
time is running away and I can't catch up with it anymore
now all that's left is to go through time's special door!!

Susan Gross

Let's Recycle Grandma

Grandma's getting old and her hair's getting gray
What do you do with an old Grandma, anyway?
Some parts are worn, but she's not rusted through
So I guess there is only one thing to do:

Let's recycle Grandma! Where do we begin?
Let's do what we can to make her useful again.
There's lots of things she can still do
So let's see if we can name just a few.

She can bake cookies, or make a good pie.
There's enough food for all if an extra comes by.
Her wit is still there, and so is her smile
So let's recycle and keep her around for a while.

There's a lot we can salvage, let's give it a whirl
For she's still quite a likeable, durable ole' girl.
No need to throw something useful away
Grandmas are in style and they're here to stay.

Nellie M. Booker

A Glimpse Of Heaven

A glorious night of ecstasy resounded,
When in dreamland, angels did come,
And they took me on a heavenly journey
Oh! the sights my eyes beheld were profound.

Angelic beings from on high
sailed me through the sky,
Like treading in on the wings of an Eagle.
And suddenly a majestic place came nigh.

I travelled over mountains and valleys of grass so green, tall trees,
and large green foliage landscaped the hills, like kites in the sky.
The Angels knew the way, as if they travelled by radar,
All around was beaming light, I knew I had reached celestial heights.

The view from on high was spectacular
A oneness with all things was dramatically felt,
Time had no meaning and a great freedom prevailed
There appeared a great golden gate and I heard a beckoning call,
And I knelt.

Amen, amen, and other praises were chanted,
The home of God was inside the gate, but sadly I'll have to leave
All this behind because when I tried to enter, St. Michael said,
"This is where you'll come when it's time."

Mary H. DuPree

Untitled

It dove from the sky where it splashed into pieces.
What fun was the fall!

It was a game - a trick.
It danced on the clouds then leaped to the earth.

What revelry — what joy!
Sheer excitement!

It was the example — the prodigy.
Others followed.

It was a party — mass hysteria.

The rejoicing was echoed by groans from the sky
and flashes of brilliant light.

For a moment I joined them — then returned.
...Where is my hair dryer?

Nancy A. Hammer

Relaxing, Like In Olden Days

When did it happen, where did they go,
What happened to the gentle folks, doesn't anybody know.
I didn't see it coming, or notice how we'd changed,
But now I see the difference, we're all in faster lanes.

We don't sit on the porch anymore, sipping cups of tea,
And talk about the olden days, the way it used to be.
When we find the time to sit awhile, on any given day,
Anxiety, unfinished work, soon steals our peace away.

When did we stop relaxing, and listening to the Katydids,
Making homemade ice cream, and enjoying life, the way we did.
What happened to family gatherings, every Sunday, come what may,
Now we're just too busy, some are working, got no time today.

What turned us into time clocks, we cannot waste a day,
Each moment has to count for something, done without delay.
Relaxing is a luxury, but it's something you can't buy,
Peace of mind, a lesson, from the olden days gone by

Vivian Moore

The Stranger

I see you walking through the shadows in the night,
What have you come for?
Are you the answer to all my prayers?
Or the villain of all my fears?
I see your eyes peering at me from beyond the trees.
Is it love or malice that fills them?
I ma curious to find out what you're thinking.
Yet afraid of what I might find out.
I can see your hands reaching for me.
They look so soft and gentle, but at the same time I fear them.
The rest of you is hidden behind the shadows.
I'm not sure I really know who you are!
At this moment, confusion fills my mind.
Maybe later I'll know how I should feel, if I should love you,
or fear you!

Leslie Sowles

The Forgotten War

We left Korea, and a lot of buddies behind.
We were not welcome when we got home but we didn't mind
Now, after all these years some of us have memories of what
We said and did, and it really effects our minds.
We wonder where these thoughts come from.
Some say "Life can be unkind".
It brings us back to Korea, and the pow's/Mia's that are still
Unaccounted for that our government left behind.
It makes us wonder if we are going to relive the things
That happened to us again
From the darkness of our mind.

William G. Webster

What If

What is it to utter these words?
What if.
Many people from all walks of life
Many people of all races and creeds
From exalted leaders, royalty and statesmen
All have said, "what if."

"What if" means to many or few of us,
Could I have listened more intently?
Could I have been born of other means?
Could my education have been better?
Could I have done better at work?
Or, could I have given to someone less fortunate?
What if I had done all of the above?

No matter the language spoken
The words, "what if"
have left their weight on so many
One ponders the power of these two words,
Their fragility or weakness.
Those two simple words,
What if.
Sally H. Garner

"Listen To Within"

It's too bad we all can't hear ....
What "It" has been trying to say to us
"It" is all too clear

We're always in a hurry
We keep the bustle, always on the move
And, we don't even know what we're trying to prove

If only, we could stop and think
And usher in the true silence
Nature is working so hard to get us in sync

To our ultimate destiny "it" desires
Every day you should always take some time out
To face your Uncertainties and all your doubts

Because "It" is all within
All the truth and enlightenment is there
Only if we could stop and listen to within
"TJ"

The Payment

Jesus was born on a cold winter's eve,
   When He came there were no friends in sight.
The people awaited their promised Messiah,
   Not a babe in the still of the night!

So His birth went unnoticed, but for a few,
   Some shepherds and magi came by;
Yet the people continued to wait for a king,
   A monarch on whom they'd rely.

Since destined to live a rather short life,
   This boy became quickly a man;
Teaching, healing, sharing His love;
   Fulfilling his God-given plan.

Amassing no riches, He owned not a thing,
   Yet taunted and jeered He would be;
Still He loved all He met, treated each with respect;
   Oh, what a man was He!

But it came down to this...His ultimate goal,
   He would lay down His own life one day
To pay a debt that He didn't owe,
   For a debt that we couldn't pay!
Ralph E. Reel

Someone Must Know...

It was a quarter 'til four,
when I awoke to the slam of the door.
Rushing down the stairs as she came in,...
I tried to catch her, but she fell again.

I see all the tracks strung up her arm,
the smell of the liquor,...
She must know the harm.

Once again, helping her up the stairs,...
sometimes I wonder if she even cares.
Routinely placing her upon the bed,
she appeared lifeless,..as if she were dead.
I sat there crying for hours it seemed,..
waiting for what morning would bring.

A promise again of a better tomorrow,...
this life of mine contains so much sorrow.
Who is this person that keeps scaring me so?,..
This is my mother.. I thought you should know.
Misty Schaefer

Daddy Where Were You?

Daddy where were you? When I first climbed a tree
When I got all those skinned knees
Daddy where were you? When I was scared at night
When I learned to ride my first bike
Daddy where were you? When I first started school
When I learned to tie my shoes,
When I just got the blues.
Daddy where were you? Those times are over,
What's done is done, you weren't there for me, Daddy,
But I'll always be your son
Sara G. Bateman-Mason

Endless Delight

When I reach for you, you're not there,
When I want to touch you, you're so far away,
To you my love, no one can compare,
Please be mine and here to stay,
Come to me throughout the night,
And fill my dreams with delight,
Be there for me, eternally,
Never stay too far away,
For my heart without you, cannot survive another day,
So when I reach for you,
Please be there,
And when I want to touch you,
Please don't go away,
For my love is here to stay,
As long as you come to me throughout the night,
And fill my dreams with endless delight.
Susan Kushnatsian

Trust In Him

There are times in everyone's life
When bitter times overtake the sweet;
That is the time when we are called
To trust in faith to keep us on our feet.
Dwell in God's love and believe in Him;
Patiently endure when the world looks grim.
For whom God loves, He does chastise;
Many times our burdens are blessings in disguise.
God does not choose for his children to cry,
That is why He sent our Savior for us to die.
God is not happy to see our suffering,
But sends us a solace that is comforting.
Be not cast down, but trust in Him;
Soon again you will find your cup filled to the brim!
Sharon Martell

You

I remember you from not so long ago,
When I was living the hell you built for me.
The walls of your home stood out with the harsh reality of your illness.
I'm sure you were never aware of me hearing the foul language, the drunken slur, the screaming of your cursed life,
These were parts of the foundation you built.
The lonely, horrified child watched the liquor pour like gallons of paint on the walls of fear.
No home was built....
with nowhere to go and no one to turn to.
You don't remember hurting me,
but I remember like a nail being driven into a wall...the pain remains.
So many years later,
I need to be away from you,
the builder of my hell.

Patricia Anne Ward

"J.R. He's Our Brightest Star"

It's been two years since that painful day,
   When my little nephew was taken away.
He was so young, only six years old,
   His love move pure than the purest gold.

They say that time will heal the pain,
   The days will shine, instead of rain.
Flowers will bloom, and birds will sing,
   Bringing back to us the spring.

It was in the spring he was called away
   By our Lord in Heaven, there to stay.
Look up to the heavens, he's not too far,
   He'll always be the brightest star.

The light will shine from this star, you'll see,
   It will be his spirit running free.
And when at night you see this star,
   It's the brightest one, that's our little "J.R."

Nancy Hodges

My "Little Man"

My "Little Man" and I had a date.
We went to dinner and had a fine steak.
I was happy with my "Little Man" and he with me.
He smiled and played with his rattle. There was no battle.
Yes, my "Little Man" was happy with me. I pleased him.

He did not look at the girth of my waist. He knows I carried him within me in comfort for nine long months.

He sees no imperfections in me.
Why can't his father see — I am still me.
Inside I remain the same, only my "Little Man" knows.

Rosina C. Varela

Hattiesburg

Hattiesburg, where vibrant history was.
Where men always walked just like men.
Hattiesburg, a Mississippi town,
where racial strife may never really end.

Hattiesburg, and a teacher's caring plan,
in loving family, church, and school.
Hattiesburg, and a hopeful Clyde Kennard,
who stood so tall against acts so cruel.

Hattiesburg, and a first born son,
serving a country strong and proud.
Hattiesburg, still working still,
And wondering, still wondering, right out loud.

Mike Murphy

"Is life Real?"

Death, is it real? Or should I say: Is life real?
When one is born, he doesn't even know if he'll see his third meal.
Jolie Watson, Dupree Tave, two high school students shot
to death. Why? No one knows.
All we know is they're gone now, due to a few deadly blows.
Many people feel life is just a game. Is this true?
And if so, who do we blame?
Everyday thousands of loved ones are killed,
and the next day they're on channel "4" news, receiving fame.
IS LIFE REAL? God, why can't there just be peace?
With your help, you can make all this violence cease.
Parents losing their children; family just isn't cool!
We can do without Clinton, just take over and let your people rule!
We can do without the wars, gangs and these stupid gang acquiring pests. God, just help us put all violence to rest. Should I continue to work hard for the future, or quit everything and rest?
I don't know what to do, because it might all end up 6 feet under, cuz' I could be next!
YOU TELL ME: "IS LIFE REALLY REAL?"

Mia Gramata-Jones

Searching For Shelter

Carefree and content we were enjoying that day at our favorite park,
When our bright, sunny day suddenly went dark.
The hot, comforting rays we felt only moment ago,
Became nonexistent as the threatening wind began to blow.

The rain began to fall with intense beats,
Cold, stinging wetness fell over our bodies in sheets.
We ran for shelter from the stinging pain,
Yet we found no quick escape from the intruding rain.

Just as the weather changed so quickly that day,
In the same swift fashion, your feelings for me went away.
The fire in your heart that has previously burned for me,
Now only smoldering, it longed to be set free.

All this you professed before me with a sympathetic look,
Then, when you walked away from me, the very best of me you took.
Since that moment when your harsh words changed my life,
They continue to stab my heart with the persistent sharpness of a knife.

She was the wind that extinguished the fire that you once had for me,
She became your shelter when from me you decided to flee.
Each and every day I continue to search for mine,
But strong wind and relentless rain are all I can seem to find.

Lisa Downs

RETIREMENT

It was a year of change —
   when I learned many things,
   when I refined every aspect of my life.
It was a year of change —
   when I discovered the seasons:
      SPRING, SUMMER, AUTUMN, WINTER;
   when I really saw
      blue sky and white clouds,
      gray sky and snowflakes.
It was a year of change —
   when old friends became new friends,
   when things I'd always wanted to do - I did!

It was a year of change -
   when I laughed and loved;
   when I cried and cared;
   when I sang and smiled.

It was a year of change —
   and so will be this year —
      And the next —
         And the next...

Priscilla A. Breth

Sorrow

While sadness feels the air and crime has its share.
When people look for tomorrow.
All it's going to bring is sorrow instead of white
or rainbow colored birds to sing those
worshipping words. They wait till morrow
because it brings a lot of sorrow. You
know that He died for you and me. What
happened to the jubilee. I guess it was the
cross that took away our lost. Why wait till
morrow? It is going to bring sorrow. Little
black boys and little black girls don't even
know their own little worlds. While little
white boys and little white girls sing those
teasing spurs. So why wait till tomorrow all
you're living is sorrow. Sorrow of yesterday
sorrow of today. Sorrow of the morrow
sorrow of sorrow.

Sarina Bracey

Many And The Flower

There was a blooming flower, merry on a tree,
When someone casually came, to pluck it free,
For the owner of the land, was he.
The one who toiled hours and helped it bloom
Dashed, for his right, even if it be his doom.
The bud, did not know, what it meant, to whom.
Then came woes of the tree
How could it possibly be,
"The blossom only belongs to me."

Now, the poor flower trembled like a leaf
For soon it would be caught, like a thief,
By the one, who could become the chief.
While this was on, there blew a strong breeze,
Which decided to prove its right, and to seize.
Thus scattered were the petals, and life did cease.
So ended the story of the flower, and many to please.

Nasrin Azeem

I Wonder

  I wonder if she thinks of me
when it's quiet and she's alone
  I wonder if she remembers my phone number
when she looks at the telephone
  I wonder if she hurts inside
when they play our song
  I wonder if she yearns for me
when a couple strolls along
  I wonder if the memories
keep her awake at night
  I wonder if she wishes
that we never had that fight
  I wonder and I question
until my wonders run out
  Yet most of all I wonder
if she wonders what I wonder about

Ronald E. Hopper

Untitled

As we argued, I saw the hurt in his eyes,
His brows quickly turning to the shade of gray.
He looked down at me and closed his eyes.
Who could have hurt him this way?

Who put this distress in his heart?
Who caused this painful wound?
As his eyes slowly opened, I felt the shame.
It was me that caused my Father's pain.

Karie Long

"Love"

Love is like a candle, the passion burns, and screams for more,
when the flames grow wild, the love explodes, then leaves you
deserted, rejection, humiliation, frustration, slowly drives you
insane, torturing, abusing, invalidating.

Love is like a drug, your mind is powerless, your heart is violated,
still you seem to beg for more, to tranquillize you, obsession is
released, it conceals and complicates you, and leaves you addicted.

Love is like a dream, reality disappoints you, and makes you diseased,
so instead you enter your dream world, everything seems to be the heat
of the night where all your wishes cease,
when your hope is at its ecstasy,
actuality wakes you,
and everything turns to stone.

Ronelle Wysockey

"The Good Ole Days"

Let's go back to the good ole days,
When things were done different ways.

When summer days were sort of lazy,
And we would run through fields of wild daisies.

Things were always lovable and fine,
You never worried about the time.

We would take the time to look at little girls,
Some with brown, blue eyes, and curls.

Also with blond, brown hair and good looks,
On the way home from school we would carry their books.

We had childhood sweethearts and love too,
and remembered we always said "thank you."

At reunions and picnics we would get together,
Sometimes we had to run from the wet weather.

We had the steam engine and threshed the wheat,
Neighbors would prepare tables with plenty to eat.

Things now have changed in many years,
Now and then we would feel sad and shed tears,

The good ole days are through,
Lots of our friends, grandpa and grandma too.

Paul Skinner

England Was Our Home

England was our home
When we ventured forth from her warm bosom
To slay the foe and return
To our mother country.

We have always been her brood.
She has always loved us and nurtures us still
With Wordsworth and Keats, Coleridge, Shakespeare and Sir
Walter Scott.

She fed us chivalry
With King Arthur and his knights of the Round Table, she
Taught us gallantry for her women as with Sir Francis Drake's cape.

We were nursed our language
Through the years and found it was the most expressive
Proudly we ventured forth to protect our mother country, but
Some of us remained with her.

In Winchester Cathedral you will see the names of her famous sons.
The walls are completely filled with their names who also had
ventured forth.

I feel a kinship with those names on the walls, but
Am trying also to quench the same feeling towards our foes -
Because we all ventured forth and were brothers in fear.

Robert Warda

Gone Are The Days

Gone are the days,
When we were we,
When the eyes of mother eagle were wide and open,
She could see an on-coming storm of enemies afar,
Oh yes, those mighty bright eyes watched her children.

Oh what a joy for those who took shelter under her brood,
What peaceful old gone by days for the yankee
Mother eagle, her arrows firmly grip,
The unfailing strength from the almighty,
Those bright ever shining thirteen stars kept her always alert,

Hoo! Hoo! Huu! Ho! Comes sounds of uninvited ghosts,
They come, they kill, they destroy,
Help! Oh help, for my eyes grow dim, I cannot see,
indeed, our fathers said so, they said,
Those peaceful zones now stays violence!

The mother land has been poisoned!
Poisoned with the germ of hollywood!
Uproot her! Uproot her from her foundation!
America! the evening watching light of the west!
has yielded to collapse and destruction!
   Robert Van-Earl Danso

To Dona, My Friend

How can I tell you, my dearest one,
When your life here on earth is done,
That I'll always cherish your love so true,
   Good night, my friend, I'll miss you.

I'll miss our daily talks we had,
Sometimes we were cheerful, sometimes sad.
You always helped when I was blue,
   Good night, my friend, I'll miss you.

We shared our joys, we shared our sorrows,
But we always hoped for a better tomorrow,
When all our dreams would soon come true,
   Good night, my friend, I'll miss you.

I'll miss you at the end of day
When all alone, a prayer I'll say,
"Dear God, please keep her close to thee,"
   Good night, my friend; someday, you I'll see.
   Ruth T. George

No One Can Hear You Scream

In the dark of night
When you're stiff from fright
'Cause you woke from a scary dream
And you think it's gone so you move right on
Just to keep from turning green.

There's a monster there
By the rocking chair
By you only can he be seen.
So he waits and lurks
With his evil smirks
For no one can hear you scream

It's an awful fright
When your throat gets tight
And the hairs on your neck all rise
'Cause you know it's true
There's no one but you
Then you come to realize
No one can hear you scream.
You're all alone, baby, by yourself, just you
You.
   J. W. Shaffer Jr.

Nellie

As I prepare for lasting sleep,
where dreams shall cease to be;
I look toward the light of Heaven,
and the promise for eternity.

Since Jesus has gone forward,
made ready a place for me;
I know I need only cross over,
for Thou art waiting patiently.

Yet, should I falter, or be afraid,
'tis naught I'd ask of Thee;
'cept I might die, as I have tried to live,
with grace and dignity.
   C. Patricia Bertrand

Building My Heavenly Home

I want to build my home next door to Jesus
Where I can look into His windows all day long,
Talk to Him and sing my song

I'll touch His pierced side, His nail-scarred hands
And thank Him for giving
His life for ME!

He died upon the Cross on Calvary
That we may live blissfully in eternity
   Lorraine Laureys

My Place

On long winter nights, I go to a place,
Where no one can find me and time has no face;
The trees are just fine to shade where I read,
My stories of princes and dragons and queens.

My path's lined with red, of roses so fine;
There's green grass like emeralds and kittens with twine.

Here I'm a child with freckles and braids,
And dresses and candies and bedrooms with maids.

Enveloped with silence, there's one thing I hear,
The beating of my heart, so real and so near.

I come here when things at home aren't so good,
And darkness looms over, a big, heavy hood.

When eyes get teary and hearts start to break.
I come here to sooth everything that may ache.

And where, do you ask, is this place so dear?
I point to my head and say, "Oh, it's up here."
   Loretta Allen

Looking Into Each Other

I know your soul,
we met on a late summer afternoon in a classroom.
It walked up on me like a naked child
pure as light, smiling from the golden brown windows of your eyes.
It said simply here I am.
You know my soul, it tumbled out of my eyes,
naked like a child to roll and play before you.
I couldn't hold it back.
Our souls have laughed and played together for a life time.
Chasing currents into waves,
chasing waves into tides,
chasing each other into somersaults and cartwheels,
below cold sprinklers,
naked like children,
below the red summer skies,
we may live a trillion times
in short moments.
   Victor Noerdlinger

The Stone

Here I lie beneath this stone;
Where people stand and moan.
I pray for you not to cry.
For in God's hands I lie.
My life on earth has come to an end;
But my life with God will now begin.
So people I pray not to moan.
Because I lie in peace beneath this stone.

S. A. Hoover

Appreciate

You must appreciate what you have
where you are and what you've learned.
Do not concentrate on what you don't have
nor what you can't be and what you don't know.
Only you have the power to change your life
and make it better by giving a better attitude.
Not only to yourself but to others around you.
Only you can drive the car that controls your life.
You are the one who decides where it goes
and how long it takes you to get there.
Make your attitude count and appreciate yourself!

Norma S. Murray

A Child's Face

What do you see in the face of a child -
Whether red, yellow, black or white -
A kind of trust, an innocence, a hope
that fills one's life with light.

What do you see when that child is lost
to abuse, neglect in an uncaring world?
A sadness that lasts a lifetime -
a blot on our country's pride, unfurled.

What could we see in the face of that child
if we each took it by the hand
and led it in paths of learning,
with promises made and honored -
a spreading wide of the branches of the tree of life?

The human spirit unburdened—
each tiny soul nurtured, joyful, carefree and pure...
For America to be known forever as
   "The Land of the Child."

Phyllis L. Risch

Untitled

Just yesterday we were introduced to be together
Which I thought would last forever
Mistakes happened that ruined us together
My fault or yours, it will always be remembered
For you and I became stronger and wiser.

Vague feelings which were hard to vent
In times like this we used to send
Needless to say we became friends
Because of someone it has to end
Ending like this I want you to know
No matter what we'll always show
True friendship, true love wherever we go

Remember how you used to call me
Out of nowhere you stopped calling me
Dreams we had for each other
One day goodbye was said in October
Love bloomed when Spring came
Followed by your wedding day
Now you and I have nothing to say

Paulette Dana Panganiban

No One Can Steal

Love is not just a piece of paper,
which one can tear
Love is not just tears,
which one can wipe
It is not so cheap,
that one can make a deal
Love in my heart is just for you,
which no one can steal.

It is a kind of happiness in my heart and in my soul,
that no one can feel
And if you think love is like a piece of cake,
then forget the flavors,
Not everyone's love is fake.
If you have true love,
then you know what pain and tears mean.
Cause love and life is not a play thing,
It's not the game of bows and arrows,
if missed, it strikes deep down in one's heart.
So make your love very strong and special
that no one can steal.

Margret Morine Singh

Confidence

No problem is too big enough,
When someone you love is here.
No responsibility is too tough,
When someone special is near.

When you hear a certain song,
Place someone special in your heart.
And not before too long,
You won't be far apart.

Some emotions you may feel,
You can't ignore.
But know that jealously cannot heal.
And your personality could become very sore.

The people in your life make up your soul and spirit,
Always have respect for the ones you love.
If happiness comes you shouldn't fear it,
Because you will feel as free as a dove.

Don't let negative feelings get in your way,
And start to stew.
Or blur your vision and lead you astray,
Remember that there is someone that loves you!

Stacie Wakeley

Watermarks

Rushing currents,
Whirlpools holding fast to life's debris,
Surging,
Placid surface that hides hidden secrets -
   Never to be seen by treasure hunters,
Eddies lazily turning, flowing into a ripple -
   Swiftly carried off to an unknown place,
Clear icy cold buffeting the scattered rocks -
   Subtly leaving a mark to be seen over time spent,
Warm murky silt sitting idle over long forgotten
   Dreams,
Channeling and branching through overgrown
   Shores of generations past,
Emptying into a broad expanse that reflects the
   Heaven's own gifts of life surrounding,
Choppy and calm jockeying for same space and time,
   Covering and revealing the
   Traveled journey of the
   Weary and rested soul of
   God's image . . . man.

Karen E. Germy

An Ode To The Times — Not Much Changin'

Retirement's my line. New York Times? Just fine.
Who am I to choose.
Good as the State Daily News!
For the extra dime.

I'll talk to you all — no prejudice. Nice fall
weather, huh? The Knicks.
That's who my smart neighbor picks.
Bet they'll drop the ball.

That crime and famine and such. There's been too much!
They'll lose it, I'd say.
That's "Evans" but with an "a."
Simply lost the touch.

No, "Steven,"..."V-E." Misspelled as you can see
in the Clarion.
Best lawn. Old man Darion
just had to agree.

Poor season back in '89. A bad sign.
Shoot'n's second rate.
Yeah! Guess it's gettin' real late.
Come back any time.
  Steven Evans

Love's Anguish

The pain that stabs me each time I turn-
Who can measure the depth?

What can a barren woman
know of a labor pain?

What can a prince
know of the pangs of poverty and starvation?

What can the unwounded
know about the pain of the wounded?

Like a knife, the pain has pierced my heart;
I write in pain, oh my love;
How can you measure my anguish?

But longing for love in your eyes, I return today
Love for hate and blessing for every blow
that I received on my heart.

I, today create in me a clean and pure heart of
longing and love and cleanse my heart of pride
and passion and wish happiness for you and
may your days grow in sweetness like that of
sugar and wherever you go the fragrance of joys
spread in your life like that of a rose.
  Mrugesh Lala

Self

Self must learn to love **self** and protect **self** from all hurt and harm.
What looks good to **self** is not always good for **self**.
When **self** acknowledges that **self** has taken the wrong road, **self** gains
insight into what avenues **self** needs to pursue to be a respectful
self person.
A wrong decision to **self** allows **self** to regain pride in **self** and become
the person **self** is supposed to be in the first place.
Self must be strong and love **self**.
Self must remember that no one will love **self** like God and family.
Self must think clearly and act appropriately.
Self must determine that **self** had great plans in the future for **self**.
Self must not allow others to determine what roads to take for **self**.
When **self** has had a loss, **self** can replant new seeds which will
reap with joy.
Self must always think of **self** before afflicting any pain to **self**.
If **self** does not, no one else will.
No matter what happens to **self** always be humble and kind, but always
do the right thing for **SELF and do the very best for SELF**.
  Rita Marks

"Children Left Alone"

This is to all you children out there,
Who come from broken homes,
A sadness that's inside you,
For you have been left alone.
Maybe for various reasons, something left unknown.
I know some of the problems that can make you feel this way.
It's a mommy or a daddy with an alcohol-drug syndrome,
Chosen for the day.
Or a world of damn war lord criminal politics blowing your life
away.
They are forgetting all about you,
Not providing you a home.
It's left you with a sadness,
Children left alone!
Now listen little children, I know just how you feel.
For I now a grown woman,
Have my childhood memory still.
We as a grown society have to come together for your sake.
We have to get together to make sure that you are safe.
So listen all you children, you children left alone!
"I am someone who Loves You, so you'll never be all alone!"
  Mida A. Moore

Tiger

He was looking for a lover
Who could teach him how to fly
He was crying for his mother
But no one ever heard him cry
  And now and then he'd pass my way
    And touch me with his smile
      I knew him as a young man
        And I knew him as a child
          He always gave his best to me
            You could say it was his style
Blowing like a hurricane a tiger growing wild

He was moving like a jet plane
Through the carnival of time
Once an artist and once a poet
Always something on his mind
  Now he's sleeping by the sunrise
    Far away from the pain
      No more sadness no more madness
        Only music and the rain
  Thomas Munoz

Opportunity Prevails

Here is the story of one man jack
who packed his bags and never went back
his dreams were that of the one great nation
and decided to get real with US Immigration

His dreams were of houses and cars as well
having a family, and stories to tell
but things changed, and he had to slow down
to a pace that scared him and made him frown

With a job in hand and plenty of ideas
he worked all day to eliminate arrears
got deeper in debt and joined others with less
who couldn't pay the bills, and became penniless

He felt rejected and could never understand
why people who are successful are only by God's hand
they are the ones that are here by grace,
they don't have to decide to change their face

But things could be worse if congress digress,
don't get off their backsides and decide to address
the flag that did it all according to key, so they say
of one country to God, it's the good old USA.
  Ray Whitelock

Terrible (None Like Him)

Who called the earth into existence?
Who set the course for the winds to blow?
Who completed all his work in just six days?
And though He sits high, yet He looks down so low!

Who set the bounds for the atmosphere?
Who made the depths for the seas?
Who caused the planets to reign for a season?
And of Heaven and Hell, Who holds the keys?

Daily, He paints the world with unmatchable colors
And makes the mountains to skip like little lambs
Before Him, even the birds hush their singing
For every living thing praises the great I Am

Truly, He is the GOD of all gods
The Alpha, the Omega, the Beginning and the End
And through Jesus, The Son, mankind communicates
With his Maker, his Deliverer, who grants freedom from sin.

Theodora Robinson

The Dancing Lines

This is the story of the Dancing Lines
   Who sing and dance their way through time.
Dancing lines can never die.
Although, once, something convinced one that
   he did die.
And there he would lie, night after night,
   day after day,
Until one dancing line flew by
   and caught the thought to be dead
   (although he never could be) line
   in the corner of his eye line.
The dead line perked up his eye
And eye to eye he could not deny
   the urge to dance *was* still inside.
The dancing line inspired him and on
   the spot said, "Dead?! You're Not!"
The once dead line smiled from
   ear to ear.
And together now they dance
   through the hemispheres!

Lorraine P. Kreimeyer

Congratulations, Dear Pamela

Your life so far has been a map
with many "states" of my mind.

Crossing highways and bridges
along the passage, your trail
has been full of detours and obstacles
and many of the routes chosen
lured you to a disappointing view.

However, this has not suspended
your voyage, instead of turning back
you have forged toward the next monument with new hope.

Today is a day when you've
climbed one of the tallest mountains!!
As you peer over the peak
I hope the canyon below hears you echo
"I did it" and repeats itself
until your journey is fulfilled.

Look forward - beyond the lights of
the city of skepticism.
There lies a town filled with the history
you are made of and the future you'll never lack.

Renee Wells

A Rhinoceros Poem

I once knew a rhino
Who was such a wino
That he drank vino by the vat!

He'd wander into a pub
And order a tub
And proceed to get fat where he sat!

Now you'd think that that "Rhine"
Would drink only diet wine
In order to hold the line on his weight!

But the calories he ignored
And his weight...it just soared!
'Til of obesity he died...Lord! What a fate!

Robert E. Howard

Why?

The church bell tolls for three more souls
   who were trying to reach their several goals.
One was an old gent, who had made his living
   stitching garments.
One was a young girl trying to find another world.
The third was a soldier fighting for an ideal.
The first two had funerals fine and grand;
   but what about the fighting man?
His funeral was nothing.
He slowly sank in a foreign swampland.
At home his mother waits.
A man in uniform walks through the gate.
She rushes to meet him, only to see -
   it's someone else - not her Billy.
Now she sits and thinks of days gone by
   when her little boy saw new-mown
   grass and a big blue sky.
She remembers the time a pet dog died.
She can still hear him cry, "Why, Mommy, why?"
Then she sighs and asks, "Why, God, oh why?"

Tina Strange

The Garden Of Pleasance

Upon a hill far away,
Where anything on earth is welcome to stay.
With rolling grass and flowered trees,
With a fresh dew smell and a sweet Spring breeze.
With creamy clouds in the bright blue sky,
And a peaceful brook with a silent cry.
With honey bees and birds in the trees,
With animals playing and branches swaying.
Then night falls and all is still,
And forever there is peace upon the hill.

Michael D. Stewart

Who Am I?

As I look around, I see people laughing, crying, living life.
Who am I?
I must know, because I have been told.
As a little girl, I was told you are a daughter to all of us
and a sister to all of them.
Who am I?
As a young lady, I was told you are a wonder to all of us,
and an unknown to all of them.
Who am I?
As a woman, I was told you are a wife to all of us,
and a mother to all of them.
Who am I?
I now know I am your daughter, sister, wife and mother,
but who am I?
I don't know, but I must be me to me and to all of them.

Linda M. Kreitz

My Daughter

Whose hand is this with tiny fingers clinging
Whose eyes fight to focus and seek recognition
An innocent smile, first tentative,
Then full blown
Squeezing my heart with tiny fingers, clinging.

Her hand sometimes rests in mine,
Sometimes not
The smile has more guile now,
Not so easy in coming
Sunlight catches the tips of her hair,
Catches my breath
Eyes still sparkle,
But not always resting on me.

No hand now to hold - it has been withdrawn
The smile has lost all innocence,
Hiding for days behind dark clouds of insolence
I look for the child, but find no evidence,
Still feel my heart being squeezed with
Seemingly tiny fingers.
  R. Marlene Stauf

God's Forgotten Souls: The "Mentally Ill"

Oh God, my Creator of the universe,
Why are we afflicted with this mental curse?
To live in loneliness and despair
Is more than our minds can ever bear.

Are drugs and seclusion our only way of life
In locked institutions of mental strife?
Behind locked doors and nearly forgotten
In a world so bitter and cold and rotten?

Are we not creatures of the human race
Who also hunger for love and grace?
Instead our minds are numbed by drugs
When all that's needed is kindness and hugs.

Why must we be God's forgotten souls
And forced to act in unwanted roles?
We did not ask for our "insanity."
Nor even more, for society's inhumanity.
  Michael A. Borilla

Saying Goodbye (But Not Forever)

Why did this have to happen?
Why did this have to be?
Why did you have to die,
I need you here with me.
I never knew how much you meant to me,
Until you went away forever.
I know you're in a special place but,
I can't help but miss the smile on your face.
I'm sorry I never got the chance
to see you in person, to say goodbye to you.
But today at your funeral I saw
your picture and I just had to cry!
I wish I could have got to know you better
And I know someday I will but,
for now, I've got to say Goodbye!
"Uncle, I love you and, I always will!"
  Tracy Wigern

'Priceless Treasure'

What priceless treasure Christ is. Which cannot be bought
with millions of earthly dollars. Yet the poorest sinner
of earthly estate may attain this free gift. As but a bended
knee, a humble heart, a cry to God for mercy and forgiveness.
  Lester Dean

The Mistake

Oh prudence what have you done to me?
Why do I sting?
My virtue cries out in pain
And I cease to question and search for thee
For it hides with fear

The tongue that struck me thrice
Hath fallen in a cup of sourly beer and of thorn
Then why must I die this death of innocence
With this past to bear?

Oh prudence what have you done to thee!?
Why does this press me deeply?
And I know that noble women before me
  Bore these marks with dignity
Why then must I sting, for all is done?

Then I too will capture myself
  In sweet fragrances and beauties of the earth
Only to survive the pains
  Of an inevitable mistake
  Susan Smeltzer

Why?

Why is it that friends are always fighting?
Why do they even get mad?
Could it be a mystery?
Or is it because they are sad?

I often wonder what would it be like
If I didn't have a friend that is always there
Where would I be?
I know one thing I'm sorry that I lost the greatest friend in the
World..........
  Nicole Olivarez

Weeping Willow

Weeping willow with your tears running down
Why do you always weep and frown
Is it because he left you one day?
Is it because he could not stay?
Weeping willow stop your tears
I know something that can calm your fears
You think that you will be always apart
But I know he'll always be in your heart.
  Cain Jarrett

Seasons

'Tis raining, the sky is gray, God is cleaning His beautiful earth.
What more can I say? Such beauty, flowers, leaves sparkling green,
warmth of the Sun, Spring is here. The sun is out, the water is warm,
people heading to the beach, people heading to the mountains. Summer
is here. Such beauty, leaves are gold, brown, yellow, red, green,
orange, to warm our hearts, halloween, what more can I say? Autumn is
here. The sun is shining, the air is clean, the storm is gone,
preparation begins to start the joyous time of the year. Thanksgiving,
Christmas, Music fills the air, a soft blanket of snow, aroma of
spices and smiles on our faces. The birth of our dear savior makes
for celebration. Seasons, God's gift to us. Seasons for all time.

C - Carols
H - Harmony
R - Royal
I - Immanuel
S - Savior
T - Trumpets
M - Magic
A - Amazing
S - Snow
  Shirley Branch

Why

Why is everyone looking at me?
Why...why can't they see?
That I want nothing more than to be left alone.
And they wonder why my frustration is always shown.
I guess they want to see how far they can get
Before my anger bursts and hits
Everything that gets in its path.
But when I let it go at last,
A deep feeling came over me.
And finally I could see
That all the trouble I went through
To make my anger come out and make people see why too,
It just wasn't worth it.
So why did I have a fit?
Don't ask me why 'cause I don't know
Why I sunk that low.
   Linda Grant

Hell To Heaven

  I'm home, but that they couldn't hear
  Why you ask, well they are yelling in each other's ear.
  I run to my room, and just wonder why, or did I cause
something to start the fight.
  This goes on till the end of the night.
  It's a relief to see another day come, and they are
still as one.
  But another night comes and my hopes of a quiet night
are gone.
  Why do they make me suffer? I can't describe the pain
arguments, fights, what in the hell is there to gain?
  A while passes, it begins to show a bright side
I'm not in my room; I don't have to hide.
  I wonder what got into them; was it for me?
No it's the love they had for each other they could
finally see.
  I say to myself it's ok, I promise Kevin
but it's hard to believe that hell all of a sudden
could become heaven.
   Kevin William Reed

Hope Springs Eternal

Tears pressed hot against my lids
With torturing force deny the struggle o'er.
A wretched and bloodied soul still bids me
Look away, leave closed a door
That portals the melancholy host of despair.
O monstrous host - chill not the wine,
Set not the table with poisonous fare,
For Hope has also bid me dine.
   Marion H. Nichols

A Moment With You

When the light began to shine and the flowers are covered
with morning dew
My heart is in prayer and I am close to you
I ask for your protection and guidance in
everything I say and do
My lips whisper sincere words to you
asking what I should do, Father, to pass a safe day and please you
Your answers come deep into my heart,
your spirit guides and calms my fears
and sorrows are appeased; you help my pains, you dry my tears
I know you are there when I need you
I hope your love reflects on me
on everything I say and do
Oh dear Lord, you have my love and respect
I couldn't pass a day without taking those moments with you
   Solange Hayward

Why Not?

Can we love God and our fellowman, too? - why not?
Will optimistic dreamers' dreams come true? - why not?
This earth that we live in, will it last for another century or
Two? - why not?
Will there be any babies left to hold or hear their cry?
Why not?
Can people who live in fear, die peaceably,
When their time is near? - Why not?
We look for an answer but - will God hear?
Why not?
   Stephanie L. Holloway

Repent

Behold the judge is standing at the door;
Will you be found guilty or cleansed forevermore;
The judgement day is nearing and no one will be overlooked;
God has all the proof written down in his history book;
So if there is any guilt at all;
Why not accept his convicting call;
Repent now, having your sins blotted out;
Reaffirm your conversion beyond a shadow of a doubt:
   Lora D. Hughes

Oklahoma City Bombing

They drove down the street and into the parking lot,
With a bomb in the back of the van.
Few had a chance to escape the blast.
Then she blew and the killers ran.

At 9:00 the children laugh,
At 9:02 the children cry.
How can a few seconds change everyone's life?
For days after that we all asked why.

Police, EMS, fire fighters, and emergency personnel,
Work with the hurt and the dead.
It must be impossible,
To get it out of their head.

They place an American Flag,
On each cleared floor.
A symbol to the waiting world,
In hopes they find no more.

We ask God for his help,
To set our lives straight.
To help us find the guilty,
And send them to their fate.
   Teresa Moon

A Gift Of Love

A simple word can break a heart, encouragement and love can
  make a new start
The hard times make us all think twice, there's more to life than
  just a price
A newborn child that two can share, a gift of love for someone you
  care
A part of me, a part of you, a person to love your whole life through
I want to give it all to you, but my loyalty and respect will have to do
Inspiration and trust should always be, an act of love that comes
  naturally
Two certain people with something to give, an outlook on life on
  how you should live
A different perspective two minds can create, expressing ideas
  enthused to relate
Compelled to touch and comfort you, in difficult times we all go
  through
And at the end of every day, I close my eyes and silently say
I love you.
   Madelyn Ambrose-Parker

Space

I am the curious of the curious
with a desire to go beyond the sky,
Higher than man has ever learned to fly.
I want to set the pace
With no limit of knowledge of outer space,
With a chance to search out there
Out beyond the earthly weather
Without man's confirming line, the tether
Where the pressures of earth ceased to be
And speed without question is a fantasy.
A view from here until recently
Has been reserved for only God to see.
  Merlin L. Lundquist

I Hate Winter

I hate winter.....
With a passion that is fashioned after good old common sense,
Give us just a few more months of sun,
This chill can make you tense,
If Hawaii doesn't need it (and I hear they get on very well)
Then take this snow and sleet and cold, and all of it can go
To....well—most of all remember...when it gets to be November...
I hate winter...
But..right in the middle of all this grief,
When every tree crieth for a leaf,
There comes a time of tranquility, when we celebrate
The nativity. Church bells ring....people sing...
And snow becomes such fun. But on December 26th
The garbage trucks play "pick-up sticks,"
And back we go to slush and slime...and colds and
Flu and grit and grime.
Whilst in our hearts a silent prayer that spring will
Still...be...there...

I hate winter.
  Malcolm Dodds

A Salesman's Prayer

I ask the Lord to start my day
With a smile for those who come my way,
Help me not to be overbearing, unfeeling, insensitive
or unjust,
To make knowledge, friendship, helpfulness a must.
To be patient with the impatient,
To be friendly to the unfriendly,
To be serving to the undeserving,
To put on a happy face even when things don't go my way,
To leave my work at the office at the end of the day.
Helping others to be my creed,
But most of all Lord, help me to be
A better testimony for Thee.
  Patricia Edwards

Memere

I remember my memere plump and sweet
With a smile on her face and rosy cheeks
When it was time to do her a chore
She was always ready with a kind reward
Hot chocolate sprinkled with love
Great memories I still think of
Never a bad word came from those lips
Except sound advice I sure will miss
Yes, she's the greatest I'll let you know
She's close to my heart and I love her so
The nicest thing I want to thank her for
Which is my mother whom I adore
The reason for this is simple to see
Without my mother there's no me
  Ronald Badger

Perplexities

I stand upon my feet and fight,
With all the strength I know,
But then, I do admit that I am weak
And time will prove that I can conquer all.
Ashamed! Why should I be,
When life is full of frailties,
And I am just a complex being,
With hidden thoughts and fears,
Some much more difficult to bear,
Perplexing to the minds of those,
Who think that I'm engulfed in doubt.
But I am woman, warm,
and memories of yesterday
Like burning embers in my soul still linger on.
The joys I live today, I treasure with my being,
Not to be wasted -
But give of self, of life, of love,
And pray that if tomorrow comes
That I will be,
everlasting company to one.
  Yvonne P. Cawley

The Aging Hourglass

Our love is an endless time that seems to strengthen
   with every turn of the hourglass

I can see the sands of time in your eyes
   and the love in your heart.

Cold is the air when the sand trickles down its last grain;
   but,
   I will bring you warmth.
   I will be with you until the hourglass
   splits and the sand shatters with my tears.
  Nova C. Ebert

Little Angel In Her Wheelchair

She came to me just ten years ago,
With eyes so brown and skin so fair.
But it was not long before I knew,
She is my little angel in her wheelchair.

She cannot walk and she cannot talk,
But she is blessed with a smile so rare,
I only have to look into her eyes to know,
She is my little angel in her wheelchair.

People say they have never seen an angel,
But I know one whose life I share.
She inspires me with a boundless love,
She is my little angel in her wheelchair.

There is one thing I know for sure,
That when God calls her home up there.
I will miss her but in my heart I'll know,
She was my little angel in her wheelchair.
  Onnie R. Cockrell

My Spirit On Wings

Fly, fly, my spirit on wings,
Your eyes are still blue,
Not hazy and gray,
Your hair is still of the sun-kissed blond,
And your ears like to hear of mystical places,
Far and beyond the imagination,
Your mind thinks only those joyful thoughts,
While reality is all but fiction to us,
Fly, fly, my spirit on wings,
For always and forever,
My angelic child.
  Katherine Benson

Untitled

Freely I chose to love you
With heart and soul I gave to you
Strengthened only by your words of love
I believed in Life - Hope - Trusting
I had the faith of a child
When listening to your words of love
All the pebbles of sand - All the greatest oceans in the Universe
Could not hold the love I have in my being for you
Reality struck - As oft it does
Darkness shadowed my world
Slowly I turned my collar to the wind
Slowly I walked - With tear streaked cheeks
   Away
   Patricia Blaylock

St. Nicholas

The Village of St. Nicholas stood on a mountain top.
With its white painted homes like snowy sheep in flock.
Standing from centuries ago, you thought it would never die,
Until that day of darkness, that nazis set their eyes.
That set their eyes on St. Nick with evil in their hearts.
And turned the lovely mountain peak into a volcano top.
They burned the Village of St. Nick with all its life content
the screaming of the lives blazed was nothing like you've heard.
And then the voice of one exceeded all the cry.
My country is still around or have you put to die?
   Sophia Demas

And Parts Is Parts

I was born, just like you,
With many parts, all brand new.
Time and circumstance worked their change,
Doctors replaced and rearranged,
Now, part of me is silver, part gold,
Part metal, part plastic, I've been told.
Plastic lenses work just right,
I can see stars on a summer night.
Gold and silver help me to chew,
Metal and plastic knees work like new.
I'm now bionic, there's no doubt,
That's what these parts are all about.
A part here, a part there, so it starts,
'Till I'm a whole with many new parts'
   And thank God,
   Parts is parts!
   Rebecca Dunny

I Stand

I stand rooted here
with my inhabitants long gone.
I see passersby of all sorts as
my branches yearn to touch the sky.
I shiver in my nakedness
but yet you see it not.
I am as still as a November wind in Carolina
and to you, I may not exist;
yet I've seen the faces of the sky
and have chatted with the stages of the moon...
have watched generations come and go;
have gleamed proudly at the creations down below,
have disapproved of the way you've treated your own...
Why not learn from me—
see how we provide comfort and warmth;
see how we provide beauty and shelter;
see how we help provide a better life for earth's inhabitants...
See how we are called just trees, yet we stand proud and tall.
I, for one, lift my branches toward Heaven
and praise the Creator of us All.
   Kimberly O. McManus

"A Toast"

With cheerful eyes I behold you.
With smiling lips I greet you.
With open arms I welcome you
To a feast fit for a king, but made for two.
As we sit and talk about old times and new,
I can't help but to express the love I feel for you.
The love that carried us through good times and bad,
The love, before I met you, I had never had.
True feelings and thoughts I confess to you.
One body of flesh, but of minds—two.
So with our wine glasses filled,
I hold it high with pride:
Here's a toast, to you—
With all my love inside.
   Ralph Slusher

My Highland Love

His eyes'll be that of the Highland sky
with strong and gentle hands.
He'll know me heart without a word
for we come from the Celtic lands.
A Scot I am till me dying day,
I come from the Donald clan,
and never again shall I entrust me heart
to that of a foreign man.
He'll wear his tartan proud and strong
protecting his family's name.
He'll love, and honor and cherish me,
he'll never bring me shame.
His soul cries out at the skirl of the pipes
for those who have gone before.
His spirit soars at the mystical sound
of the harp played before his Lord.
May the God of all the heavens and earth
protect him till we meet,
may He put the angels by his side
and the wind beneath his feet.
   Laura Mitchell

Daddy's Little Girl

The years of my childhood have long since passed
with the graduations of
swings, trikes and ten-speed bikes
to four wheel automobiles.
Lollipops, ice cream cones and gumdrops
to I'll have a Drambuie on the rocks.
Pigtails, coloring books and barbies
to pantyhose, high heals and all night parties.
Sledding and playing with Frankie, the boy next door
to I take this man forevermore.
With all the transitions in my life:
baby, child and teenybopper,
to woman, mother and wife.
Throughout all the years to learn, change and grow,
Only one thing remains the same and it's
always refreshing to know
I'M ALWAYS DADDY'S LITTLE GIRL.......
   SandyLee A. Phelps

Untitled

I will always love you, it is so hard for me, too understand
your ways and the things you do sometime and why.
I know you are grow now but to me you will always be my little
one and you will always be a part of me, I am so sorry that
you have to come down with the HIV virus I, do not know how
to help you maybe all the help you need is for me, too still
love you, and I, do and for me, to embrace you, and I will
because I, love you and you will always be a part of me.
   Larry R. Otterson

Idyllic Visions

Call me a dreamer but I am in love with the old,

The horse chariots
With the open carriages...

To go rolling
Over the hills
To feel the wind
And not have a care, a conscience,

The pretty little cottages
With blooming gardens...

To sit among trees
In branched shades
And lose myself in dreams

Mary Delfin Pereira

Pussy willow

Her roots are so deeply seated,
with veins and tendons uniformly pleated
A strong sense of balance
achieved fore and aft,
In a moment of courage
her strength shall not waft

Her legs so slender and oh so strong
Nestled in her womb,
the birds sing their song
the softness of her flesh,
the subtleness of her way
Is surely what makes her strengths
do so stay

Her bosom so firm,
its senses quite strong
Is surely where I do belong

Her neck that leads to her head and her heart
Her soft flowing mane is from where she all starts
and she and I will not part

Micheal J. Arscott

In Memorium

It seems that you were here only yesterday
Yet, now they tell me that you've gone away!
But, where could you have gone?
Back into yesterday, or into tomorrow,
To be part of its joy, or of its sorrow?
Did your voice go into a song-bird,
your beauty into a tree?
Or did you somehow, irrevocably
become a part of me?

Sylvia H. Cole

Day

As the day slowly rolls in and the sun rises
with the sweet smell of mist
overcoming the chill of the night air,
we come to a new day of surprises
and things yet to be expected.
Soon the lights throughout the city will turn off and let the new
day light their offices.
As we climb into our cars and head to school,
we feel a certain excitement as we start a new day.
But soon, as we all know, the day will be over and night will slowly
take its course.
Then we will watch the sun die from our land, as it
moves to another part of history and starts its new course all over
again.

Noah Young

The Girl Of My Dreams

You're the girl of my dreams
   With your beauty and eyes of green
I wish to sweep you off your feet
   To a place of no retreat
A place with a warm soft glow
   With a fire and the lights down low
And in the flicker of the fire light
   We shall dance into the night
Swain slowly, holding you tight
   Enjoying the perfume you're wearing that night
I find myself living in a dream come true
   As I spent that night with you
To wish upon a star that night
   I would wish to hold you every night
To love and cherish you would be a dream come true
   To keep you happy never blue
You're the sweetest thing I've seen in all my life
   I wish to make you my loving wife
To have you say the words I do!
   Would truly make my dreams come true.

Mark Wallace

Stop! Disappointing Yourself

Don't let your minds wander like a child,
With your Imagination running wild;
Following all rules and regulations,
Living up to everyone's expectations.

There are times when one has to take a stand:
All can never be the same on this land.
There are goals that we all cannot reach;
Some got to learn while others teach.

Do the things that make you comfortable,
No need yearning to drive a convertible.
Follow your hearts to the depths you can conquer.
You are the one who knows where to anchor.

It's easier to be what you want to be;
Than what others want to see.
You know what heights you can go;
That, no one else, will ever know.

Verlin Allen-White

Elegy For Terry's Dad

The man is gone who trod this place, a man to me
without a face. For while we shared this hallowed
wood, at no time in space was I where he stood.

He is a spirit as am I come to this place with but
a sword. How boldly we wield, how swiftly we strike
is not the way we find reward.

Rather to plod, to carve, to shape and scrape -
the blade pressed and moved and strained by the spirit
changes the hallowed wood to kill or to endear it.

The man is gone who trod this place, and while never
I have seen his face, I have come know his carving.

A critic of such I claim to be, so by his carving the
man in known to me. A master of the blade he worked so
hard and loved it. I regret that I can give him praise
by just this humble couplet:

The Lord of the wood hath scabbard the sword and
called the spirit to joy.

He made the hallowed wood a better place I know,
because I know his boy.

Richard T. J. Peglar

Reminiscing

Though it is 21 years since you left me
Without a good-bye, a kiss or a prayer,
Each morning I reach out my arm to caress you
Then awaken to find you're not there.
I'm still climbing the stairway
And after ninety years am nearing the door
That when I step through
I know I'll find you
And it won't be just a dream anymore.
   Selma Olson

Money For God

   Money is something you will forever need,
without it you will forever bleed.
   So now I plead take your money and
plant a seed of trust. For I am God you lust.
   Before you bust, I have a must give ten
percent and repent before your money spent.
   Ronald A. Hopkins

Untitled

I am so lonesome I could cry
Without your love I'll surely die
I love you in a special way
a way that will always stay
I thought when I met you
Your feelings were true
do you really care
because together our love could be rare
I want you to hold me in your arms
With you here my heart could never be harmed
The dreams I have made
If they come true, they will never fade.
take away my fears,
Wipe away my tears
Because I will always be there
Loving, caring, willing to share.
   Maricella Rodriguez

Part Of Me

   As I see myself now full of joy and happiness, I think back and wonder what my life would have been if I never met you. Every moment
that I see you, I feel the love and I get nearer to you.

   Because being in love with you, is like running clear water from a river that would never end, and your smile makes me feel full of life, like the flowers feel in spring time. Full of colors with the morning sun. So I'm glad you are a part of me.
   Miguel A. Melara

Inch Of Time

As I sit in this engulfing darkness
Wondering what tomorrow will be,
I am without vision as I am without light,
All dangers in my mind turn and flee.

I'll never know all I wish,
I am forever searching, questing.
So involved in this task of knowledge
I go infinitely without resting.

The universe has so much to offer
Each inch of time has its own tales
Of hate and pleasure,
But not even time itself,
Knows of its secret treasure.
   Rebecca Sanderson

Thinking Of You

Twice through the night, I saw your smile.
Words unspoken, a love worthwhile.
A glimpse of your face, and my heart starts to melt
I wish this moment was everlasting; I will try to illustrate how I felt
I can see into your essence, eager to let me know
That your heart is full of rapture, pure as the winter snow,
A suave kindness surrounds me in the air,
The sentiment I receive, gives me no doubt that you care.
You're my confidant, you're my exclusive love
It's true what people say, about blessings from above.
I can't help to wonder, what I would've done,
If I had never met you; you are the one.
Faultless devotion, some say you may never find.
I guess we got lucky, we are two of a kind.
When I'm not with you, you're in my heart.
The love that we share, I know will never part.
Read this carefully, and keep it locked inside.
Cause even after death, I will be by your side.
   Tina Thompson

Life

Sitting at a job, wondering about the future, scare of job hunting, worrying about the economy, money, housing, and suddenly realizing
that you need a vacation..... Somewhere you can rest, look at the blue ocean, wear hardly any clothes, drink pinta' colas, dance until dawn, sleep late, then sit at a job, wondering about the future,.... and so on.....
   Sandra Shelton

My Wish

If GOD would grant one wish to me,
Would I make it right away or should
I think it over for at least another day.

I might wish for wealth and power and things that money buy.
If I could wish for perfect health so that no-one ever dies.

I might wish away the wars the destroy the world today.
Or wish away all types of greed so that crime could have no stay.

I might make myself a rap star, the idol of the teens.
Or I could abolish poverty for the people of no means.

If I could wish for anything for all the world to see,
I think I'd wish for JESUS to come alive inside of me.
   Melissa Di Raffaele

"Bestseller"

Each lifetime is like a novel, a tribute and a shrine.
Written with dreams and aspirations
That only we define.

When one chapter seems concluded, another one begins.
Although some pages may be hard to write
Perseverance always wins.

If you need an answer, to what the next verse should be.
Foreshadowing in the past contains the clues
And your heart holds the key.

Where love binds two lives together, a "Bestseller" will unfold.
My love for you bloomed in chapter two
as chapter three has told.

Together we can write the script to merge our lives as one.
Working through life's ups and downs
Until our work is done.

Alone this author cannot sustain his creative literary drive.
He needs the warmth your love provides
To keep his dreams alive.
   Thomas DeMola

On Creation

Long lines of sun drawn across pale stretches of snow,
Yawning trees towards heaven grow.
Whipping winds through forest howl, while still lakes seem shallow;
Glass reflection of depth hidden,
To touch is to break what is forbidden.
I creep through this land crackling twig and breaking hallow.
　My presence here disturbs the calm; my trespass on
Consecration. The Holy Church of God around me. His
Presence here wraps and surrounds me.
He speaks through the wind, sun, and moon; I know He's
Evident, I see His work.
And yet my worship in this land is corrupting of its
Character. My presence disturbs the harmony for those to follow.
　What miracle it is how God heals, for what is broken,
He congeals, mends and fixes what is misaligned.
　Too bad for man that man is blind. With rulers and
Compass man surveys; too much disorder for to have God obeyed.
I think that it is man that sees with skewed eye, for he
Forgets that it is God who is on high.

Pericles John Lantz II

Things To Do...

Lord I Love You,
Yes I do
I am so glad that I have you!

Please forgive me
and understand where I am coming from.
I love you, yes I believe

The man upstairs I can count on for relief
when times are full of grief

Lord I love you and don't wanna part
our love will heal this broken heart!

I am trying to make amends
with the man upstairs, we're more than friends.

Please Heavenly Father please show me,
show me the way back
From that blatant Verbal Attack!

Please show me your way and this comes from my heart,
I love you and don't wanna part.

Tom Spina

His Love

In His name I was raised, and I failed to give Him praise
Yes Lord please forgive me, for I know I've sinned
But with Jesus on my side, I know I can win
Even though I was a sinner, through your love I became a winner
And I've made up my mind, Lord Jesus now is the time
And that's what I've looked for, so now I have opened up the door
So fill me up with the spirit, that others will be able to hear it
Because through you I was made, through your blood I was saved
And through your mercy I was spared, Lord no love can even compare
To the precious love you show us, that's why living for you is not
just a desire, but a must
Let my soul soar as a dove, because one day I'm coming home to the
heavens above. Because of its joy I'm crying, but I'm no longer afraid
of dying
In His name we praise and His love we adore
Dear God how could we ask for anything more
I'm no more lost, because you paid the cost
I've been found by Christ and saved by the blood, that you shed out of
your precious love. When I know you are there, my worst troubles
I can bare
I now live for you, now and forever,
how it makes me feel so much better

Ronald Ketih Goode

As My Heart Bleeds

Moments of passion; unfettered and exciting,
Yet gentle and warm as the sun in the crisp morning air.

Lips soft as velvet brush over mine; a feathery
kiss that speeds my beating heart.

Eyes, oh those beautiful eyes! Flawless and bright
with life and knowledge.

My breath is caught when they look my way, as my
lips betray me when I try to speak.

The world looked so ugly and drab, lifeless and
hopeless, filled with the corpses of broken dreams.

But you erase such ugliness from my eyes and reveal
the beauty of life that I did not see before.

Yet inside I know that you are an untouchable dream;
one that I cannot have, nor deserve, even if I tried.

And though this gives me no comfort, I will enjoy it
while it lasts...until I awake...

To my beloved Matt
Lydia C. Siciliano

In Search Of

Do you know that rich people pay a lot for it,
　yet they still don't have it?
Do you know that smart people explain all about it,
　yet they still don't have it?
Do you know that poor people know that they don't have it,
　just because they have no money to pay for it?
And do you know that foolish people think they have it,
　if only they can feel it?

Is happiness so rare that nobody can find it?
Is happiness so unreachable that nobody can even have
　a taste of it?
Or are we looking in the wrong places, that we
　can't find it?

Happiness for me is...
... waking up in the morning alive and thanking God for it
... going to work, doing my best and giving God the rest
... appreciating the simple things in life, even the
smile of a child.

Happiness is just there, within our reach.
Be at peace with your Creator and He'll do the rest.

Maria Susan L. Jael

Picture Thoughts

Life is a pathway that I walk through each day.
Whom shall I fear?
　I feel Your presence near me.
Your angels surround me.
　Your words are like sunshine
coming through the trees.

　Each ray communicates Your love to me.
So much love that I can share with others
　along the way.
The quietness of the air whispers,
　"Be still and know that I am God."
My goal set in life is to
　"Seek first the kingdom of God."
I choose to walk with You and pray
　from morn till night.
For each step takes me closer to home and
　The wonders of seeing You and hearing
You say, "Welcome home, child."
　In response I'll kneel down before You
and say, "You are my Lord and my God."

Norma Stadt

Daddy

For as long as I can remember, I sat upon your knee
You always had a special way to help and comfort me.

You always knew when I was troubled, you'd say "You can't fool your Pap,
Tell me all about it, come sit here on my lap."

You'd always sit and listen, my life you'd try to guide
I could always count on you Daddy, to be right by my side.

You were not a man of many words, but you knew just what to say
You'd say just what was needed, to brighten up my day.

I'll always be your little girl, you'll always be my dad
Having you for my father, will always make me glad.

You feared to be less a man, for crying all those tears
No greater man could be found, if I searched for all my years.

I'm sorry Daddy for being so selfish and wanting you still here
It's just so hard to give you up, when I love you so dear.

It's just so hard to say good-bye, even though I know it's best
For all that you have been through, it's time for you to rest.

There will always be a special place Daddy, inside my heart for you
I speak for Mom, Barb, and Bill, they feel the same way too.

My days are long , I close my eyes and lay me down to sleep
But first I say a little prayer, please Lord your soul to keep.
   Margie Sabat

My Favorite Flower

In the vast valley of weeds,
  you are the single flower who shines brightly,
    for the whole world to see.

As you shed your light on me,
  darkness drips away.
The environment around me clears into perfect vision.

I can see,
  I can see.

You are the ray of sunlight,
  reaching beyond the glorious skies of this Earth,

My Mother Sunflower,
  You have enlightened my mind and my heart,
    and have guided me
      through the blindness of my thoughts.

I love you.
   Lauren Fong

"Benevolent Hero"

I've found in you, a benevolent hero
You came to me when I was down below.
You are to me, a legend in your own time
A wonder to behold, and the pleasure's mine.
Intellectually you are, in a class by yourself
A prince of charm—comparable to no one else.
So dominantly strong, yet noble and kind
Your spiritual demeanor, is yet to be defined.
If ever in life there's a treasure to be found,
"My significant other,"
There's no limit to all the things, we can discover.
You're my friend to the end,
And a lover so true
I would forsake all others, just to be with you.
In my heart-of-hearts this I know
You're my greatest inspiration, benevolent hero
For to give you up, I wouldn't take zero.
   Mildred A. Stevens

To Someone as Beautiful as You... Are --

To someone as beautiful as you
you can see your beauty inside and out
it just lights up your world with love and peace
everything just falls into place
when you smile the sun shines back at you
and when you're sad there's clouds of gray
the flowers bloom in spring time
to brighten your day
if not for you my world would be gray
   Mark James

You Could Not Believe

You could not believe
You could not believe
Safely sealed in carefree smiles
and the youthful guise of rich-hued hair
that you could ever be like me
in my fortieth year of wear and tear

You could not believe
You could not believe
Alloyed 'gainst loss and seeking gain
closeted content with mate and heir
that fast fading time for you could be
a wearing down, a tearing down, something hard to bear

You could not believe
You could not believe
Till your step slowed down, your sight got dim
you covered sparse and graying hair
and saw yourself in my stoop and stare
but I no longer know and I no longer care
   Rodney J. Shapiro

I Think Of You

You fill my heart;
You fill my mind.
I was thinking of you before.
I'm thinking of you now.
I'll be thinking of you later.

I think of the full moon in October.
I think of the touch of your hand,
The smell of your hair.
I think of the taste of your lips,
The look in your eyes.
I think of the sound of your voice.

The fire that's burning is not in the fire place.
The wine I taste is not from a bottle.

How do I hold you? How do I show you?

I'd give you my world if you would take it.
All I want is a place in your heart.
   Walter S. Adamiec

Sadness

I wish that I had saw you first, because now I feel much worse. Now that I'm away from you, I really miss you through and through. I wish that you could only change, and find it in your heart to rearrange.

Sadness is something that really hurts, because you think of all the thing's that could of worked
Sadness is also what makes you cry and pull all your feelings from deep inside

So let your heart point the way, because your heart always knows what to say
So when your feelings sad in what I did think of all the things I have to give.
   Tim Buck

The Miracle

Chosen among millions of equal strength and ability,
You have been guided by the Lord to reach your destiny.
The satisfying peace and tranquility erases the toils of the agonizing journey.
You have been loved even before you have arrived.

Dreams of joyful moments, concerns of the perilous future,
Plans for record events, feelings of hope, anxiety and yearning,
Fill those who care for you.
You have been loved even before you have arrived.

Your first cry brings tears to those who have long awaited you.
Your little gentle fingers melt the hardened closed gates of our hearts.
You lift everyone's spirit even as you carelessly view the world.
You have been loved especially now that you have arrived.
Marnel Villaver

A Letter To Cory

We think of you often, our angel above
You have shown us all the true meaning of love.
The meaning of family pulling together
To ride out the difficult storms we must weather.

Mommie and daddy have been so brave
You they miss and lots of love they gave.

Grandmas and grandpas, aunts, uncles, and cousins
Miss having you here with all the cousins.
But we know you are happy in God's Holy Grace
So until we all join you in his perfect place;

We'll think of you often, especially today
And pray you will guide us through life's every way.
Mary Krippel

Gram

The sun beats down upon your summer softened ground
Your body lies beneath, but your soul has not been found
You are in Gods' hands and finally laid to peace
Your smile lingers but your heart no longer beats
We see that smile in the memories held each day
And said by Robert Frost, "Nothing Gold Can Stay"
Everyone has a time and yours has sadly passed
But the special moments shared were made to last
When my time comes, then together we will be
But for now, your soul is lost deep within me!
I LOVE YOU!
Melissa A. Dunbar

Untitled

I surveyed the distant skies the last evening
while the sun was sinking,
signaling the closure of another day
Clouds were like thick cotton balls
brushed with occasional sure swoops
of grey watercolors
Sun streaks crept silently through vacant openings
The ocean lie beneath, violet blue except
for a single patch where it shone a bright yellow
Each minute there was a change,
for as the bright, powerful glare took in its
last few seconds,
it gradually began to become as a dim oil lamp,
burning only on last drops
Then it suddenly glided at a steady pace
into the far horizon,
leaving but a trace of light pinks to be seen
And a feeling of bewilderment to all
who had watched as closely as I had.
Robin Reiland

The Midnight Hour

In the midnight hour, I hold you near,
you hold me close and whisper to my ear.
the cool breezes falling around,
the heat rises far from the ground.

Two people intertwined in a bed of joy,
just a simple attraction of a girl and boy.
If making love is such an art,
then why do we feel it in just one heart.

Tension has spread all over the room
in splendor, passion, and groom.
Too much pleasure can be too much fun,
can make a beginning for a daughter or son.

So hold on to that love and don't give it away,
'cause life can be a happiness or just another day.
Shauntell McLaurine

"Navy Life"

Hand in hand you walk to the pier.
You look in each others eyes full of tears.
You assure each other everything will be alright.
You find it hard to release one another's arms.
One last kiss that will last forever.
For you know this time will soon be over.

Hand in hand you walk to the car.
You look in each others eyes full of joy.
You assure each other everything will be back to normal.
You find it hard to believe his back in your arms.
You give him a kiss, to welcome him home.
Rebecca Hamilton

Words

You can't write a poem, I heard you say!
You really don't believe you could write this way?
It's really rather simple. How? You want to know.
Just put your thoughts on paper and watch them flow.

Take any of the words you use each day.
It's amazing to watch how they play.
Like the sound of rain on a roof of tin,
or the sound of laughter caught in the wind.

Words were created to seduce and amaze.
Sometimes used to amuse and betray.
Words used in the ways of love,
can bring two together like hand and glove.

So watch what you say and say what you mean.
Words can do wonders, depending how gleaned.
If you want to impress, influence, and inspire,
let your words speak your heart's desire.
Randy B. Bowman

Untitled

When you reach eighty-nine your life becomes a bore
You sit and reminisce about the things that are no more
But, though your face is wrinkled and your walk is slow
You may still be aware of the things that glow
I am eighty-nine today, I feel like twenty-three
I cook, I write and think a lot sitting under my apple tree
My voice and my speech are clear, my brain is bursting
for something to say
But alas! That is not the case today
The young look at you and say, "She is eighty-nine today
leave her alone!"
O please God let me keep my strength
Until the day that all this will end
Marie Cigna

To Momma

I miss you Momma
You were always there for me
I could call you for the answers I need

Now it seems I'm on my own
It's hard at times, but I make it through
By talking to you

I ache to hear your voice
For you to tell me things will be all right
For you to say "I love you"

I never knew how much I depended on you
I never knew how much I loved you
till you were gone

It's been years since you passed away
But it seems like only yesterday
The hurt is so intense

The pain has eased somewhat
But the void is ever there
The void that only Momma can fill
   Patti L. Michalik

A Grasping Melody

Look at it as if it were the last time
you were going to see it, cherish it,
experience it, then say goodbye
jump down from this …….. onto
a new foundation, taste it, hear it,
smell the young being born
walk down these lonely miles without
a footstep, your heart drips, locked inside
create the burning of the sun upon
your skin, the shining of the sky,
and when the lights grow dim
love this hour of passionate moments,
gently touch, caress life's beauties
until you see them again
hate each day when you search for
the endless answers, cradled in the corner
lost love for endless hours
I see this young peaceful poet
sleeping in search of his mind,
he sits there, questions in his hands
   Shawn Rahier

"An Ode To My Pear Tree"

Pear tree, Oh, Pear tree,
You have been with me so long.

Planted by builders, just thrown in the ground,
Your roots were all crushed and twisted around.

With mounds of peat moss and water each day,
You rooted right down for years to stay.

Your bark all cracked, your leaves fringed with black,
Looks like you are about ready for the gunny sack.

Everybody says, "That old tree should come down;"
Not so long as it has life and leaves on its crown.

This old tree is kind-a-like me,
Not much to look at, or a pretty sight to see.

"You see," in that tree is hope for me,
Here are pears this season in abundance.

It signifies new life, new hope.
And a time to renew my faith.

"Only God can make a tree;"
And that same God made me.
   Marjorie D. Jones

First Love

I was just a little girl when I first met you.
You were older, wiser and full of virtue.
Like a gentle breeze on an April morning,
Your love gently caressed my very being.
Thoughts of you always lingered in my mind
Because you were so holy and divine.

Each night I saw the moon, I thought of your face,
And the stars reminded me of your grace.
At times you seemed far out of sight,
But yet you were always close to my heart.

Each day I looked forward to our quiet time
Because I knew you were mine.
So I shared my secret thoughts,
Knowing that I had found the perfect love I sought.
Others may come and stray away,
But you would always stay.
Faithful and devoted, you would see me from above.
You will forever be, My First Love.
   Marica M. Smith

Mom

You've been there for me through thick and thin,
you were there no matter what I got in.
You are the nearest person to my heart,
there is nothing that could make us part.
You've been with me all of my life,
when you hurt it cuts me like a knife.
We will always be as one,
you are second to none.
I love to see you when you smile,
it carries me on for miles and miles.
I'm sorry if I've ever let you down,
I just pray you'll always be around.
I cherish the bond that we have,
I give you love on my behalf.
You're the one who stands by me,
I know deep inside you'll never leave.
You've always helped me when I needed you,
there's nothing for you I wouldn't do.
You always seem to keep me calm,
this is why I love you Mom.
   Kevin Boyd

Forever Mother's Day

Sweet Mother,
Why do you anger my soul…
Peck at my brain with sharp claws
Slowly making me lose all control

Dear Mother,
So cruel in your nature. . .
Striking yet another deafening blow
Helplessly blind through life you go

Mixing reds and blues, painting a warm smile
For you believe everything is fine
But Mother please heed my warning
Hopeless complaints, within four walls confined

Broadening a lack of faith
And expanding your materialistic view
Will in time obscure the Great Force
That from above watches over you

I realize it's not the traditional time,
For the calendar, it says not May
But today deep inside I'm wishing you
Peace and a Happy Mother's Day
   Ronald A. Busse

The Endless Love

If I tried to explain my love for
you, you wouldn't understand,
Don't ask questions just hold my hand.
I can feel your presence when you are near.
From my body to my mind I feel free
and clear.
Free of all evil, and clear of all hate,
You showed me how great your love was
on, our very first date.
From that point on you were always
 by my side,
I know the things you said to me
 were not lies.

So if you were ever to let go,
I don't know what I would do,
But I know deep in my heart that
I'll never stop loving you.
Shannon Goida

Beautiful Ireland

Oh Ireland! You terrible beauty,
Your country is truly unique!
Your people are grand and gentle,
With smiling voices they speak.

We thank you for sharing your shores with us,
We loved every person we met-
Your children are oh, so beautiful!
Their faces we'll never forget.

We didn't find a leprechaun;
("They'll bring you luck," we're told.)
But what we found was more profound;
Your Faith is your pot of gold!

Oh Ireland, soft and misty,
Dear land of my parents' birth,
Your faith has been rewarded;
You're a vision of Heaven on Earth.

We will come again to your Emerald Isle,
We're enamored by your charm -
May St. Patrick continue to bless you,
Each city, each county, each farm.
Una Carew

Only You!!!

Mothers are God's gift to the world
with enormous hearts and loving hands;
She can be friend and enemy rolled into one
but she is always there to understand.

She is there to support you in times of need
when only her comforting arms will do;
To protect you and hold on to you tightly
With her immense love shining through.

There may be times when she is out of sorts
and she sometimes sheds a tear;
Tears of happiness, sadness and hope
but they are for the one she holds so dear.

She looks forward to the blessed day
that she has grandchildren of her own;
To let the grandkids do all the things
that she never let you do at home.

Mothers are simply something extra special
with unconditional love and few complaints;
And you know that she'll always be there
with her special love that can't be explained.
Kim Havey

The Dead

There you lie beneath the trees, beneath the falling rain
Your flowers wither with each drop—an eeriness remains
Etched in stone your name calls out, the loneliness you hate
And though some come to seek you out, they tend to leave in haste
What must you feel when a child walks by, his eyes so filled with fear
If only we could see your face, I'm sure we'd see a tear
You lie so still among the grass—time seems to pass you by
You have no care, you're simply there, this happens when you die
A keeper wipes your gravestone clean, he does this with such care
He wipes real slow as not to fright or waken those down there
The darkness of the night does fall upon forgotten dead
The stillness lingers on and on—yet you move not from your bed
The grass does grow, the years slip by, your face we do forget
And those who keep you company...are some you never met.
Rommy Goode

Sometimes You Must Walk In The Rain

We gave you life so you could be, as strong a sapling as you want to be;

To protect you through your younger years, to help you overcome your innermost fears;

No path we lay for you to tread, only a place to rest your head;

We pointed you to mountains afar, so you be your own shooting star;

Our words to you are simple and plain, "Everyone must walk in the rain";

Carry on as I know you will, but do not stop at the first small hill;

Your success is what you'll want it to be, as long it includes your God, your family, your country;

So follow your path to fortune and fame but remember; "Everyone must walk in the rain."
Louis G. Laub

Justice For Rwanda

I have seen bits and pieces by the tens of thousands what was you.
Your mute cries falling on the deaf ears of an indifferent world.
My reviled senses assaulted and numbed by your endless mass.
My mind still reeling to comprehend how this new holocaust came
 to pass.
The lucky ones not among you shout - "give US justice."
But what now occurs is not justice.
True justice would stop this endless madness.
The victorious survivors, many boys too soon men, beastly lumber now.
The battered Kalashnikovs meting out a single sentence for any
 degree of participation.
But justice will not walk about when even one is added to your
 numbers.
Robert E. Lee Smith

Wistful Thinking...

I see children play,
Stare at them for hours I may.
The pain inside me never subsides,
I pray every day for spiritual guides.

Many questions I want to ask,
Anger and fear I do mask.
Why can't my child see, walk or talk,
The hurt inside me I try to lock.

Believing my child has a better place to go,
A place where holy waters flow.
Knowing this makes me feel better,
I do wish God would send me a letter.
Ruby Noronha

You Gave Your Smile

Dedicated to Gayla Jensen

You began at age seven to know illness and pain.
Your special glowing smile helped us all to sustain.
Your kidneys failed and you were put through many a test,
with that smile from the girl who always gave her best.
Enduring every mountain or hill,
others knew nothing of your trial.
All because you gave a smile.
You amazed medical staff the entire while,
even as they stuck you, you said "I'm sorry"
and gave a great big smile.
You lived life not in vain.
You set a great example while in pain.
You always gave others hope and went that extra mile.
With your passing, now we are sorry, but we will never forget
your wonderful smile.
  Myrna L. Rose

Frenzy

How do I read your eyes?
Your sweetness glitters, your gentleness smiles, your sensitivity
    searches.
Those watchful portholes guarding secrets
As yet to be discovered.

And what of your heart?
Your passion so coyly ever-present, your innocence so cleverly
    disguised.
Their existence crashes into my naked soul
And fragments my security.

Pulsing through my flesh and in my throbbing veins
Exhilaration and apprehension join hands.
A blushing face, colored by fanciful feelings
Of something past, yet unremembered.

Bring to me some answers or some questions
And let me discover who you are.
  Susan Ebenreck

Sonnet

Thoughts of your beauty bring but tears to me,
Your tranquil eyes deep and blue as my sorrow;
Rosy cheeks that spark naught but misery;
Gentle face making me yearn for a morrow,
Thirsting for your love no more, desire calmed;
Without the burning pain, heart laid to rest;
Ultimately slain, and with peace embalmed;
Dead love - no longer to your heart addressed;
Yet such a shallow death will not occur
While by the rules of passion I abide.
For e'en my unreturned love can stir,
A myriad of cupids to flank its side.
    For even my heartbeat serves merely to count,
    The time till my fears true love can surmount.
  Matthew Tebaldi

Untitled

Orchid crushed furrowed in those dark plebeian streets
Your exotic fragility does not belong here
Was it he that let you slip from his fingertips?
Tasted the forbidden fruit
Scared his senses mixed with your fragrant secret
Golden burgundy Orchid you truly arouse my heart
Luring me to mend your forgotten petals
Mend, make you bloom with fresh sereneness
Place you back in lust Indian Jungles
But I cannot
For I too am helpless
To this night
  Natalie Ramirez

Life

Life is a precious thing that you live day by day,
You're born, you die, and then as time goes by, you slowly fade away.
Life is a miracle with a constant change,
Life is happy, sometimes quite strange.
Our parents looked on us for things they never had,
Be smart, have fame, but never be sad.
Our parents passed on, we stayed on this earth,
With sadness and grief, we never had mirth.
As time passed by we grew old and sore,
We always had something - we always wanted more.
We got old and brittle, we needed constant care,
Once we are dead, we will soar through the air.
Without any trouble,
Without any fears,
We will always have happiness never any tears.
Life is wonderful,
Life is a sky,
We will soar through the wind and always fly by.
  Lazaro Zayas

"Question"

What secrets are you hiding away up in the sky?
You're lovely and mysterious as you go drifting by...
What stories do you cherish, things you alone have known?
Sights no one else has ever seen, just your eyes alone...
What sounds have drifted up to you of love, and hope, and fears?
Sounds that have found their way to your fluffy ears...
What do you make of mortals, who war, and fight, and die?
Do they ever find their way, with you up in the sky?
Have they found their comfort in your soft and wispy arms?
Do they know the heaven of living on cloud farms?
Is it tears that touch us, when we just think it's rain?
Are you trying to tell us, we can live without pain?
What fools you must think we are, our struggles never to cease!
When we only have to look at you, to learn of comfort, and of peace.
  Theresa McDonald

To My Wife On Valentines Day

You are more to me than just my wife.
You're my friend and partner throughout life.

You're the light that lights my way.
You're the song I sing each day.
You're the sun that's shining bright.
You're the moon on a starry night.

My love, you mean everything to me.
You're the love of my life you see.

And when this life is gone,
And we both must move along.
My love for you will never end,
For you've become my eternal friend.
  William M. Thornell

Sonnet

Dear Nightingale, you clever little thing
You're nothing much to look at; small and gray
The dying Chinese emperor heard you sing
And Death, himself, was charmed and went away.
A monster in a castle, quite concealed;
A hideous looking thing to say the least.
But one girl came to love him and revealed
A handsome prince disguised within the beast
A baby born one silent, holy night
A baby born the poorest of the poor
The Christ-child who was born of truth and light
Became the King of Kings, our savior Lord.
If you look past the surface you'll discover
There's much more to a book than just its cover.
  Susan Towson

Night

In the shiftless, dusky light
You're too scared to face the world outside
With the cold wind blowing past your face
In a sorry ditch of sad disgrace
You lie sleeping on my silk shirt sleeve
While I think about what I believe
But some seasons hold no comfort
For the night you hold inside

Watch the shadows on the wall
Paint the story of your protocol
While you wait for me to make a sound
I think of daybreak, but not aloud
Upon the morning I may be changed
Until then I see only today
For the midnight sun is set so clear
And the night inside is held so dear

Laura A. Eder

Child Of My Child

Dear child of my child, so precious and dear
You've finally arrived-I'm so glad you're here.
Ten tiny fingers and ten little toes
Those "baby blue eyes" and that sweet little nose.

I'm reminded so much as I gaze at your face
Of another time and of another place.
The pride I now feel, the joy and the love
Makes me ever so thankful to God up above.

So, new love of my life, I hope that you know
What a joy it will be to watch as you grow.
Dear child of my child, so precious and new
Please know that your "Grandma" will always love you.

Linda Brenner

Progression

My striped cat, you're growing more sedate
You've quit your ploy designed to startle me,
No longer do you crouch and hide and wait
Then jump straight up defying gravity.

When I contrive a sudden thump or scrape
You don't pretend stark terror anymore,
And feign a frantic effort to escape
With futile pawing on the polished floor.
You are less rakish now and you subdue
The fervor of your romps, you seem to sense
That gentler attributes become you too.

That lovingness brings loving recompense
I, too, am more subdued and gentler now
Our summers wane, small friend, our arbors bow.

Mona Collum

I Don't Get It

I don't understand why people are so different.
Why doesn't everybody have the same personality?
If we were all the same then our feelings wouldn't get hurt.
I don't get it.

I don't understand why people neglect each other.
Why does it take little things to make people realize life's precious?
If wars never happened we would all live in peace.
I don't get it.

I don't understand, "What ifs".
Why are there so many possibilities?
If we could all just get along...
I don't get it, that's life.

Wanielista

Fictional Cause

Wastelands of concrete and steel
Ruled by hatred
Captured by fear
Chaos rampant....
Religion lost
Fear of the government destroying us all?
Killing the innocent.....and
Blaming the Cause?

Militant Militias - without a care
Where the good of the cause means more than the cross you'll have to
bear.
Destroying innocent children
Just victims of war - what the hell!!!
Did it for justice?
Or was it for vengeance?
Or done out of just plain ignorance!

John Whitney Craft

Rosary Of Tears

To my family - Mamang, Myrna, Lex, Zaldy

At every prayertime I grope for answers
To the secrets each bead holds in my rosary of tears -
I find instead in its dewy bead I touch
The sorrows of yesteryears.
I dream of you at every prayertime;
Then dream each bead along the watery chain.
Somewhere - just somewhere - I end up at the Cross
and find nothing there!

Constancio R. Montera Sr.

The Landscaper

The landscaper is a busy man.
He does a lot of whatever he can.
He plants the trees
And makes flowers grow.
Because of this,
I love him so!
He's many things
A man should be,
And is very devoted to me and his trees.
He's the father of my children,
And makes my world glow.
Because of this,
I love him so!

Beverly Siebert

It

Consumed by desperation, I'm empty all inside.
I haven't any place to run; a place it could not find.

My empty days are endless as I grow very weak.
Night by night forever after I will never sleep.

Deep into the dead of night it calls me from within.
It fights me for my freedom but I try to force it in.

I look into the mirror yet, the reflection's not of me.
What price would it have taken to make it set me free?

I can hear it utter things when others never can.
The voice, it sounds so human, and sometimes almost man.

Listen!...Is it whispering?...Or did I hear it scream?
I'm falling through the blackness within an evil dream.

Once it started happening my mind and soul would bend.
I prayed and prayed I'd go away but why should I pretend?

Poison running through these veins, why does it have to be?
The others fought and lost their soul and now it's after me.

Gretta Pena

Thinking In The Corn

The wind whispers through the leaves
Empty promises revealed with a whore's lack of sensitivity
A lone howl rides the wind's song
Underlining the sibilance
While enhancing the solitude

Hard to believe
I came from these fields
The dirt made up
My father's dreams
The broken promises
Hardened my mother's heart
To sun-baked clay

And me
I'm the product of genetic overload
And my heart cries out
Yearning to be heard
But is smothered by the breeze
Robert Lamb

Empty Nest

Once, I had a dream,
but life got in the way.
It warned frigid nights;
brightened my dark days.

Once, I had youth,
but life got in the way.
The cares of the seasons
settled, eroding naivete!

I dreamed a dream for others,
but love got in the way.
Filtered in my mind and heart,
they grew strong anyway.

Tears are therapeutic,
and dreams are free-always.
Emerge from hidden lairs.
Before time gets in the way.
Rebecca Craig

In Praise Of The Okapi

In the vast jungles of
 Africa you dwell
With a beautiful sheen in your fur,
 Hidden to almost the whole human race
It is time I uncover you,
 your beauty and grace
The dew on you looks like diamonds
 hidden from all your predators
You are powerful from beauty,
 not strength.
Jordan Grahm

The Tea Party

Wearing hats and gloves grown women came
Knelt on the "Rock" without any shame
They laughed and hugged while sipping tea
From demitasse behind the tree.

This party was planned with elegant taste
One brought the teapot, one the lace.
Off came the petticoat, spread over the "Rock"
We turned back the pages and stopped the clock.

The woods had changed like the child, through the years
But firm stood the "Rock" as we brushed back the tears.
Will we do this again 'ere the leaves start to turn?
This time next year to the "Rock" let's return.
Helen Monroe Mundinger

One Last Day

I dream of us in the sand
Holding each other by the hand
Alone at last we swear to stay
Even if for just one day
We show our love in so many ways
Letting the sun deliver its rays
And as the sun rolls over the side
I feel as if I have just died
Seeing the tear fall from your eye
Makes it even more difficult to say good-bye
But destiny has taken hold
Leaving us felling so cold
You go your way, I go mine
Leaving without scarcely a sign
But our hearts remain locked with a key
And together one day I hope we will be
It may be years and years from now
And right now I don't know how
But yet I can dream and hope
Because for now it's how I cope.
Courtney Smith

My Love For You

As I touch a newborn babe
 I think of my love for you
  ...soft and new.

As I taste the mountain water
 I think of my love for you
  ...sweet and refreshing.

As I smell the ocean air
 I think of my love for you
  ...fresh and clean.

As I listen to the rain
 I think of my love for you
  ...steady and gentle.

As I see the clear blue sky
 I think of my love for you
  ...pure and deep.

As I feel the strength of the wind
 I think of my love for you
  ...strong and sure.

I yearn to tell you all these things
 When I think of my love for you.
L. Elaine Potter

Tis A Fantasy

Wouldn't it be wonderful instead of just a dream
a favor you ask they'd do it without putting up a scream.
Walk down the street in a city or in a little town
a friendly smile would greet you instead of any frown.
The snow would melt off the street and still stay on the ground
so kids could romp and play and have fun all around.
Wake up in the morning and there by your bed
No one else is in there but a tray of food instead.
Go to church on Sunday morn too late to find an empty pew
Then the pastor up and says I've saved a seat up front just for you.
Turn on the radio or T.V. set to get the latest news
They tell you what you like to hear without distressing blues.
A friend gives you a lottery ticket and you win aplenty
For best of all you never spent one red penny.
Lots of folks from near and far would meet you at their door
And give to you the key to their heart to keep forevermore.
This fantasy is now ending but wouldn't it be great
If all the world would pray together before it is too late.
Gilbert Hedges

The Storm

A gentle rain has polished all the green,
And trembling leaves are shining bright and clean.

The wind directs a choir of singing pines,
They bow at his command and follow well his lines.

The drums of thunder beat a timed refrain,
That marks the rhythm of the falling rain.

The storm will fill the silence as it moves around,
And keep me company.
I like the sound.
Avinelle G. Wilbourne

Future

We plan for the future, look back at the past,
Realizing that time is moving too fast,
We know that we're living on borrowed time,
So let us be wise so all our life we'll continue to climb,
Higher and higher to the pinnacle of our destiny,
We'll reach it by faith, if from sin we continue to flee,
This process is long, much like a song,
To live to do right, and hate to do wrong,
A living sacrifice is what we should be,
Our will for his, it's better you'll see,
When you've made it over to Canaan's fair land,
We'll eat hidden manna, with him we will stand,
Priests of Christ and God we shall reign,
A thousand years of peace,
And after that you must realize,
That the beast must be released,
In the end the Lord, he shall win,
And forever with his people abide,
The question we must ask ourselves,
Is just who is on the Lord's side?
Herman L. Bass III

A Thank You To Noah

God sent NOAH to Keithsburg in 1993,
We were glad to see him - I think
    we'll all agree.
It was after the flood when he arrived
Hoping to help us all survive.

He helped us through many a strife
So we could get on with the rest of our life
He, along with other men,
Help put houses together again.

We want to thank him from our hearts
Without him we may have been
    torn apart.
Goodbye, dear Noah, and thanks again
For being there and being our friend.
Sharon Leigh Scott Reason

From A Mother's Heart

I never stop thinking about the way things used to be.
I know everything changes.
Nothing can stay exactly the same.
We have lost so much along the way.
I don't think it will ever be the same.
Childhood memories are still in my heart.
I think about the love we shared.
It has somehow turned to hate.
What happened along the way to change things so drastically.
If only I could turn back the clock.
I want to recapture those wonderful memories.
We can only go forward.
Maybe someday it will be together.
Janine Ratcliff

Peace

As rockets explode and soldiers stray, craters emerge
and people pray. Such is war, the struggle the pain
but can anyone be certain it is not in vain.
Men charge gallantly, sabers raised, only to return bent
and crazed. Through the ages men had thought to wage
war, but what has it brought. Ruins and sorrow, hunger
and grief, hardship and destruction beyond belief.
Foolish are those who think it wise to plot devilish
fury, to plan demise. The greatest of warriors do not
fight on the field. They control their anger, their
hatred, their zeal. For what is a battle but soldiers
and drums hunting each other until it becomes late in
the day and through darkness vain stares, loosing sight
of his target, he stumbles and fairs no better than his
opponent, until the trumpet blares, the war is over, the
fighting desists, perhaps now will come peace.
Alexander Presniakov

From A Mother's Brood

If she were an animal, she'd stalk in like a jaguar. Beautiful
shiny hair one wants to touch but dares not because of the
growling undercurrent one senses even in silence.
Piercing eyes that at first startle you, but as you peer into them,
you melt at the twinkle of their soft gaze you find enveloping you.
She wants your touch, she needs your love but yet her cool strength
frightens you away. When she pounces upon you with her hurting
words, you wait and she calms stealthily resting like the kitten
she innately and really is. You forgive with love.
If she tries to cuddle and rub up against your leg
to show she would like to act like your kin,
her father tweaks her tail and whispers weird sounds in her ear.
She jumps away from you once again, only each time she jumps away,
the space has widened. It seems to get harder and harder to
reach out to this one who scratches you when you're down.
Who takes from you when she's hungry, but who gives you
poisonous verbal darts when you're hungry.
She's yours - she came from within you yet
she is filled with genes from the other's side.
The hurting cloud of love never lifts.
Estelle Maisel

God Cares

When life seems hard
    and the going gets rough
Don't ever look down,
    always look up.

God is faithful
    He's loyal and true
He knows how you feel
    and He cares about you.

God feels every heartache
    He's always close by
The cry of your heart
    brings Him to your side.

So cast every burden
    and all of your cares
Upon your dear Saviour
    and leave them there.

Don't be impatient
    God makes no mistakes
He answers your prayers
    and he's never to late.
Shirley Goad Austrum

Mouse

I did lots of chores in my house
Until I was scared by a mouse.
I jumped on a couch
And yelled out an ouch!
Oh I wonder where is that mouse?

It ran quickly across the floor,
Not before I got to the door.
I picked up a broom
And sweeping the room,
Caught him eating cheese from the store.

I swept him right out the front door.
Hoping he would go to the store
And eat all the cheese.
Asking for more please.
For I won't give him any more!
Joey Darrow

All Mourn

Can I trust your word?
Can I lay my life on the line by it?
Would I lose my ground?
Do you play with minds and lie to win?

Everyone who lies
Is a rusted part in the world machine.
In the end all mourn
and the lying soul will lose his dream.

So you think you got it made
Slayin' dreams of the innocent for a prize.
You really believe money talks,
The friend of heaven, the saving rock!

Someday you will shiver and cry,
And the malice you esteem so high
Will erode your vicious heart!
Glenn La Voie

Sense Of Apathy

Boredom is
A very dull and plain gray

It sounds like
A full hour of the Emergency Broadcast System
Killing your brain cells, one by one

It tastes like
Somebody else's chewed and wrinkled piece of gum
That is nearly solid as a rock

It smells like
A huge tub of popcorn with far too much butter
Oozing out the side, enough to knock someone unconscious

Boredom feels like
The glue-like sap that flows endlessly from trees
And seems impossible to wash off
Brian Kralowetz

Untitled

As Ann stands next to Paul she feels such passion burning desire,
She dreams of all her love for him as she slowly lights on fire.
She stares into his eyes not knowing what to say,
Hoping that he'll brake the silence that feels the room each day.
When she sees him in her dreams his love just shines so bright,
She'll give up her whole life to hold him just one night.
He'll kiss her lips so gently as he guides away her fears,
But when she opens up her eyes his love just disappears.
As the rain falls from the window sill like the teardrops from her face,
She knows nothing in life could ever take his place.
Cynthia Louise Shields

"Lonely"

I felt every teardrop you cried in the darkness, I smiled with all your laughter in the lights. I grieved with your pain and sorrow. I understood all your lonesome nights. I woke you to a brand new day hoping good things would come your way. I watched you as the night grew long, trying to fix the things that went wrong. I saw your confusion, when you were in distress. The late nights you spent without only rest. Throughout these times I've tried to be there for you. But still there's one thing I couldn't pursue. I couldn't take the pain away. I could only wipe the tears as they fell down your face. I couldn't make the laughter long, I could only pray things wouldn't go wrong. I couldn't heal your pain and sorrow; I could only hope for new joy tomorrow. I couldn't accompany your lonely nights; I could only be there to turn off the lights. I had to let you recognize your pain. But I promised to walk with you in good times and rain. You're my best friend and sister, I love you with all my heart, nothing could ever keep us apart.
Jolene R. Flores

He Is Your Reason

Imagine how you feel
When you open up your eyes
To find a new beginning
As the early sun will rise
And you step into the daylight
And the life you see around
With all the world's uncertainties
His presence you have found.

For you need not ask nor travel far
To find all treasures dear
When you trust in Him Your Saviour
You'll find that love is here.
Margaret Kopcho Scott

I Saw A Dove

As I was outside, I saw a dove
It reminded me of someone I love
I felt a tear trickle my cheek
As I reached out to touch its beak.

He had gorgeous eyes of black
And spots of white upon his back
The white on his back seemed to appear grey
As he flew, flew far away.

Then I decided to take a walk
I looked to my left
And then to my right
And saw a sunset in the beautiful night.
Amy Rene Solis

A Drunken Woman

I hear her laughing in my mind.
It sounds free and careless.
You wonder why I hate that sound.
It's the sound of a drunken woman.

I feel her beating on my back.
It feels angry and hurtful.
You wonder why she beats me so.
It's the rage of a drunken woman.

I hear her screaming in my mind.
It sounds pointless and scary.
You wonder if I did something wrong.
It's the pain of a drunken woman.

I hear groaning in my mind.
It sounds sick and pitiful.
You wonder why I make such noise.
It's the revenge on a drunken woman.
Cyndi Harbeson

A Gift

May He bless you with a daughter
May He bless you with a son
Either way it goes you'll be the lucky ones.
The sunshine in her laughter
The strength of his cry
The joy this child will bring you will forever
get you high.
As you grow together
Each and every day
May you teach him all life's lessons
in a gentle loving way.
You'll be the best of parents
and on that you can depend
Because you know you've always
been truly special friends.
Jeannette P. Blum

What Is Love

Love is when two people care about each other
 Love... Will keep us together
from the moment I saw you
I loved the way you looked
We we're better together, than we were apart
look, I'm falling in love with you
sometimes you're usually, incredibly warm
loving. Before I get into that, first I
have to tell you that we were perfect together
I always want to be with you
every night I think about you all the time
When you're in my arm I feel safe and secure
 Love is what come from your heart.
Cynthia Cepeda

Where Did My Daddy Go?

Where did my Daddy Go?
 I have school papers to show.
 He used to read to me,
 that's how it should still be.
Where did my Daddy go?
 We could play in the snow.
 Try out my brand new sled,
 until it's time for bed.
Where did my Daddy go?
 Doesn't he want to see me grow?
 I am changing so much,
 why can't he keep in touch?
Where did my Daddy go?
 Each day I miss him so.
 Did I behave too bad?
 Did I make him this mad?
Where did my Daddy go?
 My Mommy doesn't know!
 She said she loved him so,
 but he said he had to go.
Cathy Trump

Spun

Days are like
the weave of a basket
or a spider's web.
They go in
and out and in and out.
When the days are many in number
they become weeks, then years,
like the weave becomes a basket.
Each serves its purpose.
Baskets hold goods
and years hold memories,
of a life.
Faith A Geater

"Forgetting The Rule"

Go to the streets and look at life that's all around:
Pain, poverty and pestilence — yes, it all can be found.
Peep at the women who sell their souls
With an offer of a gratuity. You will pay their tolls.
Glare at the addicts all screaming in pain!
Craving for a needle to stick in their vein!
Stare at the winds whose home is a box,
Begging for donations to have their absolution on the rocks.
Gaze at the homeless who push belongings in a cart,
For little do they know that their minds are torn apart.
See the state facilities, where men sit in a cage.
It's a never-ending line for those filled with rage.
View the third world countries, where war and hunger are born,
And listen to their wailing for the dead children they mourn.
O Lord, what has happened to your golden rule?
For it was supposed to be a bondage - breaking tool!
Are we a race that has honestly forgotten?
Can everyone of us really be all that rotten?
I say this to you so you might tell
That you don't have to die to be in Hell!
David Steers

I Suffer In Silence

I suffer in silence, Oh Lord.
 Because no one really knows
The loneliness and pain I endure.
 They can only just suppose.

I suffer in silence, My Father.
 They haven't walked in my shoes.
They only see from the outside.
 They cannot see the bruise.

I suffer in silence, My Redeemer.
 You suffered in silence, too.
Because you prepared the way for me,
 I know I'll make it through.

I suffer in silence, Sweet Jesus.
 And try to "be of good cheer,"
And continue to trust in my heart,
 That one day you shall appear.

I suffer in silence, My Saviour.
 And when this life is through,
My suffering will not have been in vain,
 Because I'll be with you.
Donna M. Smith

English

Complicated, it might seem,
without much romanticism.
It's really up to the being
what he may want to find in it.
To me, as a loving human being,
English is filled with a wisdom
unveiled to the description.
For in this language you'll find
happiness beyond the measures
that human beings at times
will place on limited thinking.
But don't let those limitations
in any way interfere, because this wonderful,
unlimited tongue is ours to use as we please.
Just to practice with broad minds
will make us of the thought athletes.
Will encourage us to love
a completely happy life.
All we have to do is reach
and everything we shall find.
Jose Miguel De La Fuente

Cherished Mother

You make my world seem brighter and every day
You make each moment of my life special in every single way
Words cannot express the way I feel for you
Love, friendship, respect - all hold to be true
When I am ill at heart, you are there, by my side, to see me through
It is then that I realize that the mother I cherish is only
You bring out the best in everyone's life you touch
Especially my life Mom, because you've given me so much
I could never repay you for all that you've done
But I feel I must sing you praises to each and everyone
A person such as you canes along only once in a lifetime
I'm so glad God placed me within your womb to make you all mine
Your personality is different and so very rare
You have special qualities that make others take notice and stare
I may be selfish when I say
I'm glad you belong to me
But I love you Mom
And I am here for you forever and always will be

Lisa Rene Robinson

Romes

Way up there! With those steel-blue ice talons...it has
an allure few admit. But, think. Were it to nest
in the squibbed, neon arcs of our Chrysler Building...
how we'd wonder...what dark and red berry we'd use
to entice it away from the snows of its mountaintop?
What drew it down-swooping - over the streets
of our bustling metropolis? Whirlwinds of scrap
paper come slamming, vehement, one violet shear
of dawn air? And the...wings...like a crossbow of out-
stretching fingers...you say it is some kind of hawk?
Or an eagle?! D'you mind if I..use your binoculars?
Anyone know about- birds?...and the affable
populace swings down on new stands in search
of one lurider, bloodier, gauze-glossy pelt...
until all of the kiosks split open like props
in that same, silent film..see? The 'star' there, in cruel
snowstorms, chugging in rags clasped against bitter cold,
"Lily Mohawk," sees land, land, land....slow on a charred
bough, her ice-speckled skyking, collapsing his wings...
in frost or ash he's her blood and she loves him; gasps "PHOENIX."

Liza Redfield

My Summer's Child

Oh come to me, my summer's child,
as leaves turn red, and winds are wild.

Shed your cloak, like leaves that fall,
while geese in azure skies do call.

Drape your arms, around my chest,
then pierce the heart within my breast.

Silken maiden, reflect the sun,
with skin that flows, through, blouse undone.

These thoughts that pierce your silken vale,
flows down your legs, to feet so frail.

Chilly storms in distant skies,
send bashful breezes, down your thighs.

Oh come to me, my summer's child,
I am the one, you have beguiled.

Let me hold you, in lustful arms,
let me feel your love, your fragrant charms.

Radiant hand, with golden skin, fraught with pleasure, for hungry men.
And I no less, am free from sin, oh carnal fruit, so sweet within.
Beware the frost, beware the cold,
and come with me, we'll ne'er grow old.

Richard Lawrence de Gallegos

Black Girl

Struggled in the past
always chosen last
but
You p-e-r-s-e-v-e-r-e-d
and
made your name known
bLAcK GiRl
you've come so far
and
I applaud your effort
BLACK GIRL
what did I do
to
deserve an Ancestor so true?
Today, when I go out in the World
with all the things to do
I am viewed as
WOMAN (who is BLACK)
because of
You.

Buffie McCrae

Pasted Smiles And Wasted Miles

Pasted smiles and wasted miles, meant to help me find a place in
the sun
Paradise has its price to pay
The journey's long but the air is warm, like great explorers we
long to venture
Set the sail and make a getaway

Along the way we'll make some friends, lose some friends, but
who is counting
By and by they always get replaced
and we'll cry in the valleys, laugh on the mountains,
  watch dry wells spring into fountains
Guess that's how it is on pilgrim's way

We'll catch the bay wind, blowing towards summer, carrying us away
Forget tomorrow, there's plenty of sun today
We'll follow Magellan toward the sunrise, now we're stowaways
We'll find an island, stake our claim and stay

We've been here ten days and my back is burnt, rum's all gone, but
that don't matter here, sober in paradise, there, drunk in hell
And I woke up late with my stomach on fire, my head is pounding
and I'm tired
It's raining outside so I guess it's just as well

We'll catch the bay wind, blowing towards summer, carrying us away
Forget tomorrow, we've got plenty of sun today
We'll follow Magellan toward the sunrise, now we're stowaways
We'll find an island, stake our claim and stay

Andrew Knechel

Thanksgiving Prayer

I'm thankful — just to be
Alive, to live and love —
The things God has blessed me with,
Nature's own — the flowers, trees and hills
Blue skies and waters that laugh with me
And share my happiness

I'm thankful - because I have
A place to call my home
For rest for work - for prayer
A child whose questions I may answer
And grandma's book to read.

I'm thankful because I love
Each day that passes by
And brings new friends my way
To cheer, to aid, to laugh with
And just be thankful.

Eileen Klein

Where Is That Man?

A man who isn't afraid to tell the truth has a stronger awareness of wrong situations before actually getting into them -
I NEED that MAN.

A man who commits himself, then later realize the commitment is not for him, his attitude will not include: betrayal, connivance, neglect, physical or verbal abuse. He knows, showing compassion and honestly will set him free from his commitment. Yet still have captured a friend -
I NEED that MAN.

A man who base his image on material possessions, hers and his outer beauty hasn't fully developed. However, a man who is proud of his spiritual knowledge and his inner self shines free with positivity,
OH LORD -
I NEED that MAN.

Desperate isn't the case, it's about having and giving a sense of peace in this dangerous world, seeking inspirational communication to transcend the negative from the mouth of others, last but thee most important (regardless what the relationship platonic or love) we need unity between man and woman. For he who to believe, where is he? I need him - I... NEED... that MAN...

Lisa L. Jones

The Children, The Children, Where Are The Children?

A great bomb made of fertilizer and TNT,
Will the terror never end;
Men driven by hate and lust and fear,
A dangerous blend.
A monstrous explosion heard round the world,
Broken walls and fractured beams;
A mountain of rubble, the smell of death,
Broken hearts and shattered dreams.
   The children, the children, night is near,
   Where are the children? They do not appear.
Who committed this callous crime?
Dark-skinned strangers take the blame;
or was it our own, home-grown-extreme?
hate and resentment by another name.
The people pray, our President speaks;
Our grief spill over, to tears we awake,
We are told to stand strong, hold together,
To bend, but not to break.
   Will the anguish never end, twisted teddy bears, smashed toys,
   Will our hearts never mend, where are out girls and boys?

Marc Herschler

Scarlet's Letter

Stormy Skies in last year's rain
Warning me of dark clouds who flaunt
Silver linings bathing me in pain
Meekly drizzling so non-chalant
Well, I know what I want

And I think Heaven will open
Peering down upon me I imagine
They'll cast me as Hester Prynne
Deflowered on a bottle of Lanvin
Truth whispers stranger than fiction

Newton discovered gravity
To tie me to the groundling
Dirt muddied with depravity
Ruffled feathers fanned an albatross
Dressed to the teeth with sickening dross

And all that they covet
Lies hidden in my secret
Vision of future perfect
Slung from a ruby pendant
July passed without incident

Angela S. H. Garcia

"Just Listen"

I need to go home for just a little while.
To find out what happiness I've left behind.
The angels have come to tell me differ.
Only for me, to make the difference.
My mother has past on....
But is back to say
Just listen
You can hear for yourself if
you would just listen
Never before would I hear anyone
Because, being stubborn I've always been one.

The time has come only to hear
That my guardian angel has appeared.
Thank you O'Lord for having my time.
To find this right path,
How I've found.
   Believe —
   Pray —
   Follow your dreams.

I'm on my way there.

Jan Francis

The Killing Time (1972)

Little feet in trenches deep
Women and children felt the heat
Choppers buzzing in the air
Where are the people who say they care

Politics of burden cast on my soul
How many days must I go

Fear for my life I run fast
Killing fields not a blast

Run from an enemy I don't know
Kill a man and ruin my soul

My mind holds captive the faces I see
Now I remember the Killing tree

Bodies sway like leaves in the wind
Wretched memories don't come in

Surrounding my camp the spirit of death
holding my breath each night spent

Longing for shelter in my home
Knowing full well I'm not alone

Snapshots of war come to mind
Never to forget the killing time

Laura Crenshaw

"When That Star Fell"

I saw a star falling bright
I was with my love that night
We were close arm in arm
When that star fell; we were alarmed.
Wishes were made, but never came true
When that star fell, I lost you.
Dreams were lost, but we couldn't tell
Till that night when that star fell.
We were dreaming of marriage that night,
We thought our love was so very right.
I thought to myself, all is well
Till after that star fell,
Hopes and dreams faded fast
Like that star, we didn't last.
That one night, no one can take,
It belongs to us; it felt like fate.
Do you remember and will you hold tight?
That falling star we saw that night.

Louis Costanzo

Crystal Winter Wind

Crystal Winter wind
Frames this glorious eve
Precious few will see the light,
And most will not believe.

I've learned to make my fairy tales,
When my heart and soul are lost
The clouds will part on the grayest days,
But the sun won't melt this cursed frost.

These morning become hard to face
The days seem long to a lonely eye
My mistakes raise a smile to the wretched
Fates whom wage a battle on the side to time.

I spend the day in search of light
My gaze can't fall on love too soon
But I stand alone on the edge of night
Losing faith in dreams come true.

I know one night my eyes will close
In search of refuge from the day,
And if my heart survives the cold,
I might hear the words, I long to say.

Shawn Perchaluk

Be A Friend

When I wake up in the morning
to face a new day,
I wonder if there is someone
I can help along the way.
Do they need a word of comfort,
or someone to listen to?
Will they want to share their feelings,
as I know I often do?
No matter what the case may be,
We always need a friend,
who, with a little love and kindness,
can help a heart to mend.

Nellie D. Wyatt

Never Known

The fire closes around her
But she feels no heat
Voices close about her
But no face does she meet

The tears are on her face
But the face is far from wet
The dress that she was in is "full o' lace"
But a beautiful dress she hasn't met

A mask of silver and gold she shall wear
What she sees is worn with tear
With all the sadness she sees within
She will never know the kindness of man

Rashell Burnette

I Thought

I thought he loved me,
I thought it was true,
I thought he meant those words (I love you)
I thought he cared,
I thought he'd be there,
I thought he'd remember the times we shared.
I thought he'd remember the words I'd praise.
I thought he'd remember the things we'd say.
I thought he'd give his every last dime.
I thought we'd last till the end of time.

April Rolfe

In The Company Of Animals

I have found myself in the company of animals, swinging from bars
to bars, clubbing and pulling pranks, scavenging to survive. I hide
in shadows dreading the light, afraid that I might be seen, stoned
cursed or worse, laughed at. I know real fear deep pain, this
loveless existence in the company of animals.

I once loved, was loved. I knew real joy...once, I had
real friends, a family. Now my kind my specie must roam together
in order to survive. We aren't many, just a handful, all once
beautiful once babes with drooling lips, sweet to the touch.
Those days are long gone, a mere pinhead on the scope of
our memories painful and weird in the company of animals.

We do not walk, once did, forgotten how to. Our pack survives
on instinct, we claw our way around staying close to the ground,
threatened we let our fangs fly slashing growling leaving anything to
survive. People are afraid of us, they try to avoid us we
prick their conscience stir up feelings of guilt. Somewhere
inside they know they are like us in many ways, one more
drink one more obstacle, one fix another rejection and they
too will be in the company of animals.

Lilian Scarlett-Collins

Tree Of Heaven

Like the spreading chestnut tree whose taste is most desirable,
so is the fruit of spirit, they are most admirable.

Like the weeping willow that leans toward the ground,
to help someone, you too lean, for this you'll wear a crown.

The evergreen colors are ever true, it will never change,
so should one's love for Christ and others be, always the same.

Like a tree by the river that shall not be moved, storms come,
currents flow, but like the tree great strength do show.

Like the tree of heaven branches without sprays,
cluttered with winged seeds sprouted upward toward heaven,
as hands to God are raised, giving honor and praise.

They say that Jesus hung on a tree, of important significance
He carried that tree to the top of a hill, at the peak it stood still.

People all around came to see the scene there on Cavalry.
He hung on the tree to sacrifice His life for you and me.

We must never let our fruit die, continue to grow spiritually,
for Christ in us now abides that some needed soul might see reality.

Dora Penn

The Dream Of The Meat

So I was reaching into my mind only
it was a cabinet full of meat?
ground meat dead
seeming to go on for pounds
a red mound of dreaming

Meant meat, to be measured in
invisible bags and I sat on the floor
in rags
hand-scooping rations
in squeezing fascination

And I thought
I am Coleridge?
or maybe bacon
a sage a link
to mold the meat in a moment of verse
and scoop it into spoken
pages only I think
between the hurrying
up I must
have woken

Jeremy Edwards

The Land Where The Penguins Fly

When I was young, my thoughts were young
and time stood patiently by.
Watching me grow, learn, and dream
in the land where the penguins fly.

Time nudged me through the difficult years;
into a world that I could understand.
She taught me patience, respect, and love
as we traveled together she held my hand.

But time can be cruel and unyielding
as she ignores me- with a sigh.
She will take away my youth, and dreams
as she goes flouncing by.

Now I am old, my thoughts are old-
and time sits idly by.
Waiting to take me by the hand-
and lead me back to the land where the penguins fly.
Peggy J. Sparks

"Doll House"

Doll house darkness over fumes
we are people in the room,

Shadows gasp for air and have none
what's said is said -
what's wrong is done.

Use our table to sit and drink
after a long and hard week.

Pain in the doll house
what do you see
we are the people that are to be.

Cold house darkness over gloom
we are the people in the room.
Jeremy Knopka

Dry And Dusty Desert

The desert is not like a feather
silky and smooth,
It's rough and dry
No! Not thirst quenching
but thirsting for
Prickly cactus,
Hot sun,
And lots of sticky bodies
No sweet smelling flowers
No petal for a rose
All there is,
is dry and a lot of desert
Hannah Cormier

Treasures

Treasures aren't jewels or gold,
but something dear in our hearts we hold.
A poor man's dime in the gutter he found,
a deaf woman's memory of sound.
A hungry child's bread crumbs,
a tune the music lover hums.
A blind man's dream of sight,
the sun that shines so bright.
A lovesick girl's daydream fairy tale,
the lonely night's moon, blue and pale.
For some it seems, treasures are hard to find,
but they are right in front of you if you put your greed behind.
Carla Roberta Pacheco

No Greater Feeling

Your tiny little body moving gently within mine,
There is no greater feeling.

Seeing you born into my life,
There is no greater feeling.

Daddy's expression of amazement in your birth,
There is no greater feeling.

I see myself in you in so many ways,
There is no greater feeling.

All I love about daddy I see in you,
There is no greater feeling.

Your soft small hands caressing my face,
There is no greater feeling.

Your ever growing and unconditional love for me,
There is no greater feeling.

The way you greet me with such excitement each day - without fail,
There is no greater feeling.

Just knowing how many more joys you will bring my way,
There is no greater feeling.

To know that God chose me to be your Mother.
There is no greater feeling, no greater feeling - no greater feeling.
Gail E. Stashick

Summer Scene

Grasshopper taking flight
in the boundaries of my backyard
with its velvet water pool
and burnt out sun
and my heart
lying on the lounge chair
relaxed
drinking in your breath
with a thirst
like none I've ever known
and here are your fingers
walking on my back
slight tickle
that you know I enjoy
Swan dive into the deep end
without your safety wings
drowning
in the depths
of my bare skin.
Rachel Semple

Art Supplies

Until the critics
return I will
be there writhing
in my own
actions wondering
if time will ever
be the same one
portfolio of canvasses
blocked by the dusty
charcoal ashes
brushed against us
only to be
shaded by our
own colors for
we once thought we
owned the crayons
Strokes of our life
return now for
us to conform
and paint by numbers
Rebecca Ann Komara

Biographies of Poets

ABELLA, RAQUEL H.
[pen.] Raquel; [b.] November 27, 1978, Manila, Philippines; [p.] Renato C. Abella, Imelda H. Abella; [ed.] West Springfield High School, 11th Grade; [memb.] National Honor Society, National Art Honor Society, Tri-Hi-Y, Junior Math League; [hon.] 3rd Place Winner, in National Editorial Cartooning Contest, in the Philippines, 1st Place Winner, in the Reflection Contest for the whole country, 1st Place Winner in an Illustration Contest; [pers.] I write the things that I could never say; [a.] Springfield, VA

ABEYTIA, ANISA ALEXANDRA
[b.] July 12, 1972, Los Angeles, CA; [p.] Martha and Charles Canales; [ed.] Currently working on my B.A. in Creative Writing at USC; [occ.] Student; [memb.] USC's Women's Crew Team - Staff Writer for the Daily Trojan; [hon.] Daily Trojan - Most Improved Staff Writer and Award of Excellence; [oth. writ.] Imprintibals Today Magazine (Nat.) Sparrowgrass Poetry Forum, Iliad "Perspectives" USC's Daily Trojan; [a.] Alhambra, CA

ACEVEDO, JUDITH
[b.] July 17, 1948, Brooklyn, NY; [p.] John Acevedo and Epifania Vazquez; [ed.] Eli Whitney High School; [occ.] Legal Secretary; [pers.] Mankind has much to learn about the essence of life, and even more to accept.; [a.] Brooklyn, NY

ACOSTA, RAYMOND J.
[b.] February 10, 1916, El Paso, TX; [p.] Jesse and Josephine Acosta; [m.] Cleo G. Acosta, April 23, 1938; [ch.] Lydia and Irene; [ed.] Nine full years of Formal Education in Los Angeles, Balance - Self Taught; [occ.] Retired after many years of Furniture Retail Managing; [memb.] Member of Elks, Several Books Club, Active in Sports Activities; [hon.] None in Literature, Member of Seniors Coalition, Cited as Employee of Year by Firm Before Retiring; [oth. writ.] Many - none published except for several in Senior Citizen Publications; [pers.] I strive to reflect importance of full equality for all people and for International Peace.; [a.] Inglewood, CA

ADAMS, ANNETTE
[pen.] A-A; [b.] July 31, 1984, Suffern, NY; [p.] Francine and Michael Adams; [ed.] Montgomery Elementary School; [occ.] Student - 5th grade; [memb.] Girl Scouts, Timberwolves 4-H Club, Band; [hon.] Young Writers Award for Poetry, Nat'l PTA Reflections Award in Visual Arts, NYSSMA Outstanding Music Award in OBOE, MES Art Award of Excellence, Perfect Attendance, Silver Star Academic Award; [oth. writ.] Poetry published for School Functions; [pers.] My classroom teachers, my family, and nature have been a great inspiration to me. Through my poetry I try to reveal the beauty and importance of nature so that other people can respect nature as I do.; [a.] Montgomery, NY

ADAMS, WARREN J.
[pen.] Warren J. Adams; [b.] May 20, 1925, Oklahoma; [ed.] B.A. University of New Mexico; [occ.] Retired BIA Employee; [memb.] Cherokee Tribe (Native American), Masonic Lodge, AARP; [oth. writ.] Instruction Manuals, Biographical Poetry, Native American Poetry; [pers.] Freedom should not infringe on the rights of others.; [a.] Albuquerque, NM

ADAMS, KERRY W.
[b.] September 27, 1950, Norfolk, NE; [p.] William and Wilma Buss; [ch.] Jason, Tisha, Rachel, Granddaughter - Alisa; [occ.] Executive Assist., Clark Jeary Home, Lincoln, NE; [oth. writ.] Several poems published in local newspapers; [pers.] I write poetry from personal experiences in my life with the passion that comes from within me about the feelings of that experience.; [a.] Crete, NE

ADAMS, RANDY R.
[b.] April 25, 1953, Bonne Terre, MO; [p.] Floyd Adams, Isolde Masters; [ch.] Benjamin and Jaclyn Adams; [ed.] Park Hills High, Mineral Area College, Leadbelt Tech.; [occ.] Maintenance Electrician, Flat River Glass, CO; [memb.] Phi Theta Kappa Society, United Steelworkers of America; [hon.] Phi Theta Kappa Society, Dean's List; [oth. writ.] Other poems, non-published; [pers.] I'm dedicated to writing about the ambivalence of romantic feelings.; [a.] Park Hills, MO

ADLER, RONNA
[pen.] "Ronna A."; [b.] July 12, 1963, Brooklyn, NY; [p.] Lou, Mort and Irene; [ed.] M.W. Sr. High, Monroe, NY, Havat Hanoar Hatzioni, Katamon, Jerusalem "Israel" and some more...; [occ.] Writer, today; [memb.] A.A., O.A., N.A, D.A.; [hon.] Para Chaplain, Sales Awards, this contest is an honor; [oth. writ.] Numerous poems and song lyrics...; [pers.] I have been greatly influenced by life experiences. One day at a time I try to keep it simple. Just for today. Thanks to God!; [a.] Carlsbad, CA

AHERN, JOHN
[occ.] Consultant - Public Relations; [oth. writ.] Novel: "Second best's a gay goodnight," Froge/Parisbook Store, Plays: "Go out and see," cancer my shipmate, many articles for magazines including MD, America's Health, Promenade, over zoo kirkus book reviews, did political analysis and speech writing, worked for newsweek and forces magazines.; [a.] New York, NY

AKERS, KATIE DANIELLE
[pen.] Ren Hjarta; [b.] July 5, 1979, Fresno, CA; [p.] Albert C. and Loretta J. Akers; [ed.] Presently a Junior at Coalinga High School; [occ.] Student worker for Fresno Private Industry Council, Coalinga, CA; [memb.] Future Farmers of America, California Scholarship Federation, Interact Club, Drama Club, L.D.S. Church Youth Group; [hon.] Freshman 2nd High Girl Scholar, F.F.A. Prepared Public Speaking, Farm Records, and Diversified Livestock Production, High Honor Roll (3.857 G.P.A); [oth. writ.] This is the first!; [pers.] Stand for truth and righteousness.; [a.] Coalinga, CA

AKERS, ERNEST L.
[pen.] E. L. Akers; [b.] December 11, 1950, Blacksburg, SC; [p.] Ernest Akers, Lillian K. Akers; [m.] Divorced; [ch.] Sherry Akers; [ed.] Blacksburg High, John Tyler Community College; [occ.] Virginia Department of Highways and Transportation (VDOT); [oth. writ.] Book of Poetry - "American Feelings" - unpublished - Finishing first novel - Horror - "Fearless Nick"; [pers.] Whether I write horror or poems, I strive to reflect the sincerity of the human nature and leave the reader a simple message, one of hope or inspiration, and hopefully, a better understanding of our fellowman.; [a.] Petersburg, VA

ALBRECHT JR., CHARLES G.
[b.] March 24, 1940, CT; [p.] Charles and Lorraine Albrecht; [m.] Marilyn Ann (Mintell) Albrecht, November 1960; [ch.] Charles III, Mitchell and Todd Emerson Albrecht; [occ.] Business and Teaching

ALCORN, AMY MARIE
[pen.] Amy Marie, Sheyenne Star; [b.] December 11, 1975, Louisville, KY; [p.] Fred and Kathy Zessin; [hon.] Young Authors Certificates in Elementary School; [pers.] Go for it!

ALDAPE, YOLANDA
[b.] El Paso, TX; [ch.] Three sons; [memb.] Romance Writers of America and Iglesia Ni Cristo; [oth. writ.] I've had several short stories published in the monthly Monterey Bay Monarch; [pers.] If one day, I'm taken away and disappear in the wind, I wish to be remembered by my poems and short stories.; [a.] Salinas, CA

ALDRIDGE, NANCY S.
[pen.] Marcy D'Angelou; [b.] March 23, 1960, Orange, NJ; [p.] Kenneth Barsby, Ruth Barsby; [m.] Marlin Lloyd Aldridge, September 10, 1983; [ch.] Erin Patricia, Kenneth Brian, Joshua Daniel; [ed.] Allentown High, Mercer County Community College; [occ.] Administrative Assistant, Chesapeake Ability School; [memb.] Presbyterian Church; [hon.] Dean's List; [oth. writ.] A few other poems never submitted anywhere for publication; [pers.] I have been greatly influenced by the "Mother Goose" rhymes. Those were the most astounding things to me when I was young. So, I try to create a moments worth of happiness with my poems.; [a.] Springfield, VA

ALEXANDER, DEAN
[b.] June 22, 1948, New York, NY; [p.] Dale Alexander and Edith Kaye; [m.] Margrette Alexander, January 16, 1990; [ch.] Brenna and Evan (ages 3 and 1); [ed.] Northfield - Mt. Hermon, Brown University - B.A., Claremont Graduate School - M.A., Ph.D.; [occ.] Psychologist; [memb.] NAS - National Academy of Songwriters, ACCESS - Autism Coalition for Creative Educational and Social Services; [hon.] Cum Laude Society, Varsity Letter (La Crosse) - NMH Dean's List - Brown University product named in 10 Best Little Inventive Innovations - LA Times: 12/26/90; [oth. writ.] 1. Journal articles and book chapters on remedial treatment and education of people with developmental disabilities, 2. National air play: I've got the Jim and Tammy Baker Blues; [pers.] Role models - Drs. Merlin Olson and Bobby Brown, Justices Alan Page and "Whizzer" White.; [a.] Wrightwood, CA

ALI, ISHMAEL
[pen.] Ali; [m.] Medina Ali; [ch.] Caliph, Amirah, Jihan Shavannah, Naadhira, Katrina; [ed.] Graduate of Springfield Technical Community College Majored in Communication; [occ.] Educator; [memb.] Masjid AC - Tawheed and Masjid Council, Organization of African American Unity; [hon.] Award for completing foreign studies and Arabic in Istanbul, Turkey; [oth. writ.] Book on prose called "Virtues of Silence"; [pers.] Be kind to all who you meet. Through them your creator will speak.; [a.] Springfield, MA

ALISON, MARK
[pen.] John Harrison; [ed.] Petroleum Engineer, Leeds Univ., Leeds, England; [hon.] Mountain Rescue Team while at Leeds Univ.; [pers.] Hobby: Untrained tenor, History: Grandfather - Shipwrecker - Village Hilton on the River Weir near New Castle, England. Father - Skipper of the sister to the paddle wheel tug, Eppleton Hall, now berthed at the San Francisco Maritime Museum.

ALL, APRIL MICHELLE
[pen.] April or Michelle All; [b.] April 1, 1981, Thomasville, GA; [p.] Martha All and Lloyd All Sr.; [ed.] Taylor County High; [occ.] Busting Tables Roy Deals Oyster House Perry, FL; [memb.] Antioch Revival Center Perry, FL; [hon.] English Honors; [oth. writ.] None published but I have written other poems and short stories; [pers.] My poetry comes from the heart in which I think. I believe the world would be a more loving place if more people thought with their heart instead of their mind.; [a.] Perry, FL

ALLARD, LORRAINE A.
[pen.] Lorraine A. Allard; [b.] December 13, 1958, Hartford, CT; [p.] Maurille O. (Deceased), Georgette M. Allard; [ed.] High School, College Graduate; [occ.] Disabled as of 1985 prior to, multiple jobs; [memb.] The league of Night Adorers of the Sacred Heart of Jesus, The Society of the Little Flower, A Great Batman Fan; [oth. writ.] Many, non-published excepting one in senior high school graduation paper (1976' 5); [pers.] "Trust God blindly never question - for He is the one whose best is direction."; [a.] East Hartford, CT

ALLEN, KRISTINA
[b.] November 26, 1979, Rexburg, ID; [p.] Marcel Allen; [ed.] Elementary School through 9th Grade; [occ.] 10th Grade Student; [hon.] Honor Roll Presidential Academic Award; [pers.] If you want something bad enough and work hard for it you will get what you want.; [a.] Webster, WI

ALLEN, GEORGE BERT
[pen.] Gord, Sorch, Tardy, Captain and President; [b.] April 8, 1925, Doniphan, MO; [p.] Edward (Ed) Allen, and Mary Lee; [m.] Christene E. Boyles, February 29, 1948; [ch.] Kenneth E., Charlotte A., Lawrence W., Fred H., Boyd L. and Everett T.; [ed.] Eleven years; [occ.] Life time experience of manufacturing of farm and garden tool handles, Sales, U.S.A. and form countries; [oth. writ.] In poetry of providence, of his life, in the pro-verbs, through plurals, and the precepts, giving the word the complete authority over the truth, for thirty years. In Perilous times.

ALLEN, NANCY GRACE STRATTON
[pen.] Nancy Grace; [b.] February 22, 1952, Stafford Springs, CT; [p.] Roger and Etta Lucille Stratton; [m.] Newell F. Allen, October 28, 1978; [ch.] Dustin Newell Allen September 28, 1979; [ed.] Assoc. in Science, Manchester Community College, Manchester, CT; [occ.] C.O.T.A, Activities Assistant; [memb.] Bethel Mennonite Church; [oth. writ.] Poems, Children Stories, Songs; [pers.] To glorify God, my saviour, my Lord, I'll lead others to Jesus by sharing his world. To be the best wife and mother I can be, I'll bring love and laughter to those around me.; [a.] Sarasota, FL

ALLEN II, RICHARD ERNEST
[b.] December 11, 1961, Pomona, CA; [p.] Richard and Lucretta Allen; [ch.] Cassie 13, Heather 9, Lindsey Allen 7; [occ.] Fire Sprinkler Fitter; [pers.] Where in: All God's green earth will we ever find the moments to live and understand what is Gods will for us.; [a.] Encinitas, CA

ALLEN, CHARLES L.
[b.] October 5, 1937, Montevallo, AL; [p.] Armon and Lessie Allen; [m.] Dorothy G. Allen, September 30, 1960; [ch.] Lisa G. Allen (Kern) (Daughter), Charle L. Allen Jr. (Son); [ed.] Thompson High School, University of Montevallo; [occ.] Retired Accountant; [memb.] United States Army Reserve; [oth. writ.] None printed even though I have written many for fun; [pers.] I like to write poetry for fun. I look for some event in my life as an inspiration to write.; [a.] Birmingham, AL

ALLERT, LORI
[pen.] Lori Ann; [b.] April 8, 1961, Chicago, IL; [p.] Monroe DeLaughter, Jeanne DeLaughter; [m.] Steven Allert, September 26, 1981; [ch.] Nicole Jean, Steven Michael; [ed.] Addison Trail High School, Elgin Community College; [occ.] Customer Care Plan Representative - Panasonic; [hon.] Dean's List; [pers.] The Lord shows me what to write. My inspiration comes from him.; [a.] Elgin, IL

ALLSOPP, TIMOTHY
[pen.] Angel Cors; [b.] October 3, 1976, Bronx, NY; [p.] Drs. Ralph and Marshalyn Allsopp; [ed.] High School graduation 6/95 - Phillips Exeter Academy, Exeter, NH; [occ.] Student - 1st year, Williams College, Williamstown, MA (1995-1996); [hon.] Honor Student, High School, Latin and Greek Scholar, National Achievement Commendation, Boston Globe all Scholastic Track Award; [oth. writ.] Many poems, none have been published; [pers.] I have been greatly influenced by love and music that incites passion.; [a.] Atlanta, CA

ALMEIDA, REBECCA
[pen.] Jacklen Sierra Saden; [b.] October 29, 1980, MA; [p.] Robert J. Desmarais, Catherine A. Almeida; [ed.] Edgewater High School; [occ.] Honor Student; [memb.] Engineering Science Technology Program, Marching Band (Flute), Latin Club, Teen Court Volunteer; [hon.] Honors School Awards, EST Honor Student; [a.] Orlando, FL

AMBROSINI, MICHELE
[b.] November 14, 1979, Bridgeport, AL; [p.] Joseph and Marie Ambrosini; [ed.] St. Ambrose Elementary School, St. Josephs High School; [occ.] Student; [hon.] Other poem published in the school poetry book entitled "Amaranth" the poem was "When I Think of You"; [oth. writ.] "As I Think of You," "A Sudden Thought"; [pers.] I would like to dedicate my poem "Too Young To Die," to my best friend Robert Stoddard (1979-1994); [a.] Bridgeport, CT

AMER, MARY ANN
[b.] November 14, 1962, Akron, OH; [p.] Delores Bouschere and Richard Amer; [ed.] St. Sebastian/St. Vincent - St. Mary's High School; [occ.] Professional Photographer; [memb.] Hearts in Harmony, Wildlife Conservation Society; [hon.] 1989-1994 Photographer of the Year (five consecutive years), 1988 Top Notch Photographer Award (Nationwide); [oth. writ.] Poems: Healing Spirits, Growing Old, A Mother Prayer, The Sheltering Sky, Could it be, Timmmberrrr...among others not yet published; [pers.] Looking for space, when the hand comes down you must create a space in your mind for your spirit and soul to live. In order to rise from the ashes of violence. A life long happiness will be yours forever. Dedicated to John Denver!; [a.] Akron, OH

AMODEI, KENLYNN D.
[pen.] Kenlynn D. Amodei; [b.] April 3, 1964, East Stroudsburg, PA; [p.] Russell Cramer, Diana Cramer; [m.] Tino Amodei, June 12, 1988; [ch.] Giovanni Joseph, Anthony Giordano, Adrianna Maria; [ed.] Pleasant Valley High School, Slippery Rock University; [occ.] Sales - Aloette Cosmetics, Inc.; [memb.] Epsilon Epsilon Epsilon Sorority Gamma Zeta Chapter '82; [hon.] Dale Carnegie Highest Achievement Award for Public Speaking and Human Relations; [oth. writ.] Currently undertaking a Children's Literature Course; [pers.] I believe that writing is a wonderful tool of expression. I feel writing to be a great form of communication for one's thoughts and emotions.; [a.] Bethlehem, PA

AMTMANN, CHRISTINA D.
[b.] May 23, 1973, Fairchild AFB, WA; [p.] Raymond and Mary Amtmann; [pers.] I've been called a dreamer. Sweet dreams.; [a.] Temple Terrace, FL

ANDERSEN, CHRISTOPHER
[b.] July 17, 1971, Aurora, IL; [p.] Robert and Sharon Andersen; [m.] Lori Renee Andersen, October 18, 1991; [ch.] Tyler, Max; [ed.] Oswego H.S., Oswego, IL; [occ.] Miner - Galena - Plattville, No. Aurora, IL; [a.] Millbrook, IL

ANDERSEN, DONALD D.
[b.] February 16, 1968, Gray, UT; [p.] Lyle and Elsie Andersen; [m.] Holly Andersen, April 1, 1995; [ed.] B.A. in English from Whitman College (1993); [occ.] Software Systems Support; [memb.] National Parks Conservation Association, Wilderness Fund; [oth. writ.] No other published works. 200 plus poems, 20 or 50 Short Stories, 3 Novels (in progress) 1 play; [pers.] I believe my work to be primarily focused on the affirmation of the natural world. Metaphysically I drift more towards Kafka and Marquez, while philosophically I confound myself with the issues of time and morality.; [a.] Chico, CA

ANDERSON, LENA
[b.] June 18, 1908, East Liverpool, OH; [p.] John and Jessie Hendricks; [m.] Emory J. Anderson, March 17, 1924; [ch.] Emory J. Anderson Jr., Paul A. Anderson

ANDERSON, CHARMAINE A.
[pen.] Shack; [b.] December 26, 1942, Philadelphia, PA; [p.] Floyd James Sr., Daisy James; [m.] Divorced; [ch.] Charel Yvette, Bryce O. Anderson Jr.; [ed.] Antioch Univ., M.Ed Geneva College - B.A. (Religion); [occ.] Asst. Pastor, First African Bapt. Ch., and Teacher, Computer, Math, English, - Faith Tabernacle Elementary and High School; [memb.] NAACP, Historical Lincoln Day Center, First African Bapt. Church, Scholarship Committee, and Asst. Pastor; [hon.] Doctor of Divinity Degree, Doctor Divinity; [oth. writ.] Poem published in through these eyes; [pers.] I attempt to concentrate on the characteristic effect or flavor which I believe will be shared to reach the heart of mankind.; [a.] Philadelphia, PA

ANDERSON, LOUISE
[b.] October 25, 1949, Sacramento, CA; [m.] John Lee Anderson, April 7, 1973; [ed.] Napa High School, Napa Valley College; [occ.] Playwright Founder of Dreamweavers Theatre, Napa California; [oth. writ.] Numerous poems, short stories and technical material on producing and directing plays, many plays, all of which have been produced in regional theatre; [a.] Mechanicsville, MD

ANDERSON, LAUREN
[b.] June 5, 1982, Arlington Heights, IL; [p.] Mikal and Sherie Anderson; [ed.] I will be entering the 8th Grade at Carl Sandburg Junior High School in the '95 - '96 School Year; [memb.] National Geographic Society; [oth. writ.] Wrote a poem entitled "I like Reading" at the age of 7 which was performed by the Child's Play Touring Theatre in Chicago; [a.] Rolling Meadows, IL

ANDERSON, NANCY ANN
[b.] March 6, 1951, Derby, CT; [p.] Edward and Elizabeth Smith; [ch.] Bryan Keith, Keith Allen, Andrew Alan and Sara Elizabeth and 2 grandchildren Tashia Rae and Scott; [ed.] Newtown High School, Newtown, Conn. Class of 69; [occ.] Pre K Teacher - Kountry Kids/Private Duty - Home Health Aid for the Elderly; [oth. writ.] Poems for my class, several children's stories which I hope to have published one day; [pers.] I enjoy working with children and knowing that I helped to mold a young mind. I also work with the elderly. I wish to thank all my lost loves, my inspirations and Suzanne Haugh my dear friend with a computer!; [a.] York, PA

ANDREKO, MARY E.
[b.] May 6, 1952, Elizabeth, NJ; [p.] Victor and Mary Ann Andreko; [ed.] So. Brns. H.S., Middlesex Co. Comm. College; [occ.] Secretary; [hon.] Editors Choice Award - Nat. Lib. of Poetry, Award of Merit - Famous Poets Society; [oth. writ.] Several poems published in different anthologies, and church news letter; [pers.] My poems are based on memories of my deceased daughter (my only child) and memories of how life and people had affected me.; [a.] Pine Mountain, GA

ANDREWS, STASS
[b.] October 19, 1970, Marietta, GA; [p.] Dave Andrews, Susie Martel; [ch.] Zane Andrews (4); [ed.] Pinellas Park High, P. Park FL, Midlands Tech. Springdale, SC; [occ.] Asst. Mngr. Old America, W. Cola, SC; [oth. writ.] Several unpublished poems and essays; [pers.] I don't retain what I read very well, so I don't have many influences. My writings are therefore innocent. I strive to reflect life as I presents itself to us, good, bad, and indifferent.; [a.] West Colombia, SC

ANDUJOR, MIRIAM
[b.] May 29, 1943, PR; [ed.] Associate Applied Science; [occ.] Executive Secretary; [memb.] AARP, Association Female Executives New Life; [hon.] CSS 1995, Outstanding Minority Award; [oth. writ.] Hate, Beyond the River, Racing Against Time; [pers.] Live for Today, Live for Tomorrow, Help others love all.; [a.] New York, NY

ANTHONY, DEBORAH
[b.] September 8, 1978, New Kensington, PA; [p.] Nancy Anthony; [ed.] Apollo - Ridge High School; [occ.] Student; [memb.] American Quarter Horse Association, 4-H American Legion Aux.; [hon.] Honor Roll Student; [pers.] Don't let others set your goals, they may set them to low.; [a.] Apollo, PA

ANZALONE, LORRAINE
[b.] April 14, 1928, Dumont, NJ; [p.] Harold and Margaret Blauvelt; [m.] Frank Anzalone, November 6, 1975; [ch.] Robert, Mary Jane, Linda, (grandchildren) Frank, Anthony, Michael, Brenda, Ranze, Eric; [occ.] Retired Homemaker; [memb.] AARP, Veterans Village Activities Assoc.; [pers.] I have always enjoyed writing poems for family and friends. It has enriched my life. Now sharing this joy with other people, is a blessing.; [a.] Port Richey, FL

ARCHIBALD, THEODORE E.
[b.] June 21, 1919, Antigua, WI; [m.] Matilda Victoria, April 21, 1949; [ch.] Cecilia, Janice and Joyce; [ed.] Average; [occ.] Retiree; [memb.] Manor Church of the Nazarine; [hon.] The Citicorp Service, Excellence Award, U.S. Citizenship; [a.] Fort Landerdale, FL

ARDANUY, CHRISTOPHER
[b.] January 2, 1970, Frankfurt, Germany; [ed.] Orchard Park High School; [occ.] Courier - Corning Laboratories; [oth. writ.] Never showed my writings, never published any; [pers.] If you say that I have talent, or am talented, you cursed me with a false observation. If you say that God is talented, and gave me talent, then you blessed me with a true observation.; [a.] Orchard Park, NY

AREFIN, MOHAMMAD S.
[pen.] Shamsul; [b.] January 29, 1965, Dhaka; [p.] Al Haj. Wahidur Rahman, Begam M. Khanan; [ed.] S.S.C. West End H/S 1982, H.S.C. Dhaka City College 1985, B.Com. (Commerce) City College 1989, M.Com. (Accounting) (pres.) Dhaka University 1991; [occ.] General Labour; [memb.] (NICPA) National Park and Conservation Association; [oth. writ.] Several poems not yet publish; [pers.] The highway to return to Eden (paradise) is that to give up the Natural Course in G.A.P. (General Accepted Principle) of Human Beings.; [a.] Queens, NY

ARGHIERE, MARIA
[pen.] Maria Arghine; [b.] May 1, 1947, Brooklyn, NY; [p.] Amalia Arghiere Papacena; [ed.] Bay Ridge High; [occ.] Medical Asst.; [hon.] Dance and Voice; [oth. writ.] Many poems not yet published; [pers.] I was inspired to write First Kiss, for my first true love.; [a.] Brooklyn, NY

ARGUELLO, CARL
[b.] April 22, 1920, Trinidad, CO; [p.] John Arguello, Isabel Arguello; [m.] Mary Arguello, April 30, 1939; [ch.] Betty, Isabel, Kathie; [ed.] San Francisco City College, San Francisco State College; [occ.] Retired Poet and Writer; [memb.] "Sirs" - Fraternal - order of Elks; [hon.] San Francisco Pocket Billiard Champion 1984; [oth. writ.] Several poems not published - I would wish to submit. My poems and essays to a publisher or publishing house; [pers.] Most of my poetry are nostalgic reflections of my personal past life. Poetry indeed is a living language. Symmetrical words and lyrical emotions - that come like music poetry harmony to the soul from one's heart.; [a.] San Francisco, CA

ARMSTRONG, BARBARA
[pen.] Muffin; [b.] September 26, 1979, Philadelphia, PA; [p.] Morris and Joan Armstrong; [ch.] I have two sisters, Lisa and Debrah. A brother Morris; [ed.] I am a Junior at Little Flower Catholic High School for girls, I would like to attend Villanova University to pursue my writing ability; [pers.] Through my writings I put my mind at ease. And I feel relaxed. When people read my poems, I hope they feel the same.; [a.] Philadelphia, PA

ARNOLD, TIMOTHY
[pen.] Tee; [b.] January 11, 1956, Greenville, SC; [p.] Shemen Davidson, Zenolia Davidson; [ed.] High School Graduate; [occ.] Warehouse Mag.; [hon.] U.S. Army, earned National Defence Service Medal for High level Security; [pers.] I dedicate this poem to "Jackie Soto" I will always love and want her.; [a.] Brooklyn, NY

ARNOLD, ELIZABETH ANN
[b.] May 12, 1958, Salt Lake City, UT; [p.] Keith and Nancy Thompson; [m.] Robin Dale Arnold; [ch.] Rachele Brandy, Stephanie Lynn, Crystal Marie; [pers.] I only wish to be recognized as a wife, mother, daughter, sister and friend.; [a.] San Jose, CA

ARRINGTON, AUDREY C.
[pen.] Gracelyn Daniel; [b.] November 16, 1951, Atlanta, GA; [p.] Lynn Carter, Birdie Carter; [m.] Gerald Arrington Sr., October 21, 1971; [ch.] Gerald, Jr., Taurin; [ed.] West Fulton High School, Atlanta, Attended Clark College, Atlanta; [occ.] Bellsouth - Collections Representative; [memb.] Fellowship of Faith Church, Sunday School Teacher; [hon.] Received awards for Community Work; [oth. writ.] Writing's published in Church Paper; [a.] East Point, GA

ARZT, WINDY
[pen.] MJ; [b.] November 30, 1980, Oklahoma; [p.] Ronald and Kathleen Arzt; [ed.] 9th Grade, Salem Junior High; [occ.] Student; [memb.] Band, Flags, Basketball; [hon.] Principal's Honor Roll, Art Achievements, Sports Metals; [pers.] I try to get a point across about how devastating the world can be and at the same time I express my most treasured thoughts.; [a.] Salem, MO

ASBURY, KAY
[pen.] KT Lou; [b.] December 15, 1939, WV; [p.] Deceased; [m.] Doyle W. Asbury, January 24, 1958; [ch.] Kimberlee Davis (daughter); [ed.] High School Grad., DuPont High School; [occ.] Retired; [pers.] I have always had a strong love add bond for family and friends I relate this in my poem, which I wrote at age fifteen. This same love has been in my heart all my life.; [a.] Belle, WV

ASHBAUCHER, ROZELLA D.
[pen.] Ashbaucher, Rozella D.; [b.] October 5, IL; [p.] Mont and Reola Dillard; [m.] Lorin F. Ashbaucher, August 18, 1963; [ed.] Graduate of Miami High, Graduate of Southern Brothers Business College, and the University of Miami in Coral Gables, Fla., have taught and done Secretarial Work; [occ.] Retired in John Knox Village of Central Fla. in Orange City, FL; [memb.] Central Christian Church in Coral Gables, FL., and Asso. Member of First Christian Church in Dehand, Fl., Martha Chapter of O.E.S. in Miami Fl., Member of Delta Zeta National Sorority at U. of Miami; [hon.] I was an Scholarship Student of Ruth

Bryan Owen Rhode at the U. of Miami and Member of Rho Beta Omicron Public speaking fraternity of U. of Miami, Honor Roll in High; [oth. writ.] I have a book of poetry unpublished for own pleasure; [pers.] I have often expressed my feelings in poetry on special occasions. Ruth Bryan Owen Rhode read my book and liked it.; [a.] Orange City, FL

ASHLEY, CHRISTINE M.
[pen.] Lona Christi; [b.] June 20, 1914, Dextar, MO; [p.] Charles and Elizabeth Moneymaker; [m.] William Raymond, December 23, 1933; [ch.] Sharon, Monte Ray, John Kirby; [ed.] High School, some College, night classes, it is on going, never learn enough. Current, typing and Spanish, at present writing a book my first; [occ.] Retired, past to numerous, the last six years as County supervisor for Kentucky Health Dept.; [memb.] I have been district Pres. of M.Y.F. Royal Matron of Amaranth and others but there comes a time to take time for self, AT 81, it's about time. I have a God given Art ability. Never had time until now, I sold six paintings last year.; [oth. writ.] Several poems published in small county newspaper, many given away, it seem someone always wanted them and I felt honored so I gave.; [pers.] Let your light so shine with the love of Christ, that others may see and prosper.

ASHTON, JOAN
[b.] Salt Lake City, UT; [m.] R. Dennis Ashton; [ch.] Erin Kate Ashton, Brodi Shawn Ashton

ATKESON, SABRINA
[b.] September 23, 1977, Roseburg, OR; [p.] Ed and Lid Atkeson; [ed.] High School; [occ.] Work in an Amphitheatre; [memb.] I am a member of the International Thespian Society; [oth. writ.] I've written many other poems as well as a couple of short stories, and a play; [pers.] I feel people can make a difference by the things they do and the way they express themselves.; [a.] Vista, CA

ATKIN, HELEN O.
[b.] February 14, 1908, Ithaca, NY; [p.] Robert H. and Helen M. Ogle (deceased); [m.] Philip T. Atkins, June 22, 1935 (deceased); [ch.] Philip O. and Melanie C.; [ed.] B.S. Education, Howard University; [occ.] Retired Teacher; [memb.] Dunbar High School Alumni Class of 1925, Capitol Hill Poetry Club, Anawim Christian Life Community, St. Peter's Senior Citizens, Plymouth Senior Citizens, Phi Delta Kappa Sorority, "The G.P.T.'s" Social Club; [oth. writ.] Several plays and poetry for the schools where I taught and others; plays and poetry for senior citizens and other events; many speeches for programs, retirements, events, etc.; [pers.] I have loved poetry as far back as I can remember and have read, learned, recited, and written it. I have never tried to publish anything but have freely shared whatever gift I have by reciting and writing whatever was asked of me. This has enriched me and given me joy.; [a.] Washington, D.C.

AVETISSIAN, ANNA
[pen.] Anna Purple; [b.] 11-25-80, L.A., CA; [p.] Lucy & Sebuh Avetissian; [ed.] Plan to go to Columbia or Oxidental. Arshag Dickranian Armenian Private School; [occ.] High school student, age 15; [memb.] Columbia House; [hon.] Astronomy Award 2nd place; [oth. writ.] "Palm Trees," "Erase," "Salt," "Past the New," "Nothingness of a Violet," "The Noise of Falling," "Why do Angels have Wings," "Give me a Color," and "Hands Bleed." [pers.] "Never once in a silent assyulm would I find what I was looking for."; [pers.] Los Angelos, CA

AXELROD, SCOTT
[b.] April 21, 1976, Astoria, NY; [p.] Michael Axelrod and Ginny Levon; [ed.] I'm a Junior at Bloomington High School; [memb.] German National Honor Society, Delta Upsilon Phi, German Club; [hon.] I take A.B. English, I have received awards in Geometry, perfect attendance, and Principles Honor Roll, my G.P.A.B. 4.17; [pers.] I am a skilled writer. I like to write about what's going on around me. If I didn't have a skill in writing then I wouldn't be in Advanced Placement English for three years.; [a.] Rialto, CA

AYLISH, LISA ANE
[b.] Hong Kong; [m.] Scott Stovall; [ed.] B.A. in English, Majored in Creative Writing, University of Arizona, Certified Clinical Hypnotherapist; [occ.] Writer; [oth. writ.] I am currently working on a novel set in ancient Scotland; [pers.] Quality of life is important to me, the daily living of peace the giving of kindness. Treading lightly on the earth being as harmless as possible and standing in my truth. This is what is important.; [a.] Phoenix, AZ

BABBAGE, JACQUELINE
[ed.] B.S. with Honors from Rutgers University; [occ.] Registered Nurse; [hon.] Sigma Theta Tau, International Honor Society of Nursing; [oth. writ.] Poetry, Short Stories, Working on First Novel.; [pers.] Influenced by personal experiences, extensive travel, Eastern Religious, and the world of nature, Address: Lived for a time with my husband in his Homeland of Australia, we currently reside in Arizona.

BABIN, JEANETTE HOLMES
[b.] November 22, 1917, Winn Ph., LA; [p.] Joseph Wilson Holmes, Louisa McGlothin; [m.] (1) Gerald David Babin, November 8, 1936, (2) LaMar Donald; [ch.] Gerald Richard Babin, Priscilla Blake, Melanie Torbett, Deidre Babin; [ed.] Winnfield High, Louisiana Tech Rome, Largery Self-educated; [occ.] Homemaker; [memb.] Roman Catholic Church, Jonesville Woman's Club, United Daughters Confederacy, Mental Health Associations, Spiritual Frontiers Fellowship, Genealogical Associations, American Legion Auxiliary; [hon.] Service Awards, 50 years, Jonesville Woman's Club, 30 years, Catahoula Parish Library Trustee, Louisiana Soybean Festival 1961-1990, "Woman of the Year" Jonesville Jubilee Club, 1983, Modern Woodmen of American, Camp 2245, Jena, LA. 1993; [oth. writ.] Poems and articles published in local papers.; [pers.] I try to abide by the "Golden Rule", and most of my poems reflect some phase of the implications such a philosophy can foster.; [a.] Alexandria, LA

BADGER, RONALD W.
[pen.] Armand Badger; [b.] July 27, 1959, Holyoke, CO; [p.] Alice and Joseph, Marciniak and Bill Badger; [m.] Debra Lee Moroschok, March 1, 1980; [ch.] Rebecca, Priscilla and Matthew; [ed.] GEd, Some College, Intro. to Computers; [memb.] Knights of Columbus, St. Rose de Lima Church, Sacred Heart League Chiefs of Police Association; [hon.] Honorable Mention, and Golden Poet Award; [oth. writ.] Poems in American Poetry Anthology, and The Poetry of Life: A Treasury of Moments; [pers.] I would like to thank my sister Lorraine Chamberlain for getting me started, and life for making it happen.; [a.] Chicopee, MA

BAERWOLF, DEBRA
[b.] March 21, 1967; [p.] Donald and Shirley Wilken; [m.] Ricky Baerwolf, June 3, 1989; [ch.] Hunter John Baerwolf; [ed.] Fall River High, UW White Water; [a.] Fall River, WI

BAFFORD, AMALINE
[pen.] Amy; [b.] August 10, 1944, Alabama; [p.] Fred and Jerri Alley; [m.] Widow; [ch.] John, Deb, Otie, Shari and Tony; [ed.] G.E.D. attending Lincoln Land Community College in Springfield, IL; [occ.] Retired; [hon.] Local Campus Winner in Essay Contest; [pers.] Life is a poem, flowing rhyming and being created as a result of our daily actions.; [a.] Springfield, IL

BAGLEY, MARY
[pen.] Mary Rea Bagley; [b.] July 14, 1913, Frost, TX; [p.] Mr. and Mrs. W. E. Moore; [m.] Grady K. Bagley, July 14, 1985; [ch.] Dick Rea, Lonnie Rea; [ed.] Frost High School, Hillsboro Jr. College, Texas University, Austin, TX; [occ.] Retired; [memb.] Texas Retired Teachers Assoc., United Methodist Women; [hon.] Delta Kappa Gamma; [oth. writ.] Other poems, children's books, poems published local newspaper, "Uncle Sam's Story" and "The Gay Nineties" (written for local stage production); [pers.] I have enjoyed writing poetry in honor or memory of special people in my life.; [a.] Kemp, TX

BAHR, RUSS
[pen.] Russell Bahr; [b.] May 26, 1978, Dodgeville, WI; [p.] Don and Mary Bahr; [ch.] Mineral Point High School (Jr); [hon.] Best Poets Story; [oth. writ.] Poetry and story. In love to write both.; [pers.] My poems come straight from the heart. My parents are divorced and ever since then I have written poems of unbelievable power at the age of 17.; [a.] Mineral Point, WI

BAIGIS, BRIAN
[pen.] Brian Baigis; [b.] May 13, 1983, Scranton, PA; [p.] Edward and Susan Bowden Baigis; [ed.] Mid-Valley Elementary School; [occ.] Student; [memb.] 1. Boy Scouts of America (BSA) Troop #322, 2. Throop Little League - baseball, 3. Throop flag Football - football; [hon.] 1. 1993 Cub Scout or the Year Award Pack #73, 2. Physical Fitness Award 1993, 1994 and 1995, 3. Throop Little League 1994 and 1995 Champions, 4. 1994 Champions Throop Flag Football; [a.] Throop, PA

BAIRD, RICHARD
[pen.] Richard Baird; [b.] June 8, 1920, Pittsburgh, PA; [p.] Arthur Wood and Marjorie Ethel; [m.] Robbie Aletha Baird-Nee Smith, October 29, 1983; [ch.] Six mostly grown, one five years old; [ed.] High School and on Job Training Steel Industry, and Electronics; [occ.] Retired; [memb.] Church and Civic Center; [hon.] Honeywell Poet Laureate Poems Published on Cover of Periodical: (Honeywell Southern Connection) Won Grand Prize (1980) Honeywell National Contest (Winning Edge) other than Honeywell, I have not submitted entries to contests; [oth. writ.] A poetry collection approx. 80 poems: Entitled (Poetic Potpourri) A Potpourri of Poetry, Kaleidoscope of Hymn, Expression of Emotion, from the simple to sublime. Would like to discuss publication.; [pers.] I am retired (On fixed income) if you consider publishing, I can provides a manuscript.; [a.] Orange Springs, FL

BAIRD, JUDY NICOLE SOULES
[pen.] Nicole; [b.] September 29, 1958, Indiana; [p.] Joan E. Soules, Harold Soules; [m.] Joseph F. Baird, March 18, 1983; [ch.] Chase Baird, Jermaine Soules; [ed.] 2 yrs. College; [occ.] Secretary - Teacher; [memb.] PTA Boy Scotts; [hon.] Honor - having the love of Christ. Award (My family united.) (My world.); [oth. writ.] Manuscript, (ULISA), several poems, songs; [pers.] To achieve what my Lord put me here for. To bring love, and beauty to my world.; [a.] Lexington, KY

BAKER, ERIN
[pen.] Erin B.; [b.] January 4, 1974, Lewisburg; [p.] Ken Baker Jr., Melanie Russell; [ed.] Milton Area High, Penn College - (Williamsport PA); [occ.] Retail Sales Associate with Wireless one Network; [pers.] Writing poems is my way of expressing the feelings I hold inside. I write the words my heart speaks, Can you hear the meaning?; [a.] West Milton, PA

BAKER, NANCY VIOLA NELSON
[pen.] Nancy V. N. Baker; [b.] March, 1955, Washington, DC; [p.] Mr. & Mrs. William F. Nelson (biological parents), Mr. & Mrs. Arnold L. Pearson (raised by); [m.] Mr. Garrett T. Baker, 26 March 83; [ch.] Anjonette M. Brown (daughter), Antuan M. Adamson (grandson); [ed.] H.S. Diploma, some college education (6 credits); [occ.] Engineering Technician II, Fx Co. Dept. of Public Works, Project Engrg. Division; [memb.] Active member-Holy Light United Baptist Church, Member International Cake Society (ICES); [hon.] Received numerous awards of service and apprenticeship as a musician of the Holy Light United Baptist Church, Manassas, VA, Certificate of Completion of the Wilton Classes as a certified cake decorator in 1983; [oth. writ.] Many other poems that have been written, but never published, have been shared with my church family throughout the past years; [pers.] In all things I'd like to give thanks unto my Lord & Savior Jesus Christ who blesses me to be able to write the poetry I do. Because I can do all things through Him who gives me the strength, wisdom & knowledge. I give all Glory to Him. Special thanks to my pastor Rev. Barbara D. Vaughan who encourages and pushes me to be all I can be in Christ Jesus, and to my husband, a true man of God, who has always been by my side. In my writings I try to let the ears that hear and eyes that read know that "you've got to be born again by repenting of your sins, and totally selling out your soul to the Lord who gives eternal life through Jesus Christ."; [a.] Centreville, VA

BAKER, THERESA C.
[b.] July 15, 1966, Merced, CA; [p.] Cheryl Lovett, Lupe Gonzales; [m.] Jerry Baker; [ch.] Jackqueline Danyel, Alexandra Sky and Savannah Cheyenne; [pers.] We all walk thru life with one hand before us and one hand behind ready to grasp what may come and what may go. Longing for the satin touches. Tormented by the fiery touches; [a.] Atwater, CA

BALAN, TRAIAN ALEX
[b.] April 5, 1967, Romania; [p.] Teodor and Ana Balan; [m.] Simona Balan, June 27, 1992; [ch.] Victor-Alexander (1 son); [ed.] B.S. Chemical Engineering, Macromolecular Compounds Polytechnical University Bacharest, Romania, Europe; [occ.] Research Chemist Coating Industry, Chicago; [oth. writ.] Several poems published in local newspapers back in Europe, novels and short stories.; [pers.] In the chemistry of our lives money shouldn't be a catalyst, but love!; [a.] Chicago, IL

BALL, BRENDA SUE
[pen.] Kennedy, Miller, Robinson, etc.; [b.] November 28, 1957, Victoria, TX; [p.] Martha Jane McDaniel; [ch.] Micah, Trevor and goddaughter Shanna; [ed.] Various colleges (3 years); [pers.] To the giver of the gift, "Thanks". To the challenge from a friend to write again. To the support from those I worked with in Victoria, TX that helped me find myself once again. To the readers who will smile at my poem.; [a.] Fort Wingate, NM

BANERJEE, DIYA
[b.] September 30, 1986, Ontario, Canada; [p.] Dr. G. and Mrs. A. Banerjee; [ed.] 4th Grade; [occ.] Student, River Oaks Baptist School; [pers.] To do better than my best. I love piano and music.; [a.] Houston, TX

BARATELLI, JOE
[b.] May 3, 1960, Goondiwindi, Australia; [ed.] A.S., B.S. in Criminal Justice - St. John's University Queens, N.Y.; [occ.] Owner of Goondiwindi Tavern, Coram N.Y.; [oth. writ.] I've written "Skateorama" which is about a brutal roller skating game of the future. I've also written "Mama's Milk" - again a work of science fiction-tending to reinforce the tenets of La Leche League. Both writings remains unpublished.; [pers.] The process of finding a publisher still eludes me.; [a.] Coram, NY

BAREFOOT, DEBBIE
[b.] November 4, 1951, Fredricksburg, VA; [m.] Bruce Barefoot, July 31, 1983; [ch.] Seth Elliot; [ed.] Coats High School, Campbell University, BS Degree Elementary Ed.; [occ.] Teacher; [memb.] NEA - NCAF Teacher's Organization, MADD, Missing Children's Organization, American Red Cross (CPR, First Aid), Gospel Tabernade Choir; [hon.] Teacher of the Year (local), Dean's List, Gospel Tabernade Board Secretary, Sunday School Teacher for J. Luther Davis Class; [oth. writ.] Several dozens of poems published in church bulletins, school functions, local newspapers, etc.; [pers.] It is my desire to use the talent that have been given to me by God to glorify him and minister to hurting needy people.; [a.] Dunn, NC

BARKER, GINNY
[pen.] Boots McCoy; [b.] December 31, 1949, Baltimore, MD; [p.] Charles and Christine Watson; [m.] David D. Barker, August 26, 1988; [ch.] Jennifer, Thomas, Erika, Sarah and Lauren; [ed.] Dundee High, McHenry College; [occ.] Production Control Lockheed, Martin Marietta, GA; [memb.] Women in the Music Business; [oth. writ.] I have recorded a country album and wrote three songs it, plus other songs. I love singing and writing music, poetry and drawing.; [pers.] I write what I feel in my heart, on what I and others have experienced in "Life."; [a.] Marietta, GA

BARLIEB, KIRSTEN AMY
[pen.] Kirsten; [b.] February 1, 1969, Bethlehem, CT; [p.] Ned R. and Patricia A. Barlieb; [ed.] Licensed Cosmetologist, Kutztown University; [occ.] Assistant Manager at Hatboro McDonalds; [oth. writ.] Several poems written over the years; [pers.] I have enjoyed writing and sharing my poetry over the past ten years or more. Poetry is not something to be taught - it is an inborn talent.; [a.] Roslyn, PA

BARNETT, NELL JEAN
[pen.] Jean Wadsworth; [b.] October 3, 1933, Wichita Falls, TX; [p.] Otto and Pauline Wadsworth; [m.] Divorced; [ch.] Linda Gail, Phillip Brooks and Carol Jean (also four grandchildren); [ed.] Wichita Falls Senior High School; [occ.] Benefits Administrator, MBNA Information Services, Dalla, Texas; [memb.] The North Church, Beta Sigma Phi Sorority; [pers.] I want my writings to express love to others because God's love for me has been the healing power in every area of my life.; [a.] Farmers Branch, TX

BARNETT, AMANDA
[b.] March 10, 1983, Houston, TX; [p.] Pat and Jean Barnett; [ed.] Because I am 12 years of age I haven't completed High School or College, but I have graduate Atkinson Elementary and going to 7th grade; [hon.] President Academic Achievement Award, Presidential ISD Poetry Contest (Honorable Mention); [oth. writ.] Imagine Dark City, This Ocean, and Hello, which have not yet been published are same of my other work.; [pers.] I wish to achieve something positive early in my life, I find poetry a wonderful way.; [a.] Lake Jackson, TX

BARREIRO, MICHELLE LYNN
[pen.] Mishi; [b.] September 23, 1972, Lindenhurst, Long Island, NY; [p.] Thomas J. and Susan Cainflone; [m.] Frank D. Barreiro, October 9, 1994; [ed.] Certified Teacher in Computers, Insurance Agents, Network Specialist, Dance Instructor; [hon.] Dean's List Academic Honors; [oth. writ.] "Forever Holding Hands," "The Rose," "Our Miracle," "Life," "Of The Heart," "Warmth Of A Smile," "Endless Love."; [pers.] Also published by Hayden Publications, Harrisburg, PA. Thanks to Frank, my parents, grandma Louise, Tom, Jason, Scott, my in-laws, Lisa and Jennifer for giving me beautiful memories.; [a.] Naples, FL

BARRETT, ANN
[pen.] Hollen Bach; [b.] August 24, 1958, Hartford, CT; [p.] Louise Blake, Robert Hollen Bach; [m.] David Barrett, August 14, 1983; [ed.] B.A. Chemistry and English, Williams College (1980), Ph.D. - Food Engineering (1991), University of Massachusetts; [occ.] Research Engineer, US Army Natick RD and E Center, Natick, Mass; [memb.] Institute of Food Technologists, Audubon Society, Trustees of Reservations, Toastmasters Int'l.; [hon.] Army Achievement Award; [oth. writ.] Numerous scientific articles concerning food processes and physical properties; [pers.] Writing makes me view the world with greater clarity; [a.] Needham, MA

BARRIOS, MARTHA
[pen.] Martha Moore; [b.] July 5, 1971, Cuba; [p.] Martha and Reinaldo Barrios; [m.] Carlos E. Gonzales; [ch.] I'm pregnant (4 months); [ed.] High School, Medical/Office Assistant, Exec. Secretary Diploma, 1 year at college as a psychology; [occ.] Now an Executive Secretary for an stainless steel company in Miami; [memb.] American Cancer Assoc; [hon.] Two awards in my original country in the early age of 8 to 10 years, Best High School Student and I was interviewed by the Miami Herald (Newspaper); [oth. writ.] I wrote a short novels, and articles and also a 24 poems, love songs etc.; [pers.] I think that every one

is rich, because everybody here a treasure in his heart. And sometimes is the most valued thing that we can get in our lives.; [a.] Hialeah, FL

BARTLETT, BEVERLY HARRIS
[b.] 1/16/27, Atlanta, GA; [p.] H.D. and Mable Harris; [m.] Dr. G. Rayburn Bartlett, 12/19/48; [ch.] Donald Bartlett, Mike Bartlett, Glennis McDonald; [ed.] B.S. in Zoology University of GA - Athens, GA; [occ.] Homemaker; [pers.] First poem submitted. All poems inspired by the Holy Spirit usually during my prayer time 3 - 4 a.m.

BARTOSIK, SHERRY LEE ANN
[b.] September 22, 1970, Arlington, VA; [p.] Linda and John Bartosik; [ed.] Pursuing BS in Physics at California State Univ. Fresno will transfer to VC Santa Barbara for MS; [occ.] Laboratory Technician, Gymnastics Coach; [memb.] Society of Physics Students, USA Gymnastics, Central Valley Astronomy, AAAs, SPIN; [hon.] Accomplished Flutist; [pers.] My poem "Music Man" tells of a man who has strongly influenced my life because of his positive attitude, courage and talent. I hope as I live my life, I can follow in his foot steps in my chosen career.; [a.] Clovis, CA

BARWICK, DEBBIE
[b.] October 4, 1976, New Bern, NC; [p.] Carl and Mary Helen Barwick; [ed.] Pursuing a B.A. in English with a concentration in writing and a minor in Anthropology; [occ.] Full-time student at East Carolina University, Greenville, NC; [memb.] Board of Directors for wesley Foundation, member of Faith United Methodist Church; [hon.] Who's Who Among American High School Students 1991-1992, Deans List East Carolina University; [oth. writ.] Short stories, research material and several poems.; [pers.] Live out your expectations of others through yourself.; [a.] Greenville, NC

BASS, MARTHA
[b.] April 29, 1970, Phoenix, AZ; [p.] Carlson and Loretta Barnes Sr.; [m.] Darrell Bass, July 17, 1994; [ch.] Amber Liesel; [occ.] Housewife; [oth. writ.] Have written other poems but none have ever been published.; [pers.] I would like to dedicate the beginning to my husband Darrell.; [a.] Glendale, AZ

BASTEN, WILLIAM J.
[pen.] Brandon; [b.] London, England; [p.] Louise and Arthur; [m.] Yvonne, September 3, 1983; [ch.] Grant and Scott; [oth. writ.] Novel, published by Commonwealth Publications of Canada Romantic Novel "P.S. I Love You," released fall 1995.; [a.] Orlando, FL

BATES, RAY O.
[pen.] Rio Bates - Rob Roy Ray; [b.] August 17, 1941, Magnolia, MS; [p.] Enos and Wilma Bates; [ed.] Kentwood High, LA, LaSalle University; [pers.] If a new spirituality is to come on this earth, it will come as always, through poets. Most great works, including the Bible, the Vedas, the Talmud, were written by poets. Most poetry is inspired, and contains higher meaning. Since I cannot read writings by David or Daniel, or ordinary subjects, I read other poets. Same inspiration, just different expression.; [a.] Las Vegas, NV

BATEY, SHANE ROLYNN
[b.] September 2, 1969, McAlester, OK; [p.] Kenneth and Julie Batey; [m.] Crystal Batey, July 2, 1992; [ch.] Laramie Danielle; [ed.] Sasakwa High, Murray State, Seminole Jr. College, U.S. Air Force; [occ.] Truck Driver; [memb.] American Paint Horse Assoc.; [hon.] V.S. Air Force Commendation Medal, Good Conduct Medal, National Defense Service Medal; [oth. writ.] Several poems unpublished.; [pers.] I like to write about friends, family and country life.; [a.] Sasakwa, OK

BATSON, GRACE
[b.] January 13, 1968, Georgetown; [p.] Eileen Batsone, Carlyle Batson; [ch.] Jamaal Raphael Holdex, Twanda Ayiesha Holder; [ed.] New Amsterdam Multilateral Cyril Potter College of Education University of Cuyana; [hon.] Participant of World University Games 1993 Part of Cuyana, Presidents XI Female Basketball Team to barbados; [pers.] Each individual is a unique work of God. Created with great potentials, just waiting to explode. All we need is the patience to shape our destiny. Poverty is a state of the mind.

BEASLEY, KEVIN O.
[b.] March 1, 1970, Anderson, SC; [p.] Roy and Rose Beasley; [ed.] Barnwell High School, Stetson University; [memb.] Palmetto Leadership; [hon.] Dean's List; [a.] De Land, FL

BEAUBRUN, JOANNE
[pen.] Jo, Jo; [b.] October 12, 1974, Castries, St. Lucia; [p.] Eugenia and Joseph Beaubrun; [ed.] White Plains High, North Carolina Central University, Westchester Community College; [occ.] Student; [hon.] Dean's List; [oth. writ.] Published poem in School Literary Magazine called Ex-Umbra.; [pers.] I write to express my feeling like a paint brush on canvas painting a picture with many colors which becomes clearer over time with past and present experiences. I've been influenced by the writings of Edgars Allan Poe.; [a.] White Plains, NY

BECHER, DAVID L.
[pen.] Biffy; [b.] February 24, 1962, Lansing, MI; [p.] Robert and Sharon Becher; [m.] In Prayer's Carol Davis; [ch.] Amanda Rose, Kelly Michelle; [ed.] Carson City Crystal High; [occ.] Plastic Process Engineer; [oth. writ.] Several poems working for Book Publication and also Involvement with Long Ridge Writers Group.; [pers.] The gift of writing my most deepest thoughts has been mostly influenced by the best selling book - the Bible.; [a.] North Ravenna, MI

BECKER, EVA L. RODGERS
[b.] December 22, 1934, Waynesboro, PA; [p.] Leo and Becky Rodgers; [m.] Michael J. Becker Sr., August 11, 1979; [ch.] Pamala K. Theinert, Matthew Becker and Grandson Eric Pappas; [ed.] 10th Grade William Penn. Senior High School, York Penn.; [occ.] Homemaker; [hon.] First Prize of the 3 Junior Heights, York Penn, 9th Grade; [oth. writ.] Published "A Little Girl Sees God." World Book of Poetry 1980-81. Recorded two songs written, words and music by myself, in Nashville 1977. "I still can feel his hands on me" and wondering where you are"; [pers.] I write about friends, family, nature. At the present time processing a book of poetry for publication, titled "Daddy and Me" Dedicated to my Dad who inspired me to write, to "speak my heart on paper." My poem is dedicated to my grandson Eric Pappas.

BECKER, NICKI
[b.] June 13, 1979, Pottstown, PA; [p.] James Becker and Ruth Wren; [ed.] Boyertown Area Senior High 11th grade; [memb.] Key Club; [hon.] Presidential Academic Fitness Award, 2nd Place Award for Key Boarding for Future Business Leaders of America, High Honors throughout High School; [pers.] I believe individuality and uniqueness are very important in writing, and also, in people.; [a.] Boyertown, PA

BECKER, ROBERT D.
[b.] June 19, 1938, Braddock, ND; [p.] Hubert and Florence Becker; [m.] Gracia M. Becker, June 6, 1959; [ch.] Daughter 35, Bobbi Gray Becker; [ed.] Master of Arts in English California State University Los Angeles 1970; [occ.] Assistant Professor of English, Standing Rock College, Fort Yates ND; [memb.] Bismarck State College Alumnae Association; [oth. writ.] The Cloverdale Review of Criticism and Poetry Morgan, John H. Ed., Bristol IN: The Cloverdale Library, 1993, "Prints of Darkness," 123.; [pers.] Wisdom is the synthesis of truisms we all know into universal verities under which we all must live, succeeding or perishing depending upon the choosing, as we all know of the sun, but not all heed the light.; [a.] Bismarck, ND

BEDNARSKI, ANDREW
[b.] October 25, 1978, Warsaw, Poland; [p.] Janusz and Izabella Bednarski; [ed.] High School Student, Sophomore; [occ.] High School Student, Penn High School in Mishawaka, TN; [memb.] United States Fencing Association; [hon.] Finalist of United States Fencing National Championships Division II in Sabre 1995; [oth. writ.] Story published in newspaper "Gwiazda Polarna" Chicago 1989; [a.] Mishawaka, IN

BELARMINO, GINO
[b.] July 7, 1978, Manila; [p.] Norma and Gilbert; [ed.] In the 11th grade at Union Catholic in Scotch Plains; [occ.] Cashier; [hon.] Graduated Valedictorian in grade 8 constantly as at student from 1st grade to 8th grade; [oth. writ.] School Paper; [pers.] In order to be truly happy you must first be totally happy with yourself.; [a.] Irvington, NJ

BELL, DONNA M.
[b.] March 2, 1947, Woodbury, NJ; [p.] Frank T. and Lillian Smith; [m.] William G. Bell III, September 18, 1982; [ch.] Kimberly M. Bell and Thomas W. Bell; [ed.] High School; [occ.] Housewife, although currently, Home Schooling Children; [oth. writ.] Only in Church newspaper book in "Go's". Unfortunately poem was lost, had one published "Shore Mall Walkers" newsletter; [pers.] I have a strong belief in God. I write mostly about what I've felt or dealt with; [a.] Egg Harbor Township, NJ

BELL, JULIAN WARREN
[pen.] J. W.; [b.] February 13, 1986, Memphis, TN; [p.] Dianne Bullock-Bell; [m.] Divorced (Earl Bell-father); [ed.] Julian is a 4th Grader at Lorin Eden Elementary School in hay ward, CA His principle's name is Ms. Eades; [hon.] Julian received numerous Citizenship award in 3rd grade; [oth. writ.] Julian has written other poems such as "The Cat" "Mr. Man" "Black History" "Old Man" (I would like to find out

how I can get these poems published through your company-Pease write back-thank you).; [pers.] Julian was born prematurely weighing one pound. He has A.D.D. with a learning disability, but it has not stopped him from being a "fighter" with a determination to not fall through the cracks of the school system. He wants to be accepted and will let nothing stand in his way. He loves Langston Hughes "Dream Variations."; [a.] Hayward, CA

BELL, LINNEA M.
[b.] April 2, 1961, Virginia, MN; [p.] Roland Lamke and Jean Lamke; [m.] Robert L. Bell, December 10, 1994; [ed.] Gilbert High School, Gilbert, MN, Valencia Community College, Orlando, FL, AA degree, University of Central Florida, Orlando, FL, pursuing Accounting Degree (BA); [occ.] Chiropractic Assistant; [memb.] Phi Kappa Phi (National Honor Society) First Baptist Church, Orlando, FL; [oth. writ.] Many other unpublished poems; [pers.] My writings reflect the people in my life and their circumstances, as well as my own personal experiences.; [a.] Orlando, FL

BELMORE, JULIANA
[b.] September 25, 1977, Detroit, MI; [p.] Donna Jaime, James Belmore; [ed.] East Detroit H.S., just starting the University of Michigan; [occ.] Artist - currently going for a joint degree in Scientific Illustration and Biology; [hon.] Sanderlean Award, Scholastic Silver Key, Macomb Art Center, Art Craft, Varsity Letter - Softball, Warren - Janet Pierce Memorial Scholarship, Siena Heights Scholarship, Sunflower Festival Awards; [pers.] Dedicated to all the people whom have helped me. Especially Ms. Veronica Russell, Mr. Will Rohloff and Mrs. Lucy Ludwig and my grandparents. I search for something new to write about from daydreams that I had as a child, the local grocery store and almost anywhere I find people or nature. Ideas are something that you are born with, they are impossible to teach how to find.; [a.] Warren, MI

BENNETT, DEMARKO
[b.] September 4, 1977, Birmingham, AL; [p.] Nancy Bennett; [ed.] As of this year High School 1995 graduate of Tarrant High School; [occ.] College Student; [oth. writ.] Varieties of songs, poems, and raps.; [pers.] Focus on the present not the past. Because the present will forever be with you. But concerning the Past you can never do what you have done. MY philosophy in life. Feel free to make it your on.; [a.] Birmingham, AL

BENNETT, JENNIFER MARIE
[b.] August 27, 1980, Utica, NY; [p.] William Bennett, Carol S. Bennett; [ed.] Sauquoit Valley Central School; [occ.] Student, Sophomore Sauquoit Valley High School; [memb.] Christ Child Society Volunteer, Multiple Sclerosis; [hon.] National Junior Honor Society, High School Honor Roll, Who's Who Among American High School Students; [pers.] Favorite saying - "All the world is a stage, and this is not a dress rehearsal."; [a.] Sauquoit, NY

BENNETT, MICHAEL E.
[b.] October 12, 1956, Hammond, IN; [p.] Pauline and Omar Bennett; [ed.] Tulane University B.S. Graduate work University of Chicago; [occ.] Research Asst., UIC Psychiatric Institute; [memb.] The Chicago Council on Foreign Relations, the Art Institute of Chicago; [hon.] Phi Eta Sigma, Dean's List; [oth. writ.] Poems published in DMDA Anthology (1988) and AMI Newsletter 1991. Screenplays: "College Dreams" and "Summiting", a first draft work.; [pers.] I have been influenced by American poets: Emerson, Therau, Frost, E. E. Cummings and TS Eliot to name a few. My writings reflect my feelings toward nature and reactions to it.; [a.] Chicago, IL

BENNETT II, RUSSELL J.
[b.] March 22, 1984, Niagara Falls, NY; [p.] Patrice Joseph, Russell Bennett; [ed.] Currently Attending Lewiston Porter Middle School; [memb.] Member of Presti's School of Karate; [pers.] While attending Sacred Heart School, I was inspired to write this poem.; [a.] Youngstown, NY

BERG, MARCIA
[pen.] Marcia Berg; [b.] June 24, 1951, Columbia, OH; [p.] Theodore Rector and Lillian Rector; [m.] Nicholas Berg, November 19, 1977; [ch.] Traci Somerlade and Marcia Nieport; [ed.] Madonna University; [occ.] Registered Nurse, William Beaumont Hospital, Royal Oak, MI; [memb.] Oncology Nursing Society; [hon.] Sigma Theta Tau, Kappa Gamma PI, "O'Neill Award for Humanistic Nursing"; [pers.] Poetry is a vehicle of community that innately inspires reflection.; [a.] Farmington Hills, MI

BERNTSEN, THOMAS
[b.] August 6, 1965, New York; [p.] Joanne and Ragnvald Berntsen; [ed.] B.A. Utica College of Syracuse University (88) in Mathematics, M.S. Indiana University (91) Math Education, currently working on Doctorate at UMASS (University of Massachusetts) in Math, Science and Instructional Technology; [occ.] Mathematics and Science Teacher at Wilmington High School in Wilmington, VT; [pers.] Dreams become reality with hard work and God's help!; [a.] Brattleboro, VT

BERRY, DAVID H.
[b.] February 7, 1955, Columbus, OH; [p.] William O. Berry (Deceased), Dorothy L. Berry; [m.] Tina S. Berry, September 25, 1992; [ed.] Graduate 1974, Walnut Ridge High School (Columbus Ohio) - Franklin University Business Administration (Major), Journalism (Minor); [occ.] Security Officer, Burn's International; [memb.] World Harvest Church and Redeemer's Church; [oth. writ.] Twice Published in Columbus Dispatch column "Cleric's View" in Summer 85 and January 86 while serving as Lay Speaker and Youth Fellowship Leader in the United Methodist Church; [pers.] Don't give up on true love. It's well worth the wait. I proudly dedicate this poem to my wife Tina whom "true love" is all about.; [a.] Columbus, OH

BERRY, DONNA
[pen.] Donna M. Berry; [b.] February 2, 1959, Springfield, MO; [p.] Floyd and Elsie Litle; [m.] Mike Berry, June 16, 1978; [ch.] William Michael, Tonya Florane, Trina Marie; [ed.] Willard High, Rutledge College; [occ.] Bookkeeper for Mike's Ozark Mountain Express; [memb.] Del Prado Baptist Church; [hon.] Who's Who Among Student in American Junior Colleges, Summa Cum Laude, Deans List; [pers.] Being a Christian and having a loving family make life more enjoyable and also easier to face the struggles that come my away.; [a.] Springfield, MO

BERRY, SCOTT MARTIN
[b.] January 26, 1954, Cook County, IN; [p.] Keith Martin and Lois Herbert Berry; [m.] Emma Jane Berry, May 31, 1975; [ch.] Crystal Hope, Monica Jeanette, (grandson) Christian Leon; [ed.] High School Graduate, L.D.S. Seminary graduate completed 2 years of College; [occ.] Leadman; [hon.] Descendant of Jamestown Settlers, Descendant of Utah (Matin), Handicraft Pioneers; [oth. writ.] Numerous poems and short stories.; [pers.] I write to express my intermost thoughts and feelings.; [a.] Ogden, UT

BERRY JR., FRANKLIN P.
[b.] July 4, 1965, Jamaica; [p.] Bettye and Franklin Berry Sr.; [m.] Jeanette Berry, July 16, 1994; [ed.] Benjamin N. Cardozo High School, S.U.N.Y. Old Westbury, B.S. Marketing, Business Management; [occ.] Elmcor Health, Aids Coordinator; [memb.] B.A.A.M. - Vice Chairperson; [hon.] Who's Who Among American High School Students; [oth. writ.] Several poems published during employment in community based Organizations Newsletters; [pers.] In my poetic writings, I have strived to luminate truth, in hope that all of humanity returns to the creator to avoid its complete destruction.; [a.] Bronx, NY

BESS, THELMA A.
[pen.] Thelma A. Bess; [b.] April 28, 1908, McCool, MS; [p.] Walter Phillip Atteberry (Deceased); [m.] Hattie Clarke Atteberry (Deceased), December 29, 1935; [ch.] Catherine Ann Bess (Camden), Paula Gay Evans (step-daughter), have three grandchildren and four great-grand children; [ed.] 12th Grade; [occ.] Retired Legal Secretary after 52 years in Circuit Court and Springfield Court of Appeals; [memb.] Athena Study Club, retired Murray Lane Baptist Church, Sikeston, Missouri was active in Cape Girardeau, Mississippi County and Scott County Legal Secretaries until I retired from work in 1976, Office of President, Secretary and Governor; [hon.] In 1968 was selected as first Legal Secretary for the State of Missouri, Artist in Albuquerque, New Mexico

BEVELACQUA, ARMANDO
[b.] December 20, 1956, West Palm Beach, FL; [p.] Salvatore Hillian Bevelacqua; [ed.] A.S. Degree - Currently finishing a BA in Five Protection Engineering; [occ.] Lieutenant/Pavawedie; [memb.] Local Emergency Planning Committee (LEPC); [oth. writ.] Books! Prehospital Documentation Hazauduous materials Medical Technician.

BIEN-AIME, YVES
[b.] January 16, 1949, Port-Au-Prince, Haiti; [m.] Charlotte Rameua Bien-Aime, May 3, 1975; [ch.] Yves Yori Bien-Aime (19), Steve Lori Bien-Aime (13); [ed.] St. Joseph's University, Phila, PA., ED. Foreign Languages Universite' Du Quebec, Quebec, Canada, BS. Accounting Universite' D'Etat D'Haiti, P-Au-P, Haiti Law; [occ.] Auditor, Consultant, Teacher, Foreign Languages, Teacher Washington Twp, N.J.; [memb.] PICPA Pennsylvania Institute of CPA's, AIM - Association for the Improvement of Minorities, NABA National Association of Black Accountants; [oth. writ.] "UN Avant - Gout De Planification Financiere" (A Foretaste of Financial Planning) is a guide to financial planning in America. A tool for acquainting newcomers to the American Financial System.; [pers.] I have been greatly influenced and deeply marked by early extensive studies of Greek, French and Haitian literature.

BIGGS, ANNA LOU
[pen.] Anna Lou Biggs; [b.] September 1, 1910, Oklahoma; [p.] Lou and Ruth McNeill; [m.] Cecil F. Biggs, November 5, 1931; [ch.] Four living children, two deceased; [ed.] High School; [occ.] House wife; [memb.] Southern Baptist Church Woman's Missionary Union Former Sunday School Teacher, Active Class Member Senior Adult Reporter; [hon.] Many poems in Church Sr. Adult News letters. Read 2 original poems at a Church Group of 1100 people; [oth. writ.] Nothing published a large note book full of poems ad writings.; [pers.] I am 85 years old and have been a widow for 34 years, raised 6 children - now have 1 son 3 daughters, 17 grand children, 9 great grand children always lived in Okla.; [a.] Oklahoma

BILLS, MARGARET
[b.] October 23, 1916, Saint Charles, MO; [p.] Robert Beste, Margaret Beste; [m.] Fred Mentzel, February 22, 1936, (Deceased 1961), Charles Bills, October 20, 1962; [ch.] Mary Jane Mentzel, David, Allen, Fred Mentzel; [ed.] St. Charles High School, took several adult education classes several years in Typing, Shorthand Etc.; [occ.] Retired - Age 79; [memb.] Friedens U.C.C. Church in Warrenton, MO, Greater St. Louis Folk and Square Dance Assn. - Greater St. Louis League of Square Dance Clubs - First Capitol Squares of St. Charles, MO; [hon.] I took part in the Senior Olympics in St. Louis, MO, for 10 years and won Gold, Silver and Bronze Medals in Horseshoes 50-100-200 Meter Dashes, Rope Skipping-Basketball 6 Mile Walk and 1 Mile Walk; [oth. writ.] Wrote many articles for square dance publications. Presently, I am starting a book for my children, grand children and great grand children; [pers.] I enjoy people, proud of my family I believe you need youth around you to keep from growing old.; [a.] Warrenton, MO

BINGER, MARY ANNE
[b.] December 24, 1942, Utica, NY; [m.] Robert E. Binger Sr., July 5, 1975; [ch.] 3 Erin Lynn, Eric Lee and Debbie; [ed.] H.S. and Bus. College; [occ.] R.E. Broker; [memb.] American Cancer Society Humane Society; [hon.] R.E. Awards, Art Awards, Design Awards in Cosmetology; [oth. writ.] Many non-published, write for a hobby, several over the years published in local papers; [pers.] Life's greatest gifts are appreciation of nature and the love of animals from which we gain insight to our most purposeful means for over meager existence.; [a.] Vacaville, CA

BINTNER, GEORGE R.
[b.] January 14, 1961, Lansdale, PA; [p.] George Bintner and Barbra Bintner; [m.] Denise Bintner, July 25, 1981; [ch.] Jacob Matthew, Rachel Elizabeth; [ed.] North Penn High, North Montco Voltech; [occ.] Carpenter, Part Time Musician and writer; [pers.] My reflections are of the goodness of nature and the goodness of mankind on earth.; [a.] North Wales, PA

BIRD, MARY ELLEN A.
[b.] May 28, 1922, Philadelphia, PA; [p.] Martin and Catherine Kelly; [m.] Donald W. Bird, March 15, 1947; [ch.] Mary Catherine, Donna Geralyn, (5 grand kids); [ed.] St. Margaret's - Narberth PA, John W. Hallahan Catholic Girls High - Phila., PA, Pierce College of Business Phila. PA; [occ.] Retired; [memb.] Fleet Reserved Aux. 39yrs., Business and Professional Women 35 yrs., VFW - Ladies Auxiliary 5yrs., Nat'l Assoc. Retired Fed. Imply, Amer. Cancer Society (15yrs Volunteer 42yrs); [hon.] 1980 - "Woman of the year" Key West FL. Bus. and Professional Women's Club. Key to the City - Twice 1975 and 1979 - Key West. FL. Nominated for mayor Key West, FL. (1984) Refused - Due to move to Calif. Numerous Plaques and Awards from Amer cancer Society over the years. For outstanding Service to my Community; [pers.] I learn many great things in my travels with my navy (submarine service) husband. I also met some famous Personalities and some not-so-famous, who contributed to my over-all outlook on life.; [a.] San Diego, CA

BISHOP, JEANIE
[b.] October 10, 1930, Oklahoma; [p.] William W. and Anna Fiessa; [m.] Billy (Deceased), 1953; [ch.] Danny and Linda; [occ.] Retired; [oth. writ.] Numerous unpublished poems. One of my poems was published in a Los Angeles paper with a relative's wedding announcement.; [pers.] Most of my poems reflects God's presence and love in my life. I thank him daily for my talent.; [a.] Phoenix, AZ

BISHOP, MARY BAINTER
[b.] November 22, 1963, Fort Dix, NJ; [p.] Hugh T. and Dorothy J. Bainter; [m.] Alfredo C. Bishop III, March 7, 1992; [ed.] B.S. in C.S., VPI and SU, M.S. in Technical Management, the Johns Hopkins University, G.W.C. Whiting School of Engineering; [occ.] Computer Systems Annalist, Westat Inc., Rockville, MD; [memb.] Potomac valley Assembly, Germantown, MD; [a.] Fredirick, MD

BJELLAND, EVELYN GALBRAITH
[b.] February 6, 1945, Joliet, IL; [p.] Henry B., Mary F. Galbraith; [m.] Milford Bjelland, April 25, 1970; [ch.] Scott, Anne; [ed.] Coal City High School; [occ.] Housewife; [memb.] Grundy County Farm Bureau; [pers.] I plan to write for children. Childhood is the most wonderful time of life and I hope to help make it so by writing.; [a.] Morris, IL

BLACK, BRYAN ROBERT
[b.] May 26, 1977, Lisbon, ND; [p.] Robert and Barb Black; [ed.] Graduated High School at Mahnomen High School, class of 1995, currently in Basic Training, RTC, Great Lakes, IL; [occ.] United States Navy, Seaman Recruit; [oth. writ.] Other sonnets, none published.; [pers.] My motivation comes from the heart. I witness what's out there, and with my pen, I lay it out for the minds eye. Harmony with nature and the people within.; [a.] Mahnomen, MN

BLACK, DOROTHY HUNLEY MOORE
[pen.] Dorothy Hunley Moore Black; [p.] Hugh and Fanney Hunley; [m.] Delphia Moore - Clifford-Black; [ch.] Walter and David Moore; [a.] Terre Haute, IN

BLAGMON, VACHE NIERI
[pen.] Che; [b.] November 24, 1981, Washington, DC; [p.] Col. Lowell E. and Djuana B. Blagmon; [ed.] Currently a 9th grader in advanced classes at Eleanor Roosevelt High School, Science and Technology Program. I've been enrolled in the talented and gifted Program ever since 2nd grade; [occ.] Part-time baby sitter and Student Assistant at the Univ. of Ark. (at little Rock); [memb.] Super-H's 4-H teen Club, Seaton Memorial AME Church Jr. Usher Board; [hon.] Some of them are: Perfect Attendance, GPA of 4.0 or Higher, Honor Roll every year since Elementary School. (3.0 or higher), Spanish Student of the year, 1st place in (3) Regional State or Chestra Competitions, and Grand Champion in 4-H Demonstration; [oth. writ.] Some are poems, "A Grandmother to Me," "The Master Creator," "Best Friends," and "Peace, Love and Harmony," and a short story, the Permanent Grove. I also co-authored a Church Christmas play.; [pers.] The most special thing about me is I'm a God-loving, well rounded girl. I play basketball, violin, and piano. I'm involved in 4-H, and participate in many such activities. I'm an excellent student, and down-to-earth person who has been blessed with the special ability of creative writing.; [a.] Lanham, MD

BLANCHARD, CHRISTOPHER
[pen.] Chris Red; [b.] November 11, 1980, Portsmouth, VA; [p.] Cynthia Lynne Curtis, Jean O. Blanchard; [ed.] Landstown Middle School, Ocean Lakes High; [occ.] Student, Artist, Apprentice; [memb.] FEA; [hon.] Outstanding Drawing Achievement, Top Drawing and Short Story Award; [pers.] Failure as your only fear can make you the best at what you do.; [a.] Virginia Beach, VA

BLAND, CALVIN
[b.] July 6, 1948, Chicago; [p.] Edward and Margaret Bland; [m.] Renee Bland, May 24, 1985; [ed.] De La Salle, High School B.A. and B.S. Easter New Mexico University Portale New Mexico, University of Texas in ElParo B.A. Crumal Justice; [occ.] Paralejal/Specialist Legal/Medical Law; [memb.] ZBT's at Eastern New Mexico University, Volunteering American, MBA; [hon.] Criminal Justice Society of Texas, International Political Society of Foreign Affairs in New Mexico and M.D.C.; [oth. writ.] The american shut collection.; [pers.] The individual dual concepts of thought of freedom in Societies forms of change. Which helps or stop the growth of idea within American. That is the process of life throughout American.; [a.] Chicago, IL

BLAYLOCK, PATRICIA
[pen.] "T"; [b.] December 14, 1953, Betheseda, MD; [p.] Kenneth and Dona Blaylock; [ed.] Corning High School (Corning, AR), Saint Louis College Pharmacy (Saint Louis, MO); [occ.] Pharmacist-Pharmacist Consultant; [memb.] National Labor Day, Arkansas Pharmacist Association, Habitat Humanity, National Wildlife Fed.; [hon.] Young Career Woman Year (B and PW Cunning, AR, 1978); [pers.] I have faith in the American people I believe that "we" will continue, we will succeed and we will live in a world made better by our presence.; [a.] Lakeview, AR

BLINCOE, ANNA LEE
[b.] 8/1/1914, Mead County, KY; [p.] Joseph & Eva Valentine Rodgers; [m.] William C. Blincoe (deceased), January 30th, 1936; [ch.] eleven; [ed.] high school graduate with one year college at Spaulding College. Severe arthritis prevented me from continuing. [occ.] retired; [oth. writ.] Several poems published in local papers, other awards for poems with World of Poetry Contest: Gold and Silver Certificates, one essay in Trinity Mission Magazine.

BLIZZARD, KIMBERLY DIANE
[pen.] Kimberly Blizzard; [b.] February 4, 1981, Fayetteville, NC; [p.] Bardon Blizzard Jr., and Diane Blizzard; [ed.] Westridge Elementary, Woodridge Middle, Starting at Osbourn Park High School; [occ.]

Babysitter/Student; [memb.] National Junior, Honor Society; [hon.] Extra ordinary Effort in Mathematics (Algebra), and the Presidents Award for Academic Achievement, Educational Excellence; [oth. writ.] No other Published writings.; [pers.] I write to show my feelings toward life, family, and friends. I have been influenced by my parents, brother, and grandma.; [a.] Woodbridge, VA

BLOCK, JENNIFER
[pen.] Jenny Block; [b.] November 2, 1957, New York, NY; [p.] Albert Block, Peggy Block; [ed.] McBurney High School, BA Fordham University, MS Fordham University; [occ.] Student, HB Studio for acting - Newyork, NY; [hon.] 1973 - Board of Education VDC 114Q, Certificate of Merit Award 1976, McBurney School Service Pin, 1980 Lincoln Square Neighborhood Center Award Certificate; [oth. writ.] Another poem published in Memories Anthology, letter to the Editor published in writer's journal.; [pers.] The poem "My Friend" was written for my good friend Pam who is presently struggling with Leukemia who is in need of a bone morrow transplant.; [a.] New York, NY

BLOOM, RUTH ANN
[b.] January 18, 1965, NE; [p.] Arthur L. and Elsie E. Ham; [m.] Dan S. Bloom, March 26, 1988; [ch.] Jason, Nicole, Miranda, Daniel; [pers.] I wrote forever for my husband Dan who is my forever love.; [a.] Boise, ID

BODELL, JANET
[b.] October 22, 1947, Detroit, MI; [p.] Frank and Irene Parada; [m.] John E. Bodell, June 15, 1973; [ch.] Dawn Bodell; [ed.] A.D.N/R.N. Macomb County Community College; [occ.] Nurse Administrator; [memb.] Secular Franciscan Order, St. Bonaventure Fraternity; [hon.] Summa Cum Laude—MCCC; [oth. writ.] For Love...An Inspiration 1993 (a Christmas story), several articles in local newspapers; [pers.] I strive to go from Gospel to Life and from Life to Gospel in the Spirit of St. Francis of Assisi.; [a.] Grosse Ile, MI

BODINE, WILLIAM A.
[pen.] William A. Bodine; [b.] November 19, 1967, Silver Spring, MD; [p.] James C. Bodine and Mary Jane Chapman; [ed.] Frederick High, Montgomery College; [occ.] Computer Systems Analyst, AT&T; [memb.] Concerned Women for America; [oth. writ.] Several poems not published, article for USA today.; [pers.] To the glory and honor of our great God and Savior, Jesus Christ.; [a.] Rockville, MD

BOGUCKI, BARBARA
[b.] January 19, 1982, Bettendore, IA; [p.] Robert and Dawn Bogucki; [occ.] Student; [oth. writ.] Short stories and other songs and poems all non-published; [pers.] I was born with birth mark on 1/3 of my body, at age 3 became blind in on eye. There are many things people said I wouldn't be able to do so I try to do as much as I can poem writings is just one of those things.; [a.] Dawson, PA

BOJANOWSKI, GLORIA J.
[pen.] Gloria Jean Howe; [b.] February 2, 1952, Albany, NY; [p.] Warren Howe, Dolores Howe; [ch.] Phillip and Rebecca; [ed.] Maple Hill High, College credits in Data Processing; [occ.] Project Supervisor; [memb.] National Association of Female Executives (NAFE); [oth. writ.] Other personal poems - never submitted for publication; [pers.] I've learned to view each of my experiences (good and bad) as possibilities for self - improvement.; [a.] Castleton, NY

BOLYARD, CELIA W.
[b.] December 10, 1928, Middletown, NY; [p.] Deceased; [m.] Deceased; [ch.] Susan B. Miller, Curtis Bolyard, David Bolyard; [ed.] Randolph Central, 1945 Tompkins-Cortland Community College 1973. Empire State College 1976; [occ.] Real Estate Sales; [memb.] Writers Association of the Ithaca Area, First Unitarian Church, Ithaca Downtown Business Women, Women's Community Center, Ithaca Board of Realtors; [oth. writ.] First publication; [pers.] Influenced mostly by my mother, Sara Pulling Wicks, I have had a lifelong interest in poetry but recently I have found writing to be a wonderful way of expressing both joy and pain.; [a.] Ithaca, NY

BOO, JESSICA
[b.] August 17, 1983, W. Islip, NY; [p.] John, Theresa Boo; [ed.] Sylvan Ave Elementary Bayport, NY, James Wilson Young J.H. Bayport, NY; [occ.] Student 7th Grade; [memb.] Baymen Soccer League, Travel Team; [hon.] Merit Roll 6th Grade, James Wilson Young J.H.; [pers.] "Never give up."; [a.] Blue Point, NY

BOOTH, CHARLENE A.
[pen.] Char; [b.] November 5, 1947, Seattle, WA; [p.] Rita George, Charles Zissell; [m.] Bramwell G. Booth; [ch.] William C. Gallegos, Sabrina Ann, Bramwell G. Jr., Solana R.; [ed.] Got my GEd; [oth. writ.] I have written alot of my poetry and have a book that never has been published. But very much would like to have published.; [pers.] I always loved to write poetry. Alot of poetry. I write is how I feel about things and things that have occurred in my life.; [a.] Seattle, WA

BOOZE, PATRICIA
[b.] August 20, 1942, San Angelo, TX; [p.] Virginia Jennings; [m.] Widow; [ch.] Shawn P. O'Brien, Mike O'Neal; [ed.] El Reno High, El Reno Okla, Orange Coast College - L.V.N.; [occ.] Writing; [memb.] Oakridge Baptist Church - Friendly Lake Eusaula Arca Supporter (F.L.E.A.S.) V.F.W. Aux.; [oth. writ.] Poems published in get a journal - California Hwy Petrol Drug Pham., Marine Corp. Journal, Playboy, Alson Local papers.; [pers.] Most of my writings are of teachings us to accept ourselves as we are, The goodness of God's world.; [a.] Eufaula, OK

BORDELON, ROBYN
[b.] February 4, 1978, New Orleans, LA; [p.] Robert and Cindy Bordelon; [ed.] Currently a High School Senior at Destsrehan High School; [occ.] Aide in Eckerd Pharmacy; [memb.] Volley ball Team, National Honor Society, JROTC; [hon.] Military order of the World Wars Award, (ROTC) Two Years Varsity Letterman, Two Years Honor Roll; [a.] Destrehan, LA

BORILLA, MICHAEL A.
[pen.] Michael A. Barile; [b.] August 4, 1924, Fresno, CA; [p.] Angelo Barile and Julia Barile (Deceased); [m.] Virginia Borilla, May 26, 1947; [ch.] Carl James, Angelo Michael, Michael Gerard, Edward John, Howard Alan, Tamyra June Turney, Jeffrey Paul (Deceased); [ed.] California State University, Fresno, Pepperdine University, Los Angeles; [occ.] Retired teacher: Fresno Unified District Elementary and adult education, present: Senior Student Program, CSUF; [memb.] Life Member California, Scholarship, Federation, past member Phi Delta Kappa, past Education, Fresno Retired Teacher Association, California Retired Teacher Association; [hon.] Past president Phi Delta Kappa, California State University, Fresno, Recipient, Taft Fellowship, Robert A. Taft Institute of Government Seminar: Participant in NDEA English Institute, CSUF, recipient PTA Award, Master of Arts Degree SCUF, Member State Instructional Materials Advisory Committee, Master Teacher in Teacher Training Program; [oth. writ.] Poem: "Friends Forever," Booklet: The Mysterious Death of Jeffrey P. Borilla at Kern Medical Center on May 1986.; [pers.] I strive in my writing to affect the outcome, however trifling, or morally significant matters. I believe the true grandeur of humanity is found in moral elevation through words expressed from the heart, sustained, enlightened and embellished by the intellect of humankind.; [a.] Fresno, CA

BOST, BARBARA SAFRIT
[b.] November 7, 1938, Rowan, CO; [p.] Maude and Maude Safrit; [m.] Caleb Watson Bost III, October 20, 1958; [ch.] Caleb, Malaine, Deatry and Dana; [ed.] 10th grade; [occ.] Retired; [memb.] Pitts Baptist Church Concord, NC; [pers.] Influenced by poet Elizabeth Barnet Browning. I have wrote a lot of romantic poems for my husband, before his death in April 1994.; [a.] Kannapolis, NC

BOTNICK, ETHEL S.
[pen.] Eve Scrivener; [b.] July 7, 1916, Norwick, CT; [p.] Isaac and Bessie Seidman; [m.] Joseph Botnick (Deceased 1982), 1936; [ch.] Daniel, Frima (Braswell) Ralph, 10 grandchildren and 8 great-grandchildren; [ed.] B.A. University of Conn. 1967, (Part-time 6 years), Rider College 1934, University Conn. 1942, etc.; [occ.] Retired, Free-lance Writer; [memb.] Many; [hon.] Raised two Botanists, Editor-in-Chief, H.S. year book 1934, Medal English; [oth. writ.] Stringer and features Hartford courant, Jewish weekly news, column Stafford Press (40's), copy retail, real estate, movie (birth of a nation) review at age 8.; [pers.] Currently at work on two books reflecting the life and times of growing up Jewish in small-town New England. Environment and ecology are integrated in my writing.; [a.] Somers, CT

BOUTZ, CATHERINE
[pen.] Catherine Overstreet Boutz; [b.] November 20, 1951, KS; [p.] Ron and Mary Overstreet; [m.] Raymond C. Boutz, May 29, 1971; [ch.] Kirk D. Boutz; [ed.] Associate Arts Degree, Graduate Beginner and Advanced Courses - Institute of Children's Literature; [occ.] Executive Director, Arkansas River Valley Tourist Association; [memb.] Parnassus of World Poets; [hon.] Publisher's Choice Award - 1990 Watermark Press. 1992 International Who's Who in Poetry and Poet's Encyclopedia; [oth. writ.] A dozen poems published in state wide newspaper. Poems published in various anthologies. Short story in pockets. Articles in country; [pers.] I love life! I love to laugh and to help, others laugh! I try to find humor and enjoyment in everything. The creator has a wonderful sense of humor. We only must look to find it!; [a.] Dover, AK

BOWDEN, CHRIS M.
[pen.] Chris M. Bowden; [b.] November 15, 1979, Fort Falls, MT; [p.] Ron and Nora Bowden; [ed.] High School - Sophomore; [occ.] Student; [a.] Vaughu, MT

BOWEN SR., ROBERT E.
[b.] January 26, 1925, East Haven, CT; [p.] Ernest Bowen, Grace Bowen; [m.] Yolanda Dellaventura Bowen, July 17, 1948; [ch.] Robert E. Bowen Jr., Sean Mirar Bowen; [ed.] Bunniplag College, Hamden, CT; [occ.] Retired Personnel Mgr; [memb.] VFW (Life time member); [oth. writ.] Original poems on Christmas Cards or special occasions - for family members or close friends writer and editor of various company "House Organs"; [pers.] Be whatever you want to be - do whatever you want to do - just so long as it does not trespass on the rights of others; [a.] Trumbull, CT

BOWMAN, RANDY
[b.] April 26, 1957, Tulsa, OK; [p.] George and Sandra Bowman; [m.] Jennie Newport, July 21, 1989; [ch.] Christopher; [ed.] Adrian High School, Adrian, MO; [occ.] Gunnery Sergeant United States Marine Corps; [a.] Stafford, NA

BOYD, CHRISTY
[b.] April 17, 1980, Chester, PA; [p.] Thomas Boyd, Linda Boyd; [ed.] Red Lion Christian Academy and Paul M. Hodgson Vocational-Technical High School; [occ.] Full-time Student; [hon.] I achieved both Athletic and Academic Awards along with Artistic Awards as well. I've also achieved a perfect 4.0 grade point average several in School; [oth. writ.] I've kept a poetry journal since the age of seven, although this is my first publication.; [pers.] I try to use poetry, or any of my other God given talents, to the best of my ability. I've used poetry as a means of expression throughout my life.; [a.] Bear, DE

BRACK, SARAH
[pen.] Sarah Brack; [b.] April 7, 1981, Spokane, WA; [p.] Sandra and Manuel Brack; [ed.] Completed 8th Grade; [occ.] Student; [memb.] Save the Wolves Foundation; [hon.] 1. 1995 Visual Art Student of the Year, 2. 1995 Creative Writing Student of the Year, 3. President's Education Award - 1995, 4. 1993 1st Place Backstroke State Finals; [oth. writ.] Various poems and short stories; [a.] Orlando, FL

BRADFORD, PATRICIA A.
[b.] March 17, 1936, Scotland; [p.] John and Margaret Campbell; [m.] Gaylord M. Bradford, May 14, 1963; [ch.] Gaylord Bradford, David Bradford, Vicki Bradford; [ed.] High School Scotland; [occ.] Housewife; [oth. writ.] Several poems published by National Library Of Poetry.; [pers.] I strive to reflect the love God has for mankind in my poems.; [a.] Cherokee Village, AR

BRADLEY, ERIN
[b.] September 19, 1982, Maryland; [p.] Lesly Wilson and Billy Bradley; [ed.] Beauvior and Green Castle Elementary, White Oak Middle School; [occ.] Student; [memb.] Honor Roll, Softball; [hon.] Honor Roll, Writing Awards, Presidential Academic Achievement Award; [pers.] I write what I know, feel, and love. I try never to falsify my beliefs. My greatest influence is my family and the past.; [a.] Silver Spring, MD

BRADLEY, THOMAS A.
[pen.] Andrew B. Thomas; [b.] January 7, 1955, Philadelphia, PA; [p.] John J. and Ruth H. Bradley; [m.] Patricia Bradley, February 9, 1979; [ch.] Kimberly Ann and Justin; [ed.] Roxborough High, Cabrini College, Temple University; [memb.] Laubach Literacy Action/Literary Council Of Norristown, Associate Member Library of Congress, the Nature Conservancy; [oth. writ.] Several poems published in cryptic, and tree, as yet unpublished, short stories.; [pers.] My work primarily reflects an examination of my own feelings, mixed with a bit of imagination, and an abiding love of nature. Influencing poets: E.A. POE, T.S. Eliot.; [a.] West Conshohocken, PA

BRAGDON, SARAH
[pen.] Sarah Bragdon; [b.] April 21, 1981, Indianapolis, IN; [p.] Mark Bragdon and Pam Bragdon; [ed.] Lawrence Central High School (Freshman 1995); [occ.] Student; [memb.] Church at the Crossing, Indpls.; [hon.] Academic Honor Awards, First Place Music and Art Award (through school) Private Piano Contest, Superior Ratings; [oth. writ.] Poetry and fiction in my spare time.; [a.] Indianapolis, IN

BRALEY, OLETA
[pen.] Oleta Plow; [b.] July 19, 1944, Rochester, NY; [p.] Ruby and Horace Sullivan; [m.] Franklin (Deceased), 1967-1990 and 1990-1992; [ch.] James P. Plow and John P. Plow; [ed.] Charlotte High School; [occ.] Home health Aide Own Sales Business; [hon.] Certificate of merit draw me contests; [pers.] Special thanks to family and special friends who have inspired this poem.; [a.] Rochester, NY

BRAUNGER, BART
[b.] December 9, 1980, Omaha, NE; [p.] Bart and Irene Braunger; [ed.] Freshman, Millard North High School, Omaha, NE; [occ.] Student; [hon.] Duke University Talent Identification Program, Two Supervisor Honor Rolls, Joslyn Art Museum Student Art Exhibition, Student Council, Quality of the Mind Award, Martial Arts Award, Spelling Bee 2nd Place Award, United Sates President's Education Awards Program; [oth. writ.] Several poems published locally; [a.] Omaha, NE

BRENNER, LINDA S.
[b.] October 18, 1946, New Haven, CT; [p.] Francis and Evelyn Sweeney; [m.] Gregory R. Brenner, June 1966; [ch.] Amy, Lynn, Karin Sue, Richard Jason, Jason Scott, Joshua Patrick and Timothy Jared; [ed.] The Gateway School-New Haven, CT; [memb.] National Society Daughters of American Revolution; [oth. writ.] Several poems; [a.] North Guilford, CT

BREWSTER, FRANCES HOPE
[pen.] Chase Eden; [b.] December 22, 1978, Newport Beach, CA; [p.] Dennis Brewster, Nancy Brewster; [ed.] Arcadia High School; [memb.] Apache Pow Wao Newspaper; [hon.] Principal Honor Roll; [pers.] My life is my message - Ghandi; [a.] Arcadia, CA

BRIDGFORD, RICHARD K.
[b.] March 24, 1960, Anaheim, CA; [p.] Janet and Allan Bridgford; [m.] Susan Andrews Bridgford, June 18, 1988; [ch.] Allan Linley, Jacqueline Andrews, Alexander Richard; [ed.] Stanford Univ., B.A. Economics 1982, Stanford Law School, J.D. 1985; [occ.] Trial Attorney; [memb.] Orange County Bar Association, Pediatric Cancer Research, Board Member Food Distribution Center, St. Margaret's Episcopal Church, Christian Children's Fund; [hon.] High School Valedictorian, Orange County Scholar, Athlete of the Year 1978, Phi Beta Kappa Stanford 1982 graduated with 4.0 G.P.A., White House Legal Counsel's Office 1984, Board of O.C. Food Bank; [oth. writ.] Assorted poems and short stories; [pers.] Man at his highest is a creator. Man chooses. Man is responsible for his creations and the spiritual, psychological and emotional impact they have on his fellow creatures and himself. Try to create good.; [a.] Newport Beach, CA

BRIGHAM, SHIRLEY
[pen.] Shirley Conway Brigham; [b.] March 9, 1932, Amherstburg, Ontario, Canada; [p.] Annie and Lionel Conway; [m.] Aldrich Brigham; [ch.] Brian, Marilee and Douglas; [ed.] I am a graduate of General Amherst High School. Amher Stburg Ontario Canada; [occ.] Home maker; [memb.] Member of St. Paul AME affiliated with Messiah Episcopal Church; [hon.] A graduate of General Amherst High School. Amherstburg Ontario Canada; [pers.] I have been honored to receive the International Poet of Merit award by the International Society of Poetry. I strive to reflect Christian values in my writings. I have been honored to receive the International poet of Merit Award for (1995) nineteen ninety five by the International Society of Poetry.; [a.] Detroit, MI

BRIGIDI, RICHARD VINCENT
[b.] May 13, 1947, Philadelphia, PA; [p.] Frank Sr., Marian; [m.] Terri, September 21, 1974; [ch.] Vincent, Denna, Alaina; [ed.] Cardinal Dougherty High School; [occ.] Automotive Consultant; [oth. writ.] 3 poems published in the Philadelphia Daily News, 1. Contest Winner, 2. Articles Published in Automotive Magazine; [pers.] 1. Be fair to those that you meet on your way up - for you will meet those same people on your way down, 2. Timing is everything.; [a.] Huntingdon Valley, PA

BRINGHURST, STEPHEN
[b.] December 28, 1951, Boise, ID; [p.] Ron and Jeanine Bringhurst; [m.] Cora Lee (Downs) Bringhurst, April 25, 1980; [ed.] Nampa High, some College and Vo-tech, Boise State University, and Trade School, Electronic Computer Programing Institute, S.L.C. Utah; [occ.] Disabled Veteran; [hon.] 1st place in 1 of 2 Divisions - Natural Science in West Junior High, Nampa ID; [oth. writ.] Several earlier poems awarded certificates for entry in poem contest with World of Poetry, Sacramento, CA; [pers.] My poems are of personal experience and inspiration, and I frequently don't fully understand (especially long ones) my poems till I have read or recited them to others. I have done this also in Interlude tavern, 1st Thursday of month, Boise, ID with micro-phone.; [a.] Nampa, ID

BRINTON, MIGNON T.
[pen.] M'non; [b.] April 20, 1913, Salt Lake City, UT; [p.] Scott and Annie Torkeldsen; [m.] Norman J. Astle (Deceased), Elias L. Brinton, June 18, 1971, (to Elias); [ch.] Ross, Lynn, Brainna; [occ.] Retired at age of 82; [pers.] I love short to the point poetry. Become absolutely exhilarated when I discover even one word that transports my exact feeling through pen to paper. Heretofore unpublished, sister Fay McQuarrie insisted I enter contest; [a.] Salt Lake City, UT

BRIST, ED L.
[pen.] Samson Daniels; [b.] May 2, 1951, Tempe, AZ; [p.] Sid Brist and Juanita Hammerstrom; [m.] Dallas Sue Brist, July 10, 1971; [ch.] Two Great Danes; [ed.] High School Graduate; [occ.] Meteorologist; [hon.] Many Sports Awards, Phoenix Metro Area Bowling Champion 1984-1985; [oth. writ.] Short stories and poems.; [pers.] Poems was written for step father in Minneapolis, Minn. He loved the Vikings and Fran Tarkington. A big game between the Oakland raiders and Minn. Vikings was coming up with two of the best Q.B's, Kenny Stabler and Frand, to battle each other.

BROCK, ARDYTH
[pen.] A.S. Brock; [b.] August 19, 1950, Coudesport, PA; [p.] Annette Londe Brock and Walter Brock; [ed.] Allegany High School, Robert Morris College, American College in Jerusalem University of Maryland; [occ.] Counselor/Trainer; [memb.] Rotary Club of Kappa, Chamber of Commerce, HSTD, American Association of Counselors, Winners Camp Board of Advisors, Small Business Association; [hon.] Hawaii State Pookela Award for Literary; [oth. writ.] Articles for: 1) New woman magazine, 2) New age magazine, assorted collected work of poetry and prose.; [pers.] My poems are the chronicles of my heart. The magazine article I have written and published are directly from career experiences. I believe in freedom and autonomy and creative self expression.; [a.] Kapaa Kawai, HI

BROCKINTON, ASHLEY B.
[pen.] Brandi Brockinton; [b.] October 9, 1976, Shreveport, LA; [p.] Billy and Ann Brockinton; [ed.] Boston University Freshman; [memb.] National Honor Society Spanish Honor Society; [hon.] Salutatorian, CHS Class of '95, Star Student, Principal's Leadership Award, Captain's Award, Most Valuable Cheer leader, Tandy Technology Scholar All-American Scholar, Outstanding English Student Award, Far Est Cheer leading Champions, "All-Far East" Cheer Leader, Class Favorite, Best Personality, most Dependable, U.S. National Math and Science Awards, Renaissance Award, Sportsmanship Award, Reflections Contest Winner 1st place Literature, Senior Class poem "Here Together, Here Atlast."; [a.] Columbus, MS

BRODER, JOSEPH
[b.] April 9, 1923, New York City; [m.] Sylvia, June 15, 1946; [ch.] Scott, Ivy and Marcie; [occ.] Retired; [memb.] 1. 8th Air Force Historical Society, 2. 2nd Air Division, 3. DR Ahead (Navigator's Society), 4. 446th Bomb group - 707th Squadron, 5. Southern Wing, NY State; [hon.] A poem published in local newspaper, other in Membership Journals; [oth. writ.] Various poems and an as yet an unpublished Novel Contrails.; [pers.] The writer is Archives Officer of the Southern Wing. Poetry reflects world war II.; [a.] New York, NY

BRODEUR, JASON
[b.] May 4, 1972, Nashua, NH; [p.] Roger and Catherine Brodeur; [m.] Katie Brodeur, June 4, 1994; [ed.] Bishop Guertin High School, University of New Hampshire; [occ.] Printing; [memb.] Promise Keepers; [hon.] Graduated Cum Laude, BA in English; [pers.] God has given me a great gift - the ability to play with words. To him who is the author of life I give all the glory.; [a.] Nashua, NH

BROOKS, DEBORAH A.
[b.] November 8, 1947, Philadelphia, PA; [p.] Mildred and Rozell Pough; [m.] Cedric Q. Brooks, July 8, 1967; [ch.] Jacqueline R. Brooks; [ed.] Williams Penn High School; [occ.] Secretary, School District of Phila.; [pers.] Life and nature is my inspiration for writing poetry.

BROWN, AGNES MILLIE
[pen.] Bobo; [b.] March 1, 1955, Norfolk, VA; [p.] Agnes Alice Stokes; [m.] Alphonso Brown Sr., 1973; [ch.] 6, 2 girls and 4 boys; [ed.] Correspondence School graduate also took a course in Animal Care Correspondence School; [occ.] Housewife; [oth. writ.] I've also wrote other poems; [a.] Norfolk, VA

BROWN, ANN BEATRICE
[b.] August 5, 1965, Toronto, Ontario, Canada; [p.] Patricia and James Collins; [m.] Lawrence Lebeck (fiance), May 1996 upcoming; [ch.] Vanessa Lea Laurin (9), Kyle Brendon Laurin (6); [ed.] Georgian College of Applied Arts and Technology, Barrie, Ontario, Canada; [occ.] Registered Nurse, Emergency Room nurse at Texas Children's Hospital; [memb.] College of Nurses of Ontario, Canada, Board of Nurse Examiners for the State of Texas, American Heart Association; [hon.] Valedictorian, Dean's List; [pers.] To inspire we need inspiration. I attribute mire to the fact. I enjoy and appreciate life now. We don't have time to go back.; [a.] Houston, TX

BROWN, CALVIN REED
[pen.] Calvin Reed Brown; [b.] July 11, 1926, Koosharem, UT; [p.] David Acma Brown and Ethel Peterson Brown; [m.] Barbara June Jenkins Brown, December 24, 1948; [ch.] Cindy, Randy, Lisa and Tammy; [ed.] BA, MA, MD, CEPA, PhD.; [occ.] General Surgeon; [memb.] Utah Poetry Society, Screen Writers Guild, Screen Exyras Guild, Maude Man Babcock Society, Numerous Medical Organs 36 Committees; [hon.] Surgeon General NSAN, numerous writing on poetry prizes, silver beaver scouting Eagle Scout. Distinguished alumnus Snow Col; [oth. writ.] 50 Medical articles, 20 non-medical articles, 36 books, 6 published, 1. Philosopher in poetry, 2. The paradox, 3. Like the physician.; [pers.] Music and poetry make up an important part of my life. I feel sorry for anyone who had never expressed either 43 years Mormon and Absernacle Choir, 40 years barbershop singer.; [a.] Salt Lake City, UT

BROWN, DENISE
[pen.] Denise Kemery Brown; [b.] April 1, 1956, Warren, PA; [p.] Charles Kemery, Delores Redmond; [m.] Paul R. Brown, December 4, 1976; [ed.] Eisenhower High School; [occ.] Merchandising Supervisor and Housewife; [oth. writ.] I have many other poems and prose stashed in boxes and bundles around the house. None published; [pers.] Alone, yet not by myself smiling, yet crying without tears I have what I want but not what I need happy yet not content.; [a.] Russell, PA

BROWN, NICOLE
[b.] May 18, 1974, Effingham, IL; [p.] William and Mary Ann Brown; [ed.] Munford High School, University of Memphis; [occ.] Student; [hon.] National Honors Society, Dean's List; [pers.] Through writing, I try to express my thoughts and feelings - every work is a piece of myself. Poetry helps me make sense of my life and emotions.; [a.] Munford, TN

BROWN, ROBERT J.
[pen.] Peter S. Thompson; [b.] July 12, 1970, Philadelphia, PA; [p.] Joseph C. and Dorothy E. Brown; [ed.] Archbishop Wood HS, Bucks County Community College, Temple University; [occ.] Manager at McDonald's; [memb.] Temple University - WRFT AM Radio Station, DJ and Trafficking Director Secretary; [hon.] Award's from WRFT, "Most Improved DJ" and "Longevity Jack Award"; [oth. writ.] Several poems, one or two published in Temple University Literary Magazine. Several short stories: "Presence", "The Three Strangers", "Off Duty" and "Saturday Night Jamboree"; [pers.] My writings often reflect man's futile struggle against elemental forces of which he has no control over (somewhat similar to the writings of Franz Kafka and Thomas Hardy); [a.] Warrington, PA

BROWN, SHAVONNE
[pen.] Vonne Brown or Michelle Brown; [b.] September 16, 1978, Washington, DC; [p.] Sharon D. Butler; [ed.] Robert Goddard Middle School, Eleanor Roosevelt High School; [oth. writ.] Several other poems never published, unfinished stories.; [pers.] My poems reflect what's in my heart. I write about my thoughts and feelings.

BROWN, STEPHANIE J.
[b.] December 23, 1965, France; [m.] Arnold Brown; [ch.] Jereme and Heather

BRUMMETTE, LINDA L.
[b.] June 11, 1949, Idaho; [p.] Carol and Ken Glore; [m.] Divorced; [ch.] Tracy (22), Mathew (18); [ed.] Two yrs. College UT-Knoxville; [occ.] Administrative Asstistant; [a.] Knoxville, TN

BRUNETTE, RANDY
[pen.] Randar; [b.] October 20, 1961, Fargo, ND; [p.] Julian and Arlene Brunette; [m.] Wanda Norton-Brunete, July 1, 1995; [ch.] Amanda Norton, Anthony Norton; [ed.] West Fargo High School, Community College of the Air Force (Associates Degree). Morse Systems Operator and Radio Communications Analysis Technical Schools; [occ.] U.S. Air Force Intelligence Analyst; [memb.] National Security Agency, Pacific Social Committee, Non-commissioned Officers Assoc., American Heart Association; [hon.] 3 Air Force Commendation Medals, 3 Air Force Achievement Medals, 1 Joint Service Achievement Medal, 1 Humanitarian Service Medal, USAF NCO Academy Commandant's Award; [pers.] I strive to live by the affirmation: "Out of every adversity there lies a seed of equal or greater benefit." I do this with the help of my personal Lord and Savior, Jesus Christ.; [a.] Mililani, HI

BRYANT, RITA
[b.] April 14, 1937, Hall Co., TX; [p.] William and Emma Benton; [m.] Richard Bryant (Deceased), January 10, 1959; [ch.] Rhonda Lynn Golightly; [ed.] BS - Wayland Baptist U., Med. Wayland and Baptist U.; [occ.] Education Consultant for Reg XVI of Texas Ed. Agency; [memb.] Lone Star Ballet Guild, First Baptist Church Choir, Panhandle Association for the Education of Young Children, Texas Association for the Education of Young Children National Association for the Education of Young Children; [hon.] Kappa Kappa Gamma - Ed. Honor Frat., Who's Who in American Women 1987 Outstanding Service Award from TAEVC - 1987-1988, Commendation Award

from Texas Dept of Human seru 1985; [oth. writ.] Children's books in rhyme (unpublished but under consideration) but under considerations - party invitations - games in rhyme - skits and school play in rhyme.; [pers.] I enjoy writing poetry and write mostly children's poems and stories in rhyme. I also write poems for friends and organizations for invitations, found raisers etc., and skits for school.; [a.] Shamrock, TX

BUCKLES, MELISSA GAY
[pen.] Melissa G. Buckles; [b.] March 24, 1960, Cleveland, TN; [p.] James C. Melton Sr., Louise E. Sansaver Blair; [m.] Dana R. Buckles, December 19, 1992; [ch.] Wendy, Tristan, Daniel and Melissa Avon; [ed.] South Kitsap High School, Forth Peck Community College; [occ.] Indian Law Advocate and Indian Civil Rights Advocate; [memb.] Wordcraft Circle of Native Writers and Storytellers; [oth. writ.] Freelance articles published in News from Indian Country.; [pers.] I am fulfilling my Circle of Life. I thank the Creator for the gifts and dreams he has given me to share with others. I actively support Indian Civil Rights and Sovereignty of Indian Nations. The ultimate sharing is to reveal one's emotions, my poetry captures the emotion of the moment.; [a.] Wolf Point, MT

BUKOWSKY, BRETT
[pen.] Larry Noccis; [b.] August 20, 1968, Dallas, TX; [p.] Robert and Sandra Bukowsky; [ed.] Naperville Central High School, Western IL, University - BA in Journalism and Philosophy; [occ.] Sales - Square D and Courtesy Carpentry; [memb.] Team Z Fitness Center and Kick boxing, Courtesy Carpentry Crew, Theta Chi Fraternity Alumni; [hon.] Black Belt, Student of Semi Jeff Obst and the Dragon Academy; [oth. writ.] Several other poems and short stories.; [pers.] A reeling sense of urgency flows from my pen, in magic abroad. The ticking time of finalness that touches us all, is what I taste to you.; [a.] Maperville, IL

BULDRA, GABRIEL
[pen.] Spot; [b.] June 7, 1982, Tuscon, AZ; [p.] Mike and Gina Buldra; [ed.] Mesa Middle School 8th grade; [occ.] Student; [memb.] Mesa Club; [pers.] I enjoy sports, computer games, and hanging out with my friends.; [a.] Roswell, NM

BURCH, STEPHANIE
[pen.] Chris; [b.] January 13, 1980, Hayward, CA; [ed.] Sophomore at Interlake High School; [pers.] When I wrote this poem I wrote it for a love I had for a guy named Erik. And when I was writing this poem I realized that I'm the one that messed everything up.; [a.] Redmond, WA

BURCHILL, HEATHER
[b.] November 17, 1979, Baltimore, MD; [p.] Dan and Tina Burchill; [ed.] Currently going into the 10th grade at Chambersburg Area Senior High School (Cash 5); [hon.] Distinguished Honor Roll, First Honor Roll; [pers.] Happiness is hard to find. Sadness comes to you naturally.; [a.] Fayetteville, PA

BURKE, VALEN ALANE
[b.] December 6, 1983, Millen, GA; [p.] Joydine and Alvin Burke; [ed.] Completed Primary School (grade K-12), completed Elementary School (grade 3-5), beginning Middle School (grade 6-8); [memb.] 4-H Club, D.A.R.E. Program, West Millen Baptist Church; [hon.] Principals List, Honor Roll, Attendance Award, Highest Average in 5th Grade Class Award Presidential Academic Award; [oth. writ.] Farm Life, My House, My Home, On The Hill - they are all poems.; [pers.] I try to make people feel relaxed in my writing. I want them to enjoy my poems and entertain themselves with my writing.; [a.] Millen, GA

BURKE JR., DAVID U.
[pen.] Dave Burke Jr.; [b.] September 9, 1966, San Antonio, TX; [m.] Mary Beth Burke; [ed.] B.A. Norwich University; [occ.] Graduate Assistant Education Dept., Marywood College Scranton, PA; [memb.] National Eagle Scout Assoc., International Reading Association; [hon.] Graduate Assistantship, Graduate Education Dept., Marywood College. Eagle Scout 1984, Arnold Air Society, AFROTC; [pers.] I want to help children understand and overcome learning and personal problems through poem/picture books designed to build confidence, hope, and self-esteem.; [a.] Dunmore, PA

BURR, PAULA
[pen.] Bugs; [b.] March 12, 1978, Tucson, AZ; [p.] Pamela Ann Burr; [ed.] Prescott High School Vocations Unlimited Prescott Yavapai College; [memb.] Lynx Creek Cloggers a country tradition; [hon.] Track and Field Vocations Unlimited; [pers.] "To the wise, life is a problem." "To the fool a solution." "I would love to thank the G.D. members of Prescott for there inspiration" Ducky and Mom.; [a.] Prescott, AZ

BURTON, KIRK ANTHONY
[b.] August 3, 1963, Roanoke, VA; [p.] Robert E. Burton, Shirley A. Burton; [ed.] Graduated Garfield Sr. High School in Woodbridge, VA (1981), B.A. (Public Relations) Old Dominion University (1986) minor: English; [occ.] Sr. Agency Services Analyst New York State Department of Economic Development; [memb.] Active member of the Black Film makers Foundation; [hon.] Honorable Discharge from USAR 4/25/88; [oth. writ.] Several poems, short stories and scripts. None have been published. Up to now writing has been a hobby.; [pers.] Love yourself and the world will love you. My writing is about honesty and being able to put my feelings into words that others enjoy and benefit from. Honesty is the foundation, love is the message.; [a.] New York, NY

BUSCH, TINA M.
[pen.] K. C. King; [b.] October 14, 1975, Albany, NY; [p.] Mark E. Busch, Patricia A. Busch; [ed.] Albany High School, The College of Saint Rose; [occ.] Full Time Student/Graphic Design Major; [hon.] CSR Art Talent Award, CSR Athletic Talent Award; [pers.] I write for myself and no one else. All of my writing comes from within. The experiences in my life which I encounter are expressed through my words...; [a.] Albany, NY

BUSSE, RONALD A.
[pen.] Tiger; [b.] April 3, 1967; [p.] Ronald and Marylou Busse; [ed.] Nassau Community College, Massapequa High School; [occ.] Insurance Rater; [oth. writ.] I have had other poems published by the National Library of Poetry as well as some poems and articles published in School Newspaper and Company Newsletters. I also write songs and I've written several parodical advertisements as well.; [pers.] I write poetry as a means of expressing my innermost feelings. I hope my mother is able to understand the positive message conveyed in this poems. It is a feeling of hope and love.; [a.] Lindenhurst, NY

BUSTARD, MATTHEW RYAN
[b.] August 14, 1981, Baltimore, BD; [p.] Barbara and Edwin Bustard; [ed.] Attending Carver Center for the Arts and Technology Studying Culinary Arts; [occ.] Student; [a.] Owings Mills, MD

BUTCHER, MYRTLE
[pen.] Myrtle Butcher; [b.] August 17, 1916, Booneville, KY; [p.] Ed and Callie Hill; [m.] McKinly Butcher (Deceased), 1938; [ch.] Dr. Maxine Nichols; [ed.] High School; [occ.] Retired; [memb.] Republan Club, Trinity Esp. Church, N.K.R., A.A.R.P., N.K. Senior Citizens; [hon.] One poems published. T.V. Commercial in 5 state; [pers.] My poems are feelings of past and current times.; [a.] Covington, KY

BUTLER, JOSEPHINE S.
[b.] February 11, 1941, Washington, DC; [p.] George T. and Mary V. Proctor; [m.] Joseph E. Butler, October 6, 1956; [ch.] Gwendolyn Ann, Paul Jerone and Michael Terrence Butler; [ed.] Fredirick Douglas High School, Business Management; [occ.] Self Educated Scholar; [hon.] Certificates of Outstanding Achievements from the Board of Education; [pers.] Dreams do come true it can happen to you!; [a.] Camp Springs, MD

BUTLER JR., CHARLES RAY
[pen.] Charles Ray Butler Jr.; [b.] August 28, 1937, Philadelphia, PA; [p.] Charles Ray and Ray Arina Butler; [m.] Barbara L. Butler; [ch.] Kimberly Vanette and Stacy Marie; [ed.] USAF (26 years), LACC, University of Phoenix; [occ.] Owner and Operator Minimum Security Prison (Scapular House Work Furlough Program); [memb.] Air Force Sergeant's Association, AARP, Watts-Willowbrook Chamber of Commerce, Mater Dolorosa Century Club; [hon.] Air Force Achievement Medal, Living Legends Oustanding Leadership and Service Award; [oth. writ.] A wide variety of poems and I am presently composing a couple short stories; [pers.] When the clouds of darkness gather 'bout... and block out the smiling sun...Take faith in God still loving you...His unforgotten one.; [a.] Los Angeles, CA

BYRNE, ERIN E.
[b.] December 20, 1976, San Deigo, CA; [p.] Thomas and Donna Byrne; [ed.] South High School Brookdale College, OCVTS Commercial Photography School; [occ.] College Student; [hon.] Modern Woodman of America speech contest first winner 1990, runner up in 1989; [oth. writ.] Several short stories and other short poems.; [pers.] And through those times I've learned to hold on to everything I have, while I still have a grip.; [a.] Toms River, NJ

CAGLE, GERALD F.
[b.] December 12, 1940, Gillsville, GA; [p.] Albert and Mae Cagle; [m.] Brenda S., August 3, 1968; [ch.] Jonathan, Amy; [ed.] Banks County High, University of GA, BS Math; [occ.] Sales Manager, Abeo Industries Ltd; [oth. writ.] Several poems and songs not published; [pers.] Man can find his soul in poetry, and through poetry can pass the substance of his soul to another generations. This is what I would like to do.; [a.] Lawrenceville, GA

CAIN, IDA PAT
[b.] May 25, 1915, Chicago, IL; [m.] John C. Cain, 1912 - 1970; [ch.] Sally, John W., Nick, Patty, Margie, Grand-children: Marie, Erica, Bryce, Twins-Adrienne and Crystal, Joseph, Jesi, Willie, Great Grand-child: Jeannie; [hon.] Won Several Contest's of Various Kinds; [pers.] Being a life long poetry lover I feel proud, because at my first attempt to have a poem published, my poem "Life is like a dream" was one of the selected to be published in this most lovely anthology "A Delicate Balance."; [a.] Chicago, IL

CAIN, PAULETTE
[pen.] Paula; [b.] May 2, 1957, Col's, OH; [p.] Arizona and Elvin Turberville; [m.] Divorced; [ch.] James, Shilo; [ed.] GED and College course at Col's State, Data Entry course; [occ.] Own La-Paul Cleaning Company (House Cleaning); [hon.] Typing and Computer Awards; [a.] Columbus, OH

CALABRO, CHRISTINA
[b.] February 17, 1982, Pompton Plains, NJ; [p.] Dale Calabro and Mr. Pasquale Calabro; [occ.] Student; [oth. writ.] Unpublished short stories and poems, working on a novel; [pers.] I want to thank all my friends and especially Mrs. Linda Reese. Remember that being individual is what gives you an identity.; [a.] Bloomingdale, NJ

CALDERONE, MARY M.
[pen.] Mary M. Calderone; [b.] March 16, 1921, Saint Johns, Newfoundland, Canada; [p.] Phillip And Mary Healey; [m.] Ross Calderone, November 26, 1939; [ch.] Carolyn M. Quaranta, Dennis R. Calderon; [ed.] Eight years Grammar School - 4 years High School; [occ.] Retired; [memb.] The International Society of Poets; [pers.] My poetry reflects my feelings about life, family, nature and our world in general. I hope I reach the readers and they enjoy what we have written.; [a.] Las Vegas, NV

CALDWELL, MARY LEE
[pen.] "Mary Lee"; [b.] June 11, 1954, Coosa County; [p.] Reu and Mrs. Robert McKinney; [m.] Dallas Earl Caldwell, November 25, 1972; [ch.] Roelando Layawn Caldwell, Diedre Frandria Caldwell; [ed.] I completed High School in 1992, I later enter Nunnley Trading School for Cosmetologist, where I completed course; [occ.] I am a managing cosmetologist, I self employed at Caldwell Cut-n-style Salon; [memb.] I am a pray partner with Marilyn Hickey, and Kenneth Copeland. I am a partner with the Sunlight Christian Program; [hon.] I have award, in my Costomogist field in my school year I was in the Beta Club, I also graduated with class honor students. At Central High; [oth. writ.] I have completed writing a book that I title "The Book of the Laws of the Lord." I have not enter my book for publishing; [pers.] I have a personal relationship with God. I want greatly to express his love for this world. I consider myself as a chosen vessel for God. Sometimes writing, teaching and singing is good ways to express his goodness.; [a.] Goodwater, AL

CALDWELL, PAMELA S.
[b.] November 23, 1960, Los Angeles, CA; [p.] Russell B. Caldwell; [ch.] Natasha McMahan, Tiffany Cole; [occ.] Human Resource Assistant

CALHOUN, FAYE
[pen.] Faye Calhoun; [b.] May 13, 1933, Kansas City, MO; [p.] William LawFayette and Leona Wry Keeney; [m.] Robert (Deceased); [ch.] Gordon, Steven, Gilbert, Evamarie and Suzy; [ed.] Weiser High - Nampa Business College, Boise Jr. College; [occ.] Homemaker, Gardener; [memb.] Sweet Adelines International, Bowling Bags, Calvary Assembly; [hon.] President and Vice Pres. of Several Organizations - 1st Place Trophy and Cash for City of Trees (Singles) Bowling Tournament (69-70), Corresponding Secretary (2 yrs.) Sweet Adelines Int.; [oth. writ.] I've never before submitted any of my writings. I've confined them to friends and relatives.; [pers.] I've always loved to write my thoughts on paper. I have "personal" thoughts when I'm "down" but try to send uplifting thoughts to others when they are "down." My joy is in helping others find happiness. Music is magic.; [a.] Boise, ID

CALKINS, RUBY L.
[b.] Bear Spring, TN; [p.] Frank and Eva (Hudson) Pulley; [m.] Joe B. Calkins; [ch.] Joe Jr., Vivian, Frank; [ed.] B.A., M.A., Partially completed Ph.D.; [occ.] Administrative Assistant to the President of the George Washington University, Washington, D.C.; [memb.] Franconia Baptist Church, Alexandria, VA; [hon.] Valedictorian of College Class and other Academic Awards; [pers.] All things work together for good to them that love God.; [a.] Springfield, VA

CALLIN, ELOISE
[b.] June 14, 1927, Ware County, GA; [p.] Thomas L. and Olive Edenfield; [m.] Glenn Thomas Callin, October 17, 1953; [ch.] Four sons; [ed.] Elementary thru Business School; [occ.] Housewife; [memb.] National Library of Poetry Downey Memorial Church; [a.] Chuluota, FL

CALVO, ANDREA
[b.] July 13, 1977, Costa Rica; [p.] Jorge A. Calvo, Ana Ma Calvo; [ed.] Framingham High, Worcester Polytechnic Institute; [occ.] Student, WPI; [pers.] All that I have accomplished is due to the effort that my parents and I have worked for.; [a.] Framingham, MA

CAMPBELL, JEFFERY RAY
[b.] April 7, 1975, Austin, TX; [p.] Jeanette Campbell of Red Rock, TX, Leslie Campbell of Buckholts, TX; [ed.] Graduated Bastrop High School 1994; [memb.] Business Professionals of America; [hon.] Salinas Art Festival (1st place in 11th grade) 1993, Who's Who Among American High School Students 1993/1994; [pers.] Let your heart be your guide. In it all things of Heaven and Earth will be revealed.; [a.] Red Rock, TX

CANNADY, MAGGIE L.
[b.] August 16, 1947, Clairton, PA; [p.] Louis Mayo Jr., Maeola Mayo; [m.] Kenneth Cannady, August 21, 1963; [ch.] Maureen Renee, Cannady Melvin; [ed.] Clairton High; [memb.] Lillington Grove FWB, Church Gospel and Senior Choirs, Lillington Grove Home Mission; [pers.] Through my poems I try to express my hopes for a better and moral society. Especially for our younger generation.; [a.] Lillington, NC

CAPPELLO, VINCENT A.
[b.] December 5, 1951, Niagara Falls, NY; [p.] John and Margaret Cappello; [ch.] John and Starylyn; [ed.] Master of Social Work Degree; [occ.] Psychotherapist, Niagara County Dept. of Mental Health; [memb.] International Association of Counselors and Therapists National Association of Social Workers; [pers.] Helping people through poetry therapy.; [a.] Niagara Falls, NY

CAPPO, RUSSELL
[b.] April 12, 1953; [ed.] Three years College; [occ.] Nurse R.N.; [a.] Shreveport, LA

CARNER, STACY
[b.] January 13, 1959, Queens; [p.] Leonard and Carole Zeifman; [m.] Rex Carner, June 15, 1986; [ch.] Michael Andrew and Ariel Starr; [ed.] Bachelor of Arts Degree, Queens College, Master's Degree in Communications, Queens College; [occ.] Management Consultant; [memb.] Phi Beta Kappa, Sigma Chapter of New York, American Society for Training and Development; [hon.] Phi Beta Kappa, Cum Laude, Dean's List; [oth. writ.] Contributor to the Verdict published by National Library Week.; [pers.] I write to express both my inner feelings and everyday experiences. I hope to touch the lives of others.; [a.] Bayside, NY

CARNEY, RUTH
[b.] March 30, 1921, Alma, MI; [p.] Albert Davis, Olive Davis; [m.] Nimrud Carney, February 27, 1942; [ch.] Gerald Carney, Elaine Bray, Michael Carney; [ed.] Northern High, Highland Park Cumm. Unity College, (1) yr. Wayne State; [occ.] Retired; [memb.] Hope Builders/Habitat for Humanity, Museum of African American History, Detroit Inst. of Arts, United States Holocaust Memorial Museum; [oth. writ.] Several poems, one short story all unpublished, one radio show a 1/2 hour in length many years ago.; [pers.] I believe that man's spiritual force is the key to our survival.; [a.] Detroit, MI

CAROBALLO, MARIA V.
[b.] June 24, 1948, Puerto Rico; [p.] Maria Rios, Eucebio Quinones; [m.] Paco Caroballo, April 18, 1969; [ch.] Richard, Jerry, Marisol; [ed.] Washington, Irving H.S., 1 yr BMCC; [occ.] Office Worker for the Manhattan District Attorney's Office; [pers.] I dedicate this poem to my beloved, departed brother Wilfredo.; [a.] New York City, NY

CARPENTER, JEAN
[b.] February 15, 1942, AR; [p.] Deceased; [ch.] Kim, Jerry, Sean, Eric; [ed.] High School; [occ.] Waitress; [oth. writ.] I have many poems that I have written, but this will be the first one published; [pers.] I am influenced in my writings by everything. My children, the beauty of nature, good and bad things that happen in society and the world, but most of all I'm influenced by God.; [a.] Kansas City, MO

CARR, LEILANI
[pen.] Lonnie Carr; [b.] May 14, 1940, MN; [p.] Billie H. and Beatrice Noyes; [m.] Richard T. Carr, February 5, 1965; [ch.] Michael, Sheri, Penny and Rick; [ed.] Arcata High School; [occ.] Housewife; [memb.] American Cancer Society - Amvets Paralized Veterans; [hon.] My biggest Honor was to have my first poem published in "Reflections of Light" by the National Library of Poetry in 1994 and then to receive the Editor's Choice Award for outstanding achievement in poetry; [oth. writ.] I have written many poems and given them as gifts to family and friends, and I've written a few songs that my daughters and I have sang locally.; [pers.] My love for my husband and children

has been my inspiration to write poetry and songs and now they will be forever preserved in the National Library of Poetry.; [a.] Laplata, MD

CARR, NICOLE
[b.] July 25, 1980; [p.] Sylvia Chandler, James Chandler; [ed.] Bethel Elementary, Bethel Whitcomb High School; [occ.] Student; [pers.] Out of all the years that I tried to write poetry I found out one thing poetry isn't something that you have to try to do it's actually natural it comes naturally to you and it will be happen all at once.; [a.] East Bethel, VT

CARRETERO, INGRID
[b.] October 23, 1964, New York City, NY; [p.] Yvonne Carretero, Efrain Carretero; [ch.] Leah J. Davis; [ed.] St. Catharine Academy, City College; [occ.] Bookkeeper, Columbia University, New York, NY; [a.] Bronx, NY

CARROLL, CAROLYN MARIE
[b.] August 4, Houston, TX; [p.] Wanda Tomlinson and Elmer Grimes; [m.] Leroy Carroll (Deceased 1989), August 29, 1979; [ch.] Loni Marie Aranda, (deceased 1991) Tonija Lea; [ed.] 12 years/Beaumont TX; [occ.] Office Manager; [pers.] The death of my daughter was very hard my mother never left my side. She carried my burdens for me. Since then I find myself writing about what I feel in my heart.; [a.] Houston, TX

CARROLL, KAREN B.
[b.] December 23, 1957, Amory, MS; [p.] H. V. and Mary Nell Taylor Brown; [m.] W. Garry Carroll; [ch.] Nicole, Jeremy, Hope; [ed.] Hatley High School, Itawamba Jr. College, Life; [occ.] Homemaker; [memb.] Victory Baptist Church, International Society of Poets, American Family Association; [hon.] Who's Who Among American High School Students, "I Dare You" Award, Dean's List - College; [oth. writ.] Several articles published in local newspaper, Sunday School Lessons, songs and poems for church, word studies published in various religious papers; [pers.] With the Lord's help, I write truth for the purpose of honoring my saviour and edifying the family of God.; [a.] Smithville, MS

CARROLL, THOMAS W.
[b.] October 5, 1906, Barbour Court, AL; [p.] William and Annie (Adams) Carroll; [m.] Vivian (Weaver) Carroll, June 10, 1950; [ch.] Thomas W., Jr., David Arthur, Andrew Brian; [ed.] Elementary School, Barbour Co. Al., Jr. High School, Henry Co. Al, SNS, Troy, Al., Univ. of Al., Univ. of Cincinnati; [occ.] Retired; [memb.] AARP, NRTA, AEA, ARTA, NEA, TROA, American Legion, SOAR; [hon.] Tuition, Summer School, University of Cincinnati, 1940; [oth. writ.] Article on Retirement, Article on Family History, unpublished poems; [a.] Andalusia, AL

CARTER, CONSTANCE
[b.] October 19, 1933, Danville, VA; [ed.] 12th Grade, Langston High School

CARUSO, JOANNE
[p.] Eugene and Maryann Bernardine; [m.] Fred Caruso, August 23, 1969; [ch.] Darren; [ed.] Canon - McMillan High Sch., California State Univ.; [occ.] Teacher, Canon McMillan School Dist.; [memb.] PSEA, St. Mary's Church, Nemacolin Country Club; [a.] Canonsburg, PA

CARVALHO, ANNA P.
[b.] January 26, 1961, Portugal; [m.] Diamantino Carvalho, October 14, 1979; [ch.] Michael Alexander; [oth. writ.] Poem published in City River Voices, Golden Poet Award In; [pers.] My inspiration comes from all things and all people. "The Wedding Poem" was inspired as a wedding gift to my sister and her husband. May God bless you Sandra and Dave and all the couples who choose to live as one.

CASE, EVA KAYE
[pen.] Eve Connestee; [b.] March 8, 1955, Brevard, NC; [p.] Mr. and Mrs. James F. Case Jr.; [ch.] Michael Phillip Sirmans; [ed.] Brevard Senior High, Brevard Music Center, Blue Ridge Technical Institute, Catawba Valley Technical Institute; [occ.] Artist, Musician, Singer and Songwriter; [memb.] Former Co-Pastor of Light House for Christ Ministries, Daytona Beach, Florida, Women's AGLO Christian Fellowship, Several Native American Associations; [hon.] Honor Roll at Brevard Senior High, Winner of numerous piano recitals and contests, recognized Praise and Worship Leader Of Contemporary Christian Music; [oth. writ.] Several Native American Historical Ballads and Folk songs performed at Nationwide Native American Festival and Pow Wows as well as contemporary Christian Music; [pers.] My writing are dedicated to and inspired by my Celtic-Native American Ancestry and heritage of the beautiful Blue Ridge Mountains of Western North Carolina.; [a.] Bryson City, NC

CASTLEBURY, CHRIS
[b.] June 4, 1977, Nevada, MD; [p.] Joe Castlebury and Tammy Larimore; [ed.] Sheldon High School; [oth. writ.] Several poems for my personal collection; [pers.] One's happiness maybe another's sorrow. I would like to thank all of the teachers at Sheldon for never doubting anyone's ability not over my own.; [a.] Sheldon, MD

CATARINO, MIRIAM
[b.] September 21, 1980, Portugal; [p.] Julia and Francisco Catarino; [ed.] Science High School Sophomore; [occ.] Student; [memb.] Pentecostal Church; [hon.] The awards I received were honor roll, perfect attendance, music, and a reading program award; [pers.] I have lots of interests on reading and writing love and friendship poems. By writing these poems I am trying to reflect the ethic side of the humanity.; [a.] Newark, NJ

CATUZZA, ELIZABETH A.
[b.] March 23, 1957, Buffalo, NY; [p.] Edward S. Holy And Adeline M. Holy; [m.] David R., November 17, 1979; [ch.] Scott Andrew, Dawn Ellery; [ed.] Lackawanna High; [occ.] Legal Assistant, Accessory Specialist - Home Interiors; [pers.] Grew up in family with 5 boys and 2 girls. Have written many poems reflecting on my personal life and feelings. This poem was inspired by my children.; [a.] Buffalo, NY

CAVALLI, YVETTE
[b.] September 1, 1979, New Hyde Park, NY; [p.] Angela Cavalli and Mario Cavalli; [ed.] Currently attending Saint Francis Preparatory High School in Fresh Meadows, NY; [occ.] Student; [memb.] St. John's University Women in Science Society, The Seraph School Newspaper Staff, Our Lady of the Blessed Sacrament, CCD Program, Junior Great Books, (in elementary school), various other school activities such as, Save Our Planet; [hon.] Principal's List at Saint John's University awards in Science and Mathematics, Elementary School Valedictorian, Participant in a Diocesan Presidential Academic Fitness, Oratorical Contest, Award, Certificate Of Congressional Recognition; [oth. writ.] Several articles published in the Seraph, several other poems never published before.; [pers.] I believe writing is one of the best ways to express one's feelings. I strive to touch a person's inner soul through my writing about nature, the world around us and the people in it.; [a.] Bayside, NY

CAWLEY, YVONNE PATRICIA
[pen.] Pat Cawley; [b.] Jamaica, West Indies; [p.] Diego and Cecile Burke, Karl Evan Cawley (all deceased); [ch.] 4 daughters - Dianne Marie Little, Jennifer Margaret and Kathleen May Thompson, Annette Marsha Stewart; [ed.] High School (Catholic Girls) Convent of Mercy Alpha - Commercial Sch - Typing - Shorthand - Bookkeeping, College of Arts Science and Technology 2 years Cake and Pastry, Cake decorating, Management; [occ.] Life Skills Trainer, Night Supervisor - Learning Services Corp. Rehab for Acquired Brain - Damaged Clients - 5 years; [pers.] I was on vacation in Jamaica and only returned on 8-13-95 I am very excited about my poetry being in the finals, and have always been interested in writing down verses as it came to mind and have done a few pieces over the years which I still possess. I am definitely concerned about people and the terrible hardships and strife which seems to consume the universe like wars, hunger and the unwanted and untimely killing of innocent people. I pray that the almighty will touch the hearts of everyone that it will be a better place to live in for the upcoming generations.; [a.] Centreville, VA

CECCARELLI, ELIJAH
[pen.] Eli Ceccarelli; [b.] January 22, 1977, Santa Rosa, CA; [p.] Diane Ceccarelli, Robert Salinas; [m.] Deceased, April 30, 1995; [ed.] 11th Grade El Molino, Forestville, Laguna Hi Sebastopol; [hon.] Eli was an a student all through Grammar School, Middle School and the first 2 years of High School; [oth. writ.] Other short stories and final writing of tragedy of last year of life.; [pers.] Emotional conflict lead to drug experimentation including inhaling of chemicals, causing brain damage and one year later suicide by hanging.; [a.] Sebastopol, CA

CEDER, JOHN W.
[b.] July 21, 1918, Moline, IL; [p.] Louise and Hjalmer Ceder; [ed.] BA Univ. of Washington, BA Butler University, Cert. Stockholm's Hogskola, MA Indiana University, MS University of Kentucky; [occ.] Retired Teacher; [memb.] Morgan County Library Board, Prince of Peace Lutheran Church; [hon.] I was honorably discharged from the 88th Infantry Division with a Bronze Star; [oth. writ.] The Hook and Eye; [pers.] I enjoy the play on words. Robert Burns is my favorite poet.; [a.] Martinsville, IN

CEPPOS, LAURIE
[pen.] Cup Cake; [b.] February 8, 1963, Bethpage; [p.] Anita Palazzo, Nick Palazzo; [ed.] Farmingdale High School; [occ.] File Clerk; [pers.] Making up the poem was easy because Frankie is the sweetest kindest guy you'll ever want to meet.

CHAPMAN, SAMUEL L.
[pen.] Sam Chapman; [b.] January 14, 1934, Anniston, AL; [p.] Hosea Chapman, Dexer Belle Chapman; [m.] Delores Mae Means, December 16, 1955; [ch.] Patsy Jean, Winslow Hosea, James Calvin, Dexer Elizabeth, David Banard, John Mark; [ed.] Port Huron High, St. Clair County Community College, Michigan - State University with a Bachelor of Art degree in Administrative Ed.; [occ.] Intermediate School Teacher in Port Huron, Michigan; [memb.] Michigan Public School Employees, Retirement System, The First Church of God, Michigan State University Alumni, National Wildlife Federation; [hon.] Board of Education Certificate of Appreciation for 24 years of service, 1994 Spirit of Port Huron Good Neighbor Award the Grant of Letter Patents on April 25, 1961, December 15, 1964 and February 14, 1978; [oth. writ.] American Poetry Anthology volume 1, number 2 summer 1982; [pers.] Life is a struggle, and success is determine by how well you do in the struggle.; [a.] Port Huron, MI

CHAPMON, ANNISE LUCIA
[b.] January 7, 1953, Washington, DC; [p.] Lucie Chapmon; [ed.] Master of Social Work, Univ. of Maryland; [occ.] Social Worker for Health and Human Services, Montgomery County; [hon.] Interviewed by "700 Club" Television Show, December 25, 1989 - The Loving Family, Interviewed by Washington Post Newspaper 4/23/89 Love Opens Door Long Closed by Susan Deford, Interviewed by People Magazine 5/29/89 Back in the Land of the Living by Marian Holmes; [pers.] "If you think you can... you can."; [a.] Capital Heights, MD

CHAPPEL, ALVIN R.
[b.] October 30, 1947, Myrtle Point, OR; [p.] Ralph Chappel, Zelma Chappel; [ch.] Connie L. Crawford, Grandchildren: Ashley Crawford, Mathew Crawford; [ed.] Some College, Tech Schools; [occ.] Surveyors Assistant; [memb.] Vietnam Vet; [hon.] Honorab Discharge, U.S. Navy Medals; [oth. writ.] Poems, short stories, songs; [pers.] Influenced by the events of my life on this planet; [a.] Fresno, CA

CHASON, SHARRON
[pen.] Sharron, Chason; [b.] January 10, 1954, Jackson, TN; [p.] Lorraine Norton; [m.] Freddie Chason, June 22, 1985; [ed.] Associates of Nursing Degree, Northside High School; [occ.] Registered Nurse, West Tennessee Cardiology Clinic; [memb.] American Heart Association; [hon.] Editor's Choice (National Library of Poetry 1995), Semi-Finals Sparrow Grass Press 1995; [oth. writ.] Published poem - National Library of Poetry 1995.; [pers.] I feel that we are all here for a purpose. We are all on a path of self enlightenment. I have chosen a path of spiritual/ physical healing. Only by speaking out can abuse be stopped the silence broken.; [a.] Jackson, TN

CHEUNG, JULIA
[pen.] Julie; [b.] November 5, 1969, Jamaica, West Indies; [p.] Bernard and Ying Cheung; [ed.] Miami-Dade Community College, Major: Accounting; [pers.] You shouldn't try to please everyone just to please yourself. I think that it is selfish.; [a.] Miami, FL

CHIARELLA, COURTNEY ANNE
[b.] March 7, 1985, Charlotte, NC; [p.] Joseph and Dianne Chiarella; [sibling] Sister - Kerry 14 yrs. [ed.] Shallowford Falls Elementary School, 4th Grade (1994) - when poem was written; [occ.] Student - 5th Grade (1995); [a.] Marietta, GA

CHRISTIAN, STEVE
[b.] February 25, 1944, Hobbs, NM; [m.] Liz Christian; [ed.] Humboldt State University; [occ.] Production Manager, Adaptive Engineering Lab. Inc.; [memb.] Nature Conservancy, People for Puget Sound, Toastmasters; [oth. writ.] Several poems and articles published, articles for "Shamanic News"; [pers.] We are all part of the web of life. What man does to the earth, he does to himself. I feel such a pull in my soul to the rhythms of nature, I know that we are all related.; [a.] Camano Island, WA

CHRISTIANSEN, MARJORIE
[b.] May 5, 1938, Wakefield, MI; [p.] Deceased; [m.] Charles (Chris) Christiansen, October 1, 1960; [ch.] Richard S.; [ed.] Wakefield High School; [occ.] Home Maker, Volunteer on Several Local and Civic Committees i.e. Secretary, etc.; [memb.] Women of the Moose; [hon.] W.O.T.M. College of Regents; [pers.] I am, and always have been, an avid reader. I started writing poetry as a young woman, with varied themes, many as personal gifts to family and friends.; [a.] Aurora, MN

CHRYSTIE, GRACE C.
[b.] June 15, 1948, Orlando, FL; [p.] Paul C. and Dorothy N. Carpenter (both deceased); [ch.] Kathryn E. Weber, Karyn E. Christie and Kevin Michael Chrystie; [ed.] B.S, Elementary Education, Culver - Stockton College Canton, MO; [occ.] Executive Secretary and Continuing Education Coordinator, Bureau of Education and Research, Bellevue, WA; [memb.] Lake Washington Christian Church, Northshore United Church of Christ, Kate Williams Memorial Scholarship Fund (Mentor); [oth. writ.] "The visit," published in Disciples Magazine, "Slam-Dunked to Hell: Thoughts on the Journey Home"....a collection of poetry of give hope along the journey.; [pers.] Words on paper combine to dance and sing as through the eye they reach the heart. Thoughts become ink and paper etchings of my soul... Regard them as pass keys to open doors. Let them stir the sorrow of your emotions. This is my legacy, my gift to you.; [a.] Kirkland, WA

CICON JR., MICHAEL A.
[b.] August 4, 1934, Trenton, NJ; [p.] Michael A. Sr., Elizabeth B.; [m.] Jean (Pulis) Cicon, November 23, 1956; [ch.] Michael Ross, Elizabeth Ann; [ed.] St. Charles College, Maiden Choice Lane, Catonsville, MD, Mira Costa College Oceanside, CA; [occ.] Senior Chief Hospital Corpsman, U.S. Navy (Retired); [memb.] Disabled American Veterans (DAV), Fleet Reserve Association (FRA), American Registry of Radiologic Technologists, California Registry of Radiologic Technologists; [hon.] Navy Achievement Awards, Dean's List (Mira Costa College); [oth. writ.] Personal Reflection Poetry, none published; [pers.] For me... reflective poetry has a soul sustaining impact that creates a lyrical legacy of an important event or an unforgettable memory.; [a.] Vista, CA

CIRELLO, KATHY
[b.] May 5, 1950, Brooklyn, NY; [p.] Margaret (deceased), and George Miller; [m.] Frank J. Cirello, January 16, 1972; [ch.] Donna Marie, Jennifer Lynn; [memb.] Lutheran Church of Our Saviour, Patchogue, NY; [oth. writ.] Many of my poems have appeared in my church newsletter, sandpiper; [pers.] Through my poetry I strive to reach others with the message of salvation, and what is waiting for those who accept Christ as their Savior.; [a.] Holtsville, NY

CIULLA, LENA
[b.] January 7, 1940, New Orleands, LA; [p.] Cosimo and Mary Viola; [ch.] Karen, Mark, Mike; [ed.] John McDonogh High, New Orleans, LA - Class of 59; [pers.] This poem concerns my deep feelings of injustices done to my children, whom I love so much.; [a.] Holly Hill, FL

CLARK, CHUCK
[b.] May 7, 1925, Oklahoma City, OK; [m.] Mary, August 20, 1965; [ed.] AB English St. Mary's College, MA Education Cal State Univ. Northridge; [occ.] Retired educator... teacher, counselor, principal, grades K-9, now working with student teachers; [memb.] Pepperdine U; [pers.] "Poetry is the recollection of intense feelings in moments of tranquility" (Wordsworth)... it cannot be taught, but is in each of us to be released....

CLARK, JULIE LYNN
[b.] April 4, 1984, Clarksdale, MS; [p.] Bryce and Toni Clark; [ed.] K-5 2nd Grade, Strider Academy, Charleston, MS, 3rd, 6th Grade, Lee Academy Clarksdale, MS; [occ.] Student; [memb.] Voice Student of Mrs. B. L. Stribling, Piano, Student of Mrs. J. J. Webb, Member of first Baptist Church of Summer, MS GA, Member, Play Softball, at Youth, Inc.; [hon.] President Outstanding Academic Achievement Award, Honor Roll and Head Masters List Music Award, 2nd Place District Art Fair; [oth. writ.] Many other poems and stories. I have written's at school for the Young Author's fair and personal things.; [a.] Sumner, MS

CLARK, LISA
[b.] February 6, 1968, Lorain, OH; [p.] Andy and Vickie Grimm; [m.] David Clark, August 20, 1988; [ch.] Megan Nicole, Zachary David Jacob, Trevor Andrew Max; [ed.] St. Edwards Elementary, St. Peters High School; [occ.] Homemaker; [memb.] St. Edwards Church, Catholic Daughters of America; [oth. writ.] Have other poems, but none have been published. This is my first to be published.; [pers.] I believe with God, all things are possible and dreams do come true. We must take one day at a time.; [a.] Ashland, OH

CLEERE, WILLIAM G.
[b.] February 17, 1966, Lamesa, TX; [p.] Fred and Dorothy Cleere; [m.] Kylie Louise, December 16, 1995; [ed.] Robert E. Lee High School; [occ.] United States Air Force; [pers.] My family is a big inspiration in my writing. I thank them for their support of me.; [a.] Midland, TX

CLINE, MICHELLE LEE
[b.] November 10, 1966, Decatur, AL; [p.] Lloyd And Gail McCulloch; [m.] Lanny Cline, June 20, 1991; [ch.] James Adam Campbell, Chelsea Nichole Campbell and Briana Lee Cline; [ed.] Lawrence Co. High, Moulton, AL; [hon.] Graduated High School 1 yr. early with Presidential Honors; [oth. writ.] The Heart of a Child, It's Only A Dream, Summer, Oh Summer, Wherefore Art Thou, All of which are in my personal collection.; [pers.] My poetry is influenced by dreams, the love of my children and husband, and my joys and struggles in life. Special thanks goes to my Daddy and Mother who said I could do anything in life I wanted if I only tried hard enough.; [a.] Success, MO

CLOETERS, MELISSA
[pen.] Meus; [b.] September 10, 1979, Madera, CA; [p.] Dina and Ivan Cloeters; [ed.] High School Student and I graduate in 1997; [occ.] Student, Madera High School (11th); [memb.] FBLA, Future Business Leaders of America; [hon.] For volunteering at the Hospital I have certificates and awards for the hours I acquired for volunteering. Certificate for having a GPA of 3.0 or higher; [oth. writ.] A poem called the big question. That's about the love and power of Christ; [pers.] My philosophy is basically based on my relationship with and everyone should stay fit and healthy.; [a.] Madera, CA

CLOUSER JR., MARLIN MORRIS
[b.] May 9, 1960, Harrisburg, PA; [p.] Marlin Clouser, Shirley Sheaffer; [ed.] El Camino College, CA, Orange Coast College, CA, Spartan Aeronautics, OK, Newport High, PA, Institute of Children's Literature, CT; [occ.] Aviation Instrumentation/Electronics Technician; [hon.] Dean's List, United States Marine Corps; [a.] Flower Mound, TX

COATS, GEALDYNE LONG
[pen.] Geri Coats; [b.] November 2, 1932, Lufkin, TX; [p.] Floyd Sr. and Lola Long; [m.] Charles Coats, September 5, 1992; [ch.] George Perry Grimes and Holly Grimes Beall; [ed.] B.A. Degree, Stephen F. Austin State University, Post-Graduate, Studies, SFASU, Nacogdoches, Texas (High School - Redland H.S., Lufkin, TX; [occ.] Retired School Teacher; [memb.] Life Member, Texas PTA, Texas Retired Teachers Association, Nacogdoches Retired Teachers Association Calvary Baptist Church, Pianist for "The Joyful Sound" Senior Adult Choir; [hon.] Co-Valedictorian, High School 1952, Who's Who in American Colleges and Universities, selected as program presenter for SEASU at ASCD convention in Philadelphia, PA, 1972, School Board Award for "Teachers Who Make a Difference"; [oth. writ.] Songs and poems written for special people and special occasions all unpublished; [pers.] I have enjoyed writing as long as I can remember. There is always a personal "cleansing" after completing a composition - regardless of the form.; [a.] Nacogdoches, TX

COBB, ISAIAH
[pen.] Isaiah Cobb; [b.] June 21, 1959, Louisville, GA; [p.] Robert A. Cobb Sr. and Frankie Mae Cobb; [ed.] Louisville High School (Louisville GA), International Correspondence School (Scranton, Penn); [occ.] Stocker (Bilo #221); [hon.] I.C.S. (Diploma Awarded Master Art), (Lowes Commitment Award), (Self Improvement Program Award Piggly Wiggly Southern, Inc.), Poet of Merit Award Plaque, Editor's Choice Award; [oth. writ.] A writing about "Fathers" in the Augusta Chronicle, a profile in the "Augusta Focus," a poem publish in "The Garden of Life" title "Wake Up America" another poem title (Stop the Killing) to be used on an album; [pers.] I try to be very "profounded" with my writing. I want people to feel and receive something from my writing. I believe my writing is inspired by God to help people, to let them know there's still "Hope."; [a.] Augusta, GA

CODY, CLAIRE ELISABETH MARY
[b.] June 4, Bloomington, IL; [p.] Peter J. Cody and Mildred L. Cody; [ed.] Frederick High and Life's Experiences; [occ.] Student and Giant Pharmacy Technician; [memb.] National Honors Society, SGA, Girl Scouts, Frederick Regional Youth Orchestra, Saint John's Youth Ministry; [hon.] Principal's Honor Roll (1992-1995), National Honor Society Induction Ceremony (1993), Junior Student Scholar Award (1995), Award of Leadership for Frederick County Schools 1994 and 1995, Half Tuition Scholarship for Hood College Awarded for Academics (1995-1996), Award for Excellence in music (1992, 1993, 1994), Community Service Award 1994, Community Service Award 1995, Girl Scouts Leadership Award, Freshman Class President 1992-1993, Student Government Association Dedication 1992-1995, Principal's Committee (1992-1995); [oth. writ.] Several poems published in School's Literary Magazine; [pers.] With life comes many struggles and great confusion, just keep an open mind and stay true to what you believe in! I'd like to thank my parents for broadening my horizons and giving me a better understanding on life.; [a.] Frederick, MD

CODY, LOUISE CLAUDIA
[pen.] Louise Claudia Cody; [b.] July 2, 1951, Houston, TX; [p.] Dr. and Mrs. Melville Lockett Cody; [ed.] Art Major, Graduated: Lamar High School, attended Southern Methodist University for 2 years; [occ.] Real Estate Sales Artist; [memb.] Houston Tennis Assn., Art League of Houston; [hon.] 5 Years Art Scholarship to the Museum of Fine Arts in High School Poetry Award for City of Houston when 9 years old French Honor Society; [oth. writ.] Children's Book: Wrote and Illustrated: "The Adventures of Marty and Francine in Outer Space"; [pers.] Nothing is the end of the world except the end of the world.; [a.] Houston, TX

COFFMAN, CAROLYN C.
[b.] December 29, 1957, Beauford, SC; [p.] Jack Coffman, Lana Coffman; [ed.] Oceanside High, University of California at Santa Barbara - Film and Psychology; [occ.] Professional Organizer; [memb.] National Association of Professional Organizers, National Study Group Chronic Disorganization, National Speakers Assoc., San Diego Museum of Art, World Wildlife Fund; [hon.] San Francisco Academy of Art, California State Speech Champion, University of California Santa Barbara (UCSB); [oth. writ.] Poetry, fiction, articles, reviews, speeches, promotions; [a.] Carlsbad, CA

COFFMAN, JON
[b.] August 5, 1978, Anchorage, AK; [p.] Beth Coffman and Jack Coffman; [ed.] Weatherford High; [occ.] Student; [memb.] Writer's Club at School; [hon.] None to speak of yet; [oth. writ.] Several unpublished, three including "Love Is...." published in School Literary Magazine, "In the Spotlight"; [pers.] Though not always about the heart, I write from the heart in hopes that it will touch someone's heart.; [a.] Weatherford, TX

COLE, HEATH
[pen.] H.; [b.] April 10, 1970, Lincoln, NE; [p.] Jerry Cole, Deb Cole; [oth. writ.] Swing set from American Bitter (a collection of poems).; [pers.] "Walking on water was not made in a day." Jack Carawack

COLEMAN, GALE O.
[b.] October 26, 1943, GA; [p.] Archie And Cleo Odom; [m.] William M. Coleman Sr., May 11, 1963; [ch.] William M. Jr., Brian Christopher; [ed.] Savannah High School; [occ.] Housewife; [memb.] First Baptist Church Pooler, GA 3rd and 4th Grade Sunday School Teacher; [oth. writ.] Letters to the Editor of our local newspaper. Various other non-published poems.; [pers.] My writings have been inspired by God through deep tragedies in my life. He has given me an outlet through which to grieve. I hope and pray that my work may be a blessing to others.; [a.] Pooler, GA

COLEMAN, MARY ISABELL
[b.] June 23, 1946, Mecklenburg County, VA; [ch.] Zabrina Denise Coleman; [ed.] St. Clare Walker High School, USDA Graduate School; [occ.] Personnel Staffing Specialist, US Office of Personnel Management Washington, DC; [memb.] For the past 36 years, I have been in membership with the Church of the Lord Jesus Christ of the Apostolic Faith; [oth. writ.] Two poems entered in "World of Poetry" contest. Received a "Golden Poet" Certificate. One poem published in the Church's monthly magazine; [pers.] My writing extends from "direct" or "indirect" personal experience, also, I write from "in the extreme" of my imagination.; [a.] Washington, DC

COLLADO, BAMIL GUTIERREZ
[pen.] Bamil "Redwolf" Gutcoll; [b.] April 5, 1969, Aguadilla, PR; [p.] Cecilia Collado; [ed.] Alfredo Dorrington Elementary School, Ramon E. Rodriguez Dias, Dr. Pedro Perea Fajardo Vocational School and InterAmerican University, San German; [occ.] Finish Line Operator in Packaging Dept., Bristol Myers, P.R.; [memb.] ISP Distinguished Member; [hon.] Publications on (1994) "Darkside of the Moon" and "Best Poems of 1995," also recently on "Walk through Paradise" titled "Tombstoned," (1995) Solo Singing and Oratory Awards; [oth. writ.] Free Like the Wind, Reflexions, Afraid to Lose, Daughters of Freedom, The Face of the World, etc. Also I'm working on "Dreaming Heaven" poetry, which I dedicated to the late singer Selena, who tragically passed away.; [pers.] "For sure there is nowhere to hide... Outside there is nowhere to run... We'll have to keep our eyes and heart awaiting, for that giant made of stone" (1994) from (Jupitairlined), poetry by me.; [a.] Mayaguez, PR

COLLIER, CRAIG
[b.] October 16, 1977, Santa Monica, CA; [p.] Gary Collier, Davida Lambert; [ed.] Tom Clark High; [occ.] College Student at ACU (Abilene Christian Univ.); [memb.] Thespian Society; [pers.] I love cats and fuzzy things.; [a.] San Antonio, TX

COLON, TONY
[b.] December 20, 1967; [m.] Maritza Colon, January 26, 1991; [ed.] Governor Mifflin (High School) Self-Educated; [pers.] Poetry has lived with me as much as I live for poetry. I deserve no special honor, it is simply what I love, self educating has and continues to increase my knowledge, and as for influence, it is all around me.; [a.] Allentown, PA

COMNICK, LORI ANN
[b.] June 19, 1978, Mankato, MN; [p.] Kathy and Wes Comnick; [ed.] Maple River High School; [occ.] Senior in High School, Waitress at "Old Country Buffet"; [oth. writ.] This is my first poem to be published.; [a.] Good Thunder, MN

CONKLIN, JOHN D.
[b.] January 16, 1922, Columbus, OH; [p.] John William (deceased) and Rose Lee Conklin; [m.] Mary E. (Hite) Conklin, October 17, 1947; [ch.] John Harvey (44), Mary Carole (Conklin) Reville (47), William Vernon Conklin (32); [ed.] 3 yrs college, no degree Univ. of Cincinnati 39-42 (Interrupted by WW II) Numerous CEU's Trinity Univ., St. Mary's Univ. Indiana Univ., Reasalear Poly Tech. Inst.; [occ.] Retired, Self-Emp., Personal Property Appraiser; [memb.] International Society of Appraisers (ISA), Gemrogical Institute of America (GIA) Alumni, Unity School of Christianity; [hon.] Numerous Military 1942-1972, 5 Commendations ISA's 1st Marketing Award for the Promotion of the Appraising Profession. Numerous Ad and Ad Art Awards, Honorary Award SDC '39; [oth. writ.] Former Sr. Writer, the Airman (official Journal of the Airforce, '63 '67) Former Chief of Public Information, Strategic Air Commanded Base in Spain and North Africa, ADYT and PR several major ad firms. noted tech. writer 10 yrs. Military Historian, Combat Documentation Officer; [pers.] I have been writing professionally for over 50 years and have continuously marveled at the boundless creativity which flows through us.; [a.] Springfield, MD

CONNER, MERCEDES VIGIL
[b.] August 17, 1926, Fort Garland, CO; [p.] Vicente And Lucia Vigil; [m.] Richard Conner, May 3, 1947; [ch.] Claudia, Jim, Patty, Dickie Jone; [ed.] College High School, Greely, Co., Fort Garland High - Adams State College 1944-48 - B.A. Degree 1948; [occ.] Retired Teacher of 33 years. Taught in 5 states - children of many cultures and races; [memb.] International Society of Poets - AARP; [hon.] 4 yrs. Scholastic, Scholarship - Adams State College 1944-48, Editor's Choice Award for poem in Journey of the Mind; [oth. writ.] Translations: Spanish to English for Confederate Air Force, Maintenance and Pilots Manual for Vintage W.W. II Aircraft: The German Heinkel HE - III. Translations for Health Care Agency - English to Spanish; [pers.] Compassion must be for people - especially for children - we must be role models.; [a.] Greenville, TX

CONSTANTINE, JESSICA
[b.] November 9, 1980, Saint Augustine, FL; [p.] Larry Constantine; [ed.] Tate High School; [hon.] Physical Fitness Certificate; [a.] Cantonment, FL

CONSUEGRA, ALEJANDRO
[b.] October 11, 1970, Coral Gables, FL; [p.] Roger and Perla Consuegra; [ed.] St. Brendan High School, Florida International University; [occ.] English Literature Teacher; [oth. writ.] One poem published in Miami Biance - Miami - Dade - Community College, and three published in Coastlines - Florida Atlantic University

CONWAY, RHODA
[b.] June 17, 1963; [p.] Garvell and LaVelle Parmer; [m.] Basil Manley Conway III, June 20, 1981; [ch.] Basil M. Conway IV and Walter James Conway; [ed.] L. W. Higgins High School, Opelika State Technical College, Southern Union J. College; [occ.] Homemaker; [memb.] New Hope Assembly of God; [hon.] Dean's List, President's List; [pers.] For I'm only a tool to write for His Glory.; [a.] Opelika, AL

COOK, RUTH J.
[b.] December 4, 1915, Mahaska, KS; [p.] William S. Livingston, Dora Mae Fuller; [m.] Elmo E. Cook, January 14, 1940; [ch.] Sharon, Glence, Maridel Arlyn and Loren Cook; [ed.] High School Graduate, Mrs. Cook graduated with the Highest Scholastic Honors in Adult Education Classes; [occ.] Homemaker; [memb.] Capitol Christian Center, Palette Club; [a.] Sacramento, CA

COOK, STEPHANIE C.
[b.] June 5, 1964, Oakland, CA; [p.] Nancy Stotts; [m.] John T. Cook, October 24, 1987; [ch.] John Joseph, Lindsay Lee; [ed.] Hayward High, Hayward R.O.C. Program 1983 Nursing Graduate; [occ.] Nurse and Mom; [oth. writ.] Nothing published all of my writings remain in my personal journals.; [pers.] My husband, children and family are the reasons I write. They truly are the spirits in "The Soul Of Life."; [a.] Tracy, CA

COOKS, SARA S.
[b.] November 29, 1966, Philadelphia, PA; [p.] Mr. and Mrs. James and Elizabeth McCoy; [m.] Robert A. Cooks, August 7, 1994; [ch.] One stepson - Brandon Cooks; [ed.] Martin Luther King H.S., Delaware State College B.S., Morgan State University M.S.; [occ.] Teacher Grade 3; [memb.] Greater Piney Grove Baptist Church, Drama Ministry, Rowland Notes Singing Group, Kappa Delta Phi; [hon.] Dean's List, Who's Who in American Colleges and Universities, National Collegiate Award Winner, Miss Delaware State College Resident Director of the Year, Honors Day Speaker, Academic and Student Leadership Awards; [oth. writ.] Leaves, Leaves/Marcey and Me/Pepper, Pepper/A poem for Rob Long Time No See/Christmas Time/The purpose of the Black Female/The Gift of life/A Poem for Mother/A poem for Dad; [pers.] When you tried to find your reason for being, it was probably with you all of the time - it was you who didn't notice it.; [a.] Clarkston, GA

COOLEY, ALTON LEE
[pen.] Al Cooley; [b.] December 8, 1954, Warren; [m.] Emilia Pecorelli Cooley, September 10, 1977; [ch.] Natalie Marie, Michael Thomas; [ed.] Warren Western Reserve High; [occ.] Heat Treating Specialist Railroad Forgings; [memb.] Catholic Charities, American Heart, American Cancer, Toxic Waste; [oth. writ.] Several poems and songs I hope to have published soon.; [pers.] Listening to oldies on my 1995 jukebox, cruising in my 1965 mustang, making wine, spending quality time with my family "give peace a chance" - John Lennon and Paul McCartney; [a.] Warren, OH

COOPER, VALERIE M.
[b.] July 28, 1972, Benton Harbor, MI; [p.] Henry and Ernestine Cooper; [ed.] Associate Degree in Applied Science; [occ.] Registered Nurse; [oth. writ.] Several poems and songs not published; [pers.] I enjoy writing poems and songs, I would like to do it as my career. Songs and poems pop in and out of my head as many times as there are hours in the day.; [a.] Benton Harbor, MI

COPE, ESTHER
[b.] March 13, 1978, Tacoma, WA; [p.] Glenn Cope, Dorothy Cope; [ed.] Victory Christian School, A Beka Home School; [occ.] Student; [pers.] The whole purpose of writing is to express something others can relate to, and that's what I want to do.; [a.] Enon, OH

COPELAND, NORA
[b.] May 1, 1942, Darlington, CT; [p.] Willie Manship, Late Harvey Manship; [m.] Tommy Copeland, December 30, 1960; [ch.] (1) son, deceased (7-12-89), 3 daughter and 3 grandson's; [ed.] High School; [occ.] House wife, Mother and Grandmother; [oth. writ.] Seeking seasons to come; [pers.] Give God the glory and honor for what he is doing in my life.; [a.] Hartsville, SC

COPPEJANS, JOHN
[pen.] John Coppejans; [b.] September 26, 1919, Netherlands; [p.] Johannes and Anna Coppejans; [m.] Patricia Cordes; [ch.] Mark Coppejans; [ed.] In the Netherlands, MULO; [occ.] Retired; [memb.] American Philatelic Society, Smithsonian, etc.; [hon.] Never published anything. Received award for painting; [oth. writ.] Several poems; [pers.] My poems reflect my feelings about nature and several about injustices that abound in our world.; [a.] Santa Barbara, CA

CORDELL, ROBERT J.
[b.] January 7, 1917, Quincy, IL; [p.] Vail and Gertrude Cordell (both Deceased); [m.] Frances S. Cordell, September 20, 1942; [ch.] Victor, David and Peggy; [ed.] B.S. 1939 and M.S. 1940 in Geology - University of Illinois, Urbana - Champaign, Ph.D in Geology - University of Missouri in Columbia 1949; [occ.] Retired, most recent position - President of Cordell Reports, Inc., Richardson, Texas; [memb.] Geological Society of America (Sr. Fellow), American Association for the Advancement of Science (Sr. Fellow), American Association of Petroleum Geologists, Society of Sedimentary Geologists, Dallas Geological Society; [hon.] Biographical Notes in: "Who's Who in America," "Who's Who in the World," "Who's Who in the South and Southwest," "Who's Who in Science and Technology." Special Service Award - 1975 American Association of Petroleum Geologists, Special Publication Award also from AAPG - 1982. Honorary Life Membership - Dallas Geological Society 1977, Outstanding Service Award - Dallas Geological Society 1975 Research and Publication Award - Dallas Geological Society 1978; [oth. writ.] About a dozen articles in technical (Geological and Petroleum) periodicals some 20 volumes on the Geology and Hydrocarbon potential of various regions - mostly in U.S. - these are my commercial reports. In M.S. Form: "Autobiography: It's been an intriguing Voyage," "Essays: The Essence from One Man's Thoughts and Experiences," "Annals of a Global Traveler."; [pers.] I've tried to live a full life, with close family ties (wife, 3 children, 5 grandchildren), and the 50 plus year pursuit of a technical profession, but with an ample seasoning of culture along the way appreciation of the arts (paintings, literature, music, etc.) - meanwhile being an extensive traveler, and also taking an interest in current events (political, economic and social).; [a.] Richardson, TX

COREY, SHELLY
[b.] July 6, 1981, Montclair, CA; [p.] Joseph and Therese Corey; [ed.] Arrowview Middle School; [oth. writ.] I have wrote many other poems, but this is the first I have entered into a contest or had published; [pers.] I find great joy when I express my feelings into the poems I write.; [a.] San Bernardino, CA

CORREIA, ROBERT LLYOD
[b.] Homer, AL; [occ.] Commercial Fisherman and Boat Builder; [a.] Soldotna, AL

CORSO, SALVATORE J.
[b.] November 1, 1959, Brooklyn, NY; [p.] Anthony and Jean Corso; [m.] Mary Corso, May 7, 1988; [ch.] Salvatore John Jr., Christopher Anthony; [ed.] Xaverian High School, Creighton University, Suny-Downstate Medical School; [occ.] Orthopaedic Surgeon; [memb.] Alpha Omega Alpha Medical Honor Society. Arthroscopy Assn. of North America. Nassau County Medical Society. New York Medical Society.; [hon.] ADA Medical Honor Society, Magna Cum Laude Creighton U., Cum Laude - Suny - Downstate Med. Center; [oth. writ.] Publications in several orthopaedic journals; [pers.] Be happy and thankful for what you have and never look back and worry about what has happened, except to learn from mistakes, so that you can make positive adjustments for the future.; [a.] South Huntington, NY

COSAERT, KAREN
[b.] February 24, 1980, Mission Hills, CA; [p.] Tom and Shirley Cosaert; [ed.] North Valley High School; [memb.] Key Club; [hon.] Student of the Month Most Improved Student, Who's Who Among High School Students, Miss American Coed Pageants; [oth. writ.] My special friend, dream, one dream, love not hate, help, can't you see, what is love, for the one I'll always love.; [pers.] I love writing poems. It helps dealing with your feelings. You can express your feelings openly in poems, love, a friend in need is a friend in deed and time.; [a.] Grants Pass, OR

COSTA, AL
[b.] September 28, 1972, Buffalo, NY; [p.] Al Costa Sr., Eileen Szymanski; [ed.] Riverside High School; [occ.] Factory Worker, General Mills Inc.; [oth. writ.] "The Dead of Winter" a collection of poems and lyrics. Not published to date.; [pers.] We are born, and then we die, the pain in the middle is called life. No matter how short, we should all try to make some sort of positive impact on this earth.; [a.] North Evans, NY

COSTA, HORATIO
[pen.] Venerable Huei Ti; [b.] May 1, 1933, Havana, Cuba; [p.] A. Horatio Costa, Elena Costa; [m.] Divorced; [ch.] Ray and Maria; [ed.] Ph.D in Psychotherapy, Northwestern College, Univ. of Tennessee, Post-Graduate Work, Univ. of Madrid, Spain, M.A. in Music, Music Conservatory, Spain, M.A. in Journalism, Univ. of Madrid, Spain B.A. Psychology, Univ. of Navana Cuba; [occ.] Educational Consultant, Los Angeles County School Districts, former College Professor, Memphis State University; [memb.] The London Buddhist Society, London, England, The Theosophical Society in America, Wheaton IL, The Eastern Buddhist Society, Kyoto, Japan, International Zen Center, Hiroshima, Japan, The Theosophical Order of Service; [hon.] Euxcadi Institute, Basque Country, Transpersonal Psychology (1991), Mozart Award, Piano Competition, Music Conservatory of Navana, 1955 - President, The Western Buddhist Society (1992-1995) Dean Emeritus, Rutledge College, Memphis, Tenn.; [oth. writ.] Books: Behind the Mirrors of the South Pacific, The Art of Leadership, Reflecting the Sun (Collection of Haiku poems), essays, articles, poems and haiku published in local and international magazines and newspapers in America, Europe and the Far East.; [pers.] Having lived in many countries and experienced their various religious beliefs. I have come to the realization that there are many paths leading to the same ultimate truth. In my writings, I try to create the awareness that we are all one with each other, as we are one with God.; [a.] Whittier, CA

COSTANZO, LOUIS
[pen.] Louis Costanzo; [b.] April 16, 1960, Johnstown, PA; [ch.] Ashia Nicole Costanzo, Giordano Louis Costanzo; [memb.] Newport Church of the Brethern; [oth. writ.] Several poems and songs not yet published "When That Star Fell" was written from a true experience.; [pers.] Many thanks to Donna Campbell for opening my eyes to love and my inner feelings. I love you Donna.; [a.] Shenandoah, VA

COULTER, PAGE P.
[b.] April 28, 1936, Hartford, CT; [p.] Maxwell Phelps, Frances Phelps; [m.] Robert O. Coulter, January 9, 1960; [ch.] Susan, Polly, Emilie, Roger; [ed.] Sweet Briar College, A.B. French, Wesleyan Univ. Mals; [occ.] Poetry Instructor in Local Schools; [hon.] Academy of American Poets College Prize, Winner Tri-State Dance Choreography Award, Junior Year in France; [oth. writ.] The Cowbridge At Dawn by Mellen Press, poems published in Kansas Quarterly, Minnesota Review, Poetry, Poet pourri, Spectrum, and others.; [pers.] I try to show through my poetry that the survival of the human spirit depends on experiences in nature.; [a.] Guilford, CT

COVACEVICH JR., FRANK V.
[b.] February 13, 1954, New Orleans; [p.] Frank and Mary Covacevich; [m.] Janet Gifford, August 1977; [ed.] H.S. East jefferson, Metairie, LA, Lake Tahoe Community College, Personal Finance - Matting Framing P. Carpenters Intro; [occ.] Promoter; [memb.] Volunteer 18 months, Senior Nutrition Program; [hon.] Coolest Pride of New Orleans Mandigrass 1988, Famous Poets Society - asked to present poem at National Convention in Disneyland - Labor Day 1995; [oth. writ.] Several poems, also I paint and have work hanging in New Orleans and Lake Tahoe Gallery; [pers.] Be good for goodness sake - Only Love All.; [a.] South Lake Tahoe, CA

COX, JENNIFER A.
[oth. writ.] The Alphabet Tree, Sometimes Forever, I Have To Wonder, The New Tenant, Untitled, When I Have Fears, Haiku, My World If Only A Whisper, More Than A Brush Stroke, So They Say, Mel, Reflection, When I Dream..., The Darkening Of The Sight...; [a.] Honolulu, HI

COX, PATSY I.
[b.] November 5, 1954, Odessa, TX; [p.] Mr. and Mrs. W. A. Tampke; [m.] Divorced; [ch.] Christa Nicole Cox, Curtis Travis Cox; [occ.] Accountant; [hon.] Treasured Poems of America 1989 published "Its Never Enough"; [a.] Stafford, TX

CRADDOCK, ANTHONY FARRIS
[b.] July 8, 1976, Longview, TX; [p.] James and Lynn Craddock; [ed.] Pine Tree High School, Kilgare College; [occ.] Full-time Student; [memb.] International Thespian Society, Dead Poet's Society; [hon.] Delta Psi Omega, Phi Theta Kappa, Dean's List; [oth. writ.] Hundreds of unpublished poems written daily upon curious thoughts.; [pers.] Life has given me one full cup. Rather than gulping it down, I have chosen to first savor the aroma then slowly swallow life.; [a.] Longview, TX

CRAIG, GLENN E.
[b.] July 10, 1923, Galesburg, IL; [p.] Glenn and Ann Craig; [ed.] Graduate Galesburg High School, Kansas City Art Inst. (1 yr); [occ.] Retired; [pers.] Self educated beyond High School.; [a.] Houston, TX

CRAIGHEAD, SABRINA
[b.] April 8, 1980, Dover, NJ; [p.] Cindy Craighead; [ed.] Dover Middle School; [memb.] Peer Leadership; [hon.] I've made Honor Roll four times and I have an award in creative writing and a number of other awards; [oth. writ.] I have written stories in school; [pers.] I have been told by a number of teachers that I have good writing skills.; [a.] Dover, NJ

CRAMPTON, BERTHA L.
[b.] March 23, 1955, Houston, TX; [p.] Bertran and Alice Bryant; [m.] Steven E. Crampton, November 7, 1975; [ch.] Kori D'Ann, Jason Alan and Karl Steven; [ed.] Jack Yates Sr. High and Southwest Business College; [occ.] Church Financial Secretary; [pers.] There's a freeness that accompanies a thought, once put to paper. There are no limitations to express one's self. I choose to believe that creative ability is as a seventh sense that God has given man. It's up to the individual to use it.; [a.] Houston, TX

CRANE, ROBERT
[b.] April 10, 1965, Saint Croix Falls, WI; [p.] Vaemond and Bonnie Crane; [ed.] Chaparral High School 1983, Bachelor of Science Psychology, Arizona State University 1988, Master of Math Communication - ASU 1993; [occ.] Poet and Lyricist for Modern Dance Company, "Open Dance"; [hon.] "Cooper's Hawk" - Runner-up, The Writer's Workshop International Poetry Contest 1993 Ashville, NC, 1992 Scottdale Film Festival: "Another Best Narrative 'Tarot' Best Overall and Best Experimental, Scottdale, AZ, 1983 Reggent Academic Scholarship, ASU; [oth. writ.] 1992, Columnist for Press at "The State At ASU", "Challenging The Limits Of Tolerance: Artistic Expression and the First Amendment": Master's Thesis - 1993.; [pers.] Synaptic vision, a lyrical comprehension. Prurient exaltation, temporal cognition. Diminutive mensuration, impercipient apprentice in love with love, the immortal demise.; [a.] Scottsdale, AZ

CRANKSHAW, BARBARA LEE MAPLES
[pen.] Barbara Crankshaw; [b.] February 18, 1931, Imlay City, MI; [p.] Agnes and Andrew Maples; [m.] Donald Ralph Crankshaw, October 28, 1948; [ch.] Dawn Knox, Starr Luth, Marc Mica Crankshaw, Grandson Collin Michael Luth; [ed.] Imlay City High School, Mott Community College, Flint, Michigan Oakland University, Rochester, Michigan; [occ.] Retired Educator; [hon.] Outstanding Staff Member Award; [oth. writ.] Published poems, Detroit Free Press, poems in local news papers short stories published in Tampa Tribune; [pers.] I strive to reflect the love and joy of my family and friends.; [a.] Saginaw, MI

CRAWFORD, RUTH
[pen.] Ruthie; [b.] August 2, 1950, Charm Co, WV; [p.] Charles and Nellie Jones; [m.] Johnny E. Crawford, October 25, 1969; [ch.] John R. and Rebecca S. Crawford; [ed.] 10th Grade of High School took GED (Nuttall High School); [occ.] Home maker; [memb.] Hopewell Baptist Church, North American Hunting Club; [oth. writ.] Have written

over 200 poems of various titles and some songs.; [pers.] Life is a very short highway we travel. We must make everyday count. Do for others and you will have no time to feel sorry for yourself. Most important, show love.; [a.] Hico, WV

CRAWFORD, TEAL SERENITY
[pen.] Lyndon S. Byam; [b.] September 17, 1974, Norvich, NY; [p.] Rodney and Sharon Crawford; [ed.] Waterville High School, Hamilton College (Junior); [hon.] National Honor Society, Vice President, Dean's List, Hanasman Fellowship; [oth. writ.] Poetry published in High School Newspaper.; [pers.] Cherish every source of inspiration in your life, hold onto each of them and always remind them of how much you love them.; [a.] Oriskany Falls, NY

CREARY, HERMAN J.
[b.] October 28, 1927, Kingston, WI; [p.] Herman B. and Ivy E. Creary (both deceased); [m.] Audrey M. Roberts-Creary, August 8, 1953; [ch.] Marianne, Kenneth, Joseph, Martin, Eve, Rose, (Michael), Nicholas, Regina, Christin; [ed.] AB - Forham, MA, Prof. Dipl. - Columbia; [occ.] Retired teacher of French, Latin, English (as Foreign Language); [memb.] NYSTRS, Old Mill Singers, Pupal Choir; [oth. writ.] American Anthology of College Verse, Catholic World, The Maroon, Fire and Ice, Friendship House News - poems, articles; [pers.] Esse bonum supremumest our down Dei Vivat Qui Nos amat semper, totn scientia, totum bonum, tota veritas, totusamor in se.; [a.] Ossining, NY

CRENSHAW, LAURA
[b.] October 8, 1969, Mosco, ID; [p.] Bernette Ronfeld; [m.] Kerry S. Crenshaw, January 23, 1995; [ch.] One; [ed.] Certified Personal Trainer; [occ.] Personal Trainer, Owner, Badd Dang Gym; [memb.] National Health Club Assoc, N.W. Martial Arts Assoc.; [pers.] Enjoy each day - as if tomorrow will never come.; [a.] Mount Home, ID

CRINKLAW, KATHERINE
[b.] February 11, 1959, Newman, CA; [p.] John and Dorothy Menezes; [m.] Michael Crinklaw, February 22, 1986; [ch.] Mark, Morgan and Jason Crinklaw; [ed.] Gustine High School, I am a self taught artist, (Water colorist); [occ.] Artist; [memb.] Central California Art League, Turlock Golf - Country Club; [hon.] Received Major's Award, Turlock Art League - 1993 Honorable Mention, Central Calif. Art League 1992-93 Best of Catagory in Watercolors, Turlock Art League, and Mayors Award 1995 I will be included in the 19th Edition of Who's Who of American Women; [oth. writ.] I have been writing poetry since I was a young girl; [pers.] I hope that my paintings move those who see them to view the world, and nature in particular in a different light, and see the beauty in the simple things around them. With my poems I attempt to paint a picture with words.; [a.] Newman, CA

CRONE, JAMIE
[b.] March 27, 1975, Cumberland, MD; [p.] Paul Crone, Linda Crone; [ed.] Frankfort H.S., Allegany Community College, Fairmont State College; [hon.] Outstanding Electro Mechanical Technology Graduate, Dean's List, Who's Who Among Students in American Junior Colleges; [oth. writ.] None published; [pers.] It would just depress you.; [a.] Cumberland, MD

CRONIN, JOHN
[b.] Chicago, IL; [p.] Leonard and Mary Cronin; [ed.] Art Institute of Chicago, BAE - Art Institute of Chicago, MFA; [occ.] High School Teacher; [memb.] Other voices - Catholics and the arts; [hon.] Dean's List, Listed In: Who's Who Among America's Teachers 1992; [a.] Chicago, IL

CRONIN, LOIS K.
[b.] August 21, 1934, New York City, NY; [p.] Idalah Kendricks and Louis Kendricks; [m.] (Deceased) Daniel J. Cronin, November 26, 1971; [ch.] Denise - Cindy - Michele - Stephen; [ed.] Guilford High Southern Conn State Univ., B.S. English - Minor Literature Teaching Degree; [occ.] Licking County Aging Program; [memb.] Former Chairman Democratic Town Committee Branford, CT; [oth. writ.] Other poem published in Conn. State Univer. Literary Mag.; [pers.] Having survived 2 husbands with 4 children - 4 stepchildren I tend to see the dark side that everyone has but is afraid to talk about. To talk about the darkness brings in a little light.; [a.] Newark, OH

CROSON, GARY
[b.] December 7, 1963, Garfield Heights; [p.] Robert Croson Sr., Janice Croson; [ed.] High School Graduate; [occ.] Truck Driver, Over the Road; [pers.] Everybody seems so smart until you hear them whine about what they seem to be so smart about.; [a.] Concord, OH

CROUSE, LINDSAY MARIE
[b.] April 3, 1987, CA; [p.] Richard and Joanne Crouse; [ed.] I am in the Third Grade; [memb.] Junior Valley Golf Assoc., Temecula, CA, Lake Elsinore, Girls Softball, Lake Elsinore, CA, OPUS Gymnastics, Lake Elsinore Tumble Jungle, Murrieta, CA; [pers.] I enjoy writing poems and reading.; [a.] Lake Elsinore, CA

CROW, ERIN
[pen.] Erin Crow; [b.] March 28, 1980, El Paso, TX; [p.] Kenneth, Janis Crow; [ed.] Clear Brook High School; [pers.] When I write I express my feelings and what I think of the world. And think everybody should always express themselves.; [a.] Friendswood, TX

CROWDER, PAUL O.
[b.] November 10, 1956, Montgomery, AL; [p.] Mary B. Crowder; [ch.] De'Lisa Sade Crowder; [ed.] Montgomery High, University of Charleston; [hon.] Three different poems published by National Library of Poetry, published in the following books, Walk through Paradise, Mists of Enchantment, A Delicate Balance; [pers.] To try to count my fellow man as a friend, and never forgetting we all make mistakes, but leaving enough room in our hearts to be willing to forgive.; [a.] Charleston, WV

CROWELL, MARGARET
[b.] June 20, 1944, Yonkers, NY; [p.] John and Mary Crowell; [ch.] Came from large family (one of 7 children) and raised by devoted parent; [ed.] 1. Blessed Sacrament H.S., Manhattan, NY, 2. St. Clare's Hospital NY, 3. Merecy College - Dobbs Ferry - NY (B.S. in Psychology); [occ.] Working as Registered Nurse in Florida - Relocated 4 years ago, from New York; [memb.] Bronx Right To Life; [hon.] Dean's List, Mercy College, Magna Cum Laude, B.S. in Psychology, Received, B+ Art appreciation, B+ Music in College; [oth. writ.] Letters to Editor published in Catholic Hew Yorker and Long Island Tribune, have always enjoyed and been interested in all poems of art expression.; [pers.] Hope to marry and adopt a child or two in near future. Believe in you can strive and accomplish almost anything in life with God as your co-pilot and if you remain "young at heart."; [a.] Tampa, FL

CRUM, CONNIE FULTZ
[b.] July 29, 1960, Frenchburg, KY; [p.] Fred Fultz and Wanda Fultz Snider; [ch.] Freddie (15), Ashley (8), Kellie (2), Stepdaughters Heather (8), Rachel 6; [occ.] Legal Secretary; [oth. writ.] A collection of poems regarding my life experiences, some children stories about our family's experiences and the beginning of my life story.; [pers.] Writing helps me deal with emotional crises and deepens my enjoyment of pleasant events. I feel I have many personal experiences worth sharing, marriage, death of first spouse, child birth, divorce, etc.; [a.] Frenchburg, KY

CRUM, JOHN, J.
[pen.] Jerry; [b.] May 20, 1976, Cherry Hill, NJ; [p.] Theresa A. Crum; [ed.] Encinal High School; [occ.] Student; [hon.] Dean's List, Principals Award, John Philip Sousa Award; [oth. writ.] "I knew A Girl Who Threw A Shoe", "Words In The Wind", "Your Kiss", and other untitled poems for Tom; [pers.] Of all the motivational forces in life, none are as rewarding as the inspiration of true love. Thank you Charlene.; [a.] Alameda, CA

CUBIC, MARK A.
[b.] April 22, 1961, Pittsburgh, PA; [p.] Andrew Cubic, Dee Cubic; [m.] Kimberly Cubic, December 19, 1982; [ch.] Lucas Andrew, Samantha Paige; [ed.] Downers Grove North, IL, Marshall University; [occ.] Manager, Goodys Family Clothing; [memb.] United States Golf Association (U.S.G.A.); [hon.] Lettered in Soccer 1978; [oth. writ.] First publication; [pers.] I look at life through realistic eyes. I have been greatly influenced by John Lennon.; [a.] Roanoke, VA

CUCKLER, SUSAN R.
[pen.] Rose Allen; [b.] March 16, 1948, Syracuse, NY; [p.] Paul and Glen Galloway; [m.] Divorced; [ch.] Two sons; [ed.] La Fargeville High School, Watertown School of Nursing; [occ.] Nurse; [memb.] American Nurses Association; [oth. writ.] Special poems for family and friends. A few stories for my nieces and nephews. Weeping Willow was the first I've ever entered in a contest.; [pers.] Listen and you will hear, open your eyes and you will see. Some of God's most beautiful creations are glistening in the sunshine and are whispering in the wind.; [a.] Saxtons River, VT

CURRIER, ANNE B.
[pen.] Anne B. Currier; [b.] September 22, 1922, Kittery, ME; [p.] Alfred and Mathilda Charest; [m.] Joseph a Currier, May 1, 1939; [ch.] Dorothy Anne, James Alfred and Thomas Albert; [ed.] 8th Grammar School; [occ.] Retired on Soc Sec; [memb.] St. Francis Church; [hon.] N.H. Honorable State Song Six Songs on Congressional Record including California. Honorable Mention (Resolution) from CA. State Assembly. CA. State "Highlight Song" which led to the "51 State Highlight" Songs.; [oth. writ.] Several books: One done in braille, sold two, am on the second book. Enclosed find explanation of what a "Highlight" song is. This is a reference book and donated to some libraries: Our state library: Pres and

Barb, Bush.; [per.] Since I have had so little education, I would like to put something back into it, by sharing my work with others. My highest goal would be to have a highlight book in every library and home. I was told I was the only person who ever tried to replace our National Anthem.

CUTSHAW, IRENE LAVERNE
[pen.] Irene McCartney, Princess White Dove; [b.] July 11, 1957, Cleveland, OH; [p.] Arthur Davis (step-father), Patricia Dawson, Raymond McCartney; [m.] Randy Marce Cutshaw, May 26, 1993; [ch.] Adopted out in 1981, Corey Lee Howard, Joseph Michael Polleck; [ed.] Ged, Pittsburgh Job Corps, July 1979 - August 1980; [occ.] Housewife; [memb.] Job Corbs Alumni Association; [hon.] Honorable Mentions, Nominated in 1984 for Volunteer of year, many certificates of appreciation for volunteer work, volunteer for special olympics and sports, by abilities games 1983, and many other volunteer jobs; [oth. writ.] Several poems published one was with National Library of Poetry and also others.; [pers.] I write from my experiences and what is in my heart. Also God and my guardian angel are my helpers. They help me to be able to help others by my own experiences and to share this.; [a.] Cleveland, OH

D' AMPOLO, CONRAD
[b.] February 10, 1933, Boston, MA; [ed.] High School, Ed. Boston, Berklee School of Music, experienced in Music and Life.

D'ANTONIO, CHRIS
[b.] June 13, 1978, Woodstock, IL; [p.] Lonnie Farr and Don D'Antonio; [ed.] Currently a Senior in High School; [oth. writ.] A personal collection of my other poems, one of the most recent being "CHANGE" dedicated to the victims of the Oklahoma City bombing.; [pers.] I guess I am an idealist. I look toward a future where we recognize a little bit of ourselves in each other and put down the guns, shut our angry mouths, and sit down to really listen to what we have to say to each other.; [a.] Crystal Lake, IL

DAER, ROBERTA HARYDZAK
[b.] April 13, 1957, Pittsburgh; [m.] Bob Daer, May 31, 1980; [ch.] Amber Leigh, Stephen Robert; [memb.] C.G. Jung Educational Center of Pittsburgh Member of Road of Directors; [pers.] I try to priority through the and of poetry images of thought that I've encounieced on my own personal quest of my insistence the true naive of love.; [a.] Pittsburgh, PA

DAHM, ELIZABETH MCLANE
[ed.] Bowdoin College; [a.] Winchester, MA

DAIDONE, CHARES A.
[b.] April 1, 1965, Bronx, NY; [p.] Carolann, Anthony Daidone; [m.] Debra Franko; [ed.] Bergenfield High, Bergenfield N.J.; [occ.] Freelance Musician, Landscape Design; [oth. writ.] Currently working on first non-fiction novel. Have written many unpublished poems and songs.; [pers.] The mind cannot nurture and open if the book pages are left closed.; [a.] Somerset, NJ

DAILEY, DOLLY ANN
[pen.] Dolly Dailey; [b.] February 13, 1957, Saluda, SC; [p.] Blanche Bobb Croner; [m.] James Croner, May 11, 1975; [ch.] Johnny E. Nobles; [ed.] 9th grade later - Tech. to Finish Special Training in Communication with Effected Children; [occ.] Nashville Deans Singer; [memb.] Under contract currently with Holton Records Nashville as a singer; [oth. writ.] "Beyond the crooked Path" - also - "Once I knew you."; [pers.] Everything I write is a reflection of something or someone I've known. My greatest influence is life itself. Dolly Dailey.; [a.] Nashville, TN

D'AMPOLO, CONRAD
[b.] February 10, 1933, Boston, MA; [ed.] High School, Ed. Boston, Berklee School of Music experienced in Music and Life

DANIELSON, JAMES E.
[b.] February 4, 1949, Jamestown, NY; [p.] Richard and Marilyn Danielson; [ed.] Maple Grove High School 1967; [occ.] Quality Inspector (factory) Valeo Engine Cooling; [memb.] United Auto Workers Local 2231; [oth. writ.] Several poems published in College Anthology. One poem published in Company Newsletter.; [pers.] Truth in poetic form is one thing that makes life bearable. What an empty world the children of the new millennium would face without beautiful words to make their spirits soar.; [a.] Jamestown, NY

DANSO, ROBERT VAN-EARL
[pen.] R.D. Van-Earl; [b.] June 19, 1950, Ghana, West Africa; [p.] Robert Aboagye, Margaret Asiedva; [m.] Selina A. Danso, April 1, 1981; [ch.] Paul, Sarah, Rebecca, Sharon, Joseph and Doreen; [ed.] Kwahu Ridge Secondary Sch. Obo-kwahu, ghana, Abuakwa State College, Kibi Ghan., Salvation Army Primary/Middle Sch. Begordiakim Ghana; [occ.] Evangelist/Missionary (Reside in U.S.A.); [memb.] 1. Spoken word Ministry., 2. Clergy Card International; [hon.] 1. Certificate in poetry by arts council of ghana, during first ghana youth festival—1977., 2. Written 20 Gospel songs for a local singing group (The Supreme Evangelic; [oth. writ.] Published poems in a local magazine called "Ideal Woman" in the 70's.; [pers.] God gives inspiration to encourage, and to follow the footsteps to righteousness. These nuggets lies in the volumes of his word. Yet, blindness and modern science have weaken its power to protect.; [a.] New Haven, CT

DANTZLER, ANNIE HOBSON
[pen.] Annie Dantzler; [b.] November 15, 1950, Belzoni, MS; [p.] Lee and Mary Hobson; [m.] Gerald Dantzler, March 13, 1974; [ch.] Gerald II, Darion Dantzler and Ivan Dantzler; [ed.] Community College, Graduated High School, Gary Indiana's Roosevelt High; [occ.] Secretary, Detroit Edison; [memb.] Notary Public, writing for the movies; [oth. writ.] I have been writing movie scripts for last two years. I have three complete. I have ten I am working on. I need help getting them on screen.; [pers.] "You can do it." "Never give up." I have written poetry and stories since 7 years old. It helped seeing children friends (Jacksons) succeed.; [a.] Detroit, MI

DARROW, JOEY
[b.] September 27, 1985, Kansas City, MO; [p.] Tim and Virginie Darrow; [ed.] Dabney Elementary 4th Grader; [memb.] Stamp Club, Black Water Federation Indian Guides Trail, Blazers Mohawk Tribe; [hon.] Tae Kwon Do Red Belt Black Tip; [a.] Leesburg, FL

DAVIDOFF, SHERRI ELIZABETH TEMKIN
[b.] December 19, 1980, Princeton, NJ; [p.] Sheila and E. Martin Davidoff; [a.] East Brunswick, NJ

DAVIDSON, ANITA M.
[b.] October 14, 1961, Gardner, MA; [p.] Robert and Carol Davidson; [ch.] Garret T. Cara Rae Davidson; [ed.] Ged; [occ.] Mother; [oth. writ.] Poem in Worcester Telegram, poem, Mists of Enchantment.

DAVIS, BRUCE R.
[b.] January 1, 1934, NC; [m.] Donna, May 27, 1978; [ed.] BA, U. North Carolina at Chapel Hill, MA, USC, Los Angeles, Ph.d, United Status International, University San Drego; [occ.] Researcher; [memb.] Am. Educ. Research Assoc, Calif. Educ. Research Assoc, Assoc, of CA School Administrators, Phi Delta Kappa; [oth. writ.] Thirty never report of educational research and evaluation.; [pers.] Universal consciousness in God. The self craver reunion with God. Sincerity is forever.; [a.] San Diego, CA

DAVIS, DONNIE PEARLETHIA DELORES PENDARUIS
[pen.] Donna; [b.] November 25, 1956, Harleyville; [p.] Sam and Lula Pendaruis; [m.] David Lee Davis, August 18, 1983; [ed.] South Carolina State College Major Elem Ed.; [occ.] Sub-Teacher and Poet; [memb.] Mt. Zion A.M.E. Church President; [hon.] Who's Who in America College Students 1977 or 76, Most Versatile in Senior Class 1975 at Harteyville Ridge UME. Best all around in Senior Class of 1975; [oth. writ.] What do you do when It's over. (Mag soul tear 1976 or 75).; [pers.] I've Learned, that we are always learning through life's experience … It's an on going learning process.; [a.] Harleyville, SC

DAVIS, JEANETTE ESTEP
[b.] July 9, 1944, Beach Mount, NC; [m.] Walter T. Davis; [ch.] Douglas A. Davis (son); [occ.] Housewife; [pers.] Words, like musical notes, are nothing by themselves. Their arrangements together is what gives them their value. A poet simply adds harmony to their arrangements.; [a.] Huber Heights, OH

DAVIS, MARIA
[pen.] Teri Davis; [b.] July 19, 1956, Miami, AZ; [p.] Arthur D. and Elisa Montenegro; [m.] Ronald Davis, January 31, 1986; [ch.] Ernest Ralph Abraham, Jacqueline Ariel; [ed.] Jefferson High, Skyline College; [occ.] Residential Manager; [memb.] QPBC, SKL; [oth. writ.] Article in Fitness Now Magazine; [pers.] Life is a jewel of many facets, reflecting the common experiences of human kind, be they joy, sorrow, or the everyday experiences we all share.

DAVIS, MICHELLE
[pen.] Shelly D., Ms. M.; [b.] March 18, 1961, Los Angeles, CA; [p.] Carolyn and Jim Davis; [ed.] Dorsey High School, El Camino College, Lumbleau Real Estate School, U.C.L.A.; [occ.] Secretary; [memb.] ZCF Training Ctr. Alumni; [hon.] ZCF Leadership Training Graduate with highest honor (Double Pauline Award); [oth. writ.] Published locally - Hamilton Poet Review. To date most of my poems are shared with friends, family, church and other public readings.; [pers.] This is a God-given gift, and I pray it encourages and inspires, those who hear/read Dedicated to: Louise Davis and Johnnie B. Davis.; [a.] Torrance, CA

DAVIS, TABITHA S.
[b.] February 24, 1980, East Liverpool, OH; [p.] Clyde and Diann Davis; [ed.] Sophomore at East Liverpool High School, East Liverpool, Ohio 43920; [occ.] Student; [memb.] Tri-M; [hon.] Dare Outstanding Student Award Choir Letter; [oth. writ.] I have wrote other poems just to keep.; [pers.] I wrote this poem (laughing, smiling, talking, crying) in remembers of my grandmother Irene Kidder.; [a.] East Liverpool, OH

DAVIS, VIRGIE M.
[b.] October 6, 1920, Pittsburg, TX; [p.] Phillip and Irene Buchanan; [m.] Louis Thomas Davis, December 12, 1939; [ch.] Marion G. Davis, Sharion M. Patterson, Melba Wiseman; [occ.] Retired; [oth. writ.] Songs; [pers.] I love poetry, music, and art. I paint scenery pictures, and play guitar. I also love to read love stories.

DAVIS, WILLIAM R.
[b.] April 13, 1926, CA; [m.] Maria Eresa, July 24, 1965; [ch.] Robert, Peter, John, Christina, Elizabeth; [ed.] Ashland, Ore. High - Univ. of Oregon; [occ.] Sales Consultant; [memb.] Knights of Columbus Regent, St. Vincent High School, Petaluma, CA; [hon.] "Death Sentence on Communism" reviewed by President Kennedy; [oth. writ.] Many unpublished poems; [pers.] My poems reflect my own thoughts.; [a.] Petaluma, CA

DAWSON, COLIN ANDREW
[b.] October 17, 1982, Lancaster, OH; [p.] Joyce and Steve Dawson; [ed.] I am entering 7th grade at Thomas Ewing Jr. High School and have attended Kids In College which is a Summer Program for the past two years; [occ.] Student; [hon.] I am an honor student who has achieved straight A's for the past two years. I have also received numerous awards and certificates; [oth. writ.] I have published a poem in the 1994 edition of Anthology of Poetry by Young Americans. I am also working on five novels and have already completed five poems.; [pers.] Some sights and thoughts overcome feelings of mine and flood my mind with words. Through writing it is that I can express these sights and thoughts of mine best.; [a.] Lancaster, OH

DAWSON, LARRY
[pen.] Larry Dawson; [b.] December 3, 1955, San Francisco, CA; [p.] Alton and Malora Dawson; [m.] Antoinette Renee Dawson, May 5, 1990; [ch.] Morgan Ane; [ed.] Polytechnic High School, City College of San Francisco, University of San Francisco; [occ.] Local Area Network Administrator; [memb.] Progressive Missionary Baptist Church, All God's Children, Brother's Being Brothers; [oth. writ.] Several poems unpublished; [pers.] Dreams can change the world, but only you can fulfill your dream. When you don't, the world suffers. When you do, the world reaps a bountiful harvest.; [a.] Danville, CA

DAWSON, ROBERT O.
[pen.] Robby Dawson; [b.] December 5, 1977, Bend, OR; [p.] Denise Schilling, Steve Thornton and Eddy Dawson; [ed.] Timberline High School 11th grade; [occ.] Student; [memb.] Assistant Head Coach for Lolo Exceptional Athletes, Idaho Special Olympics; [hon.] 3-16-92 Award essay on Idaho, selected for display at Idaho state Capitol in Boise Math counts Award - 92, Foot ball Award 93-94, 94-95, 95-96; [oth. writ.] Oh Beautiful Idaho, snowflakes the Shadow, I'd love you just the same he saw it all...; [pers.] Thanks to my teacher Mrs. Cochran for believing in me and my family's love, but most of all for Grandpa and Grandma.; [a.] Pierce, ID

DAWSON, VICKI L.
[pen.] Victoria Scott; [b.] September 16, 1951, Magnolia, AK; [p.] E. L. and Trixie Scott; [m.] Gilbert W. Dawson, January 28, 1995; [ch.] Rachel Leigh (14), Daniel Monroe (12), Ashley Nicole (10); [ed.] Jennings High, Jennings, LA 1969, 1989 Houston Community College, Houston Texas, R.W.A Conferences 1990-1993; [occ.] President - Wild Nest Enterprises; [memb.] National Romance Writers of America, West Houston Romance Writers, Golden Triangle Writers Guild, Toastmasters; [hon.] 1993 National RWA Newsletter - 1st Place, Golden Triangle Writer's Guild, 1992 - 2nd Place Poetry, Corpus Christi by liners - poetry; [oth. writ.] 4 Romance Novels, National Newsletter for RWA, School Newsletters, article published in newspaper.; [pers.] Heart threads was written during the most heart wrenching time of my life - a divorce. In the process I learned of my own strength and also that love is possible even in extreme turmoil.; [a.] Houston, TX

DAYS, CASSANDRA D.
[pen.] Cassie; [b.] January 25, 1969, Inglewood, CA; [p.] John James and Debi Perrin; [m.] Robert B. Days, August 24, 1990; [ch.] Justin Payne, Trevyn John Beuce, Trentyn Robert Michael, Cassarina Chantelesa Dianne; [ed.] Juneau - Douglas High, SST Travel School of AK, University of AK Southeast; [occ.] Community Reg Affairs Accounting Clerk III; [memb.] Washington State Chapter, S.I.D.S., AK Resident Sport Anglers Association, 2 and 3 grade Sunday School Teacher; [oth. writ.] Publications in Shadows and Sunlight for S.I.D.S., article in Juneau Empire.; [pers.] For God's love and grace through Him, my family and my friends my poetry would not be. For their encouragement and love am I able to continue my writings.; [a.] Juneau, AK

DE GALLEGOS, RICHARD LAWRENCE
[pen.] Richard Lawrence; [b.] October 21, 1940, Albuquerque, NM; [p.] Henry and Bebe Gallegos; [m.] Deceased, December 3, 1961; [ch.] Lisa, Christina, Richard, Anna and Sarah; [ed.] BA in Chemistry Masters in Math and Bio Chemistry, JD in Law presently working on PHD; [occ.] Professor of Law; [memb.] American Bar Assoc.; [hon.] Life Time Teaching Credential Calif. Community College, Advanced Trial Advocacy Hastings College Calif, whose who in Law, Whose who in American; [oth. writ.] Have written a book of Poetry Not yet published have written a book (science fiction) not published working on fiction novel based on my life.; [pers.] Would like to infuse my scientific and legal, and teaching back ground into a flow of literature.; [a.] Anaheim, CA

DE HOOP, WILMA
[pen.] Wilma De Hoop; [b.] January 16, 1935, Randolph, WI; [p.] Carl and Winnie Hoffman; [m.] Sam De Hoop, December 4, 1951; [ch.] Don, Ron (twin sons), Sandra Kay, James Randall; [ed.] High School; [occ.] Housewife; [memb.] Bellflower Brethren Church; [oth. writ.] Poems published in local newspaper, also short stories. Articles also published in Living Magazine.; [pers.] I acknowledge the God and creator of this universe who has gifted me with talents.; [a.] Lakewood, CA

DE MARTINIS, JAMES
[pen.] Jimmy Dee; [b.] April 12, 1939, Staten Island, NY; [p.] Eleanor and James De Martinis; [m.] Joan (Divorced January 1993), May 15, 1965; [ch.] Donna, Matthew, David, Nancy, James Jr.; [ed.] AAS Nursing CPR Instructor; [occ.] Registered Nurse; [memb.] New York City Retired fire fighters (Arizona chapter); [hon.] Class B Commendation for Heroism NYC Fire Dept.; [pers.] Bring to light "Real" Human experiences at times like x'mas as seen through different eyes.; [a.] Scotts Dale, AZ

DEAN, LESTER
[b.] November 23, 1953, Florence, AL; [p.] Bruce and Ruth Dean; [m.] Randy Dean; [ed.] G.E.D, University of North Alabama, Northwest/Shoals Community College; [memb.] Rock of Faith Church Petersville, AL; [hon.] Won awards in photography at State Fairs and a local museum; [oth. writ.] Priceless Treasure poem in The Garden of Life book and on audio cassette The Sound of Poetry and There is a God in Best Poems of 96 book.; [pers.] My aim through my poetry is to gain some personal satisfaction in reaching the unconverted and be a blessing and inspiration.; [a.] Florence, AL

DEAS, DONTRELLE
[pen.] Don; [b.] September 19, 1973, Florence; [p.] Hebert and Agnes Deas; [ed.] Wilson High, Spartanburg Methodist College, Norfolk State University Greenville Technical College; [occ.] Chemical Operator C.H. Patrick and Co.; [memb.] Trinity Baptist Church; [hon.] Whose, Who Among American Athletes; [oth. writ.] Several poems; [pers.] I never thought that I had only poetic ability. This hidden talent was reviled when my grandfather died and I wrote a poem about what he meant to me. I was nineteen years old at the time.; [a.] Florence, SC

DECK, ANNIA
[b.] February 2, 1967, Chattanooga, TN; [p.] Jack Rowland, Gaynell Rowland; [m.] Thomas Deck, February 2, 1984; [ch.] Richard Jeffery, Natasha Lynn, Katrina Marie, Thomas William; [ed.] Antelope Valley High, I am currently enrolled at the Institute of Children's Literature; [occ.] Mother/Homemaker; [oth. writ.] Several other poems, one of which was also published by the National Library of Poetry.; [pers.] I dedicate this poem to my nephew David. I think that people need to forget about greed, and simply learn how to care about our fellow man.; [a.] Palmdale, CA

DECKARD, GLORIA
[b.] Philadelphia; [m.] Widow; [ch.] Two (son and daughter); [ed.] University of PA Language Major; [occ.] Self - Employed - Business Woman; [oth. writ.] Song Lyrics, Poetry and Comedy; [pers.] Civic minded, politically active.

DEGRAW, ROBERT E.
[b.] January 2, 1936, Rhode Island; [ed.] Junction City High School, University of Washington, San Diego Voctec, U.S.N. Electronics School, several Sales SChools, other continuing Ed Programs; [occ.] Building Ideas and Hiking Book Publisher; [memb.] Parents WIthout Parnters, FRiends of Mt. Si, Snoqualmie Valley Trails Club, Issaquah Alps Trails Club, Plus others; [hon.] Several Regional Publications Won Several 1st Places; [oth. writ.] Over 300 published Trail Stories, 10 Electronic Books at the

Boeing Company Book - Mate Finding Tips, 6 unpublished Joke Books, a series of semi-annual books - The Art and Craft Shows Guide of Washington, How to Write Personal Ads, Etc.; [pers.] Dreams are put to sleep with time. Experience has taught me to prosper richly in them. People rich in dreams, soon lose their ability to respond just my verse concludes.; [a.] Kirkland, WA

DELANEY, CATHY
[b.] June 21, 1950, Chicago, IL; [p.] Robert and Hazel Rado; [m.] Jerry Delaney, October 27, 1991; [ed.] A.I.C., Long Beach City College, Cerritos College; [hon.] The National Library of Poetry is the first Honor bestowed on me. The most important personal day of my life; [oth. writ.] Personal poems (unpublished); [pers.] Searching for a reconciliation between life and death, fear and courage, joy and sorrow.; [a.] Long Beach, CA

DELFYETT, DORCAS H.
[b.] July 9, 1961, Fort Walton Beach, FL; [p.] Jerry and Annie Nead; [m.] Peter J. Delfyett, September 2, 1989; [ed.] Fordham University, Lincoln CTR, NYC, UNIV. of Central Florida, Orlando FL, Valencia Com College; [occ.] Student; [memb.] UCF Women's Club; [hon.] Presidents List, Deans List; [oth. writ.] Several poems and short stories.; [pers.] I attempt to translate the beauty of nature into the written word. I have been greatly influenced by prof. Christopher Hewit Fordham Univ. in NYC. Eng. Dept.

DEMAS, SOPHIA
[pen.] Sophia Demas; [b.] March 10, 1934; [p.] Stamatea Stacey; [m.] James Demas, (Divorced); [ch.] Three College Graduates, one grand son; [ed.] High School Teacher, Graduate of Long Island University with Summa Cum Laude Degree, Highest Honors; [occ.] Disable Teacher due to Car Accident; [memb.] Historical American Honor Society and Understand in God Faith and Love Member; [hon.] Summa Cum Laude Degree, making the Dean's List, Monroe College, 2 Best Studies Teach Relationship Award, Honor by the American Parent Teacher Association; [oth. writ.] 300 Copy written poems originals in the American Library of Congress Copywright office. Sophia's Autobiography.; [pers.] By reading conscious raising books I have achieved a Cosmic Positive Conscious and intellect for common good.; [a.] Holbrook, NY

DEMATAS, WENDY VENESA
[b.] Trinidad; [p.] Victor Dematas, Ann Dematas; [pers.] I directed mind to know, to investigate and to seek wisdom and explanation... ecclesiastic 7:25. For the people that the world so greatly seeks begins from within on individuals heart by having a forgiving heart. I have yet to see the ten commandments not broken Romans 5:20 and unconditional love among people.; [a.] Gainesville, FL

DEMPSEY, SARAH FAY MORGAN
[b.] February 12, 1926, Springfield, SC; [p.] Henry Arthur and Sallie J. Morgan; [m.] Horace C. (Jack) Dempsey, July 17, 1954; [ch.] Russell Morgan Dempsey, Derek Jean Dempsey, Terrilyn Fay Dempsey- Roddy; [ed.] College Degree Winthrop - Rock Hill, S.C. Plus some Post Graduate Work; [occ.] Retired from Public School Teaching - Mathematics; [memb.] Educations (AARP) and Retirement Organizations. Club Life Resorts Inc. Interval International World and Preferred; [oth. writ.] None under publication at this time.; [pers.] Poems may form the stepping stories of the path towards a full and rewarding life to guide and direct the foot prints of the young.; [a.] Niceville, FL

DENE, PATRICIA
[b.] February 17, 1941, Brooklyn, NY; [p.] Patrick and Constance Armentano; [m.] Michael Dene, October 20, 1962; [ch.] Lydia Dene, Audrey Bregante, Carl Dene; [ed.] Fontbonne Hall Academy, H.S. Fordham Univ.; [occ.] Housewife; [pers.] My greatest desire in life is to write a novel which I am presently working on. It would give me deep gratification to fulfill this dream.; [a.] Long Beach, CA

DEPASQUALE, LOUIS A.
[b.] September 4, 1930, New York; [p.] Lucia and Felice DePasquale; [m.] Iris H. DePasquale, September 7, 1985; [ch.] Diane, Joyce, Louis Jr.; [ed.] H. S. Graduate; [occ.] Retired from New York City Fire Dept.; [memb.] B. P. O. Elks #335 Loyal Order of The Moose #708, Retired Firefighters of N.Y.C., Arizona Treasure Club, Arizona Book Association, Arizona Songwriters Association; [oth. writ.] The National Firefighters Recipe Book; [pers.] I have tried to be a Professional Songwriter for many years, I have been under contract numerous times with little success.

DERRICO, VIVIAN V. MCCLAY
[pen.] Vivian Van Lennep; [b.] June 2, 1912, New York City; [p.] Charles Alfred Van Lennep, Elizabeth Van Lennep; [m.] Widow; [ch.] Robert McClay, William McClay; [ed.] Graduate Villa Maria Academy Greentree PA, Immaculate High School, College Immaculate, PA; [occ.] Retired Pitney Bowes, New York City; [hon.] From Pitney Bowes for Creating a directory of St. Claire. All city durations for Dudes VSC; [oth. writ.] A group of poems never published I wrote interested? All written when mood come mostly under stress.; [pers.] Created feelings stress love, kindness love for all mankind grand mothers brother was Robert Fitcher Germany National Poet.; [a.] Kolbrook, NY

DESTINEE, DELIA
[b.] Virginia; [p.] Rev. and Mrs. Samuel T. Stone, (Deceased); [m.] Bruce T. Faatz, ("Fates"); [ch.] Cynthia "Sunshine" Young and Karen Maria Capo; [ed.] Drams Major Howard University - Wash. D.C., Journalist School, U.S. Navy school of Journalism Great Lakes, Ill.; [occ.] Singer-Actress Play writer-Lyricist-Composer; [memb.] (Professional Organizations), Actors Equity - Singer Actress off b'way and regional those" BMI (Broad cask music inc. as writer and publisher, dramatists guild as playwright - lyric - composer; [hon.] (High school) won 3 competitive school ships to, 1. Howard University, 2. Talladaga College, 3. Fisk University; [oth. writ.] Wrote Book, Music of Lyrics for the following, shows a dramatic play with music "Have you seen sunshine" "Lady Destiny's Top-Shelf Art" Women Jazz cobart show "under the rug" Looking for love" bed check blues" and profile of a love: Note to a black man.; [pers.] "Energy follows thought"... "Think only on that which is Good..." things are not as they appear...; [a.] New York, NY

DETILLION, LINDA L.
[pen.] Julia Love; [b.] July 6, 1947, Ohio; [ch.] Lynn E. Detillion (one daughter); [ed.] Ohio University Associate Degree in Law Enforcement Technology; [occ.] Police Retired/Disabled; [memb.] St. Mary's Roman Catholic Church; [hon.] Two Letters of Accommodation to Proficiency of Job Duties; [oth. writ.] Several writings unpublished on reflections of personal life, short stories with religious overtones.; [pers.] All that I am, all that I have, and all that I hope to be I owe to God.; [a.] Chillicothe, OH

DEVAULT, DORIS
[b.] June 10, 1917, Oak Grove, AR; [p.] Rev. Robert M. Dandridge Sr. and Bess Moulton DeVault; [ed.] Watauga Academy (Baptist High School, Butler, TN) Carson - Newman College (2 yrs.) Meredith College, B.A, WMU Training School, M.R.E.; [occ.] Retired in 1982, having been WMU youth leader in Alabama and Arkansas, 10 yrs. Woman's Missionary Union, SBC, Birmingham, AL for 27 years; [memb.] Dawson Association of Genealogists Upper E. Tenn.; [hon.] Sophomore in High School Medal for essay on "Music," senior year best-all-round student medal, Valedictorian of class - wrote and delivered talk, "Floating or Rowing?," in college society "Calliopeans" was Miss Freshman and Miss Sophomore.; [oth. writ.] Ten years articles for WMU Missionary Magazines - The Window and Royal Service, also Southern Baptist Encyclopedias, Family Genealogy in Washington Co. and Sullivan Co. Histories of East Tenn.; [pers.] Since becoming a Christian at age ten, my desire has been to follow and serve Christ. My home provide guidance and encouragement. We were not rich financially, but wealthy in terms of love, books, music, and Biblical teaching.; [a.] Birmingham, AL

DI GENNARO, ROBERT J. D.
[pen.] Bobby D; [b.] February 14, 1952, Woodbury; [p.] Elizabeth R. Di Gennaro; [ed.] A.A. Liberal Arts Gloucester County College working on B.A. in Theatre Arts Th. Edison State; [occ.] Substitute Teacher St. Path, Wdbry and Telemarketer G.L.S.; [memb.] Leetor St. Patrick Church K of C Wdbry.; [hon.] Editor's Choice Award NLP 1995 Distinguished Member ISP; [oth. writ.] Persona-a moment in time pace - best of 1996; [pers.] Strong people know how to win... "Never give up!!; [a.] Woodbury, NJ

DI MARIA, NICHOLAS
[b.] November 26, 1926, Brooklyn, NY; [p.] Pietrina and James Clemente; [m.] Rose Mary Di Maria, June 21, 1947; [ch.] Nicholas Jr., and Catherine; [ed.] P.S. 206, James Madison High School, University of Southern California New York Institute of Photography; [occ.] Retired from Southern California Gas Co.; [memb.] Evangelical free Church of moreno valley, American Association of retired people (AARP); [hon.] Past President of Bay Area Chapter of Building Industry Association; [oth. writ.] Collection of 23 Inspirational poems.; [pers.] My poems Hope to inspire people to develop their fullest potential, and to have faith in God.; [a.] Moreno Valley, CA

DI RAFFAELE, MELISSA
[b.] April 20, 1980, New York; [p.] Tony DiRaffaele, Debra Vivolo; [ed.] Brentwood High School; [pers.] In my writings I try to reflect the openness of my heart.; [a.] Brentwood, NY

DIAS, HEIDRUN MARIANNE
[pen.] Runi Kessler; [b.] February 3, 1946, Hann Muenden, Germany; [m.] Vernon F. Dias, September 21, 1985; [a.] Richmond, CA

DIAZ, BENITO R.
[pen.] Nature boy; [b.] November 12, 1942, Pontlac, MI; [p.] Candelario and Enemesia Diaz; [m.] Rachel Diaz, May 8, 1961; [ch.] Rachelle Yvonne, Tina Marie; [ed.] GED, attending Oakland Community College; [occ.] Colombiere Center Secretary part time/Disability; [pers.] Life is to be thoroughly enjoyed and appreciated. All challenges should be met with vigor. I have been a paraplegic for ten years and it has brought simple pleasures back into focus!; [a.] Davisburg, MI

DIEDERICH, RODGER
[b.] October 4, 1933, Fayette City, PA; [p.] Verna and Fred Diederich; [ed.] Brownsville High School, Brownsville, PA; [occ.] Retired; [memb.] V.F.W., Self-Help Alliance, North American Fishing Club; [hon.] Poem entitled "A Little Hug Will Do" was published in the Indiana Gazette, May 1995, to commemorate Mental Health Month; [oth. writ.] Several poems published in Self-Help Alliance's poetry collections - "Reflections: Images of Who We Are" and "Poetry in Motion."; [pers.] I try to express my feelings in my poetry for the entertainment of others.; [a.] Indiana, PA

DILLER, CLARENCE
[pen.] Alvin Clay; [b.] January 10, 1927, Berrien Springs, MI; [p.] Sanford, Esther Diller; [m.] Pura Diller (Deceased December 28, 1989) July 7, 1946; [ch.] John, Elizabeth, Margaret, Cathleen; [ed.] Emmanuel Missionary College Academy plus 2 1/2 yrs. college level; [occ.] Retired Building Contractor; [memb.] Seventh Day Adventist Church (Lifetime); [hon.] Having this poem published "Common Nails Uncommon Love" is an honor; [oth. writ.] Other poems in excess of 125 in the process of cataloguing for publication.; [pers.] I have been writing poetry for the past 25 yrs. expression my inmost thoughts on a variety of subjects with the purpose of sharing with others my philosophy of life at its best.; [a.] Forest City, FL

DINGESS, CURTISS MARSHALL
[b.] August 4, 1917, Logan Country, WA; [p.] James M. and Aussie (Heard Dingess); [m.] Betty Lou (Gunnison Dingess, December 17, 1941; [ch.] John Marshall (son) and Susan Elizabeth Flesham (daughter); [ed.] Graduate of Logan High School, Logan, W.V.A and Benjamin Franklin University, Washington, DC; [occ.] Retired Special Agent/Intelligence Division, Internal Revenue Service; [memb.] Life Member: Veterans of foreign wars and disabled American Veterans. Masons (AF and AM) Lodge, Ceredo, W.VA.; [hon.] Medals farm 2 1/2 yrs. service in southern Pacific with U.S. Army Member of Kentucky Coldness; [oth. writ.] My Childhood life bidgraph Chronological History of my Army Experience Poetry (over the years) None of above published.; [pers.] East Well, Sleep Warm, enjoy friends, and love.; [a.] Huntington, WA

DIXON, HANNAH FORSYTH
[b.] July 18, 1938, Grenada, West Indies; [p.] Both Deceased; [m.] Donald E. Dixon Sr., June 6, 1964; [ch.] Alexis, Donna, Donald Jr.; [ed.] High School Graduate Grenada, Park College B.A., Webster University M.A., Ottawa University - courses in Education and Psychology; [occ.] R.N. Consultant, Part-Time Faculty Member, Penn Valley Community College; [memb.] K.C. MO, Missouri Long Term Care Educators Association, National Association of Black Journalist, Kansas City Chapter; [hon.] Journalism Award 1993, Monetary Award for Academic Excellence - 1980, Mayors Cert. of Recognition 1994; [oth. writ.] Articles: Awakening the Human Conscience, the Denial of Human Rights to Disabled Persons, the Importance of Solitude.; [pers.] Grow towards excellence with a continuous vision of positive self-esteem.; [a.] Kansas City, MO

DOBRANSKY, PAUL
[pen.] Alec Nikto; [b.] September 30, 1967, Pittsburgh, PA; [ed.] University of Pittsburgh, B.S., M.D., University of Colorado Residency in Psychiatry; [occ.] Physician, University of Colorado Dept. of Psychiatry; [hon.] Chancellor's Scholarship Semester at Sea Scholarship, Selection for Residency Training, University of Colorado; [oth. writ.] Bridges of Relevance: The Art of Learning Tales of the Joker; [pers.] Some of my work reflects a life with the most inspiring woman I have known. I will never see her again with my eyes. Only with my heart. She lives in Shakespeare's snoot 40. As for the rest of works, and my wonderful life now, I owe only one maxim: "Never give up."; [a.] Denver, CO

DOCKSTADER, BARBIE
[b.] August 24, 1972, Berwyn, IL; [p.] Carol Barnes, Frank Dockstader; [ed.] Moose Heart H.S., Lincoln College - A.A. Degree Illinois State University; [occ.] Poet and Short Story Writer; [memb.] Phitheta Kappa; [hon.] 5 Years Academic Scholarship, National Dean's List Assoc. '92, Adelia Neibur Stickel Award (English), Memorial Day Award '90 (writing) A.A. Degree High Honors; [oth. writ.] Where it all starts (Self-published collection of over 150 poems) V-Rag (Band Newsletter) and several poems published in a Christian publication through Ill. State University.; [pers.] Dedicated to the memory of peggy Richardson. I wish she could've lived to see me in print.; [a.] McLean, IL

DODDS, MALCOLM
[b.] August 7, 1929, Brooklyn, NY; [p.] Samuel Williams, Marie Williams; [m.] Divorced; [ed.] H.S. of Music and Art, N.Y.C., Brooklyn College - New York University; [occ.] Composer, Conductor, C.E.O. Malcolm Dodds Music, Inc.; [memb.] Phi Mu Alph Sinfonia, Ascap, BMI, SAG, AFM., Music Director: ILGWV Music Director: Earth House; [hon.] [For Radio/TV Commercials] (Music), Clio awards, Internat'l Film TV Festival, Big Apple Awards, Andy Awards, Art Directors Club of N.J., Ceba Awards, Etc., N.J. State Council on the arts fellowship; [oth. writ.] Florida Symphony Orchestra (World Premier 1989), Score for "The Lawyer" (Paramount Films), "Look for the union label."; [pers.] "Which is sweeter - the song the blackbird sings - or just after?"; [a.] Kendall Park, NJ

DODSON, TAMIKO YVETTE
[b.] October 17, 1975, Boston, MA; [p.] Christine and James Dodson; [m.] Engaged to Zatic Zeus Simpson III; [ed.] Brockton High School Graduate, Student at bethune - Cookman College in Daytona Beach, Florida Majoring Business Management; [memb.] NAACP, Kwanzaa Network, Woman Holding Interest in professionalism (W.H.I.P.); [hon.] Deans List, Student Achievement Award. Most Honorable Mention Literary Award for a Short Story. Bethune - Cookman College full four year Scholarship Award and Recipient; [pers.] May a Angelou, Langston Hopes my late great- grandmother Natalie Browder's poetry, and my own life experience have always in influenced my writing. Since the age of eight I write because I love to.; [a.] Brockton, MA

DOLLAR, RUSS
[b.] February 5, 1980, Thomasville, GA; [p.] S.N. and Martha Dollar; [ed.] High School Thomas County Central Sophomore hopefully, College with Masters Degree in Marine Biology; [occ.] School Student; [memb.] Baptist Church; [hon.] Presidential Academic Fitness Award, Duke University J.L.P. Program Award; [oth. writ.] "Time," "The Pool" and "Three Souls."; [a.] Ochlocknee, GA

DOMBROWSKI, THOMAS
[pen.] "T.J."; [b.] January 27, 1965, Chicago, IL; [p.] Thomas and Marge Dombrowski; [ed.] Forest View High School, Arlington Hts., Illinois; [occ.] Writer, Seeker and Adventurer; [oth. writ.] "Endless Love," "Follow The Rainbow," "I Love The Rain" "Divination," "Spreading of the Wings," "Listen to the Wind," "Say it all," "Love and Life," "Listen to Within."; [pers.] Life is like a pond. Everything we do is like throwing a rock into the pond and creating ripples in the water. We are all in some way or another interconnected. So what we do affects all of us. So start with Love at the core spreading outwards. What a wonderful world it would be!; [a.] Elk Grove, IL

DONNELLY, JASON MICHAEL
[b.] April 10, 1970, England, UK; [p.] Elizabeth and Francis Donnelly; [ed.] Saint Mary's College for Boys, Southampton, UK. University of Warwickshire, Coventry, UK; [occ.] Freelance Artist/Writer; [memb.] Aububon Society, Green Peace, Smithsonian Institute; [hon.] Fine Art BA. English Literature Minor; [oth. writ.] "Salem" (1985)" My new shoes," (1985), Collected poems., "Prellide to the Annex" and "The Annex," (1992) Collective poems., Exhibited mixed media collections 1992-5.; [a.] Mount Sinai, NY

DORY, DOROTHA B.
[pen.] Dorotha Loewen Dory; [b.] May 15, 1921, Watonga, OK; [p.] John W. Loewen, Amelia M. Goerke; [ch.] Charles E. Spiers, Aimee Louise Tessmer, John W. Spiers; [ed.] Watonga High School, Oklahoma State University - B.F.A., University of Oklahoma M.M.E.; [occ.] Retired, part time receptionist; [memb.] American Association of Retired Persons, Moses Lake Senior Center, First Presbyterian Church; [pers.] I try to stimulate the reader's mind, and challenge her or him to think. I like to bring laughter and happiness into the lives of others. I'm finishing several musical compositions.; [a.] Moses Lake, WA

DOTSON, SANDRA L.
[b.] February 5, 1948, Baltimore; [p.] George Yarbough, Sr. (Deceased), Cynthia Campbell; [ch.] Tina Larieia, Janice Renee, Monica Ray; [ed.] High School; [occ.] Supervisor of Mentally Challenged Adults; [memb.] Maryland Chapter - The National Multiple Sclerosis Society; [hon.] 1995 Employee of the Year, Progress Unlimited. As employee of the year, recipient of a banquet, certificate, and monetary award presented by Don Scott, anchor person WJZ-13 and board member of Progress Ultd. in recognition of outstanding performance, productivity and dedicated Service; [oth. writ.] Anthology of poems entitled Inspired at this time being copy- righted in which the poem "Dreams" is included. Currently working on another anthology, yet be titled. Also developing a book of essays and short stories.; [pers.] If my poems can somehow touch the emotions of my readers, then I have accomplished my goal of giving them a precious gift.; [a.] Baltimore, MD

DOTY, HEATHER
[b.] August 2, 1976, Niles, MI; [p.] Gary and Judi Doty; [ed.] Andrews Academy; [occ.] Students at Andrews University; [a.] Berrien Springs, MI

DOUGLAS, MARY ANN
[b.] July 26, 1981, Dayton Beach, FL; [p.] Paul and Karen Douglas; [ed.] Attended Sugar Mill Elementary School, attended Silver Sands Middle School; [occ.] Full Time Student; [memb.] Student Gov't President 1994/1995, Drama Club 1995/1996; [hon.] Recipient of 4.0 awards 1993 and 1994, Recipient Courage Award 1994, Nominee Disney Dreamers and Doers Award 1994 and 1995, Recipient of Numerous Science and Social Studies Awards; [oth. writ.] Short stories published in Volusia County imprints and young author's publication, poems submitted to Volusia County imprints.; [pers.] My life experiences have helped me make my poems and stories come alive. I have been greatly influenced by the love and support of my family and friends.; [a.] Port Orange, FL

DOYLE, BERNADETTE
[pen.] Bernadette Doyle; [b.] Senior Citizen, Hull, IA; [p.] Eugene and Emma Hogan (Deceased); [m.] Bernard P. Doyle (Deceased), October 15, 1955; [ed.] Hull Public High School, Bridge Cliff College Sioux City and St. Vincent Hospital Iowa Registered horse - a specialty in Opthalmology, plus many other credits in Nursing, internal Medicine in continuing fall specialities etc. Education; [occ.] Aspiring writer retired - rin) at present; [memb.] Sodality member - retired Bible class member (at present) trinity Guild member (church) Beta Sigma Phi (in the past woman's Professional grace now fire Alpha Omega nurses group Leisure World, Laguna Hills Calif.; [hon.] Poetry winner in High School Published in School and city paper I was in stage plays when in high school - all operates and singing groups also: When in High School I won honor "Declamatory Contests"; [oth. writ.] I have written poetry can Buzza Cardoza in the past. Currently I am hoping to have my completed book - a Historical Novel published.; [pers.] Although my profession has been in medicine I retired early to wait a book (historical novel) a true story of Irish immigrants who home steadied in the middle west in the 1800s. It was accepted one time but we did not come to arms a heart warning story soothly tell me.; [a.] Orange, CA

DOYLE, JOHN
[b.] January 23, 1974, Dub, Ireland; [p.] Mick, Melly; [ed.] Leaving Cert.; [occ.] Odd Jobs, Band; [memb.] Bring me to the breeze fallen down American Roads; [oth. writ.] Songs, poem short stories etc. Leg bring me to the breeze, fallen down American Roads and other etc.; [pers.] A different one every-day.; [a.] San Francisco, CA

DRAUDT, HOLLY
[b.] April 28, 1950, NY; [p.] Robert and Julia Hartman; [m.] Glean, August 29; [ch.] Greg; [ed.] Masters in Sp. Ed.; [occ.] Sp. Ed. Teacher; [memb.] National Teacher's Assoc.; [hon.] Teacher of the year; [oth. writ.] Poems us titles; [pers.] Life is too short be happy be quiet and be witty!; [a.] Hicksville, NY

DRINKARD, DAVID
[b.] August 21, 1958, Queens, NY; [p.] Charles and Rose Drinkard; [ch.] Camille Lavone; [ed.] Beach Channel High, LaGuardia Community College; [occ.] Security Console Operator for Time Warmer Inc.; [oth. writ.] Various other writings that are being compiled for future publication.; [pers.] I endeavour to impress upon people the importance of a close relationship with God.; [a.] Jersey City, NJ

DRZEWIANOWSKI, CAROL
[b.] October 26, 1975, Springfield, MA; [p.] Cathy Drzewianowski, Zenon Drzewianowski; [ed.] Palmer High School, University of Massachusetts; [occ.] Student; [hon.] Xerox Award for Excellence in Humanities and Social Sciences; [oth. writ.] Some poems and stories published in school literary journals and the local newspaper, edit and publish various fancies.; [pers.] The pome, "Earth Angel" was written to accompany a counted cross-stitch sewed by my grandmother, Emily Drzewianowski.; [a.] Belchertown, MA

DUBOSE, GRETCHEN
[pen.] Michaelle Brannon; [b.] January 1, 1980, Orlando, FL; [p.] Jhan DuBose, Stephen DuBose; [ed.] DuBose Day School; [occ.] Assistant Manager for Forest Keeper Arabians; [memb.] Michael Jackson International Fan Club; [oth. writ.] Several songs; [pers.] I will do everything in my power to help other people and make this world a better place. I have been greatly inspired by Michael Jackson.; [a.] Hot Springs, NC

DUBOSE, JOAN
[pen.] Joan DuBose; [b.] February 12, 1951, Charleston, SC; [p.] John and Florence Hopkins; [ch.] Robert DuBose, Donna DuBose; [ed.] James Island High; [occ.] Nursing Asst.; [hon.] For perfect attendance at Rutledge College, made the Dean's List four times and President List for four times for honor student; [oth. writ.] I have written many other poems.

DUNCAN, MINDY CAROL
[b.] April 24, 1968, Atlanta, GA; [p.] Dr. and Mrs. Claude D. Duncan; [ed.] High School - Westminster in Atlanta Ga, BFA University of Ga., (Photography Major) currently working on Masters in Communication/Print Journalism at Georgia State University; [occ.] Production Manager for "Verauda" Magazine based in Atlanta GA; [a.] Atlanta, GA

DUNMIRE, JESSICA MONTAISE
[b.] February 18, 1980; [p.] Matthew Dunmire, Linda Dunmire; [ed.] Kiski Area High School; [occ.] High School Student; [oth. writ.] Several unpublished poems; [pers.] My poem thank you, is dedicated to my beautiful mother who provides my inspiration for everything I do in life.; [a.] Vandergrift, PA

DUNN, MARGARET
[pen.] Margaret Mary Dunn; [b.] August 1, 1961, Coaldale, PA; [p.] Patrick Kane, Betty (Wertman) Kane; [m.] James Dunn, May 22, 1982; [ch.] Deanna Laura, Justin Patrick; [ed.] Panther Valley High School, Lehigh Carbon Comm. College; [occ.] Cert. Nurses Aide, studying to become Respiratory Tech.; [memb.] Many Organizations; [oth. writ.] Kept personal; [pers.] My writing reflects my beliefs and my emotions. I use my writing as an avenue to express feelings and issues important to me.; [a.] Lansford, PA

DUNTON, DOROTHEA LONG
[pen.] Dorothea Long Dunton; [b.] March 2, 1914, Springfield, MA; [p.] Raymond and Delia Long; [m.] Richard Dunton, September 18, 1938; [ch.] Sondra (daughter), Kathy (granddaughter); [ed.] Gorham High, NH; [occ.] Retired; [pers.] This poem was created from my heart and the memories I have of my brother.; [a.] Westfield, MA

DYKES, KIMBERLY
[b.] March 10, 1961, New York; [p.] Elois Harrison; [ch.] Ray Shawn Thorpe, Raymond Thorpe (Twins); [ed.] High School, Beach Channel; [occ.] School Security, St. Michael's Montessori School; [oth. writ.] Several poems non-published I would just write them and keep them.; [pers.] I strive to see some of my work in a book or paper in black and white. Somewhere, my thoughts. I have been greatly influenced by.; [a.] Far Rockaway, NY

DZIADOSZ, JOSEPH D.
[b.] March 15, 1971, Milwaukee, WI; [p.] Linda Susan Heider; [ed.] Milwaukee Lutaerin H.S., University of Wesconson - Whitewater; [memb.] Phi Alpha Theta National History Honor Society, Phi Sigma Kappa International Fraternity; [hon.] Donald L. and Allene L. Graham Scholarship, Dean's List; [pers.] If a man can be responsible for himself then he can be responsible for anything and if this be the case the only thing to fear is. Not trying to be your best.; [a.] Milwaukee, WI

EASLEY, CHARLOTTE
[pen.] Cha Cha E.; [b.] October 1, 1963, Baltimore, MD; [p.] Harry and Rebecca Easley; [ed.] Crossland High School, Prince Georges Community College, The Medix School (Medical Vocational); [occ.] Bookseller at Olsson's Books and Records, Washington, DC; [oth. writ.] Third place winner of Poetry Contest, as well as receiving Honorable Mention for a second poem in Crossland High's Literary Book, 1981. Also, I had a poem published in the "Mynd", a Literary Book at PG College - 1982. I am currently writing a Novel.; [pers.] I learned that the real creator is my inner self, the Holy Spirit. The desire to write is God inside talking to me. The actual manifestation of writing is God inside talking through me.; [a.] Capital Heights, MD

EBENRECK, SUSAN
[pen.] Siouxsun; [b.] February 8, 1947, Saint Louis; [p.] Edward and Arlette Doering; [m.] Gerard Ebenreck, November 22, 1969; [ch.] Thomas Clayton Ebenreck; [ed.] Nerinx Hall High School Meramec Community College Fontbonne College; [occ.] Secretary - Fontbonne College, English Major - Fontbonne College; [pers.] Love can only truly exist if it is rooted in freedom and acceptance.; [a.] Saint Louis, MO

EBERT, NOVA
[b.] January 17, 1981, Salth Lake City, UT; [p.] Dona L. Ebert and Chuck D. Ebert; [ed.] Entering Freshman Year High School; [occ.] Student; [memb.] National Honor Society; [hon.] National Honors Society (3.9 GPA) 1995 Utah State Championship Tae Kwon Do Gold Medalist (Martial Arts); [oth. writ.] Unpublished stories and poems; [a.] Salt Lake City, UT

EBY, JACK
[b.] September 3, 1982, Traverse City, MI; [p.] James and Therese Eby; [ed.] Incomplete as of today; [occ.] Student; [memb.] Northwest Mini-Sprint Association; [hon.] Quest Gifted Education Graduate, Advanced Curriculum Education Graduate, Placed with Distinction: Johns Hopkins University Academic Talent Search, 3rd Place, Barnes and Noble Short Story Contest, 1st Place Mel Conner Look alike; [a.] Redmond, WA

EDER, LAURA A.
[b.] June 28, 1967, Chicago; [p.] Mike and Kim Miller; [m.] Daniel J. Eder, September 7, 1990; [ed.] Prospect High, Harper College AA, Northeastern Illinois University; [occ.] Community Re-Investment and Training Officer, Harris Bank Palatine; [memb.] Arlington Hts. Evangelical Free Church, Lutheran Camp Association; [hon.] Various Volunteer Award Certificates; [oth. writ.] Several poems and short stories unpublished; [pers.] If I can put words together on paper that create an image, alive in a stranger's mind, I have used well a gift from God.; [a.] Rolling Meadows, IL

EDISON, MICHAEL WILLIAM
[b.] October 8, 1958, Omaha, NE; [p.] Mardell Edison Kolle, John William Kolle; [m.] Divorced; [ch.] Jennifer Marie Edison, Michael Johnathan Edison; [ed.] Glenbrook North High School Meadow Brook Elementary, Northbrook, Junior High, IL Missouri Military Academy Mexico, MO. Villa School, Arizona; [memb.] St. James Episcopal and Tien Challenge Assembly of God; [oth. writ.] Poems, short stories journal - biographical; [a.] Prospect Height, IL

EDMOND, JEFF
[b.] NY; [occ.] Choreographer/Tap Dance and Jazz Dance Teacher; [memb.] SAG - Equity- AFTRA; [oth. writ.] Off Off Broadway Musical "Bugout", original music video "I Want To Get A Head" aired on Cinemax, USA Cable WHT cable; [a.] New York, NY

EDWARDS, KATIE E.
[pen.] Kathie Aldridge; [b.] April 15, 1920, Mount Olive, NC; [p.] Mr. and Mrs. Howel B. Aldridge; [m.] Joseph G. Edwards, December 17, 1934; [ch.] Joe Jr., Brenda and Frances Edwards; [occ.] Retired; [oth. writ.] This poem is my only writing; [pers.] I try to show God's Love for his Creation; [a.] Four Oaks, NC

EDWARDS, MARY
[b.] Chicago, IL; [p.] Frank and Carolyn Kobler; [ch.] Adam, Joshua; [ed.] Loyola University of Chicago, BA, MA; [occ.] City Planner, Chicago Plan Commission; [a.] Chicago, IL

EDWARDS, PATRICIA
[b.] August 29, 1934, Bridgeport, WV; [p.] Carl and Freda Van Horn; [m.] Edgar Edwards, November 9, 1953; [ch.] Eddie, Richard, Trina Jo; [ed.] Graduated Bridgeport High School 1953; [occ.] Secretary for husbands business's, Edwards Garage and Used Cars; [memb.] Faith Baptist Church WV Writers Assoc.; [oth. writ.] Poems read in church. Two children's books hoping to get published.; [pers.] Most of my writings are spiritual. I strive to be the best I can be and one day hear. "Well done, thou good and faithful servant."; [a.] Enterprise, WV

EDWIN, SABEEN ANN
[b.] September 23, 1980, New York; [p.] Ernest and Rita Edwin; [ed.] Student - 10th Grade; [occ.] Student at Townsend Harrish High School at Queens College; [hon.] Poetry Contest at St. Nicholas of Tolentine School - 1990 4th Grade, Won 3rd Place, 1991 - 5th Grace, Won 1st Place, 1993 -7th Grade, Won 2nd Place; [oth. writ.] 1994 - Poetry published in 'Dance on the Horizon" by the National Library of Poetry 1995. Poem journey is being published in "Best Poems of 1995" by the National Library of Poetry.; [pers.] Never let other people dictate your life. In the end, the decision is all yours.; [a.] Jamaica, NY

EGGER, AMY CATHERINE
[pen.] Amy Egger; [b.] December 15, 1977, El Paso, TX; [p.] Stephen Egger, Saundra Egger; [ed.] Eastwood High School; [occ.] Presently a student; [memb.] Eastwood Letterman's Association, Eastwood Athletic Trainers Association, United Blood Services; [hon.] Most Outstanding Sophomore Girl 1993-94, Who's Who Among American High School Students 1995-96, Head Athletic Student Trainer 1994-96; [oth. writ.] Several poems published in the High School Literary Magazine 1992-995, poems published in the Anthology of Poetry By Young Americans 1995; [pers.] I hold my writings very personal and I am inspired by my own personal experiences, observations, and feelings.; [a.] El Paso, TX

EID, ALAN L.
[b.] May 25, 1955, Patchogus, NY; [p.] Albert Eid and Jean Eid; [m.] Christina M. Eid, May 6, 1979; [ch.] Ryan Christopher, Eric Michael, and Michelle Alicia; [ed.] Patchogue-Medford High School, S.U.N.Y. at Stony Brook; [occ.] Data Processing Supervisor, Northrop-Grumman, Bethpage, NY; [pers.] My writing is built upon a strong foundation of love and support from my family.; [a.] Holtsville, NY

EISENMENGER, KERRY
[b.] October 24, 1950, Marshall, MN; [p.] Joe and Anita Van Overbeke; [m.] Thomas F. Eisenmenger, January 2, 1971; [ch.] Patrick, Michael, David; [ed.] BA from Mount Marty College, Yankton, SaOak M.A. University of Nebraska; [occ.] English Teacher, Walnut Junior High Grand Island, NE; [memb.] NEA (Nebraska Education Association) Parent Teacher Association; [pers.] My poetry reflects my past experiences that I try to make come alive to the reader; [a.] Grand Island, NE

ELLER, LINDA LANIER
[b.] November 9, 1947, Atlanta; [p.] Claud V. and Ann Lee Lanier; [m.] James Eller, August 9, 1964; [ch.] James Vincent, Julie Anne; [ed.] Brown High School Clayton Junior and Georgia State; [occ.] Legislative Secretary; [memb.] Mental Health Association, State Democratic Party, several human rights organizations; [pers.] Enlightenment, Reason and Tolerance Poetry dedicated to the beautiful souls of the friends I have known, and some I haven't met.; [a.] Douglasville, GA

ELLIOTT, DIANE E.
[b.] March 25, 1937, Chicago, IL; [p.] Kathryn and Paul Krueger; [m.] James C. Elliott, April 25, 1987; [ch.] Susan Walsh and Grand Children: Kevin Walsh Megan Walsh; [ed.] Bachelors - Elem. Educ. Teaching Masters EMH Chicago Teachers College; [occ.] Retired Elementary School Teacher 35 yrs. teaching in Chicago; [pers.] I believe that expressing yourself makes a person whole/complete. Through my music and poetry, I share parts of myself as I could not do in any other way.; [a.] Bolingbrook, IL

ELLIS, BRIAN V.
[b.] March 12, 1981, Stanford, CA; [p.] David Ellis, Judy Ellis; [ed.] Kennedy Elementary School, Menlo School; [occ.] Student entering 9th grade at Menlo School; [memb.] Junior Classical League; [hon.] Highest Academic Honors both 7th and 8th grade, Gifted and Talented Education (GATE) Student; [oth. writ.] Young Author's award winner The Chocolate Caper, Pokey the Turtle, two computer programs Lost Baseball (game) and small Window (Utility) published on SIMTEL and AMUE archives and CD Rom; [pers.] Brian lives with his parents and sister Wendy. His hobbies include outdoor sports and computers; [a.] Newark, CA

ELLY, RONALD D.
[pen.] Ron Elly; [b.] December 26, 1941, Montgomery, AL; [p.] Robert D. and Dorothea S. Elly; [m.] Ellen S. Elly, June 11, 1966; [ch.] Beth E. Baumgartner 26, Juleanne D. Elly 24, Laura K. Elly 19; [ed.] BA in History/Mary Ville College, Mary Ville, Tenn, M. Div. Louiville Presbyterian Theo. Seminary, STM, Christian Theological Seminary; [occ.] Pastoral Counselor, Family Life Minatory Director; [hon.] Magna Cum Laude, Christian Theological Seminary Indianapolis, IN; [pers.] "The power of our choice to love is increasingly important in a world of injustice, and choices made out of hopelessness, I - we cannot give in to darkness!"; [a.] Lafayette, IN

ELSEA, JUDY
[b.] November 21, 1945, Benton, IL; [p.] Helen Drannon, Denver Co.; [m.] Sam Elsea, August 21, 1980; [ch.] Karen Larington, Lee Larington and Bill Larington; [ed.] I went to W. Franfort High, W. Frankfort it quitting, in my 3rd year to finish in 1973 (GED) Lincoln, NE; [occ.] Housewife; [memb.] Relief Society Church of Jesus Christ Of L.D.S.; [hon.] Expect at Church there have been none; [oth. writ.] Just poetry I only started to write in 1986; [pers.] I feel that all talent comes from above. Each is given that which he needs to enrich his life. I feel very blessed that God smiled on me. Thank you for your time.; [a.] Fort Madison, IA

ENG, TONY
[b.] May 22, 1973, Newark, NJ; [p.] Suet Eng, Han Eng; [ed.] San Francisco State University; [occ.] Film maker "Auteur", writer; [hon.] Cum Laude Graduate, National Dean's List, University Leadership Award, University Merit Award; [oth. writ.] Numerous screenplays, treatments, memoirs, articles for local newspapers, magazines; [pers.] Honesty to your heart, with much tenacity, will break you free at your own personal menagerie.; [a.] Daly City, CA

ENGER, RICHARD
[b.] July 16, 1947, El Paso, TX; [p.] Richard H. and Mary Jane Enger; [m.] Dolores Phares Enger, October 19, 1974; [ch.] Fran Tucker, Brian and Kimberlea Enger; [ed.] Jesuit High School, El Paso Univ. of Texas at El Paso; [oth. writ.] Numerous poems, short stories and a novel - all unpublished; [pers.] There is no better motivator for creative writing than riding the pendulum of life.; [a.] Phoenix, AZ

ENGLAND, STEVEN WARREN
[pen.] S. England; [b.] February 9, 1948, Oakland, AR; [p.] William (Burt) and Bertha England; [m.] Rae Marie England, October 14, 1972; [ch.] Carolyn and Erin; [ed.] BS Business Administration, Southern California University; [occ.] Real Estate Management and Investment Advisor/Consultant; [memb.] I.E.E.E., I.C.S.C., A.S.H.R.A.E., I.R.E.M., A.E.E., Executive Board Music from Bear Valley; [oth. writ.] Professional materials for corporation use, including various multimedia presentations (video), wide variety of poems not yet released; [pers.] My writing reflects my sensitivity towards all people, an optimistic attitude towards life and the world we live it. Love of God, Nature and Life, all we see as well as the unseen.; [a.] Daly City, CA

ENGLE, REBECCA W.
[b.] November 7, 1939, Charlotte, NC; [p.] King and Helen Williams; [m.] Jack L. Engle, November 26, 1966; [ch.] William Howard M. Engle, Justin L. Engle, Tilden E. Engle; [ed.] Harry P. Harding High School The Salvation Army College for Officer Training; [occ.] Pastor; [pers.] Inspiration for writing has come from God through Holy Scripture and events in the life of my church and its people. To God be the glory.; [a.] Inman, SC

ENGLISH, MARIE
[pen.] Marie Adele English; [b.] 4/13/60, Bristol, PA; [p.] Leon & Jo English; [ed.] Trained--Classical Piano--8 years and private studies; [occ.] Musician, Songwriter; [memb.] Hands Across Houston--Hands Across The World; [hon.] Vocalist #1 Florida Champion, 1978, Awarded Best Pianist of Houston, TX, 1995; [oth. writ.] Always writing about life; [pers.] What a wonderful gift I have to express myself and have an opportunity to have had it heard. We are all wonderfully talented, special people in our Father's Eyes.; [a.] Houston, TX

ERNSTER, LAWRENCE J.
[b.] April 20, 1927, Saint Paul, MN; [p.] Nicholas and Anna Ernster; [m.] Darlene Cole, January 25, 1947; [ch.] Herbert J., Linda L., John N., Daniel A., Denise E.; [ed.] Chemical Engineering ICS; [occ.] Retired; [memb.] American Legion; [oth. writ.] Many poems, and some technical papers re: chemistry, poem "Coatings" published in the customer technical book, by Valspar Corp.

ESCARENO, RAMONA EVE
[b.] September 14, 1936, U.S.A.; [p.] Ramon and Juanita Escareno; [ch.] Ramona Kathy Eder, Wolf D. Eder Jr., Rebecca Sue Eder; [ed.] 1 Semister North Lake College; [occ.] Laundry Aide Pioneer Care Center; [memb.] CR Union; [oth. writ.] Songwriter, short scripts or short stories and song poems, manual script and character of my self.; [pers.] I love to write poetry with a little story this I will always remember my education years and kind of fun for the rest of my days!; [a.] Irving, TX

ESCOTO, KRISTINE
[b.] August 20, 1967, Tacoma, WA; [p.] Terry Coman and Paulette Miller; [m.] Gunnar Escoto, October 20, 1989; [ch.] Dylan Escoto, Nicholas Escoto; [ed.] Westmont High, De Anza College; [occ.] Writer, Waialua, Hawaii; [hon.] Article of the year, shield newspaper; [oth. writ.] Editorials published in local newspapers; [pers.] My poems reflect certain, feelings and time frames in my life. I aspire to have a book of all of my poems published.; [a.] Waialua, HI

ESPIRITU, AIDA E.
[b.] June 7, 1947, Philippines; [p.] Gonzalo Espiritu, Trinidad Espiritu; [ed.] M. Ed (TESL) University of the Philippines; [occ.] Teacher; [hon.] Pi Gamma Mu

ESTES, JAMES R.
[b.] July 28, 1932, Saint Louis, MO; [p.] Raymond and Mildres Estes; [m.] Clara Ann Estes, September 10, 1955; [ch.] Gregory and Cortney Estes; [ed.] 2 years at Washington University - St. Louis B.S. Secondary Education, English Major, SE Missouri State University; [occ.] Retired; [oth. writ.] Numerous short poems; [a.] Louisville, KY

ESTES, STACI
[b.] June 17 1980, Carson City, NV; [p.] Tim and Susan Estes; [ed.] Sophomore at Douglas High School; [hon.] National Junior Honor Society, Honor Roll; [pers.] I enjoy writing my thoughts and feelings down on paper. It gives my point of view on life a different perspective of how things go.; [a.] Gardnerville, NV

ESTOCK, JOHN MATHEW
[b.] June 20, 1977, Scranton, PA; [p.] Helen and John W. Estock; [ed.] Valley View High; [pers.] Inspiration consumes us all. You've but to stand on the edge of reality and stare into the deep dark chasm of your soul.; [a.] Blakely, PA

EVANS, NAKIA
[pen.] Kia; [b.] December 13, 1977, Brooklyn; [p.] Patricia Mapp, Cedric Evans; [ed.] Sarah Jay Hale High School for Beauty Culture; [memb.] First Baptist Church of Coney Island Willing Workers; [pers.] I love to write poems to make peoples smile. I hope people could understand I am only 17 yrs. old, but I love writing poetry; [a.] Brooklyn, NY

EVERROAD, UNA-MELINA M.
[b.] August 26, 1973, Victor, CO; [p.] Terry and Esa Everroad; [occ.] Office and Road Manager, Recording Artist, Singer, Songwriter, also in a Contemporary Christian Music Group; [oth. writ.] A piece for a newsletter with a circulation over 2000, currently have a song published and recorded, a personal collection of over 100 unpublished original works; [pers.] All my family writes music, poetry, lyrics and fiction. My parents are both excellent writers, but hey taught their children to look to the author of life for inspiration.; [a.] Saint Augustine, FL

EWEN, DENNIS
[b.] March 12, 1950, Mason City, IA; [p.] Clement Ewen, Lillian Ewen; [ed.] Rockford High School, Rockford, Iowa, North Iowa Area Community College, Mason City, Iowa, Lewis Clark State College, Lewiston, Idaho, Bachelor of Science in Chemistry and the Natural Sciences; [occ.] Chef; [a.] Lewiston, ID

FAISON, DAVID
[pen.] Dabo Dabone; [b.] December 19, 1953, El Dorado, AR; [p.] Lee Vell and Annie Lean Faison; [m.] Kimibery Michelle Faison, January 28, 1982; [ch.] David Jr., Kimisha, DeVod; [ed.] El Dorado High School Henderson State Univ.; [occ.] Locomotive Engineer Union Pacific RR; [memb.] Greater Paradise, M. Baptist Church, Omega Psi Phi Fraternity, XI Beta Chapter; [oth. writ.] Several poems, songs, and short stories; [pers.] Poetry has always been an outlet to ease and please the reader and author who enjoy the sweet sound of words in a phrase; [a.] Little Rock, AR

FALK, HOWARD
[pen.] H. S. Falk; [b.] April 24, 1964, Pomona; [p.] Martin and Marcia Falk; [ed.] Claremont High School (Class of 1983), Citrus Community College (between Sept. '83 and Jan. '85); [occ.] Part-time recording transfer engineer: Transferring old phonograph discs onto blank audio cassette tapes; [oth. writ.] Humor, Music, Plotline outlines; [pers.] The late Albert Einstein once said that: "Imagination is more important than knowledge", to which a skeptic responded by stating that: "Einstein didn't know what he was talking about: He must have been imagining things", which may be said to prove Einstein's philosophical point; [a.] Claremont, CA

FARBER, ROMA
[b.] September 12, 1974, Moscow; [p.] Lyudmila and Joseph Farber; [ed.] Calvary Chapel Bible College; [oth. writ.] "A Greater Inspiration" - a collection of my favorite poems; [pers.] Today there is a great deal of talk about individuality in all areas of life, especially arts. What I want to say was expressed best by one of my favorite writers - C.S. Lewis: "Give up yourself, and you will find your real self. Lose your life and you will save it... nothing that you have not given away will ever be really yours... but look for Christ and you will find Him, and with Him everything else thrown in."; [a.] Sarasota, FL

FAY, JUSTIN
[b.] April 30, 1980, Lawrence, MA; [p.] Diana Fay, Thomas Fay; [ed.] Graduated from The Pike School, Andover, MA. in June 1995. September, 1995: Freshman at Phillips Academy, Andover, MA; [a.] Andover, MA

FEHRMANN, EDNA
[pen.] Eddie Fehrmann; [b.] April 30, 1934, Milwaukee, WI; [p.] Inga and Arthur Ludwigsen; [ch.] Steve, Roxanne, Michael, Jeffrey, Michele; [ed.] High School; [occ.] Retired; [memb.] Outer Banks Senior Fellowship - Sweet Carolines Barber Shop, Center Front Drama Group, Church Choir; [hon.] First place in Senior Olympic Literary Arts, local competing in Raleigh, N.C. for state finals; [oth. writ.] Distance, Dreamers, Have You Ever?, Time, Goals, Private Moments; [pers.] I like to take a word, and explore my meaning of it in poetry

FELL, GAYLE WINIFRED
[pen.] Gayle Lockwood Fell; [b.] May 25, 1939, Eureka, CA; [p.] Harriett Muncy, Wilton Lockwood; [ed.] BS Home Economics, Oregon State University; [occ.] Secretary, Health Care; [memb.] Elected to Membership in Lambda Chapter of Omicron NU at OSU; [oth. writ.] "Hawaiian Impressions", Iliad Literary Award Winner CELEBRATIONS 1993, "Deep Sea Darling" 1994 Presidents Award for Literary Excellence PERCEPTIONS; [pers.] I fine release for life's great experiences through my pen.; [a.] Corona, CA

FERGUSON, MICHAEL D.
[pen.] M. D. Ferguson; [b.] April 21, 1949, San Rafael, CA; [p.] Margaret and Harvey E. Ferguson;

[m.] Susan Danielle Ferguson, May 30, 1987; [ch.] Sean Michael, Michael Patrick; [ed.] BA - California State University, BS - Southern Illinois University; [occ.] Writer; [hon.] Veteran USAF 20 years Capt, USAF Ret.; [oth. writ.] Selected poems published by Quill Books; [pers.] Drink Rum, dance in the sunlight, perfect your grin and learn from your pain.; [a.] Yuba City, CA

FERRUGIO, ROSE
[b.] October 14, 1943, Brooklyn, NY; [p.] Mary Ferulle, Salvatore Ferulle; [m.] Michael A. Ferrugio, February 28, 1965; [ch.] Michael A. Jr., Josetta Marie, Andrea Lyne, Danielle Rose; [ed.] Abraham Lincoln High; [occ.] Devoted wife and mother; [oth. writ.] Poems, short stories; [pers.] To have touched someone's heart or made a difference in any small way - will have made life worth living!; [a.] Staten Island, NY

FIELDS, JULIUS THEODORE
[b.] December 11, 1967, Philadelphia, PA; [ed.] Benjamin Franklin H.S., Community College of Philadelphia; [pers.] Learn to take responsibility for your life and learn to make it the best way you know how.; [a.] Philadelphia, PA

FIENE, KEITH E.
[b.] February 6, 1931, Council Bluffs, IA; [p.] Harry and Fayne Fiene; [m.] Betty L, March 21, 1953; [ed.] B.S. at University of Nebr.; [occ.] Retired; [memb.] Member of 1950 Nebraska Football Team; [pers.] Dr. France of V of N English Dept. raised a question in class, "Who Writes Poetry In America?" The answer — anyone, R. Frost's Definition of Poetry "— is saying something in the most beautiful way possible" is a great influence.; [a.] Richland, WA

FIGUEROA, BRIDGITTE
[pen.] Bridgitte Rhoden; [b.] August 2, 1958, Urbana, IL; [p.] Harral and Victoria Rhoden; [m.] Divorced; [ch.] Rodney M. McFarland; [ed.] Centennial High School Las Vegas Community College; [occ.] Medical Unit Secretary Carle Hospital, Urbana, IL; [pers.] To convey my innermost thoughts and feelings on paper has always been a fulfilling way of expressing myself. For many years I have kept my writing tucked away in a drawer. But with loving encouragement from my dear sisters, I have finally opened that drawer and hope that someday others will find me as talented as they have.; [a.] Urbana, IL

FIGUEROA, ROBERTO JOSE
[pen.] Jose Maria de Jesus; [b.] March 21, 1953, New York City, NY; [p.] Mr. Carlos Figueroa and Mrs. Olga Figueroa; [ed.] B.A. San Francisco State Univ. (Political Science and Speech/Communication) twice on Dean's List; [occ.] Director of Marketing at a licence private vocational training college in S.F. (Oxman College); [pers.] Of all the God given talents, qualities, and abilities poetic language is the most singular whereby one can give voice to the internal rhapsodies of the eternal heart.; [a.] San Francisco, CA

FILS-AIME, RONALD
[b.] P-au-P, Haiti; [p.] Ruth and Joseph Philocles Fils-Aime; [ed.] Majoring in Education at Medgar Evers College in Brooklyn; [oth. writ.] Angelique, A Tribute To My Mom, Ruth; [pers.] I find my poetry an excellent way to express my intimate thoughts and feelings. To challenge adversity, I must write; [a.] Brooklyn, NY

FILTER, CHRISTINE
[b.] October 21, 1979, Dover, DE; [p.] A. William Filter III, Grethe Filter; [ed.] Attending Boyertown High School; [hon.] Presidential Academic Fitness Award, Presidents Award For Educational Excellence; [oth. writ.] I have written several other poems, essays, and memoirs but have never tried to published any before.; [pers.] My writings are a way for me to express my feelings, moods, and hopes. These are the only times I allow myself to remove my protective facade.; [a.] Gilbertsville, PA

FINK, SANDY
[b.] August 9, 1935, Chicago, IL; [p.] Jeannette Walker Deike, Harry Walker; [m.] John Fink, October 15, 1987; [ch.] Perry Hornkohl; [ed.] Major in Philosophy and English, Minor in Psychology; [occ.] Retired; [memb.] Life time membership in Florida Freelance Writer's Association, annual membership in The South Florida Poetry Institute and The Rockford Writers' Guild; [hon.] Numerous competitive poetry awards including first, second, third and honorable mention in Oregon, Florida and other states; [oth. writ.] I've written and been published in newspapers, magazines, newsletters, brochures and television (t.v. commercials). Key Images, a book of poetry (with illustrations and in my calligraphy) was released by Distinctive Publications January, 1992; [pers.] I'm at my best in distillations of any kind, especially when I can apply humorous twists to material. I enjoy paradox caught within a person's life, and the individual way it plays out. I'm hooked on the writer word and go through life trying to make as much of it mine as possible.; [a.] Chiefland, FL

FISCELLA, IRMA
[b.] April 11, 1934, Manhattan; [p.] Bertha and Walter Eden; [m.] Joseph Fiscella, June 12, 1954; [ch.] Charles, Anthony, and Joseph, Christa Melnick - foster daughter, Carolyn Macarthy - foster daughter; [ed.] C.W.P. College - cont'd education in Political Science through Gov. Programs John Adams High; [occ.] Personnel Specialist, Civil Service Commission, Town of Hempstead NY 11550; [memb.] Chair: town of Hempstead - Educ. and Higher skills training program, Delegate Director of L.I. Div. of A.C.S., IMED, Distinguished Past Pres. of Town Hempstead Kiwanis, Member of Repl. National Committee, Assoc. Member of Nassau City, Police Activity League, Member of Repl. Congressional Committee, Member of Wantagh Repl. Club, Brd. of Dir. for T.O.H. Day Care Center; [hon.] Award for Pres. of A.C.S. Uniondale Unit Town of Hemp. Citation from Pres. Supervisor Award for V.P. (ACS) - Award for Daffodil Days by A.C.S. (Am. Cancer Soc.) - raised $16,000 - 1995, Award for V.P. Town Hall Kiwanis 1992/3, Award Pres. Town Hall Kiwanis - 1993-94; [oth. writ.] Newsletters for various organizations; [pers.] My heart is in all places where there is suffering, hardships, sadness and strife. I want to help by being there for anyone in need, it gives me great satisfaction. "Love for one another is like grace, there to pick us up when we fall."; [a.] Massapequa Park, NY

FISHER, JULIE A.
[pen.] Julie A. Fisher; [b.] December 28, 1963, Fort Dix, NJ; [p.] James Cox, Alice Cox; [m.] Glenn P. Fisher, October 1, 1989; [ch.] Ethan James Fisher, Jason Allen Fisher; [ed.] Pasco Comprehensive High School Dade City - Pasco Fernando Com. College; [occ.] Officer Manager - Or's Office; [hon.] HOSA - Health Occupation Students of America - Trophy, Honor Roll - 2-3 yrs.; [pers.] Life isn't always what we think it is, sometimes it's leading us on a journey only we a love can understand.; [a.] Lakeland, FL

FITZPATRICK, JOHN
[b.] October 31, 1948; [p.] John and Ilo Fitzpatrick; [m.] Carol Fitzpatrick, May 21, 1969; [ch.] John Fitzpatrick IV; [occ.] Engineered Wood Products Specialists; [memb.] American Legion - Elks - United Service Men's Organization (U.S.O.); [pers.] There is a sad lack of Love, Respect, and Compassion in our society today. Wake up America. Find humanity again.; [a.] Nannford, OK

FLANDREAU, KRISTINE LYNN
[pen.] Pooh; [b.] April 8, 1982, Rhinebeck, NY; [p.] Francis and Carol Flandreau; [ed.] 6th grade at Linden Avenue Middle School in Red Hook, NY; [hon.] Had a poem The Hero That Lies In You published in After The Storm. Also won 3rd prize in the National Poetry Contest; [oth. writ.] Wrote several poems: 1. Happy Birthday Zac, 2. Dr Crenshaw, 3. Flower Shower, 4. Summer Days, 5. The Hero That Lies In You, 6. I Can Still See You (Re: I'm The Star Twinkles In The Sky), 7. Mom And Dad, 8. Cowboys Zachary's First Halloween; [pers.] Kristine was born with a congenital heart defect. Had several open heart surgeries. Several hospital stay in Rhinebeck and Albany Medical Center. Because of her medical situation had two heart pacemakers put in. Did not attend a lot of school. Kristine was a very special, caring loving person. She died on November 4, 1994 of a massive heart attack. I am Kristine's Mother Carol Flandreau

FLOWERS, BOBBY
[b.] August 21, Hopkinsville, KY; [p.] Nathaniel and Hattie Flowers; [ed.] BA Longston University Langston, Oklahoma; [occ.] Operations Manager, Director, Technical Director; [memb.] NABJ (Nat'l Assoc of Black Journalists), Alpha Phi Alpha Fraternity Inc., Screen Actor Guild; [oth. writ.] Rain, Rose, Tabago, Time, You And Me, Clouds, Fall, Judgment Day, Love, Mad, Stormy, We The People, Weep; [pers.] My writings are inspired by my strong nature to be in tuned to and with Mother Earth and the Universe. They often reflect my moods, visuals or sounds. My spirit longs to see a time of Love, Peace and Harmony on Earth.; [a.] Silver Spring, MD

FLOYD, KATHY
[b.] Atlanta, GA; [p.] Marjorie Scott and F. M. Vandegriff; [m.] Robert Floyd; [ch.] Bonita Frey (Nee Floyd), Angela Ford (Nee Floyd), grandchildren: Chrystal Frey, Kara Frey, Samantha Ford, Savannah Ford; [memb.] Member of Rock Cut Baptist Church, Conley, Georgia as well as member of several pro-family organizations; [pers.] I believe my talent is a special gift from God. I write from inspiration in the knowledge that His words will not come back void. My poems are meant to bless hearts and make people think about their souls.

FOLEY, KENNETTH J.
[b.] July 8, 1943, Manhattan, NY; [p.] Florence and James; [m.] Nancy Ann, August 18, 1984; [ch.] Kimberly Lynn; [ed.] Queens College B.A. M.S., M.S. Pd.; [occ.] Teacher - Special Education Junior High School 72 Queens; [pers.] Every child can learn regardless of handicap; [a.] West Hempstead, NY

FONG, LAUREN M.
[b.] June 22, 1978, Oakland, CA; [p.] George and Jeanette Fong; [ed.] Alameda High School, CA Class of 1996; [occ.] Student; [memb.] Eden YOuth Group (Pres), Media Academy AHS; [hon.] My family; [oth. writ.] "My Life" chronicles: Lauren's Diary; [pers.] Poetry is my psychotic expression of sanity: Everyone needs a little crazy to stay sane.; [a.] Alameda, CA

FOREE, JOHN
[b.] July 4, 1952, Sidney, NY; [p.] Izzetta Rose and Roy B. Foree; [ed.] Gilbertsville Central Unity School of Christianity; [occ.] Contract Clerical Support; [memb.] Seed Savers Exchange Silent Unity; [pers.] I practise listening, listening to the Mystery that surrounds us and pulses thru us. The Creative speaks to those who can see with the Heart.; [a.] Magnolia, TX

FORSBERG, BRIGADIER GENERAL PAUL O.
[b.] November 14, 1928, Minneapolis, MN; [p.] Oscar and Mildred Forsberg; [m.] Nancy Jean Dvorak, June 9, 1951; [ch.] Deborah, Diane, Daniel, Katherine, Kristina, Thomas, Jon; [ed.] BA of Arts St. Olaf College, many of Theological Sem, Bth Luther, Northwestern Seminary, War College; [occ.] Counselor, Ramsey County Human Services; [memb.] National Honor Society, Association U.S. Army, Pastor, ELCA, Ret Blue Key Honor Society, Retired Officers Ass.; [hon.] Distinguished Service Medal, Legion of Merit, Bronze Star, Meritorious Service Medal, The Army Commendation Medal, World War II Victory Medal; [oth. writ.] Military Chaplain in the Correctional Institution ('69), The Young Soldier ('78); [pers.] I was an Army Chaplain (Brigadier General) for 34 years. I have written poetry for 45 years; [a.] Minneapolis, MN

FORSYTHE, VIRGINIA
[pen.] Gin Forsythe; [b.] July 14, 1935, Chicago; [p.] Anne and Ed Forsythe; [m.] Deceased, February 15, 1955; [ch.] 5; [ed.] High School; [occ.] Composer, Play Writer and Poet, Singer, Actress; [memb.] Holzer and Ridge Casting Agent. For Movies National Peoples Actions; [hon.] Outstanding Award for service for community; [oth. writ.] A Soldier Prayer, Black Tracy. A original play: 1) If You Only Knew, 2) When I Write These Love Letters, 3) Everybody's Got Somebody, 4) When I'm In A Dream With You, 5) Baby Be Mine (all are copyright); [pers.] Very creative, have produced several poems and music and looking for an opportunity for exposure. Also was in The Fugitive, Blink, I Love Trouble, Missed Person - movies; [a.] Chicago, IL

FOSTER, MARIA ELENA
[b.] June 8, 1959, El Paso, TX; [m.] Raymond Eugene Foster, August 3, 1994; [pers.] I wrote this the night I fell madly and passionately in love with my friend and lover... my husband Raymond.

FOUNTAIN, DEBORAH
[b.] September 29, 1953, Seattle, WA; [p.] Pat and Bob Fountain; [ch.] Lenny Gucinski; [ed.] Roosevelt High; [occ.] PT Stewart, Meyden Bauer Center, Bellevue WA; [memb.] On Sunday, June 26, I became a new member at the Renton Lutheran Church; [hon.] Citation of Merit for the Successful Completion of Drawing and Painting in Summer School, 1968; [oth. writ.] I've written some other poems that were to help me deal with my Mom's death on June 1, 1994. It was caused by cancer.; [pers.] I'm a divorced, single parent as of January 9, 1990. My new hobby of interest, is learning how to speak and write the cherokee language.; [a.] Seattle, WA

FOWLER, SANDRA
[b.] February 4, 1937, West Columbia, WV; [p.] Okey Fowler, Jean Fowler; [ed.] Wahama High, studied poetry with Lilith Lorraine, Founder-Director of Avalon; [occ.] Poet, Disabled; [memb.] Voices Group, Israel, Amnesty International, Salem Community Church, Charter Member, Holocaust Museum; [hon.] Woman Of The Year, American Biographical Institute in the early nineties, Honorary Member of the National Steering Committee of the Clinton, Gore '96 Campaign; [oth. writ.] My work has appeared in The United States, England, Israel, Italy, Pakistan, India, Austria, and Germany; [pers.] I strive to reflect, with God's help, the beautiful, careworn landscapes and faces of Appalachia. My soul is in the exceptional region where I was born.; [a.] West Columbia, WV

FOX, GAIL
[b.] March 28, 1968, Naperville, IL; [p.] Frank and Lorreen Richards; [m.] Andrew Fox, December 5, 1992; [ch.] Child due in September 1995; [ed.] Westmont Sr. High School, DeVry Institute of Technology; [occ.] Homemaker; [memb.] St. Paul's Lutheran Church, Epilepsy Foundation; [hon.] John Philip Sousa Award for leadership and excellence in music; [pers.] Inspired by my loving husband Andy. Without his support I never would have followed my dreams.; [a.] Naperville, IL

FRANCE, WILLIAM N.
[b.] November 5, 1949, Wisconsin; [ed.] Webb Institute of Naval Architecture, New York University School of Law; [occ.] Martime Lawyer; [oth. writ.] Incunabulum, a novel in verse (unpublished), poem in "Aldebaran", journal of Roger Williams College; [a.] Harlem, NY

FRANCIS, JAN E.
[b.] May 6, 1962, C'ville, IN; [p.] Sharon Dawson, Phil Francis; [ed.] Crawfordsville High School; [occ.] Food and Beverage Service; [memb.] Trinity Methodist Church; [hon.] Employee Of The Year 1993 at Ruby Tuesdays; [oth. writ.] Working on writing a book about coming from a large family; [pers.] The inspiration of my mothers death. And coming from a family of eleven children.; [a.] Douglasville, GA

FRANCIS, MARIAN K.
[pen.] Marian Keller Francis; [b.] November 29, 1907, Los Angeles, CA; [p.] Henry Workman Keller M. Adulain Boehme; [m.] John Huber Francis (Dec.), July 8, 1933; [ch.] John Anthony Francis, Mary Kathline Francis y O'Donnell, Robert Henry Francis (Dec.); [ed.] Catholic Elementary Schools, (First) Graduate of Marymount High School of the West (in Los Angeles, California); [occ.] Enjoying family life with children, 13 grandchildren, 10 great-grandchildren, taught contract and duplicate bridge for some years; [memb.] Life member of ACBL (American Bridge Contract League) - life member National Christ Child Society; [pers.] Family life in U.S.A. must be maintained to insure our way of life, it is being destroyed at a dizzy rate by individual greed as against, even a minimum amount of sacrifice - a mad craze of too many of our population.; [a.] Los Angeles, CA

FRANCONE, BRUCE E.
[b.] September 23, 1943, New York, NY; [p.] Edeale and Phyllis Francone; [m.] Pamela Francone, September 9, 1967; [ch.] Elizabeth; [ed.] B.S. Aeronautics and Astronautics, M.I.T., J.D. University of New Mexico; [occ.] Attorney; [memb.] New Mexico and California Bars; [pers.] There is a lesson to be learned from every living thing; [a.] Redlands, CA

FRANK, GERALD B.
[pen.] Forthright; [b.] September 22, 1928, New York, NY; [p.] Blanche Baumann Frank, Morris Henry Frank; [ch.] Daniel B. Frank, Jonathan W. Frank, Louise B. Frank; [ed.] B.A. Colby College Waterville, Maine, Class of 1950; [occ.] Retired; [memb.] The Cliff Dwellers Of Chicago; [hon.] My three children, the wives of two of them and the sons of one of them!; [oth. writ.] Lotsa advertising copy over the years... mostly in "Plain Talk"; [a.] Chicago, IL

FRANK, HARVEY
[b.] February 21, 1924, Brooklyn, NY; [p.] Martha and William; [ch.] Two children Ian and Carrie, a doctor and a lawyer; [ed.] James Madison High School, U.S. Navy Air Force, N.Y. University, Anthony Scotti Dramatic School; [occ.] Retired, was V.P. Large Textile Co.; [oth. writ.] "What Happened To The Robins' Song", "My Reservoir Of Dreams"; [pers.] Don't wait for your ship to come in - row out and meet it half way.

FRANKLIN, EMANUELL SINCLAIR
[pen.] E-man; [b.] January 30, 1981, Frot Smith, AR; [p.] Angela Franklin and Alice Franklin; [ed.] I am still in Junior High School (Kimmons); [occ.] Parker Elementary; [oth. writ.] Trapped, Milestone, The World Passes Me, and You Will Be Missed; [pers.] Although I really don't believe in astrology I keep an open mind; [a.] Fort Smith, AR

FRATIS, JOHN
[b.] February 17, 1926, Sacramento, CA; [p.] John and Pearl Fratis Sr.; [m.] Lili-Ann, August 29, 1945; [ch.] Nancy Jonas, Diane Manning; [ed.] Graduated (4 yrs), Folsom High School and 1 yr Sociology Class Sacramento State College; [occ.] Museum Manager and Semi-Retired Union Rep.; [memb.] Two Peace Officer Associations and International Lions Club Officer; [hon.] Past Presidents of one Peace Officer Association and Lions Club President 2 yrs in succession; [oth. writ.] I write articles on Folsom Prison History for the monthly "Peace Keeper" magazine of the California Correctional Peace Officers Association.; [pers.] My poem is an effort to reflect some humor resulting from eventual realization of the aging process on us all.; [a.] Sacramento, CA

FRAZIER, MATTHEW
[b.] September 3, 1976, New Jersey; [p.] Michlene Frazier; [ed.] River Dell HS, Univ. of Iowa; [occ.] Sophomore at University of Iowa; [memb.] Bard College Writing Award 1994; [pers.] I am so tired and I cannot sleep and this twist of words, burgers and cold beer seems too much a poem to be real. What is poetry? I do not know, it is too much a part of us.; [a.] Iowa City, IA

FREEBAIRN, CAROLYN JOYNER
[b.] March 31, 1934, Columbia, SC; [p.] Lottie Player Joyner, Oliver Joyner; [m.] Don R. Freebairn, December 10, 1954; [ch.] David Freebairn, Carla Freebairn, Glenn Freebairn, Dan Freebairn and 8 grandchildren; [ed.] Graduated from Columbia High School (S.C.), attended Brigham Young University, attended LDS Business College, took correspondence courses in writing; [occ.] Homemaker; [memb.] Church of Jesus Christ of Latter - Day Saints (Mormon), past President of Beacon Heights Writers' Club; [hon.] Won first place in city-wide "Cookie Lover's Festival" contest 1985. My entry was 100 brightly painted cookies in 50 shapes including one of my favorite American characters, a smiling Mickey Mouse! I've baked, painted and individually wrapped thousands of these cookies and shared with friends and family in Australia, England, Argentina, Norway, Uruguay, Canada, the Philippines, South Carolina, Georgia, Utah, Arizona, Alabama, Oregon and California; [oth. writ.] Combination of approximately 50 poems and articles in the following publications: The Salt Lake Tribune, The Ensign Magazine, The Church News (LDS Publication), The 1974 Golden Anniversary Book "Utah Sings" compiled by the Utah State poetry society; [pers.] In my writing I'd like to involve the reader's own expanded, creative thinking and emotions and share together a deeper awareness, enjoyment, and more keenly-felt appreciation for the opportunity of experiencing earth-life.; [a.] Salt Lake City, UT

FREEBODY, GARY R.
[pen.] Farmbo; [b.] September 18, 1944, USA; [p.] Ruth and Robert Freebody; [m.] Christine B. Freebody, September 13, 1969; [ed.] Ramsey High - Trinity Pauling School, Univ. of Pennsylvania BA, Univ of R.I. Masters Community Planning; [occ.] Small business owner, farmer; [memb.] Human race; [hon.] Athens Center of Ekistics Conference and Employment Invitation Accepted; [oth. writ.] Professional - technical reports published. Large pile of personal writings locally shared; [pers.] I was born shortly before I had a chance to vote on any aspect of my existence. Adapting to pre-existing patterns of imbalance energy became a 0 to 18 prerequisite. The age 18 survival celebration included the awareness that I was a Universal thing on the drag strip of life looking for the lost larger picture. I am still looking...; [a.] Camden, ME

FRENCH, MARIA S.
[b.] July 21, 1951, Managua, Nicaragua; [p.] Joseph Martin Stace French, Mary Leticia French; [ed.] Widney High School East Lost Angeles Junior College University of Southern California; [occ.] Special Education, High School Teacher; [memb.] Fiesta Educativa USC Alumni; [hon.] Elected to the Honorary Association for Women in Education at the University of Calif. May 8, 1975, 1991 Shiny Apple Award (The LA. Teacher Center Volunteer Service Award) more than 200 hours at Rancho Los Amigos Hosp. Advocate Newsletter for the LA City Council for The Handicapped - Si Se Puede Award - working with parents of the disabled; [oth. writ.] "Spirit Of The Streets" an Anthology of the International Black Experience 1975 Counseling Challenge (Chapter written called Stepping Stones), 1973 "A P.S. Couple," and "Stormy and Windy" in Stone Cloud, an intercollegiate magazine, USC, CA; [pers.] I like to make people aware of the humanness that connects us all, no matter what our differences are.; [a.] Downey, CA

FRICKER, JULIE ANN
[b.] August 3, 1961, Philadelphia, PA; [p.] Adele and William Fricker; [ed.] Cheltenham High School in Pennsylvania - Northeast Career Schools Tractor - Trailer Division; [occ.] Tractor - Trailer Operator (Professional); [pers.] My inspiration comes to me from my life experiences. As I travel throughout this country. I am privileged to witness nature at her most stunning display. I see sights of unimaginable glory.; [a.] Harleysville, PA

FRIES, STELLA MCGRADY
[b.] July 23, 1909, Hollins, VA; [p.] Ennis and Lula (Scott) McGrady; [m.] George Washington Fries (Dec'd), December 24, 1935; [ch.] Katheen, Rose Marie, George Jr.; [ed.] B.S. Shippensburg State, College, Towson Normal School U. of Md. West Nottingham Academy; [occ.] Retired School Teacher; [memb.] Zion Reformed Church, Historical Society, Order of the Eastern Star, Retired Teachers Association; [oth. writ.] 1) Greenvillage And Beyond - 100 pages, 2) Some Chambersburg Roots - 260 pages, A Black Perspective; [pers.] Constant awareness of the beauty of nature, the privilege we enjoy and God's goodness throughout. Each new day is a blessings - a poem for me to write.; [a.] Chambersburg, PA

FRISCO, MARIE
[b.] February 26, 1953, Norristown, PA; [p.] Frank Frisco and Frances Frisco; [ch.] Nicole Lynn Kramer; [pers.] Poetry is the expression of an individual, who is willing to share with the world, a part of their inner most soul. For those who care to listen.; [a.] Allentown, PA

FROST, KRISTINE
[b.] December 26, 1963, Burley, ID; [p.] Warner and Tamara Weber Frost; [ed.] Degree in Health Science from Boise State University, Boise Idaho; [occ.] Registered Respiratory Therapist Primary Children's Medical Center Salt Lake City, Utah; [pers.] Through the expression of my thoughts on paper, I seek to touch the lives of others as they have touched my life. If through my wrings, I can touch even one person, then I have succeeded.; [a.] Farmington, UT

FUDGE, PATRICIA A.
[pen.] Iman I; [b.] June 23, 1949, Connecticut; [ed.] College Courses; [occ.] Cellular Industry; [memb.] Currently researching writing, poetry associations; [hon.] Annie Fisher, English award when graduated from elementary school many years ago; [oth. writ.] Forthcoming; [pers.] At age 46, I realize life is a journey. I plan to share my feelings through writing. Maybe, just maybe, my writing can help someone on their journey.; [a.] Houston, TX

FUENTEFRIA, MELISSA
[b.] October 25, 1980, Livingston, NJ; [p.] Alice Fuentefria, Pedro Fuentefria; [occ.] Student; [oth. writ.] I wrote a couple of other poems, one of which is being published in another publication.; [a.] Union, NJ

FUENTES, CRISTA
[b.] March 26, 1985, Los Angeles, CA; [p.] Josephine and Tony Fuentes; [ed.] I am going into the fifth grade at Gardner Street Elementary School in Hollywood, CA; [hon.] School Awards: Citizen of the Month June 92, July 93, Outstanding Student '94, '95, Perfect Attendance '94, '95, Turns in Homework Daily '94, '95; [oth. writ.] Poem: "The Person Is God"; [pers.] I wrote this poem because I wanted people to see how beautiful the world really is.; [a.] Los Angeles, CA

FULLER, MAXCINE
[b.] July 31, 1940, Texas; [p.] Malissia Randolph; [ch.] Beverly, Anita, Tyrone, Crystal and 7 grand children; [ed.] HG Temple High, Valrie Hurd Beauty and Business College. State Board-Austin Texas; [occ.] Custodian - DJH School; [memb.] Perry Chapel CME Church - actively supports church fictions and community programs; [hon.] Editors Choice Award; [oth. writ.] Birth of a Hope, Cross Fire, The Hour of Power, poem that I have not published; [pers.] Poetry is like the blues you say it with feeling and emotions, the vision inside helps me with the subject.; [a.] Diboll, TX

FULTON, CRISSIE
[b.] March 12, 1970, Galax, VA; [p.] Edna and Walter Fulton; [ed.] I attend school at Fort Chiswell High in Maxmeadows, Va., where I will be a rising Junior; [pers.] I believe that poetry is a great way for people, of any age, to express their feelings through.; [a.] Maxmeadows, VA

GAFFNEY, MARCELLE
[pen.] Marcelle; [b.] December 12, 1929, Paris, France; [p.] Marcelle and Rudolf Stastnik; [m.] William N. Gaffney, April 25, 1950; [ch.] Gary O. Gaffney and Grandchild Noah O. Gaffney; [ed.] French School and conservatory of Music and Dance Vienna, Austria, (4 yrs.); [occ.] Home keeper, and various hobbies and volunteer. Musician, clothes designer.; [oth. writ.] Children stories for "Noah" (Grandchild) and over 100 poems; [pers.] As the 3 muses hold each other's hands, I have been touched and influenced by all three. Inspiration followed, then writing.; [a.] Long Beach, CA

GAGLIANO, MARYANN SMITH
[pen.] Shamrock Sea; [b.] February 23, Rockford; [p.] Vera Smith George Wallace; [m.] Frank Gagliano, August 7; [ch.] Doreen, David, Dana Dan; [ed.] Rock Valley College Rockford College; [occ.] Co-owner New Milford Refrigeration; [memb.] Irish Society Phi Theta Kappa Woman space; [hon.] Outstanding student writing award from Rock Valley College; [oth. writ.] Golden Harp. Bright morning Dove, Mother sun and the Golden bear the little flower with wings.; [pers.] When I really trust that I'll take care of myself, I can let go enough to soar; [a.] Rockford, IL

GALLAGHER, DONNA MARIA
[b.] July 10, 1952, Amarillo, TX; [p.] Salvature and Dorothy Trementozzi; [m.] Richard Gallagher, May 27, 1973; [ch.] Kimberly Marie, Shaun Michael, Brian Joseph,; [ed.] Thomas Acquinas high school - Boston. Northeastern University-Boston; [occ.] Corporate Communications Specialist - Hughes Network Systems Germantown, MD; [oth. writ.] Poems and articles published in local newsletters and newspapers. Currently working on my first book, a non-fiction called "More precious than silver - more costly than gold".; [pers.] I believe my writing talent is a gift from God for the purpose of using words and emotions to express his love. Care an concern for all of mankind. My desire is to impact my readers with truth, to touch their hearts and souls. And to reflect the goodness of God through words of hope.; [a.] Germantown, MD

GARBERINO, DENNIS CHARLES
[pen.] Dennis Charles; [b.] February 21, 1956, Saddle Brook, NJ; [p.] Charles and Dolores Garberino; [ed.] Ramapo Regional High Fairleigh Dickinson University of Teaneck and Wroxton, England, NJ; [occ.] Business Administration purchasing, education; [memb.] "National Association of purchasing managers", "Distinguished member of International society of poets", "American manager's Association"; [hon.] Dean's list and academic honors from fairleigh Dickinson University; [oth. writ.] Poem published, called "Autumn Shadows" in anthology "Beyond the Stars"; [pers.] Poetry has been for me, a creative release of my perception of life.; [a.] Saddle Brook, NJ

GARCIA, ADRIANA
[b.] May 23, 1978, Los Angeles, CA; [p.] Jesus Garcia, Marisela C.; [ed.] Morningside High, El Camino College; [occ.] Liberal Arts Student; [pers.] Mexican American, I get my inspiration from things that I see everyday and always try to show in my writings the good side of human race.; [a.] Inglewood, CA

GARCIA, ANGELA S. H.
[b.] July 28, 1954, Berlin, Germany; [p.] Hershel and Siegrid Curati; [m.] Israel Garcia (Former), May 16, 1975; [ch.] Israel C. Garcia; [ed.] Miami University,m Oxford Ohio, Black Hills State U. Spearfish SD Sough Dakota School of Mines and Technology, Rapid City SD; [occ.] Denny's Inc. Waitress; [memb.] International Thespian Society; [hon.] International Thespian Society all star cast award 1971, Best Supporting Actress 1971, Miami University Creative Writing: Second place 1973, Monogram Pictures Best Writer 1995; [oth. writ.] Ajax Space Candy Co. for the Wire, the Stubborn Sehlat for All Ways; [pers.] I am a liberal by nature. The bottom line is basically I'll tolerate your pig if it doesn't take the bloom off my rose. It falls down when you notice the other guy's pig wants to eat your rose. My fingers bleed a lot.; [a.] Miami Beach, FL

GARCIA, ZETTIE M.
[b.] July 26, 1912, Stockton, UT; [p.] John Aaron Painter and Florence Louise Niblett of G.B.; [m.] Robert Garcia, June 15, 1931; [ch.] Robert Aaron; [ed.] G.E.D; [occ.] Retired Federal Employee; [memb.] The Church of Jesus of Latter Day Saint. (L.D.S.); [oth. writ.] A Brief History of Stockton, Utah, My Wonder Book of the The Painter, Niblett and Related Families. Family connection in New Mexico articles, poems and Travel-Logs,; [pers.] Role Models: My mother who read to me and early-day school teachers who made us recite great poems. A plus for any child. I believe that every individual is worthy of recognition and deserves a written record, regardless of his fame or fortune.

GARDNER, JASON K.
[pen.] Nosaj; [b.] May 14, 1973, Cocoa, FL; [p.] Keith and Kathy Gardner; [ed.] Cocao High School Brevard Community College; [occ.] Graphic Designer; [memb.] Surf Rider Foundation Photography Guild; [oth. writ.] Several poems published in underground Magazines; [pers.] No dream is unattainable to the dreamer who walks in a waking dream.; [a.] Coca, FL

GARMA, BRENDA L.
[pen.] Brandi; [b.] January 26, 1947, Philippines; [p.] Salvadore and Carmen; [m.] Dr. Alberto M. Garma, M.D., September 1st; [ch.] Alberto "Chip" Patrick, Albert Francis, Leizl Carmencita, Anthony Andrew; [ed.] Notre Dame High, Ateneo De Zamboanga, School of Nursing-Zamboanga; [occ.] Registered Nurse; [oth. writ.] A Dream; [pers.] I would like to urge and encourage all mankind to dispose of themselves humbly to receive with all patience what GOD will to do in them, to be transformed into CHRIST by the fire of the SPIRIT through this writing.; [a.] Plano, TX

GARNER, J. H.
[b.] August 12, 1961, Kellogg, ID; [p.] J. P. Garner; [ed.] B.S., Agricultural Economics, Washington State University, M.B.A., Organizational behavior, University of Missouri; [occ.] Computer Engineer Geographic Information Systems (GIS); [oth. writ.] Numerous unpublished poems; [pers.] I began writing poetry merely as means of self-expression. Since I tend to conceptualize my relationship with the rest of the human race in the most vague terms, imagine my surprise to find others were interested in what I had to say and could even relate to it.; [a.] Grandview, MO

GARNER, SALLY
[b.] September 19, 1932, Boston, MA; [p.] Benjamin and Rebecca Davis; [ch.] Jonathan Michael Garner; [ed.] (1946-1950) Notre Dame De Pitie High School (1950-1951), Cambridge Jr. College, Took Courses for W. Peat Golden West, College and Cal State Fullerton; [occ.] Retired Dance Teacher and Retired Medical Transcriptionist; [memb.] Past member - Dance Teacher's Club of Boston - Feb 25, 1954, past member - Professional Dance, Teacher's Assoc. Inc. 12-31-71, past member - American Assoc. for Medical Transcription (#19957) 12-29-89; [hon.] Employee of the Month (6-82) VIP Award from Anaheim Gen. Hospital, (1974) VIP Award from Garden Park Hospital Graduated with honors-high school; [oth. writ.] I have written several poems and over 8 children's books, none of which have been published.; [pers.] "Writing is a creative adventure." "Poetry touches one's souls."; [a.] Norwalk, CA

GASKIN, ROBERT EDWARD
[pen.] O'Eddie; [b.] March 8, 1935, Lillington, NC; [p.] E. Peal and Reba Gaskin; [m.] I was married twice 1. M. Dr. Diane Snyder - 1960, 2. M. Janice Ogburn - August 18, 1968; [ed.] Bules Creek Public Schools, Campbell University, Durham Tech. College; [occ.] Poet, Historian, Genealogist Free-lance writer, speaker; [memb.] Oak Grove Baptist Church, Deacon, Church Association, Executive, Choir member, Masonic Lodge, Rotarian, Jaycees, Future business leader of America full Gospel Business men; [hon.] Alpha Phi Omega Fraternity Phi Beta Lamba, in Library Congress-poem anthology in Library congress- history anthology in Harnett County Hertage - History anthology, in county Library- History anthology history anthology poet Anthology in library congress and Library; [oth. writ.] 1993 Harnett Hertage wrote in county History library book that is anthology in library and Library congress write social Happening for 4 newspaper. That get published regular. I am accredited poet. Historian, genealogist.; [pers.] I am a sentimental person and a caring person and like to share my thoughts with others; [a.] Lillington, NC

GASSMANN, PAULA ROZAN
[b.] Boston; [ch.] 2 Children; [ed.] BA in Psychology, MA in writing, Certificate in Human Resource management; [occ.] Astrologer, Writer, Editor, Meditation Practitioner; [oth. writ.] 2 Collection of fiction, 4 collection of creative non-fiction, 5 collection of poetry and 28 volume of journal writing; [pers.] I believe creative development runs parallel to psycho spiritual dimension, which translates into soulful concern for people and their contribution to society.; [a.] Lexington, MA

GEIDE, MATTHEW
[b.] March 25, 1981, Red Bank, NJ; [p.] Kenneth Geide, Cherie Geide; [ed.] I have just graduated from St. Ann School on June 10, 1995. I plan on attending Gonzaga High School this year.; [pers.] I, Matthew Geide, am focusing on scaring the reader similar to Alfred Hitchcock. I have been greatly influenced by Stephen King's works.; [a.] Arlington, VA

GEIGER, DOROTHY B.
[b.] June 17, 1929, Lagrange, GA; [m.] Sidney E. Geiger, March 24, 1946; [ch.] Michael Edward, Keith Osborne; [ed.] Clift Hare High School, Opelika, Ala., Auburn University, Auburn, Al. B.S. and M.S.; [occ.] Retired Microbiologist; [memb.] Auburn First Baptist Church; [oth. writ.] None published; [pers.] My writings reflect my faith in God and my faith in my fellow-men.; [a.] Auburn, AL

GENN, ELISABETH
[b.] August 9, 1980, Moscow; [p.] Nina and Ilya Genn; [ed.] Niles North High School Student; [memb.] French National Honors Society; [hon.] School Merit Awards Two subsequent years. Graduated valedictorian from Junior high school. Have been an honor roll student for 9 years.; [pers.] In taking one step forward we may regress a thousand years. It is only by looking back at the past and evaluating the present that we can truly make progress.; [a.] Skokie, IL

GENOVESE-BUCK, ANN MARIE
[pen.] Ann Marie Genovese; [b.] June 10, 1961, Fort Jefferson, NY; [m.] Henry John Buck Jr, April 22, 1989; [ch.] Henry John Buck III; [oth. writ.] Self published book of poems titled "The Tears of My Heart." I am currently writing two children's books.; [pers.] I hav e been writing as a therapeutic tool for the purpose of healing from sexual abuse. I have enjoyed writing since I was a child. I hope that my poem may touch someone and be able in their healing in the future.; [a.] Shirley, NY

GENTRY, DERENDA
[pen.] D; [b.] December 17, 1977, Leesburg; [p.] Carol and Huland Gentry; [ed.] Senior at Leesburg High School; [memb.] Leesburg First Assembly Youth Program; [hon.] Latin State and Nationals, who's who among American High School students, Dance Tech; [oth. writ.] 2 years of yearbook, poems published in local newspapers; [pers.] This poem is dedicated to a very special person who has influenced my life a great deal. Someday I'll be with him in his new home in Alabama; [a.] Leesburg, FL

GEORGE, ANDY
[pen.] I Rock; [p.] Margret George; [ed.] St. John's RC School and St. John's Christian Secondary school; [occ.] Sailor, with Carnival Cruise lines; [memb.]

Dundee sport and culture club; [pers.] I will like to record many of my great songs I have written down on book or write songs for an excellent singer. Writing is one of my Hobbies.

GERRITZ, MARTHA
[b.] December 6, 1910, Iowa; [p.] Matt and Selma Elo; [m.] Harold Gerritz, (Deceased), July 29, 1939; [ch.] Kathleen Gerritz (quality not quantity); [ed.] Two Harbors High School Saint Cloud Teacher College University of Minnesota; [occ.] Retired Teacher; [memb.] Kappa Delta Pi-, retired teachers of Minneapolis - W.K.Y.Z - Women, Extra Young with Zeal Member of first Congregations church, United Church of Christ - Seniors of MN. Mpls English Club, Chair, 3 Education Associations Mpls Mn, Nat'l.; [hon.] Jostin's Citizenship Award - 4H Adult Leadership, chairperson for Red Cross Drive, Certificate for 25 years teaching, Mpls. - active member Search committee for next Minister, Volunteer in Nursing Home; [oth. writ.] Poetry in "Talahi" College Yearbook - News items for small town paper in Michigan. Unnamed poem in Desert Sun Article for "CHIMES" United Church of Christ monthly publication for 10 years.; [pers.] God, grant me the serenity to accept the things I cannot change, courage to change things I can and wisdom to know the differences. Serenity prayer; [a.] Minneapolis, MN

GERUT, JOHN D.
[pen.] J. D. Garrett; [b.] February 18, 1962, Chicago; [p.] Mary Gerut, John Gerut; [ed.] BA, Northwestern University MUPP University of Illinois Chicago; [occ.] City Planner; [memb.] National Returned Peace Corps Volunteer; [hon.] AICP Student Award, 1990; [oth. writ.] Public process documents, jottings; [pers.] Observe unfolding life. Sift senses and self. Let creation rein.; [a.] Chicago, IL

GIBSON, CONSTANCE RENE
[pen.] Constance Gibson; [b.] January 13, 1961, St. Louis, MO; [p.] Joseph and Shirley VarVera; [ch.] Michael James Cross, 11-13-81, Jamie Marie Cross, 1-09-84; [ed.] St. Angela 1-8, Hazelwood Central 9-12, Meramec Community College 13-15; [occ.] Homemaker; [pers.] I also would like to thank my Antonio Smith. Without his love and support, I would not write anything.; [a.] Eminence, MO

GIBSON, OPAL
[b.] March 16 1929, Cyril, OK; [p.] Claude Long and Winona Long; [m.] Oren Gibson (Dec'd), July 17, 1948; [ch.] Judy, Tienna, Connie (Dec'd), Mike, Glenda, Brenda, James, Jeff; [ed.] High School; [occ.] Retired; [oth. writ.] Several Poems; [pers.] I enjoy writing poetry of a philosophical nature and life's lessons.; [a.] Cement, OK

GIBSON JR., CALVIN T.
[b.] December 16, 1934, Choctaw, OK; [p.] Calvin T. and Opal V. Gibson; [m.] Rita C., December 16, 1992; [ch.] 2 children, 3 grandchildren, 2 stepchildren, 2 step grandchildren; [ed.] Command and General Staff College, various aviation school, B.S. in Bus. Admin, Roosevelt Univ. Chicago; [occ.] Retired Military Pilot and retired Business man; [memb.] Retired Officer's Assoc., U.S. Army Airforce mutual Aid Assoc., U.S. Army Assoc., AARP (ret. Assoc.); [hon.] NCPSSM (Nati'l seniors Assoc.), United Seniors Assoc. Certificates various poet's 1994-95 Assoc., "Diamond Homer Trophy 1995', Induction into "Homer Honor Society of Int'l. Poets", 1995, Many military decorations wartime and peacetime; [oth. writ.] 90 plus poems, short stories, bi-monthly column in local newspaper, a book of Love poems to my wife, poem "Given the Time", in "Famous Poems of Today", "Famous Poet's Society, "Hollywood, Ca.; [pers.] I write on "Today" as I see it, and one yesterday as I lived it - I "muse" and "Philosophically" Express views on many subjects as they surface, in "Laymen's" Terms.; [a.] Lawton, OK

GIGLIOTTI, DEBORAH EMERY
[b.] November 25, 1955, Rockland, ME; [p.] Gerald Emery, Alice Emery; [m.] Michael Gigliotti, April 16, 1994; [ch.] Rebecca Lynn Flood; [ed.] Medomak Valley H.S., McIntosh College, College of life long Learning; [occ.] Secretary, EHMI; [memb.] Sierra Club Northeast Riders; [oth. writ.] Several poems; [pers.] Poetry is my way of venting my feelings. My poems reflect my inner self at the time they were written.; [a.] Rochester, NH

GILL, JEANNE V.
[pen.] Jeanne V. Gill; [b.] March 31, 1958, Hattiesburg, MS; [p.] John and Marie Van; [m.] Douglas Gill, July 12, 1985; [ch.] Christopher, Michael; [ed.] Hattiesburg High, Pearl, River Vo-Tech, Jones Co. Jr. College; [occ.] Staff nurse, telemetry unti, Methodist Hospital, Hattiesburg. MS Order of the Eastern star, Hattiesburg Chapter #334, North Shore Animal League; [oth. writ.] Essay "Why American Servicemen Need Our Support" won 2nd place (7th grade - 1971) Poem "Sea of Love" published in high school newspaper (10th grade - 1974); [pers.] My writing reflects my life experiences. "Lost Treasure" was written with a piece of my heart.; [a.] Maselle, MS

GILMORE, DANIEL B.
[b.] April 3, 1963, Ridgewood, NJ; [p.] James P. and Constance Gilmore; [ed.] Jersey City State College, B.A. History, as management, Mitchell College; [occ.] Photographer; [hon.] Award of Merit Medal, Military order of World Wars; [oth. writ.] Articles in local newspapers; [a.] Columbus, NC

GLAISTER, MURIEL DYAR
[b.] January 24, 1928, Marion Co., Hamilton, AL; [p.] S. C. and Bulaf. Dyar; [m.] Joseph W. Glaister, January 26, 1952; [ch.] Ira Glaister, Jerome Glaister, Debra Glaister, Sherri G. Hendrix Melissa Glaister; [ed.] Hi Sc. Hamilton, AL, B.S. Liberal Art, BSN Nursing, Master of Arts in Education, Master of Arts Clinical Counseling, UNA-Florence AL, UAH - Huntsville, AL; [occ.] Registered Nurse Clinical Counselor, Retired; [memb.] Trinity Episcopal Church, Flo, Al,, Alabama Nurses Assoc, American Nurse Association. Medical Aux. of state of Alabama - National Med. Aux. Biology Honor Society, Educational Honor Society; [hon.] Deans list University No. Al., Flo. Al.,; [oth. writ.] "Lamentations", A Collection of poems, short stories: "My old Man and Peter Gill", "The Purple Twilight", "The Little Boy Who Could" I have never published; [pers.] As I am in the late autumn of my season I walk out of my home which is located in the North Western Hills of Alabama and I gaze into the giant. Ooh Oak Hickory trees which all a blaze in a burst of the many Hughes of colors. I then look to upward and beyond those magnificent forms of life and I am satisfied. For I have witnessed all the various hughes of color.; [a.] Florence, AL

GLEASON, LYNN MARIE
[b.] January 11, 1955, Havre De Grace, MD; [p.] Donald E. Almoney and Janet M. Ziegler; [m.] William Thomas Gleason, February 14, 1992; [ch.] Geffry M. Gorman, Johnathan R. Gorman and Karey L. Gorman; [ed.] David Glasgow Farragut High; [occ.] Housewife; [oth. writ.] I have several other writing that have not been published, but were written for my own pleasure. Most of them are about other members of my family.; [pers.] God is my strength and comforter, and so are my memories.; [a.] Tallahassee, FL

GLINTON, GRACE
[b.] Guyana; [p.] Edna Collymore; [m.] Earle Glinton, April 29, 1978; [ch.] Gavin and Duane; [ed.] St. Joseph's High University of Guyana; [occ.] Case Counselor; [pers.] Change comes from internal desire only.; [a.] Livermore, CA

GLOVER, CHRISTINA A.
[pen.] "Cee-Gee"; [b.] February 11, 1969, Florida; [p.] Helen Davis; [ed.] High school diploma presently attending Montclair State College; [occ.] Basic Skills Computer Assistant E.O.; [memb.] Lifetime Membership at Palmer video; [hon.] Award from special programs for maintaining a 3.0 or higher at Essex County College; [oth. writ.] I have several other poems that have written, also have started writing other poems.; [pers.] If you have a dreary aim higher and higher, if you love in your heart, it makes it all too easy. Behold.; [a.] East Orange, NJ

GNOTTA, DIANE MARIE
[b.] April 18, 1961, Duluth, MN; [p.] Charles and Janice; [ch.] Alex Houck, Matthew Houck; [ed.] B.S. Sociology University of MN, B.S.W. College of St. Catherine, J.D. Hamline University school of Law; [occ.] Attorney; [memb.] Minnesota State Bar Assoc., Minneapolis Legal Aid Volunteer Lawyers Network Minnesota Women Lawyers; [hon.] Clarissa L. Gray Award, Dean's List; [pers.] Creative writing and poetry has always been a source of great personal joy and satisfaction for me. Utilizing this form of self-expression has enabled me to successfully balance my personal life with a demanding professional life.; [a.] Crystal, MN

GODOSKI, CHARLES
[pen.] Charles Godoski; [b.] January 4, 1974, Warren, MI; [p.] William Godoski and Peggy Kaufman; [ed.] Oliver Wendell Holmes Jr. High Wheeling, IL., Crivitz High School, Crivitz, WI; [occ.] Truck Driver; [oth. writ.] Poems published in "Echoes from the Silence", by Quill books and "Poetic voices of America" by the Sparrow grass Poetry forum; [pers.] Often when I needed to say something to someone, the right words never come to mind until the moment had been lost. When they do, I write them down, and somehow, they become poems. I hope these people can find themselves in my writing, and I hope that others will too.; [a.] Crivitz, WI

GOLDEN, BYRON LEE
[b.] March 5, 1978, Los Angeles, CA; [p.] Norine Golden, Dennis Loranger; [ed.] High School - College planned; [occ.] Student; [oth. writ.] Poems, and thoughts "not published"; [pers.] My favorite poetry is Lord Byron and Long fellow. Writing poetry lifts me up when I am depressed.; [a.] Pomona, CA

GOLDMAN, MARTIN R. R.
[b.] October 3, 1920, New York, NY; [m.] Marian Gordon Goldman, March 30, 1947; [ed.] New York University, Harvard University, Oxford University; [occ.] Writer; [memb.] Phi Beta Kappa, American Historical Assn., Harvard Club of New York City; [hon.] B.A. Summa Cum Laude, Valedictorian, Class of '42; [oth. writ.] Verse in Harvard Magazine Prose in the New York times; [pers.] Air-combat veteran former P.O.W.; [a.] East Hampton, NY

GOLLIDAY, TAMMY
[pen.] Cory Jean Dobbs; [b.] May 3, 1963, Oakland, CA; [p.] Glen and Ellen, Michele and Micheal; [m.] Sean Golliday, October 5, 1986; [ch.] Daniel and Joshua; [occ.] Christian Counselor, Minister's Wife; [oth. writ.] 25 Lyrics, recorded by contemporary Christian artist Dayera Medor. Published on two albums "Church Arise" and "Renewal"; [pers.] This was written to my mom, Michele, on our 1st mother's Day. My search ended when I found this beautiful woman who gave me life. God has certainly blessed us!; [a.] Auburn, CA

GOMEZ, RAFAEL
[b.] August 29, 1979, Worthington; [p.] Jill Gomez and Harold Junk; [ed.] Harris-Lake Park High School; [oth. writ.] Poems I wrote for someone I cared for; [pers.] I write what I feel not what I'm taught; [a.] Lake Park, IA

GONZALEZ, BLANCA ESTELA
[b.] October 14, 1957, McAllen; [p.] Argentina Alvarado Gonzalez, Marcelo Gonzalez Jr.; [ed.] PSJA High School 1976, Pan American University 1980, Texas A and I University 1985. BA Psychology and Elementary Education, MA Reading; [occ.] Reading Teacher at PSJA North High School; [memb.] Texas Computer Education Association, The International Society of poets; [hon.] Editor's Choice Award 1994 poem published in After the Storm, First Division for two years in Ensemble Band, Second division for one year in Ensemble Band, Psychology Scholarship for tuition, President honor roll; [oth. writ.] Article published in local paper, Poem published in the following books, After the storm, Best poems of 1996, A delicate Balance; [pers.] I believe that through education anything will be achieve. A goal is accomplished and determination the stars can be reached.; [a.] San Juan, TX

GOOD, CATHERINE L.
[pen.] K. C. Copper; [b.] April 7, 1973, Pittsburgh; [p.] Carol and Samuel Good; [ed.] Gateway High School; [occ.] Self employed through Home Interiors and Gifts Inc.; [memb.] Member of the Pittsburgh Steel City Angels dance company; [hon.] Most Improved dancer 1993-1994; [oth. writ.] In the proses of full length noval "keeping the dream"; [pers.] I live to find the words I use, and hope to inspire others.; [a.] Wilmerding, PA

GOODE, ROMMY
[b.] November 22, 1965, Galveston, TX; [p.] Don Goode and Gizelle Goode; [m.] Jaime Fernandez, March 25, 1995; [ed.] Balboa High School (Panama), Panama Canal College (1985) and BS Degree in Journalism from University of Texas in Austin (1987); [occ.] Dept. of Defense Photographer in Ft. Clayton, Rep. of Panama and Co-owner of own photo business "New Age Phot" in Republic of Panama; [memb.] National League of American Pen Women, American Society of Panama; [hon.] I have won several photography contest and have had my photographs exhibited and published locally as well as internationally. I've been invited to lecture on the "History of photography" in local museums, Universities and seminars; [oth. writ.] I have a collection of poems I've written in Spanish and English, yet unpublished, in a book I've titled "La Clave Del Tiempo" (A Clue of Time); [pers.] Writing is indeed "a window into one's soul". Although I have bene greatly influenced by the early spanish romantic poets, personal experiences in my life have greatly inspired me, as well.; [a.] San Francisco, CA

GOODE JR., JOSEPH
[b.] March 1, 1969; [ed.] Graduate East Brunswick Vocational and Technical High School special subjects studied (welding); [occ.] Machine operator; [oth. writ.] I have many other writings never submitted for possible publication; [pers.] In life it only rains once. Is it our choice to remove ourselves from it? I'm inspired by Jim Morrison a truly forgotten American Poet.; [a.] Old Bridge, NJ

GOODMAN, DONALD L.
[pen.] Don Goodman; [b.] January 30, 1948, Linton, IN; [p.] Etta I. Goodman (Mother); [ed.] Indiana University, Indiana State University, City College San Francisco, Certificate in Legal Assisting; [occ.] Writer and Lega Assistant; [memb.] Broadcast Music Inc.; [oth. writ.] I write Blues Songs Hilltop Records of Hollywood, CA has recorded one of my songs titled "BAD NEWS BLUES" on cassette titled AMERICA. Hilltop is about to record another one. AmeRecords of Hollywood are recording two of my songs.; [pers.] I like to write songs about ordinary people. I like contemporary poetry. I like to lyrics written by John Lee Hooker, Van Morrison, and the Rolling Stones.; [a.] Linton, IN

GOODMAN, HEATHER
[b.] December 25, 1978, Rochester; [p.] Richard and Linda; [pers.] I can't write happy poems, but I can write love and drama poems. It doesn't mean I'm not happy. It means I owe alot to the people I once loved and still do.; [a.] Rochester Hills, MI

GOODWILL, TAMMARYN ALSTON
[pen.] T. Norman-Peed; [b.] May 13, 1961, Philadelphia; [p.] Ernestine Johnson-Avery and Herbert Peed; [m.] Filiberto J. Goodwill, February 17, 1984; [ch.] Philibert Joshua Goodwill and Raena Elyse; [ed.] Ravenhill Academy-Philadelphia, PA., Blue Mountain Academy-Hamburg PA., Columbia Union College-Takoma Park MD; [occ.] Child Care Provider Goodwills Family Day Care in Gaithersburg MD; [oth. writ.] A collection of poems called "Wandering Home" just recently Copyrighted. Have begun a second collection not yet titled and have written and composed the music to 5 songs; [pers.] My poems usually are inspirational and many deal with friendships and the human emotional experience I try to get in touch with the private feelings we all have about life and place them a paper "seeing" is just as important as "believing'!; [a.] Gaithersburg, MD

GOODWIN, LORI ANN
[b.] April 3, 1971, Skowhegan, ME; [p.] Richard and Beverly; [m.] Paul Bassett Goodwin, December 7, 1991; [ch.] Ryan Goodwin; [ed.] Carrabec High School; [occ.] Momma Baldaccis restaurant, cleaning business; [oth. writ.] Several poems that have not yet been published; [pers.] I believe that poetry is a beautiful way for an individual to both express and also create thoughts, feelings, and emotions. To be able to express myself regarding different circumstances in my life personally give me great peace, pride, and a sense of accomplishment.; [a.] Madison, ME

GORDON, BRIAN
[pen.] Jacob Casey; [b.] June 20, 1970, Chicago, IL; [ed.] Lane Tech High, Wilber Wright College; [occ.] Upholstery, Woodworking; [memb.] Current member of Writers Digest Book Club, and Shepherds Chapel for IL; [oth. writ.] The Knowledge of Time, The Old Oak, I Shed My Last Tears, Changes, Silent Stalker, Rainy Days, Desire from Within, submitted to local newspapers; [pers.] Writing is more than just an occupation or something to do to just pass the time. It is a desire from within, a challenge to the individual to strive to their greatest accomplishment and knowing that the reward is a job well done.; [a.] Chicago, IL

GORDON, I. HERBERT
[b.] Pocatello, ID; [m.] Gail, 1975; [ch.] Hilary, Rebecca; [ed.] Idaho State University, Queens College, NYC; [occ.] Free Lance Writer; [memb.] Sierra Club, Appalachian, Mountain Club, Rails to Trails, Appalachian Trail Conference, Society Professional Journalists, North American Ski Journalists, Golden Key National Honor Society; [hon.] Three Peabody Awards, for writings, producing documentaries. During 20 years with NBC News.; [oth. writ.] Author, two books on Canoeing. Freelance travel/articles in Los Angeles Times, New York Times, Readers Digest et al.; [pers.] Preserving the wilderness is as critical to our total environment as is the actual use of the wilderness by a nation threatened with losing reality by the trivia creation of a virtual reality; [a.] New York City, NY

GORDON, JANIS
[b.] August 23, 1961, Oklahoma City, OK; [p.] Dr. A.B. Carter and Carol Carter; [m.] Robert F. Gordon; [ch.] Jeff, Andy, Alan, Jenny, Toni and Jeremy; [ed.] Eaufaula High School and Eastern Okla. State College; [occ.] Registered Nurse; [memb.] Noble Assembly of God Church; [hon.] College Deans list 1989, U.S, Achievement Academy Collegiate Award winner 1989; [pers.] I give God the glory for my written words.; [a.] Noble, OK

GORGE, VINCENT JAMES
[b.] November 19, 1964; [p.] James H. Gorge, Mary Lee Gorge; [ed.] Camelback High, Phoenix Community College, Mesa Community College; [occ.] Business owner, retail manager; [memb.] Sierra Club, The nature conservancy, The cousteau society, The Walden Wood project, The Environmental Defense Fund, Green peace; [oth. writ.] Many poems and songs not published; [pers.] Searching for TRUTH, BEAUTY, JUSTICE, and LOVE... are you out there?; [a.] Mesa, AZ

GOSTEL, MARIE
[b.] March 24, 1980, Elmira, NY; [p.] John R. Gostel, Victoria Gostel; [ed.] Elementary, High School Going into the 10th grade; [occ.] Teach CCO for St. Francis secretary at really world; [memb.] SADD, ACIS St. Francis Cathedral Church; [hon.] 1991 State

twirling team champ 1995. Basketball award JR high honors many girl scout award; [oth. writ.] Written a lot of poems and stories never have been published; [pers.] I write stories and poetry about real people. All of the feelings come directly from the heart.; [a.] Edison, NJ

GOUGH, ALMA ILENE
[b.] May 14, 1928, Akron, OH; [p.] Gertrude and Victor Richard; [m.] Gerald, March 29, 1957; [ch.] Terry and Timothy, Robertson - Robert Gough; [ed.] East High - Akron, OH, Actual Business School Akron, OH; [occ.] Retired; [memb.] American Heart Assoc., American Lung Assoc., First Baptist church - Tavares; [a.] Tavares, FL

GOURDINE, KEVIN O.
[pen.] GQ; [b.] November 21, 1960, New York, NY; [p.] Samuel Gourdine, Sarah Gourdine; [m.] Grace Gourdine, August 25, 1984; [ch.] Daniel Kevin, Danielle Krystal, Deanna Krystin; [ed.] Roosevelt High, Manhattan C.C., New York, NY; [occ.] Assistant Vice President Computer Operations, Citicorp N.A.; [memb.] Tremount United Methodist Church; [oth. writ.] Other unpublished poems written in memoriam of people that have had an impact in my life; [pers.] My writings are my inner feelings expressed only after I have examined someone that has made a difference in how I live. My writings are something I give back to those special folks who helped me.; [a.] Silver Spring, MD

GRAHAM, RICHARD A.
[b.] May 24, 1956, Providence, RI; [p.] James M. Graham Priscilla M. Graham; [ch.] Christopher Alan Siravo, Jessica Michelle Siravo; [ed.] Graduated Cranston High School West 1974; [memb.] U.S. Any 1974-1977 RI. National Guards 1978-1988; [oth. writ.] Numerous other poems dealing with my past life and romantic emotions all presently unpublished. This was my first entry.; [pers.] My poems and other writings are just "things' that came to mind" and reflect my feelings of love, happiness and sadness. Christopher and Jessica, I miss you both and love you always.; [a.] Cranston, RI

GRANGER, JULIE
[b.] August 27, 1965, Co. Bluffs, IA; [p.] Robert and Sally Davis; [m.] John Granger, July 31, 1993; [ch.] Shelbie Rae; [ed.] Thomas Jefferson High, Iowa Western Community College (IWCC); [hon.] Poem published in a Delicate Balance; [oth. writ.] Several poems unpublished; [pers.] I write from personal feelings and experiences, with which I enjoy expressing them on paper.; [a.] Council Bluffs, IA

GRANOWITZ, THOMAS
[b.] November 25, 1921, Brooklyn, NY; [p.] Lottie and Stephen; [m.] Lucy (Deceased), 1946; [ch.] Thomas C,, Steven, Susan and Timothy; [ed.] BA in Phys Ed -Sci. And M.A. history, Ithaca College, Harpur College; [occ.] Retired - 13 yrs., School Teacher - taught at W.T Clarke HS - Westbury, NY for 28 yrs.; [memb.] USS San Juan Shipmates Seventy plus ski club; [hon.] Delphi and oracle societies graduated cum laude from Ithaca college 7 battle stars WW2; [oth. writ.] I have 15 good poems I would like to have published!; [pers.] Favorite poems, "The Highwayman", "The Ballad of Reading Goal" senior citizens need to be heard, especially poets; [a.] Massapequa Park, NY

GRANTHAM, ANGIE
[pen.] Angelic Grantham; [b.] June 12, 1969, Eufaula, AL; [ed.] Eufaula High School, Troy State University; [memb.] Member of Corinth Baptist Church, Sigma Alpha Sigma, and Social Work Connection; [hon.] Outstanding member of Social Work Connection in 1992; [pers.] I like to focus my thoughts on the beauty of nature and I also have learned to express my inner feelings best through my writings.; [a.] Clayton, AL

GRAY, CAROLYN S.
[pen.] Cerise; [b.] October 27, 1942, England; [ed.] Some years in a British boarding school; [pers.] Christian Mystic. I know the "Angel of his presence". (Isaiah: 63:9). The age of spirit is at hand.; [a.] Indianapolis, IN

GREEN, TISA
[b.] St. Thomas, VI; [p.] Iona and Ulric Maduro; [m.] Alfred Green, September 21, 1990; [ch.] Damall Maduro, Dekella Green; [ed.] Fairmont Heights Night Capitol Heights, Maryland; [occ.] Hairdresser (Beautician); [hon.] Student of the months employee year at: Marinello Beauty School J.T. (Jerrytone Training, Center) Sam's Club, Loin Foods Corp. Overall a hard worker trying to reach my goals.; [oth. writ.] Rainbow records wanted to record my song (poem); [pers.] One's heart contains everything one needs to know and feel to survive. One live's by the way he/she feels (whether it be sad or glad) God is our everything.; [a.] Las Vegas, NV

GRICE, KATHRYN R.
[pen.] Kathryn R. Grice; [b.] April 7, 1926, Cramerton, NC; [p.] Etta Jane and Idus Reece; [m.] John W. Grice, March 23, 1947; [ch.] Barbara, Bill; [ed.] High School - Cramerton, NC; [occ.] V. Pres. John W. Grice Co.; [memb.] New Hope Baptist Church, Eastern Star; [pers.] I love life, and people. I want to make people happy.; [a.] Gastonia, NC

GRIFFIN, CARRIE
[b.] February 17, 1982, Evanston, IL; [p.] Laura and Michael Griffin; [ed.] Cary Jr. High School; [occ.] Full time student; [memb.] United States Figure Skating Assoc.; [hon.] Won young Author's award went to the Regional Science Fair (1995) won honorary 1st place award - Figure Akating Awards - 1995 Juvenille Upper Great Lakes Intial Round Winner

GRIFFIN, MICHAEL
[b.] May 1, 1967, Torrance, CA; [p.] Michael P. Griffin, Ute MacPherson; [ed.] BFA California Institute of The Arts; [occ.] Artist; [oth. writ.] Poem published in small underground literary papers and small mags; [pers.] My work is derived from a deep dissatisfaction with consumer society and it's neglect of. Human expression and support for the Arts.; [a.] San Jose, CA

GRIFFIN, PATRICIA ANN TAYLOR WETZEL
[pen.] Patti Ann Griffin; [b.] July 24, 1940, Milwaukee, IN; [p.] Thomas J. Taylor, Ruth Agusta; [m.] Lawrence Paul Griffin; [ch.] David and Mary Wetzel, Scott Arthur Wetzel, Grandchildren, Jodelle and Cristian Wetzel Brother and sister-in-law, Thomas J. Taylor Jr., Barbara Taylor; [ed.] Riverside N.S., University of Wisconsin; [occ.] Writer; [hon.] Editor's Choice Award; [oth. writ.] Several published articles 4 poems of American Nostalgia published in "Good Old Day" and "Reminisce" magazines; [pers.] Dreams come true, they really do. It happened to me and never, never can happen to you, too. Never, Never give up on your dreams. I thank God for my blessings and all good comes from my heavenly father; [a.] Minneapolis, MN

GRIFFIN, SEAN C.
[b.] May 1, 1961, Hudson, NY; [p.] Claire Griffin, Karl Griffin; [m.] Sharron M. Griffin, June 6, 1992; [ch.] Rose Sage - yellow, Labrador Retriever; [ed.] Germantown Central, Germantown, NY (M.S. diploma) Columbia Greene Community, College, Hudson, NY (1 semester only); [occ.] Chef and Artist; [memb.] Green peace, MS PCA, Smithsonian Association; [hon.] 1st Prize Village Common's Apple Pie Baking Contest, So. Hadley, Ma., 1st prize different Drummer's Ginger Bread House Contest, Northampton, Ma.; [oth. writ.] Poetry and short stories, (as yet unpublished); [a.] South Hadley, MA

GRIMES, JASON K.
[b.] July 8, 1978, Philadelphia, PA; [p.] Johanne and James Grimes; [ed.] Sr. West Phila. High School; [occ.] Student; [pers.] My poetry reflects issues of today's urban society.; [a.] Philadelphia, PA

GROLL JR., THOMAS R.
[pen.] Tom Groll; [b.] January 20, 1950, St. Louis; [p.] Thomas Groll and Elvera Paolucci; [ed.] Graduate Student, St. Louis University; [occ.] Registered Nurse. Home Health Care: The Visiting Nurse Association and Staff builders.; [memb.] St. Louis University Alumni Association, National Association of Orthopaedic Nurses, and Intravenous Nurses Society; [hon.] Norma Jean Frank Caring Award, St. Louis University Health Sciences Center, 1989; [oth. writ.] A Heart Held Captive and The Allegory of a Thirsty Horse. Unpublished poetry.; [pers.] "To be or not to be, we decide"; [a.] Saint Louis, MO

GROSS, BELINDA D.
[pen.] Fufu; [b.] Port Norris, WI; [p.] Virginia Gross; [ch.] 2 sons, Marvin and Marcus; [ed.] Millulle Sr. High School, Licensed Real Estate Agent, Amateur Artist; [occ.] CTT at Woodbine Dev. Centr.

GRUBER, IRENE
[b.] March 4, 1949, New York; [ch.] Two; [ed.] Queens College; [pers.] Writing poetry for me is a way of sharing feelings and happenings with the world.

GUILLORY, DAMON CRAIG
[pen.] Ebony; [b.] February 13, 1967, Houston, TX; [p.] James and Lou Guillory; [m.] Beverly Devon Owens, July 1, 1994; [ch.] Tyiesha, Tarrence, Damon Jr., Kennisha, LaDeja, Antione; [ed.] Graduate of James Madison Sir. High, Class of "85" President of (FBLA) Future Business Leaders of America/(TIASA) Tx. Industrial Arts Students Asso.; [occ.] Conv. Store Supervisor/singer; [hon.] My greatest honor would have to be the love and support that my family has always given me and most of all the blessings from almighty God above.; [oth. writ.] My #1 Love, My love, Midnight Dream, Fire in My Eyes, Your the Star in my Eye; [pers.] "Fantasies are fun but, dreams come true' is dedicated to my wife Beverly Devon Owens-Guillory for the happiness she brought into my life that I never knew possible. Thanks to my wonderful parents for their love and support. My children for being a growth of wisdom and their love. A special thanks to my beautiful wife Beverly for her love support and inspiration for "Fantasies Are Fun But, dreams come true"; [a.] Houston, TX

GUINN, LAHOMA VIVIAN
[b.] February 2, 1937, Whorton, TX; [p.] B. E. Andrews, Suveller Andrews; [m.] Fred Guinn, December 2, 1955; [ch.] Richard Lloyd Guinn, Guy Steven Guinn, Terri Jeanene; [ed.] Bakersfield High School, Bakersfield College, Chabot College Hayward, B.A. Faith Bible College now Sierra Bible College; [occ.] Writer - Minister; [hon.] Real Estate Honors (17) yrs., School Achievements, Graduate Degrees AA and BA, Opening Prayer and Inspirational speech. Calif. Univ. Bakersfield Cal St. Indian Graduates ministering messages in several churches, rotary club fremont, Ca.; [oth. writ.] I have been writing 12 yrs.; [pers.] I aspire to higher spiritual and intellectual thinking for mankind. I believe we can all reach towards the betterment of one another.; [a.] Bakersfield, CA

GUNNETT, LUCRETIA A.
[b.] January 19, 1929, Jacksonville, IL; [p.] Major Ferry, Effie Ferry; [m.] Arthur M. Gunnett - (Deceased 12-18-94), September 9, 1950; [ch.] Melina Marie Schlotthaver; [ed.] Springfield (IL) High, 8 Real Estate Courses-Anthony, Schools, broker license; [occ.] Retired; [memb.] Previous member Calif. Board of Realtors; [hon.] Won 1986 Calif. voter slogan contest with "What a difference a vote makes" first and second place in flower displays at Del Mar Fair in late 60's; [pers.] This poetry contest has sparked a new interest - writing poetry, love to quilt and enter contests; [a.] Oceanside, CA

HADA, JOHN JULI
[b.] April 16, 1927, San Francisco; [p.] Jutaro Hada and Katsuyo (Noma) Hada; [m.] Mitzi Mutsumi (Equsa) Hada, May 27, 1951; [ch.] Elayne Naomi, Matthew Stuart Jun, Sterling Theodore, and Leslie Anne; [ed.] B.A., M.A., Ed.D. University of San Francisco, Ph.D., University of Tokyo; [occ.] Professor of International Affairs of East Asia - Univ. of San Francisco; [memb.] Phi Alpha Theta, Phi Delta Kappa; [hon.] Distinguished Faculty Award (June 1995) College of Arts and Science, University of San Francisco; [oth. writ.] Zen Nihon Gakusei Jichikai Sorengo (Zengakuren) (National Federation of Student Self-Government Association: Evolution and Dimensions of Japanese Student Activism) in Japanese language, 1983; [a.] San Francisco, CA

HAGETHORN, LARRY
[ed.] BFA, University of Puget Sound MA in Arts and Crafts, New Mexico Highlands University, Division Chair, Industrial Technology, Grays Harbor College, Aberdeen, Washington, Community College Educator, 24 years; [occ.] I utilize my brokership with Coldwell Banker Real Estate to support my teaching habit.; [pers.] I am a machinist by trade, but my labor is teaching people how to make a living. My passion is painting and drawing. However, I have learned that a well crafted sentence can evoke a vivid image.; [a.] Aberdeen, WA

HAGLUND, KATHLEEN
[b.] June 15, 1959, Portland, OR; [p.] William Virginia Kearney; [m.] Ole C. Haglund; [ch.] Angela Marie, Melissa LeAnn; [ed.] Marshall High Portland Oregon; [occ.] Housewife - Mother; [oth. writ.] Several poems published in - local - poet newsletter; [pers.] The written word is a small poem with a big meaning. God gave us the world. We should give Him something in return. All for the goodness in of mankind and his children.; [a.] Chandler, AZ

HAINES, TIFFANY
[b.] May 11, 1978, Ephrata Hospital; [p.] Mr. and Mrs. Robert Haines; [ed.] Conestoga Valley High School (Sophomore); [occ.] Hostess at Pizza Hut; [oth. writ.] 1 poem called "Love" that has been published twice; [a.] Ephrata, PA

HALL, CHARLES W.
[pen.] Charlie Hall; [b.] July 7, 1923, Iva, SC; [m.] Deceased 1988, June 1961; [ch.] April Ann - Allee Robin Denile Charles; [ed.] B.S. - M.A.; [occ.] Retired; [oth. writ.] Several unpublished; [pers.] A positive attitude romantic

HALL, KATHERINE
[pen.] Katherine Hall; [b.] January 21, 1980, Augusta, GA; [p.] John and Vonda Hall; [ed.] Lakeside High School; [occ.] Student (Sophomore); [memb.] Greene Street Press. Youth Group, Student Against Drunk Driving, Dramma Club; [hon.] 1st place Coca-Cola writing contest, 1st place Georgia Young Authors District and Regional Contest; [oth. writ.] No other publications; [pers.] Someday I hope I'll be able to touch a person's life in my writing.; [a.] Martinez, GA

HALL, SHARON
[pen.] Sharon Hall; [b.] October 1, 1943, Cambria, IL; [p.] Virgil Swann - Maude Swann; [m.] Wesley Hall, January 23, 1960; [ch.] Lonnie 34, Kathy 30, Tracie 24, Kelli 19; [ed.] 10 1/2 years; [occ.] I run a Continental Filler Machine at General Tire in Mt. Vernon, IL; [oth. writ.] Friends often ask me to write limericks or little verses for or about them that are humorous. I have done this in short work since I was young.; [pers.] This poem helped me to release some frustration I felt when my grandson was born. By letting me feel the guilt is overwhelming to his father now. Time: 30 min; [a.] Benton, IL

HAMMER, JILL
[b.] October 14, 1969, Chicago, IL; [p.] Dr. Leonard and Mrs. Erra Hammer; [m.] Jeremy Goldman, August 16, 1992; [ed.] Brandeis University (B.A.) University of Connecticut (Ph.D); [occ.] Rabbinical Student, Social Psychologist; [hon.] Brandeis University Sanctity of Life Award, Rose Schlow Prize; [oth. writ.] Poems published in Response, Voices Israel, Encoding, Writing for Our Lives, Harp-strings, The Lyric; [pers.] My goal is to make my work holy by illuminating it with the light of spirit, myth, and rhythm.; [a.] East Norwalk, CT

HAMMER, NANCY A.
[b.] August 20, 1967, L.I., NY; [p.] Don and Shirley Hammer; [ch.] Cat - Tulip; [memb.] East Rockaway Church of the Nazarene; [pers.] The most important thing in my life is my relationship with Jesus Christ, God's Son. He is my Lord and Savior. He is my reason for living, my inspiration! I give Him all the glory in my life.; [a.] Merrick, NY

HAMPTON, JOSEPH F.
[pen.] Jody Hampton; [b.] April 16, 1952, Levelland, TX; [p.] M. L. Hampton Sr., Wilma Hampton; [m.] Marcia D. Hampton, May 29, 1971; [ch.] Levi Hampton, Robin Hampton; [ed.] Miami High School, Miami Arizona; [occ.] Coal Miner, Longwall Coordinator; [memb.] United States Team Roping Championships, Hayden Valley Roping Club, National Cattlemen's Association; [oth. writ.] Nothing ever published; [pers.] I write best about my own experiences; [a.] Oak Creek, CO

HANDLY, MARION D.
[pen.] Grasshopper; [b.] February 8, 1917, Concordia, MO; [p.] Lee and Marie Handly; [ed.] District 93 Grade School, Lafayette County Mo. Higginsville Missouri High School; [occ.] Retired Farmer and Salvage Yard Operator; [memb.] Concordia Baptist, Church Concordia Farmer's Co-operative Company, Edgerton Chamber of Commerce; [hon.] E Honor Roll in High School; [oth. writ.] Items for St. Joseph News-press Young at Heart Section, Magazine Articles, news for local newspaper; [pers.] I try to treat others as I wish to be treated; [a.] Edgerton, MO

HANN, JENNY
[pen.] Mama Hann; [b.] December 13, 1939, Lompoc, CA; [ch.] Kellie Mize and Jennifer Hann; [ed.] Calvary Chapel Bible College, Costa Mesa, CA; [occ.] Bank Auditor; [oth. writ.] Other unpublished poems; [pers.] The Holy Bible has been my inspiration and has illuminated my soul to write poetry that reveals God's love, Mercy and Grace to this dying world. This is my hope, that man may know the truth of God.; [a.] Fountain Valley, CA

HANNA, SHERYL
[pen.] Sheryl Lynn; [b.] November 16, 1952, Los Angeles, CA; [p.] Walter and Phyllis Wong; [m.] Fouad Hanna, August 1975; [ch.] 2 Daughters, one is 14 the eldest is 16; [ed.] High School and two years in a Junior College I have an AA Degree; [occ.] Freelance writer; [hon.] Honorable Mention Award for "The Fat Person's Prayer" in the Anthology "Voices" by Iliad Press; [pers.] I believe poetry touches every one's lives at some point in time, just like everyone is different so is poetry.; [a.] Los Angeles, CA

HANNAMAN, JUDY
[b.] January 1, 1935, Parkersburg, WV; [p.] Sterrett and Marie Lloyd; [m.] Howard, August 10, 1954; [ch.] Paul, Jeff and Susann; [ed.] Parkersburg High, Ohio Volley General Hospital School of Nursing and Life; [occ.] Retires from occupations but never from life; [oth. writ.] Short stories and poems; [pers.] Let love guide your life, let the peace of heart always be present in your heart and always be thankful; [a.] Elizabeth City, NC

HANNEMAN, KAREN
[b.] December 20, 1951, Berlin, WI; [p.] Nadine Hanneman and Harlo Hanneman; [ed.] Appleton East High School University of Wis., Green Bay Extension 1 year Theater major; [occ.] 25 years in the Health Food industry - last 16 yrs at SUN flower shoppe Health foods in Ft Worth Texas; [hon.] 1 silver music metal, 1 gold music metal, Armstrong flute player. Like accoustic music. Jeni Mitchel - my favorite song writer and lyrical writer.; [oth. writ.] Lyrics for songs for personal enjoyment; [pers.] Plant good seeds in life and hope they'll be watered. Love each other unconditionally and never ever stop growing. Be thankful for our many blessings. We must all let go in order to grow.; [a.] Fort Worth, TX

HANSEN, DALENE
[pen.] Dee Hansen; [b.] June 7, 1939, Clarion, IA; [p.] Lennie and Dolores; [m.] John Lindstrom Hansen, June 6, 1958; [ch.] Laurie, Trudy; [ed.] High school

self-employed owner gift store and Candy store, Director of Retail Marketing for Shopping Centers; [occ.] Disabled; [oth. writ.] Started at age of 12 with children type poems (None Published). Continued thru marriage and children with special family type poems wrote Reg Cookbook and Published for family use.; [pers.] The submitted poem was written in memory of my niece who died at age of 29 after suffering with Hodgins Disease for 7 years. Have desire to write poems, song lyrics, children's books; [a.] Peoria, AZ

HANSON, MICHELLE JEANNE
[b.] November 22, 1966, Damariscotta, ME; [p.] Cyrus E. and Evelyn M. Bennett; [ch.] Travis Jonathan Dubord; [ed.] Lincoln Academy, Newcastle, Maine; [occ.] Musician; [memb.] Augusta Spiritualist Church; [hon.] Acknowledged by several organization for work done with special needs child; [oth. writ.] Several poems, as well as a few short stories. Currently working on a personal autobiography; [pers.] In life, you can create whatever illusions you wish to accommodate society's guest for normalcy: in the end, it all comes down to just you.; [a.] Augusta, ME

HANWAY, DEZARAI D.
[pen.] Dez Hanway; [b.] July 7, 1983, Lander, WY; [p.] Francine R. Shakespeare, John E. Hanway Sr.; [ed.] Saint Stephens Ind. Sch. going into 7th grade; [occ.] Working in Tribal Northern Arapaho Enrollments Office, Assistant; [hon.] 1st Place Excel Mini Project on Snake Pythons, Second place in Young Authors "My 9 lives Cat", Achievement of the Most Outstanding Keyboarding Student. Excellence and Recognition in Academic Excellence and Recognition in Arapahoe Language; [oth. writ.] Young Authors 2nd Place Excellent Author Award for Exceptional Writing; [pers.] I enjoy reading books and writing poems. I'm enrolled in the Northern Arapaho Tribe and reside on the Wind River Indian Reservation. I strive to do the best in my poems; [a.] Ethete, WY

HARDY, CHARLENE
[b.] April 12, 1963, Illinois; [ch.] Robert Lee Hardy III; [ed.] Southern Illinois University at Edwardsville (SIUE); [occ.] Specialized Secretary Kelly Temporary Services; [memb.] Mt. Joy Baptist Church Sigma Gamma Rho Sorority, Inc. Bone Marrow Donors; [oth. writ.] A "few" unpublished poems; [pers.] Having a passion for the Psalms, paintings, poetry and people, I am always amazed with the range of emotions evoked by them. I try to convey those feelings through my poetry.; [a.] Edwardsville, IL

HARNESS, BRADY C.
[b.] May 9, 1951, Emporia, KS; [p.] Alton and Elizabeth Harness; [m.] Divorced, July 4, 1992; [ed.] Sophomore Coll.; [memb.] Harvest Time Tabernacle Church Fort Smith, AR 72901; [oth. writ.] Philosophical writings in several newspapers in the U.S.A.; [pers.] Greatly influenced by nature and the cause of conservation. For if we break Gods chain of life there will be no life, dreams or a tomorrow; [a.] Van Buren, AR

HARRIS, BETTY L.
[pen.] B. LUE; [b.] March 23, 1944, TN; [m.] L. N. Harris, December 23, 1964; [ch.] Rebecca L., John F, and step-son Bobby Lewis; [pers.] I must write! I have a phantom voice that has made its home in me. There are times when my phantom is roaming inside my innermost being, when the words drop off the end of my pen, and I, even I, am surprised at what is has called forth.; [a.] Cookeville, TN

HARRIS, BYRON JEROME
[b.] July 23, 1962, Cincinnati, OH; [p.] Rev. Earnest and Kathleen Harris; [m.] Ann-Marie Harris, May 10, 1987; [ch.] Andwele Kwabena Akin Harris; [ed.] Dublin High School, Dublin, GA. Howard University and The University of the District of Columbia, Wash. DC; [occ.] Director of Government Affairs - Legislative Director; [memb.]The Bellemead Citizens Georges County Chamber of Commerce - Member; [hon.] Outstanding Young Man of America - 1990; [pers.] As human beings it is incumbent that we strive to understand the significance in the routine of life.; [a.] Landover Hills, MD

HARRIS, JASON
[b.] September 21, 1978, Birmingham; [p.] Angela, Billy Harris; [ed.] Tarrant High School; [occ.] Sales Associate at Wal-Mart; [oth. writ.] School poems that I have sent to contests; [pers.] I am highly influenced by my girlfriend.; [a.] Tarrant, AL

HARRIS, MARIE B.
[pen.] Rhe Harris; [b.] December 23, 1946, Kentucky; [p.] Lola and Elijah Wright; [m.] Donald William Harris, December 7, 1963; [ch.] Donna Mae Harris, Deborah Marie Harris; [ed.] High School; [occ.] Personnel Manager; [pers.] I write my poems from feelings deep in the heart for the most part. Other come to me in the middle of the night, and some simply from a title or a photograph. My wish for my poetry is to bring pleasure to others.

HARRISON, ROGER D.
[b.] March 12, 1948, Dodgeville, WI; [p.] Donald and Dorothy Harrison; [m.] Alice M. Harrison, May 5, 1989; [ch.] Julie Ann 20 yrs., Amanda Elizabeth 14 yrs.; [occ.] Fidelity Acceptance Corp. Executive Vice-President Director of Operations; [a.] Kansas City, MO

HARSH, SUZETTE
[occ.] Medical Technologist; [pers.] Never say it doesn't matter what you were in the past. What you are today is the result of what you were in the past, be it for the better or worse. To deny your past is to deny yourself the chance for self-improvement and personal growth; [a.] Tecumseh, MI

HART, PENNY ANN
[b.] August 14, 1940, Columbus, OH; [p.] Harold L. Bocook and Birdie Bianci; [m.] Dan Hart, December 24, 1976; [ch.] Kelly, Jill, Beth, Jennifer and Sally (my own little women); [ed.] Amador Valley Joint Union H.S., Pleasant California; [occ.] Foster parent and enjoying every moment; [pers.] My writings are inspired by my heart, my soul and most importantly people I love.; [a.] Lancaster, OH

HARVEY, MR. JAMES S.
[pen.] The Preachin' Poet; [b.] Arlington, VA; [p.] Mr. Hugh G. and Mrs. Patricia L. Harvey; [m.] Mrs. Nancy S. Harvey, November 8, 1975; [ch.] 1 child our daughter Rebecca C. Harvey "Becky"; [ed.] Graduate of James Madison H.S. Vienna VA, Graduate of Valley Force Christian College, Phoennville, PA; [occ.] Teacher, Woodbridge Christian School; [hon.] Licensed minister (current licensing from 1992 - present, 3rd place Junior AAU Olympics, 16-year-old division (some years back); [oth. writ.] Scores of poems "Grab that Froward (SIC) Mouth" Lyrics (to be received advance royalties soon) on album entitled "The Light Of The World" (Hilltop Rec.); [pers.] Happily married almost 20 years, play harmonica and guitar, "write" songs (not notes), am bird watcher, exercise "nut" (walking, biking, swimming); [a.] Woodbridge, VA

HASKINS, LINDSEY
[pen.] Barnabas Haskins; [b.] May 13, 1935, Beaumont, CA; [ed.] MacArthur High, Texas A&M Galveston College; [occ.] Retired; [memb.] National Honor Society, Thespian; [oth. writ.] Several poems published in college newspaper, along with a few short stories as well; [pers.] Poetry: The soul's expression of life and death through every possible view-point throughout the infinities of time.; [a.] Houston, TX

HATHEWAY, DARLENE R.
[pen.] Darlene R. Hatheway; [b.] February 6, 1947, Indianapolis, IN; [p.] Joe and Helen LuBovich; [m.] Herbert Gilbert Hatheway Sr., July 20, 1968; [ch.] Holly Darlene Hatheway, Herbert Gilbert Hatheway Jr.; [ed.] High School Graduate; [occ.] Housewife; [oth. writ.] "Brownie Troop 209" Song Non-published. Other poems or songs unfinished.; [pers.] In 1979 I learned to play the guitar, and I guess that's when I wrote "Treasures' Of His Love", I just sat and wrote it down, it was the same more or less with the "Brownie Troop Song". It's amazing to me how it all comes together; [a.] Clinton, IN

HAUGEN, MARGARET
[b.] March 7, 1939, Crown Paint, NY; [m.] Eugene K. Haugen, September 18, 1957; [ch.] Eugene III, Steven, Marlena and 53 Foster Children; [ed.] BSN; [occ.] RN, ST Joseph Hospital, Pediatric Intensive Care Unit; [memb.] Gilbert Christian Church; [pers.] As a nurse in a Children's Intensive Care Unit, I deal with many deaths. My way to cope with these deaths is to write a poem about each child and present it to the parents.; [a.] Phoenix, AZ

HAWKINS, APRIL
[b.] July 1, 1982, Jackson, AL; [p.] Phyllis Hawkins; [ed.] K-7th entering 8th at Hawkins Middle School; [memb.] Bata Club; [hon.] An reading Award; [oth. writ.] "The Meadow" published in a school Pamphlet (yearly); [pers.] I hope my being 13 does not hurt my chances at all; [a.] Forest, MS

HAWKINS, MICHELLE
[b.] March 8, 1980, Duluth, MN; [p.] Mike and Diane Hawkins; [ed.] Sophomore at Sandalwood High School; [oth. writ.] Several poems published the school paper yearbook, includes "Under The Tree" and "A Child in Need"; [pers.] I have been greatly encouraged and inspired by my teacher and friend, Mr. Robert Pierce; [a.] Jacksonville, FL

HAYES, JANICE D. FLAUTO
[b.] September 10, 1952, Queens, NY; [p.] Gilbert and Gloria Flauto; [m.] Clifford G. Hayes (Deceased); [ch.] Joanna, Jeremy, Danielle, Justin (Kessler), Clifford, Jaclyn (Hayes); [ed.] John F. Kennedy H.S., Bellmore, L.I., New York; [occ.] Homemaker; [pers.] I began writing poetry following the tragic death of my husband in January 1991. My poems often reflect that loss.; [a.] Ballston Spa, NY

HAYGOOD, FAITH GEATER
[b.] December 27, 1955, Greensbord, NC; [p.] Lawrence and Delphine Geater; [m.] Mark A. Haygood, September 25, 1994; [ed.] Dudley Sr. High, Winston Salem State U., Southern Illinois U.; [occ.] Flight attendant USAIR Baltimore based; [memb.] Sigma Gamma Rho, Inc. Who's Who in America Colleges and Universities '77; [oth. writ.] Several poems published in the annual Rama at Winston-Salem State University 1977-1978; [pers.] To Judge each person only by their humanity and on equal terms. To respect all people. It takes so little energy to be a pleasant human being and you live longer.; [a.] Baltimore, MD

HAYNES, JOHN SCOTT
[b.] December 26, 1927, Silver Grove, KY; [p.] John M. and Violah A. Haynes; [m.] Essie A. (Redman) Haynes, February 22, 1951; [ch.] 3 daughters, Della Marie, Bonnie Lynn and Mickey Sue; [ed.] BSEE, West Virginia University 1955, Electronic Major; [occ.] Retired Engineer; [hon.] ETA Kappa NU; [oth. writ.] Have written, as a hobby, two science fictions books of 300 pages each. I am new working on the third book. None of the above have been published.; [pers.] Life is meant to be a challenge, not just a free lunch. Hardship as a youth teaches self-esteem. Where is youth hardship today? Youth needs to be allowed to work to acquire self-esteem.; [a.] Chandler, AZ

HE, XINING
[b.] February 4, 1984, Guangahan, China; [p.] Xiaorong He and Li Yan; [ed.] 9/90 - 11/91 Elementary School Grade 1-2, Toronto, Canada, 11/91 - 1/94 Grade 3 - 5 PS175, NYC 9/94 - 6/95 Grade 6 - ms67. NYC; [occ.] Junior High School Student; [hon.] Awards: Awards for Excellence in Writing 6/22/94 by NYC Association of teachers of English, President's Award for Educational Excellence 6/22/94; [oth. writ.] Poem will be published by Anthology of Poetry Inc.; [pers.] There is a door, it's you who has to find it and open it.; [a.] Little Neck, NY

HEALY IV, DENNIS L.
[b.] January 27, 1950, Washington, DC; [p.] Rita C. and Dennis L. Healy III; [m.] Patricia C. Healy, March 1 1982; [ch.] Rita Colleen Healy; [ed.] Calvert Elementary, Mackin High School, GED in United States Marine Corps; [occ.] Group Leader Mail Handler with the US Postal Service; [memb.] Volunteer "Camp Jamie"; [hon.] US Marine Corps 1966 - 1970, 3 Purple hearts Bronzestar, Combat Action Ribbon, Letters of Appreciation from U.S. Postal Service; [a.] Frederick, MD

HEFFERNAN, JESSICA RACHEL
[pen.] Perika; [b.] May 13, 1973, San Diego; [p.] Becky; [m.] A would be Adam Ant, in my dreams; [ed.] Drama, Bar tending, Photography, and the UCLA Media Worship '89; [occ.] Landmark Theater in San Francisco; [memb.] In "DEBT" Club of McCoppin; [hon.] Best Laugh Awards, Scariest Halloween Costume, Best Dancer, I am the alternative to Academic Achievement; [oth. writ.] "Tener Hambre Para Amor", "Never", "Barbies", "My Theropist"; [pers.] "Soldier Boy" was written for my younger brother, Jared. However, it is for all who have misplaced their courage.; [a.] San Francisco, CA

HEITMAN, CHRIS
[b.] May 17, 1936, Big Sandy, TN; [p.] George C. Christopher and Annie M. Davis; [m.] Michael (Deceased 6-15-94), January 12, 1977; [ch.] Karen Lipford, Kent Lowry; [ed.] Big Sandy High School Memphis State University; [occ.] Freelance Decorator; [oth. writ.] "Cheated", "That Moment", "Silence", "Alone", "Lost Love" partial list published; [pers.] I've always loved to write poetry and years ago aspired to write for a greeting card Co. and do my own illustrations because I also like art. My husband's sudden unexpected death caused me to write "unfinished"; [a.] Memphis, TN

HELDMAN, CORALIE
[pen.] Coralie Heldman; [b.] May 6, 1930, Ogallala, NE; [ch.] William Vernon Andrew Jay and Thomas Theodore; [occ.] Nurse; [hon.] Nursing has its own rewards, one of my biggest "honors" is being a grandparent; [oth. writ.] None yet, I am contemplating writing a novel perhaps to be named "The Etiology and Prognosis of a Non-Optimist."; [pers.] Henry Wadsworth longfellow influenced my love of poetry at a very early age, poetry is one of my main "Love"; [a.] Aurora, CO

HENDERSHOTT, HILON JOSEPH JOAN
[pen.] Hilon; [b.] December 19, 1914, New York City, NY; [p.] Hilon and Alice Hendershott; [m.] Jacqueline Kranz, January 5, 1951; [ch.] Hilon Jr, Jacqueline, Jane Susan, Patricia; [ed.] La Salle Academy, Nyeity St. Johns University Brooklyn NY, 2 years Arts and Science, Law School L.L.B.; [occ.] Retired Lawyer; [memb.] Disabled American Veterans (My Disability Minor); [hon.] Won short contest several years ago-given by Met. Life Ins. Co. Member of my bar 1945 as Joseph J.; [oth. writ.] Many short stories and poems but only a few published; [pers.] I like to entertain Scoff at those who would destroy our republic Hope for God's Mercy.; [a.] Massapequa Park, NY

HENDRICKS, ANTHONY CHARLES
[b.] January 27, 1969, Michigan City, IN; [p.] Jacqueline and Charles Hendricks; [ed.] Bachelor Science Purdue University; [pers.] Always and forever thank you Amy; [a.] Michigan City, IN

HENDRICKS, SARAH THOMAS
[pen.] Sarah Thomas Hendricks; [b.] March 4, 1935, Walls, MS; [p.] Darrell D. and Maggie McKay Thomas (Deceased); [m.] William L. Hendricks (Deceased August 24, 1992), April 7, 1958; [ch.] Patricia Skaggs, Kim Ewing, Christie Butler; [ed.] Horn Lake High School Northwest Jr., College Senatobia, Ms.; [occ.] Retired, Data Processor; [memb.] Sacred Heart Church Walls, Ms.; [oth. writ.] 1) Poems published in Tennessee Register (a state Catholic pub.), 2) Memphis Methodist Hosp. Mo. Pub., 3) Song - "Mr. River" - recorded by the ovations; [pers.] In my work I attempt to convey God's gift of love and compassion for my fellow man.; [a.] Walls, MS

HENGESBACH, MARY JANE BELLANT
[b.] July 24, 1967, Saint Johns, MI; [p.] Richard and Judith Bellant; [m.] Louis Richard Hengesbach, Jr., May 9, 1987; [ch.] Louis III, Charles and Hillary Anne; [ed.] Lansing Eastern High School, Lansing Community College; [occ.] Homemaker; [memb.] St. Mary's Catholic Church and Sault Ste. Marie Tribe of Chippewa Indians; [oth. writ.] My poem "Our Happiness" published in win Awenen Nisitotung Newspaper; [pers.] I strive to remind people that the greatest asset in life, is ones family. I have been greatly influenced by my loving parents.; [a.] Portland, MI

HENRY, ELEANOR MICHAEL
[pen.] Eleanor Michael Henry; [b.] September 15, 1920, Dayton, OH; [p.] Herman and Myrna Michael; [m.] Clifford W. Henry, October 2, 1954; [ch.] Twins: Sally Henry, Lyle William Michael Henry; [ed.] Extensive voice study in various colleges and music schools in Dayton, Ohio, New York City, and St. Petersburg, Fla.; [occ.] Lifelong Career as Singer; [hon.] National Tours in Operettas for Shubert Productions, New York, also experience in Summer Stock, radio and TV. formerly with NBC in New York City; [oth. writ.] Currently writing autobiography titled "This is My Story, This is My Song"; [pers.] Writing poetry has been a hobby since early childhood. I strive to express in verse impressions of what I Have seen and experienced in life.; [a.] Saint Petersburg, FL

HENRY, JOHN R.
[b.] November 12, 1923, Heidelberg, MS; [p.] John A. and Estelle Henry; [m.] Alice E. Henry, July 14, 1946; [ch.] Leisa R. Mercer, Lorna D. Henry; [ed.] Heidelberg High School, East Central Junior College Miss., Mississippi State University Long Ridge Writers Group, CT; [occ.] Retired from US Dept. Agriculture after 35 years; [memb.] Windmore's Writers Club, Soil and Water Conservation Society, National Assn., Retired Fed. Employees, Rapidan Habitat for Humanity; [hon.] Eight High Performances awards from USDA, Fellow award from Soil and Water Conservation Society, Distinguished Service Award, from Property owners association; [oth. writ.] Published in two magazines, published in seven newspapers. To be published in the Windmore's Writers Club's Anthology in Fall of 1995.; [pers.] I find writing to be real pleasure. I find writing to be mv best teacher. I enjoy my best teacher.; [a.] Locust Grove, VA

HERBST, KELLY
[pen.] Annie Oakley; [b.] November 7, 1979, Golden Valley, MN; [p.] Ken and Jan Herbst; [ed.] Elk River Senior High; [occ.] Student and Camp Counselor; [hon.] National Junior Honor Society; [oth. writ.] Numerous stories for school speech competition; [pers.] "As every thread of gold is precious, so is every minute of time."; [a.] Elk River, MN

HERENSZTAT, GRETA
[pen.] Greta Herensztat; [b.] July 7, 1933, Paris, France; [p.] Yidele Herensztat, Charlottle Herensztat; [ch.] Claudine, Judith, Hannah, Charlotte; [ed.] High School Equivalency Diploma, BA Cunt Graduate Center, MLS Cunt Graduate Center; [occ.] Operations Managers Saks 5th Ave NTC; [memb.] International Women's Writing Guild. "IWWG"; [hon.] Dean's List Kappa Delta Pi, Pi Delta Phi Magna Cum Laude; [oth. writ.] Several stories published in local newspaper and magazines poems in the process of publishing; [pers.] I am a Holocaust survivor and just started to write about my unending grief of having lost

my family at the hand of the Nagrs. we have to remember what happened wonder for mankind to become human; [a.] New York, NY

HEROLD, MICHELLE
[pen.] Shelley Herold; [b.] June 1, 1953, Milwaukee, WI; [p.] James Hobbs, Janet Hobbs; [m.] Bedford (Buzz) Herold, May 13, 1982; [ch.] Lorien Sea, Starr Jennifer Lee; [ed.] Ridgewood High, Brookdale Comm. College; [occ.] Dog Groomer, Horse Trainer, Writer; [memb.] American Mustang and Burro Assoc., Florida Cracker Horse Assoc.; [oth. writ.] "Thunder" young adult horse story, other books in progress, This portion of Lady Bronc Rider II from 80 line poem, many other long horse poems, plus shorter horse and dog poetry; [pers.] I believe that God has given me a gift to communicate both with and for animals.; [a.] Davie, FL

HERREJON, THERESA SHENEA
[b.] June 26, 1970, Minnesota; [p.] Sampson and Lillie Riser; [m.] Wilfrido Herrejon; [ch.] Xadriana LeShae Herrejon; [ed.] Park Center Sr. High, Triton College, De Paul University; [occ.] Account Control Rep.; [hon.] Who's Who Among American High School Students Dean's List; [oth. writ.] Story in local paper (Brooklyn Park) when I was in 9th grade; [pers.] Poetry and writing brings out the person's inner self well as beauty.; [a.] Bensenville, IL

HERSCHLER, MARC
[pen.] Marc Dottzhle; [b.] March 10, 1939, OH; [p.] Violet and Hayes Herschler; [m.] Joan S. Herschler, June 1961; [ch.] Jeff; [ed.] BS, Penn. State, 1962; [occ.] Retired; [memb.] Int'l Pers. Mgnt. Association Atbetratur, Better Business Bureau American Institute of Indiv. Investor; [hon.] Inter Governmental Affairs Fellow 1973, Toastmaster of the Year - 1975, Meritorious Service Award 1987; [oth. writ.] A number of short fiction pieces Technical Reports; [pers.] One of my goals in pursuit of and productive retirement is to write and publish poetry and short fiction.; [a.] Rockville, MI

HERTZ, NANCY A.
[b.] August 2, 1970, McHenry, IL; [p.] Charles and Jeannine Martina; [m.] Steven Hertz, September 17, 1988; [ch.] Jenna Rose; [ed.] McHenry East Campus; [pers.] To my Angel in the sky Jeannine Martina I dedicate this to you.; [a.] McHenry, IL

HERVEY, MARY L.
[b.] March 14, 1936, Pittsburg, KS; [p.] Ray R. and May E. Beth; [m.] Alfred L. Hervey, October 31, 1975; [ch.] Steven, Danny, Dena, Buddy, Monty and Vangie; [ed.] Franklin High School; [occ.] Retired; [memb.] First Assembly Church Women's Missionary Council; [pers.] Writing poems has always given me a way to express myself during "marked events" in my life. It would give me great joy if when someone reads my poems they would say "oh, I have felt just like that."

HESKETT, JOAN
[b.] November 21, 1927, England; [p.] Tom and Nell Weston; [m.] John F. Heskett, August 3, 1946; [ch.] David Gail, Paul; [ed.] High School - England Glendale Community College Glendale. Az Associate Degree. General Studies History Political Science; [occ.] Retired; [memb.] Ariz and National Fed of Republican Women Past State President of AZ Federation, current Chmn. Chiropractic Board of Examiners AZ Foster Care Review Board Phx. AZ; [hon.] Woman of Year - 1983 AZ Business Women's Assoc. Thunderbird Chapter Honor Roll, Glendale Community College; [oth. writ.] Numerous poems and windings speeches, usually on Reflections of Life. And Patriotism. I became a U.S. citizen in May 1949 I am proud to be an American; [pers.] An open mind means an open heart. My philosophy. The future belongs to those who prepare for it. Is a quote for our children.; [a.] Phoenix, AZ

HESS, SARASVATI LORION
[pen.] Sarasvati; [b.] November 24, 1962, Los Angeles, CA; [p.] Surya and Parvati Sabaratnam; [m.] Thomas Dean Hess, March 7; [ch.] Vasanti, Usha, Arjuna ("A.J.") and Dean; [ed.] Konawaena High, Hawaii Soland Community College, Fairfield CA. Hawaii Community College Hilo, Hawaii; [occ.] Student at Hawaii Community College Hilo, HI; [memb.] Saiva Siddhanta Church Kauai, Hawaii; [oth. writ.] Numerous poems still unpublished; [pers.] For me, poetry is an art, and my inspiration comes from the heart. Beautiful things follow when you can be true to yourself!; [a.] Keaau, HI

HICKS, NAN GARCIA
[b.] April 16, 1922; [p.] Gertrude (Nee Anderson) and Tony Garcia; [ch.] Ruthmarie; [occ.] Freelance Writer; [memb.] Former Trustee Westchester County Historical Trustee, Member Charter Revision Commission of White Plains; [oth. writ.] On The Go With Garcia "diplomat Magazine Capsule Travel Tips, And Nan's Vignettes, Herald Tribune, "Tricentennial Vignettes", Gannett Newspaper Publisications interviewed over 1000 guests in my D.C. and Wor Radio Shows. Among them Billy Graham, Eleanor Roosevelt, the Dale Carnegies appeared as Professional Singer in the states, South America and Europe guest Soloist Air Force Symphony, guest at White House twice informally presented to England Queen Mother by former espionage agent captain Brian Stoneduse.; [pers.] Drawing upon my background as a writer and interviewer I am writing further vignettes concentrating on the upbeat, positive and humorous. This is my first attempt at writing a poem and I am touched and pleased that you selected it; [a.] White Plains, NY

HICKS, WANDA
[pen.] Jean McBride; [b.] April 14, 1941, Rossville, GA; [p.] Deceased; [m.] Frank F. Hicks, November 2, 1994; [ch.] Jerry Edwards Phomas, Wendell, Dale and Doyle Phomas; [ed.] King High and Hillsborough Junior College; [occ.] Retired; [memb.] AARP, Harney Baptist Church; [hon.] Red Cross Volunteer, Better than B Aug. at graduation; [oth. writ.] A non-fiction novel, non-published other poems not published; [pers.] I have a lot to live for and enjoy sharing my thought with the world. I was influenced by an English College instructor in 1982 to write here in; [a.] Tampa, FL

HIGGINBOTHAM, ONEIDA
[pen.] Anita Barrera; [b.] November 2, 1954, Houston, TX; [p.] Erasmo and Slyvia Barrera; [m.] Gordon Higginbotham, August 13, 1986; [ch.] Sabrina Susanne Schuetz, Daniel Mark Schuetz and Sarah Elizabeth Higginbotham; [ed.] Sam Houston High GED, Houston Community College, International Christian Institute Graduate and under Graduate University; [occ.] Sales, Joshua's Christian Bookstore, full time student - ICI; [memb.] Christian Certification Counselor, Art Therapy Certification for Damaged Emotions, The Escape Center CPS Parent Aide Volunteer American Cross Medical Aid and CPR Certification; [hon.] Poem place in USA distribution of the issue of the "Eagle's Wing." Spanish poetry 7th grade 4th place.; [oth. writ.] Currently writing, many writing yet unpublished books, articles poems; [pers.] The heartbeat of a person's sense of belonging the life line of being able to be a survivor no matter what the ennoblement of the power with in each person; [a.] Houston, TX

HILBERT, RANDALL ARDEANE
[pen.] Randall Ardeane Hilbert; [b.] September 6, 1948, P.N.A.S.; [p.] Crd. Ray A. and Virginia Hilbert; [m.] Divorced, September 14, 1979; [ch.] Shannon Hilbert; [ed.] Military parents, I was exposed to a diversity of Educators and Trade Schools. My trade in life is a Refrigeration Mechanic.; [occ.] Retired; [hon.] Many; [oth. writ.] Men critters I, A delicate Balance, Rah Poems 2; [pers.] Randall has always felt at home in a sea trees or in a sea of water. He now has time to bring forth stories and poetry to enjoy, ponder and wonder.; [a.] Newberry, Fl

HILDE SR., REUBEN L.
[pen.] Reuben; [b.] April 30, 1922, Gilchrist, MN; [p.] Rynart and Johanna Hilde; [m.] Charlotte Hilde, July 18, 1940; [ch.] Karen Cullen Wells B.A. R. Lynn Hilde, Jr. M.D.; [ed.] La Sierra College, A.B. Andrews University, MA University of Southern Calif. Ph.D; [occ.] Retired Educator Last position - Dean of the School of Educ. Loma Linda University; [memb.] Seventh Day Adventist Church, Emeritus Professor, La Sierra University; [hon.] M.A. with honors, Andrews University. Citation of Excellence, General Conf of S.D.A's (in educational service); [oth. writ.] Seven books of Christian Education; [pers.] Summed up in the words of Kenneth Ebel, "Learning Begins in Delight and Flourishes in Wonder!"; [a.] La Mirada, CA

HILDRETH, LIESEL
[b.] April 4, 1937, Germany; [p.] Johannes Meyer - Elisabeth Rade (both deceased); [m.] Martin A. Hildreth, March 12, 1966; [ch.] Russell B. Hildreth, published poet at age six "Claremont Courier" Calf.; [ed.] Educated in Germany and England and United States; [occ.] Retired; [memb.] Community Concert - Association Hildreth Family Association; [oth. writ.] Poems written in German - unpublished, also short stories written in German unpublished; [pers.] I have in my possession very touching poems written by my father when he was stationed at the Russian Front during World War II. I cherish these poems very much especially, nice my father never returned from the war.; [a.] Upland, CA

HILL, JOANNE KENDALL
[pen.] Joanne; [b.] May 29, 1974, Texas; [p.] Oscar Walter Kendall III; [m.] Philip M. Hill, October 6, 1994; [ed.] Tarleton State University; [occ.] Home Health; [pers.] I try to reveal the meaning and thoughts of my own personal view and hope others feel the same and know we are not alone. I have been greatly influenced by the strength of my father.; [a.] Abilene, TX

HILL, MICHAEL D.
[b.] September 7, 1942, Des Moines, IA; [p.] Jesse - Mable; [m.] Freda, April 29, 1974; [ch.] Eight (8), 2 boys and 3 girls; [ed.] AA (Early Childhood Dev); [occ.] Veterans Service Officer Merchant; [memb.] Co - Chair African-American Leadership Council. Long Island Blade Educators, Exec. Board, Office Of Econ-Devel. Co-Producer Public TV "On the Dove" Lecturer; [hon.] Many awards for community work helped 1st Monument Statue for Medal of Honor Winner; [oth. writ.] Many small newspaper articles black history column, two TV poetry readings; [pers.] The most important aspect of our being, is our "living-life". Anything that does not enhance or protect our living life...leave it alone. In order to get back to your "living life" we (you) must change the way we (you) think. Thus, you'll change the things you do.; [a.] Mastic, NY

HILL, RICHARD H.
[b.] October 23, 1964, Oxford, MS; [p.] Richard and Jane Hill; [m.] Cheryl L. Hill, February 11, 1993; [ed.] 1 yr College Univ. of Mississippi; [occ.] U.S. Army Drill Instructor; [memb.] Phi Beta Sigma Prince Hall Free Masonry (European Division); [hon.] Bronze Star for service during Persian Gulf War Dec. 26 1990, June 26 1991 (U.S. Army Award); [pers.] All of mankind has the power to save man...; [a.] Fort Knox, KY

HILL, ULRIKE B. R.
[pen.] Rikki; [b.] August 2, 1956, Germany; [p.] Otto and Ida Klar; [m.] Bruce B. Hill, September 9, 1980; [ch.] Melanie Pike, Shelia Pike, Daniell Hill; [ed.] Graduated from German Schools plus have a GED in Virginia, start in College in Fall 1995; [occ.] TAP and Sec 8 Administrator William C. Smith and Co. in Washington DC; [memb.] I have been a member of Prince William REACT Inc., in Virginia for 10 years, which is a Radio Emergency Associated Communications Team; [hon.] Gold medalist, Junior Year of School in Track and Field. Received several awards from REACT, March of dimes and DARE Program for Voluntary Communications; [oth. writ.] I wrote about 200 other poems, but never attempted to have any published. I also write about life in General.; [pers.] My writing brings me serenity and will hopefully bring the same to other. My writings came from deep within. I express on paper what most people carry inside but are afraid to bring out; [a.] Dale City, VA

HILL JR., JEFFA P.
[b.] August 24, 1921, El Paso, TX; [p.] Jeffa P. and Margaret J. Hill; [m.] Juanita B. Hill, September 4, 1943; [ch.] Jeffa D. Hill, Ormond W. Hill; [ed.] Superior High (Arizona); [occ.] Retired; [memb.] Gadsden Mid morning Kiwanis, National Geographic Society, National Wildlife Federation; [oth. writ.] Several poems; [pers.] "An Angel unawares" dedicated to Lee and Betty Beckler, Melanie and Melissa. Mary Nell, their daughter and sister, has been a blessing to them and many others she has touched; [a.] Rainbow City, AL

HILL JR., THEODORE
[pen.] T. J. Hill; [b.] March 31, 1961, Lumberton, NC; [p.] Magadlean and Theodore Hill Sr.; [m.] Rena Ann Winston Hill, October 26, 1991; [ed.] Littlefield High School, Pembroke State University; [occ.] Dyer, Westpoint Stevens, Lumberton, NC; [memb.] National Sunday School Superintendent United Pentecostal Holiness Churches of America (Southern District), Deacon, Mt. Carmel Holiness Church; [oth. writ.] Several unpublished poems; [pers.] Giving should always take precedence over receiving. If this recipe is followed through life, you will never be wanting or unfulfilled and you will have peace of mind.; [a.] Lumberton, NC

HILTON, NICOLE D.
[b.] June 30, 1981, Oswego, NY; [p.] Richard and Deborah Hilton; [ed.] St. Paul's Academy, Pre-School and grades K-6, Oswego Middle School - Gr 7 and 8, Oswego High School - Gr 9; [occ.] 9th grade high - school student; [hon.] 1994 - U.S. Achievement Award Winner for Science and Math, 1995 - Daughters of the American Revolution Award, 1995 - History 8th grade award, 1995 - US Presidential; [oth. writ.] Achievement Award. Danced Awards - 1st place for acrojazz and tap - state level 1994 and '95; [a.] Oswego, NY

HILTZ, DANIEL R.
[b.] November 23, 1952, Williamsport, PA; [p.] George W. Hiltz, Mary Jane Hollingsworth; [m.] Patricia (Deceased 1995), January 19, 1974; [ch.] Brian D. 18, Kevin L. 14; [ed.] Williamsport High (1970), Williamsport Area Comm. College (1974), Penn. State University, Electrical Engineering (1977); [occ.] Self-employed Engineering Consultant and Constructor (Printing/Publishing); [memb.]Research and Engineering Council of the Graphic Arts Inventory; [hon.] Graduated with honors from Penn. State University; [oth. writ.] Numerous short stories and poems (unpublished), many personal greeting cards with personalized messages or poems, analytical and technical writing; [pers.] Each time I write, I reach inside as far as I can, take out a little part of my individuality, lay it out on an empty piece of paper, and then simply color it in with my pencil.; [a.] Mechanksburg, PA

HINCHEY, BONNIE LYNN
[b.] November 27, 1978, Richmond, VA; [p.] Gladys V. Hinchey and the Late Hursey Hinchey S.; [ed.] I am an upcoming senior at Dinwiddie Country High School; [occ.] Cashier at Classics Supermarket; [memb.] Smyrna Baptist Youth Group, Senior Class Vice-President, Yearbook (editor-in-chief), literary magazines; [hon.] Who's Who Among American High School Students (3 Consecutive years), National Journalism Award, National Business Award, All American Scholar Academic Achievement Award; [oth. writ.] I have written over 600 poems. Several of these have been published in a school Literary Magazine.; [pers.] A smile is worth more than any amount of money, a hug is a symbol of compassion. Smile, be happy, and make sure to hug those you hold dear to you; [a.] Dinwiddie, VA

HINZ, GERALDINE
[b.] February 20, 1948, Westfield, MA; [p.] Betty J. Bly William J. Bly; [m.] William F. Hinz, September 1, 1990; [ed.] Springfield Trade High; [occ.] Care Provider for Specialized Home Care; [memb.] Special Olympics (Coach) National Rifle Association Moose Club Lutheran Brotherhood; [hon.] Care provider recognition award from Association for Community Living Honored in Dept. of Mental Retardation Statewide Compaign Families 1000 Award; [oth. writ.] "Another Kind of Love" a short story published in the compendium for the commonwealth of Pennsylvania and was the main story for a brochure for specialized home care in Spfld. Mass.; [pers.] I dedicate this poem to my unborn babies for without them I chose a path in life to help others actions clearly demonstrate the benefits of choice, dignity, respect and independence; [a.] Granby, MA

HIRSCH, DEBRA BEVINETTO
[b.] August 2, 1954, New Orleans; [p.] Anthony and Dolores Bevinetto; [m.] Richard Hirsch, September 2, 1979; [ch.] David age 9; [ed.] Bachelor of Arts, University of Georgia 1976 - major - Broadcast News Journalism, minor - Speech Communication; [occ.] Writer; [memb.] Zone Rosa, a female writing workshop Savannah led by author, Rosemary Daniell; [hon.] Quill and Scroll (High School) Dean's List - UGA; [oth. writ.] Currently working on a book of my collected writings, mostly poems about my childhood in New Orleans and my journey as a woman today.; [a.] Savannah, GA

HODGE, LEON
[pen.] The Kid Who Wonder; [b.] February 14, 1950, Valdosta, GA; [p.] Walter and Catherine Hodge; [ed.] Valdosta High School Atlanta Area Tech; [occ.] Piedmont Hospital Atlanta Georgia in Housekeep; [memb.] Church of God; [oth. writ.] I have written several poem and a song call dare; [pers.] I strive to make people happy in my written to the best of my ability hoping to bring some joy in this trouble world and my biggest influence by Maya Agglo; [a.] Atlanta, GA

HODGES, HELEN MILBURN
[b.] February 11, 1908, New Burnside, IL; [p.] L. R. Milburn, Olf Taylor Milburn; [m.] Harlan Crews Hodges (Deceased), June 10, 1930; [ch.] Nancy H. Darnell; [ed.] Illinois College, Jacksonville, Ill., B.A. U of Colo.; [occ.] Poet; [memb.] Murray, KY., Woman's Club, Christian Women's Fellowship; [hon.] Lifetime Achievement Award, Murray and Calloway County, Ky., March 2, 1993, First Place in Poetry, Northwest Division, American Pen Women, "The Two Thousand Women of Achievement," published in London, England, "Personalities of the South", "Dictionary of International Biography"; [oth. writ.] With the art of writing poetry, I hope to leave, at least, a tiny touch of what we call the true, the good and the beautiful on this troubled and bewildering world.; [pers.] Magnolia, TX

HODGES, NANCY R.
[b.] December 17, 1958, San Bernardino, CA; [p.] Sylvia Lowther and Aaron Earl Crook; [m.] Timothy M. Hodges, November 14, 1993; [ch.] Jason M. Crook, Timothy Earl Hodges Martin, Joshua Aaron Crook; [ed.] High School Graduate, Technical College (Optical Tech.); [occ.] Photo Lab. Tech.; [hon.] Poppy drawing contest for VFW, medal ribbons for Swim Club, School Letters for Academics in Jr. High School, High School Letter for Volleyball; [pers.] Wrote this poem for my Nephew who was taken from US at a very young age. This poem is dedicated to his parent (My Brother and Sister in law). In the hope that they know someday they will see there son again.; [a.] Waipahu, HI

HODGSON, SHARON R.
[b.] May 17, 1978, Chicago, IL; [p.] Sandra L. Hodgson, Robert L. Hodgson; [ed.] Currently 12th grade student at Thornwood High School; [hon.]

Charter Member Dist. 149 National Junior Honors Society; [oth. writ.] Published in 1993, 1994, and 1995 Thornwood Kaleidoscope Literary Magazine, all poetry; [pers.] I am presently in the process of putting together a full manuscript of the poetry I have done to date and am currently seeking a publisher. I look forward to a fruitful publishing career - just waiting to get started.; [a.] Calumet City, IL

HOFFMAN, KENNETH
[b.] July 20, 1934, Teaneck, NJ; [p.] Charles and June Hoffman (Deceased); [m.] Marianne, November 6, 1966; [ch.] One girl, Yvonne White; [ed.] Two years Rutgers University three accepted by magazines; [occ.] Photographer; [memb.] SPBS QSA (Singing) PPA Bergen County, NJ; [hon.] Many Photographic Awards; [oth. writ.] Over 100 poems; [pers.] I enjoy composing entertaining poems in order to share by philosophies with the rest of the world.

HOHMANN, NEIL
[pen.] Corneilius Hophmann; [b.] September 2, 1942, Clarksville, TX; [p.] Walt and Lucille Hohmann; [m.] Katherine Guilbean Hohmann, January 23, 1965; [ch.] Neil Martin H. Mark Christopher H. and Claire Emily Hohmann; [ed.] BS Geology Louis Ma. St. University, MJ Geography Univ. of Maryland; [occ.] GIS Professional; [memb.] American Association of Professional Landmen (AAPL), American Society for Photogrammetry and Remote Sensing (ASPAS) Anne Arundel Country Writers Club, Phi Delta Theta Fraternity; [hon.] Outstanding Unit Award (US Army, 1968), Mix Sigma Honor Society, GSA Meritorious Service Award (ASPRS 1994), President Councilor Science; [oth. writ.] 22 Poems text "A Source Book for Professional Landmen, Technical P. for Seminars Symposia and Professional Societies, unpublished Novella and a play; [pers.] Writing poetry has been an avocation of mine for twenty-five years. Each is written from a personal experience; [a.] Edgewater, MD

HOLBROOK, MILDRED L.
[pen.] Mildred L. Holbrook; [b.] August 27, 1912, Nashville, IL; [p.] Henry and Louisa (Grote) Hake; [m.] Raymond A. Holbrook, August 6, 1935; [ch.] Phyllis, Beverly, Herbs, Brenda; [ed.] H.S. and Bus. College Graduate; [occ.] Retired legal secretary; [memb.] A.A.R.P.; [hon.] Published poetry in newspapers in W. VA., till; [oth. writ.] "The Letters You Didn't Write" (World War II), "Mailman's Soliloquy" "After the Storm", "Remembrance"; [pers.] have patterned much of my poetry from actual experiences. Life is an real motivator!; [a.] Streator, IL

HOLBROOKS, DOROTHY RUTH
[pen.] Dot Holbrooks; [b.] May 26, 1927, Seminole, TX; [p.] Mr. and Mrs. R. W. Pittman; [m.] Ulan Iris Holbrooks (Deceased), June 30 1946; [ch.] Linda, Ginny, Larry, Cecil (twins) Dana, Dena, Samuel, Deborah, Janna, Zachary; [ed.] Music Training McMarry College Abilene, Tx. Interlocker School of Music Interlocker Mich. 18 years Activity Director in nursing homes 45 yrs. teaching music; [occ.] Private Sitter for an Alzhiemer's patient and Music Teacher; [memb.] I am a member of a Civic Orchestra in Hobbs, Nm. on B Clarinet. I am a member of the Activity Directors Association Midland, Tx. Member of Worldwide "Church of God"; [hon.] 18 music medals in high school, musical activity. Band Choir String Viola (solo vocal) tenor, Piano Sax. Bt Clarine T. Bass Clarinet etc. my compositions, at this time, are wanted in Nashville, TN; [oth. writ.] I have many poems and am a songwriter of Gospel, as well as, Country Western Music. I perform with my own piano playing. I am recording at this time!; [pers.] I want my writings to be very constructive encouraging as well as inspirational. I am carrying on family talents and tradition. Poetic and musical Gene S. My children will carry on!; [a.] Seminole, TX

HOLCOMB, STEPHANIE M.
[pen.] Pauline Girard-Montgomery; [b.] July 22, 1975, Charleston, WV; [p.] Noel and Della Holcomb; [ed.] Clay County High, West Virginia Institute of Technology; [occ.] College Student; [memb.] Tech Singers, Tech Players, Student Government Association, Community Choir, Vice-President of Alpha Psi Omega, Concert Choir; [hon.] Alpha Psi Omega, Student Director, National Honor Society, Top of the Mountain Scholar; [oth. writ.] I continuously keep a daily journal and have written over 100 poems in the past 5 years. I have also recently begun a novel.; [pers.] Within each of us lies the power to truly live or merely exist. To truly live one must posses passion and express that passion to the fullest extent. Otherwise we merely exist.; [a.] Bomont, WV

HOLDEN, SHIRLEY
[b.] March 12, 1922, Corning, NY; [p.] William and Norma Call; [m.] Harley H. Holden, 1st 1940/now 1987; [ch.] Dale, Ronald, Jason, Ted, Neil Hitchens and Daughter Valerie; [ed.] Graduated C.F.A. High School in Corning, N.Y. had some college courses thereafter; [occ.] Retired, formerly a field underwriter for New York Life Ins.; [memb.] Seventh day Adventist Church. Cinderella Softball League Inc. A joyous member of the Whitfield - Dalton Senior Center in Dalton, Ga. where I'm secretary - treasurer of the Cappes St. Cappers Drama Group and the Georgia Golden Olympics in competition; [hon.] Co-Founder of the State and National Cinderella Softball League Inc. in 1958, I give honors to our Lord and Savior. I neither ask for or have received personal honors - only my personal satisfaction.; [oth. writ.] I've written approximately 100 short stories mostly unsubmitted. A couple was printed in insignificant magazines for which I didn't receive any payment. I enjoy writing. Poetry is a new endeavor - pleasing to my soul and hopefully to God.; [pers.] I don't criticize, nor do I preach but whatever I write, even when I try not to, there is always a spiritual message or over tones. They say you are what you write so I accept this as a blessing and hope in glorifies my heavenly father.; [a.] Tunnel Hill, GA

HOLLENBECK, CATHERINE
[b.] May 1, 1960, California; [p.] Richard and Bonnie Coury; [ch.] Jaclyn Bonnie Hollenbeck; [ed.] College Degree in Business; [occ.] Operations Coordinator; [oth. writ.] Several for personal enjoyment; [pers.] I am influenced by many in my life, especially the love of my daughter, Jaclyn. I love to write about children, romance and dreams.; [a.] Orange, CA

HOLLEY, BRANDON L.
[pen.] The Black Bird; [b.] June 6, 1971, Rexburg, ID; [p.] Lynnea Holley, Ira Holley; [ed.] Communications Major, Ricks College, College of Eastern Utah, Univ. of Utah, Weber St. University; [occ.] Habilitation Therapist; [hon.] Trophied in collegiate debate at several colleges and universities; [oth. writ.] None in major publication (other in small publications, other stolen); [pers.] I don't believe poetry has rules or can be formally taught, it is picked up along the way and comes out naturally.; [a.] Sandy City, UT

HOLLIDAY, DEANA TRUMAN
[b.] April 20, 1965, Compton, CA; [p.] Charles Truman and Catherine Scriven; [m.] Rick Holliday, 1986 (Deceased 1988), currently living with companion of 6 years, Robin R. Bach; [ch.] Hallie Farmer of Summerville, SC; [ed.] California State University, Sacramento; [occ.] Mental Health Counselor, Freelance Writer; [memb.] Volunteers in Victim Assistance (VIVA), Concerned United Birthparents, Warehouse Ministries; [hon.] My greatest honor has been the privilege of giving birth to my daughter; [oth. writ.] Several other unpublished poems, occasional articles in a local, non-profit newsletter; [pers.] Out of the deep losses of life and the ensuing struggle, vast wells of emptiness are carved within us. It is from these wells that great art springs forth, until the barren space that was left becomes filled with something beautiful. To Dianne was written in 1984, in memory of my friend Dianne Culpepper, who was killed in an auto accident.; [a.] Sacramento, CA

HOLLINS, SHENEK
[b.] January 17, 1980, San Leondro; [p.] Janice Hollins, Wilbert Hollins; [ed.] Tiny Tot University St. Benard, St. Columbus Parker Elementary and But Harte Jr. High; [occ.] "We Mean Clean" (City of Oakland); [memb.] Shiloh Baptist Church Active Teen Committee and Choral; [hon.] Oakland Alliance Black Educators Award, Speech Award, MLK Jr. 1st Place Award 1994, Scholastic Achievement Award (State of California); [oth. writ.] You Don't know Me, Runaway, The War, I Took A Stand, The Argument, Mystery, Once, Gretto Life, Progress, Should Care? I'm So fine, The Man Who Walks The Streets; [pers.] Through my writing I'm speaking to mankind to help save the world for the best"; [a.] Oakland, CA

HOLMAN, MICHAEL D.
[pen.] Miles; [b.] April 12, 1961, Florence, AL; [p.] Marie B. Anderson and Albert Holman; [m.] Divorced; [ch.] Jessica, Erica, Brittnie and Mikey Jr.; [ed.] Rock Valley College (AAS) Rockford College (BS); [occ.] Investigator for the Rockford, Il. Police Depart.; [memb.] Northern Il. Jazz Society; [hon.] Rock Valley College Dean's List; [oth. writ.] Editorial promoting racial harmony and world peace. Rkfd. Reg. Star, local newspaper.; [pers.] Life is art, live it to its fullest!; [a.] Rockford, IL

HOLMAN, MYRA HILTON
[pen.] Mira; [b.] 11/3/47, Palatka, FL; [p.] Mary Frances and Luther "Rosie" Hilton; [m.] John Perrine Holman, Jr., Sept. 8, 1993; [ch.] Michel Renea Kehoe & Jai Raja Christopher Ali Sikes; [ed.] Graduate Crescent City H.S.-1965, St. John's Fine Arts 1974, Real Estate School, 1982, Century 21 Real Estate School 1984; [occ.] writer, singer (music ministry, evangelization); [memb.] Beta Sigma Phi Sorority, formerly Palatka Art League, Daytona Beach Board of Realtors Association, Cathedral Basilica of St. Augustine, FL; [hon.] FL Literary Award in "Kairo" 1974 for this poem, 2nd in Oils Azalea Art Show, Star Search Trophy for singing WAIK Radio Station for FL - GA in Top 40 in States, Art Award, 2nd in Oils Azalea Festival Poetry - Kairo, for St. John's Comm. College; [oth. writ.] Former City Editor Palatka Daily News, columnist "Myra's Mes-

sages" Health Notes, Palatka Daily News, columnist "Entertainment News," Daytona Beach News Journal, and 1st book "Jesus is Alive." [pers.] I am a Jesus Visionary and have a deep religious outlook on life and the future of the world and to put it back in the hands of Jesus and Mary. God bless the world.; [a.] Welaka, FL

HOLMES, ANGELINE
[pen.] Angie; [b.] March 2, 1964, Benton Harbor, MI; [p.] Dave Margaret Holmes; [ed.] Kettering High School A.C.T. Nursing School East Wood Nursing Center/Now Homemaker; [occ.] Help baby sit for friend sometimes; [memb.] Go tell it Church of God in Christ; [hon.] One for saying a poem in six grade; [oth. writ.] Who Am I God, "It's Like Fire Shot Up In My Bones", A River Called Jordan"; [pers.] I grew up in Detroit I've always wanted to write, so God give me the gift of poetry although I wish others see it too.; [a.] Detroit, MI

HOLTON, AGNES BLONDECK
[b.] October 7, 1931, NJ; [p.] Frances and Walter Blondek; [m.] William Holton, February 1972; [occ.] Retired; [oth. writ.] Ten published Travel-Logs in Freehold Journal; [pers.] I enjoy insperational creativity regarding serious public issues via writing.; [a.] Whiting, NJ

HOLTVLUWER, NICHOLAS
[pen.] Nicholas Holt; [b.] September 23, Grand Rapids, MI; [p.] Jack and Sue Holtvluwer; [ed.] Hope College (Sophomore); [occ.] Student; [memb.] Hope College Football Team; [pers.] I strive to find the humor in life's everyday trial and errors in my writing. Life's short. Laugh it up.; [a.] Grand Rapids, MI

HOMOLA, ROSE M.
[b.] October 24, 1922, New Castle, England; [p.] Patrick McCarron; [m.] Rose E. McCarron, May 31, 1942; [ch.] Michael - College Chemist, Jean - Beauty School, Phillip - "Mack Truck Mech.; [ed.] Through High School 2 yrs. Community College Bookkeeping - couldn't afford tuition to go for C.P.A.; [occ.] Retired was full time - full charge Bookkeeper; [memb.] CYO, PTA, AARP, "Notch" Babies; [hon.] 3 yrs Champion (CYO) Basketball, honor Roll in high school - 4 yrs.; [oth. writ.] Short story "Champ", (Carin Terrior), kids story never submitted for publication - Did - accepted New York Firm - wanted to much money to published; [pers.] Worked up from 60.00 a month to $280.00 A week now writing book of my life. Born under Roosevelt to Clinton, through depression wars - traveled all over world no country has it over Amer. Even with fault's; [a.] Haines City, FL

HONAKER, MARY ANN
[b.] May 22, 1976, Beckley, WV; [p.] James and Frankie Honaker; [ed.] Woodrow Wilson High School; [occ.] Student of West Virginia University; [hon.] Winner of the Register - Herald's Golden Pen Contest 3 times, finalist twice. All-American Scholar Award (twice) National English Merit Award, US National Mathematics Award, National Leadership and Service Award; [oth. writ.] Golden Pen winning poems: 'Art's Pond', 'In Response to Romans 6:23', and 'Speak' finalist poems. 'The Statesman' and 'A Psalm: As Day Fades'; [pers.] I strive to communicate essences, ideal forms, auras, atmospheres, and spirituality itself - to make the intangible a verbal reality, and release it with all the passion a pen can hold.; [a.] Beckley, WV

HONEA, DWAINE L.
[b.] January 19, 1965, Falls City, NC; [p.] Howard Honea, Linda Wiar; [ch.] Malinda Lee Honea; [ed.] Falls City High; [occ.] Production Worker Farmland Foods Inc. Crete NC; [memb.] Zion Lutheran Church H.O.G. Harley Owners Group National and Local, Lincoln NC; [hon.] Army Achievement Award - 1984; [oth. writ.] None published this is my first one; [pers.] I'm just a single parent in the working world who likes to jot my thoughts; [a.] Tobias, NC

HONEYCUTT, DAVID GENE
[pen.] "Big Fist"; [b.] February 22, 1925, Raleigh, NC; [p.] L. D. Honeycutt, Emma Myrtle Honeycutt; [m.] Helen Cross Honeycutt, June 7, 1947; [ch.] David Jr., Susan Annette, Robert Edward, Helen Jr., Genie; [ed.] Boylan Heights Grammar School, Hugh Morson High School, North Carolina State College, University of North Carolina, various Business course and seminars; [occ.] Retired "Big Ticket", merchandiser and National Retail Sales Manager; [memb.] Y.M.C.A., Little League, Boy Scouts of America, U.S. Marine Corps, V.F.W., A.A.R.P., Montgomery Ward and Company, Methodist Church, married forty-eight years; [hon.] High School Letters in Track, Basketball, Tennis. Coach N.C. Little League Football Champs and Raleigh baseball champs. WW II Battle Star and Presidential Unit Citation. Various Regional and National Sales and Public Speaking Awards; [oth. writ.] Commendations and awards for "Letters" and many poems, eulogies, testimonials; [pers.] I am influenced by the Italian Renaissance. The family unit must be respected and appreciated. Self reliance must be recognized and rewarded, not sacrificed to big government. The elderly, our word, the U.S. flag must always be respected.; [a.] Spring, TX

HOPKINS, RONALD A.
[b.] August 29, 1962, Hawaii; [p.] Inge DiGusto and Allen Hopkins; [ed.] GED; [occ.] Cook; [memb.] Lifetime Member of Hutt River Province of Australia; [hon.] Royal Patronage Holder of HRP of Australia. Nominated for 1994 HRP Citizen of the Year.; [pers.] A lifetime of experiences are worthy to put into writing to benefit the growing generations; [a.] Atlanta, GA

HORAN, BILL
[b.] February 24, 1933, Boston; [p.] Patrick and Mary Horan; [ch.] Bernice, Donna, Mary and William; [ed.] Suffulk Univ. Boston, Mass. Lowell Tech. Lowell Mass; [occ.] Retired; [memb.] Elks, VFW, Amen Legion; [hon.] Retired Officer U.S. Army many Combat Awards. Lowell Tech (Univ. of Mass) High Honors; [oth. writ.] None published, many written since 1950; [pers.] I have just returned from Fiji in the South Pacific where I led a movement to stop the brutality of children in the schools I was a high school teacher with "Peace Corps." Many of my poems are about the Hind, Children I taught.; [a.] Brookline, MA

HORNE, AARON
[pen.] Big Horne; [b.] February 1, 1975, Union, NC; [p.] Linda and Eugene Horne Jr.; [ed.] I have a 10th grade education and do have training in welding, automechanics, and farming. I obtained this training at Pageland Center High.; [occ.] Self-employed I do landscaping and really enjoy it; [oth. writ.] I have many other poems that I hope maybe one day to also have them published.; [pers.] My poems that I write is basically in what kind of mood that I'm in while I write. I have found that I can work through problem's and write good poems at the same time.; [a.] Mount Croghan, SC

HORNER, WENDY
[b.] November 19, 1968, Niagara Falls, NY; [p.] Carol Horner; [ch.] Joshua Ferguson; [ed.] Niagara Falls High School Niagara Country Community College (NCCC); [hon.] Dean's List; [pers.] I dedicate this poem to my son Joshua. He is the inspiration of my life.; [a.] Niagara Falls, NY

HOUCHINS, CHARLES E.
[b.] April 8, 1943, Princeton, WV; [p.] Charles E. Houchins, Ferne E. Damewood; [ed.] Graduated from John Adams High School, June 1962, Cleveland OH. Attended Kent State Univ. 1964 - 1968; [occ.] Author; [memb.] Lifetime member of A.A.R.P.; [hon.] Served in Vietnam in the U.S. Army June 1968 - June 1969 Received Army Commendation Medal Combat Infantry Badge (C.I.B.) and Vietnam Service Medal; [oth. writ.] Hard Parts (published), You Are the One (published); [pers.] I believe God's plan is to have the world evolve into a paradise.; [a.] Daytona Beach, FL

HOWARD, JIM COFFIN
[pen.] Jim Coffin; [b.] September 1, 1966, Van Nuys, CA; [p.] Don Howard, Judy Douglas, (Biological Parents) - Jill Harris, Rick Main; [m.] Bridgette Howard, August 1, 1992; [ed.] Palos Verdes High College of San Mateo (CSM) California State University, Hayward (CSUH) A.A. Degree, Journalism; [occ.] Full-time student (SCUH) part-time Furniture Mover, Writer; [memb.] World Wildlife Fund, Environmental Defense Fund, Sierra Club; [hon.] Dean's List, Managing Editor, The San Matean (CSM Newspaper); [oth. writ.] Lead story published in Enquirer - Bulletin (weekly San Mateo/Belmont Newspaper), several poems in the Bitch and Moan Blues; [pers.] Poetry, at its best, allows the reader to take an intellectual break from reality. My hope is to inspire such travels within the mind.; [a.] Belmont, CA

HOWARD, LOUISE Z.
[pen.] Louise Z. Howard; [b.] January 9, 1935, Leadwood, MO; [p.] Sylvester and Jessie Watson; [m.] David A. Howard, April 21, 1979; [ch.] Wanda, Patt Paul Bill, 2 step-children David Jr., Carla; [ed.] Some College Licensed Professional Hair Dresser; [occ.] Retired U.A.W. worker presently Beautician in Health Care for Aged; [oth. writ.] "Tribute to auto-workers" Published in River of Dreams 1994 "Dearest Mother" published in "Best Poem of 90", 1995. Also published in UAW Newspaper.; [pers.] My poetry is my way of showing those I love inside my heart. Each one is in honor of those people. That I may be remembered with love. As they are my inspiration.; [a.] Ballwin, MO

HUBBARD, THERESA
[b.] July 28, 1949, New York; [m.] John Hubbard, July 3, 1969; [ch.] Lisa and Jason; stepchildren - John, Veronica, Anne; and grandchildren - Joey, Tommy, Michelle, Debbie; [ed.] Graduated High School - Riverhead High School, 2 yrs. College - Suffolk County Community College; [occ.] Teacher

Aide at Riverhead Middle School; [memb.] Woman of the Moose Riverhead Elkettes CSEA Secretary; [pers.] I have been highly influenced by my life long circle of family and friends. Their lives give me so much to reflect on that I feel I could write endlessly.; [a.] Aquebogue, NY

HUBER, COURTNEY
[pen.] Daisy Adams; [b.] April 29, 1980, Cincinnati, OH; [p.] John and Karen Huber; [ed.] School for the Creative and Performing Arts, Cincinnati, OH; [occ.] Student; [memb.] Music Theatre Crew (school related); [hon.] Young Author's Writing Award, Technical Theater Award of Achievement; [oth. writ.] Several short stories and poetry written for creative writing classes in school; [pers.] I feel if you believe in yourself and listen to your heart, you can achieve anything, set your goals and never listen to criticism; [a.] Cincinnati, OH

HUBERT, PAUL
[b.] October 28, 1948, Denver, CO; [occ.] Systems Software Specialist State of California; [hon.] 400 or more unpublished poems; [pers.] Those poems of mini that luke the best write themselves, indeed they insist on being written. They are born out of a longing to describe the indescribable.; [a.] Carmichael, CA

HUDSON, CARL D.
[b.] December 13, 1960, Indiana; [p.] Charles and Lillian Hudson; [m.] Pamela, July 4, 1995; [ch.] Ava Dawn, Nolan, Albert Glenn; [ed.] Cabrillo Sr. High, Lompoc Cal.; [occ.] Security - Locksmith; [oth. writ.] Poems and humor pieces about and for my friends and family; [pers.] I write with the hope and intent to give people a perspective of their life and the many elements that make it special.; [a.] Red Oak, TX

HUDSON, ELLEN MATILDA
[pen.] Ellen Matilda Hudson; [b.] October 3, 1945, Atlanta, GA; [p.] Charles Hudson and Lillian Hudson; [ed.] B.A. Degree "Tift College", M.A. Degree Music and Music Ed. "Columbia University" (N.Y.) Honorary A.B. "Mercer Univ." past grad. - Emery, Ga. State, Univ. of Ga.; [occ.] Retired - Volunteer Organist and Pianist "Decatur First Bapt. CA" - 35 years; [memb.] "National League of Am. Pen Women" - "Decatur Business and Professional Women" - "The Atlanta Presidents Council" - "All Chapter American Guild of Organists" "Decatur First Baptist Ch." - "Adelphia Sunday School Class.", "Dec. A.A.R.P."; [hon.] A "Teacher of Year" plaque, Atl., schools - taught elementary - 43 1/2 yrs. "Women of Wk" - article and plaque - "Dec. News Sun", "Woman of Achievement" B. and P.W., "Who's Who in U.S.A." teacher Poet, Org., and Pianist", "Am Biographical Ins Directory", "Woman of Year" 1995 - gold filled 24 carat medallion. "Am. Biog. Inst.", by "International Research Come"; [oth. writ.] Poem in 3 Anthologies - 1, "Sparrowgrass" Not., published hard back poetry bk - 100 poems. "Secrets" 1987; [pers.] I believe you are supposed to use your God given talent, no matter what it is, to help others to achieve happy fulfilled lives.; [a.] Decatur, GA

HUDSON, HENRY T.
[pen.] "Hank"; [b.] February 3, 1923, Utah; [p.] Owen M. Hudson, M. Opal Boggs; [m.] Polly H. Bell Lynch, September 26, 1947, Eunice Mae Dewhirst Martin, March 24, 1994; [ch.] Deborah O., David W., Drusilla L., Naomi R., Paul H.; [ed.] Butte, Mt High Sch. Grad., Higher Education, General School of Hard Knocks; [occ.] Retired Farmer, Logger, Public Official; [memb.] Active LDS Church, Family History Researcher; [hon.] WW II Tech., Sgt. Army Medical Corps Awards; [oth. writ.] Special occasion stories, poems, Limericks for Enjoyment of Family and Associates; [pers.] Personal: Sort of a poor man's combination Ambrose Bierce, Ogden Nash, Richard Armour. Philosophical: "Every baby born is proof that God is not yet totally discouraged with man,"; [a.] Magna, UT

HUFFHINES, TERRY
[pen.] Andrew W. Lore; [ch.] Son: Justine Terry; [occ.] Entrepreneur, Inventor; [memb.] The Planetary Society, The Humane Society, The World Wild Life Fund; [hon.] 2 Patents; [oth. writ.] Two books (unfinished...), several poems; [pers.] Make the Magic Happen!... Love one another. We're all in this together.; [a.] Lenexa, KS

HUGENOT, IDA
[b.] May 26, 1919, Webberville, MI; [p.] Mac J. Smith, Pearl Smith; [ch.] 7 Wonderful Children, 17 Grandchildren and 4 Great-grandchildren Charlene, David, Sara, Joyce, Terrie, Kristina and Shanon; [ed.] Webberville High School, various classes of interest at Lansing CC, Logel's School of Cosmetology; [occ.] Homemaker; [memb.] Grace Lutheran Church AARP; [oth. writ.] Several letters of opinion to the editor of local newspaper; [pers.] I have had a love of poetry since I was a young girl and have enjoyed collecting the works of Edgar A. Guest. I also greatly admire the poems of Helen Stiner Rice.; [a.] Lansing, MI

HUGHES, DEMETRESS
[b.] May 13, 1969, Washington, DC; [p.] John Belk and Jarris Belk; [m.] Michael Hughes, March 16, 1995; [ch.] Ariel Michaela Hughes; [ed.] Central High School Bowie State University; [occ.] Systems Analyst; [memb.] Bowie State Women's Basketball Team; [hon.] Outstanding Freshman Rookie of the Year and two-time AL-CIAA Team; [oth. writ.] "No Fellowship with Darkness" "Demetress", "A Lesson in Maturity" and a few others; [pers.] Always be true to yourself because you are the only one who will have to face the decisions you make; [a.] Fort Washington, MD

HULME, NAOMI
[pen.] Ni Hulme; [b.] July 10, 1934, Wilson, NY; [p.] Leo and Elizabeth Colton; [m.] Thomas Hulme (Deceased), June 9, 1955; [ch.] Thomas, Karin, Margaret Joseph Johns; [ed.] Hambury, NY High School Graduate 1954 - June 22, I grew up in orphanage (Randolp Children's Home) went to foster home and went to Hamburg High School; [occ.] Candy maker; [pers.] I ask God everyday to help me live each day to the fullest. Enjoy the beauty of the sunrise to the evening sunset. Do everything possible to be "Kind", "Helpful" and "Love" all people and animals. My 14 sister and brothers are fur be sharing my life with others.; [a.] Buffalo, NY

HUMPHREY, OWEN EVERETT
[b.] October 25, 1920, Wautoma, WI; [p.] Marion and Flora (Helms) Humphrey; [m.] Billye (Cox) Humphrey (Deceased), April 6, 1946; [ch.] Reba (Humphrey) Rick, Ivye Humphrey; [ed.] B.S., Univ. of Wis./Whitewater, M.S., Univ. of Arkansas/Fayetevile Ed. Sp., Univ. of Illinois/Champaign; [occ.] Retired school teacher and school administrator; [memb.] Association for Supervision and Curriculum Development (Life Hon.), National Education Association (Life), Kappa Delta Pi Honorary Society, Phi Delta Kappa, Collinsville Area Theatrical Society; [hon.] Biog. sketches: Dictionary of International Biography, Who's Who in the Midwest, Who's Who in American Education, Two Thousand Men of Achievement, Creative and Successful Personalities of the World (Creativity Recognation Award, 1972), Granite City Area Council PTA Award, 1979), I-Search Certificate of Recognition for writing Five-County Curriculum for Prevention of Child Abduction (1987), Phi Delta Kappa Service Key Award (1983), George H. Reavis Associate Award (1991); [oth. writ.] Author, The greening of Gateway East, A History of PDK Chapter 1097, contributor, IASCD Newsletter and Illinois School Research publications (1969, 1970, 1971, 1973); [pers.] Life is too short to spend it in hate, anger and prejudice, when love and compassion are so accessible.; [a.] Granite City, IL

HUNT, ALLEN T.
[b.] July 27, 1944, South Haven, MI; [ch.] Jill and Bridget; [ed.] LC Mohr H.S. Atten. LMC Writing Courses and Seminars and classes; [memb.] Fairmount Historical Museum, NRA, Whizzer Motor Bike, International Soc. Poets; [oth. writ.] Life long passion and pursuit - writing for many occasions pub: "Reflections", Nat. Lib. of Poetry Anthology, "Sugar Plum" "Best Poems 95", "March 1958" Iliad Press; [pers.] I've always had a deep passion for rain. I hope "A Walk In The Rain" expresses that feeling.; [a.] South Haven, MI

HUNT, DEBRA W.
[b.] May 17, Oakland, CA; [m.] Divorced; [ch.] 2 sons; [ed.] Berkeley High School, College of Alameda - Dual Degree in Fashion Arts; [occ.] Admin Asst/Tailor; [oth. writ.] Currently writing a novel and always writing poems; [pers.] Almost and half is not good enough!; [a.] Berkeley, CA

HUNT, SAMUEL J.
[b.] October 4, 1972, Anderson, IN; [occ.] Restaurant Mgr.; [pers.] If, from the beginning of the world till now, my life, compared to the amount of time that has evolved from the beginning of Earth, is but a blink of an eye, then what time have eye but to know the Lord?; [a.] Indianapolis, IN

HUNTER, BARRY C.
[pen.] PP; [b.] December 13, 1951, Philadelphia; [p.] James and Rena Hunter; [m.] Liza R. Knight, May 1972; [ch.] David Demon Hunter, Lisa Nicole Hunter; [ed.] Jones Jr. High School Phila. Thomas A. Edison High State University Balt. MD; [occ.] Retired United States Air Force; [memb.] Disabled American Veterans, Kappa Alpha Kappa (Scroller) Morgan State University 1971, National Rifle Association; [hon.] Jr. High School High School Honors Awards, United States Patents For Invention, American Inventor Incorp. 82 Broad St. Westfield, Mass., USAF National Defense Medal Outstanding Unit Citation Marks Men Ship M-16; [oth. writ.] Poet Corner Phila Tribune 1971-1989 Peoples Paper Poetry Phila Daily News 1981, 1995 Vantage Press Publications 1971 New York City; [pers.] From the spirit of the heart of God, no greater gift to give than his love. In which he's given to a chosen few to share and give to mankind and womanhood from the heart on earth to heaven to Kingdom come forever more; [a.] Philadelphia, PA

HUNTER, ISABELLE
[pen.] Isabelle; [b.] February 16, 1927, Penna; [p.] Lucy and Alex Jackson; [ed.] High School Fishers Jr. College Boston State; [occ.] Retired; [memb.] Boston Public Library Museum of Science Mystic Valley Rail Road; [hon.] Life study fellowship Bartenders Award The geography of the White; [oth. writ.] I dream the learning dream; [pers.] I live from day to day; [a.] Boston, MA

HUNTER, LINDA K.
[pen.] Linda K. Hunter; [b.] November 7, 1961, Lawton, OK; [p.] Eddie and Mary McKesson, Jr.; [m.] Jay Stephen Hunter, February 17, 1990; [ch.] Kyle 13, Kyndall 11, Kallie 4; [ed.] High School Diploma, 2 yrs vocational school; [occ.] Drapery Seamstress, and installer. Sales in Interiors Design; [memb.] Faith Bible Church; [hon.] Being a mother of three wonderful children has been my biggest honor. Having Jay for the greatest husband is my biggest award.; [oth. writ.] I have written many other poems for personal or family experiences. It's a great way to express feelings.; [pers.] Always let the Lord guide your life and you will never be on the wrong path.; [a.] Lawton, OK

HURDLE, TANISHA J.
[pen.] Nisha; [b.] January 5, 1973, New York, NY; [p.] Hazel Duncan and James D; [m.] Glen Stewart; [ed.] Raysdale H.S. in North Carolina; [occ.] Assistant Tech. in Nynex; [memb.] North Bronx Mennonite Church Visions Committee; [hon.] In 12th Grade I won an award for art; [oth. writ.] Me, Lost Love, My Fate, Conceit many others; [pers.] In my poetry, I try to relate to things in a colorful and spiritual way that draws the reader in enough to feel, smell, and see.; [a.] Bronx, NY

HURLEY, ROBERT
[pen.] Rob Ediciuc; [b.] March 27, 1972; [occ.] Musician, Poet Struggling Artist; [oth. writ.] Four notebooks of unpublished poetry working on a fifth; [pers.] I hope to one day make a comfortable living with my talent and I hope when I die I can do so being content feeling I had talent that was both personal and universal, appreciated by all.; [a.] Boston, MA

HUSTON, LELIA S.
[pen.] Lilia S. Huston; [b.] December 8, 1919, Martin Creek, PA; [p.] Pierina Joseph Scar Pantonio; [m.] Joseph William Huston (Deceased), July 6, 1941; [ch.] Leilani, Barabara Cynthia, Joseph Boyd Huston; [ed.] Centerfield Grammar School (8 grades) located in lower Mt. Bethel Twsp. (actual-7 years) I was advanced 1 yr.; [occ.] Enjoying poetry writing and reading; [memb.] Recently International Society of Poets; [hon.] Never entered my writings before - only National Library of Poetry Honor's well enough! To learn (if only in an amateur way) that it is poetry!; [oth. writ.] Had a prolific season - during 1991-1995 wrote in entire times, of my interest in posey - over sixty poems. Also I have fashioned - 80 lines in a ballad - My favorite: Titled "Farewell to Princeton"; [pers.] I have always had a fascination for poetry - in grammar school it was a very large part of our schooling - My heart is overjoyed in my golden years - to learn first hand - that poetry in America - is alive! And well!; [a.] Bethlehem Penna, PA

HYATT, CHARLIE
[b.] June 19, 1964, Brooklyn; [p.] David and Eunice Hyatt; [m.] Christine Hyatt, June 20, 1995; [ed.] High School; [occ.] Investigator for Dept. of Corrections; [memb.] Masonic Order Scottish Rite; [oth. writ.] Sentimental poems of love to my wife; [pers.] Enjoying the flow of writing with a free hand and thought.

HYDE, LESLIE EVERTON
[pen.] Wiro; [b.] August 18, 1954, Jamaica; [p.] Glaslyn Hyde, Virginia Morrison; [m.] Margret Hyde, April 10, 1990; [ch.] Ewan Hyde, Rohan Hyde, Leron Hyde and Cyritah Hyde; [ed.] Grade nineth Elementary or Primary Jamaica West Indies. Also two subject in the Jamaica School Certificate; [occ.] Writing and acting; [memb.] Duane Bourough Library Cambria Hgts. Branch on Linden Buldvard; [oth. writ.] Unpublished five novels. Three movies scripts and about fifty songs, two plays and three hundred and fifty others poems including spiritual and cultural; [pers.] I must thank God and give him the Glory for what he has done for me because He is the one that gave me this gift of writing I must also thank my cousin Winniefred; [a.] Cambria Heights, NY

ILSLEY, VELMA
[pen.] Vela Ilsley; [b.] August 6, 1918, Edmonton, Alberta, Canada; [p.] Rowland Sutherland Ilsley, Lily Thomas Ilsley; [m.] James W. Ledwith, MD, May 1, 1962; [ed.] Douglas College, New Brunswick, N.J. 1936-38, Moore Institute of Art, Philadelphia, PA 1938-40, Art Students League, NYC and Woodstock, New School; [occ.] Author, Illustrator of Children's Books, Painters, Sculptor; [memb.] Authors Guild, Charter Member of the National Museum of the American Indian; [hon.] Certificate of Special Merit 1958 for book jacket: New Buy in Town (Farra Strans), Christopher Medal 1980 for Illustrations for Son for A Day (atheneum); [oth. writ.] Children picture books: The Pinkhat, A Busy Day For Chris, The Long Stocking (Lippincott), M is for Moving (Henry Z. Wakk), Baby Record Book 'Once Upon A Time' (C. R. Gibson); [pers.] The Christopher award says it all: "Better to light one candle than curse the darkness"; [a.] Huntington, NY

IMIG, ALICE M.
[pen.] Alice Marie Imig; [b.] December 31, 1914, Muskegon, MI; [p.] Hans and Karen (Hansen) Nielsen; [m.] Holger Thuesen (He died in Muskegon, MI - 1982), 1935, Donald J. Imig, January 5, 1990; [ch.] Janet M. Thuesen-Kroeger, Richard J. Thuesen (adopted), 2 step sons: David G. Imig and Dale R. Imig; [ed.] Muskegon High School grad. and Muskegon Community College; [occ.] (Retired) former co-owner of a Danish Bakery with Danish baker-husband, secretary, Danish and Spanish tutor, English and 2nd Language tutor, volunteer literary tutor; [memb.] Church organizations and Danish Sisterhood Lodge of America - local and state past pres in MI; [hon.] Central Lutheran Church (Muskegon, MI), certificate for volunteering aid to Vietnamese church - sponsored family and for outstanding Christian service. Also - an award from Mich., Bd of Education for Literacy Tutoring in Muskegon. (Later, a certificate for same in Joliet, IL); [oth. writ.] Poems and articles in Muskegon, MI, Chronicle and National Danish Newspapers and Publications; [pers.] As a 3rd Generation American Dane who speaks, reads and writes Danish (all 4 grandparents immigrated from Denmark, also my 1st husband - I am very proud of my Danish heritage.; [a.] Joliet, IL

IMPINK, SUSAN
[pen.] Sue I; [b.] October 28, 1969, Reading, PA; [p.] Thomas and Virginia Impink; [ed.] Holy Name High, Allentown College of St. Francis de Sales; [occ.] Disabled; [oth. writ.] Several poems published in a local hospital literary magazine; [pers.] I am a survivor of childhood traumas. I am able to use writing, in either poetry or short story form as a way to express my thoughts and feelings.; [a.] Baltimore, MD

INGOGLIA, ANDREW
[b.] August 6, 1967, Long Island; [m.] Clare E. Connelly, June 17, 1995; [ed.] Dowling College - BA Visual Art, Suffolk Community College: Associate of Arts; [occ.] Cartoonist; [hon.] Deans List, Phi Alpha Sigma, Human Potential FRA - Sorority Academic Fitness Award; [pers.] To conform to societies standards is to give up every human beings right to be an individual; [a.] Orlando, FL

INGRAM, JAIME L.
[b.] August 8, 1977, Akron, OH; [p.] Kim Baker, Jim Ingram; [ed.] Kenmore High School graduate June 1995; [occ.] Assistant at Associated Screen Print; [memb.] Preferred reader with Waldens Book Store; [hon.] Merit Roll through High School; [oth. writ.] Several poems published in High School poem collection, "Cardinal Creations" plus a collection of my own poems, unpublished; [a.] Akron, OH

IPPOLITO, CAREN
[b.] October 28, 1947, Columbus, GA; [m.] The late Dr. Steve C. Ippolito, June 2, 1973; [ch.] Stephen, Anna, Tess, Lara; [ed.] B.S. Physical Therapy - Univ. of Maryland - 1971; [occ.] Commercial Real Estate Management; [memb.] American Physical Therapy Association, Florida Physical Therapy Association, S.D.A. Church, Chairman Brandon Free Health, Screening Clinic 8 yrs.; [hon.] Univ. of S. Florida Honors program, American Cancer Society Volunteer award; [oth. writ.] Numerous poems published in local newsletters. Songs, and children's songs used in children's programming.; [pers.] The parables I see in nature, reassure me, when my own life seems inexplicable. The undercurrents of Creation carry, for me, a message of hope, and renewal.; [a.] Valrico, FL

IRIZARRY, LORNA
[b.] March 13, 1959, Puerto Rico; [p.] Valentina Caraballoso, Agustin Caraballoso; [ed.] Joan of Arc High School; [occ.] Student; [oth. writ.] Poetry published by the literacy class blooming date Regional Library, Spring 1992; [pers.] Even though I have a learning difficulty, I like to write down my thoughts, and things. That happen to me. I'm hoping that it can help people like me.; [a.] New York City, NY

IRVIN, MARY
[b.] August 16, 1917, Bellingham, WA; [p.] Dick and Margaret Kink; [m.] T. Patrick Irvin, June 10, 1940; [ch.] Timothy Patrick Irvin, Thomas Paul Irvin; [ed.] Fairhaven High Western Washington University; [occ.] Retired Teacher; [memb.] Retired Teachers Local - State and National, Past member Delta Kappa Gamma State and Local President of Association Childhood Education; [hon.] National Board Member - EKNE of NEA, Listed in Who's Who of American Women; [oth. writ.] Co-author "Noisy Waters", a story of Whatcom Creek for Children; [pers.] I write poetry mostly to express my feelings for people whose friendship I cherish.; [a.] Bellingham, WA

ISAAC, GEORGE
[b.] Kerala, IN; [p.] E. P. Isaac, Kunjamma Isaac; [m.] Anna Isaac; [ch.] Kochu, Priya; [a.] Flushing, NY

ISETTA, KEVIN DOMINIC
[pen.] Kevin Isetta; [b.] July 26, 1979, Fresno, CA; [p.] Andrew and Bambi; [ed.] Sophomore - Saint Vincent High School; [occ.] Student; [hon.] A. President's Award for Educational Excellence, B. Academic Achievement for Spanish I, C. Academic First Honors - Freshman Year; [oth. writ.] Numerous poems and short stories that reflect my life; [pers.] I love writing because it reflects my life as I work toward my goal of achieving academic excellence.; [a.] Petaluma, CA

IWAMURA, LANDON
[b.] August 21, 1978, Honolulu, HI; [p.] Steven and Harriet Iwamura; [ed.] Moanalua High School; [hon.] So far all the poems I've did in class each receive a A!, also many people say I should be a poet or a songwriter; [oth. writ.] Couple were posted on my teacher's (Who Taught English) wall; [pers.] So far I've touched many of my classmates and friend who read my poems, but most of all, practically all my teachers enjoy reading my poems!; [a.] Honolulu, HI

JACHIMIAK, EDWARD J.
[pen.] Eddie Jachimiak; [b.] March 10, 1975, Reno, NV; [p.] Paul Jachimiak, Judith Kynast; [ed.] Washoe County Schools; [occ.] Working for part-time temporary services - student, trucker Meadows Community College; [oth. writ.] Several poems, none as yet published; [pers.] I write my poetry to express my true feelings. It gives me great pleasure when someone reads my poetry and finds it exciting and entertaining; [a.] Sun Valley, NV

JACKSON, CONNIE SUE
[pen.] Connie Polk Jackson; [b.] September 7, 1948, Orange, TX; [p.] Roy Polk (Deceased), Jaucelle Carlton; [m.] Michael David Jackson, May 27, 1966; [ch.] Jeffrey Michael, Patricia Dianne and Christy Lynn. Four Grandchildren; [ed.] Bridge City High School, Bridge City, Texas (class of '66); [occ.] Insurance Agent for the State of Texas, Office Manager; [memb.] Active member of the 9th and Elm Street Church of Christ where I teach Sunday School for the 3rd and 4th grade and very active in a singing group. Also member of the Beaumont, TX. Association of Life Underwriters; [oth. writ.] Different types of poetry and one article for the local paper. I also write every morning in what I call my daily prayer journal, which I feel keeps me very close to God and keeps Him in the center of my life.; [pers.] I feel that whatever I am, I owe to the Lord and whatever talent that I may have, comes from Him. I try in most of my writings to focus on what moves me and I always write what feelings I have in my heart. I feel that I have been given a talent of expression.; [a.] Orange, TX

JACKSON, DELORIS LIGHTFOOT
[b.] Charlottesville, VA; [m.] Edward F. Jackson; [ch.] Michael and Rise; [ed.] B.S. with High Honors Hampton University, VA, Taught H.S. Science in Texas and VA; [memb.] National Delta Sigma Theta Sorority, Alpha Kappa MU Honor Society, Beta Kappa Chi Science Honor Society; [hon.] Featured in N.J. Record; [pers.] This poem dedicated to my mother Emily Lightfoot who showed her love in the nurturing of family: husband, Joseph, daughters: Hattie, Helen, Evelyn, Dorothy, Josephine, Alma, Deloris. I enjoy being creative in writing and painting.; [a.] Passaic, NJ

JACKSON, JENNIFER R.
[b.] September 28, 1973; [p.] Mr. and Mrs. Jerry R. Jackson; [ed.] University of Michigan Ann Arbor; [occ.] Student; [pers.] I hope that my poetry, God's gift to me, will leave a profound impact on those who open their minds to what their souls are saying.; [a.] Chicago, IL

JACKSON, LISA
[b.] November 2, 1963, Chicago, IL; [p.] Fanny Martin; [ch.] Keith, LaKrystal and Pierre Jackson; [ed.] High School, graduate; [occ.] Homemaker, Caregiver; [pers.] I like to give thanks to Jesus Christ, for my salvation and talent. Also I'd like to thank my family, Keith, La'Krystal and Pierre my grandmom, Fanny Winston, Mona, Fanny Martin, brothers and sisters, friends for their support; [a.] Saint Paul, MN

JACOBY, NANCY
[b.] June 23, 1951, Mt. Holly, NJ; [ed.] Rider College, BS Finance; [occ.] Investment Banker; [memb.] Currently employed as senior Sales Consultant of investment securities as Commerce Bank, Cherry Hill, NJ; [hon.] Magna Cum Laude; [pers.] Poetry is the only art that must come from the heart.; [a.] Pine Hill, NJ

JAEL, MARIA SUSAN L.
[pen.] Susan, San; [b.] December 21, 1957, Lucena City, Philippines; [p.] Candido Jael, Corazon Lagrosas; [ed.] B.S. Foods and Nutrition; [occ.] Cake Decorator, Eli's Chicago Finest Cheescake; [memb.] Belmont Assembly of God; [hon.] Most Promising Writer 1970-71; [oth. writ.] Prose and Poetry in English and in my native language published in our school newspaper (The Coconut); [pers.] With GOD, all things are possible. So, I give thanks to God, that my poem inspired by His goodness to me in all aspects of my life, has been included in your forthcoming anthology, a delicate balance. Thank you! Praise God!; [a.] Elmwood Park, IL

JANSEN, KAREN
[b.] March 15, 1967, Rockville Centre, NY; [p.] Helga Jansen; [m.] James Bellon, January 14, 1996; [ed.] Brentwood Sonderling H.S., New York Institute of Technology; [occ.] Product Manager, Mktg., Chemical Bank, NY; [hon.] Cum Laude, Dean's List; [oth. writ.] Several poems, short stories, documentary script - "The Interactive Highway"; [pers.] I try to make my writings enjoyable for everybody, and to improve my technique with each piece.; [a.] Brentwood, NY

JASON, JENNIFER D.
[b.] May 27, 1970, Lansing, MI; [p.] Jerry and Betty Jason; [ed.] B.A. Elementary Ed. from Michigan State University; [occ.] 2nd grade, Teacher, South Elementary, Watervliet, MI; [pers.] Children should never be afraid of who they are.; [a.] Saint Joseph, MI

JASPER, KARI MARIE
[b.] November 25, 1930, California; [p.] Daniel and Lisette Jasper; [ed.] Cox High School Sophomore. I intend to go to college; [hon.] This is my very first poem, and my first published work; [oth. writ.] None, this is my first piece of published work; [pers.] Imagination is more important than knowledge-Albert Einstein; [a.] Virginia Beach, VA

JEDLICKA, JAMIE ANN
[b.] May 16, 1976, Phoenix, AZ; [p.] Glen and Patricia Jedlicka; [ed.] Cathedral High School, Lincoln College; [occ.] Student at Lincoln College in Lincoln, IL; [memb.] First Covenant Church, Sponsor of Endangered sea turtles, Year book, Student Senate and Hall Government; [pers.] My writing comes from the inner depth of my soul, where I have been touched by pain, anger, happiness and glory. I am inspired daily by the people who have chosen to include me in their lives.; [a.] Omaha, NE

JEHS, SHAWN MICHAEL
[b.] August 4, 1983, Hayward, CA; [p.] Robert and Terry Jehs Jr.; [ed.] Ardenwood Elem. Walter Junior High; [occ.] Student; [hon.] Basketball trophy/fitness awards checkers award; [oth. writ.] First poem published have also written stories and other poems; [pers.] I am 11 years old and enjoy writing for school and in my spare time. I enjoy hurting, fishing trap shooting, and other outdoor activities. I enjoy sports especially basketball.; [a.] Fremont, CA

JEMISON, MILDRED
[pen.] Mildred Clauff Jemison; [b.] February 27, 1904, Osceolag, NE; [p.] Elizabeth Moragan and Charles Edward Clauff; [m.] Earl Jemison, 1924 and 1979; [ch.] Eugene and Darrell Adamson; [ed.] A degree to touch K-12 with extra classes along that line. A Wesleyan, Central College, and Kearney State Nebr.; [occ.] I manage my farm land. Live alone on the farm.; [memb.] Church. I go very little now. "C.T.V." and "World Wild Life."; [hon.] Nothing of importance; [oth. writ.] Nothing published; [pers.] On our farm is a strip of land where flood water runs, my husband called waste land. I call my treasure grove. I plant fruit bearing bushes, and trees, wild, native heb. flowers, and grasses, listen to warblers, see wild life.; [a.] Aurora, NE

JENKINS, EAN MICHELLE
[b.] June 30, 1984; [p.] Sue A. and Theodore J. Jenkins; [ed.] Westlake Elementary; [memb.] Singing group called "Wild flowers", Bellevue Children's Theater, Starr Dance, Westlake Playhouse; [hon.] The Presidents outstanding educational improvement award; [pers.] I know I'm only 11 years old but, I can stun many people with my singing and poetry.

JENSEN, SANDRA MARIE
[b.] November 11, 1963, Medford, MA; [p.] Charles W. Crilley, Jane R. Mitchell-Crilley; [m.] Steven Paul Jensen, February 14, 1987; [ch.] Ashley Jordan, Amanda Corinne, Mitchell Paul, Dylan Paul; [ed.] Our Lady of Nazareth Academy - Wakefield, MA; [occ.] Accounts Poyalde Assistant - Tasc, Inc. Reading, MA; [oth. writ.] Many poems based on the many aspects of childhood; [pers.] My inspiration in writing is greatly influenced by the wonder and innocence of childhood, my own as well as my children's, blessed are those who view the world through the eyes of a child.; [a.] Reading, MA

JERGENSON, BETH KRISTIN
[b.] September 10, 1978, Alamogordo, NM; [p.] Dennis and Kathleen Jergenson; [ed.] Junior at Centennial High School in Peoria, AZ; [occ.] Student and Intern at local newspaper; [hon.] Cub Reporter of the year for Arizona in 1991 for Essential News; [oth. writ.] Write a weekly column, "Adolescent Angst," for local paper; [pers.] Writing is the expression of one's inner self, it becomes worthwhile the moment my words touch the life of another person.; [a.] Peoria, AZ

JOHN, ALUN HARRIS
[b.] June 24, 1978, New York; [p.] Keith and Rita Milner; [ed.] High School; [occ.] Student; [oth. writ.] A City-Like Mind Published in the National Poetry Society's Anthology; [pers.] You know when you've written a good poem when someone else can read it and understand exactly what you're trying to say.; [a.] McHenry, IL

JOHNSON, ALICE ROSA
[pen.] Alice Rosa Johnson; [b.] April 19, 1979, Lakeland, FL; [p.] Dick and Karen Johnson; [ed.] Lakeland High School; [occ.] High School Student Community Volunteer and Sunday School teacher; [memb.] French Club-treasurer, Exploration V Children's Museum - Coordinator, St. Davids Episcopal Church, Keyettes, St. Council, Youth Action Committee Central Florida, National Honor Society, Quality Improvement Council; [hon.] Several academic awards: French, English, "Outstanding Youth" of Lakeland for Volunterism; [oth. writ.] Poetry for school contests and literary magazine; [pers.] I always try my hardest at everything I do became I believe with hope and love we can accomplish anything I love all that is beautiful.; [a.] Lakeland, FL

JOHNSON, ARLENE B.
[b.] May 23, Utah; [p.] Irene H. and Preston M. Budge; [m.] Harold S. Johnson (Deceased), July 31, 1970; [ch.] Vicki Bramel, Dan Ezell, Linda Ryan and Laura Snow; [ed.] L.D.S. (Secretarial Degree) Business College Graduate with honors Paralegal Certificate, Cal State Hayward; [occ.] Deputy City Clerk, Paralegal; [hon.] Alpha Iota Sorority Scholarship Award; [pers.] My husband, Hal (the subject of my poem), suffered his first stroke ten days after our marriage in 1970. He overcame the effects of that stroke and continued in his "no holds barred" lifestyle, living each day to the maximum as a very typical "Type-A" personality until February 1976, when he suffered the first of three massive strokes (aneurysms at the base of his neck). He was paralyzed from the neck down and spent the rest of his life in a wheelchair. He was a remarkable man, however, and wrote a book — typing it with a headwand which fit around his head. It was never published because it was determined to be too positive. He never dealt with the negative, until he was transferred to a terrible "subacute" hospital to recuperate from a staph infection in his lungs, carelessly transferred to him at a convalescent hospital where he had "lived" for 17 years. Until then, he came home every weekend and worked on his lap top computer with special programs we bought so that he could continue with his "new love" as a ham radio operator. His death, predicted in 1970, culminated on Easter Sunday 1993. I wrote a letter to Hillary Clinton in early 1993, which was published as part of the Congressional Record on Health Insurance concerning the need to consider the non-existence "lived" by so many people forced to sit in wheelchairs in convalescent hospitals including young men who fought in the Gulf War, and the need to help them keep their sanity by giving them some work to do.; [a.] Fremont, CA

JOHNSON, REV. BERTHA D.
[pen.] Pastor Johnson; [b.] March 9, 1924, New Castle, DE; [p.] The Rt Rev. and Mrs. P. Robert Brown; [m.] Deceased; [ch.] Raymond, Gloria, Angela, Rachel, Timothy, Davidia, Blanche, Mike, Mack, and Ivy Jr.; [ed.] Douglass High and Community College of Baltimore; [occ.] Retired United Methodist Minister; [memb.] NAACP, AARP; [hon.] Mother of the Year award from Luskins Store (1984), (Balto. MD) Citizen Citation from the honorable Mayor Kurt L. Schmoke Baltimore, MD, May 17, 1992 Honorary Doctorate Degree, Dean's List; [oth. writ.] Songs for Recording (Sunrise) Published Poems for Church Paper and School Paper; [pers.] If is my greatest desire to reflect God's love to all people especially to children.; [a.] San Leandro, CA

JOHNSON, BETTY J. GARNER
[pen.] Abby Brown; [b.] April 18, 1945, WS, NC; [p.] Cordella Garner, Luther Jackson; [m.] George E. Johnson (Deceased), March 9, 1982; [ch.] Sean I. Garner, Artessa M. Garner; [ed.] Carver High School, Nurse Aide Training, Unity Secretary Training, Forsyth Tech-College; [occ.] Housekeeper, At Watson Salem State University; [oth. writ.] Looking in the mirror, Married man, The Shadow, The Bottom of the Barrell, Cry Silently, A Beautiful Ache, Pain, Little Mind, I'm not Worthy of Your Love, The Greatest Artist, etc.; [pers.] Even the lowest of people can come forth with genius work, if there is a will.; [a.] Winston Salem, NC

JOHNSON, BRANDON D.
[b.] February 16, 1985, Clearwater, FL; [p.] Laurie and Dale Johnson; [ed.] 5th Grade Virginia Run Elementary School, Centreville, VA; [memb.] Centreville Methodist Church League Baseball Team; [hon.] Honor Roll

JOHNSON, DON ALVA
[ch.] Donna Alvah, Donna Lynn, Joyce, Rosemary, Lita, Dennis, Donald II, Lowell; [ed.] Master of Science (M Sc.); [occ.] Medical Bio-analyst Cal. License Drg 331; [hon.] Former Clinical Laboratory Chief Stanford Univ. Hosp. and School of Medicine; [oth. writ.] Scientific articles (Med. journals) (Hermatology, Bacteriology, Parasitology, Serology etc.); [pers.] Write it like it is!; [a.] Los Angeles, CA

JOHNSON, JOSEPH MARK
[pen.] Reverend; [b.] 10/11/62, Brooklyn, NY; [p.] Joseph & Carol Johnson; [m.] Carleen Johnson, 7/25/93; [ch.] Elijah Joseph Johnson; [ed.] Currently enrolled at York College; [occ.] Emergency Room Registration St. Vincent's Hospital; [hon.] Deacon at the church of Zoe Ministries; [pers.] May God bless those less fortunate than myself because their plight is much harder than mine.

JOHNSON, LILLIAN L.
[b.] November 15, 1947, Maspeth, NY; [p.] Walter Klee and Delia Duffy; [m.] William P. Johnson, November 4, 1984; [ch.] John Lessler, Katie Mae Johnson; [ed.] Suffolk Community College, Selden, NY; [occ.] Recertification Coordinator, Kings Park, NY; [hon.] Dean's Lists, Honor Society, Pi Alpha Sigma; [oth. writ.] Several poems from the 1960's that were never published; [pers.] Being a true romantic, I wrote from my heart to express my innermost feelings. Poetry is a soothing therapy is a pleasurable hobby for me.; [a.] Miller Place, NY

JOHNSON, MACKSINE
[b.] December 14, 1968, Kingston; [p.] Robert and Macksine McDaniels, also Lawrence Forgach; [ch.] Scott R. Johnson Jr.; [ed.] Lake Lehman High School; [pers.] My creative writing comes from within. I write about experiences, dreams and my inspirations. My heart feels, my head produces images and my hand creates the combination of the two.; [a.] Shickshinny, PA

JOHNSON, PAULINE E.
[b.] January 9, 1929, Rivers, MA; [p.] Donald, Josephine Trecartin; [m.] Clyde S. Johnson (Deceased), June 30, 1949; [ch.] Michael, Gary Irene, Patricia Ann; [ed.] Lynn Classical, attended Murray State, Paducah Jr College University of KY Conducts of Murray LPP School of Nursing; [occ.] L.P.N. Charter Ridge Behavioral Systems; [memb.] Republican Party (NI), (Past) Murray Women's Club, Member - The Espit de Camps Club, (Lourdes Hosp. Paduch, KY, Catholic Church at VA, Hoop Lex, KY; [hon.] President Altar Society, One of three authors for a Evalbody, choir - Music Dept. Murray Women's Club; [oth. writ.] Newspaper Articles; [pers.] I believe God gives us our talents and respects us to use them. I feel - I do this daily - in the nursing and volunteer work - I do on a weekly basis. God can't be out done in generosity.; [a.] Lexington, KY

JOHNSON, PHYLLIS M.
[b.] May 7, 1965, Delta, CO; [p.] Frank and Betty Bishop; [m.] Todd J. Johnson, April 27, 1984; [ch.] Justin, Cody, Clayton; [ed.] 1983 Graduate Of Olathe High School, Olathe, CO; [occ.] Home maker, Teacher Aid, Ellicott Baptist School; [memb.] Ellicott Baptist Church; [hon.] 1983 Prof. Wilson Award for Outstanding Senior Girl; [oth. writ.] I have written many poems about special people and things that happen in our every day life.; [pers.] If I were to try to set down and try to write poetry on my own, it wouldn't happen! The Lord lays things on my heart, in a form of poetry, that I need to change about myself or things to help and encourage others.; [a.] Ellicott, CO

JOHNSON, RAE SHONDA
[pen.] Cujo; [b.] July 29, 1981, Chicago, IL; [p.] Dorothy Lias, Rayford Johnson; [sib.] Divaneshia Antearia Johnson; [ed.] I have completed the eight grade, and will start the ninth grade in August; [memb.] Cheerleading squad, 4-H Club; [hon.] Awards in: Math, Science, Science Fair, English, Reading, Social Studies, Arts - Industrial Tech. Trophies - Miss Cheerleader 94-95, Principal Scholar; [oth. writ.] Poem of Love and Poem to science through the years; [pers.] When I write I try to put myself into the poems.; [a.] Fayette, MS

JOHNSON, STEPHEN
[b.] November 2, 1977, Durham, NC; [p.] Mike and June Johnson; [ed.] Senior at Orange High School in Hillsborough, NC; [memb.] Beta Club, Cross Country and Track Teams at Orange High; [pers.] "To be great is to be misunderstood."-Thoreau That says it all.; [a.] Hillsborough, NC

JOHNSTON, EARL WILSON
[b.] July 10, 1915, Carrollton, TX; [p.] James Edward and Sarah Maud Perry Johnston; [m.] Mauriece Vance Johnston, August 24, 1938; [ch.] James Robert Johnston; [ed.] A.B. Baylor University, B.D. Southern Baptist Theology Seminary, M. Div. Southern Baptist Theol Seminary, Doctor of Ministry San Francisco Theological Seminary; [occ.] Retired Minister; [memb.] Masonic Lodge (32 degrees Scottish Rite); [pers.] I aspire to apply the principles of Jesus Christ to all area of modern life.; [a.] San Antonio, TX

JOINER, ARIELL
[pen.] Air; [b.] November 18, 1986, Long Beach, NJ; [p.] Dennis and Patricia Joiner; [ed.] Currently in third grade; [occ.] Student; [hon.] Straight a student; [oth. writ.] Many stories and plays; [pers.] I love to read and write about many things.; [a.] Tinton Falls, NJ

JONES, CHRISTOPHER SCOTT
[pen.] Millard Scott; [b.] November 13, 1980, Alexandria, VA; [p.] Susan Millard, Robert Millard; [ed.] Bishop Ireton High School; [occ.] Student; [oth. writ.] Poetry Short Stories, and Children's Stories; [a.] Springfield, VA

JONES, DEAN
[pen.] Star Child; [b.] August 29, 1966, Owosso, MI; [p.] Robert Jones, Anna Marie Jones; [ed.] Corunna High, Lansing Community College, US Navy; [occ.] Student, Grocery Clerk; [memb.] "The All-seeing Eyes"; [oth. writ.] Several poems and short stories in college publication, underground newspaper; [pers.] I write what I believe to be the truth. I am always looking for a good conspiracy; [a.] Haslett, MI

JONES, KEYANA
[pen.] Nanna; [b.] April 14, 1982, Hackensack, NJ; [p.] Mr. Alban Jones Sr. Mrs. Karen Jones; [ed.] Presently attending Vernon L. Davey Junior High School; [occ.] Student of Vernon L. Davey Junior High School; [memb.] National Honor Society; [hon.] Member of the National Junior Honor Society, Received an Academic Presidential Award, 2nd runner up in East Coast Pageant; [oth. writ.] Several poems and a short story; [pers.] When I write my poetry I try to put myself in that position so my writing will be realistic. My mother is a writer who helps me accomplish; [a.] East Orange, NJ

JONES, KOURTNI E.
[b.] January 24, 1985, Washington, DC; [p.] Alphonsa and Sharon Jones; [sib.] Alphonsa A. Jones; [ed.] MacArthur Elementary School, Grade 5; [occ.] Student; [memb.] MacArthur School Orchestra; [pers.] I would like to thank my mother for entering my poem; [a.] Alexandria, VA

JONES, LISA L.
[b.] February 20, 1970, Lakewood, NJ; [p.] Emma Huff, Robert C. Brown (Deceased); [m.] Larry J. Jones, March 14, 1992; [ch.] Larry J. Jones Jr (L'Jaye); [ed.] Lakewood High, T.R. Vocational, Star Tech. Trade; [occ.] Housewife, Mom; [pers.] Your heart is made by God never second guess it. The mind play tricks, think before you repeat it.; [a.] Lakewood, NJ

JONES, LYNN M.
[pen.] Jessy Marvin; [b.] April 21, 1971, South Lake Tahoe, CA; [p.] Anne-Grethe Jones, John Jones (Deceased); [ed.] Currently going for a Bachelor's Degree in Creative Writing of University of New Mexico; [occ.] Stressed Student; [memb.] Golden Key National Honors Society (I constantly forget I am a member).; [hon.] 1989 Southeast High School Creative Writing Awards, won shortbread in Walker's Poetry contest, 1989. Tasted good.; [oth. writ.] Threw together poetry book for David Johnson's creative writing 321 course at University of New Mexico entitled My Body in Motion.; [pers.] Thank you, David.; [a.] Albuquerque, NM

JONES, MARJORIE DORMAN
[pen.] Marjorie Dorman Jones; [b.] August 2, 1933, NC; [p.] Elgie and Milford Dorman; [m.] John R. Jones, December 9, 1952; [ch.] Teresa Jones Tolliver, John Jr. and Jeffrey Jones, Granddaughter Sarah; [ed.] High School, Benson, North Carolina; [occ.] Homemaker; [memb.] St Matthews United Methodist Church; [hon.] Enjoying raising my children into well adjusted, successful adults, and caring for my 10 year old granddaughter; [oth. writ.] No other publications; [pers.] I have been a resident of the beautiful state of Md for 40 years. It is an honor to be a part of a National publication.; [a.] Bowie, MD

JONES, THOMAS A.
[pen.] Tom Jones; [b.] January 18, 1919, Brazos, TX; [p.] Thomas and Alta Jones; [m.] Dorothy, September 18, 1921; [ch.] Kathryn Marie, Thomas Mitchell; [ed.] Brazos High, G.E.D. for 2 year College; [occ.] Retired; [memb.] VFW, NRA; [hon.] Good conduct Medal (Fifth Award) Asiatic Pacific Campaign Medal (with IQ Battle Stars), World War II Victory Medal and Presidential Unit Citation; [oth. writ.] Poems for family members and friends.; [a.] Palo Pinto, TX

JORDAN, BOJANA V.
[pen.] Boji; [b.] June 19, 1930, South Africa; [m.] Barbara Ellery, May, 1985; [ed.] Doctor of Arts degree in Philosophy; [occ.] Professor African History, College of St Rose, Albany; [memb.] Was overseas diploma for liberation movement - Pro Africanist Congress, before S. Africa's freedom in 1994 President American South African People's Friendship Association; [hon.] Meritorious Award by New York African Studies Association, 1992, Governor's Award with Barbara Ellery, 1993 for distinguished work with Teachers and school children; [oth. writ.] We will be heard - a South African Exile Remembers, Quintan Press, Boston 1986, Poetry of Protest - unpublished several articles in educational magazines; [pers.] This would be a much better, world to live in if we all realized that we belonged to only one more - The Human Race - irrespective of colour or physiognomy.; [a.] Albany, NY

JORGENSEN, SUSANNAH
[pen.] Susannah; [b.] October 16, 1980, Tooele, UT; [p.] John and Susan Jorgensen; [occ.] Student; [memb.] 4-H, Derby and Denim; [hon.] Board Scholar Award, New Mexico; [oth. writ.] A few other poems; [pers.] I usually base most of my writings on my dreams and fears. Sometimes I write about fears I see in other people; [a.] Pueblo, CO

JOSEPHSON, JESSICA L.
[pen.] Jessica L. Pieplow; [b.] March 26, 1974, Kansas City; [p.] Albert Wesly and Christine Ann Pieplow; [m.] Ray L. Josephson, March 18, 1994; [ed.] Park Hill Sr. High Ground Radio Communications Technical School; [occ.] United States Air Force; [memb.] Brooks Air Force Base Honor Guard Women's History Month Planning Committee Volunteer for Texas Special Olympics; [hon.] Student Leader Honor Guard award for services rendered; [oth. writ.] Article in Brooks AFB publication numerous poems in highschool publication; [pers.] Strive for what you want in life. Don't ever let anything hold you back. Live, Learn, Love, but most important of all, feel everything inside of you to the Extreme!; [a.] Lajes Field, Portugal

JULIAN, KARL
[b.] May 28, 1979, Lexington, KY; [p.] Bruce Julian, Rachel Julian; [ed.] Presently enrolled at Vestavia Hills High School; [occ.] Student; [memb.] Teens Against A Littered State (TALS), VP; [hon.] Alabama Pennman (2nd Place, 9th Grade Division) Alabama Pennman, 1st Place; [oth. writ.] Several publications in school newspaper; [pers.] Poetry is the universal river into which each individual poet contributes, it is the unified being of endless, diverse voices in the night.; [a.] Birmingham, AL

JUNGELS, CHRISTINE MARTIN
[pen.] Christine Martin Jungles; [b.] May 30, 1952, Brooklyn, NY; [p.] John P. and Eileen Martin; [m.] Mick Jungels, March 17, 1984; [ch.] Bill Lambeth, Brian Lambeth, Dana Jungels, Britt Jungels; [ed.] Charter Oak High Saddleback College; [oth. writ.] Several poems and short stories "starring" family members "The Blabbermouth" (My niece jenee), "Christmas in the Glen" (My entire family) "Beyond a Room" (My son Brian); [pers.] Listen to the critic within yourself, not to the criticism of others.; [a.] San Clemente, CA

KAIMAKAMIAN, FERDINAND
[b.] January 16, 1916, Cilicia, Armenia; [p.] Haroutune and Haiganoush Kaimakamian; [ed.] American College of Central Turkey; [occ.] Radiation Therapy and Radiographic Technologist-Licensed; [memb.] American Legion Chaplin (New York, Post #18 Vet. WW2), Knights of Vartan Brotherhood P.C.; [hon.] John F. Kennedy Award for Libraries (1972), Knights of Vartan Outstanding Achievement 1988; [oth. writ.] First Rhythmic Translation Opera Cavalleria Rusticana into Armenian 1954, Pagan Eras of Church Music 1965, numerous articles on Middle Eastern Music and History, etc.; [pers.] From realities of life's inspiration to constructive ideals applied... [a.] Corona, NY

KAISEN, RONALD KEVIN
[b.] March 9, 1963, Huntington, NY; [p.] Ronald and Florence; [m.] Ann Marie, May 29, 1992; [ch.] Zoe Ann; [ed.] Holy Family HS, Walt Whitman HS, Farmingdale College, NYIT; [occ.] International Business Owner including business in the US, Canada, South America and The People's Republic of China; [memb.] Specialty Coffee Assoc. of the US; [hon.] Regents Diploma Graduate and Honor Student - Dean's List; [oth. writ.] Song writing, southern properties magazine (Publisher, Editor, etc.), Lyrics, and Multiple Marketing Brochures Internationally.; [pers.] Never leave to chance that you can leave to calculation.; [a.] Boca Raton, FL

KALLENBACH, FLORENCE P. BULLIS
[pen.] Victoria Rose; [b.] June 12, Lyons, NY; [p.] Harry and Edna Proseus; [m.] James D. Kallenbach, April 29, 1995; [ch.] 3 sons, 3 step daughters and 1 stepson; [ed.] College, Technical College Diploma; [occ.] LPN, Program Coordinator (on site respite care) and Personal Care; [hon.] Honorable Mention in Poetry contests. Volunteer work.; [oth. writ.] Poetry, Thru Experiences Autobiography, mostly unpublished others in church news letters one newspaper contest 3rd place; [pers.] Choose to let yourself, come to the place of blessing.; [a.] Peachtree City, GA

KALTON, DONALD
[pen.] Don Kalton; [b.] February 3, 1942, Brooklyn, NY; [p.] George and Tillie Kalton; [m.] Divorced; [ed.] Brooklyn College, Liberal Arts Degree; [occ.] Advertising Specially Sales; [memb.] Human Society, Sierra Club, The Nature Conservancy, World Wildlife Federation, National Audition Society; [hon.] Best Poet, Brooklyn Society of Poets, Honorary Member of the National Afghan Hound Society of America; [oth. writ.] "Alone", Before it Gets too Late, A Knock Upon my Door; [pers.] The poem "I sit looking upon the desert" is a cry for help, a cry to stop destroying the gift we never given, our animals. We cannot live without them!; [a.] Scottsdale, AZ

KAPLAN, MAX V.
[b.] Bialstok, Russian; [m.] Mae Klein, June 30, 1933; [ch.] Ellen, Paul; [occ.] Poet-writer; [oth. writ.] Short stories, and poems have appeared in many publications. Among them are the following: Event, the Douglas College Quarterly, Piedmont Literary Review, Yonkers Library Anthologies (1974, '76), The Villager, Suburbia section of Gannett Newspapers, Books and Company anniversary book, Rock Hill Journal in Woodstock, NY; [pers.] Goal as a writer is to explore the dimensions and problems that living provides, and that sustains some sense of purpose in life despite being a witness of despair, disease, and death.

KARAGOVALIS, JOHN
[pen.] John Kaye; [b.] June 29, 1950, Hartford, CT; [p.] Nick and Jean Karagovalis; [ed.] Hartford High School; [occ.] Furniture maker and part time singer song writer; [memb.] From 1969 to 1973, I was a member of two rock bands! "The Quiet Ones" And Liquide Lighte. Both Bands had a very big following in Connecticut, and through out the North East; [oth. writ.] Several rock songs, new age songs, novelty songs, the poem presented here! — Bird up in the sky, has words and music as well.; [pers.] I try to create a perfect balance of metaphor and imagery, accompanied by a lively rhythmic tempo.; [a.] Somerville, MA

KARDATZKE, BRENDA
[b.] February 15, 1946, Atlanta, GA; [p.] William B. and Alline Jones Bramblett; [m.] James T. Kardatzke, March 17, 1990; [ch.] Timothy M. Strickland, Deborah K. Hettiger; [ed.] Bachelor of Science Occupational Safety and Health Certificate; [occ.] Safety and Occupational Health Specialist (unemployed); [hon.] Dean's List; [oth. writ.] Safety Manual; [pers.] I care about others. If I can accomplish one thing in my life, it will be to help others.; [a.] Winter Springs, FL

KASS, MELISSA
[b.] 12-14-78, South Dakota; [p.] Brenda Kelly & Richard Kass; [ed.] North West High School (Coppell Middle & Elementary); [memb.] (Drill Team) North West Side Kicks; [pers.] My poems are the reflections of my personal feelings. I hope that when people read my poems they are influenced to take action in their feelings.; [a.] Trophy Club, TX

KATHWARI, RAFIQUE
[b.] November 11, 1948, Srinagar, Kashmir; [p.] Gulum and Maryam Kathwari; [ed.] Master of Arts, New School for Social Research, New York; [occ.] Entrepreneur, Int'l. Consultant for NGO's.; [memb.] Exhibitions (selections) 1980-International Center of Photography, NYC, 1986-The Metropolitan Museum of Art, NYC, 1991-HEIMTEXTIL, Frankfurt, Germany; [hon.] Acting and debating Society Awards during School and College in Kashmir, Captain Cricket, Hockey and Football teams; [oth. writ.] Commentaries in New York Times. Book Review's for Current History.; [pers.] Writing about my mother's paranoid schizophrenia is my true calling. Greatly influenced by Allen Ginsberg, Phillip Levine, Aghashahid Ali.

KAUFMAN, IRVING
[b.] September 16, 1917, Orange, NJ; [p.] Morris and Tillie Kaufman; [m.] Martha Buskirk Kaufman, November 30; [ch.] Stephen David Kaufman, Carol Suzanne Bittenson, Richard Paul Kaufman, James Robert Kaufman and 5 grandchildren-Jeffrey, Alice, Rose, Allen, and Paul; [ed.] 1935 grad, East Orange High School, School 1938 grad. N.Y.U., 1939 The Geo. Univers. School of Medicine 1943, Psychiatric Training, The Boston Psychoanalytical Institute, also trained as a child Psychiatrist.; [occ.] MD Psychiatrist, at age 78 semiretired from practice and teaching at Harvard Med. School, and Smith School for Soc. Work; [memb.] AM.A., AP.P.A. Int. Psychoanalytic Assoc., Boston Gerontology, The French Academy; [hon.] Black Belts in Uechy Ryu and Isshin Ryu Karate, An Honorary degree from Smith College School for Social Eork, Member of Alpha Omega Honors Society.; [oth. writ.] Many Articles in Psychiatry Washington Journals, 5 books in the Psych.; [pers.] At age 78, I am a Black Belt in Karate, play cello in a quartette, write scientific articles as well as prose, and poetry also enjoy refinishing furniture. I believe in a full and varied life despite my Parkinsons Disease which impedes my motility.; [a.] Auburndale, MA

KAYASTHA, KUMAR J.
[b.] December 27, 1979, Chicago, IL; [p.] Jasuant Kayastha, Bharati Kayastha; [educ.] Sophomore - Riverside - Brookfield High; [occ.] Student; [pers.] For one to achieve inner-peace he must have a balance of mind and soul. I strive to attain and express this balance in my poems.; [a.] North Riverside, IL

KAZIMOV, NUSHABE
[b.] February 20, 1980, Orange, NJ; [p.] Arcadia and Ferdinand Kazimov; [ed.] I am a freshman (soon to be sophomore in '95) in a local high school; [occ.] Being a good student and I stage manage and produce school plays; [oth. writ.] I have written several poems. So far, four have been published through North American and National contests.; [pers.] Life can be very tough for teenagers, and being fifteen I know that for a fact. I am fortunate though. I have, at this young age, found and strengthened my talent.; [a.] Stanhope, NJ

KEATING, NADIA N.
[b.] December 16, 1973, Jamaica; [p.] Vincent Keating, Claudette Keating; [ed.] College of New Rochelle Co-op city (campus); [occ.] Secretary Fast-Rite Refrigeration; [pers.] I always dreamed to be light as air, when I write and express my thought my dream to be light comes through.; [a.] Bronx, NY

KEELER, STEVEN T.
[b.] January 8, 1966, Queens, NY; [p.] Gustave Keeler, Christina Mardorf; [pers.] this poem is dedicated to my one and only love, Blanca I. Santiago. My bride to be, can't wait to share all of the wonderful moments life has in store for us. Mom, Dad and Grandma whom I will always cherish in my heart.; [a.] New York, NY

KEEMON, ADAM J.
[b.] July 11, 1972, Jewett City, CT; [ed.] Norwich Tech.; [pers.] Interested in reading unpublished works of other artists; [a.] Jewett City, CT

KELLER, LINN
[b.] March 30, 1955, Cleveland, OH; [p.] Harold and Patricia Keller; [ed.] Miller High, Perry County Muskingum Tech, Zanesville: Emt-Paramedic certification, Hocking Tech, nursing; [occ.] Nurse, Doctor's Hosp. and EMT, Health Pro Ambulance; [memb.] The Plains Fire Dept. and Emergency Squad, Thauncey Marshal's Office, Athens County Red Cross Disaster Services, Cmdr, 223d MP Co., Ohio Military Reserve; [hon.] 20 Years Fire Fighter/EMT, Past Paramedic Training Officer, Past Fire Chief, Past Acting Marshal, Past Firearms Instructor, Red Cross CPR and First Aid Instructor; [oth. writ.] Poems published in EMS journal, articles in police and military journals; [pers.] I've been writing since eighth grade, most of ten to express conflict, grief, or great happiness. After twenty years as a fire fighter - EMT, and seventeen of those twenty as a deputy marshal, I am compiling a book of my "war stories" and another of my families verbal history.; [a.] Athens, OH

KELSO, KATHLEEN
[b.] August 2, 1925, Lynn, MA; [p.] Francis Kain and Marguerite Kain; [m.] Richard W. Kelso (deceased), September 10, 1949; [ch.] One son, Thomas R. Kelso; [ed.] St. Petersburg High, St. Petersburg, Florida; [occ.] Retired; [memb.] Past President of Azusa Emblem Club #325; [oth. writ.] Poems not published; [pers.] To really write so all could understand the feelings that words bring to our hearts and our minds.; [a.] Rancho Cucamonga, CA

KEMP, GREGORY L.
[pen.] Amandine A. L. Dupin; [b.] April 1, 1970, Rockford, IL; [p.] Wayne and Elaine Kemp; [m.] Audra Lynn, September 29, 1996; [ch.] Madelyne Zoe, Aleksander Josef, Omega Supreme.; [ed.] PR Walleer Elementary, West High, Walter Panas, Wheaton College/The King's College.; [occ.] Behavior Counselor VCP; [memb.] Blockbuster Video, YMCA, Book of the Month Club.; [pers.] I have found that to see as Newton saw, from the shoulders of giants, one must know his strength lay in knowing how minute that actually is.; [a.] Cortlandt Manor, NY

KEMP, HAZEL VIRGINIA
[pen.] Ginger Bab; [b.] December 4, 1921, Wisconsin; [p.] G. Leslie and Millie M. Babcock; [m.] Chester Reece Kemp (deceased) August 30, 1941; [ch.] Kaye D. and Joye D.; [ed.] High School, Leader Trainer Course, Girl Scouts of America (and, if travel means anything, we have lived in every section of the USA, Japan and Europe); [occ.] Homemaker; [memb.] Order of the Easter Star, Santa Rosa Mineral and Gem Society, Calif. Mineralogical Societies, Am. Mineralogical Societies; [hon.] Worthy Matron, Order of the Easter Star, United States Air Force Wife by Sec. of USAF and President Mixon; [oth. writ.] Several poems, several articles concerning customs, political changes and life in Japan published New London, Wis. Press Republican; [pers.] I believe in old fashioned family values and that money means nothing if you do not have the love of family and friends.; [a.] Forestville, CA

KENNEPP, KELLY
[pen.] Aspen Kelsher; [b.] July 14, 1968, Chicago, IL; [p.] Doris Kennepp, Eugene Kennepp; [ed.] Wheeling High School, Harper College, McHenry County College, Columbia College (Chicago); [occ.] Broadcast Journalism Student; [memb.] Willow Creek Community Church; [oth. writ.] An essay published in school newspaper, an article written for, and published by "Controversy" magazine; [pers.] Poetry, like love, embraces the soul and guides it. There should be no room for melancholy in a world striving for beauty and love. A bright star once guided my soul until one day it just disappeared, but it still exists in my dreams.; [a.] Wonder Lake, IL

KENNEY JR., JOHN WILLIAM
[pen.] Ken Jackson; [b.] November 21, 1950, Littleton, NH; [p.] Jack and Peg Kenney; [ed.] 13.5 years Holderness School Class of '69 Middlebury College Class of '73; [occ.] Soil builder, stock farmer, logger; [memb.] Franconia Church of Christ, Trustee. American Beefalo World Registry.; [hon.] Various and Sunday athletic awards in alpine and nordic skiing, tennis, soccer and running.; [oth. writ.] Many poems unpublished short stories and two longer books in the works; [pers.] In my writing I range on two seeming extremes: love and social critique. I am bringing them together in my longer works.; [a.] Easton, NH

KERN, THOMAS J.
[b.] April 26, 1974, Everett, WA; [p.] Scott Kern, Dianne Kern; [ed.] Marysville Pilchuck High School, Business Computer Training Institute; [occ.] Student; [hon.] US Army Rifle Marksman, Master Driver's Badge, National Defence Ribbon, 8 Certificate's of Achievement Honorable Discharge (Nov. 22, 1994); [oth. Writ.] The Forever Cowboy, The Devil and Bertrain McDoogle, A Night in Pomeroy Castle, The Singing Ghoul, (all unpublished); [pers.] I saw the light at the end of the tunnel, but I didn't like what I saw. So I changed the light bulb.; [a.] Marysville, WA

KESSLER, IRENE N.
[b.] March 18, 1955, Suffern, NY; [p.] Beatrice I. Kessler; [ch.] Ashley Renee Kessler; [ed.] S.S. Seward Institute, Florida New York; [occ.] Equal Employment Opportunity Specialist; [oth. writ.] Numerous cultural pamphlets on women, African-Americans, Asian-Americans, Hispanic-Americans and Native Americans.; [pers.] Respect others for who they are not who you "think" they are. Learn about them before making your judgment.; [a.] Gloucester, VA

KETCHUM, PIERCE STITH
[ed.] Received stylebook of English as a student at the University of Illinois; [hon.] 3 poetry awards (10th, 11th, and 12th) in 1995, also nominated for International Society of Poets' Poet of the year for 1995; [oth. writ.] Include 1 poem in outstanding poets of 1994, poetry in Matrix 19, 1 poem in after the storm, 1 poem expected in best poems of 1995

KEW, ANN M.
[b.] January 11, 1944, Boston, MA; [p.] Kathryn McDermott and Arthur Hill; [m.] Harold W. Kew (deceased), December 13, 1986; [ch.] Bernadette Ferland, Robin Blanchard, Lloyd Saltzman, Scott Saltzman, Edwin Blanchard, Robert Kew, Susie Bruenckner, Cindy Baker, Dana Kew, David Kew; [ed.] Randolph High School Fisher Jr. College; [occ.] Sales-Ron Jons Surf Shop; [oth. writ.] "Two Babies" short story readers digest. Not sure if published no notice. Poem: Slender You Cord. Published in monthly National Newsletter.; [pers.] In memory of Harold W. Kew Jr., with when I spent the most special time of my life.; [a.] Cocoa Beach, FL

KHADEMZADEH, AMIR
[pen.] The Fool; [b.] April 1, 1971, Saint Cloud; [p.] Manoncher and Haydeh Khademzadeh; [ed.] University of Minnesota senior studying chemistry and communication disorder; [occ.] Psychiative Ass. at U. of M Hospital; [hon.] Pro-Midwest Scholarship winner 1990-91; [pers.] From the peaks of the center of "Being", where eyes blinded by love alone create, I say "Let there be no boundaries in our search." The Fool.; [a.] Crystal, MN

KIDD, JONATHAN
[pen.] Emanuel Brown/Rex E. Ferguson; [b.] October 6, 1974, Mansfield, OH; [p.] John and Lynda Kidd; [occ.] College Student, The University of Michigan; [memb.] Michigan Marching Band, Black Student Union, Native American Student Association; [hon.] President's List, Phi Alpha Delta; [pers.] Life is madness, utilize the insanity; [a.] Ann Arbor, MI

KIDD, THADDEUS W.
[b.] February 18, 1969, PA; [p.] Robert and Irene Kidd; [ed.] Burgettstown Area High School, Penn State University, B.S. finance Econ., Robert Morris College, MBA (not finished yet); [occ.] Business Analyst, II; [memb.] Members of: 1. Eldersville United Methodist Church, 2. National Speleological Society, 3. Fraternal Order of Bikers Everywhere; [hon.] Lambda Sigma Honors Fraternity, Sigma Iota Epsolon Honors Fraternity, President of "The Rack" House; [oth. writ.] This poem is an excerpt from my new book Ardent Heart: Rogvery, Reflections, and Life so far. Currently, I am hard at work on my next book. Call for details.; [pers.] "When life throws you a curve, lean into it." I would love to hear what you think of my work.; [a.] Pittsburg, PA

KILPATRICK, KEVIN
[b.] November 1, 1971, New London, CT; [p.] Wayne and Marcia Kilpatrick; [ed.] BA, History, Bolton High School, University of Missouri; [occ.] Soldier, U.S. Army; [hon.] 1989 Connecticut State Public Speaking Champion; [oth. writ.] Poem used in Award Winning Speech; [pers.] I want to put every reader smack, dab in the middle of everything I write. I want them to feel what I feel.; [a.] Presidio of Monterey, CA

KILTS, MATTHEW JAMES
[b.] April 19, 1980, Des Moines, IA; [p.] James and Marlene Kilts; [ed.] Will start 9th grade fall 1995 was 14 years and in 8th grade when poem was written in 1994; [occ.] Student; [pers.] Poem was written in honor of my cousin Jennifer who was raised like a sister to me, she was mentally and physically challenged and could not speak in sentences. She called me "At" and I helped care for her at times, feed, bath, diaper, play with, and care for while she was totally bedridden. She died very unexpectedly, on my brother's wedding day, Sept. 17, 1994. She gave kisses-noises made with her mouth when she was happy.

KIMMEL, SANDI
[b.] August 12, 1954, NY; [p.] Barbara Diamond, Edwin Kimmel; [ed.] Lawrence High School Rutgers University; [occ.] Songwriter and Author; [memb.] Dramatists Guild BMI; [oth. writ.] Book: Let's get personal, the complete survival guide to personal ad dating, Musical: Romanian Rhapsody and Hundreds of songs; [pers.] As I grow on my soul, journey, my writing is the vehicle through which I share my joy, my truth and my life lessons.; [a.] Tarrytown, NY

KINDSCHY, NICOLE
[pen.] Shea; [b.] November 25, 1976, Bishop, CA; [p.] Lowell and Susan Kindschy; [ed.] I have graduated from high school and am now going to Ca state San Bernardino, majoring in criminal administration; [occ.] Assistant manager at Long John Silvers; [oth. writ.] I have a lot of written poems, not published but I would like to get them published.; [pers.] I strive for my goals because my goals are all I have, one day soon I will reach these goals.; [a.] Apple Valley, CA

KING, BERNADINE
[b.] August 23, 1932, Nanticoke, PA; [p.] Jadwiga and Albin Pogorzelski; [m.] Norman King (all deceased), May 28, 1955; [ch.] Lucinda, Norman and Kristine; [ed.] 11th grade; [oth. writ.] 24 poems and prose.; [pers.] Poetry and all kinds of good music are my favorite past-times.; [a.] Sterling Heights, MI

KINNISON, MATTIE DEE
[pen.] Minnie Hacha, Sweet Pea; [b.] December 12, 1920, Waco, TX; [p.] Edward P. and Jeffie Blackwell; [m.] Brice W. Kinnison (deceased), February 10, 1946; [ch.] Weldon Presley, Erline Louise; [ed.] Didn't graduate from High School; [occ.] Retired Home Maker; [memb.] Liberty Hill Baptist Church International Association of Chiefs of Police, Providence Good Health Club.; [hon.] Awards in cooking contests. Teaching Preschoolers 23 yrs. Sunday School; [oth. writ.] Poems published in a home town newspaper in earlier years. I've written stories, lyrics, poems etc. since a very early age.; [pers.] I strive to have my writings true to life and each one better than the one before. God has given me talent which goes back many generations in my family, back to Abraham Lincoln. My third Great Uncle.; [a.] Moody, TX

KINSEY, TARA
[b.] September 4, 1982, Gilmer, TX; [p.] Rita Kinsey, John Kinsey; [ed.] Gilmer Jr. High School; [hon.] Honor Roll Student, Choir, Future Problem Solving, Math, Science; [oth. writ.] Many poems and short stories read in school activities.; [pers.] I try to express original and fun writings to interest the minds of all ages.; [a.] Gilmer, TX

KIRK, JAMIE
[b.] April 25, 1974, Chicago, IL; [p.] Eugene Kirk and Bonnie Kirk; [ed.] Riverside, Brookfield High School, Triton College; [occ.] Clerk, E.A. Meindl Insurance, Brookfield, IL; [hon.] First place poetry contest winner in grade school. Presidential dean's list. Patrons council grant.; [pers.] It doesn't matter what people think of you, knowing that you are somebody is all that counts.; [a.] Brookfield, IL

KLAUSNER, JENNIFER
[b.] November 2, 1980, Long Island, NY; [p.] Kristine and Eli Klausner; [ed.] Currently A sophomore at Lynbrook Senior High School; [occ.] Student; [memb.] Cross Country, PAC, Environmental Club, Literary Magazine; [hon.] Honor Student, Silver Leadership Award; [oth. writ.] Several poems and short stories, most of them unpublished, 2 novels, also unpublished.; [pers.] If you can't depend upon yourself, who can you depend on?; [a.] East Rockaway, NY

KLEIN, EILEEN
[b.] March 21, 1920, Owatonna, MN; [p.] Joseph Cieszinski, Alice Cieszinski; [m.] Kenneth Klein, September 9, 1949; [ch.] Kovin, Karen, Kory; [ed.] High School, 12th grade; [occ.] House wife (husband legally blind)

KLESSEN, RUTH
[b.] March 25, 1915, WV; [p.] Mary and Gelbert Brammer; [m.] William Klessen; [ed.] Required, in my parties I completed a 6 yrs correspondence, course with ambassador college, 97 percent average, world wide church of God; [occ.] Retired now but I did several different jobs; [oth. writ.] Several poems and a short story; [pers.] I always loved poetry. Never had to write things down, always memorized poems. Favorite poem was the childrens hour, and by the shows of Giecha Guma; [a.] Clarkston, WA

KLOSTER, MARGARET
[b.] March 21, 1916, Eagle Grove, IA; [p.] Dr. and Mrs. J. R. Christensen; [m.] Erling, September 23, 1941; [ch.] Leif Kloster; [ed.] University of Iowa, University of Northern Iowa, Physical Ed., Nursery, Kg. and Primary; [occ.] Retired Kg. Teacher; [memb.] AAUW, P.E.O, Lutheran Church, Tulare Co. Art League; [hon.] Honors in art shows especially collages

KLOTZ, FRIEDA D.
[b.] October 23, 1959, Fairbanks, AK; [ed.] Austin E. Lathrop High School, Fairbanks, AK, University of Alaska, Fairbanks, AK; [hon.] Cum Laude, University of Alaska, Fairbanks, AK; [oth. writ.] Other poems published in local west Michigan papers.; [pers.] To me, there is nothing more magnificent, more awe-inspiring than the natural wonders of creation and the human spirit. If by my talents, I have shared these treasures, touched your heart and rekindled your spirit, then I have succeeded in my goal.; [a.] Zeeland, MI

KNECHEL, ANDREW
[b.] March 5, 1967; [p.] Nelson and Carol Knechel; [m.] Bev Knechel, September 27, 1986; [ch.] Courtney Knechel; [ed.] South Hunterdon Regional High, Mercer County Community College; [occ.] Mail Clerk, Merrill Lynch; [oth. writ.] Other poems and several commentaries not yet published; [pers.] If we would look at the world through the eyes of a child, the heart of a poet and the mind of God, we would see each other as the wonderous creatures that we are.; [a.] Princeton, NJ

KNEHER, DOROTHEA A.
[b.] September 24, 1931, Mincola, NY; [p.] August Kneher, Dorothy Vettel Kneher; [ed.] BS King's College, MS Queens College, Additional Studies, NY University, CUNY St. Johns, Hunter College, Univ. Wisconsin, Northwestern Univ.; [occ.] Retired Teacher of English and History; [hon.] Various teaching awards; [oth. writ.] Have written poetry since age 11; [pers.] I believe the purpose of all learning is to know God and to better understand ourselves; [a.] Dix Hills, NY

KNIERIM, CARRIE A.
[b.] October 6, 1982, Coles, CO; [p.] Lloyd and Peggy Knierim; [ed.] Altamont Elementary School; [occ.] Full time 7th grade student; [memb.] Altamont Grade School Scholastic Bowl Team; [hon.] High Honors, Creative Writing Contests, National Honor Roll Academy; [oth. writ.] Several poems and stories in creatie writing books at school.; [pers.] I look up to those writers whose parents say "Why don't you get a real job?"; [a.] Altamont, IL

KNIGHTS, CARLENE
[b.] October 3, 1956, Trinidad, WI; [p.] Wilma and Stanley Knights; [ed.] BA Journalism, Media Arts, Long Island University 1980, New York City Community College 1974-77; [occ.] Administrative Assistant H.J. Russell and Co., Construction Mgrs.; [memb.] Woman In Communications 1979-80, Eastern Association of Financial Aid Counselors, NAACP Act, So Programs, Judge (Atlanta); [hon.] Long Island University's Dean's List.; [oth. writ.] Several poems in small newspapers, church newsletters, Journalism Review, 1976; [pers.] "It's never too late to try something new under God's sun. He is the supreme source."; [a.] Decatur, GA

KNISELY, BILLY
[b.] January 27, 1980, St. Joseph Hosp, Parkersburg, WV; [p.] Rhonda Butcher, John Butcher; [ed.] 10th grade education; [occ.] I am still in school; [oth. Writ.] Man On The Moon, One Night, Silence; [pers.] :Colored vision ceases common sense." "Love is a word not often meant, but to often said."; [a.] Little Hocking, OH

KNOLL-SHATSKY, JOHANNA
[b.] 1924, Holland; [ch.] I have 4 children and 8 grandchildren; [memb.] Alpha Gamma, Sigma, Sigma Psi Chapter, Honor Society; [hon.] Was on Presidents list in College in 1987. Went in 1980 to Holland to attend the crowning of Princess Beatrix, in the church in Amsterdam, and had lunch there. Went to the Inaugural Ball of President Ronald Reagan in Orange County California.; [a.] Sun City, CA

KNOUSE, EVELYN
[b.] September 23, 1935, Hershey, PA; [p.] Edwin and Bertha Hess; [m.] Stephen J. Knouse, October 19, 1954; [ch.] Sharon Rich; [occ.] Homemaker; [memb.] Church of the Brethren; [oth. writ.] Poems published in a search of the soul and a collection of poems.; [pers.] I have been interested in poetry since reciting poems in grade school. "Do unto others as you would have them do unto you" is the way I have tried to live and strive to convey that philosophy in my poems.; [a.] Hummelstown, PA

KOIVA, ENN O.
[b.] October 4, 1940, Karksi, Estonia; [m.] Aria; [ch.] Peter, Eric, Kristian; [ed.] B.A. (Honors), U. of CT, M.S., Eastern CT State U., M.A., U. of CT; [occ.] Educational Researcher/Writer; [hon.] Named "National Teacher-Scholar" 1995 by the National Endowment for the Humanities; [oth. writ.] (books) - Using the Cultural Models approach for studying the Multicultural Experience (1978), - Changing Connecticut, 1635-1980 (1980), - Lords of the Western Sea (1984), - Flames of Honor (1978), - Isle of Fire (1994)

KOMANETSKY, ALEXANDER
[pen.] Alex Komanetsky; [b.] May 27, 1955, Russia; [p.] Anatol, Zinaida Komanetsky; [m.] Nelli Gortcherova, January 23, 1985; [ed.] Moscow, Teachers University; [occ.] Customer service in warehouse. I have been lived in America for four years and I have political asylum. English is not my native language.; [oth. writ.] I'm freelance writer for the several Russian Newspapers and Magazine "Vestnik", "Panorama".; [pers.] "That harmony can't be accepted if it's basic condition becomes the suffering of child".; [a.] Atlanta, GA

KOUSIN, LOUIS
[b.] March 29, 1910, New York City; [p.] Joseph and Leah; [m.] Cerise Kousin, April 14, 1941; [ch.] Nina and Joan; [occ.] Retired, except when I remember to find peace all over the world; [hon.] Pulitzer prize nominee 1958 Newspr. Column. Brotherhood everyday and NECJ 1958, Number of East Colleges, Natl. Cong. of Christ and Jekss, Re: a number of awards for creation of peace sites int. to rate from 1980, Leading to over 1,000 peace sites in the world in hundreds of countries; [pers.] I believe poetry is the language of peace. I would be honoured to desalinate the Natl. Library of Poetry as a peace site (the first of its kind) no obligation (if approve) willing to advise no obligation.

KOZUKA, TAKASHI
[b.] December 11, 1970, Nagoya, Japan; [p.] Ms. Tomiyo Kozuka; [ed.] B.A. in English from Gonzaga University (1995); [occ.] Graduate Student (M.A. in English) at Drew University in Madison; [hon.] Gonzaga University Presidential Scholarships (1991-95), Drew University Graduate Scholarship (1995-96); [oth. writ.] "Timetable" in Best Poems of 1996, "A Blink of Time" in In Other Words.; [pers.] His great interests are in English Renaissance literature and early 20th century British literature.; [a.] Morristown, NJ

KRALL, DIANE M.
[b.] December 22, 1959, Pittsburgh; [p.] Mary Faith and Edward J. Krall; [ed.] West Mifflin South High, Steel Valley Vocational, Cosmetology - Licensed, Cosmetology Teacher Licensed; [occ.] Hairdresser; [hon.] Silver Poets Award 1985, Gold Poets Award 1986 (World Of Poetry); [oth. writ.] Poem - "Destiny" published in "Our Word's Best Loved Poems" by John Campbell; [pers.] To teach is to learn, as a teacher is a student, as one, we are all th same, we were born of the wise. Wisdom cannot exist if it has no reflection.; [a.] Jefferson Boro, PA

KRALOWETZ, BRIAN
[b.] August 21, 1980, Munster, IN; [p.] Lynn Kralowetz, Doug Kralowetz; [ed.] Durango High School; [occ.] High School Student; [hon.] State finalist in National Geography Bee 6th, 7th, and 8th grade, school champ in Spelling Bee, 6th, 7th, and 8th grade and (Clark County 7th grade champ), Academic Letter in 9th grade; [oth. writ.] 8th grade school newspaper; [a.] Las Vegas, NV

KRAMER, CARRIE
[b.] December 17, 1980, Alexandra, MN; [p.] Judy Kramer; [ed.] I'm going into 9th grade.; [oth. writ.] I've written many other poems; [pers.] I've always like poetry and enjoyed writing it. When I grow up I'd like to be a writer.; [a.] Alexandria, MN

KRAUTHAMMER, ANNA
[b.] New York City; [p.] Dr. Arnold Scheiman; [ch.] David, Jonathan; [ed.] BA, MA New York University, Doctoral Program, English, City University of New York; [occ.] English Teacher; [memb.] Modern Language Association, Association for the study of American Indian Literature; [hon.] NYC English Teacher

of the Year (1981); [oth. writ.] "September" (poem) Slant "Poems of Ancestry" (article Perspectives; [pers.] A good poem should bring beauty and understanding to the poet and the reader; [a.] New York, NY

KREIMEYER, LORRAINE P.
[pen.] Lorrainbo; [b.] December 3, Utica, NY; [p.] Robert and Barbara Kreimeyer; [ed.] BFA Syracuse University, LRT trained Rebirther; [occ.] Artist, Illustrator, Mask Portrait, Storyteller, Artist in Residence, Rebirther; [memb.] Pearl in the Egg Storytellers Guild, Rebirthers Assn. of Upstate NY, Munson Williams Proctor Museum, Kirkland Art Center; [hon.] Deans List, Full Scholarship in Masters of Fine Arts, South Eastern Mass. University, Peoples Choice Award for second consecutive yrs. during Central NY regional art show; [oth. writ.] The Heart of the River, Then Would you Know I Loved You? Is it true?; [pers.] Webster defines illustrator as "an enlightener." In all my work and play my intent is to inspire, encourage and enlighten, which to me means helping us all to "lighten up!"; [a.] Whitesboro, NY

KRESS, MARY
[b.] January 18, 1908, New Windsor; [p.] Cleavland and Maud Kress; [ed.] Graduated from Westminister High School and Western Maryland College; [occ.] Retired; [memb.] St. Johns United, Methodist Church, United Methodist, Women, and a Senior Citizen Group; [hon.] Church awards for Bible teaching and other church work; [oth. writ.] Thirty or more poems written on the entire Bible; [pers.] My entire life has been centered on God's Word, and the work I can do for Him. My poems are about my faith and joy I find in Him.; [a.] Hampstead, MD

KRUNZEL, STEPHANIE L.
[pen.] Louise Bailey; [b.] April 30, 1968, Dayton, OH; [p.] Neil and Carolyn Bailey; [m.] Robert J. Krunzel, June 24, 1989; [ch.] Kelsey Marie Krunzel Born June 19, 1990; [ed.] Centerville High School Sinclar College: Interior Design; [occ.] Sales; [hon.] Dean's List; [oth. writ.] Many short stories not yet published, as well as several poems.; [pers.] My personal statement is to be true to myself in writing not only words for enjoyment, but words which make one think.; [a.] West Carrollton, OH

KUAR, BLANCA I.
[b.] March 16, 1965, New York; [p.] Aladino and Matilde Santiago; [pers.] This poem is dedicated to my loving parents, Aladino and Matilde Santiago. Their love and Nurturing throughout my childhood days made me the avid lover of poetry I am today. May those who read my poem understand my love for life and share the pain I feel within me for our "Mother Earth".; [a.] New York, NY

KUBIAK, GREG D.
[b.] December 12, 1960, McAlester, OK; [p.] Curtis and Pearl Kubink; [ed.] Mt. St. Mary H.S., Okla. City, BA in Political Science at The University of Oklahoma, Norman; [occ.] Syndicated columnist, free lance writer; [memb.] The Authors Guild, Front Runners, San Diego, University Christian Church; [oth. writ.] Political columns printed in various newspapers, "The Gilded Dome" (Univ.. of Okla. Press); [pers.] I am working on several creative projects, including a novel, a stage-play, a collection of short stories and a compilation of my poetry.; [a.] San Diego, CA

LAATE, NOLAN
[b.] July 10, 1972, Gallup, NM; [p.] John and Charleen Laate; [m.] Gayle R. Romancito (engaged); [ch.] Karesten Alma Mary Laate; [ed.] Fort Lewis College - one year, Albuquerque - Technical Institute, three years; [occ.] Construction Worker; [memb.] Member of the Zuni Pueblo Indians of the Southwest; [pers.] Human beings have to learn how to live with Mother Earth and all her children again, if she is to survive.; [a.] Albuquerque, NM

LACEY, DEBORAH D.
[pen.] Dee-Dee; [b.] August 29, 1961, Chicago, IL; [p.] Eugene and Minnie Lacey; [occ.] Charles Harrison Mason/William Roberts Bible Institute (1992), Roosevelt University (BA, 1991), Harold Washington College (AA, 1981), William Jones Commercial High School (1979); [occ.] Legal Secretary of Schuyler, Roche and Zwirner, P.C.; [memb.] Roosevelt University Pre-Law Society, National Association of Notaries, Legal Secretaries Association, Pentecostal Temple C.O.G.I.C. Board of Directors; [hon.] National Dean's List; [oth. writ.] Getting Beyond The Trees (incomplete and unpublished book), The Sound Of A Different Drum (Poem - unpublished work), We Choose To (Poem - unpublished work); [pers.] I believe that the impetus of all writings comes from within an individual. It does not matter how talented or theoretically correct one is. Writings are inate and are in many cases born out of experience.; [a.] Calumet City, IL

LACKEY, MICHAEL
[b.] May 30, 1969, San Francisco; [p.] Curtis Ray Lackey, Catherine Joan Weaver; [ed.] Antioch Community H.S. Grad., Junior at the University of Phoenix; [occ.] Courier with D.H.L.; [pers.] Life is shorter than you think. Don't waste one second being unhappy!

LACSINA, NICOLE ANN
[b.] April 14, 1974, California; [p.] Terry Nixon and Debra Nixon; [m.] Nelson Lacsina, February 19, 1993; [ch.] Nathaniel Allen Lacsina; [ed.] 1 year of Consumers Jr. College/Graduated from Elk Grove High School '92; [occ.] Mary Kay Cosmetic Consultant; [memb.] American Red Cross, NCOA - Non Commissioned Officers Association; [pers.] My poetry writings have brought out the inner-most feelings in my life that no one else could, except my loving husband and son.

LAFRANCE, ELIZABETH
[pen.] Elizabeth LaFrance; [b.] October 1, 1951, Fort Bragg, NC; [p.] Sarah Patterson Fishburn, Randolph Eugene Fishburn; [m.] Simon Generalao, September 9, 1994; [oth. writ.] Poems: "Listen To The Wind", "Sarah And The Three Graces", "My Favorite Artist"; [pers.] Although death may separate our loved ones from us physically, they are very aware of our prayers for them, and continue to send love to us.; [a.] Gardnerville, NV

LAGLE, CARL
[b.] January 10, 1946, Long Beach, CA; [p.] Melba and Woody; [m.] Cindy Timlinson Lagle, July 31, 1971; [ch.] Kristen, Debbie and David; [ed.] BS, Education, University of Arizona, 1969, MA, Clinical Psychology, Norwich University, 1991; [occ.] Clinical Counselor; [memb.] California Association of Marriage and Family Therapists; [hon.] Department of Army, Distinguished Service Medal; [oth. writ.] "Is It You?" A book of poems, Riyadh, Saudi Arabia: Al. Farazdak Press, Library of Congress, 1986; [a.] Salinas, CA

LAIESKI SR., FRANK
[pen.] Frank Laleski Sr.; [b.] January 2, 1934, New York City; [p.] Adam and Blanche Laleski; [m.] Dorothy M. Laleski, April 7, 1956; [ch.] Frank Jr., Gary and Michael; [ed.] Honor Student High School, Two years Famingdal Univ., Assoc Degree RCA Institutes NYC., Lic. Realty of Arizona, Ordainked Minister of Salvation Cal.; [occ.] Real Estate and Apartment Manager; [memb.] Manhattan Chess CLub, Valley Cathedral Church; [hon.] Security Officer of month writer of Religious Books and Songs, Fond Properties Achievement Award, Song Pick of the month Award, first Book "For The Love Of The Father" over sixty poems.; [oth. writ.] Expositions on Revelation Teacher of Theology; [pers.] My main objective is to bring to mankind love, hope and peace. For all people Tongue and Nation. It only takes one match to set a whole woodland on fire let it start with me.; [a.] Phoenix, AZ

LAKATOS, VICTORIA
[b.] August 10, 1962, Elizabeth, NJ; [p.] Joseph and Linda; [ch.] Jamie Lee; [ed.] Woodbridge Sr. High; [occ.] Samples for Marketing Wall Trends Int.; [pers.] My poems usually reflect my life and the people around me; using the feelings of the moment is my creative force.; [a.] Port Reading, NJ

LALOMIA, MARISA ANN
[b.] January 14, 1978, NJ; [p.] Ann and Vincent Lalomia; [ed.] Elementary thru High School - Lexington School for the Deaf, Jackson Heights, N.Y.; [occ.] Student; [memb.] Student Body Vice-President, Class Vice-President, Certified Scuba Diver; [hon.] Valedictorian, Lexington School Class of '92, Capt. Math Championship Team '93, Science Team '93, H.S. Math/Science Awards '93, Spec. Science Award '92, Honor Society '92-'93-'94; [oth. writ.] School Publications; [pers.] "There are no handicaps - only excuses!

LALONE, ROSE W.
[b.] January 27, 1946, Norwalk, OH; [p.] Bonita and Walter Franklin; [m.] Junior E. LaLone, March 1, 1974; [ch.] Barbara LaLone, Chris Chattin, Davida Richards, Walter Richards, Autumn Watson; [ed.] High School Graduate; [occ.] Physical Therapy Aide; [memb.] Amvets and Veterans of Foreign Wars; [oth. writ.] Help me "O God" I'm stuck in Vietnam, Springtime; [pers.] I wrote this poem when I was feeling down and I came to realize that its best to be yourself.; [a.] Sandusky, OH

LAMEIRO, VERONICA
[b.] December 11, 1983, Puerto Rico; [p.] Sonia Lameiro and Juan Lameiro; [ed.] Lake Michigan Catholic School St. Joseph, MI; [occ.] Student - 7th grade; [hon.] Berrien County Arts and Science Expo - 1995 Honorable Mention; [oth. writ.] Poems and Songs Talent Show - 1994, Title of the Song - "If The Love I Give You"; [pers.] I want to tell the people of the world my inner feelings and my concern for other human beings.; [a.] Stevenseville, MI

LANCASTER, ABNA A.
[b.] Salisbury, NC; [p.] J. E. K. Aggrey; [m.] Spencer W. Lancaster; [ch.] Raemi L. Evans, Carol L. Meeks, Harriet L. Graves; [ed.] H.S., College (A.B.) Shaw Univ. (Raliegh, NC), (A.M.) Univ. of Conn. (Starrs, CT), Further Studies: Columbia Univ. (N.Y.), Univ. of NC at Greensboro (NC), Central Univ. of NC (Durham, NC); [occ.] Retired Associate Professor, Livingstone College; [hon.] Dean's List, Yearbooks dedicated by Price High School and Livingstone College, Dedication of The Bear's Tale (Art Magazine, Livingstone College), Soldier's Memorial Church Award, A.M.E. Zion Church Service Plaque, Spencer and Abna Lancaster Scholarships, Price Alumni; [oth. writ.] "Playing in God's Symphony," Sunshine Magazine, Articles in "The Strength of My Life," poems in "The Bears' Tale"; [a.] Salisbury, NC

LANDIS, DEBRA H.
[b.] Fort Hood, TX; [m.] Stephen L. Landis, June 25, 1977; [ch.] Matthew Maine, Katelyn Michele; [a.] Willow Street, PA

LANDRUM, TAMI JO
[b.] March 6, 1966, Sacramento; [p.] Gary and Sally Landrum; [ch.] (Pets) - Passion, River, Doc Holliday and Emmitt; [ed.] Casa Roble Fundamental High School; [occ.] Clerical/Automobile Industry; [oth. writ.] This is the first time I have had my work published; [pers.] My poetry comes directly from my heart and soul. I write what I feel. It's nice to know that people understand and relate to my work.; [a.] Orangevale, CA

LANGHAM, JANELLE
[b.] June 20, 1950, Hinton, OK; [p.] Frank and Hazel Hitt; [m.] SL Langham, January 11, 1989; [ch.] Neely and Cheyenne, and Dane; [ed.] Lookeba-Sickles High Sch., Southwestern Okla. State University; [occ.] Architect and Fine Artist; [memb.] "Feed the Children" Pardner and Cowboys for Christ; [hon.] Numerous Art Show Awards, Magazine Cover Artist, Art in Western Horseman and Rodeo News Magazines; [oth. writ.] Numerous poems in soon to be published personal book.; [pers.] My poems are gifts from the heart that can only be inspired by God.; [a.] Chickasha, OK

LANHAM, ROBERT KERMIT
[pen.] Mark Lanham; [b.] November 22, 1961, Washington, DC; [p.] Robert J. Lanham, Joan F. May; [occ.] Cabinet Maker; [pers.] I attribute this poem to Joanne Cacace, she has taught me how important it is to express my feeling and emotions. To share what's inside with others. Thank you for being a part of my life. May our love for one another burn brighter than any candle through eternity.; [a.] Rockville, MD

LANTZ II, PERICLES JOHN
[pen.] Pericles John Lantz II; [b.] March 7, 1974, New York; [p.] John P. Lantz M.D., Marie L. Lantz; [ed.] Montclair State University, BS. Magna Cum Laude, Molecular Biology Degree with Honors in Molecular Biology; [occ.] Medical Student, Mount Sinai School of Medicine; [memb.] Nat'l Honor Fraternity Phi Kappa Phi; [hon.] Outstanding Senior in Molecular Biology (Montclair State University - May '94), Phi Kappa Phi - Senior Book Award, Dean's List; [oth. writ.] Many other poems, short stories and movie scripts. Article for the Montclair - M.S.V.; [pers.] I believe in writing as a means of introspection. It is the ultimate dissection of self. Through my writing, I understand my desires, fears and beliefs. I have always enjoyed early writers such as Shakespeare and Coleridge. Through these writers I have understood writing as a tapestry of words to be woven in one's imagination.; [a.] New York City, NY

LARREGUI, DEBRA
[pen.] Debra Blake; [b.] December 30, 1958, Travis AFB, CA; [p.] Rev. Phillip Blake Sr., Herietta Blake; [m.] Richard Larregui Jr., October 8, 1988; [ch.] Frankie, Danielle; [ed.] Caesar Rodney Sr. H.S., Delaware State College; [occ.] Secretary; [hon.] Who's Who Among American H.S. Students, Dean's List, Sustained Superior Performance Award; [oth. writ.] Several poems never published before; [pers.] With Christ as the head of your life, all things are possible.; [a.] Okinawa, Japan

LARSON, FAITH CAROL
[pen.] Gueinevere; [b.] December 9, 1928, Stow, NY; [p.] Mildred and Wallace Saxton (both deceased); [m.] Marvin W. Larson, January 5, 1976; [ch.] Anne, Holly, Wally, Greg, Ron and Jay; [ed.] Chautauqua High School, Doyle Beauty School, University of Kentucky - selected classes; [occ.] Retired; [memb.] First Presbyterian Church, Lakeland Fl., Poets on the Park, Fla. State Poet's Assn., Lifetime Member International Society of Poets; [hon.] Semi-finalist ISP Conv. 1994, National Honor Society, Sportsmanship Brotherhood; [oth. writ.] Nat'l Library Poetry Poems in, In The Desert Sun, Edge of Twilight, Songs on the Wind, A Delicate Balance and Best Poems 96. Editor's Choice Award in 93 and 94. Poetic Sparrowgrass Voices of America 1995, several things Senior Times Magazine Lodger, Lakeland Fl., Church Newsletter; [pers.] Feelings are everywhere so be gentle.; [a.] Lakeland, FL

LARSON, TIMOTHY E.
[pen.] T. E. Larson; [b.] May 11, 1954, Fairmont, MN; [p.] Murlan and Darlene Larson; [ed.] Winnetonk H.S., K.C. MO; [occ.] Governor Technician, Gerhardt's Inc. Houston, TX; [memb.] American Motorcyclists Assoc., Honda Riders Club of America; [pers.] I started writing poetry to express my feelings, finding it easier than talking aloud about them.; [a.] Houston, TX

LARUE, DAVID H.
[pen.] Luc Laroux; [ed.] Wintersville High, Otterbien College; [occ.] AVP of Bank; [pers.] Want, Desire and Ambition can often overcome great obstacles.; [a.] Steubenville, OH

LARUE, JANET E.
[b.] November 6, 1938, Brockton; [p.] Joseph and Melva Lawson; [m.] Robert V. LaRue; [ch.] Linda, Cynthia, Bobby, Donald, Laurie, Andrew; [ed.] Brockton High School; [occ.] Telemarketing Operator; [oth. writ.] Poems to all my children and sisters and brothers; [pers.] I hope my writings inspire others, bring warmth within their heart, peace within their soul and takes them on a journey that one would otherwise never know.; [a.] Brockton, MA

LAUB, LARRY
[b.] April 27, 1949, Cleveland, OH; [p.] Eleanor and Sterling W. Laub; [m.] Claire R. Laub, August 26, 1972; [ed.] High School Grad., Euclid Ohio Class of '67; [occ.] Disabled Vietera

LAUZONIS, STACY
[b.] March 15, 1978; [p.] Shirley Lauzonis, Duane Lauzonis; [ed.] Lewiston-Porter High School, entering 12th grade in Fall of 1995; [memb.] Key Club, Amnesty International, Aquatic Club, Swim Team, National Honor Society; [hon.] Lamp of Learning Awards, Athlete/Scholar Pin, Xerox Award, Who's Who Among American High School Students, 1995 Lewiston-Porter Community Ambassador to Greece; [oth. writ.] Poem published in Amnesty Times and Award for contest for Flag Burning Essay; [pers.] When I write poetry, I try to reach all levels, in order that the audience can relate to the message I am trying to convey.; [a.] Ransomville, NY

LAVINGTON, RONALD
[b.] August 19, 1947, New York, NY; [p.] Sarah Lavington (deceased); [m.] Divorced; [ch.] Vance Lavington, Theresa Lavington; [ed.] Woodrow Wilson HS, U.S. Army Signal School; [occ.] Professional Typesetter, New York, NY; [oth. writ.] I had written several poems, but none of them have been published yet.; [pers.] Poetry is an art of expression. My poetry will always be written from the heart, and will always express my feelings within that subject. This poem was written for my mother who meant everything to me.; [a.] Bronx, NY

LAVOY, RACHEL MARIE
[b.] May 10, 1985, Sarasota, FL; [p.] Wilson and Georgia LaVoy; [ed.] Fifth Grade Ashton Elementary School, Sarasota, FL; [occ.] Child; [memb.] Currently study piano and dance. I am also an artist; [pers.] Poetry comes from my heart. I hope to have more creations in the near future.; [a.] Sarasota, FL

LAZINGER, MAXWELL
[pen.] Maxwell Lazinger; [b.] November 19, 1963, Neptune, NJ; [p.] Sol and Jean Lazinger; [m.] Caroline Lazinger, June 19, 1994; [ed.] Brande's University, BA 1986, Tuffs University Medical School, M.D., 1990, Residency Georgetown Univ. Hospital, 1990, Lahey Clinic Medical Center.; [occ.] Interventional, Radiologist; [memb.] Radiologic Society of North America, American Roentgen Roy Society, Society of Cardiovascular and Interventional Radiologists, Aircraft Owners and Pilot's Association; [hon.] Dean's List, Nathan and Bertha Richter Award for Excellence in research in Sciences, High Honors in Biology; [pers.] "Carpe Diem"; [a.] Waltham, MA

LAZZARESCHI, LOU
[pen.] Lulu; [b.] October 6, 1927, Arkansas; [p.] Clida, Wiley Coody; [m.] Marcel, July 10, 1920; [ch.] Linda, Larry, Bart, Lisa; [ed.] Watson Chapel, High School in Pine Bluff, Arkansas; [occ.] Housewife; [memb.] American Heart Association, National Multiple Sclerosis, Society Ambassadors, Club of University of San Francisco, Mother's Against Drunk Driving (MADD), Member of Church of God, Church, Teaching Children; [pers.] Live each day as it was your last and be the best you can be; [a.] Atherton, CA

LEATH, BARBARA MILLER
[b.] October 16, 1956, Montezuma, GA; [p.] Gracie Smith; [ch.] Lizabeth Leath; [ed.] B.A. Psychology, Teacher Certification K-4 from Brenau University; [occ.] Director After-school, Tutorial Program and Summer Academy Grace UMC.; [pers.] My influence comes from the spirit of my ancestors, and the God force that is inside all of us.; [a.] Marietta, GA

LEE, DORTHENE BETTY
[pen.] Dot; [b.] May 1, 1957, Vian, OK; [p.] Beulah Mae Harrison; [m.] Austin Edward Lee, August 1, 1982; [ch.] Stardes, Austin Jr., Natasha, Reginald Lee; [ed.] Vian High School, Connors State College.; [occ.] AT & T Operator; [oth. writ.] Lift Up Your Hand, My Love, Fantasy, Love Of My Life, Memories, Vision, Who Is Calling Me, Thirty-Fifth Avenue, Thinking Of You, The Sky Is The Limit; [pers.] My poems reflect on my feelings about life. I love romance and religion.; [a.] Phoenix, AZ

LEECH, PAUL
[b.] Ireland; [p.] Susan and Garrett Leech; [m.] Johanna, 1951 (deceased); [ch.] Gary Katherine Terrence, Brendan Dermot and (Paul F.); [pers.] Paul Leech In my 24 hours day I always try to be fair.; [a.] Sonora, CA

LEFTWICH, JUDITH EVANS
[b.] October 24, 1937, Newport News, VA; [p.] Hilliary Moorefield and Annie Brooks Evans; [m.] Ronald Edward Leftwich Sr., July 9, 1961; [ch.] Kimberly Anne, Lisa Catherine and Ron Jr.; [ed.] Harrellsville High N.C., Rex Hospital School of Nursing, Raleigh N.C.; [occ.] Registered Nurse; [memb.] Yorktown Baptist Church; [pers.] I believe that inside every human being is a soul that longs to be touched, nurtured and loved. Poetry is one way to lovingly, touch a soul.; [a.] Yorktown, VA

LEGGETT, DUANE
[b.] June 13, 1973, Mariemont, OH; [p.] Harry and Carol Leggett; [ed.] Moeller High, Goshen High; [occ.] Construction Worker; [pers.] Poetry is a reflection of reality but you can only use your imagination to see what the words are saying.; [a.] Menasha, WI

LEITER, DEBI L.
[pen.] Debi L. Leiter; [b.] January 14, 1971, NJ; [ed.] Student at Brookdale College, Lincroft NJ; [pers.] I have been greatly influenced by the poetry of Jim Morrison, and the film of Quentin Tarantino and hope to be a film maker myself one day.; [pers.] I write about how I see reality, maybe I see it different than others, but I'd rather see it my way than through anyone else's eyes.; [a.] NJ

LEKHLIFI, LYNN MARIE
[pen.] Lynn Marie Lekhlifi; [b.] September 27, 1955, USA; [p.] Albertina Young; [m.] Abdellatif Lekhlifi, November 16, 1991; [ed.] Cathedral High; [occ.] Administrative Clerk at Nynex; [memb.] Artist for Kap-2, "Good New" News Paper; [pers.] I usually write when my heart feel strongly on good or bad situations. Life is what influences me. My philosophy is if you can change whatever the situation pray to God to deal with whatever.; [a.] Bronx, NY

LEMIEUX, KAREN JEAN
[b.] June 10, 1968, Washington, DC; [p.] Clement G. A. Hartley, Bonalyn J. Hartley; [m.] Kevin L. Lemieux, January 10, 1987; [ch.] Kayleigh Jean, Andrew (Drew) Clement; [ed.] Nashua Senior High, Rivier College, BS Accounting, minor: Computer Science; [occ.] Volunteer Teacher's Aid, Charlotte Avenue Elementary School, Nashua, NH; [memb.] Y.M.C.A., Daughter's of the American Revolution; [hon.] Magna Cum Laude, Dean's List; [pers.] The simple things in life bring me the most pleasure. American poet, May Swenson, has greatly influenced my poetic works.; [a.] Nashua, NH

LEON, ANNA C.
[pen.] Anna C. Leon; [b.] February 20, 1955, San Bernardino, CA; [p.] Aurora and Sabino Carrillo; [m.] Patrick G. Leon, September 21, 1974; [ch.] Patrick A. Leon, Erika M. Leon; [ed.] High School Graduate with two years College Study, Recipient of Scholarship - 1973; [occ.] Human Resource Associate - U.S. Post Office; [memb.] K-Lord Radio Station; [hon.] Member of Outstanding Teenagers of America - 1973, G.I. Forum Queen of 1972 for San Bernardino, CA; [oth. writ.] I have written other pieces of poetry, however, only for myself, never published.; [pers.] My poetry is a reflection of true life experiences that have given meaning to my mere existence.

LEON, SARA F.
[b.] April 17, 1981, San Diego, CA; [p.] Frank Leon and Anna Quan Leon; [ed.] Mendoza Elementary School and Shepherd Junior High; [occ.] Student; [memb.] National Junior Honor Society, Student Council, Math Counts; [hon.] The Ramon S. Mendoza Award-Outstanding Citizen, Royal Schools of Music for Piano-Distinction, Arizona Music Teachers Assoc., Honorable Mention, Safety Patrol-Captian; [a.] Mesa, AZ

LEONARD, K. LEIGH
[b.] June 30, 1960, Oswego, NY; [ed.] M.S. University of Wisconsin at Madison, Urban and Regional Planning, B.A., Oberlin College, Biology; [occ.] Assoc. Environmental, Health and Safety Manager, Author, Editor; [hon.] Phi Beta Kappa; [oth. writ.] Co-editor and contributing author, Pollution Prevention and Waste Minimization Laboratories, Lewis Publishers, 1995; [pers.] Thank you Father, for believing. Thank you Mother, for your courage. Thank you Sister, for sailing in our hearts, even as you sailed "Silk" so far.; [a.] Madison, WI

LEROY, SHELBY WOOD
[pen.] Shelby Wood or Joie Long; [b.] September 30, 1960, Oconee; [p.] William B. and Lola P. Wood; [m.] Gary Leroy, November 22, 1975; [ch.] Kinnith and Jonathan Leroy; [ed.] Attended Oakway High School, Oakway, S.C.; [occ.] Machine Operator; [memb.] United Way Seneca Office; [oth. writ.] Local newspaper Seneca Journal, Seneca, S.C. Have sent my stories and poems to other magazines.; [pers.] I see life as an adventure, and a dreamer and believe in the impossible; [a.] Seneca, SC

LEVER, NORINE
[ed.] B.S. Education, M.A. Management and Human Relations, M.A. Applied Psychology from USM Center of the Study and Practice of Spiritual Psychology, Star's Edge International: Masters, Professional and Wigards trainings; [occ.] I give the "Avatar" course, an experiential self-development training in exploring consciousness; [pers.] My wish upon a poem is to align with Divine Humor - the essence penetrating to the Heart of whatever is its focus and whoever is its reader.; [a.] Glenview, IL

LEVERTON, ERIN J.
[b.] April 11, 1983, Detroit, MI; [p.] Robert and Theresa Leverton; [ed.] Central Middle School - Plymouth, Michigan; [occ.] Student - 7th grade; [memb.] Girl Scouts of America; [hon.] The Honor Roll, Principal's List; [oth. writ.] Poems published in school magazines; [pers.] I almost always base my poems on nature, because it reflects the beauty of earth.; [a.] Canton, MI

LEVY, CHRISTINA TAFT
[b.] January 30, 1970, Newburgh, NY; [p.] Lawrence Levy and Pamela Whitman; [m.] Ian Duncan Smith, March 27, 1993; [ed.] University at Idaho, B.S. Communication, Creative writing minor, 1993; [occ.] Student, seeking Idaho teaching certificate; [memb.] Trinity Group Home Board Member, Coeurd'Alene, Idaho; [hon.] Dean's List, University of Idaho, 1992; [oth. writ.] This is the first time I've ever been published; [a.] Coeurd'Alene, ID

LEVY, FRANCOIS
[b.] September 15, 1975, Haiti; [p.] Anna Louis, Yves Francois; [ed.] George W. Wingate High School; [occ.] Songwriter, Write Movies, Painter, Painted Portrait; [oth. writ.] A lots of fairy tale story, my autobiography. A lots of poems, movies, songs. But none of them have yet published. In my writing I like to show how human being react to they on kind.; [pers.] Writings is my gift from God, I like to observe nature, and develop my own work of what I've seen, and learn. Because I have a powerful imagination, I like to write and put every one of my thought on paper.; [a.] Brooklyn, NY

LEWANDOWSKI, MARY A.
[b.] September 22, 1915, Italy; [p.] Joseph and Grace Gumina; [m.] Chet Lewandowski, May 26, 1941; [ch.] Elaine, Lynn; [ed.] John Adams High, Cleveland, OH, Parliamentary Law Certificate, Creative Writing Classes; [occ.] Retired Secretary; [memb.] Parent-Teacher-Association, Maple Heights Little Theatre, Council of Catholic Women, St. Barnabas Fifty-Plus Club, St. Wenceslaus Prime Timers, St. Catherine Circle; [hon.] John Adams High School Honor Roll Pin, Honorary Life Member of Ohio Congress of Parents and Teachers, Inc.; [oth. writ.] Writings published in Cleveland newspapers, Poems published in Blackberry Press Anthology, Poem prefaced High School Fiftieth Class Reunion Memory Book.; [pers.] No matter the style, I have always been enriched by poetry. May those who read my poems derive some relaxation and perhaps a sense of nourishment.; [a.] Omaha, NE

LEWIS, ANNA LAURA
[b.] March 15, 1984, Houston; [p.] Bill and Lois Lewis; [ed.] Elementary School; [occ.] Student; [memb.] Writing Round Table, Challenge for the Gifted and Talented, Junior Great Books, T.M.A.C. Swim Club; [hon.] Numerous Ribbons, Medals and Trophies in Swimming, Reflections Winner in Literature, Academic Recognition from State of Texas; [oth. writ.] Many other poems for writing Round Table and for pleasure; [a.] Houston, TX

LEWIS, DAVID R.
[b.] January 14, 1939, Harlem; [p.] Paul and Estelle Lewis; [ed.] H.S., New School - Adult Education, YWCA Writing Course, Playwright-in-Residence Brooklyn College; [occ.] Sales; [memb.] AARP; [hon.] Service to School (Graduation), Political Science (Graduation), Award for One-Act Play; [oth. writ.] Published Poet - Adult - children; [pers.] Deep affinity for black-rural-country America, Model as poet: Jean Toomer, Model as writer: James Baldwin, Influence: Zora Hurston R. H. Tawney, Favorite Sport: Baseball! Favorite music: 50's Rock n' Roll, Broadway Musicals - George Frideric Handel; [a.] New York, NY

LEWIS, DOUGLAS E.
[b.] July 7, 1967, Fort Knox, KY; [p.] Lawrence E. Lewis Sr., Edgar and Janet Halloway; [ed.] 1985 Graduate of North Hardin High School in Radcliff KY, 1989 Graduate of Lovisville College.; [occ.] Medical Laboratory, Scientist; [oth. writ.] Mostly poems for personal enjoyment and writing songs.; [pers.] I have learned to look beyond myself. Looking inside at oneself to see what makes one happy is fine, but it's when you search beyond, you find it. Always treat your Mom like a Queen.; [a.] Radcliff, KY

LEWIS, KEVIN GERARD
[b.] January 3, 1960, San Diego, CA; [p.] Richard Lewis, Jean McDew; [ed.] Suitland Sr. High/Central Chapman University; [occ.] Security; [memb.] NCOA; [oth. writ.] Are you a weed or a rose; [pers.] Treat each other as brothers and sisters, life is too short and the world too small. For hate accomplishes little, destroys alot. Only through the spirit of cooperation can anything be done.; [a.] Clinton, MD

LEWIS, ROBERT D.
[b.] October 24, 1962, Ottawa, IL; [p.] Dr. Robert Owen and Eleanor; [m.] Laura Lewis, June 3, 1995; [ed.] BA - DaPauw Univ., MD - University of Illinois; [occ.] Plastic Surgeon; [oth. writ.] Several poems and writings preserved for personal satisfaction; [pers.] My work is influenced by the songs and music of Joni Mitchell, she is a true artist whom I envy.; [a.] Cuyahoga Falls, OH

LEYTE-VIDAL, EDUARDO J.
[pen.] E. J. Leyte-Vidal; [b.] October 13, 1935, Santiago de Cuba, Cuba; [p.] Jose J. Leyte-Vidal and Noelia Leyte-Vidal; [m.] Lilliam Leyte-Vidal, August 22, 1982; [ch.] Susana C. and Elizabeth; [ed.] Oriente University, Business Administration Santiago de Cuba Institute; [occ.] Entrepreneur; [memb.] Cuban American National Foundation; [oth. writ.] Several poems and songs, including, My Native Land, Impossible To Believe It, My Children And I; [pers.] I enjoy reflecting in my writing the wonders of sounds and natural things, and combine them with the real things in life.; [a.] Miami, FL

LIAO, REBECCA
[b.] April 14, 1986, San Francisco; [p.] Antonia Hom Liao, Lawrence Liao; [ed.] Fremont Christian School, Fremont, CA, Third Grade Student, 1995; [memb.] National Geographic World Society; [hon.] Straight A Student from 1st - 3rd grade. Principal's List, 4th place and 1st place in Spelling Bee given by Association of Christian Schools International, 1st Place three times in The Elementary Speech Meet given by the Association of Christian Schools International; [a.] Fremont, CA

LICHON, VANESSA
[b.] April 15, 1981, Park Ridge, IL; [p.] Nancy and Francis Lichon; [ed.] Prairie Elementary School, Washington Junior High School, will be attending Benet Academy as a Freshman In Fall '95; [hon.] American Legion Award Winner, 8th Grade Girl Athlete of the Year (School), Thater J. Hill Service Award, Granquist Music Competition - 1st Place 1993 (Solo), 1994 (Duet), 1995 (Solo and Duet), President's Education Award, Participation in Dupage County's Student Government Day; [oth. writ.] Publication of poem in Mists Of Enchantment; [pers.] The development of my writing over the past three years has been sensational. Teachers, family, and friends have always been there for me. Thank you for all your input and support.; [a.] Naperville, IL

LIERMAN, KYLE
[b.] September 5, 1984, Champaign, IL; [p.] Michael and Denise Lierman; [ed.] Marian Bergeson, Elementary - 4th grade; [occ.] Student; [memb.] Ayso Soccer, Rancho Niguel Little League, Saddleback Valley U.S.D. Youth Hockey, Boy Scouts of America Troop 771, Marian Bergeson Elem. Safety Patrol; [hon.] Capistrano U.S.D. Gate Program, Capistrano U.S.D. Science Fest 1994 and 1995 Entrant, P.T.A. Reflections Program, 1994 - 1995 second place winner, Ayso Division 5 Champ 1992, SV U.S.D. "C" League Champ 1995; [pers.] Being best doesn't mean being better than anyone else, it means being the best you can be.; [a.] Laguna Niguel, CA

LIFTO, MATTHEW TAIT
[pen.] Tait; [b.] November 29, 1974, Augsburg, West Germany; [p.] George and Lois Lifto; [ed.] Berkner High School, Illinois Institute of Technology; [occ.] Physician Liaison for a rehabilitation facility; [oth. writ.] Several poems yet unpublished; [pers.] I describe my poetry as a reflection in a cracked mirror of myself; [a.] Dallas, TX

LIGHT, AMY L.
[b.] November 25, 1973, Winchester, VA; [p.] Eugene and Ethel Light; [ed.] Paw Paw High School, Paw Paw WV; [occ.] Inventory Control, Specialist/ Receiver - Giant Food; [hon.] National Honor Society; [oth. writ.] None published; [pers.] Follow your heart and live each day to the fullest because tomorrow's not guaranteed!; [a.] Seabrook, MD

LIKOVETZ, BESSIE
[b.] July 23, 1933, Electric Mills, MS; [p.] Lee and Pearl Lockley; [ch.] Kay Waters, Cynthia Pearson, Donna Rice; [ed.] High School; [occ.] Retired; [oth. writ.] Poems (none pub); [pers.] I let God control my writing. My thoughts are to try to make everyone aware of the miracles of our God.; [a.] Cottondale, AL

LILES, DAVID ANDREW
[pen.] D. Andrew Liles; [b.] February 25, 1964, Andalusia, AL; [p.] Bryan and Joanne Liles; [ed.] Graduate of Red Level H.S.; [occ.] USMC; [memb.] Fairmount Baptist Church, AWANA Director, Non-Commissioned Officers Association; [hon.] Red Level H.S. English Award; [oth. writ.] Several poems published for local publications; [pers.] Life is not as hard has we perceive it to be. Living is much easier, when we view it from a simple man's mountain. Hopefully, through my writing, I can help someone see the love and laughter of life through simplicity.; [a.] Red Level, AL

LINDE, LINDA GIBSON
[b.] May 13, 1967, Melbourne, FL; [p.] Virginia I. Robinson, Frank E. Robinson; [ch.] Robert S. Linde; [ed.] Melbourne High, Brevard Community College, Keiser College; [occ.] Writer, Paralegal; [pers.] I write from my heart. I wish to thank my parents for believing in me, and for their love.; [a.] Warrensville, NC

LINDSAY, ELIZABETH
[pen.] Betty Lindsay; [p.] Julia Lindsay, Albert C. Lindsay (deceased); [m.] Bernard Georgini; [ed.] Ridley Township High, Madernella Beauty College; [occ.] Owner thrift shop; [memb.] Resurrection life church; [oth. writ.] Several articles published in local newspapers; [pers.] Praise to "Jesus" who died on the cross in our place that we can receive Him. All that was His becomes ours. We exchange death for life eternal. All I know is "Jesus Christ" and Him crucified.; [a.] Folsum, PA

LINDSEY, DOROTHY L.
[pen.] "Lulu"; [b.] Houston, TX; [occ.] Regional Secretary; [oth. writ.] Local Newspaper; [pers.] I wrote this poem for my Dad. We were only able to see each other a couple of times a year and I presented this poem to him along with a big Teddy Bear....; [a.] Houston, TX

LINDSEY, NATILLE P.
[m.] Dr. Henry C. Lindsey, 1947, (deceased 1988); [ch.] John B. Lindsey, Denise L. Peek, Mark P. Lindsey, 7 grandchildren; [ed.] B.A., M.A. Ouachita Baptist University, Arkadelphia, Arkansas; [occ.] Own a porcelain doll shop where I teach doll making and sell supplies and the finished doll.; [a.] Atlanta, TX

LIPSHETZ, TERRY ALLEN
[b.] December 30, 1975, Staten Island, NY; [p.] Jeanne and Steven Lipshetz; [ed.] Sayreville War Memorial High School (1994), Sophomore at Monmouth University as a Journalism/Communications Major; [occ.] Student, Writing Tutor at Monmouth University; [memb.] Phi Eta Sigma (Freshman Honor Society), Zeta Phi Eta (National Professional Fraternity of Communication Arts and Sciences), "The Outlook" Student Run Paper of Monmouth University; [hon.] H.S. - Excellence in History, Contributions to H.S. paper "Echolites", Honor Role, Monmouth U. - Dean's List, Phi Eta Sigma, Zeta Phi Eta; [oth. writ.] Articles for "Echolites" (H.S. Paper), "The Outlook" (Monmouth U. Paper), "The News Tribune" and "Holmdel Reporter". Currently writing first novel, a work of Science fiction.; [pers.] I do not believe in unreachable goals. If I desire something strongly, I will pay my dues and do as much as I can to achieve those goals.; [a.] Sayreville, NJ

LISENBY, LOUISE V.
[pen.] Lu Lisenby; [b.] July 9, 1932, SC; [p.] Palmer and Mable Waters; [m.] Tom Lisenby; [ch.] Shirley, Andy and Ronald; [ed.] Spartanburg High, SC, Cambridge Academy, Fla., Lincoln School of Nursing, CA; [occ.] Retired Nurse; [memb.] Eastern Star, United Methodist Woman, American Cancer Association, Cancer Survivor Association; [hon.] Critical Care Nursing Award 1982; [oth. writ.] Several poems, but none published; [pers.] I believe that each God given child is a jewel to be nurtured with love, and not tarnished with hate. God is Love.

LOCASCIO, PAT
[b.] August 20, 1929; [p.] Wallace James Minshull and Olive McEnally Minshull; [m.] Charles R. LoCascio, September 14, 1968; [ch.] Diane E., Donna M., Jaime F. and Patrick E., Also six grandchildren - Yancey, Gabriel, Megan, Meghan, Sarah

and Elizabeth; [ed.] Maury and Norview H.S., St. Vincent DePaul School of Nursing, Old Dominion College (VA). Advanced PR and publications certifications.; [occ.] Political consultant, Real Estate Associate (MD); [memb.] Democratic Party, A.A. Society for Prevention of Cruelty to Animals (SPCA), World Wildlife Fund; [hon.] Virginia and Maryland newspapers associations awards and recognitions for reportorial, editorial and photographic excellence; [oth. writ.] Feature and news articles as reporter/editor, including Norfolk Virginian Pilot, Hagerstown Morning Herald, Annapolis (MD) Evening Capital, Baltimore News American; [pers.] I have never been lied to by an animal, would that I could say the same for humans. There is no substitute for truth! I can ask no more for mankind than that we understand and practice the precepts espoused in John Lennon's "Imagine."; [a.] Annapolis, MD

LOCKE, KEITH
[pen.] Hewkjah Keith Johnson; [b.] December 25, 1948, Texas; [p.] Joseph, Gladys; [ed.] MSC, Sociology Oxford Eng., MA, Business, St. Johns Manchester, England, BS Political Science, New Castle Upon Tyne England; [occ.] Self-employed, Entertainer; [memb.] Performing Rights Society, London, England; [oth. writ.] Articles for Guardian News Paper, Manchester England, Several short books/poems reflecting God's greatness - never published; [pers.] I write as God directs striving to awaken mankind to the majesty that is life. All truly great artists, writers, painters have influenced my philosophy.; [a.] Cincinnati, OH

LODER, DALE
[pen.] Dirty Sam; [b.] December 24, 1971, McPherson, KS; [p.] Carrol Loder, Ann Classen; [m.] Amy Loder, August 1, 1992; [ch.] Allana Kay, Blake Ethan; [ed.] 2 years Degree in Farm and Ranch Management Dodge City Community College; [occ.] Feedyard Pen Rider Ford Kansas; [hon.] Phi Theta Kappa, Dean's Honor Roll; [oth. writ.] I have 30-40 original poems that have not been published; [pers.] The majority of my poems are slightly exaggerated events that happen to me. They all involve cowboys, horses and cattles with a wild west flavor.; [a.] Spearville, KS

LOIN, JOSEPH
[b.] March 6, 1918, Wallingford; [p.] Catherine and Michael Lain; [ed.] Grammer and Trade School; [occ.] Landscape Gardener; [memb.] Wallingford Senior Center; [pers.] With a clear mind and love from my heart to do my very best.; [a.] Wallingford, CO

LOMBARDO, LAWRENCE
[b.] April 5, 1960, Queens, NY; [p.] Kenneth and Prudence Bartlett; [m.] Nydia Lombardo, October 25, 1986; [ch.] Allison Justine Lombardo; [ed.] BA Sociology (Law and Criminal Justice); [occ.] Retired-Sergeant N.Y.C. Transit Police; [memb.] Executive Assistant, N.Y.C. Retired, Transit Police Assoc., Lynbrook Citizens Party, Lynbrook Civic Assoc.; [hon.] 2 Dedication Awards (N.Y.C. Transit Police and Columbian Assoc.) 2 letters of Merit Transit Police, Cop of the Month 12/88; [oth. writ.] At Water Edge, Best Poems of 1996, Mists of Enchantment Windows of the Soul, A Delicate Balance Wall Thin Paradise, staff writer Walford Cazette, writing include N.Y. Daily News, News Day, Lynbrook, U.S.A. Herald; [pers.] We must never forget those men and women who gave the ultimate sacrifice for our freedom: Dedicated to Fallen Transit Police Officers; [a.] Lynbrook, NY

LONG, CATHY
[pen.] Cat; [b.] August 28, 1952, McCray Hospital; [p.] Jim and Catherine (Hile) Bell; [m.] Kennth Long, December 10, 1994; [ch.] Ryan; [ed.] Prairie Heights High School - 1971, and Ivy Tech College - 1993; [occ.] Teller/Campbell and Fetter Bank Customer Service Representative; [memb.] Delta Theta Tau Sorority - South Milford Methodist Church; [oth. writ.] "Life Is...", poem published by you and in local newspaper; [pers.] Life is God and God is life. And we need to put prayer back in schools and also the allegiance to the flag as well. Our children need discipline and love that God's word can give.; [a.] Kendalville, IN

LONG, KARIE E.
[b.] December 8, 1978, Concord, NC; [p.] Brenda and Darrell Long; [ed.] Currently a student at Mt. Pleasant High School, (Mt. Pleasant NC), planning on attending college (hopefully at UNC at Chapel Hill); [occ.] Student at Mount Pleasant High School; [memb.] Cold Springs UMYF Officer, Senior Girl Scout, Duke Talent Identification Program (TIP); [hon.] A North Carolina State Winner of the Young Authors Project two consecutive years, Girl Scout Silver Award and Leadership Award recipient; [pers.] I believe that life is like a Choose Your Own Adventure book...the decisions you make now determine your future.; [a.] Concord, NC

LOPEZ, MICHAEL
[b.] April 10, 1984, Tarzana, CA; [p.] Lillian Ferreri, Thomas Lopez; [ed.] St. Joseph Elementary Green Chimneys School; [occ.] Student; [memb.] Little League Baseball, J.V. Basketball, Club Scouts, D.A.R.E.; [hon.] Student of the Month, Honor Roll, Drug Awakeness Award; [a.] New Windsor, NY

LOPEZ, ROSA M.
[pen.] Rosa Lopez; [b.] October 25, 1964, El Salvador; [p.] Rufino A. Pimentel, Reina Rivera; [m.] Gene S. Lopez, July 21, 1985; [ch.] Roberto C. Lopez, Marvin A. Lopez and Sylvana J. Lopez; [ed.] Herbert Hoover High, Davis Applied Technology Center; [occ.] Mother; [pers.] I am so please to know that my words can travel, and bring enjoyment to those, I can not reach; [a.] Layton, UT

LORIAUX, BARBARA J.
[b.] June 22, 1951, Philadelphia, PA; [p.] Charles Dammer Sr. and Alma Carson Dammer; [m.] Robert C. Loriaux, September 23, 1975; [ed.] Hallahan High, Pierce Junior College, Immaculata College; [occ.] Bookkeeper for a Phila. Center-City Law Firm; [memb.] Holy Innocents St. Paul's Episcopal Church Choir, Bally's Health Club; [hon.] Phi Theta Kappa, Who's Who Among Students in American Jr. Colleges, Dean's List - Peirce, Full-tuition Scholarship at Immaculata, Magna Cum Laude; [oth. writ.] Unpublished; [pers.] The purpose of my writings is to share my emotions and experiences, particularly those of love and affection.; [a.] Philadelphia, PA

LOVE, DOROTHY HUNT
[pen.] Dorothy Lotton; [b.] May 16, 1926, Clarksville, AR; [p.] Dr. and Mrs. Earle Hunt; [m.] Louis Lawrence Love, March 23, 1945; [ch.] Pamela Dee Love, Tracy Love, Dorothy Louise Love; [ed.] High School, Columbia College, College of the Ozarks, University of Arkansas; [occ.] Burns International Security Person; [memb.] First United Methodist Church, PEO sisterhood, Beta Sigma Phi, was food service Director for Clarksville Public Schools; [hon.] (1) Clarksville Public Schools, School Board, (2) Home Companion Program, I was coordinator of this program, Coordinator of Mustard Seed Program Func.; [oth. writ.] Many poems never tried to have any published. My husband teased and made fun of poetry. So I just stopped for many years, until he died.; [pers.] My main "career" was just being "Mother" and tending to their needs: (1) Pammade Wycliffe Bible Translator, (2) Tracy Chirofractor, (3) Dottie 1st Lt. in Army, now a mother and three kids; [a.] Clarksville, AR

LOWE, BLAINE
[pen.] Rad Baxter; [b.] April 21, 1947, Salmon, ID; [p.] Dutch and Afton; [ch.] Shelley, Lisa, Robyn; [ed.] Traveling through all the thresholds this life presents, seems to override and validate most book learning; [occ.] Going just as fast as I can, making money for someone else; [hon.] Shelly, Lisa, Robyn; [pers.] Of the many things I have yet to learn, that I'm OK, and the small part I play in this show has already been reviewed and acclaimed; [a.] Orange, CA

LOWE, CARLA A.
[b.] November 24, 1972, Wiesbaden, West Germany; [p.] Harry Lowe, Linda Lowe; [ed.] Westover High School, University of Georgia; [occ.] Copy Editor, The Albany Herald; [memb.] Xi Delta Sorority, Gamma Sigma Sigma, Sorority, Richard B. Russell Leadership Fellow; [hon.] Who's Who Among American Colleges and Universities 1995; [oth. writ.] Article in Athens Magazine; [pers.] Life is a series of stretching oneself from comfort zones to discomfort zones in order to achieve greatness.; [a.] Albany, GA

LOWELL, KATHRYN
[pen.] Kate Lowell; [b.] August 19, 1958, Los Angeles; [p.] Robert Lowell, Jan Lowell; [m.] Divorced; [ed.] St. Georges English School, Rome, Italy, U. of Charleston, W. Va., B.S. Criminal Psychology; [occ.] Hairstylist/Nail Technician; [memb.] American Foundation for AIDS Research (AMFAR), American Cosmetology Assoc.; [hon.] Marie Overton Award (London University, 1976) For Highest Grade on English Literature "O" level.; [oth. writ.] Altogether, 80 poems, 3 in Italian published in an Italian Journal. A novel currently in submission in a NY publishing house.; [pers.] I abide simply by the credo of do unto others as you would have them do unto you. It works all the time.; [a.] Delray Beach, FL

LOWELL, MARITA J.
[b.] March 16, 1938, Norman, OK; [p.] Arthur and Mary Bragg; [m.] Percival M. Lowell Jr., September 25, 1959; [ch.] Augustus P. Lowell, Dana M. Lowell; [ed.] University High School, University of Oklahoma, Massachusetts General Hospital Sch, of Nursing; [occ.] RN - Cashier; [memb.] Arizona Early Day Gas Engine and Tractor Association; [hon.] Alpha Lambda Delta, Who's Who Among Health Care Professionals; [pers.] I've had a long standing love affair with nature and now live in the Arizona Desert where I can enjoy it - the sky is Huge! And the lightening spectacular.; [a.] Tonopah, AZ

LOY, J. E.
[b.] June 26, 1960, KY; [p.] Preston and Faye Loy; [ed.] Russel County High; [occ.] Machinest; [oth. writ.] Several poems with deep personal meanings; [pers.] I strive to write poems based on reality and not the false illusions society teaches us to believe.; [a.] Ferguson, KY

LUCAS, MARY GERENE
[pen.] Gerene; [b.] November 8, 1943, Pittsburg, KS; [p.] Henry and Martha Henneberg; [m.] Garrick J. Lucas, March 29, 1961; [ch.] Tim, Jenny, John, William; [ed.] High School, 2 years of College in General, Computer and Art courses; [occ.] Artist beginning Writer and Poet, I illustrate many of my works, too; [oth. writ.] Published one poem in another Anthology, called "Time". A group of my equestrian poems should be ready to publish by 1996, and several children's stories in poem form and regular story form are getting ready, too!; [pers.] Thank you for providing a place for a collection of works to be gathered. I love poetry and writing in general. I feel no one will every be lonesome if they can read and write.; [a.] Los Angeles, CA

LUMKES, DR. JANET M.
[b.] Momence, FL; [p.] Diana Mulder and John Lumkes; [ed.] Bachelors degrees in both English literature and psychology, Doctoral degree in psychology; [occ.] Private practice as doctor of psychology; [memb.] Sigma Tau Delta, National English Honorary Society, TSI CHI National Honors in Psychology Society, American Psychology Association, American Organ Guild, Christian Association for Psychological Studies; [hon.] Who's Who in America; [oth. writ.] Psychological cases and briefs; [pers.] I fondly wish to dedicate this poem to Chase Kimball, who told me I had a precious mind and soul, and proved to be my mentor.; [a.] Momence, IL

LUMPKIN, TRISTA
[pen.] Trista Lumpkin; [b.] July 4, 1982, Greenville, OH; [p.] Ted and Dianna Lumpkin; [ed.] 7th grade student at Ansonia Middle School, Ansonia, OH; [occ.] Student; [hon.] Recognized by the Rotary Club of Greenville for outstanding achievement, received a superior in Darke County Writing Contest, Honor Roll Student; [pers.] In my writings, I try to show that there is a good side and a bad side to everything.; [a.] Ansonia, OH

LUNEL, GINA MARIE
[b.] October 2, 1981; [p.] Roy and Carolyn Lunel; [ed.] Deer Canyon Elementary, Vineyard Jr. High, Bancho Cucamonga High School (Class of 1999); [occ.] Student; [hon.] 1. Grand Prize for my book, The Rose, at the Book Affaire, 2. A medal for the California Junior Scholarship Federation, 3. Many writing awards; [oth. writ.] A book called The Rose belongs with my poem. It won the school's Grand Prize Ribbon for Young Adult Fiction.; [a.] Altaloma, CA

LYKINS, RYAN
[pen.] Ryan Lykins; [b.] April 7, 1973, Panama City, FL; [p.] Rick and Cindy Lykins; [ed.] Eastern High School, Louisville, Ky., University of Kentucky, Lexington Ky.; [occ.] Aspiring CPA and Entrepreneur; [hon.] Dean's List, Beta Alpha Psi; [pers.] We are limited by what we are taught. Only through unlearning can we truly free our minds.; [a.] Lexington, KY

LYNCH, ALBERTA S.
[b.] February 20, 1927, Lawrence Co., PA; [p.] Charles B. Snyder, Mary Bartle Snyder; [m.] William M. Lynch, June 20, 1964; [ch.] Jon Thomas, Joseph Michael; [ed.] Wanpum High School, New Castle Business College; [occ.] Retired Legal Secretary; [oth. writ.] A collection of lyrics entitled "23 Songs by Alberta S. Lynch" under copyright of the Library of Congress.; [a.] Glenn Dale, MD

LYNCH, JOSEPH C.
[pen.] J. E. Lynch; [b.] September 6, 1971, Springfield; [p.] Edmond J. and Sandra L.; [ed.] Agawam High, Springfield Technical Community College; [occ.] Shipping Clerk, Southworth Paper Co. Agawam, Ma.; [memb.] Phi Theta Kappa, International Honor Society; [hon.] National Dean's List '94-'95; [pers.] The ability to influence the thoughts and perceptions of others, through the written word, is the greatest tool of civilization. Television is ephemeral, writing is enduring; [a.] Agawam, MA

LYONS, JEAN
[pen.] Jonett Lowell; [b.] October 25, 1977, Walterboro, SC; [p.] Bernard and Darlene Lyons; [ed.] Walterboro High School Graduate; [occ.] Entering Clemson University; [memb.] Future Teachers of America, History Club, Spirit Club, Modeling Club; [hon.] National Spanish Award, All American Scholar, Citizenship Award, Academic Letter; [oth. writ.] Several Love Poems; [pers.] All of my poems come from deep within me and reflect my true feelings.; [a.] Walterboro, SC

MABB, JOHNDRUE
[pen.] Johndrue Mabb; [b.] October 13, 1959, Hudson NY; [p.] Leon Robert Sr., Rita Orbon; [ch.] Johndrue Pauel Mabb (6 yrs), Heather Lee Mabb (4 yrs); [ed.] Ichabod Crane High School, 1978 Dutchess College Working Toward Associate Liberal Arts Poughkeepsie N.Y.; [occ.] New York State Education Dept. (Operations); [oth. writ.] Many others not yet published; [pers.] Inspired by my girl Rene Rovere and my two children. Poetry an expression of life and inner self is only touched when shared by others.; [a.] Pleasant Valley, NY

MABERY, MARILYNE V. MOYERS
[pen.] Marilyne V. Mabery; [b.] July 6, 1952, Clayton, NM; [p.] Jim and Betty Moyers; [m.] Ken R. Mabery, September 5, 1971; [ed.] BS 1972, BA 1993, MS 1995/6; [occ.] Writer - College Instructor; [memb.] Southwest Writer's Workshop 78-Present, Archaelogical Society of New Mexico 1980-1996, Too many to list; [hon.] Who's Who Amer. Univ. and Colleges 172, 1993, 1995/6, Gallup Film Festival - 1st Documentary Award; [oth. writ.] 3 National Park Service Books, 7 Romances Novels (Unpublished), 3 Science Fiction Novels, 6 BBS Documentaries, 2 Native American Teaching Story Bks, BI-Monthly News Paper Columnist, Poetry and articles in National and International Magazines and Newspapers since 1965.; [pers.] I am a conservationist and have worked and lived with the Navajo, Zuni, and Acoma peoples during the past 20 years. I find their wholism perspective embraces my own and makes life a path of conrtinal change and beauty.; [a.] Grants, NM

MACDONALD, MAUREEN
[b.] May 13, 1985, Boston; [p.] William and Geraldine MacDonald; [ed.] 5th grader, Richard J. Murphy Elementary, Dorchester MA; [occ.] Student; [hon.] Alice J. Casey Award for achievement and conduct; [pers.] I wrote this poem in memory of my Aunt Loretta who has a very special place in my heart!; [a.] Dorchester, MA

MACK, HILDRED P.
[b.] February 11, 1933, Brooklyn, NY; [p.] Redmond Peyton, Nancy Peyton; [m.] Harry C. Mack (Deceased), May 25, 1957; [ch.] Kenneth M. Peyton, Kim T. Mack, Kevin C. Mack, Kris N. Mack, Kelly J. Mack; [ed.] Franklin K. Lane H.S., City College of New York, B.S., M.S.; [occ.] Elementary School Teacher, George E. Wibecan School, Brooklyn, New York; [hon.] Dean's List; [oth. writ.] A Lonely Lament, unpublished; [pers.] I try to reflect my African ancestry into my writing and remember who I really am. They are a legacy for a (9) grandchildren. I have been influenced by another poet, "Maya Angelou".; [a.] Brooklyn, NY

MACK JR., RICHARD
[b.] May 31, 1939, Philadelphia, PA; [p.] Richard Mack, Dolores Mack; [m.] Divorce; [ch.] Richard III, Kyle Jason, Scott Avery; [ed.] Bok High, York College, T.C. Columbia University; [occ.] Anthropologist, Sophie Davis School of Bio Med City College; [oth. Writ.] Bittersweet In Press; [pers.] I seek to express the bittersweet human condition that is life with it's ups and downs.; [a.] Hollis, NY

MACKINTOSH, STELLA M.
[pen.] Stella M. Mackintosh; [b.] February 27, 1914, Nairn, United Kingdom; [p.] Enid and Arthur K. MacLean (dec.); [m.] William E. Mackintosh; [ed.] In UK and France until age 19; [occ.] Housewife; [memb.] California Federation of Chaparall Poets; [oth. writ.] Other poems and children's stories; [a.] Riverside, CA

MACPHERSON, DAVID K.
[b.] February 19, 1956, Port Huron, MI; [p.] Kenneth and Helen MacPherson; [m.] Hyon Y. MacPherson, June 7, 1982; [ch.] Adam Kenneth; [ed.] Bad Ave High School, MI; [occ.] Video Store Owner; [memb.] Parkesburg Area Business Association; [oth. writ.] Self Published Children's Poems; [a.] Parkesburg, PA

MACQUEEN, CHER
[b.] March 20, 1952, Kansas City, MO; [p.] Peggy E. Turner; [ed.] BS - U of New York 1993, AA - LA Valley College 1982; [occ.] News/Sports Specialist (On Air Talent), Armed Forces Radio and TV (DOD); [memb.] American Business Women's Assn., Disabled American Veterans, Life Member; [hon.] Intellectual of the Year and Woman of the Year, International Who's Who of Intellectuals - 1992, 2000 Notable American Woman 1991 and 1992, Directory of Distinguished Leadership - 1992; [oth. writ.] Story sketches and outlines, other poems - none published previously.; [pers.] I've been writing poetry and short stories since elementary school. Hope to have more of my work published.; [a.] Burbank, CA

MADDI, MICHAEL
[b.] March 28, 1952, Binghamton, NY; [p.] Nicholas and Arlene Maddi; [ch.] Gina and Ryan Maddi; [ed.] Susquehanna Valley High, Broome Community College and SUNY at Binghamton; [occ.] Software Engineer; [pers.] The inspiration for "When You're

Not Near", came from the love of my life Janet Sheppard and was written for her on May 8, 1995.; [a.] Sarasota, FL

MAGEE JR., HENRY
[b.] October 30, 1948, Glasgow, Scotland; [occ.] Respiratory Therapist; [hon.] United States Citizenship; [pers.] (Visualize World Peace), I am an Ex Marine and a Viet-nam Vet.; [a.] San Diego, CA

MAGIED, LUQMAN A.
[b.] January 16, 1941, New York; [p.] Ali Bishara, Gertrude (Mother); [m.] Kemer Abdurahman, July 04, 1992; [ch.] 2 Boys, 2 Girls; [ed.] New York Institute of Technology (Biology Major), New School for Social Research NY, Visual Arts New York; [occ.] Artist, Designer for Volt information Sciences Syosset, New York; [memb.] American Museum of Natural History New York

MALABAG, CANDINA ANN
[pen.] Akuna Mutata; [b.] November 18, 1070, Oakland, CA; [p.] Sylvester and Carol Malabag; [m.] Michael DelaRiva Jr.; [ch.] Michael Gianni Castillo (7), Michael Frank Dela Riva (2); [ed.] Alameda High School Grad., also studying Health and Fitness at College of Alameda; [occ.] Student, full time mother and soon to be wife.; [hon.] Awards: Queen of Alameda for 1 yr. (7 mths.), Most Creative and Most Artistic In Junior High "1982-1983", 1st place "1983" Jesse Owens Olympics; [oth. writ.] Other personal poems: "Just For You" written for my Fiance, who I owe most of my thanks to and also "Was This Lesson Truly Learned" written for a close friend and his family.; [pers.] I would like to give a special thank also to my friends Donna and Fitz and my little brothers Joe, Jerry, and Freddy for giving me the strength to believe in myself and for them believing in me. I wish to share the knowledge I've learned from my lonely and confused past with the children of today and also my own. Hoping it will be of great use in keeping them from having to experience the pain and suffering themselves. Then I will know my struggle was not for nothing.; [a.] Alameda, CA

MALONE, ANTIONETTE IDELL
[pen.] Toni Malone; [b.] May 23, 1955, Saint Louis, MO; [p.] John C. Sampson, Pernecie Sampson; [ch.] Shaundra Danielle Malone; [occ.] Training Administrator Purina Hills, Inc.; [pers.] I reflect passion and tenderness in my writings. I am inspired by God and influenced by life.; [a.] East Saint Louis, IL

MANNING, KATHLEEN ELIZABETH
[b.] August 17, 1952, Ayer, MA; [p.] Mable and Avery Emerson; [m.] John Frederick Manning, August 23, 1992; [ch.] Holly, Shannon, Jody, John, Benjamin, Gregory and Ann; [pers.] Writing is a unique and beautiful way to express ones feelings for it comes from the inner depths of our souls.; [a.] Lyons Falls, NY

MANUEL, REV. DENNIS H.
[b.] November 24, 1934, Terre Haute, IN; [p.] Evelyn Robertson, Carl Manuel; [m.] Viola R. Manuel, May 27, 1977; [ch.] LaRita Manuel, Crystal Walden, Rhonda Phillips; [ed.] Wiley High School, Ivy Tech, Indiana State, Industrial Vocational School; [occ.] Retired; [memb.] Senior Citizens, Kitchen Band also, Pastor, Chaplian Light House Mission Board; [hon.] Prison Fellowship, Leader Development for Supervisors, Member of Mt. of Olive St. Convention, Certificate of Ordination.; [oth. writ.] Lyrics for Songs, Book of Poems; [pers.] Through the inspiration of God I like to write poems and songs.; [a.] Terre Haute, IN

MARASA, CYNTHIA MORRIS
[pen.] Cynthia Marasa; [b.] Los Angeles, CA; [p.] Chester Morris, Suzanne Redderman; [m.] S. Michael Marasa, April 21, 1972; [ch.] 6 Sons; [ed.] Beverly Hills High School plus Extensive College Courses, Secretarial College.; [occ.] Retired; [oth. writ.] Stories and poems written for the enjoyment of my family and friends.; [a.] Granada Hills, CA

MARCHAND, SUSAN
[b.] January 2, 1945, Norfold, VA; [p.] Ben McClure, Helen McClure; [m.] Henri Marchand, December 21, 1968; [ch.] Anneliese, Celine, Eric; [ed.] Chateau Beau Cedre, Switzerland, Mary Mount Int'l School, France, postgraduate Program Amer. School, Switzerland; [occ.] Charity Work, Russian Student; [memb.] Amer. Wives of European, NS - Paris, France, Centre, Puschkin - Paris, France; [oth. writ.] A collection of poetry, never published.; [pers.] I believe in the need for "Family" more and more in today's world.; [a.] New Canaan, CT

MARDRES, OTIS A.
[pen.] Brian Marders; [b.] May 21, 1965, Washington, DC; [p.] Robert Mardres and Helen Durrer; [ed.] William Monroe High; [occ.] Data Entry, Asst. Manager - Direc Tech; [pers.] Love is the key to a united world. When we can get past race and color, we can finally know paradise.; [a.] Gaithersburg, MD

MARIA, ANNETTE
[pen.] Annette Maria; [b.] 4-22-44, Irvington, NJ; [p.] Rose Stevens, Step Father Daniel Cicalease; [m.] Widow; [ch.] Thomas E. Buccine, Jr., Damian J. Buccine, Scott J. Buccine; [ed.] Some college - also attending The Clayton College of Natural Healing. Dr. of Natropathy; [occ.] "Consultant"; [memb.] Domestic Abuse Rape Crisis Center, Portland Ambulance Corp, Portland, PA; [hon.] Domestic Abuse Rape CC Vol. of the Year from 1983 through 1986; [oth. writ.] "Hello Child" published in Our World's Favorite Poems, Who's Who in Poetry, and Whispers in the Wind; [pers.] Today - "There are no slaves but the slave you make of yourself--"; [a.] Bangor, PA

MARINO, CAROL
[pen.] Carolann Marino; [b.] December 12, Brooklyn, NY; [p.] Rose and Joseph Marino; [memb.] Girl Scouts of Greater New York; [oth. writ.] Words and Music for many songs, including Spanish translations for future publication and recording. Collection of Poems for publication by Dorrance Publishing.; [pers.] Though my gift from God in my writing of music and poetry, my message to all is: "The World is very simple if we open our eyes, created with such beauty, in Perfect Balance so that all can survive". God Blessed Everyone.

MARION, JULIA
[b.] January 28, 1980, Canton, OH; [p.] Cheryl Marion; [ed.] Attending Sandy Valley High, 10th Grade, I will be 16 on January 28.; [pers.] We should all do our part in preserving the animals and forests. Death and extinction are forever, but endangerment, is a condition that can be resolved.; [a.] Waynesburg, OH

MARKS, RITA
[pen.] Rita Marks; [b.] May 31, 1953, San Mateo; [p.] Joseph and Sarah Marks; [m.] Divorce; [ch.] Lazet Howard, Tanesha Howard; [ed.] Canada College, Redwood City, CA AA College of Norte Dame, Belmont, CA - expect Computer Science degree in 1997; [occ.] Sr. Admin., Asst./Purchasing Agent at Sun Microsystems, Inc., Mountain View, CA.; [memb.] Member of Pilgrim Baptist Church in San Mateo, CA; [hon.] Dean's list - twice, American Business Women's Scholarship, Redwood City Citizen's Scholarship, Canada College Scholarship, CA Student Aid Grant, Bay Area Urban League Scholarship.; [oth. writ.] I have several new writings. None have been published. The titles are: "Waiting, What Is Love, At The Club, and My Heart."; [pers.] When I write, I write from the heart. I want to show feeling, motivation, and compassion to others along with encouragement. I thank Mr. Gary Webb for inspiration. I thank my family for their love, and God for creativity.; [a.] East Palo Alto, CA

MARLETT, ROBERT
[b.] July 11, 1973, Martinsville, IN; [p.] David and Nancy Marlett; [m.] Karen Sue Marlett, April 24, 1924; [ch.] Bethasy Sue (2 yrs.), Michael William (1 yr.); [oth. writ.] Many Poems such as: "The Everglades Daughter of the Wild", "Robin Started Day", "The Death of a Poet", and "They Thought I Was Brave."; [pers.] If a verse does not create within the reader the emotions of the author - It is merely a nursery rhyme. Poetry isn't merely literature. It's emotions in print.; [a.] Jacksonville, FL

MARNELL, DAVE
[pen.] Dave Marnell; [b.] May 6, 1978, NJ; [p.] John and Fran Kelly; [ed.] Still in High School; [oth. writ.] Several unpublished poems; [pers.] I like to write poems during boring classes in school. Hope to make a career of my writings.; [a.] Cherry Hill, NJ

MAROTTA, MARIE ELAINE
[b.] May 6, 1942, USA, New York City; [p.] Thomas and Connie Guinto; [m.] Jack Marotta; [ch.] Anthony and Thomas; [ed.] Completed High School; [occ.] Bookkeeper

MARSAC, LACEY
[b.] September 18, 1976, Long Beach, CA; [p.] Eileen Marsac; [ed.] St. Joseph High School, University of Southern California; [hon.] California Scholarship Federation Sealbearer, National Science Foundation, Young Scholar; [pers.] Everyone has poetry in their soul. Some of us just choose to write it down.; [a.] Long Beach, CA

MARTELLI, ROCCO J.
[b.] November 12, 1953, Niagara Falls, NY; [p.] Silvio and Lucy Martelli; [m.] Chiara Martelli, January 9, 1976; [ch.] Rocco, Joseph, Michelle, Christina; [ed.] Niagara County Community College; [occ.] Maintenance Worker; [oth. writ.] Many songs and poems, never submitted for publication.; [pers.] As a teenager in the 60s, I was greatly influenced by the Beatles, and still believe in peace and love.; [a.] Niagara Falls, NY

MARTIN, CARLA LAWRENCE
[pen.] Carla Lawrence; [b.] September 18, 1969; [p.] Sandra McKnight; [ch.] Briony "Kyrie" Lewis; [ed.] San Juan Senior Comprehensive School San Juan,

Trinidad W.I., St Hugh's High J.A.; [occ.] Nursing Assistant; [hon.] For general Proficiency and History in the CXC examination, 2nd Prize in School Poetry Competition at San Juan Camp.; [oth. writ.] I have written several poems and is striving to complete a book of poems.; [pers.] Words carefully put together create a most artistic picture as beautiful as an artist with his canvas and brush.; [a.] East Elmhurst Queens, NY

MARTIN, LEE
[pen.] Lee Martin; [b.] July 22, 1956, Mississippi; [p.] Ida B. Jordan; [m.] Elizabeth Martin, May 13, 1987; [ch.] Dondeleak Martin; [ed.] High School, one year off college; [occ.] Assy module; [pers.] Every person is like a Peacock, "But", some see only one color. "Yet", we all cannot fly.; [a.] Niles, MI

MARTIN, LORETTA
[pen.] Lu; [b.] July 8, 1984, Brooklyn, NY; [p.] Vincent and Ingrid Martin; [ed.] William Hughley Elementary - Grade 5. Moving up to Grade 6 in September.; [hon.] 1. Won best essay competition in my school, received an award. 2. Received many other awards for writing in my school.; [oth. writ.] Poems printed in my school's year book. Birthday Cards for family members.

MARTIN, MICHAEL A.
[b.] February 29, 1940, Akron, OH; [p.] Beatrice M. Gorcoff, Albert L. Martin; [ed.] 4 Yrs. College Equivilant - H.S. (College Entrance Boards Test), graduate - Passed College GED - received two Major Educational Awards in U.S. Air Force/Strategic Air Command - U.S. Air force Europe Conspicuous Award; [occ.] Professional Security Officer; [memb.] Master Mason-32nd Degree, Scottish Rite Mason and Shriner - Member Post #8 (American Legion) - Distinguished Member of The International Society of Poets.; [hon.] Presidential Security in U.S. Air FOrce - received several Editor's Choice Awards for Outstanding Poetry from The National Library of Poetry.; [oth. writ.] Published Author (Book) - "Atlantis Secrets Revealed" - Published Poet. Lyric Writer for Hill Top Records who recorded "To Eva My Love"/ In Best Poems of 1995. Published Poet by The National Library of Poetry - Poems In Dance On The Horizon - Echoes of Yesterday Best Poems of 1995 - Beyond the Stars - Walk Through Paradise - A Delicate Balance. Published Book: Atlantis Secrets Revealed - Published in Las Vegas, Nv. by Gorman Inc. Hill Top Records featured "To Eva My Love" in their Album "America".; [pers.] To strive for perfection in all I do. I especially want to make my Book: Atlantis Secrets Revealed very successful and to write the very best lyrics for songs. I do write book(s) - poetry - lyrics for songs.; [a.] Las Vegas, NV

MARTINEZ, RALPH W.
[b.] June 16, 1923, MA; [p.] John A. and Ella L. Martinez; [m.] Ruby S. Martinez died Nov. 25, 1994, August 26, 1946; [ch.] Robert L. Martinez, Ronald W. and Carol A. Lovelady; [ed.] High School, Carmel High School, Carmel, NY; [occ.] Retired, Melting Supt.; [memb.] Lifetime Member National Management Ass., Masonic Lodge, Easter Star (Past Patron); [oth. writ.] Several other poems; [pers.] I want to be able to help my fellow men to cope with the world problems and leave it a better place to live in.

MARTTINEN, ARJA
[b.] August 20, 1951, Helsinki, Finland; [p.] Mirjam and Aage Asola; [m.] Jaakko Marttinen, June 30, 1979; [ch.] Mikke, Kari and Kristina; [ed.] Graduated from Munkkivuoren Yhteiskoulu, Helsinki; [occ.] Flight Attendant with Delta Air Lines, Inc.; [oth. writ.] Only recently I have started to write yearly chronicles and some poems; [pers.] I want to keep a positive attitude and remember what is important in life. My motto is - If there is a will, there is a way.; [a.] Pleasantville, NY

MASCARO, NANCY C.
[b.] June 25, 1956, Lansdale, PA; [p.] Carol and Charles Jenkins; [m.] William Mascaro, September 9, 1978; [ch.] Heather Nicole and Ashley Lynne; [pers.] This poem was written for, and is dedicated to the 1995 Confirmation Class of Sanctuary United Methodist Church, North Wales, PA; [a.] Lansdale, PA

MASCHINO, JO NOBLE
[b.] December 3, 1942, Long Island, NY; [p.] Frank (dec.) and Josephine Pandolfo; [m.] Robert Maschino, May 11, 1985; [ch.] Dianajean Noble and Jennifer Jo Noble; [ed.] H. Frank Carey H.S., Franklin Square, L.I., N.Y.; [occ.] Owner, Val-Pak of Suffold County, Direct Mail Marketing Company; [memb.] Past Editor United Methodist Church Publications, Retired Licensed, and Real Estate Broker, Suffolk County, New York; [hon.] Top Production Awards, Century 21 Long Island Brokers Council, 1980-84, National Honor Society 1960; [oth. writ.] "Fires of Life", published in Great Contemporary Poems, 1978, Little Pegasus Press; [pers.] I have accumulated "thoughts" since my high school years - and put them on paper as reflections, a pool of memories precious enough to record.; [a.] Saint James, NY

MASON, TODD
[b.] March 17, 1984, Williamsburg, VA; [p.] June and Morris Mason; [ed.] 5th Grade Student at Matthew Whaley Elementary School, Williamsburg, VA; [a.] Williamsburg, VA

MASTRANGELO, DUANE
[pen.] Dwayne Range; [b.] May 27, 1930, Trenton, NJ; [p.] Albert and Jennie Mastrangelo; [ed.] T.C., Trenton, N.J. High Sch., N.Y.C., and Rensselaez, N.Y., College, Catholic Univ., Wash., D.C.; [occ.] Retired Clergyman; [memb.] Missouri Poets and Friends, The National Federation of State Poetry Societies, EFA St. Louis; [pers.] The most important poems for me, is one I'm working on presently. Soon this too will be left undone, for another more worthwhile one.; [a.] Dittmer, MO

MATHENY, JENNIFER L.
[b.] February 13, 1967, Danville, IL; [p.] Sandra Waggoner and John McCarty; [m.] James Matheny, May 28, 1988; [ch.] Amethyst Lynn and James Dalton; [hon.] Editor's Choice Award, Outstanding Performance Awards in Music; [oth. writ.] I dream of a beach in Songs on the Wind, just one more time in The Best Poets of 1996, and other unpublished poems; [pers.] I have written poems for several years now. Memories and music have greatly influenced me in my writings.; [a.] Paris, IL

MATHIS, NED L.
[b.] January 18, 1939, Oxford, FL; [p.] Curtis and Cleavie Mathis; [m.] Alice Marie Mathis, February 18, 1972; [ed.] Fort Meade High School, Fort Meade Florida; [occ.] Industrial Electrician; [memb.] Church: Grace Worship Center, Winter Garden Florida; [oth. writ.] Songs and poems performed or published locally; [pers.] My writing is all based on my Christian faith and my daily walk with a rising Savior; [a.] Winter Garden, FL

MATHIS, STEPHEN L.
[pen.] Stephen Mathis; [b.] October 27, 1947, Columbus, NE; [p.] Ken L. and Clarice J. Mathis; [ed.] BA Milligan College, Tenn., M.Ed. Univ. of Cincinnati; [occ.] Former teacher, counselor, theatrical manager, and sales management. Experienced as real estate free appraiser. Sales Manager.; [memb.] Director, Beverly Hills Board of Realtors Member, West Hollywood Chamber of Commerce; [hon.] Phi Delta Kappa, Listed in "Who's Who In California", a former candidate for City Council; [oth. writ.] "Don't Blent In" - business book manuscript, "The Grains of Paradise" - co-author of original screenplay, various poems and lyrics including: "Life Is A Cycle", "Save Tomorrow", "I thought You Knew", "Diary of An American", "What's Your Addiction, Baby?", "Celebrate Your Special Day", "A Traveler's Song", "Love Rock"; [pers.] I enjoy writing poems and song lyrics.; [a.] Los Angeles, CA

MAXWELL, PHYLLIS A.
[b.] March 8, 1949, Winnemucca, Nevada; [p.] Mr. and Mrs. Jack Harrer; [m.] George Maxwell Sr., October 18, 1969; [ch.] George Maxwell Jr., Bonnie Maxwell; [ed.] 12th Grade and Cosmetology School; [occ.] Cosmetologist; [oth. writ.] Just alot of poems I've never had any published or even tried.; [pers.] I feel every poem I write comes only with the help of our Lord. Without him I could not write a word.; [a.] Carson City, NV

MAY, SUZANNE T.
[pen.] Sue T. May; [b.] October 28, 1916, Hebron, ND; [p.] Konstantine Wachtler (Deceased); [m.] Burton F. May, August 15, 1942; [ch.] Allan A. May, Lyle J. May; [ed.] Self Educated - Grade school only, Rosecrucian, and student of all religions, and races - on my own time.; [occ.] Retired - Housewife and Homeowner; [memb.] Non at present. Unity, student, love, metaphysics and mystical. Studies - any and all comparative religious studies. Born Roman Catholic, (Love All).; [hon.] The best honor is to be born in America, and be free to be as one, believes and lives. The Lambs Book of Life is the greatest honor. Amen.; [oth. writ.] Essays of and or, on various subjects, some are critical. Write mostly on Spiritual and Religious subjects. Poetry Form, some on Political Issues.; [pers.] Will be 79 on Oct. 28, 1995. Known off 3d world poverty in a first world country. Learn by life experiences. School of hard knocks. "Love Learning", all subjects, student of all.; [a.] Chicago, IL

MAYES, ROBERT WILLIAM
[pen.] Bob Mayes; [b.] September 7, 1960, Sidney, NY; [p.] Marilyn E., William L.; [m.] Michaelene Mayes, January 13, 1993; [ch.] Lisa, Billy; [ed.] High School Diploma, 6 College Credits; [occ.] Mechanical Inspector; [memb.] N.A.B.A. (No. Amer. Baseball Assoc.); [oth. writ.] Many unpublished poems. Letter to Baseball Digest. Two quotes in local newspaper.; [pers.] I write poems of diversity. I try to reflect all moods, consequences and upbeat aspects of life. I believe I am an articulate gifted poet. (Modest too).; [a.] Kirkwood, NY

MAYO, AKIMA
[b.] May 2, 1973, Newark, NJ; [p.] Linda Mayo, Albert Mayo; [ed.] David Brearley High School, Essex County College; [memb.] Imani Baptist Church of Christ, Opportunity Project of NJ, Dial, Inc.; [pers.] I believe the most beautiful poetry is not read, it is experienced.; [a.] East Orange, NJ

MCALLISTER, SUSAN
[b.] January 3, 1934, Dayton, OH; [m.] John W. McAllister, December 3, 1955; [ch.] Miami, Matthew, Timothy; [ed.] Miami University; [memb.] Holy Trinity Church; [oth. writ.] Currently working on a manuscript for our children and grandchildren about their heritage.; [a.] Waverly, OH

MCBROOM, ANNE LAURIE
[pen.] Laurie Mc; [b.] August 29, 1935, Yoakum, TX; [m.] Joe W. McBroom, June, 1983; [ch.] Robby, Leah; [occ.] Housewife; [pers.] Novels and songs speak to the heart..... Poetry whispers to the soul..... Simple words...poetic phrases of everyday life (are the best).; [a.] Mansfield, TX

MCCARTOR, ANDREA
[b.] July 12, 1982, Mount Vernon, GA; [p.] Mr. and Mrs. James McCartor; [ed.] Attending Anacortes Middle School, West View Elementary - Burlington, 7 years; [hon.] Citizenship, Student of the Month, Safety Patrol, DARE Drug Awareness Honor Program; [oth. writ.] School Newspaper and alot of poems never entered or published; [pers.] I like to make people laugh through my poems, some of my other poems are very real I'm very Athletic.; [a.] Anacortes, WA

MCCARTY, PATRICIA
[pen.] Patricia McCarty; [b.] January 4, 1938, Adrian, MI; [p.] Ernest and Eva Spence; [m.] Dale McCarty, June 17, 1956; [ch.] Four handsome sons, three good looking grandsons, and two lovely granddaughters.; [ed.] High School Graduate of Adrian, (Michigan) High School 1956; [occ.] Homemaker and inspector of screw machine products of M.S. Mfg. of Hudson, Mich. 29 years seniority.; [memb.] Jehovah Witness-Addison Mich. Congregation; [oth. writ.] I've written short stories for my children, poems and pet obituaries for myself.; [pers.] I have brought into this world, four marvelous sons, whom I am very proud of, and I am now grandmother to their beautiful children whom I am very proud of too.; [a.] Hudson, MI

MCCLAIN, ROY
[pen.] Roy McClain; [b.] Jan. 5, 1982, Pncla, FL; [p.] Kenny & Marion McClain; [ed.] Elementary - Roy, Kenny & Marion - High School - Howard High School, John High School; [oth. writ.] Love, Friendship, Giving, Hate, Clothes, School, Drinks, Wizard, Your Love, American; [pers.] I love to write poems only when they come to my head.; [a.] Mount Pleasant, TN

MCCLEESE, AMY
[b.] October 2, 1984, Rowan Co., KY; [p.] Donald and Vickie McCleese; [ed.] 5th Grade Flemingsburg, KY Elem.; [occ.] Student; [memb.] Mason County Church of Christ, YMCA; [hon.] Selected for Exceptionally Intelligent Class.; [oth. writ.] Several L poems and short stories.; [pers.] I enjoy making poems and stories and hope to have more published in the future.; [a.] Flemingsburg, KY

MCCLINTOCK, JANET M.
[pen.] Jan McClintock; [b.] June 6, 1936, Ashtabula, OH; [p.] Charles Carey, Verna Carey; [m.] Malcolm H. McClintock, June 12, 1954; [ch.] Gregory Scott, Susan Eileen; [ed.] Ashtabula High School; [occ.] Housewife; [memb.] "Concerned Women for America"; [hon.] Golden Poet 1990 and Award of Merit Certificates with honorable mention from "World of Poetry".; [pers.] Most of my poetry is based on a wide variety of thought - provoking subjects from true personal experience or observation.; [a.] Saluda, NC

MCCOMAS, ANNE
[b.] August 29, 1983, San Antonio, TX; [p.] Christine McComas; [ed.] Cambridge Elementary School; [occ.] Student; [pers.] My inspiration comes from my loved ones and the world around me. I love writing and I am grateful for the encouragement of my family.; [a.] San Antonio, TX

MCCOY, SHARON ANN
[b.] January 11, 1974, Rome, GA; [p.] Ann and Doyle McCoy; [ed.] Armuchee High School, Floyd College, Roffler Hairstyling College; [occ.] Hairstylist; [memb.] Earth Island Institute, International Marine, Mammal Project; [oth. writ.] Wrote columns for both High School and College newspapers; [pers.] Protect the Earth. It is only loaned to us for a short period of time. The ocean is the giver of life!; [a.] Armuchee, GA

MCCRAE, BUFFIE S.
[b.] January 19, 1978, Tifton, GA; [p.] Linda Tyler and Kenneth Boone; [ed.] Valdosta High School Graduation Spring 1996; [occ.] Full time High School Student; [memb.] Future Business, Leaders of America, Olympic Dream Team, Model United Nations; [hon.] Governor's Honors Program, Youth Ambassador Olympic Dream Team, Who's Who Among American High School Students, National Youth Leadership Forum on Law and Constitution; [pers.] Do not be weary when doing good, for at the proper time you will reap a harvest if you believe.; [a.] Valdosta, GA

MCCRANIE, COURTNEY
[b.] November 4, 1982; [p.] Lury and Wayne McCranie; [ed.] Seventh Grade at Simpson Middle School; [hon.] 1st place in the Science Fair, art awards, 1st and second place in Track; [pers.] I was lonely and sad and I wanted to write at dawn, but then I started to think about how great life is, and to grow up and get old.; [a.] Flat Rock, MI

MCCRAY, MAGGIE
[pen.] Gods Messenger; [b.] March 1, 1937, North Carolina; [p.] Rosie and Allen Sanders; [m.] Robert McCray, March 13, 1955; [ch.] Fran, Jeff, Mae, Teresa Clair, Nina; [ed.] High School; [occ.] Housewife; [memb.] 1st Baptist Church of Deer Park; [hon.] Deaconess Bible Class; [oth. writ.] Mother's Love, a father to respect; [pers.] The holy spirit inspired me to write the poems that I have written to share with others the joy of Jesus.; [a.] Deerpark, NY

MCDONALD, DIANN SENGLE
[pen.] Diann St. McDonald; [b.] December 22, 1943, Alexandra, LA; [p.] (Major) Mr. and Mrs. Richard M. Sengle; [m.] William M. Thornhill, July 21, 1961, William Henry McDonald (Divorce) July 22, 1976; [ch.] Joy Diann, William Henry McDonald, Wom Mark, Stewart Edwin, Jason Eric, Susan M. Goode; [ed.] Bolton High School top 15% Academic Class 1961, Certificate for Children's Writing Institute of Children's Literature in Rodding Ridge, Conn. College Semesters at Louisiana College and LSUA; [occ.] Home-Based Leather Shop Artist, Writer, Sales; [memb.] Horseshoe Southern Baptist Church. I am first Soprano in Church Concert Choir and Librarian, Twenty Years in Girl Scouts of America between Central Louisiana and Mile High, and Rocky Mountain, GS Councils; [hon.] Reporter for Louisiana for 1959, Girl Scout International Round up in Colorado Springs, Colorado. National Honor Society - Senior H.S. Year Men Applicant I am honored with three College, Vocational School Graduate Children!; [oth. writ.] "Readers Write" publisherings for Local Civic and National Subjects - 6 years in Alexandria Daily Town Talk, 1. Specific Subjects letters to our President, Senators, Representatives. 2. Also Same members of State Legislature.; [pers.] To compose beneficial, but eager-to-read, youth and adult Christian Cause, result type stories, which can be memory, content is my main goal!; [a.] Alexandria, LA

MCDOWELL, BARBARA A.
[b.] December 23, 1933, New York, NY; [p.] Harry and Alice Schmidt (Deceased); [m.] Emery "Ed" McDowell, February 10, 1968; [ch.] Marilyn; [ed.] B.A. - Jamestown College, Jamestown, N. Daly, Major - English and Education; [occ.] Housewife, formerly Technical Writer/Editor and High School English Teacher; [memb.] Society for Technical Writers and Editors Church Affiliation: Calvary Assembly of God, Ridgecrest, Calif.; [hon.] First poet in Ridgecrest to ever have her poetry displayed at the Annual Desert Empire Fair. Also, published in Salesian Missions book, The Tree of Life.; [pers.] My poetry is primarily spiritual and nature - oriented, stressing the beauty and goodness of life. Each year I create my own Christmas cards with original poetry and photographs.; [a.] Ridgecrest, CA

MCFADDEN, RANDOLPH THOMAS
[b.] December 3, 1951; [pers.] In the ways of our lives tis not particularly how we view, thus definitively what we do. That provides enrichment to our sense of value and purpose.

MCGINTY, WILLIAM MICHAEL
[b.] December 3, 1934, Dundalk, MD; [p.] Margaret Kelley and John McGinty; [m.] Edith Virginia (Nee Durham); [ch.] Linda Carole Ferracci, William Michael Jr., Bryan Sean; [a.] Cape Canaveral, FL

MCGLASSON, CHRISTINE F.
[b.] April 27, 1915, Cincinnati; [p.] Dr. and Mrs. Frank Fee; [m.] Howard McGlasson Fee, February 1939, (Marr. 56 yrs); [ch.] Christine L. McGlasson, Mkt. Dir. Bluvk Diamond, CA., Howard A. McGlasson Jr., Computers.; [ed.] Univ. Cincinnati, Balbs graduate work/reading, Learning Disabilities, Gerontology (GA, St. Un); [occ.] Writing Book, "Retreading", Volunteering in Community."; [memb.] Trinity Episcopal, Cathedral, Sacramento, Nat. Assoc., Female Executives, Sacramento Writer's Club, Delta Zeta National Sorority, Former Teacher - Ret. from Lacity Schools and Cobb Ct., Georgia.; [hon.] March of Dimes, Amer Heart Association, United Way; [oth. writ.] Columns Local Papers, Newsletters for Corporations, Magazine Articles, Commercial Public Relations and Marketing Writing; [pers.] To do good to others through teaching, writing and volunteering my time and efforts.; [a.] Rancho Cordova, CA

MCGLUMPHY, MISTY DAWN
[pen.] Misty Dawn; [b.] February 3, 1978, Morgantown, WV; [p.] Mack McGlumphy, Susan McGlumphy; [ed.] West Springfield High; [occ.] Student; [memb.] National Honor Society, International Thespian Society, Science Honor Society; [pers.] I primarily write my poetry about problems which women deal with. I stay up late at night and try to reflect what I have either been faced with or seen in society, in my poetry.; [a.] Springfield, VA

MCGLYNN, R. RYAN
[b.] March 25, 1983, New York; [p.] William and Phyllis McGlynn; [ed.] Completed the 6th Grade, K-6 Oak Knoll School of the Holy Child, Summit New Jersey, will attend Delbarton in Morris Township New Jersey, entering the 7th grade.; [hon.] Mathematical Olympiads Awards 1993-95, National Current Events League Award 1993-95, Certificate of Achievement - Ciba Geigy Science Awards 1993-95, Presidents Environmental Youth Award 1992-95, activities outside of school: Tristar Football - 1st and 2nd place, Baseball - 1st place, Soccer - 2nd place, Vermont - snow skiing, Nastar Racing, 1992 and 1993 Goldmedal and Silver, Rumbling Brook School of Horsemanship 1988-1991 - 3 first place Ribbons, 3 second place Ribbons and 1 third place Ribbon.; [pers.] Education is like walking it will take you anywhere you want to go.

MCGRADY, BILLY
[b.] August 5, 1981, Bethesda, MD; [p.] William Sr. and Colleen; [ed.] West Frederick Middle School, Frederick, MD, 8th Grade; [occ.] Student; [memb.] West Frederick Jazz Band Ensemble; [pers.] Drummer for the (COA) Children of Anarchy heavy metal, original band. Look out world, here I come.; [a.] Frederick, MD

MCINTOSH, JUANITA
[b.] December 20, 1932, Kentucky; [p.] Ford and Ida Morris Spurlock; [m.] William J. McIntosh; [ed.] Larry, Venita, Jerry and Darlene, daughter-in-law Shirley, son-in-law Domingo, grandkids Nicolas, Emma, Brandon and Travis; [occ.] Homemaker, I love the outdoors and raising flowers, I love feeding, the birds in the winter and the little humming birds in summer.; [oth. writ.] Several poems; [pers.] I have always loved poetry. And I hope people will enjoy reading my poems, as much as I enjoy writing them.; [a.] Buckhorn, KY

MCINTYRE, DONALD M.
[b.] January 19, 1940, Winnipeg, Manitoba, Canada; [ed.] B.A. (Philosophy), 1963, St. John's College, Camarillo, California, M.A. (English), 1968, Loyola University of Los Angeles, Los Angeles, California; [occ.] International Society of Poets; [hon.] Winner of the Golden Poet Award, 1985-1992, from World of Poetry; [oth. writ.] Published in numerous anthologies and listed in "Who's Who in Poetry" by World of Poetry; [pers.] The art of poetry, as expressed by this author in his writings, is an illustration of modern existentialist philosophical theories coupled with the contemporary psychological technique of stream of consciousness.; [a.] Santa Barbara, CA

MCKEEVER, THERESA
[pen.] Theresa McKeever; [b.] September 5, 1956, W-S; [m.] Billy McKeever, June 16, 1991; [ch.] April Pouncey, Latesha Pouncey; [pers.] I want to used my poems to touch many people lives, and to put it in writing what other people couldn't spy. And to be able to bless people in such a special way. With the help of God.; [a.] Winston-Salem, NC

MCKENZIE, KATIE
[b.] November 16, 1978, New Rochelle; [p.] Nancy and Bruce; [ed.] Will be a 1996 Class Graduate of Mamaroneck High School; [occ.] Student; [hon.] Creativity and Excellence in Forensic Science, English Department Scholar; [oth. writ.] Personal poems, short stories and a Forensic Science factual murder mystery.; [pers.] Thanks to everybody who believes in me. Especially my family and my boyfriend, Mike; [a.] Larchmont, NY

MCKETHAN, ERIKA
[b.] April 27, 1972, Lexington, KY; [ch.] A beautiful Siberian Husky named Saba; [ed.] Lengdorf Grundschule, Germany, Triton High School, University of NC at Chapel Hill; [occ.] Waitress; [memb.] Delta Phi Alpha; [hon.] Delta Phi Alpha, German Honor Fraternity; [oth. writ.] "Preconceptions" - Torn Veil 1990, "Curtains" - A Time To listen - an anthology, various short stories and poems. Currently working on a book.; [pers.] After having recently exited a cult, I wish to educate people about the powers of mind control and to help those who have experienced it, currently or in the past, to be liberated from those chains.; [a.] Durham, NC

MCKINNEY, ROBBIE LEE
[b.] June 11, 1977, Melo Park; [p.] Irene Commander, Donald McKinney; [ed.] Hillside High; [oth. writ.] I also write other poems but I never sended for them to become published or anything else.; [pers.] In my poems I write from experience and I also write about a person every day life good or bad.; [a.] Yoland, CA

MCNAUGHTON, SHANE D.
[b.] January 14, 1970, Hartford, CT; [p.] Dave and Laura McNaughton; [ed.] East Hampton High School, Three Rivers College, United States Navy; [occ.] Firefighter; [oth. writ.] Several poems all kept in a personal journal.; [pers.] My writing is simply a way to vent my emotions. My greatest influence would hate to be the late Jim Morrison of The Doors.; [a.] Salem, CT

MCNEELY, JENNIFER
[b.] October 25, 1979, Kingstree, SC; [p.] Betty McNeely and Clifton McNeely; [ed.] Will Graduate High School in 1997; [occ.] Student; [hon.] Jr. Beta Club, National Honor Society, Duke University Talent Identification Program; [pers.] The majority of my writings are about "real life". My goal, when writing, is to show society it's true colors, and not to glamorize, purify, nor justify it's faults.; [a.] Raleigh, NC

MCRAE, ALEX
[b.] October 13, 1983, Miami, FL; [p.] Mitch and Anna McRae; [ed.] Entering Omni Middle School, Boca Raton, FL. Elem. School years at Pine Crest and Banyan Creek, Gifted Program; [occ.] Student; [hon.] Art Award, Banyan Creek Elem., Soccer Final Four State Team, 1995; [pers.] Wait until the end to judge your work; [a.] Boca Raton, FL

MEACHAM, MARK COLYN
[b.] August 25, 1955; Native to Arizona; [pers.] My travels through Arizona's Sycamore Canyon were what inspired me to write this, my first ever publication, which I have dedicated to my mother Connie, who is just as amazingly beautiful!

MEINZINGER, LIANNE ASHLEY
[pen.] Anna Meinzinger, Rachael Manning; [b.] January 16, 1961, Oklahoma City; [p.] Wayne and Claire Ashley, Bob and Pat Fisher; [m.] Carvel Daniel Meinzinger, October 14, 1989; [ch.] Tricia Leigh Jones, Donovan Solace, Katarina Jeanne; [ed.] Lynbrook High School, De Anza College; [occ.] Housewife; [oth. writ.] Children's stories, satire, currently writing a suspense novel; [pers.] Everything I write is dedicated with love to God, the Lord Jesus, my family, and all the wonderful people who've touched my life.; [a.] Ford, WA

MEISSNER, GEORGE A.
[pen.] George Allan Meissner; [b.] April 19, 1934, Saint Paul, MN; [p.] George E. and L. Margaret Meissner; [m.] Kirsten K. Knutsen Meissner, February 12, 1983; [ch.] Mark Allen, Maven Ruth, David Gerard, and Linda Ann... Step-children: Laura and Jonathan Mossler; [ed.] Harding High, St. Paul, MN, and College of Education, N. of Minnesota; [occ.] Insurance Agent, Meissner - State Farm Insurance, Golden Valley, MN; [memb.] Buffalo, MN, Presbyterian Church, National Assn. of Life Underwriters, U. of Minnesota - M-Club, and Twin West Chamber of Commerce...; [hon.] Past President of the Optimist Club of Golden Valley, MN... Past Director of the University of Minnesota "M" Club... Past President of the Minneton Ka Babe Ruth Baseball League, Deacon of the Presbyterian Church of Buffalo, Minnesota...; [oth. writ.] Set musical adaption to "Footprints", 1986... Published a recording for 4 songs in 1987, plus have written many songs about the State of Minnesota, many religions pieces of music plus several miscellaneous Folk Songs...; [pers.] "If you desire", Life can begin at age 50, 60 or 70, "The Good Lord Willing...!" "Many Thanks" to my creative writing College English Teacher, who told me I had some creative writing abilities. ...I'm greatly influenced by all types of music...; [a.] Maple Lake, MN

MELVIN, NICOLE ANNE
[pen.] Nikki Anne; [b.] June 29, 1978, Nashua; [p.] Michael L. Melvin Sr. and Diane M. M.; [ed.] John Stark Regional High School '97; [occ.] Baby Sitting; [memb.] I don't have any right now. But I was in the American Legion.; [hon.] Honor Roll '94/95, first place Speech Award American (Junior) legion post 48 '93/94; [oth. writ.] School's News paper; [pers.] I enjoy writing to explore my imagination and the way I see things. I've been writing since 5th grade and hopefully will continue I do so. I thank my Ma.; [a.] Weare, NH

MENCIAS, PLACIDA C.
[pen.] Pat C. Mencias; [b.] October 5, 1948, Pangasinan, Philippines; [p.] Demetrio Caliboso (Deceased), Filipina Caliboso; [m.] Ponciano S. Mencias, January 2, 1974; [ch.] Olivia, Melanie Grace, Eric, Irwin, Lorelei Mae and Valerie; [ed.] Saint Jerome's Academy, Saint Mary's College, Nueva Vizcays, Phils, Heald Business College, Oakland, CA, Hawaii Business College, Honolulu, HI; [occ.] Secretary, Child and Adolescent Psychiatry, Tripler Army Medical Center, Honolulu, HI; [memb.] Cities in Schools (CIS) Program; [hon.] Commanding General's Coin of Excellence; [pers.] Life is wonderful and it's worth living for. No matter what comes our way, live with it and live our best. Take things as they come and take it one day at a time.; [a.] Waipahu, HI

MENDEZ, ROCIO ALEXIS
[b.] October 28, 1983, New York City; [p.] Zenaida Mendez, John Mendez; [ed.] 7th Grade; [occ.] Student; [hon.] Center School 1995 Achievement Award, St. Eloysios 1994 Summer Camp Award for Reading; [oth. writ.] Several poems

MENSER, TERRI LYN
[b.] September 27, 1973, Perris, CA; [p.] Karla LeGro, Terry Menser; [m.] Kevin Charles Sherer, July 5, 1993; [ed.] Elsinore High, San Jacinto Jr. College, Lassen Community College; [occ.] CNA, or Tech. IT, Modoc Medical Center, Certified Realestate Agent; [pers.] I want people to see life as it really is. My writing sheds a little light on reality and if just one person understands this, then I have succeeded. Thank you.; [a.] Canby, CA

MERCHANT, WANDA ARGATHA
[pen.] "Gat"; [b.] December 17, 1919, Thomastown, MS; [p.] J.H. Hamilton, Annie Mae; [ed.] Graduate Thomastown HS, East Central Jr. College, University of Sau, Miss B.S. MS. 30 hrs beganda retired teacher; [occ.] Substitute Teacher in the past I have taught, Sunday School - Spoken at Nusaba County Fair Spoken at Band PW Club Women Organization; [memb.] Member Disciples of Christ Church; [hon.] Graduated Magnus Cum Laude in Class 0f 1800 was my greatest thrill 1969, University of Southern Mississippi.; [oth. writ.] I have written Articles for Educational Advance Miss State Educational Magazine.; [pers.] "If at first, you don't succeed - "Try, try again". I have many note books of poems, I've jotted down as recreational writing.; [a.] Kascusko, MS

MERRIMAN, DEBORAH
[b.] October 22, 1949, Sayannah, GA; [ch.] Trey Berton, Jamie Berton, Doyle Berton, Amber Olsen; [oth. writ.] Poem published in Songs On The Wind for The National Library of Poetry.; [a.] Alpharetta, GA

METZMEIER, JUNE
[pen.] Marlo Stanley; [b.] June 15, 1948, Lousville, KY; [p.] John Broker, Dorothy Broker; [m.] Joseph A. Metzmeier, June 6, 1970; [ch.] Joseph Stanley (Lee); [ed.] Shawnee High, University of Louisville (B of S); [pers.] I tend to write about personal life experiences. God has given each person a unique path to travel. We need to allow the experiences along the way to prepare us for readiness when the journey is over.; [a.] Lufkin, TX

MEYER, BARBARA J.
[b.] January 1, 1932, Washington, IA; [p.] Homer and Hazel Godwin; [m.] Kent R. Meyer, August 19, 1951; [ch.] Nancy and Gregory; [ed.] Washington High School, University of Northern Iowa, California State University at Fresno; [occ.] Retired Teacher; [pers.] The reading and writing of poetry gives me personal satisfaction.; [a.] Emeryville, CA

MEYER, REBEKAH
[pen.] Rebekah S. Meyer; [b.] November 9, 1983, Westlake; [p.] Jack and Susan Meyer; [a.] Simi Valley, CA

MILLER, CATHERINE A.
[b.] July 22, 1923, Pennsylvania; [p.] Deceased; [m.] Deceased; [ch.] 4; [ed.] High School; [occ.] Retired; [oth. writ.] Compose mostly hymns - none that I tried to publish.; [pers.] I enjoy reading poetry and composing music for my own enjoyment. This poem I submitted is also set to music - kind of a catchy tune.; [a.] Allentown, PA

MILLER, DESIREE L.
[pen.] Dale; [b.] January 20, 1961; [p.] Betty J. Jenkins, James McDaniel; [m.] Mr. James David Gray, 1996; [ch.] April, Destiny Radika, Markisha Michael, Tyrone; [ed.] Greer High School year '79; [occ.] Vermont American; [memb.] Poplar Spring Baptist Church, Simpsonville, S.C., Austin B Brown, Paster; [pers.] I strive to reflect other's to use their talent. It's a gift from God, He made all this possible also with special thanks from Leola Gray, and Sharon Gray for their encouragement and love.; [a.] Simpsonville, SC

MILLER, JANIS LORETTA
[b.] June 6, 1938, Tennessee Ridge; [m.] Edgar Miller, January 2, 1960; [ch.] Stephen, Michael, Susan; [ed.] Central Arizona Community College; [occ.] Retired Nurse; [pers.] I find beauty in words. Creating images and feelings through words give me a sense of place and joy.; [a.] Winslow, AZ

MILLER, JASON
[pen.] Jason Miller; [b.] July 11, 1972, Murray, UT; [p.] Louie Miller, Carol L. Bingham; [ed.] Alta High, Garfield High, Jalley High; [hon.] Certificate for Outstanding Achievements at Salt Lake Community High School 5/17/90, Publication of my poem by National Library of Poetry "1995".; [oth. writ.] Published in High School Literary/Art Magazine, 1991 Valley High School.; [pers.] I know with time I will age but my writings will stay young forever! "Influenced By Past, Present, and Today", "Dedicated to my Mom, Dad, and the rest of my family, I love you very much."; [a.] Salt Lake City, UT

MILLER, RUTH WOFFORD
[b.] January 15, 1909, Fort Smith, AR; [m.] Milton (died) 1986; [ch.] 2 Sons and Daughters; [ed.] B.A. Degree from the University of Redlands in California.; [occ.] I began teaching school after only one year in college, I taught a total of 26 years, mostly primary grades and retired in 1971.; [pers.] The Lord gave me a talent in music and I have served my church as a pianist and organist until my health failed. I had a massive coronary twelve years ago and have congestive heart failure, arthritis and all those things old people get.

MILLER, SARAH R.
[b.] November 8, 1974, Atchison, KS; [p.] Peter Miller Sr., and Patricia Miller; [ed.] Atchison High School; [oth. writ.] The Poem, "Life", in an anthology of poems titled, "Aganippe".; [pers.] If you believe in yourself and have faith in God, you can accomplish anything.; [a.] Atchison, KS

MILLICAN, HELEN
[b.] October 4, 1911, Sherman, TX; [p.] W. M. and Kathrine Sheridan; [m.] Bill C. Millican, December 24, 1932; [ch.] Sharon, Charles and Mary Lynn; [ed.] High School; [occ.] Retired; [oth. writ.] Poems; [pers.] My talent was inherited from my father, who was born in Ireland and grew up there. He acquired three college degrees, spoke seven languages, and was a great poet also.; [a.] Grapevine, TX

MIN, DAPHNE ANN
[pen.] Daphne Kaylor; [b.] October 24, 1939, Lincoln County, NC; [p.] Frank Kaylor, Edith Kaylor; [m.] Kyung Ho (Ken) Min, Ph.D., September 13, 1966; [ch.] Slyvia Min, M.D., Kwan Min, M.B.A.; [ed.] Mt. Holly High School, Contra Costa College; [occ.] Housewife and Mother; [memb.] Snow Hill Methodist Church, Doctors Hospital Volunteer; [hon.] "World's Greatest Mom", 1982, "Queen Min's Castle", 1994; [oth. writ.] Letters to Friends and Family; [pers.] If God had worked on the seventh day, would he have eliminated prejudice, war and rumors of war?; [a.] El Sobrante, CA

MINIHAN, GERARD C.
[b.] August 11, 1941, Ireland; [p.] Chalres, Joan Minihan; [m.] Dorothy Minihan, April 25, 1980; [ch.] John, Brian, William, Michael; [ed.] High School, Christian Brothers, Limerick City Ireland; [occ.] Real Estate; [memb.] Masonic Lodge 1167; [pers.] It's a good feeling to write a poem, that other people think enough off, to publish.

MISCHKE, JOSEFINA
[b.] January 19, 1924, Philippines; [ed.] Bohol High School, Philippines, University of Bohol - B.S.E., University of Superior, Superior, WI - M.A.; [occ.] Retired Teacher (a total of 42 years); [memb.] Delta Kappa Gamma, Chapter Alpha Eta; [oth. writ.] Poems published in local newspaper; [pers.] In life, if you don't create memories, there's only emptiness to look back to.; [a.] Peshtigo, WI

MITCHELL, ELEANOR STOWE
[pen.] Ellie; [b.] August 31, 1949, Charlotte, NC; [p.] William and Willie; [m.] Willie Mitchell, December 8, 1990; [ch.] Dana Johnson and Angela Johnson; [ed.] Second Ward High, Central Piedmont Community College; [occ.] Customer Service Rep., ITP Staffing Service, ATL, GA; [memb.] Forest Chapel Baptist Church, Forest Pk., GA; [oth. writ.] First time ever to enter any kind of poetry contest.; [pers.] My poetry almost always reflect my inter-most feelings during my writings. Poetry is an expression of you, and who you are. Strive to release your feelings in poetry, then you'll know who you are.; [a.] Ellenwood, GA

MITCHELL, LONA
[pen.] Katherine; [b.] August 29, 1979, Dublin; [p.] Guy and Dee Mitchell; [ed.] West Laurens High School College Prep. Student; [occ.] High School Student; [oth. writ.] Several poems printed in school newspaper along with short stories.; [pers.] I started writing poetry as a hobby, now it has become much more. Just remember to thine own self be true.; [a.] Dudley, GA

MITCHELL, SANDRA F.
[b.] April 12, 1951, Dade City, FL; [p.] Mr. Chester Martin, Mrs. Ridenour; [m.] John A. Mitchell, June 23, 1979; [ch.] (Stepchildren) Julie and George Mitchell; [ed.] Haltom HS, East Mississippi Junior College; [occ.] Full Time College Student, Domestic Home Manager; [memb.] Ladies Auxiliary (VFW); [hon.] Dean's List, I have received numerous awards and decorations since I am currently a Retired USAF Technical Sergeant; [oth. writ.] This is my First attempt at writing a Poem. This will be my first ever published writings.; [pers.] I seek to Honor the code of the USAF Sgt which is Duty, Honor, Country and the most important being Love of God and Family.; [a.] Columbus, MS

MITCHELL III, E. CAMERON
[pen.] The Poet; [b.] August 30, 1967, Bronx, NY; [p.] Earle Mitchell Jr., Shaaryn A. Mitchell; [ed.] B.A. Marketing from Morehouse College; [occ.] Sales Manager; [oth. writ.] First book titled 'Of Strength and Struggle', due to be published in 1996. Currently working on first novel titled '...And the Messiah Returns'.; [a.] Jersey City, NJ

MOHYLA, OSTAP M.
[b.] April 29, 1953, Lyons, France; [p.] John Mohyla, Anna Mohyla; [m.] Olga P. Mohyla, October 4, 1975; [ch.] Tina Marie, Michael Paul, Nicholas Jason; [ed.] St. Basil's Prep Seminary, LaSalle Academy, Pace University; [occ.] Corporate Vice Pres. - Actuarial Services, NY Life Ins.; [a.] Ridgewood, NY

MOMO, FEMAARTA ANDREA
[b.] March 28, 1979, Benson, MN; [p.] Andrew Memo, Agnes Banya; [ed.] Junior at Franklin High School; [occ.] Betty K. Hodges, Community Girls Club; [a.] Somerset, NJ

MONFORE, GERVAISE
[pen.] Gerry Monfore; [b.] February 26, 1910, Kansas; [p.] Robert and Ethel Monfore; [m.] Helen Monfore, (Deceased), September 06, 1936; [ch.] Lynne Monfore, Jennifer Sweikar; [ed.] AB Degree, 1932, Col. of Emporia, KS, Grad. Studies, 1933-34, U. of Colorado MS Degree, 1950, U. of Denver; [occ.] Retired; [memb.] Sigma Pi Sigma, Sigma XI, American Men and Women Science; [hon.] Seven Inventions including one patent; [oth. writ.] 27 Technical Publications; [pers.] "Invictus" by Henley expresses my view; [a.] Springfield, MD

MONGE, MARGIE VIADO
[pen.] Mharjz-Red; [b.] July 7, 1974, Philippines; [p.] Pedro R. Monge and Maria V. Monge; [ed.] Saint James High School, Philippines Columban College, Philippines; [occ.] Department Store Employee; [hon.] Best in English (Elem.); [pers.] I hope that the poem which I wrote will serve as a good guidance to everyone. Mostly, to the students or a working student like me, who are trying to struggle to reach their goal. "Don't say goodbye to your dreams and don't give up!"; [a.] Bellflower, CA

MONROE, ANNIE MAE
[pen.] Annie M. Monroe; [b.] May 6, 1938, Comden, SC; [p.] Annie Bell and Jimmie Davis; [m.] Harry Monroe, May 20, 1972; [ch.] Rickie and Rosa; [ed.] Matheo Academy Camden, SC, Norwalk Tech College Norwalk Ct.; [occ.] Housewife; [memb.] Calvary Baptist Church, substitute Sunday School teacher; [oth. writ.] My Graduation Class Song and Motto, first poem, A Little Star; [pers.] I have found that I am bless with the gift of Mosley poems of Comfort uplifting poems, poems of sympathy, get well poems, and love poems. I have been greatly influence by James Melden Johnson.; [a.] South Norwalk, CT

MONTAGUE, NELSON CARLTON
[pen.] Sonny or Mickey; [b.] July 12, 1929, Washington, DC; [p.] Rosmond and Nelson R. Montague; [m.] Nancy L. Montague, July 7, 1961; [ch.] Lennis Lee Montague; [ed.] B.S. Electrical Engineering, Howard Univ. Washington, D.C.; [occ.] Retired U.S. Govt., Marriage Celebrant; [memb.] Deacon First Baptist Church Chesterbrook, Life Member NAACP, Treasurer No. Va. Baptist Assoc., Pres. Albert S. Brown Scholarship Fund; [hon.] Fairfax and Arlington Counties Branch NAACP, Defense Documentation center Employee of Month April, 1980; [oth. writ.] Correspondence Bible Study Lessons; [pers.] Try talk and walk be the same.; [a.] Reston, VA

MONTERA SR., CONSTANCIO R.
[pen.] Anon Nymous; [b.] January 30, 1926, Cebu City, Philippines; [p.] Arcadia R., Agaton D. Montera; [m.] Consolacion Aquino Montera, January 30, 1952; [ch.] Maria Myrna, Lex, Constancio Jr.; [ed.] Philippines Elementary and Secondary Schools, some Philippine College; [occ.] Retiree; [memb.] And Bisaya Association, Fil-Am Association; [oth. writ.] Poem "Yesteryears", published in a High School Organ in the Philippines; [pers.] Discouragement is hope eternal, heartache - a boundless ecstasy.; [a.] Manassas, VA

MOONEY, SISTER MARY C.
[b.] December 7, 1913, Ireland; [p.] Terence and Sara; [ed.] M.A. St. John's University Queens, N.Y.; [occ.] Retired; [memb.] Religious Order of Ursuline Sisters; [pers.] Living for God and helping others in need of help.

MOORE, ANDREA
[b.] June 25, 1967, Boonton, NJ; [p.] Beverly C. and Daniel J. Conway; [m.] Edward S. Moore, September 26, 1987; [ch.] Edward Seth and Ryan Mitchell; [ed.] Hackettstown High School; [memb.] Mother, wife and poet; [oth. writ.] "Whisper" printed in "Reflections of Light" - Nat'l Library of Poetry, also, many unpublished poems.; [pers.] "Always keep a dream in mind".; [a.] Greendell, NJ

MOORE, ANNA
[b.] July 16, 1957, Claremore, OK; [p.] John and Nettie Reed; [m.] Eddie A. Moore, July 29, 1983; [ch.] Andrea Nichole James; [ed.] Claremore High School, Tulsa Junior College, San Jacinto Community College; [occ.] Computer Programmer, Houston, TX; [a.] Houston, TX

MOORE, CAROLYN
[b.] June 8, 1966, Aurora, IL; [p.] Thomas and Kathleen Reier; [m.] Robert Moore, June 10, 1989; [ch.] Stephanie Anne Moore, Robert William Moore III, and Gwendolyn Therese moore; [ed.] Aurora Central Catholic H.S., Aurora University (3 yrs.); [occ.] Housewife and Part-time Craft Maker (Independant Contractor); [memb.] Brookfield Zoo Member; [hon.] NHS (in High School), 3rd year Tennis Award (College Tennis Team), 2nd place Tennis Divisional Tournament; [oth. writ.] None that have been published - mostly poems.; [pers.] The poem Grandfather was written in honor of my grandfather, J.A. Schweisthal. He was born June 11, 1912 and passed away Dec. 27, 1994. He's very much missed by my family for he was very special to all of us.; [a.] Aurora, IL

MOORE, DAVID
[b.] August 4, 1946, New York City; [p.] Agustus and Patience Moore; [m.] Donna Rimmelin, October 24, 1993; [ch.] Brie; [ed.] High School, College; [occ.] Mental Health Counselor; [oth. writ.] Personal, many poems; [pers.] Life is like a poem. With many lines and verses like people and faces going places; [a.] Jamaica, NY

MOORE, DAVID GAMBLE
[b.] March 23, 1938, Sumter County, SC; [p.] Lloyd and Clara Moore; [m.] Naomi Strickland Moore, September 21, 1956; [ch.] Denise, David, Amy; [ed.] Clemson University, BSEE '63, Southeastern Baptist Theological seminary, M.Div. '75, D. Min '78; [occ.] Pastor, First Baptist Church, Reidsville, N.C.; [memb.] Board of Registration for Engineers and Land Surveyors, State of Alabama (Inactive Status). General Board, North Carolina Baptist State Convention.; [oth. writ.] Several poems - unpublished.; [a.] Reidsville, NC

MOORE, LEAH R.
[b.] April 24, 1945, Fort Worth, TX; [p.] M. Moore; [ch.] Two; [ed.] 2 yrs. University of Hawaii; [occ.] Advertising Mgr.; [memb.] Writers Guild, Dallas, TX; [oth. writ.] "Mountain"; [pers.] I am open minded, adventurous; [a.] Dallas, TX

MOORE, MARGARET BELL
[b.] February 3, 1958, Falfurrias, TX; [p.] Richarol and Roberta Bell; [m.] Kenneth D. Moore, August 19, 1978; [ch.] Ryan, Cameron, Sean; [ed.] Bachelor of Science in Education from the University of Houston; [occ.] Educator - Physical Education; [memb.] President - Elect for the Board of American Heart Association - Brenham, Texas Board, Society of Childrens Book Writers and Illustrator's; [hon.] Graduated Cum Laude from the University of Houston.; [pers.] I have been greatly influenced by the poets of our time Maya Angelou, Kahlil Gibran ....I choose to write about life through my eyes and share its joys as well as its tribulations; [a.] Brenham, TX

MOORE, PATRICK SHERRICK
[pen.] Patrick Sherrick Moore; [b.] June 28, 1971, Chicago; [p.] Richard S. Moore, Louise Moore, Kathy Moore; [oth. writ.] "Nickels and Dimes", was taken from an unpublished book called "20,000 Cups of Coffee." I am currently working on its follow-up, called "Better Than Coffee."; [pers.] "I'm not here to save the world, I'm here to learn from it". "Remember, no matter how hard things in life get, Life is terminal." "Nothing is forever."; [a.] Minneapolis, MN

MOORE, VIVIAN ALICE
[b.] May 15, 1952, Keyser, WV; [p.] Mr. and Mrs. Harold D. Moore; [ed.] High School (Valley High) Lonaconing and some Art School Training at Vo-Tech Center, Cumberland, MD; [occ.] Lab Technician at Westuaco Corp.; [memb.] First Assembly of God Church (Lonaconing), WM's at First Ass. of God Church; [oth. writ.] Poems published in Newspaper, poems published in National Anthology (Young America Sings) in 1970, poem published in Westuaco (Luke Mill Report); [pers.] I enjoy writing about the past, and the deep appreciation of small pleasures their were 20 or 30 years ago. Time seemed to go slower and instead of a rushing stream we were more like a quiet pool.; [a.] Lonaconing, MD

MORGAN, ELAINE V.
[pen.] Elaine V. Morgan; [b.] April, Jamaica; [p.] Amanda Wilkinson; [ed.] St. Anne's Catholic Kingston Jamaica West Indies, Great Lake Community College Washtenaw Community School Crafs College; [occ.] Ford Motor Company Saline; [oth. writ.] One poem written for the College Washtenaw; [pers.] I would love to write more poems but I have no idea where to begin. Writing has been the greatest thing for me and this was a lucky break.

MORONG, MARILYN K.
[pen.] Clarice; [b.] April 29, 1947, Chicago; [p.] Frank and Helen Muschal; [m.] James Peter Morong, October 9, 1976; [ch.] Christopher Philip Morong; [ed.] Immaculata High School, Escuela Ecuestre In Mexico, Riding in several European countries.; [occ.] Full-time mommie, part-time author.; [memb.] I belonged to the riding club in high school, and horses have been a part of my life ever since. I taught my husband to jump when I worked at a stable.; [hon.] Honorable mention for an oil painting. Numerous trophies and ribbons for showing horses.; [oth. writ.] Three children's books about horses, "Bob and Fred", "The Legend of Chocolate Chip", and "Observations and Trivial Pursuits of a Barn Cat". All are unpublished.; [pers.] Look around. The world is filled with poems and stories.; [a.] Justice, IL

MORRIS, ABBY R.
[b.] January 10, 1926, Hagerstown, MD; [m.] Dr. Morton Morris; [ch.] Susan (41), Claudia (35); [ed.] York Jr. College - 1944, Jobers Hopkins School of Radiography - 1946; [occ.] Musical Theatre Director, Piano Instructor; [memb.] Founder: "Indiana Players, Inc.", Director - "Indiana Cultural Center Fund, Inc."; [hon.] "Lifetime Achievement in the Arts", by Indiana Arts Council", nominated "Woman of the Year", mayor declared "Abby Morris Day" in Indiana, PA, April 1990; [oth. writ.] "Songs You Can Count On", (A book of 79 compositions to teach pre-math concepts to slow learners.) 13 original musical revues which raised monies for charities.; [a.] Indiana, PA

MORRIS, JOHN R.
[b.] June 8, 1955, Aiken, SC; [p.] Wilborn W. and Anne B. Morris; [m.] Anna (DiCandia) Morris, June 4, 1978; [ch.] Jennifer E., J. Richard Jr., Mary E.; [ed.] Associate Degree Nuclear Engineering; [occ.] Nuclear Power Plant Equipment Operator; [pers.] I believe in protecting the environment and striving to come up with better ways to do this.; [a.] Fuquay-Varina, NC

MORRIS, SUE
[pen.] Sue Morris; [m.] Max Morris; [ch.] Susan, Brian, Mark; [ed.] S.E. Nova University (M.S.) - Master of Science Degree; [occ.] LMHC (Licensed Mental Health Counselor); [memb.] Institute of Noetic Sciences, Nature Conservancy Green Peace; [hon.] Phi Kappa Phi - University of South Florida; [oth. writ.] Local newspaper, news letters; [pers.] The orchestration of words in a worthy poem stirs the imagination and creates a universal melody that touches the soul.; [a.] Brandon, FL

MORRISSEY, JOHN F.
[b.] April 7, 1925, Chicago, IL; [ed.] J.D., DePaul University, John Marshall Law School; [occ.] Retired Attorney; [memb.] Illinois Bar; [hon.] Editor's Choice Award for the 1995 Anthology "Songs On The Wind".; [oth. writ.] Legal Magazine Articles and published poems; [a.] Wauconda, IL

MOSELEY, ANNABELLE M.
[b.] October 7, 1979, Miller Place, NY; [p.] John Moseley, Annabelle Moseley; [ed.] Presently Attends Saint Anthony's High School; [hon.] Duns Scotus, Saint Bonaventure Awards, National Honor Society, First Prize - Eastern Suffolk Reading Council Writing Contest, First Prize - The Walt Whitman Birthplace Association Poetry Contest, Winner - Nat'l Women's History Essay Contest; [pers.] As a teenage writer, I don't think it's contradictory to say, I'm much more grounded when my "head is in the clouds".; [a.] Dix Hills, NY

MOSHIER, DOROTHY
[b.] Detroit, MI; [ch.] Sandra Parkhill and Jimmy Parkhill; [ed.] High School and Thomlinson Tech., Clearwaters and St. Petersburgh, Fl.; [memb.] Palatka, Fl. Art League; [oth. writ.] Poem published in town newspaper. Poem in Trinity Methodist news letter; [pers.] I think love and care for your self and others is the best road of life. To me writing a poem is an expression of some point or meaning.; [a.] Palatka, FL

MOSS, ALEKSA
[pen.] Aleksa Moss; [b.] April 13, 1982, Detriot, MI; [p.] Phillip Moss, Vikte Moss; [ed.] School - University Higget School, I'm going into 7th grade.; [occ.] School; [pers.] I believe in a statement I read - "Breath Deep, Seek Peace". And thank you to my Aunt Linda Moss, my dad, and my teacher Mrs. Rek.; [a.] Detroit, MI

MOYERS, KELLY
[b.] March 13, 1980, Harrisonburg, VA; [p.] Randall and Eleanor Moyers; [ed.] Currently a Sophomore at Eastern Mennonite High School; [occ.] Student; [hon.] Honor Roll, Lettered in Tennis, Most Inspirational on J.V. Basketball Team; [a.] Broadway, VA

MUCKLE, MARY HERTEL
[b.] Evanston, IL; [m.] Gary Muckle, September 29, 1984; [ed.] Attend Evanston IL School district, Grad. of Kendall College, Studied at Concordia University; [occ.] Does free lance artist; [pers.] Live now in Chicago; [a.] Chicago, IL

MULDROW, STEPHEN
[b.] October 28, 1959, Memphis, TN; [ed.] Booker T. Washington High School, Memphis, TN; [occ.] Electronics Technician - Memphis City Schools; [oth. writ.] Many other poems written, some shared with friends and acquaintances.; [pers.] My wish is that all persons try to seek and follow truth and help those in need.; [a.] Memphis, TN

MULHOLLAND, JASON
[b.] February 14, 1977, Pittsburgh, PA; [p.] Bob and Denise Mullholland; [ed.] Upper St. Clair School District; [occ.] Student (Kent State Univ.); [pers.] I believe everyone has a dark side. If one shuns it, it can never be dealt with, and balance cannot be found. My poetry is a look into my personal dark side.; [a.] Pittsburgh, PA

MUNOZ, DAVID
[pen.] D. A. Empyre; [b.] May 22, 1975, Fort Worth, TX; [pers.] Choose to know or choose to be alone.; [a.] Mission, TX

MUNOZ, THOMAS
[pen.] Thomas Munoz; [b.] September 3, 1951, Stockton, CA; [p.] Frank and Helen Munoz; [ch.] Christopher Munoz, 11 years old; [ed.] Graduate of St. Mary's High School, Stockton, CA, 1969 and University of Pacific 1974; [occ.] Insurance Underwriter; [oth. writ.] Many unpublished poems and songs. When I Was Younger, Leonardo in The Sky, The Split.; [pers.] My parents were simple people, but their love gave me a deep understanding about the romance of life. My poems and songs reflect their spirit.; [a.] Walnut Creek, CA

MURPHY, BRENDA JEAN
[pen.] B. J.; [b.] March 18, 1960, Marietta; [p.] Edward and Barb Marshall; [m.] Mark Murphy, October 26, 1978; [ch.] Bo and J. T. Murphy; [occ.] Housewife and Hog Farmer; [pers.] I love the outdoors and amazed with all of God creations.; [a.] Stockport, OH

MURPHY, FRED
[b.] April 10, 1960, Boise, Idaho; [p.] Victor and Betty Murphy; [m.] Kim H. (Jones) Murphy, August 14, 1982; [ch.] John, Nathan and Andrew Murphy; [ed.] Graduated from Fort Scott High School in 1978, attended Allen County Community College in 1993-1994, transferred to Pittsburg State University in 1994.; [occ.] Full Time Student - Major Communication Education; [memb.] Past President of the Non-Trad Club, Founder of Alpha Sigma Lambda Honor Society, Pinnacle Honor Society, Chinese Association; [hon.] Listed in the 17th Edition of the National Dean's List. Nominated for Outstanding Student of the Year 1994 at Allen Country Community College.; [oth. writ.] Misc. other Poems.; [pers.] I believe that everyone has two sides, one dark and one good. It is the task of each of us to enhance the good side.; [a.] Pittsburg, KS

MURPHY, KATHLEEN
[pen.] Kitty Murphy; [b.] April 26, 1937, New York City; [p.] James and Catherine Gallagher; [m.] James Patrick Murphy, September 20, 1958; [ch.] Maureen, James, Daniel; [ed.] Julia Richman HS, Cornell Labor College; [occ.] Ex. Asst. to Labor V.P.; [memb.] AARP, Catholic Daughters of the Americas, Local 23-25, UNITE; [oth. writ.] Copyright song, We're Unite; [a.] New York, NY

MURPHY, TAMMIE
[b.] July 22, 1958, Salt Lake City, UT; [p.] Richard and Kay Murphy; [ch.] Cory L. Murphy and Anjada M. Dominguez; [ed.] University of Utah, Brighton High; [occ.] Addiction Counselor; [memb.] NAADAC, UAADAC; [hon.] Alpha Kappa Delta, Deans List; [oth. writ.] A few other poems which have not been submitted for publishing yet.; [pers.] Although I do not believe in organized religion, my poetry is usually influenced by topics of love and spirituality.; [a.] Salt Lake City, UT

MURRAY, EVA
[pen.] Eva Murray; [b.] August 8, 1900, Nelson, CA; [p.] William, Lula Campbell; [m.] Paul Murray, June 1920; [ch.] 3 Boys, 1 Girl; [ed.] Grammer School Home Schooled; [occ.] Housewife, Retired; [memb.] Methodist Church; [oth. writ.] Several penned verses.; [a.] Hampton, VA

MURRAY, NORMA S.
[b.] September 25, 1956, Los Angeles; [p.] Angela and Ralph Montellano; [m.] Keith Murray, July 4, 1986; [ch.] Jeanine S. Montellano and Sarah Murray; [ed.] Sacred Heart of Jesus Elementary, Sacred Heart of Jesus High School, East Lost Angeles College, Southland College of Legal Careers; [occ.] Legal Secretary, Secretarial Coordinator, Notary Public, Continued Education through various seminars.; [memb.] San Gabriel Valley Legal Secretary Associa-

tion, National Notary association; [hon.] I have receive various accommodations for my writing, as well as my poetry.; [oth. writ.] Editor, major law firm (Skadden, Arps, Slate, Meagher and Flom); [pers.] My main objective is to maintain a positive attitude. I try to reflect positive thoughts to create and influence as much positive energy as can be inspired.; [a.] Los Angeles, CA

MYERS, BARBARA ZEHNER
[b.] February 17, 1949, Portland, OR; [p.] Donald Q and Jane M. Hall; [ed.] Loara High School, Anaheim, CA, Fullerton College, Fullerton, CA; [occ.] Administrative Assistant, Hughes Aircraft Company; [memb.] El Segundo Foursquare Church; [hon.] Two (2) High Performance Team Awards from Hughes Missile Systems Group; [pers.] Any writing talent I may possess is not due to any particular ability on my part, but rather a gift from Almighty God.; [a.] El Segundo, CA

MYERS, CYNTHIA C.
[b.] February 28, 1952, Jamaica; [p.] Ethel Coote and Late Lionel Coote; [ch.] Stacy Michelle and Farrah; [ed.] NYC Tech College, AD, and Long Island University, BSN - Brooklyn NY; [occ.] Registered Nurse Kaiser, Permanente Hosp., Fontana Calf.; [memb.] American Assoc. of Critical Care Nurses; [pers.] That which cannot be touched can be felt.; [a.] Alta Loma, CA

MYERS, SYBIL S.
[m.] Deceased; [ch.] Anne, Bonnie, Allen and Chris; [ed.] Strafford College and Averatte College in Virginia; [occ.] Retired - Reidsvill, City School System; [memb.] Reidsville First Baptist Church, held numerous positions, Council Member - Christian Women's Club, Hospital Auxiliary, Wycliffe Associates, Southeast Writers Assoc.; [pers.] Have great passion to write and express those feelings to others.; [a.] Reidsville, NC

MYERS, WALLIS A.
[b.] December 14, 1972, Altoona, PA; [p.] Wallis S. Myers, Nancy J. Myers; [ed.] Altoona Area High School, Penn State University; [occ.] Student, Film Production Assistant; [hon.] National Art Honor Society; [pers.] I guess I look into the shadows of everyday life and write about what I see. I usually draw from unknown places, childhood fears and roads not taken.; [a.] Altoona, PA

NADEAU, WAYNE
[b.] April 15, 1928, San Jose, CA; [ed.] A.B., A.M. Stanford; [occ.] Retired teacher of music, college and secondary schools; [memb.] Calif. Retired Teachers Ass. Music Teachers Association of Calif. Society of Composers, Inc. Stockton Piano Club, Airplane Owners and Pilots Association; [hon.] Stanford Humanities Prize For Musical Composition, Teacher of the Year, Edison High School; [oth. writ.] Songs, Choral Works, Piano Pieces, String Quintet, Poems; [pers.] I am trying to understand the musical aspects of poetry and how to marry them to its emotional content, yet by using the utmost economy of means.

NASH, JANE
[pen.] Jane Nash; [b.] January 3, 1917, Port Huron, MI; [p.] Edward R. and Mava; [ed.] Port Huron (1934) High School Practical Nursings Course - 1948; [occ.] Retired L.P.N.; [hon.] Volunteer Award Marwood Manor Nursisng Home (1989), Plague for years as L.P.N. President; [oth. writ.] I have written many poems, school songs in 7th grade I wrote a winning Slogan on voting for a Local Bank during World War II; [pers.] I accepted Jesus Christ as my Personal Savior at age 8, March of 1996 I will have taught Sunday School for 64 years; [a.] Port Huron, MI

NAZARIO, NATIVIDAD
[b.] December 25, 1949, PR; [p.] Ernesto and Antonia; [ch.] Anesdi, Ernesto and Gabriel; [ed.] B.S.P.T. University of Puerto Rico, San Juan; [occ.] Physical Therapist Consultant, N.Y.C.; [oth. writ.] Nightmare in a Hospital.; [pers.] "Build your house to fit your body. Build your body to fit your soul. Grow your soul to enter God."; [a.] New York City, NY

NEAL, DEREK
[b.] May 7, 1984, Germany; [p.] Ray and Beth Neal; [ed.] 6th grace; [occ.] Student; [mem.] Chess Club, Kung-fu; [oth. writ.] Many poems; [pers.] "Honor, Honesty and Loyalty."

NEAL I, RODNEY BEE
[pen.] King Bee; [b.] January 30, 1956, Ypsalanti; [p.] Aaron and Dorothy Neal; [m.] Kareen and Kirah King; [ed.] T.V. School, Thomlinson Elementary, McNair Elementary, Mokersky Elementary, Roosevelt J.H., Robichaud High; [occ.] King, Prince, Pimp, Author, God; [memb.] King for a Day Club, Prince Rodney Bee Neal Club of America, Pimp's Gang of East Detroit, President of R.C.A. at Detroit East, Count Von Roskie Club of the World and more; [hon.] Merit Award at R.C.A., Pimp of the Year Award, Prince of the Year Award, and King Bee of the Hive 1995 Chairperson Insect's Ink, Detroit and Inkster; [oth. writ.] A Pimps is no good, the God Rodney, does Rodney really look like Hestia, Mom and Dad, the family circus, and "You can't fool a person from Inkster"; [pers.] I believe Rodney looks like God because he is going to run for President in '95 for the White House, Love-Peace-Togetherness; [a.] Detroit, MI

NELMS, BEN S.
[b.] July 5, 1951, Augusta, GA; [ed.] GA State Univ.; [occ.] Human Services; [oth. writ.] Empathetic Synergetic Participation: On the Path to no disability; [pers.] The manifest destiny of love is legend from a dream.; [a.] Bartow, GA

NELSON, DIANE
[b.] August 27, 1948, Illinois; [ed.] Knox College, Northwestern University; [memb.] Peta, Now; [hon.] Dean's List; [a.] Chicago, IL

NELSON, SHANTAL GONZALEZ
[b.] October 2, 1980, Rio Piedras, PR; [p.] Ana J. Nelson/Otto Gonzalez Blanco; [ed.] American Military Academy; [occ.] Student; [hon.] I was honored to be in a choir and for my participation in a science fair.; [oth. writ.] Several poems were published in newspaper.; [pers.] A light from God touched my heart and soul so that I could write my poems.; [a.] Guaynabo, PR

NEWELL, DOLAN
[b.] December 10, 1978, Flagstaff, AZ; [p.] Wayne and Madeline Newell; [ed.] Junior in High School at Barry Goldwater High School; [occ.] Delivery person a manager of Flower Shop; [hon.] Honor Role; [oth. writ.] Only many poems that I have written that I have at my home.; [pers.] I enjoy reflecting the good things out of any situation in life, and show the true beauty of life.; [a.] Phoenix, AZ

NEWSOM, JAMES L.
[b.] August 31, 1967, Lakewood, NY; [p.] George E. and Bobbie J. Newsom; [m.] Sarah Diann Newsom, August 31, 1991; [ch.] Leslie Ann and Lindsey Nicole Smith; [ed.] Cascade High School, Wartrace, TN; [memb.] Hillcrest Baptist Church, Manchester, TN; [pers.] Each day rather good or bad is a blessing from God, thank Him for it and don't take it for granted.

NEWSOME, LISA M. TEWS
[pen.] Lisa M. Tews-Newsome; [b.] October 7, 1969, Mil, WI; [p.] Doris Mae and Orville Harry Tews; [m.] Kevin Newsome, August 5, 1989; [ch.] Ashton Vaughn; [ed.] Colonial High School Orlando, FL, Diploma; [occ.] Writer, Mother; [memb.] Our Lady Star of the Sea Catholic Church Ponte Vedra Beach, FL; [hon.] Modeling Academy Certificate from John Cassablanca's Modeling Agency Winter Park, FL; [oth. writ.] Romance Novel - "Ace of Hearts" and various other poems; [pers.] Pen and paper is but a mirror through which I see my true self. You've only to look past me, at the reflection to see yourself; [a.] Jacksonville, FL

NGUYEN, CHI
[pen.] Laine Christenson, Tori Ramone; [b.] August 6, 1980, Hammend, IN; [p.] Thanh Nguyen, Dao Nguyen; [ed.] Sophomore at Lake Central High School; [occ.] Student; [memb.] St. Joseph Church, Lake Central Scout, Former Cheerleader; [pers.] This is a first time experience for me, though I want to be a journalist, poetry is very important to me. The subjects of portrayal in my poems vary from darkness and pain or my feelings and experiences.; [a.] Dyer, IN

NIBLET, KAMAR A.
[pen.] Kamar Ali "Kae"; [b.] December 17, 1962, Detroit, MI; [p.] Celeste Adams, Willie Niblet; [m.] Nicole Niblet, September 29, 1990; [ch.] Dianthony K. Niblet; [ed.] Graduated Cooley High School in Detroit; [occ.] Administrative Asst City of Oakland, Parks Dept.; [oth. writ.] Several writings unsubmitted and unpublished; [pers.] National Library is my inspiration to strive for Betterment in my poetry.; [a.] Oakland, CA

NICASTRO, CAROL
[oth. writ.] Past experience: 1 1/2 years as Editorial Board member and sometime, contributor of articles to bi-county quarterly Christian newsletter, 6 years as co-editor and staff writer on local church prayer group newsletter.; [pers.] To express the unconditional love, forgiving grace, and healing power of Jesus Christ through the Holy Spirit, that blesses the normal and ordinary human experience, and is freely given to all who call upon the name of Jesus.; [a.] Huntington, NY

NICHOLS, MARION H.
[b.] May 21, 1916, Torrington, CT; [p.] Raymond Hewitt, Gladys Hewitt; [m.] Brett Selpho Nichols, March 23, 1940; [ed.] Torrington High School, Torrington Executive School; [occ.] Retired; [memb.] Daughters American Revolution, West Palm Beach Garden Club, Palm Beach Int'l Piano Competition, Ann Norton Sculpture Gardens, Mounts Horticulture

Learning Center; [hon.] Dame of Merit - Constantinian Order of St. George, First Lady Palm Beach Invitational Piano Competition; [oth. writ.] Series of Articles " Our American Flag," writings on Animals, Horticulture, Graphology, etc. No particular desire to publish...; [pers.] Writing humorously has become a lost art - let's revive it!!; [a.] West Palm Beach, FL

NICHOLS, ROBERT
[pen.] Tony Nichols; [b.] March 19, 1958, Wichita, KS; [p.] Bob and Norma Nichols; [ch.] Justin, Jeremy, Stephanie; [ed.] Rose Hill High, Butler Co. Comm. College, Kansas Newman College; [occ.] Real Estate Agent, Rodeo Cowboy, Engineer Officer; [memb.] Mason's Shrine; [hon.] Awarded a Comm. as an Officer in the U.S. Army, Engineer Officer School, Airborne School, currently a 1 Lt. Kansas Army Guard; [oth. writ.] Several Cowboy poems, a military story about my daughter and myself. Three poems on the wall of stars at Dandales Western Store; [pers.] With the military story, the English Dept. at the Engineer Center told me I had the ability to become a great novelist. I want people to experience a way of life that I experience through my writings.; [a.] Wichita, KS

NICHOLS, TARA LYNN
[pen.] Tara Nichols; [b.] August 16, 1982, Gettysburg, PA; [p.] Kathy and Tony Nichols; [ed.] New Windsor Middle School, 3 Consecutive yrs (12 Marking Periods) on the honor roll; [occ.] Student; [memb.] 7th Grade Chorus, 7th and 8th Grade Choral Ensemble; [hon.] The 1995 Mathematics and Verbal Talent Search Sponsored by John's Hopkins University; [pers.] It is better to chase a dream to live in an empty one.; [a.] Vestminster, MD

NILLES, STEPHANIE LYNN
[pen.] Stephanie Lynn; [b.] August 13, 1971, Palatine, IL; [occ.] Hair Designer; [oth. writ.] All of my poems are reflections of my personal growth from the age of 12 through 24.; [pers.] In memory of Scotty J. Nelson 1968-1994, love of beauty is taste. The creation of beauty is art - Ralph Waldo Emerson; [a.] Palatine, IL

NISTICO, JOHN MARIANO
[pen.] John (Doc) Nistico; [b.] January 15, 1956, Jamaica, NY; [p.] Frank A. and Eleanor; [ch.] John Francis Nistico; [ed.] High School Diploma and Taking evening classes at Suffolk County Community College; [occ.] Building Maintenance for the Developmentally Disabled; [oth. writ.] Several unpublished poems and an article on fishing techniques.; [pers.] I feel harmony can be reached by every individual exercising honesty, integrity and a sense of fair play toward their fellow human beings.; [a.] Farmingville, NY

NITSCH, DEBORAH A.
[b.] May 5, 1956, Kingston, NY; [p.] Edward (Deceased), Audrey H. Nitsch; [ed.] B.A. in Child Psychology from Hope College, Holland, Michigan; [occ.] Preschool Teacher, Cook, Guide, and Outdoor Recreation Activities Outfitter; [memb.] Missions Committee, Volunteer Sewing for Playfair (Duluth, Minn.), selected for Art Entry at Local Art Colony (Wooburning of Scenery on Tree Fungus); [hon.] Who's Who in American High School Students; [oth. writ.] Penpal in Sochi, Russia who also works in a Kindergarten. We exchange pictures of our students art and talent.; [pers.] Most of what I know, believe and love came from Traveling and living in 10 different states. Raised in rural NY and Education in Michigan. I went on to work in camps, national parks, and tourist towns, group homes and Indian Reserves in SD, NM, Alaska, Wyoming, Texas, and Mexico and WA, for 10 years, before moving here to the Wilderness Area of Minnesota where I've been for 12 years.; [a.] Grand Marais, MN

NIVER, KAREN ANN
[pen.] Pegasus; [b.] October 29, 1952; [p.] JoAnn Muncie, John Green; [ch.] Shannon Jo Cummings; [ed.] Graduate of Miami Killian High School, Graduate of Charron William's College Paramedical Divisions; [occ.] Dental Assistant; [memb.] Florida Dental Association, CPR Basic Life Support; [pers.] I have always found peace by writing my poems by the sea, where it brings a calming effect upon me. I was inspired by how self motivated my daughter is, and how she is forever believing in me.; [a.] Miami, FL

NIXON, ANNIE WILLARD ROBINSON
[b.] September 8, 1896, Luka, MS; [p.] James Loving and Laura Isabel Lambert Robinson; [m.] Clinton Kelly Nixon, September 10, 1911; [ch.] James Clinton Nixon, Edward Kelly Nixon, Mildred Lorene Nixon Hill, Helen Marguerite Nixon; [ed.] Graduated 8th Grade; [occ.] Deceased-Homemaker and an excellent seamstress for her family; [memb.] Methodist Church Baptism Honorary Member of NSDAR and Theta Chapter, Kappa, Kappa Iota Sorority, Associate Member of Nat'l Assn of Retired Federal Employees (NARFE) from my Dtr, Helen Nixon; [oth. writ.] Birthday Milestones and others sent to you.; [pers.] Annie Nixon died 9 Jan. 1994. Her poems were found in her personal box in her trunk. Her personal life and faith were based on Proverbs 22 verse 1, "A good name is rather to be chosen than great riches, and loving favour rather than silver and gold." She had a distinguished and honorable name.

NKOMO, THABO WILLIAM
[b.] January 12, 1959, South Africa; [p.] William F. Nkomo (Deceased), Siena K. Lebodi; [ed.] Suffern High, Hamilton College, Suffern NY 1090, Clinton, NY 13323; [occ.] Assistant Supervisor, Thea Tiedemann and Sons. Inc. Mahwah, NY; [memb.] American Society of Composers, Authors and Publishers; [oth. writ.] Lyrics set to music other Lyrics soon to be set to music Currently working on a novel.; [pers.] I try my best to reflect the spirit of the human family in my writing. My inspiration comes from watching, listening to, and talking to people.; [a.] Suffern, NY

NOLAND, NATHAN MCKAIN
[pen.] Nathan McKain Noland; [b.] January 15, 1984, Jacksonville, TX; [p.] The late Mr. K. Corey McKain and Sammy and Marcie Noland; [ed.] Haude Elem, Strack Intermediate, Spring, TX; [hon.] Nathan has been in Honor Classes since 2nd grade.; [a.] Spring, TX

NORD, CINDY
[pen.] Cindy Lou; [b.] February 7, 1963, Stockton, CA; [p.] Roger Montoya, Pauline Frank; [m.] Terry Nord, April 20, 1991; [ch.] Joshua and Billy Nord, (foster children) Chasity Romey and Charlee Dennison; [ed.] High School Graduate 1992 - Bakersfield Adult School; [occ.] Foster Parent, Kern County Dept. of Human Resources; [memb.] California Police Activities League - To keep kids off drugs; [hon.] Foster Parent Assoc./Kern County Dept. of Human Resources for specialized Training, being licensed, adopting, and caring for abused children for 12 years, since 1983, also awarded for teaching Religion classes for the 3rd grade - St. Francis School; [oth. writ.] I've been writing poems for years, in which I have over a thousand in my journal. All my special poems have been given as gifts to family and friends.; [pers.] My poetry writing is one of my hobbies. Through it I want to have all my poetic writings published to share my enjoyments with others.; [a.] Bakersfield, CA

NORINSKY, IGOR
[pen.] Igor, Norinsky; [b.] March 11, 1984, Odessa, Ukraine; [p.] Boris Norinsky, Alla Norinsky; [ed.] Elementary School PS188, 5th grace; [memb.] Member of United States Judo, Inc.; [hon.] (1) Gr 3 Winner 1993 - "Bensonhurst West end Community Council", (2) Certificates of Award for BACA's Salute to Creative Youth - 1994, (3) "Black History Art and Essay Contest" winner - 1994, (4) BACA's - 1995, (5) Bronze medal winner as Author/illustrator in the 1995 - Ezrajack kets Book contest.; [oth. writ.] Two poems - "I being a bird" and "Spring" published in local newspaper; [pers.] "I try to write of life right here most of fun but some of fear some quite firmly some quite bold, but when I grow up to be so old all the poems that I have wrote. Thanks to my parents I shall note."; [a.] Brooklyn, NY

NORONHA, RUBINA
[pen.] Ruby Noronha; [b.] May 26, 1963, Karachi, Pakistan; [p.] Mabarak and Angelina Hossain; [m.] Clifford Noronha, February 29, 1992; [ch.] Nicole Noronha; [ed.] Long Island City High School, Queens College, New York, Ultrasound Diagnostic School; [occ.] Housewife; [hon.] Honor Roll; [oth. writ.] Several poems never published; [pers.] I can only write about what I know and feel; [a.] Gaithersburg, MD

NORRIS, TALITHA EASTRIDGE
[b.] August 27, 1953, Opelika, AL; [m.] James Thomas Norris; [ch.] Jamey 22, Karen 12; [occ.] Auburn Technical Assistance Center, Auburn University, AL; [oth. writ.] Short stories and poems; [pers.] Live simply, Love honestly, Feel deeply.; [a.] Opelika, AL

NORTH, KAY
[pen.] Kay North; [b.] January 7, 1941, Salt Lake City, UT; [p.] Wes and Arlene Kuehn; [m.] Ron North, February 19, 1960; [ch.] Jay, Brent and Jill; [ed.] Olympus High Salt Lake Community College; [occ.] Auditor for the Eye Institute of Utah; [oth. writ.] This is my first published writing.; [pers.] I am very concerned about our children of today!; [a.] Salt Lake City, UT

NOWBATH, FREDDY
[b.] September 17, 1966, Trinidad; [p.] Ramharrack Nowbath, Daisy Nowbath; [ed.] Penal Junior Secondary, Siparia Senior Comprehensive, San Fernando Technical Institute, Borough of Manhattan Community College; [hon.] I was awarded a Scholarship at San Fernando Technical Institute - "Trinidad"; [pers.] Only once we pass through this life and there is no turning back. Give love, appreciate kindness and fulfill your dreams.; [a.] Brooklyn, NY

NOYES, EBBIE
[pen.] Ebbie Noyes; [b.] April 9, 1963, Bountiful, UT; [p.] Rachel B. Noyes; [ed.] 2 years College at Weber State graduated Layton High; [occ.] USA Air Force Communications; [oth. writ.] Several stories and poems written just for fun, with my sister.; [pers.] My sister and I enjoy writing poems for elementary age children. This is the first time I've sent one in to a contest or even tried to have one published.; [a.] Salt Lake, UT

O'BRIEN, CHARLYN MARIE
[pen.] Charly; [b.] February 3, 1961, Philadelphia, PA; [m.] Steven O'Brien, September 24, 1983; [ch.] Elizabeth Megan, Rebecca-Jean; [ed.] Sun Valley High, Delaware County Community College; [occ.] Child care specialist; [memb.] St Clement's Catholic Church, Active member of the Patterson Home and School Association (secretary) and Volunteer, 5th grade classroom Asst.; [oth. writ.] Several poems and quotes I have written and I am now working on them getting published.; [pers.] Learn to believe in yourself, love yourself, for you are a child of God. Once you believe, follow your dreams. And only you can make them come true... Thanks to my sister for helping me, make my dreams come true!; [a.] Philadelphia, PA

O'BRIEN, PATRICIA
[p.] Eugene Viers, Mary Viers; [m.] A. D. O'Brien, July 23, 1977; [ch.] Gary Hoffar, Holly Hoffar-Burke, Amy Hoffar Kalis; [ed.] Rocky River High (Ohio), Henry Ford Community College (Mich); [occ.] Homemaker; [a.] Scottsdale, AZ

O'DONNELL, CARL W.
[b.] June 3, 1937, Crystal, WV; [ed.] Attended Schools in Wilmington, Del. Area; [occ.] Retired from Dupont Co. and currently working as part-time mgr. of a Beach Resort; [oth. writ.] My first attempt written in 15 minutes; [pers.] A strong animal activist I believe all God's creatures have rights.

O'DONNELL, ELIZABETH VIRGINIA EDWARDS
[pen.] Bette O'Donnell, Eliz O'Donnell; [b.] May 16, 1920, Baltimore, MD; [p.] States and Helen Parker Edwards; [m.] William S. O'Donnell, September 27, 1975 (second); [ch.] David Adam Suzanne Snider, Virginia Chorpenning Mark Adam Leslie Stranko; [ed.] High School Forest Park High Courses at A.C.C. Cumlerland; [occ.] Retired Avon District Manager 1962-82; [memb.] GFWC Womans Civic Club Cumlerland Woman's Sport Club, 4 Bridge Groups Beta Signs Phi-Laurente Mw, Memorial Hosp. Aux Ladies Hercules Bowling St. Lukes Choir; [hon.] Received a Congressional Medal of Honor in Waves 1942. Earned many Awards Mgr-Avon and Trips Bermuda; [oth. writ.] Several poems written for GFWC 2nd prize winner twice; [pers.] I love people, children, grandchildren and pets. I'm a happy person and choose pleasant people for companions and believe I'm in love with love and God.

O'HAVER, REV. RUBY NINA
[b.] January 15, 1945, Keyser, WV; [p.] Olyn Elzworth and Nina Mary Tichnell; [m.] Rev. William A. O'Haver Jr., June 16, 1973; [ch.] April Ann Knisley, Nina Mary O'Haver, Ann Olyn Elzworth O'Haver; [ed.] Valley High School, Catherman's Business School; [occ.] Homemaker and Musical Ministry, Evangelistic Field; [memb.] Fellowships Evangelism, Inc., DDAL, Inc., HSUS, Inc., National Committee for the Preservation of Social Security; [hon.] Certificate of Ordination License, The Presidents Athletic Award; [oth. writ.] I have written hundreds of poems, but only on a personal level for family and friends. I have written many gospel songs.; [pers.] I always try to uplift the name of Jesus Christ and bring Glory to God in my poetry, without whom I could not write.; [a.] Barton, MD

O'NEIL, J. R.
[pen.] Presley O'Neil; [b.] June 5, 1974, Olympia, WA; [p.] Denny O'Neil Sr. and Deby O'Neil; [ed.] Graduate: Evergreen High June 1993, Graduate: Clark County Vocational Skills Center June 1993, Clark College: September 1993 - Present Major: Business; [occ.] Resident Manager at Van Mall Retirement Community Van, WA; [memb.] National Human Rights Campaign Fund; [hon.] Best Reporting on The Port of Portland Operations June '92 "Travel and Tourism" Summer School Best Fiction Story 7th Grade June 1989 Shumway Middle School; [oth. writ.] Editorials, Various Poems Current: 2 Poetry Books, 1 Screenplay Hoping to be published in 1996; [pers.] I try to write poems that help people deal with there emotions. My Mother for always being there and encouraging me. Your my devine Inspiration.; [a.] Vancouver, WA

OELSLAGER, CHRISTY
[b.] June 15, 1979, Bemiji, MN; [p.] Gene Oelslager, Kay Oelslager; [ed.] Bemidji High School; [occ.] Student at Bemidji High School; [pers.] My feelings consolidate and uphold a vivid imagination which is inspired by my spiritual environment.; [a.] Bemidji, MN

OFFENBERGER, CATHY D.
[b.] October 4, 1953, Marietta; [p.] Regis and Ruth Mollohan; [m.] Stephen P. Offenberger, November 13, 1971; [ch.] Greg, Kristi; [ed.] Waterford High; [occ.] Domestic Engineer; [memb.] Women's Club of St. Bernard's Parish; [pers.] Poems are away of getting my feelings out. You can show your creativity.; [a.] Waterford, OH

OGLESBY, PAMELA HOWARD
[b.] May 13, 1953, Savannah, GA; [p.] The late Elmer Howard Sr. and Valerie Howard; [ch.] Taiyanika Oglesby-Warner and 1 grandson Terrence L. Warner II; [ed.] Tompkins High School, Gupton-Jones College of Mortuany Science 1976, Gupton-Jones College of Funeral Service-Associate of Science degree 1987; [occ.] Mortician (Licensed embalmer and funeral director); [memb.] President of the Bethany Baptist Church Gospel Choir, West Savannah Community Organization, Pi Sigma Eta Fraternity Alumni; [hon.] Scholastic Achievement Award 1976, First licensed female embalmer in South-Chatham County, Outstanding Young Woman of America 1982, Certificate of Appreciate Iota Phi Lambda Sorority 1995; [pers.] It is my wish to share my gift with others because most of my writings are abut people in present times, events in their lives and parts of their history. Poems that are keep sakes forever.; [a.] Savannah, GA

OLSON, CAROL CECELIA
[pen.] Carol Cecelia; [b.] June 10, 1938, Cincinatti, OH; [p.] Arthur and Gunhilde; [m.] Orvin B. Olson, August 12, 1955; [ch.] Laura, Amy, Diane; [ed.] High School and experientially worked on a small local newspaper doing human interest stories, inspirational column weekly poems; [occ.] Homemaker, Secretary, Chauffer, Confidante of husband. He is a consultant semi-retired.; [memb.] Eagles Nest (A place for families); [hon.] The biggest honor of life and award are the 15 grandchildren, ages 9 months to 16 years.; [oth. writ.] I've been carrying on a personal letter writing correspondence around world for 15 yrs. Have special stories I've made up for grandchildren.; [pers.] From a little girl in an Orphanage to a Granny of 15, God has kept and given me the best of all. Including the husband I prayed to God for at 14 yrs. Soon our 40th Wedding Anniversary.; [a.] King City, OR

OLSON, MICHELLE
[pen.] Holli Adams; [b.] October 18, 1959, Fort Dodge, IA; [p.] Virginia and Phil Haaland and Larry Pigman; [ch.] Holly Mae, Adam Joseph; [ed.] Clarion High School, The Institute of Children's Literature; [occ.] Pre-School Teacher; [memb.] Wright Elementary P.T.A.; [hon.] Honor Roll in High School, Dedicated Worker for Cub Scouts - Pack 34, Devoted Volunteer Work for Wright Elementary P.T.A.; [oth. writ.] Two Lost Soles, Thoughts of the Past, You are my Savior, Dream Away, Last Farewell, You've Captured My Sole (All not yet published.); [pers.] I would like to dedicate my poem to my father, Larry Pigman. Living through the pain and grief following his death greatly inspired me to write poetry. I love you Dad!; [a.] Cedar Rapids, IA

ORIOL, CHRISSY T.
[pen.] Monkey, Chris; [b.] December 13, 1979, Brooklyn, NY; [p.] Gilbert and Marie-Carmel Oriol; [ed.] West Orange H.S.; [memb.] Girl Scouts; [hon.] Honor Roll, Super Honor Roll, Attendance, Volleyball (2nd place), United States Achievement Academy Award; [pers.] If you can't find something to live for, find something to die for.; [a.] West Orange, NJ

ORLANDO, RENA F.
[b.] January 26, 1945, Boston; [p.] Mario and Ruth D'Agostino; [m.] Robert S. Orlando, August 11, 1962; [ch.] Robert, Debra, John; [ed.] Malden High School Bradenton Beauty Academy; [occ.] Cosmetologist; [memb.] Former Board of Director (Mirror Lake Condominium), Former President Activities Committee; [oth. writ.] I have written many poems but this is my first to be entered in a contest; [pers.] A mirror image of ones feelings is beautifully said in poetry. Happiness, love and tranquility is the feeling of the heart and I hope to touch the hearts of everyone that reads my poems.; [a.] Bradenton, FL

ORR, ORENA
[b.] June 27, 1948, Kesier, AR; [p.] Priest Orr, Gladys Orr; [ed.] Graduated High School Oakpark High, Ross Medical Education Center; [occ.] Between Jobs; [memb.] Fitness U.S.A., Health Spas, Walden Books; [hon.] Medical Assistant Registered Medical Assistant; [pers.] I believe the world would be a better place to live if everyone would stop living in the past and live for the future.; [a.] Oakpark, MI

ORSINI, CHARLES
[pen.] Charlie O; [b.] July 9, 1962, Mineola; [p.] Marian and James; [ed.] N.Y.S. G.E.D.; [occ.] Unemployed; [oth. Writ.] Wrote Don't Look In The Mirror; [pers.] I am a Christian Baptist and have a loving family; [a.] Bayshor, NY

ORTIZ, MICHAEL JOHN
[b.] June 27, 1970, The Bronx; [p.] Patricia Ann Blando; [ed.] Hunter College, The Borough of Manhattan Community College, Christopher Columbus High School; [oth. writ.] Winter Solstice, Carrion Heart, Late Night Storm, When I fell In Love With You; [pers.] There exist a much deeper sight, and 'tis my heart and mind which do the viewing. Love is beautiful, but love is blind, therefore, beauty cannot be seen, noticed, experienced with the mere sense of sight alone.; [a.] Bronx, NY

ORTON, ERIS
[b.] July 15, 1923, Clay Co, IA; [p.] Walter and Lois Stewart; [m.] Criley Orton, May 13, 1951; [ch.] Mary E. Orton, Barbara Hawthorne, Kathy Garcia; [ed.] Gillett Grove, Ia. High School, Iowa Methodist Hosp. school of Nursing Des Moines, Ia.; [occ.] Retired Rin; [memb.] Nazarene Church Ridgecrest, CA; [pers.] I enjoy reading, poetry, historical novels, Zane Grey, all of his books, fairy stories for children.; [a.] Ridgecrest, CA

OTTO, DR. LUDWIG
[b.] March 15, 1934, New York City, NY; [p.] Anna Messina Otton; [m.] Maxine Knight Otto, June 10, 1992; [ch.] Matthew, Ryan, Molly, Katherine, Jeff, David; [ed.] Ph.D., D. Min, MA, M. Div, BA, LLB; [occ.] Asst. Professor and Chair, English Dept; [memb.] Association of Sports Literature, National Association of Teachers of English, Modern Language Association; [hon.] Scholarship, Dallas Institute for the Humanities and Culture; [oth. writ.] 1. In the beginning there was change, 2. Euripides, Sophocles and others, The Shock-Jocks (Howard Sterns) of literature.

OWENS, JULIE
[pen.] "Jo"; [b.] February 5, 1979, Texas; [p.] William and Linda; [ed.] I attend Mt. Pleasant High School and hope to attend Texas A and M; [memb.] I have been on Nike Club for two years, Mt. Pleasant Tiger Dolls, and arrow head the forthcoming year.; [hon.] I have been honored in softball including all stars, varsity for the past two years and first team all-district.; [oth. writ.] I have never written in a contest before, but I have received high compliments in school from teachers and peers.; [pers.] "A road to success will never end unless you stop trying."; [a.] Mount Pleasant, TX

OWENS, JOANNE LYNN
[b.] January 30, 1960, Salem, NJ; [p.] Katherine D. Wood, Charles E. Owens; [ed.] Pennsville Memorial High School, NJ, Radford University, VA; [occ.] Records Manager for the law firm of Bayard, Handelman and Murdoch, PA, Wilmington, DE; [a.] Pennsville, NJ

OWENS, MICHAEL C.
[b.] December 31, 1971, Atlanta, CA; [p.] Jack and Ann Owens; [occ.] Closing Manager, Harbourton Mortgage Co. L.P.; [oth. writ.] Other poems published locally, two plays and Fraudulent Deception, a suspense novel.; [pers.] I write to relate my feelings and to give people something to think about. My biggest influences come from my everyday experiences.; [a.] Dunwoody, GA

OYEWOLE, ABIMBOLA PETER
[pen.] Peters Oyewole; [b.] December 4, 1957, Ibadan, Nigeria; [p.] Mrs. Julie Oyewole, Moses Oyewole; [ed.] University of Ibadan, Nigeria; [occ.] Freelance Writer; [memb.] Nigerian's Writers Association, Nigerian Press, Sonithsonian; [hon.] BA and MA History, Dean's List; [oth. writ.] Several poems (unpublished), 2 novels (unpublished), several articles and writings published in two Nigaria's newspapers; [pers.] I write mostly from personal experiences and try to right many wrong.; [a.] Elizabeth, NJ

PADULA, ANTONELLA M.
[b.] June 26, 1972, Philadelphia; [p.] Filomena and Antonio Padula; [ed.] The Art Institute of Philadelphia - 10/90 - 12/92 La Salle University 1/93 - 5/95 St. Maria Goretti High School 1986-1990; [occ.] Travel Agent; [hon.] Who's Who Among American High School Students; [oth. writ.] I am in the process of writing a screenplay for motion picture and a novel. I have also written a collection of poems and two poems were printed in our high school poetry book entitled. The patroness.; [pers.] I strive to include all aspects of art into my life. My heritage as well as learning about other cultures are very important to me. I strive to achieve the highest artistic merits like the artists of my ancestry.; [a.] Philadelphia, PA

PALMER, PAT
[b.] January 1, 1938, Boston, MA; [p.] Frances and Peter; [ed.] High School and 1 yr. at University of Mass., in New York studied Solfeggio, Harmony and Theory with Carol Longone who produced "Operalogues" at the Pierre Hotel for over 50 years. I sang in those Operalogues. Voice studies with Maude D. Tweedy; [occ.] President of Pat Palmer Inc., 12 E 63, NY. 10021 (A realtor); [memb.] Member of New York Athletic Club, Real Estate Board of New York, Member of Voice Foundation founded by Dr. Wilbur J. Gould, Board member of Amato Opera; [hon.] National Honor Society while in High School, won Essay on Statewide contest "What It Means To Be An American" all high school students were eligible to enter. Won cash prizes for preceding essay, and won cash prize for essay contest in New York Journal American, "How I Found My Apartment."; [oth. writ.] Am just finishing a book on New York Real Estate which I feel will be interesting to the general public, also have started two separate biographical novels, write poetry only for myself usually.; [pers.] Studied to be an Opera Singer which was my desire since I was a child, but when opportunity knocked in Real Estate I took it. My favorite poet is Robert Browning. I love art songs by Faure, Debussy, also Lieder by Schubert and Schumann which I am still studying. Horatio Alger had an influence on me as a child. Am a student of Greek classics, my favorites are Iliad and Odyssey by (Homer); [a.] New York, NY

PALMER, TRACY M.
[b.] July 31, 1972, Holyoke, MA; [p.] Stanley A. and Barbara A. Palmer; [ed.] South Hadley High School Graduate; [occ.] Cable Systems Installer; [memb.] US Army National Guard; [hon.] Verbal presentation of my poem at the Town of South Hadley Memorial Day ceremonies May 1993; [pers.] Due to the encouragement of many special people in my life and the publication of "They Forgot", I plan to continue in my poetry endeavors with the hope of future recognition.; [a.] South Hadley, MA

PALMER, VAL
[b.] April 29, 1905; [ed.] College of Hard Knock; [occ.] Retired, donate my time tutoring Math; [oth. writ.] Misc. also book published "A New Look at the Fractions"; [pers.] Strong for education; [a.] Rockford, IL

PALMER SR., HARRY D.
[pen.] Hank; [b.] March 22, 1922, Erie, PA; [p.] George E. and Ethel B. Palmer; [m.] Madeline Jayne Palmer, September 22, 1959; [ch.] Maredith, Patricia, Donna, Joyce Deborah, Sandra, Harry Jr., Karen, Lisa; [ed.] High School, College Agriculture Doctor of Divinity; [occ.] Retired; [hon.] Doctor of Divinity, The voice in the wilderness hour radio broadcast speaker and director since 1972; [oth. writ.] 40 books 200 poems none published! Yet.; [pers.] This life is short! The next life is very long. Don't miss it's joy and pleasures!; [a.] Waterfall, PA

PAMIN, DIANA DOLHANCYK
[pen.] Diana Dolhancyk; [b.] December 13, Cleveland, OH; [p.] Peter Dolhancyk and Diana Dribus Dolhancyk; [m.] Leonard Pamin; [ch.] Louis Peter and Diana Anne; [ed.] West Tech. High, Titus College of Cosmetology; [memb.] Arthritis Foundation, International Society of Poets, and I have sponsored a young girl in India for the past 15 yrs.; [hon.] "Editors Choice Award" for outstanding achievement in poetry, for "The Parting", in "Journey of the Mind", published by the N.L.O.P. "Editors Choice Award" for "Stormy" in "Songs on the Wind", "Burnt by Love" in "East of the Sunrise" and "Shadow Side" in "At Waters Edge"; [oth. writ.] And forth coming anthology, "Best Poems of 1996". My poem "The Parting" was in The Sun Star Newspaper. I hope to publish a book of my own poems, soon.; [pers.] Always give someone a smile, you'll never know whose heart you might lighten. I wrote my first poem at the age of 12.; [a.] North Royalton, OH

PANASIEWICZ, FRANCES-BEAN
[b.] April 17, 1923, Utica; [p.] Joseph and Frances Muller; [m.] Stanley Panasiewicz, October 11, 1941; [ch.] Janet, Patricia, Stanley, Richard Frances; [ed.] High School; [occ.] Retired; [memb.] Moose Lodge; [pers.] Married twice Panasiewicz children's father; [a.] Utica, NY

PANG, MISTY
[b.] June 20, 1979, Honolulu, HI; [p.] Carlos Pang and Yung Pang; [ed.] Still in High School (Junior) McKinley High School; [occ.] Student; [pers.] When writing poetry or lyrics for my band, I try to put myself in someone else's shoes and try to imagine how and what they feel. From then on I transfer those feelings to paper.; [a.] Kapolei, HI

PANZA, PAUL NICHOLAS
[b.] May 31, 1985, Seattle, WA; [p.] Nicholas and Lucy Panza; [ed.] Entering 5th grade in Fall '95; [occ.] Student; [memb.] National In-Line Hockey Association, Kids Club-New York Rangers; [hon.] "Caldeberry" Award For Best 2nd Grade Book Pleasant Library, Pleasant, CA 1992; [oth. writ.] The Wind, If I Could Give he World a Gift; [pers.] One man's strength is another man's weakness.

PARISI, LAUREL L.
[pen.] Lura Parise; [b.] September 2, 1979; [p.] Anthony and Lynn Parisi; [ed.] Baldwin Senior High School; [occ.] Student; [hon.] Honorable Mention in Iliad Press's Summer Awards Program; [oth. writ.] Published in "Phoenix" literary magazine twice; [pers.] "Always live your life on your own terms and never try to be what you are not"; [a.] Baldwin, NY

PARKER, DONALD L.
[b.] February 9, 1952, Nampa, ID; [p.] Harlan and Myrtle Parker; [m.] Karen Parker, July 14, 1973; [ch.] Donald II (Paige), Daniel; [ed.] California Baptist College, Western Baptist Seminary, International Seminary, Southern Baptist School for Biblical Studies; [occ.] Pastor

PARKER, DONNA
[pen.] Donna Parker; [b.] April 17, 1964, Fairfax; [p.] Margaret Fox, Andrew Parker; [ed.] Wood Bridge Senior High School - Class of 1982. Woodbridge, VA; [occ.] Ladies apparel Montgomery Ward, Springfield, VA; [memb.] I am a panel member for the home testing institute PO Box 9200 Port Washington, NY (11050); [pers.] I would like to dedicate my work to "Sharon", (My roommate) and her two cats, "Willie" and "Tuna"; [a.] Woodbridge, VA

PARKER, MADELYN AMBROSE
[b.] May 20, 1958, Petaluma, CA; [p.] Don and Virginia Ambrose; [m.] Christopher John Parker, January 13, 1992; [ch.] Kristopher Kody and Madison; [sib.]; [ed.] Santa Rosa High School; [occ.] Job Coach - independent living counselor; [oth. writ.] Several poems and children's books unpublished; [pers.] Through my poetry I hope to leave the threads of the past with those of future dreams into a protective cocoon in which I will emerge like a butterfly tranquil and free. Always inspired by my sister to share my love for words.; [a.] Santa Rosa, CA

PARKINSON JR., ROBERT
[pen.] Parkinson; [b.] June 17, 1962, Rahway, NJ; [p.] Robert and Eileen Parkinson; [ed.] Quincy College IL. Berklee College of Music, Boston MA; [occ.] Director of Employment Services, Shore Training Center Morton Grove, IL; [memb.] United way Child reach; [oth. writ.] Several songs and other poems. Speeches and essays on employing persons with disabilities; [a.] Chicago, IL

PARONE, JESSIE ELAINE WEST
[b.] February 20, 1905, Crawford Town, PA; [p.] Carmello West and Maria Nalbone West; [m.] Daniel Parone, March 6, 1923; [ch.] Marilyn A. Canali, Betty Zucco, Frances J. Parone and Anthony D. Parone; [ed.] Through sixth grade and night school (business course); [occ.] Retired; [oth. writ.] Poetry; [pers.] I enjoy life to the fullest with my family. I enjoy the days as they come along, and I expect to live to at least 100 or more!; [a.] Niagara Falls, NY

PARRA, LUCY M.
[b.] June 6, 1927, Chicago; [p.] Jesus and Luis Quintana; [m.] Albert Parra (Deceased), November 13, 1948; [ch.] Elizabeth, Susan, Laura, Albert, Daniel; [ed.] St. Pauls High (San Francisco Zweegman Medical Secretarial School) San Francisco; [occ.] Medical Secretary Retired; [oth. writ.] Several poems unpublished; [pers.] The love for my children and their love for me has inspired me to put on paper my feelings for them. They have been my life.; [a.] Oregon City, OR

PARRISH, ROSEMARY
[b.] March 30, 1953, Huntington, WV; [ch.] Melissa and Amber; [ed.] Bachelor of Arts, Christian Counseling Carolina Christian University 4640 Old Linwood Rd. Linwood, NC 27299; [occ.] Prod.-General Elec.; [memb.] American Ass. Christian Counselors and Therapist, National Christian Counselors Ass. Licensed Minister, United Full Gospel Church, Ohio Ass. of Christian Counselor sand Therapists; [oth. writ.] Several other poems; [pers.] To reflect the most important influence in my life-Jesus Christ

PASTOR, ERIC ANTHONY
[pen.] Five; [b.] August 6, 1971, Oahu, HI; [ch.] Kiani Pastor; [ed.] DeWitt Clinton High; [occ.] Utleys Inc., Color Matcher; [memb.] M.R.; [oth. writ.] I have 25 others but they are yet to be read; [pers.] I write about how I live, feel and what I see, that being my surroundings one forty.; [a.] South Bronx, NY

PATTERSON, LISA
[b.] July 19, 1963, Lackawanna, NY; [p.] John P. Patterson Sr., Rita Patterson; [ed.] Lackawanna Senior High; [occ.] Health and Safety Coordinator, Trim Masters Inc., Bardstown, KY; [pers.] To my family (especially Linda) who truly believes in me, I give thanks. This poem is dedicated to the memories of the 107th-fig, Niagara Falls, NY (Nyang) I praise God for my gift of writing.; [a.] Elizabethtown, KY

PATTON, ACIE
[b.] March 6, 1933, Camden, AR; [p.] Mr. and Mrs. Embry; [ed.] 12 yrs. high school; [occ.] Retired; [memb.] Toledo Museum of Art Health mag., Decision Mag., Voice of Victory mag.; [pers.] Being about some thought for a better life in our world.; [a.] Toledo, OH

PATTON, KRISTINE ELIZABETH
[b.] September 11, 1978, Battle Creek, MI; [p.] Carol Ann Patton; [ed.] Junior of the American School Home Study Program; [pers.] Writing poetry puts me at ease. I hope it does the same for those who read it.

PATZER, TY
[pen.] Ty Patzer; [b.] February 13, 1977, Gresham, OR; [p.] Herb and Sharon; [ed.] Barlow H.S.; [occ.] Starving poet; [oth. writ.] Unpublished; [a.] Gresham, OR

PAYE, MARIA PAULINA-CHANTEL
[pen.] MPCP; [b.] November 9, 1977, Tarzana, CA; [p.] Gary Paye Sr. and Antonia Paye; [memb.] The Nature Conservancy; [oth. writ.] Untitled poem published in the anthology of poetry by young Americans troops 1994 edition; [pers.] "I'm a Romantic, with an imagination not yet complete."; [a.] Valencia, CA

PEARSON, PAULA R.
[pen.] Paula R. Massey; [b.] February 17, CA; [p.] Lillie Mick, Paul Massey; [m.] Jon Pearson Jr. (separated); [ch.] Joshua, Jeremy; [ed.] Mt. Tahoma H.S., Clover Park Voc-Tech; [occ.] Full-time mom, part-time Sales Associate; [memb.] St. Andrew Presbyterian Church; [hon.] Honorable mention: (poems) only a memory, to a special friend; [oth. writ.] To a special friend (published in 1984); [pers.] I would personally like to thank my friends and family for all their love, and to Patrick Duban for the inspiration and friendship that is never ending!; [a.] Tacoma, WA

PECCERILLO JR., JOHN
[b.] May 15, 1969, Brooklyn, NY; [p.] Giovanni and Guiseppina Peccerillo; [m.] Sheri Peccerillo, February 12, 1994; [ed.] Division Avenue High School; [occ.] Bagel Baker; [oth. writ.] Books (notebooks) of my writings, never published.; [pers.] I love to write poems, my biggest influence is and was Jim Morrison, I never read any poems, 15 years ago I just started to write, to me it's an escape.; [a.] Levittown, NY

PEDVIS, ANCA
[b.] March 5, 1946, Romania; [p.] Stella and Samuel Pedvisocar; [m.] Bogdan Borgovan, July 24, 1984; [ch.] Stephanie Borgovan; [ed.] Fine Arts Institute Bucharest, Romania; [occ.] Fine Artist, Designer and Writer; [hon.] National and International Awards as a Fine Artist.; [oth. writ.] Since 1967 poems published by the most prominent literary magazines in Romania; [pers.] I strive to translate the wonders and depth of human experience.; [a.] New York, NY

PEEPLES, SAMUEL
[b.] April 24, 1952, New York, NY; [p.] Clarence and Edna Peeples; [m.] Saundra Washington-Peeples, November 28, 1994; [ch.] Erica Lynn Peeples and Kenneth Peeples; [ed.] Graduated Brien McMahon High School South Norwalk, CT; [occ.] Telecommunications Installation Technician; [oth. writ.] Other poems include Puberty's Curse, Who Are They, My Town, and Oasis; [pers.] Everyday life is a struggle. We must all find something in our lives that will strengthen us for the battle we face each day. Love is what I seek.; [a.] Detroit, MI

PEEPLES, SAUNDRA L. WASHINGTON
[p.] Reatha and Andrew Smith; [m.] Samuel F. Peeples, November 28, 1994; [ed.] BSW, Mary Grove College MA, Wayne State University MATS, Ashland Theological Seminary D.D., Tennessee School of Religion (Hon); [occ.] Social worker, social expression writer; [memb.] American Counseling Assoc., Michigan Counselling Assoc., NAACP., Assoc. Death Education and Counselling, Assoc of Christian Therapists, Greater Detroit Interfaith Round Table; [hon.] Four Dedicated Service Awards, Who's Who Among Human Service Professionals, Who's Who in Religion, Who's Who of American Women, Distinguished Leadership Award; [oth. writ.] Poem-"Looking Out The Rear Window" published in Bereavement Magazine. Book manuscript, "Leaves of Truth" being considered for publication. Working on "Life's Love, Loss and Laughter," a collection of poems.; [pers.] My writings seek to inspire and encourage readers to move from the trivial to the significant, from the temporal to the eternal. I have been most influenced by Helen Steiner Rice.; [a.] Detroit, MI

PEGLAR, RICHARD T.
[b.] August 27, 1945, Cleveland, OH; [p.] Art and Margaretta Peglar; [m.] Barbara Peglar, April 17, 1971; [ch.] Heather Robertson, Jesse Peglar, Joey Peglar; [ed.] St Edward High School, Lakewood, Ohio, College: Inter American University, San German, Puerto Rico; [occ.] Operations Manager;

[memb.] Arkansas Municipal League, Gassville Fire Department Gassville City Council; [pers.] A prospector looks for gems with a pan or a pick. A poet uses a pen.; [a.] Gassville, AR

PENA, ABE M.
[b.] November 8, 1926, San Mateo, NM; [p.] Pablo and Pablita Pena; [m.] Viola R. Pena, August 27 1955; [ch.] Ramona, Paula, Cecilia and Marco; [ed.] B.S. Animal-Science New Mexico State University, graduate study Fulbright Scholar Univ. New South Wales, Australia; [occ.] Secretary-Treasurer D. and P. Pena Ranch, Inc. retired from Foreign Service.; [memb.] AARP, member of National Legislative Council, Chairman Rio Grande Historical Collections, Director N. Mex. Senior Golf Association, member Grants Chamber of Commerce.; [hon.] Honorary Doctor of Laws From New Mexico State University 1978, Superior Honor Award 1978. Superior Honor Award Agency for International Development Aid 1978, Frog Department of State; [oth. writ.] Write a Historical Column for local newspaper, published in Prime Time, Gaschantscvt, Panorama, Hevencia Del Norte; [pers.] I'm writing a "life" history of hispanic life is colonial and territorial time in stories "From the Past" that tell what my people did for a living... day to day.; [a.] Grants, NM

PENROD, BEN
[pen.] Raven; [b.] January 12, 1975, Dover, OH; [p.] Raymond and Joanne Penrod; [m.] Heather Penrod, December 13, 1995; [ch.] Hannah Sue Penrod; [ed.] High School Graduate and Proud and Dover High; [occ.] Factory Worker; [memb.] United Methodist Church in Mineral City Ohio; [hon.] The only honors I will be proud of (The Honor of the Penrod name); [oth. writ.] Many other poems and songs, I'm still writing and praying I achieve my goal, to become a published writer of my own poetry book.; [pers.] Fight the odds, win or lose the ultimate prize is knowledge, don't ever let anyone tell you that you can't catch your dreams.; [a.] New Philadelphia, OH

PENTECOST, THOMAS
[b.] November 12, 1950, Weinheim, Germany; [ed.] B.S., Arizona State Univeristy, M.I.M., American Graduate School of International Management, Currently Attending Baltimore International Culinary College; [occ.] U.S. Army, Retired, Consultant, CTI; [oth. writ.] Several poems published in newspapers in El Paso, TX; [pers.] For me, poetry is a way to bring myself and a reader to understand a moment.

PEOPIES, DAVIED J.
[b.] April 18, 1970, Bronx, NY; [p.] Bettye Peopies and Willie Jenkins; [ed.] John F. Kennedy High School, Bronx Community College, The City College of New York; [occ.] Student (college) seeking a BA in English; [memb.] The International Society of Poets; [hon.] 1995 Editor's Choice Awards in poetry by the National Library of Poetry; [oth. writ.] "Pungent Love" published in After The Storm, "Dead Phone" published in A Moment In Time, "You Sitting There" published in A Sea of Treasures, "Chained to the Days of Yesterday" published in Best Poems of 1996; [pers.] I hope to get better with each poem. I create.; [a.] Bronx, NY

PERDUE, JO ANN
[b.] October 31, Los Angeles, CA; [p.] Ann Marie Perdue and Leonard Rodney Perdue; [occ.] I am self-employed part-time with a gift basket and handcrafted gift business (I'm also an Administrative Asst.); [oth. writ.] This is my first publication. I have many unpublished works, that I would like to put into book from one day soon.; [pers.] My writings come from the inspiration of heaven itself. I draw great inspiration from my spiritual beliefs. I've also been inspired by the works of Helen Steiner Rice.; [a.] Los Angeles, CA

PEREA, BENJAMIN
[pen.] Ben Perea; [b.] May 12, 1930, Torreon, NM; [p.] Antonio Perea and Escolastica Perea; [m.] Celeste Zamora Perea, January 21, 1956; [ch.] Linda Celeste, Benjamin Ramon, Maria Luisa (Lisa); [ed.] Estancia High School Graduate, Two years University of New Mexico in Albuq., NM.; [occ.] Advertisement Consultant with Linda Sedillo; [memb.] Disabled American Veterans, Veterans of Foreign Wars, American Legion.; [hon.] Unbearable Plaques, and Certificates, such as the outstanding Citizen Award, from Keep America Beautiful; [oth. writ.] Many many unpublished poems and songs, and many letter and the local newspaper: "The Torrance County Citizen" here in estancia New Mexico 87016. My latest writings are professional letter writing.; [pers.] When I travel to any of the large cities, and I see the homeless, and the homeless, and the alcoholics, and the young teenage girls and boys on the streets pushing drugs and prostitution, I return home totally depressed and I feel so helpless.; [a.] Estancia, NM

PEREZ, MICHAEL
[b.] August 13, 1979, New Braunfels, TX; [p.] J.D. and Debbie Perez; [ed.] New Braunfels High School (1988 graduate); [memb.] National Honor Society, National Eagle Scout Association, Order of the Arrow (B.S.A.); [hon.] Eagle Scout, will graduate with honors in 1998, Recipient of the Presidential Academic Fitness Award; [pers.] To live, is to sleep, to die, is to awaken!; [a.] New Braunfels, TX

PERIN, ANTHONY
[b.] April 3, 1953, Windsor, Ontario, Canada; [p.] Daniel Perin, Carmella Perin; [ch.] Patrick Alan, Michael Anthony; [ed.] Peterson High, West Valley College, University of Phoenix; [occ.] Manager, High Tech Industry; [memb.] San Francisco Bay Area Artists Association; [oth. writ.] Currently working on several screenplays (unpublished as of yet); [pers.] One writes what one feels, and in this way touches all those around him.; [a.] Union City, CA

PERLOW, AUSTIN H.
[b.] June 16, 1914, New York; [m.] Mildred Stern Perlow, July 19, 1945; [ch.] Kenneth R., Ellen J.; [ed.] BA New York University; [occ.] Retired; [memb.] Workers Education Local 189 or CWA National Writers Union Local 1981 U.A.W.; [hon.] Numerous citations from trade unions as outstanding labor columnist; [oth. writ.] What have you done for me lately? Basic Communications Akills— A Handbook for Unions; [a.] Hempstead, NY

PERRI, GLORIA JEAN O.
[pen.] G. O. Perri; [b.] November 27, 1947, Philadelphia; [p.] Robt and Elvira Olivieri; [m.] Gustav S. Perri, May, 24, 1969; [ch.] Robert Jonathan, Joshua Michael; [ed.] High School Some College Dropped out of night school at St. Joe's Private Art Classes no degree; [occ.] Free Lance Artist - Homemaker; [memb.] Christian Children's Fund Pro-Life, PTA, Green Peace, Audobon Society, Brian Davies (Save the Marp Seal), Christian Coalition, Blue Army, Catholic Charismatics.; [hon.] Soccer Coach; [oth. writ.] Short stories, working on a novel, and a full diary of poems.; [pers.] Life moves very fast. Every once in a while, we must pluck out a moment. These moment's, are the times we shall cherish forever...; [a.] Philadelphia, PA

PERSAUD, JOHN W.
[b.] February 1, 1949, Guyana, SA; [p.] Hiram S. Ruth; [m.] Anita; [ch.] Nigel and Anastasia; [ed.] New York Institute of Photography, School of modern Photography, Writer's Institute of America, Gyana mining enterprise management Institute and Guyana State Corp. P.R.O. Institute; [occ.] Publisher the "West Indiana" (newspaper); [memb.] "Motion picture and television engineers of America" "Writers Institute of America"; [hon.] Awards of Special Commendation school of modern Photography May 1971 and November 1971; [oth. writ.] Nearly Completed (Novel) "The Stained Fields" The Life of an Indian family of the British Colonial End in now - "Guyana" S. America; [pers.] I believe that the basics of Mass Communication is to unite all people regardless of race, culture and religion. Tough as it is, the pen and camera can heal the pain of misunderstanding - if we strive to tell the truth.; [a.] Ozone Park Queens, NY

PETERSON, IRENE H.
[b.] April 9, 1926, Baraga, MI; [p.] Maria and Albert Bitschenaver; [m.] James T. Peterson, July 1, 1955; [ch.] Lenore Peterson, Christie Duncan, Paul Peterson; [ed.] Graduated Baraga H.S. Baraga, MI, attended Medill School of Journalism, North Western U.; [occ.] Retired; [memb.] Ctr. for Nat'l, Independence in Politics, Or Public Broadcasting, Nat'l Org. of Women, Handgun Control Inc, Council of Indian Nations, Planned Parenthood, So Poverty Law Ctr., Americans for responsible T.V.; [hon.] Detroit Free Press Award for Declamation and Oratory, Best Actress Award Spokane Civic Theatre, Best Supporting Actress Albany Civic Theatre; [oth. writ.] An unfinished childrens story, lots of print and radio advertising and years of fashion show commentary. All occasion versification.; [pers.] I am an activist for moderate politics, in behalf of the poor, poorly-educated, minorities and am saddened by the continuing mindless assault on our environment.; [a.] Vancouver, WA

PETERSEN, JAN CHORLTON
[pen.] Jan Chorlton Petersen; [b.] September 1, 1949, Seattle; [m.] Barry Petersen, February 14, 1985; [ed.] Began Post-University with serious travel...which led to postings in Tokyo, Moscow, London, Forays into 46 countries, 10 years overseas.; [occ.] Journalist; [memb.] Not a joiner by temperament, and seldom very long in one place

PETIT, JESSICA M.
[b.] September 21, 1978, Saint Louis, MO; [p.] Dr Charles D. Petit and Penny M. Petit; [ed.] Spring Valley High; [occ.] Student; [pers.] Taking the Lord's name in vain is not saying "God Damn," but saying you're a Christian and not changing to reflect Christ.; [a.] Columbia, SC

PETRIDES, CAROLINA
[b.] December 15, 1969, New York; [p.] Pavlos and Florence Xenofontos; [m.] George Petrides, July 10, 1994; [ed.] Masters in Early Childhood Education, BA. in Elementary Education; [occ.] School Teacher, John Philip Sousa Elementary, Port Washington, NY; [hon.] Dean's List; [pers.] I am very thankful to my husband who gives me many reasons to write poetry, and my dad who said I could do all that I wanted in life.; [a.] Franklin Square, NY

PEXTON, RICHARD WILLIAM
[pen.] The Noid-Dark Poet; [b.] December 29, 1971, Saltlake City, UT; [p.] Richard and Geri Pexton; [ed.] Associates Degree in Refrigeration, Heating, and Air Conditioning Western Technical Institution; [occ.] Refrigeration Tech.; [oth. writ.] As an amateur writer I've never published or entered any of my 100 plus poems. I love to express myself through my writings. I wrote walls of steel, behind 'em. Reflect my true emotions in this poem through my experience here at I.S.F.; [pers.] I'm an exceptional achiever at whatever I put my mind to do. I favor dark poetry. I'm influenced by Edgar Allen Poe, William Shakespeare, Jim Morrison, and Kurt Cobain.; [a.] El Paso, TX

PHELPS, SANDY LEE A.
[pen.] Sas; [b.] June 6, 1962, Great Barrington, MA; [p.] Alvin Stalker, Carol Stalker; [m.] Daniel Phelps, January 18, 1989; [ch.] Shauna Phelps, Brittney Phelps; [ed.] Monument Mountain Regional High School; [occ.] Business Owner Canyon County Woodworks; [memb.] Fraternal Order of Eagles, North Santiam Chamber of Commerce; [pers.] All experience becomes my whole.; [a.] Mill City, OR

PHILLIPS, MELANIE
[b.] April 3, 1978, Akron, OH; [p.] David and Patricia Phillips; [ed.] Senior year of High School; [oth. writ.] Other poetry; [pers.] "I believe art is an expression of a person's inner feelings. It has no limits or rules. But, it does have meaning and beauty. Poetry is art. (I'm greatly influenced by music); [a.] Akron, OH

PHILLIPS, SHERRI KAY
[b.] April 17, 1962, Lake Charles, LA; [p.] Phillip and Gwen Phillips; [ed.] Westlake High, Westlake, LA McNeese State University, Lake Charles, LA (BA) Speech and Communication; [memb.] Alpha Delta Pi, Alpha Psi Omega Fraternity, Alpha Chi Fellowship; [hon.] Alpha Delta Pi Best Essay, McNeese Theatre Best Performance, Played Lead Rolls in "Cat On Hot Tin Roof" - "Amelia Airhart" - "Steel Magnolias" - "Absurd Person Singular" - "Who's Got the Will" and "Best Little Whore House"; [oth. writ.] All her poems are being made into a book to help others with cancer.; [pers.] She lived life to the fullest with so much understanding for her years. Friends came to be with her from New York to Los Angeles during her short illness and departing of her soul on this earth.

PHILPITT, EDWARD T.
[b.] November 15, 1926, Washington, DC; [p.] Isabel and Richard Philpitt; [ed.] Graduate of Benjamin Franklin Univ. 1952; [occ.] Write poems, retired; [memb.] The International Society of Poets; [pers.] It's fun to play but more profitable to work. Pray for those that goes freely and expect nothing in return. Love will never suffer when greed is imposed. Abandon is there-selectivity is the key. The thoughts you bank-shows your willingness to learn. It's devotion that produces a perfect bed of roses. The clock of the mind should wind and unwind slowly. It's through individual thoughts that we can entertain the stardom within.; [a.] Washington, DC

PIANO, VICKI L.
[pen.] Walks In The Rain; [b.] August 14, 1954, Sheridan, WY; [p.] Catherine Anich and Larry Dowdell; [m.] Frank Xavier Piano, August 18, 1983; [ch.] Miranda Jean, Adam Douglas, Alyce Marie; [ed.] Longmont Senior High, Longmont, CO, Morrisville College, New York; [occ.] Bookkeeper-Eric W. Turin Contracting; [oth. writ.] Several unpublished writings on native American peoples, views of the west.; [pers.] My ancestors are Ojibwa my ancestors are Vikings - this I understand with my heart. To the Lakota people and Pineridge and the crow people in Montana-thank you for sharing wondrous gift, showing me the way home.; [a.] Quakertown, PA

PICARD, EARL J.
[pen.] Earl "Nickey" Picard; [b.] October 10, 1931, Lafayette; [p.] Henry Avery Picard and Levee Marie Durio; [m.] Cecille Jeanette Dupuis, April 3, 1949; [ch.] Leslie James Picard-Darlene Ann Picard and Timothy L. Picard; [ed.] Two years college-graduated Southern Police Institute-University of Louisville. Continuing education programs Louisiana State University-University of Southwestern Louisiana-Penn State and University of Houston, Texas. Federal Bureau of Narcotics Training Academy-Louisiana State Police Academy. Marshal, City Court of Lafayette, Louisiana; [memb.] Louisiana Peace Officers-Alumni Association University of Louisville and University of Southwestern Louisiana. Cajun Golf Association-Carencro Golf Association Lafayette Senior Men's Golf Association and Lafayette Men's Golf Association.; [hon.] Lawman of the year 1970-Louisiana-Mississippi and West Tennessee Department of Public Safety Special Recognition for poems "Did you?" and "The Kid Behind The Wheel". Army Commendation Medal and Army Achievement Medal. Appointment to rank of Command Sergeant Major-US Army. Louisiana Commendation Medal.; [oth. writ.] Several poems on traffic safety and other subjects printed in magazines, bulletins and local newspapers.; [pers.] I believe a poem should reflect true live and feelings from one's heart. There is so much goodness in our world and writings can bring out such goodness.; [a.] Lafayette, LA

PIERCE, EVELYN
[pen.] Evelyn Pierce; [b.] October 7, 1915, Jakin, GA; [p.] William B. Springer, Bula G. Springer; [m.] Clarence W. Pierce, May 10, 1945; [ch.] One; [ed.] 7th Grade; [occ.] Retired; [memb.] Calvary Baptist Church also The American Legion; [pers.] I have lived in Fla. since 1945 after leaving GA, have always wanted to write, but not time to do so the lowly; [a.] Winter Garden, FL

PILARCZYK, FRED
[b.] January 28, 1978, Varhees, NJ; [p.] Nancy Pilarczyk and Frank Pilarczyk; [ed.] Student at Cherokee High School; [occ.] Student; [memb.] Wiley Church, Cherokee High School Marching Band, Cherokee Scout (newspaper); [hon.] Honor Roll, 4 year band member, 2 year newspaper member; [oth. writ.] Written articles and poems of local magazines and newspapers; [pers.] I just want to thank all of my family and friend for their love and support for without them I wouldn't be here.; [a.] Marlton, NJ

PIPER, JO ANN CHASE
[pen.] Jo Piper; [b.] April 5, 1929, Lake City, IA; [p.] Wilber and Ella Chase; [m.] Charles M. Piper, March 23, 1951; [ch.] Steven E., Kevin C. and Alan M.; [ed.] Lake City, IA HS Graduate, University of North IA, Writing from J. Webb Rebuilding seminars, orientation for volunteers; [occ.] Retired homemaker, writer, volunteer; [memb.] UNI Sorority, Church of Christ, International Society of Poets, retired and Senior Volunteer Program, Transportation Board for Seniors; [hon.] UNI Honor society, distinguished member of ISP, 6 Editor's Choice Awards from NLP, reading authors of Loveland, CO; [oth. writ.] "The Gift", "Tribute", "A Daughter Writes Home", "Love Letter", "Simplicity's Child", "Song for the Golden Years", "Equinox", "Prodical Found", "The Candle"; [pers.] Cherishing yesterday while dreaming about tomorrow, I live today writing and resting to keep my body and my soul in good health-I just love life because God has blessed me; [a.] Loveland, CO

PIQUE, ROGER
[pen.] Roger Pique; [b.] February 1, 1941, Detroit, MI; [p.] Oliver and Eleanor Pique; [m.] Mary Edith Pique (Deceased), August 26, 1973; [ch.] Roger Oliver, Robert Rossini, Kipp Gregory; [ed.] Fulton City High School, Colorado State University National Honor Society, Quill and Scroll Society, President; [occ.] Retired Insurance Executive; [memb.] 12100 Elas, Eagles, Moose, F and AM., Masonic Temple, 1st Methodist Church; [hon.] Rotary-Citizen of year 1974, Salesman of Year 1973-1977 - BPOE. Officer 1979 Elk of the Year 1980; [oth. writ.] All poems Life's River, Blood N' Honor, What is Forgiveness, Worldly Wise, Catch A Great Iden, Understanding Behavior, Win Over Yourself, Reflections at the Grave, "My Lit'l' Boy"; [pers.] I write my poems with the appreciation of beauty of nature that God has provided that contribute to the delicate balance among the living beauty of all things.; [a.] Fulton, KY

PLICKERT, JEFF
[b.] August 18, 1970, Willoughby, OH; [p.] Tom and Nancy Plickert; [ed.] Lake Catholic H.S. Mentor, Ohio B.S.B.A. in Marketing from Bowling Green State University Bowling Green, Ohio; [occ.] Assistant Manager Arco Financial Services; [memb.] Alumni of Alpha Sigma Phi Fraternity, Lake County Farm Bureau; [oth. writ.] No other published works yet but I have a collection of personal, romantic and children poems.; [pers.] My poems are inspired by my true love Becky Kozane, and the two most beautiful twin girls Ashley and Tiffany Kozane. A special thanks also goes out for the loving support of my family (Tom, Nancy, Scott, Kelly and Mike) as well as June, Joe and Bonnie Kozane; [a.] Mentor, OH

PLUCK, MARLA
[b.] June 2, 1964, Akron, OH; [p.] Frank and Ethel Taormina; [m.] John Pluck, May 14, 1988; [ed.] Garfield High, Hammel Business College; [occ.] Technical Aide, Ohio Edison Co.; [memb.] St. John the Baptist Catholic Church; [hon.] National Honor Society, Fitness Model for HSC Tony Little, Centerfield Astrologer and Tarot Consultant, Ordained Minister; [oth. writ.] Currently writing life

story of growing up 1/2 Italian (father's blood) and 1/2 black (mother's blood) in little ole Akron, OH; [pers.] You don't have to be rich and famous to be interesting.; [a.] Akron, OH

POFF, W. CALVERIN
[pen.] Cal; [b.] Audrain Court, Mexico, MO; [p.] Larkin and Linnie Poff; [m.] Allene L. (Dollens) Poff, May 25, 1940; [ch.] Donna E. (Poff) Polis, Gary Wade Poff - Estil D. Poff; [ed.] High School, IIA at Shelter Insurance Some Religious Cources; [occ.] Retired from Insurance Company 20 Years Retired Minister; [memb.] National Honor Society; [oth. writ.] Yes - unpublished; [pers.] I have enjoyed serving the Lord as Deacon and Minister - have enjoyed written several gospel songs.; [a.] Columbia, MO

POLANCIC, FRANK P.
[pen.] Frank Polancic; [b.] August 27, 1969, Ottawa; [p.] Frank and Patricia Polancic; [ed.] Ottawa Township High School, University of Illinois-Champaign, Urbana the Players Workshop-Acting and Improvisation Lisa Saunderson and David Gaschen-Voice Instructors; [occ.] Realtor, singer, songwriter, lyricist, poet Chicago; [hon.] Dean's List; [oth. writ.] Completed between 400-500 poems, and song Lyrics in 1993-1995. A Myriad of Subject ranging from Love, Feelings, Experience to Evolution, Art and People.; [pers.] I concentrate on the abstract in order to engender, simplify, and magnify the obvious.; [a.] Chicago, IL

POLLARD, CLARICE FORTGANG
[pen.] Clarice Fortgang Pollard; [b.] August 1, Brooklyn, NY; [p.] Rose and Louis Fortgang; [m.] Monroe M. Pollard, 1969; [ch.] Avie C. Kalker, Alfred M. Pollard; [ed.] Girls Commercial H.S., WWII Veteran-Womens Army Auxiliary Corps (WAAC), Womens Army Corps (WAC), Stephen R. Austin State U., Nacogdoches, TX, Washington and Lee U., Lexington, VA; [occ.] Designer costumes, actress, interior decorator-designer Publicity for U.S. Army, author of book-WWII poetry, signing's, speaker nationally; [memb.] Womens Army Corps (WAC), Vet's Assn., American Legion-Jewish War Vet's Ass'n., Arizona Book Publishers Ass'n, Arizona Authors Ass'n-Nat'l League of American Pen Women (PEN); [oth. writ.] "Hey Lady! Uncle Sam Needs You! Articles for nemerous magazines, state offices, historical publications, newspapers etc. and other writings include poetry, 2nd stories with an eye toward keeping female contributions to history alive!; [pers.] And emphasizing the fact that the female forces in WWII, opened the doors for others to follow as we plowed through the prejudice!; [a.] Phoenix, AZ

POLLARD, TAMMIE L.
[pen.] T. L. Pollard; [b.] May 10, 1958, Avon Park, FL; [p.] Barbara O. Haege; [m.] Peter H. Pollard, November 23, 1993; [ch.] Tracy, Benjamin, Kevin, Cassandra, Ashley; [ed.] South Florida Junior College, Christopher Newport College, Northern Illinois University; [occ.] English teacher-Sebring H.S. and South Florida Community College; [memb.] Highlands Little Theatre (HLT); [hon.] Sigma Tau Delta, Dean's List, Magna Cum Laude, Best Director (HLT); [oth. writ.] Political speeches and commercial pamphlets and multimedia presentations, short subject documentaries for television; [pers.] Great literature and writing have always been my passion.; [a.] Sebring, FL

POOLE, PEGGY J.
[b.] May 5, 1954, Dixon, KY; [p.] Wess and Betty Watson; [m.] Stace Poole, March 1, 1985; [ch.] Jared and Justin; [ed.] Webster County High School; [occ.] City clerk, freelance writer; [memb.] A.R.E. of Virginia Beach; [oth. writ.] Reporter and future editor of a local paper for 8 years, articles published in area magazines, back home in Kentucky, rural Kentuckian; [pers.] I believe a good writer can touch lives, in still courage and hope, make a young mind eager to learn, or offer solace and comfort.; [a.] Dixon, KY

PORTER, ANN
[pen.] "Annie"; [b.] November 13, 1917, Granite City, IL; [p.] John and Rose Brennan; [m.] Eldon Cook, May 13, 1934; [ch.] Betty June, Edward Lee and Janette Marie; [ed.] 8th Grade

PORTER, JANE ATHALEA LANGFORD
[b.] February 21, 1986, Winston-Salem, NC; [p.] Thomas J. Jr. and Judith A. Porter; [ed.] Entering 4th grade August 1995; [occ.] Student; [memb.] Brownie Scouts, Sherwood Sharks Swim Team, Optimist Soccer, YMCA basketball; [hon.] Brunson Elementary School, Principal's Awards for Student of the Week, Superior Effort, Positive and Consistent Effort, Citizenship, Honor Roll; [pers.] I enjoy writing poems and stories for my family, friends and teacher; [a.] Winston-Salem, NC

PORTERFIELD, KYLA DANIELLE
[b.] February 20, 1980, Mission Hills, CA; [p.] Geneva Porterfield and Keith Haywood; [ed.] Just recently celebrated my culmination from Middle School and now going on to High School to prepare for college.; [occ.] Student; [hon.] North Hills Community Coordinating Council Youth Excellence Award for 100% attendance and Leadership, Second Place In Young Authors Program. Certificate of Appreciation for Volunteering 143 hours at the Hospital of the Good Samaritan and Participating in kids Care Fair 1994.; [oth. writ.] A personal collection of other poems.; [pers.] Younger Generation, remember. That even though we were not the one's who made today's world what it is. We are the one's who can change it.; [a.] Sherman Oaks, CA

PORTES, TINA MARIE
[b.] November 23, 1978, Fall River; [p.] William and Madeline; [ed.] Joseph Case High School; [oth. writ.] Listen Like a Teddy Bear, Run Away, Our Love, A Poet, Say Goodbye; [pers.] I wrote my poem to remind us of all the children that have had a tough childhood.; [a.] Swansea, MA

POST, URSULA M.
[b.] May 31, 1928, Brooklyn, NY; [p.] Bern Hard and Emmy Backermann; [m.] Donald L. Post, June 29, 1968; [ed.] High School Walton all girl school Bronx N.Y.; [occ.] Retired; [pers.] I would like to thank the spiritual guides for writing this poem. I did not know I had this gift from the spiritual guides. I found this out January 24, 1995 from the program the other side on television. Thanking you from my heart spiritual guides.

POTTS, MARGARET R.
[b.] November 20, 1920, Cumberland Furnace, TN; [p.] Bill and Maude Bentley; [m.] Buford C. Potts (Deceased), February 16, 1946; [ch.] Judy, Michael and Timothy; [ed.] 12 years; [occ.] Retired; [memb.] Azalea Baptist Church, 60-plus Senior Club, US Croquet Asso., AARP, NARFE; [hon.] An honor to have served in the WAC during WW2; [oth. writ.] "A Soldiers Sweetheart"; [a.] Norfolk, VA

POWELL, DELIA
[pen.] Delia Powell; [b.] August 17, 1952, Lillington, NC; [p.] James and Myrtle Coleman; [m.] Leon Powell, June 5, 1976; [ch.] Casey Powell, Brannon Powell; [ed.] Lillington High School, Central Carolina Community College; [occ.] Administrative Assistant; [memb.] Union United Methodist Church; [oth. writ.] Several non-published poems; [a.] Lillington, NC

POWELL, LAUREN LANE
[ed.] Bachelor's Degree in Music from Indiana University; [occ.] Composer, arranger, teacher and performer; [memb.] Passionately involved in the Arts all of her life, her credits range from concerts and opera, to jazz dance and choreography.; [oth. writ.] From "Dear Addiction" to "Angel Flying," Lauren finds her inspiration in the ordinary as well as in the unique. Collaborative efforts have produced the environmentally impassioned "Tragic Anthem" and the picturesque "Sky Ride." Lauren's music speaks to all of us about peaceful alternatives in a violent world.

POWELL, TIFFANY
[b.] April 18, 1970, Forth Worth, TX; [p.] John H. Powell Jr. and Eleanor Powell; [ed.] O.D. Wyatt High School, Tarrant County Junior College; [occ.] Unit Clerk, Tarrant County MHMR Services; [memb.] National Association For Female Executives; [oth. writ.] Poems and articles have been published in my local church newsletter, Central Arlington Church of Christ Chronicle.; [pers.] I endeavor to inspire and motivate others to think and take action through my writing.; [a.] Fort Worth, TX

POWERS, CHARLOTTE DE VANE
[pen.] Bonnik Moultnic, Ga Col-Co; [b.] July 18, 1943; [p.] Louise and Gerre De Vane; [m.] Divorced 1982, 1963; [ch.] Michael Todd Powers, Pamela Sue Hamilton; [ed.] High School Lourdes Lowndes Hi County High School, Valdoste, GA; [occ.] Self - Employed; [memb.] Northside Baptist Church, Thomasville, GA 31792; [hon.] Certificate in typing art shorthand; [pers.] I have always loved a home and family, my parents made me a wonderful home!; [a.] Thomasville, GA

POWERS, ELLA IVEY
[b.] April 29, 1924, Lumberton, NC; [p.] Mr. and Mrs. David Ivey; [m.] Bruce Powers; [ch.] John-Surveyor, Joyce-College Math Instructor, Glenn-Farm Manger, Gail-Teacher; [occ.] Housewife; [memb.] Ten Mile Baptist Church; [oth. writ.] I recently had my first poem published by the National Library of poetry. The poem is titled "A Remembrance."; [pers.] I have written for my own personal satisfaction. I write about people and things that matter to me. Writing is a way of expressing myself.; [a.] Lumberton, NC

POWERS, JESSE R.
[pen.] Jesse Powers; [b.] August 9, 1981, San Luis Opisbo, CA; [p.] Toby Powers, Carol Pflag; [ed.] Templeton High School; [occ.] Student; [oth. writ.] The Stream; [pers.] Each person needs their own special place; [a.] Templeton, CA

POYNTER, TAMMY S.
[pen.] Maddie Thomas; [b.] August 20, 1974, Cincinnati, OH; [p.] Bill Poynter and Connie Heatherly; [ed.] Middletown High, Manchester Technical Center; [occ.] Order Entry, Representative Viking Office Products Cincinnati; [oth. writ.] Article for the Middletown Journal; [pers.] My mother always said that I could do anything I wanted, she believed in me when I could not. Thank you mom.; [a.] Middletown, OH

PRATHER, LAURA A.
[b.] June 25, 1963, Detroit, MI; [p.] Kenneth and Shirley Prather; [ed.] BA, Journalism Major, Wayne State University-Detroit, MI, JD University of Detroit, Mercy Law School; [occ.] Account Manager, LDM Technologies; [pers.] The challenges can trying at times, so I find it best to keep a sense of humor.

PRATTI, MRS. GRACE E.
[pen.] Linda; [b.] January 10; [p.] Caroline, Peter; [m.] Mr. Joseph Albert Pratti, June 19, 1993; [ed.] H.S. - School of Computer School of writing Newspaper Institute of America; [occ.] U.S. Postal letter carrier Bath Beach Station 11214; [memb.] Edgar Cayce Foundation ARE "Associate Research Englightment", "Rosicruciar Fellowship Foundation"; [hon.] Republic Political - Democratic Politic's Club mostly political; [oth. writ.] Wise Guide of maine People's puzzler N.J.; [pers.] My writing is my expression of what I feel at that moment; [a.] Staten Island, NY

PRESLEY, HEATHER L.
[b.] October 18, 1950, Waukegan, IL; [p.] Rev. O. R. Littleford; [m.] J. C. Presley; [ch.] Ted Presley, Michelle Presley; [ed.] B.S. in Business Admin., Florida Southern College; [hon.] Graduated Cum Laude; [pers.] My deep love for and commitment to my Lord, Jesus Christ, has come from years of suffering with him, rejoicing in him and abiding in his Love.; [a.] Lakeland, FL

PREZIOSE, MARLENE
[pen.] Marls; [b.] July 1957, NYC; [p.] Thomas and Cora; [ed.] Associate's Degree in Applied Science Mech. Tech. Design Drafting. Baccalaureate Degree in Architectural Technology; [occ.] Engineering Technician for NYC, Dept. of Environmental Protection.; [memb.] Westchester Association of Woman Business Owners Professional Society of Inventors; [pers.] For the leased amount of disappointment in life, depend on no one and nothing except God.

PRICE, MICHAEL G.
[pen.] Michael G. Price; [b.] October 12, 1965, Oregon; [p.] Gary and Kathy Price; [ed.] BS Financial Management, Cal. Polysan Wis Obispo, CA; [occ.] Director of Sales and Marketing, B.A.C. Inc.; [oth. writ.] A Wealth of Private Material; [pers.] I strive to successfully transfer thoughts to paper-maybe one day I'll achieve this goal.; [a.] Livermore, CA

PRIMMER, LOUISE W.
[pen.] Louise W. Primmer; [b.] December 10, 1911, Clinton, IL; [p.] Herbert and Hallie Schmith; [m.] Harry Primmer, June 20, 1940; [ch.] Robert L. Primmer; [ed.] Ill. Wesleyan University, Bloomington, IN. Bachelor of Music ,Clinton, IL. Grade School and High School; [occ.] Retired, entertain Calliope and Organ, Volunteer, work with Elderly former member of Roberson Players Tent Show BT (Before Television); [oth. writ.] Poems published in newspaper, poems in balls pub in Anthology of Bells by Dorothy Moody Warren, Exposition Press, Hicksville NY. Some poems published in Show Hopse Magazines. Always a Christmas Card Poem (original); [pers.] Every thing can be expressed in poetry.; [a.] De Land, IL

PROCOPIO, MARIE
[b.] Trenton, NJ; [p.] Marie and Henry Webster; [m.] Joseph, December 6, 1958; [ch.] Joseph Jr., Jay, Frank; [ed.] Neenah H.S., Neenah, Wis, Layton Art School, Milwaukee Lincoln Prep., Philadelphia, PA.; [occ.] Retired; [hon.] Poetry, Oil Painting (sold in home)

PUGACH, BRIAN
[b.] June 20, 1987, Orange, CA; [ed.] 2nd grade, Laguna Road School, Fullerton, CA; [occ.] Student; [hon.] Runner-up Laguna Road School writing contest; [a.] Fullerton, CA

PYLE, ALICE
[pen.] Alice Pyle; [b.] September 2, 1964, Durham, NC; [p.] Donna Renner,; [m.] White Hall Morrison III, Divorced; [ed.] Brentwood Academy, Middle Tennessee State University; [pers.] Southern Literature and poetry of all kinds are of interest to me. My poems are usually about personal experiences and my reflections about those events.; [a.] Atlanta, GA

QUAST, HEATHER E.
[b.] February 9, 1979, Faribault; [p.] Debra and Phillip Enger and Robert and Ramona Quast; [ed.] Attends Waterville Elysian-Morristown Senior High; [memb.] Faribault Assemblies of God Youth Group, Future Leaders of America, Fellowship of Christian Athletes, and Speech; [hon.] Varsity letter in Cross Country Running, a Buccaneer Buddy, Gold Star for FLA Star Event, and for Informative Speaking; [pers.] My friends, family, and fellow Christians have inspired me and encourage me to continue my writing, without them, I don't know what'd happen!; [a.] Morristown, MN

QUEENE, MICHAEL J.
[b.] April 18, 1972, Cambridge; [p.] James Queene and Pat Queene; [ed.] Pentucket High School, Northern Essex Community College; [occ.] Certified Nursing Assistant-Dancer; [pers.] I wrote this poem late at night to try and relieve some anguish I was feeling from a broken relationship. It was a way to help me cope with it.; [a.] Merrimac, MA

QUINTANA, ELADIO VARGAS
[pen.] Jose Miguel De La Fuente; [b.] August 22, 1949, Mayague; [p.] Georgino Quintana and Eladio Vargas; [m.] Celia M. Antongiorgi, June, 1994; [ed.] Writers Institute of America; [occ.] Businessman; [memb.] Hollywood Artists Hill Top Records Amway Corporation; [hon.] Noche De Poesia y Romance Frente al Mar Lectures at Hostos High School; [oth. writ.] Think positive-song, My Success-song, Lujuria Mafiosa-book, The Right Kind of Prayer-song; [pers.] I believe in thinking constructive and positive action towards my goals. I believe in right action and seeking divine guidance.; [a.] Mayague, PR

RABINOVICH, MARCELLE
[pen.] Marci Meikle; [b.] August 21, 1927, New York City; [p.] David and Bertha Michaelson; [m.] Joseph Rabinovich, March 2, 1978; [ch.] Jamie, Adrienne, Matthew Daniel; [ed.] B.A. Pre-Med, Speech and Theatre. M.A. Speech Pathology and Audiology". P.D. Education; [occ.] Speech Teacher; [hon.] Award for Poetry Reading and Writing; [oth. writ.] 50 poems, book-"Sharpen Your Tongue" and "Cooking Without a Stove".; [pers.] Truth, honor and a sense of humor; [a.] New York, NY

RACKLEY, PATTI PATTERSON
[pen.] Patti J. Patterson; [b.] July 21, 1969, Union City, TN; [p.] Harold Patterson (Deceased), Brenda Cantrell; [m.] David Rackley, March 14, 1991; [ch.] Brittney Rackley; [ed.] High School-Nimitz High, Irving, TX, Cosmetology graduated both '87 (Cosmetology License '87); [occ.] Stylist-nail tech; [memb.] St. Judes Children's Hospital, 700 Club's Operation Blessing; [hon.] I am very honored to be published in such a prestige work as this; [oth. writ.] I write whenever the inspiration strikes. And I can find a pen pencil or anything to write with, never before published; [pers.] Be thankful in everything, thank God and love one another, peace be with you.; [a.] Irving, TX

RADIN, CONSTANCE E.
[b.] November 26, 1962, Missouri; [p.] Duane P. and Billie J. Huck; [m.] Anthony E. Radin, April 25, 1987; [ed.] 1981 Graduate of Festus Senior High 1983 Graduate of Arkansas State University, Jonesboro, AR; [memb.] 1994 Member of Jefferson County Writers Guild, Current Member of the International Society of Poets, and new member of the Poets Guild; [oth. writ.] Several other poems published in The National Library of Poetry's Anthologies: "Glass Garden", "Midnight Sun", "Foolish Pride", Total Poems accepted for publication: 17; [pers.] Inspirations come from the soul, ones perceptions, and intuitiveness.; [a.] Festus, MO

RAGLAND, JANIE LORETTA
[b.] June 2, 1944, Hamilton, NC; [p.] Willoughby and Maranda Jones; [m.] Sidney Ragland (Divorced), April 17, 1965; [ch.] Craig, Darrin, Deborah and Erika; [ed.] West Martin High Winston-Salem State Univ.; [occ.] Field Office Mgr. Adm. Asst. to Vice Pres.; [memb.] Jefferson-Patchen-Ralph Avenues Block Assoc.; [oth. writ.] Cordial Polysemy Midnight Melody

RAGNO, JOSEPH S.
[b.] June 6, 1919, Libya, Africa; [p.] Francesco and Josephine; [m.] Anne, June 14; [ch.] Dr. Joseph F. Ragno; [ed.] Columbia College (M.B.), University of Virginia Law School (Juris Doctor); [occ.] Retired - former Corporation Counsel - City of Mt. Vernon, N.Y.; [oth. writ.] High School and College Essays and Poetry; [pers.] I rejoice when I can evoke a long forgotten scene or act to take on reality once again.

RAIMONDO, GINA M.
[b.] October 15, 1980, Baltimore, MD; [p.] John and Shelley Raimondo; [ed.] Attending High School; [occ.] Student; [hon.] I made the "B" honor roll in school since 6th grade; [oth. writ.] "Why Me?", "None Realizes," "Our Love" all of these are other poems that I have written.; [pers.] I enjoy writing poetry it helps me express the way I feel about people and things.; [a.] Lewes, DE

RAMIREZ, MARY MICHELLE
[pen.] Shelly; [b.] May 10, 1964, Shelby, OH; [p.] Joe and Mary Bonecutter; [m.] Joe Ramirez, October 6, 1984; [ch.] Andrew Joseph, Megan Michelle; [ed.] Portage Central High School; [occ.] Housewife; [oth. writ.] A demo tape was made through starlit production company on a song I wrote called "Lay Her To Rest" dedicated to my sister and the daughter she lost named Alyssa; [pers.] I love writing poems and songs. I'm influenced by my family. I have a very supportive husband who strongly believes in my talent.; [a.] Kalamazoo, MI

RAMIREZ, XSABEIDA L.
[b.] January 11, 1985, East Meadow, NY; [p.] Miriam Ramirez and Miguel A. Ramirez; [ed.] 4 years in Bayview Ave School in Freeport, 5th grade Atkinson School in Freeport; [occ.] Student; [hon.] Writing poetry, chorus and playing violin. Writing poetry and violin; [oth. writ.] Nature poetry, her first book titled "I am...", which includes her other poems as: "I am a dolphin", "I am the sea", "I am rain forest", I am a rose", "I am a butterfly", "I am an eagle" etc...; [pers.] "Poetry should have a new horizon, it does not necessary have to rhyme to have a colorful and spiritual message".; [a.] Freeport, NY

RAMOS, PATRICIA M.
[pen.] Scarlett Anderson; [b.] December 1, 1952, Toledo, OH; [p.] Albert and Bernice Seiro; [m.] Divorced; [ch.] 2 Deceased; [ed.] Homemaker; [memb.] Echo Meadows Church of Christ, American Bowlers Association; [hon.] Simi Finalist in "The National Library of Poetry Contest"; [oth. writ.] (Sin Ruining the Kingdom of the Body, Tale of a Fool, The Repear, Treasury of Thoughts, Dearest Lord, Twilights Child, A River of Tears, Loneliness, The Rose.; [pers.] I see my Savior as the greatest being in the universe, and I feel that the world would heal itself if only we learned to live in peace and harmony.; [a.] Toledo, OH

RANJAN, DEV PRIYA
[pen.] Ranu; [b.] November 22, 1984, Wilmington, DE; [p.] Ratna and Dinesh Ranjan; [ed.] 6th grade The Lexington School Lexington, KY; [occ.] Student

RASELEY, MARY
[b.] March 18, 1945, Toledo, OH; [p.] Maxwell Roseley, Hildreth Raseley; [ed.] Phoenix Union High School, Phoenix College; [memb.] Beth El Congregation, Phoenix Guardian Angels, Association of Women's Music and Culture, Soka Gakkai International-USA.; [oth. writ.] A Special Task published in Pioneers of Tomorrow. Articles published in Women's Central News of Arizona. Letters to the Editor the Arizona Republic.; [pers.] I have been greatly influenced by NAM-MYOHO-RENGE-KYO which is the Buddhist chant for world peace.; [a.] Phoenix, AZ

RAY, HILLOL KUMAR
[pen.] Hillol Ray, HeeRay (means Diamond); [b.] Near Calcutta, India; [p.] Nibaran Chandra & Angur Lata Ray; [m.] Mrs. Manjusree Ray, December 7, 1981; [ch.] Brian, Ryan; [ed.] M.S., Enivironmental Engg., North Dakota State Univ.; B.S., Civil Engg., Univ. of Calcutta, India; [occ.] Environmental Engineer, U.S. EPA, Dallas, TX; [memb.] American Assn. for the Advancement of Science, American Chemical Society, American Industrial Hygiene Assn., American Meteorological Society, American Nuclear Society, American Society of Civil Engineers, American Water Works Assn., Instrument Society of America, Institution of Diagnostic Engineers, Great Britain (Fellow), Royal Society of Health, Great Britain (Fellow); [hon.] Poet Laureate, "Who's Who in APAC (Asian Pacific American Community)", "Earth Day" Poet - recognized by U.S. President Bill Clinton, Vice President Al Gore, Jr., and current Indian Ambassador to USA, poems published in NLP anthologies Edge of Twilight, Best Poems of 1995, received rave reviews in national newspapers and invitations for own poetry recital; [oth. writ.] "Deshantoreer Itikotha" (in Bengali) i.e. Amusing History of an Immigrant, poems (in English) regularly published in EPA and APAC newsletters, technical articles in professional journals in USA, England and India, short stories, songs, limericks, and several hundred Bengali poems published in renowned journals and magazines in Asia, Europe, Canada, and U.S.A., Award Winning Crossword Puzzle Writer (awarded by Allied Chemical Corporation, NJ and Council of Scientific and Industrial Research (C.S.I.R.), New Delhi, India; [pers.] Material possessions may be stolen or vandalized, but power of knowledge cannot be.; [a.] Garland, TX

REDD, WINNIFRED DIXON
[pen.] Winn Dixon; [b.] April 9, 1921, Toronto, ON; [p.] Thos. Kendall Burt, Alice G. Joy; [m.] Donald W. Redd, June 16, 1990; [ch.] Lawrence C. Gauer, Eugene K, Gauer, Richard E. Gauer, Lorie Woodrow; [ed.] Malvern Collegiate, Eastern High School of Commerce, Durham College; [occ.] Retired-General Motors of Canada Ltd., writer (now); [oth. writ.] Other poems published in local papers; [pers.] I love writing short stories and poems. Hope someday to publish a novel.

REDFIELD, LIZA M.
[pen.] Stephanie George, Odile Saiemt; [b.] October 22, 1957, New York, NY; [p.] William Redfield, Betsy Meade; [m.] Hans; [ed.] B.A. Columbia, M.A. Columbia; [occ.] Teacher, writer, translator, playwright; [memb.] NFE, ARS NOVA Consortium (founding member); [hon.] Stains - Berle Award (Translations from Old English) Fellow (at Columbia 1980-1) Rageants Scholar, Dean's List; [oth. writ.] Defiance (1984), "Why Anything?" (essays) (1994), Poems in P.P.J., Pivot, Anthology of Czech Poetry, (translation) Danton's Death (Baechner) for Geraldine Fitzgerald. The Fame God (play) 1994; [pers.] The "new formalism" and Irrealism are not attempts to disrupt or reverse the better aims of 20th century arts and letters but a statement of fact. The 20th century is over. ARS NOVA (Consortium) knows.; [a.] New York, NY

REECE, TERRY A.
[pen.] T. Reece (Tee Reece); [b.] 1-2-58, Texarkana, AR; [p.] Pendon and Mary Reece; [m.] Sandra M. Reece, 7-21-84; [ch.] Karoderick Jamaal Reece, Ciscorian Eugene Reece, Carlos Allen Reece, Jeremy Reece, Brandon Eugene Whitaker; [ed.] Graduated 13th in the 76 high school class, technical education in auto repair, TWU small business course, Cedar Valley College, life experiences; [occ.] service manager; [memb.] Texas Writer's Assoc., NAACP, Dallas Black Chamber of Commerce, NIBA, The National Library of Poetry; [hon.] Auto Mechanics Top Technician '76, All District Hon. Mention-Basketball, All Tournament LKtouney 75, Top Gun (sales) Safety Plus, Inc. Dec. and Jan. 91, 92; [oth. writ.] Kids beware poems, Freedom Does it Reign, Checks and Balances, books--A Life Full of Testimonies, Freedom What Prices are We Paying, Corporate Monopoly The Games People are Plying, You and Your Car - You Auto Know; [pers.] I cover a multiple of areas in my writings, and I strive to never give up. Life deals out a lot of pitfalls, but we must continue to reach for our goals.; [a.] Dallas, TX

REED, JAMES F.
[pen.] Franklin Reed; [b.] October 23, 1970, Springfield, MO; [p.] Lois Reed; [ed.] Study Zen; [occ.] General Electric employee; [oth. writ.] No published work; [pers.] I believe poetry should be an expression of emotions, of memories and of the natural world, all of which seems so ordinary, but can prove extraordinary if given a moment of appreciation.; [a.] Springfield, MO

REED, RENE
[pen.] Neh Neh; [b.] October 20, 1978, Marlborough; [p.] David Reed, Sue Delk; [ed.] 11th grade at LaVergne High School

REEL, RALPH
[b.] February 5, 1933, Youngstown, OH; [p.] Howard and Marie Reel; [m.] Patricia Anne (Wynn) Reel, June 9, 1956; [ch.] Michael, Cynthia, Pamela; [ed.] Ursuline High, Youngstown State Univ, University of Detroit; [occ.] Music Director, Retired Officer, US Army; [memb.] The Retired Officers Association (TROA), Military Order of the World Wars (MOWW), Society For the Preservation and Encouragement of Barbershop Quartet Singing in America (SPEBQSA), Toastmasters International (TI), Retired Senior Volunteer Program (RSVP), Hospital Volunteer Auxiliary, Guardian Ad Litem; [hon.] Bronze Star with Oak Leaf Cluster (Valor), Meritorious Service Medal, Toastmaster of the Year (local Chapter), Full Academic Scholarship (4 yr.); [oth. writ.] "Tiny Child", "Surround Me", "Ode To Woody", Music: "Rubbing Shoulders", "Take My Hand", "I Said A Prayer For You", "A Mother's Love", "Only a Baby Came"; [pers.] I share the views of Bessie A. Stanley in her writing "Success", part of which is here paraphrased: "He has achieved success who has...laughed often, loved much,....sought the best in others and given them his best....", to which I would add: `And done so with a song in his heart'.; [a.] Palm Coast, FL

REESE, ELENA KRISTINA
[b.] May 6, 1942, Tidaholm, Sweden; [p.] Irma Petterson; [m.] Jon D. Reese, August 29, 1971; [ed.] High School (Swedish) accredited Cont. Educ. Courses at: NAPA Jr. College, U.C. Davis at V.M.T.H. (Veterinary Med. Tech Hosp.)-certified as ACMG (by IPG), (Master Groomer) and CAH (Companion Animal Hygienist) (By WWPSA) Animal Husbandry-8 yrs. as a V.M.T. (Veterinary Med. Tech.); [occ.] Self-employed since '74, as a dog and cat (specialty) groomer with retails (Business owner and Mgr.); [memb.] N.V.A.A. (Napa Valley Art Assoc.), S.W.E.A. (Swedish Women's Educ. Assoc.) (Int. Inc) I.P.G. (International Professional Groomer), Sons of Norway (Lodge 43) (Valle Joca) American Legion Auxiliary; [pers.] With my poems, I'd like to encourage other, "Late Bloomers", like me, "It's not ever too late!" Weather you're self taught, or of the academia, "Your Achievements Are Up To You!" Some are born with a talent, others have to work hard at it! Life is a continues school, of learning, of finding your talent and finding yourself!; [a.] Napa, CA

REEVES, CATHERINE
[pen.] "Misty"; [b.] September 9, 1935, Troy, AL; [p.] Marie and Jim Bob Beck; [m.] Earl D. Reeves, December 19, 1953; [ch.] Cathy Marie, Cynthia Kaye Christopher Dean, Ricky Lee; [ed.] 12th grade diploma; [occ.] Retired Boeing Aircraft, Everett, WA, worked as a volunteer Red Cross Nurses Aid, at Clark Air Force Base in the Philippines 1968; [memb.] Member of Pacific Northwest Song Writers Ass., Lifetime member of the National Society of Poets.; [hon.] Received Editors Choice Award for all poems that have been published by the National Library of Poetry, received an Award of Merit, from Creative Arts and Sciences Entp., for the poem Just For A Friend.; [oth. writ.] Written several personal poems by request, many country songs, but has not had a chance to try and get any of them published yet.; [a.] Camano Island, WA

REEVES, KA-SON
[pen.] Scarab; [b.] September 22, 1974, Brooklyn; [p.] Denise Reeves and Philip White; [ed.] Erasmus Hall H.S., New york City Technical College; [memb.] School Newspaper's Editorial Board; [hon.] Phi Theta Kappa, Dean's List 93-94, 94-95, 2nd place winner of the Emmet Cribbs Short Story Award Contest; [oth. writ.] Short story included in College anthology called Brooklyn Bridge,various poems, drama articles for school newspaper; [pers.] Most of what I write is a mixture of personal experience and imagination. When you use your imagination, you can turn any experience into beautiful writing.; [a.] Brooklyn, NY

REHM, RHONDA K.
[pen.] Roni Mehr; [b.] April 22, 1960, Louisville, KY; [p.] Irene Keith, Ronald Keith; [m.] Brett Rehm, March 11, 1989; [ch.] William Fredrick, Joseph Eric; [occ.] Cosmetologists; [a.] Louisville, KY

REICHEL, NANCY ELLEN
[pen.] Nancy Ellen Reichel; [b.] October 16, 1933, Teaneck, NJ; [p.] Max Levinson, Lucille Levinson; [m.] Warren Reichel, January 27, 1962; [ch.] Chance Wayne, Darren Wade, Lana Michelle; [ed.] Bergenfield High, NJ, Berkeley School, NYC; [occ.] Housewife; [oth. writ.] Two other poems: "The Last Hurrah", "It's Your Birthday, My Son". I just started writing poetry, it seems to come easy, and it is a wonderful way to express my love for my children. I love doing it.; [pers.] To leave someone a gift of a poem is the ultimate gift. It will live on forever. When I wrote "My Daughter's a Mother", it was a gift for Mother's Day. My daughter had just had twin boys in February, and she also has a four year old boy. To watch her with her children is the ultimate gift to me. I know she will keep this poem forever, and when she reads it, she will always feel the love and the pride I feel for her.; [a.] Escondido, CA

REID, NEAL N.
[b.] September 1, 1906, Orangeville, UT; [p.] John Thomas Reid, Edna Neal; [m.] Anne Bachmann (she is Swiss), August 3, 1935; [ch.] Three forms of recognition pertaining to my work; [ed.] Some college but not a graduate. As part of my education my wife and I have travelled a good deal. South America, Japan, all over Europe, Russia, India, all over the US, Hawaii, Taiwan, and other places.; [occ.] Retired Personnel Director Federal Government; [memb.] Toastmaster Club; [hon.] A plack for serving 14 years directing and managing a crew of 25 people doing Genealogical Research. There are some others. I have received several awards and; [oth. writ.] My own family history. Poems about Mother, about our children, The Wide Open Spaces, One I wrote is about Freedom. "Freedom What Art Thou?", Freedom Where Art Thou" and in the 3rd verse "Freedom Answers"; [pers.] The president of our church had a motto on a little plack on his desk: "Do It". I have adopted it because I feel it has a very deep meaning and is really the reason that some people are so successful.; [a.] Springville, UT

REID, SEAN
[b.] June 8, 1979, PA; [p.] Michael and Margaret; [ed.] Eight years at St Williams School and two at Cardinal Dougherty two pending, (both Catholic); [occ.] Student; [pers.] People are like stone Pilars connected by rope bridges. When we leave a person we must cut that bridge. Be careful which bridge you cut, it could drop others; [a.] Philadelphia, PA

RENSCH, MARY ANN
[pen.] Angel; [b.] January 17, 1942, W Brownsville, PA; [p.] Ann and Paul Antonik; [m.] H. Ronald Rensch, September 3, 1965; [ch.] Bradford Rensch; [ed.] Beth-Center Sr. High, Santa Fe Community College; [occ.] Semi-retired; [pers.] I feel the greatest gift in life one can give is love for all mankind and spirituality for his soul.; [a.] Santa Fe, NM

RIBERDY, CATHERINE LYNN
[pen.] Lynnie Noboddie phd; [b.] May 7, 1954, Dearborn, MI; [p.] Louise and Joseph Riberdy; [ed.] St Joseph Academy High, Case Western Reserve University, B.A. in Psychology and Comparative Literature and Graduate work in Medical Anthropology (1979); [occ.] Free-Lance Writer-Thinker-Quasiphilosopher, Odd Jobs (i.e. Lawncare, housecleaning); [memb.] The Humane Society of The United States, PETA; [hon.] College Dean's List, Grade School Poetry and Poster Contest; [oth. writ.] Plenty, a great deal…several plastic bins and suitcases and drawers full of years of ideas, feelings, aspirations, and sometimes (being human) a dash of delusion….Poems.; [pers.] A special thank you goes out to Dr. Ellen Rie and Dr. Walter Strauss, both have given me support and alternative insights into our strange world of Life.; [a.] Cleveland, OH

RICCI, GUY
[pen.] Tobe Santini; [b.] May 21, 1957, NJ; [p.] L.G. and Shirley Ricci; [m.] Kerry, May 17, 1980; [ed.] Univ. of Maryland BSC in Elec. Eng.; [occ.] Plumber; [hon.] 2nd Ian St. James Award-1991, honor grad-USAF Air Training (TAC 1982); [oth. writ.] "Dem Bones" - story in compliltations book "Its Past Midnight" - 1992; [pers.] This writing stuff takes some amount of time!; [a.] Key Largo, FL

RICHARDSON, KRYSTAL
[b.] September 28, 1980, Wenatchee; [p.] Gordon and Nancy Richardson; [ed.] Attending Eastmont Jr High 9th Grade; [occ.] Student; [memb.] Youth Drama, School drama, Choir, Spanish; [hon.] A choir award; [oth. writ.] Several poems, stories and songs, that I never published.; [pers.] I love poetry, especially love poems I spend a lot of time reading and writing poems.; [a.] East Wenatchee, WA

RICHARDSON, FREDA L.
[b.] September 27, 1956, Texas; [p.] Lillie Lopez Brandon-stepdad; [m.] J. M. Richardson, November 20, 1971; [ch.] Rodney, Rob and Misty Richardson; [ed.] College, currently working on AAS degree.; [occ.] Administrative Tech. II Oil Spill Prevention and Response; [oth. writ.] Written 2 songs that were sung by Soloists in my church. Two other songs I've not made public yet. Numerous poems; [pers.] All things are possible through God.; [a.] Pasadena, TX

RIGGS, D. C.
[b.] March 7, 1949, Texas; [p.] Joe and Alma Riggs; [m.] Katy, September 30, 1972; [ch.] Sherry, Terry, Joey, Debby; [ed.] Bachelor's and Masters; [occ.] US Air Force; [oth. writ.] Other poetry is unpublished; [pers.] Life is not fair and people should never quit because our Creator never died; [a.] Dover, DE

RILEY, PAUL A.
[pen.] Marcus Max Cozmos; [b.] April 1, 1969, St Louis, MO; [p.] Bob and Yvonne Gerhart; [m.] Theresa Riley, June 28, 1922; [ed.] Wilson High School; [occ.] Certified Nursing Assistant, at Beverly Health Care Center; [hon.] 2nd place Winner in Alabama Creative Writing Contest in Level in 1984. Highest Grade Point Average in Senior English in 1988 Army Achievement Award; [oth. writ.] Murder at Bermuda Island, I Looked into the Worldly Waves of Wonder, The Sea's Savior, When The Sea Awakes; [pers.] We can let problems control us, or we can control the problems.; [a.] Marina, CA

RILEY, VIRGINIA NANCY
[pen.] Ginny Riley; [b.] April 23, 1946, New York; [p.] Raymond Schuhriemen and Josephine; [m.] Robert Joseph Riley, December 5, 1966; [ch.] Sandra Riley Zepperelli, Cynthia Riley; [ed.] Bryant High School, Bible Educational Studies; [occ.] Self help Care of Systematic Lupus-full time; [memb.] Member of Lupus Foundation of America; [hon.] Teaching Volunteer Children with learning Disabilities, 3 honor awards for Achievements in Teaching, I thank God for the beautiful people who came for the ill; [oth. writ.] My Garden on the Wall, Angels, Tiny Tears, Our Angel, My Garden, The Last word, The Will, The Weapon, My Poems, Little Box, Having No One, Day Break, I'll Pray, Our Down Fall Barbara, Cynthia, Sandra, Rob love for all our futures etc.; [pers.] This poem was written in honor of those who God gas blessed my life with Robert (my husband) Cynthia Sandra, Angelo Bobby, my friend and Doctor F. Swerdlow my sister Barbara, Carole Joan, Richard Annie, Nancy Co. Edward Riley Mom-the help they have given is blessed; [a.] Jackson Heights, NY

RINGE, JAMES L.
[b.] September 21, 1948, Astoria, OR; [p.] Olga Ringe, Father Milton (Deceased); [m.] Divorced; [ch.] Ben and Jason; [ed.] BS in Pharmacy, Oregon State University; [occ.] Pharmacist; [memb.] The Human Race; [oth. writ.] Personal book of poems; [pers.] Idealist in an imperfect but beautiful world-helplessly hoping!; [a.] Beaverton, OR

RIPPL, BART
[b.] 11-7-66, Fairview Park, OH; [p.] George & Eleanor Rippl; [ed.] B.A. from Wittenberg University (1989); [hon.] Pi Sigma Alpha, Omicron Delta Epsilon, Dean's List; [oth. writ.] Several unpublished poems; [pers.] Art breathes life into a culture. Without

art, a culture is destined for decay and eventual extinction.; [a.] 380 Hurst Dr. Bay Village, OH 44140

RIVERS, PATRICIA
[pen.] Trish; [b.] April 6, 1961, California; [p.] Synthia Smith; [ch.] Edwon, LeRoy; [ed.] Mt. Pleasant High School-California, John Adams Community College, San Francisco, CA, North Lake College, Texas; [occ.] Customer Service Representative for a major Pharmaceutical Company in Texas; [oth. writ.] Anthology entry in Contemporary Poets of America and Britain - (A Hundred fold and some); [pers.] Inspired by the depth of Maya Angelou, and my own life's trials and tribulations, and a true love that surpasses life it's self keeps the words flowing through my mind, heart and soul as I one day hope to turn it all into something more precious than gold.; [a.] Dallas, TX

RIX, JOSH
[b.] December 27, 1979, Kalamazoo; [p.] Jamesce Karen Rix; [ed.] High School Student, class of 1998; [memb.] High School Athletics (Football and Wrestling); [oth. writ.] First published work; [pers.] To truly do the right thing, you must always brake a few hearts; [a.] Allegan, MI

ROBERSON, MARGARET HART
[ed.] B.S. Elem. Ed. '61, Madison College, Harrisonburg, VA

ROBERTS, DARCY
[b.] February 19, 1979, Springfield, OH; [p.] Deborah and James Roberts; [ed.] Attending Ridgemont H.S.; [hon.] Who's Who Among American High School Students, United States Achievement Academy; [pers.] My poems come from my heart and help me to recognize my emotions; [a.] Ridgeway, OH

ROBERTS, RACHAEL ANN
[b.] November 6, 1978, Edmonds; [pers.] "I wrote this certain poem for my older brother Michael J. Roberts Jr. when he left home, to tell him in my own way that I'll always be here for him."; [a.] Snohomish, WA

ROBERTSON, SANDRA LACY
[pen.] Sandy Lacy; [b.] September 21, 1957, Chicago, IL; [p.] Joseph and Rosie Lacy; [ch.] LaJaunese Robertson, Dominique Robertson and Daryl T. Robertson; [ed.] John Marshall Harlan High School Chicago, IL; [pers.] I enjoy writing for the minds and souls of humanity and have them relate to the words on paper. My mentors are poetry writers everywhere and Langston Hughes.; [a.] Louisville, KY

ROBINS, SANDRA LEE
[pen.] Sandra Robins; [b.] July 6, 1948, Washington, DC; [p.] William F. and Catherine V. Meyers; [m.] Roger Dale Robins, June 27, 1987; [ch.] Billy Bready 2 grandsons - B.J. and Bo Beady; [ed.] Calvert Senior High School Prince Frederick, MD.; [occ.] Housewife; [a.] Norman, OK

ROBINSON, LEE E.
[b.] August 30, 1938, Miss; [p.] Mr and Mrs Robinson; [ch.] I have seven children and fifteen grandchildren; [ed.] Crispus Attucks High School, and Compton College; [occ.] Cosmetologist, and poet.; [oth. writ.] I'm in the process of publishing a book of poems.; [pers.] I am influenced by almighty God; [a.] Long Beach, CA

ROBINSON, LISA RENE
[b.] February 12, 1969, Culpeper, VA; [p.] George Bryant, Patricia Bryant; [m.] Michael Robinson, June 29, 1991; [ch.] Patricia Leigh Robinson; [ed.] Completed Culpeper Co. High School (1987); [occ.] Machine operator; [pers.] This poem was written as a special tribute to my mother, Patricia Lee Bryant, I love you mom.; [a.] Culpeper, VA

ROBINSON, SHARON
[pen.] Sharon Robinson; [b.] June 5, 1966, Passaic, NJ; [p.] Nelleen Underwood and Joseph Bogan; [m.] George Robinson, September 8, 1990; [ed.] Boys and Girls High School-completed 4 yrs - 1994 Diploma Kingsborough Community College-2 yrs.; [occ.] Executive Secretary; [oth. writ.] Several poems to be published in the near future; [pers.] Writing expresses my feelings, my outlook, my goals and my dreams. It soothes my mind when things are going on around me. I thank God for my gift which he has given me.; [a.] Queensvillage, NY

ROBINSON, THEODORA
[b.] April 5, 1948, Washington, DC; [p.] Ruth Robinson, Charles Robinson; [ch.] James, Tony, & Danielle; [ed.] W.T. Woodson H.S., Fairfax, VA; [occ.] Housewife; [hon.] Merit Award, Vaux Vocational School, 10-year service with Dept of Army; [oth. writ.] The Koala and Me; [pers.] I try to tell of the Most Powerful One within and out of our universe, and the most misunderstood at times, as He relates to me.; [a.] Falls Church, VA

ROBLYER, JOHN SCOTT
[b.] September 23, 1959, Vermont; [p.] Wallace L. and Barbrar Roblyer; [m.] Esther J. Roblyer, March 3, 1990; [ed.] Paralegal, Taking College courses for business and in religion; [occ.] Student; [oth. writ.] Poem - The World; [pers.] We have to learn and get along with each other.; [a.] York, PA

RODERMAN, RICHARD
[b.] July 21, 1967, Perth Amboy, NJ; [p.] Joseph and Carolyn Roderman; [m.] Marlene Roderman, February 8, 1992; [ed.] J. Frank Dobie High, San Jacinto College; [occ.] Houston Police Officer; [hon.] Dean's List; [oth. writ.] Many other unpublished poems.; [pers.] I reflect my personal feelings and experiences in my poetry; [a.] Houston, TX

RODRIGUEZ, ARLENE
[pen.] Samantha; [b.] February 28, 1980, Brooklyn, NY; [p.] Nilda and Benny Rodriguez; [ed.] Franklin K. Lane High School; [occ.] Student; [oth. writ.] Poems published in prime: A Journal of Autobiographical writing 1995 F.K. Lane H.S.; [pers.] I've always wanted to leave my footprints on the world and by having my poems published for the first time I just left my first footprint.; [a.] Ridgewood, NY

RODRIGUEZ, ARTHUR
[b.] July 12, 1950, Dallas, TX; [p.] Florentino and Alicia Rodriguez; [m.] Maria Esther Rodriguez, October 24, 1979; [ch.] Carlos V. Rodriguez; [ed.] Amador High School in Association with Parks Job Corps Center-Pleasanton, CA, Associate of Arts and Science Degree El Centro College, Dallas, TX; [occ.] Clerk-Technician Texas Scottish Rite Hospital for Child, Dallas; [memb.] Knights of Columbus Council 3593 Dallas, TX, Amer. Academy of Orthopedic Technicians Dallas, TX; [pers.] Everything happens for the best. As tragic as it may see, as big a loss as it is, as terrible as it makes you feel-whether you realize it or not, whether you accept it or not, it forces you to change, make a decision a better yourself.

RODRIGUEZ, ELIZABETH
[pen.] Liz; [b.] November 24, 1951, NY; [p.] Mary Rodriguez; [m.] Divorced; [ch.] Christina, Felix, Anthony and William; [ed.] High School, Complete in Computer on Data entry and word processing; [occ.] N.Y.C.H.A. Senior Director at Senior Citizen Center; [memb.] Assembly of the Church Body of Christ; [hon.] The Fresh Air Fund present the community Service Award in recognition outstanding service President of the United State for Grateful Services Volunteer Vista I 25 Anniversary; [pers.] May God Bless every one who likes my poem; [a.] New York, NY

ROGAN, TIMOTHY P.
[pen.] Patrick O'Flaherty; [b.] December 11, 1947, Pawtucket, RI; [p.] Francis E. Rogan, Florence M. Rogan; [ch.] Matthew Timothy Rogan Sean Patrick Rogan; [ed.] Attleboro High East Coast Aero Tech Johnson and Wales University; [occ.] Quality Assurance Specialist; [memb.] VFW, ELKS; [pers.] Life's complex questions abound, but the answers are not of this world!; [a.] South Attleboro, MA

ROGERS, JACK ALLEN
[pen.] Jack Allen Rogers; [b.] July 2, 1930, Mendota, IL; [p.] Mr. Ted Rogers and Zaida Nighswonger; [ch.] Robert Rogers, Sherry Stevens; [occ.] Retired; [oth. writ.] The Warriors to be published poetic creations 1966; [pers.] Poetry Is My Passion; [a.] Enid, OK

ROGERS, MARK REGINALD
[b.] 8/23/54, El Paso, TX; [p.] Raymond A. & Cora Ellen Rogers; [m.] divorced from Nancy Polcyn (10/6/93), was married 1/10/86; [ch.] Heather, Sara, Hannah, Susanna; [ed.] El Paso High, Texas Tech Univ. Paramedic study at Houston Community College; [occ.] Paramedic, Corpsman in Naval Reserve assigned to Marine 1st Battalion 23rd Division; [memb.] Wilcrest Baptist Church, Houston, Texas Association of Emergency Medical Technicians; [hon.] Navy Achievement Medal; [oth. writ.] Several poems written and copyrighted in 1995 as yet unpublished.; [pers.] "Father From a Distance" is dedicated to Heather, Sara, Hannah, and Susanna Rogers, from Dad with love.; [a.] Houston, TX

ROMERO, GENARO CAMORLINGA
[pen.] Camorlinga Romero; [b.] December 7, 1924, Mexico; [p.] Genaro Camorlinga O., Guadalupe Romero M.; [m.] Dolores Diaz Camorlinga; [ch.] Genaro, Diana, Rene, Guido, Brisio; [ed.] College In Mexico; [occ.] Employed in sales store; [oth. writ.] Music compositor, and other unpublished poems; [a.] El Paso, TX

ROONEY, LISA FISHER
[b.] November 17, 1962, Minneapolis, MN; [p.] Dianne and Donald Fisher; [m.] Robert T. Rooney, January 17, 1991; [ch.] Nicole Faye, Natalie Anne; [ed.] Johnson Sr. High, Bunker Hill Community College, University of Minnesota; [pers.] I write for the sheer pleasure of writing.; [a.] Burnsville, MN

ROONEY, RENATE
[b.] July 26, 1943, Rostock, Germany; [p.] Edith Franzack, Willy Franzack; [m.] Herbert L. Rooney, November 23, 1963; [ch.] Anne, Lynn; [ed.] Associate Degree - Thomas Nelson Community College, Hampton, Virginia; [occ.] Sales Associate in Fashions; [memb.] Alumni Member at Thomas Nelson Community College, Human Society of the U.S. Member, Newport News, VA SPCA Member; [hon.] National Alliance for the Mentally Ill Member, Magna cum Laude graduate at Thomas Nelson Community College, Dean's Lists.; [oth. writ.] Several short stories and poems. None ever published; [pers.] Depicting man's plight in todays world and searching for answers to the complexity of our being combined with striving for human awareness of all living creatures and their needs.; [a.] Newport News, VA

ROSA, MANUEL S.
[b.] June 28, 1961, Azores, Portugal; [p.] Francisco and Margarida; [ed.] Degree in Graphic Design and Visual Communication but I haven't stopped learning yet.; [occ.] Computer Artist-Digital Art Coordinator; [memb.] BMI, Graphic Arts Guild and a lifetime membership in the human race; [hon.] Boston Globe's "Art Merit Award" 1977; [oth. writ.] Co-wrote 2 music albums in Portuguese-directed a music video for Brazilian MTV and have countless American song lyrics waiting for music.; [pers.] Life is easy to understand if you follow a law of Physics "every action has an equal and opposite reaction." Laugh and others laugh with you. Raise your fists and others will raise fists against you.; [a.] Somerville, MA

ROSKOM, KEVIN
[b.] May 3, 1981, Green Bay, WI; [p.] Keith Roskom, Linda Banker; [ed.] Meadow Brooke Elementary Kin Howard Elementary 1-3, Forest Glen Elementary 4-5, St. John the Baptist School 6-8; [hon.] On B Honors 9 times out of 12; [pers.] In writing I try to reflect the hardships of jews during World War II; [a.] Green Bay, WI

ROSS, FLOYD
[pen.] F. Ross; [b.] April 23, 1938, Erin, TN; [m.] B. A. Ross (Diaz), January 18, 1975; [ed.] Santa Barbara High School, UCSB; [occ.] Retired; [memb.] Goleth Valley Art Ass'n.; [oth. writ.] Personal Diaries (Meanderies); [a.] Santa Barbara, CA

ROSS, KAREN
[pen.] Christian Dove; [b.] June 28, 1952, Creston, IA; [p.] Chester and Wanda Russ; [ed.] Van Meter Community School, Southwestern Community College; [occ.] Licensed Practical Nurse, Mercy Hospital Corning; [memb.] American Heart Association; [pers.] As a spur of the moment writer I put my pen on my paper and let my mind run free.; [a.] Corning, IA

ROSS, MAEA
[b.] October 17, 1981, Beverly Hills, CA; [p.] David and Malynda Boss; [ed.] 8th Grade, Churchill County Junior High; [occ.] Student; [memb.] Save the Earth Asso.; [hon.] Honor Roll student, Awards in Basketball and in track and field; [oth. writ.] I have written many poems and short stories. Some have been published in our yearbooks. This is my first national publication.; [pers.] I am influenced by my best friend, autumn yungk, my parents and the poem "footprints".; [a.] Fallon, NV

ROSS, MATT
[b.] November 14, 1980, Colombia, OH; [p.] Steve Ross and Jane McLaughlin; [ed.] 8th grade; [occ.] Student; [oth. writ.] Other poems; [pers.] I like the works of Stephen King, John Grisham, Tom Clancy; [a.] Granville, OH

ROTH, PAULINE BRAGG
[pen.] Polly or Pauline B; [b.] June 7, 1911, Hinton, WV; [p.] John Bragg, Elaine Bragg; [m.] Elmer R. (Deceased), March 17, 1934; [ch.] John William, Rhond R (Deceased); [ed.] Green Sculptor District High West Virginia University - A.B., West Georgia College M.Ed.; [occ.] Retired Biology Teacher, writing, travel, gardening; [memb.] Rehoboth Presbyterian Church, Garden Club, Atlanta Writers Club, Copper Pennies Writing Group, Honorary Member WASPS (Women Airforce Service Pilots), Circle Rehoboth Presbyterian Church.; [hon.] Phi Epsilon Phi (Botany Fraternity) W University, Scholastic many winnings Writers Club Contests, Fourth Club Trip Campvail Mass, Junior Year WVU, Trip Country Life Conference Madison, WI; [oth. writ.] Article in book Forest Service wives book, family history story in West Virginia stories in no Double Jeopardy book. Published frequently in Senior News and Senior Tribune, Travel articles (now gone); [pers.] To do all the good I can, to and for people, while I can. Keep a positive attitude.; [a.] Atlanta, GA

ROWE, MICHELLE A.
[b.] May 16, 1965, Iowa Falls, IA; [p.] Norman Iden, Mary Iden; [m.] Robert D. Rowe, April 1, 1988; [ch.] Danielle; [ed.] Brookings High School, B.S. Social Work USD, M.S. Rehabilitation Counseling, Eastern Montana College; [occ.] Rehabilitation Consultant in private practice (RRC); [memb.] Montana Mental Health Counselors Association, National Rehabilitation Association; [hon.] Magna Cum Laude, MRCC Award for Excellence in Productivity, Army Commendation Medal; [oth. writ.] Poem for High School reunion "Twenty Years Gone By" Master Thesis, "Teaching Effective Behavior Modification Techniques to Emotionally Disturbed Adolescents in a Residential Facility; [pers.] To be the best I can be. To follow my heart and dreams. Writing energizes me.; [a.] Great Falls, MT

RUCKMAN, GREGORY
[b.] April 27, 1967, Portland, OR; [p.] Joseph and Beulah Ruckman; [ed.] Tates Creek High School Lexington Community College Sullivan Business College; [occ.] United States Navy; [pers.] I would like to thank my Lord and Savior Jesus Christ for supplying me in this life I live I will always fall short without you. Thank you for your love I never want to go on without you are the same yesterday, today, and forever; [a.] Lexington, KY

RUCKMAN, LOIS A.
[b.] August 12, 1934, Shinnston, WV; [p.] Melvin and Mary Margaret (Anderson) Matheny; [m.] Robert E. Ruckman (divorced); [ch.] Susan, Pamela and Jennifer; [ed.] Shinnston High, Montgomery College, Germantown, MD; [occ.] Retired Federal Employee (FBI, Dept. of Energy); [pers.] Now that my primary career (Federal Government) has ended, I have moved away from the area of the Nation's capital, back to my hometown, and am now able to devote time to two of my great interests-painting and writing; [a.] Shinnston, WV

RUDNICK, MARLENE B.
[pen.] Marlene Baron; [b.] June 3, Brooklyn, NY; [p.] Isidore Baron, Ada Baron; [m.] Edward M. Rudnick, June 24, 1951; [ch.] Lawrence Eliot, Eric Michael; [ed.] New Utrecht High School, Brooklyn College, Empire State College; [occ.] Editor, writer; [memb.] American Association of University Women (AAUW), National Association of Female Executives (NAFE); [oth. writ.] Children's stories, book on Genetic Counseling, poetry published in several anthologies.; [pers.] My philosophy, my beliefs and my writing indicate clearly that although I am an optimist, I am also a realist. Poetry, especially Emily Dickinson's and Keats are special favorites.; [a.] Yorktown Heights, NY

RUGANI, LAUREN I.
[b.] October 21, 1985, Springfield, MA; [p.] Thomas and Kathleen Rugani; [ed.] Grade 5 Mary O. Pottenger School, Springfield, MA; [occ.] Student; [memb.] Our Lady of Hope Choir, Shelley's Dance Unlimited, M.O.P. School Chorus, P.A.C.E. (Pottenger Advocates for a Clean Environment); [hon.] Mass. State Science Poetry Contest 1991 and 1994 (second place), Presidential Academic Fitness Award 1994 and 1995, Pottenger School Representative to City Wide Spelling Bee 1995; [oth. writ.] Save the Earth, Air at Work, (Science Poetry); [pers.] I enjoy different forms of the arts, Ballet, Music, and Writing are my favorites. I hope to use my talents to make the world a better place.; [a.] Springfield, MA

RUNDBERG, BOBBY
[b.] July 25, 1977, Houston; [p.] R.C. Rundberg, Mary Helen Rundberg; [ed.] McCullough High School, The Woodlands, TX; [occ.] Student; [hon.] Magna Cum Laude, Graduate from McCullough High School 1995; [oth. writ.] Couple published in local school papers and magazines. "You Are Here" and "The Naked Eye"; [pers.] In memory, one lives forever.; [a.] The Woodlands, TX

RUNKLE, KATHERINE GATES
[b.] November 3, 1944, Cleveland, OH; [p.] Helen Hazel Gates and Charles Gates; [m.] Clifford Charles Runkle, February 1, 1975; [ch.] None living; [ed.] B.A.: 1966 Flora Stone Mather College of Western Reserve University M.S. Organic Chemistry 1981, University of California at Davis 72 Sem. Hrs. toward doctorate; [occ.] Volunteer Instructor at Solano Community College; [memb.] American Chemical Society, SHHH, President of Vallejo Ad Hoc Committee on the Handicapped, National DMDA, St. Dymphna League, Solano Republican Women Federated, Solano County Mental Health Board; [hon.] 1962: Westinghouse National Science Talent Search Finalist. 8 Summer Science Grants, Dean's List 2x at WRU, numerous graduate fellowships, Graduate Minority Fellowship at U.C. Davis Teaching Assistanceships at Kent State U., Case Institute of Technology, U.C. Davis; [oth. writ.] M.S. Thesis on Nuclear Magnetic Resonance, Two papers as spin-offs from the thesis and as junior author in J. Chem. Ed. Other poetry and fanzine writing; [pers.] Writing is an occupation in which one can indulge if one is disabled. In this way, it makes one equal to the able-bodied person.; [a.] Vallejo, CA

RUSINIAK, YVONNE LUBOV
[b.] November 16, 1945, Detroit, MI; [p.] V. Rev. Stephen and Luba Rusiniak; [ed.] Educational back-

ground in theatre, 3 seasons apprenticeship Northland Playhouse. Small roles prof. Productions, The Sound of Music with Karen Black, Good-Bye Ghost with June Allyson. Starring roles Det. Civic Center Theatre. Participant in poetry readings universities, etc. Dudley Randall's Broadside Poet's Theatre, Evening of Solitary with Native American and So. African Political Prisoners starring Ritchie Havens, Wayne State U.; [occ.] Special Activities Instructor in Creative Critics Poetry workshops for children and teens; [memb.] Detroit Recreation Dept. Poetry Society of Michigan member, Member of Poetry Workshops at Judson Jerome's Maryland farm (one time poetry columnist for the Writer's Digest); [hon.] Poem Breakfast on casette tape The Best of Yearbook of Modern Poetry 1971. Poems in various anthologies and newspapers. Books: Exotic Tea, Vantage Press, Jasmine Days, Prarie Poet; [oth. writ.] Books, on a grant from The American Poets Fellowship Society, Playground Poems, Quality Pub. Children's play Fall in a Blue Forest produced by Civic Center Children's Theatre. A chapbook of student's poems, Yes, I've Been There.; [pers.] Less and less publishing companies are publishing poetry, doesn't sell. People say they don't like to read contemporary poetry as they can't understand it. Without sacrificing quality or originality, I would like to see poetry (besides the classics) still reaching people's hearts as well as their intellects.; [a.] Detroit, MI

RUSSELL, JOSEPH K.
[pen.] Sir Joseph Kent; [b.] June 20, 1954, Pittsburgh, PA; [p.] Hayes and Caroline Russell; [m.] Karen Gabrella Russell, March 18, 1994; [ch.] Dylan, Justin, Kyle, Christopher; [ed.] B.S. Business Administration, B.S. Nuclear Medicine; [occ.] Nuclear Cardiology; [memb.] Society of Nuclear Medicine, American College of Cardiology, United Methodist Church; [hon.] 1st place Nuclear Cardiology Research Award snm 1990, 2nd place Nuclear Cardiology Research award snm 1993, 2nd place Research Pastor Society of Nuclear Med. 1995; [oth. writ.] Several research papers published; [a.] Philadelphia, PA

RUSSO, AUGUSTINE J.
[b.] August 18, 1929, Boston, MA; [p.] Angelo Russo, Leonora Russo; [m.] Junes Russo (Divorced), September 8, 1957; [ch.] Patricia, Gary, John, Christopher, Julie; [ed.] Quincy High, Fort Knox Armored School, Lincoln Institute for River Apprentice School; [occ.] Retired Dept. of Defense (Navy Dept.); [memb.] American Legion (Post 294), Disabled American Vets (Chapter 29), South Shore Singles New Beginnings (Norwell MA); [hon.] Validictorian Class of 1955 Fore River Apprentice School; [oth. writ.] A few poems, a few speeches, nothing published; [pers.] I have always had a decide to write and now I find that my age and leisure time has given me an abundance of subjects to write about with feeling and experience; [a.] Weymouth, MA

RUSSOLESI, ELIZABETH
[b.] May 9, 1985, New York City; [p.] Geri Russolesi, Leo Russolesi; [ed.] North Hills Elementary School 5th grade; [memb.] Flushing Flyers Aquatic Club, American Martyrs Swim Team; [hon.] Gold, silver, bronze at summer Junior Olympics, gold, silver, bronze at Dix Hills Invitational, Magnet Program, Brotherhood Award of Bnai Brith.; [pers.] My writings are reflected around nature for its beauty and serenity.; [a.] Hollis Hills, NY

RUTKOWSKI, JOSEPH J.
[b.] April 6, 1910, Issaquate; [p.] Stanley and Bernice Rutkowski; [m.] Rachel, April 23, 1936; [ch.] Geoffrey Rutkowski; [ed.] University of Washington, AB, MBA, Northwestern University Institute for Management.; [occ.] Retired, International Executive Service Corps Volunteer.; [memb.] Telephone Pioneers of America.; [pers.] Hoping, always, that where I have been was a little better because I was there.; [a.] Santa Barbara, CA

SABAT, MARGIE
[pen.] Maggie Rae; [b.] September 24, 1952, Mt. Pleasant, PA; [p.] William Dezort, June Dezort; [ch.] Jodie Sabat Dowden; [ed.] Southmoreland High School; [occ.] Financial Service Rep., The Scottdale Bank and Trust Co., Scottdale, PA.; [oth. writ.] Several poems written for co-workers; [pers.] My inner most thoughts and feelings are spoken through my poetry. "Daddy", a poem promised but never written, I wrote and read for him on the day of his funeral. Somehow, I know he heard me.; [a.] Scottdale, PA

SACCOCCI, DIANE
[pen.] Diane Carr; [b.] July 27, 1943, Ogdensburg, NY; [p.] Dorthy and Vincent; [m.] Phillip; [ch.] Joey and Danny; [ed.] High school - Cosmotology School acting - modeling school creative writing and business; [occ.] Day-care; [memb.] C.C.D. - Peta I.F.A.W. - Doal; [oth. writ.] Office News Letters; [pers.] I feel poetry is born in the heart and soul and inspired by the beauty of God's nature; [a.] Syracure, NY

SAK, HELEN THERESA
[pen.] Helen Theresa Sak; [b.] January 30, 1921; [p.] Deceased; [ed.] Nursery the sick for 38 years, 3 shifts amounted to 114 yrs. (don't laugh); [occ.] My last patient had an Ins. Co and a Diabetic and I really had my hands full, people still phone me. 5 years ago he had cancer of the kidney yr. later cancer of colon, yr. later cancer of the stomach, oh it was pitiful. I'm glad I could relax. He wa such a wonderful person and the way he suffered it was sad

SALAZAR, JEROME PAUL
[b.] February 28, 1975, Orange, CA; [p.] Frankie A. and Linda J.; [ed.] Taft High School, San Antonio, TX; [memb.] Music Club, Nintendo; [hon.] Gifted child in grade school, advanced classes, first choice in 8th grade band for alto saxophone. It waa a very great experience for us to have Jerome in our family, he brought joy and laughter and wisdom to our family.; [oth. writ.] Stories about his life and his accident, many poems; [pers.] Jerome loved his music, master of Nintendo and Wheel of fortune, creative and precise. When I think of my brother I remember him being a thinker and passionate person. He was a very deep thinking person, if he had been with us longer he would have used it for the benefit of us all. A real leader. His passion, a characteristic that really set men apart, you only have to look at his poetry. In which the very existence of shows that hey 'I' have something to say and have the artistic ability in which to apply it. That makes someone better than normal.

SALAZAR, MARY THERESA
[b.] November 28, 1954, Denver, CO; [ed.] East High School, University of Colorado School of Nursing; [occ.] R.N., B.S.N., Evening Shift Supervisor/ Medicare Charge Nurse, Villa Manor Care Center; [memb.] World Wildlife Fund, Friends of The Nature Conservancy, National Wildlife Federation, Boys Town, Cystic Fibrosis Foundation; [pers.] Life is like a jewel with numerous facets, providing unending opportunities for exploration within yourself and around you.; [a.] Denver, CO

SALMON, ELEANOR
[b.] January 2, 1919, Saint Croix Falls, WI; [p.] John Patrick Salmon, Nora Angeline Barrett Salmon; [ed.] 12th grade Valedictorian, Several short stories, one novel in progress, much writing in the fifty years as an office manager; [occ.] Retired - writing a novel; [memb.] Holy Redeemer Parish (precious) National Secretaries, Sodality, BVM, Catholic NAACP, Employed by council of jevish women to supervise a halfway house; [hon.] Poem published many years ago, about the death of a little boy; [oth. writ.] Many poems unpublished novel; [pers.] Both of my novels are about various kinds of prejudice which I have encountered in the six cities where I have lived (anti-senitism and towers Afro-Ames)

SALZANO, FRANK G.
[b.] May 28, 1925, Brooklyn, NY; [p.] Frank and Grace; [m.] Frances, October 18, 1947; [ch.] Frank, John, Thomas; [ed.] Chelsea Vocational HS; [occ.] Retired; [memb.] American Legion Post 507

SAMPLE, GINA MARIE
[b.] July 9, 1968, Chicago, IL; [p.] Mr. and Mrs. James Losito; [m.] Keith Joseph Sample, July 21, 1990; [ch.] Raquelle Marie Sample; [pers.] Being that I had such a troubled pregnancy, having my Raquelle was so special. This poem is dedicated to her, for I shall always love her with my whole heart and soul.; [a.] Lake in the Hills, IL

SAMS, ERVIN
[b.] March 11, 1925, Marshall; [p.] Deceased; [ed.] 8th; [occ.] Disable; [memb.] UFW Post 891; [a.] Ashville, NC

SAMULEWICZ, BETTY
[b.] July 22, 1925, Pawhuska, OK; [p.] Florence and Hobart Sinard; [m.] Hans, October 29; [ch.] Susan Davis, Joe Soboleski; [ed.] High School Grad. Delano High School Delano, CA; [occ.] Retired Accounting positions for 40 years; [oth. writ.] None entered. Just little things I wrote for the family.; [pers.] I am 70 years old always have written little poems for family never really anything big. But this just came to me as I wrote about the poor little children that died in the bombing.; [a.] Van Nuys, CA

SANDERS, DORA L.
[b.] June 21, 1911, Richland, KS; [p.] Louis H. and Maude H. Griffith; [m.] Fred C. Sanders, January 2, 1932; [ch.] one son; [ed.] Grade and some HS.; [occ.] Housewife; [memb.] Unite Methodist Church, Edsel Owner's Club (Car) and many friends there. Historical Museum at Lawrence, KS. AARP; [hon.] Many car club awards - and reading of my poetry; [oth. writ.] My personal scrapbook of poems one poem published in the Topeka Daily Capitol.; [pers.] Raised on a farm in deep country - my friends were the animals, living things, close neighbors and God. Mother read to us and father was a minister who raised us by a strict rule.; [a.] Ottawa, KS

SANDERS, HEATHER ALICIA
[b.] November 17, 1977, Alabama; [p.] Charles Dwain and Celina Sanders; [m.] Single; [ed.] Attended Roberstdale School K-12 Grade and Graduated c/o 96'; [memb.] DECA; [hon.] National Honor Society, Awarded District Competition For DECA; [oth. writ.] Poems Published in School literary magazine, "Beyond Imagination"; [pers.] Never share your feelings keep them locked within share them with yourself for you are your only friend.; [a.] Roberstdale, AL

SANDERS, JAMES E.
[b.] March 30, 1957, Corpus Christi, TX; [p.] Mattie Runchad Sowers; [m.] Sandra Sanders, August 18, 1978; [ch.] La Toya and La Teisha Sanders; [ed.] Henderson County Jr. College attended university of Texas in Tyler, graduated Roy Miller High, Corpus Christi, TX; [occ.] Lone Star Cas Company - Sr. Plant Opr.; [memb.] NAACP; [a.] Athens, TX

SANDERS, MILDRED IRENE
[pen.] Mildred Irene Sanders; [b.] April 28, 1910, Salem, IN; [p.] Louis and Elsie Bridgewater; [m.] John D. Sanders, December 16, 1925; [ch.] Donald, Dorthy, Paul, Robert; [ed.] 8th Grade; [occ.] Retired; [memb.] This and that Club; [oth. writ.] Old sayings; [pers.] Keep busy and thank the Lord for everyday.; [a.] Bismarck, IL

SANDS, RICK
[b.] October 20, 1955, Indiana; [pers.] Love is the most powerful force in the Universe. Faith is a gift.; [a.] Warsaw, IN

SANFILIPPO, CARMELA
[pen.] Carmela Sanfilippo; [b.] January 17, 1921, Trinidad, CO; [p.] James and Mary Barcelona; [m.] Frank Sanfilippo, June 15, 1946; [ch.] Ron and Judy; [ed.] Manley Senior High School; [occ.] Housewife and Mother and loving Grandmother.; [memb.] Christian Hills Full Gospel Church, Senior prayer circle member American Heart Association; [oth. writ.] Several unpublished poems mostly inspirational poetry this is my first poem to be published.; [pers.] My deep faith in our Lord, and my personal hope that my poetry might lead someone to a personal relationship with the Lord Jesus Christ.; [a.] Orland Park, IL

SANTOS, JUDITE GABRIELLE
[b.] February 17, 1980, Newark, NJ; [p.] Rosa Maria and Sidonio Santos; [ed.] Saint Cecilia's Grammar School and Queen of Peace High School; [occ.] Student in High School; [hon.] Theater, Art and pageants awards and 3rd honors through High School; [oth. writ.] I never wrote or had anything published before.; [pers.] A dream is a goal and a goal is to be achieved. Each one of us must find that "Lost Star" within ourselves and regain the courage to achieve it. ("Star of Lost Courage"); [a.] Kearny, NJ

SANTOS, MARCIA
[b.] March 11, 1976, Azores, Portugal; [p.] Florinda and Juvenal Santos; [ed.] Brown School, Powder House Community School, Somerville High School, Boston University; [occ.] Telephone Operator; [memb.] St. Anthony's Church Choir; [hon.] National Honor Student Award, Outstanding Achievement Award in Portuguese; [pers.] This poem helped me through an extremely difficult time in my life.; [a.] Somerville, MA

SARDINO, MARIANNE RUSSO
[b.] May 29, 1938, Connecticut; [p.] Leo and Mary Russo; [m.] Robert, May 30, 1962; [ch.] One daughter, two granddaughters; [ed.] RN Mt. Vernon Hospital Mt. Vernon NY ADN Palm Beach Jr. College BS. Barry University Miami Springs; [occ.] R.N.; [memb.] Florida Nurses Assoc. Hospital Access Nurses Assoc. Fla.; [pers.] My poem is about my oldest granddaugther - Sarah. My grandchildren keep me young; [a.] West Palm Beach, FL

SAROJAK, MARK
[pen.] Jackal; [b.] April 14, 1974, Saint Paul, MN; [p.] Douglas and Sandra Sarojak; [ed.] East High, UCLA, Wake Forest University; [occ.] Student; [hon.] Cool Guy Award; [oth. writ.] A hodge-podge of ecclectic ramblings.; [pers.] "From pain comes understanding."; [a.] West Chester, PA

SARRA, KRISTEN
[b.] December 25, 1980, Elizabeth, NJ; [p.] Lynda, Joseph Sarra; [occ.] Student Old Bridge High School NJ

SASS, YVONNE K.
[b.] September 22, 1942, St. Louis, MI; [p.] Josephine M. and Jame F. Alley; [m.] Gunther Sass, April 2, 1961; [ch.] Yvette, Cecilia, Eric, Page, granddaughter Kimberly Noel; [pers.] Jesus is priest, interressor, meditator, advocator, counselor, my attorney in grace, through the blood. The editor of my words.; [a.] Fort Lauderdale, FL

SATTERFIELD, FLORAETHYL
[pen.] Floraethyl Satterfield; [b.] January 21, 1913, Bloominton, IL; [p.] George and Edith Anderson; [m.] Dewey M. Satterfield, March 27, 1937; [ed.] Illinois State Normal University (Danville, Illinois High School); [occ.] Retired; [memb.] Live Oak, FL - Woman's Club - Garden Club - bridge Club.; [oth. writ.] Magazine - 1/2 page "Dog World" mag. "Tribute to Dewey Satterfield (husband) (copy in Dahlone Ganugget (GA) and 3/4 page in Suwannee Democrat FL. Book "I remember Dahlonega (GA) 1 chapter Vol 2; [pers.] "Beneath the Stars" was inspired, at age 20, to look to God at the top of the Royal Gorge, Colorado.; [a.] LiveOak, FL

SAUMELL, EVA
[pen.] Evita; [b.] Born in Puerto Rico; [p.] Abraham and Margarita Nieves; [m.] Charles Saumell, February 17, 1962; [ch.] Mara Saumell; [ed.] Bachelor of Science in Education - Mercy College Masters Degree in Education from Long Island University NY; [occ.] Bilingual Elementary School teacher in NY City; [memb.] Honor Society (foreign Languages) Phi Sigma Iota, SABE - National Bilingual Bi-Cultural Society, Metropolitan Opera Guild - National Member; [hon.] Honor Society - Foreign Languages - Phi Sigma Iota and Kappa Delta Pi - in education; [oth. writ.] I am always writing poems for my first grade bilingual students. I love writing; [a.] Yonkers, NY

SAVAGE, DANIEL RICHARD
[pen.] Rick Savage, Doc Savage; [b.] November 10, 1972, Farmington MO; [p.] Herb Savage and Ruby Savage; [ed.] Arcadia Valley High School, was tutored in Art of four years by Kip DeVoure in Ironton, MO; [occ.] Crew Leader at Ryan's family Steakhouse. One year. Farmington MO; [memb.] Word of Life Ministries, Rev. Leon Miller in Farmington, MO; [hon.] Several Awards throughout High School for Artwork Plan on becoming a Comic Book Artist.; [oth. writ.] Several drawings were published by The Democrat News in Fredericktown, MO; [a.] Farmington, MI

SAWYER JR., LEE E.
[pen.] Rambo; [b.] February 3, 1944, Elizabeth City, NC; [p.] Mr. and Mrs. Lee E. Sawyer (Both Deceased); [m.] Mrs. Annie J. Sawyer divorced 2 yrs (Deceased), April 8, 1968; [ch.] Alonzo C. Sawyer, Michael Sawyer and Ernest T. Mitchell; [ed.] 12 yr. High School and some Community college attendance) finished P.W. Moore High School in Elizabeth City, N.C. and part) college of the Albermarle; [occ.] In MD a Gen Worker and part time cook; [memb.] Was in army active 13 1/2 yrs. Nat'l guard retired 20 1/2 yrs. (total 3 yrs); [hon.] Received a number of awards from the military period 1961-1975; [oth. writ.] Wrote a few gospel songs for this gospel quartet the new mighty gospel wonders at which I am still a member guitar and keyboard player; [pers.] In closing I love poem and song writing doing my post time. I want to say to others with time on your hands let your Minds be creative in words of a song or poems. I'm temporarily in Aberdeen, MD; [a.] Aberdeen, MD

SCARBOROUGH, HELEN
[b.] August 6, 1925, Ohio; [m.] Floyd Scarborough, June 26, 1987; [occ.] Retired; [oth. writ.] Other poems sent to different places for music; [pers.] My life has always been focused on the future of our being, I have always been inspired when I think of how God created all living things; [a.] Chloride, AZ

SCARBRO, KATHY ANN
[pen.] Katco; [b.] August 5, 1950, Fayette, CO; [p.] Raymond And Deloris Hughes; [m.] James C. Scarbro, April 20, 1969; [ch.] Jamie Paul Scarbro; [ed.] Two years College in Elementary Education Dean's List. College of West Virginia.; [occ.] Housewife; [oth. writ.] I have many stuffed in drawers, this is my first published poem.; [pers.] We lived in the woods in South Carolina, we had to move away. My sorrow was so great, because I love the woods and animals. I wrote this poem to express my love for this place; [a.] Mt. Hope, WV

SCARSELLA, DON G.
[pen.] Dan G. Scarsella; [b.] May 3, 1965; [p.] Gabriel and Sunny Scarsella; [ed.] Crestwood H.S. College, (Henry Ford Comm College); [occ.] Mgr. Pyramid Guitars Redford, Mi; [hon.] Endorsed by Sharevel Jackson Guitar Outstanding Guitar Player - Yamaha Soundcheck October 10, 1989, Aquarius Theatre Los Angeles, CA

SCELZO, ANTHONY
[pen.] Anthony, Scelzo; [b.] August 29, 1915, New York City; [p.] Deceased; [m.] Dorothy Scelzo, June 6, 1936; [ch.] One; [ed.] High School; [occ.] Retired (Police Dept.); [memb.] Columbia Ass. Police Dept.; [hon.] Three commendations; [oth. writ.] Poems concerning police work. Recited at the communion breakfast of the 42 pct.; [a.] New York, NY

SCHAFER, GERALDINE E.
[pen.] Geri E. Schafer; [b.] June 15, 1940, Norwalk, CT; [p.] Stephen J. Toth, Helen J. Toth; [m.] The Rev. Thomas F. Schafer, January 28, 1961; [ed.]

Norwalk Sr. High School, Norwalk, CT, Bryant And Stratton Business Institute Syracuse, NY; [occ.] Secretary; [memb.] LaFayette Ave. United Methodist Church Syracuse, New York, Director/Hineman Handbell Choir of LaFayette Ave. United Methodist Church Syracuse, New York; [hon.] Three Time Recipient Award for Gift To Missions, by United Methodist Women (UMW), to National United Methodist Women of the United Methodist Church; [pers.] It is to share my higher thoughts amongst humanity and, in my written work, any whom I can help along life's tough road of life, is my ultimate goal; [a.] Syracuse, NY

SCHAUM, CARL
[b.] June 9, 1973, Charleroi, PA; [p.] Connie Schaum, John Schaum; [ed.] B.S. in Meteorology at California University of Pennsylvania; [memb.] Allenport United Methodist Church; [hon.] Gamma Theta Upsilon, Sigma gamma Epsilon, Dean's List; [pers.] "People that hustle by the inch and lag by the yard, get kicked by the foot."; [a.] Allenport, PA

SCHECK, JANEA
[b.] September 17, 1977, Hays, KS; [p.] Judy Scheck, Joe Scheck; [ed.] A senior at Victoria High School; [occ.] Student; [memb.] President of CYO, SADD, President of FHA, Vice-President of Future Business Leaders of America, Vice-President Pep Club, Secretary of Student Council, Secretary of V-Club; [hon.] Who's Who of High School Students, National Honor Society; [a.] Victoria, KS

SCHEUER, SUE
[pen.] Sue Scheuer; [b.] August 21, 1951, Mexico; [p.] Jesus and Maria Guzman; [m.] Ray Scheuer, August 19, 1972; [ch.] Sandra 19, Jason 12; [occ.] Housewife; [pers.] Love comes from within and I love to share it poems brings me peace of mine and beauty inside me; [a.] Beaver, UT

SCHEUERMANN, KAREN L.
[b.] October 11, 1953, Saint Louis, MO; [p.] Harold and Vesta Scheuermann; [m.] Divorced; [ch.] Brian 25, Mike 22, Greg 19; [ed.] Cleveland High School, Vocational Training - Certified Nurses Aide, my first year of High school was at "Lutheran High South" both schools in Missouri; [occ.] Cashier; [memb.] Cedar Hill Lutheran Church; [oth. writ.] Several unpublished songs and poems: One published in area newspapers.; [pers.] I write from my heart, from personal experiences and lessons learned through my life... I feel that there is a lesson to be learned, every day of our lives. We need to keep our eyes, our ears and our hearts open also it's never too late to begin again.; [a.] Dittmer, MO

SCHEXNYDER, WALLACE J.
[pen.] Lion Heart, Lonely Heart, Aaron Lark; [b.] March 22, 1964, North Carolina; [p.] Howard and Marva Schexnyder; [ed.] Berwick High School, Berwick LA.; [occ.] Licensed Practical Nurse; [memb.] American Heart Assoc. American Red Cross, Central LA. Poetry Soc., Central Louisiana Aids support services; [hon.] CPR Instructor (AWA ARC) HIV Counselor, Aids Hotline Counselor; [oth. writ.] Several poems published Bx C.L.A.S.S. also a book called (Pineville thoughts and emotions). All my original work; [pers.] If one person is moved by my writings. Then my job is done; [a.] Pineville, LA

SCHLAUGER, DAWN
[pen.] Dawn Schlauger; [b.] November 22, 1979, Fruita, CO; [p.] Alan and Cherrie Schlauger; [ed.] Sophomore in High School; [occ.] Student, Artist; [oth. writ.] Misc. Poetry; [a.] Olathe, CO

SCHLEGEL, DARA MARIE
[b.] April 27, 1973, Philadelpia, PA; [p.] Frank and Elizabeth Schlegel; [ed.] Little Flower Catholic HS, Art Institute of Philadelphia; [occ.] Dispatcher for Summit Truck Services; [pers.] Poems are my way of expressing my feeling. So others can understand and relate to me.; [a.] Pennsauken, NJ

SCHLESSER, JOHN A.
[b.] April 2, 1904, Latvia; [p.] John Schlesser, Emilia Schlesser; [ed.] Self Educated from popular educator library 10 volumes of University standard 1940, Volunteer - Official Appointment to R.N. committee policy; [occ.] Making-board, paid-up for life member.; [memb.] The American legion painters and allied trades paid-up for life, member life, member, R.N.C.; [hon.] Honorable - discharge U.S. Army 1943.; [oth. writ.] Vind Blous Through Our Blooming Shrubs (never published.) Short story (about 100 words) we all are born, Bureaucrats; [pers.] I strive to reflect whats wrong with the world and how to correct. It put to practice all ideas that work al worlds, religions and all worlds high economics morales that will tick the world in right directions...; [a.] Leesburg, FL

SCHNEIDER, CHRIS
[b.] February 5, 1955, Orlando, FL; [p.] Paul and Virginia Mikler; [m.] Arnold Schneider, June 12, 1976; [ch.] Caroline, Melissa; [ed.] B.A. Journalism, 1976; [occ.] Homemaker, Freelance Writer; [memb.] Messiah Choral Society, 5 yrs.; [oth. writ.] Poetry, lyrics, short stories; [pers.] In 1986, my husband and I brought home God's gracious gift of a baby daughter. Two and a half years later, he gave us another daughter. Since then, my pen has been busy capturing "freeze frame" moments of our family life. My other writings (including lyrics), reflect my personal spiritual journey.; [a.] Maitland, FL

SCHNEIDER, ELLEN
[b.] November 25, 1947, Newton, MA; [p.] Richard and Eleanor Clark; [m.] Daniel Schneider, June 20, 1970; [ch.] Jessica, Julia and Eli; [ed.] Needham High School U mass-Amherts - BS Boston Teachers College Masters in Teaching Science; [occ.] Health and Physical Education teacher at English High School in Boston; [memb.] First Congregational Church of Sharon; [oth. writ.] Editorials for the local newspaper, The Sharon Advocate; [pers.] I hope to published several children's stories I have written and eventually write an autobiographical account on my years of teaching in the Boston Public Schools.

SCHNITZLER, DOUGLAS C.
[b.] August 10, 1955, Marshfield, WI; [p.] Donald W., Gloria T. Schnitzler; [m.] Lorena, April 12, 1986; [ch.] Jessica, Jason, Lesley, Kristopher, Sylvia; [ed.] High School, Marshfield Sr. High; [occ.] Custodian/Laborer; [memb.] White tails Unlimited. Knights of Columbus; [hon.] Pershing Professional Certificates, letters Commendation, and Appreciation, Army Good Conduct, and Commendation Medals; [oth. writ.] None published; [a.] Chili, WI

SCHOENBERG, BARBARA
[pen.] Katherine Aviva; [b.] March 15, 1938, Brooklyn; [p.] Esther and John Lynch; [m.] Joseph Schoenberg, June 13, 1970; [ed.] St. Joseph College - BA (Brooklyn, NY) New York University Continuing School of Education, New School; [occ.] Paralegal; [memb.] Manhattan Paralegal Association LIVE - central Park Conservancy; [hon.] MPA Director's award - continuing legal education and public relations; [oth. writ.] Poems in stray dog published by Center for The Arts Teachers College - Columbia issue 2 and 3 bloodpress. Poem in Dance On The Horizons, Poems in a Moment in time; [pers.] I am always happy to hear the birds singing in the countryside and that includes NYC.; [a.] New York City, NY

SCHOTTS, RICHARD JAMES
[b.] May 22, 1934, Amsterdam, NY; [p.] Anthony F. and Amelia F. Schotts; [m.] Marlene, August 24, 1954; [ch.] Richard Jr., Julie, Thomas, Christopher; [ed.] New York State University College for Teachers - Buffalo albright Art School - Buffalo; [occ.] Consultant; [memb.] 1st prize poetry 51 judged by Robert Tristan Coffin Purlitern Poet, 1st prize textile design McHawk Carpet Mills; [oth. writ.] When seasons change novel early 50's, several business articles in druggist magazine and the insurance salesman; [pers.] My writing is not to bring one to conclusions, but to provoke one to ponder that which is beneath the surface searching for the way of it.; [a.] Big Bear Lake, CA

SCHRAMM, JANICE
[pen.] Janice Schramm; [b.] August 21, 1962, Corning, NY; [pers.] I express my feelings through poetry so that others may understand common experiences.; [a.] Needville, TX

SCHRUPP, ADELE
[b.] August 3, 1925, Perham, MN; [p.] William and Lucille (Johnson) Butzke; [m.] Milton Schrupp, August 3, 1946; [ch.] Larry Gene - Douglas Lee - Susan Renee - Kristi Lynn; [ed.] Perham High School Graduate; [occ.] Retired Postmaster; [memb.] St. John's Lutheran Church Vergas, MN, National Ass'n of Postmasters of United States; [oth. writ.] Poems for family members and friends in remembrance of special occasions; [pers.] Inspired by my love for my Lord, my family and my friends.; [a.] Vergas, MN

SCHULDT, ROSE M.
[b.] January 4, 1950, Lyons; [p.] Arthur and Anna Harrington; [m.] George R. Schuldt, December 8, 1986; [ch.] Charlotte, Earl, Josh; [ed.] I received my GED at the age of 31; [occ.] Secretary for my husband plumb. and Heat Co.; [memb.] Council of the Arts; [oth. writ.] I have several poems and short stories that were never published because I never thought they were good enough. I now believe they are!; [pers.] I find poetry as a way of expressing myself. I love to write. It's my way of escaping from the craziness in this world. My favorite poet: Edgar Alan Poe; [a.] Lyons, NY

SCHULZE SR., WILLIAM H.
[b.] November 22, 1926, Houston, TX; [p.] Herbert H. and Ethyl Kimcaid Schulze; [m.] Mary Wyatt Schulze, November 4, 1988; [ch.] James Gerard Schulze and William H. Schulze, Jr.; [ed.] LL. B. Tulsa University Law School, undergraduate (Prelaw) University of Arkansas of Fayetteville, AR; [occ.] Administration Law Judge, office of hearings and appeals, SSA; [memb.] ALJ association (national) Arkansas Bar Assoc.; [a.] Little Rock, AR

SCHUTZ, CHENEE CHRISTINE
[b.] December 19, 1983, Lafayette, IN; [p.] Scot Schutz/Susana Bernacchi; [ed.] Will be in 6th grade; [occ.] Student; [memb.] LDS Church (Mormon) Girl Scouts of America Indianapolis Children's Choir's 4-H; [hon.] First place in school art contest. Painting shown at Indianapolis Museum of Art. School Honor Roll; [oth. writ.] Book of poems for school; [pers.] I like reading poems. I think they are really neat and fun. I also like how they rhyme.; [a.] Indianapolis, IN

SCHWARTZ, CAROLYN
[b.] February 8, 1943, Brownwood, TX; [p.] V. G. New/Colene Oloffo; [m.] Richard W. Schwartz, July 11, 1979; [ch.] Ron, Phyllis, Darrell, Margie and Scott; [ed.] Attended Bakersfield College and Kelloggs Community in Battle Creek, Michigan; [occ.] Artist, Wife, and mother; [oth. writ.] Poem "My Ship Of Bitterness" Sparrowgrass poetry forum; [a.] Tecumseh, OK

SCOTT, HENRY V.
[pen.] Henry V. Scott; [b.] April 9, 1919, Phoenix, NY; [p.] Thomas Patrick Scott, Catherine Veronica McAndrew; [m.] Josephine Hanley Hayes, August 1947; [ch.] Patrick Edmon Scott, Sheila Ann Scott, Maria Theresa Scott; [ed.] Associate Arts-Business; [occ.] Hospitalized-Vancouver, Veterans Administration-Washington Vancouever; [memb.] Irish Northern Aid, New York, 5th Marine Division Association USS York Town Assoc. Survivors we were sunk near midway; [hon.] Heroism-Bronze Star Medal, Iwo Jima C-1-27- March 3, 1945, Rifle Sharp Shooter, USMC Parachutist; [oth. writ.] I like to reach - I like to write-sometimes I try poetry or plain rhymes or just nonsense, quite liberal most things; [pers.] Never circled the globe-4/5 not too bad boyhood goal. Lost left arm above elbow on 11 or 12th day on Iwo Jima - Bullet thru chest also; [a.] Portland, OR

SCOTT, JACQUELINE D.
[b.] October 6, 1935, Hampton, VA; [p.] Ada and George Deane; [m.] Robert L. Scott, March 27, 1965; [ch.] Paul Reca, Kevin Reca, Lecia Spruill, Robert Scott Jr. and Karon Pierce; [ed.] Hampton High School; [occ.] Coordinator, Human Resources Newport News, Inc., Hampton, VA.; [pers.] These words came from the bottom of my heart and were written to honor the memory of my mother who passed away October, 1990.; [a.] Hampton, VA

SEARSON, ETHEL
[b.] December 22, 1936, NY; [p.] Mary McMahon, Hugh Polland; [m.] John Searson; [ch.] John, Kevin, Karen, Christopher and James; [occ.] Para Professional in Education; [oth. writ.] A Bird With Broken Wings, A Wisper In The Wind, The Reflection Of Your Face.; [pers.] Influenced by Kahlil Gibran the poet and prophet inspired by my Lord Jesus

SEEKAMP II, CRAIG M.
[pen.] Morgan Seekamp; [b.] March 30, 1983, Victoria, TX; [p.] Craig and Helen Seekamp; [ed.] Presently a seventh grade student at Yoakum Jr. High School Yoakum, TX; [memb.] Student Council; [pers.] My "Granny" Joyce Seekamp is a wonderful lady and an inspiration to her children and grandchildren and we love her very much

SEIBERT, MRS. MAYDELL C.
[pen.] Dell Seibert; [b.] June 24, 1921, Wynona, OK; [p.] George Coker Coleman and Mary Emma/Strawn Coleman Wilson; [m.] Floyd I. (Bill) Seibert JR.., January 18, 1947; [ch.] Samuel Lawrence Seibert (adopted), Christopher Floyd Seibert; [ed.] High School (Shawnee, OK), Two Term Course in Dental Assistant; [occ.] Retired- Homemaker, Formerly - Approx. 20 yrs as a Dental Assistant; [memb.] Presbyterian Church (Dale Presby Church Dale, IN) some others but short term usually from volunteerism; [hon.] A few from my Church - or Volunteer Group (such as R.S.V.P.); [oth. writ.] "Listen" that was published in Presby Women's Magazine "Concern", and "Karatha" published in a friend's autobiography - "Ming's Roses in December" written by Mytle Huston - are the only two among many published; [pers.] Belief, faith and service in and for God and His son Jesus Christ - through the Christian family and to all mankind, I was encouraged and influence by a high school english and lit. teacher.; [a.] Washington, IN

SEIBOLD, STEPHANIE L.
[b.] October 31, 1974, Painsville, OH; [p.] Robert and June Seibold; [ed.] Riverside High School; [occ.] Factory Worker, Striving Artist; [memb.] Redcross; [hon.] Headlands Elementary Library Award; [oth. writ.] I wish to be a famous writer one day, but until then I have my own collection of my own writings which I believe are very good.; [pers.] Poetry is a way of reflecting a feeling, thought, or statement. I choose poetry because in poetry I can express my feeling's and thought to reveal my true statement.; [a.] Painsville, OH

SEITZ, MARY
[pen.] Elizabeth Lafary; [b.] December 30, 1932, Morgan County, IN; [p.] Omer and Inez Lafary; [m.] Chester Paul Seitz, August 1, 1966; [ed.] Union Twp. High and Arsenial Tech High (Valedictorian) Indpls. University; [occ.] Realtor, broker Associate with Key Associate/Jim O'Brien Reality Franklin, IN; [memb.] MIBOR, IAR, NAR; [hon.] Valedictorian; [oth. writ.] Several poems, one of them published in a book.; [pers.] In the ministry of music, poetry is a means of reaching out to those in need. I like to reflect God's great universe.; [a.] Nineveh, IN

SEITZ, MELANIE A.
[b.] June 18, 1964, Flint, MI; [ed.] Phoenix Institute of Tech. Ph.D. in Life; [occ.] Part time correspondent for local newspaper; [memb.] Museum of natural History (avid tree hugger) green peace save the planet etc....; [hon.] Golden poet award 91/92; [pers.] "Change your mind change your life."; [a.] Heppner, OR

SELTZER, HELEN ESTES
[pen.] Helen Estes Seltzer; [b.] Philadelphia, PA; [p.] May Griffith Estes and Smith William Estes; [m.] Richard Warren Seltzer Sr., June 5, 1944; [ch.] Richard Warren Seltzer, BA English, Yale, Pub. Novel and Sallie Estes Seltzer BA Russian, MA USC Film Making; [sib.] BA in English, Goddard College, Plainfield, VT, teaching certificate Penna, and VT., now ret. to where of house of Este Crest Jewelry Co; [ed.] Does acting, modeling for print and TV and all media voice overs National Society; [occ.] Colonial Dames of Americas Phila. Chapter Dark, Genealogical Societies, Episcopal Church, Mainline Antiques Club, Colonial Dames of the Century; [oth. writ.] Author - published of the cary - Estes Genealogy, Barn Hill, Huntingdon Valley, PA., 1981, Poem: Goliath and David, published Columbia record, Columbia, PA 1975; [pers.] I have enjoyed writing poetry, prose, local news and sorority columns. I still have a notebook with several poems written in fifth grade. I keep a folder of memoirs, including folklore, of East Falls, the area of Phila in which was born and plan to write a "Bio"; [a.] Philadelphia, PA

SEPULVEDA, DAMARIS
[b.] March 23, 1980, New York; [p.] Thomas Sepulveda and Delis Sepulveda; [ed.] Osceola High School; [memb.] Air Force Junior R.O.T.C. drill team and color guard, chorus and drama.; [hon.] Certificate of summer training from the Air Force, honor student, and Award of Excellence from the City of New York; [oth. writ.] Some of my poems were in my schools newspapers and yearbooks.; [pers.] The world and all it's goods are yours if you can laugh at life. "I have once read in a book and now I live by it everyday of my life".; [a.] Kissimmee, FL

SETZER, ERIN JESSICA
[b.] May 8, 1980; [p.] Patrica Setzer, Tim Setzer; [ed.] Student in High School; [occ.] Student; [hon.] Student of the month, the principals award, and all my life I've been on the honor roll.; [oth. writ.] Poems such as.... Hope and Healing, The Rose, Always and Forever, The Door, Who Knows, and Night Things, which are just a few; [pers.] Trying to find out who you really are is like trying to fly, sometimes you think you've almost got it, then its gone, one day it shall happen, so hold on to your wings and follow your heart

SEWELL, AISHA LATRICE
[pen.] Nikko Jazz; [b.] July 11, 1978, Atlanta, GA; [p.] Antoinette B. Nathaniel Sewell; [ed.] Vegetian Hills Elem. Sylvan Hills Middle School, Benjamin E. Mays High School; [occ.] Attending BE Mays High as a rising senior.; [memb.] Kappa Pearls Social Club, Dance (Ballet and Pointe and Jazz) Band, Track and NAACP.; [hon.] Various Athletic, Academic and Dance; [oth. writ.] Short stories and other poetry; [pers.] "The human heart feels things the eyes can not see, and knows what the mind can not understand."; [a.] Atlanta, GA

SEYBOLD, CLINTON C.
[b.] November 2, 1970, Salt Lake City, UT; [p.] Calvin and Roxanna Seybold; [ed.] B.A. in History from the Virginia Military Institute, Lexington, VA; [occ.] Infantry Officer, U.S. Army; [memb.] Kappa Alpha Fraternity, B.P.O. Elks; [hon.] U.S. Army Airborne - Ranger, Numerous Awards for merit and Service.; [oth. writ.] Numerous unpublished poems and short stories.; [pers.] I'm a romantic who believes in the ultimate "Good" of mankind and that "Right" will eventually triumph. That there was things worse than death, and that "Honor" is real, relevant and important of life.; [a.] Mt. Carmel, IL

SHAFFER, MICHAEL LEE
[b.] May 17, 1947, Baltimore, MD; [p.] Earl F. and Cecelia Shaffer; [m.] Debby Hook-Shaffer, July 18, 1970; [ch.] Michael Christopher, Trevor Lee; [ed.] Florida Community College at Jacksonville, Columbia College; [occ.] Fourth Generation Railroad Worker; [memb.] Baltimore and Ohio Railroad Veteran Employees Assn.; [oth. writ.] Several short stories wait-

ing for publishers and a collection of poems still being written and assembled.; [pers.] Edgar A. Poe, Taylor Caldwell and Louis L'Amour have influenced my writing... and my pleasure.; [a.] Jacksonville, FL

SHAMS, ROZALY OSI
[b.] February 24, 1942, Budapest, Hungary, Europe; [p.] Margit and Joseph Osi; [ch.] Charles R. Daniel Alberici and Lila A. Shams and Nora A. Shams; [ed.] Started in Budapest and Brussels Belgium and Canada and U.S. School - LPN and graduated hair and skin design school; [occ.] Trying to get a teaching degree at community college soon!; [oth. writ.] Wrote a book on "How To Teach Children How To Sew" on the concept of B. D. to be published in news future - I also speak 4 languages Hungarian, Spanish, French and English; [pers.] Survived WUII - saw the twilight of the most Romantic Era - wiped out by the cruel WW II - era - lived through the most famous people that ever lived from Queens to statemen to writers - music's etc... and still have a lot on a my heart to continue.

SHAPIRO, RODNEY J.
[b.] May 26, 1935, South Africa; [p.] Maurice, Matilda Shapiro; [m.] Jacqueline D. Shapiro, April 12, 1986; [ch.] Justine, Meagan Shapiro, Jennifer, Guy Reingold; [ed.] M.A., Ph. D.; [occ.] Clinical Psychologist, Clinical Professor of California; [memb.] American Psychological Association, Association of family therapist of N. California (past President), American Family Therapy Academy; [hon.] Veterans Administration Outstanding Performance Awards, Pacific Paesbyterian Medical Center Outstanding Teacher Award, Who's who in America, Human Services U.S. Israel Professional, Teaching Exchange Award; [oth. writ.] Numerous scientific writings, some published short stories in University Publications.; [pers.] I have felt the need to write since childhood. It has helped me make some sense of the vagaries of everyday life. I turn to poetry when my deepest feelings are touched - those feelings that poets have always stricken to give voice to - mystery, wonder, love, joy and sadness.; [a.] San Francisco, CA

SHAW, FANNY LEE
[pen.] Fanny Lee Baker Shaw; [b.] March 17, 1931, Binghamton, NY; [p.] Leah and Bernard Baker; [m.] Divorced; [ch.] Gerald B. Shaw - twins Daniel C. Shaw and Donna L. Shaw D. Mura; [ed.] 12th Grade; [occ.] Retired; [memb.] Because of poor health have had to give up a lot of activities.; [hon.] Was honor to be made distinguished member of ISP and to be nominated for award in Washington, D.C.; [oth. writ.] Old and alone and my shadow; [pers.] Have several poems, hope to get them published in a book - to leave to my children; [a.] Syracuse, NY

SHAW, KRISTINA
[b.] October 20, 1976, Kingston, Jamaica, WI; [p.] Sharon Shortridge, Evol Shaw; [ed.] Prospect Heights High School, soon to start Columbia University.; [memb.] New Haven Seventh Day Adventist Church; [hon.] 2 excellence in writing, and 3 scholarships in English, Principal's Award and an English Award, Regents Diploma; [oth. writ.] Several other poems honoured in Martin Luther King Poetry Contest. A novel entitled, "A Creek in the Attic," an autobiography "The Life of Laura Avendale," and short stories "Scary Tales and Short Fantasies"; [pers.] I want to thank first of all God, He played a major part in my soon to be success. I'd like to thank my mother for her support and love. And also Mrs. Evelyn Patterson for all of her encouragement and love.; [a.] Brooklyn, NY

SHAW, LUTHIA
[b.] July 14, 1961, Jasper, AL; [p.] (late) J. W. Bullocks and Dorothy Bullocks; [m.] Joseph Wayne Shaw, September 30, 1991; [ed.] High School Cordova High, 2 yrs. college - Walker Tech; [occ.] Housewife; [pers.] Prayer is my only weapon in this world as Jesus gives me the strength.; [a.] Quinton, AL

SHEETS, KRISTOPHER LEE
[b.] November 3, 1977, Elmira, NY; [p.] Edward and Gale Sheets; [ed.] Upcoming Senior at Elmira Free Academy, Elmira, NY; [occ.] Full time student; [hon.] Scholastics Award for Art Several Athletic Achievement Awards; [oth. writ.] My Morning Prayer; [pers.] Thru God, all things are possible.; [a.] Elmira, NY

SHELTON, CHRISTINA GAIL
[pen.] Christy Shelton; [b.] October 21, 1976, Memphis, TN; [p.] Thomas H. Shelton and Patricia E. Shelton; [ed.] Bolton High School, University of Memphis; [a.] Bartlett, TN

SHELTON, GLENDA WILLIS
[b.] February 22, 1952, Atlanta, GA; [p.] Glenn and Ethelyn Willis; [m.] Wayne Shelton, December 28, 1970; [ch.] April Michelle Aldridge, Joshua Lee Shelton; [ed.] Forest Park High School; [occ.] Housewife; [oth. writ.] Religious poetry; [pers.] My gift comes from God.; [a.] Jonesboro, GA

SHEPARD, VALERIA F.
[pen.] Valeria F. Seay Shepard; [b.] June 28, Brunswick, GA; [p.] Ethel Seay; [m.] Johnnie L. Shepard Sr., October 24, 1954; [ch.] Johnniel Jr., Melvin L, Harold T., Carol A.; [ed.] High School '50 Valedictorian, two years at Clark College which is now Clark Atlanta University. I attended Clark 50-51-51-52.; [occ.] Retired; [hon.] Made the deans list three semester at Clark College; [oth. writ.] Have a set of poems entitled "Pondermap"; [pers.] I will always have to give honor to Mrs. Constance the bar for putting my poems together to form ponderings which would not have been done without her.

SHEPPARD, REGINA P.
[pen.] Regina, Gina; [b.] August 8, 1958, Evergreen Park, IL; [p.] Joseph and Adele Toscano; [m.] Dan Sheppard, August 12, 1979; [ch.] Daniel (15), Dawn (10), Douglas (6), Kelly (1); [ed.] High School (Elizabeth Seton); [occ.] Service Representative Allstate Insurance; [oth. writ.] The Sky above Me..., Two Men Confusion it happens for a reason...I have to let go...Words can be hateful...; [pers.] You never know what changes will take place in your life. Life is a game. Play the game the best you can, grow from your experiences, learn from your mistakes, and always move forward.; [a.] Orland Park, IL

SHERBERT, JOHN MARK
[b.] October 21, 1967, Silver Spring, MD; [p.] Barbara and Richard L. Sherbert Jr.; [m.] Jacqueline D. Sherbert, June 18, 1994; [ed.] 3 Semesters of College, Good Council High School; [occ.] Security officer; [oth. writ.] Have had no other poem published but have many I've written since 1986.; [pers.] Most times, I write poems when they pop out in my mind. Usually I just write what the poem wants.

SHERLIN, MARY JO
[pen.] Jan Pohler; [b.] December 20, 1931, Ocoee, TN; [p.] Grady and Alma Rose; [m.] D. A. Sherlin, March 2, 1951; [ch.] Donnie Allen, Deanna Jo, Joel Bryan, also five grandchildren - Dustin, Keeona, Duran, Skylar, Kassidy; [ed.] Polk Co. High School - National School of Business - Cleveland Community State College; [occ.] Retired from Cleveland utilities after 32 years; [memb.] S Cleveland Church of God; [hon.] Salutatorian of my class; [oth. writ.] A play during high school that was chose for acting. Many poems for pleasure for class papers and friends, etc.; [pers.] I would like to leave something in writing that would influence the reader to never stop dreaming. Great things are accomplished by ideas and dreams that will not be aborted.; [a.] Cleveland, TN

SHOEMAKER, DEE
[pen.] Dee Collins; [b.] February 9, 1947, West Virginia; [m.] James Shoemaker, April 2, 1977; [ch.] Steven and Michael; [ed.] Attended Univ. of WV Western Connecticut State College; [occ.] Writer, Controller; [memb.] Boca Raton Historical Society, Morikami Museum, Connecticut Foreign Trade Alliance; [hon.] Created T Ball (for handicapped kids) team on regular league. Received a plaque and team is still playing.; [oth. writ.] The Creepa Mongo's, The Wind Monster; [pers.] My poem, "Bobby," tells of how I found out he drowned at the age of 14. I actually saw his image telling me he was ok when I had been told it was my father. This haunted me for years.; [a.] Boca Raton, FL

SHORE, ANNA V.
[pen.] Anna Virginia Shore; [b.] February 10, 1911; [p.] Deceased; [m.] Deceased, September 15, 1932; [ch.] Three sons, 1 Deceased; [ed.] High School Graduate, moralogist original material, book reviewer; [occ.] Writer and housewife. Singer volunteer; [memb.] Active member of Methodist Church, Health problems change things...; [hon.] Shakespearian Contest second acceptance by writing group placed second in state Shakesperian contest. Wrote for the school paper-autobiography; [oth. writ.] Dramatic work actress momologost writing my own material. Give talks on my spoon collection. Lead roles in plays. Have written plays when a young girl and directed. Have been writing poems and stories all.; [pers.] I try to write things that give people enjoyment. Ann early illness kept me at home. Poems written for family variety a piece on fashion printed on PCA, paper/encouragement from family and friends and grandchildren. Children book underway.; [a.] Oakland, CA

SHORT, MADELEINE
[pen.] Madeleine; [b.] October 29, 1942, England; [p.] Frank and Dee Short; [ch.] Michael, Raymond and Gregory, and Vincent; [ed.] Educated in England graduated Business College; [occ.] Desktop Publisher; [oth. writ.] A couple of story rhymes published by the Sierra Club. Have written several other story rhymes two story rhymes commissioned for "A Tribute to Mother" and a "60th Wedding Anniversary" tribute; [pers.] Started writing, story rhymes in 1994. Story rhymes have been based on facts...so far; [a.] Playa Del Rey, CA

SIBBERING, ROSEMARY ANDREWS
[pen.] Roe; [b.] August 18, 1964, New York; [p.] Clifford and Margaret Andrews; [m.] Edward Sibbering, May 27, 1989; [ed.] Santa Maria Elementary School, Saint Raymond Academy for Girls, The Wood Secretarial School; [occ.] Office Assistant; [oth. writ.] Mother of the Bride, and A mother's Day Wish.; [pers.] Writing inspires the soul captures the heart and releases the spirit.

SICKLESTEEL, KATHY
[b.] March 2, 1952, Norwood, MA; [p.] William Chapman, Ruth Chapman; [m.] Donald Sicklesteel, April 27, 1974; [ch.] Faith Lynn, Edward James; [ed.] Norwood Senior High, Cape Cod Community College; [occ.] Accounting Clerk, Nu-Hope of Highlands Country, Sebring, FL; [memb.] Sparta Road Baptist Church, National Parks and Conservation Assoc., TOPS #FL99, Sebring; [oth. writ.] Several other poems yet unpublished.; [pers.] To continue to serve and witness for the Lord.; [a.] Sebring, FL

SIGGERS, MATTIE P.
[b.] January 5, 1923, Warren County, NC; [p.] Joseph and Julia Shearin; [m.] Otis Siggers Jr., October 4, 1944; [ch.] Otis, Julia, Diane, Rita, Alan, David; [ed.] John R. Hawkins High Holliston Jr. College; [occ.] Retired; [pers.] My natural love for people, and for writing, inspires me to put the two together in the form of poetry, in defining a person, place, or thing.; [a.] Boston, MA

SILVA, MANUEL J.
[pen.] Mal Silva; [b.] March 17, 1932, San Diego, CA; [p.] Jose Joaquim Da Silva, Dina Zolezzi Silva; [m.] Joanne Holtmann Silva, Mary 11, 1957; [ch.] Catherine Marie, Anne Louise, Elizabeth Rose, Maria Joanne, Carolyn Patricia, Eileen Helen; [ed.] Sand Diego High-June '49, (Student body President), Loyola Univ. - Los Angeles - June '53, American Graduate School, Int'l Mgmt graduate (went to work to work for Procter and Gamble); [occ.] Retired Corporate Executive, last job as president Knomark Inc. Long Island New York; [memb.] Distinguished member of Int'l Society of Poets; [hon.] Alpha Sigma Nu (Jesuit University Equivalent of Phi Beta Kappa) 1952 Dean's list 1950-53, 1954 Outstanding graduate, Army Signal Corp School, Ft. Gordon, GA (Drafted Oct '53); [oth. writ.] Essays and position papers, for government officials, mostly White House chiefs of staff from 1974 thru present. Poetry, since vision restored in 1993, and birth of grandchildren.; [pers.] All of life is a balancing action between opposing extremes.; [a.] La Mesa, CA

SILVERMAN, LAURA LEE
[pen.] Laura Lee Stevens; [b.] December 3, 1963, Forest Hills, NY; [p.] Sandra Stevens Silverman, Jack Silverman; [ed.] Forest Hills High School, Queensboro Community College; [occ.] Independent Writer; [memb.] Board of Trustees for a non-profit organization located in Torrance, CA.; [hon.] Science Fair Winner; [oth. writ.] "Promise Me Everything" was my first published endeavor. I am currently in the process of circulating my second collection of poems. I am in the early stages of collaborating as a lyricist.; [pers.] Each day I strive to surpass the goals I set for myself the day before.; [a.] Torrance, CA

SILVERMAN, MEGGIN KAHN
[b.] August 5, 1973, Canada; [ed.] Andover High School, Bloomfield Hills, Michigan State University, 1995, BA., New York University, 1996, MS; [hon.] Dean's List, Nancy Thorpe Poetry Contest - National Honors, Sigma Delta Tau, Sorority Competitor, International Concert Festivals Europe, 1990; [oth. writ.] Several poems published in Voices of Youth National Publication Laurette magazine; [a.] Orchard Lake, MI

SIMMONDS, KATE
[b.] December 26, 1977, England; [ed.] Llandovery College Wales, United Kingdom; [occ.] Student; [memb.] Duke of Edinburgh Award scheme, Llandovery College Choral and Dramatic Societies.; [hon.] URDD Gobaith Cymru (Welsh Folk Festival Winner) Swansea Festival of Speech and Drama 1st place, Bronze, Silver and Gold Duke of Edinburgh Medals.; [oth. writ.] Various (unpublished) stories and poems; [pers.] I owe a lot of what I write to two people who have taught me that to have feelings is normal but to express them well is a unique gift. Thank you, Mum and Ms. Love.; [a.] Lafayette, LA

SIMMONS, NELSON JOSEPH
[b.] March 23, 1934, Scotland Co, NC; [p.] Joseph Christephor and Nellie Simmons; [m.] Joyce Lujean Mears Simmons (Deceased), September 13, 1952; [ch.] Desiree Leigh, Sabrina Robinette, Vanessa Jo, Valerie Jenel; [ed.] 12th Graduated McColl High School; [occ.] Disabled; [memb.] Mason, Schriners Presbyterian Church, McColl, SC. Honorary Member, V.F.W., McColl, SC Past City Council Member, McColl, SC; [oth. writ.] Poems enclosed never published; [a.] Pageland, SC

SIMMONS, ROBERT J.
[pen.] Robert J. Simmons; [b.] August 24, 1925, Chicago, IL; [p.] Deceased; [m.] Deceased, May 20, 1950; [ch.] Robert J, Mary C. Stephen M. Daniel J., Christopher M.; [ed.] Associate in Science with Honors.; [occ.] Retired; [memb.] Fleet reserve Assn. Int'l society of poets AARP; [hon.] Eight of eight Semesters on Deans list.; [oth. writ.] Several awaiting publication by NSP; [pers.] I write of ten about the sea having served 24 years active duty, retiring and continuing to service Navy vessels for 21 more years.; [a.] San Diego, CA

SIMMS, CARA NICOLE
[b.] August 12, 1979, Albuquerque, NM; [p.] Kenneth and Charlene Simms; [ed.] Valley High School Junior; [occ.] Student; [hon.] Valley Academy Honor and letter; [oth. writ.] Several poems for a magazine in school about life, love and relationships; [pers.] Be yourself and always write from the heart; [a.] Albuquerque, NM

SIMON, ROSENA LEE
[b.] May 29, 1955, Albany, OR; [p.] Albert and Olive Hoefer; [m.] Howard Simon, February 14, 1991; [ch.] Michele Collins, Eric and Leif Simon; [ed.] Associate of Arts in Liberal Arts, and Associate of Science in Human Resource Technology in 1977 and 1978.; [occ.] Habilitative Training Technician at Fairview Training Center; [memb.] AFSCME (American Federation of State, National Public Radio (NPR), East Salem Seventh Day Adventist Church.; [oth. writ.] At Community College poems were published in a collective student journal and booklet, in the mid-seventies, and also for another poetry contest in the eighties.; [pers.] I believe we must strive to live in harmony with the natural world. I see many metaphors between the animal kingdom and the human one.; [a.] Salem, OR

SIMONS, MARISSA A.
[b.] December 16, 1971, Detroit, MI; [p.] Thomas Lee and Christine Simons; [m.] Jonathan Omps (fiance); [ed.] Humble High Grad. '90 North Harris Community College '91 Texas School of Business Grad '92; [occ.] Registered Medical Assistant Certified Nursing Assistant; [hon.] President's list GPA 3.5 at Texas School of business the "Never say die" award in typing!; [oth. writ.] Many unpublished poems and short stories; [pers.] I try to strive for realism in my writing. Subjects and feelings that everyone has thought about a experienced. I thank God for everything especially this publication!; [a.] Stone Mountain, GA

SIMPKINS, CAROL
[pen.] Carol Simpkins; [b.] May 16, 1946, Detroit, MI; [p.] Andy and Loraine Whitaker; [ch.] Stacy simpkins Floyd, Jack Wayde Simpkins, Clifton Wayne Simpkins; [ed.] High School Bowling Green Vocational Technical School continuing Education for current occupation; [occ.] Respiratory Therapist the Medical Center Bowling Green KY; [memb.] Christian Fellowship Church KY. Board of Respiratory Care ASCAP; [hon.] Wedding poems on display at local christian bookstore - 3 songs on contract with chestnut mound recording Co.; [oth. writ.] Several poems (some personalized) Angel article submitted to guide posts prolific songwriter 3 taped albums with lyrics, melody, and vocals by Carol Simpkins; [pers.] James 1:17, every good gift and every perfect gift is from above and cometh down from the father of lights with whom is no variableness, neither shadow of turning. All thanks and all glory to Jesus, the love of my life; [a.] Bowling Green, KY

SIMPSON, MILDRED B.
[pen.] Mildred B. Simpson; [b.] December 13, 1917, Washington, DC; [p.] Carl and Laura Braunin; [m.] Leonard A. Simpson, June 12, 1962; [ch.] One daughter, 2 Stepchildren, A daughter and Son in US Navy.; [ed.] High School diploma some night school; [occ.] Retired U.S. Gov't. I worked with British Gov't. in Washington D.C. WW II; [memb.] Episcopal Church DAV, paralyzed Vets. Volunteer in Hospitals after WWII. Membership in Smithsonian Museum - Washington D.C.; [hon.] A letter for music in orchestra, High School Orchestra; [oth. writ.] Newspapers words to tunes in local shows.; [pers.] Always had a love as poetry was encouraged teachers. Was proud to have poem published about my Dads ship U.S.S. Arizona, where he was Bandmaster.; [a.] Arlington, VA

SINGER, DAVID
[b.] July 23, 1950, South Amboy, NJ; [p.] Edward and Joan Singer; [ch.] Christopher; [ed.] Rutgers University Virginia Commonwealth University; [occ.] Social Worker/Therapist; [memb.] Smithsonian; [hon.] Dean's List Martial Arts Black Belt; [oth. writ.] Other poems, one short story, newspaper articles.; [pers.] I hope to express the suffering in this world and our responsibility to alleviate it. I've been influenced by rap and Native-American poetry.; [a.] Fairfax, VA

SINGH, BALJIT
[pen.] Uncle Looks; [b.] July 7, 1942, Guyana; [p.] Sundaria, Bridgmohan Singh; [m.] Dolly Singh, 10th December 1961; [ch.] Asha, Nar Ricky and Shannie; [ed.] Non Pareil Anglican, British Gulana, S.A. 1958, Primary School dropout; [occ.] Businessman; [oth. writ.] Inspirational verses publication pending. Have on file about 300 poems.; [pers.] Life bears, the admirations and charms of a rose, gentle, tender and fragile as it petals secured, merrily wines and swings by the dependency of it's tiny but sturdy stem of course auspicious and inspiring too

SINGH, MARGRET MORINE
[pen.] Manisha Kumar; [b.] May 15, 1975, Fiji Islands; [p.] Ashok Kumar, Mayawati; [m.] Rajesh K. Singh, April 3, 1993; [ed.] Newark Memorial High, Modesto Junior College; [occ.] Certified Nursing Assistant; [memb.] International Club, Assembly of Gods Church.; [hon.] Peer Tutor; [pers.] In my writing I simply reflect what love is and how it should be.; [a.] Modesto, CA

SINGH, XENNIA GITTOES
[b.] February 8, 1948, New York, NY; [p.] Clifton Desragh Singh and Edith Gaddy; [m.] William Long, April 20, 1984; [ch.] Michael (Deceased) Derek and Nicole Tucker; [ed.] Seton Hall University, South Orange, NY; [occ.] Cable TV Producer, Writer, Poet Insurance Broker; [hon.] Dean's list, Whos who in American Colleges and Unviersity, 1976, #1 Sales in United States, Bristol-Myers Squibb 1988, Bristol-Myers, Squibb Presidents Club 1984, 1992; [oth. writ.] Gospel Music and Ministry Magazine, general manager, writer, play "It's A Riot," poetry; [pers.] Our love; [a.] Arleta, CA

SIPP, ANTHONY FRED HOOKER
[b.] April 15, 1939, Philadelphia, PA; [p.] Arthur and Frances Sipp; [m.] Nancy Yeager Sipp, March 10, 1989; [ch.] Kim, Larry, Kate, Doug, Greg, Zack, Ashlie, Keli, Genna; [ed.] Catawba College, Univ. of GA, Bread Loaf School of English, Wharton; [occ.] Journalism Teacher Cherry Hill HS East; [memb.] NEA, NJEA, Journalism Education Assoc. Association of Professional Journalists; [hon.] Kappa Tau Kappa, High School Journalism Adviser of The year (1993) from Temple Univ. Honored teacher - CHNS East, At Temple U.: Tournament Moderator; [oth. writ.] Works in progress, Si-Fi Novel Autumn Feast, Bio of F. Scott Fitzgerald Last of The Dance (with Howard Boulden), Volume of Poetry SYZYGY; [pers.] Thoreau and I believe in crushing the bone of life between our teeth and sucking out the marrow.; [a.] Cherry Hill, NJ

SISLER, HARRY H.
[b.] March 13, 1917, Ironton, OH; [p.] Minta Ann Hall and Harry Chester Sisler; [m.] (1st) Helen Elizabeth Shaver, June 29, 1940, (2nd) Hannelore Lina Wass, April 13, 1978; [ch.] Elizabeth Ann, David Franklin, Raymond Keith, Susan Carolyn; [ed.] B.Sc. Ohio State University 1936, M.Sc. University of Illinois 1937, Ph.D. University of Illinois 1939; [occ.] Retired: Distinguished Service Professor of Chemistry, Dean of the Graduate School Emeritus., Univ. of Fla.; [memb.] Phi Beta Kappa, Sigma XI, Phi Delta Kappa, American Chemical Society, Phi Kappa Phi, Phi Lambda Upsilon, United Methodist Church; [hon.] Knight of the Royal Order of the North Star (Sweden), Honorary Doctorate, University of Poznan (Poland), Southeastern Chemist Award (American Chemical Society), Southern Chemist Award (American Chemical Society), James Flack Norris Award (American Chemical Society), Centennial Achievement Award (Ohio State Univ.), Kappa Phi Kappa Award (Ohio State University, 1962 Arthur and Ruth Sloan Visiting Professor of Chemistry, Harvard Univ.; [oth. writ.] Starlight (a book of poems), Of Outer and Inner Space (a book of poems), Earth, Air, Fire, and Water (a book of poems). More than 200 articles in national and international scientific journals either authored of co-authored. Authored or co-authored a dozen books on various aspects of chemistry.; [pers.] Throughout his scientific research and teaching Dr. Sisler has been vitally concerned with the humanisic and artistic aspects of our culture, with the essential oneness of all knowledge. His poetic writings are expressions of the concern.; [a.] Jainesville, FL

SISTRUNK, JOYCE
[b.] November 8, 1942, Auburn, AL; [p.] Clyde and Mollie Golden; [m.] John Sistrunk, July 9, 1960; [ch.] Lisa Gail, Debra Joyce, Mollie Andrea; [ed.] Beauregard High; [occ.] Housewife; [oth. writ.] Several poems published in my church.; [pers.] I credit my writing to God, for letting me have the ability to do so.; [a.] Auburn, AL

SKAGGS, JENNIFER C.
[b.] August 9, 1973, Kansas; [p.] James H. Skaggs Sr. and Anna M. Skaggs; [ch.] Jacob R. Skaggs; [ed.] Bishop Ward H.S.'; [occ.] Bank Teller at Fidelity Branch of Industrial State Bank; [memb.] President of SADD, Student Council, School Choir, Drama, Pep Club, AAU Junior Olympic Basketball Team; [pers.] Life is only as hard as you make. Take life one day at a time.; [a.] Kansas City, KS

SKINNER, MARY ANN
[b.] April 27, 1966; [p.] Frank and Mary Draper; [ch.] Logan Leon, Ceaira Davoe; [occ.] Excavation subcontractor; [oth. writ.] Several poems not published; [pers.] I say my talent is a God given. Everybody has one, you just have to find yours. What appears easy for some, may not come as easily for others. But if you enjoy it, whatever it may be, don't give up. Develop it.; [a.] Lees Summit, MO

SKINNER, SHEENA
[b.] June 25, 1982, Tyler; [p.] Johnny and Jan Skinner; [ed.] 7th Grade; [occ.] School; [memb.] Sand Springs Baptist Church; [pers.] I am currently attending the Mineola Christian Academy, I will be entering the 7th Grade this year. I am the youngest of 3 children; [a.] Mineola, TX

SKOOG, CHRISTOPHER E.
[b.] March 1, 1961, Anchorage, AK; [p.] Ronald O. Skoog, Patricia A. O'Keefe; [m.] Debra C. Skoog, September 8, 1984; [ch.] Katrina, Johnathan, Robert Ronald, Therron, Kristina; [ed.] High School Diploma, Trade School - Journeyman Status in Carpentry, Masonry, Lagging and Asbestos Management; [occ.] Carpenter's Foreman; [hon.] Meritorious Service Award Central Safety Committee Alaska Pulp Corp., Certificate of Merit Asbestos Abatement Supervisor 'Voctech' Kirkland, WA.; [oth. writ.] Letters to the editor: (Sitka, Ak. and Junean, Ak. and Anchorage, Ak.) letters to congress and the white house on behalf of the Alaska timber and petroleum industries.; [pers.] Intolerance is the root of all evil. Societal ills will be resolved only when stereotypical thinking is replaced by rational thought with understanding at its nucleus.; [a.] Juneau, AK

SLADE, PAULA
[b.] Oak Park, IL; [p.] Samuel Cinman, Elsie Jeske Cinman; [m.] Barry J. Gillogly, June 24, 1984; [ch.] Samantha Alexandra; [ed.] University of Chicago, Roosevelt University, American Conservatory and Art Institute of Chicago, Niles West High School, Skokie, Illinois; [occ.] Writer; [memb.] Screen Actors Guild, American Federation of Television and Radio Artists, Actor's Equity; [hon.] Various awards for writing and art while in school.; [oth. writ.] Co-wrote with husband for radio, television and newspapers in Southern California.; [pers.] I have always found the act of writing and reading poetry to be the most loving way with words. It's the delicate tethering of heart and mind to soul that binds us all.; [a.] Martha's Vineyard Island, MA

SLADEK, ETHEL J.
[b.] June 19, 1938, Grand Rapids, MI; [p.] Stefan and Emily Kovar; [m.] Anthony Sladek, October 29, 1960; [ch.] Gary Sladek, Daryl Sladek, David Sladek, Denise and Mary Mees; [ed.] Wayland Union High School; [occ.] Secretary; [memb.] St. Alexander Catholic Church; [hon.] I had served as PTA president for two years at my children grade school and served on many committees; [pers.] Life is a gift from God - it must be lived to the fullest.; [a.] Villa Park, IL

SLAGA, JOHN
[b.] April 10, 1950, Norwich, CT; [m.] Jean Slaga, May 3, 1980; [ch.] Jeremy and Jasmine Slaga; [ed.] H.S. Norwich Free Academy, B.S. University of Southern CT., Post Grad. Munson Memorial Inst., Univ. of Connecticut; [occ.] President/owner Apature Products Inc.; [memb.] Who's Who Worldwide; [oth. writ.] Several poems; [a.] Ormond, FL

SLATER, SAMANTHA
[pen.] Samantha Slater; [b.] April 26, 1981, Nas Lemoore, CA; [p.] Dennis and Debbie Slater; [ed.] 9th Grade; [occ.] Student at Flat Rock High School; [memb.] "The Wall" (Church Organization); [hon.] "Standard School District Young Writers Fair", and "Galaxy of Young Authors"; [oth. writ.] Poems "Love," "Death" "I believe," "Dreams." Songs "Spring," "Special times," "Darkness," "Dreaming," "Day by Day," "One Person Love," "Tall, Dark, Handsome Cowboy." All poems approved for publishing no songs.; [pers.] Poems and songs are a great way to share feelings and ideas about things that otherwise would not be heard.; [a.] Flat Rock, MT

SLAUGHTER, ANDREW
[pen.] Lone Wolf; [b.] January 10, 1964; [ed.] Andrew Jackson High School; [occ.] West Lawerence Care Center Security Conway Security Officer; [memb.] El Dorado Ranch Owner, of El Dorado Ranch Estates.; [pers.] Life is full of down fall whether it be love, jobs, etc. The key is to always be strong for yourself for without that strength you are truly lost, my friend.; [a.] Hollis Queen, NY

SLAYTON, TIFFANY ANN
[b.] March 27, 1983; [p.] Robert and Susan; [oth. writ.] Yes, many, but none have been published.; [pers.] I am only 12 years old. I have one dog, two sisters, and one brother. And a special thank you to Howard Ely.; [a.] Casey, IA

SMARGISSO, DANA M.
[pen.] Maria Veronica; [b.] September 1, 1979, Philadelphia; [p.] Nicholas and Maria Smargisso; [ed.] Grade School-Green-fields Elem., Middle School-West Deptford MS, High School-West Deptford HS, plans to attend Salisbury State University in Maryland, 10th Grade; [memb.] Brownies Age 6-7, Young Life Key Club Sports - field - hockey, tennis, soccer, softball; [hon.] Student of the month 3rd, Student of the month 4th, Student of the month 6th, Presidential Award 94' WD Athletic Award for softball, field-hockey, soccer, tennis, Physical Fitness Award, "Peace" essay contest - 2nd place; [oth. writ.] What Peace means to me (poem) (came in 2nd place out of 12 school districts) - 1990; [pers.] I don't look at myself as a writer, but a person who records the precipitates of life the world leaves behind.; [a.] West Deptford, NJ

SMELTZER, SUSAN
[pen.] Susan Smeltzer; [b.] September 13, 1941, Sapulpa, OK; [p.] Mr. and Mrs. F. C. Smeltzer; [m.] Dr. Philip S. Snyder, July 14, 1973; [ed.] Tulsa Univ., Okla. City Univ., Univ. of Southern Calif., Vienna Akademie of Music; [occ.] Musician/Composer/poet/teacher; [memb.] ISP - National Guild of Piano Teachers - Tuesday Musical Club; [hon.] 12 typewritten pages of Honors in piano performance, Composition, Poetry, Painting, Teaching (fulbright grant) Poem "The Bald Eagle March" in Jimmy Carter Presidential Library NY Debut (rave reviews NY Times, European Debut "Vienna Brahms Hall"; [oth. writ.] (Poetry) books "Selected Orchestrations of poetic Expressions" "It's Funny, and Eccentric, and Halarious", "Precious Memories" (Okla. disaster) others in newspaper and magazines Incl. England; [pers.] I strive to fit the needs of mankind and cover a wide range of moods and topics; [a.] Houston, TX

SMILEY, CAMILLE
[pen.] Cami Lou; [b.] 10-28-80, Alaska; [p.] Sherry & Lawrance Camden; [ed.] Head Start, Age 2-4 Elementary, 4-11, Middle School, 11-13, High School, 13-14 (sophomore in '95 - '96); [memb.] Aid Association for Lutherans; [hon.] Various A's and Recognitions.; [oth. writ.] Various poems and short stories that evaluate my thoughts, feelings, and experiences.; [pers.] The philosophical statements I live by are: everything that goes around, comes around, and also my favorite; love hurts, but love never dies.; [a.] Chula Vista, CA

SMITH, ANITA CAROLE
[b.] October 14, Dayton, OH; [p.] Elizabeth Moore, Howard Smith; [m.] James Appling, February 14, 1983; [ch.] Kimberly Appling, Brandon Appling; [ed.] (MSW) Masters Social Worker, (LMSW) Licensed Masters Social Worker; [occ.] Human Services Provider; [memb.] College Park CME Church; [pers.] I love to write about the most beautiful feeling in the world. That feeling is love. I love God first. Love is forever.; [a.] Atlanta, GA

SMITH, BONNIE ANNE
[pen.] Bonnie A. Smith; [b.] February 14, 1947, Homer, GA; [p.] William and Elizabeth Sisk; [m.] Arthur Grady Smith, June 10, 1966; [ch.] Todd and Chris Smith; [ed.] Gainesville GA, Public Schools and Academy of Beauty College Gainesville GA; [occ.] Housewife; [oth. writ.] Modern Times printed in local newspaper; [pers.] I try to reflect my personal feelings of things that happens in my everyday life so that they may also touch someone else's life to show we're never alone.; [a.] Lula, GA

SMITH, CELESTINE H.
[pen.] Celestine, Sassy; [b.] August 31, 1938, San Francisco, CA; [p.] Frances Blake, Celestin Hourtal; [m.] Divorced; [ch.] Tami Ann, Carla Terese, James Finley, Scott Jerome; [ed.] Holy Names Academy High School, Seattle, WA; [occ.] Self Employed Care Services; [oth. writ.] First adventure into publication - have written many poems - at present, am a work in process, weaving tapestry of life a perspective; [pers.] Nourish fragmentary moments finding balance in realm of life and history. My influence has been native American Orators and Thoreau, Emerson, Dickinson, Douglas, Twain and Greek Philosophers Socrates and Plato; [a.] Wilsonville, OR

SMITH, DONNA MILES
[b.] March 14, 1952, Dayton, TN; [p.] George and Ruth Miles; [ch.] Teresa D. Brooks, Angela D. Grainger, Brian C. Smith, Collin Chase Brooks (grandson); [ed.] Dayton City School, Rhea Central High School; [occ.] Medical Secretary of Office, (EMT/IV) Alan L. Crews, M.D.; [memb.] Rhea County Rescue Squad

SMITH, ELAINE
[pers.] Poetry is something that comes from deep within. It is heartfelt emotions that are stirred in you, and consumes your whole being. It allows those around to know you briefly, yet deeply.; [a.] Jamaica, NY

SMITH, J. R. (BOB)
[pen.] J. R. Bob Smith; [b.] July 28, 1922, Birmingham, AL; [m.] Marilou, February 1946; [ch.] Douglas, Julie; [ed.] S.M.U. in Dallas, TX; [occ.] Retired from Atlantic Richfield Co. After 38 yrs.; [memb.] American Amateur Radio League, United States Golf Association, Boy Scouts of America; [oth. writ.] Book of Poetry entitled "Throught Reflections" published by quill publications; [pers.] Try to detect something good in each person you know. You will be amazed, and much happier.; [a.] Peachtree City, GA

SMITH, JACKQUELYN PICCOLA
[pen.] Piccola Smith; [b.] April 22, 1960, Augusta, GA; [p.] Clois Herndon and Mary Herndon; [m.] Leroy Smith, February 16, 1986; [ch.] Avrion Smith, Ervin Smith; [ed.] Butler High, Albany State Col. Augusta College; [occ.] Physical Education Teacher East August Middle School, Augusta, Georgia; [memb.] Delta Sigma Theta Sorority, Tabernacle Baptist Church; [hon.] Teacher of the Year 93-94, Highest Graduating Senior 1983 Albany State College, Cum Laude Graduate 81, Coach of the Year 91-92; [oth. writ.] Personal diary of poems.; [pers.] My poems reflect my need to accept myself and my place as an African American in this society in hopes that society will one day fully accept our attributes to History.; [a.] Hephzibah, GA

SMITH, JAMES E.
[b.] July 9, 1951, West Palm Beach, FL; [p.] William H. and Josephine E. Smith; [ed.] St. Lukes School for Boys (HS), Hampton University (BA), Virginia Commonwealth University (MSW), University of LaVerne (MPA) Kansas State University (PhD Student); [occ.] Outpatient Therapist Pawnee Mental Health Services, Licensed Master Social Worker, Certified Clinical Social Worker; [memb.] National Association of Social Workers, Academy of Certified Social Workers, National Council of African American Men, American Board of Medical Psychotherapists; [hon.] Who's Who Among Students in American College and Universities, Who's Who in the West, Who's Who Among Human Services Professionals, Who's Who Among Emerging Leaders in America, numerous Military Awards; [oth. writ.] "Counseling Male Sexual Abuse Survivors" The Counselor Magazine, other professional journals; [pers.] I believe that people need to have a broad vision of life and the future in order to be spiritually connected and a broad vision of love in order to love completely. All glory is fleeting, only love, true love, is eternal.; [a.] Manhattan, KS

SMITH, JOE ALLEN
[b.] September 13, 1930, Scottsburg, VA; [p.] Charlie D. and Sallie B. Smith; [ed.] Business School Diploma, Bachelor of Arts from University of Richmond, VA; [occ.] Retired from Accountant; [memb.] Champion Forest Baptist Church; [hon.] Certificate of Retirement for 36 years of Service as an accountant; [pers.] Our Highest social fulfillment is found in doing all the good we can for all the people we can in all the ways we can.; [a.] Houston, TX

SMITH, JOSHUA D.
[b.] February 23, 1974, CA; [p.] Stephen and Meilynn Smith; [pers.] Soli Deo Gloria; [a.] Santa Cruz, CA

SMITH, JOYCE DUNHAM
[b.] November 28, 1952; [ed.] Overbrook High, Temple University, Philadelphia, PA; [occ.] Paralegal; [pers.] My writing has always been inspired by personal experiences or observations that deeply affected me. My poetry is not just on expression of my emotions but, more like a release of them; [a.] Philadelphia, PA

SMITH, KRISTY D.
[b.] November 9, 1979, Albuquerque, NM; [p.] Paul and Carol Smith; [ed.] Starting 10th grade this year; [memb.] Pythian Sunshine Girls - holding office of Grand Royal Princess; [hon.] Student of the Month (95) Honor roll; [pers.] Writing poetry helps me to keep my life in hand.; [a.] Bosque Farms, NM

SMITH, LARRY L.
[b.] April 1, 1958, Baltimore, NY; [p.] Milton J. Smith Sr. and Doris M. Smith; [m.] Patricia A. Smith, November 12, 1988; [ch.] Mary-Martha, JoAnna Rachell; [ed.] Laurel Sr. High, Prince George's Community College; [occ.] Pressman; [oth. writ.] Editorials in local newspapers compilation in book form, of father's writings.; [pers.] Let God be glorified.; [a.] Strasburg, VA

SMITH, LAURIE L.
[pen.] LLS; [b.] May 4, 1960, Hobbs, NM; [p.] Howard And Rozetta Smith; [ed.] Clear Lake High School Texas Tech University; [occ.] Part of corpo-

rate America; [oth. writ.] I have written other poems, one is to be published in sparkles in the sand, and one poem in walk through paradise. All other poems I have written have not been ready by others except for a select few individuals.; [pers.] All my writings have come from my emotional feelings and experiences I have encountered due to my family, my extended family of unique friends and especially from relationships past and present. My writings are my way of dealing with life in general, as far as what I worth; [a.] Lewisville, TX

SMITH, MICHELLE K.
[b.] March 10, 1983, Allentown, PA; [p.] Lynda Haywood-Smith and William B. Smith; [ed.] 7th Grader; [occ.] Student in middle school; [a.] Ann Arbor, MI

SMITH, NANCY I.
[b.] August 25, 1959, Habana, Cuba; [p.] Mr. and Mrs. Joaquin Pinon; [m.] Michael A. Smith, May 5, 1990; [ed.] Robinson High School, Hillsborough Community College; [occ.] Executive Assistant at Vigo Importing Co., Tampa, FL; [memb.] Terrace Palms Community Church.; [hon.] National Honor Society, Spanish Honor Society, Dean's List.; [pers.] In my writing, I seek to glorify God... the giver of my talent.

SMITH, NEVA
[b.] June 25, 1911, Bloomington, IL; [p.] Rev. and Mrs. Sidney A. Guthrie (Deceased); [m.] C. Prentiss Smith, November 25, 1933; [ch.] Sidney G. Smith, M.D. (Pediatrician); [ed.] B.A. plus 26 hours graduate and in-service courses; [occ.] Retired elementary school teacher, I substituted in all grades for ten years, then taught 6th grade for 17 years. For the past 18 years I have taught an adult couples class in our church.; [memb.] The United Methodist Church, National Council for the Social Studies, Cornwall Family History Society, McLean County (IL) Genealogy Society; [hon.] Received Merit Award each year that I taught selected as Methodist Woman of the Year in our local church; [oth. writ.] I have never submitted anything for publication before. However, I have written/told some stories for children. Also I've written poetry for our Christmas greetings for many years, always on the real theme of Christmas, though different each year.; [pers.] My philosophy of life: To grow in faith, to meet each new day as a challenge, to not let a day pass without doing something for somebody, to continually gain knowledge, to attain wisdom.; [a.] Carterville, IL

SMITH, REBECCA H.
[b.] December 13, 1980, Denver, CO; [p.] Tom and Phoebe Smith; [ed.] Mukelti Elementary, Hellen Haller Elementary, Sequim Middle School, soon to be entering high school; [occ.] Volunteer poet for museum Arts newsletter (a local thing); [hon.] National geography and History Achievement Award; [oth. writ.] About 56 other poems and about twenty short stories, the longest of which is "The Dark Hour: at 65 pages; [pers.] Fun may not be the key to world power, but power is the key to eternal stress so who cares?; [a.] Sequim, WA

SMITH, SAMUEL
[pen.] The Poet; [b.] January 7, 1977, Los Angeles, CA; [p.] Abraham Lincoln Smith Sr.; [m.] Earlene Smith (Mother-Deceased); [ed.] Crenshaw High School; [occ.] Taco Bell Telecommunications Work Base Program; [memb.] African Student Union The African American Youth Arts Society of IBWA Speech and Debate Club; [hon.] Junior High Valedictorian National Junior Honor Society High School Honor Student; [pers.] Growing up in South Central L.A. has taught me the importance of keeping a positive attitude and dedicating myself to hard work. At the age of 18 I am living proof that anyone can strive and achieve.; [a.] Los Angeles, CA

SMITH, SHERRY A.
[b.] August 31, 1947, Buffalo, NY; [p.] Raymond and Frank Kenyon; [m.] David Smith, November 19, 1973; [ch.] Shawn Smith; [occ.] I'm Pending; [memb.] New Poets Society; [oth. writ.] The Awakening. Yearning, Yes, You Loved Me, My Friend, The Distinction, One Wish; [pers.] Life is not designed to be easy but the plan is simple if we choose it; [a.] Hesperia, CA

SNOW, JAMES P.
[pen.] James P. Snow; [b.] July 17, 1970, Salt Lake City, VT; [p.] James R. Snow, Patricia M. Snow; [m.] Kara H. Snow, April 6, 1996; [ch.] Eric L. Snow; [ed.] Vista High School, Mira Costa College; [occ.] Produce Clerk, Lucky Stores, Encinitas, Ca; [memb.] Lutheran Church of New Hope, Zoological Society of San Diego, Scripps Institution of Oceanography, republican National Committee; [pers.] In writing about life or death, and the feelings and emotions in between, my objective is to display the connections every human being shares.; [a.] Oceanside, CA

SNOWDEN JR., RANDALL C.
[pen.] Randall Clay II; [b.] January 4, 1980, Orlando, FL; [p.] Randall Sr., Pat Snowden; [occ.] Student - 11th Grade; [hon.] Publication in a local newspaper "The Apopka Planter", Publication in a local newspaper "The Apopka Chief"; [oth. writ.] Two unpublished collections, "the night" and "my heart, mind, and soul."; [pers.] I would like to thank God for my gift, Erin for my inspiration, and my family for their love.; [a.] Orlando, FL

SOFFLER, EDITH
[b.] April 28, 1927, New York City; [p.] Abraham and Sarah Meyerson; [m.] David Soffler, September 4, 1949; [ch.] Dr. Robert Soffler, Mrs. Rhonda Kahgan, Mrs. Lori Stillerman; [ed.] Seward High, Kingsboro College, Brooklyn College, New York City; [occ.] Retired School Secretary Board of Education, N.Y.C.; [oth. writ.] Several poems published in school newspapers, also in monthly newspaper of retirement condominium complex.; [pers.] Poetry peels back the layers of feelings derived from our complex world and reveals the poet's inner thoughts and gentle words.; [a.] Coconut Creek, FL

SOLDYN, TERESA R.
[b.] May 26, 1982, Brooklyn, NY; [p.] Edward and Miriam; [occ.] Student; [hon.] Charlotte D. Zimmerman Memorial Award, General Excellence Award, Resurrection School; [pers.] I thank the Lord for my inspiration and my family for their love and support; [a.] Brooklyn, NY

SOLIS, HERMAN
[b.] May 27, 1967, San Antonio, TX; [p.] Joe M. Solis and Mary R. Solis; [ed.] East Central High School, San Antonio College; [occ.] Director of Personnel, Unique Professional Management; [memb.] Texas State Peace Officer's Association; [pers.] Special thanks to mom and dad for being the foundation of my success!; [a.] San Antonio, TX

SOLO, RICHARD
[b.] May 18, 1936, Waterbury, CT; [p.] The late Isadore Solo and Pauline Solo; [m.] Elinor Solo; [ch.] Four sons, by first marriage; [ed.] Attended Wilby High School in Waterbury, Conn, Class of 1954; [occ.] Semi Retired Assists one of my sons in Engineering Co.; [oth. writ.] My Sea Side town, The winter Night, The Storm, The Dreamer, The Mattatuch Fife and Drum, The Fight, The Trowler; [pers.] I have wrote many poems and short stories as well as lyrics. Most of my writing deals with life experiences and reflection of an particular moment in my life.

SONOQUI, SOPHIA ANDREA
[b.] 9-24-77, Bel flower; [p.] Sally Irene Becerra, Rubin Ray Sonoqui, I am an only child; [ed.] California High School; [memb.] I belong to family fitness; [oth. writ.] I have a lot of poetry written, but it's never been published or anything like that, I kind of keep it to myself.; [pers.] I open my eyes & my mind and try to see life from a different perspective, and live my life to the fullest because one can't live forever.; [a.] Whittier, CA

SOOKDEO, NEELA
[b.] May 30, 1977, St. Thomas, VI; [p.] Lal Sookdeo, Molly Sookdeo; [ed.] Antilles School, Boston College; [occ.] Student; [memb.] Who's Who Among American High School Students, United States Achievement Academy, Community Volunteer; [hon.] Honor Roll, MKC Award, Recipient of 95-96 VI Counseling Association Scholarship, and 95-96 Rotary Scholarship; [oth. writ.] Column for School Newspaper, various poems and short stories; [pers.] Poetry brings emotions to life and paints a picture of even the deepest thoughts.; [a.] St. Thomas, VI

SORENSEN, LEIF
[b.] August 14, 1972; [p.] Nels and Pearl Sorensen; [ed.] U.C. Berkeley; [pers.] I would like to thank my friends and family and especially Ana, who inspired this and continues to inspire me daily.; [a.] Richmond, CA

SPARKS, ZACK
[b.] July 22, 1984, Owensboro, KY; [p.] Jack and Teresa Sparks; [ed.] Masonville Elementary School; [occ.] Presently in 6th grade at College View Middle School; [memb.] Buena Vista Baptist Church; [hon.] Presidential Award for Academic Fitness - All "A" Honor roll All elementary years - City swimming Champion 3 yrs. in a row - has won numerous bowling trophies; [oth. writ.] Has written several poems for school and recreation.; [a.] Owensboro, KY

SPENCE, O. CLINTON
[b.] June 6, 1924, Roswell, GA; [p.] Rev. W. D. Spence (Bessie); [m.] Carolyn; [ed.] 2 years GA. State University also Emory University; [occ.] United Methodist Minister (Retiree); [pers.] We are only going through this life one time.; [a.] Dearing, GA

SPICKERMAN, WAYNE
[b.] August 31, 1953, Catskill, NY; [m.] Virginia Spickerman, August 30, 1975; [ch.] Danielle Azure, Vanessa Erin; [ed.] Coxsackie - Athens High School, Russell Sage College, Albany - Hudson Valley Physician Assistant Program; [occ.] Physician Assistant;

[memb.] New York State Society of Physician Assistants, American Academy of Physician Assistants; [hon.] Dean's List; [oth. writ.] The Azure and Erin Tales (unpublished); [pers.] We are meant to transform the present so it preserves our children's future.; [a.] Latham, NY

SPOONER, F. E.
[pen.] Buz Spooner; [b.] February 11, 1934, Washburn, ME; [p.] Earl and Wilda Spooner; [m.] Verlie, July 17, 1954; [ch.] David, John, Steven and Daniel; [ed.] Washburn High, Univ. of Maine, Univ. of Florida, Florida Atlantic University BS, M.Ed; [occ.] Elementary School Principal; [memb.] Florida Association of School Administrators (F.A.S.A.) National Assoc. of Elementary School Principals (N.A.E.S.P.); [hon.] President - Palm Beach County Principals Assoc. President - Palm Beach County Patrol Assoc. President - Rotary Club, Runner-up - National Distinguished Principal (Elementary Division - State of Florida

ST. LOUIS, ESTHER
[b.] August 29, 1946, St. Louis, MO; [p.] Mildred Hammerstone and the late George F. Hammerstone; [m.] Robert St. Louis, September 3, 1966; [ch.] Michele Deann St. Louis-Weber and Renee Danielle St. Louis; [ed.] Riverview High School and some formal career education; [occ.] Formerly in Real Estate Sales, Farmer's wife; [memb.] Carillon Music Club, Hawk Point Community Church; [oth. writ.] I have written a few original scripts for music club performances, I was author of a local neighborhood news column, also other poetry.; [pers.] I was inspired to write this my first poem as a song (2nd vs. being the chorus) honoring the rural people of Missouri and the satisfaction of country living.; [a.] Troy, MI

ST. PIERRE, APRIL SNOW
[b.] April 10, 1982, Claremont, NH; [p.] Fred R. and Debbie E. St. Pierre; [occ.] Student; [pers.] I wrote this poem for a special someone who helped me when I needed it. I have also written many unpublished poems with the inspiration and encouragement of my family and friends. My two older sisters and my one younger brother always gave me a lot to think about. I'm just glad that I could express my opinions and creativity through my poems. They seem to make other people stop and think like I do.; [a.] North Charlestown, NH

STADTMAN, MARY A.
[b.] September 14, 1911, Nebraska; [p.] James A. and Susanna Farris; [m.] Kenneth Stadtman, May 14, 1983; [ch.] Joseph, Dennis, Judith Simon (Nee Mogis) Terance Ann Eugene Mogis; [ed.] High School - Omaha, NE Dropped out. Father considered Schooling was unnecessary for girls became self taught; [occ.] Retired - After 30 Years with Western Union Telegraph Co.; [oth. writ.] Letters to the editor in later years - controversial content. Poems for customers of Telegraph Co. IE: Birthdays, events, holidays Et Al; [pers.] Life is a challenge, full of unexpected surprises, both good and bad. Keep your sense of human and your faith in God. Nothing is impossible.; [a.] Hemet, CA

STAED, JUDITH A.
[pen.] Judith Bingley Stead; [b.] April 14, 1945, Trenton, NJ; [p.] Sherwood and Dorothy Bingley; [m.] Thomas Patrick Staed, February 17; [ch.] Lisa Staed Sprague, grandchildren - Jordan and Kaitlin; [ed.] Trenton Central High School; [occ.] Homemaker/Writer; [memb.] Hopewell United Methodist Church, Hopewell Valley Republican Club; [oth. writ.] Thirteen short Fiction stories have been published in various magazines for youth; [pers.] I believe in stopping to smell the roses along the way and encourage others to do so. There is some beauty in every day and our walk here is truly very short.; [a.] Hopewell, NJ

STAMBAUGH, DEBORAH
[b.] April 10, 1966, Amarillo, TX; [ed.] BS Environmental Science University of St. Thomas; [occ.] Health, Safety and Environmental Affairs Data Analyst, Solvay America, Inc.; [memb.] Houston World Affairs Council; [hon.] Phi Sigma Tau (International Philosophy Honor Society), Alpha Sigma Lambda, Sigma Tau Delta (International English Honor Society), Dean's List; [oth. writ.] Five published poems, songs, short stories and some books in the making; [pers.] I believe it is in everyone's best interest to seek who they really are in life and pursue their dreams in accordance with what is objectively good, regardless of their religious affiliations. Lately, my poetry seems to have a particular them: One's attempt to overcome oneself. There are so many barriers in this life: prejudice, culture, and the list goes on. True strength and true being can only be found when one is truly able to overcome this veneer and find one's meaning and purpose in life. Only them is one able to conquer one's own world and really... really live.; [a.] Houston, TX

STAMM, DOROTHY
[pen.] Dorfli; [b.] March 20, 1942, Gary, IN; [p.] Mr. and Mrs. Robert Schaus; [m.] Charles Owen Stamm, May 23, 1964; [ch.] Reverend Shawn Owen Stamm of Lutheran Church Missouri Synod; [ed.] High School Graduate Plus - 2 yrs. of College; [occ.] Homemaker; [pers.] My poems reflect my personal experiences; [a.] Granada Hills, CA

STANDFIELD, NADINE
[b.] February 3, 1931, Minneapolis, MN; [p.] Alice and Archie Austin; [ch.] Kathleen, Craig, Duane, Randy, Kevin, Donette; [ed.] South High - Institute of Childrens Literature - long ridge writers groups; [occ.] Retired; [memb.] American Legion, Int'l Society of Poets, Abiding Savior - Sunday School Teacher; [hon.] God honored me with wonderful parents and awarded me with six wonderful children.; [oth. writ.] Several poems published in anthologies - also church paper - many short stories for children; [pers.] When day is over, work is done with pen in hand, it's time for fun; [a.] Mounds View, MN

STANLEY, DAVID R.
[b.] July 29, 1961, Enid, OK; [p.] Joseph Stanley, Sonja Parks; [m.] Gaye Stanley, August 8, 1988; [ed.] Drummond Public Schools Carver Educational Ctr. Phillips University; [occ.] Habilitation Training Specialist, Enid group Homes Inc.; [memb.] Psi, Chi, Nat. Honors Society in Psychology, OPASS, OK Psych. Assc. Student Society, APASS, Am Psych. Assc. Student Society; [hon.] President Honor roll - Dean's Honor roll; [oth. writ.] Songs of the City (a collection of related poems unpublished 1995); [pers.] In my writings I attempt to bring to life both the darkest and brightest aspects of the universe. I am a spiritualist and student of all philosophies, religions and cultures.; [a.] Enid, OK

STANSBERRY, ASHLEY
[pen.] Ashley Stansberry; [b.] April 13, 1981 Gh, MI; [p.] Warren and Linda Stansberry; [occ.] Student; [oth. writ.] Several poems written never published though.; [pers.] I like to write poems about myself and my emotions and feelings. So the poem is about myself and how it feel.; [a.] Spring Lake, MI

STAPLES, MARIANNA K.
[b.] July 18, 1940, Oregon City, OR; [p.] Walter and Katherine Koch; [m.] William K. Staples, 1979; [ch.] Kecia, Trevor, Tidra (stepchidlren); [ed.] B.A. Willamette University M.A. and Ph.D. Univ. of Michigan; [occ.] Professor of French, Adrian College, Adrian, Ml; [oth. writ.] Nature and children's poems; [pers.] My poetic imagination is spurred by the beauty and mystery of nature and the pleasure of playing with words.; [a.] Adrian, MI

STARKE, BETTY
[b.] May 29, 1932, Littlefield, TX; [p.] BD and Annie Gentry; [ch.] Don and Ron Starke, Grandson Nathan Starke, (adopted grandchildren) Josh and Melanie Yarborough, Chris and Stephanie De Polis and D.J. Joos; [occ.] Decorator; [oth. writ.] Several Poems published in newspaper also several monthly publications; [pers.] All my poems are based on mine and my families and friends experiences. I have words for several songs that I need someone to put music to.; [a.] Tampa, FL

STARTUP, CHARLES A.
[pen.] Charles A. Startup; [b.] November 21, 1944, Middletown, NY; [p.] Charles and Jane; [ch.] Joshua Skyler Startup; [ed.] M.S.W.- Case-Western Reserve; [occ.] Licensed Independent Social Worker; [memb.] National Association of Social Workers, Society of Social Workers, Society of Clinical Experimental Hypnosis, American Board of Certified Managed Care Providers; [hon.] Fukiyama Travel Grant Ti Tapan, CIF Fellowship to Sweden; [pers.] I have been greatly influenced by my visit to Tagore's home in India, wordsworth's birth place at Cockermouth, England and the Cleveland Browns.; [a.] Oberlin, OH

STATHAM, GEORGE E.
[b.] July 8, 1924, Wilmington, CA; [p.] George and Anna Mae Statham; [m.] Wanda Dillon Statham, April 25, 1950; [ch.] Three-two Boys, 1 girl; [ed.] B.S. in Ed. 1967, North Texas State Univ. Graduate Work in Ed.; [occ.] Ret'd Fishery Biol. U.S. Fish and Wildlife Service; [memb.] Gamma Theta Upsilon in College; [hon.] Deans List Twice at NTSU Perf. Awds. (2) U.S. F and W.S. written Commend B.S.A.; [oth. writ.] Book of poetry to be pub. 60-90 Da. "Poetic Injustice" A Rhyme Crime, A-Book as yet unpub. on science and religion, Hope to publish this second one later; [pers.] Laugh at yourself and don't take like seriously. You must love dogs, boys and fishin "Wimmen" are truly a great gift to us.; [a.] Hiawassee, GA

STAUF, MARLENE R.
[b.] June 10, 1948, Lake City, FL; [p.] Mary Caroline Messer, Marvin Messer; [m.] Jay Stauf, February 12, 1977; [ch.] Spencer Jason Merke, Rachel Taylor Stauf; [ed.] Columbia High School Seminole Community College; [occ.] Property Manager Atlanta, GA; [oth. writ.] This is my first published writing.; [pers.] My poems are written from my own personal experiences; [a.] Atlanta, GA

STAYNER, LISA
[pen.] Asil; [b.] February 1, 1979; [p.] Linda Johnson, Rick Stayner; [ed.] Woodcrest Christian High School; [occ.] School; [hon.] M.V.P. in Volleyball; [pers.] Think with your heart, and feel with your mind.; [a.] Riverside, CA

STEARNS, RALPH H.
[b.] April 12, 1923, New York, NY; [m.] Dorothea D. Stearns, October 5, 1947; [ch.] John, Chris, and Scott; [ed.] B.S., Wharton School, Univ. of Penna., M.B.A., N.V. University; [occ.] Retired; [hon.] Ordained Presbyterian Elder Veteran, World War II U.S. Army; [oth. writ.] Co-author of books on management, finance, and history.; [pers.] One never out grow the need and comfort of poetry.; [a.] Pittsford, NY

STEELE, ALAN
[b.] October 31, 1960, Hamilton, OH; [p.] Jack and Alpha Steele; [m.] Lynn, November 16, 1985; [ch.] Bowen; [ed.] BS, Accounting from NKU; [occ.] Controller, Moore's Home Center; [hon.] Who's Who in American Executives; [oth. writ.] Short Stories, personal experience ("Grandma and hot chocolate"), poems; [pers.] The most important thing in the development of civilization is the written word, we need to keep it alive.; [a.] Fort Thomas, KY

STEELE, ORVILLE MILBOURN
[b.] March 1, 1913, New Castle, DE; [p.] Walter Wesley and Elma Milbourn Steele; [m.] Lillian Jean Ferguson Steele, October 24, 1942; [ch.] Orville M. Steele Jr., Lois Jean Steele Reynolds; [ed.] High School, College Credits in Theology courses in Public speaking.; [occ.] Retired - DuPont Company Research Center Wilm. DE; [memb.] Masonic Lodge, Royal Arch Mason 32 degree, St. John's Commandery, Bahia Temple (Shrine Club), High Twelve Club P, Pres., Grotto (Masonic), 1995 Republican National Comm. - Charter Member, Order Eastern Star 1939-1941 Past Patron; [hon.] Certified Lay Speaker Methodist church, Won 2 trophies at Toastmasters Club - Du Pont Co., Graduation Speaker at Univ. Cincinnati - 1965; [oth. writ.] Many poems, sermons and messages, wrote articles for the National Methodist Magazine.; [pers.] I have enjoyed writing poetry most of my life. I like speaking at church and pastored a church for awhile.; [a.] Tavares, FL

STEERS, DAVID A.
[b.] January 22, 1964, Hardford, CT; [p.] Frank and Sandra Steers; [m.] Maryann (Schmidt) Steers, July 25, 1992; [ch.] Samantha Ann, Kyle Alexander, and Kristopher Andrew; [ed.] East Catholic H.S. Manchester, CT; [occ.] Retail Sales; [pers.] If you think that we have arrived... think again!; [a.] Elmira Heights, NY

STEFFEK, JENNIFER
[b.] January 7, 1981, Victoria, Detar Medical Center; [p.] Albert Steffek, Carolyn Steffek; [ed.] Edna Junior High/Edna High School; [hon.] National Jr. Honor Society, Citizenship, Region Band, National Physical Fitness, U.I.L. Literary Team; [pers.] Poetry is a fabulous way to express my feelings towards a certain subject.; [a.] Edna, TX

STEGALL, CORDY
[b.] April 29, 1974, California; [p.] Calvin Stegall Jr., and Jewelene Stegall; [ed.] Graduated from Westminster High School in 1992. Currently enrolled at Orange Coast Community College in Costa Mesa, California, majoring in Theatrical Arts.; [occ.] Students and Grocery Clerk at Lucky's.; [oth. writ.] Author of "Bustin' Loose" poems of my youth, first condensed edition to be published in October 1995. (copies upon request) several poems published in local newspaper, interview article for the Orange County News.; [pers.] Through my poems I try to express my experiences in hopes of reaching and relating to others. I find that through my writings I can express my inner spirit and true self, and go beyond the everyday life into a world where my writings have no limitations.; [a.] Midway City, CA

STEGENGA, D. A. DAWN
[pen.] Dawn Stegenga or D. A. Stegenga; [b.] December 17, 1940, Michigan; [p.] Alvah and Ivah Stegenga (dec.); [m.] Jack Prince (dec.); [ch.] Jennifer Wallesz 24, Cynthia Wallesz 22; [ed.] B.A. Eastern Mich. Univ. M.A. Univ. of Michigan cont. ed. PA State Univ.; [occ.] Retired (teacher 16 yrs) self-employed Artist; [memb.] AARP, AAUW, Luth. Ch. but I'm Reform, Grey Nun Assoc. Phila. Chapters, Phila. Museum of Art; [hon.] Trueblood Scholarship Graduate School, State Scholarship undergraduate school, poems published in Anthologies source College; [oth. writ.] Advertisements, essays, short stories published in magazines (there have been many Dutch artists); [pers.] I was raised to honor my heritage in 2 arts: Poetry and painting which is what I am doing and to select and to motivate the next poet which is what I'm doing. (My father poured creativity into my veins); [a.] Upper Darby, PA

STEPHEN, VIRGINIA
[pen.] Jean Stephen; [b.] January 16, 1941, Connersville, IN; [p.] Joe D. and Frieda Redmon; [m.] James R. Stephen, December 20, 1957; [ch.] J. R. II, Joseph Edward, Lee Allen; [ed.] Greensburg IN, High School - currently taking course from Institute of Children's Literature; [occ.] Housewife (mother - grandmother); [memb.] C.I. Family worship Center; [hon.] Volunteer of the Year Award for Nursing facility, Volunteers - Possibility Poem published in Library of Congress - A Delicate Balance; [oth. writ.] I write a bi-monthly short story for a local magazine, The Rural Shopper; [pers.] I strive to reflect a Christian principle in each item I write, God's goodness to be exalted at all times.; [a.] Osgood, IN

STEPHENS, BARBARA
[pen.] Bgs; [b.] March 4, 1943, Aberdeen, MS; [p.] Loye and Bobbie Gullick; [m.] Richard Stephens, December 26, 1965; [ch.] Stacey, Richy; [ed.] Headland High, University of Georgia; [occ.] Homemaker and Musician; [memb.] Vinings Bible Study, "The Well", United Methodist Church, Antique and Classic Boat Society, Delta Delta Delta, Moody Fellowship; [hon.] UGA Valedictorian, Phi Beta Kappa, Phi Kappa Phi, Zodiac; [oth. writ.] Numerous, unpublished songs based on Christian scriptures ("lyrical narratives"); [pers.] Philippians 3:8-10; [a.] Atlanta, GA

STEVENS, MILDRED ANN COTTON
[pen.] Lois-Ann Rosenvelt; [b.] February 22, 1959, Sumter, SC; [p.] Ollie Mae Cotton, Rosavelt Bradley (Deceased); [ch.] Don Trell 20, Angiea LaToya 17; [ed.] Sumter High, Carolina Technical College, and University of Los Angeles at Clark AFB Philippines, currently will be attending Carolina Tech. again this winter.; [occ.] Switchboard Operator, Shaw AFB Sumter, SC (10 years.); [oth. writ.] Also have knack for writing short stories involving characters met through my job, which gives public relations a whole new era. People always have a story to tell, especially military people.; [pers.] I love astrology, and being a Pisces, my great challenge is to live to my great compassion and sensitivity. My creative talent has taken me to new heights of discovery. I've fallen in love with mythology, and paintings and poems from the Renaissance period. I do believe I was "born too late."; [a.] Sumter, SC

STEWARD, JOSEPH MARTIN
[pen.] Joseph M. Steward; [b.] May 30, 1947, Asheville, NC; [p.] Florence and John L. Smith (adoptive); [m.] Single; [ed.] Asheville Catholic High School U.S. Army Clinical Specialist School Allegheny College, Consolata College; [occ.] Nurse, Nurse Manager (DPH) San Francisco County Jail.; [memb.] American Heart Association Northern California Correctional Nurses Association. Holy Name Society.; [hon.] Letter of Commendation from the U.S. Military Ordinate for services rendered as organist for Catholic services.; [pers.] Poetry captures events in time. I would further classify. It as a literary snapshot that captivates, stimulates, and invigorates mankind's emotions.; [a.] San Francisco, CA

STEWART, CLARA OSCIE-OLA
[b.] August 22, 1947, Ford City, PA; [p.] Wilmer L. Stewart, Barbara A. Stewart; [ed.] Ford City High School; [pers.] I wrote this poem after my grandmother died. It was my way of venting the pain of losing her.; [a.] Ford City, PA

STEWART, LINDA
[pen.] Linda Dianne Pellerin; [b.] October 21, 1951, Houston; [p.] Willie and Lorine Pellerin; [m.] Herbert Lee Stewart, May 31, 1973; [ch.] Kevin B. Stewart, Herbert F. King, Brian W. Stewart; [ed.] Kashmere Senior High, the Bruman School for Dental Assisting; [occ.] Dental Office Insurance Clerk/Receptionist/Assistant; [memb.] Fellowship Baptist Church; [hon.] Graduated High School with group having 2nd highest of honors. Graduated 1st in my Dental assisting class.; [oth. writ.] None published. Several written for children and family members or church functions.; [pers.] Nothing stays the same in life but he unconditional love, grace, and mercy of God. Learning this early in life could possibly save us from a lot of daily emotional pain.; [a.] Houston, TX

STEWART, MICHAEL D.
[pen.] Mike Stewart; [b.] June 6, 1979, Boston, MA; [p.] Barry R. Stewart, Rebecca L. Stewart; [ed.] Stoughton High School, The Arlington School; [occ.] Student; [hon.] Great Woods Institute for the Arts Award, July 15, 1989; [a.] Stoughton, MA

STIFFEL, LISA
[ed.] BA from Sarah Lawrence College Bronxville, New York '91; [occ.] General Office Clerk in a Law Firm; [oth. writ.] One poem recently published. Polaris press; [pers.] My continued focus on the beauty of nature allows me to escape from daily pressures and frustrations and release emotional energies.; [a.] Chicago, IL

STOCKMAN, KATHY
[pen.] "Giggles"; [b.] January 18, 1979, Pennsylvania, PA; [p.] Judy and Terry Stockman; [ed.] Warren Local High School - School Colors are blue and white; [occ.] Taco Bell and want to be come either a poet or chiropractor; [memb.] Girl Scouts for 10 years; [oth. writ.] I have a bunch of other poems at home that are very, very good.; [pers.] I love writing poetry because it makes me feel free.; [a.] Belpre, OH

STOCKTON, HAROLD WAYNE
[b.] September 15, 1934, Blackwell, OK; [m.] Mary Jane Stockton; [ch.] 3 Stephen W., Linda R., Barbara J.; [ed.] High School; [occ.] Postal Service; [memb.] 1st Baptist Church Medford - Okla.; [oth. writ.] I have many poem's writing in the last 20 yrs. Most of my poetry is longer. In story form.; [pers.] I strive to reflect a spiritual message in my poetry, interlocked with nature, and every day happenings in the world around us.; [a.] Medford, OK

STODDARD, JAMES A.
[pen.] Jim, Jimmy; [b.] January 28, 1922, Nyack, NY; [p.] Jason and Alice Stoddard; [m.] Margaret Jane Stoddard, August 26, 1947; [ch.] Alice M. Stoddard PA-C David A. Stoddard, Eng.; [ed.] H.S., BA-College, 1 yr. toward for Normandy Beach WWII MA, US Army Training, Spanish Lang., Institute-Costa Rica, Boy Scouts of A. training, 12 years Scoutmaster.; [occ.] Active retirement from missionary work in Guatemala, CA, Supt. Building and Grounds, Huehue Academy one activity of many, 38 years.; [memb.] The American Legion, Poetry Club, BMV, Bradenton, FL., BMV Orchestra, BMV Drama Club; [hon.] Various US Army Medals, WW II, 50th year-Normandy Campaign Medal, The Gold Jubilee of Operation Over Lord Medal, USA 50th Anniversary of World War Medal; [oth. writ.] Many poems since 1943 poet about our flag just before landing on Normandy beach.; [pers.] I love Poetry. I love to write it, I have many books of poetry.; [a.] Bradenton, FL

STOREY, MATT
[ed.] Rochester Institute of Technology; [occ.] Electrical Engineer; [pers.] Short poems are like word puzzles, with many solutions, usually one being the best. This poem was written prior to recent media interest in Angels while courting my wife, Ruthie; [a.] Titusville, FL

STOREY, MAUDE B.
[b.] January 19, 1934, Waynesboro, GA; [p.] Bartow M. and Cassie Blount; [m.] Adrian C. Storey Jr., January 19, 1952; [ch.] Debra, Trina, Michael, and Michelle; [occ.] Previous Doctors and Merchants Credit Bureau for 32 yrs.; [oth. writ.] Various type poems never submitted for possible publication; [pers.] Although I have always loved to write, my main interest is writing country style song poems.; [a.] Augusta, GA

STORMS, DONNA
[b.] October 9, 1959, London, KY; [p.] Milford Allen, Louella Allen; [m.] Gary Storms, August 31, 1975; [ch.] Christopher Lee, Matthew Aaron, Timothy James; [sib.] Laurel County High; [occ.] Secretary - Ross Realty, Westland, MI; [memb.] Democratic Club, Wareing PTO, Security Baptist Church; [pers.] I would like to dedicate this poem to my Mother who has provided everlasting inspiration which guides me through all my days. Thank you Mom, I love you!; [a.] Taylor, MI

STRAIT, MICAH N.
[b.] October 23, 1978, Ogden, UT; [p.] Clifton E. and Karen Lund Strait; [ed.] Currently a Junior at Olympus High School Salt Lake City, Utah; [occ.] Student and Furniture Mover; [a.] Salt Lake City, UT

STRAND, MARSHA
[b.] November 19, 1951, Nampa, ID; [p.] Earl and Norma Sumner; [m.] Duane A. Strand, November 6, 1976; [ch.] Randy D. Stand; [ed.] West Valley High, Yakima, WA; [occ.] Savings Counselor, First Savings Bank, Dayton, WA; [memb.] Chamber of Commerce, Methodist Church; [oth. writ.] Just to family members; [pers.] I try to reflect my feelings in my writings and to show love to all. To continue to explore feelings and put them in writing.; [a.] Dayton, Washington

STRANGE, MS. TINA
[b.] December 7, 1952, Oskaloosa, IA; [p.] Margaret and Robert Dowling; [ch.] Jennifer Nelson, Courtney Meyer; [ed.] 1971 Graduate of Central Lee High School 1 1/2 years at Southeastern Community College; [occ.] Clerical/Secretarial at Blue Bird Midwest; [memb.] Order of Eastern Star PEO; [a.] Donnellson, IA

STRENTH, MATTHEW CLARK
[b.] November 6, 1984, Avon Park, FL; [p.] Janet and Bruce Strenth; [ed.] 5th Grade at Park Elem. Avon Park, FL.; [occ.] Student; [memb.] AWANA Club International Park Elem. Chorus Bethany Baptist Church; [hon.] Received Florida Governors Environment and Energy Award, Patriotism Awards from Veterans' Organizations; [oth. writ.] Third place winner of FL. Tropicana Speech Contest; [pers.] 1st place winner for 3rd Grade in Highlands Student Anthology; [a.] Avon Park, FL

STROBLE, AZZIE LEE
[b.] September 25, 1945, Barnwell, SC; [p.] Lueticher W. Ryans, Father (Deceased); [m.] Paul E. Stroble, September 5, 1965; [ch.] Paul A. Stroble and Konsuela Stroble Caldwell; [ed.] Associates in Arts, Bachelors of Psychology and Master's in Human Resources Management Degrees; [occ.] Director, Child Development Center (Nationally Accredited); [memb.] First Baptist Church of Hampton VA., Christian Fellowship Choir, Explorer Advisor Board, Subscriptions to Psychology Today, Ebony and my Development Center is Nationally Accredited with NAEYC. Member of Troy State University Alumni; [hon.] Generals, Colonels endorsements, noted by employers for Outstanding performances noted for Volunteer experience in CPR and First Aid as an Instructor; [oth. writ.] Poem published in best news poets of 1989 by Robert Nelson several poems, songs composed to music but not published; [pers.] My poetry conveys meaning that I am person centered and write to reach all audiences, through feeling and familiarity. I enjoy reading all types of poetry by various authors.; [a.] Hampton, VA

STRONG, CATHY M.
[pen.] Catherine Gail; [b.] January 5, 1957, Fort Worth, TX; [p.] Marty and Bonnie Martinez; [m.] Michael P. Strong, December 1, 1978; [ch.] Hollie Leigh Ann, Bridgit Nicole; [ed.] Scarborough High Tarrant County Jr. College; [occ.] Registered Nurse; [memb.] Church of God of Prophecy Texas Nurse's Association; [hon.] Phi Theta Kappa Dean's List; [oth. writ.] Many poems for family and friends.; [pers.] My writings are a mirror of everyone that has touched my soul.; [a.] TX

STUP, JOSEPH JERRY
[pen.] J. Jerry Stup; [b.] January 11, 1948, Frederick, MD; [p.] Paul E. Stup, Mary Helen Lowery; [m.] Susan C. Stup, June 14, 1975; [ed.] Approx. 3 years College, also have studied violin, piano, and composition under Harry L. Oakes III; [occ.] I sell stringed instruments, (self-employed); [memb.] Maryland Real Estate Broker's License; [oth. writ.] None published, but I have written many poems, songs, and stories over the years. I recently submitted a poem to country magazine for consideration.; [pers.] "Mr. Hank" was inspired by true life experiences, from the people who lived on the Potomac River near Point of Rocks, Maryland. Their livelihoods and philosophies are expressed in the song.; [a.] Frederick, MD

STURGES, CAROLINE
[b.] August 1, 1981, Evanston, IL; [p.] Elisabeth Sturges, Robert Sturges; [ed.] Mt. Lebanon Junior High School; [occ.] Student; [pers.] I believe that you must be at peace with yourself before you can be at peace with the rest of the world. This is very important to me.; [a.] Pittsburgh, PA

STUVE, MARY
[pen.] Mary Manzer; [b.] August 20, 1928, Hudson, WI; [p.] Ernest and Bess Samuelson; [m.] Kermitt K. Stuve, December 27, 1950; [ch.] Nancy, Mark, Jeffrey; [ed.] BA English State Teachers College, Wayne, NE, M - Sp. Ed UNM - Albuquerque, NM; [occ.] Retired Taught School - 22 years; [pers.] If you fail to plan, you are planning to fail.; [a.] Albuquerque, NM

SUSCO, RHONDA KAY
[b.] November 23, 1963, Hamilton, OH; [p.] Verlyn and Onalee Perry; [m.] Mark Steven Susco, May 25, 1985; [ch.] Lacey 13, David 10; [ed.] New Miami High School; [occ.] Self-employed; [memb.] Trenton First Church of God, Church Youth Leader Choir; [oth. writ.] Newspaper contest as a teenager; [pers.] To me, poetry has always been my way of expression, a private form of letting out a wide range of emotion, be it spiritual or just personnel reflection. Its nice to be able to share it.; [a.] Middletown, OH

SWAIN, SUE
[b.] December 3, 1962, Moltrie, GA; [p.] Raymond David, Linda Davis; [m.] Paul Swain, October 3, 1991; [ch.] Christina Marie, Gini Marie, William David; [ed.] Lowndes High, Valdosta Tech.; [occ.] Housewife; [oth. writ.] I have written many poems and songs. Forever free is the only poem I have sent in for publication.; [pers.] God is my guide through everything I write. Each poem or song speaks about Gods awesome love.; [a.] Valdosta, GA

SWAN, EDNA
[b.] March 30, 1911, East Peru, ME; [p.] Lucius V. Robinson-Oldham Gertrude; [m.] Winfred D. Swan, July 4, 1936; [ch.] William Herbert-Linda Marie-Carla Lorraine; [ed.] 8th Grade only I was crippled at age two could not walk to High School no transportation then; [occ.] I'm in a Nursing home now; [oth. writ.] My first and only poem.; [pers.] My husband

passed away August 17, 1989 Linda Marie November 22, 1945, Carla Lorraine February 17 1990, I have five grandsons two great grand children; [a.] Dixfield, ME

SWANSON, HEATHER L.
[b.] December 17, 1968, Warren, PA; [p.] Thomas Swanson and Rebecca Donato; [ed.] High School Graduate; [occ.] Self Employed; [oth. writ.] I have many other writings all of which are unpublished at this time. I have only submitted 20 lines of the road that I must follow it is a much longer poem.; [pers.] I try to reflect what I myself going through or feeling at the time and I also try to relate to others and hope that they might be in inspired and lifted up my writing also reflect my faith in God.; [a.] Russell, PA

SWARTZ, DALE
[b.] December 24, 1986, Richmond, VA; [p.] W. Bruce and Margaret W. Swartz; [ed.] The Collegiate School (3rd Grade at time of publication); [oth. writ.] Dale enjoys writing stories and poems at school and for his own pleasure. He wrote "An Eagle's View" when he was in the second grade.; [pers.] Dale plays the violin. He likes to read, swim, build things and play with his younger brothers Ben and Tim.; [a.] Richmond, VA

SWEENEY, FRANCIS J. "FRANK"
[pen.] Frank Sweeney; [b.] June 30, 1937, Berlin, NH; [p.] Francis J. and Evelyn J. Sweeney Sr.; [m.] Joy J. Sweeney, September 2, 1978; [ch.] Five (3 mine, 2 hers), Vicki, Francine, Cynthia, Robert and Laurie; [ed.] Assoc. in Arts Degree Hillsborough Community College Plant City, FL; [occ.] Realtor; [hon.] Phi Theta Kappa; [oth. writ.] Other poetry and articles published in high school and college periodicals and local newspaper.; [pers.] Although my philosophy of life is quite complex, I try to create poetry that is simple to read and understand.; [a.] Plant City, FL

SY, CHERRY LOU C.
[b.] January 18, 1981, Philippines; [p.] Manuel and Merlita Sy; [ed.] Our Lady of Mt. Carmel Montessori (Philippines), Lafayette High School (Brooklyn); [occ.] Student; [oth. writ.] Unpublished poetry, finished and unfinished short stories.; [pers.] The universe lies unbound when love and life abounds.; [a.] Brooklyn, NY

SYMONS, WILLIAM B.
[b.] February 23, 1974, MI; [p.] William C. and Flora M. Symons; [ed.] High School (Hart); [occ.] United States Navy; [pers.] My inspirations in life are my family and friends. God bless them all.; [a.] Hart, MI

SZEWCZYK, TODD
[pen.] Gale Lane; [b.] June 9, 1976, Johnstown, PA; [p.] Tony Szewczyk and Kristin Webb; [ed.] Graduate Of North Star High; [occ.] Student at Delaware Valley College; [hon.] Published in the Anthology of Poetry by Young Americans and the National Poetry Society; [oth. writ.] "A Look Outside" and "The Trial"; [a.] West Chester, PA

SZWARC, BELINDA
[b.] August 28, 1953, Illinois; [p.] Billie and Barbara Craig; [m.] Frank Szwarc; [ch.] Wesley, Kelly, Jenna; [occ.] Optical Sales; [oth. writ.] Poems, short stories unpublished; [pers.] My inspiration comes from the beauty God has created. "Whatsoever ye do in word or deed, do in the name of the Lord Jesus, giving thanks to God the Father by him". -Colossians 3:17; [a.] Florissant, MO

TABOR, VIOLA JANE
[b.] May 5, 1946, Kinston, NC; [p.] Eunice Summerlin, Silas Summerlin; [m.] Larry E. Tabor, February 29, 1972; [ch.] Cynthia, Sara, Donna; [ed.] Grainger (Kinston) High, American School, Lenoir Community College; [occ.] Self-Employed; [hon.] Volunteer of the Year Award, Elementary Schools, Polk County, FL; [oth. writ.] Book - Legend of Black Creek; [pers.] I strive to produce quality wholesome reading for young children and young adults.; [a.] Deland, FL

TALBERT, KIM M.
[b.] June 2, 1968, Philadelphia, PA; [p.] Claude and Janie Anderson; [m.] Brian A. Talbert, April 25, 1992; [ch.] Shawn E. Talbert; [ed.] University of Pgh., Bartram High School; [occ.] Milieu Therapist; [memb.] America Speech and Hearing Association (ASHA); [oth. writ.] Several poems and songs; [a.] Pittsburgh, PA

TALLENT, LISA RENEE
[b.] August 20, 1979, Hamilton, CO; [p.] Rick Tallent, Rhonda Tallent; [ed.] Soddy-Daisy High School; [oth. writ.] Several poems, yet to be published; [pers.] I write to express my feelings. I am influenced by the extra special men in my life.

TALLMAN, EVELYN T.
[b.] November 13, 1922, South Westerlo, NY; [p.] Mrs. Hazel F. Mabie; [m.] Deceased, January 23, 1940; [ch.] One; [ed.] Greenville Central High School, National Bakers School, 835 Diversey Parkway Chicago, IL; [occ.] Retired and write; [memb.] Albany County Social Service Social Security Benefits; [oth. writ.] World of Poetry

TANKSLEY, GAIL
[b.] May 29, 1949, Athens, GA; [p.] Helen Parker and Waymon Tanskley; [m.] Divorced; [ch.] Kimberly Gail and Kenneth Gary; [ed.] Joseph M. Hodgson Academy, Clarke County Junior High, Athens High School, University of Georgia; [occ.] Administrative Coordinator University of Georgia; [memb.] Professional Secretaries, International Office School and Community Clubs and Committees Hull Baptist Church; [hon.] Several Monetary Awards for Local Literary Contests, various Certificates, Pins, Honors, and Acknowledgements for Local Community, School, or Office Accomplishments; [oth. writ.] Various Office News Letter, Articles and Poems; [pers.] I am an aspiring Author, striving to be creative and versatile in my writings, hoping to spark some entertaining interests as well as educational benefits to my readers!; [a.] Athens, GA

TAYLOR, CARLENE
[pen.] Carlene Taylor; [b.] Mississippi; [p.] Thelma and Oscar King; [m.] Nevelle Cascoe; [ch.] Ida, Rickey, Gentra, Tommy, Calvin, Marcus, and Jay Taylor; [ed.] Va Shun High; [occ.] Housewife; [oth. writ.] Personal note, grandparent's raising, grand kids, newsletter; [pers.] I am very happy to be able to write a poem of, some of the things, that's happening, in the World around us in the 90's.; [a.] Avon Park, FL

TAYLOR, DOUGLAS JR.
[pen.] Douglas Taylor Jr.; [b.] June 5, 1970, Atlanta, GA; [ed.] Monroe Area Comprehensive High, De Kulb College; [occ.] Media Consultant and Disc Jockey; [pers.] I am greatly influenced by the world around me. People, music and places. Poetry is meant to be read and enjoyed by all and not dissected. Special thanks to Jim Morrison.; [a.] Monroe, GA

TAYLOR, JASON L.
[pen.] J.T.; [b.] October 2, 1985, Richmond, VA; [p.] James and Gertrude Taylor; [ed.] 5th grade; [memb.] Antioch Christian Center, Petersburg, VA; [hon.] Honor Roll, National Physical Education, Young Writers Award; [pers.] I want to be a businessman.; [a.] Ettrick, VA

TAYLOR, JESSIE
[pen.] Jessie Taylor; [b.] July 4, 1917, Wisconsin, CO; [p.] John and Jannie Read; [m.] Clyde T. Taylor (Deceased), April 24, 1971; [ch.] Anita Goddberg and Bobbie Jean Chappell; [ed.] High School several business courses LUTC Graduate; [occ.] Retired; [memb.] Lifetime member of Internal Society of Poets, Tarrant County Poetry Society, OES; [hon.] Nation Quality Award, Several International Merit Awards EIA Golden Poet 1995; [oth. writ.] Several Poems Published; [pers.] Born and raised on a farm many years worked as a waitress. Later, was in Insurance Business 15 years. Love my family, nature sewing - etc.; [a.] Aledo, TX

TAYLOR, SANDY
[pen.] Alexandra; [b.] January 8, 1943, Iowa; [p.] Merle and Rosemond Brandon; [m.] Ronald Taylor, June 14, 1992; [ch.] William Thompson, Lindsay Thompson and Tyler Thompson; [ed.] Bachelor of Arts Degree in Psychology of Learning; [occ.] Teacher; [pers.] The poem, "Oh, Daughter Of Mine" was inspired by my daughter, Pamela Lynn, born August 8, 1966. I hope someday to be her friend.; [a.] Wallace, CA

TEABOUT, LINDA
[b.] May 8, 1948, Gloversville, NY; [m.] Martin Teabout (Deceased); [ch.] Delbert-Douglas, Deborah-Kandy and 7 stepchildren; [ed.] Graduated Broadalbin, Central High School, Class of 1966; [occ.] Health Aid and Housewife; [pers.] I love writing poems and Science Fiction. I have written over 200 poems for my own enjoyment.

TEMPLETT, JOSEPH
[pen.] Poet Templett; [m.] Hattie; [ed.] 12 Grade, Conservatory of Music; [occ.] Retired; [memb.] Theatre Organ Club, Home Organ Club, Opera Club, Dixieland Music Club, Golf Tournament Club; [hon.] For a Hole in one in Golf; [pers.] After reading the Poem Contest of the Nat'l. Library of Poetry. I went to the Library and read E. Allan Poe. Because in high school he was my favorite. This inspired me and now I write a poem every other night.; [a.] San Lorenzo, CA

THIBODAUX, KATHERINE M.
[b.] November 14, 1941, New Iberia, LA; [p.] Carmen and Bo Bonini; [m.] L. P. "Bud" Thibodaux, June 6, 1964; [ed.] High school and 2 years of College; [occ.] Legal Secretary; [memb.] Former member of Lafayette Scrabble Club of Lafayette Paris Legal Secretaries; [oth. writ.] I write personal wed-

ding poems for friends and relatives and have them framed as wedding gifts; [pers.] I always wanted to write for a greeting card company. Since that never came to pass, I now write my own cards sent to relatives and friends for birthdays, weddings, graduations, get well, etc.; [a.] Lafayette, LA

THOMAS, ANGIE CARMEN
[b.] September 12, 1961, Montgomery, PA; [p.] Else and Frank Simmons; [m.] Bobby Joe Thomas Jr., May 16, 1987; [ed.] Kecoughtan High, St. Leo College; [occ.] Management Assistant; [hon.] The greatest honor is "Touch of Sand" being published... a poem inspired by Joan Gallimore; [pers.] Relieving the mind of thoughts, the heart of feelings, and the soul of dreams...is the essence of my writing.; [a.] Hampton, VA

THOMAS, ARLA
[pen.] Arla; [b.] April 7, 1949, Kokomo, IN; [m.] Deceased, November 22, 1986; [ed.] Life; [occ.] Self employed, Landscape Co.; [memb.] Phoenix zoo; [oth. writ.] Arla - Cards; [pers.] If this was the last five minutes of your life, is this how you want to spend it.; [a.] Surprise, AZ

THOMAS, CAROLYN
[pen.] Carolyn Thomas; [b.] September 29, 1935, Fulton, KS; [p.] Mary and Hillman Collier; [m.] A. R. Thomas, June 6, 1954; [ch.] Gordon Adam Thomas, John (Bing) Abbington Thomas, Joseph Andrew Thomas; [ed.] Graduated from High School in 1954, went to College at UT Mat Martin, TN and Lambuth College at Jachoo, TN; [occ.] Housewife and grandmother of five; [hon.] Alpha Beta Gama in College. Was a Golden Poet several poems of honorarily mention. I had a 3.01 in High School.; [pers.] I write poems that have something to say about myself and about her friend and animals.; [a.] West Valley City, KS

THOMAS, CASSANDRA A. SMITH
[b.] April 3, 1945, Winston-Salem, NC; [p.] Willie and Alease Smith; [ch.] Daughter-Brandy Alease Thomas; [ed.] St. Anne's Academy, Winston-Salem State University; [occ.] Registered Nurse - Winston-Salem State Univ. W-S, N.C.; [oth. writ.] "Cadeusus" - Health Services Newsletter; [pers.] My desire for nursing, as well as my love of poetry, came from the gentle souls of my mother and grand mother.; [a.] Winston-Salem, NC

THOMAS, WENDY
[b.] December 22, 1980, Oneonta, NY; [p.] Barbara Thomas, Thomas Thomas; [ed.] Delaware Academy, will graduate in the year 1999; [oth. writ.] My poem "Time" printed in a local newspaper. Two other poems which will be printed in poetry books. Short stories and books I did not have published along with more poems and plays.; [pers.] With all craziness in the world, people want inner harmony and peace. I get that through poetry.; [a.] East Meredith, NY

THOMEN, FLORENCE VINING
[pen.] Florence Vining Thomen; [b.] July 20, 1913, Colebrook, CT; [p.] Henry and Wally Vining; [m.] Alfred H. Thomen (Deceased), July 7, 1956; [ch.] Richard Vining Crump, Roger Wakefield Crump, William Henry Crump; [ed.] The Gilbert School, attended Teachers College of Connecticut also little College of Liberal Arts; [occ.] Retired. Former Amway Distributor.; [memb.] Promised Land Baptist Church and Committee's there; [hon.] Honorable mention by Edwin Markham Poetry Contest (1930's). Reading at County-Wide Meeting of Poets.; [oth. writ.] Poems and articles published locally, and in Church newsletters; [pers.] Wrote romantic and fantasy poems - 1930s. Today, mostly with a religious ending. I prefer conventional rhyming verse.; [a.] East Canaan, CT

THOMPSON, CASEY
[b.] June 30, 1979, Union County Hospital; [p.] Eddie and Dee; [ed.] Currently a Junior in the Hickory Flat High School; [oth. writ.] Several poems dealings with other topics; [pers.] I strive to help others reveal their emotions to themselves. I feel it is better to read poetry than any other literature. Poetry helps to see that vibrant characteristics of fantasy world's are just as common in our world.; [a.] Hickory Flat, MS

THOMPSON, JEFFREY C.
[b.] February 24, 1957, San Diego; [p.] Charles and Claire Thompson; [m.] Janna Thompson, March 5, 1994; [ch.] Joshua (boy-5 yrs. old), Jackie and Jessie (5 months twin girls); [ed.] Graduated Crawford High, Grossmont College and Marketing Institute, Helsinki, Finland; [occ.] CD-Broker, First National Bank, San Diego; [memb.] Skyline Church, Home Group Committee. Various Foreign Exchange Student Programs. Demolay.; [hon.] Foreign-Exchange Teacher of the Year (in Commercial English) - Helsinki Businessmen's College - Helsinki, Finland. Graduated with honors Crawford High School; [oth. writ.] Wrote and performed English Radio Spots on Finnish Radio. Designed and Marketed Language Materials for Finnish Colleges. Have drawn and scripted over 300 cards for friends and colleagues.; [pers.] I attempt to show man and his/her intricate connection with God and nature. My years of Foreign experience and love of nature have molded many of my thoughts.; [a.] Lakeside, CA

THOMPSON, MARCELLA KAY
[b.] March 6, 1963, California; [ch.] Kimberly, Markeiba, Jack, Johnny, Timothy; [ed.] Finished 11th Grade went to Adult School this year received certificate; [occ.] Housewife, Volunteer at Schools; [hon.] Management Certificate, Very important Person Certificates, Music; [oth. writ.] Write music lyrics writing a book now on my life, Autobiography or myself. Teachers Assistance for 2 1/2 years Recreational Aide also.; [pers.] Just managing my home and my five children, whom I love their father (absent) I do my best with them their my heart, I live in a housing project I'm just making it. Children are first!; [a.] Long Beach, CA

THRASH, RUTH P. STREETMAN
[b.] February 4, 1939, Augusta, GA; [p.] Leroy and Ruth Streetman; [m.] Joseph Thrash Jr., May 28, 1966; [ch.] Joi L. Thrash, Sonja Thrash Edmonds, M.D. and Brian L. Thrash; [ed.] B.S. - Paine College in Augusta, GA., M.S. - University of Iowa in Iowa City, IA; [occ.] Biology Professor Emeritus - Mott CMTY College; [memb.] Community Presbyterian CH, HAPS, NY Academy of Science; [hon.] NSOD Award for Excellence in Teaching, outstanding Teacher of Year MCC, Who's Who Among America's Teachers, 1994; [oth. writ.] Several unpublished poems and essays; [pers.] My writings reflect my own personal experiences.; [a.] Flint, MI

TIENG, JAMES FRANCIS
[b.] August 15, 1982, Ridgewood, NJ; [p.] Joseph V. Tieng, Fortunata T. Tieng; [ed.] St. Anne School, 8th Grade, Fair Lawn, New Jersey; [memb.] Unlimited Martials Arts Institute (Black Belt), Student Council (Treasurer) Fair Lawn Bantam Bowling 1992-1994, Yearbook Staff (Editor-in-Chief), Safety Patrol (Captain), United States Taek Won Do Union, Inc. (Competitor), School newspaper (reporter); [hon.] Outstanding Citation (1992-1995), Academic Excellence and Perfect Attendance (1995), Student of the Month (1992-1993), 1st Place Team Sec. B Fair Lawn Rec., 1st Place in 1st Annual St. Anne School/NJPS Poetry Contest, Silver Medal in 1st PA, Taek Won Do Governor's Cup, and more; [oth. writ.] "The Monkey and the Banana Tree" (Poem) Published in Filipino Reporter and Philippine News, "Our Earth" (Poem) published in Anthology of Poetry by Young Amcricans, 2nd Place Columbus Day essay, "Freedom: Only a Dream" pub. in Best Poems of 1996, and other writings; [pers.] Life is barren without hopes and dreams. Anyone can succeed when you reach for the sky.; [a.] Fair Lawn, NJ

TIERI, MICHAEL J.
[b.] January 26, 1958, Chicago Heights, IL; [ch.] Angela (8) and Frank (5); [occ.] Sales; [oth. writ.] "The Power In You" "To My Daughter"; [pers.] I enjoy writing about the ups and downs of my life, and all the wonderful people in it.; [a.] Crete, IL

TILLWACH, WANDA E.
[b.] October 30, 1944, West Germany; [p.] Anton and Maria Gwizdala; [m.] Paul J. Tillwach, May 23, 1964; [ch.] Wanda Maria, Paul Anthony and Jason Christopher; [ed.] Resurrection High School (2 yrs.) G.E.D. Graduate; [occ.] Examiner Tech II (Adot-Aeronautics Div.); [memb.] Taught Religion for 5 yrs. at out Church, was Vice-Pres. for 2 yrs. at our Ladies Auxiliary, also affiliated with our Church, my husband and I were taking care of the elderly from our Church. Also helped with abused children at a crisis center.; [hon.] Various Certificates of Appreciation and Acknowledgement for Volunteering at Work for various Charitable Organizations. In Germany (1st thru 4th. grade won in various Olympic Fields); [oth. writ.] Other poems, not submitted; [pers.] I wanted to share "God" with mankind, and I felt it reflected the signs of the times.; [a.] Phoenix, AZ

TJERNAGEL, DON
[b.] July 5, 1975, Oelwein, IA; [p.] Wayne and Susan Tjernagel; [ed.] Oelwein High School, currently attending University of Northern Iowa; [oth. writ.] Poem entitled "Bad Nostalgia"; [pers.] I want to redefine everything. Test every boundary and force readers to begin to possess a new image of a clear and unusual reality. I want people to learn that every detail of our lives is significant and worth acknowledgement.; [a.] Waterloo, IA

TOLSON, FRANCES E.
[b.] September 15, 1913, Licking, CO; [p.] H. H. and Mary Hoover; [m.] Melvin L. Tolson (Deceased, January 18, 1994), November 8, 1953; [ch.] One stepdaughter (Deceased), four grandchildren, four great grandchildren; [ed.] Bachelors-Ohio State University, Master's - Art Education - Kent State University; [occ.] Retired Art Teacher; [memb.] State Retired Teachers Assoc., Carroll Retired Teachers; [hon.] Who's Who in American Education, Who's

Who in the Arts 1971-1972; [oth. writ.] Christian Life Letters, The Lookout, Free press Standard, World of Poetry, Christian Evangelist; [pers.] I try to put feelings and pictures into the poetry.; [a.] Carrollton, OH

TOMMANEY, TIMOTHY J.
[b.] November 30, 1958, Albany, NY; [p.] Joseph and Reta Tommaney; [m.] Maribeth, April 21, 1926; [ch.] Todd and Katie; [ed.] Mars Area High School, Indiana University of PA; [occ.] Media Manager - Thrift Drug, Pittsburgh, PA; [memb.] Alle-Kiski Literacy Council, theta XI, Alle-Kiski and Thrift Drug Runnders Club; [oth. writ.] Poems published in school newspaper, write poems on cards for personal favors and friends.; [pers.] I like to seek the good in things that appear hopeless. Most poems of a serious nature reflect this attitude.; [a.] New Kensington, PA

TONEY, PATRICK
[b.] September 19, 1971, Phoenix; [ed.] Jesvit Education Northern Arizona University; [occ.] Assistant Registrar May Gallery Scottscdale; [memb.] Amnesty International; [hon.] Dean's List Brophy College Prep., Secondary Dean's List Northern Arizona University; [oth. writ.] Cities in Dust, Interstates in Rust; [pers.] The Romantic Notion of Love and Loss consists of scenery and circumstance. Those elements create a sovice for writing tangibly.; [a.] Phoenix, AZ

TORRES, CHRISTOPHER CURTIS
[pen.] Popo; [b.] December 29, 1975, Lubbock; [p.] Lupe and Nellie Torres; [m.] Casey Torres, June 24, 1995; [ch.] Calynne Leticia Torres; [ed.] Coronado High School, US Naval Yeoman School; [occ.] US Navy Yeoman at Pearl Harbor, Hawaii; [memb.] Our Lady of Grace Catholic Church; [hon.] Art Award by South Plains Fair Garden and Art Center Award; [oth. writ.] My writings are done only with my brother, when we write to our Mother.; [pers.] My writing represents how I feel about my Mom.; [a.] Lubbock, TX

TORRES, CHRISTIAN CURTIS
[pen.] Popo; [b.] December 29, 1975, Lubbock, TX; [p.] Lupe and Nellie Torres; [m.] Angelica M. Torres, June 17, 1995; [ed.] Coronado High School, US Naval Dental Technician, US Marine Medical Root Camp; [occ.] US Naval and US Marine Dental Tech.; [memb.] Our Lady of Grace Catholic Church, American Red Cross, Catechist Teacher; [hon.] Golden Key Art Award; [oth. writ.] Personal poems written to wife, and Mom; [pers.] When I write a poem, I write straight from my heart. My poems are or have been for my own enjoyment.; [a.] Lubbock, TX

TORREY, ARTHUR
[b.] August 2, 1939, Weymouth, MA; [p.] Charles Torrey and Esther Torrey; [m.] Eleanor Torrey, October 29, 1960; [ch.] Arthur Gregory, Wendy Lee; [ed.] Braintree High School; [pers.] Surrounded by love ones it's very easy to express your feeling, your accomplishments and of course your dreams of happiness.; [a.] Braintree, MA

TOULSON, CHRISTOPHER M.
[pen.] Chris Toulson; [b.] September 9, 1979, Milford, CT; [p.] Rodney Toulson, Carolee Toulson; [ed.] Presently enrolled as a sophomore at Pulaski Academy College Prep School; [hon.] National Junior honor society, Beta Club, Duke University T.I.P. Program; [a.] Little Rock, AR

TOWSON, SUSAN KIM
[b.] June 7, 1979, DC; [p.] Travis J. and Kyong Towson; [ed.] Currently a Junior at Bishop Treton H.S. in Alexandria, VA; [pers.] This poem is dedicated to Fr. David Meng. I owe him my life because he gave me a second chance at mine. "Man looks at the outward appearance but the Lord looks at the heart" I Sam 16:7.; [a.] Springfield, VA

TRACY, VANESSA RODGERS
[b.] 3-26-66, Pike County; [p.] Mr. & Mrs. Willie Bob Rodgers; [m.] Zane Lawrence Tracy, August 19, 1995; [ch.] Melody Shari Rodgers; [ed.] Graduate Pike County High School & 2 1/2 years Alabama State University; [occ.] Self-employed (Provisioning Coordinator); [memb.] Sweet Pilgrim Baptist Church, CLIO Elementary Parents Teachers Association; [hon.] Who's Who in Music 1984, WSFA Appreciation Award 1979, Host of Educational Awards; [pers.] I'd like to thank my husband Zane, whose love inspired me to write this poem.; [a.] Brundidge, AL

TRAPP, GENIDA TAN
[pen.] G. Diane; [b.] April 28, Davao City, Philippines; [p.] Lorenzo (Deceased) and Isabel Tan; [m.] Arthur Trapp, July 16, 1986; [ch.] Arianne Gwynevere and Arthur Guilles; [ed.] Stella Maris Academy, Ateneo de Davao College, Silliman University (All in the Philippines); [occ.] Accountant/Stay-At-Home Mom (While my kids grow); [memb.] Philippine Association of CPA's, Stella Maris Alumni Association; [hon.] Dean's List, 2nd Place-Ateneo de Davao Poetry Writing Contest 1969-70, Honors Class since Elementary; [oth. writ.] Columnist-Solidbanker, Opinions/Commentaries-Philnews, several poems published in native Philippines; [pers.] I life to write poems with universal subjects that touch the heart of people and make them appreciate humanity and our surrounding world.; [a.] Sierra Vista, AZ

TRIPPOD, IRENE
[b.] September 18, 1931, Poland; [p.] Joseph Stanistgia Lata; [m.] Joseph Trippod (Deceased), February 10, 1983; [ch.] Aldona Rossabella Kareta; [ed.] Med College of Dentistry in Poland 1964 Dental Technision; [memb.] Member of the choir at St. Vincent de Paul Catholic Church, Member of the American Heart Association; [oth. writ.] Wrote song that was not published wrote children stories that also were not published; [pers.] I moved to the United States in 1966. I feel that God has blessed me with the gift to write and I feel that I need to share that gift with the world.; [a.] Holiday, FL

TROGOLO, ANDREW M.
[b.] August 7, 1981, West Frankfort, IL; [p.] James A. Trogolo and Tammy L. West; [ed.] Christopher Elementary School; [occ.] Student (8th Grade); [a.] Christopher, IL

TROTTER, ELAINE
[b.] November 16, 1942, Detroit, MI; [p.] Monroe and Luella Neal; [m.] Calvin Trotter, November 15, 1986; [ch.] Wanda Oldham and Billy R. Morgan, II; [ed.] Northern High; [occ.] Switchboard Operator and Receptionist/Eastman Kodak Company; [pers.] Ostracized, by family and friends as a young un-wed Mother in the late 1950's. I was overwhelmed with love and pride when my Daughter reached adulthood and gave birth, three years AFTER she was married.

This pride encourage and influenced me to put my heart felt feelings on paper in the form of poetry.; [a.] Oak Park, MI

TRUITT, MAURINE I.
[b.] May 13, 1910, Idaho; [p.] William and Ida Vanvreeland; [m.] Gerald L. Truitt (Deceased, 1988), September 12, 1929; [ch.] Geraldine Jewel, Dorothy Kraft, Charles, Truitt; [ed.] Public School and High in Boise Idaho; [occ.] Retired age 85; [memb.] Church of Jesus Christ; [hon.] A few poems published, not too much. Poem "Wild Grapes" published in Famous Poets Society 1995; [oth. writ.] I have compiled a book of poems for my daughter; [pers.] I have mostly written for my family and Church. My father was Pioneer, going from Missouri to Boise, Idaho in 1886; [a.] Baldwin Park, CA

TRUPIANO, DOROTHY E.
[pen.] Dot E. Trupiano; [b.] September 23, 1913, Detroit, MI; [p.] Emma and Emile Miottel; [m.] Nick (Deceased), October 2, 1937; [ed.] High School Graduated - Eastern High School, Detroit, MI; [occ.] Retired Housewife; [memb.] St. Paul Lutheran Church, Lakeland, FL; [oth. writ.] Articles printed in the Lakeland Ledger, Voice of the people, and several poems printed in the Lakeland Ledger, and The Radio Flyer; [pers.] Have been writing poetry since I was about 17 years old.

TUCKER, HELEN M.
[pen.] Helen Palmer Tucker; [b.] Little Rock, AR; [p.] Eli Palmer, Sr., Annie Bell Palmer; [m.] Rev. George Tucker, December 17, 1947; [ch.] Carolyn Tucker Smith; [ed.] Arkansas Baptist College Philander-Smith College (both of L.R. University of Central AR, Conway, AR; [occ.] Retired Teacher - Nurse, Writer; [memb.] Now Light Baptist Church, Missionary President, Minister's Wives Club, AEA - NEA, Central High Neighborhood Association, LR. City Mission; [hon.] Dean's List-Dunbar Jr. College, MSE UCA, Conway, AR Award of Merit Certificate World of Poetry, Sacramento, CA; [oth. writ.] Poetry Book published in 1991, "Prime Time Celebrations." Many poems published in Local Newspapers and Church Bulletins; [pers.] Communication is a Vital element between family and friends. Obedience to God Everyday should be a day of Celebration. Maya Angelou's Poetry Poetry has influenced my writing.; [a.] Little Rock, AR

TUCKER, JUDITH I.
[hon.] 23 Awards of Merit Certificates, 6 Golden Poet Awards, 1 Silver Poet Awards, 6 Editor's Choice Awards, 2 Women's Inner Circle of Achievement Awards, 1 Woman of the Year 1992 Award, 2 Five Thousand Personalities of the World Awards, 1 International Cultural Diploma of Honor Award and has been awarded 2 Golden Medals for Literary Work from the USA. Also awarded The International Who's Who of Intellectuals Award, and a Silver Medal Award, The 20th Century Award for Achievement.; [oth. writ.] Several poems published in the USA, Netherlands and Greece. Two books published in England. She was published in the International Who's Who in Poetry and Poet's Encyclopaedia: Seventh Edition 1993/94. And International Who's Who of Intellectuals: Tenth Edition 1993/94.

TURNER, GLADYS M.
[b.] September 10, 1929, Tillar, AR; [p.] Nellie J., Arthur Greswold; [ch.] Clyde L. Jones; [ed.] Cook, Pre Cosmetologist; [occ.] Cosmetologist and Cook; [memb.] O.A.B no U. The Ohio Association of Beauticians, NCL Beautician by Union 868 Cooking spec.; [hon.] Beauty contest on 23-day 1980, July Canton, 17 day 1973, including 21 day 1982; [pers.] Singer, speaker; [a.] Toledo, OH

TURNER JR., THOMAS BOYD
[b.] September 15, 1974, San Francisco, CA; [p.] Frances Rankin Turner; [ed.] Graduate of Mercy High School, Red Bluff, CA, AA degree from Shasta College Redding CA; [occ.] Logger, Selfemployed; [oth. writ.] Now we will feel no rain; [pers.] I feel blessed that though my Dad died just a month before my graduation from high school, I was raised in a loving home of 2 parents. I hate traditional family values and principles. When I give you my word it is binding - that makes for good business and good personal relations. I am hard working and self supporting in the logging business and plan to enter Chico State College Fall 96 to complete a degree in business administration.; [a.] Cottonwood, CA

TUTTLE, DENNIS JOSEPH
[b.] August 23, 1946, Detroit, MI; [p.] Camille and Joseph; [m.] Peggy Nan Tuttle, August 9, 1991; [ed.] Riverside High School Dearborn Hgts., MI. Graduated 1965 Ross Business Institute 1985; [occ.] Sterile Processing Material Collector, Providence Hospital, Southfield,MI; [oth. writ.] Have wrote personal poetry off and on since 1977; [pers.] Wrote my poem "One Day I Will Join You" in honor and memory of my wife Peggy Nan Tuttle who died at age 34 on November 8, 1991.

TYSON, WYCLIFFE E.
[pen.] Wycliffe E. Tyson; [b.] January 12, 1953, Nevis, WI; [p.] Samuel Tyson, Margery Tyson; [ed.] Trinity College at Miami, FL, Miami Dada College, FL B Sci., A Sci.; [occ.] Licensed Minister; [memb.] International Society of Poets, American Naturopathic Medical Association, First United Methodist Church, Miami; [hon.] Honorable Discharge U.S. Navy, Vietnam Veteran, In honor of my mother Mrs. Margery Tyson, who recognized my educational deficiencies as a youth, and made every effort to change it.; [oth. writ.] Author of book entitled "Message, Prayers and Poetry."; [pers.] I may be blind mentally, but I can see further than you can.; [a.] Miami Beach, FL

UDDLEY, METALLICA
[b.] 11-25-85, Plainview, TX; [p.] Sophia Ponce (Mom); [ed.] 4 years in Elementary at Halverson in Albert Lea, MN 56007; [occ.] Student at Halverson Elementary; [memb.] Peer Media for Halverson Elementary; [hon.] Citizenship 1st 1994 for best poster; [oth. writ.] Book on the children in Somalia which was given to President Bill Clinton; [pers.] I believe that my mother has influenced me to write and to love to write. I think that if my mother would not encourage me to write and to let me enjoy writing, I would not have begun to write. Thank God for Mother.; [a.] Albert Lea, MN

UDING, KATHERINE
[pen.] Katy; [b.] October 21, 1984, Dallas, TX; [p.] Tom and Ginny Uding; [ed.] 4th Grade; [occ.] Student; [hon.] Honor student thru 4 years of elementary school; [oth. writ.] Personal writing's non published; [a.] Carrollton, TX

ULRICH, AUDRA
[b.] December 13, 1967, Springfield, IL; [p.] Jack and Linda Woods; [m.] Greg D. Ulrich, March 4, 1995; [ch.] One on the way; [ed.] Master of Arts Degree in Human Service Administration, Bachelor of Science Degree in Psychology; [occ.] Socialworker; [oth. writ.] This is one of my firsts; [pers.] I wrote this poem to express how I felt growing up as an identical twin. I then gave it to my sister and my parents a surprise Christmas gifts last year (1994)

UNTCH, MAXINE
[b.] December 16, 1927, Canton, OH; [p.] Frank and Lillian Welter; [m.] Frank Untch (Deceased), July 27, 1946; [ch.] Frank Untch Jr., Sharon Sandra-Hoover, and Edwards, Susan-Curry (deceased); [ed.] Gibbs Grade School and McKinley High School, (One year) Canton, Ohio; [occ.] Homemaker; [memb.] AARP - American Association of Retired Persons; [oth. writ.] No other poems published; [pers.] Although I am an uneducated woman, my family and I get much enjoyment from the few poems. I have written, inspired by events which happened in my younger days.; [a.] Canton, OH

VAHAN, RICHARD
[b.] October 23, 1927, New York, NY; [p.] V. C. Vahan and Minerva E. Vahan; [m.] Melissa Merwin, December 25, 1977; [ch.] Julia, Suzanne, Alexander, Peter, Tatiana; [ed.] B.S. Boston University; [occ.] V.P., Miami International Studios; [oth. writ.] Editor of several books, magazine articles; [a.] Miami, FL

VAHEY, CHRISTOPHER B.
[b.] December 3, 1968, Philadelphia; [p.] Celeste Vahey, Michael Vahey; [ed.] Temple University (SBA); [oth. writ.] Not published; [pers.] This poem was written for my wonderful girlfriend Dawn. It was inspired by a fire to succeed that has been kindled by my loving mother, Celeste. Thank you Mom. Your loving son always, Christopher.; [a.] Elkins Park, PA

VAINE, HONEY
[b.] July 15, 1947, Newport, NH; [p.] Lorraine and Sidney Ash; [m.] Ted Vaine Jr., December 18, 1964; [ch.] 2 daughters - Tammy and Josie, 1 son - Ted Vaine III; [ed.] Currently Attending School for Nursing, Avid Crafter, Spinner, Weaver, Quilter, pottery, Knitter, Basketry; [occ.] Medical Assistant for a Pediatrician; [oth. writ.] Working on a series of children's stories along with my son, who is doing the illustrations, and currently looking for a publisher; [pers.] I believe in sharing our past, our dreams, and our experiences with our children. This is what I try to do with my stories and sneak in little moral tidbits along the way.; [a.] Croydon, NH

VALDEZ, JANITA
[b.] October 31, 1961, Richmond, TX; [p.] Judy and Edgar Cheairs; [m.] Joe A. Valdez, August 5, 1993; [ed.] Madisonville High School, Madisonville, TX, Judson High School, Universal City, TX, Sam Houston State University, Huntsville; [occ.] Correctional Officer; [a.] Madisonville, TX

VALLIER, ERIN
[pen.] Erin, Vallier; [b.] August 21, 1980, Fort Lauderdale, FL; [p.] Mark and Connie Vallier; [ed.] I'm entering the 10th grade; [memb.] First United Methodist Youth. Appling County Show - Choir, Appling Co. Chorus.; [hon.] Outstanding Freshman in Chorus/Show Choir, Adv. Chorus Award, Show Choir Merit Award All State Chorus 2 yrs., Superior Chorus; [pers.] I greatly encourage other people to express their feelings in their writing. Then it is a great work of art.; [a.] Baxley, GA

VAN ZILE, TIM
[b.] November 9, 1967, Merced, CA; [p.] Larry and Delores Van Zile; [ed.] Merced High and Business College graduate; [occ.] Bookkeeper; [memb.] American Bowling Congress; [hon.] Two perfect games in bowling; [oth. writ.] Several writings, but none submitted for publishing; [pers.] People tend to judge without knowing what or who it is they are judging.; [a.] Merced, CA

VAN WYK, JACOB W.
[pen.] Jacob W. Van Wyk; [b.] August 2, 1920, Michigan; [p.] John Grace Van Wyk; [m.] June 7, 1941; [ch.] Margaret Ann, Merlin Jack, Judy Kay, Arthur William; [ed.] 9th grade; [occ.] Retired; [memb.] V.F.W., Republican National Committee; [oth. writ.] Footprints in the Sands of Time, Thanks to God, Children Day, Mother's Day; [pers.] I write to editor of Harold Press.; [a.] Huntington, IN

VANDERWOOD, DEBORAH M.
[pen.] Deborah M. Vanderwood; [b.] November 20, 1950, Ilion, NY; [p.] Frances Benson, Roger Newhouse; [m.] Barry S. Vanderwood (D.O.M.), September 7, 1967, Divorced, Alan R. Piotrowski (D.O.M), October 18, 1975 Divorced; [ch.] Brandy Alexanderia P., Alan Raymond P., Christopher Michel P.; [ed.] Utica Free Academy, Pikes Peuk Comm. College, College of F.I.C.S. for Journalism; [occ.] Writer/Poet, Songwriter, Dental Assistant, Preschool Teacher; [memb.] American Red Cross, YMCA, P.T.A.; [hon.] Nomination as Poet of the year 1995, Certificate of Recognition for Preschool teacher, Certificate of Recognition from USAF space command for Dental Assistant Program, Certificate of Recognition from American Red Cross for Dental workshop, Certificate of Appreciation from DeFence Commissary Agency, Pikes Peak Community College for Dental Radiology and Math Science and Health Division of Dental Assisting Program Certificate of Degree for Journalism and short story writing from College of I.C.S.; [oth. writ.] Several poems for good housekeeping and Mile High Poetry Society and the National Library of Poetry, 1. In Passing as We Meet. 2. A Poet's Dream. 3. Awakened by a Dream. 4. Mother's in the Book of Piera. 5. To Everything There is a Season, in a delicate balance and a sea of treasure.; [pers.] As a new poet I hope that poet readers will feel the emotions in my poetry, and I hope to move their emotions with their souls and their lives as life is poetry. I have been greatly influenced by Emily Dickerson.; [a.] Colorado Springs, CO

VANZANT, DOROTHY
[pen.] Dorothy Vanzant; [b.] December 24, 1919, Greenwood Springs, MS; [p.] Mr. and Mrs. John A. Gray (Deceased); [m.] David M. Vanzant, July 27, 1938; [ch.] David III (Deceased), Robert, Judith, Joy; [ed.] High School and one year nursing for LPN. Did

private duty nursing for 25 years.; [occ.] Retired; [memb.] First Baptist Church - Mount Dora, FL; [hon.] Knights of Pythias, Essay Award in High School; [oth. writ.] Many poems of nature, seasons, spiritual and everything; [pers.] I like all types of poetry, arts and crafts, oil painting (I also do oil painting) I made Raggedy Ann and Andy Dolls and lots of fancy handwork.; [a.] Mount Dora, FL

VAUGHAN, PAMILA
[pen.] Pamila Gale Vaughan; [b.] February 20, 1948, Coolville, UT; [p.] Michael A. and Elva Robinson Gale; [m.] Virgil V. Vaughan, October 19, 1968; [ch.] Denise M. Wedemeyer, Christopher M. Vaughan; [ed.] High School Granger High School, Salt Lake City, UT, Lassen Community College, Susanville, CA; [occ.] Homemaker; [oth. writ.] Family Histories, currently writing a fiction story about Mothers Younger Years. Various poems, short stories.; [pers.] I enjoy writing in poem form. I try to write about my life and members of my family for future generations. Writing gives me peace.; [a.] Doyle, CA

VAUSE, RAYNA
[b.] July 26, 1977, Philadelphia; [ed.] Episcopal Academy - class of 1995, Freshman at Haverford College; [occ.] Full-time student; [memb.] Academy of Natural Sciences; [hon.] Recognition by National Achievement Scholarship Program, Who's Who Among American High School students; [a.] Haddonfield, NJ

VEIT, LAUREL E.
[b.] February 16, 1978, Orange, CA; [p.] James Dakin Veit, Ildiko Szabo Veit; [ed.] Senior, Villa Park High School Villa Park, CA; [memb.] California Scholarship Federation, National Honor Society, Key Club, Editor and staff writer of school newspaper, the Oracle; [oth. writ.] Unpublished children's picture book, editor and staff writer on the Oracle (high school newspaper); [pers.] This poem was written for my mother in 1993 as a Mother's Day present. I hope that I can continue to publish my other works and someday become an accomplished author. However, my immediate goal is to get into a good college.; [a.] Orange, CA

VELASQUEZ, MYRA
[b.] March 4, 1963, Pearsall, TX; [p.] Imelda and Pedro Trevino; [m.] Rodolfo Velasquez II, October 22, 1992; [ch.] Pamela, Amanda and Marcus Ramirez; [ed.] 10th grade; [occ.] Housekeeper; [oth. writ.] Yes, but not published; [pers.] I wrote this poem for my daughters and husband. Who were away from home at the time it was going to be put in two Christmas cards that my son had made at school but we never gave out the cards. (It was written with my 3 children and husband in my thoughts Rodolfo, Pamela Amanda and Marcus).; [a.] Richmond, TX

VELEZ, ALEXANDRA
[pen.] Alexandra Velez; [b.] December 4, 1977, Puerto Rico; [p.] Jose A. Velez, Sylvia D. Velez; [ed.] I am in my 3rd year of High School of Fashion Industries; [occ.] Full time student; [pers.] In my writing, I try to show the truth. I hope when people read my poem, it shows them the truth about themselves or the people around them. Like God has shown me.; [a.] Jackson Heights, NY

VELOTT, JOAN M.
[b.] April 26, 1932, Gettysburg, PA; [p.] Helen V. and Joseph S. Holochwost; [m.] LaRue H. (Pete) Velott, September 1, 1956; [ch.] Patricia M. Guinter, Steven J. Velott, Gregory A. Velott; [ed.] Williamsport High School, Temple University Hospital School of Nursing, Lycoming College (R.N.) Certificate of Pastoral Studies; [occ.] Proprietor - Velott Associates Travel Agency; [memb.] St. Genevieve's Catholic Church - WIT - RV - Travelers Club; [hon.] National Honor Society; [oth. writ.] Other poems published in "Antioch" - Dalton, PA, Seminary Magazine and Diaconate Newsletter Scranton, PA; [pers.] I have been so fortunate and given so much by God. I want to give back to my fellow man all I can.; [a.] Las Cruces, NM

VIGORITO, CARMINE T.
[b.] September 25, 1935, Paterson, NJ; [p.] Carmine F. Vigorito and Helen Vigorito; [m.] Patricia M. Vigorito, October 21, 1967; [ch.] Karen Marie, Kelly Ann and Brian Michael; [ed.] Central High, Paterson, NJ, Seton Hall University-BA and LLB; [occ.] Attorney at Law; [oth. writ.] Numerous poems and short stories; [pers.] Life's challenge is to fight for what you love and believe.; [a.] North Haledon, NJ

VILAIRE, MELISSA
[b.] August 21, 1981, Philadelphia, PA; [p.] Marlene Pilet Vilaire, Gaston Vilaire; [m.] August 13, 1977; [ch.] One; [ed.] Waldron Mercy Academy Elementary School, Merion Pennsylvania; [occ.] Student at Merion Mercy Academy (Merion, PA); [oth. writ.] Several poems published in LePetit Courier, A Hatian newsletter. Also, poems published in the Anthology of Poems by young Americans 1995, and in A Celebration of Pennsylvania's Young Poets.; [pers.] Nothing ever happens if you don't show up, never repress your emotions, let them explode into your world. My parents have been a constant source of love and support.; [a.] Philadelphia, PA

VILLAREAL, STACY
[pen.] Stacee Brown; [b.] August 23, 1971, Chicago, IL; [p.] Charles and Charlotte Brown; [m.] Joseph W. Villareal, November 9, 1991; [ed.] Metcalf County High School, Edmonton, KY; [occ.] Staff Asst. Educational and Institutional Coop; [oth. writ.] A small poem about my father; [pers.] I wrote this poem on a Sunday morning. Sunday mornings were always pleasant home. Mom making breakfast before church and getting ready for Sunday School. I miss my mother more than words can say.; [a.] Justice, IL

VISEUR, RENATE
[b.] July 17, 1940, Friedberg, Hessen, Germany; [p.] Ludwig and Emma Stelz; [m.] Don Lee Viseur, September 8, 1962; [ch.] Michael Lee Viseur, Renee M. Kulick; [ed.] Europa (Germany); [occ.] Owner of Pet Grooming Shop (Groomer); [memb.] A child of God!; [hon.] Someday "I Am Waiting" for my wings; [oth. writ.] With dedication for all times to God be the Glory! As God guides me to write.; [pers.] A born hessian, by choice I came to this country and the Richard Leach Family in 1961-62 (Bamey) Today Dinosaur The #1 Family in America!!; [a.] Litchfield, IL

VOCKRODT, MARLO DEAN
[pen.] Marlo Dean; [b.] October 20, 1943, Portland; [p.] Martin and Augusta Vockrodt; [m.] Kathryn, March 21, 1970; [ch.] Kerrie - 21, Ryan - 19, Timothy - 16; [ed.] Associate Science/Sociology Clackamas Community College, Milwaukee High School; [occ.] Letter courier 25 years with U.S.P.S.; [memb.] New Hope Celebration Choir, New Hope Com. Church, some solo on fear occasions, did poetry readings; [hon.] Bone Marrow donor Mar 9, 1992, Donor of 10 gal. blood Am. Red Cross; [oth. writ.] Alderbrook, copyrighted but not published, a collection of poetry; [pers.] "Life is rich, and the finest things in it are free. Can you put your hands on laughter, put a price on a tear? Love, joy, peace and most of all eternity..."; [a.] Oregon City, OR

VOLPE, ROBERT A.
[b.] July 14, 1951, Philadelphia; [p.] Assunta Domizio, Alfred Volpe; [m.] Joanne Volpe, October 13, 1984; [ch.] Angela Volpe; [ed.] St. Thomas More H.S., Temple Univ.; [oth. writ.] "Bits of Bob"; [pers.] "My Parents Wanted `A Wit' for a Son. Half a wish is better than none."; [a.] Phoenixville, PA

VON HALLMARK, MELONY
[pen.] Melony Van Hallmark; [b.] October 28, 1966, Macon, GA; [p.] Wayne and Yvonne Davis; [m.] Horace L. Hallmark, April 12, 1991; [ch.] Ashleigh Van Hallmark; [ed.] Graduated from Winter Haven High School in 1984, Dental Technician with X-ray license; [occ.] Homemaker and taking care of my daughter; [memb.] American Cancer Society, St. John's United Methodist Church, Big Brother Big Sisters Association; [hon.] Poems printed in newspaper, spelling B Champion in my class in 1982; [oth. writ.] I've written three other poems that are all dedicated and inspired by a member of my immediate family; [pers.] I have written "The Sacrifice" and dedicated it to my daughter, Ashleigh Von Hallmark and my niece - Kialey Gail Davis so that when they are old enough they will know the true meaning of Easter.; [a.] Winter Haven, FL

VONDRELL SR., JAMES HENRY
[b.] January 28, 1950, Dayton, OH; [p.] Urban J. and Louise L. Vondrell; [m.] M. Starleyne Test Vondrell, July 7, 1973; [ch.] Jim Jr., Abigail, Lisa Lindsey, Christopher; [ed.] BBA - Business University of Cinti, Ed. M. - Education - University of Cinti, Ed. D. - Education - University of Cinti; [occ.] Associate Dean, College of Evening and Continuing Education - Univ. of Cincinnati; [memb.] Association For Continuing Higher Education, National University Continuing Education Association; [hon.] Past President ACHE, Distinguisher Services Award, Evening College Division, University of Cinti.; [oth. writ.] How to take a test and score with Memory Power - with Keith N. Haley; [a.] Cincinnati, OH

WAGNER, MARK
[pen.] Mark Wagner; [b.] February 5, 1951, Chicago, IL; [p.] Harold and Olive Wagner; [m.] Katie Metz-Wagner, June 17, 1995; [ed.] Prosser High, LaVerne College, BA; [occ.] Charter Driver; [oth. writ.] Screenplays! "Aquarius Warrior," "Bringer Of Spirit," "California Bound"; [pers.] Deeper and deeper I dive into a dark, mysterious abyss. All there threatening monsters have so far been chased into vanishing shadows. What a glorious sight! Here shines the spiritual realm!; [a.] Santa Rosa, CA

WAHNON, DENISE-MARIE
[pen.] Denise-Marie, D. M.; [b.] February 7, 1964, California; [p.] Herbert E. Wahnon, Charlie-Lynn Schiola; [ch.] William D. Jacobs II and Destiny Marie Davis; [ed.] James Monroe High and John F. Kennedy High; [occ.] Full Time Mommy and Aspiring Writer; [memb.] American Cancer Society, United Way; [oth. writ.] Several Poems and a Scripture/Writing "The Prince And The Princess"; [pers.] I am a very positive person with myself and in life. All of my poetry writing are through self expression. My dreams and my goals are to become a published writer through my poetry writings and short stories and hopefully someday write a book and also write children's books. My inspiration comes from several poets who write about love and romance, and also through the love of my children, my family, my friends, and my loved ones.; [a.] Los Angeles, CA

WAINSCOAT, JAMES PAUL
[pen.] Troy Conrad; [b.] May 8, 1941, Alameda, CA; [p.] Troy and Conrad Wainscoat; [m.] Roslynn (Rose) Wainscoat, June 3, 1990; [ch.] (1st marriage) Annette, Paula, Denise, Pamela, Amy and Racheal (2nd marriage) Judah, Ishayah and Lazarus; [ed.] School of Life and still learning; [occ.] Whatever odd job will put bread on the table and "Peace Work"; [memb.] Vietnam Veterans for Peace, Disabled Veterans of America; [hon.] Two Bronze Start with Valor, an Army Commendation Medal with Valor and a Purple Heart. Honored by those who count me among their friends.; [oth. writ.] Personal accounts of war in Vietnam.; [pers.] Poetry is the Music of Philosophy.; [a.] Corralitos, CA

WAKAMATSU, JACK K.
[b.] May 28, 1918, Los Angeles, CA; [p.] Mr. and Mrs. M. Wakamatsu; [m.] Fumiko F. Wakamatsu, September 25, 1951; [ch.] John, Mark, Peter, Kimi; [ed.] Venice High School Santa Monica City. Col. Bisttran Fine Arts, Art Center College; [occ.] Retired, Industrial Designer; [memb.] JACL, 442nd. Assoc. Life Member of Dav. Life Member of Art Center Alum. Assoc. (2) Japanese/Amer. National Museums; [hon.] WW II Decoration S.S., Purple Heart - Pres. Citation. CIA; [oth. writ.] Published, curr. Book silent warriors - vantage press. New York NY, 1995. Many Tech. Article in Scientific Area.; [pers.] Truth is the bases of our life - we all know this - then, why do we not live it - !!; [a.] Los Angeles, CA

WAKE, DAVID
[b.] September 20, 1977, Brookings, SD; [p.] Carol Wake, Richard Wake; [ed.] 3 years of High School; [occ.] High School Senior; [hon.] Previously unpublished; [pers.] I hope to obtain wisdom through introspection. Poetry is the most powerful tool for this task at my command.; [a.] Brookings, SD

WAKELEY, STACIE
[b.] September 25, 1970, Glens Falls, NY; [p.] Gary Wakeley, Linda Wakeley; [m.] Single; [ed.] South Glens Falls High School, Saratoga Boces - Cosmetology.; [occ.] Developmental Aide of the mentally disabled, Wilton Developmental Center Greenbarn Rd. IRA, Kingsbury N.Y.; [oth. writ.] Very first writing sent out.; [pers.] Although I was influenced by a tragedy in my childhood I've become more positive and I have tried to write with honesty and a variety of emotions.; [a.] Glens Falls, NY

WALKER, ETHEL CAROL
[pen.] E. C. Walker; [b.] September 15, 1947, Bel Air, MD; [p.] Walter Plummer, Lillian Plummer; [m.] Calvin Walker, October 29, 1966; [ch.] Amber Lee, Shawn Robert; [ed.] Edgewood High, Harford Community College; [occ.] Customer Service Representative; [pers.] My poems reflect feelings deep within the soul. I am on the outside looking in with great insight.; [a.] Aberdeen, MD

WALLACE, DOROTHY A.
[b.] September 11, 1942, Wright County, MO; [p.] Stephen Foster Dudley, Lois Breman Dudley; [ch.] Michael Huckaby, David Wallace; [ed.] Mansfield High School, Mansfield, MO Drury College and Southwest Missouri State University, Springfield, MO; [occ.] Director of Special Services, Mansfield Schools, Mansfield, MO; [memb.] Missouri State Teachers Association, Council of Administration of Special Education, American Salers Association, International Society of Poets; [oth. writ.] Several poems published articles for local newspapers, family histories for county history books; [a.] Seymour, MO

WALLACE, EDWARD
[b.] October 7, 1950, Philadelphia, PA; [p.] Frank and Gertrude Wallace; [m.] Sharon Wallace, October 27, 1973; [ch.] Kelly Wallace, Edward Wallace; [ed.] Bristol Twp School District Bucks Co. Community College; [occ.] Police Officer Bristol Twp, PA.; [memb.] Fraternal order of police Bristol Twp Benevolent Assoc. Loyal order of moose lodge #1169; [hon.] Served 20 months in Viet Nam with vs Marine Corps.; [a.] Levittown, PA

WALLACE, ESTHER E.
[pen.] "S" ter; [b.] August 26, 1940, New York; [p.] Esther and Dirk VanDerest; [m.] Thomas J. Wallace, July 29, 1991; [ch.] Jake and Michael Shaffer; [ed.] St. Adatha's School and Convent for Girls; [occ.] Homemaker and Grandchildren sitter; [hon.] Gloria VanDerest Tyson Stearn (my sister) honors me every time she read one of my poems; [oth. writ.] Many other poems about all sorts of times in my life, just to understand myself.; [pers.] I am constantly thinking, and writing poetry, will never let my thoughts escape me.; [a.] Philadelphia, PA

WALLACE, LARY L.
[b.] March 15, 1950, East Liverpool, OH; [p.] Harold W. and Mildred E. Wallace; [m.] Waltraud U. Wallace; [ch.] Lary L. Wallace II, Melissa S. Wallace, Christina L. Wallace; [ed.] Alva High School, Edison Jr. College; [occ.] Retail Sales, Retired U.S. Army; [memb.] German American Club; [hon.] German Army Schutzenschnur, BSA Woodbadge, Meritorious Service Medal (150 OLC), Army Commendation Medal (1 OLC), Vietnam Service Medal, Army Occupation Medal (Berlin); [oth. writ.] Many, but none published; [pers.] There are a whole lot of people in the world that have it worse than we do.

WALLACE, TORREY
[pen.] Woodstock; [b.] September 16, 1977, Muncie, IN; [p.] Jim and Char Wallace; [ed.] I attend WCHS in Winchester where I am now a senior, I'm also enrolled in a semester at ICS where I'm studying a general drafting course.; [occ.] I am a full-time student; [hon.] My sophomore year I received an award for "sharing the arts," we travelled to other schools and taught the little ones a bit of art, education, where we made ceramic pottery.; [oth. writ.] I have many other writings that I have and believe are good, but never had the courage to let them out, maybe not I will.; [pers.] I must credit myself and Edgar Allan Poe for my work. Not to be selfish but I believe that if we listen to our own thoughts a little more than other people's there might be a little more, individualism in the world, isn't that what we strive for?; [a.] Winchester, IN

WALSH, ANN SCANNELL
[pen.] Ann Scannell Walsh or A. S. Walsh; [b.] July 31, 1943, Brony, NY; [p.] Margaret and Michael Scannell; [m.] David R. Walsh, September 7, 1968; [ch.] David C. and Kenneth S. Walsh; [ed.] St. Nicholas of Tolentine, Grace Institute Business School; [occ.] Co-Owner Card and Gift Shop Irvington, NY; [memb.] Immaculate Conception Church, Irvington, NY, Chamber of Commerce, Irvington, NY; [oth. writ.] 11 other poems to date; [pers.] I believe we should love God and His image that we find in ourselves and in each other. And that the family unit should heal itself so world peace can follow.; [a.] Irvington, NY

WALSH, CATHRYN L.
[b.] July 21, 1968, Douglas, GA; [p.] Jean J. Hope and James H. Hope; [m.] Ray C. Walsh, December 7, 1991; [ch.] Rhéa Ashley Walsh; [ed.] Coffee High, South Georgia College; [occ.] Secretary, Bookkeeper; [hon.] Who's, Who Among American High School Students; [oth. writ.] Short story in college literary book, Pegasus.; [pers.] The gift of a child and the job of a mother are two of the greatest blessings from God.; [a.] Ambrose, GA

WALSH, FIONA
[b.] November 18, 1980, San Francisco, CA; [p.] Dorothy and Vincent Walsh; [ed.] St. Anne's elementary school, Mercy S.F. and Cardinal spellman high Schools; [occ.] Teacher's assistant at a Montessori school - After School; [pers.] I write because it is my truest form of expression.; [a.] San Francisco, CA

WALTERS, SHARON
[b.] January 23, 1960, Denver, CO; [p.] Fred and Teresa Boyd; [m.] Troy Walters, September 15, 1984; [ch.] Seth Joseph, Joshua Wayne; [ed.] Melbourne High, University of Florida; [occ.] Registered Nurse in Obstetrics at Wuesthoff Hospital, Rocklege; [memb.] Florida Nurses Association, Northside Presbyterian Church; [hon.] Sigma Theta Tau, National Honor Society of Nursing, Golden Key National Honor Society, Phi Kappa Phi National Honor Society; [pers.] Our children .... our most precious resource.; [a.] Melbourne, FL

WALUKONIS, CASIE J.
[b.] October 25, 1977, Anderson; [p.] John and Vicki Walukonis; [ed.] Sr. At Highland High School in Anderson; [occ.] Student in High School (12 Grade); [hon.] National Honor Society, I dare you, 2 silver metals in Latin, Key Club, Volunteers Service Award from Anderson Noon Optimist Club, Nat'l Veterinary Award; [pers.] As a young adult in America Today, it is my responsibility, to help shape future generations. Younger children look to older students as role models.; [a.] Anderson, IN

WALUS, PAIGE G.
[b.] June 14, 1985, Joliet, IL; [p.] Alan and Cindi Walus; [ed.] Joy Elementary School; [occ.] 5th Grade Student; [hon.] Minority Leadership Award, Academic Achievement Award; [oth. writ.] Two Short Stories titled "The Closet Cat" and "Rafiki And The Three Little Blobs."; [a.] Michigan, IN

WAMSLEY, ANN M.
[b.] July 15, 1981, Dayton, OH; [p.] Douglas and Karen Wamsley; [ed.] Hilsman Middle School; [occ.] High School Student; [memb.] Beta Club; [hon.] 5th Place Georgia State Spelling Bee, NE Georgia Reader of the year, Duke Talent Identification Program Principal's Academic Achievement Award 4 years; [oth. writ.] Poems published in local newspaper, recognition for an essay and a speech.; [pers.] I write from my heart.; [a.] Athens, GA

WAMSLEY, CHAD
[pen.] C. Huston Wamsley; [b.] January 18, 1969, Bethesda, MD; [p.] Raymond and Barbara Wamsley; [m.] Carrie Calimer; [ed.] Damascus High School 1987, B.A. Psychology Salisbury State University 1991; [occ.] Security Assistant redland middle school, Rockville, MD.; [memb.] Contemporary Fighting Arts, Tau Kappa Epsilon Fraternity; [oth. writ.] My Solemn Prayer, The Warmth Of Your Face, That Old Rose, If I Believe, Life, The Greatest Thing, Of Joyous Time, You Are, Come Back To Me, The Wind, I Will Show You The Way, all poems unpublished.; [pers.] My reflection in the water staring back at me, my reflection of the past the rememberance of being, by using my reflection as a mirror I search for my own person. By finding my reflection I know who I am, without my reflection I am lost.; [a.] Germantown, MD

WARD, HILDA E.
[pen.] Her Ward; [b.] March 21, 1932, Ansonia, CT; [p.] Ms. Lucinda R. Sampson; [ch.] Dureen Ward, Luanne Ward, Elnora Ward; [ed.] MA in Health Education; [occ.] Retired Health Educator; [memb.] National Black Womens Health Project International Black Womens Coalition, International Womens Writers Guild; [hon.] PTSH National Award Jenkins Award, A scholarship has been created in my honor (the martin luther king scholarship in honor of Hilda Ward) Many Service Awards; [oth. writ.] A chapbook pieces of her African American Quilt in the process of writing a book "Journey into healing through journaling" also writing a novel - contributed to a publication rising spirits - words from the Wise; [pers.] Writing has become a deep part of my soul. It's the nourishment to my soul that keeps me on my path.; [a.] Freeport, NY

WARDLAW, DONNA
[b.] April 28, 1980, Easley, SC; [p.] Billy Wardlaw and Doris Wardlaw; [ed.] Pickens High School; [occ.] Student; [memb.] The National Beta Club; [hon.] The National Beta Club, The National Honor Roll, Citizens Award; [oth. writ.] Several unpublished poems; [pers.] Believe in yourself and no matter what any one else thinks, know you are the best you can be.; [a.] Pickens, SC

WARREN, LYKEN
[pen.] Sandy Warren; [b.] June 27, 1924, Watertown, FL; [p.] Lyken Warren Sr. and Emma Warren (Both Deceased); [m.] Helen V. Warren, May 9, 1975; [ch.] Six; [ed.] 11th Grade; [occ.] Retired; [memb.] AFM Musicians Local Union 389, Nashville Song Writers Association, Int'l, CMA and BMI.; [hon.] Several songs received radio plays and write-up in Country Song Round Up" magazine. 2 songs went to number 9 and number 8 respectively on independent labels chart out of "Top 30 Indies Charts".; [pers.] Poetry, whether it be mine or not is a way for we to transcend the ills and problems of society.; [a.] South Daytona, FL

WARREN, MARK A.
[b.] May 10, 1962, Lansing, MI; [p.] Gordon Warren, Brenda Allen-Hawkins; [m.] Nola Reed-Warren, February 16, 1985; [ed.] Clio High School - Diploma University of Michigan - B.A., English Major, Michigan First Responder - Diploma/Cert.; [occ.] Paint Production Operator - DuPont Paint - Mt. Clemens; [memb.] Dupont Fire Brigade, U-M Rec. Member, Confined Space Core Team - Rescue Member; [hon.] Presidential Physical Fitness Award, Dean's List - 80-81 SUSC.; [oth. writ.] Currently compiling 1st book of poems, and attempting a novel. Working on third chapter of a fantasy called 'Crystal Deliverance'.; [pers.] For every human ailment, both of the body and mind, somewhere there is a cure found in nature. The more we destroy our world the more we doom ourselves.; [a.] Mount Morris, MI

WASHINGTON, CHARLES M.
[b.] September 4, 1954, Philadelphia, PA; [p.] Mary and Charlie Washington; [ed.] B.S., Spring Garden College, MBA, Philadelphia College Textile and Science Current Ph. D. student at the University of South Carolina; [occ.] Assistant Professor and Doctoral Student; [memb.] Is the director and founder of Tree of Life, Professional Self Development and Ldr. Training Center; [hon.] Outstanding Young Men in America 92 and 93, Outstanding Graduate Student, Outstanding Service Award at Benedict College, 1st Recipient of the Ernest Shell Memorial Achievement Award; [oth. writ.] All unpublished the Betu! Journey into manhood and to date seven books of poetry including "Synergy"; [pers.] I believe in the inherent and untapped potential of the human spirit and the challenge for each individual to recognize and develop such potential.; [a.] Columbia, SC

WATHEN, CATHY
[pen.] Zig Zag; [b.] October 5, 1981, Westminster, MD; [p.] Terry Wathen; [ed.] Currently attending Westminster High. Plans for College; [occ.] (Future poet) student; [hon.] 2nd place in DAR American Poetry Contest in 6th grade, (first place went to a schoolmate); [oth. writ.] (None published) First novel written at age 13. (Still the Father), started poetry before I could write, short stories.; [pers.] Sometimes I feel hurt and alone, but when I write I can share my life and feelings with others, and that's the best feeling in the world.; [a.] Westminster, MD

WATHEN, KAREN
[pen.] Karen Haley Wathen; [b.] September 2, 1954, Salem; [p.] Robert Eugene Haley (Deceased), Dorlene Imogene Strange; [m.] Lawrence A. Wathen, August 11, 1984; [ch.] Tammy Jo, A. J. Wathen; [ed.] Bradie M. Shrum Elem. (Salem) Parkview Jr. High (Jeff) Jeffersonville High School; [occ.] Housewife; [hon.] Bible Correspondence Course, Editors Choice Award, Awarded by the National Library Poetry; [oth. writ.] "Jesus Spared Their Lives" published in Reflections of Light anthology in 1995!; [pers.] I hope to reach the hearts of many throughout the world. To bring peace and comfort where man's sole lies!; [a.] Floyds Knobs, IN

WATSON, KAREN S.
[b.] January 12, 1951; [p.] Robert E. and Mary K. McCrate; [m.] Gerald S. Watson; [pers.] When God has blessed us in so many ways, I feel an obligation to be thankful for not just what I have, but what I have learned. Our eyes should be opened so that we can see what the love of family and understanding of faith is all about. We should be grateful for not only the ability to love, but sharing in life's commitment to love one another as well. Our contribution to it all may not be perfection, but we need to at least acknowledge that there are many wonderful people who touch our lives everyday and bring both enrichment and joy into our lives. These people may be family or just friends... perhaps they influence us now or are a treasured memory of those who've lived before... Regardless, we need to remind ourselves daily of our obligation of share in God's love and keep the commitment alive.

WATSON, S. LYRIC
[b.] January 31, Aurora, IL; [p.] Dr. and Mrs. S. B. Watson; [ed.] Classical Voice - At Interlochen School for the Arts, Michigan, Graphic Artistic Design, University of California at Davis; [occ.] Designer/ Fine Artist; [memb.] Art Institute of Chicago, Aids Action League of California, Morris Animal Foundation; [hon.] Scholarship in Classical voice/interlochen schorlarship in figurative sculpture at Univ. of CA at Humboldt; [oth. writ.] The Moon (unpublished), Cruise, You; [pers.] Life is a state of mind, and my mind does its best to make sense of it all. I agree with chaucer, when he wrote "The Life So Short, The Craft So Long To Leave" my poems reflect this logic.; [a.] Waterman, IL

WATTERS, MARILYNN
[pen.] Marilyn; [b.] September 26, 1936; [p.] Del and Norma Watters; [m.] Divorced, June 25, 1995; [ch.] Four; [ed.] High School; [occ.] Disabled Ex. Empsema on S.S.I.

WATTS JR., TOYE E.
[pen.] Dwaine Troye; [b.] July 3, 1978, Monroe, LA; [p.] Toye Watts Sr., Lynda Watts; [ed.] Evans High Class of '97; [memb.] Greater Young Zion Baptist Church, Evans High School Band, National Thespian Society; [hon.] 1995 National Credit Education Week Contest; [oth. writ.] Good Credit; [pers.] I was once told that a writer can only write about things he/she knows about. When I write my poems, I only write about things that have happened in my life.; [a.] Martinez, GA

WEAVER, DEWAYNE
[b.] January 25, 1939, Texas; [p.] Bill and Lucille Weaver; [m.] Rev. Joyce Weaver, July 18, 1988; [ed.] High School - Hempstead, TX Aviation Schools - US Army; [occ.] Retired helicopter Pilot and Technician; [memb.] Int'l Church of New Thought - VFW - Veterans Self Help Groups; [hon.] Medal of Honor 2 Purple Hearts (Viet Nam) I served in Saudi Arabia in 9091 also -; [pers.] My endeavors are to help make the world a kinder, safer place for all and to teach, or show tolerance and compassion. I know that all humankind has its own unique, creative gifts to offer to society - both on a local and on a collective basis.; [a.] Mesa, AZ

WEAVER, JEANETTE A.
[b.] November 5, 1952, Peoria, IL; [p.] Justin and Margaret Weaver; [ed.] Washington Comm. High; [occ.] Lady Custodian, Berguer's Sheridan Village, Peoria, IL; [memb.] Choir member, first Federated Church, Peoria, IL; [pers.] I'm hoping to strengthen my faith, to spread the word of God, throughout the world in my writing. I appreciate, Dr. Robert Gillogly and Rev. William Petterson at First Federated Church for encouraging me in the love of poetry.; [a.] Washington, IL

WEAVER, VERNIECA G.
[b.] May 1, 1958, Athens, TN; [p.] Roy M. (Deceased) and Iris I (Shugart) Greene of Etowah, Tennessee; [ch.] Dustin Wesley (14 yrs.) and John Clifford Weaver (11 yrs.); [ed.] 1976 Graduate of Palatka South High School, Palatka, FL, U.S. Navy 1977-1979; [occ.] Office Manager for a Medical Office; [pers.] I have been greatly influenced by the memories of my childhood that I hold so deeply within my heart.; [a.] Hollister, FL

WEAVER JR., DIXON
[b.] November 18, 1931, Darlington, SC; [p.] Dixon Weaver Sr., Lois Sansbury (Both Deceased); [m.] Eugenia Bazen Weaver, May 16, 1958; [ch.] David Weaver, Angela Weaver, Holly Wilson, Dixie Welch; [ed.] McClenaghan High, Florence, S.C. Attended University of S.C. and Spartanburg Methodist College, Graduate of Southern Baptist External Education Division - Pastoral Ministries Diploma; [occ.] Retired; [memb.] American Association of Retired Persons (AARP); [pers.] I love to write religious poetry to inspire Christians to new heights in their Christian faith, and to draw non-Christian to Christ.; [a.] Florence, SC

WEBB, CARSON
[b.] March 18, 1950, Bell, CO; [p.] Mr. and Mrs. Andy Webb; [ed.] Seventh Grade; [occ.] Enrolled in G.E.D classes; [oth. writ.] Slices of Life; [pers.] I enjoy my writing as I do playing my music. I feels every one need to have a purpose or enjoyment in Life.; [a.] Burgin, KY

WEBB, LILLIAN R.
[b.] November 9, 1947, Chicago, IL; [p.] Richard and Edna Beeker; [ch.] Timothy James Webb, Johanna Lynn Webb; [ed.] Steinmetz High, Northern Illinois University, University of Colorado Medical School; [occ.] Physical Therapist, Delnor Community Hospital Home Care, Geneva, IL; [memb.] Faith Lutheran Church; [pers.] I do my best with what the good Lord give some.; [a.] Geneva, IL

WEBER, QUINN
[b.] April 10, 1974, Salt Lake City, UT; [p.] Mike Weber, Jeane Weber; [ed.] Brighton High School, University of Puget Sound; [occ.] Student; [memb.] Phi Kappa Phi, Phi Sigma; [hon.] Trustee Scholarship, Ross Wright Scholarship, Dean's List, Freshman Chemistry Award, Scholarship Award for the Athlete with the Highest G.P.A.; [a.] Salt Lake City, UT

WEIBULL, PONTUS
[b.] May 16, 1977, Hassleholm, Sweden; [p.] Nils and Kerstin Weibull; [ed.] GMI Engineering and Management Institute; [occ.] Student, Electrical Engineering; [hon.] Eagle Scout; [oth. writ.] Poetry and Prose published in various underground magazines and papers.; [pers.] Light exists only with the help of the dark. Only by looking into the dark can we find the light.; [a.] Chapel Hill, NC

WEINSTEIN, MICHAEL
[b.] August 11, 1969; [ed.] Transferred from Golden West College in Huntington Beach California to Cal State University Fullerton. Will be in the middle of my Junior year at time of publication.; [oth. writ.] Nothing major until this, mostly personal.; [pers.] Do not over burden yourself with extra stress or hassles, learn from your experiences, successes, and mistakes, set achievable goals.; [a.] Costa Mesa, CA

WEISS, AMY L. CROCKETT
[pen.] Amy L. Crockett; [b.] July 8, 1958, Seattle, WA; [p.] Dr. and Mrs. Wayne A. Crockett; [m.] James V. Weiss, June 18, 1988; [ch.] Jared R. Weiss; [ed.] Purdue University, Doctor of Veterinary Medicine in 1982; [occ.] Veterinarian/Business owner; [memb.] CRMA, AUMA, AAHA; [hon.] Society of Phi Zeta, (Honor Society of Vet Medicine), Phi Kappa Phi, Purdue 500 Club (Top 500 students); [oth. writ.] Over 100 poems on animals and their emotions, feelings and souls, and many human issues and humor.; [pers.] I am able to dig beneath the surface of humanity and write about the struggles of the soul. Love is the current of life and the Lord guides my every word.; [a.] Ledyard, CT

WELCH, GRACE R.
[b.] November 14, 1924, Manhattan, NY; [p.] Antonio Ripa and Grazia Caccioppoli; [m.] Frank Prince Welch, September 28, 1946; [ch.] Michael, Jean, Lisa; [ed.] Newtown High School, Elmhorst Non-Matric writing Courses, Columbian - NYC; [occ.] Yoga Teacher; [memb.] L.I. Yoga Assoc. National Organization for Women Sivananda Vedanta Teacher Training; [hon.] Honor Soc. Arista Woman of the Year Amer. Ass. Bus. women 1989 L.I. Chapter; [oth. writ.] "Kimberly Grace", published in Live Poets society of Long of Island Chap. 1990 Queens Women's Center News letter 1990 South Suffolk Now Chapter Newsletter 1991 Electric Umbrella, L.D. 1991; [pers.] The joy is in the Journey.; [a.] Islandia, NY

WELLS, B. RENEE
[pen.] Jake; [b.] November 17, 1957, Tulsa, OK; [p.] George Wm. and Jeanice Marie Jakeway; [m.] Rosslyn E. Wells III, March 9, 1992; [ed.] Soquel High, Canada College, College of San Mateo; [occ.] Grants Manager, Henry J. Kaiser Family Foundation; [memb.] American Federation of Motorcyclists; [hon.] Several stories and poems published in local newspaper and put into local libraries for other to read; [oth. writ.] Publication on the Scotts Valley Fire District; [pers.] I love adventure and people. Life has brought many trials to which I make my own path. I thank my close friends Pam Jacobs and Julie Lorenzen for their confidence in me. I'd be nowhere without them.; [a.] South San Francisco, CA

WELLS, BRYAN
[b.] April 19, 1943, Detroit, MI; [p.] Deceased; [m.] Divorced; [ed.] B.A., English; [occ.] Jazz Pianist, composer and editor: adweek direction of interactive marketing; [hon.] 2 gold records, 4 Clio awards; [a.] New York, NY

WELLS, MILES
[b.] October 22, 1944, Houston, TX; [p.] Miles Erwin Wells, Julia Wells; [m.] Widowed; [ed.] Self educated; [occ.] Real estate; [pers.] I write from an inspirational feeling. I feel a phrase, idea or concept comes to me and then I have a flow of words. I appear to have some influence from the British Isles.; [a.] Houston, TX

WENDT, SUSAN E.
[b.] October 15, 1963, Erie, PA; [p.] Donald and Dorothy Wendt; [ed.] Niagara Wheatfield Senior High School, Trott Vocational High School for Nursing; [occ.] Licensed Practical Nurse in Doctor's Office; [memb.] Music Panel Member for George Fine Surveys, Member of First Assembly of God.; [hon.] First place for Sterile Technique in Nursing School. Achievement Certificate for Completion of Electrocardiogram Procedures and Operations.; [pers.] As I've walked down the path of life I realize when I place my concerns in God's hand I can rest for He works all things together for good.; [a.] Sanborn, NY

WERNER, CHRISTINA M.
[b.] April 3, 1983, Brooklyn, NY; [p.] Patricia S. Werner; [ed.] P.S. 153; [hon.] Creative Writing Art; [pers.] Writing makes me feel good and it also makes people feel happy when they read what I write, when people are happy, so am I.; [a.] Brooklyn, NY

WESSEL, CELESTE
[b.] April 12, 1920, New York City, NY; [p.] Michel and Marie Fontrier; [m.] Vincent Wessel, April 12, 1952; [ch.] David Deyo; [ed.] High School Grad, two yrs. NY University, later, College level courses in Art and Languages; [occ.] Retired P.R.; [memb.] Charter member AWRT (American Women in Radio and TV.) NYC. Other NYC and L.I. Assns. e.g. Publicity, P.R. journalistic, L.I. and NYC Social Welfare organizations; [oth. writ.] As Religious and Educational Dir. for MBS, NY wrote radio pgms, etc. NBC, NYC and far West affiliates wrote diverse pgms, etc. etc. Voluminous writings for various Media, L.I. NYC journalistic, creative, etc. and Social Welfare; [pers.] I believe achievement can be best measured in what it accomplishes for humanity.; [a.] Elizaville, NY

WESTERN, M. WAYNE
[b.] May 4, 1936, Deseret, UT; [p.] Marion and Myrtle Western; [m.] Dolores B. Western, January 19, 1985; [ch.] Ellen, Mare, Amy, James, (stepchildren) Quinn and Joe; [ed.] B.S. Chemistry, Utah State, Univ. Logan, Utah 1961, J.D. with Honors Geo. Wash. Univ. Washington D.C. 1964; [occ.] Patent Attorney - Thorpa, North and Western, Sandy, UT; [memb.] California State Bar, Utah State Bar, Registered Patent Attorney; [hon.] Scholastic Scholarships Brigham Young Univ. and Utah State Univ. and Phi Beta Sigma National Honorary Society - Runner up Patent Office Society, Student Award 1964; [oth. writ.] Patent Law Articles, unpublished Lyrics and Poems, Published Patents written for clients; [pers.] I like the outdoors and try to identity and harmonize the traits and personalities of humans with nature.; [a.] Sandy, UT

WESTON, CHRISTOPHER
[b.] January 16, 1974, Boston, MA; [p.] Lewis and Loretta Weston; [ed.] Thornton Academy, Emerson College; [occ.] Student, Emerson College; [hon.]

Who's Who Among American High School Students; [pers.] Chaos is the only constant in life. Nothing can be created until something is destroyed. Hail the predecessors of my flesh and all they shall create.; [a.] Boston, MA

WHALEN, JENNIFER A.
[b.] August 2, 1971, South Amboy, NJ; [p.] Kenneth and Susan Miller; [m.] Richard Whalen Jr., June 16, 1990; [ch.] Richard Whalen III; [ed.] Perth Amboy High School, The Berkeley College of Business, Currently enrolled in a journalism/short story writing home study program; [hon.] Dean's List; [oth. writ.] A poem published in Famous Poets Anthology; [pers.] To be happy, truly happy, is the hardest thing you'll ever have to work at being.; [a.] Perth Amboy, NJ

WHEELER, ELLEN
[pen.] Ellen Wheeler; [b.] May 7, 1920, Whitesboro, TX; [m.] Fred Wheeler, April 29, 1938; [ch.] Five children (3 boys, 2 girls) all registered nurses; [ed.] High School - St. Joe ARK Associated Degree Reg. Nurse - Kilgore Jr. College, Kilgore, TX, 1974; [occ.] Registered Nurse (Retired); [memb.] Church of Christ, Poetry Society of Texas (past), East TX Writers Ass. (past); [hon.] Dean's List in College, 1978 Lena Beatrice Morton Award, Poetry S of TX East, TX, Poetry work shop - 1st place in poetry - 1st place in short story - 2nd place in children's story.; [oth. writ.] A poem published in local newspaper at 11 years of age, hundreds of poems, several short stories.; [pers.] I am deeply religious and the central theme of many of my poems is religion and nature. My job as an RN gave me the opportunity to satisfy my need to be of service.; [a.] Longview, TX

WHITE, ANGELA
[b.] January 30, 1950, Florence, AL; [p.] Paul Butler, Dean Butler; [m.] Jimmy White (Deceased), July 25, 1972; [ch.] Rebecca Jane, Tammy Darlene; [ed.] Central High School, Columbia, TN; [occ.] Dining Room Manager, Hillcrest Country Club, Pulaski, TN; [memb.] American Humane Society, Highland Park Baptist Church; [oth. writ.] I have written poetry all my life but have never tried to have them publish before.; [pers.] I enjoy and try to reflect nature by painting on canvas. I try to reflect on the feelings of mankind and how they are influenced by certain events. I have been influenced mostly by the hardships and trials we go through in our lifetime on earth.; [a.] Pulaski, TN

WHITE, CHERYL D. BROWN
[pen.] Aquarius; [b.] February 5, 1954, Philadelphia; [p.] William and Catherine Brown; [ch.] William A. White, Desore M. White, Tyleen D. Brown-Bryont; [ed.] Dover High School - Dover, DE University of Delaware - Newark, Delaware Community College of Philadelphia, Philadelphia, Pennsylvania; [occ.] Homemaker; [oth. writ.] An Aquarius Heart (Poems of Life), Dreams Can Come True (A fantasy), Woody's Playhouse (A play); [pers.] Diamond Unique Jones - (Diamond Girl) born December 29, 1994 is my first grandchild. "Don't be afraid to dream and to go after yourself short, for a dreams can come true."; [a.] Philadelphia, PA

WHITE, JEAN
[b.] May 27, 1927, Athens, CO; [p.] Clinton and Alpha Ash Douglas; [m.] Lawrence O. White, March 13, 1950; [ch.] Craig White, Staci and Amy Beth White (Granddaughters); [ed.] High School Grad, Secretary and Accounting Courses; [occ.] Retired; [a.] Athens, OH

WHITE, JOHN EDWARD
[pen.] Jew, Eddie; [b.] February 2, 1958, Fairmont, WV; [p.] Alyce White, John L. Hood; [m.] Frances Jean White, September 24, 1983; [ch.] Dwight, Shayla, John Jr.; [ed.] 11 yrs. High School, Ged, about 1 1/2 yrs. college; [occ.] Coal Miner - Fireboss - Eastern Coal Corp. Fed mine; [memb.] United Mine Workers Union Local #1570; [hon.] Deacon - 1st Church of God - In Fairmont; [oth. writ.] I wrote another poem called Young Man, Young Man Desert Shield, even though the outcome of the war was different than the poem, I enjoyed writing it!; [pers.] I love truth, in all its applications in my writing or speaking or in just my everyday living.; [a.] Fairmont, WV

WHITEHEAD, ELIZABETH
[b.] January 4, 1983, Houston, TX; [p.] Richard and Cathy Whitehead; [ed.] Entering 7th grade (95-96) at Space Center Intermediate. Attended Ward Elementary through 5-94. (Suburban, Houston); [occ.] Student; [memb.] Activities Advanced Class Honor Student, French horn - Symphonic Band, Piano Student, Book lover, Sports fan.; [oth. writ.] Background of "Buck:" I wrote this poem as an English assignment. I was to begin each line with a preposition - a bit of a challenge! Composed "Buck" Fall, 94 - I was 11 years old at the time.; [a.] Houston, TX

WHITELOCK, RAYMOND
[pen.] Sunshine; [b.] January 8, 1943, London, United Kingdom; [p.] Mamie Whitelock, Leslie Whitelock; [m.] Ann Margaret Whitelock, June 8, 1968; [ch.] Sally Ann Whitelock; [ed.] Willesdon Tech. College London (UK); [occ.] Sales Engineer (Electronics Grp.); [memb.] Royal Television Society, Lions Club, Alpharetta; [pers.] Anything that is enjoyed by people, can only be good for everyone, and the nation.; [a.] Alpharetta, GA

WHITEMAN, ERIC
[pen.] "Grizzy" Eric; [b.] May 5, 1942, Glen Ridge, NJ; [p.] Walter H. Whiteman, Ebythel Whiteman; [ed.] High School; [occ.] Cleak, Goven; [memb.] Livingston Camar Club, Trinity Convey Church; [oth. writ.] Montana Dreams, it "The Cool" Montee Small town; [pers.] I write for the love it, because, I am a poet Irish.; [a.] Livingston, NJ

WHITFIELD, PAUL
[b.] March 18, 1972, Boston; [p.] Denise Whitfield; [ed.] High School Diploma (Brockton High School) 1 year at Massassoit Community College (Brockton); [occ.] Child care worker for Dept. of Youth Services; [oth. writ.] Never had other poems published. Although I have others written if there were to be requests.; [pers.] I feel that everyone deserve a chance in life. No matter what mistakes are made, individuals should keep their head up and keep looking for their pot of gold.; [a.] Stoughton, MA

WHITTEMORE, JOY R.
[b.] January 13, 1971, Poniac, MI; [p.] James and Juliet Whittemore; [ed.] Suncoast Community High School; [occ.] Pharmacy Technician Full-time and Receptionist Part-time; [hon.] 1981 Mathematics, 1983 Science, 1984-85 Handbell Choir, 1987 Physical Education, 1987 Honor Roll, 1988 Honor Roll, 1988-89 Home Economics, 1989 DCT Program, 1989 Outstanding and Exemplary Scholastic Achievements, 1989 Graduation, 1989 400.00 dollars Scholarship from North Area Alternative School; [oth. writ.] As an amateur I have several unpublished poems and lyrics; [pers.] My emotions inspire and stimulate me to write. My goal is to touch people with my poems and lyrics. I would like to be more than an amateur writer.; [a.] Palm Beach Gardens, FL

WIEDERKEHR, JESSICA
[b.] August 4, 1981, Pekin, IL; [p.] Stephen and Pamela Wiederkehr; [ed.] St. Paul's Lutheran School Preschool - 6th, Oklahoma Bible Academy 7th; [occ.] Jubilation Music and Drama Group, St. Paul's Lutheran Church Youth Group; [memb.] National Honor Society, National Math Society; [pers.] Thanks to Mrs. Linda Zander, My Junior High English teacher, for making me for making me write this poem!; [a.] Enid, OK

WIGHT, TARA
[b.] December 9, 1976, Huntington Beach, CA; [p.] Quintin and Vicki Wight; [ed.] Amador Valley High School in Pleasanton, CA.; [occ.] College student at Las Positas College; [pers.] This poem is dedicated to all the birds who lost their lives sin the valdez oil spill in Alaska.; [a.] Plesanton, CA

WILBUR, DONNA R.
[b.] April 13, 1942, Albion, MI; [p.] Lynnford and Charlene Hunt; [m.] Donald L. Wilbur, June 11, 1960; [ch.] Dawn Marie, Gary Lee; [ed.] High School Graduate, 1 1/2 years Community College; [occ.] Breakfast Opener for Burger King; [memb.] Community Church of God in Marshall, MI.; [hon.] Honor Student with 4. Aug. Received Scholarship Award to Kellogg Community College; [oth. writ.] Poem published in after the storm - published in April, 1995; [pers.] I love all types of poetry. I strive to live a life pleasing and tree to others. To help make this place a better world to live in. Something to hard down to my children.; [a.] Albion, MI

WILBUR, WILLIAM BREWSTER
[b.] August 25, 1909, Hanford, CA; [p.] William H. and Candace Wilbur; [m.] Charlotte H. Wilbur, March 21, 1937; [ch.] William G. and Carol Lynn Wilbur; [ed.] Tulare High School, U.C. Davis, Ext. Courses Stanford U., Salinas Jr. College; [occ.] Retired; [memb.] North Minster Pres Church, Salinas, CA; [oth. writ.] Poems and Short Stories; [pers.] Take pride in doing ones best. Take pride in doing ones best - God will do the rest; [a.] Salinas, CA

WILHELMY, GUS
[b.] February 17, 1935, Saint Paul, MN; [p.] George and Emily Wilhelmy; [m.] Mary Vallely, September 1, 1990; [ch.] Rochelle, Rebecca, Todd; [ed.] Good Counsel High, Passionist Academic Inst., Univ. of MI, Univ. of WI, Univ. of Saint Louis; [occ.] Fund Raising Consultant; [memb.] National Society of Fund Raising Executives, American Marketing Assoc., American Management Assoc., Chicago Assoc of Technical Assistance Providers; [hon.] Martin Luther King Community Leadership Award, Outstanding Young Man of America Award, Head Start Distinguished Service Award; [oth. writ.] Spirit Magazine of Poetry, Horizons - Univ. of Indiana Business School, Our Sunday Visitor, The Passionist, Louisville Courier Journal; [pers.] I strive to share the depths of my emotional experience, poetry allows me to reveal my inner being and in that come into touch with a Universal self we all share.; [a.] Chicago, IL

WILKINS, JANICE
[b.] July 7, 1948; [m.] Harry F. Wilkins III, October 21, 1972; [ch.] Patrick - 16, Ashley - 12; [ed.] BA in English; [occ.] Writer and Poet; [memb.] Arizona Lupus Foundation (Where I also do volunteer work), Arizona Humane Society; [hon.] Dean's List throughout College; [pers.] I am an avid reader and perpetual student of all literary forms, especially fiction and poetry.; [a.] Phoenix, AZ

WILKINS, JASON
[b.] September 13, 1981, Soldotna, AK; [p.] Gordon and Nancy Wilkins; [ed.] 9th Grade Student at Skyview High School Soldotna, AK; [occ.] Student; [memb.] World Tang Soo Do Assoc. - Sterling Do Jang.; [hon.] Academic Pentathalon Winner - 1st Overall - Varsity Div. and 1st, 2nd and 3rd place medals.; [a.] Sterling, AK

WILLIAMS, ALLYN LEARLENA
[b.] March 10, 1973, Peoria, IL; [p.] Barbara Williams and Alfred Williams; [m.] Stephen B. Wiley, June 1995; [ed.] Whitnall High School, Morris Brown College; [occ.] Struggling College Student and Sales Representative; [pers.] God only gives you as much as you can handle. With the love and support of God and your family.... you can accomplish anything you set your mind.; [a.] Dunwoody, GA

WILLIAMS, CLETA
[b.] December 6, 1914, Farmersville, TX; [p.] Cleve and Ollie Mae Marshall; [m.] Fred K. Williams (Deceased), January 25, 1934; [ch.] Peggy Marlene Williams (Deceased), Jackie D. N. Williams, Billy K. Williams, Michieltoe Williams; [ed.] High School; [occ.] Housewife; [memb.] Disabled American Da Va. Auxiliary; [hon.] Have won several Pins and Trophies through the years; [oth. writ.] Have written several poems and articles for Wichita Record News. One of my poems published in World's Book of Poetry at Sacramento, California.; [pers.] Have been Auxiliary Chaplain, since 1980. Have been Americanism Chairman since 1982.; [a.] Wichita Falls, TX

WILLIAMS, JONELL WARD
[b.] May 29, 1971, Wilmington, NC; [p.] Paul and Sandra Ward; [m.] John Williams, July 24, 1994; [ed.] B.A. in English from Meredith College, graduate student at NCSU in Student Development; [hon.] NC Teaching Fellow, Dean's List, Alpha Lambda Delta; [pers.] God's creation is inspiring, and I want to share what he shows me.; [a.] Raleigh, NC

WILLIAMS, JOYCE NADINE
[b.] June 10, 1932, Indiana; [p.] Russel and Mary Van Valkenburg; [m.] Ronald Williams, February 14, 1993; [ch.] Bradley, Robert and Todd McTaggart; [ed.] Britton High School; [occ.] Nurse Aide Lenawee County Dept on Aging; [memb.] Bread of Life, Ministry; [oth. writ.] Short Stories; [pers.] The Lord said pick up your pen and write. So I will put my talent down as God inspires me to do so.; [a.] Adrian, MI

WILLIAMS, LUCY L.
[b.] August 23, 1940, Guthrie, KY; [p.] Roscoe and Eddie Mary Taylor; [m.] Mr. Shirley Williams, December 30, 1960; [ch.] Adrienne Denise, Michael L., Ronald S., Bryant K., Jason L., and Marcus Scott (Adrienne's son); [ed.] Chestnut/Walnut Grd. Lincoln Elem. - Lincoln High Bramwells Business College, ISU Extension College, Lockyears Business College, U of E University; [occ.] Community Service Aide, EHA - Evansville Housing Authority; [memb.] Mt. olive Galilee Missionary Baptist Church - American Bible Society, 21st Century Parent Project - Haitian Child Survival Comm., Mt. Olive M. B. State CSacramento Ohio Valley District Association; [hon.] 2nd place Noma Business Award, Nominee of Black Women of Year Award, Winner of Valentine Contest Evansville Press, President Women's Art. of stated Convention - President Women's and of Stated District; [oth. writ.] Many discourses for Area Churches and Conventions and other cities and states - Church Bulletin; [pers.] Quote! If I can help somebody along the way, then my living has not been in vain. Praise God from whom all of my blessings flow. I started writing letter at age 10-12 for a neighbor, who asked me to write to her daughter in Ohio. The neighbor, Ms. Hazel, gave me $.25 for each letter. My family was very poor, this gave me $.25 to eat lunch at school at lease one (1) a day. I enjoy writing, it is a personal talk with one's self.; [a.] Eranville, IN

WILLIAMS, MELANIE N.
[b.] February 25, 1974, Virginia; [p.] Melvin and Irene Williams; [ch.] Jasmin T. Williams; [ed.] Highlands Springs High, VA., Virginia Union University, VA; [occ.] Full-Time Student; [hon.] Who's Who among American High School Students, Sergeant in Marine Corps Jr. ROTC; [a.] Richmond, VA

WILLIAMS, MISTIE LEA
[pen.] Mistie L. Williams; [b.] January 24, 1963, Rockford, IL; [p.] Alice M. Crisp, Henry A. Truett; [ed.] High School Grad., some college; [occ.] Certified Nurses Asst.; [pers.] I love writing poetry it helps to relieve the stress of relationships and everyday living.; [a.] Mount North Grove, MO

WILLIAMS, SUZANNE
[b.] December 10, 1962, Barberton, OH; [ch.] Charles B. Williams, Stephanie L. Williams; [ed.] Data Processing Degree; [occ.] Local Area Network Administrator; [oth. writ.] Several unpublished poems; [pers.] Poetry gives you the power to shower beauty and creativity into a remembered experience and the challenge to emotionally move the reader in its contents. It refreshes life!; [a.] Norton, OH

WILLIAMS, TRAVIS
[pen.] Travis B. Williams; [b.] September 5, 1979; [p.] Tag and Debbie Williams; [ed.] I Attend Lee Scott Academy. When I graduate I plan to attend the University of Alabama at major in LAW.; [memb.] I am a member of the LSA Band, Key Club, SGA, Basket Ball Team, Track Team, and on the Drama Team and Tennis Team; [hon.] 3rd Place in District and state drama Festival, and named to the all state cast, nominated for Who's Who, and passing the 9th grade.; [oth. writ.] I have had two poems, selected for publication, and a short story that is being considered for publication in Boy's Life; [pers.] "Emotions are often expressed as words.... so take a few minutes and write them down." I would also like to thank Mrs. P. Scott for her encouragement to write.; [a.] Hurtsboro, AL

WILLIAMS, MS. VERLYN D.
[b.] November 20, 1952, Saint Louis, MO; [oth. writ.] Several unpublished poems such as, "One-of-a-kind Dad," "Motherhood: At It's Best", "The Greatest Story Ever Told", "Saying Goodbye to Yesterday", and several others.; [pers.] I delight in sharing my faith in God through my poetry writings. God bless the written word - it is as piercing as the spoken.; [a.] Saint Louis, MO

WILLIAMSON, BILLY
[pen.] Billy Williamson; [b.] November 4, 1957, Newnan, GA; [p.] Bill Williamson Sr., Betty Johnson; [m.] Mandy Williamson, February 4, 1983; [ch.] Cathy Lynn, David Lamar, Amanda Jo, Samantha Jo; [ed.] Newnan High School; [occ.] Inmate-Rivers Correctional Institute Hardwick, GA; [pers.] I never really appreciated the beauty of life, love, or poetry until my incarceration. Now that is all that matters to me.; [a.] Newnan, GA

WILLIAMSON, LA GOLDIA
[pen.] Goldie Green; [b.] April 14, 1946, Detroit, MI; [p.] James Jeff Davis Green, Ruth Macy Faye Charles Green; [m.] Willie A. Williamson, June 13, 1964; [ch.] Trisa, Aaron, Corey, Stacey, Alaina, Rachelle; [ed.] M.S. Elem. Educ. Commerce High, University of the District of Columbia, VA. Commonwealth Univ.; [occ.] Library Media Spec. Stuart Elementary, Richmond, VA; [memb.] ALA (Library Amer. Assoc.), Bethel Temple Church Choir; [hon.] Singing Awards, Various Public Speaking Awards; [oth. writ.] Book "Pele The Great King" children's book; [pers.] I enjoy bringing joy to children through literature.; [a.] Richmond, VA

WILSON, CAROLYN MAE
[pen.] Caddie; [b.] May 5, 1939, Liberty Co, Hinesville, GA; [p.] Addie Lee Wells and William Elwyn; [m.] Robert Edward Wilson Mobley, December 20, 1958; [ch.] Kathy, Michael, Debbie, Bobby, Mary, Margaret, Jimmy and George; [ed.] H.S. 2 yr., College - GA Souther University, (Statesboro, GA) 1 quarter - Kennesaw State, Kennesaw GA.; [occ.] Deli-Manager; [memb.] St Thomas Agrinas Church Alpharetta, GA. Tops GA 273 - Woodstoch, GA.; [hon.] Honor graduate Beta Club Secretary F-H-A. President Secretary Tops Leader Tops Co-Leader Tops Wt Reonder Tops; [oth. writ.] Just Poetry; [pers.] I attribute all my accomplishments and successes to my everlasting faith in my personal savior Jesus Christ. Without him I am nothing.; [a.] Woodstock, GA

WILSON, CLYDE
[pen.] Lex Argot; [b.] November 8, 1920, Alameda, CA; [p.] Clyde Sr, and Melva; [m.] Barbara Darrimon Wilson, June 26, 1943; [ch.] Karna, Clyde III, Dean, Janinne; [ed.] Alameda High; [occ.] Retired; [memb.] International Society of Poets; [hon.] U.S. Patent #3752766 Editor's Choice Award 1994; [oth. writ.] Poems in: "Reflections of light", "East of Sunrise", "A Delicate Balance", "Best Poems of 1996"; [pers.] "May your mettle surpass the crucible of challenge and change".; [a.] Moraga, CA

WILSON, DOROTHY G.
[b.] March 1, 1944, San Diego, CA; [p.] Eugene and Dorothy Hughey; [ch.] Stacie Weber, Dorothy Tate, Thomas R. Wilson, 8 grandchildren; [ed.] Santa Ana High, Rancho Santiago Junior College; [occ.] Secretary; [oth. writ.] Several poems; [pers.] Do your best, accept your limitations, realize the possibilities.; [a.] Garden Grove, CA

WILSON, HESTER
[b.] June 19, 1925, Wayne County; [p.] William and Herder Fleming; [m.] Richard Lee Wilson, June 8, 1945; [ch.] Leevaghn Wilson; [ed.] 8th Grade; [occ.] Retired; [memb.] Parkplace Baptist Church, N.N. School Bus Service; [hon.] Ordained Minister, Certificate for Foster Kids, Work with Battered Women; [pers.] I educated myself from the eight grade. I'm inspire by God to write poems. Also the songs I write, I sing them in Church. God is my inspiration!; [a.] Hampton, VA

WILSON, JODY
[pen.] Big Cat Daddy, Knuckled Head; [b.] July 12, 1970, Newport Beach, CA; [p.] Laverne-Sherley Wilson; [m.] Angie Wilson, March 21, 1993; [ch.] Josey Michael Wilson; [ed.] Corona del Mar High Newport Beach CA, Iowa Western Community College; [occ.] Mechanic's helper; [memb.] Kirkman Methodist Church; [hon.] Awards for Football and PTTA Scholarship; [oth. writ.] For the Iowa meet people paper; [a.] Hurlan, IA

WILSON, LINDA S.
[b.] October 15, 1942, Neelyville, MO; [p.] John T. and Thelma Franklin; [ch.] Victoria Lynn Meyers, Karen Lea Jones and Brian Keith Wilson; [ed.] Hardin Jr. High - Mexico, MO, Mexico High - Mexico, MO, Roosevelt High, St Louis, MO; [occ.] Food Service Manager for Harbor Light Center (St. L.) Salvation Army; [memb.] Baptist Church - I work for a drug and alcohol Rehab. Center; [hon.] I am honored that God has awarded me the gift of poetry, from other, as well as being able to write.; [oth. writ.] Poetry for Church Bulletins. A collection of spiritual poems. "The Trail Of Tears," "Jesus Was A Carpenter," and many others.; [pers.] "What does not destroy me, strengthens me" is the motto that I try to live by. James J. Metcalf is my favorite poet.; [a.] Saint Louis, MO

WILSON, MYRTLE
[pen.] Millery Winston; [b.] April 1, 1940, Linden, TX; [p.] Grand and Arvelia Whitman; [m.] Divorced; [ch.] Pamela D. Green, Keith R. Green, Alaric D. Wilson; [ed.] James Madison High, Business Courses, Dallas County Comm. Colleges; [occ.] Self Employed, Wilson's Secretarial Service; [memb.] Member-Tabernacle of Praise Baptist Church, Member-Economic Development Ministry, Member-Sunshine Ministry; [oth. writ.] Many poems, none published; [pers.] My poetic expressions are dedicated to the memory of my deceased son Alaric D. Wilson.; [a.] Dallas, TX

WILSON, SONIA LOWIS
[b.] May 10, 1936, Sussex, England; [p.] Lallie Lee and Geoffrey Rollo Lowis; [ch.] Guy, Jonathan, Richard (Deceased) Christopher, David; [ed.] Church Missionary Society School in Limpsfield Chart Surrey, England, Cordon Blev Culinary Institute and Katinka Dress Design, London; [occ.] Wife, Hostess, Mother, Writer, Gardener, Tennis and Bridge Player, Needle Pointer; [memb.] St. Columba's Episcopal Chapel Middletown, Newport Preservation Society, English Speaking Union, Clambake Club, Spouting Rock Beach Association, Redwood Library; [hon.] None, this is the first time I've submitted anything; [oth. writ.] A novel based on my parent's lives depicting a way of life which depicting a way of life which radically changed in England after the 2nd World War. I hope to find a publisher for it and I'll completed 2nd Novel on my life.; [pers.] I try to portray people and emotions honesty to give readers a sense of recognition and comfort as they experience other's response to life's many challenges.; [a.] Newport, RI

WINCHOWKY, LAWRENCE
[b.] August 4, 1970, Milwaukee, WI; [p.] Walter and Elizabeth Winchowky; [ed.] Eisenhower High, New Berlin, WI, Marquette University, Milwaukee, University. of Wisc. - Milw., Milw.; [occ.] Marketing Secretary, Orlando, FL; [memb.] National Honor Society; [pers.] Life has been very good to me. Writing is my way of returning the favor.; [a.] Longwood, FL

WINIASZ, EDWARD
[b.] August 26, 1917, Lorain; [p.] John and Sophia Winiasz; [m.] Ethel Winiasz (Deceased, March 30, 1995), August 22, 1942; [ch.] Michael, Jerome and Thomas Winiasz; [ed.] Graduated Lorain High, Class 1935, Attended Ohio State University 1939 and 1940; [occ.] Retired President of A.D.I. Advanced Design Industries, Inc. which I started in 1955.; [pers.] As many professionals in our society, the least recognized and appreciated are the nurses. To them I dedicate my poem "Angel In White."

WISE, JOAN
[pen.] Jone; [b.] December 11, 1934, Savannah, GA; [p.] Henry and Helen Rocker; [m.] Divorced; [ch.] Stacey Wise; [ed.] Pape Girls School, Savannah, GA graduated Harwich High, Cape Cod Mass., Creative writing; [occ.] Executive Secretary at former ILGWU now UNITE; [memb.] Edgewater Ladies Auxiliary EPOC Beautification Committee, City Island Poetry Reading At Lauras; [hon.] Movie Poonis "Dress Up Your Neighborhood" Award and Grant 1994; [pers.] My early experience around the 5th and 6th grade teacher was a lasting impression and influence which I keep going back to throughout my life.; [a.] Throggs Neck Bronx, NY

WISE, SEQUOIA
[pen.] Sequoia Wise; [b.] December 17, 1979, Guthrie; [p.] Bill Wise; [ed.] Junior High; [occ.] Babysitting; [memb.] Midsouth Youth Rodeo Cowboy Association (MRCA); [hon.] MRCA Finalists; [a.] Marlow, OK

WISNIEWSKI, LILLIAN
[pen.] Lill Wise; [b.] October 3, 1933, Tyre, MI; [p.] Walter Ertman-Bektha; [m.] George Wisniewski, November 15, 1952; [ch.] Jackie Howell, Karen Gould, Teresa, Noel Sue Isken; [occ.] Housewife; [memb.] The Smithsonian, Associates - American, Museum of Natural History; [oth. writ.] Personal opinions published in Detroit Newspaper - won "Name The Story" in magazine in "56".; [pers.] My interests are totally widespread, ranging from literary to cartoons, to poetry and crossword puzzles, to opera and travelling, dancing and singing and a "fascinating neighbor", interested in everything.; [a.] Warren, MI

WITHERINGTON, MARK
[b.] February 4, 1970, Maron, GA; [p.] Willa Dean Cooper and James W. Witherington Jr.; [ed.] Raban County High School 3 yrs. College, Piedmont College, Merier University; [occ.] Mill Worker for Fruit of the Loom; [hon.] Honorary Citizen of Farmer's Branch, Texas; [oth. writ.] Currently writing a Book (Fiction) titled "A Rose, a thorn my Heart Prefers"; [pers.] I'm more conceited with the things I don't have, then the things I do have.; [a.] Clayton, GA

WOOD, BRIAN L.
[pen.] Elwood; [b.] January 18, 1973, NJ; [p.] Sandra and Sam Wood; [ed.] North Plainfield High, Raritan Valley Community College; [occ.] Student; [oth. writ.] Various poems and some short stories.; [a.] Northfield, NJ

WOODALL, THELMA MAE
[pen.] Thelma Woodall; [b.] August 11, 1971, Anchorage, AK; [p.] Fannie and William Woodall; [m.] George Raymond Thompson (common law), July 4, 1985; [ch.] Raylen Marie Thompson, Renae Alice Thompson; [ed.] King Career Center; [occ.] Oaken Keg Anchorage, AK; [pers.] I have been writing since Jr. High. I enjoy sharing my writing. I hope my writing helps people in a positive way.; [a.] Anchorage, AK

WOODMORE, PEGGY JO SMITH
[b.] December 28, 1976, Nashville, TN; [p.] Helen Silcox and John Smith; [m.] Shannon Woodmore, April 11, 1995; [ed.] Smith Country High School Graduated 1995; [occ.] Full-time wife; [memb.] Navy Wifeline Association; [hon.] Who's Who Among American High School Students, National Honor Roll, National Honor Society; [oth. writ.] Poems printed in high school annual, poem on graduation program; [pers.] I let my poems represent my feelings on subjects that are dear to my heart. My views on many of life's issues show through in my poetry.; [a.] Carthage, TN

WOODWARD SR., TYRONE E.
[pen.] Tyrone E. Woodward Sr.; [b.] April 22, 1955, Philadelphia, PA; [p.] Oreeda and Virgil Woodward; [m.] Carol A. Woodward, June 14, 1986; [ch.] Tyrone Jr. and Fontella; [ed.] Simon Gratz High, P.T.C. Career Institute, Community College of Philadelphia and Cheyney Univ.; [occ.] Nursing Asst.; [memb.] World Affairs Council of Philadelphia, WH. Pisgalt Church, The National Union of the Homeless, and V.I.P. Blood Donor for the Red Cross; [hon.] Little League M.V.P. Amateur Boxer, High School Football and Track and Field, Letters Jr. College Basketball Team Captain.; [oth. writ.] Lyrics to the song "This Love" that will be released by Hilltop Records in the Spring of 1996.; [pers.] I am a recovering addict with 15 months clean. If you do drugs stop. If you don't do drugs don't start. And whichever you go, take the Lord with you.; [a.] Philadelphia, PA

WOOLARD, DARYL NATHAN
[b.] January 25, 1979, Washington, NC; [p.] Dewey W. Woolard and LaRue H. Woolard; [ed.] Junior at Northside High School Beaufort County, NC; [occ.] Student; [memb.] A.R.T.S. Club (Northside High School), Rosemary Church of Christ; [hon.] Perfect attendance award for 7 years from North Carolina Public Schools; [oth. writ.] The Ocean of Beauty, Someone For Me, Date With An Angel, Back Off Satan; [pers.] The Lord has given everyone special talents, I guess that this is just one of mine, and I'll work on it along with the others I find when I grow older. Trust in the Lord, try your best, and everything will workout for the best.; [a.] Washington, NC

WORSHAM, MARYELLEN PERDUE
[b.] June 11, 1930, Waverly, KY; [p.] Annie and Joseph Perdue; [m.] Stanley A. Worsham, November 15, 1947; [ch.] 2 Girls (1948-1990 Becky Wilson) Lisa Jecarole Norris; [occ.] Retired; [memb.] DAR and International Society of Poets; [oth. writ.] "Death Of A Poet", "Prayer On A Hill", "Moon Vine" and 100 more poems, some have already been published.; [pers.] I can paint your canvas heart with poetry - your eyes with pictures of my life.

WRIGHT, LOUISE M.
[b.] August 31, 1931, Morgantown, WV; [p.] George and Helen Wood; [m.] Divorced; [ch.] William Kenneth Miller and Sherry Wright; [ed.] Morgantown High and two years of business college at the Stenotype Institute, Washington, D.C.; [occ.] Secretary, Government Relations Office of the Communications Workers of America. (Previous: Library of Congress, U.S. Senate and U.S. House of Representatives. Over 39 years); [memb.] Charter Member of the National Museum of Women in the Arts; [hon.] While in high School I received a monetary award and a gold "Quiz Kid" key for a poem I wrote entitled, "What America Means to Me."; [oth. writ.] I have written poetry over the years but the first one submitted for any type of consideration as an adult was 1994 when I entered the North American Open Poetry Contest for 1995 and my poem, "Sarah's Cry" was published in the National Library of Poetry Anthology entitled, Songs on the Wind.; [pers.] I enjoy writing about people and nature, creating "poetry pictures," and analogies as a special challenge. I always hope my work will inspire and strive for this.; [a.] Alexandria, VA

WRIGHT, TAMMY LEE
[b.] March 7, 1969; [p.] Marjorie Elizabeth Reck; [m.] Carlton Lee Wright, February 14, 1989; [ch.] Kayla Lee Wright; [ed.] Serrano High School, Cal State University San Bernardino; [occ.] Student, studying Physical Educ. (BS) Psychology (minor) Recreation (minor). Studying to be a, "Rec. therapist". I'm also a volunteer at the, "Center for Individuals with disabilities".; [hon.] Honor roll in H.S. (10th) received awards and patches for participating and completing "Jump Rope for Heart Contest". Finalist in," Writing Celebration" 11th grade, for a poem I wrote.; [oth. writ.] Since a young girl, I've loved to sing and write poems. In 11th grade my music talents was recognized (by my chorus director). Soon after, 3 songs that I wrote: "Scotty" "The Lonely" and "Does she remind you of me" were all recorded on a "Demo" tape in Hollywood (payed by my school).; [pers.] I'd like to thank God for blessing me with such a beautiful talent. Writing poems and songs have always allowed me to express my "deepest" feelings. Loving and caring is the greatest gift of all, and what better way to express it than with a poem or song.; [a.] San Bernardino, CA

WRIGHT, THOMAS M.
[pen.] Wizard; [b.] February 27, 1973, Kenton, OH; [p.] Deborah Cook and Michael Wright; [ch.] K. Jade Michael Wright; [ed.] Graduated from Riverdale High School; [pers.] The poem living limbo is dedicated to my father. For he taught me 'It's always darkest before the dawn.' My Iluvatar be kind to him.; [a.] Forest, OH

WRIGHT, TIKOYO DEON
[b.] May 3, 1986, Burlington, NC; [p.] Tina V. Walker; [m.] Dr. Mihaly Bartalos (Best Friend); [ed.] The Robert J. Christea School, 5550 Riverdale Avenue Riverdale, NY 10471; [occ.] Trying to get a life; [memb.] St. Margaret's Church 6000 Riverdale Ave. Riverdale, NY 10471; [hon.] To be a good boy; [pers.] I love you mama and Mihaly. You are the best.

WU, LILY T.
[b.] October 9, 1967; [p.] Carol and Michael Wu; [m.] Hoang Le, February 14, 1991; [ch.] Isabella and Alan Le; [ed.] University of Hawaii, School of Architecture; [hon.] Miss Chinatown Hawaii 1989, Miss Future Business Leader (2nd place) various scholarship to the Honolulu Academy of Art; [pers.] Besides writing poetry. I enjoy music and love to draw and paint. A world without creative expression, whether written, physical (as in dance) or visual is unthinkable!; [a.] Kaneohe, HI

YANTIS, JENNIFER ROSE
[pen.] Yenny; [b.] October 2, 1978, Hanover; [p.] Mike and Carol Yantis; [ed.] 8 years of Elementary School, still in High School (Junior); [occ.] Student; [hon.] 1st place in Essay Contest on "What Pro-life means to me." Two Basketball trophies from Grade School, Members of the #1 Club in school; [oth. writ.] Wrote a book entitled "Quest For Peace" for sophomore English class. Miscellaneous poems and compositions for school; [pers.] "This poem is my own interpretation of life itself. The cycle of life is vital to the existence of humanity and humanity's fate. Without it we would be soulless."; [a.] McSherrystown, PA

YARBROUGH, LAMONICA
[b.] August 6, 1971, Houston, TX; [ed.] Current Journalism student at University of Houston, High School at Ross S. Sterling, Houston; [occ.] U.S. Postal Service; [memb.] National Thespian Society, Disabled American Veterans, and American Postal Workers Union; [hon.] Exemplary Student Award 88-89, Best Actress (UIL - One Act Play Comp) '88-'89, and Honorable Mention (UIL - One Act Play Comp) '87; [oth. writ.] Several poems, one published due to previous entry of National Library of Poetry Contest; [pers.] My goal is to send out a message that everyone can relate to regardless of the person's cultural background.; [a.] Houston, TX

YASHARIAN, MARGARET T.
[b.] July 6, 1973; [p.] Havard and Terry; [ed.] Chenango Valley High School. Broome Community College, Binghamton, NY; [occ.] Certified Medical Assistant; [hon.] President's list, Dean's list; [oth. writ.] My own collection that has never been published; [pers.] When I started writing I was 16. It was just my own thoughts and emotions which turned out to be poems.; [a.] Binghamton, NY

YI, INKUK
[b.] August 29, 1977; [ed.] Kalani High School; [occ.] Attending Kapi'olani Community College; [oth. writ.] Poems to and about the girl I love; [pers.] I would like to think God, my teachers, and everyone who has shown, or taught me something. Most importantly my 12th grade English teacher, Michael Doran, who showed me this thing called poetry. I am influenced by what I see, hear, and feel.; [a.] Honolulu, HI

YIELDING, DANIELLE
[b.] March 22, 1986, Jackson, MI; [p.] Sandra Yielding; [ed.] 4th Grade; [occ.] Student; [memb.] Girl Scouts; [hon.] Tecumseh Rotary Club; [oth. writ.] Poem published in Anthology of Poetry by Young Americans; [pers.] I enjoy writing stories and poetry and hope someday to become a children's author.; [a.] Tecumseh, MI

YOHN, JEFFERSON D.
[b.] February 18, 1917, Urbana, MO; [p.] Leonard and Orpha Yohn; [m.] Martha Elizabeth, October 23, 1965; [ed.] Washington High, University of Portland, B.A. and M.A. degrees; [occ.] Retired Editor. Currently a columnist and editorial for a twice-a-week newspaper writer.; [memb.] Delta Epsilon Sigma. Association of American Editorial Cartoonists. 50 - year mason; [hon.] 13 Freedoms Foundation Awards. Sierra Cascade Forest Award. Christopher Gold Medal. American Medical Assn. Award. Christian and Jews Mass Media Award. Valedictorian for B.A. (Graduated Maxima Cum Laude), M.A. with Cum Laude; [oth. writ.] The Preface (University Literary Magazine); [pers.] "A poet works in the Realm of Angels".; [a.] Sacramento, CA

YOUNG, NOAH
[b.] August 26, 1978, Newark, OH; [p.] Dave and Betty Young; [ed.] High School; [occ.] Camp Counselor; [memb.] Thespian; [hon.] Eagle Scout; [pers.] I owe my beginning and slow start to Mary Kay Bocher a drama teacher at Newark High for believing in me and helping me write my first poem.; [a.] Newark, OH

YOUNG, VICKIE
[b.] June 8, 1931, Saint Charles, IL; [p.] James Smith, Lois Tranby; [ch.] Kelly and Randy; [ed.] M.A. (Special Ed.) Northeastern Illinois Univ.; [occ.] Education Specialist and Jr. College Instructor; [memb.] Northeastern Illinois, Univ. Alumni, Association of Humanistic Psychology; [hon.] National Merit Award, Dean's list; [oth. writ.] Professional papers, unpublished poems, family biography - prose published poem, "A Tear From The Sky"; [pers.] I believe all people are called to inspire one another and that doing so is both our privilege and our responsibility.; [a.] Winfield, IL

YOUNGER, MARY E.
[b.] July 10, 1933, Elmhurst, IL; [p.] John Younger, Marie Younger; [ed.] High School Equivelent, Some College Classes; [occ.] Clerk; [oth. writ.] I have written many poems and a few short stories, but I have never had anything published; [pers.] I enjoy writing very much. Most all my poems have been inspired by God. I enjoy nature, so most of my poetry reflection nature.; [a.] Villa Park, IL

YOUNGQUIST, ROSEMARY P.
[b.] October 18, 1929, Stratford, CT; [p.] George and Caroline Pickering; [m.] Robert Philip Youngquist, January 21, 1956; [ch.] Robert Varson, Nancy Stone, Susan Lea; [occ.] Housewife; [a.] Vershire, VT

YULE, JOEDY A.
[pen.] Joedy Yule; [b.] March 26, 1934, Long Branch, NJ; [m.] Thomas, October 13, 1956; [ch.] Kathi, Ippolito, Nancy, Glenn; [ed.] Long Branch Senior High. Richmond Professional Institute (College of William and Mary). Studied Fashion Design.; [occ.] Retired Mgr. of Travel Agency, Self employed, silk flower arranging paint on T's, sweats, chairs; [memb.] Church Elder, Christian Educ. Comm. member, ISP Distinguished Member, Auburndale Improvement Assoc., AARP, Arbor Day Foundation, NAFE, Women in the Arts; [hon.] Editors Choice Award for

"A Time to See" in the 1994 NLP's anthology "Echoes of Yesterday". Editors Choice Award for "Winds of Change" in NLP's anthology "Best Poems of 1995". Both poems were selected for "Sound of Poetry".; [pers.] I started writing poetry in 1994, as words from everywhere, any time and place appeared. I dreamed of writing as a child before many other dreams came to fruition. By expressing my feelings in poetry, I seek to help and inspire others to ease this journey - life I believe that if you dare to live your dreams to soar with eagles rise above the madden crowds clouds of fear and fly with his light of love...; [a.] Whitestone, NY

ZAFFINO, CONNIE K.
[b.] June 25, 1942, Detroit, MI; [p.] Joseph and Kathryn Markiewicz; [ch.] James Anthony Zaffino, Lisa Janine Siegfried, Maria Catherine Zaffino (Deceased); [ed.] Fordson High - Dearborn Michigan; [oth. writ.] Letter to the Editor in the West Orlando Times; [pers.] We are all poets if we put our true feelings in pen.

ZAMPELLA, VIRGINIA
[b.] 5/11/79, Paris, France; [p.] Chantal & Jacob Zampella; [ed.] high school so far, I'm only in 11th grade; [occ.] student; [hon.] Honor Roll, B Honor Roll-1995; [pers.] Our children are time capsules, sent to a place and time that we will never see.; [a.] Kannapolis, NC

ZARREH, MEHRDAD
[pen.] Mehrdad Zarreh; [b.] December 26, 1964, Tehran, Iran; [p.] Bahram Zarreh, Maryam Safaee-Nikoo; [ed.] Technical High School of Tehran, Technical College of Tehran; [occ.] Machinist, Tool and Mold Maker; [oth. writ.] Several poems in Persian language; [pers.] I strive to reflect the goodness of mankind and to show a real picture of life. I have been greatly influenced by the realism.; [a.] Coral Springs, FL

ZEC, ROBERT J.
[b.] February 12, 1950, Philadelphia, PA; [p.] Frank Zec Jr., Sabina Zec; [ed.] Holy Cross Elementary Caesar Rodney High School; [occ.] Truck driver; [oth. writ.] This was the only one I submitted; [pers.] In life as you take, you must give.; [a.] Magnolia, DE

ZERIN, EDWARD
[b.] May 5, 1920; [m.] Marjory Fisher, October 27, 1946; [ch.] Jonathan (Attorney), Wendy (Physician), Michael (Physician), five grandchildren; [ed.] University of Delaware, B.A., Phi Kappa Phi Honorary Scholastic Society, Hebrew Union College-Bachelor of Hebrew Letters, 1942, Master of Hebrew Letters, 1946, Ordination as Rabbi, 1946, Honorary Doctor of Divinity, 1971, University of Southern California, Master of Science in Education, 1950, University of Southern California, Ph.D. with areas of concentration in Religious Education, Psychology of Religion, Old Testament and New Testament, 1953, Boston University, Research Associate in Philosophy of Science with emphasis on the work of Sir Karl Popper, Graduate training and Licensure (1974) as a California Marriage and Family Therapist; [occ.] 1954-77 Faculty, 1946-present Founding National Chair of the Chesky Institute for Judaism and psychotherapy of the Central Conference of American Rabbis; [oth. writ.] Living Judaism, Our Jewish Neighbors, Justice and Judaism, The Birth of the Torah, "Dreams and Visions" in That Day with God, What Catholics and Other Christians should Know About Jews, The "Q" Model for the Effective Management of Personal Stress, When Your Patient has a Drinking Problem and Six Difficult Patients, 1946-present over 25 articles in professional journals; [a.] Westlake Village, CA

ZIMMERMAN, PATSY
[b.] July 28, 1951, Wauseon, OH; [p.] Orval and Marian Zimmerman; [ed.] Stryker High School, Northwest State Community College; [occ.] Account Clerk, Four County Vocational School, Archbold, OH; [memb.] Ohio Education Association; [hon.] Honor graduate from Stryker High, Dean's List; [a.] Napoleon, OH

Index of Poets

A

Abbas, Batul Jeddy 235
Abejon, Celestina F. 7
Abel II, Thomas Paul 511
Abella, Raquel 381
Abeytia, Anisa 541
Abrahim, Joseph 37
Acevedo, Judith 523
Acosta, Raymond J. 516
Adamiec, Walter S. 574
Adams, Annette 240
Adams, Cairo W. 400
Adams, Elaine M. 121
Adams, George Jacob 530
Adams, Jason 332
Adams, Kerry W. 584
Adams, Patrice 374
Adams, Ralph E. 304
Adams, Randy 500
Adams, Shawn 332
Adams, Warren J. 270
Addison, Robert T. 136
Addy, Penelope H. 393
Adler, Orrice E. 68
Adler, Ronna 173
Afinowicz, Lauren 263
Aginah, Sherry 266
Agnew, Connie 232
Agostino, Nellie 270
Ahern, John 327
Aiello, James K. 326
Ajami, Mansour J. 293
Akers, Ernest L. 20
Akers, Katie 516
Alaway, Crystal 523
Albrecht Jr., Charles G. 221
Aldape, Yolanda 306
Alderete, Rosemary 428
Aldridge, Nancy 176
Alexander, Dean 438
Alexander, Monique 71
Alford, Robert 371
Ali, Ishmael 451
Aliamus, Dixie L. 88
All, April 243
Allan, Cora Jean 317
Allard, Lorraine A. 51
Allen, Anna 333
Allen, Charles L. 526
Allen, George B. 16
Allen II, Richard E. 277
Allen, Jim 361
Allen, June Keener 329
Allen, Kristina 386
Allen, Loretta 563
Allen, Nicole 418
Allen, Ralph 43
Allen-White, Verlin 571
Allert, Lori 417
Allison, Fran 446
Allison, Monica 297
Allred, Sharon Kaye 68
Allsopp, Timothy 150
Almeida, Rebecca 48
Alston-Goodwill, Tammaryn 171
Altamirano, Ramon 487
Alvarez, José 433
Amador, Rudy 186
Ambrose-Parker, Madelyn 568
Ambrosini, Michele 419
Ambrosino, Joe 473
Amer, Mary Ann 585
Ammerman, Mark James 412
Amodei, Kenlynn D. 46
Amos, Jennifer S. 440
Amtmann, Christina D. 244
Amy, Bonnie Kerr 331
Anaya, Genia 34
Ancelet, Maude 394
and, Celia Jessy Stokes 324
Anderlini, Jaidene 92
Andersen, Christopher A. 460
Andersen, Donald D. 105
Anderson, Britta 543
Anderson, Charmaine 11
Anderson, Cheryl C. 367
Anderson, Donald 226
Anderson, Joan C. 21
Anderson, Lauren 153
Anderson, Lena H. 183
Anderson, Louise 477
Anderson, Marge 298
Anderson, Michael L. 426
Anderson, Nancy Ann 282
Anderson, Rosia 289
Anderson, Shirley L. 147
Anderson, Stephen 409
Anderson, Tracy Fowler 300
Anderson-Madsen, Judie 9
Andreko, Mary E. 297
Andrews, Paul 44
Andrews, Stass 3
Andrews-Sibbering, Rosemary 378
Andujor, Miriam 522
Angel, Miguel 142
Angelo, Nicholas 118
Angst, Kurt 487
Anthony, Deborah Lynn 457
Anthony, Frank 237
Antoniadis, Hope 16
Antonucci, John M. 238
Anzalone, Lorraine 396
Applegate, Michael 513
Apponi, Ida 466
Archer, Charles R. 348
Archibald, Theodore 408
Archuleta, Adria 471
Ardanuy, Christopher 241
Ardolino, Nicole 173
Arefin, Mohammad S. 374
Arena, Kristin Sunshine 404
Arghiere, Maria 412
Argilan, Nathan 293
Arguello, Carl 316
Armentrout, Deborah 452
Armes, William R. 547
Armstrong, Barbara 470
Arniola, Mark 63
Arnold, Elizabeth A. 369
Arnold, Nicole 184
Arnold, Timothy 553
Arriens, Cristina 247
Arrington, Audrey C. 29
Arscott, Heather J. 235
Arscott, Micheal J. 571
Arzt, Windy Ronnell 484
Asbury, Kay 61
Ascher, Ricky 550
Ashbaucher, Rozella D. 297
Ashe-Montgomery, Annette 450
Ashley, Christine Moneymaker 324
Ashton, Joan 528
Aslanian, Elizabeth 348
Atkeson, Sabrina 148
Atkins, Helen O. 367
Atkins, Nora 185
Atkinson, Joe 198
Aum, Leya 41
Aumann, Dolly 29
Austin, Robert E. 303
Austrum, Shirley G. 581
Autry, Tracy 422
Averette, Patricia A. 160
Averitt, Clyde R. 525
Avetissian, Anna 469
Awais, Muhammad J. 54
Axelrod, Scott 296
Ayers, Thelma Lee 421
Aylish, Lisa Ane 554
Azeem, Nasrin 562

B

B.LUE 103
Baarz, Ronald H. 512
Babbage, Jacqueline 235
Babcock, David 361
Babin, Jeanette Holmes 328
Backes, Michael F. 67
Bacon, Cari M. 95
Bacon, Nathaniel 405
Badger, Ronald 569
Badilla, Shakira 421
Baerwolf, Debra 434
Bafford, Amy 366
Baggarly, Renee 384
Bagley, Mary F. 269
Bahr, Russ 515
Bai, Matthew 62
Baigis, Brian 212
Bailey, Eirlys E. 360
Bailey, Fran 320
Bailey Jr., Charles M. 231
Bailey, Laura 485
Bailey, Marguerite M. 511
Bailey, Pauline E. 481
Bailo, Dyana 93
Baird, Judy N. 33
Baird, Richard 170
Baker, Betty 352
Baker, Dominique 228
Baker, Edwin C. 125
Baker, Erin 327
Baker, Estelle C. 527
Baker, Kenneth D. 303
Baker, Nancy V. N. 160
Baker, Tara Lee 291
Baker, Theresa C. 163
Baker, Victoria Ribbron 189
Bakke, Lisa Diane 486
Bakker, Francine 340
Balan, Traian Alexander 553
Balderston, Jessica 361
Balentine Sr., Lester H. 307
Bales, M. M. 146
Ball, Barbara 310
Ball, Brenda Sue 363
Balzamo, Tom J. 274
Banerjee, Diya 525
Banks, Valerie R. 262
Baptiste, Willbends 425
Baratelli, Joe 245
Barber, Monica 256
Barbour, Janet A. 452
Barefoot, Debbie T. 338
Barham, Neill Winston 427
Barker, Daniel 364
Barker, Ginny 86
Barkley, Wendy 494
Barks, Jean C. 348
Barlieb, Kirsten Amy 304
Barnes, Betty V. 332
Barnes, Gladys 443
Barnes, Joyce R. 470
Barnes, Russell 498
Barnett, Amanda 250
Barnett, Nell Jean 68
Barnhill, Jacob 470
Barno, Mark A. 305
Baron, Marlene 43
Barranca, Victor 273
Barreiro, Michelle 554
Barrera, Roberta A. 413
Barrett, Ann 6
Barrett, Katherine Chase 193
Barrett, S. Ethan 428
Barrow, Josiah 432
Barry, Rosemary J. L. 556
Barter, Susie 427
Bartlett, Benjamin 315
Bartlett, LuJuan 140
Bartlett, Nelson D. 420
Bartlett, Willie-Dean 70
Bartolome, Rolando 54
Barton, Arlene 228
Barton, Mac 277
Bartosik, Sherry L. A. 550
Barwick, Debbie 19
Basham, John 324
Baskin, Evelyn 436
Bass III, Herman L. 581
Bass, Marie 151
Bass, Martha M. 305
Bassi, Marie 73
Basten, William J. 68
Batcheller, Terri 299
Batchelor, Brad 205
Bateman-Mason, Sara G. 560
Bates, Jeffrey 10
Bates, Rio 302
Batey, Shane R. 386
Batson, Grace 89
Bauer, Nannette 71
Baughman, Jessica 345
Baumgartel, Beth 434
Bava, Angela 37
Baxter, Michael 180
Baxter, Robert T. 152
Baxter, Therese 401
Bayman, Donald J. 93
Baymiller, Paul 302
Beagle, Terry 49
Bean, Frances 104
Bean, Thomas J. 141
Bean, Winona Evans 52
Bear, Bryan 324
Beardsley, Sara Maria 380
Beasley, Kevin O. 174
Beaubrun, Joanne 442
Beaupre', Amy L. 81
Becher, David L. 214
Beck, Jeanette 101
Becker, Eva L. Rodgers 250

Becker, Howard H. 457
Becker, Nicki 182
Becker, Robert D. 298
Beckstrom, Jennifer 354
Bedell, Rose Ann 392
Bednarski, Andrew 334
Bedway, George T. 331
Begett, Gloria J. 23
Begnaud, Carrie-Ann 343
Behrman, Christine Bjorkfelt 249
Belarmino, Gino 328
Belk, Lynn 410
Belk, Nikki 409
Bell, Diana 341
Bell, Donna M. 74
Bell, Holly M. 234
Bell, Jennifer 538
Bell, Julian Warren 248
Bell, Linnea M. 293
Belmore, Juliana 463
Bender, Pauline 515
Bender, Thomas 414
Benedict, Lisa R. 173
Benepe, Wallace Lee 379
Benner, M. Sue 521
Bennett, Demarko 537
Bennett, Jeannette 212
Bennett, Jennifer Marie 359
Bennett, Michael E. 175
Bennett, Russell J., II 173
Bensch, Kathryn Eliza 515
Benso, Anne 77
Benson, Katherine 569
Berardi, Christopher L. 325
Berg, Marcia E. 425
Bergadon, Errol 248
Bergandine, Brent M. 459
Berlin Jr., Robert B. 286
Berman, Shari 513
Bernstein, Ellen 468
Berntsen, Thomas 478
Berry, David H. 224
Berry, Donna M. 199
Berry, Eileen S. 94
Berry, Franklin P. 332
Berry, Scott Martin 276
Bertrand, C. Patricia 563
Besinger, Billie S. 131
Bess, Thelma A. 148
Best, Patrica 395
Best, Stacey 304
Betts, Genienne 24
Betts, Margene 404
Betz, Betsy 429
Bevelacqua, Armando S. 234
Beyrle, Nicholas 264
Bezner, Henry 247
Bianchi, Len 179
Bibb, Holly C. 330
Bicking, Della 353
Biela, Debra Theresa 250
Bien-Aime, Yves 308
Biggs, Anna Lou 355
Bilbrey, Barbara J. 341
Biles, Ethyl 236
Bill, Jeffrey P. 249
Billheimer, Karon 177
Billings, Ted 516
Billiot, Estelle M. 101
Billman, Dana 205
Bills, Margaret H. 141

Binger, Mary Anne 53
Binion, Celious 468
Bintner, George R. 31
Bird, Mary Ellen 300
Birge, Nancy R. 409
Bishop, Billie-Jo 232
Bishop, Jeanie 229
Bishop, Mary Bainter 147
Bixby, David A. 455
Bjelland, Evelyn 111
Black, Bryan Robert 345
Black, Debbie 532
Black, Dorothy L. 529
Black, Dorothy Moore 354
Black, Brandon L. Holley 196
Blackmon, Stephanie A. 501
Blagmon, Vaché 303
Blaich, Virginia C. 414
Blair, Mary 152
Blake, Parish 280
Blalock, James 332
Blanch Sr., David F. 87
Blanchard, Christopher 355
Blanchette, Laurie Beth 182
Blanchfield, Joseph 87
Bland, Calvin 340
Blanton, Sherri 308
Blaser, Lois 546
Blaszczyk, Jessica 540
Blaylock, Patricia 570
Blevins, Larry 56
Blincoe, Anna L. Rodgers 367
Blizzard, Kimberly 499
Block, Jenny 89
Bloom, Ruth 293
Bloustine, Jennifer 204
Blum, Jeannette 583
Blumberg, Larry 547
Blythe, Donna 538
Bock, Evelyn L. 36
Bodell, Janet 131
Bodie, Jamie 472
Bodine, William A. 265
Bodkin, Norma 174
Boes, Janet Joann Butcher 510
Bogart, Darlene 195
Bogucki, Barbara E. 199
Boik, Rachel 413
Boisvert, Bonnie 236
Bojanowski, Gloria J. 125
Bolen, Charles D. 529
Bolyard, Celia 79
Bonadurer, Adelee 350
Bonfiglio, Lisa Marie 424
Bong-Ye' 88
Bonham, Charles 38
Boni, Anthony F. 333
Bonomo, Roanne 179
Boo, Jessica 370
Booker, Nellie M. 559
Boone, Dawn 80
Booth, Charlene 231
Booze, Pat 266
Bordelon, Robyn 505
Borghi, Elizabeth 133
Borgman, Beth 76
Borhman, Deborah A. 215
Borilla, Michael A. 567
Borkoski, Edward A. Jr. 452
Bosma, Anneke 100
Bosse, Lisa 186

Bost, Barbara S. 523
Bostick, Tommie 426
Botnick, Ethel S. 466
Bouchard, Karen 556
Boutz, Catherine Overstreet 107
Bowden, Chris M. 29
Bowen, Ina 351
Bowen, Robert 376
Bowen, Susan 484
Bowen, William Lawrence 398
Bower, Patricia G. 52
Bowers, Marilyn H. 63
Bowie, Doris T. 210
Bowles, Shannon M. 287
Bowman, Cathy 406
Bowman, Randy B. 575
Bowyer, Jessica 357
Boyce, Marge 502
Boyd, Bob 220
Boyd, Christy 342
Boyd, D. H. 340
Boyd, Kevin 576
Boyd, Sharon J. 421
Boyer, Amanda 119
Bozell, Pearl 264
Bracey, Sarina 562
Brack, Sarah A. 402
Bradburn, Raymond 479
Braddock, Nicole 393
Braddy Jr., Ricky 487
Bradford, Patricia A. 392
Bradford, Sharon Elisabeth 294
Bradley 190
Bradley, Erin M. W. 444
Bradley, Ora Lewis 533
Bradley, Thomas A. 180
Bradshaw, Lucy C. 425
Bradshaw, Murray C. 384
Bradshaw, Stacey 191
Brady, Donald R. 123
Brady, Peggy 515
Brae 221
Bragdon, Sarah 505
Braley, Oleta 405
Bramlett, Patricia A. 480
Branch, Shirley 567
Brand, Lisa 251
Brand, Nellie M. 292
Brandon, Marc 290
Braun, Kristen Renee 288
Braunger, Bart 245
Breedy, Valerie 307
Brenner, Linda 579
Breth, Priscilla A. 561
Brewer, Jennifer M. 105
Brewer, Justin E. 248
Brewster, Frances Hope 459
Brewton, Jeremiah 236
Bridgford, Richard 282
Bridwell, Nathan Z. 303
Briggs, Ashley 28
Brigham, Shirley Conway 182
Brigidi, Richard Vincent 425
Brill, Donald J. 352
Bringhurst, Stephen 137
Brinton, Mignon T. 276
Bristow, Ricky G. 516
Broadway, Ron 485
Brock, Ardyth 17
Brock, Sue 98

Brockinton, Brandi 158
Broder, Joseph 534
Brodeur, Jason 36
Brokhin, Mira 171
Brooks, Deborah A. 245
Brooks, Priscilla Lee 182
Brosnan, Marguerite 393
Brothers, Kris L. 409
Brotherton, Esther 81
Brotzman, Leah Betterly 478
Broude, Shirley R. 413
Brown, Agnes M. 354
Brown, Ann 471
Brown, Annette C. 326
Brown, Ause 18
Brown, Betty 232
Brown, Bill 207
Brown, Calvin Reed 340
Brown, Denise Kemery 357
Brown, Elaine 111
Brown, Kevin M. 70
Brown, Lois Jean 428
Brown, Nicole 426
Brown, Robert J. 60
Brown, Samuel J. 426
Brown, Shavonne 292
Brown Sr., William L. 67
Brown, Stephanie 185
Brown, Tiffany Miranda 491
Brown, Walter R. 144
Browne, Diana G. 222
Broz, David A. 357
Bruce, Louise 390
Bruck, Charlotte 318
Brummette, Linda L. 264
Brunette, Randy L. 557
Bruni, Mary Ann 148
Brunswick, Mary 375
Bryant, D. L. 356
Bryant, D'Eitra O. 338
Bryant, Rita 278
Buccino, Neal 278
Buchanan, Brenda S. 314
Bucinski, Billie Kelly 313
Buck, Jason 221
Buck, Tim 574
Buckingham, Elizabeth 34
Buckles, Melissa G. 518
Buckley, Susan M. 145
Buehler, Elizabeth 538
Buehler, Jade 243
Buice, Bo 347
Bukowsky, Brett R. 113
Buldra, Gabriel V. 88
Bullis, Florence 524
Burch, Stephanie 190
Burchill, Heather 230
Burckhardt, Dani 251
Burford, Bridgette 308
Burger, Janet 358
Burgess, Hope 448
Burke, Diane 246
Burke Jr., David U. 103
Burke, Julie 233
Burke, Valen Alane 260
Burkitt, Robin-Louise 54
Burksaze, Sandra L. 292
Burnam, Robin Ann 184
Burnell, Mary 494
Burnette, Rashell 586
Burns, Mary D. 502

Burr, Paula 276
Burr, Travis 62
Burton, Barbara 330
Burton, Kirk A. 406
Busch, Tina M. 177
Buss, Anne 364
Busse, Ronald A. 576
Bustard, Matthew 423
Butcher, Myrtle 375
Butler, Josephine S. 316
Butler Jr., Charles R. 459
Butterfield, David C. 309
Button, Ruby 64
Butzer, Dorothy A. 99
Buvinger, Elizabeth 323
Byers, Peggy 483
Bylsma, Wilma 392
Byrne, Erin E. 526
Byrne, J. 296

C

Caboni, Ariana 100
Cagle, Gerald 434
Cahill, Michael S. 483
Cain, Arin 214
Cain, Christy 251
Cain, Ida Pat 219
Cain, Paulette 388
Calabro, Christina L. 322
Calandro, Kristina 180
Calaor, Paula 517
Calderone, M. M. 424
Caldwell, Mary Lee 169
Caldwell, Mazlone 488
Caldwell, Pamela 137
Calhoun, Faye 431
Calhoun, Robyn C. M. 166
Calkins, Ruby L. 384
Call, Robin Elise 184
Callin, Eloise N. 539
Calloway, Arlyne 84
Calvacca, Karen Marie 413
Calvin, Carolee M. 239
Calvo, Andrea 333
Camorlinga-Romero, Genaro 317
Campbell, Bonnie Cohu 201
Campbell, Connie 205
Campbell, Dora Lee 364
Campbell, Erica 124
Campbell, Gladys Starr 23
Campbell, Jeffery Ray 226
Campbell, Pat 151
Canady, Pat 252
Cannady, Maggie L. 409
Canning, Donald Johns 538
Cannon, Sandra 398
Canonica, Stephanie S. 426
Cansing, Alexandra M. 443
Cantu, Jaybird Raul Strungbow 462
Cappello, Vincent A. 68
Cappo, Russell 174
Caraceni, Adrian 115
Caraway, Mary 309
Carbona, Dominic 201
Carchide, Jacqueline 432
Carden, Sheri 154
Carew, Una 577
Carey, Arthur W. 466
Carey, Julie 280
Carius, Naomi 282

Carlomagno, Frank 471
Carlson, Alice 238
Carlson, Chad L. 438
Carlson, Jamie 556
Carlson, Marilyn 98
Carnahan, Eric M. 435
Carner, Stacy L. 142
Carney, Ruth 410
Caroballo, Maria 515
Carol, Sandra 513
Carpeno, Linda 380
Carpenter, Jean 26
Carr, Lonnie 279
Carr, Nicole 297
Carr, Richard L. 521
Carrasco, Cyndy 529
Carretero, Ingrid 226
Carrigan, Julie Rae 316
Carriker, Zane 296
Carroll, Carolyn 533
Carroll, Karen B. 309
Carroll, Marjorie 511
Carroll, Thomas W. 493
Carson, M. Ernstine 548
Carson, Raine A. 279
Carter, Constance 200
Carter, Scott 521
Carter, Valerie 381
Caruso, Joanne 28
Carvalho, Anna P. 450
Casale, Katie 98
Casey, Jeff 212
Casselle, Kwakou 373
Castaneda, Brian T. 335
Castlebury, Chris 196
Castro, Cindy 242
Catarino, Miriam 501
Cates, Clifton 95
Cates, Kathleen N. 289
Catuzza, Elizabeth A. 246
Caudill, Angela 99
Caudle, Linda Little 547
Cavalier, Andrea 198
Cavalli, Yvette 377
Cawley, Yvonne P. 569
Cawrse, Dawn J. 94
Caylak, Turhan 157
Ceccarelli, Elijah 444
Cece, Robert J. 517
Ceder, John W. 337
Cenna, Frank J. 27
Cepeda, Cynthia 583
Ceppos, Laurie 214
Cessna, Opal M. 147
Chadwick, Leigh 373
Chamberlain, LaVerne 143
Chambers, Scott 48
Chan, Yi-Wen 283
Chandler, Chanel Narcissus 435
Chandler, Helen J. 248
Chang, Cheryl Lynn 223
Chapman, Cynthia K. 240
Chapman, David 28
Chapman, Patricia Wolf DeSanti 64
Chapman, Samuel L. 62
Chapmon, Annise Lucia 116
Chappel, Alvin R. 363
Char, Lynette Y. C. 306
Charles, Symone 500
Chase, Lisa 289
Chase, Veronica 425

Chason, Sharron 416
Chavez, Brenda 316
Chavez, David T. 349
Chavez, J. 289
Cheatham, Patrick James 273
Chen, Jemmy 88
Chen, Serena 403
Cheung, Julie 543
Chiarella, Courtney Anne 238
Chiasson, Denise 14
Chicoine, Megan K. 182
Ching, Leizel 548
Chisholm, Matthew 412
Chitty, Trevor 263
Chiuchiolo, Lisa M. 398
Chollick, Jay 351
Choung, Andrew 16
Chowdhry, Ammara 19
Christensen, Dorothy 130
Christian, Steve 282
Christiansen, Marjorie 415
Christopher, Helene 346
Chrystie, Grace C. 337
Chu, Betty 318
Churchill, Kathie 409
Churder, Jessica 213
Ciacco, Jessica 460
Cicon Jr., Michael A. 426
Ciesielski, Janice 337
Cigna, Marie 575
Cirello, Kathy 521
Ciulla, Lena 417
Clague, Jessica 434
Clark, Barbara 244
Clark, Charles R. 341
Clark, Christy 239
Clark, David A. 105
Clark, Helen Madge 314
Clark, Joni 209
Clark, Julie 440
Clark, Kelly 257
Clark, L. 188
Clark, Rod 386
Clark, Sarah 309
Clasby, Brian 326
Clauss, D. Christian 177
Clayborn, LaVerne 274
Claypool, Deborah J. 356
Clear, Patricia 293
Cleere, Cassie Jo 81
Cleere, William Gregory 501
Cline, Michelle 424
Cline, Nicole 426
Clinton, Dorothy Randle 465
Cloeters, Melissa 488
Clouser Jr., Marlin M. 308
Coaker, Linda 163
Coats, Geri 20
Cobb, Isaiah 454
Cochran, Jason Wayne 353
Cockrell, Onnie R. 569
Coddington, Russell J. 71
Cody, Claire 223
Cody, Louise Claudia 73
Coffin, Jim 85
Coffman, Carolyn C. 115
Coffman, Jon 114
Coffman, Lucia 512
Cogshall, Carlene 238
Cohen, Geri 361
Colaor, Paula A. 42

Colclough, Ted 60
Cole, Heath A. 114
Cole, Keri-Ann 265
Cole, Leslie A. 391
Cole, Sylvia H. 571
Colebrook, Sara D. 384
Coleman, D. Lynn 262
Coleman, Erica 3
Coleman, Gale Odom 237
Coleman, Margaret 177
Coleman, Mary 291
Coleman, Mary Isabell 371
Coleman, R. Brian 300
Coley, Scott 428
Collado, Bamil Gutierrez 102
Collier, Craig 327
Collier, Peggy 428
Collins, Barbara 353
Collins, Susan M. 271
Collum, Mona 579
Colon, Harold 132
Colon, Tony 184
Comnick, Lori Ann 507
Compton III, C. Garland 520
Condon, Merry 428
Conklin, John D. 246
Conley-Walters, Rita Lee 475
Connell, Judith D. 194
Conner, Mercedes 181
Connestee, Eve 128
Connors, Bob 330
Conrad, Julie M. 219
Conrad, Troy 42
Conrado, Joanne 124
Conroy, Ronald E. 415
Constantine, Jessica 88
Consuegra, Alejandro R. 11
Conway, Ozelle 389
Conway, Rhoda 477
Cook, Clara Marie 113
Cook, Robert F. 54
Cook, Roy A. 555
Cook, Ruth L. 20
Cook, Sara 286
Cook, Stephanie Colleen 72
Cooke, Dorothy Norman 318
Cooks, Sara S. 274
Cooley, Al 92
Cooley, Lauren 404
Cooper, Bill 358
Cooper, Jacqui 351
Cooper, Valerie M. 483
Cope, Esther 535
Copeland, Melissa 116
Copeland, Nora Lee 475
Coppejans, John L. 361
Copper, K. C. 22
Coppol, Brett 524
Corcoran, Paul H. 57
Cordell, Robert J. 180
Corey, Shelly 383
Corinthian, Evelyn 346
Cormier, Hannah 587
Corner, Kelley 74
Correia, Robert Lloyd 141
Corso, Salvatore 66
Cory, Darlene L. 347
Cosaert, Karen 301
Costa, Al 7
Costa, Horatio 350
Costanzo, Louis 297

Costic, Donna 311
Couch, Jan 349
Coulson, Andrea F. 92
Coulter, Page P. 553
Counselman, Robert C. 141
Courts, Alayne M. 86
Coutee, Alice 106
Couzo, Theresa A. 75
Covacevich Jr., Frank V. 37
Covas, Maria 286
Cowan, J. Patrick 184
Cowdin, Josh 315
Cowen, Eugene L. 363
Cowgill, Christopher M. 238
Cox, D. G. 256
Cox III, Leon Sergio 382
Cox, Jennifer 335
Cox, Patsy I. 49
Cox, Shelia 411
Cox, Susan Charlene 307
Cozmos, Marcus Max 549
Craddock, Anthony 233
Craft, John Whitney 579
Cragnale, Dave 437
Craig, Glenn 250
Craig, Kathleen 283
Craig, Rebecca 580
Craighead, Sabrina 495
Crampton, Bertha 455
Crandall, Mike 426
Crane, Robert 268
Crankshaw, Barbara 538
Cranston, Nichelle Anne 391
Crawford, Barbara C. 354
Crawford, Crystal 354
Crawford, Curtis 104
Crawford, Ruth 518
Crawford, Teal S. 389
Creary, Herman J. 533
Crehan, Kathleen Elizabeth 256
Crenshaw, Laura 585
Crinklaw, Katherine 391
Crobaugh, Emma 117
Crockett, Amy L. 123
Croft, Gale 338
Crone, Jamie 127
Cronin, John 81
Cronin, Lois K. 154
Cronin, Nancy 162
Crosby, Roland L. 172
Croson, Gary 351
Crouch, Teresa 74
Crouse, Lindsay 297
Crouse, Michael 522
Crow, Erin 251
Crowder, Paul O. 517
Crowder, Tom 189
Crowell, Margaret 290
Crum, Connie S. 81
Crum, John J. 472
Cubic, Mark 67
Cuckler, Susan 481
Culp, Jennifer 539
Culp, Rebecca 273
Cumbie, Christy 446
Cunningham, Alvin Robert 356
Cunningham, John 102
Cupp, Joey 340
Currier, Anne B. 89
Curtis, Keith Duane 401
Curtis, Rebecca 258
Cutlip, Barry 35
Cutlip, Pansy 403
Czopek-Knight, John 350

D

Da Roza, George 77
Da Vinci, Dr. Laura 513
Dabbs, Dawn 104
Daddona, Richard 520
Daer, Roberta Harydzak 165
Dahlgren, Marilyn Ruth 302
Dahm, Elizabeth 468
Daidone, Charles 457
Dailey, Dolly 310
Dakin, Malinda Andreasen 496
D'Ampolo, Conrad 221
Danchenko, Karen M. 150
Dande, Sylvia 192
D'Angelo, M. J. 520
D'Angelo, Valerie 98
Daniel, Angeline 117
Daniels, LaTonya 503
Daniels, Samson 163
Danielsen, Barbara 321
Danielson, James E. 95
Danso, Robert Van-Earl 563
D'Antonio, Chris 535
Dantzler, Annie 106
Darrow, Joey 582
Das, Sati Mohan 297
DasSarma, Basudeb 446
Daveler, Angie 536
Davidoff, Sherri 416
Davidson, Anita M. 472
Davies, Aaron 212
Davis, Bruce R. 37
Davis, C. R. 416
Davis, Carly Anne 3
Davis, Daniel 335
Davis, Darlene 361
Davis, Donnie 83
Davis, Jacki 86
Davis, James W. 111
Davis, Jeanette Estep 25
Davis, Joyce Ann 229
Davis, Maria T. 512
Davis, Michelle 262
Davis, Norman D. 280
Davis, Rodney W. 389
Davis, Sandra 476
Davis, Stacy Lynn MacKail 171
Davis, Tabitha S. 402
Davis, Virgie Mae 404
Davis, William 411
Dawkins, Neva 298
Dawn, Misty 482
Dawson, Barbara Nell Smith 28
Dawson, Colin 441
Dawson, Jim 406
Dawson, Larry 395
Dawson, Robby 488
Dawson, Vicki L. 299
Day, Christina 80
Day, Diana M. 239
Days, Cassandra D. 458
De Caprio, Danielle 247
de Gallegos, Richard Lawrence 66
De Hoop, Wilma 152
de Jesus, Jose Maria 46
De La Fuente, Jose Miguel 583

De Laney, Cathy 535
De Los Reyes, Yvonne 518
De Mar, Margaret H. 400
Dean, Danielle S. 36
Dean, Lester 567
Dearing, Jennifer 213
Deas, Dontrell 211
DeCair, Kimberly S. 393
DeCaro, Yvette 192
Deck, Annia 456
Deckard, Gloria 5
Decker, Marianne J. 69
DeCoteau, Mark 491
DeFrancesco, MaryAnn 54
DeGrange, Tawnie M. 285
DeGraw, Robert 177
Del Monte, Marcy 165
Delancey, Lorna E. 176
Delaney, Michelle A. 475
Delfyett, Dorcas H. 436
Dell, Irene Prater 234
Dellert, Christopher 33
DeMartinis, James J. 97
Demas, Sophia 570
Dematas, Wendy V. 510
Demetral, Ruth C. 255
DeMola, Thomas 572
Dempsey, Marjorie 414
Dempsey, Sarah 65
Dene, Patricia 253
Denham, Paige B. 160
Dennis, N. Jonathan 283
Dennison, Sean 58
DePasquale, Louis A. 507
Deriso, Doris B. 77
DeRose, Gina 314
DeRyck, Jennifer 350
Desiderio, Elio 237
DeSimone, Chrissy 473
Destinee, Delia 116
DeTonno, Theresa 514
DeVault, Doris 14
Dever, Pete 151
DeViney, John H. 4
DeVivo, Kristina 298
Di Giovanni, Frank 314
Di Maria, Nicholas 486
Di Raffaele, Melissa 572
Dia, Bocar 32
Diamond, Jennifer 202
Dias, Heidrun M. 223
Diaz, Benito R. (Nature Boy) 39
Diaz, Eileen M. 222
Diaz, Kimberly J. 422
Dibble, Paula J. 275
Dickerson, Sherri T. 345
Dieb, A. 40
Diederich, Rodger 140
Dieringer, Carina S. 359
Dietrich, Elizabeth 543
DiGennaro, Robert J. 55
Dill, Alta 313
Dillard, Toni Lee 389
Dillen, Colleen 539
Diller, Clarence A. 341
Dimmette, Megahn Elizabeth 406
Dingess, Curtiss M. 25
DiPrima, Michele 295
Dixon, Hannah Forsyth 82
Dixon III, Elliot J. 14
Dobransky, Paul 58

Dockstader, Barbie 91
Dodd-Ray, Cheryl 8
Dodds, Malcolm 569
Doderidge, James Grimsley 34
Dodge, Kevin 395
Dodimead, Marilee 375
Dodson, Robert 491
Dodson, Tamiko Y. 306
Dolejs, Doris J. 31
Dolhancyk, Diana 22
Dolinko, Frieda 227
Dollar, Russ 117
DomDera, Helen 206
Domis, Rebecca 260
Donnelly, Jason M. 25
Donovan, Patricia Lynn 52
Donovan, Ron 151
Doolin, Courtney 243
Doonan, David M. 467
Dopeman 187
Dopkin, Jennifer 92
Dorenbosch, Dell 225
Dorn, Patricia C. 263
Dorn, Yvette 57
Dory, Dorotha Loewen 83
Dotson, Sandra L. 57
Doty, Heather L. 213
Dougherty, Dennis 454
Douglas III, John 343
Douglas, Mary Ann 480
Dow, R. Sollows 517
Downey, Jacqueline 77
Downs, Lisa 561
Doyle, Bernadette C. 129
Doyle, John 336
Drake, Sheila 295
Draper, Kevin 497
Draudt, Holly 341
Dreher, Ruth 254
Dreibelbis, Lora 183
Driggers, Stephanie 496
Drinkard, David 461
Drury, Paul R. 514
Drybrae, Lynsey 414
Dryja, Eric 13
Drzewianowski, Carol 321
Dubbrin, Norma 423
DuBois, Barbara R. 89
DuBois, Jennifer 222
DuBose, Gretchin 356
DuBose, Joan 542
Duchard, Maxime 302
Duckworth, Ella 91
Dudley, Amber 93
Dugan, Henry J. 338
Dukes, K. 375
Dunbar, Melissa A. 575
Duncan, Cherylynne 355
Duncan, James W. 208
Duncan, Jeanne Aya 24
Duncan, Mildred Brown 98
Duncan, Mindy 400
Dunham-Smith, Joyce 456
Dunkelberger, Lee A. 376
Dunkin, Joe 18
Dunlap, Tim 46
Dunmire, Jessica 75
Dunn, Margaret Mary 175
Dunn, Mary 298
Dunn, Mary Lou 511
Dunny, Rebecca 570

Dunton, Dorothea 461
DuPree, Mary H. 559
DuRant, Roy C. 288
Durden, Brenda 534
Durmer, Patsy A. 291
Duteau, Arthur L. 365
Dweck, Florence 355
Dyer, Ann 76
Dyer, Lela 286
Dykes, Kimberly 331
Dykstra, Cora June 463
Dykstra, Melissa S. 387
Dymond, Jaime 235
Dziadosz, Joseph 242

E

Early, Becki 313
Earnest, Taylor H. 162
Easley, Charlotte L. 462
Eaton, Mandi 513
Ebenreck, Susan 578
Eberhard, Candice 369
Ebert, Nova C. 569
Ebright, Jessica Kelly 362
Eby, Jack 205
Eckerle, Philip A. 173
Edelman, Lynn 400
Eder, Laura A. 579
Edgar, Harvey 343
Edison, Michael William 167
Edmond, Jeff 217
Edwards, Bettie Withers 344
Edwards, Dana 76
Edwards, Ebony 471
Edwards, Jeremy 586
Edwards, Katie E. 65
Edwards, Mary 417
Edwards, Micah 50
Edwards, Patricia 569
Edwards, Yvonne 426
Edwin, Sabeen 72
Egger, Amy C. 329
Eichelkraut, Christina 18
Eid, Alan L. 20
Eikamp, Arthur 235
Eikenberry, Ferne 467
Einhellig, Veronica 145
Eisenmenger, Kerry 409
Eiser, Florence 22
Eitelmann, Brian Kenneth 101
Elder, Dixie 16
Elio, Erin Whitney 211
Elizabeth, Sharon 547
Eller, Linda Lanier 380
Elliott, Diane 364
Ellis, Brian 435
Ellis, Lenny 187
Elly, Ronald D. 476
Elsea, Judy 317
Elshout, Yvonne Linden 309
Ely, Douglas L. 455
Emadi, Baq 228
Emerson, J. A. 48
Emery-Gigliotti, Deborah 82
Emory, Priscilla 145
Eng, Tony 482
Engbretson, William E. 173
Engels, Kristen 403
Enger, Richard C. 421
England, Steven W. 474

Engle, Rebecca W. 137
English, Marie Adele 285
Epstein, Carol L. 322
Epting, Jennifer 541
Erhart, Jennifer 438
Ericksen, Garrett 135
Erickson, Ann 536
Erickson, Crystal 206
Erickson, Leslie A. 512
Ericson, Evelyn T. 107
Ernest, Joseph K. 355
Ernst, Erin 320
Ernster, L. J. 388
Error, Dalin T. 127
Ervin, Stacy 176
Erwin, Diana 449
Escareno, Ramona Eve 496
Escobar, Ely Blu 248
Escoto, Kristine 256
Espenschied, Ida 473
Espiritu, Aida E. 122
Estes, James R. 350
Estes, Keith D. 259
Estes, Staci 390
Estock, John Matthew 130
Eubanks, Juanita Lorraine 6
Evans, Dan 336
Evans, Lisa 510
Evans, Ludmilla 181
Evans, Nakia 547
Evans, Rob 283
Evans, Robert 550
Evans, Steven 565
Everroad, Una-Melina M. 64
Evers, Helen H. G. 244
Ewen, Dennis 366
Ewing, Harold 85
Ewing, Helen Ruth 339
Ezell, Teresa 143

F

Fagliano, Ann 224
Faison, David L. 331
Falk, Andrea 363
Falk, Howard 85
Falzone, Vita T. 396
Farber, Roma 512
Farda, Laurie L. 186
Farkas, R. F. 296
Farr, Mildred P. 512
Farrel 371
Farrell, Mary Esther 260
Farris, Glenn 442
Farthing, Shane 407
Fassett, Rhonda L. 75
Faucher, Gloria 312
Fauci-Morosky, Patricia A. 418
Fay, Justin 206
Feeley Jr., John J. 15
Fehrmann, Edna P. 90
Feinberg, Delores 430
Feldman, Seymour B. 482
Feliz, Guido 247
Felks, Mandy 181
Fell, Gayle Lockwood 347
Ferguson, Amanda 22
Ferguson, Michael D. 415
Ferguson, Robert H. 176
Fernandez, Sonia 504
Ferraro, John 406

Ferrugio, Rose 504
Fick, Sister Loretta 399
Field, C. Duane 458
Field, Veronica 504
Field, Wayne 175
Fielding, Aileen 451
Fields, Evelyn W. 122
Fields, Julius Theodore 134
Fiene, Keith 518
Figueroa, Bridgitte 313
Fils-Aime, Ronald 261
Filter, Christine V. 313
Finch, Donald 232
Finch, Mary R. 418
Findlay, Sandra M. 176
Fink, Sandy 521
Fiore, Carlo 111
Fiore, Christina 219
Fiscella, Irma 126
Fish, Madeline Chapman 408
Fisher, Anne T. 125
Fisher, Bonnie 351
Fisher, Carole 364
Fisher, Denise C. 511
Fisher, Jewel 96
Fisher, Julie A. 347
Fisher, Susan 392
Fishman, Lisa 553
Fitzgerald, Brent 29
Fitzpatrick, John 84
Fitzpatrick, Michael 152
Flahave, Amy 80
Flandreau, Kristine Lynn 259
Flannery, Edel 4
Flauto-Hayes, Janice 84
Fleck, Cindy 92
Fleming, Brandy 370
Fleming, Kimberly 392
Fleming, Margaret G. 287
Flemings, Sandra K. 481
Flood, Charlotte 85
Flores, Jolene R. 582
Flowers, Bobby 329
Floyd, Jonathan 229
Floyd, Kathy 289
Flynn, Polly 410
Fogle, Ron 259
Foley, Kenneth 411
Fong, Lauren 574
Ford, Anita S. 445
Ford, Daniel 528
Ford, George 461
Ford, Helen J. 231
Ford, Lena 155
Ford, Michelle E. 370
Foree, John 354
Fornaro, Andrea 471
Forsberg, Paul O. 186
Forsythe, Virginia 292
Forte, Marcel 179
Fosshage, J. W. 515
Foster, Brenda L. 460
Foster, Gina 95
Foster, Maria E. 192
Foster, Marjorie S. 262
Fountain, Deborah 372
Fowler, Amy 87
Fowler, David P. 90
Fowler, Dee 536
Fowler, Sandra 476
Fox, Bill 286

Fox, Gail A. 365
Fox, Melissa 270
Frakes, Linda 301
France, William N. 269
Frances, Mary 96
Francis, Elissa Johnson 130
Francis, Jan 450
Francis, Marian K. 181
Franco, Crystal 542
Franco, David 533
Francone, Bruce E. 541
Frank, Colleen A. 80
Frank, Frances B. 10
Frank, Gerald B. 126
Frank, Harvey 5
Frank, Lisbeth Sweet 383
Frank, Mary 517
Franklin, Emanuell Sinclair 207
Fratis, John 439
Frazer, Marjorie 175
Frazier, Matthew Timothy 391
Frazier-Means, Willerma 267
Freebairn, Carolyn Joyner 87
Freebody, Gary 361
Freed, Dana 466
Freedman, Bethany 193
Freeland, Minnie 156
Freels, Virgil 186
Freeman, Richelle M. 416
Freeman, Rudolph V. 42
Freije, Khriscinda M. 149
French, Kim 501
French, Maria S. 189
French, Rosemary 513
Fricker, Julie Ann 135
Friedman, Mort 375
Fries, Stella M. 161
Friesz, Mary Lee 146
Frisco, Marie 192
Fritz, Bradley J. 18
Frizalone, Danielle 350
Fross, Ruth Ellen 408
Frost, Kristine 149
Fudge, Patricia A. 180
Fuentefria, Melissa 274
Fuentes, Crista 88
Fuhriman, Lori 557
Fujita, Glenn W. 214
Fuller, Maxcine 284
Fuller, Shandi 66
Fullerton, Patricia 183
Fulton, Crissie 223
Fultz, Patricia Nicole 136
Funches, Precious M. 417
Fung, Becky 98

G

Gaffney, Marcelle 300
Gagliano, Mary Ann 184
Gainey, Kimberly 73
Galiza, Linda L. 178
Gallagher, Donna M. 531
Gallagher, J. R. 421
Ganatra, Jyotsom 113
Ganley, Virginia L. 182
Garberino, Dennis Charles 200
Garcia, A. K. 139
Garcia, Adriana 355
Garcia, Andrea V. 545
Garcia, Angela 585

Garcia, Catherine   23
Garcia, Kathleen   555
Garcia, Toff B.   391
Garcia, Zettie Painter   556
Gardner, Jason K.   94
Gardner, Jessi   201
Gardner, Suzanne Eva   278
Garfield, Sarah   264
Garleb, Kathy L.   423
Garma, Brenda   133
Garner, J. H.   306
Garner, Sally H.   560
Garner, Tracey Overby   304
Garone, Kelly   428
Garramone, Rose   492
Garrett, Dorothy Phyllis   354
Garrett, R. B.   372
Garvin, Patricia Ann   53
Gary, Benjamin   344
Gary, Melissa   153
Gary, Suzanne K.   40
Gaskin, Robert Edward   159
Gassmann, Paula Rozan   288
Gates, Janice P.   113
Gause, Matthew Ryan   479
Gay, Olive P.   74
Gayler, Kalman   407
Gayler, Nancy L.   308
Gayness, Linda   154
Geater, Faith A.   583
Geddes, Junko   200
Geide, Matthew   156
Geiger, Dorothy B.   231
Geisel, Dorothy M.   494
Geller, Herman S.   361
Geller, Lillian   180
Genn, Elisabeth   114
Gennari, Anthony R.   329
Genovese-Buck, Ann Marie   202
Gentry, Derenda   438
George, Michelle   295
George, Ruth T.   563
Gerardi, Dave   134
Gerber, Adele   549
Gerber, Clare B.   105
Gerber, Stacey Handler   371
Gerber, Tobias   286
Gerhard, Bonnie   327
German, Josh   312
Germy, Karen E.   564
Gerritz, Martha   294
Gerstenkorn, Jessi   537
Gerut, John D.   91
Ghiglieri, Deana   27
Ghosh, Alexandra   112
Gianadda, Nicholas A.   519
Gibboney, Daniel   94
Gibbons, Maureen   508
Gibson, Constance   467
Gibson, Joyce W.   473
Gibson Jr., Calvin T.   315
Gibson, Opal   43
Giddens, Terrance R.   144
Gill, Elizabeth S.   316
Gill, Jeanne V.   92
Gill, Jessica   213
Gilleland, Lavonia   189
Gillenwater, Shirley   412
Gillis, Loretta   146
Gilman, Sarah   172
Gilmore, Daniel Blythe   103

Gilreath, Michelle   386
Gingrich, Verda M.   59
Gittoes-Singh, Xennia   41
Glaister, Muriel D.   39
Glass, Hattie   341
Glass, Timothy A.   421
Gleason, John B.   197
Gleason, Lynn Marie   39
Glenn, Joseph   251
Glenn, Lucie   421
Glinton, Grace   439
Glover, Christina A.   208
Glover, Marian L.   119
Gloyd, Millie Faye   503
Glucksman, James   360
Glynn, John   449
Gnotta, Diane   454
Goco, Andrew   22
Godberson, Renee   169
Godoski, Charles   461
Gohman, Mandy   259
Goida, Shannon   577
Golden, Byron Lee   92
Golden, Robert   390
Goldman, Martin   380
Goldstein, Frances R.   242
Golley Jr., Howard   540
Golliday, Tammy   306
Gomez, Rafael   285
Goncalves, Elaine   527
Gonyea, Sheila   506
Gonzales, Asianita C.   9
Gonzales, Praxcedes   399
Gonzalez, Blanca Estela   225
Gonzalez, Crystal R.   368
Gonzalez, Shantal   146
Good, Margaret   372
Goode Jr., Joseph   449
Goode, Rommy   577
Goode, Ronald Ketih   573
Gooden, Diana L.   124
Gooding, Matt   139
Gooding, Rhonda   426
Goodman, Don   246
Goodman, Heather   204
Goodwin, Lori   376
Goold, Diane   225
Gordon, Brian C.   457
Gordon, Desiree   91
Gordon, Ginger   94
Gordon, Harry W.   524
Gordon, I. Herbert   412
Gordon, Janis   250
Gordon, M. Faith   435
Gordon, Ruby Coggins   299
Gorge, Vincent James   509
Goss, Suzanne   42
Gostel, Marie V.   482
Gottermeyer, Jeff   309
Gottfried, Susan   184
Goudeau, Janell Kotrice   91
Gough, Alma Ilene   128
Gouker, Tammy   488
Gould, Helen C.   232
Gould, Marilyn E.   374
Gourdine, Kevin O.   376
Gower, Cristi   456
Grable, Katie L.   306
Grace, David R.   172
Grace, Michal   519
Grace, Nancy   290

Gracey, Kelly A.   47
Graf, Lois   558
Graham, Charlene   333
Graham, Ida F.   204
Graham, Richard A.   278
Grahl, Helen   88
Grahm, Jordan   580
Gramata-Jones, Mia   561
Grandinetti, Donna K.   353
Granfeldt, N.   298
Granger, Julie   26
Granger, Michele Lynn   498
Granholm, Richard A.   510
Granowitz, Thomas   380
Grant, C. A.   413
Grant, Linda   568
Grant, Nicole   72
Grantham, Angie   446
Graves, Melanie K.   45
Gray, Carolyn S.   105
Gray, Douglas   367
Gray, Shelli J.   149
Greason, Staci   406
Green, Joan L.   233
Green, Maureen M.   191
Green, Sean   395
Green, Tisa   371
Greene, Denise   523
Greer, Dolph   28
Gregory, Wanda Lee   500
Gregson, Judy   366
Grice, Kathryn R.   262
Gries, Jason   27
Griffin, Cari D.   17
Griffin, Carrie   25
Griffin, Michael Osborne   374
Griffin, Patti Ann   278
Griffin, Sean C.   387
Griffy, David   352
Grigereit, Carolyn   107
Griggs, Richard C.   390
Grigsby, Lillian J.   393
Grimes, Jason K.   236
Grimes, Michele   257
Grinstead, Heather   83
Groll Jr., Thomas R.   558
Groomer, Verla Marlene   516
Gross, Ashley   35
Gross, Belinda   76
Gross, Susan   559
Grouf, Inez Spradling   444
Gruber, Irene   319
Grunau, Jacqueline   362
Guerin, Marlene   406
Guidry, Vanice   176
Guillory, Damon Craig   94
Guinn, Lahoma Vivian   418
Guldemann, Michael   159
Gullett, Heather   540
Gulsvig, Norris D.   385
Gunderson, Gil   325
Gunnett, Lucretia A.   508
Gurevich, Ilana   227
Gurgui, Gabriela   352
Gutheil, Scott G.   147
Guthrie, Vaughn   423
Gutierrez, Dominic E.   205
Guy, Corinee W.   357
Guyan, Linda   255
Guyler, Christine M.   110
Guzay, Alice S.   344

Guzman, Joann   34
Gypsy, Lawrence   494

H

Haag, Nicole   394
Haar, Greta M.   118
Hackl, Edda H.   95
Hackney, Marie Matthews   402
Hada, John Juji   241
Haddox, Maxine   140
Haft, Barry R.   456
Hagan, Amber L.   78
Hagethorn, Larry   283
Haglund, Kathleen   50
Hahn, Jennifer   116
Hahn, Marshall   474
Hailey, Terri   399
Haines, Norma J.   258
Haines, Tiffany   288
Haire, Betty L.   204
Hairston, Alphonso J.   357
Hale, Connie Lee   232
Hale, Dolores   470
Hale, Jody   33
Hale, Roy   46
Haley, Chris   367
Hall, Beth   542
Hall, Charles W.   121
Hall, Clarice   337
Hall, Katherine   128
Hall, Kathleen M.   271
Hall, Mary Dorothy   401
Hall, Sharon   184
Hallowell, Juli   241
Halverson, Jodi   90
Hambrick, Janice Lynn   36
Hamel, Robert W.   73
Hamilton, Evelyn   135
Hamilton, Rebecca   575
Hamilton, Rebecca J.   427
Hamilton, Ronald R.   546
Hamilton, Tyron Chad   171
Hammer, Callie   363
Hammer, Jill   462
Hammer, Nancy A.   559
Hammond, Kathy Piazza   420
Hammonds, Mary Jo   382
Hampson, Jennifer   433
Hampton, Jody   231
Hancock, Robbyn   67
Handly, Marion D.   383
Haney, Teri   170
Hann, Jenny   460
Hanna, Sheryl   284
Hannah, Ruth N.   416
Hannaman, Judy   216
Hanneman, Karen   545
Hannon, Rachel   408
Hansen, Alathea   345
Hansen, Amber   368
Hansen, Carin M.   463
Hansen, Dalene   534
Hansen, Steve   308
Hanson, Bea   81
Hanson, Michelle Jeanne   558
Hanway, Dezarai   101
Haraczka, Dayna M.   108
Harbeson, Cyndi   582
Harbeson, Jennifer   356
Harden, Benny   83

Hardesty, Stewart 41
Hardin, Noah Kory 258
Harding, Charles G. 33
Harding III, Joseph James 454
Hardy, Charlene 110
Hardy, Joe W. 534
Harlow, Ellen F. 231
Harlow, June Bailey 9
Harmdierks, Gina 209
Harmon, Amy 116
Harmon, Jennifer Elaine 19
Harms, Robert W. F. 397
Harness, Brady C. 249
Harper, Bernadette 127
Harper, John 82
Harriman, Shirley 405
Harris, Ann 438
Harris, Bernadette 230
Harris, Byron J. 133
Harris, Deborah D. 442
Harris, Jason 216
Harris, Marie B. 44
Harris, Sally J. 252
Harris-John, Alun 365
Harrison, Elizabeth A. 94
Harrison, Jemilia 317
Harrison, John 308
Harrison, Lisa 305
Harrison, Nicole 177
Harrison, Roger D. 187
Harrop-Williams, Kingsley O. 504
Harsh, Suzette 262
Harshman, Carl L. 32
Hart, Beatrice Held 26
Hart, Bonnie 463
Hart, Penny A. 407
Hartz, Susan 484
Haruvi, Jacob 345
Harvey, James S. 446
Harvey, Mark Vincent 251
Harvey, Roxanne 188
Harvey, Torrance R. 276
Harwood, Phil 507
Hasche, Susan 65
Haseltine, Robin 398
Haskett, Jeanette 194
Haskins, Lindsey 408
Hassan, Ghassan 209
Hastings, Helen 531
Hatcher, John E. 78
Hatfield, Margaret 549
Hatheway, Darlene R. 232
Hauber, Steve 558
Haugen, Margaret E. 509
Haussmann, Jan 354
Havel, Gary E. 215
Havey, Kim 577
Havranek, Gary L. 208
Hawk, Regina 301
Hawkins, April 365
Hawkins, Dustin K. 349
Hawkins, Michelle 513
Hawkins, William Alan 558
Hawley, William Keith 59
Hayes, Desiree A. 6
Haynes, April 472
Haynes, John S. 90
Hayward, Solange 568
Hazen, Laura R. 294
He, Xining 522
Heady, Sabrina 307

Healy IV, Dennis L. 38
Hedges, Gilbert 580
Hefner, Lisa K. 416
Heike, Allen D. 21
Heitman, Chris 82
Heldman, Coralie 337
Helgen, Hazel 219
Hellewell, Margaret 173
Helm, Sara Jo 370
Hempel, Charles M. 365
Hemphill, Sharon 417
Hendershot, Leroy James 39
Hendershott, Hilon 5
Henderson, Cecelia 211
Henderson, Garry L. 244
Henderson, Justin 199
Henderson, Vanessa Aspen 514
Hendricks, Anthony 330
Hendricks, Sarah Thomas 415
Hendrickson, Thelma 40
Hendryx, Andrea 436
Hengesbach, Mary Jane 164
Henry, Eleanor Michael 222
Henry, Emily 87
Henry, Jessica Ann 129
Henry, John R. 441
Henry, Sandra J. 252
Herbst, Kelly 181
Herensztat, Greta 197
Hernandez, Timothy 257
Herold, Shelley 495
Herrejon, Theresa S. 281
Herring, Jeanette 314
Herron, Harry W. 230
Herschler, Marc 585
Hertz, Nancy A. 280
Hervey, Mary 410
Heskett, Joan 110
Hess, Sarasvati Lorion 299
Heusser, A. 280
Hewett, F. H. 511
Hewitt, Fred 456
Hicks, Nan Garcia 409
Hicks, Thelma 41
Hicks, Wanda 555
Higginbotham, Oneida 374
Higgins, Henry C. 320
Hilbert, Randall Ardeane 401
Hilborn, Helen 334
Hildabrand, Chandra 199
Hilde Sr., Reuben L. 396
Hildreth, Liesel 308
Hill, Amber 350
Hill, Denise 450
Hill, Jeffa P., Jr. 241
Hill, Jessica 327
Hill, Joanne K. 355
Hill Jr., Theodore 162
Hill, LaToya R. 550
Hill, Michael 289
Hill, Rachel 137
Hill, Richard H. 374
Hill, Rikki 520
Hill, Ronald J. 270
Hill, Sandy 170
Hill, Thomas Culver 161
Hill, Thomas L. 499
Hill, Tommy 189
Hill, Vera Rush 518
Hilliard, Evelyn 335
Hilton, Nicole 65

Hiltz, Daniel R. 330
Hinchey, Bonnie Lynn 250
Hinshaw, Alice 211
Hintz, Stacy 412
Hinz, Geraldine 457
Hirsch, Debra Bevinetto 5
Hitchcock, Ernie 217
Hite, Theresa 296
Hodge, Laura 497
Hodge, Leon 477
Hodge, Mamie 55
Hodges, Erana 95
Hodges, Helen Milburn 249
Hodges, Nancy 561
Hodgson, Sharon 311
Hoell, Muriel 500
Hoffman, Ann 435
Hoffman, Helen A. 95
Hoffman, Kenneth 58
Hoffmann, Joseph 338
Hofhine, Carol 225
Hogan, Eileen 120
Hogue, Rebecca 288
Hohmann, W. Neil 288
Holbrook, Eva K. 104
Holbrook, Mildred L. 304
Holbrooks, Dot "Pittman" 218
Holcomb, Amanda L. 106
Holcomb, Stephanie M. 147
Holden, Shirley M. 60
Holder, Erin 9
Holeman, Andi 221
Holihan, Kenneth 184
Hollenbach Jr., W. A. 387
Hollenbeck, Catherine 453
Holley, Rosanne 159
Hollins, Shenek 156
Hollis, Lee 385
Holloway, Stephanie L. 568
Holly, Nicole 302
Holman, Michael 495
Holman, Mira 295
Holmes, Angeline 248
Holton, Agnes 76
Holton Sr., A. E. 517
Holtvluwer, Nicholas 66
Holtz, Danielle 545
Holtzclaw, Nathan 280
Holzer, Lorraine 259
Homan, Jean Y. 451
Homola, Rose M. 487
Honaker, Mary Ann 156
Honea, Dwaine L. 536
Honeycutt, David G. 12
Honeywell, Carmen L. 206
Hooks, Ernie 118
Hooven, Gary 543
Hoover, David Shade 243
Hoover, S. A. 564
Hopkins, Lottie 407
Hopkins, Ronald A. 572
Hopkins, Vincent S. 267
Hopkinson, Jean 122
Hopper, Ronald E. 562
Hopper, Scotty 485
Horan, Bill 119
Horne, Aaron 125
Horner, Wendy J. 276
Horsley, Timothy 267
horstmeyer, erica 28
Horton, Michael Scot 502

Horton, Walter M. 289
Hoskins, Rosie 387
Houchins, Charles E. 529
Houk, Dody 244
Houpt, Myrtie G. 512
Howard, Evelyn M. 311
Howard, Frances M. 333
Howard, Louise 502
Howard, Robert E. 566
Howard, Virginia 551
Howe, Maxine C. 394
Howie, Ellen E. 77
Howieson, Gertrude G. 135
Howton, Rhonda Carol 185
Huang, Sarah 254
Hubbard, Theresa 253
Huber, Courtney 80
hubert, paul 520
Hudson, Barbara 339
Hudson, Carl D. 218
Hudson, Ellen Matilda 465
Hudson, Henry T. 18
Hudson, Remy 465
Hudzietz, Joan M. 523
Huebl, Hubert C. 470
Huffhines, Terry W. 174
Huffman, Connie 85
Huffman, Eve 15
Hugenot, Ida 455
Hughes, Demetress M. 4
Hughes, Lora D. 568
Hughes, R. Kevin 139
Hull, Dave 22
Hulme, Naomi 63
Hummel, Heather 247
Humphrey, Owen E. 169
Humphreys, Karen 275
Hungler, Ann 213
Hunt, Allen T. 329
Hunt, Debra W. 236
Hunt, Samuel J. 509
Hunt, Stacey 481
Hunter, Barry C. 95
Hunter, Dawn Marie 229
Hunter, Isabelle 467
Hunter, Linda K. 404
Hurdle, Tanisha 150
Hurley, Robert E. 257
Hurry, Mary 70
Huseth, David O. 453
Husk, Renee 137
Hussey, Richard 475
Huston, Lilia S. 307
Hutter, Charles 469
Hutto, F. M. 546
Huwald, Fred J. 449
Huyler, Alice 89
Hyatt, Charlie 94
Hyatt, Karen 518
Hyde, Leslie E. 397

I

Ibarra, Nick J. 494
Ibe, Comfort 469
Ibert, Ellen 237
Ilsley, Velma 299
Imberi, Daniel 91
Imel, Lucille Burke 191
Imig, Alice Marie 527
Impink, Susan J. 522

Ingoglia, Andrew 472
Ingram, Jaime 127
Ingram, Ruby 265
Innis, Pauline 496
Iorlano, Maria 519
Ippolito, Caren 525
Irelan, Christine C. 233
Ireland, Vera 483
Irizarry, Lorna 514
Irvin, Cathy Lee 198
Irvin, Mary 46
Irwin, Joseph 241
Isaac, George 240
Isetta, Kevin 539
Ishkanian, Alice 5
Ivor-Smith, Randal 57
Iwamura, Landon 520

J

Jabusch, Jane 454
Jachimiak, Edward Joseph 135
Jachimowicz, Teresa 255
Jackson, Anita 98
Jackson, Connie 531
Jackson, Deloris Lightfoot 352
Jackson, Deveron B. 195
Jackson, Donald M. 214
Jackson, Elaine 443
Jackson, Frances S. 126
Jackson, Glenda K. 246
Jackson, Jayne Anne 540
Jackson, Jennifer 468
Jackson, Lisa 290
Jackson, Rachalle Denise 142
Jacobs, Debbie 79
Jacobs, Kathleen 382
Jacobs, Mara 486
Jacobs, Naomi R. 293
Jacobs, Todd M. 555
Jacobs, Wynona 294
Jacobsen, Annemarie 462
Jacoby, Nancy J. 290
Jael, Maria Susan L. 573
James Jr., Richard T. 56
James, LaShunda 275
James, Mark 574
James, Nicole 422
Janecki, Sonia M. 142
Janis, Timothy 296
Jansen, Karen 496
Janssen, Connie K. 472
January, David 13
Jarratt, Ashley 228
Jarrett, Cain 567
Jason, Jennifer D. 363
Jasper, Kari 162
Jay, Christina 133
Jaymes, Dylan 243
Jean-Pierre, Yvan 69
Jedlicka, Jamie 345
Jefferson, Jennifer 521
Jeffery, B. 255
Jeffrey, Rhea V. 190
Jehs, Shawn Michael 148
Jemison, Mildred Clauff 304
Jenkins, Ean 104
Jenkins, Erica 202
Jenkins, Jimmy 432
Jenkins, Jonelle 91
Jenkins, Karen Butler 409

Jenkins, Susie M. 261
Jennings, Ragin 266
Jensen, Carolyn H. 110
Jensen, Sandra Marie 140
Jergenson, Beth K. 30
Jessee, Dana Michelle 448
Jewell, Barbara Lee 351
Jezarian, Gregory 335
Joglar, Carl 3
Johanson, Angela 130
Johanson, Elaine 89
Johns, Ed 133
Johnson, Alice 336
Johnson, Arlene 226
Johnson, Bertha D. 444
Johnson, Betty J. Garner 224
Johnson, Brande 313
Johnson, Brandon 242
Johnson, Dana 103
Johnson, Don Alva 466
Johnson, Dora 353
Johnson, Emogene 346
Johnson, James Eric 243
Johnson, James L. 351
Johnson, Joseph Mark 435
Johnson, Kim 191
Johnson, Lillian L. 58
Johnson, Linda 491
Johnson, Macksine 164
Johnson, Marv 518
Johnson, Mary P. 388
Johnson, Monica 417
Johnson, Pauline E. 272
Johnson, Phyllis 300
Johnson, Russell 512
Johnson, Ryaja 272
Johnson, Stephanie 517
Johnson, Stephen 183
Johnston, Earl W. 120
Johnston, John M. 5
Johnston, Kenneth A. 389
Joiner, Ariell 355
Jones, Artemese B. 455
Jones, Cecilia B. 467
Jones, Christopher 440
Jones, Danica L. 107
Jones, Dean A. 248
Jones, Donna Foy 15
Jones, Florence 323
Jones, Forrest 451
Jones, G. Theresa 381
Jones, Gregory 249
Jones, Keelan 66
Jones, Keyana 184
Jones, Kimberly 190
Jones, Kourtni Elizabeth 50
Jones, Linda L. 552
Jones, Lisa L. 585
Jones, Lynn M. 274
Jones, Marjorie D. 576
Jones, Rick 182
Jones, Sharon A. 60
Jones, Tom 508
Jordan, Amanda 90
Jordan, Bojana V. 212
Jordan, Joseph A. 229
Jordon, Carl 242
Jorgensen, Susannah 557
Jorgenson, Cheryl F. 195
Joseph, Beatrice Downes 7
Josephson, Jessica 78

Jost, Christine 351
Juarez, Cathy 82
Julian, Karl 251
Julian, Marlene T. 75
Julian, Sharon 159
Juliano, Joseph 111
Jungels, Christine Martin 368
Juntz, Natalie Mitchell 485

K

Kachelriess, Audrey R. 541
Kachur, Christopher 227
Kaimakamian, Ferdinand 12
Kaisen, Ronald 149
Kalton, Donald S. 110
Kammerer, Lisa Marie 47
Kanter, Irene 448
Kantlehner, Arika 195
Kaplan, Max V. 416
Kaplan, Tillie Lewis 178
Karagovalis, John 6
Kardatzke, Brenda 315
Karlson, Dixie D. 131
Karmo, Natalie 258
Kasdan, Frances Collins 243
Kass, Melissa 299
Katemopoulos, Mildred J. 416
Kathwari, Rafique 552
Katz, Louis 266
Kaufman, Irving 316
Kaufman, Sean 514
Kawka, Josh 320
Kayastha, Kumar J. 154
Kaylor, Daphne 220
Kazimov, Nushabe 274
Kearns, Melany 308
Keating, Nadia N. 168
Keele, Cynthia Kay 194
Keeler, Robin 268
Keeler, Steven T. 49
Keemon, Adam J. 242
Keenan, Tara R. 514
Keene, Rosalie A. 384
Keetch, Barbara B. 170
Keeton, April 364
Keevey, Thomas P. 418
Keith, Jennifer 201
Keithline, Angela 231
Keller, Kathleen 377
Keller, Linn 144
Kelley, Louise 48
Kelly, Carolyn 250
Kelly, Frances 127
Kelly, Hubert P. 14
Kelly, James Timothy 466
Kelly, Kay 258
Kelly, Natalie 412
Kelm, Pat 69
Kelmenson, Amy 436
Kelso, Kathleen A. 408
Kemler, Marc 411
Kemp, Gregory L. 89
Kemp, Hazel V. 442
Kemp, Mamie 479
Ken, Klever 388
Kendricks, Dona J. 215
Kennedy, Edith M. 369
Kennedy, Evelyn 247
Kennepp, Kelly 42
Kenney, Bill 233

Kenyon, Richard 385
Keomia 387
Keown, Sienna 147
Kephart, Wendy R. 142
Kerg, Brian 234
Kerins, Martin J. 288
Kern, Thomas J. 420
Kernal, Sara N. 267
Kerr, Jack W. 468
Kerr, Jessica 77
Kerr, Stephen C. 61
Kersch, Christine E. 194
Kersting, Lisa G. 388
Kessler, Irene N. 19
Kessler, Penny Lee 423
Kestin, Alan R. 195
Ketchum, Pierce Stith 306
Kew, Ann 464
Khademzadeh, Amir 122
Khoury, Sharon E. 277
Kidd, Harriet O. 192
Kidd, Jonathan 433
Kidd, Thaddeus W. 53
Kilpatrick, Kevin 387
Kilts, Matthew 516
Kim, Young Mi 289
Kimbro, Kathryn 545
Kimbrough, Janette 216
Kimmel, Sandi 69
Kimmer, Lisa Diana 265
Kindred, Ellen M. 234
Kindschy, Nicole 159
King, Anthony 119
King, Bernadine 96
King, Eva 472
King, Sean 403
Kingsbery, Lane 189
Kingston, R. J. 271
Kinnison, Mattie Dee 394
Kinsey, Tara 423
Kirby, Robin 309
Kirchner, Jessica 340
Kirk, Jamie 110
Kirkpatrick, Anne Carr 232
Kirkwood, Lawrence C. 303
Kisala, Jennifer L. 359
Kishimoto, Carolina 254
Kitchens, Kenneth R. 73
Kittinger, Phyllis 163
Kizer, Jo 36
Klase, Marilyn C. 490
Klausner, Jennifer 106
Klausner, Jeri 220
Kleeb, Sarah 191
Klein, Eileen 584
Klein, Rebecca 520
Klement, Charles J. 359
Klessen, Ruth 420
Kloster, Margaret 48
Klotz, Frieda D. 31
Knarr, Cheryl 118
Knechel, Andrew 584
Kneher, Dorothea A. 432
Knierim, Carrie 359
Knight, Loie P. 159
Knights, Carlene A. 103
Knisely, Billy 455
Knoble, Mollie 515
Knopka, Jeremy 587
Knouse, Evelyn 287
Knowles, Char 13

Knox, Elisabeth Haylee 348
Koch, Jon 229
Koenig, Tara 50
Kohlhepp, Ellen E. 117
Koiva, Enn O. 343
Komanetsky, Alex 524
Komara, Rebecca Ann 587
Komarek, Pamela 64
Kommer, Bruce F. 11
Konen, Ryan Marie 285
Koon, Phillip 309
Kosack, Kathleen E. 537
Kostopoulos, Jessica 204
Kousin, Louis M. 428
Kovach, Roger P. 519
Kovner, Barbara F. 123
Kowalsky, Joan M. 86
Kozuka, Takashi 63
Kraemer, Michael 413
Krajeski, Courtney 230
Krall, Diane M. 35
Kralowetz, Brian 582
Kramer, Carrie 244
Kramer, Matthew D. 486
Kramer, Phyllis A. 159
Kramer, Reba R. 155
Krauthammer, Anna 464
Krebes, Carrie Jo 323
Kreimeyer, Lorraine P. 566
Kreitz, Linda M. 566
Kremer, Mary E. 281
Kress, Mary L. 419
Krigbaum, Bradley S. 535
Krippel, Mary 575
Krolack, Janice Brown 361
Krull, Sam 45
Kuar, Blanca I. 6
Kuberski, Matthew 203
Kubiak, Greg D. 442
Kuhn, Barbara 35
Kumpf, Lindsay 138
Kunco, John Joseph 467
Kunnemann, Chandra 332
Kunz, Ken 553
Kushnatsian, Susan 560
Kuster, Katie 291
Kutac, Kevin 551
Kyre, Christen 316

L

la follette, nico 491
Laate, Nolan 489
Laberge, Kate 554
LaBrake, Gregory M. 219
Lacasse, James 206
Lacey, Deborah D. 539
Lackey, Michael 40
Lacsina, Nicole Ann 178
Ladonis, Walter 156
Laflin, Robin R. 376
LaFrance, Elizabeth 133
Lagle, Carl 244
Lagoe, Lindsay 167
LaGorio, Karen 47
Laieski Sr., Frank J. 434
Lakatos, Victoria 188
Lala, Mrugesh 565
Lallave, Elba 90
Lalomia, Marisa Ann 14
LaLone, Rose W. 546

Lamb, Robert 580
Lamberg, June 312
Lambert, Allan H. 362
Lambert, Jade 76
Lambert-Dannen, Evelyn 240
Lambrecht, Elizabeth 350
Lameiro, Veronica 506
LaMonte, Bobbi 203
Lamp, Richard R. 516
Lamprecht, Cortney 91
Lanberg, Joan 451
Lancaster, Abna A. 544
Landis, Cameron S. 120
Landis, Debra H. 231
Landrum, Tami Jo 305
Lane, Harold A. 438
Lane, Tamika 142
Langeloh, Mary Jane 272
Langer, Mirth B. 382
Langham, Janelle 445
Lanham, Robert K. 556
Lanier, Sonya 373
Lankeit, Inge 324
Lannin, Joanna 93
Lannoye, Rosie Sandra 174
Lantz II, Pericles John 573
Lantz, Susan 186
Lanum, Tamra 399
Lanzendorfer, Amy 81
Lapides, Julie 106
LaPorte, Christopher M. 351
Large, Abby Jane 97
LaRosa, Donna 246
Larregui, Debra 528
Larrimore, Gene 221
Larson, Faith Carol 359
Larson, Karen R. 179
Larson, Timothy E. 254
LaRue, Brandon 436
LaRue, David H. 128
LaRue, Janet E. 24
LaSure, Reba 254
Latimer, Renee 422
Laub, Larry 192
Laub, Louis G. 577
Laughlin, Shawn T. 307
Lauletta, Dorothy J. 32
Laureys, Lorraine 563
Lauzonis, Stacy Renee 385
Laverty, Mary 58
Lavington, Ronald 548
Lavoie, Christine 545
La Voie, Glenn 582
LaVoy, Rachel 182
Lawrence, Rowena B. 390
Lawrence-Martin, Carla 77
Lawson, Julie 36
Lawter, Sharon 480
Layman, Mitchell Wayne 165
Lazinger, Maxwell 476
Lazzareschi, Lou 251
Leal, Leslie A. 306
Leamy, Kit 392
Leaton, Marcella K. 258
Leavey, Patricia 554
LeBahn, Richard Lee 428
Leboeuf, Alma Martin 78
Lecher, Angela M. 32
LeCompte, Denise 368
Lee, Anne W. 106
Lee, Bill 349

Lee, Dot 321
Lee, Heather 99
Lee, Lorri 306
Lee, Melissa 478
Lee, Te-Yi 553
Leech, Melissa 429
Leech, Paul 522
Leeds, David 358
Leftwich, Judith Evans 238
Leggett, Duane 359
Legros, Christine Dawn 105
Lehfeldt, Carl 38
Leiter, Debi 216
Leiteritz, Stephanie 294
Leitzke, Douglas J. 197
Lekhlifi, Lynn Marie 257
Lemieux, Karen Jean 298
Lendacky, Maria A. 511
Lenz, Stuart D. 276
Leon, Anna 205
Leon, Louann 375
Leon, Mary 302
Leon, Sara 263
Leonard, K. Leigh 261
Leonard, Patricia S. 170
Leroy, Shelby Wood 478
Lesch, Danyelle 473
Leslie, Connie Worden 325
Lessing, Jessica 35
Leuliette, M. E. 60
Lever, Norine 47
Leverington, Denis C. 361
Leverton, Erin Jeannine 112
Levin, Sidney 477
Levinson, Mitchell A. 185
Levy, Christina Taft 449
Levy, D. Alexander 492
Levy, Francois Petit 535
Levy, Janet 38
Lewandowski, Mary A. 304
Lewellen, Rodney Duane 295
Lewis, Anna L. 450
Lewis, Brittani W. 196
Lewis, David R. 214
Lewis, Douglas Everett 249
Lewis, Fred 217
Lewis, Joseph R. 127
Lewis, Kevin G. 192
Lewis, Robert D. 281
Leyte-Vidal, Eduardo J. 95
Liaga, Carmen 13
Liao, Rebecca 270
Licari, Sabrina 381
Lichon, Vanessa 180
Liddy, Crystal 364
Liedecke, Mindy 414
Lierman, Kyle 303
Liew, Vincent E. 482
Lifto, Matthew Tait 511
Liggett, Woody 191
Light, Amy 97
Lightfoot, Linda 479
Liguori, Jessica 231
Likes, J. Carlton 50
Likovetz, Bessie L. 470
Liles, D. Andrew 129
Lillethun, Kara L. 498
Lima, Marcos Tiberio 372
Liming, Kim Michelle 377
Lin, Esther 96
Lincoln, Leslie 301

Linde-Gibson, Linda 515
Lindsay, Elizabeth 449
Lindsay, Merrideth A. 298
Lindsey, Dorothy L. 17
Lindsey, Natille P. 410
Linkous, Belinda A. 466
Linsenmeyer, Jill 30
Lipshetz, Terry Allen 171
Lipsius, Bernard 347
Lisenby, Louise 174
Lister, William Joe 141
Little, Maxey D. 482
Littman, Emma 132
Lively, Charity 101
Livingston, Elizabeth Blair 100
Liwaj, Brianne 349
Llewellyn, Link W. 373
Lloyd, Patricia A. 488
LoCascio, Pat 163
Locke, Keith 12
Lockwood, Lisa L. 148
Loder, Dale 128
Lodico, Cheryl M. 352
Logan, Michael L. 372
Logan, Theresa Marie 301
Lohry, Jennifer 472
Loin, Joe 338
Lolley, April 78
Lombardi, Maria 140
Lombardo, Lawrence 52
Lomonte, Diana 94
Long, Arthur A. 544
Long, Barbara F. 461
Long, Cathy L. 235
Long, Karie 562
Looney, Shana 291
Lopes, Sharon M. 75
Lopez, Michael 171
Lopez, Nikki 419
Lopez, Rosa M. 113
Lord, Debra J. 239
Lord, Laura Anne 169
Loriaux, Barbara J. 315
Loschiavo, Tim 53
Lotti, Fran 489
Loudermilk, Jean 470
Loughran, Carole B. 122
Lovato, Benjamin J. 456
Love, Dorothy Hunt 22
Love Jr., James T. 38
Love, Julia 145
Lowe, Blaine 311
Lowe, Carla A. 239
Lowell, Edna Mae 470
Lowell, Kate 474
Lowell, Marita J. 58
Lowman, Helen 330
Loy, J. E. 408
Loyd, Rachel 262
Lucas, Mary Gerene 489
Lucki, Jerome 19
Luger, Sally A. 177
Lukasik, Tanya 379
Lumkes, Janet M. 360
Lumpkin, Trista 370
Lundgren, Robert 294
Lundquist, Merlin L. 569
Lunel, Gina Marie 368
Luther, Fred 11
Luthi, Ruth Morris 173
Lutz, Nancy M. 552

Luznicky, Melissa R. 166
Lychak, Marie D. 403
Lykins, Richard 481
Lykins, Ryan 98
Lynch, Alberta S. 471
Lynch, J. E. 425
Lynch, Lillian K. 396
Lynn, Wendy 296
Lyon, Laura 145
Lyons, Jacquelyn D. 471
Lyons, Jean 347
Lyons-Colichio, R. James 421
Lytle, Connie 89

M

Mabb, Johndrue 201
Mabery, Marilyne V. 289
MacDonald, Maureen 384
Mace, Tyler 519
Machalk, Amber 80
Mack, Hildred P. 101
Mack Jr., Richard 485
Mack, Sharon Grove 64
MacKintosh, Stella M. 57
MacPherson, David K. 242
MacQueen, Cher 242
Madaffari, Cristina 437
Maddalone, Marilyn 150
Maddi, Michael 378
Madeo Jr., Joseph F. 88
Madison, Maranacci 194
Madsen, Jennie W. 121
Madsen, Jessie 542
Maeder, Molly 290
Maetzold, C. Martine 257
Magan, Tina 155
Magee, Bettie M. 438
Magee, Erin 239
Magee Jr., Henry 93
Magied, Luqman A. 288
Magliano, Joelle 217
Mahon, Doris 528
Maida, Cassandra 246
Maiden, Thomas 71
Mainenti, Etty 470
Maisel, Estelle 581
Makar, Samantha 187
Makl, Claire 198
Malabag, Candina 230
Malasnik, Natasha 484
Malcom, Coralou K. 230
Maldonado, Elisa 33
Mallik, Romi 497
Malo, Daniel R. 120
Malone, Amanda S. 320
Malone, Antionette I. 31
Maltese, Laura 160
Manaker, Stella 179
Manaloto, Anna Melissa 207
Mancuso, Julia M. 459
Manning, Kathleen 49
Manning, Todd 515
Mansanales, Jeremy 439
Manuel, Dennis 119
Manuell, Jean 30
Marasa, Cynthia S. 526
Marcano, Beatriz 544
Marceau, Nineveh J. 174
Marchand, Susan 166
Marcum, Gerri 459

Mardres, Otis A. 56
Maree, Roxanne 290
Margroff, Linda Sue 517
Maria, Annette 93
Marienthal-Baumgartner, Martha 420
Marino, Carolann 89
Marion, Julia 356
Marion, S. J. 268
Marion, Sandra 309
Marioni, Frances 459
Markey, Rich 520
Markey, Shannon 268
Markey, Tim 411
Markos, Athena M. 86
Marks, Rita 565
Marlett, Robert 174
Marnell, Dave 8
Marotta, Marie 519
Marquette, J. M. 494
Marquez, Corinne 542
Marquez, Julianna 360
Marron, Rebecca A. 52
Marsac, Lacey 492
Marshall, Tim 157
Marshall-Terry, Teresa Kaye 306
Martell, Sharon 560
Martelli, Rocco 477
Martin, Brendalyn Crudup 349
Martin, Gary Saint 87
Martin Jr., Ralph W. 178
Martin, Lee 287
Martin, Loretta 388
Martin, Michael A. 421
Martin, Sarah 302
Martin, Starlet 63
Martinez, Angelica Panduro 96
Martinez Jr., Salvador 504
Martinez, Ralph Warren 254
Martinsson, James 465
Martley, Sarah 397
Marttinen, Arja 363
Martucci, Robin 131
Marut, Bruce 31
Mascaro, Nancy Carol 411
Maschino, Jo 366
Mason, Betty O. 339
Mason, Todd 297
Mastrangelo, Duane 406
Matheny, Jennifer L. 237
Mathes, Martha L. 402
Matheson, Shelby 144
Mathews, Nancy 548
Mathews, Vivian Archie 521
Mathis, Ned L. 190
Mathis, Stephen 501
Mattei, Patricia 294
Mattes, Marion Jane 189
Matthews, Elaine N. 207
Matthews, Scott B. 155
Mattingly, Daniel B. 312
Mauldin, David 196
Mauldin, Forrest A. 85
Maxey, Yaminah 184
Maxwell, Phyllis 386
May, Angie 216
May, Suzanne T. 44
Mayer, Carla 80
Mayer, Janet S. 444
Mayes, Cheree 82
Mayes, Robert W. 179
Mayne, MaryAnne 519

Mayo, Akima 104
Mc, Elaine Namara 15
McAllister, Hazel 80
McAllister, Susan 370
McBroom, Laurie A. 509
McCallum, David 362
McCarthy, Matthew W. 491
McCartney, Ann R. 218
McCartney, Fran 31
McCartney-Cutshaw, Irene L. 321
McCartor, Andrea 250
McCarty, Patricia 190
McClain, Roy 175
McClaney, Jacquelyn M. 230
McCleese, Amy 334
McClelland, Gail 334
McClintock, Camden 242
McClintock, Jan 312
McCloskey, Carole M. 122
McClure, Barbara 544
McCollum, Dani 87
McComas, Anne 246
McComb, Viva M. 505
McCord, Mary L. 255
McCormick, William J. 269
McCovey-Kelly, Janice R. 109
McCoy Jr., David 109
McCoy, Sharon Ann 307
McCrae, Buffie 584
McCranie, Courtney 368
McCray, Maggie 62
McCroy, Melissa A. 386
McCullough, Debbie 79
McDermott, Hope 472
McDermott, John 464
McDonald, Diann S. T. 108
McDonald, Ramon 405
McDonald, Theresa 578
McDonnell, Susan 53
McDowell, Audrey 16
McDowell, Barbara A. 84
McElroy, Diana L. 84
McEveney, Kelly 442
McFadden, Randolph 284
McFarland, Elva D. 366
McFarlane, Gerald J. 440
McGaha, Christen Rae 108
McGinnis, Jackie 240
McGinty, William Michael 179
McGlasson, Christine 85
McGlynn, Ryan 394
McGowan, Joann 24
McGrady II, William Allen 62
McGregor, Novia 304
McGregor, Sarah 413
McGuire, Erika C. 447
McGuire, Margaret 407
McGuyer, Marshall D. 158
McIlvaine, Jeaninne 246
McIntosh, Juanita 23
McIntyre, Donald M. 120
McIntyre, Gary 193
McKeever, Theresa 287
McKenna, Helen 94
McKenzie, Katie 484
McKethan, Erika M. 30
McKinney, F. Norris 168
McKinney, Robbie Lee 44
McKittrick, Stacey 476
McLane-Collins, Georgia Rose 430
McLaughlin, Erin 358

McLaurine, Shauntell 575
McLean, Rosell W. 345
McManus, Kimberly O. 570
McMaster, Jeanne Beckett 107
McMasters, Ruth 305
McMillen, Rebecca 415
McMillian, Wendy M. 62
McMurry, Jeremy 431
McMurtrie, Sandy 63
McNabb, D. H. 493
McNally, John H. 81
McNaughton, Shane D. 178
McNeeley, Margo 136
McNeely, Jennifer 15
McNeil, Keyana 551
McPherson, D. Jayne 174
McPherson, Elizabeth 102
McPherson, John W. 531
McPike, Keri 183
McRae, Alexander 114
McRae, Frederick K. 3
McReynolds, Tracy 425
McSwain, Suzanne 72
McVeigh, Wilda Kathryn 138
McWater, Darci 447
McWhirter, Jill 233
Meacham, Mark Colyn 301
Meagan, Jennifer 104
Medeiros, Andrea 15
Medeiros, Susan 523
Medlock Bridge 4th graders 328
Meinzinger, Lianne Ashley 490
Meissner, George Allan 342
Melara, Miguel A. 572
Melaro, Marie A. 403
Melchiori, Elizabeth A. 320
Melendez, Ieisha M. 10
Meling, Florence 81
Mellon, Rachel 170
Meltz, Rachel 485
Melvin, Nicole 271
Mencias, Placida C. 286
Mendez, Guadalupe 241
Mendez, Raymond J. 146
Mendez, Rocio 265
Mendicki, Vi 508
Menke, Roma 403
Menn, Catherine Vera 118
Menser, Terri 481
Mercer, Betty E. 523
Mercer, Melissa 389
Merchant, Argatha Hamilton 211
Merchant, Georgia 467
Mercier, Julie C. 197
Merel, Brian 203
Mergens, Judith Anne 26
Merrifield, Bambi 97
Merriman, Deborah Elizabeth 134
Merry, Maxine A. 285
Mertz, Mary A. 176
Metcalf Jr., Raymond E. 275
Metz, Debbie 207
Metzler, Janis 116
Metzmeier, June 466
Meyer, Barbara 247
Meyer, Michelle 398
Meyer, Rebekah 192
Meyers, Nola K. 557
Mezynski, Danean 349
Michael, Jeanmari 118
Michaels, Kevin P. 153

Michalik, Patti L. 576
Micheli, Ann 195
Mick, Lydia 498
Mickels, Nancy L. 40
Mickens, Eric Lamont 329
Mickey 295
Middaugh, Rebecca 422
Midkiff, Stephanie 400
Mierisch-Kracke, Suzanne L. 42
Mijatovic, Peter 308
Mikulski, Paul 548
Miles, Cynthia J. 35
Miles, Randy 164
Milford, Morgan 427
Milhoan, Jennifer 367
Miller, Andrea Lynn 349
Miller, Andrew J. 434
Miller, Barbara 202
Miller, Carl R. 96
Miller, Catherine A. 241
Miller, Dara Rebecca 132
Miller, Desiree L. 343
Miller, Florence G. 34
Miller, Florence L. 342
Miller, Janis L. 364
Miller, Jason C. 331
Miller, Joseph Martin 239
Miller, Keturah J. 54
Miller, Lilly 298
Miller, Lisa 275
Miller, Mandy Rhea 478
Miller, Max J. 552
Miller, Richard C. 190
Miller, Rita Sylvia 167
Miller, Ruth Wofford 269
Miller, Sally 75
Miller, Sarah 185
Miller, Sarah R. 302
Miller, Susan S. 387
Miller, Trunita 377
Millican, Helen 452
Mills, Zane 498
Miner, Ida L. 17
Minihan, Gerard C. 91
Mink, Florence M. 203
Minor, Harry 358
Minteer, April 441
Minthorn, Daisy 219
Miraglia, Ann 314
Mischke, Josefina 13
Mitchell, Carol 225
Mitchell, Ellie 26
Mitchell III, E. Cameron 382
Mitchell III, James T. 334
Mitchell, Laura 570
Mitchell, Lona 61
Mitchell, Marion V. 166
Mitchell, Sandra F. 499
Mitchell, Susan S. 309
Mitchem, Tara 411
Moberly, Dorothy 21
Modaressi, Marc C. 297
Mogle, Claudette M. 363
Mohler, Carol A. 223
Mohr, Lauralyn T. 172
Mohr, Marty 43
Mohr, Pat 429
Mohyla, Ostap M. 549
Mojica, Mica 502
Moler Jr., Michael H. 303
Momo, Femaarta 208

Mondragon, Tory 395
Moneyhun, Susan 183
Monfore, Gerry 112
Monge, Margie Viado 509
Mongeau, Barbara A. 473
Monroe, Annie Mae 466
Monroe, Lynn A. 160
Montague, Nelson C. 425
Montera Sr., Constancio 441, 579
Montgomery, David E. 86
Montgomery, Melody 138
Moo, Aimee 120
Moody, Anna 354
Moody, Vonna 200
Moon, Teresa 568
Mooney, Sarah 191
Moore, Andrea 115
Moore, Anna 469
Moore, Carolyn 232
Moore, David 208
Moore, David Gamble 91
Moore, Ebony 466
Moore, Ella Jane 85
Moore, Ellouise 311
Moore, Jeremy 433
Moore, Leah R. 42
Moore, Margaret Bell 155
Moore, Mida A. 565
Moore, Nikeishia M. 191
Moore, Patrick Sherrick 278
Moore, Paula 171
Moore, Roy J. 263
Moore, Vernon C. 509
Moore, Vivian 559
Moores, Mary Catherine 189
Mora, Iris M. 358
Morales, Fernando 104
Morang, Lydia E. 519
Morcy, Edith . 76
Moreno, Rhonda 422
Morgan, Catherine M. 533
Morgan, Elaine V. 469
Morgan, Griffith 535
Morin, Danielle 357
Morocco, Joyce M. 441
Morone, Christina 472
Morong, Marilyn 161
Morphew, Liz 429
Morris, Abby 249
Morris, Bridgette 234
Morris, Joanne P. 109
Morris, John R. 532
Morris, Sue 518
Morrison, Brook 440
Morrissey, John 243
Morrow, M. D. 272
Morse, David 36
Mosbacher, Joseph L. 356
Moseley, Annabelle M. 460
Moser, Louise 157
Moshier, Dorothy 213
Moss, Aleksa 244
Moss, Janice 454
Motta, Joseph 124
Motter, Norman K. 187
Mowatt, Dorene J. 97
Moya, Iris 322
Moyers, Kelly 304
Muckle, Mary 294
Muja, Kathleen A. 528
Muldrow, Stephen 385

Mulholland, Jason 531
Mulkern, Louis 137
Mullis, Timothy D. 55
Mundinger, Helen Monroe 580
Munjak, Daniel Raymond 367
Munoz, Dave Antonio 9
Munoz, Sharon D. 557
Munoz, Sonia 420
Munoz, Thomas 565
Munson, Michelle Renee 170
Murakami, Dorothy 94
Murino, Andy 25
Murphy, Brenda 361
Murphy, Dianna 117
Murphy, Fred 86
Murphy, Kaleigh 381
Murphy, Kitty 308
Murphy, Mike 561
Murphy, Tammie Kay 381
Murray, Eva B. 125
Murray, Norma S. 564
Muscarella, Janelle 80
Muscoe, Doreen 239
Musgrove, Shelly 549
Mushiana, Paul 548
Musselman, Janeen 364
Mutch, Mandi 490
Muyleart, Diane G. 336
Myers, Barbara Z. 468
Myers, Cynthia C. 218
Myers, Sybil S. 64
Myers, Wallis A. 271
Myles, Donna 468

N

Nadeau, Wayne 484
Napier, Jack 329
Nappa, Eleanor 112
Nash, Jane 118
Nash, Joyce Ann 246
Natalie 185
Natera, Sebastian 253
Nation, Chad Allen 539
Naucke, Lisa 390
Navarrete, Jeannette 132
Nazario, Natividad 253
Neal, Derek 90
Neal I, Rodney Bee 172
Nebblett, Kesiwaa 548
Nebeker, Becci 134
Needham, Florence 17
Needlman, Herbert 347
Neel, Sharon H. 414, 518
Neh 389
Neilsen, Norma 50
Nelms, Ben S. 537
Nelson, Dawn 22
Nelson, Diane 89
Nelson, Larie 150
Nelson, R. W. 143
Nelson, T. R. 298
Nereo, Lynn Marie 415
Newcombe, Lucille 277
Newell, Dolan G. 84
Newman, Gay Gaisma 123
Newman, Thomas 51
Newsom, James 235
Nguyen, Chi 436
Nguyen, Suzan 502
Nguyen, Thuy 515

Niblet, Kamar Ali 558
Nicastro, Carol 318
Nice, Michelle 178
Nicholas, Victoria G. 522
Nichols, Darrell Lee 115
Nichols, Elizabeth 312
Nichols, Lois 267
Nichols, Marion H. 568
Nichols, Rachel 43
Nichols, Robert 188
Nichols, Tara 419
Nicholson, Robert 270
Nickel, Richard E. 273
Nielsen, Melanie 394
Nilles, Stephanie 187
Nistico, John Mariano 11
Nitsch, Deborah A. 322
Niver, Karen A. 491
Nixon, Annie Willard 213
Nkomo, Thabo William 48
Noall, Eleanor Hepburn 349
Noble Sr., Clifton J. 530
Noe, Traci 188
Noerdlinger, Victor 563
Nohren, Ruby 410
Noland, Nathan McKain 502
Nord, Cindy 447
Norgaard, Melanee 417
Norgaard, Nona 183
Norinsky, Igor 360
Norman, Clayton 228
Norman, Melanie 291
Noronha, Ruby 577
Norris, Arnold L. 85
Norris, Talitha Eastridge 144
North, Kay 145
Northam, Kelley 277
Norton, Thelma C. 160
Notti, Jenna 4
Novak, Paul 283
Nowbath, Freddy 362
Noyes, Andrew 21
Noyes, Dan Ray 234
Noyes, Ebbie 200
Nunamaker, Caroline F. 199
Nunes, Trilby 39
Nuottila, Shirley A. 71
Nusser, Melisa A. 492
Nye, Suzanne M. - 1992 293

O

Obecunas, Dorothy Farrell 345
Obremski, Norman L. 522
O'Brien, Charlyn 21
O'Brien, Patricia 510
Occhiogrosso, James J. 234
Ochenduszko, Linda E. 185
O'Connell, Lindsay 148
O'Connor, Cailin 432
O'Daniel, Amber Dawn 319
O'Dell, Shannon Anne 138
Odman, Lauren 288
O'Donnell, Carl W. 536
O'Donnell, Elizabeth 196
Oelslager, Christy 245
Offenberger, Cathy 431
O'Gara, Melissa 151
Ogihara, Dorothy 102
Oglesby, Pamela H. 377
O'Hanlon, Ceane 445

O'Haver, Ruby N. 67
O'Hearn, K. 521
Olds, Isaac J. 215
Olimpio, Ruth 176
Olivarez, Nicole 567
Olivencia Jr., Frank 83
Oliver, Melissa 419
Olsen, Carrie 369
Olsen, Rebecca H. 492
Olson, Carol 358
Olson, Michelle M. 45
Olson, Selma 572
O'Neil, J. R. 175
Onnen, Clayton 208
Onyeali, Ihuoma 129
Opela, Danella 85
Orfanos, Lina 292
Oriol, Chrissy T. 3
O'Riordan, Raymond S. 420
Orlando, Rena 178
Ornstein, Martin H. 420
O'Rowe, Eileen C. 90
Orr, Orena 522
Orsini, Charles W. 343
Ortiz, Michael John 273
Orton, Eris M. 359
Oshiro, Janet R. 88
Osi, Rozaly 552
Osten, William 44
Otterson, Larry R. 570
Otto, Ludwig 185
Ouni, Mehdi 397
Ousley, Judy W. 466
Oviedo, Suzanne 152
Owen, Jenifer 365
Owens, Cindy 367
Owens, Joanne L. 336
Owens, Julie Ann 446
Owens, Michael C. 57
Owens, Willie 71
Oyewole, Abimbola P. 128
Ozdaglar, M. N. 305

P

Pacheco, Carla Roberta 587
Padrick, Charles D. 239
Padula, Antonella Maria 247
Pahl, Carole A. 205
Palincas, L. 269
Palmer, Kevin L. 191
Palmer, Pat 421
Palmer, Rachel 188
Palmer Sr., Harry D. 463
Palmer, Tracy M. 426
Palmer, Val 154
Pang, Misty 255
Panganiban, Paulette Dana 564
Panza, Paul Nicholas 397
Paolucci, Louis 424
Papania, Leonard Guy 401
Paquette, Jan 219
Paredes, J. R. 558
Parfitt, Annetta 542
Paris, Evelyn R. 465
Parish, Stacey 511
Parisi, Laurel 284
Park, Elizabeth S. 77
Parker, C. Orlando 215
Parker, Donald L. 325
Parker, Donna 349

Parker, Lisa 556
Parker, Monique 162
Parker, Pat Blackcat 479
Parker, Shannon 264
Parker, Teara 272
Parkinson Jr., Robert 178
Parks, Whitney 158
Parone, Jessie Elaine 90
Parra, Lucy 290
Parrington, Irmgard 26
Parrish, Rosemary 175
Pash, Diana M. 38
Pastor, Eric 78
Pastula, Monica 408
Paterson, Laura 551
Patri, Teresa R. A. 304
Patterson, Charles 540
Patterson, Lisa 282
Patterson, Maurice 500
Pattillo-Newman, Mary 279
Patton, Acie 215
Patton, Kristine 496
Patty, Benita J. 342
Patzer, Ty 425
Paugh, W. 301
Paulick, Sharren Ann 190
Paulsen, Helen 462
Paye, M. P. C. 149
Payne, Theresa 72
Pearlman, Edward L. 339
Pearson, Comfort 9
Pearson, Florence 347
Pearson, Paula R. 381
Peccerillo Jr., John 12
Pedescleaux, Cheka 4
Pedvis, Anca 448
Peeples, Samuel F. 496
Peglar, Richard T. J. 571
Pembeltan, Sage Michaels 190
Peña, Abe M. 353
Pena, Gretta 579
Pender, Abbie 6
Pengelly, Sylvia A. 259
Penn, Dora 586
Penrod, Ben 90
Pentecost, Gregory L. 311
Pentecost, Thomas 61
Peoples, Davied J. 221
Perchaluk, Shawn 586
Perdue, JoAnn 444
Perea, Benjamin 234
Pereira, Mary Delfin 571
Perero, Linda 139
Perez, Michael 400
Perika 431
Perin, Anthony 538
Perkins, Mary E. A. 72
Perlow, A. H. 407
Perrault, Katrina 172
Perri, G. O. 393
Perris, Colleen 193
Persaud, John 445
Peruski, Deborah R. 243
Peter, William C. 391
Peters, Jo Anne 102
Petersen, Brooke L. 461
Petersen, Jan Chorlton 311
Peterson, Holly 365
Peterson, I. Renie 3
Peterson, Irene H. 128
Peterson, Jean 112

Peterson, Marple E. 554
Peterson, Ryan P. 272
Petit, Brianne 342
Petit, Jessica 349
Petramalo, Marie Elena 474
Petrides, Carolina 206
Pettett, Muriel 419
Petts, Richard 162
Pettus, Ernest F. 369
Petty, Julie A. 110
Petulla, Joseph 217
Pexton, Richard W. 284
Pezzuti, Cathy 78
Pfaff, Brian S. 460
Pfaffly, Allan W. 226
Pfeifer, Amber 193
Pham, Henry Tuoc V. 352
Phelps, Archie G. 21
Phelps, SandyLee A. 570
Philips, Angelique M. 109
Phillips, Doris Chapman 84
Phillips, Laura 171
Phillips, Melanie 177
Phillips, Monettia 424
Phillips, Otto 59
Phillips, Scott 181
Phillips, Sherri Kay 49
Phillips, Z. W. 508
Philomena, Karie 485
Philpitt, Edward T. 92
Piano, Vicki L. 52
Picard, Earl J. 111
Pickett, Fay Ernestine Gillespie 543
Pierce, Evelyn J. 318
Piernowski, Helene D. 366
Piersen, Shirley R. 270
Pierson, Barbara 338
Pierson, Deborah A. 440
Pietila, Renee 413
Pietras, Frank J. 30
Pifko Jr., John 196
Pilarczyk, Fred 328
Pinazza, Yvette 167
Pineo, Christine A. 250
Pino, Katherine J. 293
Piper, Jo 362
Pique, Roger 53
Pitchford, Alicia 10
Pitchford, Chris 457
Pitkofsky, Bertha 115
Pizzella, Edward G. 449
Plant, Dorothy 365
Plantz, Gabriella A. 443
Plass, Elena 527
Playford, Heather 462
Plickert, Jeff 545
Pluck, Marla Lynn 165
Plummer, Alan 439
Poff, W. Calverin 498
Pogue, Ida M. 79
Pogue, Lora L. 494
Pointer, Clyde 434
Pointon, George E. 77
Polancic, Frank P. 39
Polanco, Helen 132
Poland, Tina L. 192
Pollack, Mary 274
Pollard, Clarice F. 91
Pollard, Sue 492
Pollard, Tammie L. 422
Polleck, Audrey E. 530

Pool, Robert J. 419
Poole, Peggy J. 395
Pooley, Velma A. 182
Pope, Sarah 428
Popejay, Eva 99
Poppas, William 511
Porter, Ann 360
Porter, Flora Turbyfield 348
Porter, Jane 108
Porter, Steven 189
Porterfield, Kyla 490
Post, Heidi Sue 464
Post, Thomas K. 280
Post, Ursula M. 423
Potter, L. Elaine 580
Potts, Margaret R. 161
Powderly, Ruth E. 172
Powe, Trevor 416
Powell, Adair 103
Powell, Delia 360
Powell, Felicia A. 131
Powell, Lauren Lane 254
Powell, Sarah M. 514
Powell, Tiffany 289
Powers, Charlotte 77
Powers, Ella Ivey 235
Powers, Jesse 216
Powers, Jessica 469
Poynter, Tammy S. 61
Prather, Laura 500
Pratti, Mrs. Grace E. 27
Prazen, Jared 126
Praznik, Linda 465
Presby, Laurie 62
Prescott, Cheryl C. 27
Presley, Heather 442
Presniakov, Alexander 581
Prewett, Jessica 540
Preziose, Marlene 166
Price, JoAnn 357
Price Jr., James O. 319
Price, Michael G. 136
Price, Ruby Faye Crews 385
Primmer, Louise W. 312
Primrose, Barbara A. 525
Prince, Suzanne 413
Prince, Tia Nashay 269
Pringle, William 282
Pritchett, Elveda O. 528
Pritt, Jon M. 198
Pritt, Julia 433
Procopio, Marie 475
Prokopets, Marie 121
Prout, J. 418
Pruitt, Dennis 534
Pruitt, William 498
Prygon, Kenneth 191
Pugach, Brian 97
Pugh, Robert 475
Purkey, LaVerne M. 252
Pyle, Alice 231

Q

Quast, Heather 466
Queene, Michael J. 499
Quezada, Eduardo 7
Quijano, Peggy C. 52
Quillen, Renettia K. 427
Quinn, Peter 140
Quirk, Edward S. 243

R

Rabinovich, Marcelle 187
Race, Dottie 33
Rackley, Patti J. 307
Radakovich, Anita L. 355
Radandt, Amanda 238
Radcliffe, Dorothy 239
Radin, Constance E. 350
Radke, Dylana 259
Radojcic, Elizabeth A. 465
Radt, Gwen 79
Raeheim, Renaldo 144
Rager, Kesa 155
Ragin, Angela 37
Ragland, Janie L. 541
Ragno, Joseph S. 245
Rahier, Shawn 576
Raimondo, Gina 357
Rains, Darrius 453
Ramirez, June 87
Ramirez, Natalie 578
Ramirez, Shelly 257
Ramirez, Suzanne 432
Ramirez, Xsabeida L. 175
Ramos, Patricia M. 189
Ramsay, Jean Carol 353
Randall, Monique M. 177
Randolph, Jeannine 240
Ranjan, Dev Priya 468
Raseley, Mary 409
Rastetter, D. Mae 499
Ratcliff, Janine 581
Ratliff, Bettye W. 17
Rausch, Margaret 291
Rauscher, Renee M. 158
Ray, Hillol 437
Rayner, Jeffrey A. 544
Razaqi, Asma 319
Reason, Sharon Leigh Scott 581
Rector, Fern 532
Redd, Winnifred Dixon 424
Redfield, Liza 584
Redman, Angela 129
Reece, Terry 273
Reed, Chris 116
Reed, Franklin 232
Reed, Jody 236
Reed, Kevin William 568
Reel, Ralph E. 560
Reese, Elena Kristina 369
Reeves, Catherine 127
Reeves, Kason 162
Regina, Jean 526
Regnaiere, Ray 376
Rehm, Rhonda 289
Reichel, Nancy 482
Reid, Brendolyn 93
Reid, N. N. 407
Reid, Sean 268
Reidel, Arthur 321
Reidenbach, Rene S. 172
Reider, Harold 363
Reiland, Robin 575
Reilly, Dorothy Therese 240
Reilly, Margaret B. 481
Reimer, Dora 527
Reinier, Cindy 353
Reisner, Jerry 362
Reiter, Amanda Lee 237
Rej, Walter F. 53
Remster, Myra 490
Renault, Troy D. 138
Renecke, Lillian 164
Renker, Lois 281
Rennhak, Eleanor 314
Rensch, Mary Ann 272
Replogle, Marybeth 153
Ressler, Faye E. 13
Reynolds, Jamie 88
Reynolds, Joan 362
Reynolds, Wade 173
Reznik, Theresa M. 479
Reznikov, Girsh 358
Rhoden, Laverne 51
Rhodes Jr., Robert 550
Riberdy, Catherine Lynn 99
Riccardi, Kristen 420
Ricci, Guy J. 348
Rice, Doreen K. 206
Rice, Ellen 119
Rice, Lisa 497
Rice, Mary Ann 190
Rice, Susan 266
Rich, Graham N. 122
Rich III, Charles 347
Rich, Samuel 289
Richard, Marie 547
Richardson, Betty 467
Richardson, Freda L. 453
Richardson, Krystle 518
Richardson, Linda 392
Richardson, Rita 378
Richardson, Shiloh 185
Richmond, Mary J. 513
Ricka, L. F. 234
Rickert, Becky 11
Ridgway, Thomas J. 261
Ridley, Amie R. 448
Riesbeck, Cathy 129
Riggs, D. C. 264
Riggs, Gary 126
Riley, Debby Schryer 431
Riley, Mary Wolfe 497
Riley, Virginia 514
Rimel, R. C. 279
Ring, Alex 356
Ringe, James L. 98
Riola, Sara Hewitt 411
Rippl, Bart 220
Risch, Phyllis L. 564
Rittiluechai, Choochai 366
Rivera, Rosie 51
Rivers, Patricia 402
Rix, Joshua L. 433
Robb, Joan Schipper 524
Robbins, Jennifer 33
Roberson, Margaret 284
Roberts, Darcy 310
Roberts, Dazel Mary 344
Roberts, Edna V. 309
Roberts, Erik 440
Roberts, Joanne 344
Roberts, Rachael A. 503
Roberts, Raymond L. 55
Roberts, Susan C. 178
Robertson, Christopher S. 100
Robertson, Lee 177
Robertson, Sandra Lacy 117
Robins, Sandra L. 166
Robinson, Jennie 125
Robinson, Lee Ette 56
Robinson, Lisa Rene 584
Robinson, Patricia M. 517
Robinson, Paul T. 493
Robinson, Sharon 551
Robinson, Theodora 566
Robleau, Robi M. 47
Roblyer, John S. 331
Rocha, Helen May 97
Roche, Melinda 377
Rochester, Roni 299
Rochon, Charmaine 38
Roddy, Marge 74
Roderman, Richard 45
Rodriguez, Arlene 333
Rodriguez, Arthur 532
Rodriguez, Christine 348
Rodriguez, Elizabeth 228
Rodriguez, Jenica 350
Rodriguez, Maricella 572
Roe, Ricky Ray 398
Rogan, Timothy P. 505
Rogers, Amanda 229
Rogers, Jack A. 96
Rogers, Mark Reginald 175
Rogers, Raymond F. 40
Rogers, Summer 407
Rogowski, Kristi 263
Rokeach, Gia M. 327
Rolfe, April 586
Rollins, Charlotte B. 32
Rollwitz, Frances, 28
Romanowski, Richard 380
Romer, Sandy 516
Roode, Dawn E. 7
Rooney, Lisa 384
Rooney, Renate 150
Roop, Ian 323
Roppolo, Lou 45
Rosa, Manuel 154
Rose, Christina 247
Rose, Jill 208
Rose, Linda 412
Rose, Myrna L. 578
Rose, Tania L. 409
Rosen, Morris 265
Rosenberg, Michael 47
Rosenthal, Matt 300
Roskom, Kevin 489
Ross, Artee M. 447
Ross, Floyd 246
Ross, Jeff 30
Ross, Karen 292
Ross, Leon T. 411
Ross, Linda K. 185
Ross, Maea 373
Ross, Matt 264
Ross, Sheena 187
Rossi, Natalie 303
Roth, Betsy Ross 456
Roth, Pauline B. 417
Rotkowitz, Ruth 44
Rouse, Courtney 76
Rowe, Angela 198
Rowe, Michelle A. 511
Rowland, Mary Shaw 417
Rowland, S. J. 477
Royston, Lloyd L. 256
Rozbicka, Helena 78
Ru, Susan Y. 413
Rubel, Rachel 411
Ruberg, Stephen J. 514
Ruby, Rebecca 301
Rucker, Clara Rose 322
Ruckman, Gregory 109
Ruckman, Lois A. 557
Ruddell, Bobbi 452
Rugani, Lauren I. 290
Ruggiero, Samantha 518
Ruggiero, Victoria 61
Ruhling, Thea M. 516
Rundberg, Bobby 8
Runkle, Katherine Gates 181
Ruopp, June M. 322
Rupp, Norma J. 179
Ruppert, Richard 501
Rush, Joseph A. 97
Rusiniak, Yvonne Lubov 155
Russell, Arthur 242
Russell, Casey L. 198
Russell, Doris 197
Russell, Hope L. 238
Russell, Joseph K. 360
Russian, Ashley 362
Russo, Augustine J. 310
Russolesi, Elizabeth 430
Ruth, Marian 486
Rutkowski, Joseph 492
Ruttner, E. 423
Ryan, Charlotte M. 458
Ryan, Dorothy 90
Ryan, Joann 79
Ryan, Pamela R. 513
Ryther, Frank T. 82

S

Sabat, Margie 574
Saccocci, Diane 237
Sack, Joni 24
Sadeghpour, F. 176
Sak, Helen 15
Salazar, D. O'Connor 417
Salazar, Jerome Paul 347
Salazar, Kenneth V. 157
Salazar, Mary Theresa 164
Salley, Carolyn 236
Salmen, Adam 250
Salmon, Eleanor Brigid 16
Salome, Norman 178
Salomon, Janet 458
Saltsman, Tiffanie 407
Salvanish, Jayme 83
Salyers, Roger K. 307
Salzano, Frank 93
Sample, Gina Marie 235
Sampson, DeAnna Drake 321
Sampson, Harold 87
Sampson, Wilbur 187
Sams, Ervin 212
Samuel, Jefreys K. 537
Samulewicz, Betty 310
Sanders, Dora Griffith 325
Sanders, Heather 194
Sanders, James 404
Sanders, Mildred 58
Sanders, Stephanie Paige 275
Sanderson, Rebecca 572
Sandoval, Christina 319
Sandoval, Josephine 530
Sands, Rick 372
Sandstrom, Ethel M. 352
Sanfilippo, Carmela 363

Sanguesa, Esther N. 10
Sanson, Rossilyn 171
Santiago, Eugenia 23
Santos, Claribel 461
Santos, Jacqueline 245
Santos, Judite Garbrielle 328
Santos, Marcia 261
Sarra, Kristen 358
Sardino, Marianne 172
Sargent, Flora Beth Weber 529
Sarlo, Bernadette Melissa 333
Sarmiento, Rossinia 66
Sarojak, Mark 64
Sass, Yvonne 506
Sasson, Suzanne 553
Satterfield, F. 410
Sauder, Michelle 499
Saumell, Eva 77
Saunders, Jessica C. 439
Saunders, L. 191
Savage, Daniel Richard 318
Savo, Tracy L. 268
Sawler, Danita 348
Sawyer, Lee E. 278
Saye, Sara 187
Scales, Sirena 504
Scanlan, Winnifred Hiatt 179
Scanlon, Ursula 405
Scarborough, Helen L. 83
Scarbro, Kathy 306
Scardina, Tara 99
Scarlett-Collins, Lilian 586
Scarpa, Susan 62
Scarsella, Don G. 204
Scavone, Ron D. 371
Scelzo, Anthony R. 84
Schaefer, Misty 560
Schaeffer, Katherine M. 251
Schafer, Geraldine E. 135
Schaffner, Karl 547
Schaler, Jennifer 236
Schaller, Dianne 126
Schantz, Julie E. 435
Schaum, Carl 524
Scheck, Janea 223
Scheuer, Sue 291
Scheuermann, Karen L. 479
Schexnyder, Wallace J. 141
Schickedanz, Cathy 529
Schiffman, Jason 342
Schilling, Jane 211
Schimming, Jacob Daniel 90
Schintzius-Wilt, Amy 437
Schlauger, Dawn 105
Schlegel, Dara 473
Schlesinger, Dorothy Baigle 368
Schlesser, John A. 468
Schlief, Jennifer 238
Schmidt, Eugene F. 250
Schmidt, Yvonne M. 414
Schneider, Chris 405
Schneider, Ellen 236
Schneider, Merle Ann 74
Schneiders, Sandra M. 299
Schnitzler, Douglas C. 367
Schock, Stephanie Nicole 167
Schoenberg, Barbara 88
Schoenthal, Harold G. 134
Schotts, Richard J. 419
Schramm, Christine M. 471
Schramm, Janice W. 209

Schreiner, Eloise K. 453
Schreiner, Mark S. 487
Schriever, Barbara D. 79
Schrupp, Adele 453
Schuh, Rebecca P. 186
Schuldt, Rose M. 181
Schultz, Beth 441
Schulze, Edward B. 237
Schulze, William H., Sr. 513
Schutz, Chenee' 227
Schwamberger, Mari 488
Schwartz, Carolyn 124
Schwartz, Kim 55
Schwartz, Laurence C. 161
Schwartztrauber, Toni 510
Schwickerath, Sarah Jean 186
Scoggins, Jane 135
Scott, Danielle 220
Scott, Henry Vincent 77
Scott, Jacqueline D. 131
Scott, Jeannie 245
Scott, Margaret Kopcho 582
Scott, Peggy L. 41
Scott, William H. 288
Scott, Zack 379
Scrivano, Faith 353
Scrivner, Sherry 291
Scruggs, Lillie 151
Seafarers, Andy George 474
Searles, Patrick R. 291
Searson, Ethel 544
Sebastian 429
Sedlacek, Danielle 93
Sedlock, Angi 236
Seekamp, Craig Morgan II 200
Seeliger, Ruth 308
Seibert, Maydell 59
Seibold, Stephanie L. 488
Seigle, David J. 230
Seiler, Jennifer 23
Seitz, Mary Lafary 305
Seitz, Melanie A. 425
Selfridge, Nel 260
Seltzer, Helen Estes 201
Semensohn, Jaime 102
Semple, Rachel 587
Sentino, John 543
Sepulveda, Damaris 8
Serra, Siobhan 268
Serre, Nicholas 399
Setters, Jeanne 360
Settlemyer, Terri M. 512
Setzer, Erin J. 134
Sewell, Aisha L. 446
Seybold, Clinton C. 80
Seymour, Irene 350
Sfekas, Christina 318
Shackleton, Ocean 385
Shaffer Jr., J. W. 563
Shaffer, Michael L. 506
Shaffer, Richard M. 397
Shagoury, Charles J. 524
Shanahan, George 313
Shapiro, Barbara 92
Shapiro, Kevin 186
Shapiro, Rodney J. 574
Sharon, Donald A. 78
Sharp, Carol 539
Sharp, Justin Lee 241
Sharp, Rebecca 73
Shastsky, Johanna 469

Shaw, David A. 465
Shaw, Fanny Lee Baker 229
Shaw, Kristina 506
Shaw, Luthia 71
Sheard, Melissa J. 503
Sheets, Kristopher 505
Sheldon, Keith E. 396
Shelhamer, Russell Eyre 516
Shelton, Christy 215
Shelton, Glenda Willis 369
Shelton, Mary L. 188
Shelton, Sandra 572
Shemansky, Diana M. 108
Shepard, Valeria F. Seay 585
Sheppard, Regina 493
Sherbert, John Mark 225
Sherlin, Mary Jo 421
Sherma, Arlene 444
Sherman, Dick 525
Sherr, Harry B. 12
Shervanick, Karla 277
Shields, Cynthia 582
Shima, Erica 429
Shin, John 528
Shoemaker, Dee 134
Shoemaker, Ernie 201
Shore, Anna V. 82
Short, Madeleine 56
Showers, Joanna 84
Shrubb, Teri 515
Shults, Roy L. 154
Shutt, Nora 415
Sias, Heather M. 343
Siberry, Lindsay 546
Siciliano, Lydia C. 573
Sicklesteel, Kathy 506
Siebers, Melissa 297
Siebert, Beverly 579
Siegelman, Hilda Barbara 323
Siggers, Mattie P. 413
Silberstein, Michael Wade 260
Silmon, Ne'Kilya 486
Silva, Manuel J. 476
Silverman, Laura Lee 302
Silverman, Meggin Kahn 427
Silvers, Norma 507
Simmonds, Kate 414
Simmons, Joyce 89
Simmons, Leon 285
Simmons, Nelson Joseph 285
Simmons, Robert 297
Simmons, Roberta B. 410
Simms, Cara 246
Simon, Isabella M. 85
Simon, Jessica 243
Simon, Rosena 418
Simonds, Keetah 167
Simons, Marissa 295
Simpkins, Carol 527
Simpkins, Carole 450
Simpkins, Faye 34
Simpson, Mildred B. 299
Sin, Catherine 27
Singer, David 541
Singh, Baljit 335
Singh, Margret Morine 564
Siodlarz, Stephen 61
Siple, Josephine 124
Sipp, Anthony 3
Sisler, Harry H. 227
Sissons, Ron 178

Sistrunk, Joyce 14
Skaggs, Jennifer C. 233
Skinner, Mary Ann 183
Skinner, Paul 562
Skinner, Sheena 511
Skinner, Virginia 427
Skinner, Wayne 186
Skoog, Christopher E. 317
Skrovanek, Sonja 257
Slack, David 25
Slade, Paula 415
Slade, Tim 253
Sladek, Ethel J. 525
Slaga, John 82
Slater, Samantha 291
Slaughter, Andrew 82
Slayton, Tiffany 290
Slobodnikova, Zuzana 296
Slusher, Ralph 570
Small, Rebecca 181
Smalley, Trip 73
Smargisso, Dana M. V. 230
Smeltzer, Susan 567
Smiley, Camille 210
Smith, Alma LaMothe 242
Smith, Amy 97
Smith, Anita C. 544
Smith, Bonnie A. 223
Smith, Celestine H. 86
Smith, Christine S. 116
Smith, Courtney 580
Smith, Denise 97
Smith, Donna D. 359
Smith, Donna M. 583
Smith, Elaine 334
Smith, Ella 202
Smith, Flavia V. 24
Smith, J. R. (Bob) 272
Smith, Jamel 224
Smith, James E. 536
Smith, Joe Allen 96
Smith, Joshua D. 209
Smith, Kristy 271
Smith, Larry L. 302
Smith, Laurie L. 417
Smith, Linda 145
Smith, Marcia C. 300
Smith, Marica M. 576
Smith, Mary 256
Smith, Melissa 483
Smith, Michelle 557
Smith, Nancy I. 301
Smith, Neva G. 180
Smith, Piccola 502
Smith, Rachael 495
Smith, Rebecca H. 146
Smith, Rhonda 260
Smith, Robert E. Lee 577
Smith, Samuel 507
Smith, Sherry 251
Smith, William R. 549
Smith-Thomas, Cassandra A. 460
Smith-Woodmore, Peggy Jo 515
Snouffer, Melissa 188
Snow, Crystal A. 202
Snow, James P. 102
Snow, Julee 19
Snowden Jr., Randall 516
Snyder, Rebecca 305
Snyder, Vera 522
Sobel, Mort 407

Soffler, Edith 350
Solberg, Chris 227
Soldyn, Teresa 69
Solimene, Paul 409
Solis, Amy 582
Solis, Herman 535
Solo, Richard 383
Solomon, Marcy L. 168
Sones, Christina 360
Sonoqui, Sophia A. 102
Sookdeo, Neela 281
Sorensen, Carolyn Kelley 451
Sorensen, Leif 292
Sorgeloos, Keith R. 388
Soriano, Jennie 430
Sosomen, Grace R. 9
Soto, Susan 489
Sotolongo, Francisco J. 366
Southard, Sue 292
Sowers, Joyce 108
Sowers, Sara 487
Sowles, Leslie 559
Sparks, Peggy J. 587
Sparks, Zack 412
Spaulding, Marie 260
Speakman, Margaret L. 60
Spear, Helen T. 244
Spears, Rebecca Renay 179
Spegal, Angela P. 532
Spell, Louise Simmons Thomas 62
Spence, David Leslie 214
Spence, O. Clinton 59
Spencer, Barbara F. 6
Spencer, Margaret 549
Spencer, Tyler 190
Spickerman, Wayne 383
Spilton, Maxine 160
Spina, Tom 573
Spinosi, Dotty 114
Spivery, John Damascus 30
Spivey, Tyresa 478
Spooner, Buz 464
Spratt, Luvena 265
Spratt, Rose-Marie 294
Spring-Dupres, Chantal 107
Springstead, Leroy 417
St. Jean, Faye 18
St. Louis, Esther 332
St. Pierre, April 525
Stack, D. Randall 386
Stadt, Norma 573
Stadtman, Mary A. 46
Staed, Judith A. 473
Staeven, Charles 10
Staggs, Elaine 209
Stahlmann, Sheri 509
Stambaugh, Deborah 323
Stamm, Dorothy 365
Stanczyk, Beverly 346
Standfield, Nadine 551
Stanley, Barbara C. 526
Stanley, David R. 470
Stanley, Sabrina 422
Stansberry, Ashley E. 290
Staples, Marianna K. 423
Staplins, Recina 159
Star, Sheyenne 367
Stark, David C. 239
Stark, James H. 439
Starke, Betty 314
Startup, Charles A. 243

Stashick, Gail E. 587
Statham, George E. 443
Staub, Michael S. 294
Stauf, R. Marlene 567
Stayner, Lisa 172
Stearns, Ralph H. 405
Steeby, Shayne 67
Steel, M. Thomasine 175
Steele, Alan R. 451
Steele, April 204
Steele, Margaret M. 412
Steele Sr., Orville M. 328
Steen, Eddy 20
Steers, David 583
Steffek, Jennifer 537
Stefko, Korin 424
Stegall, Cordy 217
Stegenga, D. A. Dawn 292
Steiger, Claire L. 347
Stein, Ada 317
Steinbaum, Keith 43
Stephen, Jean 158
Stephens, Barbara G. 220
Stephens, Kimberly 306
Stephenson, Therésa C. 503
Steudel, Mark 188
Stevens, Faith 231
Stevens, Mildred A. 574
Stevens, Shannon Lynn 303
Stevens, Trey 179
Stevenson, Greg 365
Stevenson, Mary 418
Steward, Joseph M. 463
Stewart, Camilla L. 339
Stewart, Clara Oscie-Ola 202
Stewart, Linda Dianne 379
Stewart, Michael D. 566
Stewart, Robert J. 394
Stiffel, Lisa 153
Stiner, Alex 32
Stisser, Betty E. 81
Stockman, Irene 24
Stockman, Kathy 293
Stockman, Kelly 514
Stockton, Harold Wayne 8
Stoddard, James A. 113
Stoeckel, Deborah 367
Stokes, Carolyn Ashe 467
Stokes, Yvonne 253
Stolting, J. 555
Stone, Matt 480
Stone, Misty N. 184
Stoner, Ashley 129
Storey, Matthew J. 302
Storey, Maude 55
Storm, Lou 150
Storms, Donna C. 203
Storrick, Jennifer 445
Stracener, Lacy 412
Strait, Micah 167
Strand, Marsha 188
Strandahl, DebraLee 123
Strange, John B. 7
Strange, Tina 566
Stratton, Betsy 130
Stratton, Robert W. 483
Strauss, Bob 221
Strayer, Jennie 470
Strehle, R. 522
Strenth, Matthew 234
Strickland, Jeremy 249

Stringfellow, Bobbie L. 86
Stroble, Azzie Lee 193
Stroman, Lucy N. 427
Strong, Cathy M. 93
Stroud, Zach 290
Strub, Christine 109
Struwe, Shannon 378
Stup, Jerry 458
Sturges, Caroline 6
Stuve, Mary 298
Stuyvesant, Elinor 531
Sugelmar, Hilda Barbara 527
Sullivan, Grace L. 229
Sullivan, Gwendolyn M. 233
Sumner, Charles F. 10
Sunukjian, Debra 82
Susco, Rhonda 292
Susky, Helen H. 80
Sutherlan-Chun, Jaime 223
Swain, Sue 252
Swan, Barbara 344
Swan, Edna A. 121
Swanson, Heather 243
Swart, Linda 422
Swartz, Dale 229
Sweeney, Amy 233
Sweeney, Frank 241
Sweerman, Wim R. 139
Swenson, Evelyn J. 441
Swinford, Pam 291
Swint, Charles 108
Switzer, Barbara A. 199
Switzer, Rebecca 399
Swope, Candy 348
Sword, Suzanne 146
Sy, Cherry Lou C. 37
Symons, Bill 115
Szasz, Jennifer 101
Szeless, Gertrud 366
Szewczyk, Todd 59
Szlosek, Sarah 45
Szwarc, Belinda 123

T

Tabor, Viola Jane 168
Tacker, Alexandria 8
Taffe, Keresia 521
Takahashi, Cynthia 237
Talbert, Kim M. 422
Tallent, Lisa 299
Talley, Bryan 334
Talley, Maxine 259
Tallman, Evelyn T. 91
Tamborello, Dean 436
Tamuccio, Joanne 218
Tan-Trapp, Genida 92
Tanksley, Gail 210
Tanner, Crystalynn 358
Tate, Jennifer S. 200
Tates, Bruce A. 215
Tavenner, Mary Hilaire 414
Taylor, Bradley 331
Taylor, Carlene 5
Taylor, Clyde Matthew 247
Taylor, Jason 349
Taylor, Jessie 454
Taylor Jr., Douglas 118
Taylor, Kenneth L. 418
Taylor, Leslie 391
Taylor, Marie D. 419

Taylor, Sandra 49
Taylor, Sarah 407
Teabout, Linda 180
Teague, Lisa 168
Tebaldi, Matthew 578
Tebay, Gayle 240
Teitelbaum, Sidney L. 140
Templett, A. Joseph 408
Tenorio, Oclides 298
Ternes, Peter 181
Terpening, Darcy 364
Terrill, Beverly 357
Terry, Christina 431
Tesh, Ruby Nifong 43
Tews-Newsome, Lisa Marie 301
Thacker, Lydia E. 459
Thames-Walton, Linda 70
Thayaparan, P. 546
Thayer, Shannon 281
Theisen, Mary 192
Theuma, Veronica 300
Thibodaux, Katherine M. 514
Thies, Valorie 164
Thigpen, Rakel 548
Thomas, Alice J. 362
Thomas, Angie 76
Thomas, Arla 235
Thomas, Candace 287
Thomas, Carolyn 473
Thomas, Diori J. 222
Thomas Jr., David U. 437
Thomas, Kirsten 295
Thomas, Robert B. 423
Thomas, Tanja S. 410
Thomas, Tomara 373
Thomas, Wendy 261
Thomen, Florence Vining 434
Thompson, Alva M. 324
Thompson, Barbara 13
Thompson, Casey Lee 455
Thompson, Diane 76
Thompson, Erin 343
Thompson, Jeffrey C. 245
Thompson, Kelly 495
Thompson, Marcella 282
Thompson, Mark Somerlyn L. 480
Thompson, Maxine 414
Thompson, Monica 253
Thompson, Roger L. 499
Thompson, Tina 572
Thompson, Virginia C. 510
Thorne, Irene 317
Thornell, William M. 578
Thornton, Ruth J. 473
Thorpe, Tiffany 48
Thrash, Ruth P. 418
Thrift, Carrie 445
Thurmond, Laura Shelton 309
Thurston, Bonnie 230
Tiberi, Primio 378
Tiemann, Georganne G. 356
Tieng, James 207
Tieri, Michael J. 300
Tierney-Hashimoto, Pat 497
Tillwach, Wanda Elizabeth 428
Tindal, Linda 182
Tindall, Thomas E. 273
Tiner, David 321
Tinsley, Emily 231
Tippin, Lily 422
Tipping, Harriet 413

"TJ" 560
Tjernagel, Don 369
Tolbert, Taniesha 57
Tolson, Frances E. 368
Tomlinson, Rick 171
Tommaney, Tim 383
Tonelli, Pat 66
Toney, Patrick 280
Toney-Regusters, Billie A. 537
Tonkin, Phyllis Ilene 189
Toomey, Dawn M. 130
Topham, Shelley A. 275
Torre, Theresa 296
Torres, Christian Curtis 132
Torres, Christopher Curtis 132
Torresson, Rebekah N. 422
Torrey, Arthur 344
Torruella, Peter 271
Toulson, Christopher M. 12
Townsley, Alice 92
Towson, Susan 578
Tracy, Amanda 100
Tracy, Vanessa Rodgers 174
Trammell, R. M. 383
Trautwein, Lisa 75
Traverse, Melanie 266
Travis, Gary D. 531
Trejos, Debbie L. 96
Trice, Cindy 236
Triolo, Michelle A. 189
Tripodi, Tony 277
Tripp, Lisette Y. 419
Trippod, Irene 369
Troesch, Susan 151
Trogolo, Andrew N. 76
Trory, Geraldine P. 233
Trotter, Elaine 540
Trotter, Marian W. 393
Truchinski, Joyce A. 96
Truitt, Maurine I. 400
Truman, Judy Strom 235
Truman-Holliday, Deana 225
Trump, Cathy 583
Trupiano, Dorothy E. 464
Trusel, Elizabeth R. 210
Trzyna, Patricia 303
Tsuji, R. T. 157
TTW 228
Tucker, Helen Palmer 356
Tucker, Judith 250
Tucker, Keith 521
Tull-Esterbrook, Karla Renee 176
Tully, Michael R. 375
Turnbull, Mark 71
Turner, Angela Michelle 529
Turner, Bill 430
Turner, Edwin Charles 366
Turner, Gladys 334
Turner, Holly DeBerry 99
Turner, Jason 213
Turner, Joann 77
Turner Jr., Thomas B. 300
Turner, Kyle 503
Turney, King V. 425
Turnquist, Gerda 512
Turovsky, Dmitry 218
Turpin, Anna F. 83
Turpin, Tracy 121
Tuttle, Dennis 545
Tyner, Pam 480
Tyson, Wycliffe E. 50

U

Uddley, Metallica 423
Uding, Katherine 183
Ulbrich, Valerie 346
Ule, Rose 55
Ulrich, Audra Woods 335
Ulrick, Richard C. 493
Ungaro, Danielle K. 218
Untch, Maxine 379
Urban, Helen 92
Urban, Irene 359
Urraca, Christa Deyanira 326
Usher, William 176
Uthes, Dorothy V. 469

V

Vaglia, Marilyn Hohn 136
Vahan, A. R. 491
Vahey, Christopher B. 446
Vaine, Honey 114
Valdez, Janita 79
Valenta, Gerald A. 418
Valiton, Martin 47
Vallas, Peter 305
Vallier, Erin 131
Van Dam, Kristen 265
Van Deest, Beatrice 124
Van Dyke, Ruth M. S. 293
Van Engen, Brooke 210
Van Horne, Colleen 100
Van Houten, Lindsay Sydney 183
Van Lennep, Vivian 166
Van Metre, Marlene 68
Van Riemsdyk, Jason 126
Van Schyndel, Kathie G. 490
Van Wyk, Jacob W. 79
Van Zile, Tim 157
Vanderwood, Deborah M. 78
Vanzant, Dorothy 327
Varela, Rosina C. 561
Vasquez, Martha 505
Vaughan, Pamila Gale 54
Vaughn, Garrett 194
Vause, Rayna A. 276
Veguilla, Damaris 463
Veit, Laurel E. 427
Velasquez, Myra 72
Velez, Alexandra 249
Velott, Joan M. 35
Velox, Shelly Todd 396
Venettozzi, Raymond 185
Verburg, Jessica 238
Viars, Ronda G. 169
Vice, Erin 450
Vickrey, Laura Davis 301
Vierra, Sylvia K. 495
Vigil, Jay 471
Vigorito, Carmine T. 341
Vilaire, Melissa 552
Villarreal, Stacy 156
Villaver, Marnel 575
Vines, John A. 237
Viney, Anita A. 541
Viseur, Renate 519
Vockrodt, Marlo Dean 152
Vogel, Charlotte 526
Volkhardt, Diane 222
Volkman, Vicki L. 382
Volpe, Robert A. 158
Von Hallmark, Melony 554
von Rummelhoff, Elisabeth 217
Von Steen, Verna 391
Vondrell Sr., James H. 359
Voors, Tara 399

W

Waddell, Brenda M. 93
Wagner, Beth J. Pauley 251
Wagner, Fred 366
Wagner, Mark 512
Wagner, Melissa 140
Wahner, Rudolph H. 373
Wahnon, Denise Marie 244
Wakamatsu, Jack 357
Wake, Dave 196
Wakeley, Stacie 564
Walker, Cheryl 130
Walker, E. C. 136
Walker, Gladys E. 239
Walker, Phylli 132
Wallace, Dorothy A. 471
Wallace, Douglas Morrison 205
Wallace, Edward 234
Wallace, Esther E. 233
Wallace, Lary L. 65
Wallace, Mark A. 571
Wallace, Torrey 551
Waller, Bonnie 95
Walsh, Ann S. 109
Walsh, Cathryn L. 115
Walsh, Fiona 195
Walsh, Herb 230
Walsh, Patrick 402
Walsh, Robin Marie 143
Walter, Howard F. 310
Walters, Rachel 296
Walters, Sharon 98
Walton-Barnett, Lula M. 278
Walukonis, Casie 431
Walus, Paige 413
Wamsley, Ann 113
Wamsley, C. Huston 29
Wang, Emily 88
Wangler, Larry L. 514
Wanielista 579
Ward, Dorothy Ethel Vancil 22
Ward, Hilda E. 245
Ward, Patricia Anne 561
Ward, Patricia Rhea 186
Ward, Shannon 161
Ward, William E. 65
Warda, Robert 562
Warder, Velma G. 176
Wardlaw, Donna 230
Warn, L. Mila 284
Warren, Dorothy 430
Warren, Lucille L. 251
Warren, Lyken L. 164
Warren, Mark A. 398
Warren, Robert L. 47
Warren, Tricia 294
Washington, Charles 240
Washington, Janet 3??
Washington, Monicole L. 307
Washington, Morrison 70
Washington-Peeples, Saundra 260
Wasserman, Sue 156
Waterman, Carrie S. 437
Waters, Helen J. 472
Wathen, Catherine 368
Wathen, Karen Haley 504
Watson, Geraldine 216
Watson Jr., Stiles T. 381
Watson, Karen S. 555
Watson, Muriel 550
Watson, S. Lyric 182
Watters, Marilynn 305
Watts Jr., Toye E. 173
Wayland Jr., Gene 245
Weaver, DeWayne M. 120
Weaver, Jeanette A. 121
Weaver Jr., Dixon 315
Weaver, Vernieca (Aunt Icea) 41
Webb, Carson 37
Webb, Lil 346
Webbert, Nicole 296
Weber, Caryl 96
Weber, Glenna 332
Weber, Marian G. 143
Weber, Pearl Ann 505
Weber, Quinn 144
Weber, William J. 379
Webster, William G. 559
Wechselberger, Joseph P. 447
Wedal, Lori 507
Wedgbury, David J. 123
Weeks, Floyd R. 530
Weems, Carl 27
Weibull, Pontus 484
Weidman, Star A. 474
Weigand-Wood, Madelyn 149
Wein, Bella 469
Weinsteiger, Dawn 10
Weinstein, Michael 51
Welborn, Shelly 480
Welch, Andrea N. 536
Welch, Donna L. 523
Welch, Grace R. 224
Welebir, Benita Slawson 197
Weller, Dannielle 433
Weller, Michelle 54
Welles, Cyril M. 81
Wells, Bryan 443
Wells, Cynthia 437
Wells Jr., Stephen Leon 304
Wells, Marcia S. 267
Wells, Miles 429
Wells, Renee 566
Wendt, Susan 394
Werner, Christina M. 336
Wesbecher, Michael 520
Wessel, Celeste 123
West, Glenda M. 20
West Jr., Walter I. 172
West-Fields, Teresa A. 258
Westergaard, Walter 183
Western, M. Wayne 489
Weston, Christopher L. 31
Whalen, Jennifer A. 327
Wheby, Ellis 544
Wheeler, Ellen 83
Whitaker, Charlotte 78
whitaker, priscilla 390
White, Amy 87
White, Angela 530
White, Cheryl D. Brown 248
White, Jean 244
White Jr., James M. 535
White, Juanita A. T. 226
White, Kelley 182
White, Leonard T. 397

White, Linda 154
White, Michelle 425
White Sr., John Edward 87
Whitehead, Elizabeth 87
Whitelock, Ray 565
Whiteman, Eric 330
Whitfield, Paul 153
Whittemore, Joy R. 95
Whitton, Louellen 412
Whybark, Bree 532
Wick, Michelle 295
Wicker, C. L. J. 253
Wiederkehr, Jessica 231
Wiener, Marc 424
Wierwille, Chloe 51
Wiesenmayer, Raymond M. 416
Wiest, Anna M. 84
Wigern, Tracy 567
Wiggins, Dana Marie 16
Wight, Tara R. 163
Wilbourne, Avinelle G. 581
Wilbur, Donna 21
Wilbur, William B. 70
Wilcock, Grant 360
Wilcox, Jean 472
Wilen, Gwendolyn 249
Wiley, Imogene 199
Wilhelmy, Gus 117
Wilke, Dorothy E. 448
Wilkerson, Eva 532
Wilkins, J. 68
Wilkins, Jason 351
Wilkins, Timmy R. 378
Will, Ruth L. 495
Williams, Agatha T. 126
Williams, Allyn L. 529
Williams, Alyce Trimm 339
Williams, Ann M. 319
Williams, Bobbie Jean 119
Williams, Caitlin M. 358
Williams, Carlton 449
Williams, Cleta 530
Williams, Diana 210
Williams, John M. 245
Williams, Jonell W. 196
Williams, Joyce Nadine 342
Williams, Karen L. 61
Williams, Kenneth 228
Williams, Kristin 279
Williams, Linda 519
Williams, Lucy L. 279
Williams, Melanie 483
Williams, Mistie L. 404
Williams, Ruth 429
Williams, Shari 153
Williams, Shari L. 294
Williams, Suzanne 137
Williams, Travis 403
Williams, Verlyn D. 375
Williams, Willie C. 429
Williamson, Billy 337
Williamson, Edith 152
Williamson, La-Goldia 155
Willis, Therese M. 501
Willis, William R. 326
Willoughby, Stephen 506
Willyard Sr., Johnnie Estle 247
Wilson, Carolyn M. 224
Wilson, Clyde 326
Wilson, Daniel Ray 23
Wilson, Dorothy 354
Wilson, Elizabeth 11
Wilson, Grandma K. 165
Wilson, Hester 203
Wilson, Jody 227
Wilson, Larry G. 423
Wilson, Linda S. 295
Wilson, Margaret S. 481
Wilson, Mrs. R. Thornton 69
Wilson, Myrtle 168
Wilson, Sonia 415
Wilson, Theresa Marie 270
Wimer, Kimothy A. 486
Winans, Caley 25
Winchowky, Lawrence I. 188
Wineland, Sara 192
Winfrey, Mick 503
Wingerter, Jason 211
Winiasz, Edward 468
Winn, Exel Dyar 348
Winn, Geoff 336
Winn, Jarret D. 357
Winterfeldt, David 111
Wintrow, Jacinda 443
Wiscomb, Kenneth K. 421
Wise, Jone 29
Wise, Sequoia 417
Wise, Virginia 520
Wismer, Loretta M. 192
Wisner, Casey E. 99
Wisniewski, Lillian 293
Witherington, Mark 181
Witt, Pamela 479
Wittenberger, Paul 173
Woan, Winston Veeraprasert 167
Wojciechowski, Holly 130
Wolfe, Mattie 168
Wolford, Carol 455
Wolfschmidt, Willi 173
Womeldorff, Sara Lynn 493
Wong, Shirley 493
Woo, Robert Hyun Wook 138
Wood, Amy 86
Wood, Brian L. 112
Wood, Frances Ely 240
Woodall, Thelma Mae 148
Woodard, James H. 106
Woodcock, Sean 169
Woodson, Pamela 554
Woodward, Johanna L. 23
Woodward Sr., Tyrone E. 138
Wooff, Marti 551
Woolard, Daryl Nathan 324
Woomer, Suzanne 276
Wormald, Beverly J. 352
Wormley, Machelle D. 547
Worsham, Maryellen 319
Woulfe, Julie 241
Wray-Scriven, Devyn 355
Wright, Bonnie 4
Wright, Carolyn 329
Wright, Denise Rae 534
Wright, Donna 469
Wright, Hal 96
Wright, Judith 229
Wright, Louise 401
Wright, Melody 179
Wright, Tammy L. 165
Wright, Thomas M. 427
Wright, Tikoyo 387
Wu, Lily T. 428
Wyatt, Nellie D. 586
Wyler, Beth 447
Wysockey, Ronelle 562

Y

Yamaguchi, Stan 424
Yamasaki, Clinton T. 200
Yancey, Susan L. 429
Yano, J. 302
Yano, John 533
Yantis, Jennifer Rose 79
Yarbrough, LaMonica 149
Yasharian, Margaret T. 520
Yasparro, Rosemary Muntz 143
Yeatts, Phyllis D. 410
Yeoman, Cheryl and 4th grade students at Medlock 328
Yi, Inkuk 212
Yielding, Danielle 241
Yohn, Jefferson D. 325
Yost, Robert G. 158
Young, Alicia 203
Young, Ardelia 238
Young, Christopher 360
Young, John 467
Young, John J. 14
Young, Joy A. 34
Young, Noah 571
Young, Ruth 521
Young, Ryanne 519
Young, Susan 297
Young, Vickie 522
Young, William K. 169
Younger, Mary E. 487
Youngquist, Rosemary P. 424
Yule, Joedy A. 92
Yurenda, Dena M. 542

Z

Zack, Michael B. 173
Zaffino, Connie Kay 194
Zampella, Virginia 288
Zane, George T. 368
Zarou II, Paul 478
Zarreh, Mehrdad 252
Zaun, Kristin Kae 139
Zayas, Lazaro 578
Zcats, Anastasia 14
Zebley, Janet L. 452
Zec, Robert J. 177
Zerin, Edward 19
Ziemkiewicz, Hope 351
Zimmerman, Charity 458
Zimmerman, Joseph 17
Zimmerman, Memie 65
Zimmerman, Patsy 56
Zino, Marielle 508
Zivkovic-Torres, Monique 299
Zogg, Melanie 295
Zuar, Donna L. 353
Zucker, Melanie 383
Zuckerman, Sandra L. 408